# THE MICHELSEN
# BOOK OF
# TABLES

**Koch and Placidus Tables of Houses**
**How to Cast a Natal Horoscope**
**Interpolation Tables**
**Time Tables**

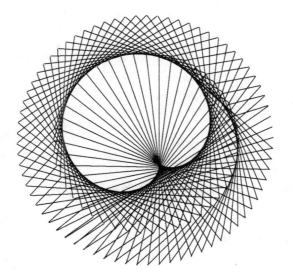

Compiled and Programmed by
Neil F. Michelsen
Revisions by Rique Pottenger

Published by
ACS Publications
5521 Ruffin Road
San Diego, CA 92123-1314

International Standard Book Number 0-935127-60-7

Published by ACS Publications
5521 Ruffin Road
San Diego, CA  92123-1314

Printed in the United States of America

First Printing, March 1997
Second Printing, March 1998
Third Printing, July 2001

# Contents

# How to Cast a Natal Horoscope

by Robert Hand and Joshua Brackett

These instructions consist of two parts: the worksheet, which is an outline used for casting a horoscope, and the notes, which explain the worksheet. The worksheet provides minimal directions for one method of casting an ordinary natal chart. The notes support the worksheet directions with theory, with alternative methods and with prescriptions for special cases. Each section of notes is headed by the lines from the worksheet to which the notes apply, with the spaces filled in with appropriate example values. A complete chart is cast as an example for the reader to follow.

We anticipate that the beginner will read through the entire text of the notes, perhaps casting a first chart as s/he goes. The experienced astrologer, on the other hand, will use the worksheet to cast charts and will select notes to read at leisure, out of curiosity rather than necessity.

In the worksheet and in the notes, the order of operations is (1) time calculations, (2) locating the planets and (3) locating the house cusps. We know that astrologers usually do the house cusps before the planets, probably because the house cusps have to be put on the horoscope wheel first. We have changed the usual order so as to help the beginner by arranging the tasks in ascending order of difficulty. Locating the planets requires only a one-way interpolation, whereas locating the house cusps requires two-way interpolation. If you prefer to calculate the house cusps first, there is nothing to prevent you from doing so.

The ephemerides referred to in the text and illustrations are from *The American Ephemeris* Series, available in paperback volumes and the *American Ephemeris for the 20th Century 1900 - 2000 at Midnight* published by ACS Publications.

---

Please refer to the last pages of this book for information on additional titles and astrological reports and calculation services available from Astro Communications Services, Inc.

# NATAL HOROSCOPE WORKSHEET

Name_____

## TIME CALCULATIONS

| | | | | | | |
|---|---|---|---|---|---|---|
| 1 | **Born** | am/pm Zone | | **Date** | | |
| 2 | **Place** | Longitude | | **Latitude** | | |
| 3 | **Standard Time** (pm: + 12h, DST: – 1h) | | **3** | h | m | |
| 4 | **Time Zone Number** (Table I) | | **4** | h | | |
| 5 | **Universal Time** (West+ East–) **Greenwich date** | | **5** | h | m | **UT** |

| | | | | | | |
|---|---|---|---|---|---|---|
| 6 | ΔT  (**5** date, Table IV) | | **6** | | | s |
| 7 | **Ephemeris Time** (add **5** + **6** = **7**) | | **7** | h | m | s  **ET** |

| | | | | | | |
|---|---|---|---|---|---|---|
| 8 | **Greenwich Sidereal Time** 00h (Ephemeris) | | **8** | h | m | s |
| 9 | **Solar-Correction** (5, Table II) | | **9** | | m | s |
| 10 | **Greenwich Sidereal Time**  (add **5** + **8** + **9** = **10**) | | **10** | h | m | s |
| 11 | **Longitude Correction** (Table III)  **degrees: 11a**  h  m | | | | | |
| | **minutes: 11b**  m  s | | | | | |
| | **total** (add **11a** + **11b** = **11c**) | **11c** | h | m | s | |
| | (WEST: Subtract **10 – 11c = 12**); East: add **10 + 11c = 12** | | | | | |
| 12 | **Local Sidereal Time** | | **12** | h | m | s  **LST** |

## LOCATING THE PLANETS

| | | | | | | |
|---|---|---|---|---|---|---|
| 13 | ☉ **Longitude** 0h **After Birth** (5 date + 1d, Ephemeris) | | **13** | ° | ' | " |
| 14 | ☉ **Longitude** 0h **Before Birth** (5 date, Ephemeris) | | **14** | ° | ' | " |
| 15 | **24h Travel** (Subtract **13 – 14 = 15**) | | **15** | ° | ' | " |
| 16 | **ET Travel** (7, 15 Table V) | **minutes** | **16a** | ° | ' | " |
| | | **hours** | **16b** | ° | ' | " |
| 17 | ☉ **Longitude At Birthtime** (add **14** + **16a** + **16b** = **17**) | | **17** | ° | ' | "  ☉ |

*If ET (7) is less than 12h:*

| | | | | | |
|---|---|---|---|---|---|
| 18 | ☽ **12h date of birth** (5 date) **18** | ° | ' | " | |
| 19 | ☽ **date of birth** (5 date)  **19** | ° | ' | " | |
| 20 | 12h **Travel** (**18 – 19 = 20**)  **20** | ° | ' | " | |
| 21 | ET (7)  **21** | h | m | s | |
| 22 | ☽ **Travel To Birthtime** (20, 21, Table VI) | | | | |
| 23 | ☽ **Longitude at Birthtime** (add **19** + **22a** + **22b** = **23**)  **23** | ° | ' | "  ☽ | |

*If ET (7) is greater than 12h:*

| | | | | | |
|---|---|---|---|---|---|
| 18 | ☽ **next day** (5 date+1d)  **18** | ° | ' | " | |
| 19 | ☽ **12h date of birth** (5 date)  **19** | ° | ' | " | |
| 20 | 12h **Travel** (**18 – 19 = 20**)  **20** | ° | ' | " | |
| 21 | ET Since Noon (**7 – 12h = 21**) **21** | h | m | s | |
| | **minutes**  **22a** | ° | ' | " | |
| | **hours**  **22b** | ° | ' | " | |

| | |
|---|---|
| 24 | **Longitude** 0h **After Birth** (5 date + 1d, Ephemeris) |
| 25 | **Longitude** 0h **Before** Birth ( 5 date, Ephemeris) |
| 26 | 24h **Travel** (Subtract **24 – 25 = 26**; If Retrograde, Subtract **25 – 24 = 26**) |
| 27 | **ET Travel** (7, 26, Table VII: minutes 27a, hours 27b, 27a + 27b = 27c) |
| 28 | **Longitude At Birthtime** (**25 + 27c = 28**; If Retrograde, **25 – 27c = 28**) |

| | Mean☊ | True☊ | ☿ | ♀ | ♂ | ♃ | ♄ | ♅ | ♆ | ♇ |
|---|---|---|---|---|---|---|---|---|---|---|---|
| 24 | | | | | | | | | | |
| 25 | | | | | | | | | | |
| 26 | | | | | | | | | | |
| 27a | | | | | | | | | | |
| 27b | | | | | | | | | | |
| 27c | | | | | | | | | | |
| 28 | | | | | | | | | | |
| | Mean☊ | True☊ | ☿ | ♀ | ♂ | ♃ | ♄ | ♅ | ♆ | ♇ |

# LOCATING HOUSE CUSPS

| | | | | |
|---|---|---|---|---|
| 29 **Local Sidereal Time (12)** | 29 | h | m | s |
| 30 **Earlier LST** (Table of Houses) | 30 | h | m | s |
| 31 **Later** LST (Table of Houses) | 31 | h | m | s |
| 32 **LST Increment** (Subtract **29 – 30 =32**) | 32 | | m | s  ΔLST |

| | | | | |
|---|---|---|---|---|
| 33 **Midheaven At Later LST** (Table of Houses) | 33 | ° | ' | |
| 34 **Midheaven At Earlier LST** (Table of Houses) | 34 | ° | ' | |
| 35 **4m Midheaven Increment** (subtract **33 – 34 = 35**) | 35 | ° | ' | |
| 36 **Midheaven Increment** (32, 35, Table XI) | 36 | ° | ' | |
| 37 **Midheaven At Birth LST** (add **34 + 36 = 37**) | 37 | ° | ' | MC |

| | | | | |
|---|---|---|---|---|
| 38 **Lower Latitude** (Table of Houses) | 38 | ° | ' | |
| 39 **Higher Latitude** (Table of Houses) | 39 | ° | ' | |
| 40 **Latitude Increment** (Subtract **Birth Latitude – 38 = 40**) | 40 | ° | ' | ΔLat |

41 **House Cusps at Later LST, Lower Latitude** (Table of Houses)
42 **House Cusps at Earlier LST, Lower Latitude** (Table of Houses)
43 **4m Cusp Intervals** (Subtract **41 – 42 = 43**)
44 **Cusp Increments** (32, 43, Table XI)
45 **House Cusps at Birth LST, Lower Latitude** (add **42 + 44 = 45**)

| | LST | Latitude | 11 | 12 | ASC | 2 | 3 |
|---|---|---|---|---|---|---|---|
| 41 | LATER | LOWER (38) | | | | | |
| 42 | EARLIER | | | | | | |
| 43 | 4m | ° | | | | | |
| 44 | LINE 32 | | | | | | |
| 45 | BIRTH | | | | | | |

46 **House Cusps at Later LST, Higher Latitude** (Table of Houses)
47 **House Cusps at Earlier LST, Higher Latitude** (Table of Houses)
48 **4m Cusp Intervals** (Subtract **46 – 47 = 48**)
49 **Cusp Increments** (32, 48, Table XI)
50 **House Cusps at Birth LST, Higher Latitude** (add **47 + 49 = 50**)

| | LST | Latitude | 11 | 12 | ASC | 2 | 3 |
|---|---|---|---|---|---|---|---|
| 46 | LATER | HIGHER (39) | | | | | |
| 47 | EARLIER | | | | | | |
| 48 | 4m | ° | | | | | |
| 49 | LINE 32 | | | | | | |
| 50 | BIRTH | | | | | | |

51 **1° Cusp Intervals**
   If **50** is greater than **45**, rewrite **45** below. Subtract **50 – 45 = 51**.
   If **50** is less than **45** mark **51** and **52** negative (–) for that house. Subtract **45 – 50 = 51**.
52 **Cusp Increments for Latitude** (40, 51, Table XII)
53 **House Cusps at Birth LST, Birth Latitude** (add **45 + 52 = 53**)

| | LST | Latitude | 11 | 12 | ASC | 2 | 3 |
|---|---|---|---|---|---|---|---|
| 45 | **BIRTH (29)** | LOWER | | | | | |
| 51 | | 1° | | | | | |
| 52 | h   m   s | LINE 40 | | | | | |
| 53 | | BIRTH | | | | | |
| | | | 11 | 12 | ASC | 2 | 3 |

## TIME CALCULATIONS

**1 Born** 8:22 **Am/Pm Zone** EASTERN **Date** MARCH 25, 1970

Using the procedure outlined on the worksheet, you can cast a chart with Sun and Moon positions accurate to the nearest second of arc, planet positions accurate to the nearest minute of arc, and house cusps accurate to the nearest three minutes of arc. Such precision is fu-

tile, however, if the original birth information is in error. Birthtime should be verified by official records – a birth certificate or hospital file. Parents' memories are notoriously unreliable.

**2 Place** HYANNIS, MA **Longitude** 70°W 15' **Latitude** 41°N 39'

If you do not find the longitude and latitude of the birthplace in the list of major cities at the back of this

book , consult *The American Atlas* or *The International Atlas*.

**3 Standard Time** (pm: + 12h, DST: – 1h) 3  8 h  22 m

**h** = hours
**m** = minutes

The recorded birthtime must be expressed as standard time, if it is not already, and in terms of the twenty-four-hour clock. This means you must add twelve hours if the birthtime is 1:00 pm or later, and also you must subtract one hour if Daylight Saving Time was in effect at

the time of birth. Remember that during World War II, 1942-45, the United States was on year-round Daylight Saving Time, called War Time. When in doubt, consult *The American Atlas* or *The International Atlas.*

**4 Time Zone Number** (Table I) 4  5 h
**5 Universal Time** (West+ East–) Greenwich date 5  13 h  22 m   **UT**

Universal time (UT) is the twenty-four-hour clock version of Greenwich Mean Time (GMT), the standard time of Great Britain, where the Greenwich Meridian, 0 longitude, is located. Time measurements in the earth sciences ordinarily use UT, as do astronomical tables.

Universal Time and all other standard times are forms of solar time in that they measure time by the changing relationship of the Sun to the meridian at a certain place on the Earth. The meridian of a place is the arc of the great circle that runs from the north point of the horizon to the zenith, directly overhead, to the south point of the horizon. At northern latitudes, when the Sun crosses the meridian, it is due south of the observer. In old books, the crossing of the meridian is called the Sun's "southing" and defines local noon.

The trouble with using the real Sun as the basis of timekeeping is that because of the elliptical shape of the Earth's orbit around the Sun, the Sun's apparent motion

is not constant. Time measurements using the southing of the Sun can vary by as much as fifteen minutes from measurements that use a constant clock. This became a problem with the invention of the mechanical clock, which was constant and could not easily be adjusted to fit the Sun's variations. So astronomers created a fictitious "mean Sun," which moves along the celestial equator at a constant rate. Noon local mean time then, is the southing of the mean Sun, which moves at the average rate of the true Sun and coincides with it twice a year.

In theory, every place on Earth could keep its own local mean time based on the angle between the local meridian and the mean Sun. In practice, the Earth has been divided into twenty-four time zones. Every place keeps the time of a nearby meridian of longitude, which is usually a multiple of 15 east or west of Greenwich. Most of these time zones are a whole number of hours ahead or behind Greenwich.

Table I (page 123) gives the number of hours for each time zone. The time in zones to the west of Greenwich is earlier than Greenwich time; therefore you add to get Greenwich time. Conversely, in zones to the east of Greenwich, you subtract the time-zone number given in Table I.

If a person is born near midnight standard time, adding or subtracting the time-zone number can put the birthtime into the preceding or following day. For example, if the birthtime is 11:15 pm eastern standard time

or 23h 15m, when we add the time-zone number 5, we get 28h 15m UT. What does that figure mean? It actually means 4h 15m of the following day. In other words, we must subtract twenty-four hours from the time and add one day to the date. The date on line 5 would then be March 26, 1970, even though the date in line 1 was March 25, 1970. That would be the date at Greenwich at the time of birth in Hyannis, Massachusetts. The corrected date on line 5 would be used from then on when you are consulting the ephemeris.

| | | | | | | |
|---|---|---|---|---|---|---|
| 6 | ΔT  (5 date, Table  IV) | 6 | | | *41* s | |
| 7 | **Ephemeris Time** (add **5** + **6** = **7**) | 7 | *13* h *22* m *41* s | | | ET |

s = seconds

The abbreviated directions on the worksheet are meant to be read, "Line 6 is for ΔT. You get it by taking the information on line 5 and going to Table IV. Line 7 is for ephemeris time. Add the values on lines 5 and 6 and write the sum on line 7."

Universal time, measured as it is by the angle between the mean Sun and the Greenwich meridian, would be perfect for astronomical and astrological purposes if the Earth turned at a perfectly uniform rate. However, because of earthquakes and other disturbances, the Earth does not rotate uniformly. Thus UT clocks, especially the newer astronomical clocks that keep time extremely precisely by measuring the disintegration of atomic nuclei, have to be reset when the Earth is fast or slow. The astronomical calculations that go into an ephemeris presuppose a constant time, independent of the Earth's variations. So astronomers have created such a time. Ephemeris time is Universal time as it would be if the Earth had rotated uniformly since the beginning of the century. It is an ideal mean solar time, used in all modern ephemerides. The difference between ET and UT, ΔT, cannot be predicted exactly, because it is the result of observations. It can only be estimated for the future. Thus Table IV (page 124), which gives ΔT in this book ends with the year 1997, with ET differing from UT by about 63 seconds.

Planetary calculations should be done in ET because the planets move independently of the Earth. House cusps, on the other hand, are closely related to the rotation of the Earth and should, therefore, be calculated based on UT. Calculating an entire chart in ET is a common error, which results in slightly misplaced house cusps.

The difference between UT and ET is only worth bothering with if you are going to locate the Sun and Moon as accurately as possible, perhaps for the purpose of solar and lunar returns. If you are satisfied with accuracy to the nearest minute of arc, forty-odd seconds of birthtime is not significant.

Universal time and ephemeris time are solar times, but to measure planetary motion, it is convenient to have a time that is related not to the Sun but to the zodiac: Sidereal Time. Instead of measuring the angle from the Sun to the meridian, Sidereal Time (ST) measures the angle from the vernal equinox (0° Aries) to the meridian. Thus at 0h 0m ST, 0° Aries is on the meridian or "southing." At 1h 0m ST, 0° Aries is 15° west of the meridian.

In the time it takes the Earth to revolve around the Sun once, a solar year, the Earth rotates on its axis 366.2422 times. Thus to us on Earth it appears that the zodiac and vernal equinox, our reference point on the zodiac, go around the Earth 366.2422 times a year. The Sun, however, rises, crosses the meridian and sets only 365.2422 times a year. Why? The Sun's apparent yearly motion through the zodiac is opposed to its apparent daily motion across the sky. Thus one yearly motion "undoes" one daily motion. Consequently a year has 366.2422 sidereal days and only 365.2422 solar days or exactly one less; a sidereal day is shorter than a solar day by 3 minutes 56 seconds; and a sidereal hour is shorter than a solar hour by 9.86 seconds. Universal Time and Sidereal Time are together on September 21 every year. Then ST pulls ahead of UT at the rate of 9.86 seconds per hour of UT until a year later on September 21, ST is exactly twenty-four hours ahead.

| | | | | |
|---|---|---|---|---|
| | 5 | *13* h | *22* m | UT |
| | 6 | | *41* s | |
| | 7 | *13* h | *22* m *41* s | ET |
| 8 **Greenwich Sidereal Time 00h** (Ephemeris) | 8 | *12* h | *8* m *9* s | |
| 9 **Solar-Correction** (5, Table II) | 9 | | *2* m *12* s | |
| 10 **Greenwich Sidereal Time** (add 5 + 8 + 9 = 10) | 10 | *25* h | *32* m *21* s | |

## MARCH 1970
### LONGITUDE

| Day | Sid.Time | ☉ | 0 hr ☽ | Noon |
|---|---|---|---|---|
| 1 Su | 10 33 32 | 9♓59 14 | 8♐38 39 | 15♐2 |
| 2 M | 10 37 29 | 10 59 27 | 22 26 15 | 29 2 |
| 3 Tu | 10 41 25 | 11 59 39 | 6♑35 14 | 13♑4 |
| 4 W | 10 45 22 | 12 59 49 | 21 4 6 | 28 2 |
| 5 Th | 10 49 18 | 13 59 57 | 5♒49 17 | 13♒1 |
| 6 F | 10 53 15 | 15 0 4 | 20 45 4 | 28 1 |
| 7 Sa | 10 57 12 | 16 0 9 | 5♓44 1 | 13♓1 |
| 8 Su | 11 1 8 | 17 0 12 | 20 37 51 | 28 |
| 9 M | 11 5 5 | 18 0 13 | 5♈18 32 | 12♈3 |
| 10 Tu | 11 9 1 | 19 0 12 | 19 39 32 | 26 4 |
| 11 W | 11 12 58 | 20 0 9 | 3♉36 27 | 10♉2 |
| 12 Th | 11 16 54 | 21 0 4 | 17 7 20 | 23 4 |
| 13 F | 11 20 51 | 21 59 57 | 0♊12 36 | 6♊3 |
| 14 Sa | 11 24 47 | 22 59 48 | 12 54 31 | 19 |
| 15 Su | 11 28 44 | 23 59 36 | 25 16 38 | 1♋2 |
| 16 M | 11 32 41 | 24 59 23 | 7♋23 19 | 13 2 |
| 17 Tu | 11 36 37 | 25 59 7 | 19 19 15 | 25 1 |
| 18 W | 11 40 34 | 26 58 48 | 1♌9 7 | 7♌ |
| 19 Th | 11 44 30 | 27 58 28 | 12 57 18 | 18 5 |
| 20 F | 11 48 27 | 28 58 5 | 24 47 45 | 0♍4 |
| 21 Sa | 11 52 23 | 29 57 40 | 6♍43 53 | 12 4 |
| 22 Su | 11 56 20 | 0♈57 13 | 18 48 26 | 24 5 |
| 23 M | 12 0 16 | 1 56 44 | 1♎3 30 | 7♎1 |
| 24 Tu | 12 4 13 | 2 56 13 | 13 30 34 | 19 4 |
| 25 W | 12 8 9 | 3 55 40 | 26 10 33 | 2♏3 |
| 26 Th | 12 12 6 | 4 55 5 | 9♏3 58 | 15 3 |
| 27 F | 12 16 3 | 5 54 28 | 22 10 58 | 28 4 |
| 28 Sa | 12 19 59 | 6 53 49 | 5♐31 37 | 12♐1 |
| 29 Su | 12 23 56 | 7 53 9 | 19 5 51 | 25 5 |
| 30 M | 12 27 52 | 8 52 27 | 2♑53 28 | 9♑5 |
| 31 Tu | 12 31 49 | 9 51 43 | 16 54 3 | 23 5 |

*The ephemeris gives Greenwich Sidereal Time
at 0h 0m UT at the beginning of every day.*

The ephemeris gives ST for 0h 0m 0s UT at the beginning of every day. Therefore, you must add 9.86 seconds for every hour of UT in order to find the correct ST. Table II (page 123) gives this correction. Read across the top to find the column for the number of hours of UT; then read down that column to the line for the number of minutes of UT. (See illustration below.) Enter the correction on line 9.

Sidereal Time, because it measures the angle between the local meridian and 0° Aries, is different for different longitudes. Since Sidereal Time has no time zones, the difference between Sidereal Time at any place and Greenwich Sidereal Time depends on the longitude of the place. Longitude divides the Earth into 360°; time measurement divides its rotation into 24 hours. Therefore, 360 ÷ 24 or 15° equals one hour. The longitude correction is given along with longitude and latitude for major cities of the United States and the world in the back of this book. If the birthplace is not listed there, use Table III (page 124). Table III gives the correction for each degree and each minute of longitude. If the longitude of birth is east of Greenwich, add the correction; if it is west, subtract it. The result is Local Sidereal Time of birth or LST. (See example on page 7.)

### Table II Solar-Sidereal Correction

| MIN | 0h m s | 1h m s | 2h m s | 3h m s | 4h m s | 5h m s | 6h m s | 7h m s | 8h m s | 9h m s | 10h m s | 11h m s | 12h m s | 13h m s | 14h m s | 15h m s | 16h m s | 17h m s | 18h m s | 19h m s | 20h m s | 21h m s | 22h m s | 23h m s |
|---|---|---|---|---|---|---|---|---|---|---|---|---|---|---|---|---|---|---|---|---|---|---|---|---|
| 0 | 0 0 | 0 10 | 0 20 | 0 30 | 0 39 | 0 49 | 0 59 | 1 9 | 1 19 | 1 29 | 1 39 | 1 48 | 1 58 | 2 8 | 2 18 | 2 28 | 2 38 | 2 48 | 2 57 | 3 7 | 3 17 | 3 27 | 3 37 | 3 47 |
| 1 | 0 0 | 0 10 | 0 20 | 0 30 | 0 40 | 0 49 | 0 59 | 1 9 | 1 19 | 1 29 | 1 39 | 1 49 | 1 58 | 2 8 | 2 18 | 2 28 | 2 38 | 2 48 | 2 58 | 3 7 | 3 17 | 3 27 | 3 37 | 3 47 |
| 2 | 0 0 | 0 10 | 0 20 | 0 30 | 0 40 | 0 50 | 0 59 | 1 9 | 1 19 | 1 29 | 1 39 | 1 49 | 1 59 | 2 8 | 2 18 | 2 28 | 2 38 | 2 48 | 2 58 | 3 8 | 3 17 | 3 27 | 3 37 | 3 47 |
| 3 | 0 0 | 0 10 | 0 20 | 0 30 | 0 40 | 0 50 | 0 60 | 1 9 | 1 19 | 1 29 | 1 39 | 1 49 | 1 59 | 2 9 | 2 18 | 2 28 | 2 38 | 2 48 | 2 58 | 3 8 | 3 18 | 3 27 | 3 37 | 3 47 |
| 20 | 0 3 | 0 13 | 0 23 | 0 33 | 0 43 | 0 53 | 1 2 | 1 12 | 1 22 | 1 32 | 1 42 | 1 52 | 2 2 | 2 11 | 2 21 | 2 31 | 2 41 | 2 51 | 3 1 | 3 11 | 3 20 | 3 30 | 3 40 | 3 50 |
| 21 | 0 3 | 0 13 | 0 23 | 0 33 | 0 43 | 0 53 | 1 3 | 1 12 | 1 22 | 1 32 | 1 42 | 1 52 | 2 2 | 2 12 | 2 21 | 2 31 | 2 41 | 2 51 | 3 1 | 3 11 | 3 21 | 3 30 | 3 40 | 3 50 |
| 22 | 0 4 | 0 13 | 0 23 | 0 33 | 0 43 | 0 53 | 1 3 | 1 13 | 1 22 | 1 32 | 1 43 | 1 52 | 2 2 | 2 12 | 2 22 | 2 31 | 2 41 | 2 51 | 3 1 | 3 11 | 3 21 | 3 31 | 3 40 | 3 50 |
| 23 | 0 4 | 0 14 | 0 24 | 0 33 | 0 43 | 0 53 | 1 3 | 1 13 | 1 23 | 1 32 | 1 42 | 1 52 | 2 2 | 2 12 | 2 22 | 2 32 | 2 41 | 2 51 | 3 1 | 3 11 | 3 21 | 3 31 | 3 41 | 3 50 |
| 24 | 0 4 | 0 14 | 0 24 | 0 34 | 0 43 | 0 53 | 1 3 | 1 13 | 1 23 | 1 33 | 1 43 | 1 52 | 2 2 | 2 12 | 2 22 | 2 32 | 2 42 | 2 51 | 3 1 | 3 11 | 3 21 | 3 31 | 3 41 | 3 50 |
| 25 | 0 4 | 0 14 | 0 24 | 0 34 | 0 44 | 0 53 | 1 3 | 1 13 | 1 23 | 1 33 | 1 43 | 1 53 | 2 2 | 2 12 | 2 22 | 2 32 | 2 42 | 2 52 | 3 2 | 3 11 | 3 21 | 3 31 | 3 41 | 3 51 |

*Table II, Solar-Sidereal correction, gives the difference between Solar and Sidereal Time since midnight UT before birth, 9.86 seconds per hour of UT.*

| | | | | | | | | |
|---|---|---|---|---|---|---|---|---|
| | | | | | | | 10 _25_ h _32_ m _21_ s | |
| **11 Longitude Correction** (Table III) | **degrees: 11a** | _4_ h _40_ m | | | | | | |
| | **minutes: 11b** | h _1_ m _0_ s | | | | | | |
| | **total** (add **11a** + **11b** = **11c**) | | | | | 11c _4_ h _41_ m _0_ s | | |
| (WEST: Subtract **10** – **11c** = **12**; East: add **10** + **11c** = **12**) | | | | | | | | |
| **12 Local Sidereal Time** | | | | | | 12 _20_ h _51_ m _21_ s | **LST** | |

## Direct Method

This method of calculating local Sidereal Time, called the direct method because it dispenses with local mean time, was first worked out by Charles Carter. The more cumbersome traditional methods are holdovers from the days before standard time zones, when all times were local. The direct method can be used even when birthtime is given in local mean time: simply reverse the longitude correction to get back to UT and proceed with steps **6** through **12**.

## Rounding Off

Although we began with a birthtime accurate only to the nearest minute, we now have a Local Sidereal Time accurate to the nearest second. In truth, 8:22 am means some time between 8:21:30 and 8:22:30. Consequently our LST is really some time between 20:50:51 and 20:51:51. Should LST then be rounded off to the nearest minute? No, because LST is only an intermediate value on the way to locating house cusps. Rounding off an intermediate value has the effect of increasing the error introduced by the approximation of birthtime. When you have the final house cusps, however, remember that they are accurate only to within ± seven minutes of arc, which is the average error caused by a one-minute error of birthtime. Only a rectified chart can be assumed to have house cusps accurate to the nearest minute of arc. Not even the chart of a birth timed with a stopwatch qualifies, because astrologers are still uncertain about what a precise moment of birth is. In spite of these uncertainties, our task here is to learn the techniques of calculation, so we will assume that birthtime is precisely 8:22:00 am EST.

## Sexagesimal Arithmetic

In casting a horoscope, you often have to add or subtract sexagesimal numbers, quantities counted by sixties, in the form of hours, minutes and seconds or degrees, minutes and seconds. It is a simple process that often can be done mentally. Perhaps the greatest problems to overcome the habits of a lifetime and remember to do it correctly.

The principle involved is the same as that used in ordinary decimal addition and subtraction: if you add and subtract equal quantities to and from a quantity, the re-

## Table III
## Longitude Correction

| | DEGREES | | | | | | MINUTES | |
|---|---|---|---|---|---|---|---|---|
| ° | h m | ° | h m | ° | h m | ′ | m s | |
| 1 | 0 4 | 61 | 4 4 | 121 | 8 4 | 1 | 0 4 | |
| 2 | 0 8 | 62 | 4 8 | 122 | 8 8 | 2 | 0 8 | |
| 3 | 0 12 | 63 | 4 12 | 123 | 8 12 | 3 | 0 12 | |
| 4 | 0 16 | 64 | 4 16 | 124 | 8 16 | 4 | 0 16 | |
| 5 | 0 20 | 65 | 4 20 | 125 | 8 20 | 5 | 0 20 | |
| 6 | 0 24 | 66 | 4 24 | 126 | 8 24 | 6 | 0 24 | |
| 7 | 0 28 | 67 | 4 28 | 127 | 8 28 | 7 | 0 28 | |
| 8 | 0 32 | 68 | 4 32 | 128 | 8 32 | 8 | 0 32 | |
| 9 | 0 36 | 69 | 4 36 | 129 | 8 36 | 9 | 0 36 | |
| 10 | 0 40 | 70 | 4 40 | 130 | 8 40 | 10 | 0 40 | |
| 11 | 0 44 | 71 | 4 44 | 131 | 8 44 | 11 | 0 44 | |
| 12 | 0 48 | 72 | 4 48 | 132 | 8 48 | 12 | 0 48 | |
| 13 | 0 52 | 73 | 4 52 | 133 | 8 52 | 13 | 0 52 | |
| 14 | 0 56 | 74 | 4 56 | 134 | 8 56 | 14 | 0 56 | |
| 15 | 1 0 | 75 | 5 0 | 135 | 9 0 | 15 | 1 0 | |

*Table III, Longitude Correction, gives the difference between Local Sidereal Time and Greenwich Sidereal Time, a function of the difference in longitude between the birthplace and Greenwich.*

sult is identical to the quantity you started with. In our example above, we had to do the following subtraction:

$$25h \quad 32m \quad 21s$$
$$-4h \quad 41m \quad 0s$$

How can we subtract 41 from 32m? By first adding and subtracting equal quantities.

$$25h \quad 32m \quad 21s$$
$$\quad \quad +60m$$
$$-1h$$
$$\overline{24h \quad 92m \quad 21s}$$

Because 1h = 60m, 25h 32m 21s = 24h 92m 21s. Now we can subtract.

$$24h \quad 92m \quad 21s$$
$$-4h \quad 41m \quad 0s$$
$$\overline{20h \quad 51m \quad 21s}$$

You can see that the principle is the same as the one we use when we "borrow" in ordinary subtraction.

Suppose that instead of subtracting, we had to add 4h 41m 0s.

| | | |
|---|---|---|
| 25h | 32m | 21s |
| +4h | 41m | 0s |
| 29h | 73m | 21s |

First we would deal with the 73m.

| | | |
|---|---|---|
| 29h | 73m | 21s |
| | − 60m | |
| +1h | | |
| 30h | 13m | 21s |

Now what about the 30h?

| | | | |
|---|---|---|---|
| | 30h | 13m | 21s |
| | -24h | | |
| +1d | | | |
| 1d | 6h | 13m | 21s |

And now what about the extra day? If we are at line 5, Universal Time, or above, we have to add the one day to the date of birth so that we go into the ephemeris with the correct date. That date matters because Greenwich Sidereal Time and the positions of the planets are different on different days. But Sidereal Time is used only for location house cusps, which are the same if the LST is the same, regardless of date. Therefore we discard the extra day and use 6h 31m 21s as our LST.

The identity principle applies to adding and subtracting angles as well. For example.

| | | | |
|---|---|---|---|
| 29° ♒ | 41' | 33" |
| + 2° | 30' | 48" |
| 31 ° ♒ | 71' | 81" |
| | | +1' | − 60" |
| +1 | −60' | |
| 32° ♒ | 12' | 21" |

This result is satisfactory except for the fact that Aquarius has only 30 degrees. So we must subtract 30 degrees and add one sign. The result is 2° ♓ 12' 21".

## LOCATING THE PLANETS

The ephemeris gives the longitudes of the Sun and the planets at midnight (0h) at the beginning of every day and the Moon at midnight and noon. The ephemeris does not give the position of any planet at any other time. So unless you are casting the chart for someone born at midnight, you have to interpolate.

The underlying principle of interpolation is quite simple. Assuming that any body, an automobile, an airplane or a planet, is moving at a constant speed, if you know how far it traveled in one period of time, you can deduce how far it traveled in another period of time. If in two hours a car goes 100 miles, in one hour it will go 50 miles because

$$\frac{1}{2} = \frac{50}{100}$$

The assumption of constant speed is much more realistic when applied to planets than to automobiles. Interpolation takes the form "If Venus moved 1° 14' in twenty-four hours, how far did it move in nine hours and thirteen minutes?" The answer is: twenty-eight minutes of arc because

$$\frac{9h\ 13m}{24h} = \frac{28}{1°\ 14'}$$

If Venus was at 8°♓10' at midnight, where was it at 9h 13m? Answer: 8°♓38' because 8°♓10' + 28' = 8°♓38'. In principle, that is all there is to it. The rest is details.

| | | |
|---|---|---|
| 13 ☉ **Longitude** 0h **After Birth** (5 date + 1d, Ephemeris) | 13 | 4°T55' 3" |
| 14 ☉ **Longitude** 0h **Before Birth** (5 date, Ephemeris) | 14 | 3°T55' 38" |
| 15 24h **Travel** (Subtract **13 – 14 = 15**) | 15 | °59' 25" |

**d** = day

By subtracting the Sun's 0h longitude at the beginning of the date of birth (given in the ephemeris) from its 0h longitude at the beginning of the following day, we find out how far the Sun traveled in twenty-four hours. Be sure to use the date from line 5 if it is different from the original birthdate.

Do not round off the Sun's twenty-four-hour travel. It is desirable to have the Sun's position accurate to within a second or two of arc in order to be able to calculate solar return charts.

## MARCH 1970
### LONGITUDE

| Day | Sid.Time | ☉ | 0 hr ☽ | Noon ☽ | True ☊ | ☿ | ♀ | ♂ | ♃ | ♄ | ♅ | ♆ | ♇ |
|---|---|---|---|---|---|---|---|---|---|---|---|---|---|
| 1 Su | 10 33 32 | 9♓59 14 | 8♐38 39 | 15♐29 46 | 11♍49.9 | 22♒9.6 | 18♒29.7 | 25♈38.7 | 5♏50.4 | 4♉48.4 | 7♎51.6 | 0♐53.4 | 26♍29.5 |
| 2 M | 10 37 29 | 10 59 27 | 22 26 15 | 29 28 7 | 11D49.9 | 23 44.8 | 19 44.6 | 26 21.9 | 5R48.6 | 4 54.0 | 7R49.4 | 0 53.4 | 26R27.9 |
| | | | | | | | | | | | | | |
| 21 Sa | 11 52 23 | 29 57 40 | 6♍43 53 | 12 44 57 | 11R51.6 | 27 23.0 | 13 23.6 | 9 55.4 | 4 40.7 | 6 50.9 | 7 3.3 | 0 48.3 | 25 57.3 |
| 22 Su | 11 56 20 | 0♈57 13 | 18 48 26 | 24 54 32 | 11 51.5 | 29 20.6 | 14 38.0 | 10 37.8 | 4 35.5 | 6 57.6 | 7 0.7 | 0 47.7 | 25 55.7 |
| 23 M | 12 0 16 | 1 56 44 | 1♎3 30 | 7♎15 28 | 11 50.4 | 1♈19.3 | 15 52.4 | 11 20.1 | 4 30.2 | 7 4.4 | 6 58.1 | 0 47.1 | 25 54.1 |
| 24 Tu | 12 4 13 | 2 56 13 | 13 30 34 | 19 48 54 | 11 48.3 | 3 19.0 | 17 6.8 | 12 2.4 | 4 24.7 | 7 11.2 | 6 55.5 | 0 46.4 | 25 52.5 |
| 25 W | 12 8 9 | 3 55 40 | 26 10 33 | 2♏35 34 | 11 45.3 | 5 19.5 | 18 21.1 | 12 44.7 | 4 19.1 | 7 18.0 | 6 52.9 | 0 45.7 | 25 50.9 |
| 26 Th | 12 12 6 | 4 55 5 | 9♏3 58 | 15 35 46 | 11 41.7 | 7 20.7 | 19 35.4 | 13 26.9 | 4 13.3 | 7 24.9 | 6 50.3 | 0 45.0 | 25 49.2 |
| 27 F | 12 16 3 | 5 54 28 | 22 10 58 | 28 49 36 | 11 38.0 | 9 22.6 | 20 49.7 | 14 9.1 | 4 7.4 | 7 31.8 | 6 47.7 | 0 44.3 | 25 47.6 |
| 28 Sa | 12 19 59 | 6 53 49 | 5♐31 37 | 12♐17 3 | 11 34.8 | 11 24.9 | 22 3.9 | 14 51.3 | 4 1.4 | 7 38.8 | 6 45.1 | 0 43.5 | 25 46.0 |

*The ephemeris gives the longitudes of the Sun, Moon and planets at 0h 0m 0s at the beginning of each day of the month.*

| | | | |
|---|---|---|---|
| 16 ET Travel (7, 15 Table V) | minutes | 16a | °0' 57" |
| | Hours | 16b | °32' 11" |

Table V, Diurnal Motion of the Sun, has two parts. The upper part gives the Sun's motion for time changes of one to 60 minutes. The bottom part gives the same thing for one to twenty-four hours. The numbers at the head of each column across the top of the page show the twenty-four hour motion of the Sun at intervals of two seconds of arc. In this section, we go down the column for 59' 24", that value being nearest to our actual twenty-four-hour travel of 59' 25". Then reading across the line for 23 minutes, which is closest to 22m 41s, we find 0'57" and enter it on line **16a**. Continuing down the 59'24" column into the hours section, we find the line for 13h and on it 32'11". We enter that on line **16b**.

### Table V Diurnal Motion of the Sun

| TIME | 59 12 | 59 14 | 59 16 | 59 18 | 59 20 | 59 22 | 59 24 | 59 26 | 59 28 | 59 30 | 59 32 | 59 34 | 59 36 | 59 38 | 59 40 | 59 42 | 59 44 | 59 46 | 59 48 | 59 50 |
|---|---|---|---|---|---|---|---|---|---|---|---|---|---|---|---|---|---|---|---|---|
| M 1 | 2 | 2 | 2 | 2 | 2 | 2 | 2 | 2 | 2 | 2 | 2 | 2 | 2 | 2 | 2 | 2 | 2 | 2 | 2 | 2 |
| I 2 | 5 | 5 | 5 | 5 | 5 | 5 | 5 | 5 | 5 | 5 | 5 | 5 | 5 | 5 | 5 | 5 | 5 | 5 | 5 | 5 |
| N 3 | 7 | 7 | 7 | 7 | 7 | 7 | 7 | 7 | 7 | 7 | 7 | 7 | 7 | 7 | 7 | 7 | 7 | 7 | 7 | 7 |
| U 4 | 10 | 10 | 10 | 10 | 10 | 10 | 10 | 10 | 10 | 10 | 10 | 10 | 10 | 10 | 10 | 10 | 10 | 10 | 10 | 10 |
| T ... | | | | | | | | | | | | | | | | | | | | |
| E 21 | 52 | 52 | 52 | 52 | 52 | 52 | 52 | 52 | 52 | 52 | 52 | 52 | 52 | 52 | 52 | 52 | 52 | 52 | 52 | 52 |
| S 22 | 54 | 54 | 54 | 54 | 54 | 54 | 54 | 54 | 55 | 55 | 55 | 55 | 55 | 55 | 55 | 55 | 55 | 55 | 55 | 55 |
| 23 | 57 | 57 | 57 | 57 | 57 | 57 | 57 | 57 | 57 | 57 | 57 | 57 | 57 | 57 | 57 | 57 | 57 | 57 | 57 | 57 |
| 24 | 59 | 59 | 59 | 59 | 59 | 59 | 59 | 59 | 59 | 1 0 | 1 0 | 1 0 | 1 0 | 1 0 | 1 0 | 1 0 | 1 0 | 1 0 | 1 0 | 1 0 |
| 25 | 1 2 | 1 2 | 1 2 | 1 2 | 1 2 | 1 2 | 1 2 | 1 2 | 1 2 | 1 2 | 1 2 | 1 2 | 1 2 | 1 2 | 1 2 | 1 2 | 1 2 | 1 2 | 1 2 | 1 2 |
| H 11 | 27 8 | 27 9 | 27 10 | 27 11 | 27 12 | 27 13 | 27 14 | 27 14 | 27 15 | 27 16 | 27 17 | 27 18 | 27 19 | 27 20 | 27 21 | 27 22 | 27 23 | 27 24 | 27 25 | 27 25 |
| O 12 | 29 36 | 29 37 | 29 38 | 29 39 | 29 41 | 29 42 | 29 43 | 29 44 | 29 45 | 29 46 | 29 47 | 29 48 | 29 49 | 29 50 | 29 51 | 29 52 | 29 53 | 29 54 | 29 55 | 29 55 |
| U 13 | 32 4 | 32 5 | 32 6 | 32 7 | 32 8 | 32 9 | 32 11 | 32 12 | 32 13 | 32 14 | 32 15 | 32 16 | 32 17 | 32 18 | 32 19 | 32 20 | 32 21 | 32 22 | 32 24 | 32 25 |
| R 14 | 34 32 | 34 33 | 34 34 | 34 36 | 34 37 | 34 38 | 34 39 | 34 9 | 34 43 | 34 44 | 34 46 | 34 47 | 34 48 | 34 50 | 34 51 | 34 52 | 34 53 | 34 54 | | |
| S 15 | 37 0 | 37 1 | 37 3 | 37 4 | 37 5 | 37 6 | 37 8 | 37 9 | 37 10 | 37 11 | 37 13 | 37 14 | 37 15 | 37 16 | 37 18 | 37 19 | 37 20 | 37 21 | 37 23 | 37 24 |

*Table V, Diurnal Motion of the Sun, gives the motion of the Sun between 0h 0m 0s and birthtime.*

Table V simply solves the following proportion for you.

$$\frac{\text{ET travel}}{\text{24h travel}} = \frac{\text{ET}}{\text{24h}}$$

In our example,

$$\frac{\text{ET travel}}{59' \ 25''} = \frac{13h \ 22m \ 41s}{24h}$$

### Direct Calculation

Some may prefer to do planetary positions on a calculator or by hand. First translate sexagesimal numbers into decimal numbers by dividing the appropriate parts by 60. ≅ means "is approximately equal to."

$$25 \div 60 \cong .42$$
$$59' \ 25'' \cong 59.42'$$
$$41 \div 60 \cong .7$$
$$22m \ 41s \cong 22.7m$$
$$22.7 \div 60 \cong .38$$
$$13h \ 22.7m \cong 13.38h$$

$$\text{ET travel} = \frac{13.38}{24} \times 59.42'$$
$$= .5575 \times 59.42'$$
$$\cong 33.13'$$
$$.13 \times 60 \cong 8$$
$$33.13' \cong 33' \ 8''$$

You will recall that using Table V we got 0' 57" and 32' 11". Together they add up to 33'8" or exactly the same result.

### Logarithms

The traditional method of interpolating planetary positions is by means of logarithms or "logs." What logs do is convert all multiplications to additions and all divisions to subtractions.

To calculate the longitude of the Sun or of the other planets by means of logs, we must find the log of the time ratio, which is constant for all planets in a chart except the Moon, and add it to the log of the twenty-four-hour travel of the planet. We get the log of the time ratio from Table IX, Diurnal Motion Logarithms, 0 to 24 hours. In our example ET is 13h 22m 41s. We read across to the column for 13h and down to the line for 23m, the closest value to 22m41s. The number we find there is the log of 13h 23m ÷ 24h, .25365. We get the log of the twenty-four-hour travel of the Sun, 0° 59' 5" in our example from Table X, Diurnal Motion Logarithms, 0 to 2 Hours/Degrees, by reading across the top to the column for 0° 59' and down to the line for 25". Where they meet we find 1.38445. Adding the two logs we get

$$
\begin{array}{lll}
\log 13h \ 23m \div 24h & = & .25365 \\
\log 0° \ 59' \ 25'' & = & 1.38445 + \\
\hline
& & 1.63810
\end{array}
$$

Working Table X backwards we find that 1.63810 is the log of 0° 33' 8". This is the same as the result we got using the two previous methods.

| | | | | | |
|---|---|---|---|---|---|
| | 14 | 3 | °♈ 55' | 38" | |
| | 15 | | ° 59' | 25" | |
| minutes | 16a | | ° 0' | 57" | |
| hours | 16b | | ° 32' | 11" | |

**17 ☉ Longitude At Birthtime** (add **14 + 16a + 16b =17**)     17   4 °♈ 28'   46 "   ☉

Whatever method you use to calculate the Sun's ET travel, you must add it to the Sun's position before birth to get the Sun's birthtime position.

| | If ET (7) is less than 12h: | | | | | If ET (7) is greater than 12h: | | | | |
|---|---|---|---|---|---|---|---|---|---|---|
| 18 | D 12h date of birth (5 date) | 18 | ° | ' | " | 18 | D next day (5 date + 1d) | 18 | 9 °M 3' 36 " |
| 19 | D date of birth (5 date) | 19 | ° | ' | " | 19 | D 12h date of birth (5 date) | 19 | 2 M 35 13 " |
| 20 | 12h Travel (18 − 19 = 20) | 20 | ° | ' | " | 20 | 12h Travel (18 − 19 = 20) | 20 | 6 ° 28' 23 " |
| 21 | ET (7) | 21 | h | m | s | 21 | ET Since Noon (7 − 12h = 21) | 21 | / h 22m 41s |
| 22 | D Travel To Birthtime (20, 21, Table VI) | | | | | | minutes 22a | ° | 12 ' 24 " |
| | | | | | | | hours 22b | ° | 32 ' 20 " |

Because the apparent motion of the Moon is faster and more erratic than that of any other planets, the ephemeris gives the Moon's position at twelve-hour instead of twenty-four-hour intervals. To find the Moon's position at birth, we must interpolate between midnight and noon if the birth took place in the morning (Universal Time) or between noon and midnight for an afternoon birth. Otherwise, the process is exactly the same as the one we followed in determining the Sun's position.

The 0h D column of the ephemeris gives the 0h position of the Moon at the beginning of each day. The noon D column gives the Moon's noon position for that day.

For a morning birth, ET less than 12h, use the left side of the worksheet. Go into Table VI (page 131) with ET and the twelve-hour travel of the Moon between 0h and noon of the date of birth.

For an afternoon birth, ET greater than 12h, use the right side of the worksheet. Go into Table VI with the ET time elapsed between noon and ET (ET - 12h) and the twelve-hour travel of the Moon between noon and 0h of the following day.

In our example, ET is 13h 22m41s, which is greater than 12h, so we use the right side of the worksheet.

## Table VI Semidiurnal Motion of the Moon

| TIME | 6° 25' | 6° 26' | 6° 27' | 6° 28' | 6° 29' | 6° 30' | 6° 31' | 6° 32' | 6° 33' | 6° 34' | 6° 35' | 6° 36' | 6° 37' | 6° 38' | 6° 39' |
|---|---|---|---|---|---|---|---|---|---|---|---|---|---|---|---|
| | ° ' | ° ' | ° ' | ° ' | ° ' | ° ' | ° ' | ° ' | ° ' | ° ' | ° ' | ° ' | ° ' | ° ' | ° ' |
| M 1 | 0 32 | 0 32 | 0 32 | 0 32 | 0 32 | 0 33 | 0 33 | 0 33 | 0 33 | 0 33 | 0 33 | 0 33 | 0 33 | 0 33 | 0 33 |
| I 2 | 1 4 | 1 4 | 1 5 | 1 5 | 1 5 | 1 5 | 1 5 | 1 5 | 1 6 | 1 6 | 1 6 | 1 6 | 1 6 | 1 6 | 1 7 |
| N 3 | 1 36 | 1 37 | 1 37 | 1 37 | 1 37 | 1 38 | 1 38 | 1 38 | 1 38 | 1 39 | 1 39 | 1 39 | 1 39 | 1 40 | 1 40 |
| U 4 | | | | | | | | | | | | | | | |
| T — | | | | | | | | | | | | | | | |
| E — | | | | | | | | | | | | | | | |
| S 21 | 11 14 | 11 16 | 11 17 | 11 19 | 11 21 | 11 23 | 11 24 | 11 26 | 11 28 | 11 30 | 11 31 | 11 33 | 11 35 | 11 37 | 11 38 |
| 22 | 11 46 | 11 48 | 11 50 | 11 51 | 11 53 | 11 55 | 11 57 | 11 59 | 12 1 | 12 2 | 12 4 | 12 6 | 12 8 | 12 10 | 12 12 |
| 23 | 12 18 | 12 20 | 12 22 | 12 24 | 12 26 | 12 28 | 12 29 | 12 31 | 12 33 | 12 35 | 12 37 | 12 39 | 12 41 | 12 43 | 12 45 |
| 24 | 12 50 | 12 52 | 12 54 | 12 56 | 12 58 | 13 0 | 13 2 | 13 4 | 13 6 | 13 8 | 13 10 | 13 12 | 13 14 | 13 16 | 13 18 |
| 25 | 13 22 | 13 24 | 13 26 | 13 28 | 13 30 | 13 33 | 13 35 | 13 37 | 13 39 | 13 41 | 13 43 | 13 45 | 13 47 | 13 49 | 13 51 |
| H 1 | 32 5 | 32 10 | 32 15 | 32 20 | 32 25 | 32 30 | 32 35 | 32 40 | 32 45 | 32 50 | 32 55 | 33 0 | 33 5 | 33 10 | 33 15 |
| O 2 | 1 4 10 | 1 4 20 | 1 4 30 | 1 4 40 | 1 4 50 | 1 5 0 | 1 5 10 | 1 5 20 | 1 5 30 | 1 5 40 | 1 5 50 | 1 6 0 | 1 6 10 | 1 6 20 | 1 6 30 |
| U 3 | 1 36 15 | 1 36 30 | 1 36 45 | 1 37 0 | 1 37 15 | 1 37 30 | 1 37 45 | 1 38 0 | 1 38 15 | 1 38 30 | 1 38 45 | 1 39 0 | 1 39 15 | 1 39 30 | 1 39 45 |
| R 4 | 2 8 20 | 2 8 40 | 2 9 0 | 2 9 20 | 2 9 40 | 2 10 0 | 2 10 20 | 2 10 40 | 2 11 0 | 2 11 20 | 2 11 40 | 2 12 0 | 2 12 20 | 2 12 40 | 2 13 0 |
| S 5 | 2 40 25 | 2 40 50 | 2 41 15 | 2 41 40 | 2 42 5 | 2 42 30 | 2 42 55 | 2 43 20 | 2 43 45 | 2 44 10 | 2 44 35 | 2 45 0 | 2 45 25 | 2 45 50 | 2 46 15 |

*Table VI, Semidiurnal Motion of the Moon, gives the Moon from noon or midnight, whichever is most recent, to birthtime.*

The Moon's travel to birthtime can be gotten from Table VI, Semidiurnal Motion of the Moon, or it can be calculated directly or by using logs. If you want to use logs, you must use a special log table based on twelve-hour instead of twenty-four-hour motion. No such log table is included in this book.

| | | | | |
|---|---|---|---|---|
| | 19 | 2 M 35 | 13 " | |
| | 20 | 6 ° 28 | 23 " | |
| | 21 | / h 22m 41s | | |
| 22a | ° | 12 ' 24 " | | |
| 22b | ° | 32 ' 20 " | | |
| **23 D Longitude at Birthtime (add 19 + 22a + 22b = 23)** | 23 | 3 ° 19 ' 57 " | | D |

After getting the Moon's travel to birthtime, we add it to the Moon's position before birth to get the Moon's position at birthtime. The result is accurate to the nearest minute of arc, and the original birth data does not allow any greater accuracy. The calculated result in our example was 3°♏ 19'57", which rounds off to 3°♏ 20'.

**24 Longitude** 0h **After Birth** (**5** date + 1d, Ephemeris)
**25 Longitude** 0h **Before** Birth ( **5** date, Ephemeris)
**26** 24h **Travel** (Subtract **24 – 25 = 26**; If Retrograde, Subtract **25 –24= 26**)
**27 ET Travel** (**7,26,** Table VII: **minutes 27a, Hours 27b, 27a + 27b=27c**)
**28 Longitude At Birthtime** (**25 + 27c = 28;** If Retrograde, **25 – 27c = 28**)

| | Mean☊ | True☊ | ☿ | ♀ | ♂ | ♃ | ♄ | ♅ | ♆ | ♇ |
|---|---|---|---|---|---|---|---|---|---|---|
| **24** | 10°♓50' | 11°♓42' | 7°♈21' | 19°♈35' | 13°♉27' | 4°♏13' | 7°♉25' | 6°♎50' | 0°♐45' | 25°♍49' |
| **25** | 10°♓53' | 11°♓45' | 5°♈19' | 18°♈21' | 12°♉45' | 4°♏19' | 7°♉18' | 6°♎53' | 0°♐46' | 25°♍51' |
| **26** | R 3' | R 3' | 2° 2' | 1° 14' | 42' | R 6' | 7' | R 3' | 1' | R 2' |
| **27a** | 0'3" | 0'3" | 1' 57" | 1' 11" | 40" | 6" | 7" | 3" | 1" | 2" |
| **27b** | 1'38" | 1'38" | 1°6' 5" | 40' 5" | 22'45" | 3' 15" | 3' 46" | 1'38" | 33" | 1' 5" |
| **27c** | 1'41" | 1'41" | 1°8' 2" | 41' 16" | 23'25" | R 3' 21" | 3' 55" | R 1' 41" | R 34" | R 1' 7" |
| **28** | 10°♓51 | 11°♓43' | 6°♈27' | 19°♈2' | 13°♉8" | 4°♏16' | 7°♉22' | 6°♎51' | 0°♐45° | 25°♍50' |

The positions of the Moon's nodes and the planets are calculated using Table VII (page 138), Diurnal Motion of the Planets, and the same interpolation methods used to calculate the positions of the Sun and the Moon.

There is only one consideration that applies to the planets and nodes and not to the Sun and Moon. When a planet is retrograde, its longitude is greater before birth than after birth. Retrograde planets are marked in the ephemeris with an R next to the planet's position on the day it goes retrograde or next to its position on the first of the month if it is already retrograde then. Its position on the day it goes direct is marked D. The mean node is, of course, always retrograde.

Whether or not a planet is retrograde, subtract the lesser longitude from the greater to get the twenty-four-hour travel. But in the case of a retrograde planet, mark the twenty-four-hour travel and the ET travel (lines **26** and **27c** with an R to remind you to subtract it from 0h longitude later instead of adding it. In our example, this has been done in the columns for Jupiter, Uranus, Neptune and Pluto.

## Second Difference Interpolation of the Moon's Position

There are times when it is desirable to obtain a more accurate position of the Moon than can be gotten with the interpolation techniques described so far. In calculating lunar returns, for example, the natal Moon must be calculated to at least ± 1' of accuracy and even more accurately if the chart has been rectified or if you are using the precise position of the Moon in directions. Most ephemerides give the position of the Moon only every twenty-four-hours, which can result in an error of ± 5' of arc. This ephemeris gives the Moon's position every twelve hours, which allows an accuracy by simple interpolation techniques of about ± 2' of arc.

Simple interpolation techniques assume that the speed of motion of a planet is constant over the period of time between two successive positions. If a body does not move at a constant speed, simple interpolation produces an error. To deal with this problem, a technique of higher-order interpolation has been developed which takes into consideration the change in the rate of motion and allows us to correct for it.

We find the Moon's position, using simple interpolation techniques but calculating directly rather than using tables. Then we apply a correction to that position based on the rate of change of the Moon's motion. We derive that correction as follows.

1. Find the two consecutive Moon positions in the ephemeris that come at twelve-hour intervals before birth and two consecutive positions after birth.
2. Find the three twelve-hour travels between each of the three pairs of successive Moon positions. These are called the first differences.
3. Find the difference between the first two twelve-hour travels and the difference between the second and third. These are called the second differences.
4. Add the two second differences and divide by two. The result is the mean second difference.

The following array should make this clearer. Let us start with the times for which Moon positions are given in the ephemeris immediately before and after birth, the times associated with lines **18** and **19** on the worksheet. Let us call them $t_2$ and $t_3$. If birthtime was before noon, $t_2$ and $t_3$ will be 0h and 12h on the date of birth; if birthtime was after noon, $t_2$ and $t_3$ will be 12h on the date of birth and 0h the following day. Let us use $t_1$ for the time twelve hours before $t_2$ and $t_4$ for the time twelve hours after $t_3$. We will use $L_1$, $L_2$, $L_3$ and $L_4$ for the Moon longitudes give in the ephemeris for $t_1$, $t_2$, $t_3$ and $t_4$ respectively.

| Times | Moon positions | First differences | Second differences | Mean second difference |
|---|---|---|---|---|
| $t_1$ | $L_1$ | | | |
| | | $L_2 - L_1 = d_1$ | | |
| $t_2$ | $L_2$ | | $d_2 - d_1 = D_1$ | |
| | | $L_3 - L_2 = d_2$ | | $\dfrac{D_1 + D_2}{2} = \text{Mean D}$ |
| $t_3$ | $L_3$ | | $d_3 - d_2 = D_2$ | |
| | | $L_4 - L_3 = d_3$ | | |
| $t_4$ | $L_4$ | | | |

We go into Table VIII with two values: the time elapsed from the ephemeris time just before birth to birthtime (birthtime – $t_2$, the time on line **21**) and the mean second difference. From the table we get a correction which we will add to or subtract from the Moon position we got by ordinary methods (line **23**).

If the second differences and the mean second difference are positive, it means that the Moon was accelerating. It had been moving slower before birthtime than at birthtime; therefore its true position was behind the position indicated by ordinary methods, which assume con-

stant speed. So we must subtract the correction that we get from the tables in order to get the true position. Conversely, if the second differences and the mean second difference are negative, we know that the Moon was decelerating. It had been moving faster before birthtime than at birthtime; therefore its true position was ahead of the position indicated by ordinary methods which assume constant speed. So we must add the correction from the tables to get the true position.

Let us now apply this technique to our sample horoscope.

| | | | |
|---|---|---|---|
| $t_1$ | = | 3/25/70 | 0h |
| $t_2$ | = | 3/25/70 | 12h |
| $t_3$ | = | 3/26/70 | 0h |
| $t_4$ | = | 3/26/70 | 12h |

| | | | | | |
|---|---|---|---|---|---|
| $L_1 =$ | 26°♎10'12" | | | | |
| | | $d_1 =$ | 6° 25' 1" | | |
| $L_2 =$ | 2°♏35'13" | | | $D_1 =$ | 3'22" |
| | | $d_2 =$ | 6° 28'23" | | |
| $L_3 =$ | 9°♏3'36" | | | $D_2 =$ | 3'25" |
| | | $d_3 =$ | 6° 31'48" | | |
| $L_4 =$ | 15°♏35'24" | | | | |

Mean D = 3'23.5"

Simple interpolation calculated directly:

| 1h 22m 41s = 1h 22.7 | = | 1.3783h |
| 6° 28' 23" = 6° 28.3833' | = | 6.4731° |
| 1.3783h ÷ 12h | = | .11486 |
| .11486 × 6.4731° | = | .7436° |
| | = | 44.616' |
| | = | 44'37" |

| 2° ♏ 35' 13" + 44' 37" | = | 3° ♏ 19' 50" |

You will recall that using table VI we got 3°♏ 19' 57", which rounded off to 3°♏ 20'. We can assume that 3°♏ 19' 50" is slightly more accurate because it was calculated directly. We now enter Table VIII (page 147) with a time of 1h 22m 41s and a mean second difference of 3'23.5". In the table, correction values are given to the nearest second for every minute of mean second difference and every hour of time.

## Table VIII Second Difference Interpolation For The Moon

| TIME INTVL | 1' | | 2' | | 3' | | 4' | | 5' | | 6' | | 7' | | 8' | | 9' | | 10' | | TIME INTVL |
|---|---|---|---|---|---|---|---|---|---|---|---|---|---|---|---|---|---|---|---|---|---|
| | ' | " | ' | " | ' | " | ' | " | ' | " | ' | " | ' | " | ' | " | ' | " | ' | " | |
| 0-1 | 0 | 1 | 0 | 2 | 0 | 4 | 0 | 5 | 0 | 6 | 0 | 7 | 0 | 8 | 0 | 10 | 0 | 11 | 0 | 12 | 11-12 |
| 1-2 | 0 | 3 | 0 | 7 | 0 | 10 | 0 | 13 | 0 | 16 | 0 | 20 | 0 | 23 | 0 | 26 | 0 | 30 | 0 | 33 | 10-11 |
| 2-3 | 0 | 5 | 0 | 10 | 0 | 15 | 0 | 20 | 0 | 25 | 0 | 30 | 0 | 35 | 0 | 40 | 0 | 45 | 0 | 49 | 9-10 |
| 3-4 | 0 | 6 | 0 | 12 | 0 | 19 | 0 | 25 | 0 | 31 | 0 | 37 | 0 | 43 | 0 | 50 | 0 | 56 | 1 | 2 | 8-9 |
| 4-5 | 0 | 7 | 0 | 14 | 0 | 21 | 0 | 28 | 0 | 35 | 0 | 42 | 0 | 49 | 0 | 56 | 1 | 3 | 1 | 10 | 7-8 |
| 5-6 | 0 | 7 | 0 | 15 | 0 | 22 | 0 | 30 | 0 | 37 | 0 | 45 | 0 | 52 | 0 | 60 | 1 | 7 | 1 | 14 | 6-7 |

We read across the top of the twelve-hour section of the table to the column for a mean second difference of 3', which is closest to 3'23.5", and read down to the line for a time interval of between one and two hours, which includes 1h 22m41s. Where the column and line meet we find 0'10", which is our correction. The Moon was accelerating, so we subtract 0'10" from the constant-speed position of 3°♏ 19'50". The result is 3°♏ 19'40".

The above method can also be used with an ephemeris that gives Moon positions only at twenty-four-hour intervals. Simply read "twenty-four hours" for "twelve-hours" in the above instructions and use the twenty-four-hour section of Table VIII. The results will be slightly less accurate than those obtained with the help of a twelve-hour Moon ephemeris but much more accurate than with constant-speed interpolation only.

## LOCATING KOCH HOUSE CUSPS

The Table of Houses in this book gives a complete set of house cusps for every four minutes of Sidereal Time for latitudes from 0° to 60°. For those readers who have access to a trigonometric calculator, the methods for extracting house cusps by trigonometry are given at the end of this section. Trigonometry gives the most accurate results, but the tables supplied here to assist in your calculations will suffice for most purposes.

Since the tables give house cusps only for every four minutes of Sidereal Time and for whole degrees of latitude, we must either be satisfied with approximate house cusps, say to the nearest degree at best, or we must interpolate. But before we get to that, let us learn more about the layout of the Table of Houses.

As you thumb through the table, you will note that the Sidereal Time is given at the top of the page, along with a zodiacal longitude. There is only one Midheaven for each Sidereal time because the Midheaven is independent of the latitude of the place. But beneath the Midheaven and the ST are five columns of positions, headed as follows: 11, 12, ASC, 2, 3. These are the cusps of the eleventh, twelfth, first, second and third houses. The first house cusp is also called the Ascendant. These house cusps are not independent of latitude and therefore must be listed for every degree of latitude. That makes finding house cusps other than the tenth (Midheaven) a bit complicated, but it doesn't require any mathematics beyond the high-school level.

The techniques outlined here for interpolating precise cusps from a table apply to any kind of house tables, even though the numbers may vary. The house division system of Koch is by no means the only system. A variety of other house systems exist, among them Placidus, Regiomontanus, Equal, Meridian, Topocentric, Porphyry and Alcabitius. You can order a report called *House Systems Comparison* from Astro Communications Services. The report lists house cusps for any horoscope in nine systems and specifies the house placements of the planets in each of the nine systems. A brief discussion of the astronomical basis of the Koch system is given later on in this section.

Our birth LST of 20h 51m 21s falls between 20h 48m 0s and 20h 52m 0s. At these two times, 9°≈ 34' and 10°≈ 33', respectively, are on the Midheaven. Our birthtime Midheaven will fall between these two values. We can roughly estimate the house cusps by observing that our birth LST is nearer to 20h 52m than to 20h 48m and that our latitude, 41 N 39', is about two thirds of the way from 41 N to 42. Our estimates would be: Midheaven: 10°≈, eleventh: 19°♓  twelfth: 1°♉, first:

5°♊, second: 0°♋, third: 21°♋. Many astrologers never go beyond this point, and you can do a great deal with approximate house cusps. If you don't like to calculate, this is a good shortcut to take until you are ready to do more. On the other hand, all predictive techniques involving directions or progressions require greater accuracy than this. So we will now find out how to get that accuracy.

## Koch Table of Houses
## for Latitudes 0° to 60° North

| 20h 48m 0s | | 312° 0' 0' | | | 20h 52m 0s | | 313° 0' 0' | | | |
| 09 ≈ 34 | | | | | 10 ≈ 33 | | | | | |
| 11 | 12 | ASC | 2 | 3 | 11 | 12 | ASC | 2 | 3 | LAT. |
|---|---|---|---|---|---|---|---|---|---|---|
| 10♓30 | 13♈03 | 14♉28 | 13♊24 | 11♋02 | 11♓34 | 14♈07 | 15♉28 | 14♊20 | 11♋58 | 0 |
| 10 57 | 14 09 | 15 58 | 14 50 | 12 00 | 12 03 | 15 16 | 16 59 | 15 47 | 12 56 | 5 |
| 11 27 | 15 22 | 17 34 | 16 20 | 12 58 | 12 34 | 16 31 | 18 37 | 17 17 | 13 54 | 10 |
| 12 00 | 16 44 | 19 19 | 17 54 | 13 56 | 13 09 | 17 55 | 20 22 | 18 52 | 14 53 | 15 |
| 12 38 | 18 18 | 21 15 | 19 34 | 14 57 | 13 49 | 19 31 | 22 21 | 20 33 | 15 54 | 20 |
| 12 47 | 18 38 | 21 40 | 19 55 | 15 09 | 13 58 | 19 51 | 22 46 | 20 55 | 16 07 | 21 |
| 12 56 | 18 59 | 22 06 | 20 17 | 15 22 | 14 07 | 20 13 | 23 12 | 21 16 | 16 19 | 22 |
| 13 05 | 19 21 | 22 32 | 20 39 | 15 35 | 14 17 | 20 35 | 23 38 | 21 38 | 16 32 | 23 |
| 13 14 | 19 44 | 22 59 | 21 01 | 15 48 | 14 27 | 20 59 | 24 06 | 22 00 | 16 45 | 24 |
| 13 24 | 20 07 | 23 26 | 21 23 | 16 01 | 14 37 | 21 23 | 24 33 | 22 23 | 16 58 | 25 |
| 13 34 | 20 31 | 23 55 | 21 46 | 16 14 | 14 48 | 21 48 | 25 02 | 22 48 | 17 11 | 26 |
| 13 45 | 20 57 | 24 24 | 22 10 | 16 27 | 14 59 | 22 13 | 25 32 | 23 10 | 17 25 | 27 |
| 13 56 | 21 23 | 24 54 | 22 34 | 16 41 | 15 11 | 22 40 | 26 02 | 23 34 | 17 38 | 28 |
| 14 08 | 21 50 | 25 25 | 22 59 | 16 54 | 15 23 | 23 08 | 26 33 | 23 59 | 17 52 | 29 |
| 14 20 | 22 19 | 25 57 | 23 24 | 17 08 | 15 36 | 23 38 | 27 06 | 24 24 | 18 06 | 30 |
| 14 33 | 22 49 | 26 31 | 23 50 | 17 23 | 15 49 | 24 08 | 27 39 | 24 50 | 18 20 | 31 |
| 14 47 | 23 20 | 27 05 | 24 16 | 17 37 | 16 04 | 24 40 | 28 14 | 25 16 | 18 35 | 32 |
| 15 01 | 23 53 | 27 41 | 24 43 | 17 52 | 16 19 | 25 14 | 28 49 | 25 43 | 18 49 | 33 |
| 15 16 | 24 28 | 28 17 | 25 11 | 18 07 | 16 34 | 25 49 | 29 27 | 26 11 | 19 04 | 34 |
| 15 32 | 25 04 | 28 56 | 25 39 | 18 22 | 16 51 | 26 26 | 00♋05 | 26 40 | 19 20 | 35 |
| 15 49 | 25 42 | 29 35 | 26 09 | 18 38 | 17 09 | 27 05 | 00 44 | 27 09 | 19 35 | 36 |
| 16 07 | 26 23 | 00♋17 | 26 39 | 18 54 | 17 28 | 27 46 | 01 27 | 27 39 | 19 51 | 37 |
| 16 27 | 27 05 | 01 00 | 27 10 | 19 10 | 17 48 | 28 29 | 02 10 | 28 10 | 20 08 | 38 |
| 16 47 | 27 50 | 01 45 | 27 42 | 19 27 | 18 10 | 29 15 | 02 55 | 28 43 | 20 24 | 39 |
| 17 10 | 28 38 | 02 32 | 28 15 | 19 44 | 18 33 | 00♉04 | 03 42 | 29 16 | 20 41 | 40 |
| 17 34 | 29 29 | 03 21 | 28 49 | 20 01 | 18 59 | 00 56 | 04 31 | 29 50 | 20 59 | 41 |
| 17 59 | 00♉24 | 04 12 | 29 25 | 20 19 | 19 26 | 01 51 | 05 22 | 00♋25 | 21 17 | 42 |
| 18 28 | 01 22 | 05 05 | 00♋01 | 20 38 | 19 55 | 02 50 | 06 16 | 01 01 | 21 35 | 43 |
| 18 58 | 02 24 | 06 02 | 00 39 | 20 57 | 20 27 | 03 53 | 07 12 | 01 39 | 21 54 | 44 |
| 19 32 | 03 31 | 07 01 | 01 19 | 21 16 | 21 02 | 05 00 | 08 11 | 02 18 | 22 14 | 45 |
| 20 09 | 04 43 | 08 03 | 01 59 | 21 37 | 21 41 | 06 13 | 09 13 | 02 59 | 22 34 | 46 |
| 20 46 | 06 00 | 09 08 | 02 42 | 21 57 | 22 24 | 07 31 | 10 18 | 03 41 | 22 55 | 47 |
| 21 35 | 07 24 | 10 17 | 03 26 | 22 19 | 23 11 | 08 56 | 11 26 | 04 25 | 23 16 | 48 |
| 22 26 | 08 55 | 11 29 | 04 12 | 22 41 | 24 04 | 10 27 | 12 38 | 05 10 | 23 38 | 49 |
| 23 23 | 10 34 | 12 46 | 04 59 | 23 04 | 25 03 | 12 07 | 13 54 | 05 58 | 24 01 | 50 |
| 24 28 | 12 22 | 14 07 | 05 49 | 23 28 | 26 11 | 13 55 | 15 15 | 06 47 | 24 24 | 51 |
| 25 42 | 14 20 | 15 33 | 06 42 | 23 54 | 27 28 | 15 53 | 16 40 | 07 39 | 24 49 | 52 |
| 27 08 | 16 29 | 17 03 | 07 36 | 24 18 | 28 58 | 18 01 | 18 10 | 08 33 | 25 14 | 53 |
| 28 48 | 18 50 | 18 40 | 08 33 | 24 45 | 00♈42 | 20 22 | 19 48 | 09 30 | 25 41 | 54 |
| 00♈46 | 21 26 | 20 22 | 09 33 | 25 13 | 02 44 | 22 57 | 21 26 | 10 29 | 26 09 | 55 |
| 03 08 | 24 17 | 22 11 | 10 36 | 25 42 | 05 11 | 25 47 | 23 13 | 11 31 | 26 37 | 56 |
| 06 01 | 27 26 | 24 06 | 11 43 | 26 12 | 08 08 | 28 53 | 25 07 | 12 37 | 27 07 | 57 |
| 09 34 | 00♊53 | 26 09 | 12 52 | 26 44 | 11 46 | 02♊17 | 27 08 | 13 46 | 27 39 | 58 |
| 14 01 | 04 40 | 28 19 | 14 06 | 27 18 | 16 19 | 06 00 | 29 16 | 14 58 | 28 12 | 59 |
| 19♈41 | 08♊49 | 00♋38 | 15♋23 | 27♋53 | 22♈03 | 10♊03 | 01♋32 | 16♋14 | 28♋47 | 60 |

*The Table of Houses gives zodiacal longitude and house cusps for every four minutes of Sidereal Time. The Midheaven, which is the same at all latitudes, is given at the top. The other house cusps are given for 0° to 60°.*

### Interpolation

Interpolation works because there is a constant proportional relationship between change of LST and change in the Midheaven and in the other house cusps. There is a similar relationship as well between change in latitude and change in house cusps.

We will call the times in the Table of Houses just before and just after birth "earlier LST" and "later LST" and enter them on lines **30** and **31** respectively. In order to interpolate, we need to know the LST increment or time change between earlier LST and birth LST. We do this by subtracting earlier LST from birth LST. The result goes on line **32**.

| | | | | | | |
|---|---|---|---|---|---|---|
| **29 Local Sidereal Time (12)** | 29 | 20 h | 51 m | 21 s | | |
| **30 Earlier LST** (Table of Houses) | 30 | 20 h | 48 m | s | | |
| **31 Later** LST (Table of Houses) | 31 | 20 h | 52 m | s | | |
| **32 LST Increment** (Subtract 29 – 30 =32) | 32 | | 3 m | 21 s | ΔLST | |

| | | | |
|---|---|---|---|
| **33 Midheaven At Later LST** (Table of Houses) | 33 | 10 °≈33 ' |
| **34 Midheaven At Earlier LST** (Table of Houses) | 34 | 9 °≈34 ' |
| **35 4m Midheaven Increment** (subtract 33 – 34 = 35) | 35 | ° 59 ' |

Next we need to know how much the Midheaven changed in the four minutes between earlier LST and later LST. We find out by reading the Midheavens at the two times from the Table of Houses and subtracting.

| | | |
|---|---|---|
| **36 Midheaven Increment (32, 35, Table XI)** | 36 | ° 49 ' |

When we know how much time elapsed between earlier LST and birth LST (LST increment) and how much the Midheaven changed in the four minutes between earlier LST and later LST (Midheaven interval), we can deduce how much the Midheaven changed between earlier LST and birth LST (Midheaven increment), using Table XI. Read across the top to find the column closest to the LST increment, then read down to find the line for the Midheaven interval. Where they meet is the Midheaven increment. In our example, the 3m 20s column is closest to our LST increment of 3m21s. The one-second difference is not significant. We read down to the 0° 59' line and find that our Midheaven increment is 49'.

## Table XI House Cusp Interpolation Between Sidereal Times

| CUSP INTVL | m 2 | s 44 | m 2 | s 48 | m 2 | s 52 | m 2 | s 56 | m 3 | s 0 | m 3 | s 4 | m 3 | s 8 | m 3 | s 12 | m 3 | s 16 | m 3 | s 20 | m 3 | s 24 | m 3 | s 28 | m 3 | s 32 | m 3 | s 36 | m 3 | s 40 | m 3 | s 44 | m 3 | s 48 | m 3 | s 52 | m 3 | s 56 | m 4 | s 0 | CUSP INTVL |
|---|---|---|---|---|---|---|---|---|---|---|---|---|---|---|---|---|---|---|---|---|---|---|---|---|---|---|---|---|---|---|---|---|---|---|---|---|---|---|---|---|---|
| ° ' | ° | ' | ° | ' | ° | ' | ° | ' | ° | ' | ° | ' | ° | ' | ° | ' | ° | ' | ° | ' | ° | ' | ° | ' | ° | ' | ° | ' | ° | ' | ° | ' | ° | ' | ° | ' | ° | ' | ° | ' | ° ' |
| 0 31 | 0 | 21 | 0 | 22 | 0 | 22 | 0 | 23 | 0 | 23 | 0 | 24 | 0 | 24 | 0 | 25 | 0 | 25 | 0 | 26 | 0 | 26 | 0 | 27 | 0 | 27 | 0 | 28 | 0 | 28 | 0 | 29 | 0 | 29 | 0 | 30 | 0 | 30 | 0 | 31 | 0 31 |
| 0 32 | 0 | 22 | 0 | 22 | 0 | 23 | 0 | 23 | 0 | 24 | 0 | 25 | 0 | 25 | 0 | 26 | 0 | 26 | 0 | 27 | 0 | 27 | 0 | 28 | 0 | 28 | 0 | 29 | 0 | 29 | 0 | 30 | 0 | 30 | 0 | 31 | 0 | 31 | 0 | 32 | 0 32 |
| 0 33 | 0 | 23 | 0 | 23 | 0 | 24 | 0 | 24 | 0 | 25 | 0 | 25 | 0 | 26 | 0 | 26 | 0 | 27 | 0 | 28 | 0 | 28 | 0 | 29 | 0 | 29 | 0 | 30 | 0 | 30 | 0 | 31 | 0 | 31 | 0 | 32 | 0 | 32 | 0 | 33 | 0 33 |
| 0 34 | | | | | | | | | | | | | | | | | | | | | | | | | | | | | | | | | | | | | | | | | 0 34 |
| 0 56 | 0 | 38 | 0 | 39 | 0 | 40 | 0 | 41 | 0 | 42 | 0 | 43 | 0 | 44 | 0 | 45 | 0 | 46 | 0 | 47 | 0 | 48 | 0 | 49 | 0 | 50 | 0 | 51 | 0 | 52 | 0 | 53 | 0 | 54 | 0 | 55 | 0 | 56 | 0 56 |
| 0 57 | 0 | 39 | 0 | 40 | 0 | 41 | 0 | 42 | 0 | 43 | 0 | 44 | 0 | 45 | 0 | 46 | 0 | 47 | 0 | 48 | 0 | 49 | 0 | 50 | 0 | 51 | 0 | 52 | 0 | 53 | 0 | 54 | 0 | 55 | 0 | 56 | 0 | 57 | 0 57 |
| 0 58 | 0 | 40 | 0 | 41 | 0 | 42 | 0 | 43 | 0 | 44 | 0 | 45 | 0 | 46 | 0 | 47 | 0 | 48 | 0 | 49 | 0 | 50 | 0 | 51 | 0 | 52 | 0 | 53 | 0 | 54 | 0 | 55 | 0 | 56 | 0 | 57 | 0 | 58 | 0 58 |
| 0 59 | 0 | 40 | 0 | 41 | 0 | 42 | 0 | 43 | 0 | 44 | 0 | 45 | 0 | 46 | 0 | 47 | 0 | 48 | 0 | 49 | 0 | 50 | 0 | 51 | 0 | 52 | 0 | 53 | 0 | 54 | 0 | 55 | 0 | 56 | 0 | 57 | 0 | 58 | 0 59 |
| 1 0 | 0 | 41 | 0 | 42 | 0 | 43 | 0 | 44 | 0 | 45 | 0 | 46 | 0 | 47 | 0 | 48 | 0 | 49 | 0 | 50 | 0 | 51 | 0 | 52 | 0 | 53 | 0 | 54 | 0 | 55 | 0 | 56 | 0 | 57 | 0 | 58 | 1 | 0 | 1 0 |

*Table XI, House Cusp Interpolation Between Sidereal Times, gives the cusp increment, the amount by which the house cusp changed from earlier LST to birth LST.*

What Table XI actually does is solve the following proportion for us

$$\frac{\text{cusp increment}}{\text{cusp interval}} = \frac{\text{LST increment}}{\text{LST interval}}$$

In our example,

$$\frac{\text{cusp increment}}{59'} = \frac{3\text{m } 21\text{s}}{4\text{m}}$$

$$\text{cusp increment} = \frac{3\text{m}21\text{s}}{4\text{m}} \times 59'$$

$$= 49'$$

## Direct Calculation

If you have a calculator, or even if you do not, you may prefer to do this calculation directly instead of using Table XI. In this case, first translate the LST increment into decimal minutes to make the arithmetic easier. Do this by dividing the seconds portion by 60 and adding it to the whole minutes. for example.

$$21 \div 60 = .35$$
$$3\text{m } 21\text{s} = 3.35\text{m}$$

Then solve the proportion as above.

$$\text{cusp increment} = (3.35 \div 4) \times 59'$$
$$= 0.8375 \times 59'$$
$$= 49.4125'$$
$$\cong 49' \text{ (rounded off)}$$

Although cusp intervals are different for different houses, the LST increment and LST interval are the same for all houses in the chart. Therefore the time ratio, 0.8375 in our example, will be the same for all houses. Note it down for later use. If you have a calculator that stores a constant multiplier, this is an opportunity to use it.

## Logarithms

House cusps can be interpolated using logarithms as well. You will recall that logs convert all multiplications into additions and all divisions into subtractions. In our example,

$$\frac{3\text{m } 21\text{s}}{4\text{m}} \times 59'$$

becomes

$$\log 3\text{m } 21\text{s} - \log 4\text{m} + \log 59'$$

In Table IX the numbers across the top are units that can be read either as hours, as degrees or even as minutes. The vertical column at the left refers to minutes if you are looking up degrees and minutes or hours and minutes, or it refers to seconds if you are looking up minutes and seconds. In other words, the column at the left gives sixtieths of the numbers along the top.

From Table IX, we get the following values. Log 3m 21s = .85517; log 4m = .77815. From Table X we get log 59' = 1.38751.

We calculate as follows.

$$
\begin{array}{r}
.85517 \\
- .77815 \\
\hline
= .07702 \\
+ 1.38751 \\
\hline
= 1.46453
\end{array}
$$

Working Table X backwards, we find that 1.46453 is the log of 49'25" +. This rounds off to 49', almost the same result we got by other methods.

No matter which method we use to get the Midheaven increment, we must add the increment to the Midheaven at earlier time to get the Midheaven at birthtime. When we know the Midheaven, we also know the cusp of the fourth house, which is opposite, that is, exactly six signs away.

| | | |
|---|---|---|
| 34 | 9° ♒ 34' | |
| 35 | ° 59' | |
| 36 | ° 49' | |
| **37 Midheaven At Birth LST** (add 34 + 36 = 37) | 37 10° ♒ 23' | MC |

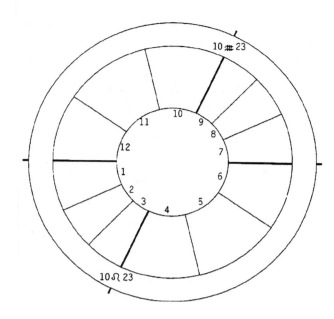

*The IC [Imum Coeli], the cusp of the fourth house, is alway exactly six signs away from the MC [Medium Coeli] or Midheaven, the cusp of the tenth house.*

| | | |
|---|---|---|
| **38 Lower Latitude** (Table of Houses) | 38 *41 ∘N* | |
| **39 Higher Latitude** (Table of Houses) | 39 *42 ∘N* | |
| **40 Latitude Increment** (Subtract **Birth Latitude** – 38 = 40) | 40 ° *39'* | Δ **Lat** |

The Midheaven at a given LST is the same at all latitudes, but the cusps of the other houses vary with latitude. The Table of Houses in this book gives the cusps of the eleventh, twelfth, first (Ascendant), second and third houses for 0°, 5°, 10°, 15° and every whole degree of latitude from 20° to 60°.

To find the house cusps at birth LST at birth latitude, our strategy will be to find the house cusps at birth LST at the two latitudes in the Table that are nearest the birth latitude, using exactly the same methods we used to find the Midheaven, and then to interpolate between latitudes. On lines **38**, **39** and **40**, we locate those two latitudes

and find the increment from the lower latitude to birth latitude, which we will need later in order to interpolate. It is a good idea at this point to fill in the **LST** and **Latitude** columns of lines **41** to **53** completely. All the values are now known, and they serve to label the lines and thereby avoid confusion.

Lines **41** to **45** of the worksheet are devoted to finding the house cusps at birth LST at the lower latitude. The method is exactly the same as the used in finding the Midheaven on lines **30** to **37**. Specific instructions for each line are given on the worksheet.

**41 House Cusps at Later LST, Lower Latitude** (Table of Houses)
**42 House Cusps at Earlier LST, Lower Latitude** (Table of Houses)
**43 4m Cusp Intervals** (Subtract **41** – **42** = **43**)
**44 Cusp Increments** (32, 43, Table XI)
**45 House Cusps at Birth LST, Lower Latitude** (add **42** + **44** = **45**)

| | LST | Latitude | 11 | 12 | ASC | 2 | 3 |
|---|---|---|---|---|---|---|---|
| 41 | LATER *20:52* | LOWER (38) | *18ℋ55'* | *0°♉56'* | *4°♊31'* | *29°♊50'* | *20°♋59'* |
| 42 | EARLIER *20:48* | | *17ℋ34'* | *29°♈29'* | *3°♊21'* | *28°♊49'* | *20°♋01'* |
| 43 | *4m* | *41°N* | *1° 25'* | *1° 27'* | *1° 10'* | *1° 1'* | *0° 58'* |
| 44 | LINE 32 *3:21* | | *1° 11'* | *1° 13'* | *0° 58'* | *0° 51'* | *0° 48'* |
| 45 | BIRTH *20:51:21* | | *18°ℋ45'* | *0°♉42'* | *4°♊19'* | *29°♊40'* | *20°♋49'* |

This part of the process of casting a chart is by far the most subject to error, not because any link in the chain of calculation is especially difficult but because the chain is so long. It is important to check your work continually so that if you make an error you will catch it and correct it before it spoils future work.

For example, line 41 should be greater than line 42. Subtracting, you should get a difference of less than two degrees in most cases, less than four degrees in extreme cases. If you do not, check to see that you have copied from the right place in the table of houses and have done the sexagesimal subtraction correctly.

Line 44 should be smaller than line 43 and in the same proportion to it as the LST increment is to the interval 4m. That is, in our example, 3m21s is about three quarters of 4m. Therefore, each increment on line 44 should be about three quarters of the interval on line 43.

Check to be sure that the cusp on line 45 for each house is between the cusps on lines 41 and 42 (greater than line 42 and less than line 41.)

## Koch Table of Houses
### for Latitudes 0° to 60° North

| 20h 48m 0s 312° 0' 0' 09 ♒ 34 | | | | | 20h 52m 0s 313° 0' 0' 10 ♒ 33 | | | | | |
|---|---|---|---|---|---|---|---|---|---|---|
| 11 | 12 | ASC | 2 | 3 | 11 | 12 | ASC | 2 | 3 | LAT. |
| 10H30 | 13T03 | 14♉28 | 13♊24 | 11♋02 | 11H34 | 14T07 | 15♉28 | 14♊20 | 11♋58 | 0 |
| 10 57 | 14 09 | 15 58 | 14 50 | 12 00 | 12 03 | 15 16 | 16 58 | 15 47 | 12 56 | 5 |
| 11 27 | 15 22 | 17 34 | 16 20 | 12 58 | 12 34 | 16 31 | 18 37 | 17 17 | 13 54 | 10 |
| 12 00 | 16 44 | 19 19 | 17 54 | 13 56 | 13 09 | 17 55 | 20 24 | 18 52 | 14 53 | 15 |
| 12 38 | 18 18 | 21 15 | 19 34 | 14 57 | 13 49 | 19 31 | 22 21 | 20 33 | 15 54 | 20 |
| 16 47 | 27 50 | 01 45 | 27 42 | 19 27 | 18 10 | 29 15 | 02 55 | 28 43 | 20 24 | 39 |
| 17 10 | 28 38 | 02 32 | 28 15 | 19 44 | 18 33 | 00♉04 | 03 42 | 29 16 | 20 41 | 40 |
| 17 34 | 29 29 | 03 21 | 28 49 | 20 01 | 18 59 | 00 56 | 04 31 | 29 50 | 20 59 | 41 |
| 17 59 | 00♉24 | 04 12 | 29 25 | 20 19 | 19 26 | 01 51 | 05 22 | 00♋25 | 21 17 | 42 |
| 18 28 | 01 22 | 05 05 | 00♋01 | 20 38 | 19 55 | 02 50 | 06 16 | 01 01 | 21 35 | 43 |
| 18 58 | 02 24 | 06 02 | 00 39 | 20 57 | 20 27 | 03 53 | 07 12 | 01 39 | 21 54 | 44 |

*The Table of Houses gives house cusps for 0°, 5°, 10°, 15° and every whole degree of latitude from 20° to 60°.*

**46** House Cusps at Later LST, Higher Latitude (Table of Houses)
**47** House Cusps at Earlier LST, Higher Latitude (Table of Houses)
**48** 4m Cusp Intervals (Subtract 46 – 47 = 48)
**49** Cusp Increments (32, 48, Table XI)
**50** House Cusps at Birth LST, Higher Latitude (add 47 + 49 = 50)

| | LST | Latitude | 11 | 12 | ASC | 2 | 3 |
|---|---|---|---|---|---|---|---|
| **46** | LATER 20:52 | HIGHER (39) | 19°H26' | 1°♉51' | 5°♊22' | 0°♉25' | 21°♉17' |
| **47** | EARLIER 20:48 | | 17°H59' | 0°♉24' | 4°♊12' | 29°♊25' | 20°♉19' |
| **48** | 4m | 42°N | 1°27' | 1°27' | 1°10' | 1°0' | 0°58' |
| **49** | LINE 32 3:21 | | 1°13' | 1°13' | 0°58' | 0°50' | 0°48' |
| **50** | BIRTH 20:51:21 | | 19°H12' | 1°♉37' | 5°♊10' | 0°♉15' | 21°♉07' |

Lines 46 to 50 of the worksheet are devoted to finding the house cusps at birthtime at the higher latitude. The method is exactly the same as that used for the lower latitude on lines 41 to 45. Check your work in the same ways. Also, compare line 48 to line 43 and line 49 to line 44. If for a given house they differ by more than a few minutes, something is wrong.

**51** 1° Cusp Intervals
   If 50 is greater than 45, rewrite 45 below. Subtract 50 – 45 = 51.
   If 50 is less than 45 mark 51 and 52 negative (–) for that house. Subtract 45 – 50 = 51.
**52** Cusp Increments for Latitude (40, 51, Table XII)
**53** House Cusps at Birth LST, Birth Latitude (add 45 + 52 = 53)

| | LST | Latitude | 11 | 12 | ASC | 2 | 3 |
|---|---|---|---|---|---|---|---|
| **45** | BIRTH (29) | LOWER 41°N | 18°H45' | 0°♉42' | 4°♊19' | 29°♊40' | 20°♉49' |
| **51** | | 1° | 0°27' | 0°55' | 0°51' | 0°35' | 0°18' |
| **52** | 20h51m21s | LINE 40 0°39' | 0°18' | 0°36' | 0°33' | 0°23' | 0°12' |
| **53** | | BIRTH 41°N39' | 19°H03' | 1°♉18' | 4°♊52' | 0°♉03' | 21°♉01' |

## Table XII House Cusp Interpolation between Latitudes

| LAT INC | HOUSE CUSP INTERVAL | | | | | | | | | | | | | | | | | | | | | | | | | | | | | | LAT INC |
|---|1|2|3|4|5|6|7|8|9|10|11|12|13|14|15|16|17|18|19|20|21|22|23|24|25|26|27|28|29|30|---|
| 1 | 0 | 0 | 0 | 0 | 0 | 0 | 0 | 0 | 0 | 0 | 0 | 0 | 0 | 0 | 0 | 1 | 1 | 0 | 0 | 0 | 0 | 0 | 0 | 0 | 0 | 0 | 0 | 0 | 0 | 1 | 1 |
| 2 | 0 | 0 | 0 | 0 | 0 | 0 | 0 | 0 | 0 | 0 | 0 | 0 | 0 | 0 | 1 | 1 | 1 | 1 | 1 | 1 | 1 | 1 | 1 | 1 | 1 | 1 | 1 | 1 | 1 | 1 | 2 |
| 3 | 0 | 0 | 0 | 0 | 0 | 0 | 0 | 0 | 1 | 1 | 1 | 1 | 1 | 1 | 1 | 1 | 1 | 1 | 1 | 1 | 1 | 1 | 1 | 1 | 1 | 1 | 1 | 1 | 1 | 2 | 3 |
| 35 | 1 | 1 | 2 | 2 | 3 | 4 | 4 | 5 | 5 | 5 | 6 | 6 | 7 | 8 | 8 | 9 | 9 | 10 | 11 | 11 | 12 | 12 | 13 | 13 | 14 | 15 | 15 | 16 | 16 | 17 | 35 |
| 36 | 1 | 1 | 2 | 2 | 3 | 4 | 4 | 5 | 5 | 6 | 7 | 7 | 8 | 8 | 9 | 10 | 10 | 11 | 11 | 12 | 13 | 13 | 14 | 14 | 15 | 16 | 16 | 17 | 17 | 18 | 36 |
| 37 | 1 | 1 | 2 | 2 | 3 | 4 | 4 | 5 | 6 | 6 | 7 | 7 | 8 | 9 | 9 | 10 | 10 | 11 | 11 | 12 | 12 | 13 | 14 | 14 | 15 | 16 | 17 | 17 | 18 | 19 | 37 |
| 38 | 1 | 1 | 2 | 3 | 3 | 4 | 4 | 5 | 6 | 6 | 7 | 8 | 8 | 9 | 10 | 10 | 11 | 11 | 12 | 13 | 13 | 14 | 15 | 15 | 16 | 16 | 17 | 18 | 18 | 19 | 38 |
| 39 | 1 | 1 | 2 | 3 | 3 | 4 | 5 | 5 | 6 | 7 | 7 | 8 | 8 | 9 | 10 | 10 | 11 | 12 | 12 | 13 | 14 | 14 | 15 | 16 | 16 | 17 | 18 | 18 | 19 | 20 | 39 |
| 40 | 1 | 1 | 2 | 3 | 3 | 4 | 5 | 5 | 6 | 7 | 7 | 8 | 9 | 9 | 10 | 10 | 11 | 11 | 12 | 13 | 13 | 14 | 15 | 15 | 16 | 17 | 17 | 18 | 19 | 20 | 40 |

*Table XII, House Cusp Interpolation between Latitudes, gives the cusp increment for latitude, the amount by which the house cusp at the birth latitude differs from the cusp at the lower whole latitude.*

When we have the birthtime cusps at the two whole latitudes, we must interpolate between them to find birthtime cusps at birth latitude. We do this on lines 51, 52 and 53, using Table XII for the interpolation.*

Sometime house cusps *increase* as latitude increases. When they do, the cusp at the higher latitude (line 50) is greater than the cusp at the lower latitude (line 45). In that case, to get the cusp interval for latitude, (line 51) you subtract line 45 from line 50. To make this easier, we have provided a place on the worksheet to rewrite line 45 below line 50. You should fill in a space on this line only if the cusp of that house is increasing, that is, if line 50 is greater than line 45 for that house. If it is, add the cusp increment from Table XII (line 52) to the cusp at lower latitude (line 45) to get the final cusp (line 53). This is the case with all the house cusps in our example.

Sometimes house cusps *decrease* as latitude increases, and the birthtime cusp at the higher latitude (line 50) is less than the cusp at the lower latitude (line 45). To get cusp interval for latitude (line 52), subtract line 50 from line 45. Line 50 is already below line 45, so there is no need to rewrite it. Mark the difference (line 51) as negative with a minus sign too, to remind you to subtract it from line 45 later instead of adding it. (If you look in the Table of Houses at a LST of 12:32:00, you will note that all the house cusps are *decreasing* with latitude.)

Once you have found the eastern house cusps, the tenth through the third, it is simple to find the western cusps, fourth through the ninth. Each of the western cusps is opposite, exactly six signs away from, one of the eastern cusps. The complete house cusps for our example are:

| Midheaven | 10° ♒ 23' | fourth | 10° ♌ 23' |
|---|---|---|---|
| eleventh | 19° ♓ 3' | fifth | 19° ♍ 3' |
| twelfth | 1° ♉ 18' | sixth | 1° ♏ 18' |
| Ascendant | 4° ♊ 52' | seventh | 4° ♐ 52' |
| second | 0° ♋ 3' | eighth | 0° ♑ 3' |
| third | 21° ♋ 1' | ninth | 21° ♑ 1' |

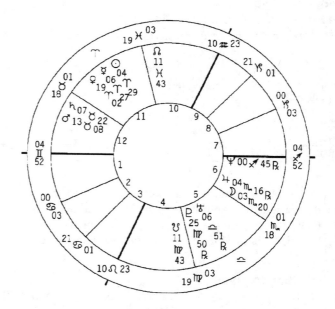

*Our sample chart completed.*

---

* If birth latitude is less than 20°, the difference between the two whole latitudes will be 5° instead of 1° and the difference between the cusps of a house at those two latitudes will be a 5° cusp interval instead of a 1° cusp interval. Two extra steps are necessary (1) To get the 1° cusp interval for each house, divide the 5° cusp interval by five. Enter the quotient on line 51. (2) If the latitude increment on line 40 is greater than 1°, the largest argument in Table XII, go into Table XII, go into Table XII with only the minutes part of the latitude increment. Add the cusp increment you get from Table XII to the product of the 1° cusp interval multiplied by the number of whole degrees in the latitude increment on line 40. The result of this calculation is the cusp increment for latitude and goes on line 52.

### South Latitudes

These Table of Houses are calculated for north latitudes only, but they can easily be used for casting charts of persons born in south latitudes. The technique is quite simple.

First find the LST that is twelve hours different from you LST of birth (line **12**). If LST of birth is less than 12h, add 12h; if it is greater than 12h, subtract 12h. Using the Table of Houses, calculate the Midheaven for that time. The Midheaven for that time is actually the IC (*Imum Coeli*), the cusp of the fourth house for your birth LST at south latitudes. Similarly, calculate the cusps of the eleventh through the third houses at birth LST ± 12h in the usual way. Actually you are calculating the cusps of the fifth through the nine houses for south latitude. In our example chart, if the native had been born at 41° S 39' the cusps would have been:

| | | | | | | |
|---|---|---|---|---|---|---|
| fourth | 10° | ♌ | 23' | Midheaven | 10° | ♒ | 23' |
| fifth | 7° | ♍ | 57' | eleventh | 7° | ♓ | 57' |
| sixth | 5° | ♎ | 47' | twelfth | 5° | ♈ | 47' |
| seventh | 3° | ♏ | 31' | Ascendant | 3° | ♉ | 31' |
| eighth | 1° | ♐ | 8' | second | 1° | ♊ | 8' |
| ninth | 1° | ♑ | 1' | third | 1° | ♋ | 1' |

### Vertex and East Point

There are two other sensitive points that have become quite popular among astrological researchers, the Vertex and the East Point. The first of these, the Vertex, is the degree and minute of the ecliptic that is exactly due west of the observer at the time of the chart. Technically it is the intersection of the prime vertical and the ecliptic. The Vertex is considered a key to relationships with others, often denoting personal qualities we find mirrored by a partner. It is especially useful in synastry (comparing contacts between charts)*. The method for determining this point from the Table of Houses is similar to the method of finding an Ascendant. Here is the procedure.

1. Add or subtract twelve hours to or from the LST of birth (line **12**) as with a south latitude birth. This is similar to the procedure for finding an Ascendant for south latitudes, but watch out for the difference.

2. Instead of using the latitude of birth, subtract the given latitude of birth from 90° to find the value known as the *colatitude*.

3. Now go into the Table of Houses and calculate an Ascendant for the colatitude using the new LST obtained in step 1. This "Ascendant" is actually the Vertex.

In our sample chart the colatitude is 48° 21'. If you perform the calculations correctly according to these rules, you should obtain a Vertex of 1°♏16'.

The East Point, also called the Equatorial Ascendant, is the zodiacal longitude of the degree of the equator that is rising at birth. It is also what the Ascendant would have been if the native had been born at the equator, hence the name, Equatorial Ascendant. Since the Table of Houses in this book gives the Ascendants for 0 latitude, the East Point can be found without calculation.

### The Koch House System

The Koch House System is one of several—including Placidus, derivatives of Placidus such as Dalton's and Alcabitius—that use a trisection of a semi-arc as the basis for calculating the cusps. A semi-arc is a quadrant of a declination circle bounded by the horizon and the meridian as shown in figure 1.

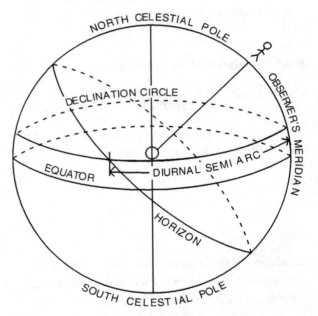

**Figure 1**

The Koch principles are:

1) Trisect the diurnal semi-arc of the MC. Call the result DSA/3.

2) Rotate the MC counter-clockwise to the horizon.

3) Then rotate the MC clockwise above the horizon by DSA/3 degrees. The Ascendant for this position is the 11th house cusp. Repeat this procedure by adding DSA/3 degrees to the MC to find, in turn, the 12th, 1st, 2nd and 3rd house cusps.

---

* See also the booklet *The East Point and the Antivertex* available through ACS Publications.

By following the above explanation, one can manually calculate the Koch cusps by using any table of houses that gives the MC and Ascendant positions.

1) Calculate the sidereal time for the given data.
2) Find the MC and Ascendant for the given latitude and calculated sidereal time.
3) Calculate the sidereal time as if the MC were the Ascendant.
4) Subtract the results of 3) from the result of 1) and divide by 3. Call this result DSA/3
5a) Add DSA/3 to the result from 3).
  b) Calculate the Ascendant as if this were the sidereal time to get the 11th house cusp.

6a) Add DSA/3 to the result from 5a).
  b) Calculate the Ascendant as if this were the sidereal time to get the 12th house cusp.
7a) Add DSA/3 to the result from 6a).
  b) Calculate the Ascendant as if this were the sidereal time to get the Ascendant (which it is). This is obviously redundant but is inserted here to further clarify how the procedure works.
8a) Add DSA/3 to the result from 7a).
  b) Calculate the Ascendant as if this were the sidereal time to get the 2nd house cusp.
9a) Add DSA/3 to the result from 8a).
  b) Calculate the Ascendant as if this were the sidereal time to get the 3rd house cusp.

### Direct Calculation of MC

Calculate the Midheaven (MC) as follows.

1) Find the right ascension of the Midheaven (RAMC) by converting ST of birth to angular measure (1h = 15°).

$$2)\ MC = \arctan \left[ \frac{\tan RAMC}{\cos OE} \right]$$

The result may be 180° off. If so, subtract 180° to place the MC in the same quadrant as the RAMC.

### Direct Calculation of the Ascendant

$$ASC = \arctan \left[ \frac{\cos RAMC}{-(\sin OBLIQUITY \times \tan LATITUDE + \cos OBLIQUITY \times \sin RAMC)} \right]$$

The quadrant of the Ascendant and any other position determined by arctan is unambiguously determined as follows:

| Longitude | = | arctan | ( a | / | b ) |
|---|---|---|---|---|---|
| ↓ | | | ↓ | | ↓ |
| 0- 90° | | | + | | + |
| 90-180° | | | + | | − |
| 180-270° | | | − | | − |
| 270-360° | | | − | | + |

### Calculation of the Intermediate House Cusps

The calculator or computer calculation procedure is as follows:

1) Calculate the Ascensional Difference of the MC
  ADMC = arcsin (sin RAMC × tan OBLIQUITY × tan LATITUDE)
2) Calculate the Oblique Ascension of the MC
  OAMC = RAMC − ADMC
3) Calculate the diurnal semi-arc of the MC
  DSAMC = 90 + ADMC
4) Divide the DSAMC by 3
  ARC = DSAMC/3

5) Calculate the Oblique Ascension of the Houses

$$OA(11) = OAMC + ARC$$
$$OA(12) = OAMC + ARC \times 2$$
$$OA(1) = OAMC + ARC \times 3$$
$$OA(2) = OAMC + ARC \times 4$$
$$OA(3) = OAMC + ARC \times 5$$

6) Calculate the longitude from the OA

$$Longitude = \arctan \left[ \frac{\sin OA}{\cos OA \, \cos OBLIQUITY - \tan LATITUDE \times \sin OBLIQUITY} \right]$$

Like the other semi-arc systems, the Ascendant is the 1st house cusp and MC is the 10th house cusp. Like the other semi-arc systems, except for Alcabitius, the calculation procedure breaks down when the MC is circumpolar since the MC cannot then be rotated through its semi-arc to the horizon.

Since the house cusps are only clearly defined on the ecliptic, a planet off the ecliptic, i.e., with latitude greater than 0° will not clearly fall in one house or another when it is close to a cusp. The greater the latitude, the more uncertain is the house position. In the current practice of astrology, when we construct a flat, two-dimensional chart we ignore the three-dimensional ramifications of house position determination.

If one draws curves from the north ecliptic pole to the south ecliptic pole though the points on the ecliptic determined by the Koch system, then the lunes defined in this way are implicitly the Koch house curves.

Supporters of the Koch system claim that the cusps are unusually sensitive to transits and directions, particularly in mundane affairs. Indeed, the "Winning" system of Joyce Wehrman is based on transiting Koch house cusps aspecting natal planets and cusps. She claims that if one used Placidian cusps one would not enjoy as frequent trips to the cashier to cash in winning tickets as one does when using Koch cusps.

Walter Koch, who first published this system, makes the misleading claim that his is the only method calculated "for the exact birthplace." Since most other systems, whether using semi-arcs or not, are also latitude dependent, they are just as "birthplace" oriented as Koch's. From the interpretation point of view, the only basis for a claim of superiority of one house system over another would be convincing evidence that the house system explained more observable data than any other. No study has been published that supports any such claim for any house system.

## LOCATING PLACIDUS HOUSE CUSPS

The Table of Houses in this book gives a complete set of house cusps for every four minutes of Sidereal Time for latitudes from 0° to 60°. For those readers who have access to a trigonometric calculator, the methods for extracting house cusps by trigonometry are given at the end of this section. Trigonometry gives the most accurate results, but the tables supplied here to assist in your calculations will suffice for most purposes.

Since the tables give house cusps only for every four minutes of Sidereal Time and for whole degrees of latitude, we must either be satisfied with approximate house cusps, say to the nearest degree at best, or we must interpolate. But before we get to that, let us learn more about the layout of the Table of Houses.

As you thumb through the table, you will note that the Sidereal Time is given at the top of the page, along with a zodiacal longitude. There is only one Midheaven for each Sidereal time because the Midheaven is independent of the latitude of the place. But beneath the Midheaven and the ST are five columns of positions, headed as follows: 11, 12, ASC, 2, 3. These are the cusps of the eleventh, twelfth, first, second and third houses. The first house cusp is also called the Ascendant. These house cusps are not independent of latitude and therefore must be listed for every degree of latitude. That makes finding house cusps other than the tenth (Midheaven) a bit complicated, but it doesn't require any mathematics beyond the high-school level.

The techniques outlined here for interpolating precise cusps from a table apply to any kind of house tables, even though the numbers may vary. The house division system of Placidus is by no means the only system. A variety of other house systems exist, among them Koch, Regiomontanus, Equal, Meridian, Topocentric, Porphyry and Alcabitius. You can order a report called *House Systems Comparison* from Astro Communications Services. The report lists house cusps for any horoscope in nine systems and specifies the house placements of the planets in each of the nine systems. A brief discussion of the astronomical basis of the Placidus is given later on in this section.

Our birth LST of 20h 51m 21s falls between 20h 48m 0s and 20h 52m 0s. At these two times, 9°≈ 34' and 10°≈ 33', respectively, are on the Midheaven. Our birthtime Midheaven will fall between these two values. We can roughly estimate the house cusps by observing that our birth LST is nearer to 20h 52m than to 20h 48m and that our latitude, 41 N 39', is about two thirds of the way from 41 N to 42. Our estimates would be: Midheaven: 10°≈, eleventh: 9°♓ twelfth: 19°♈, first:

5°♊, second: 28°♊, third: 18°♋. Many astrologers never go beyond this point, and you can do a great deal with approximate house cusps. If you don't like to calculate, this is a good shortcut to take until you are ready to do more. On the other hand, all predictive techniques involving directions or progressions require greater accuracy than this. So we will now find out how to get that accuracy.

## Placidus Table of Houses for Latitudes 0° to 60° North

| 11 | 12 | ASC | 2 | 3 | 11 | 12 | ASC | 2 | 3 | LAT. |
|---|---|---|---|---|---|---|---|---|---|---|
| 20h 48m 0s — 312° 0' 0' — 09 ≈ 34 | | | | | 20h 52m 0s — 313° 0' 0' — 10 ≈ 33 | | | | | |
| 10♓30 | 13♈03 | 14♉28 | 13♊24 | 11♋02 | 11♓34 | 14♈07 | 15♉28 | 14♊20 | 11♋58 | 0 |
| 10 15 | 13 23 | 15 58 | 14 42 | 11 41 | 11 20 | 14 29 | 16 59 | 15 38 | 12 37 | 5 |
| 10 00 | 13 44 | 17 34 | 16 01 | 12 21 | 11 06 | 14 52 | 18 37 | 16 58 | 13 16 | 10 |
| 09 44 | 14 07 | 19 19 | 17 25 | 13 02 | 10 51 | 15 17 | 20 24 | 18 21 | 13 57 | 15 |
| 09 27 | 14 33 | 21 15 | 18 53 | 13 44 | 10 34 | 15 45 | 22 21 | 19 50 | 14 39 | 20 |
| 09 23 | 14 39 | 21 40 | 19 12 | 13 53 | 10 31 | 15 51 | 22 46 | 20 09 | 14 48 | 21 |
| 09 20 | 14 44 | 22 06 | 19 31 | 14 02 | 10 28 | 15 57 | 23 12 | 20 27 | 14 57 | 22 |
| 09 16 | 14 50 | 22 32 | 19 50 | 14 11 | 10 24 | 16 04 | 23 38 | 20 47 | 15 06 | 23 |
| 09 12 | 14 56 | 22 59 | 20 09 | 14 21 | 10 20 | 16 10 | 24 06 | 21 06 | 15 15 | 24 |
| 09 08 | 15 03 | 23 26 | 20 29 | 14 30 | 10 17 | 16 17 | 24 33 | 21 26 | 15 25 | 25 |
| 09 04 | 15 09 | 23 55 | 20 50 | 14 39 | 10 13 | 16 24 | 25 02 | 21 46 | 15 34 | 26 |
| 09 00 | 15 15 | 24 24 | 21 10 | 14 49 | 10 09 | 16 31 | 25 32 | 22 07 | 15 44 | 27 |
| 08 56 | 15 22 | 24 54 | 21 31 | 14 59 | 10 05 | 16 38 | 26 02 | 22 28 | 15 54 | 28 |
| 08 51 | 15 29 | 25 25 | 21 53 | 15 09 | 10 01 | 16 46 | 26 33 | 22 49 | 16 04 | 29 |
| 08 47 | 15 37 | 25 57 | 22 15 | 15 19 | 09 56 | 16 54 | 27 06 | 23 11 | 16 14 | 30 |
| 08 42 | 15 44 | 26 31 | 22 37 | 15 30 | 09 52 | 17 02 | 27 39 | 23 34 | 16 24 | 31 |
| 08 38 | 15 52 | 27 05 | 23 01 | 15 40 | 09 48 | 17 10 | 28 14 | 23 57 | 16 35 | 32 |
| 08 33 | 16 00 | 27 41 | 23 25 | 15 51 | 09 43 | 17 19 | 28 50 | 24 21 | 16 46 | 33 |
| 08 28 | 16 08 | 28 17 | 23 49 | 16 03 | 09 38 | 17 28 | 29 27 | 24 45 | 16 57 | 34 |
| 08 23 | 16 17 | 28 56 | 24 14 | 16 14 | 09 33 | 17 37 | 00♊05 | 25 10 | 17 08 | 35 |
| 08 17 | 16 26 | 29 35 | 24 39 | 16 26 | 09 28 | 17 47 | 00 45 | 25 36 | 17 20 | 36 |
| 08 12 | 16 36 | 00♊17 | 25 06 | 16 38 | 09 23 | 17 58 | 01 27 | 26 02 | 17 32 | 37 |
| 08 06 | 16 46 | 01 00 | 25 33 | 16 50 | 09 18 | 18 09 | 02 10 | 26 29 | 17 44 | 38 |
| 08 00 | 16 57 | 01 45 | 26 01 | 17 03 | 09 12 | 18 20 | 02 55 | 26 57 | 17 57 | 39 |
| 07 54 | 17 08 | 02 32 | 26 30 | 17 16 | 09 06 | 18 32 | 03 42 | 27 26 | 18 10 | 40 |
| 07 48 | 17 19 | 03 21 | 27 01 | 17 30 | 09 00 | 18 44 | 04 31 | 27 56 | 18 23 | 41 |
| 07 41 | 17 32 | 04 12 | 27 32 | 17 44 | 08 54 | 18 58 | 05 22 | 28 27 | 18 37 | 42 |
| 07 34 | 17 45 | 05 05 | 28 04 | 17 58 | 08 47 | 19 12 | 06 16 | 28 59 | 18 52 | 43 |
| 07 27 | 17 58 | 06 02 | 28 37 | 18 13 | 08 40 | 19 26 | 07 12 | 29 32 | 19 07 | 44 |
| 07 19 | 18 13 | 07 01 | 29 12 | 18 29 | 08 33 | 19 42 | 08 11 | 00♋07 | 19 22 | 45 |
| 07 11 | 18 29 | 08 03 | 29 48 | 18 45 | 08 26 | 19 59 | 09 13 | 00 43 | 19 38 | 46 |
| 07 03 | 18 45 | 09 08 | 00♋26 | 19 02 | 08 18 | 20 17 | 10 18 | 01 21 | 19 55 | 47 |
| 06 54 | 19 03 | 10 17 | 01 06 | 19 19 | 08 09 | 20 36 | 11 26 | 02 00 | 20 12 | 48 |
| 06 45 | 19 22 | 11 29 | 01 47 | 19 37 | 08 01 | 20 56 | 12 38 | 02 41 | 20 30 | 49 |
| 06 35 | 19 42 | 12 46 | 02 30 | 19 56 | 07 51 | 21 18 | 13 54 | 03 24 | 20 49 | 50 |
| 06 25 | 20 04 | 14 07 | 03 15 | 20 16 | 07 42 | 21 42 | 15 15 | 04 08 | 21 09 | 51 |
| 06 14 | 20 28 | 15 33 | 04 02 | 20 37 | 07 31 | 22 08 | 16 40 | 04 56 | 21 29 | 52 |
| 06 02 | 20 55 | 17 03 | 04 52 | 20 59 | 07 20 | 22 36 | 18 10 | 05 45 | 21 51 | 53 |
| 05 50 | 21 23 | 18 40 | 05 45 | 21 22 | 07 08 | 23 06 | 19 45 | 06 37 | 22 14 | 54 |
| 05 37 | 21 55 | 20 22 | 06 41 | 21 47 | 06 56 | 23 40 | 21 26 | 07 32 | 22 38 | 55 |
| 05 22 | 22 29 | 22 11 | 07 39 | 22 13 | 06 42 | 24 17 | 23 13 | 08 30 | 23 04 | 56 |
| 05 07 | 23 08 | 24 06 | 08 42 | 22 40 | 06 28 | 24 59 | 25 07 | 09 32 | 23 31 | 57 |
| 04 50 | 23 51 | 26 09 | 09 48 | 23 09 | 06 12 | 25 45 | 27 08 | 10 38 | 24 00 | 58 |
| 04 32 | 24 40 | 28 19 | 10 59 | 23 41 | 05 55 | 26 38 | 29 16 | 11 48 | 24 30 | 59 |
| 04♓13 | 25♈36 | 00♊38 | 12♋15 | 24♋14 | 05♓36 | 27♈38 | 01♋32 | 13♋02 | 25♋03 | 60 |

*The Table of Houses gives zodiacal longitude and house cusps for every four minutes of Sidereal Time. The Midheaven, which is the same at all latitudes, is given at the top. The other house cusps are given for 0° to 60°.*

### Interpolation

Interpolation works because there is a constant proportional relationship between change of LST and change in the Midheaven and in the other house cusps. There is a similar relationship as well between change in latitude and change in house cusps.

We will call the times in the Table of Houses just before and just after birth "earlier LST" and "later LST" and enter them on lines **30** and **31** respectively. In order to interpolate, we need to know the LST increment or time change between earlier LST and birth LST. We do this by subtracting earlier LST from birth LST. The result goes on line **32**.

| | | |
|---|---|---|
| **29 Local Sidereal Time (12)** | 29 | *20* h *51* m *21* s |
| **30 Earlier LST** (Table of Houses) | 30 | *20* h *48* m ___ s |
| **31 Later** LST (Table of Houses) | 31 | *20* h *52* m ___ s |
| **32 LST Increment** (Subtract **29 − 30 = 32**) | 32 | *3* m *21* s  ΔLST |

| | | |
|---|---|---|
| **33 Midheaven At Later LST** (Table of Houses) | 33 | *10* °♒*33* ' |
| **34 Midheaven At Earlier LST** (Table of Houses) | 34 | *9* °♒*34* ' |
| **35 4m Midheaven Increment** (subtract **33 − 34 = 35**) | 35 | ° *59* ' |

Next we need to know how much the Midheaven changed in the four minutes between earlier LST and later LST. We find out by reading the Midheavens at the two times from the Table of Houses and subtracting.

| | | |
|---|---|---|
| **36 Midheaven Increment** (32, 35, Table XI) | 36 | ° *49* ' |

When we know how much time elapsed between earlier LST and birth LST (LST increment) and how much the Midheaven changed in the four minutes between earlier LST and later LST (Midheaven interval), we can deduce how much the Midheaven changed between earlier LST and birth LST (Midheaven increment), using Table XI. Read across the top to find the column closest to the LST increment, then read down to find the line for the Midheaven interval. Where they meet is the Midheaven increment. In our example, the 3m 20s column is closest to our LST increment of 3m21s. The one-second difference is not significant. We read down to the 0° 59' line and find that our Midheaven increment is 49'.

## Table XI House Cusp Interpolation Between Sidereal Times

| CUSP INTVL | m s 2 44 | m s 2 48 | m s 2 52 | m s 2 56 | m s 3 0 | m s 3 4 | m s 3 8 | m s 3 12 | m s 3 16 | m s 3 20 | m s 3 24 | m s 3 28 | m s 3 32 | m s 3 36 | m s 3 40 | m s 3 44 | m s 3 48 | m s 3 52 | m s 3 56 | m s 4 0 | CUSP INTVL |
|---|---|---|---|---|---|---|---|---|---|---|---|---|---|---|---|---|---|---|---|---|---|
| 0 31 | 0 21 | 0 22 | 0 22 | 0 23 | 0 23 | 0 24 | 0 24 | 0 25 | 0 25 | 0 26 | 0 26 | 0 27 | 0 27 | 0 28 | 0 28 | 0 29 | 0 29 | 0 30 | 0 30 | 0 31 | 0 31 |
| 0 32 | 0 22 | 0 22 | 0 23 | 0 23 | 0 24 | 0 25 | 0 25 | 0 26 | 0 26 | 0 27 | 0 27 | 0 28 | 0 28 | 0 29 | 0 29 | 0 30 | 0 30 | 0 31 | 0 31 | 0 32 | 0 32 |
| 0 33 | 0 23 | 0 23 | 0 24 | 0 24 | 0 25 | 0 25 | 0 26 | 0 26 | 0 27 | 0 27 | 0 28 | 0 28 | 0 29 | 0 29 | 0 30 | 0 31 | 0 31 | 0 32 | 0 32 | 0 33 | 0 33 |
| 0 34 | 0 23 | 0 24 | 0 24 | 0 25 | 0 26 | 0 26 | 0 27 | 0 27 | 0 28 | 0 28 | 0 29 | 0 30 | 0 31 | 0 31 | 0 32 | 0 32 | 0 33 | 0 34 |
| … | | | | | | | | | | | | | | | | | | | | | … |
| 0 56 | 0 38 | 0 39 | 0 40 | 0 41 | 0 42 | 0 43 | 0 44 | 0 45 | 0 46 | 0 47 | 0 48 | 0 49 | 0 49 | 0 50 | 0 51 | 0 52 | 0 53 | 0 54 | 0 55 | 0 56 | 0 56 |
| 0 57 | 0 39 | 0 40 | 0 41 | 0 42 | 0 43 | 0 44 | 0 45 | 0 46 | 0 47 | 0 48 | 0 48 | 0 49 | 0 50 | 0 51 | 0 52 | 0 53 | 0 54 | 0 55 | 0 56 | 0 57 | 0 57 |
| 0 58 | 0 40 | 0 41 | 0 42 | 0 43 | 0 44 | 0 44 | 0 45 | 0 46 | 0 47 | 0 48 | 0 49 | 0 50 | 0 51 | 0 52 | 0 53 | 0 54 | 0 55 | 0 56 | 0 57 | 0 58 | 0 58 |
| 0 59 | 0 41 | 0 42 | 0 43 | 0 44 | 0 44 | 0 45 | 0 46 | 0 47 | 0 48 | 0 49 | 0 50 | 0 51 | 0 52 | 0 53 | 0 54 | 0 55 | 0 56 | 0 57 | 0 58 | 0 59 | 0 59 |
| 1 0 | 0 41 | 0 42 | 0 43 | 0 44 | 0 45 | 0 46 | 0 47 | 0 48 | 0 49 | 0 50 | 0 51 | 0 52 | 0 53 | 0 54 | 0 55 | 0 56 | 0 57 | 0 58 | 0 59 | 1 0 | 1 0 |

*Table XI, House Cusp Interpolation Between Sidereal Times, gives the cusp increment, the amount by which the house cusp changed from earlier LST to birth LST.*

What Table XI actually does is solve the following proportion for us

$$\frac{\text{cusp increment}}{\text{cusp interval}} = \frac{\text{LST increment}}{\text{LST interval}}$$

In our example,

$$\frac{\text{cusp increment}}{59'} = \frac{3\text{m } 21\text{s}}{4\text{m}}$$

$$\text{cusp increment} = \frac{3\text{m}21\text{s}}{4\text{m}} \times 59'$$

$$= 49'$$

### Direct Calculation

If you have a calculator, or even if you do not, you may prefer to do this calculation directly instead of using Table XI. In this case, first translate the LST increment into decimal minutes to make the arithmetic easier. Do this by dividing the seconds portion by 60 and adding it to the whole minutes. for example.

$$21 \div 60 = .35$$
$$3\text{m } 21\text{s} = 3.35\text{m}$$

Then solve the proportion as above.

$$\begin{aligned}\text{cusp increment} &= (3.35 \div 4) \times 59' \\ &= 0.8375 \times 59' \\ &= 49.4125' \\ &\cong 49' \text{ (rounded off)}\end{aligned}$$

Although cusp intervals are different for different houses, the LST increment and LST interval are the same for all houses in the chart. Therefore the time ratio, 0.8375 in our example, will be the same for all houses. Note it down for later use. If you have a calculator that stores a constant multiplier, this is an opportunity to use it.

### Logarithms

House cusps can be interpolated using logarithms as well. You will recall that logs convert all multiplications into additions and all divisions into subtractions. In our example,

$$\frac{3\text{m } 21\text{s}}{4\text{m}} \times 59'$$

becomes

$$\log 3\text{m } 21\text{s} - \log 4\text{m} + \log 59'$$

In Table IX the numbers across the top are units that can be read either as hours, as degrees or even as minutes. The vertical column at the left refers to minutes if you are looking up degrees and minutes or hours and minutes, or it refers to seconds if you are looking up minutes and seconds. In other words, the column at the left gives sixtieths of the numbers along the top.

From Table IX, we get the following values. Log 3m 21s = .85517; log 4m = .77815. From Table X we get log 59' = 1.38751.

We calculate as follows.

$$\begin{aligned}&\phantom{-}.85517 \\ -&\phantom{.}.77815 \\ \hline =&\phantom{.}.07702 \\ +&1.38751 \\ \hline =&1.46453\end{aligned}$$

Working Table X backwards, we find that 1.46453 is the log of 49'25" +. This rounds off to 49', almost the same result we got by other methods.

No matter which method we use to get the Midheaven increment, we must add the increment to the Midheaven at earlier time to get the Midheaven at birthtime. When we know the Midheaven, we also know the cusp of the fourth house, which is opposite, that is, exactly six signs away.

| | | |
|---|---|---|
| 34 | 9° ≈ 34' | |
| 35 | ° 59' | |
| 36 | ° 49' | |
| **37 Midheaven At Birth LST (add 34 + 36 = 37)** | 37 10° ≈ 23' | **MC** |

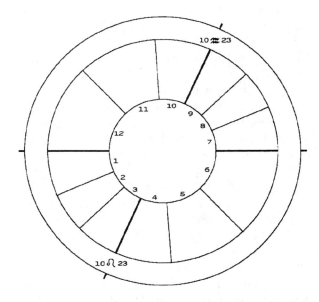

*The IC [Imum Coeli], the cusp of the fourth house, is alway exactly six signs away from the MC [Medium Coeli] or Midheaven, the cusp of the tenth house.*

| | | |
|---|---|---|
| 38 **Lower Latitude** (Table of Houses) | 38 *41 ° N* | |
| 39 **Higher Latitude** (Table of Houses) | 39 *42 ° N* | |
| 40 **Latitude Increment** (Subtract **Birth Latitude − 38 = 40**) | 40 ° *39'* | Δ **Lat** |

The Midheaven at a given LST is the same at all latitudes, but the cusps of the other houses vary with latitude. The Table of Houses in this book gives the cusps of the eleventh, twelfth, first (Ascendant), second and third houses for 0°, 5°, 10°, 15° and every whole degree of latitude from 20° to 60°.

To find the house cusps at birth LST at birth latitude, our strategy will be to find the house cusps at birth LST at the two latitudes in the Table that are nearest the birth latitude, using exactly the same methods we used to find the Midheaven, and then to interpolate between latitudes. On lines **38**, **39** and **40**, we locate those two latitudes

and find the increment from the lower latitude to birth latitude, which we will need later in order to interpolate. It is a good idea at this point to fill in the **LST** and **Latitude** columns of lines **41** to **53** completely. All the values are now known, and they serve to label the lines and thereby avoid confusion.

Lines **41** to **45** of the worksheet are devoted to finding the house cusps at birth LST at the lower latitude. The method is exactly the same as the used in finding the Midheaven on lines **30** to **37**. Specific instructions for each line are given on the worksheet.

41 **House Cusps at Later LST, Lower Latitude** (Table of Houses)
42 **House Cusps at Earlier LST, Lower Latitude** (Table of Houses)
43 **4m Cusp Intervals** (Subtract **41 − 42 = 43**)
44 **Cusp Increments** (32, 43, Table XI)
45 **House Cusps at Birth LST, Lower Latitude** (add **42 + 44 = 45**)

| | LST | Latitude | 11 | 12 | ASC | 2 | 3 |
|---|---|---|---|---|---|---|---|
| 41 | LATER *20:52* | LOWER (38) | *9° ℋ 0'* | *18° ♈ 44'* | *4° ♊ 31'* | *27° ♊ 56'* | *18° ♋ 23'* |
| 42 | EARLIER *20:48* | | *7° ℋ 48'* | *17° ♈ 19'* | *3° ♊ 21'* | *27° ♊ 1'* | *17° ♋ 30'* |
| 43 | 4m | *41° N* | *1° 12'* | *1° 25'* | *1° 10'* | *55'* | *53'* |
| 44 | LINE 32 *3:21* | | *1° 1'* | *1° 11'* | *58'* | *46'* | *44'* |
| 45 | BIRTH *20:51:21* | | *8° ℋ 49'* | *18° ♈ 30'* | *4° ♊ 19'* | *27° ♊ 47'* | *18° ♋ 14'* |

This part of the process of casting a chart is by far the most subject to error, not because any link in the chain of calculation is especially difficult but because the chain is so long. It is important to check your work continually so that if you make an error you will catch it and correct it before it spoils future work.

For example, line **41** should be greater than line **42**. Subtracting, you should get a difference of less than two degrees in most cases, less than four degrees in extreme cases. If you do not, check to see that you have copied from the right place in the table of houses and have done the sexagesimal subtraction correctly.

Line **44** should be smaller than line **43** and in the same proportion to it as the LST increment is to the interval 4m. That is, in our example, 3m21s is about three quarters of 4m. Therefore, each increment on line **44** should be about three quarters of the interval on line **43**.

Check to be sure that the cusp on line **45** for each house is between the cusps on lines **41** and **42** (greater than line **42** and less than line **41**.)

## Placidus Table of Houses
## for Latitudes 0° to 60° North

| 20h 48m 0s | | 312° 0' 0' | | | | 20h 52m 0s | | 313° 0' 0' | | | |
| 09 ≈ 34 | | | | | | 10 ≈ 33 | | | | | |
| 11 | 12 | ASC | 2 | 3 | | 11 | 12 | ASC | 2 | 3 | LAT. |
|---|---|---|---|---|---|---|---|---|---|---|---|
| 10 H30 | 13 T03 | 14 ☉28 | 13 Ⅱ24 | 11 ☉02 | | 11 H34 | 14 T07 | 15 ☉28 | 14 Ⅱ20 | 11 ☉58 | 0 |
| 10 15 | 13 23 | 15 58 | 14 42 | 11 41 | | 11 20 | 14 29 | 16 59 | 15 38 | 12 37 | 5 |
| 10 00 | 13 44 | 17 34 | 16 01 | 12 21 | | 11 06 | 14 52 | 18 37 | 16 58 | 13 16 | 10 |
| 09 44 | 14 07 | 19 19 | 17 25 | 13 02 | | 10 51 | 15 17 | 20 24 | 18 21 | 13 57 | 15 |
| 09 27 | 14 33 | 21 15 | 18 53 | 13 44 | | 10 34 | 15 45 | 22 21 | 19 50 | 14 39 | 20 |
| 07 48 | 17 19 | 03 21 | 27 01 | 17 30 | | 09 00 | 18 44 | 04 31 | 27 56 | 18 23 | 41 |
| 07 41 | 17 32 | 04 12 | 27 32 | 17 44 | | 08 54 | 18 58 | 05 22 | 28 27 | 18 37 | 42 |
| 07 34 | 17 45 | 05 05 | 28 04 | 17 58 | | 08 47 | 19 12 | 06 16 | 28 59 | 18 52 | 43 |
| 07 27 | 17 58 | 06 02 | 28 37 | 18 13 | | 08 40 | 19 26 | 07 12 | 29 33 | 19 07 | 44 |
| 07 19 | 18 13 | 07 01 | 29 12 | 18 29 | | 08 33 | 19 42 | 08 11 | 00☉07 | 19 22 | 45 |

*The Table of Houses gives house cusps for 0°, 5°, 10°, 15° and every whole degree of latitude from 20° to 60°.*

---

**46 House Cusps at Later LST, Higher Latitude** (Table of Houses)
**47 House Cusps at Earlier LST, Higher Latitude** (Table of Houses)
**48 4m Cusp Intervals** (Subtract 46 – 47 = 48)
**49 Cusp Increments** (32, 48, Table XI)
**50 House Cusps at Birth LST, Higher Latitude** (add 47 + 49 = 50)

| | LST | Latitude | 11 | 12 | ASC | 2 | 3 |
|---|---|---|---|---|---|---|---|
| 46 | LATER 20:52 | HIGHER (39) | 8° H 54' | 18° T 58' | 5° Ⅱ 22' | 28° Ⅱ 27' | 18° ☉ 37' |
| 47 | EARLIER 20:48 | | 7° H 41' | 17° T 32' | 4° Ⅱ 12' | 27° Ⅱ 32' | 17° ☉ 44' |
| 48 | 4m | 42°N | 1° 13' | 1° 26' | 1° 10' | 55' | 53' |
| 49 | LINE 32 3:21 | | 1° 1' | 1° 12' | 58' | 46' | 44' |
| 50 | BIRTH 20:51:21 | | 8° H 42' | 18° T 44' | 5° Ⅱ 10' | 28° Ⅱ 18' | 18° ☉ 28' |

Lines **46** to **50** of the worksheet are devoted to finding the house cusps at birthtime at the higher latitude. The method is exactly the same as that used for the lower latitude on lines **41** to **45**. Check your work in the same ways. Also, compare line 48 to line 43 and line 49 to line 44. If for a given house they differ by more than a few minutes, something is wrong.

---

**51 1° Cusp Intervals**
If **50** is greater than **45**, rewrite **45** below. Subtract **50 – 45 = 51**.
If **50** is less than **45** mark **51** and **52** negative (–) for that house. Subtract **45 – 50 = 51**.
**52 Cusp Increments for Latitude** (40, 51, Table XII)
**53 House Cusps at Birth LST, Birth Latitude** (add 45 + 52 = 53)

| | LST | Latitude | 11 | 12 | ASC | 2 | 3 |
|---|---|---|---|---|---|---|---|
| 45 | BIRTH (29) | LOWER 41°N | | 18° T 30' | 4° Ⅱ 19' | 27° Ⅱ 47' | 18° ☉ 14' |
| 51 | | 1° | – 7' | 14' | 51' | 31' | 14' |
| 52 | 20 h 51 m 21 s | LINE 40 39' | – 5' | 9' | 33' | 20' | 9' |
| 53 | | BIRTH 41°N 39' | 8° H 44' | 18° T 39' | 4° Ⅱ 52' | 28° Ⅱ 7' | 18° ☉ 23' |

## Table XII House Cusp Interpolation between Latitudes

| LAT INC | HOUSE CUSP INTERVAL | | | | | | | | | | | | | | | | | | | | | | | | | | | | | | LAT INC |
|---|---|---|---|---|---|---|---|---|---|---|---|---|---|---|---|---|---|---|---|---|---|---|---|---|---|---|---|---|---|---|---|
| | 1 | 2 | 3 | 4 | 5 | 6 | 7 | 8 | 9 | 10 | 11 | 12 | 13 | 14 | 15 | 16 | 17 | 18 | 19 | 20 | 21 | 22 | 23 | 24 | 25 | 26 | 27 | 28 | 29 | 30 | |
| 1 | 0 | 0 | 0 | 0 | 0 | 0 | 0 | 0 | 0 | 0 | 0 | 0 | 0 | 0 | 0 | 0 | 0 | 0 | 0 | 0 | 0 | 0 | 0 | 0 | 0 | 0 | 0 | 0 | 0 | 1 | 1 |
| 2 | 0 | 0 | 0 | 0 | 0 | 0 | 0 | 0 | 0 | 0 | 0 | 0 | 0 | 0 | 0 | 0 | 1 | 1 | 1 | 1 | 1 | 1 | 1 | 1 | 1 | 1 | 1 | 1 | 1 | 2 | 2 |
| 3 | 0 | 0 | 0 | 0 | 0 | 0 | 0 | 0 | 0 | 1 | 1 | 1 | 1 | 1 | 1 | 1 | 1 | 1 | 1 | 1 | 1 | 1 | 1 | 1 | 1 | 1 | 1 | 1 | 1 | 2 | 3 |
| 35 | 1 | 1 | 2 | 2 | 3 | 4 | 4 | 5 | 5 | 6 | 6 | 7 | 8 | 8 | 9 | 9 | 10 | 11 | 11 | 12 | 12 | 13 | 13 | 14 | 15 | 15 | 16 | 16 | 17 | 18 | 35 |
| 36 | 1 | 1 | 2 | 2 | 3 | 4 | 4 | 5 | 5 | 6 | 7 | 7 | 8 | 8 | 9 | 10 | 10 | 11 | 11 | 12 | 13 | 13 | 14 | 14 | 15 | 16 | 16 | 17 | 17 | 18 | 36 |
| 37 | 1 | 1 | 2 | 2 | 3 | 4 | 4 | 5 | 5 | 6 | 7 | 7 | 8 | 9 | 9 | 10 | 10 | 11 | 12 | 12 | 13 | 14 | 14 | 15 | 15 | 16 | 17 | 17 | 18 | 19 | 37 |
| 38 | 1 | 1 | 2 | 3 | 3 | 4 | 4 | 5 | 6 | 6 | 7 | 8 | 8 | 9 | 10 | 10 | 11 | 11 | 12 | 13 | 13 | 14 | 15 | 15 | 16 | 16 | 17 | 18 | 18 | 19 | 38 |
| 39 | 1 | 1 | 2 | 3 | 3 | 4 | 5 | 5 | 6 | 7 | 7 | 8 | 8 | 9 | 10 | 10 | 11 | 12 | 12 | 13 | 14 | 14 | 15 | 16 | 16 | 17 | 18 | 18 | 19 | 20 | 39 |
| 40 | 1 | 1 | 2 | 3 | 3 | 4 | 5 | 5 | 6 | 7 | 7 | 8 | 9 | 9 | 10 | 11 | 11 | 12 | 13 | 13 | 14 | 15 | 15 | 16 | 17 | 17 | 18 | 19 | 19 | 20 | 40 |

*Table XII, House Cusp Interpolation between Latitudes, gives the cusp increment for latitude, the amount by which the house cusp at the birth latitude differs from the cusp at the lower whole latitude.*

When we have the birthtime cusps at the two whole latitudes, we must interpolate between them to find birthtime cusps at birth latitude. We do this on lines **51**, **52** and **53**, using Table XII for the interpolation.*

Sometimes house cusps *increase* as latitude increases. When they do, the cusp at the higher latitude (line **50**) is greater than the cusp at the lower latitude (line **45**). In that case, to get the cusp interval for latitude, (line **51**) you subtract line **45** from line **50**. To make this easier, we have provided a place on the worksheet to rewrite line **45** below line **50**. You should fill in a space on this line only if the cusp of that house is increasing, that is, if line **50** is greater than line **45** for that house. If it is, add the cusp increment from Table XII (line **52**) to the cusp at the lower latitude (line **45**) to get the final cusp (line **53**). In our example, see the twelfth, Ascendant, second and third houses.

Sometimes house cusps *decrease* as latitude increases, and the birthtime cusp at the higher latitude (line **50**) is less than the cusp at the lower latitude (line **45**). To get the cusp interval for latitude (line **52**), subtract line **50** from line **45**. Line **50** is already below line **45**, so there is no need to rewrite it. Mark the difference (line **51**) as negative with a minus sign. The cusp increment (line **52**) will also be negative, so mark it with a minus sign too, to remind you to subtract it from line **45** later instead of adding it. See the eleventh house in our example.

Once you have found the eastern house cusps, the tenth through the third, it is simple to find the western cusps, the fourth through the ninth. Each of the western cusps is opposite, exactly six signs away from, one of the eastern cusps. The complete house cusps for our example are:

| | | | | | |
|---|---|---|---|---|---|
| Midheaven | 10° ♒ 23' | | fourth | 10° ♌ 23' |
| eleventh | 8° ♓ 44' | | fifth | 8° ♍ 44' |
| twelfth | 18° ♈ 39' | | sixth | 18° ♎ 39' |
| Ascendant | 4° ♊ 52' | | seventh | 4° ♐ 52' |
| second | 28° ♊ 7' | | eighth | 28° ♐ 7' |
| third | 18° ♋ 23' | | ninth | 18° ♑ 23' |

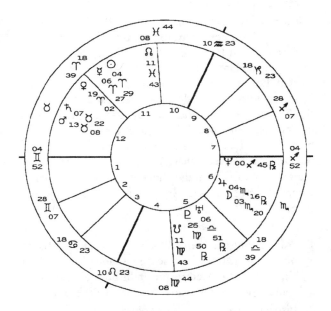

*Our sample chart completed.*

* If birth latitude is less than 20°, the difference between the two whole latitudes will be 5° instead of 1° and the difference between the cusps of a house at those two latitudes will be a 5° cusp interval instead of a 1° cusp interval. Two extra steps are necessary (1) To get the 1° cusp interval for each house, divide the 5° cusp interval by five. Enter the quotient on line **51**. (2) If the latitude increment on line **40** is greater than 1°, the largest argument in Table XII, go into Table XII, go into Table XII with only the minutes part of the latitude increment. Add the cusp increment you get from Table XII to the product of the 1° cusp interval multiplied by the number of whole degrees in the latitude increment on line **40**. The result of this calculation is the cusp increment for latitude and goes on line **52**.

### South Latitudes

These Table of Houses are calculated for north latitudes only, but they can easily be used for casting charts of persons born in south latitudes. The technique is quite simple.

First find the LST that is twelve hours different from you LST of birth (line **12**). If LST of birth is less than 12h, add 12h; if it is greater than 12h, subtract 12h. Using the Table of Houses, calculate the Midheaven for that time. The Midheaven for that time is actually the IC (*Imum Coeli*), the cusp of the fourth house for your birth LST at south latitudes. Similarly, calculate the cusps of the eleventh through the third houses at birth LST ± 12h in the usual way. Actually you are calculating the cusps of the fifth through the nine houses for south latitude. In our example chart, if the native had been born at 41° S 39' the cusps would have been:

| | | | | | | |
|---|---|---|---|---|---|---|
| fourth | 10° | ♌ | 23' | Midheaven | 10° ♒ 23' |
| fifth | 13° | ♍ | 29' | eleventh | 13° ♓ 29' |
| sixth | 11° | ♎ | 7' | twelfth | 11° ♈ 7' |
| seventh | 3° | ♏ | 31' | Ascendant | 3° ♉ 31' |
| eighth | 1° | ♐ | 57' | second | 1° ♊ 57' |
| ninth | 4° | ♑ | 52' | third | 4° ♋ 52' |

### Vertex and East Point

There are two other sensitive points that have become quite popular among astrological researchers, the Vertex and the East Point. The first of these, the Vertex, is the degree and minute of the ecliptic that is exactly due west of the observer at the time of the chart. Technically it is the intersection of the prime vertical and the ecliptic. The Vertex is considered a key to relationships with others often denoting personal qualities we find mirrored by a partner. It is especially useful in synastry (comparing contacts between charts)*. The method for determining this point from the Table of Houses is similar to the method of finding an Ascendant. Here is the procedure.

1. Add or subtract twelve hours to or from the LST of birth (line **12**) as with a south latitude birth. This is similar to the procedure for finding an Ascendant for south latitudes, but watch out for the difference.
2. Instead of using the latitude of birth, subtract the given latitude of birth from 90° to find the value known as the *colatitude*.
3. Now go into the Table of Houses and calculate an Ascendant for the colatitude using the new LST obtained in step 1. This "Ascendant" is actually the Vertex.

In our sample chart the colatitude is 48° 21'. If you perform the calculations correctly according to these rules, you should obtain a Vertex of 1° ♏ 16'.

The East Point, also called the Equatorial Ascendant, is the zodiacal longitude of the degree of the equator that is rising at birth. It is also what the Ascendant would have been if the native had been born at the equator, hence the name, Equatorial Ascendant. Since the Table of Houses in this book gives the Ascendants for 0 latitude, the East Point can be found without calculation.

### The Placidian System

The house division system of Placidus does not divide the space between the horizon and the meridian in any simple way. Nor does it divide time, as some believe. Placidus divides the individual path that each degree of the zodiac traces out in the heavens as the Earth rotates on its axis—not the paths that the planets take as they move through the zodiac, but paths apparently traced in the diurnal rotation.

As the Earth rotates daily, planets and stars appear to move from east to west. As they do, they can be thought of as tracing out circles on the celestial sphere parallel to the plane of rotation of the Earth, that is, parallel to the equator. These are declination circles and are, as the name implies, functions of the planet or star's declination, its angular distance above or below the celestial equator.

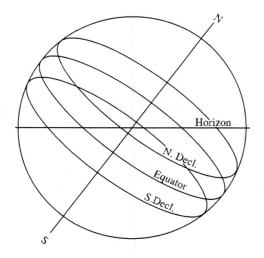

*Declination circles as seen from outside the celestial sphere.*

---

* See also the booklet *The East Point and the Antivertex* available through ACS Publications.

The portion of a declination circle that is above the horizon is called its diurnal arc. The portion below the horizon is called its nocturnal arc. Seen from north latitudes, an object of south declination has a diurnal arc shorter than its nocturnal arc. An object on the celestial equator, 0° declination, has a diurnal arc longer than its nocturnal arc. This is why day and night are of different lengths in different seasons. In the fall and winter, the Sun is in those signs that have south declination and shorter diurnal arcs. In the spring and summer, the Sun is in those signs that have north declination and longer diurnal arcs. On March 21 and September 21, approximately, the Sun is at those points of the ecliptic that cross the equator and have equal diurnal and nocturnal arcs.

The relative lengths of diurnal and nocturnal arcs are a function not only of the declination of the object being observed but also of the latitude of the observer. This explains why those who live at higher latitudes, in the Scandinavian countries, for example, have longer summer days and longer winter nights than those of us who live at lower latitudes. It also explains why house cusps, except the tenth and fourth, are different for different latitudes.

Each declination circle is bisected exactly by the meridian. Thus each diurnal and nocturnal arc is bisected by the meridian, forming two equal diurnal semiarcs and two equal nocturnal semiarcs. Each planet and each degree of the zodiac traces out its own diurnal and nocturnal semicarcs as the Earth turns. This is the basis of the Placidian system.

Every possible nocturnal and diurnal semiarc is trisected into three equal parts. What, then, are the cusps given in the Table of Houses? They are the degrees of the zodiac that, in terms of their own declination circles, are one third, two thirds or three thirds of the way through their own semiarcs at a given Local Sidereal Time.

In our example, 4°♊52' is the Ascendant because 4°♊52' was on the horizon at the time and place of birth. 10°♒23' is the Midheaven because it was on the meridian at the time and place of birth. 18°♈39' is the cusp of the twelfth house because it is the on the point of the zodiac that had traveled one third of the way along its own diurnal semiarc from the horizon to the meridian. 8°♓44' had completed two thirds of its journey to the meridian, so it is the cusp of the eleventh house.

*Declination circles as seen from a North latitude. In each case, the vertical line represents the meridian and the horizontal line the horizon.*

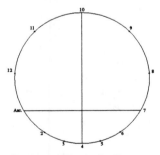

*Object at north declination*

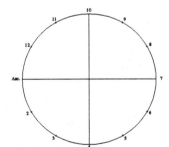

*Object on the equator*

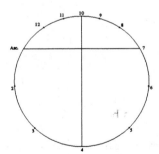

*Object at south declination*

### Calculation of House Cusps Directly

Those who have access to a trigonometric calculator may wish to use it to calculate house cusps directly. Calculating the Midheaven and the Ascendant is not difficult, but getting the intermediate house cusps can he very tedious without the help of a programmable machine because the algorithm is an iterative one: the same calculation is done over and over with increasingly accurate results. The method given here is from Hugh Rice's *American Astrology Tables of Houses*. Here are the values for the obliquity of the ecliptic (OE) and trigonometric functions of the OE that you will need.

| Year | OE | tan OE | cos OE |
|------|------|------|------|
| 1900 | 23° 27' 8.26" | .4338227 | .91739176 |
| 1925 | 23° 26' 56.55" | .43375523 | .91741436 |
| 1950 | 23° 26' 44.84" | .43368777 | .91743695 |
| 1975 | 23° 26' 33.12" | .43362031 | .91745954 |

Calculate the Midheaven (MC) as follows.

1. Find the right ascension of thc Midheaven (RAMC) by converting ST of birth to angular measure (1h = 15°).

2. $MC = \arctan \left[ \dfrac{\tan RAMC}{\cos OE} \right]$

The result may be 180° off. lf so, subtract 180° to place the MC in the same quadrant as the RAMC.

Calculate the eleventh and twelfth house cusps as follows. Lat = latitude of birth. Use these values for F and for the initial approximation of $RA_1$.

| House | Initial $RA_1$ | F |
|------|------|------|
| 11th | RAMC + 30° | 3 |
| 12th | RAMC + 60° | 1.5 |

1. $RAMC + \dfrac{\arccos\,[-(\sin RA_1)\,(\tan OE)\,(\tan Lat)]}{F} = RA_2$

2. Set $RA_1$ Equal to $RA_2$ and repeat until $RA_2$ comes out within .01° of $RA_1$.

3. Convert $RA_2$ to longitude: $\arctan \left[ \dfrac{\tan RA_2}{\cos OE} \right] = $ longitude

Calculate the Ascendant, second and third house cusps as follows.

| House | Initial $RA_1$ | F |
|------|------|------|
| Ascendant | RAMC + 90° | 1 |
| 2nd | RAMC + 120° | 1.5 |
| 3rd | RAMC + 150° | 3 |

1. $RAMC + 180 - \dfrac{\arccos\,[(\sin RA_1)\,(\tan OE)\,(\tan Lat)]}{F} = RA_2$

Steps 2 and 3 are the same as for the eleventh and twelfth house cusps.

Sidereal Time

# Koch Table of Houses for Latitudes 0° to 60° North

**0h 0m 0s — 0° 0' 0" — 00 ♈ 00**

| LAT. | 11 | 12 | ASC | 2 | 3 |
|---|---|---|---|---|---|
| 0 | 02♉11 | 02♊05 | 00♋00 | 27♋55 | 27♌49 |
| 5 | 03 21 | 03 55 | 02 00 | 29 41 | 28 55 |
| 10 | 04 37 | 05 50 | 04 01 | 01♌25 | 29 58 |
| 15 | 06 01 | 07 52 | 06 05 | 03 08 | 00♍59 |
| 20 | 07 35 | 10 05 | 08 14 | 04 52 | 01 58 |
| 21 | 07 55 | 10 32 | 08 41 | 05 13 | 02 10 |
| 22 | 08 16 | 11 01 | 09 08 | 05 35 | 02 22 |
| 23 | 08 38 | 11 30 | 09 35 | 05 56 | 02 34 |
| 24 | 09 00 | 11 59 | 10 03 | 06 17 | 02 46 |
| 25 | 09 23 | 12 30 | 10 31 | 06 39 | 02 58 |
| 26 | 09 47 | 13 00 | 10 59 | 07 00 | 03 10 |
| 27 | 10 12 | 13 32 | 11 28 | 07 22 | 03 22 |
| 28 | 10 37 | 14 04 | 11 57 | 07 44 | 03 34 |
| 29 | 11 04 | 14 37 | 12 26 | 08 07 | 03 47 |
| 30 | 11 31 | 15 11 | 12 56 | 08 29 | 03 59 |
| 31 | 12 00 | 15 46 | 13 27 | 08 52 | 04 11 |
| 32 | 12 29 | 16 22 | 13 58 | 09 14 | 04 23 |
| 33 | 13 00 | 16 59 | 14 29 | 09 38 | 04 36 |
| 34 | 13 32 | 17 36 | 15 01 | 10 01 | 04 48 |
| 35 | 14 06 | 18 15 | 15 34 | 10 25 | 05 01 |
| 36 | 14 41 | 18 55 | 16 07 | 10 49 | 05 14 |
| 37 | 15 18 | 19 36 | 16 41 | 11 13 | 05 27 |
| 38 | 15 57 | 20 19 | 17 16 | 11 38 | 05 40 |
| 39 | 16 38 | 21 02 | 17 52 | 12 03 | 05 53 |
| 40 | 17 21 | 21 48 | 18 28 | 12 28 | 06 06 |
| 41 | 18 06 | 22 35 | 19 05 | 12 54 | 06 20 |
| 42 | 18 54 | 23 23 | 19 43 | 13 20 | 06 33 |
| 43 | 19 44 | 24 13 | 20 21 | 13 46 | 06 47 |
| 44 | 20 38 | 25 05 | 21 01 | 14 14 | 07 01 |
| 45 | 21 35 | 25 59 | 21 42 | 14 41 | 07 15 |
| 46 | 22 35 | 26 55 | 22 24 | 15 09 | 07 29 |
| 47 | 23 39 | 27 53 | 23 06 | 15 38 | 07 44 |
| 48 | 24 48 | 28 53 | 23 50 | 16 07 | 07 59 |
| 49 | 26 02 | 29 56 | 24 36 | 16 37 | 08 14 |
| 50 | 27 21 | 01♋01 | 25 22 | 17 08 | 08 29 |
| 51 | 28 46 | 02 09 | 26 10 | 17 39 | 08 45 |
| 52 | 00♊18 | 03 20 | 26 59 | 18 11 | 09 01 |
| 53 | 01 56 | 04 34 | 27 50 | 18 44 | 09 17 |
| 54 | 03 43 | 05 52 | 28 42 | 19 17 | 09 34 |
| 55 | 05 39 | 07 12 | 29 36 | 19 52 | 09 51 |
| 56 | 07 44 | 08 37 | 00♌32 | 20 27 | 10 09 |
| 57 | 10 01 | 10 05 | 01 30 | 21 03 | 10 26 |
| 58 | 12 29 | 11 37 | 02 29 | 21 40 | 10 45 |
| 59 | 15 11 | 13 13 | 03 31 | 22 19 | 11 03 |
| 60 | 18♊06 | 14♋54 | 04♌34 | 22♌58 | 11♍23 |

**0h 4m 0s — 1° 0' 0" — 01 ♈ 05**

| LAT. | 11 | 12 | ASC | 2 | 3 |
|---|---|---|---|---|---|
| 0 | 03♉13 | 03♊03 | 00♋55 | 28♋52 | 28♌52 |
| 5 | 04 24 | 04 52 | 02 55 | 00♌38 | 29 57 |
| 10 | 05 40 | 06 47 | 04 56 | 02 22 | 01♍00 |
| 15 | 07 04 | 08 49 | 07 00 | 04 05 | 02 00 |
| 20 | 08 38 | 11 01 | 09 08 | 05 48 | 03 00 |
| 21 | 08 58 | 11 29 | 09 35 | 06 09 | 03 11 |
| 22 | 09 19 | 11 57 | 10 02 | 06 30 | 03 23 |
| 23 | 09 41 | 12 26 | 10 29 | 06 52 | 03 35 |
| 24 | 10 03 | 12 55 | 10 56 | 07 13 | 03 47 |
| 25 | 10 26 | 13 25 | 11 24 | 07 34 | 03 59 |
| 26 | 10 50 | 13 56 | 11 52 | 07 56 | 04 11 |
| 27 | 11 15 | 14 27 | 12 20 | 08 18 | 04 23 |
| 28 | 11 40 | 15 00 | 12 49 | 08 39 | 04 35 |
| 29 | 12 07 | 15 32 | 13 19 | 09 02 | 04 47 |
| 30 | 12 34 | 16 06 | 13 48 | 09 24 | 04 59 |
| 31 | 13 02 | 16 41 | 14 19 | 09 46 | 05 11 |
| 32 | 13 32 | 17 16 | 14 49 | 10 09 | 05 23 |
| 33 | 14 03 | 17 53 | 15 21 | 10 32 | 05 36 |
| 34 | 14 35 | 18 30 | 15 53 | 10 55 | 05 48 |
| 35 | 15 09 | 19 09 | 16 25 | 11 19 | 06 01 |
| 36 | 15 44 | 19 48 | 16 58 | 11 42 | 06 13 |
| 37 | 16 20 | 20 29 | 17 32 | 12 06 | 06 26 |
| 38 | 16 59 | 21 11 | 18 06 | 12 31 | 06 39 |
| 39 | 17 40 | 21 54 | 18 41 | 12 56 | 06 52 |
| 40 | 18 22 | 22 39 | 19 17 | 13 21 | 07 05 |
| 41 | 19 07 | 23 26 | 19 54 | 13 46 | 07 18 |
| 42 | 19 55 | 24 13 | 20 31 | 14 12 | 07 32 |
| 43 | 20 45 | 25 03 | 21 10 | 14 39 | 07 46 |
| 44 | 21 38 | 25 54 | 21 49 | 15 06 | 07 59 |
| 45 | 22 34 | 26 48 | 22 29 | 15 33 | 08 13 |
| 46 | 23 34 | 27 43 | 23 11 | 16 01 | 08 28 |
| 47 | 24 38 | 28 40 | 23 53 | 16 29 | 08 42 |
| 48 | 25 46 | 29 40 | 24 36 | 16 58 | 08 57 |
| 49 | 26 59 | 00♋42 | 25 21 | 17 28 | 09 12 |
| 50 | 28 17 | 01 46 | 26 07 | 17 58 | 09 27 |
| 51 | 29 41 | 02 53 | 26 54 | 18 29 | 09 43 |
| 52 | 01♊12 | 04 03 | 27 43 | 19 00 | 09 58 |
| 53 | 02 49 | 05 16 | 28 33 | 19 33 | 10 15 |
| 54 | 04 34 | 06 32 | 29 25 | 20 06 | 10 31 |
| 55 | 06 28 | 07 52 | 00♌18 | 20 40 | 10 48 |
| 56 | 08 32 | 09 15 | 01 13 | 21 15 | 11 05 |
| 57 | 10 46 | 10 42 | 02 10 | 21 50 | 11 23 |
| 58 | 13 12 | 12 12 | 03 08 | 22 27 | 11 41 |
| 59 | 15 50 | 13 47 | 04 09 | 23 05 | 11 59 |
| 60 | 18♊42 | 15♋26 | 05♌12 | 23♌44 | 12♍18 |

**0h 8m 0s — 2° 0' 0" — 02 ♈ 11**

| LAT. | 11 | 12 | ASC | 2 | 3 |
|---|---|---|---|---|---|
| 0 | 04♉16 | 04♊00 | 01♋50 | 29♋49 | 29♌54 |
| 5 | 05 26 | 05 49 | 03 50 | 01♌35 | 00♍59 |
| 10 | 06 42 | 07 44 | 05 50 | 03 19 | 02 02 |
| 15 | 08 06 | 09 46 | 07 54 | 05 01 | 03 02 |
| 20 | 09 41 | 11 57 | 10 02 | 06 45 | 04 01 |
| 21 | 10 01 | 12 25 | 10 28 | 07 06 | 04 13 |
| 22 | 10 22 | 12 53 | 10 55 | 07 26 | 04 24 |
| 23 | 10 44 | 13 22 | 11 22 | 07 47 | 04 36 |
| 24 | 11 06 | 13 51 | 11 49 | 08 09 | 04 48 |
| 25 | 11 29 | 14 21 | 12 17 | 08 30 | 05 00 |
| 26 | 11 53 | 14 51 | 12 45 | 08 51 | 05 11 |
| 27 | 12 17 | 15 23 | 13 13 | 09 13 | 05 23 |
| 28 | 12 43 | 15 55 | 13 42 | 09 35 | 05 35 |
| 29 | 13 09 | 16 27 | 14 11 | 09 57 | 05 47 |
| 30 | 13 36 | 17 01 | 14 41 | 10 19 | 05 59 |
| 31 | 14 05 | 17 35 | 15 11 | 10 41 | 06 11 |
| 32 | 14 34 | 18 10 | 15 41 | 11 03 | 06 23 |
| 33 | 15 05 | 18 46 | 16 12 | 11 26 | 06 36 |
| 34 | 15 37 | 19 23 | 16 44 | 11 49 | 06 48 |
| 35 | 16 11 | 20 02 | 17 16 | 12 13 | 07 00 |
| 36 | 16 45 | 20 41 | 17 49 | 12 36 | 07 13 |
| 37 | 17 22 | 21 21 | 18 22 | 13 00 | 07 26 |
| 38 | 18 00 | 22 03 | 18 56 | 13 24 | 07 38 |
| 39 | 18 41 | 22 46 | 19 31 | 13 49 | 07 51 |
| 40 | 19 23 | 23 30 | 20 06 | 14 14 | 08 04 |
| 41 | 20 08 | 24 16 | 20 43 | 14 39 | 08 17 |
| 42 | 20 55 | 25 04 | 21 20 | 15 05 | 08 31 |
| 43 | 21 45 | 25 53 | 21 58 | 15 31 | 08 44 |
| 44 | 22 37 | 26 43 | 22 37 | 15 57 | 08 58 |
| 45 | 23 33 | 27 36 | 23 17 | 16 24 | 09 12 |
| 46 | 24 33 | 28 31 | 23 57 | 16 52 | 09 26 |
| 47 | 25 36 | 29 27 | 24 39 | 17 20 | 09 40 |
| 48 | 26 43 | 00♋26 | 25 22 | 17 49 | 09 55 |
| 49 | 27 55 | 01 27 | 26 06 | 18 18 | 10 10 |
| 50 | 29 13 | 02 31 | 26 52 | 18 48 | 10 25 |
| 51 | 00♊36 | 03 37 | 27 38 | 19 18 | 10 40 |
| 52 | 02 05 | 04 46 | 28 26 | 19 50 | 10 56 |
| 53 | 03 41 | 05 58 | 29 16 | 20 22 | 11 12 |
| 54 | 05 25 | 07 13 | 00♌07 | 20 54 | 11 28 |
| 55 | 07 17 | 08 31 | 00 59 | 21 28 | 11 45 |
| 56 | 09 19 | 09 53 | 01 54 | 22 02 | 12 02 |
| 57 | 11 30 | 11 18 | 02 50 | 22 38 | 12 19 |
| 58 | 13 54 | 12 47 | 03 47 | 23 14 | 12 37 |
| 59 | 16 29 | 14 20 | 04 47 | 23 51 | 12 55 |
| 60 | 19♊18 | 15♋58 | 05♌49 | 24♌30 | 13♍14 |

**0h 12m 0s — 3° 0' 0" — 03 ♈ 16**

| LAT. | 11 | 12 | ASC | 2 | 3 |
|---|---|---|---|---|---|
| 0 | 05♉18 | 04♊57 | 02♋45 | 00♌47 | 00♍57 |
| 5 | 06 28 | 06 46 | 04 44 | 02 33 | 02 02 |
| 10 | 07 45 | 08 41 | 06 45 | 04 16 | 03 04 |
| 15 | 09 09 | 10 43 | 08 48 | 05 58 | 04 03 |
| 20 | 10 43 | 12 53 | 10 56 | 07 41 | 05 02 |
| 21 | 11 04 | 13 21 | 11 22 | 08 02 | 05 14 |
| 22 | 11 25 | 13 49 | 11 48 | 08 22 | 05 25 |
| 23 | 11 46 | 14 17 | 12 15 | 08 43 | 05 37 |
| 24 | 12 08 | 14 46 | 12 42 | 09 04 | 05 49 |
| 25 | 12 31 | 15 16 | 13 10 | 09 25 | 06 00 |
| 26 | 12 55 | 15 46 | 13 38 | 09 47 | 06 12 |
| 27 | 13 20 | 16 17 | 14 06 | 10 08 | 06 24 |
| 28 | 13 45 | 16 49 | 14 34 | 10 30 | 06 36 |
| 29 | 14 11 | 17 22 | 15 03 | 10 52 | 06 48 |
| 30 | 14 39 | 17 55 | 15 33 | 11 13 | 07 00 |
| 31 | 15 07 | 18 29 | 16 02 | 11 36 | 07 12 |
| 32 | 15 36 | 19 04 | 16 33 | 11 58 | 07 24 |
| 33 | 16 07 | 19 40 | 17 03 | 12 21 | 07 36 |
| 34 | 16 39 | 20 17 | 17 35 | 12 43 | 07 48 |
| 35 | 17 12 | 20 54 | 18 07 | 13 07 | 08 00 |
| 36 | 17 47 | 21 33 | 18 39 | 13 30 | 08 13 |
| 37 | 18 23 | 22 13 | 19 12 | 13 54 | 08 25 |
| 38 | 19 01 | 22 55 | 19 46 | 14 18 | 08 38 |
| 39 | 19 41 | 23 37 | 20 20 | 14 42 | 08 50 |
| 40 | 20 24 | 24 21 | 20 56 | 15 07 | 09 03 |
| 41 | 21 08 | 25 06 | 21 32 | 15 32 | 09 16 |
| 42 | 21 55 | 25 53 | 22 08 | 15 57 | 09 30 |
| 43 | 22 44 | 26 42 | 22 46 | 16 23 | 09 43 |
| 44 | 23 36 | 27 32 | 23 24 | 16 49 | 09 57 |
| 45 | 24 32 | 28 24 | 24 04 | 17 16 | 10 10 |
| 46 | 25 30 | 29 18 | 24 44 | 17 43 | 10 24 |
| 47 | 26 33 | 00♋14 | 25 25 | 18 11 | 10 38 |
| 48 | 27 40 | 01 12 | 26 08 | 18 40 | 10 53 |
| 49 | 28 51 | 02 12 | 26 52 | 19 08 | 11 07 |
| 50 | 00♊07 | 03 15 | 27 36 | 19 38 | 11 22 |
| 51 | 01 29 | 04 20 | 28 22 | 20 08 | 11 38 |
| 52 | 02 57 | 05 28 | 29 10 | 20 39 | 11 53 |
| 53 | 04 32 | 06 39 | 29 59 | 21 11 | 12 09 |
| 54 | 06 14 | 07 53 | 00♌49 | 21 43 | 12 25 |
| 55 | 08 05 | 09 10 | 01 41 | 22 16 | 12 41 |
| 56 | 10 04 | 10 30 | 02 34 | 22 50 | 12 58 |
| 57 | 12 14 | 11 54 | 03 29 | 23 25 | 13 15 |
| 58 | 14 35 | 13 22 | 04 26 | 24 01 | 13 33 |
| 59 | 17 08 | 14 54 | 05 25 | 24 38 | 13 51 |
| 60 | 19♊54 | 16♋29 | 06♌26 | 25♌15 | 14♍10 |

**0h 16m 0s — 4° 0' 0" — 04 ♈ 22**

| LAT. | 11 | 12 | ASC | 2 | 3 |
|---|---|---|---|---|---|
| 0 | 06♉19 | 05♊54 | 03♋40 | 01♌45 | 02♍00 |
| 5 | 07 30 | 07 43 | 05 39 | 03 30 | 03 05 |
| 10 | 08 47 | 09 38 | 07 40 | 05 13 | 04 06 |
| 15 | 10 11 | 11 39 | 09 42 | 06 55 | 05 05 |
| 20 | 11 45 | 13 49 | 11 49 | 08 37 | 06 03 |
| 21 | 12 06 | 14 16 | 12 15 | 08 58 | 06 15 |
| 22 | 12 27 | 14 44 | 12 42 | 09 18 | 06 27 |
| 23 | 12 48 | 15 13 | 13 08 | 09 39 | 06 38 |
| 24 | 13 11 | 15 42 | 13 35 | 10 00 | 06 50 |
| 25 | 13 33 | 16 11 | 14 03 | 10 21 | 07 01 |
| 26 | 13 57 | 16 41 | 14 30 | 10 42 | 07 13 |
| 27 | 14 22 | 17 12 | 14 58 | 11 04 | 07 25 |
| 28 | 14 47 | 17 44 | 15 26 | 11 25 | 07 36 |
| 29 | 15 13 | 18 16 | 15 55 | 11 47 | 07 48 |
| 30 | 15 40 | 18 49 | 16 24 | 12 08 | 08 00 |
| 31 | 16 08 | 19 23 | 16 54 | 12 30 | 08 12 |
| 32 | 16 38 | 19 57 | 17 24 | 12 53 | 08 24 |
| 33 | 17 08 | 20 33 | 17 55 | 13 15 | 08 36 |
| 34 | 17 40 | 21 09 | 18 26 | 13 38 | 08 48 |
| 35 | 18 13 | 21 47 | 18 57 | 14 00 | 09 00 |
| 36 | 18 48 | 22 25 | 19 29 | 14 24 | 09 12 |
| 37 | 19 24 | 23 05 | 20 02 | 14 47 | 09 25 |
| 38 | 20 02 | 23 46 | 20 36 | 15 11 | 09 37 |
| 39 | 20 42 | 24 28 | 21 10 | 15 35 | 09 50 |
| 40 | 21 23 | 25 12 | 21 45 | 15 59 | 10 03 |
| 41 | 22 07 | 25 56 | 22 20 | 16 24 | 10 15 |
| 42 | 22 54 | 26 43 | 22 57 | 16 50 | 10 29 |
| 43 | 23 43 | 27 31 | 23 34 | 17 15 | 10 42 |
| 44 | 24 34 | 28 20 | 24 12 | 17 41 | 10 55 |
| 45 | 25 29 | 29 12 | 24 51 | 18 08 | 11 09 |
| 46 | 26 28 | 00♋05 | 25 31 | 18 35 | 11 23 |
| 47 | 27 30 | 01 00 | 26 11 | 19 02 | 11 37 |
| 48 | 28 36 | 01 57 | 26 53 | 19 30 | 11 51 |
| 49 | 29 46 | 02 57 | 27 37 | 19 59 | 12 05 |
| 50 | 01♊01 | 03 59 | 28 21 | 20 28 | 12 20 |
| 51 | 02 22 | 05 03 | 29 06 | 20 58 | 12 35 |
| 52 | 03 49 | 06 10 | 29 53 | 21 28 | 12 50 |
| 53 | 05 23 | 07 20 | 00♌41 | 22 00 | 13 06 |
| 54 | 07 03 | 08 32 | 01 31 | 22 32 | 13 22 |
| 55 | 08 52 | 09 48 | 02 22 | 23 04 | 13 38 |
| 56 | 10 50 | 11 07 | 03 15 | 23 38 | 13 55 |
| 57 | 12 57 | 12 30 | 04 09 | 24 12 | 14 12 |
| 58 | 15 16 | 13 56 | 05 05 | 24 48 | 14 29 |
| 59 | 17 46 | 15 27 | 06 03 | 25 24 | 14 47 |
| 60 | 20♊29 | 17♋01 | 07♌03 | 26♌01 | 15♍05 |

**0h 20m 0s — 5° 0' 0" — 05 ♈ 27**

| LAT. | 11 | 12 | ASC | 2 | 3 |
|---|---|---|---|---|---|
| 0 | 07♉21 | 06♊50 | 04♋35 | 02♌43 | 03♍03 |
| 5 | 08 32 | 08 40 | 06 34 | 04 28 | 04 07 |
| 10 | 09 49 | 10 34 | 08 34 | 06 10 | 05 08 |
| 15 | 11 13 | 12 35 | 10 36 | 07 52 | 06 07 |
| 20 | 12 47 | 14 44 | 12 43 | 09 33 | 07 05 |
| 21 | 13 08 | 15 12 | 13 09 | 09 54 | 07 16 |
| 22 | 13 29 | 15 39 | 13 35 | 10 15 | 07 28 |
| 23 | 13 50 | 16 08 | 14 02 | 10 35 | 07 39 |
| 24 | 14 12 | 16 36 | 14 28 | 10 56 | 07 51 |
| 25 | 14 35 | 17 06 | 14 55 | 11 17 | 08 02 |
| 26 | 14 59 | 17 36 | 15 23 | 11 38 | 08 14 |
| 27 | 15 23 | 18 06 | 15 51 | 11 59 | 08 25 |
| 28 | 15 48 | 18 38 | 16 19 | 12 20 | 08 37 |
| 29 | 16 14 | 19 10 | 16 47 | 12 42 | 08 49 |
| 30 | 16 41 | 19 42 | 17 16 | 13 03 | 09 00 |
| 31 | 17 10 | 20 16 | 17 45 | 13 25 | 09 12 |
| 32 | 17 39 | 20 50 | 18 15 | 13 47 | 09 24 |
| 33 | 18 09 | 21 26 | 18 46 | 14 09 | 09 36 |
| 34 | 18 41 | 22 02 | 19 16 | 14 32 | 09 48 |
| 35 | 19 14 | 22 39 | 19 48 | 14 54 | 10 00 |
| 36 | 19 48 | 23 17 | 20 20 | 15 17 | 10 12 |
| 37 | 20 24 | 23 56 | 20 52 | 15 41 | 10 24 |
| 38 | 21 02 | 24 37 | 21 25 | 16 04 | 10 37 |
| 39 | 21 41 | 25 19 | 21 59 | 16 28 | 10 49 |
| 40 | 22 23 | 26 02 | 22 33 | 16 52 | 11 02 |
| 41 | 23 06 | 26 46 | 23 09 | 17 17 | 11 15 |
| 42 | 23 52 | 27 32 | 23 45 | 17 42 | 11 27 |
| 43 | 24 41 | 28 19 | 24 21 | 18 07 | 11 41 |
| 44 | 25 32 | 29 08 | 24 59 | 18 33 | 11 54 |
| 45 | 26 27 | 29 59 | 25 38 | 18 59 | 12 07 |
| 46 | 27 24 | 00♋51 | 26 17 | 19 26 | 12 21 |
| 47 | 28 25 | 01 46 | 26 57 | 19 53 | 12 35 |
| 48 | 29 31 | 02 42 | 27 39 | 20 21 | 12 49 |
| 49 | 00♊40 | 03 41 | 28 21 | 20 49 | 13 03 |
| 50 | 01 55 | 04 42 | 29 05 | 21 18 | 13 18 |
| 51 | 03 15 | 05 46 | 29 50 | 21 48 | 13 33 |
| 52 | 04 40 | 06 52 | 00♌36 | 22 18 | 13 48 |
| 53 | 06 12 | 08 00 | 01 24 | 22 48 | 14 03 |
| 54 | 07 52 | 09 12 | 02 13 | 23 20 | 14 19 |
| 55 | 09 39 | 10 27 | 03 03 | 23 52 | 14 35 |
| 56 | 11 34 | 11 44 | 03 55 | 24 26 | 14 51 |
| 57 | 13 40 | 13 06 | 04 49 | 25 00 | 15 08 |
| 58 | 15 56 | 14 31 | 05 44 | 25 34 | 15 25 |
| 59 | 18 23 | 15 59 | 06 41 | 26 10 | 15 43 |
| 60 | 21♊03 | 17♋32 | 07♌40 | 26♌47 | 16♍01 |

**0h 24m 0s — 6° 0' 0" — 06 ♈ 32**

| LAT. | 11 | 12 | ASC | 2 | 3 |
|---|---|---|---|---|---|
| 0 | 08♉23 | 07♊47 | 05♋30 | 03♌41 | 04♍07 |
| 5 | 09 34 | 09 36 | 07 29 | 05 26 | 05 10 |
| 10 | 10 51 | 11 30 | 09 29 | 07 08 | 06 11 |
| 15 | 12 15 | 13 31 | 11 31 | 08 49 | 07 09 |
| 20 | 13 49 | 15 40 | 13 36 | 10 30 | 08 06 |
| 21 | 14 09 | 16 07 | 14 02 | 10 50 | 08 18 |
| 22 | 14 30 | 16 34 | 14 28 | 11 11 | 08 29 |
| 23 | 14 52 | 17 02 | 14 55 | 11 31 | 08 40 |
| 24 | 15 14 | 17 31 | 15 21 | 11 52 | 08 52 |
| 25 | 15 37 | 18 00 | 15 48 | 12 12 | 09 03 |
| 26 | 16 00 | 18 30 | 16 15 | 12 33 | 09 15 |
| 27 | 16 24 | 19 00 | 16 43 | 12 54 | 09 26 |
| 28 | 16 49 | 19 31 | 17 11 | 13 15 | 09 38 |
| 29 | 17 15 | 20 03 | 17 39 | 13 37 | 09 49 |
| 30 | 17 42 | 20 36 | 18 08 | 13 58 | 10 01 |
| 31 | 18 10 | 21 09 | 18 37 | 14 20 | 10 12 |
| 32 | 18 39 | 21 43 | 19 06 | 14 42 | 10 24 |
| 33 | 19 10 | 22 18 | 19 36 | 15 04 | 10 36 |
| 34 | 19 41 | 22 54 | 20 07 | 15 26 | 10 48 |
| 35 | 20 14 | 23 31 | 20 38 | 15 48 | 11 00 |
| 36 | 20 48 | 24 09 | 21 10 | 16 11 | 11 12 |
| 37 | 21 24 | 24 47 | 21 42 | 16 34 | 11 24 |
| 38 | 22 01 | 25 28 | 22 15 | 16 58 | 11 36 |
| 39 | 22 40 | 26 09 | 22 48 | 17 21 | 11 48 |
| 40 | 23 21 | 26 51 | 23 22 | 17 45 | 12 01 |
| 41 | 24 05 | 27 35 | 23 57 | 18 10 | 12 14 |
| 42 | 24 50 | 28 21 | 24 33 | 18 34 | 12 26 |
| 43 | 25 38 | 29 07 | 25 09 | 18 59 | 12 39 |
| 44 | 26 29 | 29 56 | 25 46 | 19 25 | 12 52 |
| 45 | 27 23 | 00♋46 | 26 24 | 19 51 | 13 06 |
| 46 | 28 20 | 01 38 | 27 03 | 20 17 | 13 19 |
| 47 | 29 21 | 02 31 | 27 43 | 20 44 | 13 33 |
| 48 | 00♊25 | 03 27 | 28 24 | 21 12 | 13 47 |
| 49 | 01 34 | 04 25 | 29 06 | 21 40 | 14 01 |
| 50 | 02 48 | 05 25 | 29 49 | 22 08 | 14 15 |
| 51 | 04 06 | 06 28 | 00♌34 | 22 37 | 14 30 |
| 52 | 05 31 | 07 33 | 01 19 | 23 07 | 14 45 |
| 53 | 07 01 | 08 40 | 02 06 | 23 37 | 15 00 |
| 54 | 08 39 | 09 51 | 02 54 | 24 09 | 15 16 |
| 55 | 10 24 | 11 05 | 03 44 | 24 41 | 15 32 |
| 56 | 12 18 | 12 21 | 04 35 | 25 13 | 15 48 |
| 57 | 14 22 | 13 41 | 05 28 | 25 47 | 16 05 |
| 58 | 16 35 | 15 05 | 06 23 | 26 21 | 16 22 |
| 59 | 19 00 | 16 32 | 07 19 | 26 57 | 16 39 |
| 60 | 21♊37 | 18♋03 | 08♌17 | 27♌33 | 16♍57 |

**0h 28m 0s — 7° 0' 0" — 07 ♈ 37**

| LAT. | 11 | 12 | ASC | 2 | 3 |
|---|---|---|---|---|---|
| 0 | 09♉24 | 08♊43 | 06♋26 | 04♌39 | 05♍10 |
| 5 | 10 35 | 10 33 | 08 24 | 06 24 | 06 13 |
| 10 | 11 52 | 12 26 | 10 23 | 08 06 | 07 13 |
| 15 | 13 16 | 14 26 | 12 25 | 09 46 | 08 11 |
| 20 | 14 50 | 16 35 | 14 30 | 11 26 | 09 08 |
| 21 | 15 10 | 17 02 | 14 55 | 11 47 | 09 19 |
| 22 | 15 31 | 17 29 | 15 21 | 12 07 | 09 30 |
| 23 | 15 53 | 17 57 | 15 47 | 12 27 | 09 42 |
| 24 | 16 15 | 18 25 | 16 14 | 12 48 | 09 53 |
| 25 | 16 37 | 18 54 | 16 41 | 13 08 | 10 04 |
| 26 | 17 01 | 19 24 | 17 08 | 13 29 | 10 16 |
| 27 | 17 25 | 19 54 | 17 35 | 13 50 | 10 27 |
| 28 | 17 50 | 20 25 | 18 03 | 14 11 | 10 38 |
| 29 | 18 16 | 20 56 | 18 31 | 14 32 | 10 50 |
| 30 | 18 43 | 21 29 | 18 59 | 14 53 | 11 01 |
| 31 | 19 11 | 22 02 | 19 28 | 15 14 | 11 13 |
| 32 | 19 40 | 22 35 | 19 57 | 15 36 | 11 24 |
| 33 | 20 10 | 23 10 | 20 27 | 15 58 | 11 36 |
| 34 | 20 41 | 23 46 | 20 58 | 16 20 | 11 48 |
| 35 | 21 13 | 24 22 | 21 28 | 16 42 | 11 59 |
| 36 | 21 47 | 25 00 | 22 00 | 17 05 | 12 11 |
| 37 | 22 23 | 25 38 | 22 31 | 17 28 | 12 23 |
| 38 | 23 00 | 26 18 | 23 04 | 17 51 | 12 36 |
| 39 | 23 39 | 26 59 | 23 37 | 18 14 | 12 48 |
| 40 | 24 20 | 27 41 | 24 11 | 18 38 | 13 00 |
| 41 | 25 03 | 28 24 | 24 45 | 19 02 | 13 13 |
| 42 | 25 48 | 29 09 | 25 21 | 19 27 | 13 25 |
| 43 | 26 36 | 29 55 | 25 56 | 19 51 | 13 38 |
| 44 | 27 26 | 00♋43 | 26 33 | 20 17 | 13 51 |
| 45 | 28 19 | 01 32 | 27 11 | 20 42 | 14 04 |
| 46 | 29 16 | 02 24 | 27 49 | 21 08 | 14 18 |
| 47 | 00♊15 | 03 17 | 28 29 | 21 35 | 14 31 |
| 48 | 01 19 | 04 12 | 29 09 | 22 02 | 14 45 |
| 49 | 02 27 | 05 09 | 29 51 | 22 30 | 14 59 |
| 50 | 03 40 | 06 08 | 00♌33 | 22 58 | 15 13 |
| 51 | 04 57 | 07 10 | 01 17 | 23 27 | 15 28 |
| 52 | 06 21 | 08 14 | 02 02 | 23 56 | 15 42 |
| 53 | 07 50 | 09 20 | 02 48 | 24 26 | 15 57 |
| 54 | 09 26 | 10 30 | 03 36 | 24 57 | 16 13 |
| 55 | 11 10 | 11 42 | 04 25 | 25 29 | 16 29 |
| 56 | 13 02 | 12 58 | 05 16 | 26 01 | 16 45 |
| 57 | 15 03 | 14 16 | 06 08 | 26 34 | 17 01 |
| 58 | 17 14 | 15 39 | 07 01 | 27 08 | 17 18 |
| 59 | 19 36 | 17 04 | 07 57 | 27 43 | 17 35 |
| 60 | 22♊10 | 18♋34 | 08♌54 | 28♌19 | 17♍53 |

# Koch Table of Houses for Latitudes 0° to 60° North

0h 32m 0s — 8° 0' 0" — 08 ♈ 43

| LAT. | 11 | 12 | ASC | 2 | 3 |
|---|---|---|---|---|---|
| 0 | 10♉25 | 09♊40 | 07♋21 | 05♌38 | 06♍14 |
| 5 | 11 36 | 11 29 | 09 19 | 07 22 | 07 17 |
| 10 | 12 53 | 13 22 | 11 18 | 09 03 | 08 16 |
| 15 | 14 17 | 15 22 | 13 19 | 10 43 | 09 13 |
| 20 | 15 51 | 17 29 | 15 23 | 12 23 | 10 09 |
| 21 | 16 11 | 17 56 | 15 49 | 12 43 | 10 21 |
| 22 | 16 32 | 18 24 | 16 14 | 13 03 | 10 32 |
| 23 | 16 54 | 18 51 | 16 40 | 13 23 | 10 43 |
| 24 | 17 16 | 19 19 | 17 07 | 13 44 | 10 54 |
| 25 | 17 38 | 19 48 | 17 33 | 14 04 | 11 05 |
| 26 | 18 02 | 20 18 | 18 00 | 14 25 | 11 17 |
| 27 | 18 26 | 20 48 | 18 27 | 14 45 | 11 28 |
| 28 | 18 51 | 21 18 | 18 55 | 15 06 | 11 39 |
| 29 | 19 16 | 21 49 | 19 22 | 15 27 | 11 50 |
| 30 | 19 43 | 22 21 | 19 51 | 15 48 | 12 02 |
| 31 | 20 11 | 22 54 | 20 19 | 16 09 | 12 13 |
| 32 | 20 39 | 23 28 | 20 48 | 16 31 | 12 25 |
| 33 | 21 09 | 24 02 | 21 18 | 16 52 | 12 36 |
| 34 | 21 40 | 24 37 | 21 48 | 17 14 | 12 48 |
| 35 | 22 13 | 25 13 | 22 18 | 17 36 | 12 59 |
| 36 | 22 46 | 25 51 | 22 49 | 17 59 | 13 11 |
| 37 | 23 22 | 26 29 | 23 21 | 18 21 | 13 23 |
| 38 | 23 58 | 27 08 | 23 53 | 18 44 | 13 35 |
| 39 | 24 37 | 27 48 | 24 26 | 19 07 | 13 47 |
| 40 | 25 18 | 28 30 | 24 59 | 19 31 | 13 59 |
| 41 | 26 00 | 29 13 | 25 33 | 19 55 | 14 12 |
| 42 | 26 45 | 29 57 | 26 08 | 20 19 | 14 24 |
| 43 | 27 32 | 00♋43 | 26 44 | 20 44 | 14 37 |
| 44 | 28 22 | 01 30 | 27 20 | 21 08 | 14 50 |
| 45 | 29 15 | 02 19 | 27 57 | 21 34 | 15 03 |
| 46 | 00♊10 | 03 09 | 28 35 | 22 00 | 15 16 |
| 47 | 01 10 | 04 02 | 29 14 | 22 26 | 15 29 |
| 48 | 02 13 | 04 56 | 29 54 | 22 53 | 15 43 |
| 49 | 03 20 | 05 52 | 00♌35 | 23 20 | 15 57 |
| 50 | 04 31 | 06 51 | 01 17 | 23 48 | 16 11 |
| 51 | 05 48 | 07 51 | 02 01 | 24 16 | 16 25 |
| 52 | 07 10 | 08 55 | 02 45 | 24 46 | 16 40 |
| 53 | 08 38 | 10 00 | 03 31 | 25 15 | 16 55 |
| 54 | 10 12 | 11 09 | 04 18 | 25 46 | 17 10 |
| 55 | 11 54 | 12 20 | 05 06 | 26 17 | 17 25 |
| 56 | 13 45 | 13 34 | 05 56 | 26 49 | 17 41 |
| 57 | 15 44 | 14 52 | 06 47 | 27 21 | 17 57 |
| 58 | 17 52 | 16 12 | 07 40 | 27 55 | 18 14 |
| 59 | 20 12 | 17 37 | 08 35 | 28 29 | 18 31 |
| 60 | 22♊43 | 19♋05 | 09♌31 | 29♌05 | 18♍48 |

0h 36m 0s — 9° 0' 0" — 09 ♈ 48

| LAT. | 11 | 12 | ASC | 2 | 3 |
|---|---|---|---|---|---|
| 0 | 11♉26 | 10♊36 | 08♋16 | 06♌37 | 07♍18 |
| 5 | 12 37 | 12 25 | 10 14 | 08 20 | 08 20 |
| 10 | 13 54 | 14 18 | 12 12 | 10 01 | 09 19 |
| 15 | 15 18 | 16 17 | 14 13 | 11 40 | 10 16 |
| 20 | 16 52 | 18 24 | 16 16 | 13 19 | 11 11 |
| 21 | 17 12 | 18 51 | 16 42 | 13 39 | 11 22 |
| 22 | 17 33 | 19 18 | 17 07 | 13 59 | 11 33 |
| 23 | 17 54 | 19 45 | 17 33 | 14 19 | 11 44 |
| 24 | 18 16 | 20 13 | 17 59 | 14 40 | 11 55 |
| 25 | 18 38 | 20 42 | 18 26 | 15 00 | 12 06 |
| 26 | 19 02 | 21 11 | 18 52 | 15 20 | 12 18 |
| 27 | 19 26 | 21 41 | 19 19 | 15 41 | 12 29 |
| 28 | 19 51 | 22 11 | 19 46 | 16 01 | 12 40 |
| 29 | 20 16 | 22 42 | 20 14 | 16 22 | 12 51 |
| 30 | 20 43 | 23 14 | 20 42 | 16 43 | 13 02 |
| 31 | 21 10 | 23 46 | 21 10 | 17 04 | 13 13 |
| 32 | 21 39 | 24 20 | 21 39 | 17 25 | 13 25 |
| 33 | 22 08 | 24 54 | 22 09 | 17 47 | 13 36 |
| 34 | 22 39 | 25 29 | 22 38 | 18 08 | 13 48 |
| 35 | 23 11 | 26 04 | 23 08 | 18 30 | 13 59 |
| 36 | 23 45 | 26 41 | 23 39 | 18 52 | 14 11 |
| 37 | 24 20 | 27 19 | 24 10 | 19 15 | 14 23 |
| 38 | 24 56 | 27 58 | 24 42 | 19 38 | 14 35 |
| 39 | 25 35 | 28 38 | 25 15 | 20 00 | 14 46 |
| 40 | 26 15 | 29 19 | 25 48 | 20 24 | 14 59 |
| 41 | 26 57 | 00♋01 | 26 21 | 20 47 | 15 11 |
| 42 | 27 41 | 00 45 | 26 56 | 21 11 | 15 23 |
| 43 | 28 28 | 01 30 | 27 31 | 21 36 | 15 36 |
| 44 | 29 17 | 02 17 | 28 07 | 22 00 | 15 48 |
| 45 | 00♊09 | 03 05 | 28 44 | 22 25 | 16 01 |
| 46 | 01 05 | 03 55 | 29 21 | 22 51 | 16 14 |
| 47 | 02 03 | 04 46 | 00♌00 | 23 17 | 16 28 |
| 48 | 03 05 | 05 40 | 00 39 | 23 43 | 16 41 |
| 49 | 04 11 | 06 35 | 01 20 | 24 10 | 16 55 |
| 50 | 05 22 | 07 33 | 02 01 | 24 38 | 17 09 |
| 51 | 06 38 | 08 33 | 02 44 | 25 06 | 17 23 |
| 52 | 07 58 | 09 35 | 03 28 | 25 35 | 17 37 |
| 53 | 09 25 | 10 40 | 04 13 | 26 04 | 17 52 |
| 54 | 10 58 | 11 47 | 04 59 | 26 34 | 18 07 |
| 55 | 12 39 | 12 57 | 05 47 | 27 05 | 18 22 |
| 56 | 14 27 | 14 10 | 06 36 | 27 36 | 18 38 |
| 57 | 16 24 | 15 26 | 07 26 | 28 09 | 18 54 |
| 58 | 18 30 | 16 46 | 08 18 | 28 42 | 19 10 |
| 59 | 20 47 | 18 09 | 09 12 | 29 16 | 19 27 |
| 60 | 23♊16 | 19♋35 | 10♌08 | 29♌51 | 19♍44 |

0h 40m 0s — 10° 0' 0" — 10 ♈ 53

| LAT. | 11 | 12 | ASC | 2 | 3 |
|---|---|---|---|---|---|
| 0 | 12♉27 | 11♊32 | 09♋11 | 07♌35 | 08♍22 |
| 5 | 13 38 | 13 21 | 11 09 | 09 19 | 09 23 |
| 10 | 14 55 | 15 13 | 13 07 | 10 59 | 10 22 |
| 15 | 16 19 | 17 12 | 15 07 | 12 38 | 11 18 |
| 20 | 17 52 | 19 18 | 17 10 | 14 16 | 12 13 |
| 21 | 18 12 | 19 45 | 17 35 | 14 36 | 12 24 |
| 22 | 18 33 | 20 12 | 18 00 | 14 56 | 12 35 |
| 23 | 18 54 | 20 39 | 18 26 | 15 16 | 12 46 |
| 24 | 19 16 | 21 07 | 18 52 | 15 36 | 12 57 |
| 25 | 19 38 | 21 35 | 19 18 | 15 56 | 13 08 |
| 26 | 20 02 | 22 04 | 19 44 | 16 16 | 13 19 |
| 27 | 20 25 | 22 34 | 20 11 | 16 36 | 13 30 |
| 28 | 20 50 | 23 04 | 20 38 | 16 57 | 13 41 |
| 29 | 21 16 | 23 35 | 21 06 | 17 17 | 13 52 |
| 30 | 21 42 | 24 06 | 21 33 | 17 38 | 14 03 |
| 31 | 22 09 | 24 38 | 22 01 | 17 59 | 14 14 |
| 32 | 22 38 | 25 11 | 22 30 | 18 20 | 14 25 |
| 33 | 23 07 | 25 45 | 22 59 | 18 41 | 14 36 |
| 34 | 23 38 | 26 20 | 23 28 | 19 03 | 14 48 |
| 35 | 24 10 | 26 55 | 23 58 | 19 24 | 14 59 |
| 36 | 24 43 | 27 31 | 24 29 | 19 46 | 15 11 |
| 37 | 25 18 | 28 09 | 25 00 | 20 08 | 15 22 |
| 38 | 25 54 | 28 47 | 25 31 | 20 31 | 15 34 |
| 39 | 26 32 | 29 27 | 26 03 | 20 54 | 15 46 |
| 40 | 27 12 | 00♋07 | 26 36 | 21 17 | 15 58 |
| 41 | 27 53 | 00 49 | 27 09 | 21 40 | 16 10 |
| 42 | 28 37 | 01 32 | 27 43 | 22 04 | 16 22 |
| 43 | 29 24 | 02 17 | 28 18 | 22 28 | 16 34 |
| 44 | 00♊12 | 03 03 | 28 54 | 22 52 | 16 47 |
| 45 | 01 04 | 03 51 | 29 30 | 23 17 | 17 00 |
| 46 | 01 58 | 04 40 | 00♌07 | 23 42 | 17 13 |
| 47 | 02 56 | 05 31 | 00 45 | 24 08 | 17 26 |
| 48 | 03 57 | 06 24 | 01 24 | 24 34 | 17 39 |
| 49 | 05 03 | 07 18 | 02 04 | 25 01 | 17 52 |
| 50 | 06 12 | 08 15 | 02 45 | 25 28 | 18 06 |
| 51 | 07 27 | 09 14 | 03 27 | 25 56 | 18 20 |
| 52 | 08 46 | 10 15 | 04 10 | 26 24 | 18 34 |
| 53 | 10 12 | 11 19 | 04 55 | 26 53 | 18 49 |
| 54 | 11 43 | 12 25 | 05 40 | 27 23 | 19 04 |
| 55 | 13 22 | 13 34 | 06 27 | 27 53 | 19 19 |
| 56 | 15 09 | 14 46 | 07 16 | 28 24 | 19 34 |
| 57 | 17 03 | 16 01 | 08 06 | 28 56 | 19 50 |
| 58 | 19 08 | 17 19 | 08 57 | 29 29 | 20 06 |
| 59 | 21 22 | 18 41 | 09 50 | 00♍02 | 20 23 |
| 60 | 23♊48 | 20♋06 | 10♌45 | 00♍37 | 20♍40 |

0h 44m 0s — 11° 0' 0" — 11 ♈ 58

| LAT. | 11 | 12 | ASC | 2 | 3 |
|---|---|---|---|---|---|
| 0 | 13♉27 | 12♊28 | 10♋07 | 08♌34 | 09♍26 |
| 5 | 14 39 | 14 17 | 12 04 | 10 17 | 10 27 |
| 10 | 15 56 | 16 09 | 14 02 | 11 57 | 11 24 |
| 15 | 17 19 | 18 07 | 16 01 | 13 35 | 12 20 |
| 20 | 18 52 | 20 13 | 18 03 | 15 13 | 13 15 |
| 21 | 19 12 | 20 39 | 18 28 | 15 32 | 13 26 |
| 22 | 19 33 | 21 06 | 18 53 | 15 52 | 13 36 |
| 23 | 19 54 | 21 33 | 19 19 | 16 12 | 13 47 |
| 24 | 20 16 | 22 00 | 19 44 | 16 32 | 13 58 |
| 25 | 20 38 | 22 29 | 20 10 | 16 52 | 14 09 |
| 26 | 21 01 | 22 57 | 20 36 | 17 12 | 14 20 |
| 27 | 21 25 | 23 27 | 21 03 | 17 32 | 14 30 |
| 28 | 21 49 | 23 57 | 21 30 | 17 52 | 14 41 |
| 29 | 22 15 | 24 27 | 21 57 | 18 12 | 14 52 |
| 30 | 22 41 | 24 58 | 22 25 | 18 33 | 15 03 |
| 31 | 23 08 | 25 30 | 22 52 | 18 54 | 15 14 |
| 32 | 23 36 | 26 03 | 23 21 | 19 14 | 15 25 |
| 33 | 24 06 | 26 36 | 23 49 | 19 36 | 15 37 |
| 34 | 24 36 | 27 10 | 24 19 | 19 57 | 15 48 |
| 35 | 25 08 | 27 45 | 24 48 | 20 18 | 15 59 |
| 36 | 25 41 | 28 21 | 25 18 | 20 40 | 16 10 |
| 37 | 26 15 | 28 58 | 25 49 | 21 02 | 16 22 |
| 38 | 26 51 | 29 36 | 26 20 | 21 24 | 16 34 |
| 39 | 27 29 | 00♋15 | 26 52 | 21 47 | 16 45 |
| 40 | 28 08 | 00 56 | 27 24 | 22 09 | 16 57 |
| 41 | 28 49 | 01 37 | 27 57 | 22 33 | 17 09 |
| 42 | 29 33 | 02 20 | 28 31 | 22 56 | 17 21 |
| 43 | 00♊19 | 03 04 | 29 05 | 23 20 | 17 33 |
| 44 | 01 07 | 03 49 | 29 40 | 23 44 | 17 46 |
| 45 | 01 58 | 04 36 | 00♌16 | 24 08 | 17 58 |
| 46 | 02 52 | 05 25 | 00 53 | 24 33 | 18 11 |
| 47 | 03 49 | 06 15 | 01 30 | 24 59 | 18 24 |
| 48 | 04 49 | 07 07 | 02 09 | 25 25 | 18 37 |
| 49 | 05 54 | 08 01 | 02 48 | 25 51 | 18 50 |
| 50 | 07 02 | 08 57 | 03 29 | 26 18 | 19 04 |
| 51 | 08 16 | 09 55 | 04 10 | 26 45 | 19 18 |
| 52 | 09 34 | 10 55 | 04 53 | 27 13 | 19 32 |
| 53 | 10 58 | 11 58 | 05 37 | 27 42 | 19 46 |
| 54 | 12 28 | 13 03 | 06 22 | 28 11 | 20 01 |
| 55 | 14 05 | 14 11 | 07 08 | 28 41 | 20 16 |
| 56 | 15 50 | 15 22 | 07 56 | 29 12 | 20 31 |
| 57 | 17 43 | 16 35 | 08 45 | 29 43 | 20 47 |
| 58 | 19 45 | 17 52 | 09 35 | 00♍15 | 21 03 |
| 59 | 21 57 | 19 13 | 10 28 | 00 48 | 21 19 |
| 60 | 24♊20 | 20♋36 | 11♌22 | 01♍22 | 21♍36 |

0h 48m 0s — 12° 0' 0" — 13 ♈ 03

| LAT. | 11 | 12 | ASC | 2 | 3 |
|---|---|---|---|---|---|
| 0 | 14♉28 | 13♊24 | 11♋02 | 09♌34 | 10♍30 |
| 5 | 15 39 | 15 12 | 12 59 | 11 16 | 11 30 |
| 10 | 16 56 | 17 04 | 14 56 | 12 55 | 12 27 |
| 15 | 18 19 | 19 02 | 16 55 | 14 32 | 13 23 |
| 20 | 19 52 | 21 07 | 18 56 | 16 09 | 14 16 |
| 21 | 20 12 | 21 33 | 19 21 | 16 29 | 14 27 |
| 22 | 20 33 | 21 59 | 19 46 | 16 48 | 14 38 |
| 23 | 20 54 | 22 26 | 20 11 | 17 08 | 14 49 |
| 24 | 21 15 | 22 54 | 20 37 | 17 28 | 14 59 |
| 25 | 21 37 | 23 22 | 21 02 | 17 48 | 15 10 |
| 26 | 22 00 | 23 50 | 21 28 | 18 07 | 15 21 |
| 27 | 22 24 | 24 19 | 21 55 | 18 27 | 15 31 |
| 28 | 22 48 | 24 49 | 22 21 | 18 47 | 15 42 |
| 29 | 23 14 | 25 19 | 22 48 | 19 08 | 15 53 |
| 30 | 23 40 | 25 50 | 23 16 | 19 28 | 16 04 |
| 31 | 24 07 | 26 22 | 23 43 | 19 48 | 16 15 |
| 32 | 24 35 | 26 54 | 24 11 | 20 09 | 16 26 |
| 33 | 25 04 | 27 27 | 24 40 | 20 30 | 16 37 |
| 34 | 25 34 | 28 01 | 25 09 | 20 51 | 16 48 |
| 35 | 26 05 | 28 36 | 25 38 | 21 12 | 16 59 |
| 36 | 26 38 | 29 11 | 26 08 | 21 34 | 17 10 |
| 37 | 27 12 | 29 48 | 26 38 | 21 55 | 17 22 |
| 38 | 27 48 | 00♋25 | 27 09 | 22 17 | 17 33 |
| 39 | 28 25 | 01 04 | 27 40 | 22 40 | 17 45 |
| 40 | 29 04 | 01 44 | 28 12 | 23 02 | 17 56 |
| 41 | 29 45 | 02 25 | 28 45 | 23 25 | 18 08 |
| 42 | 00♊28 | 03 07 | 29 18 | 23 48 | 18 20 |
| 43 | 01 13 | 03 50 | 29 52 | 24 12 | 18 32 |
| 44 | 02 01 | 04 35 | 00♌27 | 24 36 | 18 44 |
| 45 | 02 51 | 05 21 | 01 02 | 25 00 | 18 57 |
| 46 | 03 44 | 06 09 | 01 39 | 25 25 | 19 09 |
| 47 | 04 41 | 06 59 | 02 16 | 25 50 | 19 22 |
| 48 | 05 40 | 07 50 | 02 54 | 26 15 | 19 35 |
| 49 | 06 44 | 08 43 | 03 33 | 26 41 | 19 48 |
| 50 | 07 52 | 09 38 | 04 12 | 27 08 | 20 02 |
| 51 | 09 04 | 10 36 | 04 53 | 27 35 | 20 15 |
| 52 | 10 21 | 11 35 | 05 35 | 28 02 | 20 29 |
| 53 | 11 44 | 12 37 | 06 19 | 28 31 | 20 43 |
| 54 | 13 12 | 13 41 | 07 03 | 29 00 | 20 58 |
| 55 | 14 48 | 14 48 | 07 49 | 29 29 | 21 12 |
| 56 | 16 30 | 15 57 | 08 36 | 29 59 | 21 28 |
| 57 | 18 21 | 17 10 | 09 24 | 00♍30 | 21 43 |
| 58 | 20 21 | 18 25 | 10 14 | 01 02 | 21 59 |
| 59 | 22 31 | 19 44 | 11 05 | 01 35 | 22 15 |
| 60 | 24♊51 | 21♋07 | 11♌58 | 02♍08 | 22♍32 |

0h 52m 0s — 13° 0' 0" — 14 ♈ 07

| LAT. | 11 | 12 | ASC | 2 | 3 |
|---|---|---|---|---|---|
| 0 | 15♉28 | 14♊20 | 11♋58 | 10♌33 | 11♍34 |
| 5 | 16 39 | 16 08 | 13 54 | 12 15 | 12 34 |
| 10 | 17 56 | 17 59 | 15 51 | 13 53 | 13 31 |
| 15 | 19 19 | 19 56 | 17 48 | 15 30 | 14 25 |
| 20 | 20 52 | 22 00 | 19 49 | 17 06 | 15 18 |
| 21 | 21 11 | 22 26 | 20 14 | 17 26 | 15 29 |
| 22 | 21 32 | 22 53 | 20 39 | 17 45 | 15 40 |
| 23 | 21 53 | 23 20 | 21 04 | 18 04 | 15 50 |
| 24 | 22 14 | 23 47 | 21 29 | 18 24 | 16 01 |
| 25 | 22 36 | 24 15 | 21 55 | 18 43 | 16 11 |
| 26 | 22 59 | 24 43 | 22 20 | 19 03 | 16 22 |
| 27 | 23 23 | 25 12 | 22 47 | 19 23 | 16 32 |
| 28 | 23 47 | 25 41 | 23 13 | 19 43 | 16 43 |
| 29 | 24 12 | 26 11 | 23 40 | 20 03 | 16 54 |
| 30 | 24 38 | 26 42 | 24 07 | 20 23 | 17 04 |
| 31 | 25 05 | 27 13 | 24 34 | 20 43 | 17 15 |
| 32 | 25 32 | 27 45 | 25 02 | 21 04 | 17 26 |
| 33 | 26 01 | 28 18 | 25 30 | 21 24 | 17 37 |
| 34 | 26 31 | 28 51 | 25 59 | 21 45 | 17 48 |
| 35 | 27 02 | 29 25 | 26 28 | 22 06 | 17 59 |
| 36 | 27 35 | 00♋01 | 26 57 | 22 28 | 18 10 |
| 37 | 28 09 | 00 37 | 27 27 | 22 49 | 18 21 |
| 38 | 28 44 | 01 14 | 27 58 | 23 11 | 18 33 |
| 39 | 29 21 | 01 52 | 28 29 | 23 33 | 18 44 |
| 40 | 29 59 | 02 31 | 29 00 | 23 55 | 18 55 |
| 41 | 00♊40 | 03 12 | 29 33 | 24 18 | 19 07 |
| 42 | 01 22 | 03 53 | 00♌05 | 24 41 | 19 19 |
| 43 | 02 07 | 04 36 | 00 39 | 25 04 | 19 31 |
| 44 | 02 54 | 05 21 | 01 13 | 25 27 | 19 43 |
| 45 | 03 44 | 06 06 | 01 48 | 25 51 | 19 55 |
| 46 | 04 36 | 06 54 | 02 24 | 26 16 | 20 08 |
| 47 | 05 32 | 07 42 | 03 01 | 26 41 | 20 20 |
| 48 | 06 31 | 08 33 | 03 38 | 27 06 | 20 33 |
| 49 | 07 34 | 09 25 | 04 17 | 27 31 | 20 46 |
| 50 | 08 40 | 10 20 | 04 56 | 27 58 | 20 59 |
| 51 | 09 51 | 11 16 | 05 36 | 28 24 | 21 13 |
| 52 | 11 07 | 12 15 | 06 18 | 28 52 | 21 26 |
| 53 | 12 29 | 13 15 | 07 00 | 29 20 | 21 40 |
| 54 | 13 56 | 14 18 | 07 44 | 29 48 | 21 55 |
| 55 | 15 30 | 15 24 | 08 29 | 00♍17 | 22 09 |
| 56 | 17 11 | 16 33 | 09 15 | 00 47 | 22 24 |
| 57 | 19 00 | 17 44 | 10 03 | 01 18 | 22 39 |
| 58 | 20 57 | 18 58 | 10 52 | 01 49 | 22 55 |
| 59 | 23 04 | 20 16 | 11 43 | 02 21 | 23 11 |
| 60 | 25♊22 | 21♋37 | 12♌35 | 02♍54 | 23♍27 |

0h 56m 0s — 14° 0' 0" — 15 ♈ 12

| LAT. | 11 | 12 | ASC | 2 | 3 |
|---|---|---|---|---|---|
| 0 | 16♉28 | 15♊16 | 12♋53 | 11♌32 | 12♍39 |
| 5 | 17 39 | 17 03 | 14 49 | 13 14 | 13 38 |
| 10 | 18 56 | 18 54 | 16 45 | 14 52 | 14 34 |
| 15 | 20 19 | 20 51 | 18 42 | 16 28 | 15 28 |
| 20 | 21 51 | 22 54 | 20 42 | 18 03 | 16 20 |
| 21 | 22 11 | 23 20 | 21 07 | 18 22 | 16 31 |
| 22 | 22 31 | 23 46 | 21 32 | 18 42 | 16 41 |
| 23 | 22 52 | 24 13 | 21 56 | 19 01 | 16 52 |
| 24 | 23 13 | 24 40 | 22 21 | 19 20 | 17 02 |
| 25 | 23 35 | 25 07 | 22 47 | 19 40 | 17 12 |
| 26 | 23 58 | 25 35 | 23 12 | 19 59 | 17 23 |
| 27 | 24 21 | 26 04 | 23 38 | 20 19 | 17 33 |
| 28 | 24 45 | 26 33 | 24 04 | 20 38 | 17 44 |
| 29 | 25 10 | 27 03 | 24 31 | 20 58 | 17 54 |
| 30 | 25 36 | 27 33 | 24 58 | 21 18 | 18 05 |
| 31 | 26 02 | 28 04 | 25 25 | 21 38 | 18 16 |
| 32 | 26 30 | 28 35 | 25 52 | 21 58 | 18 26 |
| 33 | 26 58 | 29 08 | 26 20 | 22 19 | 18 37 |
| 34 | 27 28 | 29 41 | 26 49 | 22 39 | 18 48 |
| 35 | 27 59 | 00♋15 | 27 17 | 23 00 | 18 59 |
| 36 | 28 31 | 00 50 | 27 46 | 23 21 | 19 10 |
| 37 | 29 05 | 01 26 | 28 16 | 23 43 | 19 21 |
| 38 | 29 40 | 02 02 | 28 46 | 24 04 | 19 32 |
| 39 | 00♊16 | 02 40 | 29 17 | 24 26 | 19 43 |
| 40 | 00 54 | 03 19 | 29 48 | 24 48 | 19 55 |
| 41 | 01 34 | 03 59 | 00♌20 | 25 10 | 20 06 |
| 42 | 02 16 | 04 40 | 00 53 | 25 33 | 20 18 |
| 43 | 03 01 | 05 22 | 01 26 | 25 56 | 20 30 |
| 44 | 03 47 | 06 06 | 02 00 | 26 20 | 20 41 |
| 45 | 04 36 | 06 51 | 02 34 | 26 43 | 20 54 |
| 46 | 05 28 | 07 38 | 03 10 | 27 07 | 21 06 |
| 47 | 06 23 | 08 26 | 03 46 | 27 31 | 21 18 |
| 48 | 07 21 | 09 16 | 04 23 | 27 56 | 21 31 |
| 49 | 08 23 | 10 07 | 05 01 | 28 22 | 21 44 |
| 50 | 09 29 | 11 01 | 05 39 | 28 48 | 21 57 |
| 51 | 10 39 | 11 56 | 06 19 | 29 14 | 22 10 |
| 52 | 11 53 | 12 54 | 07 00 | 29 41 | 22 24 |
| 53 | 13 13 | 13 54 | 07 42 | 00♍08 | 22 37 |
| 54 | 14 39 | 14 56 | 08 25 | 00 37 | 22 52 |
| 55 | 16 11 | 16 00 | 09 10 | 01 05 | 23 06 |
| 56 | 17 51 | 17 08 | 09 55 | 01 35 | 23 21 |
| 57 | 19 37 | 18 18 | 10 42 | 02 05 | 23 36 |
| 58 | 21 33 | 19 31 | 11 30 | 02 36 | 23 51 |
| 59 | 23 38 | 20 47 | 12 20 | 03 08 | 24 07 |
| 60 | 25♊53 | 22♋07 | 13♌12 | 03♍40 | 24♍23 |

1h 0m 0s — 15° 0' 0" — 16 ♈ 17

| LAT. | 11 | 12 | ASC | 2 | 3 |
|---|---|---|---|---|---|
| 0 | 17♉28 | 16♊11 | 13♋49 | 12♌32 | 13♍43 |
| 5 | 18 39 | 17 59 | 15 44 | 14 13 | 14 42 |
| 10 | 19 55 | 19 49 | 17 40 | 15 50 | 15 37 |
| 15 | 21 18 | 21 45 | 19 36 | 17 25 | 16 30 |
| 20 | 22 50 | 23 47 | 21 35 | 19 00 | 17 22 |
| 21 | 23 09 | 24 13 | 22 00 | 19 19 | 17 32 |
| 22 | 23 30 | 24 39 | 22 24 | 19 38 | 17 43 |
| 23 | 23 50 | 25 05 | 22 49 | 19 57 | 17 53 |
| 24 | 24 12 | 25 32 | 23 14 | 20 16 | 18 03 |
| 25 | 24 33 | 26 00 | 23 39 | 20 36 | 18 14 |
| 26 | 24 56 | 26 27 | 24 04 | 20 55 | 18 24 |
| 27 | 25 19 | 26 56 | 24 30 | 21 14 | 18 34 |
| 28 | 25 43 | 27 24 | 24 56 | 21 34 | 18 45 |
| 29 | 26 08 | 27 54 | 25 22 | 21 53 | 18 55 |
| 30 | 26 33 | 28 24 | 25 49 | 22 13 | 19 06 |
| 31 | 27 00 | 28 55 | 26 16 | 22 33 | 19 16 |
| 32 | 27 27 | 29 26 | 26 43 | 22 53 | 19 27 |
| 33 | 27 55 | 29 58 | 27 10 | 23 13 | 19 37 |
| 34 | 28 25 | 00♋31 | 27 38 | 23 34 | 19 48 |
| 35 | 28 55 | 01 05 | 28 07 | 23 54 | 19 59 |
| 36 | 29 27 | 01 39 | 28 36 | 24 15 | 20 10 |
| 37 | 00♊00 | 02 14 | 29 05 | 24 36 | 20 20 |
| 38 | 00 35 | 02 51 | 29 35 | 24 57 | 20 31 |
| 39 | 01 11 | 03 28 | 00♌05 | 25 19 | 20 43 |
| 40 | 01 49 | 04 06 | 00 36 | 25 41 | 20 54 |
| 41 | 02 29 | 04 46 | 01 08 | 26 03 | 21 05 |
| 42 | 03 10 | 05 26 | 01 40 | 26 25 | 21 17 |
| 43 | 03 54 | 06 08 | 02 13 | 26 48 | 21 28 |
| 44 | 04 40 | 06 51 | 02 46 | 27 11 | 21 40 |
| 45 | 05 28 | 07 36 | 03 20 | 27 34 | 21 52 |
| 46 | 06 19 | 08 22 | 03 55 | 27 58 | 22 04 |
| 47 | 07 13 | 09 09 | 04 31 | 28 22 | 22 16 |
| 48 | 08 11 | 09 58 | 05 07 | 28 47 | 22 29 |
| 49 | 09 12 | 10 49 | 05 45 | 29 12 | 22 41 |
| 50 | 10 16 | 11 42 | 06 23 | 29 37 | 22 54 |
| 51 | 11 25 | 12 36 | 07 02 | 00♍04 | 23 07 |
| 52 | 12 39 | 13 33 | 07 42 | 00 30 | 23 21 |
| 53 | 13 58 | 14 32 | 08 24 | 00 57 | 23 35 |
| 54 | 15 22 | 15 33 | 09 06 | 01 25 | 23 48 |
| 55 | 16 53 | 16 37 | 09 50 | 01 53 | 24 03 |
| 56 | 18 30 | 17 43 | 10 35 | 02 22 | 24 17 |
| 57 | 20 15 | 18 52 | 11 21 | 02 52 | 24 32 |
| 58 | 22 08 | 20 04 | 12 09 | 03 23 | 24 47 |
| 59 | 24 11 | 21 19 | 12 58 | 03 54 | 25 03 |
| 60 | 26♊23 | 22♋37 | 13♌49 | 04♍26 | 25♍19 |

# Koch Table of Houses for Latitudes 0° to 60° North

1h 4m 0s 16° 0' 0"
17 ♈ 21

| LAT. | 11 | 12 | ASC | 2 | 3 |
|---|---|---|---|---|---|
| 0 | 18♉28 | 17♊07 | 14♋44 | 13♌32 | 14♍48 |
| 5 | 19 39 | 18 54 | 16 40 | 15 12 | 15 46 |
| 10 | 20 55 | 20 44 | 18 35 | 16 49 | 16 40 |
| 15 | 22 17 | 22 39 | 20 30 | 18 23 | 17 33 |
| 20 | 23 48 | 24 41 | 22 29 | 19 57 | 18 24 |
| 21 | 24 08 | 25 06 | 22 53 | 20 16 | 18 34 |
| 22 | 24 28 | 25 32 | 23 17 | 20 35 | 18 44 |
| 23 | 24 49 | 25 58 | 23 41 | 20 54 | 18 55 |
| 24 | 25 10 | 26 25 | 24 06 | 21 13 | 19 05 |
| 25 | 25 31 | 26 52 | 24 31 | 21 32 | 19 15 |
| 26 | 25 54 | 27 19 | 24 56 | 21 51 | 19 25 |
| 27 | 26 17 | 27 47 | 25 22 | 22 10 | 19 35 |
| 28 | 26 41 | 28 16 | 25 47 | 22 29 | 19 46 |
| 29 | 27 05 | 28 45 | 26 13 | 22 49 | 19 56 |
| 30 | 27 30 | 29 15 | 26 40 | 23 08 | 20 06 |
| 31 | 27 57 | 29 45 | 27 06 | 23 28 | 20 17 |
| 32 | 28 24 | 00♋16 | 27 33 | 23 48 | 20 27 |
| 33 | 28 52 | 00 48 | 28 00 | 24 08 | 20 37 |
| 34 | 29 21 | 01 20 | 28 28 | 24 28 | 20 48 |
| 35 | 29 51 | 01 54 | 28 56 | 24 48 | 20 59 |
| 36 | 00♊23 | 02 28 | 29 25 | 25 09 | 21 09 |
| 37 | 00 56 | 03 03 | 29 54 | 25 30 | 21 20 |
| 38 | 01 30 | 03 39 | 00♌23 | 25 51 | 21 31 |
| 39 | 02 06 | 04 15 | 00 53 | 26 12 | 21 42 |
| 40 | 02 43 | 04 53 | 01 24 | 26 34 | 21 53 |
| 41 | 03 22 | 05 32 | 01 55 | 26 55 | 22 04 |
| 42 | 04 03 | 06 12 | 02 27 | 27 17 | 22 15 |
| 43 | 04 46 | 06 53 | 02 59 | 27 40 | 22 27 |
| 44 | 05 32 | 07 36 | 03 32 | 28 03 | 22 39 |
| 45 | 06 20 | 08 20 | 04 06 | 28 26 | 22 50 |
| 46 | 07 10 | 09 05 | 04 40 | 28 49 | 23 02 |
| 47 | 08 03 | 09 52 | 05 15 | 29 13 | 23 14 |
| 48 | 09 00 | 10 40 | 05 51 | 29 37 | 23 27 |
| 49 | 10 00 | 11 30 | 06 28 | 00♍02 | 23 39 |
| 50 | 11 04 | 12 22 | 07 06 | 00 27 | 23 52 |
| 51 | 12 12 | 13 16 | 07 45 | 00 53 | 24 05 |
| 52 | 13 24 | 14 12 | 08 25 | 01 19 | 24 18 |
| 53 | 14 41 | 15 10 | 09 05 | 01 46 | 24 32 |
| 54 | 16 04 | 16 10 | 09 47 | 02 13 | 24 45 |
| 55 | 17 33 | 17 13 | 10 30 | 02 41 | 24 59 |
| 56 | 19 09 | 18 18 | 11 15 | 03 10 | 25 14 |
| 57 | 20 52 | 19 26 | 12 00 | 03 39 | 25 28 |
| 58 | 22 43 | 20 36 | 12 47 | 04 10 | 25 43 |
| 59 | 24 43 | 21 50 | 13 35 | 04 40 | 25 59 |
| 60 | 26♊53 | 23♋07 | 14♌25 | 05♍12 | 26♍15 |

1h 8m 0s 17° 0' 0"
18 ♈ 26

| LAT. | 11 | 12 | ASC | 2 | 3 |
|---|---|---|---|---|---|
| 0 | 19♉27 | 18♊02 | 15♋40 | 14♌32 | 15♍53 |
| 5 | 20 38 | 19 49 | 17 35 | 16 11 | 16 50 |
| 10 | 21 54 | 21 39 | 19 29 | 17 47 | 17 44 |
| 15 | 23 16 | 23 33 | 21 24 | 19 21 | 18 35 |
| 20 | 24 47 | 25 34 | 23 22 | 20 54 | 19 26 |
| 21 | 25 06 | 25 59 | 23 46 | 21 13 | 19 36 |
| 22 | 25 26 | 26 25 | 24 10 | 21 32 | 19 46 |
| 23 | 25 47 | 26 51 | 24 34 | 21 50 | 19 56 |
| 24 | 26 08 | 27 17 | 24 58 | 22 09 | 20 06 |
| 25 | 26 29 | 27 44 | 25 23 | 22 28 | 20 16 |
| 26 | 26 51 | 28 11 | 25 48 | 22 47 | 20 26 |
| 27 | 27 14 | 28 39 | 26 13 | 23 06 | 20 36 |
| 28 | 27 38 | 29 07 | 26 39 | 23 25 | 20 46 |
| 29 | 28 02 | 29 36 | 27 04 | 23 44 | 20 57 |
| 30 | 28 27 | 00♋06 | 27 30 | 24 03 | 21 07 |
| 31 | 28 53 | 00 36 | 27 57 | 24 23 | 21 17 |
| 32 | 29 20 | 01 06 | 28 23 | 24 43 | 21 27 |
| 33 | 29 48 | 01 38 | 28 50 | 25 02 | 21 38 |
| 34 | 00♊17 | 02 10 | 29 18 | 25 22 | 21 48 |
| 35 | 00 47 | 02 43 | 29 46 | 25 42 | 21 58 |
| 36 | 01 18 | 03 16 | 00♌14 | 26 03 | 22 09 |
| 37 | 01 51 | 03 51 | 00 43 | 26 23 | 22 20 |
| 38 | 02 24 | 04 26 | 01 12 | 26 44 | 22 30 |
| 39 | 03 00 | 05 03 | 01 41 | 27 05 | 22 41 |
| 40 | 03 37 | 05 40 | 02 12 | 27 26 | 22 52 |
| 41 | 04 16 | 06 19 | 02 42 | 27 48 | 23 03 |
| 42 | 04 56 | 06 58 | 03 14 | 28 10 | 23 14 |
| 43 | 05 39 | 07 39 | 03 46 | 28 32 | 23 26 |
| 44 | 06 23 | 08 21 | 04 18 | 28 54 | 23 37 |
| 45 | 07 11 | 09 04 | 04 52 | 29 17 | 23 49 |
| 46 | 08 00 | 09 49 | 05 26 | 29 40 | 24 00 |
| 47 | 08 53 | 10 35 | 06 00 | 00♍04 | 24 12 |
| 48 | 09 49 | 11 22 | 06 36 | 00 28 | 24 24 |
| 49 | 10 48 | 12 12 | 07 12 | 00 52 | 24 37 |
| 50 | 11 51 | 13 03 | 07 49 | 01 17 | 24 49 |
| 51 | 12 57 | 13 56 | 08 28 | 01 43 | 25 02 |
| 52 | 14 09 | 14 51 | 09 07 | 02 08 | 25 15 |
| 53 | 15 25 | 15 48 | 09 47 | 02 35 | 25 28 |
| 54 | 16 46 | 16 47 | 10 28 | 03 02 | 25 42 |
| 55 | 18 14 | 17 48 | 11 11 | 03 30 | 25 56 |
| 56 | 19 48 | 18 52 | 11 54 | 03 58 | 26 10 |
| 57 | 21 29 | 19 59 | 12 39 | 04 27 | 26 25 |
| 58 | 23 18 | 21 09 | 13 25 | 04 56 | 26 39 |
| 59 | 25 16 | 22 21 | 14 13 | 05 27 | 26 55 |
| 60 | 27♊23 | 23♋36 | 15♌02 | 05♍58 | 27♍10 |

1h 12m 0s 18° 0' 0"
19 ♈ 30

| LAT. | 11 | 12 | ASC | 2 | 3 |
|---|---|---|---|---|---|
| 0 | 20♉26 | 18♊58 | 16♋36 | 15♌32 | 16♍57 |
| 5 | 21 37 | 20 44 | 18 30 | 17 11 | 17 54 |
| 10 | 22 53 | 22 33 | 20 24 | 18 46 | 18 47 |
| 15 | 24 15 | 24 27 | 22 18 | 20 19 | 19 38 |
| 20 | 25 45 | 26 27 | 24 15 | 21 51 | 20 28 |
| 21 | 26 04 | 26 52 | 24 38 | 22 10 | 20 38 |
| 22 | 26 24 | 27 17 | 25 02 | 22 28 | 20 48 |
| 23 | 26 44 | 27 43 | 25 26 | 22 47 | 20 58 |
| 24 | 27 05 | 28 09 | 25 51 | 23 05 | 21 08 |
| 25 | 27 27 | 28 36 | 26 15 | 23 24 | 21 18 |
| 26 | 27 49 | 29 03 | 26 40 | 23 43 | 21 27 |
| 27 | 28 11 | 29 30 | 27 05 | 24 02 | 21 37 |
| 28 | 28 35 | 29 58 | 27 30 | 24 21 | 21 47 |
| 29 | 28 59 | 00♋27 | 27 55 | 24 40 | 21 57 |
| 30 | 29 24 | 00 56 | 28 21 | 24 59 | 22 07 |
| 31 | 29 50 | 01 26 | 28 47 | 25 18 | 22 17 |
| 32 | 00♊16 | 01 56 | 29 14 | 25 37 | 22 28 |
| 33 | 00 44 | 02 27 | 29 40 | 25 57 | 22 38 |
| 34 | 01 12 | 02 59 | 00♌08 | 26 17 | 22 48 |
| 35 | 01 42 | 03 32 | 00 35 | 26 36 | 22 58 |
| 36 | 02 13 | 04 05 | 01 03 | 26 57 | 23 09 |
| 37 | 02 45 | 04 39 | 01 31 | 27 17 | 23 19 |
| 38 | 03 19 | 05 14 | 02 00 | 27 37 | 23 30 |
| 39 | 03 54 | 05 50 | 02 30 | 27 58 | 23 40 |
| 40 | 04 30 | 06 27 | 02 59 | 28 19 | 23 51 |
| 41 | 05 08 | 07 05 | 03 30 | 28 40 | 24 02 |
| 42 | 05 48 | 07 44 | 04 01 | 29 02 | 24 13 |
| 43 | 06 31 | 08 24 | 04 32 | 29 24 | 24 24 |
| 44 | 07 15 | 09 05 | 05 04 | 29 46 | 24 35 |
| 45 | 08 01 | 09 48 | 05 37 | 00♍09 | 24 47 |
| 46 | 08 50 | 10 32 | 06 11 | 00 31 | 24 58 |
| 47 | 09 42 | 11 17 | 06 45 | 00 55 | 25 10 |
| 48 | 10 37 | 12 04 | 07 20 | 01 18 | 25 22 |
| 49 | 11 35 | 12 53 | 07 56 | 01 42 | 25 34 |
| 50 | 12 37 | 13 43 | 08 33 | 02 07 | 25 47 |
| 51 | 13 43 | 14 35 | 09 10 | 02 32 | 25 59 |
| 52 | 14 53 | 15 29 | 09 49 | 02 58 | 26 12 |
| 53 | 16 08 | 16 25 | 10 28 | 03 24 | 26 25 |
| 54 | 17 28 | 17 24 | 11 09 | 03 50 | 26 39 |
| 55 | 18 53 | 18 24 | 11 51 | 04 18 | 26 52 |
| 56 | 20 26 | 19 27 | 12 34 | 04 45 | 27 06 |
| 57 | 22 05 | 20 33 | 13 18 | 05 14 | 27 21 |
| 58 | 23 52 | 21 41 | 14 03 | 05 43 | 27 35 |
| 59 | 25 48 | 22 52 | 14 50 | 06 13 | 27 51 |
| 60 | 27♊53 | 24♋06 | 15♌39 | 06♍44 | 28♍06 |

1h 16m 0s 19° 0' 0"
20 ♈ 34

| LAT. | 11 | 12 | ASC | 2 | 3 |
|---|---|---|---|---|---|
| 0 | 21♉26 | 19♊53 | 17♋32 | 16♌33 | 18♍02 |
| 5 | 22 36 | 21 39 | 19 26 | 18 11 | 18 58 |
| 10 | 23 52 | 23 28 | 21 19 | 19 45 | 19 50 |
| 15 | 25 13 | 25 20 | 23 12 | 21 17 | 20 41 |
| 20 | 26 43 | 27 20 | 25 08 | 22 49 | 21 30 |
| 21 | 27 02 | 27 44 | 25 31 | 23 07 | 21 40 |
| 22 | 27 22 | 28 10 | 25 55 | 23 25 | 21 50 |
| 23 | 27 42 | 28 35 | 26 19 | 23 43 | 21 59 |
| 24 | 28 03 | 29 01 | 26 43 | 24 02 | 22 09 |
| 25 | 28 24 | 29 27 | 27 07 | 24 20 | 22 19 |
| 26 | 28 46 | 29 54 | 27 32 | 24 39 | 22 29 |
| 27 | 29 08 | 00♋22 | 27 56 | 24 57 | 22 38 |
| 28 | 29 31 | 00 49 | 28 21 | 25 16 | 22 48 |
| 29 | 29 55 | 01 18 | 28 46 | 25 35 | 22 58 |
| 30 | 00♊20 | 01 46 | 29 12 | 25 54 | 23 08 |
| 31 | 00 46 | 02 16 | 29 38 | 26 13 | 23 18 |
| 32 | 01 12 | 02 46 | 00♌04 | 26 32 | 23 28 |
| 33 | 01 39 | 03 17 | 00 30 | 26 51 | 23 38 |
| 34 | 02 08 | 03 48 | 00 57 | 27 11 | 23 48 |
| 35 | 02 37 | 04 20 | 01 24 | 27 31 | 23 58 |
| 36 | 03 08 | 04 53 | 01 52 | 27 50 | 24 08 |
| 37 | 03 39 | 05 27 | 02 20 | 28 10 | 24 19 |
| 38 | 04 12 | 06 01 | 02 49 | 28 31 | 24 29 |
| 39 | 04 47 | 06 37 | 03 17 | 28 51 | 24 39 |
| 40 | 05 23 | 07 13 | 03 47 | 29 12 | 24 50 |
| 41 | 06 01 | 07 51 | 04 17 | 29 33 | 25 01 |
| 42 | 06 40 | 08 29 | 04 47 | 29 54 | 25 12 |
| 43 | 07 22 | 09 09 | 05 19 | 00♍16 | 25 23 |
| 44 | 08 06 | 09 49 | 05 50 | 00 38 | 25 34 |
| 45 | 08 51 | 10 32 | 06 23 | 01 00 | 25 45 |
| 46 | 09 40 | 11 15 | 06 56 | 01 23 | 25 57 |
| 47 | 10 31 | 12 00 | 07 30 | 01 45 | 26 08 |
| 48 | 11 25 | 12 46 | 08 04 | 02 09 | 26 20 |
| 49 | 12 22 | 13 34 | 08 40 | 02 33 | 26 32 |
| 50 | 13 23 | 14 23 | 09 16 | 02 57 | 26 44 |
| 51 | 14 28 | 15 15 | 09 53 | 03 22 | 26 57 |
| 52 | 15 37 | 16 08 | 10 31 | 03 47 | 27 09 |
| 53 | 16 50 | 17 03 | 11 10 | 04 12 | 27 22 |
| 54 | 18 09 | 18 00 | 11 50 | 04 39 | 27 35 |
| 55 | 19 33 | 19 00 | 12 31 | 05 06 | 27 49 |
| 56 | 21 04 | 20 02 | 13 13 | 05 33 | 28 03 |
| 57 | 22 41 | 21 06 | 13 57 | 06 01 | 28 17 |
| 58 | 24 26 | 22 13 | 14 42 | 06 30 | 28 31 |
| 59 | 26 19 | 23 23 | 15 28 | 07 00 | 28 46 |
| 60 | 28♊22 | 24♋36 | 16♌15 | 07♍30 | 29♍02 |

1h 20m 0s 20° 0' 0"
21 ♈ 38

| LAT. | 11 | 12 | ASC | 2 | 3 |
|---|---|---|---|---|---|
| 0 | 22♉25 | 20♊49 | 18♋28 | 17♌33 | 19♍07 |
| 5 | 23 35 | 22 34 | 20 21 | 19 10 | 20 02 |
| 10 | 24 50 | 24 22 | 22 13 | 20 44 | 20 54 |
| 15 | 26 11 | 26 14 | 24 06 | 22 15 | 21 43 |
| 20 | 27 40 | 28 12 | 26 01 | 23 46 | 22 32 |
| 21 | 27 59 | 28 37 | 26 24 | 24 04 | 22 42 |
| 22 | 28 19 | 29 02 | 26 48 | 24 22 | 22 51 |
| 23 | 28 39 | 29 27 | 27 11 | 24 40 | 23 01 |
| 24 | 29 00 | 29 53 | 27 35 | 24 58 | 23 10 |
| 25 | 29 21 | 00♋19 | 27 59 | 25 17 | 23 20 |
| 26 | 29 42 | 00 46 | 28 23 | 25 35 | 23 30 |
| 27 | 00♊05 | 01 13 | 28 48 | 25 53 | 23 39 |
| 28 | 00 28 | 01 40 | 29 12 | 26 12 | 23 49 |
| 29 | 00 51 | 02 08 | 29 37 | 26 30 | 23 59 |
| 30 | 01 16 | 02 37 | 00♌03 | 26 49 | 24 08 |
| 31 | 01 41 | 03 06 | 00 28 | 27 08 | 24 18 |
| 32 | 02 07 | 03 35 | 00 54 | 27 27 | 24 28 |
| 33 | 02 34 | 04 06 | 01 20 | 27 46 | 24 38 |
| 34 | 03 02 | 04 37 | 01 47 | 28 05 | 24 48 |
| 35 | 03 32 | 05 09 | 02 14 | 28 25 | 24 58 |
| 36 | 04 02 | 05 41 | 02 41 | 28 44 | 25 08 |
| 37 | 04 33 | 06 14 | 03 09 | 29 04 | 25 18 |
| 38 | 05 06 | 06 49 | 03 37 | 29 24 | 25 28 |
| 39 | 05 40 | 07 24 | 04 05 | 29 44 | 25 39 |
| 40 | 06 16 | 07 59 | 04 34 | 00♍05 | 25 49 |
| 41 | 06 53 | 08 36 | 05 04 | 00 25 | 26 00 |
| 42 | 07 32 | 09 14 | 05 34 | 00 46 | 26 10 |
| 43 | 08 13 | 09 53 | 06 05 | 01 08 | 26 21 |
| 44 | 08 56 | 10 34 | 06 36 | 01 29 | 26 32 |
| 45 | 09 41 | 11 15 | 07 08 | 01 51 | 26 43 |
| 46 | 10 29 | 11 58 | 07 41 | 02 14 | 26 55 |
| 47 | 11 19 | 12 42 | 08 14 | 02 36 | 27 06 |
| 48 | 12 13 | 13 27 | 08 48 | 02 59 | 27 18 |
| 49 | 13 09 | 14 15 | 09 23 | 03 23 | 27 29 |
| 50 | 14 09 | 15 03 | 09 59 | 03 47 | 27 42 |
| 51 | 15 12 | 15 54 | 10 35 | 04 11 | 27 54 |
| 52 | 16 20 | 16 46 | 11 13 | 04 36 | 28 06 |
| 53 | 17 32 | 17 40 | 11 51 | 05 01 | 28 19 |
| 54 | 18 49 | 18 37 | 12 31 | 05 27 | 28 32 |
| 55 | 20 12 | 19 35 | 13 11 | 05 54 | 28 45 |
| 56 | 21 41 | 20 36 | 13 53 | 06 21 | 28 59 |
| 57 | 23 17 | 21 39 | 14 36 | 06 48 | 29 13 |
| 58 | 25 00 | 22 45 | 15 20 | 07 17 | 29 27 |
| 59 | 26 51 | 23 54 | 16 05 | 07 46 | 29 42 |
| 60 | 28♊51 | 25♋05 | 16♌52 | 08♍16 | 29♍57 |

1h 24m 0s 21° 0' 0"
22 ♈ 42

| LAT. | 11 | 12 | ASC | 2 | 3 |
|---|---|---|---|---|---|
| 0 | 23♉23 | 21♊44 | 19♋24 | 18♌34 | 20♍12 |
| 5 | 24 34 | 23 29 | 21 17 | 20 10 | 21 06 |
| 10 | 25 48 | 25 16 | 23 08 | 21 43 | 21 57 |
| 15 | 27 09 | 27 08 | 25 00 | 23 14 | 22 46 |
| 20 | 28 38 | 29 05 | 26 54 | 24 43 | 23 34 |
| 21 | 28 57 | 29 29 | 27 17 | 25 01 | 23 43 |
| 22 | 29 16 | 29 54 | 27 40 | 25 19 | 23 53 |
| 23 | 29 36 | 00♋19 | 28 04 | 25 37 | 24 02 |
| 24 | 29 56 | 00 45 | 28 27 | 25 55 | 24 12 |
| 25 | 00♊17 | 01 10 | 28 51 | 26 13 | 24 21 |
| 26 | 00 39 | 01 37 | 29 15 | 26 31 | 24 31 |
| 27 | 01 01 | 02 03 | 29 39 | 26 49 | 24 40 |
| 28 | 01 24 | 02 31 | 00♌04 | 27 08 | 24 50 |
| 29 | 01 47 | 02 58 | 00 28 | 27 26 | 24 59 |
| 30 | 02 11 | 03 27 | 00 53 | 27 44 | 25 09 |
| 31 | 02 36 | 03 55 | 01 19 | 28 03 | 25 18 |
| 32 | 03 02 | 04 25 | 01 44 | 28 22 | 25 28 |
| 33 | 03 29 | 04 55 | 02 10 | 28 40 | 25 38 |
| 34 | 03 57 | 05 26 | 02 36 | 29 00 | 25 48 |
| 35 | 04 26 | 05 57 | 03 03 | 29 19 | 25 57 |
| 36 | 04 56 | 06 29 | 03 30 | 29 38 | 26 07 |
| 37 | 05 27 | 07 02 | 03 57 | 29 58 | 26 17 |
| 38 | 05 59 | 07 36 | 04 25 | 00♍17 | 26 28 |
| 39 | 06 33 | 08 10 | 04 53 | 00 37 | 26 38 |
| 40 | 07 08 | 08 46 | 05 22 | 00 58 | 26 48 |
| 41 | 07 45 | 09 22 | 05 51 | 01 18 | 26 58 |
| 42 | 08 23 | 09 59 | 06 21 | 01 39 | 27 09 |
| 43 | 09 04 | 10 38 | 06 51 | 02 00 | 27 20 |
| 44 | 09 46 | 11 18 | 07 22 | 02 21 | 27 30 |
| 45 | 10 31 | 11 58 | 07 54 | 02 43 | 27 41 |
| 46 | 11 18 | 12 40 | 08 26 | 03 05 | 27 52 |
| 47 | 12 07 | 13 24 | 08 59 | 03 27 | 28 04 |
| 48 | 13 00 | 14 09 | 09 32 | 03 50 | 28 15 |
| 49 | 13 55 | 14 55 | 10 07 | 04 13 | 28 27 |
| 50 | 14 54 | 15 43 | 10 42 | 04 36 | 28 39 |
| 51 | 15 56 | 16 33 | 11 18 | 05 00 | 28 51 |
| 52 | 17 03 | 17 24 | 11 55 | 05 25 | 29 03 |
| 53 | 18 14 | 18 18 | 12 33 | 05 50 | 29 16 |
| 54 | 19 30 | 19 13 | 13 11 | 06 15 | 29 29 |
| 55 | 20 51 | 20 10 | 13 51 | 06 42 | 29 42 |
| 56 | 22 18 | 21 10 | 14 32 | 07 08 | 29 55 |
| 57 | 23 52 | 22 12 | 15 14 | 07 36 | 00♎09 |
| 58 | 25 33 | 23 17 | 15 58 | 08 04 | 00 23 |
| 59 | 27 22 | 24 24 | 16 42 | 08 33 | 00 38 |
| 60 | 29♊20 | 25♋35 | 17♌28 | 09♍02 | 00♎53 |

1h 28m 0s 22° 0' 0"
23 ♈ 46

| LAT. | 11 | 12 | ASC | 2 | 3 |
|---|---|---|---|---|---|
| 0 | 24♉22 | 22♊39 | 20♋20 | 19♌35 | 21♍17 |
| 5 | 25 32 | 24 24 | 22 12 | 21 11 | 22 11 |
| 10 | 26 46 | 26 10 | 24 03 | 22 42 | 23 01 |
| 15 | 28 07 | 28 01 | 25 54 | 24 12 | 23 49 |
| 20 | 29 35 | 29 57 | 27 47 | 25 41 | 24 36 |
| 21 | 29 54 | 00♋22 | 28 10 | 25 58 | 24 45 |
| 22 | 00♊13 | 00 46 | 28 33 | 26 16 | 24 55 |
| 23 | 00 33 | 01 11 | 28 56 | 26 34 | 25 04 |
| 24 | 00 53 | 01 36 | 29 19 | 26 51 | 25 13 |
| 25 | 01 14 | 02 02 | 29 43 | 27 09 | 25 22 |
| 26 | 01 35 | 02 28 | 00♌07 | 27 27 | 25 32 |
| 27 | 01 57 | 02 54 | 00 31 | 27 45 | 25 41 |
| 28 | 02 19 | 03 21 | 00 55 | 28 03 | 25 50 |
| 29 | 02 43 | 03 49 | 01 19 | 28 21 | 26 00 |
| 30 | 03 07 | 04 16 | 01 44 | 28 40 | 26 09 |
| 31 | 03 32 | 04 45 | 02 09 | 28 58 | 26 19 |
| 32 | 03 57 | 05 14 | 02 34 | 29 16 | 26 28 |
| 33 | 04 24 | 05 44 | 03 00 | 29 35 | 26 38 |
| 34 | 04 51 | 06 14 | 03 26 | 29 54 | 26 47 |
| 35 | 05 20 | 06 45 | 03 52 | 00♍13 | 26 57 |
| 36 | 05 49 | 07 17 | 04 19 | 00 32 | 27 07 |
| 37 | 06 20 | 07 49 | 04 46 | 00 51 | 27 17 |
| 38 | 06 52 | 08 22 | 05 13 | 01 11 | 27 27 |
| 39 | 07 25 | 08 56 | 05 41 | 01 30 | 27 37 |
| 40 | 08 00 | 09 31 | 06 09 | 01 50 | 27 47 |
| 41 | 08 36 | 10 07 | 06 38 | 02 11 | 27 57 |
| 42 | 09 14 | 10 44 | 07 08 | 02 31 | 28 07 |
| 43 | 09 54 | 11 22 | 07 38 | 02 52 | 28 18 |
| 44 | 10 36 | 12 01 | 08 08 | 03 13 | 28 29 |
| 45 | 11 20 | 12 42 | 08 39 | 03 34 | 28 39 |
| 46 | 12 06 | 13 23 | 09 11 | 03 56 | 28 50 |
| 47 | 12 55 | 14 06 | 09 43 | 04 18 | 29 01 |
| 48 | 13 46 | 14 50 | 10 16 | 04 40 | 29 13 |
| 49 | 14 41 | 15 36 | 10 50 | 05 03 | 29 24 |
| 50 | 15 39 | 16 23 | 11 25 | 05 26 | 29 36 |
| 51 | 16 40 | 17 12 | 12 00 | 05 50 | 29 48 |
| 52 | 17 46 | 18 02 | 12 37 | 06 14 | 00♎00 |
| 53 | 18 55 | 18 55 | 13 14 | 06 39 | 00 12 |
| 54 | 20 10 | 19 49 | 13 52 | 07 04 | 00 25 |
| 55 | 21 30 | 20 46 | 14 31 | 07 30 | 00 38 |
| 56 | 22 55 | 21 44 | 15 12 | 07 56 | 00 51 |
| 57 | 24 27 | 22 45 | 15 53 | 08 23 | 01 05 |
| 58 | 26 06 | 23 49 | 16 36 | 08 51 | 01 19 |
| 59 | 27 54 | 24 55 | 17 20 | 09 19 | 01 33 |
| 60 | 29♊49 | 26♋04 | 18♌05 | 09♍48 | 01♎48 |

1h 32m 0s 23° 0' 0"
24 ♈ 50

| LAT. | 11 | 12 | ASC | 2 | 3 |
|---|---|---|---|---|---|
| 0 | 25♉21 | 23♊34 | 21♋17 | 20♌36 | 22♍23 |
| 5 | 26 30 | 25 18 | 23 08 | 22 11 | 23 15 |
| 10 | 27 44 | 27 04 | 24 58 | 23 42 | 24 04 |
| 15 | 29 04 | 28 54 | 26 48 | 25 10 | 24 52 |
| 20 | 00♊32 | 00♋50 | 28 40 | 26 38 | 25 38 |
| 21 | 00 50 | 01 14 | 29 03 | 26 55 | 25 47 |
| 22 | 01 09 | 01 38 | 29 26 | 27 13 | 25 56 |
| 23 | 01 29 | 02 02 | 29 49 | 27 31 | 26 05 |
| 24 | 01 49 | 02 27 | 00♌12 | 27 48 | 26 14 |
| 25 | 02 10 | 02 53 | 00 35 | 28 06 | 26 24 |
| 26 | 02 31 | 03 19 | 00 58 | 28 23 | 26 33 |
| 27 | 02 53 | 03 45 | 01 22 | 28 41 | 26 42 |
| 28 | 03 15 | 04 11 | 01 46 | 28 59 | 26 51 |
| 29 | 03 38 | 04 39 | 02 10 | 29 17 | 27 00 |
| 30 | 04 02 | 05 06 | 02 35 | 29 35 | 27 10 |
| 31 | 04 26 | 05 34 | 02 59 | 29 53 | 27 19 |
| 32 | 04 52 | 06 03 | 03 24 | 00♍11 | 27 28 |
| 33 | 05 18 | 06 32 | 03 50 | 00 30 | 27 38 |
| 34 | 05 45 | 07 02 | 04 16 | 00 48 | 27 47 |
| 35 | 06 13 | 07 33 | 04 41 | 01 07 | 27 57 |
| 36 | 06 42 | 08 04 | 05 08 | 01 26 | 28 06 |
| 37 | 07 13 | 08 36 | 05 34 | 01 45 | 28 16 |
| 38 | 07 44 | 09 09 | 06 01 | 02 04 | 28 26 |
| 39 | 08 17 | 09 43 | 06 29 | 02 23 | 28 36 |
| 40 | 08 51 | 10 17 | 06 57 | 02 43 | 28 46 |
| 41 | 09 27 | 10 53 | 07 25 | 03 03 | 28 56 |
| 42 | 10 05 | 11 29 | 07 54 | 03 23 | 29 06 |
| 43 | 10 44 | 12 06 | 08 24 | 03 44 | 29 16 |
| 44 | 11 25 | 12 45 | 08 54 | 04 04 | 29 27 |
| 45 | 12 09 | 13 25 | 09 25 | 04 25 | 29 37 |
| 46 | 12 54 | 14 05 | 09 56 | 04 47 | 29 48 |
| 47 | 13 42 | 14 48 | 10 28 | 05 08 | 29 59 |
| 48 | 14 33 | 15 31 | 11 00 | 05 31 | 00♎10 |
| 49 | 15 26 | 16 16 | 11 34 | 05 53 | 00 22 |
| 50 | 16 23 | 17 02 | 12 08 | 06 16 | 00 33 |
| 51 | 17 24 | 17 50 | 12 43 | 06 39 | 00 45 |
| 52 | 18 28 | 18 40 | 13 19 | 07 03 | 00 57 |
| 53 | 19 36 | 19 32 | 13 55 | 07 27 | 01 09 |
| 54 | 20 49 | 20 25 | 14 33 | 07 52 | 01 22 |
| 55 | 22 08 | 21 21 | 15 12 | 08 18 | 01 34 |
| 56 | 23 32 | 22 18 | 15 51 | 08 44 | 01 47 |
| 57 | 25 02 | 23 18 | 16 32 | 09 10 | 02 01 |
| 58 | 26 39 | 24 21 | 17 14 | 09 37 | 02 15 |
| 59 | 28 24 | 25 26 | 17 57 | 10 05 | 02 29 |
| 60 | 00♋17 | 26♋33 | 18♌42 | 10♍34 | 02♎44 |

# Koch Table of Houses for Latitudes 0° to 60° North

1h 36m 0s — 24° 0' 0" — 25 ♈ 53

| LAT. | 11 | 12 | ASC | 2 | 3 |
|---|---|---|---|---|---|
| 0 | 26♉19 | 24♊30 | 22♋13 | 21♌37 | 23♍28 |
| 5 | 27 28 | 26 13 | 24 04 | 23 11 | 24 19 |
| 10 | 28 42 | 27 58 | 25 53 | 24 41 | 25 08 |
| 15 | 00♊01 | 29 47 | 27 42 | 26 09 | 25 54 |
| 20 | 01 28 | 01♋42 | 29 33 | 27 36 | 26 40 |
| 21 | 01 47 | 02 06 | 29 56 | 27 53 | 26 49 |
| 22 | 02 06 | 02 30 | 00♌18 | 28 10 | 26 58 |
| 23 | 02 25 | 02 54 | 00 41 | 28 27 | 27 07 |
| 24 | 02 45 | 03 19 | 01 04 | 28 45 | 27 16 |
| 25 | 03 05 | 03 44 | 01 27 | 29 02 | 27 25 |
| 26 | 03 26 | 04 09 | 01 50 | 29 20 | 27 34 |
| 27 | 03 48 | 04 35 | 02 14 | 29 37 | 27 43 |
| 28 | 04 10 | 05 02 | 02 37 | 29 55 | 27 52 |
| 29 | 04 33 | 05 28 | 03 01 | 00♍12 | 28 01 |
| 30 | 04 56 | 05 56 | 03 25 | 00 30 | 28 10 |
| 31 | 05 21 | 06 24 | 03 50 | 00 48 | 28 19 |
| 32 | 05 46 | 06 52 | 04 14 | 01 06 | 28 28 |
| 33 | 06 12 | 07 21 | 04 39 | 01 24 | 28 38 |
| 34 | 06 38 | 07 50 | 05 05 | 01 43 | 28 47 |
| 35 | 07 06 | 08 21 | 05 30 | 02 01 | 28 56 |
| 36 | 07 35 | 08 52 | 05 56 | 02 20 | 29 06 |
| 37 | 08 05 | 09 23 | 06 23 | 02 38 | 29 15 |
| 38 | 08 36 | 09 56 | 06 49 | 02 57 | 29 25 |
| 39 | 09 09 | 10 29 | 07 17 | 03 16 | 29 35 |
| 40 | 09 43 | 11 03 | 07 44 | 03 36 | 29 44 |
| 41 | 10 18 | 11 38 | 08 12 | 03 56 | 29 54 |
| 42 | 10 55 | 12 14 | 08 41 | 04 15 | 00♎04 |
| 43 | 11 34 | 12 50 | 09 10 | 04 36 | 00 15 |
| 44 | 12 14 | 13 28 | 09 40 | 04 56 | 00 25 |
| 45 | 12 57 | 14 07 | 10 10 | 05 17 | 00 35 |
| 46 | 13 42 | 14 48 | 10 41 | 05 38 | 00 46 |
| 47 | 14 29 | 15 29 | 11 12 | 05 59 | 00 57 |
| 48 | 15 19 | 16 12 | 11 44 | 06 21 | 01 08 |
| 49 | 16 12 | 16 56 | 12 17 | 06 43 | 01 19 |
| 50 | 17 08 | 17 42 | 12 51 | 07 06 | 01 30 |
| 51 | 18 07 | 18 29 | 13 25 | 07 29 | 01 42 |
| 52 | 19 10 | 19 18 | 14 00 | 07 52 | 01 54 |
| 53 | 20 17 | 20 09 | 14 37 | 08 16 | 02 06 |
| 54 | 21 29 | 21 01 | 15 14 | 08 41 | 02 18 |
| 55 | 22 46 | 21 56 | 15 52 | 09 06 | 02 31 |
| 56 | 24 08 | 22 52 | 16 31 | 09 31 | 02 43 |
| 57 | 25 36 | 23 51 | 17 11 | 09 57 | 02 57 |
| 58 | 27 12 | 24 52 | 17 52 | 10 24 | 03 10 |
| 59 | 28 54 | 25 56 | 18 35 | 10 52 | 03 24 |
| 60 | 00♋45 | 27♋03 | 19♌18 | 11♍20 | 03♎39 |

1h 40m 0s — 25° 0' 0" — 26 ♈ 57

| LAT. | 11 | 12 | ASC | 2 | 3 |
|---|---|---|---|---|---|
| 0 | 27♉17 | 25♊25 | 23♋10 | 22♌39 | 24♍33 |
| 5 | 28 26 | 27 07 | 25 00 | 24 12 | 25 24 |
| 10 | 29 39 | 28 52 | 26 48 | 25 41 | 26 11 |
| 15 | 00♊58 | 00♋40 | 28 37 | 27 08 | 26 57 |
| 20 | 02 25 | 02 34 | 00♌26 | 28 33 | 27 42 |
| 21 | 02 43 | 02 57 | 00 49 | 28 50 | 27 50 |
| 22 | 03 02 | 03 21 | 01 11 | 29 07 | 27 59 |
| 23 | 03 21 | 03 45 | 01 33 | 29 24 | 28 08 |
| 24 | 03 41 | 04 10 | 01 56 | 29 42 | 28 17 |
| 25 | 04 01 | 04 35 | 02 19 | 29 59 | 28 26 |
| 26 | 04 22 | 05 00 | 02 42 | 00♍16 | 28 35 |
| 27 | 04 43 | 05 26 | 03 05 | 00 33 | 28 44 |
| 28 | 05 05 | 05 52 | 03 28 | 00 51 | 28 52 |
| 29 | 05 28 | 06 18 | 03 52 | 01 08 | 29 01 |
| 30 | 05 51 | 06 45 | 04 16 | 01 26 | 29 10 |
| 31 | 06 15 | 07 13 | 04 40 | 01 43 | 29 19 |
| 32 | 06 40 | 07 41 | 05 04 | 02 01 | 29 28 |
| 33 | 07 05 | 08 09 | 05 29 | 02 19 | 29 37 |
| 34 | 07 32 | 08 39 | 05 54 | 02 37 | 29 47 |
| 35 | 07 59 | 09 08 | 06 19 | 02 55 | 29 56 |
| 36 | 08 28 | 09 39 | 06 45 | 03 13 | 00♎05 |
| 37 | 08 57 | 10 10 | 07 11 | 03 32 | 00 14 |
| 38 | 09 28 | 10 42 | 07 38 | 03 51 | 00 24 |
| 39 | 10 00 | 11 15 | 08 04 | 04 10 | 00 33 |
| 40 | 10 34 | 11 48 | 08 32 | 04 29 | 00 43 |
| 41 | 11 08 | 12 23 | 08 59 | 04 48 | 00 53 |
| 42 | 11 45 | 12 58 | 09 27 | 05 08 | 01 03 |
| 43 | 12 23 | 13 34 | 09 56 | 05 27 | 01 13 |
| 44 | 13 03 | 14 12 | 10 25 | 05 48 | 01 23 |
| 45 | 13 45 | 14 50 | 10 55 | 06 08 | 01 33 |
| 46 | 14 29 | 15 30 | 11 26 | 06 29 | 01 44 |
| 47 | 15 16 | 16 11 | 11 57 | 06 50 | 01 54 |
| 48 | 16 05 | 16 53 | 12 28 | 07 11 | 02 05 |
| 49 | 16 56 | 17 36 | 13 01 | 07 33 | 02 16 |
| 50 | 17 51 | 18 21 | 13 34 | 07 55 | 02 27 |
| 51 | 18 50 | 19 07 | 14 08 | 08 18 | 02 38 |
| 52 | 19 52 | 19 55 | 14 42 | 08 41 | 02 50 |
| 53 | 20 58 | 20 45 | 15 18 | 09 05 | 03 02 |
| 54 | 22 08 | 21 37 | 15 54 | 09 29 | 03 14 |
| 55 | 23 23 | 22 30 | 16 32 | 09 53 | 03 27 |
| 56 | 24 44 | 23 26 | 17 10 | 10 19 | 03 39 |
| 57 | 26 11 | 24 24 | 17 50 | 10 44 | 03 52 |
| 58 | 27 44 | 25 24 | 18 30 | 11 11 | 04 06 |
| 59 | 29 25 | 26 27 | 19 12 | 11 38 | 04 20 |
| 60 | 01♋13 | 27♋32 | 19♌55 | 12♍06 | 04♎34 |

1h 44m 0s — 26° 0' 0" — 28 ♈ 00

| LAT. | 11 | 12 | ASC | 2 | 3 |
|---|---|---|---|---|---|
| 0 | 28♉15 | 26♊20 | 24♋06 | 23♌41 | 25♍38 |
| 5 | 29 24 | 28 02 | 25 56 | 25 13 | 26 28 |
| 10 | 00♊37 | 29 46 | 27 43 | 26 41 | 27 15 |
| 15 | 01 55 | 01♋33 | 29 31 | 28 06 | 28 00 |
| 20 | 03 21 | 03 26 | 01♌19 | 29 31 | 28 43 |
| 21 | 03 39 | 03 49 | 01 41 | 29 48 | 28 52 |
| 22 | 03 57 | 04 13 | 02 04 | 00♍04 | 29 01 |
| 23 | 04 17 | 04 37 | 02 26 | 00 21 | 29 10 |
| 24 | 04 36 | 05 01 | 02 48 | 00 38 | 29 18 |
| 25 | 04 56 | 05 25 | 03 11 | 00 55 | 29 27 |
| 26 | 05 17 | 05 50 | 03 34 | 01 12 | 29 36 |
| 27 | 05 38 | 06 16 | 03 56 | 01 29 | 29 44 |
| 28 | 06 00 | 06 42 | 04 20 | 01 46 | 29 53 |
| 29 | 06 22 | 07 08 | 04 43 | 02 04 | 00♎02 |
| 30 | 06 45 | 07 34 | 05 07 | 02 21 | 00 11 |
| 31 | 07 09 | 08 02 | 05 30 | 02 38 | 00 19 |
| 32 | 07 33 | 08 29 | 05 54 | 02 56 | 00 28 |
| 33 | 07 59 | 08 58 | 06 19 | 03 13 | 00 37 |
| 34 | 08 25 | 09 26 | 06 44 | 03 31 | 00 46 |
| 35 | 08 52 | 09 56 | 07 08 | 03 49 | 00 55 |
| 36 | 09 20 | 10 26 | 07 34 | 04 07 | 01 04 |
| 37 | 09 49 | 10 57 | 07 59 | 04 26 | 01 13 |
| 38 | 10 20 | 11 28 | 08 26 | 04 44 | 01 23 |
| 39 | 10 51 | 12 01 | 08 52 | 05 03 | 01 32 |
| 40 | 11 24 | 12 34 | 09 19 | 05 21 | 01 42 |
| 41 | 11 58 | 13 08 | 09 46 | 05 40 | 01 51 |
| 42 | 12 34 | 13 42 | 10 14 | 06 00 | 02 01 |
| 43 | 13 12 | 14 18 | 10 42 | 06 19 | 02 11 |
| 44 | 13 51 | 14 55 | 11 11 | 06 39 | 02 21 |
| 45 | 14 33 | 15 33 | 11 40 | 06 59 | 02 31 |
| 46 | 15 16 | 16 12 | 12 10 | 07 20 | 02 41 |
| 47 | 16 02 | 16 52 | 12 41 | 07 41 | 02 52 |
| 48 | 16 50 | 17 33 | 13 12 | 08 02 | 03 02 |
| 49 | 17 41 | 18 16 | 13 44 | 08 23 | 03 13 |
| 50 | 18 35 | 19 00 | 14 17 | 08 45 | 03 24 |
| 51 | 19 32 | 19 46 | 14 50 | 09 07 | 03 35 |
| 52 | 20 33 | 20 33 | 15 24 | 09 30 | 03 47 |
| 53 | 21 38 | 21 22 | 15 59 | 09 53 | 03 58 |
| 54 | 22 47 | 22 13 | 16 35 | 10 17 | 04 10 |
| 55 | 24 01 | 23 05 | 17 12 | 10 41 | 04 23 |
| 56 | 25 20 | 24 00 | 17 49 | 11 06 | 04 35 |
| 57 | 26 45 | 24 57 | 18 28 | 11 32 | 04 48 |
| 58 | 28 16 | 25 56 | 19 08 | 11 58 | 05 01 |
| 59 | 29 55 | 26 57 | 19 49 | 12 24 | 05 15 |
| 60 | 01♋41 | 28♋01 | 20♌32 | 12♍52 | 05♎29 |

1h 48m 0s — 27° 0' 0" — 29 ♈ 03

| LAT. | 11 | 12 | ASC | 2 | 3 |
|---|---|---|---|---|---|
| 0 | 29♉13 | 27♊15 | 25♋03 | 24♌42 | 26♍44 |
| 5 | 00♊21 | 28 56 | 26 52 | 26 13 | 27 32 |
| 10 | 01 34 | 00♋40 | 28 39 | 27 41 | 28 18 |
| 15 | 02 52 | 02 26 | 00♌25 | 29 05 | 29 02 |
| 20 | 04 17 | 04 18 | 02 13 | 00♍28 | 29 45 |
| 21 | 04 35 | 04 41 | 02 34 | 00 45 | 29 54 |
| 22 | 04 53 | 05 04 | 02 56 | 01 02 | 00♎02 |
| 23 | 05 12 | 05 28 | 03 18 | 01 18 | 00 11 |
| 24 | 05 31 | 05 52 | 03 40 | 01 35 | 00 19 |
| 25 | 05 51 | 06 16 | 04 03 | 01 52 | 00 28 |
| 26 | 06 11 | 06 41 | 04 25 | 02 09 | 00 36 |
| 27 | 06 32 | 07 06 | 04 48 | 02 25 | 00 45 |
| 28 | 06 54 | 07 31 | 05 11 | 02 42 | 00 53 |
| 29 | 07 16 | 07 57 | 05 34 | 02 59 | 01 02 |
| 30 | 07 39 | 08 24 | 05 57 | 03 16 | 01 11 |
| 31 | 08 02 | 08 50 | 06 21 | 03 33 | 01 19 |
| 32 | 08 26 | 09 18 | 06 44 | 03 51 | 01 28 |
| 33 | 08 52 | 09 46 | 07 09 | 04 08 | 01 37 |
| 34 | 09 17 | 10 14 | 07 33 | 04 26 | 01 46 |
| 35 | 09 44 | 10 43 | 07 58 | 04 43 | 01 55 |
| 36 | 10 12 | 11 13 | 08 23 | 05 01 | 02 03 |
| 37 | 10 41 | 11 43 | 08 48 | 05 19 | 02 13 |
| 38 | 11 11 | 12 14 | 09 14 | 05 37 | 02 22 |
| 39 | 11 42 | 12 46 | 09 40 | 05 56 | 02 31 |
| 40 | 12 14 | 13 19 | 10 06 | 06 14 | 02 40 |
| 41 | 12 48 | 13 52 | 10 33 | 06 33 | 02 50 |
| 42 | 13 24 | 14 27 | 11 00 | 06 52 | 02 59 |
| 43 | 14 01 | 15 02 | 11 28 | 07 11 | 03 09 |
| 44 | 14 39 | 15 38 | 11 57 | 07 31 | 03 19 |
| 45 | 15 20 | 16 15 | 12 26 | 07 51 | 03 28 |
| 46 | 16 03 | 16 54 | 12 55 | 08 11 | 03 39 |
| 47 | 16 48 | 17 33 | 13 25 | 08 31 | 03 49 |
| 48 | 17 35 | 18 14 | 13 56 | 08 52 | 03 59 |
| 49 | 18 25 | 18 56 | 14 27 | 09 13 | 04 10 |
| 50 | 19 18 | 19 39 | 14 59 | 09 35 | 04 21 |
| 51 | 20 14 | 20 24 | 15 32 | 09 57 | 04 32 |
| 52 | 21 14 | 21 10 | 16 06 | 10 19 | 04 43 |
| 53 | 22 18 | 21 59 | 16 40 | 10 42 | 04 55 |
| 54 | 23 25 | 22 48 | 17 15 | 11 05 | 05 06 |
| 55 | 24 38 | 23 40 | 17 52 | 11 29 | 05 18 |
| 56 | 25 55 | 24 34 | 18 29 | 11 54 | 05 31 |
| 57 | 27 18 | 25 29 | 19 07 | 12 19 | 05 44 |
| 58 | 28 48 | 26 27 | 19 46 | 12 44 | 05 57 |
| 59 | 00♋25 | 27 28 | 20 27 | 13 11 | 06 10 |
| 60 | 02♋09 | 28♋30 | 21♌08 | 13♍38 | 06♎24 |

1h 52m 0s — 28° 0' 0" — 00 ♉ 06

| LAT. | 11 | 12 | ASC | 2 | 3 |
|---|---|---|---|---|---|
| 0 | 00♊11 | 28♊10 | 26♋00 | 25♌44 | 27♍49 |
| 5 | 01 19 | 29 51 | 27 48 | 27 14 | 28 37 |
| 10 | 02 31 | 01♋33 | 29 34 | 28 40 | 29 22 |
| 15 | 03 48 | 03 19 | 01♌19 | 00♍04 | 00♎05 |
| 20 | 05 12 | 05 10 | 03 06 | 01 26 | 00 47 |
| 21 | 05 30 | 05 32 | 03 27 | 01 43 | 00 55 |
| 22 | 05 48 | 05 56 | 03 49 | 01 59 | 01 04 |
| 23 | 06 07 | 06 19 | 04 11 | 02 15 | 01 12 |
| 24 | 06 26 | 06 43 | 04 33 | 02 32 | 01 20 |
| 25 | 06 46 | 07 07 | 04 55 | 02 48 | 01 29 |
| 26 | 07 06 | 07 31 | 05 17 | 03 05 | 01 37 |
| 27 | 07 27 | 07 56 | 05 39 | 03 22 | 01 46 |
| 28 | 07 48 | 08 21 | 06 02 | 03 38 | 01 54 |
| 29 | 08 10 | 08 47 | 06 25 | 03 55 | 02 02 |
| 30 | 08 32 | 09 13 | 06 48 | 04 12 | 02 11 |
| 31 | 08 56 | 09 39 | 07 11 | 04 29 | 02 19 |
| 32 | 09 20 | 10 06 | 07 34 | 04 46 | 02 28 |
| 33 | 09 44 | 10 34 | 07 58 | 05 03 | 02 36 |
| 34 | 10 10 | 11 02 | 08 22 | 05 20 | 02 45 |
| 35 | 10 36 | 11 31 | 08 47 | 05 37 | 02 54 |
| 36 | 11 04 | 12 00 | 09 11 | 05 55 | 03 03 |
| 37 | 11 32 | 12 30 | 09 36 | 06 13 | 03 11 |
| 38 | 12 02 | 13 00 | 10 02 | 06 31 | 03 20 |
| 39 | 12 32 | 13 32 | 10 27 | 06 49 | 03 29 |
| 40 | 13 04 | 14 04 | 10 53 | 07 07 | 03 39 |
| 41 | 13 38 | 14 37 | 11 20 | 07 25 | 03 48 |
| 42 | 14 13 | 15 11 | 11 47 | 07 44 | 03 57 |
| 43 | 14 49 | 15 45 | 12 14 | 08 03 | 04 07 |
| 44 | 15 27 | 16 21 | 12 42 | 08 22 | 04 16 |
| 45 | 16 07 | 16 58 | 13 11 | 08 42 | 04 26 |
| 46 | 16 49 | 17 35 | 13 40 | 09 02 | 04 36 |
| 47 | 17 33 | 18 14 | 14 10 | 09 22 | 04 46 |
| 48 | 18 20 | 18 54 | 14 40 | 09 42 | 04 56 |
| 49 | 19 09 | 19 35 | 15 11 | 10 03 | 05 07 |
| 50 | 20 01 | 20 18 | 15 42 | 10 24 | 05 17 |
| 51 | 20 56 | 21 02 | 16 14 | 10 46 | 05 28 |
| 52 | 21 55 | 21 48 | 16 48 | 11 08 | 05 39 |
| 53 | 22 57 | 22 35 | 17 21 | 11 31 | 05 51 |
| 54 | 24 04 | 23 24 | 17 56 | 11 54 | 06 02 |
| 55 | 25 15 | 24 15 | 18 32 | 12 17 | 06 14 |
| 56 | 26 30 | 25 07 | 19 08 | 12 41 | 06 27 |
| 57 | 27 52 | 26 02 | 19 46 | 13 06 | 06 39 |
| 58 | 29 20 | 26 59 | 20 24 | 13 31 | 06 52 |
| 59 | 00♋54 | 27 58 | 21 04 | 13 57 | 07 05 |
| 60 | 02♋37 | 29♋00 | 21♌45 | 14♍24 | 07♎19 |

1h 56m 0s — 29° 0' 0" — 01 ♉ 08

| LAT. | 11 | 12 | ASC | 2 | 3 |
|---|---|---|---|---|---|
| 0 | 01♊08 | 29♊05 | 26♋57 | 26♌47 | 28♍55 |
| 5 | 02 16 | 00♋45 | 28 44 | 28 16 | 29 41 |
| 10 | 03 28 | 02 27 | 00♌29 | 29 41 | 00♎25 |
| 15 | 04 44 | 04 12 | 02 14 | 01♍03 | 01 08 |
| 20 | 06 08 | 06 01 | 03 59 | 02 24 | 01 49 |
| 21 | 06 25 | 06 24 | 04 20 | 02 40 | 01 57 |
| 22 | 06 43 | 06 47 | 04 42 | 02 56 | 02 05 |
| 23 | 07 02 | 07 10 | 05 03 | 03 13 | 02 13 |
| 24 | 07 21 | 07 33 | 05 25 | 03 29 | 02 21 |
| 25 | 07 40 | 07 57 | 05 47 | 03 45 | 02 30 |
| 26 | 08 00 | 08 21 | 06 09 | 04 01 | 02 38 |
| 27 | 08 21 | 08 46 | 06 31 | 04 18 | 02 46 |
| 28 | 08 42 | 09 11 | 06 53 | 04 34 | 02 54 |
| 29 | 09 03 | 09 36 | 07 16 | 04 51 | 03 03 |
| 30 | 09 26 | 10 02 | 07 38 | 05 07 | 03 11 |
| 31 | 09 49 | 10 28 | 08 01 | 05 24 | 03 19 |
| 32 | 10 12 | 10 54 | 08 24 | 05 41 | 03 27 |
| 33 | 10 37 | 11 22 | 08 48 | 05 57 | 03 36 |
| 34 | 11 02 | 11 49 | 09 12 | 06 14 | 03 44 |
| 35 | 11 28 | 12 18 | 09 36 | 06 31 | 03 53 |
| 36 | 11 55 | 12 47 | 10 00 | 06 49 | 04 02 |
| 37 | 12 23 | 13 16 | 10 25 | 07 06 | 04 10 |
| 38 | 12 52 | 13 46 | 10 50 | 07 24 | 04 19 |
| 39 | 13 23 | 14 17 | 11 15 | 07 42 | 04 28 |
| 40 | 13 54 | 14 49 | 11 41 | 08 00 | 04 37 |
| 41 | 14 27 | 15 21 | 12 07 | 08 18 | 04 46 |
| 42 | 15 01 | 15 54 | 12 33 | 08 36 | 04 55 |
| 43 | 15 37 | 16 29 | 13 00 | 08 55 | 05 04 |
| 44 | 16 15 | 17 04 | 13 28 | 09 14 | 05 14 |
| 45 | 16 54 | 17 40 | 13 56 | 09 33 | 05 23 |
| 46 | 17 35 | 18 17 | 14 25 | 09 53 | 05 33 |
| 47 | 18 19 | 18 55 | 14 54 | 10 12 | 05 43 |
| 48 | 19 04 | 19 34 | 15 24 | 10 33 | 05 53 |
| 49 | 19 53 | 20 15 | 15 54 | 10 53 | 06 03 |
| 50 | 20 44 | 20 57 | 16 25 | 11 14 | 06 14 |
| 51 | 21 38 | 21 40 | 16 57 | 11 35 | 06 25 |
| 52 | 22 35 | 22 25 | 17 29 | 11 57 | 06 36 |
| 53 | 23 36 | 23 11 | 18 03 | 12 19 | 06 47 |
| 54 | 24 42 | 23 59 | 18 37 | 12 42 | 06 58 |
| 55 | 25 51 | 24 49 | 19 12 | 13 05 | 07 10 |
| 56 | 27 06 | 25 41 | 19 47 | 13 29 | 07 22 |
| 57 | 28 25 | 26 34 | 20 24 | 13 53 | 07 34 |
| 58 | 29 51 | 27 30 | 21 02 | 14 18 | 07 47 |
| 59 | 01♋24 | 28 28 | 21 41 | 14 43 | 08 00 |
| 60 | 03♋04 | 29♋29 | 22♌21 | 15♍10 | 08♎14 |

2h 0m 0s — 30° 0' 0" — 02 ♉ 11

| LAT. | 11 | 12 | ASC | 2 | 3 |
|---|---|---|---|---|---|
| 0 | 02♊05 | 00♋00 | 27♋55 | 27♌49 | 00♎00 |
| 5 | 03 13 | 01 40 | 29 41 | 29 17 | 00 46 |
| 10 | 04 24 | 03 21 | 01♌25 | 00♍41 | 01 29 |
| 15 | 05 40 | 05 05 | 03 08 | 02 02 | 02 10 |
| 20 | 07 03 | 06 53 | 04 52 | 03 22 | 02 50 |
| 21 | 07 20 | 07 15 | 05 13 | 03 38 | 02 58 |
| 22 | 07 38 | 07 38 | 05 35 | 03 54 | 03 06 |
| 23 | 07 57 | 08 01 | 05 56 | 04 10 | 03 14 |
| 24 | 08 16 | 08 24 | 06 17 | 04 26 | 03 22 |
| 25 | 08 35 | 08 47 | 06 39 | 04 42 | 03 30 |
| 26 | 08 54 | 09 11 | 07 00 | 04 58 | 03 38 |
| 27 | 09 15 | 09 36 | 07 22 | 05 14 | 03 46 |
| 28 | 09 35 | 10 00 | 07 44 | 05 30 | 03 55 |
| 29 | 09 57 | 10 25 | 08 07 | 05 46 | 04 03 |
| 30 | 10 19 | 10 50 | 08 29 | 06 03 | 04 11 |
| 31 | 10 41 | 11 16 | 08 52 | 06 19 | 04 19 |
| 32 | 11 05 | 11 43 | 09 14 | 06 35 | 04 27 |
| 33 | 11 29 | 12 09 | 09 38 | 06 52 | 04 35 |
| 34 | 11 54 | 12 37 | 10 01 | 07 09 | 04 44 |
| 35 | 12 20 | 13 05 | 10 25 | 07 26 | 04 52 |
| 36 | 12 46 | 13 33 | 10 49 | 07 43 | 05 00 |
| 37 | 13 14 | 14 02 | 11 13 | 08 00 | 05 09 |
| 38 | 13 43 | 14 32 | 11 38 | 08 17 | 05 18 |
| 39 | 14 13 | 15 02 | 12 03 | 08 35 | 05 26 |
| 40 | 14 44 | 15 34 | 12 28 | 08 52 | 05 35 |
| 41 | 15 16 | 16 06 | 12 54 | 09 10 | 05 44 |
| 42 | 15 50 | 16 38 | 13 20 | 09 28 | 05 53 |
| 43 | 16 25 | 17 12 | 13 46 | 09 47 | 06 02 |
| 44 | 17 02 | 17 46 | 14 14 | 10 05 | 06 11 |
| 45 | 17 41 | 18 22 | 14 41 | 10 24 | 06 21 |
| 46 | 18 21 | 18 58 | 15 09 | 10 43 | 06 30 |
| 47 | 19 04 | 19 36 | 15 38 | 11 03 | 06 40 |
| 48 | 19 49 | 20 15 | 16 07 | 11 23 | 06 50 |
| 49 | 20 36 | 20 55 | 16 37 | 11 43 | 07 00 |
| 50 | 21 26 | 21 36 | 17 08 | 12 04 | 07 10 |
| 51 | 22 19 | 22 18 | 17 39 | 12 24 | 07 21 |
| 52 | 23 16 | 23 02 | 18 11 | 12 46 | 07 32 |
| 53 | 24 16 | 23 48 | 18 44 | 13 08 | 07 43 |
| 54 | 25 19 | 24 35 | 19 17 | 13 30 | 07 54 |
| 55 | 26 28 | 25 24 | 19 52 | 13 53 | 08 06 |
| 56 | 27 40 | 26 14 | 20 27 | 14 16 | 08 17 |
| 57 | 28 59 | 27 07 | 21 03 | 14 40 | 08 30 |
| 58 | 00♋23 | 28 02 | 21 40 | 15 04 | 08 42 |
| 59 | 01 53 | 28 59 | 22 19 | 15 30 | 08 55 |
| 60 | 03♋31 | 29♋58 | 22♌58 | 15♍56 | 09♎09 |

2h 4m 0s — 31° 0' 0" — 03 ♉ 13

| LAT. | 11 | 12 | ASC | 2 | 3 |
|---|---|---|---|---|---|
| 0 | 03♊03 | 00♋55 | 28♋52 | 28♌52 | 01♎05 |
| 5 | 04 10 | 02 34 | 00♌37 | 00♍18 | 01 50 |
| 10 | 05 20 | 04 14 | 02 20 | 01 41 | 02 32 |
| 15 | 06 36 | 05 57 | 04 03 | 03 01 | 03 13 |
| 20 | 07 58 | 07 45 | 05 46 | 04 20 | 03 52 |
| 21 | 08 15 | 08 07 | 06 06 | 04 36 | 04 00 |
| 22 | 08 33 | 08 29 | 06 27 | 04 51 | 04 08 |
| 23 | 08 51 | 08 52 | 06 48 | 05 07 | 04 16 |
| 24 | 09 10 | 09 15 | 07 10 | 05 23 | 04 23 |
| 25 | 09 29 | 09 38 | 07 31 | 05 38 | 04 31 |
| 26 | 09 48 | 10 01 | 07 52 | 05 54 | 04 39 |
| 27 | 10 08 | 10 25 | 08 14 | 06 10 | 04 47 |
| 28 | 10 29 | 10 50 | 08 36 | 06 26 | 04 55 |
| 29 | 10 50 | 11 14 | 08 57 | 06 42 | 05 03 |
| 30 | 11 12 | 11 39 | 09 20 | 06 58 | 05 11 |
| 31 | 11 34 | 12 05 | 09 42 | 07 14 | 05 19 |
| 32 | 11 57 | 12 31 | 10 04 | 07 30 | 05 27 |
| 33 | 12 21 | 12 57 | 10 27 | 07 47 | 05 35 |
| 34 | 12 45 | 13 24 | 10 50 | 08 03 | 05 43 |
| 35 | 13 11 | 13 52 | 11 14 | 08 20 | 05 51 |
| 36 | 13 37 | 14 20 | 11 37 | 08 36 | 05 59 |
| 37 | 14 04 | 14 48 | 12 01 | 08 53 | 06 08 |
| 38 | 14 33 | 15 18 | 12 25 | 09 10 | 06 16 |
| 39 | 15 02 | 15 48 | 12 50 | 09 28 | 06 25 |
| 40 | 15 33 | 16 18 | 13 15 | 09 45 | 06 33 |
| 41 | 16 05 | 16 50 | 13 40 | 10 03 | 06 42 |
| 42 | 16 38 | 17 22 | 14 06 | 10 20 | 06 51 |
| 43 | 17 13 | 17 55 | 14 32 | 10 39 | 07 00 |
| 44 | 17 49 | 18 29 | 14 59 | 10 57 | 07 09 |
| 45 | 18 27 | 19 04 | 15 26 | 11 15 | 07 18 |
| 46 | 19 07 | 19 40 | 15 54 | 11 34 | 07 27 |
| 47 | 19 49 | 20 17 | 16 22 | 11 53 | 07 37 |
| 48 | 20 33 | 20 55 | 16 51 | 12 13 | 07 47 |
| 49 | 21 19 | 21 34 | 17 20 | 12 33 | 07 57 |
| 50 | 22 09 | 22 14 | 17 50 | 12 53 | 08 07 |
| 51 | 23 01 | 22 56 | 18 21 | 13 14 | 08 17 |
| 52 | 23 56 | 23 39 | 18 53 | 13 35 | 08 28 |
| 53 | 24 54 | 24 24 | 19 25 | 13 56 | 08 38 |
| 54 | 25 57 | 25 10 | 19 58 | 14 18 | 08 50 |
| 55 | 27 04 | 25 58 | 20 31 | 14 40 | 09 01 |
| 56 | 28 15 | 26 48 | 21 06 | 15 03 | 09 13 |
| 57 | 29 32 | 27 39 | 21 42 | 15 27 | 09 25 |
| 58 | 00♋54 | 28 33 | 22 18 | 15 51 | 09 37 |
| 59 | 02 23 | 29 29 | 22 56 | 16 16 | 09 50 |
| 60 | 03♋59 | 00♌27 | 23♌35 | 16♍41 | 10♎04 |

# Koch Table of Houses for Latitudes 0° to 60° North

**2h 8m 0s — 32° 0' 0" — 04 ♉ 16**

| LAT. | 11 | 12 | ASC | 2 | 3 |
|---|---|---|---|---|---|
| 0 | 04♊00 | 01♋50 | 29♋49 | 29♌54 | 02♎11 |
| 5 | 05 07 | 03 28 | 01♌34 | 01♍20 | 02 54 |
| 10 | 06 17 | 05 08 | 03 16 | 02 41 | 03 36 |
| 15 | 07 31 | 06 50 | 04 57 | 04 00 | 04 15 |
| 20 | 08 53 | 08 36 | 06 39 | 05 18 | 04 54 |
| 21 | 09 10 | 08 58 | 07 00 | 05 33 | 05 01 |
| 22 | 09 28 | 09 20 | 07 20 | 05 49 | 05 09 |
| 23 | 09 45 | 09 42 | 07 41 | 06 04 | 05 17 |
| 24 | 10 04 | 10 05 | 08 02 | 06 20 | 05 24 |
| 25 | 10 23 | 10 28 | 08 23 | 06 35 | 05 32 |
| 26 | 10 42 | 10 51 | 08 44 | 06 51 | 05 39 |
| 27 | 11 02 | 11 15 | 09 05 | 07 06 | 05 47 |
| 28 | 11 22 | 11 39 | 09 27 | 07 22 | 05 55 |
| 29 | 11 43 | 12 03 | 09 48 | 07 38 | 06 03 |
| 30 | 12 04 | 12 28 | 10 10 | 07 53 | 06 10 |
| 31 | 12 26 | 12 53 | 10 32 | 08 09 | 06 18 |
| 32 | 12 49 | 13 19 | 10 54 | 08 25 | 06 26 |
| 33 | 13 13 | 13 45 | 11 17 | 08 41 | 06 34 |
| 34 | 13 37 | 14 11 | 11 40 | 08 57 | 06 42 |
| 35 | 14 02 | 14 38 | 12 03 | 09 14 | 06 50 |
| 36 | 14 28 | 15 06 | 12 26 | 09 30 | 06 58 |
| 37 | 14 55 | 15 34 | 12 50 | 09 47 | 07 06 |
| 38 | 15 23 | 16 03 | 13 13 | 10 04 | 07 14 |
| 39 | 15 52 | 16 33 | 13 38 | 10 21 | 07 23 |
| 40 | 16 22 | 17 03 | 14 02 | 10 38 | 07 31 |
| 41 | 16 53 | 17 34 | 14 27 | 10 55 | 07 40 |
| 42 | 17 26 | 18 06 | 14 53 | 11 13 | 07 48 |
| 43 | 18 00 | 18 38 | 15 18 | 11 30 | 07 57 |
| 44 | 18 35 | 19 12 | 15 45 | 11 48 | 08 06 |
| 45 | 19 13 | 19 46 | 16 11 | 12 07 | 08 15 |
| 46 | 19 52 | 20 21 | 16 39 | 12 25 | 08 24 |
| 47 | 20 33 | 20 57 | 17 06 | 12 44 | 08 34 |
| 48 | 21 17 | 21 35 | 17 35 | 13 03 | 08 43 |
| 49 | 22 02 | 22 13 | 18 04 | 13 23 | 08 53 |
| 50 | 22 50 | 22 53 | 18 33 | 13 43 | 09 03 |
| 51 | 23 42 | 23 34 | 19 03 | 14 03 | 09 13 |
| 52 | 24 36 | 24 16 | 19 34 | 14 23 | 09 23 |
| 53 | 25 33 | 25 00 | 20 06 | 14 45 | 09 34 |
| 54 | 26 34 | 25 46 | 20 38 | 15 06 | 09 45 |
| 55 | 27 40 | 26 33 | 21 11 | 15 28 | 09 56 |
| 56 | 28 50 | 27 21 | 21 45 | 15 51 | 10 08 |
| 57 | 00♋05 | 28 12 | 22 20 | 16 14 | 10 20 |
| 58 | 01 25 | 29 04 | 22 56 | 16 38 | 10 32 |
| 59 | 02 52 | 29 59 | 23 33 | 17 02 | 10 45 |
| 60 | 04♋26 | 00♌56 | 24♌11 | 17♍27 | 10♎58 |

**2h 12m 0s — 33° 0' 0" — 05 ♉ 18**

| LAT. | 11 | 12 | ASC | 2 | 3 |
|---|---|---|---|---|---|
| 0 | 04♊57 | 02♋45 | 00♌47 | 00♍57 | 03♎16 |
| 5 | 06 03 | 04 23 | 02 31 | 02 21 | 03 59 |
| 10 | 07 13 | 06 01 | 04 12 | 03 42 | 04 39 |
| 15 | 08 27 | 07 42 | 05 52 | 04 59 | 05 17 |
| 20 | 09 47 | 09 27 | 07 32 | 06 16 | 05 55 |
| 21 | 10 04 | 09 49 | 07 53 | 06 31 | 06 03 |
| 22 | 10 22 | 10 11 | 08 13 | 06 46 | 06 10 |
| 23 | 10 40 | 10 33 | 08 34 | 07 01 | 06 17 |
| 24 | 10 58 | 10 55 | 08 54 | 07 17 | 06 25 |
| 25 | 11 16 | 11 18 | 09 15 | 07 32 | 06 32 |
| 26 | 11 35 | 11 41 | 09 36 | 07 47 | 06 40 |
| 27 | 11 55 | 12 04 | 09 57 | 08 02 | 06 47 |
| 28 | 12 15 | 12 28 | 10 18 | 08 18 | 06 55 |
| 29 | 12 36 | 12 52 | 10 39 | 08 33 | 07 02 |
| 30 | 12 57 | 13 16 | 11 01 | 08 49 | 07 10 |
| 31 | 13 19 | 13 41 | 11 23 | 09 04 | 07 18 |
| 32 | 13 41 | 14 07 | 11 44 | 09 20 | 07 25 |
| 33 | 14 04 | 14 32 | 12 07 | 09 36 | 07 33 |
| 34 | 14 28 | 14 58 | 12 29 | 09 52 | 07 41 |
| 35 | 14 53 | 15 25 | 12 52 | 10 08 | 07 49 |
| 36 | 15 18 | 15 52 | 13 15 | 10 24 | 07 57 |
| 37 | 15 45 | 16 20 | 13 38 | 10 40 | 08 05 |
| 38 | 16 12 | 16 49 | 14 01 | 10 57 | 08 13 |
| 39 | 16 41 | 17 18 | 14 25 | 11 13 | 08 21 |
| 40 | 17 10 | 17 48 | 14 49 | 11 30 | 08 29 |
| 41 | 17 41 | 18 18 | 15 14 | 11 47 | 08 37 |
| 42 | 18 13 | 18 49 | 15 39 | 12 05 | 08 46 |
| 43 | 18 47 | 19 21 | 16 04 | 12 22 | 08 54 |
| 44 | 19 22 | 19 54 | 16 30 | 12 40 | 09 03 |
| 45 | 19 59 | 20 28 | 16 57 | 12 58 | 09 12 |
| 46 | 20 37 | 21 02 | 17 23 | 13 16 | 09 21 |
| 47 | 21 18 | 21 38 | 17 51 | 13 34 | 09 30 |
| 48 | 22 00 | 22 15 | 18 18 | 13 53 | 09 40 |
| 49 | 22 45 | 22 53 | 18 47 | 14 12 | 09 49 |
| 50 | 23 32 | 23 32 | 19 16 | 14 32 | 09 59 |
| 51 | 24 22 | 24 12 | 19 46 | 14 52 | 10 09 |
| 52 | 25 15 | 24 53 | 20 16 | 15 12 | 10 19 |
| 53 | 26 12 | 25 36 | 20 47 | 15 33 | 10 30 |
| 54 | 27 12 | 26 21 | 21 19 | 15 54 | 10 40 |
| 55 | 28 16 | 27 07 | 21 51 | 16 16 | 10 51 |
| 56 | 29 24 | 27 55 | 22 25 | 16 38 | 11 03 |
| 57 | 00♋37 | 28 44 | 22 59 | 17 01 | 11 15 |
| 58 | 01 56 | 29 36 | 23 34 | 17 24 | 11 27 |
| 59 | 03 21 | 00♌29 | 24 11 | 17 48 | 11 39 |
| 60 | 04♋53 | 01♌25 | 24♌48 | 18♍13 | 11♎53 |

**2h 16m 0s — 34° 0' 0" — 06 ♉ 19**

| LAT. | 11 | 12 | ASC | 2 | 3 |
|---|---|---|---|---|---|
| 0 | 05♊54 | 03♋40 | 01♌45 | 02♍00 | 04♎22 |
| 5 | 07 00 | 05 17 | 03 27 | 03 23 | 05 03 |
| 10 | 08 09 | 06 55 | 05 07 | 04 42 | 05 42 |
| 15 | 09 22 | 08 35 | 06 47 | 05 59 | 06 20 |
| 20 | 10 42 | 10 19 | 08 26 | 07 14 | 06 56 |
| 21 | 10 59 | 10 40 | 08 46 | 07 29 | 07 04 |
| 22 | 11 16 | 11 02 | 09 06 | 07 44 | 07 11 |
| 23 | 11 33 | 11 24 | 09 26 | 07 59 | 07 18 |
| 24 | 11 51 | 11 46 | 09 47 | 08 14 | 07 26 |
| 25 | 12 10 | 12 08 | 10 07 | 08 29 | 07 33 |
| 26 | 12 29 | 12 31 | 10 28 | 08 44 | 07 40 |
| 27 | 12 48 | 12 54 | 10 48 | 08 59 | 07 47 |
| 28 | 13 08 | 13 17 | 11 09 | 09 14 | 07 55 |
| 29 | 13 28 | 13 41 | 11 30 | 09 29 | 08 02 |
| 30 | 13 49 | 14 05 | 11 51 | 09 44 | 08 10 |
| 31 | 14 10 | 14 29 | 12 13 | 10 00 | 08 17 |
| 32 | 14 33 | 14 54 | 12 34 | 10 15 | 08 25 |
| 33 | 14 55 | 15 20 | 12 56 | 10 31 | 08 32 |
| 34 | 15 19 | 15 46 | 13 18 | 10 46 | 08 40 |
| 35 | 15 43 | 16 12 | 13 41 | 11 02 | 08 47 |
| 36 | 16 09 | 16 39 | 14 03 | 11 18 | 08 55 |
| 37 | 16 35 | 17 06 | 14 26 | 11 34 | 09 03 |
| 38 | 17 02 | 17 34 | 14 49 | 11 50 | 09 11 |
| 39 | 17 30 | 18 03 | 15 13 | 12 06 | 09 19 |
| 40 | 17 59 | 18 32 | 15 37 | 12 23 | 09 27 |
| 41 | 18 29 | 19 02 | 16 01 | 12 40 | 09 35 |
| 42 | 19 01 | 19 33 | 16 25 | 12 57 | 09 43 |
| 43 | 19 34 | 20 04 | 16 50 | 13 14 | 09 52 |
| 44 | 20 08 | 20 36 | 17 16 | 13 31 | 10 00 |
| 45 | 20 44 | 21 10 | 17 42 | 13 49 | 10 09 |
| 46 | 21 22 | 21 44 | 18 08 | 14 07 | 10 18 |
| 47 | 22 02 | 22 19 | 18 35 | 14 25 | 10 27 |
| 48 | 22 43 | 22 55 | 19 02 | 14 43 | 10 36 |
| 49 | 23 27 | 23 32 | 19 30 | 15 02 | 10 45 |
| 50 | 24 14 | 24 10 | 19 59 | 15 21 | 10 55 |
| 51 | 25 03 | 24 50 | 20 28 | 15 41 | 11 05 |
| 52 | 25 55 | 25 30 | 20 58 | 16 01 | 11 15 |
| 53 | 26 50 | 26 13 | 21 28 | 16 21 | 11 25 |
| 54 | 27 49 | 26 56 | 21 59 | 16 42 | 11 36 |
| 55 | 28 51 | 27 41 | 22 31 | 17 04 | 11 47 |
| 56 | 29 58 | 28 28 | 23 04 | 17 25 | 11 58 |
| 57 | 01♋10 | 29 17 | 23 38 | 17 48 | 12 09 |
| 58 | 02 27 | 00♌07 | 24 12 | 18 11 | 12 21 |
| 59 | 03 50 | 00 59 | 24 48 | 18 34 | 12 34 |
| 60 | 05♋19 | 01♌54 | 25♌25 | 18♍59 | 12♎47 |

**2h 20m 0s — 35° 0' 0" — 07 ♉ 21**

| LAT. | 11 | 12 | ASC | 2 | 3 |
|---|---|---|---|---|---|
| 0 | 06♊50 | 04♋35 | 02♌43 | 03♍03 | 05♎27 |
| 5 | 07 56 | 06 11 | 04 24 | 04 25 | 06 07 |
| 10 | 09 04 | 07 48 | 06 03 | 05 43 | 06 45 |
| 15 | 10 17 | 09 27 | 07 41 | 06 58 | 07 22 |
| 20 | 11 36 | 11 10 | 09 19 | 08 12 | 07 58 |
| 21 | 11 53 | 11 31 | 09 39 | 08 27 | 08 05 |
| 22 | 12 10 | 11 53 | 09 59 | 08 41 | 08 12 |
| 23 | 12 27 | 12 14 | 10 19 | 08 56 | 08 19 |
| 24 | 12 45 | 12 36 | 10 39 | 09 11 | 08 26 |
| 25 | 13 03 | 12 58 | 10 59 | 09 25 | 08 33 |
| 26 | 13 22 | 13 21 | 11 20 | 09 40 | 08 40 |
| 27 | 13 41 | 13 43 | 11 40 | 09 55 | 08 47 |
| 28 | 14 00 | 14 06 | 12 00 | 10 10 | 08 55 |
| 29 | 14 20 | 14 30 | 12 21 | 10 25 | 09 02 |
| 30 | 14 41 | 14 53 | 12 42 | 10 40 | 09 09 |
| 31 | 15 02 | 15 18 | 13 03 | 10 55 | 09 16 |
| 32 | 15 24 | 15 42 | 13 24 | 11 10 | 09 24 |
| 33 | 15 47 | 16 07 | 13 46 | 11 25 | 09 31 |
| 34 | 16 10 | 16 33 | 14 08 | 11 41 | 09 38 |
| 35 | 16 34 | 16 58 | 14 30 | 11 56 | 09 46 |
| 36 | 16 59 | 17 25 | 14 52 | 12 12 | 09 53 |
| 37 | 17 24 | 17 52 | 15 14 | 12 27 | 10 01 |
| 38 | 17 51 | 18 19 | 15 37 | 12 43 | 10 09 |
| 39 | 18 18 | 18 48 | 16 00 | 12 59 | 10 17 |
| 40 | 18 47 | 19 16 | 16 24 | 13 15 | 10 24 |
| 41 | 19 17 | 19 46 | 16 48 | 13 32 | 10 32 |
| 42 | 19 48 | 20 16 | 17 12 | 13 49 | 10 41 |
| 43 | 20 20 | 20 47 | 17 36 | 14 05 | 10 49 |
| 44 | 20 54 | 21 19 | 18 01 | 14 22 | 10 57 |
| 45 | 21 30 | 21 51 | 18 27 | 14 40 | 11 06 |
| 46 | 22 07 | 22 25 | 18 53 | 14 57 | 11 14 |
| 47 | 22 46 | 22 59 | 19 19 | 15 15 | 11 23 |
| 48 | 23 27 | 23 34 | 19 46 | 15 33 | 11 32 |
| 49 | 24 10 | 24 11 | 20 13 | 15 52 | 11 41 |
| 50 | 24 55 | 24 48 | 20 41 | 16 11 | 11 51 |
| 51 | 25 43 | 25 27 | 21 10 | 16 30 | 12 00 |
| 52 | 26 34 | 26 07 | 21 39 | 16 50 | 12 10 |
| 53 | 27 28 | 26 49 | 22 09 | 17 10 | 12 20 |
| 54 | 28 25 | 27 31 | 22 40 | 17 30 | 12 31 |
| 55 | 29 27 | 28 16 | 23 11 | 17 51 | 12 41 |
| 56 | 00♋32 | 29 01 | 23 43 | 18 13 | 12 53 |
| 57 | 01 42 | 29 49 | 24 16 | 18 35 | 13 04 |
| 58 | 02 58 | 00♌38 | 24 50 | 18 57 | 13 16 |
| 59 | 04 19 | 01 30 | 25 25 | 19 21 | 13 28 |
| 60 | 05♋46 | 02♌23 | 26♌01 | 19♍45 | 13♎41 |

**2h 24m 0s — 36° 0' 0" — 08 ♉ 23**

| LAT. | 11 | 12 | ASC | 2 | 3 |
|---|---|---|---|---|---|
| 0 | 07♊47 | 05♋30 | 03♌41 | 04♍07 | 06♎32 |
| 5 | 08 52 | 07 06 | 05 22 | 05 27 | 07 11 |
| 10 | 10 00 | 08 42 | 06 59 | 06 44 | 07 48 |
| 15 | 11 12 | 10 20 | 08 36 | 07 58 | 08 24 |
| 20 | 12 30 | 12 01 | 10 13 | 09 10 | 08 59 |
| 21 | 12 47 | 12 22 | 10 33 | 09 25 | 09 06 |
| 22 | 13 03 | 12 43 | 10 52 | 09 39 | 09 13 |
| 23 | 13 21 | 13 05 | 11 12 | 09 53 | 09 20 |
| 24 | 13 38 | 13 26 | 11 32 | 10 08 | 09 27 |
| 25 | 13 56 | 13 48 | 11 51 | 10 22 | 09 33 |
| 26 | 14 14 | 14 10 | 12 11 | 10 37 | 09 40 |
| 27 | 14 33 | 14 33 | 12 32 | 10 51 | 09 47 |
| 28 | 14 53 | 14 55 | 12 52 | 11 06 | 09 54 |
| 29 | 15 12 | 15 18 | 13 12 | 11 20 | 10 01 |
| 30 | 15 33 | 15 42 | 13 33 | 11 35 | 10 08 |
| 31 | 15 54 | 16 06 | 13 54 | 11 50 | 10 16 |
| 32 | 16 15 | 16 30 | 14 14 | 12 05 | 10 23 |
| 33 | 16 37 | 16 54 | 14 36 | 12 20 | 10 30 |
| 34 | 17 00 | 17 19 | 14 57 | 12 35 | 10 37 |
| 35 | 17 24 | 17 45 | 15 19 | 12 50 | 10 44 |
| 36 | 17 48 | 18 11 | 15 41 | 13 05 | 10 52 |
| 37 | 18 14 | 18 38 | 16 03 | 13 21 | 10 59 |
| 38 | 18 40 | 19 05 | 16 25 | 13 36 | 11 07 |
| 39 | 19 07 | 19 32 | 16 48 | 13 52 | 11 14 |
| 40 | 19 35 | 20 01 | 17 11 | 14 08 | 11 22 |
| 41 | 20 04 | 20 30 | 17 34 | 14 24 | 11 30 |
| 42 | 20 35 | 20 59 | 17 58 | 14 40 | 11 38 |
| 43 | 21 07 | 21 30 | 18 22 | 14 57 | 11 46 |
| 44 | 21 40 | 22 01 | 18 47 | 15 14 | 11 54 |
| 45 | 22 15 | 22 33 | 19 12 | 15 31 | 12 02 |
| 46 | 22 51 | 23 06 | 19 37 | 15 48 | 12 11 |
| 47 | 23 29 | 23 40 | 20 03 | 16 06 | 12 19 |
| 48 | 24 09 | 24 14 | 20 30 | 16 23 | 12 28 |
| 49 | 24 52 | 24 50 | 20 56 | 16 42 | 12 37 |
| 50 | 25 36 | 25 27 | 21 24 | 17 00 | 12 46 |
| 51 | 26 23 | 26 05 | 21 52 | 17 19 | 12 56 |
| 52 | 27 13 | 26 44 | 22 21 | 17 38 | 13 06 |
| 53 | 28 06 | 27 25 | 22 50 | 17 58 | 13 15 |
| 54 | 29 02 | 28 07 | 23 20 | 18 18 | 13 26 |
| 55 | 00♋02 | 28 50 | 23 51 | 18 39 | 13 36 |
| 56 | 01 06 | 29 35 | 24 23 | 19 00 | 13 47 |
| 57 | 02 15 | 00♌21 | 24 55 | 19 21 | 13 58 |
| 58 | 03 28 | 01 10 | 25 28 | 19 44 | 14 10 |
| 59 | 04 47 | 02 00 | 26 03 | 20 07 | 14 22 |
| 60 | 06♋13 | 02♌52 | 26♌38 | 20♍30 | 14♎35 |

**2h 28m 0s — 37° 0' 0" — 09 ♉ 24**

| LAT. | 11 | 12 | ASC | 2 | 3 |
|---|---|---|---|---|---|
| 0 | 08♊43 | 06♋26 | 04♌39 | 05♍10 | 07♎37 |
| 5 | 09 48 | 08 00 | 06 19 | 06 29 | 08 16 |
| 10 | 10 55 | 09 35 | 07 56 | 07 45 | 08 52 |
| 15 | 12 07 | 11 12 | 09 31 | 08 57 | 09 26 |
| 20 | 13 24 | 12 53 | 11 07 | 10 08 | 10 00 |
| 21 | 13 40 | 13 13 | 11 26 | 10 22 | 10 07 |
| 22 | 13 57 | 13 34 | 11 45 | 10 37 | 10 13 |
| 23 | 14 14 | 13 55 | 12 05 | 10 51 | 10 20 |
| 24 | 14 31 | 14 16 | 12 24 | 11 05 | 10 27 |
| 25 | 14 49 | 14 38 | 12 44 | 11 19 | 10 34 |
| 26 | 15 07 | 15 00 | 13 03 | 11 33 | 10 40 |
| 27 | 15 26 | 15 22 | 13 23 | 11 48 | 10 47 |
| 28 | 15 45 | 15 44 | 13 43 | 12 02 | 10 54 |
| 29 | 16 04 | 16 07 | 14 03 | 12 16 | 11 01 |
| 30 | 16 24 | 16 30 | 14 23 | 12 31 | 11 08 |
| 31 | 16 45 | 16 54 | 14 44 | 12 45 | 11 15 |
| 32 | 17 06 | 17 17 | 15 05 | 13 00 | 11 22 |
| 33 | 17 28 | 17 42 | 15 25 | 13 14 | 11 29 |
| 34 | 17 51 | 18 06 | 15 46 | 13 29 | 11 36 |
| 35 | 18 14 | 18 31 | 16 08 | 13 44 | 11 43 |
| 36 | 18 38 | 18 57 | 16 29 | 13 59 | 11 50 |
| 37 | 19 03 | 19 23 | 16 51 | 14 14 | 11 57 |
| 38 | 19 29 | 19 50 | 17 13 | 14 29 | 12 04 |
| 39 | 19 55 | 20 17 | 17 35 | 14 45 | 12 12 |
| 40 | 20 23 | 20 45 | 17 58 | 15 01 | 12 19 |
| 41 | 20 52 | 21 13 | 18 21 | 15 16 | 12 27 |
| 42 | 21 22 | 21 43 | 18 44 | 15 32 | 12 35 |
| 43 | 21 53 | 22 12 | 19 08 | 15 49 | 12 43 |
| 44 | 22 26 | 22 43 | 19 32 | 16 05 | 12 51 |
| 45 | 23 00 | 23 14 | 19 57 | 16 22 | 12 59 |
| 46 | 23 35 | 23 47 | 20 22 | 16 39 | 13 07 |
| 47 | 24 13 | 24 20 | 20 47 | 16 56 | 13 15 |
| 48 | 24 52 | 24 54 | 21 13 | 17 13 | 13 24 |
| 49 | 25 34 | 25 29 | 21 40 | 17 31 | 13 33 |
| 50 | 26 17 | 26 05 | 22 07 | 17 49 | 13 42 |
| 51 | 27 03 | 26 42 | 22 34 | 18 08 | 13 51 |
| 52 | 27 52 | 27 21 | 23 02 | 18 27 | 14 01 |
| 53 | 28 44 | 28 01 | 23 31 | 18 46 | 14 10 |
| 54 | 29 39 | 28 42 | 24 01 | 19 06 | 14 21 |
| 55 | 00♋37 | 29 24 | 24 31 | 19 26 | 14 31 |
| 56 | 01 40 | 00♌08 | 25 02 | 19 47 | 14 42 |
| 57 | 02 47 | 00 54 | 25 34 | 20 08 | 14 53 |
| 58 | 03 59 | 01 41 | 26 07 | 20 30 | 15 04 |
| 59 | 05 16 | 02 30 | 26 40 | 20 53 | 15 16 |
| 60 | 06♋40 | 03♌21 | 27♌15 | 21♍16 | 15♎29 |

**2h 32m 0s — 38° 0' 0" — 10 ♉ 25**

| LAT. | 11 | 12 | ASC | 2 | 3 |
|---|---|---|---|---|---|
| 0 | 09♊40 | 07♋21 | 05♌38 | 06♍14 | 08♎43 |
| 5 | 10 44 | 08 55 | 07 16 | 07 32 | 09 20 |
| 10 | 11 51 | 10 29 | 08 52 | 08 45 | 09 55 |
| 15 | 13 01 | 12 05 | 10 26 | 09 57 | 10 28 |
| 20 | 14 18 | 13 44 | 12 00 | 11 06 | 11 01 |
| 21 | 14 34 | 14 04 | 12 19 | 11 20 | 11 08 |
| 22 | 14 50 | 14 25 | 12 38 | 11 34 | 11 14 |
| 23 | 15 07 | 14 46 | 12 57 | 11 48 | 11 21 |
| 24 | 15 24 | 15 07 | 13 17 | 12 02 | 11 27 |
| 25 | 15 42 | 15 28 | 13 36 | 12 16 | 11 34 |
| 26 | 16 00 | 15 49 | 13 55 | 12 30 | 11 40 |
| 27 | 16 18 | 16 11 | 14 15 | 12 44 | 11 47 |
| 28 | 16 37 | 16 33 | 14 34 | 12 58 | 11 53 |
| 29 | 16 56 | 16 56 | 14 54 | 13 12 | 12 00 |
| 30 | 17 16 | 17 18 | 15 14 | 13 26 | 12 07 |
| 31 | 17 36 | 17 41 | 15 34 | 13 40 | 12 14 |
| 32 | 17 57 | 18 05 | 15 55 | 13 55 | 12 20 |
| 33 | 18 19 | 18 29 | 16 15 | 14 09 | 12 27 |
| 34 | 18 41 | 18 53 | 16 36 | 14 23 | 12 34 |
| 35 | 19 04 | 19 18 | 16 57 | 14 38 | 12 41 |
| 36 | 19 27 | 19 43 | 17 18 | 14 53 | 12 48 |
| 37 | 19 52 | 20 09 | 17 39 | 15 08 | 12 55 |
| 38 | 20 17 | 20 35 | 18 01 | 15 23 | 13 02 |
| 39 | 20 43 | 21 02 | 18 23 | 15 38 | 13 09 |
| 40 | 21 11 | 21 29 | 18 45 | 15 53 | 13 17 |
| 41 | 21 39 | 21 57 | 19 08 | 16 09 | 13 24 |
| 42 | 22 08 | 22 26 | 19 31 | 16 24 | 13 32 |
| 43 | 22 39 | 22 55 | 19 54 | 16 40 | 13 39 |
| 44 | 23 11 | 23 25 | 20 18 | 16 56 | 13 47 |
| 45 | 23 44 | 23 56 | 20 42 | 17 13 | 13 55 |
| 46 | 24 19 | 24 28 | 21 06 | 17 29 | 14 03 |
| 47 | 24 56 | 25 00 | 21 31 | 17 46 | 14 11 |
| 48 | 25 35 | 25 34 | 21 57 | 18 03 | 14 20 |
| 49 | 26 15 | 26 08 | 22 23 | 18 21 | 14 28 |
| 50 | 26 58 | 26 43 | 22 49 | 18 39 | 14 37 |
| 51 | 27 43 | 27 20 | 23 16 | 18 57 | 14 46 |
| 52 | 28 31 | 27 58 | 23 44 | 19 15 | 14 56 |
| 53 | 29 21 | 28 37 | 24 12 | 19 34 | 15 05 |
| 54 | 00♋15 | 29 17 | 24 41 | 19 54 | 15 15 |
| 55 | 01 12 | 29 58 | 25 11 | 20 14 | 15 25 |
| 56 | 02 13 | 00♌41 | 25 41 | 20 34 | 15 36 |
| 57 | 03 19 | 01 26 | 26 13 | 20 55 | 15 47 |
| 58 | 04 29 | 02 12 | 26 45 | 21 16 | 15 58 |
| 59 | 05 45 | 03 00 | 27 17 | 21 39 | 16 10 |
| 60 | 07♋06 | 03♌50 | 27♌51 | 22♍02 | 16♎23 |

**2h 36m 0s — 39° 0' 0" — 11 ♉ 26**

| LAT. | 11 | 12 | ASC | 2 | 3 |
|---|---|---|---|---|---|
| 0 | 10♊36 | 08♋16 | 06♌37 | 07♍18 | 09♎48 |
| 5 | 11 40 | 09 49 | 08 14 | 08 34 | 10 24 |
| 10 | 12 46 | 11 22 | 09 48 | 09 46 | 10 57 |
| 15 | 13 56 | 12 57 | 11 21 | 10 56 | 11 30 |
| 20 | 15 11 | 14 35 | 12 54 | 12 05 | 12 02 |
| 21 | 15 27 | 14 55 | 13 13 | 12 18 | 12 08 |
| 22 | 15 44 | 15 15 | 13 31 | 12 32 | 12 15 |
| 23 | 16 00 | 15 36 | 13 50 | 12 46 | 12 21 |
| 24 | 16 17 | 15 57 | 14 09 | 12 59 | 12 27 |
| 25 | 16 34 | 16 18 | 14 28 | 13 13 | 12 34 |
| 26 | 16 52 | 16 39 | 14 47 | 13 26 | 12 40 |
| 27 | 17 10 | 17 00 | 15 07 | 13 40 | 12 46 |
| 28 | 17 29 | 17 22 | 15 26 | 13 54 | 12 53 |
| 29 | 17 48 | 17 44 | 15 45 | 14 08 | 12 59 |
| 30 | 18 07 | 18 07 | 16 05 | 14 21 | 13 06 |
| 31 | 18 27 | 18 29 | 16 25 | 14 35 | 13 12 |
| 32 | 18 48 | 18 52 | 16 45 | 14 49 | 13 19 |
| 33 | 19 09 | 19 16 | 17 05 | 15 04 | 13 25 |
| 34 | 19 31 | 19 40 | 17 25 | 15 18 | 13 32 |
| 35 | 19 53 | 20 04 | 17 46 | 15 32 | 13 39 |
| 36 | 20 16 | 20 29 | 18 07 | 15 46 | 13 46 |
| 37 | 20 41 | 20 54 | 18 28 | 16 01 | 13 53 |
| 38 | 21 05 | 21 20 | 18 49 | 16 16 | 14 00 |
| 39 | 21 31 | 21 46 | 19 11 | 16 30 | 14 07 |
| 40 | 21 58 | 22 13 | 19 32 | 16 45 | 14 14 |
| 41 | 22 26 | 22 41 | 19 55 | 17 01 | 14 21 |
| 42 | 22 55 | 23 09 | 20 17 | 17 16 | 14 28 |
| 43 | 23 25 | 23 38 | 20 40 | 17 32 | 14 36 |
| 44 | 23 56 | 24 07 | 21 03 | 17 47 | 14 43 |
| 45 | 24 29 | 24 38 | 21 27 | 18 03 | 14 51 |
| 46 | 25 03 | 25 09 | 21 51 | 18 20 | 14 59 |
| 47 | 25 39 | 25 41 | 22 16 | 18 36 | 15 07 |
| 48 | 26 17 | 26 13 | 22 41 | 18 53 | 15 15 |
| 49 | 26 57 | 26 47 | 23 06 | 19 10 | 15 24 |
| 50 | 27 39 | 27 22 | 23 32 | 19 28 | 15 32 |
| 51 | 28 23 | 27 58 | 23 59 | 19 46 | 15 41 |
| 52 | 29 09 | 28 34 | 24 26 | 20 04 | 15 51 |
| 53 | 29 59 | 29 13 | 24 53 | 20 22 | 16 00 |
| 54 | 00♋51 | 29 52 | 25 22 | 20 41 | 16 10 |
| 55 | 01 47 | 00♌33 | 25 51 | 21 01 | 16 20 |
| 56 | 02 47 | 01 15 | 26 21 | 21 21 | 16 30 |
| 57 | 03 51 | 01 58 | 26 51 | 21 42 | 16 41 |
| 58 | 04 59 | 02 44 | 27 23 | 22 03 | 16 52 |
| 59 | 06 13 | 03 31 | 27 55 | 22 25 | 17 04 |
| 60 | 07♋33 | 04♌19 | 28♌28 | 22♍47 | 17♎16 |

# Koch Table of Houses for Latitudes 0° to 60° North

**2h 40m 0s — 40° 0' 0" — 12 ♉ 27**

| LAT. | 11 | 12 | ASC | 2 | 3 |
|---|---|---|---|---|---|
| 0 | 11♊32 | 09♋11 | 07♌35 | 08♍22 | 10♎53 |
| 5 | 12 35 | 10 43 | 09 11 | 09 36 | 11 27 |
| 10 | 13 41 | 12 16 | 10 45 | 10 47 | 12 00 |
| 15 | 14 50 | 13 50 | 12 16 | 11 56 | 12 32 |
| 20 | 16 05 | 15 26 | 13 48 | 13 03 | 13 03 |
| 21 | 16 21 | 15 46 | 14 06 | 13 16 | 13 09 |
| 22 | 16 37 | 16 06 | 14 25 | 13 30 | 13 15 |
| 23 | 16 53 | 16 26 | 14 43 | 13 43 | 13 21 |
| 24 | 17 10 | 16 47 | 15 02 | 13 56 | 13 27 |
| 25 | 17 27 | 17 07 | 15 21 | 14 10 | 13 34 |
| 26 | 17 44 | 17 28 | 15 39 | 14 23 | 13 40 |
| 27 | 18 02 | 17 49 | 15 58 | 14 36 | 13 46 |
| 28 | 18 20 | 18 11 | 16 17 | 14 50 | 13 52 |
| 29 | 18 39 | 18 33 | 16 36 | 15 03 | 13 58 |
| 30 | 18 58 | 18 55 | 16 56 | 15 17 | 14 05 |
| 31 | 19 18 | 19 17 | 17 15 | 15 31 | 14 11 |
| 32 | 19 38 | 19 40 | 17 35 | 15 44 | 14 17 |
| 33 | 19 59 | 20 03 | 17 55 | 15 58 | 14 24 |
| 34 | 20 20 | 20 27 | 18 15 | 16 12 | 14 30 |
| 35 | 20 43 | 20 51 | 18 35 | 16 26 | 14 37 |
| 36 | 21 06 | 21 15 | 18 55 | 16 40 | 14 43 |
| 37 | 21 29 | 21 40 | 19 16 | 16 54 | 14 50 |
| 38 | 21 54 | 22 05 | 19 37 | 17 09 | 14 57 |
| 39 | 22 19 | 22 31 | 19 58 | 17 23 | 15 04 |
| 40 | 22 45 | 22 57 | 20 20 | 17 38 | 15 11 |
| 41 | 23 13 | 23 24 | 20 41 | 17 53 | 15 18 |
| 42 | 23 41 | 23 52 | 21 04 | 18 08 | 15 25 |
| 43 | 24 10 | 24 20 | 21 26 | 18 23 | 15 32 |
| 44 | 24 41 | 24 49 | 21 49 | 18 39 | 15 40 |
| 45 | 25 13 | 25 19 | 22 12 | 18 54 | 15 47 |
| 46 | 25 47 | 25 49 | 22 36 | 19 10 | 15 55 |
| 47 | 26 22 | 26 21 | 23 00 | 19 26 | 16 03 |
| 48 | 26 59 | 26 53 | 23 24 | 19 43 | 16 11 |
| 49 | 27 38 | 27 26 | 23 49 | 20 00 | 16 19 |
| 50 | 28 19 | 28 00 | 24 15 | 20 17 | 16 28 |
| 51 | 29 02 | 28 35 | 24 41 | 20 34 | 16 36 |
| 52 | 29 48 | 29 11 | 25 07 | 20 52 | 16 45 |
| 53 | 00♋36 | 29 48 | 25 34 | 21 10 | 16 54 |
| 54 | 01 28 | 00♌27 | 26 02 | 21 29 | 17 04 |
| 55 | 02 22 | 01 07 | 26 31 | 21 48 | 17 14 |
| 56 | 03 21 | 01 48 | 27 00 | 22 08 | 17 24 |
| 57 | 04 23 | 02 31 | 27 30 | 22 28 | 17 35 |
| 58 | 05 30 | 03 15 | 28 01 | 22 49 | 17 46 |
| 59 | 06 42 | 04 01 | 28 32 | 23 10 | 17 57 |
| 60 | 07♋59 | 04♌48 | 29♌05 | 23♍33 | 18♎10 |

**2h 44m 0s — 41° 0' 0" — 13 ♉ 27**

| LAT. | 11 | 12 | ASC | 2 | 3 |
|---|---|---|---|---|---|
| 0 | 12♊28 | 10♋07 | 08♌34 | 09♍26 | 11♎58 |
| 5 | 13 31 | 11 38 | 10 09 | 10 39 | 12 31 |
| 10 | 14 36 | 13 09 | 11 41 | 11 49 | 13 03 |
| 15 | 15 44 | 14 42 | 13 11 | 12 56 | 13 34 |
| 20 | 16 58 | 16 17 | 14 42 | 14 01 | 14 03 |
| 21 | 17 14 | 16 37 | 15 00 | 14 14 | 14 09 |
| 22 | 17 29 | 16 57 | 15 18 | 14 27 | 14 15 |
| 23 | 17 46 | 17 17 | 15 36 | 14 40 | 14 21 |
| 24 | 18 02 | 17 37 | 15 55 | 14 53 | 14 27 |
| 25 | 18 19 | 17 57 | 16 13 | 15 06 | 14 33 |
| 26 | 18 36 | 18 18 | 16 31 | 15 20 | 14 39 |
| 27 | 18 54 | 18 39 | 16 50 | 15 33 | 14 45 |
| 28 | 19 12 | 19 00 | 17 09 | 15 46 | 14 51 |
| 29 | 19 30 | 19 21 | 17 28 | 15 59 | 14 57 |
| 30 | 19 49 | 19 43 | 17 47 | 16 12 | 15 03 |
| 31 | 20 08 | 20 05 | 18 06 | 16 26 | 15 10 |
| 32 | 20 28 | 20 27 | 18 25 | 16 39 | 15 16 |
| 33 | 20 49 | 20 50 | 18 44 | 16 53 | 15 22 |
| 34 | 21 10 | 21 13 | 19 04 | 17 06 | 15 28 |
| 35 | 21 32 | 21 37 | 19 24 | 17 20 | 15 35 |
| 36 | 21 54 | 22 01 | 19 44 | 17 34 | 15 41 |
| 37 | 22 18 | 22 25 | 20 04 | 17 48 | 15 48 |
| 38 | 22 42 | 22 50 | 20 25 | 18 02 | 15 54 |
| 39 | 23 07 | 23 16 | 20 46 | 18 16 | 16 01 |
| 40 | 23 32 | 23 41 | 21 07 | 18 30 | 16 08 |
| 41 | 23 59 | 24 08 | 21 28 | 18 45 | 16 14 |
| 42 | 24 27 | 24 35 | 21 50 | 19 00 | 16 21 |
| 43 | 24 56 | 25 03 | 22 12 | 19 14 | 16 28 |
| 44 | 25 26 | 25 31 | 22 34 | 19 30 | 16 36 |
| 45 | 25 58 | 26 00 | 22 57 | 19 45 | 16 43 |
| 46 | 26 31 | 26 30 | 23 20 | 20 01 | 16 51 |
| 47 | 27 05 | 27 01 | 23 44 | 20 16 | 16 58 |
| 48 | 27 41 | 27 32 | 24 08 | 20 33 | 17 06 |
| 49 | 28 19 | 28 05 | 24 32 | 20 49 | 17 14 |
| 50 | 28 59 | 28 38 | 24 57 | 21 06 | 17 22 |
| 51 | 29 42 | 29 13 | 25 23 | 21 23 | 17 31 |
| 52 | 00♋26 | 29 48 | 25 49 | 21 41 | 17 40 |
| 53 | 01 14 | 00♌24 | 26 16 | 21 58 | 17 49 |
| 54 | 02 04 | 01 02 | 26 43 | 22 17 | 17 58 |
| 55 | 02 57 | 01 41 | 27 11 | 22 36 | 18 08 |
| 56 | 03 54 | 02 21 | 27 39 | 22 55 | 18 18 |
| 57 | 04 55 | 03 03 | 28 09 | 23 15 | 18 28 |
| 58 | 06 00 | 03 46 | 28 39 | 23 35 | 18 39 |
| 59 | 07 10 | 04 31 | 29 10 | 23 56 | 18 51 |
| 60 | 08♋26 | 05♌18 | 29♌41 | 24♍18 | 19♎03 |

**2h 48m 0s — 42° 0' 0" — 14 ♉ 28**

| LAT. | 11 | 12 | ASC | 2 | 3 |
|---|---|---|---|---|---|
| 0 | 13♊24 | 11♋02 | 09♌34 | 10♍30 | 13♎03 |
| 5 | 14 26 | 12 32 | 11 07 | 11 42 | 13 35 |
| 10 | 15 30 | 14 03 | 12 38 | 12 50 | 14 06 |
| 15 | 16 38 | 15 34 | 14 07 | 13 55 | 14 35 |
| 20 | 17 51 | 17 09 | 15 36 | 15 00 | 15 04 |
| 21 | 18 07 | 17 28 | 15 53 | 15 12 | 15 10 |
| 22 | 18 22 | 17 47 | 16 11 | 15 25 | 15 16 |
| 23 | 18 38 | 18 07 | 16 29 | 15 38 | 15 21 |
| 24 | 18 54 | 18 27 | 16 47 | 15 51 | 15 27 |
| 25 | 19 11 | 18 47 | 17 05 | 16 03 | 15 33 |
| 26 | 19 28 | 19 07 | 17 24 | 16 16 | 15 39 |
| 27 | 19 45 | 19 28 | 17 42 | 16 29 | 15 44 |
| 28 | 20 03 | 19 49 | 18 00 | 16 42 | 15 50 |
| 29 | 20 21 | 20 10 | 18 19 | 16 55 | 15 56 |
| 30 | 20 40 | 20 31 | 18 37 | 17 08 | 16 02 |
| 31 | 20 59 | 20 53 | 18 56 | 17 21 | 16 08 |
| 32 | 21 18 | 21 15 | 19 15 | 17 34 | 16 14 |
| 33 | 21 39 | 21 37 | 19 34 | 17 47 | 16 20 |
| 34 | 22 00 | 22 00 | 19 54 | 18 00 | 16 26 |
| 35 | 22 21 | 22 23 | 20 13 | 18 14 | 16 32 |
| 36 | 22 43 | 22 47 | 20 33 | 18 27 | 16 38 |
| 37 | 23 06 | 23 11 | 20 53 | 18 41 | 16 45 |
| 38 | 23 30 | 23 35 | 21 13 | 18 55 | 16 51 |
| 39 | 23 54 | 24 00 | 21 33 | 19 09 | 16 58 |
| 40 | 24 19 | 24 26 | 21 54 | 19 23 | 17 04 |
| 41 | 24 46 | 24 52 | 22 15 | 19 37 | 17 11 |
| 42 | 25 13 | 25 18 | 22 36 | 19 51 | 17 18 |
| 43 | 25 41 | 25 45 | 22 58 | 20 06 | 17 24 |
| 44 | 26 11 | 26 13 | 23 20 | 20 21 | 17 32 |
| 45 | 26 42 | 26 42 | 23 42 | 20 36 | 17 39 |
| 46 | 27 14 | 27 11 | 24 05 | 20 51 | 17 46 |
| 47 | 27 48 | 27 41 | 24 28 | 21 07 | 17 54 |
| 48 | 28 23 | 28 12 | 24 52 | 21 22 | 18 01 |
| 49 | 29 01 | 28 44 | 25 16 | 21 38 | 18 09 |
| 50 | 29 40 | 29 16 | 25 40 | 21 55 | 18 17 |
| 51 | 00♋21 | 29 50 | 26 05 | 22 12 | 18 25 |
| 52 | 01 05 | 00♌25 | 26 31 | 22 29 | 18 34 |
| 53 | 01 51 | 01 00 | 26 57 | 22 46 | 18 43 |
| 54 | 02 40 | 01 37 | 27 23 | 23 04 | 18 52 |
| 55 | 03 32 | 02 15 | 27 51 | 23 23 | 19 02 |
| 56 | 04 27 | 02 55 | 28 19 | 23 42 | 19 11 |
| 57 | 05 27 | 03 35 | 28 47 | 24 01 | 19 22 |
| 58 | 06 30 | 04 18 | 29 17 | 24 21 | 19 33 |
| 59 | 07 39 | 05 01 | 29 47 | 24 42 | 19 44 |
| 60 | 08♋53 | 05♌47 | 00♍18 | 25♍03 | 19♎56 |

**2h 52m 0s — 43° 0' 0" — 15 ♉ 28**

| LAT. | 11 | 12 | ASC | 2 | 3 |
|---|---|---|---|---|---|
| 0 | 14♊20 | 11♋58 | 10♌33 | 11♍34 | 14♎07 |
| 5 | 15 21 | 13 27 | 12 05 | 12 44 | 14 39 |
| 10 | 16 25 | 14 56 | 13 34 | 13 51 | 15 08 |
| 15 | 17 32 | 16 27 | 15 02 | 14 55 | 15 37 |
| 20 | 18 44 | 18 00 | 16 30 | 15 58 | 16 04 |
| 21 | 18 59 | 18 19 | 16 47 | 16 10 | 16 10 |
| 22 | 19 15 | 18 38 | 17 05 | 16 23 | 16 16 |
| 23 | 19 30 | 18 57 | 17 22 | 16 35 | 16 21 |
| 24 | 19 46 | 19 17 | 17 40 | 16 48 | 16 27 |
| 25 | 20 03 | 19 37 | 17 58 | 17 00 | 16 32 |
| 26 | 20 20 | 19 57 | 18 16 | 17 13 | 16 38 |
| 27 | 20 37 | 20 17 | 18 34 | 17 25 | 16 43 |
| 28 | 20 54 | 20 37 | 18 52 | 17 38 | 16 49 |
| 29 | 21 12 | 20 58 | 19 10 | 17 50 | 16 55 |
| 30 | 21 30 | 21 19 | 19 28 | 18 03 | 17 00 |
| 31 | 21 49 | 21 40 | 19 47 | 18 16 | 17 06 |
| 32 | 22 08 | 22 02 | 20 05 | 18 29 | 17 12 |
| 33 | 22 28 | 22 24 | 20 24 | 18 42 | 17 18 |
| 34 | 22 49 | 22 46 | 20 43 | 18 55 | 17 24 |
| 35 | 23 10 | 23 09 | 21 02 | 19 08 | 17 30 |
| 36 | 23 32 | 23 32 | 21 21 | 19 21 | 17 36 |
| 37 | 23 54 | 23 56 | 21 41 | 19 34 | 17 42 |
| 38 | 24 17 | 24 20 | 22 01 | 19 48 | 17 48 |
| 39 | 24 41 | 24 45 | 22 21 | 20 01 | 17 54 |
| 40 | 25 06 | 25 10 | 22 41 | 20 15 | 18 01 |
| 41 | 25 32 | 25 35 | 23 02 | 20 29 | 18 07 |
| 42 | 25 59 | 26 01 | 23 23 | 20 43 | 18 14 |
| 43 | 26 27 | 26 28 | 23 44 | 20 57 | 18 20 |
| 44 | 26 56 | 26 55 | 24 05 | 21 12 | 18 27 |
| 45 | 27 26 | 27 23 | 24 27 | 21 26 | 18 34 |
| 46 | 27 57 | 27 52 | 24 49 | 21 41 | 18 41 |
| 47 | 28 31 | 28 21 | 25 12 | 21 56 | 18 49 |
| 48 | 29 05 | 28 52 | 25 35 | 22 12 | 18 56 |
| 49 | 29 42 | 29 23 | 25 59 | 22 28 | 19 04 |
| 50 | 00♋20 | 29 55 | 26 23 | 22 44 | 19 12 |
| 51 | 01 00 | 00♌28 | 26 47 | 23 00 | 19 20 |
| 52 | 01 43 | 01 01 | 27 12 | 23 17 | 19 28 |
| 53 | 02 28 | 01 36 | 27 38 | 23 34 | 19 37 |
| 54 | 03 16 | 02 12 | 28 04 | 23 52 | 19 46 |
| 55 | 04 06 | 02 50 | 28 31 | 24 10 | 19 55 |
| 56 | 05 01 | 03 28 | 28 58 | 24 28 | 20 05 |
| 57 | 05 58 | 04 08 | 29 26 | 24 48 | 20 15 |
| 58 | 07 00 | 04 49 | 29 55 | 25 07 | 20 26 |
| 59 | 08 07 | 05 32 | 00♍25 | 25 28 | 20 37 |
| 60 | 09♋19 | 06♌16 | 00♍55 | 25♍49 | 20♎49 |

**2h 56m 0s — 44° 0' 0" — 16 ♉ 28**

| LAT. | 11 | 12 | ASC | 2 | 3 |
|---|---|---|---|---|---|
| 0 | 15♊16 | 12♋53 | 11♌32 | 12♍39 | 15♎12 |
| 5 | 16 17 | 14 22 | 13 03 | 13 47 | 15 42 |
| 10 | 17 20 | 15 50 | 14 31 | 14 52 | 16 11 |
| 15 | 18 26 | 17 19 | 15 58 | 15 55 | 16 38 |
| 20 | 19 37 | 18 51 | 17 24 | 16 56 | 17 05 |
| 21 | 19 52 | 19 10 | 17 41 | 17 08 | 17 10 |
| 22 | 20 07 | 19 29 | 17 58 | 17 20 | 17 15 |
| 23 | 20 23 | 19 48 | 18 16 | 17 33 | 17 21 |
| 24 | 20 39 | 20 07 | 18 33 | 17 45 | 17 26 |
| 25 | 20 55 | 20 26 | 18 50 | 17 57 | 17 32 |
| 26 | 21 11 | 20 46 | 19 08 | 18 09 | 17 37 |
| 27 | 21 28 | 21 06 | 19 26 | 18 21 | 17 42 |
| 28 | 21 45 | 21 26 | 19 43 | 18 34 | 17 48 |
| 29 | 22 03 | 21 46 | 20 01 | 18 46 | 17 53 |
| 30 | 22 21 | 22 07 | 20 19 | 18 58 | 17 59 |
| 31 | 22 39 | 22 28 | 20 37 | 19 11 | 18 04 |
| 32 | 22 58 | 22 49 | 20 55 | 19 23 | 18 10 |
| 33 | 23 18 | 23 11 | 21 14 | 19 36 | 18 16 |
| 34 | 23 38 | 23 33 | 21 32 | 19 49 | 18 21 |
| 35 | 23 59 | 23 55 | 21 51 | 20 01 | 18 27 |
| 36 | 24 20 | 24 18 | 22 10 | 20 14 | 18 33 |
| 37 | 24 42 | 24 41 | 22 29 | 20 27 | 18 39 |
| 38 | 25 05 | 25 05 | 22 49 | 20 40 | 18 45 |
| 39 | 25 28 | 25 29 | 23 08 | 20 54 | 18 51 |
| 40 | 25 53 | 25 54 | 23 28 | 21 07 | 18 57 |
| 41 | 26 18 | 26 19 | 23 49 | 21 21 | 19 03 |
| 42 | 26 44 | 26 44 | 24 09 | 21 34 | 19 10 |
| 43 | 27 12 | 27 10 | 24 30 | 21 48 | 19 16 |
| 44 | 27 40 | 27 37 | 24 51 | 22 03 | 19 23 |
| 45 | 28 10 | 28 05 | 25 12 | 22 17 | 19 30 |
| 46 | 28 41 | 28 33 | 25 34 | 22 32 | 19 36 |
| 47 | 29 13 | 29 02 | 25 56 | 22 46 | 19 44 |
| 48 | 29 47 | 29 31 | 26 19 | 23 01 | 19 51 |
| 49 | 00♋22 | 00♌02 | 26 42 | 23 17 | 19 58 |
| 50 | 01 00 | 00 33 | 27 05 | 23 33 | 20 06 |
| 51 | 01 39 | 01 05 | 27 29 | 23 49 | 20 14 |
| 52 | 02 21 | 01 38 | 27 54 | 24 05 | 20 22 |
| 53 | 03 05 | 02 12 | 28 19 | 24 22 | 20 31 |
| 54 | 03 51 | 02 47 | 28 44 | 24 39 | 20 39 |
| 55 | 04 41 | 03 24 | 29 11 | 24 57 | 20 49 |
| 56 | 05 34 | 04 01 | 29 37 | 25 15 | 20 58 |
| 57 | 06 30 | 04 40 | 00♍05 | 25 34 | 21 08 |
| 58 | 07 31 | 05 20 | 00 33 | 25 53 | 21 19 |
| 59 | 08 35 | 06 02 | 01 02 | 26 13 | 21 30 |
| 60 | 09♋46 | 06♌45 | 01♍32 | 26♍34 | 21♎41 |

**3h 0m 0s — 45° 0' 0" — 17 ♉ 28**

| LAT. | 11 | 12 | ASC | 2 | 3 |
|---|---|---|---|---|---|
| 0 | 16♊11 | 13♋49 | 12♌32 | 13♍43 | 16♎17 |
| 5 | 17 12 | 15 16 | 14 02 | 14 50 | 16 46 |
| 10 | 18 14 | 16 43 | 15 28 | 15 54 | 17 13 |
| 15 | 19 20 | 18 12 | 16 53 | 16 55 | 17 39 |
| 20 | 20 30 | 19 42 | 18 18 | 17 54 | 18 05 |
| 21 | 20 45 | 20 00 | 18 35 | 18 06 | 18 10 |
| 22 | 21 00 | 20 19 | 18 52 | 18 18 | 18 15 |
| 23 | 21 15 | 20 38 | 19 09 | 18 30 | 18 20 |
| 24 | 21 30 | 20 57 | 19 26 | 18 42 | 18 26 |
| 25 | 21 46 | 21 16 | 19 43 | 18 54 | 18 31 |
| 26 | 22 02 | 21 35 | 20 00 | 19 06 | 18 36 |
| 27 | 22 19 | 21 55 | 20 17 | 19 18 | 18 41 |
| 28 | 22 36 | 22 15 | 20 35 | 19 30 | 18 46 |
| 29 | 22 53 | 22 35 | 20 52 | 19 42 | 18 52 |
| 30 | 23 11 | 22 55 | 21 10 | 19 54 | 18 57 |
| 31 | 23 29 | 23 16 | 21 28 | 20 06 | 19 02 |
| 32 | 23 48 | 23 37 | 21 46 | 20 18 | 19 08 |
| 33 | 24 07 | 23 58 | 22 04 | 20 30 | 19 13 |
| 34 | 24 27 | 24 20 | 22 22 | 20 43 | 19 19 |
| 35 | 24 47 | 24 42 | 22 40 | 20 55 | 19 24 |
| 36 | 25 08 | 25 04 | 22 59 | 21 08 | 19 30 |
| 37 | 25 30 | 25 27 | 23 18 | 21 20 | 19 36 |
| 38 | 25 52 | 25 50 | 23 37 | 21 33 | 19 41 |
| 39 | 26 15 | 26 13 | 23 56 | 21 46 | 19 47 |
| 40 | 26 39 | 26 37 | 24 16 | 21 59 | 19 53 |
| 41 | 27 04 | 27 02 | 24 35 | 22 13 | 19 59 |
| 42 | 27 30 | 27 27 | 24 55 | 22 26 | 20 05 |
| 43 | 27 57 | 27 53 | 25 16 | 22 40 | 20 12 |
| 44 | 28 24 | 28 19 | 25 36 | 22 53 | 20 18 |
| 45 | 28 53 | 28 46 | 25 57 | 23 07 | 20 25 |
| 46 | 29 24 | 29 13 | 26 19 | 23 22 | 20 31 |
| 47 | 29 55 | 29 42 | 26 40 | 23 36 | 20 38 |
| 48 | 00♋28 | 00♌11 | 27 03 | 23 51 | 20 45 |
| 49 | 01 03 | 00 40 | 27 25 | 24 06 | 20 53 |
| 50 | 01 40 | 01 11 | 27 48 | 24 21 | 21 00 |
| 51 | 02 18 | 01 42 | 28 11 | 24 37 | 21 08 |
| 52 | 02 59 | 02 15 | 28 35 | 24 53 | 21 16 |
| 53 | 03 42 | 02 48 | 29 00 | 25 10 | 21 24 |
| 54 | 04 27 | 03 23 | 29 25 | 25 27 | 21 33 |
| 55 | 05 16 | 03 58 | 29 50 | 25 44 | 21 42 |
| 56 | 06 07 | 04 35 | 00♍17 | 26 02 | 21 51 |
| 57 | 07 02 | 05 13 | 00 44 | 26 20 | 22 01 |
| 58 | 08 01 | 05 52 | 01 11 | 26 39 | 22 11 |
| 59 | 09 04 | 06 32 | 01 39 | 26 59 | 22 22 |
| 60 | 10♋12 | 07♌14 | 02♍09 | 27♍19 | 22♎34 |

**3h 4m 0s — 46° 0' 0" — 18 ♉ 28**

| LAT. | 11 | 12 | ASC | 2 | 3 |
|---|---|---|---|---|---|
| 0 | 17♊07 | 14♋44 | 13♌32 | 14♍48 | 17♎21 |
| 5 | 18 07 | 16 11 | 15 00 | 15 53 | 17 49 |
| 10 | 19 08 | 17 37 | 16 26 | 16 55 | 18 15 |
| 15 | 20 13 | 19 04 | 17 49 | 17 55 | 18 40 |
| 20 | 21 23 | 20 33 | 19 12 | 18 53 | 19 05 |
| 21 | 21 37 | 20 51 | 19 29 | 19 04 | 19 10 |
| 22 | 21 52 | 21 10 | 19 45 | 19 16 | 19 15 |
| 23 | 22 07 | 21 28 | 20 02 | 19 28 | 19 20 |
| 24 | 22 22 | 21 47 | 20 19 | 19 39 | 19 25 |
| 25 | 22 38 | 22 06 | 20 36 | 19 51 | 19 30 |
| 26 | 22 54 | 22 25 | 20 52 | 20 02 | 19 35 |
| 27 | 23 10 | 22 44 | 21 09 | 20 14 | 19 40 |
| 28 | 23 27 | 23 04 | 21 27 | 20 26 | 19 45 |
| 29 | 23 44 | 23 23 | 21 44 | 20 37 | 19 50 |
| 30 | 24 01 | 23 43 | 22 01 | 20 49 | 19 55 |
| 31 | 24 19 | 24 04 | 22 18 | 21 01 | 20 00 |
| 32 | 24 38 | 24 24 | 22 36 | 21 13 | 20 05 |
| 33 | 24 56 | 24 45 | 22 54 | 21 25 | 20 11 |
| 34 | 25 16 | 25 06 | 23 12 | 21 37 | 20 16 |
| 35 | 25 36 | 25 28 | 23 30 | 21 49 | 20 21 |
| 36 | 25 56 | 25 50 | 23 48 | 22 01 | 20 27 |
| 37 | 26 18 | 26 12 | 24 06 | 22 14 | 20 32 |
| 38 | 26 40 | 26 35 | 24 25 | 22 26 | 20 38 |
| 39 | 27 02 | 26 58 | 24 44 | 22 39 | 20 43 |
| 40 | 27 26 | 27 21 | 25 03 | 22 51 | 20 49 |
| 41 | 27 50 | 27 46 | 25 22 | 23 04 | 20 55 |
| 42 | 28 15 | 28 10 | 25 42 | 23 17 | 21 01 |
| 43 | 28 41 | 28 35 | 26 02 | 23 31 | 21 07 |
| 44 | 29 09 | 29 01 | 26 22 | 23 44 | 21 13 |
| 45 | 29 37 | 29 27 | 26 42 | 23 58 | 21 20 |
| 46 | 00♋07 | 29 54 | 27 03 | 24 12 | 21 26 |
| 47 | 00 38 | 00♌22 | 27 25 | 24 26 | 21 33 |
| 48 | 01 10 | 00 50 | 27 46 | 24 40 | 21 40 |
| 49 | 01 44 | 01 19 | 28 08 | 24 55 | 21 47 |
| 50 | 02 20 | 01 49 | 28 31 | 25 10 | 21 54 |
| 51 | 02 57 | 02 20 | 28 54 | 25 25 | 22 02 |
| 52 | 03 37 | 02 52 | 29 17 | 25 41 | 22 10 |
| 53 | 04 19 | 03 24 | 29 41 | 25 57 | 22 18 |
| 54 | 05 03 | 03 58 | 00♍05 | 26 14 | 22 26 |
| 55 | 05 50 | 04 32 | 00 30 | 26 31 | 22 35 |
| 56 | 06 40 | 05 08 | 00 56 | 26 48 | 22 44 |
| 57 | 07 34 | 05 45 | 01 22 | 27 06 | 22 54 |
| 58 | 08 31 | 06 23 | 01 49 | 27 25 | 23 04 |
| 59 | 09 32 | 07 03 | 02 17 | 27 44 | 23 15 |
| 60 | 10♋39 | 07♌44 | 02♍45 | 28♍04 | 23♎26 |

**3h 8m 0s — 47° 0' 0" — 19 ♉ 27**

| LAT. | 11 | 12 | ASC | 2 | 3 |
|---|---|---|---|---|---|
| 0 | 18♊02 | 15♋40 | 14♌32 | 15♍53 | 18♎26 |
| 5 | 19 02 | 17 06 | 15 59 | 16 56 | 18 52 |
| 10 | 20 03 | 18 31 | 17 23 | 17 56 | 19 17 |
| 15 | 21 07 | 19 57 | 18 45 | 18 54 | 19 41 |
| 20 | 22 15 | 21 24 | 20 06 | 19 51 | 20 05 |
| 21 | 22 29 | 21 42 | 20 23 | 20 02 | 20 10 |
| 22 | 22 44 | 22 00 | 20 39 | 20 14 | 20 14 |
| 23 | 22 59 | 22 18 | 20 55 | 20 25 | 20 19 |
| 24 | 23 14 | 22 37 | 21 12 | 20 36 | 20 24 |
| 25 | 23 29 | 22 55 | 21 28 | 20 47 | 20 29 |
| 26 | 23 45 | 23 14 | 21 45 | 20 59 | 20 33 |
| 27 | 24 01 | 23 33 | 22 01 | 21 10 | 20 38 |
| 28 | 24 17 | 23 52 | 22 18 | 21 21 | 20 43 |
| 29 | 24 34 | 24 12 | 22 35 | 21 33 | 20 48 |
| 30 | 24 51 | 24 31 | 22 52 | 21 44 | 20 53 |
| 31 | 25 09 | 24 51 | 23 09 | 21 56 | 20 58 |
| 32 | 25 27 | 25 11 | 23 26 | 22 07 | 21 03 |
| 33 | 25 46 | 25 32 | 23 44 | 22 19 | 21 08 |
| 34 | 26 05 | 25 53 | 24 01 | 22 31 | 21 13 |
| 35 | 26 24 | 26 14 | 24 19 | 22 43 | 21 18 |
| 36 | 26 44 | 26 35 | 24 37 | 22 55 | 21 23 |
| 37 | 27 05 | 26 57 | 24 55 | 23 07 | 21 29 |
| 38 | 27 27 | 27 20 | 25 13 | 23 19 | 21 34 |
| 39 | 27 49 | 27 42 | 25 31 | 23 31 | 21 39 |
| 40 | 28 12 | 28 05 | 25 50 | 23 43 | 21 45 |
| 41 | 28 36 | 28 29 | 26 09 | 23 56 | 21 51 |
| 42 | 29 00 | 28 53 | 26 28 | 24 09 | 21 56 |
| 43 | 29 26 | 29 18 | 26 48 | 24 22 | 22 02 |
| 44 | 29 53 | 29 43 | 27 07 | 24 35 | 22 08 |
| 45 | 00♋21 | 00♌09 | 27 28 | 24 48 | 22 15 |
| 46 | 00 49 | 00 35 | 27 48 | 25 02 | 22 21 |
| 47 | 01 20 | 01 02 | 28 09 | 25 16 | 22 27 |
| 48 | 01 51 | 01 30 | 28 30 | 25 30 | 22 34 |
| 49 | 02 25 | 01 58 | 28 51 | 25 44 | 22 41 |
| 50 | 02 59 | 02 27 | 29 13 | 25 59 | 22 48 |
| 51 | 03 36 | 02 57 | 29 36 | 26 14 | 22 55 |
| 52 | 04 15 | 03 28 | 29 59 | 26 29 | 23 03 |
| 53 | 04 55 | 04 00 | 00♍22 | 26 45 | 23 11 |
| 54 | 05 39 | 04 33 | 00 46 | 27 01 | 23 19 |
| 55 | 06 24 | 05 07 | 01 10 | 27 18 | 23 28 |
| 56 | 07 13 | 05 42 | 01 35 | 27 35 | 23 37 |
| 57 | 08 05 | 06 18 | 02 01 | 27 52 | 23 46 |
| 58 | 09 01 | 06 55 | 02 27 | 28 11 | 23 56 |
| 59 | 10 01 | 07 33 | 02 54 | 28 30 | 24 07 |
| 60 | 11♋05 | 08♌13 | 03♍22 | 28♍49 | 24♎18 |

# Koch Table of Houses for Latitudes 0° to 60° North

**3h 12m 0s — 48° 0' 0" — 20 ♉ 26**

| LAT. | 11 | 12 | ASC | 2 | 3 |
|---|---|---|---|---|---|
| 0 | 18♊58 | 16♋36 | 15♌32 | 16♍57 | 19♎30 |
| 5 | 19 57 | 18 00 | 16 58 | 17 59 | 19 55 |
| 10 | 20 57 | 19 24 | 18 20 | 18 58 | 20 19 |
| 15 | 22 00 | 20 49 | 19 41 | 19 54 | 20 42 |
| 20 | 23 07 | 22 16 | 21 01 | 20 50 | 21 05 |
| 21 | 23 22 | 22 33 | 21 17 | 21 00 | 21 09 |
| 22 | 23 36 | 22 51 | 21 33 | 21 11 | 21 14 |
| 23 | 23 51 | 23 09 | 21 49 | 21 22 | 21 18 |
| 24 | 24 05 | 23 27 | 22 05 | 21 33 | 21 23 |
| 25 | 24 21 | 23 45 | 22 21 | 21 44 | 21 27 |
| 26 | 24 36 | 24 04 | 22 37 | 21 55 | 21 32 |
| 27 | 24 52 | 24 22 | 22 54 | 22 06 | 21 37 |
| 28 | 25 08 | 24 41 | 23 10 | 22 17 | 21 41 |
| 29 | 25 24 | 25 00 | 23 26 | 22 28 | 21 46 |
| 30 | 25 41 | 25 19 | 23 43 | 22 40 | 21 51 |
| 31 | 25 59 | 25 39 | 24 00 | 22 51 | 21 55 |
| 32 | 26 16 | 25 59 | 24 17 | 23 02 | 22 00 |
| 33 | 26 35 | 26 19 | 24 34 | 23 13 | 22 05 |
| 34 | 26 53 | 26 39 | 24 51 | 23 25 | 22 10 |
| 35 | 27 13 | 27 00 | 25 08 | 23 36 | 22 15 |
| 36 | 27 32 | 27 21 | 25 26 | 23 48 | 22 20 |
| 37 | 27 53 | 27 43 | 25 43 | 24 00 | 22 25 |
| 38 | 28 14 | 28 04 | 26 01 | 24 11 | 22 30 |
| 39 | 28 36 | 28 27 | 26 19 | 24 23 | 22 35 |
| 40 | 28 58 | 28 49 | 26 37 | 24 35 | 22 41 |
| 41 | 29 21 | 29 12 | 26 56 | 24 48 | 22 46 |
| 42 | 29 46 | 29 36 | 27 15 | 25 00 | 22 52 |
| 43 | 00♋11 | 00♌00 | 27 34 | 25 13 | 22 57 |
| 44 | 00 37 | 00 25 | 27 53 | 25 26 | 23 03 |
| 45 | 01 04 | 00 50 | 28 13 | 25 39 | 23 09 |
| 46 | 01 32 | 01 16 | 28 33 | 25 52 | 23 15 |
| 47 | 02 02 | 01 42 | 28 53 | 26 05 | 23 22 |
| 48 | 02 33 | 02 09 | 29 14 | 26 19 | 23 28 |
| 49 | 03 05 | 02 37 | 29 35 | 26 33 | 23 35 |
| 50 | 03 39 | 03 06 | 29 56 | 26 47 | 23 42 |
| 51 | 04 15 | 03 35 | 00♍18 | 27 02 | 23 49 |
| 52 | 04 52 | 04 05 | 00 40 | 27 17 | 23 56 |
| 53 | 05 32 | 04 36 | 01 03 | 27 32 | 24 04 |
| 54 | 06 14 | 05 08 | 01 27 | 27 48 | 24 12 |
| 55 | 06 59 | 05 41 | 01 50 | 28 04 | 24 20 |
| 56 | 07 46 | 06 15 | 02 15 | 28 21 | 24 29 |
| 57 | 08 37 | 06 50 | 02 40 | 28 38 | 24 38 |
| 58 | 09 31 | 07 26 | 03 06 | 28 56 | 24 48 |
| 59 | 10 29 | 08 04 | 03 32 | 29 15 | 24 59 |
| 60 | 11♋32 | 08♌43 | 03♍59 | 29♍34 | 25♎10 |

**3h 16m 0s — 49° 0' 0" — 21 ♉ 26**

| LAT. | 11 | 12 | ASC | 2 | 3 |
|---|---|---|---|---|---|
| 0 | 19♊53 | 17♋32 | 16♌33 | 18♍02 | 20♎34 |
| 5 | 20 51 | 18 55 | 17 57 | 19 03 | 20 58 |
| 10 | 21 51 | 20 18 | 19 18 | 19 59 | 21 21 |
| 15 | 22 53 | 21 42 | 20 37 | 20 54 | 21 43 |
| 20 | 24 00 | 23 07 | 21 55 | 21 48 | 22 04 |
| 21 | 24 14 | 23 24 | 22 11 | 21 58 | 22 09 |
| 22 | 24 28 | 23 42 | 22 26 | 22 09 | 22 13 |
| 23 | 24 42 | 23 59 | 22 42 | 22 20 | 22 17 |
| 24 | 24 57 | 24 17 | 22 58 | 22 30 | 22 22 |
| 25 | 25 12 | 24 35 | 23 14 | 22 41 | 22 26 |
| 26 | 25 27 | 24 53 | 23 30 | 22 52 | 22 30 |
| 27 | 25 42 | 25 11 | 23 46 | 23 02 | 22 35 |
| 28 | 25 58 | 25 30 | 24 02 | 23 13 | 22 39 |
| 29 | 26 15 | 25 48 | 24 18 | 23 24 | 22 44 |
| 30 | 26 31 | 26 07 | 24 34 | 23 35 | 22 48 |
| 31 | 26 48 | 26 27 | 24 51 | 23 46 | 22 53 |
| 32 | 27 06 | 26 46 | 25 07 | 23 57 | 22 57 |
| 33 | 27 23 | 27 06 | 25 24 | 24 08 | 23 02 |
| 34 | 27 42 | 27 26 | 25 40 | 24 19 | 23 07 |
| 35 | 28 01 | 27 46 | 25 57 | 24 30 | 23 11 |
| 36 | 28 20 | 28 07 | 26 14 | 24 41 | 23 16 |
| 37 | 28 40 | 28 28 | 26 32 | 24 52 | 23 21 |
| 38 | 29 01 | 28 49 | 26 49 | 25 04 | 23 26 |
| 39 | 29 22 | 29 11 | 27 07 | 25 16 | 23 31 |
| 40 | 29 44 | 29 33 | 27 25 | 25 27 | 23 36 |
| 41 | 00♋07 | 29 56 | 27 43 | 25 39 | 23 41 |
| 42 | 00 31 | 00♌19 | 28 01 | 25 51 | 23 47 |
| 43 | 00 55 | 00 43 | 28 20 | 26 04 | 23 52 |
| 44 | 01 21 | 01 07 | 28 39 | 26 16 | 23 58 |
| 45 | 01 47 | 01 31 | 28 58 | 26 29 | 24 04 |
| 46 | 02 15 | 01 57 | 29 17 | 26 42 | 24 10 |
| 47 | 02 44 | 02 22 | 29 37 | 26 55 | 24 16 |
| 48 | 03 14 | 02 49 | 29 57 | 27 08 | 24 22 |
| 49 | 03 46 | 03 16 | 00♍18 | 27 22 | 24 28 |
| 50 | 04 19 | 03 44 | 00 39 | 27 36 | 24 35 |
| 51 | 04 54 | 04 13 | 01 00 | 27 50 | 24 42 |
| 52 | 05 30 | 04 42 | 01 22 | 28 05 | 24 49 |
| 53 | 06 09 | 05 12 | 01 44 | 28 20 | 24 57 |
| 54 | 06 50 | 05 43 | 02 07 | 28 35 | 25 04 |
| 55 | 07 33 | 06 16 | 02 30 | 28 51 | 25 13 |
| 56 | 08 20 | 06 49 | 02 54 | 29 07 | 25 21 |
| 57 | 09 09 | 07 23 | 03 19 | 29 24 | 25 31 |
| 58 | 10 01 | 07 58 | 03 44 | 29 42 | 25 40 |
| 59 | 10 58 | 08 35 | 04 09 | 00♎00 | 25 51 |
| 60 | 11♋59 | 09♌12 | 04♍36 | 00♎19 | 26♎02 |

**3h 20m 0s — 50° 0' 0" — 22 ♉ 25**

| LAT. | 11 | 12 | ASC | 2 | 3 |
|---|---|---|---|---|---|
| 0 | 20♊49 | 18♋28 | 17♌33 | 19♍07 | 21♎38 |
| 5 | 21 46 | 19 50 | 18 56 | 20 06 | 22 01 |
| 10 | 22 45 | 21 12 | 20 15 | 21 01 | 22 23 |
| 15 | 23 47 | 22 34 | 21 33 | 21 54 | 22 43 |
| 20 | 24 52 | 23 58 | 22 50 | 22 46 | 23 04 |
| 21 | 25 06 | 24 15 | 23 05 | 22 56 | 23 08 |
| 22 | 25 20 | 24 32 | 23 20 | 23 07 | 23 12 |
| 23 | 25 34 | 24 50 | 23 36 | 23 17 | 23 16 |
| 24 | 25 48 | 25 07 | 23 51 | 23 27 | 23 20 |
| 25 | 26 03 | 25 25 | 24 07 | 23 38 | 23 24 |
| 26 | 26 18 | 25 42 | 24 22 | 23 48 | 23 29 |
| 27 | 26 33 | 26 00 | 24 38 | 23 58 | 23 33 |
| 28 | 26 49 | 26 19 | 24 54 | 24 09 | 23 37 |
| 29 | 27 05 | 26 37 | 25 09 | 24 19 | 23 41 |
| 30 | 27 21 | 26 55 | 25 25 | 24 30 | 23 46 |
| 31 | 27 38 | 27 14 | 25 41 | 24 40 | 23 50 |
| 32 | 27 55 | 27 33 | 25 57 | 24 51 | 23 54 |
| 33 | 28 12 | 27 53 | 26 14 | 25 02 | 23 59 |
| 34 | 28 30 | 28 12 | 26 30 | 25 12 | 24 03 |
| 35 | 28 49 | 28 32 | 26 47 | 25 23 | 24 08 |
| 36 | 29 08 | 28 53 | 27 03 | 25 34 | 24 12 |
| 37 | 29 27 | 29 13 | 27 20 | 25 45 | 24 17 |
| 38 | 29 48 | 29 34 | 27 37 | 25 57 | 24 22 |
| 39 | 00♋09 | 29 56 | 27 54 | 26 08 | 24 27 |
| 40 | 00 30 | 00♌17 | 28 12 | 26 19 | 24 32 |
| 41 | 00 53 | 00 39 | 28 30 | 26 31 | 24 37 |
| 42 | 01 16 | 01 02 | 28 48 | 26 43 | 24 42 |
| 43 | 01 40 | 01 25 | 29 06 | 26 54 | 24 47 |
| 44 | 02 05 | 01 49 | 29 24 | 27 07 | 24 52 |
| 45 | 02 31 | 02 13 | 29 43 | 27 19 | 24 58 |
| 46 | 02 58 | 02 37 | 00♍02 | 27 31 | 25 04 |
| 47 | 03 26 | 03 03 | 00 21 | 27 44 | 25 09 |
| 48 | 03 55 | 03 29 | 00 41 | 27 57 | 25 15 |
| 49 | 04 26 | 03 55 | 01 01 | 28 10 | 25 22 |
| 50 | 04 58 | 04 22 | 01 22 | 28 24 | 25 28 |
| 51 | 05 32 | 04 50 | 01 42 | 28 38 | 25 35 |
| 52 | 06 08 | 05 19 | 02 04 | 28 52 | 25 42 |
| 53 | 06 46 | 05 48 | 02 25 | 29 07 | 25 49 |
| 54 | 07 26 | 06 19 | 02 48 | 29 22 | 25 57 |
| 55 | 08 08 | 06 50 | 03 10 | 29 37 | 26 05 |
| 56 | 08 53 | 07 22 | 03 34 | 29 53 | 26 13 |
| 57 | 09 40 | 07 56 | 03 57 | 00♎10 | 26 22 |
| 58 | 10 32 | 08 30 | 04 22 | 00 27 | 26 32 |
| 59 | 11 26 | 09 05 | 04 47 | 00 45 | 26 42 |
| 60 | 12♋25 | 09♌42 | 05♍13 | 01♎04 | 26♎53 |

**3h 24m 0s — 51° 0' 0" — 23 ♉ 23**

| LAT. | 11 | 12 | ASC | 2 | 3 |
|---|---|---|---|---|---|
| 0 | 21♊44 | 19♋24 | 18♌34 | 20♍12 | 22♎42 |
| 5 | 22 41 | 20 45 | 19 55 | 21 09 | 23 04 |
| 10 | 23 39 | 22 06 | 21 13 | 22 03 | 23 24 |
| 15 | 24 40 | 23 27 | 22 29 | 22 54 | 23 44 |
| 20 | 25 44 | 24 49 | 23 44 | 23 44 | 24 03 |
| 21 | 25 58 | 25 06 | 23 59 | 23 54 | 24 07 |
| 22 | 26 11 | 25 23 | 24 14 | 24 04 | 24 11 |
| 23 | 26 25 | 25 40 | 24 29 | 24 14 | 24 15 |
| 24 | 26 39 | 25 57 | 24 44 | 24 24 | 24 19 |
| 25 | 26 54 | 26 14 | 25 00 | 24 34 | 24 23 |
| 26 | 27 09 | 26 32 | 25 15 | 24 44 | 24 27 |
| 27 | 27 24 | 26 49 | 25 30 | 24 55 | 24 31 |
| 28 | 27 39 | 27 07 | 25 45 | 25 05 | 24 35 |
| 29 | 27 55 | 27 25 | 26 01 | 25 15 | 24 39 |
| 30 | 28 11 | 27 44 | 26 16 | 25 25 | 24 43 |
| 31 | 28 27 | 28 02 | 26 32 | 25 35 | 24 47 |
| 32 | 28 44 | 28 21 | 26 48 | 25 45 | 24 51 |
| 33 | 29 01 | 28 40 | 27 04 | 25 56 | 24 55 |
| 34 | 29 19 | 28 59 | 27 20 | 26 06 | 25 00 |
| 35 | 29 37 | 29 19 | 27 36 | 26 17 | 25 04 |
| 36 | 29 55 | 29 38 | 27 52 | 26 27 | 25 08 |
| 37 | 00♋15 | 29 59 | 28 09 | 26 38 | 25 13 |
| 38 | 00 34 | 00♌19 | 28 25 | 26 49 | 25 17 |
| 39 | 00 55 | 00 40 | 28 42 | 27 00 | 25 22 |
| 40 | 01 16 | 01 01 | 28 59 | 27 11 | 25 27 |
| 41 | 01 38 | 01 23 | 29 17 | 27 22 | 25 31 |
| 42 | 02 01 | 01 45 | 29 34 | 27 34 | 25 36 |
| 43 | 02 24 | 02 08 | 29 52 | 27 45 | 25 41 |
| 44 | 02 48 | 02 31 | 00♍10 | 27 57 | 25 47 |
| 45 | 03 14 | 02 54 | 00 28 | 28 09 | 25 52 |
| 46 | 03 40 | 03 18 | 00 47 | 28 21 | 25 57 |
| 47 | 04 08 | 03 43 | 01 06 | 28 34 | 26 03 |
| 48 | 04 36 | 04 08 | 01 25 | 28 46 | 26 09 |
| 49 | 05 06 | 04 34 | 01 44 | 28 59 | 26 15 |
| 50 | 05 38 | 05 01 | 02 04 | 29 12 | 26 21 |
| 51 | 06 11 | 05 28 | 02 25 | 29 26 | 26 28 |
| 52 | 06 46 | 05 56 | 02 45 | 29 40 | 26 34 |
| 53 | 07 22 | 06 25 | 03 07 | 29 54 | 26 42 |
| 54 | 08 01 | 06 54 | 03 28 | 00♎09 | 26 49 |
| 55 | 08 42 | 07 25 | 03 50 | 00 24 | 26 57 |
| 56 | 09 26 | 07 56 | 04 13 | 00 40 | 27 05 |
| 57 | 10 12 | 08 28 | 04 36 | 00 56 | 27 14 |
| 58 | 11 02 | 09 02 | 05 00 | 01 13 | 27 23 |
| 59 | 11 55 | 09 36 | 05 25 | 01 30 | 27 34 |
| 60 | 12♋52 | 10♌11 | 05♍50 | 01♎49 | 27♎44 |

**3h 28m 0s — 52° 0' 0" — 24 ♉ 22**

| LAT. | 11 | 12 | ASC | 2 | 3 |
|---|---|---|---|---|---|
| 0 | 22♊39 | 20♋20 | 19♌35 | 21♍17 | 23♎46 |
| 5 | 23 35 | 21 41 | 20 54 | 22 12 | 24 06 |
| 10 | 24 33 | 23 00 | 22 11 | 23 04 | 24 25 |
| 15 | 25 33 | 24 20 | 23 25 | 23 54 | 24 44 |
| 20 | 26 36 | 25 41 | 24 39 | 24 43 | 25 02 |
| 21 | 26 50 | 25 57 | 24 53 | 24 52 | 25 06 |
| 22 | 27 03 | 26 14 | 25 08 | 25 02 | 25 10 |
| 23 | 27 17 | 26 30 | 25 23 | 25 12 | 25 13 |
| 24 | 27 31 | 26 47 | 25 38 | 25 21 | 25 17 |
| 25 | 27 45 | 27 04 | 25 53 | 25 31 | 25 21 |
| 26 | 27 59 | 27 21 | 26 07 | 25 41 | 25 25 |
| 27 | 28 14 | 27 39 | 26 22 | 25 51 | 25 28 |
| 28 | 28 29 | 27 56 | 26 37 | 26 00 | 25 32 |
| 29 | 28 44 | 28 14 | 26 52 | 26 10 | 25 36 |
| 30 | 29 00 | 28 32 | 27 08 | 26 20 | 25 40 |
| 31 | 29 16 | 28 50 | 27 23 | 26 30 | 25 44 |
| 32 | 29 33 | 29 08 | 27 38 | 26 40 | 25 48 |
| 33 | 29 50 | 29 27 | 27 54 | 26 50 | 25 52 |
| 34 | 00♋07 | 29 46 | 28 09 | 27 00 | 25 56 |
| 35 | 00 25 | 00♌05 | 28 25 | 27 10 | 26 00 |
| 36 | 00 43 | 00 24 | 28 41 | 27 20 | 26 04 |
| 37 | 01 02 | 00 44 | 28 57 | 27 31 | 26 08 |
| 38 | 01 21 | 01 04 | 29 14 | 27 41 | 26 13 |
| 39 | 01 41 | 01 24 | 29 30 | 27 52 | 26 17 |
| 40 | 02 02 | 01 45 | 29 47 | 28 03 | 26 22 |
| 41 | 02 23 | 02 06 | 00♍03 | 28 14 | 26 26 |
| 42 | 02 45 | 02 28 | 00 21 | 28 25 | 26 31 |
| 43 | 03 08 | 02 50 | 00 38 | 28 36 | 26 36 |
| 44 | 03 32 | 03 13 | 00 55 | 28 47 | 26 41 |
| 45 | 03 57 | 03 36 | 01 13 | 28 59 | 26 46 |
| 46 | 04 23 | 03 59 | 01 31 | 29 11 | 26 51 |
| 47 | 04 49 | 04 23 | 01 50 | 29 23 | 26 56 |
| 48 | 05 17 | 04 48 | 02 09 | 29 35 | 27 02 |
| 49 | 05 47 | 05 13 | 02 28 | 29 48 | 27 08 |
| 50 | 06 17 | 05 39 | 02 47 | 00♎00 | 27 14 |
| 51 | 06 50 | 06 05 | 03 07 | 00 14 | 27 20 |
| 52 | 07 23 | 06 33 | 03 27 | 00 27 | 27 27 |
| 53 | 07 59 | 07 01 | 03 48 | 00 41 | 27 34 |
| 54 | 08 37 | 07 30 | 04 09 | 00 55 | 27 41 |
| 55 | 09 17 | 07 59 | 04 30 | 01 10 | 27 49 |
| 56 | 09 59 | 08 30 | 04 53 | 01 25 | 27 57 |
| 57 | 10 44 | 09 01 | 05 15 | 01 41 | 28 05 |
| 58 | 11 32 | 09 33 | 05 38 | 01 58 | 28 15 |
| 59 | 12 24 | 10 07 | 06 02 | 02 15 | 28 25 |
| 60 | 13♋19 | 10♌41 | 06♍27 | 02♎33 | 28♎35 |

**3h 32m 0s — 53° 0' 0" — 25 ♉ 21**

| LAT. | 11 | 12 | ASC | 2 | 3 |
|---|---|---|---|---|---|
| 0 | 23♊34 | 21♋17 | 20♌36 | 22♍23 | 24♎50 |
| 5 | 24 30 | 22 36 | 21 54 | 23 16 | 25 09 |
| 10 | 25 27 | 23 54 | 23 09 | 24 06 | 25 27 |
| 15 | 26 26 | 25 12 | 24 21 | 24 54 | 25 44 |
| 20 | 27 28 | 26 32 | 25 33 | 25 41 | 26 01 |
| 21 | 27 41 | 26 48 | 25 48 | 25 50 | 26 05 |
| 22 | 27 55 | 27 04 | 26 02 | 26 00 | 26 08 |
| 23 | 28 08 | 27 21 | 26 17 | 26 09 | 26 12 |
| 24 | 28 22 | 27 37 | 26 31 | 26 18 | 26 15 |
| 25 | 28 36 | 27 54 | 26 46 | 26 28 | 26 19 |
| 26 | 28 50 | 28 11 | 27 00 | 26 37 | 26 22 |
| 27 | 29 04 | 28 28 | 27 15 | 26 47 | 26 26 |
| 28 | 29 19 | 28 45 | 27 29 | 26 56 | 26 29 |
| 29 | 29 34 | 29 02 | 27 44 | 27 05 | 26 33 |
| 30 | 29 50 | 29 20 | 27 59 | 27 15 | 26 37 |
| 31 | 00♋05 | 29 38 | 28 14 | 27 25 | 26 40 |
| 32 | 00 21 | 29 56 | 28 29 | 27 34 | 26 44 |
| 33 | 00 38 | 00♌14 | 28 44 | 27 44 | 26 48 |
| 34 | 00 55 | 00 32 | 28 59 | 27 54 | 26 52 |
| 35 | 01 12 | 00 51 | 29 15 | 28 04 | 26 56 |
| 36 | 01 30 | 01 10 | 29 30 | 28 13 | 27 00 |
| 37 | 01 49 | 01 29 | 29 46 | 28 24 | 27 04 |
| 38 | 02 08 | 01 49 | 00♍02 | 28 34 | 27 08 |
| 39 | 02 27 | 02 09 | 00 18 | 28 44 | 27 12 |
| 40 | 02 48 | 02 29 | 00 34 | 28 54 | 27 16 |
| 41 | 03 09 | 02 50 | 00 50 | 29 05 | 27 21 |
| 42 | 03 30 | 03 11 | 01 07 | 29 16 | 27 25 |
| 43 | 03 53 | 03 33 | 01 24 | 29 27 | 27 30 |
| 44 | 04 16 | 03 55 | 01 41 | 29 38 | 27 35 |
| 45 | 04 40 | 04 17 | 01 58 | 29 49 | 27 39 |
| 46 | 05 05 | 04 40 | 02 16 | 00♎00 | 27 44 |
| 47 | 05 31 | 05 03 | 02 34 | 00 12 | 27 50 |
| 48 | 05 59 | 05 28 | 02 52 | 00 24 | 27 55 |
| 49 | 06 27 | 05 52 | 03 11 | 00 36 | 28 01 |
| 50 | 06 57 | 06 17 | 03 30 | 00 49 | 28 07 |
| 51 | 07 28 | 06 43 | 03 49 | 01 01 | 28 13 |
| 52 | 08 01 | 07 10 | 04 09 | 01 15 | 28 19 |
| 53 | 08 36 | 07 37 | 04 29 | 01 28 | 28 26 |
| 54 | 09 13 | 08 05 | 04 49 | 01 42 | 28 33 |
| 55 | 09 51 | 08 34 | 05 10 | 01 56 | 28 40 |
| 56 | 10 32 | 09 03 | 05 32 | 02 11 | 28 48 |
| 57 | 11 16 | 09 34 | 05 54 | 02 27 | 28 57 |
| 58 | 12 03 | 10 05 | 06 17 | 02 43 | 29 06 |
| 59 | 12 52 | 10 38 | 06 40 | 03 00 | 29 16 |
| 60 | 13♋46 | 11♌11 | 07♍04 | 03♎17 | 29♎26 |

**3h 36m 0s — 54° 0' 0" — 26 ♉ 19**

| LAT. | 11 | 12 | ASC | 2 | 3 |
|---|---|---|---|---|---|
| 0 | 24♊30 | 22♋13 | 21♌37 | 23♍28 | 25♎53 |
| 5 | 25 24 | 23 31 | 22 54 | 24 19 | 26 11 |
| 10 | 26 20 | 24 48 | 24 07 | 25 07 | 26 28 |
| 15 | 27 19 | 26 05 | 25 18 | 25 54 | 26 44 |
| 20 | 28 20 | 27 23 | 26 28 | 26 39 | 27 00 |
| 21 | 28 33 | 27 39 | 26 42 | 26 48 | 27 03 |
| 22 | 28 46 | 27 55 | 26 56 | 26 57 | 27 07 |
| 23 | 28 59 | 28 11 | 27 10 | 27 06 | 27 10 |
| 24 | 29 13 | 28 27 | 27 24 | 27 15 | 27 13 |
| 25 | 29 26 | 28 44 | 27 39 | 27 24 | 27 17 |
| 26 | 29 40 | 29 00 | 27 53 | 27 33 | 27 20 |
| 27 | 29 55 | 29 17 | 28 07 | 27 42 | 27 23 |
| 28 | 00♋09 | 29 34 | 28 21 | 27 52 | 27 27 |
| 29 | 00 24 | 29 51 | 28 36 | 28 01 | 27 30 |
| 30 | 00 39 | 00♌08 | 28 50 | 28 10 | 27 34 |
| 31 | 00 54 | 00 25 | 29 05 | 28 19 | 27 37 |
| 32 | 01 10 | 00 43 | 29 19 | 28 28 | 27 41 |
| 33 | 01 27 | 01 01 | 29 34 | 28 38 | 27 44 |
| 34 | 01 43 | 01 19 | 29 49 | 28 47 | 27 48 |
| 35 | 02 00 | 01 37 | 00♍04 | 28 57 | 27 51 |
| 36 | 02 18 | 01 56 | 00 19 | 29 06 | 27 55 |
| 37 | 02 36 | 02 15 | 00 34 | 29 16 | 27 59 |
| 38 | 02 54 | 02 34 | 00 50 | 29 26 | 28 03 |
| 39 | 03 14 | 02 53 | 01 06 | 29 36 | 28 07 |
| 40 | 03 33 | 03 13 | 01 21 | 29 46 | 28 11 |
| 41 | 03 54 | 03 34 | 01 37 | 29 56 | 28 15 |
| 42 | 04 15 | 03 54 | 01 54 | 00♎07 | 28 19 |
| 43 | 04 37 | 04 15 | 02 10 | 00 17 | 28 24 |
| 44 | 04 59 | 04 37 | 02 27 | 00 28 | 28 28 |
| 45 | 05 23 | 04 59 | 02 44 | 00 39 | 28 33 |
| 46 | 05 47 | 05 21 | 03 01 | 00 50 | 28 38 |
| 47 | 06 13 | 05 44 | 03 18 | 01 01 | 28 43 |
| 48 | 06 40 | 06 07 | 03 36 | 01 13 | 28 48 |
| 49 | 07 07 | 06 31 | 03 54 | 01 24 | 28 53 |
| 50 | 07 36 | 06 56 | 04 13 | 01 37 | 28 59 |
| 51 | 08 07 | 07 21 | 04 31 | 01 49 | 29 05 |
| 52 | 08 39 | 07 47 | 04 51 | 02 02 | 29 11 |
| 53 | 09 13 | 08 13 | 05 10 | 02 15 | 29 17 |
| 54 | 09 48 | 08 41 | 05 30 | 02 28 | 29 24 |
| 55 | 10 26 | 09 09 | 05 51 | 02 42 | 29 31 |
| 56 | 11 06 | 09 37 | 06 11 | 02 57 | 29 39 |
| 57 | 11 48 | 10 07 | 06 33 | 03 12 | 29 47 |
| 58 | 12 33 | 10 37 | 06 55 | 03 28 | 29 56 |
| 59 | 13 21 | 11 09 | 07 17 | 03 44 | 00♏06 |
| 60 | 14♋13 | 11♌41 | 07♍40 | 04♎02 | 00♏17 |

**3h 40m 0s — 55° 0' 0" — 27 ♉ 17**

| LAT. | 11 | 12 | ASC | 2 | 3 |
|---|---|---|---|---|---|
| 0 | 25♊25 | 23♋10 | 22♌39 | 24♍33 | 26♎57 |
| 5 | 26 19 | 24 27 | 23 54 | 25 22 | 27 13 |
| 10 | 27 14 | 25 42 | 25 05 | 26 09 | 27 29 |
| 15 | 28 11 | 26 58 | 26 14 | 26 54 | 27 44 |
| 20 | 29 12 | 28 15 | 27 23 | 27 37 | 27 59 |
| 21 | 29 25 | 28 30 | 27 37 | 27 46 | 28 02 |
| 22 | 29 37 | 28 46 | 27 50 | 27 55 | 28 05 |
| 23 | 29 50 | 29 02 | 28 04 | 28 04 | 28 08 |
| 24 | 00♋04 | 29 18 | 28 18 | 28 12 | 28 11 |
| 25 | 00 17 | 29 34 | 28 32 | 28 21 | 28 14 |
| 26 | 00 31 | 29 50 | 28 46 | 28 30 | 28 17 |
| 27 | 00 45 | 00♌06 | 28 59 | 28 38 | 28 20 |
| 28 | 00 59 | 00 23 | 29 13 | 28 47 | 28 24 |
| 29 | 01 13 | 00 39 | 29 27 | 28 56 | 28 27 |
| 30 | 01 28 | 00 56 | 29 42 | 29 05 | 28 30 |
| 31 | 01 43 | 01 13 | 29 56 | 29 14 | 28 33 |
| 32 | 01 59 | 01 30 | 00♍10 | 29 23 | 28 37 |
| 33 | 02 15 | 01 48 | 00 24 | 29 32 | 28 40 |
| 34 | 02 31 | 02 05 | 00 39 | 29 41 | 28 43 |
| 35 | 02 48 | 02 23 | 00 53 | 29 50 | 28 47 |
| 36 | 03 05 | 02 42 | 01 08 | 29 59 | 28 50 |
| 37 | 03 23 | 03 00 | 01 23 | 00♎09 | 28 54 |
| 38 | 03 41 | 03 19 | 01 38 | 00 18 | 28 58 |
| 39 | 04 00 | 03 38 | 01 53 | 00 28 | 29 01 |
| 40 | 04 19 | 03 57 | 02 09 | 00 37 | 29 05 |
| 41 | 04 39 | 04 17 | 02 24 | 00 47 | 29 09 |
| 42 | 05 00 | 04 37 | 02 40 | 00 57 | 29 13 |
| 43 | 05 21 | 04 58 | 02 56 | 01 07 | 29 17 |
| 44 | 05 43 | 05 19 | 03 12 | 01 18 | 29 22 |
| 45 | 06 06 | 05 40 | 03 29 | 01 28 | 29 26 |
| 46 | 06 30 | 06 02 | 03 46 | 01 39 | 29 31 |
| 47 | 06 55 | 06 24 | 04 03 | 01 50 | 29 36 |
| 48 | 07 21 | 06 47 | 04 20 | 02 01 | 29 40 |
| 49 | 07 48 | 07 10 | 04 37 | 02 13 | 29 46 |
| 50 | 08 16 | 07 34 | 04 55 | 02 24 | 29 51 |
| 51 | 08 46 | 07 59 | 05 14 | 02 36 | 29 57 |
| 52 | 09 17 | 08 24 | 05 32 | 02 49 | 00♏03 |
| 53 | 09 49 | 08 50 | 05 51 | 03 02 | 00 09 |
| 54 | 10 24 | 09 16 | 06 11 | 03 15 | 00 15 |
| 55 | 11 00 | 09 43 | 06 31 | 03 28 | 00 23 |
| 56 | 11 39 | 10 11 | 06 51 | 03 43 | 00 30 |
| 57 | 12 20 | 10 40 | 07 12 | 03 57 | 00 38 |
| 58 | 13 04 | 11 09 | 07 33 | 04 13 | 00 47 |
| 59 | 13 50 | 11 40 | 07 55 | 04 29 | 00 56 |
| 60 | 14♋40 | 12♌11 | 08♍17 | 04♎46 | 01♏07 |

# Koch Table of Houses for Latitudes 0° to 60° North

**3h 44m 0s — 56° 0' 0" — 28 ♉ 15**

| LAT. | 11 | 12 | ASC | 2 | 3 |
|---|---|---|---|---|---|
| 0 | 26♊20 | 24♋06 | 23♌41 | 25♍38 | 28♎00 |
| 5 | 27 13 | 25 22 | 24 53 | 26 26 | 28 15 |
| 10 | 28 08 | 26 37 | 26 03 | 27 11 | 28 29 |
| 15 | 29 04 | 27 51 | 27 11 | 27 54 | 28 43 |
| 20 | 00♋04 | 29 06 | 28 18 | 28 36 | 28 57 |
| 21 | 00 16 | 29 22 | 28 31 | 28 44 | 29 00 |
| 22 | 00 29 | 29 37 | 28 45 | 28 52 | 29 03 |
| 23 | 00 42 | 29 52 | 28 58 | 29 01 | 29 06 |
| 24 | 00 55 | 00♌08 | 29 11 | 29 09 | 29 09 |
| 25 | 01 08 | 00 24 | 29 25 | 29 17 | 29 12 |
| 26 | 01 21 | 00 39 | 29 38 | 29 26 | 29 15 |
| 27 | 01 35 | 00 55 | 29 52 | 29 34 | 29 18 |
| 28 | 01 49 | 01 12 | 00♍06 | 29 43 | 29 20 |
| 29 | 02 03 | 01 28 | 00 19 | 29 51 | 29 23 |
| 30 | 02 18 | 01 44 | 00 33 | 00♎00 | 29 26 |
| 31 | 02 32 | 02 01 | 00 47 | 00 08 | 29 30 |
| 32 | 02 48 | 02 18 | 01 01 | 00 17 | 29 33 |
| 33 | 03 03 | 02 35 | 01 15 | 00 26 | 29 36 |
| 34 | 03 19 | 02 52 | 01 29 | 00 34 | 29 39 |
| 35 | 03 36 | 03 10 | 01 43 | 00 43 | 29 42 |
| 36 | 03 52 | 03 28 | 01 57 | 00 52 | 29 46 |
| 37 | 04 10 | 03 46 | 02 12 | 01 01 | 29 49 |
| 38 | 04 27 | 04 04 | 02 26 | 01 10 | 29 52 |
| 39 | 04 46 | 04 23 | 02 41 | 01 19 | 29 56 |
| 40 | 05 05 | 04 41 | 02 56 | 01 29 | 00♏00 |
| 41 | 05 24 | 05 01 | 03 11 | 01 38 | 00 03 |
| 42 | 05 44 | 05 20 | 03 27 | 01 48 | 00 07 |
| 43 | 06 05 | 05 40 | 03 42 | 01 58 | 00 11 |
| 44 | 06 27 | 06 01 | 03 58 | 02 08 | 00 15 |
| 45 | 06 49 | 06 22 | 04 14 | 02 18 | 00 19 |
| 46 | 07 12 | 06 43 | 04 30 | 02 28 | 00 24 |
| 47 | 07 36 | 07 05 | 04 47 | 02 39 | 00 28 |
| 48 | 08 02 | 07 27 | 05 04 | 02 50 | 00 33 |
| 49 | 08 28 | 07 50 | 05 21 | 03 01 | 00 38 |
| 50 | 08 55 | 08 13 | 05 38 | 03 12 | 00 43 |
| 51 | 09 24 | 08 37 | 05 56 | 03 24 | 00 48 |
| 52 | 09 54 | 09 01 | 06 14 | 03 36 | 00 54 |
| 53 | 10 26 | 09 26 | 06 32 | 03 48 | 01 00 |
| 54 | 11 00 | 09 52 | 06 51 | 04 01 | 01 06 |
| 55 | 11 35 | 10 18 | 07 11 | 04 14 | 01 13 |
| 56 | 12 12 | 10 45 | 07 30 | 04 28 | 01 21 |
| 57 | 12 52 | 11 13 | 07 51 | 04 43 | 01 29 |
| 58 | 13 34 | 11 42 | 08 11 | 04 58 | 01 37 |
| 59 | 14 19 | 12 11 | 08 33 | 05 13 | 01 47 |
| 60 | 15♋08 | 12♌41 | 08♍54 | 05♎30 | 01♏57 |

**3h 48m 0s — 57° 0' 0" — 29 ♉ 13**

| LAT. | 11 | 12 | ASC | 2 | 3 |
|---|---|---|---|---|---|
| 0 | 27♊15 | 25♋03 | 24♌42 | 26♍44 | 29♎03 |
| 5 | 28 08 | 26 18 | 25 54 | 27 29 | 29 17 |
| 10 | 29 01 | 27 31 | 27 02 | 28 12 | 29 30 |
| 15 | 29 57 | 28 44 | 28 08 | 28 53 | 29 43 |
| 20 | 00♋56 | 29 58 | 29 13 | 29 34 | 29 56 |
| 21 | 01 08 | 00♌13 | 29 26 | 29 42 | 29 58 |
| 22 | 01 20 | 00 28 | 29 39 | 29 50 | 00♏01 |
| 23 | 01 33 | 00 43 | 29 52 | 29 58 | 00 04 |
| 24 | 01 45 | 00 58 | 00♍05 | 00♎06 | 00 06 |
| 25 | 01 58 | 01 14 | 00 18 | 00 14 | 00 09 |
| 26 | 02 12 | 01 29 | 00 31 | 00 22 | 00 12 |
| 27 | 02 25 | 01 45 | 00 44 | 00 30 | 00 14 |
| 28 | 02 39 | 02 01 | 00 58 | 00 38 | 00 17 |
| 29 | 02 53 | 02 17 | 01 11 | 00 46 | 00 20 |
| 30 | 03 07 | 02 33 | 01 24 | 00 54 | 00 23 |
| 31 | 03 21 | 02 49 | 01 38 | 01 03 | 00 26 |
| 32 | 03 36 | 03 05 | 01 51 | 01 11 | 00 28 |
| 33 | 03 52 | 03 22 | 02 05 | 01 19 | 00 31 |
| 34 | 04 07 | 03 39 | 02 19 | 01 28 | 00 34 |
| 35 | 04 23 | 03 56 | 02 32 | 01 36 | 00 37 |
| 36 | 04 40 | 04 13 | 02 46 | 01 45 | 00 40 |
| 37 | 04 56 | 04 31 | 03 00 | 01 53 | 00 44 |
| 38 | 05 14 | 04 49 | 03 15 | 02 02 | 00 47 |
| 39 | 05 32 | 05 07 | 03 29 | 02 11 | 00 50 |
| 40 | 05 50 | 05 26 | 03 44 | 02 20 | 00 54 |
| 41 | 06 09 | 05 44 | 03 58 | 02 29 | 00 57 |
| 42 | 06 29 | 06 04 | 04 13 | 02 39 | 01 01 |
| 43 | 06 49 | 06 23 | 04 28 | 02 48 | 01 04 |
| 44 | 07 10 | 06 43 | 04 44 | 02 58 | 01 08 |
| 45 | 07 32 | 07 03 | 04 59 | 03 07 | 01 12 |
| 46 | 07 55 | 07 24 | 05 15 | 03 17 | 01 16 |
| 47 | 08 18 | 07 45 | 05 31 | 03 28 | 01 21 |
| 48 | 08 43 | 08 07 | 05 47 | 03 38 | 01 25 |
| 49 | 09 08 | 08 29 | 06 04 | 03 49 | 01 30 |
| 50 | 09 35 | 08 51 | 06 21 | 04 00 | 01 35 |
| 51 | 10 03 | 09 15 | 06 38 | 04 11 | 01 40 |
| 52 | 10 32 | 09 38 | 06 56 | 04 23 | 01 45 |
| 53 | 11 03 | 10 03 | 07 14 | 04 35 | 01 51 |
| 54 | 11 35 | 10 28 | 07 32 | 04 47 | 01 57 |
| 55 | 12 10 | 10 53 | 07 51 | 05 00 | 02 04 |
| 56 | 12 46 | 11 19 | 08 10 | 05 14 | 02 11 |
| 57 | 13 24 | 11 46 | 08 30 | 05 28 | 02 19 |
| 58 | 14 05 | 12 14 | 08 50 | 05 42 | 02 27 |
| 59 | 14 49 | 12 42 | 09 10 | 05 58 | 02 36 |
| 60 | 15♋35 | 13♌11 | 09♍31 | 06♎14 | 02♏47 |

**3h 52m 0s — 58° 0' 0" — 00 ♊ 11**

| LAT. | 11 | 12 | ASC | 2 | 3 |
|---|---|---|---|---|---|
| 0 | 28♊10 | 26♋00 | 25♌44 | 27♍49 | 00♏06 |
| 5 | 29 02 | 27 13 | 26 54 | 28 33 | 00 18 |
| 10 | 29 55 | 28 25 | 28 00 | 29 14 | 00 30 |
| 15 | 00♋50 | 29 37 | 29 05 | 29 53 | 00 42 |
| 20 | 01 47 | 00♌49 | 00♍08 | 00♎32 | 00 54 |
| 21 | 01 59 | 01 04 | 00 21 | 00 40 | 00 56 |
| 22 | 02 11 | 01 19 | 00 33 | 00 47 | 00 59 |
| 23 | 02 24 | 01 34 | 00 46 | 00 55 | 01 01 |
| 24 | 02 36 | 01 49 | 00 59 | 01 03 | 01 04 |
| 25 | 02 49 | 02 04 | 01 11 | 01 10 | 01 06 |
| 26 | 03 02 | 02 19 | 01 24 | 01 18 | 01 09 |
| 27 | 03 15 | 02 34 | 01 37 | 01 26 | 01 11 |
| 28 | 03 28 | 02 50 | 01 50 | 01 33 | 01 14 |
| 29 | 03 42 | 03 05 | 02 03 | 01 41 | 01 16 |
| 30 | 03 56 | 03 21 | 02 16 | 01 49 | 01 19 |
| 31 | 04 10 | 03 37 | 02 29 | 01 57 | 01 21 |
| 32 | 04 25 | 03 53 | 02 42 | 02 05 | 01 24 |
| 33 | 04 40 | 04 09 | 02 55 | 02 13 | 01 27 |
| 34 | 04 55 | 04 26 | 03 08 | 02 21 | 01 29 |
| 35 | 05 11 | 04 42 | 03 22 | 02 29 | 01 32 |
| 36 | 05 27 | 04 59 | 03 35 | 02 37 | 01 35 |
| 37 | 05 43 | 05 17 | 03 49 | 02 46 | 01 38 |
| 38 | 06 00 | 05 34 | 04 03 | 02 54 | 01 41 |
| 39 | 06 18 | 05 52 | 04 17 | 03 03 | 01 44 |
| 40 | 06 36 | 06 10 | 04 31 | 03 11 | 01 47 |
| 41 | 06 54 | 06 28 | 04 45 | 03 20 | 01 51 |
| 42 | 07 13 | 06 47 | 05 00 | 03 29 | 01 54 |
| 43 | 07 33 | 07 06 | 05 15 | 03 38 | 01 57 |
| 44 | 07 54 | 07 25 | 05 29 | 03 47 | 02 01 |
| 45 | 08 15 | 07 45 | 05 44 | 03 57 | 02 05 |
| 46 | 08 37 | 08 05 | 06 00 | 04 06 | 02 09 |
| 47 | 09 00 | 08 26 | 06 15 | 04 16 | 02 13 |
| 48 | 09 24 | 08 47 | 06 31 | 04 26 | 02 17 |
| 49 | 09 49 | 09 08 | 06 47 | 04 37 | 02 21 |
| 50 | 10 14 | 09 30 | 07 04 | 04 47 | 02 26 |
| 51 | 10 42 | 09 53 | 07 20 | 04 58 | 02 31 |
| 52 | 11 10 | 10 16 | 07 38 | 05 10 | 02 36 |
| 53 | 11 40 | 10 39 | 07 55 | 05 21 | 02 42 |
| 54 | 12 11 | 11 03 | 08 13 | 05 33 | 02 48 |
| 55 | 12 44 | 11 28 | 08 31 | 05 46 | 02 54 |
| 56 | 13 19 | 11 54 | 08 49 | 05 59 | 03 01 |
| 57 | 13 57 | 12 20 | 09 08 | 06 12 | 03 09 |
| 58 | 14 36 | 12 46 | 09 28 | 06 27 | 03 17 |
| 59 | 15 18 | 13 14 | 09 48 | 06 42 | 03 26 |
| 60 | 16♋03 | 13♌42 | 10♍08 | 06♎58 | 03♏36 |

**3h 56m 0s — 59° 0' 0" — 01 ♊ 08**

| LAT. | 11 | 12 | ASC | 2 | 3 |
|---|---|---|---|---|---|
| 0 | 29♊05 | 26♋57 | 26♌47 | 28♍55 | 01♏08 |
| 5 | 29 56 | 28 09 | 27 54 | 29 36 | 01 20 |
| 10 | 00♋48 | 29 20 | 28 59 | 00♎15 | 01 31 |
| 15 | 01 42 | 00♌30 | 00♍02 | 00 53 | 01 41 |
| 20 | 02 39 | 01 41 | 01 03 | 01 30 | 01 52 |
| 21 | 02 51 | 01 56 | 01 16 | 01 37 | 01 54 |
| 22 | 03 03 | 02 10 | 01 28 | 01 45 | 01 56 |
| 23 | 03 15 | 02 24 | 01 40 | 01 52 | 01 59 |
| 24 | 03 27 | 02 39 | 01 52 | 01 59 | 02 01 |
| 25 | 03 39 | 02 54 | 02 05 | 02 07 | 02 03 |
| 26 | 03 52 | 03 09 | 02 17 | 02 14 | 02 05 |
| 27 | 04 05 | 03 24 | 02 30 | 02 21 | 02 08 |
| 28 | 04 18 | 03 39 | 02 42 | 02 29 | 02 10 |
| 29 | 04 31 | 03 54 | 02 55 | 02 36 | 02 12 |
| 30 | 04 45 | 04 09 | 03 07 | 02 44 | 02 15 |
| 31 | 04 59 | 04 25 | 03 20 | 02 51 | 02 17 |
| 32 | 05 13 | 04 41 | 03 33 | 02 59 | 02 19 |
| 33 | 05 28 | 04 56 | 03 46 | 03 07 | 02 22 |
| 34 | 05 43 | 05 13 | 03 58 | 03 14 | 02 24 |
| 35 | 05 58 | 05 29 | 04 11 | 03 22 | 02 27 |
| 36 | 06 14 | 05 45 | 04 25 | 03 30 | 02 30 |
| 37 | 06 30 | 06 02 | 04 38 | 03 38 | 02 32 |
| 38 | 06 47 | 06 19 | 04 51 | 03 46 | 02 35 |
| 39 | 07 04 | 06 37 | 05 05 | 03 54 | 02 38 |
| 40 | 07 21 | 06 54 | 05 19 | 04 03 | 02 41 |
| 41 | 07 39 | 07 12 | 05 32 | 04 11 | 02 44 |
| 42 | 07 58 | 07 30 | 05 46 | 04 20 | 02 47 |
| 43 | 08 17 | 07 49 | 06 01 | 04 28 | 02 50 |
| 44 | 08 37 | 08 07 | 06 15 | 04 37 | 02 54 |
| 45 | 08 58 | 08 27 | 06 30 | 04 46 | 02 57 |
| 46 | 09 19 | 08 46 | 06 45 | 04 55 | 03 01 |
| 47 | 09 42 | 09 06 | 07 00 | 05 05 | 03 05 |
| 48 | 10 05 | 09 27 | 07 15 | 05 15 | 03 09 |
| 49 | 10 29 | 09 48 | 07 31 | 05 25 | 03 13 |
| 50 | 10 54 | 10 09 | 07 47 | 05 35 | 03 17 |
| 51 | 11 20 | 10 31 | 08 03 | 05 45 | 03 22 |
| 52 | 11 48 | 10 53 | 08 19 | 05 56 | 03 27 |
| 53 | 12 17 | 11 16 | 08 36 | 06 07 | 03 32 |
| 54 | 12 47 | 11 39 | 08 53 | 06 19 | 03 38 |
| 55 | 13 19 | 12 03 | 09 11 | 06 31 | 03 44 |
| 56 | 13 53 | 12 28 | 09 29 | 06 44 | 03 51 |
| 57 | 14 29 | 12 53 | 09 47 | 06 57 | 03 58 |
| 58 | 15 07 | 13 19 | 10 06 | 07 11 | 04 06 |
| 59 | 15 47 | 13 45 | 10 26 | 07 26 | 04 15 |
| 60 | 16♋31 | 14♌12 | 10♍46 | 07♎41 | 04♏25 |

**4h 0m 0s — 60° 0' 0" — 02 ♊ 05**

| LAT. | 11 | 12 | ASC | 2 | 3 |
|---|---|---|---|---|---|
| 0 | 00♋00 | 27♋55 | 27♌49 | 00♎00 | 02♏11 |
| 5 | 00 51 | 29 05 | 28 55 | 00 40 | 02 21 |
| 10 | 01 42 | 00♌15 | 29 58 | 01 17 | 02 31 |
| 15 | 02 35 | 01 23 | 00♍59 | 01 53 | 02 40 |
| 20 | 03 31 | 02 33 | 01 58 | 02 28 | 02 50 |
| 21 | 03 42 | 02 47 | 02 10 | 02 35 | 02 52 |
| 22 | 03 54 | 03 01 | 02 22 | 02 42 | 02 54 |
| 23 | 04 06 | 03 15 | 02 34 | 02 49 | 02 56 |
| 24 | 04 18 | 03 30 | 02 46 | 02 56 | 02 58 |
| 25 | 04 30 | 03 44 | 02 58 | 03 03 | 03 00 |
| 26 | 04 42 | 03 58 | 03 10 | 03 10 | 03 02 |
| 27 | 04 55 | 04 13 | 03 22 | 03 17 | 03 04 |
| 28 | 05 08 | 04 28 | 03 34 | 03 24 | 03 06 |
| 29 | 05 21 | 04 43 | 03 47 | 03 31 | 03 08 |
| 30 | 05 34 | 04 58 | 03 59 | 03 38 | 03 10 |
| 31 | 05 48 | 05 13 | 04 11 | 03 46 | 03 12 |
| 32 | 06 02 | 05 28 | 04 23 | 03 53 | 03 15 |
| 33 | 06 16 | 05 44 | 04 36 | 04 00 | 03 17 |
| 34 | 06 31 | 05 59 | 04 48 | 04 07 | 03 19 |
| 35 | 06 46 | 06 15 | 05 01 | 04 15 | 03 22 |
| 36 | 07 01 | 06 31 | 05 14 | 04 22 | 03 24 |
| 37 | 07 17 | 06 48 | 05 27 | 04 30 | 03 26 |
| 38 | 07 33 | 07 04 | 05 40 | 04 38 | 03 29 |
| 39 | 07 49 | 07 21 | 05 53 | 04 46 | 03 32 |
| 40 | 08 07 | 07 38 | 06 06 | 04 54 | 03 34 |
| 41 | 08 24 | 07 56 | 06 20 | 05 02 | 03 37 |
| 42 | 08 42 | 08 13 | 06 33 | 05 10 | 03 40 |
| 43 | 09 01 | 08 31 | 06 47 | 05 18 | 03 43 |
| 44 | 09 21 | 08 50 | 07 01 | 05 27 | 03 46 |
| 45 | 09 41 | 09 09 | 07 15 | 05 35 | 03 49 |
| 46 | 10 02 | 09 28 | 07 29 | 05 44 | 03 53 |
| 47 | 10 23 | 09 47 | 07 44 | 05 53 | 03 56 |
| 48 | 10 46 | 10 07 | 07 59 | 06 03 | 04 00 |
| 49 | 11 09 | 10 27 | 08 14 | 06 12 | 04 04 |
| 50 | 11 34 | 10 48 | 08 29 | 06 22 | 04 08 |
| 51 | 11 59 | 11 09 | 08 45 | 06 32 | 04 13 |
| 52 | 12 26 | 11 31 | 09 01 | 06 43 | 04 18 |
| 53 | 12 54 | 11 53 | 09 17 | 06 54 | 04 23 |
| 54 | 13 23 | 12 15 | 09 34 | 07 05 | 04 28 |
| 55 | 13 54 | 12 39 | 09 51 | 07 17 | 04 34 |
| 56 | 14 27 | 13 02 | 10 09 | 07 29 | 04 41 |
| 57 | 15 01 | 13 27 | 10 26 | 07 42 | 04 48 |
| 58 | 15 38 | 13 51 | 10 45 | 07 55 | 04 56 |
| 59 | 16 17 | 14 17 | 11 03 | 08 10 | 05 04 |
| 60 | 16♋59 | 14♌43 | 11♍23 | 08♎25 | 05♏14 |

**4h 4m 0s — 61° 0' 0" — 03 ♊ 03**

| LAT. | 11 | 12 | ASC | 2 | 3 |
|---|---|---|---|---|---|
| 0 | 00♋55 | 28♋52 | 28♌52 | 01♎05 | 03♏13 |
| 5 | 01 45 | 00♌01 | 29 56 | 01 43 | 03 22 |
| 10 | 02 35 | 01 09 | 00♍57 | 02 18 | 03 31 |
| 15 | 03 28 | 02 17 | 01 56 | 02 53 | 03 39 |
| 20 | 04 22 | 03 25 | 02 54 | 03 26 | 03 48 |
| 21 | 04 33 | 03 38 | 03 05 | 03 33 | 03 49 |
| 22 | 04 45 | 03 52 | 03 17 | 03 39 | 03 51 |
| 23 | 04 56 | 04 06 | 03 28 | 03 46 | 03 53 |
| 24 | 05 08 | 04 20 | 03 40 | 03 52 | 03 55 |
| 25 | 05 20 | 04 34 | 03 52 | 03 59 | 03 56 |
| 26 | 05 32 | 04 48 | 04 03 | 04 06 | 03 58 |
| 27 | 05 45 | 05 03 | 04 15 | 04 12 | 04 00 |
| 28 | 05 57 | 05 17 | 04 27 | 04 19 | 04 02 |
| 29 | 06 10 | 05 32 | 04 39 | 04 26 | 04 04 |
| 30 | 06 23 | 05 46 | 04 50 | 04 33 | 04 06 |
| 31 | 06 37 | 06 01 | 05 02 | 04 40 | 04 08 |
| 32 | 06 50 | 06 16 | 05 14 | 04 47 | 04 10 |
| 33 | 07 04 | 06 31 | 05 26 | 04 54 | 04 12 |
| 34 | 07 18 | 06 46 | 05 38 | 05 01 | 04 14 |
| 35 | 07 33 | 07 02 | 05 51 | 05 08 | 04 16 |
| 36 | 07 48 | 07 18 | 06 03 | 05 15 | 04 18 |
| 37 | 08 03 | 07 34 | 06 15 | 05 22 | 04 20 |
| 38 | 08 19 | 07 50 | 06 28 | 05 29 | 04 23 |
| 39 | 08 35 | 08 06 | 06 41 | 05 37 | 04 25 |
| 40 | 08 52 | 08 23 | 06 54 | 05 45 | 04 28 |
| 41 | 09 09 | 08 40 | 07 07 | 05 52 | 04 30 |
| 42 | 09 27 | 08 57 | 07 20 | 06 00 | 04 33 |
| 43 | 09 45 | 09 14 | 07 33 | 06 08 | 04 36 |
| 44 | 10 04 | 09 32 | 07 47 | 06 16 | 04 38 |
| 45 | 10 24 | 09 50 | 08 00 | 06 24 | 04 41 |
| 46 | 10 44 | 10 09 | 08 14 | 06 33 | 04 45 |
| 47 | 11 05 | 10 28 | 08 28 | 06 42 | 04 48 |
| 48 | 11 27 | 10 47 | 08 43 | 06 51 | 04 51 |
| 49 | 11 50 | 11 07 | 08 57 | 07 00 | 04 55 |
| 50 | 12 13 | 11 27 | 09 12 | 07 09 | 04 59 |
| 51 | 12 38 | 11 47 | 09 27 | 07 19 | 05 03 |
| 52 | 13 04 | 12 08 | 09 43 | 07 29 | 05 08 |
| 53 | 13 31 | 12 30 | 09 59 | 07 40 | 05 13 |
| 54 | 13 59 | 12 51 | 10 15 | 07 50 | 05 18 |
| 55 | 14 29 | 13 14 | 10 31 | 08 02 | 05 24 |
| 56 | 15 01 | 13 37 | 10 48 | 08 14 | 05 30 |
| 57 | 15 34 | 14 00 | 11 05 | 08 26 | 05 37 |
| 58 | 16 09 | 14 24 | 11 23 | 08 39 | 05 44 |
| 59 | 16 47 | 14 48 | 11 41 | 08 53 | 05 53 |
| 60 | 17♋27 | 15♌13 | 12♍00 | 09♎08 | 06♏03 |

**4h 8m 0s — 62° 0' 0" — 04 ♊ 00**

| LAT. | 11 | 12 | ASC | 2 | 3 |
|---|---|---|---|---|---|
| 0 | 01♋50 | 29♋49 | 29♌54 | 02♎11 | 04♏16 |
| 5 | 02 39 | 00♌58 | 00♍56 | 02 46 | 04 23 |
| 10 | 03 29 | 02 04 | 01 56 | 03 20 | 04 31 |
| 15 | 04 20 | 03 10 | 02 53 | 03 52 | 04 38 |
| 20 | 05 14 | 04 17 | 03 49 | 04 24 | 04 45 |
| 21 | 05 25 | 04 30 | 04 00 | 04 30 | 04 47 |
| 22 | 05 36 | 04 44 | 04 12 | 04 36 | 04 48 |
| 23 | 05 47 | 04 57 | 04 23 | 04 43 | 04 50 |
| 24 | 05 59 | 05 11 | 04 34 | 04 49 | 04 51 |
| 25 | 06 11 | 05 24 | 04 45 | 04 55 | 04 53 |
| 26 | 06 23 | 05 38 | 04 56 | 05 02 | 04 54 |
| 27 | 06 35 | 05 52 | 05 08 | 05 08 | 04 56 |
| 28 | 06 47 | 06 06 | 05 19 | 05 14 | 04 58 |
| 29 | 07 00 | 06 20 | 05 31 | 05 21 | 04 59 |
| 30 | 07 12 | 06 35 | 05 42 | 05 27 | 05 01 |
| 31 | 07 25 | 06 49 | 05 54 | 05 34 | 05 03 |
| 32 | 07 39 | 07 04 | 06 05 | 05 40 | 05 05 |
| 33 | 07 52 | 07 18 | 06 17 | 05 47 | 05 06 |
| 34 | 08 06 | 07 33 | 06 28 | 05 54 | 05 08 |
| 35 | 08 21 | 07 49 | 06 40 | 06 00 | 05 10 |
| 36 | 08 35 | 08 04 | 06 52 | 06 07 | 05 12 |
| 37 | 08 50 | 08 19 | 07 04 | 06 14 | 05 14 |
| 38 | 09 05 | 08 35 | 07 16 | 06 21 | 05 16 |
| 39 | 09 21 | 08 51 | 07 29 | 06 28 | 05 18 |
| 40 | 09 38 | 09 07 | 07 41 | 06 35 | 05 21 |
| 41 | 09 54 | 09 24 | 07 54 | 06 43 | 05 23 |
| 42 | 10 11 | 09 40 | 08 06 | 06 50 | 05 25 |
| 43 | 10 29 | 09 57 | 08 19 | 06 58 | 05 28 |
| 44 | 10 48 | 10 15 | 08 32 | 07 06 | 05 30 |
| 45 | 11 07 | 10 32 | 08 46 | 07 13 | 05 33 |
| 46 | 11 26 | 10 50 | 08 59 | 07 22 | 05 36 |
| 47 | 11 47 | 11 09 | 09 13 | 07 30 | 05 39 |
| 48 | 12 08 | 11 27 | 09 27 | 07 38 | 05 42 |
| 49 | 12 30 | 11 46 | 09 41 | 07 47 | 05 46 |
| 50 | 12 53 | 12 06 | 09 55 | 07 56 | 05 50 |
| 51 | 13 17 | 12 26 | 10 10 | 08 06 | 05 54 |
| 52 | 13 42 | 12 46 | 10 25 | 08 15 | 05 58 |
| 53 | 14 08 | 13 07 | 10 40 | 08 25 | 06 02 |
| 54 | 14 36 | 13 28 | 10 56 | 08 36 | 06 07 |
| 55 | 15 04 | 13 49 | 11 11 | 08 47 | 06 13 |
| 56 | 15 35 | 14 11 | 11 28 | 08 58 | 06 19 |
| 57 | 16 07 | 14 34 | 11 44 | 09 10 | 06 26 |
| 58 | 16 41 | 14 57 | 12 01 | 09 23 | 06 33 |
| 59 | 17 17 | 15 20 | 12 19 | 09 37 | 06 41 |
| 60 | 17♋55 | 15♌44 | 12♍37 | 09♎51 | 06♏51 |

**4h 12m 0s — 63° 0' 0" — 04 ♊ 57**

| LAT. | 11 | 12 | ASC | 2 | 3 |
|---|---|---|---|---|---|
| 0 | 02♋45 | 00♌47 | 00♍57 | 03♎16 | 05♏18 |
| 5 | 03 34 | 01 54 | 01 57 | 03 50 | 05 24 |
| 10 | 04 22 | 02 59 | 02 55 | 04 21 | 05 30 |
| 15 | 05 13 | 04 04 | 03 50 | 04 52 | 05 36 |
| 20 | 06 05 | 05 09 | 04 45 | 05 22 | 05 43 |
| 21 | 06 16 | 05 22 | 04 55 | 05 28 | 05 44 |
| 22 | 06 27 | 05 35 | 05 06 | 05 33 | 05 45 |
| 23 | 06 38 | 05 48 | 05 17 | 05 39 | 05 46 |
| 24 | 06 50 | 06 01 | 05 28 | 05 45 | 05 48 |
| 25 | 07 01 | 06 15 | 05 39 | 05 51 | 05 49 |
| 26 | 07 13 | 06 28 | 05 50 | 05 57 | 05 51 |
| 27 | 07 25 | 06 42 | 06 01 | 06 03 | 05 52 |
| 28 | 07 37 | 06 56 | 06 12 | 06 09 | 05 53 |
| 29 | 07 49 | 07 09 | 06 23 | 06 15 | 05 55 |
| 30 | 08 01 | 07 23 | 06 34 | 06 22 | 05 56 |
| 31 | 08 14 | 07 37 | 06 45 | 06 28 | 05 58 |
| 32 | 08 27 | 07 52 | 06 56 | 06 34 | 05 59 |
| 33 | 08 40 | 08 06 | 07 07 | 06 40 | 06 01 |
| 34 | 08 54 | 08 20 | 07 19 | 06 46 | 06 02 |
| 35 | 09 08 | 08 35 | 07 30 | 06 53 | 06 04 |
| 36 | 09 22 | 08 50 | 07 42 | 06 59 | 06 06 |
| 37 | 09 37 | 09 05 | 07 53 | 07 06 | 06 08 |
| 38 | 09 52 | 09 20 | 08 05 | 07 13 | 06 09 |
| 39 | 10 07 | 09 36 | 08 17 | 07 19 | 06 11 |
| 40 | 10 23 | 09 52 | 08 29 | 07 26 | 06 13 |
| 41 | 10 39 | 10 08 | 08 41 | 07 33 | 06 15 |
| 42 | 10 56 | 10 24 | 08 53 | 07 40 | 06 18 |
| 43 | 11 13 | 10 40 | 09 06 | 07 47 | 06 20 |
| 44 | 11 31 | 10 57 | 09 18 | 07 55 | 06 22 |
| 45 | 11 50 | 11 14 | 09 31 | 08 02 | 06 25 |
| 46 | 12 09 | 11 32 | 09 44 | 08 10 | 06 27 |
| 47 | 12 29 | 11 49 | 09 57 | 08 18 | 06 30 |
| 48 | 12 49 | 12 08 | 10 11 | 08 26 | 06 33 |
| 49 | 13 10 | 12 26 | 10 24 | 08 35 | 06 37 |
| 50 | 13 33 | 12 45 | 10 38 | 08 43 | 06 40 |
| 51 | 13 56 | 13 04 | 10 52 | 08 52 | 06 44 |
| 52 | 14 20 | 13 24 | 11 07 | 09 01 | 06 48 |
| 53 | 14 45 | 13 44 | 11 21 | 09 11 | 06 52 |
| 54 | 15 12 | 14 04 | 11 36 | 09 21 | 06 57 |
| 55 | 15 40 | 14 25 | 11 52 | 09 32 | 07 02 |
| 56 | 16 09 | 14 46 | 12 07 | 09 43 | 07 08 |
| 57 | 16 40 | 15 08 | 12 23 | 09 55 | 07 14 |
| 58 | 17 12 | 15 30 | 12 40 | 10 07 | 07 21 |
| 59 | 17 47 | 15 52 | 12 57 | 10 20 | 07 30 |
| 60 | 18♋23 | 16♌15 | 13♍14 | 10♎34 | 07♏39 |

# Koch Table of Houses for Latitudes 0° to 60° North

4h 16m 0s — 64° 0' 0" — 05 ♊ 54

| LAT. | 11 | 12 | ASC | 2 | 3 |
|---|---|---|---|---|---|
| 0 | 03♋40 | 01♌45 | 02♍00 | 04♎22 | 06♏19 |
| 5 | 04 28 | 02 50 | 02 58 | 04 53 | 06 25 |
| 10 | 05 16 | 03 54 | 03 54 | 05 23 | 06 30 |
| 15 | 06 05 | 04 57 | 04 47 | 05 51 | 06 35 |
| 20 | 06 57 | 06 01 | 05 40 | 06 19 | 06 40 |
| 21 | 07 07 | 06 13 | 05 50 | 06 25 | 06 41 |
| 22 | 07 18 | 06 26 | 06 01 | 06 31 | 06 42 |
| 23 | 07 29 | 06 39 | 06 11 | 06 36 | 06 43 |
| 24 | 07 40 | 06 52 | 06 22 | 06 42 | 06 44 |
| 25 | 07 51 | 07 05 | 06 32 | 06 47 | 06 45 |
| 26 | 08 03 | 07 18 | 06 43 | 06 53 | 06 46 |
| 27 | 08 14 | 07 32 | 06 53 | 06 59 | 06 48 |
| 28 | 08 26 | 07 45 | 07 04 | 07 04 | 06 49 |
| 29 | 08 38 | 07 58 | 07 15 | 07 10 | 06 50 |
| 30 | 08 50 | 08 12 | 07 25 | 07 16 | 06 51 |
| 31 | 09 03 | 08 26 | 07 36 | 07 22 | 06 52 |
| 32 | 09 16 | 08 40 | 07 47 | 07 27 | 06 54 |
| 33 | 09 29 | 08 53 | 07 58 | 07 33 | 06 55 |
| 34 | 09 42 | 09 08 | 08 09 | 07 39 | 06 56 |
| 35 | 09 55 | 09 22 | 08 20 | 07 45 | 06 58 |
| 36 | 10 09 | 09 36 | 08 31 | 07 51 | 06 59 |
| 37 | 10 23 | 09 51 | 08 42 | 07 58 | 07 01 |
| 38 | 10 38 | 10 06 | 08 53 | 08 04 | 07 03 |
| 39 | 10 53 | 10 21 | 09 05 | 08 10 | 07 04 |
| 40 | 11 08 | 10 36 | 09 16 | 08 17 | 07 06 |
| 41 | 11 24 | 10 52 | 09 28 | 08 23 | 07 08 |
| 42 | 11 41 | 11 08 | 09 40 | 08 30 | 07 10 |
| 43 | 11 57 | 11 24 | 09 52 | 08 37 | 07 12 |
| 44 | 12 15 | 11 40 | 10 04 | 08 44 | 07 14 |
| 45 | 12 33 | 11 56 | 10 16 | 08 51 | 07 16 |
| 46 | 12 51 | 12 13 | 10 29 | 08 58 | 07 19 |
| 47 | 13 10 | 12 30 | 10 42 | 09 06 | 07 21 |
| 48 | 13 30 | 12 48 | 10 54 | 09 14 | 07 24 |
| 49 | 13 51 | 13 06 | 11 08 | 09 22 | 07 27 |
| 50 | 14 13 | 13 24 | 11 21 | 09 30 | 07 30 |
| 51 | 14 35 | 13 43 | 11 35 | 09 39 | 07 33 |
| 52 | 14 58 | 14 01 | 11 48 | 09 47 | 07 37 |
| 53 | 15 23 | 14 21 | 12 03 | 09 57 | 07 41 |
| 54 | 15 48 | 14 40 | 12 17 | 10 06 | 07 46 |
| 55 | 16 15 | 15 00 | 12 32 | 10 17 | 07 51 |
| 56 | 16 43 | 15 21 | 12 47 | 10 27 | 07 56 |
| 57 | 17 13 | 15 42 | 13 02 | 10 39 | 08 02 |
| 58 | 17 44 | 16 03 | 13 18 | 10 51 | 08 09 |
| 59 | 18 17 | 16 24 | 13 34 | 11 03 | 08 17 |
| 60 | 18♋52 | 16♌46 | 13♍51 | 11♎17 | 08♏27 |

4h 20m 0s — 65° 0' 0" — 06 ♊ 50

| LAT. | 11 | 12 | ASC | 2 | 3 |
|---|---|---|---|---|---|
| 0 | 04♋35 | 02♌43 | 03♍03 | 05♎27 | 07♏21 |
| 5 | 05 22 | 03 47 | 04 00 | 05 56 | 07 25 |
| 10 | 06 09 | 04 49 | 04 53 | 06 24 | 07 29 |
| 15 | 06 58 | 05 51 | 05 45 | 06 51 | 07 33 |
| 20 | 07 48 | 06 53 | 06 36 | 07 17 | 07 37 |
| 21 | 07 59 | 07 05 | 06 46 | 07 22 | 07 38 |
| 22 | 08 09 | 07 18 | 06 56 | 07 27 | 07 39 |
| 23 | 08 20 | 07 30 | 07 06 | 07 33 | 07 39 |
| 24 | 08 31 | 07 43 | 07 16 | 07 38 | 07 40 |
| 25 | 08 42 | 07 56 | 07 26 | 07 43 | 07 41 |
| 26 | 08 53 | 08 09 | 07 36 | 07 49 | 07 42 |
| 27 | 09 04 | 08 21 | 07 46 | 07 54 | 07 43 |
| 28 | 09 16 | 08 34 | 07 57 | 07 59 | 07 44 |
| 29 | 09 28 | 08 48 | 08 07 | 08 05 | 07 45 |
| 30 | 09 39 | 09 01 | 08 17 | 08 10 | 07 46 |
| 31 | 09 52 | 09 14 | 08 27 | 08 15 | 07 47 |
| 32 | 10 04 | 09 27 | 08 38 | 08 21 | 07 48 |
| 33 | 10 17 | 09 41 | 08 48 | 08 26 | 07 49 |
| 34 | 10 30 | 09 55 | 08 59 | 08 32 | 07 50 |
| 35 | 10 43 | 10 09 | 09 09 | 08 38 | 07 52 |
| 36 | 10 56 | 10 23 | 09 20 | 08 43 | 07 53 |
| 37 | 11 10 | 10 37 | 09 31 | 08 49 | 07 54 |
| 38 | 11 24 | 10 51 | 09 42 | 08 55 | 07 55 |
| 39 | 11 39 | 11 06 | 09 53 | 09 01 | 07 57 |
| 40 | 11 54 | 11 21 | 10 04 | 09 07 | 07 58 |
| 41 | 12 09 | 11 36 | 10 15 | 09 13 | 08 00 |
| 42 | 12 25 | 11 51 | 10 27 | 09 20 | 08 02 |
| 43 | 12 41 | 12 07 | 10 38 | 09 26 | 08 03 |
| 44 | 12 58 | 12 22 | 10 50 | 09 33 | 08 05 |
| 45 | 13 16 | 12 39 | 11 02 | 09 40 | 08 07 |
| 46 | 13 34 | 12 55 | 11 14 | 09 47 | 08 09 |
| 47 | 13 52 | 13 11 | 11 26 | 09 54 | 08 12 |
| 48 | 14 12 | 13 28 | 11 38 | 10 01 | 08 14 |
| 49 | 14 32 | 13 46 | 11 51 | 10 09 | 08 17 |
| 50 | 14 52 | 14 03 | 12 04 | 10 17 | 08 20 |
| 51 | 15 14 | 14 21 | 12 17 | 10 25 | 08 23 |
| 52 | 15 37 | 14 39 | 12 30 | 10 33 | 08 26 |
| 53 | 16 00 | 14 58 | 12 44 | 10 42 | 08 30 |
| 54 | 16 25 | 15 17 | 12 58 | 10 51 | 08 35 |
| 55 | 16 51 | 15 36 | 13 12 | 11 01 | 08 39 |
| 56 | 17 18 | 15 56 | 13 26 | 11 11 | 08 44 |
| 57 | 17 46 | 16 16 | 13 41 | 11 22 | 08 50 |
| 58 | 18 16 | 16 36 | 13 57 | 11 34 | 08 57 |
| 59 | 18 48 | 16 57 | 14 12 | 11 46 | 09 05 |
| 60 | 19♋21 | 17♌17 | 14♍28 | 12♎00 | 09♏14 |

4h 24m 0s — 66° 0' 0" — 07 ♊ 47

| LAT. | 11 | 12 | ASC | 2 | 3 |
|---|---|---|---|---|---|
| 0 | 05♋30 | 03♌41 | 04♍07 | 06♎32 | 08♏23 |
| 5 | 06 17 | 04 44 | 05 01 | 06 59 | 08 25 |
| 10 | 07 03 | 05 45 | 05 53 | 07 25 | 08 28 |
| 15 | 07 50 | 06 45 | 06 42 | 07 50 | 08 31 |
| 20 | 08 40 | 07 45 | 07 31 | 08 15 | 08 34 |
| 21 | 08 50 | 07 57 | 07 41 | 08 20 | 08 34 |
| 22 | 09 00 | 08 09 | 07 51 | 08 24 | 08 35 |
| 23 | 09 11 | 08 22 | 08 00 | 08 29 | 08 36 |
| 24 | 09 21 | 08 34 | 08 10 | 08 34 | 08 36 |
| 25 | 09 32 | 08 46 | 08 20 | 08 39 | 08 37 |
| 26 | 09 43 | 08 59 | 08 30 | 08 44 | 08 38 |
| 27 | 09 54 | 09 11 | 08 39 | 08 49 | 08 38 |
| 28 | 10 05 | 09 24 | 08 49 | 08 54 | 08 39 |
| 29 | 10 17 | 09 37 | 08 59 | 08 59 | 08 40 |
| 30 | 10 28 | 09 50 | 09 09 | 09 04 | 08 41 |
| 31 | 10 40 | 10 02 | 09 19 | 09 09 | 08 41 |
| 32 | 10 52 | 10 16 | 09 29 | 09 14 | 08 42 |
| 33 | 11 05 | 10 29 | 09 39 | 09 19 | 08 43 |
| 34 | 11 17 | 10 42 | 09 49 | 09 25 | 08 44 |
| 35 | 11 30 | 10 56 | 09 59 | 09 30 | 08 45 |
| 36 | 11 43 | 11 09 | 10 10 | 09 35 | 08 46 |
| 37 | 11 57 | 11 23 | 10 20 | 09 41 | 08 47 |
| 38 | 12 11 | 11 37 | 10 30 | 09 46 | 08 48 |
| 39 | 12 25 | 11 51 | 10 41 | 09 52 | 08 49 |
| 40 | 12 39 | 12 06 | 10 52 | 09 58 | 08 51 |
| 41 | 12 54 | 12 20 | 11 02 | 10 04 | 08 52 |
| 42 | 13 10 | 12 35 | 11 13 | 10 09 | 08 53 |
| 43 | 13 26 | 12 50 | 11 24 | 10 16 | 08 55 |
| 44 | 13 42 | 13 05 | 11 36 | 10 22 | 08 57 |
| 45 | 13 59 | 13 21 | 11 47 | 10 28 | 08 58 |
| 46 | 14 16 | 13 37 | 11 59 | 10 35 | 09 00 |
| 47 | 14 34 | 13 53 | 12 10 | 10 42 | 09 02 |
| 48 | 14 53 | 14 09 | 12 22 | 10 49 | 09 04 |
| 49 | 15 12 | 14 26 | 12 34 | 10 56 | 09 07 |
| 50 | 15 32 | 14 43 | 12 47 | 11 03 | 09 09 |
| 51 | 15 53 | 15 00 | 12 59 | 11 11 | 09 12 |
| 52 | 16 15 | 15 17 | 13 12 | 11 19 | 09 16 |
| 53 | 16 38 | 15 35 | 13 25 | 11 27 | 09 19 |
| 54 | 17 01 | 15 54 | 13 39 | 11 36 | 09 23 |
| 55 | 17 26 | 16 12 | 13 52 | 11 46 | 09 27 |
| 56 | 17 52 | 16 31 | 14 06 | 11 56 | 09 32 |
| 57 | 18 19 | 16 50 | 14 20 | 12 06 | 09 38 |
| 58 | 18 48 | 17 10 | 14 35 | 12 17 | 09 45 |
| 59 | 19 18 | 17 29 | 14 50 | 12 29 | 09 52 |
| 60 | 19♋50 | 17♌49 | 15♍05 | 12♎43 | 10♏01 |

4h 28m 0s — 67° 0' 0" — 08 ♊ 43

| LAT. | 11 | 12 | ASC | 2 | 3 |
|---|---|---|---|---|---|
| 0 | 06♋26 | 04♌39 | 05♍10 | 07♎37 | 09♏24 |
| 5 | 07 11 | 05 41 | 06 02 | 08 03 | 09 25 |
| 10 | 07 56 | 06 40 | 06 52 | 08 27 | 09 27 |
| 15 | 08 43 | 07 39 | 07 40 | 08 50 | 09 29 |
| 20 | 09 31 | 08 37 | 08 27 | 09 12 | 09 30 |
| 21 | 09 41 | 08 49 | 08 36 | 09 17 | 09 31 |
| 22 | 09 51 | 09 01 | 08 46 | 09 21 | 09 31 |
| 23 | 10 02 | 09 13 | 08 55 | 09 26 | 09 32 |
| 24 | 10 12 | 09 25 | 09 04 | 09 30 | 09 32 |
| 25 | 10 23 | 09 37 | 09 14 | 09 35 | 09 32 |
| 26 | 10 33 | 09 49 | 09 23 | 09 39 | 09 33 |
| 27 | 10 44 | 10 01 | 09 32 | 09 44 | 09 33 |
| 28 | 10 55 | 10 14 | 09 42 | 09 49 | 09 34 |
| 29 | 11 06 | 10 26 | 09 51 | 09 53 | 09 34 |
| 30 | 11 17 | 10 38 | 10 01 | 09 58 | 09 35 |
| 31 | 11 29 | 10 51 | 10 10 | 10 03 | 09 36 |
| 32 | 11 41 | 11 04 | 10 20 | 10 07 | 09 36 |
| 33 | 11 53 | 11 16 | 10 30 | 10 12 | 09 37 |
| 34 | 12 05 | 11 29 | 10 39 | 10 17 | 09 37 |
| 35 | 12 18 | 11 43 | 10 49 | 10 22 | 09 38 |
| 36 | 12 31 | 11 56 | 10 59 | 10 27 | 09 39 |
| 37 | 12 44 | 12 09 | 11 09 | 10 32 | 09 40 |
| 38 | 12 57 | 12 23 | 11 19 | 10 37 | 09 41 |
| 39 | 13 11 | 12 36 | 11 29 | 10 43 | 09 42 |
| 40 | 13 25 | 12 50 | 11 39 | 10 48 | 09 43 |
| 41 | 13 40 | 13 04 | 11 50 | 10 53 | 09 44 |
| 42 | 13 54 | 13 19 | 12 00 | 10 59 | 09 45 |
| 43 | 14 10 | 13 33 | 12 11 | 11 05 | 09 46 |
| 44 | 14 26 | 13 48 | 12 22 | 11 11 | 09 48 |
| 45 | 14 42 | 14 03 | 12 32 | 11 17 | 09 49 |
| 46 | 14 59 | 14 18 | 12 44 | 11 23 | 09 51 |
| 47 | 15 16 | 14 34 | 12 55 | 11 29 | 09 52 |
| 48 | 15 34 | 14 50 | 13 06 | 11 36 | 09 54 |
| 49 | 15 53 | 15 06 | 13 18 | 11 43 | 09 56 |
| 50 | 16 12 | 15 22 | 13 30 | 11 50 | 09 59 |
| 51 | 16 33 | 15 39 | 13 42 | 11 57 | 10 01 |
| 52 | 16 54 | 15 56 | 13 54 | 12 05 | 10 04 |
| 53 | 17 15 | 16 13 | 14 07 | 12 13 | 10 08 |
| 54 | 17 38 | 16 30 | 14 19 | 12 21 | 10 11 |
| 55 | 18 02 | 16 48 | 14 32 | 12 30 | 10 15 |
| 56 | 18 27 | 17 06 | 14 46 | 12 39 | 10 20 |
| 57 | 18 53 | 17 25 | 14 59 | 12 49 | 10 25 |
| 58 | 19 20 | 17 43 | 15 13 | 13 00 | 10 32 |
| 59 | 19 49 | 18 02 | 15 28 | 13 12 | 10 39 |
| 60 | 20♋20 | 18♌20 | 15♍42 | 13♎25 | 10♏48 |

4h 32m 0s — 68° 0' 0" — 09 ♊ 40

| LAT. | 11 | 12 | ASC | 2 | 3 |
|---|---|---|---|---|---|
| 0 | 07♋21 | 05♌38 | 06♍14 | 08♎43 | 10♏25 |
| 5 | 08 05 | 06 38 | 07 04 | 09 06 | 10 25 |
| 10 | 08 50 | 07 36 | 07 52 | 09 28 | 10 26 |
| 15 | 09 36 | 08 33 | 08 38 | 09 49 | 10 26 |
| 20 | 10 23 | 09 30 | 09 23 | 10 10 | 10 27 |
| 21 | 10 33 | 09 41 | 09 32 | 10 14 | 10 27 |
| 22 | 10 43 | 09 53 | 09 41 | 10 18 | 10 27 |
| 23 | 10 53 | 10 04 | 09 49 | 10 22 | 10 27 |
| 24 | 11 03 | 10 16 | 09 58 | 10 26 | 10 28 |
| 25 | 11 13 | 10 28 | 10 07 | 10 31 | 10 28 |
| 26 | 11 23 | 10 40 | 10 16 | 10 35 | 10 28 |
| 27 | 11 34 | 10 51 | 10 25 | 10 39 | 10 28 |
| 28 | 11 45 | 11 03 | 10 34 | 10 43 | 10 29 |
| 29 | 11 55 | 11 15 | 10 43 | 10 48 | 10 29 |
| 30 | 12 07 | 11 27 | 10 53 | 10 52 | 10 29 |
| 31 | 12 18 | 11 40 | 11 02 | 10 56 | 10 30 |
| 32 | 12 29 | 11 52 | 11 11 | 11 01 | 10 30 |
| 33 | 12 41 | 12 04 | 11 20 | 11 05 | 10 30 |
| 34 | 12 53 | 12 17 | 11 29 | 11 10 | 10 31 |
| 35 | 13 05 | 12 30 | 11 39 | 11 14 | 10 31 |
| 36 | 13 18 | 12 42 | 11 48 | 11 19 | 10 32 |
| 37 | 13 30 | 12 55 | 11 58 | 11 24 | 10 32 |
| 38 | 13 43 | 13 08 | 12 07 | 11 28 | 10 33 |
| 39 | 13 57 | 13 22 | 12 17 | 11 33 | 10 34 |
| 40 | 14 11 | 13 35 | 12 27 | 11 38 | 10 34 |
| 41 | 14 25 | 13 49 | 12 37 | 11 43 | 10 35 |
| 42 | 14 39 | 14 03 | 12 47 | 11 48 | 10 36 |
| 43 | 14 54 | 14 17 | 12 57 | 11 54 | 10 37 |
| 44 | 15 09 | 14 31 | 13 07 | 11 59 | 10 38 |
| 45 | 15 25 | 14 46 | 13 18 | 12 05 | 10 40 |
| 46 | 15 42 | 15 00 | 13 29 | 12 11 | 10 41 |
| 47 | 15 58 | 15 15 | 13 39 | 12 17 | 10 42 |
| 48 | 16 16 | 15 30 | 13 50 | 12 23 | 10 44 |
| 49 | 16 34 | 15 46 | 14 01 | 12 29 | 10 46 |
| 50 | 16 53 | 16 02 | 14 13 | 12 36 | 10 48 |
| 51 | 17 12 | 16 18 | 14 24 | 12 43 | 10 50 |
| 52 | 17 32 | 16 34 | 14 36 | 12 50 | 10 53 |
| 53 | 17 53 | 16 50 | 14 48 | 12 58 | 10 56 |
| 54 | 18 15 | 17 07 | 15 00 | 13 06 | 10 59 |
| 55 | 18 38 | 17 24 | 15 13 | 13 14 | 11 03 |
| 56 | 19 02 | 17 42 | 15 25 | 13 23 | 11 07 |
| 57 | 19 27 | 17 59 | 15 38 | 13 33 | 11 13 |
| 58 | 19 53 | 18 17 | 15 52 | 13 43 | 11 19 |
| 59 | 20 20 | 18 34 | 16 06 | 13 55 | 11 26 |
| 60 | 20♋49 | 18♌52 | 16♍20 | 14♎07 | 11♏34 |

4h 36m 0s — 69° 0' 0" — 10 ♊ 36

| LAT. | 11 | 12 | ASC | 2 | 3 |
|---|---|---|---|---|---|
| 0 | 08♋16 | 06♌37 | 07♍18 | 09♎48 | 11♏26 |
| 5 | 09 00 | 07 35 | 08 06 | 10 09 | 11 25 |
| 10 | 09 44 | 08 31 | 08 51 | 10 29 | 11 24 |
| 15 | 10 28 | 09 27 | 09 35 | 10 48 | 11 24 |
| 20 | 11 15 | 10 22 | 10 18 | 11 07 | 11 23 |
| 21 | 11 24 | 10 34 | 10 27 | 11 11 | 11 23 |
| 22 | 11 34 | 10 45 | 10 36 | 11 15 | 11 23 |
| 23 | 11 43 | 10 56 | 10 44 | 11 18 | 11 23 |
| 24 | 11 53 | 11 07 | 10 53 | 11 22 | 11 23 |
| 25 | 12 03 | 11 19 | 11 01 | 11 26 | 11 23 |
| 26 | 12 13 | 11 30 | 11 10 | 11 30 | 11 23 |
| 27 | 12 24 | 11 42 | 11 18 | 11 34 | 11 23 |
| 28 | 12 34 | 11 53 | 11 27 | 11 38 | 11 23 |
| 29 | 12 45 | 12 05 | 11 36 | 11 42 | 11 23 |
| 30 | 12 56 | 12 16 | 11 44 | 11 46 | 11 23 |
| 31 | 13 07 | 12 28 | 11 53 | 11 50 | 11 23 |
| 32 | 13 18 | 12 40 | 12 02 | 11 54 | 11 24 |
| 33 | 13 29 | 12 52 | 12 11 | 11 58 | 11 24 |
| 34 | 13 41 | 13 04 | 12 20 | 12 02 | 11 24 |
| 35 | 13 53 | 13 17 | 12 29 | 12 06 | 11 24 |
| 36 | 14 05 | 13 29 | 12 38 | 12 10 | 11 24 |
| 37 | 14 17 | 13 42 | 12 47 | 12 15 | 11 25 |
| 38 | 14 30 | 13 54 | 12 56 | 12 19 | 11 25 |
| 39 | 14 43 | 14 07 | 13 05 | 12 24 | 11 26 |
| 40 | 14 56 | 14 20 | 13 15 | 12 28 | 11 26 |
| 41 | 15 10 | 14 33 | 13 24 | 12 33 | 11 27 |
| 42 | 15 24 | 14 47 | 13 34 | 12 38 | 11 27 |
| 43 | 15 38 | 15 00 | 13 44 | 12 43 | 11 28 |
| 44 | 15 53 | 15 14 | 13 53 | 12 48 | 11 29 |
| 45 | 16 08 | 15 28 | 14 03 | 12 53 | 11 30 |
| 46 | 16 24 | 15 42 | 14 13 | 12 58 | 11 31 |
| 47 | 16 41 | 15 57 | 14 24 | 13 04 | 11 32 |
| 48 | 16 57 | 16 11 | 14 34 | 13 10 | 11 33 |
| 49 | 17 15 | 16 26 | 14 45 | 13 16 | 11 35 |
| 50 | 17 33 | 16 41 | 14 56 | 13 22 | 11 37 |
| 51 | 17 52 | 16 57 | 15 07 | 13 28 | 11 39 |
| 52 | 18 11 | 17 12 | 15 18 | 13 35 | 11 41 |
| 53 | 18 31 | 17 28 | 15 29 | 13 42 | 11 44 |
| 54 | 18 52 | 17 44 | 15 41 | 13 50 | 11 47 |
| 55 | 19 14 | 18 01 | 15 53 | 13 58 | 11 50 |
| 56 | 19 37 | 18 17 | 16 05 | 14 07 | 11 55 |
| 57 | 20 01 | 18 34 | 16 18 | 14 16 | 11 59 |
| 58 | 20 26 | 18 51 | 16 30 | 14 26 | 12 05 |
| 59 | 20 52 | 19 07 | 16 43 | 14 37 | 12 12 |
| 60 | 21♋19 | 19♌24 | 16♍57 | 14♎49 | 12♏20 |

4h 40m 0s — 70° 0' 0" — 11 ♊ 32

| LAT. | 11 | 12 | ASC | 2 | 3 |
|---|---|---|---|---|---|
| 0 | 09♋11 | 07♌35 | 08♍22 | 10♎53 | 12♏27 |
| 5 | 09 54 | 08 32 | 09 08 | 11 12 | 12 25 |
| 10 | 10 37 | 09 27 | 09 51 | 11 30 | 12 23 |
| 15 | 11 21 | 10 21 | 10 33 | 11 47 | 12 21 |
| 20 | 12 06 | 11 15 | 11 14 | 12 04 | 12 19 |
| 21 | 12 15 | 11 26 | 11 23 | 12 08 | 12 19 |
| 22 | 12 25 | 11 37 | 11 31 | 12 11 | 12 19 |
| 23 | 12 34 | 11 48 | 11 39 | 12 15 | 12 19 |
| 24 | 12 44 | 11 59 | 11 47 | 12 18 | 12 18 |
| 25 | 12 54 | 12 10 | 11 55 | 12 22 | 12 18 |
| 26 | 13 04 | 12 21 | 12 03 | 12 25 | 12 18 |
| 27 | 13 14 | 12 32 | 12 12 | 12 29 | 12 18 |
| 28 | 13 24 | 12 43 | 12 20 | 12 32 | 12 17 |
| 29 | 13 34 | 12 54 | 12 28 | 12 36 | 12 17 |
| 30 | 13 45 | 13 06 | 12 36 | 12 39 | 12 17 |
| 31 | 13 55 | 13 17 | 12 45 | 12 43 | 12 17 |
| 32 | 14 06 | 13 29 | 12 53 | 12 47 | 12 17 |
| 33 | 14 17 | 13 40 | 13 02 | 12 50 | 12 17 |
| 34 | 14 29 | 13 52 | 13 10 | 12 54 | 12 17 |
| 35 | 14 40 | 14 04 | 13 19 | 12 58 | 12 17 |
| 36 | 14 52 | 14 16 | 13 27 | 13 02 | 12 17 |
| 37 | 15 04 | 14 28 | 13 36 | 13 06 | 12 17 |
| 38 | 15 16 | 14 40 | 13 45 | 13 10 | 12 17 |
| 39 | 15 29 | 14 53 | 13 53 | 13 14 | 12 17 |
| 40 | 15 42 | 15 05 | 14 02 | 13 18 | 12 18 |
| 41 | 15 55 | 15 18 | 14 11 | 13 23 | 12 18 |
| 42 | 16 09 | 15 31 | 14 21 | 13 27 | 12 18 |
| 43 | 16 23 | 15 44 | 14 30 | 13 32 | 12 19 |
| 44 | 16 37 | 15 57 | 14 39 | 13 36 | 12 19 |
| 45 | 16 52 | 16 11 | 14 49 | 13 41 | 12 20 |
| 46 | 17 07 | 16 24 | 14 58 | 13 46 | 12 21 |
| 47 | 17 23 | 16 38 | 15 08 | 13 51 | 12 22 |
| 48 | 17 39 | 16 52 | 15 18 | 13 57 | 12 23 |
| 49 | 17 56 | 17 07 | 15 28 | 14 02 | 12 24 |
| 50 | 18 13 | 17 21 | 15 39 | 14 08 | 12 25 |
| 51 | 18 31 | 17 36 | 15 49 | 14 14 | 12 27 |
| 52 | 18 50 | 17 51 | 16 00 | 14 20 | 12 29 |
| 53 | 19 09 | 18 06 | 16 11 | 14 27 | 12 31 |
| 54 | 19 29 | 18 21 | 16 22 | 14 34 | 12 34 |
| 55 | 19 50 | 18 37 | 16 33 | 14 42 | 12 37 |
| 56 | 20 12 | 18 53 | 16 45 | 14 50 | 12 41 |
| 57 | 20 35 | 19 09 | 16 57 | 14 59 | 12 46 |
| 58 | 20 59 | 19 25 | 17 09 | 15 08 | 12 51 |
| 59 | 21 23 | 19 40 | 17 21 | 15 19 | 12 58 |
| 60 | 21♋49 | 19♌56 | 17♍34 | 15♎31 | 13♏06 |

4h 44m 0s — 71° 0' 0" — 12 ♊ 28

| LAT. | 11 | 12 | ASC | 2 | 3 |
|---|---|---|---|---|---|
| 0 | 10♋07 | 08♌34 | 09♍26 | 11♎58 | 13♏27 |
| 5 | 10 49 | 09 30 | 10 10 | 12 15 | 13 24 |
| 10 | 11 31 | 10 23 | 10 51 | 12 31 | 13 21 |
| 15 | 12 14 | 11 15 | 11 31 | 12 46 | 13 18 |
| 20 | 12 58 | 12 08 | 12 10 | 13 02 | 13 15 |
| 21 | 13 07 | 12 18 | 12 18 | 13 05 | 13 15 |
| 22 | 13 16 | 12 29 | 12 26 | 13 08 | 13 14 |
| 23 | 13 25 | 12 39 | 12 34 | 13 11 | 13 14 |
| 24 | 13 35 | 12 50 | 12 41 | 13 14 | 13 13 |
| 25 | 13 44 | 13 01 | 12 49 | 13 17 | 13 13 |
| 26 | 13 54 | 13 11 | 12 57 | 13 20 | 13 13 |
| 27 | 14 04 | 13 22 | 13 05 | 13 23 | 13 12 |
| 28 | 14 14 | 13 33 | 13 13 | 13 26 | 13 12 |
| 29 | 14 24 | 13 44 | 13 20 | 13 30 | 13 11 |
| 30 | 14 34 | 13 55 | 13 28 | 13 33 | 13 11 |
| 31 | 14 44 | 14 06 | 13 36 | 13 36 | 13 11 |
| 32 | 14 55 | 14 17 | 13 44 | 13 40 | 13 10 |
| 33 | 15 06 | 14 28 | 13 52 | 13 43 | 13 10 |
| 34 | 15 17 | 14 40 | 14 00 | 13 46 | 13 10 |
| 35 | 15 28 | 14 51 | 14 08 | 13 50 | 13 09 |
| 36 | 15 39 | 15 03 | 14 17 | 13 53 | 13 09 |
| 37 | 15 51 | 15 14 | 14 25 | 13 57 | 13 09 |
| 38 | 16 03 | 15 26 | 14 33 | 14 01 | 13 09 |
| 39 | 16 15 | 15 38 | 14 42 | 14 04 | 13 09 |
| 40 | 16 28 | 15 50 | 14 50 | 14 08 | 13 09 |
| 41 | 16 40 | 16 03 | 14 59 | 14 12 | 13 09 |
| 42 | 16 54 | 16 15 | 15 07 | 14 16 | 13 09 |
| 43 | 17 07 | 16 28 | 15 16 | 14 20 | 13 09 |
| 44 | 17 21 | 16 40 | 15 25 | 14 24 | 13 09 |
| 45 | 17 35 | 16 53 | 15 34 | 14 29 | 13 10 |
| 46 | 17 50 | 17 07 | 15 43 | 14 33 | 13 10 |
| 47 | 18 05 | 17 20 | 15 53 | 14 38 | 13 11 |
| 48 | 18 21 | 17 33 | 16 02 | 14 43 | 13 12 |
| 49 | 18 37 | 17 47 | 16 12 | 14 48 | 13 13 |
| 50 | 18 54 | 18 01 | 16 22 | 14 54 | 13 14 |
| 51 | 19 11 | 18 15 | 16 32 | 14 59 | 13 15 |
| 52 | 19 29 | 18 30 | 16 42 | 15 05 | 13 17 |
| 53 | 19 48 | 18 44 | 16 52 | 15 12 | 13 19 |
| 54 | 20 07 | 18 59 | 17 03 | 15 18 | 13 21 |
| 55 | 20 27 | 19 14 | 17 13 | 15 26 | 13 24 |
| 56 | 20 48 | 19 29 | 17 24 | 15 33 | 13 28 |
| 57 | 21 09 | 19 44 | 17 36 | 15 42 | 13 32 |
| 58 | 21 32 | 19 59 | 17 47 | 15 51 | 13 37 |
| 59 | 21 55 | 20 14 | 17 59 | 16 01 | 13 43 |
| 60 | 22♋20 | 20♌28 | 18♍11 | 16♎12 | 13♏51 |

# Koch Table of Houses for Latitudes 0° to 60° North

**4h 48m 0s — 72° 0' 0" — 13 ♊ 24**

| LAT. | 11 | 12 | ASC | 2 | 3 |
|---|---|---|---|---|---|
| 0 | 11♋02 | 09♌34 | 10♍30 | 13♎03 | 14♏28 |
| 5 | 11 43 | 10 27 | 11 12 | 13 18 | 14 23 |
| 10 | 12 24 | 11 19 | 11 51 | 13 32 | 14 19 |
| 15 | 13 06 | 12 10 | 12 29 | 13 45 | 14 15 |
| 20 | 13 49 | 13 01 | 13 06 | 13 59 | 14 11 |
| 21 | 13 58 | 13 11 | 13 14 | 14 01 | 14 10 |
| 22 | 14 07 | 13 21 | 13 21 | 14 04 | 14 10 |
| 23 | 14 16 | 13 31 | 13 28 | 14 07 | 14 09 |
| 24 | 14 25 | 13 41 | 13 36 | 14 10 | 14 08 |
| 25 | 14 35 | 13 52 | 13 43 | 14 12 | 14 08 |
| 26 | 14 44 | 14 02 | 13 51 | 14 15 | 14 07 |
| 27 | 14 54 | 14 13 | 13 58 | 14 18 | 14 06 |
| 28 | 15 03 | 14 23 | 14 05 | 14 21 | 14 06 |
| 29 | 15 13 | 14 34 | 14 13 | 14 24 | 14 05 |
| 30 | 15 23 | 14 44 | 14 20 | 14 26 | 14 04 |
| 31 | 15 33 | 14 55 | 14 28 | 14 29 | 14 04 |
| 32 | 15 43 | 15 06 | 14 35 | 14 32 | 14 03 |
| 33 | 15 54 | 15 16 | 14 43 | 14 35 | 14 03 |
| 34 | 16 04 | 15 27 | 14 51 | 14 38 | 14 02 |
| 35 | 16 15 | 15 39 | 14 58 | 14 41 | 14 02 |
| 36 | 16 26 | 15 50 | 15 06 | 14 45 | 14 01 |
| 37 | 16 38 | 16 01 | 15 14 | 14 48 | 14 01 |
| 38 | 16 49 | 16 12 | 15 22 | 14 51 | 14 00 |
| 39 | 17 01 | 16 24 | 15 30 | 14 54 | 14 00 |
| 40 | 17 13 | 16 36 | 15 38 | 14 58 | 14 00 |
| 41 | 17 26 | 16 47 | 15 46 | 15 01 | 14 00 |
| 42 | 17 38 | 16 59 | 15 54 | 15 05 | 13 59 |
| 43 | 17 52 | 17 11 | 16 03 | 15 09 | 13 59 |
| 44 | 18 05 | 17 24 | 16 11 | 15 13 | 13 59 |
| 45 | 18 19 | 17 36 | 16 20 | 15 17 | 13 59 |
| 46 | 18 33 | 17 49 | 16 28 | 15 21 | 14 00 |
| 47 | 18 48 | 18 02 | 16 37 | 15 25 | 14 00 |
| 48 | 19 03 | 18 15 | 16 46 | 15 30 | 14 00 |
| 49 | 19 18 | 18 28 | 16 55 | 15 34 | 14 01 |
| 50 | 19 34 | 18 41 | 17 05 | 15 39 | 14 02 |
| 51 | 19 51 | 18 55 | 17 14 | 15 45 | 14 03 |
| 52 | 20 08 | 19 08 | 17 24 | 15 50 | 14 04 |
| 53 | 20 26 | 19 22 | 17 33 | 15 56 | 14 06 |
| 54 | 20 44 | 19 36 | 17 43 | 16 02 | 14 08 |
| 55 | 21 04 | 19 50 | 17 54 | 16 09 | 14 11 |
| 56 | 21 23 | 20 05 | 18 04 | 16 16 | 14 14 |
| 57 | 21 44 | 20 19 | 18 15 | 16 24 | 14 18 |
| 58 | 22 05 | 20 33 | 18 26 | 16 33 | 14 23 |
| 59 | 22 27 | 20 47 | 18 37 | 16 43 | 14 29 |
| 60 | 22♋50 | 21♌01 | 18♍48 | 16♎54 | 14♏36 |

**4h 52m 0s — 73° 0' 0" — 14 ♊ 20**

| LAT. | 11 | 12 | ASC | 2 | 3 |
|---|---|---|---|---|---|
| 0 | 11♋58 | 10♌33 | 11♍34 | 14♎07 | 15♏28 |
| 5 | 12 38 | 11 25 | 12 14 | 14 20 | 15 22 |
| 10 | 13 18 | 12 15 | 12 51 | 14 32 | 15 17 |
| 15 | 13 59 | 13 04 | 13 27 | 14 44 | 15 12 |
| 20 | 14 41 | 13 54 | 14 02 | 14 56 | 15 07 |
| 21 | 14 50 | 14 03 | 14 09 | 14 58 | 15 06 |
| 22 | 14 58 | 14 13 | 14 16 | 15 00 | 15 05 |
| 23 | 15 07 | 14 23 | 14 23 | 15 03 | 15 04 |
| 24 | 15 16 | 14 33 | 14 30 | 15 05 | 15 03 |
| 25 | 15 25 | 14 43 | 14 37 | 15 08 | 15 02 |
| 26 | 15 34 | 14 53 | 14 44 | 15 10 | 15 01 |
| 27 | 15 44 | 15 03 | 14 51 | 15 12 | 15 00 |
| 28 | 15 53 | 15 13 | 14 58 | 15 15 | 14 59 |
| 29 | 16 02 | 15 23 | 15 05 | 15 17 | 14 59 |
| 30 | 16 12 | 15 34 | 15 12 | 15 20 | 14 58 |
| 31 | 16 22 | 15 44 | 15 19 | 15 22 | 14 57 |
| 32 | 16 32 | 15 54 | 15 27 | 15 25 | 14 56 |
| 33 | 16 42 | 16 05 | 15 34 | 15 28 | 14 55 |
| 34 | 16 52 | 16 15 | 15 41 | 15 30 | 14 55 |
| 35 | 17 03 | 16 26 | 15 48 | 15 33 | 14 54 |
| 36 | 17 14 | 16 37 | 15 56 | 15 36 | 14 53 |
| 37 | 17 25 | 16 48 | 16 03 | 15 39 | 14 52 |
| 38 | 17 36 | 16 59 | 16 11 | 15 41 | 14 52 |
| 39 | 17 47 | 17 10 | 16 18 | 15 44 | 14 51 |
| 40 | 17 59 | 17 21 | 16 26 | 15 47 | 14 51 |
| 41 | 18 11 | 17 32 | 16 33 | 15 51 | 14 50 |
| 42 | 18 23 | 17 44 | 16 41 | 15 54 | 14 50 |
| 43 | 18 36 | 17 55 | 16 49 | 15 57 | 14 49 |
| 44 | 18 49 | 18 07 | 16 57 | 16 01 | 14 49 |
| 45 | 19 02 | 18 19 | 17 05 | 16 04 | 14 49 |
| 46 | 19 16 | 18 31 | 17 13 | 16 08 | 14 49 |
| 47 | 19 30 | 18 44 | 17 22 | 16 12 | 14 49 |
| 48 | 19 45 | 18 56 | 17 30 | 16 16 | 14 49 |
| 49 | 20 00 | 19 09 | 17 39 | 16 20 | 14 49 |
| 50 | 20 15 | 19 21 | 17 48 | 16 25 | 14 50 |
| 51 | 20 31 | 19 34 | 17 57 | 16 30 | 14 51 |
| 52 | 20 47 | 19 47 | 18 06 | 16 35 | 14 52 |
| 53 | 21 05 | 20 00 | 18 15 | 16 40 | 14 53 |
| 54 | 21 22 | 20 14 | 18 24 | 16 46 | 14 55 |
| 55 | 21 40 | 20 27 | 18 34 | 16 52 | 14 57 |
| 56 | 21 59 | 20 41 | 18 44 | 16 59 | 15 00 |
| 57 | 22 19 | 20 54 | 18 54 | 17 07 | 15 03 |
| 58 | 22 39 | 21 08 | 19 04 | 17 15 | 15 08 |
| 59 | 23 00 | 21 21 | 19 15 | 17 24 | 15 13 |
| 60 | 23♋21 | 21♌34 | 19♍26 | 17♎35 | 15♏21 |

**4h 56m 0s — 74° 0' 0" — 15 ♊ 16**

| LAT. | 11 | 12 | ASC | 2 | 3 |
|---|---|---|---|---|---|
| 0 | 12♋53 | 11♌32 | 12♍39 | 15♎12 | 16♏28 |
| 5 | 13 33 | 12 23 | 13 16 | 15 23 | 16 21 |
| 10 | 14 12 | 13 11 | 13 51 | 15 33 | 16 15 |
| 15 | 14 52 | 13 59 | 14 25 | 15 43 | 16 08 |
| 20 | 15 33 | 14 47 | 14 58 | 15 53 | 16 02 |
| 21 | 15 41 | 14 56 | 15 05 | 15 55 | 16 01 |
| 22 | 15 50 | 15 06 | 15 12 | 15 57 | 16 00 |
| 23 | 15 58 | 15 15 | 15 18 | 15 59 | 15 59 |
| 24 | 16 07 | 15 25 | 15 25 | 16 01 | 15 58 |
| 25 | 16 16 | 15 34 | 15 31 | 16 03 | 15 57 |
| 26 | 16 25 | 15 44 | 15 38 | 16 05 | 15 55 |
| 27 | 16 34 | 15 54 | 15 44 | 16 07 | 15 54 |
| 28 | 16 43 | 16 03 | 15 51 | 16 09 | 15 53 |
| 29 | 16 52 | 16 13 | 15 58 | 16 11 | 15 52 |
| 30 | 17 01 | 16 23 | 16 04 | 16 13 | 15 51 |
| 31 | 17 11 | 16 33 | 16 11 | 16 15 | 15 50 |
| 32 | 17 21 | 16 43 | 16 18 | 16 17 | 15 49 |
| 33 | 17 30 | 16 53 | 16 25 | 16 20 | 15 48 |
| 34 | 17 40 | 17 03 | 16 31 | 16 22 | 15 47 |
| 35 | 17 51 | 17 14 | 16 38 | 16 24 | 15 46 |
| 36 | 18 01 | 17 24 | 16 45 | 16 27 | 15 45 |
| 37 | 18 12 | 17 34 | 16 52 | 16 29 | 15 44 |
| 38 | 18 23 | 17 45 | 16 59 | 16 32 | 15 43 |
| 39 | 18 34 | 17 56 | 17 06 | 16 34 | 15 42 |
| 40 | 18 45 | 18 06 | 17 14 | 16 37 | 15 41 |
| 41 | 18 57 | 18 17 | 17 21 | 16 40 | 15 40 |
| 42 | 19 09 | 18 28 | 17 28 | 16 43 | 15 40 |
| 43 | 19 21 | 18 39 | 17 36 | 16 45 | 15 39 |
| 44 | 19 33 | 18 51 | 17 43 | 16 49 | 15 39 |
| 45 | 19 46 | 19 02 | 17 51 | 16 52 | 15 38 |
| 46 | 19 59 | 19 14 | 17 58 | 16 55 | 15 38 |
| 47 | 20 13 | 19 26 | 18 06 | 16 59 | 15 37 |
| 48 | 20 27 | 19 37 | 18 14 | 17 02 | 15 37 |
| 49 | 20 41 | 19 49 | 18 22 | 17 06 | 15 37 |
| 50 | 20 56 | 20 02 | 18 31 | 17 10 | 15 37 |
| 51 | 21 11 | 20 14 | 18 39 | 17 15 | 15 38 |
| 52 | 21 27 | 20 26 | 18 48 | 17 19 | 15 39 |
| 53 | 21 43 | 20 39 | 18 56 | 17 24 | 15 40 |
| 54 | 22 00 | 20 52 | 19 05 | 17 30 | 15 41 |
| 55 | 22 17 | 21 04 | 19 14 | 17 35 | 15 43 |
| 56 | 22 35 | 21 17 | 19 24 | 17 42 | 15 45 |
| 57 | 22 54 | 21 30 | 19 33 | 17 49 | 15 49 |
| 58 | 23 13 | 21 42 | 19 43 | 17 57 | 15 53 |
| 59 | 23 33 | 21 55 | 19 53 | 18 06 | 15 58 |
| 60 | 23♋53 | 22♌06 | 20♍03 | 18♎16 | 16♏05 |

**5h 0m 0s — 75° 0' 0" — 16 ♊ 11**

| LAT. | 11 | 12 | ASC | 2 | 3 |
|---|---|---|---|---|---|
| 0 | 13♋49 | 12♌32 | 13♍43 | 16♎17 | 17♏28 |
| 5 | 14 27 | 13 21 | 14 18 | 16 25 | 17 20 |
| 10 | 15 06 | 14 08 | 14 51 | 16 34 | 17 12 |
| 15 | 15 45 | 14 54 | 15 23 | 16 42 | 17 05 |
| 20 | 16 25 | 15 40 | 15 54 | 16 49 | 16 58 |
| 21 | 16 33 | 15 49 | 16 01 | 16 51 | 16 56 |
| 22 | 16 41 | 15 58 | 16 07 | 16 53 | 16 55 |
| 23 | 16 49 | 16 07 | 16 13 | 16 54 | 16 54 |
| 24 | 16 58 | 16 17 | 16 19 | 16 56 | 16 52 |
| 25 | 17 06 | 16 26 | 16 25 | 16 58 | 16 51 |
| 26 | 17 15 | 16 35 | 16 32 | 16 59 | 16 49 |
| 27 | 17 24 | 16 44 | 16 38 | 17 01 | 16 48 |
| 28 | 17 33 | 16 54 | 16 44 | 17 03 | 16 47 |
| 29 | 17 42 | 17 03 | 16 50 | 17 04 | 16 45 |
| 30 | 17 51 | 17 13 | 16 57 | 17 06 | 16 44 |
| 31 | 18 00 | 17 22 | 17 03 | 17 08 | 16 43 |
| 32 | 18 09 | 17 32 | 17 09 | 17 10 | 16 41 |
| 33 | 18 19 | 17 42 | 17 15 | 17 12 | 16 40 |
| 34 | 18 29 | 17 51 | 17 22 | 17 14 | 16 39 |
| 35 | 18 38 | 18 01 | 17 28 | 17 16 | 16 38 |
| 36 | 18 49 | 18 11 | 17 35 | 17 18 | 16 36 |
| 37 | 18 59 | 18 21 | 17 41 | 17 20 | 16 35 |
| 38 | 19 09 | 18 31 | 17 48 | 17 22 | 16 34 |
| 39 | 19 20 | 18 42 | 17 55 | 17 24 | 16 33 |
| 40 | 19 31 | 18 52 | 18 01 | 17 26 | 16 32 |
| 41 | 19 42 | 19 02 | 18 08 | 17 29 | 16 31 |
| 42 | 19 54 | 19 13 | 18 15 | 17 31 | 16 30 |
| 43 | 20 05 | 19 24 | 18 22 | 17 34 | 16 29 |
| 44 | 20 17 | 19 34 | 18 29 | 17 36 | 16 28 |
| 45 | 20 30 | 19 45 | 18 36 | 17 39 | 16 27 |
| 46 | 20 43 | 19 56 | 18 43 | 17 42 | 16 26 |
| 47 | 20 56 | 20 08 | 18 51 | 17 45 | 16 26 |
| 48 | 21 09 | 20 19 | 18 58 | 17 48 | 16 25 |
| 49 | 21 23 | 20 30 | 19 06 | 17 52 | 16 25 |
| 50 | 21 37 | 20 42 | 19 14 | 17 55 | 16 25 |
| 51 | 21 52 | 20 54 | 19 22 | 17 59 | 16 25 |
| 52 | 22 07 | 21 06 | 19 30 | 18 04 | 16 25 |
| 53 | 22 22 | 21 17 | 19 38 | 18 08 | 16 26 |
| 54 | 22 38 | 21 29 | 19 46 | 18 13 | 16 27 |
| 55 | 22 55 | 21 41 | 19 55 | 18 18 | 16 29 |
| 56 | 23 12 | 21 53 | 20 03 | 18 24 | 16 31 |
| 57 | 23 29 | 22 05 | 20 12 | 18 31 | 16 34 |
| 58 | 23 47 | 22 17 | 20 21 | 18 38 | 16 37 |
| 59 | 24 06 | 22 29 | 20 31 | 18 47 | 16 42 |
| 60 | 24♋24 | 22♌39 | 20♍40 | 18♎56 | 16♏49 |

**5h 4m 0s — 76° 0' 0" — 17 ♊ 07**

| LAT. | 11 | 12 | ASC | 2 | 3 |
|---|---|---|---|---|---|
| 0 | 14♋44 | 13♌32 | 14♍48 | 17♎21 | 18♏28 |
| 5 | 15 22 | 14 19 | 15 21 | 17 28 | 18 18 |
| 10 | 16 00 | 15 05 | 15 52 | 17 34 | 18 10 |
| 15 | 16 38 | 15 49 | 16 21 | 17 40 | 18 01 |
| 20 | 17 16 | 16 33 | 16 51 | 17 46 | 17 53 |
| 21 | 17 24 | 16 42 | 16 56 | 17 47 | 17 51 |
| 22 | 17 32 | 16 51 | 17 02 | 17 49 | 17 50 |
| 23 | 17 41 | 17 00 | 17 08 | 17 50 | 17 48 |
| 24 | 17 49 | 17 08 | 17 14 | 17 51 | 17 46 |
| 25 | 17 57 | 17 17 | 17 20 | 17 53 | 17 45 |
| 26 | 18 05 | 17 26 | 17 25 | 17 54 | 17 43 |
| 27 | 18 14 | 17 35 | 17 31 | 17 55 | 17 42 |
| 28 | 18 22 | 17 44 | 17 37 | 17 57 | 17 40 |
| 29 | 18 31 | 17 53 | 17 43 | 17 58 | 17 38 |
| 30 | 18 40 | 18 02 | 17 49 | 17 59 | 17 37 |
| 31 | 18 49 | 18 12 | 17 54 | 18 01 | 17 35 |
| 32 | 18 58 | 18 21 | 18 00 | 18 02 | 17 34 |
| 33 | 19 07 | 18 30 | 18 06 | 18 04 | 17 32 |
| 34 | 19 17 | 18 40 | 18 12 | 18 05 | 17 31 |
| 35 | 19 26 | 18 49 | 18 18 | 18 07 | 17 29 |
| 36 | 19 36 | 18 58 | 18 24 | 18 08 | 17 28 |
| 37 | 19 46 | 19 08 | 18 31 | 18 10 | 17 26 |
| 38 | 19 56 | 19 18 | 18 37 | 18 12 | 17 25 |
| 39 | 20 06 | 19 28 | 18 43 | 18 14 | 17 23 |
| 40 | 20 17 | 19 38 | 18 49 | 18 16 | 17 22 |
| 41 | 20 28 | 19 48 | 18 56 | 18 18 | 17 21 |
| 42 | 20 39 | 19 58 | 19 02 | 18 20 | 17 19 |
| 43 | 20 50 | 20 08 | 19 08 | 18 22 | 17 18 |
| 44 | 21 02 | 20 18 | 19 15 | 18 24 | 17 17 |
| 45 | 21 14 | 20 29 | 19 22 | 18 26 | 17 16 |
| 46 | 21 26 | 20 39 | 19 29 | 18 29 | 17 15 |
| 47 | 21 38 | 20 50 | 19 35 | 18 31 | 17 14 |
| 48 | 21 51 | 21 01 | 19 42 | 18 34 | 17 13 |
| 49 | 22 04 | 21 12 | 19 49 | 18 37 | 17 12 |
| 50 | 22 18 | 21 23 | 19 57 | 18 40 | 17 12 |
| 51 | 22 32 | 21 34 | 20 04 | 18 44 | 17 12 |
| 52 | 22 46 | 21 45 | 20 12 | 18 48 | 17 12 |
| 53 | 23 01 | 21 56 | 20 19 | 18 52 | 17 12 |
| 54 | 23 16 | 22 07 | 20 27 | 18 56 | 17 13 |
| 55 | 23 32 | 22 19 | 20 35 | 19 01 | 17 14 |
| 56 | 23 48 | 22 30 | 20 43 | 19 07 | 17 16 |
| 57 | 24 05 | 22 41 | 20 51 | 19 13 | 17 18 |
| 58 | 24 22 | 22 52 | 21 00 | 19 20 | 17 21 |
| 59 | 24 39 | 23 03 | 21 09 | 19 27 | 17 26 |
| 60 | 24♋56 | 23♌13 | 21♍17 | 19♎37 | 17♏32 |

**5h 8m 0s — 77° 0' 0" — 18 ♊ 02**

| LAT. | 11 | 12 | ASC | 2 | 3 |
|---|---|---|---|---|---|
| 0 | 15♋40 | 14♌32 | 15♍53 | 18♎26 | 19♏27 |
| 5 | 16 17 | 15 17 | 16 23 | 18 30 | 19 17 |
| 10 | 16 54 | 16 01 | 16 52 | 18 34 | 19 07 |
| 15 | 17 30 | 16 44 | 17 20 | 18 39 | 18 57 |
| 20 | 18 08 | 17 26 | 17 47 | 18 43 | 18 48 |
| 21 | 18 16 | 17 35 | 17 52 | 18 44 | 18 46 |
| 22 | 18 24 | 17 43 | 17 58 | 18 45 | 18 44 |
| 23 | 18 32 | 17 52 | 18 03 | 18 45 | 18 42 |
| 24 | 18 40 | 18 00 | 18 08 | 18 46 | 18 41 |
| 25 | 18 48 | 18 09 | 18 14 | 18 47 | 18 39 |
| 26 | 18 56 | 18 18 | 18 19 | 18 48 | 18 37 |
| 27 | 19 04 | 18 26 | 18 24 | 18 49 | 18 35 |
| 28 | 19 12 | 18 35 | 18 30 | 18 50 | 18 33 |
| 29 | 19 21 | 18 44 | 18 35 | 18 51 | 18 31 |
| 30 | 19 29 | 18 52 | 18 41 | 18 52 | 18 30 |
| 31 | 19 38 | 19 01 | 18 46 | 18 53 | 18 28 |
| 32 | 19 47 | 19 10 | 18 52 | 18 54 | 18 26 |
| 33 | 19 56 | 19 19 | 18 57 | 18 56 | 18 24 |
| 34 | 20 05 | 19 28 | 19 03 | 18 57 | 18 22 |
| 35 | 20 14 | 19 37 | 19 08 | 18 58 | 18 21 |
| 36 | 20 24 | 19 46 | 19 14 | 18 59 | 18 19 |
| 37 | 20 33 | 19 55 | 19 20 | 19 00 | 18 17 |
| 38 | 20 43 | 20 04 | 19 25 | 19 02 | 18 15 |
| 39 | 20 53 | 20 14 | 19 31 | 19 03 | 18 14 |
| 40 | 21 03 | 20 23 | 19 37 | 19 05 | 18 12 |
| 41 | 21 14 | 20 33 | 19 43 | 19 06 | 18 10 |
| 42 | 21 24 | 20 42 | 19 49 | 19 08 | 18 09 |
| 43 | 21 35 | 20 52 | 19 55 | 19 10 | 18 07 |
| 44 | 21 46 | 21 02 | 20 01 | 19 11 | 18 06 |
| 45 | 21 58 | 21 12 | 20 07 | 19 13 | 18 04 |
| 46 | 22 09 | 21 22 | 20 14 | 19 15 | 18 03 |
| 47 | 22 21 | 21 32 | 20 20 | 19 18 | 18 02 |
| 48 | 22 34 | 21 42 | 20 26 | 19 20 | 18 01 |
| 49 | 22 46 | 21 53 | 20 33 | 19 23 | 18 00 |
| 50 | 22 59 | 22 03 | 20 40 | 19 25 | 17 59 |
| 51 | 23 13 | 22 14 | 20 47 | 19 28 | 17 58 |
| 52 | 23 26 | 22 24 | 20 54 | 19 32 | 17 58 |
| 53 | 23 41 | 22 35 | 21 01 | 19 35 | 17 58 |
| 54 | 23 55 | 22 46 | 21 08 | 19 39 | 17 58 |
| 55 | 24 10 | 22 56 | 21 15 | 19 44 | 17 59 |
| 56 | 24 25 | 23 07 | 21 23 | 19 49 | 18 00 |
| 57 | 24 41 | 23 17 | 21 30 | 19 54 | 18 02 |
| 58 | 24 56 | 23 27 | 21 38 | 20 01 | 18 05 |
| 59 | 25 12 | 23 37 | 21 46 | 20 08 | 18 09 |
| 60 | 25♋28 | 23♌46 | 21♍55 | 20♎17 | 18♏15 |

**5h 12m 0s — 78° 0' 0" — 18 ♊ 58**

| LAT. | 11 | 12 | ASC | 2 | 3 |
|---|---|---|---|---|---|
| 0 | 16♋36 | 15♌32 | 16♍57 | 19♎30 | 20♏26 |
| 5 | 17 12 | 16 16 | 17 26 | 19 32 | 20 15 |
| 10 | 17 48 | 16 58 | 17 52 | 19 35 | 20 04 |
| 15 | 18 23 | 17 39 | 18 18 | 19 37 | 19 53 |
| 20 | 19 00 | 18 20 | 18 43 | 19 39 | 19 43 |
| 21 | 19 08 | 18 28 | 18 48 | 19 40 | 19 41 |
| 22 | 19 15 | 18 36 | 18 53 | 19 40 | 19 39 |
| 23 | 19 23 | 18 44 | 18 58 | 19 41 | 19 37 |
| 24 | 19 31 | 18 53 | 19 03 | 19 41 | 19 34 |
| 25 | 19 39 | 19 01 | 19 08 | 19 42 | 19 32 |
| 26 | 19 46 | 19 09 | 19 13 | 19 43 | 19 30 |
| 27 | 19 54 | 19 17 | 19 18 | 19 43 | 19 28 |
| 28 | 20 02 | 19 25 | 19 23 | 19 44 | 19 26 |
| 29 | 20 11 | 19 34 | 19 28 | 19 44 | 19 24 |
| 30 | 20 19 | 19 42 | 19 33 | 19 45 | 19 22 |
| 31 | 20 27 | 19 51 | 19 38 | 19 46 | 19 20 |
| 32 | 20 36 | 19 59 | 19 43 | 19 46 | 19 18 |
| 33 | 20 44 | 20 08 | 19 48 | 19 47 | 19 16 |
| 34 | 20 53 | 20 16 | 19 53 | 19 48 | 19 14 |
| 35 | 21 02 | 20 25 | 19 58 | 19 49 | 19 12 |
| 36 | 21 11 | 20 34 | 20 04 | 19 50 | 19 10 |
| 37 | 21 21 | 20 42 | 20 09 | 19 51 | 19 08 |
| 38 | 21 30 | 20 51 | 20 14 | 19 52 | 19 06 |
| 39 | 21 40 | 21 00 | 20 20 | 19 53 | 19 04 |
| 40 | 21 49 | 21 09 | 20 25 | 19 54 | 19 02 |
| 41 | 21 59 | 21 18 | 20 30 | 19 55 | 19 00 |
| 42 | 22 10 | 21 27 | 20 36 | 19 56 | 18 58 |
| 43 | 22 20 | 21 37 | 20 41 | 19 57 | 18 56 |
| 44 | 22 31 | 21 46 | 20 47 | 19 59 | 18 55 |
| 45 | 22 42 | 21 56 | 20 53 | 20 00 | 18 53 |
| 46 | 22 53 | 22 05 | 20 59 | 20 02 | 18 51 |
| 47 | 23 05 | 22 15 | 21 05 | 20 04 | 18 50 |
| 48 | 23 16 | 22 24 | 21 11 | 20 06 | 18 48 |
| 49 | 23 28 | 22 34 | 21 17 | 20 08 | 18 47 |
| 50 | 23 41 | 22 44 | 21 23 | 20 10 | 18 46 |
| 51 | 23 54 | 22 54 | 21 29 | 20 13 | 18 45 |
| 52 | 24 07 | 23 04 | 21 36 | 20 16 | 18 44 |
| 53 | 24 20 | 23 14 | 21 42 | 20 19 | 18 44 |
| 54 | 24 34 | 23 24 | 21 49 | 20 22 | 18 43 |
| 55 | 24 48 | 23 34 | 21 56 | 20 26 | 18 44 |
| 56 | 25 02 | 23 44 | 22 03 | 20 31 | 18 45 |
| 57 | 25 17 | 23 53 | 22 10 | 20 36 | 18 46 |
| 58 | 25 31 | 24 03 | 22 17 | 20 42 | 18 49 |
| 59 | 25 46 | 24 12 | 22 24 | 20 49 | 18 52 |
| 60 | 26♋01 | 24♌20 | 22♍32 | 20♎57 | 18♏58 |

**5h 16m 0s — 79° 0' 0" — 19 ♊ 53**

| LAT. | 11 | 12 | ASC | 2 | 3 |
|---|---|---|---|---|---|
| 0 | 17♋32 | 16♌33 | 18♍02 | 20♎34 | 21♏26 |
| 5 | 18 07 | 17 15 | 18 28 | 20 35 | 21 13 |
| 10 | 18 42 | 17 55 | 18 53 | 20 35 | 21 01 |
| 15 | 19 17 | 18 35 | 19 16 | 20 35 | 20 49 |
| 20 | 19 52 | 19 14 | 19 39 | 20 36 | 20 37 |
| 21 | 20 00 | 19 21 | 19 44 | 20 36 | 20 35 |
| 22 | 20 07 | 19 29 | 19 48 | 20 36 | 20 33 |
| 23 | 20 14 | 19 37 | 19 53 | 20 36 | 20 31 |
| 24 | 20 22 | 19 45 | 19 58 | 20 36 | 20 28 |
| 25 | 20 29 | 19 53 | 20 02 | 20 37 | 20 26 |
| 26 | 20 37 | 20 00 | 20 07 | 20 37 | 20 24 |
| 27 | 20 45 | 20 08 | 20 11 | 20 37 | 20 21 |
| 28 | 20 53 | 20 16 | 20 16 | 20 37 | 20 19 |
| 29 | 21 00 | 20 24 | 20 20 | 20 37 | 20 17 |
| 30 | 21 08 | 20 32 | 20 25 | 20 38 | 20 14 |
| 31 | 21 17 | 20 40 | 20 30 | 20 38 | 20 12 |
| 32 | 21 25 | 20 48 | 20 34 | 20 38 | 20 10 |
| 33 | 21 33 | 20 56 | 20 39 | 20 39 | 20 08 |
| 34 | 21 42 | 21 05 | 20 44 | 20 39 | 20 05 |
| 35 | 21 50 | 21 13 | 20 49 | 20 40 | 20 03 |
| 36 | 21 59 | 21 21 | 20 53 | 20 40 | 20 01 |
| 37 | 22 08 | 21 30 | 20 58 | 20 41 | 19 58 |
| 38 | 22 17 | 21 38 | 21 03 | 20 41 | 19 56 |
| 39 | 22 26 | 21 46 | 21 08 | 20 42 | 19 54 |
| 40 | 22 36 | 21 55 | 21 13 | 20 43 | 19 52 |
| 41 | 22 45 | 22 04 | 21 18 | 20 43 | 19 49 |
| 42 | 22 55 | 22 12 | 21 23 | 20 44 | 19 47 |
| 43 | 23 05 | 22 21 | 21 28 | 20 45 | 19 45 |
| 44 | 23 16 | 22 30 | 21 33 | 20 46 | 19 43 |
| 45 | 23 26 | 22 39 | 21 38 | 20 47 | 19 41 |
| 46 | 23 37 | 22 48 | 21 44 | 20 48 | 19 39 |
| 47 | 23 48 | 22 57 | 21 49 | 20 50 | 19 37 |
| 48 | 23 59 | 23 06 | 21 55 | 20 51 | 19 35 |
| 49 | 24 11 | 23 16 | 22 00 | 20 53 | 19 34 |
| 50 | 24 22 | 23 25 | 22 06 | 20 55 | 19 32 |
| 51 | 24 35 | 23 34 | 22 12 | 20 57 | 19 31 |
| 52 | 24 47 | 23 44 | 22 18 | 20 59 | 19 30 |
| 53 | 25 00 | 23 53 | 22 24 | 21 02 | 19 29 |
| 54 | 25 13 | 24 03 | 22 30 | 21 05 | 19 28 |
| 55 | 25 26 | 24 12 | 22 36 | 21 08 | 19 28 |
| 56 | 25 39 | 24 21 | 22 42 | 21 12 | 19 29 |
| 57 | 25 53 | 24 30 | 22 49 | 21 17 | 19 30 |
| 58 | 26 07 | 24 38 | 22 55 | 21 22 | 19 32 |
| 59 | 26 21 | 24 47 | 23 02 | 21 29 | 19 35 |
| 60 | 26♋34 | 24♌54 | 23♍09 | 21♎36 | 19♏40 |

# Koch Table of Houses for Latitudes 0° to 60° North

5h 20m 0s — 80° 0' 0" — 20 ♊ 49

| LAT. | 11 | 12 | ASC | 2 | 3 |
|---|---|---|---|---|---|
| 0 | 18♋28 | 17♌33 | 19♍07 | 21♎38 | 22♏25 |
| 5 | 19 02 | 18 14 | 19 31 | 21 37 | 22 11 |
| 10 | 19 36 | 18 52 | 19 53 | 21 35 | 21 58 |
| 15 | 20 10 | 19 30 | 20 15 | 21 33 | 21 45 |
| 20 | 20 44 | 20 07 | 20 36 | 21 32 | 21 32 |
| 21 | 20 51 | 20 15 | 20 40 | 21 32 | 21 30 |
| 22 | 20 59 | 20 22 | 20 44 | 21 32 | 21 27 |
| 23 | 21 06 | 20 30 | 20 48 | 21 31 | 21 24 |
| 24 | 21 13 | 20 37 | 20 52 | 21 31 | 21 22 |
| 25 | 21 20 | 20 45 | 20 56 | 21 31 | 21 19 |
| 26 | 21 28 | 20 52 | 21 01 | 21 31 | 21 17 |
| 27 | 21 35 | 21 00 | 21 05 | 21 31 | 21 14 |
| 28 | 21 43 | 21 07 | 21 09 | 21 31 | 21 12 |
| 29 | 21 50 | 21 15 | 21 13 | 21 30 | 21 09 |
| 30 | 21 58 | 21 22 | 21 17 | 21 30 | 21 07 |
| 31 | 22 06 | 21 30 | 21 21 | 21 30 | 21 04 |
| 32 | 22 14 | 21 38 | 21 26 | 21 30 | 21 02 |
| 33 | 22 22 | 21 45 | 21 30 | 21 30 | 20 59 |
| 34 | 22 30 | 21 53 | 21 34 | 21 30 | 20 56 |
| 35 | 22 38 | 22 01 | 21 39 | 21 30 | 20 54 |
| 36 | 22 47 | 22 09 | 21 43 | 21 30 | 20 51 |
| 37 | 22 55 | 22 17 | 21 47 | 21 31 | 20 49 |
| 38 | 23 04 | 22 25 | 21 52 | 21 31 | 20 46 |
| 39 | 23 13 | 22 33 | 21 56 | 21 31 | 20 44 |
| 40 | 23 22 | 22 41 | 22 01 | 21 31 | 20 41 |
| 41 | 23 31 | 22 49 | 22 05 | 21 32 | 20 39 |
| 42 | 23 41 | 22 58 | 22 10 | 21 32 | 20 36 |
| 43 | 23 51 | 23 06 | 22 14 | 21 32 | 20 34 |
| 44 | 24 00 | 23 14 | 22 19 | 21 33 | 20 31 |
| 45 | 24 10 | 23 23 | 22 24 | 21 34 | 20 29 |
| 46 | 24 21 | 23 31 | 22 29 | 21 35 | 20 27 |
| 47 | 24 31 | 23 40 | 22 34 | 21 35 | 20 24 |
| 48 | 24 42 | 23 49 | 22 39 | 21 36 | 20 22 |
| 49 | 24 53 | 23 57 | 22 44 | 21 38 | 20 20 |
| 50 | 25 04 | 24 06 | 22 49 | 21 39 | 20 18 |
| 51 | 25 16 | 24 15 | 22 54 | 21 41 | 20 17 |
| 52 | 25 28 | 24 24 | 23 00 | 21 43 | 20 15 |
| 53 | 25 40 | 24 33 | 23 05 | 21 45 | 20 14 |
| 54 | 25 52 | 24 41 | 23 11 | 21 47 | 20 13 |
| 55 | 26 04 | 24 50 | 23 16 | 21 50 | 20 12 |
| 56 | 26 17 | 24 58 | 23 22 | 21 54 | 20 12 |
| 57 | 26 30 | 25 06 | 23 28 | 21 58 | 20 13 |
| 58 | 26 42 | 25 14 | 23 34 | 22 03 | 20 15 |
| 59 | 26 55 | 25 22 | 23 40 | 22 09 | 20 18 |
| 60 | 27♋07 | 25♌28 | 23♍47 | 22♎16 | 20♏22 |

5h 24m 0s — 81° 0' 0" — 21 ♊ 44

| LAT. | 11 | 12 | ASC | 2 | 3 |
|---|---|---|---|---|---|
| 0 | 19♋24 | 18♌34 | 20♍12 | 22♎42 | 23♏23 |
| 5 | 19 57 | 19 13 | 20 34 | 22 38 | 23 09 |
| 10 | 20 30 | 19 50 | 20 54 | 22 35 | 22 54 |
| 15 | 21 03 | 20 26 | 21 13 | 22 31 | 22 40 |
| 20 | 21 37 | 21 01 | 21 32 | 22 28 | 22 26 |
| 21 | 21 43 | 21 08 | 21 36 | 22 28 | 22 24 |
| 22 | 21 50 | 21 15 | 21 40 | 22 27 | 22 21 |
| 23 | 21 57 | 21 22 | 21 43 | 22 26 | 22 18 |
| 24 | 22 04 | 21 30 | 21 47 | 22 26 | 22 15 |
| 25 | 22 11 | 21 37 | 21 51 | 22 25 | 22 13 |
| 26 | 22 18 | 21 44 | 21 54 | 22 25 | 22 10 |
| 27 | 22 26 | 21 51 | 21 58 | 22 24 | 22 07 |
| 28 | 22 33 | 21 58 | 22 02 | 22 24 | 22 04 |
| 29 | 22 40 | 22 05 | 22 06 | 22 23 | 22 01 |
| 30 | 22 48 | 22 13 | 22 10 | 22 23 | 21 59 |
| 31 | 22 55 | 22 20 | 22 13 | 22 22 | 21 56 |
| 32 | 23 03 | 22 27 | 22 17 | 22 22 | 21 53 |
| 33 | 23 11 | 22 35 | 22 21 | 22 22 | 21 50 |
| 34 | 23 19 | 22 42 | 22 25 | 22 21 | 21 47 |
| 35 | 23 27 | 22 49 | 22 29 | 22 21 | 21 45 |
| 36 | 23 35 | 22 57 | 22 33 | 22 21 | 21 42 |
| 37 | 23 43 | 23 04 | 22 37 | 22 20 | 21 39 |
| 38 | 23 51 | 23 12 | 22 41 | 22 20 | 21 36 |
| 39 | 24 00 | 23 20 | 22 45 | 22 20 | 21 33 |
| 40 | 24 09 | 23 27 | 22 49 | 22 20 | 21 30 |
| 41 | 24 18 | 23 35 | 22 53 | 22 20 | 21 28 |
| 42 | 24 27 | 23 43 | 22 57 | 22 20 | 21 25 |
| 43 | 24 36 | 23 51 | 23 01 | 22 20 | 21 22 |
| 44 | 24 45 | 23 59 | 23 05 | 22 20 | 21 19 |
| 45 | 24 55 | 24 07 | 23 10 | 22 20 | 21 17 |
| 46 | 25 05 | 24 15 | 23 14 | 22 21 | 21 14 |
| 47 | 25 15 | 24 23 | 23 18 | 22 21 | 21 11 |
| 48 | 25 25 | 24 31 | 23 23 | 22 22 | 21 09 |
| 49 | 25 36 | 24 39 | 23 27 | 22 22 | 21 07 |
| 50 | 25 46 | 24 47 | 23 32 | 22 23 | 21 04 |
| 51 | 25 57 | 24 56 | 23 37 | 22 25 | 21 02 |
| 52 | 26 08 | 25 04 | 23 42 | 22 26 | 21 00 |
| 53 | 26 20 | 25 12 | 23 46 | 22 28 | 20 59 |
| 54 | 26 31 | 25 20 | 23 51 | 22 30 | 20 57 |
| 55 | 26 43 | 25 28 | 23 57 | 22 32 | 20 56 |
| 56 | 26 55 | 25 36 | 24 02 | 22 35 | 20 56 |
| 57 | 27 07 | 25 43 | 24 07 | 22 39 | 20 56 |
| 58 | 27 18 | 25 50 | 24 13 | 22 43 | 20 57 |
| 59 | 27 30 | 25 57 | 24 18 | 22 49 | 20 59 |
| 60 | 27♋41 | 26♌02 | 24♍24 | 22♎55 | 21♏03 |

5h 28m 0s — 82° 0' 0" — 22 ♊ 39

| LAT. | 11 | 12 | ASC | 2 | 3 |
|---|---|---|---|---|---|
| 0 | 20♋20 | 19♌35 | 21♍17 | 23♎46 | 24♏22 |
| 5 | 20 53 | 20 12 | 21 36 | 23 40 | 24 06 |
| 10 | 21 24 | 20 47 | 21 54 | 23 35 | 23 51 |
| 15 | 21 56 | 21 21 | 22 12 | 23 29 | 23 36 |
| 20 | 22 29 | 21 55 | 22 28 | 23 24 | 23 21 |
| 21 | 22 35 | 22 02 | 22 32 | 23 23 | 23 18 |
| 22 | 22 42 | 22 09 | 22 35 | 23 22 | 23 15 |
| 23 | 22 49 | 22 15 | 22 38 | 23 21 | 23 12 |
| 24 | 22 56 | 22 22 | 22 42 | 23 20 | 23 09 |
| 25 | 23 02 | 22 29 | 22 45 | 23 20 | 23 06 |
| 26 | 23 09 | 22 36 | 22 48 | 23 19 | 23 03 |
| 27 | 23 16 | 22 42 | 22 52 | 23 18 | 23 00 |
| 28 | 23 23 | 22 49 | 22 55 | 23 17 | 22 57 |
| 29 | 23 30 | 22 56 | 22 58 | 23 16 | 22 54 |
| 30 | 23 38 | 23 03 | 23 02 | 23 15 | 22 51 |
| 31 | 23 45 | 23 10 | 23 05 | 23 14 | 22 47 |
| 32 | 23 52 | 23 17 | 23 09 | 23 14 | 22 44 |
| 33 | 24 00 | 23 24 | 23 12 | 23 13 | 22 41 |
| 34 | 24 07 | 23 31 | 23 15 | 23 12 | 22 38 |
| 35 | 24 15 | 23 38 | 23 19 | 23 11 | 22 35 |
| 36 | 24 23 | 23 45 | 23 22 | 23 11 | 22 32 |
| 37 | 24 31 | 23 52 | 23 26 | 23 10 | 22 29 |
| 38 | 24 39 | 23 59 | 23 29 | 23 09 | 22 26 |
| 39 | 24 47 | 24 06 | 23 33 | 23 09 | 22 23 |
| 40 | 24 55 | 24 14 | 23 36 | 23 08 | 22 20 |
| 41 | 25 04 | 24 21 | 23 40 | 23 08 | 22 17 |
| 42 | 25 13 | 24 28 | 23 44 | 23 07 | 22 13 |
| 43 | 25 21 | 24 36 | 23 48 | 23 07 | 22 10 |
| 44 | 25 30 | 24 43 | 23 51 | 23 07 | 22 07 |
| 45 | 25 40 | 24 51 | 23 55 | 23 07 | 22 04 |
| 46 | 25 49 | 24 58 | 23 59 | 23 07 | 22 01 |
| 47 | 25 59 | 25 06 | 24 03 | 23 07 | 21 58 |
| 48 | 26 08 | 25 14 | 24 07 | 23 07 | 21 55 |
| 49 | 26 18 | 25 21 | 24 11 | 23 07 | 21 53 |
| 50 | 26 28 | 25 29 | 24 15 | 23 07 | 21 50 |
| 51 | 26 39 | 25 36 | 24 19 | 23 08 | 21 47 |
| 52 | 26 49 | 25 44 | 24 24 | 23 09 | 21 45 |
| 53 | 27 00 | 25 52 | 24 28 | 23 10 | 21 43 |
| 54 | 27 11 | 25 59 | 24 32 | 23 12 | 21 41 |
| 55 | 27 22 | 26 06 | 24 37 | 23 14 | 21 40 |
| 56 | 27 33 | 26 14 | 24 42 | 23 16 | 21 39 |
| 57 | 27 44 | 26 20 | 24 46 | 23 19 | 21 39 |
| 58 | 27 55 | 26 27 | 24 51 | 23 23 | 21 39 |
| 59 | 28 05 | 26 32 | 24 56 | 23 28 | 21 41 |
| 60 | 28♋15 | 26♌37 | 25♍01 | 23♎34 | 21♏44 |

5h 32m 0s — 83° 0' 0" — 23 ♊ 34

| LAT. | 11 | 12 | ASC | 2 | 3 |
|---|---|---|---|---|---|
| 0 | 21♋17 | 20♌36 | 22♍23 | 24♎50 | 25♏21 |
| 5 | 21 48 | 21 11 | 22 39 | 24 42 | 25 04 |
| 10 | 22 19 | 21 45 | 22 55 | 24 34 | 24 47 |
| 15 | 22 50 | 22 17 | 23 10 | 24 27 | 24 31 |
| 20 | 23 21 | 22 49 | 23 25 | 24 20 | 24 15 |
| 21 | 23 28 | 22 56 | 23 28 | 24 19 | 24 12 |
| 22 | 23 34 | 23 02 | 23 31 | 24 18 | 24 08 |
| 23 | 23 40 | 23 08 | 23 34 | 24 16 | 24 05 |
| 24 | 23 47 | 23 15 | 23 36 | 24 15 | 24 02 |
| 25 | 23 54 | 23 21 | 23 39 | 24 14 | 23 59 |
| 26 | 24 00 | 23 28 | 23 42 | 24 12 | 23 55 |
| 27 | 24 07 | 23 34 | 23 45 | 24 11 | 23 52 |
| 28 | 24 14 | 23 40 | 23 48 | 24 10 | 23 49 |
| 29 | 24 21 | 23 47 | 23 51 | 24 09 | 23 46 |
| 30 | 24 27 | 23 53 | 23 54 | 24 07 | 23 42 |
| 31 | 24 34 | 24 00 | 23 57 | 24 06 | 23 39 |
| 32 | 24 42 | 24 07 | 24 00 | 24 05 | 23 36 |
| 33 | 24 49 | 24 13 | 24 03 | 24 04 | 23 32 |
| 34 | 24 56 | 24 20 | 24 06 | 24 03 | 23 29 |
| 35 | 25 03 | 24 26 | 24 09 | 24 02 | 23 26 |
| 36 | 25 11 | 24 33 | 24 12 | 24 01 | 23 22 |
| 37 | 25 19 | 24 40 | 24 15 | 24 00 | 23 19 |
| 38 | 25 26 | 24 46 | 24 18 | 23 59 | 23 15 |
| 39 | 25 34 | 24 53 | 24 21 | 23 58 | 23 12 |
| 40 | 25 42 | 25 00 | 24 24 | 23 57 | 23 09 |
| 41 | 25 50 | 25 07 | 24 28 | 23 56 | 23 05 |
| 42 | 25 59 | 25 14 | 24 31 | 23 55 | 23 02 |
| 43 | 26 07 | 25 21 | 24 34 | 23 54 | 22 58 |
| 44 | 26 16 | 25 28 | 24 37 | 23 53 | 22 55 |
| 45 | 26 24 | 25 35 | 24 41 | 23 53 | 22 52 |
| 46 | 26 33 | 25 42 | 24 44 | 23 52 | 22 48 |
| 47 | 26 42 | 25 49 | 24 48 | 23 52 | 22 45 |
| 48 | 26 52 | 25 56 | 24 51 | 23 52 | 22 42 |
| 49 | 27 01 | 26 03 | 24 55 | 23 51 | 22 39 |
| 50 | 27 11 | 26 10 | 24 58 | 23 51 | 22 36 |
| 51 | 27 20 | 26 17 | 25 02 | 23 52 | 22 33 |
| 52 | 27 30 | 26 25 | 25 06 | 23 52 | 22 30 |
| 53 | 27 40 | 26 31 | 25 09 | 23 53 | 22 27 |
| 54 | 27 51 | 26 38 | 25 13 | 23 54 | 22 25 |
| 55 | 28 01 | 26 45 | 25 17 | 23 55 | 22 23 |
| 56 | 28 11 | 26 51 | 25 21 | 23 57 | 22 22 |
| 57 | 28 21 | 26 57 | 25 26 | 24 00 | 22 21 |
| 58 | 28 31 | 27 03 | 25 30 | 24 03 | 22 21 |
| 59 | 28 41 | 27 08 | 25 34 | 24 07 | 22 22 |
| 60 | 28♋50 | 27♌12 | 25♍39 | 24♎13 | 22♏25 |

5h 36m 0s — 84° 0' 0" — 24 ♊ 30

| LAT. | 11 | 12 | ASC | 2 | 3 |
|---|---|---|---|---|---|
| 0 | 22♋13 | 21♌37 | 23♍28 | 25♎53 | 26♏19 |
| 5 | 22 43 | 22 11 | 23 42 | 25 43 | 26 01 |
| 10 | 23 13 | 22 42 | 23 56 | 25 34 | 25 43 |
| 15 | 23 43 | 23 13 | 24 09 | 25 25 | 25 26 |
| 20 | 24 14 | 23 43 | 24 21 | 25 16 | 25 09 |
| 21 | 24 20 | 23 50 | 24 24 | 25 14 | 25 05 |
| 22 | 24 26 | 23 56 | 24 26 | 25 13 | 25 02 |
| 23 | 24 32 | 24 02 | 24 29 | 25 11 | 24 58 |
| 24 | 24 38 | 24 08 | 24 31 | 25 09 | 24 55 |
| 25 | 24 45 | 24 14 | 24 34 | 25 08 | 24 51 |
| 26 | 24 51 | 24 20 | 24 36 | 25 06 | 24 48 |
| 27 | 24 58 | 24 26 | 24 39 | 25 04 | 24 44 |
| 28 | 25 04 | 24 32 | 24 41 | 25 03 | 24 41 |
| 29 | 25 11 | 24 38 | 24 44 | 25 01 | 24 37 |
| 30 | 25 17 | 24 44 | 24 46 | 25 00 | 24 34 |
| 31 | 25 24 | 24 50 | 24 49 | 24 58 | 24 30 |
| 32 | 25 31 | 24 56 | 24 51 | 24 57 | 24 27 |
| 33 | 25 38 | 25 03 | 24 54 | 24 55 | 24 23 |
| 34 | 25 45 | 25 09 | 24 56 | 24 53 | 24 20 |
| 35 | 25 52 | 25 15 | 24 59 | 24 52 | 24 16 |
| 36 | 25 59 | 25 21 | 25 02 | 24 50 | 24 12 |
| 37 | 26 06 | 25 28 | 25 04 | 24 49 | 24 09 |
| 38 | 26 14 | 25 34 | 25 07 | 24 48 | 24 05 |
| 39 | 26 21 | 25 40 | 25 10 | 24 46 | 24 01 |
| 40 | 26 29 | 25 47 | 25 12 | 24 45 | 23 57 |
| 41 | 26 37 | 25 53 | 25 15 | 24 44 | 23 54 |
| 42 | 26 45 | 26 00 | 25 18 | 24 42 | 23 50 |
| 43 | 26 53 | 26 06 | 25 21 | 24 41 | 23 46 |
| 44 | 27 01 | 26 13 | 25 23 | 24 40 | 23 43 |
| 45 | 27 09 | 26 19 | 25 26 | 24 39 | 23 39 |
| 46 | 27 18 | 26 26 | 25 29 | 24 38 | 23 35 |
| 47 | 27 26 | 26 32 | 25 32 | 24 37 | 23 31 |
| 48 | 27 35 | 26 39 | 25 35 | 24 36 | 23 28 |
| 49 | 27 44 | 26 46 | 25 38 | 24 36 | 23 24 |
| 50 | 27 53 | 26 52 | 25 41 | 24 35 | 23 21 |
| 51 | 28 02 | 26 59 | 25 44 | 24 35 | 23 17 |
| 52 | 28 12 | 27 05 | 25 48 | 24 35 | 23 14 |
| 53 | 28 21 | 27 11 | 25 51 | 24 35 | 23 11 |
| 54 | 28 31 | 27 18 | 25 54 | 24 36 | 23 09 |
| 55 | 28 40 | 27 24 | 25 58 | 24 36 | 23 06 |
| 56 | 28 50 | 27 29 | 26 01 | 24 38 | 23 04 |
| 57 | 28 59 | 27 35 | 26 05 | 24 40 | 23 03 |
| 58 | 29 08 | 27 40 | 26 08 | 24 43 | 23 02 |
| 59 | 29 17 | 27 44 | 26 12 | 24 46 | 23 03 |
| 60 | 29♋25 | 27♌47 | 26♍16 | 24♎51 | 23♏05 |

5h 40m 0s — 85° 0' 0" — 25 ♊ 25

| LAT. | 11 | 12 | ASC | 2 | 3 |
|---|---|---|---|---|---|
| 0 | 23♋10 | 22♌39 | 24♍33 | 26♎57 | 27♏17 |
| 5 | 23 39 | 23 10 | 24 45 | 26 45 | 26 58 |
| 10 | 24 08 | 23 40 | 24 56 | 26 33 | 26 39 |
| 15 | 24 37 | 24 09 | 25 07 | 26 22 | 26 21 |
| 20 | 25 06 | 24 38 | 25 18 | 26 12 | 26 03 |
| 21 | 25 12 | 24 44 | 25 20 | 26 10 | 25 59 |
| 22 | 25 18 | 24 49 | 25 22 | 26 08 | 25 55 |
| 23 | 25 24 | 24 55 | 25 24 | 26 06 | 25 52 |
| 24 | 25 30 | 25 01 | 25 26 | 26 04 | 25 48 |
| 25 | 25 36 | 25 06 | 25 28 | 26 02 | 25 44 |
| 26 | 25 42 | 25 12 | 25 30 | 26 00 | 25 40 |
| 27 | 25 49 | 25 18 | 25 32 | 25 58 | 25 37 |
| 28 | 25 55 | 25 23 | 25 34 | 25 56 | 25 33 |
| 29 | 26 01 | 25 29 | 25 36 | 25 54 | 25 29 |
| 30 | 26 07 | 25 35 | 25 39 | 25 52 | 25 25 |
| 31 | 26 14 | 25 41 | 25 41 | 25 50 | 25 21 |
| 32 | 26 20 | 25 46 | 25 43 | 25 48 | 25 18 |
| 33 | 26 27 | 25 52 | 25 45 | 25 46 | 25 14 |
| 34 | 26 34 | 25 58 | 25 47 | 25 44 | 25 10 |
| 35 | 26 41 | 26 04 | 25 49 | 25 42 | 25 06 |
| 36 | 26 47 | 26 10 | 25 51 | 25 40 | 25 02 |
| 37 | 26 54 | 26 15 | 25 54 | 25 38 | 24 58 |
| 38 | 27 02 | 26 21 | 25 56 | 25 37 | 24 54 |
| 39 | 27 09 | 26 27 | 25 58 | 25 35 | 24 50 |
| 40 | 27 16 | 26 33 | 26 00 | 25 33 | 24 46 |
| 41 | 27 23 | 26 39 | 26 03 | 25 31 | 24 42 |
| 42 | 27 31 | 26 45 | 26 05 | 25 30 | 24 38 |
| 43 | 27 39 | 26 51 | 26 07 | 25 28 | 24 34 |
| 44 | 27 46 | 26 57 | 26 10 | 25 26 | 24 30 |
| 45 | 27 54 | 27 04 | 26 12 | 25 25 | 24 26 |
| 46 | 28 02 | 27 10 | 26 14 | 25 23 | 24 22 |
| 47 | 28 11 | 27 16 | 26 17 | 25 22 | 24 18 |
| 48 | 28 19 | 27 22 | 26 19 | 25 21 | 24 14 |
| 49 | 28 27 | 27 28 | 26 22 | 25 20 | 24 10 |
| 50 | 28 36 | 27 34 | 26 24 | 25 19 | 24 06 |
| 51 | 28 45 | 27 40 | 26 27 | 25 18 | 24 02 |
| 52 | 28 53 | 27 46 | 26 30 | 25 17 | 23 58 |
| 53 | 29 02 | 27 52 | 26 32 | 25 17 | 23 55 |
| 54 | 29 11 | 27 57 | 26 35 | 25 17 | 23 52 |
| 55 | 29 20 | 28 03 | 26 38 | 25 18 | 23 49 |
| 56 | 29 29 | 28 08 | 26 41 | 25 18 | 23 46 |
| 57 | 29 37 | 28 12 | 26 44 | 25 20 | 23 45 |
| 58 | 29 45 | 28 17 | 26 47 | 25 22 | 23 44 |
| 59 | 29 53 | 28 20 | 26 50 | 25 25 | 23 44 |
| 60 | 00♌00 | 28♌23 | 26♍53 | 25♎30 | 23♏45 |

5h 44m 0s — 86° 0' 0" — 26 ♊ 20

| LAT. | 11 | 12 | ASC | 2 | 3 |
|---|---|---|---|---|---|
| 0 | 24♋06 | 23♌41 | 25♍38 | 28♎00 | 28♏15 |
| 5 | 24 35 | 24 10 | 25 48 | 27 46 | 27 55 |
| 10 | 25 03 | 24 38 | 25 57 | 27 32 | 27 35 |
| 15 | 25 31 | 25 06 | 26 06 | 27 20 | 27 16 |
| 20 | 25 59 | 25 32 | 26 14 | 27 07 | 26 56 |
| 21 | 26 04 | 25 38 | 26 16 | 27 05 | 26 52 |
| 22 | 26 10 | 25 43 | 26 17 | 27 03 | 26 48 |
| 23 | 26 16 | 25 48 | 26 19 | 27 00 | 26 45 |
| 24 | 26 22 | 25 54 | 26 21 | 26 58 | 26 41 |
| 25 | 26 28 | 25 59 | 26 22 | 26 55 | 26 37 |
| 26 | 26 34 | 26 04 | 26 24 | 26 53 | 26 33 |
| 27 | 26 39 | 26 10 | 26 26 | 26 51 | 26 29 |
| 28 | 26 45 | 26 15 | 26 27 | 26 48 | 26 25 |
| 29 | 26 52 | 26 20 | 26 29 | 26 46 | 26 21 |
| 30 | 26 58 | 26 26 | 26 31 | 26 44 | 26 17 |
| 31 | 27 04 | 26 31 | 26 32 | 26 41 | 26 13 |
| 32 | 27 10 | 26 36 | 26 34 | 26 39 | 26 08 |
| 33 | 27 16 | 26 42 | 26 36 | 26 37 | 26 04 |
| 34 | 27 23 | 26 47 | 26 38 | 26 34 | 26 00 |
| 35 | 27 29 | 26 53 | 26 39 | 26 32 | 25 56 |
| 36 | 27 36 | 26 58 | 26 41 | 26 30 | 25 52 |
| 37 | 27 43 | 27 04 | 26 43 | 26 28 | 25 47 |
| 38 | 27 49 | 27 09 | 26 45 | 26 25 | 25 43 |
| 39 | 27 56 | 27 15 | 26 46 | 26 23 | 25 39 |
| 40 | 28 03 | 27 20 | 26 48 | 26 21 | 25 35 |
| 41 | 28 10 | 27 26 | 26 50 | 26 19 | 25 30 |
| 42 | 28 17 | 27 31 | 26 52 | 26 17 | 25 26 |
| 43 | 28 25 | 27 37 | 26 54 | 26 15 | 25 21 |
| 44 | 28 32 | 27 42 | 26 56 | 26 13 | 25 17 |
| 45 | 28 40 | 27 48 | 26 58 | 26 11 | 25 13 |
| 46 | 28 47 | 27 54 | 26 59 | 26 09 | 25 08 |
| 47 | 28 55 | 27 59 | 27 01 | 26 07 | 25 04 |
| 48 | 29 03 | 28 05 | 27 03 | 26 05 | 24 59 |
| 49 | 29 11 | 28 10 | 27 05 | 26 04 | 24 55 |
| 50 | 29 19 | 28 16 | 27 08 | 26 02 | 24 51 |
| 51 | 29 27 | 28 21 | 27 10 | 26 01 | 24 46 |
| 52 | 29 35 | 28 27 | 27 12 | 26 00 | 24 42 |
| 53 | 29 43 | 28 32 | 27 14 | 25 59 | 24 38 |
| 54 | 29 52 | 28 37 | 27 16 | 25 59 | 24 35 |
| 55 | 00♌00 | 28 42 | 27 18 | 25 58 | 24 31 |
| 56 | 00 08 | 28 46 | 27 21 | 25 59 | 24 28 |
| 57 | 00 16 | 28 50 | 27 23 | 26 00 | 24 26 |
| 58 | 00 23 | 28 54 | 27 26 | 26 01 | 24 24 |
| 59 | 00 30 | 28 56 | 27 28 | 26 04 | 24 24 |
| 60 | 00♌36 | 28♌58 | 27♍31 | 26♎08 | 24♏24 |

5h 48m 0s — 87° 0' 0" — 27 ♊ 15

| LAT. | 11 | 12 | ASC | 2 | 3 |
|---|---|---|---|---|---|
| 0 | 25♋03 | 24♌42 | 26♍44 | 29♎03 | 29♏13 |
| 5 | 25 31 | 25 10 | 26 51 | 28 47 | 28 52 |
| 10 | 25 58 | 25 36 | 26 58 | 28 32 | 28 31 |
| 15 | 26 24 | 26 02 | 27 04 | 28 17 | 28 10 |
| 20 | 26 51 | 26 27 | 27 11 | 28 03 | 27 50 |
| 21 | 26 57 | 26 32 | 27 12 | 28 00 | 27 46 |
| 22 | 27 02 | 26 37 | 27 13 | 27 57 | 27 42 |
| 23 | 27 08 | 26 42 | 27 14 | 27 54 | 27 37 |
| 24 | 27 14 | 26 47 | 27 16 | 27 52 | 27 33 |
| 25 | 27 19 | 26 52 | 27 17 | 27 49 | 27 29 |
| 26 | 27 25 | 26 57 | 27 18 | 27 46 | 27 25 |
| 27 | 27 31 | 27 02 | 27 19 | 27 43 | 27 21 |
| 28 | 27 36 | 27 07 | 27 21 | 27 41 | 27 16 |
| 29 | 27 42 | 27 12 | 27 22 | 27 38 | 27 12 |
| 30 | 27 48 | 27 17 | 27 23 | 27 35 | 27 08 |
| 31 | 27 54 | 27 22 | 27 24 | 27 33 | 27 03 |
| 32 | 28 00 | 27 27 | 27 26 | 27 30 | 26 59 |
| 33 | 28 06 | 27 32 | 27 27 | 27 27 | 26 55 |
| 34 | 28 12 | 27 37 | 27 28 | 27 25 | 26 50 |
| 35 | 28 18 | 27 42 | 27 30 | 27 22 | 26 46 |
| 36 | 28 25 | 27 47 | 27 31 | 27 19 | 26 41 |
| 37 | 28 31 | 27 52 | 27 32 | 27 17 | 26 37 |
| 38 | 28 37 | 27 57 | 27 33 | 27 14 | 26 32 |
| 39 | 28 44 | 28 02 | 27 35 | 27 11 | 26 28 |
| 40 | 28 50 | 28 07 | 27 36 | 27 09 | 26 23 |
| 41 | 28 57 | 28 12 | 27 38 | 27 06 | 26 18 |
| 42 | 29 04 | 28 17 | 27 39 | 27 04 | 26 13 |
| 43 | 29 11 | 28 22 | 27 40 | 27 01 | 26 09 |
| 44 | 29 18 | 28 28 | 27 42 | 26 59 | 26 04 |
| 45 | 29 25 | 28 33 | 27 43 | 26 56 | 25 59 |
| 46 | 29 32 | 28 38 | 27 45 | 26 54 | 25 54 |
| 47 | 29 39 | 28 43 | 27 46 | 26 52 | 25 50 |
| 48 | 29 47 | 28 48 | 27 48 | 26 50 | 25 45 |
| 49 | 29 54 | 28 53 | 27 49 | 26 47 | 25 40 |
| 50 | 00♌02 | 28 58 | 27 51 | 26 46 | 25 35 |
| 51 | 00 09 | 29 03 | 27 52 | 26 44 | 25 31 |
| 52 | 00 17 | 29 08 | 27 54 | 26 42 | 25 26 |
| 53 | 00 25 | 29 12 | 27 55 | 26 41 | 25 22 |
| 54 | 00 32 | 29 17 | 27 57 | 26 40 | 25 17 |
| 55 | 00 40 | 29 21 | 27 59 | 26 39 | 25 13 |
| 56 | 00 47 | 29 25 | 28 01 | 26 39 | 25 10 |
| 57 | 00 54 | 29 28 | 28 02 | 26 39 | 25 07 |
| 58 | 01 01 | 29 31 | 28 04 | 26 40 | 25 05 |
| 59 | 01 07 | 29 33 | 28 06 | 26 42 | 25 03 |
| 60 | 01♌12 | 29♌34 | 28♍08 | 26♎45 | 25♏03 |

# Koch Table of Houses for Latitudes 0° to 60° North

| 5h 52m 0s | 88° 0' 0" | 28 ♊ 10 | | | |
|---|---|---|---|---|---|
| LAT. | 11 | 12 | ASC | 2 | 3 |
| 0 | 26♋00 | 25♌44 | 27♍49 | 00♏06 | 00♐11 |
| 5 | 26 27 | 26 10 | 27 54 | 29♎48 | 29♏48 |
| 10 | 26 53 | 26 35 | 27 58 | 29 31 | 29 26 |
| 15 | 27 18 | 26 58 | 28 03 | 29 14 | 29 05 |
| 20 | 27 44 | 27 22 | 28 07 | 28 58 | 28 43 |
| 21 | 27 50 | 27 26 | 28 08 | 28 55 | 28 39 |
| 22 | 27 55 | 27 31 | 28 09 | 28 52 | 28 35 |
| 23 | 28 00 | 27 35 | 28 10 | 28 49 | 28 30 |
| 24 | 28 05 | 27 40 | 28 10 | 28 46 | 28 26 |
| 25 | 28 11 | 27 45 | 28 11 | 28 42 | 28 21 |
| 26 | 28 16 | 27 49 | 28 12 | 28 39 | 28 17 |
| 27 | 28 22 | 27 54 | 28 13 | 28 36 | 28 12 |
| 28 | 28 27 | 27 58 | 28 14 | 28 33 | 28 08 |
| 29 | 28 33 | 28 03 | 28 15 | 28 30 | 28 03 |
| 30 | 28 38 | 28 08 | 28 15 | 28 27 | 27 59 |
| 31 | 28 44 | 28 12 | 28 16 | 28 24 | 27 54 |
| 32 | 28 50 | 28 17 | 28 17 | 28 21 | 27 50 |
| 33 | 28 56 | 28 21 | 28 18 | 28 18 | 27 45 |
| 34 | 29 01 | 28 26 | 28 19 | 28 15 | 27 40 |
| 35 | 29 07 | 28 31 | 28 20 | 28 12 | 27 35 |
| 36 | 29 13 | 28 35 | 28 21 | 28 09 | 27 31 |
| 37 | 29 19 | 28 40 | 28 21 | 28 06 | 27 26 |
| 38 | 29 25 | 28 45 | 28 22 | 28 02 | 27 21 |
| 39 | 29 32 | 28 49 | 28 23 | 27 59 | 27 16 |
| 40 | 29 38 | 28 54 | 28 24 | 27 56 | 27 11 |
| 41 | 29 44 | 28 59 | 28 25 | 27 53 | 27 06 |
| 42 | 29 51 | 29 03 | 28 26 | 27 50 | 27 01 |
| 43 | 29 57 | 29 08 | 28 27 | 27 48 | 26 56 |
| 44 | 00♌04 | 29 13 | 28 28 | 27 45 | 26 51 |
| 45 | 00 11 | 29 18 | 28 29 | 27 42 | 26 46 |
| 46 | 00 17 | 29 22 | 28 30 | 27 39 | 26 40 |
| 47 | 00 24 | 29 27 | 28 31 | 27 36 | 26 35 |
| 48 | 00 31 | 29 31 | 28 32 | 27 34 | 26 30 |
| 49 | 00 38 | 29 36 | 28 33 | 27 31 | 26 25 |
| 50 | 00 45 | 29 40 | 28 34 | 27 29 | 26 20 |
| 51 | 00 52 | 29 45 | 28 35 | 27 26 | 26 14 |
| 52 | 00 59 | 29 49 | 28 36 | 27 24 | 26 09 |
| 53 | 01 06 | 29 53 | 28 37 | 27 22 | 26 04 |
| 54 | 01 13 | 29 57 | 28 38 | 27 21 | 26 00 |
| 55 | 01 20 | 00♍01 | 28 39 | 27 20 | 25 55 |
| 56 | 01 27 | 00 04 | 28 40 | 27 19 | 25 51 |
| 57 | 01 33 | 00 07 | 28 42 | 27 18 | 25 47 |
| 58 | 01 39 | 00 09 | 28 43 | 27 19 | 25 45 |
| 59 | 01 44 | 00 10 | 28 44 | 27 20 | 25 43 |
| 60 | 01♌48 | 00♍10 | 28♍45 | 27♎23 | 25♏42 |

| 5h 56m 0s | 89° 0' 0" | 29 ♊ 05 | | | |
|---|---|---|---|---|---|
| LAT. | 11 | 12 | ASC | 2 | 3 |
| 0 | 26♋57 | 26♌47 | 28♍55 | 01♏08 | 01♐08 |
| 5 | 27 23 | 27 11 | 28 57 | 00 48 | 00 45 |
| 10 | 27 48 | 27 33 | 28 59 | 00 29 | 00 22 |
| 15 | 28 12 | 27 55 | 29 01 | 00 11 | 29♏59 |
| 20 | 28 37 | 28 17 | 29 04 | 29♎53 | 29 37 |
| 21 | 28 42 | 28 21 | 29 04 | 29 50 | 29 32 |
| 22 | 28 47 | 28 25 | 29 04 | 29 46 | 29 27 |
| 23 | 28 52 | 28 29 | 29 05 | 29 43 | 29 23 |
| 24 | 28 57 | 28 33 | 29 05 | 29 39 | 29 18 |
| 25 | 29 03 | 28 38 | 29 06 | 29 36 | 29 13 |
| 26 | 29 08 | 28 42 | 29 06 | 29 32 | 29 09 |
| 27 | 29 13 | 28 46 | 29 06 | 29 29 | 29 04 |
| 28 | 29 18 | 28 50 | 29 07 | 29 25 | 28 59 |
| 29 | 29 24 | 28 55 | 29 07 | 29 22 | 28 55 |
| 30 | 29 29 | 28 59 | 29 08 | 29 19 | 28 50 |
| 31 | 29 34 | 29 03 | 29 08 | 29 15 | 28 45 |
| 32 | 29 40 | 29 07 | 29 09 | 29 12 | 28 40 |
| 33 | 29 45 | 29 11 | 29 09 | 29 08 | 28 35 |
| 34 | 29 51 | 29 16 | 29 09 | 29 05 | 28 30 |
| 35 | 29 56 | 29 20 | 29 10 | 29 01 | 28 25 |
| 36 | 00♌02 | 29 24 | 29 10 | 28 58 | 28 20 |
| 37 | 00 08 | 29 28 | 29 11 | 28 54 | 28 15 |
| 38 | 00 14 | 29 33 | 29 11 | 28 51 | 28 10 |
| 39 | 00 19 | 29 37 | 29 12 | 28 47 | 28 04 |
| 40 | 00 25 | 29 41 | 29 12 | 28 44 | 27 59 |
| 41 | 00 31 | 29 46 | 29 13 | 28 41 | 27 54 |
| 42 | 00 38 | 29 50 | 29 13 | 28 37 | 27 48 |
| 43 | 00 44 | 29 54 | 29 13 | 28 34 | 27 43 |
| 44 | 00 50 | 29 58 | 29 14 | 28 30 | 27 37 |
| 45 | 00 56 | 00♍03 | 29 14 | 28 27 | 27 32 |
| 46 | 01 03 | 00 07 | 29 15 | 28 24 | 27 26 |
| 47 | 01 09 | 00 11 | 29 15 | 28 21 | 27 21 |
| 48 | 01 16 | 00 15 | 29 16 | 28 18 | 27 15 |
| 49 | 01 22 | 00 19 | 29 16 | 28 15 | 27 09 |
| 50 | 01 29 | 00 23 | 29 17 | 28 12 | 27 04 |
| 51 | 01 35 | 00 27 | 29 17 | 28 09 | 26 58 |
| 52 | 01 42 | 00 30 | 29 18 | 28 06 | 26 53 |
| 53 | 01 48 | 00 34 | 29 18 | 28 04 | 26 47 |
| 54 | 01 55 | 00 37 | 29 19 | 28 02 | 26 42 |
| 55 | 02 01 | 00 40 | 29 20 | 28 00 | 26 37 |
| 56 | 02 07 | 00 43 | 29 20 | 27 58 | 26 32 |
| 57 | 02 13 | 00 45 | 29 21 | 27 57 | 26 28 |
| 58 | 02 18 | 00 46 | 29 21 | 27 57 | 26 24 |
| 59 | 02 22 | 00 47 | 29 22 | 27 58 | 26 21 |
| 60 | 02♌25 | 00♍47 | 29♍23 | 28♎00 | 26♏20 |

| 6h 0m 0s | 90° 0' 0" | 00 ♋ 00 | | | |
|---|---|---|---|---|---|
| LAT. | 11 | 12 | ASC | 2 | 3 |
| 0 | 27♋55 | 27♌49 | 00♎00 | 02♏11 | 02♐05 |
| 5 | 28 19 | 28 11 | 00 00 | 01 49 | 01 41 |
| 10 | 28 43 | 28 32 | 00 00 | 01 28 | 01 17 |
| 15 | 29 06 | 28 52 | 00 00 | 01 08 | 00 54 |
| 20 | 29 30 | 29 11 | 00 00 | 00 49 | 00 30 |
| 21 | 29 35 | 29 15 | 00 00 | 00 45 | 00 25 |
| 22 | 29 40 | 29 19 | 00 00 | 00 41 | 00 20 |
| 23 | 29 45 | 29 23 | 00 00 | 00 37 | 00 15 |
| 24 | 29 50 | 29 27 | 00 00 | 00 33 | 00 10 |
| 25 | 29 55 | 29 31 | 00 00 | 00 29 | 00 05 |
| 26 | 29 59 | 29 35 | 00 00 | 00 25 | 00 01 |
| 27 | 00♌04 | 29 39 | 00 00 | 00 21 | 29♏56 |
| 28 | 00 09 | 29 42 | 00 00 | 00 18 | 29 51 |
| 29 | 00 14 | 29 46 | 00 00 | 00 14 | 29 46 |
| 30 | 00 20 | 29 50 | 00 00 | 00 10 | 29 40 |
| 31 | 00 25 | 29 54 | 00 00 | 00 06 | 29 35 |
| 32 | 00 30 | 29 58 | 00 00 | 00 02 | 29 30 |
| 33 | 00 35 | 00♍02 | 00 00 | 29♎58 | 29 25 |
| 34 | 00 40 | 00 05 | 00 00 | 29 55 | 29 20 |
| 35 | 00 46 | 00 09 | 00 00 | 29 51 | 29 14 |
| 36 | 00 51 | 00 13 | 00 00 | 29 47 | 29 09 |
| 37 | 00 56 | 00 17 | 00 00 | 29 43 | 29 04 |
| 38 | 01 02 | 00 21 | 00 00 | 29 39 | 28 58 |
| 39 | 01 08 | 00 25 | 00 00 | 29 35 | 28 52 |
| 40 | 01 13 | 00 29 | 00 00 | 29 31 | 28 47 |
| 41 | 01 19 | 00 32 | 00 00 | 29 28 | 28 41 |
| 42 | 01 25 | 00 36 | 00 00 | 29 24 | 28 35 |
| 43 | 01 30 | 00 40 | 00 00 | 29 20 | 28 30 |
| 44 | 01 36 | 00 44 | 00 00 | 29 16 | 28 24 |
| 45 | 01 42 | 00 48 | 00 00 | 29 12 | 28 18 |
| 46 | 01 48 | 00 51 | 00 00 | 29 09 | 28 12 |
| 47 | 01 54 | 00 55 | 00 00 | 29 05 | 28 06 |
| 48 | 02 00 | 00 59 | 00 00 | 29 01 | 28 00 |
| 49 | 02 06 | 01 02 | 00 00 | 28 58 | 27 54 |
| 50 | 02 12 | 01 06 | 00 00 | 28 54 | 27 48 |
| 51 | 02 18 | 01 09 | 00 00 | 28 51 | 27 42 |
| 52 | 02 25 | 01 12 | 00 00 | 28 48 | 27 35 |
| 53 | 02 30 | 01 15 | 00 00 | 28 45 | 27 30 |
| 54 | 02 36 | 01 18 | 00 00 | 28 42 | 27 24 |
| 55 | 02 42 | 01 20 | 00 00 | 28 40 | 27 18 |
| 56 | 02 47 | 01 22 | 00 00 | 28 38 | 27 13 |
| 57 | 02 52 | 01 24 | 00 00 | 28 36 | 27 08 |
| 58 | 02 57 | 01 24 | 00 00 | 28 36 | 27 03 |
| 59 | 03 00 | 01 24 | 00 00 | 28 36 | 27 00 |
| 60 | 03♌02 | 01♍23 | 00♎00 | 28♎37 | 26♏58 |

| 6h 4m 0s | 91° 0' 0" | 00 ♋ 55 | | | |
|---|---|---|---|---|---|
| LAT. | 11 | 12 | ASC | 2 | 3 |
| 0 | 28♋52 | 28♌52 | 01♎05 | 03♏13 | 03♐03 |
| 5 | 29 15 | 29 12 | 01 03 | 02 49 | 02 37 |
| 10 | 29 38 | 29 31 | 01 01 | 02 27 | 02 12 |
| 15 | 00♌01 | 29 49 | 00 59 | 02 05 | 01 48 |
| 20 | 00 23 | 00♍07 | 00 56 | 01 43 | 01 23 |
| 21 | 00 28 | 00 10 | 00 56 | 01 39 | 01 18 |
| 22 | 00 33 | 00 14 | 00 56 | 01 35 | 01 13 |
| 23 | 00 37 | 00 17 | 00 55 | 01 31 | 01 08 |
| 24 | 00 42 | 00 21 | 00 55 | 01 27 | 01 03 |
| 25 | 00 47 | 00 24 | 00 54 | 01 22 | 00 57 |
| 26 | 00 51 | 00 28 | 00 54 | 01 18 | 00 52 |
| 27 | 00 56 | 00 31 | 00 54 | 01 14 | 00 47 |
| 28 | 01 01 | 00 35 | 00 53 | 01 10 | 00 42 |
| 29 | 01 05 | 00 38 | 00 53 | 01 05 | 00 36 |
| 30 | 01 10 | 00 41 | 00 52 | 01 01 | 00 31 |
| 31 | 01 15 | 00 45 | 00 52 | 00 57 | 00 26 |
| 32 | 01 20 | 00 48 | 00 51 | 00 53 | 00 20 |
| 33 | 01 25 | 00 52 | 00 51 | 00 49 | 00 15 |
| 34 | 01 30 | 00 55 | 00 51 | 00 44 | 00 09 |
| 35 | 01 35 | 00 59 | 00 50 | 00 40 | 00 04 |
| 36 | 01 40 | 01 02 | 00 50 | 00 36 | 29♏58 |
| 37 | 01 45 | 01 06 | 00 49 | 00 32 | 29 52 |
| 38 | 01 50 | 01 09 | 00 49 | 00 27 | 29 46 |
| 39 | 01 56 | 01 13 | 00 48 | 00 23 | 29 41 |
| 40 | 02 01 | 01 16 | 00 48 | 00 19 | 29 35 |
| 41 | 02 06 | 01 19 | 00 47 | 00 14 | 29 29 |
| 42 | 02 12 | 01 23 | 00 47 | 00 10 | 29 22 |
| 43 | 02 17 | 01 26 | 00 47 | 00 06 | 29 16 |
| 44 | 02 23 | 01 30 | 00 46 | 00 02 | 29 10 |
| 45 | 02 28 | 01 33 | 00 46 | 29♎57 | 29 04 |
| 46 | 02 34 | 01 36 | 00 45 | 29 53 | 28 57 |
| 47 | 02 39 | 01 39 | 00 45 | 29 49 | 28 51 |
| 48 | 02 45 | 01 42 | 00 44 | 29 45 | 28 44 |
| 49 | 02 51 | 01 45 | 00 44 | 29 41 | 28 38 |
| 50 | 02 56 | 01 48 | 00 43 | 29 37 | 28 31 |
| 51 | 03 02 | 01 51 | 00 43 | 29 33 | 28 25 |
| 52 | 03 07 | 01 54 | 00 42 | 29 30 | 28 18 |
| 53 | 03 13 | 01 56 | 00 42 | 29 26 | 28 12 |
| 54 | 03 18 | 01 58 | 00 41 | 29 23 | 28 05 |
| 55 | 03 23 | 02 00 | 00 40 | 29 20 | 27 59 |
| 56 | 03 28 | 02 02 | 00 40 | 29 17 | 27 53 |
| 57 | 03 32 | 02 03 | 00 39 | 29 15 | 27 47 |
| 58 | 03 36 | 02 03 | 00 39 | 29 14 | 27 42 |
| 59 | 03 39 | 02 02 | 00 38 | 29 13 | 27 38 |
| 60 | 03♌40 | 02♍00 | 00♎37 | 29♎13 | 27♏35 |

| 6h 8m 0s | 92° 0' 0" | 01 ♋ 50 | | | |
|---|---|---|---|---|---|
| LAT. | 11 | 12 | ASC | 2 | 3 |
| 0 | 29♋49 | 29♌54 | 02♎11 | 04♏16 | 04♐00 |
| 5 | 00♌12 | 00♍12 | 02 06 | 03 50 | 03 33 |
| 10 | 00 34 | 00 29 | 02 02 | 03 25 | 03 07 |
| 15 | 00 55 | 00 46 | 01 57 | 03 02 | 02 42 |
| 20 | 01 17 | 01 02 | 01 53 | 02 38 | 02 16 |
| 21 | 01 21 | 01 05 | 01 52 | 02 34 | 02 10 |
| 22 | 01 25 | 01 08 | 01 51 | 02 29 | 02 05 |
| 23 | 01 30 | 01 11 | 01 50 | 02 25 | 02 00 |
| 24 | 01 34 | 01 14 | 01 50 | 02 20 | 01 55 |
| 25 | 01 39 | 01 18 | 01 49 | 02 15 | 01 49 |
| 26 | 01 43 | 01 21 | 01 48 | 02 11 | 01 44 |
| 27 | 01 48 | 01 24 | 01 47 | 02 06 | 01 38 |
| 28 | 01 52 | 01 27 | 01 46 | 02 02 | 01 33 |
| 29 | 01 57 | 01 30 | 01 45 | 01 57 | 01 27 |
| 30 | 02 01 | 01 33 | 01 45 | 01 52 | 01 22 |
| 31 | 02 06 | 01 36 | 01 44 | 01 48 | 01 16 |
| 32 | 02 10 | 01 39 | 01 43 | 01 43 | 01 10 |
| 33 | 02 15 | 01 42 | 01 42 | 01 39 | 01 04 |
| 34 | 02 20 | 01 45 | 01 41 | 01 34 | 00 59 |
| 35 | 02 25 | 01 48 | 01 40 | 01 29 | 00 53 |
| 36 | 02 29 | 01 51 | 01 39 | 01 25 | 00 47 |
| 37 | 02 34 | 01 54 | 01 39 | 01 20 | 00 41 |
| 38 | 02 39 | 01 58 | 01 38 | 01 15 | 00 35 |
| 39 | 02 44 | 02 01 | 01 37 | 01 11 | 00 28 |
| 40 | 02 49 | 02 04 | 01 36 | 01 06 | 00 22 |
| 41 | 02 54 | 02 07 | 01 35 | 01 01 | 00 16 |
| 42 | 02 59 | 02 10 | 01 34 | 00 57 | 00 09 |
| 43 | 03 04 | 02 12 | 01 33 | 00 52 | 00 03 |
| 44 | 03 09 | 02 15 | 01 32 | 00 47 | 29♏56 |
| 45 | 03 14 | 02 18 | 01 31 | 00 42 | 29 49 |
| 46 | 03 20 | 02 21 | 01 30 | 00 38 | 29 43 |
| 47 | 03 25 | 02 24 | 01 29 | 00 33 | 29 36 |
| 48 | 03 30 | 02 26 | 01 28 | 00 29 | 29 29 |
| 49 | 03 35 | 02 29 | 01 27 | 00 24 | 29 22 |
| 50 | 03 40 | 02 31 | 01 26 | 00 20 | 29 15 |
| 51 | 03 46 | 02 34 | 01 25 | 00 15 | 29 08 |
| 52 | 03 51 | 02 36 | 01 24 | 00 11 | 29 01 |
| 53 | 03 56 | 02 38 | 01 23 | 00 07 | 28 54 |
| 54 | 04 00 | 02 39 | 01 22 | 00 03 | 28 47 |
| 55 | 04 05 | 02 40 | 01 21 | 29♎59 | 28 40 |
| 56 | 04 09 | 02 41 | 01 20 | 29 56 | 28 33 |
| 57 | 04 13 | 02 42 | 01 18 | 29 53 | 28 27 |
| 58 | 04 15 | 02 41 | 01 17 | 29 51 | 28 21 |
| 59 | 04 17 | 02 40 | 01 16 | 29 50 | 28 16 |
| 60 | 04♌18 | 02♍37 | 01♎15 | 29♎50 | 28♏12 |

| 6h 12m 0s | 93° 0' 0" | 02 ♋ 45 | | | |
|---|---|---|---|---|---|
| LAT. | 11 | 12 | ASC | 2 | 3 |
| 0 | 00♌47 | 00♍57 | 03♎16 | 05♏18 | 04♐57 |
| 5 | 01 08 | 01 13 | 03 09 | 04 50 | 04 29 |
| 10 | 01 29 | 01 28 | 03 02 | 04 24 | 04 02 |
| 15 | 01 50 | 01 43 | 02 56 | 03 58 | 03 36 |
| 20 | 02 10 | 01 57 | 02 49 | 03 33 | 03 09 |
| 21 | 02 14 | 02 00 | 02 48 | 03 28 | 03 03 |
| 22 | 02 18 | 02 03 | 02 47 | 03 23 | 02 58 |
| 23 | 02 23 | 02 06 | 02 46 | 03 18 | 02 52 |
| 24 | 02 27 | 02 08 | 02 44 | 03 13 | 02 46 |
| 25 | 02 31 | 02 11 | 02 43 | 03 08 | 02 41 |
| 26 | 02 35 | 02 14 | 02 42 | 03 03 | 02 35 |
| 27 | 02 39 | 02 17 | 02 41 | 02 58 | 02 29 |
| 28 | 02 44 | 02 19 | 02 39 | 02 53 | 02 24 |
| 29 | 02 48 | 02 22 | 02 38 | 02 48 | 02 18 |
| 30 | 02 52 | 02 25 | 02 37 | 02 43 | 02 12 |
| 31 | 02 57 | 02 27 | 02 36 | 02 38 | 02 06 |
| 32 | 03 01 | 02 30 | 02 34 | 02 33 | 02 00 |
| 33 | 03 05 | 02 33 | 02 33 | 02 28 | 01 54 |
| 34 | 03 10 | 02 35 | 02 32 | 02 23 | 01 48 |
| 35 | 03 14 | 02 38 | 02 30 | 02 18 | 01 42 |
| 36 | 03 19 | 02 41 | 02 29 | 02 13 | 01 35 |
| 37 | 03 23 | 02 43 | 02 28 | 02 08 | 01 29 |
| 38 | 03 28 | 02 46 | 02 27 | 02 03 | 01 23 |
| 39 | 03 32 | 02 49 | 02 25 | 01 58 | 01 16 |
| 40 | 03 37 | 02 51 | 02 24 | 01 53 | 01 10 |
| 41 | 03 42 | 02 54 | 02 22 | 01 48 | 01 03 |
| 42 | 03 47 | 02 56 | 02 21 | 01 43 | 00 56 |
| 43 | 03 51 | 02 59 | 02 20 | 01 38 | 00 49 |
| 44 | 03 56 | 03 01 | 02 18 | 01 32 | 00 42 |
| 45 | 04 01 | 03 04 | 02 17 | 01 27 | 00 35 |
| 46 | 04 06 | 03 06 | 02 15 | 01 22 | 00 28 |
| 47 | 04 10 | 03 08 | 02 14 | 01 17 | 00 21 |
| 48 | 04 15 | 03 10 | 02 12 | 01 12 | 00 13 |
| 49 | 04 20 | 03 13 | 02 11 | 01 07 | 00 06 |
| 50 | 04 25 | 03 14 | 02 09 | 01 02 | 29♏58 |
| 51 | 04 29 | 03 16 | 02 08 | 00 57 | 29 51 |
| 52 | 04 34 | 03 18 | 02 06 | 00 52 | 29 43 |
| 53 | 04 38 | 03 19 | 02 05 | 00 48 | 29 35 |
| 54 | 04 43 | 03 20 | 02 03 | 00 43 | 29 28 |
| 55 | 04 47 | 03 21 | 02 01 | 00 39 | 29 20 |
| 56 | 04 50 | 03 21 | 01 59 | 00 35 | 29 13 |
| 57 | 04 53 | 03 21 | 01 58 | 00 32 | 29 06 |
| 58 | 04 55 | 03 20 | 01 56 | 00 29 | 28 59 |
| 59 | 04 57 | 03 18 | 01 54 | 00 27 | 28 53 |
| 60 | 04♌57 | 03♍15 | 01♎52 | 00♏26 | 28♏48 |

| 6h 16m 0s | 94° 0' 0" | 03 ♋ 40 | | | |
|---|---|---|---|---|---|
| LAT. | 11 | 12 | ASC | 2 | 3 |
| 0 | 01♌45 | 02♍00 | 04♎22 | 06♏19 | 05♐54 |
| 5 | 02 05 | 02 14 | 04 12 | 05 50 | 05 25 |
| 10 | 02 25 | 02 28 | 04 03 | 05 22 | 04 57 |
| 15 | 02 44 | 02 40 | 03 54 | 04 54 | 04 29 |
| 20 | 03 04 | 02 53 | 03 46 | 04 28 | 04 01 |
| 21 | 03 08 | 02 55 | 03 44 | 04 22 | 03 56 |
| 22 | 03 12 | 02 57 | 03 43 | 04 17 | 03 50 |
| 23 | 03 15 | 03 00 | 03 41 | 04 12 | 03 44 |
| 24 | 03 19 | 03 02 | 03 39 | 04 06 | 03 38 |
| 25 | 03 23 | 03 05 | 03 38 | 04 01 | 03 32 |
| 26 | 03 27 | 03 07 | 03 36 | 03 56 | 03 26 |
| 27 | 03 31 | 03 09 | 03 34 | 03 50 | 03 21 |
| 28 | 03 35 | 03 12 | 03 33 | 03 45 | 03 15 |
| 29 | 03 39 | 03 14 | 03 31 | 03 40 | 03 08 |
| 30 | 03 43 | 03 16 | 03 29 | 03 34 | 03 02 |
| 31 | 03 47 | 03 19 | 03 28 | 03 29 | 02 56 |
| 32 | 03 52 | 03 21 | 03 26 | 03 24 | 02 50 |
| 33 | 03 56 | 03 23 | 03 24 | 03 18 | 02 44 |
| 34 | 04 00 | 03 26 | 03 22 | 03 13 | 02 37 |
| 35 | 04 04 | 03 28 | 03 21 | 03 07 | 02 31 |
| 36 | 04 08 | 03 30 | 03 19 | 03 02 | 02 24 |
| 37 | 04 13 | 03 32 | 03 17 | 02 56 | 02 17 |
| 38 | 04 17 | 03 35 | 03 15 | 02 51 | 02 11 |
| 39 | 04 21 | 03 37 | 03 14 | 02 45 | 02 04 |
| 40 | 04 25 | 03 39 | 03 12 | 02 40 | 01 57 |
| 41 | 04 30 | 03 41 | 03 10 | 02 34 | 01 50 |
| 42 | 04 34 | 03 43 | 03 08 | 02 29 | 01 43 |
| 43 | 04 39 | 03 45 | 03 06 | 02 23 | 01 35 |
| 44 | 04 43 | 03 47 | 03 04 | 02 18 | 01 28 |
| 45 | 04 47 | 03 49 | 03 02 | 02 12 | 01 20 |
| 46 | 04 52 | 03 51 | 03 01 | 02 06 | 01 13 |
| 47 | 04 56 | 03 53 | 02 59 | 02 01 | 01 05 |
| 48 | 05 01 | 03 55 | 02 57 | 01 55 | 00 57 |
| 49 | 05 05 | 03 56 | 02 55 | 01 50 | 00 49 |
| 50 | 05 09 | 03 58 | 02 52 | 01 44 | 00 41 |
| 51 | 05 14 | 03 59 | 02 50 | 01 39 | 00 33 |
| 52 | 05 18 | 04 00 | 02 48 | 01 33 | 00 25 |
| 53 | 05 22 | 04 01 | 02 46 | 01 28 | 00 17 |
| 54 | 05 25 | 04 01 | 02 44 | 01 23 | 00 08 |
| 55 | 05 29 | 04 02 | 02 42 | 01 18 | 00 00 |
| 56 | 05 32 | 04 01 | 02 39 | 01 14 | 29♏52 |
| 57 | 05 34 | 04 00 | 02 37 | 01 10 | 29 44 |
| 58 | 05 36 | 03 59 | 02 34 | 01 06 | 29 37 |
| 59 | 05 36 | 03 56 | 02 32 | 01 04 | 29 30 |
| 60 | 05♌36 | 03♍52 | 02♎29 | 01♏02 | 29♏24 |

| 6h 20m 0s | 95° 0' 0" | 04 ♋ 35 | | | |
|---|---|---|---|---|---|
| LAT. | 11 | 12 | ASC | 2 | 3 |
| 0 | 02♌43 | 03♍03 | 05♎27 | 07♏21 | 06♐50 |
| 5 | 03 02 | 03 15 | 05 15 | 06 50 | 06 21 |
| 10 | 03 21 | 03 27 | 05 04 | 06 20 | 05 52 |
| 15 | 03 39 | 03 38 | 04 53 | 05 51 | 05 23 |
| 20 | 03 57 | 03 48 | 04 42 | 05 22 | 04 54 |
| 21 | 04 01 | 03 50 | 04 40 | 05 16 | 04 48 |
| 22 | 04 05 | 03 52 | 04 38 | 05 11 | 04 42 |
| 23 | 04 08 | 03 54 | 04 36 | 05 05 | 04 36 |
| 24 | 04 12 | 03 56 | 04 34 | 04 59 | 04 30 |
| 25 | 04 16 | 03 58 | 04 32 | 04 54 | 04 24 |
| 26 | 04 20 | 04 00 | 04 30 | 04 48 | 04 18 |
| 27 | 04 23 | 04 02 | 04 28 | 04 42 | 04 11 |
| 28 | 04 27 | 04 04 | 04 26 | 04 37 | 04 05 |
| 29 | 04 31 | 04 06 | 04 24 | 04 31 | 03 59 |
| 30 | 04 35 | 04 08 | 04 21 | 04 25 | 03 53 |
| 31 | 04 39 | 04 10 | 04 19 | 04 19 | 03 46 |
| 32 | 04 42 | 04 12 | 04 17 | 04 14 | 03 40 |
| 33 | 04 46 | 04 14 | 04 15 | 04 08 | 03 33 |
| 34 | 04 50 | 04 16 | 04 13 | 04 02 | 03 26 |
| 35 | 04 54 | 04 18 | 04 11 | 03 56 | 03 19 |
| 36 | 04 58 | 04 20 | 04 09 | 03 50 | 03 13 |
| 37 | 05 02 | 04 22 | 04 06 | 03 45 | 03 06 |
| 38 | 05 06 | 04 23 | 04 04 | 03 39 | 02 58 |
| 39 | 05 10 | 04 25 | 04 02 | 03 33 | 02 51 |
| 40 | 05 14 | 04 27 | 04 00 | 03 27 | 02 44 |
| 41 | 05 18 | 04 29 | 03 57 | 03 21 | 02 37 |
| 42 | 05 22 | 04 30 | 03 55 | 03 15 | 02 29 |
| 43 | 05 26 | 04 32 | 03 53 | 03 09 | 02 21 |
| 44 | 05 30 | 04 34 | 03 50 | 03 03 | 02 14 |
| 45 | 05 34 | 04 35 | 03 48 | 02 56 | 02 06 |
| 46 | 05 38 | 04 37 | 03 46 | 02 50 | 01 58 |
| 47 | 05 42 | 04 38 | 03 43 | 02 44 | 01 49 |
| 48 | 05 46 | 04 39 | 03 41 | 02 38 | 01 41 |
| 49 | 05 50 | 04 40 | 03 38 | 02 32 | 01 33 |
| 50 | 05 54 | 04 41 | 03 36 | 02 26 | 01 24 |
| 51 | 05 58 | 04 42 | 03 33 | 02 20 | 01 15 |
| 52 | 06 02 | 04 43 | 03 30 | 02 14 | 01 07 |
| 53 | 06 05 | 04 43 | 03 28 | 02 08 | 00 58 |
| 54 | 06 08 | 04 43 | 03 25 | 02 03 | 00 49 |
| 55 | 06 11 | 04 42 | 03 22 | 01 57 | 00 40 |
| 56 | 06 14 | 04 42 | 03 19 | 01 52 | 00 31 |
| 57 | 06 15 | 04 40 | 03 16 | 01 48 | 00 23 |
| 58 | 06 16 | 04 38 | 03 13 | 01 43 | 00 15 |
| 59 | 06 16 | 04 35 | 03 10 | 01 40 | 00 07 |
| 60 | 06♌15 | 04♍30 | 03♎07 | 01♏37 | 00♐00 |

# Koch Table of Houses for Latitudes 0° to 60° North

6h 24m 0s — 96° 0' 0" — 05 ♋ 30

| LAT. | 11 | 12 | ASC | 2 | 3 |
|---|---|---|---|---|---|
| 0 | 03♌41 | 04♍07 | 06♎32 | 08♏23 | 07♐47 |
| 5 | 03 59 | 04 17 | 06 18 | 07 49 | 07 17 |
| 10 | 04 17 | 04 26 | 06 04 | 07 18 | 06 47 |
| 15 | 04 34 | 04 35 | 05 51 | 06 47 | 06 17 |
| 20 | 04 51 | 04 44 | 05 39 | 06 17 | 05 46 |
| 21 | 04 55 | 04 46 | 05 36 | 06 10 | 05 40 |
| 22 | 04 58 | 04 47 | 05 34 | 06 04 | 05 34 |
| 23 | 05 02 | 04 49 | 05 31 | 05 58 | 05 28 |
| 24 | 05 05 | 04 51 | 05 29 | 05 52 | 05 22 |
| 25 | 05 09 | 04 52 | 05 26 | 05 46 | 05 15 |
| 26 | 05 12 | 04 54 | 05 24 | 05 40 | 05 09 |
| 27 | 05 16 | 04 56 | 05 21 | 05 34 | 05 02 |
| 28 | 05 19 | 04 57 | 05 19 | 05 28 | 04 56 |
| 29 | 05 23 | 04 59 | 05 16 | 05 22 | 04 49 |
| 30 | 05 26 | 05 00 | 05 14 | 05 16 | 04 43 |
| 31 | 05 30 | 05 02 | 05 11 | 05 10 | 04 36 |
| 32 | 05 33 | 05 03 | 05 09 | 05 04 | 04 29 |
| 33 | 05 37 | 05 05 | 05 06 | 04 57 | 04 22 |
| 34 | 05 40 | 05 07 | 05 04 | 04 51 | 04 15 |
| 35 | 05 44 | 05 08 | 05 01 | 04 45 | 04 08 |
| 36 | 05 48 | 05 10 | 04 58 | 04 39 | 04 01 |
| 37 | 05 51 | 05 11 | 04 56 | 04 32 | 03 54 |
| 38 | 05 55 | 05 12 | 04 53 | 04 26 | 03 46 |
| 39 | 05 59 | 05 14 | 04 50 | 04 20 | 03 39 |
| 40 | 06 03 | 05 15 | 04 48 | 04 13 | 03 31 |
| 41 | 06 06 | 05 16 | 04 45 | 04 07 | 03 23 |
| 42 | 06 10 | 05 18 | 04 42 | 04 00 | 03 15 |
| 43 | 06 14 | 05 19 | 04 39 | 03 54 | 03 07 |
| 44 | 06 17 | 05 20 | 04 37 | 03 47 | 02 59 |
| 45 | 06 21 | 05 21 | 04 34 | 03 41 | 02 51 |
| 46 | 06 25 | 05 22 | 04 31 | 03 34 | 02 42 |
| 47 | 06 29 | 05 23 | 04 28 | 03 28 | 02 34 |
| 48 | 06 32 | 05 24 | 04 25 | 03 21 | 02 25 |
| 49 | 06 36 | 05 24 | 04 22 | 03 14 | 02 16 |
| 50 | 06 39 | 05 25 | 04 19 | 03 08 | 02 07 |
| 51 | 06 43 | 05 25 | 04 16 | 03 01 | 01 58 |
| 52 | 06 46 | 05 25 | 04 12 | 02 55 | 01 48 |
| 53 | 06 49 | 05 25 | 04 09 | 02 49 | 01 39 |
| 54 | 06 51 | 05 24 | 04 06 | 02 42 | 01 29 |
| 55 | 06 54 | 05 24 | 04 02 | 02 36 | 01 20 |
| 56 | 06 56 | 05 22 | 03 59 | 02 31 | 01 10 |
| 57 | 06 57 | 05 20 | 03 55 | 02 25 | 01 01 |
| 58 | 06 58 | 05 17 | 03 52 | 02 20 | 00 52 |
| 59 | 06 57 | 05 14 | 03 48 | 02 16 | 00 43 |
| 60 | 06♌55 | 05♍09 | 03♎44 | 02♏13 | 00♐35 |

6h 28m 0s — 97° 0' 0" — 06 ♋ 26

| LAT. | 11 | 12 | ASC | 2 | 3 |
|---|---|---|---|---|---|
| 0 | 04♌39 | 05♍10 | 07♎37 | 09♏24 | 08♐43 |
| 5 | 04 56 | 05 18 | 07 21 | 08 49 | 08 12 |
| 10 | 05 13 | 05 26 | 07 05 | 08 15 | 07 41 |
| 15 | 05 29 | 05 33 | 06 50 | 07 43 | 07 10 |
| 20 | 05 45 | 05 40 | 06 35 | 07 11 | 06 39 |
| 21 | 05 48 | 05 41 | 06 32 | 07 04 | 06 32 |
| 22 | 05 52 | 05 42 | 06 29 | 06 58 | 06 26 |
| 23 | 05 55 | 05 44 | 06 26 | 06 52 | 06 20 |
| 24 | 05 58 | 05 45 | 06 24 | 06 45 | 06 13 |
| 25 | 06 01 | 05 46 | 06 21 | 06 39 | 06 06 |
| 26 | 06 05 | 05 48 | 06 18 | 06 32 | 06 00 |
| 27 | 06 08 | 05 49 | 06 15 | 06 26 | 05 53 |
| 28 | 06 11 | 05 50 | 06 12 | 06 20 | 05 46 |
| 29 | 06 14 | 05 51 | 06 09 | 06 13 | 05 39 |
| 30 | 06 18 | 05 53 | 06 06 | 06 07 | 05 33 |
| 31 | 06 21 | 05 54 | 06 03 | 06 00 | 05 26 |
| 32 | 06 24 | 05 55 | 06 00 | 05 53 | 05 18 |
| 33 | 06 28 | 05 56 | 05 57 | 05 47 | 05 11 |
| 34 | 06 31 | 05 57 | 05 54 | 05 40 | 05 04 |
| 35 | 06 34 | 05 58 | 05 51 | 05 34 | 04 57 |
| 36 | 06 38 | 05 59 | 05 48 | 05 27 | 04 49 |
| 37 | 06 41 | 06 00 | 05 45 | 05 20 | 04 41 |
| 38 | 06 45 | 06 01 | 05 42 | 05 14 | 04 34 |
| 39 | 06 48 | 06 02 | 05 39 | 05 07 | 04 26 |
| 40 | 06 51 | 06 03 | 05 36 | 05 00 | 04 18 |
| 41 | 06 55 | 06 04 | 05 32 | 04 53 | 04 10 |
| 42 | 06 58 | 06 05 | 05 29 | 04 46 | 04 01 |
| 43 | 07 02 | 06 06 | 05 26 | 04 39 | 03 53 |
| 44 | 07 05 | 06 07 | 05 23 | 04 32 | 03 44 |
| 45 | 07 08 | 06 07 | 05 19 | 04 25 | 03 36 |
| 46 | 07 12 | 06 08 | 05 16 | 04 18 | 03 27 |
| 47 | 07 15 | 06 08 | 05 12 | 04 11 | 03 18 |
| 48 | 07 18 | 06 08 | 05 09 | 04 04 | 03 08 |
| 49 | 07 21 | 06 09 | 05 05 | 03 57 | 02 59 |
| 50 | 07 24 | 06 09 | 05 02 | 03 50 | 02 49 |
| 51 | 07 27 | 06 08 | 04 58 | 03 43 | 02 40 |
| 52 | 07 30 | 06 08 | 04 54 | 03 35 | 02 30 |
| 53 | 07 33 | 06 07 | 04 51 | 03 29 | 02 20 |
| 54 | 07 35 | 06 06 | 04 47 | 03 22 | 02 09 |
| 55 | 07 37 | 06 05 | 04 43 | 03 15 | 01 59 |
| 56 | 07 38 | 06 03 | 04 39 | 03 09 | 01 49 |
| 57 | 07 39 | 06 00 | 04 34 | 03 03 | 01 39 |
| 58 | 07 39 | 05 57 | 04 30 | 02 57 | 01 29 |
| 59 | 07 38 | 05 53 | 04 26 | 02 52 | 01 19 |
| 60 | 07♌35 | 05♍47 | 04♎21 | 02♏48 | 01♐10 |

6h 32m 0s — 98° 0' 0" — 07 ♋ 21

| LAT. | 11 | 12 | ASC | 2 | 3 |
|---|---|---|---|---|---|
| 0 | 05♌38 | 06♍14 | 08♎43 | 10♏25 | 09♐40 |
| 5 | 05 54 | 06 20 | 08 24 | 09 48 | 09 07 |
| 10 | 06 09 | 06 25 | 08 06 | 09 13 | 08 36 |
| 15 | 06 24 | 06 31 | 07 48 | 08 39 | 08 04 |
| 20 | 06 39 | 06 36 | 07 32 | 08 05 | 07 31 |
| 21 | 06 42 | 06 37 | 07 28 | 07 58 | 07 25 |
| 22 | 06 45 | 06 38 | 07 25 | 07 51 | 07 18 |
| 23 | 06 48 | 06 39 | 07 22 | 07 45 | 07 11 |
| 24 | 06 51 | 06 40 | 07 18 | 07 38 | 07 04 |
| 25 | 06 54 | 06 40 | 07 15 | 07 31 | 06 58 |
| 26 | 06 57 | 06 41 | 07 12 | 07 24 | 06 51 |
| 27 | 07 00 | 06 42 | 07 08 | 07 18 | 06 44 |
| 28 | 07 03 | 06 43 | 07 05 | 07 11 | 06 37 |
| 29 | 07 06 | 06 44 | 07 02 | 07 04 | 06 30 |
| 30 | 07 09 | 06 45 | 06 58 | 06 57 | 06 22 |
| 31 | 07 13 | 06 46 | 06 55 | 06 50 | 06 15 |
| 32 | 07 16 | 06 46 | 06 51 | 06 43 | 06 08 |
| 33 | 07 19 | 06 47 | 06 48 | 06 36 | 06 00 |
| 34 | 07 22 | 06 48 | 06 45 | 06 29 | 05 53 |
| 35 | 07 25 | 06 49 | 06 41 | 06 22 | 05 45 |
| 36 | 07 28 | 06 49 | 06 38 | 06 15 | 05 37 |
| 37 | 07 31 | 06 50 | 06 34 | 06 08 | 05 29 |
| 38 | 07 34 | 06 51 | 06 31 | 06 01 | 05 21 |
| 39 | 07 37 | 06 51 | 06 27 | 05 54 | 05 13 |
| 40 | 07 40 | 06 52 | 06 24 | 05 46 | 05 05 |
| 41 | 07 43 | 06 52 | 06 20 | 05 39 | 04 56 |
| 42 | 07 47 | 06 53 | 06 16 | 05 32 | 04 47 |
| 43 | 07 50 | 06 53 | 06 12 | 05 24 | 04 39 |
| 44 | 07 53 | 06 53 | 06 09 | 05 17 | 04 30 |
| 45 | 07 56 | 06 53 | 06 05 | 05 09 | 04 20 |
| 46 | 07 59 | 06 53 | 06 01 | 05 02 | 04 11 |
| 47 | 08 02 | 06 53 | 05 57 | 04 54 | 04 01 |
| 48 | 08 05 | 06 53 | 05 53 | 04 46 | 03 52 |
| 49 | 08 07 | 06 53 | 05 49 | 04 39 | 03 42 |
| 50 | 08 10 | 06 53 | 05 45 | 04 31 | 03 32 |
| 51 | 08 13 | 06 52 | 05 41 | 04 24 | 03 21 |
| 52 | 08 15 | 06 51 | 05 36 | 04 16 | 03 11 |
| 53 | 08 17 | 06 50 | 05 32 | 04 08 | 03 00 |
| 54 | 08 19 | 06 48 | 05 28 | 04 01 | 02 49 |
| 55 | 08 20 | 06 46 | 05 23 | 03 54 | 02 38 |
| 56 | 08 21 | 06 44 | 05 18 | 03 46 | 02 27 |
| 57 | 08 21 | 06 41 | 05 14 | 03 40 | 02 16 |
| 58 | 08 21 | 06 37 | 05 09 | 03 33 | 02 05 |
| 59 | 08 19 | 06 32 | 05 04 | 03 28 | 01 55 |
| 60 | 08♌16 | 06♍26 | 04♎59 | 03♏23 | 01♐45 |

6h 36m 0s — 99° 0' 0" — 08 ♋ 16

| LAT. | 11 | 12 | ASC | 2 | 3 |
|---|---|---|---|---|---|
| 0 | 06♌37 | 07♍18 | 09♎48 | 11♏26 | 10♐36 |
| 5 | 06 51 | 07 22 | 09 26 | 10 47 | 10 03 |
| 10 | 07 06 | 07 25 | 09 06 | 10 10 | 09 30 |
| 15 | 07 20 | 07 29 | 08 47 | 09 34 | 08 57 |
| 20 | 07 34 | 07 32 | 08 28 | 08 59 | 08 23 |
| 21 | 07 36 | 07 32 | 08 24 | 08 52 | 08 17 |
| 22 | 07 39 | 07 33 | 08 20 | 08 45 | 08 10 |
| 23 | 07 42 | 07 34 | 08 17 | 08 38 | 08 03 |
| 24 | 07 45 | 07 34 | 08 13 | 08 30 | 07 56 |
| 25 | 07 47 | 07 35 | 08 09 | 08 23 | 07 49 |
| 26 | 07 50 | 07 35 | 08 06 | 08 16 | 07 42 |
| 27 | 07 53 | 07 36 | 08 02 | 08 09 | 07 34 |
| 28 | 07 56 | 07 36 | 07 58 | 08 02 | 07 27 |
| 29 | 07 59 | 07 37 | 07 54 | 07 55 | 07 20 |
| 30 | 08 01 | 07 37 | 07 50 | 07 47 | 07 12 |
| 31 | 08 04 | 07 38 | 07 47 | 07 40 | 07 05 |
| 32 | 08 07 | 07 38 | 07 43 | 07 33 | 06 57 |
| 33 | 08 10 | 07 38 | 07 39 | 07 25 | 06 49 |
| 34 | 08 13 | 07 39 | 07 35 | 07 18 | 06 41 |
| 35 | 08 15 | 07 39 | 07 31 | 07 11 | 06 33 |
| 36 | 08 18 | 07 39 | 07 27 | 07 03 | 06 25 |
| 37 | 08 21 | 07 40 | 07 23 | 06 56 | 06 17 |
| 38 | 08 24 | 07 40 | 07 19 | 06 48 | 06 09 |
| 39 | 08 27 | 07 40 | 07 15 | 06 40 | 06 00 |
| 40 | 08 30 | 07 40 | 07 11 | 06 33 | 05 51 |
| 41 | 08 32 | 07 40 | 07 07 | 06 25 | 05 42 |
| 42 | 08 35 | 07 40 | 07 03 | 06 17 | 05 33 |
| 43 | 08 38 | 07 40 | 06 59 | 06 09 | 05 24 |
| 44 | 08 41 | 07 40 | 06 55 | 06 01 | 05 15 |
| 45 | 08 43 | 07 40 | 06 50 | 05 53 | 05 05 |
| 46 | 08 46 | 07 39 | 06 46 | 05 45 | 04 55 |
| 47 | 08 49 | 07 39 | 06 42 | 05 37 | 04 45 |
| 48 | 08 51 | 07 38 | 06 37 | 05 29 | 04 35 |
| 49 | 08 53 | 07 38 | 06 33 | 05 21 | 04 24 |
| 50 | 08 56 | 07 37 | 06 28 | 05 13 | 04 14 |
| 51 | 08 58 | 07 35 | 06 23 | 05 04 | 04 03 |
| 52 | 09 00 | 07 34 | 06 18 | 04 56 | 03 52 |
| 53 | 09 01 | 07 32 | 06 14 | 04 48 | 03 40 |
| 54 | 09 03 | 07 30 | 06 09 | 04 40 | 03 29 |
| 55 | 09 04 | 07 28 | 06 03 | 04 32 | 03 17 |
| 56 | 09 04 | 07 25 | 05 58 | 04 24 | 03 05 |
| 57 | 09 04 | 07 21 | 05 53 | 04 17 | 02 53 |
| 58 | 09 03 | 07 17 | 05 47 | 04 10 | 02 42 |
| 59 | 09 01 | 07 11 | 05 42 | 04 03 | 02 30 |
| 60 | 08♌57 | 07♍05 | 05♎36 | 03♏58 | 02♐19 |

6h 40m 0s — 100° 0' 0" — 09 ♋ 11

| LAT. | 11 | 12 | ASC | 2 | 3 |
|---|---|---|---|---|---|
| 0 | 07♌35 | 08♍22 | 10♎53 | 12♏27 | 11♐32 |
| 5 | 07 49 | 08 23 | 10 29 | 11 46 | 10 58 |
| 10 | 08 02 | 08 25 | 10 07 | 11 08 | 10 24 |
| 15 | 08 15 | 08 27 | 09 45 | 10 30 | 09 50 |
| 20 | 08 28 | 08 28 | 09 24 | 09 53 | 09 16 |
| 21 | 08 30 | 08 28 | 09 20 | 09 45 | 09 09 |
| 22 | 08 33 | 08 28 | 09 16 | 09 38 | 09 01 |
| 23 | 08 36 | 08 29 | 09 12 | 09 30 | 08 54 |
| 24 | 08 38 | 08 29 | 09 08 | 09 23 | 08 47 |
| 25 | 08 41 | 08 29 | 09 04 | 09 15 | 08 40 |
| 26 | 08 43 | 08 29 | 08 59 | 09 08 | 08 32 |
| 27 | 08 46 | 08 29 | 08 55 | 09 00 | 08 25 |
| 28 | 08 48 | 08 29 | 08 51 | 08 53 | 08 17 |
| 29 | 08 51 | 08 30 | 08 47 | 08 45 | 08 10 |
| 30 | 08 53 | 08 30 | 08 43 | 08 38 | 08 02 |
| 31 | 08 56 | 08 30 | 08 39 | 08 30 | 07 54 |
| 32 | 08 58 | 08 30 | 08 34 | 08 22 | 07 46 |
| 33 | 09 01 | 08 30 | 08 30 | 08 15 | 07 38 |
| 34 | 09 04 | 08 30 | 08 26 | 08 07 | 07 30 |
| 35 | 09 06 | 08 30 | 08 21 | 07 59 | 07 22 |
| 36 | 09 09 | 08 30 | 08 17 | 07 51 | 07 13 |
| 37 | 09 11 | 08 29 | 08 13 | 07 43 | 07 05 |
| 38 | 09 14 | 08 29 | 08 08 | 07 35 | 06 56 |
| 39 | 09 16 | 08 29 | 08 04 | 07 27 | 06 47 |
| 40 | 09 19 | 08 29 | 07 59 | 07 19 | 06 38 |
| 41 | 09 21 | 08 28 | 07 55 | 07 11 | 06 29 |
| 42 | 09 24 | 08 28 | 07 50 | 07 02 | 06 19 |
| 43 | 09 26 | 08 28 | 07 46 | 06 54 | 06 09 |
| 44 | 09 29 | 08 27 | 07 41 | 06 46 | 06 00 |
| 45 | 09 31 | 08 26 | 07 36 | 06 37 | 05 50 |
| 46 | 09 33 | 08 25 | 07 31 | 06 29 | 05 39 |
| 47 | 09 36 | 08 25 | 07 26 | 06 20 | 05 29 |
| 48 | 09 38 | 08 24 | 07 21 | 06 11 | 05 18 |
| 49 | 09 40 | 08 22 | 07 16 | 06 03 | 05 07 |
| 50 | 09 42 | 08 21 | 07 11 | 05 54 | 04 56 |
| 51 | 09 43 | 08 19 | 07 06 | 05 45 | 04 44 |
| 52 | 09 45 | 08 17 | 07 00 | 05 36 | 04 32 |
| 53 | 09 46 | 08 15 | 06 55 | 05 27 | 04 20 |
| 54 | 09 47 | 08 13 | 06 49 | 05 19 | 04 08 |
| 55 | 09 48 | 08 10 | 06 44 | 05 10 | 03 56 |
| 56 | 09 48 | 08 06 | 06 38 | 05 02 | 03 43 |
| 57 | 09 47 | 08 02 | 06 32 | 04 54 | 03 30 |
| 58 | 09 45 | 07 57 | 06 26 | 04 46 | 03 18 |
| 59 | 09 42 | 07 51 | 06 20 | 04 38 | 03 05 |
| 60 | 09♌38 | 07♍44 | 06♎13 | 04♏32 | 02♐53 |

6h 44m 0s — 101° 0' 0" — 10 ♋ 07

| LAT. | 11 | 12 | ASC | 2 | 3 |
|---|---|---|---|---|---|
| 0 | 08♌34 | 09♍26 | 11♎58 | 13♏27 | 12♐28 |
| 5 | 08 47 | 09 25 | 11 32 | 12 45 | 11 53 |
| 10 | 08 59 | 09 25 | 11 07 | 12 05 | 11 18 |
| 15 | 09 11 | 09 25 | 10 44 | 11 25 | 10 43 |
| 20 | 09 23 | 09 24 | 10 21 | 10 46 | 10 08 |
| 21 | 09 25 | 09 24 | 10 16 | 10 39 | 10 00 |
| 22 | 09 27 | 09 24 | 10 12 | 10 31 | 09 53 |
| 23 | 09 29 | 09 24 | 10 07 | 10 23 | 09 46 |
| 24 | 09 32 | 09 24 | 10 02 | 10 15 | 09 38 |
| 25 | 09 34 | 09 23 | 09 58 | 10 07 | 09 31 |
| 26 | 09 36 | 09 23 | 09 53 | 10 00 | 09 23 |
| 27 | 09 39 | 09 23 | 09 49 | 09 52 | 09 15 |
| 28 | 09 41 | 09 23 | 09 44 | 09 44 | 09 07 |
| 29 | 09 43 | 09 23 | 09 40 | 09 36 | 09 00 |
| 30 | 09 46 | 09 22 | 09 35 | 09 28 | 08 52 |
| 31 | 09 48 | 09 22 | 09 30 | 09 20 | 08 43 |
| 32 | 09 50 | 09 22 | 09 26 | 09 12 | 08 35 |
| 33 | 09 52 | 09 21 | 09 21 | 09 04 | 08 27 |
| 34 | 09 55 | 09 21 | 09 16 | 08 55 | 08 18 |
| 35 | 09 57 | 09 20 | 09 11 | 08 47 | 08 10 |
| 36 | 09 59 | 09 20 | 09 07 | 08 39 | 08 01 |
| 37 | 10 02 | 09 19 | 09 02 | 08 30 | 07 52 |
| 38 | 10 04 | 09 19 | 08 57 | 08 22 | 07 43 |
| 39 | 10 06 | 09 18 | 08 52 | 08 14 | 07 34 |
| 40 | 10 08 | 09 17 | 08 47 | 08 05 | 07 24 |
| 41 | 10 11 | 09 17 | 08 42 | 07 56 | 07 15 |
| 42 | 10 13 | 09 16 | 08 37 | 07 48 | 07 05 |
| 43 | 10 15 | 09 15 | 08 32 | 07 39 | 06 55 |
| 44 | 10 17 | 09 14 | 08 27 | 07 30 | 06 44 |
| 45 | 10 19 | 09 13 | 08 22 | 07 21 | 06 34 |
| 46 | 10 21 | 09 12 | 08 16 | 07 12 | 06 23 |
| 47 | 10 23 | 09 10 | 08 11 | 07 03 | 06 12 |
| 48 | 10 25 | 09 09 | 08 05 | 06 54 | 06 01 |
| 49 | 10 26 | 09 07 | 08 00 | 06 44 | 05 49 |
| 50 | 10 28 | 09 05 | 07 54 | 06 35 | 05 38 |
| 51 | 10 29 | 09 03 | 07 48 | 06 26 | 05 25 |
| 52 | 10 30 | 09 01 | 07 42 | 06 16 | 05 13 |
| 53 | 10 31 | 08 58 | 07 36 | 06 07 | 05 00 |
| 54 | 10 32 | 08 55 | 07 30 | 05 57 | 04 47 |
| 55 | 10 32 | 08 52 | 07 24 | 05 48 | 04 34 |
| 56 | 10 31 | 08 48 | 07 18 | 05 39 | 04 21 |
| 57 | 10 30 | 08 43 | 07 11 | 05 30 | 04 07 |
| 58 | 10 28 | 08 38 | 07 05 | 05 22 | 03 53 |
| 59 | 10 25 | 08 31 | 06 58 | 05 13 | 03 39 |
| 60 | 10♌20 | 08♍24 | 06♎51 | 05♏06 | 03♐26 |

6h 48m 0s — 102° 0' 0" — 11 ♋ 02

| LAT. | 11 | 12 | ASC | 2 | 3 |
|---|---|---|---|---|---|
| 0 | 09♌34 | 10♍30 | 13♎03 | 14♏28 | 13♐24 |
| 5 | 09 45 | 10 28 | 12 34 | 13 44 | 12 48 |
| 10 | 09 56 | 10 25 | 12 08 | 13 02 | 12 12 |
| 15 | 10 07 | 10 23 | 11 42 | 12 21 | 11 37 |
| 20 | 10 17 | 10 21 | 11 17 | 11 40 | 11 00 |
| 21 | 10 19 | 10 20 | 11 12 | 11 32 | 10 52 |
| 22 | 10 21 | 10 20 | 11 07 | 11 24 | 10 45 |
| 23 | 10 23 | 10 19 | 11 02 | 11 16 | 10 37 |
| 24 | 10 26 | 10 19 | 10 57 | 11 07 | 10 29 |
| 25 | 10 28 | 10 18 | 10 52 | 10 59 | 10 21 |
| 26 | 10 30 | 10 17 | 10 47 | 10 51 | 10 14 |
| 27 | 10 32 | 10 17 | 10 42 | 10 43 | 10 06 |
| 28 | 10 34 | 10 16 | 10 37 | 10 35 | 09 58 |
| 29 | 10 36 | 10 16 | 10 32 | 10 26 | 09 49 |
| 30 | 10 38 | 10 15 | 10 27 | 10 18 | 09 41 |
| 31 | 10 40 | 10 14 | 10 22 | 10 09 | 09 33 |
| 32 | 10 42 | 10 14 | 10 17 | 10 01 | 09 24 |
| 33 | 10 44 | 10 13 | 10 12 | 09 52 | 09 16 |
| 34 | 10 46 | 10 12 | 10 07 | 09 44 | 09 07 |
| 35 | 10 48 | 10 11 | 10 02 | 09 35 | 08 58 |
| 36 | 10 50 | 10 10 | 09 56 | 09 26 | 08 49 |
| 37 | 10 52 | 10 09 | 09 51 | 09 18 | 08 39 |
| 38 | 10 54 | 10 08 | 09 46 | 09 09 | 08 30 |
| 39 | 10 56 | 10 07 | 09 40 | 09 00 | 08 20 |
| 40 | 10 58 | 10 06 | 09 35 | 08 51 | 08 11 |
| 41 | 11 00 | 10 05 | 09 30 | 08 42 | 08 01 |
| 42 | 11 02 | 10 04 | 09 24 | 08 33 | 07 50 |
| 43 | 11 04 | 10 03 | 09 19 | 08 23 | 07 40 |
| 44 | 11 05 | 10 01 | 09 13 | 08 14 | 07 29 |
| 45 | 11 07 | 10 00 | 09 07 | 08 04 | 07 18 |
| 46 | 11 09 | 09 58 | 09 01 | 07 55 | 07 07 |
| 47 | 11 10 | 09 56 | 08 55 | 07 45 | 06 55 |
| 48 | 11 12 | 09 54 | 08 49 | 07 36 | 06 44 |
| 49 | 11 13 | 09 52 | 08 43 | 07 26 | 06 32 |
| 50 | 11 14 | 09 50 | 08 37 | 07 16 | 06 19 |
| 51 | 11 15 | 09 47 | 08 31 | 07 06 | 06 06 |
| 52 | 11 16 | 09 44 | 08 24 | 06 56 | 05 53 |
| 53 | 11 16 | 09 41 | 08 18 | 06 46 | 05 40 |
| 54 | 11 17 | 09 38 | 08 11 | 06 36 | 05 26 |
| 55 | 11 16 | 09 34 | 08 04 | 06 26 | 05 12 |
| 56 | 11 15 | 09 29 | 07 57 | 06 16 | 04 58 |
| 57 | 11 14 | 09 24 | 07 50 | 06 07 | 04 43 |
| 58 | 11 11 | 09 18 | 07 43 | 05 57 | 04 29 |
| 59 | 11 08 | 09 11 | 07 36 | 05 48 | 04 14 |
| 60 | 11♌02 | 09♍03 | 07♎28 | 05♏40 | 03♐59 |

6h 52m 0s — 103° 0' 0" — 11 ♋ 58

| LAT. | 11 | 12 | ASC | 2 | 3 |
|---|---|---|---|---|---|
| 0 | 10♌33 | 11♍34 | 14♎07 | 15♏28 | 14♐20 |
| 5 | 10 43 | 11 30 | 13 37 | 14 43 | 13 43 |
| 10 | 10 53 | 11 26 | 13 08 | 13 59 | 13 06 |
| 15 | 11 03 | 11 21 | 12 40 | 13 16 | 12 30 |
| 20 | 11 12 | 11 17 | 12 13 | 12 34 | 11 52 |
| 21 | 11 14 | 11 16 | 12 08 | 12 25 | 11 44 |
| 22 | 11 16 | 11 15 | 12 02 | 12 17 | 11 36 |
| 23 | 11 18 | 11 15 | 11 57 | 12 08 | 11 28 |
| 24 | 11 19 | 11 14 | 11 52 | 12 00 | 11 20 |
| 25 | 11 21 | 11 13 | 11 46 | 11 51 | 11 12 |
| 26 | 11 23 | 11 12 | 11 41 | 11 42 | 11 04 |
| 27 | 11 25 | 11 11 | 11 36 | 11 34 | 10 56 |
| 28 | 11 27 | 11 10 | 11 30 | 11 25 | 10 48 |
| 29 | 11 29 | 11 09 | 11 25 | 11 16 | 10 39 |
| 30 | 11 30 | 11 08 | 11 19 | 11 08 | 10 31 |
| 31 | 11 32 | 11 07 | 11 14 | 10 59 | 10 22 |
| 32 | 11 34 | 11 06 | 11 08 | 10 50 | 10 13 |
| 33 | 11 36 | 11 04 | 11 03 | 10 41 | 10 04 |
| 34 | 11 38 | 11 03 | 10 57 | 10 32 | 09 55 |
| 35 | 11 39 | 11 02 | 10 52 | 10 23 | 09 46 |
| 36 | 11 41 | 11 01 | 10 46 | 10 14 | 09 36 |
| 37 | 11 43 | 11 00 | 10 40 | 10 05 | 09 27 |
| 38 | 11 45 | 10 58 | 10 35 | 09 56 | 09 17 |
| 39 | 11 46 | 10 57 | 10 29 | 09 46 | 09 07 |
| 40 | 11 48 | 10 55 | 10 23 | 09 37 | 08 57 |
| 41 | 11 50 | 10 54 | 10 17 | 09 27 | 08 46 |
| 42 | 11 51 | 10 52 | 10 11 | 09 18 | 08 36 |
| 43 | 11 53 | 10 50 | 10 05 | 09 08 | 08 25 |
| 44 | 11 54 | 10 49 | 09 59 | 08 58 | 08 14 |
| 45 | 11 56 | 10 47 | 09 53 | 08 48 | 08 02 |
| 46 | 11 57 | 10 45 | 09 46 | 08 38 | 07 51 |
| 47 | 11 58 | 10 42 | 09 40 | 08 28 | 07 39 |
| 48 | 11 59 | 10 40 | 09 34 | 08 18 | 07 26 |
| 49 | 12 00 | 10 37 | 09 27 | 08 07 | 07 14 |
| 50 | 12 01 | 10 35 | 09 20 | 07 57 | 07 01 |
| 51 | 12 02 | 10 32 | 09 13 | 07 46 | 06 47 |
| 52 | 12 02 | 10 28 | 09 06 | 07 36 | 06 34 |
| 53 | 12 02 | 10 25 | 08 59 | 07 25 | 06 19 |
| 54 | 12 02 | 10 21 | 08 52 | 07 14 | 06 05 |
| 55 | 12 01 | 10 16 | 08 45 | 07 04 | 05 50 |
| 56 | 12 00 | 10 11 | 08 37 | 06 53 | 05 35 |
| 57 | 11 58 | 10 06 | 08 30 | 06 43 | 05 19 |
| 58 | 11 55 | 09 59 | 08 22 | 06 33 | 05 04 |
| 59 | 11 51 | 09 52 | 08 14 | 06 23 | 04 48 |
| 60 | 11♌45 | 09♍43 | 08♎05 | 06♏14 | 04♐32 |

# Koch Table of Houses for Latitudes 0° to 60° North

6h 56m 0s — 104° 0' 0" — 12 ♋ 53

| LAT. | 11 | 12 | ASC | 2 | 3 |
|---|---|---|---|---|---|
| 0 | 11♌32 | 12♍39 | 15♎12 | 16♏28 | 15♐16 |
| 5 | 11 42 | 12 32 | 14 39 | 15 41 | 14 38 |
| 10 | 11 50 | 12 26 | 14 08 | 14 55 | 14 00 |
| 15 | 11 59 | 12 20 | 13 39 | 14 11 | 13 22 |
| 20 | 12 07 | 12 14 | 13 09 | 13 27 | 12 44 |
| 21 | 12 09 | 12 13 | 13 04 | 13 18 | 12 36 |
| 22 | 12 10 | 12 11 | 12 58 | 13 09 | 12 28 |
| 23 | 12 12 | 12 10 | 12 52 | 13 00 | 12 19 |
| 24 | 12 14 | 12 09 | 12 46 | 12 52 | 12 11 |
| 25 | 12 15 | 12 07 | 12 40 | 12 43 | 12 03 |
| 26 | 12 17 | 12 06 | 12 35 | 12 34 | 11 55 |
| 27 | 12 18 | 12 05 | 12 29 | 12 25 | 11 46 |
| 28 | 12 20 | 12 03 | 12 23 | 12 16 | 11 38 |
| 29 | 12 22 | 12 02 | 12 17 | 12 07 | 11 29 |
| 30 | 12 23 | 12 01 | 12 11 | 11 58 | 11 20 |
| 31 | 12 25 | 11 59 | 12 06 | 11 48 | 11 11 |
| 32 | 12 26 | 11 58 | 12 00 | 11 39 | 11 02 |
| 33 | 12 28 | 11 56 | 11 54 | 11 30 | 10 53 |
| 34 | 12 29 | 11 55 | 11 48 | 11 20 | 10 43 |
| 35 | 12 31 | 11 53 | 11 42 | 11 11 | 10 34 |
| 36 | 12 32 | 11 52 | 11 36 | 11 02 | 10 24 |
| 37 | 12 34 | 11 50 | 11 29 | 10 52 | 10 14 |
| 38 | 12 35 | 11 48 | 11 23 | 10 42 | 10 04 |
| 39 | 12 37 | 11 46 | 11 17 | 10 32 | 09 54 |
| 40 | 12 38 | 11 44 | 11 11 | 10 22 | 09 43 |
| 41 | 12 39 | 11 42 | 11 04 | 10 12 | 09 32 |
| 42 | 12 41 | 11 40 | 10 58 | 10 02 | 09 21 |
| 43 | 12 42 | 11 38 | 10 52 | 09 52 | 09 10 |
| 44 | 12 43 | 11 36 | 10 45 | 09 42 | 08 58 |
| 45 | 12 44 | 11 34 | 10 38 | 09 31 | 08 46 |
| 46 | 12 45 | 11 31 | 10 31 | 09 21 | 08 34 |
| 47 | 12 46 | 11 29 | 10 25 | 09 10 | 08 22 |
| 48 | 12 47 | 11 26 | 10 18 | 08 59 | 08 09 |
| 49 | 12 48 | 11 23 | 10 11 | 08 48 | 07 56 |
| 50 | 12 48 | 11 20 | 10 03 | 08 37 | 07 42 |
| 51 | 12 48 | 11 16 | 09 56 | 08 26 | 07 28 |
| 52 | 12 48 | 11 12 | 09 48 | 08 15 | 07 14 |
| 53 | 12 48 | 11 08 | 09 41 | 08 04 | 06 59 |
| 54 | 12 47 | 11 04 | 09 33 | 07 53 | 06 44 |
| 55 | 12 46 | 10 59 | 09 25 | 07 41 | 06 28 |
| 56 | 12 44 | 10 53 | 09 17 | 07 30 | 06 12 |
| 57 | 12 42 | 10 47 | 09 09 | 07 19 | 05 55 |
| 58 | 12 39 | 10 40 | 09 00 | 07 08 | 05 38 |
| 59 | 12 34 | 10 33 | 08 51 | 06 57 | 05 21 |
| 60 | 12♌28 | 10♍23 | 08♎43 | 06♏47 | 05♐04 |

7h 0m 0s — 105° 0' 0" — 13 ♋ 49

| LAT. | 11 | 12 | ASC | 2 | 3 |
|---|---|---|---|---|---|
| 0 | 12♌32 | 13♍43 | 16♎17 | 17♏28 | 16♐11 |
| 5 | 12 40 | 13 35 | 15 42 | 16 39 | 15 33 |
| 10 | 12 48 | 13 26 | 15 09 | 15 52 | 14 54 |
| 15 | 12 55 | 13 18 | 14 37 | 15 06 | 14 15 |
| 20 | 13 02 | 13 11 | 14 06 | 14 20 | 13 35 |
| 21 | 13 04 | 13 09 | 13 59 | 14 11 | 13 27 |
| 22 | 13 05 | 13 07 | 13 53 | 14 02 | 13 19 |
| 23 | 13 06 | 13 06 | 13 47 | 13 53 | 13 11 |
| 24 | 13 08 | 13 04 | 13 41 | 13 43 | 13 02 |
| 25 | 13 09 | 13 02 | 13 35 | 13 34 | 12 54 |
| 26 | 13 11 | 13 01 | 13 28 | 13 25 | 12 45 |
| 27 | 13 12 | 12 59 | 13 22 | 13 16 | 12 36 |
| 28 | 13 13 | 12 57 | 13 16 | 13 06 | 12 27 |
| 29 | 13 15 | 12 56 | 13 10 | 12 57 | 12 18 |
| 30 | 13 16 | 12 54 | 13 03 | 12 47 | 12 09 |
| 31 | 13 17 | 12 52 | 12 57 | 12 38 | 12 00 |
| 32 | 13 19 | 12 50 | 12 51 | 12 28 | 11 51 |
| 33 | 13 20 | 12 48 | 12 45 | 12 18 | 11 41 |
| 34 | 13 21 | 12 46 | 12 38 | 12 09 | 11 31 |
| 35 | 13 22 | 12 44 | 12 32 | 11 59 | 11 22 |
| 36 | 13 24 | 12 42 | 12 25 | 11 49 | 11 11 |
| 37 | 13 25 | 12 40 | 12 19 | 11 39 | 11 01 |
| 38 | 13 26 | 12 38 | 12 12 | 11 29 | 10 51 |
| 39 | 13 27 | 12 36 | 12 05 | 11 18 | 10 40 |
| 40 | 13 28 | 12 34 | 11 59 | 11 08 | 10 29 |
| 41 | 13 29 | 12 31 | 11 52 | 10 58 | 10 18 |
| 42 | 13 30 | 12 29 | 11 45 | 10 47 | 10 06 |
| 43 | 13 31 | 12 26 | 11 38 | 10 36 | 09 55 |
| 44 | 13 32 | 12 24 | 11 31 | 10 26 | 09 43 |
| 45 | 13 33 | 12 21 | 11 24 | 10 15 | 09 30 |
| 46 | 13 34 | 12 18 | 11 17 | 10 04 | 09 17 |
| 47 | 13 34 | 12 15 | 11 09 | 09 52 | 09 04 |
| 48 | 13 35 | 12 12 | 11 02 | 09 41 | 08 51 |
| 49 | 13 35 | 12 08 | 10 54 | 09 30 | 08 37 |
| 50 | 13 35 | 12 05 | 10 46 | 09 18 | 08 23 |
| 51 | 13 35 | 12 01 | 10 38 | 09 06 | 08 08 |
| 52 | 13 35 | 11 56 | 10 30 | 08 54 | 07 53 |
| 53 | 13 34 | 11 52 | 10 22 | 08 43 | 07 38 |
| 54 | 13 33 | 11 47 | 10 14 | 08 31 | 07 22 |
| 55 | 13 31 | 11 42 | 10 05 | 08 19 | 07 05 |
| 56 | 13 29 | 11 36 | 09 57 | 08 07 | 06 48 |
| 57 | 13 26 | 11 29 | 09 48 | 07 55 | 06 31 |
| 58 | 13 23 | 11 22 | 09 39 | 07 43 | 06 13 |
| 59 | 13 18 | 11 13 | 09 29 | 07 31 | 05 54 |
| 60 | 13♌11 | 11♍04 | 09♎20 | 07♏21 | 05♐36 |

7h 4m 0s — 106° 0' 0" — 14 ♋ 44

| LAT. | 11 | 12 | ASC | 2 | 3 |
|---|---|---|---|---|---|
| 0 | 13♌32 | 14♍48 | 17♎21 | 18♏28 | 17♐07 |
| 5 | 13 39 | 14 37 | 16 44 | 17 37 | 16 27 |
| 10 | 13 45 | 14 27 | 16 09 | 16 49 | 15 48 |
| 15 | 13 52 | 14 17 | 15 35 | 16 01 | 15 08 |
| 20 | 13 58 | 14 07 | 15 02 | 15 13 | 14 27 |
| 21 | 13 59 | 14 05 | 14 55 | 15 04 | 14 19 |
| 22 | 14 00 | 14 03 | 14 48 | 14 54 | 14 10 |
| 23 | 14 01 | 14 01 | 14 42 | 14 45 | 14 02 |
| 24 | 14 02 | 13 59 | 14 35 | 14 35 | 13 53 |
| 25 | 14 03 | 13 57 | 14 29 | 14 26 | 13 44 |
| 26 | 14 05 | 13 55 | 14 22 | 14 16 | 13 35 |
| 27 | 14 06 | 13 53 | 14 16 | 14 06 | 13 26 |
| 28 | 14 07 | 13 51 | 14 09 | 13 57 | 13 17 |
| 29 | 14 08 | 13 49 | 14 02 | 13 47 | 13 08 |
| 30 | 14 09 | 13 47 | 13 56 | 13 37 | 12 59 |
| 31 | 14 10 | 13 45 | 13 49 | 13 27 | 12 49 |
| 32 | 14 11 | 13 43 | 13 42 | 13 17 | 12 39 |
| 33 | 14 12 | 13 40 | 13 35 | 13 07 | 12 30 |
| 34 | 14 13 | 13 38 | 13 29 | 12 57 | 12 20 |
| 35 | 14 14 | 13 36 | 13 22 | 12 46 | 12 09 |
| 36 | 14 15 | 13 33 | 13 15 | 12 36 | 11 59 |
| 37 | 14 16 | 13 31 | 13 08 | 12 26 | 11 48 |
| 38 | 14 17 | 13 28 | 13 01 | 12 15 | 11 37 |
| 39 | 14 18 | 13 26 | 12 54 | 12 04 | 11 26 |
| 40 | 14 19 | 13 23 | 12 46 | 11 54 | 11 15 |
| 41 | 14 20 | 13 20 | 12 39 | 11 43 | 11 03 |
| 42 | 14 20 | 13 17 | 12 32 | 11 32 | 10 51 |
| 43 | 14 21 | 13 15 | 12 24 | 11 21 | 10 39 |
| 44 | 14 21 | 13 11 | 12 17 | 11 09 | 10 27 |
| 45 | 14 22 | 13 08 | 12 09 | 10 58 | 10 14 |
| 46 | 14 22 | 13 05 | 12 02 | 10 46 | 10 01 |
| 47 | 14 23 | 13 01 | 11 54 | 10 34 | 09 47 |
| 48 | 14 23 | 12 58 | 11 46 | 10 23 | 09 33 |
| 49 | 14 23 | 12 54 | 11 38 | 10 11 | 09 19 |
| 50 | 14 23 | 12 50 | 11 29 | 09 58 | 09 04 |
| 51 | 14 22 | 12 45 | 11 21 | 09 46 | 08 49 |
| 52 | 14 21 | 12 41 | 11 12 | 09 34 | 08 33 |
| 53 | 14 20 | 12 36 | 11 04 | 09 21 | 08 17 |
| 54 | 14 19 | 12 30 | 10 55 | 09 08 | 08 00 |
| 55 | 14 17 | 12 25 | 10 46 | 08 56 | 07 43 |
| 56 | 14 15 | 12 18 | 10 36 | 08 43 | 07 25 |
| 57 | 14 11 | 12 11 | 10 27 | 08 30 | 07 06 |
| 58 | 14 07 | 12 03 | 10 17 | 08 18 | 06 47 |
| 59 | 14 02 | 11 54 | 10 07 | 08 05 | 06 27 |
| 60 | 13♌55 | 11♍44 | 09♎57 | 07♏54 | 06♐07 |

7h 8m 0s — 107° 0' 0" — 15 ♋ 40

| LAT. | 11 | 12 | ASC | 2 | 3 |
|---|---|---|---|---|---|
| 0 | 14♌32 | 15♍53 | 18♎26 | 19♏27 | 18♐02 |
| 5 | 14 38 | 15 40 | 17 46 | 18 35 | 17 22 |
| 10 | 14 43 | 15 28 | 17 09 | 17 45 | 16 42 |
| 15 | 14 48 | 15 16 | 16 33 | 16 56 | 16 01 |
| 20 | 14 53 | 15 04 | 15 58 | 16 06 | 15 19 |
| 21 | 14 54 | 15 02 | 15 51 | 15 57 | 15 10 |
| 22 | 14 55 | 15 00 | 15 44 | 15 47 | 15 02 |
| 23 | 14 56 | 14 57 | 15 37 | 15 37 | 14 53 |
| 24 | 14 57 | 14 55 | 15 30 | 15 27 | 14 44 |
| 25 | 14 58 | 14 52 | 15 23 | 15 17 | 14 35 |
| 26 | 14 59 | 14 50 | 15 16 | 15 07 | 14 26 |
| 27 | 15 00 | 14 48 | 15 09 | 14 57 | 14 16 |
| 28 | 15 01 | 14 45 | 15 02 | 14 47 | 14 07 |
| 29 | 15 01 | 14 43 | 14 55 | 14 37 | 13 58 |
| 30 | 15 02 | 14 40 | 14 48 | 14 26 | 13 48 |
| 31 | 15 03 | 14 38 | 14 41 | 14 16 | 13 38 |
| 32 | 15 04 | 14 35 | 14 33 | 14 06 | 13 28 |
| 33 | 15 05 | 14 32 | 14 26 | 13 55 | 13 18 |
| 34 | 15 05 | 14 30 | 14 19 | 13 45 | 13 08 |
| 35 | 15 06 | 14 27 | 14 12 | 13 34 | 12 57 |
| 36 | 15 07 | 14 24 | 14 04 | 13 23 | 12 46 |
| 37 | 15 08 | 14 21 | 13 57 | 13 12 | 12 35 |
| 38 | 15 08 | 14 19 | 13 49 | 13 01 | 12 24 |
| 39 | 15 09 | 14 16 | 13 42 | 12 50 | 12 13 |
| 40 | 15 09 | 14 13 | 13 34 | 12 39 | 12 01 |
| 41 | 15 10 | 14 09 | 13 27 | 12 28 | 11 49 |
| 42 | 15 10 | 14 06 | 13 19 | 12 16 | 11 37 |
| 43 | 15 11 | 14 03 | 13 11 | 12 05 | 11 24 |
| 44 | 15 11 | 13 59 | 13 03 | 11 53 | 11 11 |
| 45 | 15 11 | 13 56 | 12 55 | 11 41 | 10 58 |
| 46 | 15 11 | 13 52 | 12 47 | 11 29 | 10 44 |
| 47 | 15 11 | 13 48 | 12 38 | 11 16 | 10 30 |
| 48 | 15 11 | 13 44 | 12 30 | 11 04 | 10 15 |
| 49 | 15 11 | 13 40 | 12 21 | 10 51 | 10 00 |
| 50 | 15 10 | 13 35 | 12 12 | 10 39 | 09 45 |
| 51 | 15 09 | 13 30 | 12 03 | 10 26 | 09 29 |
| 52 | 15 08 | 13 25 | 11 54 | 10 13 | 09 13 |
| 53 | 15 07 | 13 20 | 11 45 | 10 00 | 08 55 |
| 54 | 15 05 | 13 14 | 11 36 | 09 46 | 08 38 |
| 55 | 15 03 | 13 08 | 11 26 | 09 33 | 08 20 |
| 56 | 15 00 | 13 01 | 11 16 | 09 19 | 08 01 |
| 57 | 14 57 | 12 53 | 11 06 | 09 06 | 07 41 |
| 58 | 14 52 | 12 45 | 10 56 | 08 52 | 07 21 |
| 59 | 14 47 | 12 36 | 10 45 | 08 39 | 07 00 |
| 60 | 14♌39 | 12♍25 | 10♎34 | 08♏26 | 06♐39 |

7h 12m 0s — 108° 0' 0" — 16 ♋ 36

| LAT. | 11 | 12 | ASC | 2 | 3 |
|---|---|---|---|---|---|
| 0 | 15♌32 | 16♍57 | 19♎30 | 20♏26 | 18♐58 |
| 5 | 15 37 | 16 42 | 18 48 | 19 33 | 18 17 |
| 10 | 15 41 | 16 28 | 18 09 | 18 41 | 17 36 |
| 15 | 15 45 | 16 15 | 17 31 | 17 50 | 16 54 |
| 20 | 15 49 | 16 01 | 16 54 | 16 59 | 16 11 |
| 21 | 15 50 | 15 59 | 16 46 | 16 49 | 16 02 |
| 22 | 15 50 | 15 56 | 16 39 | 16 39 | 15 53 |
| 23 | 15 51 | 15 53 | 16 32 | 16 29 | 15 44 |
| 24 | 15 52 | 15 50 | 16 24 | 16 19 | 15 35 |
| 25 | 15 52 | 15 48 | 16 17 | 16 08 | 15 25 |
| 26 | 15 53 | 15 45 | 16 09 | 15 58 | 15 16 |
| 27 | 15 54 | 15 42 | 16 02 | 15 47 | 15 06 |
| 28 | 15 54 | 15 39 | 15 55 | 15 37 | 14 57 |
| 29 | 15 55 | 15 36 | 15 47 | 15 26 | 14 47 |
| 30 | 15 56 | 15 34 | 15 40 | 15 16 | 14 37 |
| 31 | 15 56 | 15 31 | 15 32 | 15 05 | 14 27 |
| 32 | 15 57 | 15 28 | 15 25 | 14 54 | 14 17 |
| 33 | 15 57 | 15 25 | 15 17 | 14 44 | 14 06 |
| 34 | 15 58 | 15 22 | 15 09 | 14 33 | 13 56 |
| 35 | 15 58 | 15 19 | 15 02 | 14 21 | 13 45 |
| 36 | 15 59 | 15 15 | 14 54 | 14 10 | 13 34 |
| 37 | 15 59 | 15 12 | 14 46 | 13 59 | 13 22 |
| 38 | 16 00 | 15 09 | 14 38 | 13 48 | 13 11 |
| 39 | 16 00 | 15 06 | 14 30 | 13 36 | 12 59 |
| 40 | 16 00 | 15 02 | 14 22 | 13 24 | 12 47 |
| 41 | 16 00 | 14 59 | 14 14 | 13 13 | 12 34 |
| 42 | 16 01 | 14 55 | 14 06 | 13 01 | 12 22 |
| 43 | 16 01 | 14 51 | 13 57 | 12 49 | 12 08 |
| 44 | 16 01 | 14 47 | 13 49 | 12 36 | 11 55 |
| 45 | 16 01 | 14 43 | 13 40 | 12 24 | 11 41 |
| 46 | 16 00 | 14 39 | 13 32 | 12 11 | 11 27 |
| 47 | 16 00 | 14 35 | 13 23 | 11 58 | 11 12 |
| 48 | 16 00 | 14 30 | 13 14 | 11 45 | 10 57 |
| 49 | 15 59 | 14 26 | 13 05 | 11 32 | 10 42 |
| 50 | 15 58 | 14 21 | 12 55 | 11 19 | 10 26 |
| 51 | 15 57 | 14 15 | 12 46 | 11 05 | 10 09 |
| 52 | 15 56 | 14 10 | 12 36 | 10 52 | 09 52 |
| 53 | 15 54 | 14 04 | 12 27 | 10 38 | 09 34 |
| 54 | 15 52 | 13 58 | 12 17 | 10 24 | 09 16 |
| 55 | 15 49 | 13 51 | 12 06 | 10 10 | 08 56 |
| 56 | 15 46 | 13 44 | 11 56 | 09 55 | 08 37 |
| 57 | 15 42 | 13 36 | 11 45 | 09 41 | 08 16 |
| 58 | 15 37 | 13 27 | 11 34 | 09 27 | 07 55 |
| 59 | 15 31 | 13 17 | 11 23 | 09 13 | 07 33 |
| 60 | 15♌24 | 13♍06 | 11♎12 | 08♏59 | 07♐10 |

7h 16m 0s — 109° 0' 0" — 17 ♋ 32

| LAT. | 11 | 12 | ASC | 2 | 3 |
|---|---|---|---|---|---|
| 0 | 16♌33 | 18♍02 | 20♎34 | 21♏26 | 19♐53 |
| 5 | 16 36 | 17 45 | 19 50 | 20 30 | 19 11 |
| 10 | 16 39 | 17 29 | 19 09 | 19 37 | 18 29 |
| 15 | 16 42 | 17 14 | 18 29 | 18 45 | 17 46 |
| 20 | 16 45 | 16 58 | 17 50 | 17 52 | 17 02 |
| 21 | 16 45 | 16 55 | 17 42 | 17 42 | 16 53 |
| 22 | 16 46 | 16 52 | 17 34 | 17 31 | 16 44 |
| 23 | 16 46 | 16 49 | 17 26 | 17 21 | 16 35 |
| 24 | 16 47 | 16 46 | 17 19 | 17 10 | 16 25 |
| 25 | 16 47 | 16 43 | 17 11 | 16 59 | 16 16 |
| 26 | 16 47 | 16 40 | 17 03 | 16 49 | 16 06 |
| 27 | 16 48 | 16 37 | 16 55 | 16 38 | 15 56 |
| 28 | 16 48 | 16 34 | 16 47 | 16 27 | 15 46 |
| 29 | 16 49 | 16 30 | 16 40 | 16 16 | 15 36 |
| 30 | 16 49 | 16 27 | 16 32 | 16 05 | 15 26 |
| 31 | 16 49 | 16 24 | 16 24 | 15 54 | 15 16 |
| 32 | 16 50 | 16 20 | 16 16 | 15 43 | 15 05 |
| 33 | 16 50 | 16 17 | 16 08 | 15 32 | 14 54 |
| 34 | 16 50 | 16 14 | 16 00 | 15 20 | 14 43 |
| 35 | 16 51 | 16 10 | 15 52 | 15 09 | 14 32 |
| 36 | 16 51 | 16 07 | 15 43 | 14 57 | 14 21 |
| 37 | 16 51 | 16 03 | 15 35 | 14 46 | 14 09 |
| 38 | 16 51 | 15 59 | 15 27 | 14 34 | 13 57 |
| 39 | 16 51 | 15 56 | 15 18 | 14 22 | 13 45 |
| 40 | 16 51 | 15 52 | 15 10 | 14 10 | 13 32 |
| 41 | 16 51 | 15 48 | 15 01 | 13 57 | 13 20 |
| 42 | 16 51 | 15 44 | 14 53 | 13 45 | 13 06 |
| 43 | 16 51 | 15 40 | 14 44 | 13 32 | 12 53 |
| 44 | 16 51 | 15 36 | 14 35 | 13 20 | 12 39 |
| 45 | 16 50 | 15 31 | 14 26 | 13 07 | 12 25 |
| 46 | 16 50 | 15 27 | 14 17 | 12 53 | 12 10 |
| 47 | 16 49 | 15 22 | 14 07 | 12 40 | 11 55 |
| 48 | 16 48 | 15 17 | 13 58 | 12 27 | 11 39 |
| 49 | 16 47 | 15 12 | 13 48 | 12 13 | 11 23 |
| 50 | 16 46 | 15 06 | 13 38 | 11 59 | 11 06 |
| 51 | 16 45 | 15 01 | 13 28 | 11 45 | 10 49 |
| 52 | 16 43 | 14 55 | 13 18 | 11 30 | 10 31 |
| 53 | 16 41 | 14 48 | 13 08 | 11 16 | 10 12 |
| 54 | 16 39 | 14 42 | 12 57 | 11 01 | 09 53 |
| 55 | 16 36 | 14 34 | 12 47 | 10 46 | 09 33 |
| 56 | 16 32 | 14 27 | 12 36 | 10 31 | 09 12 |
| 57 | 16 28 | 14 18 | 12 24 | 10 16 | 08 51 |
| 58 | 16 23 | 14 09 | 12 13 | 10 01 | 08 28 |
| 59 | 16 17 | 13 59 | 12 01 | 09 46 | 08 05 |
| 60 | 16♌09 | 13♍48 | 11♎49 | 09♏32 | 07♐40 |

7h 20m 0s — 110° 0' 0" — 18 ♋ 28

| LAT. | 11 | 12 | ASC | 2 | 3 |
|---|---|---|---|---|---|
| 0 | 17♌33 | 19♍07 | 21♎38 | 22♏25 | 20♐49 |
| 5 | 17 35 | 18 48 | 20 52 | 21 28 | 20 06 |
| 10 | 17 37 | 18 30 | 20 09 | 20 33 | 19 23 |
| 15 | 17 39 | 18 13 | 19 27 | 19 39 | 18 39 |
| 20 | 17 41 | 17 56 | 18 46 | 18 45 | 17 54 |
| 21 | 17 41 | 17 52 | 18 37 | 18 34 | 17 45 |
| 22 | 17 41 | 17 49 | 18 29 | 18 23 | 17 35 |
| 23 | 17 41 | 17 45 | 18 21 | 18 12 | 17 26 |
| 24 | 17 42 | 17 42 | 18 13 | 18 01 | 17 16 |
| 25 | 17 42 | 17 38 | 18 05 | 17 50 | 17 06 |
| 26 | 17 42 | 17 35 | 17 57 | 17 39 | 16 56 |
| 27 | 17 42 | 17 31 | 17 48 | 17 28 | 16 46 |
| 28 | 17 43 | 17 28 | 17 40 | 17 17 | 16 36 |
| 29 | 17 43 | 17 24 | 17 32 | 17 06 | 16 26 |
| 30 | 17 43 | 17 21 | 17 24 | 16 54 | 16 15 |
| 31 | 17 43 | 17 17 | 17 15 | 16 43 | 16 05 |
| 32 | 17 43 | 17 13 | 17 07 | 16 31 | 15 54 |
| 33 | 17 43 | 17 10 | 16 58 | 16 20 | 15 43 |
| 34 | 17 43 | 17 06 | 16 50 | 16 08 | 15 31 |
| 35 | 17 43 | 17 02 | 16 41 | 15 56 | 15 20 |
| 36 | 17 43 | 16 58 | 16 33 | 15 44 | 15 08 |
| 37 | 17 43 | 16 54 | 16 24 | 15 32 | 14 56 |
| 38 | 17 43 | 16 50 | 16 15 | 15 20 | 14 44 |
| 39 | 17 43 | 16 46 | 16 07 | 15 07 | 14 31 |
| 40 | 17 42 | 16 42 | 15 58 | 14 55 | 14 18 |
| 41 | 17 42 | 16 37 | 15 49 | 14 42 | 14 05 |
| 42 | 17 42 | 16 33 | 15 39 | 14 29 | 13 51 |
| 43 | 17 41 | 16 28 | 15 30 | 14 16 | 13 37 |
| 44 | 17 41 | 16 24 | 15 21 | 14 03 | 13 23 |
| 45 | 17 40 | 16 19 | 15 11 | 13 49 | 13 08 |
| 46 | 17 39 | 16 14 | 15 02 | 13 36 | 12 53 |
| 47 | 17 38 | 16 09 | 14 52 | 13 22 | 12 37 |
| 48 | 17 37 | 16 03 | 14 42 | 13 08 | 12 21 |
| 49 | 17 36 | 15 58 | 14 32 | 12 53 | 12 04 |
| 50 | 17 35 | 15 52 | 14 21 | 12 39 | 11 47 |
| 51 | 17 33 | 15 46 | 14 11 | 12 24 | 11 29 |
| 52 | 17 31 | 15 40 | 14 00 | 12 09 | 11 10 |
| 53 | 17 29 | 15 33 | 13 49 | 11 54 | 10 51 |
| 54 | 17 26 | 15 26 | 13 38 | 11 39 | 10 31 |
| 55 | 17 23 | 15 18 | 13 27 | 11 23 | 10 10 |
| 56 | 17 19 | 15 10 | 13 15 | 11 07 | 09 48 |
| 57 | 17 14 | 15 01 | 13 03 | 10 51 | 09 25 |
| 58 | 17 09 | 14 52 | 12 51 | 10 35 | 09 01 |
| 59 | 17 02 | 14 41 | 12 39 | 10 20 | 08 37 |
| 60 | 16♌54 | 14♍29 | 12♎26 | 10♏04 | 08♐11 |

7h 24m 0s — 111° 0' 0" — 19 ♋ 24

| LAT. | 11 | 12 | ASC | 2 | 3 |
|---|---|---|---|---|---|
| 0 | 18♌34 | 20♍12 | 22♎42 | 23♏23 | 21♐44 |
| 5 | 18 35 | 19 51 | 21 54 | 22 25 | 21 00 |
| 10 | 18 36 | 19 31 | 21 09 | 21 29 | 20 16 |
| 15 | 18 36 | 19 12 | 20 25 | 20 33 | 19 32 |
| 20 | 18 37 | 18 53 | 19 42 | 19 38 | 18 45 |
| 21 | 18 37 | 18 49 | 19 33 | 19 26 | 18 36 |
| 22 | 18 37 | 18 45 | 19 24 | 19 15 | 18 26 |
| 23 | 18 37 | 18 42 | 19 16 | 19 04 | 18 17 |
| 24 | 18 37 | 18 38 | 19 07 | 18 53 | 18 07 |
| 25 | 18 37 | 18 34 | 18 59 | 18 41 | 17 57 |
| 26 | 18 37 | 18 30 | 18 50 | 18 30 | 17 47 |
| 27 | 18 37 | 18 26 | 18 42 | 18 18 | 17 36 |
| 28 | 18 37 | 18 22 | 18 33 | 18 07 | 17 26 |
| 29 | 18 37 | 18 18 | 18 24 | 17 55 | 17 15 |
| 30 | 18 37 | 18 14 | 18 16 | 17 44 | 17 04 |
| 31 | 18 37 | 18 10 | 18 07 | 17 32 | 16 53 |
| 32 | 18 36 | 18 06 | 17 58 | 17 20 | 16 42 |
| 33 | 18 36 | 18 02 | 17 49 | 17 08 | 16 31 |
| 34 | 18 36 | 17 58 | 17 40 | 16 56 | 16 19 |
| 35 | 18 36 | 17 54 | 17 31 | 16 43 | 16 07 |
| 36 | 18 36 | 17 50 | 17 22 | 16 31 | 15 55 |
| 37 | 18 35 | 17 45 | 17 13 | 16 18 | 15 43 |
| 38 | 18 35 | 17 41 | 17 04 | 16 06 | 15 30 |
| 39 | 18 34 | 17 36 | 16 55 | 15 53 | 15 17 |
| 40 | 18 34 | 17 32 | 16 45 | 15 40 | 15 04 |
| 41 | 18 33 | 17 27 | 16 36 | 15 27 | 14 50 |
| 42 | 18 33 | 17 22 | 16 26 | 15 13 | 14 36 |
| 43 | 18 32 | 17 17 | 16 16 | 15 00 | 14 22 |
| 44 | 18 31 | 17 12 | 16 07 | 14 46 | 14 07 |
| 45 | 18 30 | 17 07 | 15 57 | 14 32 | 13 52 |
| 46 | 18 29 | 17 02 | 15 47 | 14 18 | 13 36 |
| 47 | 18 28 | 16 56 | 15 36 | 14 03 | 13 19 |
| 48 | 18 27 | 16 50 | 15 26 | 13 49 | 13 03 |
| 49 | 18 25 | 16 44 | 15 15 | 13 34 | 12 45 |
| 50 | 18 23 | 16 38 | 15 04 | 13 19 | 12 27 |
| 51 | 18 21 | 16 32 | 14 53 | 13 03 | 12 08 |
| 52 | 18 19 | 16 25 | 14 42 | 12 48 | 11 49 |
| 53 | 18 16 | 16 18 | 14 31 | 12 32 | 11 29 |
| 54 | 18 13 | 16 10 | 14 19 | 12 16 | 11 08 |
| 55 | 18 10 | 16 02 | 14 07 | 11 59 | 10 46 |
| 56 | 18 05 | 15 53 | 13 55 | 11 43 | 10 23 |
| 57 | 18 01 | 15 44 | 13 42 | 11 26 | 09 59 |
| 58 | 17 55 | 15 34 | 13 30 | 11 09 | 09 34 |
| 59 | 17 48 | 15 23 | 13 17 | 10 53 | 09 08 |
| 60 | 17♌40 | 15♍11 | 13♎03 | 10♏36 | 08♐41 |

# Koch Table of Houses for Latitudes 0° to 60° North

| 7h 28m 0s | 112° 0' 0" | 20 ♋ 20 | | | |
|---|---|---|---|---|---|
| LAT. | 11 | 12 | ASC | 2 | 3 |
| 0 | 19♌35 | 21♍17 | 23♎46 | 24♏22 | 22♐39 |
| 5 | 19 35 | 20 54 | 22 56 | 23 22 | 21 55 |
| 10 | 19 34 | 20 32 | 22 08 | 22 24 | 21 10 |
| 15 | 19 34 | 20 11 | 21 22 | 21 27 | 20 24 |
| 20 | 19 33 | 19 50 | 20 37 | 20 30 | 19 37 |
| 21 | 19 33 | 19 46 | 20 28 | 20 19 | 19 27 |
| 22 | 19 33 | 19 42 | 20 19 | 20 07 | 19 17 |
| 23 | 19 33 | 19 38 | 20 11 | 19 56 | 19 07 |
| 24 | 19 32 | 19 34 | 20 02 | 19 44 | 18 57 |
| 25 | 19 32 | 19 29 | 19 53 | 19 32 | 18 47 |
| 26 | 19 32 | 19 25 | 19 44 | 19 20 | 18 37 |
| 27 | 19 32 | 19 21 | 19 35 | 19 09 | 18 26 |
| 28 | 19 31 | 19 17 | 19 26 | 18 57 | 18 15 |
| 29 | 19 31 | 19 12 | 19 17 | 18 45 | 18 05 |
| 30 | 19 31 | 19 08 | 19 07 | 18 33 | 17 53 |
| 31 | 19 30 | 19 04 | 18 58 | 18 20 | 17 42 |
| 32 | 19 30 | 18 59 | 18 49 | 18 08 | 17 31 |
| 33 | 19 30 | 18 55 | 18 40 | 17 56 | 17 19 |
| 34 | 19 29 | 18 50 | 18 31 | 17 43 | 17 07 |
| 35 | 19 29 | 18 46 | 18 21 | 17 30 | 16 55 |
| 36 | 19 28 | 18 41 | 18 12 | 17 18 | 16 42 |
| 37 | 19 28 | 18 36 | 18 02 | 17 05 | 16 30 |
| 38 | 19 27 | 18 32 | 17 53 | 16 52 | 16 17 |
| 39 | 19 26 | 18 27 | 17 43 | 16 38 | 16 03 |
| 40 | 19 26 | 18 22 | 17 33 | 16 25 | 15 49 |
| 41 | 19 25 | 18 17 | 17 23 | 16 11 | 15 35 |
| 42 | 19 24 | 18 12 | 17 13 | 15 57 | 15 21 |
| 43 | 19 23 | 18 06 | 17 03 | 15 43 | 15 06 |
| 44 | 19 22 | 18 01 | 16 53 | 15 29 | 14 51 |
| 45 | 19 20 | 17 55 | 16 42 | 15 14 | 14 35 |
| 46 | 19 19 | 17 49 | 16 31 | 15 00 | 14 18 |
| 47 | 19 18 | 17 43 | 16 21 | 14 45 | 14 02 |
| 48 | 19 16 | 17 37 | 16 10 | 14 30 | 13 44 |
| 49 | 19 14 | 17 31 | 15 59 | 14 14 | 13 26 |
| 50 | 19 12 | 17 24 | 15 47 | 13 58 | 13 07 |
| 51 | 19 10 | 17 17 | 15 36 | 13 42 | 12 48 |
| 52 | 19 07 | 17 10 | 15 24 | 13 26 | 12 28 |
| 53 | 19 04 | 17 02 | 15 12 | 13 10 | 12 07 |
| 54 | 19 01 | 16 54 | 15 00 | 12 53 | 11 45 |
| 55 | 18 57 | 16 46 | 14 47 | 12 36 | 11 22 |
| 56 | 18 53 | 16 37 | 14 35 | 12 18 | 10 58 |
| 57 | 18 47 | 16 27 | 14 22 | 12 01 | 10 33 |
| 58 | 18 41 | 16 17 | 14 08 | 11 43 | 10 07 |
| 59 | 18 34 | 16 05 | 13 54 | 11 26 | 09 40 |
| 60 | 18♌26 | 15♍53 | 13♎40 | 11♏08 | 09♐11 |

| 7h 32m 0s | 113° 0' 0" | 21 ♋ 17 | | | |
|---|---|---|---|---|---|
| LAT. | 11 | 12 | ASC | 2 | 3 |
| 0 | 20♌36 | 22♍23 | 24♎50 | 25♏21 | 23♐34 |
| 5 | 20 35 | 21 57 | 23 58 | 24 19 | 22 49 |
| 10 | 20 33 | 21 33 | 23 08 | 23 20 | 22 04 |
| 15 | 20 31 | 21 10 | 22 20 | 22 21 | 21 17 |
| 20 | 20 30 | 20 48 | 21 33 | 21 23 | 20 29 |
| 21 | 20 29 | 20 43 | 21 24 | 21 11 | 20 19 |
| 22 | 20 29 | 20 39 | 21 14 | 20 59 | 20 09 |
| 23 | 20 28 | 20 34 | 21 05 | 20 47 | 19 58 |
| 24 | 20 28 | 20 30 | 20 56 | 20 35 | 19 48 |
| 25 | 20 28 | 20 25 | 20 46 | 20 23 | 19 37 |
| 26 | 20 27 | 20 21 | 20 37 | 20 11 | 19 27 |
| 27 | 20 27 | 20 16 | 20 28 | 19 59 | 19 16 |
| 28 | 20 26 | 20 11 | 20 18 | 19 46 | 19 05 |
| 29 | 20 26 | 20 07 | 20 09 | 19 34 | 18 54 |
| 30 | 20 25 | 20 02 | 19 59 | 19 22 | 18 43 |
| 31 | 20 24 | 19 57 | 19 50 | 19 09 | 18 31 |
| 32 | 20 24 | 19 53 | 19 40 | 18 56 | 18 19 |
| 33 | 20 23 | 19 48 | 19 30 | 18 44 | 18 07 |
| 34 | 20 23 | 19 43 | 19 21 | 18 31 | 17 55 |
| 35 | 20 22 | 19 38 | 19 11 | 18 17 | 17 42 |
| 36 | 20 21 | 19 33 | 19 01 | 18 04 | 17 29 |
| 37 | 20 20 | 19 28 | 18 51 | 17 51 | 17 16 |
| 38 | 20 19 | 19 23 | 18 41 | 17 37 | 17 03 |
| 39 | 20 18 | 19 17 | 18 31 | 17 24 | 16 49 |
| 40 | 20 17 | 19 12 | 18 21 | 17 10 | 16 35 |
| 41 | 20 16 | 19 07 | 18 10 | 16 56 | 16 20 |
| 42 | 20 15 | 19 01 | 18 00 | 16 41 | 16 06 |
| 43 | 20 14 | 18 55 | 17 49 | 16 27 | 15 50 |
| 44 | 20 12 | 18 49 | 17 38 | 16 12 | 15 34 |
| 45 | 20 11 | 18 43 | 17 28 | 15 57 | 15 18 |
| 46 | 20 09 | 18 37 | 17 16 | 15 42 | 15 01 |
| 47 | 20 08 | 18 31 | 17 05 | 15 26 | 14 44 |
| 48 | 20 06 | 18 24 | 16 54 | 15 10 | 14 26 |
| 49 | 20 04 | 18 17 | 16 42 | 14 54 | 14 07 |
| 50 | 20 01 | 18 10 | 16 30 | 14 38 | 13 48 |
| 51 | 19 59 | 18 03 | 16 18 | 14 21 | 13 27 |
| 52 | 19 56 | 17 55 | 16 06 | 14 04 | 13 06 |
| 53 | 19 52 | 17 47 | 15 53 | 13 47 | 12 45 |
| 54 | 19 49 | 17 39 | 15 41 | 13 30 | 12 22 |
| 55 | 19 45 | 17 30 | 15 28 | 13 12 | 11 58 |
| 56 | 19 40 | 17 21 | 15 14 | 12 54 | 11 33 |
| 57 | 19 35 | 17 11 | 15 01 | 12 35 | 11 07 |
| 58 | 19 28 | 17 00 | 14 47 | 12 17 | 10 40 |
| 59 | 19 21 | 16 48 | 14 32 | 11 58 | 10 11 |
| 60 | 19♌12 | 16♍35 | 14♎18 | 11♏40 | 09♐40 |

| 7h 36m 0s | 114° 0' 0" | 22 ♋ 13 | | | |
|---|---|---|---|---|---|
| LAT. | 11 | 12 | ASC | 2 | 3 |
| 0 | 21♌37 | 23♍28 | 25♎53 | 26♏19 | 24♐30 |
| 5 | 21 35 | 23 01 | 24 59 | 25 16 | 23 43 |
| 10 | 21 32 | 22 35 | 24 07 | 24 15 | 22 57 |
| 15 | 21 29 | 22 10 | 23 18 | 23 15 | 22 10 |
| 20 | 21 26 | 21 45 | 22 29 | 22 15 | 21 20 |
| 21 | 21 26 | 21 40 | 22 19 | 22 03 | 21 10 |
| 22 | 21 25 | 21 36 | 22 09 | 21 51 | 21 00 |
| 23 | 21 24 | 21 31 | 22 00 | 21 38 | 20 49 |
| 24 | 21 24 | 21 26 | 21 50 | 21 26 | 20 39 |
| 25 | 21 23 | 21 21 | 21 40 | 21 14 | 20 28 |
| 26 | 21 22 | 21 16 | 21 30 | 21 01 | 20 17 |
| 27 | 21 22 | 21 11 | 21 21 | 20 49 | 20 06 |
| 28 | 21 21 | 21 06 | 21 11 | 20 36 | 19 55 |
| 29 | 21 20 | 21 01 | 21 01 | 20 23 | 19 43 |
| 30 | 21 19 | 20 56 | 20 51 | 20 10 | 19 32 |
| 31 | 21 19 | 20 51 | 20 41 | 19 58 | 19 20 |
| 32 | 21 18 | 20 46 | 20 31 | 19 44 | 19 08 |
| 33 | 21 17 | 20 41 | 20 21 | 19 31 | 18 55 |
| 34 | 21 16 | 20 35 | 20 11 | 19 18 | 18 43 |
| 35 | 21 15 | 20 30 | 20 01 | 19 04 | 18 30 |
| 36 | 21 14 | 20 25 | 19 50 | 18 51 | 18 17 |
| 37 | 21 13 | 20 19 | 19 40 | 18 37 | 18 03 |
| 38 | 21 12 | 20 14 | 19 30 | 18 23 | 17 49 |
| 39 | 21 11 | 20 08 | 19 19 | 18 09 | 17 35 |
| 40 | 21 09 | 20 02 | 19 08 | 17 54 | 17 21 |
| 41 | 21 08 | 19 56 | 18 58 | 17 40 | 17 06 |
| 42 | 21 07 | 19 51 | 18 47 | 17 25 | 16 50 |
| 43 | 21 05 | 19 44 | 18 36 | 17 10 | 16 34 |
| 44 | 21 03 | 19 38 | 18 24 | 16 55 | 16 18 |
| 45 | 21 02 | 19 32 | 18 13 | 16 39 | 16 01 |
| 46 | 21 00 | 19 25 | 18 01 | 16 23 | 15 44 |
| 47 | 20 58 | 19 18 | 17 50 | 16 07 | 15 26 |
| 48 | 20 56 | 19 11 | 17 38 | 15 51 | 15 07 |
| 49 | 20 53 | 19 04 | 17 26 | 15 34 | 14 48 |
| 50 | 20 51 | 18 57 | 17 13 | 15 17 | 14 28 |
| 51 | 20 48 | 18 49 | 17 01 | 15 00 | 14 07 |
| 52 | 20 44 | 18 41 | 16 48 | 14 43 | 13 45 |
| 53 | 20 41 | 18 33 | 16 35 | 14 25 | 13 22 |
| 54 | 20 37 | 18 24 | 16 21 | 14 06 | 12 59 |
| 55 | 20 33 | 18 14 | 16 08 | 13 48 | 12 34 |
| 56 | 20 28 | 18 04 | 15 54 | 13 29 | 12 08 |
| 57 | 20 22 | 17 54 | 15 40 | 13 10 | 11 41 |
| 58 | 20 15 | 17 43 | 15 25 | 12 50 | 11 12 |
| 59 | 20 08 | 17 31 | 15 10 | 12 31 | 10 42 |
| 60 | 19♌59 | 17♍17 | 14♎55 | 12♏11 | 10♐10 |

| 7h 40m 0s | 115° 0' 0" | 23 ♋ 10 | | | |
|---|---|---|---|---|---|
| LAT. | 11 | 12 | ASC | 2 | 3 |
| 0 | 22♌39 | 24♍33 | 26♎57 | 27♏17 | 25♐25 |
| 5 | 22 35 | 24 04 | 26 00 | 26 13 | 24 38 |
| 10 | 22 31 | 23 36 | 25 07 | 25 11 | 23 51 |
| 15 | 22 27 | 23 09 | 24 15 | 24 09 | 23 02 |
| 20 | 22 23 | 22 43 | 23 24 | 23 07 | 22 12 |
| 21 | 22 22 | 22 38 | 23 14 | 22 55 | 22 01 |
| 22 | 22 21 | 22 33 | 23 04 | 22 42 | 21 51 |
| 23 | 22 21 | 22 27 | 22 54 | 22 30 | 21 40 |
| 24 | 22 20 | 22 22 | 22 44 | 22 17 | 21 29 |
| 25 | 22 19 | 22 17 | 22 34 | 22 04 | 21 18 |
| 26 | 22 18 | 22 11 | 22 24 | 21 51 | 21 07 |
| 27 | 22 17 | 22 06 | 22 14 | 21 39 | 20 56 |
| 28 | 22 16 | 22 01 | 22 03 | 21 26 | 20 44 |
| 29 | 22 15 | 21 55 | 21 53 | 21 12 | 20 32 |
| 30 | 22 14 | 21 50 | 21 43 | 20 59 | 20 21 |
| 31 | 22 13 | 21 45 | 21 33 | 20 46 | 20 08 |
| 32 | 22 12 | 21 39 | 21 22 | 20 33 | 19 56 |
| 33 | 22 11 | 21 34 | 21 12 | 20 19 | 19 43 |
| 34 | 22 10 | 21 28 | 21 01 | 20 05 | 19 30 |
| 35 | 22 08 | 21 22 | 20 51 | 19 51 | 19 17 |
| 36 | 22 07 | 21 17 | 20 40 | 19 37 | 19 04 |
| 37 | 22 06 | 21 11 | 20 29 | 19 23 | 18 50 |
| 38 | 22 05 | 21 05 | 20 18 | 19 09 | 18 36 |
| 39 | 22 03 | 20 59 | 20 07 | 18 54 | 18 21 |
| 40 | 22 02 | 20 53 | 19 56 | 18 39 | 18 06 |
| 41 | 22 00 | 20 47 | 19 45 | 18 24 | 17 51 |
| 42 | 21 58 | 20 40 | 19 33 | 18 09 | 17 35 |
| 43 | 21 57 | 20 34 | 19 22 | 17 53 | 17 19 |
| 44 | 21 55 | 20 27 | 19 10 | 17 38 | 17 02 |
| 45 | 21 53 | 20 20 | 18 58 | 17 21 | 16 44 |
| 46 | 21 51 | 20 13 | 18 46 | 17 05 | 16 26 |
| 47 | 21 48 | 20 06 | 18 34 | 16 49 | 16 08 |
| 48 | 21 46 | 19 59 | 18 22 | 16 32 | 15 48 |
| 49 | 21 43 | 19 51 | 18 09 | 16 14 | 15 28 |
| 50 | 21 40 | 19 43 | 17 56 | 15 57 | 15 08 |
| 51 | 21 37 | 19 35 | 17 43 | 15 39 | 14 46 |
| 52 | 21 34 | 19 27 | 17 30 | 15 21 | 14 23 |
| 53 | 21 30 | 19 18 | 17 16 | 15 02 | 14 00 |
| 54 | 21 25 | 19 09 | 17 02 | 14 43 | 13 35 |
| 55 | 21 21 | 18 59 | 16 48 | 14 24 | 13 09 |
| 56 | 21 16 | 18 49 | 16 34 | 14 04 | 12 42 |
| 57 | 21 10 | 18 38 | 16 19 | 13 44 | 12 14 |
| 58 | 21 03 | 18 26 | 16 03 | 13 24 | 11 44 |
| 59 | 20 55 | 18 14 | 15 48 | 13 03 | 11 12 |
| 60 | 20♌46 | 18♍00 | 15♎32 | 12♏43 | 10♐39 |

| 7h 44m 0s | 116° 0' 0" | 24 ♋ 06 | | | |
|---|---|---|---|---|---|
| LAT. | 11 | 12 | ASC | 2 | 3 |
| 0 | 23♌41 | 25♍38 | 28♎00 | 28♏15 | 26♐20 |
| 5 | 23 35 | 25 07 | 27 02 | 27 10 | 25 32 |
| 10 | 23 30 | 24 37 | 26 06 | 26 06 | 24 44 |
| 15 | 23 25 | 24 09 | 25 13 | 25 03 | 23 55 |
| 20 | 23 20 | 23 41 | 24 20 | 23 59 | 23 03 |
| 21 | 23 19 | 23 35 | 24 10 | 23 47 | 22 53 |
| 22 | 23 18 | 23 29 | 23 59 | 23 34 | 22 42 |
| 23 | 23 17 | 23 24 | 23 49 | 23 21 | 22 31 |
| 24 | 23 16 | 23 18 | 23 38 | 23 08 | 22 20 |
| 25 | 23 15 | 23 13 | 23 28 | 22 55 | 22 09 |
| 26 | 23 14 | 23 07 | 23 17 | 22 42 | 21 57 |
| 27 | 23 12 | 23 01 | 23 07 | 22 28 | 21 46 |
| 28 | 23 11 | 22 56 | 22 56 | 22 15 | 21 34 |
| 29 | 23 10 | 22 50 | 22 45 | 22 02 | 21 22 |
| 30 | 23 09 | 22 44 | 22 35 | 21 48 | 21 10 |
| 31 | 23 08 | 22 38 | 22 24 | 21 34 | 20 57 |
| 32 | 23 06 | 22 33 | 22 13 | 21 20 | 20 44 |
| 33 | 23 05 | 22 27 | 22 02 | 21 07 | 20 31 |
| 34 | 23 04 | 22 21 | 21 51 | 20 52 | 20 18 |
| 35 | 23 02 | 22 15 | 21 40 | 20 38 | 20 05 |
| 36 | 23 01 | 22 09 | 21 29 | 20 24 | 19 51 |
| 37 | 22 59 | 22 02 | 21 18 | 20 09 | 19 37 |
| 38 | 22 57 | 21 56 | 21 07 | 19 54 | 19 22 |
| 39 | 22 56 | 21 50 | 20 55 | 19 39 | 19 07 |
| 40 | 22 54 | 21 43 | 20 44 | 19 24 | 18 52 |
| 41 | 22 52 | 21 37 | 20 32 | 19 08 | 18 36 |
| 42 | 22 50 | 21 30 | 20 20 | 18 52 | 18 19 |
| 43 | 22 48 | 21 23 | 20 08 | 18 36 | 18 03 |
| 44 | 22 46 | 21 16 | 19 56 | 18 20 | 17 45 |
| 45 | 22 44 | 21 09 | 19 44 | 18 04 | 17 27 |
| 46 | 22 41 | 21 02 | 19 31 | 17 47 | 17 09 |
| 47 | 22 39 | 20 54 | 19 18 | 17 30 | 16 50 |
| 48 | 22 36 | 20 46 | 19 06 | 17 12 | 16 30 |
| 49 | 22 33 | 20 38 | 18 52 | 16 54 | 16 09 |
| 50 | 22 30 | 20 30 | 18 39 | 16 36 | 15 47 |
| 51 | 22 27 | 20 21 | 18 25 | 16 17 | 15 25 |
| 52 | 22 23 | 20 13 | 18 12 | 15 59 | 15 02 |
| 53 | 22 19 | 20 03 | 17 57 | 15 39 | 14 37 |
| 54 | 22 14 | 19 54 | 17 43 | 15 20 | 14 12 |
| 55 | 22 09 | 19 43 | 17 28 | 15 00 | 13 45 |
| 56 | 22 04 | 19 33 | 17 13 | 14 39 | 13 17 |
| 57 | 21 58 | 19 21 | 16 58 | 14 18 | 12 47 |
| 58 | 21 51 | 19 09 | 16 42 | 13 57 | 12 16 |
| 59 | 21 43 | 18 57 | 16 26 | 13 36 | 11 43 |
| 60 | 21♌33 | 18♍43 | 16♎09 | 13♏14 | 11♐08 |

| 7h 48m 0s | 117° 0' 0" | 25 ♋ 03 | | | |
|---|---|---|---|---|---|
| LAT. | 11 | 12 | ASC | 2 | 3 |
| 0 | 24♌42 | 26♍44 | 29♎03 | 29♏13 | 27♐15 |
| 5 | 24 36 | 26 10 | 28 03 | 28 06 | 26 26 |
| 10 | 24 30 | 25 39 | 27 05 | 27 01 | 25 38 |
| 15 | 24 24 | 25 08 | 26 10 | 25 56 | 24 47 |
| 20 | 24 17 | 24 38 | 25 15 | 24 51 | 23 55 |
| 21 | 24 16 | 24 32 | 25 05 | 24 38 | 23 44 |
| 22 | 24 15 | 24 27 | 24 54 | 24 25 | 23 33 |
| 23 | 24 14 | 24 21 | 24 43 | 24 12 | 23 22 |
| 24 | 24 12 | 24 15 | 24 32 | 23 59 | 23 10 |
| 25 | 24 11 | 24 09 | 24 21 | 23 45 | 22 59 |
| 26 | 24 09 | 24 03 | 24 10 | 23 32 | 22 47 |
| 27 | 24 08 | 23 57 | 23 59 | 23 18 | 22 35 |
| 28 | 24 07 | 23 51 | 23 48 | 23 04 | 22 23 |
| 29 | 24 05 | 23 45 | 23 37 | 22 51 | 22 11 |
| 30 | 24 04 | 23 38 | 23 26 | 22 37 | 21 59 |
| 31 | 24 02 | 23 32 | 23 15 | 22 23 | 21 46 |
| 32 | 24 01 | 23 26 | 23 04 | 22 08 | 21 33 |
| 33 | 23 59 | 23 20 | 22 53 | 21 54 | 21 20 |
| 34 | 23 58 | 23 14 | 22 41 | 21 40 | 21 06 |
| 35 | 23 56 | 23 07 | 22 30 | 21 25 | 20 52 |
| 36 | 23 54 | 23 01 | 22 18 | 21 10 | 20 38 |
| 37 | 23 52 | 22 54 | 22 07 | 20 55 | 20 23 |
| 38 | 23 51 | 22 47 | 21 55 | 20 40 | 20 08 |
| 39 | 23 49 | 22 41 | 21 43 | 20 24 | 19 53 |
| 40 | 23 47 | 22 34 | 21 31 | 20 08 | 19 37 |
| 41 | 23 45 | 22 27 | 21 19 | 19 52 | 19 21 |
| 42 | 23 42 | 22 20 | 21 07 | 19 36 | 19 04 |
| 43 | 23 40 | 22 13 | 20 54 | 19 20 | 18 47 |
| 44 | 23 38 | 22 05 | 20 42 | 19 03 | 18 29 |
| 45 | 23 35 | 21 58 | 20 29 | 18 46 | 18 10 |
| 46 | 23 33 | 21 50 | 20 16 | 18 28 | 17 51 |
| 47 | 23 30 | 21 42 | 20 03 | 18 11 | 17 31 |
| 48 | 23 27 | 21 34 | 19 49 | 17 52 | 17 11 |
| 49 | 23 23 | 21 25 | 19 36 | 17 34 | 16 50 |
| 50 | 23 20 | 21 17 | 19 22 | 17 15 | 16 27 |
| 51 | 23 16 | 21 08 | 19 08 | 16 56 | 16 04 |
| 52 | 23 12 | 20 59 | 18 53 | 16 36 | 15 40 |
| 53 | 23 08 | 20 49 | 18 39 | 16 16 | 15 15 |
| 54 | 23 03 | 20 39 | 18 24 | 15 56 | 14 48 |
| 55 | 22 58 | 20 28 | 18 08 | 15 35 | 14 20 |
| 56 | 22 52 | 20 17 | 17 53 | 15 14 | 13 51 |
| 57 | 22 46 | 20 05 | 17 37 | 14 52 | 13 20 |
| 58 | 22 39 | 19 53 | 17 20 | 14 30 | 12 48 |
| 59 | 22 30 | 19 40 | 17 03 | 14 08 | 12 13 |
| 60 | 22♌21 | 19♍26 | 16♎46 | 13♏45 | 11♐37 |

| 7h 52m 0s | 118° 0' 0" | 26 ♋ 00 | | | |
|---|---|---|---|---|---|
| LAT. | 11 | 12 | ASC | 2 | 3 |
| 0 | 25♌44 | 27♍49 | 00♏06 | 00♐11 | 28♐10 |
| 5 | 25 37 | 27 14 | 29♎04 | 29♏02 | 27 21 |
| 10 | 25 29 | 26 40 | 28 04 | 27 56 | 26 31 |
| 15 | 25 22 | 26 08 | 27 07 | 26 50 | 25 40 |
| 20 | 25 15 | 25 36 | 26 11 | 25 43 | 24 46 |
| 21 | 25 13 | 25 30 | 26 00 | 25 30 | 24 35 |
| 22 | 25 12 | 25 24 | 25 48 | 25 16 | 24 24 |
| 23 | 25 10 | 25 17 | 25 37 | 25 03 | 24 13 |
| 24 | 25 09 | 25 11 | 25 26 | 24 49 | 24 01 |
| 25 | 25 07 | 25 05 | 25 15 | 24 36 | 23 49 |
| 26 | 25 06 | 24 58 | 25 04 | 24 22 | 23 37 |
| 27 | 25 04 | 24 52 | 24 52 | 24 08 | 23 25 |
| 28 | 25 02 | 24 46 | 24 41 | 23 54 | 23 13 |
| 29 | 25 01 | 24 39 | 24 29 | 23 40 | 23 00 |
| 30 | 24 59 | 24 33 | 24 18 | 23 25 | 22 48 |
| 31 | 24 57 | 24 26 | 24 06 | 23 11 | 22 35 |
| 32 | 24 55 | 24 20 | 23 55 | 22 56 | 22 21 |
| 33 | 24 54 | 24 13 | 23 43 | 22 42 | 22 08 |
| 34 | 24 52 | 24 06 | 23 32 | 22 27 | 21 54 |
| 35 | 24 50 | 24 00 | 23 20 | 22 11 | 21 39 |
| 36 | 24 48 | 23 53 | 23 08 | 21 56 | 21 25 |
| 37 | 24 46 | 23 46 | 22 56 | 21 41 | 21 10 |
| 38 | 24 44 | 23 39 | 22 44 | 21 25 | 20 55 |
| 39 | 24 42 | 23 32 | 22 31 | 21 09 | 20 39 |
| 40 | 24 39 | 23 25 | 22 19 | 20 53 | 20 22 |
| 41 | 24 37 | 23 17 | 22 06 | 20 36 | 20 06 |
| 42 | 24 35 | 23 10 | 21 54 | 20 20 | 19 49 |
| 43 | 24 32 | 23 02 | 21 41 | 20 03 | 19 31 |
| 44 | 24 30 | 22 54 | 21 28 | 19 45 | 19 12 |
| 45 | 24 27 | 22 47 | 21 14 | 19 28 | 18 53 |
| 46 | 24 24 | 22 38 | 21 01 | 19 10 | 18 34 |
| 47 | 24 21 | 22 30 | 20 47 | 18 51 | 18 13 |
| 48 | 24 18 | 22 22 | 20 33 | 18 33 | 17 52 |
| 49 | 24 14 | 22 13 | 20 19 | 18 14 | 17 30 |
| 50 | 24 10 | 22 04 | 20 05 | 17 54 | 17 07 |
| 51 | 24 06 | 21 54 | 19 50 | 17 34 | 16 43 |
| 52 | 24 02 | 21 45 | 19 35 | 17 14 | 16 18 |
| 53 | 23 58 | 21 35 | 19 20 | 16 53 | 15 52 |
| 54 | 23 53 | 21 24 | 19 04 | 16 32 | 15 24 |
| 55 | 23 47 | 21 13 | 18 49 | 16 11 | 14 56 |
| 56 | 23 41 | 21 02 | 18 32 | 15 49 | 14 25 |
| 57 | 23 34 | 20 50 | 18 16 | 15 26 | 13 53 |
| 58 | 23 27 | 20 37 | 17 59 | 15 03 | 13 19 |
| 59 | 23 19 | 20 23 | 17 41 | 14 40 | 12 43 |
| 60 | 23♌09 | 20♍09 | 17♎23 | 14♏16 | 12♐05 |

| 7h 56m 0s | 119° 0' 0" | 26 ♋ 57 | | | |
|---|---|---|---|---|---|
| LAT. | 11 | 12 | ASC | 2 | 3 |
| 0 | 26♌47 | 28♍55 | 01♏08 | 01♐08 | 29♐05 |
| 5 | 26 38 | 28 17 | 00 04 | 29♏59 | 28 15 |
| 10 | 26 29 | 27 42 | 29♎03 | 28 51 | 27 25 |
| 15 | 26 21 | 27 07 | 28 04 | 27 43 | 26 32 |
| 20 | 26 12 | 26 34 | 27 06 | 26 35 | 25 38 |
| 21 | 26 11 | 26 27 | 26 55 | 26 22 | 25 27 |
| 22 | 26 09 | 26 21 | 26 43 | 26 08 | 25 15 |
| 23 | 26 07 | 26 14 | 26 32 | 25 54 | 25 04 |
| 24 | 26 05 | 26 08 | 26 20 | 25 40 | 24 52 |
| 25 | 26 04 | 26 01 | 26 08 | 25 26 | 24 40 |
| 26 | 26 02 | 25 54 | 25 57 | 25 12 | 24 28 |
| 27 | 26 00 | 25 48 | 25 45 | 24 57 | 24 15 |
| 28 | 25 58 | 25 41 | 25 33 | 24 43 | 24 03 |
| 29 | 25 56 | 25 34 | 25 21 | 24 28 | 23 50 |
| 30 | 25 54 | 25 27 | 25 10 | 24 14 | 23 37 |
| 31 | 25 52 | 25 20 | 24 58 | 23 59 | 23 23 |
| 32 | 25 50 | 25 13 | 24 46 | 23 44 | 23 10 |
| 33 | 25 48 | 25 06 | 24 34 | 23 29 | 22 56 |
| 34 | 25 46 | 24 59 | 24 22 | 23 14 | 22 42 |
| 35 | 25 44 | 24 52 | 24 09 | 22 58 | 22 27 |
| 36 | 25 42 | 24 45 | 23 57 | 22 42 | 22 12 |
| 37 | 25 40 | 24 38 | 23 45 | 22 26 | 21 57 |
| 38 | 25 37 | 24 31 | 23 32 | 22 10 | 21 41 |
| 39 | 25 35 | 24 23 | 23 19 | 21 54 | 21 25 |
| 40 | 25 32 | 24 15 | 23 06 | 21 37 | 21 08 |
| 41 | 25 30 | 24 08 | 22 53 | 21 20 | 20 51 |
| 42 | 25 27 | 24 00 | 22 40 | 21 03 | 20 33 |
| 43 | 25 24 | 23 52 | 22 27 | 20 46 | 20 15 |
| 44 | 25 22 | 23 44 | 22 13 | 20 28 | 19 56 |
| 45 | 25 19 | 23 36 | 22 00 | 20 10 | 19 36 |
| 46 | 25 15 | 23 27 | 21 46 | 19 51 | 19 16 |
| 47 | 25 12 | 23 18 | 21 32 | 19 32 | 18 55 |
| 48 | 25 09 | 23 09 | 21 17 | 19 13 | 18 33 |
| 49 | 25 05 | 23 00 | 21 03 | 18 53 | 18 10 |
| 50 | 25 01 | 22 51 | 20 48 | 18 33 | 17 47 |
| 51 | 24 57 | 22 41 | 20 33 | 18 13 | 17 22 |
| 52 | 24 52 | 22 31 | 20 17 | 17 52 | 16 56 |
| 53 | 24 47 | 22 20 | 20 01 | 17 30 | 16 29 |
| 54 | 24 42 | 22 10 | 19 45 | 17 09 | 16 01 |
| 55 | 24 36 | 21 58 | 19 29 | 16 46 | 15 31 |
| 56 | 24 30 | 21 46 | 19 12 | 16 23 | 14 59 |
| 57 | 24 23 | 21 34 | 18 55 | 16 00 | 14 26 |
| 58 | 24 16 | 21 21 | 18 37 | 15 36 | 13 51 |
| 59 | 24 07 | 21 07 | 18 19 | 15 12 | 13 13 |
| 60 | 23♌57 | 20♍52 | 18♎00 | 14♏47 | 12♐33 |

# Koch Table of Houses for Latitudes 0° to 60° North

**8h 0m 0s — 120° 0' 0" — 27 ♋ 55**

| LAT. | 11 | 12 | ASC | 2 | 3 |
|---|---|---|---|---|---|
| 0 | 27♌49 | 00♎00 | 02♏11 | 02♐05 | 00♑00 |
| 5 | 27 39 | 29♍20 | 01 05 | 00 55 | 29♐09 |
| 10 | 27 29 | 28 43 | 00 02 | 29♏45 | 28 18 |
| 15 | 27 20 | 28 07 | 29♎01 | 28 37 | 27 25 |
| 20 | 27 10 | 27 32 | 28 02 | 27 27 | 26 29 |
| 21 | 27 08 | 27 25 | 27 50 | 27 13 | 26 18 |
| 22 | 27 06 | 27 18 | 27 38 | 26 59 | 26 06 |
| 23 | 27 04 | 27 11 | 27 26 | 26 45 | 25 54 |
| 24 | 27 02 | 27 04 | 27 14 | 26 30 | 25 42 |
| 25 | 27 00 | 26 57 | 27 02 | 26 16 | 25 30 |
| 26 | 26 58 | 26 50 | 26 50 | 26 02 | 25 18 |
| 27 | 26 56 | 26 43 | 26 38 | 25 47 | 25 05 |
| 28 | 26 54 | 26 36 | 26 26 | 25 32 | 24 52 |
| 29 | 26 52 | 26 29 | 26 13 | 25 17 | 24 39 |
| 30 | 26 50 | 26 22 | 26 01 | 25 02 | 24 26 |
| 31 | 26 48 | 26 14 | 25 49 | 24 47 | 24 12 |
| 32 | 26 45 | 26 07 | 25 37 | 24 32 | 23 58 |
| 33 | 26 43 | 26 00 | 25 24 | 24 16 | 23 44 |
| 34 | 26 41 | 25 53 | 25 12 | 24 01 | 23 29 |
| 35 | 26 38 | 25 45 | 24 59 | 23 45 | 23 14 |
| 36 | 26 36 | 25 38 | 24 46 | 23 29 | 22 59 |
| 37 | 26 34 | 25 30 | 24 33 | 23 12 | 22 43 |
| 38 | 26 31 | 25 22 | 24 20 | 22 56 | 22 27 |
| 39 | 26 28 | 25 14 | 24 07 | 22 39 | 22 11 |
| 40 | 26 26 | 25 06 | 23 54 | 22 22 | 21 53 |
| 41 | 26 23 | 24 58 | 23 40 | 22 04 | 21 36 |
| 42 | 26 20 | 24 50 | 23 27 | 21 47 | 21 18 |
| 43 | 26 17 | 24 42 | 23 13 | 21 29 | 20 59 |
| 44 | 26 14 | 24 33 | 22 59 | 21 10 | 20 39 |
| 45 | 26 11 | 24 25 | 22 45 | 20 51 | 20 19 |
| 46 | 26 07 | 24 16 | 22 31 | 20 32 | 19 58 |
| 47 | 26 04 | 24 07 | 22 16 | 20 13 | 19 37 |
| 48 | 26 00 | 23 57 | 22 01 | 19 53 | 19 14 |
| 49 | 25 56 | 23 48 | 21 46 | 19 33 | 18 51 |
| 50 | 25 52 | 23 38 | 21 31 | 19 12 | 18 26 |
| 51 | 25 47 | 23 28 | 21 15 | 18 51 | 18 01 |
| 52 | 25 42 | 23 17 | 20 59 | 18 29 | 17 34 |
| 53 | 25 37 | 23 06 | 20 43 | 18 07 | 17 06 |
| 54 | 25 32 | 22 55 | 20 26 | 17 45 | 16 37 |
| 55 | 25 26 | 22 43 | 20 09 | 17 21 | 16 06 |
| 56 | 25 19 | 22 31 | 19 51 | 16 58 | 15 33 |
| 57 | 25 12 | 22 18 | 19 34 | 16 33 | 14 59 |
| 58 | 25 04 | 22 05 | 19 15 | 16 09 | 14 22 |
| 59 | 24 56 | 21 50 | 18 57 | 15 43 | 13 43 |
| 60 | 24♌46 | 21♍35 | 18♎37 | 15♏17 | 13♐01 |

**8h 4m 0s — 121° 0' 0" — 28 ♋ 52**

| LAT. | 11 | 12 | ASC | 2 | 3 |
|---|---|---|---|---|---|
| 0 | 28♌52 | 01♎05 | 03♏13 | 03♐03 | 00♑55 |
| 5 | 28 40 | 00 24 | 02 06 | 01 51 | 00 04 |
| 10 | 28 29 | 29♍45 | 01 01 | 00 40 | 29♐12 |
| 15 | 28 19 | 29 07 | 29♎58 | 29♏30 | 28 18 |
| 20 | 28 08 | 28 30 | 28 57 | 28 19 | 27 21 |
| 21 | 28 06 | 28 23 | 28 44 | 28 04 | 27 09 |
| 22 | 28 04 | 28 15 | 28 32 | 27 50 | 26 57 |
| 23 | 28 01 | 28 08 | 28 20 | 27 36 | 26 45 |
| 24 | 27 59 | 28 01 | 28 08 | 27 21 | 26 33 |
| 25 | 27 57 | 27 53 | 27 55 | 27 06 | 26 21 |
| 26 | 27 55 | 27 46 | 27 43 | 26 51 | 26 08 |
| 27 | 27 52 | 27 39 | 27 30 | 26 36 | 25 55 |
| 28 | 27 50 | 27 31 | 27 18 | 26 21 | 25 42 |
| 29 | 27 48 | 27 24 | 27 05 | 26 06 | 25 29 |
| 30 | 27 45 | 27 16 | 26 53 | 25 51 | 25 15 |
| 31 | 27 43 | 27 09 | 26 40 | 25 35 | 25 01 |
| 32 | 27 41 | 27 01 | 26 27 | 25 19 | 24 47 |
| 33 | 27 38 | 26 53 | 26 14 | 25 04 | 24 32 |
| 34 | 27 36 | 26 46 | 26 02 | 24 47 | 24 17 |
| 35 | 27 33 | 26 38 | 25 49 | 24 31 | 24 02 |
| 36 | 27 30 | 26 30 | 25 35 | 24 15 | 23 46 |
| 37 | 27 28 | 26 22 | 25 22 | 23 58 | 23 30 |
| 38 | 27 25 | 26 14 | 25 09 | 23 41 | 23 13 |
| 39 | 27 22 | 26 06 | 24 55 | 23 23 | 22 56 |
| 40 | 27 19 | 25 57 | 24 41 | 23 06 | 22 39 |
| 41 | 27 16 | 25 49 | 24 28 | 22 48 | 22 21 |
| 42 | 27 13 | 25 40 | 24 14 | 22 30 | 22 02 |
| 43 | 27 10 | 25 32 | 23 59 | 22 11 | 21 43 |
| 44 | 27 06 | 25 23 | 23 45 | 21 53 | 21 23 |
| 45 | 27 03 | 25 14 | 23 30 | 21 33 | 21 02 |
| 46 | 26 59 | 25 05 | 23 15 | 21 14 | 20 41 |
| 47 | 26 55 | 24 55 | 23 00 | 20 54 | 20 18 |
| 48 | 26 51 | 24 45 | 22 45 | 20 33 | 19 55 |
| 49 | 26 47 | 24 35 | 22 29 | 20 12 | 19 31 |
| 50 | 26 43 | 24 25 | 22 13 | 19 51 | 19 06 |
| 51 | 26 38 | 24 15 | 21 57 | 19 29 | 18 40 |
| 52 | 26 33 | 24 04 | 21 41 | 19 07 | 18 12 |
| 53 | 26 28 | 23 53 | 21 24 | 18 44 | 17 43 |
| 54 | 26 22 | 23 41 | 21 07 | 18 21 | 17 13 |
| 55 | 26 16 | 23 29 | 20 49 | 17 57 | 16 41 |
| 56 | 26 09 | 23 16 | 20 31 | 17 32 | 16 07 |
| 57 | 26 02 | 23 03 | 20 13 | 17 07 | 15 31 |
| 58 | 25 54 | 22 49 | 19 54 | 16 41 | 14 53 |
| 59 | 25 45 | 22 34 | 19 34 | 16 15 | 14 13 |
| 60 | 25♌35 | 22♍19 | 19♎14 | 15♏48 | 13♐29 |

**8h 8m 0s — 122° 0' 0" — 29 ♋ 49**

| LAT. | 11 | 12 | ASC | 2 | 3 |
|---|---|---|---|---|---|
| 0 | 29♌54 | 02♎11 | 04♏16 | 04♐00 | 01♑50 |
| 5 | 29 42 | 01 27 | 03 06 | 02 47 | 00 58 |
| 10 | 29 30 | 00 46 | 02 00 | 01 35 | 00 05 |
| 15 | 29 18 | 00 07 | 00 55 | 00 23 | 29♐10 |
| 20 | 29 06 | 29♍28 | 29♎52 | 29♏11 | 28 13 |
| 21 | 29 04 | 29 20 | 29 39 | 28 56 | 28 01 |
| 22 | 29 01 | 29 13 | 29 27 | 28 41 | 27 49 |
| 23 | 28 59 | 29 05 | 29 14 | 28 26 | 27 36 |
| 24 | 28 56 | 28 57 | 29 01 | 28 11 | 27 24 |
| 25 | 28 54 | 28 50 | 28 49 | 27 56 | 27 11 |
| 26 | 28 51 | 28 42 | 28 36 | 27 41 | 26 58 |
| 27 | 28 49 | 28 34 | 28 23 | 27 26 | 26 45 |
| 28 | 28 46 | 28 27 | 28 10 | 27 10 | 26 32 |
| 29 | 28 44 | 28 19 | 27 57 | 26 55 | 26 18 |
| 30 | 28 41 | 28 11 | 27 44 | 26 39 | 26 04 |
| 31 | 28 39 | 28 03 | 27 31 | 26 23 | 25 50 |
| 32 | 28 36 | 27 55 | 27 18 | 26 07 | 25 35 |
| 33 | 28 33 | 27 47 | 27 05 | 25 51 | 25 20 |
| 34 | 28 31 | 27 39 | 26 52 | 25 34 | 25 05 |
| 35 | 28 28 | 27 31 | 26 38 | 25 18 | 24 49 |
| 36 | 28 25 | 27 23 | 26 25 | 25 01 | 24 33 |
| 37 | 28 22 | 27 14 | 26 11 | 24 43 | 24 17 |
| 38 | 28 19 | 27 06 | 25 57 | 24 26 | 24 00 |
| 39 | 28 16 | 26 57 | 25 43 | 24 08 | 23 42 |
| 40 | 28 13 | 26 49 | 25 29 | 23 50 | 23 24 |
| 41 | 28 09 | 26 40 | 25 15 | 23 32 | 23 06 |
| 42 | 28 06 | 26 31 | 25 00 | 23 13 | 22 47 |
| 43 | 28 03 | 26 22 | 24 45 | 22 54 | 22 27 |
| 44 | 27 59 | 26 13 | 24 31 | 22 35 | 22 06 |
| 45 | 27 55 | 26 03 | 24 16 | 22 15 | 21 45 |
| 46 | 27 51 | 25 54 | 24 00 | 21 55 | 21 23 |
| 47 | 27 47 | 25 44 | 23 45 | 21 34 | 21 00 |
| 48 | 27 43 | 25 34 | 23 29 | 21 13 | 20 36 |
| 49 | 27 39 | 25 23 | 23 13 | 20 52 | 20 11 |
| 50 | 27 34 | 25 13 | 22 56 | 20 30 | 19 46 |
| 51 | 27 29 | 25 02 | 22 40 | 20 07 | 19 18 |
| 52 | 27 24 | 24 50 | 22 22 | 19 44 | 18 50 |
| 53 | 27 18 | 24 39 | 22 05 | 19 21 | 18 20 |
| 54 | 27 12 | 24 27 | 21 47 | 18 57 | 17 49 |
| 55 | 27 06 | 24 14 | 21 29 | 18 32 | 17 16 |
| 56 | 26 59 | 24 01 | 21 11 | 18 06 | 16 41 |
| 57 | 26 51 | 23 48 | 20 52 | 17 40 | 16 03 |
| 58 | 26 43 | 23 33 | 20 32 | 17 14 | 15 24 |
| 59 | 26 34 | 23 18 | 20 12 | 16 46 | 14 42 |
| 60 | 26♌24 | 23♍02 | 19♎52 | 16♏18 | 13♐57 |

**8h 12m 0s — 123° 0' 0" — 00 ♌ 47**

| LAT. | 11 | 12 | ASC | 2 | 3 |
|---|---|---|---|---|---|
| 0 | 00♍57 | 03♎16 | 05♏18 | 04♐57 | 02♑45 |
| 5 | 00 43 | 02 31 | 04 06 | 03 42 | 01 52 |
| 10 | 00 30 | 01 48 | 02 58 | 02 29 | 00 59 |
| 15 | 00 17 | 01 07 | 01 52 | 01 16 | 00 03 |
| 20 | 00 04 | 00 26 | 00 47 | 00 02 | 29♐04 |
| 21 | 00 02 | 00 18 | 00 34 | 29♏47 | 28 52 |
| 22 | 29♌59 | 00 10 | 00 21 | 29 32 | 28 40 |
| 23 | 29 56 | 00 02 | 00 08 | 29 17 | 28 27 |
| 24 | 29 54 | 29♍54 | 29♎55 | 29 02 | 28 15 |
| 25 | 29 51 | 29 46 | 29 42 | 28 46 | 28 02 |
| 26 | 29 48 | 29 38 | 29 29 | 28 31 | 27 48 |
| 27 | 29 46 | 29 30 | 29 16 | 28 15 | 27 35 |
| 28 | 29 43 | 29 22 | 29 02 | 27 59 | 27 21 |
| 29 | 29 40 | 29 14 | 28 49 | 27 43 | 27 07 |
| 30 | 29 37 | 29 06 | 28 36 | 27 27 | 26 53 |
| 31 | 29 34 | 28 57 | 28 22 | 27 11 | 26 39 |
| 32 | 29 32 | 28 49 | 28 09 | 26 55 | 26 24 |
| 33 | 29 29 | 28 41 | 27 55 | 26 38 | 26 08 |
| 34 | 29 26 | 28 32 | 27 41 | 26 21 | 25 53 |
| 35 | 29 23 | 28 24 | 27 28 | 26 04 | 25 37 |
| 36 | 29 20 | 28 15 | 27 14 | 25 47 | 25 20 |
| 37 | 29 16 | 28 07 | 27 00 | 25 29 | 25 04 |
| 38 | 29 13 | 27 58 | 26 45 | 25 11 | 24 46 |
| 39 | 29 10 | 27 49 | 26 31 | 24 53 | 24 28 |
| 40 | 29 06 | 27 40 | 26 16 | 24 34 | 24 10 |
| 41 | 29 03 | 27 31 | 26 02 | 24 16 | 23 51 |
| 42 | 28 59 | 27 21 | 25 47 | 23 56 | 23 31 |
| 43 | 28 56 | 27 12 | 25 32 | 23 37 | 23 11 |
| 44 | 28 52 | 27 02 | 25 16 | 23 17 | 22 50 |
| 45 | 28 48 | 26 53 | 25 01 | 22 57 | 22 28 |
| 46 | 28 44 | 26 43 | 24 45 | 22 36 | 22 05 |
| 47 | 28 39 | 26 32 | 24 29 | 22 15 | 21 42 |
| 48 | 28 35 | 26 22 | 24 13 | 21 53 | 21 17 |
| 49 | 28 30 | 26 11 | 23 56 | 21 31 | 20 52 |
| 50 | 28 25 | 26 00 | 23 39 | 21 09 | 20 25 |
| 51 | 28 20 | 25 49 | 23 22 | 20 45 | 19 57 |
| 52 | 28 15 | 25 37 | 23 04 | 20 22 | 19 28 |
| 53 | 28 09 | 25 25 | 22 46 | 19 57 | 18 57 |
| 54 | 28 03 | 25 13 | 22 28 | 19 32 | 18 25 |
| 55 | 27 56 | 25 00 | 22 09 | 19 07 | 17 50 |
| 56 | 27 49 | 24 46 | 21 50 | 18 41 | 17 14 |
| 57 | 27 41 | 24 32 | 21 30 | 18 14 | 16 36 |
| 58 | 27 33 | 24 18 | 21 10 | 17 46 | 15 55 |
| 59 | 27 24 | 24 02 | 20 50 | 17 18 | 15 11 |
| 60 | 27♌13 | 23♍46 | 20♎29 | 16♏49 | 14♐25 |

**8h 16m 0s — 124° 0' 0" — 01 ♌ 45**

| LAT. | 11 | 12 | ASC | 2 | 3 |
|---|---|---|---|---|---|
| 0 | 02♍00 | 04♎22 | 06♏19 | 05♐54 | 03♑40 |
| 5 | 01 45 | 03 34 | 05 07 | 04 38 | 02 47 |
| 10 | 01 31 | 02 49 | 03 57 | 03 23 | 01 52 |
| 15 | 01 17 | 02 06 | 02 49 | 02 09 | 00 56 |
| 20 | 01 03 | 01 24 | 01 42 | 00 54 | 29♐56 |
| 21 | 01 00 | 01 16 | 01 29 | 00 38 | 29 44 |
| 22 | 00 57 | 01 08 | 01 15 | 00 23 | 29 31 |
| 23 | 00 54 | 00 59 | 01 02 | 00 08 | 29 18 |
| 24 | 00 51 | 00 51 | 00 49 | 29♏52 | 29 05 |
| 25 | 00 48 | 00 43 | 00 35 | 29 36 | 28 52 |
| 26 | 00 45 | 00 34 | 00 22 | 29 21 | 28 39 |
| 27 | 00 42 | 00 26 | 00 08 | 29 05 | 28 25 |
| 28 | 00 40 | 00 17 | 29♎54 | 28 48 | 28 11 |
| 29 | 00 37 | 00 09 | 29 41 | 28 32 | 27 57 |
| 30 | 00 34 | 00 00 | 29 27 | 28 16 | 27 42 |
| 31 | 00 30 | 29♍52 | 29 13 | 27 59 | 27 28 |
| 32 | 00 27 | 29 43 | 28 59 | 27 42 | 27 12 |
| 33 | 00 24 | 29 34 | 28 45 | 27 25 | 26 57 |
| 34 | 00 21 | 29 26 | 28 31 | 27 08 | 26 41 |
| 35 | 00 18 | 29 17 | 28 17 | 26 50 | 26 24 |
| 36 | 00 14 | 29 08 | 28 03 | 26 32 | 26 08 |
| 37 | 00 11 | 28 59 | 27 48 | 26 14 | 25 50 |
| 38 | 00 08 | 28 50 | 27 34 | 25 56 | 25 33 |
| 39 | 00 04 | 28 41 | 27 19 | 25 37 | 25 14 |
| 40 | 00 00 | 28 31 | 27 04 | 25 19 | 24 55 |
| 41 | 29♌57 | 28 22 | 26 49 | 24 59 | 24 36 |
| 42 | 29 53 | 28 12 | 26 33 | 24 40 | 24 16 |
| 43 | 29 49 | 28 02 | 26 18 | 24 20 | 23 55 |
| 44 | 29 45 | 27 52 | 26 02 | 23 59 | 23 33 |
| 45 | 29 41 | 27 42 | 25 46 | 23 38 | 23 11 |
| 46 | 29 36 | 27 32 | 25 30 | 23 17 | 22 48 |
| 47 | 29 32 | 27 21 | 25 13 | 22 55 | 22 24 |
| 48 | 29 27 | 27 10 | 24 56 | 22 33 | 21 58 |
| 49 | 29 22 | 26 59 | 24 39 | 22 10 | 21 32 |
| 50 | 29 17 | 26 48 | 24 22 | 21 47 | 21 05 |
| 51 | 29 12 | 26 36 | 24 04 | 21 23 | 20 36 |
| 52 | 29 06 | 26 24 | 23 46 | 20 59 | 20 06 |
| 53 | 29 00 | 26 12 | 23 28 | 20 34 | 19 34 |
| 54 | 28 54 | 25 59 | 23 09 | 20 08 | 19 00 |
| 55 | 28 47 | 25 46 | 22 49 | 19 42 | 18 25 |
| 56 | 28 39 | 25 32 | 22 30 | 19 15 | 17 48 |
| 57 | 28 31 | 25 17 | 22 09 | 18 47 | 17 08 |
| 58 | 28 23 | 25 02 | 21 49 | 18 18 | 16 26 |
| 59 | 28 13 | 24 47 | 21 27 | 17 49 | 15 41 |
| 60 | 28♌03 | 24♍30 | 21♎06 | 17♏19 | 14♐52 |

**8h 20m 0s — 125° 0' 0" — 02 ♌ 43**

| LAT. | 11 | 12 | ASC | 2 | 3 |
|---|---|---|---|---|---|
| 0 | 03♍03 | 05♎27 | 07♏21 | 06♐50 | 04♑35 |
| 5 | 02 47 | 04 38 | 06 06 | 05 33 | 03 41 |
| 10 | 02 31 | 03 51 | 04 55 | 04 18 | 02 46 |
| 15 | 02 16 | 03 06 | 03 46 | 03 02 | 01 49 |
| 20 | 02 01 | 02 23 | 02 37 | 01 45 | 00 48 |
| 21 | 01 58 | 02 14 | 02 23 | 01 30 | 00 35 |
| 22 | 01 55 | 02 05 | 02 10 | 01 14 | 00 23 |
| 23 | 01 52 | 01 56 | 01 56 | 00 58 | 00 10 |
| 24 | 01 49 | 01 48 | 01 42 | 00 42 | 29♐56 |
| 25 | 01 46 | 01 39 | 01 28 | 00 26 | 29 43 |
| 26 | 01 43 | 01 30 | 01 14 | 00 10 | 29 29 |
| 27 | 01 40 | 01 22 | 01 01 | 29♏54 | 29 15 |
| 28 | 01 36 | 01 13 | 00 47 | 29 37 | 29 01 |
| 29 | 01 33 | 01 04 | 00 33 | 29 21 | 28 47 |
| 30 | 01 30 | 00 55 | 00 18 | 29 04 | 28 32 |
| 31 | 01 27 | 00 46 | 00 04 | 28 47 | 28 17 |
| 32 | 01 23 | 00 37 | 29♎50 | 28 30 | 28 01 |
| 33 | 01 20 | 00 28 | 29 36 | 28 12 | 27 45 |
| 34 | 01 17 | 00 19 | 29 21 | 27 55 | 27 29 |
| 35 | 01 13 | 00 10 | 29 07 | 27 37 | 27 12 |
| 36 | 01 10 | 00 01 | 28 52 | 27 18 | 26 55 |
| 37 | 01 06 | 29♍51 | 28 37 | 27 00 | 26 37 |
| 38 | 01 02 | 29 42 | 28 22 | 26 41 | 26 19 |
| 39 | 00 59 | 29 32 | 28 07 | 26 22 | 26 00 |
| 40 | 00 55 | 29 23 | 27 51 | 26 03 | 25 41 |
| 41 | 00 51 | 29 13 | 27 36 | 25 43 | 25 21 |
| 42 | 00 47 | 29 03 | 27 20 | 25 23 | 25 00 |
| 43 | 00 43 | 28 53 | 27 04 | 25 02 | 24 39 |
| 44 | 00 38 | 28 42 | 26 48 | 24 41 | 24 17 |
| 45 | 00 34 | 28 32 | 26 31 | 24 20 | 23 54 |
| 46 | 00 29 | 28 21 | 26 14 | 23 58 | 23 30 |
| 47 | 00 24 | 28 10 | 25 57 | 23 36 | 23 05 |
| 48 | 00 20 | 27 59 | 25 40 | 23 13 | 22 39 |
| 49 | 00 14 | 27 47 | 25 23 | 22 50 | 22 12 |
| 50 | 00 09 | 27 36 | 25 05 | 22 26 | 21 44 |
| 51 | 00 03 | 27 24 | 24 46 | 22 01 | 21 14 |
| 52 | 29♌57 | 27 11 | 24 28 | 21 36 | 20 43 |
| 53 | 29 51 | 26 58 | 24 09 | 21 10 | 20 11 |
| 54 | 29 45 | 26 45 | 23 49 | 20 44 | 19 36 |
| 55 | 29 37 | 26 32 | 23 29 | 20 17 | 19 00 |
| 56 | 29 30 | 26 17 | 23 09 | 19 49 | 18 21 |
| 57 | 29 22 | 26 03 | 22 48 | 19 20 | 17 40 |
| 58 | 29 13 | 25 47 | 22 27 | 18 51 | 16 56 |
| 59 | 29 04 | 25 31 | 22 05 | 18 20 | 16 10 |
| 60 | 28♌53 | 25♍14 | 21♎43 | 17♏49 | 15♐20 |

**8h 24m 0s — 126° 0' 0" — 03 ♌ 41**

| LAT. | 11 | 12 | ASC | 2 | 3 |
|---|---|---|---|---|---|
| 0 | 04♍07 | 06♎32 | 08♏23 | 07♐47 | 05♑30 |
| 5 | 03 49 | 05 41 | 07 06 | 06 29 | 04 36 |
| 10 | 03 32 | 04 53 | 05 53 | 05 12 | 03 40 |
| 15 | 03 16 | 04 06 | 04 42 | 03 55 | 02 41 |
| 20 | 03 00 | 03 21 | 03 32 | 02 37 | 01 40 |
| 21 | 02 57 | 03 12 | 03 18 | 02 21 | 01 27 |
| 22 | 02 53 | 03 03 | 03 04 | 02 05 | 01 14 |
| 23 | 02 50 | 02 54 | 02 50 | 01 49 | 01 01 |
| 24 | 02 47 | 02 45 | 02 36 | 01 33 | 00 47 |
| 25 | 02 43 | 02 36 | 02 21 | 01 16 | 00 34 |
| 26 | 02 40 | 02 27 | 02 07 | 01 00 | 00 20 |
| 27 | 02 37 | 02 18 | 01 53 | 00 43 | 00 05 |
| 28 | 02 33 | 02 08 | 01 39 | 00 26 | 29♐51 |
| 29 | 02 30 | 01 59 | 01 24 | 00 09 | 29 36 |
| 30 | 02 26 | 01 50 | 01 10 | 29♏52 | 29 21 |
| 31 | 02 23 | 01 41 | 00 55 | 29 35 | 29 06 |
| 32 | 02 19 | 01 32 | 00 41 | 29 17 | 28 50 |
| 33 | 02 16 | 01 22 | 00 26 | 28 59 | 28 33 |
| 34 | 02 12 | 01 13 | 00 11 | 28 41 | 28 17 |
| 35 | 02 09 | 01 03 | 29♎56 | 28 23 | 28 00 |
| 36 | 02 05 | 00 54 | 29 41 | 28 04 | 27 42 |
| 37 | 02 01 | 00 44 | 29 26 | 27 45 | 27 24 |
| 38 | 01 57 | 00 34 | 29 10 | 27 26 | 27 06 |
| 39 | 01 53 | 00 24 | 28 54 | 27 07 | 26 46 |
| 40 | 01 49 | 00 14 | 28 39 | 26 47 | 26 27 |
| 41 | 01 45 | 00 04 | 28 23 | 26 26 | 26 06 |
| 42 | 01 41 | 29♍53 | 28 06 | 26 06 | 25 45 |
| 43 | 01 36 | 29 43 | 27 50 | 25 45 | 25 23 |
| 44 | 01 32 | 29 32 | 27 33 | 25 23 | 25 01 |
| 45 | 01 27 | 29 21 | 27 16 | 25 01 | 24 37 |
| 46 | 01 22 | 29 10 | 26 59 | 24 39 | 24 13 |
| 47 | 01 17 | 28 59 | 26 42 | 24 16 | 23 47 |
| 48 | 01 12 | 28 47 | 26 24 | 23 53 | 23 20 |
| 49 | 01 07 | 28 36 | 26 06 | 23 29 | 22 53 |
| 50 | 01 01 | 28 23 | 25 47 | 23 04 | 22 24 |
| 51 | 00 55 | 28 11 | 25 29 | 22 39 | 21 53 |
| 52 | 00 49 | 27 58 | 25 09 | 22 13 | 21 21 |
| 53 | 00 43 | 27 45 | 24 50 | 21 47 | 20 47 |
| 54 | 00 36 | 27 32 | 24 30 | 21 20 | 20 12 |
| 55 | 00 29 | 27 18 | 24 09 | 20 51 | 19 34 |
| 56 | 00 21 | 27 03 | 23 49 | 20 23 | 18 54 |
| 57 | 00 13 | 26 48 | 23 27 | 19 53 | 18 12 |
| 58 | 00 04 | 26 32 | 23 05 | 19 23 | 17 27 |
| 59 | 29♌54 | 26 16 | 22 43 | 18 51 | 16 39 |
| 60 | 29♌43 | 25♍58 | 22♎20 | 18♏19 | 15♐47 |

**8h 28m 0s — 127° 0' 0" — 04 ♌ 39**

| LAT. | 11 | 12 | ASC | 2 | 3 |
|---|---|---|---|---|---|
| 0 | 05♍10 | 07♎37 | 09♏24 | 08♐43 | 06♑26 |
| 5 | 04 51 | 06 44 | 08 06 | 07 24 | 05 30 |
| 10 | 04 33 | 05 54 | 06 51 | 06 06 | 04 33 |
| 15 | 04 16 | 05 06 | 05 39 | 04 48 | 03 34 |
| 20 | 03 59 | 04 19 | 04 27 | 03 28 | 02 32 |
| 21 | 03 55 | 04 10 | 04 12 | 03 12 | 02 19 |
| 22 | 03 52 | 04 00 | 03 58 | 02 56 | 02 05 |
| 23 | 03 48 | 03 51 | 03 43 | 02 39 | 01 52 |
| 24 | 03 45 | 03 42 | 03 29 | 02 23 | 01 38 |
| 25 | 03 41 | 03 32 | 03 14 | 02 06 | 01 24 |
| 26 | 03 38 | 03 23 | 03 00 | 01 49 | 01 10 |
| 27 | 03 34 | 03 13 | 02 45 | 01 32 | 00 56 |
| 28 | 03 31 | 03 04 | 02 31 | 01 15 | 00 41 |
| 29 | 03 27 | 02 55 | 02 16 | 00 58 | 00 26 |
| 30 | 03 23 | 02 45 | 02 01 | 00 40 | 00 10 |
| 31 | 03 20 | 02 35 | 01 46 | 00 22 | 29♐55 |
| 32 | 03 16 | 02 26 | 01 31 | 00 04 | 29 39 |
| 33 | 03 12 | 02 16 | 01 16 | 29♏46 | 29 22 |
| 34 | 03 08 | 02 06 | 01 01 | 29 28 | 29 05 |
| 35 | 03 04 | 01 56 | 00 45 | 29 09 | 28 48 |
| 36 | 03 00 | 01 47 | 00 30 | 28 50 | 28 30 |
| 37 | 02 56 | 01 36 | 00 14 | 28 31 | 28 11 |
| 38 | 02 52 | 01 26 | 29♎58 | 28 11 | 27 52 |
| 39 | 02 48 | 01 16 | 29 42 | 27 51 | 27 33 |
| 40 | 02 44 | 01 06 | 29 26 | 27 31 | 27 12 |
| 41 | 02 39 | 00 55 | 29 10 | 27 10 | 26 51 |
| 42 | 02 35 | 00 44 | 28 53 | 26 49 | 26 30 |
| 43 | 02 30 | 00 33 | 28 36 | 26 27 | 26 07 |
| 44 | 02 25 | 00 22 | 28 19 | 26 05 | 25 44 |
| 45 | 02 21 | 00 11 | 28 02 | 25 43 | 25 20 |
| 46 | 02 16 | 00 00 | 27 44 | 25 20 | 24 55 |
| 47 | 02 10 | 29♍48 | 27 26 | 24 57 | 24 29 |
| 48 | 02 05 | 29 36 | 27 08 | 24 32 | 24 01 |
| 49 | 01 59 | 29 24 | 26 49 | 24 08 | 23 33 |
| 50 | 01 53 | 29 11 | 26 30 | 23 43 | 23 03 |
| 51 | 01 47 | 28 59 | 26 11 | 23 17 | 22 32 |
| 52 | 01 41 | 28 45 | 25 51 | 22 50 | 21 59 |
| 53 | 01 34 | 28 32 | 25 31 | 22 23 | 21 24 |
| 54 | 01 27 | 28 18 | 25 11 | 21 55 | 20 47 |
| 55 | 01 20 | 28 04 | 24 50 | 21 26 | 20 09 |
| 56 | 01 12 | 27 49 | 24 28 | 20 57 | 19 28 |
| 57 | 01 03 | 27 33 | 24 06 | 20 26 | 18 44 |
| 58 | 00 54 | 27 17 | 23 43 | 19 55 | 17 57 |
| 59 | 00 44 | 27 00 | 23 20 | 19 22 | 17 08 |
| 60 | 00♍34 | 26♍43 | 22♎56 | 18♏49 | 16♐14 |

# Koch Table of Houses for Latitudes 0° to 60° North

**8h 32m 0s — 128° 0' 0" — 05 ♌ 38**

| LAT. | 11 | 12 | ASC | 2 | 3 |
|---|---|---|---|---|---|
| 0 | 06♍14 | 08♎43 | 10♏25 | 09♐40 | 07♑21 |
| 5 | 05 54 | 07 48 | 09 06 | 08 19 | 06 25 |
| 10 | 05 35 | 06 56 | 07 49 | 07 00 | 05 27 |
| 15 | 05 16 | 06 06 | 06 35 | 05 40 | 04 27 |
| 20 | 04 58 | 05 17 | 05 21 | 04 19 | 03 24 |
| 21 | 04 54 | 05 08 | 05 07 | 04 03 | 03 10 |
| 22 | 04 50 | 04 58 | 04 52 | 03 46 | 02 57 |
| 23 | 04 47 | 04 48 | 04 37 | 03 30 | 02 43 |
| 24 | 04 43 | 04 39 | 04 22 | 03 13 | 02 29 |
| 25 | 04 39 | 04 29 | 04 07 | 02 56 | 02 15 |
| 26 | 04 35 | 04 19 | 03 53 | 02 39 | 02 01 |
| 27 | 04 32 | 04 09 | 03 38 | 02 21 | 01 46 |
| 28 | 04 28 | 04 00 | 03 23 | 02 04 | 01 31 |
| 29 | 04 24 | 03 50 | 03 08 | 01 46 | 01 16 |
| 30 | 04 20 | 03 40 | 02 52 | 01 28 | 01 00 |
| 31 | 04 16 | 03 30 | 02 37 | 01 10 | 00 44 |
| 32 | 04 12 | 03 20 | 02 22 | 00 52 | 00 27 |
| 33 | 04 08 | 03 10 | 02 06 | 00 33 | 00 10 |
| 34 | 04 04 | 03 00 | 01 51 | 00 14 | 29♐53 |
| 35 | 04 00 | 02 50 | 01 35 | 29♏55 | 29 35 |
| 36 | 03 56 | 02 40 | 01 19 | 29 36 | 29 17 |
| 37 | 03 52 | 02 29 | 01 03 | 29 16 | 28 58 |
| 38 | 03 47 | 02 19 | 00 46 | 28 56 | 28 39 |
| 39 | 03 43 | 02 08 | 00 30 | 28 36 | 28 19 |
| 40 | 03 38 | 01 57 | 00 13 | 28 15 | 27 58 |
| 41 | 03 34 | 01 46 | 29♎57 | 27 54 | 27 37 |
| 42 | 03 29 | 01 35 | 29 39 | 27 32 | 27 15 |
| 43 | 03 24 | 01 24 | 29 22 | 27 10 | 26 52 |
| 44 | 03 19 | 01 13 | 29 05 | 26 47 | 26 28 |
| 45 | 03 14 | 01 01 | 28 47 | 26 24 | 26 03 |
| 46 | 03 09 | 00 49 | 28 29 | 26 01 | 25 37 |
| 47 | 03 04 | 00 37 | 28 10 | 25 37 | 25 11 |
| 48 | 02 58 | 00 25 | 27 51 | 25 12 | 24 43 |
| 49 | 02 52 | 00 12 | 27 32 | 24 47 | 24 13 |
| 50 | 02 46 | 00 00 | 27 13 | 24 21 | 23 43 |
| 51 | 02 40 | 29♍46 | 26 53 | 23 55 | 23 10 |
| 52 | 02 33 | 29 33 | 26 33 | 23 27 | 22 37 |
| 53 | 02 26 | 29 19 | 26 12 | 22 59 | 22 01 |
| 54 | 02 19 | 29 05 | 25 51 | 22 30 | 21 23 |
| 55 | 02 11 | 28 50 | 25 30 | 22 01 | 20 43 |
| 56 | 02 03 | 28 35 | 25 07 | 21 30 | 20 01 |
| 57 | 01 55 | 28 19 | 24 45 | 20 59 | 19 16 |
| 58 | 01 45 | 28 02 | 24 22 | 20 27 | 18 28 |
| 59 | 01 35 | 27 45 | 23 58 | 19 53 | 17 36 |
| 60 | 01♍25 | 27♍27 | 23♎33 | 19♏19 | 16♐41 |

**8h 36m 0s — 129° 0' 0" — 06 ♌ 37**

| LAT. | 11 | 12 | ASC | 2 | 3 |
|---|---|---|---|---|---|
| 0 | 07♍18 | 09♎48 | 11♏26 | 10♐36 | 08♑16 |
| 5 | 06 56 | 08 51 | 10 05 | 09 15 | 07 19 |
| 10 | 06 36 | 07 57 | 08 47 | 07 54 | 06 21 |
| 15 | 06 16 | 07 06 | 07 31 | 06 33 | 05 20 |
| 20 | 05 57 | 06 16 | 06 16 | 05 11 | 04 16 |
| 21 | 05 53 | 06 06 | 06 01 | 04 54 | 04 02 |
| 22 | 05 49 | 05 56 | 05 46 | 04 37 | 03 49 |
| 23 | 05 45 | 05 46 | 05 31 | 04 20 | 03 35 |
| 24 | 05 41 | 05 36 | 05 16 | 04 03 | 03 21 |
| 25 | 05 37 | 05 26 | 05 00 | 03 46 | 03 06 |
| 26 | 05 33 | 05 16 | 04 45 | 03 28 | 02 51 |
| 27 | 05 29 | 05 05 | 04 30 | 03 11 | 02 36 |
| 28 | 05 25 | 04 55 | 04 15 | 02 53 | 02 21 |
| 29 | 05 21 | 04 45 | 03 59 | 02 35 | 02 05 |
| 30 | 05 17 | 04 35 | 03 44 | 02 16 | 01 49 |
| 31 | 05 13 | 04 25 | 03 28 | 01 58 | 01 33 |
| 32 | 05 09 | 04 15 | 03 12 | 01 39 | 01 16 |
| 33 | 05 05 | 04 04 | 02 56 | 01 20 | 00 59 |
| 34 | 05 00 | 03 54 | 02 40 | 01 01 | 00 41 |
| 35 | 04 56 | 03 43 | 02 24 | 00 41 | 00 23 |
| 36 | 04 52 | 03 33 | 02 08 | 00 22 | 00 05 |
| 37 | 04 47 | 03 22 | 01 51 | 00 01 | 29♐45 |
| 38 | 04 43 | 03 11 | 01 35 | 29♏41 | 29 26 |
| 39 | 04 38 | 03 00 | 01 18 | 29 20 | 29 05 |
| 40 | 04 33 | 02 49 | 01 01 | 28 59 | 28 44 |
| 41 | 04 29 | 02 38 | 00 43 | 28 37 | 28 22 |
| 42 | 04 24 | 02 26 | 00 26 | 28 15 | 27 59 |
| 43 | 04 19 | 02 15 | 00 08 | 27 52 | 27 36 |
| 44 | 04 13 | 02 03 | 29♎50 | 27 29 | 27 12 |
| 45 | 04 08 | 01 51 | 29 32 | 27 06 | 26 46 |
| 46 | 04 03 | 01 39 | 29 13 | 26 42 | 26 20 |
| 47 | 03 57 | 01 26 | 28 54 | 26 17 | 25 52 |
| 48 | 03 51 | 01 14 | 28 35 | 25 52 | 25 24 |
| 49 | 03 45 | 01 01 | 28 16 | 25 26 | 24 54 |
| 50 | 03 39 | 00 48 | 27 56 | 24 59 | 24 22 |
| 51 | 03 32 | 00 34 | 27 35 | 24 32 | 23 49 |
| 52 | 03 26 | 00 20 | 27 15 | 24 04 | 23 14 |
| 53 | 03 18 | 00 06 | 26 53 | 23 35 | 22 38 |
| 54 | 03 11 | 29♍51 | 26 32 | 23 06 | 21 59 |
| 55 | 03 03 | 29 36 | 26 10 | 22 35 | 21 18 |
| 56 | 02 55 | 29 20 | 25 47 | 22 04 | 20 34 |
| 57 | 02 46 | 29 04 | 25 24 | 21 32 | 19 48 |
| 58 | 02 37 | 28 47 | 25 00 | 20 58 | 18 58 |
| 59 | 02 26 | 28 30 | 24 35 | 20 24 | 18 05 |
| 60 | 02♍16 | 28♍11 | 24♎10 | 19♏49 | 17♐08 |

**8h 40m 0s — 130° 0' 0" — 07 ♌ 35**

| LAT. | 11 | 12 | ASC | 2 | 3 |
|---|---|---|---|---|---|
| 0 | 08♍22 | 10♎53 | 12♏27 | 11♐32 | 09♑11 |
| 5 | 07 59 | 09 54 | 11 04 | 10 10 | 08 14 |
| 10 | 07 37 | 08 59 | 09 45 | 08 48 | 07 15 |
| 15 | 07 17 | 08 06 | 08 27 | 07 26 | 06 13 |
| 20 | 06 56 | 07 14 | 07 10 | 06 02 | 05 08 |
| 21 | 06 52 | 07 04 | 06 55 | 05 45 | 04 54 |
| 22 | 06 48 | 06 53 | 06 40 | 05 28 | 04 40 |
| 23 | 06 44 | 06 43 | 06 24 | 05 10 | 04 26 |
| 24 | 06 40 | 06 33 | 06 09 | 04 53 | 04 12 |
| 25 | 06 36 | 06 22 | 05 53 | 04 35 | 03 57 |
| 26 | 06 31 | 06 12 | 05 38 | 04 18 | 03 42 |
| 27 | 06 27 | 06 02 | 05 22 | 04 00 | 03 27 |
| 28 | 06 23 | 05 51 | 05 06 | 03 41 | 03 11 |
| 29 | 06 19 | 05 41 | 04 51 | 03 23 | 02 55 |
| 30 | 06 14 | 05 30 | 04 35 | 03 05 | 02 39 |
| 31 | 06 10 | 05 20 | 04 19 | 02 46 | 02 22 |
| 32 | 06 06 | 05 09 | 04 03 | 02 27 | 02 05 |
| 33 | 06 01 | 04 58 | 03 46 | 02 07 | 01 48 |
| 34 | 05 57 | 04 48 | 03 30 | 01 48 | 01 30 |
| 35 | 05 52 | 04 37 | 03 13 | 01 28 | 01 11 |
| 36 | 05 48 | 04 26 | 02 57 | 01 07 | 00 52 |
| 37 | 05 43 | 04 15 | 02 40 | 00 47 | 00 33 |
| 38 | 05 38 | 04 03 | 02 23 | 00 26 | 00 12 |
| 39 | 05 33 | 03 52 | 02 06 | 00 04 | 29♐51 |
| 40 | 05 28 | 03 41 | 01 48 | 29♏43 | 29 30 |
| 41 | 05 23 | 03 29 | 01 30 | 29 21 | 29 07 |
| 42 | 05 18 | 03 17 | 01 12 | 28 58 | 28 44 |
| 43 | 05 13 | 03 06 | 00 54 | 28 35 | 28 20 |
| 44 | 05 08 | 02 53 | 00 36 | 28 11 | 27 55 |
| 45 | 05 02 | 02 41 | 00 17 | 27 47 | 27 29 |
| 46 | 04 56 | 02 29 | 29♎58 | 27 23 | 27 02 |
| 47 | 04 51 | 02 16 | 29 39 | 26 57 | 26 34 |
| 48 | 04 45 | 02 03 | 29 19 | 26 31 | 26 05 |
| 49 | 04 38 | 01 50 | 28 59 | 26 05 | 25 34 |
| 50 | 04 32 | 01 36 | 28 38 | 25 38 | 25 02 |
| 51 | 04 25 | 01 22 | 28 18 | 25 10 | 24 28 |
| 52 | 04 18 | 01 08 | 27 56 | 24 41 | 23 52 |
| 53 | 04 11 | 00 53 | 27 35 | 24 12 | 23 14 |
| 54 | 04 03 | 00 38 | 27 12 | 23 41 | 22 34 |
| 55 | 03 55 | 00 23 | 26 50 | 23 10 | 21 52 |
| 56 | 03 47 | 00 07 | 26 26 | 22 38 | 21 07 |
| 57 | 03 38 | 29♍50 | 26 03 | 22 04 | 20 20 |
| 58 | 03 28 | 29 33 | 25 38 | 21 30 | 19 28 |
| 59 | 03 18 | 29 15 | 25 13 | 20 55 | 18 34 |
| 60 | 03♍07 | 28♍56 | 24♎47 | 20♏18 | 17♐35 |

**8h 44m 0s — 131° 0' 0" — 08 ♌ 34**

| LAT. | 11 | 12 | ASC | 2 | 3 |
|---|---|---|---|---|---|
| 0 | 09♍26 | 11♎58 | 13♏27 | 12♐28 | 10♑07 |
| 5 | 09 02 | 10 57 | 12 03 | 11 05 | 09 09 |
| 10 | 08 39 | 10 01 | 10 42 | 09 42 | 08 09 |
| 15 | 08 17 | 09 06 | 09 23 | 08 18 | 07 07 |
| 20 | 07 56 | 08 12 | 08 05 | 06 53 | 06 00 |
| 21 | 07 51 | 08 02 | 07 49 | 06 36 | 05 46 |
| 22 | 07 47 | 07 51 | 07 34 | 06 18 | 05 32 |
| 23 | 07 43 | 07 40 | 07 18 | 06 01 | 05 18 |
| 24 | 07 38 | 07 30 | 07 02 | 05 43 | 05 03 |
| 25 | 07 34 | 07 19 | 06 46 | 05 25 | 04 48 |
| 26 | 07 30 | 07 08 | 06 30 | 05 07 | 04 33 |
| 27 | 07 25 | 06 58 | 06 14 | 04 49 | 04 18 |
| 28 | 07 21 | 06 47 | 05 58 | 04 30 | 04 02 |
| 29 | 07 16 | 06 36 | 05 42 | 04 12 | 03 45 |
| 30 | 07 12 | 06 25 | 05 26 | 03 53 | 03 29 |
| 31 | 07 07 | 06 14 | 05 09 | 03 33 | 03 12 |
| 32 | 07 03 | 06 03 | 04 53 | 03 14 | 02 54 |
| 33 | 06 58 | 05 52 | 04 36 | 02 54 | 02 37 |
| 34 | 06 53 | 05 41 | 04 20 | 02 34 | 02 18 |
| 35 | 06 49 | 05 30 | 04 03 | 02 14 | 01 59 |
| 36 | 06 44 | 05 19 | 03 46 | 01 53 | 01 40 |
| 37 | 06 39 | 05 08 | 03 28 | 01 32 | 01 20 |
| 38 | 06 34 | 04 56 | 03 11 | 01 11 | 00 59 |
| 39 | 06 29 | 04 44 | 02 53 | 00 49 | 00 38 |
| 40 | 06 24 | 04 33 | 02 35 | 00 27 | 00 16 |
| 41 | 06 19 | 04 21 | 02 17 | 00 04 | 29♐53 |
| 42 | 06 13 | 04 09 | 01 59 | 29♏41 | 29 29 |
| 43 | 06 08 | 03 56 | 01 40 | 29 17 | 29 05 |
| 44 | 06 02 | 03 44 | 01 21 | 28 53 | 28 39 |
| 45 | 05 56 | 03 31 | 01 02 | 28 29 | 28 13 |
| 46 | 05 50 | 03 18 | 00 43 | 28 03 | 27 45 |
| 47 | 05 44 | 03 05 | 00 23 | 27 38 | 27 16 |
| 48 | 05 38 | 02 52 | 00 03 | 27 11 | 26 46 |
| 49 | 05 32 | 02 38 | 29♎42 | 26 44 | 26 14 |
| 50 | 05 25 | 02 24 | 29 21 | 26 16 | 25 41 |
| 51 | 05 18 | 02 10 | 29 00 | 25 47 | 25 06 |
| 52 | 05 11 | 01 55 | 28 38 | 25 18 | 24 30 |
| 53 | 05 03 | 01 40 | 28 16 | 24 48 | 23 51 |
| 54 | 04 56 | 01 25 | 27 53 | 24 17 | 23 10 |
| 55 | 04 47 | 01 09 | 27 30 | 23 44 | 22 27 |
| 56 | 04 39 | 00 53 | 27 06 | 23 11 | 21 40 |
| 57 | 04 29 | 00 36 | 26 41 | 22 37 | 20 51 |
| 58 | 04 20 | 00 18 | 26 16 | 22 02 | 19 59 |
| 59 | 04 09 | 00 00 | 25 51 | 21 25 | 19 02 |
| 60 | 03♍58 | 29♍41 | 25♎24 | 20♏48 | 18♐01 |

**8h 48m 0s — 132° 0' 0" — 09 ♌ 34**

| LAT. | 11 | 12 | ASC | 2 | 3 |
|---|---|---|---|---|---|
| 0 | 10♍30 | 13♎03 | 14♏28 | 13♐24 | 11♑02 |
| 5 | 10 05 | 12 01 | 13 02 | 12 00 | 10 03 |
| 10 | 09 41 | 11 02 | 11 40 | 10 36 | 09 03 |
| 15 | 09 18 | 10 06 | 10 19 | 09 11 | 08 00 |
| 20 | 08 55 | 09 10 | 08 59 | 07 44 | 06 53 |
| 21 | 08 51 | 09 00 | 08 43 | 07 27 | 06 38 |
| 22 | 08 46 | 08 49 | 08 27 | 07 09 | 06 24 |
| 23 | 08 42 | 08 38 | 08 11 | 06 51 | 06 09 |
| 24 | 08 37 | 08 27 | 07 55 | 06 33 | 05 55 |
| 25 | 08 33 | 08 16 | 07 39 | 06 15 | 05 39 |
| 26 | 08 28 | 08 05 | 07 23 | 05 56 | 05 24 |
| 27 | 08 23 | 07 54 | 07 06 | 05 38 | 05 08 |
| 28 | 08 19 | 07 43 | 06 50 | 05 19 | 04 52 |
| 29 | 08 14 | 07 32 | 06 34 | 05 00 | 04 36 |
| 30 | 08 09 | 07 20 | 06 17 | 04 41 | 04 19 |
| 31 | 08 05 | 07 09 | 06 00 | 04 21 | 04 01 |
| 32 | 08 00 | 06 58 | 05 43 | 04 01 | 03 44 |
| 33 | 07 55 | 06 47 | 05 26 | 03 41 | 03 25 |
| 34 | 07 50 | 06 35 | 05 09 | 03 21 | 03 07 |
| 35 | 07 45 | 06 24 | 04 52 | 03 00 | 02 47 |
| 36 | 07 40 | 06 12 | 04 34 | 02 39 | 02 28 |
| 37 | 07 35 | 06 00 | 04 17 | 02 17 | 02 07 |
| 38 | 07 30 | 05 49 | 03 59 | 01 56 | 01 46 |
| 39 | 07 25 | 05 37 | 03 41 | 01 33 | 01 24 |
| 40 | 07 19 | 05 25 | 03 23 | 01 11 | 01 02 |
| 41 | 07 14 | 05 12 | 03 04 | 00 48 | 00 39 |
| 42 | 07 08 | 05 00 | 02 45 | 00 24 | 00 14 |
| 43 | 07 03 | 04 47 | 02 26 | 00 00 | 29♐49 |
| 44 | 06 57 | 04 34 | 02 07 | 29♏35 | 29 23 |
| 45 | 06 51 | 04 21 | 01 47 | 29 10 | 28 56 |
| 46 | 06 45 | 04 08 | 01 27 | 28 44 | 28 28 |
| 47 | 06 38 | 03 55 | 01 07 | 28 18 | 27 58 |
| 48 | 06 32 | 03 41 | 00 46 | 27 51 | 27 27 |
| 49 | 06 25 | 03 27 | 00 25 | 27 23 | 26 55 |
| 50 | 06 18 | 03 13 | 00 04 | 26 54 | 26 21 |
| 51 | 06 11 | 02 58 | 29♎42 | 26 25 | 25 45 |
| 52 | 06 04 | 02 43 | 29 20 | 25 55 | 25 08 |
| 53 | 05 56 | 02 28 | 28 57 | 25 24 | 24 28 |
| 54 | 05 48 | 02 12 | 28 33 | 24 52 | 23 46 |
| 55 | 05 40 | 01 56 | 28 10 | 24 19 | 23 01 |
| 56 | 05 31 | 01 39 | 27 45 | 23 45 | 22 14 |
| 57 | 05 22 | 01 22 | 27 20 | 23 10 | 21 23 |
| 58 | 05 12 | 01 04 | 26 54 | 22 34 | 20 29 |
| 59 | 05 01 | 00 45 | 26 28 | 21 56 | 19 31 |
| 60 | 04♍50 | 00♎26 | 26♎01 | 21♏17 | 18♐28 |

**8h 52m 0s — 133° 0' 0" — 10 ♌ 33**

| LAT. | 11 | 12 | ASC | 2 | 3 |
|---|---|---|---|---|---|
| 0 | 11♍34 | 14♎07 | 15♏28 | 14♐20 | 11♑58 |
| 5 | 11 08 | 13 04 | 14 01 | 12 54 | 10 58 |
| 10 | 10 43 | 12 04 | 12 37 | 11 29 | 09 57 |
| 15 | 10 19 | 11 06 | 11 15 | 10 03 | 08 53 |
| 20 | 09 55 | 10 09 | 09 54 | 08 36 | 07 45 |
| 21 | 09 50 | 09 58 | 09 37 | 08 18 | 07 31 |
| 22 | 09 46 | 09 46 | 09 21 | 08 00 | 07 16 |
| 23 | 09 41 | 09 35 | 09 05 | 07 42 | 07 01 |
| 24 | 09 36 | 09 24 | 08 48 | 07 23 | 06 46 |
| 25 | 09 31 | 09 13 | 08 32 | 07 05 | 06 31 |
| 26 | 09 27 | 09 01 | 08 15 | 06 46 | 06 15 |
| 27 | 09 22 | 08 50 | 07 59 | 06 27 | 05 59 |
| 28 | 09 17 | 08 39 | 07 42 | 06 08 | 05 43 |
| 29 | 09 12 | 08 27 | 07 25 | 05 48 | 05 26 |
| 30 | 09 07 | 08 16 | 07 08 | 05 29 | 05 09 |
| 31 | 09 02 | 08 04 | 06 51 | 05 09 | 04 51 |
| 32 | 08 57 | 07 53 | 06 34 | 04 49 | 04 33 |
| 33 | 08 52 | 07 41 | 06 16 | 04 28 | 04 14 |
| 34 | 08 47 | 07 29 | 05 59 | 04 07 | 03 55 |
| 35 | 08 42 | 07 17 | 05 41 | 03 46 | 03 36 |
| 36 | 08 37 | 07 05 | 05 23 | 03 25 | 03 16 |
| 37 | 08 31 | 06 53 | 05 05 | 03 03 | 02 55 |
| 38 | 08 26 | 06 41 | 04 47 | 02 40 | 02 33 |
| 39 | 08 21 | 06 29 | 04 29 | 02 18 | 02 11 |
| 40 | 08 15 | 06 17 | 04 10 | 01 55 | 01 48 |
| 41 | 08 09 | 06 04 | 03 51 | 01 31 | 01 24 |
| 42 | 08 04 | 05 51 | 03 32 | 01 07 | 01 00 |
| 43 | 07 58 | 05 38 | 03 12 | 00 42 | 00 34 |
| 44 | 07 52 | 05 25 | 02 53 | 00 17 | 00 07 |
| 45 | 07 45 | 05 12 | 02 32 | 29♏51 | 29♐39 |
| 46 | 07 39 | 04 58 | 02 12 | 29 25 | 29 11 |
| 47 | 07 33 | 04 44 | 01 51 | 28 58 | 28 40 |
| 48 | 07 26 | 04 30 | 01 30 | 28 30 | 28 09 |
| 49 | 07 19 | 04 16 | 01 09 | 28 02 | 27 35 |
| 50 | 07 12 | 04 01 | 00 47 | 27 33 | 27 01 |
| 51 | 07 05 | 03 46 | 00 24 | 27 03 | 26 24 |
| 52 | 06 57 | 03 31 | 00 01 | 26 32 | 25 45 |
| 53 | 06 49 | 03 15 | 29♎38 | 26 00 | 25 05 |
| 54 | 06 41 | 02 59 | 29 14 | 25 27 | 24 21 |
| 55 | 06 32 | 02 42 | 28 50 | 24 53 | 23 36 |
| 56 | 06 23 | 02 25 | 28 25 | 24 18 | 22 47 |
| 57 | 06 14 | 02 08 | 27 59 | 23 42 | 21 55 |
| 58 | 06 04 | 01 49 | 27 33 | 23 05 | 20 59 |
| 59 | 05 53 | 01 30 | 27 06 | 22 27 | 19 59 |
| 60 | 05♍42 | 01♎11 | 26♎38 | 21♏47 | 18♐55 |

**8h 56m 0s — 134° 0' 0" — 11 ♌ 32**

| LAT. | 11 | 12 | ASC | 2 | 3 |
|---|---|---|---|---|---|
| 0 | 12♍39 | 15♎12 | 16♏28 | 15♐16 | 12♑53 |
| 5 | 12 11 | 14 07 | 15 00 | 13 49 | 11 53 |
| 10 | 11 45 | 13 05 | 13 34 | 12 23 | 10 52 |
| 15 | 11 20 | 12 05 | 12 11 | 10 56 | 09 47 |
| 20 | 10 55 | 11 07 | 10 48 | 09 27 | 08 37 |
| 21 | 10 50 | 10 56 | 10 31 | 09 09 | 08 23 |
| 22 | 10 45 | 10 44 | 10 15 | 08 50 | 08 08 |
| 23 | 10 40 | 10 32 | 09 58 | 08 32 | 07 53 |
| 24 | 10 35 | 10 21 | 09 41 | 08 13 | 07 38 |
| 25 | 10 30 | 10 09 | 09 24 | 07 54 | 07 22 |
| 26 | 10 25 | 09 58 | 09 08 | 07 35 | 07 06 |
| 27 | 10 20 | 09 46 | 08 51 | 07 16 | 06 50 |
| 28 | 10 15 | 09 34 | 08 33 | 06 56 | 06 33 |
| 29 | 10 10 | 09 23 | 08 16 | 06 37 | 06 16 |
| 30 | 10 05 | 09 11 | 07 59 | 06 17 | 05 59 |
| 31 | 10 00 | 08 59 | 07 42 | 05 56 | 05 41 |
| 32 | 09 55 | 08 47 | 07 24 | 05 36 | 05 22 |
| 33 | 09 49 | 08 35 | 07 06 | 05 15 | 05 04 |
| 34 | 09 44 | 08 23 | 06 48 | 04 54 | 04 44 |
| 35 | 09 39 | 08 11 | 06 30 | 04 32 | 04 24 |
| 36 | 09 33 | 07 59 | 06 12 | 04 10 | 04 04 |
| 37 | 09 28 | 07 46 | 05 54 | 03 48 | 03 42 |
| 38 | 09 22 | 07 34 | 05 35 | 03 25 | 03 20 |
| 39 | 09 17 | 07 21 | 05 16 | 03 02 | 02 58 |
| 40 | 09 11 | 07 09 | 04 57 | 02 39 | 02 34 |
| 41 | 09 05 | 06 56 | 04 38 | 02 14 | 02 10 |
| 42 | 08 59 | 06 43 | 04 18 | 01 50 | 01 45 |
| 43 | 08 53 | 06 29 | 03 58 | 01 25 | 01 19 |
| 44 | 08 47 | 06 16 | 03 38 | 00 59 | 00 51 |
| 45 | 08 40 | 06 02 | 03 18 | 00 33 | 00 23 |
| 46 | 08 34 | 05 48 | 02 57 | 00 06 | 29♐53 |
| 47 | 08 27 | 05 34 | 02 35 | 29♏38 | 29 22 |
| 48 | 08 20 | 05 20 | 02 14 | 29 10 | 28 50 |
| 49 | 08 13 | 05 05 | 01 52 | 28 41 | 28 16 |
| 50 | 08 06 | 04 50 | 01 29 | 28 11 | 27 40 |
| 51 | 07 58 | 04 35 | 01 06 | 27 40 | 27 03 |
| 52 | 07 50 | 04 19 | 00 43 | 27 08 | 26 23 |
| 53 | 07 42 | 04 03 | 00 19 | 26 36 | 25 41 |
| 54 | 07 34 | 03 46 | 29♎55 | 26 02 | 24 57 |
| 55 | 07 25 | 03 29 | 29 30 | 25 28 | 24 10 |
| 56 | 07 16 | 03 12 | 29 04 | 24 52 | 23 20 |
| 57 | 07 06 | 02 54 | 28 38 | 24 15 | 22 26 |
| 58 | 06 56 | 02 35 | 28 11 | 23 37 | 21 29 |
| 59 | 06 45 | 02 16 | 27 43 | 22 57 | 20 28 |
| 60 | 06♍34 | 01♎56 | 27♎15 | 22♏16 | 19♐21 |

**9h 0m 0s — 135° 0' 0" — 12 ♌ 32**

| LAT. | 11 | 12 | ASC | 2 | 3 |
|---|---|---|---|---|---|
| 0 | 13♍43 | 16♎17 | 17♏28 | 16♐11 | 13♑49 |
| 5 | 13 14 | 15 10 | 15 58 | 14 44 | 12 48 |
| 10 | 12 47 | 14 06 | 14 32 | 13 17 | 11 46 |
| 15 | 12 21 | 13 05 | 13 07 | 11 48 | 10 40 |
| 20 | 11 55 | 12 06 | 11 42 | 10 18 | 09 30 |
| 21 | 11 50 | 11 54 | 11 25 | 10 00 | 09 15 |
| 22 | 11 45 | 11 42 | 11 08 | 09 41 | 09 00 |
| 23 | 11 40 | 11 30 | 10 51 | 09 22 | 08 45 |
| 24 | 11 34 | 11 18 | 10 34 | 09 03 | 08 30 |
| 25 | 11 29 | 11 06 | 10 17 | 08 44 | 08 14 |
| 26 | 11 24 | 10 54 | 10 00 | 08 25 | 07 58 |
| 27 | 11 19 | 10 42 | 09 43 | 08 05 | 07 41 |
| 28 | 11 14 | 10 30 | 09 25 | 07 45 | 07 24 |
| 29 | 11 08 | 10 18 | 09 08 | 07 25 | 07, 07 |
| 30 | 11 03 | 10 06 | 08 50 | 07 05 | 06 49 |
| 31 | 10 58 | 09 54 | 08 32 | 06 44 | 06 31 |
| 32 | 10 52 | 09 42 | 08 14 | 06 23 | 06 12 |
| 33 | 10 47 | 09 30 | 07 56 | 06 02 | 05 53 |
| 34 | 10 41 | 09 17 | 07 38 | 05 40 | 05 33 |
| 35 | 10 36 | 09 05 | 07 20 | 05 18 | 05 13 |
| 36 | 10 30 | 08 52 | 07 01 | 04 56 | 04 52 |
| 37 | 10 24 | 08 40 | 06 42 | 04 33 | 04 30 |
| 38 | 10 19 | 08 27 | 06 23 | 04 10 | 04 08 |
| 39 | 10 13 | 08 14 | 06 04 | 03 47 | 03 45 |
| 40 | 10 07 | 08 01 | 05 44 | 03 23 | 03 21 |
| 41 | 10 01 | 07 47 | 05 25 | 02 58 | 02 56 |
| 42 | 09 55 | 07 34 | 05 05 | 02 33 | 02 30 |
| 43 | 09 48 | 07 20 | 04 44 | 02 07 | 02 03 |
| 44 | 09 42 | 07 07 | 04 24 | 01 41 | 01 36 |
| 45 | 09 35 | 06 53 | 04 03 | 01 14 | 01 07 |
| 46 | 09 29 | 06 38 | 03 41 | 00 47 | 00 36 |
| 47 | 09 22 | 06 24 | 03 20 | 00 18 | 00 05 |
| 48 | 09 15 | 06 09 | 02 57 | 29♏49 | 29♐32 |
| 49 | 09 07 | 05 54 | 02 35 | 29 20 | 28 57 |
| 50 | 09 00 | 05 39 | 02 12 | 28 49 | 28 20 |
| 51 | 08 52 | 05 23 | 01 49 | 28 18 | 27 42 |
| 52 | 08 44 | 05 07 | 01 25 | 27 45 | 27 01 |
| 53 | 08 36 | 04 50 | 01 00 | 27 12 | 26 18 |
| 54 | 08 27 | 04 33 | 00 35 | 26 37 | 25 33 |
| 55 | 08 18 | 04 16 | 00 10 | 26 02 | 24 44 |
| 56 | 08 09 | 03 58 | 29♎43 | 25 25 | 23 53 |
| 57 | 07 59 | 03 40 | 29 16 | 24 47 | 22 58 |
| 58 | 07 49 | 03 21 | 28 49 | 24 08 | 21 59 |
| 59 | 07 38 | 03 01 | 28 21 | 23 28 | 20 56 |
| 60 | 07♍26 | 02♎41 | 27♎51 | 22♏46 | 19♐48 |

# Koch Table of Houses for Latitudes 0° to 60° North

**9h 4m 0s — 136° 0' 0" — 13 ♌ 32**

| LAT. | 11 | 12 | ASC | 2 | 3 |
|---|---|---|---|---|---|
| 0 | 14♍48 | 17♎21 | 18♏28 | 17♐07 | 14♑44 |
| 5 | 14 18 | 16 13 | 16 57 | 15 38 | 13 43 |
| 10 | 13 49 | 15 08 | 15 29 | 14 10 | 12 40 |
| 15 | 13 22 | 14 05 | 14 02 | 12 41 | 11 34 |
| 20 | 12 55 | 13 04 | 12 36 | 11 09 | 10 23 |
| 21 | 12 50 | 12 52 | 12 19 | 10 50 | 10 08 |
| 22 | 12 45 | 12 40 | 12 02 | 10 31 | 09 53 |
| 23 | 12 39 | 12 27 | 11 44 | 10 12 | 09 37 |
| 24 | 12 34 | 12 15 | 11 27 | 09 53 | 09 21 |
| 25 | 12 28 | 12 03 | 11 10 | 09 34 | 09 05 |
| 26 | 12 23 | 11 51 | 10 52 | 09 14 | 08 49 |
| 27 | 12 18 | 11 39 | 10 34 | 08 54 | 08 32 |
| 28 | 12 12 | 11 26 | 10 17 | 08 34 | 08 15 |
| 29 | 12 07 | 11 14 | 09 59 | 08 14 | 07 57 |
| 30 | 12 01 | 11 02 | 09 41 | 07 53 | 07 39 |
| 31 | 11 56 | 10 49 | 09 23 | 07 32 | 07 21 |
| 32 | 11 50 | 10 37 | 09 05 | 07 11 | 07 02 |
| 33 | 11 44 | 10 24 | 08 46 | 06 49 | 06 42 |
| 34 | 11 39 | 10 11 | 08 28 | 06 27 | 06 22 |
| 35 | 11 33 | 09 59 | 08 09 | 06 05 | 06 01 |
| 36 | 11 27 | 09 46 | 07 50 | 05 42 | 05 40 |
| 37 | 11 21 | 09 33 | 07 31 | 05 19 | 05 18 |
| 38 | 11 15 | 09 20 | 07 11 | 04 55 | 04 55 |
| 39 | 11 09 | 09 06 | 06 52 | 04 31 | 04 32 |
| 40 | 11 03 | 08 53 | 06 32 | 04 06 | 04 07 |
| 41 | 10 57 | 08 39 | 06 11 | 03 41 | 03 42 |
| 42 | 10 50 | 08 26 | 05 51 | 03 16 | 03 16 |
| 43 | 10 44 | 08 12 | 05 30 | 02 50 | 02 48 |
| 44 | 10 37 | 07 57 | 05 09 | 02 23 | 02 20 |
| 45 | 10 30 | 07 43 | 04 48 | 01 55 | 01 50 |
| 46 | 10 24 | 07 28 | 04 26 | 01 27 | 01 19 |
| 47 | 10 16 | 07 14 | 04 04 | 00 58 | 00 47 |
| 48 | 10 09 | 06 59 | 03 41 | 00 29 | 00 13 |
| 49 | 10 02 | 06 43 | 03 18 | 29♏58 | 29♐38 |
| 50 | 09 54 | 06 27 | 02 55 | 29 27 | 29 00 |
| 51 | 09 46 | 06 11 | 02 31 | 28 55 | 28 21 |
| 52 | 09 38 | 05 55 | 02 06 | 28 22 | 27 39 |
| 53 | 09 29 | 05 38 | 01 41 | 27 48 | 26 55 |
| 54 | 09 21 | 05 21 | 01 16 | 27 13 | 26 09 |
| 55 | 09 11 | 05 03 | 00 49 | 26 36 | 25 19 |
| 56 | 09 02 | 04 45 | 00 23 | 25 59 | 24 26 |
| 57 | 08 52 | 04 26 | 29♎55 | 25 20 | 23 30 |
| 58 | 08 41 | 04 07 | 29 27 | 24 40 | 22 29 |
| 59 | 08 30 | 03 47 | 28 58 | 23 58 | 21 25 |
| 60 | 08♍19 | 03♎26 | 28♎28 | 23♏15 | 20♐14 |

**9h 8m 0s — 137° 0' 0" — 14 ♌ 32**

| LAT. | 11 | 12 | ASC | 2 | 3 |
|---|---|---|---|---|---|
| 0 | 15♍53 | 18♎26 | 19♏27 | 18♐02 | 15♑40 |
| 5 | 15 21 | 17 16 | 17 55 | 16 33 | 14 39 |
| 10 | 14 52 | 16 09 | 16 26 | 15 04 | 13 35 |
| 15 | 14 23 | 15 05 | 14 58 | 13 33 | 12 28 |
| 20 | 13 56 | 14 02 | 13 30 | 12 00 | 11 16 |
| 21 | 13 50 | 13 50 | 13 13 | 11 41 | 11 01 |
| 22 | 13 44 | 13 37 | 12 55 | 11 22 | 10 45 |
| 23 | 13 39 | 13 25 | 12 38 | 11 03 | 10 30 |
| 24 | 13 33 | 13 12 | 12 20 | 10 43 | 10 14 |
| 25 | 13 28 | 13 00 | 12 02 | 10 23 | 09 57 |
| 26 | 13 22 | 12 47 | 11 44 | 10 03 | 09 40 |
| 27 | 13 17 | 12 35 | 11 26 | 09 43 | 09 23 |
| 28 | 13 11 | 12 22 | 11 08 | 09 23 | 09 06 |
| 29 | 13 05 | 12 10 | 10 50 | 09 02 | 08 48 |
| 30 | 13 00 | 11 57 | 10 32 | 08 41 | 08 30 |
| 31 | 12 54 | 11 44 | 10 13 | 08 20 | 08 11 |
| 32 | 12 48 | 11 31 | 09 55 | 07 58 | 07 52 |
| 33 | 12 42 | 11 18 | 09 36 | 07 36 | 07 32 |
| 34 | 12 36 | 11 05 | 09 17 | 07 14 | 07 11 |
| 35 | 12 30 | 10 52 | 08 58 | 06 51 | 06 50 |
| 36 | 12 24 | 10 39 | 08 39 | 06 28 | 06 28 |
| 37 | 12 18 | 10 26 | 08 19 | 06 04 | 06 06 |
| 38 | 12 12 | 10 12 | 07 59 | 05 40 | 05 43 |
| 39 | 12 06 | 09 59 | 07 39 | 05 15 | 05 19 |
| 40 | 11 59 | 09 45 | 07 19 | 04 50 | 04 54 |
| 41 | 11 53 | 09 31 | 06 58 | 04 25 | 04 28 |
| 42 | 11 46 | 09 17 | 06 37 | 03 59 | 04 01 |
| 43 | 11 40 | 09 03 | 06 16 | 03 32 | 03 33 |
| 44 | 11 33 | 08 48 | 05 55 | 03 05 | 03 04 |
| 45 | 11 26 | 08 34 | 05 33 | 02 37 | 02 34 |
| 46 | 11 19 | 08 19 | 05 11 | 02 08 | 02 03 |
| 47 | 11 11 | 08 04 | 04 48 | 01 39 | 01 29 |
| 48 | 11 04 | 07 48 | 04 25 | 01 08 | 00 55 |
| 49 | 10 56 | 07 32 | 04 01 | 00 37 | 00 18 |
| 50 | 10 48 | 07 16 | 03 37 | 00 05 | 29♐40 |
| 51 | 10 40 | 07 00 | 03 13 | 29♏32 | 29 00 |
| 52 | 10 32 | 06 43 | 02 48 | 28 59 | 28 17 |
| 53 | 10 23 | 06 26 | 02 22 | 28 24 | 27 32 |
| 54 | 10 14 | 06 08 | 01 56 | 27 48 | 26 44 |
| 55 | 10 05 | 05 50 | 01 29 | 27 10 | 25 54 |
| 56 | 09 55 | 05 32 | 01 02 | 26 32 | 24 59 |
| 57 | 09 45 | 05 12 | 00 34 | 25 52 | 24 02 |
| 58 | 09 34 | 04 53 | 00 05 | 25 11 | 23 00 |
| 59 | 09 23 | 04 32 | 29♎35 | 24 28 | 21 53 |
| 60 | 09♍11 | 04♎11 | 29♎05 | 23♏44 | 20♐41 |

**9h 12m 0s — 138° 0' 0" — 15 ♌ 32**

| LAT. | 11 | 12 | ASC | 2 | 3 |
|---|---|---|---|---|---|
| 0 | 16♍57 | 19♎30 | 20♏26 | 18♐58 | 16♑36 |
| 5 | 16 25 | 18 18 | 18 53 | 17 28 | 15 34 |
| 10 | 15 54 | 17 10 | 17 22 | 15 57 | 14 30 |
| 15 | 15 25 | 16 05 | 15 53 | 14 26 | 13 22 |
| 20 | 14 56 | 15 00 | 14 24 | 12 51 | 12 09 |
| 21 | 14 50 | 14 48 | 14 07 | 12 32 | 11 53 |
| 22 | 14 44 | 14 35 | 13 49 | 12 13 | 11 38 |
| 23 | 14 39 | 14 22 | 13 31 | 11 53 | 11 22 |
| 24 | 14 33 | 14 09 | 13 13 | 11 33 | 11 06 |
| 25 | 14 27 | 13 57 | 12 55 | 11 13 | 10 49 |
| 26 | 14 21 | 13 44 | 12 36 | 10 53 | 10 32 |
| 27 | 14 16 | 13 31 | 12 18 | 10 32 | 10 15 |
| 28 | 14 10 | 13 18 | 12 00 | 10 11 | 09 57 |
| 29 | 14 04 | 13 05 | 11 41 | 09 50 | 09 39 |
| 30 | 13 58 | 12 52 | 11 23 | 09 29 | 09 20 |
| 31 | 13 52 | 12 39 | 11 04 | 09 07 | 09 01 |
| 32 | 13 46 | 12 26 | 10 45 | 08 45 | 08 42 |
| 33 | 13 40 | 12 13 | 10 26 | 08 23 | 08 21 |
| 34 | 13 34 | 12 00 | 10 06 | 08 00 | 08 00 |
| 35 | 13 28 | 11 46 | 09 47 | 07 37 | 07 39 |
| 36 | 13 22 | 11 33 | 09 27 | 07 13 | 07 17 |
| 37 | 13 15 | 11 19 | 09 07 | 06 49 | 06 54 |
| 38 | 13 09 | 11 05 | 08 47 | 06 25 | 06 30 |
| 39 | 13 02 | 10 51 | 08 27 | 06 00 | 06 06 |
| 40 | 12 56 | 10 37 | 08 06 | 05 34 | 05 41 |
| 41 | 12 49 | 10 23 | 07 45 | 05 08 | 05 14 |
| 42 | 12 42 | 10 09 | 07 24 | 04 42 | 04 47 |
| 43 | 12 36 | 09 54 | 07 02 | 04 15 | 04 19 |
| 44 | 12 28 | 09 39 | 06 40 | 03 47 | 03 49 |
| 45 | 12 21 | 09 24 | 06 18 | 03 18 | 03 18 |
| 46 | 12 14 | 09 09 | 05 55 | 02 49 | 02 46 |
| 47 | 12 06 | 08 53 | 05 32 | 02 19 | 02 12 |
| 48 | 11 59 | 08 38 | 05 08 | 01 48 | 01 37 |
| 49 | 11 51 | 08 22 | 04 44 | 01 16 | 00 59 |
| 50 | 11 43 | 08 05 | 04 20 | 00 44 | 00 20 |
| 51 | 11 35 | 07 48 | 03 55 | 00 10 | 29♐39 |
| 52 | 11 26 | 07 31 | 03 29 | 29♏35 | 28 55 |
| 53 | 11 17 | 07 14 | 03 03 | 29 00 | 28 09 |
| 54 | 11 08 | 06 56 | 02 37 | 28 23 | 27 20 |
| 55 | 10 58 | 06 37 | 02 09 | 27 45 | 26 28 |
| 56 | 10 49 | 06 18 | 01 41 | 27 05 | 25 33 |
| 57 | 10 38 | 05 59 | 01 13 | 26 25 | 24 33 |
| 58 | 10 27 | 05 39 | 00 43 | 25 42 | 23 30 |
| 59 | 10 16 | 05 18 | 00 13 | 24 59 | 22 21 |
| 60 | 10♍04 | 04♎57 | 29♎42 | 24♏13 | 21♐07 |

**9h 16m 0s — 139° 0' 0" — 16 ♌ 33**

| LAT. | 11 | 12 | ASC | 2 | 3 |
|---|---|---|---|---|---|
| 0 | 18♍02 | 20♎34 | 21♏26 | 19♐53 | 17♑32 |
| 5 | 17 29 | 19 21 | 19 51 | 18 22 | 16 29 |
| 10 | 16 57 | 18 11 | 18 19 | 16 51 | 15 24 |
| 15 | 16 26 | 17 04 | 16 49 | 15 18 | 14 16 |
| 20 | 15 57 | 15 59 | 15 18 | 13 43 | 13 02 |
| 21 | 15 51 | 15 46 | 15 00 | 13 23 | 12 46 |
| 22 | 15 45 | 15 33 | 14 42 | 13 03 | 12 31 |
| 23 | 15 39 | 15 20 | 14 24 | 12 43 | 12 14 |
| 24 | 15 33 | 15 07 | 14 05 | 12 23 | 11 58 |
| 25 | 15 27 | 14 54 | 13 47 | 12 03 | 11 41 |
| 26 | 15 21 | 14 40 | 13 29 | 11 42 | 11 24 |
| 27 | 15 15 | 14 27 | 13 10 | 11 21 | 11 06 |
| 28 | 15 09 | 14 14 | 12 51 | 11 00 | 10 48 |
| 29 | 15 03 | 14 01 | 12 32 | 10 39 | 10 30 |
| 30 | 14 57 | 13 48 | 12 13 | 10 17 | 10 11 |
| 31 | 14 50 | 13 34 | 11 54 | 09 55 | 09 52 |
| 32 | 14 44 | 13 21 | 11 35 | 09 33 | 09 32 |
| 33 | 14 38 | 13 07 | 11 16 | 09 10 | 09 11 |
| 34 | 14 32 | 12 54 | 10 56 | 08 47 | 08 50 |
| 35 | 14 25 | 12 40 | 10 36 | 08 23 | 08 28 |
| 36 | 14 19 | 12 26 | 10 16 | 07 59 | 08 06 |
| 37 | 14 12 | 12 12 | 09 56 | 07 35 | 07 42 |
| 38 | 14 06 | 11 58 | 09 35 | 07 10 | 07 18 |
| 39 | 13 59 | 11 44 | 09 14 | 06 44 | 06 53 |
| 40 | 13 52 | 11 30 | 08 53 | 06 19 | 06 28 |
| 41 | 13 46 | 11 15 | 08 32 | 05 52 | 06 01 |
| 42 | 13 39 | 11 00 | 08 10 | 05 25 | 05 33 |
| 43 | 13 32 | 10 46 | 07 48 | 04 57 | 05 04 |
| 44 | 13 24 | 10 30 | 07 26 | 04 29 | 04 34 |
| 45 | 13 17 | 10 15 | 07 03 | 04 00 | 04 02 |
| 46 | 13 09 | 09 59 | 06 40 | 03 30 | 03 29 |
| 47 | 13 02 | 09 44 | 06 16 | 02 59 | 02 55 |
| 48 | 12 54 | 09 27 | 05 52 | 02 28 | 02 19 |
| 49 | 12 46 | 09 11 | 05 28 | 01 55 | 01 41 |
| 50 | 12 38 | 08 54 | 05 03 | 01 22 | 01 01 |
| 51 | 12 29 | 08 37 | 04 37 | 00 47 | 00 18 |
| 52 | 12 20 | 08 19 | 04 11 | 00 12 | 29♐34 |
| 53 | 12 11 | 08 02 | 03 44 | 29♏36 | 28 46 |
| 54 | 12 02 | 07 43 | 03 17 | 28 58 | 27 56 |
| 55 | 11 52 | 07 24 | 02 49 | 28 19 | 27 03 |
| 56 | 11 42 | 07 05 | 02 21 | 27 39 | 26 06 |
| 57 | 11 32 | 06 45 | 01 51 | 26 57 | 25 05 |
| 58 | 11 21 | 06 25 | 01 21 | 26 14 | 24 00 |
| 59 | 11 09 | 06 04 | 00 50 | 25 29 | 22 50 |
| 60 | 10♍57 | 05♎42 | 00♏19 | 24♏42 | 21♐34 |

**9h 20m 0s — 140° 0' 0" — 17 ♌ 33**

| LAT. | 11 | 12 | ASC | 2 | 3 |
|---|---|---|---|---|---|
| 0 | 19♍07 | 21♎38 | 22♏25 | 20♐49 | 18♑28 |
| 5 | 18 33 | 20 24 | 20 49 | 19 17 | 17 25 |
| 10 | 18 00 | 19 13 | 19 15 | 17 44 | 16 19 |
| 15 | 17 28 | 18 04 | 17 44 | 16 10 | 15 10 |
| 20 | 16 57 | 16 57 | 16 12 | 14 34 | 13 55 |
| 21 | 16 51 | 16 44 | 15 54 | 14 14 | 13 39 |
| 22 | 16 45 | 16 30 | 15 35 | 13 54 | 13 23 |
| 23 | 16 39 | 16 17 | 15 17 | 13 34 | 13 07 |
| 24 | 16 33 | 16 04 | 14 58 | 13 13 | 12 50 |
| 25 | 16 26 | 15 50 | 14 39 | 12 53 | 12 33 |
| 26 | 16 20 | 15 37 | 14 21 | 12 32 | 12 16 |
| 27 | 16 14 | 15 24 | 14 02 | 12 11 | 11 58 |
| 28 | 16 08 | 15 10 | 13 43 | 11 49 | 11 40 |
| 29 | 16 02 | 14 57 | 13 24 | 11 27 | 11 21 |
| 30 | 15 55 | 14 43 | 13 04 | 11 05 | 11 02 |
| 31 | 15 49 | 14 29 | 12 45 | 10 43 | 10 42 |
| 32 | 15 43 | 14 16 | 12 25 | 10 20 | 10 22 |
| 33 | 15 36 | 14 02 | 12 05 | 09 57 | 10 01 |
| 34 | 15 30 | 13 48 | 11 45 | 09 33 | 09 40 |
| 35 | 15 23 | 13 34 | 11 25 | 09 09 | 09 17 |
| 36 | 15 17 | 13 20 | 11 05 | 08 45 | 08 54 |
| 37 | 15 10 | 13 06 | 10 44 | 08 20 | 08 31 |
| 38 | 15 03 | 12 51 | 10 23 | 07 55 | 08 06 |
| 39 | 14 56 | 12 37 | 10 02 | 07 29 | 07 41 |
| 40 | 14 49 | 12 22 | 09 40 | 07 03 | 07 15 |
| 41 | 14 42 | 12 07 | 09 19 | 06 36 | 06 47 |
| 42 | 14 35 | 11 52 | 08 56 | 06 08 | 06 19 |
| 43 | 14 28 | 11 37 | 08 34 | 05 40 | 05 50 |
| 44 | 14 20 | 11 21 | 08 11 | 05 11 | 05 19 |
| 45 | 14 13 | 11 06 | 07 48 | 04 41 | 04 47 |
| 46 | 14 05 | 10 50 | 07 24 | 04 11 | 04 13 |
| 47 | 13 57 | 10 34 | 07 00 | 03 39 | 03 38 |
| 48 | 13 49 | 10 17 | 06 36 | 03 07 | 03 01 |
| 49 | 13 41 | 10 00 | 06 11 | 02 34 | 02 22 |
| 50 | 13 32 | 09 43 | 05 45 | 02 00 | 01 41 |
| 51 | 13 24 | 09 26 | 05 19 | 01 25 | 00 58 |
| 52 | 13 15 | 09 08 | 04 53 | 00 49 | 00 12 |
| 53 | 13 06 | 08 50 | 04 26 | 00 12 | 29♐24 |
| 54 | 12 56 | 08 31 | 03 58 | 29♏33 | 28 32 |
| 55 | 12 46 | 08 12 | 03 29 | 28 53 | 27 38 |
| 56 | 12 36 | 07 52 | 03 00 | 28 12 | 26 39 |
| 57 | 12 25 | 07 32 | 02 30 | 27 29 | 25 37 |
| 58 | 12 14 | 07 11 | 01 59 | 26 45 | 24 30 |
| 59 | 12 03 | 06 50 | 01 28 | 25 59 | 23 18 |
| 60 | 11♍50 | 06♎27 | 00♏55 | 25♏12 | 22♐01 |

**9h 24m 0s — 141° 0' 0" — 18 ♌ 34**

| LAT. | 11 | 12 | ASC | 2 | 3 |
|---|---|---|---|---|---|
| 0 | 20♍12 | 22♎42 | 23♏23 | 21♐44 | 19♑24 |
| 5 | 19 36 | 21 26 | 21 46 | 20 11 | 18 20 |
| 10 | 19 03 | 20 14 | 20 12 | 18 38 | 17 14 |
| 15 | 18 30 | 19 04 | 18 39 | 17 03 | 16 04 |
| 20 | 17 58 | 17 55 | 17 06 | 15 25 | 14 49 |
| 21 | 17 52 | 17 42 | 16 47 | 15 05 | 14 33 |
| 22 | 17 45 | 17 28 | 16 29 | 14 45 | 14 16 |
| 23 | 17 39 | 17 14 | 16 10 | 14 24 | 14 00 |
| 24 | 17 33 | 17 01 | 15 51 | 14 03 | 13 43 |
| 25 | 17 26 | 16 47 | 15 32 | 13 42 | 13 26 |
| 26 | 17 20 | 16 34 | 15 13 | 13 21 | 13 08 |
| 27 | 17 14 | 16 20 | 14 53 | 13 00 | 12 50 |
| 28 | 17 07 | 16 06 | 14 34 | 12 38 | 12 31 |
| 29 | 17 01 | 15 52 | 14 15 | 12 16 | 12 12 |
| 30 | 16 54 | 15 39 | 13 55 | 11 53 | 11 53 |
| 31 | 16 48 | 15 25 | 13 35 | 11 31 | 11 33 |
| 32 | 16 41 | 15 11 | 13 15 | 11 08 | 11 12 |
| 33 | 16 35 | 14 56 | 12 55 | 10 44 | 10 51 |
| 34 | 16 28 | 14 42 | 12 35 | 10 20 | 10 29 |
| 35 | 16 21 | 14 28 | 12 14 | 09 56 | 10 07 |
| 36 | 16 14 | 14 14 | 11 53 | 09 31 | 09 44 |
| 37 | 16 07 | 13 59 | 11 32 | 09 06 | 09 19 |
| 38 | 16 00 | 13 44 | 11 11 | 08 40 | 08 55 |
| 39 | 15 53 | 13 30 | 10 49 | 08 14 | 08 29 |
| 40 | 15 46 | 13 15 | 10 28 | 07 47 | 08 02 |
| 41 | 15 39 | 12 59 | 10 05 | 07 19 | 07 34 |
| 42 | 15 32 | 12 44 | 09 43 | 06 51 | 07 05 |
| 43 | 15 24 | 12 28 | 09 20 | 06 22 | 06 35 |
| 44 | 15 17 | 12 13 | 08 57 | 05 53 | 06 04 |
| 45 | 15 09 | 11 57 | 08 33 | 05 22 | 05 31 |
| 46 | 15 01 | 11 40 | 08 09 | 04 51 | 04 57 |
| 47 | 14 53 | 11 24 | 07 44 | 04 19 | 04 21 |
| 48 | 14 45 | 11 07 | 07 19 | 03 47 | 03 43 |
| 49 | 14 36 | 10 50 | 06 54 | 03 13 | 03 03 |
| 50 | 14 28 | 10 32 | 06 28 | 02 38 | 02 21 |
| 51 | 14 19 | 10 14 | 06 01 | 02 02 | 01 37 |
| 52 | 14 09 | 09 56 | 05 34 | 01 26 | 00 51 |
| 53 | 14 00 | 09 38 | 05 07 | 00 47 | 00 01 |
| 54 | 13 50 | 09 19 | 04 38 | 00 08 | 29♐09 |
| 55 | 13 40 | 08 59 | 04 09 | 29♏27 | 28 13 |
| 56 | 13 30 | 08 39 | 03 39 | 28 45 | 27 13 |
| 57 | 13 19 | 08 18 | 03 09 | 28 02 | 26 09 |
| 58 | 13 08 | 07 57 | 02 37 | 27 16 | 25 01 |
| 59 | 12 56 | 07 35 | 02 05 | 26 29 | 23 47 |
| 60 | 12♍44 | 07♎13 | 01♏32 | 25♏41 | 22♐27 |

**9h 28m 0s — 142° 0' 0" — 19 ♌ 35**

| LAT. | 11 | 12 | ASC | 2 | 3 |
|---|---|---|---|---|---|
| 0 | 21♍17 | 23♎46 | 24♏22 | 22♐39 | 20♑20 |
| 5 | 20 40 | 22 28 | 22 44 | 21 05 | 19 16 |
| 10 | 20 05 | 21 15 | 21 08 | 19 31 | 18 09 |
| 15 | 19 32 | 20 03 | 19 34 | 17 55 | 16 59 |
| 20 | 18 59 | 18 54 | 18 00 | 16 16 | 15 42 |
| 21 | 18 52 | 18 40 | 17 41 | 15 56 | 15 26 |
| 22 | 18 46 | 18 26 | 17 22 | 15 35 | 15 10 |
| 23 | 18 39 | 18 12 | 17 03 | 15 14 | 14 53 |
| 24 | 18 33 | 17 58 | 16 43 | 14 53 | 14 36 |
| 25 | 18 26 | 17 44 | 16 24 | 14 32 | 14 18 |
| 26 | 18 20 | 17 30 | 16 05 | 14 11 | 14 00 |
| 27 | 18 13 | 17 16 | 15 45 | 13 49 | 13 42 |
| 28 | 18 07 | 17 02 | 15 26 | 13 27 | 13 23 |
| 29 | 18 00 | 16 48 | 15 06 | 13 04 | 13 04 |
| 30 | 17 53 | 16 34 | 14 46 | 12 42 | 12 44 |
| 31 | 17 46 | 16 20 | 14 26 | 12 19 | 12 24 |
| 32 | 17 40 | 16 05 | 14 05 | 11 55 | 12 03 |
| 33 | 17 33 | 15 51 | 13 45 | 11 31 | 11 41 |
| 34 | 17 26 | 15 37 | 13 24 | 11 07 | 11 19 |
| 35 | 17 19 | 15 22 | 13 03 | 10 42 | 10 56 |
| 36 | 17 12 | 15 07 | 12 42 | 10 17 | 10 33 |
| 37 | 17 05 | 14 52 | 12 21 | 09 51 | 10 08 |
| 38 | 16 58 | 14 37 | 11 59 | 09 25 | 09 43 |
| 39 | 16 51 | 14 22 | 11 37 | 08 58 | 09 17 |
| 40 | 16 43 | 14 07 | 11 15 | 08 31 | 08 49 |
| 41 | 16 36 | 13 51 | 10 52 | 08 03 | 08 21 |
| 42 | 16 28 | 13 36 | 10 29 | 07 34 | 07 52 |
| 43 | 16 21 | 13 20 | 10 06 | 07 05 | 07 21 |
| 44 | 16 13 | 13 04 | 09 42 | 06 35 | 06 49 |
| 45 | 16 05 | 12 47 | 09 18 | 06 04 | 06 16 |
| 46 | 15 57 | 12 31 | 08 54 | 05 32 | 05 41 |
| 47 | 15 49 | 12 14 | 08 29 | 05 00 | 05 04 |
| 48 | 15 40 | 11 57 | 08 03 | 04 26 | 04 25 |
| 49 | 15 32 | 11 39 | 07 37 | 03 52 | 03 45 |
| 50 | 15 23 | 11 21 | 07 11 | 03 17 | 03 02 |
| 51 | 15 14 | 11 03 | 06 44 | 02 40 | 02 17 |
| 52 | 15 04 | 10 45 | 06 16 | 02 02 | 01 29 |
| 53 | 14 55 | 10 26 | 05 48 | 01 23 | 00 39 |
| 54 | 14 45 | 10 06 | 05 19 | 00 43 | 29♐45 |
| 55 | 14 35 | 09 46 | 04 49 | 00 02 | 28 48 |
| 56 | 14 24 | 09 26 | 04 19 | 29♏19 | 27 47 |
| 57 | 14 13 | 09 05 | 03 47 | 28 34 | 26 41 |
| 58 | 14 02 | 08 44 | 03 15 | 27 48 | 25 31 |
| 59 | 13 50 | 08 21 | 02 43 | 27 00 | 24 15 |
| 60 | 13♍37 | 07♎58 | 02♏09 | 26♏10 | 22♐54 |

**9h 32m 0s — 143° 0' 0" — 20 ♌ 36**

| LAT. | 11 | 12 | ASC | 2 | 3 |
|---|---|---|---|---|---|
| 0 | 22♍23 | 24♎50 | 25♏21 | 23♐34 | 21♑17 |
| 5 | 21 44 | 23 31 | 23 41 | 22 00 | 20 12 |
| 10 | 21 08 | 22 15 | 22 04 | 20 25 | 19 05 |
| 15 | 20 34 | 21 03 | 20 29 | 18 48 | 17 53 |
| 20 | 20 00 | 19 52 | 18 53 | 17 07 | 16 36 |
| 21 | 19 53 | 19 38 | 18 34 | 16 47 | 16 20 |
| 22 | 19 47 | 19 23 | 18 15 | 16 26 | 16 03 |
| 23 | 19 40 | 19 09 | 17 55 | 16 05 | 15 46 |
| 24 | 19 33 | 18 55 | 17 36 | 15 44 | 15 29 |
| 25 | 19 26 | 18 41 | 17 16 | 15 22 | 15 11 |
| 26 | 19 20 | 18 27 | 16 57 | 15 00 | 14 53 |
| 27 | 19 13 | 18 12 | 16 37 | 14 38 | 14 34 |
| 28 | 19 06 | 17 58 | 16 17 | 14 16 | 14 15 |
| 29 | 18 59 | 17 44 | 15 57 | 13 53 | 13 56 |
| 30 | 18 52 | 17 29 | 15 37 | 13 30 | 13 36 |
| 31 | 18 45 | 17 15 | 15 16 | 13 06 | 13 15 |
| 32 | 18 38 | 17 00 | 14 55 | 12 43 | 12 54 |
| 33 | 18 31 | 16 46 | 14 35 | 12 18 | 12 32 |
| 34 | 18 24 | 16 31 | 14 14 | 11 54 | 12 09 |
| 35 | 18 17 | 16 16 | 13 52 | 11 29 | 11 46 |
| 36 | 18 10 | 16 01 | 13 31 | 11 03 | 11 22 |
| 37 | 18 03 | 15 46 | 13 09 | 10 37 | 10 57 |
| 38 | 17 56 | 15 31 | 12 47 | 10 10 | 10 31 |
| 39 | 17 48 | 15 15 | 12 25 | 09 43 | 10 05 |
| 40 | 17 41 | 14 59 | 12 02 | 09 15 | 09 37 |
| 41 | 17 33 | 14 44 | 11 39 | 08 47 | 09 08 |
| 42 | 17 25 | 14 28 | 11 16 | 08 17 | 08 38 |
| 43 | 17 17 | 14 11 | 10 52 | 07 48 | 08 07 |
| 44 | 17 09 | 13 55 | 10 28 | 07 17 | 07 34 |
| 45 | 17 01 | 13 38 | 10 03 | 06 46 | 07 00 |
| 46 | 16 53 | 13 21 | 09 38 | 06 13 | 06 25 |
| 47 | 16 45 | 13 04 | 09 13 | 05 40 | 05 47 |
| 48 | 16 36 | 12 47 | 08 47 | 05 06 | 05 08 |
| 49 | 16 27 | 12 29 | 08 20 | 04 31 | 04 26 |
| 50 | 16 18 | 12 11 | 07 53 | 03 55 | 03 43 |
| 51 | 16 09 | 11 52 | 07 26 | 03 18 | 02 57 |
| 52 | 15 59 | 11 33 | 06 58 | 02 39 | 02 08 |
| 53 | 15 50 | 11 14 | 06 29 | 01 59 | 01 16 |
| 54 | 15 39 | 10 54 | 05 59 | 01 18 | 00 21 |
| 55 | 15 29 | 10 34 | 05 29 | 00 36 | 29♐23 |
| 56 | 15 18 | 10 13 | 04 58 | 29♏52 | 28 20 |
| 57 | 15 07 | 09 52 | 04 26 | 29 06 | 27 13 |
| 58 | 14 56 | 09 30 | 03 53 | 28 19 | 26 01 |
| 59 | 14 44 | 09 07 | 03 20 | 27 30 | 24 44 |
| 60 | 14♍31 | 08♎44 | 02♏45 | 26♏39 | 23♐20 |

# Koch Table of Houses for Latitudes 0° to 60° North

**9h 36m 0s — 144° 0' 0" — 21 ♌ 37**

| LAT. | 11 | 12 | ASC | 2 | 3 |
|---|---|---|---|---|---|
| 0 | 23♍28 | 25♎53 | 26♏19 | 24♐30 | 22♑13 |
| 5 | 22 49 | 24 33 | 24 38 | 22 54 | 21 08 |
| 10 | 22 12 | 23 16 | 23 01 | 21 18 | 20 00 |
| 15 | 21 36 | 22 02 | 21 24 | 19 40 | 18 48 |
| 20 | 21 01 | 20 50 | 19 47 | 17 59 | 17 30 |
| 21 | 20 54 | 20 35 | 19 27 | 17 38 | 17 13 |
| 22 | 20 47 | 20 21 | 19 08 | 17 17 | 16 57 |
| 23 | 20 40 | 20 07 | 18 48 | 16 55 | 16 39 |
| 24 | 20 33 | 19 52 | 18 28 | 16 34 | 16 22 |
| 25 | 20 27 | 19 38 | 18 09 | 16 12 | 16 04 |
| 26 | 20 20 | 19 23 | 17 49 | 15 50 | 15 46 |
| 27 | 20 13 | 19 09 | 17 28 | 15 27 | 15 27 |
| 28 | 20 06 | 18 54 | 17 08 | 15 05 | 15 07 |
| 29 | 19 59 | 18 40 | 16 48 | 14 42 | 14 48 |
| 30 | 19 52 | 18 25 | 16 27 | 14 18 | 14 27 |
| 31 | 19 44 | 18 10 | 16 06 | 13 54 | 14 06 |
| 32 | 19 37 | 17 55 | 15 46 | 13 30 | 13 45 |
| 33 | 19 30 | 17 40 | 15 24 | 13 06 | 13 23 |
| 34 | 19 23 | 17 25 | 15 03 | 12 41 | 13 00 |
| 35 | 19 16 | 17 10 | 14 41 | 12 15 | 12 36 |
| 36 | 19 08 | 16 55 | 14 19 | 11 49 | 12 12 |
| 37 | 19 01 | 16 39 | 13 57 | 11 22 | 11 46 |
| 38 | 18 53 | 16 24 | 13 35 | 10 55 | 11 20 |
| 39 | 18 46 | 16 08 | 13 12 | 10 28 | 10 53 |
| 40 | 18 38 | 15 52 | 12 49 | 09 59 | 10 25 |
| 41 | 18 30 | 15 36 | 12 26 | 09 30 | 09 56 |
| 42 | 18 22 | 15 20 | 12 02 | 09 01 | 09 25 |
| 43 | 18 14 | 15 03 | 11 38 | 08 30 | 08 53 |
| 44 | 18 06 | 14 46 | 11 13 | 07 59 | 08 20 |
| 45 | 17 58 | 14 29 | 10 48 | 07 27 | 07 45 |
| 46 | 17 49 | 14 12 | 10 23 | 06 54 | 07 09 |
| 47 | 17 41 | 13 54 | 09 57 | 06 20 | 06 31 |
| 48 | 17 32 | 13 37 | 09 30 | 05 46 | 05 51 |
| 49 | 17 23 | 13 18 | 09 04 | 05 10 | 05 08 |
| 50 | 17 14 | 13 00 | 08 36 | 04 33 | 04 24 |
| 51 | 17 04 | 12 41 | 08 08 | 03 55 | 03 37 |
| 52 | 16 54 | 12 22 | 07 39 | 03 16 | 02 47 |
| 53 | 16 45 | 12 02 | 07 10 | 02 35 | 01 54 |
| 54 | 16 34 | 11 42 | 06 40 | 01 53 | 00 58 |
| 55 | 16 24 | 11 21 | 06 09 | 01 10 | 29♐58 |
| 56 | 16 13 | 11 00 | 05 37 | 00 25 | 28 54 |
| 57 | 16 02 | 10 39 | 05 05 | 29♏39 | 27 45 |
| 58 | 15 50 | 10 16 | 04 32 | 28 50 | 26 32 |
| 59 | 15 38 | 09 53 | 03 57 | 28 00 | 25 13 |
| 60 | 15♍25 | 09♎30 | 03♏22 | 27♏08 | 23♐47 |

**9h 40m 0s — 145° 0' 0" — 22 ♌ 39**

| LAT. | 11 | 12 | ASC | 2 | 3 |
|---|---|---|---|---|---|
| 0 | 24♍33 | 26♎57 | 27♏17 | 25♐25 | 23♑10 |
| 5 | 23 53 | 25 35 | 25 36 | 23 49 | 22 04 |
| 10 | 23 15 | 24 17 | 23 57 | 22 12 | 20 56 |
| 15 | 22 38 | 23 02 | 22 19 | 20 33 | 19 43 |
| 20 | 22 02 | 21 48 | 20 41 | 18 50 | 18 24 |
| 21 | 21 55 | 21 33 | 20 21 | 18 29 | 18 07 |
| 22 | 21 48 | 21 19 | 20 01 | 18 07 | 17 50 |
| 23 | 21 41 | 21 04 | 19 41 | 17 46 | 17 33 |
| 24 | 21 34 | 20 49 | 19 21 | 17 24 | 17 15 |
| 25 | 21 27 | 20 35 | 19 01 | 17 02 | 16 57 |
| 26 | 21 20 | 20 20 | 18 40 | 16 39 | 16 38 |
| 27 | 21 13 | 20 05 | 18 20 | 16 17 | 16 19 |
| 28 | 21 05 | 19 50 | 18 00 | 15 54 | 16 00 |
| 29 | 20 58 | 19 35 | 17 39 | 15 30 | 15 40 |
| 30 | 20 51 | 19 20 | 17 18 | 15 07 | 15 19 |
| 31 | 20 44 | 19 05 | 16 57 | 14 42 | 14 58 |
| 32 | 20 36 | 18 50 | 16 36 | 14 18 | 14 36 |
| 33 | 20 29 | 18 35 | 16 14 | 13 53 | 14 13 |
| 34 | 20 22 | 18 19 | 15 52 | 13 27 | 13 50 |
| 35 | 20 14 | 18 04 | 15 30 | 13 02 | 13 26 |
| 36 | 20 07 | 17 48 | 15 08 | 12 35 | 13 01 |
| 37 | 19 59 | 17 33 | 14 46 | 12 08 | 12 36 |
| 38 | 19 51 | 17 17 | 14 23 | 11 41 | 12 09 |
| 39 | 19 43 | 17 01 | 14 00 | 11 12 | 11 42 |
| 40 | 19 36 | 16 45 | 13 36 | 10 44 | 11 13 |
| 41 | 19 28 | 16 28 | 13 12 | 10 14 | 10 43 |
| 42 | 19 19 | 16 11 | 12 48 | 09 44 | 10 12 |
| 43 | 19 11 | 15 55 | 12 24 | 09 13 | 09 40 |
| 44 | 19 03 | 15 38 | 11 59 | 08 41 | 09 06 |
| 45 | 18 54 | 15 20 | 11 33 | 08 09 | 08 30 |
| 46 | 18 46 | 15 03 | 11 07 | 07 35 | 07 53 |
| 47 | 18 37 | 14 45 | 10 41 | 07 01 | 07 14 |
| 48 | 18 28 | 14 27 | 10 14 | 06 26 | 06 33 |
| 49 | 18 19 | 14 08 | 09 47 | 05 49 | 05 50 |
| 50 | 18 09 | 13 49 | 09 19 | 05 12 | 05 05 |
| 51 | 18 00 | 13 30 | 08 50 | 04 33 | 04 17 |
| 52 | 17 50 | 13 10 | 08 21 | 03 53 | 03 26 |
| 53 | 17 40 | 12 50 | 07 51 | 03 11 | 02 32 |
| 54 | 17 29 | 12 30 | 07 20 | 02 29 | 01 35 |
| 55 | 17 19 | 12 09 | 06 49 | 01 44 | 00 33 |
| 56 | 17 07 | 11 47 | 06 17 | 00 59 | 29♐28 |
| 57 | 16 56 | 11 25 | 05 44 | 00 11 | 28 18 |
| 58 | 16 44 | 11 03 | 05 10 | 29♏22 | 27 02 |
| 59 | 16 32 | 10 39 | 04 35 | 28 30 | 25 41 |
| 60 | 16♍19 | 10♎15 | 03♏59 | 27♏37 | 24♐14 |

**9h 44m 0s — 146° 0' 0" — 23 ♌ 41**

| LAT. | 11 | 12 | ASC | 2 | 3 |
|---|---|---|---|---|---|
| 0 | 25♍38 | 28♎00 | 28♏15 | 26♐20 | 24♑06 |
| 5 | 24 57 | 26 37 | 26 33 | 24 43 | 23 00 |
| 10 | 24 18 | 25 18 | 24 53 | 23 05 | 21 51 |
| 15 | 23 40 | 24 01 | 23 13 | 21 25 | 20 38 |
| 20 | 23 04 | 22 46 | 21 34 | 19 41 | 19 18 |
| 21 | 22 56 | 22 31 | 21 14 | 19 20 | 19 01 |
| 22 | 22 49 | 22 16 | 20 54 | 18 58 | 18 44 |
| 23 | 22 42 | 22 01 | 20 34 | 18 36 | 18 27 |
| 24 | 22 34 | 21 46 | 20 13 | 18 14 | 18 09 |
| 25 | 22 27 | 21 31 | 19 53 | 17 52 | 17 50 |
| 26 | 22 20 | 21 16 | 19 32 | 17 29 | 17 31 |
| 27 | 22 13 | 21 01 | 19 12 | 17 06 | 17 12 |
| 28 | 22 05 | 20 46 | 18 51 | 16 43 | 16 52 |
| 29 | 21 58 | 20 31 | 18 30 | 16 19 | 16 32 |
| 30 | 21 50 | 20 16 | 18 09 | 15 55 | 16 11 |
| 31 | 21 43 | 20 00 | 17 47 | 15 31 | 15 50 |
| 32 | 21 35 | 19 45 | 17 26 | 15 06 | 15 27 |
| 33 | 21 28 | 19 29 | 17 04 | 14 40 | 15 05 |
| 34 | 21 20 | 19 14 | 16 42 | 14 14 | 14 41 |
| 35 | 21 13 | 18 58 | 16 19 | 13 48 | 14 17 |
| 36 | 21 05 | 18 42 | 15 57 | 13 21 | 13 51 |
| 37 | 20 57 | 18 26 | 15 34 | 12 54 | 13 25 |
| 38 | 20 49 | 18 10 | 15 11 | 12 26 | 12 58 |
| 39 | 20 41 | 17 54 | 14 47 | 11 57 | 12 30 |
| 40 | 20 33 | 17 37 | 14 23 | 11 28 | 12 01 |
| 41 | 20 25 | 17 20 | 13 59 | 10 58 | 11 31 |
| 42 | 20 17 | 17 03 | 13 35 | 10 27 | 10 59 |
| 43 | 20 08 | 16 46 | 13 10 | 09 56 | 10 26 |
| 44 | 20 00 | 16 29 | 12 44 | 09 24 | 09 52 |
| 45 | 19 51 | 16 11 | 12 18 | 08 50 | 09 16 |
| 46 | 19 42 | 15 53 | 11 52 | 08 16 | 08 38 |
| 47 | 19 33 | 15 35 | 11 25 | 07 41 | 07 58 |
| 48 | 19 24 | 15 17 | 10 58 | 07 05 | 07 17 |
| 49 | 19 15 | 14 58 | 10 30 | 06 28 | 06 33 |
| 50 | 19 05 | 14 39 | 10 01 | 05 50 | 05 46 |
| 51 | 18 55 | 14 19 | 09 32 | 05 10 | 04 57 |
| 52 | 18 45 | 13 59 | 09 02 | 04 30 | 04 05 |
| 53 | 18 35 | 13 39 | 08 32 | 03 47 | 03 10 |
| 54 | 18 24 | 13 18 | 08 01 | 03 04 | 02 11 |
| 55 | 18 13 | 12 56 | 07 29 | 02 19 | 01 09 |
| 56 | 18 02 | 12 35 | 06 56 | 01 32 | 00 02 |
| 57 | 17 51 | 12 12 | 06 22 | 00 43 | 28♐50 |
| 58 | 17 39 | 11 49 | 05 48 | 29♏53 | 27 33 |
| 59 | 17 26 | 11 26 | 05 12 | 29 01 | 26 10 |
| 60 | 17♍13 | 11♎01 | 04♏35 | 28♏06 | 24♐41 |

**9h 48m 0s — 147° 0' 0" — 24 ♌ 42**

| LAT. | 11 | 12 | ASC | 2 | 3 |
|---|---|---|---|---|---|
| 0 | 26♍44 | 29♎03 | 29♏13 | 27♐15 | 25♑03 |
| 5 | 26 01 | 27 39 | 27 29 | 25 37 | 23 57 |
| 10 | 25 21 | 26 18 | 25 48 | 23 59 | 22 47 |
| 15 | 24 43 | 25 01 | 24 08 | 22 18 | 21 33 |
| 20 | 24 05 | 23 44 | 22 28 | 20 33 | 20 13 |
| 21 | 23 57 | 23 29 | 22 07 | 20 11 | 19 56 |
| 22 | 23 50 | 23 14 | 21 47 | 19 49 | 19 38 |
| 23 | 23 43 | 22 59 | 21 26 | 19 27 | 19 20 |
| 24 | 23 35 | 22 43 | 21 06 | 19 05 | 19 02 |
| 25 | 23 28 | 22 28 | 20 45 | 18 42 | 18 44 |
| 26 | 23 20 | 22 13 | 20 24 | 18 19 | 18 25 |
| 27 | 23 13 | 21 58 | 20 03 | 17 56 | 18 05 |
| 28 | 23 05 | 21 42 | 19 42 | 17 32 | 17 45 |
| 29 | 22 58 | 21 27 | 19 21 | 17 08 | 17 24 |
| 30 | 22 50 | 21 11 | 18 59 | 16 44 | 17 03 |
| 31 | 22 42 | 20 56 | 18 37 | 16 19 | 16 41 |
| 32 | 22 35 | 20 40 | 18 16 | 15 53 | 16 19 |
| 33 | 22 27 | 20 24 | 17 53 | 15 28 | 15 56 |
| 34 | 22 19 | 20 08 | 17 31 | 15 02 | 15 32 |
| 35 | 22 11 | 19 52 | 17 08 | 14 35 | 15 07 |
| 36 | 22 03 | 19 36 | 16 45 | 14 08 | 14 42 |
| 37 | 21 55 | 19 20 | 16 22 | 13 40 | 14 15 |
| 38 | 21 47 | 19 03 | 15 59 | 13 11 | 13 48 |
| 39 | 21 39 | 18 47 | 15 35 | 12 42 | 13 19 |
| 40 | 21 31 | 18 30 | 15 11 | 12 12 | 12 50 |
| 41 | 21 23 | 18 13 | 14 46 | 11 42 | 12 19 |
| 42 | 21 14 | 17 55 | 14 21 | 11 11 | 11 47 |
| 43 | 21 06 | 17 38 | 13 56 | 10 39 | 11 13 |
| 44 | 20 57 | 17 20 | 13 30 | 10 06 | 10 38 |
| 45 | 20 48 | 17 02 | 13 03 | 09 32 | 10 01 |
| 46 | 20 39 | 16 44 | 12 37 | 08 58 | 09 23 |
| 47 | 20 30 | 16 26 | 12 09 | 08 22 | 08 42 |
| 48 | 20 20 | 16 07 | 11 42 | 07 45 | 08 00 |
| 49 | 20 11 | 15 48 | 11 13 | 07 07 | 07 15 |
| 50 | 20 01 | 15 28 | 10 44 | 06 28 | 06 28 |
| 51 | 19 51 | 15 08 | 10 14 | 05 48 | 05 38 |
| 52 | 19 41 | 14 48 | 09 44 | 05 07 | 04 45 |
| 53 | 19 30 | 14 27 | 09 13 | 04 24 | 03 48 |
| 54 | 19 20 | 14 06 | 08 41 | 03 39 | 02 48 |
| 55 | 19 09 | 13 44 | 08 09 | 02 53 | 01 44 |
| 56 | 18 57 | 13 22 | 07 35 | 02 05 | 00 36 |
| 57 | 18 45 | 12 59 | 07 01 | 01 16 | 29♐23 |
| 58 | 18 33 | 12 36 | 06 26 | 00 24 | 28 04 |
| 59 | 18 21 | 12 12 | 05 49 | 29♏31 | 26 39 |
| 60 | 18♍07 | 11♎47 | 05♏12 | 28♏35 | 25♐07 |

**9h 52m 0s — 148° 0' 0" — 25 ♌ 44**

| LAT. | 11 | 12 | ASC | 2 | 3 |
|---|---|---|---|---|---|
| 0 | 27♍49 | 00♏06 | 00♐11 | 28♐10 | 26♑00 |
| 5 | 27 06 | 28♎40 | 28♏26 | 26 32 | 24 53 |
| 10 | 26 24 | 27 19 | 26 44 | 24 52 | 23 43 |
| 15 | 25 45 | 26 00 | 25 03 | 23 10 | 22 29 |
| 20 | 25 06 | 24 42 | 23 21 | 21 24 | 21 07 |
| 21 | 24 59 | 24 27 | 23 00 | 21 02 | 20 50 |
| 22 | 24 51 | 24 11 | 22 40 | 20 40 | 20 32 |
| 23 | 24 43 | 23 56 | 22 19 | 20 18 | 20 15 |
| 24 | 24 36 | 23 40 | 21 58 | 19 55 | 19 56 |
| 25 | 24 28 | 23 25 | 21 37 | 19 32 | 19 37 |
| 26 | 24 21 | 23 09 | 21 16 | 19 09 | 19 18 |
| 27 | 24 13 | 22 54 | 20 55 | 18 45 | 18 58 |
| 28 | 24 05 | 22 38 | 20 33 | 18 21 | 18 38 |
| 29 | 23 57 | 22 22 | 20 12 | 17 57 | 18 17 |
| 30 | 23 50 | 22 07 | 19 50 | 17 32 | 17 56 |
| 31 | 23 42 | 21 51 | 19 28 | 17 07 | 17 34 |
| 32 | 23 34 | 21 35 | 19 06 | 16 41 | 17 11 |
| 33 | 23 26 | 21 19 | 18 43 | 16 15 | 16 47 |
| 34 | 23 18 | 21 03 | 18 20 | 15 49 | 16 23 |
| 35 | 23 10 | 20 46 | 17 57 | 15 22 | 15 58 |
| 36 | 23 02 | 20 30 | 17 34 | 14 54 | 15 32 |
| 37 | 22 54 | 20 13 | 17 10 | 14 26 | 15 05 |
| 38 | 22 46 | 19 56 | 16 47 | 13 57 | 14 37 |
| 39 | 22 37 | 19 39 | 16 22 | 13 27 | 14 08 |
| 40 | 22 29 | 19 22 | 15 58 | 12 57 | 13 38 |
| 41 | 22 20 | 19 05 | 15 33 | 12 26 | 13 07 |
| 42 | 22 12 | 18 47 | 15 07 | 11 54 | 12 34 |
| 43 | 22 03 | 18 30 | 14 42 | 11 22 | 12 00 |
| 44 | 21 54 | 18 12 | 14 15 | 10 48 | 11 25 |
| 45 | 21 45 | 17 53 | 13 49 | 10 14 | 10 47 |
| 46 | 21 36 | 17 35 | 13 21 | 09 39 | 10 08 |
| 47 | 21 26 | 17 16 | 12 54 | 09 03 | 09 27 |
| 48 | 21 17 | 16 57 | 12 25 | 08 25 | 08 43 |
| 49 | 21 07 | 16 37 | 11 56 | 07 47 | 07 58 |
| 50 | 20 57 | 16 17 | 11 27 | 07 07 | 07 10 |
| 51 | 20 47 | 15 57 | 10 57 | 06 26 | 06 18 |
| 52 | 20 37 | 15 37 | 10 26 | 05 44 | 05 24 |
| 53 | 20 26 | 15 15 | 09 54 | 05 00 | 04 27 |
| 54 | 20 15 | 14 54 | 09 22 | 04 14 | 03 26 |
| 55 | 20 04 | 14 32 | 08 49 | 03 27 | 02 20 |
| 56 | 19 52 | 14 09 | 08 15 | 02 39 | 01 10 |
| 57 | 19 40 | 13 46 | 07 40 | 01 48 | 29♐55 |
| 58 | 19 28 | 13 22 | 07 04 | 00 56 | 28 35 |
| 59 | 19 15 | 12 58 | 06 27 | 00 01 | 27 08 |
| 60 | 19♍02 | 12♎33 | 05♏49 | 29♏04 | 25♐34 |

**9h 56m 0s — 149° 0' 0" — 26 ♌ 47**

| LAT. | 11 | 12 | ASC | 2 | 3 |
|---|---|---|---|---|---|
| 0 | 28♍55 | 01♏08 | 01♐08 | 29♐05 | 26♑57 |
| 5 | 28 10 | 29♎42 | 29♏23 | 27 26 | 25 50 |
| 10 | 27 28 | 28 19 | 27 40 | 25 46 | 24 40 |
| 15 | 26 47 | 26 59 | 25 57 | 24 03 | 23 24 |
| 20 | 26 08 | 25 40 | 24 14 | 22 15 | 22 02 |
| 21 | 26 00 | 25 24 | 23 54 | 21 53 | 21 45 |
| 22 | 25 52 | 25 09 | 23 33 | 21 31 | 21 27 |
| 23 | 25 44 | 24 53 | 23 12 | 21 08 | 21 09 |
| 24 | 25 37 | 24 37 | 22 50 | 20 45 | 20 50 |
| 25 | 25 29 | 24 22 | 22 29 | 20 22 | 20 31 |
| 26 | 25 21 | 24 06 | 22 08 | 19 59 | 20 12 |
| 27 | 25 13 | 23 50 | 21 46 | 19 35 | 19 52 |
| 28 | 25 05 | 23 34 | 21 24 | 19 10 | 19 31 |
| 29 | 24 57 | 23 18 | 21 03 | 18 46 | 19 10 |
| 30 | 24 49 | 23 02 | 20 40 | 18 21 | 18 48 |
| 31 | 24 41 | 22 46 | 20 18 | 17 55 | 18 26 |
| 32 | 24 33 | 22 30 | 19 56 | 17 29 | 18 03 |
| 33 | 24 25 | 22 13 | 19 33 | 17 03 | 17 39 |
| 34 | 24 17 | 21 57 | 19 10 | 16 36 | 17 15 |
| 35 | 24 09 | 21 40 | 18 46 | 16 08 | 16 49 |
| 36 | 24 01 | 21 24 | 18 23 | 15 40 | 16 23 |
| 37 | 23 52 | 21 07 | 17 59 | 15 12 | 15 56 |
| 38 | 23 44 | 20 50 | 17 35 | 14 42 | 15 27 |
| 39 | 23 35 | 20 32 | 17 10 | 14 12 | 14 58 |
| 40 | 23 27 | 20 15 | 16 45 | 13 42 | 14 27 |
| 41 | 23 18 | 19 57 | 16 20 | 13 10 | 13 55 |
| 42 | 23 09 | 19 40 | 15 54 | 12 38 | 13 22 |
| 43 | 23 00 | 19 21 | 15 28 | 12 05 | 12 47 |
| 44 | 22 51 | 19 03 | 15 01 | 11 31 | 12 11 |
| 45 | 22 42 | 18 45 | 14 34 | 10 56 | 11 33 |
| 46 | 22 33 | 18 26 | 14 06 | 10 20 | 10 53 |
| 47 | 22 23 | 18 07 | 13 38 | 09 43 | 10 11 |
| 48 | 22 13 | 17 47 | 13 09 | 09 05 | 09 27 |
| 49 | 22 03 | 17 27 | 12 40 | 08 26 | 08 41 |
| 50 | 21 53 | 17 07 | 12 10 | 07 46 | 07 51 |
| 51 | 21 43 | 16 46 | 11 39 | 07 04 | 06 59 |
| 52 | 21 32 | 16 25 | 11 07 | 06 21 | 06 04 |
| 53 | 21 22 | 16 04 | 10 35 | 05 36 | 05 06 |
| 54 | 21 10 | 15 42 | 10 02 | 04 50 | 04 03 |
| 55 | 20 59 | 15 20 | 09 29 | 04 02 | 02 56 |
| 56 | 20 47 | 14 57 | 08 54 | 03 12 | 01 45 |
| 57 | 20 35 | 14 33 | 08 18 | 02 21 | 00 28 |
| 58 | 20 23 | 14 09 | 07 42 | 01 27 | 29♐06 |
| 59 | 20 10 | 13 44 | 07 04 | 00 31 | 27 37 |
| 60 | 19♍56 | 13♎19 | 06♏25 | 29♏33 | 26♐01 |

**10h 0m 0s — 150° 0' 0" — 27 ♌ 49**

| LAT. | 11 | 12 | ASC | 2 | 3 |
|---|---|---|---|---|---|
| 0 | 00♎00 | 02♏11 | 02♐05 | 00♑00 | 27♑55 |
| 5 | 29♍14 | 00 43 | 00 19 | 28♐20 | 26 47 |
| 10 | 28 31 | 29♎19 | 28♏35 | 26 39 | 25 36 |
| 15 | 27 50 | 27 58 | 26 52 | 24 55 | 24 20 |
| 20 | 27 10 | 26 38 | 25 08 | 23 07 | 22 57 |
| 21 | 27 02 | 26 22 | 24 47 | 22 45 | 22 40 |
| 22 | 26 54 | 26 06 | 24 25 | 22 22 | 22 22 |
| 23 | 26 46 | 25 50 | 24 04 | 21 59 | 22 03 |
| 24 | 26 38 | 25 34 | 23 43 | 21 36 | 21 44 |
| 25 | 26 30 | 25 18 | 23 21 | 21 13 | 21 25 |
| 26 | 26 22 | 25 02 | 23 00 | 20 49 | 21 06 |
| 27 | 26 14 | 24 46 | 22 38 | 20 24 | 20 45 |
| 28 | 26 05 | 24 30 | 22 16 | 20 00 | 20 25 |
| 29 | 25 57 | 24 14 | 21 53 | 19 35 | 20 03 |
| 30 | 25 49 | 23 57 | 21 31 | 19 10 | 19 41 |
| 31 | 25 41 | 23 41 | 21 08 | 18 44 | 19 19 |
| 32 | 25 33 | 23 25 | 20 46 | 18 17 | 18 55 |
| 33 | 25 25 | 23 08 | 20 22 | 17 51 | 18 31 |
| 34 | 25 16 | 22 51 | 19 59 | 17 23 | 18 06 |
| 35 | 25 08 | 22 34 | 19 35 | 16 55 | 17 40 |
| 36 | 25 00 | 22 17 | 19 11 | 16 27 | 17 14 |
| 37 | 24 51 | 22 00 | 18 47 | 15 58 | 16 46 |
| 38 | 24 42 | 21 43 | 18 22 | 15 28 | 16 17 |
| 39 | 24 34 | 21 25 | 17 57 | 14 58 | 15 47 |
| 40 | 24 25 | 21 08 | 17 32 | 14 26 | 15 16 |
| 41 | 24 16 | 20 50 | 17 06 | 13 54 | 14 44 |
| 42 | 24 07 | 20 32 | 16 40 | 13 22 | 14 10 |
| 43 | 23 58 | 20 13 | 16 14 | 12 48 | 13 35 |
| 44 | 23 49 | 19 55 | 15 46 | 12 14 | 12 58 |
| 45 | 23 39 | 19 36 | 15 19 | 11 38 | 12 19 |
| 46 | 23 30 | 19 17 | 14 51 | 11 02 | 11 39 |
| 47 | 23 20 | 18 57 | 14 22 | 10 24 | 10 56 |
| 48 | 23 10 | 18 37 | 13 53 | 09 45 | 10 11 |
| 49 | 23 00 | 18 17 | 13 23 | 09 05 | 09 24 |
| 50 | 22 50 | 17 56 | 12 52 | 08 24 | 08 34 |
| 51 | 22 39 | 17 36 | 12 21 | 07 42 | 07 41 |
| 52 | 22 28 | 17 14 | 11 49 | 06 58 | 06 44 |
| 53 | 22 17 | 16 52 | 11 16 | 06 12 | 05 44 |
| 54 | 22 06 | 16 30 | 10 43 | 05 25 | 04 41 |
| 55 | 21 54 | 16 07 | 10 08 | 04 36 | 03 32 |
| 56 | 21 43 | 15 44 | 09 33 | 03 46 | 02 20 |
| 57 | 21 30 | 15 20 | 08 57 | 02 53 | 01 01 |
| 58 | 21 18 | 14 56 | 08 20 | 01 58 | 29♐37 |
| 59 | 21 05 | 14 30 | 07 41 | 01 01 | 28 07 |
| 60 | 20♍51 | 14♎04 | 07♏02 | 00♐02 | 26♐29 |

**10h 4m 0s — 151° 0' 0" — 28 ♌ 52**

| LAT. | 11 | 12 | ASC | 2 | 3 |
|---|---|---|---|---|---|
| 0 | 01♎05 | 03♏13 | 03♐03 | 00♑55 | 28♑52 |
| 5 | 00 19 | 01 44 | 01 16 | 29♐15 | 27 44 |
| 10 | 29♍35 | 00 19 | 29♏31 | 27 33 | 26 32 |
| 15 | 28 52 | 28♎57 | 27 46 | 25 48 | 25 16 |
| 20 | 28 11 | 27 36 | 26 01 | 23 59 | 23 52 |
| 21 | 28 03 | 27 20 | 25 40 | 23 36 | 23 35 |
| 22 | 27 55 | 27 04 | 25 18 | 23 13 | 23 17 |
| 23 | 27 47 | 26 47 | 24 57 | 22 50 | 22 58 |
| 24 | 27 39 | 26 31 | 24 35 | 22 27 | 22 39 |
| 25 | 27 30 | 26 15 | 24 13 | 22 03 | 22 20 |
| 26 | 27 22 | 25 59 | 23 51 | 21 39 | 22 00 |
| 27 | 27 14 | 25 42 | 23 29 | 21 14 | 21 39 |
| 28 | 27 06 | 25 26 | 23 07 | 20 49 | 21 18 |
| 29 | 26 57 | 25 09 | 22 44 | 20 24 | 20 57 |
| 30 | 26 49 | 24 53 | 22 22 | 19 58 | 20 34 |
| 31 | 26 41 | 24 36 | 21 59 | 19 32 | 20 11 |
| 32 | 26 33 | 24 19 | 21 36 | 19 06 | 19 48 |
| 33 | 26 24 | 24 03 | 21 12 | 18 38 | 19 23 |
| 34 | 26 16 | 23 46 | 20 48 | 18 11 | 18 58 |
| 35 | 26 07 | 23 29 | 20 24 | 17 42 | 18 32 |
| 36 | 25 58 | 23 11 | 20 00 | 17 13 | 18 05 |
| 37 | 25 50 | 22 54 | 19 35 | 16 44 | 17 37 |
| 38 | 25 41 | 22 36 | 19 10 | 16 14 | 17 08 |
| 39 | 25 32 | 22 18 | 18 45 | 15 43 | 16 37 |
| 40 | 25 23 | 22 00 | 18 19 | 15 11 | 16 06 |
| 41 | 25 14 | 21 42 | 17 53 | 14 39 | 15 33 |
| 42 | 25 05 | 21 24 | 17 27 | 14 06 | 14 59 |
| 43 | 24 56 | 21 05 | 17 00 | 13 31 | 14 23 |
| 44 | 24 46 | 20 46 | 16 32 | 12 56 | 13 45 |
| 45 | 24 37 | 20 27 | 16 04 | 12 20 | 13 06 |
| 46 | 24 27 | 20 07 | 15 35 | 11 43 | 12 25 |
| 47 | 24 17 | 19 48 | 15 06 | 11 05 | 11 41 |
| 48 | 24 07 | 19 27 | 14 36 | 10 26 | 10 56 |
| 49 | 23 57 | 19 07 | 14 06 | 09 45 | 10 07 |
| 50 | 23 46 | 18 46 | 13 35 | 09 03 | 09 16 |
| 51 | 23 35 | 18 25 | 13 03 | 08 20 | 08 22 |
| 52 | 23 24 | 18 03 | 12 31 | 07 35 | 07 25 |
| 53 | 23 13 | 17 41 | 11 57 | 06 49 | 06 24 |
| 54 | 23 02 | 17 18 | 11 23 | 06 01 | 05 18 |
| 55 | 22 50 | 16 55 | 10 48 | 05 11 | 04 09 |
| 56 | 22 38 | 16 31 | 10 13 | 04 19 | 02 54 |
| 57 | 22 26 | 16 07 | 09 36 | 03 26 | 01 35 |
| 58 | 22 13 | 15 42 | 08 58 | 02 30 | 00 09 |
| 59 | 22 00 | 15 17 | 08 19 | 01 32 | 28♐36 |
| 60 | 21♍46 | 14♎50 | 07♏39 | 00♐31 | 26♐56 |

# Koch Table of Houses for Latitudes 0° to 60° North

**10h 8m 0s — 152° 0' 0" — 29 ♌ 54**

| LAT. | 11 | 12 | ASC | 2 | 3 |
|---|---|---|---|---|---|
| 0 | 02♎11 | 04♏16 | 04♐00 | 01♑50 | 29♑49 |
| 5 | 01 23 | 02 46 | 02 12 | 00 09 | 28 41 |
| 10 | 00 38 | 01 20 | 00 26 | 28♐27 | 27 29 |
| 15 | 29♍55 | 29♎56 | 28♏41 | 26 41 | 26 12 |
| 20 | 29 13 | 28 34 | 26 54 | 24 50 | 24 48 |
| 21 | 29 05 | 28 17 | 26 33 | 24 28 | 24 30 |
| 22 | 28 56 | 28 01 | 26 11 | 24 04 | 24 12 |
| 23 | 28 48 | 27 45 | 25 49 | 23 41 | 23 53 |
| 24 | 28 40 | 27 28 | 25 27 | 23 17 | 23 34 |
| 25 | 28 31 | 27 12 | 25 05 | 22 53 | 23 14 |
| 26 | 28 23 | 26 55 | 24 43 | 22 29 | 22 54 |
| 27 | 28 14 | 26 38 | 24 21 | 22 04 | 22 33 |
| 28 | 28 06 | 26 22 | 23 58 | 21 39 | 22 12 |
| 29 | 27 58 | 26 05 | 23 35 | 21 13 | 21 50 |
| 30 | 27 49 | 25 48 | 23 12 | 20 47 | 21 28 |
| 31 | 27 41 | 25 31 | 22 49 | 20 21 | 21 04 |
| 32 | 27 32 | 25 14 | 22 26 | 19 54 | 20 40 |
| 33 | 27 24 | 24 57 | 22 02 | 19 26 | 20 16 |
| 34 | 27 15 | 24 40 | 21 38 | 18 58 | 19 50 |
| 35 | 27 06 | 24 23 | 21 13 | 18 29 | 19 24 |
| 36 | 26 57 | 24 05 | 20 49 | 18 00 | 18 56 |
| 37 | 26 49 | 23 47 | 20 24 | 17 30 | 18 28 |
| 38 | 26 40 | 23 29 | 19 58 | 17 00 | 17 58 |
| 39 | 26 31 | 23 11 | 19 33 | 16 28 | 17 28 |
| 40 | 26 21 | 22 53 | 19 07 | 15 56 | 16 56 |
| 41 | 26 12 | 22 35 | 18 40 | 15 23 | 16 22 |
| 42 | 26 03 | 22 16 | 18 13 | 14 49 | 15 47 |
| 43 | 25 53 | 21 57 | 17 46 | 14 15 | 15 11 |
| 44 | 25 44 | 21 38 | 17 18 | 13 39 | 14 33 |
| 45 | 25 34 | 21 18 | 16 49 | 13 02 | 13 53 |
| 46 | 25 24 | 20 58 | 16 20 | 12 25 | 13 11 |
| 47 | 25 14 | 20 38 | 15 50 | 11 46 | 12 27 |
| 48 | 25 04 | 20 18 | 15 20 | 11 06 | 11 40 |
| 49 | 24 53 | 19 57 | 14 49 | 10 25 | 10 51 |
| 50 | 24 43 | 19 36 | 14 18 | 09 42 | 09 59 |
| 51 | 24 32 | 19 14 | 13 46 | 08 58 | 09 04 |
| 52 | 24 21 | 18 52 | 13 12 | 08 12 | 08 05 |
| 53 | 24 09 | 18 29 | 12 39 | 07 25 | 07 03 |
| 54 | 23 58 | 18 06 | 12 04 | 06 36 | 05 56 |
| 55 | 23 46 | 17 43 | 11 28 | 05 45 | 04 45 |
| 56 | 23 33 | 17 19 | 10 52 | 04 53 | 03 30 |
| 57 | 23 21 | 16 54 | 10 14 | 03 58 | 02 08 |
| 58 | 23 08 | 16 29 | 09 36 | 03 01 | 00 40 |
| 59 | 22 55 | 16 03 | 08 56 | 02 02 | 29♐06 |
| 60 | 22♍41 | 15♎36 | 08♏15 | 01♐00 | 27♐23 |

**10h 12m 0s — 153° 0' 0" — 00 ♍ 57**

| LAT. | 11 | 12 | ASC | 2 | 3 |
|---|---|---|---|---|---|
| 0 | 03♎16 | 05♏18 | 04♐57 | 02♑45 | 00♒47 |
| 5 | 02 28 | 03 47 | 03 08 | 01 04 | 29♑39 |
| 10 | 01 42 | 02 19 | 01 21 | 29♐20 | 28 26 |
| 15 | 00 58 | 00 55 | 29♏35 | 27 34 | 27 08 |
| 20 | 00 15 | 29♎32 | 27 47 | 25 42 | 25 43 |
| 21 | 00 06 | 29 15 | 27 26 | 25 19 | 25 25 |
| 22 | 29♍58 | 28 58 | 27 04 | 24 56 | 25 07 |
| 23 | 29 49 | 28 42 | 26 42 | 24 32 | 24 48 |
| 24 | 29 41 | 28 25 | 26 20 | 24 08 | 24 29 |
| 25 | 29 32 | 28 08 | 25 57 | 23 44 | 24 09 |
| 26 | 29 24 | 27 51 | 25 35 | 23 19 | 23 49 |
| 27 | 29 15 | 27 35 | 25 12 | 22 54 | 23 28 |
| 28 | 29 07 | 27 18 | 24 49 | 22 29 | 23 06 |
| 29 | 28 58 | 27 01 | 24 26 | 22 03 | 22 44 |
| 30 | 28 49 | 26 44 | 24 03 | 21 36 | 22 21 |
| 31 | 28 41 | 26 27 | 23 39 | 21 10 | 21 58 |
| 32 | 28 32 | 26 09 | 23 16 | 20 42 | 21 34 |
| 33 | 28 23 | 25 52 | 22 51 | 20 14 | 21 08 |
| 34 | 28 14 | 25 34 | 22 27 | 19 46 | 20 43 |
| 35 | 28 05 | 25 17 | 22 02 | 19 17 | 20 16 |
| 36 | 27 57 | 24 59 | 21 37 | 18 47 | 19 48 |
| 37 | 27 47 | 24 41 | 21 12 | 18 17 | 19 19 |
| 38 | 27 38 | 24 23 | 20 46 | 17 46 | 18 49 |
| 39 | 27 29 | 24 04 | 20 20 | 17 14 | 18 18 |
| 40 | 27 20 | 23 46 | 19 54 | 16 41 | 17 46 |
| 41 | 27 10 | 23 27 | 19 27 | 16 08 | 17 12 |
| 42 | 27 01 | 23 08 | 19 00 | 15 33 | 16 36 |
| 43 | 26 51 | 22 49 | 18 32 | 14 58 | 15 59 |
| 44 | 26 41 | 22 29 | 18 03 | 14 22 | 15 21 |
| 45 | 26 32 | 22 09 | 17 34 | 13 45 | 14 40 |
| 46 | 26 21 | 21 49 | 17 05 | 13 06 | 13 57 |
| 47 | 26 11 | 21 29 | 16 35 | 12 27 | 13 12 |
| 48 | 26 01 | 21 08 | 16 04 | 11 46 | 12 25 |
| 49 | 25 50 | 20 47 | 15 33 | 11 04 | 11 35 |
| 50 | 25 39 | 20 25 | 15 01 | 10 21 | 10 42 |
| 51 | 25 28 | 20 03 | 14 28 | 09 36 | 09 46 |
| 52 | 25 17 | 19 41 | 13 54 | 08 50 | 08 46 |
| 53 | 25 05 | 19 18 | 13 20 | 08 01 | 07 42 |
| 54 | 24 54 | 18 55 | 12 45 | 07 12 | 06 35 |
| 55 | 24 42 | 18 31 | 12 08 | 06 20 | 05 22 |
| 56 | 24 29 | 18 06 | 11 31 | 05 26 | 04 05 |
| 57 | 24 16 | 17 41 | 10 53 | 04 31 | 02 42 |
| 58 | 24 03 | 17 16 | 10 14 | 03 33 | 01 12 |
| 59 | 23 50 | 16 49 | 09 33 | 02 32 | 29♐35 |
| 60 | 23♍36 | 16♎22 | 08♏52 | 01♐30 | 27♐51 |

**10h 16m 0s — 154° 0' 0" — 02 ♍ 00**

| LAT. | 11 | 12 | ASC | 2 | 3 |
|---|---|---|---|---|---|
| 0 | 04♎22 | 06♏19 | 05♐54 | 03♑40 | 01♒45 |
| 5 | 03 32 | 04 47 | 04 04 | 01 58 | 00 36 |
| 10 | 02 45 | 03 19 | 02 17 | 00 14 | 29♑23 |
| 15 | 02 00 | 01 54 | 00 29 | 28♐27 | 28 05 |
| 20 | 01 17 | 00 29 | 28♏41 | 26 34 | 26 39 |
| 21 | 01 08 | 00 12 | 28 19 | 26 11 | 26 21 |
| 22 | 00 59 | 29♎56 | 27 56 | 25 47 | 26 03 |
| 23 | 00 50 | 29 39 | 27 34 | 25 23 | 25 43 |
| 24 | 00 42 | 29 22 | 27 12 | 24 59 | 25 24 |
| 25 | 00 33 | 29 05 | 26 49 | 24 35 | 25 04 |
| 26 | 00 24 | 28 48 | 26 26 | 24 10 | 24 43 |
| 27 | 00 16 | 28 31 | 26 04 | 23 44 | 24 22 |
| 28 | 00 07 | 28 14 | 25 40 | 23 18 | 24 00 |
| 29 | 29♍58 | 27 56 | 25 17 | 22 52 | 23 38 |
| 30 | 29 49 | 27 39 | 24 53 | 22 26 | 23 15 |
| 31 | 29 41 | 27 22 | 24 30 | 21 58 | 22 51 |
| 32 | 29 32 | 27 04 | 24 06 | 21 31 | 22 27 |
| 33 | 29 23 | 26 47 | 23 41 | 21 02 | 22 01 |
| 34 | 29 14 | 26 29 | 23 16 | 20 34 | 21 35 |
| 35 | 29 05 | 26 11 | 22 52 | 20 04 | 21 08 |
| 36 | 28 56 | 25 53 | 22 26 | 19 34 | 20 40 |
| 37 | 28 47 | 25 34 | 22 01 | 19 03 | 20 11 |
| 38 | 28 37 | 25 16 | 21 34 | 18 32 | 19 40 |
| 39 | 28 28 | 24 57 | 21 08 | 17 59 | 19 09 |
| 40 | 28 18 | 24 39 | 20 41 | 17 26 | 18 36 |
| 41 | 28 09 | 24 20 | 20 14 | 16 52 | 18 02 |
| 42 | 27 59 | 24 00 | 19 46 | 16 18 | 17 26 |
| 43 | 27 49 | 23 41 | 19 18 | 15 42 | 16 48 |
| 44 | 27 39 | 23 21 | 18 49 | 15 05 | 16 09 |
| 45 | 27 29 | 23 01 | 18 20 | 14 27 | 15 27 |
| 46 | 27 19 | 22 40 | 17 50 | 13 48 | 14 44 |
| 47 | 27 08 | 22 19 | 17 19 | 13 08 | 13 58 |
| 48 | 26 58 | 21 58 | 16 48 | 12 27 | 13 10 |
| 49 | 26 47 | 21 37 | 16 16 | 11 44 | 12 19 |
| 50 | 26 36 | 21 15 | 15 43 | 11 00 | 11 25 |
| 51 | 26 25 | 20 53 | 15 10 | 10 14 | 10 28 |
| 52 | 26 13 | 20 30 | 14 36 | 09 27 | 09 27 |
| 53 | 26 02 | 20 07 | 14 01 | 08 38 | 08 22 |
| 54 | 25 50 | 19 43 | 13 25 | 07 47 | 07 13 |
| 55 | 25 37 | 19 19 | 12 48 | 06 55 | 05 59 |
| 56 | 25 25 | 18 54 | 12 11 | 06 00 | 04 40 |
| 57 | 25 12 | 18 28 | 11 32 | 05 03 | 03 15 |
| 58 | 24 59 | 18 02 | 10 52 | 04 04 | 01 44 |
| 59 | 24 45 | 17 36 | 10 11 | 03 03 | 00 05 |
| 60 | 24♍31 | 17♎08 | 09♏28 | 01♐59 | 28♐19 |

**10h 20m 0s — 155° 0' 0" — 03 ♍ 03**

| LAT. | 11 | 12 | ASC | 2 | 3 |
|---|---|---|---|---|---|
| 0 | 05♎27 | 07♏21 | 06♐50 | 04♑35 | 02♒43 |
| 5 | 04 36 | 05 48 | 05 00 | 02 53 | 01 34 |
| 10 | 03 49 | 04 19 | 03 12 | 01 08 | 00 21 |
| 15 | 03 03 | 02 52 | 01 23 | 29♐20 | 29♑02 |
| 20 | 02 18 | 01 27 | 29♏34 | 27 26 | 27 35 |
| 21 | 02 10 | 01 10 | 29 11 | 27 03 | 27 17 |
| 22 | 02 01 | 00 53 | 28 49 | 26 39 | 26 58 |
| 23 | 01 52 | 00 36 | 28 27 | 26 15 | 26 39 |
| 24 | 01 43 | 00 18 | 28 04 | 25 50 | 26 19 |
| 25 | 01 34 | 00 01 | 27 41 | 25 25 | 25 59 |
| 26 | 01 25 | 29♎44 | 27 18 | 25 00 | 25 38 |
| 27 | 01 16 | 29 27 | 26 55 | 24 34 | 25 17 |
| 28 | 01 08 | 29 09 | 26 32 | 24 08 | 24 55 |
| 29 | 00 59 | 28 52 | 26 08 | 23 42 | 24 32 |
| 30 | 00 50 | 28 34 | 25 44 | 23 15 | 24 09 |
| 31 | 00 41 | 28 17 | 25 20 | 22 47 | 23 45 |
| 32 | 00 32 | 27 59 | 24 56 | 22 19 | 23 20 |
| 33 | 00 23 | 27 41 | 24 31 | 21 51 | 22 55 |
| 34 | 00 13 | 27 23 | 24 06 | 21 21 | 22 28 |
| 35 | 00 04 | 27 05 | 23 41 | 20 52 | 22 01 |
| 36 | 29♍55 | 26 47 | 23 15 | 20 21 | 21 32 |
| 37 | 29 46 | 26 28 | 22 49 | 19 50 | 21 03 |
| 38 | 29 36 | 26 09 | 22 22 | 19 18 | 20 32 |
| 39 | 29 27 | 25 50 | 21 56 | 18 45 | 20 00 |
| 40 | 29 17 | 25 31 | 21 28 | 18 12 | 19 26 |
| 41 | 29 07 | 25 12 | 21 01 | 17 37 | 18 52 |
| 42 | 28 57 | 24 52 | 20 33 | 17 02 | 18 15 |
| 43 | 28 47 | 24 33 | 20 04 | 16 26 | 17 37 |
| 44 | 28 37 | 24 12 | 19 35 | 15 48 | 16 57 |
| 45 | 28 27 | 23 52 | 19 05 | 15 10 | 16 15 |
| 46 | 28 16 | 23 31 | 18 34 | 14 30 | 15 31 |
| 47 | 28 06 | 23 10 | 18 03 | 13 49 | 14 44 |
| 48 | 27 55 | 22 49 | 17 32 | 13 07 | 13 55 |
| 49 | 27 44 | 22 27 | 16 59 | 12 24 | 13 04 |
| 50 | 27 33 | 22 05 | 16 26 | 11 39 | 12 09 |
| 51 | 27 22 | 21 42 | 15 52 | 10 53 | 11 10 |
| 52 | 27 10 | 21 19 | 15 18 | 10 05 | 10 08 |
| 53 | 26 58 | 20 55 | 14 42 | 09 15 | 09 02 |
| 54 | 26 46 | 20 31 | 14 06 | 08 23 | 07 52 |
| 55 | 26 33 | 20 07 | 13 28 | 07 30 | 06 37 |
| 56 | 26 21 | 19 41 | 12 50 | 06 34 | 05 16 |
| 57 | 26 08 | 19 16 | 12 10 | 05 36 | 03 49 |
| 58 | 25 54 | 18 49 | 11 30 | 04 36 | 02 16 |
| 59 | 25 40 | 18 22 | 10 48 | 03 33 | 00 35 |
| 60 | 25♍26 | 17♎54 | 10♏05 | 02♐28 | 28♐47 |

**10h 24m 0s — 156° 0' 0" — 04 ♍ 07**

| LAT. | 11 | 12 | ASC | 2 | 3 |
|---|---|---|---|---|---|
| 0 | 06♎32 | 08♏23 | 07♐47 | 05♑30 | 03♒41 |
| 5 | 05 41 | 06 49 | 05 56 | 03 47 | 02 32 |
| 10 | 04 52 | 05 19 | 04 07 | 02 02 | 01 18 |
| 15 | 04 06 | 03 51 | 02 18 | 00 13 | 29♑59 |
| 20 | 03 20 | 02 24 | 00 27 | 28♐18 | 28 32 |
| 21 | 03 11 | 02 07 | 00 04 | 27 54 | 28 13 |
| 22 | 03 02 | 01 50 | 29♏42 | 27 30 | 27 54 |
| 23 | 02 53 | 01 33 | 29 19 | 27 06 | 27 35 |
| 24 | 02 44 | 01 15 | 28 56 | 26 41 | 27 15 |
| 25 | 02 35 | 00 58 | 28 33 | 26 16 | 26 55 |
| 26 | 02 26 | 00 40 | 28 10 | 25 51 | 26 34 |
| 27 | 02 17 | 00 23 | 27 46 | 25 25 | 26 12 |
| 28 | 02 08 | 00 05 | 27 23 | 24 58 | 25 50 |
| 29 | 01 59 | 29♎48 | 26 59 | 24 32 | 25 27 |
| 30 | 01 50 | 29 30 | 26 35 | 24 04 | 25 04 |
| 31 | 01 41 | 29 12 | 26 10 | 23 36 | 24 39 |
| 32 | 01 32 | 28 54 | 25 46 | 23 08 | 24 14 |
| 33 | 01 22 | 28 36 | 25 21 | 22 39 | 23 48 |
| 34 | 01 13 | 28 17 | 24 55 | 22 10 | 23 22 |
| 35 | 01 04 | 27 59 | 24 30 | 21 39 | 22 54 |
| 36 | 00 54 | 27 40 | 24 04 | 21 08 | 22 25 |
| 37 | 00 45 | 27 22 | 23 37 | 20 37 | 21 55 |
| 38 | 00 35 | 27 03 | 23 11 | 20 04 | 21 24 |
| 39 | 00 25 | 26 44 | 22 43 | 19 31 | 20 51 |
| 40 | 00 16 | 26 24 | 22 16 | 18 57 | 20 17 |
| 41 | 00 06 | 26 04 | 21 48 | 18 22 | 19 42 |
| 42 | 29♍56 | 25 45 | 21 19 | 17 46 | 19 05 |
| 43 | 29 45 | 25 24 | 20 50 | 17 10 | 18 26 |
| 44 | 29 35 | 25 04 | 20 20 | 16 32 | 17 46 |
| 45 | 29 25 | 24 43 | 19 50 | 15 53 | 17 03 |
| 46 | 29 14 | 24 22 | 19 19 | 15 12 | 16 18 |
| 47 | 29 03 | 24 01 | 18 48 | 14 31 | 15 31 |
| 48 | 28 52 | 23 39 | 18 16 | 13 48 | 14 41 |
| 49 | 28 41 | 23 17 | 17 43 | 13 04 | 13 48 |
| 50 | 28 30 | 22 54 | 17 09 | 12 18 | 12 52 |
| 51 | 28 18 | 22 31 | 16 35 | 11 31 | 11 53 |
| 52 | 28 06 | 22 08 | 16 00 | 10 42 | 10 50 |
| 53 | 27 54 | 21 44 | 15 23 | 09 51 | 09 43 |
| 54 | 27 42 | 21 19 | 14 46 | 08 59 | 08 31 |
| 55 | 27 29 | 20 54 | 14 08 | 08 04 | 07 14 |
| 56 | 27 17 | 20 29 | 13 29 | 07 08 | 05 52 |
| 57 | 27 03 | 20 03 | 12 49 | 06 09 | 04 24 |
| 58 | 26 50 | 19 36 | 12 08 | 05 08 | 02 48 |
| 59 | 26 36 | 19 08 | 11 25 | 04 04 | 01 06 |
| 60 | 26♍21 | 18♎40 | 10♏42 | 02♐57 | 29♐15 |

**10h 28m 0s — 157° 0' 0" — 05 ♍ 10**

| LAT. | 11 | 12 | ASC | 2 | 3 |
|---|---|---|---|---|---|
| 0 | 07♎37 | 09♏24 | 08♐43 | 06♑26 | 04♒39 |
| 5 | 06 45 | 07 49 | 06 52 | 04 42 | 03 30 |
| 10 | 05 56 | 06 18 | 05 02 | 02 56 | 02 16 |
| 15 | 05 08 | 04 50 | 03 12 | 01 06 | 00 56 |
| 20 | 04 22 | 03 22 | 01 20 | 29♐10 | 29♑28 |
| 21 | 04 13 | 03 05 | 00 57 | 28 46 | 29 10 |
| 22 | 04 04 | 02 47 | 00 34 | 28 22 | 28 51 |
| 23 | 03 55 | 02 29 | 00 11 | 27 58 | 28 31 |
| 24 | 03 46 | 02 12 | 29♏48 | 27 33 | 28 11 |
| 25 | 03 36 | 01 54 | 29 25 | 27 07 | 27 50 |
| 26 | 03 27 | 01 37 | 29 02 | 26 41 | 27 29 |
| 27 | 03 18 | 01 19 | 28 38 | 26 15 | 27 07 |
| 28 | 03 09 | 01 01 | 28 14 | 25 49 | 26 45 |
| 29 | 03 00 | 00 43 | 27 50 | 25 21 | 26 22 |
| 30 | 02 50 | 00 25 | 27 25 | 24 54 | 25 58 |
| 31 | 02 41 | 00 07 | 27 01 | 24 26 | 25 34 |
| 32 | 02 32 | 29♎49 | 26 36 | 23 57 | 25 08 |
| 33 | 02 22 | 29 30 | 26 10 | 23 28 | 24 42 |
| 34 | 02 13 | 29 12 | 25 45 | 22 58 | 24 15 |
| 35 | 02 03 | 28 53 | 25 19 | 22 27 | 23 47 |
| 36 | 01 54 | 28 34 | 24 52 | 21 56 | 23 18 |
| 37 | 01 44 | 28 15 | 24 26 | 21 24 | 22 47 |
| 38 | 01 34 | 27 56 | 23 59 | 20 51 | 22 16 |
| 39 | 01 24 | 27 37 | 23 31 | 20 17 | 21 43 |
| 40 | 01 14 | 27 17 | 23 03 | 19 43 | 21 09 |
| 41 | 01 04 | 26 57 | 22 35 | 19 07 | 20 33 |
| 42 | 00 54 | 26 37 | 22 06 | 18 31 | 19 55 |
| 43 | 00 44 | 26 16 | 21 36 | 17 54 | 19 16 |
| 44 | 00 33 | 25 56 | 21 06 | 17 15 | 18 35 |
| 45 | 00 23 | 25 35 | 20 35 | 16 35 | 17 51 |
| 46 | 00 12 | 25 13 | 20 04 | 15 55 | 17 06 |
| 47 | 00 01 | 24 52 | 19 32 | 15 12 | 16 18 |
| 48 | 29♍50 | 24 29 | 19 00 | 14 29 | 15 27 |
| 49 | 29 38 | 24 07 | 18 26 | 13 44 | 14 34 |
| 50 | 29 27 | 23 44 | 17 52 | 12 58 | 13 37 |
| 51 | 29 15 | 23 21 | 17 17 | 12 10 | 12 36 |
| 52 | 29 03 | 22 57 | 16 41 | 11 20 | 11 32 |
| 53 | 28 51 | 22 33 | 16 05 | 10 28 | 10 24 |
| 54 | 28 38 | 22 08 | 15 27 | 09 35 | 09 11 |
| 55 | 28 26 | 21 42 | 14 48 | 08 39 | 07 52 |
| 56 | 28 13 | 21 16 | 14 09 | 07 42 | 06 28 |
| 57 | 27 59 | 20 50 | 13 28 | 06 42 | 04 58 |
| 58 | 27 45 | 20 23 | 12 46 | 05 39 | 03 21 |
| 59 | 27 31 | 19 55 | 12 03 | 04 34 | 01 36 |
| 60 | 27♍16 | 19♎26 | 11♏18 | 03♐27 | 29♐43 |

**10h 32m 0s — 158° 0' 0" — 06 ♍ 14**

| LAT. | 11 | 12 | ASC | 2 | 3 |
|---|---|---|---|---|---|
| 0 | 08♎43 | 10♏25 | 09♐40 | 07♑21 | 05♒38 |
| 5 | 07 49 | 08 49 | 07 48 | 05 36 | 04 28 |
| 10 | 06 59 | 07 18 | 05 57 | 03 50 | 03 14 |
| 15 | 06 11 | 05 48 | 04 06 | 01 59 | 01 53 |
| 20 | 05 24 | 04 19 | 02 13 | 00 03 | 00 25 |
| 21 | 05 15 | 04 02 | 01 50 | 29♐38 | 00 06 |
| 22 | 05 05 | 03 44 | 01 27 | 29 14 | 29♑47 |
| 23 | 04 56 | 03 26 | 01 04 | 28 49 | 29 27 |
| 24 | 04 47 | 03 09 | 00 41 | 28 24 | 29 07 |
| 25 | 04 38 | 02 51 | 00 17 | 27 58 | 28 46 |
| 26 | 04 28 | 02 33 | 29♏53 | 27 32 | 28 25 |
| 27 | 04 19 | 02 15 | 29 29 | 27 06 | 28 03 |
| 28 | 04 10 | 01 57 | 29 05 | 26 39 | 27 41 |
| 29 | 04 00 | 01 39 | 28 41 | 26 11 | 27 17 |
| 30 | 03 51 | 01 20 | 28 16 | 25 44 | 26 53 |
| 31 | 03 41 | 01 02 | 27 51 | 25 15 | 26 28 |
| 32 | 03 32 | 00 44 | 27 26 | 24 46 | 26 03 |
| 33 | 03 22 | 00 25 | 27 00 | 24 16 | 25 36 |
| 34 | 03 13 | 00 06 | 26 34 | 23 46 | 25 09 |
| 35 | 03 03 | 29♎47 | 26 08 | 23 15 | 24 40 |
| 36 | 02 53 | 29 28 | 25 41 | 22 43 | 24 11 |
| 37 | 02 43 | 29 09 | 25 14 | 22 11 | 23 40 |
| 38 | 02 33 | 28 49 | 24 47 | 21 38 | 23 08 |
| 39 | 02 23 | 28 30 | 24 19 | 21 04 | 22 35 |
| 40 | 02 13 | 28 10 | 23 51 | 20 29 | 22 00 |
| 41 | 02 03 | 27 49 | 23 22 | 19 53 | 21 24 |
| 42 | 01 53 | 27 29 | 22 52 | 19 16 | 20 46 |
| 43 | 01 42 | 27 08 | 22 22 | 18 38 | 20 06 |
| 44 | 01 31 | 26 47 | 21 52 | 17 59 | 19 24 |
| 45 | 01 21 | 26 26 | 21 21 | 17 18 | 18 40 |
| 46 | 01 10 | 26 04 | 20 49 | 16 37 | 17 54 |
| 47 | 00 59 | 25 42 | 20 17 | 15 54 | 17 05 |
| 48 | 00 47 | 25 20 | 19 44 | 15 10 | 16 14 |
| 49 | 00 36 | 24 57 | 19 10 | 14 24 | 15 19 |
| 50 | 00 24 | 24 34 | 18 35 | 13 37 | 14 21 |
| 51 | 00 12 | 24 10 | 18 00 | 12 48 | 13 20 |
| 52 | 00 00 | 23 46 | 17 23 | 11 58 | 12 14 |
| 53 | 29♍48 | 23 21 | 16 46 | 11 05 | 11 05 |
| 54 | 29 35 | 22 56 | 16 08 | 10 11 | 09 50 |
| 55 | 29 22 | 22 30 | 15 29 | 09 14 | 08 30 |
| 56 | 29 09 | 22 04 | 14 48 | 08 16 | 07 05 |
| 57 | 28 55 | 21 37 | 14 07 | 07 15 | 05 33 |
| 58 | 28 41 | 21 09 | 13 24 | 06 11 | 03 54 |
| 59 | 28 27 | 20 41 | 12 40 | 05 05 | 02 07 |
| 60 | 28♍12 | 20♎12 | 11♏55 | 03♐56 | 00♑11 |

**10h 36m 0s — 159° 0' 0" — 07 ♍ 18**

| LAT. | 11 | 12 | ASC | 2 | 3 |
|---|---|---|---|---|---|
| 0 | 09♎48 | 11♏26 | 10♐36 | 08♑16 | 06♒37 |
| 5 | 08 54 | 09 50 | 08 43 | 06 31 | 05 26 |
| 10 | 08 03 | 08 17 | 06 52 | 04 44 | 04 12 |
| 15 | 07 14 | 06 46 | 05 00 | 02 52 | 02 51 |
| 20 | 06 26 | 05 17 | 03 06 | 00 55 | 01 22 |
| 21 | 06 17 | 04 59 | 02 43 | 00 31 | 01 03 |
| 22 | 06 07 | 04 41 | 02 20 | 00 06 | 00 44 |
| 23 | 05 58 | 04 23 | 01 56 | 29♐41 | 00 24 |
| 24 | 05 48 | 04 05 | 01 33 | 29 15 | 00 04 |
| 25 | 05 39 | 03 47 | 01 09 | 28 50 | 29♑43 |
| 26 | 05 29 | 03 29 | 00 45 | 28 23 | 29 21 |
| 27 | 05 20 | 03 11 | 00 21 | 27 57 | 28 59 |
| 28 | 05 10 | 02 52 | 29♏56 | 27 29 | 28 36 |
| 29 | 05 01 | 02 34 | 29 32 | 27 02 | 28 13 |
| 30 | 04 51 | 02 16 | 29 07 | 26 33 | 27 49 |
| 31 | 04 42 | 01 57 | 28 41 | 26 05 | 27 24 |
| 32 | 04 32 | 01 38 | 28 16 | 25 35 | 26 58 |
| 33 | 04 22 | 01 20 | 27 50 | 25 05 | 26 31 |
| 34 | 04 12 | 01 00 | 27 24 | 24 34 | 26 03 |
| 35 | 04 03 | 00 41 | 26 57 | 24 03 | 25 34 |
| 36 | 03 53 | 00 22 | 26 30 | 23 31 | 25 04 |
| 37 | 03 43 | 00 02 | 26 03 | 22 58 | 24 33 |
| 38 | 03 32 | 29♎43 | 25 35 | 22 24 | 24 01 |
| 39 | 03 22 | 29 23 | 25 07 | 21 50 | 23 27 |
| 40 | 03 12 | 29 02 | 24 38 | 21 14 | 22 52 |
| 41 | 03 02 | 28 42 | 24 09 | 20 38 | 22 15 |
| 42 | 02 51 | 28 21 | 23 39 | 20 01 | 21 37 |
| 43 | 02 40 | 28 00 | 23 09 | 19 22 | 20 56 |
| 44 | 02 30 | 27 39 | 22 38 | 18 42 | 20 14 |
| 45 | 02 19 | 27 17 | 22 06 | 18 02 | 19 29 |
| 46 | 02 08 | 26 55 | 21 34 | 17 20 | 18 42 |
| 47 | 01 56 | 26 33 | 21 01 | 16 36 | 17 53 |
| 48 | 01 45 | 26 10 | 20 28 | 15 51 | 17 00 |
| 49 | 01 33 | 25 47 | 19 53 | 15 05 | 16 05 |
| 50 | 01 21 | 25 24 | 19 18 | 14 17 | 15 06 |
| 51 | 01 09 | 25 00 | 18 42 | 13 27 | 14 04 |
| 52 | 00 57 | 24 35 | 18 05 | 12 36 | 12 57 |
| 53 | 00 44 | 24 10 | 17 27 | 11 42 | 11 46 |
| 54 | 00 31 | 23 45 | 16 49 | 10 47 | 10 30 |
| 55 | 00 18 | 23 18 | 16 09 | 09 50 | 09 09 |
| 56 | 00 05 | 22 52 | 15 28 | 08 50 | 07 42 |
| 57 | 29♍51 | 22 24 | 14 46 | 07 48 | 06 08 |
| 58 | 29 37 | 21 56 | 14 02 | 06 43 | 04 27 |
| 59 | 29 22 | 21 27 | 13 18 | 05 36 | 02 38 |
| 60 | 29♍07 | 20♎58 | 12♏32 | 04♐25 | 00♑40 |

# Koch Table of Houses for Latitudes 0° to 60° North

10h 40m 0s — 160° 0' 0" — 08 ♍ 22

| LAT. | 11 | 12 | ASC | 2 | 3 |
|---|---|---|---|---|---|
| 0 | 10♎53 | 12♏27 | 11♐32 | 09♑11 | 07♒35 |
| 5 | 09 58 | 10 50 | 09 39 | 07 26 | 06 25 |
| 10 | 09 06 | 09 16 | 07 47 | 05 38 | 05 10 |
| 15 | 08 17 | 07 45 | 05 54 | 03 46 | 03 49 |
| 20 | 07 28 | 06 14 | 03 59 | 01 48 | 02 20 |
| 21 | 07 18 | 05 56 | 03 36 | 01 23 | 02 01 |
| 22 | 07 09 | 05 38 | 03 12 | 00 58 | 01 41 |
| 23 | 06 59 | 05 20 | 02 49 | 00 33 | 01 21 |
| 24 | 06 50 | 05 02 | 02 25 | 00 07 | 01 00 |
| 25 | 06 40 | 04 43 | 02 01 | 29♐41 | 00 39 |
| 26 | 06 30 | 04 25 | 01 37 | 29 14 | 00 18 |
| 27 | 06 21 | 04 07 | 01 12 | 28 47 | 29♑55 |
| 28 | 06 11 | 03 48 | 00 48 | 28 20 | 29 32 |
| 29 | 06 01 | 03 30 | 00 23 | 27 52 | 29 09 |
| 30 | 05 52 | 03 11 | 29♏57 | 27 23 | 28 44 |
| 31 | 05 42 | 02 52 | 29 32 | 26 54 | 28 19 |
| 32 | 05 32 | 02 33 | 29 06 | 26 25 | 27 53 |
| 33 | 05 22 | 02 14 | 28 40 | 25 54 | 27 26 |
| 34 | 05 12 | 01 55 | 28 13 | 25 23 | 26 58 |
| 35 | 05 02 | 01 35 | 27 46 | 24 51 | 26 28 |
| 36 | 04 52 | 01 16 | 27 19 | 24 19 | 25 58 |
| 37 | 04 42 | 00 56 | 26 51 | 23 46 | 25 27 |
| 38 | 04 32 | 00 36 | 26 23 | 23 11 | 24 54 |
| 39 | 04 21 | 00 16 | 25 55 | 22 36 | 24 20 |
| 40 | 04 11 | 29♎55 | 25 26 | 22 01 | 23 44 |
| 41 | 04 00 | 29 35 | 24 56 | 21 24 | 23 07 |
| 42 | 03 50 | 29 14 | 24 26 | 20 46 | 22 28 |
| 43 | 03 39 | 28 52 | 23 55 | 20 07 | 21 47 |
| 44 | 03 28 | 28 31 | 23 24 | 19 26 | 21 04 |
| 45 | 03 17 | 28 09 | 22 52 | 18 45 | 20 19 |
| 46 | 03 05 | 27 46 | 22 19 | 18 02 | 19 31 |
| 47 | 02 54 | 27 24 | 21 46 | 17 18 | 18 41 |
| 48 | 02 42 | 27 01 | 21 12 | 16 33 | 17 47 |
| 49 | 02 31 | 26 37 | 20 37 | 15 45 | 16 51 |
| 50 | 02 18 | 26 13 | 20 01 | 14 57 | 15 51 |
| 51 | 02 06 | 25 49 | 19 25 | 14 06 | 14 48 |
| 52 | 01 54 | 25 24 | 18 47 | 13 14 | 13 40 |
| 53 | 01 41 | 24 59 | 18 09 | 12 20 | 12 28 |
| 54 | 01 28 | 24 33 | 17 29 | 11 23 | 11 11 |
| 55 | 01 15 | 24 06 | 16 49 | 10 25 | 09 48 |
| 56 | 01 01 | 23 39 | 16 07 | 09 24 | 08 19 |
| 57 | 00 47 | 23 12 | 15 24 | 08 21 | 06 43 |
| 58 | 00 33 | 22 43 | 14 40 | 07 15 | 05 00 |
| 59 | 00 18 | 22 14 | 13 55 | 06 06 | 03 09 |
| 60 | 00♎03 | 21♎44 | 13♏08 | 04♐55 | 01♑09 |

10h 44m 0s — 161° 0' 0" — 09 ♍ 26

| LAT. | 11 | 12 | ASC | 2 | 3 |
|---|---|---|---|---|---|
| 0 | 11♎58 | 13♏27 | 12♐28 | 10♑07 | 08♒34 |
| 5 | 11 02 | 11 49 | 10 34 | 08 21 | 07 24 |
| 10 | 10 10 | 10 15 | 08 41 | 06 32 | 06 08 |
| 15 | 09 19 | 08 43 | 06 48 | 04 40 | 04 47 |
| 20 | 08 30 | 07 11 | 04 52 | 02 40 | 03 17 |
| 21 | 08 20 | 06 53 | 04 29 | 02 16 | 02 58 |
| 22 | 08 10 | 06 35 | 04 05 | 01 50 | 02 38 |
| 23 | 08 01 | 06 17 | 03 41 | 01 25 | 02 18 |
| 24 | 07 51 | 05 58 | 03 17 | 00 59 | 01 57 |
| 25 | 07 41 | 05 40 | 02 53 | 00 33 | 01 36 |
| 26 | 07 31 | 05 21 | 02 28 | 00 06 | 01 14 |
| 27 | 07 22 | 05 03 | 02 04 | 29♐38 | 00 52 |
| 28 | 07 12 | 04 44 | 01 39 | 29 11 | 00 29 |
| 29 | 07 02 | 04 25 | 01 14 | 28 42 | 00 05 |
| 30 | 06 52 | 04 06 | 00 48 | 28 14 | 29♑40 |
| 31 | 06 42 | 03 47 | 00 22 | 27 44 | 29 14 |
| 32 | 06 32 | 03 28 | 29♏56 | 27 14 | 28 48 |
| 33 | 06 22 | 03 09 | 29 30 | 26 43 | 28 21 |
| 34 | 06 12 | 02 49 | 29 03 | 26 12 | 27 52 |
| 35 | 06 02 | 02 29 | 28 36 | 25 40 | 27 23 |
| 36 | 05 52 | 02 10 | 28 08 | 25 07 | 26 52 |
| 37 | 05 41 | 01 50 | 27 40 | 24 33 | 26 21 |
| 38 | 05 31 | 01 29 | 27 11 | 23 59 | 25 48 |
| 39 | 05 21 | 01 09 | 26 43 | 23 23 | 25 13 |
| 40 | 05 10 | 00 48 | 26 13 | 22 47 | 24 37 |
| 41 | 04 59 | 00 27 | 25 43 | 22 09 | 23 59 |
| 42 | 04 48 | 00 06 | 25 13 | 21 31 | 23 20 |
| 43 | 04 37 | 29♎44 | 24 41 | 20 51 | 22 38 |
| 44 | 04 26 | 29 22 | 24 10 | 20 11 | 21 54 |
| 45 | 04 15 | 29 00 | 23 37 | 19 28 | 21 09 |
| 46 | 04 03 | 28 37 | 23 04 | 18 45 | 20 20 |
| 47 | 03 52 | 28 15 | 22 30 | 18 00 | 19 29 |
| 48 | 03 40 | 27 51 | 21 56 | 17 14 | 18 35 |
| 49 | 03 28 | 27 27 | 21 20 | 16 26 | 17 38 |
| 50 | 03 16 | 27 03 | 20 44 | 15 37 | 16 37 |
| 51 | 03 03 | 26 38 | 20 07 | 14 45 | 15 32 |
| 52 | 02 51 | 26 13 | 19 29 | 13 52 | 14 23 |
| 53 | 02 38 | 25 48 | 18 50 | 12 57 | 13 10 |
| 54 | 02 25 | 25 21 | 18 10 | 12 00 | 11 51 |
| 55 | 02 11 | 24 54 | 17 29 | 11 00 | 10 27 |
| 56 | 01 57 | 24 27 | 16 47 | 09 58 | 08 56 |
| 57 | 01 43 | 23 59 | 16 03 | 08 54 | 07 19 |
| 58 | 01 29 | 23 30 | 15 18 | 07 47 | 05 34 |
| 59 | 01 14 | 23 00 | 14 32 | 06 37 | 03 41 |
| 60 | 00♎58 | 22♎30 | 13♏45 | 05♐24 | 01♑38 |

10h 48m 0s — 162° 0' 0" — 10 ♍ 30

| LAT. | 11 | 12 | ASC | 2 | 3 |
|---|---|---|---|---|---|
| 0 | 13♎03 | 14♏28 | 13♐24 | 11♑02 | 09♒34 |
| 5 | 12 06 | 12 49 | 11 30 | 09 16 | 08 23 |
| 10 | 11 13 | 11 14 | 09 36 | 07 27 | 07 07 |
| 15 | 10 22 | 09 41 | 07 42 | 05 33 | 05 45 |
| 20 | 09 32 | 08 09 | 05 45 | 03 33 | 04 15 |
| 21 | 09 22 | 07 50 | 05 22 | 03 08 | 03 56 |
| 22 | 09 12 | 07 32 | 04 58 | 02 43 | 03 36 |
| 23 | 09 02 | 07 13 | 04 34 | 02 17 | 03 16 |
| 24 | 08 52 | 06 55 | 04 09 | 01 51 | 02 55 |
| 25 | 08 42 | 06 36 | 03 45 | 01 24 | 02 33 |
| 26 | 08 33 | 06 17 | 03 20 | 00 57 | 02 11 |
| 27 | 08 23 | 05 58 | 02 55 | 00 30 | 01 49 |
| 28 | 08 13 | 05 39 | 02 30 | 00 02 | 01 25 |
| 29 | 08 03 | 05 20 | 02 05 | 29♐33 | 01 01 |
| 30 | 07 53 | 05 01 | 01 39 | 29 04 | 00 36 |
| 31 | 07 43 | 04 42 | 01 13 | 28 34 | 00 10 |
| 32 | 07 32 | 04 23 | 00 46 | 28 04 | 29♑44 |
| 33 | 07 22 | 04 03 | 00 20 | 27 33 | 29 16 |
| 34 | 07 12 | 03 43 | 29♏52 | 27 01 | 28 48 |
| 35 | 07 02 | 03 24 | 29 25 | 26 28 | 28 18 |
| 36 | 06 51 | 03 03 | 28 57 | 25 55 | 27 47 |
| 37 | 06 41 | 02 43 | 28 29 | 25 21 | 27 15 |
| 38 | 06 30 | 02 23 | 28 00 | 24 46 | 26 41 |
| 39 | 06 20 | 02 02 | 27 30 | 24 10 | 26 06 |
| 40 | 06 09 | 01 41 | 27 01 | 23 33 | 25 30 |
| 41 | 05 58 | 01 20 | 26 30 | 22 55 | 24 52 |
| 42 | 05 47 | 00 58 | 25 59 | 22 16 | 24 12 |
| 43 | 05 36 | 00 36 | 25 28 | 21 36 | 23 29 |
| 44 | 05 25 | 00 14 | 24 56 | 20 55 | 22 45 |
| 45 | 05 13 | 29♎51 | 24 23 | 20 12 | 21 59 |
| 46 | 05 02 | 29 29 | 23 49 | 19 28 | 21 10 |
| 47 | 04 50 | 29 05 | 23 15 | 18 43 | 20 18 |
| 48 | 04 38 | 28 42 | 22 40 | 17 56 | 19 23 |
| 49 | 04 26 | 28 18 | 22 04 | 17 07 | 18 25 |
| 50 | 04 13 | 27 53 | 21 27 | 16 17 | 17 23 |
| 51 | 04 01 | 27 28 | 20 50 | 15 25 | 16 17 |
| 52 | 03 48 | 27 02 | 20 11 | 14 31 | 15 07 |
| 53 | 03 35 | 26 36 | 19 32 | 13 35 | 13 52 |
| 54 | 03 21 | 26 10 | 18 51 | 12 36 | 12 32 |
| 55 | 03 08 | 25 42 | 18 09 | 11 36 | 11 07 |
| 56 | 02 54 | 25 15 | 17 26 | 10 33 | 09 34 |
| 57 | 02 39 | 24 46 | 16 42 | 09 27 | 07 55 |
| 58 | 02 25 | 24 17 | 15 57 | 08 19 | 06 08 |
| 59 | 02 09 | 23 47 | 15 10 | 07 08 | 04 12 |
| 60 | 01♎54 | 23♎16 | 14♏21 | 05♐54 | 02♑07 |

10h 52m 0s — 163° 0' 0" — 11 ♍ 34

| LAT. | 11 | 12 | ASC | 2 | 3 |
|---|---|---|---|---|---|
| 0 | 14♎07 | 15♏28 | 14♐20 | 11♑58 | 10♒33 |
| 5 | 13 10 | 13 49 | 12 25 | 10 11 | 09 22 |
| 10 | 12 16 | 12 13 | 10 31 | 08 21 | 08 06 |
| 15 | 11 25 | 10 39 | 08 36 | 06 27 | 06 44 |
| 20 | 10 34 | 09 06 | 06 38 | 04 26 | 05 13 |
| 21 | 10 24 | 08 47 | 06 14 | 04 01 | 04 54 |
| 22 | 10 14 | 08 28 | 05 50 | 03 35 | 04 34 |
| 23 | 10 04 | 08 10 | 05 26 | 03 09 | 04 13 |
| 24 | 09 54 | 07 51 | 05 02 | 02 43 | 03 52 |
| 25 | 09 44 | 07 32 | 04 37 | 02 16 | 03 31 |
| 26 | 09 34 | 07 13 | 04 12 | 01 49 | 03 09 |
| 27 | 09 24 | 06 54 | 03 47 | 01 21 | 02 46 |
| 28 | 09 14 | 06 35 | 03 21 | 00 53 | 02 22 |
| 29 | 09 03 | 06 16 | 02 56 | 00 24 | 01 58 |
| 30 | 08 53 | 05 57 | 02 30 | 29♐54 | 01 33 |
| 31 | 08 43 | 05 37 | 02 03 | 29 24 | 01 07 |
| 32 | 08 33 | 05 17 | 01 37 | 28 54 | 00 40 |
| 33 | 08 22 | 04 58 | 01 10 | 28 22 | 00 12 |
| 34 | 08 12 | 04 38 | 00 42 | 27 50 | 29♑43 |
| 35 | 08 02 | 04 18 | 00 14 | 27 17 | 29 13 |
| 36 | 07 51 | 03 57 | 29♏46 | 26 44 | 28 42 |
| 37 | 07 40 | 03 37 | 29 17 | 26 09 | 28 09 |
| 38 | 07 30 | 03 16 | 28 48 | 25 34 | 27 36 |
| 39 | 07 19 | 02 55 | 28 19 | 24 57 | 27 00 |
| 40 | 07 08 | 02 34 | 27 48 | 24 20 | 26 23 |
| 41 | 06 57 | 02 12 | 27 18 | 23 41 | 25 44 |
| 42 | 06 46 | 01 50 | 26 46 | 23 02 | 25 04 |
| 43 | 06 34 | 01 28 | 26 14 | 22 21 | 24 21 |
| 44 | 06 23 | 01 06 | 25 42 | 21 39 | 23 37 |
| 45 | 06 11 | 00 43 | 25 08 | 20 56 | 22 49 |
| 46 | 06 00 | 00 20 | 24 34 | 20 11 | 22 00 |
| 47 | 05 48 | 29♎56 | 24 00 | 19 25 | 21 07 |
| 48 | 05 36 | 29 32 | 23 24 | 18 38 | 20 11 |
| 49 | 05 23 | 29 08 | 22 48 | 17 48 | 19 12 |
| 50 | 05 11 | 28 43 | 22 11 | 16 57 | 18 09 |
| 51 | 04 58 | 28 17 | 21 32 | 16 04 | 17 03 |
| 52 | 04 45 | 27 52 | 20 53 | 15 09 | 15 51 |
| 53 | 04 32 | 27 25 | 20 13 | 14 12 | 14 35 |
| 54 | 04 18 | 26 58 | 19 32 | 13 13 | 13 14 |
| 55 | 04 04 | 26 30 | 18 49 | 12 12 | 11 46 |
| 56 | 03 50 | 26 02 | 18 06 | 11 08 | 10 12 |
| 57 | 03 35 | 25 33 | 17 21 | 10 01 | 08 31 |
| 58 | 03 21 | 25 04 | 16 35 | 08 51 | 06 42 |
| 59 | 03 05 | 24 33 | 15 47 | 07 39 | 04 44 |
| 60 | 02♎50 | 24♎02 | 14♏58 | 06♐24 | 02♑37 |

10h 56m 0s — 164° 0' 0" — 12 ♍ 39

| LAT. | 11 | 12 | ASC | 2 | 3 |
|---|---|---|---|---|---|
| 0 | 15♎12 | 16♏28 | 15♐16 | 12♑53 | 11♒32 |
| 5 | 14 14 | 14 48 | 13 20 | 11 06 | 10 21 |
| 10 | 13 20 | 13 11 | 11 25 | 09 16 | 09 05 |
| 15 | 12 27 | 11 37 | 09 30 | 07 21 | 07 43 |
| 20 | 11 36 | 10 03 | 07 31 | 05 19 | 06 12 |
| 21 | 11 26 | 09 44 | 07 07 | 04 54 | 05 52 |
| 22 | 11 16 | 09 25 | 06 43 | 04 28 | 05 32 |
| 23 | 11 05 | 09 06 | 06 19 | 04 02 | 05 11 |
| 24 | 10 55 | 08 47 | 05 54 | 03 35 | 04 50 |
| 25 | 10 45 | 08 28 | 05 29 | 03 08 | 04 29 |
| 26 | 10 35 | 08 09 | 05 04 | 02 41 | 04 06 |
| 27 | 10 25 | 07 50 | 04 38 | 02 13 | 03 43 |
| 28 | 10 14 | 07 31 | 04 13 | 01 44 | 03 19 |
| 29 | 10 04 | 07 11 | 03 47 | 01 15 | 02 55 |
| 30 | 09 54 | 06 52 | 03 20 | 00 45 | 02 30 |
| 31 | 09 43 | 06 32 | 02 54 | 00 15 | 02 03 |
| 32 | 09 33 | 06 12 | 02 27 | 29♐44 | 01 36 |
| 33 | 09 23 | 05 52 | 02 00 | 29 12 | 01 08 |
| 34 | 09 12 | 05 32 | 01 32 | 28 40 | 00 39 |
| 35 | 09 01 | 05 12 | 01 04 | 28 06 | 00 09 |
| 36 | 08 51 | 04 51 | 00 35 | 27 32 | 29♑37 |
| 37 | 08 40 | 04 30 | 00 06 | 26 57 | 29 04 |
| 38 | 08 29 | 04 09 | 29♏37 | 26 21 | 28 30 |
| 39 | 08 18 | 03 48 | 29 07 | 25 45 | 27 54 |
| 40 | 08 07 | 03 26 | 28 36 | 25 07 | 27 17 |
| 41 | 07 56 | 03 05 | 28 05 | 24 28 | 26 38 |
| 42 | 07 45 | 02 43 | 27 33 | 23 48 | 25 57 |
| 43 | 07 33 | 02 20 | 27 01 | 23 07 | 25 14 |
| 44 | 07 21 | 01 57 | 26 28 | 22 24 | 24 28 |
| 45 | 07 10 | 01 34 | 25 54 | 21 40 | 23 40 |
| 46 | 06 58 | 01 11 | 25 20 | 20 55 | 22 50 |
| 47 | 06 46 | 00 47 | 24 45 | 20 08 | 21 57 |
| 48 | 06 33 | 00 23 | 24 09 | 19 20 | 21 00 |
| 49 | 06 21 | 29♎58 | 23 32 | 18 30 | 20 00 |
| 50 | 06 08 | 29 33 | 22 54 | 17 38 | 18 56 |
| 51 | 05 55 | 29 07 | 22 15 | 16 44 | 17 48 |
| 52 | 05 42 | 28 41 | 21 35 | 15 48 | 16 36 |
| 53 | 05 28 | 28 14 | 20 55 | 14 50 | 15 19 |
| 54 | 05 15 | 27 47 | 20 13 | 13 50 | 13 56 |
| 55 | 05 01 | 27 19 | 19 30 | 12 47 | 12 27 |
| 56 | 04 46 | 26 50 | 18 45 | 11 42 | 10 51 |
| 57 | 04 32 | 26 21 | 18 00 | 10 34 | 09 08 |
| 58 | 04 17 | 25 50 | 17 13 | 09 24 | 07 17 |
| 59 | 04 01 | 25 20 | 16 25 | 08 10 | 05 17 |
| 60 | 03♎45 | 24♎48 | 15♏35 | 06♐53 | 03♑07 |

11h 0m 0s — 165° 0' 0" — 13 ♍ 43

| LAT. | 11 | 12 | ASC | 2 | 3 |
|---|---|---|---|---|---|
| 0 | 16♎17 | 17♏28 | 16♐11 | 13♑49 | 12♒32 |
| 5 | 15 18 | 15 47 | 14 16 | 12 01 | 11 21 |
| 10 | 14 23 | 14 10 | 12 20 | 10 11 | 10 05 |
| 15 | 13 30 | 12 35 | 10 24 | 08 15 | 08 42 |
| 20 | 12 38 | 11 00 | 08 25 | 06 13 | 07 10 |
| 21 | 12 28 | 10 41 | 08 00 | 05 47 | 06 51 |
| 22 | 12 17 | 10 22 | 07 36 | 05 21 | 06 30 |
| 23 | 12 07 | 10 03 | 07 11 | 04 55 | 06 10 |
| 24 | 11 57 | 09 44 | 06 46 | 04 28 | 05 48 |
| 25 | 11 46 | 09 24 | 06 21 | 04 00 | 05 27 |
| 26 | 11 36 | 09 05 | 05 56 | 03 33 | 05 04 |
| 27 | 11 26 | 08 46 | 05 30 | 03 04 | 04 41 |
| 28 | 11 15 | 08 26 | 05 04 | 02 36 | 04 17 |
| 29 | 11 05 | 08 07 | 04 38 | 02 06 | 03 52 |
| 30 | 10 54 | 07 47 | 04 11 | 01 36 | 03 27 |
| 31 | 10 44 | 07 27 | 03 44 | 01 05 | 03 00 |
| 32 | 10 33 | 07 07 | 03 17 | 00 34 | 02 33 |
| 33 | 10 23 | 06 47 | 02 50 | 00 02 | 02 05 |
| 34 | 10 12 | 06 26 | 02 22 | 29♐29 | 01 35 |
| 35 | 10 01 | 06 06 | 01 53 | 28 55 | 01 05 |
| 36 | 09 50 | 05 45 | 01 24 | 28 21 | 00 33 |
| 37 | 09 40 | 05 24 | 00 55 | 27 46 | 00 00 |
| 38 | 09 29 | 05 03 | 00 25 | 27 09 | 29♑25 |
| 39 | 09 17 | 04 41 | 29♏55 | 26 32 | 28 49 |
| 40 | 09 06 | 04 19 | 29 24 | 25 54 | 28 11 |
| 41 | 08 55 | 03 57 | 28 52 | 25 14 | 27 31 |
| 42 | 08 43 | 03 35 | 28 20 | 24 34 | 26 50 |
| 43 | 08 32 | 03 12 | 27 47 | 23 52 | 26 06 |
| 44 | 08 20 | 02 49 | 27 14 | 23 09 | 25 20 |
| 45 | 08 08 | 02 26 | 26 40 | 22 24 | 24 32 |
| 46 | 07 56 | 02 02 | 26 05 | 21 38 | 23 41 |
| 47 | 07 44 | 01 38 | 25 29 | 20 51 | 22 47 |
| 48 | 07 31 | 01 13 | 24 53 | 20 02 | 21 49 |
| 49 | 07 19 | 00 48 | 24 15 | 19 11 | 20 48 |
| 50 | 07 06 | 00 23 | 23 37 | 18 18 | 19 44 |
| 51 | 06 53 | 29♎56 | 22 58 | 17 24 | 18 35 |
| 52 | 06 39 | 29 30 | 22 18 | 16 27 | 17 21 |
| 53 | 06 25 | 29 03 | 21 36 | 15 28 | 16 02 |
| 54 | 06 12 | 28 35 | 20 54 | 14 27 | 14 38 |
| 55 | 05 57 | 28 07 | 20 10 | 13 23 | 13 07 |
| 56 | 05 43 | 27 38 | 19 25 | 12 17 | 11 30 |
| 57 | 05 28 | 27 08 | 18 39 | 11 08 | 09 45 |
| 58 | 05 13 | 26 37 | 17 51 | 09 56 | 07 52 |
| 59 | 04 57 | 26 06 | 17 02 | 08 41 | 05 49 |
| 60 | 04♎41 | 25♎34 | 16♏11 | 07♐23 | 03♑37 |

11h 4m 0s — 166° 0' 0" — 14 ♍ 48

| LAT. | 11 | 12 | ASC | 2 | 3 |
|---|---|---|---|---|---|
| 0 | 17♎21 | 18♏28 | 17♐07 | 14♑44 | 13♒32 |
| 5 | 16 22 | 16 46 | 15 11 | 12 57 | 12 21 |
| 10 | 15 26 | 15 08 | 13 15 | 11 06 | 11 04 |
| 15 | 14 32 | 13 32 | 11 18 | 09 09 | 09 41 |
| 20 | 13 40 | 11 57 | 09 18 | 07 06 | 08 09 |
| 21 | 13 29 | 11 38 | 08 53 | 06 40 | 07 49 |
| 22 | 13 19 | 11 18 | 08 28 | 06 14 | 07 29 |
| 23 | 13 08 | 10 59 | 08 04 | 05 47 | 07 08 |
| 24 | 12 58 | 10 40 | 07 39 | 05 20 | 06 47 |
| 25 | 12 48 | 10 20 | 07 13 | 04 53 | 06 25 |
| 26 | 12 37 | 10 01 | 06 48 | 04 25 | 06 02 |
| 27 | 12 27 | 09 41 | 06 22 | 03 56 | 05 39 |
| 28 | 12 16 | 09 22 | 05 56 | 03 27 | 05 15 |
| 29 | 12 06 | 09 02 | 05 29 | 02 57 | 04 50 |
| 30 | 11 55 | 08 42 | 05 02 | 02 27 | 04 24 |
| 31 | 11 44 | 08 22 | 04 35 | 01 56 | 03 58 |
| 32 | 11 34 | 08 02 | 04 08 | 01 25 | 03 30 |
| 33 | 11 23 | 07 41 | 03 40 | 00 52 | 03 02 |
| 34 | 11 12 | 07 21 | 03 11 | 00 19 | 02 32 |
| 35 | 11 01 | 07 00 | 02 43 | 29♐45 | 02 01 |
| 36 | 10 50 | 06 39 | 02 14 | 29 10 | 01 29 |
| 37 | 10 39 | 06 17 | 01 44 | 28 34 | 00 55 |
| 38 | 10 28 | 05 56 | 01 14 | 27 58 | 00 20 |
| 39 | 10 17 | 05 34 | 00 43 | 27 20 | 29♑44 |
| 40 | 10 05 | 05 12 | 00 12 | 26 41 | 29 06 |
| 41 | 09 54 | 04 50 | 29♏40 | 26 01 | 28 26 |
| 42 | 09 42 | 04 27 | 29 07 | 25 20 | 27 44 |
| 43 | 09 30 | 04 04 | 28 34 | 24 38 | 26 59 |
| 44 | 09 19 | 03 41 | 28 00 | 23 54 | 26 13 |
| 45 | 09 06 | 03 17 | 27 26 | 23 09 | 25 24 |
| 46 | 08 54 | 02 53 | 26 50 | 22 22 | 24 32 |
| 47 | 08 42 | 02 29 | 26 14 | 21 34 | 23 37 |
| 48 | 08 29 | 02 04 | 25 37 | 20 44 | 22 39 |
| 49 | 08 16 | 01 38 | 24 59 | 19 53 | 21 37 |
| 50 | 08 03 | 01 12 | 24 21 | 18 59 | 20 31 |
| 51 | 07 50 | 00 46 | 23 41 | 18 04 | 19 21 |
| 52 | 07 36 | 00 19 | 23 00 | 17 06 | 18 07 |
| 53 | 07 23 | 29♎52 | 22 18 | 16 06 | 16 47 |
| 54 | 07 08 | 29 23 | 21 35 | 15 04 | 15 21 |
| 55 | 06 54 | 28 55 | 20 50 | 14 00 | 13 49 |
| 56 | 06 39 | 28 25 | 20 05 | 12 52 | 12 09 |
| 57 | 06 24 | 27 55 | 19 18 | 11 42 | 10 23 |
| 58 | 06 09 | 27 24 | 18 30 | 10 29 | 08 27 |
| 59 | 05 53 | 26 52 | 17 40 | 09 13 | 06 22 |
| 60 | 05♎37 | 26♎20 | 16♏48 | 07♐53 | 04♑07 |

11h 8m 0s — 167° 0' 0" — 15 ♍ 53

| LAT. | 11 | 12 | ASC | 2 | 3 |
|---|---|---|---|---|---|
| 0 | 18♎26 | 19♏27 | 18♐02 | 15♑40 | 14♒32 |
| 5 | 17 26 | 17 45 | 16 06 | 13 52 | 13 21 |
| 10 | 16 29 | 16 07 | 14 09 | 12 01 | 12 04 |
| 15 | 15 35 | 14 30 | 12 12 | 10 04 | 10 41 |
| 20 | 14 42 | 12 54 | 10 11 | 08 00 | 09 08 |
| 21 | 14 31 | 12 34 | 09 46 | 07 34 | 08 49 |
| 22 | 14 20 | 12 15 | 09 21 | 07 07 | 08 28 |
| 23 | 14 10 | 11 56 | 08 56 | 06 40 | 08 07 |
| 24 | 13 59 | 11 36 | 08 31 | 06 13 | 07 46 |
| 25 | 13 49 | 11 17 | 08 05 | 05 45 | 07 24 |
| 26 | 13 38 | 10 57 | 07 40 | 05 17 | 07 01 |
| 27 | 13 28 | 10 37 | 07 13 | 04 48 | 06 37 |
| 28 | 13 17 | 10 17 | 06 47 | 04 19 | 06 13 |
| 29 | 13 06 | 09 57 | 06 20 | 03 49 | 05 48 |
| 30 | 12 56 | 09 37 | 05 53 | 03 18 | 05 22 |
| 31 | 12 45 | 09 17 | 05 26 | 02 47 | 04 55 |
| 32 | 12 34 | 08 56 | 04 58 | 02 15 | 04 28 |
| 33 | 12 23 | 08 36 | 04 30 | 01 42 | 03 59 |
| 34 | 12 12 | 08 15 | 04 01 | 01 09 | 03 29 |
| 35 | 12 01 | 07 54 | 03 32 | 00 35 | 02 58 |
| 36 | 11 50 | 07 32 | 03 03 | 29♐59 | 02 25 |
| 37 | 11 39 | 07 11 | 02 33 | 29 23 | 01 51 |
| 38 | 11 27 | 06 49 | 02 02 | 28 46 | 01 16 |
| 39 | 11 16 | 06 27 | 01 31 | 28 08 | 00 39 |
| 40 | 11 05 | 06 05 | 01 00 | 27 29 | 00 01 |
| 41 | 10 53 | 05 42 | 00 27 | 26 48 | 29♑20 |
| 42 | 10 41 | 05 19 | 29♏55 | 26 07 | 28 38 |
| 43 | 10 29 | 04 56 | 29 21 | 25 24 | 27 53 |
| 44 | 10 17 | 04 33 | 28 47 | 24 39 | 27 06 |
| 45 | 10 05 | 04 09 | 28 12 | 23 54 | 26 16 |
| 46 | 09 52 | 03 44 | 27 36 | 23 06 | 25 24 |
| 47 | 09 40 | 03 19 | 26 59 | 22 18 | 24 28 |
| 48 | 09 27 | 02 54 | 26 22 | 21 27 | 23 29 |
| 49 | 09 14 | 02 29 | 25 43 | 20 35 | 22 26 |
| 50 | 09 01 | 02 02 | 25 04 | 19 40 | 21 20 |
| 51 | 08 47 | 01 36 | 24 24 | 18 44 | 20 09 |
| 52 | 08 34 | 01 08 | 23 42 | 17 45 | 18 53 |
| 53 | 08 20 | 00 40 | 23 00 | 16 45 | 17 31 |
| 54 | 08 05 | 00 12 | 22 16 | 15 42 | 16 04 |
| 55 | 07 51 | 29♎43 | 21 31 | 14 36 | 14 30 |
| 56 | 07 36 | 29 13 | 20 45 | 13 27 | 12 49 |
| 57 | 07 21 | 28 42 | 19 57 | 12 16 | 11 00 |
| 58 | 07 05 | 28 11 | 19 08 | 11 02 | 09 03 |
| 59 | 06 49 | 27 39 | 18 17 | 09 44 | 06 56 |
| 60 | 06♎33 | 27♎06 | 17♏25 | 08♐23 | 04♑38 |

# Koch Table of Houses for Latitudes 0° to 60° North

**11h 12m 0s — 16 ♍ 57 — 168° 0' 0"**

| LAT. | 11 | 12 | ASC | 2 | 3 |
|---|---|---|---|---|---|
| 0 | 19♎30 | 20♏26 | 18♐58 | 16♑36 | 15♒32 |
| 5 | 18 30 | 18 44 | 17 01 | 14 48 | 14 21 |
| 10 | 17 33 | 17 05 | 15 04 | 12 56 | 13 04 |
| 15 | 16 37 | 15 28 | 13 05 | 10 58 | 11 41 |
| 20 | 15 44 | 13 51 | 11 04 | 08 53 | 10 08 |
| 21 | 15 33 | 13 31 | 10 39 | 08 27 | 09 48 |
| 22 | 15 22 | 13 12 | 10 14 | 08 01 | 09 27 |
| 23 | 15 11 | 12 52 | 09 49 | 07 34 | 09 06 |
| 24 | 15 01 | 12 32 | 09 23 | 07 06 | 08 45 |
| 25 | 14 50 | 12 12 | 08 58 | 06 38 | 08 23 |
| 26 | 14 39 | 11 53 | 08 32 | 06 10 | 08 00 |
| 27 | 14 29 | 11 33 | 08 05 | 05 41 | 07 36 |
| 28 | 14 18 | 11 13 | 07 39 | 05 11 | 07 12 |
| 29 | 14 07 | 10 52 | 07 12 | 04 41 | 06 46 |
| 30 | 13 56 | 10 32 | 06 44 | 04 10 | 06 20 |
| 31 | 13 45 | 10 12 | 06 17 | 03 38 | 05 53 |
| 32 | 13 34 | 09 51 | 05 49 | 03 06 | 05 25 |
| 33 | 13 23 | 09 30 | 05 20 | 02 33 | 04 56 |
| 34 | 13 12 | 09 09 | 04 51 | 01 59 | 04 26 |
| 35 | 13 01 | 08 48 | 04 22 | 01 24 | 03 55 |
| 36 | 12 50 | 08 26 | 03 52 | 00 49 | 03 22 |
| 37 | 12 38 | 08 05 | 03 22 | 00 12 | 02 48 |
| 38 | 12 27 | 07 43 | 02 51 | 29♐35 | 02 12 |
| 39 | 12 15 | 07 20 | 02 20 | 28 56 | 01 35 |
| 40 | 12 04 | 06 58 | 01 48 | 28 16 | 00 56 |
| 41 | 11 52 | 06 35 | 01 15 | 27 35 | 00 15 |
| 42 | 11 40 | 06 12 | 00 42 | 26 53 | 29♑32 |
| 43 | 11 28 | 05 48 | 00 08 | 26 10 | 28 47 |
| 44 | 11 16 | 05 24 | 29♏33 | 25 25 | 27 59 |
| 45 | 11 03 | 05 00 | 28 58 | 24 39 | 27 09 |
| 46 | 10 51 | 04 35 | 28 21 | 23 51 | 26 16 |
| 47 | 10 38 | 04 10 | 27 44 | 23 01 | 25 19 |
| 48 | 10 25 | 03 45 | 27 06 | 22 10 | 24 20 |
| 49 | 10 12 | 03 19 | 26 27 | 21 17 | 23 16 |
| 50 | 09 58 | 02 52 | 25 48 | 20 22 | 22 08 |
| 51 | 09 45 | 02 25 | 25 07 | 19 24 | 20 56 |
| 52 | 09 31 | 01 58 | 24 25 | 18 25 | 19 39 |
| 53 | 09 17 | 01 29 | 23 41 | 17 23 | 18 16 |
| 54 | 09 02 | 01 00 | 22 57 | 16 19 | 16 48 |
| 55 | 08 48 | 00 31 | 22 11 | 15 12 | 15 12 |
| 56 | 08 32 | 00 01 | 21 24 | 14 03 | 13 30 |
| 57 | 08 17 | 29♎30 | 20 36 | 12 50 | 11 39 |
| 58 | 08 01 | 28 58 | 19 46 | 11 35 | 09 39 |
| 59 | 07 45 | 28 25 | 18 55 | 10 16 | 07 29 |
| 60 | 07♎28 | 27♎52 | 18♏02 | 08♐53 | 05♑09 |

**11h 16m 0s — 18 ♍ 02 — 169° 0' 0"**

| LAT. | 11 | 12 | ASC | 2 | 3 |
|---|---|---|---|---|---|
| 0 | 20♎34 | 21♏26 | 19♐53 | 17♑32 | 16♒33 |
| 5 | 19 33 | 19 43 | 17 56 | 15 43 | 15 21 |
| 10 | 18 36 | 18 03 | 15 58 | 13 51 | 14 04 |
| 15 | 17 40 | 16 25 | 13 59 | 11 53 | 12 41 |
| 20 | 16 45 | 14 47 | 11 57 | 09 47 | 11 08 |
| 21 | 16 34 | 14 28 | 11 32 | 09 21 | 10 48 |
| 22 | 16 24 | 14 08 | 11 07 | 08 54 | 10 27 |
| 23 | 16 13 | 13 48 | 10 41 | 08 27 | 10 06 |
| 24 | 16 02 | 13 28 | 10 16 | 08 00 | 09 44 |
| 25 | 15 51 | 13 08 | 09 50 | 07 31 | 09 22 |
| 26 | 15 40 | 12 48 | 09 24 | 07 03 | 08 59 |
| 27 | 15 30 | 12 28 | 08 57 | 06 33 | 08 35 |
| 28 | 15 19 | 12 08 | 08 30 | 06 03 | 08 11 |
| 29 | 15 08 | 11 48 | 08 03 | 05 33 | 07 45 |
| 30 | 14 57 | 11 27 | 07 35 | 05 02 | 07 19 |
| 31 | 14 46 | 11 06 | 07 08 | 04 30 | 06 52 |
| 32 | 14 35 | 10 46 | 06 39 | 03 57 | 06 24 |
| 33 | 14 23 | 10 24 | 06 11 | 03 24 | 05 54 |
| 34 | 14 12 | 10 03 | 05 41 | 02 50 | 05 24 |
| 35 | 14 01 | 09 42 | 05 12 | 02 15 | 04 52 |
| 36 | 13 50 | 09 20 | 04 42 | 01 39 | 04 19 |
| 37 | 13 38 | 08 58 | 04 11 | 01 02 | 03 45 |
| 38 | 13 26 | 08 36 | 03 40 | 00 24 | 03 09 |
| 39 | 13 15 | 08 13 | 03 08 | 29♐45 | 02 31 |
| 40 | 13 03 | 07 51 | 02 36 | 29 04 | 01 52 |
| 41 | 12 51 | 07 27 | 02 03 | 28 23 | 01 11 |
| 42 | 12 39 | 07 04 | 01 29 | 27 40 | 00 27 |
| 43 | 12 27 | 06 40 | 00 55 | 26 56 | 29♑41 |
| 44 | 12 14 | 06 16 | 00 20 | 26 11 | 28 53 |
| 45 | 12 02 | 05 52 | 29♏44 | 25 24 | 28 02 |
| 46 | 11 49 | 05 27 | 29 07 | 24 35 | 27 08 |
| 47 | 11 36 | 05 01 | 28 30 | 23 45 | 26 11 |
| 48 | 11 23 | 04 35 | 27 51 | 22 53 | 25 11 |
| 49 | 11 10 | 04 09 | 27 12 | 21 59 | 24 06 |
| 50 | 10 56 | 03 42 | 26 31 | 21 03 | 22 58 |
| 51 | 10 42 | 03 15 | 25 50 | 20 05 | 21 44 |
| 52 | 10 28 | 02 47 | 25 07 | 19 05 | 20 26 |
| 53 | 10 14 | 02 18 | 24 23 | 18 02 | 19 02 |
| 54 | 09 59 | 01 49 | 23 38 | 16 57 | 17 32 |
| 55 | 09 44 | 01 19 | 22 52 | 15 49 | 15 55 |
| 56 | 09 29 | 00 48 | 22 04 | 14 38 | 14 10 |
| 57 | 09 13 | 00 17 | 21 15 | 13 25 | 12 17 |
| 58 | 08 57 | 29♎45 | 20 25 | 12 08 | 10 15 |
| 59 | 08 41 | 29 12 | 19 32 | 10 47 | 08 03 |
| 60 | 08♎24 | 28♎38 | 18♏38 | 09♐24 | 05♑40 |

**11h 20m 0s — 19 ♍ 07 — 170° 0' 0"**

| LAT. | 11 | 12 | ASC | 2 | 3 |
|---|---|---|---|---|---|
| 0 | 21♎38 | 22♏25 | 20♐49 | 18♑28 | 17♒33 |
| 5 | 20 37 | 20 41 | 18 51 | 16 39 | 16 22 |
| 10 | 19 38 | 19 01 | 16 53 | 14 47 | 15 05 |
| 15 | 18 42 | 17 22 | 14 53 | 12 48 | 13 41 |
| 20 | 17 47 | 15 44 | 12 50 | 10 42 | 12 08 |
| 21 | 17 36 | 15 24 | 12 25 | 10 15 | 11 48 |
| 22 | 17 25 | 15 04 | 12 00 | 09 48 | 11 27 |
| 23 | 17 14 | 14 44 | 11 34 | 09 21 | 11 06 |
| 24 | 17 03 | 14 24 | 11 08 | 08 53 | 10 44 |
| 25 | 16 52 | 14 04 | 10 42 | 08 25 | 10 22 |
| 26 | 16 41 | 13 44 | 10 16 | 07 56 | 09 58 |
| 27 | 16 30 | 13 24 | 09 49 | 07 26 | 09 35 |
| 28 | 16 19 | 13 03 | 09 22 | 06 56 | 09 10 |
| 29 | 16 08 | 12 43 | 08 54 | 06 25 | 08 44 |
| 30 | 15 57 | 12 22 | 08 27 | 05 54 | 08 18 |
| 31 | 15 46 | 12 01 | 07 59 | 05 22 | 07 51 |
| 32 | 15 35 | 11 40 | 07 30 | 04 49 | 07 22 |
| 33 | 15 24 | 11 19 | 07 01 | 04 15 | 06 53 |
| 34 | 15 12 | 10 57 | 06 32 | 03 40 | 06 22 |
| 35 | 15 01 | 10 36 | 06 02 | 03 05 | 05 50 |
| 36 | 14 49 | 10 14 | 05 31 | 02 29 | 05 17 |
| 37 | 14 38 | 09 52 | 05 00 | 01 51 | 04 42 |
| 38 | 14 26 | 09 29 | 04 29 | 01 13 | 04 06 |
| 39 | 14 14 | 09 06 | 03 57 | 00 33 | 03 28 |
| 40 | 14 02 | 08 43 | 03 24 | 29♐53 | 02 48 |
| 41 | 13 50 | 08 20 | 02 51 | 29 11 | 02 07 |
| 42 | 13 38 | 07 56 | 02 17 | 28 28 | 01 23 |
| 43 | 13 26 | 07 32 | 01 42 | 27 43 | 00 36 |
| 44 | 13 13 | 07 08 | 01 06 | 26 57 | 29♑48 |
| 45 | 13 00 | 06 43 | 00 30 | 26 09 | 28 56 |
| 46 | 12 47 | 06 18 | 29♏53 | 25 20 | 28 02 |
| 47 | 12 34 | 05 52 | 29 15 | 24 29 | 27 04 |
| 48 | 12 21 | 05 26 | 28 36 | 23 36 | 26 03 |
| 49 | 12 08 | 04 59 | 27 56 | 22 42 | 24 57 |
| 50 | 11 54 | 04 32 | 27 15 | 21 45 | 23 48 |
| 51 | 11 40 | 04 04 | 26 33 | 20 46 | 22 33 |
| 52 | 11 26 | 03 36 | 25 50 | 19 45 | 21 14 |
| 53 | 11 11 | 03 07 | 25 05 | 18 41 | 19 48 |
| 54 | 10 56 | 02 37 | 24 20 | 17 35 | 18 17 |
| 55 | 10 41 | 02 07 | 23 33 | 16 26 | 16 38 |
| 56 | 10 26 | 01 36 | 22 44 | 15 14 | 14 51 |
| 57 | 10 10 | 01 04 | 21 54 | 13 59 | 12 57 |
| 58 | 09 54 | 00 31 | 21 03 | 12 41 | 10 52 |
| 59 | 09 37 | 29♎58 | 20 10 | 11 19 | 08 38 |
| 60 | 09♎20 | 29♎23 | 19♏15 | 09♐54 | 06♑12 |

**11h 24m 0s — 20 ♍ 12 — 171° 0' 0"**

| LAT. | 11 | 12 | ASC | 2 | 3 |
|---|---|---|---|---|---|
| 0 | 22♎42 | 23♏23 | 21♐44 | 19♑24 | 18♒34 |
| 5 | 21 40 | 21 40 | 19 46 | 17 35 | 17 23 |
| 10 | 20 41 | 19 59 | 17 48 | 15 42 | 16 06 |
| 15 | 19 44 | 18 20 | 15 47 | 13 43 | 14 42 |
| 20 | 18 49 | 16 41 | 13 44 | 11 36 | 13 08 |
| 21 | 18 38 | 16 21 | 13 18 | 11 09 | 12 48 |
| 22 | 18 27 | 16 01 | 12 53 | 10 42 | 12 27 |
| 23 | 18 16 | 15 41 | 12 27 | 10 15 | 12 06 |
| 24 | 18 05 | 15 20 | 12 01 | 09 47 | 11 44 |
| 25 | 17 54 | 15 00 | 11 34 | 09 18 | 11 22 |
| 26 | 17 42 | 14 40 | 11 08 | 08 49 | 10 58 |
| 27 | 17 31 | 14 19 | 10 41 | 08 19 | 10 34 |
| 28 | 17 20 | 13 59 | 10 14 | 07 49 | 10 09 |
| 29 | 17 09 | 13 38 | 09 46 | 07 18 | 09 44 |
| 30 | 16 58 | 13 17 | 09 18 | 06 46 | 09 17 |
| 31 | 16 47 | 12 56 | 08 50 | 06 14 | 08 50 |
| 32 | 16 35 | 12 35 | 08 21 | 05 40 | 08 21 |
| 33 | 16 24 | 12 13 | 07 51 | 05 06 | 07 52 |
| 34 | 16 12 | 11 52 | 07 22 | 04 31 | 07 21 |
| 35 | 16 01 | 11 30 | 06 52 | 03 56 | 06 49 |
| 36 | 15 49 | 11 08 | 06 21 | 03 19 | 06 15 |
| 37 | 15 37 | 10 45 | 05 50 | 02 41 | 05 40 |
| 38 | 15 25 | 10 22 | 05 18 | 02 02 | 05 04 |
| 39 | 15 14 | 10 00 | 04 45 | 01 22 | 04 25 |
| 40 | 15 01 | 09 36 | 04 12 | 00 41 | 03 45 |
| 41 | 14 49 | 09 13 | 03 39 | 29♐59 | 03 03 |
| 42 | 14 37 | 08 49 | 03 04 | 29 15 | 02 19 |
| 43 | 14 24 | 08 24 | 02 29 | 28 30 | 01 32 |
| 44 | 14 12 | 08 00 | 01 53 | 27 43 | 00 43 |
| 45 | 13 59 | 07 35 | 01 16 | 26 55 | 29♑51 |
| 46 | 13 46 | 07 09 | 00 39 | 26 05 | 28 55 |
| 47 | 13 32 | 06 43 | 00 00 | 25 14 | 27 57 |
| 48 | 13 19 | 06 17 | 29♏21 | 24 20 | 26 55 |
| 49 | 13 05 | 05 50 | 28 40 | 23 25 | 25 49 |
| 50 | 12 51 | 05 22 | 27 59 | 22 27 | 24 38 |
| 51 | 12 37 | 04 54 | 27 16 | 21 27 | 23 22 |
| 52 | 12 23 | 04 25 | 26 32 | 20 25 | 22 02 |
| 53 | 12 08 | 03 56 | 25 47 | 19 20 | 20 35 |
| 54 | 11 53 | 03 26 | 25 01 | 18 13 | 19 02 |
| 55 | 11 38 | 02 55 | 24 13 | 17 03 | 17 21 |
| 56 | 11 22 | 02 24 | 23 24 | 15 50 | 15 33 |
| 57 | 11 06 | 01 51 | 22 34 | 14 34 | 13 36 |
| 58 | 10 50 | 01 18 | 21 42 | 13 14 | 11 30 |
| 59 | 10 33 | 00 44 | 20 48 | 11 51 | 09 13 |
| 60 | 10♎16 | 00♏09 | 19♏52 | 10♐25 | 06♑44 |

**11h 28m 0s — 21 ♍ 17 — 172° 0' 0"**

| LAT. | 11 | 12 | ASC | 2 | 3 |
|---|---|---|---|---|---|
| 0 | 23♎46 | 24♏22 | 22♐39 | 20♑20 | 19♒35 |
| 5 | 22 43 | 22 38 | 20 41 | 18 31 | 18 24 |
| 10 | 21 44 | 20 57 | 18 42 | 16 38 | 17 07 |
| 15 | 20 47 | 19 17 | 16 41 | 14 38 | 15 43 |
| 20 | 19 51 | 17 37 | 14 37 | 12 31 | 14 09 |
| 21 | 19 39 | 17 17 | 14 11 | 12 04 | 13 49 |
| 22 | 19 28 | 16 57 | 13 46 | 11 36 | 13 28 |
| 23 | 19 17 | 16 37 | 13 20 | 11 09 | 13 06 |
| 24 | 19 06 | 16 16 | 12 53 | 10 41 | 12 44 |
| 25 | 18 55 | 15 56 | 12 27 | 10 12 | 12 22 |
| 26 | 18 43 | 15 35 | 12 00 | 09 42 | 11 58 |
| 27 | 18 32 | 15 15 | 11 33 | 09 12 | 11 34 |
| 28 | 18 21 | 14 54 | 11 05 | 08 42 | 11 09 |
| 29 | 18 10 | 14 33 | 10 38 | 08 11 | 10 44 |
| 30 | 17 58 | 14 12 | 10 09 | 07 39 | 10 17 |
| 31 | 17 47 | 13 51 | 09 41 | 07 06 | 09 49 |
| 32 | 17 35 | 13 29 | 09 12 | 06 32 | 09 21 |
| 33 | 17 24 | 13 08 | 08 42 | 05 58 | 08 51 |
| 34 | 17 12 | 12 46 | 08 12 | 05 23 | 08 20 |
| 35 | 17 01 | 12 24 | 07 42 | 04 47 | 07 47 |
| 36 | 16 49 | 12 01 | 07 11 | 04 09 | 07 14 |
| 37 | 16 37 | 11 39 | 06 39 | 03 31 | 06 38 |
| 38 | 16 25 | 11 16 | 06 07 | 02 52 | 06 02 |
| 39 | 16 13 | 10 53 | 05 34 | 02 12 | 05 23 |
| 40 | 16 01 | 10 29 | 05 01 | 01 30 | 04 42 |
| 41 | 15 48 | 10 05 | 04 27 | 00 47 | 04 00 |
| 42 | 15 36 | 09 41 | 03 52 | 00 03 | 03 15 |
| 43 | 15 23 | 09 16 | 03 16 | 29♐17 | 02 28 |
| 44 | 15 10 | 08 52 | 02 40 | 28 30 | 01 38 |
| 45 | 14 57 | 08 26 | 02 03 | 27 41 | 00 45 |
| 46 | 14 44 | 08 00 | 01 25 | 26 51 | 29♑50 |
| 47 | 14 31 | 07 34 | 00 46 | 25 58 | 28 50 |
| 48 | 14 17 | 07 07 | 00 06 | 25 04 | 27 47 |
| 49 | 14 03 | 06 40 | 29♏25 | 24 08 | 26 40 |
| 50 | 13 49 | 06 12 | 28 43 | 23 09 | 25 29 |
| 51 | 13 35 | 05 44 | 27 59 | 22 09 | 24 12 |
| 52 | 13 20 | 05 14 | 27 15 | 21 05 | 22 50 |
| 53 | 13 05 | 04 45 | 26 29 | 20 00 | 21 22 |
| 54 | 12 50 | 04 14 | 25 42 | 18 51 | 19 48 |
| 55 | 12 35 | 03 43 | 24 54 | 17 40 | 18 06 |
| 56 | 12 19 | 03 11 | 24 04 | 16 26 | 16 15 |
| 57 | 12 03 | 02 39 | 23 13 | 15 08 | 14 16 |
| 58 | 11 46 | 02 05 | 22 20 | 13 48 | 12 08 |
| 59 | 11 29 | 01 31 | 21 25 | 12 23 | 09 48 |
| 60 | 11♎12 | 00♏55 | 20♏29 | 10♐55 | 07♑17 |

**11h 32m 0s — 22 ♍ 23 — 173° 0' 0"**

| LAT. | 11 | 12 | ASC | 2 | 3 |
|---|---|---|---|---|---|
| 0 | 24♎50 | 25♏21 | 23♐34 | 21♑17 | 20♒36 |
| 5 | 23 47 | 23 36 | 21 36 | 19 27 | 19 25 |
| 10 | 22 47 | 21 54 | 19 37 | 17 34 | 18 08 |
| 15 | 21 49 | 20 14 | 17 35 | 15 34 | 16 44 |
| 20 | 20 52 | 18 34 | 15 30 | 13 25 | 15 10 |
| 21 | 20 41 | 18 13 | 15 05 | 12 58 | 14 50 |
| 22 | 20 30 | 17 53 | 14 39 | 12 31 | 14 29 |
| 23 | 20 18 | 17 33 | 14 13 | 12 03 | 14 07 |
| 24 | 20 07 | 17 12 | 13 46 | 11 35 | 13 45 |
| 25 | 19 56 | 16 52 | 13 19 | 11 06 | 13 23 |
| 26 | 19 44 | 16 31 | 12 52 | 10 36 | 12 59 |
| 27 | 19 33 | 16 10 | 12 25 | 10 06 | 12 35 |
| 28 | 19 22 | 15 49 | 11 57 | 09 35 | 12 10 |
| 29 | 19 10 | 15 28 | 11 29 | 09 04 | 11 44 |
| 30 | 18 59 | 15 07 | 11 01 | 08 31 | 11 17 |
| 31 | 18 47 | 14 46 | 10 32 | 07 58 | 10 49 |
| 32 | 18 36 | 14 24 | 10 03 | 07 25 | 10 20 |
| 33 | 18 24 | 14 02 | 09 33 | 06 50 | 09 50 |
| 34 | 18 12 | 13 40 | 09 02 | 06 14 | 09 19 |
| 35 | 18 01 | 13 18 | 08 32 | 05 38 | 08 47 |
| 36 | 17 49 | 12 55 | 08 00 | 05 00 | 08 13 |
| 37 | 17 37 | 12 32 | 07 29 | 04 22 | 07 37 |
| 38 | 17 24 | 12 09 | 06 56 | 03 42 | 07 00 |
| 39 | 17 12 | 11 46 | 06 23 | 03 01 | 06 21 |
| 40 | 17 00 | 11 22 | 05 49 | 02 19 | 05 40 |
| 41 | 16 47 | 10 58 | 05 15 | 01 36 | 04 57 |
| 42 | 16 35 | 10 33 | 04 39 | 00 51 | 04 12 |
| 43 | 16 22 | 10 09 | 04 04 | 00 05 | 03 24 |
| 44 | 16 09 | 09 43 | 03 27 | 29♐17 | 02 34 |
| 45 | 15 56 | 09 18 | 02 49 | 28 28 | 01 41 |
| 46 | 15 42 | 08 52 | 02 11 | 27 36 | 00 44 |
| 47 | 15 29 | 08 25 | 01 31 | 26 43 | 29♑45 |
| 48 | 15 15 | 07 58 | 00 51 | 25 48 | 28 41 |
| 49 | 15 01 | 07 30 | 00 09 | 24 51 | 27 33 |
| 50 | 14 47 | 07 02 | 29♏27 | 23 52 | 26 20 |
| 51 | 14 32 | 06 33 | 28 43 | 22 50 | 25 03 |
| 52 | 14 18 | 06 04 | 27 58 | 21 46 | 23 39 |
| 53 | 14 03 | 05 34 | 27 12 | 20 40 | 22 10 |
| 54 | 13 47 | 05 03 | 26 24 | 19 30 | 20 34 |
| 55 | 13 31 | 04 31 | 25 35 | 18 18 | 18 50 |
| 56 | 13 15 | 03 59 | 24 44 | 17 02 | 16 58 |
| 57 | 12 59 | 03 26 | 23 52 | 15 44 | 14 57 |
| 58 | 12 42 | 02 52 | 22 59 | 14 21 | 12 46 |
| 59 | 12 25 | 02 17 | 22 03 | 12 56 | 10 24 |
| 60 | 12♎07 | 01♏41 | 21♏06 | 11♐26 | 07♑50 |

**11h 36m 0s — 23 ♍ 28 — 174° 0' 0"**

| LAT. | 11 | 12 | ASC | 2 | 3 |
|---|---|---|---|---|---|
| 0 | 25♎53 | 26♏19 | 24♐30 | 22♑13 | 21♒37 |
| 5 | 24 50 | 24 34 | 22 31 | 20 24 | 20 26 |
| 10 | 23 49 | 22 52 | 20 31 | 18 30 | 19 09 |
| 15 | 22 51 | 21 11 | 18 29 | 16 29 | 17 45 |
| 20 | 21 54 | 19 30 | 16 24 | 14 20 | 16 11 |
| 21 | 21 42 | 19 10 | 15 58 | 13 53 | 15 51 |
| 22 | 21 31 | 18 49 | 15 32 | 13 26 | 15 30 |
| 23 | 21 20 | 18 29 | 15 05 | 12 58 | 15 08 |
| 24 | 21 08 | 18 08 | 14 39 | 12 29 | 14 46 |
| 25 | 20 57 | 17 48 | 14 12 | 12 00 | 14 24 |
| 26 | 20 45 | 17 27 | 13 45 | 11 30 | 14 00 |
| 27 | 20 34 | 17 06 | 13 17 | 11 00 | 13 36 |
| 28 | 20 22 | 16 45 | 12 49 | 10 29 | 13 11 |
| 29 | 20 11 | 16 23 | 12 21 | 09 57 | 12 45 |
| 30 | 19 59 | 16 02 | 11 52 | 09 24 | 12 18 |
| 31 | 19 48 | 15 40 | 11 23 | 08 51 | 11 50 |
| 32 | 19 36 | 15 18 | 10 54 | 08 17 | 11 21 |
| 33 | 19 24 | 14 56 | 10 24 | 07 42 | 10 50 |
| 34 | 19 12 | 14 34 | 09 53 | 07 06 | 10 19 |
| 35 | 19 00 | 14 12 | 09 22 | 06 29 | 09 46 |
| 36 | 18 48 | 13 49 | 08 50 | 05 51 | 09 12 |
| 37 | 18 36 | 13 26 | 08 18 | 05 13 | 08 36 |
| 38 | 18 24 | 13 02 | 07 45 | 04 32 | 07 59 |
| 39 | 18 12 | 12 39 | 07 12 | 03 51 | 07 20 |
| 40 | 17 59 | 12 15 | 06 38 | 03 09 | 06 39 |
| 41 | 17 46 | 11 50 | 06 03 | 02 25 | 05 55 |
| 42 | 17 34 | 11 26 | 05 27 | 01 39 | 05 10 |
| 43 | 17 21 | 11 01 | 04 51 | 00 53 | 04 22 |
| 44 | 17 08 | 10 35 | 04 14 | 00 04 | 03 31 |
| 45 | 16 54 | 10 09 | 03 36 | 29♐14 | 02 37 |
| 46 | 16 41 | 09 43 | 02 57 | 28 22 | 01 40 |
| 47 | 16 27 | 09 16 | 02 17 | 27 29 | 00 39 |
| 48 | 16 13 | 08 48 | 01 36 | 26 33 | 29♑35 |
| 49 | 15 59 | 08 20 | 00 54 | 25 35 | 28 26 |
| 50 | 15 45 | 07 52 | 00 11 | 24 35 | 27 12 |
| 51 | 15 30 | 07 23 | 29♏26 | 23 32 | 25 54 |
| 52 | 15 15 | 06 53 | 28 41 | 22 27 | 24 29 |
| 53 | 15 00 | 06 23 | 27 54 | 21 20 | 22 59 |
| 54 | 14 44 | 05 51 | 27 06 | 20 09 | 21 21 |
| 55 | 14 28 | 05 19 | 26 16 | 18 55 | 19 36 |
| 56 | 14 12 | 04 47 | 25 25 | 17 39 | 17 42 |
| 57 | 13 55 | 04 13 | 24 32 | 16 19 | 15 38 |
| 58 | 13 38 | 03 39 | 23 37 | 14 55 | 13 25 |
| 59 | 13 21 | 03 03 | 22 41 | 13 28 | 11 00 |
| 60 | 13♎03 | 02♏27 | 21♏43 | 11♐57 | 08♑23 |

**11h 40m 0s — 24 ♍ 33 — 175° 0' 0"**

| LAT. | 11 | 12 | ASC | 2 | 3 |
|---|---|---|---|---|---|
| 0 | 26♎57 | 27♏17 | 25♐25 | 23♑10 | 22♒39 |
| 5 | 25 53 | 25 32 | 23 26 | 21 20 | 21 28 |
| 10 | 24 52 | 23 50 | 21 26 | 19 26 | 20 11 |
| 15 | 23 53 | 22 08 | 19 24 | 17 24 | 18 47 |
| 20 | 22 55 | 20 27 | 17 17 | 15 16 | 17 13 |
| 21 | 22 44 | 20 06 | 16 51 | 14 48 | 16 52 |
| 22 | 22 32 | 19 45 | 16 25 | 14 21 | 16 31 |
| 23 | 22 21 | 19 25 | 15 58 | 13 52 | 16 10 |
| 24 | 22 09 | 19 04 | 15 32 | 13 24 | 15 48 |
| 25 | 21 58 | 18 43 | 15 05 | 12 54 | 15 25 |
| 26 | 21 46 | 18 22 | 14 37 | 12 24 | 15 01 |
| 27 | 21 35 | 18 01 | 14 09 | 11 54 | 14 37 |
| 28 | 21 23 | 17 40 | 13 41 | 11 22 | 14 12 |
| 29 | 21 11 | 17 18 | 13 13 | 10 50 | 13 46 |
| 30 | 21 00 | 16 57 | 12 44 | 10 18 | 13 19 |
| 31 | 20 48 | 16 35 | 12 15 | 09 44 | 12 50 |
| 32 | 20 36 | 16 13 | 11 45 | 09 10 | 12 21 |
| 33 | 20 24 | 15 51 | 11 14 | 08 34 | 11 51 |
| 34 | 20 12 | 15 28 | 10 44 | 07 58 | 11 19 |
| 35 | 20 00 | 15 06 | 10 12 | 07 21 | 10 46 |
| 36 | 19 48 | 14 43 | 09 40 | 06 43 | 10 12 |
| 37 | 19 36 | 14 19 | 09 08 | 06 04 | 09 36 |
| 38 | 19 23 | 13 56 | 08 35 | 05 23 | 08 58 |
| 39 | 19 11 | 13 32 | 08 01 | 04 41 | 08 19 |
| 40 | 18 58 | 13 08 | 07 27 | 03 58 | 07 37 |
| 41 | 18 45 | 12 43 | 06 51 | 03 14 | 06 54 |
| 42 | 18 33 | 12 18 | 06 15 | 02 28 | 06 08 |
| 43 | 18 19 | 11 53 | 05 39 | 01 41 | 05 19 |
| 44 | 18 06 | 11 27 | 05 01 | 00 52 | 04 28 |
| 45 | 17 53 | 11 01 | 04 22 | 00 01 | 03 33 |
| 46 | 17 39 | 10 34 | 03 43 | 29♐09 | 02 36 |
| 47 | 17 25 | 10 07 | 03 03 | 28 14 | 01 35 |
| 48 | 17 11 | 09 39 | 02 21 | 27 18 | 00 29 |
| 49 | 16 57 | 09 11 | 01 39 | 26 19 | 29♑20 |
| 50 | 16 42 | 08 42 | 00 55 | 25 18 | 28 05 |
| 51 | 16 27 | 08 12 | 00 10 | 24 14 | 26 45 |
| 52 | 16 12 | 07 42 | 29♏24 | 23 08 | 25 20 |
| 53 | 15 57 | 07 12 | 28 36 | 22 00 | 23 48 |
| 54 | 15 41 | 06 40 | 27 47 | 20 48 | 22 08 |
| 55 | 15 25 | 06 08 | 26 57 | 19 33 | 20 21 |
| 56 | 15 09 | 05 34 | 26 05 | 18 16 | 18 26 |
| 57 | 14 52 | 05 00 | 25 11 | 16 54 | 16 20 |
| 58 | 14 35 | 04 26 | 24 16 | 15 29 | 14 04 |
| 59 | 14 17 | 03 50 | 23 19 | 14 01 | 11 37 |
| 60 | 13♎59 | 03♏13 | 22♏20 | 12♐28 | 08♑57 |

# Koch Table of Houses for Latitudes 0° to 60° North

**11h 44m 0s — 25 ♍ 38 — 176° 0' 0"**

| LAT. | 11 | 12 | ASC | 2 | 3 |
|---|---|---|---|---|---|
| 0 | 28≏00 | 28♏15 | 26♐20 | 24♑06 | 23♒41 |
| 5 | 26 55 | 26 30 | 24 21 | 22 17 | 22 30 |
| 10 | 25 54 | 24 47 | 22 20 | 20 22 | 21 13 |
| 15 | 24 55 | 23 05 | 20 18 | 18 21 | 19 49 |
| 20 | 23 57 | 21 23 | 18 11 | 16 11 | 18 15 |
| 21 | 23 45 | 21 02 | 17 45 | 15 44 | 17 54 |
| 22 | 23 33 | 20 42 | 17 18 | 15 16 | 17 33 |
| 23 | 23 22 | 20 21 | 16 52 | 14 47 | 17 12 |
| 24 | 23 10 | 20 00 | 16 25 | 14 18 | 16 49 |
| 25 | 22 59 | 19 39 | 15 57 | 13 49 | 16 27 |
| 26 | 22 47 | 19 18 | 15 30 | 13 19 | 16 03 |
| 27 | 22 35 | 18 56 | 15 02 | 12 48 | 15 38 |
| 28 | 22 24 | 18 35 | 14 34 | 12 16 | 15 13 |
| 29 | 22 12 | 18 13 | 14 05 | 11 44 | 14 47 |
| 30 | 22 00 | 17 52 | 13 36 | 11 11 | 14 20 |
| 31 | 21 48 | 17 30 | 13 06 | 10 37 | 13 52 |
| 32 | 21 36 | 17 07 | 12 36 | 10 03 | 13 22 |
| 33 | 21 24 | 16 45 | 12 05 | 09 27 | 12 52 |
| 34 | 21 12 | 16 22 | 11 34 | 08 51 | 12 20 |
| 35 | 21 00 | 16 00 | 11 03 | 08 13 | 11 47 |
| 36 | 20 48 | 15 36 | 10 31 | 07 35 | 11 12 |
| 37 | 20 35 | 15 13 | 09 58 | 06 55 | 10 36 |
| 38 | 20 23 | 14 49 | 09 24 | 06 14 | 09 58 |
| 39 | 20 10 | 14 25 | 08 50 | 05 32 | 09 18 |
| 40 | 19 57 | 14 01 | 08 15 | 04 48 | 08 37 |
| 41 | 19 45 | 13 36 | 07 40 | 04 04 | 07 53 |
| 42 | 19 31 | 13 10 | 07 03 | 03 17 | 07 06 |
| 43 | 19 18 | 12 45 | 06 26 | 02 29 | 06 17 |
| 44 | 19 05 | 12 19 | 05 48 | 01 40 | 05 26 |
| 45 | 18 51 | 11 52 | 05 09 | 00 48 | 04 31 |
| 46 | 18 37 | 11 25 | 04 29 | 29♐55 | 03 32 |
| 47 | 18 23 | 10 58 | 03 49 | 29 00 | 02 30 |
| 48 | 18 09 | 10 30 | 03 07 | 28 03 | 01 24 |
| 49 | 17 55 | 10 01 | 02 23 | 27 03 | 00 14 |
| 50 | 17 40 | 09 32 | 01 39 | 26 01 | 28♑59 |
| 51 | 17 25 | 09 02 | 00 54 | 24 57 | 27 38 |
| 52 | 17 10 | 08 32 | 00 07 | 23 50 | 26 11 |
| 53 | 16 54 | 08 00 | 29♏19 | 22 40 | 24 37 |
| 54 | 16 38 | 07 28 | 28 29 | 21 28 | 22 57 |
| 55 | 16 22 | 06 56 | 27 38 | 20 12 | 21 08 |
| 56 | 16 05 | 06 22 | 26 45 | 18 53 | 19 10 |
| 57 | 15 48 | 05 48 | 25 51 | 17 30 | 17 03 |
| 58 | 15 31 | 05 12 | 24 55 | 16 04 | 14 44 |
| 59 | 15 13 | 04 36 | 23 57 | 14 33 | 12 14 |
| 60 | 14≏55 | 03♏59 | 22♏57 | 12♐59 | 09♑31 |

**11h 48m 0s — 26 ♍ 44 — 177° 0' 0"**

| LAT. | 11 | 12 | ASC | 2 | 3 |
|---|---|---|---|---|---|
| 0 | 29≏03 | 29♏13 | 27♐15 | 25♑03 | 24♒42 |
| 5 | 27 58 | 27 27 | 25 16 | 23 14 | 23 32 |
| 10 | 26 56 | 25 44 | 23 15 | 21 19 | 22 15 |
| 15 | 25 57 | 24 02 | 21 12 | 19 17 | 20 51 |
| 20 | 24 58 | 22 19 | 19 04 | 17 07 | 19 17 |
| 21 | 24 46 | 21 58 | 18 38 | 16 39 | 18 56 |
| 22 | 24 35 | 21 38 | 18 12 | 16 11 | 18 35 |
| 23 | 24 23 | 21 17 | 17 45 | 15 43 | 18 14 |
| 24 | 24 11 | 20 56 | 17 18 | 15 14 | 17 52 |
| 25 | 24 00 | 20 35 | 16 50 | 14 44 | 17 29 |
| 26 | 23 48 | 20 13 | 16 22 | 14 14 | 17 05 |
| 27 | 23 36 | 19 52 | 15 54 | 13 43 | 16 40 |
| 28 | 23 24 | 19 30 | 15 26 | 13 11 | 16 15 |
| 29 | 23 12 | 19 08 | 14 57 | 12 38 | 15 49 |
| 30 | 23 00 | 18 47 | 14 27 | 12 05 | 15 21 |
| 31 | 22 48 | 18 24 | 13 58 | 11 31 | 14 53 |
| 32 | 22 36 | 18 02 | 13 27 | 10 56 | 14 24 |
| 33 | 22 24 | 17 39 | 12 57 | 10 20 | 13 53 |
| 34 | 22 12 | 17 17 | 12 25 | 09 43 | 13 21 |
| 35 | 22 00 | 16 53 | 11 53 | 09 06 | 12 48 |
| 36 | 21 47 | 16 30 | 11 21 | 08 27 | 12 13 |
| 37 | 21 35 | 16 06 | 10 48 | 07 47 | 11 37 |
| 38 | 21 22 | 15 42 | 10 14 | 07 05 | 10 59 |
| 39 | 21 10 | 15 18 | 09 40 | 06 23 | 10 19 |
| 40 | 20 57 | 14 53 | 09 04 | 05 39 | 09 36 |
| 41 | 20 44 | 14 28 | 08 28 | 04 54 | 08 52 |
| 42 | 20 30 | 14 03 | 07 52 | 04 07 | 08 05 |
| 43 | 20 17 | 13 37 | 07 14 | 03 18 | 07 16 |
| 44 | 20 03 | 13 11 | 06 36 | 02 28 | 06 24 |
| 45 | 19 50 | 12 44 | 05 56 | 01 36 | 05 28 |
| 46 | 19 36 | 12 17 | 05 16 | 00 42 | 04 30 |
| 47 | 19 22 | 11 49 | 04 35 | 29♐46 | 03 27 |
| 48 | 19 07 | 11 20 | 03 52 | 28 48 | 02 20 |
| 49 | 18 53 | 10 52 | 03 08 | 27 48 | 01 09 |
| 50 | 18 38 | 10 22 | 02 24 | 26 45 | 29♑53 |
| 51 | 18 22 | 09 52 | 01 38 | 25 40 | 28 31 |
| 52 | 18 07 | 09 21 | 00 50 | 24 32 | 27 03 |
| 53 | 17 51 | 08 49 | 00 01 | 23 21 | 25 28 |
| 54 | 17 35 | 08 17 | 29♏11 | 22 07 | 23 46 |
| 55 | 17 19 | 07 44 | 28 19 | 20 50 | 21 55 |
| 56 | 17 02 | 07 10 | 27 26 | 19 30 | 19 56 |
| 57 | 16 45 | 06 35 | 26 31 | 18 06 | 17 46 |
| 58 | 16 27 | 05 59 | 25 34 | 16 38 | 15 25 |
| 59 | 16 09 | 05 22 | 24 35 | 15 06 | 12 52 |
| 60 | 15≏50 | 04♏45 | 23♏34 | 13♐31 | 10♑06 |

**11h 52m 0s — 27 ♍ 49 — 178° 0' 0"**

| LAT. | 11 | 12 | ASC | 2 | 3 |
|---|---|---|---|---|---|
| 0 | 00♏06 | 00♐11 | 28♐10 | 26♑00 | 25♒44 |
| 5 | 29≏01 | 28♏25 | 26 10 | 24 11 | 24 34 |
| 10 | 27 58 | 26 41 | 24 10 | 22 16 | 23 18 |
| 15 | 26 58 | 24 59 | 22 06 | 20 14 | 21 54 |
| 20 | 25 59 | 23 15 | 19 58 | 18 03 | 20 19 |
| 21 | 25 47 | 22 54 | 19 32 | 17 35 | 19 59 |
| 22 | 25 36 | 22 34 | 19 05 | 17 07 | 19 38 |
| 23 | 25 24 | 22 13 | 18 38 | 16 38 | 19 16 |
| 24 | 25 12 | 21 51 | 18 11 | 16 09 | 18 54 |
| 25 | 25 00 | 21 30 | 17 43 | 15 39 | 18 31 |
| 26 | 24 49 | 21 09 | 17 15 | 15 09 | 18 07 |
| 27 | 24 37 | 20 47 | 16 47 | 14 37 | 17 43 |
| 28 | 24 25 | 20 25 | 16 18 | 14 05 | 17 17 |
| 29 | 24 13 | 20 03 | 15 49 | 13 33 | 16 51 |
| 30 | 24 01 | 19 41 | 15 19 | 12 59 | 16 24 |
| 31 | 23 49 | 19 19 | 14 49 | 12 25 | 15 55 |
| 32 | 23 37 | 18 57 | 14 19 | 11 50 | 15 26 |
| 33 | 23 24 | 18 34 | 13 48 | 11 14 | 14 55 |
| 34 | 23 12 | 18 11 | 13 16 | 10 37 | 14 23 |
| 35 | 23 00 | 17 47 | 12 44 | 09 58 | 13 49 |
| 36 | 22 47 | 17 24 | 12 11 | 09 19 | 13 15 |
| 37 | 22 34 | 17 00 | 11 38 | 08 39 | 12 38 |
| 38 | 22 22 | 16 36 | 11 04 | 07 57 | 12 00 |
| 39 | 22 09 | 16 11 | 10 29 | 07 14 | 11 19 |
| 40 | 21 56 | 15 46 | 09 54 | 06 30 | 10 37 |
| 41 | 21 43 | 15 21 | 09 17 | 05 44 | 09 52 |
| 42 | 21 29 | 14 55 | 08 40 | 04 56 | 09 05 |
| 43 | 21 16 | 14 29 | 08 02 | 04 07 | 08 15 |
| 44 | 21 02 | 14 03 | 07 23 | 03 17 | 07 23 |
| 45 | 20 48 | 13 36 | 06 43 | 02 24 | 06 27 |
| 46 | 20 34 | 13 08 | 06 03 | 01 29 | 05 27 |
| 47 | 20 20 | 12 40 | 05 21 | 00 33 | 04 24 |
| 48 | 20 05 | 12 11 | 04 38 | 29♐34 | 03 17 |
| 49 | 19 50 | 11 42 | 03 54 | 28 33 | 02 05 |
| 50 | 19 35 | 11 12 | 03 08 | 27 29 | 00 47 |
| 51 | 19 20 | 10 42 | 02 22 | 26 23 | 29♑24 |
| 52 | 19 04 | 10 10 | 01 34 | 25 14 | 27 55 |
| 53 | 18 48 | 09 38 | 00 44 | 24 02 | 26 19 |
| 54 | 18 32 | 09 06 | 29♏53 | 22 47 | 24 35 |
| 55 | 18 15 | 08 32 | 29 01 | 21 29 | 22 43 |
| 56 | 17 58 | 07 58 | 28 06 | 20 07 | 20 41 |
| 57 | 17 41 | 07 22 | 27 10 | 18 42 | 18 30 |
| 58 | 17 23 | 06 46 | 26 13 | 17 13 | 16 06 |
| 59 | 17 05 | 06 09 | 25 13 | 15 40 | 13 31 |
| 60 | 16≏46 | 05♏30 | 24♏11 | 14♐02 | 10♑42 |

**11h 56m 0s — 28 ♍ 55 — 179° 0' 0"**

| LAT. | 11 | 12 | ASC | 2 | 3 |
|---|---|---|---|---|---|
| 0 | 01♏08 | 01♐08 | 29♐05 | 26♑57 | 26♒47 |
| 5 | 00 03 | 29♏22 | 27 05 | 25 08 | 25 36 |
| 10 | 29≏00 | 27 38 | 25 04 | 23 13 | 24 20 |
| 15 | 28 00 | 25 55 | 23 00 | 21 11 | 22 56 |
| 20 | 27 00 | 24 12 | 20 52 | 18 59 | 21 22 |
| 21 | 26 49 | 23 51 | 20 25 | 18 31 | 21 02 |
| 22 | 26 37 | 23 30 | 19 58 | 18 03 | 20 41 |
| 23 | 26 25 | 23 08 | 19 31 | 17 34 | 20 19 |
| 24 | 26 13 | 22 47 | 19 04 | 17 05 | 19 57 |
| 25 | 26 01 | 22 26 | 18 36 | 16 35 | 19 34 |
| 26 | 25 49 | 22 04 | 18 08 | 16 04 | 19 10 |
| 27 | 25 37 | 21 42 | 17 40 | 15 33 | 18 45 |
| 28 | 25 25 | 21 21 | 17 11 | 15 00 | 18 20 |
| 29 | 25 13 | 20 58 | 16 41 | 14 28 | 17 53 |
| 30 | 25 01 | 20 36 | 16 12 | 13 54 | 17 26 |
| 31 | 24 49 | 20 14 | 15 41 | 13 19 | 16 58 |
| 32 | 24 37 | 19 51 | 15 11 | 12 44 | 16 28 |
| 33 | 24 24 | 19 28 | 14 39 | 12 07 | 15 57 |
| 34 | 24 12 | 19 05 | 14 07 | 11 30 | 15 25 |
| 35 | 23 59 | 18 41 | 13 35 | 10 51 | 14 51 |
| 36 | 23 47 | 18 18 | 13 02 | 10 12 | 14 16 |
| 37 | 23 34 | 17 54 | 12 28 | 09 31 | 13 40 |
| 38 | 23 21 | 17 29 | 11 54 | 08 49 | 13 01 |
| 39 | 23 08 | 17 04 | 11 19 | 08 06 | 12 20 |
| 40 | 22 55 | 16 39 | 10 43 | 07 21 | 11 38 |
| 41 | 22 42 | 16 14 | 10 06 | 06 34 | 10 53 |
| 42 | 22 28 | 15 48 | 09 29 | 05 47 | 10 05 |
| 43 | 22 14 | 15 21 | 08 50 | 04 57 | 09 15 |
| 44 | 22 01 | 14 54 | 08 11 | 04 06 | 08 22 |
| 45 | 21 47 | 14 27 | 07 31 | 03 12 | 07 26 |
| 46 | 21 32 | 13 59 | 06 49 | 02 17 | 06 26 |
| 47 | 21 18 | 13 31 | 06 07 | 01 20 | 05 22 |
| 48 | 21 03 | 13 02 | 05 24 | 00 20 | 04 14 |
| 49 | 20 48 | 12 32 | 04 39 | 29♐18 | 03 01 |
| 50 | 20 33 | 12 02 | 03 53 | 28 14 | 01 43 |
| 51 | 20 17 | 11 31 | 03 06 | 27 07 | 00 19 |
| 52 | 20 02 | 11 00 | 02 17 | 25 57 | 28♑48 |
| 53 | 19 45 | 10 27 | 01 27 | 24 44 | 27 11 |
| 54 | 19 29 | 09 54 | 00 35 | 23 28 | 25 26 |
| 55 | 19 12 | 09 20 | 29♏42 | 22 08 | 23 32 |
| 56 | 18 55 | 08 45 | 28 47 | 20 45 | 21 28 |
| 57 | 18 37 | 08 10 | 27 50 | 19 18 | 19 14 |
| 58 | 18 19 | 07 33 | 26 52 | 17 48 | 16 48 |
| 59 | 18 01 | 06 55 | 25 51 | 16 13 | 14 10 |
| 60 | 17≏42 | 06♏16 | 24♏48 | 14♐34 | 11♑18 |

**12h 0m 0s — 00 ≏ 00 — 180° 0' 0"**

| LAT. | 11 | 12 | ASC | 2 | 3 |
|---|---|---|---|---|---|
| 0 | 02♏11 | 02♐05 | 00♑00 | 27♑55 | 27♒49 |
| 5 | 01 05 | 00 19 | 28♐00 | 26 05 | 26 39 |
| 10 | 00 02 | 28♏35 | 25 59 | 24 10 | 25 23 |
| 15 | 29≏01 | 26 52 | 23 55 | 22 08 | 23 59 |
| 20 | 28 02 | 25 08 | 21 46 | 19 55 | 22 25 |
| 21 | 27 50 | 24 47 | 21 19 | 19 28 | 22 05 |
| 22 | 27 38 | 24 25 | 20 52 | 18 59 | 21 44 |
| 23 | 27 26 | 24 04 | 20 25 | 18 30 | 21 22 |
| 24 | 27 14 | 23 43 | 19 57 | 18 01 | 21 00 |
| 25 | 27 02 | 23 21 | 19 29 | 17 30 | 20 37 |
| 26 | 26 50 | 23 00 | 19 01 | 17 00 | 20 13 |
| 27 | 26 38 | 22 38 | 18 32 | 16 28 | 19 48 |
| 28 | 26 26 | 22 16 | 18 03 | 15 56 | 19 23 |
| 29 | 26 13 | 21 53 | 17 34 | 15 23 | 18 56 |
| 30 | 26 01 | 21 31 | 17 04 | 14 49 | 18 29 |
| 31 | 25 49 | 21 08 | 16 33 | 14 14 | 18 00 |
| 32 | 25 37 | 20 46 | 16 02 | 13 38 | 17 31 |
| 33 | 25 24 | 20 22 | 15 31 | 13 01 | 17 00 |
| 34 | 25 12 | 19 59 | 14 59 | 12 24 | 16 28 |
| 35 | 24 59 | 19 35 | 14 26 | 11 45 | 15 54 |
| 36 | 24 46 | 19 11 | 13 53 | 11 05 | 15 19 |
| 37 | 24 33 | 18 47 | 13 19 | 10 24 | 14 42 |
| 38 | 24 20 | 18 22 | 12 44 | 09 41 | 14 03 |
| 39 | 24 07 | 17 57 | 12 08 | 08 58 | 13 22 |
| 40 | 23 54 | 17 32 | 11 32 | 08 12 | 12 39 |
| 41 | 23 40 | 17 06 | 10 55 | 07 25 | 11 54 |
| 42 | 23 27 | 16 40 | 10 17 | 06 37 | 11 06 |
| 43 | 23 13 | 16 14 | 09 39 | 05 47 | 10 16 |
| 44 | 22 59 | 15 46 | 08 59 | 04 55 | 09 22 |
| 45 | 22 45 | 15 19 | 08 18 | 04 01 | 08 25 |
| 46 | 22 31 | 14 51 | 07 36 | 03 05 | 07 25 |
| 47 | 22 16 | 14 22 | 06 54 | 02 07 | 06 21 |
| 48 | 22 01 | 13 53 | 06 10 | 01 07 | 05 12 |
| 49 | 21 46 | 13 23 | 05 24 | 00 04 | 03 58 |
| 50 | 21 31 | 12 52 | 04 38 | 28♐59 | 02 39 |
| 51 | 21 15 | 12 21 | 03 50 | 27 51 | 01 14 |
| 52 | 20 59 | 11 49 | 03 01 | 26 40 | 29♑42 |
| 53 | 20 43 | 11 16 | 02 10 | 25 26 | 28 04 |
| 54 | 20 26 | 10 43 | 01 18 | 24 08 | 26 17 |
| 55 | 20 09 | 10 08 | 00 24 | 22 48 | 24 21 |
| 56 | 19 51 | 09 33 | 29♏28 | 21 23 | 22 16 |
| 57 | 19 34 | 08 57 | 28 30 | 19 55 | 19 59 |
| 58 | 19 15 | 08 20 | 27 31 | 18 23 | 17 31 |
| 59 | 18 57 | 07 41 | 26 29 | 16 47 | 14 49 |
| 60 | 18≏37 | 07♏02 | 25♏26 | 15♐06 | 11♑54 |

**12h 4m 0s — 01 ≏ 05 — 181° 0' 0"**

| LAT. | 11 | 12 | ASC | 2 | 3 |
|---|---|---|---|---|---|
| 0 | 03♏13 | 03♐03 | 00♑55 | 28♑52 | 28♒52 |
| 5 | 02 07 | 01 16 | 28♐55 | 27 02 | 27 42 |
| 10 | 01 04 | 29♏32 | 26 54 | 25 07 | 26 26 |
| 15 | 00 03 | 27 48 | 24 49 | 23 05 | 25 03 |
| 20 | 29≏03 | 26 04 | 22 40 | 20 52 | 23 29 |
| 21 | 28 51 | 25 43 | 22 13 | 20 24 | 23 08 |
| 22 | 28 39 | 25 21 | 21 46 | 19 56 | 22 47 |
| 23 | 28 27 | 25 00 | 21 18 | 19 27 | 22 26 |
| 24 | 28 14 | 24 38 | 20 51 | 18 57 | 22 03 |
| 25 | 28 02 | 24 17 | 20 23 | 18 27 | 21 40 |
| 26 | 27 50 | 23 55 | 19 54 | 17 56 | 21 16 |
| 27 | 27 38 | 23 33 | 19 25 | 17 24 | 20 52 |
| 28 | 27 26 | 23 11 | 18 56 | 16 51 | 20 26 |
| 29 | 27 14 | 22 48 | 18 26 | 16 18 | 20 00 |
| 30 | 27 01 | 22 26 | 17 56 | 15 44 | 19 32 |
| 31 | 26 49 | 22 03 | 17 25 | 15 09 | 19 04 |
| 32 | 26 36 | 21 40 | 16 54 | 14 33 | 18 34 |
| 33 | 26 24 | 21 17 | 16 22 | 13 56 | 18 03 |
| 34 | 26 11 | 20 53 | 15 50 | 13 18 | 17 31 |
| 35 | 25 59 | 20 29 | 15 17 | 12 39 | 16 57 |
| 36 | 25 46 | 20 05 | 14 43 | 11 58 | 16 21 |
| 37 | 25 33 | 19 41 | 14 09 | 11 17 | 15 44 |
| 38 | 25 20 | 19 16 | 13 34 | 10 34 | 15 05 |
| 39 | 25 06 | 18 51 | 12 58 | 09 50 | 14 24 |
| 40 | 24 53 | 18 25 | 12 22 | 09 04 | 13 41 |
| 41 | 24 39 | 17 59 | 11 45 | 08 17 | 12 56 |
| 42 | 24 26 | 17 33 | 11 06 | 07 28 | 12 08 |
| 43 | 24 12 | 17 06 | 10 27 | 06 37 | 11 17 |
| 44 | 23 58 | 16 38 | 09 47 | 05 45 | 10 23 |
| 45 | 23 43 | 16 10 | 09 06 | 04 50 | 09 26 |
| 46 | 23 29 | 15 42 | 08 24 | 03 54 | 08 25 |
| 47 | 23 14 | 15 13 | 07 40 | 02 55 | 07 20 |
| 48 | 22 59 | 14 44 | 06 56 | 01 54 | 06 10 |
| 49 | 22 44 | 14 13 | 06 10 | 00 50 | 04 56 |
| 50 | 22 28 | 13 42 | 05 23 | 29♐44 | 03 36 |
| 51 | 22 12 | 13 11 | 04 34 | 28 35 | 02 10 |
| 52 | 21 56 | 12 38 | 03 44 | 27 23 | 00 37 |
| 53 | 21 40 | 12 05 | 02 53 | 26 08 | 28♑57 |
| 54 | 21 23 | 11 31 | 02 00 | 24 49 | 27 09 |
| 55 | 21 06 | 10 57 | 01 05 | 23 27 | 25 11 |
| 56 | 20 48 | 10 21 | 00 09 | 22 02 | 23 04 |
| 57 | 20 30 | 09 44 | 29♏10 | 20 32 | 20 45 |
| 58 | 20 12 | 09 07 | 28 10 | 18 59 | 18 14 |
| 59 | 19 52 | 08 28 | 27 08 | 17 21 | 15 30 |
| 60 | 19≏33 | 07♏48 | 26♏03 | 15♐38 | 12♑31 |

**12h 8m 0s — 02 ≏ 11 — 182° 0' 0"**

| LAT. | 11 | 12 | ASC | 2 | 3 |
|---|---|---|---|---|---|
| 0 | 04♏16 | 04♐00 | 01♑50 | 29♑49 | 29♒54 |
| 5 | 03 09 | 02 13 | 29♐50 | 28 00 | 28 45 |
| 10 | 02 06 | 00 29 | 27 49 | 26 05 | 27 29 |
| 15 | 01 04 | 28♏45 | 25 44 | 24 02 | 26 06 |
| 20 | 00 04 | 27 00 | 23 34 | 21 49 | 24 32 |
| 21 | 29≏51 | 26 39 | 23 07 | 21 21 | 24 12 |
| 22 | 29 39 | 26 17 | 22 40 | 20 53 | 23 51 |
| 23 | 29 27 | 25 56 | 22 12 | 20 23 | 23 29 |
| 24 | 29 15 | 25 34 | 21 44 | 19 53 | 23 07 |
| 25 | 29 03 | 25 12 | 21 16 | 19 23 | 22 44 |
| 26 | 28 51 | 24 50 | 20 47 | 18 52 | 22 20 |
| 27 | 28 38 | 24 28 | 20 18 | 18 20 | 21 56 |
| 28 | 28 26 | 24 06 | 19 49 | 17 47 | 21 30 |
| 29 | 28 14 | 23 43 | 19 19 | 17 14 | 21 04 |
| 30 | 28 01 | 23 21 | 18 49 | 16 39 | 20 36 |
| 31 | 27 49 | 22 58 | 18 18 | 16 04 | 20 07 |
| 32 | 27 36 | 22 35 | 17 46 | 15 28 | 19 38 |
| 33 | 27 24 | 22 11 | 17 14 | 14 51 | 19 07 |
| 34 | 27 11 | 21 47 | 16 42 | 14 13 | 18 34 |
| 35 | 26 58 | 21 23 | 16 08 | 13 33 | 18 00 |
| 36 | 26 45 | 20 59 | 15 35 | 12 52 | 17 25 |
| 37 | 26 32 | 20 34 | 15 00 | 12 10 | 16 48 |
| 38 | 26 19 | 20 09 | 14 25 | 11 27 | 16 08 |
| 39 | 26 05 | 19 44 | 13 49 | 10 43 | 15 27 |
| 40 | 25 52 | 19 18 | 13 12 | 09 56 | 14 44 |
| 41 | 25 38 | 18 52 | 12 34 | 09 09 | 13 58 |
| 42 | 25 24 | 18 25 | 11 55 | 08 19 | 13 10 |
| 43 | 25 10 | 17 58 | 11 16 | 07 28 | 12 19 |
| 44 | 24 56 | 17 30 | 10 35 | 06 35 | 11 24 |
| 45 | 24 42 | 17 02 | 09 54 | 05 40 | 10 27 |
| 46 | 24 27 | 16 34 | 09 11 | 04 43 | 09 25 |
| 47 | 24 12 | 16 04 | 08 27 | 03 43 | 08 20 |
| 48 | 23 57 | 15 34 | 07 42 | 02 41 | 07 09 |
| 49 | 23 41 | 15 04 | 06 56 | 01 37 | 05 54 |
| 50 | 23 26 | 14 33 | 06 08 | 00 29 | 04 33 |
| 51 | 23 10 | 14 01 | 05 19 | 29♐19 | 03 06 |
| 52 | 22 53 | 13 28 | 04 28 | 28 06 | 01 33 |
| 53 | 22 37 | 12 54 | 03 36 | 26 50 | 29♑51 |
| 54 | 22 20 | 12 20 | 02 42 | 25 31 | 28 01 |
| 55 | 22 02 | 11 45 | 01 47 | 24 07 | 26 02 |
| 56 | 21 44 | 11 09 | 00 50 | 22 40 | 23 53 |
| 57 | 21 26 | 10 32 | 29♏51 | 21 09 | 21 32 |
| 58 | 21 07 | 09 53 | 28 49 | 19 34 | 18 58 |
| 59 | 20 48 | 09 14 | 27 46 | 17 55 | 16 11 |
| 60 | 20≏29 | 08♏34 | 26♏40 | 16♐11 | 13♑09 |

**12h 12m 0s — 03 ≏ 16 — 183° 0' 0"**

| LAT. | 11 | 12 | ASC | 2 | 3 |
|---|---|---|---|---|---|
| 0 | 05♏18 | 04♐57 | 02♑45 | 00♒47 | 00♓57 |
| 5 | 04 11 | 03 10 | 00 45 | 28♑58 | 29♒48 |
| 10 | 03 07 | 01 26 | 28♐44 | 27 03 | 28 33 |
| 15 | 02 05 | 29♏41 | 26 39 | 25 00 | 27 10 |
| 20 | 01 04 | 27 56 | 24 28 | 22 46 | 25 36 |
| 21 | 00 52 | 27 34 | 24 01 | 22 18 | 25 16 |
| 22 | 00 40 | 27 13 | 23 34 | 21 50 | 24 55 |
| 23 | 00 28 | 26 51 | 23 06 | 21 20 | 24 33 |
| 24 | 00 16 | 26 30 | 22 38 | 20 50 | 24 11 |
| 25 | 00 03 | 26 08 | 22 10 | 20 20 | 23 48 |
| 26 | 29≏51 | 25 46 | 21 41 | 19 48 | 23 24 |
| 27 | 29 39 | 25 23 | 21 12 | 19 16 | 23 00 |
| 28 | 29 26 | 25 01 | 20 42 | 18 43 | 22 34 |
| 29 | 29 14 | 24 38 | 20 12 | 18 10 | 22 08 |
| 30 | 29 01 | 24 16 | 19 41 | 17 35 | 21 40 |
| 31 | 28 49 | 23 52 | 19 10 | 17 00 | 21 12 |
| 32 | 28 36 | 23 29 | 18 38 | 16 23 | 20 42 |
| 33 | 28 23 | 23 05 | 18 06 | 15 46 | 20 11 |
| 34 | 28 11 | 22 42 | 17 33 | 15 07 | 19 38 |
| 35 | 27 58 | 22 17 | 17 00 | 14 28 | 19 04 |
| 36 | 27 45 | 21 53 | 16 26 | 13 47 | 18 29 |
| 37 | 27 31 | 21 28 | 15 51 | 13 04 | 17 51 |
| 38 | 27 18 | 21 03 | 15 15 | 12 21 | 17 12 |
| 39 | 27 05 | 20 37 | 14 39 | 11 36 | 16 31 |
| 40 | 26 51 | 20 11 | 14 02 | 10 49 | 15 47 |
| 41 | 26 37 | 19 45 | 13 24 | 10 01 | 15 01 |
| 42 | 26 23 | 19 18 | 12 45 | 09 11 | 14 13 |
| 43 | 26 09 | 18 50 | 12 05 | 08 19 | 13 21 |
| 44 | 25 55 | 18 22 | 11 24 | 07 25 | 12 27 |
| 45 | 25 40 | 17 54 | 10 42 | 06 30 | 11 28 |
| 46 | 25 25 | 17 25 | 09 58 | 05 32 | 10 26 |
| 47 | 25 10 | 16 55 | 09 14 | 04 32 | 09 20 |
| 48 | 24 55 | 16 25 | 08 28 | 03 29 | 08 09 |
| 49 | 24 39 | 15 54 | 07 42 | 02 24 | 06 54 |
| 50 | 24 23 | 15 23 | 06 53 | 01 16 | 05 32 |
| 51 | 24 07 | 14 50 | 06 04 | 00 05 | 04 04 |
| 52 | 23 51 | 14 17 | 05 13 | 28♐50 | 02 29 |
| 53 | 23 34 | 13 44 | 04 20 | 27 33 | 00 46 |
| 54 | 23 17 | 13 09 | 03 25 | 26 12 | 28♑55 |
| 55 | 22 59 | 12 33 | 02 29 | 24 48 | 26 54 |
| 56 | 22 41 | 11 57 | 01 31 | 23 19 | 24 42 |
| 57 | 22 22 | 11 19 | 00 31 | 21 47 | 22 19 |
| 58 | 22 03 | 10 40 | 29♏29 | 20 10 | 19 43 |
| 59 | 21 44 | 10 00 | 28 24 | 18 29 | 16 53 |
| 60 | 21≏24 | 09♏19 | 27♏18 | 16♐43 | 13♑47 |

# Koch Table of Houses for Latitudes 0° to 60° North

12h 16m 0s 184° 0' 0" 04 ♎ 22

| LAT. | 11 | 12 | ASC | 2 | 3 |
|---|---|---|---|---|---|
| 0 | 06♏19 | 05♐54 | 03♑40 | 01♒45 | 02♓00 |
| 5 | 05 13 | 04 07 | 01 41 | 29♑56 | 00 51 |
| 10 | 04 09 | 02 22 | 29♐39 | 28 01 | 29♒37 |
| 15 | 03 06 | 00 38 | 27 33 | 25 58 | 28 14 |
| 20 | 02 05 | 28♏52 | 25 22 | 23 44 | 26 41 |
| 21 | 01 53 | 28 30 | 24 55 | 23 16 | 26 20 |
| 22 | 01 41 | 28 09 | 24 28 | 22 47 | 25 59 |
| 23 | 01 28 | 27 47 | 24 00 | 22 18 | 25 38 |
| 24 | 01 16 | 27 25 | 23 32 | 21 48 | 25 16 |
| 25 | 01 04 | 27 03 | 23 03 | 21 17 | 24 53 |
| 26 | 00 51 | 26 41 | 22 34 | 20 45 | 24 29 |
| 27 | 00 39 | 26 19 | 22 05 | 20 13 | 24 04 |
| 28 | 00 27 | 25 56 | 21 35 | 19 40 | 23 39 |
| 29 | 00 14 | 25 33 | 21 05 | 19 06 | 23 12 |
| 30 | 00 01 | 25 10 | 20 34 | 18 31 | 22 45 |
| 31 | 29♎49 | 24 47 | 20 03 | 17 56 | 22 16 |
| 32 | 29 36 | 24 24 | 19 31 | 17 19 | 21 46 |
| 33 | 29 23 | 24 00 | 18 58 | 16 41 | 21 15 |
| 34 | 29 10 | 23 36 | 18 25 | 16 03 | 20 43 |
| 35 | 28 57 | 23 11 | 17 52 | 15 22 | 20 09 |
| 36 | 28 44 | 22 47 | 17 17 | 14 41 | 19 33 |
| 37 | 28 31 | 22 22 | 16 42 | 13 59 | 18 55 |
| 38 | 28 17 | 21 56 | 16 06 | 13 15 | 18 16 |
| 39 | 28 04 | 21 30 | 15 29 | 12 29 | 17 35 |
| 40 | 27 50 | 21 04 | 14 52 | 11 42 | 16 51 |
| 41 | 27 36 | 20 37 | 14 13 | 10 54 | 16 05 |
| 42 | 27 22 | 20 10 | 13 34 | 10 03 | 15 16 |
| 43 | 27 07 | 19 43 | 12 54 | 09 11 | 14 24 |
| 44 | 26 53 | 19 14 | 12 12 | 08 17 | 13 29 |
| 45 | 26 38 | 18 46 | 11 30 | 07 20 | 12 31 |
| 46 | 26 23 | 18 16 | 10 46 | 06 22 | 11 28 |
| 47 | 26 08 | 17 47 | 10 01 | 05 21 | 10 22 |
| 48 | 25 53 | 17 16 | 09 15 | 04 17 | 09 10 |
| 49 | 25 37 | 16 45 | 08 28 | 03 11 | 07 54 |
| 50 | 25 21 | 16 13 | 07 39 | 02 02 | 06 31 |
| 51 | 25 04 | 15 40 | 06 49 | 00 50 | 05 02 |
| 52 | 24 48 | 15 07 | 05 57 | 29♐35 | 03 26 |
| 53 | 24 31 | 14 33 | 05 03 | 28 16 | 01 42 |
| 54 | 24 13 | 13 57 | 04 08 | 26 54 | 29♑49 |
| 55 | 23 55 | 13 21 | 03 11 | 25 29 | 27 47 |
| 56 | 23 37 | 12 44 | 02 12 | 23 59 | 25 33 |
| 57 | 23 19 | 12 06 | 01 11 | 22 25 | 23 07 |
| 58 | 22 59 | 11 27 | 00 08 | 20 47 | 20 28 |
| 59 | 22 40 | 10 47 | 29♏03 | 19 04 | 17 35 |
| 60 | 22♎20 | 10♏05 | 27♏56 | 17♐16 | 14♑26 |

12h 20m 0s 185° 0' 0" 05 ♎ 27

| LAT. | 11 | 12 | ASC | 2 | 3 |
|---|---|---|---|---|---|
| 0 | 07♏21 | 06♐50 | 04♑35 | 02♒43 | 03♓03 |
| 5 | 06 14 | 05 04 | 02 36 | 00 54 | 01 55 |
| 10 | 05 10 | 03 19 | 00 34 | 28♑59 | 00 41 |
| 15 | 04 07 | 01 34 | 28♐28 | 26 56 | 29♒18 |
| 20 | 03 06 | 29♏48 | 26 17 | 24 42 | 27 45 |
| 21 | 02 53 | 29 26 | 25 49 | 24 14 | 27 25 |
| 22 | 02 41 | 29 04 | 25 22 | 23 45 | 27 04 |
| 23 | 02 29 | 28 43 | 24 54 | 23 15 | 26 43 |
| 24 | 02 16 | 28 21 | 24 26 | 22 45 | 26 21 |
| 25 | 02 04 | 27 59 | 23 57 | 22 14 | 25 58 |
| 26 | 01 52 | 27 36 | 23 28 | 21 43 | 25 34 |
| 27 | 01 39 | 27 14 | 22 58 | 21 10 | 25 09 |
| 28 | 01 27 | 26 51 | 22 28 | 20 37 | 24 44 |
| 29 | 01 14 | 26 28 | 21 58 | 20 03 | 24 17 |
| 30 | 01 01 | 26 05 | 21 27 | 19 28 | 23 50 |
| 31 | 00 49 | 25 42 | 20 56 | 18 52 | 23 21 |
| 32 | 00 36 | 25 18 | 20 23 | 18 15 | 22 51 |
| 33 | 00 23 | 24 54 | 19 51 | 17 37 | 22 20 |
| 34 | 00 10 | 24 30 | 19 17 | 16 58 | 21 48 |
| 35 | 29♎57 | 24 05 | 18 43 | 16 18 | 21 13 |
| 36 | 29 43 | 23 41 | 18 09 | 15 36 | 20 38 |
| 37 | 29 30 | 23 15 | 17 33 | 14 53 | 20 00 |
| 38 | 29 16 | 22 50 | 16 57 | 14 09 | 19 21 |
| 39 | 29 03 | 22 24 | 16 20 | 13 23 | 18 39 |
| 40 | 28 49 | 21 57 | 15 42 | 12 36 | 17 55 |
| 41 | 28 35 | 21 30 | 15 03 | 11 47 | 17 09 |
| 42 | 28 20 | 21 03 | 14 24 | 10 56 | 16 20 |
| 43 | 28 06 | 20 35 | 13 43 | 10 03 | 15 28 |
| 44 | 27 51 | 20 07 | 13 01 | 09 08 | 14 33 |
| 45 | 27 36 | 19 38 | 12 18 | 08 11 | 13 34 |
| 46 | 27 21 | 19 08 | 11 34 | 07 12 | 12 31 |
| 47 | 27 06 | 18 38 | 10 49 | 06 10 | 11 24 |
| 48 | 26 50 | 18 07 | 10 02 | 05 06 | 10 12 |
| 49 | 26 34 | 17 35 | 09 14 | 03 59 | 08 55 |
| 50 | 26 18 | 17 03 | 08 25 | 02 49 | 07 31 |
| 51 | 26 02 | 16 30 | 07 34 | 01 36 | 06 01 |
| 52 | 25 45 | 15 56 | 06 41 | 00 20 | 04 24 |
| 53 | 25 28 | 15 22 | 05 47 | 29♐00 | 02 39 |
| 54 | 25 10 | 14 46 | 04 51 | 27 37 | 00 44 |
| 55 | 24 52 | 14 10 | 03 53 | 26 10 | 28♑40 |
| 56 | 24 34 | 13 32 | 02 54 | 24 39 | 26 24 |
| 57 | 24 15 | 12 54 | 01 52 | 23 03 | 23 56 |
| 58 | 23 55 | 12 14 | 00 48 | 21 23 | 21 15 |
| 59 | 23 35 | 11 33 | 29♏42 | 19 39 | 18 19 |
| 60 | 23♎15 | 10♏51 | 28♏33 | 17♐49 | 15♑06 |

12h 24m 0s 186° 0' 0" 06 ♎ 32

| LAT. | 11 | 12 | ASC | 2 | 3 |
|---|---|---|---|---|---|
| 0 | 08♏23 | 07♐47 | 05♑30 | 03♒41 | 04♓07 |
| 5 | 07 15 | 06 00 | 03 31 | 01 52 | 02 59 |
| 10 | 06 11 | 04 15 | 01 29 | 29♑57 | 01 45 |
| 15 | 05 08 | 02 30 | 29♐23 | 27 54 | 00 23 |
| 20 | 04 06 | 00 44 | 27 11 | 25 40 | 28♒50 |
| 21 | 03 54 | 00 22 | 26 44 | 25 12 | 28 30 |
| 22 | 03 42 | 00 00 | 26 16 | 24 43 | 28 09 |
| 23 | 03 29 | 29♏38 | 25 48 | 24 13 | 27 48 |
| 24 | 03 17 | 29 16 | 25 20 | 23 43 | 27 26 |
| 25 | 03 04 | 28 54 | 24 51 | 23 12 | 27 03 |
| 26 | 02 52 | 28 32 | 24 22 | 22 40 | 26 39 |
| 27 | 02 39 | 28 09 | 23 52 | 22 08 | 26 15 |
| 28 | 02 27 | 27 46 | 23 22 | 21 34 | 25 49 |
| 29 | 02 14 | 27 23 | 22 51 | 21 00 | 25 23 |
| 30 | 02 01 | 27 00 | 22 20 | 20 25 | 24 55 |
| 31 | 01 48 | 26 36 | 21 48 | 19 49 | 24 27 |
| 32 | 01 35 | 26 13 | 21 16 | 19 12 | 23 57 |
| 33 | 01 22 | 25 49 | 20 43 | 18 34 | 23 26 |
| 34 | 01 09 | 25 24 | 20 10 | 17 54 | 22 53 |
| 35 | 00 56 | 24 59 | 19 35 | 17 14 | 22 19 |
| 36 | 00 43 | 24 34 | 19 00 | 16 32 | 21 43 |
| 37 | 00 29 | 24 09 | 18 25 | 15 49 | 21 06 |
| 38 | 00 15 | 23 43 | 17 48 | 15 04 | 20 26 |
| 39 | 00 02 | 23 17 | 17 11 | 14 18 | 19 44 |
| 40 | 29♎48 | 22 50 | 16 33 | 13 30 | 19 00 |
| 41 | 29 33 | 22 23 | 15 55 | 12 40 | 18 14 |
| 42 | 29 19 | 21 55 | 15 13 | 11 49 | 17 25 |
| 43 | 29 04 | 21 27 | 14 32 | 10 55 | 16 32 |
| 44 | 28 50 | 20 59 | 13 50 | 10 00 | 15 37 |
| 45 | 28 35 | 20 29 | 13 07 | 09 02 | 14 38 |
| 46 | 28 19 | 20 00 | 12 22 | 08 02 | 13 35 |
| 47 | 28 04 | 19 29 | 11 36 | 07 00 | 12 27 |
| 48 | 27 48 | 18 58 | 10 49 | 05 55 | 11 14 |
| 49 | 27 32 | 18 26 | 10 01 | 04 47 | 09 56 |
| 50 | 27 16 | 17 54 | 09 11 | 03 36 | 08 32 |
| 51 | 26 59 | 17 20 | 08 19 | 02 22 | 07 01 |
| 52 | 26 42 | 16 46 | 07 26 | 01 05 | 05 23 |
| 53 | 26 25 | 16 11 | 06 31 | 29♐44 | 03 37 |
| 54 | 26 07 | 15 35 | 05 34 | 28 20 | 01 41 |
| 55 | 25 49 | 14 58 | 04 36 | 26 51 | 29♑34 |
| 56 | 25 30 | 14 20 | 03 35 | 25 19 | 27 17 |
| 57 | 25 11 | 13 41 | 02 33 | 23 42 | 24 47 |
| 58 | 24 51 | 13 01 | 01 28 | 22 00 | 22 02 |
| 59 | 24 31 | 12 19 | 00 21 | 20 14 | 19 03 |
| 60 | 24♎10 | 11♏37 | 29♏11 | 18♐23 | 15♑47 |

12h 28m 0s 187° 0' 0" 07 ♎ 37

| LAT. | 11 | 12 | ASC | 2 | 3 |
|---|---|---|---|---|---|
| 0 | 09♏24 | 08♐43 | 06♑26 | 04♒39 | 05♓10 |
| 5 | 08 17 | 06 57 | 04 26 | 02 51 | 04 03 |
| 10 | 07 12 | 05 12 | 02 24 | 00 56 | 02 49 |
| 15 | 06 09 | 03 26 | 00 18 | 28♑53 | 01 28 |
| 20 | 05 07 | 01 39 | 28♐06 | 26 39 | 29♒55 |
| 21 | 04 54 | 01 18 | 27 38 | 26 10 | 29 35 |
| 22 | 04 42 | 00 56 | 27 11 | 25 41 | 29 15 |
| 23 | 04 29 | 00 34 | 26 43 | 25 11 | 28 53 |
| 24 | 04 17 | 00 12 | 26 14 | 24 41 | 28 31 |
| 25 | 04 04 | 29♏50 | 25 45 | 24 10 | 28 08 |
| 26 | 03 52 | 29 27 | 25 16 | 23 38 | 27 45 |
| 27 | 03 39 | 29 04 | 24 46 | 23 05 | 27 20 |
| 28 | 03 26 | 28 41 | 24 16 | 22 32 | 26 55 |
| 29 | 03 14 | 28 18 | 23 45 | 21 58 | 26 28 |
| 30 | 03 01 | 27 55 | 23 14 | 21 22 | 26 01 |
| 31 | 02 48 | 27 31 | 22 42 | 20 46 | 25 32 |
| 32 | 02 35 | 27 07 | 22 09 | 20 09 | 25 03 |
| 33 | 02 22 | 26 43 | 21 36 | 19 30 | 24 31 |
| 34 | 02 09 | 26 18 | 21 02 | 18 51 | 23 59 |
| 35 | 01 55 | 25 54 | 20 28 | 18 10 | 23 25 |
| 36 | 01 42 | 25 28 | 19 52 | 17 28 | 22 49 |
| 37 | 01 28 | 25 03 | 19 16 | 16 44 | 22 11 |
| 38 | 01 14 | 24 37 | 18 40 | 15 59 | 21 32 |
| 39 | 01 00 | 24 10 | 18 02 | 15 12 | 20 50 |
| 40 | 00 46 | 23 43 | 17 23 | 14 24 | 20 06 |
| 41 | 00 32 | 23 16 | 16 44 | 13 34 | 19 19 |
| 42 | 00 18 | 22 48 | 16 03 | 12 42 | 18 30 |
| 43 | 00 03 | 22 20 | 15 22 | 11 48 | 17 38 |
| 44 | 29♎48 | 21 51 | 14 39 | 10 52 | 16 42 |
| 45 | 29 33 | 21 21 | 13 55 | 09 54 | 15 42 |
| 46 | 29 17 | 20 51 | 13 10 | 08 54 | 14 39 |
| 47 | 29 02 | 20 20 | 12 24 | 07 50 | 13 31 |
| 48 | 28 46 | 19 49 | 11 36 | 06 45 | 12 17 |
| 49 | 28 30 | 19 17 | 10 47 | 05 36 | 10 59 |
| 50 | 28 13 | 18 44 | 09 57 | 04 24 | 09 34 |
| 51 | 27 56 | 18 10 | 09 04 | 03 09 | 08 02 |
| 52 | 27 39 | 17 36 | 08 11 | 01 51 | 06 23 |
| 53 | 27 21 | 17 00 | 07 15 | 00 29 | 04 35 |
| 54 | 27 03 | 16 24 | 06 18 | 29♐03 | 02 38 |
| 55 | 26 45 | 15 46 | 05 18 | 27 33 | 00 30 |
| 56 | 26 26 | 15 08 | 04 17 | 25 59 | 28♑10 |
| 57 | 26 07 | 14 28 | 03 13 | 24 21 | 25 38 |
| 58 | 25 47 | 13 48 | 02 08 | 22 38 | 22 50 |
| 59 | 25 27 | 13 06 | 00 59 | 20 49 | 19 48 |
| 60 | 25♎06 | 12♏22 | 29♏49 | 18♐56 | 16♑28 |

12h 32m 0s 188° 0' 0" 08 ♎ 43

| LAT. | 11 | 12 | ASC | 2 | 3 |
|---|---|---|---|---|---|
| 0 | 10♏25 | 09♐40 | 07♑21 | 05♒38 | 06♓14 |
| 5 | 09 18 | 07 53 | 05 21 | 03 49 | 05 07 |
| 10 | 08 13 | 06 08 | 03 19 | 01 55 | 03 54 |
| 15 | 07 10 | 04 22 | 01 13 | 29♑52 | 02 33 |
| 20 | 06 07 | 02 35 | 29♐01 | 27 37 | 01 01 |
| 21 | 05 55 | 02 14 | 28 33 | 27 09 | 00 41 |
| 22 | 05 42 | 01 52 | 28 05 | 26 40 | 00 20 |
| 23 | 05 30 | 01 30 | 27 37 | 26 10 | 29♒59 |
| 24 | 05 17 | 01 07 | 27 08 | 25 40 | 29 37 |
| 25 | 05 04 | 00 45 | 26 39 | 25 08 | 29 14 |
| 26 | 04 52 | 00 22 | 26 10 | 24 36 | 28 51 |
| 27 | 04 39 | 00 00 | 25 40 | 24 04 | 28 26 |
| 28 | 04 26 | 29♏36 | 25 10 | 23 30 | 28 01 |
| 29 | 04 13 | 29 13 | 24 39 | 22 56 | 27 35 |
| 30 | 04 01 | 28 50 | 24 07 | 22 20 | 27 07 |
| 31 | 03 48 | 28 26 | 23 35 | 21 44 | 26 39 |
| 32 | 03 34 | 28 02 | 23 02 | 21 06 | 26 09 |
| 33 | 03 21 | 27 37 | 22 29 | 20 27 | 25 38 |
| 34 | 03 08 | 27 13 | 21 55 | 19 48 | 25 05 |
| 35 | 02 54 | 26 48 | 21 20 | 19 07 | 24 31 |
| 36 | 02 41 | 26 22 | 20 45 | 18 24 | 23 55 |
| 37 | 02 27 | 25 56 | 20 08 | 17 40 | 23 18 |
| 38 | 02 13 | 25 30 | 19 31 | 16 55 | 22 38 |
| 39 | 01 59 | 25 04 | 18 53 | 16 08 | 21 56 |
| 40 | 01 45 | 24 36 | 18 14 | 15 19 | 21 12 |
| 41 | 01 31 | 24 09 | 17 34 | 14 29 | 20 26 |
| 42 | 01 16 | 23 41 | 16 54 | 13 36 | 19 36 |
| 43 | 01 01 | 23 12 | 16 12 | 12 42 | 18 43 |
| 44 | 00 46 | 22 43 | 15 29 | 11 45 | 17 47 |
| 45 | 00 31 | 22 13 | 14 44 | 10 46 | 16 48 |
| 46 | 00 15 | 21 43 | 13 59 | 09 45 | 15 44 |
| 47 | 00 00 | 21 12 | 13 12 | 08 41 | 14 35 |
| 48 | 29♎44 | 20 40 | 12 24 | 07 35 | 13 22 |
| 49 | 29 27 | 20 08 | 11 34 | 06 25 | 12 02 |
| 50 | 29 10 | 19 34 | 10 43 | 05 12 | 10 37 |
| 51 | 28 53 | 19 00 | 09 50 | 03 57 | 09 04 |
| 52 | 28 36 | 18 25 | 08 56 | 02 37 | 07 24 |
| 53 | 28 18 | 17 49 | 07 59 | 01 14 | 05 35 |
| 54 | 28 00 | 17 13 | 07 01 | 29♐47 | 03 36 |
| 55 | 27 41 | 16 35 | 06 01 | 28 16 | 01 26 |
| 56 | 27 22 | 15 56 | 04 59 | 26 40 | 29♑05 |
| 57 | 27 03 | 15 16 | 03 54 | 25 00 | 26 29 |
| 58 | 26 43 | 14 34 | 02 48 | 23 15 | 23 40 |
| 59 | 26 22 | 13 52 | 01 39 | 21 25 | 20 34 |
| 60 | 26♎01 | 13♏08 | 00♐27 | 19♐30 | 17♑10 |

12h 36m 0s 189° 0' 0" 09 ♎ 48

| LAT. | 11 | 12 | ASC | 2 | 3 |
|---|---|---|---|---|---|
| 0 | 11♏26 | 10♐36 | 08♑16 | 06♒37 | 07♓18 |
| 5 | 10 18 | 08 50 | 06 17 | 04 48 | 06 11 |
| 10 | 09 13 | 07 04 | 04 15 | 02 54 | 04 59 |
| 15 | 08 10 | 05 19 | 02 08 | 00 51 | 03 38 |
| 20 | 07 07 | 03 31 | 29♐55 | 28♑36 | 02 07 |
| 21 | 06 55 | 03 09 | 29 28 | 28 08 | 01 47 |
| 22 | 06 42 | 02 47 | 29 00 | 27 39 | 01 26 |
| 23 | 06 30 | 02 25 | 28 32 | 27 09 | 01 05 |
| 24 | 06 17 | 02 03 | 28 03 | 26 38 | 00 43 |
| 25 | 06 04 | 01 40 | 27 34 | 26 07 | 00 21 |
| 26 | 05 52 | 01 18 | 27 04 | 25 35 | 29♒57 |
| 27 | 05 39 | 00 55 | 26 34 | 25 02 | 29 33 |
| 28 | 05 26 | 00 32 | 26 04 | 24 29 | 29 08 |
| 29 | 05 13 | 00 08 | 25 32 | 23 54 | 28 41 |
| 30 | 05 00 | 29♏45 | 25 01 | 23 18 | 28 14 |
| 31 | 04 47 | 29 21 | 24 28 | 22 42 | 27 45 |
| 32 | 04 34 | 28 56 | 23 56 | 22 04 | 27 16 |
| 33 | 04 21 | 28 32 | 23 22 | 21 25 | 26 45 |
| 34 | 04 07 | 28 07 | 22 48 | 20 45 | 26 12 |
| 35 | 03 54 | 27 42 | 22 13 | 20 04 | 25 38 |
| 36 | 03 40 | 27 16 | 21 37 | 19 21 | 25 02 |
| 37 | 03 26 | 26 50 | 21 00 | 18 37 | 24 24 |
| 38 | 03 12 | 26 24 | 20 23 | 17 51 | 23 45 |
| 39 | 02 58 | 25 57 | 19 45 | 17 04 | 23 03 |
| 40 | 02 44 | 25 30 | 19 06 | 16 15 | 22 19 |
| 41 | 02 29 | 25 02 | 18 25 | 15 24 | 21 32 |
| 42 | 02 14 | 24 34 | 17 44 | 14 31 | 20 43 |
| 43 | 02 00 | 24 05 | 17 02 | 13 36 | 19 50 |
| 44 | 01 44 | 23 35 | 16 18 | 12 39 | 18 54 |
| 45 | 01 29 | 23 05 | 15 33 | 11 39 | 17 54 |
| 46 | 01 13 | 22 35 | 14 48 | 10 37 | 16 49 |
| 47 | 00 57 | 22 03 | 14 00 | 09 33 | 15 40 |
| 48 | 00 41 | 21 31 | 13 11 | 08 25 | 14 26 |
| 49 | 00 25 | 20 58 | 12 21 | 07 15 | 13 07 |
| 50 | 00 08 | 20 25 | 11 29 | 06 01 | 11 40 |
| 51 | 29♎51 | 19 50 | 10 36 | 04 44 | 10 07 |
| 52 | 29 33 | 19 15 | 09 41 | 03 24 | 08 26 |
| 53 | 29 15 | 18 39 | 08 44 | 02 00 | 06 35 |
| 54 | 28 57 | 18 01 | 07 45 | 00 31 | 04 35 |
| 55 | 28 38 | 17 23 | 06 44 | 28♐59 | 02 24 |
| 56 | 28 19 | 16 44 | 05 41 | 27 22 | 00 00 |
| 57 | 27 59 | 16 03 | 04 36 | 25 40 | 27♑22 |
| 58 | 27 39 | 15 21 | 03 28 | 23 53 | 24 30 |
| 59 | 27 18 | 14 38 | 02 18 | 22 01 | 21 20 |
| 60 | 26♎56 | 13♏54 | 01♐05 | 20♐04 | 17♑53 |

12h 40m 0s 190° 0' 0" 10 ♎ 53

| LAT. | 11 | 12 | ASC | 2 | 3 |
|---|---|---|---|---|---|
| 0 | 12♏27 | 11♐32 | 09♑11 | 07♒35 | 08♓22 |
| 5 | 11 19 | 09 46 | 07 12 | 05 48 | 07 16 |
| 10 | 10 14 | 08 00 | 05 10 | 03 53 | 06 04 |
| 15 | 09 11 | 06 15 | 03 04 | 01 50 | 04 44 |
| 20 | 08 08 | 04 27 | 00 51 | 29♑36 | 03 13 |
| 21 | 07 55 | 04 05 | 00 23 | 29 07 | 02 53 |
| 22 | 07 42 | 03 43 | 29♐55 | 28 38 | 02 33 |
| 23 | 07 30 | 03 21 | 29 27 | 28 08 | 02 12 |
| 24 | 07 17 | 02 58 | 28 58 | 27 38 | 01 50 |
| 25 | 07 04 | 02 36 | 28 28 | 27 06 | 01 27 |
| 26 | 06 51 | 02 13 | 27 59 | 26 34 | 01 04 |
| 27 | 06 39 | 01 50 | 27 29 | 26 01 | 00 40 |
| 28 | 06 26 | 01 27 | 26 58 | 25 27 | 00 14 |
| 29 | 06 13 | 01 03 | 26 27 | 24 53 | 29♒48 |
| 30 | 06 00 | 00 39 | 25 55 | 24 17 | 29 21 |
| 31 | 05 46 | 00 15 | 25 22 | 23 40 | 28 53 |
| 32 | 05 33 | 29♏51 | 24 49 | 23 02 | 28 23 |
| 33 | 05 20 | 29 26 | 24 15 | 22 23 | 27 52 |
| 34 | 05 06 | 29 01 | 23 41 | 21 43 | 27 20 |
| 35 | 04 53 | 28 36 | 23 06 | 21 01 | 26 46 |
| 36 | 04 39 | 28 10 | 22 30 | 20 18 | 26 10 |
| 37 | 04 25 | 27 44 | 21 53 | 19 34 | 25 32 |
| 38 | 04 11 | 27 17 | 21 15 | 18 48 | 24 53 |
| 39 | 03 57 | 26 50 | 20 37 | 18 00 | 24 11 |
| 40 | 03 42 | 26 23 | 19 57 | 17 11 | 23 27 |
| 41 | 03 28 | 25 55 | 19 16 | 16 19 | 22 40 |
| 42 | 03 13 | 25 26 | 18 35 | 15 26 | 21 50 |
| 43 | 02 58 | 24 57 | 17 52 | 14 30 | 20 57 |
| 44 | 02 43 | 24 28 | 17 08 | 13 33 | 20 01 |
| 45 | 02 27 | 23 57 | 16 23 | 12 33 | 19 00 |
| 46 | 02 11 | 23 26 | 15 36 | 11 30 | 17 56 |
| 47 | 01 55 | 22 55 | 14 49 | 10 25 | 16 47 |
| 48 | 01 39 | 22 22 | 13 59 | 09 16 | 15 32 |
| 49 | 01 22 | 21 49 | 13 09 | 08 05 | 14 12 |
| 50 | 01 05 | 21 15 | 12 16 | 06 51 | 12 45 |
| 51 | 00 48 | 20 40 | 11 22 | 05 33 | 11 11 |
| 52 | 00 30 | 20 05 | 10 26 | 04 11 | 09 28 |
| 53 | 00 12 | 19 28 | 09 28 | 02 46 | 07 37 |
| 54 | 29♎53 | 18 50 | 08 29 | 01 16 | 05 35 |
| 55 | 29 34 | 18 12 | 07 27 | 29♐42 | 03 22 |
| 56 | 29 15 | 17 32 | 06 23 | 28 03 | 00 57 |
| 57 | 28 55 | 16 51 | 05 17 | 26 20 | 28♑17 |
| 58 | 28 34 | 16 08 | 04 08 | 24 32 | 25 21 |
| 59 | 28 13 | 15 25 | 02 57 | 22 38 | 22 08 |
| 60 | 27♎51 | 14♏40 | 01♐43 | 20♐39 | 18♑37 |

12h 44m 0s 191° 0' 0" 11 ♎ 58

| LAT. | 11 | 12 | ASC | 2 | 3 |
|---|---|---|---|---|---|
| 0 | 13♏27 | 12♐28 | 10♑07 | 08♒34 | 09♓26 |
| 5 | 12 20 | 10 42 | 08 08 | 06 47 | 08 20 |
| 10 | 11 14 | 08 57 | 06 06 | 04 53 | 07 09 |
| 15 | 10 11 | 07 11 | 03 59 | 02 50 | 05 50 |
| 20 | 09 08 | 05 23 | 01 46 | 00 36 | 04 19 |
| 21 | 08 55 | 05 01 | 01 18 | 00 07 | 04 00 |
| 22 | 08 42 | 04 39 | 00 50 | 29♑38 | 03 39 |
| 23 | 08 30 | 04 16 | 00 22 | 29 08 | 03 18 |
| 24 | 08 17 | 03 54 | 29♐53 | 28 37 | 02 57 |
| 25 | 08 04 | 03 31 | 29 23 | 28 06 | 02 34 |
| 26 | 07 51 | 03 08 | 28 53 | 27 34 | 02 11 |
| 27 | 07 38 | 02 45 | 28 23 | 27 01 | 01 47 |
| 28 | 07 25 | 02 22 | 27 52 | 26 27 | 01 22 |
| 29 | 07 12 | 01 58 | 27 21 | 25 52 | 00 56 |
| 30 | 06 59 | 01 34 | 26 49 | 25 16 | 00 29 |
| 31 | 06 46 | 01 10 | 26 16 | 24 39 | 00 00 |
| 32 | 06 32 | 00 46 | 25 43 | 24 01 | 29♒31 |
| 33 | 06 19 | 00 21 | 25 09 | 23 22 | 29 00 |
| 34 | 06 05 | 29♏56 | 24 34 | 22 41 | 28 27 |
| 35 | 05 52 | 29 30 | 23 59 | 21 59 | 27 53 |
| 36 | 05 38 | 29 04 | 23 22 | 21 16 | 27 18 |
| 37 | 05 24 | 28 38 | 22 45 | 20 31 | 26 40 |
| 38 | 05 10 | 28 11 | 22 07 | 19 45 | 26 01 |
| 39 | 04 55 | 27 44 | 21 29 | 18 57 | 25 19 |
| 40 | 04 41 | 27 16 | 20 49 | 18 07 | 24 35 |
| 41 | 04 26 | 26 48 | 20 08 | 17 15 | 23 48 |
| 42 | 04 11 | 26 19 | 19 26 | 16 21 | 22 58 |
| 43 | 03 56 | 25 50 | 18 43 | 15 26 | 22 05 |
| 44 | 03 41 | 25 20 | 17 58 | 14 27 | 21 09 |
| 45 | 03 25 | 24 49 | 17 13 | 13 27 | 20 08 |
| 46 | 03 09 | 24 18 | 16 26 | 12 23 | 19 03 |
| 47 | 02 53 | 23 46 | 15 37 | 11 17 | 17 54 |
| 48 | 02 36 | 23 13 | 14 48 | 10 08 | 16 39 |
| 49 | 02 19 | 22 40 | 13 56 | 08 56 | 15 18 |
| 50 | 02 02 | 22 06 | 13 03 | 07 41 | 13 51 |
| 51 | 01 45 | 21 31 | 12 08 | 06 22 | 12 16 |
| 52 | 01 27 | 20 54 | 11 12 | 04 59 | 10 32 |
| 53 | 01 08 | 20 17 | 10 13 | 03 32 | 08 40 |
| 54 | 00 50 | 19 39 | 09 13 | 02 01 | 06 37 |
| 55 | 00 30 | 19 00 | 08 10 | 00 26 | 04 22 |
| 56 | 00 11 | 18 20 | 07 05 | 28♐46 | 01 54 |
| 57 | 29♎51 | 17 38 | 05 58 | 27 01 | 29♑12 |
| 58 | 29 30 | 16 55 | 04 49 | 25 11 | 26 13 |
| 59 | 29 08 | 16 11 | 03 36 | 23 15 | 22 57 |
| 60 | 28♎46 | 15♏25 | 02♐21 | 21♐14 | 19♑22 |

# Koch Table of Houses for Latitudes 0° to 60° North

12h 48m 0s — 192° 0' 0" — 13 ♎ 03

| LAT. | 11 | 12 | ASC | 2 | 3 |
|---|---|---|---|---|---|
| 0 | 14♏28 | 13♐24 | 11♑02 | 09♒34 | 10♓30 |
| 5 | 13 20 | 11 38 | 09 03 | 07 46 | 09 25 |
| 10 | 12 15 | 09 53 | 07 02 | 05 53 | 08 14 |
| 15 | 11 11 | 08 07 | 04 55 | 03 50 | 06 56 |
| 20 | 10 08 | 06 19 | 02 41 | 01 36 | 05 26 |
| 21 | 09 55 | 05 57 | 02 14 | 01 07 | 05 06 |
| 22 | 09 42 | 05 34 | 01 45 | 00 38 | 04 46 |
| 23 | 09 29 | 05 12 | 01 17 | 00 08 | 04 25 |
| 24 | 09 17 | 04 49 | 00 48 | 29♑37 | 04 04 |
| 25 | 09 04 | 04 27 | 00 18 | 29 06 | 03 42 |
| 26 | 08 51 | 04 04 | 29♐48 | 28 33 | 03 18 |
| 27 | 08 38 | 03 41 | 29 18 | 28 00 | 02 54 |
| 28 | 08 25 | 03 17 | 28 47 | 27 26 | 02 29 |
| 29 | 08 12 | 02 53 | 28 15 | 26 51 | 02 04 |
| 30 | 07 58 | 02 29 | 27 43 | 26 15 | 01 36 |
| 31 | 07 45 | 02 05 | 27 10 | 25 38 | 01 08 |
| 32 | 07 32 | 01 40 | 26 37 | 25 00 | 00 39 |
| 33 | 07 18 | 01 16 | 26 03 | 24 21 | 00 08 |
| 34 | 07 05 | 00 50 | 25 28 | 23 40 | 29♒36 |
| 35 | 06 51 | 00 25 | 24 52 | 22 58 | 29 02 |
| 36 | 06 37 | 29♏58 | 24 16 | 22 14 | 28 26 |
| 37 | 06 23 | 29 32 | 23 38 | 21 29 | 27 49 |
| 38 | 06 08 | 29 05 | 23 00 | 20 43 | 27 09 |
| 39 | 05 54 | 28 38 | 22 21 | 19 54 | 26 28 |
| 40 | 05 39 | 28 10 | 21 41 | 19 04 | 25 43 |
| 41 | 05 25 | 27 41 | 20 59 | 18 12 | 24 57 |
| 42 | 05 09 | 27 12 | 20 17 | 17 18 | 24 07 |
| 43 | 04 54 | 26 43 | 19 33 | 16 21 | 23 14 |
| 44 | 04 39 | 26 12 | 18 49 | 15 22 | 22 17 |
| 45 | 04 23 | 25 42 | 18 03 | 14 21 | 21 16 |
| 46 | 04 07 | 25 10 | 17 15 | 13 17 | 20 12 |
| 47 | 03 50 | 24 38 | 16 26 | 12 10 | 19 02 |
| 48 | 03 34 | 24 05 | 15 36 | 11 01 | 17 46 |
| 49 | 03 17 | 23 31 | 14 44 | 09 48 | 16 25 |
| 50 | 02 59 | 22 56 | 13 50 | 08 31 | 14 57 |
| 51 | 02 42 | 22 21 | 12 55 | 07 11 | 13 21 |
| 52 | 02 24 | 21 44 | 11 58 | 05 47 | 11 37 |
| 53 | 02 05 | 21 07 | 10 59 | 04 19 | 09 44 |
| 54 | 01 46 | 20 28 | 09 57 | 02 47 | 07 39 |
| 55 | 01 27 | 19 49 | 08 54 | 01 10 | 05 23 |
| 56 | 01 07 | 19 08 | 07 48 | 29♐29 | 02 53 |
| 57 | 00 46 | 18 26 | 06 40 | 27 42 | 00 08 |
| 58 | 00 25 | 17 42 | 05 29 | 25 50 | 27♑07 |
| 59 | 00 04 | 16 57 | 04 16 | 23 52 | 23 47 |
| 60 | 29♎41 | 16♏11 | 03♐00 | 21♐49 | 20♑08 |

12h 52m 0s — 193° 0' 0" — 14 ♎ 07

| LAT. | 11 | 12 | ASC | 2 | 3 |
|---|---|---|---|---|---|
| 0 | 15♏28 | 14♐20 | 11♑58 | 10♒33 | 11♓34 |
| 5 | 14 20 | 12 34 | 09 59 | 08 46 | 10 30 |
| 10 | 13 15 | 10 49 | 07 58 | 06 53 | 09 20 |
| 15 | 12 11 | 09 03 | 05 51 | 04 50 | 08 02 |
| 20 | 11 07 | 07 14 | 03 37 | 02 36 | 06 33 |
| 21 | 10 55 | 06 52 | 03 09 | 02 07 | 06 13 |
| 22 | 10 42 | 06 30 | 02 41 | 01 38 | 05 53 |
| 23 | 10 29 | 06 08 | 02 12 | 01 08 | 05 33 |
| 24 | 10 16 | 05 45 | 01 43 | 00 38 | 05 11 |
| 25 | 10 03 | 05 22 | 01 14 | 00 06 | 04 49 |
| 26 | 09 50 | 04 59 | 00 43 | 29♑34 | 04 26 |
| 27 | 09 37 | 04 36 | 00 13 | 29 01 | 04 02 |
| 28 | 09 24 | 04 12 | 29♐42 | 28 26 | 03 38 |
| 29 | 09 11 | 03 48 | 29 10 | 27 51 | 03 12 |
| 30 | 08 58 | 03 24 | 28 38 | 27 15 | 02 45 |
| 31 | 08 44 | 03 00 | 28 05 | 26 38 | 02 17 |
| 32 | 08 31 | 02 35 | 27 31 | 26 00 | 01 47 |
| 33 | 08 17 | 02 10 | 26 57 | 25 20 | 01 17 |
| 34 | 08 04 | 01 45 | 26 22 | 24 39 | 00 45 |
| 35 | 07 50 | 01 19 | 25 46 | 23 57 | 00 11 |
| 36 | 07 36 | 00 53 | 25 09 | 23 13 | 29♒35 |
| 37 | 07 21 | 00 26 | 24 31 | 22 28 | 28 58 |
| 38 | 07 07 | 29♏59 | 23 53 | 21 41 | 28 19 |
| 39 | 06 53 | 29 31 | 23 13 | 20 52 | 27 37 |
| 40 | 06 38 | 29 03 | 22 33 | 20 02 | 26 53 |
| 41 | 06 23 | 28 34 | 21 51 | 19 09 | 26 06 |
| 42 | 06 08 | 28 05 | 21 08 | 18 14 | 25 16 |
| 43 | 05 52 | 27 35 | 20 25 | 17 17 | 24 23 |
| 44 | 05 37 | 27 05 | 19 39 | 16 18 | 23 26 |
| 45 | 05 21 | 26 34 | 18 53 | 15 16 | 22 26 |
| 46 | 05 05 | 26 02 | 18 05 | 14 12 | 21 21 |
| 47 | 04 48 | 25 29 | 17 16 | 13 04 | 20 10 |
| 48 | 04 31 | 24 56 | 16 25 | 11 54 | 18 55 |
| 49 | 04 14 | 24 22 | 15 32 | 10 40 | 17 33 |
| 50 | 03 57 | 23 47 | 14 38 | 09 22 | 16 05 |
| 51 | 03 39 | 23 11 | 13 42 | 08 01 | 14 28 |
| 52 | 03 20 | 22 34 | 12 44 | 06 36 | 12 43 |
| 53 | 03 02 | 21 56 | 11 44 | 05 07 | 10 48 |
| 54 | 02 43 | 21 17 | 10 42 | 03 33 | 08 43 |
| 55 | 02 23 | 20 37 | 09 38 | 01 55 | 06 25 |
| 56 | 02 03 | 19 56 | 08 31 | 00 12 | 03 53 |
| 57 | 01 42 | 19 13 | 07 22 | 28♐23 | 01 06 |
| 58 | 01 21 | 18 29 | 06 10 | 26 30 | 28♑01 |
| 59 | 00 59 | 17 44 | 04 56 | 24 30 | 24 38 |
| 60 | 00♏36 | 16♏57 | 03♐39 | 22♐25 | 20♑55 |

12h 56m 0s — 194° 0' 0" — 15 ♎ 12

| LAT. | 11 | 12 | ASC | 2 | 3 |
|---|---|---|---|---|---|
| 0 | 16♏28 | 15♐16 | 12♑53 | 11♒32 | 12♓39 |
| 5 | 15 20 | 13 30 | 10 55 | 09 46 | 11 35 |
| 10 | 14 15 | 11 45 | 08 53 | 07 53 | 10 26 |
| 15 | 13 11 | 09 59 | 06 47 | 05 51 | 09 08 |
| 20 | 12 07 | 08 10 | 04 33 | 03 37 | 07 40 |
| 21 | 11 54 | 07 48 | 04 05 | 03 08 | 07 21 |
| 22 | 11 41 | 07 26 | 03 37 | 02 39 | 07 01 |
| 23 | 11 29 | 07 03 | 03 08 | 02 09 | 06 40 |
| 24 | 11 16 | 06 41 | 02 39 | 01 38 | 06 19 |
| 25 | 11 03 | 06 18 | 02 09 | 01 07 | 05 57 |
| 26 | 10 50 | 05 55 | 01 39 | 00 34 | 05 34 |
| 27 | 10 37 | 05 31 | 01 08 | 00 01 | 05 11 |
| 28 | 10 24 | 05 08 | 00 37 | 29♑27 | 04 46 |
| 29 | 10 10 | 04 44 | 00 05 | 28 52 | 04 20 |
| 30 | 09 57 | 04 19 | 29♐32 | 28 16 | 03 54 |
| 31 | 09 43 | 03 55 | 28 59 | 27 38 | 03 26 |
| 32 | 09 30 | 03 30 | 28 26 | 27 00 | 02 56 |
| 33 | 09 16 | 03 05 | 27 51 | 26 20 | 02 26 |
| 34 | 09 02 | 02 39 | 27 16 | 25 39 | 01 54 |
| 35 | 08 48 | 02 13 | 26 40 | 24 56 | 01 20 |
| 36 | 08 34 | 01 47 | 26 03 | 24 12 | 00 45 |
| 37 | 08 20 | 01 20 | 25 25 | 23 27 | 00 08 |
| 38 | 08 06 | 00 53 | 24 46 | 22 40 | 29♒28 |
| 39 | 07 51 | 00 25 | 24 06 | 21 51 | 28 47 |
| 40 | 07 36 | 29♏57 | 23 25 | 21 00 | 28 03 |
| 41 | 07 21 | 29 28 | 22 43 | 20 07 | 27 16 |
| 42 | 07 06 | 28 58 | 22 00 | 19 12 | 26 26 |
| 43 | 06 50 | 28 28 | 21 16 | 18 14 | 25 33 |
| 44 | 06 35 | 27 57 | 20 30 | 17 14 | 24 36 |
| 45 | 06 19 | 27 26 | 19 43 | 16 12 | 23 36 |
| 46 | 06 02 | 26 54 | 18 55 | 15 07 | 22 30 |
| 47 | 05 46 | 26 21 | 18 05 | 13 58 | 21 20 |
| 48 | 05 29 | 25 48 | 17 14 | 12 47 | 20 04 |
| 49 | 05 11 | 25 13 | 16 21 | 11 32 | 18 42 |
| 50 | 04 54 | 24 38 | 15 26 | 10 14 | 17 13 |
| 51 | 04 36 | 24 01 | 14 29 | 08 52 | 15 36 |
| 52 | 04 17 | 23 24 | 13 30 | 07 26 | 13 50 |
| 53 | 03 58 | 22 46 | 12 30 | 05 55 | 11 55 |
| 54 | 03 39 | 22 06 | 11 27 | 04 20 | 09 48 |
| 55 | 03 19 | 21 26 | 10 22 | 02 41 | 07 28 |
| 56 | 02 59 | 20 44 | 09 14 | 00 56 | 04 54 |
| 57 | 02 38 | 20 01 | 08 04 | 29♐05 | 02 04 |
| 58 | 02 16 | 19 16 | 06 51 | 27 10 | 28♑57 |
| 59 | 01 54 | 18 30 | 05 36 | 25 08 | 25 30 |
| 60 | 01♏31 | 17♏43 | 04♐17 | 23♐01 | 21♑43 |

13h 0m 0s — 195° 0' 0" — 16 ♎ 17

| LAT. | 11 | 12 | ASC | 2 | 3 |
|---|---|---|---|---|---|
| 0 | 17♏28 | 16♐11 | 13♑49 | 12♒32 | 13♓43 |
| 5 | 16 20 | 14 26 | 11 51 | 10 46 | 12 40 |
| 10 | 15 15 | 12 41 | 09 50 | 08 54 | 11 32 |
| 15 | 14 11 | 10 55 | 07 43 | 06 52 | 10 15 |
| 20 | 13 07 | 09 06 | 05 29 | 04 38 | 08 48 |
| 21 | 12 54 | 08 44 | 05 01 | 04 09 | 08 28 |
| 22 | 12 41 | 08 21 | 04 32 | 03 40 | 08 09 |
| 23 | 12 28 | 07 59 | 04 04 | 03 10 | 07 48 |
| 24 | 12 15 | 07 36 | 03 34 | 02 39 | 07 27 |
| 25 | 12 02 | 07 13 | 03 05 | 02 08 | 07 05 |
| 26 | 11 49 | 06 50 | 02 34 | 01 35 | 06 43 |
| 27 | 11 36 | 06 27 | 02 04 | 01 02 | 06 19 |
| 28 | 11 23 | 06 03 | 01 32 | 00 28 | 05 55 |
| 29 | 11 09 | 05 39 | 01 00 | 29♑53 | 05 29 |
| 30 | 10 56 | 05 14 | 00 28 | 29 16 | 05 03 |
| 31 | 10 43 | 04 50 | 29♐54 | 28 39 | 04 35 |
| 32 | 10 29 | 04 25 | 29 20 | 28 00 | 04 06 |
| 33 | 10 15 | 04 00 | 28 45 | 27 20 | 03 36 |
| 34 | 10 01 | 03 34 | 28 10 | 26 39 | 03 04 |
| 35 | 09 47 | 03 08 | 27 34 | 25 57 | 02 30 |
| 36 | 09 33 | 02 41 | 26 56 | 25 12 | 01 55 |
| 37 | 09 19 | 02 14 | 26 18 | 24 27 | 01 18 |
| 38 | 09 04 | 01 47 | 25 39 | 23 39 | 00 39 |
| 39 | 08 49 | 01 19 | 24 59 | 22 50 | 29♒57 |
| 40 | 08 34 | 00 50 | 24 18 | 21 58 | 29 13 |
| 41 | 08 19 | 00 21 | 23 36 | 21 05 | 28 27 |
| 42 | 08 04 | 29♏51 | 22 52 | 20 10 | 27 37 |
| 43 | 07 48 | 29 21 | 22 08 | 19 12 | 26 44 |
| 44 | 07 32 | 28 50 | 21 22 | 18 11 | 25 47 |
| 45 | 07 16 | 28 18 | 20 34 | 17 08 | 24 46 |
| 46 | 07 00 | 27 46 | 19 45 | 16 02 | 23 41 |
| 47 | 06 43 | 27 13 | 18 55 | 14 53 | 22 31 |
| 48 | 06 26 | 26 39 | 18 03 | 13 41 | 21 15 |
| 49 | 06 08 | 26 04 | 17 09 | 12 26 | 19 52 |
| 50 | 05 51 | 25 29 | 16 14 | 11 06 | 18 23 |
| 51 | 05 32 | 24 52 | 15 16 | 09 43 | 16 45 |
| 52 | 05 14 | 24 14 | 14 17 | 08 16 | 14 59 |
| 53 | 04 55 | 23 35 | 13 16 | 06 44 | 13 02 |
| 54 | 04 35 | 22 56 | 12 12 | 05 08 | 10 54 |
| 55 | 04 15 | 22 14 | 11 06 | 03 27 | 08 32 |
| 56 | 03 55 | 21 32 | 09 57 | 01 40 | 05 57 |
| 57 | 03 33 | 20 48 | 08 46 | 29♐48 | 03 04 |
| 58 | 03 12 | 20 03 | 07 32 | 27 50 | 29♑54 |
| 59 | 02 49 | 19 17 | 06 16 | 25 47 | 26 24 |
| 60 | 02♏26 | 18♏29 | 04♐56 | 23♐37 | 22♑32 |

13h 4m 0s — 196° 0' 0" — 17 ♎ 21

| LAT. | 11 | 12 | ASC | 2 | 3 |
|---|---|---|---|---|---|
| 0 | 18♏28 | 17♐07 | 14♑44 | 13♒32 | 14♓48 |
| 5 | 17 20 | 15 22 | 12 47 | 11 47 | 13 46 |
| 10 | 16 14 | 13 37 | 10 46 | 09 55 | 12 38 |
| 15 | 15 10 | 11 51 | 08 39 | 07 53 | 11 22 |
| 20 | 14 06 | 10 02 | 06 25 | 05 39 | 09 55 |
| 21 | 13 53 | 09 40 | 05 57 | 05 11 | 09 36 |
| 22 | 13 40 | 09 17 | 05 28 | 04 42 | 09 17 |
| 23 | 13 28 | 08 55 | 05 00 | 04 12 | 08 57 |
| 24 | 13 15 | 08 32 | 04 30 | 03 41 | 08 36 |
| 25 | 13 01 | 08 09 | 04 00 | 03 09 | 08 14 |
| 26 | 12 48 | 07 45 | 03 30 | 02 37 | 07 52 |
| 27 | 12 35 | 07 22 | 02 59 | 02 04 | 07 28 |
| 28 | 12 22 | 06 58 | 02 28 | 01 29 | 07 04 |
| 29 | 12 09 | 06 34 | 01 56 | 00 54 | 06 39 |
| 30 | 11 55 | 06 10 | 01 23 | 00 18 | 06 12 |
| 31 | 11 42 | 05 45 | 00 49 | 29♑40 | 05 45 |
| 32 | 11 28 | 05 20 | 00 15 | 29 01 | 05 16 |
| 33 | 11 14 | 04 54 | 29♐40 | 28 21 | 04 46 |
| 34 | 11 00 | 04 28 | 29 05 | 27 40 | 04 14 |
| 35 | 10 46 | 04 02 | 28 28 | 26 57 | 03 41 |
| 36 | 10 32 | 03 35 | 27 51 | 26 13 | 03 06 |
| 37 | 10 17 | 03 08 | 27 12 | 25 27 | 02 29 |
| 38 | 10 03 | 02 41 | 26 33 | 24 39 | 01 50 |
| 39 | 09 48 | 02 12 | 25 53 | 23 49 | 01 08 |
| 40 | 09 33 | 01 44 | 25 11 | 22 58 | 00 25 |
| 41 | 09 17 | 01 14 | 24 28 | 22 04 | 29♒38 |
| 42 | 09 02 | 00 45 | 23 45 | 21 08 | 28 49 |
| 43 | 08 46 | 00 14 | 23 00 | 20 10 | 27 56 |
| 44 | 08 30 | 29♏43 | 22 13 | 19 09 | 26 59 |
| 45 | 08 14 | 29 11 | 21 25 | 18 05 | 25 58 |
| 46 | 07 57 | 28 38 | 20 36 | 16 59 | 24 53 |
| 47 | 07 40 | 28 05 | 19 45 | 15 49 | 23 42 |
| 48 | 07 23 | 27 31 | 18 53 | 14 36 | 22 26 |
| 49 | 07 06 | 26 55 | 17 58 | 13 20 | 21 03 |
| 50 | 06 48 | 26 19 | 17 02 | 12 00 | 19 33 |
| 51 | 06 29 | 25 42 | 16 04 | 10 35 | 17 55 |
| 52 | 06 10 | 25 04 | 15 04 | 09 07 | 16 08 |
| 53 | 05 51 | 24 25 | 14 02 | 07 34 | 14 10 |
| 54 | 05 31 | 23 45 | 12 57 | 05 56 | 12 01 |
| 55 | 05 11 | 23 03 | 11 50 | 04 13 | 09 38 |
| 56 | 04 50 | 22 20 | 10 41 | 02 25 | 07 00 |
| 57 | 04 29 | 21 36 | 09 29 | 00 31 | 04 06 |
| 58 | 04 07 | 20 51 | 08 14 | 28♐32 | 00 53 |
| 59 | 03 44 | 20 03 | 06 56 | 26 26 | 27♑19 |
| 60 | 03♏21 | 19♏15 | 05♐35 | 24♐14 | 23♑23 |

13h 8m 0s — 197° 0' 0" — 18 ♎ 26

| LAT. | 11 | 12 | ASC | 2 | 3 |
|---|---|---|---|---|---|
| 0 | 19♏27 | 18♐02 | 15♑40 | 14♒32 | 15♓53 |
| 5 | 18 19 | 16 17 | 13 43 | 12 47 | 14 51 |
| 10 | 17 14 | 14 33 | 11 42 | 10 56 | 13 44 |
| 15 | 16 10 | 12 47 | 09 36 | 08 55 | 12 29 |
| 20 | 15 06 | 10 58 | 07 21 | 06 41 | 11 03 |
| 21 | 14 53 | 10 35 | 06 53 | 06 13 | 10 44 |
| 22 | 14 40 | 10 13 | 06 25 | 05 43 | 10 25 |
| 23 | 14 27 | 09 50 | 05 56 | 05 14 | 10 05 |
| 24 | 14 14 | 09 27 | 05 26 | 04 43 | 09 44 |
| 25 | 14 01 | 09 04 | 04 57 | 04 11 | 09 23 |
| 26 | 13 48 | 08 41 | 04 26 | 03 39 | 09 01 |
| 27 | 13 34 | 08 17 | 03 55 | 03 05 | 08 37 |
| 28 | 13 21 | 07 53 | 03 24 | 02 31 | 08 13 |
| 29 | 13 08 | 07 29 | 02 51 | 01 56 | 07 48 |
| 30 | 12 54 | 07 05 | 02 18 | 01 19 | 07 22 |
| 31 | 12 40 | 06 40 | 01 45 | 00 42 | 06 55 |
| 32 | 12 27 | 06 15 | 01 10 | 00 03 | 06 26 |
| 33 | 12 13 | 05 49 | 00 35 | 29♑23 | 05 56 |
| 34 | 11 59 | 05 23 | 29♐59 | 28 41 | 05 25 |
| 35 | 11 45 | 04 57 | 29 23 | 27 58 | 04 52 |
| 36 | 11 30 | 04 30 | 28 45 | 27 14 | 04 17 |
| 37 | 11 16 | 04 03 | 28 06 | 26 28 | 03 40 |
| 38 | 11 01 | 03 35 | 27 27 | 25 40 | 03 01 |
| 39 | 10 46 | 03 06 | 26 46 | 24 50 | 02 20 |
| 40 | 10 31 | 02 37 | 26 04 | 23 58 | 01 37 |
| 41 | 10 16 | 02 08 | 25 22 | 23 04 | 00 50 |
| 42 | 10 00 | 01 38 | 24 37 | 22 07 | 00 01 |
| 43 | 09 44 | 01 07 | 23 52 | 21 09 | 29♒08 |
| 44 | 09 28 | 00 36 | 23 05 | 20 07 | 28 11 |
| 45 | 09 12 | 00 04 | 22 17 | 19 03 | 27 11 |
| 46 | 08 55 | 29♏31 | 21 27 | 17 56 | 26 05 |
| 47 | 08 38 | 28 57 | 20 36 | 16 46 | 24 55 |
| 48 | 08 20 | 28 22 | 19 42 | 15 32 | 23 38 |
| 49 | 08 03 | 27 47 | 18 48 | 14 14 | 22 15 |
| 50 | 07 45 | 27 10 | 17 51 | 12 53 | 20 45 |
| 51 | 07 26 | 26 33 | 16 52 | 11 28 | 19 07 |
| 52 | 07 07 | 25 54 | 15 51 | 09 58 | 17 19 |
| 53 | 06 48 | 25 15 | 14 48 | 08 24 | 15 20 |
| 54 | 06 28 | 24 34 | 13 43 | 06 45 | 13 09 |
| 55 | 06 07 | 23 52 | 12 35 | 05 01 | 10 45 |
| 56 | 05 46 | 23 09 | 11 25 | 03 11 | 08 06 |
| 57 | 05 24 | 22 24 | 10 11 | 01 15 | 05 09 |
| 58 | 05 02 | 21 38 | 08 56 | 29♐13 | 01 52 |
| 59 | 04 39 | 20 50 | 07 37 | 27 05 | 28♑15 |
| 60 | 04♏16 | 20♏00 | 06♐15 | 24♐51 | 24♑14 |

13h 12m 0s — 198° 0' 0" — 19 ♎ 30

| LAT. | 11 | 12 | ASC | 2 | 3 |
|---|---|---|---|---|---|
| 0 | 20♏26 | 18♐58 | 16♑36 | 15♒32 | 16♓57 |
| 5 | 19 19 | 17 13 | 14 39 | 13 48 | 15 57 |
| 10 | 18 13 | 15 29 | 12 39 | 11 57 | 14 50 |
| 15 | 17 09 | 13 42 | 10 32 | 09 57 | 13 36 |
| 20 | 16 05 | 11 53 | 08 18 | 07 43 | 12 11 |
| 21 | 15 52 | 11 31 | 07 50 | 07 15 | 11 53 |
| 22 | 15 39 | 11 09 | 07 21 | 06 46 | 11 34 |
| 23 | 15 26 | 10 46 | 06 52 | 06 16 | 11 14 |
| 24 | 15 13 | 10 23 | 06 23 | 05 45 | 10 53 |
| 25 | 15 00 | 10 00 | 05 53 | 05 14 | 10 32 |
| 26 | 14 47 | 09 37 | 05 22 | 04 41 | 10 10 |
| 27 | 14 33 | 09 13 | 04 51 | 04 08 | 09 47 |
| 28 | 14 20 | 08 49 | 04 20 | 03 33 | 09 23 |
| 29 | 14 07 | 08 25 | 03 47 | 02 58 | 08 58 |
| 30 | 13 53 | 08 00 | 03 14 | 02 22 | 08 32 |
| 31 | 13 39 | 07 35 | 02 40 | 01 44 | 08 05 |
| 32 | 13 25 | 07 10 | 02 06 | 01 05 | 07 37 |
| 33 | 13 11 | 06 44 | 01 31 | 00 25 | 07 07 |
| 34 | 12 57 | 06 18 | 00 55 | 29♑43 | 06 36 |
| 35 | 12 43 | 05 51 | 00 18 | 29 00 | 06 03 |
| 36 | 12 29 | 05 24 | 29♐40 | 28 15 | 05 29 |
| 37 | 12 14 | 04 57 | 29 01 | 27 29 | 04 52 |
| 38 | 11 59 | 04 29 | 28 21 | 26 41 | 04 13 |
| 39 | 11 44 | 04 00 | 27 40 | 25 50 | 03 32 |
| 40 | 11 29 | 03 31 | 26 58 | 24 58 | 02 49 |
| 41 | 11 14 | 03 02 | 26 15 | 24 04 | 02 03 |
| 42 | 10 58 | 02 31 | 25 30 | 23 07 | 01 14 |
| 43 | 10 42 | 02 00 | 24 45 | 22 08 | 00 21 |
| 44 | 10 26 | 01 29 | 23 57 | 21 06 | 29♒24 |
| 45 | 10 09 | 00 56 | 23 09 | 20 01 | 28 24 |
| 46 | 09 52 | 00 23 | 22 18 | 18 54 | 27 19 |
| 47 | 09 35 | 29♏49 | 21 26 | 17 43 | 26 08 |
| 48 | 09 18 | 29 14 | 20 33 | 16 28 | 24 52 |
| 49 | 09 00 | 28 38 | 19 37 | 15 10 | 23 28 |
| 50 | 08 41 | 28 01 | 18 40 | 13 48 | 21 58 |
| 51 | 08 23 | 27 24 | 17 40 | 12 21 | 20 19 |
| 52 | 08 04 | 26 45 | 16 39 | 10 51 | 18 30 |
| 53 | 07 44 | 26 05 | 15 35 | 09 15 | 16 31 |
| 54 | 07 24 | 25 24 | 14 29 | 07 34 | 14 19 |
| 55 | 07 03 | 24 41 | 13 20 | 05 48 | 11 54 |
| 56 | 06 42 | 23 57 | 12 09 | 03 57 | 09 12 |
| 57 | 06 20 | 23 12 | 10 54 | 01 59 | 06 13 |
| 58 | 05 57 | 22 25 | 09 37 | 29♐56 | 02 54 |
| 59 | 05 34 | 21 37 | 08 17 | 27 46 | 29♑13 |
| 60 | 05♏10 | 20♏46 | 06♐54 | 25♐29 | 25♑07 |

13h 16m 0s — 199° 0' 0" — 20 ♎ 34

| LAT. | 11 | 12 | ASC | 2 | 3 |
|---|---|---|---|---|---|
| 0 | 21♏26 | 19♐53 | 17♑32 | 16♒33 | 18♓02 |
| 5 | 20 18 | 18 09 | 15 36 | 14 49 | 17 02 |
| 10 | 19 13 | 16 24 | 13 35 | 12 59 | 15 57 |
| 15 | 18 08 | 14 38 | 11 29 | 10 59 | 14 44 |
| 20 | 17 04 | 12 49 | 09 15 | 08 46 | 13 20 |
| 21 | 16 51 | 12 27 | 08 47 | 08 18 | 13 02 |
| 22 | 16 38 | 12 05 | 08 18 | 07 48 | 12 43 |
| 23 | 16 25 | 11 42 | 07 49 | 07 19 | 12 23 |
| 24 | 16 12 | 11 19 | 07 19 | 06 48 | 12 03 |
| 25 | 15 59 | 10 56 | 06 49 | 06 16 | 11 42 |
| 26 | 15 46 | 10 32 | 06 19 | 05 44 | 11 20 |
| 27 | 15 32 | 10 08 | 05 48 | 05 11 | 10 57 |
| 28 | 15 19 | 09 44 | 05 16 | 04 36 | 10 33 |
| 29 | 15 05 | 09 20 | 04 43 | 04 01 | 10 09 |
| 30 | 14 52 | 08 55 | 04 10 | 03 24 | 09 43 |
| 31 | 14 38 | 08 30 | 03 36 | 02 47 | 09 16 |
| 32 | 14 24 | 08 05 | 03 02 | 02 08 | 08 48 |
| 33 | 14 10 | 07 39 | 02 26 | 01 27 | 08 19 |
| 34 | 13 56 | 07 13 | 01 50 | 00 46 | 07 48 |
| 35 | 13 42 | 06 46 | 01 13 | 00 02 | 07 15 |
| 36 | 13 27 | 06 19 | 00 35 | 29♑17 | 06 41 |
| 37 | 13 12 | 05 51 | 29♐56 | 28 31 | 06 04 |
| 38 | 12 58 | 05 23 | 29 16 | 27 42 | 05 26 |
| 39 | 12 42 | 04 54 | 28 35 | 26 52 | 04 45 |
| 40 | 12 27 | 04 25 | 27 52 | 25 59 | 04 02 |
| 41 | 12 12 | 03 55 | 27 09 | 25 05 | 03 16 |
| 42 | 11 56 | 03 25 | 26 24 | 24 08 | 02 27 |
| 43 | 11 40 | 02 54 | 25 37 | 23 08 | 01 35 |
| 44 | 11 23 | 02 22 | 24 50 | 22 06 | 00 38 |
| 45 | 11 07 | 01 49 | 24 01 | 21 00 | 29♒38 |
| 46 | 10 50 | 01 15 | 23 10 | 19 52 | 28 33 |
| 47 | 10 32 | 00 41 | 22 17 | 18 40 | 27 22 |
| 48 | 10 15 | 00 06 | 21 23 | 17 25 | 26 06 |
| 49 | 09 57 | 29♏30 | 20 27 | 16 06 | 24 43 |
| 50 | 09 38 | 28 53 | 19 29 | 14 43 | 23 12 |
| 51 | 09 19 | 28 14 | 18 29 | 13 16 | 21 33 |
| 52 | 09 00 | 27 35 | 17 27 | 11 44 | 19 44 |
| 53 | 08 40 | 26 55 | 16 22 | 10 07 | 17 43 |
| 54 | 08 20 | 26 13 | 15 15 | 08 25 | 15 31 |
| 55 | 07 59 | 25 30 | 14 05 | 06 37 | 13 04 |
| 56 | 07 37 | 24 46 | 12 53 | 04 44 | 10 20 |
| 57 | 07 15 | 24 00 | 11 38 | 02 44 | 07 19 |
| 58 | 06 52 | 23 12 | 10 20 | 00 39 | 03 57 |
| 59 | 06 29 | 22 23 | 08 58 | 28♐26 | 00 12 |
| 60 | 06♏05 | 21♏32 | 07♐34 | 26♐07 | 26♑02 |

# Koch Table of Houses for Latitudes 0° to 60° North

13h 20m 0s — 200° 0' 0" — 21 ♎ 38

| LAT. | 11 | 12 | ASC | 2 | 3 |
|---|---|---|---|---|---|
| 0 | 22♏25 | 20♐49 | 18♑28 | 17♒33 | 19♓07 |
| 5 | 21 17 | 19 05 | 16 32 | 15 51 | 18 08 |
| 10 | 20 12 | 17 20 | 14 32 | 14 01 | 17 04 |
| 15 | 19 07 | 15 34 | 12 26 | 12 01 | 15 51 |
| 20 | 18 03 | 13 45 | 10 12 | 09 49 | 14 29 |
| 21 | 17 50 | 13 23 | 09 44 | 09 21 | 14 10 |
| 22 | 17 37 | 13 00 | 09 15 | 08 51 | 13 52 |
| 23 | 17 24 | 12 38 | 08 46 | 08 22 | 13 32 |
| 24 | 17 11 | 12 15 | 08 16 | 07 51 | 13 12 |
| 25 | 16 58 | 11 51 | 07 46 | 07 20 | 12 51 |
| 26 | 16 45 | 11 28 | 07 16 | 06 47 | 12 30 |
| 27 | 16 31 | 11 04 | 06 44 | 06 14 | 12 07 |
| 28 | 16 18 | 10 40 | 06 13 | 05 39 | 11 44 |
| 29 | 16 04 | 10 15 | 05 40 | 05 04 | 11 20 |
| 30 | 15 50 | 09 51 | 05 07 | 04 28 | 10 54 |
| 31 | 15 37 | 09 26 | 04 33 | 03 50 | 10 28 |
| 32 | 15 23 | 09 00 | 03 58 | 03 11 | 10 00 |
| 33 | 15 09 | 08 34 | 03 22 | 02 30 | 09 30 |
| 34 | 14 54 | 08 08 | 02 46 | 01 49 | 09 00 |
| 35 | 14 40 | 07 41 | 02 09 | 01 05 | 08 27 |
| 36 | 14 26 | 07 14 | 01 30 | 00 20 | 07 53 |
| 37 | 14 11 | 06 46 | 00 51 | 29♑33 | 07 17 |
| 38 | 13 56 | 06 18 | 00 11 | 28 45 | 06 39 |
| 39 | 13 41 | 05 49 | 29♐29 | 27 54 | 05 59 |
| 40 | 13 25 | 05 19 | 28 47 | 27 01 | 05 16 |
| 41 | 13 10 | 04 49 | 28 03 | 26 06 | 04 30 |
| 42 | 12 54 | 04 18 | 27 17 | 25 09 | 03 41 |
| 43 | 12 37 | 03 47 | 26 31 | 24 09 | 02 49 |
| 44 | 12 21 | 03 15 | 25 43 | 23 06 | 01 53 |
| 45 | 12 04 | 02 42 | 24 53 | 22 00 | 00 53 |
| 46 | 11 47 | 02 08 | 24 02 | 20 51 | 29♒48 |
| 47 | 11 30 | 01 33 | 23 09 | 19 39 | 28 37 |
| 48 | 11 12 | 00 58 | 22 14 | 18 23 | 27 21 |
| 49 | 10 54 | 00 21 | 21 18 | 17 03 | 25 58 |
| 50 | 10 35 | 29♏44 | 20 19 | 15 39 | 24 27 |
| 51 | 10 16 | 29 05 | 19 18 | 14 11 | 22 47 |
| 52 | 09 56 | 28 26 | 18 15 | 12 37 | 20 58 |
| 53 | 09 36 | 27 45 | 17 09 | 10 59 | 18 57 |
| 54 | 09 16 | 27 03 | 16 02 | 09 16 | 16 43 |
| 55 | 08 55 | 26 19 | 14 51 | 07 27 | 14 15 |
| 56 | 08 33 | 25 34 | 13 38 | 05 31 | 11 30 |
| 57 | 08 11 | 24 48 | 12 21 | 03 30 | 08 26 |
| 58 | 07 48 | 24 00 | 11 02 | 01 22 | 05 01 |
| 59 | 07 24 | 23 10 | 09 39 | 29♐07 | 01 12 |
| 60 | 06♏59 | 22♏18 | 08♐14 | 26♐46 | 26♑58 |

13h 24m 0s — 201° 0' 0" — 22 ♎ 42

| LAT. | 11 | 12 | ASC | 2 | 3 |
|---|---|---|---|---|---|
| 0 | 23♏23 | 21♐44 | 19♑24 | 18♒34 | 20♓12 |
| 5 | 22 16 | 20 00 | 17 29 | 16 52 | 19 14 |
| 10 | 21 11 | 18 16 | 15 29 | 15 03 | 18 10 |
| 15 | 20 07 | 16 30 | 13 23 | 13 04 | 16 59 |
| 20 | 19 02 | 14 41 | 11 09 | 10 52 | 15 37 |
| 21 | 18 49 | 14 19 | 10 41 | 10 24 | 15 20 |
| 22 | 18 36 | 13 56 | 10 12 | 09 55 | 15 01 |
| 23 | 18 23 | 13 33 | 09 43 | 09 25 | 14 42 |
| 24 | 18 10 | 13 10 | 09 14 | 08 55 | 14 22 |
| 25 | 17 57 | 12 47 | 08 43 | 08 23 | 14 02 |
| 26 | 17 43 | 12 24 | 08 13 | 07 51 | 13 40 |
| 27 | 17 30 | 12 00 | 07 41 | 07 18 | 13 18 |
| 28 | 17 16 | 11 35 | 07 09 | 06 43 | 12 55 |
| 29 | 17 03 | 11 11 | 06 37 | 06 08 | 12 31 |
| 30 | 16 49 | 10 46 | 06 03 | 05 31 | 12 06 |
| 31 | 16 35 | 10 21 | 05 29 | 04 54 | 11 39 |
| 32 | 16 21 | 09 55 | 04 54 | 04 14 | 11 12 |
| 33 | 16 07 | 09 29 | 04 19 | 03 34 | 10 43 |
| 34 | 15 53 | 09 03 | 03 42 | 02 52 | 10 12 |
| 35 | 15 38 | 08 36 | 03 05 | 02 09 | 09 40 |
| 36 | 15 24 | 08 08 | 02 26 | 01 24 | 09 06 |
| 37 | 15 09 | 07 40 | 01 47 | 00 37 | 08 31 |
| 38 | 14 54 | 07 12 | 01 06 | 29♑48 | 07 53 |
| 39 | 14 39 | 06 43 | 00 24 | 28 57 | 07 13 |
| 40 | 14 23 | 06 13 | 29♐41 | 28 04 | 06 30 |
| 41 | 14 07 | 05 43 | 28 57 | 27 09 | 05 45 |
| 42 | 13 51 | 05 12 | 28 12 | 26 11 | 04 56 |
| 43 | 13 35 | 04 40 | 27 25 | 25 10 | 04 04 |
| 44 | 13 19 | 04 08 | 26 36 | 24 07 | 03 09 |
| 45 | 13 02 | 03 35 | 25 46 | 23 01 | 02 09 |
| 46 | 12 44 | 03 01 | 24 54 | 21 51 | 01 04 |
| 47 | 12 27 | 02 26 | 24 01 | 20 38 | 29♒53 |
| 48 | 12 09 | 01 50 | 23 06 | 19 22 | 28 37 |
| 49 | 11 51 | 01 13 | 22 08 | 18 01 | 27 14 |
| 50 | 11 32 | 00 35 | 21 09 | 16 36 | 25 43 |
| 51 | 11 13 | 29♏56 | 20 07 | 15 06 | 24 03 |
| 52 | 10 53 | 29 16 | 19 03 | 13 32 | 22 14 |
| 53 | 10 33 | 28 35 | 17 57 | 11 52 | 20 12 |
| 54 | 10 12 | 27 52 | 16 48 | 10 07 | 17 58 |
| 55 | 09 50 | 27 08 | 15 37 | 08 17 | 15 28 |
| 56 | 09 28 | 26 23 | 14 22 | 06 20 | 12 41 |
| 57 | 09 06 | 25 36 | 13 05 | 04 16 | 09 35 |
| 58 | 08 43 | 24 47 | 11 45 | 02 06 | 06 07 |
| 59 | 08 19 | 23 57 | 10 21 | 29♐49 | 02 15 |
| 60 | 07♏54 | 23♏04 | 08♐54 | 27♐25 | 27♑55 |

13h 28m 0s — 202° 0' 0" — 23 ♎ 46

| LAT. | 11 | 12 | ASC | 2 | 3 |
|---|---|---|---|---|---|
| 0 | 24♏22 | 22♐39 | 20♑20 | 19♒35 | 21♓17 |
| 5 | 23 15 | 20 56 | 18 25 | 17 54 | 20 20 |
| 10 | 22 10 | 19 12 | 16 26 | 16 05 | 19 17 |
| 15 | 21 05 | 17 26 | 14 21 | 14 07 | 18 07 |
| 20 | 20 01 | 15 37 | 12 06 | 11 56 | 16 47 |
| 21 | 19 48 | 15 15 | 11 38 | 11 28 | 16 29 |
| 22 | 19 35 | 14 52 | 11 10 | 10 59 | 16 11 |
| 23 | 19 22 | 14 29 | 10 41 | 10 29 | 15 52 |
| 24 | 19 09 | 14 06 | 10 11 | 09 59 | 15 32 |
| 25 | 18 55 | 13 43 | 09 41 | 09 27 | 15 12 |
| 26 | 18 42 | 13 19 | 09 10 | 08 55 | 14 51 |
| 27 | 18 29 | 12 55 | 08 39 | 08 22 | 14 29 |
| 28 | 18 15 | 12 31 | 08 07 | 07 47 | 14 06 |
| 29 | 18 01 | 12 07 | 07 34 | 07 12 | 13 42 |
| 30 | 17 48 | 11 42 | 07 00 | 06 36 | 13 17 |
| 31 | 17 34 | 11 16 | 06 26 | 05 58 | 12 51 |
| 32 | 17 20 | 10 51 | 05 51 | 05 19 | 12 24 |
| 33 | 17 06 | 10 24 | 05 15 | 04 38 | 11 55 |
| 34 | 16 51 | 09 58 | 04 39 | 03 56 | 11 25 |
| 35 | 16 37 | 09 31 | 04 01 | 03 13 | 10 53 |
| 36 | 16 22 | 09 03 | 03 22 | 02 27 | 10 20 |
| 37 | 16 07 | 08 35 | 02 42 | 01 40 | 09 45 |
| 38 | 15 52 | 08 07 | 02 02 | 00 51 | 09 07 |
| 39 | 15 37 | 07 37 | 01 20 | 00 00 | 08 28 |
| 40 | 15 21 | 07 08 | 00 36 | 29♑07 | 07 45 |
| 41 | 15 05 | 06 37 | 29♐52 | 28 12 | 07 00 |
| 42 | 14 49 | 06 06 | 29 06 | 27 14 | 06 12 |
| 43 | 14 33 | 05 34 | 28 19 | 26 13 | 05 20 |
| 44 | 14 16 | 05 01 | 27 30 | 25 09 | 04 25 |
| 45 | 13 59 | 04 28 | 26 39 | 24 02 | 03 25 |
| 46 | 13 42 | 03 54 | 25 47 | 22 52 | 02 21 |
| 47 | 13 24 | 03 18 | 24 53 | 21 38 | 01 11 |
| 48 | 13 06 | 02 42 | 23 57 | 20 21 | 29♒54 |
| 49 | 12 47 | 02 05 | 22 59 | 18 59 | 28 31 |
| 50 | 12 28 | 01 27 | 21 59 | 17 34 | 27 00 |
| 51 | 12 09 | 00 48 | 20 57 | 16 03 | 25 21 |
| 52 | 11 49 | 00 07 | 19 52 | 14 27 | 23 30 |
| 53 | 11 29 | 29♏25 | 18 45 | 12 47 | 21 29 |
| 54 | 11 08 | 28 42 | 17 36 | 11 00 | 19 13 |
| 55 | 10 46 | 27 58 | 16 23 | 09 08 | 16 43 |
| 56 | 10 24 | 27 11 | 15 08 | 07 09 | 13 54 |
| 57 | 10 01 | 26 24 | 13 49 | 05 03 | 10 46 |
| 58 | 09 38 | 25 35 | 12 28 | 02 51 | 07 15 |
| 59 | 09 13 | 24 44 | 11 02 | 00 32 | 03 19 |
| 60 | 08♏48 | 23♏51 | 09♐34 | 28♐05 | 28♑55 |

13h 32m 0s — 203° 0' 0" — 24 ♎ 50

| LAT. | 11 | 12 | ASC | 2 | 3 |
|---|---|---|---|---|---|
| 0 | 25♏21 | 23♐34 | 21♑17 | 20♒36 | 22♓23 |
| 5 | 24 14 | 21 51 | 19 22 | 18 56 | 21 26 |
| 10 | 23 09 | 20 08 | 17 23 | 17 08 | 20 24 |
| 15 | 22 04 | 18 22 | 15 18 | 15 11 | 19 15 |
| 20 | 21 00 | 16 33 | 13 04 | 13 00 | 17 56 |
| 21 | 20 47 | 16 11 | 12 36 | 12 32 | 17 38 |
| 22 | 20 34 | 15 48 | 12 07 | 12 03 | 17 20 |
| 23 | 20 21 | 15 25 | 11 38 | 11 33 | 17 02 |
| 24 | 20 07 | 15 02 | 11 09 | 11 03 | 16 43 |
| 25 | 19 54 | 14 39 | 10 38 | 10 32 | 16 22 |
| 26 | 19 41 | 14 15 | 10 08 | 10 00 | 16 02 |
| 27 | 19 27 | 13 51 | 09 36 | 09 26 | 15 40 |
| 28 | 19 14 | 13 27 | 09 04 | 08 52 | 15 17 |
| 29 | 19 00 | 13 02 | 08 31 | 08 17 | 14 54 |
| 30 | 18 46 | 12 37 | 07 58 | 07 40 | 14 29 |
| 31 | 18 32 | 12 12 | 07 23 | 07 03 | 14 04 |
| 32 | 18 18 | 11 46 | 06 48 | 06 24 | 13 37 |
| 33 | 18 04 | 11 20 | 06 12 | 05 43 | 13 08 |
| 34 | 17 50 | 10 53 | 05 35 | 05 01 | 12 39 |
| 35 | 17 35 | 10 26 | 04 58 | 04 17 | 12 07 |
| 36 | 17 20 | 09 58 | 04 19 | 03 32 | 11 34 |
| 37 | 17 05 | 09 30 | 03 39 | 02 45 | 10 59 |
| 38 | 16 50 | 09 01 | 02 58 | 01 56 | 10 22 |
| 39 | 16 35 | 08 32 | 02 15 | 01 05 | 09 43 |
| 40 | 16 19 | 08 02 | 01 32 | 00 11 | 09 01 |
| 41 | 16 03 | 07 31 | 00 47 | 29♑15 | 08 16 |
| 42 | 15 47 | 07 00 | 00 01 | 28 17 | 07 28 |
| 43 | 15 30 | 06 28 | 29♐13 | 27 16 | 06 37 |
| 44 | 15 14 | 05 55 | 28 24 | 26 12 | 05 42 |
| 45 | 14 56 | 05 21 | 27 33 | 25 04 | 04 43 |
| 46 | 14 39 | 04 47 | 26 40 | 23 54 | 03 38 |
| 47 | 14 21 | 04 11 | 25 46 | 22 39 | 02 29 |
| 48 | 14 03 | 03 35 | 24 49 | 21 21 | 01 13 |
| 49 | 13 44 | 02 57 | 23 51 | 19 59 | 29♒50 |
| 50 | 13 25 | 02 18 | 22 50 | 18 32 | 28 19 |
| 51 | 13 06 | 01 39 | 21 47 | 17 00 | 26 39 |
| 52 | 12 45 | 00 58 | 20 42 | 15 24 | 24 49 |
| 53 | 12 25 | 00 16 | 19 34 | 13 42 | 22 46 |
| 54 | 12 04 | 29♏32 | 18 23 | 11 54 | 20 30 |
| 55 | 11 42 | 28 47 | 17 10 | 09 59 | 17 59 |
| 56 | 11 19 | 28 00 | 15 53 | 07 59 | 15 09 |
| 57 | 10 56 | 27 12 | 14 34 | 05 51 | 11 58 |
| 58 | 10 32 | 26 22 | 13 11 | 03 37 | 08 25 |
| 59 | 10 08 | 25 30 | 11 44 | 01 15 | 04 24 |
| 60 | 09♏42 | 24♏37 | 10♐14 | 28♐45 | 29♑56 |

13h 36m 0s — 204° 0' 0" — 25 ♎ 53

| LAT. | 11 | 12 | ASC | 2 | 3 |
|---|---|---|---|---|---|
| 0 | 26♏19 | 24♐30 | 22♑13 | 21♒37 | 23♓28 |
| 5 | 25 12 | 22 47 | 20 19 | 19 58 | 22 32 |
| 10 | 24 07 | 21 04 | 18 21 | 18 11 | 21 32 |
| 15 | 23 03 | 19 18 | 16 16 | 16 14 | 20 24 |
| 20 | 21 58 | 17 29 | 14 02 | 14 04 | 19 05 |
| 21 | 21 45 | 17 07 | 13 34 | 13 36 | 18 48 |
| 22 | 21 32 | 16 44 | 13 05 | 13 08 | 18 30 |
| 23 | 21 19 | 16 21 | 12 36 | 12 38 | 18 12 |
| 24 | 21 06 | 15 58 | 12 07 | 12 08 | 17 53 |
| 25 | 20 53 | 15 35 | 11 36 | 11 37 | 17 33 |
| 26 | 20 39 | 15 11 | 11 06 | 11 05 | 17 13 |
| 27 | 20 26 | 14 47 | 10 34 | 10 32 | 16 51 |
| 28 | 20 12 | 14 23 | 10 02 | 09 57 | 16 29 |
| 29 | 19 58 | 13 58 | 09 29 | 09 22 | 16 06 |
| 30 | 19 45 | 13 33 | 08 55 | 08 46 | 15 42 |
| 31 | 19 31 | 13 07 | 08 21 | 08 08 | 15 16 |
| 32 | 19 17 | 12 42 | 07 46 | 07 29 | 14 50 |
| 33 | 19 02 | 12 15 | 07 10 | 06 48 | 14 22 |
| 34 | 18 48 | 11 48 | 06 33 | 06 06 | 13 52 |
| 35 | 18 33 | 11 21 | 05 55 | 05 23 | 13 21 |
| 36 | 18 18 | 10 53 | 05 16 | 04 37 | 12 49 |
| 37 | 18 03 | 10 25 | 04 35 | 03 50 | 12 14 |
| 38 | 17 48 | 09 56 | 03 54 | 03 01 | 11 37 |
| 39 | 17 33 | 09 27 | 03 12 | 02 10 | 10 58 |
| 40 | 17 17 | 08 56 | 02 28 | 01 16 | 10 17 |
| 41 | 17 01 | 08 26 | 01 43 | 00 20 | 09 33 |
| 42 | 16 44 | 07 54 | 00 56 | 29♑21 | 08 45 |
| 43 | 16 28 | 07 22 | 00 08 | 28 20 | 07 54 |
| 44 | 16 11 | 06 49 | 29♐18 | 27 15 | 07 00 |
| 45 | 15 54 | 06 15 | 28 27 | 26 07 | 06 01 |
| 46 | 15 36 | 05 40 | 27 34 | 24 56 | 04 57 |
| 47 | 15 18 | 05 04 | 26 39 | 23 41 | 03 47 |
| 48 | 15 00 | 04 27 | 25 42 | 22 22 | 02 32 |
| 49 | 14 41 | 03 49 | 24 43 | 20 59 | 01 09 |
| 50 | 14 22 | 03 10 | 23 41 | 19 32 | 29♒39 |
| 51 | 14 02 | 02 30 | 22 38 | 17 59 | 27 59 |
| 52 | 13 42 | 01 49 | 21 32 | 16 21 | 26 08 |
| 53 | 13 21 | 01 06 | 20 23 | 14 37 | 24 06 |
| 54 | 12 59 | 00 22 | 19 11 | 12 48 | 21 49 |
| 55 | 12 37 | 29♏36 | 17 57 | 10 52 | 19 16 |
| 56 | 12 15 | 28 49 | 16 39 | 08 49 | 16 25 |
| 57 | 11 51 | 28 00 | 15 18 | 06 40 | 13 13 |
| 58 | 11 27 | 27 10 | 13 54 | 04 23 | 09 36 |
| 59 | 11 02 | 26 17 | 12 27 | 01 58 | 05 32 |
| 60 | 10♏37 | 25♏23 | 10♐55 | 29♐26 | 00♒58 |

13h 40m 0s — 205° 0' 0" — 26 ♎ 57

| LAT. | 11 | 12 | ASC | 2 | 3 |
|---|---|---|---|---|---|
| 0 | 27♏17 | 25♐25 | 23♑10 | 22♒39 | 24♓33 |
| 5 | 26 11 | 23 43 | 21 17 | 21 00 | 23 39 |
| 10 | 25 06 | 22 00 | 19 19 | 19 14 | 22 39 |
| 15 | 24 01 | 20 14 | 17 14 | 17 18 | 21 32 |
| 20 | 22 57 | 18 25 | 15 00 | 15 09 | 20 15 |
| 21 | 22 44 | 18 03 | 14 32 | 14 41 | 19 58 |
| 22 | 22 31 | 17 40 | 14 04 | 14 13 | 19 41 |
| 23 | 22 18 | 17 17 | 13 34 | 13 43 | 19 23 |
| 24 | 22 04 | 16 54 | 13 05 | 13 13 | 19 04 |
| 25 | 21 51 | 16 31 | 12 35 | 12 42 | 18 44 |
| 26 | 21 38 | 16 07 | 12 04 | 12 10 | 18 24 |
| 27 | 21 24 | 15 43 | 11 32 | 11 37 | 18 03 |
| 28 | 21 11 | 15 19 | 11 00 | 11 03 | 17 41 |
| 29 | 20 57 | 14 54 | 10 27 | 10 28 | 17 18 |
| 30 | 20 43 | 14 29 | 09 53 | 09 52 | 16 54 |
| 31 | 20 29 | 14 03 | 09 19 | 09 14 | 16 29 |
| 32 | 20 15 | 13 37 | 08 44 | 08 35 | 16 03 |
| 33 | 20 00 | 13 11 | 08 07 | 07 54 | 15 36 |
| 34 | 19 46 | 12 44 | 07 30 | 07 12 | 15 07 |
| 35 | 19 31 | 12 17 | 06 52 | 06 29 | 14 36 |
| 36 | 19 16 | 11 49 | 06 13 | 05 43 | 14 04 |
| 37 | 19 01 | 11 20 | 05 32 | 04 56 | 13 29 |
| 38 | 18 46 | 10 51 | 04 51 | 04 07 | 12 53 |
| 39 | 18 30 | 10 21 | 04 08 | 03 15 | 12 15 |
| 40 | 18 15 | 09 51 | 03 24 | 02 21 | 11 34 |
| 41 | 17 58 | 09 20 | 02 39 | 01 25 | 10 50 |
| 42 | 17 42 | 08 48 | 01 52 | 00 26 | 10 03 |
| 43 | 17 25 | 08 16 | 01 03 | 29♑24 | 09 12 |
| 44 | 17 08 | 07 42 | 00 13 | 28 19 | 08 18 |
| 45 | 16 51 | 07 08 | 29♐21 | 27 11 | 07 20 |
| 46 | 16 33 | 06 33 | 28 28 | 26 00 | 06 16 |
| 47 | 16 15 | 05 57 | 27 32 | 24 44 | 05 07 |
| 48 | 15 57 | 05 20 | 26 35 | 23 25 | 03 52 |
| 49 | 15 38 | 04 42 | 25 35 | 22 01 | 02 30 |
| 50 | 15 18 | 04 02 | 24 33 | 20 32 | 00 59 |
| 51 | 14 58 | 03 22 | 23 29 | 18 58 | 29♒20 |
| 52 | 14 38 | 02 40 | 22 22 | 17 19 | 27 29 |
| 53 | 14 17 | 01 57 | 21 12 | 15 34 | 25 26 |
| 54 | 13 55 | 01 12 | 20 00 | 13 43 | 23 09 |
| 55 | 13 33 | 00 26 | 18 44 | 11 46 | 20 36 |
| 56 | 13 10 | 29♏38 | 17 26 | 09 41 | 17 43 |
| 57 | 12 46 | 28 49 | 16 04 | 07 29 | 14 29 |
| 58 | 12 22 | 27 58 | 14 38 | 05 10 | 10 49 |
| 59 | 11 57 | 27 05 | 13 09 | 02 43 | 06 42 |
| 60 | 11♏31 | 26♏09 | 11♐36 | 00♑08 | 02♒03 |

13h 44m 0s — 206° 0' 0" — 28 ♎ 00

| LAT. | 11 | 12 | ASC | 2 | 3 |
|---|---|---|---|---|---|
| 0 | 28♏15 | 26♐20 | 24♑06 | 23♒41 | 25♓38 |
| 5 | 27 09 | 24 38 | 22 14 | 22 03 | 24 45 |
| 10 | 26 04 | 22 55 | 20 16 | 20 18 | 23 46 |
| 15 | 25 00 | 21 10 | 18 12 | 18 23 | 22 40 |
| 20 | 23 55 | 19 22 | 15 59 | 16 14 | 21 25 |
| 21 | 23 42 | 18 59 | 15 31 | 15 47 | 21 08 |
| 22 | 23 29 | 18 37 | 15 02 | 15 18 | 20 51 |
| 23 | 23 16 | 18 14 | 14 33 | 14 49 | 20 33 |
| 24 | 23 03 | 17 50 | 14 03 | 14 19 | 20 15 |
| 25 | 22 50 | 17 27 | 13 33 | 13 48 | 19 56 |
| 26 | 22 36 | 17 03 | 13 02 | 13 16 | 19 36 |
| 27 | 22 23 | 16 39 | 12 31 | 12 43 | 19 15 |
| 28 | 22 09 | 16 15 | 11 58 | 12 09 | 18 54 |
| 29 | 21 55 | 15 50 | 11 25 | 11 34 | 18 31 |
| 30 | 21 41 | 15 25 | 10 52 | 10 58 | 18 07 |
| 31 | 21 27 | 14 59 | 10 17 | 10 20 | 17 43 |
| 32 | 21 13 | 14 33 | 09 42 | 09 41 | 17 17 |
| 33 | 20 59 | 14 07 | 09 05 | 09 01 | 16 50 |
| 34 | 20 44 | 13 40 | 08 28 | 08 19 | 16 21 |
| 35 | 20 29 | 13 12 | 07 50 | 07 35 | 15 51 |
| 36 | 20 14 | 12 44 | 07 10 | 06 50 | 15 19 |
| 37 | 19 59 | 12 15 | 06 30 | 06 02 | 14 45 |
| 38 | 19 44 | 11 46 | 05 48 | 05 13 | 14 10 |
| 39 | 19 28 | 11 16 | 05 05 | 04 21 | 13 31 |
| 40 | 19 12 | 10 46 | 04 21 | 03 28 | 12 51 |
| 41 | 18 56 | 10 15 | 03 35 | 02 31 | 12 08 |
| 42 | 18 40 | 09 43 | 02 48 | 01 32 | 11 21 |
| 43 | 18 23 | 09 10 | 01 59 | 00 30 | 10 31 |
| 44 | 18 06 | 08 36 | 01 09 | 29♑25 | 09 38 |
| 45 | 17 48 | 08 02 | 00 16 | 28 16 | 08 39 |
| 46 | 17 30 | 07 26 | 29♐22 | 27 04 | 07 36 |
| 47 | 17 12 | 06 50 | 28 26 | 25 48 | 06 28 |
| 48 | 16 53 | 06 12 | 27 28 | 24 28 | 05 13 |
| 49 | 16 34 | 05 34 | 26 28 | 23 03 | 03 51 |
| 50 | 16 15 | 04 54 | 25 25 | 21 33 | 02 21 |
| 51 | 15 55 | 04 13 | 24 20 | 19 58 | 00 42 |
| 52 | 15 34 | 03 31 | 23 12 | 18 18 | 28♒52 |
| 53 | 15 13 | 02 47 | 22 02 | 16 32 | 26 49 |
| 54 | 14 51 | 02 02 | 20 48 | 14 39 | 24 31 |
| 55 | 14 29 | 01 16 | 19 32 | 12 40 | 21 57 |
| 56 | 14 05 | 00 27 | 18 12 | 10 34 | 19 03 |
| 57 | 13 41 | 29♏37 | 16 49 | 08 20 | 15 47 |
| 58 | 13 17 | 28 46 | 15 22 | 05 58 | 12 05 |
| 59 | 12 51 | 27 52 | 13 52 | 03 28 | 07 53 |
| 60 | 12♏25 | 26♏56 | 12♐18 | 00♑50 | 03♒10 |

13h 48m 0s — 207° 0' 0" — 29 ♎ 03

| LAT. | 11 | 12 | ASC | 2 | 3 |
|---|---|---|---|---|---|
| 0 | 29♏13 | 27♐15 | 25♑03 | 24♒42 | 26♓44 |
| 5 | 28 07 | 25 34 | 23 11 | 23 06 | 25 51 |
| 10 | 27 02 | 23 51 | 21 15 | 21 22 | 24 54 |
| 15 | 25 58 | 22 07 | 19 11 | 19 28 | 23 49 |
| 20 | 24 54 | 20 18 | 16 57 | 17 20 | 22 35 |
| 21 | 24 41 | 19 55 | 16 29 | 16 52 | 22 19 |
| 22 | 24 28 | 19 33 | 16 01 | 16 24 | 22 02 |
| 23 | 24 14 | 19 10 | 15 32 | 15 55 | 21 44 |
| 24 | 24 01 | 18 47 | 15 02 | 15 25 | 21 26 |
| 25 | 23 48 | 18 23 | 14 32 | 14 54 | 21 07 |
| 26 | 23 34 | 17 59 | 14 01 | 14 23 | 20 48 |
| 27 | 23 21 | 17 35 | 13 30 | 13 50 | 20 27 |
| 28 | 23 07 | 17 11 | 12 57 | 13 16 | 20 06 |
| 29 | 22 53 | 16 46 | 12 24 | 12 41 | 19 44 |
| 30 | 22 39 | 16 21 | 11 50 | 12 05 | 19 21 |
| 31 | 22 25 | 15 55 | 11 16 | 11 27 | 18 56 |
| 32 | 22 11 | 15 29 | 10 40 | 10 48 | 18 31 |
| 33 | 21 57 | 15 02 | 10 04 | 10 08 | 18 04 |
| 34 | 21 42 | 14 35 | 09 26 | 09 26 | 17 36 |
| 35 | 21 27 | 14 08 | 08 48 | 08 43 | 17 06 |
| 36 | 21 12 | 13 39 | 08 08 | 07 57 | 16 35 |
| 37 | 20 57 | 13 11 | 07 28 | 07 10 | 16 02 |
| 38 | 20 42 | 12 41 | 06 46 | 06 20 | 15 26 |
| 39 | 20 26 | 12 11 | 06 03 | 05 29 | 14 49 |
| 40 | 20 10 | 11 41 | 05 18 | 04 35 | 14 09 |
| 41 | 19 54 | 11 09 | 04 32 | 03 38 | 13 26 |
| 42 | 19 37 | 10 37 | 03 44 | 02 38 | 12 40 |
| 43 | 19 20 | 10 04 | 02 55 | 01 36 | 11 51 |
| 44 | 19 03 | 09 30 | 02 04 | 00 31 | 10 57 |
| 45 | 18 45 | 08 56 | 01 12 | 29♑22 | 10 00 |
| 46 | 18 27 | 08 20 | 00 17 | 28 09 | 08 58 |
| 47 | 18 09 | 07 43 | 29♐21 | 26 52 | 07 50 |
| 48 | 17 50 | 07 05 | 28 22 | 25 32 | 06 35 |
| 49 | 17 31 | 06 27 | 27 21 | 24 06 | 05 14 |
| 50 | 17 11 | 05 46 | 26 18 | 22 36 | 03 44 |
| 51 | 16 51 | 05 05 | 25 12 | 21 00 | 02 05 |
| 52 | 16 30 | 04 23 | 24 03 | 19 18 | 00 15 |
| 53 | 16 09 | 03 38 | 22 52 | 17 31 | 28♒12 |
| 54 | 15 47 | 02 53 | 21 38 | 15 37 | 25 55 |
| 55 | 15 24 | 02 06 | 20 20 | 13 36 | 23 20 |
| 56 | 15 01 | 01 17 | 18 59 | 11 27 | 20 25 |
| 57 | 14 36 | 00 26 | 17 35 | 09 11 | 17 07 |
| 58 | 14 11 | 29♏34 | 16 07 | 06 47 | 13 22 |
| 59 | 13 46 | 28 39 | 14 35 | 04 14 | 09 07 |
| 60 | 13♏19 | 27♏42 | 12♐59 | 01♑33 | 04♒19 |

# Koch Table of Houses for Latitudes 0° to 60° North

**13h 52m 0s — 208° 0' 0" — 00 ♏ 06**

| LAT. | 11 | 12 | ASC | 2 | 3 |
|---|---|---|---|---|---|
| 0 | 00♐11 | 28♐10 | 26♑00 | 25♒44 | 27♓49 |
| 5 | 29♏05 | 26 29 | 24 09 | 24 09 | 26 58 |
| 10 | 28 00 | 24 47 | 22 13 | 22 26 | 26 01 |
| 15 | 26 56 | 23 03 | 20 09 | 20 33 | 24 58 |
| 20 | 25 52 | 21 14 | 17 57 | 18 26 | 23 45 |
| 21 | 25 39 | 20 52 | 17 29 | 17 58 | 23 29 |
| 22 | 25 26 | 20 29 | 17 00 | 17 30 | 23 12 |
| 23 | 25 13 | 20 06 | 16 31 | 17 02 | 22 55 |
| 24 | 24 59 | 19 43 | 16 01 | 16 32 | 22 37 |
| 25 | 24 46 | 19 20 | 15 31 | 16 01 | 22 19 |
| 26 | 24 33 | 18 56 | 15 00 | 15 30 | 22 00 |
| 27 | 24 19 | 18 32 | 14 29 | 14 57 | 21 40 |
| 28 | 24 05 | 18 07 | 13 56 | 14 23 | 21 19 |
| 29 | 23 52 | 17 42 | 13 23 | 13 48 | 20 57 |
| 30 | 23 38 | 17 17 | 12 49 | 13 12 | 20 34 |
| 31 | 23 23 | 16 51 | 12 15 | 12 35 | 20 10 |
| 32 | 23 09 | 16 25 | 11 39 | 11 56 | 19 45 |
| 33 | 22 55 | 15 58 | 11 03 | 11 16 | 19 19 |
| 34 | 22 40 | 15 31 | 10 25 | 10 34 | 18 51 |
| 35 | 22 25 | 15 03 | 09 46 | 09 50 | 18 22 |
| 36 | 22 10 | 14 35 | 09 07 | 09 05 | 17 51 |
| 37 | 21 55 | 14 06 | 08 26 | 08 18 | 17 18 |
| 38 | 21 39 | 13 37 | 07 44 | 07 28 | 16 44 |
| 39 | 21 24 | 13 07 | 07 00 | 06 36 | 16 07 |
| 40 | 21 08 | 12 36 | 06 16 | 05 42 | 15 27 |
| 41 | 20 51 | 12 04 | 05 29 | 04 46 | 14 45 |
| 42 | 20 35 | 11 32 | 04 41 | 03 46 | 13 59 |
| 43 | 20 18 | 10 59 | 03 52 | 02 43 | 13 11 |
| 44 | 20 00 | 10 25 | 03 01 | 01 38 | 12 18 |
| 45 | 19 43 | 09 50 | 02 08 | 00 28 | 11 21 |
| 46 | 19 24 | 09 14 | 01 13 | 29♑15 | 10 20 |
| 47 | 19 06 | 08 37 | 00 16 | 27 58 | 09 12 |
| 48 | 18 47 | 07 59 | 29♐16 | 26 36 | 07 59 |
| 49 | 18 28 | 07 19 | 28 15 | 25 10 | 06 38 |
| 50 | 18 08 | 06 39 | 27 11 | 23 39 | 05 09 |
| 51 | 17 47 | 05 57 | 26 04 | 22 02 | 03 30 |
| 52 | 17 26 | 05 14 | 24 55 | 20 19 | 01 40 |
| 53 | 17 05 | 04 30 | 23 43 | 18 31 | 29♒38 |
| 54 | 16 42 | 03 43 | 22 27 | 16 35 | 27 20 |
| 55 | 16 19 | 02 56 | 21 09 | 14 32 | 24 45 |
| 56 | 15 56 | 02 06 | 19 47 | 12 22 | 21 49 |
| 57 | 15 31 | 01 15 | 18 21 | 10 03 | 18 29 |
| 58 | 15 06 | 00 22 | 16 52 | 07 36 | 14 42 |
| 59 | 14 40 | 29♏26 | 15 19 | 05 01 | 10 23 |
| 60 | 14♏13 | 28♏29 | 13♐41 | 02♑17 | 05♒30 |

**13h 56m 0s — 209° 0' 0" — 01 ♏ 08**

| LAT. | 11 | 12 | ASC | 2 | 3 |
|---|---|---|---|---|---|
| 0 | 01♐08 | 29♐05 | 26♑57 | 26♒47 | 28♓55 |
| 5 | 00 03 | 27 25 | 25 07 | 25 12 | 28 04 |
| 10 | 28♏58 | 25 43 | 23 11 | 23 30 | 27 09 |
| 15 | 27 55 | 23 59 | 21 08 | 21 38 | 26 07 |
| 20 | 26 50 | 22 11 | 18 56 | 19 32 | 24 55 |
| 21 | 26 37 | 21 48 | 18 28 | 19 05 | 24 40 |
| 22 | 26 24 | 21 26 | 17 59 | 18 37 | 24 23 |
| 23 | 26 11 | 21 03 | 17 30 | 18 08 | 24 07 |
| 24 | 25 58 | 20 39 | 17 01 | 17 39 | 23 49 |
| 25 | 25 44 | 20 16 | 16 31 | 17 08 | 23 31 |
| 26 | 25 31 | 19 52 | 16 00 | 16 37 | 23 12 |
| 27 | 25 17 | 19 28 | 15 28 | 16 05 | 22 52 |
| 28 | 25 04 | 19 03 | 14 56 | 15 31 | 22 32 |
| 29 | 24 50 | 18 38 | 14 23 | 14 56 | 22 11 |
| 30 | 24 36 | 18 13 | 13 49 | 14 20 | 21 48 |
| 31 | 24 22 | 17 47 | 13 14 | 13 43 | 21 25 |
| 32 | 24 07 | 17 21 | 12 38 | 13 05 | 21 00 |
| 33 | 23 53 | 16 54 | 12 02 | 12 24 | 20 34 |
| 34 | 23 38 | 16 27 | 11 24 | 11 43 | 20 07 |
| 35 | 23 23 | 15 59 | 10 45 | 10 59 | 19 38 |
| 36 | 23 08 | 15 31 | 10 06 | 10 14 | 19 08 |
| 37 | 22 53 | 15 02 | 09 25 | 09 26 | 18 36 |
| 38 | 22 37 | 14 32 | 08 42 | 08 37 | 18 01 |
| 39 | 22 21 | 14 02 | 07 59 | 07 45 | 17 25 |
| 40 | 22 05 | 13 31 | 07 14 | 06 51 | 16 46 |
| 41 | 21 49 | 12 59 | 06 27 | 05 54 | 16 04 |
| 42 | 21 32 | 12 27 | 05 39 | 04 54 | 15 20 |
| 43 | 21 15 | 11 53 | 04 49 | 03 52 | 14 31 |
| 44 | 20 57 | 11 19 | 03 58 | 02 45 | 13 40 |
| 45 | 20 40 | 10 44 | 03 04 | 01 36 | 12 43 |
| 46 | 20 21 | 10 08 | 02 09 | 00 22 | 11 42 |
| 47 | 20 03 | 09 30 | 01 11 | 29♑05 | 10 36 |
| 48 | 19 44 | 08 52 | 00 11 | 27 43 | 09 23 |
| 49 | 19 24 | 08 12 | 29♐09 | 26 16 | 08 03 |
| 50 | 19 04 | 07 31 | 28 05 | 24 43 | 06 34 |
| 51 | 18 43 | 06 49 | 26 57 | 23 06 | 04 56 |
| 52 | 18 22 | 06 06 | 25 47 | 21 22 | 03 07 |
| 53 | 18 01 | 05 21 | 24 34 | 19 31 | 01 04 |
| 54 | 17 38 | 04 34 | 23 18 | 17 34 | 28♒47 |
| 55 | 17 15 | 03 46 | 21 58 | 15 30 | 26 11 |
| 56 | 16 51 | 02 56 | 20 35 | 13 17 | 23 15 |
| 57 | 16 26 | 02 04 | 19 08 | 10 56 | 19 54 |
| 58 | 16 01 | 01 10 | 17 37 | 08 27 | 16 04 |
| 59 | 15 34 | 00 14 | 16 02 | 05 49 | 11 42 |
| 60 | 15♏07 | 29♏15 | 14♐23 | 03♑02 | 06♒43 |

**14h 0m 0s — 210° 0' 0" — 02 ♏ 11**

| LAT. | 11 | 12 | ASC | 2 | 3 |
|---|---|---|---|---|---|
| 0 | 02♐05 | 00♑00 | 27♑55 | 27♒49 | 00♈00 |
| 5 | 01 00 | 28♐20 | 26 05 | 26 16 | 29♓11 |
| 10 | 29♏56 | 26 39 | 24 10 | 24 35 | 28 17 |
| 15 | 28 53 | 24 55 | 22 08 | 22 44 | 27 16 |
| 20 | 27 48 | 23 07 | 19 55 | 20 39 | 26 06 |
| 21 | 27 35 | 22 45 | 19 28 | 20 12 | 25 50 |
| 22 | 27 22 | 22 22 | 18 59 | 19 44 | 25 34 |
| 23 | 27 09 | 21 59 | 18 30 | 19 16 | 25 18 |
| 24 | 26 56 | 21 36 | 18 01 | 18 46 | 25 01 |
| 25 | 26 42 | 21 13 | 17 30 | 18 16 | 24 43 |
| 26 | 26 29 | 20 49 | 17 00 | 17 45 | 24 25 |
| 27 | 26 15 | 20 24 | 16 28 | 17 13 | 24 05 |
| 28 | 26 02 | 20 00 | 15 56 | 16 39 | 23 45 |
| 29 | 25 48 | 19 35 | 15 23 | 16 05 | 23 24 |
| 30 | 25 34 | 19 10 | 14 49 | 15 29 | 23 02 |
| 31 | 25 19 | 18 44 | 14 14 | 14 52 | 22 39 |
| 32 | 25 05 | 18 17 | 13 38 | 14 13 | 22 15 |
| 33 | 24 51 | 17 51 | 13 01 | 13 33 | 21 50 |
| 34 | 24 36 | 17 23 | 12 24 | 12 52 | 21 23 |
| 35 | 24 21 | 16 55 | 11 45 | 12 08 | 20 55 |
| 36 | 24 06 | 16 27 | 11 05 | 11 23 | 20 25 |
| 37 | 23 50 | 15 58 | 10 24 | 10 36 | 19 53 |
| 38 | 23 35 | 15 28 | 09 41 | 09 46 | 19 19 |
| 39 | 23 19 | 14 58 | 08 58 | 08 55 | 18 44 |
| 40 | 23 03 | 14 26 | 08 12 | 08 00 | 18 05 |
| 41 | 22 46 | 13 54 | 07 25 | 07 03 | 17 24 |
| 42 | 22 29 | 13 22 | 06 37 | 06 03 | 16 40 |
| 43 | 22 12 | 12 48 | 05 47 | 05 01 | 15 53 |
| 44 | 21 55 | 12 14 | 04 55 | 03 54 | 15 02 |
| 45 | 21 37 | 11 38 | 04 01 | 02 44 | 14 06 |
| 46 | 21 18 | 11 02 | 03 05 | 01 30 | 13 06 |
| 47 | 21 00 | 10 24 | 02 07 | 00 12 | 12 00 |
| 48 | 20 40 | 09 45 | 01 07 | 28♑50 | 10 48 |
| 49 | 20 21 | 09 05 | 00 04 | 27 22 | 09 28 |
| 50 | 20 00 | 08 24 | 28♐59 | 25 49 | 08 01 |
| 51 | 19 40 | 07 42 | 27 51 | 24 10 | 06 23 |
| 52 | 19 18 | 06 58 | 26 40 | 22 25 | 04 34 |
| 53 | 18 56 | 06 12 | 25 26 | 20 34 | 02 33 |
| 54 | 18 34 | 05 25 | 24 08 | 18 35 | 00 15 |
| 55 | 18 10 | 04 36 | 22 48 | 16 28 | 27♒39 |
| 56 | 17 46 | 03 46 | 21 23 | 14 14 | 24 42 |
| 57 | 17 21 | 02 53 | 19 55 | 11 51 | 21 20 |
| 58 | 16 55 | 01 58 | 18 23 | 09 19 | 17 28 |
| 59 | 16 28 | 01 01 | 16 47 | 06 38 | 13 03 |
| 60 | 16♏01 | 00♐02 | 15♐06 | 03♑47 | 07♒59 |

**14h 4m 0s — 211° 0' 0" — 03 ♏ 13**

| LAT. | 11 | 12 | ASC | 2 | 3 |
|---|---|---|---|---|---|
| 0 | 03♐03 | 00♑55 | 28♑52 | 28♒52 | 01♈05 |
| 5 | 01 58 | 29♐16 | 27 03 | 27 19 | 00 17 |
| 10 | 00 54 | 27 35 | 25 09 | 25 39 | 29♓24 |
| 15 | 29♏51 | 25 52 | 23 07 | 23 49 | 28 25 |
| 20 | 28 46 | 24 04 | 20 55 | 21 46 | 27 16 |
| 21 | 28 33 | 23 41 | 20 28 | 21 19 | 27 01 |
| 22 | 28 20 | 23 19 | 19 59 | 20 52 | 26 46 |
| 23 | 28 07 | 22 56 | 19 30 | 20 24 | 26 29 |
| 24 | 27 54 | 22 33 | 19 01 | 19 54 | 26 13 |
| 25 | 27 40 | 22 09 | 18 31 | 19 24 | 25 55 |
| 26 | 27 27 | 21 45 | 18 00 | 18 53 | 25 37 |
| 27 | 27 13 | 21 21 | 17 28 | 18 21 | 25 18 |
| 28 | 27 00 | 20 57 | 16 56 | 17 48 | 24 59 |
| 29 | 26 46 | 20 31 | 16 23 | 17 14 | 24 38 |
| 30 | 26 32 | 20 06 | 15 49 | 16 38 | 24 17 |
| 31 | 26 17 | 19 40 | 15 14 | 16 01 | 23 54 |
| 32 | 26 03 | 19 14 | 14 38 | 15 23 | 23 30 |
| 33 | 25 48 | 18 47 | 14 02 | 14 43 | 23 05 |
| 34 | 25 34 | 18 20 | 13 24 | 14 02 | 22 39 |
| 35 | 25 19 | 17 52 | 12 45 | 13 18 | 22 11 |
| 36 | 25 04 | 17 23 | 12 05 | 12 33 | 21 42 |
| 37 | 24 48 | 16 54 | 11 23 | 11 46 | 21 11 |
| 38 | 24 32 | 16 24 | 10 41 | 10 56 | 20 38 |
| 39 | 24 16 | 15 53 | 09 57 | 10 05 | 20 03 |
| 40 | 24 00 | 15 22 | 09 11 | 09 10 | 19 25 |
| 41 | 23 44 | 14 50 | 08 24 | 08 14 | 18 45 |
| 42 | 23 27 | 14 17 | 07 36 | 07 14 | 18 01 |
| 43 | 23 09 | 13 43 | 06 45 | 06 11 | 17 15 |
| 44 | 22 52 | 13 08 | 05 53 | 05 04 | 16 24 |
| 45 | 22 34 | 12 33 | 04 59 | 03 54 | 15 30 |
| 46 | 22 15 | 11 56 | 04 02 | 02 40 | 14 30 |
| 47 | 21 56 | 11 18 | 03 04 | 01 21 | 13 25 |
| 48 | 21 37 | 10 39 | 02 03 | 29♑58 | 12 14 |
| 49 | 21 17 | 09 59 | 00 59 | 28 29 | 10 55 |
| 50 | 20 57 | 09 17 | 29♐53 | 26 56 | 09 28 |
| 51 | 20 36 | 08 34 | 28 45 | 25 16 | 07 52 |
| 52 | 20 14 | 07 50 | 27 33 | 23 30 | 06 04 |
| 53 | 19 52 | 07 04 | 26 18 | 21 37 | 04 02 |
| 54 | 19 29 | 06 16 | 24 59 | 19 37 | 01 45 |
| 55 | 19 06 | 05 27 | 23 38 | 17 28 | 29♒10 |
| 56 | 18 41 | 04 36 | 22 12 | 15 12 | 26 12 |
| 57 | 18 16 | 03 42 | 20 43 | 12 46 | 22 49 |
| 58 | 17 50 | 02 47 | 19 09 | 10 12 | 18 55 |
| 59 | 17 23 | 01 49 | 17 31 | 07 27 | 14 26 |
| 60 | 16♏55 | 00♐49 | 15♐49 | 04♑33 | 09♒17 |

**14h 8m 0s — 212° 0' 0" — 04 ♏ 16**

| LAT. | 11 | 12 | ASC | 2 | 3 |
|---|---|---|---|---|---|
| 0 | 04♐00 | 01♑50 | 29♑49 | 29♒54 | 02♈11 |
| 5 | 02 55 | 00 12 | 28 01 | 28 23 | 01 24 |
| 10 | 01 52 | 28♐31 | 26 08 | 26 45 | 00 32 |
| 15 | 00 48 | 26 48 | 24 07 | 24 56 | 29♓34 |
| 20 | 29♏44 | 25 00 | 21 56 | 22 53 | 28 27 |
| 21 | 29 31 | 24 38 | 21 28 | 22 27 | 28 12 |
| 22 | 29 18 | 24 15 | 21 00 | 22 00 | 27 57 |
| 23 | 29 05 | 23 53 | 20 31 | 21 32 | 27 41 |
| 24 | 28 52 | 23 29 | 20 01 | 21 03 | 27 25 |
| 25 | 28 38 | 23 06 | 19 31 | 20 33 | 27 08 |
| 26 | 28 25 | 22 42 | 19 00 | 20 02 | 26 50 |
| 27 | 28 11 | 22 18 | 18 29 | 19 30 | 26 32 |
| 28 | 27 57 | 21 53 | 17 57 | 18 58 | 26 12 |
| 29 | 27 44 | 21 28 | 17 23 | 18 23 | 25 52 |
| 30 | 27 30 | 21 03 | 16 50 | 17 48 | 25 31 |
| 31 | 27 15 | 20 37 | 16 15 | 17 11 | 25 09 |
| 32 | 27 01 | 20 10 | 15 39 | 16 33 | 24 46 |
| 33 | 26 46 | 19 43 | 15 02 | 15 53 | 24 21 |
| 34 | 26 32 | 19 16 | 14 24 | 15 12 | 23 56 |
| 35 | 26 16 | 18 48 | 13 45 | 14 29 | 23 29 |
| 36 | 26 01 | 18 19 | 13 05 | 13 44 | 23 00 |
| 37 | 25 46 | 17 50 | 12 24 | 12 57 | 22 29 |
| 38 | 25 30 | 17 20 | 11 41 | 12 07 | 21 57 |
| 39 | 25 14 | 16 49 | 10 57 | 11 16 | 21 22 |
| 40 | 24 58 | 16 18 | 10 11 | 10 22 | 20 45 |
| 41 | 24 41 | 15 45 | 09 24 | 09 25 | 20 06 |
| 42 | 24 24 | 15 12 | 08 35 | 08 25 | 19 23 |
| 43 | 24 07 | 14 38 | 07 44 | 07 21 | 18 37 |
| 44 | 23 49 | 14 03 | 06 51 | 06 15 | 17 48 |
| 45 | 23 31 | 13 27 | 05 57 | 05 04 | 16 54 |
| 46 | 23 12 | 12 50 | 05 00 | 03 50 | 15 55 |
| 47 | 22 53 | 12 12 | 04 01 | 02 31 | 14 51 |
| 48 | 22 34 | 11 33 | 02 59 | 01 07 | 13 41 |
| 49 | 22 14 | 10 52 | 01 55 | 29♑38 | 12 23 |
| 50 | 21 53 | 10 10 | 00 49 | 28 04 | 10 57 |
| 51 | 21 32 | 09 27 | 29♐39 | 26 23 | 09 21 |
| 52 | 21 10 | 08 42 | 28 26 | 24 36 | 07 34 |
| 53 | 20 48 | 07 56 | 27 11 | 22 41 | 05 34 |
| 54 | 20 25 | 07 08 | 25 51 | 20 39 | 03 17 |
| 55 | 20 01 | 06 18 | 24 28 | 18 29 | 00 42 |
| 56 | 19 36 | 05 26 | 23 02 | 16 11 | 27♒44 |
| 57 | 19 11 | 04 32 | 21 31 | 13 43 | 24 20 |
| 58 | 18 44 | 03 36 | 19 56 | 11 06 | 20 24 |
| 59 | 18 17 | 02 37 | 18 16 | 08 18 | 15 52 |
| 60 | 17♏48 | 01♐36 | 16♐32 | 05♑21 | 10♒39 |

**14h 12m 0s — 213° 0' 0" — 05 ♏ 18**

| LAT. | 11 | 12 | ASC | 2 | 3 |
|---|---|---|---|---|---|
| 0 | 04♐57 | 02♑45 | 00♒47 | 00♓57 | 03♈16 |
| 5 | 03 52 | 01 07 | 29♑00 | 29♒27 | 02 30 |
| 10 | 02 49 | 29♐28 | 27 07 | 27 50 | 01 40 |
| 15 | 01 46 | 27 45 | 25 07 | 26 02 | 00 43 |
| 20 | 00 42 | 25 57 | 22 56 | 24 01 | 29♓38 |
| 21 | 00 29 | 25 35 | 22 28 | 23 35 | 29 23 |
| 22 | 00 16 | 25 12 | 22 00 | 23 08 | 29 08 |
| 23 | 00 03 | 24 49 | 21 31 | 22 40 | 28 53 |
| 24 | 29♏50 | 24 26 | 21 02 | 22 12 | 28 37 |
| 25 | 29 36 | 24 03 | 20 32 | 21 42 | 28 20 |
| 26 | 29 23 | 23 39 | 20 01 | 21 12 | 28 03 |
| 27 | 29 09 | 23 15 | 19 30 | 20 40 | 27 45 |
| 28 | 28 55 | 22 50 | 18 58 | 20 07 | 27 26 |
| 29 | 28 41 | 22 25 | 18 24 | 19 34 | 27 07 |
| 30 | 28 27 | 22 00 | 17 51 | 18 58 | 26 46 |
| 31 | 28 13 | 21 34 | 17 16 | 18 22 | 26 24 |
| 32 | 27 59 | 21 07 | 16 40 | 17 44 | 26 02 |
| 33 | 27 44 | 20 40 | 16 03 | 17 04 | 25 38 |
| 34 | 27 29 | 20 13 | 15 25 | 16 23 | 25 13 |
| 35 | 27 14 | 19 44 | 14 46 | 15 40 | 24 46 |
| 36 | 26 59 | 19 16 | 14 06 | 14 55 | 24 18 |
| 37 | 26 43 | 18 46 | 13 24 | 14 08 | 23 48 |
| 38 | 26 28 | 18 16 | 12 41 | 13 19 | 23 16 |
| 39 | 26 11 | 17 45 | 11 57 | 12 28 | 22 42 |
| 40 | 25 55 | 17 14 | 11 11 | 11 34 | 22 06 |
| 41 | 25 38 | 16 41 | 10 24 | 10 37 | 21 27 |
| 42 | 25 21 | 16 08 | 09 34 | 09 37 | 20 45 |
| 43 | 25 04 | 15 34 | 08 43 | 08 33 | 20 00 |
| 44 | 24 46 | 14 59 | 07 50 | 07 27 | 19 12 |
| 45 | 24 28 | 14 22 | 06 55 | 06 16 | 18 19 |
| 46 | 24 09 | 13 45 | 05 58 | 05 01 | 17 21 |
| 47 | 23 50 | 13 07 | 04 58 | 03 42 | 16 18 |
| 48 | 23 30 | 12 27 | 03 56 | 02 18 | 15 09 |
| 49 | 23 10 | 11 46 | 02 52 | 00 48 | 13 52 |
| 50 | 22 50 | 11 04 | 01 44 | 29♑13 | 12 27 |
| 51 | 22 28 | 10 20 | 00 34 | 27 31 | 10 52 |
| 52 | 22 06 | 09 35 | 29♐21 | 25 43 | 09 06 |
| 53 | 21 44 | 08 48 | 28 04 | 23 47 | 07 06 |
| 54 | 21 20 | 07 59 | 26 44 | 21 44 | 04 50 |
| 55 | 20 56 | 07 09 | 25 20 | 19 32 | 02 16 |
| 56 | 20 31 | 06 16 | 23 52 | 17 11 | 29♒18 |
| 57 | 20 06 | 05 21 | 22 20 | 14 41 | 25 53 |
| 58 | 19 39 | 04 24 | 20 43 | 12 01 | 21 56 |
| 59 | 19 11 | 03 25 | 19 02 | 09 10 | 17 21 |
| 60 | 18♏42 | 02♐23 | 17♐16 | 06♑09 | 12♒03 |

**14h 16m 0s — 214° 0' 0" — 06 ♏ 19**

| LAT. | 11 | 12 | ASC | 2 | 3 |
|---|---|---|---|---|---|
| 0 | 05♐54 | 03♑40 | 01♒45 | 02♓00 | 04♈22 |
| 5 | 04 50 | 02 03 | 29♑59 | 00 32 | 03 37 |
| 10 | 03 47 | 00 24 | 28 07 | 28♒56 | 02 48 |
| 15 | 02 44 | 28♐41 | 26 07 | 27 09 | 01 52 |
| 20 | 01 40 | 26 54 | 23 57 | 25 10 | 00 48 |
| 21 | 01 27 | 26 32 | 23 29 | 24 44 | 00 34 |
| 22 | 01 14 | 26 09 | 23 01 | 24 17 | 00 20 |
| 23 | 01 01 | 25 46 | 22 33 | 23 49 | 00 05 |
| 24 | 00 47 | 25 23 | 22 03 | 23 21 | 29♓49 |
| 25 | 00 34 | 25 00 | 21 33 | 22 52 | 29 33 |
| 26 | 00 21 | 24 36 | 21 03 | 22 22 | 29 16 |
| 27 | 00 07 | 24 12 | 20 31 | 21 50 | 28 59 |
| 28 | 29♏53 | 23 47 | 19 59 | 21 18 | 28 40 |
| 29 | 29 39 | 23 22 | 19 26 | 20 44 | 28 21 |
| 30 | 29 25 | 22 57 | 18 52 | 20 09 | 28 01 |
| 31 | 29 11 | 22 31 | 18 17 | 19 33 | 27 40 |
| 32 | 28 56 | 22 04 | 17 41 | 18 55 | 27 18 |
| 33 | 28 42 | 21 37 | 17 04 | 18 16 | 26 54 |
| 34 | 28 27 | 21 09 | 16 26 | 17 35 | 26 30 |
| 35 | 28 12 | 20 41 | 15 47 | 16 52 | 26 04 |
| 36 | 27 57 | 20 12 | 15 07 | 16 08 | 25 36 |
| 37 | 27 41 | 19 43 | 14 25 | 15 21 | 25 07 |
| 38 | 27 25 | 19 13 | 13 42 | 14 32 | 24 36 |
| 39 | 27 09 | 18 42 | 12 58 | 13 40 | 24 03 |
| 40 | 26 52 | 18 10 | 12 12 | 12 46 | 23 27 |
| 41 | 26 36 | 17 37 | 11 24 | 11 49 | 22 49 |
| 42 | 26 19 | 17 04 | 10 34 | 10 49 | 22 08 |
| 43 | 26 01 | 16 29 | 09 43 | 09 46 | 21 24 |
| 44 | 25 43 | 15 54 | 08 50 | 08 39 | 20 36 |
| 45 | 25 25 | 15 18 | 07 54 | 07 29 | 19 44 |
| 46 | 25 06 | 14 40 | 06 57 | 06 13 | 18 47 |
| 47 | 24 47 | 14 01 | 05 57 | 04 54 | 17 45 |
| 48 | 24 27 | 13 21 | 04 54 | 03 29 | 16 37 |
| 49 | 24 07 | 12 40 | 03 49 | 01 59 | 15 22 |
| 50 | 23 46 | 11 57 | 02 41 | 00 23 | 13 58 |
| 51 | 23 24 | 11 13 | 01 30 | 28♑41 | 12 24 |
| 52 | 23 02 | 10 28 | 00 16 | 26 51 | 10 39 |
| 53 | 22 39 | 09 40 | 28♐58 | 24 54 | 08 40 |
| 54 | 22 16 | 08 51 | 27 37 | 22 49 | 06 26 |
| 55 | 21 52 | 08 00 | 26 11 | 20 36 | 03 51 |
| 56 | 21 26 | 07 07 | 24 42 | 18 13 | 00 54 |
| 57 | 21 00 | 06 11 | 23 09 | 15 40 | 27♒29 |
| 58 | 20 33 | 05 14 | 21 31 | 12 57 | 23 31 |
| 59 | 20 05 | 04 13 | 19 48 | 10 03 | 18 53 |
| 60 | 19♏36 | 03♐11 | 18♐00 | 06♑59 | 13♒30 |

**14h 20m 0s — 215° 0' 0" — 07 ♏ 21**

| LAT. | 11 | 12 | ASC | 2 | 3 |
|---|---|---|---|---|---|
| 0 | 06♐50 | 04♑35 | 02♒43 | 03♓03 | 05♈27 |
| 5 | 05 47 | 02 59 | 00 58 | 01 36 | 04 43 |
| 10 | 04 44 | 01 20 | 29♑06 | 00 01 | 03 55 |
| 15 | 03 41 | 29♐38 | 27 07 | 28♒17 | 03 01 |
| 20 | 02 38 | 27 51 | 24 58 | 26 18 | 01 59 |
| 21 | 02 25 | 27 29 | 24 31 | 25 53 | 01 46 |
| 22 | 02 12 | 27 06 | 24 03 | 25 26 | 01 32 |
| 23 | 01 58 | 26 44 | 23 34 | 24 59 | 01 17 |
| 24 | 01 45 | 26 21 | 23 05 | 24 31 | 01 02 |
| 25 | 01 32 | 25 57 | 22 35 | 24 02 | 00 46 |
| 26 | 01 18 | 25 33 | 22 04 | 23 32 | 00 29 |
| 27 | 01 05 | 25 09 | 21 33 | 23 01 | 00 12 |
| 28 | 00 51 | 24 44 | 21 01 | 22 29 | 29♓54 |
| 29 | 00 37 | 24 19 | 20 28 | 21 55 | 29 36 |
| 30 | 00 23 | 23 54 | 19 54 | 21 21 | 29 16 |
| 31 | 00 09 | 23 28 | 19 19 | 20 45 | 28 55 |
| 32 | 29♏54 | 23 01 | 18 43 | 20 07 | 28 34 |
| 33 | 29 40 | 22 34 | 18 06 | 19 28 | 28 11 |
| 34 | 29 25 | 22 06 | 17 28 | 18 48 | 27 47 |
| 35 | 29 10 | 21 38 | 16 49 | 18 05 | 27 22 |
| 36 | 28 54 | 21 09 | 16 09 | 17 21 | 26 55 |
| 37 | 28 38 | 20 40 | 15 27 | 16 34 | 26 26 |
| 38 | 28 23 | 20 09 | 14 44 | 15 45 | 25 56 |
| 39 | 28 06 | 19 38 | 13 59 | 14 54 | 25 23 |
| 40 | 27 50 | 19 06 | 13 13 | 14 00 | 24 49 |
| 41 | 27 33 | 18 34 | 12 25 | 13 03 | 24 11 |
| 42 | 27 16 | 18 00 | 11 35 | 12 03 | 23 31 |
| 43 | 26 58 | 17 25 | 10 44 | 11 00 | 22 48 |
| 44 | 26 40 | 16 50 | 09 50 | 09 53 | 22 01 |
| 45 | 26 22 | 16 13 | 08 54 | 08 42 | 21 10 |
| 46 | 26 03 | 15 35 | 07 56 | 07 27 | 20 15 |
| 47 | 25 43 | 14 56 | 06 56 | 06 07 | 19 14 |
| 48 | 25 24 | 14 16 | 05 53 | 04 42 | 18 07 |
| 49 | 25 03 | 13 34 | 04 47 | 03 11 | 16 52 |
| 50 | 24 42 | 12 51 | 03 38 | 01 35 | 15 30 |
| 51 | 24 21 | 12 07 | 02 26 | 29♑52 | 13 57 |
| 52 | 23 58 | 11 21 | 01 11 | 28 01 | 12 14 |
| 53 | 23 35 | 10 33 | 29♐53 | 26 03 | 10 16 |
| 54 | 23 11 | 09 43 | 28 30 | 23 57 | 08 02 |
| 55 | 22 47 | 08 51 | 27 04 | 21 41 | 05 29 |
| 56 | 22 21 | 07 57 | 25 33 | 19 16 | 02 32 |
| 57 | 21 55 | 07 01 | 23 58 | 16 41 | 29♒07 |
| 58 | 21 28 | 06 03 | 22 19 | 13 55 | 25 08 |
| 59 | 20 59 | 05 02 | 20 35 | 10 58 | 20 28 |
| 60 | 20♏29 | 03♐58 | 18♐45 | 07♑49 | 15♒00 |

# Koch Table of Houses for Latitudes 0° to 60° North

**14h 24m 0s — 216° 0' 0" — 08 ♏ 23**

| LAT. | 11 | 12 | ASC | 2 | 3 |
|---|---|---|---|---|---|
| 0 | 07♐47 | 05♑30 | 03♒41 | 04♓07 | 06♈32 |
| 5 | 06 44 | 03 54 | 01 57 | 02 41 | 05 50 |
| 10 | 05 41 | 02 16 | 00 06 | 01 07 | 05 03 |
| 15 | 04 39 | 00 35 | 28♑08 | 29♒24 | 04 11 |
| 20 | 03 35 | 28♐48 | 26 00 | 27 27 | 03 10 |
| 21 | 03 22 | 28 26 | 25 32 | 27 02 | 02 57 |
| 22 | 03 09 | 28 04 | 25 04 | 26 36 | 02 43 |
| 23 | 02 56 | 27 41 | 24 36 | 26 09 | 02 29 |
| 24 | 02 43 | 27 18 | 24 07 | 25 41 | 02 14 |
| 25 | 02 30 | 26 54 | 23 37 | 25 12 | 01 59 |
| 26 | 02 16 | 26 31 | 23 06 | 24 43 | 01 43 |
| 27 | 02 02 | 26 06 | 22 35 | 24 12 | 01 26 |
| 28 | 01 49 | 25 42 | 22 03 | 23 40 | 01 09 |
| 29 | 01 35 | 25 17 | 21 30 | 23 07 | 00 50 |
| 30 | 01 21 | 24 51 | 20 56 | 22 33 | 00 31 |
| 31 | 01 06 | 24 25 | 20 21 | 21 57 | 00 11 |
| 32 | 00 52 | 23 58 | 19 46 | 21 20 | 29♓50 |
| 33 | 00 37 | 23 31 | 19 09 | 20 41 | 29 28 |
| 34 | 00 22 | 23 04 | 18 31 | 20 01 | 29 04 |
| 35 | 00 07 | 22 35 | 17 52 | 19 19 | 28 40 |
| 36 | 29♏52 | 22 06 | 17 11 | 18 34 | 28 13 |
| 37 | 29 36 | 21 37 | 16 29 | 17 46 | 27 46 |
| 38 | 29 20 | 21 06 | 15 46 | 16 59 | 27 16 |
| 39 | 29 04 | 20 35 | 15 01 | 16 08 | 26 44 |
| 40 | 28 47 | 20 03 | 14 15 | 15 15 | 26 10 |
| 41 | 28 30 | 19 30 | 13 27 | 14 18 | 25 34 |
| 42 | 28 13 | 18 56 | 12 37 | 13 18 | 24 55 |
| 43 | 27 55 | 18 22 | 11 45 | 12 15 | 24 13 |
| 44 | 27 37 | 17 46 | 10 51 | 11 08 | 23 27 |
| 45 | 27 19 | 17 09 | 09 55 | 09 57 | 22 37 |
| 46 | 27 00 | 16 31 | 08 56 | 08 42 | 21 42 |
| 47 | 26 40 | 15 51 | 07 55 | 07 22 | 20 43 |
| 48 | 26 20 | 15 11 | 06 52 | 05 56 | 19 37 |
| 49 | 26 00 | 14 29 | 05 45 | 04 25 | 18 24 |
| 50 | 25 38 | 13 45 | 04 36 | 02 48 | 17 03 |
| 51 | 25 17 | 13 00 | 03 23 | 01 04 | 15 32 |
| 52 | 24 54 | 12 14 | 02 07 | 29♑12 | 13 49 |
| 53 | 24 31 | 11 25 | 00 48 | 27 13 | 11 53 |
| 54 | 24 07 | 10 35 | 29♐24 | 25 05 | 09 41 |
| 55 | 23 42 | 09 43 | 27 57 | 22 48 | 07 09 |
| 56 | 23 16 | 08 48 | 26 25 | 20 21 | 04 13 |
| 57 | 22 50 | 07 51 | 24 49 | 17 43 | 00 48 |
| 58 | 22 22 | 06 52 | 23 08 | 14 54 | 26♒48 |
| 59 | 21 53 | 05 50 | 21 22 | 11 53 | 22 05 |
| 60 | 21♏23 | 04♐46 | 19♐30 | 08♑41 | 16♒34 |

**14h 28m 0s — 217° 0' 0" — 09 ♏ 24**

| LAT. | 11 | 12 | ASC | 2 | 3 |
|---|---|---|---|---|---|
| 0 | 08♐43 | 06♑26 | 04♒39 | 05♓10 | 07♈37 |
| 5 | 07 41 | 04 50 | 02 56 | 03 46 | 06 56 |
| 10 | 06 38 | 03 13 | 01 07 | 02 14 | 06 11 |
| 15 | 05 36 | 01 32 | 29♑09 | 00 32 | 05 20 |
| 20 | 04 33 | 29♐45 | 27 01 | 28♒37 | 04 21 |
| 21 | 04 20 | 29 23 | 26 34 | 28 12 | 04 08 |
| 22 | 04 07 | 29 01 | 26 06 | 27 46 | 03 55 |
| 23 | 03 54 | 28 38 | 25 38 | 27 19 | 03 41 |
| 24 | 03 41 | 28 15 | 25 09 | 26 52 | 03 27 |
| 25 | 03 27 | 27 52 | 24 39 | 26 23 | 03 12 |
| 26 | 03 14 | 27 28 | 24 09 | 25 54 | 02 56 |
| 27 | 03 00 | 27 04 | 23 38 | 25 24 | 02 40 |
| 28 | 02 46 | 26 39 | 23 06 | 24 52 | 02 23 |
| 29 | 02 32 | 26 14 | 22 33 | 24 19 | 02 05 |
| 30 | 02 18 | 25 49 | 21 59 | 23 45 | 01 47 |
| 31 | 02 04 | 25 23 | 21 24 | 23 10 | 01 27 |
| 32 | 01 50 | 24 56 | 20 48 | 22 33 | 01 07 |
| 33 | 01 35 | 24 29 | 20 12 | 21 55 | 00 45 |
| 34 | 01 20 | 24 01 | 19 34 | 21 15 | 00 22 |
| 35 | 01 05 | 23 33 | 18 54 | 20 33 | 29♓58 |
| 36 | 00 49 | 23 04 | 18 14 | 19 49 | 29 33 |
| 37 | 00 34 | 22 34 | 17 32 | 19 03 | 29 05 |
| 38 | 00 18 | 22 03 | 16 49 | 18 15 | 28 37 |
| 39 | 00 01 | 21 32 | 16 04 | 17 24 | 28 06 |
| 40 | 29♏45 | 21 00 | 15 17 | 16 30 | 27 33 |
| 41 | 29 28 | 20 27 | 14 29 | 15 34 | 26 57 |
| 42 | 29 10 | 19 53 | 13 39 | 14 34 | 26 19 |
| 43 | 28 52 | 19 18 | 12 47 | 13 31 | 25 38 |
| 44 | 28 34 | 18 42 | 11 52 | 12 24 | 24 53 |
| 45 | 28 16 | 18 05 | 10 56 | 11 13 | 24 04 |
| 46 | 27 57 | 17 26 | 09 57 | 09 58 | 23 11 |
| 47 | 27 37 | 16 47 | 08 56 | 08 37 | 22 12 |
| 48 | 27 17 | 16 06 | 07 52 | 07 12 | 21 08 |
| 49 | 26 56 | 15 24 | 06 45 | 05 40 | 19 56 |
| 50 | 26 35 | 14 40 | 05 34 | 04 02 | 18 37 |
| 51 | 26 13 | 13 54 | 04 21 | 02 18 | 17 07 |
| 52 | 25 50 | 13 07 | 03 04 | 00 25 | 15 26 |
| 53 | 25 27 | 12 18 | 01 44 | 28♑25 | 13 30 |
| 54 | 25 02 | 11 28 | 00 19 | 26 15 | 11 21 |
| 55 | 24 37 | 10 35 | 28♐51 | 23 56 | 08 50 |
| 56 | 24 11 | 09 39 | 27 18 | 21 27 | 05 55 |
| 57 | 23 44 | 08 42 | 25 40 | 18 46 | 02 31 |
| 58 | 23 16 | 07 42 | 23 57 | 15 54 | 28♒30 |
| 59 | 22 47 | 06 39 | 22 09 | 12 50 | 23 46 |
| 60 | 22♏17 | 05♐34 | 20♐16 | 09♑34 | 18♒11 |

**14h 32m 0s — 218° 0' 0" — 10 ♏ 25**

| LAT. | 11 | 12 | ASC | 2 | 3 |
|---|---|---|---|---|---|
| 0 | 09♐40 | 07♑21 | 05♒38 | 06♓14 | 08♈43 |
| 5 | 08 37 | 05 46 | 03 56 | 04 51 | 08 03 |
| 10 | 07 36 | 04 09 | 02 07 | 03 20 | 07 19 |
| 15 | 06 34 | 02 29 | 00 11 | 01 40 | 06 29 |
| 20 | 05 30 | 00 43 | 28♑03 | 29♒46 | 05 32 |
| 21 | 05 17 | 00 21 | 27 36 | 29 22 | 05 20 |
| 22 | 05 04 | 29♐59 | 27 09 | 28 56 | 05 07 |
| 23 | 04 51 | 29 36 | 26 41 | 28 30 | 04 53 |
| 24 | 04 38 | 29 13 | 26 12 | 28 03 | 04 39 |
| 25 | 04 25 | 28 50 | 25 42 | 27 35 | 04 25 |
| 26 | 04 11 | 28 26 | 25 12 | 27 06 | 04 10 |
| 27 | 03 58 | 28 02 | 24 41 | 26 36 | 03 54 |
| 28 | 03 44 | 27 37 | 24 09 | 26 05 | 03 37 |
| 29 | 03 30 | 27 12 | 23 36 | 25 32 | 03 20 |
| 30 | 03 16 | 26 46 | 23 02 | 24 59 | 03 02 |
| 31 | 03 02 | 26 20 | 22 28 | 24 24 | 02 43 |
| 32 | 02 47 | 25 54 | 21 52 | 23 47 | 02 23 |
| 33 | 02 32 | 25 27 | 21 15 | 23 09 | 02 02 |
| 34 | 02 17 | 24 59 | 20 37 | 22 29 | 01 40 |
| 35 | 02 02 | 24 30 | 19 58 | 21 48 | 01 17 |
| 36 | 01 47 | 24 01 | 19 17 | 21 04 | 00 52 |
| 37 | 01 31 | 23 31 | 18 35 | 20 18 | 00 25 |
| 38 | 01 15 | 23 01 | 17 52 | 19 30 | 29♓57 |
| 39 | 00 59 | 22 29 | 17 07 | 18 40 | 29 27 |
| 40 | 00 42 | 21 57 | 16 20 | 17 47 | 28 55 |
| 41 | 00 25 | 21 24 | 15 32 | 16 50 | 28 21 |
| 42 | 00 07 | 20 50 | 14 41 | 15 51 | 27 43 |
| 43 | 29♏50 | 20 15 | 13 49 | 14 48 | 27 03 |
| 44 | 29 31 | 19 38 | 12 55 | 13 41 | 26 19 |
| 45 | 29 13 | 19 01 | 11 58 | 12 30 | 25 32 |
| 46 | 28 53 | 18 22 | 10 58 | 11 15 | 24 40 |
| 47 | 28 34 | 17 43 | 09 57 | 09 54 | 23 43 |
| 48 | 28 13 | 17 01 | 08 52 | 08 28 | 22 40 |
| 49 | 27 53 | 16 19 | 07 44 | 06 57 | 21 29 |
| 50 | 27 31 | 15 35 | 06 34 | 05 18 | 20 11 |
| 51 | 27 09 | 14 49 | 05 20 | 03 33 | 18 44 |
| 52 | 26 46 | 14 01 | 04 02 | 01 40 | 17 05 |
| 53 | 26 22 | 13 12 | 02 41 | 29♑38 | 15 12 |
| 54 | 25 58 | 12 20 | 01 15 | 27 27 | 13 03 |
| 55 | 25 33 | 11 27 | 29♐45 | 25 06 | 10 33 |
| 56 | 25 06 | 10 31 | 28 11 | 22 35 | 07 40 |
| 57 | 24 39 | 09 33 | 26 31 | 19 52 | 04 16 |
| 58 | 24 11 | 08 32 | 24 47 | 16 57 | 00 16 |
| 59 | 23 41 | 07 28 | 22 57 | 13 49 | 25♒30 |
| 60 | 23♏10 | 06♐22 | 21♐02 | 10♑29 | 19♒51 |

**14h 36m 0s — 219° 0' 0" — 11 ♏ 26**

| LAT. | 11 | 12 | ASC | 2 | 3 |
|---|---|---|---|---|---|
| 0 | 10♐36 | 08♑16 | 06♒37 | 07♓18 | 09♈48 |
| 5 | 09 34 | 06 42 | 04 55 | 05 56 | 09 09 |
| 10 | 08 33 | 05 06 | 03 08 | 04 27 | 08 26 |
| 15 | 07 31 | 03 26 | 01 12 | 02 48 | 07 39 |
| 20 | 06 28 | 01 40 | 29♑06 | 00 56 | 06 43 |
| 21 | 06 15 | 01 18 | 28 39 | 00 32 | 06 31 |
| 22 | 06 02 | 00 56 | 28 12 | 00 07 | 06 19 |
| 23 | 05 49 | 00 34 | 27 44 | 29♒41 | 06 06 |
| 24 | 05 36 | 00 11 | 27 15 | 29 14 | 05 52 |
| 25 | 05 22 | 29♐47 | 26 45 | 28 47 | 05 38 |
| 26 | 05 09 | 29 24 | 26 15 | 28 18 | 05 23 |
| 27 | 04 55 | 28 59 | 25 44 | 27 48 | 05 08 |
| 28 | 04 42 | 28 35 | 25 12 | 27 18 | 04 52 |
| 29 | 04 28 | 28 10 | 24 40 | 26 46 | 04 35 |
| 30 | 04 14 | 27 44 | 24 06 | 26 12 | 04 18 |
| 31 | 03 59 | 27 18 | 23 31 | 25 38 | 03 59 |
| 32 | 03 45 | 26 52 | 22 56 | 25 02 | 03 40 |
| 33 | 03 30 | 26 24 | 22 19 | 24 24 | 03 20 |
| 34 | 03 15 | 25 57 | 21 41 | 23 45 | 02 58 |
| 35 | 03 00 | 25 28 | 21 02 | 23 03 | 02 35 |
| 36 | 02 44 | 24 59 | 20 21 | 22 20 | 02 11 |
| 37 | 02 29 | 24 29 | 19 39 | 21 35 | 01 46 |
| 38 | 02 12 | 23 58 | 18 56 | 20 47 | 01 18 |
| 39 | 01 56 | 23 27 | 18 11 | 19 57 | 00 49 |
| 40 | 01 39 | 22 54 | 17 24 | 19 04 | 00 18 |
| 41 | 01 22 | 22 21 | 16 35 | 18 08 | 29♓44 |
| 42 | 01 05 | 21 47 | 15 45 | 17 09 | 29 08 |
| 43 | 00 47 | 21 12 | 14 52 | 16 06 | 28 29 |
| 44 | 00 28 | 20 35 | 13 57 | 14 59 | 27 46 |
| 45 | 00 10 | 19 58 | 13 00 | 13 49 | 27 00 |
| 46 | 29♏50 | 19 19 | 12 01 | 12 33 | 26 09 |
| 47 | 29 30 | 18 39 | 10 58 | 11 13 | 25 14 |
| 48 | 29 10 | 17 57 | 09 53 | 09 47 | 24 12 |
| 49 | 28 49 | 17 14 | 08 45 | 08 14 | 23 03 |
| 50 | 28 27 | 16 30 | 07 34 | 06 36 | 21 47 |
| 51 | 28 05 | 15 43 | 06 19 | 04 50 | 20 21 |
| 52 | 27 42 | 14 55 | 05 00 | 02 56 | 18 44 |
| 53 | 27 18 | 14 05 | 03 38 | 00 53 | 16 53 |
| 54 | 26 54 | 13 13 | 02 11 | 28♑40 | 14 46 |
| 55 | 26 28 | 12 19 | 00 40 | 26 18 | 12 18 |
| 56 | 26 01 | 11 23 | 29♐05 | 23 44 | 09 27 |
| 57 | 25 34 | 10 24 | 27 24 | 20 58 | 06 04 |
| 58 | 25 05 | 09 22 | 25 38 | 18 00 | 02 04 |
| 59 | 24 35 | 08 18 | 23 46 | 14 49 | 27♒18 |
| 60 | 24♏04 | 07♐10 | 21♐49 | 11♑24 | 21♒36 |

**14h 40m 0s — 220° 0' 0" — 12 ♏ 27**

| LAT. | 11 | 12 | ASC | 2 | 3 |
|---|---|---|---|---|---|
| 0 | 11♐32 | 09♑11 | 07♒35 | 08♓22 | 10♈53 |
| 5 | 10 31 | 07 38 | 05 55 | 07 01 | 10 15 |
| 10 | 09 29 | 06 03 | 04 09 | 05 34 | 09 34 |
| 15 | 08 28 | 04 23 | 02 14 | 03 57 | 08 48 |
| 20 | 07 25 | 02 38 | 00 09 | 02 07 | 07 54 |
| 21 | 07 12 | 02 16 | 29♑42 | 01 43 | 07 43 |
| 22 | 06 59 | 01 54 | 29 15 | 01 18 | 07 30 |
| 23 | 06 46 | 01 31 | 28 47 | 00 53 | 07 18 |
| 24 | 06 33 | 01 09 | 28 18 | 00 26 | 07 05 |
| 25 | 06 20 | 00 45 | 27 49 | 29♒59 | 06 51 |
| 26 | 06 07 | 00 22 | 27 19 | 29 31 | 06 37 |
| 27 | 05 53 | 29♐58 | 26 48 | 29 02 | 06 22 |
| 28 | 05 39 | 29 33 | 26 16 | 28 31 | 06 07 |
| 29 | 05 25 | 29 08 | 25 44 | 28 00 | 05 50 |
| 30 | 05 11 | 28 42 | 25 10 | 27 27 | 05 33 |
| 31 | 04 57 | 28 16 | 24 36 | 26 53 | 05 16 |
| 32 | 04 42 | 27 50 | 24 00 | 26 17 | 04 57 |
| 33 | 04 28 | 27 23 | 23 23 | 25 40 | 04 37 |
| 34 | 04 13 | 26 55 | 22 45 | 25 01 | 04 16 |
| 35 | 03 57 | 26 26 | 22 06 | 24 20 | 03 54 |
| 36 | 03 42 | 25 57 | 21 26 | 23 37 | 03 31 |
| 37 | 03 26 | 25 27 | 20 44 | 22 52 | 03 06 |
| 38 | 03 10 | 24 56 | 20 00 | 22 05 | 02 40 |
| 39 | 02 53 | 24 25 | 19 15 | 21 15 | 02 11 |
| 40 | 02 37 | 23 52 | 18 28 | 20 22 | 01 41 |
| 41 | 02 19 | 23 19 | 17 39 | 19 27 | 01 08 |
| 42 | 02 02 | 22 44 | 16 49 | 18 28 | 00 33 |
| 43 | 01 44 | 22 09 | 15 56 | 17 25 | 29♓55 |
| 44 | 01 25 | 21 32 | 15 01 | 16 19 | 29 14 |
| 45 | 01 07 | 20 54 | 14 04 | 15 08 | 28 29 |
| 46 | 00 47 | 20 15 | 13 04 | 13 53 | 27 39 |
| 47 | 00 27 | 19 35 | 12 01 | 12 32 | 26 45 |
| 48 | 00 07 | 18 53 | 10 55 | 11 06 | 25 45 |
| 49 | 29♏46 | 18 10 | 09 47 | 09 34 | 24 38 |
| 50 | 29 24 | 17 25 | 08 35 | 07 55 | 23 23 |
| 51 | 29 01 | 16 38 | 07 19 | 06 08 | 21 59 |
| 52 | 28 38 | 15 50 | 06 00 | 04 13 | 20 24 |
| 53 | 28 14 | 14 59 | 04 36 | 02 09 | 18 36 |
| 54 | 27 49 | 14 07 | 03 09 | 29♑56 | 16 30 |
| 55 | 27 23 | 13 12 | 01 36 | 27 31 | 14 05 |
| 56 | 26 56 | 12 15 | 29♐59 | 24 55 | 11 15 |
| 57 | 26 29 | 11 15 | 28 17 | 22 07 | 07 55 |
| 58 | 26 00 | 10 12 | 26 29 | 19 06 | 03 55 |
| 59 | 25 29 | 09 07 | 24 36 | 15 51 | 29♒09 |
| 60 | 24♏58 | 07♐59 | 22♐36 | 12♑22 | 23♒24 |

**14h 44m 0s — 221° 0' 0" — 13 ♏ 27**

| LAT. | 11 | 12 | ASC | 2 | 3 |
|---|---|---|---|---|---|
| 0 | 12♐28 | 10♑07 | 08♒34 | 09♓26 | 11♈58 |
| 5 | 11 27 | 08 34 | 06 55 | 08 07 | 11 22 |
| 10 | 10 26 | 06 59 | 05 10 | 06 41 | 10 42 |
| 15 | 09 25 | 05 20 | 03 17 | 05 06 | 09 57 |
| 20 | 08 23 | 03 36 | 01 12 | 03 18 | 09 05 |
| 21 | 08 10 | 03 14 | 00 46 | 02 54 | 08 54 |
| 22 | 07 57 | 02 52 | 00 19 | 02 30 | 08 42 |
| 23 | 07 44 | 02 30 | 29♑51 | 02 05 | 08 30 |
| 24 | 07 31 | 02 07 | 29 22 | 01 39 | 08 17 |
| 25 | 07 17 | 01 44 | 28 53 | 01 12 | 08 04 |
| 26 | 07 04 | 01 20 | 28 23 | 00 44 | 07 51 |
| 27 | 06 51 | 00 56 | 27 52 | 00 15 | 07 36 |
| 28 | 06 37 | 00 31 | 27 21 | 29♒45 | 07 21 |
| 29 | 06 23 | 00 06 | 26 48 | 29 14 | 07 06 |
| 30 | 06 09 | 29♐41 | 26 15 | 28 42 | 06 49 |
| 31 | 05 54 | 29 15 | 25 41 | 28 08 | 06 32 |
| 32 | 05 40 | 28 48 | 25 05 | 27 33 | 06 14 |
| 33 | 05 25 | 28 21 | 24 28 | 26 56 | 05 55 |
| 34 | 05 10 | 27 53 | 23 50 | 26 17 | 05 35 |
| 35 | 04 55 | 27 24 | 23 11 | 25 37 | 05 13 |
| 36 | 04 39 | 26 55 | 22 31 | 24 54 | 04 51 |
| 37 | 04 24 | 26 25 | 21 49 | 24 10 | 04 27 |
| 38 | 04 07 | 25 54 | 21 05 | 23 23 | 04 01 |
| 39 | 03 51 | 25 23 | 20 20 | 22 34 | 03 34 |
| 40 | 03 34 | 24 50 | 19 33 | 21 41 | 03 04 |
| 41 | 03 17 | 24 16 | 18 44 | 20 46 | 02 33 |
| 42 | 02 59 | 23 42 | 17 53 | 19 48 | 01 58 |
| 43 | 02 41 | 23 06 | 17 01 | 18 45 | 01 22 |
| 44 | 02 23 | 22 30 | 16 05 | 17 39 | 00 41 |
| 45 | 02 04 | 21 52 | 15 08 | 16 29 | 29♓58 |
| 46 | 01 44 | 21 12 | 14 07 | 15 14 | 29 10 |
| 47 | 01 24 | 20 32 | 13 04 | 13 53 | 28 17 |
| 48 | 01 03 | 19 49 | 11 58 | 12 27 | 27 18 |
| 49 | 00 42 | 19 06 | 10 49 | 10 55 | 26 13 |
| 50 | 00 20 | 18 21 | 09 36 | 09 15 | 25 01 |
| 51 | 29♏57 | 17 33 | 08 20 | 07 28 | 23 39 |
| 52 | 29 34 | 16 44 | 07 00 | 05 32 | 22 06 |
| 53 | 29 10 | 15 53 | 05 35 | 03 28 | 20 19 |
| 54 | 28 45 | 15 00 | 04 07 | 01 13 | 18 16 |
| 55 | 28 19 | 14 05 | 02 33 | 28♑47 | 15 54 |
| 56 | 27 52 | 13 07 | 00 55 | 26 09 | 13 06 |
| 57 | 27 23 | 12 07 | 29♐11 | 23 18 | 09 47 |
| 58 | 26 54 | 11 03 | 27 21 | 20 13 | 05 50 |
| 59 | 26 23 | 09 57 | 25 26 | 16 54 | 01 03 |
| 60 | 25♏51 | 08♐47 | 23♐24 | 13♑21 | 25♒16 |

**14h 48m 0s — 222° 0' 0" — 14 ♏ 28**

| LAT. | 11 | 12 | ASC | 2 | 3 |
|---|---|---|---|---|---|
| 0 | 13♐24 | 11♑02 | 09♒34 | 10♓30 | 13♈03 |
| 5 | 12 23 | 09 30 | 07 56 | 09 13 | 12 28 |
| 10 | 11 23 | 07 56 | 06 11 | 07 49 | 11 49 |
| 15 | 10 22 | 06 18 | 04 19 | 06 15 | 11 06 |
| 20 | 09 20 | 04 34 | 02 16 | 04 29 | 10 16 |
| 21 | 09 07 | 04 12 | 01 49 | 04 06 | 10 05 |
| 22 | 08 54 | 03 50 | 01 22 | 03 42 | 09 54 |
| 23 | 08 41 | 03 28 | 00 55 | 03 17 | 09 42 |
| 24 | 08 28 | 03 05 | 00 27 | 02 52 | 09 30 |
| 25 | 08 15 | 02 42 | 29♑58 | 02 25 | 09 17 |
| 26 | 08 02 | 02 18 | 29 28 | 01 58 | 09 04 |
| 27 | 07 48 | 01 54 | 28 57 | 01 29 | 08 50 |
| 28 | 07 34 | 01 30 | 28 26 | 01 00 | 08 36 |
| 29 | 07 20 | 01 05 | 27 53 | 00 29 | 08 21 |
| 30 | 07 06 | 00 39 | 27 20 | 29♒57 | 08 05 |
| 31 | 06 52 | 00 13 | 26 46 | 29 24 | 07 48 |
| 32 | 06 37 | 29♐47 | 26 10 | 28 49 | 07 31 |
| 33 | 06 23 | 29 19 | 25 34 | 28 13 | 07 12 |
| 34 | 06 08 | 28 52 | 24 56 | 27 35 | 06 53 |
| 35 | 05 52 | 28 23 | 24 17 | 26 55 | 06 32 |
| 36 | 05 37 | 27 54 | 23 37 | 26 13 | 06 11 |
| 37 | 05 21 | 27 24 | 22 55 | 25 29 | 05 47 |
| 38 | 05 05 | 26 53 | 22 11 | 24 42 | 05 23 |
| 39 | 04 48 | 26 21 | 21 26 | 23 53 | 04 56 |
| 40 | 04 31 | 25 48 | 20 39 | 23 01 | 04 28 |
| 41 | 04 14 | 25 15 | 19 50 | 22 07 | 03 57 |
| 42 | 03 56 | 24 40 | 18 59 | 21 09 | 03 24 |
| 43 | 03 38 | 24 04 | 18 06 | 20 07 | 02 48 |
| 44 | 03 20 | 23 27 | 17 10 | 19 01 | 02 09 |
| 45 | 03 01 | 22 49 | 16 12 | 17 51 | 01 27 |
| 46 | 02 41 | 22 09 | 15 12 | 16 36 | 00 41 |
| 47 | 02 21 | 21 29 | 14 08 | 15 16 | 29♓49 |
| 48 | 02 00 | 20 46 | 13 02 | 13 50 | 28 53 |
| 49 | 01 39 | 20 02 | 11 52 | 12 17 | 27 49 |
| 50 | 01 17 | 19 16 | 10 39 | 10 37 | 26 39 |
| 51 | 00 54 | 18 29 | 09 22 | 08 50 | 25 19 |
| 52 | 00 30 | 17 40 | 08 01 | 06 54 | 23 48 |
| 53 | 00 06 | 16 48 | 06 36 | 04 48 | 22 04 |
| 54 | 29♏40 | 15 54 | 05 06 | 02 32 | 20 04 |
| 55 | 29 14 | 14 58 | 03 31 | 00 04 | 17 44 |
| 56 | 28 47 | 14 00 | 01 51 | 27♑24 | 14 59 |
| 57 | 28 18 | 12 58 | 00 06 | 24 30 | 11 43 |
| 58 | 27 48 | 11 54 | 28♐14 | 21 23 | 07 47 |
| 59 | 27 17 | 10 47 | 26 17 | 18 00 | 03 01 |
| 60 | 26♏45 | 09♐36 | 24♐13 | 14♑22 | 27♒12 |

**14h 52m 0s — 223° 0' 0" — 15 ♏ 28**

| LAT. | 11 | 12 | ASC | 2 | 3 |
|---|---|---|---|---|---|
| 0 | 14♐20 | 11♑58 | 10♒33 | 11♓34 | 14♈07 |
| 5 | 13 20 | 10 27 | 08 56 | 10 19 | 13 34 |
| 10 | 12 20 | 08 53 | 07 13 | 08 56 | 12 57 |
| 15 | 11 19 | 07 16 | 05 22 | 07 25 | 12 15 |
| 20 | 10 17 | 05 32 | 03 20 | 05 40 | 11 27 |
| 21 | 10 04 | 05 10 | 02 53 | 05 18 | 11 17 |
| 22 | 09 52 | 04 49 | 02 27 | 04 54 | 11 06 |
| 23 | 09 39 | 04 26 | 01 59 | 04 30 | 10 55 |
| 24 | 09 26 | 04 04 | 01 31 | 04 05 | 10 43 |
| 25 | 09 12 | 03 40 | 01 02 | 03 39 | 10 31 |
| 26 | 08 59 | 03 17 | 00 33 | 03 12 | 10 18 |
| 27 | 08 46 | 02 53 | 00 03 | 02 44 | 10 05 |
| 28 | 08 32 | 02 29 | 29♑31 | 02 15 | 09 51 |
| 29 | 08 18 | 02 04 | 28 59 | 01 45 | 09 36 |
| 30 | 08 04 | 01 38 | 28 26 | 01 13 | 09 21 |
| 31 | 07 50 | 01 12 | 27 52 | 00 40 | 09 05 |
| 32 | 07 35 | 00 46 | 27 16 | 00 06 | 08 48 |
| 33 | 07 20 | 00 18 | 26 40 | 29♒30 | 08 30 |
| 34 | 07 05 | 29♐50 | 26 02 | 28 53 | 08 11 |
| 35 | 06 50 | 29 22 | 25 23 | 28 13 | 07 52 |
| 36 | 06 34 | 28 53 | 24 43 | 27 32 | 07 31 |
| 37 | 06 18 | 28 22 | 24 01 | 26 48 | 07 08 |
| 38 | 06 02 | 27 51 | 23 17 | 26 02 | 06 44 |
| 39 | 05 46 | 27 20 | 22 32 | 25 14 | 06 19 |
| 40 | 05 29 | 26 47 | 21 45 | 24 23 | 05 51 |
| 41 | 05 11 | 26 13 | 20 56 | 23 28 | 05 22 |
| 42 | 04 54 | 25 38 | 20 05 | 22 31 | 04 50 |
| 43 | 04 35 | 25 02 | 19 12 | 21 29 | 04 15 |
| 44 | 04 17 | 24 25 | 18 16 | 20 24 | 03 38 |
| 45 | 03 58 | 23 47 | 17 18 | 19 14 | 02 57 |
| 46 | 03 38 | 23 07 | 16 17 | 17 59 | 02 12 |
| 47 | 03 18 | 22 26 | 15 13 | 16 39 | 01 22 |
| 48 | 02 57 | 21 43 | 14 06 | 15 13 | 00 27 |
| 49 | 02 35 | 20 59 | 12 56 | 13 41 | 29♓26 |
| 50 | 02 13 | 20 13 | 11 42 | 12 01 | 28 17 |
| 51 | 01 50 | 19 25 | 10 25 | 10 13 | 27 00 |
| 52 | 01 26 | 18 35 | 09 03 | 08 16 | 25 31 |
| 53 | 01 02 | 17 43 | 07 36 | 06 10 | 23 50 |
| 54 | 00 36 | 16 49 | 06 06 | 03 52 | 21 53 |
| 55 | 00 09 | 15 52 | 04 30 | 01 23 | 19 36 |
| 56 | 29♏42 | 14 53 | 02 48 | 28♑41 | 16 54 |
| 57 | 29 13 | 13 51 | 01 01 | 25 45 | 13 40 |
| 58 | 28 43 | 12 46 | 29♐08 | 22 34 | 09 47 |
| 59 | 28 11 | 11 37 | 27 09 | 19 07 | 05 02 |
| 60 | 27♏38 | 10♐25 | 25♐02 | 15♑25 | 29♒13 |

# Koch Table of Houses for Latitudes 0° to 60° North

**14h 56m 0s — 224° 0' 0" — 16 ♏ 28**

| LAT. | 11 | 12 | ASC | 2 | 3 |
|---|---|---|---|---|---|
| 0 | 15♐16 | 12♑53 | 11♒32 | 12♓39 | 15♈12 |
| 5 | 14 16 | 11 23 | 09 57 | 11 25 | 14 40 |
| 10 | 13 16 | 09 50 | 08 15 | 10 04 | 14 04 |
| 15 | 12 16 | 08 13 | 06 25 | 08 34 | 13 24 |
| 20 | 11 14 | 06 30 | 04 24 | 06 52 | 12 38 |
| 21 | 11 02 | 06 09 | 03 58 | 06 30 | 12 28 |
| 22 | 10 49 | 05 47 | 03 31 | 06 07 | 12 18 |
| 23 | 10 36 | 05 25 | 03 04 | 05 43 | 12 07 |
| 24 | 10 23 | 05 02 | 02 36 | 05 18 | 11 56 |
| 25 | 10 10 | 04 39 | 02 08 | 04 53 | 11 44 |
| 26 | 09 57 | 04 16 | 01 38 | 04 26 | 11 32 |
| 27 | 09 43 | 03 52 | 01 08 | 03 59 | 11 19 |
| 28 | 09 29 | 03 28 | 00 37 | 03 30 | 11 05 |
| 29 | 09 15 | 03 03 | 00 05 | 03 01 | 10 51 |
| 30 | 09 01 | 02 37 | 29♑32 | 02 30 | 10 37 |
| 31 | 08 47 | 02 11 | 28 58 | 01 57 | 10 21 |
| 32 | 08 33 | 01 45 | 28 23 | 01 24 | 10 05 |
| 33 | 08 18 | 01 17 | 27 47 | 00 48 | 09 48 |
| 34 | 08 03 | 00 50 | 27 09 | 00 11 | 09 30 |
| 35 | 07 48 | 00 21 | 26 30 | 29♒32 | 09 11 |
| 36 | 07 32 | 29♐52 | 25 50 | 28 51 | 08 51 |
| 37 | 07 16 | 29 21 | 25 08 | 28 08 | 08 29 |
| 38 | 07 00 | 28 50 | 24 25 | 27 23 | 08 06 |
| 39 | 06 43 | 28 19 | 23 39 | 26 35 | 07 41 |
| 40 | 06 26 | 27 46 | 22 52 | 25 45 | 07 15 |
| 41 | 06 09 | 27 12 | 22 03 | 24 51 | 06 46 |
| 42 | 05 51 | 26 37 | 21 12 | 23 54 | 06 16 |
| 43 | 05 33 | 26 01 | 20 19 | 22 53 | 05 42 |
| 44 | 05 14 | 25 24 | 19 23 | 21 48 | 05 06 |
| 45 | 04 55 | 24 45 | 18 25 | 20 39 | 04 27 |
| 46 | 04 35 | 24 05 | 17 23 | 19 24 | 03 43 |
| 47 | 04 15 | 23 24 | 16 19 | 18 05 | 02 55 |
| 48 | 03 54 | 22 41 | 15 12 | 16 39 | 02 02 |
| 49 | 03 32 | 21 56 | 14 01 | 15 06 | 01 03 |
| 50 | 03 09 | 21 10 | 12 47 | 13 27 | 29♓56 |
| 51 | 02 46 | 20 21 | 11 28 | 11 38 | 28 41 |
| 52 | 02 22 | 19 31 | 10 06 | 09 41 | 27 15 |
| 53 | 01 57 | 18 38 | 08 38 | 07 34 | 25 37 |
| 54 | 01 32 | 17 44 | 07 06 | 05 15 | 23 43 |
| 55 | 01 05 | 16 46 | 05 29 | 02 45 | 21 29 |
| 56 | 00 37 | 15 46 | 03 46 | 00 01 | 18 50 |
| 57 | 00 08 | 14 43 | 01 58 | 27♑02 | 15 40 |
| 58 | 29♏37 | 13 37 | 00 03 | 23 48 | 11 49 |
| 59 | 29 05 | 12 28 | 28♐01 | 20 17 | 07 07 |
| 60 | 28♏32 | 11♐15 | 25♐53 | 16♑29 | 01♓17 |

**15h 0m 0s — 225° 0' 0" — 17 ♏ 28**

| LAT. | 11 | 12 | ASC | 2 | 3 |
|---|---|---|---|---|---|
| 0 | 16♐11 | 13♑49 | 12♒32 | 13♓43 | 16♈17 |
| 5 | 15 12 | 12 20 | 10 58 | 12 31 | 15 46 |
| 10 | 14 13 | 10 48 | 09 17 | 11 12 | 15 12 |
| 15 | 13 13 | 09 11 | 07 29 | 09 44 | 14 33 |
| 20 | 12 12 | 07 29 | 05 28 | 08 04 | 13 49 |
| 21 | 11 59 | 07 08 | 05 03 | 07 42 | 13 40 |
| 22 | 11 46 | 06 46 | 04 37 | 07 20 | 13 30 |
| 23 | 11 33 | 06 24 | 04 10 | 06 56 | 13 19 |
| 24 | 11 20 | 06 01 | 03 42 | 06 32 | 13 08 |
| 25 | 11 07 | 05 38 | 03 14 | 06 07 | 12 57 |
| 26 | 10 54 | 05 15 | 02 44 | 05 41 | 12 45 |
| 27 | 10 41 | 04 51 | 02 14 | 05 14 | 12 33 |
| 28 | 10 27 | 04 27 | 01 44 | 04 46 | 12 20 |
| 29 | 10 13 | 04 02 | 01 12 | 04 17 | 12 07 |
| 30 | 09 59 | 03 37 | 00 39 | 03 47 | 11 53 |
| 31 | 09 45 | 03 11 | 00 05 | 03 15 | 11 38 |
| 32 | 09 30 | 02 44 | 29♑30 | 02 42 | 11 22 |
| 33 | 09 15 | 02 17 | 28 54 | 02 07 | 11 06 |
| 34 | 09 00 | 01 49 | 28 17 | 01 30 | 10 48 |
| 35 | 08 45 | 01 20 | 27 38 | 00 52 | 10 30 |
| 36 | 08 29 | 00 51 | 26 58 | 00 12 | 10 11 |
| 37 | 08 14 | 00 21 | 26 16 | 29♒30 | 09 50 |
| 38 | 07 57 | 29♐50 | 25 32 | 28 45 | 09 28 |
| 39 | 07 41 | 29 18 | 24 47 | 27 58 | 09 04 |
| 40 | 07 24 | 28 45 | 24 00 | 27 07 | 08 39 |
| 41 | 07 06 | 28 11 | 23 11 | 26 14 | 08 11 |
| 42 | 06 48 | 27 36 | 22 20 | 25 18 | 07 42 |
| 43 | 06 30 | 27 00 | 21 26 | 24 17 | 07 10 |
| 44 | 06 11 | 26 22 | 20 31 | 23 13 | 06 35 |
| 45 | 05 52 | 25 44 | 19 32 | 22 04 | 05 57 |
| 46 | 05 32 | 25 03 | 18 30 | 20 51 | 05 15 |
| 47 | 05 12 | 24 22 | 17 26 | 19 31 | 04 29 |
| 48 | 04 50 | 23 38 | 16 18 | 18 06 | 03 38 |
| 49 | 04 29 | 22 53 | 15 07 | 16 34 | 02 40 |
| 50 | 04 06 | 22 07 | 13 52 | 14 54 | 01 36 |
| 51 | 03 43 | 21 18 | 12 33 | 13 06 | 00 23 |
| 52 | 03 19 | 20 27 | 11 09 | 11 08 | 29♓00 |
| 53 | 02 53 | 19 34 | 09 41 | 09 00 | 27 25 |
| 54 | 02 27 | 18 39 | 08 08 | 06 41 | 25 34 |
| 55 | 02 00 | 17 41 | 06 30 | 04 08 | 23 23 |
| 56 | 01 32 | 16 40 | 04 45 | 01 22 | 20 48 |
| 57 | 01 03 | 15 36 | 02 55 | 28♑21 | 17 42 |
| 58 | 00 32 | 14 29 | 00 58 | 25 04 | 13 55 |
| 59 | 00 00 | 13 19 | 28♐55 | 21 29 | 09 15 |
| 60 | 29♏26 | 12♐05 | 26♐44 | 17♑36 | 03♓26 |

**15h 4m 0s — 226° 0' 0" — 18 ♏ 28**

| LAT. | 11 | 12 | ASC | 2 | 3 |
|---|---|---|---|---|---|
| 0 | 17♐07 | 14♑44 | 13♒32 | 14♓48 | 17♈21 |
| 5 | 16 08 | 13 16 | 11 59 | 13 38 | 16 52 |
| 10 | 15 09 | 11 45 | 10 20 | 12 21 | 16 19 |
| 15 | 14 10 | 10 09 | 08 32 | 10 55 | 15 42 |
| 20 | 13 09 | 08 28 | 06 34 | 09 17 | 15 00 |
| 21 | 12 56 | 08 06 | 06 08 | 08 55 | 14 51 |
| 22 | 12 44 | 07 45 | 05 42 | 08 33 | 14 41 |
| 23 | 12 31 | 07 23 | 05 15 | 08 10 | 14 31 |
| 24 | 12 18 | 07 00 | 04 48 | 07 47 | 14 21 |
| 25 | 12 05 | 06 37 | 04 20 | 07 22 | 14 10 |
| 26 | 11 51 | 06 14 | 03 51 | 06 57 | 13 59 |
| 27 | 11 38 | 05 50 | 03 21 | 06 30 | 13 47 |
| 28 | 11 24 | 05 26 | 02 50 | 06 03 | 13 35 |
| 29 | 11 11 | 05 01 | 02 19 | 05 34 | 13 22 |
| 30 | 10 56 | 04 36 | 01 46 | 05 04 | 13 08 |
| 31 | 10 42 | 04 10 | 01 13 | 04 33 | 12 54 |
| 32 | 10 28 | 03 44 | 00 38 | 04 00 | 12 39 |
| 33 | 10 13 | 03 17 | 00 02 | 03 26 | 12 24 |
| 34 | 09 58 | 02 49 | 29♑25 | 02 50 | 12 07 |
| 35 | 09 43 | 02 20 | 28 46 | 02 13 | 11 49 |
| 36 | 09 27 | 01 51 | 28 06 | 01 33 | 11 31 |
| 37 | 09 11 | 01 21 | 27 24 | 00 51 | 11 11 |
| 38 | 08 55 | 00 49 | 26 41 | 00 07 | 10 50 |
| 39 | 08 38 | 00 17 | 25 56 | 29♒21 | 10 27 |
| 40 | 08 21 | 29♐44 | 25 09 | 28 31 | 10 03 |
| 41 | 08 04 | 29 10 | 24 20 | 27 39 | 09 36 |
| 42 | 07 46 | 28 35 | 23 29 | 26 43 | 09 08 |
| 43 | 07 27 | 27 59 | 22 35 | 25 43 | 08 37 |
| 44 | 07 08 | 27 21 | 21 39 | 24 40 | 08 04 |
| 45 | 06 49 | 26 42 | 20 40 | 23 31 | 07 27 |
| 46 | 06 29 | 26 02 | 19 39 | 22 18 | 06 47 |
| 47 | 06 08 | 25 20 | 18 34 | 20 59 | 06 03 |
| 48 | 05 47 | 24 37 | 17 26 | 19 34 | 05 13 |
| 49 | 05 25 | 23 51 | 16 14 | 18 02 | 04 18 |
| 50 | 05 03 | 23 04 | 14 58 | 16 23 | 03 16 |
| 51 | 04 39 | 22 15 | 13 39 | 14 34 | 02 06 |
| 52 | 04 15 | 21 24 | 12 14 | 12 37 | 00 46 |
| 53 | 03 49 | 20 30 | 10 45 | 10 28 | 29♓13 |
| 54 | 03 23 | 19 34 | 09 11 | 08 08 | 27 26 |
| 55 | 02 56 | 18 36 | 07 31 | 05 34 | 25 19 |
| 56 | 02 27 | 17 34 | 05 46 | 02 47 | 22 48 |
| 57 | 01 58 | 16 30 | 03 54 | 29♑43 | 19 46 |
| 58 | 01 26 | 15 22 | 01 55 | 26 22 | 16 03 |
| 59 | 00 54 | 14 10 | 29♐49 | 22 43 | 11 26 |
| 60 | 00♐19 | 12♐55 | 27♐36 | 18♑45 | 05♓40 |

**15h 8m 0s — 227° 0' 0" — 19 ♏ 27**

| LAT. | 11 | 12 | ASC | 2 | 3 |
|---|---|---|---|---|---|
| 0 | 18♐02 | 15♑40 | 14♒32 | 15♓53 | 18♈26 |
| 5 | 17 04 | 14 13 | 13 01 | 14 44 | 17 57 |
| 10 | 16 06 | 12 43 | 11 23 | 13 29 | 17 26 |
| 15 | 15 07 | 11 08 | 09 36 | 12 05 | 16 51 |
| 20 | 14 06 | 09 27 | 07 39 | 10 29 | 16 11 |
| 21 | 13 53 | 09 05 | 07 14 | 10 09 | 16 02 |
| 22 | 13 41 | 08 44 | 06 48 | 09 47 | 15 53 |
| 23 | 13 28 | 08 22 | 06 22 | 09 25 | 15 43 |
| 24 | 13 15 | 08 00 | 05 54 | 09 01 | 15 33 |
| 25 | 13 02 | 07 37 | 05 27 | 08 37 | 15 23 |
| 26 | 12 49 | 07 14 | 04 58 | 08 12 | 15 12 |
| 27 | 12 35 | 06 50 | 04 28 | 07 47 | 15 01 |
| 28 | 12 22 | 06 26 | 03 58 | 07 20 | 14 49 |
| 29 | 12 08 | 06 01 | 03 27 | 06 52 | 14 37 |
| 30 | 11 54 | 05 36 | 02 54 | 06 22 | 14 24 |
| 31 | 11 40 | 05 10 | 02 21 | 05 52 | 14 11 |
| 32 | 11 25 | 04 44 | 01 46 | 05 20 | 13 56 |
| 33 | 11 11 | 04 17 | 01 10 | 04 46 | 13 41 |
| 34 | 10 56 | 03 49 | 00 33 | 04 11 | 13 26 |
| 35 | 10 40 | 03 20 | 29♑55 | 03 34 | 13 09 |
| 36 | 10 25 | 02 51 | 29 15 | 02 55 | 12 51 |
| 37 | 10 09 | 02 21 | 28 33 | 02 14 | 12 32 |
| 38 | 09 52 | 01 50 | 27 50 | 01 31 | 12 12 |
| 39 | 09 36 | 01 17 | 27 05 | 00 45 | 11 50 |
| 40 | 09 19 | 00 44 | 26 18 | 29♒56 | 11 27 |
| 41 | 09 01 | 00 10 | 25 29 | 29 04 | 11 01 |
| 42 | 08 43 | 29♐35 | 24 38 | 28 09 | 10 34 |
| 43 | 08 25 | 28 59 | 23 44 | 27 10 | 10 05 |
| 44 | 08 06 | 28 21 | 22 48 | 26 07 | 09 33 |
| 45 | 07 46 | 27 42 | 21 49 | 25 00 | 08 58 |
| 46 | 07 26 | 27 01 | 20 47 | 23 47 | 08 19 |
| 47 | 07 06 | 26 19 | 19 42 | 22 29 | 07 36 |
| 48 | 06 44 | 25 35 | 18 34 | 21 04 | 06 49 |
| 49 | 06 22 | 24 50 | 17 22 | 19 33 | 05 56 |
| 50 | 05 59 | 24 02 | 16 06 | 17 53 | 04 57 |
| 51 | 05 36 | 23 13 | 14 45 | 16 05 | 03 49 |
| 52 | 05 11 | 22 21 | 13 20 | 14 07 | 02 32 |
| 53 | 04 46 | 21 27 | 11 50 | 11 59 | 01 02 |
| 54 | 04 19 | 20 30 | 10 15 | 09 38 | 29♓18 |
| 55 | 03 51 | 19 31 | 08 34 | 07 03 | 27 16 |
| 56 | 03 23 | 18 29 | 06 47 | 04 13 | 24 49 |
| 57 | 02 53 | 17 23 | 04 53 | 01 07 | 21 52 |
| 58 | 02 21 | 16 14 | 02 52 | 27♑43 | 18 14 |
| 59 | 01 48 | 15 02 | 00 44 | 24 00 | 13 41 |
| 60 | 01♐13 | 13♐46 | 28♐28 | 19♑57 | 07♓57 |

**15h 12m 0s — 228° 0' 0" — 20 ♏ 26**

| LAT. | 11 | 12 | ASC | 2 | 3 |
|---|---|---|---|---|---|
| 0 | 18♐58 | 16♑36 | 15♒32 | 16♓57 | 19♈30 |
| 5 | 18 00 | 15 10 | 14 02 | 15 51 | 19 03 |
| 10 | 17 02 | 13 40 | 12 26 | 14 38 | 18 33 |
| 15 | 16 04 | 12 06 | 10 41 | 13 16 | 18 00 |
| 20 | 15 03 | 10 26 | 08 45 | 11 42 | 17 22 |
| 21 | 14 51 | 10 05 | 08 20 | 11 22 | 17 13 |
| 22 | 14 38 | 09 43 | 07 54 | 11 01 | 17 04 |
| 23 | 14 25 | 09 21 | 07 28 | 10 39 | 16 55 |
| 24 | 14 12 | 08 59 | 07 01 | 10 16 | 16 46 |
| 25 | 13 59 | 08 37 | 06 34 | 09 53 | 16 36 |
| 26 | 13 46 | 08 14 | 06 05 | 09 29 | 16 26 |
| 27 | 13 33 | 07 50 | 05 36 | 09 03 | 16 15 |
| 28 | 13 19 | 07 26 | 05 06 | 08 37 | 16 04 |
| 29 | 13 06 | 07 01 | 04 35 | 08 10 | 15 52 |
| 30 | 12 52 | 06 36 | 04 03 | 07 41 | 15 40 |
| 31 | 12 37 | 06 10 | 03 29 | 07 11 | 15 27 |
| 32 | 12 23 | 05 44 | 02 55 | 06 40 | 15 13 |
| 33 | 12 08 | 05 17 | 02 19 | 06 07 | 14 59 |
| 34 | 11 53 | 04 49 | 01 43 | 05 32 | 14 44 |
| 35 | 11 38 | 04 21 | 01 04 | 04 56 | 14 28 |
| 36 | 11 22 | 03 51 | 00 25 | 04 18 | 14 11 |
| 37 | 11 06 | 03 21 | 29♑43 | 03 37 | 13 53 |
| 38 | 10 50 | 02 50 | 29 00 | 02 55 | 13 33 |
| 39 | 10 33 | 02 18 | 28 15 | 02 10 | 13 13 |
| 40 | 10 16 | 01 45 | 27 28 | 01 22 | 12 50 |
| 41 | 09 59 | 01 11 | 26 39 | 00 31 | 12 26 |
| 42 | 09 41 | 00 35 | 25 48 | 29♒36 | 12 01 |
| 43 | 09 22 | 29♐59 | 24 55 | 28 38 | 11 32 |
| 44 | 09 03 | 29 21 | 23 58 | 27 36 | 11 02 |
| 45 | 08 44 | 28 41 | 22 59 | 26 29 | 10 28 |
| 46 | 08 23 | 28 01 | 21 57 | 25 17 | 09 51 |
| 47 | 08 03 | 27 18 | 20 52 | 24 00 | 09 11 |
| 48 | 07 41 | 26 34 | 19 43 | 22 36 | 08 25 |
| 49 | 07 19 | 25 48 | 18 31 | 21 05 | 07 34 |
| 50 | 06 56 | 25 01 | 17 14 | 19 26 | 06 37 |
| 51 | 06 32 | 24 11 | 15 53 | 17 38 | 05 32 |
| 52 | 06 08 | 23 18 | 14 27 | 15 40 | 04 18 |
| 53 | 05 42 | 22 24 | 12 57 | 13 31 | 02 52 |
| 54 | 05 15 | 21 27 | 11 20 | 11 10 | 01 12 |
| 55 | 04 47 | 20 27 | 09 38 | 08 34 | 29♓14 |
| 56 | 04 18 | 19 24 | 07 49 | 05 43 | 26 52 |
| 57 | 03 48 | 18 17 | 05 54 | 02 34 | 23 59 |
| 58 | 03 16 | 17 08 | 03 51 | 29♑07 | 20 26 |
| 59 | 02 42 | 15 54 | 01 41 | 25 20 | 15 59 |
| 60 | 02♐07 | 14♐37 | 29♐22 | 21♑11 | 10♓19 |

**15h 16m 0s — 229° 0' 0" — 21 ♏ 26**

| LAT. | 11 | 12 | ASC | 2 | 3 |
|---|---|---|---|---|---|
| 0 | 19♐53 | 17♑32 | 16♒33 | 18♓02 | 20♈34 |
| 5 | 18 56 | 16 06 | 15 04 | 16 57 | 20 09 |
| 10 | 17 59 | 14 38 | 13 29 | 15 46 | 19 40 |
| 15 | 17 00 | 13 05 | 11 46 | 14 27 | 19 09 |
| 20 | 16 00 | 11 25 | 09 51 | 12 56 | 18 32 |
| 21 | 15 48 | 11 04 | 09 26 | 12 36 | 18 24 |
| 22 | 15 35 | 10 43 | 09 01 | 12 15 | 18 16 |
| 23 | 15 23 | 10 21 | 08 35 | 11 54 | 18 07 |
| 24 | 15 10 | 09 59 | 08 09 | 11 32 | 17 58 |
| 25 | 14 57 | 09 37 | 07 41 | 11 09 | 17 49 |
| 26 | 14 44 | 09 14 | 07 13 | 10 45 | 17 39 |
| 27 | 14 30 | 08 50 | 06 44 | 10 20 | 17 29 |
| 28 | 14 17 | 08 26 | 06 14 | 09 55 | 17 18 |
| 29 | 14 03 | 08 02 | 05 43 | 09 28 | 17 07 |
| 30 | 13 49 | 07 37 | 05 12 | 09 00 | 16 56 |
| 31 | 13 35 | 07 11 | 04 39 | 08 31 | 16 43 |
| 32 | 13 21 | 06 45 | 04 05 | 08 00 | 16 30 |
| 33 | 13 06 | 06 18 | 03 29 | 07 28 | 16 17 |
| 34 | 12 51 | 05 50 | 02 53 | 06 54 | 16 02 |
| 35 | 12 36 | 05 21 | 02 14 | 06 19 | 15 47 |
| 36 | 12 20 | 04 52 | 01 35 | 05 41 | 15 31 |
| 37 | 12 04 | 04 22 | 00 54 | 05 02 | 15 14 |
| 38 | 11 48 | 03 51 | 00 11 | 04 20 | 14 55 |
| 39 | 11 31 | 03 19 | 29♑26 | 03 35 | 14 36 |
| 40 | 11 14 | 02 45 | 28 39 | 02 48 | 14 14 |
| 41 | 10 56 | 02 11 | 27 51 | 01 58 | 13 52 |
| 42 | 10 38 | 01 36 | 26 59 | 01 05 | 13 27 |
| 43 | 10 20 | 00 59 | 26 06 | 00 07 | 13 00 |
| 44 | 10 01 | 00 21 | 25 10 | 29♒06 | 12 31 |
| 45 | 09 41 | 29♐42 | 24 11 | 28 00 | 11 59 |
| 46 | 09 21 | 29 01 | 23 08 | 26 49 | 11 24 |
| 47 | 09 00 | 28 18 | 22 03 | 25 32 | 10 45 |
| 48 | 08 38 | 27 34 | 20 54 | 24 09 | 10 01 |
| 49 | 08 16 | 26 48 | 19 41 | 22 39 | 09 13 |
| 50 | 07 53 | 25 59 | 18 24 | 21 00 | 08 18 |
| 51 | 07 29 | 25 09 | 17 02 | 19 13 | 07 16 |
| 52 | 07 04 | 24 17 | 15 36 | 17 15 | 06 05 |
| 53 | 06 38 | 23 21 | 14 04 | 15 06 | 04 43 |
| 54 | 06 11 | 22 24 | 12 27 | 12 44 | 03 06 |
| 55 | 05 43 | 21 23 | 10 43 | 10 08 | 01 12 |
| 56 | 05 14 | 20 19 | 08 53 | 07 15 | 28♓55 |
| 57 | 04 43 | 19 12 | 06 56 | 04 04 | 26 08 |
| 58 | 04 11 | 18 01 | 04 50 | 00 34 | 22 42 |
| 59 | 03 37 | 16 47 | 02 38 | 26♑42 | 18 20 |
| 60 | 03♐01 | 15♐28 | 00♑17 | 22♑28 | 12♓45 |

**15h 20m 0s — 230° 0' 0" — 22 ♏ 25**

| LAT. | 11 | 12 | ASC | 2 | 3 |
|---|---|---|---|---|---|
| 0 | 20♐49 | 18♑28 | 17♒33 | 19♓07 | 21♈38 |
| 5 | 19 52 | 17 04 | 16 06 | 18 04 | 21 14 |
| 10 | 18 55 | 15 36 | 14 33 | 16 55 | 20 47 |
| 15 | 17 57 | 14 03 | 12 51 | 15 38 | 20 17 |
| 20 | 16 57 | 12 24 | 10 58 | 14 09 | 19 43 |
| 21 | 16 45 | 12 04 | 10 33 | 13 50 | 19 35 |
| 22 | 16 33 | 11 43 | 10 08 | 13 30 | 19 27 |
| 23 | 16 20 | 11 21 | 09 43 | 13 09 | 19 19 |
| 24 | 16 07 | 10 59 | 09 17 | 12 48 | 19 10 |
| 25 | 15 54 | 10 37 | 08 49 | 12 25 | 19 02 |
| 26 | 15 41 | 10 14 | 08 22 | 12 02 | 18 52 |
| 27 | 15 28 | 09 51 | 07 53 | 11 38 | 18 43 |
| 28 | 15 14 | 09 27 | 07 23 | 11 13 | 18 33 |
| 29 | 15 01 | 09 02 | 06 53 | 10 47 | 18 22 |
| 30 | 14 47 | 08 37 | 06 21 | 10 19 | 18 11 |
| 31 | 14 33 | 08 12 | 05 48 | 09 51 | 17 59 |
| 32 | 14 18 | 07 45 | 05 15 | 09 21 | 17 47 |
| 33 | 14 04 | 07 18 | 04 40 | 08 49 | 17 34 |
| 34 | 13 49 | 06 51 | 04 03 | 08 16 | 17 21 |
| 35 | 13 33 | 06 22 | 03 25 | 07 42 | 17 06 |
| 36 | 13 18 | 05 53 | 02 46 | 07 05 | 16 51 |
| 37 | 13 02 | 05 23 | 02 05 | 06 26 | 16 35 |
| 38 | 12 45 | 04 52 | 01 22 | 05 45 | 16 17 |
| 39 | 12 29 | 04 20 | 00 38 | 05 02 | 15 58 |
| 40 | 12 12 | 03 46 | 29♑51 | 04 16 | 15 38 |
| 41 | 11 54 | 03 12 | 29 03 | 03 26 | 15 17 |
| 42 | 11 36 | 02 37 | 28 12 | 02 34 | 14 53 |
| 43 | 11 17 | 02 00 | 27 18 | 01 37 | 14 28 |
| 44 | 10 58 | 01 22 | 26 22 | 00 37 | 14 00 |
| 45 | 10 38 | 00 42 | 25 23 | 29♒32 | 13 29 |
| 46 | 10 18 | 00 01 | 24 20 | 28 22 | 12 56 |
| 47 | 09 57 | 29♐18 | 23 15 | 27 06 | 12 19 |
| 48 | 09 35 | 28 34 | 22 06 | 25 44 | 11 38 |
| 49 | 09 13 | 27 47 | 20 52 | 24 14 | 10 52 |
| 50 | 08 50 | 26 59 | 19 35 | 22 37 | 09 59 |
| 51 | 08 26 | 26 08 | 18 13 | 20 50 | 09 00 |
| 52 | 08 01 | 25 15 | 16 45 | 18 53 | 07 52 |
| 53 | 07 34 | 24 19 | 15 13 | 16 44 | 06 34 |
| 54 | 07 07 | 23 21 | 13 34 | 14 21 | 05 01 |
| 55 | 06 39 | 22 20 | 11 49 | 11 44 | 03 12 |
| 56 | 06 09 | 21 15 | 09 58 | 08 50 | 01 00 |
| 57 | 05 38 | 20 07 | 07 59 | 05 37 | 28♓19 |
| 58 | 05 05 | 18 56 | 05 52 | 02 03 | 24 59 |
| 59 | 04 31 | 17 40 | 03 37 | 28♑08 | 20 44 |
| 60 | 03♐55 | 16♐20 | 01♑13 | 23♑48 | 15♓15 |

**15h 24m 0s — 231° 0' 0" — 23 ♏ 23**

| LAT. | 11 | 12 | ASC | 2 | 3 |
|---|---|---|---|---|---|
| 0 | 21♐44 | 19♑24 | 18♒34 | 20♓12 | 22♈42 |
| 5 | 20 48 | 18 01 | 17 08 | 19 11 | 22 19 |
| 10 | 19 51 | 16 34 | 15 36 | 18 04 | 21 54 |
| 15 | 18 54 | 15 02 | 13 56 | 16 49 | 21 26 |
| 20 | 17 54 | 13 24 | 12 05 | 15 23 | 20 53 |
| 21 | 17 42 | 13 04 | 11 41 | 15 04 | 20 46 |
| 22 | 17 30 | 12 43 | 11 16 | 14 45 | 20 38 |
| 23 | 17 17 | 12 21 | 10 51 | 14 25 | 20 31 |
| 24 | 17 05 | 11 59 | 10 25 | 14 04 | 20 23 |
| 25 | 16 52 | 11 37 | 09 58 | 13 42 | 20 14 |
| 26 | 16 39 | 11 14 | 09 30 | 13 19 | 20 06 |
| 27 | 16 25 | 10 51 | 09 02 | 12 56 | 19 56 |
| 28 | 16 12 | 10 27 | 08 33 | 12 32 | 19 47 |
| 29 | 15 58 | 10 03 | 08 03 | 12 06 | 19 37 |
| 30 | 15 44 | 09 38 | 07 31 | 11 39 | 19 27 |
| 31 | 15 30 | 09 13 | 06 59 | 11 12 | 19 16 |
| 32 | 15 16 | 08 47 | 06 25 | 10 42 | 19 04 |
| 33 | 15 01 | 08 20 | 05 51 | 10 12 | 18 52 |
| 34 | 14 46 | 07 52 | 05 14 | 09 39 | 18 39 |
| 35 | 14 31 | 07 24 | 04 37 | 09 06 | 18 25 |
| 36 | 14 15 | 06 54 | 03 58 | 08 30 | 18 11 |
| 37 | 13 59 | 06 24 | 03 17 | 07 52 | 17 55 |
| 38 | 13 43 | 05 53 | 02 35 | 07 12 | 17 39 |
| 39 | 13 26 | 05 21 | 01 50 | 06 29 | 17 21 |
| 40 | 13 09 | 04 48 | 01 04 | 05 44 | 17 02 |
| 41 | 12 52 | 04 14 | 00 15 | 04 56 | 16 41 |
| 42 | 12 34 | 03 38 | 29♑25 | 04 04 | 16 19 |
| 43 | 12 15 | 03 01 | 28 31 | 03 09 | 15 55 |
| 44 | 11 56 | 02 23 | 27 35 | 02 09 | 15 29 |
| 45 | 11 36 | 01 43 | 26 36 | 01 05 | 15 00 |
| 46 | 11 16 | 01 02 | 25 34 | 29♒56 | 14 28 |
| 47 | 10 55 | 00 19 | 24 28 | 28 42 | 13 53 |
| 48 | 10 33 | 29♐34 | 23 18 | 27 20 | 13 14 |
| 49 | 10 10 | 28 48 | 22 05 | 25 52 | 12 30 |
| 50 | 09 47 | 27 59 | 20 47 | 24 15 | 11 41 |
| 51 | 09 23 | 27 08 | 19 24 | 22 29 | 10 44 |
| 52 | 08 57 | 26 14 | 17 56 | 20 32 | 09 40 |
| 53 | 08 31 | 25 18 | 16 23 | 18 23 | 08 25 |
| 54 | 08 04 | 24 19 | 14 43 | 16 01 | 06 57 |
| 55 | 07 35 | 23 17 | 12 57 | 13 23 | 05 12 |
| 56 | 07 05 | 22 12 | 11 04 | 10 28 | 03 06 |
| 57 | 06 33 | 21 03 | 09 03 | 07 13 | 00 31 |
| 58 | 06 00 | 19 50 | 06 54 | 03 37 | 27♓17 |
| 59 | 05 26 | 18 33 | 04 37 | 29♑37 | 23 11 |
| 60 | 04♐49 | 17♐12 | 02♑10 | 25♑12 | 17♓49 |

# Koch Table of Houses for Latitudes 0° to 60° North

**15h 28m 0s — 232° 0' 0" — 24 ♏ 22**

| LAT. | 11 | 12 | ASC | 2 | 3 |
|---|---|---|---|---|---|
| 0 | 22♐39 | 20♑20 | 19♒35 | 21♓17 | 23♈46 |
| 5 | 21 44 | 18 58 | 18 11 | 20 18 | 23 24 |
| 10 | 20 48 | 17 32 | 16 41 | 19 13 | 23 01 |
| 15 | 19 51 | 16 02 | 15 02 | 18 01 | 22 34 |
| 20 | 18 52 | 14 24 | 13 12 | 16 37 | 22 03 |
| 21 | 18 39 | 14 04 | 12 48 | 16 19 | 21 56 |
| 22 | 18 27 | 13 43 | 12 24 | 16 00 | 21 49 |
| 23 | 18 15 | 13 22 | 11 59 | 15 40 | 21 42 |
| 24 | 18 02 | 13 00 | 11 33 | 15 20 | 21 35 |
| 25 | 17 49 | 12 38 | 11 07 | 14 59 | 21 27 |
| 26 | 17 36 | 12 15 | 10 40 | 14 37 | 21 19 |
| 27 | 17 23 | 11 52 | 10 12 | 14 14 | 21 10 |
| 28 | 17 10 | 11 29 | 09 43 | 13 50 | 21 01 |
| 29 | 16 56 | 11 04 | 09 13 | 13 26 | 20 52 |
| 30 | 16 42 | 10 40 | 08 42 | 13 00 | 20 42 |
| 31 | 16 28 | 10 14 | 08 10 | 12 33 | 20 31 |
| 32 | 16 14 | 09 48 | 07 37 | 12 04 | 20 21 |
| 33 | 15 59 | 09 21 | 07 02 | 11 34 | 20 09 |
| 34 | 15 44 | 08 54 | 06 26 | 11 03 | 19 57 |
| 35 | 15 29 | 08 25 | 05 49 | 10 30 | 19 44 |
| 36 | 15 13 | 07 56 | 05 10 | 09 55 | 19 30 |
| 37 | 14 57 | 07 26 | 04 30 | 09 18 | 19 16 |
| 38 | 14 41 | 06 55 | 03 48 | 08 39 | 19 00 |
| 39 | 14 24 | 06 23 | 03 04 | 07 57 | 18 44 |
| 40 | 14 07 | 05 50 | 02 18 | 07 13 | 18 26 |
| 41 | 13 49 | 05 16 | 01 29 | 06 26 | 18 06 |
| 42 | 13 31 | 04 40 | 00 38 | 05 35 | 17 45 |
| 43 | 13 13 | 04 03 | 29♑45 | 04 41 | 17 23 |
| 44 | 12 53 | 03 25 | 28 49 | 03 43 | 16 58 |
| 45 | 12 34 | 02 45 | 27 50 | 02 40 | 16 31 |
| 46 | 12 13 | 02 04 | 26 48 | 01 32 | 16 01 |
| 47 | 11 52 | 01 20 | 25 42 | 00 18 | 15 27 |
| 48 | 11 30 | 00 35 | 24 32 | 28♒58 | 14 50 |
| 49 | 11 07 | 29♐48 | 23 18 | 27 31 | 14 09 |
| 50 | 10 44 | 28 59 | 22 00 | 25 55 | 13 22 |
| 51 | 10 20 | 28 08 | 20 37 | 24 10 | 12 29 |
| 52 | 09 54 | 27 14 | 19 08 | 22 14 | 11 27 |
| 53 | 09 28 | 26 17 | 17 34 | 20 06 | 10 16 |
| 54 | 09 00 | 25 18 | 15 54 | 17 43 | 08 52 |
| 55 | 08 31 | 24 15 | 14 06 | 15 05 | 07 12 |
| 56 | 08 01 | 23 09 | 12 12 | 12 09 | 05 12 |
| 57 | 07 29 | 21 59 | 10 09 | 08 52 | 02 44 |
| 58 | 06 55 | 20 46 | 07 58 | 05 13 | 29♓38 |
| 59 | 06 20 | 19 27 | 05 38 | 01 09 | 25 40 |
| 60 | 05♐43 | 18♐05 | 03♑09 | 26♑39 | 20♓27 |

**15h 32m 0s — 233° 0' 0" — 25 ♏ 21**

| LAT. | 11 | 12 | ASC | 2 | 3 |
|---|---|---|---|---|---|
| 0 | 23♐34 | 21♑17 | 20♒36 | 22♓23 | 24♈50 |
| 5 | 22 39 | 19 55 | 19 14 | 21 25 | 24 29 |
| 10 | 21 44 | 18 31 | 17 45 | 20 23 | 24 07 |
| 15 | 20 48 | 17 01 | 16 08 | 19 12 | 23 42 |
| 20 | 19 49 | 15 24 | 14 20 | 17 51 | 23 13 |
| 21 | 19 37 | 15 04 | 13 56 | 17 34 | 23 07 |
| 22 | 19 24 | 14 43 | 13 33 | 17 15 | 23 00 |
| 23 | 19 12 | 14 22 | 13 08 | 16 56 | 22 54 |
| 24 | 18 59 | 14 01 | 12 43 | 16 37 | 22 46 |
| 25 | 18 47 | 13 39 | 12 17 | 16 16 | 22 39 |
| 26 | 18 34 | 13 16 | 11 50 | 15 55 | 22 31 |
| 27 | 18 21 | 12 53 | 11 22 | 15 33 | 22 23 |
| 28 | 18 07 | 12 30 | 10 53 | 15 10 | 22 15 |
| 29 | 17 54 | 12 06 | 10 24 | 14 46 | 22 06 |
| 30 | 17 40 | 11 41 | 09 53 | 14 21 | 21 57 |
| 31 | 17 26 | 11 16 | 09 22 | 13 54 | 21 47 |
| 32 | 17 12 | 10 50 | 08 49 | 13 27 | 21 37 |
| 33 | 16 57 | 10 23 | 08 15 | 12 58 | 21 26 |
| 34 | 16 42 | 09 56 | 07 39 | 12 27 | 21 15 |
| 35 | 16 27 | 09 28 | 07 02 | 11 55 | 21 03 |
| 36 | 16 11 | 08 58 | 06 24 | 11 21 | 20 50 |
| 37 | 15 55 | 08 28 | 05 44 | 10 45 | 20 36 |
| 38 | 15 39 | 07 57 | 05 02 | 10 07 | 20 22 |
| 39 | 15 22 | 07 25 | 04 18 | 09 26 | 20 06 |
| 40 | 15 05 | 06 52 | 03 32 | 08 43 | 19 49 |
| 41 | 14 47 | 06 18 | 02 44 | 07 57 | 19 31 |
| 42 | 14 29 | 05 42 | 01 53 | 07 07 | 19 11 |
| 43 | 14 11 | 05 05 | 01 00 | 06 14 | 18 50 |
| 44 | 13 51 | 04 27 | 00 04 | 05 17 | 18 27 |
| 45 | 13 31 | 03 47 | 29♑05 | 04 16 | 18 01 |
| 46 | 13 11 | 03 06 | 28 03 | 03 09 | 17 33 |
| 47 | 12 50 | 02 22 | 26 57 | 01 57 | 17 01 |
| 48 | 12 28 | 01 37 | 25 47 | 00 38 | 16 26 |
| 49 | 12 05 | 00 50 | 24 33 | 29♒12 | 15 47 |
| 50 | 11 41 | 00 00 | 23 15 | 27 37 | 15 03 |
| 51 | 11 17 | 29♐08 | 21 51 | 25 53 | 14 13 |
| 52 | 10 51 | 28 14 | 20 22 | 23 58 | 13 15 |
| 53 | 10 24 | 27 17 | 18 47 | 21 50 | 12 07 |
| 54 | 09 56 | 26 17 | 17 06 | 19 29 | 10 48 |
| 55 | 09 27 | 25 14 | 15 17 | 16 50 | 09 13 |
| 56 | 08 57 | 24 07 | 13 21 | 13 53 | 07 19 |
| 57 | 08 25 | 22 56 | 11 17 | 10 35 | 04 57 |
| 58 | 07 51 | 21 41 | 09 04 | 06 54 | 01 59 |
| 59 | 07 15 | 20 22 | 06 41 | 02 46 | 28♓10 |
| 60 | 06♐37 | 18♐58 | 04♑08 | 28♑09 | 23♓07 |

**15h 36m 0s — 234° 0' 0" — 26 ♏ 19**

| LAT. | 11 | 12 | ASC | 2 | 3 |
|---|---|---|---|---|---|
| 0 | 24♐30 | 22♑13 | 21♒37 | 23♓28 | 25♈53 |
| 5 | 23 35 | 20 53 | 20 17 | 22 33 | 25 34 |
| 10 | 22 40 | 19 29 | 18 50 | 21 32 | 25 13 |
| 15 | 21 44 | 18 00 | 17 14 | 20 24 | 24 50 |
| 20 | 20 46 | 16 25 | 15 28 | 19 06 | 24 23 |
| 21 | 20 34 | 16 05 | 15 05 | 18 49 | 24 17 |
| 22 | 20 22 | 15 44 | 14 41 | 18 31 | 24 11 |
| 23 | 20 09 | 15 23 | 14 17 | 18 13 | 24 05 |
| 24 | 19 57 | 15 02 | 13 52 | 17 54 | 23 58 |
| 25 | 19 44 | 14 40 | 13 27 | 17 34 | 23 51 |
| 26 | 19 31 | 14 18 | 13 00 | 17 13 | 23 44 |
| 27 | 19 18 | 13 55 | 12 33 | 16 52 | 23 37 |
| 28 | 19 05 | 13 32 | 12 05 | 16 30 | 23 29 |
| 29 | 18 51 | 13 08 | 11 35 | 16 06 | 23 21 |
| 30 | 18 38 | 12 43 | 11 05 | 15 42 | 23 12 |
| 31 | 18 24 | 12 18 | 10 34 | 15 16 | 23 03 |
| 32 | 18 09 | 11 52 | 10 01 | 14 49 | 22 53 |
| 33 | 17 55 | 11 26 | 09 28 | 14 21 | 22 43 |
| 34 | 17 40 | 10 58 | 08 52 | 13 52 | 22 33 |
| 35 | 17 25 | 10 30 | 08 16 | 13 20 | 22 21 |
| 36 | 17 09 | 10 01 | 07 38 | 12 47 | 22 09 |
| 37 | 16 53 | 09 31 | 06 58 | 12 12 | 21 57 |
| 38 | 16 37 | 09 00 | 06 16 | 11 35 | 21 43 |
| 39 | 16 20 | 08 28 | 05 33 | 10 56 | 21 28 |
| 40 | 16 03 | 07 55 | 04 47 | 10 14 | 21 12 |
| 41 | 15 45 | 07 21 | 04 00 | 09 29 | 20 55 |
| 42 | 15 27 | 06 45 | 03 09 | 08 41 | 20 37 |
| 43 | 15 08 | 06 08 | 02 16 | 07 49 | 20 17 |
| 44 | 14 49 | 05 30 | 01 21 | 06 53 | 19 55 |
| 45 | 14 29 | 04 50 | 00 22 | 05 53 | 19 31 |
| 46 | 14 09 | 04 08 | 29♑20 | 04 48 | 19 05 |
| 47 | 13 47 | 03 25 | 28 14 | 03 37 | 18 35 |
| 48 | 13 25 | 02 39 | 27 04 | 02 19 | 18 02 |
| 49 | 13 02 | 01 52 | 25 50 | 00 54 | 17 26 |
| 50 | 12 39 | 01 02 | 24 31 | 29♒21 | 16 44 |
| 51 | 12 14 | 00 10 | 23 07 | 27 38 | 15 57 |
| 52 | 11 48 | 29♐15 | 21 37 | 25 44 | 15 02 |
| 53 | 11 21 | 28 17 | 20 01 | 23 38 | 13 58 |
| 54 | 10 53 | 27 17 | 18 19 | 21 16 | 12 43 |
| 55 | 10 24 | 26 13 | 16 29 | 18 38 | 11 14 |
| 56 | 09 53 | 25 05 | 14 32 | 15 41 | 09 26 |
| 57 | 09 20 | 23 54 | 12 26 | 12 22 | 07 11 |
| 58 | 08 46 | 22 38 | 10 10 | 08 38 | 04 22 |
| 59 | 08 10 | 21 17 | 07 45 | 04 26 | 00 43 |
| 60 | 07♐32 | 19♐52 | 05♑10 | 29♑44 | 25♓51 |

**15h 40m 0s — 235° 0' 0" — 27 ♏ 17**

| LAT. | 11 | 12 | ASC | 2 | 3 |
|---|---|---|---|---|---|
| 0 | 25♐25 | 23♑10 | 22♒39 | 24♓33 | 26♈57 |
| 5 | 24 31 | 21 51 | 21 20 | 23 40 | 26 39 |
| 10 | 23 37 | 20 28 | 19 55 | 22 42 | 26 20 |
| 15 | 22 41 | 19 00 | 18 21 | 21 36 | 25 58 |
| 20 | 21 43 | 17 26 | 16 36 | 20 21 | 25 33 |
| 21 | 21 31 | 17 06 | 16 14 | 20 04 | 25 28 |
| 22 | 21 19 | 16 45 | 15 51 | 19 47 | 25 22 |
| 23 | 21 07 | 16 25 | 15 27 | 19 29 | 25 16 |
| 24 | 20 54 | 16 03 | 15 02 | 19 11 | 25 10 |
| 25 | 20 42 | 15 42 | 14 37 | 18 52 | 25 03 |
| 26 | 20 29 | 15 20 | 14 11 | 18 32 | 24 57 |
| 27 | 20 16 | 14 57 | 13 44 | 18 11 | 24 50 |
| 28 | 20 03 | 14 34 | 13 16 | 17 50 | 24 43 |
| 29 | 19 49 | 14 10 | 12 47 | 17 27 | 24 35 |
| 30 | 19 35 | 13 46 | 12 18 | 17 03 | 24 27 |
| 31 | 19 22 | 13 21 | 11 47 | 16 39 | 24 18 |
| 32 | 19 07 | 12 55 | 11 15 | 16 13 | 24 10 |
| 33 | 18 53 | 12 28 | 10 41 | 15 45 | 24 00 |
| 34 | 18 38 | 12 01 | 10 07 | 15 17 | 23 50 |
| 35 | 18 23 | 11 33 | 09 30 | 14 46 | 23 40 |
| 36 | 18 07 | 11 04 | 08 53 | 14 14 | 23 29 |
| 37 | 17 51 | 10 34 | 08 13 | 13 40 | 23 17 |
| 38 | 17 35 | 10 03 | 07 32 | 13 04 | 23 04 |
| 39 | 17 18 | 09 31 | 06 49 | 12 26 | 22 50 |
| 40 | 17 01 | 08 58 | 06 04 | 11 45 | 22 36 |
| 41 | 16 43 | 08 24 | 05 16 | 11 01 | 22 20 |
| 42 | 16 25 | 07 48 | 04 26 | 10 15 | 22 03 |
| 43 | 16 07 | 07 11 | 03 34 | 09 24 | 21 44 |
| 44 | 15 47 | 06 33 | 02 38 | 08 30 | 21 23 |
| 45 | 15 27 | 05 53 | 01 39 | 07 31 | 21 01 |
| 46 | 15 07 | 05 11 | 00 37 | 06 27 | 20 36 |
| 47 | 14 45 | 04 27 | 29♑32 | 05 18 | 20 09 |
| 48 | 14 23 | 03 42 | 28 22 | 04 02 | 19 38 |
| 49 | 14 00 | 02 54 | 27 07 | 02 38 | 19 04 |
| 50 | 13 36 | 02 04 | 25 48 | 01 07 | 18 25 |
| 51 | 13 11 | 01 12 | 24 24 | 29♒25 | 17 40 |
| 52 | 12 45 | 00 16 | 22 54 | 27 33 | 16 49 |
| 53 | 12 18 | 29♐18 | 21 17 | 25 28 | 15 49 |
| 54 | 11 50 | 28 17 | 19 34 | 23 07 | 14 39 |
| 55 | 11 20 | 27 12 | 17 43 | 20 30 | 13 15 |
| 56 | 10 49 | 26 04 | 15 44 | 17 32 | 11 33 |
| 57 | 10 16 | 24 52 | 13 36 | 14 12 | 09 26 |
| 58 | 09 42 | 23 35 | 11 19 | 10 26 | 06 45 |
| 59 | 09 05 | 22 13 | 08 51 | 06 10 | 03 16 |
| 60 | 08♐26 | 20♐46 | 06♑12 | 01♒23 | 28♓37 |

**15h 44m 0s — 236° 0' 0" — 28 ♏ 15**

| LAT. | 11 | 12 | ASC | 2 | 3 |
|---|---|---|---|---|---|
| 0 | 26♐20 | 24♑06 | 23♒41 | 25♓38 | 28♈00 |
| 5 | 25 27 | 22 48 | 22 23 | 24 47 | 27 44 |
| 10 | 24 33 | 21 27 | 21 00 | 23 51 | 27 26 |
| 15 | 23 38 | 20 00 | 19 28 | 22 48 | 27 06 |
| 20 | 22 40 | 18 27 | 17 45 | 21 36 | 26 43 |
| 21 | 22 28 | 18 07 | 17 23 | 21 20 | 26 38 |
| 22 | 22 16 | 17 47 | 17 00 | 21 03 | 26 32 |
| 23 | 22 04 | 17 26 | 16 37 | 20 46 | 26 27 |
| 24 | 21 52 | 17 05 | 16 13 | 20 28 | 26 21 |
| 25 | 21 39 | 16 44 | 15 48 | 20 10 | 26 15 |
| 26 | 21 27 | 16 22 | 15 22 | 19 51 | 26 09 |
| 27 | 21 14 | 15 59 | 14 56 | 19 31 | 26 03 |
| 28 | 21 00 | 15 36 | 14 28 | 19 10 | 25 56 |
| 29 | 20 47 | 15 13 | 14 00 | 18 48 | 25 49 |
| 30 | 20 33 | 14 48 | 13 31 | 18 25 | 25 42 |
| 31 | 20 19 | 14 23 | 13 00 | 18 01 | 25 34 |
| 32 | 20 05 | 13 58 | 12 29 | 17 36 | 25 26 |
| 33 | 19 51 | 13 32 | 11 56 | 17 10 | 25 17 |
| 34 | 19 36 | 13 04 | 11 21 | 16 42 | 25 08 |
| 35 | 19 21 | 12 36 | 10 46 | 16 13 | 24 58 |
| 36 | 19 05 | 12 08 | 10 08 | 15 42 | 24 48 |
| 37 | 18 50 | 11 38 | 09 29 | 15 09 | 24 37 |
| 38 | 18 33 | 11 07 | 08 48 | 14 34 | 24 25 |
| 39 | 18 17 | 10 35 | 08 06 | 13 57 | 24 12 |
| 40 | 17 59 | 10 02 | 07 21 | 13 17 | 23 59 |
| 41 | 17 42 | 09 28 | 06 34 | 12 35 | 23 44 |
| 42 | 17 23 | 08 52 | 05 44 | 11 49 | 23 28 |
| 43 | 17 05 | 08 15 | 04 52 | 11 00 | 23 11 |
| 44 | 16 45 | 07 37 | 03 57 | 10 08 | 22 52 |
| 45 | 16 25 | 06 57 | 02 58 | 09 10 | 22 31 |
| 46 | 16 05 | 06 15 | 01 56 | 08 08 | 22 08 |
| 47 | 15 43 | 05 31 | 00 51 | 07 00 | 21 42 |
| 48 | 15 21 | 04 45 | 29♑41 | 05 46 | 21 14 |
| 49 | 14 58 | 03 57 | 28 26 | 04 24 | 20 42 |
| 50 | 14 34 | 03 07 | 27 07 | 02 54 | 20 05 |
| 51 | 14 09 | 02 14 | 25 43 | 01 15 | 19 24 |
| 52 | 13 43 | 01 19 | 24 12 | 29♒24 | 18 36 |
| 53 | 13 15 | 00 20 | 22 35 | 27 20 | 17 40 |
| 54 | 12 47 | 29♐18 | 20 51 | 25 01 | 16 34 |
| 55 | 12 17 | 28 13 | 18 59 | 22 24 | 15 16 |
| 56 | 11 45 | 27 04 | 16 59 | 19 27 | 13 40 |
| 57 | 11 12 | 25 50 | 14 49 | 16 06 | 11 40 |
| 58 | 10 37 | 24 33 | 12 29 | 12 18 | 09 09 |
| 59 | 10 00 | 23 10 | 09 59 | 08 00 | 05 51 |
| 60 | 09♐21 | 21♐41 | 07♑17 | 03♒07 | 01♈25 |

**15h 48m 0s — 237° 0' 0" — 29 ♏ 13**

| LAT. | 11 | 12 | ASC | 2 | 3 |
|---|---|---|---|---|---|
| 0 | 27♐15 | 25♑03 | 24♒42 | 26♓44 | 29♈03 |
| 5 | 26 22 | 23 46 | 23 27 | 25 55 | 28 48 |
| 10 | 25 29 | 22 26 | 22 05 | 25 01 | 28 32 |
| 15 | 24 35 | 21 00 | 20 35 | 24 00 | 28 13 |
| 20 | 23 37 | 19 28 | 18 55 | 22 51 | 27 52 |
| 21 | 23 26 | 19 08 | 18 33 | 22 35 | 27 47 |
| 22 | 23 14 | 18 48 | 18 11 | 22 19 | 27 43 |
| 23 | 23 02 | 18 28 | 17 48 | 22 03 | 27 38 |
| 24 | 22 49 | 18 07 | 17 24 | 21 46 | 27 32 |
| 25 | 22 37 | 17 46 | 17 00 | 21 28 | 27 27 |
| 26 | 22 24 | 17 24 | 16 34 | 21 10 | 27 21 |
| 27 | 22 11 | 17 02 | 16 08 | 20 51 | 27 15 |
| 28 | 21 58 | 16 39 | 15 41 | 20 31 | 27 09 |
| 29 | 21 45 | 16 15 | 15 13 | 20 10 | 27 03 |
| 30 | 21 31 | 15 51 | 14 44 | 19 48 | 26 56 |
| 31 | 21 18 | 15 27 | 14 14 | 19 25 | 26 49 |
| 32 | 21 03 | 15 01 | 13 43 | 19 00 | 26 41 |
| 33 | 20 49 | 14 35 | 13 11 | 18 35 | 26 33 |
| 34 | 20 34 | 14 08 | 12 37 | 18 08 | 26 25 |
| 35 | 20 19 | 13 40 | 12 02 | 17 40 | 26 16 |
| 36 | 20 04 | 13 12 | 11 25 | 17 10 | 26 06 |
| 37 | 19 48 | 12 42 | 10 46 | 16 38 | 25 56 |
| 38 | 19 32 | 12 11 | 10 06 | 16 05 | 25 45 |
| 39 | 19 15 | 11 39 | 09 23 | 15 29 | 25 34 |
| 40 | 18 58 | 11 06 | 08 39 | 14 50 | 25 21 |
| 41 | 18 40 | 10 32 | 07 52 | 14 09 | 25 08 |
| 42 | 18 22 | 09 57 | 07 03 | 13 25 | 24 53 |
| 43 | 18 03 | 09 20 | 06 11 | 12 38 | 24 37 |
| 44 | 17 44 | 08 41 | 05 16 | 11 46 | 24 19 |
| 45 | 17 24 | 08 01 | 04 18 | 10 51 | 24 00 |
| 46 | 17 03 | 07 19 | 03 16 | 09 50 | 23 39 |
| 47 | 16 41 | 06 35 | 02 11 | 08 44 | 23 15 |
| 48 | 16 19 | 05 49 | 01 01 | 07 32 | 22 49 |
| 49 | 15 56 | 05 01 | 29♑47 | 06 12 | 22 19 |
| 50 | 15 32 | 04 11 | 28 28 | 04 44 | 21 46 |
| 51 | 15 07 | 03 17 | 27 03 | 03 06 | 21 07 |
| 52 | 14 40 | 02 21 | 25 32 | 01 17 | 20 23 |
| 53 | 14 13 | 01 22 | 23 54 | 29♒15 | 19 31 |
| 54 | 13 44 | 00 20 | 22 09 | 26 58 | 18 29 |
| 55 | 13 14 | 29♐14 | 20 16 | 24 22 | 17 16 |
| 56 | 12 42 | 28 04 | 18 15 | 21 26 | 15 46 |
| 57 | 12 09 | 26 50 | 16 03 | 18 05 | 13 55 |
| 58 | 11 33 | 25 31 | 13 41 | 14 15 | 11 33 |
| 59 | 10 56 | 24 07 | 11 08 | 09 54 | 08 26 |
| 60 | 10♐16 | 22♐37 | 08♑23 | 04♒56 | 04♈14 |

**15h 52m 0s — 238° 0' 0" — 00 ♐ 11**

| LAT. | 11 | 12 | ASC | 2 | 3 |
|---|---|---|---|---|---|
| 0 | 28♐10 | 26♑00 | 25♒44 | 27♓49 | 00♉06 |
| 5 | 27 18 | 24 45 | 24 31 | 27 02 | 29♈52 |
| 10 | 26 25 | 23 25 | 23 11 | 26 11 | 29 37 |
| 15 | 25 31 | 22 01 | 21 43 | 25 13 | 29 21 |
| 20 | 24 35 | 20 29 | 20 04 | 24 06 | 29 01 |
| 21 | 24 23 | 20 10 | 19 43 | 23 51 | 28 57 |
| 22 | 24 11 | 19 50 | 19 21 | 23 36 | 28 53 |
| 23 | 23 59 | 19 30 | 18 59 | 23 20 | 28 48 |
| 24 | 23 47 | 19 09 | 18 35 | 23 04 | 28 43 |
| 25 | 23 35 | 18 48 | 18 11 | 22 47 | 28 39 |
| 26 | 23 22 | 18 27 | 17 47 | 22 29 | 28 33 |
| 27 | 23 09 | 18 05 | 17 21 | 22 11 | 28 28 |
| 28 | 22 56 | 17 42 | 16 55 | 21 51 | 28 22 |
| 29 | 22 43 | 17 19 | 16 27 | 21 31 | 28 16 |
| 30 | 22 29 | 16 55 | 15 59 | 21 10 | 28 10 |
| 31 | 22 16 | 16 30 | 15 29 | 20 48 | 28 04 |
| 32 | 22 02 | 16 05 | 14 58 | 20 25 | 27 57 |
| 33 | 21 47 | 15 39 | 14 26 | 20 00 | 27 50 |
| 34 | 21 32 | 15 12 | 13 53 | 19 35 | 27 42 |
| 35 | 21 17 | 14 44 | 13 18 | 19 08 | 27 34 |
| 36 | 21 02 | 14 16 | 12 42 | 18 39 | 27 25 |
| 37 | 20 46 | 13 46 | 12 04 | 18 08 | 27 16 |
| 38 | 20 30 | 13 16 | 11 24 | 17 36 | 27 06 |
| 39 | 20 13 | 12 44 | 10 42 | 17 01 | 26 55 |
| 40 | 19 56 | 12 11 | 09 58 | 16 24 | 26 44 |
| 41 | 19 38 | 11 37 | 09 12 | 15 44 | 26 31 |
| 42 | 19 20 | 11 02 | 08 23 | 15 02 | 26 18 |
| 43 | 19 01 | 10 25 | 07 32 | 14 16 | 26 03 |
| 44 | 18 42 | 09 46 | 06 37 | 13 26 | 25 47 |
| 45 | 18 22 | 09 06 | 05 39 | 12 32 | 25 29 |
| 46 | 18 01 | 08 24 | 04 38 | 11 33 | 25 10 |
| 47 | 17 40 | 07 40 | 03 33 | 10 29 | 24 48 |
| 48 | 17 17 | 06 54 | 02 23 | 09 19 | 24 24 |
| 49 | 16 54 | 06 06 | 01 09 | 08 01 | 23 56 |
| 50 | 16 30 | 05 15 | 29♑50 | 06 35 | 23 25 |
| 51 | 16 04 | 04 21 | 28 25 | 05 00 | 22 50 |
| 52 | 15 38 | 03 25 | 26 54 | 03 13 | 22 09 |
| 53 | 15 10 | 02 26 | 25 16 | 01 13 | 21 21 |
| 54 | 14 41 | 01 23 | 23 30 | 28♒57 | 20 24 |
| 55 | 14 11 | 00 16 | 21 36 | 26 23 | 19 16 |
| 56 | 13 39 | 29♐05 | 19 33 | 23 28 | 17 52 |
| 57 | 13 05 | 27 50 | 17 20 | 20 07 | 16 09 |
| 58 | 12 29 | 26 30 | 14 56 | 16 17 | 13 56 |
| 59 | 11 51 | 25 05 | 12 20 | 11 53 | 11 02 |
| 60 | 11♐11 | 23♐34 | 09♑31 | 06♒50 | 07♈04 |

**15h 56m 0s — 239° 0' 0" — 01 ♐ 08**

| LAT. | 11 | 12 | ASC | 2 | 3 |
|---|---|---|---|---|---|
| 0 | 29♐05 | 26♑57 | 26♒47 | 28♓55 | 01♉08 |
| 5 | 28 14 | 25 43 | 25 35 | 28 10 | 00 56 |
| 10 | 27 22 | 24 25 | 24 17 | 27 20 | 00 43 |
| 15 | 26 28 | 23 01 | 22 51 | 26 25 | 00 28 |
| 20 | 25 32 | 21 31 | 21 15 | 25 21 | 00 10 |
| 21 | 25 20 | 21 12 | 20 54 | 25 07 | 00 07 |
| 22 | 25 09 | 20 52 | 20 32 | 24 53 | 00 03 |
| 23 | 24 57 | 20 32 | 20 10 | 24 38 | 29♈59 |
| 24 | 24 45 | 20 12 | 19 47 | 24 22 | 29 54 |
| 25 | 24 32 | 19 51 | 19 24 | 24 06 | 29 50 |
| 26 | 24 20 | 19 30 | 19 00 | 23 49 | 29 45 |
| 27 | 24 07 | 19 08 | 18 34 | 23 31 | 29 40 |
| 28 | 23 54 | 18 45 | 18 08 | 23 13 | 29 35 |
| 29 | 23 41 | 18 22 | 17 41 | 22 53 | 29 30 |
| 30 | 23 28 | 17 59 | 17 14 | 22 33 | 29 24 |
| 31 | 23 14 | 17 34 | 16 44 | 22 12 | 29 18 |
| 32 | 23 00 | 17 09 | 16 14 | 21 50 | 29 12 |
| 33 | 22 45 | 16 43 | 15 43 | 21 26 | 29 06 |
| 34 | 22 31 | 16 17 | 15 10 | 21 01 | 28 59 |
| 35 | 22 16 | 15 49 | 14 36 | 20 35 | 28 51 |
| 36 | 22 00 | 15 21 | 14 00 | 20 08 | 28 43 |
| 37 | 21 45 | 14 51 | 13 22 | 19 38 | 28 35 |
| 38 | 21 28 | 14 21 | 12 43 | 19 07 | 28 26 |
| 39 | 21 12 | 13 49 | 12 02 | 18 34 | 28 16 |
| 40 | 20 55 | 13 17 | 11 18 | 17 58 | 28 06 |
| 41 | 20 37 | 12 42 | 10 32 | 17 20 | 27 54 |
| 42 | 20 19 | 12 07 | 09 44 | 16 39 | 27 42 |
| 43 | 20 00 | 11 30 | 08 53 | 15 55 | 27 29 |
| 44 | 19 41 | 10 52 | 07 59 | 15 07 | 27 14 |
| 45 | 19 21 | 10 11 | 07 02 | 14 15 | 26 58 |
| 46 | 19 00 | 09 29 | 06 01 | 13 18 | 26 40 |
| 47 | 18 38 | 08 45 | 04 56 | 12 16 | 26 20 |
| 48 | 18 16 | 07 59 | 03 47 | 11 07 | 25 58 |
| 49 | 17 52 | 07 11 | 02 33 | 09 52 | 25 33 |
| 50 | 17 28 | 06 20 | 01 13 | 08 28 | 25 04 |
| 51 | 17 03 | 05 26 | 29♑48 | 06 55 | 24 32 |
| 52 | 16 36 | 04 29 | 28 17 | 05 11 | 23 54 |
| 53 | 16 08 | 03 30 | 26 39 | 03 13 | 23 10 |
| 54 | 15 39 | 02 26 | 24 52 | 01 00 | 22 18 |
| 55 | 15 08 | 01 19 | 22 57 | 28♒28 | 21 15 |
| 56 | 14 36 | 00 07 | 20 53 | 25 34 | 19 58 |
| 57 | 14 02 | 28♐51 | 18 38 | 22 14 | 18 22 |
| 58 | 13 25 | 27 30 | 16 12 | 18 24 | 16 19 |
| 59 | 12 47 | 26 04 | 13 34 | 13 57 | 13 37 |
| 60 | 12♐06 | 24♐31 | 10♑42 | 08♒50 | 09♈55 |

# Koch Table of Houses for Latitudes 0° to 60° North

16h 0m 0s — 240° 0' 0" — 02 ♐ 05

| LAT. | 11 | 12 | ASC | 2 | 3 |
|---|---|---|---|---|---|
| 0 | 00♑00 | 27♑55 | 27♒49 | 00♈00 | 02♉11 |
| 5 | 29♐09 | 26 41 | 26 39 | 29♓17 | 02 00 |
| 10 | 28 18 | 25 24 | 25 23 | 28 30 | 01 48 |
| 15 | 27 25 | 24 02 | 23 59 | 27 38 | 01 35 |
| 20 | 26 29 | 22 33 | 22 25 | 26 37 | 01 19 |
| 21 | 26 18 | 22 14 | 22 05 | 26 23 | 01 16 |
| 22 | 26 06 | 21 55 | 21 44 | 26 09 | 01 12 |
| 23 | 25 54 | 21 35 | 21 22 | 25 55 | 01 09 |
| 24 | 25 42 | 21 15 | 21 00 | 25 40 | 01 05 |
| 25 | 25 30 | 20 54 | 20 37 | 25 25 | 01 01 |
| 26 | 25 18 | 20 33 | 20 13 | 25 08 | 00 57 |
| 27 | 25 05 | 20 11 | 19 48 | 24 51 | 00 52 |
| 28 | 24 52 | 19 49 | 19 23 | 24 34 | 00 48 |
| 29 | 24 39 | 19 26 | 18 56 | 24 15 | 00 43 |
| 30 | 24 26 | 19 03 | 18 29 | 23 56 | 00 38 |
| 31 | 24 12 | 18 39 | 18 00 | 23 36 | 00 33 |
| 32 | 23 58 | 18 14 | 17 31 | 23 15 | 00 27 |
| 33 | 23 44 | 17 48 | 17 00 | 22 52 | 00 21 |
| 34 | 23 29 | 17 22 | 16 28 | 22 29 | 00 15 |
| 35 | 23 14 | 16 54 | 15 54 | 22 04 | 00 08 |
| 36 | 22 59 | 16 26 | 15 19 | 21 37 | 00 01 |
| 37 | 22 43 | 15 57 | 14 42 | 21 09 | 29♈54 |
| 38 | 22 27 | 15 26 | 14 03 | 20 39 | 29 46 |
| 39 | 22 11 | 14 55 | 13 22 | 20 07 | 29 37 |
| 40 | 21 53 | 14 22 | 12 39 | 19 33 | 29 27 |
| 41 | 21 36 | 13 48 | 11 54 | 18 56 | 29 17 |
| 42 | 21 18 | 13 13 | 11 06 | 18 17 | 29 06 |
| 43 | 20 59 | 12 36 | 10 16 | 17 34 | 28 54 |
| 44 | 20 39 | 11 58 | 09 22 | 16 48 | 28 41 |
| 45 | 20 19 | 11 18 | 08 25 | 15 58 | 28 26 |
| 46 | 19 58 | 10 36 | 07 25 | 15 03 | 28 10 |
| 47 | 19 37 | 09 52 | 06 21 | 14 03 | 27 52 |
| 48 | 19 14 | 09 05 | 05 12 | 12 57 | 27 32 |
| 49 | 18 51 | 08 17 | 03 58 | 11 44 | 27 09 |
| 50 | 18 26 | 07 26 | 02 39 | 10 23 | 26 43 |
| 51 | 18 01 | 06 32 | 01 14 | 08 52 | 26 14 |
| 52 | 17 34 | 05 35 | 29♑42 | 07 11 | 25 39 |
| 53 | 17 06 | 04 34 | 28 04 | 05 16 | 24 59 |
| 54 | 16 37 | 03 30 | 26 17 | 03 05 | 24 11 |
| 55 | 16 06 | 02 23 | 24 21 | 00 36 | 23 13 |
| 56 | 15 33 | 01 10 | 22 16 | 27♒44 | 22 03 |
| 57 | 14 59 | 29♐53 | 19 59 | 24 26 | 20 35 |
| 58 | 14 22 | 28 31 | 17 31 | 20 35 | 18 41 |
| 59 | 13 43 | 27 03 | 14 49 | 16 07 | 16 11 |
| 60 | 13♐01 | 25♐29 | 11♑54 | 10♒56 | 12♈45 |

16h 4m 0s — 241° 0' 0" — 03 ♐ 03

| LAT. | 11 | 12 | ASC | 2 | 3 |
|---|---|---|---|---|---|
| 0 | 00♑55 | 28♑52 | 28♒52 | 01♈05 | 03♉13 |
| 5 | 00 05 | 27 40 | 27 43 | 00 25 | 03 04 |
| 10 | 29♐14 | 26 24 | 26 30 | 29♓40 | 02 53 |
| 15 | 28 22 | 25 03 | 25 08 | 28 50 | 02 42 |
| 20 | 27 27 | 23 35 | 23 36 | 27 52 | 02 28 |
| 21 | 27 15 | 23 17 | 23 16 | 27 40 | 02 25 |
| 22 | 27 04 | 22 58 | 22 56 | 27 26 | 02 22 |
| 23 | 26 52 | 22 38 | 22 34 | 27 13 | 02 19 |
| 24 | 26 40 | 22 18 | 22 13 | 26 58 | 02 15 |
| 25 | 26 28 | 21 58 | 21 50 | 26 44 | 02 12 |
| 26 | 26 16 | 21 37 | 21 27 | 26 28 | 02 08 |
| 27 | 26 03 | 21 15 | 21 03 | 26 12 | 02 04 |
| 28 | 25 50 | 20 53 | 20 38 | 25 55 | 02 00 |
| 29 | 25 37 | 20 31 | 20 12 | 25 38 | 01 56 |
| 30 | 25 24 | 20 07 | 19 45 | 25 20 | 01 52 |
| 31 | 25 10 | 19 43 | 19 17 | 25 00 | 01 47 |
| 32 | 24 57 | 19 19 | 18 48 | 24 40 | 01 42 |
| 33 | 24 42 | 18 53 | 18 18 | 24 19 | 01 37 |
| 34 | 24 28 | 18 27 | 17 46 | 23 56 | 01 31 |
| 35 | 24 13 | 18 00 | 17 13 | 23 32 | 01 25 |
| 36 | 23 58 | 17 32 | 16 38 | 23 07 | 01 19 |
| 37 | 23 42 | 17 03 | 16 02 | 22 40 | 01 12 |
| 38 | 23 26 | 16 33 | 15 24 | 22 12 | 01 05 |
| 39 | 23 09 | 16 01 | 14 44 | 21 41 | 00 57 |
| 40 | 22 52 | 15 29 | 14 01 | 21 08 | 00 49 |
| 41 | 22 35 | 14 55 | 13 17 | 20 33 | 00 40 |
| 42 | 22 17 | 14 20 | 12 30 | 19 55 | 00 30 |
| 43 | 21 58 | 13 43 | 11 40 | 19 15 | 00 19 |
| 44 | 21 38 | 13 05 | 10 47 | 18 30 | 00 07 |
| 45 | 21 18 | 12 25 | 09 51 | 17 42 | 29♈54 |
| 46 | 20 57 | 11 43 | 08 51 | 16 50 | 29 40 |
| 47 | 20 36 | 10 58 | 07 47 | 15 52 | 29 23 |
| 48 | 20 13 | 10 12 | 06 38 | 14 48 | 29 05 |
| 49 | 19 50 | 09 23 | 05 25 | 13 38 | 28 45 |
| 50 | 19 25 | 08 32 | 04 06 | 12 19 | 28 21 |
| 51 | 18 59 | 07 38 | 02 41 | 10 52 | 27 54 |
| 52 | 18 33 | 06 41 | 01 10 | 09 13 | 27 23 |
| 53 | 18 04 | 05 40 | 29♑31 | 07 21 | 26 47 |
| 54 | 17 35 | 04 36 | 27 43 | 05 13 | 26 03 |
| 55 | 17 04 | 03 27 | 25 47 | 02 47 | 25 11 |
| 56 | 16 31 | 02 14 | 23 40 | 29♒58 | 24 07 |
| 57 | 15 56 | 00 56 | 21 22 | 26 42 | 22 46 |
| 58 | 15 19 | 29♐33 | 18 52 | 22 52 | 21 02 |
| 59 | 14 39 | 28 04 | 16 08 | 18 24 | 18 45 |
| 60 | 13♐57 | 26♐28 | 13♑09 | 13♒09 | 15♈35 |

16h 8m 0s — 242° 0' 0" — 04 ♐ 00

| LAT. | 11 | 12 | ASC | 2 | 3 |
|---|---|---|---|---|---|
| 0 | 01♑50 | 29♑49 | 29♒54 | 02♈11 | 04♉16 |
| 5 | 01 01 | 28 39 | 28 48 | 01 32 | 04 07 |
| 10 | 00 11 | 27 24 | 27 36 | 00 50 | 03 58 |
| 15 | 29♐19 | 26 05 | 26 17 | 00 03 | 03 48 |
| 20 | 28 24 | 24 38 | 24 47 | 29♓08 | 03 37 |
| 21 | 28 13 | 24 19 | 24 28 | 28 56 | 03 34 |
| 22 | 28 02 | 24 01 | 24 08 | 28 43 | 03 31 |
| 23 | 27 50 | 23 41 | 23 47 | 28 30 | 03 28 |
| 24 | 27 38 | 23 22 | 23 26 | 28 17 | 03 26 |
| 25 | 27 26 | 23 01 | 23 04 | 28 03 | 03 22 |
| 26 | 27 14 | 22 41 | 22 41 | 27 48 | 03 19 |
| 27 | 27 01 | 22 20 | 22 18 | 27 33 | 03 16 |
| 28 | 26 49 | 21 58 | 21 53 | 27 17 | 03 12 |
| 29 | 26 36 | 21 35 | 21 28 | 27 01 | 03 09 |
| 30 | 26 22 | 21 12 | 21 02 | 26 43 | 03 05 |
| 31 | 26 09 | 20 49 | 20 34 | 26 25 | 03 01 |
| 32 | 25 55 | 20 24 | 20 06 | 26 06 | 02 57 |
| 33 | 25 41 | 19 59 | 19 36 | 25 45 | 02 52 |
| 34 | 25 27 | 19 33 | 19 05 | 25 24 | 02 47 |
| 35 | 25 12 | 19 06 | 18 33 | 25 01 | 02 42 |
| 36 | 24 57 | 18 38 | 17 59 | 24 37 | 02 36 |
| 37 | 24 41 | 18 09 | 17 23 | 24 12 | 02 31 |
| 38 | 24 25 | 17 39 | 16 45 | 23 44 | 02 24 |
| 39 | 24 08 | 17 08 | 16 06 | 23 15 | 02 17 |
| 40 | 23 51 | 16 36 | 15 24 | 22 44 | 02 10 |
| 41 | 23 34 | 16 02 | 14 41 | 22 11 | 02 02 |
| 42 | 23 16 | 15 27 | 13 54 | 21 35 | 01 53 |
| 43 | 22 57 | 14 50 | 13 05 | 20 56 | 01 44 |
| 44 | 22 37 | 14 12 | 12 13 | 20 13 | 01 33 |
| 45 | 22 17 | 13 32 | 11 17 | 19 27 | 01 21 |
| 46 | 21 56 | 12 50 | 10 18 | 18 37 | 01 09 |
| 47 | 21 35 | 12 06 | 09 14 | 17 42 | 00 54 |
| 48 | 21 12 | 11 20 | 08 06 | 16 40 | 00 38 |
| 49 | 20 48 | 10 31 | 06 53 | 15 33 | 00 20 |
| 50 | 20 24 | 09 39 | 05 35 | 14 17 | 29♈59 |
| 51 | 19 58 | 08 45 | 04 10 | 12 53 | 29 35 |
| 52 | 19 31 | 07 47 | 02 39 | 11 17 | 29 07 |
| 53 | 19 03 | 06 46 | 01 00 | 09 29 | 28 34 |
| 54 | 18 33 | 05 42 | 29♑12 | 07 25 | 27 55 |
| 55 | 18 02 | 04 33 | 27 15 | 05 02 | 27 08 |
| 56 | 17 28 | 03 19 | 25 07 | 02 16 | 26 09 |
| 57 | 16 53 | 02 00 | 22 48 | 29♒02 | 24 56 |
| 58 | 16 16 | 00 36 | 20 16 | 25 15 | 23 22 |
| 59 | 15 36 | 29♐05 | 17 29 | 20 46 | 21 17 |
| 60 | 14♐53 | 27♐28 | 14♑26 | 15♒28 | 18♈23 |

16h 12m 0s — 243° 0' 0" — 04 ♐ 57

| LAT. | 11 | 12 | ASC | 2 | 3 |
|---|---|---|---|---|---|
| 0 | 02♑45 | 00♒47 | 00♓57 | 03♈16 | 05♉18 |
| 5 | 01 57 | 29♑38 | 29♒53 | 02 40 | 05 11 |
| 10 | 01 07 | 28 25 | 28 43 | 02 00 | 05 03 |
| 15 | 00 16 | 27 06 | 27 26 | 01 15 | 04 55 |
| 20 | 29♐22 | 25 41 | 25 59 | 00 24 | 04 45 |
| 21 | 29 11 | 25 23 | 25 40 | 00 12 | 04 43 |
| 22 | 28 59 | 25 04 | 25 21 | 00 00 | 04 40 |
| 23 | 28 48 | 24 45 | 25 00 | 29♓48 | 04 38 |
| 24 | 28 36 | 24 26 | 24 40 | 29 36 | 04 35 |
| 25 | 28 24 | 24 06 | 24 18 | 29 22 | 04 33 |
| 26 | 28 12 | 23 45 | 23 56 | 29 08 | 04 30 |
| 27 | 28 00 | 23 24 | 23 33 | 28 54 | 04 27 |
| 28 | 27 47 | 23 03 | 23 09 | 28 39 | 04 24 |
| 29 | 27 34 | 22 41 | 22 45 | 28 23 | 04 21 |
| 30 | 27 21 | 22 18 | 22 19 | 28 07 | 04 18 |
| 31 | 27 08 | 21 54 | 21 52 | 27 50 | 04 14 |
| 32 | 26 54 | 21 30 | 21 24 | 27 31 | 04 11 |
| 33 | 26 40 | 21 05 | 20 55 | 27 12 | 04 07 |
| 34 | 26 25 | 20 39 | 20 25 | 26 52 | 04 03 |
| 35 | 26 11 | 20 13 | 19 53 | 26 30 | 03 58 |
| 36 | 25 56 | 19 45 | 19 20 | 26 08 | 03 54 |
| 37 | 25 40 | 19 16 | 18 45 | 25 43 | 03 48 |
| 38 | 25 24 | 18 47 | 18 08 | 25 18 | 03 43 |
| 39 | 25 07 | 18 16 | 17 29 | 24 50 | 03 37 |
| 40 | 24 51 | 17 43 | 16 48 | 24 20 | 03 31 |
| 41 | 24 33 | 17 10 | 16 05 | 23 49 | 03 24 |
| 42 | 24 15 | 16 35 | 15 20 | 23 14 | 03 16 |
| 43 | 23 56 | 15 59 | 14 31 | 22 37 | 03 08 |
| 44 | 23 37 | 15 20 | 13 40 | 21 57 | 02 59 |
| 45 | 23 17 | 14 40 | 12 45 | 21 13 | 02 48 |
| 46 | 22 56 | 13 58 | 11 46 | 20 25 | 02 37 |
| 47 | 22 34 | 13 14 | 10 43 | 19 32 | 02 24 |
| 48 | 22 11 | 12 28 | 09 36 | 18 34 | 02 10 |
| 49 | 21 48 | 11 39 | 08 24 | 17 29 | 01 54 |
| 50 | 21 23 | 10 48 | 07 06 | 16 17 | 01 36 |
| 51 | 20 57 | 09 53 | 05 41 | 14 55 | 01 14 |
| 52 | 20 30 | 08 55 | 04 10 | 13 23 | 00 49 |
| 53 | 20 02 | 07 54 | 02 31 | 11 38 | 00 20 |
| 54 | 19 32 | 06 49 | 00 43 | 09 38 | 29♈45 |
| 55 | 19 00 | 05 39 | 28♑46 | 07 19 | 29 03 |
| 56 | 18 26 | 04 25 | 26 37 | 04 37 | 28 11 |
| 57 | 17 51 | 03 05 | 24 17 | 01 27 | 27 05 |
| 58 | 17 13 | 01 40 | 21 42 | 27♒42 | 25 40 |
| 59 | 16 33 | 00 08 | 18 53 | 23 15 | 23 47 |
| 60 | 15♐49 | 28♐29 | 15♑47 | 17♒55 | 21♈09 |

16h 16m 0s — 244° 0' 0" — 05 ♐ 54

| LAT. | 11 | 12 | ASC | 2 | 3 |
|---|---|---|---|---|---|
| 0 | 03♑40 | 01♒45 | 02♓00 | 04♈22 | 06♉19 |
| 5 | 02 52 | 00 37 | 00 58 | 03 48 | 06 14 |
| 10 | 02 04 | 29♑25 | 29♒50 | 03 10 | 06 08 |
| 15 | 01 13 | 28 08 | 28 36 | 02 28 | 06 01 |
| 20 | 00 20 | 26 44 | 27 11 | 01 39 | 05 53 |
| 21 | 00 08 | 26 26 | 26 53 | 01 29 | 05 51 |
| 22 | 29♐57 | 26 08 | 26 34 | 01 18 | 05 49 |
| 23 | 29 46 | 25 49 | 26 14 | 01 06 | 05 47 |
| 24 | 29 34 | 25 30 | 25 54 | 00 54 | 05 45 |
| 25 | 29 22 | 25 10 | 25 33 | 00 42 | 05 43 |
| 26 | 29 10 | 24 50 | 25 11 | 00 29 | 05 41 |
| 27 | 28 58 | 24 29 | 24 49 | 00 15 | 05 39 |
| 28 | 28 45 | 24 08 | 24 26 | 00 01 | 05 36 |
| 29 | 28 33 | 23 46 | 24 02 | 29♓46 | 05 33 |
| 30 | 28 20 | 23 24 | 23 37 | 29 31 | 05 31 |
| 31 | 28 06 | 23 00 | 23 11 | 29 14 | 05 28 |
| 32 | 27 53 | 22 36 | 22 43 | 28 57 | 05 25 |
| 33 | 27 39 | 22 12 | 22 15 | 28 39 | 05 21 |
| 34 | 27 24 | 21 46 | 21 45 | 28 20 | 05 18 |
| 35 | 27 10 | 21 20 | 21 14 | 28 00 | 05 14 |
| 36 | 26 55 | 20 52 | 20 42 | 27 38 | 05 10 |
| 37 | 26 39 | 20 24 | 20 08 | 27 15 | 05 06 |
| 38 | 26 23 | 19 54 | 19 32 | 26 51 | 05 01 |
| 39 | 26 07 | 19 24 | 18 54 | 26 25 | 04 56 |
| 40 | 25 50 | 18 52 | 18 14 | 25 57 | 04 51 |
| 41 | 25 32 | 18 18 | 17 31 | 25 27 | 04 45 |
| 42 | 25 14 | 17 44 | 16 46 | 24 55 | 04 38 |
| 43 | 24 56 | 17 07 | 15 59 | 24 19 | 04 31 |
| 44 | 24 36 | 16 29 | 15 08 | 23 41 | 04 23 |
| 45 | 24 16 | 15 49 | 14 14 | 23 00 | 04 15 |
| 46 | 23 55 | 15 08 | 13 16 | 22 14 | 04 05 |
| 47 | 23 33 | 14 24 | 12 14 | 21 24 | 03 54 |
| 48 | 23 11 | 13 37 | 11 07 | 20 28 | 03 42 |
| 49 | 22 47 | 12 48 | 09 56 | 19 26 | 03 28 |
| 50 | 22 22 | 11 57 | 08 38 | 18 17 | 03 12 |
| 51 | 21 56 | 11 02 | 07 14 | 16 59 | 02 53 |
| 52 | 21 29 | 10 04 | 05 44 | 15 31 | 02 31 |
| 53 | 21 01 | 09 02 | 04 05 | 13 51 | 02 05 |
| 54 | 20 30 | 07 57 | 02 17 | 11 55 | 01 35 |
| 55 | 19 58 | 06 47 | 00 19 | 09 40 | 00 57 |
| 56 | 19 25 | 05 31 | 28♑10 | 07 03 | 00 11 |
| 57 | 18 49 | 04 11 | 25 48 | 03 57 | 29♈13 |
| 58 | 18 11 | 02 45 | 23 12 | 00 16 | 27 57 |
| 59 | 17 30 | 01 11 | 20 20 | 25♒50 | 26 15 |
| 60 | 16♐46 | 29♐31 | 17♑10 | 20♒30 | 23♈54 |

16h 20m 0s — 245° 0' 0" — 06 ♐ 50

| LAT. | 11 | 12 | ASC | 2 | 3 |
|---|---|---|---|---|---|
| 0 | 04♑35 | 02♒43 | 03♓03 | 05♈27 | 07♉21 |
| 5 | 03 48 | 01 36 | 02 03 | 04 55 | 07 17 |
| 10 | 03 00 | 00 26 | 00 58 | 04 20 | 07 12 |
| 15 | 02 10 | 29♑10 | 29♒45 | 03 41 | 07 07 |
| 20 | 01 17 | 27 47 | 28 23 | 02 55 | 07 01 |
| 21 | 01 06 | 27 30 | 28 06 | 02 45 | 06 59 |
| 22 | 00 55 | 27 12 | 27 47 | 02 35 | 06 58 |
| 23 | 00 44 | 26 53 | 27 28 | 02 24 | 06 56 |
| 24 | 00 32 | 26 34 | 27 09 | 02 13 | 06 55 |
| 25 | 00 21 | 26 15 | 26 48 | 02 01 | 06 53 |
| 26 | 00 09 | 25 55 | 26 27 | 01 49 | 06 51 |
| 27 | 29♐56 | 25 35 | 26 06 | 01 36 | 06 49 |
| 28 | 29 44 | 25 14 | 25 43 | 01 23 | 06 47 |
| 29 | 29 31 | 24 52 | 25 20 | 01 09 | 06 45 |
| 30 | 29 18 | 24 30 | 24 55 | 00 55 | 06 43 |
| 31 | 29 05 | 24 07 | 24 30 | 00 39 | 06 41 |
| 32 | 28 52 | 23 43 | 24 03 | 00 23 | 06 38 |
| 33 | 28 38 | 23 19 | 23 36 | 00 06 | 06 36 |
| 34 | 28 24 | 22 54 | 23 07 | 29♓48 | 06 33 |
| 35 | 28 09 | 22 27 | 22 36 | 29 29 | 06 30 |
| 36 | 27 54 | 22 00 | 22 05 | 29 09 | 06 27 |
| 37 | 27 39 | 21 32 | 21 31 | 28 48 | 06 23 |
| 38 | 27 23 | 21 03 | 20 56 | 28 25 | 06 19 |
| 39 | 27 06 | 20 32 | 20 19 | 28 00 | 06 15 |
| 40 | 26 49 | 20 01 | 19 40 | 27 34 | 06 11 |
| 41 | 26 32 | 19 27 | 18 58 | 27 06 | 06 06 |
| 42 | 26 14 | 18 53 | 18 14 | 26 35 | 06 00 |
| 43 | 25 55 | 18 17 | 17 27 | 26 02 | 05 55 |
| 44 | 25 36 | 17 39 | 16 37 | 25 26 | 05 48 |
| 45 | 25 16 | 16 59 | 15 44 | 24 47 | 05 41 |
| 46 | 24 55 | 16 18 | 14 47 | 24 04 | 05 32 |
| 47 | 24 33 | 15 34 | 13 46 | 23 16 | 05 23 |
| 48 | 24 10 | 14 47 | 12 40 | 22 24 | 05 13 |
| 49 | 23 47 | 13 59 | 11 29 | 21 25 | 05 01 |
| 50 | 23 22 | 13 07 | 10 13 | 20 19 | 04 47 |
| 51 | 22 56 | 12 12 | 08 50 | 19 05 | 04 31 |
| 52 | 22 29 | 11 14 | 07 19 | 17 41 | 04 12 |
| 53 | 22 00 | 10 12 | 05 41 | 16 05 | 03 50 |
| 54 | 21 29 | 09 06 | 03 53 | 14 13 | 03 23 |
| 55 | 20 57 | 07 55 | 01 55 | 12 04 | 02 50 |
| 56 | 20 23 | 06 39 | 29♑45 | 09 32 | 02 10 |
| 57 | 19 47 | 05 18 | 27 22 | 06 31 | 01 18 |
| 58 | 19 09 | 03 51 | 24 44 | 02 54 | 00 11 |
| 59 | 18 27 | 02 16 | 21 50 | 28♒32 | 28♈41 |
| 60 | 17♐43 | 00♑34 | 18♑37 | 23♒13 | 26♈35 |

16h 24m 0s — 246° 0' 0" — 07 ♐ 47

| LAT. | 11 | 12 | ASC | 2 | 3 |
|---|---|---|---|---|---|
| 0 | 05♑30 | 03♒41 | 04♓07 | 06♈32 | 08♉23 |
| 5 | 04 44 | 02 36 | 03 09 | 06 03 | 08 20 |
| 10 | 03 57 | 01 27 | 02 06 | 05 30 | 08 16 |
| 15 | 03 07 | 00 13 | 00 55 | 04 54 | 08 13 |
| 20 | 02 15 | 28♑51 | 29♒36 | 04 11 | 08 08 |
| 21 | 02 04 | 28 34 | 29 19 | 04 02 | 08 07 |
| 22 | 01 53 | 28 16 | 29 01 | 03 52 | 08 06 |
| 23 | 01 42 | 27 58 | 28 43 | 03 42 | 08 05 |
| 24 | 01 31 | 27 39 | 28 24 | 03 32 | 08 04 |
| 25 | 01 19 | 27 20 | 28 04 | 03 21 | 08 03 |
| 26 | 01 07 | 27 01 | 27 44 | 03 10 | 08 01 |
| 27 | 00 55 | 26 41 | 27 23 | 02 58 | 08 00 |
| 28 | 00 43 | 26 20 | 27 01 | 02 45 | 07 59 |
| 29 | 00 30 | 25 59 | 26 38 | 02 32 | 07 57 |
| 30 | 00 17 | 25 37 | 26 14 | 02 19 | 07 55 |
| 31 | 00 04 | 25 14 | 25 49 | 02 05 | 07 54 |
| 32 | 29♐51 | 24 51 | 25 24 | 01 50 | 07 52 |
| 33 | 29 37 | 24 26 | 24 57 | 01 34 | 07 50 |
| 34 | 29 23 | 24 01 | 24 29 | 01 17 | 07 48 |
| 35 | 29 08 | 23 35 | 23 59 | 00 59 | 07 45 |
| 36 | 28 53 | 23 09 | 23 28 | 00 40 | 07 43 |
| 37 | 28 38 | 22 41 | 22 56 | 00 20 | 07 40 |
| 38 | 28 22 | 22 12 | 22 21 | 29♓59 | 07 37 |
| 39 | 28 06 | 21 42 | 21 45 | 29 36 | 07 34 |
| 40 | 27 49 | 21 10 | 21 07 | 29 11 | 07 30 |
| 41 | 27 32 | 20 37 | 20 26 | 28 45 | 07 26 |
| 42 | 27 14 | 20 03 | 19 43 | 28 16 | 07 22 |
| 43 | 26 55 | 19 27 | 18 57 | 27 45 | 07 17 |
| 44 | 26 36 | 18 49 | 18 08 | 27 11 | 07 12 |
| 45 | 26 16 | 18 10 | 17 16 | 26 35 | 07 06 |
| 46 | 25 55 | 17 28 | 16 20 | 25 54 | 06 59 |
| 47 | 25 33 | 16 45 | 15 20 | 25 09 | 06 51 |
| 48 | 25 10 | 15 58 | 14 15 | 24 20 | 06 43 |
| 49 | 24 47 | 15 10 | 13 05 | 23 24 | 06 33 |
| 50 | 24 22 | 14 18 | 11 49 | 22 22 | 06 21 |
| 51 | 23 56 | 13 23 | 10 27 | 21 12 | 06 08 |
| 52 | 23 28 | 12 25 | 08 57 | 19 52 | 05 52 |
| 53 | 22 59 | 11 22 | 07 19 | 18 21 | 05 33 |
| 54 | 22 29 | 10 16 | 05 32 | 16 35 | 05 10 |
| 55 | 21 57 | 09 05 | 03 34 | 14 31 | 04 42 |
| 56 | 21 22 | 07 49 | 01 24 | 12 04 | 04 07 |
| 57 | 20 46 | 06 27 | 29♑00 | 09 09 | 03 22 |
| 58 | 20 07 | 04 58 | 26 20 | 05 38 | 02 24 |
| 59 | 19 25 | 03 22 | 23 23 | 01 21 | 01 05 |
| 60 | 18♐40 | 01♑38 | 20♑07 | 26♒05 | 29♈14 |

16h 28m 0s — 247° 0' 0" — 08 ♐ 43

| LAT. | 11 | 12 | ASC | 2 | 3 |
|---|---|---|---|---|---|
| 0 | 06♑26 | 04♒39 | 05♓10 | 07♈37 | 09♉24 |
| 5 | 05 40 | 03 36 | 04 14 | 07 10 | 09 22 |
| 10 | 04 53 | 02 28 | 03 13 | 06 40 | 09 20 |
| 15 | 04 05 | 01 15 | 02 06 | 06 06 | 09 18 |
| 20 | 03 13 | 29♑55 | 00 49 | 05 27 | 09 16 |
| 21 | 03 02 | 29 38 | 00 32 | 05 18 | 09 15 |
| 22 | 02 51 | 29 21 | 00 15 | 05 10 | 09 14 |
| 23 | 02 40 | 29 03 | 29♒57 | 05 00 | 09 14 |
| 24 | 02 29 | 28 45 | 29 39 | 04 51 | 09 13 |
| 25 | 02 17 | 28 26 | 29 20 | 04 41 | 09 12 |
| 26 | 02 06 | 28 07 | 29 00 | 04 30 | 09 11 |
| 27 | 01 54 | 27 47 | 28 40 | 04 19 | 09 10 |
| 28 | 01 42 | 27 26 | 28 19 | 04 08 | 09 09 |
| 29 | 01 29 | 27 05 | 27 57 | 03 56 | 09 08 |
| 30 | 01 16 | 26 44 | 27 34 | 03 43 | 09 07 |
| 31 | 01 03 | 26 21 | 27 10 | 03 30 | 09 06 |
| 32 | 00 50 | 25 58 | 26 45 | 03 16 | 09 05 |
| 33 | 00 36 | 25 34 | 26 19 | 03 01 | 09 03 |
| 34 | 00 22 | 25 10 | 25 51 | 02 46 | 09 02 |
| 35 | 00 08 | 24 44 | 25 23 | 02 29 | 09 00 |
| 36 | 29♐53 | 24 18 | 24 52 | 02 12 | 08 58 |
| 37 | 29 38 | 23 50 | 24 21 | 01 53 | 08 56 |
| 38 | 29 22 | 23 21 | 23 47 | 01 33 | 08 54 |
| 39 | 29 06 | 22 51 | 23 12 | 01 12 | 08 52 |
| 40 | 28 49 | 22 20 | 22 35 | 00 49 | 08 49 |
| 41 | 28 32 | 21 48 | 21 55 | 00 24 | 08 46 |
| 42 | 28 14 | 21 14 | 21 13 | 29♓58 | 08 43 |
| 43 | 27 55 | 20 38 | 20 28 | 29 29 | 08 39 |
| 44 | 27 36 | 20 01 | 19 40 | 28 57 | 08 35 |
| 45 | 27 16 | 19 21 | 18 49 | 28 23 | 08 31 |
| 46 | 26 55 | 18 40 | 17 54 | 27 45 | 08 25 |
| 47 | 26 33 | 17 56 | 16 55 | 27 03 | 08 19 |
| 48 | 26 11 | 17 10 | 15 51 | 26 16 | 08 12 |
| 49 | 25 47 | 16 22 | 14 43 | 25 25 | 08 04 |
| 50 | 25 22 | 15 30 | 13 28 | 24 26 | 07 55 |
| 51 | 24 56 | 14 35 | 12 07 | 23 20 | 07 44 |
| 52 | 24 28 | 13 37 | 10 38 | 22 05 | 07 31 |
| 53 | 23 59 | 12 34 | 09 00 | 20 38 | 07 15 |
| 54 | 23 29 | 11 27 | 07 14 | 18 58 | 06 56 |
| 55 | 22 56 | 10 16 | 05 16 | 17 00 | 06 32 |
| 56 | 22 22 | 08 59 | 03 05 | 14 40 | 06 02 |
| 57 | 21 45 | 07 36 | 00 41 | 11 52 | 05 24 |
| 58 | 21 05 | 06 07 | 28♑00 | 08 28 | 04 34 |
| 59 | 20 23 | 04 30 | 25 01 | 04 17 | 03 26 |
| 60 | 19♐38 | 02♑44 | 21♑41 | 29♒05 | 01♉49 |

# Koch Table of Houses for Latitudes 0° to 60° North

**16h 32m 0s — 248° 0' 0" — 09 ♐ 40**

| LAT. | 11 | 12 | ASC | 2 | 3 |
|---|---|---|---|---|---|
| 0 | 07♑21 | 05♒38 | 06♓14 | 08♈43 | 10♉25 |
| 5 | 06 36 | 04 36 | 05 20 | 08 18 | 10 25 |
| 10 | 05 50 | 03 29 | 04 22 | 07 50 | 10 24 |
| 15 | 05 02 | 02 18 | 03 17 | 07 19 | 10 24 |
| 20 | 04 11 | 01 00 | 02 03 | 06 43 | 10 23 |
| 21 | 04 00 | 00 43 | 01 46 | 06 35 | 10 22 |
| 22 | 03 50 | 00 26 | 01 30 | 06 27 | 10 22 |
| 23 | 03 39 | 00 08 | 01 13 | 06 18 | 10 22 |
| 24 | 03 27 | 29♑50 | 00 55 | 06 09 | 10 22 |
| 25 | 03 16 | 29 32 | 00 37 | 06 00 | 10 21 |
| 26 | 03 04 | 29 13 | 00 18 | 05 51 | 10 21 |
| 27 | 02 53 | 28 53 | 29♒58 | 05 40 | 10 20 |
| 28 | 02 41 | 28 33 | 29 37 | 05 30 | 10 20 |
| 29 | 02 28 | 28 13 | 29 16 | 05 19 | 10 19 |
| 30 | 02 16 | 27 51 | 28 54 | 05 07 | 10 19 |
| 31 | 02 03 | 27 29 | 28 31 | 04 55 | 10 18 |
| 32 | 01 49 | 27 07 | 28 06 | 04 42 | 10 17 |
| 33 | 01 36 | 26 43 | 27 41 | 04 29 | 10 17 |
| 34 | 01 22 | 26 19 | 27 15 | 04 14 | 10 16 |
| 35 | 01 08 | 25 53 | 26 47 | 03 59 | 10 15 |
| 36 | 00 53 | 25 27 | 26 18 | 03 43 | 10 14 |
| 37 | 00 38 | 25 00 | 25 47 | 03 26 | 10 12 |
| 38 | 00 22 | 24 32 | 25 14 | 03 08 | 10 11 |
| 39 | 00 06 | 24 02 | 24 40 | 02 48 | 10 10 |
| 40 | 29♐49 | 23 31 | 24 04 | 02 27 | 10 08 |
| 41 | 29 32 | 22 59 | 23 25 | 02 04 | 10 06 |
| 42 | 29 14 | 22 25 | 22 44 | 01 39 | 10 04 |
| 43 | 28 56 | 21 50 | 22 00 | 01 12 | 10 01 |
| 44 | 28 36 | 21 13 | 21 14 | 00 43 | 09 58 |
| 45 | 28 16 | 20 34 | 20 24 | 00 11 | 09 55 |
| 46 | 27 56 | 19 52 | 19 30 | 29♓36 | 09 51 |
| 47 | 27 34 | 19 09 | 18 32 | 28 57 | 09 46 |
| 48 | 27 11 | 18 23 | 17 30 | 28 14 | 09 41 |
| 49 | 26 47 | 17 35 | 16 22 | 27 25 | 09 35 |
| 50 | 26 23 | 16 43 | 15 08 | 26 31 | 09 27 |
| 51 | 25 56 | 15 48 | 13 48 | 25 29 | 09 19 |
| 52 | 25 29 | 14 50 | 12 21 | 24 19 | 09 08 |
| 53 | 25 00 | 13 47 | 10 44 | 22 57 | 08 56 |
| 54 | 24 29 | 12 40 | 08 58 | 21 23 | 08 40 |
| 55 | 23 56 | 11 28 | 07 01 | 19 31 | 08 20 |
| 56 | 23 21 | 10 11 | 04 50 | 17 19 | 07 56 |
| 57 | 22 44 | 08 47 | 02 25 | 14 38 | 07 24 |
| 58 | 22 05 | 07 17 | 29♑44 | 11 22 | 06 41 |
| 59 | 21 22 | 05 38 | 26 42 | 07 19 | 05 43 |
| 60 | 20♐36 | 03♑51 | 23♑19 | 02♓13 | 04♉21 |

**16h 36m 0s — 249° 0' 0" — 10 ♐ 36**

| LAT. | 11 | 12 | ASC | 2 | 3 |
|---|---|---|---|---|---|
| 0 | 08♑16 | 06♒37 | 07♓18 | 09♈48 | 11♉26 |
| 5 | 07 32 | 05 36 | 06 26 | 09 25 | 11 27 |
| 10 | 06 47 | 04 31 | 05 30 | 09 00 | 11 28 |
| 15 | 05 59 | 03 21 | 04 27 | 08 32 | 11 29 |
| 20 | 05 09 | 02 04 | 03 16 | 07 59 | 11 30 |
| 21 | 04 59 | 01 48 | 03 01 | 07 52 | 11 30 |
| 22 | 04 48 | 01 31 | 02 45 | 07 44 | 11 30 |
| 23 | 04 37 | 01 14 | 02 28 | 07 36 | 11 30 |
| 24 | 04 26 | 00 56 | 02 11 | 07 28 | 11 30 |
| 25 | 04 15 | 00 38 | 01 54 | 07 20 | 11 30 |
| 26 | 04 03 | 00 20 | 01 35 | 07 11 | 11 30 |
| 27 | 03 52 | 00 00 | 01 16 | 07 02 | 11 30 |
| 28 | 03 40 | 29♑41 | 00 56 | 06 52 | 11 30 |
| 29 | 03 27 | 29 20 | 00 36 | 06 42 | 11 30 |
| 30 | 03 15 | 28 59 | 00 14 | 06 32 | 11 30 |
| 31 | 03 02 | 28 38 | 29♒52 | 06 20 | 11 30 |
| 32 | 02 49 | 28 15 | 29 29 | 06 09 | 11 30 |
| 33 | 02 36 | 27 52 | 29 04 | 05 56 | 11 30 |
| 34 | 02 22 | 27 28 | 28 39 | 05 43 | 11 29 |
| 35 | 02 08 | 27 03 | 28 12 | 05 29 | 11 29 |
| 36 | 01 53 | 26 37 | 27 43 | 05 15 | 11 29 |
| 37 | 01 38 | 26 10 | 27 14 | 04 59 | 11 28 |
| 38 | 01 22 | 25 42 | 26 42 | 04 42 | 11 28 |
| 39 | 01 06 | 25 13 | 26 09 | 04 24 | 11 27 |
| 40 | 00 50 | 24 43 | 25 34 | 04 05 | 11 26 |
| 41 | 00 33 | 24 11 | 24 56 | 03 44 | 11 25 |
| 42 | 00 15 | 23 37 | 24 16 | 03 21 | 11 24 |
| 43 | 29♐56 | 23 02 | 23 34 | 02 56 | 11 22 |
| 44 | 29 37 | 22 25 | 22 48 | 02 29 | 11 20 |
| 45 | 29 17 | 21 47 | 22 00 | 02 00 | 11 18 |
| 46 | 28 56 | 21 06 | 21 07 | 01 28 | 11 16 |
| 47 | 28 35 | 20 23 | 20 11 | 00 52 | 11 13 |
| 48 | 28 12 | 19 37 | 19 10 | 00 12 | 11 09 |
| 49 | 27 48 | 18 49 | 18 03 | 29♓27 | 11 05 |
| 50 | 27 23 | 17 57 | 16 51 | 28 37 | 10 59 |
| 51 | 26 57 | 17 02 | 15 32 | 27 39 | 10 53 |
| 52 | 26 29 | 16 04 | 14 06 | 26 34 | 10 45 |
| 53 | 26 00 | 15 01 | 12 31 | 25 18 | 10 35 |
| 54 | 25 29 | 13 54 | 10 45 | 23 49 | 10 23 |
| 55 | 24 57 | 12 42 | 08 49 | 22 05 | 10 08 |
| 56 | 24 22 | 11 24 | 06 39 | 20 00 | 09 48 |
| 57 | 23 44 | 10 00 | 04 14 | 17 28 | 09 22 |
| 58 | 23 04 | 08 28 | 01 31 | 14 22 | 08 47 |
| 59 | 22 21 | 06 49 | 28♑28 | 10 28 | 07 58 |
| 60 | 21♐34 | 05♑00 | 25♑02 | 05♓31 | 06♉49 |

**16h 40m 0s — 250° 0' 0" — 11 ♐ 32**

| LAT. | 11 | 12 | ASC | 2 | 3 |
|---|---|---|---|---|---|
| 0 | 09♑11 | 07♒35 | 08♓22 | 10♈53 | 12♉27 |
| 5 | 08 28 | 06 36 | 07 32 | 10 32 | 12 29 |
| 10 | 07 43 | 05 33 | 06 39 | 10 10 | 12 31 |
| 15 | 06 57 | 04 25 | 05 39 | 09 44 | 12 34 |
| 20 | 06 07 | 03 09 | 04 30 | 09 15 | 12 36 |
| 21 | 05 57 | 02 53 | 04 16 | 09 08 | 12 37 |
| 22 | 05 46 | 02 37 | 04 00 | 09 01 | 12 37 |
| 23 | 05 36 | 02 20 | 03 44 | 08 54 | 12 38 |
| 24 | 05 25 | 02 03 | 03 28 | 08 47 | 12 38 |
| 25 | 05 14 | 01 45 | 03 11 | 08 39 | 12 39 |
| 26 | 05 02 | 01 27 | 02 53 | 08 31 | 12 39 |
| 27 | 04 51 | 01 08 | 02 35 | 08 23 | 12 40 |
| 28 | 04 39 | 00 49 | 02 16 | 08 14 | 12 40 |
| 29 | 04 27 | 00 29 | 01 56 | 08 05 | 12 41 |
| 30 | 04 14 | 00 08 | 01 36 | 07 56 | 12 41 |
| 31 | 04 02 | 29♑47 | 01 14 | 07 46 | 12 41 |
| 32 | 03 49 | 29 25 | 00 52 | 07 35 | 12 42 |
| 33 | 03 35 | 29 02 | 00 28 | 07 24 | 12 42 |
| 34 | 03 22 | 28 38 | 00 03 | 07 12 | 12 43 |
| 35 | 03 08 | 28 14 | 29♒37 | 06 59 | 12 43 |
| 36 | 02 53 | 27 48 | 29 10 | 06 46 | 12 43 |
| 37 | 02 38 | 27 22 | 28 41 | 06 32 | 12 43 |
| 38 | 02 23 | 26 54 | 28 11 | 06 16 | 12 43 |
| 39 | 02 07 | 26 25 | 27 39 | 06 00 | 12 44 |
| 40 | 01 50 | 25 55 | 27 05 | 05 42 | 12 44 |
| 41 | 01 33 | 25 23 | 26 28 | 05 23 | 12 43 |
| 42 | 01 16 | 24 50 | 25 50 | 05 03 | 12 43 |
| 43 | 00 57 | 24 16 | 25 09 | 04 40 | 12 43 |
| 44 | 00 38 | 23 39 | 24 25 | 04 16 | 12 42 |
| 45 | 00 18 | 23 01 | 23 37 | 03 49 | 12 41 |
| 46 | 29♐58 | 22 20 | 22 46 | 03 19 | 12 40 |
| 47 | 29 36 | 21 37 | 21 51 | 02 46 | 12 38 |
| 48 | 29 13 | 20 52 | 20 51 | 02 10 | 12 36 |
| 49 | 28 49 | 20 04 | 19 47 | 01 29 | 12 34 |
| 50 | 28 25 | 19 12 | 18 36 | 00 43 | 12 30 |
| 51 | 27 58 | 18 18 | 17 19 | 29♓50 | 12 26 |
| 52 | 27 31 | 17 19 | 15 54 | 28 49 | 12 21 |
| 53 | 27 01 | 16 17 | 14 20 | 27 39 | 12 14 |
| 54 | 26 30 | 15 09 | 12 36 | 26 17 | 12 05 |
| 55 | 25 57 | 13 57 | 10 40 | 24 40 | 11 53 |
| 56 | 25 22 | 12 39 | 08 31 | 22 44 | 11 38 |
| 57 | 24 44 | 11 14 | 06 06 | 20 21 | 11 17 |
| 58 | 24 04 | 09 41 | 03 23 | 17 25 | 10 49 |
| 59 | 23 20 | 08 01 | 00 18 | 13 43 | 10 10 |
| 60 | 22♐33 | 06♑10 | 26♑50 | 08♓56 | 09♉13 |

**16h 44m 0s — 251° 0' 0" — 12 ♐ 28**

| LAT. | 11 | 12 | ASC | 2 | 3 |
|---|---|---|---|---|---|
| 0 | 10♑07 | 08♒34 | 09♓26 | 11♈58 | 13♉27 |
| 5 | 09 24 | 07 37 | 08 39 | 11 39 | 13 31 |
| 10 | 08 40 | 06 35 | 07 47 | 11 19 | 13 35 |
| 15 | 07 54 | 05 28 | 06 50 | 10 57 | 13 38 |
| 20 | 07 06 | 04 15 | 05 45 | 10 30 | 13 43 |
| 21 | 06 55 | 03 59 | 05 31 | 10 25 | 13 43 |
| 22 | 06 45 | 03 43 | 05 16 | 10 19 | 13 44 |
| 23 | 06 34 | 03 27 | 05 01 | 10 12 | 13 45 |
| 24 | 06 24 | 03 10 | 04 45 | 10 06 | 13 46 |
| 25 | 06 13 | 02 52 | 04 29 | 09 59 | 13 47 |
| 26 | 06 01 | 02 34 | 04 12 | 09 52 | 13 48 |
| 27 | 05 50 | 02 16 | 03 54 | 09 44 | 13 49 |
| 28 | 05 38 | 01 57 | 03 36 | 09 37 | 13 50 |
| 29 | 05 26 | 01 37 | 03 17 | 09 29 | 13 51 |
| 30 | 05 14 | 01 17 | 02 57 | 09 20 | 13 52 |
| 31 | 05 02 | 00 56 | 02 37 | 09 11 | 13 53 |
| 32 | 04 49 | 00 34 | 02 15 | 09 01 | 13 54 |
| 33 | 04 35 | 00 12 | 01 52 | 08 51 | 13 55 |
| 34 | 04 22 | 29♑49 | 01 29 | 08 41 | 13 55 |
| 35 | 04 08 | 29 25 | 01 04 | 08 30 | 13 56 |
| 36 | 03 54 | 28 59 | 00 37 | 08 18 | 13 57 |
| 37 | 03 39 | 28 33 | 00 10 | 08 05 | 13 58 |
| 38 | 03 23 | 28 06 | 29♒41 | 07 51 | 13 59 |
| 39 | 03 08 | 27 38 | 29 10 | 07 36 | 14 00 |
| 40 | 02 51 | 27 08 | 28 37 | 07 20 | 14 01 |
| 41 | 02 34 | 26 37 | 28 02 | 07 03 | 14 01 |
| 42 | 02 17 | 26 04 | 27 24 | 06 45 | 14 02 |
| 43 | 01 58 | 25 30 | 26 45 | 06 24 | 14 03 |
| 44 | 01 39 | 24 54 | 26 02 | 06 02 | 14 03 |
| 45 | 01 20 | 24 16 | 25 16 | 05 38 | 14 03 |
| 46 | 00 59 | 23 35 | 24 26 | 05 11 | 14 03 |
| 47 | 00 37 | 22 53 | 23 33 | 04 41 | 14 03 |
| 48 | 00 15 | 22 08 | 22 35 | 04 08 | 14 03 |
| 49 | 29♐51 | 21 20 | 21 32 | 03 31 | 14 02 |
| 50 | 29 26 | 20 29 | 20 23 | 02 49 | 14 00 |
| 51 | 29 00 | 19 34 | 19 07 | 02 01 | 13 58 |
| 52 | 28 32 | 18 36 | 17 44 | 01 06 | 13 55 |
| 53 | 28 03 | 17 33 | 16 12 | 00 02 | 13 51 |
| 54 | 27 32 | 16 26 | 14 29 | 28♓46 | 13 45 |
| 55 | 26 58 | 15 13 | 12 35 | 27 17 | 13 37 |
| 56 | 26 23 | 13 55 | 10 27 | 25 29 | 13 26 |
| 57 | 25 45 | 12 29 | 08 03 | 23 17 | 13 11 |
| 58 | 25 04 | 10 56 | 05 19 | 20 32 | 12 50 |
| 59 | 24 20 | 09 14 | 02 14 | 17 03 | 12 19 |
| 60 | 23♐33 | 07♑22 | 28♑42 | 12♓30 | 11♉33 |

**16h 48m 0s — 252° 0' 0" — 13 ♐ 24**

| LAT. | 11 | 12 | ASC | 2 | 3 |
|---|---|---|---|---|---|
| 0 | 11♑02 | 09♒34 | 10♓30 | 13♈03 | 14♉28 |
| 5 | 10 20 | 08 37 | 09 45 | 12 47 | 14 33 |
| 10 | 09 37 | 07 37 | 08 56 | 12 29 | 14 38 |
| 15 | 08 52 | 06 32 | 08 02 | 12 09 | 14 43 |
| 20 | 08 04 | 05 21 | 07 00 | 11 46 | 14 49 |
| 21 | 07 54 | 05 05 | 06 46 | 11 41 | 14 50 |
| 22 | 07 44 | 04 49 | 06 32 | 11 36 | 14 51 |
| 23 | 07 33 | 04 33 | 06 17 | 11 30 | 14 52 |
| 24 | 07 23 | 04 17 | 06 02 | 11 24 | 14 54 |
| 25 | 07 12 | 04 00 | 05 47 | 11 18 | 14 55 |
| 26 | 07 01 | 03 42 | 05 31 | 11 12 | 14 56 |
| 27 | 06 49 | 03 24 | 05 14 | 11 06 | 14 58 |
| 28 | 06 38 | 03 05 | 04 57 | 10 59 | 14 59 |
| 29 | 06 26 | 02 46 | 04 38 | 10 52 | 15 00 |
| 30 | 06 14 | 02 26 | 04 20 | 10 44 | 15 02 |
| 31 | 06 01 | 02 06 | 04 00 | 10 36 | 15 03 |
| 32 | 05 49 | 01 45 | 03 39 | 10 28 | 15 05 |
| 33 | 05 36 | 01 23 | 03 17 | 10 19 | 15 06 |
| 34 | 05 22 | 01 00 | 02 55 | 10 10 | 15 08 |
| 35 | 05 08 | 00 36 | 02 31 | 10 00 | 15 09 |
| 36 | 04 54 | 00 11 | 02 06 | 09 49 | 15 11 |
| 37 | 04 39 | 29♑46 | 01 39 | 09 38 | 15 13 |
| 38 | 04 24 | 29 19 | 01 11 | 09 25 | 15 14 |
| 39 | 04 09 | 28 51 | 00 41 | 09 12 | 15 16 |
| 40 | 03 52 | 28 22 | 00 10 | 08 58 | 15 17 |
| 41 | 03 35 | 27 51 | 29♒36 | 08 43 | 15 19 |
| 42 | 03 18 | 27 19 | 29 00 | 08 26 | 15 20 |
| 43 | 03 00 | 26 45 | 28 22 | 08 08 | 15 22 |
| 44 | 02 41 | 26 09 | 27 40 | 07 49 | 15 23 |
| 45 | 02 21 | 25 31 | 26 56 | 07 27 | 15 25 |
| 46 | 02 01 | 24 52 | 26 08 | 07 03 | 15 26 |
| 47 | 01 39 | 24 09 | 25 16 | 06 37 | 15 27 |
| 48 | 01 17 | 23 25 | 24 20 | 06 07 | 15 28 |
| 49 | 00 53 | 22 37 | 23 19 | 05 33 | 15 29 |
| 50 | 00 28 | 21 46 | 22 12 | 04 56 | 15 29 |
| 51 | 00 02 | 20 52 | 20 58 | 04 12 | 15 29 |
| 52 | 29♐34 | 19 54 | 19 37 | 03 22 | 15 28 |
| 53 | 29 05 | 18 52 | 18 07 | 02 24 | 15 27 |
| 54 | 28 33 | 17 44 | 16 25 | 01 16 | 15 24 |
| 55 | 28 00 | 16 32 | 14 34 | 29♓55 | 15 19 |
| 56 | 27 25 | 15 13 | 12 27 | 28 16 | 15 12 |
| 57 | 26 46 | 13 47 | 10 04 | 26 15 | 15 02 |
| 58 | 26 05 | 12 13 | 07 21 | 23 43 | 14 47 |
| 59 | 25 21 | 10 30 | 04 15 | 20 28 | 14 25 |
| 60 | 24♐33 | 08♑36 | 00♒41 | 16♓11 | 13♉50 |

**16h 52m 0s — 253° 0' 0" — 14 ♐ 20**

| LAT. | 11 | 12 | ASC | 2 | 3 |
|---|---|---|---|---|---|
| 0 | 11♑58 | 10♒33 | 11♓34 | 14♈07 | 15♉28 |
| 5 | 11 17 | 09 38 | 10 52 | 13 54 | 15 34 |
| 10 | 10 34 | 08 40 | 10 05 | 13 39 | 15 40 |
| 15 | 09 50 | 07 37 | 09 14 | 13 22 | 15 47 |
| 20 | 09 03 | 06 27 | 08 15 | 13 02 | 15 55 |
| 21 | 08 53 | 06 12 | 08 02 | 12 57 | 15 56 |
| 22 | 08 43 | 05 56 | 07 48 | 12 53 | 15 58 |
| 23 | 08 32 | 05 41 | 07 34 | 12 48 | 15 59 |
| 24 | 08 22 | 05 24 | 07 20 | 12 43 | 16 01 |
| 25 | 08 11 | 05 08 | 07 05 | 12 38 | 16 03 |
| 26 | 08 00 | 04 50 | 06 50 | 12 32 | 16 05 |
| 27 | 07 49 | 04 33 | 06 34 | 12 27 | 16 06 |
| 28 | 07 38 | 04 15 | 06 18 | 12 21 | 16 08 |
| 29 | 07 26 | 03 56 | 06 00 | 12 15 | 16 10 |
| 30 | 07 14 | 03 36 | 05 42 | 12 08 | 16 12 |
| 31 | 07 02 | 03 16 | 05 23 | 12 01 | 16 14 |
| 32 | 06 49 | 02 55 | 05 04 | 11 54 | 16 16 |
| 33 | 06 36 | 02 34 | 04 43 | 11 46 | 16 18 |
| 34 | 06 23 | 02 12 | 04 21 | 11 38 | 16 20 |
| 35 | 06 09 | 01 48 | 03 58 | 11 29 | 16 22 |
| 36 | 05 55 | 01 24 | 03 34 | 11 20 | 16 24 |
| 37 | 05 40 | 00 59 | 03 09 | 11 10 | 16 27 |
| 38 | 05 25 | 00 32 | 02 42 | 11 00 | 16 29 |
| 39 | 05 10 | 00 05 | 02 14 | 10 48 | 16 31 |
| 40 | 04 54 | 29♑36 | 01 43 | 10 36 | 16 33 |
| 41 | 04 37 | 29 06 | 01 11 | 10 23 | 16 36 |
| 42 | 04 20 | 28 34 | 00 37 | 10 08 | 16 38 |
| 43 | 04 02 | 28 01 | 00 00 | 09 52 | 16 41 |
| 44 | 03 43 | 27 25 | 29♒20 | 09 35 | 16 43 |
| 45 | 03 23 | 26 48 | 28 38 | 09 16 | 16 46 |
| 46 | 03 03 | 26 09 | 27 52 | 08 55 | 16 48 |
| 47 | 02 41 | 25 27 | 27 02 | 08 32 | 16 51 |
| 48 | 02 19 | 24 43 | 26 07 | 08 05 | 16 53 |
| 49 | 01 55 | 23 56 | 25 08 | 07 36 | 16 55 |
| 50 | 01 30 | 23 05 | 24 03 | 07 02 | 16 57 |
| 51 | 01 04 | 22 11 | 22 52 | 06 24 | 16 59 |
| 52 | 00 36 | 21 14 | 21 32 | 05 39 | 17 00 |
| 53 | 00 07 | 20 11 | 20 04 | 04 48 | 17 01 |
| 54 | 29♐36 | 19 04 | 18 26 | 03 46 | 17 01 |
| 55 | 29 02 | 17 51 | 16 36 | 02 33 | 17 00 |
| 56 | 28 27 | 16 32 | 14 31 | 01 05 | 16 57 |
| 57 | 27 48 | 15 06 | 12 09 | 29♓15 | 16 51 |
| 58 | 27 07 | 13 31 | 09 27 | 26 56 | 16 42 |
| 59 | 26 22 | 11 47 | 06 21 | 23 57 | 16 27 |
| 60 | 25♐33 | 09♑53 | 02♒46 | 19♓58 | 16♉02 |

**16h 56m 0s — 254° 0' 0" — 15 ♐ 16**

| LAT. | 11 | 12 | ASC | 2 | 3 |
|---|---|---|---|---|---|
| 0 | 12♑53 | 11♒32 | 12♓39 | 15♈12 | 16♉28 |
| 5 | 12 13 | 10 39 | 11 59 | 15 01 | 16 35 |
| 10 | 11 31 | 09 43 | 11 15 | 14 48 | 16 43 |
| 15 | 10 48 | 08 41 | 10 26 | 14 34 | 16 51 |
| 20 | 10 01 | 07 33 | 09 30 | 14 17 | 17 00 |
| 21 | 09 51 | 07 18 | 09 18 | 14 13 | 17 02 |
| 22 | 09 42 | 07 03 | 09 05 | 14 10 | 17 04 |
| 23 | 09 31 | 06 48 | 08 52 | 14 06 | 17 06 |
| 24 | 09 21 | 06 32 | 08 38 | 14 01 | 17 08 |
| 25 | 09 10 | 06 16 | 08 24 | 13 57 | 17 10 |
| 26 | 09 00 | 05 59 | 08 10 | 13 53 | 17 12 |
| 27 | 08 49 | 05 42 | 07 55 | 13 48 | 17 15 |
| 28 | 08 37 | 05 24 | 07 39 | 13 43 | 17 17 |
| 29 | 08 26 | 05 06 | 07 22 | 13 38 | 17 19 |
| 30 | 08 14 | 04 47 | 07 05 | 13 32 | 17 22 |
| 31 | 08 02 | 04 27 | 06 47 | 13 26 | 17 24 |
| 32 | 07 50 | 04 07 | 06 29 | 13 20 | 17 27 |
| 33 | 07 37 | 03 46 | 06 09 | 13 14 | 17 29 |
| 34 | 07 24 | 03 24 | 05 48 | 13 07 | 17 32 |
| 35 | 07 10 | 03 01 | 05 27 | 12 59 | 17 34 |
| 36 | 06 56 | 02 37 | 05 04 | 12 51 | 17 37 |
| 37 | 06 42 | 02 12 | 04 40 | 12 43 | 17 40 |
| 38 | 06 27 | 01 47 | 04 14 | 12 34 | 17 43 |
| 39 | 06 11 | 01 20 | 03 47 | 12 24 | 17 46 |
| 40 | 05 55 | 00 51 | 03 18 | 12 14 | 17 49 |
| 41 | 05 39 | 00 21 | 02 47 | 12 02 | 17 52 |
| 42 | 05 22 | 29♑50 | 02 14 | 11 50 | 17 56 |
| 43 | 05 04 | 29 17 | 01 39 | 11 36 | 17 59 |
| 44 | 04 45 | 28 43 | 01 01 | 11 21 | 18 02 |
| 45 | 04 25 | 28 06 | 00 20 | 11 05 | 18 06 |
| 46 | 04 05 | 27 27 | 29♒36 | 10 47 | 18 10 |
| 47 | 03 44 | 26 46 | 28 48 | 10 26 | 18 13 |
| 48 | 03 21 | 26 02 | 27 56 | 10 04 | 18 17 |
| 49 | 02 58 | 25 15 | 26 59 | 09 38 | 18 21 |
| 50 | 02 33 | 24 25 | 25 56 | 09 09 | 18 24 |
| 51 | 02 07 | 23 32 | 24 47 | 08 35 | 18 28 |
| 52 | 01 39 | 22 34 | 23 31 | 07 56 | 18 31 |
| 53 | 01 10 | 21 33 | 22 05 | 07 11 | 18 34 |
| 54 | 00 38 | 20 25 | 20 29 | 06 17 | 18 37 |
| 55 | 00 05 | 19 13 | 18 42 | 05 12 | 18 39 |
| 56 | 29♐29 | 17 54 | 16 39 | 03 53 | 18 40 |
| 57 | 28 51 | 16 27 | 14 19 | 02 15 | 18 38 |
| 58 | 28 09 | 14 52 | 11 39 | 00 11 | 18 35 |
| 59 | 27 24 | 13 07 | 08 34 | 27♓29 | 18 26 |
| 60 | 26♐34 | 11♑11 | 04♒58 | 23♓51 | 18♉10 |

**17h 0m 0s — 255° 0' 0" — 16 ♐ 11**

| LAT. | 11 | 12 | ASC | 2 | 3 |
|---|---|---|---|---|---|
| 0 | 13♑49 | 12♒32 | 13♓43 | 16♈17 | 17♉28 |
| 5 | 13 09 | 11 41 | 13 05 | 16 08 | 17 36 |
| 10 | 12 29 | 10 46 | 12 24 | 15 57 | 17 45 |
| 15 | 11 46 | 09 46 | 11 38 | 15 46 | 17 55 |
| 20 | 11 00 | 08 40 | 10 45 | 15 32 | 18 06 |
| 21 | 10 50 | 08 26 | 10 34 | 15 29 | 18 08 |
| 22 | 10 41 | 08 11 | 10 22 | 15 26 | 18 10 |
| 23 | 10 31 | 07 56 | 10 10 | 15 23 | 18 13 |
| 24 | 10 20 | 07 41 | 09 57 | 15 20 | 18 15 |
| 25 | 10 10 | 07 25 | 09 44 | 15 16 | 18 18 |
| 26 | 10 00 | 07 08 | 09 30 | 15 13 | 18 20 |
| 27 | 09 49 | 06 52 | 09 16 | 15 09 | 18 23 |
| 28 | 09 38 | 06 34 | 09 01 | 15 05 | 18 25 |
| 29 | 09 26 | 06 16 | 08 45 | 15 00 | 18 28 |
| 30 | 09 15 | 05 58 | 08 29 | 14 56 | 18 31 |
| 31 | 09 03 | 05 39 | 08 12 | 14 51 | 18 34 |
| 32 | 08 50 | 05 19 | 07 54 | 14 46 | 18 37 |
| 33 | 08 38 | 04 58 | 07 36 | 14 41 | 18 40 |
| 34 | 08 25 | 04 37 | 07 16 | 14 35 | 18 43 |
| 35 | 08 11 | 04 14 | 06 56 | 14 29 | 18 46 |
| 36 | 07 57 | 03 51 | 06 34 | 14 22 | 18 50 |
| 37 | 07 43 | 03 27 | 06 11 | 14 15 | 18 53 |
| 38 | 07 28 | 03 01 | 05 47 | 14 08 | 18 57 |
| 39 | 07 13 | 02 35 | 05 21 | 14 00 | 19 00 |
| 40 | 06 57 | 02 07 | 04 54 | 13 51 | 19 04 |
| 41 | 06 41 | 01 38 | 04 24 | 13 41 | 19 08 |
| 42 | 06 24 | 01 07 | 03 53 | 13 31 | 19 12 |
| 43 | 06 06 | 00 35 | 03 19 | 13 19 | 19 17 |
| 44 | 05 47 | 00 01 | 02 43 | 13 07 | 19 21 |
| 45 | 05 28 | 29♑25 | 02 04 | 12 53 | 19 26 |
| 46 | 05 08 | 28 46 | 01 22 | 12 38 | 19 30 |
| 47 | 04 47 | 28 06 | 00 37 | 12 21 | 19 35 |
| 48 | 04 24 | 27 23 | 29♒47 | 12 02 | 19 40 |
| 49 | 04 01 | 26 36 | 28 52 | 11 40 | 19 45 |
| 50 | 03 36 | 25 47 | 27 52 | 11 15 | 19 50 |
| 51 | 03 10 | 24 54 | 26 45 | 10 46 | 19 56 |
| 52 | 02 42 | 23 57 | 25 31 | 10 13 | 20 01 |
| 53 | 02 13 | 22 55 | 24 09 | 09 34 | 20 06 |
| 54 | 01 42 | 21 49 | 22 36 | 08 47 | 20 11 |
| 55 | 01 08 | 20 36 | 20 51 | 07 51 | 20 16 |
| 56 | 00 32 | 19 17 | 18 52 | 06 42 | 20 20 |
| 57 | 29♐53 | 17 50 | 16 35 | 05 16 | 20 23 |
| 58 | 29 12 | 16 15 | 13 57 | 03 27 | 20 24 |
| 59 | 28 26 | 14 29 | 10 52 | 01 03 | 20 22 |
| 60 | 27♐36 | 12♑32 | 07♒17 | 27♓47 | 20♉15 |

# Koch Table of Houses for Latitudes 0° to 60° North

**17h 4m 0s — 256° 0' 0" — 17 ♐ 07**

| LAT. | 11 | 12 | ASC | 2 | 3 |
|---|---|---|---|---|---|
| 0 | 14♑44 | 13♒32 | 14♓48 | 17♈21 | 18♉28 |
| 5 | 14 06 | 12 42 | 14 12 | 17 14 | 18 37 |
| 10 | 13 26 | 11 49 | 13 34 | 17 07 | 18 48 |
| 15 | 12 44 | 10 51 | 12 51 | 16 58 | 18 59 |
| 20 | 11 59 | 09 47 | 12 01 | 16 48 | 19 11 |
| 21 | 11 50 | 09 33 | 11 50 | 16 45 | 19 13 |
| 22 | 11 40 | 09 19 | 11 39 | 16 43 | 19 16 |
| 23 | 11 30 | 09 04 | 11 28 | 16 41 | 19 19 |
| 24 | 11 20 | 08 49 | 11 16 | 16 38 | 19 22 |
| 25 | 11 10 | 08 34 | 11 03 | 16 35 | 19 24 |
| 26 | 10 59 | 08 18 | 10 50 | 16 32 | 19 27 |
| 27 | 10 49 | 08 02 | 10 37 | 16 29 | 19 30 |
| 28 | 10 38 | 07 45 | 10 23 | 16 26 | 19 33 |
| 29 | 10 27 | 07 27 | 10 08 | 16 23 | 19 37 |
| 30 | 10 15 | 07 09 | 09 53 | 16 19 | 19 40 |
| 31 | 10 03 | 06 51 | 09 37 | 16 16 | 19 43 |
| 32 | 09 51 | 06 31 | 09 20 | 16 12 | 19 47 |
| 33 | 09 39 | 06 11 | 09 03 | 16 07 | 19 50 |
| 34 | 09 26 | 05 50 | 08 44 | 16 03 | 19 54 |
| 35 | 09 13 | 05 28 | 08 25 | 15 58 | 19 58 |
| 36 | 08 59 | 05 06 | 08 05 | 15 53 | 20 02 |
| 37 | 08 45 | 04 42 | 07 43 | 15 47 | 20 06 |
| 38 | 08 30 | 04 17 | 07 20 | 15 42 | 20 10 |
| 39 | 08 15 | 03 51 | 06 56 | 15 35 | 20 14 |
| 40 | 08 00 | 03 24 | 06 30 | 15 28 | 20 19 |
| 41 | 07 43 | 02 55 | 06 02 | 15 20 | 20 24 |
| 42 | 07 26 | 02 25 | 05 33 | 15 12 | 20 29 |
| 43 | 07 09 | 01 54 | 05 01 | 15 03 | 20 34 |
| 44 | 06 50 | 01 20 | 04 27 | 14 53 | 20 39 |
| 45 | 06 31 | 00 45 | 03 50 | 14 42 | 20 44 |
| 46 | 06 11 | 00 07 | 03 10 | 14 29 | 20 50 |
| 47 | 05 50 | 29♑27 | 02 26 | 14 15 | 20 56 |
| 48 | 05 28 | 28 44 | 01 39 | 13 59 | 21 02 |
| 49 | 05 04 | 27 59 | 00 47 | 13 41 | 21 09 |
| 50 | 04 40 | 27 10 | 29♒49 | 13 21 | 21 16 |
| 51 | 04 14 | 26 17 | 28 46 | 12 57 | 21 23 |
| 52 | 03 46 | 25 21 | 27 35 | 12 29 | 21 30 |
| 53 | 03 17 | 24 20 | 26 16 | 11 56 | 21 37 |
| 54 | 02 45 | 23 13 | 24 46 | 11 17 | 21 45 |
| 55 | 02 12 | 22 01 | 23 05 | 10 29 | 21 52 |
| 56 | 01 36 | 20 42 | 21 09 | 09 31 | 21 59 |
| 57 | 00 57 | 19 15 | 18 55 | 08 17 | 22 06 |
| 58 | 00 15 | 17 40 | 16 20 | 06 43 | 22 12 |
| 59 | 29♐29 | 15 53 | 13 18 | 04 37 | 22 15 |
| 60 | 28♐39 | 13♑55 | 09♒44 | 01♈46 | 22♉15 |

**17h 8m 0s — 257° 0' 0" — 18 ♐ 02**

| LAT. | 11 | 12 | ASC | 2 | 3 |
|---|---|---|---|---|---|
| 0 | 15♑40 | 14♒32 | 15♓53 | 18♈26 | 19♉27 |
| 5 | 15 02 | 13 44 | 15 20 | 18 21 | 19 38 |
| 10 | 14 23 | 12 53 | 14 44 | 18 16 | 19 50 |
| 15 | 13 42 | 11 57 | 14 03 | 18 10 | 20 02 |
| 20 | 12 58 | 10 54 | 13 17 | 18 03 | 20 16 |
| 21 | 12 49 | 10 41 | 13 07 | 18 01 | 20 19 |
| 22 | 12 39 | 10 27 | 12 57 | 17 59 | 20 22 |
| 23 | 12 30 | 10 13 | 12 46 | 17 58 | 20 25 |
| 24 | 12 20 | 09 58 | 12 35 | 17 56 | 20 28 |
| 25 | 12 10 | 09 43 | 12 23 | 17 54 | 20 31 |
| 26 | 12 00 | 09 28 | 12 11 | 17 52 | 20 34 |
| 27 | 11 49 | 09 12 | 11 58 | 17 50 | 20 38 |
| 28 | 11 38 | 08 56 | 11 45 | 17 48 | 20 41 |
| 29 | 11 27 | 08 39 | 11 32 | 17 45 | 20 45 |
| 30 | 11 16 | 08 21 | 11 17 | 17 43 | 20 49 |
| 31 | 11 04 | 08 03 | 11 03 | 17 40 | 20 52 |
| 32 | 10 52 | 07 44 | 10 47 | 17 37 | 20 56 |
| 33 | 10 40 | 07 25 | 10 31 | 17 34 | 21 00 |
| 34 | 10 27 | 07 04 | 10 13 | 17 31 | 21 05 |
| 35 | 10 14 | 06 43 | 09 55 | 17 27 | 21 09 |
| 36 | 10 01 | 06 21 | 09 36 | 17 23 | 21 13 |
| 37 | 09 47 | 05 58 | 09 16 | 17 19 | 21 18 |
| 38 | 09 33 | 05 33 | 08 54 | 17 15 | 21 23 |
| 39 | 09 18 | 05 08 | 08 31 | 17 10 | 21 28 |
| 40 | 09 02 | 04 41 | 08 07 | 17 05 | 21 33 |
| 41 | 08 46 | 04 14 | 07 41 | 16 59 | 21 39 |
| 42 | 08 29 | 03 44 | 07 13 | 16 53 | 21 44 |
| 43 | 08 12 | 03 13 | 06 43 | 16 46 | 21 50 |
| 44 | 07 54 | 02 40 | 06 11 | 16 38 | 21 56 |
| 45 | 07 35 | 02 05 | 05 36 | 16 29 | 22 03 |
| 46 | 07 15 | 01 28 | 04 59 | 16 20 | 22 09 |
| 47 | 06 54 | 00 49 | 04 18 | 16 09 | 22 17 |
| 48 | 06 32 | 00 07 | 03 33 | 15 56 | 22 24 |
| 49 | 06 08 | 29♑22 | 02 43 | 15 42 | 22 32 |
| 50 | 05 44 | 28 34 | 01 49 | 15 26 | 22 40 |
| 51 | 05 18 | 27 42 | 00 48 | 15 07 | 22 48 |
| 52 | 04 50 | 26 47 | 29♒41 | 14 44 | 22 57 |
| 53 | 04 21 | 25 46 | 28 25 | 14 18 | 23 06 |
| 54 | 03 50 | 24 40 | 27 00 | 13 46 | 23 16 |
| 55 | 03 16 | 23 28 | 25 22 | 13 07 | 23 26 |
| 56 | 02 40 | 22 10 | 23 30 | 12 19 | 23 36 |
| 57 | 02 01 | 20 43 | 21 21 | 11 17 | 23 47 |
| 58 | 01 19 | 19 07 | 18 49 | 09 58 | 23 57 |
| 59 | 00 33 | 17 20 | 15 51 | 08 12 | 24 06 |
| 60 | 29♐42 | 15♑21 | 12♒19 | 05♈45 | 24♉12 |

**17h 12m 0s — 258° 0' 0" — 18 ♐ 58**

| LAT. | 11 | 12 | ASC | 2 | 3 |
|---|---|---|---|---|---|
| 0 | 16♑36 | 15♒32 | 16♓57 | 19♈30 | 20♉26 |
| 5 | 15 59 | 14 46 | 16 27 | 19 28 | 20 38 |
| 10 | 15 21 | 13 56 | 15 54 | 19 25 | 20 51 |
| 15 | 14 41 | 13 02 | 15 16 | 19 22 | 21 05 |
| 20 | 13 57 | 12 02 | 14 33 | 19 18 | 21 20 |
| 21 | 13 48 | 11 49 | 14 24 | 19 17 | 21 24 |
| 22 | 13 39 | 11 36 | 14 14 | 19 16 | 21 27 |
| 23 | 13 30 | 11 22 | 14 04 | 19 15 | 21 30 |
| 24 | 13 20 | 11 08 | 13 54 | 19 14 | 21 34 |
| 25 | 13 10 | 10 53 | 13 43 | 19 13 | 21 37 |
| 26 | 13 00 | 10 39 | 13 32 | 19 11 | 21 41 |
| 27 | 12 50 | 10 23 | 13 20 | 19 10 | 21 45 |
| 28 | 12 39 | 10 07 | 13 08 | 19 09 | 21 49 |
| 29 | 12 28 | 09 51 | 12 55 | 19 07 | 21 53 |
| 30 | 12 17 | 09 34 | 12 42 | 19 06 | 21 57 |
| 31 | 12 06 | 09 16 | 12 28 | 19 04 | 22 01 |
| 32 | 11 54 | 08 58 | 12 14 | 19 02 | 22 06 |
| 33 | 11 42 | 08 39 | 11 59 | 19 00 | 22 10 |
| 34 | 11 29 | 08 19 | 11 43 | 18 58 | 22 15 |
| 35 | 11 16 | 07 58 | 11 26 | 18 56 | 22 20 |
| 36 | 11 03 | 07 37 | 11 08 | 18 54 | 22 25 |
| 37 | 10 49 | 07 14 | 10 49 | 18 51 | 22 30 |
| 38 | 10 35 | 06 51 | 10 29 | 18 48 | 22 35 |
| 39 | 10 20 | 06 26 | 10 08 | 18 45 | 22 41 |
| 40 | 10 05 | 06 00 | 09 45 | 18 41 | 22 47 |
| 41 | 09 49 | 05 33 | 09 21 | 18 37 | 22 53 |
| 42 | 09 32 | 05 04 | 08 55 | 18 33 | 22 59 |
| 43 | 09 15 | 04 33 | 08 27 | 18 28 | 23 06 |
| 44 | 08 57 | 04 01 | 07 57 | 18 23 | 23 13 |
| 45 | 08 38 | 03 27 | 07 24 | 18 17 | 23 20 |
| 46 | 08 18 | 02 51 | 06 49 | 18 10 | 23 28 |
| 47 | 07 58 | 02 13 | 06 10 | 18 02 | 23 36 |
| 48 | 07 36 | 01 31 | 05 28 | 17 53 | 23 45 |
| 49 | 07 13 | 00 47 | 04 42 | 17 42 | 23 54 |
| 50 | 06 48 | 00 00 | 03 50 | 17 30 | 24 03 |
| 51 | 06 23 | 29♑09 | 02 53 | 17 16 | 24 13 |
| 52 | 05 55 | 28 14 | 01 49 | 16 59 | 24 24 |
| 53 | 05 26 | 27 14 | 00 38 | 16 38 | 24 35 |
| 54 | 04 55 | 26 09 | 29♒16 | 16 14 | 24 46 |
| 55 | 04 21 | 24 58 | 27 43 | 15 43 | 24 59 |
| 56 | 03 45 | 23 39 | 25 56 | 15 05 | 25 12 |
| 57 | 03 06 | 22 13 | 23 52 | 14 16 | 25 25 |
| 58 | 02 24 | 20 37 | 21 25 | 13 12 | 25 39 |
| 59 | 01 37 | 18 50 | 18 31 | 11 45 | 25 53 |
| 60 | 00♑46 | 16♑50 | 15♒03 | 09♈44 | 26♉06 |

**17h 16m 0s — 259° 0' 0" — 19 ♐ 53**

| LAT. | 11 | 12 | ASC | 2 | 3 |
|---|---|---|---|---|---|
| 0 | 17♑32 | 16♒33 | 18♓02 | 20♈34 | 21♉26 |
| 5 | 16 56 | 15 48 | 17 34 | 20 34 | 21 39 |
| 10 | 16 19 | 15 00 | 17 04 | 20 34 | 21 53 |
| 15 | 15 39 | 14 08 | 16 29 | 20 33 | 22 08 |
| 20 | 14 57 | 13 10 | 15 50 | 20 32 | 22 25 |
| 21 | 14 48 | 12 58 | 15 41 | 20 32 | 22 28 |
| 22 | 14 39 | 12 45 | 15 32 | 20 32 | 22 32 |
| 23 | 14 30 | 12 31 | 15 23 | 20 32 | 22 36 |
| 24 | 14 20 | 12 18 | 15 13 | 20 31 | 22 40 |
| 25 | 14 10 | 12 04 | 15 04 | 20 31 | 22 43 |
| 26 | 14 00 | 11 49 | 14 53 | 20 31 | 22 48 |
| 27 | 13 50 | 11 34 | 14 42 | 20 30 | 22 52 |
| 28 | 13 40 | 11 19 | 14 31 | 20 30 | 22 56 |
| 29 | 13 29 | 11 03 | 14 20 | 20 29 | 23 00 |
| 30 | 13 18 | 10 47 | 14 07 | 20 29 | 23 05 |
| 31 | 13 07 | 10 30 | 13 55 | 20 28 | 23 10 |
| 32 | 12 55 | 10 12 | 13 41 | 20 27 | 23 14 |
| 33 | 12 44 | 09 53 | 13 27 | 20 27 | 23 19 |
| 34 | 12 31 | 09 34 | 13 12 | 20 26 | 23 25 |
| 35 | 12 19 | 09 14 | 12 57 | 20 25 | 23 30 |
| 36 | 12 05 | 08 53 | 12 40 | 20 24 | 23 35 |
| 37 | 11 52 | 08 31 | 12 23 | 20 22 | 23 41 |
| 38 | 11 38 | 08 08 | 12 04 | 20 21 | 23 47 |
| 39 | 11 23 | 07 44 | 11 45 | 20 19 | 23 53 |
| 40 | 11 08 | 07 19 | 11 24 | 20 17 | 24 00 |
| 41 | 10 52 | 06 52 | 11 01 | 20 15 | 24 07 |
| 42 | 10 36 | 06 24 | 10 37 | 20 13 | 24 14 |
| 43 | 10 19 | 05 55 | 10 11 | 20 10 | 24 21 |
| 44 | 10 01 | 05 24 | 09 43 | 20 07 | 24 29 |
| 45 | 09 42 | 04 50 | 09 13 | 20 03 | 24 37 |
| 46 | 09 23 | 04 15 | 08 40 | 19 59 | 24 46 |
| 47 | 09 02 | 03 37 | 08 04 | 19 54 | 24 55 |
| 48 | 08 41 | 02 57 | 07 25 | 19 49 | 25 05 |
| 49 | 08 18 | 02 14 | 06 41 | 19 42 | 25 15 |
| 50 | 07 53 | 01 27 | 05 54 | 19 34 | 25 25 |
| 51 | 07 28 | 00 37 | 05 00 | 19 24 | 25 37 |
| 52 | 07 01 | 29♑43 | 04 00 | 19 12 | 25 49 |
| 53 | 06 31 | 28 44 | 02 53 | 18 58 | 26 02 |
| 54 | 06 00 | 27 40 | 01 36 | 18 40 | 26 15 |
| 55 | 05 27 | 26 29 | 00 08 | 18 18 | 26 30 |
| 56 | 04 51 | 25 11 | 28♒27 | 17 50 | 26 45 |
| 57 | 04 12 | 23 46 | 26 28 | 17 13 | 27 02 |
| 58 | 03 29 | 22 10 | 24 08 | 16 24 | 27 19 |
| 59 | 02 43 | 20 23 | 21 20 | 15 16 | 27 37 |
| 60 | 01♑51 | 18♑22 | 17♒56 | 13♈40 | 27♉56 |

**17h 20m 0s — 260° 0' 0" — 20 ♐ 49**

| LAT. | 11 | 12 | ASC | 2 | 3 |
|---|---|---|---|---|---|
| 0 | 18♑28 | 17♒33 | 19♓07 | 21♈38 | 22♉25 |
| 5 | 17 53 | 16 51 | 18 42 | 21 40 | 22 39 |
| 10 | 17 17 | 16 05 | 18 14 | 21 42 | 22 54 |
| 15 | 16 38 | 15 14 | 17 42 | 21 45 | 23 11 |
| 20 | 15 56 | 14 18 | 17 06 | 21 47 | 23 29 |
| 21 | 15 48 | 14 06 | 16 59 | 21 47 | 23 33 |
| 22 | 15 39 | 13 54 | 16 50 | 21 48 | 23 37 |
| 23 | 15 30 | 13 41 | 16 42 | 21 48 | 23 41 |
| 24 | 15 20 | 13 28 | 16 33 | 21 49 | 23 45 |
| 25 | 15 11 | 13 15 | 16 24 | 21 49 | 23 49 |
| 26 | 15 01 | 13 01 | 16 15 | 21 50 | 23 54 |
| 27 | 14 51 | 12 46 | 16 05 | 21 50 | 23 58 |
| 28 | 14 41 | 12 31 | 15 55 | 21 50 | 24 03 |
| 29 | 14 31 | 12 16 | 15 44 | 21 51 | 24 08 |
| 30 | 14 20 | 12 00 | 15 33 | 21 51 | 24 13 |
| 31 | 14 09 | 11 44 | 15 21 | 21 52 | 24 18 |
| 32 | 13 57 | 11 26 | 15 09 | 21 52 | 24 23 |
| 33 | 13 46 | 11 08 | 14 56 | 21 52 | 24 28 |
| 34 | 13 34 | 10 50 | 14 43 | 21 53 | 24 34 |
| 35 | 13 21 | 10 30 | 14 28 | 21 53 | 24 40 |
| 36 | 13 08 | 10 10 | 14 13 | 21 53 | 24 46 |
| 37 | 12 55 | 09 49 | 13 57 | 21 53 | 24 52 |
| 38 | 12 41 | 09 27 | 13 40 | 21 53 | 24 59 |
| 39 | 12 27 | 09 04 | 13 22 | 21 53 | 25 05 |
| 40 | 12 12 | 08 39 | 13 03 | 21 53 | 25 13 |
| 41 | 11 56 | 08 13 | 12 42 | 21 53 | 25 20 |
| 42 | 11 40 | 07 46 | 12 20 | 21 52 | 25 28 |
| 43 | 11 23 | 07 17 | 11 56 | 21 52 | 25 36 |
| 44 | 11 05 | 06 47 | 11 31 | 21 51 | 25 45 |
| 45 | 10 47 | 06 14 | 11 03 | 21 49 | 25 54 |
| 46 | 10 28 | 05 40 | 10 32 | 21 48 | 26 03 |
| 47 | 10 07 | 05 03 | 09 59 | 21 46 | 26 13 |
| 48 | 09 46 | 04 24 | 09 23 | 21 43 | 26 24 |
| 49 | 09 23 | 03 42 | 08 43 | 21 40 | 26 35 |
| 50 | 08 59 | 02 56 | 07 59 | 21 36 | 26 47 |
| 51 | 08 34 | 02 07 | 07 09 | 21 31 | 26 59 |
| 52 | 08 06 | 01 14 | 06 14 | 21 24 | 27 13 |
| 53 | 07 38 | 00 16 | 05 11 | 21 16 | 27 27 |
| 54 | 07 07 | 29♑12 | 03 59 | 21 05 | 27 43 |
| 55 | 06 33 | 28 03 | 02 37 | 20 51 | 27 59 |
| 56 | 05 57 | 26 46 | 01 02 | 20 32 | 28 17 |
| 57 | 05 18 | 25 21 | 29♒09 | 20 07 | 28 36 |
| 58 | 04 36 | 23 46 | 26 56 | 19 32 | 28 57 |
| 59 | 03 49 | 21 59 | 24 16 | 18 44 | 29 19 |
| 60 | 02♑57 | 19♑58 | 20♒59 | 17♈33 | 29♉42 |

**17h 24m 0s — 261° 0' 0" — 21 ♐ 44**

| LAT. | 11 | 12 | ASC | 2 | 3 |
|---|---|---|---|---|---|
| 0 | 19♑24 | 18♒34 | 20♓12 | 22♈42 | 23♉23 |
| 5 | 18 50 | 17 53 | 19 49 | 22 46 | 23 39 |
| 10 | 18 14 | 17 09 | 19 24 | 22 51 | 23 55 |
| 15 | 17 37 | 16 21 | 18 56 | 22 56 | 24 13 |
| 20 | 16 56 | 15 27 | 18 23 | 23 01 | 24 33 |
| 21 | 16 48 | 15 16 | 18 16 | 23 02 | 24 37 |
| 22 | 16 39 | 15 04 | 18 09 | 23 04 | 24 41 |
| 23 | 16 30 | 14 51 | 18 01 | 23 05 | 24 46 |
| 24 | 16 21 | 14 39 | 17 53 | 23 06 | 24 50 |
| 25 | 16 12 | 14 26 | 17 45 | 23 07 | 24 55 |
| 26 | 16 02 | 14 12 | 17 37 | 23 08 | 24 59 |
| 27 | 15 52 | 13 59 | 17 28 | 23 10 | 25 04 |
| 28 | 15 42 | 13 44 | 17 18 | 23 11 | 25 09 |
| 29 | 15 32 | 13 29 | 17 09 | 23 12 | 25 15 |
| 30 | 15 21 | 13 14 | 16 59 | 23 14 | 25 20 |
| 31 | 15 11 | 12 58 | 16 48 | 23 15 | 25 25 |
| 32 | 14 59 | 12 42 | 16 37 | 23 16 | 25 31 |
| 33 | 14 48 | 12 24 | 16 25 | 23 18 | 25 37 |
| 34 | 14 36 | 12 06 | 16 13 | 23 19 | 25 43 |
| 35 | 14 24 | 11 48 | 16 00 | 23 21 | 25 49 |
| 36 | 14 11 | 11 28 | 15 46 | 23 22 | 25 56 |
| 37 | 13 58 | 11 08 | 15 32 | 23 24 | 26 03 |
| 38 | 13 44 | 10 46 | 15 17 | 23 25 | 26 10 |
| 39 | 13 30 | 10 24 | 15 00 | 23 27 | 26 17 |
| 40 | 13 16 | 10 00 | 14 43 | 23 28 | 26 25 |
| 41 | 13 00 | 09 35 | 14 24 | 23 30 | 26 33 |
| 42 | 12 44 | 09 09 | 14 04 | 23 31 | 26 41 |
| 43 | 12 28 | 08 41 | 13 42 | 23 32 | 26 50 |
| 44 | 12 10 | 08 11 | 13 19 | 23 34 | 26 59 |
| 45 | 11 52 | 07 40 | 12 54 | 23 35 | 27 09 |
| 46 | 11 33 | 07 06 | 12 26 | 23 36 | 27 19 |
| 47 | 11 13 | 06 30 | 11 56 | 23 37 | 27 30 |
| 48 | 10 51 | 05 52 | 11 23 | 23 37 | 27 42 |
| 49 | 10 29 | 05 11 | 10 46 | 23 38 | 27 54 |
| 50 | 10 05 | 04 26 | 10 06 | 23 38 | 28 07 |
| 51 | 09 40 | 03 38 | 09 20 | 23 37 | 28 21 |
| 52 | 09 13 | 02 46 | 08 29 | 23 35 | 28 36 |
| 53 | 08 44 | 01 49 | 07 32 | 23 32 | 28 52 |
| 54 | 08 13 | 00 47 | 06 26 | 23 28 | 29 09 |
| 55 | 07 40 | 29♑39 | 05 09 | 23 22 | 29 27 |
| 56 | 07 04 | 28 23 | 03 41 | 23 12 | 29 47 |
| 57 | 06 25 | 26 59 | 01 56 | 22 58 | 00♊09 |
| 58 | 05 43 | 25 25 | 29♒51 | 22 38 | 00 32 |
| 59 | 04 56 | 23 38 | 27 20 | 22 07 | 00 58 |
| 60 | 04♑04 | 21♑38 | 24♒13 | 21♈20 | 01♊26 |

**17h 28m 0s — 262° 0' 0" — 22 ♐ 39**

| LAT. | 11 | 12 | ASC | 2 | 3 |
|---|---|---|---|---|---|
| 0 | 20♑20 | 19♒35 | 21♓17 | 23♈46 | 24♉22 |
| 5 | 19 47 | 18 56 | 20 57 | 23 52 | 24 39 |
| 10 | 19 13 | 18 14 | 20 34 | 23 59 | 24 56 |
| 15 | 18 36 | 17 28 | 20 09 | 24 07 | 25 16 |
| 20 | 17 56 | 16 36 | 19 40 | 24 15 | 25 36 |
| 21 | 17 48 | 16 25 | 19 34 | 24 17 | 25 41 |
| 22 | 17 39 | 16 14 | 19 27 | 24 19 | 25 46 |
| 23 | 17 31 | 16 02 | 19 21 | 24 21 | 25 50 |
| 24 | 17 22 | 15 50 | 19 14 | 24 23 | 25 55 |
| 25 | 17 13 | 15 37 | 19 06 | 24 25 | 26 00 |
| 26 | 17 03 | 15 25 | 18 59 | 24 27 | 26 05 |
| 27 | 16 54 | 15 11 | 18 51 | 24 29 | 26 10 |
| 28 | 16 44 | 14 58 | 18 42 | 24 31 | 26 16 |
| 29 | 16 34 | 14 43 | 18 34 | 24 33 | 26 21 |
| 30 | 16 23 | 14 29 | 18 25 | 24 36 | 26 27 |
| 31 | 16 13 | 14 13 | 18 15 | 24 38 | 26 33 |
| 32 | 16 02 | 13 57 | 18 05 | 24 40 | 26 39 |
| 33 | 15 51 | 13 41 | 17 55 | 24 43 | 26 45 |
| 34 | 15 39 | 13 23 | 17 44 | 24 45 | 26 52 |
| 35 | 15 27 | 13 05 | 17 32 | 24 48 | 26 58 |
| 36 | 15 14 | 12 47 | 17 20 | 24 51 | 27 05 |
| 37 | 15 02 | 12 27 | 17 07 | 24 54 | 27 13 |
| 38 | 14 48 | 12 06 | 16 53 | 24 56 | 27 20 |
| 39 | 14 34 | 11 44 | 16 39 | 24 59 | 27 28 |
| 40 | 14 20 | 11 22 | 16 23 | 25 03 | 27 36 |
| 41 | 14 05 | 10 57 | 16 06 | 25 06 | 27 45 |
| 42 | 13 49 | 10 32 | 15 48 | 25 09 | 27 54 |
| 43 | 13 33 | 10 05 | 15 29 | 25 12 | 28 04 |
| 44 | 13 15 | 09 36 | 15 08 | 25 16 | 28 14 |
| 45 | 12 57 | 09 06 | 14 45 | 25 19 | 28 24 |
| 46 | 12 39 | 08 33 | 14 20 | 25 23 | 28 35 |
| 47 | 12 19 | 07 59 | 13 53 | 25 27 | 28 47 |
| 48 | 11 58 | 07 22 | 13 24 | 25 30 | 28 59 |
| 49 | 11 35 | 06 42 | 12 51 | 25 34 | 29 13 |
| 50 | 11 12 | 05 58 | 12 14 | 25 38 | 29 27 |
| 51 | 10 47 | 05 12 | 11 33 | 25 41 | 29 42 |
| 52 | 10 20 | 04 21 | 10 47 | 25 44 | 29 58 |
| 53 | 09 52 | 03 25 | 09 55 | 25 47 | 00♊15 |
| 54 | 09 21 | 02 24 | 08 55 | 25 49 | 00 34 |
| 55 | 08 48 | 01 17 | 07 45 | 25 50 | 00 54 |
| 56 | 08 12 | 00 03 | 06 24 | 25 50 | 01 16 |
| 57 | 07 33 | 28♑40 | 04 48 | 25 46 | 01 40 |
| 58 | 06 51 | 27 07 | 02 53 | 25 39 | 02 06 |
| 59 | 06 04 | 25 22 | 00 32 | 25 25 | 02 34 |
| 60 | 05♑12 | 23♑21 | 27♒36 | 25♈01 | 03♊06 |

**17h 32m 0s — 263° 0' 0" — 23 ♐ 34**

| LAT. | 11 | 12 | ASC | 2 | 3 |
|---|---|---|---|---|---|
| 0 | 21♑17 | 20♒36 | 22♓23 | 24♈50 | 25♉21 |
| 5 | 20 44 | 19 59 | 22 05 | 24 58 | 25 38 |
| 10 | 20 11 | 19 19 | 21 45 | 25 08 | 25 57 |
| 15 | 19 35 | 18 35 | 21 23 | 25 18 | 26 18 |
| 20 | 18 56 | 17 46 | 20 57 | 25 29 | 26 40 |
| 21 | 18 48 | 17 35 | 20 52 | 25 32 | 26 45 |
| 22 | 18 40 | 17 24 | 20 46 | 25 34 | 26 50 |
| 23 | 18 31 | 17 13 | 20 40 | 25 37 | 26 55 |
| 24 | 18 23 | 17 01 | 20 34 | 25 39 | 27 00 |
| 25 | 18 14 | 16 49 | 20 28 | 25 42 | 27 05 |
| 26 | 18 05 | 16 37 | 20 21 | 25 45 | 27 10 |
| 27 | 17 55 | 16 24 | 20 14 | 25 48 | 27 16 |
| 28 | 17 46 | 16 11 | 20 07 | 25 51 | 27 22 |
| 29 | 17 36 | 15 58 | 19 59 | 25 54 | 27 27 |
| 30 | 17 26 | 15 43 | 19 51 | 25 57 | 27 33 |
| 31 | 17 15 | 15 29 | 19 43 | 26 01 | 27 40 |
| 32 | 17 05 | 15 14 | 19 34 | 26 04 | 27 46 |
| 33 | 16 53 | 14 58 | 19 25 | 26 08 | 27 53 |
| 34 | 16 42 | 14 41 | 19 15 | 26 11 | 28 00 |
| 35 | 16 30 | 14 24 | 19 05 | 26 15 | 28 07 |
| 36 | 16 18 | 14 06 | 18 54 | 26 19 | 28 14 |
| 37 | 16 05 | 13 47 | 18 43 | 26 23 | 28 22 |
| 38 | 15 52 | 13 27 | 18 31 | 26 27 | 28 30 |
| 39 | 15 39 | 13 06 | 18 18 | 26 32 | 28 39 |
| 40 | 15 24 | 12 44 | 18 04 | 26 37 | 28 48 |
| 41 | 15 10 | 12 21 | 17 49 | 26 41 | 28 57 |
| 42 | 14 54 | 11 56 | 17 33 | 26 46 | 29 06 |
| 43 | 14 38 | 11 30 | 17 16 | 26 52 | 29 17 |
| 44 | 14 21 | 11 03 | 16 58 | 26 57 | 29 27 |
| 45 | 14 03 | 10 33 | 16 38 | 27 03 | 29 38 |
| 46 | 13 45 | 10 02 | 16 16 | 27 09 | 29 50 |
| 47 | 13 25 | 09 29 | 15 52 | 27 16 | 00♊03 |
| 48 | 13 04 | 08 53 | 15 26 | 27 22 | 00 16 |
| 49 | 12 42 | 08 14 | 14 56 | 27 29 | 00 30 |
| 50 | 12 19 | 07 32 | 14 24 | 27 37 | 00 45 |
| 51 | 11 54 | 06 47 | 13 48 | 27 44 | 01 01 |
| 52 | 11 28 | 05 57 | 13 07 | 27 52 | 01 19 |
| 53 | 11 00 | 05 03 | 12 20 | 28 00 | 01 37 |
| 54 | 10 29 | 04 04 | 11 26 | 28 08 | 01 57 |
| 55 | 09 57 | 02 59 | 10 24 | 28 16 | 02 19 |
| 56 | 09 21 | 01 46 | 09 12 | 28 24 | 02 43 |
| 57 | 08 42 | 00 24 | 07 45 | 28 31 | 03 08 |
| 58 | 08 00 | 28♑53 | 06 01 | 28 36 | 03 37 |
| 59 | 07 13 | 27 09 | 03 52 | 28 38 | 04 08 |
| 60 | 06♑21 | 25♑09 | 01♓10 | 28♈34 | 04♊43 |

# Koch Table of Houses for Latitudes 0° to 60° North

**17h 36m 0s — 264° 0' 0" — 24 ♐ 30**

| LAT. | 11 | 12 | ASC | 2 | 3 |
|---|---|---|---|---|---|
| 0 | 22♑13 | 21♒37 | 23♓28 | 25♈53 | 26♉19 |
| 5 | 21 42 | 21 02 | 23 12 | 26 04 | 26 38 |
| 10 | 21 09 | 20 24 | 22 56 | 26 16 | 26 58 |
| 15 | 20 34 | 19 42 | 22 37 | 26 28 | 27 19 |
| 20 | 19 57 | 18 56 | 22 15 | 26 43 | 27 43 |
| 21 | 19 49 | 18 45 | 22 10 | 26 46 | 27 48 |
| 22 | 19 41 | 18 35 | 22 05 | 26 49 | 27 53 |
| 23 | 19 32 | 18 24 | 22 00 | 26 52 | 27 59 |
| 24 | 19 24 | 18 13 | 21 55 | 26 56 | 28 04 |
| 25 | 19 15 | 18 02 | 21 49 | 26 59 | 28 10 |
| 26 | 19 06 | 17 50 | 21 43 | 27 03 | 28 15 |
| 27 | 18 57 | 17 38 | 21 37 | 27 07 | 28 21 |
| 28 | 18 48 | 17 25 | 21 31 | 27 10 | 28 27 |
| 29 | 18 38 | 17 12 | 21 25 | 27 14 | 28 33 |
| 30 | 18 28 | 16 59 | 21 18 | 27 19 | 28 40 |
| 31 | 18 18 | 16 45 | 21 11 | 27 23 | 28 46 |
| 32 | 18 07 | 16 30 | 21 03 | 27 27 | 28 53 |
| 33 | 17 57 | 16 15 | 20 55 | 27 32 | 29 00 |
| 34 | 17 45 | 15 59 | 20 47 | 27 37 | 29 08 |
| 35 | 17 34 | 15 43 | 20 38 | 27 42 | 29 15 |
| 36 | 17 22 | 15 26 | 20 29 | 27 47 | 29 23 |
| 37 | 17 10 | 15 07 | 20 19 | 27 52 | 29 31 |
| 38 | 16 57 | 14 48 | 20 09 | 27 58 | 29 40 |
| 39 | 16 43 | 14 28 | 19 57 | 28 04 | 29 49 |
| 40 | 16 29 | 14 07 | 19 46 | 28 10 | 29 58 |
| 41 | 16 15 | 13 45 | 19 33 | 28 16 | 00♊08 |
| 42 | 16 00 | 13 22 | 19 19 | 28 23 | 00 18 |
| 43 | 15 44 | 12 57 | 19 04 | 28 30 | 00 29 |
| 44 | 15 27 | 12 30 | 18 48 | 28 38 | 00 40 |
| 45 | 15 10 | 12 02 | 18 31 | 28 46 | 00 52 |
| 46 | 14 51 | 11 32 | 18 12 | 28 54 | 01 05 |
| 47 | 14 32 | 11 00 | 17 51 | 29 03 | 01 18 |
| 48 | 14 12 | 10 25 | 17 28 | 29 13 | 01 32 |
| 49 | 13 50 | 09 48 | 17 03 | 29 23 | 01 47 |
| 50 | 13 27 | 09 07 | 16 35 | 29 34 | 02 03 |
| 51 | 13 03 | 08 24 | 16 04 | 29 45 | 02 20 |
| 52 | 12 37 | 07 36 | 15 28 | 29 58 | 02 38 |
| 53 | 12 09 | 06 44 | 14 47 | 00♉11 | 02 58 |
| 54 | 11 39 | 05 46 | 14 01 | 00 25 | 03 19 |
| 55 | 11 06 | 04 42 | 13 06 | 00 39 | 03 43 |
| 56 | 10 31 | 03 31 | 12 03 | 00 55 | 04 08 |
| 57 | 09 52 | 02 12 | 10 46 | 01 11 | 04 36 |
| 58 | 09 10 | 00 42 | 09 14 | 01 28 | 05 06 |
| 59 | 08 23 | 29♑00 | 07 20 | 01 45 | 05 40 |
| 60 | 07♑31 | 27♑02 | 04♓55 | 02♉00 | 06♊18 |

**17h 40m 0s — 265° 0' 0" — 25 ♐ 25**

| LAT. | 11 | 12 | ASC | 2 | 3 |
|---|---|---|---|---|---|
| 0 | 23♑10 | 22♒39 | 24♓33 | 26♈57 | 27♉17 |
| 5 | 22 39 | 22 06 | 24 20 | 27 09 | 27 37 |
| 10 | 22 08 | 21 30 | 24 06 | 27 23 | 27 58 |
| 15 | 21 34 | 20 50 | 23 50 | 27 39 | 28 21 |
| 20 | 20 57 | 20 06 | 23 32 | 27 56 | 28 46 |
| 21 | 20 49 | 19 56 | 23 28 | 28 00 | 28 51 |
| 22 | 20 42 | 19 46 | 23 24 | 28 04 | 28 57 |
| 23 | 20 33 | 19 36 | 23 20 | 28 08 | 29 02 |
| 24 | 20 25 | 19 26 | 23 15 | 28 12 | 29 08 |
| 25 | 20 17 | 19 15 | 23 11 | 28 16 | 29 14 |
| 26 | 20 08 | 19 04 | 23 06 | 28 20 | 29 20 |
| 27 | 19 59 | 18 52 | 23 01 | 28 25 | 29 26 |
| 28 | 19 50 | 18 40 | 22 56 | 28 30 | 29 33 |
| 29 | 19 41 | 18 28 | 22 50 | 28 34 | 29 39 |
| 30 | 19 31 | 18 15 | 22 44 | 28 39 | 29 46 |
| 31 | 19 21 | 18 02 | 22 38 | 28 45 | 29 53 |
| 32 | 19 11 | 17 48 | 22 32 | 28 50 | 00♊00 |
| 33 | 19 00 | 17 33 | 22 26 | 28 56 | 00 07 |
| 34 | 18 49 | 17 18 | 22 19 | 29 01 | 00 15 |
| 35 | 18 38 | 17 03 | 22 11 | 29 08 | 00 23 |
| 36 | 18 26 | 16 46 | 22 04 | 29 14 | 00 32 |
| 37 | 18 14 | 16 29 | 21 55 | 29 21 | 00 40 |
| 38 | 18 01 | 16 11 | 21 47 | 29 28 | 00 49 |
| 39 | 17 48 | 15 52 | 21 37 | 29 35 | 00 59 |
| 40 | 17 35 | 15 32 | 21 27 | 29 43 | 01 08 |
| 41 | 17 20 | 15 10 | 21 17 | 29 51 | 01 19 |
| 42 | 17 06 | 14 48 | 21 05 | 29 59 | 01 29 |
| 43 | 16 50 | 14 24 | 20 53 | 00♉08 | 01 41 |
| 44 | 16 34 | 13 59 | 20 39 | 00 18 | 01 53 |
| 45 | 16 17 | 13 32 | 20 25 | 00 28 | 02 05 |
| 46 | 15 59 | 13 03 | 20 09 | 00 39 | 02 18 |
| 47 | 15 40 | 12 32 | 19 52 | 00 50 | 02 32 |
| 48 | 15 20 | 11 59 | 19 32 | 01 02 | 02 47 |
| 49 | 14 58 | 11 23 | 19 11 | 01 16 | 03 03 |
| 50 | 14 36 | 10 44 | 18 47 | 01 30 | 03 20 |
| 51 | 14 12 | 10 02 | 18 21 | 01 45 | 03 38 |
| 52 | 13 46 | 09 16 | 17 51 | 02 01 | 03 57 |
| 53 | 13 18 | 08 26 | 17 16 | 02 19 | 04 18 |
| 54 | 12 48 | 07 30 | 16 37 | 02 38 | 04 40 |
| 55 | 12 16 | 06 29 | 15 51 | 03 00 | 05 05 |
| 56 | 11 41 | 05 20 | 14 57 | 03 23 | 05 32 |
| 57 | 11 03 | 04 03 | 13 52 | 03 48 | 06 01 |
| 58 | 10 21 | 02 35 | 12 33 | 04 15 | 06 34 |
| 59 | 09 35 | 00 55 | 10 54 | 04 45 | 07 10 |
| 60 | 08♑43 | 29♑00 | 08♓48 | 05♉18 | 07♊50 |

**17h 44m 0s — 266° 0' 0" — 26 ♐ 20**

| LAT. | 11 | 12 | ASC | 2 | 3 |
|---|---|---|---|---|---|
| 0 | 24♑06 | 23♒41 | 25♓38 | 28♈00 | 28♉15 |
| 5 | 23 37 | 23 09 | 25 28 | 28 15 | 28 36 |
| 10 | 23 06 | 22 35 | 25 17 | 28 31 | 28 58 |
| 15 | 22 34 | 21 58 | 25 04 | 28 49 | 29 22 |
| 20 | 21 58 | 21 16 | 24 50 | 29 09 | 29 49 |
| 21 | 21 50 | 21 07 | 24 46 | 29 14 | 29 54 |
| 22 | 21 43 | 20 58 | 24 43 | 29 18 | 00♊00 |
| 23 | 21 35 | 20 48 | 24 40 | 29 23 | 00 06 |
| 24 | 21 27 | 20 38 | 24 36 | 29 28 | 00 12 |
| 25 | 21 19 | 20 28 | 24 32 | 29 33 | 00 18 |
| 26 | 21 10 | 20 17 | 24 28 | 29 38 | 00 24 |
| 27 | 21 01 | 20 07 | 24 24 | 29 43 | 00 31 |
| 28 | 20 52 | 19 55 | 24 20 | 29 48 | 00 38 |
| 29 | 20 43 | 19 44 | 24 16 | 29 54 | 00 44 |
| 30 | 20 34 | 19 31 | 24 11 | 00♉00 | 00 52 |
| 31 | 20 24 | 19 19 | 24 07 | 00 06 | 00 59 |
| 32 | 20 14 | 19 06 | 24 02 | 00 12 | 01 06 |
| 33 | 20 04 | 18 52 | 23 56 | 00 19 | 01 14 |
| 34 | 19 53 | 18 38 | 23 51 | 00 26 | 01 22 |
| 35 | 19 42 | 18 23 | 23 45 | 00 33 | 01 31 |
| 36 | 19 31 | 18 07 | 23 39 | 00 41 | 01 39 |
| 37 | 19 19 | 17 51 | 23 32 | 00 48 | 01 49 |
| 38 | 19 07 | 17 34 | 23 25 | 00 57 | 01 58 |
| 39 | 18 54 | 17 16 | 23 17 | 01 05 | 02 08 |
| 40 | 18 40 | 16 57 | 23 09 | 01 15 | 02 18 |
| 41 | 18 27 | 16 36 | 23 01 | 01 24 | 02 29 |
| 42 | 18 12 | 16 15 | 22 52 | 01 34 | 02 40 |
| 43 | 17 57 | 15 52 | 22 42 | 01 45 | 02 52 |
| 44 | 17 41 | 15 28 | 22 31 | 01 57 | 03 04 |
| 45 | 17 24 | 15 03 | 22 19 | 02 09 | 03 18 |
| 46 | 17 06 | 14 35 | 22 06 | 02 22 | 03 31 |
| 47 | 16 48 | 14 06 | 21 52 | 02 36 | 03 46 |
| 48 | 16 28 | 13 34 | 21 37 | 02 51 | 04 02 |
| 49 | 16 07 | 13 00 | 21 20 | 03 07 | 04 18 |
| 50 | 15 45 | 12 23 | 21 01 | 03 24 | 04 36 |
| 51 | 15 21 | 11 43 | 20 39 | 03 43 | 04 55 |
| 52 | 14 56 | 10 59 | 20 15 | 04 03 | 05 15 |
| 53 | 14 29 | 10 11 | 19 47 | 04 26 | 05 37 |
| 54 | 13 59 | 09 17 | 19 15 | 04 50 | 06 00 |
| 55 | 13 27 | 08 18 | 18 38 | 05 17 | 06 26 |
| 56 | 12 53 | 07 12 | 17 54 | 05 47 | 06 54 |
| 57 | 12 15 | 05 58 | 17 01 | 06 20 | 07 25 |
| 58 | 11 34 | 04 33 | 15 56 | 06 57 | 07 59 |
| 59 | 10 48 | 02 56 | 14 35 | 07 39 | 08 37 |
| 60 | 09♑56 | 01♒03 | 12♓51 | 08♉27 | 09♊20 |

**17h 48m 0s — 267° 0' 0" — 27 ♐ 15**

| LAT. | 11 | 12 | ASC | 2 | 3 |
|---|---|---|---|---|---|
| 0 | 25♑03 | 24♒42 | 26♓44 | 29♈03 | 29♉13 |
| 5 | 24 35 | 24 13 | 26 36 | 29 20 | 29 35 |
| 10 | 24 05 | 23 41 | 26 28 | 29 39 | 29 58 |
| 15 | 23 33 | 23 06 | 26 18 | 29 59 | 00♊24 |
| 20 | 22 59 | 22 27 | 26 07 | 00♉22 | 00 51 |
| 21 | 22 52 | 22 18 | 26 05 | 00 27 | 00 57 |
| 22 | 22 44 | 22 10 | 26 02 | 00 32 | 01 03 |
| 23 | 22 36 | 22 00 | 26 00 | 00 38 | 01 09 |
| 24 | 22 29 | 21 51 | 25 57 | 00 43 | 01 15 |
| 25 | 22 21 | 21 42 | 25 54 | 00 49 | 01 22 |
| 26 | 22 12 | 21 32 | 25 51 | 00 55 | 01 28 |
| 27 | 22 04 | 21 21 | 25 48 | 01 01 | 01 35 |
| 28 | 21 55 | 21 11 | 25 45 | 01 07 | 01 42 |
| 29 | 21 46 | 21 00 | 25 42 | 01 13 | 01 49 |
| 30 | 21 37 | 20 48 | 25 38 | 01 20 | 01 57 |
| 31 | 21 28 | 20 36 | 25 35 | 01 27 | 02 05 |
| 32 | 21 18 | 20 24 | 25 31 | 01 34 | 02 12 |
| 33 | 21 08 | 20 11 | 25 27 | 01 42 | 02 21 |
| 34 | 20 58 | 19 58 | 25 23 | 01 50 | 02 29 |
| 35 | 20 47 | 19 44 | 25 18 | 01 58 | 02 38 |
| 36 | 20 36 | 19 29 | 25 14 | 02 07 | 02 47 |
| 37 | 20 24 | 19 14 | 25 09 | 02 16 | 02 57 |
| 38 | 20 12 | 18 57 | 25 04 | 02 25 | 03 06 |
| 39 | 20 00 | 18 40 | 24 58 | 02 35 | 03 17 |
| 40 | 19 47 | 18 22 | 24 52 | 02 46 | 03 27 |
| 41 | 19 33 | 18 03 | 24 45 | 02 57 | 03 39 |
| 42 | 19 19 | 17 43 | 24 38 | 03 09 | 03 50 |
| 43 | 19 04 | 17 22 | 24 31 | 03 21 | 04 03 |
| 44 | 18 48 | 16 59 | 24 23 | 03 35 | 04 16 |
| 45 | 18 32 | 16 35 | 24 14 | 03 49 | 04 29 |
| 46 | 18 15 | 16 09 | 24 04 | 04 04 | 04 44 |
| 47 | 17 56 | 15 41 | 23 54 | 04 20 | 04 59 |
| 48 | 17 37 | 15 11 | 23 42 | 04 37 | 05 15 |
| 49 | 17 16 | 14 39 | 23 29 | 04 56 | 05 33 |
| 50 | 16 55 | 14 04 | 23 15 | 05 17 | 05 51 |
| 51 | 16 31 | 13 25 | 22 59 | 05 39 | 06 11 |
| 52 | 16 06 | 12 44 | 22 40 | 06 03 | 06 32 |
| 53 | 15 40 | 11 58 | 22 19 | 06 29 | 06 54 |
| 54 | 15 11 | 11 07 | 21 55 | 06 59 | 07 19 |
| 55 | 14 40 | 10 10 | 21 27 | 07 31 | 07 46 |
| 56 | 14 06 | 09 07 | 20 53 | 08 07 | 08 15 |
| 57 | 13 28 | 07 56 | 20 13 | 08 48 | 08 47 |
| 58 | 12 47 | 06 35 | 19 24 | 09 34 | 09 23 |
| 59 | 12 02 | 05 01 | 18 21 | 10 27 | 10 03 |
| 60 | 11♑10 | 03♒12 | 17♓01 | 11♉28 | 10♊47 |

**17h 52m 0s — 268° 0' 0" — 28 ♐ 10**

| LAT. | 11 | 12 | ASC | 2 | 3 |
|---|---|---|---|---|---|
| 0 | 26♑00 | 25♒44 | 27♓49 | 00♉06 | 00♊11 |
| 5 | 25 33 | 25 17 | 27 44 | 00 25 | 00 34 |
| 10 | 25 04 | 24 47 | 27 38 | 00 46 | 00 58 |
| 15 | 24 33 | 24 15 | 27 32 | 01 09 | 01 25 |
| 20 | 24 00 | 23 38 | 27 25 | 01 35 | 01 53 |
| 21 | 23 53 | 23 30 | 27 23 | 01 40 | 01 59 |
| 22 | 23 46 | 23 22 | 27 21 | 01 46 | 02 06 |
| 23 | 23 38 | 23 13 | 27 20 | 01 52 | 02 12 |
| 24 | 23 31 | 23 05 | 27 18 | 01 58 | 02 19 |
| 25 | 23 23 | 22 56 | 27 16 | 02 05 | 02 25 |
| 26 | 23 15 | 22 46 | 27 14 | 02 11 | 02 32 |
| 27 | 23 07 | 22 37 | 27 12 | 02 18 | 02 39 |
| 28 | 22 58 | 22 27 | 27 10 | 02 25 | 02 47 |
| 29 | 22 50 | 22 16 | 27 08 | 02 32 | 02 54 |
| 30 | 22 41 | 22 06 | 27 06 | 02 40 | 03 02 |
| 31 | 22 32 | 21 55 | 27 03 | 02 48 | 03 10 |
| 32 | 22 22 | 21 43 | 27 01 | 02 56 | 03 18 |
| 33 | 22 12 | 21 31 | 26 58 | 03 04 | 03 27 |
| 34 | 22 02 | 21 18 | 26 55 | 03 13 | 03 36 |
| 35 | 21 52 | 21 05 | 26 52 | 03 23 | 03 45 |
| 36 | 21 41 | 20 52 | 26 49 | 03 32 | 03 54 |
| 37 | 21 30 | 20 37 | 26 46 | 03 42 | 04 04 |
| 38 | 21 18 | 20 22 | 26 42 | 03 53 | 04 14 |
| 39 | 21 06 | 20 06 | 26 38 | 04 05 | 04 25 |
| 40 | 20 53 | 19 49 | 26 34 | 04 16 | 04 36 |
| 41 | 20 40 | 19 31 | 26 30 | 04 29 | 04 48 |
| 42 | 20 26 | 19 12 | 26 26 | 04 42 | 05 00 |
| 43 | 20 12 | 18 52 | 26 21 | 04 56 | 05 13 |
| 44 | 19 56 | 18 31 | 26 15 | 05 12 | 05 26 |
| 45 | 19 40 | 18 08 | 26 09 | 05 28 | 05 41 |
| 46 | 19 23 | 17 44 | 26 03 | 05 45 | 05 56 |
| 47 | 19 06 | 17 18 | 25 56 | 06 03 | 06 11 |
| 48 | 18 47 | 16 49 | 25 48 | 06 23 | 06 28 |
| 49 | 18 27 | 16 19 | 25 39 | 06 44 | 06 46 |
| 50 | 18 05 | 15 46 | 25 30 | 07 08 | 07 05 |
| 51 | 17 42 | 15 10 | 25 19 | 07 33 | 07 26 |
| 52 | 17 18 | 14 30 | 25 06 | 08 01 | 07 48 |
| 53 | 16 52 | 13 47 | 24 52 | 08 31 | 08 11 |
| 54 | 16 23 | 12 59 | 24 36 | 09 05 | 08 37 |
| 55 | 15 53 | 12 06 | 24 17 | 09 42 | 09 04 |
| 56 | 15 19 | 11 06 | 23 54 | 10 24 | 09 35 |
| 57 | 14 42 | 09 58 | 23 27 | 11 11 | 10 08 |
| 58 | 14 02 | 08 41 | 22 54 | 12 05 | 10 45 |
| 59 | 13 17 | 07 12 | 22 12 | 13 08 | 11 26 |
| 60 | 12♑26 | 05♒27 | 21♓17 | 14♉20 | 12♊13 |

**17h 56m 0s — 269° 0' 0" — 29 ♐ 05**

| LAT. | 11 | 12 | ASC | 2 | 3 |
|---|---|---|---|---|---|
| 0 | 26♑57 | 26♒47 | 28♓55 | 01♉08 | 01♊08 |
| 5 | 26 31 | 26 21 | 28 52 | 01 30 | 01 32 |
| 10 | 26 03 | 25 54 | 28 49 | 01 53 | 01 58 |
| 15 | 25 34 | 25 23 | 28 46 | 02 18 | 02 25 |
| 20 | 25 01 | 24 49 | 28 42 | 02 47 | 02 55 |
| 21 | 24 54 | 24 42 | 28 42 | 02 53 | 03 02 |
| 22 | 24 47 | 24 34 | 28 41 | 03 00 | 03 08 |
| 23 | 24 40 | 24 26 | 28 40 | 03 06 | 03 15 |
| 24 | 24 33 | 24 18 | 28 39 | 03 13 | 03 22 |
| 25 | 24 25 | 24 10 | 28 38 | 03 20 | 03 29 |
| 26 | 24 18 | 24 01 | 28 37 | 03 27 | 03 36 |
| 27 | 24 10 | 23 52 | 28 36 | 03 35 | 03 43 |
| 28 | 24 02 | 23 43 | 28 35 | 03 43 | 03 51 |
| 29 | 23 53 | 23 34 | 28 34 | 03 51 | 03 59 |
| 30 | 23 45 | 23 24 | 28 33 | 03 59 | 04 07 |
| 31 | 23 36 | 23 13 | 28 32 | 04 08 | 04 15 |
| 32 | 23 27 | 23 03 | 28 30 | 04 17 | 04 24 |
| 33 | 23 17 | 22 51 | 28 29 | 04 26 | 04 32 |
| 34 | 23 07 | 22 40 | 28 28 | 04 36 | 04 42 |
| 35 | 22 57 | 22 27 | 28 26 | 04 46 | 04 51 |
| 36 | 22 47 | 22 15 | 28 25 | 04 57 | 05 01 |
| 37 | 22 36 | 22 01 | 28 23 | 05 09 | 05 11 |
| 38 | 22 24 | 21 47 | 28 21 | 05 20 | 05 22 |
| 39 | 22 13 | 21 32 | 28 19 | 05 33 | 05 33 |
| 40 | 22 00 | 21 16 | 28 17 | 05 46 | 05 44 |
| 41 | 21 47 | 21 00 | 28 15 | 06 00 | 05 57 |
| 42 | 21 34 | 20 42 | 28 13 | 06 15 | 06 09 |
| 43 | 21 20 | 20 24 | 28 10 | 06 31 | 06 23 |
| 44 | 21 05 | 20 04 | 28 07 | 06 47 | 06 37 |
| 45 | 20 49 | 19 42 | 28 05 | 07 05 | 06 51 |
| 46 | 20 33 | 19 20 | 28 01 | 07 24 | 07 07 |
| 47 | 20 15 | 18 55 | 27 58 | 07 45 | 07 23 |
| 48 | 19 57 | 18 29 | 27 54 | 08 07 | 07 41 |
| 49 | 19 37 | 18 01 | 27 50 | 08 31 | 07 59 |
| 50 | 19 16 | 17 30 | 27 45 | 08 57 | 08 19 |
| 51 | 18 54 | 16 56 | 27 39 | 09 25 | 08 40 |
| 52 | 18 30 | 16 19 | 27 33 | 09 56 | 09 02 |
| 53 | 18 05 | 15 39 | 27 26 | 10 30 | 09 27 |
| 54 | 17 37 | 14 54 | 27 18 | 11 08 | 09 53 |
| 55 | 17 07 | 14 04 | 27 08 | 11 50 | 10 22 |
| 56 | 16 34 | 13 08 | 26 57 | 12 37 | 10 53 |
| 57 | 15 58 | 12 05 | 26 43 | 13 30 | 11 27 |
| 58 | 15 18 | 10 52 | 26 26 | 14 31 | 12 05 |
| 59 | 14 34 | 09 28 | 26 05 | 15 42 | 12 48 |
| 60 | 13♑44 | 07♒49 | 25♓38 | 17♉05 | 13♊36 |

**18h 0m 0s — 270° 0' 0" — 00 ♑ 00**

| LAT. | 11 | 12 | ASC | 2 | 3 |
|---|---|---|---|---|---|
| 0 | 27♑55 | 27♒49 | 00♈00 | 02♉11 | 02♊05 |
| 5 | 27 29 | 27 26 | 00 00 | 02 34 | 02 31 |
| 10 | 27 03 | 27 00 | 00 00 | 03 00 | 02 57 |
| 15 | 26 34 | 26 32 | 00 00 | 03 28 | 03 26 |
| 20 | 26 03 | 26 01 | 00 00 | 03 59 | 03 57 |
| 21 | 25 56 | 25 54 | 00 00 | 04 06 | 04 04 |
| 22 | 25 49 | 25 47 | 00 00 | 04 13 | 04 11 |
| 23 | 25 43 | 25 40 | 00 00 | 04 20 | 04 17 |
| 24 | 25 35 | 25 32 | 00 00 | 04 28 | 04 25 |
| 25 | 25 28 | 25 25 | 00 00 | 04 35 | 04 32 |
| 26 | 25 21 | 25 17 | 00 00 | 04 43 | 04 39 |
| 27 | 25 13 | 25 09 | 00 00 | 04 51 | 04 47 |
| 28 | 25 05 | 25 00 | 00 00 | 05 00 | 04 55 |
| 29 | 24 57 | 24 51 | 00 00 | 05 09 | 05 03 |
| 30 | 24 49 | 24 42 | 00 00 | 05 18 | 05 11 |
| 31 | 24 40 | 24 33 | 00 00 | 05 27 | 05 20 |
| 32 | 24 31 | 24 23 | 00 00 | 05 37 | 05 29 |
| 33 | 24 22 | 24 12 | 00 00 | 05 48 | 05 38 |
| 34 | 24 13 | 24 01 | 00 00 | 05 59 | 05 47 |
| 35 | 24 03 | 23 50 | 00 00 | 06 10 | 05 57 |
| 36 | 23 53 | 23 38 | 00 00 | 06 22 | 06 07 |
| 37 | 23 42 | 23 26 | 00 00 | 06 34 | 06 18 |
| 38 | 23 31 | 23 13 | 00 00 | 06 47 | 06 29 |
| 39 | 23 20 | 22 59 | 00 00 | 07 01 | 06 40 |
| 40 | 23 08 | 22 45 | 00 00 | 07 15 | 06 52 |
| 41 | 22 55 | 22 29 | 00 00 | 07 31 | 07 05 |
| 42 | 22 42 | 22 13 | 00 00 | 07 47 | 07 18 |
| 43 | 22 28 | 21 56 | 00 00 | 08 04 | 07 32 |
| 44 | 22 14 | 21 38 | 00 00 | 08 22 | 07 46 |
| 45 | 21 59 | 21 18 | 00 00 | 08 42 | 08 01 |
| 46 | 21 43 | 20 57 | 00 00 | 09 03 | 08 17 |
| 47 | 21 26 | 20 35 | 00 00 | 09 25 | 08 34 |
| 48 | 21 08 | 20 10 | 00 00 | 09 50 | 08 52 |
| 49 | 20 49 | 19 44 | 00 00 | 10 16 | 09 11 |
| 50 | 20 28 | 19 16 | 00 00 | 10 44 | 09 32 |
| 51 | 20 07 | 18 45 | 00 00 | 11 15 | 09 53 |
| 52 | 19 43 | 18 11 | 00 00 | 11 49 | 10 17 |
| 53 | 19 18 | 17 33 | 00 00 | 12 27 | 10 42 |
| 54 | 18 51 | 16 52 | 00 00 | 13 08 | 11 09 |
| 55 | 18 22 | 16 06 | 00 00 | 13 54 | 11 38 |
| 56 | 17 50 | 15 14 | 00 00 | 14 46 | 12 10 |
| 57 | 17 15 | 14 15 | 00 00 | 15 45 | 12 45 |
| 58 | 16 36 | 13 08 | 00 00 | 16 52 | 13 24 |
| 59 | 15 52 | 11 50 | 00 00 | 18 10 | 14 08 |
| 60 | 15♑03 | 10♒19 | 00♈00 | 19♉41 | 14♊57 |

**18h 4m 0s — 271° 0' 0" — 00 ♑ 55**

| LAT. | 11 | 12 | ASC | 2 | 3 |
|---|---|---|---|---|---|
| 0 | 28♑52 | 28♒52 | 01♈05 | 03♉13 | 03♊03 |
| 5 | 28 28 | 28 30 | 01 08 | 03 39 | 03 29 |
| 10 | 28 02 | 28 07 | 01 11 | 04 06 | 03 57 |
| 15 | 27 35 | 27 42 | 01 14 | 04 37 | 04 26 |
| 20 | 27 05 | 27 13 | 01 18 | 05 11 | 04 59 |
| 21 | 26 58 | 27 07 | 01 18 | 05 18 | 05 06 |
| 22 | 26 52 | 27 00 | 01 19 | 05 26 | 05 13 |
| 23 | 26 45 | 26 54 | 01 20 | 05 34 | 05 20 |
| 24 | 26 38 | 26 47 | 01 21 | 05 42 | 05 27 |
| 25 | 26 31 | 26 40 | 01 22 | 05 50 | 05 35 |
| 26 | 26 24 | 26 33 | 01 23 | 05 59 | 05 42 |
| 27 | 26 17 | 26 25 | 01 24 | 06 08 | 05 50 |
| 28 | 26 09 | 26 17 | 01 25 | 06 17 | 05 58 |
| 29 | 26 01 | 26 09 | 01 26 | 06 26 | 06 07 |
| 30 | 25 53 | 26 01 | 01 27 | 06 36 | 06 15 |
| 31 | 25 45 | 25 52 | 01 28 | 06 47 | 06 24 |
| 32 | 25 36 | 25 43 | 01 30 | 06 57 | 06 33 |
| 33 | 25 28 | 25 34 | 01 31 | 07 09 | 06 43 |
| 34 | 25 18 | 25 24 | 01 32 | 07 20 | 06 53 |
| 35 | 25 09 | 25 14 | 01 34 | 07 33 | 07 03 |
| 36 | 24 59 | 25 03 | 01 35 | 07 45 | 07 13 |
| 37 | 24 49 | 24 51 | 01 37 | 07 59 | 07 24 |
| 38 | 24 38 | 24 40 | 01 39 | 08 13 | 07 36 |
| 39 | 24 27 | 24 27 | 01 41 | 08 28 | 07 47 |
| 40 | 24 16 | 24 14 | 01 43 | 08 44 | 08 00 |
| 41 | 24 03 | 24 00 | 01 45 | 09 00 | 08 13 |
| 42 | 23 51 | 23 45 | 01 47 | 09 18 | 08 26 |
| 43 | 23 37 | 23 29 | 01 50 | 09 36 | 08 40 |
| 44 | 23 23 | 23 13 | 01 53 | 09 56 | 08 55 |
| 45 | 23 09 | 22 55 | 01 55 | 10 18 | 09 11 |
| 46 | 22 53 | 22 36 | 01 59 | 10 40 | 09 27 |
| 47 | 22 37 | 22 15 | 02 02 | 11 05 | 09 45 |
| 48 | 22 19 | 21 53 | 02 06 | 11 31 | 10 03 |
| 49 | 22 01 | 21 29 | 02 10 | 11 59 | 10 23 |
| 50 | 21 41 | 21 03 | 02 15 | 12 30 | 10 44 |
| 51 | 21 20 | 20 35 | 02 21 | 13 04 | 11 06 |
| 52 | 20 58 | 20 04 | 02 27 | 13 41 | 11 30 |
| 53 | 20 33 | 19 30 | 02 34 | 14 21 | 11 55 |
| 54 | 20 07 | 18 52 | 02 42 | 15 06 | 12 23 |
| 55 | 19 38 | 18 10 | 02 52 | 15 56 | 12 53 |
| 56 | 19 07 | 17 23 | 03 03 | 16 52 | 13 26 |
| 57 | 18 33 | 16 30 | 03 17 | 17 55 | 14 02 |
| 58 | 17 55 | 15 29 | 03 34 | 19 08 | 14 42 |
| 59 | 17 12 | 14 18 | 03 55 | 20 32 | 15 26 |
| 60 | 16♑24 | 12♒55 | 04♈22 | 22♉11 | 16♊16 |

# Koch Table of Houses for Latitudes 0° to 60° North

**18h 8m 0s — 272° 0' 0' — 01 ♑ 50**

| LAT. | 11 | 12 | ASC | 2 | 3 |
|---|---|---|---|---|---|
| 0 | 29♑49 | 29♒54 | 02♈11 | 04♉16 | 04♊00 |
| 5 | 29 26 | 29 35 | 02 16 | 04 43 | 04 27 |
| 10 | 29 02 | 29 14 | 02 22 | 05 13 | 04 56 |
| 15 | 28 35 | 28 51 | 02 28 | 05 45 | 05 27 |
| 20 | 28 07 | 28 25 | 02 35 | 06 22 | 06 00 |
| 21 | 28 01 | 28 20 | 02 37 | 06 30 | 06 07 |
| 22 | 27 54 | 28 14 | 02 39 | 06 38 | 06 14 |
| 23 | 27 48 | 28 08 | 02 40 | 06 47 | 06 22 |
| 24 | 27 41 | 28 02 | 02 42 | 06 55 | 06 29 |
| 25 | 27 35 | 27 55 | 02 44 | 07 04 | 06 37 |
| 26 | 27 28 | 27 49 | 02 46 | 07 14 | 06 45 |
| 27 | 27 21 | 27 42 | 02 48 | 07 23 | 06 53 |
| 28 | 27 13 | 27 35 | 02 50 | 07 33 | 07 02 |
| 29 | 27 06 | 27 28 | 02 52 | 07 44 | 07 10 |
| 30 | 26 58 | 27 20 | 02 54 | 07 54 | 07 19 |
| 31 | 26 50 | 27 12 | 02 57 | 08 05 | 07 28 |
| 32 | 26 42 | 27 04 | 02 59 | 08 17 | 07 38 |
| 33 | 26 33 | 26 56 | 03 02 | 08 29 | 07 48 |
| 34 | 26 24 | 26 47 | 03 05 | 08 42 | 07 58 |
| 35 | 26 15 | 26 37 | 03 08 | 08 55 | 08 08 |
| 36 | 26 06 | 26 28 | 03 11 | 09 08 | 08 19 |
| 37 | 25 56 | 26 18 | 03 14 | 09 23 | 08 30 |
| 38 | 25 46 | 26 07 | 03 18 | 09 38 | 08 42 |
| 39 | 25 35 | 25 55 | 03 22 | 09 54 | 08 54 |
| 40 | 25 24 | 25 44 | 03 26 | 10 11 | 09 07 |
| 41 | 25 12 | 25 31 | 03 30 | 10 29 | 09 20 |
| 42 | 25 00 | 25 18 | 03 34 | 10 48 | 09 34 |
| 43 | 24 47 | 25 04 | 03 39 | 11 08 | 09 48 |
| 44 | 24 34 | 24 48 | 03 45 | 11 29 | 10 04 |
| 45 | 24 19 | 24 32 | 03 51 | 11 52 | 10 20 |
| 46 | 24 04 | 24 15 | 03 57 | 12 16 | 10 37 |
| 47 | 23 49 | 23 57 | 04 04 | 12 42 | 10 54 |
| 48 | 23 32 | 23 37 | 04 12 | 13 11 | 11 13 |
| 49 | 23 14 | 23 16 | 04 21 | 13 41 | 11 33 |
| 50 | 22 55 | 22 52 | 04 30 | 14 14 | 11 55 |
| 51 | 22 34 | 22 27 | 04 41 | 14 50 | 12 18 |
| 52 | 22 12 | 21 59 | 04 54 | 15 30 | 12 42 |
| 53 | 21 49 | 21 29 | 05 08 | 16 13 | 13 08 |
| 54 | 21 23 | 20 55 | 05 24 | 17 01 | 13 37 |
| 55 | 20 56 | 20 18 | 05 43 | 17 54 | 14 07 |
| 56 | 20 25 | 19 36 | 06 06 | 18 54 | 14 41 |
| 57 | 19 52 | 18 49 | 06 33 | 20 02 | 15 18 |
| 58 | 19 15 | 17 55 | 07 06 | 21 19 | 15 58 |
| 59 | 18 34 | 16 52 | 07 48 | 22 48 | 16 43 |
| 60 | 17♑47 | 15♒40 | 08♈43 | 24♉33 | 17♊34 |

**18h 12m 0s — 273° 0' 0' — 02 ♑ 45**

| LAT. | 11 | 12 | ASC | 2 | 3 |
|---|---|---|---|---|---|
| 0 | 00♒47 | 00♓57 | 03♈16 | 05♉18 | 04♊57 |
| 5 | 00 25 | 00 40 | 03 24 | 05 47 | 05 25 |
| 10 | 00 02 | 00 21 | 03 32 | 06 19 | 05 55 |
| 15 | 29♑36 | 00 01 | 03 42 | 06 54 | 06 27 |
| 20 | 29 09 | 29♒38 | 03 53 | 07 33 | 07 01 |
| 21 | 29 03 | 29 33 | 03 55 | 07 42 | 07 08 |
| 22 | 28 57 | 29 28 | 03 58 | 07 50 | 07 16 |
| 23 | 28 51 | 29 22 | 04 00 | 08 00 | 07 24 |
| 24 | 28 45 | 29 17 | 04 03 | 08 09 | 07 31 |
| 25 | 28 38 | 29 11 | 04 06 | 08 18 | 07 39 |
| 26 | 28 32 | 29 05 | 04 09 | 08 28 | 07 48 |
| 27 | 28 25 | 28 59 | 04 12 | 08 39 | 07 56 |
| 28 | 28 18 | 28 53 | 04 15 | 08 49 | 08 05 |
| 29 | 28 11 | 28 47 | 04 18 | 09 00 | 08 14 |
| 30 | 28 03 | 28 40 | 04 22 | 09 12 | 08 23 |
| 31 | 27 55 | 28 33 | 04 25 | 09 24 | 08 32 |
| 32 | 27 48 | 28 26 | 04 29 | 09 36 | 08 42 |
| 33 | 27 39 | 28 18 | 04 33 | 09 49 | 08 52 |
| 34 | 27 31 | 28 10 | 04 37 | 10 02 | 09 02 |
| 35 | 27 22 | 28 02 | 04 42 | 10 16 | 09 13 |
| 36 | 27 13 | 27 53 | 04 46 | 10 31 | 09 24 |
| 37 | 27 03 | 27 44 | 04 51 | 10 46 | 09 36 |
| 38 | 26 54 | 27 35 | 04 56 | 11 03 | 09 48 |
| 39 | 26 43 | 27 25 | 05 02 | 11 20 | 10 00 |
| 40 | 26 33 | 27 14 | 05 08 | 11 38 | 10 13 |
| 41 | 26 21 | 27 03 | 05 15 | 11 57 | 10 27 |
| 42 | 26 10 | 26 51 | 05 22 | 12 17 | 10 41 |
| 43 | 25 57 | 26 39 | 05 29 | 12 38 | 10 56 |
| 44 | 25 44 | 26 25 | 05 37 | 13 01 | 11 12 |
| 45 | 25 31 | 26 11 | 05 46 | 13 25 | 11 28 |
| 46 | 25 16 | 25 56 | 05 56 | 13 51 | 11 45 |
| 47 | 25 01 | 25 40 | 06 06 | 14 19 | 12 04 |
| 48 | 24 45 | 25 23 | 06 18 | 14 49 | 12 23 |
| 49 | 24 27 | 25 04 | 06 31 | 15 21 | 12 44 |
| 50 | 24 09 | 24 43 | 06 45 | 15 56 | 13 05 |
| 51 | 23 49 | 24 21 | 07 01 | 16 35 | 13 29 |
| 52 | 23 28 | 23 57 | 07 20 | 17 16 | 13 54 |
| 53 | 23 06 | 23 31 | 07 41 | 18 02 | 14 20 |
| 54 | 22 41 | 23 01 | 08 05 | 18 53 | 14 49 |
| 55 | 22 14 | 22 29 | 08 33 | 19 50 | 15 20 |
| 56 | 21 45 | 21 53 | 09 07 | 20 53 | 15 54 |
| 57 | 21 13 | 21 12 | 09 47 | 22 04 | 16 32 |
| 58 | 20 37 | 20 26 | 10 36 | 23 25 | 17 13 |
| 59 | 19 57 | 19 33 | 11 39 | 24 59 | 17 58 |
| 60 | 19♑13 | 18♒32 | 12♈59 | 26♉48 | 18♊50 |

**18h 16m 0s — 274° 0' 0' — 03 ♑ 40**

| LAT. | 11 | 12 | ASC | 2 | 3 |
|---|---|---|---|---|---|
| 0 | 01♒45 | 02♓00 | 04♈22 | 06♉19 | 05♊54 |
| 5 | 01 24 | 01 45 | 04 32 | 06 51 | 06 23 |
| 10 | 01 02 | 01 29 | 04 43 | 07 25 | 06 54 |
| 15 | 00 38 | 01 11 | 04 56 | 08 02 | 07 26 |
| 20 | 00 11 | 00 51 | 05 10 | 08 44 | 08 02 |
| 21 | 00 06 | 00 46 | 05 14 | 08 53 | 08 10 |
| 22 | 00 00 | 00 42 | 05 17 | 09 02 | 08 17 |
| 23 | 29♑54 | 00 37 | 05 20 | 09 12 | 08 25 |
| 24 | 29 48 | 00 32 | 05 24 | 09 22 | 08 33 |
| 25 | 29 42 | 00 27 | 05 28 | 09 32 | 08 41 |
| 26 | 29 36 | 00 22 | 05 32 | 09 43 | 08 50 |
| 27 | 29 29 | 00 17 | 05 36 | 09 53 | 08 59 |
| 28 | 29 22 | 00 12 | 05 40 | 10 05 | 09 08 |
| 29 | 29 16 | 00 06 | 05 44 | 10 16 | 09 17 |
| 30 | 29 08 | 00 00 | 05 49 | 10 29 | 09 26 |
| 31 | 29 01 | 29♒54 | 05 53 | 10 41 | 09 36 |
| 32 | 28 54 | 29 48 | 05 58 | 10 54 | 09 46 |
| 33 | 28 46 | 29 41 | 06 04 | 11 08 | 09 56 |
| 34 | 28 38 | 29 34 | 06 09 | 11 22 | 10 07 |
| 35 | 28 29 | 29 27 | 06 15 | 11 37 | 10 18 |
| 36 | 28 21 | 29 19 | 06 21 | 11 53 | 10 29 |
| 37 | 28 11 | 29 12 | 06 28 | 12 09 | 10 41 |
| 38 | 28 02 | 29 03 | 06 35 | 12 26 | 10 53 |
| 39 | 27 52 | 28 55 | 06 43 | 12 44 | 11 06 |
| 40 | 27 42 | 28 45 | 06 51 | 13 03 | 11 20 |
| 41 | 27 31 | 28 36 | 06 59 | 13 24 | 11 33 |
| 42 | 27 20 | 28 26 | 07 08 | 13 45 | 11 48 |
| 43 | 27 08 | 28 15 | 07 18 | 14 08 | 12 03 |
| 44 | 26 56 | 28 03 | 07 29 | 14 32 | 12 19 |
| 45 | 26 42 | 27 51 | 07 41 | 14 57 | 12 36 |
| 46 | 26 29 | 27 38 | 07 54 | 15 25 | 12 54 |
| 47 | 26 14 | 27 24 | 08 08 | 15 54 | 13 12 |
| 48 | 25 58 | 27 09 | 08 23 | 16 26 | 13 32 |
| 49 | 25 42 | 26 53 | 08 40 | 17 00 | 13 53 |
| 50 | 25 24 | 26 36 | 08 59 | 17 37 | 14 15 |
| 51 | 25 05 | 26 17 | 09 21 | 18 17 | 14 39 |
| 52 | 24 45 | 25 57 | 09 45 | 19 01 | 15 04 |
| 53 | 24 23 | 25 35 | 10 13 | 19 49 | 15 31 |
| 54 | 24 00 | 25 10 | 10 45 | 20 43 | 16 01 |
| 55 | 23 34 | 24 43 | 11 22 | 21 42 | 16 33 |
| 56 | 23 06 | 24 13 | 12 06 | 22 48 | 17 07 |
| 57 | 22 35 | 23 40 | 12 59 | 24 02 | 17 45 |
| 58 | 22 01 | 23 03 | 14 04 | 25 27 | 18 26 |
| 59 | 21 23 | 22 21 | 15 25 | 27 04 | 19 12 |
| 60 | 20♑40 | 21♒33 | 17♈09 | 28♉57 | 20♊04 |

**18h 20m 0s — 275° 0' 0' — 04 ♑ 35**

| LAT. | 11 | 12 | ASC | 2 | 3 |
|---|---|---|---|---|---|
| 0 | 02♒43 | 03♓03 | 05♈27 | 07♉21 | 06♊50 |
| 5 | 02 23 | 02 51 | 05 40 | 07 54 | 07 21 |
| 10 | 02 02 | 02 37 | 05 54 | 08 30 | 07 52 |
| 15 | 01 39 | 02 21 | 06 10 | 09 10 | 08 26 |
| 20 | 01 14 | 02 04 | 06 28 | 09 54 | 09 03 |
| 21 | 01 09 | 02 00 | 06 32 | 10 04 | 09 11 |
| 22 | 01 03 | 01 56 | 06 36 | 10 14 | 09 18 |
| 23 | 00 58 | 01 52 | 06 40 | 10 24 | 09 27 |
| 24 | 00 52 | 01 48 | 06 45 | 10 34 | 09 35 |
| 25 | 00 46 | 01 44 | 06 49 | 10 45 | 09 43 |
| 26 | 00 40 | 01 40 | 06 54 | 10 56 | 09 52 |
| 27 | 00 34 | 01 35 | 06 59 | 11 08 | 10 01 |
| 28 | 00 27 | 01 30 | 07 04 | 11 20 | 10 10 |
| 29 | 00 21 | 01 26 | 07 10 | 11 32 | 10 19 |
| 30 | 00 14 | 01 21 | 07 16 | 11 45 | 10 29 |
| 31 | 00 07 | 01 15 | 07 22 | 11 58 | 10 39 |
| 32 | 00 00 | 01 10 | 07 28 | 12 12 | 10 49 |
| 33 | 29♑53 | 01 04 | 07 34 | 12 27 | 11 00 |
| 34 | 29 45 | 00 59 | 07 41 | 12 42 | 11 11 |
| 35 | 29 37 | 00 52 | 07 49 | 12 57 | 11 22 |
| 36 | 29 28 | 00 46 | 07 56 | 13 14 | 11 34 |
| 37 | 29 20 | 00 39 | 08 05 | 13 31 | 11 46 |
| 38 | 29 11 | 00 32 | 08 13 | 13 49 | 11 59 |
| 39 | 29 01 | 00 25 | 08 23 | 14 08 | 12 12 |
| 40 | 28 52 | 00 17 | 08 33 | 14 28 | 12 25 |
| 41 | 28 41 | 00 09 | 08 43 | 14 50 | 12 40 |
| 42 | 28 31 | 00 01 | 08 55 | 15 12 | 12 54 |
| 43 | 28 19 | 29♒52 | 09 07 | 15 36 | 13 10 |
| 44 | 28 07 | 29 42 | 09 21 | 16 01 | 13 26 |
| 45 | 27 55 | 29 32 | 09 35 | 16 28 | 13 43 |
| 46 | 27 42 | 29 21 | 09 51 | 16 57 | 14 01 |
| 47 | 27 28 | 29 10 | 10 08 | 17 28 | 14 20 |
| 48 | 27 13 | 28 58 | 10 28 | 18 01 | 14 40 |
| 49 | 26 57 | 28 44 | 10 49 | 18 37 | 15 02 |
| 50 | 26 40 | 28 30 | 11 13 | 19 16 | 15 24 |
| 51 | 26 22 | 28 15 | 11 39 | 19 58 | 15 48 |
| 52 | 26 03 | 27 59 | 12 09 | 20 44 | 16 14 |
| 53 | 25 42 | 27 41 | 12 44 | 21 34 | 16 42 |
| 54 | 25 20 | 27 22 | 13 23 | 22 30 | 17 12 |
| 55 | 24 55 | 27 00 | 14 09 | 23 31 | 17 44 |
| 56 | 24 28 | 26 37 | 15 03 | 24 40 | 18 19 |
| 57 | 23 59 | 26 12 | 16 08 | 25 57 | 18 57 |
| 58 | 23 26 | 25 45 | 17 27 | 27 25 | 19 39 |
| 59 | 22 50 | 25 15 | 19 06 | 29 05 | 20 25 |
| 60 | 22♑10 | 24♒42 | 21♈12 | 01♊00 | 21♊17 |

**18h 24m 0s — 276° 0' 0' — 05 ♑ 30**

| LAT. | 11 | 12 | ASC | 2 | 3 |
|---|---|---|---|---|---|
| 0 | 03♒41 | 04♓07 | 06♈32 | 08♉23 | 07♊47 |
| 5 | 03 22 | 03 56 | 06 48 | 08 58 | 08 18 |
| 10 | 03 02 | 03 44 | 07 04 | 09 36 | 08 51 |
| 15 | 02 41 | 03 32 | 07 23 | 10 18 | 09 26 |
| 20 | 02 17 | 03 17 | 07 45 | 11 04 | 10 03 |
| 21 | 02 12 | 03 14 | 07 50 | 11 15 | 10 11 |
| 22 | 02 07 | 03 11 | 07 55 | 11 25 | 10 19 |
| 23 | 02 01 | 03 08 | 08 00 | 11 36 | 10 28 |
| 24 | 01 56 | 03 04 | 08 05 | 11 47 | 10 36 |
| 25 | 01 50 | 03 01 | 08 11 | 11 58 | 10 45 |
| 26 | 01 45 | 02 57 | 08 17 | 12 10 | 10 54 |
| 27 | 01 39 | 02 53 | 08 23 | 12 22 | 11 03 |
| 28 | 01 33 | 02 50 | 08 29 | 12 35 | 11 12 |
| 29 | 01 27 | 02 46 | 08 35 | 12 48 | 11 22 |
| 30 | 01 20 | 02 41 | 08 42 | 13 01 | 11 32 |
| 31 | 01 14 | 02 37 | 08 49 | 13 15 | 11 42 |
| 32 | 01 07 | 02 33 | 08 57 | 13 30 | 11 53 |
| 33 | 01 00 | 02 28 | 09 05 | 13 45 | 12 03 |
| 34 | 00 52 | 02 23 | 09 13 | 14 01 | 12 15 |
| 35 | 00 45 | 02 18 | 09 22 | 14 17 | 12 26 |
| 36 | 00 37 | 02 13 | 09 31 | 14 34 | 12 38 |
| 37 | 00 29 | 02 08 | 09 41 | 14 53 | 12 50 |
| 38 | 00 20 | 02 02 | 09 51 | 15 12 | 13 03 |
| 39 | 00 11 | 01 56 | 10 03 | 15 32 | 13 17 |
| 40 | 00 02 | 01 50 | 10 14 | 15 53 | 13 31 |
| 41 | 29♑52 | 01 44 | 10 27 | 16 15 | 13 45 |
| 42 | 29 42 | 01 37 | 10 41 | 16 38 | 14 00 |
| 43 | 29 31 | 01 30 | 10 56 | 17 03 | 14 16 |
| 44 | 29 20 | 01 22 | 11 12 | 17 30 | 14 33 |
| 45 | 29 08 | 01 14 | 11 29 | 17 58 | 14 50 |
| 46 | 28 55 | 01 06 | 11 48 | 18 28 | 15 09 |
| 47 | 28 42 | 00 57 | 12 09 | 19 00 | 15 28 |
| 48 | 28 28 | 00 47 | 12 32 | 19 35 | 15 48 |
| 49 | 28 13 | 00 37 | 12 57 | 20 12 | 16 10 |
| 50 | 27 57 | 00 26 | 13 25 | 20 53 | 16 33 |
| 51 | 27 40 | 00 15 | 13 56 | 21 36 | 16 57 |
| 52 | 27 22 | 00 02 | 14 32 | 22 24 | 17 23 |
| 53 | 27 02 | 29♒49 | 15 13 | 23 16 | 17 51 |
| 54 | 26 41 | 29 35 | 15 59 | 24 14 | 18 21 |
| 55 | 26 17 | 29 21 | 16 54 | 25 18 | 18 54 |
| 56 | 25 52 | 29 05 | 17 57 | 26 29 | 19 29 |
| 57 | 25 24 | 28 49 | 19 14 | 27 48 | 20 08 |
| 58 | 24 54 | 28 32 | 20 46 | 29 18 | 20 50 |
| 59 | 24 20 | 28 15 | 22 40 | 01♊00 | 21 37 |
| 60 | 23♑42 | 28♒00 | 25♈05 | 02♊58 | 22♊29 |

**18h 28m 0s — 277° 0' 0' — 06 ♑ 26**

| LAT. | 11 | 12 | ASC | 2 | 3 |
|---|---|---|---|---|---|
| 0 | 04♒39 | 05♓10 | 07♈37 | 09♉24 | 08♊43 |
| 5 | 04 22 | 05 02 | 07 55 | 10 01 | 09 16 |
| 10 | 04 03 | 04 52 | 08 15 | 10 41 | 09 49 |
| 15 | 03 42 | 04 42 | 08 37 | 11 25 | 10 25 |
| 20 | 03 20 | 04 31 | 09 03 | 12 14 | 11 04 |
| 21 | 03 15 | 04 28 | 09 08 | 12 25 | 11 12 |
| 22 | 03 10 | 04 26 | 09 14 | 12 36 | 11 20 |
| 23 | 03 05 | 04 23 | 09 20 | 12 47 | 11 29 |
| 24 | 03 00 | 04 21 | 09 26 | 12 59 | 11 37 |
| 25 | 02 55 | 04 18 | 09 32 | 13 11 | 11 46 |
| 26 | 02 50 | 04 15 | 09 39 | 13 23 | 11 55 |
| 27 | 02 44 | 04 12 | 09 46 | 13 36 | 12 05 |
| 28 | 02 38 | 04 09 | 09 53 | 13 49 | 12 14 |
| 29 | 02 33 | 04 06 | 10 01 | 14 02 | 12 24 |
| 30 | 02 27 | 04 03 | 10 09 | 14 17 | 12 34 |
| 31 | 02 20 | 03 59 | 10 17 | 14 31 | 12 45 |
| 32 | 02 14 | 03 56 | 10 26 | 14 46 | 12 55 |
| 33 | 02 07 | 03 52 | 10 35 | 15 02 | 13 07 |
| 34 | 02 00 | 03 49 | 10 45 | 15 19 | 13 18 |
| 35 | 01 53 | 03 45 | 10 55 | 15 36 | 13 30 |
| 36 | 01 46 | 03 41 | 11 06 | 15 54 | 13 42 |
| 37 | 01 38 | 03 37 | 11 17 | 16 13 | 13 55 |
| 38 | 01 30 | 03 33 | 11 29 | 16 33 | 14 08 |
| 39 | 01 21 | 03 28 | 11 42 | 16 54 | 14 22 |
| 40 | 01 12 | 03 23 | 11 56 | 17 16 | 14 36 |
| 41 | 01 03 | 03 19 | 12 11 | 17 39 | 14 50 |
| 42 | 00 54 | 03 14 | 12 27 | 18 04 | 15 06 |
| 43 | 00 43 | 03 08 | 12 44 | 18 30 | 15 22 |
| 44 | 00 33 | 03 03 | 13 02 | 18 57 | 15 39 |
| 45 | 00 22 | 02 57 | 13 22 | 19 27 | 15 57 |
| 46 | 00 10 | 02 51 | 13 44 | 19 58 | 16 15 |
| 47 | 29♑57 | 02 44 | 14 08 | 20 31 | 16 35 |
| 48 | 29 44 | 02 38 | 14 34 | 21 07 | 16 56 |
| 49 | 29 30 | 02 31 | 15 04 | 21 46 | 17 18 |
| 50 | 29 15 | 02 23 | 15 36 | 22 28 | 17 41 |
| 51 | 28 59 | 02 16 | 16 12 | 23 13 | 18 06 |
| 52 | 28 41 | 02 08 | 16 53 | 24 03 | 18 32 |
| 53 | 28 23 | 02 00 | 17 40 | 24 57 | 19 00 |
| 54 | 28 03 | 01 52 | 18 34 | 25 56 | 19 31 |
| 55 | 27 41 | 01 44 | 19 36 | 27 01 | 20 03 |
| 56 | 27 17 | 01 36 | 20 48 | 28 14 | 20 39 |
| 57 | 26 52 | 01 29 | 22 15 | 29 36 | 21 18 |
| 58 | 26 23 | 01 24 | 23 59 | 01♊07 | 22 00 |
| 59 | 25 52 | 01 22 | 26 08 | 02 51 | 22 47 |
| 60 | 25♑17 | 01♓26 | 28♈50 | 04♊51 | 23♊39 |

**18h 32m 0s — 278° 0' 0' — 07 ♑ 21**

| LAT. | 11 | 12 | ASC | 2 | 3 |
|---|---|---|---|---|---|
| 0 | 05♒38 | 06♓14 | 08♈43 | 10♉25 | 09♊40 |
| 5 | 05 21 | 06 08 | 09 03 | 11 04 | 10 13 |
| 10 | 05 04 | 06 01 | 09 26 | 11 46 | 10 47 |
| 15 | 04 44 | 05 53 | 09 51 | 12 32 | 11 24 |
| 20 | 04 24 | 05 45 | 10 20 | 13 24 | 12 04 |
| 21 | 04 19 | 05 43 | 10 26 | 13 35 | 12 12 |
| 22 | 04 14 | 05 41 | 10 33 | 13 46 | 12 21 |
| 23 | 04 10 | 05 39 | 10 39 | 13 58 | 12 29 |
| 24 | 04 05 | 05 37 | 10 46 | 14 10 | 12 38 |
| 25 | 04 00 | 05 35 | 10 54 | 14 23 | 12 47 |
| 26 | 03 55 | 05 33 | 11 01 | 14 35 | 12 57 |
| 27 | 03 50 | 05 31 | 11 09 | 14 49 | 13 06 |
| 28 | 03 44 | 05 29 | 11 18 | 15 02 | 13 16 |
| 29 | 03 39 | 05 27 | 11 26 | 15 17 | 13 26 |
| 30 | 03 33 | 05 24 | 11 35 | 15 31 | 13 37 |
| 31 | 03 27 | 05 22 | 11 45 | 15 47 | 13 47 |
| 32 | 03 21 | 05 20 | 11 55 | 16 03 | 13 58 |
| 33 | 03 15 | 05 17 | 12 05 | 16 19 | 14 09 |
| 34 | 03 08 | 05 15 | 12 16 | 16 37 | 14 21 |
| 35 | 03 02 | 05 12 | 12 28 | 16 55 | 14 33 |
| 36 | 02 55 | 05 09 | 12 40 | 17 13 | 14 46 |
| 37 | 02 47 | 05 06 | 12 53 | 17 33 | 14 58 |
| 38 | 02 40 | 05 04 | 13 07 | 17 54 | 15 12 |
| 39 | 02 32 | 05 01 | 13 21 | 18 16 | 15 26 |
| 40 | 02 24 | 04 57 | 13 37 | 18 38 | 15 40 |
| 41 | 02 15 | 04 54 | 13 54 | 19 03 | 15 55 |
| 42 | 02 06 | 04 51 | 14 12 | 19 28 | 16 11 |
| 43 | 01 56 | 04 48 | 14 31 | 19 55 | 16 27 |
| 44 | 01 46 | 04 44 | 14 52 | 20 24 | 16 45 |
| 45 | 01 36 | 04 41 | 15 15 | 20 54 | 17 03 |
| 46 | 01 25 | 04 37 | 15 40 | 21 27 | 17 21 |
| 47 | 01 13 | 04 33 | 16 07 | 22 01 | 17 41 |
| 48 | 01 01 | 04 30 | 16 36 | 22 38 | 18 02 |
| 49 | 00 47 | 04 26 | 17 09 | 23 18 | 18 25 |
| 50 | 00 33 | 04 22 | 17 46 | 24 02 | 18 48 |
| 51 | 00 18 | 04 19 | 18 27 | 24 48 | 19 13 |
| 52 | 00 02 | 04 16 | 19 13 | 25 39 | 19 40 |
| 53 | 29♑45 | 04 13 | 20 05 | 26 35 | 20 08 |
| 54 | 29 26 | 04 11 | 21 05 | 27 36 | 20 39 |
| 55 | 29 06 | 04 10 | 22 15 | 28 43 | 21 12 |
| 56 | 28 44 | 04 10 | 23 36 | 29 57 | 21 48 |
| 57 | 28 20 | 04 14 | 25 12 | 01♊20 | 22 27 |
| 58 | 27 54 | 04 21 | 27 07 | 02 53 | 23 09 |
| 59 | 27 26 | 04 35 | 29 28 | 04 38 | 23 56 |
| 60 | 26♑54 | 04♓59 | 02♉24 | 06♊39 | 24♊48 |

**18h 36m 0s — 279° 0' 0' — 08 ♑ 16**

| LAT. | 11 | 12 | ASC | 2 | 3 |
|---|---|---|---|---|---|
| 0 | 06♒37 | 07♓18 | 09♈48 | 11♉26 | 10♊36 |
| 5 | 06 21 | 07 14 | 10 11 | 12 07 | 11 10 |
| 10 | 06 05 | 07 09 | 10 36 | 12 51 | 11 46 |
| 15 | 05 47 | 07 04 | 11 04 | 13 39 | 12 23 |
| 20 | 05 27 | 06 59 | 11 37 | 14 33 | 13 04 |
| 21 | 05 23 | 06 58 | 11 44 | 14 44 | 13 12 |
| 22 | 05 19 | 06 56 | 11 51 | 14 56 | 13 21 |
| 23 | 05 14 | 06 55 | 11 59 | 15 09 | 13 30 |
| 24 | 05 10 | 06 54 | 12 07 | 15 21 | 13 39 |
| 25 | 05 05 | 06 53 | 12 15 | 15 34 | 13 48 |
| 26 | 05 01 | 06 52 | 12 23 | 15 48 | 13 58 |
| 27 | 04 56 | 06 50 | 12 32 | 16 01 | 14 08 |
| 28 | 04 51 | 06 49 | 12 42 | 16 16 | 14 18 |
| 29 | 04 45 | 06 48 | 12 51 | 16 31 | 14 28 |
| 30 | 04 40 | 06 46 | 13 01 | 16 46 | 14 39 |
| 31 | 04 35 | 06 45 | 13 12 | 17 02 | 14 49 |
| 32 | 04 29 | 06 44 | 13 23 | 17 18 | 15 01 |
| 33 | 04 23 | 06 42 | 13 35 | 17 36 | 15 12 |
| 34 | 04 17 | 06 41 | 13 47 | 17 54 | 15 24 |
| 35 | 04 11 | 06 39 | 14 00 | 18 12 | 15 36 |
| 36 | 04 04 | 06 38 | 14 14 | 18 32 | 15 49 |
| 37 | 03 57 | 06 36 | 14 28 | 18 52 | 16 02 |
| 38 | 03 50 | 06 35 | 14 43 | 19 14 | 16 16 |
| 39 | 03 43 | 06 33 | 15 00 | 19 36 | 16 30 |
| 40 | 03 35 | 06 32 | 15 17 | 20 00 | 16 44 |
| 41 | 03 27 | 06 30 | 15 36 | 20 25 | 17 00 |
| 42 | 03 19 | 06 29 | 15 56 | 20 51 | 17 16 |
| 43 | 03 10 | 06 28 | 16 18 | 21 19 | 17 32 |
| 44 | 03 01 | 06 26 | 16 41 | 21 49 | 17 50 |
| 45 | 02 51 | 06 25 | 17 06 | 22 20 | 18 08 |
| 46 | 02 41 | 06 24 | 17 34 | 22 54 | 18 27 |
| 47 | 02 30 | 06 23 | 18 04 | 23 30 | 18 47 |
| 48 | 02 18 | 06 23 | 18 37 | 24 08 | 19 09 |
| 49 | 02 06 | 06 22 | 19 14 | 24 49 | 19 31 |
| 50 | 01 53 | 06 22 | 19 54 | 25 34 | 19 55 |
| 51 | 01 39 | 06 23 | 20 40 | 26 22 | 20 20 |
| 52 | 01 24 | 06 25 | 21 31 | 27 14 | 20 47 |
| 53 | 01 08 | 06 28 | 22 28 | 28 11 | 21 16 |
| 54 | 00 51 | 06 32 | 23 34 | 29 13 | 21 47 |
| 55 | 00 33 | 06 38 | 24 51 | 00♊21 | 22 20 |
| 56 | 00 13 | 06 48 | 26 19 | 01 37 | 22 56 |
| 57 | 29♑51 | 07 02 | 28 04 | 03 01 | 23 35 |
| 58 | 29 28 | 07 22 | 00♉09 | 04 35 | 24 17 |
| 59 | 29 02 | 07 53 | 02 40 | 06 22 | 25 04 |
| 60 | 28♑34 | 08♓40 | 05♉47 | 08♊22 | 25♊56 |

# Koch Table of Houses for Latitudes 0° to 60° North

| 18h 40m 0s | 280° 0' 0" | 09 ♑ 11 | | | |
|---|---|---|---|---|---|
| LAT. | 11 | 12 | ASC | 2 | 3 |
| 0 | 07♒35 | 08♓22 | 10♈53 | 12♉27 | 11♊32 |
| 5 | 07 21 | 08 20 | 11 18 | 13 09 | 12 07 |
| 10 | 07 06 | 08 18 | 11 46 | 13 55 | 12 43 |
| 15 | 06 49 | 08 15 | 12 18 | 14 46 | 13 22 |
| 20 | 06 31 | 08 13 | 12 54 | 15 42 | 14 04 |
| 21 | 06 27 | 08 13 | 13 01 | 15 54 | 14 12 |
| 22 | 06 23 | 08 12 | 13 10 | 16 06 | 14 21 |
| 23 | 06 19 | 08 12 | 13 18 | 16 19 | 14 30 |
| 24 | 06 15 | 08 11 | 13 27 | 16 32 | 14 40 |
| 25 | 06 11 | 08 11 | 13 36 | 16 45 | 14 49 |
| 26 | 06 06 | 08 10 | 13 45 | 16 59 | 14 59 |
| 27 | 06 02 | 08 10 | 13 55 | 17 14 | 15 09 |
| 28 | 05 57 | 08 10 | 14 05 | 17 29 | 15 19 |
| 29 | 05 52 | 08 09 | 14 16 | 17 44 | 15 29 |
| 30 | 05 47 | 08 09 | 14 27 | 18 00 | 15 40 |
| 31 | 05 42 | 08 08 | 14 39 | 18 16 | 15 51 |
| 32 | 05 37 | 08 08 | 14 51 | 18 34 | 16 03 |
| 33 | 05 32 | 08 08 | 15 04 | 18 52 | 16 14 |
| 34 | 05 26 | 08 07 | 15 17 | 19 10 | 16 26 |
| 35 | 05 20 | 08 07 | 15 32 | 19 30 | 16 39 |
| 36 | 05 14 | 08 07 | 15 47 | 19 50 | 16 52 |
| 37 | 05 08 | 08 07 | 16 03 | 20 11 | 17 05 |
| 38 | 05 01 | 08 07 | 16 20 | 20 33 | 17 19 |
| 39 | 04 55 | 08 07 | 16 38 | 20 56 | 17 33 |
| 40 | 04 47 | 08 07 | 16 57 | 21 21 | 17 48 |
| 41 | 04 40 | 08 07 | 17 18 | 21 47 | 18 04 |
| 42 | 04 32 | 08 08 | 17 40 | 22 14 | 18 20 |
| 43 | 04 24 | 08 08 | 18 04 | 22 43 | 18 37 |
| 44 | 04 15 | 08 09 | 18 29 | 23 13 | 18 55 |
| 45 | 04 06 | 08 11 | 18 57 | 23 46 | 19 13 |
| 46 | 03 57 | 08 12 | 19 28 | 24 20 | 19 32 |
| 47 | 03 47 | 08 14 | 20 01 | 24 57 | 19 53 |
| 48 | 03 36 | 08 17 | 20 37 | 25 36 | 20 14 |
| 49 | 03 25 | 08 20 | 21 17 | 26 18 | 20 37 |
| 50 | 03 13 | 08 24 | 22 01 | 27 04 | 21 01 |
| 51 | 03 01 | 08 29 | 22 51 | 27 53 | 21 26 |
| 52 | 02 47 | 08 36 | 23 46 | 28 46 | 21 54 |
| 53 | 02 33 | 08 44 | 24 49 | 29 44 | 22 22 |
| 54 | 02 17 | 08 55 | 26 01 | 00♊48 | 22 53 |
| 55 | 02 01 | 09 09 | 27 23 | 01 57 | 23 27 |
| 56 | 01 43 | 09 28 | 28 58 | 03 14 | 24 03 |
| 57 | 01 24 | 09 53 | 00♉51 | 04 39 | 24 42 |
| 58 | 01 03 | 10 28 | 03 04 | 06 14 | 25 24 |
| 59 | 00 41 | 11 16 | 05 44 | 08 01 | 26 11 |
| 60 | 00♒18 | 12♓27 | 09♉01 | 10♊02 | 27♊03 |

| 18h 44m 0s | 281° 0' 0" | 10 ♑ 07 | | | |
|---|---|---|---|---|---|
| LAT. | 11 | 12 | ASC | 2 | 3 |
| 0 | 08♒34 | 09♓26 | 11♈58 | 13♉27 | 12♊28 |
| 5 | 08 21 | 09 26 | 12 26 | 14 12 | 13 04 |
| 10 | 08 07 | 09 26 | 12 56 | 15 00 | 13 41 |
| 15 | 07 52 | 09 27 | 13 31 | 15 52 | 14 21 |
| 20 | 07 35 | 09 28 | 14 10 | 16 50 | 15 03 |
| 21 | 07 32 | 09 28 | 14 19 | 17 02 | 15 12 |
| 22 | 07 28 | 09 28 | 14 28 | 17 15 | 15 21 |
| 23 | 07 24 | 09 28 | 14 37 | 17 29 | 15 30 |
| 24 | 07 20 | 09 29 | 14 47 | 17 42 | 15 40 |
| 25 | 07 17 | 09 29 | 14 56 | 17 56 | 15 50 |
| 26 | 07 12 | 09 29 | 15 07 | 18 11 | 16 00 |
| 27 | 07 08 | 09 30 | 15 18 | 18 26 | 16 10 |
| 28 | 07 04 | 09 30 | 15 29 | 18 41 | 16 20 |
| 29 | 07 00 | 09 31 | 15 40 | 18 57 | 16 31 |
| 30 | 06 55 | 09 31 | 15 53 | 19 13 | 16 42 |
| 31 | 06 50 | 09 32 | 16 05 | 19 30 | 16 53 |
| 32 | 06 46 | 09 33 | 16 19 | 19 48 | 17 05 |
| 33 | 06 41 | 09 33 | 16 33 | 20 07 | 17 16 |
| 34 | 06 35 | 09 34 | 16 48 | 20 26 | 17 29 |
| 35 | 06 30 | 09 35 | 17 03 | 20 46 | 17 41 |
| 36 | 06 25 | 09 36 | 17 20 | 21 07 | 17 55 |
| 37 | 06 19 | 09 38 | 17 37 | 21 29 | 18 08 |
| 38 | 06 13 | 09 39 | 17 56 | 21 52 | 18 22 |
| 39 | 06 07 | 09 41 | 18 15 | 22 16 | 18 37 |
| 40 | 06 00 | 09 43 | 18 36 | 22 41 | 18 52 |
| 41 | 05 53 | 09 45 | 18 59 | 23 08 | 19 08 |
| 42 | 05 46 | 09 47 | 19 23 | 23 36 | 19 24 |
| 43 | 05 39 | 09 50 | 19 49 | 24 05 | 19 41 |
| 44 | 05 31 | 09 53 | 20 17 | 24 36 | 19 59 |
| 45 | 05 23 | 09 57 | 20 47 | 25 10 | 20 18 |
| 46 | 05 14 | 10 01 | 21 20 | 25 45 | 20 37 |
| 47 | 05 05 | 10 06 | 21 56 | 26 23 | 20 58 |
| 48 | 04 55 | 10 11 | 22 35 | 27 03 | 21 19 |
| 49 | 04 45 | 10 18 | 23 19 | 27 46 | 21 42 |
| 50 | 04 35 | 10 26 | 24 06 | 28 33 | 22 07 |
| 51 | 04 23 | 10 36 | 25 00 | 29 23 | 22 32 |
| 52 | 04 11 | 10 48 | 26 00 | 00♊17 | 22 59 |
| 53 | 03 58 | 11 02 | 27 07 | 01 16 | 23 29 |
| 54 | 03 45 | 11 20 | 28 24 | 02 20 | 24 00 |
| 55 | 03 30 | 11 42 | 29 52 | 03 31 | 24 33 |
| 56 | 03 15 | 12 10 | 01♉33 | 04 49 | 25 09 |
| 57 | 02 58 | 12 47 | 03 32 | 06 14 | 25 48 |
| 58 | 02 41 | 13 36 | 05 52 | 07 50 | 26 31 |
| 59 | 02 23 | 14 44 | 08 40 | 09 37 | 27 17 |
| 60 | 02♒04 | 16♓20 | 12♉04 | 11♊38 | 28♊09 |

| 18h 48m 0s | 282° 0' 0" | 11 ♑ 02 | | | |
|---|---|---|---|---|---|
| LAT. | 11 | 12 | ASC | 2 | 3 |
| 0 | 09♒34 | 10♓30 | 13♈03 | 14♉28 | 13♊24 |
| 5 | 09 22 | 10 32 | 13 33 | 15 14 | 14 01 |
| 10 | 09 09 | 10 35 | 14 06 | 16 04 | 14 39 |
| 15 | 08 55 | 10 38 | 14 44 | 16 58 | 15 19 |
| 20 | 08 40 | 10 42 | 15 27 | 17 58 | 16 03 |
| 21 | 08 36 | 10 43 | 15 36 | 18 11 | 16 12 |
| 22 | 08 33 | 10 44 | 15 46 | 18 24 | 16 21 |
| 23 | 08 30 | 10 45 | 15 56 | 18 38 | 16 30 |
| 24 | 08 26 | 10 46 | 16 06 | 18 52 | 16 40 |
| 25 | 08 23 | 10 47 | 16 17 | 19 07 | 16 50 |
| 26 | 08 19 | 10 49 | 16 28 | 19 21 | 17 00 |
| 27 | 08 15 | 10 50 | 16 40 | 19 37 | 17 10 |
| 28 | 08 11 | 10 51 | 16 52 | 19 53 | 17 21 |
| 29 | 08 07 | 10 53 | 17 05 | 20 09 | 17 32 |
| 30 | 08 03 | 10 54 | 17 18 | 20 26 | 17 43 |
| 31 | 07 59 | 10 56 | 17 32 | 20 44 | 17 54 |
| 32 | 07 54 | 10 58 | 17 46 | 21 02 | 18 06 |
| 33 | 07 50 | 11 00 | 18 01 | 21 21 | 18 18 |
| 34 | 07 45 | 11 02 | 18 17 | 21 41 | 18 31 |
| 35 | 07 40 | 11 04 | 18 34 | 22 02 | 18 44 |
| 36 | 07 35 | 11 06 | 18 52 | 22 23 | 18 57 |
| 37 | 07 30 | 11 09 | 19 11 | 22 46 | 19 11 |
| 38 | 07 25 | 11 12 | 19 31 | 23 09 | 19 25 |
| 39 | 07 19 | 11 15 | 19 52 | 23 34 | 19 40 |
| 40 | 07 13 | 11 19 | 20 15 | 24 00 | 19 55 |
| 41 | 07 07 | 11 23 | 20 39 | 24 27 | 20 11 |
| 42 | 07 01 | 11 27 | 21 05 | 24 56 | 20 28 |
| 43 | 06 54 | 11 32 | 21 33 | 25 27 | 20 45 |
| 44 | 06 47 | 11 37 | 22 03 | 25 59 | 21 03 |
| 45 | 06 40 | 11 43 | 22 36 | 26 33 | 21 22 |
| 46 | 06 32 | 11 50 | 23 11 | 27 09 | 21 42 |
| 47 | 06 24 | 11 58 | 23 50 | 27 47 | 22 02 |
| 48 | 06 15 | 12 07 | 24 32 | 28 29 | 22 24 |
| 49 | 06 06 | 12 18 | 25 18 | 29 13 | 22 47 |
| 50 | 05 57 | 12 30 | 26 10 | 00♊00 | 23 12 |
| 51 | 05 47 | 12 44 | 27 07 | 00 51 | 23 37 |
| 52 | 05 36 | 13 01 | 28 11 | 01 46 | 24 05 |
| 53 | 05 25 | 13 22 | 29 22 | 02 46 | 24 34 |
| 54 | 05 14 | 13 46 | 00♉44 | 03 51 | 25 05 |
| 55 | 05 01 | 14 17 | 02 17 | 05 02 | 25 39 |
| 56 | 04 48 | 14 55 | 04 04 | 06 21 | 26 15 |
| 57 | 04 35 | 15 44 | 06 08 | 07 47 | 26 54 |
| 58 | 04 21 | 16 48 | 08 35 | 09 23 | 27 36 |
| 59 | 04 07 | 18 15 | 11 29 | 11 10 | 28 23 |
| 60 | 03♒54 | 20♓16 | 14♉57 | 13♊10 | 29♊14 |

| 18h 52m 0s | 283° 0' 0" | 11 ♑ 58 | | | |
|---|---|---|---|---|---|
| LAT. | 11 | 12 | ASC | 2 | 3 |
| 0 | 10♒33 | 11♓34 | 14♈07 | 15♉28 | 14♊20 |
| 5 | 10 22 | 11 39 | 14 40 | 16 16 | 14 58 |
| 10 | 10 10 | 11 44 | 15 16 | 17 07 | 15 37 |
| 15 | 09 58 | 11 50 | 15 57 | 18 03 | 16 18 |
| 20 | 09 44 | 11 57 | 16 43 | 19 06 | 17 02 |
| 21 | 09 41 | 11 59 | 16 53 | 19 19 | 17 11 |
| 22 | 09 38 | 12 01 | 17 03 | 19 33 | 17 21 |
| 23 | 09 35 | 12 02 | 17 14 | 19 47 | 17 30 |
| 24 | 09 32 | 12 04 | 17 25 | 20 02 | 17 40 |
| 25 | 09 29 | 12 06 | 17 37 | 20 17 | 17 50 |
| 26 | 09 26 | 12 08 | 17 49 | 20 32 | 18 00 |
| 27 | 09 22 | 12 10 | 18 02 | 20 48 | 18 11 |
| 28 | 09 19 | 12 12 | 18 15 | 21 04 | 18 22 |
| 29 | 09 15 | 12 15 | 18 28 | 21 21 | 18 33 |
| 30 | 09 11 | 12 17 | 18 43 | 21 39 | 18 44 |
| 31 | 09 08 | 12 20 | 18 57 | 21 57 | 18 56 |
| 32 | 09 04 | 12 23 | 19 13 | 22 16 | 19 08 |
| 33 | 09 00 | 12 26 | 19 29 | 22 35 | 19 20 |
| 34 | 08 55 | 12 29 | 19 47 | 22 56 | 19 33 |
| 35 | 08 51 | 12 33 | 20 05 | 23 17 | 19 46 |
| 36 | 08 47 | 12 37 | 20 24 | 23 39 | 19 59 |
| 37 | 08 42 | 12 41 | 20 44 | 24 02 | 20 13 |
| 38 | 08 37 | 12 45 | 21 06 | 24 27 | 20 27 |
| 39 | 08 32 | 12 50 | 21 29 | 24 52 | 20 42 |
| 40 | 08 27 | 12 55 | 21 53 | 25 19 | 20 58 |
| 41 | 08 21 | 13 01 | 22 19 | 25 46 | 21 14 |
| 42 | 08 16 | 13 07 | 22 47 | 26 16 | 21 31 |
| 43 | 08 10 | 13 14 | 23 17 | 26 47 | 21 48 |
| 44 | 08 04 | 13 22 | 23 49 | 27 20 | 22 06 |
| 45 | 07 57 | 13 31 | 24 24 | 27 55 | 22 25 |
| 46 | 07 51 | 13 40 | 25 01 | 28 32 | 22 45 |
| 47 | 07 43 | 13 51 | 25 42 | 29 11 | 23 06 |
| 48 | 07 36 | 14 04 | 26 27 | 29 53 | 23 28 |
| 49 | 07 28 | 14 18 | 27 17 | 00♊38 | 23 52 |
| 50 | 07 20 | 14 34 | 28 11 | 01 26 | 24 16 |
| 51 | 07 12 | 14 53 | 29 12 | 02 18 | 24 42 |
| 52 | 07 03 | 15 16 | 00♉19 | 03 13 | 25 10 |
| 53 | 06 54 | 15 42 | 01 35 | 04 14 | 25 39 |
| 54 | 06 44 | 16 14 | 03 00 | 05 20 | 26 10 |
| 55 | 06 34 | 16 53 | 04 38 | 06 32 | 26 44 |
| 56 | 06 24 | 17 41 | 06 30 | 07 50 | 27 20 |
| 57 | 06 13 | 18 43 | 08 39 | 09 17 | 27 59 |
| 58 | 06 03 | 20 02 | 11 11 | 10 53 | 28 41 |
| 59 | 05 54 | 21 48 | 14 09 | 12 40 | 29 27 |
| 60 | 05♒48 | 24♓15 | 17♉41 | 14♊39 | 00♋18 |

| 18h 56m 0s | 284° 0' 0" | 12 ♑ 53 | | | |
|---|---|---|---|---|---|
| LAT. | 11 | 12 | ASC | 2 | 3 |
| 0 | 11♒32 | 12♓39 | 15♈12 | 16♉28 | 15♊16 |
| 5 | 11 23 | 12 46 | 15 48 | 17 18 | 15 54 |
| 10 | 11 12 | 12 53 | 16 26 | 18 11 | 16 34 |
| 15 | 11 01 | 13 02 | 17 09 | 19 09 | 17 16 |
| 20 | 10 49 | 13 12 | 17 59 | 20 13 | 18 01 |
| 21 | 10 47 | 13 15 | 18 10 | 20 27 | 18 10 |
| 22 | 10 44 | 13 17 | 18 21 | 20 41 | 18 20 |
| 23 | 10 41 | 13 19 | 18 32 | 20 56 | 18 30 |
| 24 | 10 38 | 13 22 | 18 44 | 21 11 | 18 40 |
| 25 | 10 36 | 13 25 | 18 57 | 21 26 | 18 50 |
| 26 | 10 33 | 13 28 | 19 10 | 21 42 | 19 01 |
| 27 | 10 30 | 13 31 | 19 23 | 21 58 | 19 11 |
| 28 | 10 27 | 13 34 | 19 37 | 22 15 | 19 22 |
| 29 | 10 23 | 13 37 | 19 52 | 22 33 | 19 33 |
| 30 | 10 20 | 13 41 | 20 07 | 22 51 | 19 45 |
| 31 | 10 17 | 13 44 | 20 23 | 23 09 | 19 57 |
| 32 | 10 13 | 13 48 | 20 40 | 23 29 | 20 09 |
| 33 | 10 10 | 13 53 | 20 57 | 23 49 | 20 21 |
| 34 | 10 06 | 13 57 | 21 16 | 24 10 | 20 34 |
| 35 | 10 02 | 14 02 | 21 35 | 24 32 | 20 47 |
| 36 | 09 58 | 14 07 | 21 55 | 24 54 | 21 01 |
| 37 | 09 54 | 14 13 | 22 17 | 25 18 | 21 15 |
| 38 | 09 50 | 14 18 | 22 40 | 25 43 | 21 30 |
| 39 | 09 46 | 14 25 | 23 04 | 26 09 | 21 45 |
| 40 | 09 41 | 14 32 | 23 30 | 26 36 | 22 00 |
| 41 | 09 36 | 14 40 | 23 58 | 27 05 | 22 17 |
| 42 | 09 31 | 14 48 | 24 27 | 27 35 | 22 34 |
| 43 | 09 26 | 14 57 | 24 59 | 28 06 | 22 51 |
| 44 | 09 21 | 15 07 | 25 33 | 28 40 | 23 10 |
| 45 | 09 16 | 15 18 | 26 10 | 29 15 | 23 29 |
| 46 | 09 10 | 15 31 | 26 50 | 29 53 | 23 49 |
| 47 | 09 04 | 15 45 | 27 34 | 00♊33 | 24 10 |
| 48 | 08 58 | 16 01 | 28 21 | 01 16 | 24 32 |
| 49 | 08 51 | 16 19 | 29 13 | 02 01 | 24 56 |
| 50 | 08 44 | 16 39 | 00♉11 | 02 50 | 25 20 |
| 51 | 08 37 | 17 03 | 01 14 | 03 43 | 25 46 |
| 52 | 08 30 | 17 31 | 02 25 | 04 39 | 26 14 |
| 53 | 08 23 | 18 04 | 03 44 | 05 40 | 26 43 |
| 54 | 08 15 | 18 43 | 05 14 | 06 47 | 27 15 |
| 55 | 08 08 | 19 31 | 06 55 | 07 59 | 27 48 |
| 56 | 08 01 | 20 29 | 08 51 | 09 18 | 28 24 |
| 57 | 07 54 | 21 43 | 11 05 | 10 45 | 29 03 |
| 58 | 07 48 | 23 17 | 13 40 | 12 20 | 29 45 |
| 59 | 07 45 | 25 23 | 16 42 | 14 07 | 00♋31 |
| 60 | 07♒45 | 28♓14 | 20♉16 | 16♊05 | 01♋21 |

| 19h 0m 0s | 285° 0' 0" | 13 ♑ 49 | | | |
|---|---|---|---|---|---|
| LAT. | 11 | 12 | ASC | 2 | 3 |
| 0 | 12♒32 | 13♓43 | 16♈17 | 17♉28 | 16♊11 |
| 5 | 12 24 | 13 52 | 16 55 | 18 19 | 16 51 |
| 10 | 12 15 | 14 03 | 17 36 | 19 14 | 17 31 |
| 15 | 12 05 | 14 14 | 18 22 | 20 14 | 18 14 |
| 20 | 11 54 | 14 28 | 19 15 | 21 20 | 19 00 |
| 21 | 11 52 | 14 31 | 19 26 | 21 34 | 19 10 |
| 22 | 11 50 | 14 34 | 19 38 | 21 49 | 19 19 |
| 23 | 11 47 | 14 37 | 19 50 | 22 04 | 19 29 |
| 24 | 11 45 | 14 40 | 20 03 | 22 19 | 19 40 |
| 25 | 11 42 | 14 44 | 20 16 | 22 35 | 19 50 |
| 26 | 11 40 | 14 47 | 20 30 | 22 52 | 20 00 |
| 27 | 11 37 | 14 51 | 20 44 | 23 08 | 20 11 |
| 28 | 11 35 | 14 55 | 20 59 | 23 26 | 20 22 |
| 29 | 11 32 | 15 00 | 21 15 | 23 44 | 20 34 |
| 30 | 11 29 | 15 04 | 21 31 | 24 02 | 20 45 |
| 31 | 11 26 | 15 09 | 21 48 | 24 21 | 20 57 |
| 32 | 11 23 | 15 14 | 22 06 | 24 41 | 21 10 |
| 33 | 11 20 | 15 19 | 22 24 | 25 02 | 21 22 |
| 34 | 11 17 | 15 25 | 22 44 | 25 23 | 21 35 |
| 35 | 11 14 | 15 31 | 23 04 | 25 46 | 21 49 |
| 36 | 11 10 | 15 38 | 23 26 | 26 09 | 22 03 |
| 37 | 11 07 | 15 45 | 23 49 | 26 33 | 22 17 |
| 38 | 11 03 | 15 52 | 24 13 | 26 59 | 22 32 |
| 39 | 11 00 | 16 00 | 24 39 | 27 25 | 22 47 |
| 40 | 10 56 | 16 09 | 25 06 | 27 53 | 23 03 |
| 41 | 10 52 | 16 19 | 25 36 | 28 22 | 23 19 |
| 42 | 10 48 | 16 29 | 26 07 | 28 53 | 23 36 |
| 43 | 10 43 | 16 40 | 26 41 | 29 25 | 23 54 |
| 44 | 10 39 | 16 53 | 27 17 | 29 59 | 24 13 |
| 45 | 10 34 | 17 07 | 27 56 | 00♊35 | 24 32 |
| 46 | 10 30 | 17 22 | 28 38 | 01 14 | 24 52 |
| 47 | 10 25 | 17 39 | 29 23 | 01 54 | 25 13 |
| 48 | 10 20 | 17 58 | 00♉13 | 02 37 | 25 36 |
| 49 | 10 15 | 18 20 | 01 08 | 03 24 | 25 59 |
| 50 | 10 10 | 18 45 | 02 08 | 04 13 | 26 24 |
| 51 | 10 04 | 19 14 | 03 15 | 05 06 | 26 50 |
| 52 | 09 59 | 19 47 | 04 29 | 06 03 | 27 18 |
| 53 | 09 54 | 20 26 | 05 51 | 07 05 | 27 47 |
| 54 | 09 49 | 21 13 | 07 24 | 08 11 | 28 18 |
| 55 | 09 44 | 22 09 | 09 09 | 09 24 | 28 52 |
| 56 | 09 40 | 23 18 | 11 08 | 10 43 | 29 28 |
| 57 | 09 37 | 24 44 | 13 25 | 12 10 | 00♋07 |
| 58 | 09 36 | 26 33 | 16 03 | 13 45 | 00 48 |
| 59 | 09 38 | 28 57 | 19 08 | 15 31 | 01 34 |
| 60 | 09♒45 | 02♈13 | 22♉43 | 17♊28 | 02♋24 |

| 19h 4m 0s | 286° 0' 0" | 14 ♑ 44 | | | |
|---|---|---|---|---|---|
| LAT. | 11 | 12 | ASC | 2 | 3 |
| 0 | 13♒32 | 14♓48 | 17♈21 | 18♉28 | 17♊07 |
| 5 | 13 25 | 14 59 | 18 01 | 19 21 | 17 47 |
| 10 | 13 17 | 15 12 | 18 45 | 20 17 | 18 29 |
| 15 | 13 09 | 15 26 | 19 34 | 21 19 | 19 12 |
| 20 | 13 00 | 15 43 | 20 30 | 22 27 | 19 59 |
| 21 | 12 58 | 15 47 | 20 42 | 22 42 | 20 09 |
| 22 | 12 56 | 15 50 | 20 55 | 22 57 | 20 18 |
| 23 | 12 54 | 15 54 | 21 08 | 23 12 | 20 29 |
| 24 | 12 52 | 15 59 | 21 22 | 23 28 | 20 39 |
| 25 | 12 50 | 16 03 | 21 36 | 23 44 | 20 50 |
| 26 | 12 48 | 16 07 | 21 50 | 24 01 | 21 00 |
| 27 | 12 45 | 16 12 | 22 05 | 24 18 | 21 11 |
| 28 | 12 43 | 16 17 | 22 21 | 24 36 | 21 23 |
| 29 | 12 41 | 16 22 | 22 38 | 24 54 | 21 34 |
| 30 | 12 38 | 16 28 | 22 55 | 25 13 | 21 46 |
| 31 | 12 36 | 16 34 | 23 13 | 25 33 | 21 58 |
| 32 | 12 33 | 16 40 | 23 31 | 25 53 | 22 10 |
| 33 | 12 31 | 16 46 | 23 51 | 26 14 | 22 23 |
| 34 | 12 28 | 16 53 | 24 12 | 26 36 | 22 36 |
| 35 | 12 26 | 17 01 | 24 33 | 26 59 | 22 50 |
| 36 | 12 23 | 17 09 | 24 56 | 27 23 | 23 04 |
| 37 | 12 20 | 17 17 | 25 20 | 27 48 | 23 18 |
| 38 | 12 17 | 17 26 | 25 46 | 28 13 | 23 33 |
| 39 | 12 14 | 17 36 | 26 13 | 28 40 | 23 49 |
| 40 | 12 11 | 17 46 | 26 42 | 29 09 | 24 05 |
| 41 | 12 08 | 17 58 | 27 13 | 29 39 | 24 21 |
| 42 | 12 04 | 18 10 | 27 46 | 00♊10 | 24 38 |
| 43 | 12 01 | 18 24 | 28 21 | 00 43 | 24 56 |
| 44 | 11 58 | 18 39 | 28 59 | 01 17 | 25 15 |
| 45 | 11 54 | 18 55 | 29 40 | 01 54 | 25 35 |
| 46 | 11 50 | 19 13 | 00♉24 | 02 33 | 25 55 |
| 47 | 11 47 | 19 34 | 01 12 | 03 14 | 26 16 |
| 48 | 11 43 | 19 56 | 02 04 | 03 58 | 26 39 |
| 49 | 11 39 | 20 22 | 03 01 | 04 45 | 27 02 |
| 50 | 11 36 | 20 51 | 04 04 | 05 35 | 27 27 |
| 51 | 11 32 | 21 25 | 05 13 | 06 28 | 27 53 |
| 52 | 11 29 | 22 04 | 06 29 | 07 26 | 28 21 |
| 53 | 11 26 | 22 49 | 07 55 | 08 27 | 28 50 |
| 54 | 11 23 | 23 43 | 09 31 | 09 35 | 29 22 |
| 55 | 11 21 | 24 48 | 11 18 | 10 47 | 29 55 |
| 56 | 11 20 | 26 07 | 13 21 | 12 06 | 00♋31 |
| 57 | 11 22 | 27 45 | 15 41 | 13 33 | 01 09 |
| 58 | 11 25 | 29 49 | 18 21 | 15 08 | 01 51 |
| 59 | 11 34 | 02♈31 | 21 26 | 16 53 | 02 36 |
| 60 | 11♒50 | 06♈09 | 25♉02 | 18♊49 | 03♋26 |

| 19h 8m 0s | 287° 0' 0" | 15 ♑ 40 | | | |
|---|---|---|---|---|---|
| LAT. | 11 | 12 | ASC | 2 | 3 |
| 0 | 14♒32 | 15♓53 | 18♈26 | 19♉27 | 18♊02 |
| 5 | 14 26 | 16 06 | 19 08 | 20 22 | 18 43 |
| 10 | 14 20 | 16 21 | 19 55 | 21 20 | 19 26 |
| 15 | 14 13 | 16 38 | 20 46 | 22 23 | 20 10 |
| 20 | 14 05 | 16 58 | 21 45 | 23 33 | 20 57 |
| 21 | 14 04 | 17 03 | 21 58 | 23 48 | 21 07 |
| 22 | 14 02 | 17 07 | 22 12 | 24 04 | 21 17 |
| 23 | 14 01 | 17 12 | 22 26 | 24 19 | 21 28 |
| 24 | 13 59 | 17 17 | 22 40 | 24 36 | 21 38 |
| 25 | 13 57 | 17 22 | 22 55 | 24 52 | 21 49 |
| 26 | 13 55 | 17 28 | 23 10 | 25 10 | 22 00 |
| 27 | 13 54 | 17 33 | 23 26 | 25 27 | 22 11 |
| 28 | 13 52 | 17 39 | 23 42 | 25 45 | 22 22 |
| 29 | 13 50 | 17 45 | 24 00 | 26 04 | 22 34 |
| 30 | 13 48 | 17 52 | 24 18 | 26 24 | 22 46 |
| 31 | 13 46 | 17 59 | 24 37 | 26 44 | 22 58 |
| 32 | 13 44 | 18 06 | 24 56 | 27 05 | 23 11 |
| 33 | 13 42 | 18 14 | 25 17 | 27 26 | 23 24 |
| 34 | 13 40 | 18 22 | 25 39 | 27 48 | 23 37 |
| 35 | 13 38 | 18 31 | 26 02 | 28 12 | 23 51 |
| 36 | 13 36 | 18 40 | 26 26 | 28 36 | 24 05 |
| 37 | 13 33 | 18 50 | 26 51 | 29 01 | 24 20 |
| 38 | 13 31 | 19 00 | 27 18 | 29 28 | 24 35 |
| 39 | 13 29 | 19 12 | 27 46 | 29 55 | 24 50 |
| 40 | 13 27 | 19 24 | 28 17 | 00♊24 | 25 06 |
| 41 | 13 24 | 19 37 | 28 49 | 00 54 | 25 23 |
| 42 | 13 22 | 19 52 | 29 23 | 01 26 | 25 40 |
| 43 | 13 19 | 20 08 | 00♉00 | 01 59 | 25 58 |
| 44 | 13 17 | 20 25 | 00 40 | 02 35 | 26 17 |
| 45 | 13 14 | 20 44 | 01 22 | 03 12 | 26 37 |
| 46 | 13 12 | 21 05 | 02 08 | 03 51 | 26 57 |
| 47 | 13 09 | 21 28 | 02 58 | 04 33 | 27 19 |
| 48 | 13 07 | 21 55 | 03 53 | 05 17 | 27 41 |
| 49 | 13 05 | 22 24 | 04 52 | 06 04 | 28 05 |
| 50 | 13 03 | 22 58 | 05 57 | 06 55 | 28 30 |
| 51 | 13 01 | 23 36 | 07 08 | 07 49 | 28 56 |
| 52 | 13 00 | 24 21 | 08 28 | 08 46 | 29 24 |
| 53 | 12 59 | 25 12 | 09 56 | 09 49 | 29 53 |
| 54 | 12 59 | 26 14 | 11 34 | 10 56 | 00♋24 |
| 55 | 13 00 | 27 27 | 13 24 | 12 09 | 00 58 |
| 56 | 13 03 | 28 55 | 15 29 | 13 28 | 01 33 |
| 57 | 13 09 | 00♈45 | 17 51 | 14 54 | 02 12 |
| 58 | 13 18 | 03 04 | 20 33 | 16 29 | 02 53 |
| 59 | 13 33 | 06 03 | 23 39 | 18 13 | 03 38 |
| 60 | 13♒58 | 10♈02 | 27♉14 | 20♊07 | 04♋27 |

# Koch Table of Houses for Latitudes 0° to 60° North

**19h 12m 0s — 288° 0' 0" — 16 ♑ 36**

| LAT. | 11 | 12 | ASC | 2 | 3 |
|---|---|---|---|---|---|
| 0 | 15♒32 | 16♓57 | 19♈30 | 20♉26 | 18♊58 |
| 5 | 15 27 | 17 13 | 20 15 | 21 23 | 19 40 |
| 10 | 15 22 | 17 31 | 21 04 | 22 23 | 20 23 |
| 15 | 15 17 | 17 51 | 21 58 | 23 28 | 21 08 |
| 20 | 15 11 | 18 14 | 23 00 | 24 39 | 21 56 |
| 21 | 15 10 | 18 19 | 23 14 | 24 55 | 22 06 |
| 22 | 15 09 | 18 24 | 23 28 | 25 11 | 22 16 |
| 23 | 15 08 | 18 30 | 23 43 | 25 27 | 22 27 |
| 24 | 15 06 | 18 36 | 23 58 | 25 43 | 22 37 |
| 25 | 15 05 | 18 42 | 24 13 | 26 00 | 22 48 |
| 26 | 15 04 | 18 48 | 24 29 | 26 18 | 22 59 |
| 27 | 15 02 | 18 54 | 24 46 | 26 36 | 23 11 |
| 28 | 15 01 | 19 01 | 25 03 | 26 55 | 23 22 |
| 29 | 14 59 | 19 08 | 25 22 | 27 14 | 23 34 |
| 30 | 14 58 | 19 16 | 25 40 | 27 34 | 23 46 |
| 31 | 14 57 | 19 24 | 26 00 | 27 54 | 23 59 |
| 32 | 14 55 | 19 32 | 26 21 | 28 15 | 24 11 |
| 33 | 14 54 | 19 41 | 26 43 | 28 37 | 24 24 |
| 34 | 14 52 | 19 50 | 27 05 | 29 00 | 24 38 |
| 35 | 14 51 | 20 00 | 27 29 | 29 24 | 24 52 |
| 36 | 14 49 | 20 11 | 27 54 | 29 49 | 25 06 |
| 37 | 14 47 | 20 22 | 28 21 | 00♊14 | 25 21 |
| 38 | 14 46 | 20 35 | 28 49 | 00 41 | 25 36 |
| 39 | 14 44 | 20 48 | 29 19 | 01 09 | 25 51 |
| 40 | 14 43 | 21 02 | 29 50 | 01 38 | 26 08 |
| 41 | 14 41 | 21 17 | 00♉24 | 02 09 | 26 25 |
| 42 | 14 40 | 21 34 | 01 00 | 02 41 | 26 42 |
| 43 | 14 38 | 21 52 | 01 38 | 03 15 | 27 00 |
| 44 | 14 37 | 22 11 | 02 20 | 03 51 | 27 19 |
| 45 | 14 35 | 22 33 | 03 04 | 04 29 | 27 39 |
| 46 | 14 34 | 22 57 | 03 52 | 05 08 | 27 59 |
| 47 | 14 33 | 23 23 | 04 44 | 05 51 | 28 21 |
| 48 | 14 32 | 23 53 | 05 40 | 06 35 | 28 43 |
| 49 | 14 31 | 24 27 | 06 41 | 07 23 | 29 07 |
| 50 | 14 31 | 25 04 | 07 48 | 08 14 | 29 32 |
| 51 | 14 31 | 25 48 | 09 02 | 09 08 | 29 58 |
| 52 | 14 32 | 26 38 | 10 23 | 10 06 | 00♋26 |
| 53 | 14 33 | 27 36 | 11 53 | 11 08 | 00 55 |
| 54 | 14 36 | 28 44 | 13 34 | 12 16 | 01 27 |
| 55 | 14 41 | 00♈05 | 15 26 | 13 28 | 02 00 |
| 56 | 14 48 | 01 44 | 17 33 | 14 47 | 02 35 |
| 57 | 14 58 | 03 45 | 19 56 | 16 13 | 03 14 |
| 58 | 15 13 | 06 17 | 22 39 | 17 47 | 03 55 |
| 59 | 15 35 | 09 32 | 25 45 | 19 30 | 04 39 |
| 60 | 16♒10 | 13♈49 | 29♉19 | 21♊24 | 05♋27 |

**19h 16m 0s — 289° 0' 0" — 17 ♑ 32**

| LAT. | 11 | 12 | ASC | 2 | 3 |
|---|---|---|---|---|---|
| 0 | 16♒33 | 18♓02 | 20♈34 | 21♉26 | 19♊53 |
| 5 | 16 29 | 18 21 | 21 21 | 22 23 | 20 36 |
| 10 | 16 25 | 18 41 | 22 13 | 23 25 | 21 20 |
| 15 | 16 22 | 19 03 | 23 10 | 24 32 | 22 06 |
| 20 | 16 17 | 19 30 | 24 15 | 25 45 | 22 54 |
| 21 | 16 17 | 19 35 | 24 29 | 26 01 | 23 05 |
| 22 | 16 16 | 19 41 | 24 44 | 26 17 | 23 15 |
| 23 | 16 15 | 19 48 | 24 59 | 26 33 | 23 26 |
| 24 | 16 14 | 19 54 | 25 15 | 26 50 | 23 36 |
| 25 | 16 13 | 20 01 | 25 31 | 27 08 | 23 47 |
| 26 | 16 12 | 20 08 | 25 48 | 27 26 | 23 59 |
| 27 | 16 11 | 20 16 | 26 06 | 27 44 | 24 10 |
| 28 | 16 10 | 20 23 | 26 24 | 28 03 | 24 22 |
| 29 | 16 09 | 20 31 | 26 43 | 28 23 | 24 34 |
| 30 | 16 08 | 20 40 | 27 03 | 28 43 | 24 46 |
| 31 | 16 07 | 20 49 | 27 23 | 29 04 | 24 58 |
| 32 | 16 06 | 20 59 | 27 45 | 29 26 | 25 11 |
| 33 | 16 05 | 21 09 | 28 08 | 29 48 | 25 25 |
| 34 | 16 05 | 21 19 | 28 31 | 00♊11 | 25 38 |
| 35 | 16 04 | 21 30 | 28 56 | 00 35 | 25 52 |
| 36 | 16 03 | 21 42 | 29 23 | 01 01 | 26 06 |
| 37 | 16 02 | 21 55 | 29 50 | 01 27 | 26 21 |
| 38 | 16 01 | 22 09 | 00♉19 | 01 54 | 26 37 |
| 39 | 16 00 | 22 24 | 00 50 | 02 22 | 26 52 |
| 40 | 15 59 | 22 40 | 01 23 | 02 52 | 27 09 |
| 41 | 15 59 | 22 57 | 01 58 | 03 23 | 27 26 |
| 42 | 15 58 | 23 15 | 02 36 | 03 56 | 27 43 |
| 43 | 15 57 | 23 36 | 03 15 | 04 30 | 28 02 |
| 44 | 15 57 | 23 58 | 03 58 | 05 06 | 28 21 |
| 45 | 15 57 | 24 22 | 04 44 | 05 44 | 28 40 |
| 46 | 15 57 | 24 49 | 05 34 | 06 25 | 29 01 |
| 47 | 15 57 | 25 19 | 06 27 | 07 07 | 29 23 |
| 48 | 15 57 | 25 52 | 07 25 | 07 52 | 29 45 |
| 49 | 15 58 | 26 29 | 08 28 | 08 40 | 00♋09 |
| 50 | 16 00 | 27 11 | 09 37 | 09 31 | 00 34 |
| 51 | 16 02 | 27 59 | 10 53 | 10 26 | 01 00 |
| 52 | 16 05 | 28 54 | 12 16 | 11 24 | 01 28 |
| 53 | 16 09 | 29 58 | 13 48 | 12 27 | 01 57 |
| 54 | 16 15 | 01♈14 | 15 31 | 13 34 | 02 28 |
| 55 | 16 23 | 02 43 | 17 25 | 14 47 | 03 02 |
| 56 | 16 34 | 04 31 | 19 33 | 16 05 | 03 37 |
| 57 | 16 49 | 06 43 | 21 57 | 17 31 | 04 15 |
| 58 | 17 10 | 09 28 | 24 41 | 19 04 | 04 56 |
| 59 | 17 41 | 12 57 | 27 46 | 20 46 | 05 40 |
| 60 | 18♒27 | 17♈30 | 01♊18 | 22♊38 | 06♋27 |

**19h 20m 0s — 290° 0' 0" — 18 ♑ 28**

| LAT. | 11 | 12 | ASC | 2 | 3 |
|---|---|---|---|---|---|
| 0 | 17♒33 | 19♓07 | 21♈38 | 22♉25 | 20♊49 |
| 5 | 17 31 | 19 28 | 22 28 | 23 24 | 21 32 |
| 10 | 17 29 | 19 50 | 23 21 | 24 27 | 22 17 |
| 15 | 17 26 | 20 16 | 24 21 | 25 35 | 23 03 |
| 20 | 17 24 | 20 45 | 25 30 | 26 51 | 23 53 |
| 21 | 17 23 | 20 52 | 25 44 | 27 07 | 24 03 |
| 22 | 17 23 | 20 59 | 26 00 | 27 23 | 24 14 |
| 23 | 17 22 | 21 06 | 26 16 | 27 40 | 24 24 |
| 24 | 17 22 | 21 13 | 26 32 | 27 57 | 24 35 |
| 25 | 17 21 | 21 21 | 26 49 | 28 15 | 24 46 |
| 26 | 17 21 | 21 29 | 27 07 | 28 33 | 24 58 |
| 27 | 17 20 | 21 37 | 27 25 | 28 52 | 25 09 |
| 28 | 17 20 | 21 46 | 27 44 | 29 11 | 25 21 |
| 29 | 17 19 | 21 55 | 28 04 | 29 31 | 25 33 |
| 30 | 17 19 | 22 04 | 28 24 | 29 52 | 25 46 |
| 31 | 17 19 | 22 14 | 28 46 | 00♊13 | 25 58 |
| 32 | 17 18 | 22 25 | 29 08 | 00 35 | 26 11 |
| 33 | 17 18 | 22 36 | 29 32 | 00 58 | 26 25 |
| 34 | 17 17 | 22 48 | 29 57 | 01 22 | 26 38 |
| 35 | 17 17 | 23 01 | 00♉23 | 01 46 | 26 52 |
| 36 | 17 17 | 23 14 | 00 50 | 02 12 | 27 07 |
| 37 | 17 17 | 23 28 | 01 19 | 02 38 | 27 22 |
| 38 | 17 17 | 23 44 | 01 49 | 03 06 | 27 37 |
| 39 | 17 16 | 24 00 | 02 21 | 03 35 | 27 53 |
| 40 | 17 16 | 24 18 | 02 55 | 04 05 | 28 10 |
| 41 | 17 17 | 24 37 | 03 32 | 04 37 | 28 27 |
| 42 | 17 17 | 24 57 | 04 10 | 05 10 | 28 44 |
| 43 | 17 17 | 25 20 | 04 51 | 05 44 | 29 03 |
| 44 | 17 18 | 25 44 | 05 35 | 06 21 | 29 22 |
| 45 | 17 19 | 26 11 | 06 23 | 06 59 | 29 42 |
| 46 | 17 20 | 26 41 | 07 14 | 07 40 | 00♋02 |
| 47 | 17 22 | 27 14 | 08 09 | 08 23 | 00 24 |
| 48 | 17 24 | 27 50 | 09 09 | 09 08 | 00 47 |
| 49 | 17 26 | 28 31 | 10 13 | 09 56 | 01 11 |
| 50 | 17 30 | 29 17 | 11 24 | 10 48 | 01 35 |
| 51 | 17 34 | 00♈10 | 12 41 | 11 42 | 02 02 |
| 52 | 17 39 | 01 11 | 14 06 | 12 41 | 02 29 |
| 53 | 17 46 | 02 21 | 15 40 | 13 43 | 02 59 |
| 54 | 17 55 | 03 43 | 17 24 | 14 51 | 03 30 |
| 55 | 18 07 | 05 20 | 19 20 | 16 03 | 04 03 |
| 56 | 18 22 | 07 16 | 21 29 | 17 21 | 04 38 |
| 57 | 18 43 | 09 39 | 23 54 | 18 46 | 05 16 |
| 58 | 19 11 | 12 35 | 26 37 | 20 19 | 05 56 |
| 59 | 19 50 | 16 17 | 29 42 | 21 59 | 06 40 |
| 60 | 20♒47 | 21♈04 | 03♊10 | 23♊50 | 07♋27 |

**19h 24m 0s — 291° 0' 0" — 19 ♑ 24**

| LAT. | 11 | 12 | ASC | 2 | 3 |
|---|---|---|---|---|---|
| 0 | 18♒34 | 20♓12 | 22♈42 | 23♉23 | 21♊44 |
| 5 | 18 33 | 20 35 | 23 34 | 24 24 | 22 28 |
| 10 | 18 32 | 21 00 | 24 30 | 25 29 | 23 13 |
| 15 | 18 31 | 21 28 | 25 33 | 26 39 | 24 01 |
| 20 | 18 30 | 22 01 | 26 44 | 27 56 | 24 51 |
| 21 | 18 30 | 22 08 | 26 59 | 28 12 | 25 01 |
| 22 | 18 30 | 22 16 | 27 15 | 28 29 | 25 12 |
| 23 | 18 30 | 22 24 | 27 32 | 28 46 | 25 23 |
| 24 | 18 30 | 22 32 | 27 49 | 29 04 | 25 34 |
| 25 | 18 30 | 22 40 | 28 06 | 29 22 | 25 45 |
| 26 | 18 30 | 22 49 | 28 25 | 29 40 | 25 57 |
| 27 | 18 30 | 22 58 | 28 44 | 00♊00 | 26 08 |
| 28 | 18 30 | 23 08 | 29 04 | 00 19 | 26 20 |
| 29 | 18 30 | 23 18 | 29 24 | 00 40 | 26 33 |
| 30 | 18 30 | 23 28 | 29 46 | 01 01 | 26 45 |
| 31 | 18 30 | 23 40 | 00♉08 | 01 22 | 26 58 |
| 32 | 18 30 | 23 51 | 00 31 | 01 45 | 27 11 |
| 33 | 18 30 | 24 04 | 00 56 | 02 08 | 27 24 |
| 34 | 18 31 | 24 17 | 01 21 | 02 32 | 27 38 |
| 35 | 18 31 | 24 31 | 01 48 | 02 57 | 27 52 |
| 36 | 18 31 | 24 45 | 02 17 | 03 23 | 28 07 |
| 37 | 18 32 | 25 01 | 02 46 | 03 50 | 28 22 |
| 38 | 18 32 | 25 18 | 03 18 | 04 18 | 28 38 |
| 39 | 18 33 | 25 36 | 03 51 | 04 47 | 28 54 |
| 40 | 18 34 | 25 55 | 04 26 | 05 17 | 29 10 |
| 41 | 18 35 | 26 16 | 05 04 | 05 49 | 29 27 |
| 42 | 18 36 | 26 39 | 05 44 | 06 23 | 29 45 |
| 43 | 18 38 | 27 04 | 06 26 | 06 58 | 00♋04 |
| 44 | 18 40 | 27 31 | 07 12 | 07 35 | 00 23 |
| 45 | 18 42 | 28 00 | 08 00 | 08 13 | 00 43 |
| 46 | 18 44 | 28 32 | 08 53 | 08 54 | 01 04 |
| 47 | 18 47 | 29 08 | 09 49 | 09 37 | 01 25 |
| 48 | 18 51 | 29 48 | 10 50 | 10 23 | 01 48 |
| 49 | 18 55 | 00♈33 | 11 57 | 11 11 | 02 12 |
| 50 | 19 01 | 01 23 | 13 09 | 12 03 | 02 37 |
| 51 | 19 07 | 02 21 | 14 28 | 12 58 | 03 03 |
| 52 | 19 15 | 03 26 | 15 54 | 13 56 | 03 31 |
| 53 | 19 25 | 04 42 | 17 29 | 14 59 | 04 00 |
| 54 | 19 37 | 06 11 | 19 15 | 16 06 | 04 31 |
| 55 | 19 52 | 07 55 | 21 11 | 17 18 | 05 03 |
| 56 | 20 12 | 10 00 | 23 21 | 18 36 | 05 38 |
| 57 | 20 38 | 12 32 | 25 46 | 20 00 | 06 16 |
| 58 | 21 13 | 15 38 | 28 29 | 21 32 | 06 56 |
| 59 | 22 02 | 19 32 | 01♊32 | 23 11 | 07 39 |
| 60 | 23♒11 | 24♈29 | 04♊58 | 25♊00 | 08♋26 |

**19h 28m 0s — 292° 0' 0" — 20 ♑ 20**

| LAT. | 11 | 12 | ASC | 2 | 3 |
|---|---|---|---|---|---|
| 0 | 19♒35 | 21♓17 | 23♈46 | 24♉22 | 22♊39 |
| 5 | 19 35 | 21 42 | 24 40 | 25 24 | 23 24 |
| 10 | 19 36 | 22 10 | 25 38 | 26 31 | 24 10 |
| 15 | 19 36 | 22 41 | 26 43 | 27 42 | 24 58 |
| 20 | 19 37 | 23 17 | 27 57 | 29 00 | 25 49 |
| 21 | 19 38 | 23 25 | 28 14 | 29 17 | 26 00 |
| 22 | 19 38 | 23 33 | 28 30 | 29 34 | 26 10 |
| 23 | 19 38 | 23 42 | 28 47 | 29 52 | 26 21 |
| 24 | 19 38 | 23 51 | 29 05 | 00♊10 | 26 33 |
| 25 | 19 39 | 24 00 | 29 23 | 00 28 | 26 44 |
| 26 | 19 39 | 24 09 | 29 42 | 00 47 | 26 56 |
| 27 | 19 40 | 24 20 | 00♉02 | 01 07 | 27 07 |
| 28 | 19 40 | 24 30 | 00 23 | 01 27 | 27 19 |
| 29 | 19 41 | 24 41 | 00 44 | 01 47 | 27 32 |
| 30 | 19 41 | 24 53 | 01 06 | 02 09 | 27 44 |
| 31 | 19 42 | 25 05 | 01 29 | 02 31 | 27 57 |
| 32 | 19 43 | 25 18 | 01 54 | 02 53 | 28 11 |
| 33 | 19 43 | 25 31 | 02 19 | 03 17 | 28 24 |
| 34 | 19 44 | 25 46 | 02 45 | 03 41 | 28 38 |
| 35 | 19 45 | 26 01 | 03 13 | 04 07 | 28 52 |
| 36 | 19 46 | 26 17 | 03 42 | 04 33 | 29 07 |
| 37 | 19 48 | 26 34 | 04 13 | 05 00 | 29 22 |
| 38 | 19 49 | 26 52 | 04 46 | 05 28 | 29 38 |
| 39 | 19 50 | 27 12 | 05 20 | 05 58 | 29 54 |
| 40 | 19 52 | 27 33 | 05 56 | 06 29 | 00♋11 |
| 41 | 19 54 | 27 56 | 06 35 | 07 01 | 00 28 |
| 42 | 19 56 | 28 21 | 07 16 | 07 35 | 00 46 |
| 43 | 19 59 | 28 48 | 08 00 | 08 10 | 01 04 |
| 44 | 20 02 | 29 17 | 08 46 | 08 47 | 01 24 |
| 45 | 20 05 | 29 49 | 09 36 | 09 26 | 01 44 |
| 46 | 20 09 | 00♈24 | 10 30 | 10 08 | 02 04 |
| 47 | 20 14 | 01 03 | 11 28 | 10 51 | 02 26 |
| 48 | 20 19 | 01 46 | 12 30 | 11 37 | 02 49 |
| 49 | 20 25 | 02 35 | 13 38 | 12 25 | 03 13 |
| 50 | 20 33 | 03 29 | 14 52 | 13 17 | 03 37 |
| 51 | 20 41 | 04 31 | 16 12 | 14 12 | 04 04 |
| 52 | 20 52 | 05 41 | 17 39 | 15 10 | 04 31 |
| 53 | 21 04 | 07 03 | 19 16 | 16 13 | 05 00 |
| 54 | 21 20 | 08 37 | 21 02 | 17 20 | 05 31 |
| 55 | 21 40 | 10 29 | 22 59 | 18 32 | 06 04 |
| 56 | 22 04 | 12 41 | 25 10 | 19 49 | 06 39 |
| 57 | 22 36 | 15 22 | 27 35 | 21 13 | 07 16 |
| 58 | 23 19 | 18 38 | 00♊16 | 22 43 | 07 55 |
| 59 | 24 17 | 22 41 | 03 18 | 24 22 | 08 38 |
| 60 | 25♒39 | 27♈47 | 06♊41 | 26♊09 | 09♋24 |

**19h 32m 0s — 293° 0' 0" — 21 ♑ 17**

| LAT. | 11 | 12 | ASC | 2 | 3 |
|---|---|---|---|---|---|
| 0 | 20♒36 | 22♓23 | 24♈50 | 25♉21 | 23♊34 |
| 5 | 20 38 | 22 50 | 25 46 | 26 24 | 24 20 |
| 10 | 20 40 | 23 20 | 26 47 | 27 32 | 25 07 |
| 15 | 20 42 | 23 54 | 27 54 | 28 45 | 25 56 |
| 20 | 20 44 | 24 33 | 29 11 | 00♊05 | 26 47 |
| 21 | 20 45 | 24 42 | 29 28 | 00 22 | 26 58 |
| 22 | 20 46 | 24 50 | 29 45 | 00 39 | 27 09 |
| 23 | 20 46 | 25 00 | 00♉03 | 00 57 | 27 20 |
| 24 | 20 47 | 25 09 | 00 21 | 01 15 | 27 31 |
| 25 | 20 48 | 25 19 | 00 40 | 01 34 | 27 43 |
| 26 | 20 49 | 25 30 | 01 00 | 01 53 | 27 54 |
| 27 | 20 50 | 25 41 | 01 20 | 02 13 | 28 06 |
| 28 | 20 51 | 25 52 | 01 41 | 02 34 | 28 18 |
| 29 | 20 52 | 26 04 | 02 03 | 02 55 | 28 31 |
| 30 | 20 53 | 26 17 | 02 26 | 03 16 | 28 44 |
| 31 | 20 54 | 26 30 | 02 50 | 03 39 | 28 57 |
| 32 | 20 55 | 26 44 | 03 15 | 04 02 | 29 10 |
| 33 | 20 57 | 26 59 | 03 41 | 04 26 | 29 24 |
| 34 | 20 58 | 27 14 | 04 09 | 04 50 | 29 38 |
| 35 | 21 00 | 27 31 | 04 37 | 05 16 | 29 52 |
| 36 | 21 02 | 27 48 | 05 08 | 05 42 | 00♋07 |
| 37 | 21 04 | 28 07 | 05 39 | 06 10 | 00 22 |
| 38 | 21 06 | 28 27 | 06 13 | 06 39 | 00 38 |
| 39 | 21 08 | 28 48 | 06 48 | 07 09 | 00 54 |
| 40 | 21 11 | 29 11 | 07 25 | 07 40 | 01 11 |
| 41 | 21 14 | 29 36 | 08 05 | 08 12 | 01 28 |
| 42 | 21 17 | 00♈02 | 08 47 | 08 46 | 01 46 |
| 43 | 21 21 | 00 31 | 09 32 | 09 22 | 02 05 |
| 44 | 21 25 | 01 03 | 10 20 | 09 59 | 02 24 |
| 45 | 21 29 | 01 37 | 11 11 | 10 39 | 02 44 |
| 46 | 21 35 | 02 15 | 12 06 | 11 20 | 03 05 |
| 47 | 21 41 | 02 57 | 13 05 | 12 04 | 03 27 |
| 48 | 21 48 | 03 44 | 14 09 | 12 50 | 03 49 |
| 49 | 21 56 | 04 35 | 15 17 | 13 38 | 04 13 |
| 50 | 22 05 | 05 34 | 16 32 | 14 30 | 04 38 |
| 51 | 22 16 | 06 40 | 17 53 | 15 25 | 05 04 |
| 52 | 22 29 | 07 55 | 19 22 | 16 23 | 05 32 |
| 53 | 22 45 | 09 22 | 21 00 | 17 26 | 06 01 |
| 54 | 23 04 | 11 02 | 22 46 | 18 33 | 06 31 |
| 55 | 23 28 | 13 00 | 24 44 | 19 44 | 07 04 |
| 56 | 23 58 | 15 20 | 26 55 | 21 01 | 07 38 |
| 57 | 24 36 | 18 08 | 29 19 | 22 24 | 08 15 |
| 58 | 25 26 | 21 32 | 02♊00 | 23 53 | 08 55 |
| 59 | 26 34 | 25 43 | 04 59 | 25 30 | 09 37 |
| 60 | 28♒11 | 00♉55 | 08♊19 | 27♊16 | 10♋22 |

**19h 36m 0s — 294° 0' 0" — 22 ♑ 13**

| LAT. | 11 | 12 | ASC | 2 | 3 |
|---|---|---|---|---|---|
| 0 | 21♒37 | 23♓28 | 25♈53 | 26♉19 | 24♊30 |
| 5 | 21 40 | 23 57 | 26 51 | 27 24 | 25 16 |
| 10 | 21 44 | 24 30 | 27 54 | 28 33 | 26 03 |
| 15 | 21 47 | 25 06 | 29 05 | 29 47 | 26 53 |
| 20 | 21 52 | 25 49 | 00♉24 | 01♊09 | 27 45 |
| 21 | 21 53 | 25 58 | 00 41 | 01 26 | 27 56 |
| 22 | 21 54 | 26 08 | 00 59 | 01 44 | 28 07 |
| 23 | 21 55 | 26 18 | 01 17 | 02 02 | 28 18 |
| 24 | 21 56 | 26 28 | 01 36 | 02 21 | 28 29 |
| 25 | 21 57 | 26 39 | 01 56 | 02 40 | 28 41 |
| 26 | 21 59 | 26 50 | 02 16 | 02 59 | 28 53 |
| 27 | 22 00 | 27 02 | 02 37 | 03 19 | 29 05 |
| 28 | 22 01 | 27 15 | 02 59 | 03 40 | 29 17 |
| 29 | 22 03 | 27 28 | 03 22 | 04 01 | 29 30 |
| 30 | 22 05 | 27 41 | 03 46 | 04 23 | 29 43 |
| 31 | 22 06 | 27 55 | 04 11 | 04 46 | 29 56 |
| 32 | 22 08 | 28 10 | 04 36 | 05 09 | 00♋09 |
| 33 | 22 10 | 28 26 | 05 03 | 05 34 | 00 23 |
| 34 | 22 12 | 28 43 | 05 31 | 05 59 | 00 37 |
| 35 | 22 15 | 29 01 | 06 01 | 06 25 | 00 52 |
| 36 | 22 17 | 29 20 | 06 32 | 06 51 | 01 07 |
| 37 | 22 20 | 29 40 | 07 04 | 07 19 | 01 22 |
| 38 | 22 23 | 00♈01 | 07 39 | 07 48 | 01 38 |
| 39 | 22 26 | 00 24 | 08 15 | 08 18 | 01 54 |
| 40 | 22 30 | 00 49 | 08 53 | 08 50 | 02 11 |
| 41 | 22 34 | 01 15 | 09 34 | 09 23 | 02 28 |
| 42 | 22 38 | 01 44 | 10 17 | 09 57 | 02 46 |
| 43 | 22 43 | 02 15 | 11 03 | 10 33 | 03 05 |
| 44 | 22 48 | 02 49 | 11 52 | 11 11 | 03 24 |
| 45 | 22 54 | 03 25 | 12 44 | 11 50 | 03 44 |
| 46 | 23 01 | 04 06 | 13 40 | 12 32 | 04 05 |
| 47 | 23 09 | 04 51 | 14 40 | 13 15 | 04 27 |
| 48 | 23 17 | 05 40 | 15 45 | 14 02 | 04 50 |
| 49 | 23 27 | 06 36 | 16 55 | 14 50 | 05 13 |
| 50 | 23 39 | 07 38 | 18 11 | 15 42 | 05 38 |
| 51 | 23 52 | 08 48 | 19 33 | 16 37 | 06 04 |
| 52 | 24 08 | 10 08 | 21 03 | 17 35 | 06 32 |
| 53 | 24 27 | 11 39 | 22 41 | 18 38 | 07 01 |
| 54 | 24 50 | 13 25 | 24 28 | 19 44 | 07 31 |
| 55 | 25 18 | 15 29 | 26 26 | 20 55 | 08 03 |
| 56 | 25 53 | 17 56 | 28 36 | 22 11 | 08 38 |
| 57 | 26 38 | 20 51 | 01♊00 | 23 33 | 09 14 |
| 58 | 27 36 | 24 22 | 03 40 | 25 02 | 09 53 |
| 59 | 28 55 | 28 39 | 06 37 | 26 38 | 10 35 |
| 60 | 00♓46 | 03♉55 | 09♊53 | 28♊22 | 11♋20 |

**19h 40m 0s — 295° 0' 0" — 23 ♑ 10**

| LAT. | 11 | 12 | ASC | 2 | 3 |
|---|---|---|---|---|---|
| 0 | 22♒39 | 24♓33 | 26♈57 | 27♉17 | 25♊25 |
| 5 | 22 43 | 25 05 | 27 57 | 28 24 | 26 12 |
| 10 | 22 48 | 25 40 | 29 02 | 29 34 | 27 00 |
| 15 | 22 53 | 26 19 | 00♉15 | 00♊50 | 27 50 |
| 20 | 22 59 | 27 05 | 01 37 | 02 13 | 28 43 |
| 21 | 23 01 | 27 15 | 01 54 | 02 30 | 28 54 |
| 22 | 23 02 | 27 25 | 02 13 | 02 48 | 29 05 |
| 23 | 23 04 | 27 36 | 02 32 | 03 07 | 29 16 |
| 24 | 23 05 | 27 47 | 02 51 | 03 26 | 29 28 |
| 25 | 23 07 | 27 59 | 03 12 | 03 45 | 29 39 |
| 26 | 23 09 | 28 11 | 03 33 | 04 05 | 29 51 |
| 27 | 23 11 | 28 24 | 03 54 | 04 25 | 00♋04 |
| 28 | 23 13 | 28 37 | 04 17 | 04 46 | 00 16 |
| 29 | 23 15 | 28 51 | 04 40 | 05 08 | 00 29 |
| 30 | 23 17 | 29 05 | 05 05 | 05 30 | 00 42 |
| 31 | 23 19 | 29 21 | 05 30 | 05 53 | 00 55 |
| 32 | 23 22 | 29 37 | 05 57 | 06 17 | 01 08 |
| 33 | 23 24 | 29 54 | 06 24 | 06 41 | 01 22 |
| 34 | 23 27 | 00♈12 | 06 53 | 07 06 | 01 36 |
| 35 | 23 30 | 00 31 | 07 24 | 07 33 | 01 51 |
| 36 | 23 33 | 00 51 | 07 55 | 08 00 | 02 06 |
| 37 | 23 37 | 01 12 | 08 29 | 08 28 | 02 21 |
| 38 | 23 41 | 01 35 | 09 04 | 08 57 | 02 37 |
| 39 | 23 45 | 02 00 | 09 41 | 09 28 | 02 54 |
| 40 | 23 49 | 02 26 | 10 20 | 09 59 | 03 11 |
| 41 | 23 54 | 02 54 | 11 02 | 10 33 | 03 28 |
| 42 | 24 00 | 03 25 | 11 46 | 11 07 | 03 46 |
| 43 | 24 05 | 03 58 | 12 33 | 11 43 | 04 05 |
| 44 | 24 12 | 04 34 | 13 23 | 12 21 | 04 24 |
| 45 | 24 19 | 05 13 | 14 16 | 13 01 | 04 44 |
| 46 | 24 28 | 05 56 | 15 13 | 13 42 | 05 05 |
| 47 | 24 37 | 06 44 | 16 14 | 14 26 | 05 27 |
| 48 | 24 47 | 07 36 | 17 20 | 15 13 | 05 50 |
| 49 | 24 59 | 08 35 | 18 31 | 16 01 | 06 13 |
| 50 | 25 13 | 09 41 | 19 47 | 16 53 | 06 38 |
| 51 | 25 29 | 10 55 | 21 10 | 17 48 | 07 04 |
| 52 | 25 48 | 12 19 | 22 41 | 18 46 | 07 31 |
| 53 | 26 10 | 13 55 | 24 19 | 19 48 | 08 00 |
| 54 | 26 37 | 15 47 | 26 07 | 20 54 | 08 31 |
| 55 | 27 10 | 17 56 | 28 05 | 22 05 | 09 03 |
| 56 | 27 50 | 20 28 | 00♊15 | 23 21 | 09 37 |
| 57 | 28 42 | 23 29 | 02 38 | 24 42 | 10 13 |
| 58 | 29 49 | 27 06 | 05 16 | 26 09 | 10 51 |
| 59 | 01♓19 | 01♉28 | 08 10 | 27 44 | 11 33 |
| 60 | 03♓25 | 06♉47 | 11♊23 | 29♊26 | 12♋17 |

# Koch Table of Houses for Latitudes 0° to 60° North

**19h 44m 0s — 296° 0' 0" — 24 ♑ 06**

| LAT. | 11 | 12 | ASC | 2 | 3 |
|---|---|---|---|---|---|
| 0 | 23♒41 | 25♓38 | 28♈00 | 28♉15 | 26♊20 |
| 5 | 23 46 | 26 12 | 29 02 | 29 23 | 27 08 |
| 10 | 23 52 | 26 50 | 00♉10 | 00♊35 | 27 56 |
| 15 | 23 59 | 27 32 | 01 24 | 01 52 | 28 47 |
| 20 | 24 07 | 28 21 | 02 49 | 03 16 | 29 40 |
| 21 | 24 09 | 28 31 | 03 07 | 03 34 | 29 52 |
| 22 | 24 11 | 28 42 | 03 26 | 03 52 | 00♋03 |
| 23 | 24 13 | 28 54 | 03 46 | 04 11 | 00 14 |
| 24 | 24 15 | 29 06 | 04 06 | 04 30 | 00 26 |
| 25 | 24 17 | 29 18 | 04 27 | 04 50 | 00 38 |
| 26 | 24 19 | 29 31 | 04 49 | 05 10 | 00 50 |
| 27 | 24 21 | 29 45 | 05 11 | 05 31 | 01 02 |
| 28 | 24 24 | 29 59 | 05 34 | 05 52 | 01 15 |
| 29 | 24 27 | 00♈14 | 05 58 | 06 14 | 01 27 |
| 30 | 24 29 | 00 29 | 06 23 | 06 36 | 01 40 |
| 31 | 24 32 | 00 46 | 06 49 | 07 00 | 01 54 |
| 32 | 24 35 | 01 03 | 07 17 | 07 24 | 02 07 |
| 33 | 24 39 | 01 21 | 07 45 | 07 48 | 02 21 |
| 34 | 24 42 | 01 40 | 08 15 | 08 14 | 02 36 |
| 35 | 24 46 | 02 00 | 08 46 | 08 40 | 02 50 |
| 36 | 24 50 | 02 22 | 09 18 | 09 08 | 03 05 |
| 37 | 24 54 | 02 45 | 09 52 | 09 36 | 03 21 |
| 38 | 24 59 | 03 09 | 10 28 | 10 06 | 03 37 |
| 39 | 25 04 | 03 35 | 11 06 | 10 36 | 03 53 |
| 40 | 25 09 | 04 03 | 11 46 | 11 08 | 04 10 |
| 41 | 25 15 | 04 33 | 12 29 | 11 42 | 04 28 |
| 42 | 25 22 | 05 05 | 13 14 | 12 16 | 04 46 |
| 43 | 25 29 | 05 41 | 14 01 | 12 53 | 05 04 |
| 44 | 25 37 | 06 19 | 14 52 | 13 31 | 05 24 |
| 45 | 25 45 | 07 00 | 15 46 | 14 11 | 05 44 |
| 46 | 25 55 | 07 46 | 16 44 | 14 52 | 06 05 |
| 47 | 26 06 | 08 36 | 17 46 | 15 36 | 06 27 |
| 48 | 26 18 | 09 32 | 18 53 | 16 23 | 06 49 |
| 49 | 26 32 | 10 34 | 20 04 | 17 12 | 07 13 |
| 50 | 26 48 | 11 43 | 21 22 | 18 03 | 07 38 |
| 51 | 27 07 | 13 01 | 22 46 | 18 58 | 08 04 |
| 52 | 27 29 | 14 29 | 24 16 | 19 56 | 08 31 |
| 53 | 27 55 | 16 09 | 25 55 | 20 58 | 08 59 |
| 54 | 28 25 | 18 05 | 27 43 | 22 03 | 09 30 |
| 55 | 29 03 | 20 20 | 29 41 | 23 13 | 10 02 |
| 56 | 29 49 | 22 57 | 01♊50 | 24 29 | 10 35 |
| 57 | 00♓47 | 26 03 | 04 12 | 25 49 | 11 11 |
| 58 | 02 03 | 29 44 | 06 48 | 27 15 | 11 49 |
| 59 | 03 45 | 04♉10 | 09 40 | 28 49 | 12 30 |
| 60 | 06♓06 | 09♉30 | 12♊50 | 00♋29 | 13♋14 |

**19h 48m 0s — 297° 0' 0" — 25 ♑ 03**

| LAT. | 11 | 12 | ASC | 2 | 3 |
|---|---|---|---|---|---|
| 0 | 24♒42 | 26♓44 | 29♈03 | 29♉13 | 27♊15 |
| 5 | 24 49 | 27 20 | 00♉07 | 00♊22 | 28 03 |
| 10 | 24 57 | 28 00 | 01 17 | 01 35 | 28 53 |
| 15 | 25 05 | 28 45 | 02 34 | 02 54 | 29 44 |
| 20 | 25 15 | 29 36 | 04 01 | 04 19 | 00♋38 |
| 21 | 25 17 | 29 48 | 04 20 | 04 37 | 00 49 |
| 22 | 25 20 | 00♈00 | 04 39 | 04 56 | 01 01 |
| 23 | 25 22 | 00 12 | 05 00 | 05 15 | 01 12 |
| 24 | 25 25 | 00 24 | 05 20 | 05 34 | 01 24 |
| 25 | 25 27 | 00 38 | 05 42 | 05 54 | 01 36 |
| 26 | 25 30 | 00 52 | 06 04 | 06 15 | 01 48 |
| 27 | 25 33 | 01 06 | 06 27 | 06 36 | 02 00 |
| 28 | 25 36 | 01 21 | 06 51 | 06 57 | 02 13 |
| 29 | 25 39 | 01 37 | 07 15 | 07 19 | 02 26 |
| 30 | 25 42 | 01 53 | 07 41 | 07 42 | 02 39 |
| 31 | 25 46 | 02 10 | 08 08 | 08 06 | 02 52 |
| 32 | 25 49 | 02 29 | 08 36 | 08 30 | 03 06 |
| 33 | 25 53 | 02 48 | 09 05 | 08 55 | 03 20 |
| 34 | 25 57 | 03 08 | 09 35 | 09 21 | 03 35 |
| 35 | 26 02 | 03 30 | 10 07 | 09 47 | 03 49 |
| 36 | 26 06 | 03 52 | 10 40 | 10 15 | 04 04 |
| 37 | 26 12 | 04 17 | 11 15 | 10 44 | 04 20 |
| 38 | 26 17 | 04 42 | 11 52 | 11 13 | 04 36 |
| 39 | 26 23 | 05 10 | 12 31 | 11 44 | 04 53 |
| 40 | 26 29 | 05 40 | 13 12 | 12 17 | 05 09 |
| 41 | 26 36 | 06 11 | 13 55 | 12 50 | 05 27 |
| 42 | 26 44 | 06 46 | 14 40 | 13 25 | 05 45 |
| 43 | 26 52 | 07 23 | 15 29 | 14 01 | 06 04 |
| 44 | 27 01 | 08 03 | 16 20 | 14 40 | 06 23 |
| 45 | 27 12 | 08 47 | 17 15 | 15 20 | 06 43 |
| 46 | 27 23 | 09 35 | 18 14 | 16 02 | 07 04 |
| 47 | 27 36 | 10 28 | 19 17 | 16 46 | 07 26 |
| 48 | 27 50 | 11 26 | 20 24 | 17 32 | 07 49 |
| 49 | 28 06 | 12 31 | 21 36 | 18 21 | 08 12 |
| 50 | 28 24 | 13 43 | 22 54 | 19 12 | 08 37 |
| 51 | 28 46 | 15 05 | 24 19 | 20 07 | 09 03 |
| 52 | 29 11 | 16 37 | 25 50 | 21 05 | 09 30 |
| 53 | 29 40 | 18 22 | 27 29 | 22 06 | 09 58 |
| 54 | 00♓15 | 20 22 | 29 17 | 23 11 | 10 28 |
| 55 | 00 57 | 22 41 | 01♊14 | 24 21 | 11 00 |
| 56 | 01 49 | 25 23 | 03 23 | 25 35 | 11 34 |
| 57 | 02 55 | 28 33 | 05 43 | 26 55 | 12 09 |
| 58 | 04 20 | 02♉18 | 08 18 | 28 20 | 12 47 |
| 59 | 06 13 | 06 45 | 11 07 | 29 52 | 13 27 |
| 60 | 08♓51 | 12♉05 | 14♊13 | 01♋31 | 14♋11 |

**19h 52m 0s — 298° 0' 0" — 26 ♑ 00**

| LAT. | 11 | 12 | ASC | 2 | 3 |
|---|---|---|---|---|---|
| 0 | 25♒44 | 27♓49 | 00♉06 | 00♊11 | 28♊10 |
| 5 | 25 53 | 28 28 | 01 12 | 01 21 | 28 59 |
| 10 | 26 02 | 29 10 | 02 24 | 02 36 | 29 49 |
| 15 | 26 12 | 29 57 | 03 43 | 03 55 | 00♋41 |
| 20 | 26 23 | 00♈52 | 05 13 | 05 22 | 01 36 |
| 21 | 26 26 | 01 04 | 05 32 | 05 41 | 01 47 |
| 22 | 26 29 | 01 17 | 05 52 | 05 59 | 01 58 |
| 23 | 26 32 | 01 30 | 06 13 | 06 19 | 02 10 |
| 24 | 26 34 | 01 43 | 06 34 | 06 38 | 02 22 |
| 25 | 26 38 | 01 57 | 06 56 | 06 59 | 02 34 |
| 26 | 26 41 | 02 12 | 07 19 | 07 19 | 02 46 |
| 27 | 26 44 | 02 27 | 07 42 | 07 40 | 02 59 |
| 28 | 26 48 | 02 43 | 08 06 | 08 02 | 03 11 |
| 29 | 26 51 | 02 59 | 08 32 | 08 25 | 03 24 |
| 30 | 26 55 | 03 17 | 08 58 | 08 48 | 03 38 |
| 31 | 26 59 | 03 35 | 09 26 | 09 11 | 03 51 |
| 32 | 27 03 | 03 54 | 09 54 | 09 36 | 04 05 |
| 33 | 27 08 | 04 15 | 10 24 | 10 01 | 04 19 |
| 34 | 27 13 | 04 36 | 10 55 | 10 27 | 04 33 |
| 35 | 27 18 | 04 59 | 11 27 | 10 54 | 04 48 |
| 36 | 27 24 | 05 23 | 12 01 | 11 22 | 05 03 |
| 37 | 27 29 | 05 48 | 12 37 | 11 51 | 05 19 |
| 38 | 27 36 | 06 16 | 13 15 | 12 21 | 05 35 |
| 39 | 27 43 | 06 45 | 13 54 | 12 52 | 05 52 |
| 40 | 27 50 | 07 16 | 14 36 | 13 24 | 06 09 |
| 41 | 27 58 | 07 49 | 15 19 | 13 58 | 06 26 |
| 42 | 28 07 | 08 25 | 16 06 | 14 33 | 06 44 |
| 43 | 28 16 | 09 04 | 16 55 | 15 10 | 07 03 |
| 44 | 28 27 | 09 47 | 17 47 | 15 48 | 07 23 |
| 45 | 28 39 | 10 33 | 18 43 | 16 28 | 07 43 |
| 46 | 28 51 | 11 23 | 19 42 | 17 10 | 08 04 |
| 47 | 29 06 | 12 18 | 20 46 | 17 54 | 08 25 |
| 48 | 29 22 | 13 20 | 21 54 | 18 40 | 08 48 |
| 49 | 29 40 | 14 27 | 23 07 | 19 29 | 09 12 |
| 50 | 00♓01 | 15 43 | 24 25 | 20 21 | 09 36 |
| 51 | 00 25 | 17 07 | 25 50 | 21 15 | 10 02 |
| 52 | 00 53 | 18 43 | 27 21 | 22 13 | 10 29 |
| 53 | 01 26 | 20 31 | 29 00 | 23 14 | 10 57 |
| 54 | 02 05 | 22 35 | 00♊48 | 24 18 | 11 27 |
| 55 | 02 52 | 24 58 | 02 45 | 25 27 | 11 58 |
| 56 | 03 51 | 27 44 | 04 53 | 26 41 | 12 32 |
| 57 | 05 04 | 00♉58 | 07 12 | 28 00 | 13 07 |
| 58 | 06 38 | 04 45 | 09 44 | 29 24 | 13 44 |
| 59 | 08 43 | 09 14 | 12 31 | 00♋55 | 14 24 |
| 60 | 11♓37 | 14♉32 | 15♊34 | 02♋32 | 15♋07 |

**19h 56m 0s — 299° 0' 0" — 26 ♑ 57**

| LAT. | 11 | 12 | ASC | 2 | 3 |
|---|---|---|---|---|---|
| 0 | 26♒47 | 28♓55 | 01♉08 | 01♊08 | 29♊05 |
| 5 | 26 56 | 29 35 | 02 17 | 02 20 | 29 55 |
| 10 | 27 07 | 00♈20 | 03 30 | 03 36 | 00♋46 |
| 15 | 27 18 | 01 10 | 04 52 | 04 57 | 01 38 |
| 20 | 27 32 | 02 08 | 06 24 | 06 25 | 02 33 |
| 21 | 27 35 | 02 20 | 06 44 | 06 43 | 02 45 |
| 22 | 27 38 | 02 34 | 07 04 | 07 02 | 02 56 |
| 23 | 27 41 | 02 47 | 07 26 | 07 22 | 03 08 |
| 24 | 27 45 | 03 02 | 07 47 | 07 42 | 03 20 |
| 25 | 27 48 | 03 16 | 08 10 | 08 02 | 03 32 |
| 26 | 27 52 | 03 32 | 08 33 | 08 23 | 03 44 |
| 27 | 27 56 | 03 48 | 08 57 | 08 45 | 03 57 |
| 28 | 28 00 | 04 05 | 09 22 | 09 07 | 04 10 |
| 29 | 28 04 | 04 22 | 09 48 | 09 29 | 04 23 |
| 30 | 28 08 | 04 40 | 10 15 | 09 53 | 04 36 |
| 31 | 28 13 | 05 00 | 10 43 | 10 17 | 04 50 |
| 32 | 28 18 | 05 20 | 11 12 | 10 41 | 05 03 |
| 33 | 28 23 | 05 41 | 11 42 | 11 07 | 05 18 |
| 34 | 28 29 | 06 04 | 12 14 | 11 33 | 05 32 |
| 35 | 28 35 | 06 28 | 12 47 | 12 00 | 05 47 |
| 36 | 28 41 | 06 53 | 13 22 | 12 28 | 06 02 |
| 37 | 28 48 | 07 20 | 13 58 | 12 57 | 06 18 |
| 38 | 28 55 | 07 48 | 14 36 | 13 27 | 06 34 |
| 39 | 29 03 | 08 19 | 15 16 | 13 59 | 06 51 |
| 40 | 29 11 | 08 52 | 15 59 | 14 31 | 07 08 |
| 41 | 29 20 | 09 27 | 16 43 | 15 05 | 07 25 |
| 42 | 29 30 | 10 05 | 17 30 | 15 40 | 07 43 |
| 43 | 29 41 | 10 45 | 18 20 | 16 17 | 08 02 |
| 44 | 29 53 | 11 30 | 19 13 | 16 55 | 08 22 |
| 45 | 00♓06 | 12 18 | 20 09 | 17 35 | 08 42 |
| 46 | 00 20 | 13 10 | 21 09 | 18 17 | 09 03 |
| 47 | 00 37 | 14 08 | 22 13 | 19 02 | 09 24 |
| 48 | 00 55 | 15 12 | 23 22 | 19 48 | 09 47 |
| 49 | 01 15 | 16 22 | 24 35 | 20 37 | 10 10 |
| 50 | 01 39 | 17 41 | 25 54 | 21 28 | 10 35 |
| 51 | 02 06 | 19 08 | 27 19 | 22 22 | 11 01 |
| 52 | 02 37 | 20 47 | 28 50 | 23 19 | 11 27 |
| 53 | 03 13 | 22 39 | 00♊29 | 24 20 | 11 56 |
| 54 | 03 57 | 24 47 | 02 17 | 25 24 | 12 25 |
| 55 | 04 49 | 27 13 | 04 13 | 26 33 | 12 56 |
| 56 | 05 53 | 00♉02 | 06 20 | 27 46 | 13 29 |
| 57 | 07 14 | 03 18 | 08 38 | 29 04 | 14 04 |
| 58 | 08 58 | 07 08 | 11 08 | 00♋27 | 14 41 |
| 59 | 11 15 | 11 36 | 13 52 | 01 56 | 15 21 |
| 60 | 14♓25 | 16♉51 | 16♊51 | 03♋32 | 16♋03 |

**20h 0m 0s — 300° 0' 0" — 27 ♑ 55**

| LAT. | 11 | 12 | ASC | 2 | 3 |
|---|---|---|---|---|---|
| 0 | 27♒49 | 00♈00 | 02♉11 | 02♊05 | 00♋00 |
| 5 | 28 00 | 00 43 | 03 21 | 03 19 | 00 51 |
| 10 | 28 12 | 01 30 | 04 37 | 04 36 | 01 42 |
| 15 | 28 25 | 02 22 | 06 01 | 05 58 | 02 35 |
| 20 | 28 41 | 03 23 | 07 35 | 07 27 | 03 31 |
| 21 | 28 44 | 03 37 | 07 55 | 07 46 | 03 42 |
| 22 | 28 48 | 03 51 | 08 16 | 08 05 | 03 54 |
| 23 | 28 51 | 04 05 | 08 38 | 08 25 | 04 06 |
| 24 | 28 55 | 04 20 | 09 00 | 08 45 | 04 18 |
| 25 | 28 59 | 04 35 | 09 23 | 09 06 | 04 30 |
| 26 | 29 03 | 04 52 | 09 47 | 09 27 | 04 42 |
| 27 | 29 08 | 05 09 | 10 12 | 09 49 | 04 55 |
| 28 | 29 12 | 05 26 | 10 37 | 10 11 | 05 08 |
| 29 | 29 17 | 05 45 | 11 04 | 10 34 | 05 21 |
| 30 | 29 22 | 06 04 | 11 31 | 10 57 | 05 34 |
| 31 | 29 27 | 06 24 | 12 00 | 11 21 | 05 48 |
| 32 | 29 33 | 06 45 | 12 29 | 11 46 | 06 02 |
| 33 | 29 39 | 07 08 | 13 00 | 12 12 | 06 16 |
| 34 | 29 45 | 07 31 | 13 32 | 12 38 | 06 31 |
| 35 | 29 52 | 07 56 | 14 06 | 13 06 | 06 46 |
| 36 | 29 59 | 08 23 | 14 41 | 13 34 | 07 01 |
| 37 | 00♓06 | 08 51 | 15 18 | 14 03 | 07 17 |
| 38 | 00 14 | 09 21 | 15 57 | 14 34 | 07 33 |
| 39 | 00 23 | 09 53 | 16 38 | 15 05 | 07 49 |
| 40 | 00 33 | 10 27 | 17 21 | 15 38 | 08 07 |
| 41 | 00 43 | 11 04 | 18 06 | 16 12 | 08 24 |
| 42 | 00 54 | 11 43 | 18 54 | 16 47 | 08 42 |
| 43 | 01 06 | 12 26 | 19 44 | 17 24 | 09 01 |
| 44 | 01 19 | 13 12 | 20 38 | 18 02 | 09 21 |
| 45 | 01 34 | 14 02 | 21 35 | 18 42 | 09 41 |
| 46 | 01 50 | 14 57 | 22 35 | 19 24 | 10 02 |
| 47 | 02 08 | 15 57 | 23 39 | 20 08 | 10 23 |
| 48 | 02 28 | 17 03 | 24 48 | 20 55 | 10 46 |
| 49 | 02 51 | 18 16 | 26 02 | 21 43 | 11 09 |
| 50 | 03 17 | 19 37 | 27 21 | 22 34 | 11 34 |
| 51 | 03 46 | 21 08 | 28 46 | 23 28 | 11 59 |
| 52 | 04 21 | 22 49 | 00♊18 | 24 25 | 12 26 |
| 53 | 05 01 | 24 44 | 01 56 | 25 26 | 12 54 |
| 54 | 05 49 | 26 55 | 03 43 | 26 30 | 13 23 |
| 55 | 06 47 | 29 24 | 05 39 | 27 37 | 13 54 |
| 56 | 07 57 | 02♉16 | 07 44 | 28 50 | 14 27 |
| 57 | 09 25 | 05 34 | 10 01 | 00♋07 | 15 01 |
| 58 | 11 19 | 09 25 | 12 29 | 01 29 | 15 38 |
| 59 | 13 49 | 13 53 | 15 11 | 02 57 | 16 17 |
| 60 | 17♓15 | 19♉04 | 18♊06 | 04♋31 | 16♋59 |

**20h 4m 0s — 301° 0' 0" — 28 ♑ 52**

| LAT. | 11 | 12 | ASC | 2 | 3 |
|---|---|---|---|---|---|
| 0 | 28♒52 | 01♈05 | 03♉13 | 03♊03 | 00♋55 |
| 5 | 29 04 | 01 50 | 04 25 | 04 17 | 01 46 |
| 10 | 29 17 | 02 40 | 05 43 | 05 35 | 02 38 |
| 15 | 29 32 | 03 35 | 07 09 | 06 59 | 03 32 |
| 20 | 29 50 | 04 39 | 08 45 | 08 29 | 04 28 |
| 21 | 29 53 | 04 53 | 09 06 | 08 48 | 04 40 |
| 22 | 29 57 | 05 07 | 09 28 | 09 08 | 04 51 |
| 23 | 00♓01 | 05 22 | 09 50 | 09 28 | 05 03 |
| 24 | 00 06 | 05 38 | 10 13 | 09 48 | 05 15 |
| 25 | 00 10 | 05 54 | 10 36 | 10 09 | 05 28 |
| 26 | 00 15 | 06 11 | 11 00 | 10 30 | 05 40 |
| 27 | 00 20 | 06 29 | 11 26 | 10 52 | 05 53 |
| 28 | 00 25 | 06 47 | 11 52 | 11 15 | 06 06 |
| 29 | 00 30 | 07 07 | 12 19 | 11 38 | 06 19 |
| 30 | 00 36 | 07 27 | 12 46 | 12 01 | 06 32 |
| 31 | 00 42 | 07 48 | 13 16 | 12 26 | 06 46 |
| 32 | 00 48 | 08 10 | 13 46 | 12 51 | 07 00 |
| 33 | 00 54 | 08 34 | 14 17 | 13 17 | 07 15 |
| 34 | 01 01 | 08 59 | 14 50 | 13 43 | 07 29 |
| 35 | 01 09 | 09 25 | 15 24 | 14 11 | 07 44 |
| 36 | 01 17 | 09 52 | 16 00 | 14 39 | 08 00 |
| 37 | 01 25 | 10 22 | 16 38 | 15 09 | 08 15 |
| 38 | 01 34 | 10 53 | 17 17 | 15 39 | 08 32 |
| 39 | 01 44 | 11 26 | 17 58 | 16 11 | 08 48 |
| 40 | 01 54 | 12 02 | 18 42 | 16 43 | 09 05 |
| 41 | 02 06 | 12 40 | 19 28 | 17 18 | 09 23 |
| 42 | 02 18 | 13 21 | 20 16 | 17 53 | 09 41 |
| 43 | 02 31 | 14 05 | 21 07 | 18 30 | 10 00 |
| 44 | 02 46 | 14 53 | 22 01 | 19 08 | 10 19 |
| 45 | 03 02 | 15 45 | 22 58 | 19 49 | 10 39 |
| 46 | 03 20 | 16 42 | 23 59 | 20 31 | 11 00 |
| 47 | 03 40 | 17 44 | 25 04 | 21 15 | 11 22 |
| 48 | 04 02 | 18 53 | 26 13 | 22 01 | 11 44 |
| 49 | 04 27 | 20 08 | 27 27 | 22 49 | 12 08 |
| 50 | 04 56 | 21 32 | 28 47 | 23 40 | 12 32 |
| 51 | 05 28 | 23 05 | 00♊12 | 24 34 | 12 57 |
| 52 | 06 06 | 24 49 | 01 43 | 25 31 | 13 24 |
| 53 | 06 50 | 26 47 | 03 21 | 26 30 | 13 52 |
| 54 | 07 42 | 29 00 | 05 08 | 27 34 | 14 21 |
| 55 | 08 45 | 01♉32 | 07 03 | 28 41 | 14 52 |
| 56 | 10 02 | 04 26 | 09 07 | 29 53 | 15 24 |
| 57 | 11 38 | 07 46 | 11 22 | 01♋09 | 15 58 |
| 58 | 13 41 | 11 36 | 13 48 | 02 30 | 16 35 |
| 59 | 16 23 | 16 03 | 16 26 | 03 56 | 17 13 |
| 60 | 20♓05 | 21♉10 | 19♊18 | 05♋29 | 17♋54 |

**20h 8m 0s — 302° 0' 0" — 29 ♑ 49**

| LAT. | 11 | 12 | ASC | 2 | 3 |
|---|---|---|---|---|---|
| 0 | 29♒54 | 02♈11 | 04♉16 | 04♊00 | 01♋50 |
| 5 | 00♓08 | 02 58 | 05 29 | 05 15 | 02 42 |
| 10 | 00 23 | 03 49 | 06 49 | 06 35 | 03 35 |
| 15 | 00 39 | 04 47 | 08 17 | 07 59 | 04 29 |
| 20 | 00 59 | 05 54 | 09 56 | 09 31 | 05 25 |
| 21 | 01 03 | 06 09 | 10 17 | 09 50 | 05 37 |
| 22 | 01 07 | 06 24 | 10 39 | 10 10 | 05 49 |
| 23 | 01 12 | 06 40 | 11 01 | 10 30 | 06 01 |
| 24 | 01 17 | 06 56 | 11 25 | 10 51 | 06 13 |
| 25 | 01 21 | 07 13 | 11 49 | 11 12 | 06 25 |
| 26 | 01 27 | 07 31 | 12 13 | 11 33 | 06 38 |
| 27 | 01 32 | 07 49 | 12 39 | 11 55 | 06 51 |
| 28 | 01 38 | 08 09 | 13 05 | 12 18 | 07 04 |
| 29 | 01 44 | 08 29 | 13 33 | 12 41 | 07 17 |
| 30 | 01 50 | 08 50 | 14 01 | 13 05 | 07 31 |
| 31 | 01 56 | 09 12 | 14 31 | 13 30 | 07 44 |
| 32 | 02 03 | 09 35 | 15 02 | 13 55 | 07 58 |
| 33 | 02 10 | 10 00 | 15 34 | 14 21 | 08 13 |
| 34 | 02 18 | 10 25 | 16 07 | 14 48 | 08 28 |
| 35 | 02 26 | 10 52 | 16 42 | 15 16 | 08 43 |
| 36 | 02 35 | 11 21 | 17 18 | 15 44 | 08 58 |
| 37 | 02 44 | 11 52 | 17 56 | 16 14 | 09 14 |
| 38 | 02 54 | 12 24 | 18 36 | 16 44 | 09 30 |
| 39 | 03 05 | 12 59 | 19 18 | 17 16 | 09 47 |
| 40 | 03 16 | 13 36 | 20 02 | 17 49 | 10 04 |
| 41 | 03 29 | 14 16 | 20 48 | 18 23 | 10 22 |
| 42 | 03 42 | 14 58 | 21 37 | 18 58 | 10 40 |
| 43 | 03 57 | 15 44 | 22 28 | 19 35 | 10 59 |
| 44 | 04 13 | 16 34 | 23 23 | 20 14 | 11 18 |
| 45 | 04 31 | 17 28 | 24 21 | 20 54 | 11 38 |
| 46 | 04 50 | 18 27 | 25 22 | 21 36 | 11 59 |
| 47 | 05 12 | 19 31 | 26 27 | 22 20 | 12 20 |
| 48 | 05 36 | 20 41 | 27 37 | 23 06 | 12 43 |
| 49 | 06 04 | 21 59 | 28 51 | 23 54 | 13 06 |
| 50 | 06 35 | 23 25 | 00♊10 | 24 45 | 13 30 |
| 51 | 07 10 | 25 00 | 01 35 | 25 39 | 13 56 |
| 52 | 07 51 | 26 47 | 03 06 | 26 35 | 14 22 |
| 53 | 08 39 | 28 47 | 04 44 | 27 35 | 14 50 |
| 54 | 09 36 | 01♉03 | 06 30 | 28 37 | 15 19 |
| 55 | 10 44 | 03 37 | 08 24 | 29 44 | 15 49 |
| 56 | 12 08 | 06 32 | 10 27 | 00♋55 | 16 21 |
| 57 | 13 51 | 09 53 | 12 40 | 02 10 | 16 55 |
| 58 | 16 04 | 13 43 | 15 04 | 03 30 | 17 31 |
| 59 | 18 58 | 18 07 | 17 40 | 04 55 | 18 09 |
| 60 | 22♓56 | 23♉10 | 20♊29 | 06♋26 | 18♋49 |

**20h 12m 0s — 303° 0' 0" — 00 ♒ 47**

| LAT. | 11 | 12 | ASC | 2 | 3 |
|---|---|---|---|---|---|
| 0 | 00♓57 | 03♈16 | 05♉18 | 04♊57 | 02♋45 |
| 5 | 01 12 | 04 05 | 06 33 | 06 14 | 03 38 |
| 10 | 01 28 | 04 59 | 07 55 | 07 34 | 04 31 |
| 15 | 01 47 | 06 00 | 09 25 | 09 00 | 05 25 |
| 20 | 02 08 | 07 09 | 11 05 | 10 32 | 06 23 |
| 21 | 02 13 | 07 25 | 11 27 | 10 52 | 06 34 |
| 22 | 02 17 | 07 41 | 11 49 | 11 12 | 06 46 |
| 23 | 02 22 | 07 57 | 12 12 | 11 32 | 06 58 |
| 24 | 02 28 | 08 14 | 12 36 | 11 53 | 07 11 |
| 25 | 02 33 | 08 32 | 13 00 | 12 14 | 07 23 |
| 26 | 02 39 | 08 50 | 13 26 | 12 36 | 07 36 |
| 27 | 02 45 | 09 09 | 13 52 | 12 58 | 07 49 |
| 28 | 02 51 | 09 29 | 14 19 | 13 21 | 08 02 |
| 29 | 02 57 | 09 50 | 14 47 | 13 45 | 08 15 |
| 30 | 03 04 | 10 12 | 15 16 | 14 09 | 08 29 |
| 31 | 03 11 | 10 35 | 15 46 | 14 33 | 08 42 |
| 32 | 03 19 | 11 00 | 16 17 | 14 59 | 08 57 |
| 33 | 03 27 | 11 25 | 16 49 | 15 25 | 09 11 |
| 34 | 03 35 | 11 52 | 17 23 | 15 52 | 09 26 |
| 35 | 03 44 | 12 20 | 17 58 | 16 20 | 09 41 |
| 36 | 03 54 | 12 50 | 18 35 | 16 48 | 09 56 |
| 37 | 04 04 | 13 22 | 19 14 | 17 18 | 10 12 |
| 38 | 04 15 | 13 55 | 19 54 | 17 49 | 10 28 |
| 39 | 04 26 | 14 31 | 20 37 | 18 21 | 10 45 |
| 40 | 04 39 | 15 10 | 21 21 | 18 54 | 11 02 |
| 41 | 04 52 | 15 51 | 22 08 | 19 28 | 11 20 |
| 42 | 05 07 | 16 35 | 22 57 | 20 03 | 11 38 |
| 43 | 05 23 | 17 22 | 23 49 | 20 40 | 11 57 |
| 44 | 05 41 | 18 14 | 24 44 | 21 19 | 12 16 |
| 45 | 06 00 | 19 09 | 25 42 | 21 59 | 12 36 |
| 46 | 06 21 | 20 10 | 26 44 | 22 41 | 12 57 |
| 47 | 06 45 | 21 16 | 27 49 | 23 25 | 13 19 |
| 48 | 07 11 | 22 28 | 28 59 | 24 11 | 13 41 |
| 49 | 07 41 | 23 48 | 00♊13 | 24 59 | 14 04 |
| 50 | 08 14 | 25 16 | 01 32 | 25 49 | 14 28 |
| 51 | 08 53 | 26 54 | 02 57 | 26 43 | 14 53 |
| 52 | 09 37 | 28 43 | 04 28 | 27 39 | 15 20 |
| 53 | 10 29 | 00♉45 | 06 06 | 28 38 | 15 47 |
| 54 | 11 31 | 03 02 | 07 51 | 29 40 | 16 16 |
| 55 | 12 44 | 05 38 | 09 44 | 00♋46 | 16 46 |
| 56 | 14 14 | 08 34 | 11 45 | 01 56 | 17 18 |
| 57 | 16 05 | 11 55 | 13 57 | 03 10 | 17 51 |
| 58 | 18 27 | 15 45 | 16 19 | 04 29 | 18 27 |
| 59 | 21 34 | 20 06 | 18 52 | 05 53 | 19 04 |
| 60 | 25♓46 | 25♉04 | 21♊37 | 07♋23 | 19♋44 |

# Koch Table of Houses for Latitudes 0° to 60° North

**20h 16m 0s — 304° 0' 0" — 01 ♒ 45**

| LAT. | 11 | 12 | ASC | 2 | 3 |
|---|---|---|---|---|---|
| 0 | 02♓00 | 04♈22 | 06♉19 | 05♊54 | 03♋40 |
| 5 | 02 16 | 05 13 | 07 37 | 07 12 | 04 33 |
| 10 | 02 34 | 06 09 | 09 00 | 08 33 | 05 27 |
| 15 | 02 54 | 07 12 | 10 32 | 10 00 | 06 22 |
| 20 | 03 17 | 08 24 | 12 15 | 11 33 | 07 20 |
| 21 | 03 22 | 08 40 | 12 37 | 11 53 | 07 32 |
| 22 | 03 28 | 08 57 | 13 00 | 12 13 | 07 44 |
| 23 | 03 33 | 09 14 | 13 23 | 12 34 | 07 56 |
| 24 | 03 39 | 09 32 | 13 47 | 12 55 | 08 08 |
| 25 | 03 45 | 09 50 | 14 12 | 13 16 | 08 21 |
| 26 | 03 51 | 10 09 | 14 38 | 13 38 | 08 33 |
| 27 | 03 57 | 10 29 | 15 04 | 14 01 | 08 46 |
| 28 | 04 04 | 10 50 | 15 32 | 14 24 | 09 00 |
| 29 | 04 11 | 11 12 | 16 00 | 14 47 | 09 13 |
| 30 | 04 18 | 11 35 | 16 29 | 15 12 | 09 27 |
| 31 | 04 26 | 11 59 | 17 00 | 15 37 | 09 41 |
| 32 | 04 34 | 12 24 | 17 31 | 16 02 | 09 55 |
| 33 | 04 43 | 12 50 | 18 04 | 16 28 | 10 09 |
| 34 | 04 52 | 13 18 | 18 39 | 16 56 | 10 24 |
| 35 | 05 02 | 13 47 | 19 14 | 17 24 | 10 39 |
| 36 | 05 12 | 14 18 | 19 52 | 17 52 | 10 55 |
| 37 | 05 23 | 14 51 | 20 31 | 18 22 | 11 10 |
| 38 | 05 35 | 15 26 | 21 12 | 18 53 | 11 27 |
| 39 | 05 48 | 16 03 | 21 54 | 19 25 | 11 43 |
| 40 | 06 01 | 16 43 | 22 39 | 19 58 | 12 01 |
| 41 | 06 16 | 17 25 | 23 26 | 20 32 | 12 18 |
| 42 | 06 32 | 18 11 | 24 16 | 21 08 | 12 37 |
| 43 | 06 49 | 19 00 | 25 08 | 21 45 | 12 55 |
| 44 | 07 08 | 19 52 | 26 03 | 22 23 | 13 15 |
| 45 | 07 29 | 20 50 | 27 02 | 23 03 | 13 35 |
| 46 | 07 52 | 21 52 | 28 04 | 23 45 | 13 55 |
| 47 | 08 18 | 23 00 | 29 09 | 24 29 | 14 17 |
| 48 | 08 46 | 24 14 | 00♊19 | 25 15 | 14 39 |
| 49 | 09 18 | 25 36 | 01 34 | 26 03 | 15 02 |
| 50 | 09 55 | 27 06 | 02 53 | 26 53 | 15 26 |
| 51 | 10 36 | 28 45 | 04 17 | 27 46 | 15 51 |
| 52 | 11 24 | 00♉36 | 05 48 | 28 41 | 16 17 |
| 53 | 12 20 | 02 40 | 07 25 | 29 40 | 16 45 |
| 54 | 13 26 | 04 59 | 09 09 | 00♋42 | 17 14 |
| 55 | 14 44 | 07 36 | 11 01 | 01 47 | 17 43 |
| 56 | 16 20 | 10 33 | 13 01 | 02 56 | 18 15 |
| 57 | 18 20 | 13 54 | 15 11 | 04 10 | 18 48 |
| 58 | 20 51 | 17 42 | 17 31 | 05 27 | 19 23 |
| 59 | 24 09 | 22 00 | 20 01 | 06 50 | 20 00 |
| 60 | 28♓35 | 26♉53 | 22♊43 | 08♋19 | 20♋39 |

**20h 20m 0s — 305° 0' 0" — 02 ♒ 43**

| LAT. | 11 | 12 | ASC | 2 | 3 |
|---|---|---|---|---|---|
| 0 | 03♓03 | 05♈27 | 07♉21 | 06♊50 | 04♋35 |
| 5 | 03 21 | 06 20 | 08 40 | 08 09 | 05 29 |
| 10 | 03 40 | 07 18 | 10 05 | 09 32 | 06 23 |
| 15 | 04 02 | 08 24 | 11 39 | 11 00 | 07 19 |
| 20 | 04 27 | 09 39 | 13 24 | 12 34 | 08 17 |
| 21 | 04 32 | 09 56 | 13 46 | 12 54 | 08 29 |
| 22 | 04 38 | 10 13 | 14 09 | 13 15 | 08 41 |
| 23 | 04 44 | 10 31 | 14 33 | 13 35 | 08 53 |
| 24 | 04 50 | 10 49 | 14 58 | 13 57 | 09 06 |
| 25 | 04 57 | 11 08 | 15 23 | 14 18 | 09 18 |
| 26 | 05 03 | 11 28 | 15 49 | 14 40 | 09 31 |
| 27 | 05 10 | 11 49 | 16 16 | 15 03 | 09 44 |
| 28 | 05 17 | 12 10 | 16 44 | 15 26 | 09 57 |
| 29 | 05 25 | 12 33 | 17 13 | 15 50 | 10 11 |
| 30 | 05 33 | 12 57 | 17 42 | 16 14 | 10 25 |
| 31 | 05 42 | 13 21 | 18 13 | 16 39 | 10 38 |
| 32 | 05 50 | 13 47 | 18 45 | 17 05 | 10 53 |
| 33 | 06 00 | 14 15 | 19 19 | 17 32 | 11 07 |
| 34 | 06 10 | 14 43 | 19 53 | 17 59 | 11 22 |
| 35 | 06 20 | 15 14 | 20 30 | 18 27 | 11 37 |
| 36 | 06 31 | 15 46 | 21 07 | 18 56 | 11 53 |
| 37 | 06 43 | 16 20 | 21 47 | 19 26 | 12 09 |
| 38 | 06 56 | 16 56 | 22 28 | 19 57 | 12 25 |
| 39 | 07 10 | 17 34 | 23 11 | 20 29 | 12 42 |
| 40 | 07 24 | 18 15 | 23 56 | 21 02 | 12 59 |
| 41 | 07 40 | 18 59 | 24 44 | 21 36 | 13 17 |
| 42 | 07 57 | 19 45 | 25 34 | 22 12 | 13 35 |
| 43 | 08 16 | 20 36 | 26 26 | 22 49 | 13 53 |
| 44 | 08 37 | 21 30 | 27 22 | 23 27 | 14 13 |
| 45 | 08 59 | 22 29 | 28 21 | 24 07 | 14 33 |
| 46 | 09 24 | 23 33 | 29 23 | 24 49 | 14 53 |
| 47 | 09 51 | 24 42 | 00♊28 | 25 33 | 15 15 |
| 48 | 10 22 | 25 58 | 01 38 | 26 18 | 15 37 |
| 49 | 10 56 | 27 22 | 02 53 | 27 06 | 16 00 |
| 50 | 11 35 | 28 53 | 04 12 | 27 56 | 16 24 |
| 51 | 12 20 | 00♉35 | 05 36 | 28 48 | 16 49 |
| 52 | 13 11 | 02 27 | 07 06 | 29 44 | 17 15 |
| 53 | 14 11 | 04 32 | 08 43 | 00♋42 | 17 42 |
| 54 | 15 21 | 06 53 | 10 26 | 01 43 | 18 10 |
| 55 | 16 45 | 09 30 | 12 17 | 02 48 | 18 40 |
| 56 | 18 27 | 12 28 | 14 16 | 03 56 | 19 11 |
| 57 | 20 34 | 15 48 | 16 24 | 05 08 | 19 44 |
| 58 | 23 15 | 19 34 | 18 41 | 06 25 | 20 18 |
| 59 | 26 44 | 23 50 | 21 09 | 07 47 | 20 55 |
| 60 | 01♈23 | 28♉37 | 23♊48 | 09♋14 | 21♋34 |

**20h 24m 0s — 306° 0' 0" — 03 ♒ 41**

| LAT. | 11 | 12 | ASC | 2 | 3 |
|---|---|---|---|---|---|
| 0 | 04♓07 | 06♈32 | 08♉23 | 07♊47 | 05♋30 |
| 5 | 04 26 | 07 27 | 09 43 | 09 07 | 06 25 |
| 10 | 04 47 | 08 28 | 11 10 | 10 31 | 07 20 |
| 15 | 05 10 | 09 36 | 12 46 | 12 00 | 08 16 |
| 20 | 05 37 | 10 54 | 14 32 | 13 35 | 09 14 |
| 21 | 05 43 | 11 11 | 14 55 | 13 55 | 09 26 |
| 22 | 05 49 | 11 29 | 15 19 | 14 16 | 09 38 |
| 23 | 05 55 | 11 47 | 15 43 | 14 37 | 09 51 |
| 24 | 06 02 | 12 06 | 16 08 | 14 58 | 10 03 |
| 25 | 06 09 | 12 26 | 16 33 | 15 20 | 10 16 |
| 26 | 06 16 | 12 47 | 17 00 | 15 42 | 10 29 |
| 27 | 06 23 | 13 08 | 17 27 | 16 05 | 10 42 |
| 28 | 06 31 | 13 30 | 17 55 | 16 28 | 10 55 |
| 29 | 06 39 | 13 54 | 18 25 | 16 52 | 11 09 |
| 30 | 06 48 | 14 18 | 18 55 | 17 17 | 11 22 |
| 31 | 06 57 | 14 44 | 19 26 | 17 42 | 11 36 |
| 32 | 07 07 | 15 11 | 19 59 | 18 08 | 11 51 |
| 33 | 07 17 | 15 39 | 20 32 | 18 34 | 12 05 |
| 34 | 07 27 | 16 08 | 21 08 | 19 02 | 12 20 |
| 35 | 07 39 | 16 40 | 21 44 | 19 30 | 12 35 |
| 36 | 07 51 | 17 13 | 22 22 | 19 59 | 12 51 |
| 37 | 08 03 | 17 48 | 23 02 | 20 29 | 13 07 |
| 38 | 08 17 | 18 25 | 23 44 | 21 00 | 13 23 |
| 39 | 08 32 | 19 04 | 24 27 | 21 32 | 13 40 |
| 40 | 08 48 | 19 46 | 25 13 | 22 05 | 13 57 |
| 41 | 09 05 | 20 31 | 26 00 | 22 39 | 14 15 |
| 42 | 09 23 | 21 19 | 26 51 | 23 15 | 14 33 |
| 43 | 09 43 | 22 11 | 27 44 | 23 52 | 14 52 |
| 44 | 10 05 | 23 07 | 28 39 | 24 30 | 15 11 |
| 45 | 10 29 | 24 07 | 29 38 | 25 10 | 15 31 |
| 46 | 10 55 | 25 12 | 00♊40 | 25 52 | 15 51 |
| 47 | 11 25 | 26 23 | 01 46 | 26 35 | 16 13 |
| 48 | 11 58 | 27 41 | 02 56 | 27 21 | 16 35 |
| 49 | 12 34 | 29 06 | 04 10 | 28 08 | 16 58 |
| 50 | 13 16 | 00♉39 | 05 29 | 28 58 | 17 21 |
| 51 | 14 03 | 02 22 | 06 53 | 29 50 | 17 46 |
| 52 | 14 58 | 04 16 | 08 23 | 00♋45 | 18 12 |
| 53 | 16 02 | 06 22 | 09 59 | 01 43 | 18 39 |
| 54 | 17 17 | 08 44 | 11 41 | 02 43 | 19 07 |
| 55 | 18 46 | 11 22 | 13 31 | 03 47 | 19 36 |
| 56 | 20 34 | 14 19 | 15 28 | 04 55 | 20 07 |
| 57 | 22 49 | 17 38 | 17 34 | 06 06 | 20 40 |
| 58 | 25 38 | 21 22 | 19 50 | 07 22 | 21 14 |
| 59 | 29 17 | 25 34 | 22 15 | 08 43 | 21 50 |
| 60 | 04♈09 | 00♊16 | 24♊50 | 10♋08 | 22♋28 |

**20h 28m 0s — 307° 0' 0" — 04 ♒ 39**

| LAT. | 11 | 12 | ASC | 2 | 3 |
|---|---|---|---|---|---|
| 0 | 05♓10 | 07♈37 | 09♉24 | 08♊43 | 06♋26 |
| 5 | 05 31 | 08 35 | 10 46 | 10 05 | 07 21 |
| 10 | 05 53 | 09 37 | 12 15 | 11 29 | 08 16 |
| 15 | 06 18 | 10 48 | 13 52 | 12 59 | 09 12 |
| 20 | 06 47 | 12 09 | 15 40 | 14 36 | 10 11 |
| 21 | 06 53 | 12 26 | 16 04 | 14 56 | 10 23 |
| 22 | 07 00 | 12 45 | 16 27 | 15 17 | 10 36 |
| 23 | 07 06 | 13 04 | 16 52 | 15 38 | 10 48 |
| 24 | 07 14 | 13 23 | 17 17 | 15 59 | 11 01 |
| 25 | 07 21 | 13 44 | 17 43 | 16 21 | 11 13 |
| 26 | 07 29 | 14 05 | 18 10 | 16 44 | 11 26 |
| 27 | 07 37 | 14 27 | 18 38 | 17 07 | 11 39 |
| 28 | 07 45 | 14 50 | 19 07 | 17 30 | 11 53 |
| 29 | 07 54 | 15 14 | 19 36 | 17 54 | 12 06 |
| 30 | 08 03 | 15 39 | 20 07 | 18 19 | 12 20 |
| 31 | 08 13 | 16 06 | 20 38 | 18 44 | 12 34 |
| 32 | 08 23 | 16 33 | 21 11 | 19 10 | 12 48 |
| 33 | 08 34 | 17 02 | 21 45 | 19 37 | 13 03 |
| 34 | 08 45 | 17 33 | 22 21 | 20 04 | 13 18 |
| 35 | 08 57 | 18 05 | 22 58 | 20 32 | 13 33 |
| 36 | 09 10 | 18 39 | 23 36 | 21 02 | 13 49 |
| 37 | 09 24 | 19 15 | 24 16 | 21 32 | 14 05 |
| 38 | 09 38 | 19 53 | 24 58 | 22 03 | 14 21 |
| 39 | 09 54 | 20 34 | 25 42 | 22 35 | 14 38 |
| 40 | 10 11 | 21 17 | 26 28 | 23 08 | 14 55 |
| 41 | 10 29 | 22 03 | 27 16 | 23 42 | 15 13 |
| 42 | 10 49 | 22 53 | 28 07 | 24 18 | 15 31 |
| 43 | 11 10 | 23 46 | 29 00 | 24 55 | 15 49 |
| 44 | 11 33 | 24 43 | 29 56 | 25 33 | 16 09 |
| 45 | 11 59 | 25 44 | 00♊55 | 26 13 | 16 29 |
| 46 | 12 27 | 26 51 | 01 57 | 26 54 | 16 49 |
| 47 | 12 59 | 28 03 | 03 03 | 27 38 | 17 10 |
| 48 | 13 34 | 29 22 | 04 13 | 28 23 | 17 32 |
| 49 | 14 13 | 00♉48 | 05 27 | 29 10 | 17 55 |
| 50 | 14 57 | 02 23 | 06 45 | 00♋00 | 18 19 |
| 51 | 15 47 | 04 07 | 08 09 | 00 52 | 18 43 |
| 52 | 16 45 | 06 02 | 09 38 | 01 46 | 19 09 |
| 53 | 17 53 | 08 10 | 11 13 | 02 43 | 19 36 |
| 54 | 19 12 | 10 31 | 12 54 | 03 43 | 20 04 |
| 55 | 20 47 | 13 10 | 14 43 | 04 46 | 20 33 |
| 56 | 22 41 | 16 07 | 16 39 | 05 53 | 21 03 |
| 57 | 25 03 | 19 25 | 18 43 | 07 04 | 21 35 |
| 58 | 28 01 | 23 06 | 20 56 | 08 19 | 22 09 |
| 59 | 01♈50 | 27 14 | 23 19 | 09 38 | 22 45 |
| 60 | 06♈53 | 01♊51 | 25♊52 | 11♋02 | 23♋23 |

**20h 32m 0s — 308° 0' 0" — 05 ♒ 38**

| LAT. | 11 | 12 | ASC | 2 | 3 |
|---|---|---|---|---|---|
| 0 | 06♓14 | 08♈43 | 10♉25 | 09♊40 | 07♋21 |
| 5 | 06 36 | 09 42 | 11 49 | 11 02 | 08 16 |
| 10 | 06 59 | 10 47 | 13 19 | 12 28 | 09 12 |
| 15 | 07 26 | 11 59 | 14 58 | 13 58 | 10 09 |
| 20 | 07 57 | 13 23 | 16 48 | 15 36 | 11 08 |
| 21 | 08 04 | 13 41 | 17 12 | 15 56 | 11 21 |
| 22 | 08 11 | 14 00 | 17 36 | 16 17 | 11 33 |
| 23 | 08 18 | 14 20 | 18 01 | 16 38 | 11 45 |
| 24 | 08 25 | 14 40 | 18 27 | 17 00 | 11 58 |
| 25 | 08 33 | 15 01 | 18 53 | 17 22 | 12 11 |
| 26 | 08 41 | 15 23 | 19 20 | 17 45 | 12 24 |
| 27 | 08 50 | 15 46 | 19 48 | 18 08 | 12 37 |
| 28 | 08 59 | 16 10 | 20 17 | 18 31 | 12 50 |
| 29 | 09 08 | 16 34 | 20 47 | 18 56 | 13 04 |
| 30 | 09 18 | 17 00 | 21 18 | 19 20 | 13 18 |
| 31 | 09 29 | 17 27 | 21 50 | 19 46 | 13 32 |
| 32 | 09 39 | 17 56 | 22 23 | 20 12 | 13 46 |
| 33 | 09 51 | 18 26 | 22 58 | 20 39 | 14 01 |
| 34 | 10 03 | 18 57 | 23 34 | 21 06 | 14 16 |
| 35 | 10 16 | 19 30 | 24 11 | 21 35 | 14 31 |
| 36 | 10 30 | 20 05 | 24 50 | 22 04 | 14 47 |
| 37 | 10 44 | 20 42 | 25 30 | 22 34 | 15 03 |
| 38 | 11 00 | 21 21 | 26 12 | 23 05 | 15 19 |
| 39 | 11 16 | 22 03 | 26 56 | 23 37 | 15 36 |
| 40 | 11 34 | 22 47 | 27 42 | 24 10 | 15 53 |
| 41 | 11 54 | 23 34 | 28 31 | 24 44 | 16 11 |
| 42 | 12 15 | 24 25 | 29 22 | 25 20 | 16 29 |
| 43 | 12 37 | 25 19 | 00♊15 | 25 57 | 16 47 |
| 44 | 13 02 | 26 17 | 01 11 | 26 35 | 17 07 |
| 45 | 13 29 | 27 20 | 02 10 | 27 15 | 17 26 |
| 46 | 13 59 | 28 28 | 03 12 | 27 56 | 17 47 |
| 47 | 14 33 | 29 42 | 04 18 | 28 40 | 18 08 |
| 48 | 15 10 | 01♉02 | 05 28 | 29 25 | 18 30 |
| 49 | 15 51 | 02 29 | 06 42 | 00♋12 | 18 53 |
| 50 | 16 38 | 04 05 | 08 00 | 01 01 | 19 16 |
| 51 | 17 31 | 05 50 | 09 23 | 01 52 | 19 40 |
| 52 | 18 33 | 07 46 | 10 52 | 02 46 | 20 06 |
| 53 | 19 44 | 09 54 | 12 26 | 03 43 | 20 32 |
| 54 | 21 08 | 12 17 | 14 06 | 04 42 | 21 00 |
| 55 | 22 48 | 14 55 | 15 54 | 05 45 | 21 29 |
| 56 | 24 48 | 17 51 | 17 48 | 06 51 | 21 59 |
| 57 | 27 16 | 21 08 | 19 51 | 08 01 | 22 31 |
| 58 | 00♈22 | 24 47 | 22 02 | 09 14 | 23 05 |
| 59 | 04 20 | 28 51 | 24 22 | 10 33 | 23 40 |
| 60 | 09♈33 | 03♊21 | 26♊51 | 11♋55 | 24♋17 |

**20h 36m 0s — 309° 0' 0" — 06 ♒ 37**

| LAT. | 11 | 12 | ASC | 2 | 3 |
|---|---|---|---|---|---|
| 0 | 07♓18 | 09♈48 | 11♉26 | 10♊36 | 08♋16 |
| 5 | 07 41 | 10 49 | 12 52 | 11 59 | 09 12 |
| 10 | 08 06 | 11 56 | 14 24 | 13 26 | 10 09 |
| 15 | 08 34 | 13 11 | 16 04 | 14 58 | 11 06 |
| 20 | 09 07 | 14 37 | 17 55 | 16 36 | 12 06 |
| 21 | 09 14 | 14 56 | 18 19 | 16 56 | 12 18 |
| 22 | 09 22 | 15 15 | 18 44 | 17 17 | 12 30 |
| 23 | 09 29 | 15 35 | 19 09 | 17 39 | 12 43 |
| 24 | 09 37 | 15 56 | 19 35 | 18 01 | 12 55 |
| 25 | 09 46 | 16 18 | 20 02 | 18 23 | 13 08 |
| 26 | 09 54 | 16 41 | 20 30 | 18 46 | 13 21 |
| 27 | 10 04 | 17 04 | 20 58 | 19 09 | 13 35 |
| 28 | 10 13 | 17 28 | 21 27 | 19 33 | 13 48 |
| 29 | 10 23 | 17 54 | 21 57 | 19 57 | 14 02 |
| 30 | 10 33 | 18 21 | 22 29 | 20 22 | 14 16 |
| 31 | 10 44 | 18 48 | 23 01 | 20 47 | 14 30 |
| 32 | 10 56 | 19 18 | 23 35 | 21 13 | 14 44 |
| 33 | 11 08 | 19 48 | 24 09 | 21 40 | 14 59 |
| 34 | 11 21 | 20 21 | 24 46 | 22 08 | 15 14 |
| 35 | 11 35 | 20 54 | 25 23 | 22 36 | 15 29 |
| 36 | 11 49 | 21 30 | 26 02 | 23 06 | 15 45 |
| 37 | 12 05 | 22 08 | 26 43 | 23 36 | 16 01 |
| 38 | 12 21 | 22 48 | 27 25 | 24 07 | 16 17 |
| 39 | 12 39 | 23 31 | 28 10 | 24 39 | 16 34 |
| 40 | 12 58 | 24 16 | 28 56 | 25 12 | 16 51 |
| 41 | 13 19 | 25 04 | 29 45 | 25 46 | 17 08 |
| 42 | 13 41 | 25 56 | 00♊35 | 26 22 | 17 26 |
| 43 | 14 05 | 26 51 | 01 29 | 26 59 | 17 45 |
| 44 | 14 31 | 27 51 | 02 25 | 27 37 | 18 04 |
| 45 | 15 00 | 28 55 | 03 24 | 28 17 | 18 24 |
| 46 | 15 32 | 00♉04 | 04 26 | 28 58 | 18 44 |
| 47 | 16 07 | 01 18 | 05 32 | 29 41 | 19 05 |
| 48 | 16 46 | 02 40 | 06 42 | 00♋26 | 19 27 |
| 49 | 17 30 | 04 08 | 07 55 | 01 12 | 19 50 |
| 50 | 18 19 | 05 45 | 09 13 | 02 01 | 20 13 |
| 51 | 19 16 | 07 31 | 10 36 | 02 52 | 20 37 |
| 52 | 20 20 | 09 28 | 12 04 | 03 46 | 21 03 |
| 53 | 21 35 | 11 37 | 13 37 | 04 42 | 21 29 |
| 54 | 23 03 | 13 59 | 15 17 | 05 41 | 21 56 |
| 55 | 24 48 | 16 37 | 17 03 | 06 43 | 22 25 |
| 56 | 26 54 | 19 32 | 18 56 | 07 48 | 22 55 |
| 57 | 29 29 | 22 47 | 20 57 | 08 57 | 23 27 |
| 58 | 02♈43 | 26 23 | 23 06 | 10 10 | 24 00 |
| 59 | 06 49 | 00♊23 | 25 23 | 11 27 | 24 34 |
| 60 | 12♈11 | 04♊48 | 27♊50 | 12♋48 | 25♋11 |

**20h 40m 0s — 310° 0' 0" — 07 ♒ 35**

| LAT. | 11 | 12 | ASC | 2 | 3 |
|---|---|---|---|---|---|
| 0 | 08♓22 | 10♈53 | 12♉27 | 11♊32 | 09♋11 |
| 5 | 08 46 | 11 56 | 13 54 | 12 56 | 10 08 |
| 10 | 09 13 | 13 05 | 15 27 | 14 24 | 11 05 |
| 15 | 09 43 | 14 22 | 17 09 | 15 57 | 12 03 |
| 20 | 10 17 | 15 51 | 19 02 | 17 36 | 13 03 |
| 21 | 10 25 | 16 10 | 19 27 | 17 56 | 13 15 |
| 22 | 10 33 | 16 30 | 19 52 | 18 17 | 13 27 |
| 23 | 10 41 | 16 51 | 20 17 | 18 39 | 13 40 |
| 24 | 10 50 | 17 12 | 20 43 | 19 01 | 13 53 |
| 25 | 10 58 | 17 35 | 21 11 | 19 23 | 14 06 |
| 26 | 11 08 | 17 58 | 21 38 | 19 46 | 14 19 |
| 27 | 11 17 | 18 22 | 22 07 | 20 09 | 14 32 |
| 28 | 11 27 | 18 47 | 22 37 | 20 33 | 14 46 |
| 29 | 11 38 | 19 13 | 23 07 | 20 58 | 14 59 |
| 30 | 11 49 | 19 41 | 23 39 | 21 23 | 15 13 |
| 31 | 12 01 | 20 09 | 24 12 | 21 48 | 15 27 |
| 32 | 12 13 | 20 39 | 24 45 | 22 15 | 15 42 |
| 33 | 12 26 | 21 11 | 25 20 | 22 42 | 15 56 |
| 34 | 12 39 | 21 44 | 25 57 | 23 09 | 16 11 |
| 35 | 12 54 | 22 18 | 26 35 | 23 38 | 16 27 |
| 36 | 13 09 | 22 55 | 27 14 | 24 07 | 16 42 |
| 37 | 13 25 | 23 34 | 27 55 | 24 37 | 16 58 |
| 38 | 13 43 | 24 15 | 28 38 | 25 08 | 17 15 |
| 39 | 14 02 | 24 58 | 29 22 | 25 40 | 17 31 |
| 40 | 14 22 | 25 44 | 00♊09 | 26 14 | 17 48 |
| 41 | 14 43 | 26 34 | 00 57 | 26 48 | 18 06 |
| 42 | 15 07 | 27 26 | 01 48 | 27 23 | 18 24 |
| 43 | 15 32 | 28 23 | 02 42 | 28 00 | 18 43 |
| 44 | 16 00 | 29 23 | 03 38 | 28 38 | 19 02 |
| 45 | 16 31 | 00♉28 | 04 37 | 29 18 | 19 22 |
| 46 | 17 04 | 01 38 | 05 40 | 29 59 | 19 42 |
| 47 | 17 41 | 02 54 | 06 45 | 00♋42 | 20 03 |
| 48 | 18 22 | 04 16 | 07 54 | 01 26 | 20 25 |
| 49 | 19 08 | 05 46 | 09 08 | 02 13 | 20 47 |
| 50 | 20 01 | 07 23 | 10 25 | 03 01 | 21 10 |
| 51 | 21 00 | 09 10 | 11 47 | 03 52 | 21 34 |
| 52 | 22 08 | 11 07 | 13 15 | 04 45 | 21 59 |
| 53 | 23 26 | 13 16 | 14 47 | 05 41 | 22 26 |
| 54 | 24 59 | 15 39 | 16 26 | 06 39 | 22 53 |
| 55 | 26 48 | 18 16 | 18 11 | 07 40 | 23 21 |
| 56 | 29 00 | 21 10 | 20 02 | 08 45 | 23 51 |
| 57 | 01♈41 | 24 23 | 22 01 | 09 53 | 24 22 |
| 58 | 05 01 | 27 57 | 24 08 | 11 04 | 24 55 |
| 59 | 09 16 | 01♊52 | 26 23 | 12 20 | 25 29 |
| 60 | 14♈45 | 06♊12 | 28♊47 | 13♋40 | 26♋05 |

**20h 44m 0s — 311° 0' 0" — 08 ♒ 34**

| LAT. | 11 | 12 | ASC | 2 | 3 |
|---|---|---|---|---|---|
| 0 | 09♓26 | 11♈58 | 13♉28 | 12♊28 | 10♋07 |
| 5 | 09 51 | 13 03 | 14 56 | 13 54 | 11 04 |
| 10 | 10 20 | 14 14 | 16 31 | 15 22 | 12 01 |
| 15 | 10 51 | 15 33 | 18 14 | 16 55 | 13 00 |
| 20 | 11 28 | 17 04 | 20 09 | 18 35 | 14 00 |
| 21 | 11 36 | 17 24 | 20 34 | 18 56 | 14 12 |
| 22 | 11 44 | 17 45 | 20 59 | 19 17 | 14 25 |
| 23 | 11 53 | 18 06 | 21 25 | 19 39 | 14 37 |
| 24 | 12 02 | 18 28 | 21 51 | 20 01 | 14 50 |
| 25 | 12 11 | 18 51 | 22 19 | 20 23 | 15 03 |
| 26 | 12 21 | 19 15 | 22 47 | 20 46 | 15 16 |
| 27 | 12 31 | 19 40 | 23 16 | 21 10 | 15 30 |
| 28 | 12 42 | 20 05 | 23 46 | 21 34 | 15 43 |
| 29 | 12 53 | 20 32 | 24 17 | 21 58 | 15 57 |
| 30 | 13 04 | 21 00 | 24 48 | 22 23 | 16 11 |
| 31 | 13 17 | 21 29 | 25 21 | 22 49 | 16 25 |
| 32 | 13 30 | 22 00 | 25 55 | 23 15 | 16 39 |
| 33 | 13 43 | 22 32 | 26 31 | 23 42 | 16 54 |
| 34 | 13 58 | 23 06 | 27 07 | 24 10 | 17 09 |
| 35 | 14 13 | 23 41 | 27 46 | 24 39 | 17 24 |
| 36 | 14 29 | 24 19 | 28 25 | 25 08 | 17 40 |
| 37 | 14 46 | 24 58 | 29 06 | 25 38 | 17 56 |
| 38 | 15 05 | 25 40 | 29 49 | 26 09 | 18 12 |
| 39 | 15 24 | 26 25 | 00♊34 | 26 41 | 18 29 |
| 40 | 15 46 | 27 12 | 01 21 | 27 15 | 18 46 |
| 41 | 16 08 | 28 02 | 02 09 | 27 49 | 19 04 |
| 42 | 16 33 | 28 55 | 03 01 | 28 24 | 19 22 |
| 43 | 17 00 | 29 53 | 03 54 | 29 01 | 19 40 |
| 44 | 17 29 | 00♉54 | 04 50 | 29 39 | 19 59 |
| 45 | 18 01 | 02 00 | 05 49 | 00♋18 | 20 19 |
| 46 | 18 36 | 03 11 | 06 52 | 00 59 | 20 39 |
| 47 | 19 15 | 04 28 | 07 57 | 01 42 | 21 00 |
| 48 | 19 59 | 05 51 | 09 06 | 02 26 | 21 22 |
| 49 | 20 47 | 07 21 | 10 19 | 03 12 | 21 44 |
| 50 | 21 42 | 09 00 | 11 36 | 04 01 | 22 07 |
| 51 | 22 44 | 10 47 | 12 58 | 04 51 | 22 31 |
| 52 | 23 55 | 12 45 | 14 24 | 05 43 | 22 56 |
| 53 | 25 17 | 14 54 | 15 56 | 06 39 | 23 22 |
| 54 | 26 54 | 17 16 | 17 33 | 07 36 | 23 49 |
| 55 | 28 48 | 19 52 | 19 17 | 08 37 | 24 17 |
| 56 | 01♈05 | 22 45 | 21 07 | 09 41 | 24 46 |
| 57 | 03 52 | 25 56 | 23 04 | 10 48 | 25 17 |
| 58 | 07 18 | 29 26 | 25 09 | 11 59 | 25 49 |
| 59 | 11 40 | 03♊18 | 27 22 | 13 13 | 26 23 |
| 60 | 17♈15 | 07♊32 | 29♊43 | 14♋32 | 26♋59 |

# Koch Table of Houses for Latitudes 0° to 60° North

**20h 48m 0s — 312° 0' 0" — 09 ♒ 34**

| LAT. | 11 | 12 | ASC | 2 | 3 |
|---|---|---|---|---|---|
| 0 | 10♓30 | 13♈03 | 14♉28 | 13♊24 | 11♋02 |
| 5 | 10 57 | 14 09 | 15 58 | 14 50 | 12 00 |
| 10 | 11 27 | 15 22 | 17 34 | 16 20 | 12 58 |
| 15 | 12 00 | 16 44 | 19 19 | 17 54 | 13 56 |
| 20 | 12 38 | 18 18 | 21 15 | 19 34 | 14 57 |
| 21 | 12 47 | 18 38 | 21 40 | 19 55 | 15 09 |
| 22 | 12 56 | 18 59 | 22 06 | 20 17 | 15 22 |
| 23 | 13 05 | 19 21 | 22 32 | 20 39 | 15 35 |
| 24 | 13 14 | 19 44 | 22 59 | 21 01 | 15 48 |
| 25 | 13 24 | 20 07 | 23 26 | 21 23 | 16 01 |
| 26 | 13 34 | 20 31 | 23 55 | 21 46 | 16 14 |
| 27 | 13 45 | 20 57 | 24 24 | 22 10 | 16 27 |
| 28 | 13 56 | 21 23 | 24 54 | 22 34 | 16 41 |
| 29 | 14 08 | 21 50 | 25 25 | 22 59 | 16 54 |
| 30 | 14 20 | 22 19 | 25 57 | 23 24 | 17 08 |
| 31 | 14 33 | 22 49 | 26 31 | 23 50 | 17 23 |
| 32 | 14 47 | 23 20 | 27 05 | 24 16 | 17 37 |
| 33 | 15 01 | 23 53 | 27 41 | 24 43 | 17 52 |
| 34 | 15 16 | 24 28 | 28 17 | 25 11 | 18 07 |
| 35 | 15 32 | 25 04 | 28 56 | 25 39 | 18 22 |
| 36 | 15 49 | 25 42 | 29 35 | 26 09 | 18 38 |
| 37 | 16 07 | 26 23 | 00♊17 | 26 39 | 18 54 |
| 38 | 16 27 | 27 05 | 01 00 | 27 10 | 19 10 |
| 39 | 16 47 | 27 50 | 01 45 | 27 42 | 19 27 |
| 40 | 17 10 | 28 38 | 02 32 | 28 15 | 19 44 |
| 41 | 17 34 | 29 29 | 03 21 | 28 49 | 20 01 |
| 42 | 17 59 | 00♉24 | 04 12 | 29 25 | 20 19 |
| 43 | 18 28 | 01 22 | 05 05 | 00♋01 | 20 38 |
| 44 | 18 58 | 02 24 | 06 02 | 00 39 | 20 57 |
| 45 | 19 32 | 03 31 | 07 01 | 01 19 | 21 16 |
| 46 | 20 09 | 04 43 | 08 03 | 01 59 | 21 37 |
| 47 | 20 49 | 06 00 | 09 08 | 02 42 | 21 57 |
| 48 | 21 35 | 07 24 | 10 17 | 03 26 | 22 19 |
| 49 | 22 26 | 08 55 | 11 29 | 04 12 | 22 41 |
| 50 | 23 23 | 10 34 | 12 46 | 04 59 | 23 04 |
| 51 | 24 28 | 12 22 | 14 07 | 05 49 | 23 28 |
| 52 | 25 42 | 14 20 | 15 33 | 06 42 | 23 52 |
| 53 | 27 08 | 16 29 | 17 03 | 07 36 | 24 18 |
| 54 | 28 48 | 18 50 | 18 40 | 08 33 | 24 45 |
| 55 | 00♈46 | 21 26 | 20 22 | 09 33 | 25 13 |
| 56 | 03 08 | 24 17 | 22 10 | 10 36 | 25 42 |
| 57 | 06 01 | 27 26 | 24 06 | 11 43 | 26 12 |
| 58 | 09 34 | 00♊53 | 26 09 | 12 52 | 26 44 |
| 59 | 14 01 | 04 40 | 28 19 | 14 06 | 27 18 |
| 60 | 19♈41 | 08♊49 | 00♋38 | 15♋23 | 27♋53 |

**20h 52m 0s — 313° 0' 0" — 10 ♒ 33**

| LAT. | 11 | 12 | ASC | 2 | 3 |
|---|---|---|---|---|---|
| 0 | 11♓34 | 14♈07 | 15♉28 | 14♊20 | 11♋58 |
| 5 | 12 03 | 15 16 | 16 59 | 15 47 | 12 56 |
| 10 | 12 34 | 16 31 | 18 37 | 17 17 | 13 54 |
| 15 | 13 09 | 17 55 | 20 24 | 18 52 | 14 53 |
| 20 | 13 49 | 19 31 | 22 21 | 20 33 | 15 54 |
| 21 | 13 58 | 19 51 | 22 46 | 20 55 | 16 07 |
| 22 | 14 07 | 20 13 | 23 12 | 21 16 | 16 19 |
| 23 | 14 17 | 20 35 | 23 38 | 21 38 | 16 32 |
| 24 | 14 27 | 20 59 | 24 06 | 22 00 | 16 45 |
| 25 | 14 37 | 21 23 | 24 33 | 22 23 | 16 58 |
| 26 | 14 48 | 21 48 | 25 02 | 22 46 | 17 11 |
| 27 | 14 59 | 22 13 | 25 32 | 23 10 | 17 25 |
| 28 | 15 11 | 22 40 | 26 02 | 23 34 | 17 38 |
| 29 | 15 23 | 23 08 | 26 33 | 23 59 | 17 52 |
| 30 | 15 36 | 23 38 | 27 06 | 24 24 | 18 06 |
| 31 | 15 49 | 24 08 | 27 39 | 24 50 | 18 20 |
| 32 | 16 04 | 24 40 | 28 14 | 25 16 | 18 35 |
| 33 | 16 19 | 25 14 | 28 50 | 25 43 | 18 49 |
| 34 | 16 34 | 25 49 | 29 27 | 26 11 | 19 04 |
| 35 | 16 51 | 26 26 | 00♊05 | 26 40 | 19 20 |
| 36 | 17 09 | 27 05 | 00 45 | 27 09 | 19 35 |
| 37 | 17 28 | 27 46 | 01 27 | 27 39 | 19 51 |
| 38 | 17 48 | 28 29 | 02 10 | 28 10 | 20 08 |
| 39 | 18 10 | 29 15 | 02 55 | 28 43 | 20 24 |
| 40 | 18 33 | 00♉04 | 03 42 | 29 16 | 20 41 |
| 41 | 18 59 | 00 56 | 04 31 | 29 50 | 20 59 |
| 42 | 19 26 | 01 51 | 05 22 | 00♋25 | 21 17 |
| 43 | 19 55 | 02 50 | 06 16 | 01 01 | 21 35 |
| 44 | 20 27 | 03 53 | 07 12 | 01 39 | 21 54 |
| 45 | 21 02 | 05 00 | 08 11 | 02 18 | 22 14 |
| 46 | 21 41 | 06 13 | 09 13 | 02 59 | 22 34 |
| 47 | 22 24 | 07 31 | 10 18 | 03 41 | 22 54 |
| 48 | 23 11 | 08 56 | 11 26 | 04 25 | 23 16 |
| 49 | 24 04 | 10 27 | 12 38 | 05 10 | 23 38 |
| 50 | 25 03 | 12 07 | 13 54 | 05 58 | 24 01 |
| 51 | 26 11 | 13 55 | 15 15 | 06 47 | 24 24 |
| 52 | 27 28 | 15 53 | 16 40 | 07 39 | 24 49 |
| 53 | 28 58 | 18 01 | 18 10 | 08 33 | 25 14 |
| 54 | 00♈42 | 20 22 | 19 45 | 09 30 | 25 41 |
| 55 | 02 44 | 22 57 | 21 26 | 10 29 | 26 09 |
| 56 | 05 11 | 25 47 | 23 13 | 11 31 | 26 37 |
| 57 | 08 08 | 28 53 | 25 07 | 12 37 | 27 07 |
| 58 | 11 46 | 02♊17 | 27 08 | 13 46 | 27 39 |
| 59 | 16 19 | 06 00 | 29 16 | 14 58 | 28 12 |
| 60 | 22♈03 | 10♊03 | 01♋32 | 16♋14 | 28♋47 |

**20h 56m 0s — 314° 0' 0" — 11 ♒ 32**

| LAT. | 11 | 12 | ASC | 2 | 3 |
|---|---|---|---|---|---|
| 0 | 12♓39 | 15♈12 | 16♉28 | 15♊16 | 12♋53 |
| 5 | 13 08 | 16 22 | 18 01 | 16 44 | 13 52 |
| 10 | 13 41 | 17 39 | 19 40 | 18 15 | 14 51 |
| 15 | 14 18 | 19 05 | 21 28 | 19 51 | 15 50 |
| 20 | 15 00 | 20 43 | 23 26 | 21 32 | 16 51 |
| 21 | 15 09 | 21 05 | 23 52 | 21 54 | 17 04 |
| 22 | 15 19 | 21 27 | 24 18 | 22 15 | 17 16 |
| 23 | 15 29 | 21 50 | 24 45 | 22 37 | 17 29 |
| 24 | 15 39 | 22 13 | 25 12 | 23 00 | 17 42 |
| 25 | 15 50 | 22 38 | 25 40 | 23 23 | 17 55 |
| 26 | 16 01 | 23 03 | 26 09 | 23 46 | 18 09 |
| 27 | 16 13 | 23 30 | 26 39 | 24 10 | 18 22 |
| 28 | 16 25 | 23 57 | 27 10 | 24 34 | 18 36 |
| 29 | 16 38 | 24 26 | 27 41 | 24 59 | 18 49 |
| 30 | 16 52 | 24 56 | 28 14 | 25 24 | 19 04 |
| 31 | 17 06 | 25 27 | 28 47 | 25 50 | 19 18 |
| 32 | 17 21 | 26 00 | 29 22 | 26 16 | 19 32 |
| 33 | 17 36 | 26 34 | 29 58 | 26 43 | 19 47 |
| 34 | 17 53 | 27 10 | 00♊35 | 27 11 | 20 02 |
| 35 | 18 11 | 27 47 | 01 14 | 27 40 | 20 17 |
| 36 | 18 29 | 28 27 | 01 54 | 28 09 | 20 33 |
| 37 | 18 49 | 29 09 | 02 36 | 28 39 | 20 49 |
| 38 | 19 10 | 29 53 | 03 19 | 29 11 | 21 05 |
| 39 | 19 33 | 00♉39 | 04 04 | 29 43 | 21 22 |
| 40 | 19 57 | 01 29 | 04 51 | 00♋16 | 21 39 |
| 41 | 20 24 | 02 21 | 05 40 | 00 50 | 21 56 |
| 42 | 20 52 | 03 17 | 06 31 | 01 25 | 22 14 |
| 43 | 21 23 | 04 17 | 07 25 | 02 01 | 22 33 |
| 44 | 21 56 | 05 20 | 08 21 | 02 39 | 22 52 |
| 45 | 22 33 | 06 29 | 09 20 | 03 18 | 23 11 |
| 46 | 23 13 | 07 42 | 10 21 | 03 58 | 23 31 |
| 47 | 23 57 | 09 01 | 11 26 | 04 40 | 23 52 |
| 48 | 24 47 | 10 26 | 12 34 | 05 23 | 24 13 |
| 49 | 25 42 | 11 58 | 13 46 | 06 09 | 24 35 |
| 50 | 26 44 | 13 37 | 15 02 | 06 56 | 24 57 |
| 51 | 27 54 | 15 26 | 16 21 | 07 45 | 25 21 |
| 52 | 29 14 | 17 23 | 17 46 | 08 36 | 25 45 |
| 53 | 00♈47 | 19 32 | 19 15 | 09 30 | 26 11 |
| 54 | 02 34 | 21 52 | 20 49 | 10 26 | 26 37 |
| 55 | 04 41 | 24 26 | 22 29 | 11 24 | 27 04 |
| 56 | 07 12 | 27 13 | 24 14 | 12 26 | 27 33 |
| 57 | 10 14 | 00♊17 | 26 06 | 13 30 | 28 02 |
| 58 | 13 57 | 03 38 | 28 05 | 14 38 | 28 34 |
| 59 | 18 34 | 07 17 | 00♋11 | 15 50 | 29 06 |
| 60 | 24♈20 | 11♊15 | 02♋24 | 17♋05 | 29♋41 |

**21h 0m 0s — 315° 0' 0" — 12 ♒ 32**

| LAT. | 11 | 12 | ASC | 2 | 3 |
|---|---|---|---|---|---|
| 0 | 13♓43 | 16♈17 | 17♉28 | 16♊11 | 13♋49 |
| 5 | 14 14 | 17 29 | 19 02 | 17 40 | 14 48 |
| 10 | 14 48 | 18 48 | 20 43 | 19 12 | 15 47 |
| 15 | 15 27 | 20 16 | 22 31 | 20 49 | 16 47 |
| 20 | 16 11 | 21 56 | 24 32 | 22 31 | 17 48 |
| 21 | 16 20 | 22 18 | 24 57 | 22 52 | 18 01 |
| 22 | 16 30 | 22 40 | 25 23 | 23 14 | 18 14 |
| 23 | 16 41 | 23 04 | 25 50 | 23 36 | 18 27 |
| 24 | 16 52 | 23 28 | 26 18 | 23 59 | 18 40 |
| 25 | 17 03 | 23 53 | 26 46 | 24 22 | 18 53 |
| 26 | 17 15 | 24 19 | 27 16 | 24 45 | 19 06 |
| 27 | 17 27 | 24 46 | 27 46 | 25 09 | 19 19 |
| 28 | 17 40 | 25 14 | 28 16 | 25 33 | 19 33 |
| 29 | 17 53 | 25 43 | 28 48 | 25 58 | 19 47 |
| 30 | 18 07 | 26 13 | 29 21 | 26 23 | 20 01 |
| 31 | 18 22 | 26 45 | 29 55 | 26 49 | 20 15 |
| 32 | 18 38 | 27 18 | 00♊30 | 27 16 | 20 30 |
| 33 | 18 54 | 27 53 | 01 06 | 27 43 | 20 45 |
| 34 | 19 12 | 28 30 | 01 43 | 28 11 | 21 00 |
| 35 | 19 30 | 29 08 | 02 22 | 28 40 | 21 15 |
| 36 | 19 49 | 29 48 | 03 02 | 29 09 | 21 31 |
| 37 | 20 10 | 00♉30 | 03 44 | 29 39 | 21 46 |
| 38 | 20 32 | 01 15 | 04 28 | 00♋10 | 22 03 |
| 39 | 20 56 | 02 02 | 05 13 | 00 42 | 22 19 |
| 40 | 21 21 | 02 53 | 06 00 | 01 15 | 22 36 |
| 41 | 21 49 | 03 46 | 06 49 | 01 49 | 22 54 |
| 42 | 22 18 | 04 42 | 07 40 | 02 24 | 23 12 |
| 43 | 22 50 | 05 43 | 08 34 | 03 00 | 23 30 |
| 44 | 23 25 | 06 47 | 09 29 | 03 38 | 23 49 |
| 45 | 24 03 | 07 56 | 10 28 | 04 16 | 24 08 |
| 46 | 24 45 | 09 09 | 11 30 | 04 57 | 24 28 |
| 47 | 25 31 | 10 29 | 12 34 | 05 38 | 24 48 |
| 48 | 26 22 | 11 54 | 13 42 | 06 22 | 25 10 |
| 49 | 27 20 | 13 26 | 14 53 | 07 07 | 25 31 |
| 50 | 28 24 | 15 06 | 16 08 | 07 53 | 25 54 |
| 51 | 29 37 | 16 54 | 17 27 | 08 42 | 26 17 |
| 52 | 01♈00 | 18 52 | 18 51 | 09 33 | 26 41 |
| 53 | 02 35 | 21 00 | 20 19 | 10 26 | 27 07 |
| 54 | 04 26 | 23 19 | 21 52 | 11 21 | 27 33 |
| 55 | 06 37 | 25 52 | 23 30 | 12 19 | 28 00 |
| 56 | 09 12 | 28 38 | 25 15 | 13 20 | 28 28 |
| 57 | 12 18 | 01♊39 | 27 05 | 14 24 | 28 57 |
| 58 | 16 05 | 04 56 | 29 02 | 15 31 | 29 28 |
| 59 | 20 45 | 08 31 | 01♋05 | 16 41 | 00♌00 |
| 60 | 26♈34 | 12♊24 | 03♋16 | 17♋55 | 00♌34 |

**21h 4m 0s — 316° 0' 0" — 13 ♒ 32**

| LAT. | 11 | 12 | ASC | 2 | 3 |
|---|---|---|---|---|---|
| 0 | 14♓48 | 17♈21 | 18♉28 | 17♊07 | 14♋44 |
| 5 | 15 20 | 18 35 | 20 03 | 18 37 | 15 44 |
| 10 | 15 56 | 19 56 | 21 45 | 20 10 | 16 44 |
| 15 | 16 36 | 21 26 | 23 35 | 21 47 | 17 44 |
| 20 | 17 22 | 23 08 | 25 36 | 23 30 | 18 46 |
| 21 | 17 32 | 23 30 | 26 02 | 23 51 | 18 58 |
| 22 | 17 42 | 23 53 | 26 29 | 24 13 | 19 11 |
| 23 | 17 53 | 24 17 | 26 56 | 24 35 | 19 24 |
| 24 | 18 04 | 24 42 | 27 24 | 24 58 | 19 37 |
| 25 | 18 16 | 25 07 | 27 52 | 25 21 | 19 50 |
| 26 | 18 28 | 25 34 | 28 22 | 25 44 | 20 03 |
| 27 | 18 41 | 26 01 | 28 52 | 26 08 | 20 17 |
| 28 | 18 55 | 26 30 | 29 23 | 26 32 | 20 31 |
| 29 | 19 09 | 26 59 | 29 55 | 26 57 | 20 45 |
| 30 | 19 23 | 27 30 | 00♊28 | 27 23 | 20 59 |
| 31 | 19 39 | 28 03 | 01 02 | 27 49 | 21 13 |
| 32 | 19 55 | 28 36 | 01 37 | 28 15 | 21 27 |

**21h 8m 0s — 317° 0' 0" — 14 ♒ 32**

| LAT. | 11 | 12 | ASC | 2 | 3 |
|---|---|---|---|---|---|
| 0 | 15♓53 | 18♈26 | 19♉27 | 18♊02 | 15♋40 |
| 5 | 16 26 | 19 41 | 21 04 | 19 33 | 16 40 |
| 10 | 17 03 | 21 04 | 22 47 | 21 07 | 17 40 |
| 15 | 17 45 | 22 35 | 24 38 | 22 44 | 18 41 |
| 20 | 18 33 | 24 20 | 26 40 | 24 28 | 19 43 |
| 21 | 18 43 | 24 42 | 27 07 | 24 50 | 19 56 |
| 22 | 18 54 | 25 06 | 27 33 | 25 11 | 20 08 |
| 23 | 19 05 | 25 30 | 28 01 | 25 34 | 20 21 |
| 24 | 19 17 | 25 55 | 28 29 | 25 56 | 20 34 |
| 25 | 19 29 | 26 21 | 28 58 | 26 20 | 20 48 |
| 26 | 19 42 | 26 48 | 29 27 | 26 43 | 21 01 |
| 27 | 19 55 | 27 16 | 29 57 | 27 07 | 21 14 |
| 28 | 20 09 | 27 45 | 00♊29 | 27 31 | 21 28 |
| 29 | 20 24 | 28 15 | 01 01 | 27 56 | 21 42 |
| 30 | 20 39 | 28 47 | 01 34 | 28 22 | 21 56 |
| 31 | 20 55 | 29 20 | 02 08 | 28 48 | 22 10 |
| 32 | 21 12 | 29 54 | 02 44 | 29 14 | 22 25 |
| 33 | [illegible] | [illegible] | [illegible] 20 | 29 42 | 22 40 |
| 34 | [illegible] | [illegible] | [illegible] 58 | 00♋10 | 22 55 |
| 35 | [illegible] | [illegible] | [illegible] 37 | 00 38 | 23 10 |
| 36 | [illegible] | [illegible] | [illegible] 17 | 01 07 | 23 26 |
| 37 | [illegible] | [illegible] | [illegible] 59 | 01 38 | 23 42 |
| 38 | [illegible] | [illegible] | [illegible] 43 | 02 09 | 23 58 |
| 39 | [illegible] | [illegible] | [illegible] 28 | 02 40 | 24 14 |
| 40 | [illegible] | [illegible] | [illegible] 15 | 03 13 | 24 31 |
| 41 | [illegible] | [illegible] | [illegible] 04 | 03 47 | 24 49 |
| 42 | [illegible] | [illegible] | [illegible] 55 | 04 22 | 25 06 |
| 43 | [illegible] | [illegible] | [illegible] 48 | 04 58 | 25 25 |
| 44 | [illegible] | [illegible] | [illegible] 44 | 05 35 | 25 43 |
| 45 | [illegible] | [illegible] | [illegible] 42 | 06 13 | 26 02 |
| 46 | [illegible] | [illegible] | [illegible] 43 | 06 53 | 26 22 |
| 47 | [illegible] | [illegible] | [illegible] 47 | 07 34 | 26 42 |
| 48 | [illegible] | [illegible] | [illegible] 54 | 08 17 | 27 03 |
| 49 | [illegible] | [illegible] | [illegible] 04 | 09 01 | 27 25 |
| 50 | [illegible] | [illegible] | [illegible] 18 | 09 47 | 27 47 |
| 51 | [illegible] | [illegible] | [illegible] 35 | 10 35 | 28 10 |
| 52 | [illegible] | [illegible] | [illegible] 57 | 11 25 | 28 34 |
| 53 | [illegible] | [illegible] | [illegible] 24 | 12 17 | 28 58 |
| 54 | [illegible] | [illegible] | [illegible] 54 | 13 11 | 29 24 |
| 55 | [illegible] | [illegible] | [illegible] 30 | 14 08 | 29 51 |
| 56 | [illegible] | [illegible] | [illegible] 12 | 15 07 | 00♌18 |
| 57 | [illegible] | [illegible] | [illegible] 59 | 16 09 | 00 47 |
| 58 | [illegible] | [illegible] | [illegible] 52 | 17 14 | 01 17 |
| 59 | [illegible] | [illegible] | [illegible] 51 | 18 23 | 01 49 |
| 60 | [illegible] | [illegible] | [illegible] 58 | 19♋35 | 02♌22 |

**21h 12m 0s — 318° 0' 0" — 15 ♒ 32**

| LAT. | 11 | 12 | ASC | 2 | 3 |
|---|---|---|---|---|---|
| 0 | 16♓57 | 19♈30 | 20♉26 | 18♊58 | 16♋36 |
| 5 | 17 32 | 20 47 | 22 04 | 20 30 | 17 37 |
| 10 | 18 11 | 22 11 | 23 49 | 22 04 | 18 37 |
| 15 | 18 54 | 23 45 | 25 41 | 23 43 | 19 38 |
| 20 | 19 44 | 25 31 | 27 44 | 25 26 | 20 40 |
| 21 | 19 55 | 25 54 | 28 11 | 25 48 | 20 53 |
| 22 | 20 06 | 26 18 | 28 38 | 26 10 | 21 06 |
| 23 | 20 18 | 26 43 | 29 05 | 26 32 | 21 19 |
| 24 | 20 30 | 27 08 | 29 33 | 26 55 | 21 32 |
| 25 | 20 43 | 27 35 | 00♊02 | 27 18 | 21 45 |
| 26 | 20 56 | 28 02 | 00 32 | 27 42 | 21 58 |
| 27 | 21 10 | 28 31 | 01 03 | 28 06 | 22 12 |
| 28 | 21 24 | 29 00 | 01 34 | 28 30 | 22 26 |
| 29 | 21 39 | 29 31 | 02 07 | 28 55 | 22 40 |
| 30 | 21 55 | 00♉03 | 02 40 | 29 21 | 22 54 |
| 31 | 22 12 | 00 36 | 03 14 | 29 47 | 23 08 |
| 32 | 22 29 | 01 11 | 03 50 | 00♋13 | 23 23 |
| 33 | 22 48 | 01 47 | 04 26 | 00 41 | 23 37 |
| 34 | 23 07 | 02 25 | 05 04 | 01 08 | 23 52 |
| 35 | 23 28 | 03 05 | 05 43 | 01 37 | 24 08 |
| 36 | 23 49 | 03 47 | 06 23 | 02 06 | 24 23 |
| 37 | 24 13 | 04 31 | 07 05 | 02 36 | 24 39 |
| 38 | 24 37 | 05 18 | 07 49 | 03 07 | 24 55 |
| 39 | 25 04 | 06 07 | 08 34 | 03 39 | 25 12 |
| 40 | 25 32 | 06 59 | 09 21 | 04 12 | 25 29 |
| 41 | 26 03 | 07 53 | 10 10 | 04 45 | 25 46 |
| 42 | 26 36 | 08 51 | 11 01 | 05 20 | 26 04 |
| 43 | 27 12 | 09 53 | 11 54 | 05 56 | 26 22 |
| 44 | 27 51 | 10 59 | 12 50 | 06 33 | 26 40 |
| 45 | 28 33 | 12 09 | 13 48 | 07 11 | 26 59 |
| 46 | 29 19 | 13 24 | 14 48 | 07 51 | 27 19 |
| 47 | 00♈11 | 14 44 | 15 52 | 08 31 | 27 39 |
| 48 | 01 07 | 16 10 | 16 58 | 09 14 | 28 00 |
| 49 | 02 11 | 17 43 | 18 08 | 09 58 | 28 21 |
| 50 | 03 21 | 19 23 | 19 21 | 10 44 | 28 43 |
| 51 | 04 41 | 21 10 | 20 38 | 11 31 | 29 06 |
| 52 | 06 12 | 23 06 | 21 59 | 12 20 | 29 30 |
| 53 | 07 56 | 25 12 | 23 24 | 13 12 | 29 54 |
| 54 | 09 56 | 27 28 | 24 54 | 14 06 | 00♌20 |
| 55 | 12 16 | 29 56 | 26 29 | 15 02 | 00 46 |
| 56 | 15 01 | 02♊36 | 28 09 | 16 00 | 01 13 |
| 57 | 18 17 | 05 30 | 29 54 | 17 02 | 01 42 |
| 58 | 22 13 | 08 37 | 01♋46 | 18 06 | 02 12 |
| 59 | 26 59 | 12 00 | 03 43 | 19 13 | 02 43 |
| 60 | 02♉48 | 15♊38 | 05♋47 | 20♋24 | 03♌15 |

**21h 16m 0s — 319° 0' 0" — 16 ♒ 33**

| LAT. | 11 | 12 | ASC | 2 | 3 |
|---|---|---|---|---|---|
| 0 | 18♓02 | 20♈34 | 21♉26 | 19♊53 | 17♋32 |
| 5 | 18 38 | 21 53 | 23 05 | 21 26 | 18 33 |
| 10 | 19 18 | 23 19 | 24 50 | 23 01 | 19 34 |
| 15 | 20 03 | 24 54 | 26 43 | 24 40 | 20 35 |
| 20 | 20 55 | 26 42 | 28 48 | 26 24 | 21 37 |
| 21 | 21 06 | 27 06 | 29 14 | 26 46 | 21 50 |
| 22 | 21 18 | 27 30 | 29 42 | 27 08 | 22 03 |
| 23 | 21 30 | 27 55 | 00♊09 | 27 30 | 22 16 |
| 24 | 21 43 | 28 21 | 00 38 | 27 53 | 22 29 |
| 25 | 21 56 | 28 48 | 01 07 | 28 16 | 22 43 |
| 26 | 22 09 | 29 16 | 01 37 | 28 40 | 22 56 |
| 27 | 22 24 | 29 45 | 02 08 | 29 04 | 23 09 |
| 28 | 22 39 | 00♉15 | 02 39 | 29 29 | 23 23 |
| 29 | 22 54 | 00 46 | 03 12 | 29 54 | 23 37 |
| 30 | 23 11 | 01 18 | 03 45 | 00♋19 | 23 51 |
| 31 | 23 28 | 01 52 | 04 19 | 00 45 | 24 06 |
| 32 | 23 46 | 02 27 | 04 55 | 01 12 | 24 20 |
| 33 | 24 05 | 03 04 | 05 32 | 01 39 | 24 35 |
| 34 | 24 25 | 03 43 | 06 10 | 02 07 | 24 50 |
| 35 | 24 47 | 04 23 | 06 49 | 02 36 | 25 05 |
| 36 | 25 09 | 05 06 | 07 29 | 03 05 | 25 21 |
| 37 | 25 33 | 05 50 | 08 11 | 03 35 | 25 36 |
| 38 | 25 59 | 06 37 | 08 55 | 04 06 | 25 53 |
| 39 | 26 26 | 07 26 | 09 40 | 04 37 | 26 09 |
| 40 | 26 56 | 08 19 | 10 27 | 05 10 | 26 26 |
| 41 | 27 27 | 09 14 | 11 16 | 05 44 | 26 43 |
| 42 | 28 02 | 10 12 | 12 07 | 06 18 | 27 01 |
| 43 | 28 38 | 11 15 | 12 59 | 06 54 | 27 19 |
| 44 | 29 19 | 12 21 | 13 55 | 07 30 | 27 37 |
| 45 | 00♈02 | 13 31 | 14 52 | 08 08 | 27 56 |
| 46 | 00 50 | 14 46 | 15 53 | 08 48 | 28 16 |
| 47 | 01 43 | 16 07 | 16 56 | 09 28 | 28 36 |
| 48 | 02 42 | 17 33 | 18 02 | 10 11 | 28 57 |
| 49 | 03 47 | 19 05 | 19 11 | 10 54 | 29 18 |
| 50 | 04 59 | 20 45 | 20 24 | 11 39 | 29 40 |
| 51 | 06 21 | 22 32 | 21 40 | 12 27 | 00♌03 |
| 52 | 07 54 | 24 28 | 23 01 | 13 16 | 00 26 |
| 53 | 09 41 | 26 32 | 24 25 | 14 07 | 00 50 |
| 54 | 11 44 | 28 47 | 25 53 | 15 00 | 01 15 |
| 55 | 14 06 | 01♊13 | 27 27 | 15 55 | 01 41 |
| 56 | 16 54 | 03 51 | 29 05 | 16 53 | 02 08 |
| 57 | 20 13 | 06 42 | 00♋49 | 17 53 | 02 37 |
| 58 | 24 10 | 09 47 | 02 39 | 18 57 | 03 06 |
| 59 | 28 57 | 13 06 | 04 34 | 20 03 | 03 37 |
| 60 | 04♉44 | 16♊39 | 06♋36 | 21♋13 | 04♌09 |

# Koch Table of Houses for Latitudes 0° to 60° North

**21h 20m 0s — 320° 0' 0" — 17 ♒ 33**

| LAT. | 11 | 12 | ASC | 2 | 3 |
|---|---|---|---|---|---|
| 0 | 19♓07 | 21♈38 | 22♉25 | 20♊49 | 18♋28 |
| 5 | 19 45 | 22 59 | 24 05 | 22 22 | 19 29 |
| 10 | 20 26 | 24 26 | 25 51 | 23 57 | 20 31 |
| 15 | 21 12 | 26 03 | 27 46 | 25 37 | 21 32 |
| 20 | 22 06 | 27 53 | 29 51 | 27 22 | 22 35 |
| 21 | 22 17 | 28 17 | 00♊18 | 27 44 | 22 48 |
| 22 | 22 30 | 28 42 | 00 45 | 28 06 | 23 01 |
| 23 | 22 42 | 29 07 | 01 13 | 28 29 | 23 14 |
| 24 | 22 55 | 29 34 | 01 42 | 28 51 | 23 27 |
| 25 | 23 09 | 00♉01 | 02 11 | 29 15 | 23 40 |
| 26 | 23 23 | 00 29 | 02 41 | 29 38 | 23 53 |
| 27 | 23 38 | 00 58 | 03 12 | 00♋02 | 24 07 |
| 28 | 23 53 | 01 29 | 03 44 | 00 27 | 24 21 |
| 29 | 24 10 | 02 00 | 04 16 | 00 52 | 24 35 |
| 30 | 24 27 | 02 33 | 04 50 | 01 18 | 24 49 |
| 31 | 24 44 | 03 07 | 05 24 | 01 44 | 25 03 |
| 32 | 25 03 | 03 43 | 06 00 | 02 10 | 25 18 |
| 33 | 25 23 | 04 20 | 06 37 | 02 37 | 25 32 |
| 34 | 25 44 | 04 59 | 07 15 | 03 05 | 25 47 |
| 35 | 26 06 | 05 40 | 07 54 | 03 34 | 26 03 |
| 36 | 26 29 | 06 23 | 08 34 | 04 03 | 26 18 |
| 37 | 26 54 | 07 08 | 09 16 | 04 33 | 26 34 |
| 38 | 27 20 | 07 55 | 10 00 | 05 04 | 26 50 |
| 39 | 27 49 | 08 45 | 10 45 | 05 35 | 27 07 |
| 40 | 28 19 | 09 38 | 11 32 | 06 08 | 27 23 |
| 41 | 28 52 | 10 33 | 12 21 | 06 41 | 27 41 |
| 42 | 29 27 | 11 32 | 13 11 | 07 16 | 27 58 |
| 43 | 00♈05 | 12 35 | 14 04 | 07 51 | 28 16 |
| 44 | 00 46 | 13 41 | 14 59 | 08 28 | 28 35 |
| 45 | 01 31 | 14 52 | 15 56 | 09 06 | 28 53 |
| 46 | 02 21 | 16 07 | 16 56 | 09 45 | 29 13 |
| 47 | 03 15 | 17 28 | 17 59 | 10 25 | 29 33 |
| 48 | 04 15 | 18 54 | 19 05 | 11 07 | 29 53 |
| 49 | 05 22 | 20 26 | 20 13 | 11 50 | 00♌14 |
| 50 | 06 37 | 22 05 | 21 25 | 12 35 | 00 36 |
| 51 | 08 01 | 23 52 | 22 41 | 13 22 | 00 59 |
| 52 | 09 36 | 25 47 | 24 00 | 14 10 | 01 22 |
| 53 | 11 24 | 27 51 | 25 24 | 15 01 | 01 46 |
| 54 | 13 30 | 00♊04 | 26 51 | 15 53 | 02 11 |
| 55 | 15 55 | 02 29 | 28 24 | 16 48 | 02 37 |
| 56 | 18 45 | 05 05 | 00♋01 | 17 45 | 03 04 |
| 57 | 22 05 | 07 53 | 01 43 | 18 45 | 03 31 |
| 58 | 26 05 | 10 54 | 03 31 | 19 48 | 04 00 |
| 59 | 00♉51 | 14 09 | 05 24 | 20 53 | 04 31 |
| 60 | 06♉36 | 17♊38 | 07♋24 | 22♋01 | 05♌02 |

**21h 24m 0s — 321° 0' 0" — 18 ♒ 34**

| LAT. | 11 | 12 | ASC | 2 | 3 |
|---|---|---|---|---|---|
| 0 | 20♓12 | 22♈42 | 23♉23 | 21♊44 | 19♋24 |
| 5 | 20 51 | 24 04 | 25 05 | 23 18 | 20 26 |
| 10 | 21 34 | 25 33 | 26 52 | 24 54 | 21 27 |
| 15 | 22 21 | 27 12 | 28 48 | 26 34 | 22 29 |
| 20 | 23 17 | 29 04 | 00♊54 | 28 20 | 23 32 |
| 21 | 23 29 | 29 28 | 01 21 | 28 42 | 23 45 |
| 22 | 23 41 | 29 53 | 01 48 | 29 04 | 23 58 |
| 23 | 23 54 | 00♉19 | 02 16 | 29 26 | 24 11 |
| 24 | 24 08 | 00 46 | 02 45 | 29 49 | 24 24 |
| 25 | 24 22 | 01 13 | 03 15 | 00♋13 | 24 38 |
| 26 | 24 37 | 01 42 | 03 45 | 00 36 | 24 51 |
| 27 | 24 52 | 02 12 | 04 16 | 01 01 | 25 05 |
| 28 | 25 08 | 02 42 | 04 48 | 01 25 | 25 18 |
| 29 | 25 25 | 03 14 | 05 20 | 01 50 | 25 32 |
| 30 | 25 42 | 03 48 | 05 54 | 02 16 | 25 46 |
| 31 | 26 01 | 04 22 | 06 29 | 02 42 | 26 01 |
| 32 | 26 20 | 04 58 | 07 04 | 03 08 | 26 15 |
| 33 | 26 40 | 05 36 | 07 41 | 03 36 | 26 30 |
| 34 | 27 02 | 06 15 | 08 19 | 04 03 | 26 45 |
| 35 | 27 25 | 06 57 | 08 58 | 04 32 | 27 00 |
| 36 | 27 49 | 07 40 | 09 39 | 05 01 | 27 16 |
| 37 | 28 14 | 08 25 | 10 21 | 05 31 | 27 31 |
| 38 | 28 42 | 09 13 | 11 04 | 06 02 | 27 48 |
| 39 | 29 11 | 10 03 | 11 49 | 06 33 | 28 04 |
| 40 | 29 42 | 10 56 | 12 36 | 07 06 | 28 21 |
| 41 | 00♈16 | 11 52 | 13 25 | 07 39 | 28 38 |
| 42 | 00 52 | 12 51 | 14 15 | 08 13 | 28 55 |
| 43 | 01 31 | 13 54 | 15 08 | 08 48 | 29 13 |
| 44 | 02 14 | 15 01 | 16 03 | 09 25 | 29 32 |
| 45 | 03 00 | 16 11 | 17 00 | 10 02 | 29 50 |
| 46 | 03 51 | 17 27 | 17 59 | 10 41 | 00♌10 |
| 47 | 04 46 | 18 47 | 19 02 | 11 21 | 00 30 |
| 48 | 05 48 | 20 13 | 20 07 | 12 03 | 00 50 |
| 49 | 06 57 | 21 46 | 21 15 | 12 46 | 01 11 |
| 50 | 08 13 | 23 24 | 22 26 | 13 30 | 01 33 |
| 51 | 09 39 | 25 10 | 23 41 | 14 17 | 01 55 |
| 52 | 11 16 | 27 04 | 25 00 | 15 05 | 02 18 |
| 53 | 13 07 | 29 07 | 26 22 | 15 55 | 02 42 |
| 54 | 15 14 | 01♊20 | 27 49 | 16 47 | 03 06 |
| 55 | 17 42 | 03 42 | 29 20 | 17 41 | 03 32 |
| 56 | 20 33 | 06 16 | 00♋55 | 18 37 | 03 59 |
| 57 | 23 56 | 09 02 | 02 36 | 19 36 | 04 26 |
| 58 | 27 56 | 12 00 | 04 22 | 20 38 | 04 55 |
| 59 | 02♉42 | 15 11 | 06 14 | 21 42 | 05 25 |
| 60 | 08♉24 | 18♊36 | 08♋11 | 22♋50 | 05♌56 |

**21h 28m 0s — 322° 0' 0" — 19 ♒ 35**

| LAT. | 11 | 12 | ASC | 2 | 3 |
|---|---|---|---|---|---|
| 0 | 21♓17 | 23♈46 | 24♉22 | 22♊39 | 20♋20 |
| 5 | 21 57 | 25 09 | 26 04 | 24 14 | 21 23 |
| 10 | 22 41 | 26 40 | 27 53 | 25 51 | 22 24 |
| 15 | 23 31 | 28 20 | 29 49 | 27 31 | 23 26 |
| 20 | 24 28 | 00♉14 | 01♊57 | 29 17 | 24 30 |
| 21 | 24 40 | 00 38 | 02 24 | 29 39 | 24 43 |
| 22 | 24 53 | 01 04 | 02 51 | 00♋01 | 24 56 |
| 23 | 25 07 | 01 30 | 03 19 | 00 24 | 25 09 |
| 24 | 25 21 | 01 57 | 03 48 | 00 47 | 25 22 |
| 25 | 25 35 | 02 25 | 04 18 | 01 10 | 25 35 |
| 26 | 25 50 | 02 54 | 04 48 | 01 34 | 25 49 |
| 27 | 26 06 | 03 24 | 05 19 | 01 58 | 26 02 |
| 28 | 26 23 | 03 55 | 05 51 | 02 23 | 26 16 |
| 29 | 26 40 | 04 28 | 06 24 | 02 48 | 26 30 |
| 30 | 26 58 | 05 01 | 06 58 | 03 14 | 26 44 |
| 31 | 27 17 | 05 36 | 07 32 | 03 40 | 26 58 |
| 32 | 27 37 | 06 13 | 08 08 | 04 06 | 27 13 |
| 33 | 27 58 | 06 51 | 08 45 | 04 33 | 27 28 |
| 34 | 28 20 | 07 31 | 09 23 | 05 01 | 27 43 |
| 35 | 28 43 | 08 12 | 10 02 | 05 30 | 27 58 |
| 36 | 29 08 | 08 56 | 10 43 | 05 59 | 28 13 |
| 37 | 29 35 | 09 42 | 11 25 | 06 29 | 28 29 |
| 38 | 00♈03 | 10 30 | 12 08 | 06 59 | 28 45 |
| 39 | 00 33 | 11 20 | 12 53 | 07 31 | 29 01 |
| 40 | 01 05 | 12 13 | 13 40 | 08 03 | 29 18 |
| 41 | 01 39 | 13 10 | 14 28 | 08 36 | 29 35 |
| 42 | 02 17 | 14 09 | 15 19 | 09 10 | 29 53 |
| 43 | 02 57 | 15 12 | 16 11 | 09 45 | 00♌10 |
| 44 | 03 41 | 16 19 | 17 05 | 10 22 | 00 29 |
| 45 | 04 28 | 17 30 | 18 02 | 10 59 | 00 47 |
| 46 | 05 20 | 18 45 | 19 02 | 11 38 | 01 07 |
| 47 | 06 17 | 20 06 | 20 03 | 12 17 | 01 26 |
| 48 | 07 20 | 21 32 | 21 08 | 12 59 | 01 47 |
| 49 | 08 31 | 23 03 | 22 16 | 13 41 | 02 07 |
| 50 | 09 49 | 24 42 | 23 26 | 14 25 | 02 29 |
| 51 | 11 16 | 26 27 | 24 40 | 15 11 | 02 51 |
| 52 | 12 55 | 28 20 | 25 58 | 15 59 | 03 14 |
| 53 | 14 48 | 00♊22 | 27 19 | 16 48 | 03 38 |
| 54 | 16 57 | 02 33 | 28 45 | 17 40 | 04 02 |
| 55 | 19 27 | 04 54 | 00♋15 | 18 33 | 04 27 |
| 56 | 22 20 | 07 25 | 01 49 | 19 29 | 04 54 |
| 57 | 25 44 | 10 08 | 03 29 | 20 27 | 05 21 |
| 58 | 29 44 | 13 03 | 05 13 | 21 28 | 05 49 |
| 59 | 04♉30 | 16 11 | 07 03 | 22 32 | 06 19 |
| 60 | 10♉09 | 19♊31 | 08♋58 | 23♋38 | 06♌50 |

**21h 32m 0s — 323° 0' 0" — 20 ♒ 36**

| LAT. | 11 | 12 | ASC | 2 | 3 |
|---|---|---|---|---|---|
| 0 | 22♓23 | 24♈50 | 25♉21 | 23♊34 | 21♋17 |
| 5 | 23 04 | 26 14 | 27 04 | 25 10 | 22 19 |
| 10 | 23 49 | 27 46 | 28 53 | 26 47 | 23 22 |
| 15 | 24 40 | 29 28 | 00♊51 | 28 28 | 24 24 |
| 20 | 25 39 | 01♉23 | 02 59 | 00♋15 | 25 27 |
| 21 | 25 52 | 01 48 | 03 26 | 00 37 | 25 40 |
| 22 | 26 05 | 02 14 | 03 54 | 00 59 | 25 53 |
| 23 | 26 19 | 02 41 | 04 22 | 01 22 | 26 06 |
| 24 | 26 33 | 03 08 | 04 51 | 01 45 | 26 19 |
| 25 | 26 48 | 03 37 | 05 21 | 02 08 | 26 33 |
| 26 | 27 04 | 04 06 | 05 51 | 02 32 | 26 46 |
| 27 | 27 20 | 04 36 | 06 22 | 02 56 | 27 00 |
| 28 | 27 37 | 05 08 | 06 54 | 03 21 | 27 14 |
| 29 | 27 55 | 05 41 | 07 27 | 03 46 | 27 28 |
| 30 | 28 13 | 06 15 | 08 01 | 04 11 | 27 42 |
| 31 | 28 33 | 06 50 | 08 36 | 04 37 | 27 56 |
| 32 | 28 53 | 07 27 | 09 12 | 05 04 | 28 10 |
| 33 | 29 15 | 08 05 | 09 48 | 05 31 | 28 25 |
| 34 | 29 38 | 08 45 | 10 26 | 05 59 | 28 40 |
| 35 | 00♈02 | 09 27 | 11 06 | 06 27 | 28 55 |
| 36 | 00 27 | 10 11 | 11 46 | 06 56 | 29 11 |
| 37 | 00 55 | 10 57 | 12 28 | 07 26 | 29 26 |
| 38 | 01 23 | 11 45 | 13 11 | 07 57 | 29 42 |
| 39 | 01 54 | 12 36 | 13 56 | 08 28 | 29 59 |
| 40 | 02 27 | 13 30 | 14 43 | 09 00 | 00♌15 |
| 41 | 03 03 | 14 26 | 15 31 | 09 33 | 00 32 |
| 42 | 03 41 | 15 26 | 16 21 | 10 07 | 00 50 |
| 43 | 04 22 | 16 29 | 17 13 | 10 42 | 01 08 |
| 44 | 05 07 | 17 36 | 18 08 | 11 18 | 01 26 |
| 45 | 05 56 | 18 47 | 19 04 | 11 55 | 01 44 |
| 46 | 06 49 | 20 02 | 20 03 | 12 34 | 02 03 |
| 47 | 07 48 | 21 23 | 21 04 | 13 13 | 02 23 |
| 48 | 08 52 | 22 48 | 22 08 | 13 54 | 02 43 |
| 49 | 10 04 | 24 20 | 23 15 | 14 36 | 03 04 |
| 50 | 11 23 | 25 58 | 24 26 | 15 20 | 03 25 |
| 51 | 12 53 | 27 42 | 25 39 | 16 06 | 03 47 |
| 52 | 14 34 | 29 35 | 26 56 | 16 53 | 04 10 |
| 53 | 16 28 | 01♊35 | 28 16 | 17 42 | 04 33 |
| 54 | 18 39 | 03 45 | 29 41 | 18 32 | 04 58 |
| 55 | 21 10 | 06 04 | 01♋09 | 19 25 | 05 23 |
| 56 | 24 05 | 08 33 | 02 42 | 20 21 | 05 49 |
| 57 | 27 29 | 11 14 | 04 20 | 21 18 | 06 16 |
| 58 | 01♉30 | 14 06 | 06 03 | 22 18 | 06 44 |
| 59 | 06 14 | 17 10 | 07 51 | 23 21 | 07 13 |
| 60 | 11♉49 | 20♊26 | 09♋44 | 24♋26 | 07♌43 |

**21h 36m 0s — 324° 0' 0" — 21 ♒ 37**

| LAT. | 11 | 12 | ASC | 2 | 3 |
|---|---|---|---|---|---|
| 0 | 23♓28 | 25♈53 | 26♉19 | 24♊30 | 22♋13 |
| 5 | 24 10 | 27 19 | 28 03 | 26 06 | 23 16 |
| 10 | 24 57 | 28 53 | 29 54 | 27 44 | 24 19 |
| 15 | 25 49 | 00♉36 | 01♊52 | 29 25 | 25 21 |
| 20 | 26 50 | 02 33 | 04 00 | 01♋12 | 26 25 |
| 21 | 27 03 | 02 58 | 04 28 | 01 34 | 26 38 |
| 22 | 27 17 | 03 24 | 04 56 | 01 56 | 26 51 |
| 23 | 27 31 | 03 51 | 05 24 | 02 19 | 27 04 |
| 24 | 27 46 | 04 19 | 05 53 | 02 42 | 27 17 |
| 25 | 28 01 | 04 48 | 06 23 | 03 06 | 27 30 |
| 26 | 28 17 | 05 17 | 06 54 | 03 29 | 27 44 |
| 27 | 28 34 | 05 48 | 07 25 | 03 54 | 27 58 |
| 28 | 28 51 | 06 20 | 07 57 | 04 18 | 28 11 |
| 29 | 29 10 | 06 53 | 08 30 | 04 43 | 28 25 |
| 30 | 29 29 | 07 27 | 09 04 | 05 09 | 28 39 |
| 31 | 29 49 | 08 03 | 09 39 | 05 35 | 28 54 |
| 32 | 00♈10 | 08 40 | 10 14 | 06 02 | 29 08 |
| 33 | 00 32 | 09 19 | 10 51 | 06 29 | 29 23 |
| 34 | 00 56 | 09 59 | 11 29 | 06 56 | 29 38 |
| 35 | 01 20 | 10 41 | 12 08 | 07 25 | 29 53 |
| 36 | 01 47 | 11 26 | 12 49 | 07 54 | 00♌08 |
| 37 | 02 14 | 12 12 | 13 31 | 08 23 | 00 24 |
| 38 | 02 44 | 13 01 | 14 14 | 08 54 | 00 40 |
| 39 | 03 16 | 13 52 | 14 59 | 09 25 | 00 56 |
| 40 | 03 50 | 14 45 | 15 45 | 09 57 | 01 13 |
| 41 | 04 26 | 15 42 | 16 33 | 10 30 | 01 30 |
| 42 | 05 05 | 16 42 | 17 23 | 11 04 | 01 47 |
| 43 | 05 47 | 17 45 | 18 15 | 11 38 | 02 05 |
| 44 | 06 33 | 18 52 | 19 09 | 12 14 | 02 23 |
| 45 | 07 23 | 20 03 | 20 05 | 12 51 | 02 41 |
| 46 | 08 18 | 21 18 | 21 04 | 13 29 | 03 00 |
| 47 | 09 17 | 22 38 | 22 05 | 14 09 | 03 20 |
| 48 | 10 23 | 24 04 | 23 08 | 14 49 | 03 40 |
| 49 | 11 36 | 25 35 | 24 15 | 15 31 | 04 00 |
| 50 | 12 57 | 27 12 | 25 24 | 16 15 | 04 22 |
| 51 | 14 28 | 28 56 | 26 37 | 17 00 | 04 43 |
| 52 | 16 11 | 00♊48 | 27 53 | 17 46 | 05 06 |
| 53 | 18 07 | 02 47 | 29 12 | 18 35 | 05 29 |
| 54 | 20 19 | 04 55 | 00♋36 | 19 25 | 05 53 |
| 55 | 22 51 | 07 12 | 02 03 | 20 17 | 06 18 |
| 56 | 25 47 | 09 39 | 03 35 | 21 12 | 06 44 |
| 57 | 29 12 | 12 17 | 05 11 | 22 09 | 07 10 |
| 58 | 03♉12 | 15 06 | 06 52 | 23 08 | 07 38 |
| 59 | 07 55 | 18 07 | 08 38 | 24 10 | 08 07 |
| 60 | 13♉26 | 21♊19 | 10♋30 | 25♋14 | 08♌37 |

**21h 40m 0s — 325° 0' 0" — 22 ♒ 39**

| LAT. | 11 | 12 | ASC | 2 | 3 |
|---|---|---|---|---|---|
| 0 | 24♓33 | 26♈57 | 27♉17 | 25♊25 | 23♋10 |
| 5 | 25 17 | 28 24 | 29 02 | 27 01 | 24 13 |
| 10 | 26 05 | 29 59 | 00♊54 | 28 40 | 25 16 |
| 15 | 26 59 | 01♉43 | 02 53 | 00♋22 | 26 19 |
| 20 | 28 01 | 03 42 | 05 02 | 02 09 | 27 22 |
| 21 | 28 14 | 04 07 | 05 29 | 02 31 | 27 35 |
| 22 | 28 28 | 04 34 | 05 57 | 02 54 | 27 48 |
| 23 | 28 43 | 05 01 | 06 26 | 03 16 | 28 02 |
| 24 | 28 58 | 05 29 | 06 55 | 03 39 | 28 15 |
| 25 | 29 14 | 05 58 | 07 25 | 04 03 | 28 28 |
| 26 | 29 31 | 06 28 | 07 56 | 04 27 | 28 42 |
| 27 | 29 48 | 06 59 | 08 27 | 04 51 | 28 55 |
| 28 | 00♈06 | 07 31 | 08 59 | 05 16 | 29 09 |
| 29 | 00 24 | 08 05 | 09 32 | 05 41 | 29 23 |
| 30 | 00 44 | 08 39 | 10 06 | 06 06 | 29 37 |
| 31 | 01 05 | 09 15 | 10 41 | 06 32 | 29 51 |
| 32 | 01 26 | 09 53 | 11 17 | 06 59 | 00♌06 |
| 33 | 01 49 | 10 32 | 11 54 | 07 26 | 00 20 |
| 34 | 02 13 | 11 12 | 12 32 | 07 54 | 00 35 |
| 35 | 02 38 | 11 55 | 13 11 | 08 22 | 00 50 |
| 36 | 03 05 | 12 39 | 13 51 | 08 51 | 01 06 |
| 37 | 03 34 | 13 26 | 14 33 | 09 20 | 01 22 |
| 38 | 04 04 | 14 15 | 15 16 | 09 51 | 01 37 |
| 39 | 04 37 | 15 06 | 16 01 | 10 22 | 01 54 |
| 40 | 05 11 | 16 00 | 16 47 | 10 54 | 02 10 |
| 41 | 05 49 | 16 57 | 17 35 | 11 26 | 02 27 |
| 42 | 06 29 | 17 57 | 18 25 | 12 00 | 02 44 |
| 43 | 07 12 | 19 00 | 19 16 | 12 35 | 03 02 |
| 44 | 07 59 | 20 07 | 20 10 | 13 10 | 03 20 |
| 45 | 08 50 | 21 18 | 21 06 | 13 47 | 03 38 |
| 46 | 09 45 | 22 33 | 22 04 | 14 25 | 03 57 |
| 47 | 10 46 | 23 53 | 23 04 | 15 04 | 04 17 |
| 48 | 11 53 | 25 18 | 24 07 | 15 44 | 04 36 |
| 49 | 13 08 | 26 49 | 25 13 | 16 26 | 04 57 |
| 50 | 14 30 | 28 25 | 26 22 | 17 09 | 05 18 |
| 51 | 16 03 | 00♊08 | 27 34 | 17 53 | 05 39 |
| 52 | 17 46 | 01 59 | 28 49 | 18 39 | 06 02 |
| 53 | 19 44 | 03 57 | 00♋07 | 19 27 | 06 25 |
| 54 | 21 58 | 06 03 | 01 30 | 20 17 | 06 49 |
| 55 | 24 31 | 08 19 | 02 56 | 21 09 | 07 13 |
| 56 | 27 28 | 10 44 | 04 27 | 22 03 | 07 39 |
| 57 | 00♉53 | 13 19 | 06 02 | 22 59 | 08 05 |
| 58 | 04 52 | 16 05 | 07 41 | 23 57 | 08 32 |
| 59 | 09 32 | 19 02 | 09 25 | 24 58 | 09 01 |
| 60 | 15♉00 | 22♊11 | 11♋15 | 26♋02 | 09♌31 |

**21h 44m 0s — 326° 0' 0" — 23 ♒ 41**

| LAT. | 11 | 12 | ASC | 2 | 3 |
|---|---|---|---|---|---|
| 0 | 25♓38 | 28♈00 | 28♉15 | 26♊20 | 24♋06 |
| 5 | 26 23 | 29 28 | 00♊01 | 27 57 | 25 10 |
| 10 | 27 12 | 01♉04 | 01 53 | 29 36 | 26 13 |
| 15 | 28 08 | 02 51 | 03 53 | 01♋19 | 27 16 |
| 20 | 29 12 | 04 50 | 06 03 | 03 06 | 28 20 |
| 21 | 29 26 | 05 16 | 06 31 | 03 28 | 28 33 |
| 22 | 29 40 | 05 43 | 06 59 | 03 51 | 28 46 |
| 23 | 29 55 | 06 11 | 07 27 | 04 14 | 28 59 |
| 24 | 00♈11 | 06 39 | 07 57 | 04 37 | 29 13 |
| 25 | 00 27 | 07 08 | 08 27 | 05 00 | 29 26 |
| 26 | 00 44 | 07 38 | 08 57 | 05 24 | 29 39 |
| 27 | 01 01 | 08 10 | 09 29 | 05 48 | 29 53 |
| 28 | 01 20 | 08 42 | 10 01 | 06 13 | 00♌07 |
| 29 | 01 39 | 09 16 | 10 34 | 06 38 | 00 21 |
| 30 | 01 59 | 09 51 | 11 08 | 07 03 | 00 35 |
| 31 | 02 20 | 10 27 | 11 43 | 07 29 | 00 49 |
| 32 | 02 42 | 11 05 | 12 19 | 07 56 | 01 04 |
| 33 | 03 06 | 11 44 | 12 56 | 08 23 | 01 18 |
| 34 | 03 30 | 12 25 | 13 34 | 08 51 | 01 33 |
| 35 | 03 56 | 13 08 | 14 13 | 09 19 | 01 48 |
| 36 | 04 24 | 13 52 | 14 53 | 09 48 | 02 03 |
| 37 | 04 53 | 14 39 | 15 35 | 10 17 | 02 19 |
| 38 | 05 24 | 15 28 | 16 18 | 10 47 | 02 35 |
| 39 | 05 57 | 16 20 | 17 02 | 11 18 | 02 51 |
| 40 | 06 33 | 17 14 | 17 48 | 11 50 | 03 08 |
| 41 | 07 11 | 18 11 | 18 36 | 12 23 | 03 24 |
| 42 | 07 52 | 19 11 | 19 26 | 12 56 | 03 41 |
| 43 | 08 36 | 20 14 | 20 17 | 13 31 | 03 59 |
| 44 | 09 24 | 21 21 | 21 10 | 14 06 | 04 17 |
| 45 | 10 16 | 22 31 | 22 06 | 14 42 | 04 35 |
| 46 | 11 13 | 23 47 | 23 03 | 15 20 | 04 54 |
| 47 | 12 15 | 25 06 | 24 03 | 15 59 | 05 13 |
| 48 | 13 23 | 26 31 | 25 06 | 16 39 | 05 33 |
| 49 | 14 38 | 28 01 | 26 11 | 17 20 | 05 53 |
| 50 | 16 02 | 29 37 | 27 19 | 18 03 | 06 14 |
| 51 | 17 36 | 01♊19 | 28 30 | 18 47 | 06 36 |
| 52 | 19 21 | 03 09 | 29 44 | 19 32 | 06 58 |
| 53 | 21 20 | 05 06 | 01♋02 | 20 20 | 07 21 |
| 54 | 23 34 | 07 11 | 02 23 | 21 09 | 07 44 |
| 55 | 26 09 | 09 24 | 03 49 | 22 00 | 08 08 |
| 56 | 29 06 | 11 47 | 05 18 | 22 53 | 08 34 |
| 57 | 02♉31 | 14 20 | 06 51 | 23 49 | 09 00 |
| 58 | 06 29 | 17 03 | 08 29 | 24 46 | 09 27 |
| 59 | 11 07 | 19 57 | 10 12 | 25 47 | 09 55 |
| 60 | 16♉30 | 23♊01 | 12♋00 | 26♋49 | 10♌24 |

**21h 48m 0s — 327° 0' 0" — 24 ♒ 42**

| LAT. | 11 | 12 | ASC | 2 | 3 |
|---|---|---|---|---|---|
| 0 | 26♓44 | 29♈03 | 29♉13 | 27♊15 | 25♋03 |
| 5 | 27 30 | 00♉33 | 01♊00 | 28 53 | 26 08 |
| 10 | 28 20 | 02 10 | 02 53 | 00♋32 | 27 11 |
| 15 | 29 17 | 03 58 | 04 53 | 02 15 | 28 14 |
| 20 | 00♈22 | 05 59 | 07 04 | 04 03 | 29 18 |
| 21 | 00 37 | 06 25 | 07 32 | 04 25 | 29 31 |
| 22 | 00 52 | 06 52 | 08 00 | 04 48 | 29 44 |
| 23 | 01 07 | 07 20 | 08 29 | 05 11 | 29 57 |
| 24 | 01 23 | 07 48 | 08 58 | 05 34 | 00♌10 |
| 25 | 01 40 | 08 18 | 09 28 | 05 57 | 00 24 |
| 26 | 01 57 | 08 48 | 09 59 | 06 21 | 00 37 |
| 27 | 02 15 | 09 20 | 10 30 | 06 45 | 00 51 |
| 28 | 02 34 | 09 53 | 11 02 | 07 10 | 01 05 |
| 29 | 02 53 | 10 26 | 11 36 | 07 35 | 01 19 |
| 30 | 03 14 | 11 02 | 12 09 | 08 00 | 01 33 |
| 31 | 03 36 | 11 38 | 12 44 | 08 26 | 01 47 |
| 32 | 03 58 | 12 16 | 13 20 | 08 53 | 02 01 |
| 33 | 04 22 | 12 56 | 13 57 | 09 20 | 02 16 |
| 34 | 04 47 | 13 37 | 14 35 | 09 47 | 02 31 |
| 35 | 05 14 | 14 20 | 15 14 | 10 16 | 02 46 |
| 36 | 05 42 | 15 05 | 15 54 | 10 44 | 03 01 |
| 37 | 06 12 | 15 52 | 16 36 | 11 14 | 03 17 |
| 38 | 06 44 | 16 41 | 17 19 | 11 44 | 03 32 |
| 39 | 07 18 | 17 32 | 18 03 | 12 15 | 03 49 |
| 40 | 07 54 | 18 26 | 18 49 | 12 46 | 04 05 |
| 41 | 08 33 | 19 23 | 19 36 | 13 19 | 04 22 |
| 42 | 09 15 | 20 23 | 20 26 | 13 52 | 04 39 |
| 43 | 10 00 | 21 27 | 21 17 | 14 26 | 04 56 |
| 44 | 10 48 | 22 33 | 22 10 | 15 01 | 05 14 |
| 45 | 11 41 | 23 44 | 23 05 | 15 38 | 05 32 |
| 46 | 12 39 | 24 59 | 24 02 | 16 15 | 05 51 |
| 47 | 13 42 | 26 18 | 25 02 | 16 53 | 06 10 |
| 48 | 14 51 | 27 42 | 26 04 | 17 33 | 06 30 |
| 49 | 16 08 | 29 12 | 27 08 | 18 14 | 06 50 |
| 50 | 17 33 | 00♊47 | 28 16 | 18 56 | 07 10 |
| 51 | 19 08 | 02 29 | 29 26 | 19 40 | 07 32 |
| 52 | 20 54 | 04 17 | 00♋39 | 20 25 | 07 54 |
| 53 | 22 54 | 06 13 | 01 56 | 21 12 | 08 16 |
| 54 | 25 10 | 08 16 | 03 16 | 22 01 | 08 40 |
| 55 | 27 44 | 10 28 | 04 40 | 22 51 | 09 04 |
| 56 | 00♉42 | 12 49 | 06 08 | 23 44 | 09 29 |
| 57 | 04 07 | 15 19 | 07 40 | 24 39 | 09 54 |
| 58 | 08 04 | 17 59 | 09 17 | 25 36 | 10 21 |
| 59 | 12 39 | 20 50 | 10 58 | 26 35 | 10 49 |
| 60 | 17♉57 | 23♊51 | 12♋44 | 27♋37 | 11♌18 |

# Koch Table of Houses for Latitudes 0° to 60° North

**21h 52m 0s — 328° 0' 0" — 25 ♒ 44**

| LAT. | 11 | 12 | ASC | 2 | 3 |
|---|---|---|---|---|---|
| 0 | 27♓49 | 00♉06 | 00♊11 | 28♊10 | 26♋00 |
| 5 | 28 36 | 01 37 | 01 59 | 29 48 | 27 05 |
| 10 | 29 28 | 03 15 | 03 52 | 01♋29 | 28 08 |
| 15 | 00♈26 | 05 04 | 05 53 | 03 12 | 29 12 |
| 20 | 01 33 | 07 07 | 08 04 | 05 00 | 00♌16 |
| 21 | 01 48 | 07 33 | 08 32 | 05 22 | 00 29 |
| 22 | 02 03 | 08 00 | 09 00 | 05 45 | 00 42 |
| 23 | 02 19 | 08 28 | 09 29 | 06 07 | 00 55 |
| 24 | 02 35 | 08 57 | 09 59 | 06 31 | 01 08 |
| 25 | 02 52 | 09 27 | 10 29 | 06 54 | 01 22 |
| 26 | 03 10 | 09 58 | 11 00 | 07 18 | 01 35 |
| 27 | 03 28 | 10 30 | 11 31 | 07 42 | 01 49 |
| 28 | 03 48 | 11 02 | 12 03 | 08 07 | 02 03 |
| 29 | 04 08 | 11 37 | 12 37 | 08 32 | 02 16 |
| 30 | 04 29 | 12 12 | 13 10 | 08 57 | 02 30 |
| 31 | 04 51 | 12 49 | 13 45 | 09 23 | 02 45 |
| 32 | 05 14 | 13 27 | 14 21 | 09 50 | 02 59 |
| 33 | 05 39 | 14 07 | 14 58 | 10 17 | 03 14 |
| 34 | 06 04 | 14 48 | 15 36 | 10 44 | 03 28 |
| 35 | 06 31 | 15 31 | 16 15 | 11 12 | 03 44 |
| 36 | 07 00 | 16 16 | 16 55 | 11 41 | 03 59 |
| 37 | 07 31 | 17 03 | 17 36 | 12 10 | 04 14 |
| 38 | 08 03 | 17 53 | 18 19 | 12 40 | 04 30 |
| 39 | 08 38 | 18 44 | 19 03 | 13 11 | 04 46 |
| 40 | 09 15 | 19 38 | 19 49 | 13 42 | 05 02 |
| 41 | 09 54 | 20 35 | 20 36 | 14 15 | 05 19 |
| 42 | 10 37 | 21 35 | 21 25 | 14 48 | 05 36 |
| 43 | 11 23 | 22 39 | 22 16 | 15 22 | 05 53 |
| 44 | 12 12 | 23 45 | 23 09 | 15 57 | 06 11 |
| 45 | 13 06 | 24 56 | 24 03 | 16 33 | 06 29 |
| 46 | 14 05 | 26 10 | 25 00 | 17 10 | 06 48 |
| 47 | 15 09 | 27 29 | 25 59 | 17 48 | 07 07 |
| 48 | 16 19 | 28 53 | 27 01 | 18 27 | 07 26 |
| 49 | 17 37 | 00♊22 | 28 05 | 19 08 | 07 46 |
| 50 | 19 03 | 01 56 | 29 11 | 19 50 | 08 07 |
| 51 | 20 39 | 03 37 | 00♋21 | 20 33 | 08 28 |
| 52 | 22 26 | 05 24 | 01 34 | 21 18 | 08 50 |
| 53 | 24 26 | 07 19 | 02 49 | 22 04 | 09 12 |
| 54 | 26 43 | 09 21 | 04 09 | 22 52 | 09 35 |
| 55 | 29 18 | 11 31 | 05 32 | 23 42 | 09 59 |
| 56 | 02♉16 | 13 49 | 06 58 | 24 34 | 10 24 |
| 57 | 05 40 | 16 17 | 08 29 | 25 28 | 10 49 |
| 58 | 09 36 | 18 54 | 10 04 | 26 24 | 11 16 |
| 59 | 14 08 | 21 42 | 11 44 | 27 23 | 11 43 |
| 60 | 19♉21 | 24♊39 | 13♋28 | 28♋24 | 12♌12 |

**21h 56m 0s — 329° 0' 0" — 26 ♒ 47**

| LAT. | 11 | 12 | ASC | 2 | 3 |
|---|---|---|---|---|---|
| 0 | 28♓55 | 01♉08 | 01♊08 | 29♊05 | 26♋57 |
| 5 | 29 43 | 02 41 | 02 57 | 00♋44 | 28 02 |
| 10 | 00♈36 | 04 21 | 04 51 | 02 25 | 29 06 |
| 15 | 01 35 | 06 11 | 06 53 | 04 08 | 00♌09 |
| 20 | 02 44 | 08 14 | 09 05 | 05 56 | 01 14 |
| 21 | 02 59 | 08 41 | 09 32 | 06 19 | 01 27 |
| 22 | 03 14 | 09 08 | 10 01 | 06 41 | 01 40 |
| 23 | 03 31 | 09 36 | 10 30 | 07 04 | 01 53 |
| 24 | 03 47 | 10 06 | 10 59 | 07 27 | 02 06 |
| 25 | 04 05 | 10 36 | 11 29 | 07 51 | 02 20 |
| 26 | 04 23 | 11 07 | 12 00 | 08 15 | 02 33 |
| 27 | 04 42 | 11 39 | 12 32 | 08 39 | 02 47 |
| 28 | 05 01 | 12 12 | 13 04 | 09 03 | 03 00 |
| 29 | 05 22 | 12 46 | 13 37 | 09 29 | 03 14 |
| 30 | 05 43 | 13 22 | 14 11 | 09 54 | 03 28 |
| 31 | 06 06 | 13 59 | 14 46 | 10 20 | 03 43 |
| 32 | 06 30 | 14 37 | 15 22 | 10 46 | 03 57 |
| 33 | 06 55 | 15 17 | 15 58 | 11 13 | 04 12 |
| 34 | 07 21 | 15 58 | 16 36 | 11 40 | 04 26 |
| 35 | 07 49 | 16 42 | 17 15 | 12 08 | 04 41 |
| 36 | 08 18 | 17 27 | 17 55 | 12 37 | 04 56 |
| 37 | 08 49 | 18 14 | 18 37 | 13 06 | 05 12 |
| 38 | 09 22 | 19 04 | 19 19 | 13 36 | 05 28 |
| 39 | 09 57 | 19 55 | 20 03 | 14 07 | 05 44 |
| 40 | 10 35 | 20 50 | 20 49 | 14 38 | 06 00 |
| 41 | 11 15 | 21 46 | 21 36 | 15 10 | 06 16 |
| 42 | 11 59 | 22 46 | 22 24 | 15 43 | 06 33 |
| 43 | 12 45 | 23 49 | 23 15 | 16 17 | 06 51 |
| 44 | 13 36 | 24 56 | 24 07 | 16 52 | 07 08 |
| 45 | 14 30 | 26 06 | 25 01 | 17 27 | 07 26 |
| 46 | 15 30 | 27 20 | 25 58 | 18 04 | 07 45 |
| 47 | 16 35 | 28 39 | 26 56 | 18 42 | 08 04 |
| 48 | 17 46 | 00♊02 | 27 57 | 19 21 | 08 23 |
| 49 | 19 05 | 01 31 | 29 01 | 20 01 | 08 43 |
| 50 | 20 32 | 03 04 | 00♋07 | 20 43 | 09 03 |
| 51 | 22 08 | 04 44 | 01 15 | 21 26 | 09 24 |
| 52 | 23 56 | 06 30 | 02 27 | 22 10 | 09 46 |
| 53 | 25 58 | 08 23 | 03 42 | 22 56 | 10 08 |
| 54 | 28 15 | 10 23 | 05 01 | 23 44 | 10 31 |
| 55 | 00♉50 | 12 32 | 06 22 | 24 33 | 10 54 |
| 56 | 03 48 | 14 48 | 07 48 | 25 24 | 11 19 |
| 57 | 07 11 | 17 14 | 09 17 | 26 18 | 11 44 |
| 58 | 11 05 | 19 48 | 10 51 | 27 13 | 12 10 |
| 59 | 15 34 | 22 33 | 12 29 | 28 11 | 12 37 |
| 60 | 20♉43 | 25♊27 | 14♋11 | 29♋11 | 13♌05 |

**22h 0m 0s — 330° 0' 0" — 27 ♒ 49**

| LAT. | 11 | 12 | ASC | 2 | 3 |
|---|---|---|---|---|---|
| 0 | 00♈00 | 02♉11 | 02♊05 | 00♋00 | 27♋55 |
| 5 | 00 49 | 03 44 | 03 55 | 01 40 | 29 00 |
| 10 | 01 43 | 05 25 | 05 50 | 03 21 | 00♌04 |
| 15 | 02 44 | 07 16 | 07 52 | 05 05 | 01 07 |
| 20 | 03 54 | 09 21 | 10 05 | 06 53 | 02 12 |
| 21 | 04 10 | 09 48 | 10 32 | 07 15 | 02 25 |
| 22 | 04 26 | 10 16 | 11 01 | 07 38 | 02 38 |
| 23 | 04 42 | 10 44 | 11 30 | 08 01 | 02 51 |
| 24 | 04 59 | 11 14 | 11 59 | 08 24 | 03 04 |
| 25 | 05 17 | 11 44 | 12 30 | 08 47 | 03 18 |
| 26 | 05 35 | 12 15 | 13 00 | 09 11 | 03 31 |
| 27 | 05 55 | 12 47 | 13 32 | 09 36 | 03 45 |
| 28 | 06 15 | 13 21 | 14 04 | 10 00 | 03 58 |
| 29 | 06 36 | 13 55 | 14 37 | 10 25 | 04 12 |
| 30 | 06 58 | 14 31 | 15 11 | 10 50 | 04 26 |
| 31 | 07 21 | 15 08 | 15 46 | 11 16 | 04 41 |
| 32 | 07 45 | 15 47 | 16 22 | 11 43 | 04 55 |
| 33 | 08 10 | 16 27 | 16 59 | 12 09 | 05 09 |
| 34 | 08 37 | 17 08 | 17 36 | 12 37 | 05 24 |
| 35 | 09 05 | 17 52 | 18 15 | 13 05 | 05 39 |
| 36 | 09 35 | 18 37 | 18 55 | 13 33 | 05 54 |
| 37 | 10 07 | 19 24 | 19 36 | 14 02 | 06 10 |
| 38 | 10 41 | 20 14 | 20 19 | 14 32 | 06 25 |
| 39 | 11 16 | 21 05 | 21 02 | 15 02 | 06 41 |
| 40 | 11 55 | 22 00 | 21 48 | 15 34 | 06 57 |
| 41 | 12 36 | 22 57 | 22 35 | 16 06 | 07 14 |
| 42 | 13 20 | 23 57 | 23 23 | 16 38 | 07 31 |
| 43 | 14 07 | 24 59 | 24 13 | 17 12 | 07 48 |
| 44 | 14 58 | 26 06 | 25 05 | 17 46 | 08 05 |
| 45 | 15 54 | 27 16 | 25 59 | 18 22 | 08 23 |
| 46 | 16 54 | 28 30 | 26 55 | 18 58 | 08 42 |
| 47 | 18 00 | 29 48 | 27 53 | 19 36 | 09 00 |
| 48 | 19 12 | 01♊10 | 28 53 | 20 15 | 09 20 |
| 49 | 20 32 | 02 38 | 29 56 | 20 55 | 09 39 |
| 50 | 21 59 | 04 11 | 01♋01 | 21 36 | 10 00 |
| 51 | 23 37 | 05 50 | 02 09 | 22 18 | 10 20 |
| 52 | 25 26 | 07 35 | 03 20 | 23 02 | 10 42 |
| 53 | 27 27 | 09 26 | 04 34 | 23 48 | 11 04 |
| 54 | 29 45 | 11 25 | 05 52 | 24 35 | 11 26 |
| 55 | 02♉21 | 13 32 | 07 12 | 25 24 | 11 50 |
| 56 | 05 18 | 15 46 | 08 37 | 26 14 | 12 14 |
| 57 | 08 40 | 18 09 | 10 05 | 27 07 | 12 39 |
| 58 | 12 32 | 20 41 | 11 37 | 28 02 | 13 05 |
| 59 | 16 57 | 23 22 | 13 13 | 28 59 | 13 32 |
| 60 | 22♉01 | 26♊13 | 14♋54 | 29♋58 | 13♌59 |

**22h 4m 0s — 331° 0' 0" — 28 ♒ 52**

| LAT. | 11 | 12 | ASC | 2 | 3 |
|---|---|---|---|---|---|
| 0 | 01♈05 | 03♉13 | 03♊03 | 00♋55 | 28♋52 |
| 5 | 01 56 | 04 48 | 04 53 | 02 35 | 29 57 |
| 10 | 02 51 | 06 30 | 06 49 | 04 17 | 01♌02 |
| 15 | 03 53 | 08 22 | 08 52 | 06 01 | 02 05 |
| 20 | 05 05 | 10 28 | 11 04 | 07 49 | 03 10 |
| 21 | 05 20 | 10 55 | 11 32 | 08 12 | 03 23 |
| 22 | 05 37 | 11 23 | 12 01 | 08 34 | 03 36 |
| 23 | 05 53 | 11 52 | 12 30 | 08 57 | 03 49 |
| 24 | 06 11 | 12 21 | 12 59 | 09 21 | 04 02 |
| 25 | 06 29 | 12 52 | 13 29 | 09 44 | 04 16 |
| 26 | 06 48 | 13 23 | 14 00 | 10 08 | 04 29 |
| 27 | 07 08 | 13 55 | 14 32 | 10 32 | 04 43 |
| 28 | 07 28 | 14 29 | 15 04 | 10 57 | 04 56 |
| 29 | 07 49 | 15 04 | 15 37 | 11 22 | 05 10 |
| 30 | 08 12 | 15 40 | 16 11 | 11 47 | 05 24 |
| 31 | 08 35 | 16 17 | 16 46 | 12 13 | 05 38 |
| 32 | 09 00 | 16 55 | 17 22 | 12 39 | 05 53 |
| 33 | 09 26 | 17 36 | 17 58 | 13 06 | 06 07 |
| 34 | 09 53 | 18 17 | 18 36 | 13 33 | 06 22 |
| 35 | 10 22 | 19 01 | 19 15 | 14 01 | 06 37 |
| 36 | 10 52 | 19 46 | 19 54 | 14 29 | 06 52 |
| 37 | 11 24 | 20 34 | 20 35 | 14 58 | 07 07 |
| 38 | 11 59 | 21 23 | 21 18 | 15 28 | 07 23 |
| 39 | 12 35 | 22 15 | 22 01 | 15 58 | 07 39 |
| 40 | 13 14 | 23 09 | 22 46 | 16 29 | 07 55 |
| 41 | 13 56 | 24 06 | 23 33 | 17 01 | 08 11 |
| 42 | 14 40 | 25 06 | 24 21 | 17 33 | 08 28 |
| 43 | 15 29 | 26 08 | 25 11 | 18 07 | 08 45 |
| 44 | 16 20 | 27 15 | 26 02 | 18 41 | 09 03 |
| 45 | 17 17 | 28 24 | 26 56 | 19 16 | 09 20 |
| 46 | 18 18 | 29 38 | 27 51 | 19 52 | 09 39 |
| 47 | 19 24 | 00♊55 | 28 49 | 20 30 | 09 57 |
| 48 | 20 37 | 02 17 | 29 49 | 21 08 | 10 16 |
| 49 | 21 57 | 03 44 | 00♋51 | 21 48 | 10 36 |
| 50 | 23 26 | 05 17 | 01 55 | 22 29 | 10 56 |
| 51 | 25 04 | 06 54 | 03 03 | 23 11 | 11 17 |
| 52 | 26 53 | 08 38 | 04 13 | 23 54 | 11 38 |
| 53 | 28 56 | 10 29 | 05 26 | 24 39 | 11 59 |
| 54 | 01♉13 | 12 26 | 06 42 | 25 26 | 12 22 |
| 55 | 03 49 | 14 30 | 08 02 | 26 14 | 12 45 |
| 56 | 06 45 | 16 43 | 09 25 | 27 04 | 13 09 |
| 57 | 10 06 | 19 04 | 10 52 | 27 56 | 13 34 |
| 58 | 13 56 | 21 33 | 12 23 | 28 50 | 13 59 |
| 59 | 18 18 | 24 11 | 13 58 | 29 46 | 14 26 |
| 60 | 23♉17 | 26♊58 | 15♋37 | 00♌45 | 14♌53 |

**22h 8m 0s — 332° 0' 0" — 29 ♒ 54**

| LAT. | 11 | 12 | ASC | 2 | 3 |
|---|---|---|---|---|---|
| 0 | 02♈11 | 04♉16 | 04♊00 | 01♋50 | 29♋49 |
| 5 | 03 02 | 05 51 | 05 51 | 03 31 | 00♌55 |
| 10 | 03 59 | 07 34 | 07 47 | 05 13 | 02 00 |
| 15 | 05 02 | 09 27 | 09 51 | 06 57 | 03 04 |
| 20 | 06 15 | 11 34 | 12 03 | 08 46 | 04 08 |
| 21 | 06 31 | 12 02 | 12 31 | 09 08 | 04 21 |
| 22 | 06 48 | 12 30 | 13 00 | 09 31 | 04 34 |
| 23 | 07 05 | 12 58 | 13 29 | 09 54 | 04 47 |
| 24 | 07 23 | 13 28 | 13 59 | 10 17 | 05 01 |
| 25 | 07 41 | 13 59 | 14 29 | 10 40 | 05 14 |
| 26 | 08 00 | 14 30 | 15 00 | 11 04 | 05 27 |
| 27 | 08 20 | 15 03 | 15 31 | 11 28 | 05 41 |
| 28 | 08 41 | 15 37 | 16 04 | 11 53 | 05 55 |
| 29 | 09 03 | 16 12 | 16 37 | 12 18 | 06 08 |
| 30 | 09 26 | 16 48 | 17 11 | 12 43 | 06 22 |
| 31 | 09 50 | 17 25 | 17 45 | 13 09 | 06 37 |
| 32 | 10 15 | 18 04 | 18 21 | 13 35 | 06 51 |
| 33 | 10 41 | 18 44 | 18 57 | 14 02 | 07 05 |
| 34 | 11 09 | 19 26 | 19 35 | 14 29 | 07 20 |
| 35 | 11 38 | 20 10 | 20 14 | 14 57 | 07 35 |
| 36 | 12 09 | 20 55 | 20 53 | 15 25 | 07 50 |
| 37 | 12 42 | 21 42 | 21 34 | 15 54 | 08 05 |
| 38 | 13 16 | 22 32 | 22 16 | 16 23 | 08 21 |
| 39 | 13 53 | 23 24 | 23 00 | 16 53 | 08 36 |
| 40 | 14 33 | 24 18 | 23 44 | 17 24 | 08 52 |
| 41 | 15 15 | 25 14 | 24 31 | 17 56 | 09 09 |
| 42 | 16 01 | 26 14 | 25 19 | 18 28 | 09 25 |
| 43 | 16 49 | 27 17 | 26 08 | 19 01 | 09 42 |
| 44 | 17 42 | 28 22 | 26 59 | 19 35 | 10 00 |
| 45 | 18 39 | 29 32 | 27 52 | 20 10 | 10 17 |
| 46 | 19 40 | 00♊45 | 28 47 | 20 46 | 10 36 |
| 47 | 20 48 | 02 02 | 29 44 | 21 23 | 10 54 |
| 48 | 22 01 | 03 24 | 00♋44 | 22 01 | 11 13 |
| 49 | 23 22 | 04 50 | 01 45 | 22 41 | 11 32 |
| 50 | 24 51 | 06 21 | 02 49 | 23 21 | 11 52 |
| 51 | 26 30 | 07 58 | 03 56 | 24 03 | 12 13 |
| 52 | 28 20 | 09 41 | 05 05 | 24 46 | 12 34 |
| 53 | 00♉22 | 11 29 | 06 17 | 25 30 | 12 55 |
| 54 | 02 40 | 13 25 | 07 32 | 26 17 | 13 18 |
| 55 | 05 15 | 15 28 | 08 51 | 27 04 | 13 41 |
| 56 | 08 11 | 17 38 | 10 13 | 27 54 | 14 04 |
| 57 | 11 31 | 19 57 | 11 39 | 28 45 | 14 29 |
| 58 | 15 18 | 22 24 | 13 08 | 29 38 | 14 54 |
| 59 | 19 37 | 24 59 | 14 41 | 00♌34 | 15 20 |
| 60 | 24♉30 | 27♊43 | 16♋19 | 01♌31 | 15♌47 |

**22h 12m 0s — 333° 0' 0" — 00 ♓ 57**

| LAT. | 11 | 12 | ASC | 2 | 3 |
|---|---|---|---|---|---|
| 0 | 03♈16 | 05♉18 | 04♊57 | 02♋45 | 00♌47 |
| 5 | 04 09 | 06 54 | 06 49 | 04 26 | 01 53 |
| 10 | 05 06 | 08 38 | 08 45 | 06 09 | 02 58 |
| 15 | 06 11 | 10 32 | 10 49 | 07 53 | 04 02 |
| 20 | 07 25 | 12 40 | 13 03 | 09 42 | 05 06 |
| 21 | 07 41 | 13 08 | 13 31 | 10 05 | 05 19 |
| 22 | 07 58 | 13 36 | 13 59 | 10 27 | 05 32 |
| 23 | 08 16 | 14 05 | 14 28 | 10 50 | 05 46 |
| 24 | 08 34 | 14 35 | 14 58 | 11 13 | 05 59 |
| 25 | 08 53 | 15 06 | 15 28 | 11 37 | 06 12 |
| 26 | 09 12 | 15 37 | 15 59 | 12 01 | 06 26 |
| 27 | 09 33 | 16 10 | 16 30 | 12 25 | 06 39 |
| 28 | 09 54 | 16 44 | 17 03 | 12 49 | 06 53 |
| 29 | 10 16 | 17 19 | 17 36 | 13 14 | 07 07 |
| 30 | 10 39 | 17 55 | 18 10 | 13 39 | 07 21 |
| 31 | 11 04 | 18 33 | 18 44 | 14 05 | 07 35 |
| 32 | 11 29 | 19 12 | 19 20 | 14 31 | 07 49 |
| 33 | 11 56 | 19 52 | 19 56 | 14 58 | 08 03 |
| 34 | 12 24 | 20 34 | 20 34 | 15 25 | 08 18 |
| 35 | 12 54 | 21 17 | 21 12 | 15 52 | 08 33 |
| 36 | 13 25 | 22 03 | 21 52 | 16 21 | 08 48 |
| 37 | 13 58 | 22 50 | 22 32 | 16 49 | 09 03 |
| 38 | 14 34 | 23 40 | 23 14 | 17 19 | 09 19 |
| 39 | 15 11 | 24 31 | 23 57 | 17 49 | 09 34 |
| 40 | 15 51 | 25 25 | 24 42 | 18 19 | 09 50 |
| 41 | 16 34 | 26 22 | 25 28 | 18 51 | 10 06 |
| 42 | 17 20 | 27 22 | 26 16 | 19 23 | 10 23 |
| 43 | 18 09 | 28 24 | 27 05 | 19 56 | 10 40 |
| 44 | 19 03 | 29 29 | 27 56 | 20 30 | 10 57 |
| 45 | 20 00 | 00♊38 | 28 48 | 21 04 | 11 15 |
| 46 | 21 02 | 01 51 | 29 43 | 21 40 | 11 33 |
| 47 | 22 10 | 03 08 | 00♋39 | 22 17 | 11 51 |
| 48 | 23 25 | 04 28 | 01 38 | 22 55 | 12 10 |
| 49 | 24 46 | 05 54 | 02 39 | 23 33 | 12 29 |
| 50 | 26 16 | 07 24 | 03 42 | 24 14 | 12 49 |
| 51 | 27 55 | 09 00 | 04 48 | 24 55 | 13 09 |
| 52 | 29 45 | 10 42 | 05 57 | 25 37 | 13 30 |
| 53 | 01♉48 | 12 29 | 07 08 | 26 22 | 13 51 |
| 54 | 04 05 | 14 23 | 08 22 | 27 07 | 14 13 |
| 55 | 06 40 | 16 24 | 09 40 | 27 54 | 14 36 |
| 56 | 09 35 | 18 33 | 11 01 | 28 43 | 14 59 |
| 57 | 12 53 | 20 49 | 12 25 | 29 34 | 15 24 |
| 58 | 16 38 | 23 13 | 13 53 | 00♌26 | 15 49 |
| 59 | 20 53 | 25 46 | 15 25 | 01 21 | 16 14 |
| 60 | 25♉41 | 28♊27 | 17♋01 | 02♌18 | 16♌41 |

**22h 16m 0s — 334° 0' 0" — 02 ♓ 00**

| LAT. | 11 | 12 | ASC | 2 | 3 |
|---|---|---|---|---|---|
| 0 | 04♈22 | 06♉19 | 05♊54 | 03♋40 | 01♌45 |
| 5 | 05 15 | 07 57 | 07 46 | 05 22 | 02 51 |
| 10 | 06 14 | 09 42 | 09 44 | 07 05 | 03 56 |
| 15 | 07 20 | 11 37 | 11 48 | 08 50 | 05 00 |
| 20 | 08 35 | 13 46 | 14 01 | 10 38 | 06 05 |
| 21 | 08 52 | 14 13 | 14 29 | 11 01 | 06 18 |
| 22 | 09 09 | 14 42 | 14 58 | 11 23 | 06 31 |
| 23 | 09 27 | 15 11 | 15 27 | 11 46 | 06 44 |
| 24 | 09 45 | 15 41 | 15 57 | 12 10 | 06 57 |
| 25 | 10 04 | 16 12 | 16 27 | 12 33 | 07 10 |
| 26 | 10 24 | 16 44 | 16 58 | 12 57 | 07 24 |
| 27 | 10 45 | 17 17 | 17 29 | 13 21 | 07 37 |
| 28 | 11 06 | 17 51 | 18 02 | 13 45 | 07 51 |
| 29 | 11 29 | 18 26 | 18 35 | 14 10 | 08 05 |
| 30 | 11 53 | 19 02 | 19 08 | 14 35 | 08 19 |
| 31 | 12 17 | 19 40 | 19 43 | 15 01 | 08 33 |
| 32 | 12 43 | 20 19 | 20 18 | 15 27 | 08 47 |
| 33 | 13 10 | 20 59 | 20 55 | 15 53 | 09 01 |
| 34 | 13 39 | 21 41 | 21 32 | 16 20 | 09 16 |
| 35 | 14 09 | 22 25 | 22 10 | 16 48 | 09 31 |
| 36 | 14 41 | 23 10 | 22 50 | 17 16 | 09 46 |
| 37 | 15 15 | 23 58 | 23 30 | 17 45 | 10 01 |
| 38 | 15 50 | 24 47 | 24 12 | 18 14 | 10 16 |
| 39 | 16 29 | 25 39 | 24 55 | 18 44 | 10 32 |
| 40 | 17 09 | 26 32 | 25 39 | 19 14 | 10 48 |
| 41 | 17 52 | 27 29 | 26 25 | 19 45 | 11 04 |
| 42 | 18 39 | 28 28 | 27 12 | 20 17 | 11 20 |
| 43 | 19 29 | 29 30 | 28 01 | 20 50 | 11 37 |
| 44 | 20 22 | 00♊35 | 28 51 | 21 24 | 11 54 |
| 45 | 21 21 | 01 44 | 29 44 | 21 58 | 12 12 |
| 46 | 22 24 | 02 56 | 00♋38 | 22 34 | 12 30 |
| 47 | 23 32 | 04 12 | 01 34 | 23 10 | 12 48 |
| 48 | 24 47 | 05 32 | 02 32 | 23 48 | 13 07 |
| 49 | 26 09 | 06 57 | 03 32 | 24 26 | 13 26 |
| 50 | 27 39 | 08 27 | 04 35 | 25 06 | 13 45 |
| 51 | 29 18 | 10 02 | 05 40 | 25 47 | 14 05 |
| 52 | 01♉08 | 11 42 | 06 48 | 26 29 | 14 26 |
| 53 | 03 11 | 13 28 | 07 58 | 27 13 | 14 47 |
| 54 | 05 29 | 15 21 | 09 12 | 27 58 | 15 09 |
| 55 | 08 03 | 17 20 | 10 28 | 28 44 | 15 31 |
| 56 | 10 57 | 19 26 | 11 48 | 29 33 | 15 55 |
| 57 | 14 13 | 21 40 | 13 11 | 00♌23 | 16 19 |
| 58 | 17 55 | 24 02 | 14 38 | 01 14 | 16 43 |
| 59 | 22 07 | 26 32 | 16 08 | 02 08 | 17 09 |
| 60 | 26♉50 | 29♊10 | 17♋42 | 03♌04 | 17♌35 |

**22h 20m 0s — 335° 0' 0" — 03 ♓ 03**

| LAT. | 11 | 12 | ASC | 2 | 3 |
|---|---|---|---|---|---|
| 0 | 05♈27 | 07♉21 | 06♊50 | 04♋35 | 02♌43 |
| 5 | 06 21 | 09 00 | 08 43 | 06 17 | 03 49 |
| 10 | 07 21 | 10 46 | 10 41 | 08 00 | 04 54 |
| 15 | 08 28 | 12 42 | 12 46 | 09 46 | 05 59 |
| 20 | 09 45 | 14 51 | 15 00 | 11 35 | 07 03 |
| 21 | 10 02 | 15 19 | 15 28 | 11 57 | 07 16 |
| 22 | 10 19 | 15 47 | 15 56 | 12 20 | 07 29 |
| 23 | 10 37 | 16 17 | 16 26 | 12 43 | 07 42 |
| 24 | 10 56 | 16 47 | 16 55 | 13 06 | 07 56 |
| 25 | 11 16 | 17 18 | 17 25 | 13 29 | 08 09 |
| 26 | 11 36 | 17 50 | 17 56 | 13 53 | 08 22 |
| 27 | 11 57 | 18 23 | 18 28 | 14 17 | 08 36 |
| 28 | 12 19 | 18 57 | 19 00 | 14 41 | 08 49 |
| 29 | 12 42 | 19 32 | 19 33 | 15 06 | 09 03 |
| 30 | 13 06 | 20 08 | 20 07 | 15 31 | 09 17 |
| 31 | 13 31 | 20 46 | 20 41 | 15 57 | 09 31 |
| 32 | 13 57 | 21 25 | 21 16 | 16 23 | 09 45 |
| 33 | 14 24 | 22 06 | 21 53 | 16 49 | 10 00 |
| 34 | 14 53 | 22 48 | 22 30 | 17 16 | 10 14 |
| 35 | 15 24 | 23 31 | 23 08 | 17 43 | 10 29 |
| 36 | 15 56 | 24 17 | 23 47 | 18 11 | 10 44 |
| 37 | 16 31 | 25 04 | 24 28 | 18 40 | 10 59 |
| 38 | 17 07 | 25 53 | 25 09 | 19 09 | 11 14 |
| 39 | 17 45 | 26 45 | 25 52 | 19 39 | 11 30 |
| 40 | 18 26 | 27 39 | 26 36 | 20 09 | 11 45 |
| 41 | 19 10 | 28 35 | 27 21 | 20 40 | 12 02 |
| 42 | 19 57 | 29 34 | 28 08 | 21 12 | 12 18 |
| 43 | 20 48 | 00♊36 | 28 57 | 21 44 | 12 35 |
| 44 | 21 42 | 01 41 | 29 47 | 22 18 | 12 52 |
| 45 | 22 40 | 02 49 | 00♋39 | 22 52 | 13 09 |
| 46 | 23 44 | 04 00 | 01 32 | 23 27 | 13 27 |
| 47 | 24 53 | 05 16 | 02 28 | 24 03 | 13 45 |
| 48 | 26 08 | 06 35 | 03 25 | 24 40 | 14 03 |
| 49 | 27 30 | 07 59 | 04 25 | 25 18 | 14 22 |
| 50 | 29 01 | 09 28 | 05 27 | 25 58 | 14 42 |
| 51 | 00♉40 | 11 02 | 06 31 | 26 38 | 15 02 |
| 52 | 02 31 | 12 41 | 07 38 | 27 20 | 15 22 |
| 53 | 04 34 | 14 26 | 08 48 | 28 03 | 15 43 |
| 54 | 06 51 | 16 17 | 10 00 | 28 48 | 16 05 |
| 55 | 09 24 | 18 14 | 11 16 | 29 34 | 16 27 |
| 56 | 12 17 | 20 19 | 12 34 | 00♌22 | 16 50 |
| 57 | 15 31 | 22 31 | 13 56 | 01 11 | 17 14 |
| 58 | 19 11 | 24 50 | 15 22 | 02 02 | 17 38 |
| 59 | 23 18 | 27 17 | 16 51 | 02 55 | 18 03 |
| 60 | 27♉57 | 29♊52 | 18♋24 | 03♌51 | 18♌29 |

# Koch Table of Houses for Latitudes 0° to 60° North

**22h 24m 0s — 336° 0' 0' — 04 ♓ 07**

| LAT. | 11 | 12 | ASC | 2 | 3 |
|---|---|---|---|---|---|
| 0 | 06♈32 | 08♉23 | 07♊47 | 05♋30 | 03♌41 |
| 5 | 07 28 | 10 02 | 09 41 | 07 13 | 04 48 |
| 10 | 08 28 | 11 49 | 11 39 | 08 56 | 05 53 |
| 15 | 09 36 | 13 46 | 13 44 | 10 42 | 06 57 |
| 20 | 10 55 | 15 56 | 15 58 | 12 31 | 08 02 |
| 21 | 11 12 | 16 24 | 16 26 | 12 53 | 08 15 |
| 22 | 11 30 | 16 52 | 16 55 | 13 16 | 08 28 |
| 23 | 11 48 | 17 22 | 17 24 | 13 39 | 08 41 |
| 24 | 12 07 | 17 52 | 17 53 | 14 02 | 08 54 |
| 25 | 12 27 | 18 23 | 18 24 | 14 25 | 09 07 |
| 26 | 12 47 | 18 55 | 18 54 | 14 49 | 09 21 |
| 27 | 13 09 | 19 28 | 19 26 | 15 13 | 09 34 |
| 28 | 13 31 | 20 03 | 19 58 | 15 37 | 09 48 |
| 29 | 13 54 | 20 38 | 20 31 | 16 02 | 10 02 |
| 30 | 14 18 | 21 14 | 21 05 | 16 27 | 10 15 |
| 31 | 14 44 | 21 52 | 21 39 | 16 53 | 10 29 |
| 32 | 15 10 | 22 31 | 22 14 | 17 18 | 10 43 |
| 33 | 15 38 | 23 12 | 22 50 | 17 45 | 10 58 |
| 34 | 16 08 | 23 54 | 23 27 | 18 12 | 11 12 |
| 35 | 16 39 | 24 37 | 24 05 | 18 39 | 11 27 |
| 36 | 17 11 | 25 23 | 24 44 | 19 07 | 11 42 |
| 37 | 17 46 | 26 10 | 25 25 | 19 35 | 11 57 |
| 38 | 18 23 | 26 59 | 26 06 | 20 04 | 12 12 |
| 39 | 19 02 | 27 50 | 26 48 | 20 33 | 12 27 |
| 40 | 19 43 | 28 44 | 27 32 | 21 04 | 12 43 |
| 41 | 20 27 | 29 40 | 28 17 | 21 34 | 12 59 |
| 42 | 21 15 | 00♊39 | 29 04 | 22 06 | 13 16 |
| 43 | 22 06 | 01 40 | 29 52 | 22 38 | 13 32 |
| 44 | 23 00 | 02 45 | 00♋42 | 23 11 | 13 49 |
| 45 | 23 59 | 03 53 | 01 33 | 23 45 | 14 06 |
| 46 | 25 03 | 05 04 | 02 26 | 24 20 | 14 24 |
| 47 | 26 13 | 06 19 | 03 21 | 24 56 | 14 42 |
| 48 | 27 28 | 07 38 | 04 18 | 25 33 | 15 00 |
| 49 | 28 51 | 09 01 | 05 17 | 26 11 | 15 19 |
| 50 | 00♉21 | 10 28 | 06 19 | 26 50 | 15 38 |
| 51 | 02 01 | 12 01 | 07 22 | 27 30 | 15 58 |
| 52 | 03 52 | 13 39 | 08 28 | 28 11 | 16 18 |
| 53 | 05 54 | 15 23 | 09 37 | 28 54 | 16 39 |
| 54 | 08 11 | 17 12 | 10 49 | 29 38 | 17 01 |
| 55 | 10 44 | 19 08 | 12 03 | 00♌24 | 17 23 |
| 56 | 13 35 | 21 11 | 13 21 | 01 11 | 17 45 |
| 57 | 16 47 | 23 20 | 14 42 | 02 00 | 18 09 |
| 58 | 20 24 | 25 37 | 16 06 | 02 50 | 18 33 |
| 59 | 24 28 | 28 02 | 17 33 | 03 43 | 18 58 |
| 60 | 29♉02 | 00♋34 | 19♋05 | 04♌37 | 19♌23 |

**22h 28m 0s — 337° 0' 0' — 05 ♓ 10**

| LAT. | 11 | 12 | ASC | 2 | 3 |
|---|---|---|---|---|---|
| 0 | 07♈37 | 09♉24 | 08♊43 | 06♋26 | 04♌39 |
| 5 | 08 34 | 11 04 | 10 38 | 08 09 | 05 46 |
| 10 | 09 36 | 12 52 | 12 37 | 09 52 | 06 51 |
| 15 | 10 45 | 14 49 | 14 42 | 11 38 | 07 56 |
| 20 | 12 04 | 17 00 | 16 56 | 13 27 | 09 00 |
| 21 | 12 22 | 17 28 | 17 24 | 13 49 | 09 13 |
| 22 | 12 40 | 17 57 | 17 53 | 14 12 | 09 26 |
| 23 | 12 58 | 18 27 | 18 22 | 14 35 | 09 39 |
| 24 | 13 17 | 18 57 | 18 51 | 14 58 | 09 53 |
| 25 | 13 38 | 19 28 | 19 22 | 15 21 | 10 06 |
| 26 | 13 58 | 20 00 | 19 52 | 15 45 | 10 19 |
| 27 | 14 20 | 20 34 | 20 24 | 16 09 | 10 33 |
| 28 | 14 43 | 21 08 | 20 56 | 16 33 | 10 46 |
| 29 | 15 06 | 21 43 | 21 29 | 16 58 | 11 00 |
| 30 | 15 31 | 22 20 | 22 02 | 17 23 | 11 14 |
| 31 | 15 56 | 22 57 | 22 37 | 17 48 | 11 28 |
| 32 | 16 23 | 23 36 | 23 12 | 18 14 | 11 42 |
| 33 | 16 52 | 24 17 | 23 48 | 18 40 | 11 56 |
| 34 | 17 21 | 24 59 | 24 25 | 19 07 | 12 10 |
| 35 | 17 53 | 25 43 | 25 02 | 19 34 | 12 25 |
| 36 | 18 26 | 26 28 | 25 41 | 20 02 | 12 40 |
| 37 | 19 01 | 27 15 | 26 21 | 20 30 | 12 55 |
| 38 | 19 38 | 28 04 | 27 02 | 20 59 | 13 10 |
| 39 | 20 17 | 28 55 | 27 45 | 21 28 | 13 25 |
| 40 | 20 59 | 29 49 | 28 28 | 21 58 | 13 41 |
| 41 | 21 44 | 00♊45 | 29 13 | 22 29 | 13 57 |
| 42 | 22 32 | 01 43 | 29 59 | 23 00 | 14 13 |
| 43 | 23 23 | 02 44 | 00♋47 | 23 32 | 14 30 |
| 44 | 24 18 | 03 48 | 01 36 | 24 05 | 14 46 |
| 45 | 25 17 | 04 56 | 02 27 | 24 39 | 15 04 |
| 46 | 26 22 | 06 06 | 03 20 | 25 13 | 15 21 |
| 47 | 27 31 | 07 21 | 04 14 | 25 49 | 15 39 |
| 48 | 28 47 | 08 39 | 05 11 | 26 25 | 15 57 |
| 49 | 00♉10 | 10 01 | 06 09 | 27 03 | 16 16 |
| 50 | 01 41 | 11 28 | 07 10 | 27 42 | 16 35 |
| 51 | 03 21 | 13 00 | 08 13 | 28 21 | 16 54 |
| 52 | 05 11 | 14 36 | 09 18 | 29 02 | 17 15 |
| 53 | 07 14 | 16 18 | 10 26 | 29 44 | 17 35 |
| 54 | 09 30 | 18 06 | 11 37 | 00♌28 | 17 56 |
| 55 | 12 01 | 20 01 | 12 50 | 01 13 | 18 18 |
| 56 | 14 51 | 22 01 | 14 07 | 02 00 | 18 41 |
| 57 | 18 02 | 24 09 | 15 26 | 02 48 | 19 04 |
| 58 | 21 35 | 26 23 | 16 49 | 03 38 | 19 28 |
| 59 | 25 36 | 28 45 | 18 16 | 04 30 | 19 52 |
| 60 | 00♊04 | 01♋15 | 19♋46 | 05♌23 | 20♌18 |

**22h 32m 0s — 338° 0' 0' — 06 ♓ 14**

| LAT. | 11 | 12 | ASC | 2 | 3 |
|---|---|---|---|---|---|
| 0 | 08♈43 | 10♉25 | 09♊40 | 07♋21 | 05♌38 |
| 5 | 09 40 | 12 06 | 11 35 | 09 04 | 06 45 |
| 10 | 10 43 | 13 55 | 13 34 | 10 48 | 07 50 |
| 15 | 11 53 | 15 53 | 15 39 | 12 34 | 08 55 |
| 20 | 13 13 | 18 04 | 17 54 | 14 23 | 09 59 |
| 21 | 13 31 | 18 32 | 18 22 | 14 45 | 10 12 |
| 22 | 13 49 | 19 01 | 18 50 | 15 08 | 10 25 |
| 23 | 14 08 | 19 31 | 19 19 | 15 31 | 10 38 |
| 24 | 14 28 | 20 01 | 19 49 | 15 54 | 10 51 |
| 25 | 14 48 | 20 33 | 20 19 | 16 17 | 11 05 |
| 26 | 15 09 | 21 05 | 20 50 | 16 41 | 11 18 |
| 27 | 15 31 | 21 38 | 21 21 | 17 05 | 11 31 |
| 28 | 15 54 | 22 13 | 21 53 | 17 29 | 11 45 |
| 29 | 16 18 | 22 48 | 22 26 | 17 53 | 11 59 |
| 30 | 16 43 | 23 24 | 23 00 | 18 18 | 12 12 |
| 31 | 17 09 | 24 02 | 23 34 | 18 44 | 12 26 |
| 32 | 17 36 | 24 41 | 24 09 | 19 09 | 12 40 |
| 33 | 18 05 | 25 22 | 24 45 | 19 36 | 12 54 |
| 34 | 18 35 | 26 04 | 25 21 | 20 02 | 13 09 |
| 35 | 19 07 | 26 47 | 25 59 | 20 29 | 13 23 |
| 36 | 19 40 | 27 33 | 26 38 | 20 57 | 13 38 |
| 37 | 20 15 | 28 20 | 27 18 | 21 25 | 13 53 |
| 38 | 20 53 | 29 09 | 27 58 | 21 53 | 14 08 |
| 39 | 21 32 | 00♊00 | 28 40 | 22 23 | 14 23 |
| 40 | 22 15 | 00 53 | 29 24 | 22 52 | 14 39 |
| 41 | 23 00 | 01 48 | 00♋08 | 23 23 | 14 55 |
| 42 | 23 48 | 02 46 | 00 54 | 23 54 | 15 11 |
| 43 | 24 40 | 03 47 | 01 41 | 24 26 | 15 27 |
| 44 | 25 35 | 04 51 | 02 30 | 24 59 | 15 44 |
| 45 | 26 35 | 05 58 | 03 21 | 25 32 | 16 01 |
| 46 | 27 39 | 07 08 | 04 13 | 26 06 | 16 18 |
| 47 | 28 49 | 08 22 | 05 07 | 26 42 | 16 36 |
| 48 | 00♉06 | 09 39 | 06 03 | 27 18 | 16 54 |
| 49 | 01 29 | 11 01 | 07 01 | 27 55 | 17 13 |
| 50 | 03 00 | 12 26 | 08 01 | 28 33 | 17 32 |
| 51 | 04 39 | 13 57 | 09 03 | 29 12 | 17 51 |
| 52 | 06 30 | 15 33 | 10 08 | 29 53 | 18 11 |
| 53 | 08 31 | 17 13 | 11 15 | 00♌35 | 18 31 |
| 54 | 10 47 | 19 00 | 12 24 | 01 18 | 18 52 |
| 55 | 13 17 | 20 52 | 13 37 | 02 02 | 19 14 |
| 56 | 16 06 | 22 51 | 14 52 | 02 49 | 19 36 |
| 57 | 19 14 | 24 57 | 16 11 | 03 36 | 19 59 |
| 58 | 22 45 | 27 09 | 17 32 | 04 25 | 20 22 |
| 59 | 26 41 | 29 28 | 18 58 | 05 16 | 20 47 |
| 60 | 01♊05 | 01♋55 | 20♋26 | 06♌09 | 21♌12 |

**22h 36m 0s — 339° 0' 0' — 07 ♓ 18**

| LAT. | 11 | 12 | ASC | 2 | 3 |
|---|---|---|---|---|---|
| 0 | 09♈48 | 11♉26 | 10♊36 | 08♋16 | 06♌37 |
| 5 | 10 46 | 13 08 | 12 31 | 10 00 | 07 44 |
| 10 | 11 50 | 14 57 | 14 31 | 11 44 | 08 49 |
| 15 | 13 01 | 16 56 | 16 37 | 13 30 | 09 53 |
| 20 | 14 23 | 19 08 | 18 51 | 15 19 | 10 58 |
| 21 | 14 40 | 19 36 | 19 19 | 15 41 | 11 11 |
| 22 | 14 59 | 20 05 | 19 48 | 16 04 | 11 24 |
| 23 | 15 18 | 20 35 | 20 17 | 16 27 | 11 37 |
| 24 | 15 38 | 21 05 | 20 46 | 16 50 | 11 50 |
| 25 | 15 58 | 21 37 | 21 17 | 17 13 | 12 03 |
| 26 | 16 20 | 22 09 | 21 47 | 17 36 | 12 17 |
| 27 | 16 42 | 22 42 | 22 19 | 18 00 | 12 30 |
| 28 | 17 05 | 23 17 | 22 51 | 18 25 | 12 44 |
| 29 | 17 29 | 23 52 | 23 23 | 18 49 | 12 57 |
| 30 | 17 54 | 24 29 | 23 57 | 19 14 | 13 11 |
| 31 | 18 21 | 25 06 | 24 31 | 19 39 | 13 25 |
| 32 | 18 48 | 25 46 | 25 06 | 20 05 | 13 39 |
| 33 | 19 17 | 26 26 | 25 41 | 20 31 | 13 53 |
| 34 | 19 48 | 27 08 | 26 18 | 20 57 | 14 07 |
| 35 | 20 20 | 27 51 | 26 55 | 21 24 | 14 22 |
| 36 | 20 54 | 28 36 | 27 34 | 21 52 | 14 36 |
| 37 | 21 29 | 29 23 | 28 13 | 22 20 | 14 51 |
| 38 | 22 07 | 00♊12 | 28 54 | 22 48 | 15 06 |
| 39 | 22 47 | 01 03 | 29 36 | 23 17 | 15 21 |
| 40 | 23 30 | 01 56 | 00♋19 | 23 47 | 15 37 |
| 41 | 24 15 | 02 51 | 01 03 | 24 17 | 15 53 |
| 42 | 25 04 | 03 49 | 01 48 | 24 48 | 16 09 |
| 43 | 25 56 | 04 50 | 02 35 | 25 20 | 16 25 |
| 44 | 26 51 | 05 53 | 03 24 | 25 52 | 16 41 |
| 45 | 27 51 | 06 59 | 04 14 | 26 25 | 16 58 |
| 46 | 28 56 | 08 09 | 05 06 | 26 59 | 17 16 |
| 47 | 00♉07 | 09 22 | 05 59 | 27 34 | 17 33 |
| 48 | 01 23 | 10 38 | 06 54 | 28 10 | 17 51 |
| 49 | 02 46 | 11 59 | 07 52 | 28 47 | 18 09 |
| 50 | 04 17 | 13 24 | 08 51 | 29 25 | 18 28 |
| 51 | 05 57 | 14 54 | 09 53 | 00♌04 | 18 47 |
| 52 | 07 46 | 16 28 | 10 57 | 00 44 | 19 07 |
| 53 | 09 48 | 18 08 | 12 03 | 01 25 | 19 27 |
| 54 | 12 02 | 19 53 | 13 12 | 02 08 | 19 48 |
| 55 | 14 32 | 21 43 | 14 23 | 02 52 | 20 10 |
| 56 | 17 19 | 23 40 | 15 38 | 03 37 | 20 32 |
| 57 | 20 25 | 25 44 | 16 55 | 04 24 | 20 54 |
| 58 | 23 53 | 27 54 | 18 15 | 05 13 | 21 17 |
| 59 | 27 45 | 00♋11 | 19 39 | 06 03 | 21 41 |
| 60 | 02♊05 | 02♋35 | 21♋06 | 06♌56 | 22♌06 |

**22h 40m 0s — 340° 0' 0' — 08 ♓ 22**

| LAT. | 11 | 12 | ASC | 2 | 3 |
|---|---|---|---|---|---|
| 0 | 10♈53 | 12♉27 | 11♊32 | 09♋11 | 07♌35 |
| 5 | 11 52 | 14 09 | 13 28 | 10 55 | 08 43 |
| 10 | 12 56 | 15 59 | 15 28 | 12 40 | 09 48 |
| 15 | 14 09 | 17 59 | 17 34 | 14 26 | 10 53 |
| 20 | 15 31 | 20 11 | 19 48 | 16 15 | 11 57 |
| 21 | 15 50 | 20 39 | 20 16 | 16 37 | 12 10 |
| 22 | 16 08 | 21 09 | 20 45 | 17 00 | 12 23 |
| 23 | 16 28 | 21 38 | 21 14 | 17 22 | 12 36 |
| 24 | 16 48 | 22 09 | 21 44 | 17 45 | 12 49 |
| 25 | 17 09 | 22 40 | 22 14 | 18 09 | 13 02 |
| 26 | 17 30 | 23 13 | 22 44 | 18 32 | 13 15 |
| 27 | 17 53 | 23 46 | 23 16 | 18 56 | 13 29 |
| 28 | 18 16 | 24 21 | 23 47 | 19 20 | 13 42 |
| 29 | 18 40 | 24 56 | 24 20 | 19 45 | 13 56 |
| 30 | 19 06 | 25 32 | 24 53 | 20 09 | 14 10 |
| 31 | 19 32 | 26 10 | 25 27 | 20 34 | 14 23 |
| 32 | 20 00 | 26 49 | 26 02 | 21 00 | 14 37 |
| 33 | 20 30 | 27 30 | 26 38 | 21 26 | 14 51 |
| 34 | 21 00 | 28 11 | 27 14 | 21 52 | 15 06 |
| 35 | 21 33 | 28 55 | 27 51 | 22 19 | 15 20 |
| 36 | 22 07 | 29 40 | 28 30 | 22 46 | 15 34 |
| 37 | 22 43 | 00♊27 | 29 09 | 23 14 | 15 49 |
| 38 | 23 21 | 01 15 | 29 49 | 23 42 | 16 04 |
| 39 | 24 01 | 02 06 | 00♋31 | 24 11 | 16 19 |
| 40 | 24 44 | 02 59 | 01 13 | 24 41 | 16 35 |
| 41 | 25 30 | 03 54 | 01 57 | 25 11 | 16 50 |
| 42 | 26 19 | 04 51 | 02 43 | 25 42 | 17 06 |
| 43 | 27 11 | 05 51 | 03 29 | 26 13 | 17 23 |
| 44 | 28 07 | 06 54 | 04 17 | 26 45 | 17 39 |
| 45 | 29 07 | 08 00 | 05 07 | 27 18 | 17 56 |
| 46 | 00♉12 | 09 09 | 05 58 | 27 52 | 18 13 |
| 47 | 01 23 | 10 21 | 06 51 | 28 27 | 18 30 |
| 48 | 02 39 | 11 37 | 07 46 | 29 02 | 18 48 |
| 49 | 04 02 | 12 57 | 08 42 | 29 39 | 19 06 |
| 50 | 05 33 | 14 21 | 09 41 | 00♌16 | 19 25 |
| 51 | 07 13 | 15 49 | 10 42 | 00 55 | 19 44 |
| 52 | 09 02 | 17 23 | 11 45 | 01 34 | 20 04 |
| 53 | 11 03 | 19 01 | 12 51 | 02 15 | 20 24 |
| 54 | 13 17 | 20 44 | 13 58 | 02 57 | 20 44 |
| 55 | 15 45 | 22 33 | 15 09 | 03 41 | 21 05 |
| 56 | 18 30 | 24 29 | 16 22 | 04 26 | 21 27 |
| 57 | 21 34 | 26 30 | 17 39 | 05 12 | 21 49 |
| 58 | 24 59 | 28 38 | 18 58 | 06 00 | 22 12 |
| 59 | 28 48 | 00♋53 | 20 21 | 06 50 | 22 36 |
| 60 | 03♊02 | 03♋14 | 21♋46 | 07♌42 | 23♌01 |

**22h 44m 0s — 341° 0' 0' — 09 ♓ 26**

| LAT. | 11 | 12 | ASC | 2 | 3 |
|---|---|---|---|---|---|
| 0 | 11♈58 | 13♉27 | 12♊28 | 10♋07 | 08♌34 |
| 5 | 12 58 | 15 11 | 14 24 | 11 51 | 09 42 |
| 10 | 14 03 | 17 01 | 16 25 | 13 36 | 10 47 |
| 15 | 15 16 | 19 01 | 18 31 | 15 22 | 11 52 |
| 20 | 16 40 | 21 14 | 20 45 | 17 11 | 12 56 |
| 21 | 16 58 | 21 42 | 21 13 | 17 33 | 13 09 |
| 22 | 17 17 | 22 12 | 21 42 | 17 55 | 13 22 |
| 23 | 17 37 | 22 41 | 22 11 | 18 18 | 13 35 |
| 24 | 17 57 | 23 12 | 22 41 | 18 41 | 13 48 |
| 25 | 18 18 | 23 44 | 23 11 | 19 04 | 14 01 |
| 26 | 18 40 | 24 16 | 23 41 | 19 28 | 14 14 |
| 27 | 19 03 | 24 49 | 24 12 | 19 52 | 14 28 |
| 28 | 19 27 | 25 24 | 24 44 | 20 16 | 14 41 |
| 29 | 19 51 | 25 59 | 25 17 | 20 40 | 14 55 |
| 30 | 20 17 | 26 36 | 25 50 | 21 05 | 15 08 |
| 31 | 20 44 | 27 13 | 26 24 | 21 30 | 15 22 |
| 32 | 21 12 | 27 52 | 26 58 | 21 55 | 15 36 |
| 33 | 21 41 | 28 33 | 27 34 | 22 21 | 15 50 |
| 34 | 22 12 | 29 14 | 28 10 | 22 47 | 16 04 |
| 35 | 22 45 | 29 58 | 28 47 | 23 14 | 16 18 |
| 36 | 23 19 | 00♊43 | 29 25 | 23 41 | 16 33 |
| 37 | 23 56 | 01 29 | 00♋04 | 24 09 | 16 48 |
| 38 | 24 34 | 02 18 | 00 44 | 24 37 | 17 02 |
| 39 | 25 15 | 03 08 | 01 25 | 25 06 | 17 18 |
| 40 | 25 58 | 04 01 | 02 08 | 25 35 | 17 33 |
| 41 | 26 44 | 04 55 | 02 51 | 26 05 | 17 48 |
| 42 | 27 33 | 05 52 | 03 36 | 26 35 | 18 04 |
| 43 | 28 25 | 06 52 | 04 23 | 27 06 | 18 20 |
| 44 | 29 22 | 07 54 | 05 10 | 27 38 | 18 37 |
| 45 | 00♉22 | 09 00 | 05 59 | 28 11 | 18 53 |
| 46 | 01 27 | 10 08 | 06 50 | 28 45 | 19 10 |
| 47 | 02 38 | 11 20 | 07 43 | 29 19 | 19 28 |
| 48 | 03 54 | 12 35 | 08 37 | 29 54 | 19 45 |
| 49 | 05 17 | 13 54 | 09 33 | 00♌30 | 20 03 |
| 50 | 06 48 | 15 17 | 10 31 | 01 07 | 20 22 |
| 51 | 08 27 | 16 44 | 11 31 | 01 46 | 20 41 |
| 52 | 10 16 | 18 16 | 12 33 | 02 25 | 21 00 |
| 53 | 12 17 | 19 53 | 13 38 | 03 05 | 21 20 |
| 54 | 14 29 | 21 35 | 14 45 | 03 47 | 21 40 |
| 55 | 16 56 | 23 23 | 15 55 | 04 30 | 22 01 |
| 56 | 19 40 | 25 16 | 17 07 | 05 14 | 22 23 |
| 57 | 22 41 | 27 16 | 18 22 | 06 00 | 22 45 |
| 58 | 26 03 | 29 21 | 19 40 | 06 48 | 23 08 |
| 59 | 29 48 | 01♋34 | 21 02 | 07 37 | 23 31 |
| 60 | 03♊58 | 03♋53 | 22♋26 | 08♌28 | 23♌55 |

**22h 48m 0s — 342° 0' 0' — 10 ♓ 30**

| LAT. | 11 | 12 | ASC | 2 | 3 |
|---|---|---|---|---|---|
| 0 | 13♈03 | 14♉28 | 13♊24 | 11♋02 | 09♌34 |
| 5 | 14 03 | 16 12 | 15 21 | 12 47 | 10 41 |
| 10 | 15 10 | 18 03 | 17 21 | 14 31 | 11 47 |
| 15 | 16 24 | 20 03 | 19 28 | 16 18 | 12 51 |
| 20 | 17 49 | 22 17 | 21 42 | 18 07 | 13 55 |
| 21 | 18 07 | 22 45 | 22 10 | 18 29 | 14 08 |
| 22 | 18 26 | 23 14 | 22 39 | 18 51 | 14 21 |
| 23 | 18 46 | 23 44 | 23 08 | 19 14 | 14 34 |
| 24 | 19 07 | 24 15 | 23 37 | 19 37 | 14 47 |
| 25 | 19 28 | 24 46 | 24 07 | 20 00 | 15 00 |
| 26 | 19 50 | 25 19 | 24 38 | 20 23 | 15 13 |
| 27 | 20 13 | 25 52 | 25 09 | 20 47 | 15 27 |
| 28 | 20 37 | 26 27 | 25 40 | 21 11 | 15 40 |
| 29 | 21 02 | 27 02 | 26 13 | 21 35 | 15 53 |
| 30 | 21 28 | 27 38 | 26 46 | 22 00 | 16 07 |
| 31 | 21 55 | 28 16 | 27 20 | 22 25 | 16 21 |
| 32 | 22 23 | 28 55 | 27 54 | 22 50 | 16 35 |
| 33 | 22 53 | 29 35 | 28 29 | 23 16 | 16 49 |
| 34 | 23 24 | 00♊17 | 29 05 | 23 42 | 17 03 |
| 35 | 23 57 | 01 00 | 29 42 | 24 09 | 17 17 |
| 36 | 24 31 | 01 45 | 00♋20 | 24 36 | 17 31 |
| 37 | 25 08 | 02 31 | 00 59 | 25 03 | 17 46 |
| 38 | 25 47 | 03 19 | 01 39 | 25 31 | 18 01 |
| 39 | 26 28 | 04 10 | 02 20 | 26 00 | 18 16 |
| 40 | 27 11 | 05 02 | 03 02 | 26 29 | 18 31 |
| 41 | 27 57 | 05 56 | 03 45 | 26 58 | 18 46 |
| 42 | 28 46 | 06 53 | 04 30 | 27 29 | 19 02 |
| 43 | 29 39 | 07 52 | 05 15 | 28 00 | 19 18 |
| 44 | 00♉36 | 08 54 | 06 02 | 28 31 | 19 34 |
| 45 | 01 36 | 09 59 | 06 51 | 29 04 | 19 51 |
| 46 | 02 41 | 11 06 | 07 42 | 29 37 | 20 08 |
| 47 | 03 52 | 12 17 | 08 34 | 00♌11 | 20 25 |
| 48 | 05 08 | 13 32 | 09 27 | 00 46 | 20 42 |
| 49 | 06 32 | 14 50 | 10 23 | 01 22 | 21 00 |
| 50 | 08 02 | 16 12 | 11 20 | 01 59 | 21 19 |
| 51 | 09 41 | 17 39 | 12 20 | 02 36 | 21 37 |
| 52 | 11 30 | 19 09 | 13 21 | 03 15 | 21 56 |
| 53 | 13 29 | 20 45 | 14 25 | 03 55 | 22 16 |
| 54 | 15 41 | 22 26 | 15 31 | 04 36 | 22 36 |
| 55 | 18 06 | 24 12 | 16 40 | 05 19 | 22 57 |
| 56 | 20 48 | 26 03 | 17 51 | 06 03 | 23 18 |
| 57 | 23 47 | 28 01 | 19 06 | 06 48 | 23 40 |
| 58 | 27 06 | 00♋04 | 20 23 | 07 35 | 24 03 |
| 59 | 00♊47 | 02 14 | 21 43 | 08 23 | 24 26 |
| 60 | 04♊53 | 04♋31 | 23♋06 | 09♌14 | 24♌50 |

**22h 52m 0s — 343° 0' 0' — 11 ♓ 34**

| LAT. | 11 | 12 | ASC | 2 | 3 |
|---|---|---|---|---|---|
| 0 | 14♈07 | 15♉28 | 14♊20 | 11♋58 | 10♌33 |
| 5 | 15 09 | 17 13 | 16 17 | 13 43 | 11 41 |
| 10 | 16 16 | 19 04 | 18 18 | 15 27 | 12 46 |
| 15 | 17 31 | 21 05 | 20 24 | 17 13 | 13 50 |
| 20 | 18 57 | 23 19 | 22 39 | 19 02 | 14 54 |
| 21 | 19 16 | 23 47 | 23 07 | 19 25 | 15 07 |
| 22 | 19 35 | 24 17 | 23 35 | 19 47 | 15 20 |
| 23 | 19 55 | 24 46 | 24 04 | 20 10 | 15 33 |
| 24 | 20 16 | 25 17 | 24 34 | 20 33 | 15 46 |
| 25 | 20 37 | 25 49 | 25 03 | 20 56 | 15 59 |
| 26 | 20 59 | 26 21 | 25 34 | 21 19 | 16 12 |
| 27 | 21 23 | 26 55 | 26 05 | 21 43 | 16 26 |
| 28 | 21 47 | 27 29 | 26 36 | 22 07 | 16 39 |
| 29 | 22 12 | 28 04 | 27 09 | 22 31 | 16 52 |
| 30 | 22 38 | 28 41 | 27 42 | 22 55 | 17 06 |
| 31 | 23 05 | 29 18 | 28 15 | 23 20 | 17 20 |
| 32 | 23 34 | 29 57 | 28 50 | 23 45 | 17 33 |
| 33 | 24 04 | 00♊37 | 29 25 | 24 11 | 17 47 |
| 34 | 24 35 | 01 19 | 00♋01 | 24 37 | 18 01 |
| 35 | 25 08 | 02 02 | 00 37 | 25 03 | 18 15 |
| 36 | 25 43 | 02 46 | 01 15 | 25 30 | 18 30 |
| 37 | 26 20 | 03 32 | 01 54 | 25 57 | 18 44 |
| 38 | 26 59 | 04 20 | 02 33 | 26 25 | 18 59 |
| 39 | 27 40 | 05 10 | 03 14 | 26 54 | 19 14 |
| 40 | 28 23 | 06 02 | 03 56 | 27 23 | 19 29 |
| 41 | 29 10 | 06 56 | 04 38 | 27 52 | 19 44 |
| 42 | 29 59 | 07 53 | 05 23 | 28 22 | 20 00 |
| 43 | 00♉52 | 08 51 | 06 08 | 28 53 | 20 16 |
| 44 | 01 49 | 09 53 | 06 55 | 29 24 | 20 32 |
| 45 | 02 49 | 10 57 | 07 43 | 29 56 | 20 48 |
| 46 | 03 55 | 12 04 | 08 33 | 00♌29 | 21 05 |
| 47 | 05 05 | 13 14 | 09 24 | 01 03 | 21 22 |
| 48 | 06 22 | 14 28 | 10 18 | 01 38 | 21 40 |
| 49 | 07 45 | 15 46 | 11 12 | 02 13 | 21 57 |
| 50 | 09 15 | 17 07 | 12 09 | 02 50 | 22 15 |
| 51 | 10 53 | 18 32 | 13 08 | 03 27 | 22 34 |
| 52 | 12 41 | 20 02 | 14 09 | 04 06 | 22 53 |
| 53 | 14 40 | 21 36 | 15 12 | 04 45 | 23 12 |
| 54 | 16 51 | 23 15 | 16 17 | 05 26 | 23 32 |
| 55 | 19 15 | 24 59 | 17 25 | 06 08 | 23 53 |
| 56 | 21 54 | 26 49 | 18 35 | 06 51 | 24 14 |
| 57 | 24 51 | 28 45 | 19 49 | 07 36 | 24 36 |
| 58 | 28 08 | 00♋47 | 21 04 | 08 22 | 24 58 |
| 59 | 01♊45 | 02 55 | 22 23 | 09 10 | 25 21 |
| 60 | 05♊46 | 05♋09 | 23♋45 | 10♌00 | 25♌44 |

# Koch Table of Houses for Latitudes 0° to 60° North

| 22h 56m 0s — 344° 0' 0" — 12 ♓ 39 | | | | | |
|---|---|---|---|---|---|
| LAT. | 11 | 12 | ASC | 2 | 3 |
| 0 | 15♈12 | 16♉28 | 15♊16 | 12♋53 | 11♌32 |
| 5 | 16 14 | 18 13 | 17 13 | 14 38 | 12 40 |
| 10 | 17 22 | 20 05 | 19 14 | 16 23 | 13 46 |
| 15 | 18 38 | 22 07 | 21 21 | 18 09 | 14 50 |
| 20 | 20 05 | 24 21 | 23 35 | 19 58 | 15 54 |
| 21 | 20 24 | 24 49 | 24 03 | 20 20 | 16 07 |
| 22 | 20 43 | 25 18 | 24 32 | 20 43 | 16 20 |
| 23 | 21 03 | 25 48 | 25 00 | 21 05 | 16 32 |
| 24 | 21 24 | 26 19 | 25 30 | 21 28 | 16 45 |
| 25 | 21 46 | 26 51 | 26 00 | 21 51 | 16 59 |
| 26 | 22 08 | 27 23 | 26 30 | 22 15 | 17 12 |
| 27 | 22 32 | 27 56 | 27 01 | 22 38 | 17 25 |
| 28 | 22 56 | 28 31 | 27 32 | 23 02 | 17 38 |
| 29 | 23 21 | 29 06 | 28 04 | 23 26 | 17 51 |
| 30 | 23 48 | 29 42 | 28 37 | 23 50 | 18 05 |
| 31 | 24 15 | 00♊20 | 29 11 | 24 15 | 18 18 |
| 32 | 24 44 | 00 59 | 29 45 | 24 40 | 18 32 |
| 33 | 25 14 | 01 39 | 00♋20 | 25 06 | 18 46 |
| 34 | 25 46 | 02 20 | 00 55 | 25 32 | 19 00 |
| 35 | 26 19 | 03 03 | 01 32 | 25 58 | 19 14 |
| 36 | 26 54 | 03 47 | 02 09 | 26 25 | 19 28 |
| 37 | 27 31 | 04 33 | 02 48 | 26 52 | 19 43 |
| 38 | 28 10 | 05 21 | 03 27 | 27 19 | 19 57 |
| 39 | 28 52 | 06 11 | 04 07 | 27 48 | 20 12 |
| 40 | 29 35 | 07 02 | 04 49 | 28 16 | 20 27 |
| 41 | 00♉22 | 07 56 | 05 32 | 28 46 | 20 43 |
| 42 | 01 11 | 08 52 | 06 15 | 29 15 | 20 58 |
| 43 | 02 04 | 09 50 | 07 00 | 29 46 | 21 14 |
| 44 | 03 01 | 10 51 | 07 47 | 00♌17 | 21 30 |
| 45 | 04 02 | 11 55 | 08 35 | 00 49 | 21 46 |
| 46 | 05 07 | 13 01 | 09 24 | 01 22 | 22 03 |
| 47 | 06 18 | 14 11 | 10 15 | 01 55 | 22 20 |
| 48 | 07 34 | 15 24 | 11 07 | 02 29 | 22 37 |
| 49 | 08 57 | 16 40 | 12 02 | 03 05 | 22 54 |
| 50 | 10 27 | 18 00 | 12 58 | 03 41 | 23 12 |
| 51 | 12 05 | 19 25 | 13 56 | 04 18 | 23 31 |
| 52 | 13 52 | 20 53 | 14 56 | 04 56 | 23 50 |
| 53 | 15 50 | 22 26 | 15 58 | 05 35 | 24 09 |
| 54 | 17 59 | 24 04 | 17 03 | 06 15 | 24 29 |
| 55 | 20 22 | 25 47 | 18 10 | 06 57 | 24 49 |
| 56 | 23 00 | 27 35 | 19 19 | 07 40 | 25 10 |
| 57 | 25 54 | 29 29 | 20 31 | 08 24 | 25 31 |
| 58 | 29 07 | 01♋28 | 21 46 | 09 09 | 25 53 |
| 59 | 02♊41 | 03 34 | 23 04 | 09 57 | 26 16 |
| 60 | 06♊37 | 05♋46 | 24♋25 | 10♌45 | 26♌39 |

| 23h 0m 0s — 345° 0' 0" — 13 ♓ 43 | | | | | |
|---|---|---|---|---|---|
| LAT. | 11 | 12 | ASC | 2 | 3 |
| 0 | 16♈17 | 17♉28 | 16♊11 | 13♋49 | 12♌32 |
| 5 | 17 20 | 19 14 | 18 09 | 15 34 | 13 40 |
| 10 | 18 28 | 21 06 | 20 10 | 17 19 | 14 45 |
| 15 | 19 45 | 23 08 | 22 17 | 19 05 | 15 49 |
| 20 | 21 12 | 25 22 | 24 31 | 20 54 | 16 53 |
| 21 | 21 32 | 25 51 | 24 59 | 21 16 | 17 06 |
| 22 | 21 51 | 26 20 | 25 28 | 21 39 | 17 19 |
| 23 | 22 12 | 26 50 | 25 56 | 22 01 | 17 32 |
| 24 | 22 33 | 27 21 | 26 26 | 22 24 | 17 45 |
| 25 | 22 55 | 27 52 | 26 55 | 22 47 | 17 58 |
| 26 | 23 17 | 28 25 | 27 26 | 23 10 | 18 11 |
| 27 | 23 41 | 28 58 | 27 56 | 23 33 | 18 24 |
| 28 | 24 05 | 29 32 | 28 28 | 23 57 | 18 37 |
| 29 | 24 31 | 00♊07 | 29 00 | 24 21 | 18 51 |
| 30 | 24 57 | 00 44 | 29 32 | 24 46 | 19 04 |
| 31 | 25 25 | 01 21 | 00♋06 | 25 10 | 19 17 |
| 32 | 25 54 | 02 00 | 00 40 | 25 35 | 19 31 |
| 33 | 26 24 | 02 40 | 01 15 | 26 00 | 19 45 |
| 34 | 26 56 | 03 21 | 01 50 | 26 26 | 19 59 |
| 35 | 27 30 | 04 03 | 02 26 | 26 52 | 20 13 |
| 36 | 28 05 | 04 48 | 03 04 | 27 19 | 20 27 |
| 37 | 28 42 | 05 33 | 03 42 | 27 46 | 20 41 |
| 38 | 29 21 | 06 21 | 04 21 | 28 13 | 20 56 |
| 39 | 00♉03 | 07 10 | 05 01 | 28 41 | 21 11 |
| 40 | 00 47 | 08 02 | 05 42 | 29 10 | 21 26 |
| 41 | 01 33 | 08 55 | 06 24 | 29 39 | 21 41 |
| 42 | 02 23 | 09 50 | 07 08 | 00♌09 | 21 56 |
| 43 | 03 16 | 10 48 | 07 52 | 00 39 | 22 12 |
| 44 | 04 13 | 11 49 | 08 38 | 01 10 | 22 28 |
| 45 | 05 14 | 12 52 | 09 26 | 01 42 | 22 44 |
| 46 | 06 19 | 13 58 | 10 15 | 02 14 | 23 00 |
| 47 | 07 29 | 15 07 | 11 05 | 02 47 | 23 17 |
| 48 | 08 45 | 16 19 | 11 57 | 03 21 | 23 34 |
| 49 | 10 08 | 17 34 | 12 51 | 03 56 | 23 52 |
| 50 | 11 37 | 18 54 | 13 46 | 04 31 | 24 09 |
| 51 | 13 15 | 20 17 | 14 44 | 05 08 | 24 28 |
| 52 | 15 01 | 21 44 | 15 43 | 05 46 | 24 46 |
| 53 | 16 58 | 23 16 | 16 44 | 06 25 | 25 05 |
| 54 | 19 06 | 24 52 | 17 48 | 07 04 | 25 25 |
| 55 | 21 28 | 26 33 | 18 54 | 07 46 | 25 45 |
| 56 | 24 03 | 28 20 | 20 03 | 08 28 | 26 05 |
| 57 | 26 56 | 00♋12 | 21 14 | 09 12 | 26 27 |
| 58 | 00♊06 | 02 10 | 22 28 | 09 57 | 26 48 |
| 59 | 03 36 | 04 13 | 23 44 | 10 43 | 27 11 |
| 60 | 07♊28 | 06♋23 | 25♋04 | 11♌31 | 27♌34 |

| 23h 4m 0s — 346° 0' 0" — 14 ♓ 48 | | | | | |
|---|---|---|---|---|---|
| LAT. | 11 | 12 | ASC | 2 | 3 |
| 0 | 17♈21 | 18♉28 | 17♊07 | 14♋44 | 13♌32 |
| 5 | 18 25 | 20 14 | 19 05 | 16 30 | 14 40 |
| 10 | 19 34 | 22 07 | 21 07 | 18 15 | 15 45 |
| 15 | 20 52 | 24 09 | 23 13 | 20 01 | 16 49 |
| 20 | 22 20 | 26 23 | 25 27 | 21 50 | 17 53 |
| 21 | 22 39 | 26 52 | 25 55 | 22 12 | 18 06 |
| 22 | 22 59 | 27 21 | 26 23 | 22 34 | 18 19 |
| 23 | 23 20 | 27 51 | 26 52 | 22 57 | 18 31 |
| 24 | 23 41 | 28 22 | 27 21 | 23 19 | 18 44 |
| 25 | 24 03 | 28 53 | 27 51 | 23 42 | 18 57 |
| 26 | 24 26 | 29 26 | 28 21 | 24 05 | 19 10 |
| 27 | 24 49 | 29 59 | 28 52 | 24 29 | 19 23 |
| 28 | 25 14 | 00♊33 | 29 23 | 24 52 | 19 36 |
| 29 | 25 40 | 01 08 | 29 55 | 25 16 | 19 50 |
| 30 | 26 06 | 01 44 | 00♋28 | 25 41 | 20 03 |
| 31 | 26 34 | 02 22 | 01 01 | 26 05 | 20 17 |
| 32 | 27 04 | 03 00 | 01 34 | 26 30 | 20 30 |
| 33 | 27 34 | 03 40 | 02 09 | 26 55 | 20 44 |
| 34 | 28 06 | 04 21 | 02 44 | 27 21 | 20 58 |
| 35 | 28 40 | 05 04 | 03 20 | 27 47 | 21 12 |
| 36 | 29 15 | 05 48 | 03 57 | 28 13 | 21 26 |
| 37 | 29 52 | 06 33 | 04 35 | 28 40 | 21 40 |
| 38 | 00♉32 | 07 20 | 05 14 | 29 07 | 21 54 |
| 39 | 01 13 | 08 09 | 05 54 | 29 35 | 22 09 |
| 40 | 01 57 | 09 00 | 06 35 | 00♌03 | 22 24 |
| 41 | 02 44 | 09 53 | 07 17 | 00 32 | 22 39 |
| 42 | 03 34 | 10 48 | 08 00 | 01 02 | 22 54 |
| 43 | 04 27 | 11 46 | 08 44 | 01 32 | 23 10 |
| 44 | 05 24 | 12 46 | 09 30 | 02 03 | 23 25 |
| 45 | 06 24 | 13 48 | 10 17 | 02 34 | 23 41 |
| 46 | 07 30 | 14 53 | 11 05 | 03 06 | 23 58 |
| 47 | 08 40 | 16 02 | 11 55 | 03 39 | 24 14 |
| 48 | 09 56 | 17 13 | 12 46 | 04 12 | 24 31 |
| 49 | 11 18 | 18 28 | 13 39 | 04 47 | 24 49 |
| 50 | 12 47 | 19 46 | 14 34 | 05 22 | 25 06 |
| 51 | 14 24 | 21 08 | 15 31 | 05 59 | 25 24 |
| 52 | 16 10 | 22 34 | 16 30 | 06 36 | 25 43 |
| 53 | 18 05 | 24 05 | 17 30 | 07 14 | 26 02 |
| 54 | 20 12 | 25 40 | 18 33 | 07 54 | 26 21 |
| 55 | 22 32 | 27 19 | 19 38 | 08 34 | 26 41 |
| 56 | 25 06 | 29 04 | 20 46 | 09 16 | 27 01 |
| 57 | 27 56 | 00♋55 | 21 56 | 09 59 | 27 22 |
| 58 | 01♊03 | 02 50 | 23 09 | 10 44 | 27 44 |
| 59 | 04 30 | 04 52 | 24 24 | 11 30 | 28 06 |
| 60 | 08♊17 | 06♋59 | 25♋43 | 12♌17 | 28♌29 |

| 23h 8m 0s — 347° 0' 0" — 15 ♓ 53 | | | | | |
|---|---|---|---|---|---|
| LAT. | 11 | 12 | ASC | 2 | 3 |
| 0 | 18♈26 | 19♉27 | 18♊02 | 15♋40 | 14♌32 |
| 5 | 19 30 | 21 14 | 20 01 | 17 26 | 15 40 |
| 10 | 20 40 | 23 07 | 22 02 | 19 11 | 16 45 |
| 15 | 21 58 | 25 10 | 24 09 | 20 57 | 17 49 |
| 20 | 23 27 | 27 24 | 26 23 | 22 46 | 18 53 |
| 21 | 23 47 | 27 53 | 26 51 | 23 08 | 19 05 |
| 22 | 24 07 | 28 22 | 27 19 | 23 30 | 19 18 |
| 23 | 24 27 | 28 52 | 27 48 | 23 52 | 19 31 |
| 24 | 24 49 | 29 22 | 28 17 | 24 15 | 19 44 |
| 25 | 25 11 | 29 54 | 28 46 | 24 38 | 19 57 |
| 26 | 25 34 | 00♊26 | 29 17 | 25 01 | 20 10 |
| 27 | 25 58 | 00 59 | 29 47 | 25 24 | 20 23 |
| 28 | 26 22 | 01 34 | 00♋18 | 25 48 | 20 36 |
| 29 | 26 48 | 02 09 | 00 50 | 26 12 | 20 49 |
| 30 | 27 15 | 02 45 | 01 22 | 26 36 | 21 02 |
| 31 | 27 43 | 03 22 | 01 55 | 27 00 | 21 16 |
| 32 | 28 13 | 04 00 | 02 29 | 27 25 | 21 29 |
| 33 | 28 43 | 04 40 | 03 03 | 27 50 | 21 43 |
| 34 | 29 15 | 05 21 | 03 38 | 28 15 | 21 56 |
| 35 | 29 49 | 06 03 | 04 14 | 28 41 | 22 10 |
| 36 | 00♉25 | 06 47 | 04 51 | 29 07 | 22 24 |
| 37 | 01 02 | 07 32 | 05 29 | 29 34 | 22 39 |
| 38 | 01 41 | 08 19 | 06 07 | 00♌01 | 22 53 |
| 39 | 02 23 | 09 08 | 06 47 | 00 29 | 23 07 |
| 40 | 03 07 | 09 58 | 07 27 | 00 57 | 23 22 |
| 41 | 03 54 | 10 51 | 08 09 | 01 26 | 23 37 |
| 42 | 04 44 | 11 46 | 08 52 | 01 55 | 23 52 |
| 43 | 05 37 | 12 43 | 09 35 | 02 25 | 24 08 |
| 44 | 06 34 | 13 42 | 10 21 | 02 55 | 24 23 |
| 45 | 07 34 | 14 44 | 11 07 | 03 26 | 24 39 |
| 46 | 08 39 | 15 48 | 11 55 | 03 58 | 24 55 |
| 47 | 09 50 | 16 56 | 12 44 | 04 31 | 25 12 |
| 48 | 11 05 | 18 06 | 13 35 | 05 04 | 25 29 |
| 49 | 12 27 | 19 20 | 14 28 | 05 38 | 25 46 |
| 50 | 13 55 | 20 38 | 15 22 | 06 13 | 26 03 |
| 51 | 15 32 | 21 59 | 16 18 | 06 49 | 26 21 |
| 52 | 17 17 | 23 24 | 17 16 | 07 26 | 26 40 |
| 53 | 19 12 | 24 53 | 18 16 | 08 04 | 26 58 |
| 54 | 21 17 | 26 27 | 19 18 | 08 43 | 27 17 |
| 55 | 23 35 | 28 05 | 20 22 | 09 23 | 27 37 |
| 56 | 26 07 | 29 48 | 21 29 | 10 04 | 27 57 |
| 57 | 28 54 | 01♋37 | 22 38 | 10 47 | 28 18 |
| 58 | 01♊59 | 03 30 | 23 50 | 11 31 | 28 39 |
| 59 | 05 22 | 05 30 | 25 04 | 12 16 | 29 01 |
| 60 | 09♊05 | 07♋35 | 26♋21 | 13♌03 | 29♌24 |

| 23h 12m 0s — 348° 0' 0" — 16 ♓ 57 | | | | | |
|---|---|---|---|---|---|
| LAT. | 11 | 12 | ASC | 2 | 3 |
| 0 | 19♈30 | 20♉26 | 18♊58 | 16♋36 | 15♌32 |
| 5 | 20 35 | 22 14 | 20 57 | 18 22 | 16 40 |
| 10 | 21 46 | 24 07 | 22 58 | 20 07 | 17 45 |
| 15 | 23 04 | 26 10 | 25 05 | 21 53 | 18 49 |
| 20 | 24 34 | 28 24 | 27 19 | 23 41 | 19 52 |
| 21 | 24 54 | 28 53 | 27 46 | 24 03 | 20 05 |
| 22 | 25 14 | 29 22 | 28 15 | 24 26 | 20 18 |
| 23 | 25 35 | 29 52 | 28 43 | 24 48 | 20 31 |
| 24 | 25 56 | 00♊23 | 29 12 | 25 11 | 20 43 |
| 25 | 26 18 | 00 54 | 29 42 | 25 33 | 20 56 |
| 26 | 26 42 | 01 27 | 00♋12 | 25 56 | 21 09 |
| 27 | 27 06 | 02 00 | 00 42 | 26 19 | 21 22 |
| 28 | 27 31 | 02 34 | 01 13 | 26 43 | 21 35 |
| 29 | 27 56 | 03 09 | 01 45 | 27 07 | 21 48 |
| 30 | 28 24 | 03 45 | 02 17 | 27 31 | 22 02 |
| 31 | 28 52 | 04 22 | 02 50 | 27 55 | 22 15 |
| 32 | 29 21 | 05 00 | 03 23 | 28 20 | 22 28 |
| 33 | 29 52 | 05 39 | 03 57 | 28 44 | 22 42 |
| 34 | 00♉24 | 06 20 | 04 32 | 29 10 | 22 55 |
| 35 | 00 58 | 07 02 | 05 08 | 29 35 | 23 09 |
| 36 | 01 34 | 07 46 | 05 44 | 00♌02 | 23 23 |
| 37 | 02 11 | 08 31 | 06 22 | 00 28 | 23 37 |
| 38 | 02 51 | 09 17 | 07 00 | 00 55 | 23 52 |
| 39 | 03 32 | 10 06 | 07 39 | 01 22 | 24 06 |
| 40 | 04 17 | 10 56 | 08 19 | 01 50 | 24 21 |
| 41 | 05 03 | 11 48 | 09 01 | 02 19 | 24 35 |
| 42 | 05 53 | 12 42 | 09 43 | 02 48 | 24 51 |
| 43 | 06 46 | 13 39 | 10 27 | 03 17 | 25 06 |
| 44 | 07 43 | 14 38 | 11 11 | 03 48 | 25 21 |
| 45 | 08 44 | 15 39 | 11 57 | 04 18 | 25 37 |
| 46 | 09 48 | 16 43 | 12 45 | 04 50 | 25 53 |
| 47 | 10 58 | 17 50 | 13 34 | 05 22 | 26 10 |
| 48 | 12 14 | 18 59 | 14 24 | 05 55 | 26 26 |
| 49 | 13 35 | 20 12 | 15 16 | 06 29 | 26 43 |
| 50 | 15 03 | 21 29 | 16 10 | 07 04 | 27 01 |
| 51 | 16 39 | 22 49 | 17 05 | 07 39 | 27 18 |
| 52 | 18 23 | 24 13 | 18 02 | 08 16 | 27 36 |
| 53 | 20 16 | 25 41 | 19 01 | 08 53 | 27 55 |
| 54 | 22 21 | 27 13 | 20 03 | 09 32 | 28 14 |
| 55 | 24 37 | 28 50 | 21 06 | 10 11 | 28 33 |
| 56 | 27 07 | 00♋31 | 22 12 | 10 52 | 28 53 |
| 57 | 29 52 | 02 18 | 23 20 | 11 34 | 29 14 |
| 58 | 02♊53 | 04 10 | 24 31 | 12 18 | 29 35 |
| 59 | 06 13 | 06 08 | 25 44 | 13 03 | 29 56 |
| 60 | 09♊52 | 08♋11 | 27♋00 | 13♌49 | 00♍19 |

| 23h 16m 0s — 349° 0' 0" — 18 ♓ 02 | | | | | |
|---|---|---|---|---|---|
| LAT. | 11 | 12 | ASC | 2 | 3 |
| 0 | 20♈34 | 21♉26 | 19♊53 | 17♋32 | 16♌33 |
| 5 | 21 40 | 23 13 | 21 52 | 19 18 | 17 40 |
| 10 | 22 51 | 25 07 | 23 54 | 21 03 | 18 46 |
| 15 | 24 10 | 27 10 | 26 01 | 22 49 | 19 49 |
| 20 | 25 41 | 29 24 | 28 14 | 24 37 | 20 52 |
| 21 | 26 00 | 29 53 | 28 42 | 24 59 | 21 05 |
| 22 | 26 21 | 00♊22 | 29 10 | 25 21 | 21 18 |
| 23 | 26 42 | 00 52 | 29 38 | 25 44 | 21 30 |
| 24 | 27 03 | 01 23 | 00♋07 | 26 06 | 21 43 |
| 25 | 27 26 | 01 54 | 00 37 | 26 29 | 21 56 |
| 26 | 27 49 | 02 26 | 01 07 | 26 52 | 22 09 |
| 27 | 28 13 | 02 59 | 01 37 | 27 15 | 22 22 |
| 28 | 28 38 | 03 33 | 02 08 | 27 38 | 22 35 |
| 29 | 29 04 | 04 08 | 02 39 | 28 02 | 22 48 |
| 30 | 29 31 | 04 44 | 03 11 | 28 26 | 23 01 |
| 31 | 00♉00 | 05 21 | 03 44 | 28 50 | 23 14 |
| 32 | 00 29 | 05 59 | 04 17 | 29 14 | 23 28 |
| 33 | 01 00 | 06 38 | 04 51 | 29 39 | 23 41 |
| 34 | 01 33 | 07 19 | 05 26 | 00♌04 | 23 55 |
| 35 | 02 07 | 08 01 | 06 01 | 00 30 | 24 08 |
| 36 | 02 42 | 08 44 | 06 38 | 00 56 | 24 22 |
| 37 | 03 20 | 09 29 | 07 15 | 01 22 | 24 36 |
| 38 | 03 59 | 10 15 | 07 53 | 01 49 | 24 50 |
| 39 | 04 41 | 11 03 | 08 31 | 02 16 | 25 05 |
| 40 | 05 25 | 11 53 | 09 11 | 02 44 | 25 19 |
| 41 | 06 12 | 12 45 | 09 52 | 03 12 | 25 34 |
| 42 | 07 02 | 13 39 | 10 34 | 03 41 | 25 49 |
| 43 | 07 55 | 14 34 | 11 17 | 04 10 | 26 04 |
| 44 | 08 51 | 15 33 | 12 02 | 04 40 | 26 19 |
| 45 | 09 52 | 16 33 | 12 47 | 05 11 | 26 35 |
| 46 | 10 57 | 17 37 | 13 34 | 05 42 | 26 51 |
| 47 | 12 06 | 18 43 | 14 23 | 06 14 | 27 07 |
| 48 | 13 21 | 19 52 | 15 12 | 06 47 | 27 24 |
| 49 | 14 42 | 21 04 | 16 04 | 07 20 | 27 41 |
| 50 | 16 09 | 22 19 | 16 57 | 07 54 | 27 58 |
| 51 | 17 44 | 23 38 | 17 52 | 08 29 | 28 15 |
| 52 | 19 28 | 25 01 | 18 48 | 09 06 | 28 33 |
| 53 | 21 20 | 26 28 | 19 47 | 09 43 | 28 52 |
| 54 | 23 23 | 27 59 | 20 47 | 10 21 | 29 10 |
| 55 | 25 38 | 29 34 | 21 50 | 11 00 | 29 30 |
| 56 | 28 06 | 01♋14 | 22 55 | 11 40 | 29 49 |
| 57 | 00♊48 | 02 59 | 24 02 | 12 22 | 00♍09 |
| 58 | 03 47 | 04 49 | 25 11 | 13 05 | 00 30 |
| 59 | 07 03 | 06 45 | 26 24 | 13 49 | 00 52 |
| 60 | 10♊38 | 08♋46 | 27♋39 | 14♌35 | 01♍14 |

| 23h 20m 0s — 350° 0' 0" — 19 ♓ 07 | | | | | |
|---|---|---|---|---|---|
| LAT. | 11 | 12 | ASC | 2 | 3 |
| 0 | 21♈38 | 22♉25 | 20♊49 | 18♋28 | 17♌33 |
| 5 | 22 44 | 24 12 | 22 48 | 20 14 | 18 41 |
| 10 | 23 56 | 26 07 | 24 50 | 22 00 | 19 46 |
| 15 | 25 16 | 28 10 | 26 56 | 23 45 | 20 49 |
| 20 | 26 47 | 00♊24 | 29 09 | 25 33 | 21 52 |
| 21 | 27 07 | 00 53 | 29 37 | 25 55 | 22 05 |
| 22 | 27 27 | 01 22 | 00♋05 | 26 17 | 22 18 |
| 23 | 27 48 | 01 52 | 00 33 | 26 39 | 22 30 |
| 24 | 28 10 | 02 22 | 01 02 | 27 02 | 22 43 |
| 25 | 28 33 | 02 54 | 01 32 | 27 24 | 22 56 |
| 26 | 28 56 | 03 26 | 02 01 | 27 47 | 23 09 |
| 27 | 29 20 | 03 59 | 02 31 | 28 10 | 23 21 |
| 28 | 29 46 | 04 33 | 03 02 | 28 33 | 23 34 |
| 29 | 00♉12 | 05 07 | 03 33 | 28 57 | 23 47 |
| 30 | 00 39 | 05 43 | 04 05 | 29 21 | 24 00 |
| 31 | 01 07 | 06 20 | 04 38 | 29 45 | 24 14 |
| 32 | 01 37 | 06 58 | 05 11 | 00♌09 | 24 27 |
| 33 | 02 08 | 07 37 | 05 45 | 00 34 | 24 40 |
| 34 | 02 40 | 08 17 | 06 19 | 00 59 | 24 54 |
| 35 | 03 14 | 08 59 | 06 54 | 01 24 | 25 07 |
| 36 | 03 50 | 09 42 | 07 30 | 01 50 | 25 21 |
| 37 | 04 28 | 10 26 | 08 07 | 02 16 | 25 35 |
| 38 | 05 07 | 11 12 | 08 45 | 02 43 | 25 49 |
| 39 | 05 49 | 12 00 | 09 23 | 03 10 | 26 03 |
| 40 | 06 33 | 12 49 | 10 03 | 03 37 | 26 18 |
| 41 | 07 20 | 13 41 | 10 44 | 04 05 | 26 32 |
| 42 | 08 10 | 14 34 | 11 25 | 04 34 | 26 47 |
| 43 | 09 03 | 15 30 | 12 08 | 05 03 | 27 02 |
| 44 | 09 59 | 16 27 | 12 52 | 05 32 | 27 17 |
| 45 | 11 00 | 17 27 | 13 37 | 06 03 | 27 33 |
| 46 | 12 04 | 18 30 | 14 24 | 06 34 | 27 49 |
| 47 | 13 13 | 19 35 | 15 11 | 07 05 | 28 05 |
| 48 | 14 28 | 20 44 | 16 01 | 07 38 | 28 21 |
| 49 | 15 48 | 21 55 | 16 51 | 08 11 | 28 38 |
| 50 | 17 15 | 23 09 | 17 44 | 08 45 | 28 55 |
| 51 | 18 49 | 24 27 | 18 38 | 09 20 | 29 12 |
| 52 | 20 32 | 25 49 | 19 34 | 09 55 | 29 30 |
| 53 | 22 23 | 27 14 | 20 32 | 10 32 | 29 48 |
| 54 | 24 25 | 28 44 | 21 31 | 11 10 | 00♍07 |
| 55 | 26 38 | 00♋18 | 22 33 | 11 48 | 00 26 |
| 56 | 29 03 | 01 57 | 23 37 | 12 28 | 00 45 |
| 57 | 01♊43 | 03 40 | 24 43 | 13 09 | 01 05 |
| 58 | 04 39 | 05 28 | 25 52 | 13 52 | 01 26 |
| 59 | 07 52 | 07 22 | 27 03 | 14 35 | 01 47 |
| 60 | 11♊23 | 09♋21 | 28♋17 | 15♌20 | 02♍09 |

| 23h 24m 0s — 351° 0' 0" — 20 ♓ 12 | | | | | |
|---|---|---|---|---|---|
| LAT. | 11 | 12 | ASC | 2 | 3 |
| 0 | 22♈42 | 23♉23 | 21♊44 | 19♋24 | 18♌34 |
| 5 | 23 49 | 25 12 | 23 43 | 21 10 | 19 42 |
| 10 | 25 01 | 27 06 | 25 45 | 22 56 | 20 47 |
| 15 | 26 22 | 29 09 | 27 52 | 24 41 | 21 50 |
| 20 | 27 53 | 01♊24 | 00♋05 | 26 29 | 22 53 |
| 21 | 28 13 | 01 52 | 00 32 | 26 51 | 23 05 |
| 22 | 28 34 | 02 21 | 01 00 | 27 13 | 23 18 |
| 23 | 28 55 | 02 51 | 01 28 | 27 35 | 23 30 |
| 24 | 29 17 | 03 22 | 01 57 | 27 57 | 23 43 |
| 25 | 29 39 | 03 53 | 02 26 | 28 20 | 23 56 |
| 26 | 00♉03 | 04 25 | 02 56 | 28 42 | 24 08 |
| 27 | 00 27 | 04 58 | 03 26 | 29 05 | 24 21 |
| 28 | 00 52 | 05 31 | 03 56 | 29 28 | 24 34 |
| 29 | 01 19 | 06 06 | 04 28 | 29 52 | 24 47 |
| 30 | 01 46 | 06 42 | 04 59 | 00♌15 | 25 00 |
| 31 | 02 15 | 07 18 | 05 32 | 00 39 | 25 13 |
| 32 | 02 44 | 07 56 | 06 04 | 01 04 | 25 26 |
| 33 | 03 15 | 08 35 | 06 38 | 01 28 | 25 39 |
| 34 | 03 48 | 09 15 | 07 12 | 01 53 | 25 53 |
| 35 | 04 22 | 09 56 | 07 47 | 02 18 | 26 06 |
| 36 | 04 58 | 10 39 | 08 23 | 02 44 | 26 20 |
| 37 | 05 35 | 11 23 | 09 00 | 03 10 | 26 34 |
| 38 | 06 15 | 12 09 | 09 37 | 03 36 | 26 48 |
| 39 | 06 57 | 12 56 | 10 15 | 04 03 | 27 02 |
| 40 | 07 41 | 13 45 | 10 54 | 04 30 | 27 16 |
| 41 | 08 28 | 14 36 | 11 35 | 04 58 | 27 31 |
| 42 | 09 17 | 15 29 | 12 16 | 05 26 | 27 46 |
| 43 | 10 10 | 16 24 | 12 58 | 05 55 | 28 00 |
| 44 | 11 06 | 17 21 | 13 42 | 06 25 | 28 16 |
| 45 | 12 06 | 18 21 | 14 27 | 06 55 | 28 31 |
| 46 | 13 11 | 19 23 | 15 12 | 07 25 | 28 47 |
| 47 | 14 20 | 20 27 | 16 00 | 07 57 | 29 03 |
| 48 | 15 34 | 21 35 | 16 49 | 08 29 | 29 19 |
| 49 | 16 53 | 22 45 | 17 39 | 09 02 | 29 35 |
| 50 | 18 20 | 23 59 | 18 31 | 09 35 | 29 52 |
| 51 | 19 53 | 25 16 | 19 24 | 10 10 | 00♍09 |
| 52 | 21 34 | 26 36 | 20 19 | 10 45 | 00 27 |
| 53 | 23 25 | 28 00 | 21 16 | 11 21 | 00 45 |
| 54 | 25 25 | 29 29 | 22 15 | 11 59 | 01 03 |
| 55 | 27 36 | 01♋01 | 23 16 | 12 37 | 01 22 |
| 56 | 00♊00 | 02 38 | 24 19 | 13 16 | 01 41 |
| 57 | 02 38 | 04 20 | 25 24 | 13 57 | 02 01 |
| 58 | 05 30 | 06 07 | 26 32 | 14 39 | 02 21 |
| 59 | 08 40 | 07 58 | 27 42 | 15 22 | 02 42 |
| 60 | 12♊07 | 09♋56 | 28♋55 | 16♌06 | 03♍04 |

# Koch Table of Houses for Latitudes 0° to 60° North

**23h 28m 0s — 352° 0' 0" — 21 ♓ 17**

| LAT. | 11 | 12 | ASC | 2 | 3 |
|---|---|---|---|---|---|
| 0 | 23♈46 | 24♉22 | 22♊39 | 20♋20 | 19♌35 |
| 5 | 24 53 | 26 11 | 24 39 | 22 07 | 20 42 |
| 10 | 26 06 | 28 05 | 26 41 | 23 52 | 21 47 |
| 15 | 27 27 | 00♊08 | 28 47 | 25 38 | 22 50 |
| 20 | 28 59 | 02 23 | 00♋59 | 27 25 | 23 53 |
| 21 | 29 19 | 02 51 | 01 27 | 27 46 | 24 05 |
| 22 | 29 40 | 03 20 | 01 55 | 28 08 | 24 18 |
| 23 | 00♉01 | 03 50 | 02 23 | 28 30 | 24 30 |
| 24 | 00 23 | 04 20 | 02 52 | 28 53 | 24 43 |
| 25 | 00 46 | 04 52 | 03 21 | 29 15 | 24 56 |
| 26 | 01 09 | 05 24 | 03 50 | 29 38 | 25 08 |
| 27 | 01 34 | 05 56 | 04 20 | 00♌00 | 25 21 |
| 28 | 01 59 | 06 30 | 04 50 | 00 24 | 25 34 |
| 29 | 02 25 | 07 04 | 05 21 | 00 47 | 25 47 |
| 30 | 02 53 | 07 40 | 05 53 | 01 10 | 25 59 |
| 31 | 03 21 | 08 16 | 06 25 | 01 34 | 26 12 |
| 32 | 03 51 | 08 54 | 06 58 | 01 58 | 26 26 |
| 33 | 04 22 | 09 33 | 07 31 | 02 23 | 26 39 |
| 34 | 04 55 | 10 12 | 08 05 | 02 47 | 26 52 |
| 35 | 05 29 | 10 53 | 08 40 | 03 12 | 27 06 |
| 36 | 06 05 | 11 36 | 09 15 | 03 38 | 27 19 |
| 37 | 06 42 | 12 20 | 09 52 | 04 04 | 27 33 |
| 38 | 07 22 | 13 05 | 10 29 | 04 30 | 27 47 |
| 39 | 08 04 | 13 52 | 11 07 | 04 56 | 28 01 |
| 40 | 08 48 | 14 41 | 11 46 | 05 24 | 28 15 |
| 41 | 09 34 | 15 31 | 12 26 | 05 51 | 28 29 |
| 42 | 10 24 | 16 24 | 13 06 | 06 19 | 28 44 |
| 43 | 11 17 | 17 18 | 13 48 | 06 48 | 28 59 |
| 44 | 12 13 | 18 15 | 14 31 | 07 17 | 29 14 |
| 45 | 13 12 | 19 14 | 15 16 | 07 47 | 29 29 |
| 46 | 14 16 | 20 15 | 16 01 | 08 17 | 29 45 |
| 47 | 15 25 | 21 19 | 16 48 | 08 48 | 00♍00 |
| 48 | 16 38 | 22 25 | 17 36 | 09 20 | 00 16 |
| 49 | 17 58 | 23 35 | 18 26 | 09 52 | 00 33 |
| 50 | 19 23 | 24 48 | 19 17 | 10 26 | 00 50 |
| 51 | 20 56 | 26 03 | 20 10 | 11 00 | 01 07 |
| 52 | 22 36 | 27 23 | 21 04 | 11 35 | 01 24 |
| 53 | 24 25 | 28 46 | 22 01 | 12 11 | 01 42 |
| 54 | 26 24 | 00♋13 | 22 59 | 12 47 | 02 00 |
| 55 | 28 34 | 01 44 | 23 59 | 13 25 | 02 19 |
| 56 | 00♊55 | 03 20 | 25 01 | 14 04 | 02 38 |
| 57 | 03 31 | 05 00 | 26 06 | 14 44 | 02 57 |
| 58 | 06 20 | 06 45 | 27 12 | 15 26 | 03 17 |
| 59 | 09 26 | 08 35 | 28 21 | 16 08 | 03 38 |
| 60 | 12♊50 | 10♋30 | 29♋33 | 16♌52 | 03♍59 |

**23h 32m 0s — 353° 0' 0" — 22 ♓ 23**

| LAT. | 11 | 12 | ASC | 2 | 3 |
|---|---|---|---|---|---|
| 0 | 24♈50 | 25♉21 | 23♊34 | 21♋17 | 20♌36 |
| 5 | 25 57 | 27 09 | 25 34 | 23 03 | 21 43 |
| 10 | 27 11 | 29 04 | 27 36 | 24 48 | 22 48 |
| 15 | 28 32 | 01♊07 | 29 42 | 26 34 | 23 51 |
| 20 | 00♉05 | 03 21 | 01♋54 | 28 21 | 24 53 |
| 21 | 00 25 | 03 50 | 02 22 | 28 42 | 25 06 |
| 22 | 00 45 | 04 19 | 02 49 | 29 04 | 25 18 |
| 23 | 01 07 | 04 49 | 03 17 | 29 26 | 25 31 |
| 24 | 01 29 | 05 19 | 03 46 | 29 48 | 25 43 |
| 25 | 01 52 | 05 50 | 04 15 | 00♌10 | 25 56 |
| 26 | 02 15 | 06 22 | 04 44 | 00 33 | 26 08 |
| 27 | 02 40 | 06 55 | 05 14 | 00 56 | 26 21 |
| 28 | 03 05 | 07 28 | 05 44 | 01 19 | 26 34 |
| 29 | 03 32 | 08 02 | 06 15 | 01 42 | 26 46 |
| 30 | 03 59 | 08 38 | 06 46 | 02 05 | 26 59 |
| 31 | 04 28 | 09 14 | 07 18 | 02 29 | 27 12 |
| 32 | 04 57 | 09 51 | 07 51 | 02 53 | 27 25 |
| 33 | 05 29 | 10 30 | 08 24 | 03 17 | 27 38 |
| 34 | 06 01 | 11 09 | 08 58 | 03 42 | 27 51 |
| 35 | 06 35 | 11 50 | 09 32 | 04 06 | 28 05 |
| 36 | 07 11 | 12 32 | 10 08 | 04 32 | 28 18 |
| 37 | 07 49 | 13 16 | 10 44 | 04 57 | 28 32 |
| 38 | 08 28 | 14 01 | 11 20 | 05 23 | 28 46 |
| 39 | 09 10 | 14 48 | 11 58 | 05 50 | 29 00 |
| 40 | 09 54 | 15 36 | 12 37 | 06 17 | 29 14 |
| 41 | 10 41 | 16 26 | 13 16 | 06 44 | 29 28 |
| 42 | 11 30 | 17 18 | 13 57 | 07 12 | 29 42 |
| 43 | 12 22 | 18 12 | 14 38 | 07 40 | 29 57 |
| 44 | 13 18 | 19 08 | 15 21 | 08 09 | 00♍12 |
| 45 | 14 18 | 20 06 | 16 05 | 08 39 | 00 27 |
| 46 | 15 21 | 21 06 | 16 50 | 09 09 | 00 43 |
| 47 | 16 29 | 22 10 | 17 36 | 09 40 | 00 58 |
| 48 | 17 43 | 23 15 | 18 24 | 10 11 | 01 14 |
| 49 | 19 01 | 24 24 | 19 13 | 10 43 | 01 30 |
| 50 | 20 26 | 25 36 | 20 03 | 11 16 | 01 47 |
| 51 | 21 58 | 26 51 | 20 56 | 11 50 | 02 04 |
| 52 | 23 37 | 28 09 | 21 49 | 12 24 | 02 21 |
| 53 | 25 25 | 29 31 | 22 45 | 13 00 | 02 39 |
| 54 | 27 22 | 00♋57 | 23 42 | 13 36 | 02 57 |
| 55 | 29 30 | 02 27 | 24 42 | 14 14 | 03 15 |
| 56 | 01♊50 | 04 01 | 25 43 | 14 52 | 03 34 |
| 57 | 04 22 | 05 39 | 26 47 | 15 32 | 03 53 |
| 58 | 07 10 | 07 22 | 27 52 | 16 12 | 04 13 |
| 59 | 10 12 | 09 11 | 29 01 | 16 54 | 04 33 |
| 60 | 13♊32 | 11♋04 | 00♌11 | 17♌38 | 04♍54 |

**23h 36m 0s — 354° 0' 0" — 23 ♓ 28**

| LAT. | 11 | 12 | ASC | 2 | 3 |
|---|---|---|---|---|---|
| 0 | 25♈53 | 26♉19 | 24♊30 | 22♋13 | 21♌37 |
| 5 | 27 01 | 28 08 | 26 29 | 24 00 | 22 45 |
| 10 | 28 15 | 00♊03 | 28 31 | 25 45 | 23 49 |
| 15 | 29 37 | 02 06 | 00♋37 | 27 30 | 24 52 |
| 20 | 01♉10 | 04 20 | 02 49 | 29 16 | 25 54 |
| 21 | 01 30 | 04 48 | 03 16 | 29 38 | 26 06 |
| 22 | 01 51 | 05 17 | 03 44 | 00♌00 | 26 18 |
| 23 | 02 12 | 05 47 | 04 12 | 00 22 | 26 31 |
| 24 | 02 34 | 06 17 | 04 40 | 00 44 | 26 43 |
| 25 | 02 57 | 06 48 | 05 09 | 01 06 | 26 56 |
| 26 | 03 21 | 07 20 | 05 38 | 01 28 | 27 08 |
| 27 | 03 45 | 07 52 | 06 08 | 01 51 | 27 21 |
| 28 | 04 11 | 08 26 | 06 38 | 02 14 | 27 33 |
| 29 | 04 37 | 09 00 | 07 09 | 02 37 | 27 46 |
| 30 | 05 05 | 09 35 | 07 40 | 03 00 | 27 59 |
| 31 | 05 33 | 10 11 | 08 12 | 03 24 | 28 12 |
| 32 | 06 03 | 10 48 | 08 44 | 03 47 | 28 25 |
| 33 | 06 34 | 11 26 | 09 17 | 04 11 | 28 38 |
| 34 | 07 07 | 12 06 | 09 50 | 04 36 | 28 51 |
| 35 | 07 41 | 12 46 | 10 25 | 05 01 | 29 04 |
| 36 | 08 17 | 13 28 | 11 00 | 05 26 | 29 17 |
| 37 | 08 54 | 14 11 | 11 35 | 05 51 | 29 31 |
| 38 | 09 34 | 14 56 | 12 12 | 06 17 | 29 45 |
| 39 | 10 16 | 15 42 | 12 49 | 06 43 | 29 58 |
| 40 | 11 00 | 16 30 | 13 27 | 07 10 | 00♍12 |
| 41 | 11 46 | 17 20 | 14 07 | 07 37 | 00 27 |
| 42 | 12 35 | 18 11 | 14 47 | 08 05 | 00 41 |
| 43 | 13 28 | 19 05 | 15 28 | 08 33 | 00 56 |
| 44 | 14 23 | 20 00 | 16 10 | 09 01 | 01 10 |
| 45 | 15 22 | 20 58 | 16 53 | 09 31 | 01 25 |
| 46 | 16 25 | 21 58 | 17 38 | 10 00 | 01 41 |
| 47 | 17 33 | 23 00 | 18 24 | 10 31 | 01 56 |
| 48 | 18 46 | 24 05 | 19 11 | 11 02 | 02 12 |
| 49 | 20 04 | 25 13 | 19 59 | 11 34 | 02 28 |
| 50 | 21 28 | 26 24 | 20 49 | 12 06 | 02 44 |
| 51 | 22 59 | 27 38 | 21 41 | 12 40 | 03 01 |
| 52 | 24 37 | 28 55 | 22 34 | 13 14 | 03 18 |
| 53 | 26 23 | 00♋16 | 23 29 | 13 49 | 03 35 |
| 54 | 28 19 | 01 40 | 24 26 | 14 25 | 03 53 |
| 55 | 00♊26 | 03 09 | 25 24 | 15 02 | 04 11 |
| 56 | 02 43 | 04 41 | 26 25 | 15 40 | 04 30 |
| 57 | 05 13 | 06 18 | 27 27 | 16 19 | 04 49 |
| 58 | 07 58 | 08 00 | 28 32 | 16 59 | 05 09 |
| 59 | 10 57 | 09 46 | 29 39 | 17 41 | 05 29 |
| 60 | 14♊13 | 11♋37 | 00♌49 | 18♌23 | 05♍50 |

**23h 40m 0s — 355° 0' 0" — 24 ♓ 33**

| LAT. | 11 | 12 | ASC | 2 | 3 |
|---|---|---|---|---|---|
| 0 | 26♈57 | 27♉17 | 25♊25 | 23♋10 | 22♌39 |
| 5 | 28 05 | 29 06 | 27 24 | 24 56 | 23 46 |
| 10 | 29 19 | 01♊01 | 29 26 | 26 41 | 24 50 |
| 15 | 00♉42 | 03 04 | 01♋32 | 28 26 | 25 53 |
| 20 | 02 15 | 05 18 | 03 43 | 00♌12 | 26 54 |
| 21 | 02 35 | 05 46 | 04 11 | 00 34 | 27 07 |
| 22 | 02 56 | 06 15 | 04 38 | 00 56 | 27 19 |
| 23 | 03 17 | 06 45 | 05 06 | 01 17 | 27 31 |
| 24 | 03 39 | 07 15 | 05 34 | 01 39 | 27 44 |
| 25 | 04 02 | 07 46 | 06 03 | 02 01 | 27 56 |
| 26 | 04 26 | 08 17 | 06 32 | 02 24 | 28 08 |
| 27 | 04 51 | 08 50 | 07 02 | 02 46 | 28 21 |
| 28 | 05 16 | 09 23 | 07 32 | 03 09 | 28 33 |
| 29 | 05 43 | 09 57 | 08 02 | 03 32 | 28 46 |
| 30 | 06 10 | 10 32 | 08 33 | 03 55 | 28 59 |
| 31 | 06 39 | 11 08 | 09 04 | 04 18 | 29 11 |
| 32 | 07 09 | 11 45 | 09 37 | 04 42 | 29 24 |
| 33 | 07 40 | 12 23 | 10 09 | 05 06 | 29 37 |
| 34 | 08 12 | 13 02 | 10 43 | 05 30 | 29 50 |
| 35 | 08 47 | 13 42 | 11 17 | 05 55 | 00♍03 |
| 36 | 09 22 | 14 24 | 11 51 | 06 19 | 00 17 |
| 37 | 10 00 | 15 07 | 12 27 | 06 45 | 00 30 |
| 38 | 10 39 | 15 51 | 13 03 | 07 10 | 00 44 |
| 39 | 11 21 | 16 37 | 13 40 | 07 36 | 00 57 |
| 40 | 12 05 | 17 24 | 14 18 | 08 03 | 01 11 |
| 41 | 12 51 | 18 13 | 14 57 | 08 30 | 01 25 |
| 42 | 13 40 | 19 04 | 15 36 | 08 57 | 01 40 |
| 43 | 14 32 | 19 57 | 16 17 | 09 25 | 01 54 |
| 44 | 15 27 | 20 52 | 16 59 | 09 53 | 02 09 |
| 45 | 16 26 | 21 49 | 17 42 | 10 22 | 02 24 |
| 46 | 17 29 | 22 48 | 18 26 | 10 52 | 02 39 |
| 47 | 18 36 | 23 50 | 19 11 | 11 22 | 02 54 |
| 48 | 19 48 | 24 54 | 19 58 | 11 53 | 03 10 |
| 49 | 21 05 | 26 01 | 20 46 | 12 25 | 03 26 |
| 50 | 22 29 | 27 11 | 21 35 | 12 57 | 03 42 |
| 51 | 23 59 | 28 24 | 22 26 | 13 30 | 03 58 |
| 52 | 25 36 | 29 40 | 23 19 | 14 04 | 04 15 |
| 53 | 27 21 | 01♋00 | 24 13 | 14 38 | 04 32 |
| 54 | 29 16 | 02 23 | 25 09 | 15 14 | 04 50 |
| 55 | 01♊20 | 03 50 | 26 07 | 15 50 | 05 08 |
| 56 | 03 36 | 05 21 | 27 06 | 16 28 | 05 26 |
| 57 | 06 04 | 06 57 | 28 08 | 17 06 | 05 45 |
| 58 | 08 45 | 08 37 | 29 12 | 17 46 | 06 05 |
| 59 | 11 41 | 10 21 | 00♌18 | 18 27 | 06 25 |
| 60 | 14♊54 | 12♋11 | 01♌27 | 19♌09 | 06♍45 |

**23h 44m 0s — 356° 0' 0" — 25 ♓ 38**

| LAT. | 11 | 12 | ASC | 2 | 3 |
|---|---|---|---|---|---|
| 0 | 28♈00 | 28♉15 | 26♊20 | 24♋06 | 23♌41 |
| 5 | 29 09 | 00♊04 | 28 19 | 25 53 | 24 47 |
| 10 | 00♉23 | 01 59 | 00♋21 | 27 38 | 25 51 |
| 15 | 01 46 | 04 02 | 02 27 | 29 22 | 26 54 |
| 20 | 03 19 | 06 16 | 04 38 | 01♌08 | 27 55 |
| 21 | 03 40 | 06 44 | 05 05 | 01 30 | 28 07 |
| 22 | 04 01 | 07 13 | 05 32 | 01 51 | 28 19 |
| 23 | 04 22 | 07 42 | 06 00 | 02 13 | 28 32 |
| 24 | 04 44 | 08 12 | 06 28 | 02 35 | 28 44 |
| 25 | 05 07 | 08 43 | 06 57 | 02 57 | 28 56 |
| 26 | 05 31 | 09 15 | 07 26 | 03 19 | 29 09 |
| 27 | 05 56 | 09 47 | 07 55 | 03 41 | 29 21 |
| 28 | 06 21 | 10 20 | 08 25 | 04 04 | 29 33 |
| 29 | 06 48 | 10 54 | 08 55 | 04 27 | 29 46 |
| 30 | 07 15 | 11 29 | 09 26 | 04 50 | 29 59 |
| 31 | 07 44 | 12 04 | 09 57 | 05 13 | 00♍11 |
| 32 | 08 14 | 12 41 | 10 29 | 05 36 | 00 24 |
| 33 | 08 45 | 13 19 | 11 02 | 06 00 | 00 37 |
| 34 | 09 17 | 13 57 | 11 35 | 06 24 | 00 50 |
| 35 | 09 51 | 14 38 | 12 08 | 06 49 | 01 03 |
| 36 | 10 27 | 15 19 | 12 43 | 07 13 | 01 16 |
| 37 | 11 05 | 16 01 | 13 18 | 07 38 | 01 29 |
| 38 | 11 44 | 16 45 | 13 54 | 08 04 | 01 43 |
| 39 | 12 25 | 17 31 | 14 31 | 08 30 | 01 56 |
| 40 | 13 09 | 18 18 | 15 08 | 08 56 | 02 10 |
| 41 | 13 55 | 19 06 | 15 47 | 09 23 | 02 24 |
| 42 | 14 44 | 19 57 | 16 26 | 09 50 | 02 38 |
| 43 | 15 36 | 20 49 | 17 06 | 10 17 | 02 53 |
| 44 | 16 31 | 21 43 | 17 48 | 10 46 | 03 07 |
| 45 | 17 29 | 22 40 | 18 30 | 11 14 | 03 22 |
| 46 | 18 32 | 23 38 | 19 14 | 11 44 | 03 37 |
| 47 | 19 38 | 24 39 | 19 59 | 12 13 | 03 52 |
| 48 | 20 50 | 25 43 | 20 45 | 12 44 | 04 07 |
| 49 | 22 06 | 26 49 | 21 32 | 13 15 | 04 23 |
| 50 | 23 29 | 27 58 | 22 21 | 13 47 | 04 39 |
| 51 | 24 58 | 29 10 | 23 11 | 14 20 | 04 56 |
| 52 | 26 34 | 00♋25 | 24 03 | 14 53 | 05 12 |
| 53 | 28 18 | 01 44 | 24 57 | 15 27 | 05 29 |
| 54 | 00♊11 | 03 06 | 25 52 | 16 03 | 05 47 |
| 55 | 02 13 | 04 31 | 26 49 | 16 39 | 06 05 |
| 56 | 04 27 | 06 01 | 27 48 | 17 16 | 06 23 |
| 57 | 06 53 | 07 35 | 28 49 | 17 54 | 06 41 |
| 58 | 09 32 | 09 13 | 29 52 | 18 33 | 07 01 |
| 59 | 12 25 | 10 56 | 00♌57 | 19 13 | 07 20 |
| 60 | 15♊34 | 12♋44 | 02♌04 | 19♌55 | 07♍40 |

**23h 48m 0s — 357° 0' 0" — 26 ♓ 44**

| LAT. | 11 | 12 | ASC | 2 | 3 |
|---|---|---|---|---|---|
| 0 | 29♈03 | 29♉13 | 27♊15 | 25♋03 | 24♌42 |
| 5 | 00♉12 | 01♊02 | 29 15 | 26 50 | 25 49 |
| 10 | 01 27 | 02 57 | 01♋16 | 28 34 | 26 53 |
| 15 | 02 50 | 05 00 | 03 21 | 00♌19 | 27 55 |
| 20 | 04 24 | 07 14 | 05 32 | 02 04 | 28 56 |
| 21 | 04 44 | 07 42 | 05 59 | 02 26 | 29 08 |
| 22 | 05 05 | 08 10 | 06 26 | 02 47 | 29 20 |
| 23 | 05 27 | 08 40 | 06 54 | 03 09 | 29 32 |
| 24 | 05 49 | 09 10 | 07 22 | 03 30 | 29 44 |
| 25 | 06 12 | 09 40 | 07 50 | 03 52 | 29 57 |
| 26 | 06 36 | 10 12 | 08 19 | 04 14 | 00♍09 |
| 27 | 07 00 | 10 44 | 08 48 | 04 37 | 00 21 |
| 28 | 07 26 | 11 17 | 09 18 | 04 59 | 00 34 |
| 29 | 07 52 | 11 50 | 09 48 | 05 22 | 00 46 |
| 30 | 08 20 | 12 25 | 10 19 | 05 44 | 00 59 |
| 31 | 08 48 | 13 00 | 10 50 | 06 08 | 01 11 |
| 32 | 09 18 | 13 37 | 11 22 | 06 31 | 01 24 |
| 33 | 09 49 | 14 14 | 11 54 | 06 55 | 01 37 |
| 34 | 10 22 | 14 53 | 12 27 | 07 18 | 01 49 |
| 35 | 10 56 | 15 32 | 13 00 | 07 43 | 02 02 |
| 36 | 11 31 | 16 13 | 13 34 | 08 07 | 02 15 |
| 37 | 12 09 | 16 56 | 14 09 | 08 32 | 02 29 |
| 38 | 12 48 | 17 39 | 14 45 | 08 57 | 02 42 |
| 39 | 13 29 | 18 24 | 15 21 | 09 23 | 02 55 |
| 40 | 14 13 | 19 11 | 15 58 | 09 49 | 03 09 |
| 41 | 14 59 | 19 59 | 16 36 | 10 15 | 03 23 |
| 42 | 15 47 | 20 49 | 17 15 | 10 42 | 03 37 |
| 43 | 16 39 | 21 41 | 17 55 | 11 10 | 03 51 |
| 44 | 17 33 | 22 35 | 18 36 | 11 38 | 04 05 |
| 45 | 18 32 | 23 30 | 19 18 | 12 06 | 04 20 |
| 46 | 19 34 | 24 28 | 20 02 | 12 35 | 04 35 |
| 47 | 20 40 | 25 28 | 20 46 | 13 05 | 04 50 |
| 48 | 21 51 | 26 31 | 21 32 | 13 35 | 05 05 |
| 49 | 23 06 | 27 36 | 22 18 | 14 06 | 05 21 |
| 50 | 24 28 | 28 44 | 23 07 | 14 37 | 05 37 |
| 51 | 25 56 | 29 55 | 23 56 | 15 10 | 05 53 |
| 52 | 27 31 | 01♋10 | 24 47 | 15 43 | 06 09 |
| 53 | 29 14 | 02 27 | 25 40 | 16 16 | 06 26 |
| 54 | 01♊05 | 03 48 | 26 35 | 16 51 | 06 43 |
| 55 | 03 06 | 05 12 | 27 31 | 17 27 | 07 01 |
| 56 | 05 18 | 06 41 | 28 29 | 18 03 | 07 19 |
| 57 | 07 41 | 08 13 | 29 29 | 18 41 | 07 38 |
| 58 | 10 17 | 09 50 | 00♌31 | 19 20 | 07 57 |
| 59 | 13 07 | 11 31 | 01 36 | 20 00 | 08 16 |
| 60 | 16♊13 | 13♋17 | 02♌42 | 20♌41 | 08♍36 |

**23h 52m 0s — 358° 0' 0" — 27 ♓ 49**

| LAT. | 11 | 12 | ASC | 2 | 3 |
|---|---|---|---|---|---|
| 0 | 00♉06 | 00♊11 | 28♊10 | 26♋00 | 25♌44 |
| 5 | 01 15 | 02 00 | 00♋10 | 27 47 | 26 51 |
| 10 | 02 31 | 03 55 | 02 11 | 29 31 | 27 54 |
| 15 | 03 54 | 05 58 | 04 16 | 01♌15 | 28 56 |
| 20 | 05 28 | 08 11 | 06 26 | 03 00 | 29 56 |
| 21 | 05 48 | 08 39 | 06 53 | 03 21 | 00♍09 |
| 22 | 06 09 | 09 07 | 07 20 | 03 43 | 00 21 |
| 23 | 06 31 | 09 37 | 07 48 | 04 04 | 00 33 |
| 24 | 06 53 | 10 07 | 08 16 | 04 26 | 00 45 |
| 25 | 07 16 | 10 37 | 08 44 | 04 48 | 00 57 |
| 26 | 07 40 | 11 08 | 09 13 | 05 10 | 01 09 |
| 27 | 08 04 | 11 40 | 09 42 | 05 32 | 01 22 |
| 28 | 08 30 | 12 13 | 10 11 | 05 54 | 01 34 |
| 29 | 08 56 | 12 46 | 10 41 | 06 17 | 01 46 |
| 30 | 09 24 | 13 21 | 11 11 | 06 39 | 01 59 |
| 31 | 09 53 | 13 56 | 11 42 | 07 02 | 02 11 |
| 32 | 10 22 | 14 32 | 12 14 | 07 25 | 02 24 |
| 33 | 10 53 | 15 09 | 12 46 | 07 49 | 02 36 |
| 34 | 11 26 | 15 48 | 13 18 | 08 13 | 02 49 |
| 35 | 12 00 | 16 27 | 13 52 | 08 37 | 03 02 |
| 36 | 12 35 | 17 08 | 14 25 | 09 01 | 03 15 |
| 37 | 13 12 | 17 50 | 15 00 | 09 26 | 03 28 |
| 38 | 13 52 | 18 33 | 15 35 | 09 51 | 03 41 |
| 39 | 14 33 | 19 17 | 16 11 | 10 16 | 03 55 |
| 40 | 15 16 | 20 04 | 16 48 | 10 42 | 04 08 |
| 41 | 16 02 | 20 51 | 17 26 | 11 08 | 04 22 |
| 42 | 16 50 | 21 41 | 18 05 | 11 35 | 04 36 |
| 43 | 17 41 | 22 32 | 18 44 | 12 02 | 04 50 |
| 44 | 18 36 | 23 25 | 19 25 | 12 30 | 05 04 |
| 45 | 19 33 | 24 20 | 20 06 | 12 58 | 05 18 |
| 46 | 20 35 | 25 17 | 20 49 | 13 26 | 05 33 |
| 47 | 21 40 | 26 17 | 21 33 | 13 56 | 05 48 |
| 48 | 22 51 | 27 19 | 22 18 | 14 26 | 06 03 |
| 49 | 24 06 | 28 23 | 23 04 | 14 56 | 06 19 |
| 50 | 25 27 | 29 31 | 23 52 | 15 27 | 06 34 |
| 51 | 26 54 | 00♋41 | 24 41 | 15 59 | 06 50 |
| 52 | 28 27 | 01 54 | 25 32 | 16 32 | 07 07 |
| 53 | 00♊09 | 03 10 | 26 24 | 17 06 | 07 23 |
| 54 | 01 59 | 04 29 | 27 17 | 17 40 | 07 40 |
| 55 | 03 58 | 05 53 | 28 13 | 18 15 | 07 58 |
| 56 | 06 07 | 07 20 | 29 10 | 18 51 | 08 16 |
| 57 | 08 28 | 08 51 | 00♌09 | 19 28 | 08 34 |
| 58 | 11 02 | 10 26 | 01 11 | 20 07 | 08 53 |
| 59 | 13 49 | 12 05 | 02 14 | 20 46 | 09 12 |
| 60 | 16♊51 | 13♋49 | 03♌20 | 21♌26 | 09♍31 |

**23h 56m 0s — 359° 0' 0" — 28 ♓ 55**

| LAT. | 11 | 12 | ASC | 2 | 3 |
|---|---|---|---|---|---|
| 0 | 01♉08 | 01♊08 | 29♊05 | 26♋57 | 26♌47 |
| 5 | 02 18 | 02 58 | 01♋05 | 28 44 | 27 53 |
| 10 | 03 34 | 04 53 | 03 06 | 00♌28 | 28 56 |
| 15 | 04 57 | 06 55 | 05 11 | 02 12 | 29 57 |
| 20 | 06 31 | 09 08 | 07 20 | 03 56 | 00♍57 |
| 21 | 06 52 | 09 36 | 07 47 | 04 17 | 01 09 |
| 22 | 07 13 | 10 04 | 08 14 | 04 39 | 01 21 |
| 23 | 07 34 | 10 33 | 08 42 | 05 00 | 01 33 |
| 24 | 07 57 | 11 03 | 09 09 | 05 22 | 01 46 |
| 25 | 08 20 | 11 33 | 09 37 | 05 43 | 01 58 |
| 26 | 08 44 | 12 04 | 10 06 | 06 05 | 02 10 |
| 27 | 09 08 | 12 36 | 10 35 | 06 27 | 02 22 |
| 28 | 09 34 | 13 09 | 11 04 | 06 49 | 02 34 |
| 29 | 10 00 | 13 42 | 11 34 | 07 12 | 02 46 |
| 30 | 10 28 | 14 16 | 12 04 | 07 34 | 02 59 |
| 31 | 10 56 | 14 51 | 12 35 | 07 57 | 03 11 |
| 32 | 11 26 | 15 27 | 13 06 | 08 20 | 03 24 |
| 33 | 11 57 | 16 04 | 13 38 | 08 43 | 03 36 |
| 34 | 12 29 | 16 42 | 14 10 | 09 07 | 03 49 |
| 35 | 13 03 | 17 21 | 14 43 | 09 31 | 04 01 |
| 36 | 13 39 | 18 02 | 15 17 | 09 55 | 04 14 |
| 37 | 14 16 | 18 43 | 15 51 | 10 19 | 04 27 |
| 38 | 14 55 | 19 26 | 16 26 | 10 44 | 04 40 |
| 39 | 15 36 | 20 10 | 17 02 | 11 09 | 04 54 |
| 40 | 16 19 | 20 56 | 17 38 | 11 35 | 05 07 |
| 41 | 17 04 | 21 43 | 18 15 | 12 01 | 05 21 |
| 42 | 17 52 | 22 32 | 18 54 | 12 27 | 05 34 |
| 43 | 18 43 | 23 23 | 19 33 | 12 54 | 05 48 |
| 44 | 19 37 | 24 15 | 20 13 | 13 22 | 06 02 |
| 45 | 20 34 | 25 10 | 20 54 | 13 50 | 06 17 |
| 46 | 21 35 | 26 06 | 21 36 | 14 18 | 06 31 |
| 47 | 22 40 | 27 05 | 22 20 | 14 47 | 06 46 |
| 48 | 23 50 | 28 06 | 23 04 | 15 16 | 07 01 |
| 49 | 25 04 | 29 10 | 23 50 | 15 47 | 07 16 |
| 50 | 26 24 | 00♋16 | 24 37 | 16 18 | 07 32 |
| 51 | 27 50 | 01 25 | 25 26 | 16 49 | 07 48 |
| 52 | 29 23 | 02 37 | 26 16 | 17 22 | 08 04 |
| 53 | 01♊03 | 03 52 | 27 07 | 17 55 | 08 20 |
| 54 | 02 51 | 05 11 | 28 00 | 18 29 | 08 37 |
| 55 | 04 49 | 06 33 | 28 55 | 19 03 | 08 54 |
| 56 | 06 56 | 07 58 | 29 51 | 19 39 | 09 12 |
| 57 | 09 15 | 09 28 | 00♌50 | 20 16 | 09 30 |
| 58 | 11 46 | 11 01 | 01 50 | 20 53 | 09 49 |
| 59 | 14 30 | 12 39 | 02 52 | 21 32 | 10 08 |
| 60 | 17♊29 | 14♋22 | 03♌57 | 22♌12 | 10♍27 |

# Placidus Table of Houses for Latitudes 0° to 60° North

| 0h 0m 0s | 0° 0' 0" | 00 ♈ 00 | | | |
|---|---|---|---|---|---|
| LAT. | 11 | 12 | ASC | 2 | 3 |
| 0 | 02♉11 | 02♊05 | 00♋00 | 27♋55 | 27♌49 |
| 5 | 02 34 | 03 18 | 02 00 | 29 06 | 28 11 |
| 10 | 02 58 | 04 34 | 04 01 | 00♌16 | 28 34 |
| 15 | 03 23 | 05 53 | 06 05 | 01 28 | 28 56 |
| 20 | 03 49 | 07 19 | 08 14 | 02 40 | 29 19 |
| 21 | 03 55 | 07 37 | 08 41 | 02 55 | 29 24 |
| 22 | 04 01 | 07 55 | 09 08 | 03 10 | 29 29 |
| 23 | 04 07 | 08 14 | 09 35 | 03 25 | 29 34 |
| 24 | 04 13 | 08 33 | 10 03 | 03 41 | 29 38 |
| 25 | 04 19 | 08 52 | 10 31 | 03 56 | 29 43 |
| 26 | 04 25 | 09 12 | 10 59 | 04 12 | 29 48 |
| 27 | 04 32 | 09 33 | 11 28 | 04 27 | 29 53 |
| 28 | 04 38 | 09 53 | 11 57 | 04 43 | 29 59 |
| 29 | 04 45 | 10 15 | 12 26 | 05 00 | 00♍04 |
| 30 | 04 52 | 10 37 | 12 56 | 05 16 | 00 09 |
| 31 | 04 59 | 10 59 | 13 27 | 05 33 | 00 14 |
| 32 | 05 06 | 11 22 | 13 58 | 05 50 | 00 20 |
| 33 | 05 14 | 11 46 | 14 29 | 06 07 | 00 25 |
| 34 | 05 21 | 12 10 | 15 01 | 06 24 | 00 31 |
| 35 | 05 29 | 12 36 | 15 34 | 06 42 | 00 37 |
| 36 | 05 38 | 13 02 | 16 07 | 07 00 | 00 42 |
| 37 | 05 46 | 13 28 | 16 41 | 07 18 | 00 48 |
| 38 | 05 55 | 13 56 | 17 16 | 07 37 | 00 54 |
| 39 | 06 04 | 14 25 | 17 52 | 07 56 | 01 00 |
| 40 | 06 13 | 14 55 | 18 28 | 08 15 | 01 07 |
| 41 | 06 23 | 15 26 | 19 05 | 08 35 | 01 13 |
| 42 | 06 34 | 15 58 | 19 43 | 08 56 | 01 20 |
| 43 | 06 44 | 16 31 | 20 21 | 09 17 | 01 27 |
| 44 | 06 55 | 17 06 | 21 01 | 09 38 | 01 34 |
| 45 | 07 07 | 17 42 | 21 42 | 10 00 | 01 41 |
| 46 | 07 19 | 18 20 | 22 24 | 10 22 | 01 48 |
| 47 | 07 32 | 19 00 | 23 06 | 10 45 | 01 56 |
| 48 | 07 46 | 19 42 | 23 50 | 11 09 | 02 04 |
| 49 | 08 00 | 20 26 | 24 36 | 11 33 | 02 12 |
| 50 | 08 15 | 21 12 | 25 22 | 11 58 | 02 20 |
| 51 | 08 31 | 22 01 | 26 10 | 12 24 | 02 29 |
| 52 | 08 48 | 22 53 | 26 59 | 12 51 | 02 38 |
| 53 | 09 06 | 23 47 | 27 50 | 13 19 | 02 47 |
| 54 | 09 25 | 24 46 | 28 42 | 13 47 | 02 57 |
| 55 | 09 46 | 25 48 | 29 36 | 14 17 | 03 07 |
| 56 | 10 08 | 26 54 | 00♌32 | 14 47 | 03 17 |
| 57 | 10 32 | 28 05 | 01 30 | 15 19 | 03 28 |
| 58 | 10 58 | 29 21 | 02 29 | 15 52 | 03 39 |
| 59 | 11 26 | 00♋44 | 03 31 | 16 26 | 03 51 |
| 60 | 11♉58 | 02♋13 | 04♌34 | 17♌01 | 04♍03 |

| 0h 4m 0s | 1° 0' 0" | 01 ♈ 05 | | | |
|---|---|---|---|---|---|
| LAT. | 11 | 12 | ASC | 2 | 3 |
| 0 | 03♉13 | 03♊03 | 00♋55 | 28♋52 | 28♌52 |
| 5 | 03 37 | 04 16 | 02 55 | 00♌03 | 29 13 |
| 10 | 04 01 | 05 32 | 04 56 | 01 13 | 29 35 |
| 15 | 04 27 | 06 52 | 07 00 | 02 23 | 29 57 |
| 20 | 04 54 | 08 18 | 09 08 | 03 35 | 00♍19 |
| 21 | 05 00 | 08 36 | 09 35 | 03 50 | 00 24 |
| 22 | 05 06 | 08 54 | 10 02 | 04 05 | 00 29 |
| 23 | 05 12 | 09 13 | 10 29 | 04 20 | 00 33 |
| 24 | 05 18 | 09 32 | 10 56 | 04 35 | 00 38 |
| 25 | 05 25 | 09 52 | 11 24 | 04 50 | 00 43 |
| 26 | 05 31 | 10 12 | 11 52 | 05 05 | 00 48 |
| 27 | 05 38 | 10 32 | 12 20 | 05 21 | 00 52 |
| 28 | 05 44 | 10 53 | 12 49 | 05 37 | 00 57 |
| 29 | 05 51 | 11 14 | 13 19 | 05 53 | 01 02 |
| 30 | 05 58 | 11 36 | 13 48 | 06 09 | 01 07 |
| 31 | 06 06 | 11 59 | 14 19 | 06 25 | 01 13 |
| 32 | 06 13 | 12 22 | 14 49 | 06 42 | 01 18 |
| 33 | 06 21 | 12 46 | 15 21 | 06 59 | 01 23 |
| 34 | 06 29 | 13 10 | 15 53 | 07 16 | 01 29 |
| 35 | 06 37 | 13 35 | 16 25 | 07 34 | 01 34 |
| 36 | 06 45 | 14 01 | 16 58 | 07 52 | 01 40 |
| 37 | 06 54 | 14 28 | 17 32 | 08 10 | 01 46 |
| 38 | 07 03 | 14 56 | 18 06 | 08 28 | 01 51 |
| 39 | 07 12 | 15 25 | 18 41 | 08 47 | 01 57 |
| 40 | 07 22 | 15 55 | 19 17 | 09 06 | 02 04 |
| 41 | 07 32 | 16 26 | 19 54 | 09 26 | 02 10 |
| 42 | 07 43 | 16 58 | 20 31 | 09 46 | 02 16 |
| 43 | 07 54 | 17 31 | 21 10 | 10 06 | 02 23 |
| 44 | 08 05 | 18 06 | 21 49 | 10 27 | 02 30 |
| 45 | 08 17 | 18 42 | 22 29 | 10 49 | 02 37 |
| 46 | 08 30 | 19 20 | 23 11 | 11 11 | 02 44 |
| 47 | 08 43 | 20 00 | 23 53 | 11 34 | 02 51 |
| 48 | 08 57 | 20 41 | 24 36 | 11 57 | 02 59 |
| 49 | 09 11 | 21 25 | 25 21 | 12 21 | 03 07 |
| 50 | 09 27 | 22 11 | 26 07 | 12 46 | 03 15 |
| 51 | 09 43 | 23 00 | 26 54 | 13 11 | 03 23 |
| 52 | 10 01 | 23 51 | 27 43 | 13 38 | 03 32 |
| 53 | 10 19 | 24 46 | 28 33 | 14 05 | 03 41 |
| 54 | 10 39 | 25 43 | 29 25 | 14 33 | 03 50 |
| 55 | 11 00 | 26 45 | 00♌18 | 15 02 | 04 00 |
| 56 | 11 23 | 27 51 | 01 13 | 15 32 | 04 10 |
| 57 | 11 47 | 29 01 | 02 10 | 16 03 | 04 20 |
| 58 | 12 14 | 00♋17 | 03 08 | 16 35 | 04 31 |
| 59 | 12 43 | 01 38 | 04 09 | 17 09 | 04 42 |
| 60 | 13♉15 | 03♋06 | 05♌12 | 17♌44 | 04♍54 |

| 0h 8m 0s | 2° 0' 0" | 02 ♈ 11 | | | |
|---|---|---|---|---|---|
| LAT. | 11 | 12 | ASC | 2 | 3 |
| 0 | 04♉16 | 04♊00 | 01♋50 | 29♋49 | 29♌54 |
| 5 | 04 40 | 05 14 | 03 50 | 00♌59 | 00♍15 |
| 10 | 05 05 | 06 30 | 05 50 | 02 09 | 00 36 |
| 15 | 05 31 | 07 51 | 07 54 | 03 19 | 00 58 |
| 20 | 05 59 | 09 17 | 10 02 | 04 30 | 01 19 |
| 21 | 06 05 | 09 35 | 10 28 | 04 45 | 01 24 |
| 22 | 06 11 | 09 53 | 10 55 | 04 59 | 01 28 |
| 23 | 06 17 | 10 12 | 11 22 | 05 14 | 01 33 |
| 24 | 06 24 | 10 31 | 11 49 | 05 29 | 01 37 |
| 25 | 06 30 | 10 51 | 12 17 | 05 44 | 01 42 |
| 26 | 06 37 | 11 11 | 12 45 | 05 59 | 01 47 |
| 27 | 06 43 | 11 31 | 13 13 | 06 15 | 01 52 |
| 28 | 06 50 | 11 52 | 13 42 | 06 30 | 01 56 |
| 29 | 06 57 | 12 14 | 14 11 | 06 46 | 02 01 |
| 30 | 07 05 | 12 36 | 14 41 | 07 02 | 02 06 |
| 31 | 07 12 | 12 58 | 15 11 | 07 18 | 02 11 |
| 32 | 07 20 | 13 22 | 15 41 | 07 35 | 02 16 |
| 33 | 07 28 | 13 45 | 16 12 | 07 51 | 02 21 |
| 34 | 07 36 | 14 10 | 16 44 | 08 08 | 02 27 |
| 35 | 07 44 | 14 35 | 17 16 | 08 26 | 02 32 |
| 36 | 07 53 | 15 01 | 17 49 | 08 43 | 02 38 |
| 37 | 08 02 | 15 28 | 18 22 | 09 01 | 02 43 |
| 38 | 08 11 | 15 56 | 18 56 | 09 19 | 02 49 |
| 39 | 08 21 | 16 24 | 19 31 | 09 38 | 02 55 |
| 40 | 08 31 | 16 54 | 20 06 | 09 57 | 03 01 |
| 41 | 08 41 | 17 25 | 20 43 | 10 16 | 03 07 |
| 42 | 08 52 | 17 57 | 21 20 | 10 36 | 03 13 |
| 43 | 09 03 | 18 30 | 21 58 | 10 56 | 03 19 |
| 44 | 09 15 | 19 05 | 22 37 | 11 17 | 03 26 |
| 45 | 09 27 | 19 41 | 23 17 | 11 38 | 03 32 |
| 46 | 09 40 | 20 19 | 23 57 | 12 00 | 03 39 |
| 47 | 09 53 | 20 59 | 24 39 | 12 22 | 03 47 |
| 48 | 10 07 | 21 40 | 25 22 | 12 45 | 03 54 |
| 49 | 10 22 | 22 24 | 26 06 | 13 09 | 04 01 |
| 50 | 10 38 | 23 10 | 26 52 | 13 33 | 04 09 |
| 51 | 10 55 | 23 58 | 27 38 | 13 58 | 04 17 |
| 52 | 11 13 | 24 49 | 28 26 | 14 24 | 04 26 |
| 53 | 11 32 | 25 43 | 29 16 | 14 51 | 04 34 |
| 54 | 11 52 | 26 40 | 00♌07 | 15 18 | 04 43 |
| 55 | 12 14 | 27 42 | 00 59 | 15 47 | 04 53 |
| 56 | 12 37 | 28 47 | 01 54 | 16 16 | 05 02 |
| 57 | 13 02 | 29 56 | 02 50 | 16 47 | 05 12 |
| 58 | 13 30 | 01♋11 | 03 47 | 17 19 | 05 23 |
| 59 | 13 59 | 02 32 | 04 47 | 17 52 | 05 34 |
| 60 | 14♉32 | 03♋59 | 05♌49 | 18♌26 | 05♍46 |

| 0h 12m 0s | 3° 0' 0" | 03 ♈ 16 | | | |
|---|---|---|---|---|---|
| LAT. | 11 | 12 | ASC | 2 | 3 |
| 0 | 05♉18 | 04♊57 | 02♋45 | 00♌47 | 00♍57 |
| 5 | 05 42 | 06 11 | 04 44 | 01 57 | 01 18 |
| 10 | 06 08 | 07 28 | 06 45 | 03 05 | 01 38 |
| 15 | 06 35 | 08 49 | 08 48 | 04 14 | 01 59 |
| 20 | 07 04 | 10 15 | 10 56 | 05 25 | 02 20 |
| 21 | 07 10 | 10 34 | 11 22 | 05 39 | 02 24 |
| 22 | 07 16 | 10 52 | 11 48 | 05 54 | 02 28 |
| 23 | 07 22 | 11 11 | 12 15 | 06 08 | 02 33 |
| 24 | 07 29 | 11 30 | 12 42 | 06 23 | 02 37 |
| 25 | 07 35 | 11 50 | 13 10 | 06 38 | 02 42 |
| 26 | 07 42 | 12 10 | 13 38 | 06 53 | 02 46 |
| 27 | 07 49 | 12 30 | 14 06 | 07 08 | 02 51 |
| 28 | 07 56 | 12 51 | 14 34 | 07 24 | 02 55 |
| 29 | 08 03 | 13 13 | 15 03 | 07 39 | 03 00 |
| 30 | 08 11 | 13 35 | 15 33 | 07 55 | 03 05 |
| 31 | 08 18 | 13 58 | 16 02 | 08 11 | 03 10 |
| 32 | 08 26 | 14 21 | 16 33 | 08 27 | 03 15 |
| 33 | 08 34 | 14 45 | 17 03 | 08 44 | 03 20 |
| 34 | 08 43 | 15 09 | 17 35 | 09 01 | 03 25 |
| 35 | 08 51 | 15 34 | 18 07 | 09 18 | 03 30 |
| 36 | 09 00 | 16 00 | 18 39 | 09 35 | 03 35 |
| 37 | 09 09 | 16 27 | 19 12 | 09 53 | 03 41 |
| 38 | 09 19 | 16 55 | 19 46 | 10 11 | 03 46 |
| 39 | 09 28 | 17 24 | 20 20 | 10 29 | 03 52 |
| 40 | 09 39 | 17 53 | 20 56 | 10 48 | 03 57 |
| 41 | 09 49 | 18 24 | 21 32 | 11 07 | 04 03 |
| 42 | 10 00 | 18 56 | 22 08 | 11 26 | 04 09 |
| 43 | 10 12 | 19 29 | 22 46 | 11 46 | 04 16 |
| 44 | 10 24 | 20 04 | 23 24 | 12 07 | 04 22 |
| 45 | 10 36 | 20 40 | 24 04 | 12 27 | 04 28 |
| 46 | 10 49 | 21 18 | 24 44 | 12 49 | 04 35 |
| 47 | 11 03 | 21 57 | 25 25 | 13 11 | 04 42 |
| 48 | 11 18 | 22 39 | 26 08 | 13 33 | 04 49 |
| 49 | 11 33 | 23 22 | 26 52 | 13 57 | 04 56 |
| 50 | 11 49 | 24 08 | 27 36 | 14 21 | 05 04 |
| 51 | 12 06 | 24 56 | 28 22 | 14 45 | 05 12 |
| 52 | 12 25 | 25 46 | 29 10 | 15 11 | 05 20 |
| 53 | 12 44 | 26 40 | 29 59 | 15 37 | 05 28 |
| 54 | 13 05 | 27 37 | 00♌49 | 16 04 | 05 37 |
| 55 | 13 27 | 28 38 | 01 41 | 16 32 | 05 46 |
| 56 | 13 51 | 29 42 | 02 34 | 17 01 | 05 55 |
| 57 | 14 16 | 00♋51 | 03 29 | 17 31 | 06 05 |
| 58 | 14 45 | 02 05 | 04 26 | 18 02 | 06 15 |
| 59 | 15 15 | 03 25 | 05 25 | 18 34 | 06 26 |
| 60 | 15♉49 | 04♋51 | 06♌26 | 19♌08 | 06♍37 |

| 0h 16m 0s | 4° 0' 0" | 04 ♈ 22 | | | |
|---|---|---|---|---|---|
| LAT. | 11 | 12 | ASC | 2 | 3 |
| 0 | 06♉19 | 05♊54 | 03♋40 | 01♌45 | 02♍00 |
| 5 | 06 45 | 07 08 | 05 39 | 02 54 | 02 20 |
| 10 | 07 11 | 08 26 | 07 40 | 04 02 | 02 40 |
| 15 | 07 39 | 09 47 | 09 42 | 05 10 | 03 00 |
| 20 | 08 08 | 11 14 | 11 49 | 06 20 | 03 20 |
| 21 | 08 14 | 11 32 | 12 15 | 06 34 | 03 24 |
| 22 | 08 21 | 11 51 | 12 42 | 06 48 | 03 28 |
| 23 | 08 27 | 12 10 | 13 08 | 07 03 | 03 33 |
| 24 | 08 34 | 12 29 | 13 35 | 07 17 | 03 37 |
| 25 | 08 40 | 12 49 | 14 03 | 07 32 | 03 41 |
| 26 | 08 47 | 13 09 | 14 30 | 07 47 | 03 46 |
| 27 | 08 54 | 13 29 | 14 58 | 08 02 | 03 50 |
| 28 | 09 02 | 13 50 | 15 26 | 08 17 | 03 55 |
| 29 | 09 09 | 14 12 | 15 55 | 08 33 | 03 59 |
| 30 | 09 17 | 14 34 | 16 24 | 08 48 | 04 04 |
| 31 | 09 24 | 14 56 | 16 54 | 09 04 | 04 08 |
| 32 | 09 32 | 15 20 | 17 24 | 09 20 | 04 13 |
| 33 | 09 41 | 15 43 | 17 55 | 09 36 | 04 18 |
| 34 | 09 49 | 16 08 | 18 26 | 09 53 | 04 23 |
| 35 | 09 58 | 16 33 | 18 57 | 10 10 | 04 28 |
| 36 | 10 07 | 16 59 | 19 29 | 10 27 | 04 33 |
| 37 | 10 16 | 17 26 | 20 02 | 10 44 | 04 38 |
| 38 | 10 26 | 17 54 | 20 36 | 11 02 | 04 44 |
| 39 | 10 36 | 18 22 | 21 10 | 11 20 | 04 49 |
| 40 | 10 46 | 18 52 | 21 45 | 11 38 | 04 55 |
| 41 | 10 57 | 19 23 | 22 20 | 11 57 | 05 00 |
| 42 | 11 08 | 19 55 | 22 57 | 12 16 | 05 06 |
| 43 | 11 20 | 20 28 | 23 34 | 12 36 | 05 12 |
| 44 | 11 32 | 21 03 | 24 12 | 12 56 | 05 18 |
| 45 | 11 45 | 21 39 | 24 51 | 13 17 | 05 24 |
| 46 | 11 59 | 22 16 | 25 31 | 13 38 | 05 31 |
| 47 | 12 13 | 22 56 | 26 11 | 13 59 | 05 37 |
| 48 | 12 28 | 23 37 | 26 53 | 14 22 | 05 44 |
| 49 | 12 43 | 24 20 | 27 37 | 14 44 | 05 51 |
| 50 | 13 00 | 25 05 | 28 21 | 15 08 | 05 59 |
| 51 | 13 17 | 25 53 | 29 06 | 15 32 | 06 06 |
| 52 | 13 36 | 26 43 | 29 53 | 15 57 | 06 14 |
| 53 | 13 56 | 27 37 | 00♌41 | 16 23 | 06 22 |
| 54 | 14 17 | 28 33 | 01 31 | 16 49 | 06 30 |
| 55 | 14 39 | 29 33 | 02 22 | 17 17 | 06 39 |
| 56 | 15 04 | 00♋37 | 03 15 | 17 45 | 06 48 |
| 57 | 15 30 | 01 45 | 04 09 | 18 15 | 06 57 |
| 58 | 15 59 | 02 58 | 05 05 | 18 46 | 07 07 |
| 59 | 16 30 | 04 17 | 06 03 | 19 17 | 07 18 |
| 60 | 17♉05 | 05♋42 | 07♌03 | 19♌50 | 07♍28 |

| 0h 20m 0s | 5° 0' 0" | 05 ♈ 27 | | | |
|---|---|---|---|---|---|
| LAT. | 11 | 12 | ASC | 2 | 3 |
| 0 | 07♉21 | 06♊50 | 04♋35 | 02♌43 | 03♍03 |
| 5 | 07 47 | 08 05 | 06 34 | 03 51 | 03 23 |
| 10 | 08 14 | 09 23 | 08 34 | 04 58 | 03 42 |
| 15 | 08 42 | 10 45 | 10 36 | 06 06 | 04 01 |
| 20 | 09 12 | 12 12 | 12 43 | 07 15 | 04 21 |
| 21 | 09 19 | 12 30 | 13 09 | 07 29 | 04 25 |
| 22 | 09 25 | 12 49 | 13 35 | 07 43 | 04 29 |
| 23 | 09 32 | 13 08 | 14 02 | 07 57 | 04 33 |
| 24 | 09 38 | 13 27 | 14 28 | 08 12 | 04 37 |
| 25 | 09 45 | 13 47 | 14 55 | 08 26 | 04 41 |
| 26 | 09 52 | 14 07 | 15 23 | 08 41 | 04 45 |
| 27 | 10 00 | 14 28 | 15 51 | 08 56 | 04 50 |
| 28 | 10 07 | 14 49 | 16 19 | 09 11 | 04 54 |
| 29 | 10 14 | 15 10 | 16 47 | 09 26 | 04 58 |
| 30 | 10 22 | 15 32 | 17 16 | 09 41 | 05 03 |
| 31 | 10 30 | 15 55 | 17 45 | 09 57 | 05 07 |
| 32 | 10 38 | 16 18 | 18 15 | 10 13 | 05 12 |
| 33 | 10 47 | 16 42 | 18 46 | 10 29 | 05 16 |
| 34 | 10 55 | 17 07 | 19 16 | 10 45 | 05 21 |
| 35 | 11 04 | 17 32 | 19 48 | 11 02 | 05 26 |
| 36 | 11 14 | 17 58 | 20 20 | 11 19 | 05 31 |
| 37 | 11 23 | 18 25 | 20 52 | 11 36 | 05 36 |
| 38 | 11 33 | 18 52 | 21 25 | 11 53 | 05 41 |
| 39 | 11 43 | 19 21 | 21 59 | 12 11 | 05 46 |
| 40 | 11 54 | 19 51 | 22 33 | 12 29 | 05 52 |
| 41 | 12 05 | 20 21 | 23 09 | 12 48 | 05 57 |
| 42 | 12 16 | 20 53 | 23 45 | 13 06 | 06 03 |
| 43 | 12 28 | 21 26 | 24 21 | 13 26 | 06 09 |
| 44 | 12 41 | 22 01 | 24 59 | 13 46 | 06 14 |
| 45 | 12 54 | 22 37 | 25 38 | 14 06 | 06 20 |
| 46 | 13 08 | 23 14 | 26 17 | 14 27 | 06 27 |
| 47 | 13 22 | 23 53 | 26 57 | 14 48 | 06 33 |
| 48 | 13 37 | 24 34 | 27 39 | 15 10 | 06 40 |
| 49 | 13 53 | 25 17 | 28 21 | 15 32 | 06 46 |
| 50 | 14 10 | 26 02 | 29 05 | 15 55 | 06 53 |
| 51 | 14 28 | 26 50 | 29 50 | 16 19 | 07 01 |
| 52 | 14 47 | 27 40 | 00♌36 | 16 44 | 07 08 |
| 53 | 15 07 | 28 33 | 01 24 | 17 09 | 07 16 |
| 54 | 15 29 | 29 29 | 02 13 | 17 35 | 07 24 |
| 55 | 15 52 | 00♋28 | 03 03 | 18 02 | 07 32 |
| 56 | 16 17 | 01 32 | 03 55 | 18 30 | 07 41 |
| 57 | 16 44 | 02 39 | 04 49 | 18 59 | 07 50 |
| 58 | 17 13 | 03 51 | 05 44 | 19 29 | 08 00 |
| 59 | 17 45 | 05 09 | 06 41 | 20 00 | 08 09 |
| 60 | 18♉20 | 06♋33 | 07♌40 | 20♌33 | 08♍20 |

| 0h 24m 0s | 6° 0' 0" | 06 ♈ 32 | | | |
|---|---|---|---|---|---|
| LAT. | 11 | 12 | ASC | 2 | 3 |
| 0 | 08♉23 | 07♊47 | 05♋30 | 03♌41 | 04♍07 |
| 5 | 08 49 | 09 02 | 07 29 | 04 49 | 04 25 |
| 10 | 09 16 | 10 20 | 09 29 | 05 55 | 04 44 |
| 15 | 09 45 | 11 42 | 11 31 | 07 02 | 05 02 |
| 20 | 10 16 | 13 10 | 13 36 | 08 10 | 05 21 |
| 21 | 10 23 | 13 28 | 14 02 | 08 24 | 05 25 |
| 22 | 10 29 | 13 47 | 14 28 | 08 38 | 05 29 |
| 23 | 10 36 | 14 06 | 14 55 | 08 52 | 05 33 |
| 24 | 10 43 | 14 25 | 15 21 | 09 06 | 05 37 |
| 25 | 10 50 | 14 45 | 15 48 | 09 21 | 05 41 |
| 26 | 10 57 | 15 05 | 16 15 | 09 35 | 05 45 |
| 27 | 11 04 | 15 26 | 16 43 | 09 50 | 05 49 |
| 28 | 11 12 | 15 47 | 17 11 | 10 05 | 05 53 |
| 29 | 11 20 | 16 09 | 17 39 | 10 20 | 05 57 |
| 30 | 11 27 | 16 31 | 18 08 | 10 35 | 06 02 |
| 31 | 11 36 | 16 53 | 18 37 | 10 50 | 06 06 |
| 32 | 11 44 | 17 16 | 19 06 | 11 06 | 06 11 |
| 33 | 11 52 | 17 40 | 19 36 | 11 21 | 06 15 |
| 34 | 12 01 | 18 05 | 20 07 | 11 38 | 06 20 |
| 35 | 12 10 | 18 30 | 20 38 | 11 54 | 06 24 |
| 36 | 12 20 | 18 56 | 21 10 | 12 10 | 06 29 |
| 37 | 12 30 | 19 23 | 21 42 | 12 27 | 06 34 |
| 38 | 12 40 | 19 51 | 22 15 | 12 44 | 06 39 |
| 39 | 12 50 | 20 19 | 22 48 | 13 02 | 06 44 |
| 40 | 13 01 | 20 49 | 23 22 | 13 20 | 06 49 |
| 41 | 13 12 | 21 19 | 23 57 | 13 38 | 06 54 |
| 42 | 13 24 | 21 51 | 24 33 | 13 57 | 07 00 |
| 43 | 13 36 | 22 24 | 25 09 | 14 16 | 07 05 |
| 44 | 13 49 | 22 58 | 25 46 | 14 35 | 07 11 |
| 45 | 14 02 | 23 34 | 26 24 | 14 55 | 07 17 |
| 46 | 14 16 | 24 12 | 27 03 | 15 16 | 07 23 |
| 47 | 14 31 | 24 50 | 27 43 | 15 36 | 07 29 |
| 48 | 14 46 | 25 31 | 28 24 | 15 58 | 07 35 |
| 49 | 15 02 | 26 14 | 29 06 | 16 20 | 07 42 |
| 50 | 15 20 | 26 59 | 29 49 | 16 43 | 07 48 |
| 51 | 15 38 | 27 46 | 00♌34 | 17 06 | 07 55 |
| 52 | 15 57 | 28 36 | 01 19 | 17 30 | 08 03 |
| 53 | 16 18 | 29 28 | 02 06 | 17 55 | 08 10 |
| 54 | 16 40 | 00♋24 | 02 54 | 18 21 | 08 18 |
| 55 | 17 03 | 01 23 | 03 44 | 18 47 | 08 26 |
| 56 | 17 29 | 02 25 | 04 35 | 19 15 | 08 34 |
| 57 | 17 56 | 03 32 | 05 28 | 19 43 | 08 43 |
| 58 | 18 26 | 04 44 | 06 23 | 20 13 | 08 52 |
| 59 | 18 59 | 06 00 | 07 19 | 20 43 | 09 01 |
| 60 | 19♉35 | 07♋23 | 08♌17 | 21♌15 | 09♍11 |

| 0h 28m 0s | 7° 0' 0" | 07 ♈ 37 | | | |
|---|---|---|---|---|---|
| LAT. | 11 | 12 | ASC | 2 | 3 |
| 0 | 09♉24 | 08♊43 | 06♋26 | 04♌39 | 05♍10 |
| 5 | 09 51 | 09 59 | 08 24 | 05 46 | 05 28 |
| 10 | 10 19 | 11 18 | 10 23 | 06 52 | 05 46 |
| 15 | 10 48 | 12 40 | 12 25 | 07 58 | 06 04 |
| 20 | 11 20 | 14 08 | 14 30 | 09 05 | 06 22 |
| 21 | 11 26 | 14 26 | 14 55 | 09 19 | 06 26 |
| 22 | 11 33 | 14 45 | 15 21 | 09 33 | 06 29 |
| 23 | 11 40 | 15 04 | 15 47 | 09 47 | 06 33 |
| 24 | 11 47 | 15 23 | 16 14 | 10 01 | 06 37 |
| 25 | 11 54 | 15 43 | 16 41 | 10 15 | 06 41 |
| 26 | 12 01 | 16 03 | 17 08 | 10 29 | 06 45 |
| 27 | 12 09 | 16 24 | 17 35 | 10 44 | 06 49 |
| 28 | 12 17 | 16 45 | 18 03 | 10 58 | 06 53 |
| 29 | 12 24 | 17 07 | 18 31 | 11 13 | 06 57 |
| 30 | 12 32 | 17 29 | 18 59 | 11 28 | 07 01 |
| 31 | 12 41 | 17 51 | 19 28 | 11 43 | 07 05 |
| 32 | 12 49 | 18 14 | 19 57 | 11 58 | 07 09 |
| 33 | 12 58 | 18 38 | 20 27 | 12 14 | 07 14 |
| 34 | 13 07 | 19 03 | 20 58 | 12 30 | 07 18 |
| 35 | 13 16 | 19 28 | 21 28 | 12 46 | 07 23 |
| 36 | 13 26 | 19 54 | 22 00 | 13 02 | 07 27 |
| 37 | 13 36 | 20 21 | 22 31 | 13 19 | 07 32 |
| 38 | 13 46 | 20 48 | 23 04 | 13 36 | 07 36 |
| 39 | 13 57 | 21 17 | 23 37 | 13 53 | 07 41 |
| 40 | 14 08 | 21 46 | 24 11 | 14 11 | 07 46 |
| 41 | 14 19 | 22 17 | 24 45 | 14 29 | 07 51 |
| 42 | 14 31 | 22 49 | 25 21 | 14 47 | 07 56 |
| 43 | 14 44 | 23 22 | 25 56 | 15 06 | 08 02 |
| 44 | 14 56 | 23 56 | 26 33 | 15 25 | 08 07 |
| 45 | 15 10 | 24 31 | 27 11 | 15 44 | 08 13 |
| 46 | 15 24 | 25 09 | 27 49 | 16 04 | 08 19 |
| 47 | 15 39 | 25 47 | 28 29 | 16 25 | 08 24 |
| 48 | 15 55 | 26 28 | 29 09 | 16 46 | 08 31 |
| 49 | 16 12 | 27 10 | 29 51 | 17 08 | 08 37 |
| 50 | 16 29 | 27 55 | 00♌33 | 17 30 | 08 43 |
| 51 | 16 48 | 28 42 | 01 17 | 17 53 | 08 50 |
| 52 | 17 07 | 29 31 | 02 02 | 18 17 | 08 57 |
| 53 | 17 28 | 00♋23 | 02 48 | 18 41 | 09 04 |
| 54 | 17 51 | 01 18 | 03 36 | 19 06 | 09 11 |
| 55 | 18 15 | 02 17 | 04 25 | 19 32 | 09 19 |
| 56 | 18 41 | 03 19 | 05 16 | 19 59 | 09 27 |
| 57 | 19 09 | 04 25 | 06 08 | 20 27 | 09 35 |
| 58 | 19 39 | 05 36 | 07 01 | 20 56 | 09 44 |
| 59 | 20 13 | 06 51 | 07 57 | 21 26 | 09 53 |
| 60 | 20♉50 | 08♋13 | 08♌54 | 21♌57 | 10♍03 |

# Placidus Table of Houses for Latitudes 0° to 60° North

**0h 32m 0s — 8° 0' 0" — 08 ♈ 43**

| LAT. | 11 | 12 | ASC | 2 | 3 |
|---|---|---|---|---|---|
| 0 | 10♉25 | 09♊40 | 07♋21 | 05♌38 | 06♍14 |
| 5 | 10 53 | 10 56 | 09 19 | 06 44 | 06 31 |
| 10 | 11 21 | 12 15 | 11 18 | 07 49 | 06 48 |
| 15 | 11 51 | 13 37 | 13 19 | 08 54 | 07 05 |
| 20 | 12 23 | 15 05 | 15 23 | 10 01 | 07 23 |
| 21 | 12 30 | 15 24 | 15 49 | 10 14 | 07 26 |
| 22 | 12 37 | 15 42 | 16 14 | 10 28 | 07 30 |
| 23 | 12 44 | 16 01 | 16 40 | 10 42 | 07 33 |
| 24 | 12 51 | 16 21 | 17 07 | 10 55 | 07 37 |
| 25 | 12 58 | 16 41 | 17 33 | 11 09 | 07 41 |
| 26 | 13 06 | 17 01 | 18 00 | 11 23 | 07 45 |
| 27 | 13 13 | 17 22 | 18 27 | 11 38 | 07 48 |
| 28 | 13 21 | 17 43 | 18 55 | 11 52 | 07 52 |
| 29 | 13 29 | 18 04 | 19 22 | 12 07 | 07 56 |
| 30 | 13 37 | 18 26 | 19 51 | 12 21 | 08 00 |
| 31 | 13 46 | 18 49 | 20 19 | 12 36 | 08 04 |
| 32 | 13 54 | 19 12 | 20 48 | 12 51 | 08 08 |
| 33 | 14 03 | 19 36 | 21 18 | 13 07 | 08 12 |
| 34 | 14 12 | 20 01 | 21 48 | 13 22 | 08 17 |
| 35 | 14 22 | 20 26 | 22 18 | 13 38 | 08 21 |
| 36 | 14 32 | 20 52 | 22 49 | 13 54 | 08 25 |
| 37 | 14 42 | 21 18 | 23 21 | 14 11 | 08 30 |
| 38 | 14 52 | 21 46 | 23 53 | 14 27 | 08 34 |
| 39 | 15 03 | 22 14 | 24 26 | 14 44 | 08 39 |
| 40 | 15 14 | 22 44 | 24 59 | 15 01 | 08 44 |
| 41 | 15 26 | 23 14 | 25 33 | 15 19 | 08 48 |
| 42 | 15 38 | 23 46 | 26 08 | 15 37 | 08 53 |
| 43 | 15 51 | 24 19 | 26 44 | 15 56 | 08 59 |
| 44 | 16 04 | 24 53 | 27 20 | 16 14 | 09 04 |
| 45 | 16 18 | 25 28 | 27 57 | 16 34 | 09 09 |
| 46 | 16 32 | 26 05 | 28 35 | 16 53 | 09 15 |
| 47 | 16 47 | 26 44 | 29 14 | 17 14 | 09 20 |
| 48 | 17 03 | 27 24 | 29 54 | 17 34 | 09 26 |
| 49 | 17 20 | 28 06 | 00♌35 | 17 56 | 09 32 |
| 50 | 17 38 | 28 51 | 01 17 | 18 18 | 09 38 |
| 51 | 17 57 | 29 37 | 02 01 | 18 40 | 09 45 |
| 52 | 18 17 | 00♋26 | 02 45 | 19 03 | 09 51 |
| 53 | 18 38 | 01 18 | 03 31 | 19 27 | 09 58 |
| 54 | 19 01 | 02 13 | 04 18 | 19 52 | 10 05 |
| 55 | 19 26 | 03 10 | 05 06 | 20 18 | 10 13 |
| 56 | 19 52 | 04 12 | 05 56 | 20 44 | 10 20 |
| 57 | 20 21 | 05 17 | 06 47 | 21 11 | 10 28 |
| 58 | 20 52 | 06 27 | 07 40 | 21 40 | 10 37 |
| 59 | 21 26 | 07 42 | 08 35 | 22 09 | 10 45 |
| 60 | 22♉03 | 09♋02 | 09♌31 | 22♌40 | 10♍54 |

**0h 36m 0s — 9° 0' 0" — 09 ♈ 48**

| LAT. | 11 | 12 | ASC | 2 | 3 |
|---|---|---|---|---|---|
| 0 | 11♉26 | 10♊36 | 08♋16 | 06♌37 | 07♍18 |
| 5 | 11 54 | 11 53 | 10 14 | 07 42 | 07 34 |
| 10 | 12 23 | 13 12 | 12 12 | 08 46 | 07 50 |
| 15 | 12 54 | 14 34 | 14 13 | 09 51 | 08 07 |
| 20 | 13 26 | 16 03 | 16 16 | 10 56 | 08 24 |
| 21 | 13 33 | 16 21 | 16 42 | 11 09 | 08 27 |
| 22 | 13 40 | 16 40 | 17 07 | 11 23 | 08 30 |
| 23 | 13 47 | 16 59 | 17 33 | 11 36 | 08 34 |
| 24 | 13 54 | 17 18 | 17 59 | 11 50 | 08 37 |
| 25 | 14 02 | 17 38 | 18 26 | 12 04 | 08 41 |
| 26 | 14 09 | 17 58 | 18 52 | 12 18 | 08 45 |
| 27 | 14 17 | 18 19 | 19 19 | 12 32 | 08 48 |
| 28 | 14 25 | 18 40 | 19 46 | 12 46 | 08 52 |
| 29 | 14 33 | 19 02 | 20 14 | 13 00 | 08 56 |
| 30 | 14 42 | 19 24 | 20 42 | 13 15 | 08 59 |
| 31 | 14 50 | 19 46 | 21 10 | 13 29 | 09 03 |
| 32 | 14 59 | 20 10 | 21 39 | 13 44 | 09 07 |
| 33 | 15 08 | 20 33 | 22 09 | 13 59 | 09 11 |
| 34 | 15 17 | 20 58 | 22 38 | 14 15 | 09 15 |
| 35 | 15 27 | 21 23 | 23 08 | 14 30 | 09 19 |
| 36 | 15 37 | 21 49 | 23 39 | 14 46 | 09 24 |
| 37 | 15 47 | 22 16 | 24 10 | 15 02 | 09 28 |
| 38 | 15 58 | 22 43 | 24 42 | 15 19 | 09 32 |
| 39 | 16 09 | 23 12 | 25 15 | 15 35 | 09 37 |
| 40 | 16 20 | 23 41 | 25 48 | 15 52 | 09 41 |
| 41 | 16 32 | 24 11 | 26 21 | 16 10 | 09 46 |
| 42 | 16 44 | 24 43 | 26 56 | 16 27 | 09 50 |
| 43 | 16 57 | 25 16 | 27 31 | 16 45 | 09 55 |
| 44 | 17 11 | 25 49 | 28 07 | 17 04 | 10 00 |
| 45 | 17 25 | 26 25 | 28 44 | 17 23 | 10 05 |
| 46 | 17 39 | 27 02 | 29 21 | 17 42 | 10 11 |
| 47 | 17 55 | 27 40 | 00♌00 | 18 02 | 10 16 |
| 48 | 18 11 | 28 20 | 00 39 | 18 23 | 10 22 |
| 49 | 18 28 | 29 02 | 01 20 | 18 44 | 10 27 |
| 50 | 18 46 | 29 46 | 02 01 | 19 05 | 10 33 |
| 51 | 19 06 | 00♋32 | 02 44 | 19 27 | 10 39 |
| 52 | 19 26 | 01 21 | 03 28 | 19 50 | 10 46 |
| 53 | 19 48 | 02 12 | 04 13 | 20 13 | 10 52 |
| 54 | 20 11 | 03 06 | 04 59 | 20 38 | 10 59 |
| 55 | 20 36 | 04 04 | 05 47 | 21 03 | 11 06 |
| 56 | 21 03 | 05 04 | 06 36 | 21 29 | 11 14 |
| 57 | 21 32 | 06 09 | 07 26 | 21 55 | 11 21 |
| 58 | 22 04 | 07 18 | 08 18 | 22 23 | 11 29 |
| 59 | 22 38 | 08 32 | 09 12 | 22 52 | 11 37 |
| 60 | 23♉17 | 09♋51 | 10♌08 | 23♌22 | 11♍46 |

**0h 40m 0s — 10° 0' 0" — 10 ♈ 53**

| LAT. | 11 | 12 | ASC | 2 | 3 |
|---|---|---|---|---|---|
| 0 | 12♉27 | 11♊32 | 09♋11 | 07♌35 | 08♍22 |
| 5 | 12 55 | 12 49 | 11 09 | 08 40 | 08 37 |
| 10 | 13 25 | 14 08 | 13 07 | 09 43 | 08 53 |
| 15 | 13 56 | 15 31 | 15 07 | 10 47 | 09 09 |
| 20 | 14 29 | 17 00 | 17 10 | 11 52 | 09 25 |
| 21 | 14 36 | 17 18 | 17 35 | 12 05 | 09 28 |
| 22 | 14 43 | 17 37 | 18 00 | 12 18 | 09 31 |
| 23 | 14 50 | 17 56 | 18 26 | 12 31 | 09 34 |
| 24 | 14 58 | 18 16 | 18 52 | 12 45 | 09 38 |
| 25 | 15 05 | 18 35 | 19 18 | 12 58 | 09 41 |
| 26 | 15 13 | 18 56 | 19 44 | 13 12 | 09 45 |
| 27 | 15 21 | 19 16 | 20 11 | 13 26 | 09 48 |
| 28 | 15 29 | 19 37 | 20 38 | 13 40 | 09 52 |
| 29 | 15 37 | 19 59 | 21 06 | 13 54 | 09 55 |
| 30 | 15 46 | 20 21 | 21 33 | 14 08 | 09 59 |
| 31 | 15 55 | 20 44 | 22 01 | 14 23 | 10 03 |
| 32 | 16 03 | 21 07 | 22 30 | 14 37 | 10 06 |
| 33 | 16 13 | 21 31 | 22 59 | 14 52 | 10 10 |
| 34 | 16 22 | 21 55 | 23 28 | 15 07 | 10 14 |
| 35 | 16 32 | 22 20 | 23 58 | 15 23 | 10 18 |
| 36 | 16 42 | 22 46 | 24 29 | 15 38 | 10 22 |
| 37 | 16 52 | 23 13 | 25 00 | 15 54 | 10 26 |
| 38 | 17 03 | 23 40 | 25 31 | 16 10 | 10 30 |
| 39 | 17 14 | 24 08 | 26 03 | 16 27 | 10 34 |
| 40 | 17 26 | 24 38 | 26 36 | 16 43 | 10 39 |
| 41 | 17 38 | 25 08 | 27 09 | 17 00 | 10 43 |
| 42 | 17 51 | 25 39 | 27 43 | 17 18 | 10 48 |
| 43 | 18 04 | 26 12 | 28 18 | 17 35 | 10 52 |
| 44 | 18 17 | 26 46 | 28 54 | 17 54 | 10 57 |
| 45 | 18 32 | 27 21 | 29 30 | 18 12 | 11 02 |
| 46 | 18 47 | 27 58 | 00♌07 | 18 31 | 11 07 |
| 47 | 19 02 | 28 36 | 00 45 | 18 51 | 11 12 |
| 48 | 19 19 | 29 16 | 01 24 | 19 11 | 11 17 |
| 49 | 19 36 | 29 57 | 02 04 | 19 31 | 11 23 |
| 50 | 19 55 | 00♋41 | 02 45 | 19 52 | 11 29 |
| 51 | 20 14 | 01 27 | 03 27 | 20 14 | 11 34 |
| 52 | 20 35 | 02 15 | 04 10 | 20 37 | 11 40 |
| 53 | 20 57 | 03 06 | 04 55 | 21 00 | 11 47 |
| 54 | 21 20 | 04 00 | 05 40 | 21 23 | 11 53 |
| 55 | 21 46 | 04 56 | 06 27 | 21 48 | 12 00 |
| 56 | 22 13 | 05 56 | 07 16 | 22 13 | 12 07 |
| 57 | 22 43 | 07 00 | 08 06 | 22 40 | 12 14 |
| 58 | 23 15 | 08 09 | 08 57 | 23 07 | 12 22 |
| 59 | 23 50 | 09 21 | 09 50 | 23 35 | 12 29 |
| 60 | 24♉29 | 10♋39 | 10♌45 | 24♌04 | 12♍38 |

**0h 44m 0s — 11° 0' 0" — 11 ♈ 58**

| LAT. | 11 | 12 | ASC | 2 | 3 |
|---|---|---|---|---|---|
| 0 | 13♉27 | 12♊28 | 10♋07 | 08♌34 | 09♍26 |
| 5 | 13 56 | 13 45 | 12 04 | 09 38 | 09 41 |
| 10 | 14 26 | 15 05 | 14 02 | 10 41 | 09 55 |
| 15 | 14 58 | 16 28 | 16 01 | 11 44 | 10 10 |
| 20 | 15 32 | 17 57 | 18 03 | 12 47 | 10 26 |
| 21 | 15 39 | 18 15 | 18 28 | 13 00 | 10 29 |
| 22 | 15 46 | 18 34 | 18 53 | 13 13 | 10 32 |
| 23 | 15 53 | 18 53 | 19 19 | 13 26 | 10 35 |
| 24 | 16 01 | 19 13 | 19 44 | 13 40 | 10 38 |
| 25 | 16 09 | 19 32 | 20 10 | 13 53 | 10 42 |
| 26 | 16 16 | 19 53 | 20 36 | 14 06 | 10 45 |
| 27 | 16 24 | 20 13 | 21 03 | 14 20 | 10 48 |
| 28 | 16 33 | 20 34 | 21 30 | 14 34 | 10 52 |
| 29 | 16 41 | 20 56 | 21 57 | 14 48 | 10 55 |
| 30 | 16 50 | 21 18 | 22 25 | 15 02 | 10 58 |
| 31 | 16 59 | 21 41 | 22 52 | 15 16 | 11 02 |
| 32 | 17 08 | 22 04 | 23 21 | 15 30 | 11 05 |
| 33 | 17 17 | 22 28 | 23 49 | 15 45 | 11 09 |
| 34 | 17 27 | 22 52 | 24 19 | 16 00 | 11 13 |
| 35 | 17 37 | 23 17 | 24 48 | 16 15 | 11 16 |
| 36 | 17 47 | 23 43 | 25 18 | 16 30 | 11 20 |
| 37 | 17 57 | 24 09 | 25 49 | 16 46 | 11 24 |
| 38 | 18 08 | 24 37 | 26 20 | 17 02 | 11 28 |
| 39 | 18 20 | 25 05 | 26 52 | 17 18 | 11 32 |
| 40 | 18 31 | 25 34 | 27 24 | 17 34 | 11 36 |
| 41 | 18 44 | 26 04 | 27 57 | 17 51 | 11 40 |
| 42 | 18 56 | 26 36 | 28 31 | 18 08 | 11 45 |
| 43 | 19 10 | 27 08 | 29 05 | 18 25 | 11 49 |
| 44 | 19 24 | 27 42 | 29 40 | 18 43 | 11 54 |
| 45 | 19 38 | 28 17 | 00♌16 | 19 02 | 11 58 |
| 46 | 19 53 | 28 53 | 00 53 | 19 20 | 12 03 |
| 47 | 20 09 | 29 31 | 01 30 | 19 39 | 12 08 |
| 48 | 20 26 | 00♋11 | 02 09 | 19 59 | 12 13 |
| 49 | 20 44 | 00 52 | 02 48 | 20 19 | 12 18 |
| 50 | 21 02 | 01 36 | 03 29 | 20 40 | 12 24 |
| 51 | 21 22 | 02 21 | 04 10 | 21 01 | 12 29 |
| 52 | 21 43 | 03 09 | 04 53 | 21 23 | 12 35 |
| 53 | 22 05 | 03 59 | 05 37 | 21 46 | 12 41 |
| 54 | 22 29 | 04 52 | 06 22 | 22 09 | 12 47 |
| 55 | 22 55 | 05 49 | 07 08 | 22 33 | 12 53 |
| 56 | 23 23 | 06 48 | 07 56 | 22 58 | 13 00 |
| 57 | 23 53 | 07 51 | 08 45 | 23 24 | 13 07 |
| 58 | 24 26 | 08 59 | 09 35 | 23 50 | 13 14 |
| 59 | 25 02 | 10 10 | 10 28 | 24 18 | 13 22 |
| 60 | 25♉41 | 11♋27 | 11♌22 | 24♌47 | 13♍30 |

**0h 48m 0s — 12° 0' 0" — 13 ♈ 03**

| LAT. | 11 | 12 | ASC | 2 | 3 |
|---|---|---|---|---|---|
| 0 | 14♉28 | 13♊24 | 11♋02 | 09♌34 | 10♍30 |
| 5 | 14 57 | 14 42 | 12 59 | 10 36 | 10 44 |
| 10 | 15 28 | 16 01 | 14 56 | 11 38 | 10 58 |
| 15 | 16 00 | 17 25 | 16 55 | 12 40 | 11 12 |
| 20 | 16 34 | 18 53 | 18 56 | 13 43 | 11 27 |
| 21 | 16 41 | 19 12 | 19 21 | 13 56 | 11 30 |
| 22 | 16 49 | 19 31 | 19 46 | 14 08 | 11 33 |
| 23 | 16 56 | 19 50 | 20 11 | 14 21 | 11 36 |
| 24 | 17 04 | 20 09 | 20 37 | 14 34 | 11 39 |
| 25 | 17 12 | 20 29 | 21 02 | 14 48 | 11 42 |
| 26 | 17 20 | 20 50 | 21 28 | 15 01 | 11 45 |
| 27 | 17 28 | 21 10 | 21 55 | 15 14 | 11 48 |
| 28 | 17 36 | 21 31 | 22 21 | 15 28 | 11 51 |
| 29 | 17 45 | 21 53 | 22 48 | 15 41 | 11 55 |
| 30 | 17 53 | 22 15 | 23 16 | 15 55 | 11 58 |
| 31 | 18 02 | 22 37 | 23 43 | 16 09 | 12 01 |
| 32 | 18 12 | 23 01 | 24 11 | 16 23 | 12 05 |
| 33 | 18 21 | 23 24 | 24 40 | 16 38 | 12 08 |
| 34 | 18 31 | 23 49 | 25 09 | 16 52 | 12 12 |
| 35 | 18 41 | 24 14 | 25 38 | 17 07 | 12 15 |
| 36 | 18 51 | 24 39 | 26 08 | 17 22 | 12 19 |
| 37 | 19 02 | 25 06 | 26 38 | 17 38 | 12 22 |
| 38 | 19 13 | 25 33 | 27 09 | 17 53 | 12 26 |
| 39 | 19 25 | 26 01 | 27 40 | 18 09 | 12 30 |
| 40 | 19 37 | 26 30 | 28 12 | 18 25 | 12 34 |
| 41 | 19 49 | 27 01 | 28 45 | 18 42 | 12 38 |
| 42 | 20 02 | 27 32 | 29 18 | 18 58 | 12 42 |
| 43 | 20 15 | 28 04 | 29 52 | 19 16 | 12 46 |
| 44 | 20 29 | 28 37 | 00♌27 | 19 33 | 12 51 |
| 45 | 20 44 | 29 12 | 01 02 | 19 51 | 12 55 |
| 46 | 20 59 | 29 48 | 01 39 | 20 09 | 12 59 |
| 47 | 21 16 | 00♋26 | 02 16 | 20 28 | 13 04 |
| 48 | 21 33 | 01 06 | 02 54 | 20 47 | 13 09 |
| 49 | 21 51 | 01 47 | 03 33 | 21 07 | 13 14 |
| 50 | 22 10 | 02 30 | 04 12 | 21 27 | 13 19 |
| 51 | 22 30 | 03 15 | 04 53 | 21 48 | 13 24 |
| 52 | 22 51 | 04 02 | 05 35 | 22 10 | 13 30 |
| 53 | 23 14 | 04 52 | 06 19 | 22 32 | 13 35 |
| 54 | 23 38 | 05 45 | 07 03 | 22 55 | 13 41 |
| 55 | 24 04 | 06 41 | 07 49 | 23 18 | 13 47 |
| 56 | 24 32 | 07 39 | 08 36 | 23 43 | 13 53 |
| 57 | 25 03 | 08 42 | 09 24 | 24 08 | 14 00 |
| 58 | 25 36 | 09 48 | 10 14 | 24 34 | 14 07 |
| 59 | 26 12 | 10 59 | 11 05 | 25 01 | 14 14 |
| 60 | 26♉53 | 12♋15 | 11♌58 | 25♌29 | 14♍21 |

**0h 52m 0s — 13° 0' 0" — 14 ♈ 07**

| LAT. | 11 | 12 | ASC | 2 | 3 |
|---|---|---|---|---|---|
| 0 | 15♉28 | 14♊20 | 11♋58 | 10♌33 | 11♍34 |
| 5 | 15 58 | 15 38 | 13 54 | 11 35 | 11 48 |
| 10 | 16 29 | 16 58 | 15 51 | 12 36 | 12 01 |
| 15 | 17 02 | 18 21 | 17 48 | 13 37 | 12 14 |
| 20 | 17 36 | 19 50 | 19 49 | 14 39 | 12 28 |
| 21 | 17 44 | 20 09 | 20 14 | 14 51 | 12 31 |
| 22 | 17 51 | 20 27 | 20 39 | 15 04 | 12 34 |
| 23 | 17 59 | 20 47 | 21 04 | 15 17 | 12 37 |
| 24 | 18 06 | 21 06 | 21 29 | 15 29 | 12 40 |
| 25 | 18 14 | 21 26 | 21 55 | 15 42 | 12 43 |
| 26 | 18 22 | 21 46 | 22 20 | 15 55 | 12 45 |
| 27 | 18 31 | 22 07 | 22 47 | 16 09 | 12 48 |
| 28 | 18 39 | 22 28 | 23 13 | 16 22 | 12 51 |
| 29 | 18 48 | 22 49 | 23 40 | 16 35 | 12 55 |
| 30 | 18 57 | 23 11 | 24 07 | 16 49 | 12 58 |
| 31 | 19 06 | 23 34 | 24 34 | 17 03 | 13 01 |
| 32 | 19 15 | 23 57 | 25 02 | 17 17 | 13 04 |
| 33 | 19 25 | 24 21 | 25 30 | 17 31 | 13 07 |
| 34 | 19 35 | 24 45 | 25 59 | 17 45 | 13 11 |
| 35 | 19 45 | 25 10 | 26 28 | 18 00 | 13 14 |
| 36 | 19 55 | 25 36 | 26 57 | 18 14 | 13 17 |
| 37 | 20 06 | 26 02 | 27 27 | 18 29 | 13 21 |
| 38 | 20 18 | 26 29 | 27 58 | 18 45 | 13 24 |
| 39 | 20 29 | 26 57 | 28 29 | 19 00 | 13 28 |
| 40 | 20 41 | 27 26 | 29 00 | 19 16 | 13 32 |
| 41 | 20 54 | 27 56 | 29 33 | 19 32 | 13 35 |
| 42 | 21 07 | 28 27 | 00♌05 | 19 49 | 13 39 |
| 43 | 21 21 | 28 59 | 00 39 | 20 06 | 13 43 |
| 44 | 21 35 | 29 33 | 01 13 | 20 23 | 13 47 |
| 45 | 21 50 | 00♋07 | 01 48 | 20 40 | 13 52 |
| 46 | 22 05 | 00 43 | 02 24 | 20 58 | 13 56 |
| 47 | 22 22 | 01 21 | 03 01 | 21 17 | 14 00 |
| 48 | 22 39 | 02 00 | 03 38 | 21 36 | 14 05 |
| 49 | 22 57 | 02 41 | 04 17 | 21 55 | 14 09 |
| 50 | 23 16 | 03 24 | 04 56 | 22 15 | 14 14 |
| 51 | 23 37 | 04 08 | 05 36 | 22 35 | 14 19 |
| 52 | 23 58 | 04 56 | 06 18 | 22 56 | 14 24 |
| 53 | 24 21 | 05 45 | 07 00 | 23 18 | 14 30 |
| 54 | 24 46 | 06 37 | 07 44 | 23 41 | 14 35 |
| 55 | 25 13 | 07 32 | 08 29 | 24 04 | 14 41 |
| 56 | 25 41 | 08 30 | 09 15 | 24 27 | 14 47 |
| 57 | 26 12 | 09 32 | 10 03 | 24 52 | 14 53 |
| 58 | 26 46 | 10 38 | 10 52 | 25 18 | 14 59 |
| 59 | 27 23 | 11 48 | 11 43 | 25 44 | 15 06 |
| 60 | 28♉04 | 13♋02 | 12♌35 | 26♌12 | 15♍13 |

**0h 56m 0s — 14° 0' 0" — 15 ♈ 12**

| LAT. | 11 | 12 | ASC | 2 | 3 |
|---|---|---|---|---|---|
| 0 | 16♉28 | 15♊16 | 12♋53 | 11♌32 | 12♍39 |
| 5 | 16 59 | 16 34 | 14 49 | 12 34 | 12 51 |
| 10 | 17 30 | 17 54 | 16 45 | 13 34 | 13 04 |
| 15 | 18 03 | 19 18 | 18 42 | 14 34 | 13 17 |
| 20 | 18 38 | 20 47 | 20 42 | 15 35 | 13 30 |
| 21 | 18 46 | 21 05 | 21 07 | 15 47 | 13 32 |
| 22 | 18 53 | 21 24 | 21 32 | 15 59 | 13 35 |
| 23 | 19 01 | 21 43 | 21 56 | 16 12 | 13 38 |
| 24 | 19 09 | 22 03 | 22 21 | 16 24 | 13 40 |
| 25 | 19 17 | 22 22 | 22 47 | 16 37 | 13 43 |
| 26 | 19 25 | 22 43 | 23 12 | 16 50 | 13 46 |
| 27 | 19 33 | 23 03 | 23 38 | 17 03 | 13 49 |
| 28 | 19 42 | 23 24 | 24 04 | 17 16 | 13 52 |
| 29 | 19 51 | 23 46 | 24 31 | 17 29 | 13 54 |
| 30 | 20 00 | 24 08 | 24 58 | 17 43 | 13 57 |
| 31 | 20 09 | 24 30 | 25 25 | 17 56 | 14 00 |
| 32 | 20 18 | 24 53 | 25 52 | 18 10 | 14 03 |
| 33 | 20 28 | 25 17 | 26 20 | 18 24 | 14 06 |
| 34 | 20 38 | 25 41 | 26 49 | 18 38 | 14 10 |
| 35 | 20 49 | 26 06 | 27 17 | 18 52 | 14 13 |
| 36 | 20 59 | 26 32 | 27 46 | 19 07 | 14 16 |
| 37 | 21 10 | 26 58 | 28 16 | 19 21 | 14 19 |
| 38 | 21 22 | 27 25 | 28 46 | 19 36 | 14 23 |
| 39 | 21 34 | 27 53 | 29 17 | 19 52 | 14 26 |
| 40 | 21 46 | 28 22 | 29 48 | 20 07 | 14 29 |
| 41 | 21 59 | 28 52 | 00♌20 | 20 23 | 14 33 |
| 42 | 22 12 | 29 23 | 00 53 | 20 39 | 14 37 |
| 43 | 22 26 | 29 55 | 01 26 | 20 56 | 14 40 |
| 44 | 22 40 | 00♋28 | 02 00 | 21 13 | 14 44 |
| 45 | 22 55 | 01 02 | 02 34 | 21 30 | 14 48 |
| 46 | 23 11 | 01 38 | 03 10 | 21 47 | 14 52 |
| 47 | 23 28 | 02 15 | 03 46 | 22 05 | 14 56 |
| 48 | 23 45 | 02 54 | 04 23 | 22 24 | 15 01 |
| 49 | 24 03 | 03 35 | 05 01 | 22 43 | 15 05 |
| 50 | 24 23 | 04 17 | 05 39 | 23 03 | 15 10 |
| 51 | 24 43 | 05 02 | 06 19 | 23 23 | 15 14 |
| 52 | 25 05 | 05 48 | 07 00 | 23 43 | 15 19 |
| 53 | 25 29 | 06 37 | 07 42 | 24 04 | 15 24 |
| 54 | 25 54 | 07 29 | 08 25 | 24 26 | 15 29 |
| 55 | 26 20 | 08 23 | 09 10 | 24 49 | 15 35 |
| 56 | 26 49 | 09 21 | 09 55 | 25 12 | 15 40 |
| 57 | 27 21 | 10 22 | 10 42 | 25 36 | 15 46 |
| 58 | 27 55 | 11 27 | 11 30 | 26 01 | 15 52 |
| 59 | 28 32 | 12 36 | 12 20 | 26 27 | 15 59 |
| 60 | 29♉14 | 13♋49 | 13♌12 | 26♌54 | 16♍05 |

**1h 0m 0s — 15° 0' 0" — 16 ♈ 17**

| LAT. | 11 | 12 | ASC | 2 | 3 |
|---|---|---|---|---|---|
| 0 | 17♉28 | 16♊11 | 13♋49 | 12♌32 | 13♍43 |
| 5 | 17 59 | 17 30 | 15 44 | 13 32 | 13 55 |
| 10 | 18 31 | 18 50 | 17 40 | 14 32 | 14 07 |
| 15 | 19 04 | 20 14 | 19 36 | 15 31 | 14 19 |
| 20 | 19 40 | 21 43 | 21 35 | 16 31 | 14 31 |
| 21 | 19 48 | 22 01 | 22 00 | 16 43 | 14 34 |
| 22 | 19 55 | 22 20 | 22 24 | 16 55 | 14 36 |
| 23 | 20 03 | 22 39 | 22 49 | 17 07 | 14 39 |
| 24 | 20 11 | 22 59 | 23 14 | 17 20 | 14 41 |
| 25 | 20 19 | 23 19 | 23 39 | 17 32 | 14 44 |
| 26 | 20 27 | 23 39 | 24 04 | 17 45 | 14 46 |
| 27 | 20 36 | 23 59 | 24 30 | 17 57 | 14 49 |
| 28 | 20 45 | 24 20 | 24 56 | 18 10 | 14 52 |
| 29 | 20 53 | 24 42 | 25 22 | 18 23 | 14 54 |
| 30 | 21 03 | 25 04 | 25 49 | 18 36 | 14 57 |
| 31 | 21 12 | 25 26 | 26 16 | 18 50 | 15 00 |
| 32 | 21 21 | 25 49 | 26 43 | 19 03 | 15 03 |
| 33 | 21 31 | 26 13 | 27 10 | 19 17 | 15 06 |
| 34 | 21 42 | 26 37 | 27 38 | 19 31 | 15 09 |
| 35 | 21 52 | 27 02 | 28 07 | 19 45 | 15 12 |
| 36 | 22 03 | 27 27 | 28 36 | 19 59 | 15 15 |
| 37 | 22 14 | 27 54 | 29 05 | 20 13 | 15 18 |
| 38 | 22 26 | 28 21 | 29 35 | 20 28 | 15 21 |
| 39 | 22 38 | 28 49 | 00♌05 | 20 43 | 15 24 |
| 40 | 22 50 | 29 17 | 00 36 | 20 58 | 15 27 |
| 41 | 23 03 | 29 47 | 01 08 | 21 14 | 15 31 |
| 42 | 23 16 | 00♋18 | 01 40 | 21 30 | 15 34 |
| 43 | 23 30 | 00 50 | 02 13 | 21 46 | 15 38 |
| 44 | 23 45 | 01 23 | 02 46 | 22 02 | 15 41 |
| 45 | 24 00 | 01 57 | 03 20 | 22 19 | 15 45 |
| 46 | 24 16 | 02 32 | 03 55 | 22 37 | 15 49 |
| 47 | 24 33 | 03 09 | 04 31 | 22 54 | 15 53 |
| 48 | 24 51 | 03 48 | 05 07 | 23 12 | 15 57 |
| 49 | 25 09 | 04 28 | 05 45 | 23 31 | 16 01 |
| 50 | 25 29 | 05 10 | 06 23 | 23 50 | 16 05 |
| 51 | 25 50 | 05 54 | 07 02 | 24 10 | 16 09 |
| 52 | 26 12 | 06 41 | 07 42 | 24 30 | 16 14 |
| 53 | 26 36 | 07 29 | 08 24 | 24 51 | 16 19 |
| 54 | 27 01 | 08 20 | 09 06 | 25 12 | 16 24 |
| 55 | 27 28 | 09 14 | 09 50 | 25 34 | 16 29 |
| 56 | 27 57 | 10 11 | 10 35 | 25 57 | 16 34 |
| 57 | 28 29 | 11 11 | 11 21 | 26 21 | 16 39 |
| 58 | 29 04 | 12 15 | 12 09 | 26 45 | 16 45 |
| 59 | 29 42 | 13 23 | 12 58 | 27 10 | 16 51 |
| 60 | 00♊24 | 14♋36 | 13♌49 | 27♌37 | 16♍57 |

# Placidus Table of Houses for Latitudes 0° to 60° North

**1h 4m 0s — 16° 0' 0" — 17 ♈ 21**

| LAT. | 11 | 12 | ASC | 2 | 3 |
|---|---|---|---|---|---|
| 0 | 18♉28 | 17♊07 | 14♋44 | 13♌32 | 14♍48 |
| 5 | 18 59 | 18 25 | 16 40 | 14 31 | 14 59 |
| 10 | 19 31 | 19 46 | 18 35 | 15 30 | 15 10 |
| 15 | 20 05 | 21 10 | 20 30 | 16 28 | 15 21 |
| 20 | 20 42 | 22 39 | 22 29 | 17 27 | 15 33 |
| 21 | 20 49 | 22 57 | 22 53 | 17 39 | 15 35 |
| 22 | 20 57 | 23 16 | 23 17 | 17 51 | 15 37 |
| 23 | 21 05 | 23 35 | 23 41 | 18 03 | 15 40 |
| 24 | 21 13 | 23 55 | 24 06 | 18 15 | 15 42 |
| 25 | 21 21 | 24 15 | 24 31 | 18 27 | 15 45 |
| 26 | 21 29 | 24 35 | 24 56 | 18 39 | 15 47 |
| 27 | 21 38 | 24 55 | 25 22 | 18 52 | 15 49 |
| 28 | 21 47 | 25 16 | 25 47 | 19 05 | 15 52 |
| 29 | 21 56 | 25 38 | 26 13 | 19 17 | 15 55 |
| 30 | 22 05 | 26 00 | 26 40 | 19 30 | 15 57 |
| 31 | 22 15 | 26 22 | 27 06 | 19 43 | 16 00 |
| 32 | 22 24 | 26 45 | 27 33 | 19 56 | 16 02 |
| 33 | 22 34 | 27 09 | 28 00 | 20 10 | 16 05 |
| 34 | 22 45 | 27 33 | 28 28 | 20 23 | 16 08 |
| 35 | 22 55 | 27 58 | 28 56 | 20 37 | 16 11 |
| 36 | 23 06 | 28 23 | 29 25 | 20 51 | 16 13 |
| 37 | 23 17 | 28 49 | 29 54 | 21 05 | 16 16 |
| 38 | 23 29 | 29 16 | 00♌23 | 21 20 | 16 19 |
| 39 | 23 41 | 29 44 | 00 53 | 21 34 | 16 22 |
| 40 | 23 54 | 00♋12 | 01 24 | 21 49 | 16 25 |
| 41 | 24 07 | 00 42 | 01 55 | 22 05 | 16 28 |
| 42 | 24 20 | 01 13 | 02 27 | 22 20 | 16 32 |
| 43 | 24 35 | 01 44 | 02 59 | 22 36 | 16 35 |
| 44 | 24 49 | 02 17 | 03 32 | 22 52 | 16 38 |
| 45 | 25 05 | 02 51 | 04 06 | 23 09 | 16 42 |
| 46 | 25 21 | 03 26 | 04 40 | 23 26 | 16 45 |
| 47 | 25 38 | 04 03 | 05 15 | 23 43 | 16 49 |
| 48 | 25 56 | 04 42 | 05 51 | 24 01 | 16 53 |
| 49 | 26 15 | 05 22 | 06 28 | 24 19 | 16 56 |
| 50 | 26 35 | 06 03 | 07 06 | 24 38 | 17 00 |
| 51 | 26 56 | 06 47 | 07 45 | 24 57 | 17 05 |
| 52 | 27 18 | 07 33 | 08 25 | 25 17 | 17 09 |
| 53 | 27 42 | 08 21 | 09 05 | 25 37 | 17 13 |
| 54 | 28 07 | 09 12 | 09 47 | 25 58 | 17 18 |
| 55 | 28 35 | 10 05 | 10 30 | 26 20 | 17 22 |
| 56 | 29 05 | 11 01 | 11 15 | 26 42 | 17 27 |
| 57 | 29 37 | 12 01 | 12 00 | 27 05 | 17 32 |
| 58 | 00♊12 | 13 04 | 12 47 | 27 29 | 17 38 |
| 59 | 00 50 | 14 11 | 13 35 | 27 54 | 17 43 |
| 60 | 01♊33 | 15♋22 | 14♌25 | 28♌19 | 17♍49 |

**1h 8m 0s — 17° 0' 0" — 18 ♈ 26**

| LAT. | 11 | 12 | ASC | 2 | 3 |
|---|---|---|---|---|---|
| 0 | 19♉27 | 18♊02 | 15♋40 | 14♌32 | 15♍53 |
| 5 | 19 59 | 19 21 | 17 35 | 15 30 | 16 03 |
| 10 | 20 32 | 20 42 | 19 29 | 16 28 | 16 13 |
| 15 | 21 06 | 22 06 | 21 24 | 17 25 | 16 24 |
| 20 | 21 43 | 23 35 | 23 22 | 18 23 | 16 34 |
| 21 | 21 50 | 23 53 | 23 46 | 18 35 | 16 36 |
| 22 | 21 58 | 24 12 | 24 10 | 18 46 | 16 39 |
| 23 | 22 06 | 24 31 | 24 34 | 18 58 | 16 41 |
| 24 | 22 14 | 24 51 | 24 58 | 19 10 | 16 43 |
| 25 | 22 23 | 25 11 | 25 23 | 19 22 | 16 45 |
| 26 | 22 31 | 25 31 | 25 48 | 19 34 | 16 48 |
| 27 | 22 40 | 25 51 | 26 13 | 19 47 | 16 50 |
| 28 | 22 49 | 26 12 | 26 39 | 19 59 | 16 52 |
| 29 | 22 58 | 26 34 | 27 04 | 20 11 | 16 55 |
| 30 | 23 07 | 26 56 | 27 30 | 20 24 | 16 57 |
| 31 | 23 17 | 27 18 | 27 57 | 20 37 | 16 59 |
| 32 | 23 27 | 27 41 | 28 23 | 20 50 | 17 02 |
| 33 | 23 37 | 28 04 | 28 50 | 21 03 | 17 04 |
| 34 | 23 47 | 28 28 | 29 18 | 21 16 | 17 07 |
| 35 | 23 58 | 28 53 | 29 46 | 21 30 | 17 10 |
| 36 | 24 09 | 29 18 | 00♌14 | 21 43 | 17 12 |
| 37 | 24 20 | 29 44 | 00 43 | 21 57 | 17 15 |
| 38 | 24 32 | 00♋11 | 01 12 | 22 12 | 17 18 |
| 39 | 24 45 | 00 39 | 01 41 | 22 26 | 17 20 |
| 40 | 24 57 | 01 07 | 02 12 | 22 41 | 17 23 |
| 41 | 25 10 | 01 37 | 02 42 | 22 55 | 17 26 |
| 42 | 25 24 | 02 07 | 03 14 | 23 11 | 17 29 |
| 43 | 25 38 | 02 39 | 03 46 | 23 26 | 17 32 |
| 44 | 25 53 | 03 11 | 04 18 | 23 42 | 17 35 |
| 45 | 26 09 | 03 45 | 04 52 | 23 58 | 17 38 |
| 46 | 26 25 | 04 20 | 05 26 | 24 15 | 17 42 |
| 47 | 26 43 | 04 57 | 06 00 | 24 32 | 17 45 |
| 48 | 27 01 | 05 35 | 06 36 | 24 49 | 17 49 |
| 49 | 27 20 | 06 14 | 07 12 | 25 07 | 17 52 |
| 50 | 27 40 | 06 56 | 07 49 | 25 25 | 17 56 |
| 51 | 28 01 | 07 39 | 08 28 | 25 44 | 18 00 |
| 52 | 28 24 | 08 25 | 09 07 | 26 03 | 18 04 |
| 53 | 28 48 | 09 12 | 09 47 | 26 23 | 18 08 |
| 54 | 29 14 | 10 02 | 10 28 | 26 44 | 18 12 |
| 55 | 29 42 | 10 55 | 11 11 | 27 05 | 18 16 |
| 56 | 00♊11 | 11 51 | 11 54 | 27 27 | 18 21 |
| 57 | 00 44 | 12 49 | 12 39 | 27 49 | 18 26 |
| 58 | 01 19 | 13 52 | 13 25 | 28 13 | 18 31 |
| 59 | 01 58 | 14 58 | 14 13 | 28 37 | 18 36 |
| 60 | 02♊42 | 16♋08 | 15♌02 | 29♌02 | 18♍41 |

**1h 12m 0s — 18° 0' 0" — 19 ♈ 30**

| LAT. | 11 | 12 | ASC | 2 | 3 |
|---|---|---|---|---|---|
| 0 | 20♉26 | 18♊58 | 16♋36 | 15♌32 | 16♍57 |
| 5 | 20 59 | 20 17 | 18 30 | 16 30 | 17 07 |
| 10 | 21 32 | 21 38 | 20 24 | 17 26 | 17 17 |
| 15 | 22 07 | 23 02 | 22 18 | 18 22 | 17 26 |
| 20 | 22 44 | 24 31 | 24 15 | 19 19 | 17 36 |
| 21 | 22 52 | 24 49 | 24 38 | 19 31 | 17 38 |
| 22 | 23 00 | 25 08 | 25 02 | 19 42 | 17 40 |
| 23 | 23 08 | 25 27 | 25 26 | 19 54 | 17 42 |
| 24 | 23 16 | 25 47 | 25 51 | 20 06 | 17 44 |
| 25 | 23 24 | 26 06 | 26 15 | 20 17 | 17 46 |
| 26 | 23 33 | 26 26 | 26 40 | 20 29 | 17 48 |
| 27 | 23 42 | 26 47 | 27 05 | 20 41 | 17 50 |
| 28 | 23 51 | 27 08 | 27 30 | 20 53 | 17 53 |
| 29 | 24 00 | 27 29 | 27 55 | 21 06 | 17 55 |
| 30 | 24 09 | 27 51 | 28 21 | 21 18 | 17 57 |
| 31 | 24 19 | 28 13 | 28 47 | 21 31 | 17 59 |
| 32 | 24 29 | 28 36 | 29 14 | 21 43 | 18 02 |
| 33 | 24 39 | 29 00 | 29 40 | 21 56 | 18 04 |
| 34 | 24 50 | 29 24 | 00♌08 | 22 09 | 18 06 |
| 35 | 25 00 | 29 48 | 00 35 | 22 22 | 18 09 |
| 36 | 25 12 | 00♋13 | 01 03 | 22 36 | 18 11 |
| 37 | 25 23 | 00 39 | 01 31 | 22 49 | 18 13 |
| 38 | 25 35 | 01 06 | 02 00 | 23 03 | 18 16 |
| 39 | 25 48 | 01 34 | 02 30 | 23 17 | 18 19 |
| 40 | 26 00 | 02 02 | 02 59 | 23 32 | 18 21 |
| 41 | 26 14 | 02 31 | 03 30 | 23 46 | 18 24 |
| 42 | 26 28 | 03 02 | 04 01 | 24 01 | 18 27 |
| 43 | 26 42 | 03 33 | 04 32 | 24 16 | 18 30 |
| 44 | 26 57 | 04 05 | 05 04 | 24 32 | 18 32 |
| 45 | 27 13 | 04 39 | 05 37 | 24 48 | 18 35 |
| 46 | 27 29 | 05 14 | 06 11 | 25 04 | 18 38 |
| 47 | 27 47 | 05 50 | 06 45 | 25 21 | 18 42 |
| 48 | 28 05 | 06 28 | 07 20 | 25 38 | 18 45 |
| 49 | 28 24 | 07 07 | 07 56 | 25 55 | 18 48 |
| 50 | 28 45 | 07 48 | 08 33 | 26 13 | 18 51 |
| 51 | 29 06 | 08 31 | 09 10 | 26 31 | 18 55 |
| 52 | 29 29 | 09 16 | 09 49 | 26 50 | 18 59 |
| 53 | 29 53 | 10 03 | 10 28 | 27 10 | 19 02 |
| 54 | 00♊20 | 10 53 | 11 09 | 27 30 | 19 06 |
| 55 | 00 48 | 11 45 | 11 51 | 27 50 | 19 10 |
| 56 | 01 18 | 12 40 | 12 34 | 28 12 | 19 15 |
| 57 | 01 51 | 13 38 | 13 18 | 28 34 | 19 19 |
| 58 | 02 27 | 14 40 | 14 03 | 28 56 | 19 24 |
| 59 | 03 06 | 15 45 | 14 50 | 29 20 | 19 28 |
| 60 | 03♊50 | 16♋54 | 15♌39 | 29♌44 | 19♍33 |

**1h 16m 0s — 19° 0' 0" — 20 ♈ 34**

| LAT. | 11 | 12 | ASC | 2 | 3 |
|---|---|---|---|---|---|
| 0 | 21♉26 | 19♊53 | 17♋32 | 16♌33 | 18♍02 |
| 5 | 21 58 | 21 12 | 19 26 | 17 29 | 18 11 |
| 10 | 22 32 | 22 33 | 21 19 | 18 25 | 18 20 |
| 15 | 23 07 | 23 58 | 23 12 | 19 20 | 18 29 |
| 20 | 23 45 | 25 26 | 25 08 | 20 15 | 18 38 |
| 21 | 23 52 | 25 45 | 25 31 | 20 27 | 18 40 |
| 22 | 24 01 | 26 04 | 25 55 | 20 38 | 18 41 |
| 23 | 24 09 | 26 23 | 26 19 | 20 49 | 18 43 |
| 24 | 24 17 | 26 42 | 26 43 | 21 01 | 18 45 |
| 25 | 24 26 | 27 02 | 27 07 | 21 13 | 18 47 |
| 26 | 24 34 | 27 22 | 27 32 | 21 24 | 18 49 |
| 27 | 24 43 | 27 43 | 27 56 | 21 36 | 18 51 |
| 28 | 24 52 | 28 03 | 28 21 | 21 48 | 18 53 |
| 29 | 25 01 | 28 25 | 28 46 | 22 00 | 18 55 |
| 30 | 25 11 | 28 46 | 29 12 | 22 12 | 18 57 |
| 31 | 25 21 | 29 09 | 29 38 | 22 24 | 18 59 |
| 32 | 25 31 | 29 31 | 00♌04 | 22 37 | 19 01 |
| 33 | 25 41 | 29 55 | 00 30 | 22 49 | 19 03 |
| 34 | 25 52 | 00♋19 | 00 57 | 23 02 | 19 05 |
| 35 | 26 03 | 00 43 | 01 24 | 23 15 | 19 08 |
| 36 | 26 14 | 01 08 | 01 52 | 23 28 | 19 10 |
| 37 | 26 26 | 01 34 | 02 20 | 23 42 | 19 12 |
| 38 | 26 38 | 02 01 | 02 49 | 23 55 | 19 15 |
| 39 | 26 50 | 02 28 | 03 17 | 24 09 | 19 17 |
| 40 | 27 03 | 02 56 | 03 47 | 24 23 | 19 19 |
| 41 | 27 17 | 03 25 | 04 17 | 24 37 | 19 22 |
| 42 | 27 31 | 03 56 | 04 47 | 24 52 | 19 24 |
| 43 | 27 45 | 04 27 | 05 19 | 25 07 | 19 27 |
| 44 | 28 01 | 04 59 | 05 50 | 25 22 | 19 30 |
| 45 | 28 17 | 05 32 | 06 23 | 25 37 | 19 32 |
| 46 | 28 33 | 06 07 | 06 56 | 25 53 | 19 35 |
| 47 | 28 51 | 06 43 | 07 30 | 26 09 | 19 38 |
| 48 | 29 09 | 07 20 | 08 04 | 26 26 | 19 41 |
| 49 | 29 29 | 07 59 | 08 40 | 26 43 | 19 44 |
| 50 | 29 49 | 08 40 | 09 16 | 27 01 | 19 47 |
| 51 | 00♊11 | 09 23 | 09 53 | 27 19 | 19 50 |
| 52 | 00 34 | 10 07 | 10 31 | 27 37 | 19 54 |
| 53 | 00 59 | 10 54 | 11 10 | 27 56 | 19 57 |
| 54 | 01 25 | 11 43 | 11 50 | 28 16 | 20 01 |
| 55 | 01 53 | 12 35 | 12 31 | 28 36 | 20 04 |
| 56 | 02 24 | 13 29 | 13 13 | 28 56 | 20 08 |
| 57 | 02 57 | 14 26 | 13 57 | 29 18 | 20 12 |
| 58 | 03 33 | 15 27 | 14 42 | 29 40 | 20 16 |
| 59 | 04 13 | 16 31 | 15 28 | 00♍03 | 20 21 |
| 60 | 04♊57 | 17♋40 | 16♌15 | 00♍27 | 20♍25 |

**1h 20m 0s — 20° 0' 0" — 21 ♈ 38**

| LAT. | 11 | 12 | ASC | 2 | 3 |
|---|---|---|---|---|---|
| 0 | 22♉25 | 20♊49 | 18♋28 | 17♌33 | 19♍07 |
| 5 | 22 58 | 22 08 | 20 21 | 18 29 | 19 15 |
| 10 | 23 32 | 23 29 | 22 13 | 19 23 | 19 23 |
| 15 | 24 07 | 24 53 | 24 06 | 20 17 | 19 31 |
| 20 | 24 45 | 26 22 | 26 01 | 21 12 | 19 40 |
| 21 | 24 53 | 26 40 | 26 24 | 21 23 | 19 41 |
| 22 | 25 01 | 26 59 | 26 48 | 21 34 | 19 43 |
| 23 | 25 10 | 27 18 | 27 11 | 21 45 | 19 45 |
| 24 | 25 18 | 27 38 | 27 35 | 21 57 | 19 46 |
| 25 | 25 27 | 27 57 | 27 59 | 22 08 | 19 48 |
| 26 | 25 35 | 28 17 | 28 23 | 22 19 | 19 50 |
| 27 | 25 44 | 28 38 | 28 48 | 22 31 | 19 52 |
| 28 | 25 53 | 28 59 | 29 12 | 22 43 | 19 53 |
| 29 | 26 03 | 29 20 | 29 37 | 22 54 | 19 55 |
| 30 | 26 12 | 29 42 | 00♌03 | 23 06 | 19 57 |
| 31 | 26 22 | 00♋04 | 00 28 | 23 18 | 19 59 |
| 32 | 26 32 | 00 27 | 00 54 | 23 30 | 20 01 |
| 33 | 26 43 | 00 50 | 01 20 | 23 43 | 20 03 |
| 34 | 26 54 | 01 14 | 01 47 | 23 55 | 20 05 |
| 35 | 27 05 | 01 38 | 02 14 | 24 08 | 20 07 |
| 36 | 27 16 | 02 03 | 02 41 | 24 21 | 20 09 |
| 37 | 27 28 | 02 29 | 03 09 | 24 34 | 20 11 |
| 38 | 27 40 | 02 55 | 03 37 | 24 47 | 20 13 |
| 39 | 27 53 | 03 22 | 04 05 | 25 01 | 20 15 |
| 40 | 28 06 | 03 51 | 04 34 | 25 14 | 20 17 |
| 41 | 28 19 | 04 20 | 05 04 | 25 28 | 20 20 |
| 42 | 28 34 | 04 49 | 05 34 | 25 43 | 20 22 |
| 43 | 28 48 | 05 20 | 06 05 | 25 57 | 20 24 |
| 44 | 29 04 | 05 52 | 06 36 | 26 12 | 20 27 |
| 45 | 29 20 | 06 26 | 07 08 | 26 27 | 20 29 |
| 46 | 29 37 | 07 00 | 07 41 | 26 43 | 20 32 |
| 47 | 29 54 | 07 36 | 08 14 | 26 58 | 20 34 |
| 48 | 00♊13 | 08 13 | 08 48 | 27 15 | 20 37 |
| 49 | 00 32 | 08 52 | 09 23 | 27 31 | 20 40 |
| 50 | 00 53 | 09 32 | 09 59 | 27 48 | 20 43 |
| 51 | 01 15 | 10 14 | 10 35 | 28 06 | 20 46 |
| 52 | 01 38 | 10 58 | 11 13 | 28 24 | 20 49 |
| 53 | 02 03 | 11 44 | 11 51 | 28 42 | 20 52 |
| 54 | 02 30 | 12 33 | 12 31 | 29 01 | 20 55 |
| 55 | 02 58 | 13 24 | 13 11 | 29 21 | 20 58 |
| 56 | 03 29 | 14 18 | 13 53 | 29 41 | 21 02 |
| 57 | 04 03 | 15 14 | 14 36 | 00♍02 | 21 06 |
| 58 | 04 39 | 16 14 | 15 20 | 00 24 | 21 09 |
| 59 | 05 19 | 17 18 | 16 05 | 00 46 | 21 13 |
| 60 | 06♊04 | 18♋25 | 16♌52 | 01♍10 | 21♍17 |

**1h 24m 0s — 21° 0' 0" — 22 ♈ 42**

| LAT. | 11 | 12 | ASC | 2 | 3 |
|---|---|---|---|---|---|
| 0 | 23♉23 | 21♊44 | 19♋24 | 18♌34 | 20♍12 |
| 5 | 23 57 | 23 03 | 21 17 | 19 29 | 20 20 |
| 10 | 24 31 | 24 24 | 23 08 | 20 22 | 20 27 |
| 15 | 25 07 | 25 49 | 25 00 | 21 15 | 20 34 |
| 20 | 25 46 | 27 17 | 26 54 | 22 08 | 20 42 |
| 21 | 25 54 | 27 36 | 27 17 | 22 19 | 20 43 |
| 22 | 26 02 | 27 55 | 27 40 | 22 30 | 20 45 |
| 23 | 26 10 | 28 14 | 28 04 | 22 41 | 20 46 |
| 24 | 26 19 | 28 33 | 28 27 | 22 52 | 20 48 |
| 25 | 26 27 | 28 53 | 28 51 | 23 03 | 20 49 |
| 26 | 26 36 | 29 13 | 29 15 | 23 15 | 20 51 |
| 27 | 26 45 | 29 33 | 29 39 | 23 26 | 20 52 |
| 28 | 26 54 | 29 54 | 00♌04 | 23 37 | 20 54 |
| 29 | 27 04 | 00♋15 | 00 28 | 23 49 | 20 56 |
| 30 | 27 14 | 00 37 | 00 53 | 24 00 | 20 57 |
| 31 | 27 24 | 00 59 | 01 19 | 24 12 | 20 59 |
| 32 | 27 34 | 01 21 | 01 44 | 24 24 | 21 01 |
| 33 | 27 44 | 01 45 | 02 10 | 24 36 | 21 02 |
| 34 | 27 55 | 02 08 | 02 36 | 24 48 | 21 04 |
| 35 | 28 06 | 02 33 | 03 03 | 25 01 | 21 06 |
| 36 | 28 18 | 02 58 | 03 30 | 25 13 | 21 08 |
| 37 | 28 30 | 03 23 | 03 57 | 25 26 | 21 10 |
| 38 | 28 42 | 03 49 | 04 25 | 25 39 | 21 12 |
| 39 | 28 55 | 04 17 | 04 53 | 25 52 | 21 14 |
| 40 | 29 08 | 04 45 | 05 22 | 26 06 | 21 16 |
| 41 | 29 22 | 05 13 | 05 51 | 26 19 | 21 18 |
| 42 | 29 36 | 05 43 | 06 21 | 26 33 | 21 20 |
| 43 | 29 51 | 06 14 | 06 51 | 26 47 | 21 22 |
| 44 | 00♊06 | 06 46 | 07 22 | 27 02 | 21 24 |
| 45 | 00 23 | 07 18 | 07 54 | 27 17 | 21 26 |
| 46 | 00 40 | 07 53 | 08 26 | 27 32 | 21 28 |
| 47 | 00 57 | 08 28 | 08 59 | 27 47 | 21 31 |
| 48 | 01 16 | 09 05 | 09 32 | 28 03 | 21 33 |
| 49 | 01 36 | 09 43 | 10 07 | 28 19 | 21 36 |
| 50 | 01 57 | 10 23 | 10 42 | 28 36 | 21 38 |
| 51 | 02 19 | 11 05 | 11 18 | 28 53 | 21 41 |
| 52 | 02 42 | 11 49 | 11 55 | 29 11 | 21 44 |
| 53 | 03 07 | 12 35 | 12 33 | 29 29 | 21 47 |
| 54 | 03 34 | 13 23 | 13 11 | 29 47 | 21 49 |
| 55 | 04 03 | 14 13 | 13 51 | 00♍07 | 21 52 |
| 56 | 04 34 | 15 06 | 14 32 | 00 26 | 21 56 |
| 57 | 05 08 | 16 02 | 15 14 | 00 47 | 21 59 |
| 58 | 05 45 | 17 01 | 15 58 | 01 08 | 22 02 |
| 59 | 06 25 | 18 04 | 16 42 | 01 30 | 22 06 |
| 60 | 07♊10 | 19♋10 | 17♌28 | 01♍52 | 22♍10 |

**1h 28m 0s — 22° 0' 0" — 23 ♈ 46**

| LAT. | 11 | 12 | ASC | 2 | 3 |
|---|---|---|---|---|---|
| 0 | 24♉22 | 22♊39 | 20♋20 | 19♌35 | 21♍17 |
| 5 | 24 56 | 23 59 | 22 12 | 20 28 | 21 24 |
| 10 | 25 30 | 25 20 | 24 03 | 21 21 | 21 30 |
| 15 | 26 07 | 26 44 | 25 54 | 22 13 | 21 37 |
| 20 | 26 46 | 28 13 | 27 47 | 23 05 | 21 43 |
| 21 | 26 54 | 28 31 | 28 10 | 23 16 | 21 45 |
| 22 | 27 02 | 28 50 | 28 33 | 23 26 | 21 46 |
| 23 | 27 10 | 29 09 | 28 56 | 23 37 | 21 48 |
| 24 | 27 19 | 29 28 | 29 19 | 23 48 | 21 49 |
| 25 | 27 28 | 29 48 | 29 43 | 23 59 | 21 50 |
| 26 | 27 37 | 00♋08 | 00♌07 | 24 10 | 21 52 |
| 27 | 27 46 | 00 28 | 00 31 | 24 21 | 21 53 |
| 28 | 27 55 | 00 49 | 00 55 | 24 32 | 21 55 |
| 29 | 28 05 | 01 10 | 01 19 | 24 43 | 21 56 |
| 30 | 28 15 | 01 32 | 01 44 | 24 55 | 21 58 |
| 31 | 28 25 | 01 54 | 02 09 | 25 06 | 21 59 |
| 32 | 28 35 | 02 16 | 02 34 | 25 18 | 22 01 |
| 33 | 28 46 | 02 39 | 03 00 | 25 30 | 22 02 |
| 34 | 28 57 | 03 03 | 03 26 | 25 42 | 22 04 |
| 35 | 29 08 | 03 27 | 03 52 | 25 54 | 22 05 |
| 36 | 29 19 | 03 52 | 04 19 | 26 06 | 22 07 |
| 37 | 29 31 | 04 17 | 04 46 | 26 18 | 22 09 |
| 38 | 29 44 | 04 44 | 05 13 | 26 31 | 22 10 |
| 39 | 29 57 | 05 10 | 05 41 | 26 44 | 22 12 |
| 40 | 00♊10 | 05 38 | 06 09 | 26 57 | 22 14 |
| 41 | 00 24 | 06 07 | 06 38 | 27 10 | 22 16 |
| 42 | 00 38 | 06 36 | 07 08 | 27 24 | 22 17 |
| 43 | 00 53 | 07 07 | 07 38 | 27 38 | 22 19 |
| 44 | 01 09 | 07 39 | 08 08 | 27 52 | 22 21 |
| 45 | 01 25 | 08 11 | 08 39 | 28 06 | 22 23 |
| 46 | 01 42 | 08 45 | 09 11 | 28 21 | 22 25 |
| 47 | 02 00 | 09 20 | 09 43 | 28 36 | 22 27 |
| 48 | 02 19 | 09 57 | 10 16 | 28 52 | 22 29 |
| 49 | 02 39 | 10 35 | 10 50 | 29 08 | 22 32 |
| 50 | 03 00 | 11 15 | 11 25 | 29 24 | 22 34 |
| 51 | 03 22 | 11 56 | 12 00 | 29 40 | 22 36 |
| 52 | 03 46 | 12 39 | 12 37 | 29 58 | 22 39 |
| 53 | 04 11 | 13 25 | 13 14 | 00♍15 | 22 41 |
| 54 | 04 38 | 14 12 | 13 52 | 00 33 | 22 44 |
| 55 | 05 07 | 15 02 | 14 31 | 00 52 | 22 47 |
| 56 | 05 39 | 15 54 | 15 12 | 01 11 | 22 49 |
| 57 | 06 13 | 16 50 | 15 53 | 01 31 | 22 52 |
| 58 | 06 50 | 17 48 | 16 36 | 01 52 | 22 55 |
| 59 | 07 31 | 18 49 | 17 20 | 02 13 | 22 59 |
| 60 | 08♊16 | 19♋55 | 18♌05 | 02♍35 | 23♍02 |

**1h 32m 0s — 23° 0' 0" — 24 ♈ 50**

| LAT. | 11 | 12 | ASC | 2 | 3 |
|---|---|---|---|---|---|
| 0 | 25♉21 | 23♊34 | 21♋17 | 20♌36 | 22♍23 |
| 5 | 25 55 | 24 54 | 23 08 | 21 28 | 22 28 |
| 10 | 26 30 | 26 15 | 24 58 | 22 20 | 22 34 |
| 15 | 27 06 | 27 39 | 26 48 | 23 11 | 22 40 |
| 20 | 27 46 | 29 08 | 28 40 | 24 02 | 22 45 |
| 21 | 27 54 | 29 26 | 29 03 | 24 12 | 22 47 |
| 22 | 28 02 | 29 45 | 29 26 | 24 23 | 22 48 |
| 23 | 28 11 | 00♋04 | 29 49 | 24 33 | 22 49 |
| 24 | 28 19 | 00 23 | 00♌12 | 24 44 | 22 50 |
| 25 | 28 28 | 00 43 | 00 35 | 24 54 | 22 51 |
| 26 | 28 37 | 01 03 | 00 58 | 25 05 | 22 53 |
| 27 | 28 46 | 01 23 | 01 22 | 25 16 | 22 54 |
| 28 | 28 56 | 01 44 | 01 46 | 25 27 | 22 55 |
| 29 | 29 05 | 02 05 | 02 10 | 25 38 | 22 56 |
| 30 | 29 15 | 02 26 | 02 35 | 25 49 | 22 58 |
| 31 | 29 25 | 02 48 | 02 59 | 26 00 | 22 59 |
| 32 | 29 36 | 03 11 | 03 24 | 26 12 | 23 00 |
| 33 | 29 47 | 03 34 | 03 50 | 26 23 | 23 02 |
| 34 | 29 58 | 03 57 | 04 15 | 26 35 | 23 03 |
| 35 | 00♊09 | 04 21 | 04 41 | 26 47 | 23 05 |
| 36 | 00 21 | 04 46 | 05 08 | 26 59 | 23 06 |
| 37 | 00 33 | 05 11 | 05 34 | 27 11 | 23 07 |
| 38 | 00 45 | 05 37 | 06 01 | 27 23 | 23 09 |
| 39 | 00 58 | 06 04 | 06 29 | 27 36 | 23 10 |
| 40 | 01 12 | 06 32 | 06 57 | 27 48 | 23 12 |
| 41 | 01 26 | 07 00 | 07 25 | 28 01 | 23 14 |
| 42 | 01 40 | 07 30 | 07 54 | 28 15 | 23 15 |
| 43 | 01 55 | 08 00 | 08 24 | 28 28 | 23 17 |
| 44 | 02 11 | 08 31 | 08 54 | 28 42 | 23 18 |
| 45 | 02 27 | 09 04 | 09 25 | 28 56 | 23 20 |
| 46 | 02 45 | 09 37 | 09 56 | 29 11 | 23 22 |
| 47 | 03 03 | 10 12 | 10 28 | 29 25 | 23 24 |
| 48 | 03 22 | 10 49 | 11 00 | 29 40 | 23 26 |
| 49 | 03 42 | 11 26 | 11 34 | 29 56 | 23 28 |
| 50 | 04 03 | 12 06 | 12 08 | 00♍12 | 23 30 |
| 51 | 04 25 | 12 47 | 12 43 | 00 28 | 23 32 |
| 52 | 04 49 | 13 29 | 13 19 | 00 45 | 23 34 |
| 53 | 05 15 | 14 14 | 13 55 | 01 02 | 23 36 |
| 54 | 05 42 | 15 01 | 14 33 | 01 19 | 23 38 |
| 55 | 06 11 | 15 50 | 15 12 | 01 38 | 23 41 |
| 56 | 06 43 | 16 42 | 15 51 | 01 56 | 23 43 |
| 57 | 07 17 | 17 37 | 16 32 | 02 16 | 23 46 |
| 58 | 07 54 | 18 34 | 17 14 | 02 36 | 23 48 |
| 59 | 08 36 | 19 35 | 17 57 | 02 56 | 23 51 |
| 60 | 09♊21 | 20♋39 | 18♌42 | 03♍18 | 23♍54 |

# Placidus Table of Houses for Latitudes 0° to 60° North

**1h 36m 0s — 25 ♈ 53 — 24° 0' 0"**

| LAT. | 11 | 12 | ASC | 2 | 3 |
|---|---|---|---|---|---|
| 0 | 26♉19 | 24♊30 | 22♋13 | 21♌37 | 23♍28 |
| 5 | 26 53 | 25 49 | 24 04 | 22 29 | 23 33 |
| 10 | 27 29 | 27 10 | 25 53 | 23 19 | 23 38 |
| 15 | 28 06 | 28 35 | 27 42 | 24 09 | 23 42 |
| 20 | 28 45 | 00♋03 | 29 33 | 24 59 | 23 47 |
| 21 | 28 53 | 00 21 | 29 56 | 25 09 | 23 48 |
| 22 | 29 02 | 00 40 | 00♌18 | 25 19 | 23 49 |
| 23 | 29 10 | 00 59 | 00 41 | 25 29 | 23 50 |
| 24 | 29 19 | 01 18 | 01 04 | 25 40 | 23 52 |
| 25 | 29 28 | 01 38 | 01 27 | 25 50 | 23 53 |
| 26 | 29 37 | 01 58 | 01 50 | 26 01 | 23 54 |
| 27 | 29 47 | 02 18 | 02 14 | 26 11 | 23 55 |
| 28 | 29 56 | 02 38 | 02 37 | 26 22 | 23 56 |
| 29 | 00♊06 | 02 59 | 03 01 | 26 33 | 23 57 |
| 30 | 00 16 | 03 21 | 03 25 | 26 43 | 23 58 |
| 31 | 00 26 | 03 43 | 03 50 | 26 54 | 23 59 |
| 32 | 00 36 | 04 05 | 04 14 | 27 05 | 24 00 |
| 33 | 00 47 | 04 28 | 04 39 | 27 17 | 24 01 |
| 34 | 00 58 | 04 51 | 05 05 | 27 28 | 24 03 |
| 35 | 01 10 | 05 15 | 05 30 | 27 40 | 24 04 |
| 36 | 01 22 | 05 40 | 05 56 | 27 51 | 24 05 |
| 37 | 01 34 | 06 05 | 06 23 | 28 03 | 24 06 |
| 38 | 01 46 | 06 31 | 06 49 | 28 15 | 24 08 |
| 39 | 01 59 | 06 58 | 07 17 | 28 28 | 24 09 |
| 40 | 02 13 | 07 25 | 07 44 | 28 40 | 24 10 |
| 41 | 02 27 | 07 53 | 08 12 | 28 53 | 24 12 |
| 42 | 02 42 | 08 23 | 08 41 | 29 06 | 24 13 |
| 43 | 02 57 | 08 53 | 09 10 | 29 19 | 24 14 |
| 44 | 03 13 | 09 24 | 09 40 | 29 32 | 24 16 |
| 45 | 03 29 | 09 56 | 10 10 | 29 46 | 24 17 |
| 46 | 03 47 | 10 29 | 10 41 | 00♍00 | 24 19 |
| 47 | 04 05 | 11 04 | 11 12 | 00 14 | 24 20 |
| 48 | 04 24 | 11 40 | 11 44 | 00 29 | 24 22 |
| 49 | 04 44 | 12 17 | 12 17 | 00 44 | 24 24 |
| 50 | 05 05 | 12 56 | 12 51 | 00 59 | 24 25 |
| 51 | 05 28 | 13 37 | 13 25 | 01 15 | 24 27 |
| 52 | 05 52 | 14 19 | 14 00 | 01 32 | 24 29 |
| 53 | 06 18 | 15 04 | 14 37 | 01 48 | 24 31 |
| 54 | 06 45 | 15 50 | 15 14 | 02 05 | 24 33 |
| 55 | 07 15 | 16 39 | 15 52 | 02 23 | 24 35 |
| 56 | 07 46 | 17 30 | 16 31 | 02 41 | 24 37 |
| 57 | 08 21 | 18 24 | 17 11 | 03 00 | 24 39 |
| 58 | 08 58 | 19 21 | 17 52 | 03 20 | 24 41 |
| 59 | 09 40 | 20 20 | 18 35 | 03 40 | 24 44 |
| 60 | 10♊26 | 21♋24 | 19♌18 | 04♍01 | 24♍46 |

**1h 40m 0s — 26 ♈ 57 — 25° 0' 0"**

| LAT. | 11 | 12 | ASC | 2 | 3 |
|---|---|---|---|---|---|
| 0 | 27♉17 | 25♊25 | 23♋10 | 22♌39 | 24♍33 |
| 5 | 27 52 | 26 44 | 25 00 | 23 29 | 24 37 |
| 10 | 28 27 | 28 06 | 26 48 | 24 18 | 24 41 |
| 15 | 29 05 | 29 30 | 28 37 | 25 07 | 24 45 |
| 20 | 29 45 | 00♋58 | 00♌26 | 25 56 | 24 49 |
| 21 | 29 53 | 01 16 | 00 49 | 26 06 | 24 50 |
| 22 | 00♊02 | 01 35 | 01 11 | 26 16 | 24 51 |
| 23 | 00 10 | 01 54 | 01 33 | 26 26 | 24 52 |
| 24 | 00 19 | 02 13 | 01 56 | 26 36 | 24 53 |
| 25 | 00 28 | 02 32 | 02 19 | 26 46 | 24 54 |
| 26 | 00 37 | 02 52 | 02 42 | 26 56 | 24 55 |
| 27 | 00 46 | 03 12 | 03 05 | 27 06 | 24 56 |
| 28 | 00 56 | 03 33 | 03 28 | 27 17 | 24 56 |
| 29 | 01 06 | 03 54 | 03 52 | 27 27 | 24 57 |
| 30 | 01 16 | 04 15 | 04 16 | 27 38 | 24 58 |
| 31 | 01 26 | 04 37 | 04 40 | 27 49 | 24 59 |
| 32 | 01 37 | 04 59 | 05 04 | 27 59 | 25 00 |
| 33 | 01 48 | 05 22 | 05 29 | 28 10 | 25 01 |
| 34 | 01 59 | 05 45 | 05 54 | 28 21 | 25 02 |
| 35 | 02 10 | 06 09 | 06 19 | 28 33 | 25 03 |
| 36 | 02 22 | 06 34 | 06 45 | 28 44 | 25 04 |
| 37 | 02 35 | 06 59 | 07 11 | 28 56 | 25 05 |
| 38 | 02 47 | 07 25 | 07 38 | 29 07 | 25 06 |
| 39 | 03 00 | 07 51 | 08 04 | 29 19 | 25 07 |
| 40 | 03 14 | 08 18 | 08 32 | 29 32 | 25 08 |
| 41 | 03 28 | 08 46 | 08 59 | 29 44 | 25 10 |
| 42 | 03 43 | 09 15 | 09 27 | 29 56 | 25 11 |
| 43 | 03 58 | 09 45 | 09 56 | 00♍09 | 25 12 |
| 44 | 04 14 | 10 16 | 10 25 | 00 22 | 25 13 |
| 45 | 04 31 | 10 48 | 10 55 | 00 36 | 25 14 |
| 46 | 04 48 | 11 21 | 11 26 | 00 49 | 25 16 |
| 47 | 05 07 | 11 56 | 11 57 | 01 03 | 25 17 |
| 48 | 05 26 | 12 31 | 12 28 | 01 18 | 25 18 |
| 49 | 05 46 | 13 08 | 13 01 | 01 32 | 25 20 |
| 50 | 06 08 | 13 47 | 13 34 | 01 47 | 25 21 |
| 51 | 06 30 | 14 27 | 14 08 | 02 03 | 25 23 |
| 52 | 06 55 | 15 09 | 14 42 | 02 19 | 25 24 |
| 53 | 07 20 | 15 53 | 15 18 | 02 35 | 25 26 |
| 54 | 07 48 | 16 39 | 15 54 | 02 51 | 25 27 |
| 55 | 08 17 | 17 27 | 16 32 | 03 09 | 25 29 |
| 56 | 08 49 | 18 18 | 17 10 | 03 26 | 25 31 |
| 57 | 09 24 | 19 11 | 17 50 | 03 45 | 25 33 |
| 58 | 10 02 | 20 07 | 18 30 | 04 04 | 25 35 |
| 59 | 10 44 | 21 06 | 19 12 | 04 23 | 25 36 |
| 60 | 11♊30 | 22♋08 | 19♌55 | 04♍44 | 25♍39 |

**1h 44m 0s — 28 ♈ 00 — 26° 0' 0"**

| LAT. | 11 | 12 | ASC | 2 | 3 |
|---|---|---|---|---|---|
| 0 | 28♉15 | 26♊20 | 24♋06 | 23♌41 | 25♍38 |
| 5 | 28 50 | 27 40 | 25 56 | 24 30 | 25 42 |
| 10 | 29 26 | 29 01 | 27 43 | 25 18 | 25 45 |
| 15 | 00♊04 | 00♋25 | 29 31 | 26 05 | 25 48 |
| 20 | 00 44 | 01 53 | 01♌19 | 26 53 | 25 52 |
| 21 | 00 52 | 02 11 | 01 41 | 27 03 | 25 52 |
| 22 | 01 01 | 02 30 | 02 04 | 27 12 | 25 53 |
| 23 | 01 10 | 02 49 | 02 26 | 27 22 | 25 54 |
| 24 | 01 18 | 03 08 | 02 48 | 27 32 | 25 54 |
| 25 | 01 28 | 03 27 | 03 11 | 27 42 | 25 55 |
| 26 | 01 37 | 03 47 | 03 34 | 27 52 | 25 56 |
| 27 | 01 46 | 04 07 | 03 56 | 28 02 | 25 56 |
| 28 | 01 56 | 04 27 | 04 20 | 28 12 | 25 57 |
| 29 | 02 06 | 04 48 | 04 43 | 28 22 | 25 58 |
| 30 | 02 16 | 05 09 | 05 07 | 28 32 | 25 59 |
| 31 | 02 26 | 05 31 | 05 30 | 28 43 | 25 59 |
| 32 | 02 37 | 05 53 | 05 54 | 28 53 | 26 00 |
| 33 | 02 48 | 06 16 | 06 19 | 29 04 | 26 01 |
| 34 | 02 59 | 06 39 | 06 44 | 29 15 | 26 02 |
| 35 | 03 11 | 07 03 | 07 08 | 29 26 | 26 02 |
| 36 | 03 23 | 07 27 | 07 34 | 29 37 | 26 03 |
| 37 | 03 35 | 07 52 | 07 59 | 29 48 | 26 04 |
| 38 | 03 48 | 08 18 | 08 26 | 00♍00 | 26 05 |
| 39 | 04 01 | 08 44 | 08 52 | 00 11 | 26 06 |
| 40 | 04 15 | 09 11 | 09 19 | 00 23 | 26 07 |
| 41 | 04 29 | 09 39 | 09 46 | 00 35 | 26 08 |
| 42 | 04 44 | 10 08 | 10 14 | 00 47 | 26 09 |
| 43 | 04 59 | 10 38 | 10 42 | 01 00 | 26 10 |
| 44 | 05 15 | 11 08 | 11 11 | 01 13 | 26 10 |
| 45 | 05 32 | 11 40 | 11 40 | 01 26 | 26 11 |
| 46 | 05 50 | 12 13 | 12 10 | 01 39 | 26 13 |
| 47 | 06 08 | 12 47 | 12 41 | 01 52 | 26 14 |
| 48 | 06 27 | 13 22 | 13 12 | 02 06 | 26 15 |
| 49 | 06 48 | 13 59 | 13 44 | 02 21 | 26 16 |
| 50 | 07 09 | 14 37 | 14 17 | 02 35 | 26 17 |
| 51 | 07 32 | 15 17 | 14 50 | 02 50 | 26 18 |
| 52 | 07 57 | 15 59 | 15 24 | 03 06 | 26 19 |
| 53 | 08 23 | 16 42 | 15 59 | 03 21 | 26 21 |
| 54 | 08 50 | 17 27 | 16 35 | 03 38 | 26 22 |
| 55 | 09 20 | 18 15 | 17 12 | 03 54 | 26 23 |
| 56 | 09 52 | 19 05 | 17 49 | 04 12 | 26 25 |
| 57 | 10 27 | 19 57 | 18 28 | 04 29 | 26 26 |
| 58 | 11 05 | 20 52 | 19 08 | 04 48 | 26 28 |
| 59 | 11 47 | 21 51 | 19 49 | 05 07 | 26 29 |
| 60 | 12♊33 | 22♋52 | 20♌32 | 05♍27 | 26♍31 |

**1h 48m 0s — 29 ♈ 03 — 27° 0' 0"**

| LAT. | 11 | 12 | ASC | 2 | 3 |
|---|---|---|---|---|---|
| 0 | 29♉13 | 27♊15 | 25♋03 | 24♌42 | 26♍44 |
| 5 | 29 48 | 28 35 | 26 52 | 25 30 | 26 46 |
| 10 | 00♊24 | 29 56 | 28 39 | 26 17 | 26 49 |
| 15 | 01 03 | 01♋20 | 00♌25 | 27 03 | 26 51 |
| 20 | 01 43 | 02 48 | 02 13 | 27 50 | 26 54 |
| 21 | 01 51 | 03 06 | 02 34 | 27 59 | 26 54 |
| 22 | 02 00 | 03 24 | 02 56 | 28 09 | 26 55 |
| 23 | 02 09 | 03 43 | 03 18 | 28 18 | 26 55 |
| 24 | 02 18 | 04 02 | 03 40 | 28 28 | 26 56 |
| 25 | 02 27 | 04 22 | 04 03 | 28 38 | 26 56 |
| 26 | 02 36 | 04 41 | 04 25 | 28 47 | 26 57 |
| 27 | 02 46 | 05 01 | 04 48 | 28 57 | 26 57 |
| 28 | 02 55 | 05 22 | 05 11 | 29 07 | 26 58 |
| 29 | 03 05 | 05 42 | 05 34 | 29 17 | 26 58 |
| 30 | 03 16 | 06 04 | 05 57 | 29 27 | 26 59 |
| 31 | 03 26 | 06 25 | 06 21 | 29 37 | 27 00 |
| 32 | 03 37 | 06 47 | 06 44 | 29 47 | 27 00 |
| 33 | 03 48 | 07 10 | 07 09 | 29 58 | 27 01 |
| 34 | 03 59 | 07 33 | 07 33 | 00♍08 | 27 01 |
| 35 | 04 11 | 07 57 | 07 58 | 00 19 | 27 02 |
| 36 | 04 23 | 08 21 | 08 23 | 00 30 | 27 02 |
| 37 | 04 35 | 08 46 | 08 48 | 00 41 | 27 03 |
| 38 | 04 48 | 09 11 | 09 14 | 00 52 | 27 04 |
| 39 | 05 01 | 09 37 | 09 40 | 01 03 | 27 04 |
| 40 | 05 15 | 10 04 | 10 06 | 01 15 | 27 05 |
| 41 | 05 30 | 10 32 | 10 33 | 01 26 | 27 06 |
| 42 | 05 44 | 11 01 | 11 00 | 01 38 | 27 06 |
| 43 | 06 00 | 11 30 | 11 28 | 01 50 | 27 07 |
| 44 | 06 16 | 12 00 | 11 57 | 02 03 | 27 08 |
| 45 | 06 33 | 12 32 | 12 26 | 02 16 | 27 09 |
| 46 | 06 51 | 13 04 | 12 55 | 02 28 | 27 09 |
| 47 | 07 09 | 13 38 | 13 25 | 02 42 | 27 10 |
| 48 | 07 29 | 14 13 | 13 56 | 02 55 | 27 11 |
| 49 | 07 49 | 14 50 | 14 27 | 03 09 | 27 12 |
| 50 | 08 11 | 15 27 | 14 59 | 03 23 | 27 13 |
| 51 | 08 34 | 16 07 | 15 32 | 03 38 | 27 14 |
| 52 | 08 58 | 16 48 | 16 06 | 03 53 | 27 14 |
| 53 | 09 24 | 17 31 | 16 40 | 04 08 | 27 15 |
| 54 | 09 52 | 18 16 | 17 15 | 04 24 | 27 16 |
| 55 | 10 22 | 19 03 | 17 52 | 04 40 | 27 17 |
| 56 | 10 54 | 19 52 | 18 29 | 04 57 | 27 18 |
| 57 | 11 29 | 20 44 | 19 07 | 05 14 | 27 20 |
| 58 | 12 08 | 21 38 | 19 46 | 05 32 | 27 21 |
| 59 | 12 50 | 22 36 | 20 27 | 05 50 | 27 22 |
| 60 | 13♊37 | 23♋36 | 21♌08 | 06♍09 | 27♍23 |

**1h 52m 0s — 00 ♉ 06 — 28° 0' 0"**

| LAT. | 11 | 12 | ASC | 2 | 3 |
|---|---|---|---|---|---|
| 0 | 00♊11 | 28♊10 | 26♋00 | 25♌44 | 27♍49 |
| 5 | 00 46 | 29 30 | 27 48 | 26 31 | 27 51 |
| 10 | 01 23 | 00♋51 | 29 34 | 27 17 | 27 52 |
| 15 | 02 01 | 02 15 | 01♌19 | 28 02 | 27 54 |
| 20 | 02 42 | 03 42 | 03 06 | 28 47 | 27 56 |
| 21 | 02 50 | 04 01 | 03 27 | 28 57 | 27 56 |
| 22 | 02 59 | 04 19 | 03 49 | 29 06 | 27 56 |
| 23 | 03 08 | 04 38 | 04 11 | 29 15 | 27 57 |
| 24 | 03 17 | 04 57 | 04 33 | 29 24 | 27 57 |
| 25 | 03 26 | 05 16 | 04 55 | 29 34 | 27 57 |
| 26 | 03 35 | 05 36 | 05 17 | 29 43 | 27 58 |
| 27 | 03 45 | 05 56 | 05 39 | 29 53 | 27 58 |
| 28 | 03 55 | 06 16 | 06 02 | 00♍02 | 27 59 |
| 29 | 04 05 | 06 37 | 06 25 | 00 12 | 27 59 |
| 30 | 04 15 | 06 58 | 06 48 | 00 22 | 27 59 |
| 31 | 04 26 | 07 19 | 07 11 | 00 32 | 28 00 |
| 32 | 04 36 | 07 41 | 07 34 | 00 42 | 28 00 |
| 33 | 04 47 | 08 04 | 07 58 | 00 52 | 28 00 |
| 34 | 04 59 | 08 27 | 08 22 | 01 02 | 28 01 |
| 35 | 05 11 | 08 50 | 08 47 | 01 12 | 28 01 |
| 36 | 05 23 | 09 14 | 09 11 | 01 23 | 28 02 |
| 37 | 05 35 | 09 39 | 09 36 | 01 33 | 28 02 |
| 38 | 05 48 | 10 04 | 10 02 | 01 44 | 28 02 |
| 39 | 06 02 | 10 30 | 10 27 | 01 55 | 28 03 |
| 40 | 06 15 | 10 57 | 10 53 | 02 06 | 28 03 |
| 41 | 06 30 | 11 24 | 11 20 | 02 18 | 28 04 |
| 42 | 06 45 | 11 53 | 11 47 | 02 29 | 28 04 |
| 43 | 07 00 | 12 22 | 12 14 | 02 41 | 28 05 |
| 44 | 07 17 | 12 52 | 12 42 | 02 53 | 28 05 |
| 45 | 07 34 | 13 23 | 13 11 | 03 05 | 28 06 |
| 46 | 07 51 | 13 56 | 13 40 | 03 18 | 28 06 |
| 47 | 08 10 | 14 29 | 14 10 | 03 31 | 28 07 |
| 48 | 08 30 | 15 04 | 14 40 | 03 44 | 28 07 |
| 49 | 08 50 | 15 40 | 15 11 | 03 57 | 28 08 |
| 50 | 09 12 | 16 17 | 15 42 | 04 11 | 28 08 |
| 51 | 09 35 | 16 56 | 16 14 | 04 25 | 28 09 |
| 52 | 10 00 | 17 37 | 16 48 | 04 40 | 28 10 |
| 53 | 10 26 | 18 19 | 17 21 | 04 55 | 28 10 |
| 54 | 10 54 | 19 04 | 17 56 | 05 10 | 28 11 |
| 55 | 11 24 | 19 50 | 18 32 | 05 26 | 28 12 |
| 56 | 11 56 | 20 39 | 19 08 | 05 42 | 28 12 |
| 57 | 12 31 | 21 30 | 19 46 | 05 59 | 28 13 |
| 58 | 13 10 | 22 24 | 20 24 | 06 16 | 28 14 |
| 59 | 13 52 | 23 20 | 21 04 | 06 34 | 28 15 |
| 60 | 14♊39 | 24♋20 | 21♌45 | 06♍52 | 28♍15 |

**1h 56m 0s — 01 ♉ 08 — 29° 0' 0"**

| LAT. | 11 | 12 | ASC | 2 | 3 |
|---|---|---|---|---|---|
| 0 | 01♊08 | 29♊05 | 26♋57 | 26♌47 | 28♍55 |
| 5 | 01 44 | 00♋25 | 28 44 | 27 32 | 28 55 |
| 10 | 02 21 | 01 46 | 00♌29 | 28 17 | 28 56 |
| 15 | 02 59 | 03 09 | 02 14 | 29 01 | 28 57 |
| 20 | 03 41 | 04 37 | 03 59 | 29 45 | 28 58 |
| 21 | 03 49 | 04 55 | 04 20 | 29 54 | 28 58 |
| 22 | 03 58 | 05 14 | 04 42 | 00♍03 | 28 58 |
| 23 | 04 07 | 05 32 | 05 03 | 00 12 | 28 58 |
| 24 | 04 16 | 05 51 | 05 25 | 00 21 | 28 59 |
| 25 | 04 25 | 06 10 | 05 47 | 00 30 | 28 59 |
| 26 | 04 34 | 06 30 | 06 09 | 00 39 | 28 59 |
| 27 | 04 44 | 06 50 | 06 31 | 00 48 | 28 59 |
| 28 | 04 54 | 07 10 | 06 53 | 00 58 | 28 59 |
| 29 | 05 04 | 07 31 | 07 16 | 01 07 | 28 59 |
| 30 | 05 14 | 07 52 | 07 38 | 01 16 | 29 00 |
| 31 | 05 25 | 08 13 | 08 01 | 01 26 | 29 00 |
| 32 | 05 36 | 08 35 | 08 24 | 01 36 | 29 00 |
| 33 | 05 47 | 08 57 | 08 48 | 01 46 | 29 00 |
| 34 | 05 58 | 09 20 | 09 12 | 01 55 | 29 00 |
| 35 | 06 10 | 09 43 | 09 36 | 02 06 | 29 01 |
| 36 | 06 22 | 10 07 | 10 00 | 02 16 | 29 01 |
| 37 | 06 35 | 10 32 | 10 25 | 02 26 | 29 01 |
| 38 | 06 48 | 10 57 | 10 50 | 02 37 | 29 01 |
| 39 | 07 01 | 11 23 | 11 15 | 02 47 | 29 01 |
| 40 | 07 15 | 11 49 | 11 41 | 02 58 | 29 02 |
| 41 | 07 30 | 12 17 | 12 07 | 03 09 | 29 02 |
| 42 | 07 45 | 12 45 | 12 33 | 03 20 | 29 02 |
| 43 | 08 01 | 13 14 | 13 00 | 03 32 | 29 02 |
| 44 | 08 17 | 13 44 | 13 28 | 03 44 | 29 03 |
| 45 | 08 34 | 14 15 | 13 56 | 03 55 | 29 03 |
| 46 | 08 52 | 14 47 | 14 25 | 04 08 | 29 03 |
| 47 | 09 10 | 15 20 | 14 54 | 04 20 | 29 03 |
| 48 | 09 30 | 15 54 | 15 24 | 04 33 | 29 04 |
| 49 | 09 51 | 16 30 | 15 54 | 04 46 | 29 04 |
| 50 | 10 13 | 17 07 | 16 25 | 04 59 | 29 04 |
| 51 | 10 36 | 17 46 | 16 57 | 05 13 | 29 05 |
| 52 | 11 01 | 18 26 | 17 29 | 05 27 | 29 05 |
| 53 | 11 27 | 19 08 | 18 03 | 05 41 | 29 05 |
| 54 | 11 55 | 19 52 | 18 37 | 05 56 | 29 05 |
| 55 | 12 25 | 20 38 | 19 12 | 06 11 | 29 06 |
| 56 | 12 58 | 21 26 | 19 47 | 06 27 | 29 06 |
| 57 | 13 33 | 22 16 | 20 24 | 06 43 | 29 07 |
| 58 | 14 11 | 23 09 | 21 02 | 07 00 | 29 07 |
| 59 | 14 54 | 24 05 | 21 41 | 07 17 | 29 07 |
| 60 | 15♊41 | 25♋04 | 22♌21 | 07♍35 | 29♍08 |

**2h 0m 0s — 02 ♉ 11 — 30° 0' 0"**

| LAT. | 11 | 12 | ASC | 2 | 3 |
|---|---|---|---|---|---|
| 0 | 02♊05 | 00♋00 | 27♋55 | 27♌49 | 00♎00 |
| 5 | 02 42 | 01 20 | 29 41 | 28 33 | 00 00 |
| 10 | 03 19 | 02 41 | 01♌25 | 29 17 | 00 00 |
| 15 | 03 58 | 04 04 | 03 08 | 29 59 | 00 00 |
| 20 | 04 39 | 05 32 | 04 52 | 00♍42 | 00 00 |
| 21 | 04 48 | 05 50 | 05 13 | 00 51 | 00 00 |
| 22 | 04 56 | 06 08 | 05 35 | 01 00 | 00 00 |
| 23 | 05 05 | 06 27 | 05 56 | 01 08 | 00 00 |
| 24 | 05 14 | 06 46 | 06 17 | 01 17 | 00 00 |
| 25 | 05 24 | 07 05 | 06 39 | 01 26 | 00 00 |
| 26 | 05 33 | 07 24 | 07 00 | 01 35 | 00 00 |
| 27 | 05 43 | 07 44 | 07 22 | 01 44 | 00 00 |
| 28 | 05 53 | 08 04 | 07 44 | 01 53 | 00 00 |
| 29 | 06 03 | 08 25 | 08 07 | 02 02 | 00 00 |
| 30 | 06 13 | 08 45 | 08 29 | 02 11 | 00 00 |
| 31 | 06 24 | 09 07 | 08 52 | 02 21 | 00 00 |
| 32 | 06 35 | 09 28 | 09 14 | 02 30 | 00 00 |
| 33 | 06 46 | 09 51 | 09 38 | 02 40 | 00 00 |
| 34 | 06 58 | 10 13 | 10 01 | 02 49 | 00 00 |
| 35 | 07 10 | 10 37 | 10 25 | 02 59 | 00 00 |
| 36 | 07 22 | 11 00 | 10 49 | 03 09 | 00 00 |
| 37 | 07 34 | 11 25 | 11 13 | 03 19 | 00 00 |
| 38 | 07 48 | 11 50 | 11 38 | 03 29 | 00 00 |
| 39 | 08 01 | 12 15 | 12 03 | 03 39 | 00 00 |
| 40 | 08 15 | 12 42 | 12 28 | 03 50 | 00 00 |
| 41 | 08 30 | 13 09 | 12 54 | 04 01 | 00 00 |
| 42 | 08 45 | 13 37 | 13 20 | 04 12 | 00 00 |
| 43 | 09 00 | 14 06 | 13 46 | 04 23 | 00 00 |
| 44 | 09 17 | 14 35 | 14 14 | 04 34 | 00 00 |
| 45 | 09 34 | 15 06 | 14 41 | 04 45 | 00 00 |
| 46 | 09 52 | 15 38 | 15 09 | 04 57 | 00 00 |
| 47 | 10 11 | 16 11 | 15 38 | 05 09 | 00 00 |
| 48 | 10 30 | 16 45 | 16 07 | 05 22 | 00 00 |
| 49 | 10 51 | 17 20 | 16 37 | 05 34 | 00 00 |
| 50 | 11 13 | 17 57 | 17 08 | 05 47 | 00 00 |
| 51 | 11 36 | 18 35 | 17 39 | 06 00 | 00 00 |
| 52 | 12 01 | 19 15 | 18 11 | 06 14 | 00 00 |
| 53 | 12 27 | 19 56 | 18 44 | 06 28 | 00 00 |
| 54 | 12 56 | 20 40 | 19 17 | 06 42 | 00 00 |
| 55 | 13 26 | 21 25 | 19 52 | 06 57 | 00 00 |
| 56 | 13 59 | 22 12 | 20 27 | 07 12 | 00 00 |
| 57 | 14 34 | 23 02 | 21 03 | 07 28 | 00 00 |
| 58 | 15 13 | 23 54 | 21 40 | 07 44 | 00 00 |
| 59 | 15 55 | 24 49 | 22 19 | 08 01 | 00 00 |
| 60 | 16♊42 | 25♋47 | 22♌58 | 08♍18 | 00♎00 |

**2h 4m 0s — 03 ♉ 13 — 31° 0' 0"**

| LAT. | 11 | 12 | ASC | 2 | 3 |
|---|---|---|---|---|---|
| 0 | 03♊03 | 00♋55 | 28♋52 | 28♌52 | 01♎05 |
| 5 | 03 39 | 02 15 | 00♌37 | 29 35 | 01 05 |
| 10 | 04 17 | 03 36 | 02 20 | 00♍17 | 01 04 |
| 15 | 04 56 | 04 59 | 04 03 | 00 58 | 01 03 |
| 20 | 05 37 | 06 26 | 05 46 | 01 40 | 01 02 |
| 21 | 05 46 | 06 44 | 06 06 | 01 48 | 01 02 |
| 22 | 05 55 | 07 02 | 06 27 | 01 57 | 01 02 |
| 23 | 06 04 | 07 21 | 06 48 | 02 05 | 01 02 |
| 24 | 06 13 | 07 40 | 07 10 | 02 14 | 01 01 |
| 25 | 06 22 | 07 59 | 07 31 | 02 22 | 01 01 |
| 26 | 06 32 | 08 18 | 07 52 | 02 31 | 01 01 |
| 27 | 06 42 | 08 38 | 08 14 | 02 40 | 01 01 |
| 28 | 06 52 | 08 58 | 08 36 | 02 48 | 01 01 |
| 29 | 07 02 | 09 18 | 08 57 | 02 57 | 01 01 |
| 30 | 07 12 | 09 39 | 09 20 | 03 06 | 01 00 |
| 31 | 07 23 | 10 00 | 09 42 | 03 15 | 01 00 |
| 32 | 07 34 | 10 22 | 10 04 | 03 24 | 01 00 |
| 33 | 07 45 | 10 44 | 10 27 | 03 34 | 01 00 |
| 34 | 07 57 | 11 07 | 10 50 | 03 43 | 01 00 |
| 35 | 08 09 | 11 30 | 11 14 | 03 52 | 00 59 |
| 36 | 08 21 | 11 53 | 11 37 | 04 02 | 00 59 |
| 37 | 08 34 | 12 18 | 12 01 | 04 12 | 00 59 |
| 38 | 08 47 | 12 42 | 12 25 | 04 22 | 00 59 |
| 39 | 09 00 | 13 08 | 12 50 | 04 32 | 00 59 |
| 40 | 09 14 | 13 34 | 13 15 | 04 42 | 00 58 |
| 41 | 09 29 | 14 01 | 13 40 | 04 52 | 00 58 |
| 42 | 09 44 | 14 29 | 14 06 | 05 03 | 00 58 |
| 43 | 10 00 | 14 57 | 14 32 | 05 13 | 00 58 |
| 44 | 10 16 | 15 27 | 14 59 | 05 24 | 00 57 |
| 45 | 10 34 | 15 57 | 15 26 | 05 36 | 00 57 |
| 46 | 10 52 | 16 29 | 15 54 | 05 47 | 00 57 |
| 47 | 11 11 | 17 01 | 16 22 | 05 59 | 00 57 |
| 48 | 11 30 | 17 35 | 16 51 | 06 10 | 00 56 |
| 49 | 11 51 | 18 10 | 17 20 | 06 23 | 00 56 |
| 50 | 12 13 | 18 46 | 17 50 | 06 35 | 00 56 |
| 51 | 12 37 | 19 24 | 18 21 | 06 48 | 00 55 |
| 52 | 13 01 | 20 03 | 18 53 | 07 01 | 00 55 |
| 53 | 13 28 | 20 44 | 19 25 | 07 15 | 00 55 |
| 54 | 13 56 | 21 27 | 19 58 | 07 29 | 00 55 |
| 55 | 14 26 | 22 12 | 20 31 | 07 43 | 00 54 |
| 56 | 14 59 | 22 59 | 21 06 | 07 58 | 00 54 |
| 57 | 15 35 | 23 48 | 21 42 | 08 13 | 00 53 |
| 58 | 16 13 | 24 39 | 22 18 | 08 28 | 00 53 |
| 59 | 16 56 | 25 33 | 22 56 | 08 45 | 00 53 |
| 60 | 17♊43 | 26♋30 | 23♌35 | 09♍01 | 00♎52 |

# Placidus Table of Houses for Latitudes 0° to 60° North

**2h 8m 0s — 32° 0' 0" — 04 ♉ 16**

| LAT. | 11 | 12 | ASC | 2 | 3 |
|---|---|---|---|---|---|
| 0 | 04♊00 | 01♋50 | 29♋49 | 29♌54 | 02♎11 |
| 5 | 04 36 | 03 10 | 01♌34 | 00♍36 | 02 09 |
| 10 | 05 14 | 04 31 | 03 16 | 01 17 | 02 08 |
| 15 | 05 54 | 05 54 | 04 57 | 01 57 | 02 06 |
| 20 | 06 35 | 07 21 | 06 39 | 02 37 | 02 04 |
| 21 | 06 44 | 07 39 | 07 00 | 02 46 | 02 04 |
| 22 | 06 53 | 07 57 | 07 20 | 02 54 | 02 04 |
| 23 | 07 02 | 08 15 | 07 41 | 03 02 | 02 03 |
| 24 | 07 11 | 08 34 | 08 02 | 03 10 | 02 03 |
| 25 | 07 21 | 08 53 | 08 23 | 03 19 | 02 03 |
| 26 | 07 30 | 09 12 | 08 44 | 03 27 | 02 02 |
| 27 | 07 40 | 09 32 | 09 05 | 03 35 | 02 02 |
| 28 | 07 50 | 09 52 | 09 27 | 03 44 | 02 01 |
| 29 | 08 00 | 10 12 | 09 48 | 03 52 | 02 01 |
| 30 | 08 11 | 10 33 | 10 10 | 04 01 | 02 01 |
| 31 | 08 21 | 10 54 | 10 32 | 04 10 | 02 00 |
| 32 | 08 33 | 11 15 | 10 54 | 04 19 | 02 00 |
| 33 | 08 44 | 11 37 | 11 17 | 04 28 | 02 00 |
| 34 | 08 56 | 12 00 | 11 40 | 04 37 | 01 59 |
| 35 | 09 08 | 12 23 | 12 03 | 04 46 | 01 59 |
| 36 | 09 20 | 12 46 | 12 26 | 04 55 | 01 58 |
| 37 | 09 33 | 13 10 | 12 50 | 05 05 | 01 58 |
| 38 | 09 46 | 13 35 | 13 13 | 05 14 | 01 58 |
| 39 | 09 59 | 14 00 | 13 38 | 05 24 | 01 57 |
| 40 | 10 14 | 14 26 | 14 02 | 05 34 | 01 57 |
| 41 | 10 28 | 14 53 | 14 27 | 05 44 | 01 56 |
| 42 | 10 43 | 15 20 | 14 53 | 05 54 | 01 56 |
| 43 | 10 59 | 15 49 | 15 18 | 06 04 | 01 55 |
| 44 | 11 16 | 16 18 | 15 45 | 06 15 | 01 55 |
| 45 | 11 33 | 16 48 | 16 11 | 06 26 | 01 54 |
| 46 | 11 51 | 17 19 | 16 39 | 06 37 | 01 54 |
| 47 | 12 10 | 17 52 | 17 06 | 06 48 | 01 53 |
| 48 | 12 30 | 18 25 | 17 35 | 06 59 | 01 53 |
| 49 | 12 51 | 19 00 | 18 04 | 07 11 | 01 52 |
| 50 | 13 13 | 19 36 | 18 33 | 07 23 | 01 52 |
| 51 | 13 36 | 20 13 | 19 03 | 07 36 | 01 51 |
| 52 | 14 01 | 20 52 | 19 34 | 07 48 | 01 50 |
| 53 | 14 28 | 21 32 | 20 06 | 08 01 | 01 50 |
| 54 | 14 56 | 22 15 | 20 38 | 08 15 | 01 49 |
| 55 | 15 26 | 22 59 | 21 11 | 08 29 | 01 48 |
| 56 | 15 59 | 23 45 | 21 45 | 08 43 | 01 48 |
| 57 | 16 35 | 24 33 | 22 20 | 08 58 | 01 47 |
| 58 | 17 14 | 25 24 | 22 56 | 09 13 | 01 46 |
| 59 | 17 56 | 26 18 | 23 33 | 09 28 | 01 45 |
| 60 | 18♊44 | 27♋14 | 24♌11 | 09♍45 | 01♎45 |

**2h 12m 0s — 33° 0' 0" — 05 ♉ 18**

| LAT. | 11 | 12 | ASC | 2 | 3 |
|---|---|---|---|---|---|
| 0 | 04♊57 | 02♋45 | 00♌47 | 00♍57 | 03♎16 |
| 5 | 05 34 | 04 05 | 02 31 | 01 38 | 03 14 |
| 10 | 06 12 | 05 25 | 04 12 | 02 17 | 03 11 |
| 15 | 06 51 | 06 48 | 05 52 | 02 56 | 03 09 |
| 20 | 07 33 | 08 15 | 07 32 | 03 35 | 03 06 |
| 21 | 07 42 | 08 33 | 07 53 | 03 43 | 03 06 |
| 22 | 07 51 | 08 51 | 08 13 | 03 51 | 03 05 |
| 23 | 08 00 | 09 09 | 08 34 | 03 59 | 03 05 |
| 24 | 08 09 | 09 28 | 08 54 | 04 07 | 03 04 |
| 25 | 08 19 | 09 47 | 09 15 | 04 15 | 03 04 |
| 26 | 08 28 | 10 06 | 09 36 | 04 23 | 03 03 |
| 27 | 08 38 | 10 26 | 09 57 | 04 31 | 03 03 |
| 28 | 08 48 | 10 45 | 10 18 | 04 39 | 03 02 |
| 29 | 08 59 | 11 06 | 10 39 | 04 48 | 03 02 |
| 30 | 09 09 | 11 26 | 11 01 | 04 56 | 03 01 |
| 31 | 09 20 | 11 47 | 11 23 | 05 05 | 03 00 |
| 32 | 09 31 | 12 09 | 11 44 | 05 13 | 03 00 |
| 33 | 09 42 | 12 30 | 12 07 | 05 22 | 02 59 |
| 34 | 09 54 | 12 53 | 12 29 | 05 30 | 02 59 |
| 35 | 10 06 | 13 15 | 12 52 | 05 39 | 02 58 |
| 36 | 10 19 | 13 39 | 13 15 | 05 48 | 02 58 |
| 37 | 10 31 | 14 03 | 13 38 | 05 57 | 02 57 |
| 38 | 10 45 | 14 27 | 14 01 | 06 07 | 02 56 |
| 39 | 10 58 | 14 52 | 14 25 | 06 16 | 02 56 |
| 40 | 11 12 | 15 18 | 14 49 | 06 26 | 02 55 |
| 41 | 11 27 | 15 45 | 15 14 | 06 35 | 02 54 |
| 42 | 11 42 | 16 12 | 15 39 | 06 45 | 02 54 |
| 43 | 11 58 | 16 40 | 16 04 | 06 55 | 02 53 |
| 44 | 12 15 | 17 09 | 16 30 | 07 05 | 02 52 |
| 45 | 12 32 | 17 39 | 16 57 | 07 16 | 02 51 |
| 46 | 12 50 | 18 10 | 17 23 | 07 26 | 02 51 |
| 47 | 13 09 | 18 42 | 17 51 | 07 37 | 02 50 |
| 48 | 13 29 | 19 15 | 18 18 | 07 48 | 02 49 |
| 49 | 13 50 | 19 49 | 18 47 | 08 00 | 02 48 |
| 50 | 14 12 | 20 25 | 19 16 | 08 11 | 02 47 |
| 51 | 14 36 | 21 02 | 19 46 | 08 23 | 02 46 |
| 52 | 15 01 | 21 40 | 20 16 | 08 36 | 02 46 |
| 53 | 15 27 | 22 20 | 20 47 | 08 48 | 02 45 |
| 54 | 15 56 | 23 02 | 21 19 | 09 01 | 02 44 |
| 55 | 16 26 | 23 45 | 21 51 | 09 14 | 02 43 |
| 56 | 16 59 | 24 31 | 22 25 | 09 28 | 02 42 |
| 57 | 17 35 | 25 19 | 22 59 | 09 42 | 02 40 |
| 58 | 18 13 | 26 09 | 23 34 | 09 57 | 02 39 |
| 59 | 18 56 | 27 02 | 24 11 | 10 12 | 02 38 |
| 60 | 19♊44 | 27♋57 | 24♌48 | 10♍28 | 02♎37 |

**2h 16m 0s — 34° 0' 0" — 06 ♉ 19**

| LAT. | 11 | 12 | ASC | 2 | 3 |
|---|---|---|---|---|---|
| 0 | 05♊54 | 03♋40 | 01♌45 | 02♍00 | 04♎22 |
| 5 | 06 31 | 05 00 | 03 27 | 02 39 | 04 18 |
| 10 | 07 09 | 06 20 | 05 07 | 03 18 | 04 15 |
| 15 | 07 49 | 07 43 | 06 47 | 03 55 | 04 12 |
| 20 | 08 31 | 09 09 | 08 26 | 04 33 | 04 08 |
| 21 | 08 40 | 09 27 | 08 46 | 04 41 | 04 08 |
| 22 | 08 49 | 09 45 | 09 06 | 04 48 | 04 07 |
| 23 | 08 58 | 10 03 | 09 26 | 04 56 | 04 06 |
| 24 | 09 07 | 10 22 | 09 47 | 05 04 | 04 06 |
| 25 | 09 17 | 10 41 | 10 07 | 05 11 | 04 05 |
| 26 | 09 26 | 11 00 | 10 28 | 05 19 | 04 04 |
| 27 | 09 36 | 11 19 | 10 48 | 05 27 | 04 04 |
| 28 | 09 46 | 11 39 | 11 09 | 05 35 | 04 03 |
| 29 | 09 57 | 11 59 | 11 30 | 05 43 | 04 02 |
| 30 | 10 07 | 12 20 | 11 51 | 05 51 | 04 01 |
| 31 | 10 18 | 12 40 | 12 13 | 05 59 | 04 01 |
| 32 | 10 29 | 13 02 | 12 34 | 06 08 | 04 00 |
| 33 | 10 41 | 13 23 | 12 56 | 06 16 | 03 59 |
| 34 | 10 52 | 13 46 | 13 18 | 06 24 | 03 58 |
| 35 | 11 05 | 14 08 | 13 41 | 06 33 | 03 58 |
| 36 | 11 17 | 14 31 | 14 03 | 06 42 | 03 57 |
| 37 | 11 30 | 14 55 | 14 26 | 06 50 | 03 56 |
| 38 | 11 43 | 15 19 | 14 49 | 06 59 | 03 55 |
| 39 | 11 57 | 15 44 | 15 13 | 07 08 | 03 54 |
| 40 | 12 11 | 16 10 | 15 37 | 07 17 | 03 53 |
| 41 | 12 26 | 16 36 | 16 01 | 07 27 | 03 52 |
| 42 | 12 41 | 17 03 | 16 25 | 07 36 | 03 51 |
| 43 | 12 57 | 17 31 | 16 50 | 07 46 | 03 50 |
| 44 | 13 14 | 18 00 | 17 16 | 07 56 | 03 50 |
| 45 | 13 31 | 18 30 | 17 42 | 08 06 | 03 49 |
| 46 | 13 49 | 19 00 | 18 08 | 08 16 | 03 47 |
| 47 | 14 08 | 19 32 | 18 35 | 08 27 | 03 46 |
| 48 | 14 28 | 20 05 | 19 02 | 08 37 | 03 45 |
| 49 | 14 49 | 20 38 | 19 30 | 08 48 | 03 44 |
| 50 | 15 12 | 21 14 | 19 59 | 09 00 | 03 43 |
| 51 | 15 35 | 21 50 | 20 28 | 09 11 | 03 42 |
| 52 | 16 00 | 22 28 | 20 58 | 09 23 | 03 41 |
| 53 | 16 27 | 23 08 | 21 28 | 09 35 | 03 39 |
| 54 | 16 55 | 23 49 | 21 59 | 09 48 | 03 38 |
| 55 | 17 25 | 24 32 | 22 31 | 10 00 | 03 37 |
| 56 | 17 58 | 25 17 | 23 04 | 10 14 | 03 35 |
| 57 | 18 34 | 26 04 | 23 38 | 10 27 | 03 34 |
| 58 | 19 13 | 26 54 | 24 12 | 10 41 | 03 32 |
| 59 | 19 56 | 27 45 | 24 48 | 10 56 | 03 31 |
| 60 | 20♊43 | 28♋40 | 25♌25 | 11♍11 | 03♎29 |

**2h 20m 0s — 35° 0' 0" — 07 ♉ 21**

| LAT. | 11 | 12 | ASC | 2 | 3 |
|---|---|---|---|---|---|
| 0 | 06♊50 | 04♋35 | 02♌43 | 03♍03 | 05♎27 |
| 5 | 07 28 | 05 55 | 04 24 | 03 41 | 05 23 |
| 10 | 08 06 | 07 15 | 06 03 | 04 18 | 05 19 |
| 15 | 08 46 | 08 38 | 07 41 | 04 55 | 05 15 |
| 20 | 09 29 | 10 04 | 09 19 | 05 31 | 05 11 |
| 21 | 09 37 | 10 21 | 09 39 | 05 38 | 05 10 |
| 22 | 09 46 | 10 39 | 09 59 | 05 46 | 05 09 |
| 23 | 09 56 | 10 58 | 10 19 | 05 53 | 05 08 |
| 24 | 10 05 | 11 16 | 10 39 | 06 01 | 05 07 |
| 25 | 10 14 | 11 35 | 10 59 | 06 08 | 05 06 |
| 26 | 10 24 | 11 54 | 11 20 | 06 16 | 05 05 |
| 27 | 10 34 | 12 13 | 11 40 | 06 23 | 05 04 |
| 28 | 10 44 | 12 33 | 12 00 | 06 31 | 05 04 |
| 29 | 10 55 | 12 53 | 12 21 | 06 39 | 05 03 |
| 30 | 11 05 | 13 13 | 12 42 | 06 46 | 05 02 |
| 31 | 11 16 | 13 34 | 13 03 | 06 54 | 05 01 |
| 32 | 11 27 | 13 55 | 13 24 | 07 02 | 05 00 |
| 33 | 11 39 | 14 16 | 13 46 | 07 10 | 04 59 |
| 34 | 11 51 | 14 38 | 14 08 | 07 18 | 04 58 |
| 35 | 12 03 | 15 01 | 14 30 | 07 27 | 04 57 |
| 36 | 12 15 | 15 24 | 14 52 | 07 35 | 04 56 |
| 37 | 12 28 | 15 47 | 15 14 | 07 43 | 04 55 |
| 38 | 12 41 | 16 12 | 15 37 | 07 52 | 04 54 |
| 39 | 12 55 | 16 36 | 16 00 | 08 01 | 04 53 |
| 40 | 13 09 | 17 02 | 16 24 | 08 09 | 04 52 |
| 41 | 13 24 | 17 28 | 16 48 | 08 18 | 04 50 |
| 42 | 13 40 | 17 55 | 17 12 | 08 28 | 04 49 |
| 43 | 13 56 | 18 22 | 17 36 | 08 37 | 04 48 |
| 44 | 14 12 | 18 51 | 18 01 | 08 46 | 04 47 |
| 45 | 14 30 | 19 20 | 18 27 | 08 56 | 04 46 |
| 46 | 14 48 | 19 50 | 18 53 | 09 06 | 04 44 |
| 47 | 15 07 | 20 22 | 19 19 | 09 16 | 04 43 |
| 48 | 15 27 | 20 54 | 19 46 | 09 26 | 04 42 |
| 49 | 15 48 | 21 28 | 20 13 | 09 37 | 04 40 |
| 50 | 16 10 | 22 03 | 20 41 | 09 48 | 04 39 |
| 51 | 16 34 | 22 39 | 21 10 | 09 59 | 04 37 |
| 52 | 16 59 | 23 16 | 21 39 | 10 10 | 04 36 |
| 53 | 17 26 | 23 55 | 22 09 | 10 22 | 04 34 |
| 54 | 17 54 | 24 36 | 22 40 | 10 34 | 04 33 |
| 55 | 18 24 | 25 19 | 23 11 | 10 46 | 04 31 |
| 56 | 18 57 | 26 03 | 23 43 | 10 59 | 04 29 |
| 57 | 19 33 | 26 49 | 24 16 | 11 12 | 04 27 |
| 58 | 20 12 | 27 38 | 24 50 | 11 26 | 04 25 |
| 59 | 20 55 | 28 29 | 25 25 | 11 40 | 04 24 |
| 60 | 21♊42 | 29♋23 | 26♌01 | 11♍54 | 04♎21 |

**2h 24m 0s — 36° 0' 0" — 08 ♉ 23**

| LAT. | 11 | 12 | ASC | 2 | 3 |
|---|---|---|---|---|---|
| 0 | 07♊47 | 05♋30 | 03♌41 | 04♍07 | 06♎32 |
| 5 | 08 24 | 06 50 | 05 22 | 04 43 | 06 27 |
| 10 | 09 03 | 08 10 | 06 59 | 05 19 | 06 22 |
| 15 | 09 43 | 09 32 | 08 36 | 05 54 | 06 18 |
| 20 | 10 26 | 10 58 | 10 13 | 06 29 | 06 13 |
| 21 | 10 35 | 11 15 | 10 33 | 06 36 | 06 12 |
| 22 | 10 44 | 11 33 | 10 52 | 06 43 | 06 11 |
| 23 | 10 53 | 11 52 | 11 12 | 06 50 | 06 10 |
| 24 | 11 03 | 12 10 | 11 32 | 06 57 | 06 08 |
| 25 | 11 12 | 12 29 | 11 51 | 07 05 | 06 07 |
| 26 | 11 22 | 12 47 | 12 11 | 07 12 | 06 06 |
| 27 | 11 32 | 13 07 | 12 32 | 07 19 | 06 05 |
| 28 | 11 42 | 13 26 | 12 52 | 07 27 | 06 04 |
| 29 | 11 52 | 13 46 | 13 12 | 07 34 | 06 03 |
| 30 | 12 03 | 14 06 | 13 33 | 07 42 | 06 02 |
| 31 | 12 14 | 14 27 | 13 54 | 07 49 | 06 01 |
| 32 | 12 25 | 14 48 | 14 14 | 07 57 | 06 00 |
| 33 | 12 37 | 15 09 | 14 36 | 08 05 | 05 59 |
| 34 | 12 49 | 15 31 | 14 57 | 08 12 | 05 57 |
| 35 | 13 01 | 15 53 | 15 19 | 08 20 | 05 56 |
| 36 | 13 13 | 16 16 | 15 41 | 08 28 | 05 55 |
| 37 | 13 26 | 16 40 | 16 03 | 08 36 | 05 54 |
| 38 | 13 40 | 17 04 | 16 25 | 08 45 | 05 52 |
| 39 | 13 53 | 17 28 | 16 48 | 08 53 | 05 51 |
| 40 | 14 08 | 17 53 | 17 11 | 09 02 | 05 50 |
| 41 | 14 22 | 18 19 | 17 34 | 09 10 | 05 48 |
| 42 | 14 38 | 18 46 | 17 58 | 09 19 | 05 47 |
| 43 | 14 54 | 19 13 | 18 22 | 09 28 | 05 46 |
| 44 | 15 11 | 19 41 | 18 47 | 09 37 | 05 44 |
| 45 | 15 28 | 20 11 | 19 12 | 09 46 | 05 43 |
| 46 | 15 46 | 20 41 | 19 37 | 09 56 | 05 41 |
| 47 | 16 05 | 21 12 | 20 03 | 10 06 | 05 40 |
| 48 | 16 25 | 21 44 | 20 30 | 10 15 | 05 38 |
| 49 | 16 47 | 22 17 | 20 56 | 10 26 | 05 36 |
| 50 | 17 09 | 22 51 | 21 24 | 10 36 | 05 35 |
| 51 | 17 32 | 23 27 | 21 52 | 10 47 | 05 33 |
| 52 | 17 57 | 24 04 | 22 21 | 10 58 | 05 31 |
| 53 | 18 24 | 24 43 | 22 50 | 11 09 | 05 29 |
| 54 | 18 53 | 25 23 | 23 20 | 11 20 | 05 27 |
| 55 | 19 23 | 26 05 | 23 51 | 11 32 | 05 25 |
| 56 | 19 56 | 26 49 | 24 23 | 11 44 | 05 23 |
| 57 | 20 32 | 27 35 | 24 55 | 11 57 | 05 21 |
| 58 | 21 10 | 28 23 | 25 28 | 12 10 | 05 19 |
| 59 | 21 53 | 29 13 | 26 03 | 12 23 | 05 16 |
| 60 | 22♊40 | 00♌06 | 26♌38 | 12♍37 | 05♎14 |

**2h 28m 0s — 37° 0' 0" — 09 ♉ 24**

| LAT. | 11 | 12 | ASC | 2 | 3 |
|---|---|---|---|---|---|
| 0 | 08♊43 | 06♋26 | 04♌39 | 05♍10 | 07♎37 |
| 5 | 09 21 | 07 45 | 06 19 | 05 45 | 07 32 |
| 10 | 10 00 | 09 05 | 07 56 | 06 20 | 07 26 |
| 15 | 10 40 | 10 27 | 09 31 | 06 53 | 07 20 |
| 20 | 11 23 | 11 52 | 11 07 | 07 27 | 07 15 |
| 21 | 11 32 | 12 10 | 11 26 | 07 34 | 07 13 |
| 22 | 11 41 | 12 27 | 11 45 | 07 41 | 07 12 |
| 23 | 11 50 | 12 45 | 12 05 | 07 48 | 07 11 |
| 24 | 12 00 | 13 04 | 12 24 | 07 54 | 07 10 |
| 25 | 12 09 | 13 22 | 12 44 | 08 01 | 07 09 |
| 26 | 12 19 | 13 41 | 13 03 | 08 08 | 07 07 |
| 27 | 12 29 | 14 00 | 13 23 | 08 15 | 07 06 |
| 28 | 12 39 | 14 20 | 13 43 | 08 23 | 07 05 |
| 29 | 12 50 | 14 39 | 14 03 | 08 30 | 07 04 |
| 30 | 13 01 | 14 59 | 14 23 | 08 37 | 07 02 |
| 31 | 13 12 | 15 20 | 14 44 | 08 44 | 07 01 |
| 32 | 13 23 | 15 41 | 15 05 | 08 51 | 07 00 |
| 33 | 13 34 | 16 02 | 15 25 | 08 59 | 06 58 |
| 34 | 13 46 | 16 24 | 15 46 | 09 06 | 06 57 |
| 35 | 13 58 | 16 46 | 16 08 | 09 14 | 06 55 |
| 36 | 14 11 | 17 09 | 16 29 | 09 22 | 06 54 |
| 37 | 14 24 | 17 32 | 16 51 | 09 30 | 06 53 |
| 38 | 14 37 | 17 56 | 17 13 | 09 37 | 06 51 |
| 39 | 14 51 | 18 20 | 17 35 | 09 45 | 06 50 |
| 40 | 15 06 | 18 45 | 17 58 | 09 54 | 06 48 |
| 41 | 15 20 | 19 11 | 18 21 | 10 02 | 06 46 |
| 42 | 15 36 | 19 37 | 18 44 | 10 10 | 06 45 |
| 43 | 15 52 | 20 04 | 19 08 | 10 19 | 06 43 |
| 44 | 16 09 | 20 32 | 19 32 | 10 28 | 06 42 |
| 45 | 16 26 | 21 01 | 19 57 | 10 37 | 06 40 |
| 46 | 16 44 | 21 31 | 20 22 | 10 46 | 06 38 |
| 47 | 17 04 | 22 01 | 20 47 | 10 55 | 06 36 |
| 48 | 17 24 | 22 33 | 21 13 | 11 05 | 06 34 |
| 49 | 17 45 | 23 06 | 21 40 | 11 14 | 06 32 |
| 50 | 18 07 | 23 40 | 22 07 | 11 24 | 06 30 |
| 51 | 18 31 | 24 15 | 22 34 | 11 34 | 06 28 |
| 52 | 18 56 | 24 52 | 23 02 | 11 45 | 06 26 |
| 53 | 19 22 | 25 30 | 23 31 | 11 56 | 06 24 |
| 54 | 19 51 | 26 10 | 24 01 | 12 07 | 06 22 |
| 55 | 20 21 | 26 51 | 24 31 | 12 18 | 06 19 |
| 56 | 20 54 | 27 34 | 25 02 | 12 30 | 06 17 |
| 57 | 21 30 | 28 20 | 25 34 | 12 42 | 06 14 |
| 58 | 22 09 | 29 07 | 26 07 | 12 54 | 06 12 |
| 59 | 22 51 | 29 56 | 26 40 | 13 07 | 06 09 |
| 60 | 23♊38 | 00♌49 | 27♌15 | 13♍20 | 06♎06 |

**2h 32m 0s — 38° 0' 0" — 10 ♉ 25**

| LAT. | 11 | 12 | ASC | 2 | 3 |
|---|---|---|---|---|---|
| 0 | 09♊40 | 07♋21 | 05♌38 | 06♍14 | 08♎43 |
| 5 | 10 18 | 08 40 | 07 16 | 06 48 | 08 36 |
| 10 | 10 57 | 10 00 | 08 52 | 07 21 | 08 30 |
| 15 | 11 37 | 11 21 | 10 26 | 07 53 | 08 23 |
| 20 | 12 20 | 12 46 | 12 00 | 08 25 | 08 17 |
| 21 | 12 29 | 13 04 | 12 19 | 08 32 | 08 15 |
| 22 | 12 38 | 13 21 | 12 38 | 08 38 | 08 14 |
| 23 | 12 48 | 13 39 | 12 57 | 08 45 | 08 12 |
| 24 | 12 57 | 13 58 | 13 17 | 08 52 | 08 11 |
| 25 | 13 07 | 14 16 | 13 36 | 08 58 | 08 10 |
| 26 | 13 17 | 14 35 | 13 55 | 09 05 | 08 08 |
| 27 | 13 27 | 14 54 | 14 15 | 09 12 | 08 07 |
| 28 | 13 37 | 15 13 | 14 34 | 09 18 | 08 05 |
| 29 | 13 47 | 15 33 | 14 54 | 09 25 | 08 04 |
| 30 | 13 58 | 15 53 | 15 14 | 09 32 | 08 02 |
| 31 | 14 09 | 16 13 | 15 34 | 09 39 | 08 01 |
| 32 | 14 20 | 16 34 | 15 55 | 09 46 | 07 59 |
| 33 | 14 32 | 16 55 | 16 15 | 09 53 | 07 58 |
| 34 | 14 44 | 17 16 | 16 36 | 10 01 | 07 56 |
| 35 | 14 56 | 17 38 | 16 57 | 10 08 | 07 55 |
| 36 | 15 09 | 18 01 | 17 18 | 10 15 | 07 53 |
| 37 | 15 22 | 18 24 | 17 39 | 10 23 | 07 51 |
| 38 | 15 35 | 18 47 | 18 01 | 10 30 | 07 50 |
| 39 | 15 49 | 19 12 | 18 23 | 10 38 | 07 48 |
| 40 | 16 03 | 19 36 | 18 45 | 10 46 | 07 46 |
| 41 | 16 18 | 20 02 | 19 08 | 10 54 | 07 44 |
| 42 | 16 34 | 20 28 | 19 31 | 11 02 | 07 43 |
| 43 | 16 50 | 20 55 | 19 54 | 11 10 | 07 41 |
| 44 | 17 06 | 21 23 | 20 18 | 11 18 | 07 39 |
| 45 | 17 24 | 21 51 | 20 42 | 11 27 | 07 37 |
| 46 | 17 42 | 22 20 | 21 06 | 11 36 | 07 35 |
| 47 | 18 01 | 22 51 | 21 31 | 11 45 | 07 33 |
| 48 | 18 22 | 23 22 | 21 57 | 11 54 | 07 31 |
| 49 | 18 43 | 23 55 | 22 23 | 12 03 | 07 28 |
| 50 | 19 05 | 24 28 | 22 49 | 12 13 | 07 26 |
| 51 | 19 29 | 25 03 | 23 16 | 12 22 | 07 24 |
| 52 | 19 54 | 25 40 | 23 44 | 12 32 | 07 21 |
| 53 | 20 20 | 26 17 | 24 12 | 12 43 | 07 19 |
| 54 | 20 49 | 26 56 | 24 41 | 12 53 | 07 16 |
| 55 | 21 19 | 27 37 | 25 11 | 13 04 | 07 13 |
| 56 | 21 52 | 28 20 | 25 41 | 13 15 | 07 11 |
| 57 | 22 28 | 29 05 | 26 13 | 13 27 | 07 08 |
| 58 | 23 06 | 29 51 | 26 45 | 13 39 | 07 05 |
| 59 | 23 49 | 00♌40 | 27 17 | 13 51 | 07 01 |
| 60 | 24♊36 | 01♌31 | 27♌51 | 14♍04 | 06♎58 |

**2h 36m 0s — 39° 0' 0" — 11 ♉ 26**

| LAT. | 11 | 12 | ASC | 2 | 3 |
|---|---|---|---|---|---|
| 0 | 10♊36 | 08♋16 | 06♌37 | 07♍18 | 09♎48 |
| 5 | 11 14 | 09 35 | 08 14 | 07 50 | 09 40 |
| 10 | 11 53 | 10 54 | 09 48 | 08 22 | 09 33 |
| 15 | 12 34 | 12 16 | 11 21 | 08 53 | 09 26 |
| 20 | 13 17 | 13 40 | 12 54 | 09 24 | 09 18 |
| 21 | 13 26 | 13 58 | 13 13 | 09 30 | 09 17 |
| 22 | 13 35 | 14 15 | 13 31 | 09 36 | 09 15 |
| 23 | 13 45 | 14 33 | 13 50 | 09 42 | 09 14 |
| 24 | 13 54 | 14 51 | 14 09 | 09 49 | 09 12 |
| 25 | 14 04 | 15 10 | 14 28 | 09 55 | 09 11 |
| 26 | 14 14 | 15 28 | 14 47 | 10 01 | 09 09 |
| 27 | 14 24 | 15 47 | 15 07 | 10 08 | 09 08 |
| 28 | 14 34 | 16 06 | 15 26 | 10 14 | 09 06 |
| 29 | 14 44 | 16 26 | 15 45 | 10 21 | 09 04 |
| 30 | 14 55 | 16 46 | 16 05 | 10 28 | 09 03 |
| 31 | 15 06 | 17 06 | 16 25 | 10 34 | 09 01 |
| 32 | 15 18 | 17 26 | 16 45 | 10 41 | 08 59 |
| 33 | 15 29 | 17 47 | 17 05 | 10 48 | 08 58 |
| 34 | 15 41 | 18 09 | 17 25 | 10 55 | 08 56 |
| 35 | 15 53 | 18 31 | 17 46 | 11 02 | 08 54 |
| 36 | 16 06 | 18 53 | 18 07 | 11 09 | 08 52 |
| 37 | 16 19 | 19 16 | 18 28 | 11 16 | 08 50 |
| 38 | 16 32 | 19 39 | 18 49 | 11 23 | 08 48 |
| 39 | 16 46 | 20 03 | 19 11 | 11 30 | 08 46 |
| 40 | 17 01 | 20 28 | 19 32 | 11 38 | 08 44 |
| 41 | 17 16 | 20 53 | 19 55 | 11 46 | 08 42 |
| 42 | 17 31 | 21 19 | 20 17 | 11 53 | 08 40 |
| 43 | 17 47 | 21 46 | 20 40 | 12 01 | 08 38 |
| 44 | 18 04 | 22 13 | 21 03 | 12 09 | 08 36 |
| 45 | 18 22 | 22 41 | 21 27 | 12 17 | 08 34 |
| 46 | 18 40 | 23 10 | 21 51 | 12 26 | 08 32 |
| 47 | 18 59 | 23 40 | 22 16 | 12 34 | 08 29 |
| 48 | 19 19 | 24 11 | 22 41 | 12 43 | 08 27 |
| 49 | 19 40 | 24 44 | 23 06 | 12 52 | 08 24 |
| 50 | 20 03 | 25 17 | 23 32 | 13 01 | 08 22 |
| 51 | 20 26 | 25 51 | 23 59 | 13 10 | 08 19 |
| 52 | 20 51 | 26 27 | 24 26 | 13 20 | 08 16 |
| 53 | 21 18 | 27 04 | 24 53 | 13 30 | 08 13 |
| 54 | 21 46 | 27 43 | 25 22 | 13 40 | 08 11 |
| 55 | 22 17 | 28 23 | 25 51 | 13 50 | 08 08 |
| 56 | 22 50 | 29 05 | 26 21 | 14 01 | 08 04 |
| 57 | 23 25 | 29 49 | 26 51 | 14 12 | 08 01 |
| 58 | 24 04 | 00♌35 | 27 23 | 14 23 | 07 58 |
| 59 | 24 46 | 01 23 | 27 55 | 14 35 | 07 54 |
| 60 | 25♊33 | 02♌14 | 28♌28 | 14♍47 | 07♎50 |

# Placidus Table of Houses for Latitudes 0° to 60° North

| 2h 40m 0s | 12 ♉ 27 | | 40° 0' 0" | | |
|---|---|---|---|---|---|
| LAT. | 11 | 12 | ASC | 2 | 3 |
| 0 | 11♊32 | 09♋11 | 07♌35 | 08♍22 | 10♎53 |
| 5 | 12 10 | 10 30 | 09 11 | 08 53 | 10 45 |
| 10 | 12 50 | 11 49 | 10 45 | 09 23 | 10 37 |
| 15 | 13 31 | 13 10 | 12 16 | 09 52 | 10 29 |
| 20 | 14 14 | 14 34 | 13 48 | 10 22 | 10 20 |
| 21 | 14 23 | 14 52 | 14 06 | 10 28 | 10 19 |
| 22 | 14 32 | 15 09 | 14 25 | 10 34 | 10 17 |
| 23 | 14 41 | 15 27 | 14 43 | 10 40 | 10 15 |
| 24 | 14 51 | 15 45 | 15 02 | 10 46 | 10 14 |
| 25 | 15 01 | 16 03 | 15 21 | 10 52 | 10 12 |
| 26 | 15 11 | 16 22 | 15 39 | 10 58 | 10 10 |
| 27 | 15 21 | 16 41 | 15 58 | 11 04 | 10 08 |
| 28 | 15 31 | 17 00 | 16 17 | 11 10 | 10 07 |
| 29 | 15 42 | 17 19 | 16 36 | 11 17 | 10 05 |
| 30 | 15 52 | 17 39 | 16 56 | 11 23 | 10 03 |
| 31 | 16 03 | 17 59 | 17 15 | 11 29 | 10 01 |
| 32 | 16 15 | 18 19 | 17 35 | 11 36 | 09 59 |
| 33 | 16 26 | 18 40 | 17 55 | 11 42 | 09 57 |
| 34 | 16 38 | 19 01 | 18 15 | 11 49 | 09 55 |
| 35 | 16 51 | 19 23 | 18 35 | 11 56 | 09 53 |
| 36 | 17 03 | 19 45 | 18 55 | 12 02 | 09 51 |
| 37 | 17 16 | 20 08 | 19 16 | 12 09 | 09 49 |
| 38 | 17 30 | 20 31 | 19 37 | 12 16 | 09 47 |
| 39 | 17 44 | 20 55 | 19 58 | 12 23 | 09 45 |
| 40 | 17 58 | 21 19 | 20 20 | 12 30 | 09 43 |
| 41 | 18 13 | 21 44 | 20 41 | 12 37 | 09 40 |
| 42 | 18 28 | 22 10 | 21 04 | 12 45 | 09 38 |
| 43 | 18 45 | 22 36 | 21 26 | 12 52 | 09 36 |
| 44 | 19 01 | 23 03 | 21 49 | 13 00 | 09 33 |
| 45 | 19 19 | 23 31 | 22 12 | 13 08 | 09 31 |
| 46 | 19 37 | 24 00 | 22 36 | 13 16 | 09 28 |
| 47 | 19 56 | 24 30 | 23 00 | 13 24 | 09 26 |
| 48 | 20 17 | 25 00 | 23 24 | 13 32 | 09 23 |
| 49 | 20 38 | 25 32 | 23 49 | 13 40 | 09 20 |
| 50 | 21 00 | 26 05 | 24 15 | 13 49 | 09 17 |
| 51 | 21 24 | 26 39 | 24 41 | 13 58 | 09 14 |
| 52 | 21 49 | 27 15 | 25 07 | 14 07 | 09 11 |
| 53 | 22 15 | 27 51 | 25 34 | 14 17 | 09 08 |
| 54 | 22 44 | 28 29 | 26 02 | 14 26 | 09 05 |
| 55 | 23 14 | 29 09 | 26 31 | 14 36 | 09 02 |
| 56 | 23 47 | 29 51 | 27 00 | 14 46 | 08 58 |
| 57 | 24 22 | 00♌34 | 27 30 | 14 57 | 08 54 |
| 58 | 25 01 | 01 19 | 28 01 | 15 08 | 08 51 |
| 59 | 25 43 | 02 07 | 28 32 | 15 19 | 08 47 |
| 60 | 26♊30 | 02♌56 | 29♌05 | 15♍30 | 08♎43 |

| 2h 44m 0s | 13 ♉ 27 | | 41° 0' 0" | | |
|---|---|---|---|---|---|
| LAT. | 11 | 12 | ASC | 2 | 3 |
| 0 | 12♊28 | 10♋07 | 08♌34 | 09♍26 | 11♎58 |
| 5 | 13 07 | 11 25 | 10 09 | 09 55 | 11 49 |
| 10 | 13 46 | 12 44 | 11 41 | 10 24 | 11 40 |
| 15 | 14 27 | 14 05 | 13 11 | 10 52 | 11 31 |
| 20 | 15 11 | 15 29 | 14 42 | 11 20 | 11 22 |
| 21 | 15 20 | 15 46 | 15 00 | 11 26 | 11 20 |
| 22 | 15 29 | 16 03 | 15 18 | 11 32 | 11 19 |
| 23 | 15 38 | 16 21 | 15 36 | 11 37 | 11 17 |
| 24 | 15 48 | 16 39 | 15 55 | 11 43 | 11 15 |
| 25 | 15 57 | 16 57 | 16 13 | 11 49 | 11 13 |
| 26 | 16 07 | 17 15 | 16 31 | 11 55 | 11 11 |
| 27 | 16 17 | 17 34 | 16 50 | 12 01 | 11 09 |
| 28 | 16 28 | 17 53 | 17 09 | 12 07 | 11 07 |
| 29 | 16 38 | 18 12 | 17 28 | 12 13 | 11 05 |
| 30 | 16 49 | 18 32 | 17 47 | 12 19 | 11 03 |
| 31 | 17 00 | 18 52 | 18 06 | 12 25 | 11 01 |
| 32 | 17 12 | 19 12 | 18 25 | 12 31 | 10 59 |
| 33 | 17 23 | 19 33 | 18 44 | 12 37 | 10 57 |
| 34 | 17 35 | 19 54 | 19 04 | 12 43 | 10 55 |
| 35 | 17 48 | 20 15 | 19 24 | 12 49 | 10 52 |
| 36 | 18 00 | 20 37 | 19 44 | 12 56 | 10 50 |
| 37 | 18 13 | 21 00 | 20 04 | 13 02 | 10 48 |
| 38 | 18 27 | 21 23 | 20 25 | 13 09 | 10 45 |
| 39 | 18 41 | 21 46 | 20 46 | 13 16 | 10 43 |
| 40 | 18 55 | 22 10 | 21 07 | 13 22 | 10 41 |
| 41 | 19 10 | 22 35 | 21 28 | 13 29 | 10 38 |
| 42 | 19 26 | 23 00 | 21 50 | 13 36 | 10 36 |
| 43 | 19 42 | 23 27 | 22 12 | 13 43 | 10 33 |
| 44 | 19 59 | 23 53 | 22 34 | 13 51 | 10 30 |
| 45 | 20 16 | 24 21 | 22 57 | 13 58 | 10 28 |
| 46 | 20 34 | 24 50 | 23 20 | 14 06 | 10 25 |
| 47 | 20 54 | 25 19 | 23 44 | 14 13 | 10 22 |
| 48 | 21 14 | 25 49 | 24 08 | 14 21 | 10 19 |
| 49 | 21 35 | 26 21 | 24 32 | 14 29 | 10 16 |
| 50 | 21 57 | 26 53 | 24 57 | 14 38 | 10 13 |
| 51 | 22 21 | 27 27 | 25 23 | 14 46 | 10 10 |
| 52 | 22 46 | 28 02 | 25 49 | 14 55 | 10 06 |
| 53 | 23 12 | 28 38 | 26 16 | 15 04 | 10 03 |
| 54 | 23 41 | 29 16 | 26 43 | 15 13 | 09 59 |
| 55 | 24 11 | 29 55 | 27 11 | 15 22 | 09 56 |
| 56 | 24 44 | 00♌36 | 27 39 | 15 32 | 09 52 |
| 57 | 25 19 | 01 19 | 28 09 | 15 42 | 09 48 |
| 58 | 25 58 | 02 03 | 28 39 | 15 52 | 09 44 |
| 59 | 26 40 | 02 50 | 29 10 | 16 03 | 09 39 |
| 60 | 27♊26 | 03♌39 | 29♌41 | 16♍14 | 09♎35 |

| 2h 48m 0s | 14 ♉ 28 | | 42° 0' 0" | | |
|---|---|---|---|---|---|
| LAT. | 11 | 12 | ASC | 2 | 3 |
| 0 | 13♊24 | 11♋02 | 09♌34 | 10♍30 | 13♎03 |
| 5 | 14 03 | 12 20 | 11 07 | 10 58 | 12 53 |
| 10 | 14 42 | 13 39 | 12 38 | 11 25 | 12 43 |
| 15 | 15 23 | 14 59 | 14 07 | 11 52 | 12 34 |
| 20 | 16 07 | 16 23 | 15 36 | 12 19 | 12 24 |
| 21 | 16 16 | 16 40 | 15 53 | 12 24 | 12 22 |
| 22 | 16 25 | 16 57 | 16 11 | 12 30 | 12 20 |
| 23 | 16 35 | 17 15 | 16 29 | 12 35 | 12 18 |
| 24 | 16 44 | 17 33 | 16 47 | 12 41 | 12 16 |
| 25 | 16 54 | 17 51 | 17 05 | 12 46 | 12 14 |
| 26 | 17 04 | 18 09 | 17 24 | 12 52 | 12 12 |
| 27 | 17 14 | 18 27 | 17 42 | 12 57 | 12 10 |
| 28 | 17 24 | 18 46 | 18 00 | 13 03 | 12 07 |
| 29 | 17 35 | 19 05 | 18 19 | 13 08 | 12 05 |
| 30 | 17 46 | 19 25 | 18 37 | 13 14 | 12 03 |
| 31 | 17 57 | 19 44 | 18 56 | 13 20 | 12 01 |
| 32 | 18 08 | 20 05 | 19 15 | 13 26 | 11 58 |
| 33 | 18 20 | 20 25 | 19 34 | 13 31 | 11 56 |
| 34 | 18 32 | 20 46 | 19 54 | 13 37 | 11 54 |
| 35 | 18 44 | 21 07 | 20 13 | 13 43 | 11 51 |
| 36 | 18 57 | 21 29 | 20 33 | 13 49 | 11 49 |
| 37 | 19 10 | 21 51 | 20 53 | 13 56 | 11 47 |
| 38 | 19 24 | 22 14 | 21 13 | 14 02 | 11 44 |
| 39 | 19 38 | 22 38 | 21 33 | 14 08 | 11 41 |
| 40 | 19 52 | 23 01 | 21 54 | 14 15 | 11 39 |
| 41 | 20 07 | 23 26 | 22 15 | 14 21 | 11 36 |
| 42 | 20 22 | 23 51 | 22 36 | 14 28 | 11 33 |
| 43 | 20 39 | 24 17 | 22 58 | 14 35 | 11 30 |
| 44 | 20 55 | 24 44 | 23 20 | 14 42 | 11 28 |
| 45 | 21 13 | 25 11 | 23 42 | 14 49 | 11 25 |
| 46 | 21 31 | 25 39 | 24 05 | 14 56 | 11 22 |
| 47 | 21 50 | 26 08 | 24 28 | 15 03 | 11 18 |
| 48 | 22 11 | 26 38 | 24 52 | 15 10 | 11 15 |
| 49 | 22 32 | 27 09 | 25 16 | 15 18 | 11 12 |
| 50 | 22 54 | 27 41 | 25 40 | 15 26 | 11 09 |
| 51 | 23 18 | 28 15 | 26 05 | 15 34 | 11 05 |
| 52 | 23 43 | 28 49 | 26 31 | 15 42 | 11 01 |
| 53 | 24 09 | 29 25 | 26 57 | 15 51 | 10 58 |
| 54 | 24 37 | 00♌02 | 27 23 | 15 59 | 10 54 |
| 55 | 25 08 | 00 41 | 27 51 | 16 08 | 10 50 |
| 56 | 25 40 | 01 21 | 28 19 | 16 17 | 10 45 |
| 57 | 26 16 | 02 03 | 28 47 | 16 27 | 10 41 |
| 58 | 26 54 | 02 47 | 29 17 | 16 36 | 10 36 |
| 59 | 27 36 | 03 33 | 29 47 | 16 47 | 10 32 |
| 60 | 28♊22 | 04♌21 | 00♍18 | 16♍57 | 10♎27 |

| 2h 52m 0s | 15 ♉ 28 | | 43° 0' 0" | | |
|---|---|---|---|---|---|
| LAT. | 11 | 12 | ASC | 2 | 3 |
| 0 | 14♊20 | 11♋58 | 10♌33 | 11♍34 | 14♎07 |
| 5 | 14 59 | 13 16 | 12 05 | 12 01 | 13 57 |
| 10 | 15 38 | 14 34 | 13 34 | 12 27 | 13 47 |
| 15 | 16 20 | 15 54 | 15 02 | 12 52 | 13 36 |
| 20 | 17 03 | 17 17 | 16 30 | 13 17 | 13 26 |
| 21 | 17 12 | 17 34 | 16 47 | 13 23 | 13 24 |
| 22 | 17 22 | 17 51 | 17 05 | 13 28 | 13 21 |
| 23 | 17 31 | 18 09 | 17 22 | 13 33 | 13 19 |
| 24 | 17 41 | 18 26 | 17 40 | 13 38 | 13 17 |
| 25 | 17 51 | 18 44 | 17 58 | 13 43 | 13 15 |
| 26 | 18 00 | 19 02 | 18 16 | 13 48 | 13 12 |
| 27 | 18 11 | 19 21 | 18 34 | 13 54 | 13 10 |
| 28 | 18 21 | 19 39 | 18 52 | 13 59 | 13 08 |
| 29 | 18 32 | 19 58 | 19 10 | 14 04 | 13 05 |
| 30 | 18 42 | 20 18 | 19 28 | 14 10 | 13 03 |
| 31 | 18 54 | 20 37 | 19 47 | 14 15 | 13 01 |
| 32 | 19 05 | 20 57 | 20 05 | 14 21 | 12 58 |
| 33 | 19 17 | 21 18 | 20 24 | 14 26 | 12 56 |
| 34 | 19 29 | 21 38 | 20 43 | 14 32 | 12 53 |
| 35 | 19 41 | 21 59 | 21 02 | 14 37 | 12 50 |
| 36 | 19 54 | 22 21 | 21 21 | 14 43 | 12 48 |
| 37 | 20 07 | 22 43 | 21 41 | 14 49 | 12 45 |
| 38 | 20 20 | 23 06 | 22 01 | 14 55 | 12 42 |
| 39 | 20 34 | 23 29 | 22 21 | 15 01 | 12 40 |
| 40 | 20 49 | 23 53 | 22 41 | 15 07 | 12 37 |
| 41 | 21 04 | 24 17 | 23 02 | 15 13 | 12 34 |
| 42 | 21 19 | 24 42 | 23 23 | 15 19 | 12 31 |
| 43 | 21 35 | 25 07 | 23 44 | 15 26 | 12 28 |
| 44 | 21 52 | 25 34 | 24 05 | 15 32 | 12 25 |
| 45 | 22 10 | 26 01 | 24 27 | 15 39 | 12 22 |
| 46 | 22 28 | 26 29 | 24 49 | 15 46 | 12 18 |
| 47 | 22 47 | 26 57 | 25 12 | 15 53 | 12 15 |
| 48 | 23 07 | 27 27 | 25 35 | 16 00 | 12 11 |
| 49 | 23 28 | 27 58 | 25 59 | 16 07 | 12 08 |
| 50 | 23 51 | 28 29 | 26 23 | 16 14 | 12 04 |
| 51 | 24 14 | 29 02 | 26 47 | 16 22 | 12 00 |
| 52 | 24 39 | 29 36 | 27 12 | 16 30 | 11 56 |
| 53 | 25 06 | 00♌12 | 27 38 | 16 38 | 11 52 |
| 54 | 25 34 | 00 48 | 28 04 | 16 46 | 11 48 |
| 55 | 26 04 | 01 27 | 28 31 | 16 54 | 11 44 |
| 56 | 26 37 | 02 06 | 28 58 | 17 03 | 11 39 |
| 57 | 27 12 | 02 48 | 29 26 | 17 12 | 11 34 |
| 58 | 27 50 | 03 31 | 29 55 | 17 21 | 11 29 |
| 59 | 28 32 | 04 16 | 00♍25 | 17 30 | 11 24 |
| 60 | 29♊18 | 05♌04 | 00♍55 | 17♍40 | 11♎19 |

| 2h 56m 0s | 16 ♉ 28 | | 44° 0' 0" | | |
|---|---|---|---|---|---|
| LAT. | 11 | 12 | ASC | 2 | 3 |
| 0 | 15♊16 | 12♋53 | 11♌32 | 12♍39 | 15♎12 |
| 5 | 15 55 | 14 11 | 13 03 | 13 04 | 15 01 |
| 10 | 16 34 | 15 29 | 14 31 | 13 28 | 14 50 |
| 15 | 17 16 | 16 48 | 15 58 | 13 52 | 14 39 |
| 20 | 18 00 | 18 11 | 17 24 | 14 16 | 14 27 |
| 21 | 18 09 | 18 28 | 17 41 | 14 21 | 14 25 |
| 22 | 18 18 | 18 45 | 17 58 | 14 26 | 14 23 |
| 23 | 18 27 | 19 02 | 18 16 | 14 31 | 14 20 |
| 24 | 18 37 | 19 20 | 18 33 | 14 35 | 14 18 |
| 25 | 18 47 | 19 38 | 18 50 | 14 40 | 14 15 |
| 26 | 18 57 | 19 56 | 19 08 | 14 45 | 14 13 |
| 27 | 19 07 | 20 14 | 19 26 | 14 50 | 14 11 |
| 28 | 19 17 | 20 33 | 19 43 | 14 55 | 14 08 |
| 29 | 19 28 | 20 51 | 20 01 | 15 00 | 14 05 |
| 30 | 19 39 | 21 10 | 20 19 | 15 05 | 14 03 |
| 31 | 19 50 | 21 30 | 20 37 | 15 10 | 14 00 |
| 32 | 20 01 | 21 50 | 20 55 | 15 16 | 13 58 |
| 33 | 20 13 | 22 10 | 21 14 | 15 21 | 13 55 |
| 34 | 20 25 | 22 31 | 21 32 | 15 26 | 13 52 |
| 35 | 20 37 | 22 51 | 21 51 | 15 31 | 13 49 |
| 36 | 20 50 | 23 13 | 22 10 | 15 37 | 13 47 |
| 37 | 21 03 | 23 35 | 22 29 | 15 42 | 13 44 |
| 38 | 21 17 | 23 57 | 22 49 | 15 48 | 13 41 |
| 39 | 21 31 | 24 20 | 23 08 | 15 54 | 13 38 |
| 40 | 21 45 | 24 44 | 23 28 | 15 59 | 13 35 |
| 41 | 22 00 | 25 08 | 23 49 | 16 05 | 13 32 |
| 42 | 22 16 | 25 32 | 24 09 | 16 11 | 13 28 |
| 43 | 22 32 | 25 58 | 24 30 | 16 17 | 13 25 |
| 44 | 22 49 | 26 24 | 24 51 | 16 23 | 13 22 |
| 45 | 23 06 | 26 50 | 25 12 | 16 29 | 13 18 |
| 46 | 23 24 | 27 18 | 25 34 | 16 36 | 13 15 |
| 47 | 23 44 | 27 46 | 25 56 | 16 42 | 13 11 |
| 48 | 24 04 | 28 16 | 26 19 | 16 49 | 13 07 |
| 49 | 24 25 | 28 46 | 26 42 | 16 56 | 13 04 |
| 50 | 24 47 | 29 17 | 27 05 | 17 03 | 13 00 |
| 51 | 25 10 | 29 50 | 27 29 | 17 10 | 12 55 |
| 52 | 25 35 | 00♌23 | 27 54 | 17 17 | 12 51 |
| 53 | 26 02 | 00 58 | 28 19 | 17 25 | 12 47 |
| 54 | 26 30 | 01 35 | 28 44 | 17 32 | 12 42 |
| 55 | 27 00 | 02 12 | 29 11 | 17 40 | 12 38 |
| 56 | 27 32 | 02 51 | 29 37 | 17 48 | 12 33 |
| 57 | 28 07 | 03 32 | 00♍05 | 17 57 | 12 28 |
| 58 | 28 45 | 04 15 | 00 33 | 18 06 | 12 22 |
| 59 | 29 27 | 05 00 | 01 02 | 18 14 | 12 17 |
| 60 | 00♋13 | 05♌46 | 01♍32 | 18♍24 | 12♎11 |

| 3h 0m 0s | 17 ♉ 28 | | 45° 0' 0" | | |
|---|---|---|---|---|---|
| LAT. | 11 | 12 | ASC | 2 | 3 |
| 0 | 16♊11 | 13♋49 | 12♌32 | 13♍43 | 16♎17 |
| 5 | 16 50 | 15 06 | 14 02 | 14 07 | 16 05 |
| 10 | 17 30 | 16 24 | 15 28 | 14 30 | 15 53 |
| 15 | 18 12 | 17 43 | 16 53 | 14 52 | 15 41 |
| 20 | 18 56 | 19 05 | 18 18 | 15 15 | 15 29 |
| 21 | 19 05 | 19 22 | 18 35 | 15 19 | 15 26 |
| 22 | 19 14 | 19 39 | 18 52 | 15 24 | 15 24 |
| 23 | 19 24 | 19 56 | 19 09 | 15 28 | 15 21 |
| 24 | 19 33 | 20 14 | 19 26 | 15 33 | 15 19 |
| 25 | 19 43 | 20 31 | 19 43 | 15 38 | 15 16 |
| 26 | 19 53 | 20 49 | 20 00 | 15 42 | 15 14 |
| 27 | 20 03 | 21 07 | 20 17 | 15 47 | 15 11 |
| 28 | 20 14 | 21 26 | 20 35 | 15 52 | 15 08 |
| 29 | 20 24 | 21 44 | 20 52 | 15 56 | 15 06 |
| 30 | 20 35 | 22 03 | 21 10 | 16 01 | 15 03 |
| 31 | 20 46 | 22 23 | 21 28 | 16 06 | 15 00 |
| 32 | 20 58 | 22 42 | 21 46 | 16 11 | 14 57 |
| 33 | 21 09 | 23 02 | 22 04 | 16 16 | 14 54 |
| 34 | 21 21 | 23 23 | 22 22 | 16 21 | 14 51 |
| 35 | 21 34 | 23 44 | 22 40 | 16 26 | 14 48 |
| 36 | 21 46 | 24 05 | 22 59 | 16 31 | 14 45 |
| 37 | 22 00 | 24 26 | 23 18 | 16 36 | 14 42 |
| 38 | 22 13 | 24 49 | 23 37 | 16 41 | 14 39 |
| 39 | 22 27 | 25 11 | 23 56 | 16 46 | 14 36 |
| 40 | 22 41 | 25 34 | 24 16 | 16 52 | 14 33 |
| 41 | 22 56 | 25 58 | 24 35 | 16 57 | 14 29 |
| 42 | 23 12 | 26 23 | 24 55 | 17 03 | 14 26 |
| 43 | 23 28 | 26 48 | 25 16 | 17 08 | 14 22 |
| 44 | 23 45 | 27 14 | 25 36 | 17 14 | 14 19 |
| 45 | 24 02 | 27 40 | 25 57 | 17 20 | 14 15 |
| 46 | 24 21 | 28 07 | 26 19 | 17 26 | 14 11 |
| 47 | 24 40 | 28 35 | 26 40 | 17 32 | 14 07 |
| 48 | 25 00 | 29 04 | 27 03 | 17 38 | 14 03 |
| 49 | 25 21 | 29 34 | 27 25 | 17 45 | 13 59 |
| 50 | 25 43 | 00♌05 | 27 48 | 17 51 | 13 55 |
| 51 | 26 07 | 00 37 | 28 11 | 17 58 | 13 51 |
| 52 | 26 31 | 01 11 | 28 35 | 18 05 | 13 46 |
| 53 | 26 58 | 01 45 | 29 00 | 18 12 | 13 41 |
| 54 | 27 26 | 02 21 | 29 25 | 18 19 | 13 36 |
| 55 | 27 56 | 02 58 | 29 50 | 18 26 | 13 31 |
| 56 | 28 28 | 03 36 | 00♍17 | 18 34 | 13 26 |
| 57 | 29 03 | 04 17 | 00 44 | 18 42 | 13 21 |
| 58 | 29 41 | 04 59 | 01 11 | 18 50 | 13 15 |
| 59 | 00♋22 | 05 43 | 01 39 | 18 58 | 13 09 |
| 60 | 01♋07 | 06♌29 | 02♍09 | 19♍07 | 13♎03 |

| 3h 4m 0s | 18 ♉ 28 | | 46° 0' 0" | | |
|---|---|---|---|---|---|
| LAT. | 11 | 12 | ASC | 2 | 3 |
| 0 | 17♊07 | 14♋44 | 13♌32 | 14♍48 | 17♎21 |
| 5 | 17 46 | 16 01 | 15 00 | 15 10 | 17 09 |
| 10 | 18 26 | 17 19 | 16 26 | 15 31 | 16 56 |
| 15 | 19 08 | 18 38 | 17 49 | 15 52 | 16 43 |
| 20 | 19 52 | 19 59 | 19 12 | 16 13 | 16 30 |
| 21 | 20 01 | 20 16 | 19 29 | 16 18 | 16 28 |
| 22 | 20 10 | 20 33 | 19 45 | 16 22 | 16 25 |
| 23 | 20 20 | 20 50 | 20 02 | 16 26 | 16 22 |
| 24 | 20 29 | 21 07 | 20 19 | 16 30 | 16 20 |
| 25 | 20 39 | 21 25 | 20 36 | 16 35 | 16 17 |
| 26 | 20 49 | 21 43 | 20 52 | 16 39 | 16 14 |
| 27 | 20 59 | 22 01 | 21 09 | 16 43 | 16 11 |
| 28 | 21 10 | 22 19 | 21 27 | 16 48 | 16 08 |
| 29 | 21 20 | 22 37 | 21 44 | 16 52 | 16 06 |
| 30 | 21 31 | 22 56 | 22 01 | 16 57 | 16 03 |
| 31 | 21 42 | 23 15 | 22 18 | 17 01 | 16 00 |
| 32 | 21 54 | 23 35 | 22 36 | 17 06 | 15 57 |
| 33 | 22 05 | 23 55 | 22 54 | 17 10 | 15 54 |
| 34 | 22 17 | 24 15 | 23 12 | 17 15 | 15 50 |
| 35 | 22 30 | 24 35 | 23 30 | 17 20 | 15 47 |
| 36 | 22 43 | 24 57 | 23 48 | 17 24 | 15 44 |
| 37 | 22 56 | 25 18 | 24 06 | 17 29 | 15 41 |
| 38 | 23 09 | 25 40 | 24 25 | 17 34 | 15 37 |
| 39 | 23 23 | 26 02 | 24 44 | 17 39 | 15 34 |
| 40 | 23 38 | 26 25 | 25 03 | 17 44 | 15 31 |
| 41 | 23 53 | 26 49 | 25 22 | 17 49 | 15 27 |
| 42 | 24 08 | 27 13 | 25 42 | 17 54 | 15 23 |
| 43 | 24 24 | 27 38 | 26 02 | 18 00 | 15 20 |
| 44 | 24 41 | 28 03 | 26 22 | 18 05 | 15 16 |
| 45 | 24 58 | 28 30 | 26 42 | 18 11 | 15 12 |
| 46 | 25 17 | 28 57 | 27 03 | 18 16 | 15 08 |
| 47 | 25 36 | 29 24 | 27 25 | 18 22 | 15 04 |
| 48 | 25 56 | 29 53 | 27 46 | 18 28 | 14 59 |
| 49 | 26 17 | 00♌23 | 28 08 | 18 34 | 14 55 |
| 50 | 26 39 | 00 53 | 28 31 | 18 40 | 14 50 |
| 51 | 27 02 | 01 25 | 28 54 | 18 46 | 14 46 |
| 52 | 27 27 | 01 58 | 29 17 | 18 52 | 14 41 |
| 53 | 27 53 | 02 31 | 29 41 | 18 59 | 14 36 |
| 54 | 28 21 | 03 07 | 00♍05 | 19 06 | 14 31 |
| 55 | 28 51 | 03 43 | 00 30 | 19 13 | 14 25 |
| 56 | 29 23 | 04 21 | 00 56 | 19 20 | 14 20 |
| 57 | 29 58 | 05 01 | 01 22 | 19 27 | 14 14 |
| 58 | 00♋36 | 05 42 | 01 49 | 19 35 | 14 08 |
| 59 | 01 17 | 06 26 | 02 17 | 19 42 | 14 01 |
| 60 | 02♋02 | 07♌11 | 02♍45 | 19♍51 | 13♎55 |

| 3h 8m 0s | 19 ♉ 27 | | 47° 0' 0" | | |
|---|---|---|---|---|---|
| LAT. | 11 | 12 | ASC | 2 | 3 |
| 0 | 18♊02 | 15♋40 | 14♌32 | 15♍53 | 18♎26 |
| 5 | 18 42 | 16 57 | 15 59 | 16 13 | 18 12 |
| 10 | 19 22 | 18 14 | 17 23 | 16 33 | 17 59 |
| 15 | 20 04 | 19 32 | 18 45 | 16 53 | 17 46 |
| 20 | 20 48 | 20 53 | 20 06 | 17 12 | 17 32 |
| 21 | 20 57 | 21 10 | 20 23 | 17 16 | 17 29 |
| 22 | 21 06 | 21 27 | 20 39 | 17 20 | 17 26 |
| 23 | 21 16 | 21 44 | 20 55 | 17 24 | 17 23 |
| 24 | 21 25 | 22 01 | 21 12 | 17 28 | 17 20 |
| 25 | 21 35 | 22 18 | 21 28 | 17 32 | 17 17 |
| 26 | 21 45 | 22 36 | 21 45 | 17 36 | 17 15 |
| 27 | 21 55 | 22 54 | 22 01 | 17 40 | 17 12 |
| 28 | 22 06 | 23 12 | 22 18 | 17 44 | 17 09 |
| 29 | 22 16 | 23 30 | 22 35 | 17 48 | 17 05 |
| 30 | 22 27 | 23 49 | 22 52 | 17 53 | 17 02 |
| 31 | 22 38 | 24 08 | 23 09 | 17 57 | 16 59 |
| 32 | 22 50 | 24 27 | 23 26 | 18 01 | 16 56 |
| 33 | 23 01 | 24 47 | 23 44 | 18 05 | 16 53 |
| 34 | 23 13 | 25 07 | 24 01 | 18 10 | 16 49 |
| 35 | 23 26 | 25 27 | 24 19 | 18 14 | 16 46 |
| 36 | 23 39 | 25 48 | 24 37 | 18 18 | 16 43 |
| 37 | 23 52 | 26 10 | 24 55 | 18 23 | 16 39 |
| 38 | 24 05 | 26 31 | 25 13 | 18 27 | 16 36 |
| 39 | 24 19 | 26 54 | 25 31 | 18 32 | 16 32 |
| 40 | 24 34 | 27 16 | 25 50 | 18 37 | 16 28 |
| 41 | 24 49 | 27 40 | 26 09 | 18 41 | 16 25 |
| 42 | 25 04 | 28 03 | 26 28 | 18 46 | 16 21 |
| 43 | 25 20 | 28 28 | 26 48 | 18 51 | 16 17 |
| 44 | 25 37 | 28 53 | 27 07 | 18 56 | 16 13 |
| 45 | 25 54 | 29 19 | 27 28 | 19 01 | 16 08 |
| 46 | 26 13 | 29 46 | 27 48 | 19 06 | 16 04 |
| 47 | 26 32 | 00♌13 | 28 09 | 19 12 | 16 00 |
| 48 | 26 52 | 00 42 | 28 30 | 19 17 | 15 55 |
| 49 | 27 13 | 01 11 | 28 51 | 19 23 | 15 51 |
| 50 | 27 35 | 01 41 | 29 13 | 19 28 | 15 46 |
| 51 | 27 58 | 02 12 | 29 36 | 19 34 | 15 41 |
| 52 | 28 23 | 02 44 | 29 59 | 19 40 | 15 36 |
| 53 | 28 49 | 03 18 | 00♍22 | 19 46 | 15 30 |
| 54 | 29 17 | 03 53 | 00 46 | 19 52 | 15 25 |
| 55 | 29 47 | 04 29 | 01 10 | 19 59 | 15 19 |
| 56 | 00♋19 | 05 06 | 01 35 | 20 05 | 15 13 |
| 57 | 00 53 | 05 45 | 02 01 | 20 12 | 15 07 |
| 58 | 01 30 | 06 26 | 02 27 | 20 19 | 15 01 |
| 59 | 02 11 | 07 09 | 02 54 | 20 26 | 14 54 |
| 60 | 02♋56 | 07♌53 | 03♍22 | 20♍34 | 14♎47 |

# Placidus Table of Houses for Latitudes 0° to 60° North

**3h 12m 0s — 48° 0' 0" — 20 ♉ 26**

| LAT. | 11 | 12 | ASC | 2 | 3 |
|---|---|---|---|---|---|
| 0 | 18♊58 | 16♋36 | 15♌32 | 16♍57 | 19♎30 |
| 5 | 19 37 | 17 52 | 16 58 | 17 16 | 19 16 |
| 10 | 20 18 | 19 09 | 18 20 | 17 35 | 19 02 |
| 15 | 20 59 | 20 27 | 19 41 | 17 53 | 18 48 |
| 20 | 21 43 | 21 48 | 21 01 | 18 11 | 18 33 |
| 21 | 21 53 | 22 04 | 21 17 | 18 15 | 18 30 |
| 22 | 22 02 | 22 21 | 21 33 | 18 18 | 18 27 |
| 23 | 22 11 | 22 38 | 21 49 | 18 22 | 18 24 |
| 24 | 22 21 | 22 55 | 22 05 | 18 26 | 18 21 |
| 25 | 22 31 | 23 12 | 22 21 | 18 29 | 18 18 |
| 26 | 22 41 | 23 29 | 22 37 | 18 33 | 18 15 |
| 27 | 22 51 | 23 47 | 22 54 | 18 37 | 18 12 |
| 28 | 23 02 | 24 05 | 23 10 | 18 41 | 18 09 |
| 29 | 23 12 | 24 23 | 23 26 | 18 44 | 18 05 |
| 30 | 23 23 | 24 42 | 23 43 | 18 48 | 18 02 |
| 31 | 23 34 | 25 01 | 24 00 | 18 52 | 17 59 |
| 32 | 23 46 | 25 20 | 24 17 | 18 56 | 17 55 |
| 33 | 23 57 | 25 39 | 24 34 | 19 00 | 17 52 |
| 34 | 24 09 | 25 59 | 24 51 | 19 04 | 17 48 |
| 35 | 24 22 | 26 19 | 25 08 | 19 08 | 17 45 |
| 36 | 24 34 | 26 40 | 25 26 | 19 12 | 17 41 |
| 37 | 24 48 | 27 01 | 25 43 | 19 16 | 17 38 |
| 38 | 25 01 | 27 23 | 26 01 | 19 20 | 17 34 |
| 39 | 25 15 | 27 45 | 26 19 | 19 25 | 17 30 |
| 40 | 25 29 | 28 07 | 26 37 | 19 29 | 17 26 |
| 41 | 25 44 | 28 30 | 26 56 | 19 33 | 17 22 |
| 42 | 26 00 | 28 54 | 27 15 | 19 38 | 17 18 |
| 43 | 26 16 | 29 18 | 27 34 | 19 42 | 17 14 |
| 44 | 26 33 | 29 43 | 27 53 | 19 47 | 17 09 |
| 45 | 26 50 | 00♌09 | 28 13 | 19 52 | 17 05 |
| 46 | 27 08 | 00 35 | 28 33 | 19 57 | 17 01 |
| 47 | 27 27 | 01 02 | 28 53 | 20 01 | 16 56 |
| 48 | 27 47 | 01 30 | 29 14 | 20 06 | 16 51 |
| 49 | 28 08 | 01 59 | 29 35 | 20 12 | 16 46 |
| 50 | 28 30 | 02 29 | 29 56 | 20 17 | 16 41 |
| 51 | 28 53 | 02 59 | 00♍18 | 20 22 | 16 36 |
| 52 | 29 18 | 03 31 | 00 40 | 20 28 | 16 30 |
| 53 | 29 44 | 04 04 | 01 03 | 20 33 | 16 25 |
| 54 | 00♋12 | 04 39 | 01 27 | 20 39 | 16 19 |
| 55 | 00 42 | 05 14 | 01 50 | 20 45 | 16 13 |
| 56 | 01 13 | 05 51 | 02 15 | 20 51 | 16 07 |
| 57 | 01 48 | 06 30 | 02 40 | 20 57 | 16 00 |
| 58 | 02 25 | 07 10 | 03 06 | 21 04 | 15 53 |
| 59 | 03 05 | 07 52 | 03 32 | 21 11 | 15 46 |
| 60 | 03♋50 | 08♌35 | 03♍59 | 21♍17 | 15♎39 |

**3h 16m 0s — 49° 0' 0" — 21 ♉ 26**

| LAT. | 11 | 12 | ASC | 2 | 3 |
|---|---|---|---|---|---|
| 0 | 19♊53 | 17♋32 | 16♌33 | 18♍02 | 20♎34 |
| 5 | 20 33 | 18 48 | 17 57 | 18 20 | 20 19 |
| 10 | 21 13 | 20 04 | 19 18 | 18 37 | 20 05 |
| 15 | 21 55 | 21 22 | 20 37 | 18 53 | 19 50 |
| 20 | 22 39 | 22 42 | 21 55 | 19 10 | 19 34 |
| 21 | 22 48 | 22 58 | 22 11 | 19 13 | 19 31 |
| 22 | 22 58 | 23 15 | 22 26 | 19 17 | 19 28 |
| 23 | 23 07 | 23 31 | 22 42 | 19 20 | 19 25 |
| 24 | 23 17 | 23 48 | 22 58 | 19 23 | 19 22 |
| 25 | 23 27 | 24 05 | 23 14 | 19 27 | 19 18 |
| 26 | 23 37 | 24 23 | 23 30 | 19 30 | 19 15 |
| 27 | 23 47 | 24 40 | 23 46 | 19 34 | 19 12 |
| 28 | 23 57 | 24 58 | 24 02 | 19 37 | 19 08 |
| 29 | 24 08 | 25 16 | 24 18 | 19 41 | 19 05 |
| 30 | 24 19 | 25 35 | 24 34 | 19 44 | 19 02 |
| 31 | 24 30 | 25 53 | 24 51 | 19 48 | 18 58 |
| 32 | 24 41 | 26 12 | 25 07 | 19 51 | 18 55 |
| 33 | 24 53 | 26 32 | 25 24 | 19 55 | 18 51 |
| 34 | 25 05 | 26 51 | 25 40 | 19 59 | 18 47 |
| 35 | 25 17 | 27 11 | 25 57 | 20 02 | 18 44 |
| 36 | 25 30 | 27 32 | 26 14 | 20 06 | 18 40 |
| 37 | 25 43 | 27 53 | 26 32 | 20 10 | 18 36 |
| 38 | 25 57 | 28 14 | 26 49 | 20 14 | 18 32 |
| 39 | 26 11 | 28 36 | 27 07 | 20 18 | 18 28 |
| 40 | 26 25 | 28 58 | 27 25 | 20 22 | 18 24 |
| 41 | 26 40 | 29 21 | 27 43 | 20 26 | 18 20 |
| 42 | 26 55 | 29 44 | 28 01 | 20 30 | 18 15 |
| 43 | 27 12 | 00♌08 | 28 20 | 20 34 | 18 11 |
| 44 | 27 28 | 00 33 | 28 39 | 20 38 | 18 06 |
| 45 | 27 46 | 00 58 | 28 58 | 20 42 | 18 02 |
| 46 | 28 04 | 01 24 | 29 17 | 20 47 | 17 57 |
| 47 | 28 23 | 01 51 | 29 37 | 20 51 | 17 52 |
| 48 | 28 43 | 02 18 | 29 57 | 20 56 | 17 47 |
| 49 | 29 04 | 02 47 | 00♍18 | 21 01 | 17 42 |
| 50 | 29 25 | 03 16 | 00 39 | 21 05 | 17 36 |
| 51 | 29 49 | 03 47 | 01 00 | 21 10 | 17 31 |
| 52 | 00♋13 | 04 18 | 01 22 | 21 15 | 17 25 |
| 53 | 00 39 | 04 51 | 01 44 | 21 20 | 17 19 |
| 54 | 01 07 | 05 24 | 02 07 | 21 26 | 17 13 |
| 55 | 01 36 | 06 00 | 02 30 | 21 31 | 17 07 |
| 56 | 02 08 | 06 36 | 02 54 | 21 37 | 17 00 |
| 57 | 02 42 | 07 14 | 03 19 | 21 43 | 16 53 |
| 58 | 03 19 | 07 53 | 03 44 | 21 48 | 16 46 |
| 59 | 03 59 | 08 35 | 04 09 | 21 55 | 16 38 |
| 60 | 04♋43 | 09♌18 | 04♍36 | 22♍01 | 16♎30 |

**3h 20m 0s — 50° 0' 0" — 22 ♉ 25**

| LAT. | 11 | 12 | ASC | 2 | 3 |
|---|---|---|---|---|---|
| 0 | 20♊49 | 18♋28 | 17♌33 | 19♍07 | 21♎38 |
| 5 | 21 28 | 19 44 | 18 56 | 19 23 | 21 23 |
| 10 | 22 09 | 21 00 | 20 15 | 19 39 | 21 07 |
| 15 | 22 50 | 22 17 | 21 33 | 19 54 | 20 51 |
| 20 | 23 35 | 23 36 | 22 50 | 20 09 | 20 35 |
| 21 | 23 44 | 23 52 | 23 05 | 20 12 | 20 32 |
| 22 | 23 53 | 24 09 | 23 20 | 20 15 | 20 29 |
| 23 | 24 03 | 24 25 | 23 36 | 20 18 | 20 26 |
| 24 | 24 12 | 24 42 | 23 51 | 20 21 | 20 22 |
| 25 | 24 22 | 24 59 | 24 07 | 20 24 | 20 19 |
| 26 | 24 32 | 25 16 | 24 22 | 20 27 | 20 15 |
| 27 | 24 42 | 25 34 | 24 38 | 20 31 | 20 12 |
| 28 | 24 53 | 25 51 | 24 54 | 20 34 | 20 08 |
| 29 | 25 03 | 26 09 | 25 09 | 20 37 | 20 05 |
| 30 | 25 14 | 26 27 | 25 25 | 20 40 | 20 01 |
| 31 | 25 26 | 26 46 | 25 41 | 20 43 | 19 57 |
| 32 | 25 37 | 27 05 | 25 57 | 20 47 | 19 54 |
| 33 | 25 49 | 27 24 | 26 14 | 20 50 | 19 50 |
| 34 | 26 01 | 27 43 | 26 30 | 20 53 | 19 46 |
| 35 | 26 13 | 28 03 | 26 47 | 20 57 | 19 42 |
| 36 | 26 26 | 28 23 | 27 03 | 21 00 | 19 38 |
| 37 | 26 39 | 28 44 | 27 20 | 21 03 | 19 34 |
| 38 | 26 52 | 29 05 | 27 37 | 21 07 | 19 30 |
| 39 | 27 06 | 29 27 | 27 54 | 21 10 | 19 26 |
| 40 | 27 21 | 29 49 | 28 12 | 21 14 | 19 21 |
| 41 | 27 35 | 00♌11 | 28 30 | 21 18 | 19 17 |
| 42 | 27 51 | 00 34 | 28 48 | 21 21 | 19 12 |
| 43 | 28 07 | 00 58 | 29 06 | 21 25 | 19 08 |
| 44 | 28 24 | 01 22 | 29 24 | 21 29 | 19 03 |
| 45 | 28 41 | 01 47 | 29 43 | 21 33 | 18 58 |
| 46 | 28 59 | 02 13 | 00♍02 | 21 37 | 18 53 |
| 47 | 29 18 | 02 40 | 00 21 | 21 41 | 18 48 |
| 48 | 29 38 | 03 07 | 00 41 | 21 45 | 18 43 |
| 49 | 29 59 | 03 35 | 01 01 | 21 49 | 18 37 |
| 50 | 00♋21 | 04 04 | 01 21 | 21 54 | 18 31 |
| 51 | 00 44 | 04 34 | 01 42 | 21 58 | 18 26 |
| 52 | 01 08 | 05 05 | 02 04 | 22 03 | 18 20 |
| 53 | 01 34 | 05 37 | 02 25 | 22 08 | 18 13 |
| 54 | 02 01 | 06 10 | 02 48 | 22 12 | 18 07 |
| 55 | 02 31 | 06 45 | 03 10 | 22 17 | 18 00 |
| 56 | 03 02 | 07 21 | 03 34 | 22 22 | 17 53 |
| 57 | 03 36 | 07 58 | 03 57 | 22 28 | 17 46 |
| 58 | 04 13 | 08 37 | 04 22 | 22 33 | 17 38 |
| 59 | 04 53 | 09 17 | 04 47 | 22 39 | 17 31 |
| 60 | 05♋36 | 10♌00 | 05♍13 | 22♍44 | 17♎22 |

**3h 24m 0s — 51° 0' 0" — 23 ♉ 23**

| LAT. | 11 | 12 | ASC | 2 | 3 |
|---|---|---|---|---|---|
| 0 | 21♊44 | 19♋24 | 18♌34 | 20♍12 | 22♎42 |
| 5 | 22 24 | 20 39 | 19 55 | 20 27 | 22 26 |
| 10 | 23 04 | 21 55 | 21 13 | 20 41 | 22 10 |
| 15 | 23 46 | 23 11 | 22 29 | 20 54 | 21 53 |
| 20 | 24 30 | 24 30 | 23 44 | 21 08 | 21 36 |
| 21 | 24 39 | 24 46 | 23 59 | 21 11 | 21 33 |
| 22 | 24 49 | 25 03 | 24 14 | 21 13 | 21 30 |
| 23 | 24 58 | 25 19 | 24 29 | 21 16 | 21 26 |
| 24 | 25 08 | 25 36 | 24 44 | 21 19 | 21 23 |
| 25 | 25 18 | 25 53 | 25 00 | 21 22 | 21 19 |
| 26 | 25 28 | 26 10 | 25 15 | 21 25 | 21 15 |
| 27 | 25 38 | 26 27 | 25 30 | 21 27 | 21 12 |
| 28 | 25 48 | 26 44 | 25 45 | 21 30 | 21 08 |
| 29 | 25 59 | 27 02 | 26 01 | 21 33 | 21 04 |
| 30 | 26 10 | 27 20 | 26 16 | 21 36 | 21 01 |
| 31 | 26 21 | 27 39 | 26 32 | 21 39 | 20 57 |
| 32 | 26 32 | 27 57 | 26 48 | 21 42 | 20 53 |
| 33 | 26 44 | 28 16 | 27 04 | 21 45 | 20 49 |
| 34 | 26 56 | 28 35 | 27 20 | 21 48 | 20 45 |
| 35 | 27 08 | 28 55 | 27 36 | 21 51 | 20 41 |
| 36 | 27 21 | 29 15 | 27 52 | 21 54 | 20 36 |
| 37 | 27 34 | 29 35 | 28 09 | 21 57 | 20 32 |
| 38 | 27 48 | 29 56 | 28 25 | 22 00 | 20 28 |
| 39 | 28 02 | 00♌18 | 28 42 | 22 03 | 20 23 |
| 40 | 28 16 | 00 39 | 28 59 | 22 07 | 20 19 |
| 41 | 28 31 | 01 02 | 29 17 | 22 10 | 20 14 |
| 42 | 28 46 | 01 25 | 29 34 | 22 13 | 20 10 |
| 43 | 29 02 | 01 48 | 29 52 | 22 17 | 20 05 |
| 44 | 29 19 | 02 12 | 00♍10 | 22 20 | 20 00 |
| 45 | 29 36 | 02 37 | 00 28 | 22 24 | 19 55 |
| 46 | 29 54 | 03 02 | 00 47 | 22 27 | 19 49 |
| 47 | 00♋13 | 03 28 | 01 06 | 22 31 | 19 44 |
| 48 | 00 33 | 03 55 | 01 25 | 22 35 | 19 38 |
| 49 | 00 54 | 04 23 | 01 44 | 22 39 | 19 33 |
| 50 | 01 15 | 04 51 | 02 04 | 22 42 | 19 27 |
| 51 | 01 38 | 05 21 | 02 25 | 22 46 | 19 21 |
| 52 | 02 03 | 05 52 | 02 45 | 22 51 | 19 14 |
| 53 | 02 28 | 06 23 | 03 07 | 22 55 | 19 08 |
| 54 | 02 56 | 06 56 | 03 28 | 22 59 | 19 01 |
| 55 | 03 25 | 07 30 | 03 50 | 23 04 | 18 54 |
| 56 | 03 56 | 08 05 | 04 13 | 23 08 | 18 46 |
| 57 | 04 30 | 08 42 | 04 36 | 23 13 | 18 39 |
| 58 | 05 06 | 09 20 | 05 00 | 23 18 | 18 31 |
| 59 | 05 46 | 10 00 | 05 25 | 23 23 | 18 23 |
| 60 | 06♋29 | 10♌42 | 05♍50 | 23♍28 | 18♎14 |

**3h 28m 0s — 52° 0' 0" — 24 ♉ 22**

| LAT. | 11 | 12 | ASC | 2 | 3 |
|---|---|---|---|---|---|
| 0 | 22♊39 | 20♋20 | 19♌35 | 21♍17 | 23♎46 |
| 5 | 23 19 | 21 35 | 20 54 | 21 30 | 23 29 |
| 10 | 23 59 | 22 50 | 22 11 | 21 43 | 23 12 |
| 15 | 24 41 | 24 06 | 23 25 | 21 55 | 22 55 |
| 20 | 25 26 | 25 24 | 24 39 | 22 07 | 22 37 |
| 21 | 25 35 | 25 40 | 24 53 | 22 09 | 22 34 |
| 22 | 25 44 | 25 57 | 25 08 | 22 12 | 22 30 |
| 23 | 25 54 | 26 13 | 25 23 | 22 14 | 22 27 |
| 24 | 26 03 | 26 29 | 25 38 | 22 17 | 22 23 |
| 25 | 26 13 | 26 46 | 25 53 | 22 19 | 22 19 |
| 26 | 26 23 | 27 03 | 26 07 | 22 22 | 22 15 |
| 27 | 26 33 | 27 20 | 26 22 | 22 24 | 22 12 |
| 28 | 26 44 | 27 38 | 26 37 | 22 27 | 22 08 |
| 29 | 26 54 | 27 55 | 26 52 | 22 29 | 22 04 |
| 30 | 27 05 | 28 13 | 27 08 | 22 32 | 22 00 |
| 31 | 27 16 | 28 31 | 27 23 | 22 34 | 21 56 |
| 32 | 27 28 | 28 50 | 27 38 | 22 37 | 21 52 |
| 33 | 27 39 | 29 08 | 27 54 | 22 40 | 21 48 |
| 34 | 27 51 | 29 27 | 28 09 | 22 42 | 21 43 |
| 35 | 28 04 | 29 47 | 28 25 | 22 45 | 21 39 |
| 36 | 28 16 | 00♌07 | 28 41 | 22 48 | 21 35 |
| 37 | 28 29 | 00 27 | 28 57 | 22 51 | 21 30 |
| 38 | 28 43 | 00 47 | 29 14 | 22 53 | 21 26 |
| 39 | 28 57 | 01 09 | 29 30 | 22 56 | 21 21 |
| 40 | 29 11 | 01 30 | 29 47 | 22 59 | 21 16 |
| 41 | 29 26 | 01 52 | 00♍03 | 23 02 | 21 12 |
| 42 | 29 41 | 02 15 | 00 21 | 23 05 | 21 07 |
| 43 | 29 57 | 02 38 | 00 38 | 23 08 | 21 01 |
| 44 | 00♋14 | 03 02 | 00 55 | 23 11 | 20 56 |
| 45 | 00 31 | 03 26 | 01 13 | 23 14 | 20 51 |
| 46 | 00 49 | 03 51 | 01 31 | 23 18 | 20 45 |
| 47 | 01 08 | 04 17 | 01 50 | 23 21 | 20 40 |
| 48 | 01 28 | 04 43 | 02 09 | 23 24 | 20 34 |
| 49 | 01 48 | 05 11 | 02 28 | 23 28 | 20 28 |
| 50 | 02 10 | 05 39 | 02 47 | 23 31 | 20 22 |
| 51 | 02 33 | 06 08 | 03 07 | 23 35 | 20 15 |
| 52 | 02 57 | 06 38 | 03 27 | 23 38 | 20 09 |
| 53 | 03 23 | 07 10 | 03 48 | 23 42 | 20 02 |
| 54 | 03 50 | 07 42 | 04 09 | 23 46 | 19 55 |
| 55 | 04 19 | 08 15 | 04 30 | 23 50 | 19 47 |
| 56 | 04 50 | 08 50 | 04 53 | 23 54 | 19 40 |
| 57 | 05 24 | 09 26 | 05 15 | 23 58 | 19 32 |
| 58 | 06 00 | 10 04 | 05 38 | 24 02 | 19 23 |
| 59 | 06 39 | 10 43 | 06 02 | 24 07 | 19 15 |
| 60 | 07♋22 | 11♌24 | 06♍27 | 24♍11 | 19♎06 |

**3h 32m 0s — 53° 0' 0" — 25 ♉ 21**

| LAT. | 11 | 12 | ASC | 2 | 3 |
|---|---|---|---|---|---|
| 0 | 23♊34 | 21♋17 | 20♌36 | 22♍23 | 24♎50 |
| 5 | 24 14 | 22 31 | 21 54 | 22 34 | 24 32 |
| 10 | 24 55 | 23 46 | 23 09 | 22 45 | 24 14 |
| 15 | 25 37 | 25 01 | 24 21 | 22 55 | 23 56 |
| 20 | 26 21 | 26 19 | 25 33 | 23 06 | 23 38 |
| 21 | 26 30 | 26 35 | 25 48 | 23 08 | 23 34 |
| 22 | 26 39 | 26 51 | 26 02 | 23 10 | 23 31 |
| 23 | 26 49 | 27 07 | 26 17 | 23 13 | 23 27 |
| 24 | 26 59 | 27 23 | 26 31 | 23 15 | 23 23 |
| 25 | 27 08 | 27 40 | 26 46 | 23 17 | 23 19 |
| 26 | 27 18 | 27 57 | 27 00 | 23 19 | 23 15 |
| 27 | 27 29 | 28 13 | 27 15 | 23 21 | 23 11 |
| 28 | 27 39 | 28 31 | 27 29 | 23 23 | 23 07 |
| 29 | 27 50 | 28 48 | 27 44 | 23 26 | 23 03 |
| 30 | 28 01 | 29 06 | 27 59 | 23 28 | 22 59 |
| 31 | 28 12 | 29 24 | 28 14 | 23 30 | 22 55 |
| 32 | 28 23 | 29 42 | 28 29 | 23 32 | 22 51 |
| 33 | 28 35 | 00♌01 | 28 44 | 23 35 | 22 46 |
| 34 | 28 47 | 00 19 | 28 59 | 23 37 | 22 42 |
| 35 | 28 59 | 00 39 | 29 15 | 23 39 | 22 37 |
| 36 | 29 12 | 00 58 | 29 30 | 23 42 | 22 33 |
| 37 | 29 25 | 01 18 | 29 46 | 23 44 | 22 28 |
| 38 | 29 38 | 01 39 | 00♍02 | 23 47 | 22 24 |
| 39 | 29 52 | 02 00 | 00 18 | 23 49 | 22 19 |
| 40 | 00♋06 | 02 21 | 00 34 | 23 52 | 22 14 |
| 41 | 00 21 | 02 43 | 00 50 | 23 54 | 22 09 |
| 42 | 00 36 | 03 05 | 01 07 | 23 57 | 22 04 |
| 43 | 00 52 | 03 28 | 01 24 | 24 00 | 21 58 |
| 44 | 01 09 | 03 51 | 01 41 | 24 02 | 21 53 |
| 45 | 01 26 | 04 15 | 01 58 | 24 05 | 21 47 |
| 46 | 01 44 | 04 40 | 02 16 | 24 08 | 21 41 |
| 47 | 02 03 | 05 05 | 02 34 | 24 11 | 21 36 |
| 48 | 02 22 | 05 32 | 02 52 | 24 14 | 21 29 |
| 49 | 02 43 | 05 59 | 03 11 | 24 17 | 21 23 |
| 50 | 03 05 | 06 27 | 03 30 | 24 20 | 21 17 |
| 51 | 03 27 | 06 55 | 03 49 | 24 23 | 21 10 |
| 52 | 03 52 | 07 25 | 04 09 | 24 26 | 21 03 |
| 53 | 04 17 | 07 56 | 04 29 | 24 29 | 20 56 |
| 54 | 04 44 | 08 28 | 04 49 | 24 33 | 20 49 |
| 55 | 05 13 | 09 01 | 05 10 | 24 36 | 20 41 |
| 56 | 05 44 | 09 35 | 05 32 | 24 40 | 20 33 |
| 57 | 06 17 | 10 10 | 05 54 | 24 43 | 20 25 |
| 58 | 06 53 | 10 47 | 06 17 | 24 47 | 20 16 |
| 59 | 07 32 | 11 26 | 06 40 | 24 51 | 20 07 |
| 60 | 08♋14 | 12♌06 | 07♍04 | 24♍55 | 19♎57 |

**3h 36m 0s — 54° 0' 0" — 26 ♉ 19**

| LAT. | 11 | 12 | ASC | 2 | 3 |
|---|---|---|---|---|---|
| 0 | 24♊30 | 22♋13 | 21♌37 | 23♍28 | 25♎53 |
| 5 | 25 09 | 23 27 | 22 54 | 23 38 | 25 35 |
| 10 | 25 50 | 24 41 | 24 07 | 23 47 | 25 16 |
| 15 | 26 32 | 25 56 | 25 18 | 23 56 | 24 58 |
| 20 | 27 16 | 27 13 | 26 28 | 24 05 | 24 39 |
| 21 | 27 25 | 27 29 | 26 42 | 24 07 | 24 35 |
| 22 | 27 35 | 27 45 | 26 56 | 24 09 | 24 31 |
| 23 | 27 44 | 28 01 | 27 10 | 24 11 | 24 27 |
| 24 | 27 54 | 28 17 | 27 24 | 24 12 | 24 23 |
| 25 | 28 04 | 28 33 | 27 39 | 24 14 | 24 19 |
| 26 | 28 14 | 28 50 | 27 53 | 24 16 | 24 15 |
| 27 | 28 24 | 29 07 | 28 07 | 24 18 | 24 11 |
| 28 | 28 34 | 29 24 | 28 21 | 24 20 | 24 07 |
| 29 | 28 45 | 29 41 | 28 36 | 24 22 | 24 03 |
| 30 | 28 56 | 29 59 | 28 50 | 24 24 | 23 58 |
| 31 | 29 07 | 00♌16 | 29 05 | 24 26 | 23 54 |
| 32 | 29 18 | 00 34 | 29 19 | 24 28 | 23 49 |
| 33 | 29 30 | 00 53 | 29 34 | 24 30 | 23 45 |
| 34 | 29 42 | 01 12 | 29 49 | 24 32 | 23 40 |
| 35 | 29 54 | 01 31 | 00♍04 | 24 34 | 23 36 |
| 36 | 00♋07 | 01 50 | 00 19 | 24 36 | 23 31 |
| 37 | 00 20 | 02 10 | 00 34 | 24 38 | 23 26 |
| 38 | 00 33 | 02 30 | 00 50 | 24 40 | 23 21 |
| 39 | 00 47 | 02 50 | 01 06 | 24 42 | 23 16 |
| 40 | 01 01 | 03 11 | 01 21 | 24 44 | 23 11 |
| 41 | 01 16 | 03 33 | 01 37 | 24 46 | 23 06 |
| 42 | 01 31 | 03 55 | 01 54 | 24 49 | 23 00 |
| 43 | 01 47 | 04 18 | 02 10 | 24 51 | 22 55 |
| 44 | 02 04 | 04 41 | 02 27 | 24 53 | 22 49 |
| 45 | 02 21 | 05 05 | 02 44 | 24 56 | 22 43 |
| 46 | 02 39 | 05 29 | 03 01 | 24 58 | 22 37 |
| 47 | 02 57 | 05 54 | 03 18 | 25 01 | 22 31 |
| 48 | 03 17 | 06 20 | 03 36 | 25 03 | 22 25 |
| 49 | 03 37 | 06 47 | 03 54 | 25 06 | 22 18 |
| 50 | 03 59 | 07 14 | 04 13 | 25 08 | 22 12 |
| 51 | 04 22 | 07 42 | 04 31 | 25 11 | 22 05 |
| 52 | 04 46 | 08 12 | 04 51 | 25 14 | 21 57 |
| 53 | 05 11 | 08 42 | 05 10 | 25 16 | 21 50 |
| 54 | 05 38 | 09 13 | 05 30 | 25 19 | 21 42 |
| 55 | 06 07 | 09 46 | 05 51 | 25 22 | 21 34 |
| 56 | 06 37 | 10 19 | 06 11 | 25 25 | 21 26 |
| 57 | 07 10 | 10 55 | 06 33 | 25 29 | 21 17 |
| 58 | 07 46 | 11 31 | 06 55 | 25 32 | 21 08 |
| 59 | 08 24 | 12 09 | 07 17 | 25 35 | 20 59 |
| 60 | 09♋06 | 12♌48 | 07♍40 | 25♍39 | 20♎49 |

**3h 40m 0s — 55° 0' 0" — 27 ♉ 17**

| LAT. | 11 | 12 | ASC | 2 | 3 |
|---|---|---|---|---|---|
| 0 | 25♊25 | 23♋10 | 22♌39 | 24♍33 | 26♎57 |
| 5 | 26 04 | 24 23 | 23 54 | 24 41 | 26 37 |
| 10 | 26 45 | 25 37 | 25 05 | 24 49 | 26 18 |
| 15 | 27 27 | 26 51 | 26 14 | 24 57 | 25 59 |
| 20 | 28 11 | 28 08 | 27 23 | 25 04 | 25 39 |
| 21 | 28 21 | 28 23 | 27 37 | 25 06 | 25 35 |
| 22 | 28 30 | 28 39 | 27 50 | 25 07 | 25 31 |
| 23 | 28 39 | 28 55 | 28 04 | 25 09 | 25 27 |
| 24 | 28 49 | 29 11 | 28 18 | 25 10 | 25 23 |
| 25 | 28 59 | 29 27 | 28 32 | 25 12 | 25 19 |
| 26 | 29 09 | 29 44 | 28 46 | 25 13 | 25 15 |
| 27 | 29 19 | 00♌00 | 28 59 | 25 15 | 25 10 |
| 28 | 29 29 | 00 17 | 29 13 | 25 17 | 25 06 |
| 29 | 29 40 | 00 34 | 29 27 | 25 18 | 25 02 |
| 30 | 29 51 | 00 51 | 29 42 | 25 20 | 24 57 |
| 31 | 00♋02 | 01 09 | 29 56 | 25 21 | 24 53 |
| 32 | 00 13 | 01 27 | 00♍10 | 25 23 | 24 48 |
| 33 | 00 25 | 01 45 | 00 24 | 25 25 | 24 44 |
| 34 | 00 37 | 02 04 | 00 39 | 25 26 | 24 39 |
| 35 | 00 49 | 02 22 | 00 53 | 25 28 | 24 34 |
| 36 | 01 02 | 02 42 | 01 08 | 25 30 | 24 29 |
| 37 | 01 15 | 03 01 | 01 23 | 25 32 | 24 24 |
| 38 | 01 28 | 03 21 | 01 38 | 25 33 | 24 19 |
| 39 | 01 42 | 03 41 | 01 53 | 25 35 | 24 14 |
| 40 | 01 56 | 04 02 | 02 09 | 25 37 | 24 08 |
| 41 | 02 11 | 04 23 | 02 24 | 25 39 | 24 03 |
| 42 | 02 26 | 04 45 | 02 40 | 25 41 | 23 57 |
| 43 | 02 42 | 05 07 | 02 56 | 25 42 | 23 51 |
| 44 | 02 58 | 05 30 | 03 12 | 25 44 | 23 46 |
| 45 | 03 15 | 05 54 | 03 29 | 25 46 | 23 40 |
| 46 | 03 33 | 06 18 | 03 46 | 25 48 | 23 33 |
| 47 | 03 52 | 06 43 | 04 03 | 25 50 | 23 27 |
| 48 | 04 11 | 07 08 | 04 20 | 25 53 | 23 20 |
| 49 | 04 32 | 07 34 | 04 37 | 25 55 | 23 14 |
| 50 | 04 53 | 08 01 | 04 55 | 25 57 | 23 07 |
| 51 | 05 16 | 08 29 | 05 14 | 25 59 | 22 59 |
| 52 | 05 40 | 08 58 | 05 32 | 26 01 | 22 52 |
| 53 | 06 05 | 09 28 | 05 51 | 26 04 | 22 44 |
| 54 | 06 32 | 09 59 | 06 11 | 26 06 | 22 36 |
| 55 | 07 00 | 10 31 | 06 31 | 26 09 | 22 28 |
| 56 | 07 31 | 11 04 | 06 51 | 26 11 | 22 19 |
| 57 | 08 03 | 11 39 | 07 12 | 26 14 | 22 10 |
| 58 | 08 38 | 12 14 | 07 33 | 26 16 | 22 00 |
| 59 | 09 17 | 12 52 | 07 55 | 26 19 | 21 51 |
| 60 | 09♋58 | 13♌31 | 08♍17 | 26♍22 | 21♎40 |

# Placidus Table of Houses for Latitudes 0° to 60° North

3h 44m 0s — 56° 0' 0" — 28 ♉ 15

| LAT. | 11 | 12 | ASC | 2 | 3 |
|---|---|---|---|---|---|
| 0 | 26♊20 | 24♋06 | 23♌41 | 25♍38 | 28♎00 |
| 5 | 27 00 | 25 20 | 24 53 | 25 45 | 27 40 |
| 10 | 27 40 | 26 33 | 26 03 | 25 51 | 27 20 |
| 15 | 28 22 | 27 46 | 27 11 | 25 57 | 27 00 |
| 20 | 29 06 | 29 02 | 28 18 | 26 03 | 26 40 |
| 21 | 29 16 | 29 17 | 28 31 | 26 05 | 26 36 |
| 22 | 29 25 | 29 33 | 28 45 | 26 06 | 26 32 |
| 23 | 29 34 | 29 49 | 28 58 | 26 07 | 26 27 |
| 24 | 29 44 | 00♌05 | 29 11 | 26 08 | 26 23 |
| 25 | 29 54 | 00 21 | 29 25 | 26 10 | 26 19 |
| 26 | 00♋04 | 00 37 | 29 38 | 26 11 | 26 14 |
| 27 | 00 14 | 00 54 | 29 52 | 26 12 | 26 10 |
| 28 | 00 24 | 01 10 | 00♍06 | 26 13 | 26 05 |
| 29 | 00 35 | 01 27 | 00 19 | 26 15 | 26 01 |
| 30 | 00 46 | 01 44 | 00 33 | 26 16 | 25 56 |
| 31 | 00 57 | 02 02 | 00 47 | 26 17 | 25 52 |
| 32 | 01 08 | 02 19 | 01 01 | 26 18 | 25 47 |
| 33 | 01 20 | 02 37 | 01 15 | 26 20 | 25 42 |
| 34 | 01 32 | 02 56 | 01 29 | 26 21 | 25 37 |
| 35 | 01 44 | 03 14 | 01 43 | 26 22 | 25 32 |
| 36 | 01 57 | 03 33 | 01 57 | 26 24 | 25 27 |
| 37 | 02 10 | 03 52 | 02 12 | 26 25 | 25 22 |
| 38 | 02 23 | 04 12 | 02 26 | 26 27 | 25 16 |
| 39 | 02 37 | 04 32 | 02 41 | 26 28 | 25 11 |
| 40 | 02 51 | 04 53 | 02 56 | 26 29 | 25 05 |
| 41 | 03 05 | 05 14 | 03 11 | 26 31 | 25 00 |
| 42 | 03 21 | 05 35 | 03 27 | 26 32 | 24 54 |
| 43 | 03 36 | 05 57 | 03 42 | 26 34 | 24 48 |
| 44 | 03 53 | 06 20 | 03 58 | 26 36 | 24 42 |
| 45 | 04 10 | 06 43 | 04 14 | 26 37 | 24 36 |
| 46 | 04 28 | 07 07 | 04 30 | 26 39 | 24 29 |
| 47 | 04 46 | 07 31 | 04 47 | 26 40 | 24 23 |
| 48 | 05 06 | 07 56 | 05 04 | 26 42 | 24 16 |
| 49 | 05 26 | 08 22 | 05 21 | 26 44 | 24 09 |
| 50 | 05 47 | 08 49 | 05 38 | 26 45 | 24 01 |
| 51 | 06 10 | 09 16 | 05 56 | 26 47 | 23 54 |
| 52 | 06 33 | 09 45 | 06 14 | 26 49 | 23 46 |
| 53 | 06 58 | 10 14 | 06 32 | 26 51 | 23 38 |
| 54 | 07 25 | 10 45 | 06 51 | 26 53 | 23 30 |
| 55 | 07 53 | 11 16 | 07 11 | 26 55 | 23 21 |
| 56 | 08 24 | 11 49 | 07 30 | 26 57 | 23 12 |
| 57 | 08 56 | 12 23 | 07 51 | 26 59 | 23 03 |
| 58 | 09 31 | 12 58 | 08 11 | 27 01 | 22 53 |
| 59 | 10 09 | 13 35 | 08 33 | 27 03 | 22 42 |
| 60 | 10♋50 | 14♌13 | 08♍54 | 27♍06 | 22♎32 |

3h 48m 0s — 57° 0' 0" — 29 ♉ 13

| LAT. | 11 | 12 | ASC | 2 | 3 |
|---|---|---|---|---|---|
| 0 | 27♊15 | 25♋03 | 24♌42 | 26♍44 | 29♎03 |
| 5 | 27 55 | 26 16 | 25 54 | 26 49 | 28 42 |
| 10 | 28 35 | 27 28 | 27 02 | 26 53 | 28 22 |
| 15 | 29 17 | 28 42 | 28 08 | 26 58 | 28 01 |
| 20 | 00♋02 | 29 56 | 29 13 | 27 03 | 27 40 |
| 21 | 00 11 | 00♌12 | 29 26 | 27 03 | 27 36 |
| 22 | 00 20 | 00 27 | 29 39 | 27 04 | 27 32 |
| 23 | 00 29 | 00 43 | 29 52 | 27 05 | 27 27 |
| 24 | 00 39 | 00 59 | 00♍05 | 27 06 | 27 23 |
| 25 | 00 49 | 01 15 | 00 18 | 27 07 | 27 18 |
| 26 | 00 59 | 01 31 | 00 31 | 27 08 | 27 14 |
| 27 | 01 09 | 01 47 | 00 44 | 27 09 | 27 09 |
| 28 | 01 19 | 02 04 | 00 58 | 27 10 | 27 05 |
| 29 | 01 30 | 02 20 | 01 11 | 27 11 | 27 00 |
| 30 | 01 41 | 02 37 | 01 24 | 27 12 | 26 55 |
| 31 | 01 52 | 02 54 | 01 38 | 27 13 | 26 50 |
| 32 | 02 03 | 03 12 | 01 51 | 27 14 | 26 45 |
| 33 | 02 15 | 03 30 | 02 05 | 27 15 | 26 40 |
| 34 | 02 27 | 03 48 | 02 19 | 27 16 | 26 35 |
| 35 | 02 39 | 04 06 | 02 32 | 27 17 | 26 30 |
| 36 | 02 51 | 04 25 | 02 46 | 27 18 | 26 25 |
| 37 | 03 04 | 04 44 | 03 00 | 27 19 | 26 19 |
| 38 | 03 18 | 05 03 | 03 15 | 27 20 | 26 14 |
| 39 | 03 31 | 05 23 | 03 29 | 27 21 | 26 08 |
| 40 | 03 45 | 05 43 | 03 44 | 27 22 | 26 03 |
| 41 | 04 00 | 06 04 | 03 58 | 27 23 | 25 57 |
| 42 | 04 15 | 06 25 | 04 13 | 27 24 | 25 51 |
| 43 | 04 31 | 06 47 | 04 28 | 27 25 | 25 44 |
| 44 | 04 47 | 07 09 | 04 44 | 27 27 | 25 38 |
| 45 | 05 04 | 07 32 | 04 59 | 27 28 | 25 32 |
| 46 | 05 22 | 07 56 | 05 15 | 27 29 | 25 25 |
| 47 | 05 40 | 08 20 | 05 31 | 27 30 | 25 18 |
| 48 | 06 00 | 08 45 | 05 47 | 27 31 | 25 11 |
| 49 | 06 20 | 09 10 | 06 04 | 27 33 | 25 04 |
| 50 | 06 41 | 09 36 | 06 21 | 27 34 | 24 56 |
| 51 | 07 03 | 10 03 | 06 38 | 27 35 | 24 48 |
| 52 | 07 27 | 10 31 | 06 56 | 27 37 | 24 40 |
| 53 | 07 52 | 11 00 | 07 14 | 27 38 | 24 32 |
| 54 | 08 18 | 11 30 | 07 32 | 27 40 | 24 23 |
| 55 | 08 46 | 12 01 | 07 51 | 27 41 | 24 14 |
| 56 | 09 16 | 12 33 | 08 10 | 27 43 | 24 05 |
| 57 | 09 49 | 13 07 | 08 30 | 27 44 | 23 55 |
| 58 | 10 23 | 13 41 | 08 50 | 27 46 | 23 45 |
| 59 | 11 01 | 14 17 | 09 10 | 27 48 | 23 34 |
| 60 | 11♋41 | 14♌55 | 09♍31 | 27♍49 | 23♎23 |

3h 52m 0s — 58° 0' 0" — 00 ♊ 11

| LAT. | 11 | 12 | ASC | 2 | 3 |
|---|---|---|---|---|---|
| 0 | 28♊10 | 26♋00 | 25♌44 | 27♍49 | 00♏06 |
| 5 | 28 50 | 27 12 | 26 54 | 27 52 | 29♎45 |
| 10 | 29 30 | 28 24 | 28 00 | 27 56 | 29 24 |
| 15 | 00♋12 | 29 37 | 29 05 | 27 59 | 29 02 |
| 20 | 00 57 | 00♌51 | 00♍08 | 28 02 | 28 41 |
| 21 | 01 06 | 01 06 | 00 21 | 28 02 | 28 36 |
| 22 | 01 15 | 01 22 | 00 33 | 28 03 | 28 32 |
| 23 | 01 24 | 01 37 | 00 46 | 28 04 | 28 27 |
| 24 | 01 34 | 01 53 | 00 59 | 28 04 | 28 23 |
| 25 | 01 44 | 02 08 | 01 11 | 28 05 | 28 18 |
| 26 | 01 54 | 02 24 | 01 24 | 28 05 | 28 13 |
| 27 | 02 04 | 02 40 | 01 37 | 28 06 | 28 08 |
| 28 | 02 14 | 02 57 | 01 50 | 28 07 | 28 04 |
| 29 | 02 25 | 03 13 | 02 03 | 28 07 | 27 59 |
| 30 | 02 36 | 03 30 | 02 16 | 28 08 | 27 54 |
| 31 | 02 47 | 03 47 | 02 29 | 28 09 | 27 49 |
| 32 | 02 58 | 04 04 | 02 42 | 28 09 | 27 44 |
| 33 | 03 10 | 04 22 | 02 55 | 28 10 | 27 39 |
| 34 | 03 21 | 04 40 | 03 08 | 28 11 | 27 33 |
| 35 | 03 34 | 04 58 | 03 22 | 28 11 | 27 28 |
| 36 | 03 46 | 05 16 | 03 35 | 28 12 | 27 22 |
| 37 | 03 59 | 05 35 | 03 49 | 28 13 | 27 17 |
| 38 | 04 12 | 05 55 | 04 03 | 28 13 | 27 11 |
| 39 | 04 26 | 06 14 | 04 17 | 28 14 | 27 05 |
| 40 | 04 40 | 06 34 | 04 31 | 28 15 | 26 59 |
| 41 | 04 55 | 06 55 | 04 45 | 28 15 | 26 53 |
| 42 | 05 10 | 07 16 | 05 00 | 28 16 | 26 47 |
| 43 | 05 25 | 07 37 | 05 15 | 28 17 | 26 41 |
| 44 | 05 42 | 07 59 | 05 29 | 28 18 | 26 34 |
| 45 | 05 58 | 08 21 | 05 44 | 28 19 | 26 28 |
| 46 | 06 16 | 08 45 | 06 00 | 28 19 | 26 21 |
| 47 | 06 34 | 09 08 | 06 15 | 28 20 | 26 13 |
| 48 | 06 54 | 09 33 | 06 31 | 28 21 | 26 06 |
| 49 | 07 14 | 09 58 | 06 47 | 28 22 | 25 59 |
| 50 | 07 35 | 10 24 | 07 04 | 28 23 | 25 51 |
| 51 | 07 57 | 10 50 | 07 20 | 28 24 | 25 43 |
| 52 | 08 20 | 11 18 | 07 38 | 28 25 | 25 34 |
| 53 | 08 45 | 11 46 | 07 55 | 28 25 | 25 26 |
| 54 | 09 11 | 12 16 | 08 13 | 28 26 | 25 17 |
| 55 | 09 39 | 12 46 | 08 31 | 28 27 | 25 07 |
| 56 | 10 09 | 13 18 | 08 49 | 28 28 | 24 58 |
| 57 | 10 41 | 13 51 | 09 08 | 28 29 | 24 48 |
| 58 | 11 15 | 14 25 | 09 28 | 28 31 | 24 37 |
| 59 | 11 52 | 15 00 | 09 48 | 28 32 | 24 26 |
| 60 | 12♋32 | 15♌37 | 10♍08 | 28♍33 | 24♎14 |

3h 56m 0s — 59° 0' 0" — 01 ♊ 08

| LAT. | 11 | 12 | ASC | 2 | 3 |
|---|---|---|---|---|---|
| 0 | 29♊05 | 26♋57 | 26♌47 | 28♍55 | 01♏08 |
| 5 | 29 45 | 28 09 | 27 54 | 28 56 | 00 47 |
| 10 | 00♋25 | 29 20 | 28 59 | 28 58 | 00 25 |
| 15 | 01 07 | 00♌32 | 00♍02 | 28 59 | 00 03 |
| 20 | 01 52 | 01 46 | 01 03 | 29 01 | 29♎41 |
| 21 | 02 01 | 02 01 | 01 16 | 29 01 | 29 36 |
| 22 | 02 10 | 02 16 | 01 28 | 29 01 | 29 31 |
| 23 | 02 19 | 02 31 | 01 40 | 29 02 | 29 27 |
| 24 | 02 29 | 02 47 | 01 52 | 29 02 | 29 22 |
| 25 | 02 39 | 03 02 | 02 05 | 29 02 | 29 17 |
| 26 | 02 49 | 03 18 | 02 17 | 29 03 | 29 12 |
| 27 | 02 59 | 03 34 | 02 30 | 29 03 | 29 08 |
| 28 | 03 09 | 03 50 | 02 42 | 29 03 | 29 03 |
| 29 | 03 20 | 04 06 | 02 55 | 29 04 | 28 58 |
| 30 | 03 30 | 04 23 | 03 07 | 29 04 | 28 53 |
| 31 | 03 41 | 04 40 | 03 20 | 29 04 | 28 47 |
| 32 | 03 53 | 04 57 | 03 33 | 29 05 | 28 42 |
| 33 | 04 04 | 05 14 | 03 46 | 29 05 | 28 37 |
| 34 | 04 16 | 05 32 | 03 58 | 29 05 | 28 31 |
| 35 | 04 28 | 05 50 | 04 11 | 29 06 | 28 26 |
| 36 | 04 41 | 06 08 | 04 25 | 29 06 | 28 20 |
| 37 | 04 54 | 06 27 | 04 38 | 29 06 | 28 14 |
| 38 | 05 07 | 06 46 | 04 51 | 29 07 | 28 09 |
| 39 | 05 20 | 07 05 | 05 05 | 29 07 | 28 03 |
| 40 | 05 34 | 07 25 | 05 19 | 29 07 | 27 56 |
| 41 | 05 49 | 07 45 | 05 32 | 29 08 | 27 50 |
| 42 | 06 04 | 08 06 | 05 46 | 29 08 | 27 44 |
| 43 | 06 20 | 08 27 | 06 01 | 29 08 | 27 37 |
| 44 | 06 36 | 08 48 | 06 15 | 29 09 | 27 30 |
| 45 | 06 53 | 09 11 | 06 30 | 29 09 | 27 23 |
| 46 | 07 10 | 09 33 | 06 45 | 29 10 | 27 16 |
| 47 | 07 28 | 09 57 | 07 00 | 29 10 | 27 09 |
| 48 | 07 48 | 10 21 | 07 15 | 29 10 | 27 01 |
| 49 | 08 08 | 10 46 | 07 31 | 29 11 | 26 53 |
| 50 | 08 28 | 11 11 | 07 47 | 29 11 | 26 45 |
| 51 | 08 51 | 11 37 | 08 03 | 29 12 | 26 37 |
| 52 | 09 14 | 12 04 | 08 19 | 29 12 | 26 28 |
| 53 | 09 38 | 12 32 | 08 36 | 29 13 | 26 19 |
| 54 | 10 04 | 13 01 | 08 53 | 29 13 | 26 10 |
| 55 | 10 32 | 13 31 | 09 11 | 29 14 | 26 00 |
| 56 | 11 02 | 14 03 | 09 29 | 29 14 | 25 50 |
| 57 | 11 33 | 14 35 | 09 47 | 29 15 | 25 40 |
| 58 | 12 07 | 15 08 | 10 06 | 29 15 | 25 29 |
| 59 | 12 44 | 15 43 | 10 26 | 29 16 | 25 18 |
| 60 | 13♋23 | 16♌19 | 10♍46 | 29♍16 | 25♎06 |

4h 0m 0s — 60° 0' 0" — 02 ♊ 05

| LAT. | 11 | 12 | ASC | 2 | 3 |
|---|---|---|---|---|---|
| 0 | 00♋00 | 27♋55 | 27♌49 | 00♎00 | 02♏11 |
| 5 | 00 40 | 29 06 | 28 55 | 00 00 | 01 49 |
| 10 | 01 20 | 00♌16 | 29 58 | 00 00 | 01 26 |
| 15 | 02 02 | 01 28 | 00♍59 | 00 00 | 01 04 |
| 20 | 02 46 | 02 40 | 01 58 | 00 00 | 00 41 |
| 21 | 02 56 | 02 55 | 02 10 | 00 00 | 00 36 |
| 22 | 03 05 | 03 10 | 02 22 | 00 00 | 00 31 |
| 23 | 03 14 | 03 25 | 02 34 | 00 00 | 00 26 |
| 24 | 03 24 | 03 41 | 02 46 | 00 00 | 00 22 |
| 25 | 03 34 | 03 56 | 02 58 | 00 00 | 00 17 |
| 26 | 03 44 | 04 12 | 03 10 | 00 00 | 00 12 |
| 27 | 03 54 | 04 27 | 03 22 | 00 00 | 00 07 |
| 28 | 04 04 | 04 43 | 03 34 | 00 00 | 00 01 |
| 29 | 04 14 | 05 00 | 03 47 | 00 00 | 29♎56 |
| 30 | 04 25 | 05 16 | 03 59 | 00 00 | 29 51 |
| 31 | 04 36 | 05 33 | 04 11 | 00 00 | 29 46 |
| 32 | 04 47 | 05 50 | 04 23 | 00 00 | 29 40 |
| 33 | 04 59 | 06 07 | 04 36 | 00 00 | 29 35 |
| 34 | 05 11 | 06 24 | 04 48 | 00 00 | 29 29 |
| 35 | 05 23 | 06 42 | 05 01 | 00 00 | 29 23 |
| 36 | 05 35 | 07 00 | 05 14 | 00 00 | 29 18 |
| 37 | 05 48 | 07 18 | 05 27 | 00 00 | 29 12 |
| 38 | 06 01 | 07 37 | 05 40 | 00 00 | 29 06 |
| 39 | 06 15 | 07 56 | 05 53 | 00 00 | 29 00 |
| 40 | 06 29 | 08 15 | 06 06 | 00 00 | 28 53 |
| 41 | 06 43 | 08 35 | 06 20 | 00 00 | 28 47 |
| 42 | 06 58 | 08 56 | 06 33 | 00 00 | 28 40 |
| 43 | 07 14 | 09 17 | 06 47 | 00 00 | 28 33 |
| 44 | 07 30 | 09 38 | 07 01 | 00 00 | 28 26 |
| 45 | 07 47 | 10 00 | 07 15 | 00 00 | 28 19 |
| 46 | 08 04 | 10 22 | 07 29 | 00 00 | 28 12 |
| 47 | 08 22 | 10 45 | 07 44 | 00 00 | 28 04 |
| 48 | 08 41 | 11 09 | 07 59 | 00 00 | 27 56 |
| 49 | 09 01 | 11 33 | 08 14 | 00 00 | 27 48 |
| 50 | 09 22 | 11 58 | 08 29 | 00 00 | 27 40 |
| 51 | 09 44 | 12 24 | 08 45 | 00 00 | 27 31 |
| 52 | 10 07 | 12 51 | 09 01 | 00 00 | 27 22 |
| 53 | 10 31 | 13 19 | 09 17 | 00 00 | 27 13 |
| 54 | 10 57 | 13 47 | 09 34 | 00 00 | 27 03 |
| 55 | 11 25 | 14 17 | 09 51 | 00 00 | 26 53 |
| 56 | 11 54 | 14 47 | 10 09 | 00 00 | 26 43 |
| 57 | 12 25 | 15 19 | 10 26 | 00 00 | 26 32 |
| 58 | 12 59 | 15 52 | 10 45 | 00 00 | 26 21 |
| 59 | 13 35 | 16 26 | 11 03 | 00 00 | 26 09 |
| 60 | 14♋14 | 17♌01 | 11♍23 | 00♎00 | 25♎57 |

4h 4m 0s — 61° 0' 0" — 03 ♊ 03

| LAT. | 11 | 12 | ASC | 2 | 3 |
|---|---|---|---|---|---|
| 0 | 00♋55 | 28♋52 | 28♌52 | 01♎05 | 03♏13 |
| 5 | 01 35 | 00♌03 | 29 56 | 01 04 | 02 50 |
| 10 | 02 15 | 01 13 | 00♍57 | 01 02 | 02 27 |
| 15 | 02 57 | 02 23 | 01 56 | 01 01 | 02 04 |
| 20 | 03 41 | 03 35 | 02 54 | 00 59 | 01 41 |
| 21 | 03 50 | 03 50 | 03 05 | 00 59 | 01 36 |
| 22 | 04 00 | 04 05 | 03 17 | 00 59 | 01 31 |
| 23 | 04 09 | 04 20 | 03 28 | 00 58 | 01 26 |
| 24 | 04 19 | 04 35 | 03 40 | 00 58 | 01 21 |
| 25 | 04 28 | 04 50 | 03 52 | 00 58 | 01 16 |
| 26 | 04 38 | 05 05 | 04 03 | 00 57 | 01 11 |
| 27 | 04 48 | 05 21 | 04 15 | 00 57 | 01 05 |
| 28 | 04 59 | 05 37 | 04 27 | 00 57 | 01 00 |
| 29 | 05 09 | 05 53 | 04 39 | 00 56 | 00 55 |
| 30 | 05 20 | 06 09 | 04 50 | 00 56 | 00 49 |
| 31 | 05 31 | 06 25 | 05 02 | 00 56 | 00 44 |
| 32 | 05 42 | 06 42 | 05 14 | 00 55 | 00 38 |
| 33 | 05 53 | 06 59 | 05 26 | 00 55 | 00 33 |
| 34 | 06 05 | 07 16 | 05 38 | 00 55 | 00 27 |
| 35 | 06 17 | 07 34 | 05 51 | 00 54 | 00 21 |
| 36 | 06 30 | 07 52 | 06 03 | 00 54 | 00 15 |
| 37 | 06 42 | 08 10 | 06 15 | 00 54 | 00 09 |
| 38 | 06 56 | 08 28 | 06 28 | 00 53 | 00 03 |
| 39 | 07 09 | 08 47 | 06 41 | 00 53 | 29♎56 |
| 40 | 07 23 | 09 06 | 06 54 | 00 53 | 29 50 |
| 41 | 07 37 | 09 26 | 07 07 | 00 52 | 29 43 |
| 42 | 07 52 | 09 46 | 07 20 | 00 52 | 29 36 |
| 43 | 08 08 | 10 06 | 07 33 | 00 52 | 29 29 |
| 44 | 08 24 | 10 27 | 07 47 | 00 51 | 29 22 |
| 45 | 08 41 | 10 49 | 08 00 | 00 51 | 29 15 |
| 46 | 08 58 | 11 11 | 08 14 | 00 50 | 29 07 |
| 47 | 09 16 | 11 34 | 08 28 | 00 50 | 28 59 |
| 48 | 09 35 | 11 57 | 08 43 | 00 50 | 28 51 |
| 49 | 09 55 | 12 21 | 08 57 | 00 49 | 28 43 |
| 50 | 10 15 | 12 46 | 09 12 | 00 49 | 28 34 |
| 51 | 10 37 | 13 11 | 09 27 | 00 48 | 28 25 |
| 52 | 11 00 | 13 38 | 09 43 | 00 48 | 28 16 |
| 53 | 11 24 | 14 05 | 09 59 | 00 47 | 28 07 |
| 54 | 11 50 | 14 33 | 10 15 | 00 47 | 27 57 |
| 55 | 12 17 | 15 02 | 10 31 | 00 46 | 27 46 |
| 56 | 12 46 | 15 32 | 10 48 | 00 46 | 27 36 |
| 57 | 13 17 | 16 03 | 11 05 | 00 45 | 27 25 |
| 58 | 13 50 | 16 35 | 11 23 | 00 45 | 27 13 |
| 59 | 14 26 | 17 09 | 11 41 | 00 44 | 27 01 |
| 60 | 15♋05 | 17♌44 | 12♍00 | 00♎44 | 26♎48 |

4h 8m 0s — 62° 0' 0" — 04 ♊ 00

| LAT. | 11 | 12 | ASC | 2 | 3 |
|---|---|---|---|---|---|
| 0 | 01♋50 | 29♋49 | 29♌54 | 02♎11 | 04♏16 |
| 5 | 02 30 | 00♌59 | 00♍56 | 02 08 | 03 52 |
| 10 | 03 10 | 02 09 | 01 56 | 02 04 | 03 28 |
| 15 | 03 52 | 03 19 | 02 53 | 02 01 | 03 05 |
| 20 | 04 36 | 04 30 | 03 49 | 01 58 | 02 40 |
| 21 | 04 45 | 04 45 | 04 00 | 01 58 | 02 35 |
| 22 | 04 55 | 04 59 | 04 12 | 01 57 | 02 30 |
| 23 | 05 04 | 05 14 | 04 23 | 01 56 | 02 25 |
| 24 | 05 14 | 05 29 | 04 34 | 01 56 | 02 20 |
| 25 | 05 23 | 05 44 | 04 45 | 01 55 | 02 15 |
| 26 | 05 33 | 05 59 | 04 56 | 01 55 | 02 10 |
| 27 | 05 43 | 06 15 | 05 08 | 01 54 | 02 04 |
| 28 | 05 53 | 06 30 | 05 19 | 01 53 | 01 59 |
| 29 | 06 04 | 06 46 | 05 31 | 01 53 | 01 53 |
| 30 | 06 15 | 07 02 | 05 42 | 01 52 | 01 48 |
| 31 | 06 25 | 07 18 | 05 54 | 01 51 | 01 42 |
| 32 | 06 37 | 07 35 | 06 05 | 01 51 | 01 36 |
| 33 | 06 48 | 07 51 | 06 17 | 01 50 | 01 31 |
| 34 | 07 00 | 08 08 | 06 28 | 01 49 | 01 25 |
| 35 | 07 12 | 08 26 | 06 40 | 01 49 | 01 19 |
| 36 | 07 24 | 08 43 | 06 52 | 01 48 | 01 12 |
| 37 | 07 37 | 09 01 | 07 04 | 01 47 | 01 06 |
| 38 | 07 50 | 09 19 | 07 16 | 01 47 | 01 00 |
| 39 | 08 03 | 09 38 | 07 29 | 01 46 | 00 53 |
| 40 | 08 17 | 09 57 | 07 41 | 01 45 | 00 47 |
| 41 | 08 32 | 10 16 | 07 54 | 01 45 | 00 40 |
| 42 | 08 46 | 10 36 | 08 06 | 01 44 | 00 33 |
| 43 | 09 02 | 10 56 | 08 19 | 01 43 | 00 25 |
| 44 | 09 18 | 11 17 | 08 32 | 01 42 | 00 18 |
| 45 | 09 34 | 11 38 | 08 46 | 01 41 | 00 10 |
| 46 | 09 52 | 12 00 | 08 59 | 01 41 | 00 03 |
| 47 | 10 10 | 12 22 | 09 13 | 01 40 | 29♎54 |
| 48 | 10 28 | 12 45 | 09 27 | 01 39 | 29 46 |
| 49 | 10 48 | 13 09 | 09 41 | 01 38 | 29 38 |
| 50 | 11 09 | 13 33 | 09 55 | 01 37 | 29 29 |
| 51 | 11 30 | 13 58 | 10 10 | 01 36 | 29 20 |
| 52 | 11 53 | 14 24 | 10 25 | 01 35 | 29 10 |
| 53 | 12 17 | 14 51 | 10 40 | 01 35 | 29 00 |
| 54 | 12 42 | 15 18 | 10 56 | 01 34 | 28 50 |
| 55 | 13 09 | 15 47 | 11 11 | 01 33 | 28 39 |
| 56 | 13 38 | 16 16 | 11 28 | 01 32 | 28 28 |
| 57 | 14 09 | 16 47 | 11 44 | 01 31 | 28 17 |
| 58 | 14 42 | 17 19 | 12 01 | 01 29 | 28 05 |
| 59 | 15 17 | 17 52 | 12 19 | 01 28 | 27 52 |
| 60 | 15♋56 | 18♌26 | 12♍37 | 01♎27 | 27♎39 |

4h 12m 0s — 63° 0' 0" — 04 ♊ 57

| LAT. | 11 | 12 | ASC | 2 | 3 |
|---|---|---|---|---|---|
| 0 | 02♋45 | 00♌47 | 00♍57 | 03♎16 | 05♏18 |
| 5 | 03 25 | 01 57 | 01 57 | 03 11 | 04 53 |
| 10 | 04 05 | 03 05 | 02 55 | 03 07 | 04 29 |
| 15 | 04 47 | 04 14 | 03 50 | 03 02 | 04 05 |
| 20 | 05 31 | 05 25 | 04 45 | 02 57 | 03 40 |
| 21 | 05 40 | 05 39 | 04 55 | 02 57 | 03 35 |
| 22 | 05 49 | 05 54 | 05 06 | 02 56 | 03 30 |
| 23 | 05 59 | 06 08 | 05 17 | 02 55 | 03 24 |
| 24 | 06 08 | 06 23 | 05 28 | 02 54 | 03 19 |
| 25 | 06 18 | 06 38 | 05 39 | 02 53 | 03 14 |
| 26 | 06 28 | 06 53 | 05 50 | 02 52 | 03 08 |
| 27 | 06 38 | 07 08 | 06 01 | 02 51 | 03 03 |
| 28 | 06 48 | 07 24 | 06 12 | 02 50 | 02 57 |
| 29 | 06 58 | 07 39 | 06 23 | 02 49 | 02 52 |
| 30 | 07 09 | 07 55 | 06 34 | 02 48 | 02 46 |
| 31 | 07 20 | 08 11 | 06 45 | 02 47 | 02 40 |
| 32 | 07 31 | 08 27 | 06 56 | 02 46 | 02 34 |
| 33 | 07 43 | 08 44 | 07 07 | 02 45 | 02 28 |
| 34 | 07 54 | 09 01 | 07 19 | 02 44 | 02 22 |
| 35 | 08 06 | 09 18 | 07 30 | 02 43 | 02 16 |
| 36 | 08 18 | 09 35 | 07 42 | 02 42 | 02 10 |
| 37 | 08 31 | 09 53 | 07 53 | 02 41 | 02 03 |
| 38 | 08 44 | 10 11 | 08 05 | 02 40 | 01 57 |
| 39 | 08 58 | 10 29 | 08 17 | 02 39 | 01 50 |
| 40 | 09 11 | 10 48 | 08 29 | 02 38 | 01 43 |
| 41 | 09 26 | 11 07 | 08 41 | 02 37 | 01 36 |
| 42 | 09 40 | 11 26 | 08 53 | 02 36 | 01 29 |
| 43 | 09 56 | 11 46 | 09 06 | 02 35 | 01 21 |
| 44 | 10 12 | 12 07 | 09 18 | 02 33 | 01 14 |
| 45 | 10 28 | 12 27 | 09 31 | 02 32 | 01 06 |
| 46 | 10 45 | 12 49 | 09 44 | 02 31 | 00 58 |
| 47 | 11 03 | 13 11 | 09 57 | 02 30 | 00 50 |
| 48 | 11 22 | 13 33 | 10 11 | 02 29 | 00 41 |
| 49 | 11 41 | 13 57 | 10 24 | 02 27 | 00 32 |
| 50 | 12 02 | 14 21 | 10 38 | 02 26 | 00 23 |
| 51 | 12 23 | 14 45 | 10 52 | 02 25 | 00 14 |
| 52 | 12 46 | 15 11 | 11 07 | 02 23 | 00 04 |
| 53 | 13 10 | 15 37 | 11 21 | 02 22 | 29♎54 |
| 54 | 13 35 | 16 04 | 11 36 | 02 20 | 29 43 |
| 55 | 14 02 | 16 32 | 11 52 | 02 19 | 29 32 |
| 56 | 14 30 | 17 01 | 12 07 | 02 17 | 29 21 |
| 57 | 15 00 | 17 31 | 12 23 | 02 16 | 29 09 |
| 58 | 15 33 | 18 02 | 12 40 | 02 14 | 28 56 |
| 59 | 16 08 | 18 34 | 12 57 | 02 12 | 28 44 |
| 60 | 16♋46 | 19♌08 | 13♍14 | 02♎11 | 28♎30 |

# Placidus Table of Houses for Latitudes 0° to 60° North

**4h 16m 0s — 64° 0' 0" — 05 ♊ 54**

| LAT. | 11 | 12 | ASC | 2 | 3 |
|---|---|---|---|---|---|
| 0 | 03♋40 | 01♌45 | 02♍00 | 04♎22 | 06♏19 |
| 5 | 04 20 | 02 54 | 02 58 | 04 15 | 05 55 |
| 10 | 05 00 | 04 02 | 03 54 | 04 09 | 05 30 |
| 15 | 05 42 | 05 10 | 04 47 | 04 03 | 05 05 |
| 20 | 06 26 | 06 20 | 05 40 | 03 57 | 04 39 |
| 21 | 06 35 | 06 34 | 05 50 | 03 55 | 04 34 |
| 22 | 06 44 | 06 48 | 06 01 | 03 54 | 04 29 |
| 23 | 06 54 | 07 03 | 06 11 | 03 53 | 04 23 |
| 24 | 07 03 | 07 17 | 06 22 | 03 52 | 04 18 |
| 25 | 07 13 | 07 32 | 06 32 | 03 50 | 04 13 |
| 26 | 07 22 | 07 47 | 06 43 | 03 49 | 04 07 |
| 27 | 07 32 | 08 02 | 06 53 | 03 48 | 04 01 |
| 28 | 07 43 | 08 17 | 07 04 | 03 47 | 03 56 |
| 29 | 07 53 | 08 33 | 07 15 | 03 45 | 03 50 |
| 30 | 08 04 | 08 48 | 07 25 | 03 44 | 03 44 |
| 31 | 08 15 | 09 04 | 07 36 | 03 43 | 03 38 |
| 32 | 08 26 | 09 20 | 07 47 | 03 42 | 03 32 |
| 33 | 08 37 | 09 36 | 07 58 | 03 40 | 03 26 |
| 34 | 08 49 | 09 53 | 08 09 | 03 39 | 03 20 |
| 35 | 09 00 | 10 10 | 08 20 | 03 38 | 03 13 |
| 36 | 09 13 | 10 27 | 08 31 | 03 36 | 03 07 |
| 37 | 09 25 | 10 44 | 08 42 | 03 35 | 03 00 |
| 38 | 09 38 | 11 02 | 08 53 | 03 33 | 02 53 |
| 39 | 09 52 | 11 20 | 09 05 | 03 32 | 02 47 |
| 40 | 10 05 | 11 38 | 09 16 | 03 31 | 02 39 |
| 41 | 10 20 | 11 57 | 09 28 | 03 29 | 02 32 |
| 42 | 10 34 | 12 16 | 09 40 | 03 28 | 02 25 |
| 43 | 10 50 | 12 36 | 09 52 | 03 26 | 02 17 |
| 44 | 11 05 | 12 56 | 10 04 | 03 24 | 02 09 |
| 45 | 11 22 | 13 17 | 10 16 | 03 23 | 02 01 |
| 46 | 11 39 | 13 38 | 10 29 | 03 21 | 01 53 |
| 47 | 11 57 | 13 59 | 10 42 | 03 20 | 01 44 |
| 48 | 12 15 | 14 22 | 10 54 | 03 18 | 01 36 |
| 49 | 12 35 | 14 44 | 11 08 | 03 16 | 01 27 |
| 50 | 12 55 | 15 08 | 11 21 | 03 15 | 01 17 |
| 51 | 13 16 | 15 32 | 11 35 | 03 13 | 01 08 |
| 52 | 13 39 | 15 57 | 11 48 | 03 11 | 00 57 |
| 53 | 14 02 | 16 23 | 12 03 | 03 09 | 00 47 |
| 54 | 14 27 | 16 49 | 12 17 | 03 07 | 00 36 |
| 55 | 14 54 | 17 17 | 12 32 | 03 05 | 00 25 |
| 56 | 15 22 | 17 45 | 12 47 | 03 03 | 00 13 |
| 57 | 15 52 | 18 15 | 13 02 | 03 01 | 00 01 |
| 58 | 16 24 | 18 46 | 13 18 | 02 59 | 29♎48 |
| 59 | 16 59 | 19 17 | 13 34 | 02 57 | 29 35 |
| 60 | 17♋36 | 19♌50 | 13♍51 | 02♎54 | 29♎21 |

**4h 20m 0s — 65° 0' 0" — 06 ♊ 50**

| LAT. | 11 | 12 | ASC | 2 | 3 |
|---|---|---|---|---|---|
| 0 | 04♋35 | 02♌43 | 03♍03 | 05♎27 | 07♏21 |
| 5 | 05 15 | 03 51 | 04 00 | 05 19 | 06 56 |
| 10 | 05 55 | 04 58 | 04 53 | 05 11 | 06 30 |
| 15 | 06 37 | 06 06 | 05 45 | 05 03 | 06 05 |
| 20 | 07 21 | 07 15 | 06 36 | 04 56 | 05 39 |
| 21 | 07 30 | 07 29 | 06 46 | 04 54 | 05 33 |
| 22 | 07 39 | 07 43 | 06 56 | 04 53 | 05 28 |
| 23 | 07 48 | 07 57 | 07 06 | 04 51 | 05 22 |
| 24 | 07 58 | 08 12 | 07 16 | 04 50 | 05 17 |
| 25 | 08 07 | 08 26 | 07 26 | 04 48 | 05 11 |
| 26 | 08 17 | 08 41 | 07 36 | 04 47 | 05 06 |
| 27 | 08 27 | 08 56 | 07 46 | 04 45 | 05 00 |
| 28 | 08 37 | 09 11 | 07 57 | 04 43 | 04 54 |
| 29 | 08 48 | 09 26 | 08 07 | 04 42 | 04 48 |
| 30 | 08 58 | 09 41 | 08 17 | 04 40 | 04 42 |
| 31 | 09 09 | 09 57 | 08 27 | 04 39 | 04 36 |
| 32 | 09 20 | 10 13 | 08 38 | 04 37 | 04 30 |
| 33 | 09 31 | 10 29 | 08 48 | 04 35 | 04 24 |
| 34 | 09 43 | 10 45 | 08 59 | 04 34 | 04 17 |
| 35 | 09 55 | 11 02 | 09 09 | 04 32 | 04 11 |
| 36 | 10 07 | 11 19 | 09 20 | 04 30 | 04 04 |
| 37 | 10 20 | 11 36 | 09 31 | 04 28 | 03 57 |
| 38 | 10 32 | 11 53 | 09 42 | 04 27 | 03 50 |
| 39 | 10 46 | 12 11 | 09 53 | 04 25 | 03 43 |
| 40 | 10 59 | 12 29 | 10 04 | 04 23 | 03 36 |
| 41 | 11 14 | 12 48 | 10 15 | 04 21 | 03 28 |
| 42 | 11 28 | 13 06 | 10 27 | 04 19 | 03 21 |
| 43 | 11 43 | 13 26 | 10 38 | 04 18 | 03 13 |
| 44 | 11 59 | 13 46 | 10 50 | 04 16 | 03 05 |
| 45 | 12 15 | 14 06 | 11 02 | 04 14 | 02 57 |
| 46 | 12 32 | 14 27 | 11 14 | 04 12 | 02 48 |
| 47 | 12 50 | 14 48 | 11 26 | 04 10 | 02 39 |
| 48 | 13 08 | 15 10 | 11 38 | 04 07 | 02 30 |
| 49 | 13 28 | 15 32 | 11 51 | 04 05 | 02 21 |
| 50 | 13 48 | 15 55 | 12 04 | 04 03 | 02 11 |
| 51 | 14 09 | 16 19 | 12 17 | 04 01 | 02 01 |
| 52 | 14 31 | 16 44 | 12 30 | 03 59 | 01 51 |
| 53 | 14 55 | 17 09 | 12 44 | 03 56 | 01 40 |
| 54 | 15 19 | 17 35 | 12 58 | 03 54 | 01 29 |
| 55 | 15 46 | 18 02 | 13 12 | 03 51 | 01 18 |
| 56 | 16 14 | 18 30 | 13 26 | 03 49 | 01 06 |
| 57 | 16 43 | 18 59 | 13 41 | 03 46 | 00 53 |
| 58 | 17 15 | 19 29 | 13 57 | 03 44 | 00 40 |
| 59 | 17 49 | 20 00 | 14 12 | 03 41 | 00 26 |
| 60 | 18♋26 | 20♌33 | 14♍28 | 03♎38 | 00♏12 |

**4h 24m 0s — 66° 0' 0" — 07 ♊ 47**

| LAT. | 11 | 12 | ASC | 2 | 3 |
|---|---|---|---|---|---|
| 0 | 05♋30 | 03♌41 | 04♍07 | 06♎32 | 08♏23 |
| 5 | 06 10 | 04 49 | 05 01 | 06 22 | 07 57 |
| 10 | 06 50 | 05 55 | 05 53 | 06 13 | 07 31 |
| 15 | 07 32 | 07 02 | 06 42 | 06 04 | 07 05 |
| 20 | 08 15 | 08 10 | 07 31 | 05 55 | 06 38 |
| 21 | 08 25 | 08 24 | 07 41 | 05 53 | 06 32 |
| 22 | 08 34 | 08 38 | 07 51 | 05 51 | 06 27 |
| 23 | 08 43 | 08 52 | 08 00 | 05 49 | 06 21 |
| 24 | 08 52 | 09 06 | 08 10 | 05 48 | 06 16 |
| 25 | 09 02 | 09 21 | 08 20 | 05 46 | 06 10 |
| 26 | 09 12 | 09 35 | 08 30 | 05 44 | 06 04 |
| 27 | 09 22 | 09 50 | 08 39 | 05 42 | 05 58 |
| 28 | 09 32 | 10 05 | 08 49 | 05 40 | 05 52 |
| 29 | 09 42 | 10 20 | 08 59 | 05 38 | 05 46 |
| 30 | 09 53 | 10 35 | 09 09 | 05 36 | 05 40 |
| 31 | 10 03 | 10 50 | 09 19 | 05 34 | 05 34 |
| 32 | 10 14 | 11 06 | 09 29 | 05 32 | 05 27 |
| 33 | 10 26 | 11 21 | 09 39 | 05 30 | 05 21 |
| 34 | 10 37 | 11 38 | 09 49 | 05 28 | 05 14 |
| 35 | 10 49 | 11 54 | 09 59 | 05 26 | 05 08 |
| 36 | 11 01 | 12 10 | 10 10 | 05 24 | 05 01 |
| 37 | 11 14 | 12 27 | 10 20 | 05 22 | 04 54 |
| 38 | 11 27 | 12 44 | 10 30 | 05 20 | 04 47 |
| 39 | 11 40 | 13 02 | 10 41 | 05 18 | 04 39 |
| 40 | 11 53 | 13 20 | 10 52 | 05 16 | 04 32 |
| 41 | 12 07 | 13 38 | 11 02 | 05 14 | 04 24 |
| 42 | 12 22 | 13 57 | 11 13 | 05 11 | 04 17 |
| 43 | 12 37 | 14 16 | 11 24 | 05 09 | 04 09 |
| 44 | 12 53 | 14 35 | 11 36 | 05 07 | 04 00 |
| 45 | 13 09 | 14 55 | 11 47 | 05 04 | 03 52 |
| 46 | 13 26 | 15 16 | 11 59 | 05 02 | 03 43 |
| 47 | 13 43 | 15 36 | 12 10 | 04 59 | 03 34 |
| 48 | 14 02 | 15 58 | 12 22 | 04 57 | 03 25 |
| 49 | 14 21 | 16 20 | 12 34 | 04 54 | 03 15 |
| 50 | 14 41 | 16 43 | 12 47 | 04 52 | 03 05 |
| 51 | 15 02 | 17 06 | 12 59 | 04 49 | 02 55 |
| 52 | 15 24 | 17 30 | 13 12 | 04 46 | 02 45 |
| 53 | 15 47 | 17 55 | 13 25 | 04 44 | 02 34 |
| 54 | 16 11 | 18 21 | 13 39 | 04 41 | 02 22 |
| 55 | 16 37 | 18 47 | 13 52 | 04 38 | 02 10 |
| 56 | 17 05 | 19 15 | 14 06 | 04 35 | 01 58 |
| 57 | 17 35 | 19 43 | 14 20 | 04 31 | 01 45 |
| 58 | 18 06 | 20 13 | 14 35 | 04 28 | 01 31 |
| 59 | 18 40 | 20 43 | 14 50 | 04 25 | 01 17 |
| 60 | 19♋16 | 21♌15 | 15♍05 | 04♎21 | 01♏02 |

**4h 28m 0s — 67° 0' 0" — 08 ♊ 43**

| LAT. | 11 | 12 | ASC | 2 | 3 |
|---|---|---|---|---|---|
| 0 | 06♋26 | 04♌39 | 05♍10 | 07♎37 | 09♏24 |
| 5 | 07 05 | 05 46 | 06 02 | 07 26 | 08 57 |
| 10 | 07 45 | 06 52 | 06 52 | 07 15 | 08 31 |
| 15 | 08 27 | 07 58 | 07 40 | 07 05 | 08 04 |
| 20 | 09 10 | 09 05 | 08 27 | 06 54 | 07 37 |
| 21 | 09 19 | 09 19 | 08 36 | 06 52 | 07 31 |
| 22 | 09 28 | 09 33 | 08 46 | 06 50 | 07 26 |
| 23 | 09 38 | 09 47 | 08 55 | 06 48 | 07 20 |
| 24 | 09 47 | 10 01 | 09 04 | 06 45 | 07 14 |
| 25 | 09 57 | 10 15 | 09 14 | 06 43 | 07 08 |
| 26 | 10 06 | 10 29 | 09 23 | 06 41 | 07 02 |
| 27 | 10 16 | 10 44 | 09 32 | 06 39 | 06 56 |
| 28 | 10 26 | 10 58 | 09 42 | 06 37 | 06 50 |
| 29 | 10 37 | 11 13 | 09 51 | 06 34 | 06 44 |
| 30 | 10 47 | 11 28 | 10 01 | 06 32 | 06 38 |
| 31 | 10 58 | 11 43 | 10 10 | 06 30 | 06 31 |
| 32 | 11 09 | 11 58 | 10 20 | 06 28 | 06 25 |
| 33 | 11 20 | 12 14 | 10 30 | 06 25 | 06 18 |
| 34 | 11 32 | 12 30 | 10 39 | 06 23 | 06 12 |
| 35 | 11 43 | 12 46 | 10 49 | 06 21 | 06 05 |
| 36 | 11 55 | 13 02 | 10 59 | 06 18 | 05 58 |
| 37 | 12 08 | 13 19 | 11 09 | 06 16 | 05 51 |
| 38 | 12 21 | 13 36 | 11 19 | 06 13 | 05 43 |
| 39 | 12 34 | 13 53 | 11 29 | 06 11 | 05 36 |
| 40 | 12 47 | 14 11 | 11 39 | 06 08 | 05 28 |
| 41 | 13 01 | 14 29 | 11 50 | 06 06 | 05 20 |
| 42 | 13 16 | 14 47 | 12 00 | 06 03 | 05 12 |
| 43 | 13 31 | 15 06 | 12 11 | 06 00 | 05 04 |
| 44 | 13 46 | 15 25 | 12 22 | 05 58 | 04 56 |
| 45 | 14 02 | 15 44 | 12 32 | 05 55 | 04 47 |
| 46 | 14 19 | 16 04 | 12 44 | 05 52 | 04 38 |
| 47 | 14 36 | 16 25 | 12 55 | 05 49 | 04 29 |
| 48 | 14 55 | 16 46 | 13 06 | 05 46 | 04 19 |
| 49 | 15 14 | 17 08 | 13 18 | 05 43 | 04 10 |
| 50 | 15 33 | 17 30 | 13 30 | 05 40 | 03 59 |
| 51 | 15 54 | 17 53 | 13 42 | 05 37 | 03 49 |
| 52 | 16 16 | 18 17 | 13 54 | 05 34 | 03 38 |
| 53 | 16 39 | 18 41 | 14 07 | 05 31 | 03 27 |
| 54 | 17 03 | 19 06 | 14 19 | 05 27 | 03 15 |
| 55 | 17 29 | 19 32 | 14 32 | 05 24 | 03 03 |
| 56 | 17 57 | 19 59 | 14 46 | 05 20 | 02 50 |
| 57 | 18 26 | 20 27 | 14 59 | 05 17 | 02 37 |
| 58 | 18 57 | 20 56 | 15 13 | 05 13 | 02 23 |
| 59 | 19 30 | 21 26 | 15 28 | 05 09 | 02 08 |
| 60 | 20♋06 | 21♌57 | 15♍42 | 05♎05 | 01♏53 |

**4h 32m 0s — 68° 0' 0" — 09 ♊ 40**

| LAT. | 11 | 12 | ASC | 2 | 3 |
|---|---|---|---|---|---|
| 0 | 07♋21 | 05♌38 | 06♍14 | 08♎43 | 10♏25 |
| 5 | 08 00 | 06 44 | 07 04 | 08 30 | 09 58 |
| 10 | 08 40 | 07 49 | 07 52 | 08 17 | 09 31 |
| 15 | 09 22 | 08 54 | 08 38 | 08 05 | 09 04 |
| 20 | 10 05 | 10 01 | 09 23 | 07 53 | 08 36 |
| 21 | 10 14 | 10 14 | 09 32 | 07 51 | 08 30 |
| 22 | 10 23 | 10 28 | 09 41 | 07 48 | 08 24 |
| 23 | 10 32 | 10 42 | 09 49 | 07 46 | 08 18 |
| 24 | 10 42 | 10 55 | 09 58 | 07 43 | 08 13 |
| 25 | 10 51 | 11 09 | 10 07 | 07 41 | 08 07 |
| 26 | 11 01 | 11 23 | 10 16 | 07 38 | 08 00 |
| 27 | 11 11 | 11 38 | 10 25 | 07 36 | 07 54 |
| 28 | 11 21 | 11 52 | 10 34 | 07 33 | 07 48 |
| 29 | 11 31 | 12 07 | 10 43 | 07 31 | 07 42 |
| 30 | 11 42 | 12 21 | 10 53 | 07 28 | 07 35 |
| 31 | 11 52 | 12 36 | 11 02 | 07 26 | 07 29 |
| 32 | 12 03 | 12 51 | 11 11 | 07 23 | 07 22 |
| 33 | 12 14 | 13 07 | 11 20 | 07 20 | 07 15 |
| 34 | 12 26 | 13 22 | 11 29 | 07 18 | 07 09 |
| 35 | 12 37 | 13 38 | 11 39 | 07 15 | 07 02 |
| 36 | 12 49 | 13 54 | 11 48 | 07 12 | 06 54 |
| 37 | 13 02 | 14 11 | 11 58 | 07 09 | 06 47 |
| 38 | 13 15 | 14 27 | 12 07 | 07 07 | 06 40 |
| 39 | 13 28 | 14 44 | 12 17 | 07 04 | 06 32 |
| 40 | 13 41 | 15 01 | 12 27 | 07 01 | 06 24 |
| 41 | 13 55 | 15 19 | 12 37 | 06 58 | 06 16 |
| 42 | 14 09 | 15 37 | 12 47 | 06 55 | 06 08 |
| 43 | 14 24 | 15 56 | 12 57 | 06 52 | 06 00 |
| 44 | 14 40 | 16 14 | 13 07 | 06 49 | 05 51 |
| 45 | 14 56 | 16 34 | 13 18 | 06 46 | 05 42 |
| 46 | 15 12 | 16 53 | 13 29 | 06 42 | 05 33 |
| 47 | 15 30 | 17 14 | 13 39 | 06 39 | 05 24 |
| 48 | 15 48 | 17 34 | 13 50 | 06 36 | 05 14 |
| 49 | 16 06 | 17 56 | 14 01 | 06 32 | 05 04 |
| 50 | 16 26 | 18 18 | 14 13 | 06 29 | 04 53 |
| 51 | 16 47 | 18 40 | 14 24 | 06 25 | 04 43 |
| 52 | 17 08 | 19 03 | 14 36 | 06 22 | 04 31 |
| 53 | 17 31 | 19 27 | 14 48 | 06 18 | 04 20 |
| 54 | 17 55 | 19 52 | 15 00 | 06 14 | 04 08 |
| 55 | 18 21 | 20 18 | 15 13 | 06 10 | 03 55 |
| 56 | 18 48 | 20 44 | 15 25 | 06 06 | 03 42 |
| 57 | 19 17 | 21 11 | 15 38 | 06 02 | 03 29 |
| 58 | 19 47 | 21 40 | 15 52 | 05 58 | 03 14 |
| 59 | 20 20 | 22 09 | 16 06 | 05 53 | 02 59 |
| 60 | 20♋56 | 22♌40 | 16♍20 | 05♎49 | 02♏44 |

**4h 36m 0s — 69° 0' 0" — 10 ♊ 36**

| LAT. | 11 | 12 | ASC | 2 | 3 |
|---|---|---|---|---|---|
| 0 | 08♋16 | 06♌37 | 07♍18 | 09♎48 | 11♏26 |
| 5 | 08 56 | 07 42 | 08 06 | 09 33 | 10 59 |
| 10 | 09 36 | 08 46 | 08 51 | 09 19 | 10 31 |
| 15 | 10 17 | 09 51 | 09 35 | 09 06 | 10 03 |
| 20 | 11 00 | 10 56 | 10 18 | 08 52 | 09 35 |
| 21 | 11 09 | 11 09 | 10 27 | 08 49 | 09 29 |
| 22 | 11 18 | 11 23 | 10 36 | 08 47 | 09 23 |
| 23 | 11 27 | 11 36 | 10 44 | 08 44 | 09 17 |
| 24 | 11 36 | 11 50 | 10 53 | 08 41 | 09 11 |
| 25 | 11 46 | 12 04 | 11 01 | 08 38 | 09 05 |
| 26 | 11 56 | 12 18 | 11 10 | 08 35 | 08 59 |
| 27 | 12 05 | 12 32 | 11 18 | 08 33 | 08 52 |
| 28 | 12 15 | 12 46 | 11 27 | 08 30 | 08 46 |
| 29 | 12 26 | 13 00 | 11 36 | 08 27 | 08 39 |
| 30 | 12 36 | 13 15 | 11 44 | 08 24 | 08 33 |
| 31 | 12 47 | 13 29 | 11 53 | 08 21 | 08 26 |
| 32 | 12 57 | 13 44 | 12 02 | 08 18 | 08 19 |
| 33 | 13 09 | 13 59 | 12 11 | 08 15 | 08 13 |
| 34 | 13 20 | 14 15 | 12 20 | 08 12 | 08 06 |
| 35 | 13 32 | 14 30 | 12 29 | 08 09 | 07 58 |
| 36 | 13 44 | 14 46 | 12 38 | 08 06 | 07 51 |
| 37 | 13 56 | 15 02 | 12 47 | 08 03 | 07 44 |
| 38 | 14 09 | 15 19 | 12 56 | 08 00 | 07 36 |
| 39 | 14 22 | 15 35 | 13 05 | 07 57 | 07 28 |
| 40 | 14 35 | 15 52 | 13 15 | 07 53 | 07 20 |
| 41 | 14 49 | 16 10 | 13 24 | 07 50 | 07 12 |
| 42 | 15 03 | 16 27 | 13 34 | 07 47 | 07 04 |
| 43 | 15 18 | 16 45 | 13 44 | 07 43 | 06 55 |
| 44 | 15 33 | 17 04 | 13 53 | 07 40 | 06 46 |
| 45 | 15 49 | 17 23 | 14 03 | 07 36 | 06 37 |
| 46 | 16 06 | 17 42 | 14 13 | 07 33 | 06 28 |
| 47 | 16 23 | 18 02 | 14 24 | 07 29 | 06 18 |
| 48 | 16 41 | 18 23 | 14 34 | 07 25 | 06 08 |
| 49 | 16 59 | 18 44 | 14 45 | 07 21 | 05 58 |
| 50 | 17 19 | 19 05 | 14 56 | 07 18 | 05 47 |
| 51 | 17 39 | 19 27 | 15 07 | 07 14 | 05 36 |
| 52 | 18 01 | 19 50 | 15 18 | 07 09 | 05 25 |
| 53 | 18 23 | 20 13 | 15 29 | 07 05 | 05 13 |
| 54 | 18 47 | 20 38 | 15 41 | 07 01 | 05 01 |
| 55 | 19 12 | 21 03 | 15 53 | 06 56 | 04 48 |
| 56 | 19 39 | 21 29 | 16 05 | 06 52 | 04 34 |
| 57 | 20 08 | 21 55 | 16 18 | 06 47 | 04 20 |
| 58 | 20 38 | 22 23 | 16 30 | 06 42 | 04 06 |
| 59 | 21 11 | 22 52 | 16 43 | 06 37 | 03 50 |
| 60 | 21♋46 | 23♌22 | 16♍57 | 06♎32 | 03♏34 |

**4h 40m 0s — 70° 0' 0" — 11 ♊ 32**

| LAT. | 11 | 12 | ASC | 2 | 3 |
|---|---|---|---|---|---|
| 0 | 09♋11 | 07♌35 | 08♍22 | 10♎53 | 12♏27 |
| 5 | 09 51 | 08 40 | 09 08 | 10 37 | 11 59 |
| 10 | 10 31 | 09 43 | 09 51 | 10 21 | 11 31 |
| 15 | 11 12 | 10 47 | 10 33 | 10 06 | 11 02 |
| 20 | 11 55 | 11 52 | 11 14 | 09 51 | 10 33 |
| 21 | 12 04 | 12 05 | 11 23 | 09 48 | 10 27 |
| 22 | 12 13 | 12 18 | 11 31 | 09 45 | 10 21 |
| 23 | 12 22 | 12 31 | 11 39 | 09 42 | 10 15 |
| 24 | 12 31 | 12 45 | 11 47 | 09 39 | 10 09 |
| 25 | 12 41 | 12 58 | 11 55 | 09 36 | 10 03 |
| 26 | 12 50 | 13 12 | 12 03 | 09 33 | 09 56 |
| 27 | 13 00 | 13 26 | 12 12 | 09 29 | 09 50 |
| 28 | 13 10 | 13 40 | 12 20 | 09 26 | 09 44 |
| 29 | 13 20 | 13 54 | 12 28 | 09 23 | 09 37 |
| 30 | 13 30 | 14 08 | 12 36 | 09 20 | 09 30 |
| 31 | 13 41 | 14 23 | 12 45 | 09 17 | 09 23 |
| 32 | 13 52 | 14 37 | 12 53 | 09 13 | 09 17 |
| 33 | 14 03 | 14 52 | 13 02 | 09 10 | 09 10 |
| 34 | 14 14 | 15 07 | 13 10 | 09 07 | 09 02 |
| 35 | 14 26 | 15 23 | 13 19 | 09 03 | 08 55 |
| 36 | 14 38 | 15 38 | 13 27 | 09 00 | 08 48 |
| 37 | 14 50 | 15 54 | 13 36 | 08 57 | 08 40 |
| 38 | 15 02 | 16 10 | 13 45 | 08 53 | 08 32 |
| 39 | 15 15 | 16 27 | 13 53 | 08 50 | 08 24 |
| 40 | 15 29 | 16 43 | 14 02 | 08 46 | 08 16 |
| 41 | 15 42 | 17 00 | 14 11 | 08 42 | 08 08 |
| 42 | 15 57 | 17 18 | 14 21 | 08 39 | 07 59 |
| 43 | 16 11 | 17 35 | 14 30 | 08 35 | 07 50 |
| 44 | 16 27 | 17 54 | 14 39 | 08 31 | 07 41 |
| 45 | 16 42 | 18 12 | 14 49 | 08 27 | 07 32 |
| 46 | 16 59 | 18 31 | 14 58 | 08 23 | 07 22 |
| 47 | 17 16 | 18 51 | 15 08 | 08 19 | 07 13 |
| 48 | 17 33 | 19 11 | 15 18 | 08 15 | 07 02 |
| 49 | 17 52 | 19 31 | 15 28 | 08 11 | 06 52 |
| 50 | 18 11 | 19 52 | 15 39 | 08 06 | 06 41 |
| 51 | 18 32 | 20 14 | 15 49 | 08 02 | 06 30 |
| 52 | 18 53 | 20 37 | 16 00 | 07 57 | 06 18 |
| 53 | 19 15 | 21 00 | 16 11 | 07 52 | 06 06 |
| 54 | 19 39 | 21 23 | 16 22 | 07 48 | 05 53 |
| 55 | 20 04 | 21 48 | 16 33 | 07 43 | 05 40 |
| 56 | 20 30 | 22 13 | 16 45 | 07 38 | 05 26 |
| 57 | 20 59 | 22 40 | 16 57 | 07 32 | 05 12 |
| 58 | 21 29 | 23 07 | 17 09 | 07 27 | 04 57 |
| 59 | 22 01 | 23 35 | 17 21 | 07 21 | 04 41 |
| 60 | 22♋35 | 24♌04 | 17♍34 | 07♎16 | 04♏25 |

**4h 44m 0s — 71° 0' 0" — 12 ♊ 28**

| LAT. | 11 | 12 | ASC | 2 | 3 |
|---|---|---|---|---|---|
| 0 | 10♋07 | 08♌34 | 09♍26 | 11♎58 | 13♏27 |
| 5 | 10 46 | 09 38 | 10 10 | 11 40 | 12 59 |
| 10 | 11 26 | 10 41 | 10 51 | 11 23 | 12 30 |
| 15 | 12 07 | 11 44 | 11 31 | 11 07 | 12 02 |
| 20 | 12 50 | 12 47 | 12 10 | 10 50 | 11 32 |
| 21 | 12 58 | 13 00 | 12 18 | 10 47 | 11 26 |
| 22 | 13 07 | 13 13 | 12 26 | 10 43 | 11 20 |
| 23 | 13 17 | 13 26 | 12 34 | 10 40 | 11 13 |
| 24 | 13 26 | 13 40 | 12 41 | 10 37 | 11 07 |
| 25 | 13 35 | 13 53 | 12 49 | 10 33 | 11 01 |
| 26 | 13 45 | 14 06 | 12 57 | 10 30 | 10 54 |
| 27 | 13 55 | 14 20 | 13 05 | 10 26 | 10 48 |
| 28 | 14 04 | 14 34 | 13 13 | 10 23 | 10 41 |
| 29 | 14 15 | 14 48 | 13 20 | 10 19 | 10 34 |
| 30 | 14 25 | 15 02 | 13 28 | 10 16 | 10 28 |
| 31 | 14 35 | 15 16 | 13 36 | 10 12 | 10 21 |
| 32 | 14 46 | 15 30 | 13 44 | 10 09 | 10 14 |
| 33 | 14 57 | 15 45 | 13 52 | 10 05 | 10 06 |
| 34 | 15 08 | 16 00 | 14 00 | 10 01 | 09 59 |
| 35 | 15 20 | 16 15 | 14 08 | 09 58 | 09 52 |
| 36 | 15 32 | 16 30 | 14 17 | 09 54 | 09 44 |
| 37 | 15 44 | 16 46 | 14 25 | 09 50 | 09 36 |
| 38 | 15 56 | 17 02 | 14 33 | 09 46 | 09 28 |
| 39 | 16 09 | 17 18 | 14 42 | 09 42 | 09 20 |
| 40 | 16 22 | 17 34 | 14 50 | 09 38 | 09 12 |
| 41 | 16 36 | 17 51 | 14 59 | 09 34 | 09 03 |
| 42 | 16 50 | 18 08 | 15 07 | 09 30 | 08 55 |
| 43 | 17 05 | 18 25 | 15 16 | 09 26 | 08 46 |
| 44 | 17 20 | 18 43 | 15 25 | 09 22 | 08 36 |
| 45 | 17 36 | 19 02 | 15 34 | 09 18 | 08 27 |
| 46 | 17 52 | 19 20 | 15 43 | 09 13 | 08 17 |
| 47 | 18 09 | 19 39 | 15 53 | 09 09 | 08 07 |
| 48 | 18 26 | 19 59 | 16 02 | 09 04 | 07 57 |
| 49 | 18 45 | 20 19 | 16 12 | 08 59 | 07 46 |
| 50 | 19 04 | 20 40 | 16 22 | 08 55 | 07 35 |
| 51 | 19 24 | 21 01 | 16 32 | 08 50 | 07 23 |
| 52 | 19 45 | 21 23 | 16 42 | 08 45 | 07 11 |
| 53 | 20 07 | 21 46 | 16 52 | 08 40 | 06 59 |
| 54 | 20 31 | 22 09 | 17 03 | 08 34 | 06 46 |
| 55 | 20 55 | 22 33 | 17 13 | 08 29 | 06 32 |
| 56 | 21 22 | 22 58 | 17 24 | 08 23 | 06 18 |
| 57 | 21 49 | 23 24 | 17 36 | 08 17 | 06 03 |
| 58 | 22 19 | 23 50 | 17 47 | 08 12 | 05 48 |
| 59 | 22 51 | 24 18 | 17 59 | 08 05 | 05 32 |
| 60 | 23♋25 | 24♌47 | 18♍11 | 07♎59 | 05♏15 |

# Placidus Table of Houses for Latitudes 0° to 60° North

**4h 48m 0s — 72° 0' 0" — 13 ♊ 24**

| LAT. | 11 | 12 | ASC | 2 | 3 |
|---|---|---|---|---|---|
| 0 | 11♋02 | 09♌34 | 10♍30 | 13♎03 | 14♏28 |
| 5 | 11 41 | 10 36 | 11 12 | 12 44 | 13 59 |
| 10 | 12 21 | 11 38 | 11 51 | 12 25 | 13 30 |
| 15 | 13 02 | 12 40 | 12 29 | 12 07 | 13 00 |
| 20 | 13 44 | 13 43 | 13 06 | 11 49 | 12 30 |
| 21 | 13 53 | 13 56 | 13 14 | 11 45 | 12 24 |
| 22 | 14 02 | 14 08 | 13 21 | 11 42 | 12 18 |
| 23 | 14 11 | 14 21 | 13 28 | 11 38 | 12 11 |
| 24 | 14 21 | 14 34 | 13 36 | 11 34 | 12 05 |
| 25 | 14 30 | 14 48 | 13 43 | 11 31 | 11 59 |
| 26 | 14 39 | 15 01 | 13 51 | 11 27 | 11 52 |
| 27 | 14 49 | 15 14 | 13 58 | 11 23 | 11 45 |
| 28 | 14 59 | 15 28 | 14 05 | 11 19 | 11 39 |
| 29 | 15 09 | 15 41 | 14 13 | 11 16 | 11 32 |
| 30 | 15 19 | 15 55 | 14 20 | 11 12 | 11 25 |
| 31 | 15 30 | 16 09 | 14 28 | 11 08 | 11 18 |
| 32 | 15 40 | 16 23 | 14 35 | 11 04 | 11 10 |
| 33 | 15 51 | 16 38 | 14 43 | 11 00 | 11 03 |
| 34 | 16 03 | 16 52 | 14 51 | 10 56 | 10 56 |
| 35 | 16 14 | 17 07 | 14 58 | 10 52 | 10 48 |
| 36 | 16 26 | 17 22 | 15 06 | 10 48 | 10 40 |
| 37 | 16 38 | 17 38 | 15 14 | 10 44 | 10 32 |
| 38 | 16 50 | 17 53 | 15 22 | 10 40 | 10 24 |
| 39 | 17 03 | 18 09 | 15 30 | 10 35 | 10 16 |
| 40 | 17 16 | 18 25 | 15 38 | 10 31 | 10 08 |
| 41 | 17 30 | 18 42 | 15 46 | 10 27 | 09 59 |
| 42 | 17 44 | 18 58 | 15 54 | 10 22 | 09 50 |
| 43 | 17 58 | 19 16 | 16 03 | 10 18 | 09 41 |
| 44 | 18 13 | 19 33 | 16 11 | 10 13 | 09 31 |
| 45 | 18 29 | 19 51 | 16 20 | 10 08 | 09 22 |
| 46 | 18 45 | 20 09 | 16 28 | 10 03 | 09 12 |
| 47 | 19 02 | 20 28 | 16 37 | 09 59 | 09 01 |
| 48 | 19 19 | 20 47 | 16 46 | 09 54 | 08 51 |
| 49 | 19 37 | 21 07 | 16 55 | 09 48 | 08 40 |
| 50 | 19 56 | 21 27 | 17 05 | 09 43 | 08 28 |
| 51 | 20 16 | 21 48 | 17 14 | 09 38 | 08 16 |
| 52 | 20 37 | 22 10 | 17 24 | 09 32 | 08 04 |
| 53 | 20 59 | 22 32 | 17 33 | 09 27 | 07 51 |
| 54 | 21 22 | 22 55 | 17 43 | 09 21 | 07 38 |
| 55 | 21 47 | 23 18 | 17 54 | 09 15 | 07 24 |
| 56 | 22 13 | 23 43 | 18 04 | 09 09 | 07 10 |
| 57 | 22 40 | 24 08 | 18 15 | 09 03 | 06 55 |
| 58 | 23 09 | 24 34 | 18 26 | 08 56 | 06 39 |
| 59 | 23 41 | 25 01 | 18 37 | 08 49 | 06 23 |
| 60 | 24♋14 | 25♌29 | 18♍48 | 08♎43 | 06♏05 |

**4h 52m 0s — 73° 0' 0" — 14 ♊ 20**

| LAT. | 11 | 12 | ASC | 2 | 3 |
|---|---|---|---|---|---|
| 0 | 11♋58 | 10♌33 | 11♍34 | 14♎07 | 15♏28 |
| 5 | 12 37 | 11 35 | 12 14 | 13 47 | 14 59 |
| 10 | 13 16 | 12 36 | 12 51 | 13 27 | 14 29 |
| 15 | 13 57 | 13 37 | 13 27 | 13 07 | 13 59 |
| 20 | 14 39 | 14 39 | 14 02 | 12 48 | 13 28 |
| 21 | 14 48 | 14 51 | 14 09 | 12 44 | 13 22 |
| 22 | 14 57 | 15 04 | 14 16 | 12 40 | 13 16 |
| 23 | 15 06 | 15 17 | 14 23 | 12 36 | 13 09 |
| 24 | 15 15 | 15 29 | 14 30 | 12 32 | 13 03 |
| 25 | 15 25 | 15 42 | 14 37 | 12 28 | 12 56 |
| 26 | 15 34 | 15 55 | 14 44 | 12 24 | 12 50 |
| 27 | 15 44 | 16 09 | 14 51 | 12 20 | 12 43 |
| 28 | 15 54 | 16 22 | 14 58 | 12 16 | 12 36 |
| 29 | 16 04 | 16 35 | 15 05 | 12 12 | 12 29 |
| 30 | 16 14 | 16 49 | 15 12 | 12 07 | 12 22 |
| 31 | 16 24 | 17 03 | 15 19 | 12 03 | 12 15 |
| 32 | 16 35 | 17 17 | 15 27 | 11 59 | 12 07 |
| 33 | 16 46 | 17 31 | 15 34 | 11 55 | 12 00 |
| 34 | 16 57 | 17 45 | 15 41 | 11 50 | 11 52 |
| 35 | 17 08 | 18 00 | 15 48 | 11 46 | 11 44 |
| 36 | 17 20 | 18 14 | 15 56 | 11 42 | 11 37 |
| 37 | 17 32 | 18 29 | 16 03 | 11 37 | 11 28 |
| 38 | 17 44 | 18 45 | 16 11 | 11 33 | 11 20 |
| 39 | 17 57 | 19 00 | 16 18 | 11 28 | 11 12 |
| 40 | 18 10 | 19 16 | 16 26 | 11 23 | 11 03 |
| 41 | 18 23 | 19 32 | 16 33 | 11 19 | 10 54 |
| 42 | 18 37 | 19 49 | 16 41 | 11 14 | 10 45 |
| 43 | 18 52 | 20 06 | 16 49 | 11 09 | 10 36 |
| 44 | 19 07 | 20 23 | 16 57 | 11 04 | 10 26 |
| 45 | 19 22 | 20 40 | 17 05 | 10 59 | 10 16 |
| 46 | 19 38 | 20 58 | 17 13 | 10 54 | 10 06 |
| 47 | 19 55 | 21 17 | 17 22 | 10 48 | 09 55 |
| 48 | 20 12 | 21 36 | 17 30 | 10 43 | 09 45 |
| 49 | 20 30 | 21 55 | 17 39 | 10 37 | 09 33 |
| 50 | 20 49 | 22 15 | 17 48 | 10 32 | 09 22 |
| 51 | 21 09 | 22 35 | 17 57 | 10 26 | 09 10 |
| 52 | 21 29 | 22 56 | 18 06 | 10 20 | 08 57 |
| 53 | 21 51 | 23 18 | 18 15 | 10 14 | 08 44 |
| 54 | 22 14 | 23 41 | 18 24 | 10 08 | 08 31 |
| 55 | 22 38 | 24 04 | 18 34 | 10 01 | 08 17 |
| 56 | 23 04 | 24 27 | 18 44 | 09 55 | 08 02 |
| 57 | 23 31 | 24 52 | 18 54 | 09 48 | 07 46 |
| 58 | 24 00 | 25 18 | 19 04 | 09 41 | 07 30 |
| 59 | 24 30 | 25 44 | 19 15 | 09 34 | 07 13 |
| 60 | 25♋03 | 26♌12 | 19♍26 | 09♎26 | 06♏56 |

**4h 56m 0s — 74° 0' 0" — 15 ♊ 16**

| LAT. | 11 | 12 | ASC | 2 | 3 |
|---|---|---|---|---|---|
| 0 | 12♋53 | 11♌32 | 12♍39 | 15♎12 | 16♏28 |
| 5 | 13 32 | 12 34 | 13 16 | 14 50 | 15 58 |
| 10 | 14 11 | 13 34 | 13 51 | 14 29 | 15 28 |
| 15 | 14 52 | 14 34 | 14 25 | 14 08 | 14 58 |
| 20 | 15 34 | 15 35 | 14 58 | 13 47 | 14 27 |
| 21 | 15 43 | 15 47 | 15 05 | 13 42 | 14 20 |
| 22 | 15 52 | 15 59 | 15 12 | 13 38 | 14 14 |
| 23 | 16 01 | 16 12 | 15 18 | 13 34 | 14 07 |
| 24 | 16 10 | 16 24 | 15 25 | 13 30 | 14 00 |
| 25 | 16 19 | 16 37 | 15 31 | 13 25 | 13 54 |
| 26 | 16 29 | 16 50 | 15 38 | 13 21 | 13 47 |
| 27 | 16 38 | 17 03 | 15 44 | 13 17 | 13 40 |
| 28 | 16 48 | 17 16 | 15 51 | 13 12 | 13 33 |
| 29 | 16 58 | 17 29 | 15 58 | 13 08 | 13 26 |
| 30 | 17 08 | 17 43 | 16 04 | 13 03 | 13 19 |
| 31 | 17 19 | 17 56 | 16 11 | 12 59 | 13 11 |
| 32 | 17 29 | 18 10 | 16 18 | 12 54 | 13 04 |
| 33 | 17 40 | 18 24 | 16 25 | 12 50 | 12 56 |
| 34 | 17 51 | 18 38 | 16 31 | 12 45 | 12 49 |
| 35 | 18 02 | 18 52 | 16 38 | 12 40 | 12 41 |
| 36 | 18 14 | 19 07 | 16 45 | 12 36 | 12 33 |
| 37 | 18 26 | 19 21 | 16 52 | 12 31 | 12 24 |
| 38 | 18 38 | 19 36 | 16 59 | 12 26 | 12 16 |
| 39 | 18 51 | 19 52 | 17 06 | 12 21 | 12 07 |
| 40 | 19 04 | 20 07 | 17 14 | 12 16 | 11 59 |
| 41 | 19 17 | 20 23 | 17 21 | 12 11 | 11 50 |
| 42 | 19 31 | 20 39 | 17 28 | 12 06 | 11 40 |
| 43 | 19 45 | 20 56 | 17 36 | 12 00 | 11 31 |
| 44 | 20 00 | 21 13 | 17 43 | 11 55 | 11 21 |
| 45 | 20 15 | 21 30 | 17 51 | 11 49 | 11 11 |
| 46 | 20 31 | 21 47 | 17 58 | 11 44 | 11 00 |
| 47 | 20 48 | 22 05 | 18 06 | 11 38 | 10 50 |
| 48 | 21 05 | 22 24 | 18 14 | 11 32 | 10 39 |
| 49 | 21 23 | 22 43 | 18 22 | 11 26 | 10 27 |
| 50 | 21 41 | 23 03 | 18 31 | 11 20 | 10 15 |
| 51 | 22 01 | 23 23 | 18 39 | 11 14 | 10 03 |
| 52 | 22 21 | 23 43 | 18 48 | 11 08 | 09 50 |
| 53 | 22 43 | 24 04 | 18 56 | 11 01 | 09 37 |
| 54 | 23 05 | 24 26 | 19 05 | 10 54 | 09 23 |
| 55 | 23 29 | 24 49 | 19 14 | 10 47 | 09 09 |
| 56 | 23 55 | 25 12 | 19 24 | 10 40 | 08 54 |
| 57 | 24 21 | 25 36 | 19 33 | 10 33 | 08 38 |
| 58 | 24 50 | 26 01 | 19 43 | 10 25 | 08 21 |
| 59 | 25 20 | 26 27 | 19 53 | 10 18 | 08 04 |
| 60 | 25♋53 | 26♌54 | 20♍03 | 10♎09 | 07♏46 |

**5h 0m 0s — 75° 0' 0" — 16 ♊ 11**

| LAT. | 11 | 12 | ASC | 2 | 3 |
|---|---|---|---|---|---|
| 0 | 13♋49 | 12♌32 | 13♍43 | 16♎17 | 17♏28 |
| 5 | 14 27 | 13 32 | 14 18 | 15 53 | 16 58 |
| 10 | 15 07 | 14 32 | 14 51 | 15 30 | 16 27 |
| 15 | 15 47 | 15 31 | 15 23 | 15 08 | 15 56 |
| 20 | 16 29 | 16 31 | 15 54 | 14 45 | 15 25 |
| 21 | 16 38 | 16 43 | 16 01 | 14 41 | 15 18 |
| 22 | 16 47 | 16 55 | 16 07 | 14 36 | 15 11 |
| 23 | 16 56 | 17 07 | 16 13 | 14 32 | 15 05 |
| 24 | 17 05 | 17 20 | 16 19 | 14 27 | 14 58 |
| 25 | 17 14 | 17 32 | 16 25 | 14 22 | 14 51 |
| 26 | 17 23 | 17 45 | 16 32 | 14 18 | 14 44 |
| 27 | 17 33 | 17 57 | 16 38 | 14 13 | 14 37 |
| 28 | 17 43 | 18 10 | 16 44 | 14 08 | 14 30 |
| 29 | 17 53 | 18 23 | 16 50 | 14 04 | 14 23 |
| 30 | 18 03 | 18 36 | 16 57 | 13 59 | 14 16 |
| 31 | 18 13 | 18 50 | 17 03 | 13 54 | 14 08 |
| 32 | 18 23 | 19 03 | 17 09 | 13 49 | 14 01 |
| 33 | 18 34 | 19 17 | 17 15 | 13 44 | 13 53 |
| 34 | 18 45 | 19 31 | 17 22 | 13 39 | 13 45 |
| 35 | 18 56 | 19 45 | 17 28 | 13 34 | 13 37 |
| 36 | 19 08 | 19 59 | 17 35 | 13 29 | 13 29 |
| 37 | 19 20 | 20 13 | 17 41 | 13 24 | 13 20 |
| 38 | 19 32 | 20 28 | 17 48 | 13 19 | 13 12 |
| 39 | 19 44 | 20 43 | 17 55 | 13 14 | 13 03 |
| 40 | 19 57 | 20 58 | 18 01 | 13 08 | 12 54 |
| 41 | 20 11 | 21 14 | 18 08 | 13 03 | 12 45 |
| 42 | 20 24 | 21 30 | 18 15 | 12 57 | 12 35 |
| 43 | 20 38 | 21 46 | 18 22 | 12 52 | 12 26 |
| 44 | 20 53 | 22 02 | 18 29 | 12 46 | 12 16 |
| 45 | 21 08 | 22 19 | 18 36 | 12 40 | 12 05 |
| 46 | 21 24 | 22 37 | 18 43 | 12 34 | 11 55 |
| 47 | 21 40 | 22 54 | 18 51 | 12 28 | 11 44 |
| 48 | 21 57 | 23 12 | 18 58 | 12 22 | 11 32 |
| 49 | 22 15 | 23 31 | 19 06 | 12 15 | 11 21 |
| 50 | 22 34 | 23 50 | 19 14 | 12 09 | 11 09 |
| 51 | 22 53 | 24 10 | 19 22 | 12 02 | 10 56 |
| 52 | 23 13 | 24 30 | 19 30 | 11 55 | 10 43 |
| 53 | 23 35 | 24 51 | 19 38 | 11 48 | 10 29 |
| 54 | 23 57 | 25 12 | 19 46 | 11 41 | 10 15 |
| 55 | 24 21 | 25 34 | 19 55 | 11 34 | 10 01 |
| 56 | 24 45 | 25 57 | 20 03 | 11 26 | 09 45 |
| 57 | 25 12 | 26 21 | 20 12 | 11 18 | 09 29 |
| 58 | 25 40 | 26 45 | 20 21 | 11 10 | 09 12 |
| 59 | 26 10 | 27 10 | 20 31 | 11 02 | 08 55 |
| 60 | 26♋42 | 27♌37 | 20♍40 | 10♎53 | 08♏36 |

**5h 4m 0s — 76° 0' 0" — 17 ♊ 07**

| LAT. | 11 | 12 | ASC | 2 | 3 |
|---|---|---|---|---|---|
| 0 | 14♋44 | 13♌32 | 14♍48 | 17♎21 | 18♏28 |
| 5 | 15 23 | 14 31 | 15 21 | 16 56 | 17 57 |
| 10 | 16 02 | 15 30 | 15 52 | 16 32 | 17 26 |
| 15 | 16 42 | 16 28 | 16 21 | 16 08 | 16 55 |
| 20 | 17 24 | 17 27 | 16 51 | 15 44 | 16 22 |
| 21 | 17 33 | 17 39 | 16 56 | 15 39 | 16 16 |
| 22 | 17 42 | 17 51 | 17 02 | 15 34 | 16 09 |
| 23 | 17 51 | 18 03 | 17 08 | 15 29 | 16 02 |
| 24 | 18 00 | 18 15 | 17 14 | 15 25 | 15 55 |
| 25 | 18 09 | 18 27 | 17 20 | 15 20 | 15 48 |
| 26 | 18 18 | 18 39 | 17 25 | 15 15 | 15 41 |
| 27 | 18 28 | 18 52 | 17 31 | 15 10 | 15 34 |
| 28 | 18 37 | 19 05 | 17 37 | 15 05 | 15 27 |
| 29 | 18 47 | 19 17 | 17 43 | 15 00 | 15 20 |
| 30 | 18 57 | 19 30 | 17 49 | 14 55 | 15 12 |
| 31 | 19 07 | 19 43 | 17 54 | 14 50 | 15 05 |
| 32 | 19 18 | 19 56 | 18 00 | 14 44 | 14 57 |
| 33 | 19 28 | 20 10 | 18 06 | 14 39 | 14 49 |
| 34 | 19 39 | 20 23 | 18 12 | 14 34 | 14 41 |
| 35 | 19 51 | 20 37 | 18 18 | 14 29 | 14 33 |
| 36 | 20 02 | 20 51 | 18 24 | 14 23 | 14 25 |
| 37 | 20 14 | 21 05 | 18 31 | 14 18 | 14 16 |
| 38 | 20 26 | 21 20 | 18 37 | 14 12 | 14 07 |
| 39 | 20 38 | 21 34 | 18 43 | 14 06 | 13 58 |
| 40 | 20 51 | 21 49 | 18 49 | 14 01 | 13 49 |
| 41 | 21 04 | 22 05 | 18 56 | 13 55 | 13 40 |
| 42 | 21 18 | 22 20 | 19 02 | 13 49 | 13 30 |
| 43 | 21 32 | 22 36 | 19 08 | 13 43 | 13 20 |
| 44 | 21 46 | 22 52 | 19 15 | 13 37 | 13 10 |
| 45 | 22 01 | 23 09 | 19 22 | 13 31 | 13 00 |
| 46 | 22 17 | 23 26 | 19 29 | 13 24 | 12 49 |
| 47 | 22 33 | 23 43 | 19 35 | 13 18 | 12 38 |
| 48 | 22 50 | 24 01 | 19 42 | 13 11 | 12 26 |
| 49 | 23 08 | 24 19 | 19 49 | 13 04 | 12 14 |
| 50 | 23 26 | 24 38 | 19 57 | 12 57 | 12 02 |
| 51 | 23 45 | 24 57 | 20 04 | 12 50 | 11 49 |
| 52 | 24 05 | 25 17 | 20 12 | 12 43 | 11 36 |
| 53 | 24 26 | 25 37 | 20 19 | 12 35 | 11 22 |
| 54 | 24 48 | 25 58 | 20 27 | 12 28 | 11 07 |
| 55 | 25 12 | 26 20 | 20 35 | 12 20 | 10 52 |
| 56 | 25 36 | 26 42 | 20 43 | 12 12 | 10 37 |
| 57 | 26 02 | 27 05 | 20 51 | 12 03 | 10 20 |
| 58 | 26 30 | 27 29 | 21 00 | 11 54 | 10 03 |
| 59 | 27 00 | 27 54 | 21 09 | 11 46 | 09 45 |
| 60 | 27♋31 | 28♌19 | 21♍17 | 11♎36 | 09♏26 |

**5h 8m 0s — 77° 0' 0" — 18 ♊ 02**

| LAT. | 11 | 12 | ASC | 2 | 3 |
|---|---|---|---|---|---|
| 0 | 15♋40 | 14♌32 | 15♍53 | 18♎26 | 19♏27 |
| 5 | 16 19 | 15 30 | 16 23 | 17 59 | 18 56 |
| 10 | 16 58 | 16 28 | 16 52 | 17 33 | 18 25 |
| 15 | 17 38 | 17 25 | 17 20 | 17 08 | 17 53 |
| 20 | 18 19 | 18 23 | 17 47 | 16 43 | 17 20 |
| 21 | 18 28 | 18 35 | 17 52 | 16 37 | 17 13 |
| 22 | 18 37 | 18 46 | 17 58 | 16 32 | 17 07 |
| 23 | 18 46 | 18 58 | 18 03 | 16 27 | 17 00 |
| 24 | 18 55 | 19 10 | 18 08 | 16 22 | 16 53 |
| 25 | 19 04 | 19 22 | 18 14 | 16 17 | 16 46 |
| 26 | 19 13 | 19 34 | 18 19 | 16 12 | 16 39 |
| 27 | 19 22 | 19 47 | 18 24 | 16 06 | 16 31 |
| 28 | 19 32 | 19 59 | 18 30 | 16 01 | 16 24 |
| 29 | 19 42 | 20 11 | 18 35 | 15 56 | 16 16 |
| 30 | 19 52 | 20 24 | 18 41 | 15 50 | 16 09 |
| 31 | 20 02 | 20 37 | 18 46 | 15 45 | 16 01 |
| 32 | 20 12 | 20 50 | 18 52 | 15 39 | 15 53 |
| 33 | 20 23 | 21 03 | 18 57 | 15 34 | 15 45 |
| 34 | 20 34 | 21 16 | 19 03 | 15 28 | 15 37 |
| 35 | 20 45 | 21 30 | 19 08 | 15 23 | 15 29 |
| 36 | 20 56 | 21 43 | 19 14 | 15 17 | 15 20 |
| 37 | 21 08 | 21 57 | 19 20 | 15 11 | 15 12 |
| 38 | 21 20 | 22 12 | 19 25 | 15 05 | 15 03 |
| 39 | 21 32 | 22 26 | 19 31 | 14 59 | 14 54 |
| 40 | 21 45 | 22 41 | 19 37 | 14 53 | 14 44 |
| 41 | 21 58 | 22 55 | 19 43 | 14 47 | 14 35 |
| 42 | 22 11 | 23 11 | 19 49 | 14 41 | 14 25 |
| 43 | 22 25 | 23 26 | 19 55 | 14 34 | 14 15 |
| 44 | 22 40 | 23 42 | 20 01 | 14 28 | 14 05 |
| 45 | 22 55 | 23 58 | 20 07 | 14 21 | 13 54 |
| 46 | 23 10 | 24 15 | 20 14 | 14 14 | 13 43 |
| 47 | 23 26 | 24 32 | 20 20 | 14 07 | 13 32 |
| 48 | 23 43 | 24 49 | 20 26 | 14 00 | 13 20 |
| 49 | 24 00 | 25 07 | 20 33 | 13 53 | 13 08 |
| 50 | 24 18 | 25 25 | 20 40 | 13 46 | 12 55 |
| 51 | 24 37 | 25 44 | 20 47 | 13 38 | 12 42 |
| 52 | 24 57 | 26 03 | 20 54 | 13 30 | 12 28 |
| 53 | 25 18 | 26 23 | 21 01 | 13 22 | 12 14 |
| 54 | 25 40 | 26 44 | 21 08 | 13 14 | 12 00 |
| 55 | 26 03 | 27 05 | 21 15 | 13 06 | 11 44 |
| 56 | 26 27 | 27 27 | 21 23 | 12 57 | 11 28 |
| 57 | 26 53 | 27 49 | 21 30 | 12 48 | 11 11 |
| 58 | 27 20 | 28 13 | 21 38 | 12 39 | 10 54 |
| 59 | 27 49 | 28 37 | 21 46 | 12 30 | 10 35 |
| 60 | 28♋21 | 29♌02 | 21♍55 | 12♎20 | 10♏16 |

**5h 12m 0s — 78° 0' 0" — 18 ♊ 58**

| LAT. | 11 | 12 | ASC | 2 | 3 |
|---|---|---|---|---|---|
| 0 | 16♋36 | 15♌32 | 16♍57 | 19♎30 | 20♏26 |
| 5 | 17 14 | 16 30 | 17 26 | 19 02 | 19 55 |
| 10 | 17 53 | 17 26 | 17 52 | 18 35 | 19 23 |
| 15 | 18 33 | 18 22 | 18 18 | 18 08 | 18 51 |
| 20 | 19 14 | 19 19 | 18 43 | 17 41 | 18 18 |
| 21 | 19 23 | 19 31 | 18 48 | 17 36 | 18 11 |
| 22 | 19 32 | 19 42 | 18 53 | 17 30 | 18 04 |
| 23 | 19 40 | 19 54 | 18 58 | 17 25 | 17 57 |
| 24 | 19 49 | 20 06 | 19 03 | 17 19 | 17 50 |
| 25 | 19 58 | 20 17 | 19 08 | 17 14 | 17 43 |
| 26 | 20 08 | 20 29 | 19 13 | 17 08 | 17 35 |
| 27 | 20 17 | 20 41 | 19 18 | 17 03 | 17 28 |
| 28 | 20 27 | 20 53 | 19 23 | 16 57 | 17 21 |
| 29 | 20 36 | 21 06 | 19 28 | 16 52 | 17 13 |
| 30 | 20 46 | 21 18 | 19 33 | 16 46 | 17 05 |
| 31 | 20 56 | 21 31 | 19 38 | 16 40 | 16 58 |
| 32 | 21 07 | 21 43 | 19 43 | 16 34 | 16 50 |
| 33 | 21 17 | 21 56 | 19 48 | 16 29 | 16 41 |
| 34 | 21 28 | 22 09 | 19 53 | 16 23 | 16 33 |
| 35 | 21 39 | 22 22 | 19 58 | 16 17 | 16 25 |
| 36 | 21 50 | 22 36 | 20 04 | 16 11 | 16 16 |
| 37 | 22 02 | 22 49 | 20 09 | 16 04 | 16 07 |
| 38 | 22 14 | 23 03 | 20 14 | 15 58 | 15 58 |
| 39 | 22 26 | 23 17 | 20 20 | 15 52 | 15 49 |
| 40 | 22 38 | 23 32 | 20 25 | 15 45 | 15 40 |
| 41 | 22 51 | 23 46 | 20 30 | 15 39 | 15 30 |
| 42 | 23 05 | 24 01 | 20 36 | 15 32 | 15 20 |
| 43 | 23 19 | 24 16 | 20 41 | 15 25 | 15 10 |
| 44 | 23 33 | 24 32 | 20 47 | 15 18 | 14 59 |
| 45 | 23 48 | 24 48 | 20 53 | 15 11 | 14 48 |
| 46 | 24 03 | 25 04 | 20 59 | 15 04 | 14 37 |
| 47 | 24 19 | 25 21 | 21 05 | 14 57 | 14 25 |
| 48 | 24 35 | 25 38 | 21 11 | 14 50 | 14 13 |
| 49 | 24 53 | 25 55 | 21 17 | 14 42 | 14 01 |
| 50 | 25 11 | 26 13 | 21 23 | 14 34 | 13 48 |
| 51 | 25 29 | 26 31 | 21 29 | 14 26 | 13 35 |
| 52 | 25 49 | 26 50 | 21 36 | 14 18 | 13 21 |
| 53 | 26 10 | 27 10 | 21 42 | 14 09 | 13 07 |
| 54 | 26 31 | 27 30 | 21 49 | 14 01 | 12 52 |
| 55 | 26 54 | 27 50 | 21 56 | 13 52 | 12 36 |
| 56 | 27 18 | 28 12 | 22 03 | 13 43 | 12 20 |
| 57 | 27 43 | 28 34 | 22 10 | 13 33 | 12 03 |
| 58 | 28 10 | 28 56 | 22 17 | 13 24 | 11 45 |
| 59 | 28 39 | 29 20 | 22 24 | 13 13 | 11 26 |
| 60 | 29♋10 | 29♌44 | 22♍32 | 13♎03 | 11♏06 |

**5h 16m 0s — 79° 0' 0" — 19 ♊ 53**

| LAT. | 11 | 12 | ASC | 2 | 3 |
|---|---|---|---|---|---|
| 0 | 17♋32 | 16♌33 | 18♍02 | 20♎34 | 21♏26 |
| 5 | 18 10 | 17 29 | 18 28 | 20 05 | 20 54 |
| 10 | 18 49 | 18 25 | 18 53 | 19 36 | 20 21 |
| 15 | 19 28 | 19 20 | 19 16 | 19 08 | 19 49 |
| 20 | 20 10 | 20 15 | 19 39 | 18 40 | 19 15 |
| 21 | 20 18 | 20 27 | 19 44 | 18 34 | 19 08 |
| 22 | 20 27 | 20 38 | 19 48 | 18 28 | 19 01 |
| 23 | 20 35 | 20 49 | 19 53 | 18 23 | 18 54 |
| 24 | 20 44 | 21 01 | 19 58 | 18 17 | 18 47 |
| 25 | 20 53 | 21 13 | 20 02 | 18 11 | 18 40 |
| 26 | 21 03 | 21 24 | 20 07 | 18 05 | 18 32 |
| 27 | 21 12 | 21 36 | 20 11 | 17 59 | 18 25 |
| 28 | 21 21 | 21 48 | 20 16 | 17 53 | 18 17 |
| 29 | 21 31 | 22 00 | 20 20 | 17 47 | 18 10 |
| 30 | 21 41 | 22 12 | 20 25 | 17 41 | 18 02 |
| 31 | 21 51 | 22 24 | 20 30 | 17 35 | 17 54 |
| 32 | 22 01 | 22 37 | 20 34 | 17 29 | 17 46 |
| 33 | 22 11 | 22 49 | 20 39 | 17 23 | 17 38 |
| 34 | 22 22 | 23 02 | 20 44 | 17 17 | 17 29 |
| 35 | 22 33 | 23 15 | 20 49 | 17 11 | 17 21 |
| 36 | 22 44 | 23 28 | 20 53 | 17 04 | 17 12 |
| 37 | 22 56 | 23 42 | 20 58 | 16 58 | 17 03 |
| 38 | 23 08 | 23 55 | 21 03 | 16 51 | 16 54 |
| 39 | 23 20 | 24 09 | 21 08 | 16 44 | 16 44 |
| 40 | 23 32 | 24 23 | 21 13 | 16 38 | 16 35 |
| 41 | 23 45 | 24 37 | 21 18 | 16 31 | 16 25 |
| 42 | 23 58 | 24 52 | 21 23 | 16 24 | 16 15 |
| 43 | 24 12 | 25 07 | 21 28 | 16 17 | 16 04 |
| 44 | 24 26 | 25 22 | 21 33 | 16 09 | 15 53 |
| 45 | 24 41 | 25 37 | 21 38 | 16 02 | 15 42 |
| 46 | 24 56 | 25 53 | 21 44 | 15 54 | 15 31 |
| 47 | 25 12 | 26 09 | 21 49 | 15 47 | 15 19 |
| 48 | 25 28 | 26 26 | 21 55 | 15 39 | 15 07 |
| 49 | 25 45 | 26 43 | 22 00 | 15 31 | 14 54 |
| 50 | 26 03 | 27 01 | 22 06 | 15 22 | 14 41 |
| 51 | 26 21 | 27 19 | 22 12 | 15 14 | 14 28 |
| 52 | 26 41 | 27 37 | 22 18 | 15 05 | 14 14 |
| 53 | 27 01 | 27 56 | 22 24 | 14 56 | 13 59 |
| 54 | 27 23 | 28 16 | 22 30 | 14 47 | 13 44 |
| 55 | 27 45 | 28 36 | 22 36 | 14 38 | 13 28 |
| 56 | 28 09 | 28 56 | 22 42 | 14 28 | 13 11 |
| 57 | 28 34 | 29 18 | 22 49 | 14 18 | 12 54 |
| 58 | 29 00 | 29 40 | 22 55 | 14 08 | 12 35 |
| 59 | 29 29 | 00♍03 | 23 02 | 13 57 | 12 16 |
| 60 | 29♋59 | 00♍27 | 23♍09 | 13♎46 | 11♏56 |

# Placidus Table of Houses for Latitudes 0° to 60° North

**5h 20m 0s — 80° 0' 0" — 20 ♊ 49**

| LAT. | 11 | 12 | ASC | 2 | 3 |
|---|---|---|---|---|---|
| 0 | 18♋28 | 17♌33 | 19♍07 | 21♎38 | 22♏25 |
| 5 | 19 06 | 18 29 | 19 31 | 21 07 | 21 52 |
| 10 | 19 44 | 19 23 | 19 53 | 20 37 | 21 20 |
| 15 | 20 24 | 20 17 | 20 15 | 20 08 | 20 47 |
| 20 | 21 05 | 21 12 | 20 36 | 19 38 | 20 12 |
| 21 | 21 13 | 21 23 | 20 40 | 19 32 | 20 05 |
| 22 | 21 22 | 21 34 | 20 44 | 19 26 | 19 58 |
| 23 | 21 31 | 21 45 | 20 48 | 19 20 | 19 51 |
| 24 | 21 39 | 21 57 | 20 52 | 19 14 | 19 44 |
| 25 | 21 48 | 22 08 | 20 56 | 19 08 | 19 36 |
| 26 | 21 57 | 22 19 | 21 01 | 19 02 | 19 29 |
| 27 | 22 07 | 22 31 | 21 05 | 18 56 | 19 21 |
| 28 | 22 16 | 22 43 | 21 09 | 18 50 | 19 14 |
| 29 | 22 26 | 22 54 | 21 13 | 18 43 | 19 06 |
| 30 | 22 35 | 23 06 | 21 17 | 18 37 | 18 58 |
| 31 | 22 45 | 23 18 | 21 21 | 18 31 | 18 50 |
| 32 | 22 55 | 23 30 | 21 26 | 18 24 | 18 42 |
| 33 | 23 06 | 23 43 | 21 30 | 18 18 | 18 33 |
| 34 | 23 16 | 23 55 | 21 34 | 18 11 | 18 25 |
| 35 | 23 27 | 24 08 | 21 39 | 18 04 | 18 16 |
| 36 | 23 38 | 24 21 | 21 43 | 17 58 | 18 07 |
| 37 | 23 50 | 24 34 | 21 47 | 17 51 | 17 58 |
| 38 | 24 02 | 24 47 | 21 52 | 17 44 | 17 49 |
| 39 | 24 14 | 25 01 | 21 56 | 17 37 | 17 39 |
| 40 | 24 26 | 25 14 | 22 01 | 17 30 | 17 30 |
| 41 | 24 39 | 25 28 | 22 05 | 17 23 | 17 20 |
| 42 | 24 52 | 25 43 | 22 10 | 17 15 | 17 09 |
| 43 | 25 05 | 25 57 | 22 14 | 17 08 | 16 59 |
| 44 | 25 19 | 26 12 | 22 19 | 17 00 | 16 48 |
| 45 | 25 34 | 26 27 | 22 24 | 16 52 | 16 36 |
| 46 | 25 49 | 26 43 | 22 29 | 16 44 | 16 25 |
| 47 | 26 05 | 26 58 | 22 34 | 16 36 | 16 13 |
| 48 | 26 21 | 27 15 | 22 39 | 16 28 | 16 01 |
| 49 | 26 38 | 27 31 | 22 44 | 16 20 | 15 48 |
| 50 | 26 55 | 27 48 | 22 49 | 16 11 | 15 34 |
| 51 | 27 13 | 28 06 | 22 54 | 16 02 | 15 21 |
| 52 | 27 33 | 28 24 | 23 00 | 15 53 | 15 06 |
| 53 | 27 53 | 28 42 | 23 05 | 15 43 | 14 51 |
| 54 | 28 14 | 29 01 | 23 11 | 15 34 | 14 36 |
| 55 | 28 36 | 29 21 | 23 16 | 15 24 | 14 19 |
| 56 | 28 59 | 29 41 | 23 22 | 15 14 | 14 02 |
| 57 | 29 24 | 00♍02 | 23 28 | 15 03 | 13 45 |
| 58 | 29 50 | 00 24 | 23 34 | 14 52 | 13 26 |
| 59 | 00♌18 | 00 46 | 23 40 | 14 41 | 13 06 |
| 60 | 00♌48 | 01♍10 | 23♍47 | 14♎30 | 12♏46 |

**5h 24m 0s — 81° 0' 0" — 21 ♊ 44**

| LAT. | 11 | 12 | ASC | 2 | 3 |
|---|---|---|---|---|---|
| 0 | 19♋24 | 18♌34 | 20♍12 | 22♎42 | 23♏23 |
| 5 | 20 02 | 19 29 | 20 34 | 22 10 | 22 51 |
| 10 | 20 40 | 20 22 | 20 54 | 21 38 | 22 18 |
| 15 | 21 19 | 21 15 | 21 13 | 21 07 | 21 44 |
| 20 | 22 00 | 22 08 | 21 32 | 20 36 | 21 10 |
| 21 | 22 08 | 22 19 | 21 36 | 20 30 | 21 02 |
| 22 | 22 17 | 22 30 | 21 40 | 20 24 | 20 55 |
| 23 | 22 26 | 22 41 | 21 43 | 20 18 | 20 48 |
| 24 | 22 34 | 22 52 | 21 47 | 20 11 | 20 41 |
| 25 | 22 43 | 23 03 | 21 51 | 20 05 | 20 33 |
| 26 | 22 52 | 23 15 | 21 54 | 19 59 | 20 26 |
| 27 | 23 02 | 23 26 | 21 58 | 19 52 | 20 18 |
| 28 | 23 11 | 23 37 | 22 02 | 19 46 | 20 10 |
| 29 | 23 20 | 23 49 | 22 06 | 19 39 | 20 02 |
| 30 | 23 30 | 24 00 | 22 10 | 19 32 | 19 54 |
| 31 | 23 40 | 24 12 | 22 13 | 19 26 | 19 46 |
| 32 | 23 50 | 24 24 | 22 17 | 19 19 | 19 38 |
| 33 | 24 00 | 24 36 | 22 21 | 19 12 | 19 29 |
| 34 | 24 11 | 24 48 | 22 25 | 19 05 | 19 21 |
| 35 | 24 22 | 25 01 | 22 29 | 18 58 | 19 12 |
| 36 | 24 33 | 25 13 | 22 33 | 18 51 | 19 03 |
| 37 | 24 44 | 25 26 | 22 37 | 18 44 | 18 53 |
| 38 | 24 56 | 25 39 | 22 41 | 18 37 | 18 44 |
| 39 | 25 07 | 25 52 | 22 45 | 18 30 | 18 34 |
| 40 | 25 20 | 26 06 | 22 49 | 18 22 | 18 24 |
| 41 | 25 32 | 26 19 | 22 53 | 18 14 | 18 14 |
| 42 | 25 45 | 26 33 | 22 57 | 18 07 | 18 04 |
| 43 | 25 59 | 26 47 | 23 01 | 17 59 | 17 53 |
| 44 | 26 13 | 27 02 | 23 05 | 17 51 | 17 42 |
| 45 | 26 27 | 27 17 | 23 10 | 17 43 | 17 30 |
| 46 | 26 42 | 27 32 | 23 14 | 17 34 | 17 19 |
| 47 | 26 57 | 27 47 | 23 18 | 17 26 | 17 07 |
| 48 | 27 13 | 28 03 | 23 23 | 17 17 | 16 54 |
| 49 | 27 30 | 28 19 | 23 27 | 17 08 | 16 41 |
| 50 | 27 47 | 28 36 | 23 32 | 16 59 | 16 27 |
| 51 | 28 06 | 28 53 | 23 37 | 16 50 | 16 13 |
| 52 | 28 25 | 29 11 | 23 42 | 16 40 | 15 59 |
| 53 | 28 44 | 29 29 | 23 46 | 16 30 | 15 43 |
| 54 | 29 05 | 29 47 | 23 51 | 16 20 | 15 28 |
| 55 | 29 27 | 00♍07 | 23 57 | 16 10 | 15 11 |
| 56 | 29 50 | 00 26 | 24 02 | 15 59 | 14 54 |
| 57 | 00♌15 | 00 47 | 24 07 | 15 48 | 14 36 |
| 58 | 00 40 | 01 08 | 24 13 | 15 37 | 14 16 |
| 59 | 01 08 | 01 30 | 24 18 | 15 25 | 13 56 |
| 60 | 01♌37 | 01♍52 | 24♍24 | 15♎13 | 13♏35 |

**5h 28m 0s — 82° 0' 0" — 22 ♊ 39**

| LAT. | 11 | 12 | ASC | 2 | 3 |
|---|---|---|---|---|---|
| 0 | 20♋20 | 19♌35 | 21♍17 | 23♎46 | 24♏22 |
| 5 | 20 58 | 20 28 | 21 36 | 23 12 | 23 49 |
| 10 | 21 36 | 21 21 | 21 54 | 22 39 | 23 16 |
| 15 | 22 15 | 22 13 | 22 12 | 22 07 | 22 42 |
| 20 | 22 55 | 23 05 | 22 28 | 21 35 | 22 07 |
| 21 | 23 04 | 23 16 | 22 32 | 21 28 | 21 59 |
| 22 | 23 12 | 23 26 | 22 35 | 21 22 | 21 52 |
| 23 | 23 21 | 23 37 | 22 38 | 21 15 | 21 45 |
| 24 | 23 30 | 23 48 | 22 42 | 21 08 | 21 37 |
| 25 | 23 38 | 23 59 | 22 45 | 21 02 | 21 30 |
| 26 | 23 47 | 24 10 | 22 48 | 20 55 | 21 22 |
| 27 | 23 56 | 24 21 | 22 52 | 20 48 | 21 14 |
| 28 | 24 06 | 24 32 | 22 55 | 20 42 | 21 06 |
| 29 | 24 15 | 24 43 | 22 58 | 20 35 | 20 58 |
| 30 | 24 25 | 24 55 | 23 02 | 20 28 | 20 50 |
| 31 | 24 35 | 25 06 | 23 05 | 20 21 | 20 42 |
| 32 | 24 45 | 25 18 | 23 09 | 20 14 | 20 34 |
| 33 | 24 55 | 25 30 | 23 12 | 20 07 | 20 25 |
| 34 | 25 05 | 25 42 | 23 15 | 19 59 | 20 16 |
| 35 | 25 16 | 25 54 | 23 19 | 19 52 | 20 07 |
| 36 | 25 27 | 26 06 | 23 22 | 19 45 | 19 58 |
| 37 | 25 38 | 26 18 | 23 26 | 19 37 | 19 49 |
| 38 | 25 50 | 26 31 | 23 29 | 19 30 | 19 39 |
| 39 | 26 01 | 26 44 | 23 33 | 19 22 | 19 29 |
| 40 | 26 14 | 26 57 | 23 36 | 19 14 | 19 19 |
| 41 | 26 26 | 27 10 | 23 40 | 19 06 | 19 09 |
| 42 | 26 39 | 27 24 | 23 44 | 18 58 | 18 58 |
| 43 | 26 52 | 27 38 | 23 48 | 18 50 | 18 47 |
| 44 | 27 06 | 27 52 | 23 51 | 18 42 | 18 36 |
| 45 | 27 20 | 28 06 | 23 55 | 18 33 | 18 24 |
| 46 | 27 35 | 28 21 | 23 59 | 18 24 | 18 12 |
| 47 | 27 50 | 28 36 | 24 03 | 18 15 | 18 00 |
| 48 | 28 06 | 28 52 | 24 07 | 18 06 | 17 47 |
| 49 | 28 23 | 29 08 | 24 11 | 17 57 | 17 34 |
| 50 | 28 40 | 29 24 | 24 15 | 17 47 | 17 20 |
| 51 | 28 58 | 29 40 | 24 19 | 17 38 | 17 06 |
| 52 | 29 16 | 29 58 | 24 24 | 17 28 | 16 51 |
| 53 | 29 36 | 00♍15 | 24 28 | 17 17 | 16 36 |
| 54 | 29 57 | 00 33 | 24 32 | 17 07 | 16 19 |
| 55 | 00♌18 | 00 52 | 24 37 | 16 56 | 16 03 |
| 56 | 00 41 | 01 11 | 24 42 | 16 45 | 15 45 |
| 57 | 01 05 | 01 31 | 24 46 | 16 33 | 15 26 |
| 58 | 01 30 | 01 52 | 24 51 | 16 21 | 15 07 |
| 59 | 01 57 | 02 13 | 24 56 | 16 09 | 14 47 |
| 60 | 02♌26 | 02♍35 | 25♍01 | 15♎56 | 14♏25 |

**5h 32m 0s — 83° 0' 0" — 23 ♊ 34**

| LAT. | 11 | 12 | ASC | 2 | 3 |
|---|---|---|---|---|---|
| 0 | 21♋17 | 20♌36 | 22♍23 | 24♎50 | 25♏21 |
| 5 | 21 54 | 21 28 | 22 39 | 24 15 | 24 47 |
| 10 | 22 32 | 22 20 | 22 55 | 23 40 | 24 13 |
| 15 | 23 11 | 23 11 | 23 10 | 23 07 | 23 39 |
| 20 | 23 51 | 24 02 | 23 25 | 22 33 | 23 04 |
| 21 | 23 59 | 24 12 | 23 28 | 22 26 | 22 56 |
| 22 | 24 08 | 24 23 | 23 31 | 22 19 | 22 49 |
| 23 | 24 16 | 24 33 | 23 34 | 22 12 | 22 41 |
| 24 | 24 25 | 24 44 | 23 36 | 22 06 | 22 34 |
| 25 | 24 33 | 24 54 | 23 39 | 21 59 | 22 26 |
| 26 | 24 42 | 25 05 | 23 42 | 21 52 | 22 19 |
| 27 | 24 51 | 25 16 | 23 45 | 21 45 | 22 11 |
| 28 | 25 01 | 25 27 | 23 48 | 21 37 | 22 03 |
| 29 | 25 10 | 25 38 | 23 51 | 21 30 | 21 55 |
| 30 | 25 20 | 25 49 | 23 54 | 21 23 | 21 46 |
| 31 | 25 29 | 26 00 | 23 57 | 21 16 | 21 38 |
| 32 | 25 39 | 26 12 | 24 00 | 21 09 | 21 29 |
| 33 | 25 49 | 26 23 | 24 03 | 21 01 | 21 21 |
| 34 | 26 00 | 26 35 | 24 06 | 20 54 | 21 12 |
| 35 | 26 10 | 26 47 | 24 09 | 20 46 | 21 03 |
| 36 | 26 21 | 26 59 | 24 12 | 20 38 | 20 53 |
| 37 | 26 32 | 27 11 | 24 15 | 20 30 | 20 44 |
| 38 | 26 44 | 27 23 | 24 18 | 20 23 | 20 34 |
| 39 | 26 55 | 27 36 | 24 21 | 20 15 | 20 24 |
| 40 | 27 07 | 27 48 | 24 24 | 20 06 | 20 14 |
| 41 | 27 20 | 28 01 | 24 28 | 19 58 | 20 03 |
| 42 | 27 33 | 28 15 | 24 31 | 19 50 | 19 53 |
| 43 | 27 46 | 28 28 | 24 34 | 19 41 | 19 42 |
| 44 | 27 59 | 28 42 | 24 37 | 19 32 | 19 30 |
| 45 | 28 13 | 28 56 | 24 41 | 19 23 | 19 18 |
| 46 | 28 28 | 29 11 | 24 44 | 19 14 | 19 06 |
| 47 | 28 43 | 29 25 | 24 48 | 19 05 | 18 54 |
| 48 | 28 59 | 29 40 | 24 51 | 18 55 | 18 41 |
| 49 | 29 15 | 29 56 | 24 55 | 18 46 | 18 27 |
| 50 | 29 32 | 00♍12 | 24 58 | 18 36 | 18 13 |
| 51 | 29 50 | 00 28 | 25 02 | 18 26 | 17 59 |
| 52 | 00♌08 | 00 45 | 25 06 | 18 15 | 17 43 |
| 53 | 00 28 | 01 02 | 25 09 | 18 04 | 17 28 |
| 54 | 00 48 | 01 19 | 25 13 | 17 53 | 17 11 |
| 55 | 01 09 | 01 38 | 25 17 | 17 42 | 16 54 |
| 56 | 01 32 | 01 56 | 25 21 | 17 30 | 16 36 |
| 57 | 01 55 | 02 16 | 25 26 | 17 18 | 16 17 |
| 58 | 02 20 | 02 36 | 25 30 | 17 06 | 15 57 |
| 59 | 02 47 | 02 56 | 25 34 | 16 53 | 15 37 |
| 60 | 03♌15 | 03♍18 | 25♍39 | 16♎40 | 15♏15 |

**5h 36m 0s — 84° 0' 0" — 24 ♊ 30**

| LAT. | 11 | 12 | ASC | 2 | 3 |
|---|---|---|---|---|---|
| 0 | 22♋13 | 21♌37 | 23♍28 | 25♎53 | 26♏19 |
| 5 | 22 50 | 22 29 | 23 42 | 25 17 | 25 45 |
| 10 | 23 28 | 23 19 | 23 56 | 24 41 | 25 11 |
| 15 | 24 06 | 24 09 | 24 09 | 24 06 | 24 36 |
| 20 | 24 46 | 24 59 | 24 21 | 23 31 | 24 00 |
| 21 | 24 55 | 25 09 | 24 24 | 23 24 | 23 53 |
| 22 | 25 03 | 25 19 | 24 26 | 23 17 | 23 46 |
| 23 | 25 11 | 25 29 | 24 29 | 23 10 | 23 38 |
| 24 | 25 20 | 25 40 | 24 31 | 23 03 | 23 30 |
| 25 | 25 29 | 25 50 | 24 34 | 22 55 | 23 23 |
| 26 | 25 37 | 26 01 | 24 36 | 22 48 | 23 15 |
| 27 | 25 46 | 26 11 | 24 39 | 22 41 | 23 07 |
| 28 | 25 56 | 26 22 | 24 41 | 22 33 | 22 59 |
| 29 | 26 05 | 26 33 | 24 44 | 22 26 | 22 50 |
| 30 | 26 14 | 26 43 | 24 46 | 22 18 | 22 42 |
| 31 | 26 24 | 26 54 | 24 49 | 22 11 | 22 34 |
| 32 | 26 34 | 27 05 | 24 51 | 22 03 | 22 25 |
| 33 | 26 44 | 27 17 | 24 54 | 21 55 | 22 16 |
| 34 | 26 54 | 27 28 | 24 56 | 21 48 | 22 07 |
| 35 | 27 05 | 27 40 | 24 59 | 21 40 | 21 58 |
| 36 | 27 15 | 27 51 | 25 02 | 21 32 | 21 48 |
| 37 | 27 26 | 28 03 | 25 04 | 21 24 | 21 39 |
| 38 | 27 38 | 28 15 | 25 07 | 21 15 | 21 29 |
| 39 | 27 49 | 28 28 | 25 10 | 21 07 | 21 19 |
| 40 | 28 01 | 28 40 | 25 12 | 20 58 | 21 09 |
| 41 | 28 13 | 28 53 | 25 15 | 20 50 | 20 58 |
| 42 | 28 26 | 29 06 | 25 18 | 20 41 | 20 47 |
| 43 | 28 39 | 29 19 | 25 21 | 20 32 | 20 36 |
| 44 | 28 53 | 29 32 | 25 23 | 20 23 | 20 24 |
| 45 | 29 07 | 29 46 | 25 26 | 20 14 | 20 12 |
| 46 | 29 21 | 00♍00 | 25 29 | 20 04 | 20 00 |
| 47 | 29 36 | 00 14 | 25 32 | 19 54 | 19 47 |
| 48 | 29 51 | 00 29 | 25 35 | 19 45 | 19 34 |
| 49 | 00♌08 | 00 44 | 25 38 | 19 34 | 19 20 |
| 50 | 00 24 | 00 59 | 25 41 | 19 24 | 19 06 |
| 51 | 00 42 | 01 15 | 25 44 | 19 13 | 18 51 |
| 52 | 01 00 | 01 32 | 25 48 | 19 02 | 18 36 |
| 53 | 01 19 | 01 48 | 25 51 | 18 51 | 18 20 |
| 54 | 01 39 | 02 05 | 25 54 | 18 40 | 18 03 |
| 55 | 02 00 | 02 23 | 25 58 | 18 28 | 17 46 |
| 56 | 02 22 | 02 41 | 26 01 | 18 16 | 17 27 |
| 57 | 02 46 | 03 00 | 26 05 | 18 03 | 17 08 |
| 58 | 03 10 | 03 20 | 26 08 | 17 50 | 16 48 |
| 59 | 03 37 | 03 40 | 26 12 | 17 37 | 16 27 |
| 60 | 04♌04 | 04♍01 | 26♍16 | 17♎23 | 16♏04 |

**5h 40m 0s — 85° 0' 0" — 25 ♊ 25**

| LAT. | 11 | 12 | ASC | 2 | 3 |
|---|---|---|---|---|---|
| 0 | 23♋10 | 22♌39 | 24♍33 | 26♎57 | 27♏17 |
| 5 | 23 47 | 23 29 | 24 45 | 26 19 | 26 43 |
| 10 | 24 24 | 24 18 | 24 56 | 25 42 | 26 08 |
| 15 | 25 02 | 25 07 | 25 07 | 25 05 | 25 33 |
| 20 | 25 42 | 25 56 | 25 18 | 24 29 | 24 57 |
| 21 | 25 50 | 26 06 | 25 20 | 24 22 | 24 50 |
| 22 | 25 58 | 26 16 | 25 22 | 24 14 | 24 42 |
| 23 | 26 07 | 26 26 | 25 24 | 24 07 | 24 34 |
| 24 | 26 15 | 26 36 | 25 26 | 23 59 | 24 27 |
| 25 | 26 24 | 26 46 | 25 28 | 23 52 | 24 19 |
| 26 | 26 33 | 26 56 | 25 30 | 23 44 | 24 11 |
| 27 | 26 42 | 27 06 | 25 32 | 23 37 | 24 03 |
| 28 | 26 51 | 27 17 | 25 34 | 23 29 | 23 55 |
| 29 | 27 00 | 27 27 | 25 36 | 23 21 | 23 46 |
| 30 | 27 09 | 27 38 | 25 39 | 23 14 | 23 38 |
| 31 | 27 19 | 27 49 | 25 41 | 23 06 | 23 29 |
| 32 | 27 29 | 27 59 | 25 43 | 22 58 | 23 21 |
| 33 | 27 38 | 28 10 | 25 45 | 22 50 | 23 12 |
| 34 | 27 49 | 28 21 | 25 47 | 22 42 | 23 02 |
| 35 | 27 59 | 28 33 | 25 49 | 22 33 | 22 53 |
| 36 | 28 10 | 28 44 | 25 51 | 22 25 | 22 44 |
| 37 | 28 21 | 28 56 | 25 54 | 22 17 | 22 34 |
| 38 | 28 32 | 29 07 | 25 56 | 22 08 | 22 24 |
| 39 | 28 43 | 29 19 | 25 58 | 21 59 | 22 14 |
| 40 | 28 55 | 29 32 | 26 00 | 21 51 | 22 03 |
| 41 | 29 07 | 29 44 | 26 03 | 21 42 | 21 52 |
| 42 | 29 20 | 29 56 | 26 05 | 21 32 | 21 41 |
| 43 | 29 33 | 00♍09 | 26 07 | 21 23 | 21 30 |
| 44 | 29 46 | 00 22 | 26 10 | 21 14 | 21 18 |
| 45 | 00♌00 | 00 36 | 26 12 | 21 04 | 21 06 |
| 46 | 00 14 | 00 49 | 26 14 | 20 54 | 20 53 |
| 47 | 00 29 | 01 03 | 26 17 | 20 44 | 20 40 |
| 48 | 00 44 | 01 18 | 26 19 | 20 34 | 20 27 |
| 49 | 01 00 | 01 32 | 26 22 | 20 23 | 20 13 |
| 50 | 01 17 | 01 47 | 26 24 | 20 12 | 19 59 |
| 51 | 01 34 | 02 03 | 26 27 | 20 01 | 19 44 |
| 52 | 01 52 | 02 19 | 26 30 | 19 50 | 19 28 |
| 53 | 02 11 | 02 35 | 26 32 | 19 38 | 19 12 |
| 54 | 02 31 | 02 51 | 26 35 | 19 26 | 18 55 |
| 55 | 02 51 | 03 09 | 26 38 | 19 14 | 18 37 |
| 56 | 03 13 | 03 26 | 26 41 | 19 01 | 18 18 |
| 57 | 03 36 | 03 45 | 26 44 | 18 48 | 17 59 |
| 58 | 04 00 | 04 04 | 26 47 | 18 34 | 17 38 |
| 59 | 04 26 | 04 23 | 26 50 | 18 20 | 17 16 |
| 60 | 04♌54 | 04♍44 | 26♍53 | 18♎06 | 16♏54 |

**5h 44m 0s — 86° 0' 0" — 26 ♊ 20**

| LAT. | 11 | 12 | ASC | 2 | 3 |
|---|---|---|---|---|---|
| 0 | 24♋06 | 23♌41 | 25♍38 | 28♎00 | 28♏15 |
| 5 | 24 43 | 24 30 | 25 48 | 27 21 | 27 40 |
| 10 | 25 20 | 25 18 | 25 57 | 26 42 | 27 06 |
| 15 | 25 58 | 26 05 | 26 06 | 26 05 | 26 30 |
| 20 | 26 38 | 26 53 | 26 14 | 25 27 | 25 54 |
| 21 | 26 46 | 27 03 | 26 16 | 25 19 | 25 46 |
| 22 | 26 54 | 27 12 | 26 17 | 25 12 | 25 39 |
| 23 | 27 02 | 27 22 | 26 19 | 25 04 | 25 31 |
| 24 | 27 11 | 27 32 | 26 21 | 24 56 | 25 23 |
| 25 | 27 19 | 27 42 | 26 22 | 24 49 | 25 15 |
| 26 | 27 28 | 27 52 | 26 24 | 24 41 | 25 07 |
| 27 | 27 37 | 28 02 | 26 26 | 24 33 | 24 59 |
| 28 | 27 46 | 28 12 | 26 27 | 24 25 | 24 51 |
| 29 | 27 55 | 28 22 | 26 29 | 24 17 | 24 42 |
| 30 | 28 04 | 28 32 | 26 31 | 24 09 | 24 34 |
| 31 | 28 14 | 28 43 | 26 32 | 24 01 | 24 25 |
| 32 | 28 23 | 28 53 | 26 34 | 23 52 | 24 16 |
| 33 | 28 33 | 29 04 | 26 36 | 23 44 | 24 07 |
| 34 | 28 43 | 29 15 | 26 38 | 23 36 | 23 58 |
| 35 | 28 54 | 29 26 | 26 39 | 23 27 | 23 48 |
| 36 | 29 04 | 29 37 | 26 41 | 23 18 | 23 39 |
| 37 | 29 15 | 29 48 | 26 43 | 23 10 | 23 29 |
| 38 | 29 26 | 00♍00 | 26 45 | 23 01 | 23 19 |
| 39 | 29 37 | 00 11 | 26 46 | 22 52 | 23 08 |
| 40 | 29 49 | 00 23 | 26 48 | 22 43 | 22 58 |
| 41 | 00♌01 | 00 35 | 26 50 | 22 33 | 22 47 |
| 42 | 00 13 | 00 47 | 26 52 | 22 24 | 22 35 |
| 43 | 00 26 | 01 00 | 26 54 | 22 14 | 22 24 |
| 44 | 00 39 | 01 13 | 26 56 | 22 04 | 22 12 |
| 45 | 00 53 | 01 26 | 26 58 | 21 54 | 22 00 |
| 46 | 01 07 | 01 39 | 26 59 | 21 44 | 21 47 |
| 47 | 01 22 | 01 52 | 27 01 | 21 33 | 21 34 |
| 48 | 01 37 | 02 06 | 27 03 | 21 23 | 21 20 |
| 49 | 01 53 | 02 21 | 27 05 | 21 12 | 21 06 |
| 50 | 02 09 | 02 35 | 27 08 | 21 00 | 20 51 |
| 51 | 02 26 | 02 50 | 27 10 | 20 49 | 20 36 |
| 52 | 02 44 | 03 06 | 27 12 | 20 37 | 20 20 |
| 53 | 03 02 | 03 21 | 27 14 | 20 25 | 20 04 |
| 54 | 03 22 | 03 38 | 27 16 | 20 12 | 19 46 |
| 55 | 03 42 | 03 54 | 27 18 | 20 00 | 19 28 |
| 56 | 04 04 | 04 12 | 27 21 | 19 46 | 19 09 |
| 57 | 04 27 | 04 29 | 27 23 | 19 33 | 18 49 |
| 58 | 04 50 | 04 48 | 27 26 | 19 19 | 18 28 |
| 59 | 05 16 | 05 07 | 27 28 | 19 04 | 18 06 |
| 60 | 05♌43 | 05♍27 | 27♍31 | 18♎49 | 17♏43 |

**5h 48m 0s — 87° 0' 0" — 27 ♊ 15**

| LAT. | 11 | 12 | ASC | 2 | 3 |
|---|---|---|---|---|---|
| 0 | 25♋03 | 24♌42 | 26♍44 | 29♎03 | 29♏13 |
| 5 | 25 40 | 25 30 | 26 51 | 28 22 | 28 38 |
| 10 | 26 17 | 26 17 | 26 58 | 27 43 | 28 03 |
| 15 | 26 54 | 27 03 | 27 04 | 27 04 | 27 27 |
| 20 | 27 33 | 27 50 | 27 11 | 26 25 | 26 50 |
| 21 | 27 41 | 27 59 | 27 12 | 26 17 | 26 43 |
| 22 | 27 50 | 28 09 | 27 13 | 26 09 | 26 35 |
| 23 | 27 58 | 28 18 | 27 14 | 26 01 | 26 27 |
| 24 | 28 06 | 28 28 | 27 16 | 25 53 | 26 19 |
| 25 | 28 15 | 28 38 | 27 17 | 25 45 | 26 11 |
| 26 | 28 23 | 28 47 | 27 18 | 25 37 | 26 03 |
| 27 | 28 32 | 28 57 | 27 19 | 25 29 | 25 55 |
| 28 | 28 41 | 29 07 | 27 21 | 25 21 | 25 46 |
| 29 | 28 50 | 29 17 | 27 22 | 25 12 | 25 38 |
| 30 | 28 59 | 29 27 | 27 23 | 25 04 | 25 29 |
| 31 | 29 09 | 29 37 | 27 24 | 24 55 | 25 20 |
| 32 | 29 18 | 29 47 | 27 26 | 24 47 | 25 11 |
| 33 | 29 28 | 29 58 | 27 27 | 24 38 | 25 02 |
| 34 | 29 38 | 00♍08 | 27 28 | 24 30 | 24 53 |
| 35 | 29 48 | 00 19 | 27 30 | 24 21 | 24 43 |
| 36 | 29 59 | 00 30 | 27 31 | 24 12 | 24 33 |
| 37 | 00♌09 | 00 41 | 27 32 | 24 03 | 24 23 |
| 38 | 00 20 | 00 52 | 27 33 | 23 53 | 24 13 |
| 39 | 00 31 | 01 03 | 27 35 | 23 44 | 24 03 |
| 40 | 00 43 | 01 15 | 27 36 | 23 34 | 23 52 |
| 41 | 00 55 | 01 26 | 27 38 | 23 25 | 23 41 |
| 42 | 01 07 | 01 38 | 27 39 | 23 15 | 23 29 |
| 43 | 01 20 | 01 50 | 27 40 | 23 05 | 23 18 |
| 44 | 01 33 | 02 03 | 27 42 | 22 55 | 23 06 |
| 45 | 01 46 | 02 16 | 27 43 | 22 44 | 22 53 |
| 46 | 02 00 | 02 28 | 27 45 | 22 34 | 22 40 |
| 47 | 02 15 | 02 42 | 27 46 | 22 23 | 22 27 |
| 48 | 02 30 | 02 55 | 27 48 | 22 12 | 22 13 |
| 49 | 02 45 | 03 09 | 27 49 | 22 00 | 21 59 |
| 50 | 03 01 | 03 23 | 27 51 | 21 49 | 21 44 |
| 51 | 03 18 | 03 38 | 27 52 | 21 37 | 21 28 |
| 52 | 03 36 | 03 53 | 27 54 | 21 24 | 21 12 |
| 53 | 03 54 | 04 08 | 27 55 | 21 12 | 20 55 |
| 54 | 04 13 | 04 24 | 27 57 | 20 59 | 20 38 |
| 55 | 04 33 | 04 40 | 27 59 | 20 46 | 20 20 |
| 56 | 04 55 | 04 57 | 28 01 | 20 32 | 20 00 |
| 57 | 05 17 | 05 14 | 28 02 | 20 18 | 19 40 |
| 58 | 05 41 | 05 32 | 28 04 | 20 03 | 19 19 |
| 59 | 06 05 | 05 50 | 28 06 | 19 48 | 18 56 |
| 60 | 06♌32 | 06♍09 | 28♍08 | 19♎32 | 18♏32 |

# Placidus Table of Houses for Latitudes 0° to 60° North

**5h 52m 0s — 28 ♊ 10 — 88° 0' 0"**

| LAT. | 11 | 12 | ASC | 2 | 3 |
|---|---|---|---|---|---|
| 0 | 26♋00 | 25♌44 | 27♍49 | 00♏06 | 00♐11 |
| 5 | 26 37 | 26 31 | 27 54 | 29♎24 | 29♏35 |
| 10 | 27 13 | 27 17 | 27 58 | 28 43 | 29 00 |
| 15 | 27 50 | 28 02 | 28 03 | 28 03 | 28 24 |
| 20 | 28 29 | 28 47 | 28 07 | 27 23 | 27 46 |
| 21 | 28 37 | 28 57 | 28 08 | 27 14 | 27 39 |
| 22 | 28 45 | 29 06 | 28 09 | 27 06 | 27 31 |
| 23 | 28 53 | 29 15 | 28 10 | 26 58 | 27 23 |
| 24 | 29 02 | 29 24 | 28 10 | 26 50 | 27 15 |
| 25 | 29 10 | 29 34 | 28 11 | 26 41 | 27 07 |
| 26 | 29 19 | 29 43 | 28 12 | 26 33 | 26 59 |
| 27 | 29 27 | 29 53 | 28 13 | 26 25 | 26 50 |
| 28 | 29 36 | 00♍02 | 28 14 | 26 16 | 26 42 |
| 29 | 29 45 | 00 12 | 28 15 | 26 08 | 26 33 |
| 30 | 29 54 | 00 22 | 28 15 | 25 59 | 26 25 |
| 31 | 00♌04 | 00 32 | 28 16 | 25 50 | 26 16 |
| 32 | 00 13 | 00 42 | 28 17 | 25 41 | 26 07 |
| 33 | 00 23 | 00 52 | 28 18 | 25 32 | 25 57 |
| 34 | 00 33 | 01 02 | 28 19 | 25 23 | 25 48 |
| 35 | 00 43 | 01 12 | 28 20 | 25 14 | 25 38 |
| 36 | 00 53 | 01 23 | 28 21 | 25 05 | 25 28 |
| 37 | 01 04 | 01 33 | 28 21 | 24 55 | 25 18 |
| 38 | 01 14 | 01 44 | 28 22 | 24 46 | 25 08 |
| 39 | 01 26 | 01 55 | 28 23 | 24 36 | 24 57 |
| 40 | 01 37 | 02 06 | 28 24 | 24 26 | 24 46 |
| 41 | 01 49 | 02 18 | 28 25 | 24 16 | 24 35 |
| 42 | 02 01 | 02 29 | 28 26 | 24 06 | 24 23 |
| 43 | 02 13 | 02 41 | 28 27 | 23 56 | 24 12 |
| 44 | 02 26 | 02 53 | 28 28 | 23 45 | 23 59 |
| 45 | 02 40 | 03 05 | 28 29 | 23 34 | 23 47 |
| 46 | 02 53 | 03 18 | 28 30 | 23 23 | 23 34 |
| 47 | 03 08 | 03 31 | 28 31 | 23 12 | 23 20 |
| 48 | 03 22 | 03 44 | 28 32 | 23 01 | 23 06 |
| 49 | 03 38 | 03 57 | 28 33 | 22 49 | 22 52 |
| 50 | 03 54 | 04 11 | 28 34 | 22 37 | 22 36 |
| 51 | 04 10 | 04 25 | 28 35 | 22 24 | 22 21 |
| 52 | 04 28 | 04 40 | 28 36 | 22 12 | 22 04 |
| 53 | 04 46 | 04 55 | 28 37 | 21 59 | 21 47 |
| 54 | 05 05 | 05 10 | 28 38 | 21 45 | 21 29 |
| 55 | 05 25 | 05 26 | 28 39 | 21 31 | 21 11 |
| 56 | 05 45 | 05 42 | 28 40 | 21 17 | 20 51 |
| 57 | 06 07 | 05 59 | 28 42 | 21 02 | 20 31 |
| 58 | 06 31 | 06 16 | 28 43 | 20 47 | 20 09 |
| 59 | 06 55 | 06 34 | 28 44 | 20 32 | 19 46 |
| 60 | 07♌21 | 06♍52 | 28♍45 | 20♎15 | 19♏22 |

**5h 56m 0s — 29 ♊ 05 — 89° 0' 0"**

| LAT. | 11 | 12 | ASC | 2 | 3 |
|---|---|---|---|---|---|
| 0 | 26♋57 | 26♌47 | 28♍55 | 01♏08 | 01♐08 |
| 5 | 27 33 | 27 32 | 28 57 | 00 25 | 00 33 |
| 10 | 28 10 | 28 17 | 28 59 | 29♎43 | 29♏57 |
| 15 | 28 47 | 29 01 | 29 01 | 29 02 | 29 21 |
| 20 | 29 25 | 29 45 | 29 04 | 28 20 | 28 43 |
| 21 | 29 33 | 29 54 | 29 04 | 28 12 | 28 35 |
| 22 | 29 41 | 00♍03 | 29 04 | 28 03 | 28 27 |
| 23 | 29 49 | 00 12 | 29 05 | 27 55 | 28 19 |
| 24 | 29 57 | 00 21 | 29 05 | 27 46 | 28 11 |
| 25 | 00♌06 | 00 30 | 29 06 | 27 38 | 28 03 |
| 26 | 00 14 | 00 39 | 29 06 | 27 29 | 27 55 |
| 27 | 00 23 | 00 48 | 29 06 | 27 20 | 27 46 |
| 28 | 00 31 | 00 58 | 29 07 | 27 12 | 27 38 |
| 29 | 00 40 | 01 07 | 29 07 | 27 03 | 27 29 |
| 30 | 00 49 | 01 16 | 29 08 | 26 54 | 27 20 |
| 31 | 00 59 | 01 26 | 29 08 | 26 45 | 27 11 |
| 32 | 01 08 | 01 36 | 29 09 | 26 36 | 27 02 |
| 33 | 01 18 | 01 46 | 29 09 | 26 26 | 26 52 |
| 34 | 01 27 | 01 55 | 29 09 | 26 17 | 26 43 |
| 35 | 01 37 | 02 06 | 29 10 | 26 08 | 26 33 |
| 36 | 01 48 | 02 16 | 29 10 | 25 58 | 26 23 |
| 37 | 01 58 | 02 26 | 29 11 | 25 48 | 26 13 |
| 38 | 02 09 | 02 37 | 29 11 | 25 38 | 26 02 |
| 39 | 02 20 | 02 47 | 29 12 | 25 28 | 25 52 |
| 40 | 02 31 | 02 58 | 29 12 | 25 18 | 25 41 |
| 41 | 02 43 | 03 09 | 29 13 | 25 08 | 25 29 |
| 42 | 02 55 | 03 20 | 29 13 | 24 57 | 25 17 |
| 43 | 03 07 | 03 32 | 29 13 | 24 47 | 25 05 |
| 44 | 03 20 | 03 44 | 29 14 | 24 36 | 24 53 |
| 45 | 03 33 | 03 55 | 29 14 | 24 24 | 24 40 |
| 46 | 03 47 | 04 08 | 29 15 | 24 13 | 24 27 |
| 47 | 04 01 | 04 20 | 29 15 | 24 01 | 24 13 |
| 48 | 04 15 | 04 33 | 29 16 | 23 50 | 23 59 |
| 49 | 04 30 | 04 46 | 29 16 | 23 37 | 23 44 |
| 50 | 04 46 | 04 59 | 29 17 | 23 25 | 23 29 |
| 51 | 05 02 | 05 13 | 29 17 | 23 12 | 23 13 |
| 52 | 05 20 | 05 27 | 29 18 | 22 59 | 22 56 |
| 53 | 05 37 | 05 41 | 29 18 | 22 45 | 22 39 |
| 54 | 05 56 | 05 56 | 29 19 | 22 31 | 22 21 |
| 55 | 06 16 | 06 11 | 29 20 | 22 17 | 22 02 |
| 56 | 06 36 | 06 27 | 29 20 | 22 02 | 21 42 |
| 57 | 06 58 | 06 43 | 29 21 | 21 47 | 21 21 |
| 58 | 07 21 | 07 00 | 29 21 | 21 32 | 20 59 |
| 59 | 07 45 | 07 17 | 29 22 | 21 15 | 20 36 |
| 60 | 08♌10 | 07♍35 | 29♍23 | 20♎59 | 20♏11 |

**6h 0m 0s — 00 ♋ 00 — 90° 0' 0"**

| LAT. | 11 | 12 | ASC | 2 | 3 |
|---|---|---|---|---|---|
| 0 | 27♋55 | 27♌49 | 00♎00 | 02♏11 | 02♐05 |
| 5 | 28 30 | 28 33 | 00 00 | 01 27 | 01 30 |
| 10 | 29 06 | 29 17 | 00 00 | 00 43 | 00 54 |
| 15 | 29 43 | 29 59 | 00 00 | 00 01 | 00 17 |
| 20 | 00♌21 | 00♍42 | 00 00 | 29♎18 | 29♏39 |
| 21 | 00 29 | 00 51 | 00 00 | 29 09 | 29 31 |
| 22 | 00 37 | 01 00 | 00 00 | 29 00 | 29 23 |
| 23 | 00 45 | 01 08 | 00 00 | 28 52 | 29 15 |
| 24 | 00 53 | 01 17 | 00 00 | 28 43 | 29 07 |
| 25 | 01 01 | 01 26 | 00 00 | 28 34 | 28 59 |
| 26 | 01 10 | 01 35 | 00 00 | 28 25 | 28 50 |
| 27 | 01 18 | 01 44 | 00 00 | 28 16 | 28 42 |
| 28 | 01 27 | 01 53 | 00 00 | 28 07 | 28 33 |
| 29 | 01 36 | 02 02 | 00 00 | 27 58 | 28 24 |
| 30 | 01 45 | 02 11 | 00 00 | 27 49 | 28 15 |
| 31 | 01 54 | 02 21 | 00 00 | 27 39 | 28 06 |
| 32 | 02 03 | 02 30 | 00 00 | 27 30 | 27 57 |
| 33 | 02 13 | 02 40 | 00 00 | 27 20 | 27 47 |
| 34 | 02 22 | 02 49 | 00 00 | 27 11 | 27 38 |
| 35 | 02 32 | 02 59 | 00 00 | 27 01 | 27 28 |
| 36 | 02 42 | 03 09 | 00 00 | 26 51 | 27 18 |
| 37 | 02 53 | 03 19 | 00 00 | 26 41 | 27 07 |
| 38 | 03 03 | 03 29 | 00 00 | 26 31 | 26 57 |
| 39 | 03 14 | 03 39 | 00 00 | 26 21 | 26 46 |
| 40 | 03 25 | 03 50 | 00 00 | 26 10 | 26 35 |
| 41 | 03 37 | 04 01 | 00 00 | 25 59 | 26 23 |
| 42 | 03 49 | 04 12 | 00 00 | 25 48 | 26 11 |
| 43 | 04 01 | 04 23 | 00 00 | 25 37 | 25 59 |
| 44 | 04 13 | 04 34 | 00 00 | 25 26 | 25 47 |
| 45 | 04 26 | 04 45 | 00 00 | 25 15 | 25 34 |
| 46 | 04 40 | 04 57 | 00 00 | 25 03 | 25 20 |
| 47 | 04 54 | 05 09 | 00 00 | 24 51 | 25 06 |
| 48 | 05 08 | 05 22 | 00 00 | 24 38 | 24 52 |
| 49 | 05 23 | 05 34 | 00 00 | 24 26 | 24 37 |
| 50 | 05 39 | 05 47 | 00 00 | 24 13 | 24 21 |
| 51 | 05 55 | 06 00 | 00 00 | 24 00 | 24 05 |
| 52 | 06 12 | 06 14 | 00 00 | 23 46 | 23 48 |
| 53 | 06 29 | 06 28 | 00 00 | 23 32 | 23 31 |
| 54 | 06 48 | 06 42 | 00 00 | 23 18 | 23 12 |
| 55 | 07 07 | 06 57 | 00 00 | 23 03 | 22 53 |
| 56 | 07 27 | 07 12 | 00 00 | 22 48 | 22 33 |
| 57 | 07 48 | 07 28 | 00 00 | 22 32 | 22 12 |
| 58 | 08 11 | 07 44 | 00 00 | 22 16 | 21 49 |
| 59 | 08 34 | 08 01 | 00 00 | 21 59 | 21 26 |
| 60 | 09♌00 | 08♍18 | 00♎00 | 21♎42 | 21♏00 |

**6h 4m 0s — 00 ♋ 55 — 91° 0' 0"**

| LAT. | 11 | 12 | ASC | 2 | 3 |
|---|---|---|---|---|---|
| 0 | 28♋52 | 28♌52 | 01♎05 | 03♏13 | 03♐03 |
| 5 | 29 27 | 29 35 | 01 03 | 02 28 | 02 27 |
| 10 | 00♌03 | 00♍17 | 01 01 | 01 43 | 01 50 |
| 15 | 00 39 | 00 58 | 00 59 | 00 59 | 01 13 |
| 20 | 01 17 | 01 40 | 00 56 | 00 15 | 00 35 |
| 21 | 01 25 | 01 48 | 00 56 | 00 06 | 00 27 |
| 22 | 01 33 | 01 57 | 00 56 | 29♎57 | 00 19 |
| 23 | 01 41 | 02 05 | 00 55 | 29 48 | 00 11 |
| 24 | 01 49 | 02 14 | 00 55 | 29 39 | 00 03 |
| 25 | 01 57 | 02 22 | 00 54 | 29 30 | 29♏54 |
| 26 | 02 05 | 02 31 | 00 54 | 29 21 | 29 46 |
| 27 | 02 14 | 02 40 | 00 54 | 29 12 | 29 37 |
| 28 | 02 22 | 02 48 | 00 53 | 29 02 | 29 29 |
| 29 | 02 31 | 02 57 | 00 53 | 28 53 | 29 20 |
| 30 | 02 40 | 03 06 | 00 52 | 28 44 | 29 11 |
| 31 | 02 49 | 03 15 | 00 52 | 28 34 | 29 01 |
| 32 | 02 58 | 03 24 | 00 51 | 28 24 | 28 52 |
| 33 | 03 08 | 03 34 | 00 51 | 28 14 | 28 42 |
| 34 | 03 17 | 03 43 | 00 51 | 28 05 | 28 33 |
| 35 | 03 27 | 03 52 | 00 50 | 27 54 | 28 23 |
| 36 | 03 37 | 04 02 | 00 50 | 27 44 | 28 12 |
| 37 | 03 47 | 04 12 | 00 49 | 27 34 | 28 02 |
| 38 | 03 58 | 04 22 | 00 49 | 27 23 | 27 51 |
| 39 | 04 08 | 04 32 | 00 48 | 27 13 | 27 40 |
| 40 | 04 19 | 04 42 | 00 48 | 27 02 | 27 29 |
| 41 | 04 31 | 04 52 | 00 47 | 26 51 | 27 17 |
| 42 | 04 43 | 05 03 | 00 47 | 26 40 | 27 05 |
| 43 | 04 55 | 05 13 | 00 47 | 26 28 | 26 53 |
| 44 | 05 07 | 05 24 | 00 46 | 26 16 | 26 40 |
| 45 | 05 20 | 05 36 | 00 46 | 26 05 | 26 27 |
| 46 | 05 33 | 05 47 | 00 45 | 25 52 | 26 13 |
| 47 | 05 47 | 05 59 | 00 45 | 25 40 | 25 59 |
| 48 | 06 01 | 06 10 | 00 44 | 25 27 | 25 45 |
| 49 | 06 16 | 06 23 | 00 44 | 25 14 | 25 30 |
| 50 | 06 31 | 06 35 | 00 43 | 25 01 | 25 14 |
| 51 | 06 47 | 06 48 | 00 43 | 24 47 | 24 58 |
| 52 | 07 04 | 07 01 | 00 42 | 24 33 | 24 40 |
| 53 | 07 21 | 07 15 | 00 42 | 24 19 | 24 23 |
| 54 | 07 39 | 07 29 | 00 41 | 24 04 | 24 04 |
| 55 | 07 58 | 07 43 | 00 40 | 23 49 | 23 44 |
| 56 | 08 18 | 07 58 | 00 40 | 23 33 | 23 24 |
| 57 | 08 39 | 08 13 | 00 39 | 23 17 | 23 02 |
| 58 | 09 01 | 08 28 | 00 39 | 23 00 | 22 39 |
| 59 | 09 24 | 08 45 | 00 38 | 22 43 | 22 15 |
| 60 | 09♌49 | 09♍01 | 00♎37 | 22♎25 | 21♏50 |

**6h 8m 0s — 01 ♋ 50 — 92° 0' 0"**

| LAT. | 11 | 12 | ASC | 2 | 3 |
|---|---|---|---|---|---|
| 0 | 29♋49 | 29♌54 | 02♎11 | 04♏16 | 04♐00 |
| 5 | 00♌25 | 00♍36 | 02 06 | 03 29 | 03 23 |
| 10 | 01 00 | 01 17 | 02 02 | 02 43 | 02 47 |
| 15 | 01 36 | 01 57 | 01 57 | 01 58 | 02 10 |
| 20 | 02 14 | 02 37 | 01 53 | 01 13 | 01 31 |
| 21 | 02 21 | 02 46 | 01 52 | 01 03 | 01 23 |
| 22 | 02 29 | 02 54 | 01 51 | 00 54 | 01 15 |
| 23 | 02 37 | 03 02 | 01 50 | 00 45 | 01 07 |
| 24 | 02 45 | 03 10 | 01 50 | 00 36 | 00 58 |
| 25 | 02 53 | 03 19 | 01 49 | 00 26 | 00 50 |
| 26 | 03 01 | 03 27 | 01 48 | 00 17 | 00 41 |
| 27 | 03 10 | 03 35 | 01 47 | 00 07 | 00 33 |
| 28 | 03 18 | 03 44 | 01 46 | 29♎58 | 00 24 |
| 29 | 03 27 | 03 52 | 01 45 | 29 48 | 00 15 |
| 30 | 03 35 | 04 01 | 01 45 | 29 38 | 00 06 |
| 31 | 03 44 | 04 10 | 01 44 | 29 28 | 29♏56 |
| 32 | 03 53 | 04 19 | 01 43 | 29 18 | 29 47 |
| 33 | 04 03 | 04 28 | 01 42 | 29 08 | 29 37 |
| 34 | 04 12 | 04 37 | 01 41 | 28 58 | 29 27 |
| 35 | 04 22 | 04 46 | 01 40 | 28 48 | 29 17 |
| 36 | 04 32 | 04 55 | 01 39 | 28 37 | 29 07 |
| 37 | 04 42 | 05 05 | 01 39 | 28 27 | 28 56 |
| 38 | 04 52 | 05 14 | 01 38 | 28 16 | 28 46 |
| 39 | 05 03 | 05 24 | 01 37 | 28 05 | 28 34 |
| 40 | 05 14 | 05 34 | 01 36 | 27 54 | 28 23 |
| 41 | 05 25 | 05 44 | 01 35 | 27 42 | 28 11 |
| 42 | 05 37 | 05 54 | 01 34 | 27 31 | 27 59 |
| 43 | 05 48 | 06 04 | 01 33 | 27 19 | 27 47 |
| 44 | 06 01 | 06 15 | 01 32 | 27 07 | 27 34 |
| 45 | 06 13 | 06 26 | 01 31 | 26 55 | 27 20 |
| 46 | 06 26 | 06 37 | 01 30 | 26 42 | 27 07 |
| 47 | 06 40 | 06 48 | 01 29 | 26 29 | 26 52 |
| 48 | 06 54 | 06 59 | 01 28 | 26 16 | 26 38 |
| 49 | 07 08 | 07 11 | 01 27 | 26 03 | 26 22 |
| 50 | 07 24 | 07 23 | 01 26 | 25 49 | 26 06 |
| 51 | 07 39 | 07 36 | 01 25 | 25 35 | 25 50 |
| 52 | 07 56 | 07 48 | 01 24 | 25 20 | 25 32 |
| 53 | 08 13 | 08 01 | 01 23 | 25 05 | 25 14 |
| 54 | 08 31 | 08 15 | 01 22 | 24 50 | 24 55 |
| 55 | 08 49 | 08 29 | 01 21 | 24 34 | 24 35 |
| 56 | 09 09 | 08 43 | 01 20 | 24 18 | 24 15 |
| 57 | 09 29 | 08 58 | 01 18 | 24 01 | 23 53 |
| 58 | 09 51 | 09 13 | 01 17 | 23 44 | 23 29 |
| 59 | 10 14 | 09 28 | 01 16 | 23 26 | 23 05 |
| 60 | 10♌38 | 09♍45 | 01♎15 | 23♎08 | 22♏39 |

**6h 12m 0s — 02 ♋ 45 — 93° 0' 0"**

| LAT. | 11 | 12 | ASC | 2 | 3 |
|---|---|---|---|---|---|
| 0 | 00♌47 | 00♍57 | 03♎16 | 05♏18 | 04♐57 |
| 5 | 01 22 | 01 38 | 03 09 | 04 30 | 04 20 |
| 10 | 01 57 | 02 17 | 03 02 | 03 43 | 03 43 |
| 15 | 02 33 | 02 56 | 02 56 | 02 57 | 03 06 |
| 20 | 03 10 | 03 35 | 02 49 | 02 10 | 02 27 |
| 21 | 03 17 | 03 43 | 02 48 | 02 01 | 02 19 |
| 22 | 03 25 | 03 51 | 02 47 | 01 51 | 02 10 |
| 23 | 03 33 | 03 59 | 02 46 | 01 42 | 02 02 |
| 24 | 03 41 | 04 07 | 02 44 | 01 32 | 01 54 |
| 25 | 03 49 | 04 15 | 02 43 | 01 22 | 01 45 |
| 26 | 03 57 | 04 23 | 02 42 | 01 13 | 01 37 |
| 27 | 04 05 | 04 31 | 02 41 | 01 03 | 01 28 |
| 28 | 04 14 | 04 39 | 02 39 | 00 53 | 01 19 |
| 29 | 04 22 | 04 48 | 02 38 | 00 43 | 01 10 |
| 30 | 04 31 | 04 56 | 02 37 | 00 33 | 01 01 |
| 31 | 04 40 | 05 05 | 02 36 | 00 23 | 00 51 |
| 32 | 04 49 | 05 13 | 02 34 | 00 13 | 00 42 |
| 33 | 04 58 | 05 22 | 02 33 | 00 02 | 00 32 |
| 34 | 05 07 | 05 30 | 02 32 | 29♎52 | 00 22 |
| 35 | 05 17 | 05 39 | 02 30 | 29 41 | 00 12 |
| 36 | 05 27 | 05 48 | 02 29 | 29 30 | 00 01 |
| 37 | 05 37 | 05 57 | 02 28 | 29 19 | 29♏51 |
| 38 | 05 47 | 06 07 | 02 27 | 29 08 | 29 40 |
| 39 | 05 57 | 06 16 | 02 25 | 28 57 | 29 29 |
| 40 | 06 08 | 06 26 | 02 24 | 28 45 | 29 17 |
| 41 | 06 19 | 06 35 | 02 22 | 28 34 | 29 05 |
| 42 | 06 31 | 06 45 | 02 21 | 28 22 | 28 53 |
| 43 | 06 42 | 06 55 | 02 20 | 28 10 | 28 40 |
| 44 | 06 54 | 07 05 | 02 18 | 27 57 | 28 27 |
| 45 | 07 07 | 07 16 | 02 17 | 27 44 | 28 14 |
| 46 | 07 20 | 07 26 | 02 15 | 27 32 | 28 00 |
| 47 | 07 33 | 07 37 | 02 14 | 27 18 | 27 45 |
| 48 | 07 47 | 07 48 | 02 12 | 27 05 | 27 30 |
| 49 | 08 01 | 08 00 | 02 11 | 26 51 | 27 15 |
| 50 | 08 16 | 08 11 | 02 09 | 26 37 | 26 59 |
| 51 | 08 32 | 08 23 | 02 08 | 26 22 | 26 42 |
| 52 | 08 48 | 08 36 | 02 06 | 26 07 | 26 24 |
| 53 | 09 05 | 08 48 | 02 05 | 25 52 | 26 06 |
| 54 | 09 22 | 09 01 | 02 03 | 25 36 | 25 47 |
| 55 | 09 40 | 09 14 | 02 01 | 25 20 | 25 27 |
| 56 | 10 00 | 09 28 | 01 59 | 25 03 | 25 05 |
| 57 | 10 20 | 09 42 | 01 58 | 24 46 | 24 43 |
| 58 | 10 41 | 09 57 | 01 56 | 24 28 | 24 19 |
| 59 | 11 04 | 10 12 | 01 54 | 24 10 | 23 55 |
| 60 | 11♌28 | 10♍28 | 01♎52 | 23♎51 | 23♏28 |

**6h 16m 0s — 03 ♋ 40 — 94° 0' 0"**

| LAT. | 11 | 12 | ASC | 2 | 3 |
|---|---|---|---|---|---|
| 0 | 01♌45 | 02♍00 | 04♎22 | 06♏19 | 05♐54 |
| 5 | 02 20 | 02 39 | 04 12 | 05 30 | 05 17 |
| 10 | 02 54 | 03 18 | 04 03 | 04 42 | 04 40 |
| 15 | 03 30 | 03 55 | 03 54 | 03 55 | 04 02 |
| 20 | 04 06 | 04 33 | 03 46 | 03 07 | 03 22 |
| 21 | 04 14 | 04 41 | 03 44 | 02 57 | 03 14 |
| 22 | 04 21 | 04 48 | 03 43 | 02 48 | 03 06 |
| 23 | 04 29 | 04 56 | 03 41 | 02 38 | 02 58 |
| 24 | 04 37 | 05 04 | 03 39 | 02 28 | 02 49 |
| 25 | 04 45 | 05 11 | 03 38 | 02 18 | 02 41 |
| 26 | 04 53 | 05 19 | 03 36 | 02 08 | 02 32 |
| 27 | 05 01 | 05 27 | 03 34 | 01 58 | 02 23 |
| 28 | 05 09 | 05 35 | 03 33 | 01 48 | 02 14 |
| 29 | 05 18 | 05 43 | 03 31 | 01 38 | 02 05 |
| 30 | 05 26 | 05 51 | 03 29 | 01 28 | 01 56 |
| 31 | 05 35 | 05 59 | 03 28 | 01 17 | 01 46 |
| 32 | 05 44 | 06 08 | 03 26 | 01 07 | 01 37 |
| 33 | 05 53 | 06 16 | 03 24 | 00 56 | 01 27 |
| 34 | 06 02 | 06 24 | 03 22 | 00 45 | 01 17 |
| 35 | 06 12 | 06 33 | 03 21 | 00 34 | 01 06 |
| 36 | 06 21 | 06 42 | 03 19 | 00 23 | 00 56 |
| 37 | 06 31 | 06 50 | 03 17 | 00 12 | 00 45 |
| 38 | 06 41 | 06 59 | 03 15 | 00 00 | 00 34 |
| 39 | 06 52 | 07 08 | 03 14 | 29♎49 | 00 23 |
| 40 | 07 02 | 07 17 | 03 12 | 29 37 | 00 11 |
| 41 | 07 13 | 07 27 | 03 10 | 29 25 | 29♏59 |
| 42 | 07 25 | 07 36 | 03 08 | 29 13 | 29 47 |
| 43 | 07 36 | 07 46 | 03 06 | 29 00 | 29 34 |
| 44 | 07 48 | 07 56 | 03 04 | 28 47 | 29 21 |
| 45 | 08 00 | 08 06 | 03 02 | 28 34 | 29 07 |
| 46 | 08 13 | 08 16 | 03 01 | 28 21 | 28 53 |
| 47 | 08 26 | 08 27 | 02 59 | 28 08 | 28 38 |
| 48 | 08 40 | 08 37 | 02 57 | 27 54 | 28 23 |
| 49 | 08 54 | 08 48 | 02 55 | 27 39 | 28 07 |
| 50 | 09 09 | 09 00 | 02 52 | 27 25 | 27 51 |
| 51 | 09 24 | 09 11 | 02 50 | 27 10 | 27 34 |
| 52 | 09 40 | 09 23 | 02 48 | 26 54 | 27 16 |
| 53 | 09 56 | 09 35 | 02 46 | 26 39 | 26 58 |
| 54 | 10 14 | 09 48 | 02 44 | 26 22 | 26 38 |
| 55 | 10 32 | 10 00 | 02 42 | 26 06 | 26 18 |
| 56 | 10 51 | 10 14 | 02 39 | 25 48 | 25 56 |
| 57 | 11 11 | 10 27 | 02 37 | 25 31 | 25 33 |
| 58 | 11 32 | 10 41 | 02 34 | 25 12 | 25 10 |
| 59 | 11 54 | 10 56 | 02 32 | 24 53 | 24 44 |
| 60 | 12♌17 | 11♍11 | 02♎29 | 24♎33 | 24♏17 |

**6h 20m 0s — 04 ♋ 35 — 95° 0' 0"**

| LAT. | 11 | 12 | ASC | 2 | 3 |
|---|---|---|---|---|---|
| 0 | 02♌43 | 03♍03 | 05♎27 | 07♏21 | 06♐50 |
| 5 | 03 17 | 03 41 | 05 15 | 06 31 | 06 13 |
| 10 | 03 52 | 04 18 | 05 04 | 05 42 | 05 36 |
| 15 | 04 27 | 04 55 | 04 53 | 04 53 | 04 58 |
| 20 | 05 03 | 05 31 | 04 42 | 04 04 | 04 18 |
| 21 | 05 10 | 05 38 | 04 40 | 03 54 | 04 10 |
| 22 | 05 18 | 05 46 | 04 38 | 03 44 | 04 02 |
| 23 | 05 26 | 05 53 | 04 36 | 03 34 | 03 53 |
| 24 | 05 33 | 06 01 | 04 34 | 03 24 | 03 45 |
| 25 | 05 41 | 06 08 | 04 32 | 03 14 | 03 36 |
| 26 | 05 49 | 06 16 | 04 30 | 03 04 | 03 27 |
| 27 | 05 57 | 06 23 | 04 28 | 02 54 | 03 18 |
| 28 | 06 05 | 06 31 | 04 26 | 02 43 | 03 09 |
| 29 | 06 14 | 06 39 | 04 24 | 02 33 | 03 00 |
| 30 | 06 22 | 06 46 | 04 21 | 02 22 | 02 51 |
| 31 | 06 31 | 06 54 | 04 19 | 02 11 | 02 41 |
| 32 | 06 39 | 07 02 | 04 17 | 02 01 | 02 31 |
| 33 | 06 48 | 07 10 | 04 15 | 01 50 | 02 22 |
| 34 | 06 58 | 07 18 | 04 13 | 01 39 | 02 11 |
| 35 | 07 07 | 07 27 | 04 11 | 01 27 | 02 01 |
| 36 | 07 16 | 07 35 | 04 09 | 01 16 | 01 50 |
| 37 | 07 26 | 07 43 | 04 06 | 01 04 | 01 39 |
| 38 | 07 36 | 07 52 | 04 04 | 00 53 | 01 28 |
| 39 | 07 46 | 08 01 | 04 02 | 00 41 | 01 17 |
| 40 | 07 57 | 08 09 | 04 00 | 00 28 | 01 05 |
| 41 | 08 08 | 08 18 | 03 57 | 00 16 | 00 53 |
| 42 | 08 19 | 08 28 | 03 55 | 00 04 | 00 40 |
| 43 | 08 30 | 08 37 | 03 53 | 29♎51 | 00 27 |
| 44 | 08 42 | 08 46 | 03 50 | 29 38 | 00 14 |
| 45 | 08 54 | 08 56 | 03 48 | 29 24 | 00 00 |
| 46 | 09 07 | 09 06 | 03 46 | 29 11 | 29♏46 |
| 47 | 09 20 | 09 16 | 03 43 | 28 57 | 29 31 |
| 48 | 09 33 | 09 26 | 03 41 | 28 42 | 29 16 |
| 49 | 09 47 | 09 37 | 03 38 | 28 28 | 29 00 |
| 50 | 10 01 | 09 48 | 03 36 | 28 13 | 28 43 |
| 51 | 10 16 | 09 59 | 03 33 | 27 57 | 28 26 |
| 52 | 10 32 | 10 10 | 03 30 | 27 41 | 28 08 |
| 53 | 10 48 | 10 22 | 03 28 | 27 25 | 27 49 |
| 54 | 11 05 | 10 34 | 03 25 | 27 09 | 27 29 |
| 55 | 11 23 | 10 46 | 03 22 | 26 51 | 27 09 |
| 56 | 11 42 | 10 59 | 03 19 | 26 34 | 26 47 |
| 57 | 12 01 | 11 12 | 03 16 | 26 15 | 26 24 |
| 58 | 12 22 | 11 26 | 03 13 | 25 56 | 26 00 |
| 59 | 12 44 | 11 40 | 03 10 | 25 37 | 25 34 |
| 60 | 13♌06 | 11♍54 | 03♎07 | 25♎16 | 25♏06 |

# Placidus Table of Houses for Latitudes 0° to 60° North

**6h 24m 0s — 96° 0' 0" — 05 ♋ 30**

| LAT. | 11 | 12 | ASC | 2 | 3 |
|---|---|---|---|---|---|
| 0 | 03♌41 | 04♍07 | 06♎32 | 08♏23 | 07♐47 |
| 5 | 04 15 | 04 43 | 06 18 | 07 31 | 07 10 |
| 10 | 04 49 | 05 19 | 06 04 | 06 41 | 06 32 |
| 15 | 05 24 | 05 54 | 05 51 | 05 51 | 05 54 |
| 20 | 06 00 | 06 29 | 05 39 | 05 01 | 05 14 |
| 21 | 06 07 | 06 36 | 05 36 | 04 51 | 05 05 |
| 22 | 06 14 | 06 43 | 05 34 | 04 41 | 04 57 |
| 23 | 06 22 | 06 50 | 05 31 | 04 31 | 04 49 |
| 24 | 06 30 | 06 57 | 05 29 | 04 20 | 04 40 |
| 25 | 06 37 | 07 05 | 05 26 | 04 10 | 04 31 |
| 26 | 06 45 | 07 12 | 05 24 | 03 59 | 04 23 |
| 27 | 06 53 | 07 19 | 05 21 | 03 49 | 04 14 |
| 28 | 07 01 | 07 27 | 05 19 | 03 38 | 04 04 |
| 29 | 07 10 | 07 34 | 05 16 | 03 27 | 03 55 |
| 30 | 07 18 | 07 42 | 05 14 | 03 17 | 03 46 |
| 31 | 07 26 | 07 49 | 05 11 | 03 06 | 03 36 |
| 32 | 07 35 | 07 57 | 05 09 | 02 55 | 03 26 |
| 33 | 07 44 | 08 05 | 05 06 | 02 43 | 03 16 |
| 34 | 07 53 | 08 12 | 05 04 | 02 32 | 03 06 |
| 35 | 08 02 | 08 20 | 05 01 | 02 20 | 02 55 |
| 36 | 08 12 | 08 28 | 04 58 | 02 09 | 02 45 |
| 37 | 08 21 | 08 36 | 04 56 | 01 57 | 02 34 |
| 38 | 08 31 | 08 45 | 04 53 | 01 45 | 02 22 |
| 39 | 08 41 | 08 53 | 04 50 | 01 32 | 02 11 |
| 40 | 08 51 | 09 02 | 04 48 | 01 20 | 01 59 |
| 41 | 09 02 | 09 10 | 04 45 | 01 07 | 01 47 |
| 42 | 09 13 | 09 19 | 04 42 | 00 54 | 01 34 |
| 43 | 09 24 | 09 28 | 04 39 | 00 41 | 01 21 |
| 44 | 09 36 | 09 37 | 04 37 | 00 28 | 01 07 |
| 45 | 09 48 | 09 46 | 04 34 | 00 14 | 00 53 |
| 46 | 10 00 | 09 56 | 04 31 | 00 00 | 00 39 |
| 47 | 10 13 | 10 06 | 04 28 | 29♎46 | 00 24 |
| 48 | 10 26 | 10 15 | 04 25 | 29 31 | 00 09 |
| 49 | 10 40 | 10 26 | 04 22 | 29 16 | 29♏52 |
| 50 | 10 54 | 10 36 | 04 19 | 29 01 | 29 36 |
| 51 | 11 09 | 10 47 | 04 16 | 28 45 | 29 18 |
| 52 | 11 24 | 10 58 | 04 12 | 28 28 | 29 00 |
| 53 | 11 40 | 11 09 | 04 09 | 28 12 | 28 41 |
| 54 | 11 57 | 11 20 | 04 06 | 27 55 | 28 21 |
| 55 | 12 14 | 11 32 | 04 02 | 27 37 | 28 00 |
| 56 | 12 33 | 11 44 | 03 59 | 27 19 | 27 38 |
| 57 | 12 52 | 11 57 | 03 55 | 27 00 | 27 14 |
| 58 | 13 12 | 12 10 | 03 52 | 26 40 | 26 50 |
| 59 | 13 33 | 12 23 | 03 48 | 26 20 | 26 23 |
| 60 | 13♌56 | 12♍37 | 03♎44 | 25♎59 | 25♏56 |

**6h 28m 0s — 97° 0' 0" — 06 ♋ 26**

| LAT. | 11 | 12 | ASC | 2 | 3 |
|---|---|---|---|---|---|
| 0 | 04♌39 | 05♍10 | 07♎37 | 09♏24 | 08♐43 |
| 5 | 05 13 | 05 45 | 07 21 | 08 32 | 08 06 |
| 10 | 05 47 | 06 20 | 07 05 | 07 40 | 07 28 |
| 15 | 06 21 | 06 53 | 06 50 | 06 49 | 06 49 |
| 20 | 06 56 | 07 27 | 06 35 | 05 58 | 06 09 |
| 21 | 07 04 | 07 34 | 06 32 | 05 48 | 06 01 |
| 22 | 07 11 | 07 41 | 06 29 | 05 37 | 05 52 |
| 23 | 07 19 | 07 48 | 06 26 | 05 27 | 05 44 |
| 24 | 07 26 | 07 54 | 06 24 | 05 16 | 05 35 |
| 25 | 07 34 | 08 01 | 06 21 | 05 06 | 05 27 |
| 26 | 07 41 | 08 08 | 06 18 | 04 55 | 05 18 |
| 27 | 07 49 | 08 15 | 06 15 | 04 44 | 05 09 |
| 28 | 07 57 | 08 23 | 06 12 | 04 33 | 04 59 |
| 29 | 08 05 | 08 30 | 06 09 | 04 22 | 04 50 |
| 30 | 08 14 | 08 37 | 06 06 | 04 11 | 04 40 |
| 31 | 08 22 | 08 44 | 06 03 | 04 00 | 04 31 |
| 32 | 08 31 | 08 51 | 06 00 | 03 48 | 04 21 |
| 33 | 08 39 | 08 59 | 05 57 | 03 37 | 04 11 |
| 34 | 08 48 | 09 06 | 05 54 | 03 25 | 04 00 |
| 35 | 08 57 | 09 14 | 05 51 | 03 13 | 03 50 |
| 36 | 09 07 | 09 22 | 05 48 | 03 01 | 03 39 |
| 37 | 09 16 | 09 30 | 05 45 | 02 49 | 03 28 |
| 38 | 09 26 | 09 37 | 05 42 | 02 37 | 03 16 |
| 39 | 09 36 | 09 45 | 05 39 | 02 24 | 03 05 |
| 40 | 09 46 | 09 54 | 05 36 | 02 12 | 02 53 |
| 41 | 09 57 | 10 02 | 05 32 | 01 59 | 02 40 |
| 42 | 10 07 | 10 10 | 05 29 | 01 45 | 02 27 |
| 43 | 10 18 | 10 19 | 05 26 | 01 32 | 02 14 |
| 44 | 10 30 | 10 28 | 05 23 | 01 18 | 02 01 |
| 45 | 10 42 | 10 37 | 05 19 | 01 04 | 01 47 |
| 46 | 10 54 | 10 46 | 05 16 | 00 49 | 01 32 |
| 47 | 11 06 | 10 55 | 05 12 | 00 35 | 01 17 |
| 48 | 11 19 | 11 05 | 05 09 | 00 20 | 01 01 |
| 49 | 11 33 | 11 14 | 05 05 | 00 04 | 00 45 |
| 50 | 11 47 | 11 24 | 05 02 | 29♎48 | 00 28 |
| 51 | 12 01 | 11 34 | 04 58 | 29 32 | 00 10 |
| 52 | 12 17 | 11 45 | 04 54 | 29 15 | 29♏52 |
| 53 | 12 32 | 11 56 | 04 51 | 28 58 | 29 32 |
| 54 | 12 49 | 12 07 | 04 47 | 28 41 | 29 12 |
| 55 | 13 06 | 12 18 | 04 43 | 28 22 | 28 51 |
| 56 | 13 24 | 12 30 | 04 39 | 28 04 | 28 28 |
| 57 | 13 43 | 12 42 | 04 34 | 27 44 | 28 05 |
| 58 | 14 03 | 12 54 | 04 30 | 27 24 | 27 40 |
| 59 | 14 23 | 13 07 | 04 26 | 27 04 | 27 13 |
| 60 | 14♌45 | 13♍20 | 04♎21 | 26♎42 | 26♏45 |

**6h 32m 0s — 98° 0' 0" — 07 ♋ 21**

| LAT. | 11 | 12 | ASC | 2 | 3 |
|---|---|---|---|---|---|
| 0 | 05♌38 | 06♍14 | 08♎43 | 10♏25 | 09♐40 |
| 5 | 06 11 | 06 48 | 08 24 | 09 32 | 09 02 |
| 10 | 06 44 | 07 21 | 08 06 | 08 39 | 08 24 |
| 15 | 07 18 | 07 53 | 07 48 | 07 47 | 07 45 |
| 20 | 07 53 | 08 25 | 07 32 | 06 55 | 07 05 |
| 21 | 08 01 | 08 32 | 07 28 | 06 44 | 06 56 |
| 22 | 08 08 | 08 38 | 07 25 | 06 34 | 06 48 |
| 23 | 08 15 | 08 45 | 07 22 | 06 23 | 06 39 |
| 24 | 08 23 | 08 52 | 07 18 | 06 12 | 06 30 |
| 25 | 08 30 | 08 58 | 07 15 | 06 01 | 06 22 |
| 26 | 08 38 | 09 05 | 07 12 | 05 50 | 06 13 |
| 27 | 08 46 | 09 12 | 07 08 | 05 39 | 06 04 |
| 28 | 08 54 | 09 18 | 07 05 | 05 28 | 05 54 |
| 29 | 09 02 | 09 25 | 07 02 | 05 17 | 05 45 |
| 30 | 09 10 | 09 32 | 06 58 | 05 05 | 05 35 |
| 31 | 09 18 | 09 39 | 06 55 | 04 54 | 05 25 |
| 32 | 09 26 | 09 46 | 06 51 | 04 42 | 05 15 |
| 33 | 09 35 | 09 53 | 06 48 | 04 30 | 05 05 |
| 34 | 09 44 | 10 01 | 06 45 | 04 18 | 04 55 |
| 35 | 09 53 | 10 08 | 06 41 | 04 06 | 04 44 |
| 36 | 10 02 | 10 15 | 06 38 | 03 54 | 04 33 |
| 37 | 10 11 | 10 23 | 06 34 | 03 42 | 04 22 |
| 38 | 10 21 | 10 30 | 06 31 | 03 29 | 04 10 |
| 39 | 10 31 | 10 38 | 06 27 | 03 16 | 03 59 |
| 40 | 10 41 | 10 46 | 06 24 | 03 03 | 03 46 |
| 41 | 10 51 | 10 54 | 06 20 | 02 50 | 03 34 |
| 42 | 11 02 | 11 02 | 06 16 | 02 36 | 03 21 |
| 43 | 11 13 | 11 10 | 06 12 | 02 22 | 03 08 |
| 44 | 11 24 | 11 18 | 06 09 | 02 08 | 02 54 |
| 45 | 11 36 | 11 27 | 06 05 | 01 54 | 02 40 |
| 46 | 11 48 | 11 36 | 06 01 | 01 39 | 02 25 |
| 47 | 12 00 | 11 45 | 05 57 | 01 24 | 02 10 |
| 48 | 12 13 | 11 54 | 05 53 | 01 08 | 01 54 |
| 49 | 12 26 | 12 03 | 05 49 | 00 52 | 01 37 |
| 50 | 12 40 | 12 13 | 05 45 | 00 36 | 01 20 |
| 51 | 12 54 | 12 22 | 05 41 | 00 20 | 01 02 |
| 52 | 13 09 | 12 32 | 05 36 | 00 02 | 00 44 |
| 53 | 13 24 | 12 43 | 05 32 | 29♎45 | 00 24 |
| 54 | 13 41 | 12 53 | 05 28 | 29 27 | 00 03 |
| 55 | 13 57 | 13 04 | 05 23 | 29 08 | 29♏42 |
| 56 | 14 15 | 13 15 | 05 18 | 28 49 | 29 19 |
| 57 | 14 34 | 13 27 | 05 14 | 28 29 | 28 55 |
| 58 | 14 53 | 13 39 | 05 09 | 28 08 | 28 30 |
| 59 | 15 13 | 13 51 | 05 04 | 27 47 | 28 03 |
| 60 | 15♌35 | 14♍04 | 04♎59 | 27♎25 | 27♏34 |

**6h 36m 0s — 99° 0' 0" — 08 ♋ 16**

| LAT. | 11 | 12 | ASC | 2 | 3 |
|---|---|---|---|---|---|
| 0 | 06♌37 | 07♍18 | 09♎48 | 11♏26 | 10♐36 |
| 5 | 07 09 | 07 50 | 09 26 | 10 31 | 09 58 |
| 10 | 07 42 | 08 22 | 09 06 | 09 38 | 09 20 |
| 15 | 08 16 | 08 53 | 08 47 | 08 45 | 08 41 |
| 20 | 08 50 | 09 24 | 08 28 | 07 52 | 08 00 |
| 21 | 08 58 | 09 30 | 08 24 | 07 41 | 07 52 |
| 22 | 09 05 | 09 36 | 08 20 | 07 30 | 07 43 |
| 23 | 09 12 | 09 42 | 08 17 | 07 19 | 07 34 |
| 24 | 09 19 | 09 49 | 08 13 | 07 08 | 07 26 |
| 25 | 09 27 | 09 55 | 08 09 | 06 57 | 07 17 |
| 26 | 09 34 | 10 01 | 08 06 | 06 45 | 07 08 |
| 27 | 09 42 | 10 08 | 08 02 | 06 34 | 06 58 |
| 28 | 09 50 | 10 14 | 07 58 | 06 23 | 06 49 |
| 29 | 09 58 | 10 21 | 07 54 | 06 11 | 06 40 |
| 30 | 10 06 | 10 28 | 07 50 | 06 00 | 06 30 |
| 31 | 10 14 | 10 34 | 07 47 | 05 48 | 06 20 |
| 32 | 10 22 | 10 41 | 07 43 | 05 36 | 06 10 |
| 33 | 10 31 | 10 48 | 07 39 | 05 24 | 06 00 |
| 34 | 10 39 | 10 55 | 07 35 | 05 12 | 05 49 |
| 35 | 10 48 | 11 02 | 07 31 | 04 59 | 05 38 |
| 36 | 10 57 | 11 09 | 07 27 | 04 47 | 05 27 |
| 37 | 11 07 | 11 16 | 07 23 | 04 34 | 05 16 |
| 38 | 11 16 | 11 23 | 07 19 | 04 21 | 05 04 |
| 39 | 11 26 | 11 30 | 07 15 | 04 08 | 04 53 |
| 40 | 11 36 | 11 38 | 07 11 | 03 54 | 04 40 |
| 41 | 11 46 | 11 46 | 07 07 | 03 41 | 04 28 |
| 42 | 11 56 | 11 53 | 07 03 | 03 27 | 04 15 |
| 43 | 12 07 | 12 01 | 06 59 | 03 13 | 04 01 |
| 44 | 12 18 | 12 09 | 06 55 | 02 58 | 03 47 |
| 45 | 12 30 | 12 17 | 06 50 | 02 43 | 03 33 |
| 46 | 12 41 | 12 26 | 06 46 | 02 28 | 03 18 |
| 47 | 12 53 | 12 34 | 06 42 | 02 13 | 03 03 |
| 48 | 13 06 | 12 43 | 06 37 | 01 57 | 02 47 |
| 49 | 13 19 | 12 52 | 06 33 | 01 41 | 02 30 |
| 50 | 13 33 | 13 01 | 06 28 | 01 24 | 02 13 |
| 51 | 13 47 | 13 10 | 06 23 | 01 07 | 01 54 |
| 52 | 14 01 | 13 20 | 06 18 | 00 49 | 01 35 |
| 53 | 14 17 | 13 30 | 06 14 | 00 31 | 01 16 |
| 54 | 14 32 | 13 40 | 06 09 | 00 13 | 00 55 |
| 55 | 14 49 | 13 50 | 06 03 | 29♎53 | 00 33 |
| 56 | 15 06 | 14 01 | 05 58 | 29 34 | 00 10 |
| 57 | 15 24 | 14 12 | 05 53 | 29 13 | 29♏45 |
| 58 | 15 44 | 14 23 | 05 47 | 28 52 | 29 20 |
| 59 | 16 04 | 14 35 | 05 42 | 28 30 | 28 52 |
| 60 | 16♌25 | 14♍47 | 05♎36 | 28♎08 | 28♏23 |

**6h 40m 0s — 100° 0' 0" — 09 ♋ 11**

| LAT. | 11 | 12 | ASC | 2 | 3 |
|---|---|---|---|---|---|
| 0 | 07♌35 | 08♍22 | 10♎53 | 12♏27 | 11♐32 |
| 5 | 08 08 | 08 53 | 10 29 | 11 31 | 10 54 |
| 10 | 08 40 | 09 23 | 10 07 | 10 37 | 10 16 |
| 15 | 09 13 | 09 52 | 09 45 | 09 43 | 09 36 |
| 20 | 09 48 | 10 22 | 09 24 | 08 48 | 08 55 |
| 21 | 09 55 | 10 28 | 09 20 | 08 37 | 08 47 |
| 22 | 10 02 | 10 34 | 09 16 | 08 26 | 08 38 |
| 23 | 10 09 | 10 40 | 09 12 | 08 15 | 08 29 |
| 24 | 10 16 | 10 46 | 09 08 | 08 03 | 08 21 |
| 25 | 10 24 | 10 52 | 09 04 | 07 52 | 08 12 |
| 26 | 10 31 | 10 58 | 08 59 | 07 41 | 08 03 |
| 27 | 10 39 | 11 04 | 08 55 | 07 29 | 07 53 |
| 28 | 10 46 | 11 10 | 08 51 | 07 17 | 07 44 |
| 29 | 10 54 | 11 17 | 08 47 | 07 06 | 07 34 |
| 30 | 11 02 | 11 23 | 08 43 | 06 54 | 07 25 |
| 31 | 11 10 | 11 29 | 08 39 | 06 42 | 07 15 |
| 32 | 11 18 | 11 36 | 08 34 | 06 30 | 07 05 |
| 33 | 11 27 | 11 42 | 08 30 | 06 17 | 06 54 |
| 34 | 11 35 | 11 49 | 08 26 | 06 05 | 06 44 |
| 35 | 11 44 | 11 56 | 08 21 | 05 52 | 06 33 |
| 36 | 11 53 | 12 02 | 08 17 | 05 39 | 06 22 |
| 37 | 12 02 | 12 09 | 08 13 | 05 26 | 06 10 |
| 38 | 12 11 | 12 16 | 08 08 | 05 13 | 05 58 |
| 39 | 12 21 | 12 23 | 08 04 | 04 59 | 05 46 |
| 40 | 12 30 | 12 30 | 07 59 | 04 46 | 05 34 |
| 41 | 12 40 | 12 37 | 07 55 | 04 32 | 05 21 |
| 42 | 12 51 | 12 45 | 07 50 | 04 17 | 05 08 |
| 43 | 13 01 | 12 52 | 07 46 | 04 03 | 04 55 |
| 44 | 13 12 | 13 00 | 07 41 | 03 48 | 04 41 |
| 45 | 13 24 | 13 08 | 07 36 | 03 33 | 04 26 |
| 46 | 13 35 | 13 16 | 07 31 | 03 17 | 04 11 |
| 47 | 13 47 | 13 24 | 07 26 | 03 02 | 03 55 |
| 48 | 13 59 | 13 32 | 07 21 | 02 45 | 03 39 |
| 49 | 14 12 | 13 40 | 07 16 | 02 29 | 03 22 |
| 50 | 14 26 | 13 49 | 07 11 | 02 12 | 03 05 |
| 51 | 14 39 | 13 58 | 07 06 | 01 54 | 02 47 |
| 52 | 14 54 | 14 07 | 07 00 | 01 36 | 02 27 |
| 53 | 15 09 | 14 17 | 06 55 | 01 18 | 02 07 |
| 54 | 15 24 | 14 26 | 06 49 | 00 59 | 01 46 |
| 55 | 15 41 | 14 36 | 06 44 | 00 39 | 01 24 |
| 56 | 15 58 | 14 46 | 06 38 | 00 19 | 01 01 |
| 57 | 16 15 | 14 57 | 06 32 | 29♎58 | 00 36 |
| 58 | 16 34 | 15 08 | 06 26 | 29 36 | 00 10 |
| 59 | 16 54 | 15 19 | 06 20 | 29 14 | 29♏42 |
| 60 | 17♌14 | 15♍30 | 06♎13 | 28♎50 | 29♏12 |

**6h 44m 0s — 101° 0' 0" — 10 ♋ 07**

| LAT. | 11 | 12 | ASC | 2 | 3 |
|---|---|---|---|---|---|
| 0 | 08♌34 | 09♍26 | 11♎58 | 13♏27 | 12♐28 |
| 5 | 09 06 | 09 55 | 11 32 | 12 31 | 11 50 |
| 10 | 09 39 | 10 24 | 11 07 | 11 35 | 11 11 |
| 15 | 10 11 | 10 52 | 10 44 | 10 40 | 10 32 |
| 20 | 10 45 | 11 20 | 10 21 | 09 45 | 09 50 |
| 21 | 10 52 | 11 26 | 10 16 | 09 33 | 09 42 |
| 22 | 10 59 | 11 32 | 10 12 | 09 22 | 09 33 |
| 23 | 11 06 | 11 37 | 10 07 | 09 11 | 09 25 |
| 24 | 11 13 | 11 43 | 10 02 | 08 59 | 09 16 |
| 25 | 11 20 | 11 49 | 09 58 | 08 47 | 09 07 |
| 26 | 11 28 | 11 55 | 09 53 | 08 36 | 08 57 |
| 27 | 11 35 | 12 01 | 09 49 | 08 24 | 08 48 |
| 28 | 11 43 | 12 07 | 09 44 | 08 12 | 08 39 |
| 29 | 11 50 | 12 13 | 09 40 | 08 00 | 08 29 |
| 30 | 11 58 | 12 19 | 09 35 | 07 48 | 08 19 |
| 31 | 12 06 | 12 25 | 09 30 | 07 36 | 08 09 |
| 32 | 12 14 | 12 31 | 09 26 | 07 23 | 07 59 |
| 33 | 12 22 | 12 37 | 09 21 | 07 11 | 07 49 |
| 34 | 12 31 | 12 43 | 09 16 | 06 58 | 07 38 |
| 35 | 12 39 | 12 49 | 09 11 | 06 45 | 07 27 |
| 36 | 12 48 | 12 56 | 09 07 | 06 32 | 07 16 |
| 37 | 12 57 | 13 02 | 09 02 | 06 18 | 07 04 |
| 38 | 13 06 | 13 09 | 08 57 | 06 05 | 06 52 |
| 39 | 13 16 | 13 16 | 08 52 | 05 51 | 06 40 |
| 40 | 13 25 | 13 22 | 08 47 | 05 37 | 06 28 |
| 41 | 13 35 | 13 29 | 08 42 | 05 23 | 06 15 |
| 42 | 13 45 | 13 36 | 08 37 | 05 08 | 06 02 |
| 43 | 13 56 | 13 43 | 08 32 | 04 53 | 05 48 |
| 44 | 14 07 | 13 51 | 08 27 | 04 38 | 05 34 |
| 45 | 14 18 | 13 58 | 08 22 | 04 23 | 05 19 |
| 46 | 14 29 | 14 06 | 08 16 | 04 07 | 05 04 |
| 47 | 14 41 | 14 13 | 08 11 | 03 51 | 04 48 |
| 48 | 14 53 | 14 21 | 08 05 | 03 34 | 04 32 |
| 49 | 15 06 | 14 29 | 08 00 | 03 17 | 04 15 |
| 50 | 15 19 | 14 38 | 07 54 | 02 59 | 03 57 |
| 51 | 15 32 | 14 46 | 07 48 | 02 41 | 03 39 |
| 52 | 15 46 | 14 55 | 07 42 | 02 23 | 03 19 |
| 53 | 16 01 | 15 04 | 07 36 | 02 04 | 02 59 |
| 54 | 16 16 | 15 13 | 07 30 | 01 44 | 02 37 |
| 55 | 16 32 | 15 22 | 07 24 | 01 24 | 02 15 |
| 56 | 16 49 | 15 32 | 07 18 | 01 04 | 01 51 |
| 57 | 17 06 | 15 42 | 07 11 | 00 42 | 01 26 |
| 58 | 17 25 | 15 52 | 07 05 | 00 20 | 01 00 |
| 59 | 17 44 | 16 03 | 06 58 | 29♎57 | 00 31 |
| 60 | 18♌04 | 16♍14 | 06♎51 | 29♎33 | 00♐01 |

**6h 48m 0s — 102° 0' 0" — 11 ♋ 02**

| LAT. | 11 | 12 | ASC | 2 | 3 |
|---|---|---|---|---|---|
| 0 | 09♌34 | 10♍30 | 13♎03 | 14♏28 | 13♐24 |
| 5 | 10 05 | 10 58 | 12 34 | 13 30 | 12 46 |
| 10 | 10 37 | 11 25 | 12 08 | 12 34 | 12 07 |
| 15 | 11 09 | 11 52 | 11 42 | 11 38 | 11 27 |
| 20 | 11 42 | 12 19 | 11 17 | 10 41 | 10 46 |
| 21 | 11 49 | 12 24 | 11 12 | 10 29 | 10 37 |
| 22 | 11 56 | 12 30 | 11 07 | 10 18 | 10 28 |
| 23 | 12 03 | 12 35 | 11 02 | 10 06 | 10 20 |
| 24 | 12 10 | 12 41 | 10 57 | 09 54 | 10 11 |
| 25 | 12 17 | 12 46 | 10 52 | 09 43 | 10 02 |
| 26 | 12 25 | 12 52 | 10 47 | 09 31 | 09 52 |
| 27 | 12 32 | 12 57 | 10 42 | 09 19 | 09 43 |
| 28 | 12 39 | 13 03 | 10 37 | 09 07 | 09 33 |
| 29 | 12 47 | 13 08 | 10 32 | 08 54 | 09 24 |
| 30 | 12 55 | 13 14 | 10 27 | 08 42 | 09 14 |
| 31 | 13 02 | 13 20 | 10 22 | 08 29 | 09 04 |
| 32 | 13 10 | 13 26 | 10 17 | 08 17 | 08 53 |
| 33 | 13 19 | 13 31 | 10 12 | 08 04 | 08 43 |
| 34 | 13 27 | 13 37 | 10 07 | 07 51 | 08 32 |
| 35 | 13 35 | 13 43 | 10 02 | 07 38 | 08 21 |
| 36 | 13 44 | 13 49 | 09 56 | 07 24 | 08 10 |
| 37 | 13 53 | 13 56 | 09 51 | 07 11 | 07 58 |
| 38 | 14 02 | 14 02 | 09 46 | 06 57 | 07 46 |
| 39 | 14 11 | 14 08 | 09 40 | 06 43 | 07 34 |
| 40 | 14 20 | 14 15 | 09 35 | 06 28 | 07 22 |
| 41 | 14 30 | 14 21 | 09 30 | 06 14 | 07 09 |
| 42 | 14 40 | 14 28 | 09 24 | 05 59 | 06 55 |
| 43 | 14 50 | 14 35 | 09 19 | 05 44 | 06 41 |
| 44 | 15 01 | 14 42 | 09 13 | 05 28 | 06 27 |
| 45 | 15 12 | 14 49 | 09 07 | 05 12 | 06 12 |
| 46 | 15 23 | 14 56 | 09 01 | 04 56 | 05 57 |
| 47 | 15 35 | 15 03 | 08 55 | 04 39 | 05 41 |
| 48 | 15 47 | 15 10 | 08 49 | 04 22 | 05 25 |
| 49 | 15 59 | 15 18 | 08 43 | 04 05 | 05 07 |
| 50 | 16 12 | 15 26 | 08 37 | 03 47 | 04 49 |
| 51 | 16 25 | 15 34 | 08 31 | 03 29 | 04 31 |
| 52 | 16 39 | 15 42 | 08 24 | 03 10 | 04 11 |
| 53 | 16 53 | 15 51 | 08 18 | 02 50 | 03 50 |
| 54 | 17 08 | 15 59 | 08 11 | 02 30 | 03 29 |
| 55 | 17 24 | 16 08 | 08 04 | 02 10 | 03 06 |
| 56 | 17 40 | 16 17 | 07 57 | 01 48 | 02 42 |
| 57 | 17 57 | 16 27 | 07 50 | 01 26 | 02 17 |
| 58 | 18 15 | 16 36 | 07 43 | 01 04 | 01 50 |
| 59 | 18 34 | 16 47 | 07 36 | 00 40 | 01 21 |
| 60 | 18♌54 | 16♍57 | 07♎28 | 00♏16 | 00♐50 |

**6h 52m 0s — 103° 0' 0" — 11 ♋ 58**

| LAT. | 11 | 12 | ASC | 2 | 3 |
|---|---|---|---|---|---|
| 0 | 10♌33 | 11♍34 | 14♎07 | 15♏28 | 14♐20 |
| 5 | 11 04 | 12 01 | 13 37 | 14 30 | 13 41 |
| 10 | 11 35 | 12 27 | 13 08 | 13 32 | 13 02 |
| 15 | 12 07 | 12 52 | 12 40 | 12 35 | 12 22 |
| 20 | 12 40 | 13 17 | 12 13 | 11 37 | 11 41 |
| 21 | 12 47 | 13 23 | 12 08 | 11 25 | 11 32 |
| 22 | 12 53 | 13 28 | 12 02 | 11 14 | 11 23 |
| 23 | 13 00 | 13 33 | 11 57 | 11 02 | 11 14 |
| 24 | 13 07 | 13 38 | 11 52 | 10 50 | 11 05 |
| 25 | 13 14 | 13 43 | 11 46 | 10 38 | 10 56 |
| 26 | 13 21 | 13 48 | 11 41 | 10 26 | 10 47 |
| 27 | 13 29 | 13 54 | 11 36 | 10 13 | 10 38 |
| 28 | 13 36 | 13 59 | 11 30 | 10 01 | 10 28 |
| 29 | 13 44 | 14 04 | 11 25 | 09 49 | 10 18 |
| 30 | 13 51 | 14 10 | 11 19 | 09 36 | 10 08 |
| 31 | 13 59 | 14 15 | 11 14 | 09 23 | 09 58 |
| 32 | 14 07 | 14 21 | 11 08 | 09 10 | 09 48 |
| 33 | 14 15 | 14 26 | 11 03 | 08 57 | 09 37 |
| 34 | 14 23 | 14 32 | 10 57 | 08 44 | 09 26 |
| 35 | 14 31 | 14 37 | 10 52 | 08 30 | 09 15 |
| 36 | 14 40 | 14 43 | 10 46 | 08 17 | 09 04 |
| 37 | 14 48 | 14 49 | 10 40 | 08 03 | 08 52 |
| 38 | 14 57 | 14 55 | 10 35 | 07 48 | 08 40 |
| 39 | 15 06 | 15 01 | 10 29 | 07 34 | 08 28 |
| 40 | 15 16 | 15 07 | 10 23 | 07 19 | 08 15 |
| 41 | 15 25 | 15 13 | 10 17 | 07 05 | 08 02 |
| 42 | 15 35 | 15 19 | 10 11 | 06 49 | 07 49 |
| 43 | 15 45 | 15 26 | 10 05 | 06 34 | 07 35 |
| 44 | 15 55 | 15 32 | 09 59 | 06 18 | 07 20 |
| 45 | 16 06 | 15 39 | 09 53 | 06 02 | 07 05 |
| 46 | 16 17 | 15 46 | 09 46 | 05 45 | 06 50 |
| 47 | 16 28 | 15 53 | 09 40 | 05 28 | 06 34 |
| 48 | 16 40 | 16 00 | 09 34 | 05 11 | 06 17 |
| 49 | 16 52 | 16 07 | 09 27 | 04 53 | 06 00 |
| 50 | 17 05 | 16 14 | 09 20 | 04 35 | 05 42 |
| 51 | 17 18 | 16 22 | 09 13 | 04 16 | 05 23 |
| 52 | 17 32 | 16 30 | 09 06 | 03 57 | 05 03 |
| 53 | 17 46 | 16 38 | 08 59 | 03 37 | 04 42 |
| 54 | 18 00 | 16 46 | 08 52 | 03 16 | 04 20 |
| 55 | 18 16 | 16 54 | 08 45 | 02 55 | 03 57 |
| 56 | 18 32 | 17 03 | 08 37 | 02 33 | 03 33 |
| 57 | 18 49 | 17 12 | 08 30 | 02 11 | 03 07 |
| 58 | 19 06 | 17 21 | 08 22 | 01 47 | 02 40 |
| 59 | 19 25 | 17 30 | 08 14 | 01 23 | 02 11 |
| 60 | 19♌44 | 17♍40 | 08♎05 | 00♏58 | 01♐39 |

# Placidus Table of Houses for Latitudes 0° to 60° North

**6h 56m 0s — 104° 0' 0" — 12 ♋ 53**

| LAT. | 11 | 12 | ASC | 2 | 3 |
|---|---|---|---|---|---|
| 0 | 11♌32 | 12♍39 | 15♎12 | 16♏28 | 15♐16 |
| 5 | 12 03 | 13 04 | 14 39 | 15 29 | 14 37 |
| 10 | 12 34 | 13 28 | 14 08 | 14 30 | 13 58 |
| 15 | 13 05 | 13 52 | 13 39 | 13 32 | 13 18 |
| 20 | 13 38 | 14 16 | 13 09 | 12 33 | 12 36 |
| 21 | 13 44 | 14 21 | 13 04 | 12 21 | 12 27 |
| 22 | 13 51 | 14 26 | 12 58 | 12 09 | 12 18 |
| 23 | 13 58 | 14 31 | 12 52 | 11 57 | 12 09 |
| 24 | 14 05 | 14 35 | 12 46 | 11 45 | 12 00 |
| 25 | 14 12 | 14 40 | 12 40 | 11 33 | 11 51 |
| 26 | 14 19 | 14 45 | 12 35 | 11 21 | 11 42 |
| 27 | 14 26 | 14 50 | 12 29 | 11 08 | 11 32 |
| 28 | 14 33 | 14 55 | 12 23 | 10 55 | 11 23 |
| 29 | 14 40 | 15 00 | 12 17 | 10 43 | 11 13 |
| 30 | 14 48 | 15 05 | 12 11 | 10 30 | 11 03 |
| 31 | 14 55 | 15 10 | 12 06 | 10 17 | 10 53 |
| 32 | 15 03 | 15 16 | 12 00 | 10 04 | 10 42 |
| 33 | 15 11 | 15 21 | 11 54 | 09 50 | 10 32 |
| 34 | 15 19 | 15 26 | 11 48 | 09 37 | 10 21 |
| 35 | 15 27 | 15 31 | 11 42 | 09 23 | 10 09 |
| 36 | 15 35 | 15 37 | 11 36 | 09 09 | 09 58 |
| 37 | 15 44 | 15 42 | 11 29 | 08 55 | 09 46 |
| 38 | 15 53 | 15 48 | 11 23 | 08 40 | 09 34 |
| 39 | 16 02 | 15 54 | 11 17 | 08 26 | 09 22 |
| 40 | 16 11 | 15 59 | 11 11 | 08 11 | 09 09 |
| 41 | 16 20 | 16 05 | 11 04 | 07 55 | 08 56 |
| 42 | 16 30 | 16 11 | 10 58 | 07 40 | 08 42 |
| 43 | 16 40 | 16 17 | 10 52 | 07 24 | 08 28 |
| 44 | 16 50 | 16 23 | 10 45 | 07 08 | 08 14 |
| 45 | 17 00 | 16 29 | 10 38 | 06 51 | 07 59 |
| 46 | 17 11 | 16 36 | 10 31 | 06 34 | 07 43 |
| 47 | 17 22 | 16 42 | 10 25 | 06 17 | 07 27 |
| 48 | 17 34 | 16 49 | 10 18 | 05 59 | 07 10 |
| 49 | 17 46 | 16 56 | 10 11 | 05 41 | 06 52 |
| 50 | 17 58 | 17 03 | 10 03 | 05 22 | 06 34 |
| 51 | 18 11 | 17 10 | 09 56 | 05 03 | 06 15 |
| 52 | 18 24 | 17 17 | 09 48 | 04 43 | 05 55 |
| 53 | 18 38 | 17 25 | 09 41 | 04 23 | 05 34 |
| 54 | 18 53 | 17 32 | 09 33 | 04 02 | 05 12 |
| 55 | 19 08 | 17 40 | 09 25 | 03 40 | 04 48 |
| 56 | 19 23 | 17 48 | 09 17 | 03 18 | 04 24 |
| 57 | 19 40 | 17 57 | 09 09 | 02 55 | 03 58 |
| 58 | 19 57 | 18 06 | 09 00 | 02 31 | 03 30 |
| 59 | 20 15 | 18 14 | 08 51 | 02 06 | 03 00 |
| 60 | 20♌34 | 18♍24 | 08♎43 | 01♏41 | 02♐29 |

**7h 0m 0s — 105° 0' 0" — 13 ♋ 49**

| LAT. | 11 | 12 | ASC | 2 | 3 |
|---|---|---|---|---|---|
| 0 | 12♌32 | 13♍43 | 16♎17 | 17♏28 | 16♐11 |
| 5 | 13 02 | 14 07 | 15 42 | 16 28 | 15 33 |
| 10 | 13 33 | 14 30 | 15 09 | 15 28 | 14 53 |
| 15 | 14 04 | 14 52 | 14 37 | 14 29 | 14 13 |
| 20 | 14 35 | 15 15 | 14 06 | 13 29 | 13 31 |
| 21 | 14 42 | 15 19 | 13 59 | 13 17 | 13 22 |
| 22 | 14 49 | 15 24 | 13 53 | 13 05 | 13 13 |
| 23 | 14 55 | 15 28 | 13 47 | 12 53 | 13 04 |
| 24 | 15 02 | 15 33 | 13 41 | 12 40 | 12 55 |
| 25 | 15 09 | 15 38 | 13 35 | 12 28 | 12 46 |
| 26 | 15 16 | 15 42 | 13 28 | 12 15 | 12 37 |
| 27 | 15 23 | 15 47 | 13 22 | 12 03 | 12 27 |
| 28 | 15 30 | 15 52 | 13 16 | 11 50 | 12 17 |
| 29 | 15 37 | 15 56 | 13 10 | 11 37 | 12 07 |
| 30 | 15 44 | 16 01 | 13 03 | 11 24 | 11 57 |
| 31 | 15 52 | 16 06 | 12 57 | 11 10 | 11 47 |
| 32 | 15 59 | 16 11 | 12 51 | 10 57 | 11 37 |
| 33 | 16 07 | 16 16 | 12 45 | 10 43 | 11 26 |
| 34 | 16 15 | 16 21 | 12 38 | 10 29 | 11 15 |
| 35 | 16 23 | 16 26 | 12 32 | 10 15 | 11 04 |
| 36 | 16 31 | 16 31 | 12 25 | 10 01 | 10 52 |
| 37 | 16 40 | 16 36 | 12 19 | 09 47 | 10 40 |
| 38 | 16 48 | 16 41 | 12 12 | 09 32 | 10 28 |
| 39 | 16 57 | 16 46 | 12 05 | 09 17 | 10 16 |
| 40 | 17 06 | 16 52 | 11 59 | 09 02 | 10 03 |
| 41 | 17 15 | 16 57 | 11 52 | 08 46 | 09 49 |
| 42 | 17 25 | 17 03 | 11 45 | 08 30 | 09 36 |
| 43 | 17 34 | 17 08 | 11 38 | 08 14 | 09 22 |
| 44 | 17 44 | 17 14 | 11 31 | 07 58 | 09 07 |
| 45 | 17 55 | 17 20 | 11 24 | 07 41 | 08 52 |
| 46 | 18 05 | 17 26 | 11 17 | 07 23 | 08 36 |
| 47 | 18 16 | 17 32 | 11 09 | 07 06 | 08 20 |
| 48 | 18 28 | 17 38 | 11 02 | 06 48 | 08 03 |
| 49 | 18 39 | 17 45 | 10 54 | 06 29 | 07 45 |
| 50 | 18 51 | 17 51 | 10 46 | 06 10 | 07 26 |
| 51 | 19 04 | 17 58 | 10 38 | 05 50 | 07 07 |
| 52 | 19 17 | 18 05 | 10 30 | 05 30 | 06 47 |
| 53 | 19 31 | 18 12 | 10 22 | 05 09 | 06 25 |
| 54 | 19 45 | 18 19 | 10 14 | 04 48 | 06 03 |
| 55 | 19 59 | 18 26 | 10 05 | 04 26 | 05 39 |
| 56 | 20 15 | 18 34 | 09 57 | 04 03 | 05 15 |
| 57 | 20 31 | 18 42 | 09 48 | 03 39 | 04 48 |
| 58 | 20 48 | 18 50 | 09 39 | 03 15 | 04 20 |
| 59 | 21 05 | 18 58 | 09 29 | 02 50 | 03 50 |
| 60 | 21♌24 | 19♍07 | 09♎20 | 02♏23 | 03♐18 |

**7h 4m 0s — 106° 0' 0" — 14 ♋ 44**

| LAT. | 11 | 12 | ASC | 2 | 3 |
|---|---|---|---|---|---|
| 0 | 13♌32 | 14♍48 | 17♎21 | 18♏28 | 17♐07 |
| 5 | 14 02 | 15 10 | 16 44 | 17 26 | 16 28 |
| 10 | 14 32 | 15 31 | 16 09 | 16 26 | 15 49 |
| 15 | 15 02 | 15 52 | 15 35 | 15 26 | 15 08 |
| 20 | 15 33 | 16 13 | 15 02 | 14 25 | 14 26 |
| 21 | 15 40 | 16 18 | 14 55 | 14 13 | 14 17 |
| 22 | 15 46 | 16 22 | 14 48 | 14 01 | 14 08 |
| 23 | 15 53 | 16 26 | 14 42 | 13 48 | 13 59 |
| 24 | 16 00 | 16 30 | 14 35 | 13 36 | 13 50 |
| 25 | 16 06 | 16 35 | 14 29 | 13 23 | 13 41 |
| 26 | 16 13 | 16 39 | 14 22 | 13 10 | 13 31 |
| 27 | 16 20 | 16 43 | 14 16 | 12 57 | 13 22 |
| 28 | 16 27 | 16 48 | 14 09 | 12 44 | 13 12 |
| 29 | 16 34 | 16 52 | 14 02 | 12 31 | 13 02 |
| 30 | 16 41 | 16 57 | 13 56 | 12 17 | 12 52 |
| 31 | 16 49 | 17 01 | 13 49 | 12 04 | 12 41 |
| 32 | 16 56 | 17 06 | 13 42 | 11 50 | 12 31 |
| 33 | 17 04 | 17 10 | 13 35 | 11 36 | 12 20 |
| 34 | 17 11 | 17 15 | 13 29 | 11 22 | 12 09 |
| 35 | 17 19 | 17 20 | 13 22 | 11 08 | 11 58 |
| 36 | 17 27 | 17 24 | 13 15 | 10 53 | 11 46 |
| 37 | 17 36 | 17 29 | 13 08 | 10 39 | 11 34 |
| 38 | 17 44 | 17 34 | 13 01 | 10 24 | 11 22 |
| 39 | 17 53 | 17 39 | 12 54 | 10 08 | 11 09 |
| 40 | 18 01 | 17 44 | 12 46 | 09 53 | 10 56 |
| 41 | 18 10 | 17 49 | 12 39 | 09 37 | 10 43 |
| 42 | 18 20 | 17 54 | 12 32 | 09 21 | 10 29 |
| 43 | 18 29 | 18 00 | 12 24 | 09 04 | 10 15 |
| 44 | 18 39 | 18 05 | 12 17 | 08 47 | 10 00 |
| 45 | 18 49 | 18 11 | 12 09 | 08 30 | 09 45 |
| 46 | 19 00 | 18 16 | 12 02 | 08 13 | 09 29 |
| 47 | 19 10 | 18 22 | 11 54 | 07 55 | 09 12 |
| 48 | 19 21 | 18 28 | 11 46 | 07 36 | 08 55 |
| 49 | 19 33 | 18 34 | 11 38 | 07 17 | 08 37 |
| 50 | 19 45 | 18 40 | 11 29 | 06 57 | 08 19 |
| 51 | 19 57 | 18 46 | 11 21 | 06 37 | 07 59 |
| 52 | 20 10 | 18 52 | 11 12 | 06 17 | 07 39 |
| 53 | 20 23 | 18 59 | 11 04 | 05 56 | 07 17 |
| 54 | 20 37 | 19 06 | 10 55 | 05 34 | 06 55 |
| 55 | 20 51 | 19 13 | 10 46 | 05 11 | 06 31 |
| 56 | 21 06 | 19 20 | 10 36 | 04 48 | 06 05 |
| 57 | 21 22 | 19 27 | 10 27 | 04 24 | 05 39 |
| 58 | 21 39 | 19 35 | 10 17 | 03 59 | 05 10 |
| 59 | 21 56 | 19 42 | 10 07 | 03 33 | 04 40 |
| 60 | 22♌14 | 19♍51 | 09♎57 | 03♏06 | 04♐07 |

**7h 8m 0s — 107° 0' 0" — 15 ♋ 40**

| LAT. | 11 | 12 | ASC | 2 | 3 |
|---|---|---|---|---|---|
| 0 | 14♌32 | 15♍53 | 18♎26 | 19♏27 | 18♐02 |
| 5 | 15 01 | 16 13 | 17 46 | 18 25 | 17 23 |
| 10 | 15 31 | 16 33 | 17 09 | 17 24 | 16 44 |
| 15 | 16 01 | 16 53 | 16 33 | 16 23 | 16 03 |
| 20 | 16 32 | 17 12 | 15 58 | 15 21 | 15 21 |
| 21 | 16 38 | 17 16 | 15 51 | 15 09 | 15 12 |
| 22 | 16 44 | 17 20 | 15 44 | 14 56 | 15 03 |
| 23 | 16 51 | 17 24 | 15 37 | 14 43 | 14 54 |
| 24 | 16 57 | 17 28 | 15 30 | 14 31 | 14 45 |
| 25 | 17 04 | 17 32 | 15 23 | 14 18 | 14 35 |
| 26 | 17 10 | 17 36 | 15 16 | 14 05 | 14 26 |
| 27 | 17 17 | 17 40 | 15 09 | 13 51 | 14 16 |
| 28 | 17 24 | 17 44 | 15 02 | 13 38 | 14 06 |
| 29 | 17 31 | 17 48 | 14 55 | 13 25 | 13 56 |
| 30 | 17 38 | 17 53 | 14 48 | 13 11 | 13 46 |
| 31 | 17 45 | 17 57 | 14 41 | 12 57 | 13 36 |
| 32 | 17 53 | 18 01 | 14 33 | 12 43 | 13 25 |
| 33 | 18 00 | 18 05 | 14 26 | 12 29 | 13 14 |
| 34 | 18 08 | 18 10 | 14 19 | 12 15 | 13 03 |
| 35 | 18 16 | 18 14 | 14 12 | 12 00 | 12 52 |
| 36 | 18 23 | 18 18 | 14 04 | 11 46 | 12 40 |
| 37 | 18 32 | 18 23 | 13 57 | 11 31 | 12 28 |
| 38 | 18 40 | 18 27 | 13 49 | 11 15 | 12 16 |
| 39 | 18 48 | 18 32 | 13 42 | 11 00 | 12 03 |
| 40 | 18 57 | 18 37 | 13 34 | 10 44 | 11 50 |
| 41 | 19 06 | 18 41 | 13 27 | 10 28 | 11 37 |
| 42 | 19 15 | 18 46 | 13 19 | 10 11 | 11 23 |
| 43 | 19 24 | 18 51 | 13 11 | 09 54 | 11 08 |
| 44 | 19 34 | 18 56 | 13 03 | 09 37 | 10 53 |
| 45 | 19 44 | 19 01 | 12 55 | 09 20 | 10 38 |
| 46 | 19 54 | 19 06 | 12 47 | 09 02 | 10 22 |
| 47 | 20 05 | 19 12 | 12 38 | 08 43 | 10 05 |
| 48 | 20 15 | 19 17 | 12 30 | 08 24 | 09 48 |
| 49 | 20 27 | 19 23 | 12 21 | 08 05 | 09 30 |
| 50 | 20 38 | 19 28 | 12 12 | 07 45 | 09 11 |
| 51 | 20 50 | 19 34 | 12 03 | 07 25 | 08 51 |
| 52 | 21 03 | 19 40 | 11 54 | 07 04 | 08 31 |
| 53 | 21 16 | 19 46 | 11 45 | 06 42 | 08 09 |
| 54 | 21 29 | 19 52 | 11 36 | 06 19 | 07 46 |
| 55 | 21 43 | 19 59 | 11 26 | 05 56 | 07 22 |
| 56 | 21 58 | 20 05 | 11 16 | 05 33 | 06 56 |
| 57 | 22 14 | 20 12 | 11 06 | 05 08 | 06 29 |
| 58 | 22 30 | 20 19 | 10 56 | 04 42 | 06 00 |
| 59 | 22 47 | 20 26 | 10 45 | 04 16 | 05 30 |
| 60 | 23♌04 | 20♍34 | 10♎34 | 03♏48 | 04♐57 |

**7h 12m 0s — 108° 0' 0" — 16 ♋ 36**

| LAT. | 11 | 12 | ASC | 2 | 3 |
|---|---|---|---|---|---|
| 0 | 15♌32 | 16♍57 | 19♎30 | 20♏26 | 18♐58 |
| 5 | 16 01 | 17 16 | 18 48 | 19 24 | 18 19 |
| 10 | 16 30 | 17 35 | 18 09 | 18 22 | 17 39 |
| 15 | 17 00 | 17 53 | 17 31 | 17 20 | 16 58 |
| 20 | 17 30 | 18 11 | 16 54 | 16 17 | 16 16 |
| 21 | 17 36 | 18 15 | 16 46 | 16 04 | 16 07 |
| 22 | 17 42 | 18 18 | 16 39 | 15 52 | 15 58 |
| 23 | 17 49 | 18 22 | 16 32 | 15 39 | 15 49 |
| 24 | 17 55 | 18 26 | 16 24 | 15 26 | 15 39 |
| 25 | 18 01 | 18 29 | 16 17 | 15 12 | 15 30 |
| 26 | 18 08 | 18 33 | 16 09 | 14 59 | 15 21 |
| 27 | 18 15 | 18 37 | 16 02 | 14 46 | 15 11 |
| 28 | 18 21 | 18 41 | 15 55 | 14 32 | 15 01 |
| 29 | 18 28 | 18 44 | 15 47 | 14 19 | 14 51 |
| 30 | 18 35 | 18 48 | 15 40 | 14 05 | 14 41 |
| 31 | 18 42 | 18 52 | 15 32 | 13 51 | 14 30 |
| 32 | 18 50 | 18 56 | 15 25 | 13 37 | 14 20 |
| 33 | 18 57 | 19 00 | 15 17 | 13 22 | 14 09 |
| 34 | 19 04 | 19 04 | 15 09 | 13 08 | 13 57 |
| 35 | 19 12 | 19 08 | 15 02 | 12 53 | 13 46 |
| 36 | 19 20 | 19 12 | 14 54 | 12 38 | 13 34 |
| 37 | 19 28 | 19 16 | 14 46 | 12 22 | 13 22 |
| 38 | 19 36 | 19 20 | 14 38 | 12 07 | 13 10 |
| 39 | 19 44 | 19 25 | 14 30 | 11 51 | 12 57 |
| 40 | 19 52 | 19 29 | 14 22 | 11 35 | 12 44 |
| 41 | 20 01 | 19 33 | 14 14 | 11 18 | 12 30 |
| 42 | 20 10 | 19 38 | 14 06 | 11 02 | 12 16 |
| 43 | 20 19 | 19 42 | 13 57 | 10 44 | 12 02 |
| 44 | 20 29 | 19 47 | 13 49 | 10 27 | 11 47 |
| 45 | 20 38 | 19 52 | 13 40 | 10 09 | 11 31 |
| 46 | 20 48 | 19 57 | 13 32 | 09 51 | 11 15 |
| 47 | 20 59 | 20 01 | 13 23 | 09 32 | 10 58 |
| 48 | 21 09 | 20 06 | 13 14 | 09 13 | 10 41 |
| 49 | 21 20 | 20 12 | 13 05 | 08 53 | 10 23 |
| 50 | 21 32 | 20 17 | 12 55 | 08 33 | 10 04 |
| 51 | 21 44 | 20 22 | 12 46 | 08 12 | 09 44 |
| 52 | 21 56 | 20 28 | 12 36 | 07 50 | 09 23 |
| 53 | 22 09 | 20 33 | 12 27 | 07 28 | 09 01 |
| 54 | 22 22 | 20 39 | 12 17 | 07 05 | 08 38 |
| 55 | 22 36 | 20 45 | 12 06 | 06 42 | 08 13 |
| 56 | 22 50 | 20 51 | 11 56 | 06 17 | 07 47 |
| 57 | 23 05 | 20 57 | 11 45 | 05 52 | 07 20 |
| 58 | 23 21 | 21 04 | 11 34 | 05 26 | 06 51 |
| 59 | 23 37 | 21 11 | 11 23 | 04 59 | 06 19 |
| 60 | 23♌55 | 21♍17 | 11♎12 | 04♏31 | 05♐46 |

**7h 16m 0s — 109° 0' 0" — 17 ♋ 32**

| LAT. | 11 | 12 | ASC | 2 | 3 |
|---|---|---|---|---|---|
| 0 | 16♌33 | 18♍02 | 20♎34 | 21♏25 | 19♐53 |
| 5 | 17 01 | 18 20 | 19 50 | 20 22 | 19 14 |
| 10 | 17 30 | 18 37 | 19 09 | 19 19 | 18 34 |
| 15 | 17 58 | 18 53 | 18 29 | 18 16 | 17 53 |
| 20 | 18 28 | 19 10 | 17 50 | 17 13 | 17 10 |
| 21 | 18 34 | 19 13 | 17 42 | 17 00 | 17 02 |
| 22 | 18 40 | 19 17 | 17 34 | 16 47 | 16 53 |
| 23 | 18 47 | 19 20 | 17 26 | 16 34 | 16 43 |
| 24 | 18 53 | 19 23 | 17 19 | 16 20 | 16 34 |
| 25 | 18 59 | 19 27 | 17 11 | 16 07 | 16 25 |
| 26 | 19 06 | 19 30 | 17 03 | 15 54 | 16 15 |
| 27 | 19 12 | 19 34 | 16 55 | 15 40 | 16 05 |
| 28 | 19 19 | 19 37 | 16 47 | 15 26 | 15 56 |
| 29 | 19 26 | 19 41 | 16 40 | 15 12 | 15 45 |
| 30 | 19 32 | 19 44 | 16 32 | 14 58 | 15 35 |
| 31 | 19 39 | 19 48 | 16 24 | 14 44 | 15 25 |
| 32 | 19 46 | 19 51 | 16 16 | 14 30 | 15 14 |
| 33 | 19 54 | 19 55 | 16 08 | 14 15 | 15 03 |
| 34 | 20 01 | 19 59 | 16 00 | 14 00 | 14 52 |
| 35 | 20 08 | 20 02 | 15 52 | 13 45 | 14 40 |
| 36 | 20 16 | 20 06 | 15 43 | 13 30 | 14 28 |
| 37 | 20 24 | 20 10 | 15 35 | 13 14 | 14 16 |
| 38 | 20 32 | 20 14 | 15 27 | 12 58 | 14 04 |
| 39 | 20 40 | 20 18 | 15 18 | 12 42 | 13 51 |
| 40 | 20 48 | 20 22 | 15 10 | 12 26 | 13 38 |
| 41 | 20 57 | 20 26 | 15 01 | 12 09 | 13 24 |
| 42 | 21 05 | 20 30 | 14 53 | 11 52 | 13 10 |
| 43 | 21 14 | 20 34 | 14 44 | 11 35 | 12 55 |
| 44 | 21 24 | 20 38 | 14 35 | 11 17 | 12 40 |
| 45 | 21 33 | 20 42 | 14 26 | 10 58 | 12 24 |
| 46 | 21 43 | 20 47 | 14 17 | 10 40 | 12 08 |
| 47 | 21 53 | 20 51 | 14 07 | 10 21 | 11 51 |
| 48 | 22 03 | 20 56 | 13 58 | 10 01 | 11 34 |
| 49 | 22 14 | 21 01 | 13 48 | 09 41 | 11 15 |
| 50 | 22 25 | 21 05 | 13 38 | 09 20 | 10 56 |
| 51 | 22 37 | 21 10 | 13 28 | 08 59 | 10 36 |
| 52 | 22 49 | 21 15 | 13 18 | 08 37 | 10 15 |
| 53 | 23 01 | 21 20 | 13 08 | 08 14 | 09 53 |
| 54 | 23 14 | 21 26 | 12 57 | 07 51 | 09 29 |
| 55 | 23 28 | 21 31 | 12 47 | 07 27 | 09 05 |
| 56 | 23 42 | 21 37 | 12 36 | 07 02 | 08 38 |
| 57 | 23 57 | 21 43 | 12 24 | 06 36 | 08 11 |
| 58 | 24 12 | 21 48 | 12 13 | 06 10 | 07 41 |
| 59 | 24 28 | 21 55 | 12 01 | 05 42 | 07 09 |
| 60 | 24♌45 | 22♍01 | 11♎49 | 05♏13 | 06♐35 |

**7h 20m 0s — 110° 0' 0" — 18 ♋ 28**

| LAT. | 11 | 12 | ASC | 2 | 3 |
|---|---|---|---|---|---|
| 0 | 17♌33 | 19♍07 | 21♎38 | 22♏25 | 20♐49 |
| 5 | 18 01 | 19 23 | 20 52 | 21 20 | 20 09 |
| 10 | 18 29 | 19 39 | 20 09 | 20 17 | 19 29 |
| 15 | 18 58 | 19 54 | 19 27 | 19 13 | 18 48 |
| 20 | 19 27 | 20 09 | 18 46 | 18 08 | 18 05 |
| 21 | 19 33 | 20 12 | 18 37 | 17 55 | 17 56 |
| 22 | 19 39 | 20 15 | 18 29 | 17 42 | 17 47 |
| 23 | 19 45 | 20 18 | 18 21 | 17 29 | 17 38 |
| 24 | 19 51 | 20 21 | 18 13 | 17 15 | 17 29 |
| 25 | 19 57 | 20 24 | 18 05 | 17 02 | 17 19 |
| 26 | 20 04 | 20 27 | 17 57 | 16 48 | 17 10 |
| 27 | 20 10 | 20 31 | 17 48 | 16 34 | 17 00 |
| 28 | 20 16 | 20 34 | 17 40 | 16 20 | 16 50 |
| 29 | 20 23 | 20 37 | 17 32 | 16 06 | 16 40 |
| 30 | 20 30 | 20 40 | 17 24 | 15 52 | 16 30 |
| 31 | 20 37 | 20 43 | 17 15 | 15 37 | 16 19 |
| 32 | 20 43 | 20 47 | 17 07 | 15 23 | 16 08 |
| 33 | 20 50 | 20 50 | 16 58 | 15 08 | 15 57 |
| 34 | 20 58 | 20 53 | 16 50 | 14 53 | 15 46 |
| 35 | 21 05 | 20 57 | 16 41 | 14 37 | 15 34 |
| 36 | 21 12 | 21 00 | 16 33 | 14 22 | 15 22 |
| 37 | 21 20 | 21 03 | 16 24 | 14 06 | 15 10 |
| 38 | 21 28 | 21 07 | 16 15 | 13 50 | 14 58 |
| 39 | 21 36 | 21 10 | 16 07 | 13 33 | 14 45 |
| 40 | 21 44 | 21 14 | 15 58 | 13 17 | 14 31 |
| 41 | 21 52 | 21 18 | 15 49 | 13 00 | 14 18 |
| 42 | 22 01 | 21 21 | 15 39 | 12 42 | 14 03 |
| 43 | 22 10 | 21 25 | 15 30 | 12 25 | 13 49 |
| 44 | 22 19 | 21 29 | 15 21 | 12 06 | 13 33 |
| 45 | 22 28 | 21 33 | 15 11 | 11 48 | 13 18 |
| 46 | 22 38 | 21 37 | 15 02 | 11 29 | 13 01 |
| 47 | 22 47 | 21 41 | 14 52 | 11 09 | 12 44 |
| 48 | 22 58 | 21 45 | 14 42 | 10 49 | 12 27 |
| 49 | 23 08 | 21 49 | 14 32 | 10 29 | 12 08 |
| 50 | 23 19 | 21 54 | 14 21 | 10 08 | 11 49 |
| 51 | 23 30 | 21 58 | 14 11 | 09 46 | 11 28 |
| 52 | 23 42 | 22 03 | 14 00 | 09 23 | 11 07 |
| 53 | 23 54 | 22 08 | 13 49 | 09 00 | 10 45 |
| 54 | 24 07 | 22 12 | 13 38 | 08 37 | 10 21 |
| 55 | 24 20 | 22 17 | 13 27 | 08 12 | 09 56 |
| 56 | 24 34 | 22 22 | 13 15 | 07 47 | 09 30 |
| 57 | 24 48 | 22 28 | 13 03 | 07 20 | 09 01 |
| 58 | 25 03 | 22 33 | 12 51 | 06 53 | 08 31 |
| 59 | 25 19 | 22 39 | 12 39 | 06 25 | 07 59 |
| 60 | 25♌35 | 22♍44 | 12♎26 | 05♏56 | 07♐25 |

**7h 24m 0s — 111° 0' 0" — 19 ♋ 24**

| LAT. | 11 | 12 | ASC | 2 | 3 |
|---|---|---|---|---|---|
| 0 | 18♌34 | 20♍12 | 22♎42 | 23♏23 | 21♐44 |
| 5 | 19 01 | 20 27 | 21 54 | 22 18 | 21 04 |
| 10 | 19 29 | 20 41 | 21 09 | 21 14 | 20 24 |
| 15 | 19 57 | 20 54 | 20 25 | 20 09 | 19 43 |
| 20 | 20 25 | 21 08 | 19 42 | 19 04 | 19 00 |
| 21 | 20 31 | 21 11 | 19 33 | 18 51 | 18 51 |
| 22 | 20 37 | 21 13 | 19 24 | 18 37 | 18 42 |
| 23 | 20 43 | 21 16 | 19 16 | 18 24 | 18 33 |
| 24 | 20 49 | 21 19 | 19 07 | 18 10 | 18 24 |
| 25 | 20 55 | 21 22 | 18 59 | 17 56 | 18 14 |
| 26 | 21 01 | 21 25 | 18 50 | 17 42 | 18 04 |
| 27 | 21 08 | 21 27 | 18 42 | 17 28 | 17 55 |
| 28 | 21 14 | 21 30 | 18 33 | 17 14 | 17 45 |
| 29 | 21 21 | 21 33 | 18 24 | 17 00 | 17 34 |
| 30 | 21 27 | 21 36 | 18 16 | 16 45 | 17 24 |
| 31 | 21 34 | 21 39 | 18 07 | 16 31 | 17 13 |
| 32 | 21 41 | 21 42 | 17 58 | 16 16 | 17 03 |
| 33 | 21 47 | 21 45 | 17 49 | 16 01 | 16 51 |
| 34 | 21 54 | 21 48 | 17 40 | 15 45 | 16 40 |
| 35 | 22 02 | 21 51 | 17 31 | 15 30 | 16 28 |
| 36 | 22 09 | 21 54 | 17 22 | 15 14 | 16 16 |
| 37 | 22 16 | 21 57 | 17 13 | 14 58 | 16 04 |
| 38 | 22 24 | 22 00 | 17 04 | 14 41 | 15 51 |
| 39 | 22 32 | 22 03 | 16 55 | 14 25 | 15 38 |
| 40 | 22 40 | 22 07 | 16 45 | 14 08 | 15 25 |
| 41 | 22 48 | 22 10 | 16 36 | 13 50 | 15 11 |
| 42 | 22 56 | 22 13 | 16 26 | 13 33 | 14 57 |
| 43 | 23 05 | 22 17 | 16 16 | 13 15 | 14 42 |
| 44 | 23 14 | 22 20 | 16 07 | 12 56 | 14 27 |
| 45 | 23 23 | 22 24 | 15 57 | 12 37 | 14 11 |
| 46 | 23 32 | 22 27 | 15 47 | 12 18 | 13 54 |
| 47 | 23 42 | 22 31 | 15 36 | 11 58 | 13 37 |
| 48 | 23 52 | 22 35 | 15 26 | 11 37 | 13 19 |
| 49 | 24 02 | 22 39 | 15 15 | 11 16 | 13 01 |
| 50 | 24 13 | 22 42 | 15 04 | 10 55 | 12 41 |
| 51 | 24 24 | 22 46 | 14 53 | 10 33 | 12 21 |
| 52 | 24 35 | 22 51 | 14 42 | 10 10 | 11 59 |
| 53 | 24 47 | 22 55 | 14 31 | 09 47 | 11 37 |
| 54 | 24 59 | 22 59 | 14 19 | 09 22 | 11 13 |
| 55 | 25 12 | 23 04 | 14 07 | 08 57 | 10 48 |
| 56 | 25 26 | 23 08 | 13 55 | 08 31 | 10 21 |
| 57 | 25 40 | 23 13 | 13 42 | 08 05 | 09 52 |
| 58 | 25 54 | 23 18 | 13 30 | 07 37 | 09 22 |
| 59 | 26 10 | 23 23 | 13 17 | 07 08 | 08 49 |
| 60 | 26♌26 | 23♍28 | 13♎03 | 06♏38 | 08♐14 |

# Placidus Table of Houses for Latitudes 0° to 60° North

7h 28m 0s — 112° 0' 0" — 20 ♋ 20

| LAT. | 11 | 12 | ASC | 2 | 3 |
|---|---|---|---|---|---|
| 0 | 19♌35 | 21♍17 | 23♎46 | 24♏22 | 22♐39 |
| 5 | 20 02 | 21 30 | 22 56 | 23 16 | 22 00 |
| 10 | 20 29 | 21 43 | 22 08 | 22 11 | 21 20 |
| 15 | 20 56 | 21 55 | 21 22 | 21 06 | 20 38 |
| 20 | 21 24 | 22 07 | 20 37 | 19 59 | 19 55 |
| 21 | 21 30 | 22 09 | 20 28 | 19 46 | 19 46 |
| 22 | 21 36 | 22 12 | 20 19 | 19 32 | 19 37 |
| 23 | 21 42 | 22 14 | 20 11 | 19 18 | 19 28 |
| 24 | 21 47 | 22 17 | 20 02 | 19 05 | 19 18 |
| 25 | 21 53 | 22 19 | 19 53 | 18 51 | 19 09 |
| 26 | 22 00 | 22 22 | 19 44 | 18 37 | 18 59 |
| 27 | 22 06 | 22 24 | 19 35 | 18 22 | 18 49 |
| 28 | 22 12 | 22 27 | 19 26 | 18 08 | 18 39 |
| 29 | 22 18 | 22 29 | 19 17 | 17 53 | 18 29 |
| 30 | 22 25 | 22 32 | 19 07 | 17 39 | 18 18 |
| 31 | 22 31 | 22 34 | 18 58 | 17 24 | 18 08 |
| 32 | 22 38 | 22 37 | 18 49 | 17 09 | 17 57 |
| 33 | 22 45 | 22 40 | 18 40 | 16 53 | 17 46 |
| 34 | 22 51 | 22 42 | 18 31 | 16 38 | 17 34 |
| 35 | 22 58 | 22 45 | 18 21 | 16 22 | 17 23 |
| 36 | 23 06 | 22 48 | 18 12 | 16 06 | 17 11 |
| 37 | 23 13 | 22 51 | 18 02 | 15 49 | 16 58 |
| 38 | 23 20 | 22 53 | 17 53 | 15 33 | 16 45 |
| 39 | 23 28 | 22 56 | 17 43 | 15 16 | 16 32 |
| 40 | 23 36 | 22 59 | 17 33 | 14 59 | 16 19 |
| 41 | 23 44 | 23 02 | 17 23 | 14 41 | 16 05 |
| 42 | 23 52 | 23 05 | 17 13 | 14 23 | 15 51 |
| 43 | 24 00 | 23 08 | 17 03 | 14 04 | 15 36 |
| 44 | 24 09 | 23 11 | 16 53 | 13 46 | 15 20 |
| 45 | 24 18 | 23 14 | 16 42 | 13 26 | 15 04 |
| 46 | 24 27 | 23 18 | 16 31 | 13 07 | 14 48 |
| 47 | 24 36 | 23 21 | 16 21 | 12 46 | 14 30 |
| 48 | 24 46 | 23 24 | 16 10 | 12 26 | 14 12 |
| 49 | 24 56 | 23 28 | 15 59 | 12 04 | 13 54 |
| 50 | 25 07 | 23 31 | 15 47 | 11 42 | 13 34 |
| 51 | 25 17 | 23 35 | 15 36 | 11 20 | 13 13 |
| 52 | 25 29 | 23 38 | 15 24 | 10 57 | 12 52 |
| 53 | 25 40 | 23 42 | 15 12 | 10 33 | 12 29 |
| 54 | 25 52 | 23 46 | 15 00 | 10 08 | 12 05 |
| 55 | 26 05 | 23 50 | 14 47 | 09 42 | 11 39 |
| 56 | 26 18 | 23 54 | 14 35 | 09 16 | 11 12 |
| 57 | 26 31 | 23 58 | 14 22 | 08 49 | 10 43 |
| 58 | 26 46 | 24 02 | 14 08 | 08 20 | 10 13 |
| 59 | 27 01 | 24 07 | 13 54 | 07 51 | 09 40 |
| 60 | 27♌16 | 24♍11 | 13♎40 | 07♏20 | 09♐04 |

7h 32m 0s — 113° 0' 0" — 21 ♋ 17

| LAT. | 11 | 12 | ASC | 2 | 3 |
|---|---|---|---|---|---|
| 0 | 20♌36 | 22♍23 | 24♎50 | 25♏21 | 23♐34 |
| 5 | 21 03 | 22 34 | 23 58 | 24 14 | 22 55 |
| 10 | 21 29 | 22 45 | 23 08 | 23 08 | 22 15 |
| 15 | 21 56 | 22 55 | 22 20 | 22 02 | 21 33 |
| 20 | 22 23 | 23 06 | 21 33 | 20 55 | 20 50 |
| 21 | 22 29 | 23 08 | 21 24 | 20 41 | 20 41 |
| 22 | 22 34 | 23 10 | 21 14 | 20 27 | 20 32 |
| 23 | 22 40 | 23 12 | 21 05 | 20 13 | 20 22 |
| 24 | 22 46 | 23 15 | 20 56 | 19 59 | 20 13 |
| 25 | 22 52 | 23 17 | 20 46 | 19 45 | 20 03 |
| 26 | 22 58 | 23 19 | 20 37 | 19 31 | 19 54 |
| 27 | 23 04 | 23 21 | 20 28 | 19 16 | 19 44 |
| 28 | 23 10 | 23 23 | 20 18 | 19 02 | 19 34 |
| 29 | 23 16 | 23 26 | 20 09 | 18 47 | 19 23 |
| 30 | 23 22 | 23 28 | 19 59 | 18 32 | 19 13 |
| 31 | 23 29 | 23 30 | 19 50 | 18 17 | 19 02 |
| 32 | 23 35 | 23 32 | 19 40 | 18 02 | 18 51 |
| 33 | 23 42 | 23 35 | 19 30 | 17 46 | 18 40 |
| 34 | 23 48 | 23 37 | 19 21 | 17 30 | 18 28 |
| 35 | 23 55 | 23 39 | 19 11 | 17 14 | 18 17 |
| 36 | 24 02 | 23 42 | 19 01 | 16 58 | 18 05 |
| 37 | 24 09 | 23 44 | 18 51 | 16 41 | 17 52 |
| 38 | 24 17 | 23 47 | 18 41 | 16 24 | 17 39 |
| 39 | 24 24 | 23 49 | 18 31 | 16 07 | 17 26 |
| 40 | 24 32 | 23 52 | 18 21 | 15 49 | 17 13 |
| 41 | 24 40 | 23 54 | 18 10 | 15 31 | 16 59 |
| 42 | 24 48 | 23 57 | 18 00 | 15 13 | 16 44 |
| 43 | 24 56 | 24 00 | 17 49 | 14 54 | 16 29 |
| 44 | 25 04 | 24 02 | 17 38 | 14 35 | 16 14 |
| 45 | 25 13 | 24 05 | 17 28 | 14 16 | 15 58 |
| 46 | 25 22 | 24 08 | 17 16 | 13 56 | 15 41 |
| 47 | 25 31 | 24 11 | 17 05 | 13 35 | 15 24 |
| 48 | 25 41 | 24 14 | 16 54 | 13 14 | 15 05 |
| 49 | 25 50 | 24 17 | 16 42 | 12 52 | 14 46 |
| 50 | 26 01 | 24 20 | 16 30 | 12 30 | 14 27 |
| 51 | 26 11 | 24 23 | 16 18 | 12 07 | 14 06 |
| 52 | 26 22 | 24 26 | 16 06 | 11 43 | 13 44 |
| 53 | 26 33 | 24 29 | 15 53 | 11 19 | 13 21 |
| 54 | 26 45 | 24 33 | 15 41 | 10 54 | 12 57 |
| 55 | 26 57 | 24 36 | 15 28 | 10 28 | 12 31 |
| 56 | 27 10 | 24 40 | 15 14 | 10 01 | 12 03 |
| 57 | 27 23 | 24 43 | 15 01 | 09 33 | 11 34 |
| 58 | 27 37 | 24 47 | 14 47 | 09 04 | 11 03 |
| 59 | 27 52 | 24 51 | 14 32 | 08 34 | 10 30 |
| 60 | 28♌07 | 24♍55 | 14♎18 | 08♏03 | 09♐54 |

7h 36m 0s — 114° 0' 0" — 22 ♋ 13

| LAT. | 11 | 12 | ASC | 2 | 3 |
|---|---|---|---|---|---|
| 0 | 21♌37 | 23♍28 | 25♎53 | 26♏19 | 24♐30 |
| 5 | 22 03 | 23 38 | 24 59 | 25 11 | 23 50 |
| 10 | 22 29 | 23 47 | 24 07 | 24 05 | 23 10 |
| 15 | 22 55 | 23 56 | 23 18 | 22 58 | 22 28 |
| 20 | 23 22 | 24 05 | 22 29 | 21 50 | 21 45 |
| 21 | 23 28 | 24 07 | 22 19 | 21 36 | 21 35 |
| 22 | 23 33 | 24 09 | 22 09 | 21 22 | 21 26 |
| 23 | 23 39 | 24 11 | 22 00 | 21 08 | 21 17 |
| 24 | 23 44 | 24 12 | 21 50 | 20 54 | 21 08 |
| 25 | 23 50 | 24 14 | 21 40 | 20 39 | 20 58 |
| 26 | 23 56 | 24 16 | 21 30 | 20 25 | 20 48 |
| 27 | 24 02 | 24 18 | 21 21 | 20 10 | 20 38 |
| 28 | 24 08 | 24 20 | 21 11 | 19 55 | 20 28 |
| 29 | 24 14 | 24 22 | 21 01 | 19 40 | 20 18 |
| 30 | 24 20 | 24 24 | 20 51 | 19 25 | 20 07 |
| 31 | 24 26 | 24 26 | 20 41 | 19 10 | 19 57 |
| 32 | 24 33 | 24 28 | 20 31 | 18 54 | 19 46 |
| 33 | 24 39 | 24 30 | 20 21 | 18 39 | 19 34 |
| 34 | 24 46 | 24 32 | 20 11 | 18 22 | 19 23 |
| 35 | 24 52 | 24 34 | 20 01 | 18 06 | 19 11 |
| 36 | 24 59 | 24 36 | 19 50 | 17 50 | 18 59 |
| 37 | 25 06 | 24 38 | 19 40 | 17 33 | 18 46 |
| 38 | 25 13 | 24 40 | 19 30 | 17 16 | 18 33 |
| 39 | 25 21 | 24 42 | 19 19 | 16 58 | 18 20 |
| 40 | 25 28 | 24 44 | 19 08 | 16 40 | 18 07 |
| 41 | 25 36 | 24 46 | 18 58 | 16 22 | 17 53 |
| 42 | 25 43 | 24 49 | 18 47 | 16 03 | 17 38 |
| 43 | 25 51 | 24 51 | 18 36 | 15 44 | 17 23 |
| 44 | 26 00 | 24 53 | 18 24 | 15 25 | 17 07 |
| 45 | 26 08 | 24 56 | 18 13 | 15 05 | 16 51 |
| 46 | 26 17 | 24 58 | 18 01 | 14 44 | 16 34 |
| 47 | 26 26 | 25 01 | 17 50 | 14 24 | 16 17 |
| 48 | 26 35 | 25 03 | 17 38 | 14 02 | 15 58 |
| 49 | 26 45 | 25 06 | 17 26 | 13 40 | 15 39 |
| 50 | 26 55 | 25 08 | 17 13 | 13 17 | 15 19 |
| 51 | 27 05 | 25 11 | 17 01 | 12 54 | 14 58 |
| 52 | 27 15 | 25 14 | 16 48 | 12 30 | 14 36 |
| 53 | 27 26 | 25 16 | 16 35 | 12 05 | 14 13 |
| 54 | 27 38 | 25 19 | 16 21 | 11 39 | 13 49 |
| 55 | 27 50 | 25 22 | 16 08 | 11 13 | 13 23 |
| 56 | 28 02 | 25 25 | 15 54 | 10 45 | 12 55 |
| 57 | 28 15 | 25 29 | 15 40 | 10 17 | 12 25 |
| 58 | 28 29 | 25 32 | 15 25 | 09 47 | 11 54 |
| 59 | 28 43 | 25 35 | 15 10 | 09 17 | 11 20 |
| 60 | 28♌58 | 25♍39 | 14♎55 | 08♏45 | 10♐44 |

7h 40m 0s — 115° 0' 0" — 23 ♋ 10

| LAT. | 11 | 12 | ASC | 2 | 3 |
|---|---|---|---|---|---|
| 0 | 22♌39 | 24♍33 | 26♎57 | 27♏17 | 25♐25 |
| 5 | 23 04 | 24 41 | 26 00 | 26 09 | 24 45 |
| 10 | 23 30 | 24 49 | 25 07 | 25 02 | 24 05 |
| 15 | 23 55 | 24 57 | 24 15 | 23 54 | 23 23 |
| 20 | 24 21 | 25 04 | 23 24 | 22 45 | 22 39 |
| 21 | 24 27 | 25 06 | 23 14 | 22 31 | 22 30 |
| 22 | 24 32 | 25 07 | 23 04 | 22 17 | 22 21 |
| 23 | 24 38 | 25 09 | 22 54 | 22 03 | 22 12 |
| 24 | 24 43 | 25 10 | 22 44 | 21 48 | 22 02 |
| 25 | 24 49 | 25 12 | 22 34 | 21 34 | 21 53 |
| 26 | 24 54 | 25 13 | 22 24 | 21 19 | 21 43 |
| 27 | 25 00 | 25 15 | 22 14 | 21 04 | 21 33 |
| 28 | 25 06 | 25 17 | 22 03 | 20 49 | 21 23 |
| 29 | 25 12 | 25 18 | 21 53 | 20 34 | 21 12 |
| 30 | 25 18 | 25 20 | 21 43 | 20 19 | 21 02 |
| 31 | 25 24 | 25 21 | 21 33 | 20 03 | 20 51 |
| 32 | 25 30 | 25 23 | 21 22 | 19 47 | 20 40 |
| 33 | 25 36 | 25 25 | 21 12 | 19 31 | 20 29 |
| 34 | 25 43 | 25 26 | 21 01 | 19 15 | 20 17 |
| 35 | 25 49 | 25 28 | 20 51 | 18 58 | 20 05 |
| 36 | 25 56 | 25 30 | 20 40 | 18 41 | 19 53 |
| 37 | 26 03 | 25 32 | 20 29 | 18 24 | 19 40 |
| 38 | 26 10 | 25 33 | 20 18 | 18 07 | 19 28 |
| 39 | 26 17 | 25 35 | 20 07 | 17 49 | 19 14 |
| 40 | 26 24 | 25 37 | 19 56 | 17 31 | 19 01 |
| 41 | 26 32 | 25 39 | 19 45 | 17 12 | 18 46 |
| 42 | 26 39 | 25 41 | 19 33 | 16 54 | 18 32 |
| 43 | 26 47 | 25 42 | 19 22 | 16 34 | 18 17 |
| 44 | 26 55 | 25 44 | 19 10 | 16 14 | 18 01 |
| 45 | 27 03 | 25 46 | 18 58 | 15 54 | 17 45 |
| 46 | 27 12 | 25 48 | 18 46 | 15 33 | 17 28 |
| 47 | 27 21 | 25 50 | 18 34 | 15 12 | 17 10 |
| 48 | 27 30 | 25 53 | 18 22 | 14 50 | 16 52 |
| 49 | 27 39 | 25 55 | 18 09 | 14 28 | 16 32 |
| 50 | 27 49 | 25 57 | 17 56 | 14 05 | 16 12 |
| 51 | 27 59 | 25 59 | 17 43 | 13 41 | 15 51 |
| 52 | 28 09 | 26 01 | 17 30 | 13 16 | 15 29 |
| 53 | 28 20 | 26 04 | 17 16 | 12 51 | 15 05 |
| 54 | 28 31 | 26 06 | 17 02 | 12 25 | 14 41 |
| 55 | 28 42 | 26 09 | 16 48 | 11 58 | 14 14 |
| 56 | 28 54 | 26 11 | 16 34 | 11 30 | 13 46 |
| 57 | 29 07 | 26 14 | 16 19 | 11 01 | 13 17 |
| 58 | 29 20 | 26 16 | 16 03 | 10 31 | 12 45 |
| 59 | 29 34 | 26 19 | 15 48 | 10 00 | 12 11 |
| 60 | 29♌48 | 26♍22 | 15♎32 | 09♏27 | 11♐34 |

7h 44m 0s — 116° 0' 0" — 24 ♋ 06

| LAT. | 11 | 12 | ASC | 2 | 3 |
|---|---|---|---|---|---|
| 0 | 23♌41 | 25♍38 | 28♎00 | 28♏15 | 26♐20 |
| 5 | 24 05 | 25 45 | 27 02 | 27 06 | 25 40 |
| 10 | 24 30 | 25 51 | 26 06 | 25 58 | 25 00 |
| 15 | 24 55 | 25 57 | 25 13 | 24 50 | 24 18 |
| 20 | 25 21 | 26 03 | 24 20 | 23 40 | 23 34 |
| 21 | 25 26 | 26 05 | 24 10 | 23 26 | 23 25 |
| 22 | 25 31 | 26 06 | 23 59 | 23 12 | 23 16 |
| 23 | 25 37 | 26 07 | 23 49 | 22 57 | 23 06 |
| 24 | 25 42 | 26 08 | 23 38 | 22 43 | 22 57 |
| 25 | 25 47 | 26 10 | 23 28 | 22 28 | 22 47 |
| 26 | 25 53 | 26 11 | 23 17 | 22 13 | 22 38 |
| 27 | 25 59 | 26 12 | 23 07 | 21 58 | 22 28 |
| 28 | 26 04 | 26 13 | 22 56 | 21 43 | 22 17 |
| 29 | 26 10 | 26 15 | 22 45 | 21 27 | 22 07 |
| 30 | 26 16 | 26 16 | 22 35 | 21 12 | 21 56 |
| 31 | 26 22 | 26 17 | 22 24 | 20 56 | 21 45 |
| 32 | 26 28 | 26 18 | 22 13 | 20 40 | 21 34 |
| 33 | 26 34 | 26 20 | 22 02 | 20 24 | 21 23 |
| 34 | 26 40 | 26 21 | 21 51 | 20 07 | 21 11 |
| 35 | 26 47 | 26 22 | 21 40 | 19 50 | 21 00 |
| 36 | 26 53 | 26 24 | 21 29 | 19 33 | 20 47 |
| 37 | 27 00 | 26 25 | 21 18 | 19 16 | 20 35 |
| 38 | 27 07 | 26 27 | 21 07 | 18 58 | 20 22 |
| 39 | 27 13 | 26 28 | 20 55 | 18 40 | 20 08 |
| 40 | 27 21 | 26 29 | 20 44 | 18 22 | 19 55 |
| 41 | 27 28 | 26 31 | 20 32 | 18 03 | 19 40 |
| 42 | 27 35 | 26 32 | 20 20 | 17 44 | 19 26 |
| 43 | 27 43 | 26 34 | 20 08 | 17 24 | 19 10 |
| 44 | 27 51 | 26 36 | 19 56 | 17 04 | 18 55 |
| 45 | 27 59 | 26 37 | 19 44 | 16 43 | 18 38 |
| 46 | 28 07 | 26 39 | 19 31 | 16 22 | 18 21 |
| 47 | 28 16 | 26 40 | 19 18 | 16 01 | 18 03 |
| 48 | 28 24 | 26 42 | 19 06 | 15 38 | 17 45 |
| 49 | 28 33 | 26 44 | 18 52 | 15 16 | 17 25 |
| 50 | 28 43 | 26 45 | 18 39 | 14 52 | 17 05 |
| 51 | 28 52 | 26 47 | 18 25 | 14 28 | 16 44 |
| 52 | 29 03 | 26 49 | 18 12 | 14 03 | 16 21 |
| 53 | 29 13 | 26 51 | 17 57 | 13 37 | 15 58 |
| 54 | 29 24 | 26 53 | 17 43 | 13 11 | 15 33 |
| 55 | 29 35 | 26 55 | 17 28 | 12 43 | 15 06 |
| 56 | 29 47 | 26 57 | 17 13 | 12 15 | 14 38 |
| 57 | 29 59 | 26 59 | 16 58 | 11 45 | 14 08 |
| 58 | 00♍12 | 27 01 | 16 42 | 11 14 | 13 36 |
| 59 | 00 25 | 27 03 | 16 26 | 10 43 | 13 01 |
| 60 | 00♍39 | 27♍06 | 16♎09 | 10♏10 | 12♐24 |

7h 48m 0s — 117° 0' 0" — 25 ♋ 03

| LAT. | 11 | 12 | ASC | 2 | 3 |
|---|---|---|---|---|---|
| 0 | 24♌42 | 26♍44 | 29♎03 | 29♏13 | 27♐15 |
| 5 | 25 07 | 26 49 | 28 03 | 28 03 | 26 35 |
| 10 | 25 31 | 26 53 | 27 05 | 26 55 | 25 55 |
| 15 | 25 55 | 26 58 | 26 10 | 25 46 | 25 13 |
| 20 | 26 20 | 27 03 | 25 15 | 24 35 | 24 29 |
| 21 | 26 25 | 27 03 | 25 05 | 24 21 | 24 20 |
| 22 | 26 30 | 27 04 | 24 54 | 24 06 | 24 11 |
| 23 | 26 36 | 27 05 | 24 43 | 23 52 | 24 01 |
| 24 | 26 41 | 27 06 | 24 32 | 23 37 | 23 52 |
| 25 | 26 46 | 27 07 | 24 21 | 23 22 | 23 42 |
| 26 | 26 52 | 27 08 | 24 10 | 23 07 | 23 32 |
| 27 | 26 57 | 27 09 | 23 59 | 22 52 | 23 22 |
| 28 | 27 03 | 27 10 | 23 48 | 22 36 | 23 12 |
| 29 | 27 08 | 27 11 | 23 37 | 22 21 | 23 02 |
| 30 | 27 14 | 27 12 | 23 26 | 22 05 | 22 51 |
| 31 | 27 20 | 27 13 | 23 15 | 21 49 | 22 40 |
| 32 | 27 26 | 27 14 | 23 04 | 21 33 | 22 29 |
| 33 | 27 32 | 27 15 | 22 53 | 21 16 | 22 17 |
| 34 | 27 38 | 27 16 | 22 41 | 20 59 | 22 06 |
| 35 | 27 44 | 27 17 | 22 30 | 20 42 | 21 54 |
| 36 | 27 50 | 27 18 | 22 18 | 20 25 | 21 42 |
| 37 | 27 57 | 27 19 | 22 07 | 20 07 | 21 29 |
| 38 | 28 03 | 27 20 | 21 55 | 19 49 | 21 16 |
| 39 | 28 10 | 27 21 | 21 43 | 19 31 | 21 02 |
| 40 | 28 17 | 27 22 | 21 31 | 19 12 | 20 49 |
| 41 | 28 24 | 27 23 | 21 19 | 18 53 | 20 34 |
| 42 | 28 31 | 27 24 | 21 07 | 18 34 | 20 20 |
| 43 | 28 39 | 27 25 | 20 54 | 18 14 | 20 04 |
| 44 | 28 46 | 27 27 | 20 42 | 17 53 | 19 48 |
| 45 | 28 54 | 27 28 | 20 29 | 17 33 | 19 32 |
| 46 | 29 02 | 27 29 | 20 16 | 17 11 | 19 15 |
| 47 | 29 10 | 27 30 | 20 03 | 16 49 | 18 57 |
| 48 | 29 19 | 27 31 | 19 49 | 16 27 | 18 38 |
| 49 | 29 28 | 27 33 | 19 36 | 16 03 | 18 19 |
| 50 | 29 37 | 27 34 | 19 22 | 15 39 | 17 58 |
| 51 | 29 46 | 27 35 | 19 08 | 15 15 | 17 37 |
| 52 | 29 56 | 27 37 | 18 53 | 14 49 | 17 14 |
| 53 | 00♍06 | 27 38 | 18 39 | 14 23 | 16 50 |
| 54 | 00 17 | 27 40 | 18 24 | 13 56 | 16 25 |
| 55 | 00 28 | 27 41 | 18 08 | 13 28 | 15 58 |
| 56 | 00 39 | 27 43 | 17 53 | 12 59 | 15 30 |
| 57 | 00 51 | 27 44 | 17 37 | 12 29 | 15 00 |
| 58 | 01 04 | 27 46 | 17 20 | 11 58 | 14 28 |
| 59 | 01 16 | 27 48 | 17 03 | 11 26 | 13 52 |
| 60 | 01♍30 | 27♍49 | 16♎46 | 10♏52 | 13♐14 |

7h 52m 0s — 118° 0' 0" — 26 ♋ 00

| LAT. | 11 | 12 | ASC | 2 | 3 |
|---|---|---|---|---|---|
| 0 | 25♌44 | 27♍49 | 00♏06 | 00♐11 | 28♐10 |
| 5 | 26 08 | 27 52 | 29♎04 | 29♏01 | 27 30 |
| 10 | 26 32 | 27 56 | 28 04 | 27 51 | 26 50 |
| 15 | 26 55 | 27 59 | 27 07 | 26 41 | 26 08 |
| 20 | 27 20 | 28 02 | 26 11 | 25 30 | 25 24 |
| 21 | 27 25 | 28 02 | 26 00 | 25 15 | 25 15 |
| 22 | 27 30 | 28 03 | 25 48 | 25 01 | 25 05 |
| 23 | 27 35 | 28 04 | 25 37 | 24 46 | 24 56 |
| 24 | 27 40 | 28 04 | 25 26 | 24 31 | 24 46 |
| 25 | 27 45 | 28 05 | 25 15 | 24 16 | 24 37 |
| 26 | 27 50 | 28 05 | 25 04 | 24 01 | 24 27 |
| 27 | 27 56 | 28 06 | 24 52 | 23 45 | 24 17 |
| 28 | 28 01 | 28 07 | 24 41 | 23 30 | 24 07 |
| 29 | 28 07 | 28 07 | 24 29 | 23 14 | 23 56 |
| 30 | 28 12 | 28 08 | 24 18 | 22 58 | 23 45 |
| 31 | 28 18 | 28 09 | 24 06 | 22 42 | 23 35 |
| 32 | 28 24 | 28 09 | 23 55 | 22 25 | 23 23 |
| 33 | 28 29 | 28 10 | 23 43 | 22 09 | 23 12 |
| 34 | 28 35 | 28 11 | 23 32 | 21 52 | 23 00 |
| 35 | 28 41 | 28 11 | 23 20 | 21 34 | 22 48 |
| 36 | 28 48 | 28 12 | 23 08 | 21 17 | 22 36 |
| 37 | 28 54 | 28 13 | 22 56 | 20 59 | 22 23 |
| 38 | 29 00 | 28 13 | 22 44 | 20 41 | 22 10 |
| 39 | 29 07 | 28 14 | 22 31 | 20 22 | 21 57 |
| 40 | 29 13 | 28 15 | 22 19 | 20 03 | 21 43 |
| 41 | 29 20 | 28 15 | 22 06 | 19 44 | 21 28 |
| 42 | 29 27 | 28 16 | 21 54 | 19 24 | 21 14 |
| 43 | 29 35 | 28 17 | 21 41 | 19 04 | 20 58 |
| 44 | 29 42 | 28 18 | 21 28 | 18 43 | 20 42 |
| 45 | 29 50 | 28 19 | 21 14 | 18 22 | 20 26 |
| 46 | 29 57 | 28 19 | 21 01 | 18 00 | 20 08 |
| 47 | 00♍06 | 28 20 | 20 47 | 17 38 | 19 50 |
| 48 | 00 14 | 28 21 | 20 33 | 17 15 | 19 32 |
| 49 | 00 22 | 28 22 | 20 19 | 16 51 | 19 12 |
| 50 | 00 31 | 28 23 | 20 05 | 16 27 | 18 51 |
| 51 | 00 40 | 28 24 | 19 50 | 16 02 | 18 30 |
| 52 | 00 50 | 28 25 | 19 35 | 15 36 | 18 07 |
| 53 | 01 00 | 28 25 | 19 20 | 15 09 | 17 43 |
| 54 | 01 10 | 28 26 | 19 04 | 14 42 | 17 18 |
| 55 | 01 21 | 28 27 | 18 49 | 14 13 | 16 51 |
| 56 | 01 32 | 28 28 | 18 32 | 13 44 | 16 22 |
| 57 | 01 43 | 28 29 | 18 16 | 13 13 | 15 51 |
| 58 | 01 55 | 28 31 | 17 59 | 12 41 | 15 18 |
| 59 | 02 08 | 28 32 | 17 41 | 12 08 | 14 43 |
| 60 | 02♍21 | 28♍33 | 17♎23 | 11♏34 | 14♐04 |

7h 56m 0s — 119° 0' 0" — 26 ♋ 57

| LAT. | 11 | 12 | ASC | 2 | 3 |
|---|---|---|---|---|---|
| 0 | 26♌47 | 28♍55 | 01♏08 | 01♐08 | 29♐05 |
| 5 | 27 10 | 28 56 | 00 04 | 29♏57 | 28 25 |
| 10 | 27 33 | 28 58 | 29♎03 | 28 47 | 27 45 |
| 15 | 27 56 | 28 59 | 28 04 | 27 37 | 27 03 |
| 20 | 28 19 | 29 01 | 27 06 | 26 25 | 26 19 |
| 21 | 28 24 | 29 01 | 26 55 | 26 10 | 26 10 |
| 22 | 28 29 | 29 01 | 26 43 | 25 55 | 26 00 |
| 23 | 28 34 | 29 02 | 26 32 | 25 40 | 25 51 |
| 24 | 28 39 | 29 02 | 26 20 | 25 25 | 25 41 |
| 25 | 28 44 | 29 02 | 26 08 | 25 10 | 25 32 |
| 26 | 28 49 | 29 03 | 25 57 | 24 55 | 25 22 |
| 27 | 28 55 | 29 03 | 25 45 | 24 39 | 25 12 |
| 28 | 29 00 | 29 03 | 25 33 | 24 23 | 25 01 |
| 29 | 29 05 | 29 04 | 25 21 | 24 07 | 24 51 |
| 30 | 29 11 | 29 04 | 25 10 | 23 51 | 24 40 |
| 31 | 29 16 | 29 04 | 24 58 | 23 35 | 24 29 |
| 32 | 29 22 | 29 05 | 24 46 | 23 18 | 24 18 |
| 33 | 29 27 | 29 05 | 24 34 | 23 01 | 24 07 |
| 34 | 29 33 | 29 05 | 24 22 | 22 44 | 23 55 |
| 35 | 29 39 | 29 06 | 24 09 | 22 26 | 23 43 |
| 36 | 29 45 | 29 06 | 23 57 | 22 08 | 23 30 |
| 37 | 29 51 | 29 06 | 23 45 | 21 50 | 23 18 |
| 38 | 29 57 | 29 07 | 23 32 | 21 32 | 23 04 |
| 39 | 00♍04 | 29 07 | 23 19 | 21 13 | 22 51 |
| 40 | 00 10 | 29 07 | 23 06 | 20 54 | 22 37 |
| 41 | 00 17 | 29 08 | 22 53 | 20 34 | 22 23 |
| 42 | 00 24 | 29 08 | 22 40 | 20 14 | 22 08 |
| 43 | 00 31 | 29 08 | 22 27 | 19 54 | 21 52 |
| 44 | 00 38 | 29 09 | 22 13 | 19 33 | 21 36 |
| 45 | 00 45 | 29 09 | 22 00 | 19 11 | 21 19 |
| 46 | 00 53 | 29 10 | 21 46 | 18 49 | 21 02 |
| 47 | 01 01 | 29 10 | 21 32 | 18 26 | 20 44 |
| 48 | 01 09 | 29 10 | 21 17 | 18 03 | 20 25 |
| 49 | 01 17 | 29 11 | 21 03 | 17 39 | 20 05 |
| 50 | 01 26 | 29 11 | 20 48 | 17 14 | 19 45 |
| 51 | 01 35 | 29 12 | 20 33 | 16 49 | 19 23 |
| 52 | 01 44 | 29 12 | 20 17 | 16 22 | 19 00 |
| 53 | 01 53 | 29 13 | 20 01 | 15 55 | 18 36 |
| 54 | 02 03 | 29 13 | 19 45 | 15 27 | 18 10 |
| 55 | 02 14 | 29 14 | 19 29 | 14 58 | 17 43 |
| 56 | 02 24 | 29 14 | 19 12 | 14 28 | 17 14 |
| 57 | 02 35 | 29 15 | 18 55 | 13 57 | 16 43 |
| 58 | 02 47 | 29 15 | 18 37 | 13 25 | 16 10 |
| 59 | 02 59 | 29 16 | 18 19 | 12 51 | 15 34 |
| 60 | 03♍12 | 29♍16 | 18♎00 | 12♏16 | 14♐55 |

# Placidus Table of Houses for Latitudes 0° to 60° North

8h 0m 0s — 120° 0' 0" — 27 ♋ 55

| LAT. | 11 | 12 | ASC | 2 | 3 |
|---|---|---|---|---|---|
| 0 | 27♌49 | 00♎00 | 02♏11 | 02♐05 | 00♑00 |
| 5 | 28 11 | 00 00 | 01 05 | 00 54 | 29♐20 |
| 10 | 28 34 | 00 00 | 00 02 | 29♏44 | 28 40 |
| 15 | 28 56 | 00 00 | 29♎01 | 28 32 | 27 58 |
| 20 | 29 19 | 00 00 | 28 02 | 27 20 | 27 14 |
| 21 | 29 24 | 00 00 | 27 50 | 27 05 | 27 04 |
| 22 | 29 29 | 00 00 | 27 38 | 26 50 | 26 55 |
| 23 | 29 34 | 00 00 | 27 26 | 26 35 | 26 46 |
| 24 | 29 38 | 00 00 | 27 14 | 26 19 | 26 36 |
| 25 | 29 43 | 00 00 | 27 02 | 26 04 | 26 26 |
| 26 | 29 48 | 00 00 | 26 50 | 25 48 | 26 16 |
| 27 | 29 53 | 00 00 | 26 38 | 25 33 | 26 06 |
| 28 | 29 59 | 00 00 | 26 26 | 25 17 | 25 56 |
| 29 | 00♍04 | 00 00 | 26 13 | 25 00 | 25 46 |
| 30 | 00 09 | 00 00 | 26 01 | 24 44 | 25 35 |
| 31 | 00 14 | 00 00 | 25 49 | 24 27 | 25 24 |
| 32 | 00 20 | 00 00 | 25 37 | 24 10 | 25 13 |
| 33 | 00 25 | 00 00 | 25 24 | 23 53 | 25 01 |
| 34 | 00 31 | 00 00 | 25 12 | 23 36 | 24 49 |
| 35 | 00 37 | 00 00 | 24 59 | 23 18 | 24 37 |
| 36 | 00 42 | 00 00 | 24 46 | 23 00 | 24 25 |
| 37 | 00 48 | 00 00 | 24 33 | 22 42 | 24 12 |
| 38 | 00 54 | 00 00 | 24 20 | 22 23 | 23 59 |
| 39 | 01 00 | 00 00 | 24 07 | 22 04 | 23 45 |
| 40 | 01 07 | 00 00 | 23 54 | 21 45 | 23 31 |
| 41 | 01 13 | 00 00 | 23 40 | 21 25 | 23 17 |
| 42 | 01 20 | 00 00 | 23 27 | 21 04 | 23 02 |
| 43 | 01 27 | 00 00 | 23 13 | 20 43 | 22 46 |
| 44 | 01 34 | 00 00 | 22 59 | 20 22 | 22 30 |
| 45 | 01 41 | 00 00 | 22 45 | 20 00 | 22 13 |
| 46 | 01 48 | 00 00 | 22 31 | 19 38 | 21 56 |
| 47 | 01 56 | 00 00 | 22 16 | 19 15 | 21 38 |
| 48 | 02 04 | 00 00 | 22 01 | 18 51 | 21 19 |
| 49 | 02 12 | 00 00 | 21 46 | 18 27 | 20 59 |
| 50 | 02 20 | 00 00 | 21 31 | 18 02 | 20 38 |
| 51 | 02 29 | 00 00 | 21 15 | 17 36 | 20 16 |
| 52 | 02 38 | 00 00 | 20 59 | 17 09 | 19 53 |
| 53 | 02 47 | 00 00 | 20 43 | 16 41 | 19 29 |
| 54 | 02 57 | 00 00 | 20 26 | 16 13 | 19 03 |
| 55 | 03 07 | 00 00 | 20 09 | 15 43 | 18 35 |
| 56 | 03 17 | 00 00 | 19 51 | 15 13 | 18 06 |
| 57 | 03 28 | 00 00 | 19 34 | 14 41 | 17 35 |
| 58 | 03 39 | 00 00 | 19 15 | 14 08 | 17 01 |
| 59 | 03 51 | 00 00 | 18 57 | 13 34 | 16 25 |
| 60 | 04♍03 | 00♎00 | 18♎37 | 12♏59 | 15♐46 |

8h 4m 0s — 121° 0' 0" — 28 ♋ 52

| LAT. | 11 | 12 | ASC | 2 | 3 |
|---|---|---|---|---|---|
| 0 | 28♌52 | 01♎05 | 03♏13 | 03♐03 | 00♑55 |
| 5 | 29 13 | 01 04 | 02 06 | 01 51 | 00 15 |
| 10 | 29 35 | 01 02 | 01 01 | 00 40 | 29♐35 |
| 15 | 29 57 | 01 01 | 29♎58 | 29♏28 | 28 53 |
| 20 | 00♍19 | 00 59 | 28 57 | 28 14 | 28 08 |
| 21 | 00 24 | 00 59 | 28 44 | 27 59 | 27 59 |
| 22 | 00 29 | 00 59 | 28 32 | 27 44 | 27 50 |
| 23 | 00 33 | 00 58 | 28 20 | 27 29 | 27 41 |
| 24 | 00 38 | 00 58 | 28 08 | 27 13 | 27 31 |
| 25 | 00 43 | 00 58 | 27 55 | 26 58 | 27 21 |
| 26 | 00 48 | 00 57 | 27 43 | 26 42 | 27 11 |
| 27 | 00 52 | 00 57 | 27 30 | 26 26 | 27 01 |
| 28 | 00 57 | 00 57 | 27 18 | 26 10 | 26 51 |
| 29 | 01 02 | 00 56 | 27 05 | 25 54 | 26 40 |
| 30 | 01 07 | 00 56 | 26 53 | 25 37 | 26 30 |
| 31 | 01 13 | 00 56 | 26 40 | 25 20 | 26 19 |
| 32 | 01 18 | 00 55 | 26 27 | 25 03 | 26 07 |
| 33 | 01 23 | 00 55 | 26 14 | 24 46 | 25 56 |
| 34 | 01 29 | 00 55 | 26 02 | 24 28 | 25 44 |
| 35 | 01 34 | 00 54 | 25 49 | 24 10 | 25 32 |
| 36 | 01 40 | 00 54 | 25 35 | 23 52 | 25 19 |
| 37 | 01 46 | 00 54 | 25 22 | 23 33 | 25 06 |
| 38 | 01 51 | 00 53 | 25 09 | 23 14 | 24 53 |
| 39 | 01 57 | 00 53 | 24 55 | 22 55 | 24 40 |
| 40 | 02 04 | 00 53 | 24 41 | 22 35 | 24 26 |
| 41 | 02 10 | 00 52 | 24 28 | 22 15 | 24 11 |
| 42 | 02 16 | 00 52 | 24 14 | 21 54 | 23 56 |
| 43 | 02 23 | 00 52 | 23 59 | 21 33 | 23 40 |
| 44 | 02 30 | 00 51 | 23 45 | 21 12 | 23 24 |
| 45 | 02 37 | 00 51 | 23 30 | 20 49 | 23 07 |
| 46 | 02 44 | 00 50 | 23 15 | 20 27 | 22 50 |
| 47 | 02 51 | 00 50 | 23 00 | 20 03 | 22 32 |
| 48 | 02 59 | 00 50 | 22 45 | 19 39 | 22 12 |
| 49 | 03 07 | 00 49 | 22 29 | 19 14 | 21 52 |
| 50 | 03 15 | 00 49 | 22 13 | 18 49 | 21 32 |
| 51 | 03 23 | 00 48 | 21 57 | 18 23 | 21 09 |
| 52 | 03 32 | 00 48 | 21 41 | 17 56 | 20 46 |
| 53 | 03 41 | 00 47 | 21 24 | 17 28 | 20 22 |
| 54 | 03 50 | 00 47 | 21 07 | 16 59 | 19 56 |
| 55 | 04 00 | 00 46 | 20 49 | 16 29 | 19 28 |
| 56 | 04 10 | 00 46 | 20 31 | 15 57 | 18 58 |
| 57 | 04 20 | 00 45 | 20 13 | 15 25 | 18 27 |
| 58 | 04 31 | 00 45 | 19 54 | 14 52 | 17 53 |
| 59 | 04 42 | 00 44 | 19 34 | 14 17 | 17 16 |
| 60 | 04♍54 | 00♎44 | 19♎14 | 13♏41 | 16♐37 |

8h 8m 0s — 122° 0' 0" — 29 ♋ 49

| LAT. | 11 | 12 | ASC | 2 | 3 |
|---|---|---|---|---|---|
| 0 | 29♌54 | 02♎11 | 04♏16 | 04♐00 | 01♑50 |
| 5 | 00♍15 | 02 08 | 03 06 | 02 48 | 01 10 |
| 10 | 00 36 | 02 04 | 02 00 | 01 36 | 00 30 |
| 15 | 00 58 | 02 01 | 00 55 | 00 23 | 29♐48 |
| 20 | 01 19 | 01 58 | 29♎52 | 29♏09 | 29 03 |
| 21 | 01 24 | 01 58 | 29 39 | 28 54 | 28 54 |
| 22 | 01 28 | 01 57 | 29 27 | 28 38 | 28 45 |
| 23 | 01 33 | 01 56 | 29 14 | 28 23 | 28 36 |
| 24 | 01 37 | 01 56 | 29 01 | 28 07 | 28 26 |
| 25 | 01 42 | 01 55 | 28 49 | 27 52 | 28 16 |
| 26 | 01 47 | 01 55 | 28 36 | 27 36 | 28 06 |
| 27 | 01 52 | 01 54 | 28 23 | 27 20 | 27 56 |
| 28 | 01 56 | 01 53 | 28 10 | 27 03 | 27 46 |
| 29 | 02 01 | 01 53 | 27 57 | 26 47 | 27 35 |
| 30 | 02 06 | 01 52 | 27 44 | 26 30 | 27 24 |
| 31 | 02 11 | 01 51 | 27 31 | 26 13 | 27 13 |
| 32 | 02 16 | 01 51 | 27 18 | 25 56 | 27 02 |
| 33 | 02 21 | 01 50 | 27 05 | 25 38 | 26 50 |
| 34 | 02 27 | 01 49 | 26 52 | 25 20 | 26 39 |
| 35 | 02 32 | 01 49 | 26 38 | 25 02 | 26 26 |
| 36 | 02 38 | 01 48 | 26 25 | 24 44 | 26 14 |
| 37 | 02 43 | 01 47 | 26 11 | 24 25 | 26 01 |
| 38 | 02 49 | 01 47 | 25 57 | 24 05 | 25 48 |
| 39 | 02 55 | 01 46 | 25 43 | 23 46 | 25 34 |
| 40 | 03 01 | 01 45 | 25 29 | 23 26 | 25 20 |
| 41 | 03 07 | 01 45 | 25 15 | 23 05 | 25 05 |
| 42 | 03 13 | 01 44 | 25 00 | 22 44 | 24 50 |
| 43 | 03 19 | 01 43 | 24 45 | 22 23 | 24 35 |
| 44 | 03 26 | 01 42 | 24 31 | 22 01 | 24 18 |
| 45 | 03 32 | 01 41 | 24 16 | 21 39 | 24 02 |
| 46 | 03 39 | 01 41 | 24 00 | 21 15 | 23 44 |
| 47 | 03 47 | 01 40 | 23 45 | 20 52 | 23 26 |
| 48 | 03 54 | 01 39 | 23 29 | 20 27 | 23 06 |
| 49 | 04 01 | 01 38 | 23 13 | 20 02 | 22 46 |
| 50 | 04 09 | 01 37 | 22 56 | 19 36 | 22 25 |
| 51 | 04 17 | 01 36 | 22 40 | 19 10 | 22 03 |
| 52 | 04 26 | 01 35 | 22 22 | 18 42 | 21 40 |
| 53 | 04 34 | 01 35 | 22 05 | 18 14 | 21 15 |
| 54 | 04 43 | 01 34 | 21 47 | 17 44 | 20 49 |
| 55 | 04 53 | 01 33 | 21 29 | 17 14 | 20 21 |
| 56 | 05 02 | 01 32 | 21 11 | 16 42 | 19 51 |
| 57 | 05 12 | 01 31 | 20 52 | 16 09 | 19 19 |
| 58 | 05 23 | 01 29 | 20 32 | 15 35 | 18 45 |
| 59 | 05 34 | 01 28 | 20 12 | 15 00 | 18 08 |
| 60 | 05♍46 | 01♎27 | 19♎52 | 14♏23 | 17♐28 |

8h 12m 0s — 123° 0' 0" — 00 ♌ 47

| LAT. | 11 | 12 | ASC | 2 | 3 |
|---|---|---|---|---|---|
| 0 | 00♍57 | 03♎16 | 05♏18 | 04♐57 | 02♑45 |
| 5 | 01 18 | 03 11 | 04 06 | 03 44 | 02 05 |
| 10 | 01 38 | 03 07 | 02 58 | 02 32 | 01 25 |
| 15 | 01 59 | 03 02 | 01 52 | 01 18 | 00 43 |
| 20 | 02 20 | 02 57 | 00 47 | 00 04 | 29♐58 |
| 21 | 02 24 | 02 57 | 00 34 | 29♏48 | 29 49 |
| 22 | 02 28 | 02 56 | 00 21 | 29 33 | 29 40 |
| 23 | 02 33 | 02 55 | 00 08 | 29 17 | 29 31 |
| 24 | 02 37 | 02 54 | 29♎55 | 29 01 | 29 21 |
| 25 | 02 42 | 02 53 | 29 42 | 28 45 | 29 11 |
| 26 | 02 46 | 02 52 | 29 29 | 28 29 | 29 01 |
| 27 | 02 51 | 02 51 | 29 16 | 28 13 | 28 51 |
| 28 | 02 55 | 02 50 | 29 02 | 27 56 | 28 41 |
| 29 | 03 00 | 02 49 | 28 49 | 27 40 | 28 30 |
| 30 | 03 05 | 02 48 | 28 36 | 27 23 | 28 19 |
| 31 | 03 10 | 02 47 | 28 22 | 27 06 | 28 08 |
| 32 | 03 15 | 02 46 | 28 09 | 26 48 | 27 57 |
| 33 | 03 20 | 02 45 | 27 55 | 26 30 | 27 45 |
| 34 | 03 25 | 02 44 | 27 41 | 26 12 | 27 33 |
| 35 | 03 30 | 02 43 | 27 28 | 25 54 | 27 21 |
| 36 | 03 35 | 02 42 | 27 14 | 25 35 | 27 09 |
| 37 | 03 41 | 02 41 | 27 00 | 25 16 | 26 56 |
| 38 | 03 46 | 02 40 | 26 45 | 24 57 | 26 42 |
| 39 | 03 52 | 02 39 | 26 31 | 24 37 | 26 29 |
| 40 | 03 57 | 02 38 | 26 16 | 24 17 | 26 15 |
| 41 | 04 03 | 02 37 | 26 02 | 23 56 | 26 00 |
| 42 | 04 09 | 02 36 | 25 47 | 23 35 | 25 45 |
| 43 | 04 16 | 02 35 | 25 32 | 23 13 | 25 29 |
| 44 | 04 22 | 02 33 | 25 16 | 22 51 | 25 13 |
| 45 | 04 28 | 02 32 | 25 01 | 22 28 | 24 56 |
| 46 | 04 35 | 02 31 | 24 45 | 22 04 | 24 38 |
| 47 | 04 42 | 02 30 | 24 29 | 21 40 | 24 20 |
| 48 | 04 49 | 02 29 | 24 13 | 21 15 | 24 00 |
| 49 | 04 56 | 02 27 | 23 56 | 20 50 | 23 40 |
| 50 | 05 04 | 02 26 | 23 39 | 20 24 | 23 19 |
| 51 | 05 12 | 02 25 | 23 22 | 19 57 | 22 57 |
| 52 | 05 20 | 02 23 | 23 04 | 19 29 | 22 33 |
| 53 | 05 28 | 02 22 | 22 46 | 19 00 | 22 08 |
| 54 | 05 37 | 02 20 | 22 28 | 18 30 | 21 42 |
| 55 | 05 46 | 02 19 | 22 09 | 17 59 | 21 14 |
| 56 | 05 55 | 02 17 | 21 50 | 17 27 | 20 44 |
| 57 | 06 05 | 02 16 | 21 30 | 16 53 | 20 11 |
| 58 | 06 15 | 02 14 | 21 10 | 16 19 | 19 37 |
| 59 | 06 26 | 02 12 | 20 50 | 15 43 | 18 59 |
| 60 | 06♍37 | 02♎11 | 20♎29 | 15♏05 | 18♐19 |

8h 16m 0s — 124° 0' 0" — 01 ♌ 45

| LAT. | 11 | 12 | ASC | 2 | 3 |
|---|---|---|---|---|---|
| 0 | 02♍00 | 04♎22 | 06♏19 | 05♐54 | 03♑40 |
| 5 | 02 20 | 04 15 | 05 07 | 04 40 | 03 00 |
| 10 | 02 40 | 04 09 | 03 57 | 03 27 | 02 20 |
| 15 | 03 00 | 04 03 | 02 49 | 02 14 | 01 38 |
| 20 | 03 20 | 03 57 | 01 42 | 00 58 | 00 54 |
| 21 | 03 24 | 03 55 | 01 29 | 00 43 | 00 44 |
| 22 | 03 28 | 03 54 | 01 15 | 00 27 | 00 35 |
| 23 | 03 33 | 03 53 | 01 02 | 00 11 | 00 26 |
| 24 | 03 37 | 03 52 | 00 49 | 29♏55 | 00 16 |
| 25 | 03 41 | 03 50 | 00 35 | 29 39 | 00 06 |
| 26 | 03 46 | 03 49 | 00 22 | 29 23 | 29♐56 |
| 27 | 03 50 | 03 48 | 00 08 | 29 06 | 29 46 |
| 28 | 03 55 | 03 47 | 29♎54 | 28 50 | 29 36 |
| 29 | 03 59 | 03 45 | 29 41 | 28 33 | 29 25 |
| 30 | 04 04 | 03 44 | 29 27 | 28 16 | 29 14 |
| 31 | 04 08 | 03 43 | 29 13 | 27 58 | 29 03 |
| 32 | 04 13 | 03 42 | 28 59 | 27 41 | 28 52 |
| 33 | 04 18 | 03 40 | 28 45 | 27 23 | 28 40 |
| 34 | 04 23 | 03 39 | 28 31 | 27 04 | 28 28 |
| 35 | 04 28 | 03 38 | 28 17 | 26 46 | 28 16 |
| 36 | 04 33 | 03 36 | 28 03 | 26 27 | 28 03 |
| 37 | 04 38 | 03 35 | 27 48 | 26 08 | 27 50 |
| 38 | 04 44 | 03 33 | 27 34 | 25 48 | 27 37 |
| 39 | 04 49 | 03 32 | 27 19 | 25 28 | 27 23 |
| 40 | 04 55 | 03 31 | 27 04 | 25 07 | 27 09 |
| 41 | 05 00 | 03 29 | 26 49 | 24 46 | 26 55 |
| 42 | 05 06 | 03 28 | 26 33 | 24 25 | 26 39 |
| 43 | 05 12 | 03 26 | 26 18 | 24 03 | 26 24 |
| 44 | 05 18 | 03 24 | 26 02 | 23 40 | 26 07 |
| 45 | 05 24 | 03 23 | 25 46 | 23 17 | 25 50 |
| 46 | 05 31 | 03 21 | 25 30 | 22 53 | 25 32 |
| 47 | 05 37 | 03 20 | 25 13 | 22 29 | 25 14 |
| 48 | 05 44 | 03 18 | 24 56 | 22 04 | 24 54 |
| 49 | 05 51 | 03 16 | 24 39 | 21 38 | 24 34 |
| 50 | 05 59 | 03 15 | 24 22 | 21 11 | 24 13 |
| 51 | 06 06 | 03 13 | 24 04 | 20 44 | 23 50 |
| 52 | 06 14 | 03 11 | 23 46 | 20 15 | 23 27 |
| 53 | 06 22 | 03 09 | 23 28 | 19 46 | 23 02 |
| 54 | 06 30 | 03 07 | 23 09 | 19 15 | 22 35 |
| 55 | 06 39 | 03 05 | 22 49 | 18 44 | 22 07 |
| 56 | 06 48 | 03 03 | 22 30 | 18 11 | 21 36 |
| 57 | 06 57 | 03 01 | 22 09 | 17 37 | 21 04 |
| 58 | 07 07 | 02 59 | 21 49 | 17 02 | 20 29 |
| 59 | 07 18 | 02 57 | 21 27 | 16 25 | 19 51 |
| 60 | 07♍28 | 02♎54 | 21♎06 | 15♏47 | 19♐10 |

8h 20m 0s — 125° 0' 0" — 02 ♌ 43

| LAT. | 11 | 12 | ASC | 2 | 3 |
|---|---|---|---|---|---|
| 0 | 03♍03 | 05♎27 | 07♏21 | 06♐50 | 04♑35 |
| 5 | 03 23 | 05 19 | 06 06 | 05 37 | 03 56 |
| 10 | 03 42 | 05 11 | 04 55 | 04 23 | 03 15 |
| 15 | 04 01 | 05 03 | 03 46 | 03 09 | 02 33 |
| 20 | 04 21 | 04 56 | 02 37 | 01 52 | 01 49 |
| 21 | 04 25 | 04 54 | 02 23 | 01 37 | 01 39 |
| 22 | 04 29 | 04 53 | 02 10 | 01 21 | 01 30 |
| 23 | 04 33 | 04 51 | 01 56 | 01 05 | 01 21 |
| 24 | 04 37 | 04 50 | 01 42 | 00 49 | 01 11 |
| 25 | 04 41 | 04 48 | 01 28 | 00 33 | 01 01 |
| 26 | 04 45 | 04 47 | 01 14 | 00 16 | 00 51 |
| 27 | 04 50 | 04 45 | 01 01 | 00 00 | 00 41 |
| 28 | 04 54 | 04 43 | 00 47 | 29♏43 | 00 31 |
| 29 | 04 58 | 04 42 | 00 33 | 29 26 | 00 20 |
| 30 | 05 03 | 04 40 | 00 18 | 29 09 | 00 09 |
| 31 | 05 07 | 04 39 | 00 04 | 28 51 | 29♐58 |
| 32 | 05 12 | 04 37 | 29♎50 | 28 33 | 29 47 |
| 33 | 05 16 | 04 35 | 29 36 | 28 15 | 29 35 |
| 34 | 05 21 | 04 34 | 29 21 | 27 56 | 29 23 |
| 35 | 05 26 | 04 32 | 29 07 | 27 38 | 29 11 |
| 36 | 05 31 | 04 30 | 28 52 | 27 18 | 28 58 |
| 37 | 05 36 | 04 28 | 28 37 | 26 59 | 28 45 |
| 38 | 05 41 | 04 27 | 28 22 | 26 39 | 28 32 |
| 39 | 05 46 | 04 25 | 28 07 | 26 19 | 28 18 |
| 40 | 05 52 | 04 23 | 27 51 | 25 58 | 28 04 |
| 41 | 05 57 | 04 21 | 27 36 | 25 37 | 27 49 |
| 42 | 06 03 | 04 19 | 27 20 | 25 15 | 27 34 |
| 43 | 06 09 | 04 18 | 27 04 | 24 53 | 27 18 |
| 44 | 06 14 | 04 16 | 26 48 | 24 30 | 27 02 |
| 45 | 06 20 | 04 14 | 26 31 | 24 06 | 26 45 |
| 46 | 06 27 | 04 12 | 26 14 | 23 42 | 26 27 |
| 47 | 06 33 | 04 10 | 25 57 | 23 17 | 26 08 |
| 48 | 06 40 | 04 07 | 25 40 | 22 52 | 25 49 |
| 49 | 06 46 | 04 05 | 25 23 | 22 26 | 25 28 |
| 50 | 06 53 | 04 03 | 25 05 | 21 59 | 25 07 |
| 51 | 07 01 | 04 01 | 24 46 | 21 31 | 24 44 |
| 52 | 07 08 | 03 59 | 24 28 | 21 02 | 24 20 |
| 53 | 07 16 | 03 56 | 24 09 | 20 32 | 23 55 |
| 54 | 07 24 | 03 54 | 23 49 | 20 01 | 23 28 |
| 55 | 07 32 | 03 51 | 23 29 | 19 29 | 23 00 |
| 56 | 07 41 | 03 49 | 23 09 | 18 56 | 22 29 |
| 57 | 07 50 | 03 46 | 22 48 | 18 21 | 21 57 |
| 58 | 08 00 | 03 44 | 22 27 | 17 46 | 21 22 |
| 59 | 08 09 | 03 41 | 22 05 | 17 08 | 20 43 |
| 60 | 08♍20 | 03♎38 | 21♎43 | 16♏29 | 20♐02 |

8h 24m 0s — 126° 0' 0" — 03 ♌ 41

| LAT. | 11 | 12 | ASC | 2 | 3 |
|---|---|---|---|---|---|
| 0 | 04♍07 | 06♎32 | 08♏23 | 07♐47 | 05♑30 |
| 5 | 04 25 | 06 22 | 07 06 | 06 33 | 04 51 |
| 10 | 04 44 | 06 13 | 05 53 | 05 19 | 04 10 |
| 15 | 05 02 | 06 04 | 04 42 | 04 04 | 03 28 |
| 20 | 05 21 | 05 55 | 03 32 | 02 47 | 02 44 |
| 21 | 05 25 | 05 53 | 03 18 | 02 31 | 02 35 |
| 22 | 05 29 | 05 51 | 03 04 | 02 15 | 02 25 |
| 23 | 05 33 | 05 49 | 02 50 | 01 59 | 02 16 |
| 24 | 05 37 | 05 48 | 02 36 | 01 43 | 02 06 |
| 25 | 05 41 | 05 46 | 02 21 | 01 27 | 01 56 |
| 26 | 05 45 | 05 44 | 02 07 | 01 10 | 01 46 |
| 27 | 05 49 | 05 42 | 01 53 | 00 53 | 01 36 |
| 28 | 05 53 | 05 40 | 01 39 | 00 36 | 01 26 |
| 29 | 05 57 | 05 38 | 01 24 | 00 19 | 01 15 |
| 30 | 06 02 | 05 36 | 01 10 | 00 01 | 01 04 |
| 31 | 06 06 | 05 34 | 00 55 | 29♏44 | 00 53 |
| 32 | 06 11 | 05 32 | 00 41 | 29 26 | 00 42 |
| 33 | 06 15 | 05 30 | 00 26 | 29 07 | 00 30 |
| 34 | 06 20 | 05 28 | 00 11 | 28 48 | 00 18 |
| 35 | 06 24 | 05 26 | 29♎56 | 28 29 | 00 06 |
| 36 | 06 29 | 05 24 | 29 41 | 28 10 | 29♐53 |
| 37 | 06 34 | 05 22 | 29 26 | 27 50 | 29 40 |
| 38 | 06 39 | 05 20 | 29 10 | 27 30 | 29 27 |
| 39 | 06 44 | 05 18 | 28 54 | 27 10 | 29 13 |
| 40 | 06 49 | 05 16 | 28 39 | 26 49 | 28 59 |
| 41 | 06 54 | 05 14 | 28 23 | 26 27 | 28 44 |
| 42 | 07 00 | 05 11 | 28 06 | 26 05 | 28 29 |
| 43 | 07 05 | 05 09 | 27 50 | 25 42 | 28 13 |
| 44 | 07 11 | 05 07 | 27 33 | 25 19 | 27 56 |
| 45 | 07 17 | 05 04 | 27 16 | 24 55 | 27 39 |
| 46 | 07 23 | 05 02 | 26 59 | 24 31 | 27 21 |
| 47 | 07 29 | 04 59 | 26 42 | 24 06 | 27 03 |
| 48 | 07 35 | 04 57 | 26 24 | 23 40 | 26 43 |
| 49 | 07 42 | 04 54 | 26 06 | 23 13 | 26 23 |
| 50 | 07 48 | 04 52 | 25 47 | 22 46 | 26 01 |
| 51 | 07 55 | 04 49 | 25 29 | 22 18 | 25 38 |
| 52 | 08 03 | 04 46 | 25 09 | 21 48 | 25 14 |
| 53 | 08 10 | 04 44 | 24 50 | 21 18 | 24 49 |
| 54 | 08 18 | 04 41 | 24 30 | 20 47 | 24 22 |
| 55 | 08 26 | 04 38 | 24 09 | 20 14 | 23 53 |
| 56 | 08 34 | 04 35 | 23 49 | 19 41 | 23 23 |
| 57 | 08 43 | 04 31 | 23 27 | 19 05 | 22 50 |
| 58 | 08 52 | 04 28 | 23 05 | 18 29 | 22 14 |
| 59 | 09 01 | 04 25 | 22 43 | 17 51 | 21 36 |
| 60 | 09♍11 | 04♎21 | 22♎20 | 17♏12 | 20♐54 |

8h 28m 0s — 127° 0' 0" — 04 ♌ 39

| LAT. | 11 | 12 | ASC | 2 | 3 |
|---|---|---|---|---|---|
| 0 | 05♍10 | 07♎37 | 09♏24 | 08♐43 | 06♑26 |
| 5 | 05 28 | 07 26 | 08 06 | 07 29 | 05 46 |
| 10 | 05 46 | 07 15 | 06 51 | 06 14 | 05 05 |
| 15 | 06 04 | 07 05 | 05 39 | 04 59 | 04 23 |
| 20 | 06 22 | 06 54 | 04 27 | 03 41 | 03 39 |
| 21 | 06 26 | 06 52 | 04 12 | 03 25 | 03 30 |
| 22 | 06 29 | 06 50 | 03 58 | 03 09 | 03 21 |
| 23 | 06 33 | 06 48 | 03 43 | 02 53 | 03 11 |
| 24 | 06 37 | 06 45 | 03 29 | 02 37 | 03 01 |
| 25 | 06 41 | 06 43 | 03 14 | 02 20 | 02 52 |
| 26 | 06 45 | 06 41 | 03 00 | 02 03 | 02 42 |
| 27 | 06 49 | 06 39 | 02 45 | 01 47 | 02 31 |
| 28 | 06 53 | 06 37 | 02 31 | 01 29 | 02 21 |
| 29 | 06 57 | 06 34 | 02 16 | 01 12 | 02 10 |
| 30 | 07 01 | 06 32 | 02 01 | 00 54 | 01 59 |
| 31 | 07 05 | 06 30 | 01 46 | 00 36 | 01 48 |
| 32 | 07 09 | 06 28 | 01 31 | 00 18 | 01 37 |
| 33 | 07 14 | 06 25 | 01 16 | 29♏59 | 01 25 |
| 34 | 07 18 | 06 23 | 01 01 | 29 41 | 01 13 |
| 35 | 07 23 | 06 21 | 00 45 | 29 21 | 01 01 |
| 36 | 07 27 | 06 18 | 00 30 | 29 02 | 00 48 |
| 37 | 07 32 | 06 16 | 00 14 | 28 42 | 00 35 |
| 38 | 07 36 | 06 13 | 29♎58 | 28 21 | 00 22 |
| 39 | 07 41 | 06 11 | 29 42 | 28 00 | 00 08 |
| 40 | 07 46 | 06 08 | 29 26 | 27 39 | 29♐54 |
| 41 | 07 51 | 06 06 | 29 10 | 27 17 | 29 39 |
| 42 | 07 56 | 06 03 | 28 53 | 26 55 | 29 24 |
| 43 | 08 02 | 06 00 | 28 36 | 26 32 | 29 08 |
| 44 | 08 07 | 05 58 | 28 19 | 26 09 | 28 51 |
| 45 | 08 13 | 05 55 | 28 02 | 25 45 | 28 34 |
| 46 | 08 19 | 05 52 | 27 44 | 25 20 | 28 16 |
| 47 | 08 24 | 05 49 | 27 26 | 24 55 | 27 57 |
| 48 | 08 31 | 05 46 | 27 08 | 24 28 | 27 38 |
| 49 | 08 37 | 05 43 | 26 49 | 24 01 | 27 17 |
| 50 | 08 43 | 05 40 | 26 30 | 23 33 | 26 55 |
| 51 | 08 50 | 05 37 | 26 11 | 23 05 | 26 33 |
| 52 | 08 57 | 05 34 | 25 51 | 22 35 | 26 08 |
| 53 | 09 04 | 05 31 | 25 31 | 22 04 | 25 43 |
| 54 | 09 11 | 05 27 | 25 11 | 21 32 | 25 16 |
| 55 | 09 19 | 05 24 | 24 50 | 20 59 | 24 47 |
| 56 | 09 27 | 05 20 | 24 28 | 20 25 | 24 16 |
| 57 | 09 35 | 05 17 | 24 06 | 19 50 | 23 43 |
| 58 | 09 44 | 05 13 | 23 43 | 19 13 | 23 07 |
| 59 | 09 53 | 05 09 | 23 20 | 18 34 | 22 28 |
| 60 | 10♍03 | 05♎05 | 22♎56 | 17♏54 | 21♐46 |

# Placidus Table of Houses for Latitudes 0° to 60° North

**8h 32m 0s — 128° 0' 0" — 05 ♌ 38**

| LAT. | 11 | 12 | ASC | 2 | 3 |
|---|---|---|---|---|---|
| 0 | 06♍14 | 08♎43 | 10♏25 | 09♐40 | 07♑21 |
| 5 | 06 31 | 08 30 | 09 06 | 08 25 | 06 41 |
| 10 | 06 48 | 08 17 | 07 49 | 07 10 | 06 01 |
| 15 | 07 05 | 08 05 | 06 35 | 05 54 | 05 19 |
| 20 | 07 23 | 07 53 | 05 21 | 04 36 | 04 34 |
| 21 | 07 26 | 07 51 | 05 07 | 04 20 | 04 25 |
| 22 | 07 30 | 07 48 | 04 52 | 04 03 | 04 16 |
| 23 | 07 33 | 07 46 | 04 37 | 03 47 | 04 06 |
| 24 | 07 37 | 07 43 | 04 22 | 03 31 | 03 57 |
| 25 | 07 41 | 07 41 | 04 07 | 03 14 | 03 47 |
| 26 | 07 45 | 07 38 | 03 53 | 02 57 | 03 37 |
| 27 | 07 48 | 07 36 | 03 38 | 02 40 | 03 27 |
| 28 | 07 52 | 07 33 | 03 23 | 02 22 | 03 16 |
| 29 | 07 56 | 07 31 | 03 08 | 02 05 | 03 06 |
| 30 | 08 00 | 07 28 | 02 52 | 01 47 | 02 55 |
| 31 | 08 04 | 07 26 | 02 37 | 01 29 | 02 44 |
| 32 | 08 08 | 07 23 | 02 22 | 01 10 | 02 32 |
| 33 | 08 12 | 07 20 | 02 06 | 00 52 | 02 21 |
| 34 | 08 17 | 07 18 | 01 51 | 00 33 | 02 09 |
| 35 | 08 21 | 07 15 | 01 35 | 00 13 | 01 56 |
| 36 | 08 25 | 07 12 | 01 19 | 29♏53 | 01 44 |
| 37 | 08 30 | 07 09 | 01 03 | 29 33 | 01 31 |
| 38 | 08 34 | 07 07 | 00 46 | 29 13 | 01 17 |
| 39 | 08 39 | 07 04 | 00 30 | 28 51 | 01 03 |
| 40 | 08 44 | 07 01 | 00 13 | 28 30 | 00 49 |
| 41 | 08 48 | 06 58 | 29♎57 | 28 08 | 00 34 |
| 42 | 08 53 | 06 55 | 29 39 | 27 45 | 00 19 |
| 43 | 08 59 | 06 52 | 29 22 | 27 22 | 00 03 |
| 44 | 09 04 | 06 49 | 29 05 | 26 58 | 29♐46 |
| 45 | 09 09 | 06 46 | 28 47 | 26 34 | 29 29 |
| 46 | 09 15 | 06 42 | 28 29 | 26 09 | 29 11 |
| 47 | 09 20 | 06 39 | 28 10 | 25 43 | 28 52 |
| 48 | 09 26 | 06 36 | 27 51 | 25 17 | 28 32 |
| 49 | 09 32 | 06 32 | 27 32 | 24 49 | 28 12 |
| 50 | 09 38 | 06 29 | 27 13 | 24 21 | 27 50 |
| 51 | 09 45 | 06 25 | 26 53 | 23 52 | 27 27 |
| 52 | 09 51 | 06 22 | 26 33 | 23 22 | 27 03 |
| 53 | 09 58 | 06 18 | 26 12 | 22 50 | 26 37 |
| 54 | 10 05 | 06 14 | 25 51 | 22 18 | 26 10 |
| 55 | 10 13 | 06 10 | 25 30 | 21 45 | 25 41 |
| 56 | 10 20 | 06 06 | 25 07 | 21 10 | 25 10 |
| 57 | 10 28 | 06 02 | 24 45 | 20 34 | 24 36 |
| 58 | 10 37 | 05 58 | 24 22 | 19 56 | 24 00 |
| 59 | 10 45 | 05 53 | 23 58 | 19 17 | 23 21 |
| 60 | 10♍54 | 05♎49 | 23♎33 | 18♏36 | 22♐38 |

**8h 36m 0s — 129° 0' 0" — 06 ♌ 37**

| LAT. | 11 | 12 | ASC | 2 | 3 |
|---|---|---|---|---|---|
| 0 | 07♍18 | 09♎48 | 11♏26 | 10♐36 | 08♑16 |
| 5 | 07 34 | 09 33 | 10 05 | 09 21 | 07 36 |
| 10 | 07 50 | 09 19 | 08 47 | 08 05 | 06 56 |
| 15 | 08 07 | 09 06 | 07 31 | 06 49 | 06 14 |
| 20 | 08 24 | 08 52 | 06 16 | 05 30 | 05 30 |
| 21 | 08 27 | 08 49 | 06 01 | 05 14 | 05 21 |
| 22 | 08 30 | 08 47 | 05 46 | 04 57 | 05 11 |
| 23 | 08 34 | 08 44 | 05 31 | 04 41 | 05 02 |
| 24 | 08 37 | 08 41 | 05 16 | 04 24 | 04 52 |
| 25 | 08 41 | 08 38 | 05 00 | 04 07 | 04 42 |
| 26 | 08 45 | 08 35 | 04 45 | 03 50 | 04 32 |
| 27 | 08 48 | 08 33 | 04 30 | 03 33 | 04 22 |
| 28 | 08 52 | 08 30 | 04 15 | 03 16 | 04 12 |
| 29 | 08 56 | 08 27 | 03 59 | 02 58 | 04 01 |
| 30 | 08 59 | 08 24 | 03 44 | 02 40 | 03 50 |
| 31 | 09 03 | 08 21 | 03 28 | 02 21 | 03 39 |
| 32 | 09 07 | 08 18 | 03 12 | 02 03 | 03 28 |
| 33 | 09 11 | 08 15 | 02 56 | 01 44 | 03 16 |
| 34 | 09 15 | 08 12 | 02 40 | 01 25 | 03 04 |
| 35 | 09 19 | 08 09 | 02 24 | 01 05 | 02 52 |
| 36 | 09 24 | 08 06 | 02 08 | 00 45 | 02 39 |
| 37 | 09 28 | 08 03 | 01 51 | 00 25 | 02 26 |
| 38 | 09 32 | 08 00 | 01 35 | 00 04 | 02 12 |
| 39 | 09 37 | 07 57 | 01 18 | 29♏42 | 01 58 |
| 40 | 09 41 | 07 53 | 01 01 | 29 21 | 01 44 |
| 41 | 09 46 | 07 50 | 00 43 | 28 58 | 01 29 |
| 42 | 09 50 | 07 47 | 00 26 | 28 35 | 01 14 |
| 43 | 09 55 | 07 43 | 00 08 | 28 12 | 00 58 |
| 44 | 10 00 | 07 40 | 29♎50 | 27 48 | 00 41 |
| 45 | 10 05 | 07 36 | 29 32 | 27 23 | 00 24 |
| 46 | 10 11 | 07 33 | 29 13 | 26 58 | 00 06 |
| 47 | 10 16 | 07 29 | 28 54 | 26 32 | 29♐47 |
| 48 | 10 22 | 07 25 | 28 35 | 26 05 | 29 27 |
| 49 | 10 27 | 07 21 | 28 16 | 25 37 | 29 06 |
| 50 | 10 33 | 07 18 | 27 56 | 25 09 | 28 45 |
| 51 | 10 39 | 07 14 | 27 35 | 24 39 | 28 22 |
| 52 | 10 46 | 07 09 | 27 15 | 24 08 | 27 57 |
| 53 | 10 52 | 07 05 | 26 53 | 23 37 | 27 32 |
| 54 | 10 59 | 07 01 | 26 32 | 23 04 | 27 04 |
| 55 | 11 06 | 06 56 | 26 10 | 22 30 | 26 35 |
| 56 | 11 14 | 06 52 | 25 47 | 21 55 | 26 04 |
| 57 | 11 21 | 06 47 | 25 24 | 21 18 | 25 30 |
| 58 | 11 29 | 06 42 | 25 00 | 20 40 | 24 54 |
| 59 | 11 37 | 06 37 | 24 35 | 20 00 | 24 14 |
| 60 | 11♍46 | 06♎32 | 24♎10 | 19♏18 | 23♐31 |

**8h 40m 0s — 130° 0' 0" — 07 ♌ 35**

| LAT. | 11 | 12 | ASC | 2 | 3 |
|---|---|---|---|---|---|
| 0 | 08♍22 | 10♎53 | 12♏27 | 11♐32 | 09♑11 |
| 5 | 08 37 | 10 37 | 11 04 | 10 16 | 08 32 |
| 10 | 08 53 | 10 21 | 09 45 | 09 00 | 07 51 |
| 15 | 09 09 | 10 06 | 08 27 | 07 43 | 07 10 |
| 20 | 09 25 | 09 51 | 07 10 | 06 24 | 06 25 |
| 21 | 09 28 | 09 48 | 06 55 | 06 08 | 06 16 |
| 22 | 09 31 | 09 45 | 06 40 | 05 51 | 06 07 |
| 23 | 09 34 | 09 42 | 06 24 | 05 35 | 05 57 |
| 24 | 09 38 | 09 39 | 06 09 | 05 18 | 05 48 |
| 25 | 09 41 | 09 36 | 05 53 | 05 01 | 05 38 |
| 26 | 09 45 | 09 33 | 05 38 | 04 44 | 05 28 |
| 27 | 09 48 | 09 29 | 05 22 | 04 26 | 05 18 |
| 28 | 09 52 | 09 26 | 05 06 | 04 09 | 05 07 |
| 29 | 09 55 | 09 23 | 04 51 | 03 51 | 04 57 |
| 30 | 09 59 | 09 20 | 04 35 | 03 33 | 04 46 |
| 31 | 10 03 | 09 17 | 04 19 | 03 14 | 04 34 |
| 32 | 10 06 | 09 13 | 04 03 | 02 55 | 04 23 |
| 33 | 10 10 | 09 10 | 03 46 | 02 36 | 04 11 |
| 34 | 10 14 | 09 07 | 03 30 | 02 17 | 03 59 |
| 35 | 10 18 | 09 03 | 03 13 | 01 57 | 03 47 |
| 36 | 10 22 | 09 00 | 02 57 | 01 37 | 03 34 |
| 37 | 10 26 | 08 57 | 02 40 | 01 16 | 03 21 |
| 38 | 10 30 | 08 53 | 02 23 | 00 55 | 03 08 |
| 39 | 10 34 | 08 50 | 02 06 | 00 33 | 02 54 |
| 40 | 10 39 | 08 46 | 01 48 | 00 11 | 02 39 |
| 41 | 10 43 | 08 42 | 01 30 | 29♏49 | 02 25 |
| 42 | 10 48 | 08 39 | 01 12 | 29 26 | 02 09 |
| 43 | 10 52 | 08 35 | 00 54 | 29 02 | 01 53 |
| 44 | 10 57 | 08 31 | 00 36 | 28 38 | 01 36 |
| 45 | 11 02 | 08 27 | 00 17 | 28 13 | 01 19 |
| 46 | 11 07 | 08 23 | 29♎58 | 27 47 | 01 01 |
| 47 | 11 12 | 08 19 | 29 39 | 27 20 | 00 42 |
| 48 | 11 17 | 08 15 | 29 19 | 26 53 | 00 22 |
| 49 | 11 23 | 08 11 | 28 59 | 26 25 | 00 01 |
| 50 | 11 29 | 08 06 | 28 38 | 25 56 | 29♐39 |
| 51 | 11 34 | 08 02 | 28 18 | 25 26 | 29 16 |
| 52 | 11 40 | 07 57 | 27 56 | 24 55 | 28 52 |
| 53 | 11 47 | 07 52 | 27 35 | 24 23 | 28 26 |
| 54 | 11 53 | 07 48 | 27 12 | 23 50 | 27 59 |
| 55 | 12 00 | 07 43 | 26 50 | 23 15 | 27 29 |
| 56 | 12 07 | 07 38 | 26 26 | 22 39 | 26 58 |
| 57 | 12 14 | 07 32 | 26 03 | 22 02 | 26 24 |
| 58 | 12 22 | 07 27 | 25 38 | 21 23 | 25 47 |
| 59 | 12 29 | 07 21 | 25 13 | 20 43 | 25 07 |
| 60 | 12♍38 | 07♎16 | 24♎47 | 20♏00 | 24♐24 |

**8h 44m 0s — 131° 0' 0" — 08 ♌ 34**

| LAT. | 11 | 12 | ASC | 2 | 3 |
|---|---|---|---|---|---|
| 0 | 09♍26 | 11♎58 | 13♏27 | 12♐28 | 10♑07 |
| 5 | 09 41 | 11 40 | 12 03 | 11 12 | 09 27 |
| 10 | 09 55 | 11 23 | 10 42 | 09 56 | 08 47 |
| 15 | 10 10 | 11 07 | 09 23 | 08 38 | 08 05 |
| 20 | 10 26 | 10 50 | 08 05 | 07 18 | 07 21 |
| 21 | 10 29 | 10 47 | 07 49 | 07 02 | 07 12 |
| 22 | 10 32 | 10 43 | 07 34 | 06 45 | 07 02 |
| 23 | 10 35 | 10 40 | 07 18 | 06 29 | 06 53 |
| 24 | 10 38 | 10 37 | 07 02 | 06 12 | 06 43 |
| 25 | 10 42 | 10 33 | 06 46 | 05 55 | 06 33 |
| 26 | 10 45 | 10 30 | 06 30 | 05 37 | 06 23 |
| 27 | 10 48 | 10 26 | 06 14 | 05 20 | 06 13 |
| 28 | 10 52 | 10 23 | 05 58 | 05 02 | 06 03 |
| 29 | 10 55 | 10 19 | 05 42 | 04 44 | 05 52 |
| 30 | 10 58 | 10 16 | 05 26 | 04 25 | 05 41 |
| 31 | 11 02 | 10 12 | 05 09 | 04 07 | 05 30 |
| 32 | 11 05 | 10 09 | 04 53 | 03 48 | 05 19 |
| 33 | 11 09 | 10 05 | 04 36 | 03 28 | 05 07 |
| 34 | 11 13 | 10 01 | 04 20 | 03 09 | 04 55 |
| 35 | 11 16 | 09 58 | 04 03 | 02 49 | 04 43 |
| 36 | 11 20 | 09 54 | 03 46 | 02 28 | 04 30 |
| 37 | 11 24 | 09 50 | 03 28 | 02 07 | 04 17 |
| 38 | 11 28 | 09 46 | 03 11 | 01 46 | 04 03 |
| 39 | 11 32 | 09 42 | 02 53 | 01 24 | 03 49 |
| 40 | 11 36 | 09 38 | 02 35 | 01 02 | 03 35 |
| 41 | 11 40 | 09 34 | 02 17 | 00 39 | 03 20 |
| 42 | 11 45 | 09 30 | 01 59 | 00 16 | 03 05 |
| 43 | 11 49 | 09 26 | 01 40 | 29♏52 | 02 48 |
| 44 | 11 54 | 09 22 | 01 21 | 29 27 | 02 32 |
| 45 | 11 58 | 09 18 | 01 02 | 29 02 | 02 14 |
| 46 | 12 03 | 09 13 | 00 43 | 28 36 | 01 56 |
| 47 | 12 08 | 09 09 | 00 23 | 28 09 | 01 37 |
| 48 | 12 13 | 09 04 | 00 03 | 27 42 | 01 17 |
| 49 | 12 18 | 08 59 | 29♎42 | 27 13 | 00 56 |
| 50 | 12 24 | 08 55 | 29 21 | 26 44 | 00 35 |
| 51 | 12 29 | 08 50 | 29 00 | 26 13 | 00 11 |
| 52 | 12 35 | 08 45 | 28 38 | 25 42 | 29♐47 |
| 53 | 12 41 | 08 40 | 28 16 | 25 09 | 29 21 |
| 54 | 12 47 | 08 34 | 27 53 | 24 36 | 28 53 |
| 55 | 12 53 | 08 29 | 27 30 | 24 00 | 28 24 |
| 56 | 13 00 | 08 23 | 27 06 | 23 24 | 27 52 |
| 57 | 13 07 | 08 17 | 26 41 | 22 46 | 27 18 |
| 58 | 13 14 | 08 12 | 26 16 | 22 07 | 26 41 |
| 59 | 13 22 | 08 05 | 25 51 | 21 25 | 26 01 |
| 60 | 13♍30 | 07♎59 | 25♎24 | 20♏42 | 25♐17 |

**8h 48m 0s — 132° 0' 0" — 09 ♌ 34**

| LAT. | 11 | 12 | ASC | 2 | 3 |
|---|---|---|---|---|---|
| 0 | 10♍30 | 13♎03 | 14♏28 | 13♐24 | 11♑02 |
| 5 | 10 44 | 12 44 | 13 02 | 12 08 | 10 23 |
| 10 | 10 58 | 12 25 | 11 40 | 10 51 | 09 42 |
| 15 | 11 12 | 12 07 | 10 19 | 09 33 | 09 01 |
| 20 | 11 27 | 11 49 | 08 59 | 08 12 | 08 17 |
| 21 | 11 30 | 11 45 | 08 43 | 07 56 | 08 07 |
| 22 | 11 33 | 11 42 | 08 27 | 07 39 | 07 58 |
| 23 | 11 36 | 11 38 | 08 11 | 07 22 | 07 49 |
| 24 | 11 39 | 11 34 | 07 55 | 07 05 | 07 39 |
| 25 | 11 42 | 11 31 | 07 39 | 06 48 | 07 29 |
| 26 | 11 45 | 11 27 | 07 23 | 06 31 | 07 19 |
| 27 | 11 48 | 11 23 | 07 06 | 06 13 | 07 09 |
| 28 | 11 51 | 11 19 | 06 50 | 05 55 | 06 58 |
| 29 | 11 55 | 11 16 | 06 34 | 05 37 | 06 48 |
| 30 | 11 58 | 11 12 | 06 17 | 05 18 | 06 37 |
| 31 | 12 01 | 11 08 | 06 00 | 04 59 | 06 26 |
| 32 | 12 05 | 11 04 | 05 43 | 04 40 | 06 14 |
| 33 | 12 08 | 11 00 | 05 26 | 04 21 | 06 03 |
| 34 | 12 12 | 10 56 | 05 09 | 04 01 | 05 51 |
| 35 | 12 15 | 10 52 | 04 52 | 03 41 | 05 38 |
| 36 | 12 19 | 10 48 | 04 34 | 03 20 | 05 26 |
| 37 | 12 22 | 10 44 | 04 17 | 02 59 | 05 12 |
| 38 | 12 26 | 10 40 | 03 59 | 02 37 | 04 59 |
| 39 | 12 30 | 10 35 | 03 41 | 02 15 | 04 45 |
| 40 | 12 34 | 10 31 | 03 23 | 01 53 | 04 31 |
| 41 | 12 38 | 10 27 | 03 04 | 01 30 | 04 16 |
| 42 | 12 42 | 10 22 | 02 45 | 01 06 | 04 00 |
| 43 | 12 46 | 10 18 | 02 26 | 00 42 | 03 44 |
| 44 | 12 51 | 10 13 | 02 07 | 00 17 | 03 27 |
| 45 | 12 55 | 10 08 | 01 47 | 29♏51 | 03 10 |
| 46 | 12 59 | 10 03 | 01 27 | 29 25 | 02 52 |
| 47 | 13 04 | 09 59 | 01 07 | 28 58 | 02 33 |
| 48 | 13 09 | 09 54 | 00 46 | 28 30 | 02 13 |
| 49 | 13 14 | 09 48 | 00 25 | 28 01 | 01 52 |
| 50 | 13 19 | 09 43 | 00 04 | 27 31 | 01 30 |
| 51 | 13 24 | 09 38 | 29♎42 | 27 01 | 01 07 |
| 52 | 13 30 | 09 32 | 29 20 | 26 29 | 00 42 |
| 53 | 13 35 | 09 27 | 28 57 | 25 56 | 00 16 |
| 54 | 13 41 | 09 21 | 28 33 | 25 21 | 29♐48 |
| 55 | 13 47 | 09 15 | 28 10 | 24 46 | 29 18 |
| 56 | 13 53 | 09 09 | 27 45 | 24 09 | 28 47 |
| 57 | 14 00 | 09 03 | 27 20 | 23 30 | 28 12 |
| 58 | 14 07 | 08 56 | 26 54 | 22 50 | 27 35 |
| 59 | 14 14 | 08 49 | 26 28 | 22 08 | 26 55 |
| 60 | 14♍21 | 08♎43 | 26♎01 | 21♏25 | 26♐10 |

**8h 52m 0s — 133° 0' 0" — 10 ♌ 33**

| LAT. | 11 | 12 | ASC | 2 | 3 |
|---|---|---|---|---|---|
| 0 | 11♍34 | 14♎07 | 15♏28 | 14♐20 | 11♑58 |
| 5 | 11 48 | 13 47 | 14 01 | 13 03 | 11 18 |
| 10 | 12 01 | 13 27 | 12 37 | 11 46 | 10 38 |
| 15 | 12 14 | 13 07 | 11 15 | 10 28 | 09 56 |
| 20 | 12 28 | 12 48 | 09 54 | 09 07 | 09 12 |
| 21 | 12 31 | 12 44 | 09 37 | 08 50 | 09 03 |
| 22 | 12 34 | 12 40 | 09 21 | 08 33 | 08 54 |
| 23 | 12 37 | 12 36 | 09 05 | 08 16 | 08 44 |
| 24 | 12 40 | 12 32 | 08 48 | 07 59 | 08 35 |
| 25 | 12 43 | 12 28 | 08 32 | 07 42 | 08 25 |
| 26 | 12 45 | 12 24 | 08 15 | 07 24 | 08 15 |
| 27 | 12 48 | 12 20 | 07 59 | 07 06 | 08 05 |
| 28 | 12 51 | 12 16 | 07 42 | 06 48 | 07 54 |
| 29 | 12 55 | 12 12 | 07 25 | 06 30 | 07 44 |
| 30 | 12 58 | 12 07 | 07 08 | 06 11 | 07 33 |
| 31 | 13 01 | 12 03 | 06 51 | 05 52 | 07 22 |
| 32 | 13 04 | 11 59 | 06 34 | 05 33 | 07 10 |
| 33 | 13 07 | 11 55 | 06 16 | 05 13 | 06 59 |
| 34 | 13 11 | 11 50 | 05 59 | 04 53 | 06 47 |
| 35 | 13 14 | 11 46 | 05 41 | 04 33 | 06 34 |
| 36 | 13 17 | 11 42 | 05 23 | 04 12 | 06 21 |
| 37 | 13 21 | 11 37 | 05 05 | 03 50 | 06 08 |
| 38 | 13 24 | 11 33 | 04 47 | 03 29 | 05 55 |
| 39 | 13 28 | 11 28 | 04 29 | 03 06 | 05 41 |
| 40 | 13 32 | 11 23 | 04 10 | 02 44 | 05 26 |
| 41 | 13 35 | 11 19 | 03 51 | 02 20 | 05 11 |
| 42 | 13 39 | 11 14 | 03 32 | 01 57 | 04 56 |
| 43 | 13 43 | 11 09 | 03 12 | 01 32 | 04 40 |
| 44 | 13 47 | 11 04 | 02 53 | 01 07 | 04 23 |
| 45 | 13 52 | 10 59 | 02 32 | 00 41 | 04 06 |
| 46 | 13 56 | 10 54 | 02 12 | 00 14 | 03 47 |
| 47 | 14 00 | 10 48 | 01 51 | 29♏47 | 03 28 |
| 48 | 14 05 | 10 43 | 01 30 | 29 18 | 03 08 |
| 49 | 14 09 | 10 37 | 01 09 | 28 49 | 02 47 |
| 50 | 14 14 | 10 32 | 00 47 | 28 19 | 02 25 |
| 51 | 14 19 | 10 26 | 00 24 | 27 48 | 02 02 |
| 52 | 14 24 | 10 20 | 00 01 | 27 16 | 01 37 |
| 53 | 14 30 | 10 14 | 29♎38 | 26 42 | 01 11 |
| 54 | 14 35 | 10 08 | 29 14 | 26 07 | 00 43 |
| 55 | 14 41 | 10 01 | 28 50 | 25 31 | 00 13 |
| 56 | 14 47 | 09 55 | 28 25 | 24 54 | 29♐41 |
| 57 | 14 53 | 09 48 | 27 59 | 24 15 | 29 07 |
| 58 | 14 59 | 09 41 | 27 33 | 23 34 | 28 30 |
| 59 | 15 06 | 09 34 | 27 06 | 22 51 | 27 49 |
| 60 | 15♍13 | 09♎26 | 26♎38 | 22♏07 | 27♐04 |

**8h 56m 0s — 134° 0' 0" — 11 ♌ 32**

| LAT. | 11 | 12 | ASC | 2 | 3 |
|---|---|---|---|---|---|
| 0 | 12♍39 | 15♎12 | 16♏28 | 15♐16 | 12♑53 |
| 5 | 12 51 | 14 50 | 15 00 | 13 59 | 12 14 |
| 10 | 13 04 | 14 29 | 13 34 | 12 41 | 11 34 |
| 15 | 13 17 | 14 08 | 12 11 | 11 22 | 10 52 |
| 20 | 13 30 | 13 47 | 10 48 | 10 01 | 10 08 |
| 21 | 13 32 | 13 42 | 10 31 | 09 44 | 09 59 |
| 22 | 13 35 | 13 38 | 10 15 | 09 27 | 09 50 |
| 23 | 13 38 | 13 34 | 09 58 | 09 10 | 09 40 |
| 24 | 13 40 | 13 30 | 09 41 | 08 53 | 09 31 |
| 25 | 13 43 | 13 25 | 09 24 | 08 35 | 09 21 |
| 26 | 13 46 | 13 21 | 09 08 | 08 17 | 09 11 |
| 27 | 13 49 | 13 17 | 08 51 | 07 59 | 09 01 |
| 28 | 13 52 | 13 12 | 08 33 | 07 41 | 08 50 |
| 29 | 13 54 | 13 08 | 08 16 | 07 23 | 08 40 |
| 30 | 13 57 | 13 03 | 07 59 | 07 04 | 08 29 |
| 31 | 14 00 | 12 59 | 07 42 | 06 45 | 08 18 |
| 32 | 14 03 | 12 54 | 07 24 | 06 25 | 08 06 |
| 33 | 14 06 | 12 50 | 07 06 | 06 05 | 07 55 |
| 34 | 14 10 | 12 45 | 06 48 | 05 45 | 07 43 |
| 35 | 14 13 | 12 40 | 06 30 | 05 25 | 07 30 |
| 36 | 14 16 | 12 36 | 06 12 | 05 03 | 07 17 |
| 37 | 14 19 | 12 31 | 05 54 | 04 42 | 07 04 |
| 38 | 14 23 | 12 26 | 05 35 | 04 20 | 06 51 |
| 39 | 14 26 | 12 21 | 05 16 | 03 58 | 06 37 |
| 40 | 14 29 | 12 16 | 04 57 | 03 35 | 06 22 |
| 41 | 14 33 | 12 11 | 04 38 | 03 11 | 06 07 |
| 42 | 14 37 | 12 06 | 04 18 | 02 47 | 05 52 |
| 43 | 14 40 | 12 00 | 03 58 | 02 22 | 05 36 |
| 44 | 14 44 | 11 55 | 03 38 | 01 57 | 05 19 |
| 45 | 14 48 | 11 49 | 03 18 | 01 30 | 05 02 |
| 46 | 14 52 | 11 44 | 02 57 | 01 03 | 04 43 |
| 47 | 14 56 | 11 38 | 02 35 | 00 36 | 04 24 |
| 48 | 15 01 | 11 32 | 02 14 | 00 07 | 04 04 |
| 49 | 15 05 | 11 26 | 01 52 | 29♏37 | 03 43 |
| 50 | 15 10 | 11 20 | 01 29 | 29 07 | 03 21 |
| 51 | 15 14 | 11 14 | 01 06 | 28 35 | 02 58 |
| 52 | 15 19 | 11 08 | 00 43 | 28 02 | 02 33 |
| 53 | 15 24 | 11 01 | 00 19 | 27 29 | 02 07 |
| 54 | 15 29 | 10 54 | 29♎55 | 26 53 | 01 39 |
| 55 | 15 35 | 10 47 | 29 30 | 26 17 | 01 09 |
| 56 | 15 40 | 10 40 | 29 04 | 25 39 | 00 37 |
| 57 | 15 46 | 10 33 | 28 38 | 24 59 | 00 02 |
| 58 | 15 52 | 10 25 | 28 11 | 24 18 | 29♐24 |
| 59 | 15 59 | 10 18 | 27 43 | 23 34 | 28 43 |
| 60 | 16♍05 | 10♎09 | 27♎15 | 22♏49 | 27♐58 |

**9h 0m 0s — 135° 0' 0" — 12 ♌ 32**

| LAT. | 11 | 12 | ASC | 2 | 3 |
|---|---|---|---|---|---|
| 0 | 13♍43 | 16♎17 | 17♏28 | 16♐11 | 13♑49 |
| 5 | 13 55 | 15 53 | 15 58 | 14 54 | 13 10 |
| 10 | 14 07 | 15 30 | 14 32 | 13 36 | 12 30 |
| 15 | 14 19 | 15 08 | 13 07 | 12 17 | 11 48 |
| 20 | 14 31 | 14 45 | 11 42 | 10 55 | 11 04 |
| 21 | 14 34 | 14 41 | 11 25 | 10 38 | 10 55 |
| 22 | 14 36 | 14 36 | 11 08 | 10 21 | 10 46 |
| 23 | 14 39 | 14 32 | 10 51 | 10 04 | 10 36 |
| 24 | 14 41 | 14 27 | 10 34 | 09 46 | 10 27 |
| 25 | 14 44 | 14 22 | 10 17 | 09 29 | 10 17 |
| 26 | 14 46 | 14 18 | 10 00 | 09 11 | 10 07 |
| 27 | 14 49 | 14 13 | 09 43 | 08 53 | 09 57 |
| 28 | 14 52 | 14 08 | 09 25 | 08 34 | 09 46 |
| 29 | 14 54 | 14 04 | 09 08 | 08 16 | 09 36 |
| 30 | 14 57 | 13 59 | 08 50 | 07 57 | 09 25 |
| 31 | 15 00 | 13 54 | 08 32 | 07 37 | 09 14 |
| 32 | 15 03 | 13 49 | 08 14 | 07 18 | 09 02 |
| 33 | 15 06 | 13 44 | 07 56 | 06 58 | 08 51 |
| 34 | 15 09 | 13 39 | 07 38 | 06 37 | 08 39 |
| 35 | 15 12 | 13 34 | 07 20 | 06 16 | 08 26 |
| 36 | 15 15 | 13 29 | 07 01 | 05 55 | 08 14 |
| 37 | 15 18 | 13 24 | 06 42 | 05 34 | 08 00 |
| 38 | 15 21 | 13 19 | 06 23 | 05 11 | 07 47 |
| 39 | 15 24 | 13 14 | 06 04 | 04 49 | 07 33 |
| 40 | 15 27 | 13 08 | 05 44 | 04 26 | 07 19 |
| 41 | 15 31 | 13 03 | 05 25 | 04 02 | 07 04 |
| 42 | 15 34 | 12 57 | 05 05 | 03 37 | 06 48 |
| 43 | 15 38 | 12 52 | 04 44 | 03 12 | 06 32 |
| 44 | 15 41 | 12 46 | 04 24 | 02 46 | 06 15 |
| 45 | 15 45 | 12 40 | 04 03 | 02 20 | 05 58 |
| 46 | 15 49 | 12 34 | 03 41 | 01 53 | 05 39 |
| 47 | 15 53 | 12 28 | 03 20 | 01 25 | 05 20 |
| 48 | 15 57 | 12 22 | 02 57 | 00 56 | 05 00 |
| 49 | 16 01 | 12 15 | 02 35 | 00 26 | 04 39 |
| 50 | 16 05 | 12 09 | 02 12 | 29♏55 | 04 17 |
| 51 | 16 09 | 12 02 | 01 49 | 29 23 | 03 53 |
| 52 | 16 14 | 11 55 | 01 25 | 28 49 | 03 29 |
| 53 | 16 19 | 11 48 | 01 00 | 28 15 | 03 02 |
| 54 | 16 24 | 11 41 | 00 35 | 27 39 | 02 34 |
| 55 | 16 29 | 11 34 | 00 10 | 27 02 | 02 04 |
| 56 | 16 34 | 11 26 | 29♎43 | 26 24 | 01 32 |
| 57 | 16 39 | 11 18 | 29 16 | 25 43 | 00 57 |
| 58 | 16 45 | 11 10 | 28 49 | 25 01 | 00 19 |
| 59 | 16 51 | 11 02 | 28 21 | 24 17 | 29♐38 |
| 60 | 16♍57 | 10♎53 | 27♎51 | 23♏31 | 28♐53 |

# Placidus Table of Houses for Latitudes 0° to 60° North

9h 4m 0s — 136° 0' 0" — 13 ♌ 32

| LAT. | 11 | 12 | ASC | 2 | 3 |
|---|---|---|---|---|---|
| 0 | 14♍48 | 17♎21 | 18♏28 | 17♐07 | 14♑44 |
| 5 | 14 59 | 16 56 | 16 57 | 15 49 | 14 05 |
| 10 | 15 10 | 16 32 | 15 29 | 14 31 | 13 26 |
| 15 | 15 21 | 16 08 | 14 02 | 13 12 | 12 44 |
| 20 | 15 33 | 15 44 | 12 36 | 11 49 | 12 00 |
| 21 | 15 35 | 15 39 | 12 19 | 11 32 | 11 51 |
| 22 | 15 37 | 15 34 | 12 02 | 11 15 | 11 42 |
| 23 | 15 40 | 15 29 | 11 44 | 10 58 | 11 33 |
| 24 | 15 42 | 15 25 | 11 27 | 10 40 | 11 23 |
| 25 | 15 45 | 15 20 | 11 10 | 10 22 | 11 13 |
| 26 | 15 47 | 15 15 | 10 52 | 10 04 | 11 03 |
| 27 | 15 49 | 15 10 | 10 34 | 09 46 | 10 53 |
| 28 | 15 52 | 15 05 | 10 17 | 09 27 | 10 43 |
| 29 | 15 55 | 15 00 | 09 59 | 09 09 | 10 32 |
| 30 | 15 57 | 14 55 | 09 41 | 08 50 | 10 21 |
| 31 | 16 00 | 14 50 | 09 23 | 08 30 | 10 10 |
| 32 | 16 02 | 14 44 | 09 05 | 08 10 | 09 59 |
| 33 | 16 05 | 14 39 | 08 46 | 07 50 | 09 47 |
| 34 | 16 08 | 14 34 | 08 28 | 07 29 | 09 35 |
| 35 | 16 11 | 14 29 | 08 09 | 07 09 | 09 23 |
| 36 | 16 13 | 14 23 | 07 50 | 06 47 | 09 10 |
| 37 | 16 16 | 14 18 | 07 31 | 06 25 | 08 57 |
| 38 | 16 19 | 14 12 | 07 11 | 06 03 | 08 43 |
| 39 | 16 22 | 14 06 | 06 52 | 05 40 | 08 29 |
| 40 | 16 25 | 14 01 | 06 32 | 05 16 | 08 15 |
| 41 | 16 28 | 13 55 | 06 11 | 04 52 | 08 00 |
| 42 | 16 32 | 13 49 | 05 51 | 04 28 | 07 44 |
| 43 | 16 35 | 13 43 | 05 30 | 04 02 | 07 28 |
| 44 | 16 38 | 13 37 | 05 09 | 03 36 | 07 11 |
| 45 | 16 42 | 13 31 | 04 48 | 03 10 | 06 54 |
| 46 | 16 45 | 13 24 | 04 26 | 02 42 | 06 36 |
| 47 | 16 49 | 13 18 | 04 04 | 02 14 | 06 16 |
| 48 | 16 53 | 13 11 | 03 41 | 01 44 | 05 56 |
| 49 | 16 56 | 13 04 | 03 18 | 01 14 | 05 35 |
| 50 | 17 00 | 12 57 | 02 55 | 00 43 | 05 13 |
| 51 | 17 05 | 12 50 | 02 31 | 00 10 | 04 50 |
| 52 | 17 09 | 12 43 | 02 06 | 29♏37 | 04 25 |
| 53 | 17 13 | 12 35 | 01 41 | 29 02 | 03 58 |
| 54 | 17 18 | 12 28 | 01 16 | 28 25 | 03 30 |
| 55 | 17 22 | 12 20 | 00 49 | 27 48 | 03 00 |
| 56 | 17 27 | 12 12 | 00 23 | 27 09 | 02 28 |
| 57 | 17 32 | 12 03 | 29♎55 | 26 28 | 01 53 |
| 58 | 17 38 | 11 54 | 29 27 | 25 45 | 01 15 |
| 59 | 17 43 | 11 46 | 28 58 | 25 00 | 00 33 |
| 60 | 17♍49 | 11♎36 | 28♎28 | 24♏14 | 29♐47 |

9h 8m 0s — 137° 0' 0" — 14 ♌ 32

| LAT. | 11 | 12 | ASC | 2 | 3 |
|---|---|---|---|---|---|
| 0 | 15♍53 | 18♎26 | 19♏27 | 18♐02 | 15♑40 |
| 5 | 16 03 | 17 59 | 17 55 | 16 44 | 15 01 |
| 10 | 16 13 | 17 33 | 16 26 | 15 26 | 14 22 |
| 15 | 16 24 | 17 08 | 14 58 | 14 06 | 13 40 |
| 20 | 16 34 | 16 43 | 13 30 | 12 43 | 12 57 |
| 21 | 16 36 | 16 37 | 13 13 | 12 26 | 12 48 |
| 22 | 16 39 | 16 32 | 12 55 | 12 09 | 12 38 |
| 23 | 16 41 | 16 27 | 12 38 | 11 51 | 12 29 |
| 24 | 16 43 | 16 22 | 12 20 | 11 34 | 12 19 |
| 25 | 16 45 | 16 17 | 12 02 | 11 16 | 12 09 |
| 26 | 16 48 | 16 12 | 11 44 | 10 58 | 12 00 |
| 27 | 16 50 | 16 06 | 11 26 | 10 39 | 11 49 |
| 28 | 16 52 | 16 01 | 11 08 | 10 21 | 11 39 |
| 29 | 16 55 | 15 56 | 10 50 | 10 02 | 11 28 |
| 30 | 16 57 | 15 50 | 10 32 | 09 42 | 11 18 |
| 31 | 16 59 | 15 45 | 10 13 | 09 23 | 11 06 |
| 32 | 17 02 | 15 39 | 09 55 | 09 03 | 10 55 |
| 33 | 17 04 | 15 34 | 09 36 | 08 42 | 10 43 |
| 34 | 17 07 | 15 28 | 09 17 | 08 22 | 10 31 |
| 35 | 17 10 | 15 23 | 08 58 | 08 01 | 10 19 |
| 36 | 17 12 | 15 17 | 08 39 | 07 39 | 10 06 |
| 37 | 17 15 | 15 11 | 08 19 | 07 17 | 09 53 |
| 38 | 17 18 | 15 05 | 07 59 | 06 54 | 09 40 |
| 39 | 17 20 | 14 59 | 07 39 | 06 31 | 09 26 |
| 40 | 17 23 | 14 53 | 07 19 | 06 07 | 09 11 |
| 41 | 17 26 | 14 47 | 06 58 | 05 43 | 08 56 |
| 42 | 17 29 | 14 41 | 06 37 | 05 18 | 08 41 |
| 43 | 17 32 | 14 34 | 06 16 | 04 53 | 08 25 |
| 44 | 17 35 | 14 28 | 05 55 | 04 26 | 08 08 |
| 45 | 17 38 | 14 21 | 05 33 | 03 59 | 07 50 |
| 46 | 17 42 | 14 14 | 05 11 | 03 31 | 07 32 |
| 47 | 17 45 | 14 07 | 04 48 | 03 03 | 07 13 |
| 48 | 17 49 | 14 00 | 04 25 | 02 33 | 06 53 |
| 49 | 17 52 | 13 53 | 04 01 | 02 02 | 06 32 |
| 50 | 17 56 | 13 46 | 03 37 | 01 31 | 06 09 |
| 51 | 18 00 | 13 38 | 03 13 | 00 58 | 05 46 |
| 52 | 18 04 | 13 30 | 02 48 | 00 24 | 05 21 |
| 53 | 18 08 | 13 22 | 02 22 | 29♏48 | 04 54 |
| 54 | 18 12 | 13 14 | 01 56 | 29 12 | 04 26 |
| 55 | 18 16 | 13 06 | 01 29 | 28 33 | 03 56 |
| 56 | 18 21 | 12 57 | 01 02 | 27 54 | 03 23 |
| 57 | 18 26 | 12 48 | 00 34 | 27 12 | 02 48 |
| 58 | 18 31 | 12 39 | 00 05 | 26 29 | 02 10 |
| 59 | 18 36 | 12 30 | 29♎35 | 25 44 | 01 28 |
| 60 | 18♍41 | 12♎20 | 29♎05 | 24♏56 | 00♑42 |

9h 12m 0s — 138° 0' 0" — 15 ♌ 32

| LAT. | 11 | 12 | ASC | 2 | 3 |
|---|---|---|---|---|---|
| 0 | 16♍57 | 19♎30 | 20♏26 | 18♐58 | 16♑36 |
| 5 | 17 07 | 19 02 | 18 53 | 17 40 | 15 57 |
| 10 | 17 17 | 18 35 | 17 22 | 16 21 | 15 18 |
| 15 | 17 26 | 18 08 | 15 53 | 15 01 | 14 37 |
| 20 | 17 36 | 17 41 | 14 24 | 13 37 | 13 53 |
| 21 | 17 38 | 17 36 | 14 07 | 13 20 | 13 44 |
| 22 | 17 40 | 17 30 | 13 49 | 13 03 | 13 35 |
| 23 | 17 42 | 17 25 | 13 31 | 12 45 | 13 25 |
| 24 | 17 44 | 17 19 | 13 13 | 12 27 | 13 16 |
| 25 | 17 46 | 17 14 | 12 55 | 12 09 | 13 06 |
| 26 | 17 48 | 17 08 | 12 36 | 11 51 | 12 56 |
| 27 | 17 50 | 17 03 | 12 18 | 11 33 | 12 46 |
| 28 | 17 53 | 16 57 | 12 00 | 11 14 | 12 36 |
| 29 | 17 55 | 16 52 | 11 41 | 10 55 | 12 25 |
| 30 | 17 57 | 16 46 | 11 23 | 10 35 | 12 14 |
| 31 | 17 59 | 16 40 | 11 04 | 10 16 | 12 03 |
| 32 | 18 02 | 16 34 | 10 45 | 09 55 | 11 52 |
| 33 | 18 04 | 16 29 | 10 26 | 09 35 | 11 40 |
| 34 | 18 06 | 16 23 | 10 06 | 09 14 | 11 28 |
| 35 | 18 09 | 16 17 | 09 47 | 08 53 | 11 16 |
| 36 | 18 11 | 16 11 | 09 27 | 08 31 | 11 03 |
| 37 | 18 13 | 16 04 | 09 07 | 08 09 | 10 50 |
| 38 | 18 16 | 15 58 | 08 47 | 07 46 | 10 36 |
| 39 | 18 19 | 15 52 | 08 27 | 07 22 | 10 22 |
| 40 | 18 21 | 15 45 | 08 06 | 06 59 | 10 08 |
| 41 | 18 24 | 15 39 | 07 45 | 06 34 | 09 53 |
| 42 | 18 27 | 15 32 | 07 24 | 06 09 | 09 38 |
| 43 | 18 30 | 15 25 | 07 02 | 05 43 | 09 21 |
| 44 | 18 32 | 15 18 | 06 40 | 05 16 | 09 05 |
| 45 | 18 35 | 15 11 | 06 18 | 04 49 | 08 47 |
| 46 | 18 38 | 15 04 | 05 55 | 04 21 | 08 29 |
| 47 | 18 42 | 14 57 | 05 32 | 03 52 | 08 10 |
| 48 | 18 45 | 14 50 | 05 08 | 03 22 | 07 49 |
| 49 | 18 48 | 14 42 | 04 44 | 02 51 | 07 28 |
| 50 | 18 51 | 14 34 | 04 20 | 02 19 | 07 06 |
| 51 | 18 55 | 14 26 | 03 55 | 01 45 | 06 42 |
| 52 | 18 59 | 14 18 | 03 29 | 01 11 | 06 17 |
| 53 | 19 02 | 14 09 | 03 03 | 00 35 | 05 51 |
| 54 | 19 06 | 14 01 | 02 37 | 29♏58 | 05 23 |
| 55 | 19 10 | 13 52 | 02 09 | 29 19 | 04 52 |
| 56 | 19 15 | 13 43 | 01 41 | 28 39 | 04 20 |
| 57 | 19 19 | 13 33 | 01 13 | 27 57 | 03 44 |
| 58 | 19 24 | 13 24 | 00 43 | 27 13 | 03 06 |
| 59 | 19 28 | 13 13 | 00 13 | 26 27 | 02 24 |
| 60 | 19♍33 | 13♎03 | 29♎42 | 25♏39 | 01♑38 |

9h 16m 0s — 139° 0' 0" — 16 ♌ 33

| LAT. | 11 | 12 | ASC | 2 | 3 |
|---|---|---|---|---|---|
| 0 | 18♍02 | 20♎34 | 21♏26 | 19♐53 | 17♑32 |
| 5 | 18 11 | 20 05 | 19 51 | 18 35 | 16 53 |
| 10 | 18 20 | 19 36 | 18 19 | 17 16 | 16 14 |
| 15 | 18 29 | 19 08 | 16 49 | 15 55 | 15 33 |
| 20 | 18 38 | 18 40 | 15 18 | 14 31 | 14 49 |
| 21 | 18 40 | 18 34 | 15 00 | 14 14 | 14 40 |
| 22 | 18 41 | 18 28 | 14 42 | 13 57 | 14 31 |
| 23 | 18 43 | 18 23 | 14 24 | 13 39 | 14 22 |
| 24 | 18 45 | 18 17 | 14 05 | 13 21 | 14 12 |
| 25 | 18 47 | 18 11 | 13 47 | 13 03 | 14 03 |
| 26 | 18 49 | 18 05 | 13 29 | 12 45 | 13 53 |
| 27 | 18 51 | 17 59 | 13 10 | 12 26 | 13 43 |
| 28 | 18 53 | 17 53 | 12 51 | 12 07 | 13 32 |
| 29 | 18 55 | 17 47 | 12 32 | 11 48 | 13 22 |
| 30 | 18 57 | 17 41 | 12 13 | 11 28 | 13 11 |
| 31 | 18 59 | 17 35 | 11 54 | 11 08 | 13 00 |
| 32 | 19 01 | 17 29 | 11 35 | 10 48 | 12 48 |
| 33 | 19 03 | 17 23 | 11 16 | 10 27 | 12 37 |
| 34 | 19 05 | 17 17 | 10 56 | 10 06 | 12 25 |
| 35 | 19 08 | 17 11 | 10 36 | 09 45 | 12 12 |
| 36 | 19 10 | 17 04 | 10 16 | 09 23 | 12 00 |
| 37 | 19 12 | 16 58 | 09 56 | 09 00 | 11 47 |
| 38 | 19 15 | 16 51 | 09 35 | 08 37 | 11 33 |
| 39 | 19 17 | 16 44 | 09 14 | 08 14 | 11 19 |
| 40 | 19 19 | 16 38 | 08 53 | 07 50 | 11 05 |
| 41 | 19 22 | 16 31 | 08 32 | 07 25 | 10 50 |
| 42 | 19 24 | 16 24 | 08 10 | 07 00 | 10 34 |
| 43 | 19 27 | 16 17 | 07 48 | 06 33 | 10 18 |
| 44 | 19 30 | 16 09 | 07 26 | 06 07 | 10 01 |
| 45 | 19 32 | 16 02 | 07 03 | 05 39 | 09 44 |
| 46 | 19 35 | 15 54 | 06 40 | 05 10 | 09 26 |
| 47 | 19 38 | 15 47 | 06 16 | 04 41 | 09 06 |
| 48 | 19 41 | 15 39 | 05 52 | 04 11 | 08 46 |
| 49 | 19 44 | 15 31 | 05 28 | 03 39 | 08 25 |
| 50 | 19 47 | 15 22 | 05 03 | 03 07 | 08 03 |
| 51 | 19 50 | 15 14 | 04 37 | 02 33 | 07 39 |
| 52 | 19 54 | 15 05 | 04 11 | 01 58 | 07 14 |
| 53 | 19 57 | 14 56 | 03 44 | 01 22 | 06 48 |
| 54 | 20 01 | 14 47 | 03 17 | 00 44 | 06 19 |
| 55 | 20 04 | 14 38 | 02 49 | 00 05 | 05 49 |
| 56 | 20 08 | 14 28 | 02 21 | 29♏24 | 05 16 |
| 57 | 20 12 | 14 18 | 01 51 | 28 41 | 04 41 |
| 58 | 20 16 | 14 08 | 01 21 | 27 57 | 04 02 |
| 59 | 20 21 | 13 57 | 00 50 | 27 10 | 03 20 |
| 60 | 20♍25 | 13♎46 | 00♏19 | 26♏21 | 02♑34 |

9h 20m 0s — 140° 0' 0" — 17 ♌ 33

| LAT. | 11 | 12 | ASC | 2 | 3 |
|---|---|---|---|---|---|
| 0 | 19♍07 | 21♎38 | 22♏25 | 20♐49 | 18♑28 |
| 5 | 19 15 | 21 07 | 20 49 | 19 30 | 17 50 |
| 10 | 19 23 | 20 37 | 19 15 | 18 11 | 17 10 |
| 15 | 19 31 | 20 08 | 17 44 | 16 50 | 16 29 |
| 20 | 19 40 | 19 38 | 16 12 | 15 26 | 15 46 |
| 21 | 19 41 | 19 32 | 15 54 | 15 08 | 15 37 |
| 22 | 19 43 | 19 26 | 15 35 | 14 51 | 15 28 |
| 23 | 19 45 | 19 20 | 15 17 | 14 33 | 15 19 |
| 24 | 19 46 | 19 14 | 14 58 | 14 15 | 15 09 |
| 25 | 19 48 | 19 08 | 14 39 | 13 57 | 14 59 |
| 26 | 19 50 | 19 02 | 14 21 | 13 38 | 14 49 |
| 27 | 19 52 | 18 56 | 14 02 | 13 19 | 14 39 |
| 28 | 19 53 | 18 50 | 13 43 | 13 00 | 14 29 |
| 29 | 19 55 | 18 43 | 13 24 | 12 41 | 14 18 |
| 30 | 19 57 | 18 37 | 13 04 | 12 21 | 14 08 |
| 31 | 19 59 | 18 31 | 12 45 | 12 01 | 13 57 |
| 32 | 20 01 | 18 24 | 12 25 | 11 41 | 13 45 |
| 33 | 20 03 | 18 18 | 12 05 | 11 20 | 13 34 |
| 34 | 20 05 | 18 11 | 11 45 | 10 59 | 13 22 |
| 35 | 20 07 | 18 04 | 11 25 | 10 37 | 13 09 |
| 36 | 20 09 | 17 58 | 11 05 | 10 15 | 12 57 |
| 37 | 20 11 | 17 51 | 10 44 | 09 52 | 12 44 |
| 38 | 20 13 | 17 44 | 10 23 | 09 29 | 12 30 |
| 39 | 20 15 | 17 37 | 10 02 | 09 05 | 12 16 |
| 40 | 20 17 | 17 30 | 09 40 | 08 41 | 12 02 |
| 41 | 20 20 | 17 23 | 09 19 | 08 16 | 11 47 |
| 42 | 20 22 | 17 15 | 08 56 | 07 50 | 11 32 |
| 43 | 20 24 | 17 08 | 08 34 | 07 24 | 11 15 |
| 44 | 20 27 | 17 00 | 08 11 | 06 57 | 10 59 |
| 45 | 20 29 | 16 52 | 07 48 | 06 29 | 10 41 |
| 46 | 20 32 | 16 44 | 07 24 | 06 00 | 10 23 |
| 47 | 20 34 | 16 36 | 07 00 | 05 30 | 10 04 |
| 48 | 20 37 | 16 28 | 06 36 | 05 00 | 09 43 |
| 49 | 20 40 | 16 20 | 06 11 | 04 28 | 09 22 |
| 50 | 20 43 | 16 11 | 05 45 | 03 55 | 09 00 |
| 51 | 20 46 | 16 02 | 05 19 | 03 21 | 08 36 |
| 52 | 20 49 | 15 53 | 04 53 | 02 45 | 08 11 |
| 53 | 20 52 | 15 43 | 04 26 | 02 09 | 07 45 |
| 54 | 20 55 | 15 34 | 03 58 | 01 31 | 07 16 |
| 55 | 20 58 | 15 24 | 03 29 | 00 51 | 06 46 |
| 56 | 21 02 | 15 14 | 03 00 | 00 09 | 06 13 |
| 57 | 21 06 | 15 03 | 02 30 | 29♏26 | 05 38 |
| 58 | 21 09 | 14 52 | 01 59 | 28 41 | 04 59 |
| 59 | 21 13 | 14 41 | 01 28 | 27 53 | 04 17 |
| 60 | 21♍17 | 14♎30 | 00♏55 | 27♏04 | 03♑30 |

9h 24m 0s — 141° 0' 0" — 18 ♌ 34

| LAT. | 11 | 12 | ASC | 2 | 3 |
|---|---|---|---|---|---|
| 0 | 20♍12 | 22♎42 | 23♏23 | 21♐44 | 19♑24 |
| 5 | 20 20 | 22 10 | 21 46 | 20 25 | 18 46 |
| 10 | 20 27 | 21 38 | 20 12 | 19 06 | 18 07 |
| 15 | 20 34 | 21 07 | 18 39 | 17 44 | 17 26 |
| 20 | 20 42 | 20 36 | 17 06 | 16 20 | 16 43 |
| 21 | 20 43 | 20 30 | 16 47 | 16 02 | 16 34 |
| 22 | 20 45 | 20 24 | 16 29 | 15 45 | 16 25 |
| 23 | 20 46 | 20 18 | 16 10 | 15 27 | 16 15 |
| 24 | 20 48 | 20 11 | 15 51 | 15 09 | 16 06 |
| 25 | 20 49 | 20 05 | 15 32 | 14 50 | 15 56 |
| 26 | 20 51 | 19 59 | 15 13 | 14 32 | 15 46 |
| 27 | 20 52 | 19 52 | 14 53 | 14 13 | 15 36 |
| 28 | 20 54 | 19 46 | 14 34 | 13 54 | 15 26 |
| 29 | 20 56 | 19 39 | 14 15 | 13 34 | 15 16 |
| 30 | 20 57 | 19 32 | 13 55 | 13 14 | 15 05 |
| 31 | 20 59 | 19 26 | 13 35 | 12 54 | 14 54 |
| 32 | 21 01 | 19 19 | 13 15 | 12 34 | 14 42 |
| 33 | 21 02 | 19 12 | 12 55 | 12 13 | 14 31 |
| 34 | 21 04 | 19 05 | 12 35 | 11 51 | 14 19 |
| 35 | 21 06 | 18 58 | 12 14 | 11 29 | 14 07 |
| 36 | 21 08 | 18 51 | 11 53 | 11 07 | 13 54 |
| 37 | 21 10 | 18 44 | 11 32 | 10 44 | 13 41 |
| 38 | 21 12 | 18 37 | 11 11 | 10 21 | 13 28 |
| 39 | 21 14 | 18 30 | 10 49 | 09 57 | 13 14 |
| 40 | 21 16 | 18 22 | 10 28 | 09 32 | 12 59 |
| 41 | 21 18 | 18 14 | 10 05 | 09 07 | 12 44 |
| 42 | 21 20 | 18 07 | 09 43 | 08 41 | 12 29 |
| 43 | 21 22 | 17 59 | 09 20 | 08 14 | 12 13 |
| 44 | 21 24 | 17 51 | 08 57 | 07 47 | 11 56 |
| 45 | 21 26 | 17 43 | 08 33 | 07 19 | 11 38 |
| 46 | 21 28 | 17 34 | 08 09 | 06 50 | 11 20 |
| 47 | 21 31 | 17 26 | 07 44 | 06 20 | 11 01 |
| 48 | 21 33 | 17 17 | 07 19 | 05 49 | 10 41 |
| 49 | 21 36 | 17 08 | 06 54 | 05 16 | 10 20 |
| 50 | 21 38 | 16 59 | 06 28 | 04 43 | 09 57 |
| 51 | 21 41 | 16 50 | 06 01 | 04 09 | 09 34 |
| 52 | 21 44 | 16 40 | 05 34 | 03 33 | 09 09 |
| 53 | 21 47 | 16 30 | 05 07 | 02 56 | 08 42 |
| 54 | 21 49 | 16 20 | 04 38 | 02 17 | 08 14 |
| 55 | 21 52 | 16 10 | 04 09 | 01 37 | 07 43 |
| 56 | 21 56 | 15 59 | 03 39 | 00 55 | 07 10 |
| 57 | 21 59 | 15 48 | 03 09 | 00 11 | 06 35 |
| 58 | 22 02 | 15 37 | 02 37 | 29♏25 | 05 56 |
| 59 | 22 06 | 15 25 | 02 05 | 28 37 | 05 14 |
| 60 | 22♍10 | 15♎13 | 01♏32 | 27♏46 | 04♑27 |

9h 28m 0s — 142° 0' 0" — 19 ♌ 35

| LAT. | 11 | 12 | ASC | 2 | 3 |
|---|---|---|---|---|---|
| 0 | 21♍17 | 23♎46 | 24♏22 | 22♐39 | 20♑20 |
| 5 | 21 24 | 23 12 | 22 44 | 21 20 | 19 42 |
| 10 | 21 30 | 22 39 | 21 08 | 20 00 | 19 03 |
| 15 | 21 37 | 22 07 | 19 34 | 18 39 | 18 23 |
| 20 | 21 43 | 21 35 | 18 00 | 17 14 | 17 40 |
| 21 | 21 45 | 21 28 | 17 41 | 16 56 | 17 31 |
| 22 | 21 46 | 21 22 | 17 22 | 16 39 | 17 22 |
| 23 | 21 48 | 21 15 | 17 03 | 16 21 | 17 12 |
| 24 | 21 49 | 21 08 | 16 43 | 16 02 | 17 03 |
| 25 | 21 50 | 21 02 | 16 24 | 15 44 | 16 53 |
| 26 | 21 52 | 20 55 | 16 05 | 15 25 | 16 43 |
| 27 | 21 53 | 20 48 | 15 45 | 15 06 | 16 33 |
| 28 | 21 55 | 20 42 | 15 26 | 14 47 | 16 23 |
| 29 | 21 56 | 20 35 | 15 06 | 14 27 | 16 13 |
| 30 | 21 58 | 20 28 | 14 46 | 14 07 | 16 02 |
| 31 | 21 59 | 20 21 | 14 26 | 13 47 | 15 51 |
| 32 | 22 01 | 20 14 | 14 05 | 13 26 | 15 40 |
| 33 | 22 02 | 20 07 | 13 45 | 13 05 | 15 28 |
| 34 | 22 04 | 19 59 | 13 24 | 12 44 | 15 16 |
| 35 | 22 05 | 19 52 | 13 03 | 12 22 | 15 04 |
| 36 | 22 07 | 19 45 | 12 42 | 11 59 | 14 51 |
| 37 | 22 09 | 19 37 | 12 21 | 11 36 | 14 38 |
| 38 | 22 10 | 19 30 | 11 59 | 11 13 | 14 25 |
| 39 | 22 12 | 19 22 | 11 37 | 10 48 | 14 11 |
| 40 | 22 14 | 19 14 | 11 15 | 10 24 | 13 57 |
| 41 | 22 16 | 19 06 | 10 52 | 09 58 | 13 42 |
| 42 | 22 17 | 18 58 | 10 29 | 09 32 | 13 26 |
| 43 | 22 19 | 18 50 | 10 06 | 09 05 | 13 10 |
| 44 | 22 21 | 18 42 | 09 42 | 08 37 | 12 54 |
| 45 | 22 23 | 18 33 | 09 18 | 08 09 | 12 36 |
| 46 | 22 25 | 18 24 | 08 54 | 07 40 | 12 18 |
| 47 | 22 27 | 18 15 | 08 29 | 07 09 | 11 59 |
| 48 | 22 29 | 18 06 | 08 03 | 06 38 | 11 38 |
| 49 | 22 32 | 17 57 | 07 37 | 06 05 | 11 17 |
| 50 | 22 34 | 17 47 | 07 11 | 05 32 | 10 55 |
| 51 | 22 36 | 17 38 | 06 44 | 04 57 | 10 31 |
| 52 | 22 39 | 17 28 | 06 16 | 04 20 | 10 06 |
| 53 | 22 41 | 17 17 | 05 48 | 03 43 | 09 40 |
| 54 | 22 44 | 17 07 | 05 19 | 03 04 | 09 11 |
| 55 | 22 47 | 16 56 | 04 49 | 02 23 | 08 41 |
| 56 | 22 49 | 16 45 | 04 19 | 01 40 | 08 08 |
| 57 | 22 52 | 16 33 | 03 47 | 00 55 | 07 32 |
| 58 | 22 55 | 16 21 | 03 15 | 00 09 | 06 54 |
| 59 | 22 59 | 16 09 | 02 43 | 29♏20 | 06 11 |
| 60 | 23♍02 | 15♎56 | 02♏09 | 28♏29 | 05♑24 |

9h 32m 0s — 143° 0' 0" — 20 ♌ 36

| LAT. | 11 | 12 | ASC | 2 | 3 |
|---|---|---|---|---|---|
| 0 | 22♍23 | 24♎50 | 25♏21 | 23♐34 | 21♑17 |
| 5 | 22 28 | 24 15 | 23 41 | 22 15 | 20 39 |
| 10 | 22 34 | 23 40 | 22 04 | 20 55 | 20 00 |
| 15 | 22 40 | 23 07 | 20 29 | 19 33 | 19 20 |
| 20 | 22 45 | 22 33 | 18 53 | 18 08 | 18 37 |
| 21 | 22 47 | 22 26 | 18 34 | 17 50 | 18 28 |
| 22 | 22 48 | 22 19 | 18 15 | 17 33 | 18 19 |
| 23 | 22 49 | 22 12 | 17 55 | 17 15 | 18 10 |
| 24 | 22 50 | 22 06 | 17 36 | 16 56 | 18 00 |
| 25 | 22 51 | 21 59 | 17 16 | 16 38 | 17 51 |
| 26 | 22 53 | 21 52 | 16 57 | 16 19 | 17 41 |
| 27 | 22 54 | 21 45 | 16 37 | 16 00 | 17 31 |
| 28 | 22 55 | 21 37 | 16 17 | 15 40 | 17 21 |
| 29 | 22 56 | 21 30 | 15 57 | 15 21 | 17 10 |
| 30 | 22 58 | 21 23 | 15 37 | 15 01 | 16 59 |
| 31 | 22 59 | 21 16 | 15 16 | 14 40 | 16 48 |
| 32 | 23 00 | 21 09 | 14 55 | 14 19 | 16 37 |
| 33 | 23 02 | 21 01 | 14 35 | 13 58 | 16 26 |
| 34 | 23 03 | 20 54 | 14 14 | 13 36 | 16 14 |
| 35 | 23 05 | 20 46 | 13 52 | 13 14 | 16 02 |
| 36 | 23 06 | 20 38 | 13 31 | 12 51 | 15 49 |
| 37 | 23 07 | 20 30 | 13 09 | 12 28 | 15 36 |
| 38 | 23 09 | 20 23 | 12 47 | 12 04 | 15 23 |
| 39 | 23 10 | 20 15 | 12 25 | 11 40 | 15 09 |
| 40 | 23 12 | 20 06 | 12 02 | 11 15 | 14 54 |
| 41 | 23 14 | 19 58 | 11 39 | 10 49 | 14 40 |
| 42 | 23 15 | 19 50 | 11 16 | 10 23 | 14 24 |
| 43 | 23 17 | 19 41 | 10 52 | 09 56 | 14 08 |
| 44 | 23 18 | 19 32 | 10 28 | 09 28 | 13 51 |
| 45 | 23 20 | 19 23 | 10 03 | 08 59 | 13 34 |
| 46 | 23 22 | 19 14 | 09 38 | 08 29 | 13 16 |
| 47 | 23 24 | 19 05 | 09 13 | 07 59 | 12 56 |
| 48 | 23 26 | 18 55 | 08 47 | 07 27 | 12 36 |
| 49 | 23 28 | 18 46 | 08 20 | 06 54 | 12 15 |
| 50 | 23 30 | 18 36 | 07 53 | 06 20 | 11 53 |
| 51 | 23 32 | 18 26 | 07 26 | 05 45 | 11 29 |
| 52 | 23 34 | 18 15 | 06 58 | 05 08 | 11 04 |
| 53 | 23 36 | 18 04 | 06 29 | 04 30 | 10 38 |
| 54 | 23 38 | 17 53 | 05 59 | 03 50 | 10 09 |
| 55 | 23 41 | 17 42 | 05 29 | 03 09 | 09 39 |
| 56 | 23 43 | 17 30 | 04 58 | 02 26 | 09 06 |
| 57 | 23 46 | 17 18 | 04 26 | 01 40 | 08 30 |
| 58 | 23 48 | 17 06 | 03 53 | 00 53 | 07 51 |
| 59 | 23 51 | 16 53 | 03 20 | 00 04 | 07 09 |
| 60 | 23♍54 | 16♎40 | 02♏45 | 29♏11 | 06♑22 |

# Placidus Table of Houses for Latitudes 0° to 60° North

**9h 36m 0s — 144° 0' 0" — 21 ♌ 37**

| LAT. | 11 | 12 | ASC | 2 | 3 |
|---|---|---|---|---|---|
| 0 | 23♍28 | 25♎53 | 26♏19 | 24♐30 | 22♑13 |
| 5 | 23 33 | 25 17 | 24 38 | 23 10 | 21 36 |
| 10 | 23 38 | 24 41 | 23 01 | 21 50 | 20 57 |
| 15 | 23 42 | 24 06 | 21 24 | 20 28 | 20 17 |
| 20 | 23 47 | 23 31 | 19 47 | 19 02 | 19 34 |
| 21 | 23 48 | 23 24 | 19 27 | 18 45 | 19 25 |
| 22 | 23 49 | 23 17 | 19 08 | 18 27 | 19 16 |
| 23 | 23 50 | 23 10 | 18 48 | 18 08 | 19 07 |
| 24 | 23 52 | 23 03 | 18 28 | 17 50 | 18 57 |
| 25 | 23 53 | 22 55 | 18 09 | 17 31 | 18 48 |
| 26 | 23 54 | 22 48 | 17 49 | 17 13 | 18 38 |
| 27 | 23 55 | 22 41 | 17 28 | 16 53 | 18 28 |
| 28 | 23 56 | 22 33 | 17 08 | 16 34 | 18 18 |
| 29 | 23 57 | 22 26 | 16 48 | 16 14 | 18 08 |
| 30 | 23 58 | 22 18 | 16 27 | 15 54 | 17 57 |
| 31 | 23 59 | 22 11 | 16 06 | 15 33 | 17 46 |
| 32 | 24 00 | 22 03 | 15 46 | 15 12 | 17 35 |
| 33 | 24 01 | 21 55 | 15 24 | 14 51 | 17 23 |
| 34 | 24 03 | 21 48 | 15 03 | 14 29 | 17 11 |
| 35 | 24 04 | 21 40 | 14 41 | 14 07 | 16 59 |
| 36 | 24 05 | 21 32 | 14 19 | 13 44 | 16 47 |
| 37 | 24 06 | 21 24 | 13 57 | 13 20 | 16 34 |
| 38 | 24 08 | 21 15 | 13 35 | 12 56 | 16 20 |
| 39 | 24 09 | 21 07 | 13 12 | 12 32 | 16 07 |
| 40 | 24 10 | 20 58 | 12 49 | 12 07 | 15 52 |
| 41 | 24 12 | 20 50 | 12 26 | 11 41 | 15 38 |
| 42 | 24 13 | 20 41 | 12 02 | 11 14 | 15 22 |
| 43 | 24 14 | 20 32 | 11 38 | 10 47 | 15 06 |
| 44 | 24 16 | 20 23 | 11 13 | 10 19 | 14 49 |
| 45 | 24 17 | 20 14 | 10 48 | 09 49 | 14 32 |
| 46 | 24 19 | 20 04 | 10 23 | 09 19 | 14 14 |
| 47 | 24 20 | 19 54 | 09 57 | 08 48 | 13 55 |
| 48 | 24 22 | 19 45 | 09 30 | 08 16 | 13 35 |
| 49 | 24 24 | 19 34 | 09 04 | 07 43 | 13 13 |
| 50 | 24 25 | 19 24 | 08 36 | 07 09 | 12 51 |
| 51 | 24 27 | 19 13 | 08 08 | 06 33 | 12 28 |
| 52 | 24 29 | 19 02 | 07 39 | 05 56 | 12 03 |
| 53 | 24 31 | 18 51 | 07 10 | 05 17 | 11 36 |
| 54 | 24 33 | 18 40 | 06 40 | 04 37 | 11 07 |
| 55 | 24 35 | 18 28 | 06 09 | 03 55 | 10 37 |
| 56 | 24 37 | 18 16 | 05 37 | 03 11 | 10 04 |
| 57 | 24 39 | 18 03 | 05 05 | 02 25 | 09 28 |
| 58 | 24 41 | 17 50 | 04 32 | 01 37 | 08 50 |
| 59 | 24 44 | 17 37 | 03 57 | 00 47 | 08 07 |
| 60 | 24♍46 | 17♎23 | 03♏22 | 29♏54 | 07♑20 |

**9h 40m 0s — 145° 0' 0" — 22 ♌ 39**

| LAT. | 11 | 12 | ASC | 2 | 3 |
|---|---|---|---|---|---|
| 0 | 24♍33 | 26♎57 | 27♏17 | 25♐25 | 23♑10 |
| 5 | 24 37 | 26 19 | 25 36 | 24 05 | 22 32 |
| 10 | 24 41 | 25 42 | 23 57 | 22 45 | 21 54 |
| 15 | 24 45 | 25 05 | 22 19 | 21 22 | 21 14 |
| 20 | 24 49 | 24 29 | 20 41 | 19 56 | 20 31 |
| 21 | 24 50 | 24 22 | 20 21 | 19 39 | 20 23 |
| 22 | 24 51 | 24 14 | 20 01 | 19 21 | 20 14 |
| 23 | 24 52 | 24 07 | 19 41 | 19 02 | 20 04 |
| 24 | 24 53 | 23 59 | 19 21 | 18 44 | 19 55 |
| 25 | 24 54 | 23 52 | 19 01 | 18 25 | 19 46 |
| 26 | 24 55 | 23 44 | 18 40 | 18 06 | 19 36 |
| 27 | 24 56 | 23 37 | 18 20 | 17 47 | 19 26 |
| 28 | 24 56 | 23 29 | 18 00 | 17 27 | 19 16 |
| 29 | 24 57 | 23 21 | 17 39 | 17 07 | 19 05 |
| 30 | 24 58 | 23 14 | 17 18 | 16 47 | 18 55 |
| 31 | 24 59 | 23 06 | 16 57 | 16 26 | 18 44 |
| 32 | 25 00 | 22 58 | 16 36 | 16 05 | 18 33 |
| 33 | 25 01 | 22 50 | 16 14 | 15 44 | 18 21 |
| 34 | 25 02 | 22 42 | 15 52 | 15 22 | 18 09 |
| 35 | 25 03 | 22 33 | 15 30 | 14 59 | 17 57 |
| 36 | 25 04 | 22 25 | 15 08 | 14 36 | 17 45 |
| 37 | 25 05 | 22 17 | 14 46 | 14 13 | 17 32 |
| 38 | 25 06 | 22 08 | 14 23 | 13 48 | 17 19 |
| 39 | 25 07 | 21 59 | 14 00 | 13 24 | 17 05 |
| 40 | 25 08 | 21 51 | 13 36 | 12 58 | 16 51 |
| 41 | 25 10 | 21 42 | 13 12 | 12 32 | 16 36 |
| 42 | 25 11 | 21 32 | 12 48 | 12 05 | 16 20 |
| 43 | 25 12 | 21 23 | 12 24 | 11 38 | 16 04 |
| 44 | 25 13 | 21 14 | 11 59 | 11 09 | 15 48 |
| 45 | 25 14 | 21 04 | 11 33 | 10 40 | 15 30 |
| 46 | 25 16 | 20 54 | 11 07 | 10 10 | 15 12 |
| 47 | 25 17 | 20 44 | 10 41 | 09 38 | 14 53 |
| 48 | 25 18 | 20 34 | 10 14 | 09 06 | 14 33 |
| 49 | 25 20 | 20 23 | 09 47 | 08 32 | 14 12 |
| 50 | 25 21 | 20 12 | 09 19 | 07 57 | 13 50 |
| 51 | 25 23 | 20 01 | 08 50 | 07 21 | 13 26 |
| 52 | 25 24 | 19 50 | 08 21 | 06 44 | 13 01 |
| 53 | 25 26 | 19 38 | 07 51 | 06 05 | 12 34 |
| 54 | 25 27 | 19 26 | 07 20 | 05 24 | 12 06 |
| 55 | 25 29 | 19 14 | 06 49 | 04 41 | 11 36 |
| 56 | 25 31 | 19 01 | 06 17 | 03 57 | 11 03 |
| 57 | 25 33 | 18 48 | 05 44 | 03 11 | 10 27 |
| 58 | 25 35 | 18 34 | 05 10 | 02 22 | 09 48 |
| 59 | 25 36 | 18 20 | 04 35 | 01 31 | 09 05 |
| 60 | 25♍39 | 18♎06 | 03♏59 | 00♐37 | 08♑18 |

**9h 44m 0s — 146° 0' 0" — 23 ♌ 41**

| LAT. | 11 | 12 | ASC | 2 | 3 |
|---|---|---|---|---|---|
| 0 | 25♍38 | 28♎00 | 28♏15 | 26♐20 | 24♑06 |
| 5 | 25 42 | 27 21 | 26 33 | 25 00 | 23 29 |
| 10 | 25 45 | 26 42 | 24 53 | 23 40 | 22 51 |
| 15 | 25 48 | 26 05 | 23 13 | 22 17 | 22 11 |
| 20 | 25 52 | 25 27 | 21 34 | 20 51 | 21 29 |
| 21 | 25 52 | 25 19 | 21 14 | 20 33 | 21 20 |
| 22 | 25 53 | 25 12 | 20 54 | 20 15 | 21 11 |
| 23 | 25 54 | 25 04 | 20 34 | 19 57 | 21 02 |
| 24 | 25 54 | 24 56 | 20 13 | 19 38 | 20 53 |
| 25 | 25 55 | 24 49 | 19 53 | 19 19 | 20 43 |
| 26 | 25 56 | 24 41 | 19 32 | 19 00 | 20 34 |
| 27 | 25 56 | 24 33 | 19 12 | 18 41 | 20 24 |
| 28 | 25 57 | 24 25 | 18 51 | 18 21 | 20 14 |
| 29 | 25 58 | 24 17 | 18 30 | 18 01 | 20 03 |
| 30 | 25 59 | 24 09 | 18 09 | 17 40 | 19 53 |
| 31 | 25 59 | 24 01 | 17 47 | 17 20 | 19 42 |
| 32 | 26 00 | 23 52 | 17 26 | 16 58 | 19 31 |
| 33 | 26 01 | 23 44 | 17 04 | 16 37 | 19 19 |
| 34 | 26 02 | 23 36 | 16 42 | 16 14 | 19 08 |
| 35 | 26 02 | 23 27 | 16 19 | 15 52 | 18 55 |
| 36 | 26 03 | 23 18 | 15 57 | 15 29 | 18 43 |
| 37 | 26 04 | 23 10 | 15 34 | 15 05 | 18 30 |
| 38 | 26 05 | 23 01 | 15 11 | 14 41 | 18 17 |
| 39 | 26 06 | 22 52 | 14 47 | 14 16 | 18 03 |
| 40 | 26 07 | 22 43 | 14 23 | 13 50 | 17 49 |
| 41 | 26 08 | 22 33 | 13 59 | 13 24 | 17 34 |
| 42 | 26 09 | 22 24 | 13 35 | 12 57 | 17 19 |
| 43 | 26 10 | 22 14 | 13 10 | 12 29 | 17 03 |
| 44 | 26 10 | 22 04 | 12 44 | 12 00 | 16 46 |
| 45 | 26 11 | 21 54 | 12 18 | 11 30 | 16 29 |
| 46 | 26 13 | 21 44 | 11 52 | 11 00 | 16 11 |
| 47 | 26 14 | 21 33 | 11 25 | 10 28 | 15 52 |
| 48 | 26 15 | 21 23 | 10 58 | 09 55 | 15 32 |
| 49 | 26 16 | 21 12 | 10 30 | 09 22 | 15 11 |
| 50 | 26 17 | 21 00 | 10 01 | 08 46 | 14 48 |
| 51 | 26 18 | 20 49 | 09 32 | 08 10 | 14 25 |
| 52 | 26 19 | 20 37 | 09 02 | 07 32 | 14 00 |
| 53 | 26 21 | 20 25 | 08 32 | 06 52 | 13 33 |
| 54 | 26 22 | 20 12 | 08 01 | 06 11 | 13 05 |
| 55 | 26 23 | 20 00 | 07 29 | 05 28 | 12 35 |
| 56 | 26 25 | 19 46 | 06 56 | 04 43 | 12 02 |
| 57 | 26 26 | 19 33 | 06 22 | 03 56 | 11 26 |
| 58 | 26 28 | 19 19 | 05 48 | 03 06 | 10 47 |
| 59 | 26 29 | 19 04 | 05 12 | 02 15 | 10 04 |
| 60 | 26♍31 | 18♎49 | 04♏35 | 01♐20 | 09♑17 |

**9h 48m 0s — 147° 0' 0" — 24 ♌ 42**

| LAT. | 11 | 12 | ASC | 2 | 3 |
|---|---|---|---|---|---|
| 0 | 26♍44 | 29♎03 | 29♏13 | 27♐15 | 25♑03 |
| 5 | 26 46 | 28 22 | 27 29 | 25 55 | 24 26 |
| 10 | 26 49 | 27 43 | 25 48 | 24 35 | 23 48 |
| 15 | 26 51 | 27 04 | 24 08 | 23 12 | 23 09 |
| 20 | 26 54 | 26 25 | 22 28 | 21 45 | 22 27 |
| 21 | 26 54 | 26 17 | 22 07 | 21 27 | 22 18 |
| 22 | 26 55 | 26 09 | 21 47 | 21 09 | 22 09 |
| 23 | 26 55 | 26 01 | 21 26 | 20 51 | 22 00 |
| 24 | 26 56 | 25 53 | 21 06 | 20 32 | 21 51 |
| 25 | 26 56 | 25 45 | 20 45 | 20 13 | 21 41 |
| 26 | 26 57 | 25 37 | 20 24 | 19 54 | 21 32 |
| 27 | 26 57 | 25 29 | 20 03 | 19 34 | 21 22 |
| 28 | 26 58 | 25 21 | 19 42 | 19 15 | 21 12 |
| 29 | 26 58 | 25 12 | 19 21 | 18 54 | 21 01 |
| 30 | 26 59 | 25 04 | 18 59 | 18 34 | 20 51 |
| 31 | 27 00 | 24 55 | 18 37 | 18 13 | 20 40 |
| 32 | 27 00 | 24 47 | 18 16 | 17 51 | 20 29 |
| 33 | 27 01 | 24 38 | 17 53 | 17 30 | 20 18 |
| 34 | 27 01 | 24 30 | 17 31 | 17 07 | 20 06 |
| 35 | 27 02 | 24 21 | 17 08 | 16 45 | 19 54 |
| 36 | 27 02 | 24 12 | 16 45 | 16 21 | 19 41 |
| 37 | 27 03 | 24 03 | 16 22 | 15 57 | 19 29 |
| 38 | 27 04 | 23 53 | 15 59 | 15 33 | 19 15 |
| 39 | 27 04 | 23 44 | 15 35 | 15 08 | 19 02 |
| 40 | 27 05 | 23 34 | 15 11 | 14 42 | 18 48 |
| 41 | 27 06 | 23 25 | 14 46 | 14 15 | 18 33 |
| 42 | 27 06 | 23 15 | 14 21 | 13 48 | 18 18 |
| 43 | 27 07 | 23 05 | 13 56 | 13 20 | 18 02 |
| 44 | 27 08 | 22 55 | 13 30 | 12 51 | 17 45 |
| 45 | 27 09 | 22 44 | 13 03 | 12 21 | 17 28 |
| 46 | 27 09 | 22 34 | 12 37 | 11 50 | 17 10 |
| 47 | 27 10 | 22 23 | 12 09 | 11 18 | 16 51 |
| 48 | 27 11 | 22 12 | 11 42 | 10 45 | 16 31 |
| 49 | 27 12 | 22 00 | 11 13 | 10 11 | 16 10 |
| 50 | 27 13 | 21 49 | 10 44 | 09 35 | 15 48 |
| 51 | 27 14 | 21 37 | 10 14 | 08 58 | 15 24 |
| 52 | 27 14 | 21 24 | 09 44 | 08 20 | 14 59 |
| 53 | 27 15 | 21 12 | 09 13 | 07 40 | 14 33 |
| 54 | 27 16 | 20 59 | 08 41 | 06 58 | 14 04 |
| 55 | 27 17 | 20 46 | 08 09 | 06 15 | 13 34 |
| 56 | 27 18 | 20 32 | 07 35 | 05 29 | 13 01 |
| 57 | 27 20 | 20 18 | 07 01 | 04 41 | 12 25 |
| 58 | 27 21 | 20 03 | 06 26 | 03 51 | 11 47 |
| 59 | 27 22 | 19 48 | 05 49 | 02 58 | 11 04 |
| 60 | 27♍23 | 19♎32 | 05♏12 | 02♐03 | 10♑16 |

**9h 52m 0s — 148° 0' 0" — 25 ♌ 44**

| LAT. | 11 | 12 | ASC | 2 | 3 |
|---|---|---|---|---|---|
| 0 | 27♍49 | 00♏06 | 00♐11 | 28♐10 | 26♑00 |
| 5 | 27 51 | 29♎24 | 28♏26 | 26 50 | 25 24 |
| 10 | 27 52 | 28 43 | 26 44 | 25 29 | 24 46 |
| 15 | 27 54 | 28 03 | 25 03 | 24 06 | 24 06 |
| 20 | 27 56 | 27 23 | 23 21 | 22 39 | 23 25 |
| 21 | 27 56 | 27 14 | 23 00 | 22 21 | 23 16 |
| 22 | 27 56 | 27 06 | 22 40 | 22 03 | 23 07 |
| 23 | 27 57 | 26 58 | 22 19 | 21 45 | 22 58 |
| 24 | 27 57 | 26 50 | 21 58 | 21 26 | 22 49 |
| 25 | 27 57 | 26 41 | 21 37 | 21 07 | 22 39 |
| 26 | 27 58 | 26 33 | 21 16 | 20 48 | 22 30 |
| 27 | 27 58 | 26 25 | 20 55 | 20 28 | 22 20 |
| 28 | 27 59 | 26 16 | 20 33 | 20 08 | 22 10 |
| 29 | 27 59 | 26 08 | 20 12 | 19 48 | 22 00 |
| 30 | 27 59 | 25 59 | 19 50 | 19 27 | 21 49 |
| 31 | 28 00 | 25 50 | 19 28 | 19 06 | 21 39 |
| 32 | 28 00 | 25 41 | 19 06 | 18 45 | 21 27 |
| 33 | 28 00 | 25 32 | 18 43 | 18 23 | 21 16 |
| 34 | 28 01 | 25 23 | 18 20 | 18 00 | 21 04 |
| 35 | 28 01 | 25 14 | 17 57 | 17 37 | 20 52 |
| 36 | 28 02 | 25 05 | 17 34 | 17 14 | 20 40 |
| 37 | 28 02 | 24 55 | 17 10 | 16 50 | 20 27 |
| 38 | 28 02 | 24 46 | 16 47 | 16 25 | 20 14 |
| 39 | 28 03 | 24 36 | 16 22 | 16 00 | 20 01 |
| 40 | 28 03 | 24 26 | 15 58 | 15 34 | 19 46 |
| 41 | 28 04 | 24 16 | 15 33 | 15 07 | 19 32 |
| 42 | 28 04 | 24 06 | 15 07 | 14 40 | 19 17 |
| 43 | 28 05 | 23 56 | 14 42 | 14 11 | 19 01 |
| 44 | 28 05 | 23 45 | 14 15 | 13 42 | 18 44 |
| 45 | 28 06 | 23 34 | 13 49 | 13 12 | 18 27 |
| 46 | 28 06 | 23 23 | 13 21 | 12 41 | 18 09 |
| 47 | 28 07 | 23 12 | 12 54 | 12 08 | 17 50 |
| 48 | 28 07 | 23 01 | 12 25 | 11 35 | 17 30 |
| 49 | 28 08 | 22 49 | 11 56 | 11 00 | 17 09 |
| 50 | 28 08 | 22 37 | 11 27 | 10 24 | 16 47 |
| 51 | 28 09 | 22 24 | 10 57 | 09 47 | 16 24 |
| 52 | 28 10 | 22 12 | 10 26 | 09 08 | 15 59 |
| 53 | 28 10 | 21 59 | 09 54 | 08 28 | 15 32 |
| 54 | 28 11 | 21 45 | 09 22 | 07 45 | 15 04 |
| 55 | 28 12 | 21 31 | 08 49 | 07 01 | 14 34 |
| 56 | 28 12 | 21 17 | 08 15 | 06 15 | 14 01 |
| 57 | 28 13 | 21 02 | 07 40 | 05 27 | 13 25 |
| 58 | 28 14 | 20 47 | 07 04 | 04 36 | 12 46 |
| 59 | 28 15 | 20 32 | 06 27 | 03 42 | 12 04 |
| 60 | 28♍15 | 20♎15 | 05♏49 | 02♐46 | 11♑16 |

**9h 56m 0s — 149° 0' 0" — 26 ♌ 47**

| LAT. | 11 | 12 | ASC | 2 | 3 |
|---|---|---|---|---|---|
| 0 | 28♍55 | 01♏08 | 01♐08 | 29♐05 | 26♑57 |
| 5 | 28 55 | 00 25 | 29♏23 | 27 45 | 26 21 |
| 10 | 28 56 | 29♎43 | 27 40 | 26 24 | 25 43 |
| 15 | 28 57 | 29 02 | 25 57 | 25 01 | 25 04 |
| 20 | 28 58 | 28 20 | 24 14 | 23 34 | 24 23 |
| 21 | 28 58 | 28 12 | 23 54 | 23 16 | 24 14 |
| 22 | 28 58 | 28 03 | 23 33 | 22 58 | 24 05 |
| 23 | 28 58 | 27 55 | 23 12 | 22 39 | 23 56 |
| 24 | 28 59 | 27 46 | 22 50 | 22 20 | 23 47 |
| 25 | 28 59 | 27 38 | 22 29 | 22 01 | 23 38 |
| 26 | 28 59 | 27 29 | 22 08 | 21 42 | 23 28 |
| 27 | 28 59 | 27 20 | 21 46 | 21 22 | 23 18 |
| 28 | 28 59 | 27 12 | 21 24 | 21 02 | 23 08 |
| 29 | 28 59 | 27 03 | 21 03 | 20 42 | 22 58 |
| 30 | 29 00 | 26 54 | 20 40 | 20 21 | 22 48 |
| 31 | 29 00 | 26 45 | 20 18 | 20 00 | 22 37 |
| 32 | 29 00 | 26 36 | 19 56 | 19 38 | 22 26 |
| 33 | 29 00 | 26 26 | 19 33 | 19 16 | 22 15 |
| 34 | 29 00 | 26 17 | 19 10 | 18 53 | 22 03 |
| 35 | 29 01 | 26 08 | 18 46 | 18 30 | 21 51 |
| 36 | 29 01 | 25 58 | 18 23 | 18 07 | 21 39 |
| 37 | 29 01 | 25 48 | 17 59 | 17 42 | 21 26 |
| 38 | 29 01 | 25 38 | 17 35 | 17 18 | 21 13 |
| 39 | 29 01 | 25 28 | 17 10 | 16 52 | 21 00 |
| 40 | 29 02 | 25 18 | 16 45 | 16 26 | 20 46 |
| 41 | 29 02 | 25 08 | 16 20 | 15 59 | 20 31 |
| 42 | 29 02 | 24 57 | 15 54 | 15 31 | 20 16 |
| 43 | 29 02 | 24 47 | 15 28 | 15 03 | 20 00 |
| 44 | 29 03 | 24 36 | 15 01 | 14 33 | 19 44 |
| 45 | 29 03 | 24 24 | 14 34 | 14 03 | 19 26 |
| 46 | 29 03 | 24 13 | 14 06 | 13 31 | 19 08 |
| 47 | 29 03 | 24 01 | 13 38 | 12 59 | 18 49 |
| 48 | 29 04 | 23 50 | 13 09 | 12 25 | 18 30 |
| 49 | 29 04 | 23 37 | 12 40 | 11 50 | 18 09 |
| 50 | 29 04 | 23 25 | 12 10 | 11 14 | 17 47 |
| 51 | 29 05 | 23 12 | 11 39 | 10 36 | 17 23 |
| 52 | 29 05 | 22 59 | 11 07 | 09 57 | 16 59 |
| 53 | 29 05 | 22 45 | 10 35 | 09 16 | 16 32 |
| 54 | 29 05 | 22 31 | 10 02 | 08 33 | 16 04 |
| 55 | 29 06 | 22 17 | 09 29 | 07 48 | 15 34 |
| 56 | 29 06 | 22 02 | 08 54 | 07 01 | 15 01 |
| 57 | 29 07 | 21 47 | 08 18 | 06 12 | 14 25 |
| 58 | 29 07 | 21 32 | 07 42 | 05 21 | 13 47 |
| 59 | 29 07 | 21 15 | 07 04 | 04 27 | 13 04 |
| 60 | 29♍08 | 20♎59 | 06♏25 | 03♐30 | 12♑17 |

**10h 0m 0s — 150° 0' 0" — 27 ♌ 49**

| LAT. | 11 | 12 | ASC | 2 | 3 |
|---|---|---|---|---|---|
| 0 | 00♎00 | 02♏11 | 02♐05 | 00♑00 | 27♑55 |
| 5 | 00 00 | 01 27 | 00 19 | 28♐40 | 27 18 |
| 10 | 00 00 | 00 43 | 28♏35 | 27 19 | 26 41 |
| 15 | 00 00 | 00 01 | 26 52 | 25 56 | 26 02 |
| 20 | 00 00 | 29♎18 | 25 08 | 24 28 | 25 21 |
| 21 | 00 00 | 29 09 | 24 47 | 24 10 | 25 12 |
| 22 | 00 00 | 29 00 | 24 25 | 23 52 | 25 04 |
| 23 | 00 00 | 28 52 | 24 04 | 23 33 | 24 55 |
| 24 | 00 00 | 28 43 | 23 43 | 23 14 | 24 46 |
| 25 | 00 00 | 28 34 | 23 21 | 22 55 | 24 36 |
| 26 | 00 00 | 28 25 | 23 00 | 22 36 | 24 27 |
| 27 | 00 00 | 28 16 | 22 38 | 22 16 | 24 17 |
| 28 | 00 00 | 28 07 | 22 16 | 21 56 | 24 07 |
| 29 | 00 00 | 27 58 | 21 53 | 21 35 | 23 57 |
| 30 | 00 00 | 27 49 | 21 31 | 21 15 | 23 47 |
| 31 | 00 00 | 27 39 | 21 08 | 20 53 | 23 36 |
| 32 | 00 00 | 27 30 | 20 46 | 20 32 | 23 25 |
| 33 | 00 00 | 27 20 | 20 22 | 20 09 | 23 14 |
| 34 | 00 00 | 27 11 | 19 59 | 19 47 | 23 02 |
| 35 | 00 00 | 27 01 | 19 35 | 19 23 | 22 50 |
| 36 | 00 00 | 26 51 | 19 11 | 19 00 | 22 38 |
| 37 | 00 00 | 26 41 | 18 47 | 18 35 | 22 26 |
| 38 | 00 00 | 26 31 | 18 22 | 18 10 | 22 12 |
| 39 | 00 00 | 26 21 | 17 57 | 17 45 | 21 59 |
| 40 | 00 00 | 26 10 | 17 32 | 17 18 | 21 45 |
| 41 | 00 00 | 25 59 | 17 06 | 16 51 | 21 30 |
| 42 | 00 00 | 25 48 | 16 40 | 16 23 | 21 15 |
| 43 | 00 00 | 25 37 | 16 14 | 15 54 | 21 00 |
| 44 | 00 00 | 25 26 | 15 46 | 15 25 | 20 43 |
| 45 | 00 00 | 25 15 | 15 19 | 14 54 | 20 26 |
| 46 | 00 00 | 25 03 | 14 51 | 14 22 | 20 08 |
| 47 | 00 00 | 24 51 | 14 22 | 13 49 | 19 49 |
| 48 | 00 00 | 24 38 | 13 53 | 13 15 | 19 30 |
| 49 | 00 00 | 24 26 | 13 23 | 12 40 | 19 09 |
| 50 | 00 00 | 24 13 | 12 52 | 12 03 | 18 47 |
| 51 | 00 00 | 24 00 | 12 21 | 11 25 | 18 24 |
| 52 | 00 00 | 23 46 | 11 49 | 10 45 | 17 59 |
| 53 | 00 00 | 23 32 | 11 16 | 10 04 | 17 33 |
| 54 | 00 00 | 23 18 | 10 43 | 09 20 | 17 04 |
| 55 | 00 00 | 23 03 | 10 08 | 08 35 | 16 34 |
| 56 | 00 00 | 22 48 | 09 33 | 07 48 | 16 01 |
| 57 | 00 00 | 22 32 | 08 57 | 06 58 | 15 26 |
| 58 | 00 00 | 22 16 | 08 20 | 06 06 | 14 47 |
| 59 | 00 00 | 21 59 | 07 41 | 05 11 | 14 05 |
| 60 | 00♎00 | 21♎42 | 07♏02 | 04♐13 | 13♑18 |

**10h 4m 0s — 151° 0' 0" — 28 ♌ 52**

| LAT. | 11 | 12 | ASC | 2 | 3 |
|---|---|---|---|---|---|
| 0 | 01♎05 | 03♏13 | 03♐03 | 00♑55 | 28♑52 |
| 5 | 01 05 | 02 28 | 01 16 | 29♐35 | 28 16 |
| 10 | 01 04 | 01 43 | 29♏31 | 28 14 | 27 39 |
| 15 | 01 03 | 00 59 | 27 46 | 26 51 | 27 01 |
| 20 | 01 02 | 00 15 | 26 01 | 25 23 | 26 19 |
| 21 | 01 02 | 00 06 | 25 40 | 25 05 | 26 11 |
| 22 | 01 02 | 29♎57 | 25 18 | 24 46 | 26 02 |
| 23 | 01 02 | 29 48 | 24 57 | 24 28 | 25 53 |
| 24 | 01 01 | 29 39 | 24 35 | 24 09 | 25 44 |
| 25 | 01 01 | 29 30 | 24 13 | 23 50 | 25 35 |
| 26 | 01 01 | 29 21 | 23 51 | 23 30 | 25 26 |
| 27 | 01 01 | 29 12 | 23 29 | 23 10 | 25 16 |
| 28 | 01 01 | 29 02 | 23 07 | 22 50 | 25 06 |
| 29 | 01 01 | 28 53 | 22 44 | 22 29 | 24 56 |
| 30 | 01 00 | 28 44 | 22 22 | 22 08 | 24 46 |
| 31 | 01 00 | 28 34 | 21 59 | 21 47 | 24 35 |
| 32 | 01 00 | 28 24 | 21 36 | 21 25 | 24 24 |
| 33 | 01 00 | 28 14 | 21 12 | 21 03 | 24 13 |
| 34 | 01 00 | 28 05 | 20 48 | 20 40 | 24 02 |
| 35 | 00 59 | 27 54 | 20 24 | 20 17 | 23 50 |
| 36 | 00 59 | 27 44 | 20 00 | 19 53 | 23 38 |
| 37 | 00 59 | 27 34 | 19 35 | 19 28 | 23 25 |
| 38 | 00 59 | 27 23 | 19 10 | 19 03 | 23 12 |
| 39 | 00 59 | 27 13 | 18 45 | 18 37 | 22 59 |
| 40 | 00 58 | 27 02 | 18 19 | 18 11 | 22 45 |
| 41 | 00 58 | 26 51 | 17 53 | 17 43 | 22 30 |
| 42 | 00 58 | 26 40 | 17 27 | 17 15 | 22 15 |
| 43 | 00 58 | 26 28 | 17 00 | 16 46 | 21 59 |
| 44 | 00 57 | 26 16 | 16 32 | 16 16 | 21 43 |
| 45 | 00 57 | 26 05 | 16 04 | 15 45 | 21 26 |
| 46 | 00 57 | 25 52 | 15 35 | 15 13 | 21 08 |
| 47 | 00 57 | 25 40 | 15 06 | 14 40 | 20 50 |
| 48 | 00 56 | 25 27 | 14 36 | 14 06 | 20 30 |
| 49 | 00 56 | 25 14 | 14 06 | 13 30 | 20 09 |
| 50 | 00 56 | 25 01 | 13 35 | 12 53 | 19 47 |
| 51 | 00 55 | 24 47 | 13 03 | 12 14 | 19 24 |
| 52 | 00 55 | 24 33 | 12 31 | 11 34 | 18 59 |
| 53 | 00 55 | 24 19 | 11 57 | 10 52 | 18 33 |
| 54 | 00 55 | 24 04 | 11 23 | 10 08 | 18 05 |
| 55 | 00 54 | 23 49 | 10 48 | 09 22 | 17 35 |
| 56 | 00 54 | 23 33 | 10 13 | 08 34 | 17 02 |
| 57 | 00 53 | 23 17 | 09 36 | 07 44 | 16 27 |
| 58 | 00 53 | 23 00 | 08 58 | 06 51 | 15 49 |
| 59 | 00 53 | 22 43 | 08 19 | 05 55 | 15 06 |
| 60 | 00♎52 | 22♎25 | 07♏39 | 04♐56 | 14♑19 |

# Placidus Table of Houses for Latitudes 0° to 60° North

10h 8m 0s — 152° 0' 0" — 29 ♌ 54

| 11 | 12 | ASC | 2 | 3 | LAT. |
|---|---|---|---|---|---|
| 02♎11 | 04♏16 | 04♐00 | 01♑50 | 29♑49 | 0 |
| 02 09 | 03 29 | 02 12 | 00 30 | 29 14 | 5 |
| 02 08 | 02 43 | 00 26 | 29♐09 | 28 37 | 10 |
| 02 06 | 01 58 | 28♏41 | 27 45 | 27 59 | 15 |
| 02 04 | 01 13 | 26 54 | 26 18 | 27 18 | 20 |
| 02 04 | 01 03 | 26 33 | 25 59 | 27 10 | 21 |
| 02 04 | 00 54 | 26 11 | 25 41 | 27 01 | 22 |
| 02 03 | 00 45 | 25 49 | 25 22 | 26 52 | 23 |
| 02 03 | 00 36 | 25 27 | 25 03 | 26 43 | 24 |
| 02 03 | 00 26 | 25 05 | 24 44 | 26 34 | 25 |
| 02 02 | 00 17 | 24 43 | 24 24 | 26 25 | 26 |
| 02 02 | 00 07 | 24 21 | 24 04 | 26 15 | 27 |
| 02 01 | 29♎58 | 23 58 | 23 44 | 26 05 | 28 |
| 02 01 | 29 48 | 23 35 | 23 23 | 25 55 | 29 |
| 02 01 | 29 38 | 23 12 | 23 02 | 25 45 | 30 |
| 02 00 | 29 28 | 22 49 | 22 41 | 25 34 | 31 |
| 02 00 | 29 18 | 22 26 | 22 19 | 25 24 | 32 |
| 02 00 | 29 08 | 22 02 | 21 56 | 25 13 | 33 |
| 01 59 | 28 58 | 21 38 | 21 33 | 25 01 | 34 |
| 01 59 | 28 48 | 21 13 | 21 10 | 24 49 | 35 |
| 01 58 | 28 37 | 20 49 | 20 46 | 24 37 | 36 |
| 01 58 | 28 27 | 20 24 | 20 21 | 24 25 | 37 |
| 01 58 | 28 16 | 19 58 | 19 56 | 24 12 | 38 |
| 01 57 | 28 05 | 19 33 | 19 30 | 23 58 | 39 |
| 01 57 | 27 54 | 19 07 | 19 03 | 23 45 | 40 |
| 01 56 | 27 42 | 18 40 | 18 36 | 23 30 | 41 |
| 01 56 | 27 31 | 18 13 | 18 07 | 23 15 | 42 |
| 01 55 | 27 19 | 17 46 | 17 38 | 23 00 | 43 |
| 01 55 | 27 07 | 17 18 | 17 08 | 22 43 | 44 |
| 01 54 | 26 55 | 16 49 | 16 37 | 22 26 | 45 |
| 01 54 | 26 42 | 16 20 | 16 04 | 22 09 | 46 |
| 01 53 | 26 29 | 15 50 | 15 31 | 21 50 | 47 |
| 01 53 | 26 16 | 15 20 | 14 56 | 21 30 | 48 |
| 01 52 | 26 03 | 14 49 | 14 20 | 21 10 | 49 |
| 01 52 | 25 49 | 14 18 | 13 43 | 20 48 | 50 |
| 01 51 | 25 35 | 13 46 | 13 04 | 20 25 | 51 |
| 01 50 | 25 20 | 13 12 | 12 23 | 20 00 | 52 |
| 01 50 | 25 05 | 12 39 | 11 41 | 19 34 | 53 |
| 01 49 | 24 50 | 12 04 | 10 56 | 19 06 | 54 |
| 01 48 | 24 34 | 11 28 | 10 10 | 18 36 | 55 |
| 01 48 | 24 18 | 10 52 | 09 21 | 18 04 | 56 |
| 01 47 | 24 01 | 10 14 | 08 30 | 17 29 | 57 |
| 01 46 | 23 44 | 09 36 | 07 36 | 16 50 | 58 |
| 01 45 | 23 26 | 08 56 | 06 40 | 16 08 | 59 |
| 01♎45 | 23♎08 | 08♏15 | 05♐40 | 15♑21 | 60 |

10h 12m 0s — 153° 0' 0" — 00 ♍ 57

| LAT. | 11 | 12 | ASC | 2 | 3 |
|---|---|---|---|---|---|
| 0 | 03♎16 | 05♏18 | 04♐57 | 02♑45 | 00♒47 |
| 5 | 03 14 | 04 30 | 03 08 | 01 25 | 00 12 |
| 10 | 03 11 | 03 43 | 01 21 | 00 04 | 29♑36 |
| 15 | 03 09 | 02 57 | 29♏35 | 28♐40 | 28 57 |
| 20 | 03 06 | 02 10 | 27 47 | 27 12 | 28 17 |
| 21 | 03 06 | 02 01 | 27 26 | 26 54 | 28 09 |
| 22 | 03 05 | 01 51 | 27 04 | 26 36 | 28 00 |
| 23 | 03 05 | 01 42 | 26 42 | 26 17 | 27 51 |
| 24 | 03 04 | 01 32 | 26 20 | 25 58 | 27 42 |
| 25 | 03 04 | 01 22 | 25 57 | 25 38 | 27 33 |
| 26 | 03 03 | 01 13 | 25 35 | 25 19 | 27 24 |
| 27 | 03 03 | 01 03 | 25 12 | 24 59 | 27 14 |
| 28 | 03 02 | 00 53 | 24 49 | 24 38 | 27 05 |
| 29 | 03 02 | 00 43 | 24 26 | 24 18 | 26 55 |
| 30 | 03 01 | 00 33 | 24 03 | 23 56 | 26 44 |
| 31 | 03 00 | 00 23 | 23 39 | 23 35 | 26 34 |
| 32 | 03 00 | 00 13 | 23 16 | 23 13 | 26 23 |
| 33 | 02 59 | 00 02 | 22 51 | 22 50 | 26 12 |
| 34 | 02 59 | 29♎52 | 22 27 | 22 27 | 26 01 |
| 35 | 02 58 | 29 41 | 22 02 | 22 03 | 25 49 |
| 36 | 02 58 | 29 30 | 21 37 | 21 39 | 25 37 |
| 37 | 02 57 | 29 19 | 21 12 | 21 14 | 25 25 |
| 38 | 02 56 | 29 08 | 20 46 | 20 49 | 25 12 |
| 39 | 02 56 | 28 57 | 20 20 | 20 23 | 24 59 |
| 40 | 02 55 | 28 45 | 19 54 | 19 56 | 24 45 |
| 41 | 02 54 | 28 34 | 19 27 | 19 28 | 24 30 |
| 42 | 02 54 | 28 22 | 19 00 | 18 59 | 24 16 |
| 43 | 02 53 | 28 10 | 18 32 | 18 30 | 24 00 |
| 44 | 02 52 | 27 57 | 18 03 | 18 00 | 23 44 |
| 45 | 02 51 | 27 44 | 17 34 | 17 28 | 23 27 |
| 46 | 02 51 | 27 32 | 17 05 | 16 56 | 23 09 |
| 47 | 02 50 | 27 18 | 16 35 | 16 22 | 22 51 |
| 48 | 02 49 | 27 05 | 16 04 | 15 47 | 22 31 |
| 49 | 02 48 | 26 51 | 15 33 | 15 10 | 22 11 |
| 50 | 02 47 | 26 37 | 15 01 | 14 33 | 21 49 |
| 51 | 02 46 | 26 22 | 14 28 | 13 53 | 21 26 |
| 52 | 02 46 | 26 07 | 13 54 | 13 12 | 21 02 |
| 53 | 02 45 | 25 52 | 13 20 | 12 29 | 20 36 |
| 54 | 02 44 | 25 36 | 12 45 | 11 44 | 20 08 |
| 55 | 02 43 | 25 20 | 12 08 | 10 57 | 19 38 |
| 56 | 02 42 | 25 03 | 11 31 | 10 08 | 19 06 |
| 57 | 02 40 | 24 46 | 10 53 | 09 16 | 18 31 |
| 58 | 02 39 | 24 28 | 10 14 | 08 22 | 17 52 |
| 59 | 02 38 | 24 10 | 09 33 | 07 24 | 17 10 |
| 60 | 02♎37 | 23♎51 | 08♏52 | 06♐24 | 16♑23 |

10h 16m 0s — 154° 0' 0" — 02 ♍ 00

| LAT. | 11 | 12 | ASC | 2 | 3 |
|---|---|---|---|---|---|
| 0 | 04♎22 | 06♏19 | 05♐54 | 03♑40 | 01♒45 |
| 5 | 04 18 | 05 30 | 04 04 | 02 20 | 01 10 |
| 10 | 04 15 | 04 42 | 02 17 | 00 59 | 00 34 |
| 15 | 04 12 | 03 55 | 00 29 | 29♐35 | 29♑56 |
| 20 | 04 08 | 03 07 | 28♏41 | 28 07 | 29 16 |
| 21 | 04 08 | 02 57 | 28 19 | 27 49 | 29 08 |
| 22 | 04 07 | 02 48 | 27 56 | 27 30 | 28 59 |
| 23 | 04 06 | 02 38 | 27 34 | 27 11 | 28 50 |
| 24 | 04 06 | 02 28 | 27 12 | 26 52 | 28 42 |
| 25 | 04 05 | 02 18 | 26 49 | 26 33 | 28 32 |
| 26 | 04 04 | 02 08 | 26 26 | 26 13 | 28 23 |
| 27 | 04 04 | 01 58 | 26 04 | 25 53 | 28 14 |
| 28 | 04 03 | 01 48 | 25 40 | 25 33 | 28 04 |
| 29 | 04 02 | 01 38 | 25 17 | 25 12 | 27 54 |
| 30 | 04 01 | 01 28 | 24 53 | 24 51 | 27 44 |
| 31 | 04 01 | 01 17 | 24 30 | 24 29 | 27 34 |
| 32 | 04 00 | 01 07 | 24 06 | 24 07 | 27 23 |
| 33 | 03 59 | 00 56 | 23 41 | 23 44 | 27 12 |
| 34 | 03 58 | 00 45 | 23 16 | 23 21 | 27 01 |
| 35 | 03 58 | 00 34 | 22 52 | 22 57 | 26 49 |
| 36 | 03 57 | 00 23 | 22 26 | 22 33 | 26 37 |
| 37 | 03 56 | 00 12 | 22 01 | 22 08 | 26 25 |
| 38 | 03 55 | 00 00 | 21 34 | 21 42 | 26 12 |
| 39 | 03 54 | 29♎49 | 21 08 | 21 16 | 25 59 |
| 40 | 03 53 | 29 37 | 20 41 | 20 49 | 25 45 |
| 41 | 03 52 | 29 25 | 20 14 | 20 21 | 25 31 |
| 42 | 03 51 | 29 13 | 19 46 | 19 52 | 25 16 |
| 43 | 03 50 | 29 00 | 19 18 | 19 22 | 25 01 |
| 44 | 03 50 | 28 47 | 18 49 | 18 52 | 24 45 |
| 45 | 03 49 | 28 34 | 18 20 | 18 20 | 24 28 |
| 46 | 03 47 | 28 21 | 17 50 | 17 47 | 24 10 |
| 47 | 03 46 | 28 08 | 17 19 | 17 13 | 23 52 |
| 48 | 03 45 | 27 54 | 16 48 | 16 38 | 23 33 |
| 49 | 03 44 | 27 39 | 16 16 | 16 01 | 23 12 |
| 50 | 03 43 | 27 25 | 15 43 | 15 23 | 22 51 |
| 51 | 03 42 | 27 10 | 15 10 | 14 43 | 22 28 |
| 52 | 03 41 | 26 54 | 14 36 | 14 01 | 22 03 |
| 53 | 03 39 | 26 39 | 14 01 | 13 18 | 21 37 |
| 54 | 03 38 | 26 22 | 13 25 | 12 33 | 21 10 |
| 55 | 03 37 | 26 06 | 12 48 | 11 45 | 20 40 |
| 56 | 03 35 | 25 48 | 12 11 | 10 55 | 20 08 |
| 57 | 03 34 | 25 31 | 11 32 | 10 03 | 19 33 |
| 58 | 03 32 | 25 12 | 10 52 | 09 08 | 18 55 |
| 59 | 03 31 | 24 53 | 10 11 | 08 09 | 18 13 |
| 60 | 03♎29 | 24♎33 | 09♏28 | 07♐08 | 17♑27 |

10h 20m 0s — 155° 0' 0" — 03 ♍ 03

| LAT. | 11 | 12 | ASC | 2 | 3 |
|---|---|---|---|---|---|
| 0 | 05♎27 | 07♏21 | 06♐50 | 04♑35 | 02♒43 |
| 5 | 05 23 | 06 31 | 05 00 | 03 16 | 02 08 |
| 10 | 05 19 | 05 42 | 03 12 | 01 54 | 01 33 |
| 15 | 05 15 | 04 53 | 01 23 | 00 30 | 00 55 |
| 20 | 05 11 | 04 04 | 29♏34 | 29♐02 | 00 15 |
| 21 | 05 10 | 03 54 | 29 11 | 28 44 | 00 07 |
| 22 | 05 09 | 03 44 | 28 49 | 28 25 | 29♑58 |
| 23 | 05 08 | 03 34 | 28 27 | 28 06 | 29 50 |
| 24 | 05 07 | 03 24 | 28 04 | 27 47 | 29 41 |
| 25 | 05 06 | 03 14 | 27 41 | 27 28 | 29 32 |
| 26 | 05 05 | 03 04 | 27 18 | 27 08 | 29 23 |
| 27 | 05 04 | 02 54 | 26 55 | 26 48 | 29 14 |
| 28 | 05 04 | 02 43 | 26 32 | 26 27 | 29 04 |
| 29 | 05 03 | 02 33 | 26 08 | 26 06 | 28 54 |
| 30 | 05 02 | 02 22 | 25 44 | 25 45 | 28 44 |
| 31 | 05 01 | 02 11 | 25 20 | 25 23 | 28 34 |
| 32 | 05 00 | 02 01 | 24 56 | 25 01 | 28 23 |
| 33 | 04 59 | 01 50 | 24 31 | 24 38 | 28 12 |
| 34 | 04 58 | 01 39 | 24 06 | 24 15 | 28 01 |
| 35 | 04 57 | 01 27 | 23 41 | 23 51 | 27 50 |
| 36 | 04 56 | 01 16 | 23 15 | 23 26 | 27 38 |
| 37 | 04 55 | 01 04 | 22 49 | 23 01 | 27 25 |
| 38 | 04 54 | 00 53 | 22 22 | 22 35 | 27 13 |
| 39 | 04 53 | 00 41 | 21 56 | 22 09 | 27 00 |
| 40 | 04 52 | 00 28 | 21 28 | 21 42 | 26 46 |
| 41 | 04 50 | 00 16 | 21 01 | 21 14 | 26 32 |
| 42 | 04 49 | 00 04 | 20 33 | 20 45 | 26 17 |
| 43 | 04 48 | 29♎51 | 20 04 | 20 15 | 26 02 |
| 44 | 04 47 | 29 38 | 19 35 | 19 44 | 25 46 |
| 45 | 04 46 | 29 24 | 19 05 | 19 12 | 25 29 |
| 46 | 04 44 | 29 11 | 18 34 | 18 39 | 25 12 |
| 47 | 04 43 | 28 57 | 18 03 | 18 04 | 24 53 |
| 48 | 04 42 | 28 42 | 17 32 | 17 29 | 24 34 |
| 49 | 04 40 | 28 28 | 16 59 | 16 52 | 24 14 |
| 50 | 04 39 | 28 13 | 16 26 | 16 13 | 23 52 |
| 51 | 04 37 | 27 57 | 15 52 | 15 33 | 23 30 |
| 52 | 04 36 | 27 41 | 15 18 | 14 51 | 23 05 |
| 53 | 04 34 | 27 25 | 14 42 | 14 07 | 22 40 |
| 54 | 04 33 | 27 09 | 14 06 | 13 21 | 22 12 |
| 55 | 04 31 | 26 51 | 13 28 | 12 33 | 21 43 |
| 56 | 04 29 | 26 34 | 12 50 | 11 42 | 21 11 |
| 57 | 04 27 | 26 15 | 12 10 | 10 49 | 20 36 |
| 58 | 04 25 | 25 56 | 11 30 | 09 53 | 19 58 |
| 59 | 04 24 | 25 37 | 10 48 | 08 54 | 19 16 |
| 60 | 04♎21 | 25♎16 | 10♏05 | 07♐52 | 18♑30 |

10h 24m 0s — 156° 0' 0" — 04 ♍ 07

| 11 | 12 | ASC | 2 | 3 | LAT. |
|---|---|---|---|---|---|
| 06♎32 | 08♏23 | 07♐47 | 05♑30 | 03♒41 | 0 |
| 06 27 | 07 31 | 05 56 | 04 11 | 03 07 | 5 |
| 06 22 | 06 41 | 04 07 | 02 50 | 02 31 | 10 |
| 06 18 | 05 51 | 02 18 | 01 25 | 01 54 | 15 |
| 06 13 | 05 01 | 00 27 | 29♐57 | 01 15 | 20 |
| 06 12 | 04 51 | 00 04 | 29 39 | 01 07 | 21 |
| 06 11 | 04 41 | 29♏42 | 29 20 | 00 58 | 22 |
| 06 10 | 04 31 | 29 19 | 29 01 | 00 50 | 23 |
| 06 08 | 04 20 | 28 56 | 28 42 | 00 41 | 24 |
| 06 07 | 04 10 | 28 33 | 28 22 | 00 32 | 25 |
| 06 06 | 03 59 | 28 10 | 28 02 | 00 23 | 26 |
| 06 05 | 03 49 | 27 46 | 27 42 | 00 13 | 27 |
| 06 04 | 03 38 | 27 23 | 27 22 | 00 04 | 28 |
| 06 03 | 03 27 | 26 59 | 27 01 | 29♑54 | 29 |
| 06 02 | 03 17 | 26 35 | 26 39 | 29 44 | 30 |
| 06 01 | 03 06 | 26 10 | 26 17 | 29 34 | 31 |
| 06 00 | 02 55 | 25 46 | 25 55 | 29 24 | 32 |
| 05 59 | 02 43 | 25 21 | 25 32 | 29 13 | 33 |
| 05 57 | 02 32 | 24 55 | 25 09 | 29 02 | 34 |
| 05 56 | 02 20 | 24 30 | 24 45 | 28 50 | 35 |
| 05 55 | 02 09 | 24 04 | 24 20 | 28 38 | 36 |
| 05 54 | 01 57 | 23 37 | 23 55 | 28 26 | 37 |
| 05 52 | 01 45 | 23 11 | 23 29 | 28 14 | 38 |
| 05 51 | 01 32 | 22 43 | 23 02 | 28 01 | 39 |
| 05 50 | 01 20 | 22 16 | 22 35 | 27 47 | 40 |
| 05 48 | 01 07 | 21 48 | 22 07 | 27 33 | 41 |
| 05 47 | 00 54 | 21 19 | 21 37 | 27 18 | 42 |
| 05 46 | 00 41 | 20 50 | 21 07 | 27 03 | 43 |
| 05 44 | 00 28 | 20 20 | 20 36 | 26 47 | 44 |
| 05 43 | 00 14 | 19 50 | 20 04 | 26 31 | 45 |
| 05 41 | 00 00 | 19 19 | 19 31 | 26 13 | 46 |
| 05 40 | 29♎46 | 18 48 | 18 56 | 25 55 | 47 |
| 05 38 | 29 31 | 18 16 | 18 20 | 25 36 | 48 |
| 05 36 | 29 16 | 17 43 | 17 43 | 25 16 | 49 |
| 05 35 | 29 01 | 17 09 | 17 04 | 24 55 | 50 |
| 05 33 | 28 45 | 16 35 | 16 23 | 24 32 | 51 |
| 05 31 | 28 28 | 16 00 | 15 41 | 24 08 | 52 |
| 05 29 | 28 12 | 15 23 | 14 56 | 23 42 | 53 |
| 05 27 | 27 55 | 14 46 | 14 10 | 23 15 | 54 |
| 05 25 | 27 37 | 14 08 | 13 21 | 22 45 | 55 |
| 05 23 | 27 19 | 13 29 | 12 30 | 22 14 | 56 |
| 05 21 | 27 00 | 12 49 | 11 36 | 21 39 | 57 |
| 05 19 | 26 40 | 12 08 | 10 39 | 21 02 | 58 |
| 05 16 | 26 20 | 11 25 | 09 40 | 20 20 | 59 |
| 05♎14 | 25♎59 | 10♏42 | 08♐36 | 19♑34 | 60 |

10h 28m 0s — 157° 0' 0" — 05 ♍ 10

| LAT. | 11 | 12 | ASC | 2 | 3 |
|---|---|---|---|---|---|
| 0 | 07♎37 | 09♏24 | 08♐43 | 06♑26 | 04♒39 |
| 5 | 07 32 | 08 32 | 06 52 | 05 06 | 04 05 |
| 10 | 07 26 | 07 40 | 05 02 | 03 45 | 03 30 |
| 15 | 07 20 | 06 49 | 03 12 | 02 21 | 02 54 |
| 20 | 07 15 | 05 58 | 01 20 | 00 52 | 02 14 |
| 21 | 07 13 | 05 48 | 00 57 | 00 34 | 02 06 |
| 22 | 07 12 | 05 37 | 00 34 | 00 15 | 01 58 |
| 23 | 07 11 | 05 27 | 00 11 | 29♐56 | 01 49 |
| 24 | 07 10 | 05 16 | 29♏48 | 29 37 | 01 41 |
| 25 | 07 09 | 05 06 | 29 25 | 29 17 | 01 32 |
| 26 | 07 07 | 04 55 | 29 02 | 28 57 | 01 23 |
| 27 | 07 06 | 04 44 | 28 38 | 28 37 | 01 14 |
| 28 | 07 05 | 04 33 | 28 14 | 28 16 | 01 04 |
| 29 | 07 04 | 04 22 | 27 50 | 27 55 | 00 55 |
| 30 | 07 02 | 04 11 | 27 25 | 27 34 | 00 45 |
| 31 | 07 01 | 04 00 | 27 01 | 27 12 | 00 35 |
| 32 | 07 00 | 03 48 | 26 36 | 26 49 | 00 24 |
| 33 | 06 58 | 03 37 | 26 10 | 26 26 | 00 13 |
| 34 | 06 57 | 03 25 | 25 45 | 26 03 | 00 02 |
| 35 | 06 55 | 03 13 | 25 19 | 25 39 | 29♑51 |
| 36 | 06 54 | 03 01 | 24 52 | 25 14 | 29 39 |
| 37 | 06 53 | 02 49 | 24 26 | 24 49 | 29 27 |
| 38 | 06 51 | 02 37 | 23 59 | 24 23 | 29 15 |
| 39 | 06 50 | 02 24 | 23 31 | 23 56 | 29 02 |
| 40 | 06 48 | 02 12 | 23 03 | 23 28 | 28 48 |
| 41 | 06 46 | 01 59 | 22 35 | 23 00 | 28 34 |
| 42 | 06 45 | 01 45 | 22 06 | 22 30 | 28 20 |
| 43 | 06 43 | 01 32 | 21 36 | 22 00 | 28 05 |
| 44 | 06 42 | 01 18 | 21 06 | 21 29 | 27 49 |
| 45 | 06 40 | 01 04 | 20 35 | 20 56 | 27 33 |
| 46 | 06 38 | 00 49 | 20 04 | 20 23 | 27 15 |
| 47 | 06 36 | 00 35 | 19 32 | 19 48 | 26 57 |
| 48 | 06 34 | 00 20 | 19 00 | 19 11 | 26 38 |
| 49 | 06 32 | 00 04 | 18 26 | 18 34 | 26 18 |
| 50 | 06 30 | 29♎48 | 17 52 | 17 54 | 25 57 |
| 51 | 06 28 | 29 32 | 17 17 | 17 13 | 25 35 |
| 52 | 06 26 | 29 15 | 16 41 | 16 31 | 25 11 |
| 53 | 06 24 | 28 58 | 16 05 | 15 46 | 24 45 |
| 54 | 06 22 | 28 41 | 15 27 | 14 59 | 24 18 |
| 55 | 06 19 | 28 22 | 14 48 | 14 10 | 23 49 |
| 56 | 06 17 | 28 04 | 14 09 | 13 18 | 23 17 |
| 57 | 06 14 | 27 44 | 13 28 | 12 23 | 22 43 |
| 58 | 06 12 | 27 24 | 12 46 | 11 26 | 22 06 |
| 59 | 06 09 | 27 04 | 12 03 | 10 25 | 21 24 |
| 60 | 06♎06 | 26♎42 | 11♏18 | 09♐21 | 20♑39 |

10h 32m 0s — 158° 0' 0" — 06 ♍ 14

| LAT. | 11 | 12 | ASC | 2 | 3 |
|---|---|---|---|---|---|
| 0 | 08♎43 | 10♏25 | 09♐40 | 07♑21 | 05♒38 |
| 5 | 08 36 | 09 32 | 07 48 | 06 01 | 05 04 |
| 10 | 08 30 | 08 39 | 05 57 | 04 40 | 04 30 |
| 15 | 08 23 | 07 47 | 04 06 | 03 16 | 03 53 |
| 20 | 08 17 | 06 55 | 02 13 | 01 47 | 03 14 |
| 21 | 08 15 | 06 44 | 01 50 | 01 29 | 03 06 |
| 22 | 08 14 | 06 34 | 01 27 | 01 10 | 02 58 |
| 23 | 08 12 | 06 23 | 01 04 | 00 51 | 02 50 |
| 24 | 08 11 | 06 12 | 00 41 | 00 32 | 02 41 |
| 25 | 08 10 | 06 01 | 00 17 | 00 12 | 02 32 |
| 26 | 08 08 | 05 50 | 29♏53 | 29♐52 | 02 23 |
| 27 | 08 07 | 05 39 | 29 29 | 29 32 | 02 14 |
| 28 | 08 05 | 05 28 | 29 05 | 29 11 | 02 05 |
| 29 | 08 04 | 05 17 | 28 41 | 28 50 | 01 55 |
| 30 | 08 02 | 05 05 | 28 16 | 28 28 | 01 45 |
| 31 | 08 01 | 04 54 | 27 51 | 28 06 | 01 35 |
| 32 | 07 59 | 04 42 | 27 26 | 27 44 | 01 25 |
| 33 | 07 58 | 04 30 | 27 00 | 27 21 | 01 14 |
| 34 | 07 56 | 04 18 | 26 34 | 26 57 | 01 03 |
| 35 | 07 55 | 04 06 | 26 08 | 26 33 | 00 52 |
| 36 | 07 53 | 03 54 | 25 41 | 26 08 | 00 41 |
| 37 | 07 51 | 03 42 | 25 14 | 25 43 | 00 29 |
| 38 | 07 50 | 03 29 | 24 47 | 25 16 | 00 16 |
| 39 | 07 48 | 03 16 | 24 19 | 24 50 | 00 03 |
| 40 | 07 46 | 03 03 | 23 51 | 24 22 | 29♑50 |
| 41 | 07 44 | 02 50 | 23 22 | 23 53 | 29 36 |
| 42 | 07 43 | 02 36 | 22 52 | 23 24 | 29 22 |
| 43 | 07 41 | 02 22 | 22 22 | 22 53 | 29 07 |
| 44 | 07 39 | 02 08 | 21 52 | 22 21 | 28 51 |
| 45 | 07 37 | 01 54 | 21 21 | 21 49 | 28 35 |
| 46 | 07 35 | 01 39 | 20 49 | 21 15 | 28 18 |
| 47 | 07 33 | 01 24 | 20 17 | 20 40 | 28 00 |
| 48 | 07 31 | 01 08 | 19 44 | 20 03 | 27 41 |
| 49 | 07 28 | 00 52 | 19 10 | 19 25 | 27 21 |
| 50 | 07 26 | 00 36 | 18 35 | 18 45 | 27 00 |
| 51 | 07 24 | 00 20 | 18 00 | 18 04 | 26 38 |
| 52 | 07 21 | 00 02 | 17 23 | 17 21 | 26 14 |
| 53 | 07 19 | 29♎45 | 16 46 | 16 35 | 25 49 |
| 54 | 07 16 | 29 27 | 16 08 | 15 48 | 25 22 |
| 55 | 07 13 | 29 08 | 15 29 | 14 58 | 24 53 |
| 56 | 07 11 | 28 49 | 14 48 | 14 06 | 24 21 |
| 57 | 07 08 | 28 29 | 14 07 | 13 10 | 23 47 |
| 58 | 07 05 | 28 08 | 13 24 | 12 12 | 23 10 |
| 59 | 07 01 | 27 47 | 12 40 | 11 11 | 22 29 |
| 60 | 06♎58 | 27♎25 | 11♏55 | 10♐05 | 21♑44 |

10h 36m 0s — 159° 0' 0" — 07 ♍ 18

| LAT. | 11 | 12 | ASC | 2 | 3 |
|---|---|---|---|---|---|
| 0 | 09♎48 | 11♏26 | 10♐36 | 08♑16 | 06♒37 |
| 5 | 09 40 | 10 31 | 08 43 | 06 57 | 06 03 |
| 10 | 09 33 | 09 38 | 06 52 | 05 36 | 05 29 |
| 15 | 09 26 | 08 45 | 05 00 | 04 11 | 04 53 |
| 20 | 09 18 | 07 52 | 03 06 | 02 43 | 04 14 |
| 21 | 09 17 | 07 41 | 02 43 | 02 24 | 04 06 |
| 22 | 09 15 | 07 30 | 02 20 | 02 05 | 03 58 |
| 23 | 09 14 | 07 19 | 01 56 | 01 46 | 03 50 |
| 24 | 09 12 | 07 08 | 01 33 | 01 27 | 03 41 |
| 25 | 09 11 | 06 57 | 01 09 | 01 07 | 03 33 |
| 26 | 09 09 | 06 45 | 00 45 | 00 47 | 03 24 |
| 27 | 09 08 | 06 34 | 00 21 | 00 27 | 03 15 |
| 28 | 09 06 | 06 23 | 29♏56 | 00 06 | 03 06 |
| 29 | 09 04 | 06 11 | 29 32 | 29♐45 | 02 56 |
| 30 | 09 03 | 06 00 | 29 07 | 29 23 | 02 46 |
| 31 | 09 01 | 05 48 | 28 41 | 29 01 | 02 36 |
| 32 | 08 59 | 05 36 | 28 16 | 28 39 | 02 26 |
| 33 | 08 58 | 05 24 | 27 50 | 28 15 | 02 16 |
| 34 | 08 56 | 05 12 | 27 24 | 27 52 | 02 05 |
| 35 | 08 54 | 04 59 | 26 57 | 27 27 | 01 54 |
| 36 | 08 52 | 04 47 | 26 30 | 27 02 | 01 42 |
| 37 | 08 50 | 04 34 | 26 03 | 26 37 | 01 30 |
| 38 | 08 48 | 04 21 | 25 35 | 26 11 | 01 18 |
| 39 | 08 46 | 04 08 | 25 07 | 25 43 | 01 05 |
| 40 | 08 44 | 03 54 | 24 38 | 25 15 | 00 52 |
| 41 | 08 42 | 03 41 | 24 09 | 24 47 | 00 38 |
| 42 | 08 40 | 03 27 | 23 39 | 24 17 | 00 24 |
| 43 | 08 38 | 03 13 | 23 09 | 23 46 | 00 09 |
| 44 | 08 36 | 02 58 | 22 38 | 23 14 | 29♑54 |
| 45 | 08 34 | 02 43 | 22 06 | 22 42 | 29 37 |
| 46 | 08 32 | 02 28 | 21 34 | 22 07 | 29 20 |
| 47 | 08 29 | 02 13 | 21 01 | 21 32 | 29 03 |
| 48 | 08 27 | 01 57 | 20 28 | 20 55 | 28 44 |
| 49 | 08 24 | 01 41 | 19 53 | 20 17 | 28 24 |
| 50 | 08 22 | 01 24 | 19 18 | 19 37 | 28 03 |
| 51 | 08 19 | 01 07 | 18 42 | 18 55 | 27 41 |
| 52 | 08 16 | 00 49 | 18 05 | 18 11 | 27 18 |
| 53 | 08 13 | 00 31 | 17 27 | 17 25 | 26 53 |
| 54 | 08 11 | 00 13 | 16 49 | 16 37 | 26 26 |
| 55 | 08 08 | 29♎53 | 16 09 | 15 47 | 25 57 |
| 56 | 08 04 | 29 34 | 15 28 | 14 54 | 25 26 |
| 57 | 08 01 | 29 13 | 14 46 | 13 58 | 24 52 |
| 58 | 07 58 | 28 52 | 14 02 | 12 59 | 24 15 |
| 59 | 07 54 | 28 30 | 13 18 | 11 56 | 23 35 |
| 60 | 07♎50 | 28♎08 | 12♏32 | 10♐50 | 22♑50 |

# Placidus Table of Houses for Latitudes 0° to 60° North

10h 40m 0s — 160° 0' 0" — 08 ♍ 22

| LAT. | 11 | 12 | ASC | 2 | 3 |
|---|---|---|---|---|---|
| 0 | 10♎53 | 12♏27 | 11♐32 | 09♑11 | 07♒35 |
| 5 | 10 45 | 11 31 | 09 39 | 07 52 | 07 02 |
| 10 | 10 37 | 10 37 | 07 47 | 06 31 | 06 28 |
| 15 | 10 29 | 09 43 | 05 54 | 05 07 | 05 53 |
| 20 | 10 20 | 08 48 | 03 59 | 03 38 | 05 15 |
| 21 | 10 19 | 08 37 | 03 36 | 03 20 | 05 07 |
| 22 | 10 17 | 08 26 | 03 12 | 03 01 | 04 59 |
| 23 | 10 15 | 08 15 | 02 49 | 02 42 | 04 50 |
| 24 | 10 14 | 08 03 | 02 25 | 02 22 | 04 42 |
| 25 | 10 12 | 07 52 | 02 01 | 02 03 | 04 33 |
| 26 | 10 10 | 07 41 | 01 37 | 01 43 | 04 25 |
| 27 | 10 08 | 07 29 | 01 12 | 01 22 | 04 16 |
| 28 | 10 07 | 07 17 | 00 48 | 01 01 | 04 07 |
| 29 | 10 05 | 07 06 | 00 23 | 00 40 | 03 57 |
| 30 | 10 03 | 06 54 | 29♏57 | 00 18 | 03 48 |
| 31 | 10 01 | 06 42 | 29 32 | 29♐56 | 03 38 |
| 32 | 09 59 | 06 30 | 29 06 | 29 33 | 03 28 |
| 33 | 09 57 | 06 17 | 28 40 | 29 10 | 03 17 |
| 34 | 09 55 | 06 05 | 28 13 | 28 46 | 03 06 |
| 35 | 09 53 | 05 52 | 27 46 | 28 22 | 02 55 |
| 36 | 09 51 | 05 39 | 27 19 | 27 57 | 02 44 |
| 37 | 09 49 | 05 26 | 26 51 | 27 31 | 02 32 |
| 38 | 09 47 | 05 13 | 26 23 | 27 05 | 02 20 |
| 39 | 09 45 | 04 59 | 25 55 | 26 38 | 02 07 |
| 40 | 09 43 | 04 46 | 25 26 | 26 09 | 01 54 |
| 41 | 09 40 | 04 32 | 24 56 | 25 40 | 01 41 |
| 42 | 09 38 | 04 17 | 24 26 | 25 11 | 01 26 |
| 43 | 09 36 | 04 03 | 23 55 | 24 40 | 01 12 |
| 44 | 09 33 | 03 48 | 23 24 | 24 08 | 00 56 |
| 45 | 09 31 | 03 33 | 22 52 | 23 34 | 00 40 |
| 46 | 09 28 | 03 17 | 22 19 | 23 00 | 00 23 |
| 47 | 09 26 | 03 02 | 21 46 | 22 24 | 00 06 |
| 48 | 09 23 | 02 45 | 21 12 | 21 47 | 29♑47 |
| 49 | 09 20 | 02 29 | 20 37 | 21 08 | 29 28 |
| 50 | 09 17 | 02 12 | 20 01 | 20 28 | 29 07 |
| 51 | 09 14 | 01 54 | 19 25 | 19 46 | 28 45 |
| 52 | 09 11 | 01 36 | 18 47 | 19 02 | 28 22 |
| 53 | 09 08 | 01 18 | 18 09 | 18 16 | 27 57 |
| 54 | 09 05 | 00 59 | 17 29 | 17 27 | 27 30 |
| 55 | 09 02 | 00 39 | 16 49 | 16 36 | 27 02 |
| 56 | 08 58 | 00 19 | 16 07 | 15 42 | 26 31 |
| 57 | 08 54 | 29♎58 | 15 24 | 14 46 | 25 57 |
| 58 | 08 51 | 29 36 | 14 40 | 13 46 | 25 21 |
| 59 | 08 47 | 29 14 | 13 55 | 12 42 | 24 41 |
| 60 | 08♎43 | 28♎50 | 13♏08 | 11♐35 | 23♑56 |

10h 44m 0s — 161° 0' 0" — 09 ♍ 26

| LAT. | 11 | 12 | ASC | 2 | 3 |
|---|---|---|---|---|---|
| 0 | 11♎58 | 13♏27 | 12♐28 | 10♑07 | 08♒34 |
| 5 | 11 49 | 12 31 | 10 34 | 08 48 | 08 02 |
| 10 | 11 40 | 11 35 | 08 41 | 07 27 | 07 28 |
| 15 | 11 31 | 10 40 | 06 48 | 06 02 | 06 53 |
| 20 | 11 22 | 09 45 | 04 52 | 04 34 | 06 15 |
| 21 | 11 20 | 09 33 | 04 29 | 04 15 | 06 08 |
| 22 | 11 19 | 09 22 | 04 05 | 03 56 | 05 59 |
| 23 | 11 17 | 09 11 | 03 41 | 03 37 | 05 51 |
| 24 | 11 15 | 08 59 | 03 17 | 03 18 | 05 43 |
| 25 | 11 13 | 08 47 | 02 53 | 02 58 | 05 34 |
| 26 | 11 11 | 08 36 | 02 28 | 02 38 | 05 26 |
| 27 | 11 09 | 08 24 | 02 04 | 02 17 | 05 17 |
| 28 | 11 07 | 08 12 | 01 39 | 01 57 | 05 08 |
| 29 | 11 05 | 08 00 | 01 14 | 01 35 | 04 59 |
| 30 | 11 03 | 07 48 | 00 48 | 01 14 | 04 49 |
| 31 | 11 01 | 07 36 | 00 22 | 00 51 | 04 39 |
| 32 | 10 59 | 07 23 | 29♏56 | 00 29 | 04 29 |
| 33 | 10 57 | 07 11 | 29 30 | 00 05 | 04 19 |
| 34 | 10 55 | 06 58 | 29 03 | 29♐41 | 04 08 |
| 35 | 10 52 | 06 45 | 28 36 | 29 17 | 03 57 |
| 36 | 10 50 | 06 32 | 28 08 | 28 52 | 03 46 |
| 37 | 10 48 | 06 18 | 27 40 | 28 26 | 03 34 |
| 38 | 10 45 | 06 05 | 27 11 | 27 59 | 03 22 |
| 39 | 10 43 | 05 51 | 26 43 | 27 32 | 03 10 |
| 40 | 10 41 | 05 37 | 26 13 | 27 04 | 02 57 |
| 41 | 10 38 | 05 23 | 25 43 | 26 35 | 02 43 |
| 42 | 10 36 | 05 08 | 25 13 | 26 04 | 02 29 |
| 43 | 10 33 | 04 53 | 24 41 | 25 33 | 02 15 |
| 44 | 10 30 | 04 38 | 24 10 | 25 01 | 01 59 |
| 45 | 10 28 | 04 23 | 23 37 | 24 28 | 01 43 |
| 46 | 10 25 | 04 07 | 23 04 | 23 53 | 01 27 |
| 47 | 10 22 | 03 51 | 22 30 | 23 17 | 01 09 |
| 48 | 10 19 | 03 34 | 21 56 | 22 40 | 00 51 |
| 49 | 10 16 | 03 17 | 21 20 | 22 01 | 00 31 |
| 50 | 10 13 | 02 59 | 20 44 | 21 20 | 00 11 |
| 51 | 10 10 | 02 41 | 20 07 | 20 37 | 29♑49 |
| 52 | 10 06 | 02 23 | 19 29 | 19 53 | 29 26 |
| 53 | 10 03 | 02 04 | 18 50 | 19 06 | 29 01 |
| 54 | 09 59 | 01 44 | 18 10 | 18 17 | 28 35 |
| 55 | 09 56 | 01 24 | 17 29 | 17 25 | 28 07 |
| 56 | 09 52 | 01 04 | 16 47 | 16 31 | 27 36 |
| 57 | 09 48 | 00 42 | 16 03 | 15 34 | 27 03 |
| 58 | 09 44 | 00 20 | 15 18 | 14 33 | 26 27 |
| 59 | 09 39 | 29♎57 | 14 32 | 13 29 | 25 47 |
| 60 | 09♎35 | 29♎33 | 13♏45 | 12♐20 | 25♑03 |

10h 48m 0s — 162° 0' 0" — 10 ♍ 30

| LAT. | 11 | 12 | ASC | 2 | 3 |
|---|---|---|---|---|---|
| 0 | 13♎03 | 14♏28 | 13♐24 | 11♑02 | 09♒34 |
| 5 | 12 53 | 13 30 | 11 30 | 09 43 | 09 01 |
| 10 | 12 43 | 12 34 | 09 36 | 08 22 | 08 28 |
| 15 | 12 34 | 11 38 | 07 42 | 06 58 | 07 53 |
| 20 | 12 24 | 10 41 | 05 45 | 05 29 | 07 16 |
| 21 | 12 22 | 10 29 | 05 22 | 05 11 | 07 08 |
| 22 | 12 20 | 10 18 | 04 58 | 04 52 | 07 00 |
| 23 | 12 18 | 10 06 | 04 34 | 04 33 | 06 52 |
| 24 | 12 16 | 09 54 | 04 09 | 04 13 | 06 44 |
| 25 | 12 14 | 09 43 | 03 45 | 03 54 | 06 36 |
| 26 | 12 12 | 09 31 | 03 20 | 03 34 | 06 27 |
| 27 | 12 10 | 09 19 | 02 55 | 03 13 | 06 18 |
| 28 | 12 07 | 09 07 | 02 30 | 02 52 | 06 09 |
| 29 | 12 05 | 08 54 | 02 05 | 02 31 | 06 00 |
| 30 | 12 03 | 08 42 | 01 39 | 02 09 | 05 51 |
| 31 | 12 01 | 08 29 | 01 13 | 01 47 | 05 41 |
| 32 | 11 58 | 08 17 | 00 46 | 01 24 | 05 31 |
| 33 | 11 56 | 08 04 | 00 20 | 01 00 | 05 21 |
| 34 | 11 54 | 07 51 | 29♏52 | 00 36 | 05 10 |
| 35 | 11 51 | 07 38 | 29 25 | 00 12 | 05 00 |
| 36 | 11 49 | 07 24 | 28 57 | 29♐47 | 04 48 |
| 37 | 11 47 | 07 11 | 28 29 | 29 21 | 04 37 |
| 38 | 11 44 | 06 57 | 28 00 | 28 54 | 04 25 |
| 39 | 11 41 | 06 43 | 27 30 | 28 26 | 04 12 |
| 40 | 11 39 | 06 28 | 27 01 | 27 58 | 04 00 |
| 41 | 11 36 | 06 14 | 26 30 | 27 29 | 03 46 |
| 42 | 11 33 | 05 59 | 25 59 | 26 58 | 03 32 |
| 43 | 11 30 | 05 44 | 25 28 | 26 27 | 03 18 |
| 44 | 11 28 | 05 28 | 24 56 | 25 55 | 03 03 |
| 45 | 11 25 | 05 12 | 24 23 | 25 21 | 02 47 |
| 46 | 11 22 | 04 56 | 23 49 | 24 46 | 02 31 |
| 47 | 11 18 | 04 39 | 23 15 | 24 10 | 02 13 |
| 48 | 11 15 | 04 22 | 22 40 | 23 32 | 01 55 |
| 49 | 11 12 | 04 05 | 22 04 | 22 53 | 01 36 |
| 50 | 11 09 | 03 47 | 21 27 | 22 12 | 01 15 |
| 51 | 11 05 | 03 29 | 20 50 | 21 29 | 00 54 |
| 52 | 11 01 | 03 10 | 20 11 | 20 44 | 00 31 |
| 53 | 10 58 | 02 50 | 19 32 | 19 57 | 00 07 |
| 54 | 10 54 | 02 30 | 18 51 | 19 07 | 29♑40 |
| 55 | 10 50 | 02 10 | 18 09 | 18 15 | 29 12 |
| 56 | 10 45 | 01 48 | 17 26 | 17 20 | 28 42 |
| 57 | 10 41 | 01 26 | 16 42 | 16 22 | 28 09 |
| 58 | 10 36 | 01 04 | 15 57 | 15 20 | 27 33 |
| 59 | 10 32 | 00 40 | 15 10 | 14 15 | 26 54 |
| 60 | 10♎27 | 00♏16 | 14♏21 | 13♐06 | 26♑10 |

10h 52m 0s — 163° 0' 0" — 11 ♍ 34

| LAT. | 11 | 12 | ASC | 2 | 3 |
|---|---|---|---|---|---|
| 0 | 14♎07 | 15♏28 | 14♐20 | 11♑58 | 10♒33 |
| 5 | 13 57 | 14 30 | 12 25 | 10 39 | 10 01 |
| 10 | 13 47 | 13 32 | 10 31 | 09 18 | 09 28 |
| 15 | 13 36 | 12 35 | 08 36 | 07 54 | 08 54 |
| 20 | 13 26 | 11 37 | 06 38 | 06 25 | 08 17 |
| 21 | 13 24 | 11 25 | 06 14 | 06 07 | 08 10 |
| 22 | 13 21 | 11 14 | 05 50 | 05 48 | 08 02 |
| 23 | 13 19 | 11 02 | 05 26 | 05 29 | 07 54 |
| 24 | 13 17 | 10 50 | 05 02 | 05 09 | 07 46 |
| 25 | 13 15 | 10 38 | 04 37 | 04 49 | 07 37 |
| 26 | 13 12 | 10 26 | 04 12 | 04 29 | 07 29 |
| 27 | 13 10 | 10 13 | 03 47 | 04 09 | 07 20 |
| 28 | 13 08 | 10 01 | 03 21 | 03 48 | 07 11 |
| 29 | 13 05 | 09 49 | 02 56 | 03 26 | 07 02 |
| 30 | 13 03 | 09 36 | 02 30 | 03 04 | 06 53 |
| 31 | 13 01 | 09 23 | 02 03 | 02 42 | 06 43 |
| 32 | 12 58 | 09 10 | 01 37 | 02 19 | 06 33 |
| 33 | 12 56 | 08 57 | 01 10 | 01 56 | 06 23 |
| 34 | 12 53 | 08 44 | 00 42 | 01 32 | 06 13 |
| 35 | 12 50 | 08 30 | 00 14 | 01 07 | 06 02 |
| 36 | 12 48 | 08 17 | 29♏46 | 00 42 | 05 51 |
| 37 | 12 45 | 08 03 | 29 17 | 00 16 | 05 40 |
| 38 | 12 42 | 07 48 | 28 48 | 29♐49 | 05 28 |
| 39 | 12 40 | 07 34 | 28 19 | 29 21 | 05 15 |
| 40 | 12 37 | 07 19 | 27 48 | 28 53 | 05 03 |
| 41 | 12 34 | 07 05 | 27 18 | 28 23 | 04 50 |
| 42 | 12 31 | 06 49 | 26 46 | 27 53 | 04 36 |
| 43 | 12 28 | 06 34 | 26 14 | 27 21 | 04 22 |
| 44 | 12 25 | 06 18 | 25 42 | 26 49 | 04 07 |
| 45 | 12 22 | 06 02 | 25 08 | 26 15 | 03 51 |
| 46 | 12 18 | 05 45 | 24 34 | 25 40 | 03 35 |
| 47 | 12 15 | 05 28 | 24 00 | 25 03 | 03 17 |
| 48 | 12 11 | 05 11 | 23 24 | 24 25 | 02 59 |
| 49 | 12 08 | 04 53 | 22 48 | 23 46 | 02 40 |
| 50 | 12 04 | 04 35 | 22 11 | 23 04 | 02 20 |
| 51 | 12 00 | 04 16 | 21 32 | 22 21 | 01 59 |
| 52 | 11 56 | 03 57 | 20 53 | 21 35 | 01 36 |
| 53 | 11 52 | 03 37 | 20 13 | 20 48 | 01 12 |
| 54 | 11 48 | 03 16 | 19 32 | 19 58 | 00 46 |
| 55 | 11 44 | 02 55 | 18 49 | 19 05 | 00 18 |
| 56 | 11 39 | 02 33 | 18 06 | 18 09 | 29♑49 |
| 57 | 11 34 | 02 11 | 17 21 | 17 11 | 29 16 |
| 58 | 11 29 | 01 47 | 16 35 | 16 08 | 28 41 |
| 59 | 11 24 | 01 23 | 15 47 | 15 02 | 28 02 |
| 60 | 11♎19 | 00♏58 | 14♏58 | 13♐52 | 27♑18 |

10h 56m 0s — 164° 0' 0" — 12 ♍ 39

| LAT. | 11 | 12 | ASC | 2 | 3 |
|---|---|---|---|---|---|
| 0 | 15♎12 | 16♏28 | 15♐16 | 12♑53 | 11♒32 |
| 5 | 15 01 | 15 29 | 13 20 | 11 35 | 11 01 |
| 10 | 14 50 | 14 30 | 11 25 | 10 14 | 10 29 |
| 15 | 14 39 | 13 32 | 09 30 | 08 50 | 09 55 |
| 20 | 14 27 | 12 33 | 07 31 | 07 21 | 09 18 |
| 21 | 14 25 | 12 21 | 07 07 | 07 03 | 09 11 |
| 22 | 14 23 | 12 09 | 06 43 | 06 44 | 09 03 |
| 23 | 14 20 | 11 57 | 06 19 | 06 25 | 08 55 |
| 24 | 14 18 | 11 45 | 05 54 | 06 05 | 08 47 |
| 25 | 14 15 | 11 33 | 05 29 | 05 45 | 08 39 |
| 26 | 14 13 | 11 21 | 05 04 | 05 25 | 08 31 |
| 27 | 14 11 | 11 08 | 04 38 | 05 05 | 08 22 |
| 28 | 14 08 | 10 55 | 04 13 | 04 44 | 08 13 |
| 29 | 14 05 | 10 43 | 03 47 | 04 22 | 08 04 |
| 30 | 14 03 | 10 30 | 03 20 | 04 00 | 07 55 |
| 31 | 14 00 | 10 17 | 02 54 | 03 38 | 07 45 |
| 32 | 13 58 | 10 04 | 02 27 | 03 15 | 07 36 |
| 33 | 13 55 | 09 50 | 02 00 | 02 51 | 07 26 |
| 34 | 13 52 | 09 37 | 01 32 | 02 27 | 07 15 |
| 35 | 13 49 | 09 23 | 01 04 | 02 02 | 07 05 |
| 36 | 13 47 | 09 09 | 00 35 | 01 37 | 06 54 |
| 37 | 13 44 | 08 55 | 00 06 | 01 11 | 06 43 |
| 38 | 13 41 | 08 40 | 29♏37 | 00 44 | 06 31 |
| 39 | 13 38 | 08 26 | 29 07 | 00 16 | 06 19 |
| 40 | 13 35 | 08 11 | 28 36 | 29♐48 | 06 06 |
| 41 | 13 32 | 07 55 | 28 05 | 29 18 | 05 53 |
| 42 | 13 28 | 07 40 | 27 33 | 28 47 | 05 40 |
| 43 | 13 25 | 07 24 | 27 01 | 28 16 | 05 25 |
| 44 | 13 22 | 07 08 | 26 28 | 27 43 | 05 11 |
| 45 | 13 18 | 06 51 | 25 54 | 27 09 | 04 55 |
| 46 | 13 15 | 06 34 | 25 20 | 26 34 | 04 39 |
| 47 | 13 11 | 06 17 | 24 45 | 25 57 | 04 22 |
| 48 | 13 07 | 05 59 | 24 09 | 25 18 | 04 04 |
| 49 | 13 04 | 05 41 | 23 32 | 24 38 | 03 45 |
| 50 | 13 00 | 05 22 | 22 54 | 23 57 | 03 25 |
| 51 | 12 55 | 05 03 | 22 15 | 23 13 | 03 04 |
| 52 | 12 51 | 04 43 | 21 35 | 22 27 | 02 42 |
| 53 | 12 47 | 04 23 | 20 55 | 21 39 | 02 18 |
| 54 | 12 42 | 04 02 | 20 13 | 20 48 | 01 53 |
| 55 | 12 38 | 03 40 | 19 30 | 19 55 | 01 25 |
| 56 | 12 33 | 03 18 | 18 45 | 18 59 | 00 55 |
| 57 | 12 28 | 02 55 | 18 00 | 17 59 | 00 23 |
| 58 | 12 22 | 02 31 | 17 13 | 16 56 | 29♑48 |
| 59 | 12 17 | 02 06 | 16 25 | 15 49 | 29 10 |
| 60 | 12♎11 | 01♏41 | 15♏35 | 14♐38 | 28♑27 |

11h 0m 0s — 165° 0' 0" — 13 ♍ 43

| LAT. | 11 | 12 | ASC | 2 | 3 |
|---|---|---|---|---|---|
| 0 | 16♎17 | 17♏28 | 16♐11 | 13♑49 | 12♒32 |
| 5 | 16 05 | 16 28 | 14 16 | 12 30 | 12 01 |
| 10 | 15 53 | 15 28 | 12 20 | 11 10 | 11 29 |
| 15 | 15 41 | 14 29 | 10 24 | 09 46 | 10 56 |
| 20 | 15 29 | 13 29 | 08 25 | 08 17 | 10 20 |
| 21 | 15 26 | 13 17 | 08 00 | 07 59 | 10 12 |
| 22 | 15 24 | 13 05 | 07 36 | 07 40 | 10 05 |
| 23 | 15 21 | 12 53 | 07 11 | 07 21 | 09 57 |
| 24 | 15 19 | 12 40 | 06 46 | 07 01 | 09 49 |
| 25 | 15 16 | 12 28 | 06 21 | 06 41 | 09 41 |
| 26 | 15 14 | 12 15 | 05 56 | 06 21 | 09 33 |
| 27 | 15 11 | 12 03 | 05 30 | 06 01 | 09 24 |
| 28 | 15 08 | 11 50 | 05 04 | 05 40 | 09 15 |
| 29 | 15 06 | 11 37 | 04 38 | 05 18 | 09 07 |
| 30 | 15 03 | 11 24 | 04 11 | 04 56 | 08 57 |
| 31 | 15 00 | 11 10 | 03 44 | 04 34 | 08 48 |
| 32 | 14 57 | 10 57 | 03 17 | 04 11 | 08 39 |
| 33 | 14 54 | 10 43 | 02 50 | 03 47 | 08 28 |
| 34 | 14 51 | 10 29 | 02 22 | 03 23 | 08 18 |
| 35 | 14 48 | 10 15 | 01 53 | 02 58 | 08 08 |
| 36 | 14 45 | 10 01 | 01 24 | 02 33 | 07 57 |
| 37 | 14 42 | 09 47 | 00 55 | 02 06 | 07 46 |
| 38 | 14 39 | 09 32 | 00 25 | 01 39 | 07 34 |
| 39 | 14 36 | 09 17 | 29♏55 | 01 11 | 07 22 |
| 40 | 14 33 | 09 02 | 29 24 | 00 43 | 07 10 |
| 41 | 14 29 | 08 46 | 28 52 | 00 13 | 06 57 |
| 42 | 14 26 | 08 30 | 28 20 | 29♐42 | 06 44 |
| 43 | 14 22 | 08 14 | 27 47 | 29 10 | 06 30 |
| 44 | 14 19 | 07 58 | 27 14 | 28 37 | 06 15 |
| 45 | 14 15 | 07 41 | 26 40 | 28 03 | 06 00 |
| 46 | 14 11 | 07 23 | 26 05 | 27 28 | 05 44 |
| 47 | 14 07 | 07 06 | 25 29 | 26 51 | 05 27 |
| 48 | 14 03 | 06 48 | 24 53 | 26 12 | 05 09 |
| 49 | 13 59 | 06 29 | 24 15 | 25 32 | 04 51 |
| 50 | 13 55 | 06 10 | 23 37 | 24 50 | 04 31 |
| 51 | 13 51 | 05 50 | 22 58 | 24 06 | 04 10 |
| 52 | 13 46 | 05 30 | 22 18 | 23 19 | 03 48 |
| 53 | 13 41 | 05 09 | 21 36 | 22 31 | 03 24 |
| 54 | 13 36 | 04 48 | 20 54 | 21 40 | 02 59 |
| 55 | 13 31 | 04 26 | 20 10 | 20 46 | 02 32 |
| 56 | 13 26 | 04 03 | 19 25 | 19 49 | 02 03 |
| 57 | 13 21 | 03 39 | 18 39 | 18 49 | 01 31 |
| 58 | 13 15 | 03 15 | 17 51 | 17 45 | 00 56 |
| 59 | 13 09 | 02 50 | 17 02 | 16 37 | 00 18 |
| 60 | 13♎03 | 02♏23 | 16♏11 | 15♐24 | 29♑36 |

11h 4m 0s — 166° 0' 0" — 14 ♍ 48

| LAT. | 11 | 12 | ASC | 2 | 3 |
|---|---|---|---|---|---|
| 0 | 17♎21 | 18♏28 | 17♐07 | 14♑44 | 13♒32 |
| 5 | 17 09 | 17 26 | 15 11 | 13 26 | 13 01 |
| 10 | 16 56 | 16 26 | 13 15 | 12 06 | 12 30 |
| 15 | 16 43 | 15 26 | 11 18 | 10 42 | 11 57 |
| 20 | 16 30 | 14 25 | 09 18 | 09 13 | 11 22 |
| 21 | 16 28 | 14 13 | 08 53 | 08 55 | 11 14 |
| 22 | 16 25 | 14 01 | 08 28 | 08 36 | 11 07 |
| 23 | 16 22 | 13 48 | 08 04 | 08 17 | 10 59 |
| 24 | 16 20 | 13 36 | 07 39 | 07 57 | 10 51 |
| 25 | 16 17 | 13 23 | 07 13 | 07 38 | 10 43 |
| 26 | 16 14 | 13 10 | 06 48 | 07 17 | 10 35 |
| 27 | 16 11 | 12 57 | 06 22 | 06 57 | 10 27 |
| 28 | 16 08 | 12 44 | 05 56 | 06 36 | 10 18 |
| 29 | 16 06 | 12 31 | 05 29 | 06 14 | 10 09 |
| 30 | 16 03 | 12 17 | 05 02 | 05 52 | 10 00 |
| 31 | 16 00 | 12 04 | 04 35 | 05 30 | 09 51 |
| 32 | 15 57 | 11 50 | 04 08 | 05 07 | 09 42 |
| 33 | 15 54 | 11 36 | 03 40 | 04 43 | 09 32 |
| 34 | 15 50 | 11 22 | 03 11 | 04 19 | 09 22 |
| 35 | 15 47 | 11 08 | 02 43 | 03 54 | 09 11 |
| 36 | 15 44 | 10 53 | 02 14 | 03 28 | 09 01 |
| 37 | 15 41 | 10 39 | 01 44 | 03 02 | 08 50 |
| 38 | 15 37 | 10 24 | 01 14 | 02 35 | 08 38 |
| 39 | 15 34 | 10 08 | 00 43 | 02 07 | 08 26 |
| 40 | 15 31 | 09 53 | 00 12 | 01 38 | 08 14 |
| 41 | 15 27 | 09 37 | 29♏40 | 01 08 | 08 01 |
| 42 | 15 23 | 09 21 | 29 07 | 00 37 | 07 48 |
| 43 | 15 20 | 09 04 | 28 34 | 00 06 | 07 34 |
| 44 | 15 16 | 08 47 | 28 00 | 29♐32 | 07 20 |
| 45 | 15 12 | 08 30 | 27 26 | 28 58 | 07 05 |
| 46 | 15 08 | 08 13 | 26 50 | 28 22 | 06 49 |
| 47 | 15 04 | 07 55 | 26 14 | 27 45 | 06 32 |
| 48 | 14 59 | 07 36 | 25 37 | 27 06 | 06 15 |
| 49 | 14 55 | 07 17 | 24 59 | 26 25 | 05 57 |
| 50 | 14 50 | 06 57 | 24 21 | 25 43 | 05 37 |
| 51 | 14 46 | 06 37 | 23 41 | 24 58 | 05 17 |
| 52 | 14 41 | 06 17 | 23 00 | 24 12 | 04 55 |
| 53 | 14 36 | 05 56 | 22 18 | 23 23 | 04 31 |
| 54 | 14 31 | 05 34 | 21 35 | 22 31 | 04 06 |
| 55 | 14 25 | 05 11 | 20 50 | 21 37 | 03 40 |
| 56 | 14 20 | 04 48 | 20 05 | 20 39 | 03 11 |
| 57 | 14 14 | 04 24 | 19 18 | 19 38 | 02 39 |
| 58 | 14 08 | 03 59 | 18 30 | 18 33 | 02 05 |
| 59 | 14 01 | 03 33 | 17 40 | 17 24 | 01 28 |
| 60 | 13♎55 | 03♏06 | 16♏48 | 16♐11 | 00♒46 |

11h 8m 0s — 167° 0' 0" — 15 ♍ 53

| LAT. | 11 | 12 | ASC | 2 | 3 |
|---|---|---|---|---|---|
| 0 | 18♎26 | 19♏27 | 18♐02 | 15♑40 | 14♒32 |
| 5 | 18 12 | 18 25 | 16 06 | 14 22 | 14 02 |
| 10 | 17 59 | 17 24 | 14 09 | 13 02 | 13 31 |
| 15 | 17 46 | 16 23 | 12 12 | 11 39 | 12 58 |
| 20 | 17 32 | 15 21 | 10 11 | 10 10 | 12 24 |
| 21 | 17 29 | 15 09 | 09 46 | 09 51 | 12 16 |
| 22 | 17 26 | 14 56 | 09 21 | 09 33 | 12 09 |
| 23 | 17 23 | 14 43 | 08 56 | 09 13 | 12 01 |
| 24 | 17 20 | 14 31 | 08 31 | 08 54 | 11 54 |
| 25 | 17 17 | 14 18 | 08 05 | 08 34 | 11 46 |
| 26 | 17 15 | 14 05 | 07 40 | 08 14 | 11 38 |
| 27 | 17 12 | 13 51 | 07 13 | 07 53 | 11 29 |
| 28 | 17 09 | 13 38 | 06 47 | 07 32 | 11 21 |
| 29 | 17 05 | 13 25 | 06 20 | 07 11 | 11 12 |
| 30 | 17 02 | 13 11 | 05 53 | 06 49 | 11 03 |
| 31 | 16 59 | 12 57 | 05 26 | 06 26 | 10 54 |
| 32 | 16 56 | 12 43 | 04 58 | 06 03 | 10 45 |
| 33 | 16 53 | 12 29 | 04 30 | 05 39 | 10 35 |
| 34 | 16 49 | 12 15 | 04 01 | 05 15 | 10 25 |
| 35 | 16 46 | 12 00 | 03 32 | 04 50 | 10 15 |
| 36 | 16 43 | 11 46 | 03 03 | 04 24 | 10 05 |
| 37 | 16 39 | 11 31 | 02 33 | 03 58 | 09 54 |
| 38 | 16 36 | 11 15 | 02 02 | 03 31 | 09 42 |
| 39 | 16 32 | 11 00 | 01 31 | 03 03 | 09 31 |
| 40 | 16 28 | 10 44 | 01 00 | 02 34 | 09 19 |
| 41 | 16 25 | 10 28 | 00 27 | 02 04 | 09 06 |
| 42 | 16 21 | 10 11 | 29♏55 | 01 33 | 08 53 |
| 43 | 16 17 | 09 54 | 29 21 | 01 01 | 08 39 |
| 44 | 16 13 | 09 37 | 28 47 | 00 27 | 08 25 |
| 45 | 16 08 | 09 20 | 28 12 | 29♐53 | 08 10 |
| 46 | 16 04 | 09 02 | 27 36 | 29 17 | 07 55 |
| 47 | 16 00 | 08 43 | 26 59 | 28 39 | 07 38 |
| 48 | 15 55 | 08 24 | 26 22 | 28 00 | 07 21 |
| 49 | 15 51 | 08 05 | 25 43 | 27 19 | 07 03 |
| 50 | 15 46 | 07 45 | 25 04 | 26 36 | 06 44 |
| 51 | 15 41 | 07 25 | 24 24 | 25 52 | 06 23 |
| 52 | 15 36 | 07 04 | 23 42 | 25 04 | 06 02 |
| 53 | 15 30 | 06 42 | 23 00 | 24 15 | 05 39 |
| 54 | 15 25 | 06 19 | 22 16 | 23 23 | 05 14 |
| 55 | 15 19 | 05 56 | 21 31 | 22 28 | 04 47 |
| 56 | 15 13 | 05 33 | 20 45 | 21 30 | 04 19 |
| 57 | 15 07 | 05 08 | 19 57 | 20 28 | 03 48 |
| 58 | 15 01 | 04 42 | 19 08 | 19 22 | 03 14 |
| 59 | 14 54 | 04 16 | 18 17 | 18 12 | 02 37 |
| 60 | 14♎47 | 03♏48 | 17♏25 | 16♐58 | 01♒56 |

# Placidus Table of Houses for Latitudes 0° to 60° North

**11h 12m 0s — 168° 0' 0" — 16 ♍ 57**

| LAT. | 11 | 12 | ASC | 2 | 3 |
|---|---|---|---|---|---|
| 0 | 19♎30 | 20♏26 | 18♐58 | 16♑36 | 15♒32 |
| 5 | 19 16 | 19 24 | 17 01 | 15 18 | 15 03 |
| 10 | 19 02 | 18 22 | 15 04 | 13 59 | 14 32 |
| 15 | 18 48 | 17 20 | 13 05 | 12 35 | 14 00 |
| 20 | 18 33 | 16 17 | 11 04 | 11 07 | 13 26 |
| 21 | 18 30 | 16 04 | 10 39 | 10 48 | 13 19 |
| 22 | 18 27 | 15 52 | 10 14 | 10 29 | 13 11 |
| 23 | 18 24 | 15 39 | 09 49 | 10 10 | 13 04 |
| 24 | 18 21 | 15 26 | 09 23 | 09 51 | 12 56 |
| 25 | 18 18 | 15 12 | 08 58 | 09 31 | 12 48 |
| 26 | 18 15 | 14 59 | 08 32 | 09 10 | 12 40 |
| 27 | 18 12 | 14 46 | 08 05 | 08 50 | 12 32 |
| 28 | 18 09 | 14 32 | 07 39 | 08 29 | 12 24 |
| 29 | 18 05 | 14 19 | 07 12 | 08 07 | 12 15 |
| 30 | 18 02 | 14 05 | 06 44 | 07 45 | 12 07 |
| 31 | 17 59 | 13 51 | 06 17 | 07 23 | 11 58 |
| 32 | 17 55 | 13 37 | 05 49 | 06 59 | 11 48 |
| 33 | 17 52 | 13 22 | 05 20 | 06 36 | 11 39 |
| 34 | 17 48 | 13 08 | 04 51 | 06 11 | 11 29 |
| 35 | 17 45 | 12 53 | 04 22 | 05 46 | 11 19 |
| 36 | 17 41 | 12 38 | 03 52 | 05 21 | 11 09 |
| 37 | 17 38 | 12 22 | 03 22 | 04 54 | 10 58 |
| 38 | 17 34 | 12 07 | 02 51 | 04 27 | 10 47 |
| 39 | 17 30 | 11 51 | 02 20 | 03 59 | 10 35 |
| 40 | 17 26 | 11 35 | 01 48 | 03 30 | 10 23 |
| 41 | 17 22 | 11 18 | 01 15 | 02 59 | 10 11 |
| 42 | 17 18 | 11 02 | 00 42 | 02 28 | 09 58 |
| 43 | 17 14 | 10 44 | 00 08 | 01 56 | 09 45 |
| 44 | 17 09 | 10 27 | 29♏33 | 01 23 | 09 31 |
| 45 | 17 05 | 10 09 | 28 58 | 00 48 | 09 16 |
| 46 | 17 01 | 09 51 | 28 21 | 00 12 | 09 01 |
| 47 | 16 56 | 09 32 | 27 44 | 29♐34 | 08 44 |
| 48 | 16 51 | 09 13 | 27 06 | 28 54 | 08 27 |
| 49 | 16 46 | 08 53 | 26 27 | 28 13 | 08 09 |
| 50 | 16 41 | 08 33 | 25 48 | 27 30 | 07 50 |
| 51 | 16 36 | 08 12 | 25 07 | 26 45 | 07 30 |
| 52 | 16 30 | 07 50 | 24 25 | 25 58 | 07 09 |
| 53 | 16 25 | 07 28 | 23 41 | 25 08 | 06 46 |
| 54 | 16 19 | 07 05 | 22 57 | 24 15 | 06 22 |
| 55 | 16 13 | 06 42 | 22 11 | 23 19 | 05 56 |
| 56 | 16 07 | 06 17 | 21 24 | 22 21 | 05 28 |
| 57 | 16 00 | 05 52 | 20 36 | 21 18 | 04 57 |
| 58 | 15 53 | 05 26 | 19 46 | 20 12 | 04 24 |
| 59 | 15 46 | 04 59 | 18 55 | 19 01 | 03 48 |
| 60 | 15♎39 | 04♏31 | 18♏02 | 17♐45 | 03♒07 |

**11h 16m 0s — 169° 0' 0" — 18 ♍ 02**

| LAT. | 11 | 12 | ASC | 2 | 3 |
|---|---|---|---|---|---|
| 0 | 20♎34 | 21♏26 | 19♐53 | 17♑32 | 16♒33 |
| 5 | 20 19 | 20 22 | 17 56 | 16 15 | 16 04 |
| 10 | 20 05 | 19 19 | 15 58 | 14 55 | 15 34 |
| 15 | 19 50 | 18 16 | 13 59 | 13 32 | 15 02 |
| 20 | 19 34 | 17 13 | 11 57 | 12 03 | 14 28 |
| 21 | 19 31 | 17 00 | 11 32 | 11 45 | 14 21 |
| 22 | 19 28 | 16 47 | 11 07 | 11 26 | 14 14 |
| 23 | 19 25 | 16 34 | 10 41 | 11 07 | 14 07 |
| 24 | 19 22 | 16 20 | 10 16 | 10 47 | 13 59 |
| 25 | 19 18 | 16 07 | 09 50 | 10 28 | 13 51 |
| 26 | 19 15 | 15 54 | 09 24 | 10 07 | 13 44 |
| 27 | 19 12 | 15 40 | 08 57 | 09 47 | 13 36 |
| 28 | 19 08 | 15 26 | 08 30 | 09 26 | 13 27 |
| 29 | 19 05 | 15 12 | 08 03 | 09 04 | 13 19 |
| 30 | 19 02 | 14 58 | 07 35 | 08 42 | 13 10 |
| 31 | 18 58 | 14 44 | 07 08 | 08 19 | 13 01 |
| 32 | 18 55 | 14 30 | 06 39 | 07 56 | 12 52 |
| 33 | 18 51 | 14 15 | 06 11 | 07 32 | 12 43 |
| 34 | 18 47 | 14 00 | 05 41 | 07 08 | 12 33 |
| 35 | 18 44 | 13 45 | 05 12 | 06 43 | 12 23 |
| 36 | 18 40 | 13 30 | 04 42 | 06 17 | 12 13 |
| 37 | 18 36 | 13 14 | 04 11 | 05 51 | 12 03 |
| 38 | 18 32 | 12 58 | 03 40 | 05 23 | 11 52 |
| 39 | 18 28 | 12 42 | 03 08 | 04 55 | 11 40 |
| 40 | 18 24 | 12 26 | 02 36 | 04 26 | 11 29 |
| 41 | 18 20 | 12 09 | 02 03 | 03 56 | 11 16 |
| 42 | 18 15 | 11 52 | 01 29 | 03 24 | 11 04 |
| 43 | 18 11 | 11 35 | 00 55 | 02 52 | 10 50 |
| 44 | 18 06 | 11 17 | 00 20 | 02 18 | 10 36 |
| 45 | 18 02 | 10 58 | 29♏44 | 01 43 | 10 22 |
| 46 | 17 57 | 10 40 | 29 07 | 01 07 | 10 07 |
| 47 | 17 52 | 10 21 | 28 30 | 00 29 | 09 51 |
| 48 | 17 47 | 10 01 | 27 51 | 29♐49 | 09 34 |
| 49 | 17 42 | 09 41 | 27 12 | 29 08 | 09 16 |
| 50 | 17 36 | 09 20 | 26 31 | 28 24 | 08 58 |
| 51 | 17 31 | 08 59 | 25 50 | 27 39 | 08 38 |
| 52 | 17 25 | 08 37 | 25 07 | 26 51 | 08 17 |
| 53 | 17 19 | 08 14 | 24 23 | 26 01 | 07 55 |
| 54 | 17 13 | 07 51 | 23 38 | 25 08 | 07 31 |
| 55 | 17 07 | 07 27 | 22 52 | 24 11 | 07 05 |
| 56 | 17 00 | 07 02 | 22 04 | 23 12 | 06 37 |
| 57 | 16 53 | 06 36 | 21 15 | 22 09 | 06 07 |
| 58 | 16 46 | 06 10 | 20 25 | 21 01 | 05 34 |
| 59 | 16 38 | 05 42 | 19 32 | 19 50 | 04 58 |
| 60 | 16♎30 | 05♏13 | 18♏38 | 18♐33 | 04♒19 |

**11h 20m 0s — 170° 0' 0" — 19 ♍ 07**

| LAT. | 11 | 12 | ASC | 2 | 3 |
|---|---|---|---|---|---|
| 0 | 21♎38 | 22♏25 | 20♐49 | 18♑28 | 17♒33 |
| 5 | 21 23 | 21 20 | 18 51 | 17 11 | 17 05 |
| 10 | 21 07 | 20 17 | 16 53 | 15 52 | 16 35 |
| 15 | 20 51 | 19 13 | 14 53 | 14 29 | 16 04 |
| 20 | 20 35 | 18 08 | 12 50 | 13 00 | 15 31 |
| 21 | 20 32 | 17 55 | 12 25 | 12 42 | 15 24 |
| 22 | 20 29 | 17 42 | 12 00 | 12 23 | 15 17 |
| 23 | 20 26 | 17 29 | 11 34 | 12 04 | 15 10 |
| 24 | 20 22 | 17 15 | 11 08 | 11 44 | 15 02 |
| 25 | 20 19 | 17 02 | 10 42 | 11 25 | 14 55 |
| 26 | 20 15 | 16 48 | 10 16 | 11 04 | 14 47 |
| 27 | 20 12 | 16 34 | 09 49 | 10 44 | 14 39 |
| 28 | 20 08 | 16 20 | 09 22 | 10 23 | 14 31 |
| 29 | 20 05 | 16 06 | 08 54 | 10 01 | 14 23 |
| 30 | 20 01 | 15 52 | 08 27 | 09 39 | 14 14 |
| 31 | 19 57 | 15 37 | 07 59 | 09 16 | 14 05 |
| 32 | 19 54 | 15 23 | 07 30 | 08 53 | 13 57 |
| 33 | 19 50 | 15 08 | 07 01 | 08 29 | 13 47 |
| 34 | 19 46 | 14 53 | 06 32 | 08 05 | 13 38 |
| 35 | 19 42 | 14 37 | 06 02 | 07 40 | 13 28 |
| 36 | 19 38 | 14 22 | 05 31 | 07 14 | 13 18 |
| 37 | 19 34 | 14 06 | 05 00 | 06 47 | 13 08 |
| 38 | 19 30 | 13 50 | 04 29 | 06 20 | 12 57 |
| 39 | 19 26 | 13 33 | 03 57 | 05 52 | 12 46 |
| 40 | 19 21 | 13 17 | 03 24 | 05 22 | 12 34 |
| 41 | 19 17 | 13 00 | 02 51 | 04 52 | 12 22 |
| 42 | 19 12 | 12 42 | 02 17 | 04 21 | 12 09 |
| 43 | 19 08 | 12 25 | 01 42 | 03 48 | 11 56 |
| 44 | 19 03 | 12 06 | 01 06 | 03 14 | 11 43 |
| 45 | 18 58 | 11 48 | 00 30 | 02 39 | 11 28 |
| 46 | 18 53 | 11 29 | 29♏53 | 02 02 | 11 13 |
| 47 | 18 48 | 11 09 | 29 15 | 01 24 | 10 58 |
| 48 | 18 43 | 10 49 | 28 36 | 00 44 | 10 41 |
| 49 | 18 37 | 10 29 | 27 56 | 00 03 | 10 24 |
| 50 | 18 31 | 10 08 | 27 15 | 29♐19 | 10 05 |
| 51 | 18 26 | 09 46 | 26 33 | 28 33 | 09 46 |
| 52 | 18 20 | 09 23 | 25 50 | 27 45 | 09 25 |
| 53 | 18 13 | 09 00 | 25 05 | 26 54 | 09 03 |
| 54 | 18 07 | 08 37 | 24 20 | 26 00 | 08 40 |
| 55 | 18 00 | 08 12 | 23 33 | 25 04 | 08 14 |
| 56 | 17 53 | 07 47 | 22 44 | 24 04 | 07 47 |
| 57 | 17 46 | 07 20 | 21 54 | 23 00 | 07 17 |
| 58 | 17 38 | 06 53 | 21 03 | 21 51 | 06 45 |
| 59 | 17 31 | 06 25 | 20 10 | 20 39 | 06 10 |
| 60 | 17♎22 | 05♏56 | 19♏15 | 19♐21 | 05♒31 |

**11h 24m 0s — 171° 0' 0" — 20 ♍ 12**

| LAT. | 11 | 12 | ASC | 2 | 3 |
|---|---|---|---|---|---|
| 0 | 22♎42 | 23♏23 | 21♐44 | 19♑24 | 18♒34 |
| 5 | 22 26 | 22 18 | 19 46 | 18 07 | 18 06 |
| 10 | 22 10 | 21 14 | 17 48 | 16 48 | 17 37 |
| 15 | 21 53 | 20 09 | 15 47 | 15 26 | 17 06 |
| 20 | 21 36 | 19 04 | 13 44 | 13 57 | 16 34 |
| 21 | 21 33 | 18 51 | 13 18 | 13 39 | 16 27 |
| 22 | 21 30 | 18 37 | 12 53 | 13 20 | 16 20 |
| 23 | 21 26 | 18 24 | 12 27 | 13 01 | 16 13 |
| 24 | 21 23 | 18 10 | 12 01 | 12 42 | 16 06 |
| 25 | 21 19 | 17 56 | 11 34 | 12 22 | 15 58 |
| 26 | 21 15 | 17 42 | 11 08 | 12 02 | 15 51 |
| 27 | 21 12 | 17 28 | 10 41 | 11 41 | 15 43 |
| 28 | 21 08 | 17 14 | 10 14 | 11 20 | 15 35 |
| 29 | 21 04 | 17 00 | 09 46 | 10 58 | 15 27 |
| 30 | 21 01 | 16 45 | 09 18 | 10 36 | 15 18 |
| 31 | 20 57 | 16 31 | 08 50 | 10 14 | 15 10 |
| 32 | 20 53 | 16 16 | 08 21 | 09 50 | 15 01 |
| 33 | 20 49 | 16 01 | 07 51 | 09 27 | 14 52 |
| 34 | 20 45 | 15 45 | 07 22 | 09 02 | 14 43 |
| 35 | 20 41 | 15 30 | 06 52 | 08 37 | 14 33 |
| 36 | 20 36 | 15 14 | 06 21 | 08 11 | 14 23 |
| 37 | 20 32 | 14 58 | 05 50 | 07 44 | 14 13 |
| 38 | 20 28 | 14 41 | 05 18 | 07 17 | 14 02 |
| 39 | 20 23 | 14 25 | 04 45 | 06 48 | 13 51 |
| 40 | 20 19 | 14 08 | 04 12 | 06 19 | 13 40 |
| 41 | 20 14 | 13 50 | 03 39 | 05 49 | 13 28 |
| 42 | 20 10 | 13 33 | 03 04 | 05 17 | 13 16 |
| 43 | 20 05 | 13 15 | 02 29 | 04 44 | 13 03 |
| 44 | 20 00 | 12 56 | 01 53 | 04 11 | 12 49 |
| 45 | 19 55 | 12 37 | 01 16 | 03 35 | 12 35 |
| 46 | 19 49 | 12 18 | 00 39 | 02 58 | 12 21 |
| 47 | 19 44 | 11 58 | 00 00 | 02 20 | 12 05 |
| 48 | 19 38 | 11 37 | 29♏21 | 01 40 | 11 49 |
| 49 | 19 33 | 11 16 | 28 40 | 00 58 | 11 32 |
| 50 | 19 27 | 10 55 | 27 59 | 00 14 | 11 14 |
| 51 | 19 21 | 10 33 | 27 16 | 29♐28 | 10 54 |
| 52 | 19 14 | 10 10 | 26 32 | 28 39 | 10 34 |
| 53 | 19 08 | 09 47 | 25 47 | 27 48 | 10 12 |
| 54 | 19 01 | 09 22 | 25 01 | 26 54 | 09 49 |
| 55 | 18 54 | 08 57 | 24 13 | 25 56 | 09 24 |
| 56 | 18 46 | 08 31 | 23 24 | 24 56 | 08 57 |
| 57 | 18 39 | 08 05 | 22 34 | 23 51 | 08 28 |
| 58 | 18 31 | 07 37 | 21 42 | 22 42 | 07 56 |
| 59 | 18 23 | 07 08 | 20 48 | 21 28 | 07 22 |
| 60 | 18♎14 | 06♏38 | 19♏52 | 20♐09 | 06♒43 |

**11h 28m 0s — 172° 0' 0" — 21 ♍ 17**

| LAT. | 11 | 12 | ASC | 2 | 3 |
|---|---|---|---|---|---|
| 0 | 23♎46 | 24♏22 | 22♐39 | 20♑20 | 19♒35 |
| 5 | 23 29 | 23 16 | 20 41 | 19 04 | 19 07 |
| 10 | 23 12 | 22 11 | 18 42 | 17 45 | 18 39 |
| 15 | 22 55 | 21 06 | 16 41 | 16 23 | 18 09 |
| 20 | 22 37 | 19 59 | 14 37 | 14 55 | 17 37 |
| 21 | 22 34 | 19 46 | 14 11 | 14 36 | 17 30 |
| 22 | 22 30 | 19 32 | 13 46 | 14 18 | 17 23 |
| 23 | 22 27 | 19 18 | 13 20 | 13 59 | 17 16 |
| 24 | 22 23 | 19 05 | 12 53 | 13 39 | 17 09 |
| 25 | 22 19 | 18 51 | 12 27 | 13 19 | 17 02 |
| 26 | 22 15 | 18 37 | 12 00 | 12 59 | 16 54 |
| 27 | 22 12 | 18 22 | 11 33 | 12 38 | 16 47 |
| 28 | 22 08 | 18 08 | 11 05 | 12 17 | 16 39 |
| 29 | 22 04 | 17 53 | 10 38 | 11 56 | 16 31 |
| 30 | 22 00 | 17 39 | 10 09 | 11 34 | 16 23 |
| 31 | 21 56 | 17 24 | 09 41 | 11 11 | 16 14 |
| 32 | 21 52 | 17 09 | 09 12 | 10 48 | 16 06 |
| 33 | 21 48 | 16 53 | 08 42 | 10 24 | 15 57 |
| 34 | 21 43 | 16 38 | 08 12 | 09 59 | 15 48 |
| 35 | 21 39 | 16 22 | 07 42 | 09 34 | 15 38 |
| 36 | 21 35 | 16 06 | 07 11 | 09 08 | 15 28 |
| 37 | 21 30 | 15 49 | 06 39 | 08 42 | 15 18 |
| 38 | 21 26 | 15 33 | 06 07 | 08 14 | 15 08 |
| 39 | 21 21 | 15 16 | 05 34 | 07 46 | 14 57 |
| 40 | 21 16 | 14 59 | 05 01 | 07 16 | 14 46 |
| 41 | 21 12 | 14 41 | 04 27 | 06 46 | 14 34 |
| 42 | 21 07 | 14 23 | 03 52 | 06 14 | 14 22 |
| 43 | 21 01 | 14 04 | 03 16 | 05 41 | 14 09 |
| 44 | 20 56 | 13 46 | 02 40 | 05 07 | 13 56 |
| 45 | 20 51 | 13 26 | 02 03 | 04 32 | 13 42 |
| 46 | 20 45 | 13 07 | 01 25 | 03 55 | 13 28 |
| 47 | 20 40 | 12 46 | 00 46 | 03 16 | 13 13 |
| 48 | 20 34 | 12 26 | 00 06 | 02 36 | 12 57 |
| 49 | 20 28 | 12 04 | 29♏25 | 01 54 | 12 40 |
| 50 | 20 22 | 11 42 | 28 43 | 01 09 | 12 22 |
| 51 | 20 15 | 11 20 | 27 59 | 00 23 | 12 03 |
| 52 | 20 09 | 10 57 | 27 15 | 29♐34 | 11 43 |
| 53 | 20 02 | 10 33 | 26 29 | 28 42 | 11 22 |
| 54 | 19 55 | 10 08 | 25 42 | 27 47 | 10 59 |
| 55 | 19 47 | 09 42 | 24 54 | 26 50 | 10 34 |
| 56 | 19 40 | 09 16 | 24 04 | 25 48 | 10 08 |
| 57 | 19 32 | 08 49 | 23 13 | 24 43 | 09 39 |
| 58 | 19 23 | 08 20 | 22 20 | 23 33 | 09 08 |
| 59 | 19 15 | 07 51 | 21 25 | 22 18 | 08 34 |
| 60 | 19♎06 | 07♏20 | 20♏29 | 20♐58 | 07♒57 |

**11h 32m 0s — 173° 0' 0" — 22 ♍ 23**

| LAT. | 11 | 12 | ASC | 2 | 3 |
|---|---|---|---|---|---|
| 0 | 24♎50 | 25♏21 | 23♐34 | 21♑17 | 20♒36 |
| 5 | 24 32 | 24 14 | 21 36 | 20 01 | 20 09 |
| 10 | 24 14 | 23 08 | 19 37 | 18 42 | 19 41 |
| 15 | 23 56 | 22 02 | 17 35 | 17 20 | 19 12 |
| 20 | 23 38 | 20 55 | 15 30 | 15 52 | 18 40 |
| 21 | 23 34 | 20 41 | 15 05 | 15 34 | 18 34 |
| 22 | 23 31 | 20 27 | 14 39 | 15 15 | 18 27 |
| 23 | 23 27 | 20 13 | 14 13 | 14 56 | 18 20 |
| 24 | 23 23 | 19 59 | 13 46 | 14 37 | 18 13 |
| 25 | 23 19 | 19 45 | 13 19 | 14 17 | 18 06 |
| 26 | 23 15 | 19 31 | 12 52 | 13 57 | 17 59 |
| 27 | 23 11 | 19 16 | 12 25 | 13 36 | 17 51 |
| 28 | 23 07 | 19 02 | 11 57 | 13 15 | 17 43 |
| 29 | 23 03 | 18 47 | 11 29 | 12 53 | 17 36 |
| 30 | 22 59 | 18 32 | 11 01 | 12 31 | 17 28 |
| 31 | 22 55 | 18 17 | 10 32 | 12 09 | 17 19 |
| 32 | 22 51 | 18 02 | 10 03 | 11 46 | 17 11 |
| 33 | 22 46 | 17 46 | 09 33 | 11 22 | 17 02 |
| 34 | 22 42 | 17 30 | 09 02 | 10 57 | 16 53 |
| 35 | 22 37 | 17 14 | 08 32 | 10 32 | 16 44 |
| 36 | 22 33 | 16 58 | 08 00 | 10 06 | 16 34 |
| 37 | 22 28 | 16 41 | 07 29 | 09 39 | 16 24 |
| 38 | 22 24 | 16 24 | 06 56 | 09 12 | 16 14 |
| 39 | 22 19 | 16 07 | 06 23 | 08 43 | 16 03 |
| 40 | 22 14 | 15 49 | 05 49 | 08 14 | 15 52 |
| 41 | 22 09 | 15 31 | 05 15 | 07 43 | 15 41 |
| 42 | 22 04 | 15 13 | 04 39 | 07 11 | 15 29 |
| 43 | 21 58 | 14 54 | 04 04 | 06 38 | 15 16 |
| 44 | 21 53 | 14 35 | 03 27 | 06 04 | 15 04 |
| 45 | 21 47 | 14 16 | 02 49 | 05 29 | 14 50 |
| 46 | 21 41 | 13 56 | 02 11 | 04 51 | 14 36 |
| 47 | 21 36 | 13 35 | 01 31 | 04 13 | 14 21 |
| 48 | 21 29 | 13 14 | 00 51 | 03 32 | 14 05 |
| 49 | 21 23 | 12 52 | 00 09 | 02 50 | 13 48 |
| 50 | 21 17 | 12 30 | 29♏27 | 02 05 | 13 31 |
| 51 | 21 10 | 12 07 | 28 43 | 01 18 | 13 12 |
| 52 | 21 03 | 11 43 | 27 58 | 00 29 | 12 53 |
| 53 | 20 56 | 11 19 | 27 12 | 29♐37 | 12 32 |
| 54 | 20 49 | 10 54 | 26 24 | 28 42 | 12 09 |
| 55 | 20 41 | 10 28 | 25 35 | 27 43 | 11 45 |
| 56 | 20 33 | 10 01 | 24 44 | 26 41 | 11 19 |
| 57 | 20 25 | 09 33 | 23 52 | 25 35 | 10 51 |
| 58 | 20 16 | 09 04 | 22 59 | 24 24 | 10 21 |
| 59 | 20 07 | 08 34 | 22 03 | 23 09 | 09 47 |
| 60 | 19♎57 | 08♏03 | 21♏06 | 21♐47 | 09♒10 |

**11h 36m 0s — 174° 0' 0" — 23 ♍ 28**

| LAT. | 11 | 12 | ASC | 2 | 3 |
|---|---|---|---|---|---|
| 0 | 25♎53 | 26♏19 | 24♐30 | 22♑13 | 21♒37 |
| 5 | 25 35 | 25 11 | 22 31 | 20 58 | 21 11 |
| 10 | 25 16 | 24 05 | 20 31 | 19 40 | 20 44 |
| 15 | 24 58 | 22 58 | 18 29 | 18 18 | 20 15 |
| 20 | 24 39 | 21 50 | 16 24 | 16 50 | 19 44 |
| 21 | 24 35 | 21 36 | 15 58 | 16 32 | 19 37 |
| 22 | 24 31 | 21 22 | 15 32 | 16 13 | 19 31 |
| 23 | 24 27 | 21 08 | 15 05 | 15 54 | 19 24 |
| 24 | 24 23 | 20 54 | 14 39 | 15 35 | 19 17 |
| 25 | 24 19 | 20 39 | 14 12 | 15 15 | 19 10 |
| 26 | 24 15 | 20 25 | 13 45 | 14 55 | 19 03 |
| 27 | 24 11 | 20 10 | 13 17 | 14 34 | 18 56 |
| 28 | 24 07 | 19 55 | 12 49 | 14 13 | 18 48 |
| 29 | 24 03 | 19 40 | 12 21 | 13 51 | 18 40 |
| 30 | 23 58 | 19 25 | 11 52 | 13 29 | 18 33 |
| 31 | 23 54 | 19 10 | 11 23 | 13 07 | 18 24 |
| 32 | 23 49 | 18 54 | 10 54 | 12 44 | 18 16 |
| 33 | 23 45 | 18 39 | 10 24 | 12 20 | 18 08 |
| 34 | 23 40 | 18 22 | 09 53 | 11 55 | 17 59 |
| 35 | 23 36 | 18 06 | 09 22 | 11 30 | 17 50 |
| 36 | 23 31 | 17 50 | 08 50 | 11 04 | 17 40 |
| 37 | 23 26 | 17 33 | 08 18 | 10 37 | 17 30 |
| 38 | 23 21 | 17 16 | 07 45 | 10 09 | 17 20 |
| 39 | 23 16 | 16 58 | 07 12 | 09 41 | 17 10 |
| 40 | 23 11 | 16 40 | 06 38 | 09 11 | 16 59 |
| 41 | 23 06 | 16 22 | 06 03 | 08 41 | 16 48 |
| 42 | 23 00 | 16 03 | 05 27 | 08 09 | 16 36 |
| 43 | 22 55 | 15 44 | 04 51 | 07 36 | 16 24 |
| 44 | 22 49 | 15 25 | 04 14 | 07 02 | 16 11 |
| 45 | 22 43 | 15 05 | 03 36 | 06 26 | 15 58 |
| 46 | 22 37 | 14 44 | 02 57 | 05 48 | 15 44 |
| 47 | 22 31 | 14 24 | 02 17 | 05 10 | 15 29 |
| 48 | 22 25 | 14 02 | 01 36 | 04 29 | 15 14 |
| 49 | 22 18 | 13 40 | 00 54 | 03 46 | 14 58 |
| 50 | 22 12 | 13 17 | 00 11 | 03 01 | 14 40 |
| 51 | 22 05 | 12 54 | 29♏26 | 02 14 | 14 22 |
| 52 | 21 57 | 12 30 | 28 41 | 01 24 | 14 03 |
| 53 | 21 50 | 12 05 | 27 54 | 00 32 | 13 42 |
| 54 | 21 42 | 11 39 | 27 06 | 29♐36 | 13 20 |
| 55 | 21 34 | 11 13 | 26 16 | 28 37 | 12 57 |
| 56 | 21 26 | 10 45 | 25 25 | 27 35 | 12 31 |
| 57 | 21 17 | 10 17 | 24 32 | 26 28 | 12 04 |
| 58 | 21 08 | 09 47 | 23 37 | 25 16 | 11 34 |
| 59 | 20 59 | 09 17 | 22 41 | 24 00 | 11 01 |
| 60 | 20♎49 | 08♏45 | 21♏43 | 22♐37 | 10♒25 |

**11h 40m 0s — 175° 0' 0" — 24 ♍ 33**

| LAT. | 11 | 12 | ASC | 2 | 3 |
|---|---|---|---|---|---|
| 0 | 26♎57 | 27♏17 | 25♐25 | 23♑10 | 22♒39 |
| 5 | 26 37 | 26 09 | 23 26 | 21 55 | 22 13 |
| 10 | 26 18 | 25 02 | 21 26 | 20 37 | 21 46 |
| 15 | 25 59 | 23 54 | 19 24 | 19 15 | 21 18 |
| 20 | 25 39 | 22 45 | 17 17 | 17 48 | 20 48 |
| 21 | 25 35 | 22 31 | 16 51 | 17 30 | 20 41 |
| 22 | 25 31 | 22 17 | 16 25 | 17 11 | 20 35 |
| 23 | 25 27 | 22 03 | 15 58 | 16 52 | 20 28 |
| 24 | 25 23 | 21 48 | 15 32 | 16 33 | 20 22 |
| 25 | 25 19 | 21 34 | 15 05 | 16 13 | 20 15 |
| 26 | 25 15 | 21 19 | 14 37 | 15 53 | 20 08 |
| 27 | 25 10 | 21 04 | 14 09 | 15 32 | 20 00 |
| 28 | 25 06 | 20 49 | 13 41 | 15 11 | 19 53 |
| 29 | 25 02 | 20 34 | 13 13 | 14 50 | 19 46 |
| 30 | 24 57 | 20 19 | 12 44 | 14 28 | 19 38 |
| 31 | 24 53 | 20 03 | 12 15 | 14 05 | 19 30 |
| 32 | 24 48 | 19 47 | 11 45 | 13 42 | 19 22 |
| 33 | 24 44 | 19 31 | 11 14 | 13 18 | 19 13 |
| 34 | 24 39 | 19 15 | 10 44 | 12 53 | 19 05 |
| 35 | 24 34 | 18 58 | 10 12 | 12 28 | 18 56 |
| 36 | 24 29 | 18 41 | 09 40 | 12 02 | 18 46 |
| 37 | 24 24 | 18 24 | 09 08 | 11 35 | 18 37 |
| 38 | 24 19 | 18 07 | 08 35 | 11 08 | 18 27 |
| 39 | 24 14 | 17 49 | 08 01 | 10 39 | 18 17 |
| 40 | 24 08 | 17 31 | 07 27 | 10 09 | 18 06 |
| 41 | 24 03 | 17 12 | 06 51 | 09 39 | 17 55 |
| 42 | 23 57 | 16 54 | 06 15 | 09 07 | 17 44 |
| 43 | 23 51 | 16 34 | 05 39 | 08 34 | 17 32 |
| 44 | 23 46 | 16 14 | 05 01 | 07 59 | 17 19 |
| 45 | 23 40 | 15 54 | 04 22 | 07 23 | 17 06 |
| 46 | 23 33 | 15 33 | 03 43 | 06 46 | 16 52 |
| 47 | 23 27 | 15 12 | 03 03 | 06 07 | 16 38 |
| 48 | 23 20 | 14 50 | 02 21 | 05 26 | 16 23 |
| 49 | 23 14 | 14 28 | 01 39 | 04 43 | 16 07 |
| 50 | 23 07 | 14 05 | 00 55 | 03 58 | 15 50 |
| 51 | 22 59 | 13 41 | 00 10 | 03 10 | 15 32 |
| 52 | 22 52 | 13 16 | 29♏24 | 02 20 | 15 13 |
| 53 | 22 44 | 12 51 | 28 36 | 01 27 | 14 53 |
| 54 | 22 36 | 12 25 | 27 47 | 00 31 | 14 31 |
| 55 | 22 28 | 11 58 | 26 57 | 29♐32 | 14 08 |
| 56 | 22 19 | 11 30 | 26 05 | 28 28 | 13 43 |
| 57 | 22 10 | 11 01 | 25 11 | 27 21 | 13 16 |
| 58 | 22 00 | 10 31 | 24 16 | 26 09 | 12 47 |
| 59 | 21 51 | 10 00 | 23 19 | 24 51 | 12 15 |
| 60 | 21♎40 | 09♏27 | 22♏20 | 23♐27 | 11♒40 |

# Placidus Table of Houses for Latitudes 0° to 60° North

**11h 44m 0s — 176° 0' 0" — 25 ♍ 38**

| LAT. | 11 | 12 | ASC | 2 | 3 |
|---|---|---|---|---|---|
| 0 | 28♎00 | 28♏15 | 26♐20 | 24♑06 | 23♒41 |
| 5 | 27 40 | 27 06 | 24 21 | 22 52 | 23 15 |
| 10 | 27 20 | 25 58 | 22 20 | 21 34 | 22 49 |
| 15 | 27 00 | 24 50 | 20 18 | 20 13 | 22 21 |
| 20 | 26 40 | 23 40 | 18 11 | 18 46 | 21 52 |
| 21 | 26 36 | 23 26 | 17 45 | 18 28 | 21 46 |
| 22 | 26 32 | 23 12 | 17 18 | 18 09 | 21 39 |
| 23 | 26 27 | 22 57 | 16 52 | 17 50 | 21 33 |
| 24 | 26 23 | 22 43 | 16 25 | 17 31 | 21 26 |
| 25 | 26 19 | 22 28 | 15 57 | 17 11 | 21 20 |
| 26 | 26 14 | 22 13 | 15 30 | 16 51 | 21 13 |
| 27 | 26 10 | 21 58 | 15 02 | 16 31 | 21 06 |
| 28 | 26 05 | 21 43 | 14 34 | 16 10 | 20 58 |
| 29 | 26 01 | 21 27 | 14 06 | 15 48 | 20 51 |
| 30 | 25 56 | 21 12 | 13 36 | 15 26 | 20 43 |
| 31 | 25 52 | 20 56 | 13 06 | 15 04 | 20 36 |
| 32 | 25 47 | 20 40 | 12 36 | 14 40 | 20 28 |
| 33 | 25 42 | 20 24 | 12 05 | 14 17 | 20 19 |
| 34 | 25 37 | 20 07 | 11 34 | 13 52 | 20 11 |
| 35 | 25 32 | 19 50 | 11 03 | 13 27 | 20 02 |
| 36 | 25 27 | 19 33 | 10 31 | 13 01 | 19 53 |
| 37 | 25 22 | 19 16 | 09 58 | 12 34 | 19 44 |
| 38 | 25 16 | 18 58 | 09 24 | 12 06 | 19 34 |
| 39 | 25 11 | 18 40 | 08 50 | 11 38 | 19 24 |
| 40 | 25 05 | 18 22 | 08 15 | 11 08 | 19 14 |
| 41 | 25 00 | 18 03 | 07 40 | 10 37 | 19 03 |
| 42 | 24 54 | 17 44 | 07 03 | 10 05 | 18 52 |
| 43 | 24 48 | 17 24 | 06 26 | 09 32 | 18 40 |
| 44 | 24 42 | 17 04 | 05 48 | 08 57 | 18 28 |
| 45 | 24 36 | 16 43 | 05 09 | 08 21 | 18 15 |
| 46 | 24 29 | 16 22 | 04 29 | 07 44 | 18 01 |
| 47 | 24 23 | 16 01 | 03 49 | 07 04 | 17 47 |
| 48 | 24 16 | 15 38 | 03 07 | 06 23 | 17 32 |
| 49 | 24 09 | 15 16 | 02 23 | 05 40 | 17 17 |
| 50 | 24 01 | 14 52 | 01 39 | 04 55 | 17 00 |
| 51 | 23 54 | 14 28 | 00 54 | 04 07 | 16 43 |
| 52 | 23 46 | 14 03 | 00 07 | 03 17 | 16 24 |
| 53 | 23 38 | 13 37 | 29♏19 | 02 23 | 16 04 |
| 54 | 23 30 | 13 11 | 28 29 | 01 27 | 15 43 |
| 55 | 23 21 | 12 43 | 27 38 | 00 27 | 15 21 |
| 56 | 23 12 | 12 15 | 26 45 | 29♐23 | 14 56 |
| 57 | 23 03 | 11 45 | 25 51 | 28 15 | 14 30 |
| 58 | 22 53 | 11 14 | 24 55 | 27 02 | 14 01 |
| 59 | 22 42 | 10 43 | 23 57 | 25 43 | 13 30 |
| 60 | 22♎32 | 10♏10 | 22♏57 | 24♐18 | 12♒55 |

**11h 48m 0s — 177° 0' 0" — 26 ♍ 44**

| LAT. | 11 | 12 | ASC | 2 | 3 |
|---|---|---|---|---|---|
| 0 | 29♎03 | 29♏13 | 27♐15 | 25♑03 | 24♒42 |
| 5 | 28 42 | 28 03 | 25 16 | 23 49 | 24 18 |
| 10 | 28 22 | 26 55 | 23 15 | 22 32 | 23 52 |
| 15 | 28 01 | 25 46 | 21 12 | 21 11 | 23 25 |
| 20 | 27 40 | 24 35 | 19 04 | 19 45 | 22 56 |
| 21 | 27 36 | 24 21 | 18 38 | 19 26 | 22 50 |
| 22 | 27 32 | 24 06 | 18 12 | 19 08 | 22 44 |
| 23 | 27 27 | 23 52 | 17 45 | 18 49 | 22 38 |
| 24 | 27 23 | 23 37 | 17 18 | 18 30 | 22 31 |
| 25 | 27 18 | 23 22 | 16 50 | 18 10 | 22 25 |
| 26 | 27 14 | 23 07 | 16 22 | 17 50 | 22 18 |
| 27 | 27 09 | 22 52 | 15 54 | 17 30 | 22 11 |
| 28 | 27 05 | 22 36 | 15 26 | 17 09 | 22 04 |
| 29 | 27 00 | 22 21 | 14 57 | 16 47 | 21 57 |
| 30 | 26 55 | 22 05 | 14 27 | 16 25 | 21 49 |
| 31 | 26 50 | 21 49 | 13 58 | 16 02 | 21 42 |
| 32 | 26 45 | 21 33 | 13 27 | 15 39 | 21 34 |
| 33 | 26 40 | 21 16 | 12 57 | 15 15 | 21 26 |
| 34 | 26 35 | 20 59 | 12 25 | 14 51 | 21 17 |
| 35 | 26 30 | 20 42 | 11 53 | 14 26 | 21 09 |
| 36 | 26 25 | 20 25 | 11 21 | 14 00 | 21 00 |
| 37 | 26 19 | 20 07 | 10 48 | 13 33 | 20 51 |
| 38 | 26 14 | 19 49 | 10 14 | 13 05 | 20 41 |
| 39 | 26 08 | 19 31 | 09 40 | 12 36 | 20 32 |
| 40 | 26 03 | 19 12 | 09 04 | 12 07 | 20 21 |
| 41 | 25 57 | 18 53 | 08 28 | 11 36 | 20 11 |
| 42 | 25 51 | 18 34 | 07 52 | 11 04 | 20 00 |
| 43 | 25 44 | 18 14 | 07 14 | 10 31 | 19 48 |
| 44 | 25 38 | 17 53 | 06 36 | 09 56 | 19 36 |
| 45 | 25 32 | 17 33 | 05 56 | 09 20 | 19 24 |
| 46 | 25 25 | 17 11 | 05 16 | 08 42 | 19 11 |
| 47 | 25 18 | 16 49 | 04 35 | 08 03 | 18 57 |
| 48 | 25 11 | 16 27 | 03 52 | 07 21 | 18 42 |
| 49 | 25 04 | 16 03 | 03 08 | 06 38 | 18 27 |
| 50 | 24 56 | 15 39 | 02 24 | 05 52 | 18 11 |
| 51 | 24 48 | 15 15 | 01 38 | 05 04 | 17 54 |
| 52 | 24 40 | 14 49 | 00 50 | 04 14 | 17 35 |
| 53 | 24 32 | 14 23 | 00 01 | 03 20 | 17 16 |
| 54 | 24 23 | 13 56 | 29♏11 | 02 23 | 16 55 |
| 55 | 24 14 | 13 28 | 28 19 | 01 22 | 16 33 |
| 56 | 24 05 | 12 59 | 27 26 | 00 18 | 16 09 |
| 57 | 23 55 | 12 29 | 26 31 | 29♐09 | 15 44 |
| 58 | 23 45 | 11 58 | 25 34 | 27 55 | 15 15 |
| 59 | 23 34 | 11 26 | 24 35 | 26 35 | 14 45 |
| 60 | 23♎23 | 10♏52 | 23♏34 | 25♐09 | 14♒11 |

**11h 52m 0s — 178° 0' 0" — 27 ♍ 49**

| LAT. | 11 | 12 | ASC | 2 | 3 |
|---|---|---|---|---|---|
| 0 | 00♏06 | 00♐11 | 28♐10 | 26♑00 | 25♒44 |
| 5 | 29♎45 | 29♏01 | 26 10 | 24 46 | 25 20 |
| 10 | 29 24 | 27 51 | 24 10 | 23 30 | 24 55 |
| 15 | 29 02 | 26 41 | 22 06 | 22 09 | 24 29 |
| 20 | 28 41 | 25 30 | 19 58 | 20 43 | 24 01 |
| 21 | 28 36 | 25 15 | 19 32 | 20 25 | 23 55 |
| 22 | 28 32 | 25 01 | 19 05 | 20 07 | 23 49 |
| 23 | 28 27 | 24 46 | 18 38 | 19 48 | 23 43 |
| 24 | 28 23 | 24 31 | 18 11 | 19 29 | 23 36 |
| 25 | 28 18 | 24 16 | 17 43 | 19 09 | 23 30 |
| 26 | 28 13 | 24 01 | 17 15 | 18 49 | 23 23 |
| 27 | 28 08 | 23 45 | 16 47 | 18 29 | 23 17 |
| 28 | 28 04 | 23 30 | 16 18 | 18 08 | 23 10 |
| 29 | 27 59 | 23 14 | 15 49 | 17 46 | 23 03 |
| 30 | 27 54 | 22 58 | 15 19 | 17 24 | 22 55 |
| 31 | 27 49 | 22 42 | 14 49 | 17 02 | 22 48 |
| 32 | 27 44 | 22 25 | 14 19 | 16 38 | 22 40 |
| 33 | 27 39 | 22 09 | 13 48 | 16 15 | 22 32 |
| 34 | 27 33 | 21 52 | 13 16 | 15 50 | 22 24 |
| 35 | 27 28 | 21 34 | 12 44 | 15 25 | 22 16 |
| 36 | 27 22 | 21 17 | 12 11 | 14 59 | 22 07 |
| 37 | 27 17 | 20 59 | 11 38 | 14 32 | 21 58 |
| 38 | 27 11 | 20 41 | 11 04 | 14 04 | 21 49 |
| 39 | 27 05 | 20 22 | 10 29 | 13 36 | 21 39 |
| 40 | 26 59 | 20 03 | 09 54 | 13 06 | 21 29 |
| 41 | 26 53 | 19 44 | 09 17 | 12 35 | 21 19 |
| 42 | 26 47 | 19 24 | 08 40 | 12 03 | 21 08 |
| 43 | 26 41 | 19 04 | 08 02 | 11 30 | 20 57 |
| 44 | 26 34 | 18 43 | 07 23 | 10 55 | 20 45 |
| 45 | 26 28 | 18 22 | 06 43 | 10 19 | 20 33 |
| 46 | 26 21 | 18 00 | 06 03 | 09 41 | 20 20 |
| 47 | 26 13 | 17 38 | 05 21 | 09 01 | 20 07 |
| 48 | 26 06 | 17 15 | 04 38 | 08 20 | 19 53 |
| 49 | 25 59 | 16 51 | 03 54 | 07 36 | 19 38 |
| 50 | 25 51 | 16 27 | 03 08 | 06 50 | 19 22 |
| 51 | 25 43 | 16 02 | 02 22 | 06 02 | 19 05 |
| 52 | 25 34 | 15 36 | 01 34 | 05 11 | 18 47 |
| 53 | 25 26 | 15 09 | 00 44 | 04 17 | 18 28 |
| 54 | 25 17 | 14 42 | 29♏53 | 03 20 | 18 08 |
| 55 | 25 07 | 14 13 | 29 01 | 02 18 | 17 46 |
| 56 | 24 58 | 13 44 | 28 06 | 01 13 | 17 23 |
| 57 | 24 48 | 13 13 | 27 10 | 00 04 | 16 58 |
| 58 | 24 37 | 12 41 | 26 13 | 28♐49 | 16 30 |
| 59 | 24 26 | 12 08 | 25 13 | 27 28 | 16 01 |
| 60 | 24♎14 | 11♏34 | 24♏11 | 26♐01 | 15♒28 |

**11h 56m 0s — 179° 0' 0" — 28 ♍ 55**

| LAT. | 11 | 12 | ASC | 2 | 3 |
|---|---|---|---|---|---|
| 0 | 01♏08 | 01♐08 | 29♐05 | 26♑57 | 26♒47 |
| 5 | 00 47 | 29♏57 | 27 05 | 25 44 | 26 23 |
| 10 | 00 25 | 28 47 | 25 04 | 24 28 | 25 59 |
| 15 | 00 03 | 27 37 | 23 00 | 23 08 | 25 33 |
| 20 | 29♎41 | 26 25 | 20 52 | 21 42 | 25 06 |
| 21 | 29 36 | 26 10 | 20 25 | 21 24 | 25 00 |
| 22 | 29 31 | 25 55 | 19 58 | 21 06 | 24 54 |
| 23 | 29 27 | 25 40 | 19 31 | 20 47 | 24 48 |
| 24 | 29 22 | 25 25 | 19 04 | 20 28 | 24 42 |
| 25 | 29 17 | 25 10 | 18 36 | 20 08 | 24 35 |
| 26 | 29 12 | 24 55 | 18 08 | 19 48 | 24 29 |
| 27 | 29 08 | 24 39 | 17 40 | 19 28 | 24 22 |
| 28 | 29 03 | 24 23 | 17 11 | 19 07 | 24 16 |
| 29 | 28 58 | 24 07 | 16 41 | 18 46 | 24 09 |
| 30 | 28 53 | 23 51 | 16 12 | 18 24 | 24 02 |
| 31 | 28 47 | 23 35 | 15 41 | 18 01 | 23 54 |
| 32 | 28 42 | 23 18 | 15 11 | 17 38 | 23 47 |
| 33 | 28 37 | 23 01 | 14 39 | 17 14 | 23 39 |
| 34 | 28 31 | 22 44 | 14 07 | 16 50 | 23 31 |
| 35 | 28 26 | 22 26 | 13 35 | 16 25 | 23 23 |
| 36 | 28 20 | 22 08 | 13 02 | 15 59 | 23 15 |
| 37 | 28 14 | 21 50 | 12 28 | 15 32 | 23 06 |
| 38 | 28 09 | 21 32 | 11 54 | 15 04 | 22 57 |
| 39 | 28 03 | 21 13 | 11 19 | 14 35 | 22 48 |
| 40 | 27 56 | 20 54 | 10 43 | 14 05 | 22 38 |
| 41 | 27 50 | 20 34 | 10 06 | 13 34 | 22 28 |
| 42 | 27 44 | 20 14 | 09 29 | 13 02 | 22 17 |
| 43 | 27 37 | 19 54 | 08 50 | 12 29 | 22 06 |
| 44 | 27 30 | 19 33 | 08 11 | 11 54 | 21 55 |
| 45 | 27 23 | 19 11 | 07 31 | 11 18 | 21 43 |
| 46 | 27 16 | 18 49 | 06 49 | 10 40 | 21 30 |
| 47 | 27 09 | 18 26 | 06 07 | 10 00 | 21 17 |
| 48 | 27 01 | 18 03 | 05 24 | 09 19 | 21 03 |
| 49 | 26 53 | 17 39 | 04 39 | 08 35 | 20 49 |
| 50 | 26 45 | 17 14 | 03 53 | 07 49 | 20 33 |
| 51 | 26 37 | 16 49 | 03 06 | 07 00 | 20 17 |
| 52 | 26 28 | 16 22 | 02 17 | 06 09 | 19 59 |
| 53 | 26 19 | 15 55 | 01 27 | 05 14 | 19 41 |
| 54 | 26 10 | 15 27 | 00 35 | 04 17 | 19 21 |
| 55 | 26 00 | 14 58 | 29♏42 | 03 15 | 19 00 |
| 56 | 25 50 | 14 28 | 28 47 | 02 09 | 18 37 |
| 57 | 25 40 | 13 57 | 27 50 | 00 59 | 18 13 |
| 58 | 25 29 | 13 25 | 26 52 | 29♐43 | 17 46 |
| 59 | 25 18 | 12 51 | 25 51 | 28 22 | 17 17 |
| 60 | 25♎06 | 12♏16 | 24♏48 | 26♐54 | 16♒45 |

**12h 0m 0s — 180° 0' 0" — 00 ♎ 00**

| LAT. | 11 | 12 | ASC | 2 | 3 |
|---|---|---|---|---|---|
| 0 | 02♏11 | 02♐05 | 00♑00 | 27♑55 | 27♒49 |
| 5 | 01 49 | 00 54 | 28♐00 | 26 42 | 27 26 |
| 10 | 01 26 | 29♏44 | 25 59 | 25 26 | 27 02 |
| 15 | 01 04 | 28 32 | 23 55 | 24 07 | 26 37 |
| 20 | 00 41 | 27 20 | 21 46 | 22 41 | 26 11 |
| 21 | 00 36 | 27 05 | 21 19 | 22 23 | 26 05 |
| 22 | 00 31 | 26 50 | 20 52 | 22 05 | 25 59 |
| 23 | 00 26 | 26 35 | 20 25 | 21 46 | 25 53 |
| 24 | 00 22 | 26 19 | 19 57 | 21 27 | 25 47 |
| 25 | 00 17 | 26 04 | 19 29 | 21 08 | 25 41 |
| 26 | 00 12 | 25 48 | 19 01 | 20 48 | 25 35 |
| 27 | 00 07 | 25 33 | 18 32 | 20 27 | 25 28 |
| 28 | 00 01 | 25 17 | 18 03 | 20 07 | 25 22 |
| 29 | 29♎56 | 25 00 | 17 34 | 19 45 | 25 15 |
| 30 | 29 51 | 24 44 | 17 04 | 19 23 | 25 08 |
| 31 | 29 46 | 24 27 | 16 33 | 19 01 | 25 01 |
| 32 | 29 40 | 24 10 | 16 02 | 18 38 | 24 54 |
| 33 | 29 35 | 23 53 | 15 31 | 18 14 | 24 46 |
| 34 | 29 29 | 23 36 | 14 59 | 17 50 | 24 39 |
| 35 | 29 23 | 23 18 | 14 26 | 17 24 | 24 31 |
| 36 | 29 18 | 23 00 | 13 53 | 16 58 | 24 22 |
| 37 | 29 12 | 22 42 | 13 19 | 16 32 | 24 14 |
| 38 | 29 06 | 22 23 | 12 44 | 16 04 | 24 05 |
| 39 | 29 00 | 22 04 | 12 08 | 15 35 | 23 56 |
| 40 | 28 53 | 21 45 | 11 32 | 15 05 | 23 47 |
| 41 | 28 47 | 21 25 | 10 55 | 14 34 | 23 37 |
| 42 | 28 40 | 21 04 | 10 17 | 14 02 | 23 26 |
| 43 | 28 33 | 20 43 | 09 39 | 13 29 | 23 16 |
| 44 | 28 26 | 20 22 | 08 59 | 12 54 | 23 05 |
| 45 | 28 19 | 20 00 | 08 18 | 12 18 | 22 53 |
| 46 | 28 12 | 19 38 | 07 36 | 11 40 | 22 41 |
| 47 | 28 04 | 19 15 | 06 54 | 11 00 | 22 28 |
| 48 | 27 56 | 18 51 | 06 10 | 10 18 | 22 14 |
| 49 | 27 48 | 18 27 | 05 24 | 09 34 | 22 00 |
| 50 | 27 40 | 18 02 | 04 38 | 08 48 | 21 45 |
| 51 | 27 31 | 17 36 | 03 50 | 07 59 | 21 29 |
| 52 | 27 22 | 17 09 | 03 01 | 07 07 | 21 12 |
| 53 | 27 13 | 16 41 | 02 10 | 06 13 | 20 54 |
| 54 | 27 03 | 16 13 | 01 18 | 05 16 | 20 35 |
| 55 | 26 53 | 15 43 | 00 24 | 04 12 | 20 14 |
| 56 | 26 43 | 15 13 | 29♏28 | 03 06 | 19 52 |
| 57 | 26 32 | 14 41 | 28 30 | 01 55 | 19 28 |
| 58 | 26 21 | 14 08 | 27 31 | 00 39 | 19 02 |
| 59 | 26 09 | 13 34 | 26 29 | 29♐16 | 18 34 |
| 60 | 25♎57 | 12♏59 | 25♏26 | 27♐47 | 18♒02 |

**12h 4m 0s — 181° 0' 0" — 01 ♎ 05**

| LAT. | 11 | 12 | ASC | 2 | 3 |
|---|---|---|---|---|---|
| 0 | 03♏13 | 03♐03 | 00♑55 | 28♑52 | 28♒52 |
| 5 | 02 50 | 01 51 | 28♐55 | 27 40 | 28 29 |
| 10 | 02 27 | 00 40 | 26 54 | 26 25 | 28 06 |
| 15 | 02 04 | 29♏28 | 24 49 | 25 05 | 27 42 |
| 20 | 01 41 | 28 14 | 22 40 | 23 40 | 27 16 |
| 21 | 01 36 | 27 59 | 22 13 | 23 22 | 27 10 |
| 22 | 01 31 | 27 44 | 21 46 | 23 04 | 27 05 |
| 23 | 01 26 | 27 29 | 21 18 | 22 46 | 26 59 |
| 24 | 01 21 | 27 13 | 20 51 | 22 27 | 26 53 |
| 25 | 01 16 | 26 58 | 20 23 | 22 07 | 26 47 |
| 26 | 01 11 | 26 42 | 19 54 | 21 47 | 26 41 |
| 27 | 01 05 | 26 26 | 19 25 | 21 27 | 26 35 |
| 28 | 01 00 | 26 10 | 18 56 | 21 06 | 26 28 |
| 29 | 00 55 | 25 54 | 18 26 | 20 45 | 26 22 |
| 30 | 00 49 | 25 37 | 17 56 | 20 23 | 26 15 |
| 31 | 00 44 | 25 20 | 17 25 | 20 01 | 26 08 |
| 32 | 00 38 | 25 03 | 16 54 | 19 38 | 26 01 |
| 33 | 00 33 | 24 46 | 16 22 | 19 14 | 25 54 |
| 34 | 00 27 | 24 28 | 15 50 | 18 50 | 25 46 |
| 35 | 00 21 | 24 10 | 15 17 | 18 25 | 25 39 |
| 36 | 00 15 | 23 52 | 14 43 | 17 59 | 25 31 |
| 37 | 00 09 | 23 33 | 14 09 | 17 32 | 25 22 |
| 38 | 00 03 | 23 14 | 13 34 | 17 04 | 25 14 |
| 39 | 29♎56 | 22 55 | 12 58 | 16 35 | 25 05 |
| 40 | 29 50 | 22 35 | 12 22 | 16 06 | 24 56 |
| 41 | 29 43 | 22 15 | 11 45 | 15 35 | 24 46 |
| 42 | 29 36 | 21 54 | 11 06 | 15 03 | 24 36 |
| 43 | 29 29 | 21 33 | 10 27 | 14 29 | 24 26 |
| 44 | 29 22 | 21 12 | 09 47 | 13 54 | 24 15 |
| 45 | 29 15 | 20 49 | 09 06 | 13 18 | 24 04 |
| 46 | 29 07 | 20 27 | 08 24 | 12 40 | 23 51 |
| 47 | 28 59 | 20 03 | 07 40 | 12 00 | 23 39 |
| 48 | 28 51 | 19 39 | 06 56 | 11 18 | 23 26 |
| 49 | 28 43 | 19 14 | 06 10 | 10 34 | 23 12 |
| 50 | 28 34 | 18 49 | 05 23 | 09 47 | 22 57 |
| 51 | 28 25 | 18 23 | 04 34 | 08 58 | 22 42 |
| 52 | 28 16 | 17 56 | 03 44 | 08 06 | 22 25 |
| 53 | 28 07 | 17 28 | 02 53 | 07 11 | 22 08 |
| 54 | 27 57 | 16 59 | 02 00 | 06 13 | 21 49 |
| 55 | 27 46 | 16 29 | 01 05 | 05 10 | 21 29 |
| 56 | 27 36 | 15 57 | 00 09 | 04 03 | 21 07 |
| 57 | 27 25 | 15 25 | 29♏10 | 02 52 | 20 44 |
| 58 | 27 13 | 14 52 | 28 10 | 01 34 | 20 18 |
| 59 | 27 01 | 14 17 | 27 08 | 00 11 | 19 51 |
| 60 | 26♎48 | 13♏41 | 26♏03 | 28♐40 | 19♒21 |

**12h 8m 0s — 182° 0' 0" — 02 ♎ 11**

| LAT. | 11 | 12 | ASC | 2 | 3 |
|---|---|---|---|---|---|
| 0 | 04♏16 | 04♐00 | 01♑50 | 29♑49 | 29♒54 |
| 5 | 03 52 | 02 48 | 29♐50 | 28 38 | 29 33 |
| 10 | 03 28 | 01 36 | 27 49 | 27 23 | 29 10 |
| 15 | 03 05 | 00 23 | 25 44 | 26 05 | 28 47 |
| 20 | 02 40 | 29♏09 | 23 34 | 24 40 | 28 21 |
| 21 | 02 35 | 28 54 | 23 07 | 24 22 | 28 16 |
| 22 | 02 30 | 28 38 | 22 40 | 24 04 | 28 10 |
| 23 | 02 25 | 28 23 | 22 12 | 23 45 | 28 05 |
| 24 | 02 20 | 28 07 | 21 44 | 23 27 | 27 59 |
| 25 | 02 15 | 27 52 | 21 16 | 23 07 | 27 53 |
| 26 | 02 10 | 27 36 | 20 47 | 22 48 | 27 47 |
| 27 | 02 04 | 27 20 | 20 18 | 22 27 | 27 41 |
| 28 | 01 59 | 27 03 | 19 49 | 22 07 | 27 35 |
| 29 | 01 53 | 26 47 | 19 19 | 21 45 | 27 29 |
| 30 | 01 48 | 26 30 | 18 49 | 21 24 | 27 22 |
| 31 | 01 42 | 26 13 | 18 18 | 21 01 | 27 16 |
| 32 | 01 36 | 25 56 | 17 46 | 20 38 | 27 09 |
| 33 | 01 31 | 25 38 | 17 14 | 20 15 | 27 02 |
| 34 | 01 25 | 25 20 | 16 42 | 19 50 | 26 54 |
| 35 | 01 19 | 25 02 | 16 08 | 19 25 | 26 47 |
| 36 | 01 12 | 24 44 | 15 35 | 18 59 | 26 39 |
| 37 | 01 06 | 24 25 | 15 00 | 18 33 | 26 31 |
| 38 | 01 00 | 24 05 | 14 25 | 18 05 | 26 23 |
| 39 | 00 53 | 23 46 | 13 49 | 17 36 | 26 14 |
| 40 | 00 47 | 23 26 | 13 12 | 17 06 | 26 05 |
| 41 | 00 40 | 23 05 | 12 34 | 16 35 | 25 56 |
| 42 | 00 33 | 22 44 | 11 55 | 16 03 | 25 46 |
| 43 | 00 25 | 22 23 | 11 16 | 15 30 | 25 36 |
| 44 | 00 18 | 22 01 | 10 35 | 14 55 | 25 25 |
| 45 | 00 10 | 21 39 | 09 54 | 14 18 | 25 14 |
| 46 | 00 03 | 21 15 | 09 11 | 13 40 | 25 02 |
| 47 | 29♎54 | 20 52 | 08 27 | 13 00 | 24 50 |
| 48 | 29 46 | 20 27 | 07 42 | 12 18 | 24 37 |
| 49 | 29 38 | 20 02 | 06 56 | 11 34 | 24 24 |
| 50 | 29 29 | 19 36 | 06 08 | 10 47 | 24 10 |
| 51 | 29 20 | 19 10 | 05 19 | 09 58 | 23 55 |
| 52 | 29 10 | 18 42 | 04 28 | 09 06 | 23 39 |
| 53 | 29 00 | 18 14 | 03 36 | 08 10 | 23 21 |
| 54 | 28 50 | 17 44 | 02 43 | 07 12 | 23 03 |
| 55 | 28 39 | 17 14 | 01 47 | 06 09 | 22 44 |
| 56 | 28 28 | 16 42 | 00 50 | 05 01 | 22 23 |
| 57 | 28 17 | 16 09 | 29♏51 | 03 49 | 22 00 |
| 58 | 28 05 | 15 35 | 28 49 | 02 31 | 21 35 |
| 59 | 27 52 | 15 00 | 27 46 | 01 06 | 21 09 |
| 60 | 27♎39 | 14♏23 | 26♏40 | 29♐35 | 20♒39 |

**12h 12m 0s — 183° 0' 0" — 03 ♎ 16**

| LAT. | 11 | 12 | ASC | 2 | 3 |
|---|---|---|---|---|---|
| 0 | 05♏18 | 04♐57 | 02♑45 | 00♒47 | 00♓57 |
| 5 | 04 53 | 03 44 | 00 45 | 29♑36 | 00 36 |
| 10 | 04 29 | 02 32 | 28♐44 | 28 22 | 00 15 |
| 15 | 04 05 | 01 18 | 26 39 | 27 04 | 29♒52 |
| 20 | 03 40 | 00 04 | 24 28 | 25 40 | 29 27 |
| 21 | 03 35 | 29♏48 | 24 01 | 25 22 | 29 22 |
| 22 | 03 30 | 29 33 | 23 34 | 25 04 | 29 16 |
| 23 | 03 24 | 29 17 | 23 06 | 24 46 | 29 11 |
| 24 | 03 19 | 29 01 | 22 38 | 24 27 | 29 06 |
| 25 | 03 14 | 28 45 | 22 10 | 24 08 | 29 00 |
| 26 | 03 08 | 28 29 | 21 41 | 23 48 | 28 54 |
| 27 | 03 03 | 28 13 | 21 12 | 23 28 | 28 48 |
| 28 | 02 57 | 27 56 | 20 42 | 23 07 | 28 42 |
| 29 | 02 52 | 27 40 | 20 12 | 22 46 | 28 36 |
| 30 | 02 46 | 27 23 | 19 41 | 22 24 | 28 30 |
| 31 | 02 40 | 27 06 | 19 10 | 22 02 | 28 23 |
| 32 | 02 34 | 26 48 | 18 38 | 21 39 | 28 16 |
| 33 | 02 28 | 26 30 | 18 06 | 21 16 | 28 10 |
| 34 | 02 22 | 26 12 | 17 33 | 20 51 | 28 02 |
| 35 | 02 16 | 25 54 | 17 00 | 20 26 | 27 55 |
| 36 | 02 10 | 25 35 | 16 26 | 20 00 | 27 48 |
| 37 | 02 03 | 25 16 | 15 51 | 19 34 | 27 40 |
| 38 | 01 57 | 24 57 | 15 15 | 19 06 | 27 32 |
| 39 | 01 50 | 24 37 | 14 39 | 18 37 | 27 23 |
| 40 | 01 43 | 24 17 | 14 02 | 18 08 | 27 15 |
| 41 | 01 36 | 23 56 | 13 24 | 17 37 | 27 05 |
| 42 | 01 29 | 23 35 | 12 45 | 17 05 | 26 56 |
| 43 | 01 21 | 23 13 | 12 05 | 16 31 | 26 46 |
| 44 | 01 14 | 22 51 | 11 24 | 15 56 | 26 36 |
| 45 | 01 06 | 22 28 | 10 42 | 15 19 | 26 25 |
| 46 | 00 58 | 22 04 | 09 58 | 14 41 | 26 14 |
| 47 | 00 50 | 21 40 | 09 14 | 14 01 | 26 02 |
| 48 | 00 41 | 21 15 | 08 28 | 13 19 | 25 50 |
| 49 | 00 32 | 20 50 | 07 42 | 12 35 | 25 36 |
| 50 | 00 23 | 20 24 | 06 53 | 11 48 | 25 23 |
| 51 | 00 14 | 19 57 | 06 04 | 10 58 | 25 08 |
| 52 | 00 04 | 19 29 | 05 13 | 10 06 | 24 52 |
| 53 | 29♎54 | 19 00 | 04 20 | 09 10 | 24 36 |
| 54 | 29 43 | 18 30 | 03 25 | 08 11 | 24 18 |
| 55 | 29 32 | 17 59 | 02 29 | 07 08 | 23 59 |
| 56 | 29 21 | 17 27 | 01 31 | 06 00 | 23 39 |
| 57 | 29 09 | 16 53 | 00 31 | 04 47 | 23 17 |
| 58 | 28 56 | 16 19 | 29♏29 | 03 28 | 22 53 |
| 59 | 28 44 | 15 43 | 28 24 | 02 03 | 22 27 |
| 60 | 28♎30 | 15♏05 | 27♏18 | 00♑30 | 21♒59 |

# Placidus Table of Houses for Latitudes 0° to 60° North

12h 16m 0s — 184° 0' 0" — 04 ♎ 22

| LAT. | 11 | 12 | ASC | 2 | 3 |
|---|---|---|---|---|---|
| 0 | 06♏19 | 05♐54 | 03♑40 | 01♒45 | 02♓00 |
| 5 | 05 55 | 04 40 | 01 41 | 00 35 | 01 40 |
| 10 | 05 30 | 03 27 | 29♐39 | 29♑21 | 01 19 |
| 15 | 05 05 | 02 14 | 27 33 | 28 03 | 00 57 |
| 20 | 04 39 | 00 58 | 25 22 | 26 40 | 00 33 |
| 21 | 04 34 | 00 43 | 24 55 | 26 22 | 00 28 |
| 22 | 04 29 | 00 27 | 24 28 | 26 04 | 00 23 |
| 23 | 04 23 | 00 11 | 24 00 | 25 46 | 00 17 |
| 24 | 04 18 | 29♏55 | 23 32 | 25 27 | 00 12 |
| 25 | 04 13 | 29 39 | 23 03 | 25 08 | 00 07 |
| 26 | 04 07 | 29 23 | 22 34 | 24 49 | 00 01 |
| 27 | 04 01 | 29 06 | 22 05 | 24 28 | 29♒55 |
| 28 | 03 56 | 28 50 | 21 35 | 24 08 | 29 49 |
| 29 | 03 50 | 28 33 | 21 05 | 23 47 | 29 43 |
| 30 | 03 44 | 28 16 | 20 34 | 23 25 | 29 37 |
| 31 | 03 38 | 27 58 | 20 03 | 23 03 | 29 31 |
| 32 | 03 32 | 27 41 | 19 31 | 22 40 | 29 25 |
| 33 | 03 26 | 27 23 | 18 58 | 22 17 | 29 18 |
| 34 | 03 20 | 27 04 | 18 25 | 21 53 | 29 11 |
| 35 | 03 13 | 26 46 | 17 52 | 21 28 | 29 04 |
| 36 | 03 07 | 26 27 | 17 17 | 21 02 | 28 57 |
| 37 | 03 00 | 26 08 | 16 42 | 20 35 | 28 49 |
| 38 | 02 53 | 25 48 | 16 06 | 20 08 | 28 41 |
| 39 | 02 47 | 25 28 | 15 29 | 19 39 | 28 33 |
| 40 | 02 39 | 25 07 | 14 52 | 19 09 | 28 24 |
| 41 | 02 32 | 24 46 | 14 13 | 18 38 | 28 16 |
| 42 | 02 25 | 24 25 | 13 34 | 18 06 | 28 06 |
| 43 | 02 17 | 24 03 | 12 54 | 17 33 | 27 57 |
| 44 | 02 09 | 23 40 | 12 12 | 16 58 | 27 47 |
| 45 | 02 01 | 23 17 | 11 30 | 16 21 | 27 37 |
| 46 | 01 53 | 22 53 | 10 46 | 15 43 | 27 26 |
| 47 | 01 44 | 22 29 | 10 01 | 15 03 | 27 14 |
| 48 | 01 36 | 22 04 | 09 15 | 14 20 | 27 02 |
| 49 | 01 27 | 21 38 | 08 28 | 13 36 | 26 49 |
| 50 | 01 17 | 21 11 | 07 39 | 12 49 | 26 36 |
| 51 | 01 08 | 20 44 | 06 49 | 11 59 | 26 22 |
| 52 | 00 57 | 20 15 | 05 57 | 11 07 | 26 07 |
| 53 | 00 47 | 19 46 | 05 03 | 10 11 | 25 51 |
| 54 | 00 36 | 19 15 | 04 08 | 09 11 | 25 33 |
| 55 | 00 25 | 18 44 | 03 11 | 08 07 | 25 15 |
| 56 | 00 13 | 18 11 | 02 12 | 06 59 | 24 55 |
| 57 | 00 01 | 17 37 | 01 11 | 05 45 | 24 34 |
| 58 | 29♎48 | 17 02 | 00 08 | 04 26 | 24 11 |
| 59 | 29 35 | 16 25 | 29♏03 | 03 00 | 23 46 |
| 60 | 29♎21 | 15♏47 | 27♏56 | 01♑26 | 23♒18 |

12h 20m 0s — 185° 0' 0" — 05 ♎ 27

| LAT. | 11 | 12 | ASC | 2 | 3 |
|---|---|---|---|---|---|
| 0 | 07♏21 | 06♐50 | 04♑35 | 02♒43 | 03♓03 |
| 5 | 06 56 | 05 37 | 02 36 | 01 33 | 02 44 |
| 10 | 06 30 | 04 23 | 00 34 | 00 20 | 02 23 |
| 15 | 06 05 | 03 09 | 28♐28 | 29♑03 | 02 02 |
| 20 | 05 39 | 01 52 | 26 17 | 27 40 | 01 39 |
| 21 | 05 33 | 01 37 | 25 49 | 27 23 | 01 34 |
| 22 | 05 28 | 01 21 | 25 22 | 27 05 | 01 29 |
| 23 | 05 22 | 01 05 | 24 54 | 26 47 | 01 24 |
| 24 | 05 17 | 00 49 | 24 26 | 26 28 | 01 19 |
| 25 | 05 11 | 00 33 | 23 57 | 26 09 | 01 14 |
| 26 | 05 06 | 00 16 | 23 28 | 25 49 | 01 08 |
| 27 | 05 00 | 00 00 | 22 58 | 25 30 | 01 03 |
| 28 | 04 54 | 29♏43 | 22 28 | 25 09 | 00 57 |
| 29 | 04 48 | 29 26 | 21 58 | 24 48 | 00 51 |
| 30 | 04 42 | 29 09 | 21 27 | 24 27 | 00 45 |
| 31 | 04 36 | 28 51 | 20 56 | 24 05 | 00 39 |
| 32 | 04 30 | 28 33 | 20 23 | 23 42 | 00 33 |
| 33 | 04 24 | 28 15 | 19 51 | 23 18 | 00 26 |
| 34 | 04 17 | 27 56 | 19 17 | 22 54 | 00 20 |
| 35 | 04 11 | 27 38 | 18 43 | 22 29 | 00 13 |
| 36 | 04 04 | 27 18 | 18 09 | 22 04 | 00 06 |
| 37 | 03 57 | 26 59 | 17 33 | 21 37 | 29♒58 |
| 38 | 03 50 | 26 39 | 16 57 | 21 09 | 29 51 |
| 39 | 03 43 | 26 19 | 16 20 | 20 41 | 29 43 |
| 40 | 03 36 | 25 58 | 15 42 | 20 11 | 29 35 |
| 41 | 03 28 | 25 37 | 15 03 | 19 40 | 29 26 |
| 42 | 03 21 | 25 15 | 14 24 | 19 08 | 29 17 |
| 43 | 03 13 | 24 53 | 13 43 | 18 35 | 29 08 |
| 44 | 03 05 | 24 30 | 13 01 | 18 00 | 28 58 |
| 45 | 02 57 | 24 06 | 12 18 | 17 23 | 28 48 |
| 46 | 02 48 | 23 42 | 11 34 | 16 45 | 28 38 |
| 47 | 02 39 | 23 17 | 10 49 | 16 05 | 28 27 |
| 48 | 02 30 | 22 52 | 10 02 | 15 22 | 28 15 |
| 49 | 02 21 | 22 26 | 09 14 | 14 38 | 28 03 |
| 50 | 02 11 | 21 59 | 08 25 | 13 51 | 27 50 |
| 51 | 02 01 | 21 31 | 07 34 | 13 01 | 27 36 |
| 52 | 01 51 | 21 02 | 06 41 | 12 08 | 27 21 |
| 53 | 01 40 | 20 32 | 05 47 | 11 12 | 27 06 |
| 54 | 01 29 | 20 01 | 04 51 | 10 12 | 26 49 |
| 55 | 01 18 | 19 29 | 03 53 | 09 08 | 26 31 |
| 56 | 01 06 | 18 56 | 02 54 | 07 59 | 26 12 |
| 57 | 00 53 | 18 21 | 01 52 | 06 45 | 25 52 |
| 58 | 00 40 | 17 46 | 00 48 | 05 25 | 25 29 |
| 59 | 00 26 | 17 08 | 29♏42 | 03 57 | 25 05 |
| 60 | 00♏12 | 16♏29 | 28♏33 | 02♑22 | 24♒38 |

12h 24m 0s — 186° 0' 0" — 06 ♎ 32

| LAT. | 11 | 12 | ASC | 2 | 3 |
|---|---|---|---|---|---|
| 0 | 08♏23 | 07♐47 | 05♑30 | 03♒41 | 04♓07 |
| 5 | 07 57 | 06 33 | 03 31 | 02 32 | 03 48 |
| 10 | 07 31 | 05 19 | 01 29 | 01 20 | 03 28 |
| 15 | 07 05 | 04 04 | 29♐23 | 00 03 | 03 07 |
| 20 | 06 38 | 02 47 | 27 11 | 28♑41 | 02 45 |
| 21 | 06 32 | 02 31 | 26 44 | 28 23 | 02 40 |
| 22 | 06 27 | 02 15 | 26 16 | 28 06 | 02 36 |
| 23 | 06 21 | 01 59 | 25 48 | 27 47 | 02 31 |
| 24 | 06 16 | 01 43 | 25 20 | 27 29 | 02 26 |
| 25 | 06 10 | 01 27 | 24 51 | 27 10 | 02 21 |
| 26 | 06 04 | 01 10 | 24 22 | 26 51 | 02 16 |
| 27 | 05 58 | 00 53 | 23 52 | 26 31 | 02 10 |
| 28 | 05 52 | 00 36 | 23 22 | 26 11 | 02 05 |
| 29 | 05 46 | 00 19 | 22 51 | 25 50 | 01 59 |
| 30 | 05 40 | 00 01 | 22 20 | 25 28 | 01 53 |
| 31 | 05 34 | 29♏44 | 21 48 | 25 06 | 01 47 |
| 32 | 05 27 | 29 26 | 21 16 | 24 44 | 01 41 |
| 33 | 05 21 | 29 07 | 20 43 | 24 20 | 01 35 |
| 34 | 05 14 | 28 48 | 20 10 | 23 56 | 01 29 |
| 35 | 05 08 | 28 29 | 19 35 | 23 31 | 01 22 |
| 36 | 05 01 | 28 10 | 19 00 | 23 06 | 01 15 |
| 37 | 04 54 | 27 50 | 18 25 | 22 39 | 01 08 |
| 38 | 04 47 | 27 30 | 17 48 | 22 12 | 01 01 |
| 39 | 04 39 | 27 10 | 17 11 | 21 43 | 00 53 |
| 40 | 04 32 | 26 49 | 16 33 | 21 14 | 00 45 |
| 41 | 04 24 | 26 27 | 15 53 | 20 43 | 00 37 |
| 42 | 04 17 | 26 05 | 15 13 | 20 11 | 00 28 |
| 43 | 04 09 | 25 42 | 14 32 | 19 37 | 00 19 |
| 44 | 04 00 | 25 19 | 13 50 | 19 02 | 00 10 |
| 45 | 03 52 | 24 55 | 13 07 | 18 26 | 00 00 |
| 46 | 03 43 | 24 31 | 12 22 | 17 47 | 29♒50 |
| 47 | 03 34 | 24 06 | 11 36 | 17 07 | 29 39 |
| 48 | 03 25 | 23 40 | 10 49 | 16 25 | 29 28 |
| 49 | 03 15 | 23 13 | 10 01 | 15 40 | 29 16 |
| 50 | 03 05 | 22 46 | 09 11 | 14 53 | 29 04 |
| 51 | 02 55 | 22 18 | 08 19 | 14 03 | 28 50 |
| 52 | 02 45 | 21 48 | 07 26 | 13 10 | 28 36 |
| 53 | 02 34 | 21 18 | 06 31 | 12 14 | 28 21 |
| 54 | 02 22 | 20 47 | 05 34 | 11 13 | 28 05 |
| 55 | 02 10 | 20 14 | 04 36 | 10 09 | 27 48 |
| 56 | 01 58 | 19 41 | 03 35 | 09 00 | 27 30 |
| 57 | 01 45 | 19 05 | 02 33 | 07 45 | 27 10 |
| 58 | 01 31 | 18 29 | 01 28 | 06 24 | 26 48 |
| 59 | 01 17 | 17 51 | 00 21 | 04 56 | 26 25 |
| 60 | 01♏02 | 17♏12 | 29♏11 | 03♑20 | 25♒59 |

12h 28m 0s — 187° 0' 0" — 07 ♎ 37

| LAT. | 11 | 12 | ASC | 2 | 3 |
|---|---|---|---|---|---|
| 0 | 09♏24 | 08♐43 | 06♑26 | 04♒39 | 05♓10 |
| 5 | 08 57 | 07 29 | 04 26 | 03 31 | 04 52 |
| 10 | 08 31 | 06 14 | 02 24 | 02 19 | 04 33 |
| 15 | 08 04 | 04 59 | 00 18 | 01 04 | 04 13 |
| 20 | 07 37 | 03 41 | 28♐06 | 29♑42 | 03 52 |
| 21 | 07 31 | 03 25 | 27 38 | 29 24 | 03 47 |
| 22 | 07 26 | 03 09 | 27 11 | 29 07 | 03 43 |
| 23 | 07 20 | 02 53 | 26 43 | 28 49 | 03 38 |
| 24 | 07 14 | 02 37 | 26 14 | 28 30 | 03 33 |
| 25 | 07 08 | 02 20 | 25 45 | 28 12 | 03 28 |
| 26 | 07 02 | 02 03 | 25 16 | 27 52 | 03 23 |
| 27 | 06 56 | 01 47 | 24 46 | 27 33 | 03 18 |
| 28 | 06 50 | 01 29 | 24 16 | 27 12 | 03 13 |
| 29 | 06 44 | 01 12 | 23 45 | 26 52 | 03 07 |
| 30 | 06 38 | 00 54 | 23 14 | 26 30 | 03 02 |
| 31 | 06 31 | 00 36 | 22 42 | 26 08 | 02 56 |
| 32 | 06 25 | 00 18 | 22 09 | 25 46 | 02 50 |
| 33 | 06 18 | 29♏59 | 21 36 | 25 23 | 02 44 |
| 34 | 06 12 | 29 41 | 21 02 | 24 59 | 02 38 |
| 35 | 06 05 | 29 21 | 20 28 | 24 34 | 02 32 |
| 36 | 05 58 | 29 02 | 19 52 | 24 08 | 02 25 |
| 37 | 05 51 | 28 42 | 19 16 | 23 42 | 02 18 |
| 38 | 05 43 | 28 21 | 18 40 | 23 15 | 02 11 |
| 39 | 05 36 | 28 00 | 18 02 | 22 46 | 02 04 |
| 40 | 05 28 | 27 39 | 17 23 | 22 17 | 01 56 |
| 41 | 05 20 | 27 17 | 16 44 | 21 46 | 01 48 |
| 42 | 05 12 | 26 55 | 16 03 | 21 14 | 01 40 |
| 43 | 05 04 | 26 32 | 15 22 | 20 40 | 01 31 |
| 44 | 04 56 | 26 09 | 14 39 | 20 06 | 01 22 |
| 45 | 04 47 | 25 45 | 13 55 | 19 29 | 01 13 |
| 46 | 04 38 | 25 20 | 13 10 | 18 51 | 01 03 |
| 47 | 04 29 | 24 55 | 12 24 | 18 10 | 00 53 |
| 48 | 04 19 | 24 28 | 11 36 | 17 28 | 00 42 |
| 49 | 04 10 | 24 01 | 10 47 | 16 43 | 00 30 |
| 50 | 03 59 | 23 33 | 09 57 | 15 56 | 00 18 |
| 51 | 03 49 | 23 05 | 09 04 | 15 06 | 00 05 |
| 52 | 03 38 | 22 35 | 08 11 | 14 13 | 29♒52 |
| 53 | 03 27 | 22 04 | 07 15 | 13 16 | 29 37 |
| 54 | 03 15 | 21 32 | 06 18 | 12 16 | 29 22 |
| 55 | 03 03 | 20 59 | 05 18 | 11 11 | 29 05 |
| 56 | 02 50 | 20 25 | 04 17 | 10 01 | 28 47 |
| 57 | 02 37 | 19 50 | 03 13 | 08 46 | 28 28 |
| 58 | 02 23 | 19 13 | 02 08 | 07 24 | 28 07 |
| 59 | 02 08 | 18 34 | 00 59 | 05 55 | 27 45 |
| 60 | 01♏53 | 17♏54 | 29♏49 | 04♑18 | 27♒20 |

12h 32m 0s — 188° 0' 0" — 08 ♎ 43

| LAT. | 11 | 12 | ASC | 2 | 3 |
|---|---|---|---|---|---|
| 0 | 10♏25 | 09♐40 | 07♑21 | 05♒38 | 06♓14 |
| 5 | 09 58 | 08 25 | 05 21 | 04 30 | 05 56 |
| 10 | 09 31 | 07 10 | 03 19 | 03 19 | 05 38 |
| 15 | 09 04 | 05 54 | 01 13 | 02 04 | 05 19 |
| 20 | 08 36 | 04 36 | 29♐01 | 00 43 | 04 58 |
| 21 | 08 30 | 04 20 | 28 33 | 00 26 | 04 54 |
| 22 | 08 24 | 04 03 | 28 05 | 00 08 | 04 50 |
| 23 | 08 18 | 03 47 | 27 37 | 29♑50 | 04 45 |
| 24 | 08 13 | 03 31 | 27 08 | 29 32 | 04 40 |
| 25 | 08 07 | 03 14 | 26 39 | 29 13 | 04 36 |
| 26 | 08 00 | 02 57 | 26 10 | 28 54 | 04 31 |
| 27 | 07 54 | 02 40 | 25 40 | 28 35 | 04 26 |
| 28 | 07 48 | 02 22 | 25 10 | 28 15 | 04 21 |
| 29 | 07 42 | 02 05 | 24 39 | 27 54 | 04 16 |
| 30 | 07 35 | 01 47 | 24 07 | 27 33 | 04 10 |
| 31 | 07 29 | 01 29 | 23 35 | 27 11 | 04 05 |
| 32 | 07 22 | 01 10 | 23 02 | 26 48 | 03 59 |
| 33 | 07 15 | 00 52 | 22 29 | 26 25 | 03 53 |
| 34 | 07 09 | 00 33 | 21 55 | 26 02 | 03 47 |
| 35 | 07 02 | 00 13 | 21 20 | 25 37 | 03 41 |
| 36 | 06 54 | 29♏53 | 20 45 | 25 11 | 03 35 |
| 37 | 06 47 | 29 33 | 20 08 | 24 45 | 03 28 |
| 38 | 06 40 | 29 13 | 19 31 | 24 18 | 03 21 |
| 39 | 06 32 | 28 51 | 18 53 | 23 49 | 03 14 |
| 40 | 06 24 | 28 30 | 18 14 | 23 20 | 03 07 |
| 41 | 06 16 | 28 08 | 17 34 | 22 49 | 02 59 |
| 42 | 06 08 | 27 45 | 16 54 | 22 17 | 02 51 |
| 43 | 06 00 | 27 22 | 16 12 | 21 44 | 02 43 |
| 44 | 05 51 | 26 58 | 15 29 | 21 09 | 02 35 |
| 45 | 05 42 | 26 34 | 14 44 | 20 33 | 02 25 |
| 46 | 05 33 | 26 09 | 13 59 | 19 54 | 02 16 |
| 47 | 05 24 | 25 43 | 13 12 | 19 14 | 02 06 |
| 48 | 05 14 | 25 17 | 12 24 | 18 32 | 01 56 |
| 49 | 05 04 | 24 49 | 11 34 | 17 47 | 01 45 |
| 50 | 04 53 | 24 21 | 10 43 | 17 00 | 01 33 |
| 51 | 04 43 | 23 52 | 09 50 | 16 09 | 01 21 |
| 52 | 04 31 | 23 22 | 08 56 | 15 16 | 01 07 |
| 53 | 04 20 | 22 50 | 07 59 | 14 19 | 00 53 |
| 54 | 04 08 | 22 18 | 07 01 | 13 19 | 00 39 |
| 55 | 03 55 | 21 45 | 06 01 | 12 13 | 00 23 |
| 56 | 03 42 | 21 10 | 04 59 | 11 03 | 00 06 |
| 57 | 03 29 | 20 34 | 03 54 | 09 48 | 29♒47 |
| 58 | 03 14 | 19 56 | 02 48 | 08 25 | 29 27 |
| 59 | 02 59 | 19 17 | 01 39 | 06 56 | 29 06 |
| 60 | 02♏44 | 18♏36 | 00♐27 | 05♑17 | 28♒42 |

12h 36m 0s — 189° 0' 0" — 09 ♎ 48

| LAT. | 11 | 12 | ASC | 2 | 3 |
|---|---|---|---|---|---|
| 0 | 11♏26 | 10♐36 | 08♑16 | 06♒37 | 07♓18 |
| 5 | 10 59 | 09 21 | 06 17 | 05 29 | 07 01 |
| 10 | 10 31 | 08 05 | 04 15 | 04 19 | 06 43 |
| 15 | 10 03 | 06 49 | 02 08 | 03 05 | 06 25 |
| 20 | 09 35 | 05 30 | 29♐55 | 01 44 | 06 05 |
| 21 | 09 29 | 05 14 | 29 28 | 01 27 | 06 01 |
| 22 | 09 23 | 04 57 | 29 00 | 01 10 | 05 57 |
| 23 | 09 17 | 04 41 | 28 32 | 00 52 | 05 52 |
| 24 | 09 11 | 04 24 | 28 03 | 00 34 | 05 48 |
| 25 | 09 05 | 04 07 | 27 34 | 00 15 | 05 43 |
| 26 | 08 59 | 03 50 | 27 04 | 29♑56 | 05 39 |
| 27 | 08 52 | 03 33 | 26 34 | 29 37 | 05 34 |
| 28 | 08 46 | 03 16 | 26 04 | 29 17 | 05 29 |
| 29 | 08 39 | 02 58 | 25 32 | 28 56 | 05 24 |
| 30 | 08 33 | 02 40 | 25 01 | 28 35 | 05 19 |
| 31 | 08 26 | 02 21 | 24 28 | 28 14 | 05 14 |
| 32 | 08 19 | 02 03 | 23 56 | 27 51 | 05 08 |
| 33 | 08 13 | 01 44 | 23 22 | 27 28 | 05 03 |
| 34 | 08 06 | 01 25 | 22 48 | 27 05 | 04 57 |
| 35 | 07 58 | 01 05 | 22 13 | 26 40 | 04 51 |
| 36 | 07 51 | 00 45 | 21 37 | 26 15 | 04 45 |
| 37 | 07 44 | 00 25 | 21 00 | 25 49 | 04 39 |
| 38 | 07 36 | 00 04 | 20 23 | 25 21 | 04 32 |
| 39 | 07 28 | 29♏42 | 19 45 | 24 53 | 04 25 |
| 40 | 07 20 | 29 21 | 19 06 | 24 24 | 04 18 |
| 41 | 07 12 | 28 58 | 18 25 | 23 53 | 04 11 |
| 42 | 07 04 | 28 35 | 17 44 | 23 21 | 04 03 |
| 43 | 06 55 | 28 12 | 17 02 | 22 48 | 03 55 |
| 44 | 06 46 | 27 48 | 16 18 | 22 13 | 03 47 |
| 45 | 06 37 | 27 23 | 15 33 | 21 37 | 03 38 |
| 46 | 06 28 | 26 58 | 14 48 | 20 59 | 03 29 |
| 47 | 06 18 | 26 32 | 14 00 | 20 18 | 03 20 |
| 48 | 06 08 | 26 05 | 13 11 | 19 36 | 03 10 |
| 49 | 05 58 | 25 37 | 12 21 | 18 51 | 02 59 |
| 50 | 05 47 | 25 09 | 11 29 | 18 04 | 02 48 |
| 51 | 05 36 | 24 39 | 10 36 | 17 14 | 02 36 |
| 52 | 05 25 | 24 08 | 09 41 | 16 20 | 02 24 |
| 53 | 05 13 | 23 37 | 08 44 | 15 23 | 02 10 |
| 54 | 05 01 | 23 04 | 07 45 | 14 22 | 01 56 |
| 55 | 04 48 | 22 30 | 06 44 | 13 17 | 01 41 |
| 56 | 04 34 | 21 55 | 05 41 | 12 06 | 01 24 |
| 57 | 04 20 | 21 18 | 04 36 | 10 50 | 01 06 |
| 58 | 04 06 | 20 40 | 03 28 | 09 27 | 00 47 |
| 59 | 03 50 | 20 00 | 02 18 | 07 57 | 00 27 |
| 60 | 03♏34 | 19♏18 | 01♐05 | 06♑17 | 00♓04 |

12h 40m 0s — 190° 0' 0" — 10 ♎ 53

| LAT. | 11 | 12 | ASC | 2 | 3 |
|---|---|---|---|---|---|
| 0 | 12♏27 | 11♐32 | 09♑11 | 07♒35 | 08♓22 |
| 5 | 11 59 | 10 16 | 07 12 | 06 29 | 08 06 |
| 10 | 11 31 | 09 00 | 05 10 | 05 20 | 07 49 |
| 15 | 11 02 | 07 43 | 03 04 | 04 06 | 07 31 |
| 20 | 10 33 | 06 24 | 00 51 | 02 46 | 07 12 |
| 21 | 10 27 | 06 08 | 00 23 | 02 29 | 07 08 |
| 22 | 10 21 | 05 51 | 29♐55 | 02 12 | 07 04 |
| 23 | 10 15 | 05 35 | 29 27 | 01 54 | 07 00 |
| 24 | 10 09 | 05 18 | 28 58 | 01 36 | 06 56 |
| 25 | 10 03 | 05 01 | 28 28 | 01 18 | 06 51 |
| 26 | 09 56 | 04 44 | 27 59 | 00 59 | 06 47 |
| 27 | 09 50 | 04 26 | 27 29 | 00 40 | 06 42 |
| 28 | 09 44 | 04 09 | 26 58 | 00 20 | 06 38 |
| 29 | 09 37 | 03 51 | 26 27 | 29♑59 | 06 33 |
| 30 | 09 30 | 03 33 | 25 55 | 29 39 | 06 28 |
| 31 | 09 23 | 03 14 | 25 22 | 29 17 | 06 23 |
| 32 | 09 17 | 02 55 | 24 49 | 28 55 | 06 18 |
| 33 | 09 10 | 02 36 | 24 15 | 28 32 | 06 13 |
| 34 | 09 02 | 02 17 | 23 41 | 28 08 | 06 07 |
| 35 | 08 55 | 01 57 | 23 06 | 27 44 | 06 01 |
| 36 | 08 48 | 01 37 | 22 30 | 27 19 | 05 56 |
| 37 | 08 40 | 01 16 | 21 53 | 26 53 | 05 50 |
| 38 | 08 32 | 00 55 | 21 15 | 26 26 | 05 43 |
| 39 | 08 24 | 00 33 | 20 37 | 25 57 | 05 37 |
| 40 | 08 16 | 00 11 | 19 57 | 25 28 | 05 30 |
| 41 | 08 08 | 29♏49 | 19 16 | 24 58 | 05 23 |
| 42 | 07 59 | 29 26 | 18 35 | 24 26 | 05 16 |
| 43 | 07 50 | 29 02 | 17 52 | 23 53 | 05 08 |
| 44 | 07 41 | 28 38 | 17 08 | 23 18 | 05 00 |
| 45 | 07 32 | 28 13 | 16 23 | 22 42 | 04 52 |
| 46 | 07 22 | 27 47 | 15 36 | 22 03 | 04 43 |
| 47 | 07 13 | 27 20 | 14 49 | 21 23 | 04 34 |
| 48 | 07 02 | 26 53 | 13 59 | 20 41 | 04 24 |
| 49 | 06 52 | 26 25 | 13 09 | 19 56 | 04 14 |
| 50 | 06 41 | 25 56 | 12 16 | 19 09 | 04 03 |
| 51 | 06 30 | 25 26 | 11 22 | 18 19 | 03 52 |
| 52 | 06 18 | 24 55 | 10 26 | 17 25 | 03 40 |
| 53 | 06 06 | 24 23 | 09 28 | 16 28 | 03 27 |
| 54 | 05 53 | 23 50 | 08 29 | 15 27 | 03 13 |
| 55 | 05 40 | 23 15 | 07 27 | 14 21 | 02 59 |
| 56 | 05 26 | 22 39 | 06 23 | 13 10 | 02 43 |
| 57 | 05 12 | 22 02 | 05 17 | 11 53 | 02 26 |
| 58 | 04 57 | 21 23 | 04 08 | 10 30 | 02 08 |
| 59 | 04 41 | 20 43 | 02 57 | 08 59 | 01 48 |
| 60 | 04♏25 | 20♏00 | 01♐43 | 07♑18 | 01♓26 |

12h 44m 0s — 191° 0' 0" — 11 ♎ 58

| LAT. | 11 | 12 | ASC | 2 | 3 |
|---|---|---|---|---|---|
| 0 | 13♏27 | 12♐28 | 10♑07 | 08♒34 | 09♓26 |
| 5 | 12 59 | 11 12 | 08 08 | 07 29 | 09 10 |
| 10 | 12 30 | 09 56 | 06 06 | 06 20 | 08 54 |
| 15 | 12 02 | 08 38 | 03 59 | 05 07 | 08 38 |
| 20 | 11 32 | 07 18 | 01 46 | 03 48 | 08 20 |
| 21 | 11 26 | 07 02 | 01 18 | 03 31 | 08 16 |
| 22 | 11 20 | 06 45 | 00 50 | 03 14 | 08 12 |
| 23 | 11 13 | 06 29 | 00 22 | 02 57 | 08 08 |
| 24 | 11 07 | 06 12 | 29♐53 | 02 39 | 08 04 |
| 25 | 11 01 | 05 55 | 29 23 | 02 21 | 08 00 |
| 26 | 10 54 | 05 37 | 28 53 | 02 02 | 07 55 |
| 27 | 10 48 | 05 20 | 28 23 | 01 43 | 07 51 |
| 28 | 10 41 | 05 02 | 27 52 | 01 23 | 07 47 |
| 29 | 10 34 | 04 44 | 27 21 | 01 03 | 07 42 |
| 30 | 10 28 | 04 25 | 26 49 | 00 42 | 07 37 |
| 31 | 10 21 | 04 07 | 26 16 | 00 21 | 07 33 |
| 32 | 10 14 | 03 48 | 25 43 | 29♑59 | 07 28 |
| 33 | 10 06 | 03 28 | 25 09 | 29 36 | 07 23 |
| 34 | 09 59 | 03 09 | 24 34 | 29 12 | 07 17 |
| 35 | 09 52 | 02 49 | 23 59 | 28 48 | 07 12 |
| 36 | 09 44 | 02 28 | 23 22 | 28 23 | 07 06 |
| 37 | 09 36 | 02 07 | 22 45 | 27 57 | 07 01 |
| 38 | 09 28 | 01 46 | 22 07 | 27 30 | 06 55 |
| 39 | 09 20 | 01 24 | 21 29 | 27 02 | 06 48 |
| 40 | 09 12 | 01 02 | 20 49 | 26 33 | 06 42 |
| 41 | 09 03 | 00 39 | 20 08 | 26 03 | 06 35 |
| 42 | 08 55 | 00 16 | 19 26 | 25 31 | 06 28 |
| 43 | 08 46 | 29♏52 | 18 43 | 24 58 | 06 21 |
| 44 | 08 36 | 29 27 | 17 58 | 24 23 | 06 13 |
| 45 | 08 27 | 29 02 | 17 13 | 23 47 | 06 05 |
| 46 | 08 17 | 28 36 | 16 26 | 23 09 | 05 57 |
| 47 | 08 07 | 28 09 | 15 37 | 22 29 | 05 48 |
| 48 | 07 57 | 27 42 | 14 48 | 21 46 | 05 39 |
| 49 | 07 46 | 27 13 | 13 56 | 21 02 | 05 29 |
| 50 | 07 35 | 26 44 | 13 03 | 20 14 | 05 19 |
| 51 | 07 23 | 26 13 | 12 08 | 19 24 | 05 08 |
| 52 | 07 11 | 25 42 | 11 12 | 18 31 | 04 57 |
| 53 | 06 59 | 25 09 | 10 13 | 17 33 | 04 45 |
| 54 | 06 46 | 24 36 | 09 13 | 16 32 | 04 31 |
| 55 | 06 32 | 24 00 | 08 10 | 15 26 | 04 18 |
| 56 | 06 18 | 23 24 | 07 05 | 14 15 | 04 03 |
| 57 | 06 03 | 22 46 | 05 58 | 12 58 | 03 46 |
| 58 | 05 48 | 22 07 | 04 49 | 11 34 | 03 29 |
| 59 | 05 32 | 21 25 | 03 36 | 10 02 | 03 10 |
| 60 | 05♏15 | 20♏42 | 02♐21 | 08♑20 | 02♓49 |

# Placidus Table of Houses for Latitudes 0° to 60° North

**12h 48m 0s — 192° 0' 0" — 13 ♎ 03**

| LAT. | 11 | 12 | ASC | 2 | 3 |
|---|---|---|---|---|---|
| 0 | 14♏28 | 13♐24 | 11♑02 | 09♒34 | 10♓30 |
| 5 | 13 59 | 12 08 | 09 03 | 08 29 | 10 15 |
| 10 | 13 30 | 10 51 | 07 02 | 07 21 | 10 00 |
| 15 | 13 00 | 09 33 | 04 55 | 06 09 | 09 44 |
| 20 | 12 30 | 08 12 | 02 41 | 04 50 | 09 27 |
| 21 | 12 24 | 07 56 | 02 14 | 04 34 | 09 23 |
| 22 | 12 18 | 07 39 | 01 45 | 04 17 | 09 20 |
| 23 | 12 11 | 07 22 | 01 17 | 03 59 | 09 16 |
| 24 | 12 05 | 07 05 | 00 48 | 03 42 | 09 12 |
| 25 | 11 59 | 06 48 | 00 18 | 03 24 | 09 08 |
| 26 | 11 52 | 06 31 | 29♐48 | 03 05 | 09 04 |
| 27 | 11 45 | 06 13 | 29 18 | 02 46 | 09 00 |
| 28 | 11 39 | 05 55 | 28 47 | 02 26 | 08 56 |
| 29 | 11 32 | 05 37 | 28 15 | 02 06 | 08 51 |
| 30 | 11 25 | 05 18 | 27 43 | 01 46 | 08 47 |
| 31 | 11 18 | 04 59 | 27 10 | 01 25 | 08 42 |
| 32 | 11 10 | 04 40 | 26 37 | 01 03 | 08 38 |
| 33 | 11 03 | 04 21 | 26 03 | 00 40 | 08 33 |
| 34 | 10 56 | 04 01 | 25 28 | 00 17 | 08 28 |
| 35 | 10 48 | 03 41 | 24 52 | 29♑53 | 08 23 |
| 36 | 10 40 | 03 20 | 24 16 | 29 28 | 08 17 |
| 37 | 10 32 | 02 59 | 23 38 | 29 02 | 08 12 |
| 38 | 10 24 | 02 37 | 23 00 | 28 35 | 08 06 |
| 39 | 10 16 | 02 15 | 22 21 | 28 07 | 08 00 |
| 40 | 10 08 | 01 53 | 21 41 | 27 38 | 07 54 |
| 41 | 09 59 | 01 30 | 20 59 | 27 08 | 07 48 |
| 42 | 09 50 | 01 06 | 20 17 | 26 37 | 07 41 |
| 43 | 09 41 | 00 42 | 19 33 | 26 04 | 07 34 |
| 44 | 09 31 | 00 17 | 18 49 | 25 29 | 07 27 |
| 45 | 09 22 | 29♏51 | 18 03 | 24 53 | 07 19 |
| 46 | 09 12 | 29 25 | 17 15 | 24 15 | 07 11 |
| 47 | 09 01 | 28 58 | 16 26 | 23 35 | 07 03 |
| 48 | 08 51 | 28 30 | 15 36 | 22 53 | 06 54 |
| 49 | 08 40 | 28 01 | 14 44 | 22 08 | 06 45 |
| 50 | 08 28 | 27 31 | 13 50 | 21 21 | 06 35 |
| 51 | 08 16 | 27 01 | 12 55 | 20 30 | 06 25 |
| 52 | 08 04 | 26 29 | 11 58 | 19 37 | 06 14 |
| 53 | 07 51 | 25 56 | 10 59 | 18 39 | 06 02 |
| 54 | 07 38 | 25 21 | 09 57 | 17 38 | 05 50 |
| 55 | 07 24 | 24 46 | 08 54 | 16 32 | 05 37 |
| 56 | 07 10 | 24 09 | 07 48 | 15 21 | 05 22 |
| 57 | 06 55 | 23 30 | 06 40 | 14 03 | 05 07 |
| 58 | 06 39 | 22 50 | 05 29 | 12 39 | 04 50 |
| 59 | 06 23 | 22 08 | 04 16 | 11 06 | 04 32 |
| 60 | 06♏05 | 21♏25 | 03♐00 | 09♑24 | 04♓13 |

**12h 52m 0s — 193° 0' 0" — 14 ♎ 07**

| LAT. | 11 | 12 | ASC | 2 | 3 |
|---|---|---|---|---|---|
| 0 | 15♏28 | 14♐20 | 11♑58 | 10♒33 | 11♓34 |
| 5 | 14 59 | 13 03 | 09 59 | 09 29 | 11 20 |
| 10 | 14 29 | 11 46 | 07 58 | 08 22 | 11 06 |
| 15 | 13 59 | 10 28 | 05 51 | 07 10 | 10 51 |
| 20 | 13 28 | 09 07 | 03 37 | 05 53 | 10 34 |
| 21 | 13 22 | 08 50 | 03 09 | 05 36 | 10 31 |
| 22 | 13 16 | 08 33 | 02 41 | 05 20 | 10 28 |
| 23 | 13 09 | 08 16 | 02 12 | 05 02 | 10 24 |
| 24 | 13 03 | 07 59 | 01 43 | 04 45 | 10 20 |
| 25 | 12 56 | 07 42 | 01 14 | 04 27 | 10 17 |
| 26 | 12 50 | 07 24 | 00 43 | 04 09 | 10 13 |
| 27 | 12 43 | 07 06 | 00 13 | 03 50 | 10 09 |
| 28 | 12 36 | 06 48 | 29♐42 | 03 30 | 10 05 |
| 29 | 12 29 | 06 30 | 29 10 | 03 10 | 10 01 |
| 30 | 12 22 | 06 11 | 28 38 | 02 50 | 09 56 |
| 31 | 12 15 | 05 52 | 28 05 | 02 29 | 09 52 |
| 32 | 12 07 | 05 33 | 27 31 | 02 07 | 09 48 |
| 33 | 12 00 | 05 13 | 26 57 | 01 45 | 09 43 |
| 34 | 11 52 | 04 53 | 26 22 | 01 22 | 09 38 |
| 35 | 11 44 | 04 33 | 25 46 | 00 58 | 09 33 |
| 36 | 11 37 | 04 12 | 25 09 | 00 33 | 09 28 |
| 37 | 11 28 | 03 50 | 24 31 | 00 07 | 09 23 |
| 38 | 11 20 | 03 29 | 23 53 | 29♑41 | 09 18 |
| 39 | 11 12 | 03 06 | 23 13 | 29 13 | 09 12 |
| 40 | 11 03 | 02 44 | 22 33 | 28 44 | 09 06 |
| 41 | 10 54 | 02 20 | 21 51 | 28 14 | 09 00 |
| 42 | 10 45 | 01 57 | 21 08 | 27 43 | 08 54 |
| 43 | 10 36 | 01 32 | 20 25 | 27 10 | 08 47 |
| 44 | 10 26 | 01 07 | 19 39 | 26 36 | 08 40 |
| 45 | 10 16 | 00 41 | 18 53 | 26 00 | 08 33 |
| 46 | 10 06 | 00 14 | 18 05 | 25 22 | 08 26 |
| 47 | 09 55 | 29♏47 | 17 16 | 24 42 | 08 18 |
| 48 | 09 45 | 29 18 | 16 25 | 24 00 | 08 09 |
| 49 | 09 33 | 28 49 | 15 32 | 23 15 | 08 01 |
| 50 | 09 22 | 28 19 | 14 38 | 22 28 | 07 51 |
| 51 | 09 10 | 27 48 | 13 42 | 21 37 | 07 42 |
| 52 | 08 57 | 27 16 | 12 44 | 20 44 | 07 31 |
| 53 | 08 44 | 26 42 | 11 44 | 19 46 | 07 20 |
| 54 | 08 31 | 26 07 | 10 42 | 18 45 | 07 08 |
| 55 | 08 17 | 25 31 | 09 38 | 17 39 | 06 56 |
| 56 | 08 02 | 24 54 | 08 31 | 16 27 | 06 42 |
| 57 | 07 46 | 24 15 | 07 22 | 15 09 | 06 28 |
| 58 | 07 30 | 23 34 | 06 10 | 13 44 | 06 12 |
| 59 | 07 13 | 22 51 | 04 56 | 12 11 | 05 55 |
| 60 | 06♏56 | 22♏07 | 03♐39 | 10♑28 | 05♓36 |

**12h 56m 0s — 194° 0' 0" — 15 ♎ 12**

| LAT. | 11 | 12 | ASC | 2 | 3 |
|---|---|---|---|---|---|
| 0 | 16♏28 | 15♐16 | 12♑53 | 11♒32 | 12♓39 |
| 5 | 15 58 | 13 59 | 10 55 | 10 29 | 12 26 |
| 10 | 15 28 | 12 41 | 08 53 | 09 23 | 12 12 |
| 15 | 14 58 | 11 22 | 06 47 | 08 12 | 11 58 |
| 20 | 14 27 | 10 01 | 04 33 | 06 56 | 11 42 |
| 21 | 14 20 | 09 44 | 04 05 | 06 39 | 11 39 |
| 22 | 14 14 | 09 27 | 03 37 | 06 23 | 11 36 |
| 23 | 14 07 | 09 10 | 03 08 | 06 06 | 11 32 |
| 24 | 14 00 | 08 53 | 02 39 | 05 48 | 11 29 |
| 25 | 13 54 | 08 35 | 02 09 | 05 31 | 11 25 |
| 26 | 13 47 | 08 17 | 01 39 | 05 12 | 11 22 |
| 27 | 13 40 | 07 59 | 01 08 | 04 54 | 11 18 |
| 28 | 13 33 | 07 41 | 00 37 | 04 35 | 11 14 |
| 29 | 13 26 | 07 23 | 00 05 | 04 15 | 11 10 |
| 30 | 13 19 | 07 04 | 29♐32 | 03 55 | 11 06 |
| 31 | 13 11 | 06 45 | 28 59 | 03 34 | 11 02 |
| 32 | 13 04 | 06 25 | 28 26 | 03 12 | 10 58 |
| 33 | 12 56 | 06 05 | 27 51 | 02 50 | 10 54 |
| 34 | 12 49 | 05 45 | 27 16 | 02 27 | 10 49 |
| 35 | 12 41 | 05 25 | 26 40 | 02 03 | 10 44 |
| 36 | 12 33 | 05 03 | 26 03 | 01 39 | 10 40 |
| 37 | 12 24 | 04 42 | 25 25 | 01 13 | 10 35 |
| 38 | 12 16 | 04 20 | 24 46 | 00 47 | 10 30 |
| 39 | 12 07 | 03 58 | 24 06 | 00 19 | 10 24 |
| 40 | 11 59 | 03 35 | 23 25 | 29♑51 | 10 19 |
| 41 | 11 50 | 03 11 | 22 43 | 29 21 | 10 13 |
| 42 | 11 40 | 02 47 | 22 00 | 28 49 | 10 07 |
| 43 | 11 31 | 02 22 | 21 16 | 28 17 | 10 01 |
| 44 | 11 21 | 01 57 | 20 30 | 27 43 | 09 54 |
| 45 | 11 11 | 01 30 | 19 43 | 27 07 | 09 48 |
| 46 | 11 00 | 01 03 | 18 55 | 26 29 | 09 40 |
| 47 | 10 50 | 00 36 | 18 05 | 25 49 | 09 33 |
| 48 | 10 39 | 00 07 | 17 14 | 25 07 | 09 25 |
| 49 | 10 27 | 29♏37 | 16 21 | 24 23 | 09 17 |
| 50 | 10 15 | 29 07 | 15 26 | 23 35 | 09 08 |
| 51 | 10 03 | 28 35 | 14 29 | 22 45 | 08 59 |
| 52 | 09 50 | 28 02 | 13 30 | 21 52 | 08 49 |
| 53 | 09 37 | 27 29 | 12 30 | 20 54 | 08 39 |
| 54 | 09 23 | 26 53 | 11 27 | 19 53 | 08 27 |
| 55 | 09 09 | 26 17 | 10 22 | 18 46 | 08 16 |
| 56 | 08 54 | 25 39 | 09 14 | 17 35 | 08 03 |
| 57 | 08 38 | 24 59 | 08 04 | 16 16 | 07 49 |
| 58 | 08 21 | 24 18 | 06 51 | 14 51 | 07 34 |
| 59 | 08 04 | 23 34 | 05 36 | 13 17 | 07 18 |
| 60 | 07♏46 | 22♏49 | 04♐17 | 11♑33 | 07♓00 |

**13h 0m 0s — 195° 0' 0" — 16 ♎ 17**

| LAT. | 11 | 12 | ASC | 2 | 3 |
|---|---|---|---|---|---|
| 0 | 17♏28 | 16♐11 | 13♑49 | 12♒32 | 13♓43 |
| 5 | 16 58 | 14 54 | 11 51 | 11 30 | 13 31 |
| 10 | 16 27 | 13 36 | 09 50 | 10 24 | 13 18 |
| 15 | 15 56 | 12 17 | 07 43 | 09 15 | 13 05 |
| 20 | 15 25 | 10 55 | 05 29 | 07 59 | 12 50 |
| 21 | 15 18 | 10 38 | 05 01 | 07 43 | 12 47 |
| 22 | 15 11 | 10 21 | 04 32 | 07 26 | 12 44 |
| 23 | 15 05 | 10 04 | 04 04 | 07 10 | 12 41 |
| 24 | 14 58 | 09 46 | 03 34 | 06 52 | 12 37 |
| 25 | 14 51 | 09 29 | 03 05 | 06 35 | 12 34 |
| 26 | 14 44 | 09 11 | 02 34 | 06 17 | 12 31 |
| 27 | 14 37 | 08 53 | 02 04 | 05 58 | 12 27 |
| 28 | 14 30 | 08 34 | 01 32 | 05 39 | 12 24 |
| 29 | 14 23 | 08 16 | 01 00 | 05 20 | 12 20 |
| 30 | 14 16 | 07 57 | 00 28 | 05 00 | 12 16 |
| 31 | 14 08 | 07 37 | 29♐54 | 04 39 | 12 12 |
| 32 | 14 01 | 07 18 | 29 20 | 04 18 | 12 08 |
| 33 | 13 53 | 06 58 | 28 45 | 03 56 | 12 04 |
| 34 | 13 45 | 06 37 | 28 10 | 03 33 | 12 00 |
| 35 | 13 37 | 06 16 | 27 34 | 03 09 | 11 56 |
| 36 | 13 29 | 05 55 | 26 56 | 02 45 | 11 51 |
| 37 | 13 20 | 05 34 | 26 18 | 02 20 | 11 47 |
| 38 | 13 12 | 05 11 | 25 39 | 01 53 | 11 42 |
| 39 | 13 03 | 04 49 | 24 59 | 01 26 | 11 37 |
| 40 | 12 54 | 04 26 | 24 18 | 00 57 | 11 32 |
| 41 | 12 45 | 04 02 | 23 36 | 00 28 | 11 26 |
| 42 | 12 35 | 03 37 | 22 52 | 29♑57 | 11 21 |
| 43 | 12 26 | 03 12 | 22 08 | 29 24 | 11 15 |
| 44 | 12 16 | 02 46 | 21 22 | 28 50 | 11 09 |
| 45 | 12 05 | 02 20 | 20 34 | 28 14 | 11 02 |
| 46 | 11 55 | 01 53 | 19 45 | 27 37 | 10 55 |
| 47 | 11 44 | 01 25 | 18 55 | 26 57 | 10 48 |
| 48 | 11 32 | 00 56 | 18 03 | 26 15 | 10 41 |
| 49 | 11 21 | 00 26 | 17 09 | 25 31 | 10 33 |
| 50 | 11 09 | 29♏55 | 16 14 | 24 44 | 10 25 |
| 51 | 10 56 | 29 23 | 15 16 | 23 54 | 10 16 |
| 52 | 10 43 | 28 49 | 14 17 | 23 00 | 10 07 |
| 53 | 10 29 | 28 15 | 13 16 | 22 03 | 09 57 |
| 54 | 10 15 | 27 39 | 12 12 | 21 01 | 09 47 |
| 55 | 10 01 | 27 02 | 11 06 | 19 55 | 09 35 |
| 56 | 09 45 | 26 24 | 09 57 | 18 43 | 09 23 |
| 57 | 09 29 | 25 43 | 08 46 | 17 25 | 09 10 |
| 58 | 09 12 | 25 01 | 07 32 | 15 59 | 08 57 |
| 59 | 08 55 | 24 17 | 06 16 | 14 25 | 08 41 |
| 60 | 08♏36 | 23♏31 | 04♐56 | 12♑40 | 08♓25 |

**13h 4m 0s — 196° 0' 0" — 17 ♎ 21**

| LAT. | 11 | 12 | ASC | 2 | 3 |
|---|---|---|---|---|---|
| 0 | 18♏28 | 17♐07 | 14♑44 | 13♒32 | 14♓48 |
| 5 | 17 57 | 15 49 | 12 47 | 12 31 | 14 36 |
| 10 | 17 26 | 14 31 | 10 46 | 11 26 | 14 24 |
| 15 | 16 55 | 13 12 | 08 39 | 10 17 | 14 12 |
| 20 | 16 22 | 11 49 | 06 25 | 09 02 | 13 58 |
| 21 | 16 16 | 11 32 | 05 57 | 08 46 | 13 55 |
| 22 | 16 09 | 11 15 | 05 28 | 08 30 | 13 52 |
| 23 | 16 02 | 10 58 | 05 00 | 08 14 | 13 49 |
| 24 | 15 55 | 10 40 | 04 30 | 07 57 | 13 46 |
| 25 | 15 48 | 10 22 | 04 00 | 07 39 | 13 43 |
| 26 | 15 41 | 10 04 | 03 30 | 07 21 | 13 40 |
| 27 | 15 34 | 09 46 | 02 59 | 07 03 | 13 37 |
| 28 | 15 27 | 09 27 | 02 28 | 06 44 | 13 33 |
| 29 | 15 20 | 09 09 | 01 56 | 06 25 | 13 30 |
| 30 | 15 12 | 08 50 | 01 23 | 06 05 | 13 26 |
| 31 | 15 05 | 08 30 | 00 49 | 05 45 | 13 23 |
| 32 | 14 57 | 08 10 | 00 15 | 05 23 | 13 19 |
| 33 | 14 49 | 07 50 | 29♐40 | 05 02 | 13 15 |
| 34 | 14 41 | 07 29 | 29 05 | 04 39 | 13 11 |
| 35 | 14 33 | 07 09 | 28 28 | 04 16 | 13 07 |
| 36 | 14 25 | 06 47 | 27 51 | 03 51 | 13 03 |
| 37 | 14 16 | 06 25 | 27 12 | 03 26 | 12 59 |
| 38 | 14 07 | 06 03 | 26 33 | 03 00 | 12 54 |
| 39 | 13 58 | 05 40 | 25 53 | 02 33 | 12 49 |
| 40 | 13 49 | 05 16 | 25 11 | 02 05 | 12 45 |
| 41 | 13 40 | 04 52 | 24 28 | 01 35 | 12 39 |
| 42 | 13 30 | 04 28 | 23 45 | 01 05 | 12 34 |
| 43 | 13 20 | 04 02 | 23 00 | 00 32 | 12 29 |
| 44 | 13 10 | 03 36 | 22 13 | 29♑58 | 12 23 |
| 45 | 13 00 | 03 10 | 21 25 | 29 23 | 12 17 |
| 46 | 12 49 | 02 42 | 20 36 | 28 45 | 12 11 |
| 47 | 12 38 | 02 14 | 19 45 | 28 06 | 12 04 |
| 48 | 12 26 | 01 44 | 18 53 | 27 24 | 11 57 |
| 49 | 12 14 | 01 14 | 17 58 | 26 40 | 11 50 |
| 50 | 12 02 | 00 43 | 17 02 | 25 53 | 11 42 |
| 51 | 11 49 | 00 10 | 16 04 | 25 03 | 11 34 |
| 52 | 11 36 | 29♏37 | 15 04 | 24 10 | 11 25 |
| 53 | 11 22 | 29 02 | 14 02 | 23 13 | 11 16 |
| 54 | 11 07 | 28 25 | 12 57 | 22 11 | 11 06 |
| 55 | 10 52 | 27 48 | 11 50 | 21 05 | 10 56 |
| 56 | 10 37 | 27 09 | 10 41 | 19 52 | 10 44 |
| 57 | 10 20 | 26 28 | 09 29 | 18 34 | 10 32 |
| 58 | 10 03 | 25 45 | 08 14 | 17 08 | 10 19 |
| 59 | 09 45 | 25 00 | 06 56 | 15 33 | 10 05 |
| 60 | 09♏26 | 24♏14 | 05♐35 | 13♑48 | 09♓50 |

**13h 8m 0s — 197° 0' 0" — 18 ♎ 26**

| LAT. | 11 | 12 | ASC | 2 | 3 |
|---|---|---|---|---|---|
| 0 | 19♏27 | 18♐02 | 15♑40 | 14♒32 | 15♓53 |
| 5 | 18 56 | 16 44 | 13 43 | 13 32 | 15 42 |
| 10 | 18 25 | 15 26 | 11 42 | 12 28 | 15 31 |
| 15 | 17 53 | 14 06 | 09 36 | 11 20 | 15 19 |
| 20 | 17 20 | 12 43 | 07 21 | 10 06 | 15 06 |
| 21 | 17 13 | 12 26 | 06 53 | 09 50 | 15 04 |
| 22 | 17 07 | 12 09 | 06 25 | 09 34 | 15 01 |
| 23 | 17 00 | 11 51 | 05 56 | 09 18 | 14 58 |
| 24 | 16 53 | 11 34 | 05 26 | 09 01 | 14 55 |
| 25 | 16 46 | 11 16 | 04 57 | 08 44 | 14 52 |
| 26 | 16 39 | 10 58 | 04 26 | 08 26 | 14 49 |
| 27 | 16 31 | 10 39 | 03 55 | 08 08 | 14 46 |
| 28 | 16 24 | 10 21 | 03 24 | 07 50 | 14 43 |
| 29 | 16 16 | 10 02 | 02 51 | 07 30 | 14 40 |
| 30 | 16 09 | 09 42 | 02 18 | 07 11 | 14 37 |
| 31 | 16 01 | 09 23 | 01 45 | 06 51 | 14 33 |
| 32 | 15 53 | 09 03 | 01 10 | 06 30 | 14 30 |
| 33 | 15 45 | 08 42 | 00 35 | 06 08 | 14 26 |
| 34 | 15 37 | 08 22 | 29♐59 | 05 46 | 14 23 |
| 35 | 15 29 | 08 01 | 29 23 | 05 22 | 14 19 |
| 36 | 15 20 | 07 39 | 28 45 | 04 59 | 14 15 |
| 37 | 15 12 | 07 17 | 28 06 | 04 34 | 14 11 |
| 38 | 15 03 | 06 54 | 27 27 | 04 08 | 14 07 |
| 39 | 14 54 | 06 31 | 26 46 | 03 41 | 14 02 |
| 40 | 14 44 | 06 07 | 26 04 | 03 13 | 13 58 |
| 41 | 14 35 | 05 43 | 25 22 | 02 44 | 13 53 |
| 42 | 14 25 | 05 18 | 24 37 | 02 13 | 13 48 |
| 43 | 14 15 | 04 53 | 23 52 | 01 41 | 13 43 |
| 44 | 14 05 | 04 26 | 23 05 | 01 07 | 13 38 |
| 45 | 13 54 | 03 59 | 22 17 | 00 32 | 13 32 |
| 46 | 13 43 | 03 31 | 21 27 | 29♑55 | 13 26 |
| 47 | 13 32 | 03 03 | 20 36 | 29 15 | 13 20 |
| 48 | 13 20 | 02 33 | 19 42 | 28 34 | 13 14 |
| 49 | 13 08 | 02 02 | 18 48 | 27 50 | 13 07 |
| 50 | 12 55 | 01 31 | 17 51 | 27 03 | 13 00 |
| 51 | 12 42 | 00 58 | 16 52 | 26 13 | 12 52 |
| 52 | 12 28 | 00 24 | 15 51 | 25 20 | 12 44 |
| 53 | 12 14 | 29♏48 | 14 48 | 24 23 | 12 35 |
| 54 | 12 00 | 29 12 | 13 43 | 23 21 | 12 26 |
| 55 | 11 44 | 28 33 | 12 35 | 22 15 | 12 16 |
| 56 | 11 28 | 27 54 | 11 25 | 21 03 | 12 06 |
| 57 | 11 11 | 27 12 | 10 11 | 19 44 | 11 54 |
| 58 | 10 54 | 26 29 | 08 56 | 18 18 | 11 42 |
| 59 | 10 35 | 25 44 | 07 37 | 16 43 | 11 29 |
| 60 | 10♏16 | 24♏56 | 06♐15 | 14♑57 | 11♓15 |

**13h 12m 0s — 198° 0' 0" — 19 ♎ 30**

| LAT. | 11 | 12 | ASC | 2 | 3 |
|---|---|---|---|---|---|
| 0 | 20♏26 | 18♐58 | 16♑36 | 15♒32 | 16♓57 |
| 5 | 19 55 | 17 40 | 14 39 | 14 33 | 16 47 |
| 10 | 19 23 | 16 21 | 12 39 | 13 30 | 16 37 |
| 15 | 18 51 | 15 01 | 10 32 | 12 23 | 16 26 |
| 20 | 18 18 | 13 37 | 08 18 | 11 10 | 16 14 |
| 21 | 18 11 | 13 20 | 07 50 | 10 55 | 16 12 |
| 22 | 18 04 | 13 03 | 07 21 | 10 39 | 16 09 |
| 23 | 17 57 | 12 45 | 06 52 | 10 23 | 16 07 |
| 24 | 17 50 | 12 27 | 06 23 | 10 06 | 16 04 |
| 25 | 17 43 | 12 09 | 05 53 | 09 49 | 16 02 |
| 26 | 17 35 | 11 51 | 05 22 | 09 32 | 15 59 |
| 27 | 17 28 | 11 33 | 04 51 | 09 14 | 15 56 |
| 28 | 17 21 | 11 14 | 04 20 | 08 55 | 15 53 |
| 29 | 17 13 | 10 55 | 03 47 | 08 36 | 15 50 |
| 30 | 17 05 | 10 35 | 03 14 | 08 17 | 15 47 |
| 31 | 16 58 | 10 16 | 02 40 | 07 57 | 15 44 |
| 32 | 16 50 | 09 55 | 02 06 | 07 36 | 15 41 |
| 33 | 16 41 | 09 35 | 01 31 | 07 15 | 15 37 |
| 34 | 16 33 | 09 14 | 00 55 | 06 53 | 15 34 |
| 35 | 16 25 | 08 53 | 00 18 | 06 30 | 15 31 |
| 36 | 16 16 | 08 31 | 29♐40 | 06 06 | 15 27 |
| 37 | 16 07 | 08 09 | 29 01 | 05 41 | 15 23 |
| 38 | 15 58 | 07 46 | 28 21 | 05 16 | 15 19 |
| 39 | 15 49 | 07 22 | 27 40 | 04 49 | 15 15 |
| 40 | 15 40 | 06 59 | 26 58 | 04 21 | 15 11 |
| 41 | 15 30 | 06 34 | 26 15 | 03 52 | 15 07 |
| 42 | 15 20 | 06 09 | 25 30 | 03 22 | 15 02 |
| 43 | 15 10 | 05 43 | 24 45 | 02 50 | 14 57 |
| 44 | 14 59 | 05 16 | 23 57 | 02 17 | 14 52 |
| 45 | 14 48 | 04 49 | 23 09 | 01 42 | 14 47 |
| 46 | 14 37 | 04 21 | 22 18 | 01 05 | 14 42 |
| 47 | 14 25 | 03 52 | 21 26 | 00 26 | 14 36 |
| 48 | 14 13 | 03 22 | 20 33 | 29♑44 | 14 30 |
| 49 | 14 01 | 02 51 | 19 37 | 29 01 | 14 24 |
| 50 | 13 48 | 02 19 | 18 40 | 28 14 | 14 17 |
| 51 | 13 35 | 01 45 | 17 40 | 27 24 | 14 10 |
| 52 | 13 21 | 01 11 | 16 39 | 26 31 | 14 03 |
| 53 | 13 07 | 00 35 | 15 35 | 25 34 | 13 55 |
| 54 | 12 52 | 29♏58 | 14 29 | 24 33 | 13 46 |
| 55 | 12 36 | 29 19 | 13 20 | 23 27 | 13 37 |
| 56 | 12 20 | 28 39 | 12 09 | 22 14 | 13 27 |
| 57 | 12 03 | 27 57 | 10 54 | 20 56 | 13 17 |
| 58 | 11 45 | 27 13 | 09 37 | 19 29 | 13 06 |
| 59 | 11 26 | 26 27 | 08 17 | 17 54 | 12 53 |
| 60 | 11♏06 | 25♏39 | 06♐54 | 16♑08 | 12♓40 |

**13h 16m 0s — 199° 0' 0" — 20 ♎ 34**

| LAT. | 11 | 12 | ASC | 2 | 3 |
|---|---|---|---|---|---|
| 0 | 21♏26 | 19♐53 | 17♑32 | 16♒33 | 18♓02 |
| 5 | 20 54 | 18 35 | 15 36 | 15 34 | 17 53 |
| 10 | 20 21 | 17 16 | 13 35 | 14 32 | 17 44 |
| 15 | 19 49 | 15 55 | 11 29 | 13 26 | 17 34 |
| 20 | 19 15 | 14 31 | 09 15 | 12 14 | 17 23 |
| 21 | 19 08 | 14 14 | 08 47 | 11 59 | 17 21 |
| 22 | 19 01 | 13 57 | 08 18 | 11 44 | 17 18 |
| 23 | 18 54 | 13 39 | 07 49 | 11 28 | 17 16 |
| 24 | 18 47 | 13 21 | 07 19 | 11 11 | 17 13 |
| 25 | 18 40 | 13 03 | 06 49 | 10 54 | 17 11 |
| 26 | 18 32 | 12 45 | 06 19 | 10 37 | 17 08 |
| 27 | 18 25 | 12 26 | 05 48 | 10 20 | 17 06 |
| 28 | 18 17 | 12 07 | 05 16 | 10 01 | 17 03 |
| 29 | 18 10 | 11 48 | 04 43 | 09 43 | 17 01 |
| 30 | 18 02 | 11 28 | 04 10 | 09 24 | 16 58 |
| 31 | 17 54 | 11 08 | 03 36 | 09 04 | 16 55 |
| 32 | 17 46 | 10 48 | 03 02 | 08 43 | 16 52 |
| 33 | 17 38 | 10 27 | 02 26 | 08 22 | 16 49 |
| 34 | 17 29 | 10 06 | 01 50 | 08 00 | 16 46 |
| 35 | 17 21 | 09 45 | 01 13 | 07 38 | 16 42 |
| 36 | 17 12 | 09 23 | 00 35 | 07 14 | 16 39 |
| 37 | 17 03 | 09 00 | 29♐56 | 06 50 | 16 36 |
| 38 | 16 54 | 08 37 | 29 16 | 06 24 | 16 32 |
| 39 | 16 44 | 08 14 | 28 35 | 05 58 | 16 28 |
| 40 | 16 35 | 07 50 | 27 52 | 05 30 | 16 24 |
| 41 | 16 25 | 07 25 | 27 09 | 05 02 | 16 20 |
| 42 | 16 15 | 07 00 | 26 24 | 04 31 | 16 16 |
| 43 | 16 04 | 06 33 | 25 37 | 04 00 | 16 12 |
| 44 | 15 53 | 06 07 | 24 50 | 03 27 | 16 07 |
| 45 | 15 42 | 05 39 | 24 01 | 02 52 | 16 03 |
| 46 | 15 31 | 05 10 | 23 10 | 02 15 | 15 58 |
| 47 | 15 19 | 04 41 | 22 17 | 01 37 | 15 52 |
| 48 | 15 07 | 04 11 | 21 23 | 00 55 | 15 47 |
| 49 | 14 54 | 03 39 | 20 27 | 00 12 | 15 41 |
| 50 | 14 41 | 03 07 | 19 29 | 29♑26 | 15 35 |
| 51 | 14 28 | 02 33 | 18 29 | 28 36 | 15 28 |
| 52 | 14 14 | 01 58 | 17 27 | 27 43 | 15 22 |
| 53 | 13 59 | 01 22 | 16 22 | 26 47 | 15 14 |
| 54 | 13 44 | 00 44 | 15 15 | 25 45 | 15 06 |
| 55 | 13 28 | 00 05 | 14 05 | 24 39 | 14 58 |
| 56 | 13 11 | 29♏24 | 12 53 | 23 27 | 14 49 |
| 57 | 12 54 | 28 41 | 11 38 | 22 08 | 14 40 |
| 58 | 12 35 | 27 57 | 10 20 | 20 42 | 14 29 |
| 59 | 12 16 | 27 10 | 08 58 | 19 06 | 14 18 |
| 60 | 11♏56 | 26♏21 | 07♐34 | 17♑20 | 14♓06 |

# Placidus Table of Houses for Latitudes 0° to 60° North

**13h 20m 0s — 200° 0' 0" — 21 ♎ 38**

| LAT. | 11 | 12 | ASC | 2 | 3 |
|---|---|---|---|---|---|
| 0 | 22♏25 | 20♐49 | 18♑28 | 17♒33 | 19♓07 |
| 5 | 21 52 | 19 30 | 16 32 | 16 36 | 18 59 |
| 10 | 21 20 | 18 11 | 14 32 | 15 35 | 18 50 |
| 15 | 20 47 | 16 50 | 12 26 | 14 30 | 18 41 |
| 20 | 20 12 | 15 26 | 10 12 | 13 19 | 18 31 |
| 21 | 20 05 | 15 08 | 09 44 | 13 04 | 18 29 |
| 22 | 19 58 | 14 51 | 09 15 | 12 49 | 18 27 |
| 23 | 19 51 | 14 33 | 08 46 | 12 33 | 18 25 |
| 24 | 19 44 | 14 15 | 08 16 | 12 17 | 18 23 |
| 25 | 19 36 | 13 57 | 07 46 | 12 00 | 18 21 |
| 26 | 19 29 | 13 38 | 07 16 | 11 43 | 18 18 |
| 27 | 19 21 | 13 19 | 06 44 | 11 26 | 18 16 |
| 28 | 19 14 | 13 00 | 06 13 | 11 08 | 18 13 |
| 29 | 19 06 | 12 41 | 05 40 | 10 50 | 18 11 |
| 30 | 18 58 | 12 21 | 05 07 | 10 31 | 18 08 |
| 31 | 18 50 | 12 01 | 04 33 | 10 11 | 18 06 |
| 32 | 18 42 | 11 41 | 03 58 | 09 51 | 18 03 |
| 33 | 18 33 | 11 20 | 03 22 | 09 30 | 18 00 |
| 34 | 18 25 | 10 59 | 02 46 | 09 08 | 17 57 |
| 35 | 18 16 | 10 37 | 02 09 | 08 46 | 17 55 |
| 36 | 18 07 | 10 15 | 01 30 | 08 23 | 17 51 |
| 37 | 17 58 | 09 52 | 00 51 | 07 58 | 17 48 |
| 38 | 17 49 | 09 29 | 00 11 | 07 33 | 17 45 |
| 39 | 17 39 | 09 05 | 29♐29 | 07 07 | 17 42 |
| 40 | 17 30 | 08 41 | 28 47 | 06 40 | 17 38 |
| 41 | 17 20 | 08 16 | 28 03 | 06 11 | 17 34 |
| 42 | 17 09 | 07 50 | 27 17 | 05 42 | 17 31 |
| 43 | 16 59 | 07 24 | 26 31 | 05 10 | 17 27 |
| 44 | 16 48 | 06 57 | 25 43 | 04 38 | 17 23 |
| 45 | 16 36 | 06 29 | 24 53 | 04 03 | 17 18 |
| 46 | 16 25 | 06 00 | 24 02 | 03 27 | 17 14 |
| 47 | 16 13 | 05 30 | 23 09 | 02 48 | 17 09 |
| 48 | 16 01 | 05 00 | 22 14 | 02 07 | 17 04 |
| 49 | 15 48 | 04 28 | 21 18 | 01 24 | 16 59 |
| 50 | 15 34 | 03 55 | 20 19 | 00 38 | 16 53 |
| 51 | 15 21 | 03 21 | 19 18 | 29♑49 | 16 47 |
| 52 | 15 06 | 02 45 | 18 15 | 28 56 | 16 41 |
| 53 | 14 51 | 02 09 | 17 09 | 28 00 | 16 34 |
| 54 | 14 36 | 01 31 | 16 02 | 26 59 | 16 27 |
| 55 | 14 19 | 00 51 | 14 51 | 25 53 | 16 19 |
| 56 | 14 02 | 00 09 | 13 38 | 24 41 | 16 11 |
| 57 | 13 45 | 29♏26 | 12 21 | 23 22 | 16 02 |
| 58 | 13 26 | 28 41 | 11 02 | 21 56 | 15 53 |
| 59 | 13 06 | 27 53 | 09 39 | 20 20 | 15 43 |
| 60 | 12♏46 | 27♏04 | 08♐14 | 18♑33 | 15♓32 |

**13h 24m 0s — 201° 0' 0" — 22 ♎ 42**

| LAT. | 11 | 12 | ASC | 2 | 3 |
|---|---|---|---|---|---|
| 0 | 23♏23 | 21♐44 | 19♑24 | 18♒34 | 20♓12 |
| 5 | 22 51 | 20 25 | 17 29 | 17 37 | 20 05 |
| 10 | 22 18 | 19 06 | 15 29 | 16 38 | 19 57 |
| 15 | 21 44 | 17 44 | 13 23 | 15 34 | 19 49 |
| 20 | 21 10 | 16 20 | 11 09 | 14 24 | 19 40 |
| 21 | 21 02 | 16 02 | 10 41 | 14 09 | 19 38 |
| 22 | 20 55 | 15 45 | 10 12 | 13 54 | 19 36 |
| 23 | 20 48 | 15 27 | 09 43 | 13 39 | 19 34 |
| 24 | 20 41 | 15 09 | 09 14 | 13 23 | 19 32 |
| 25 | 20 33 | 14 50 | 08 43 | 13 06 | 19 30 |
| 26 | 20 26 | 14 32 | 08 13 | 12 50 | 19 28 |
| 27 | 20 18 | 14 13 | 07 41 | 12 33 | 19 26 |
| 28 | 20 10 | 13 54 | 07 09 | 12 15 | 19 24 |
| 29 | 20 02 | 13 34 | 06 37 | 11 57 | 19 22 |
| 30 | 19 54 | 13 14 | 06 03 | 11 38 | 19 19 |
| 31 | 19 46 | 12 54 | 05 29 | 11 19 | 19 17 |
| 32 | 19 38 | 12 34 | 04 54 | 10 59 | 19 14 |
| 33 | 19 29 | 12 13 | 04 19 | 10 38 | 19 12 |
| 34 | 19 21 | 11 51 | 03 42 | 10 17 | 19 09 |
| 35 | 19 12 | 11 29 | 03 05 | 09 55 | 19 07 |
| 36 | 19 03 | 11 07 | 02 26 | 09 32 | 19 04 |
| 37 | 18 53 | 10 44 | 01 47 | 09 08 | 19 01 |
| 38 | 18 44 | 10 21 | 01 06 | 08 43 | 18 58 |
| 39 | 18 34 | 09 57 | 00 24 | 08 17 | 18 55 |
| 40 | 18 24 | 09 32 | 29♐41 | 07 50 | 18 52 |
| 41 | 18 14 | 09 07 | 28 57 | 07 22 | 18 49 |
| 42 | 18 04 | 08 41 | 28 12 | 06 52 | 18 45 |
| 43 | 17 53 | 08 14 | 27 25 | 06 21 | 18 42 |
| 44 | 17 42 | 07 47 | 26 36 | 05 49 | 18 38 |
| 45 | 17 30 | 07 19 | 25 46 | 05 15 | 18 34 |
| 46 | 17 19 | 06 50 | 24 54 | 04 39 | 18 30 |
| 47 | 17 07 | 06 20 | 24 01 | 04 00 | 18 25 |
| 48 | 16 54 | 05 49 | 23 06 | 03 20 | 18 21 |
| 49 | 16 41 | 05 16 | 22 08 | 02 37 | 18 16 |
| 50 | 16 27 | 04 43 | 21 09 | 01 51 | 18 11 |
| 51 | 16 13 | 04 09 | 20 07 | 01 02 | 18 06 |
| 52 | 15 59 | 03 33 | 19 03 | 00 10 | 18 00 |
| 53 | 15 43 | 02 56 | 17 57 | 29♑14 | 17 54 |
| 54 | 15 28 | 02 17 | 16 48 | 28 13 | 17 48 |
| 55 | 15 11 | 01 37 | 15 37 | 27 07 | 17 41 |
| 56 | 14 54 | 00 55 | 14 22 | 25 56 | 17 33 |
| 57 | 14 36 | 00 11 | 13 05 | 24 37 | 17 26 |
| 58 | 14 16 | 29♏25 | 11 45 | 23 11 | 17 17 |
| 59 | 13 56 | 28 37 | 10 21 | 21 35 | 17 08 |
| 60 | 13♏35 | 27♏46 | 08♐54 | 19♑48 | 16♓58 |

**13h 28m 0s — 202° 0' 0" — 23 ♎ 46**

| LAT. | 11 | 12 | ASC | 2 | 3 |
|---|---|---|---|---|---|
| 0 | 24♏22 | 22♐39 | 20♑20 | 19♒35 | 21♓17 |
| 5 | 23 49 | 21 20 | 18 25 | 18 39 | 21 11 |
| 10 | 23 16 | 20 00 | 16 26 | 17 41 | 21 04 |
| 15 | 22 42 | 18 39 | 14 21 | 16 38 | 20 57 |
| 20 | 22 07 | 17 14 | 12 06 | 15 29 | 20 49 |
| 21 | 21 59 | 16 56 | 11 38 | 15 15 | 20 47 |
| 22 | 21 52 | 16 39 | 11 10 | 15 00 | 20 45 |
| 23 | 21 45 | 16 21 | 10 41 | 14 45 | 20 43 |
| 24 | 21 37 | 16 02 | 10 11 | 14 29 | 20 42 |
| 25 | 21 30 | 15 44 | 09 41 | 14 13 | 20 40 |
| 26 | 21 22 | 15 25 | 09 10 | 13 56 | 20 38 |
| 27 | 21 14 | 15 06 | 08 39 | 13 40 | 20 36 |
| 28 | 21 06 | 14 47 | 08 07 | 13 22 | 20 34 |
| 29 | 20 58 | 14 27 | 07 34 | 13 04 | 20 32 |
| 30 | 20 50 | 14 07 | 07 00 | 12 46 | 20 30 |
| 31 | 20 42 | 13 47 | 06 26 | 12 27 | 20 28 |
| 32 | 20 34 | 13 26 | 05 51 | 12 07 | 20 26 |
| 33 | 20 25 | 13 05 | 05 15 | 11 47 | 20 24 |
| 34 | 20 16 | 12 44 | 04 39 | 11 26 | 20 21 |
| 35 | 20 07 | 12 22 | 04 01 | 11 04 | 20 19 |
| 36 | 19 58 | 11 59 | 03 22 | 10 41 | 20 17 |
| 37 | 19 49 | 11 36 | 02 42 | 10 18 | 20 14 |
| 38 | 19 39 | 11 13 | 02 02 | 09 53 | 20 11 |
| 39 | 19 29 | 10 48 | 01 20 | 09 27 | 20 09 |
| 40 | 19 19 | 10 24 | 00 36 | 09 01 | 20 06 |
| 41 | 19 09 | 09 58 | 29♐52 | 08 33 | 20 03 |
| 42 | 18 58 | 09 32 | 29 06 | 08 04 | 20 00 |
| 43 | 18 47 | 09 05 | 28 19 | 07 33 | 19 57 |
| 44 | 18 36 | 08 37 | 27 30 | 07 01 | 19 53 |
| 45 | 18 24 | 08 09 | 26 39 | 06 27 | 19 50 |
| 46 | 18 12 | 07 40 | 25 47 | 05 51 | 19 46 |
| 47 | 18 00 | 07 09 | 24 53 | 05 13 | 19 42 |
| 48 | 17 47 | 06 38 | 23 57 | 04 33 | 19 38 |
| 49 | 17 34 | 06 05 | 22 59 | 03 51 | 19 34 |
| 50 | 17 20 | 05 32 | 21 59 | 03 05 | 19 29 |
| 51 | 17 06 | 04 57 | 20 57 | 02 17 | 19 25 |
| 52 | 16 51 | 04 20 | 19 52 | 01 25 | 19 20 |
| 53 | 16 36 | 03 43 | 18 45 | 00 29 | 19 14 |
| 54 | 16 19 | 03 04 | 17 36 | 29♑29 | 19 09 |
| 55 | 16 03 | 02 23 | 16 23 | 28 23 | 19 02 |
| 56 | 15 45 | 01 40 | 15 08 | 27 12 | 18 56 |
| 57 | 15 26 | 00 55 | 13 49 | 25 53 | 18 49 |
| 58 | 15 07 | 00 09 | 12 28 | 24 27 | 18 41 |
| 59 | 14 47 | 29♏20 | 11 02 | 22 51 | 18 33 |
| 60 | 14♏25 | 28♏29 | 09♐34 | 21♑04 | 18♓24 |

**13h 32m 0s — 203° 0' 0" — 24 ♎ 50**

| LAT. | 11 | 12 | ASC | 2 | 3 |
|---|---|---|---|---|---|
| 0 | 25♏21 | 23♐34 | 21♑17 | 20♒36 | 22♓23 |
| 5 | 24 47 | 22 15 | 19 22 | 19 42 | 22 17 |
| 10 | 24 13 | 20 55 | 17 23 | 18 44 | 22 11 |
| 15 | 23 39 | 19 33 | 15 18 | 17 43 | 22 04 |
| 20 | 23 04 | 18 08 | 13 04 | 16 35 | 21 57 |
| 21 | 22 56 | 17 50 | 12 36 | 16 21 | 21 56 |
| 22 | 22 49 | 17 33 | 12 07 | 16 06 | 21 54 |
| 23 | 22 41 | 17 15 | 11 38 | 15 51 | 21 53 |
| 24 | 22 34 | 16 56 | 11 09 | 15 36 | 21 51 |
| 25 | 22 26 | 16 38 | 10 38 | 15 20 | 21 50 |
| 26 | 22 19 | 16 19 | 10 08 | 15 04 | 21 48 |
| 27 | 22 11 | 16 00 | 09 36 | 14 47 | 21 46 |
| 28 | 22 03 | 15 40 | 09 04 | 14 30 | 21 45 |
| 29 | 21 55 | 15 21 | 08 31 | 14 12 | 21 43 |
| 30 | 21 46 | 15 01 | 07 58 | 13 54 | 21 41 |
| 31 | 21 38 | 14 40 | 07 23 | 13 35 | 21 39 |
| 32 | 21 29 | 14 19 | 06 48 | 13 16 | 21 37 |
| 33 | 21 21 | 13 58 | 06 12 | 12 56 | 21 35 |
| 34 | 21 12 | 13 36 | 05 35 | 12 35 | 21 33 |
| 35 | 21 03 | 13 14 | 04 58 | 12 13 | 21 31 |
| 36 | 20 53 | 12 51 | 04 19 | 11 51 | 21 29 |
| 37 | 20 44 | 12 28 | 03 39 | 11 28 | 21 27 |
| 38 | 20 34 | 12 04 | 02 58 | 11 04 | 21 25 |
| 39 | 20 24 | 11 40 | 02 15 | 10 38 | 21 22 |
| 40 | 20 14 | 11 15 | 01 32 | 10 12 | 21 20 |
| 41 | 20 03 | 10 49 | 00 47 | 09 45 | 21 17 |
| 42 | 19 53 | 10 23 | 00 01 | 09 16 | 21 15 |
| 43 | 19 42 | 09 56 | 29♐13 | 08 45 | 21 12 |
| 44 | 19 30 | 09 28 | 28 24 | 08 14 | 21 09 |
| 45 | 19 18 | 08 59 | 27 33 | 07 40 | 21 06 |
| 46 | 19 06 | 08 29 | 26 40 | 07 05 | 21 03 |
| 47 | 18 54 | 07 59 | 25 46 | 06 27 | 20 59 |
| 48 | 18 41 | 07 27 | 24 49 | 05 48 | 20 56 |
| 49 | 18 27 | 06 54 | 23 51 | 05 05 | 20 52 |
| 50 | 18 13 | 06 20 | 22 50 | 04 20 | 20 48 |
| 51 | 17 59 | 05 45 | 21 47 | 03 32 | 20 44 |
| 52 | 17 43 | 05 08 | 20 42 | 02 41 | 20 39 |
| 53 | 17 28 | 04 30 | 19 34 | 01 45 | 20 35 |
| 54 | 17 11 | 03 50 | 18 23 | 00 45 | 20 30 |
| 55 | 16 54 | 03 09 | 17 10 | 29♑40 | 20 24 |
| 56 | 16 36 | 02 26 | 15 53 | 28 29 | 20 19 |
| 57 | 16 17 | 01 40 | 14 34 | 27 11 | 20 12 |
| 58 | 15 57 | 00 53 | 13 11 | 25 45 | 20 06 |
| 59 | 15 37 | 00 04 | 11 44 | 24 09 | 19 59 |
| 60 | 15♏15 | 29♏11 | 10♐14 | 22♑22 | 19♓51 |

**13h 36m 0s — 204° 0' 0" — 25 ♎ 53**

| LAT. | 11 | 12 | ASC | 2 | 3 |
|---|---|---|---|---|---|
| 0 | 26♏19 | 24♐30 | 22♑13 | 21♒37 | 23♓28 |
| 5 | 25 45 | 23 10 | 20 19 | 20 44 | 23 23 |
| 10 | 25 11 | 21 50 | 18 21 | 19 48 | 23 18 |
| 15 | 24 36 | 20 28 | 16 16 | 18 47 | 23 12 |
| 20 | 24 00 | 19 02 | 14 02 | 17 41 | 23 06 |
| 21 | 23 53 | 18 45 | 13 34 | 17 27 | 23 05 |
| 22 | 23 46 | 18 27 | 13 05 | 17 12 | 23 04 |
| 23 | 23 38 | 18 08 | 12 36 | 16 58 | 23 02 |
| 24 | 23 30 | 17 50 | 12 07 | 16 43 | 23 01 |
| 25 | 23 23 | 17 31 | 11 36 | 16 27 | 23 00 |
| 26 | 23 15 | 17 13 | 11 06 | 16 11 | 22 58 |
| 27 | 23 07 | 16 53 | 10 34 | 15 55 | 22 57 |
| 28 | 22 59 | 16 34 | 10 02 | 15 38 | 22 55 |
| 29 | 22 50 | 16 14 | 09 29 | 15 20 | 22 54 |
| 30 | 22 42 | 15 54 | 08 55 | 15 03 | 22 52 |
| 31 | 22 34 | 15 33 | 08 21 | 14 44 | 22 51 |
| 32 | 22 25 | 15 12 | 07 46 | 14 25 | 22 49 |
| 33 | 22 16 | 14 51 | 07 10 | 14 05 | 22 47 |
| 34 | 22 07 | 14 29 | 06 33 | 13 45 | 22 46 |
| 35 | 21 58 | 14 07 | 05 55 | 13 24 | 22 44 |
| 36 | 21 48 | 13 44 | 05 16 | 13 02 | 22 42 |
| 37 | 21 39 | 13 20 | 04 35 | 12 39 | 22 40 |
| 38 | 21 29 | 12 56 | 03 54 | 12 15 | 22 38 |
| 39 | 21 19 | 12 32 | 03 12 | 11 50 | 22 36 |
| 40 | 21 09 | 12 07 | 02 28 | 11 24 | 22 34 |
| 41 | 20 58 | 11 41 | 01 43 | 10 57 | 22 32 |
| 42 | 20 47 | 11 14 | 00 56 | 10 28 | 22 29 |
| 43 | 20 36 | 10 47 | 00 08 | 09 58 | 22 27 |
| 44 | 20 24 | 10 19 | 29♐18 | 09 27 | 22 25 |
| 45 | 20 12 | 09 49 | 28 27 | 08 54 | 22 22 |
| 46 | 20 00 | 09 19 | 27 34 | 08 19 | 22 19 |
| 47 | 19 47 | 08 48 | 26 39 | 07 42 | 22 16 |
| 48 | 19 34 | 08 16 | 25 42 | 07 03 | 22 13 |
| 49 | 19 20 | 07 43 | 24 43 | 06 21 | 22 10 |
| 50 | 19 06 | 07 09 | 23 41 | 05 36 | 22 07 |
| 51 | 18 51 | 06 33 | 22 38 | 04 49 | 22 03 |
| 52 | 18 36 | 05 56 | 21 32 | 03 57 | 21 59 |
| 53 | 18 20 | 05 17 | 20 23 | 03 02 | 21 55 |
| 54 | 18 03 | 04 37 | 19 11 | 02 03 | 21 51 |
| 55 | 17 46 | 03 55 | 17 57 | 00 58 | 21 46 |
| 56 | 17 27 | 03 11 | 16 39 | 29♑47 | 21 41 |
| 57 | 17 08 | 02 25 | 15 18 | 28 30 | 21 36 |
| 58 | 16 48 | 01 37 | 13 54 | 27 04 | 21 30 |
| 59 | 16 27 | 00 47 | 12 27 | 25 29 | 21 24 |
| 60 | 16♏04 | 29♏54 | 10♐55 | 23♑41 | 21♓17 |

**13h 40m 0s — 205° 0' 0" — 26 ♎ 57**

| LAT. | 11 | 12 | ASC | 2 | 3 |
|---|---|---|---|---|---|
| 0 | 27♏17 | 25♐25 | 23♑10 | 22♒39 | 24♓33 |
| 5 | 26 43 | 24 05 | 21 17 | 21 47 | 24 29 |
| 10 | 26 08 | 22 45 | 19 19 | 20 52 | 24 25 |
| 15 | 25 33 | 21 22 | 17 14 | 19 52 | 24 20 |
| 20 | 24 57 | 19 56 | 15 00 | 18 47 | 24 15 |
| 21 | 24 50 | 19 39 | 14 32 | 18 33 | 24 14 |
| 22 | 24 42 | 19 21 | 14 04 | 18 19 | 24 13 |
| 23 | 24 34 | 19 02 | 13 34 | 18 05 | 24 12 |
| 24 | 24 27 | 18 44 | 13 05 | 17 50 | 24 11 |
| 25 | 24 19 | 18 25 | 12 35 | 17 35 | 24 10 |
| 26 | 24 11 | 18 06 | 12 04 | 17 19 | 24 08 |
| 27 | 24 03 | 17 47 | 11 32 | 17 03 | 24 07 |
| 28 | 23 55 | 17 27 | 11 00 | 16 46 | 24 06 |
| 29 | 23 46 | 17 07 | 10 27 | 16 29 | 24 05 |
| 30 | 23 38 | 16 47 | 09 53 | 16 12 | 24 03 |
| 31 | 23 29 | 16 26 | 09 19 | 15 53 | 24 02 |
| 32 | 23 21 | 16 05 | 08 44 | 15 35 | 24 01 |
| 33 | 23 12 | 15 44 | 08 07 | 15 15 | 23 59 |
| 34 | 23 02 | 15 22 | 07 30 | 14 55 | 23 58 |
| 35 | 22 53 | 14 59 | 06 52 | 14 34 | 23 56 |
| 36 | 22 44 | 14 36 | 06 13 | 14 13 | 23 55 |
| 37 | 22 34 | 14 13 | 05 32 | 13 50 | 23 53 |
| 38 | 22 24 | 13 48 | 04 51 | 13 26 | 23 52 |
| 39 | 22 14 | 13 24 | 04 08 | 13 02 | 23 50 |
| 40 | 22 03 | 12 58 | 03 24 | 12 36 | 23 48 |
| 41 | 21 52 | 12 32 | 02 39 | 12 10 | 23 46 |
| 42 | 21 41 | 12 05 | 01 52 | 11 41 | 23 44 |
| 43 | 21 30 | 11 38 | 01 03 | 11 12 | 23 42 |
| 44 | 21 18 | 11 09 | 00 13 | 10 41 | 23 40 |
| 45 | 21 06 | 10 40 | 29♐21 | 10 08 | 23 38 |
| 46 | 20 53 | 10 10 | 28 28 | 09 34 | 23 36 |
| 47 | 20 40 | 09 38 | 27 32 | 08 57 | 23 33 |
| 48 | 20 27 | 09 06 | 26 35 | 08 18 | 23 31 |
| 49 | 20 13 | 08 32 | 25 35 | 07 37 | 23 28 |
| 50 | 19 59 | 07 57 | 24 33 | 06 53 | 23 25 |
| 51 | 19 44 | 07 21 | 23 29 | 06 06 | 23 22 |
| 52 | 19 28 | 06 44 | 22 22 | 05 15 | 23 19 |
| 53 | 19 12 | 06 05 | 21 12 | 04 20 | 23 16 |
| 54 | 18 55 | 05 24 | 20 00 | 03 21 | 23 12 |
| 55 | 18 37 | 04 41 | 18 44 | 02 17 | 23 08 |
| 56 | 18 18 | 03 57 | 17 26 | 01 07 | 23 04 |
| 57 | 17 59 | 03 11 | 16 04 | 29♑50 | 23 00 |
| 58 | 17 38 | 02 22 | 14 38 | 28 24 | 22 55 |
| 59 | 17 16 | 01 31 | 13 09 | 26 49 | 22 50 |
| 60 | 16♏54 | 00♐37 | 11♐36 | 25♑03 | 22♓44 |

**13h 44m 0s — 206° 0' 0" — 28 ♎ 00**

| LAT. | 11 | 12 | ASC | 2 | 3 |
|---|---|---|---|---|---|
| 0 | 28♏15 | 26♐20 | 24♑06 | 23♒41 | 25♓38 |
| 5 | 27 40 | 25 00 | 22 14 | 22 50 | 25 35 |
| 10 | 27 06 | 23 40 | 20 16 | 21 56 | 25 32 |
| 15 | 26 30 | 22 17 | 18 12 | 20 57 | 25 28 |
| 20 | 25 54 | 20 51 | 15 59 | 19 54 | 25 24 |
| 21 | 25 46 | 20 33 | 15 31 | 19 40 | 25 23 |
| 22 | 25 39 | 20 15 | 15 02 | 19 26 | 25 22 |
| 23 | 25 31 | 19 57 | 14 33 | 19 12 | 25 21 |
| 24 | 25 23 | 19 38 | 14 03 | 18 57 | 25 21 |
| 25 | 25 15 | 19 19 | 13 33 | 18 43 | 25 20 |
| 26 | 25 07 | 19 00 | 13 02 | 18 27 | 25 19 |
| 27 | 24 59 | 18 41 | 12 31 | 18 11 | 25 18 |
| 28 | 24 51 | 18 21 | 11 58 | 17 55 | 25 17 |
| 29 | 24 42 | 18 01 | 11 25 | 17 38 | 25 16 |
| 30 | 24 34 | 17 40 | 10 52 | 17 21 | 25 15 |
| 31 | 24 25 | 17 20 | 10 17 | 17 03 | 25 14 |
| 32 | 24 16 | 16 58 | 09 42 | 16 45 | 25 13 |
| 33 | 24 07 | 16 37 | 09 05 | 16 26 | 25 11 |
| 34 | 23 58 | 16 14 | 08 28 | 16 06 | 25 10 |
| 35 | 23 48 | 15 52 | 07 50 | 15 45 | 25 09 |
| 36 | 23 39 | 15 29 | 07 10 | 15 24 | 25 08 |
| 37 | 23 29 | 15 05 | 06 30 | 15 02 | 25 07 |
| 38 | 23 19 | 14 41 | 05 48 | 14 39 | 25 05 |
| 39 | 23 08 | 14 16 | 05 05 | 14 15 | 25 04 |
| 40 | 22 58 | 13 50 | 04 21 | 13 49 | 25 02 |
| 41 | 22 47 | 13 24 | 03 35 | 13 23 | 25 01 |
| 42 | 22 35 | 12 57 | 02 48 | 12 55 | 24 59 |
| 43 | 22 24 | 12 29 | 01 59 | 12 26 | 24 58 |
| 44 | 22 12 | 12 00 | 01 09 | 11 56 | 24 56 |
| 45 | 22 00 | 11 30 | 00 16 | 11 23 | 24 54 |
| 46 | 21 47 | 11 00 | 29♐22 | 10 49 | 24 53 |
| 47 | 21 34 | 10 28 | 28 26 | 10 13 | 24 51 |
| 48 | 21 20 | 09 55 | 27 28 | 09 35 | 24 49 |
| 49 | 21 06 | 09 22 | 26 28 | 08 54 | 24 46 |
| 50 | 20 51 | 08 46 | 25 25 | 08 10 | 24 44 |
| 51 | 20 36 | 08 10 | 24 20 | 07 24 | 24 42 |
| 52 | 20 20 | 07 32 | 23 12 | 06 34 | 24 39 |
| 53 | 20 04 | 06 52 | 22 02 | 05 40 | 24 37 |
| 54 | 19 46 | 06 11 | 20 48 | 04 41 | 24 34 |
| 55 | 19 28 | 05 28 | 19 32 | 03 37 | 24 31 |
| 56 | 19 09 | 04 43 | 18 12 | 02 28 | 24 27 |
| 57 | 18 49 | 03 56 | 16 49 | 01 11 | 24 24 |
| 58 | 18 28 | 03 06 | 15 22 | 29♑46 | 24 20 |
| 59 | 18 06 | 02 15 | 13 52 | 28 12 | 24 16 |
| 60 | 17♏43 | 01♐20 | 12♐18 | 26♑25 | 24♓11 |

**13h 48m 0s — 207° 0' 0" — 29 ♎ 03**

| LAT. | 11 | 12 | ASC | 2 | 3 |
|---|---|---|---|---|---|
| 0 | 29♏13 | 27♐15 | 25♑03 | 24♒42 | 26♓44 |
| 5 | 28 38 | 25 55 | 23 11 | 23 53 | 26 41 |
| 10 | 28 03 | 24 35 | 21 15 | 23 00 | 26 39 |
| 15 | 27 27 | 23 12 | 19 11 | 22 03 | 26 36 |
| 20 | 26 50 | 21 45 | 16 57 | 21 01 | 26 33 |
| 21 | 26 43 | 21 27 | 16 29 | 20 47 | 26 32 |
| 22 | 26 35 | 21 09 | 16 01 | 20 34 | 26 32 |
| 23 | 26 27 | 20 51 | 15 32 | 20 20 | 26 31 |
| 24 | 26 19 | 20 32 | 15 02 | 20 05 | 26 30 |
| 25 | 26 11 | 20 13 | 14 32 | 19 51 | 26 30 |
| 26 | 26 03 | 19 54 | 14 01 | 19 36 | 26 29 |
| 27 | 25 55 | 19 34 | 13 30 | 19 20 | 26 28 |
| 28 | 25 46 | 19 15 | 12 57 | 19 04 | 26 28 |
| 29 | 25 38 | 18 54 | 12 24 | 18 48 | 26 27 |
| 30 | 25 29 | 18 34 | 11 50 | 18 31 | 26 26 |
| 31 | 25 20 | 18 13 | 11 16 | 18 13 | 26 25 |
| 32 | 25 11 | 17 51 | 10 40 | 17 55 | 26 24 |
| 33 | 25 02 | 17 30 | 10 04 | 17 37 | 26 24 |
| 34 | 24 53 | 17 07 | 09 26 | 17 17 | 26 23 |
| 35 | 24 43 | 16 45 | 08 48 | 16 57 | 26 22 |
| 36 | 24 33 | 16 21 | 08 08 | 16 36 | 26 21 |
| 37 | 24 23 | 15 57 | 07 28 | 16 14 | 26 20 |
| 38 | 24 13 | 15 33 | 06 46 | 15 51 | 26 19 |
| 39 | 24 03 | 15 08 | 06 03 | 15 28 | 26 18 |
| 40 | 23 52 | 14 42 | 05 18 | 15 03 | 26 17 |
| 41 | 23 41 | 14 15 | 04 32 | 14 37 | 26 16 |
| 42 | 23 29 | 13 48 | 03 44 | 14 10 | 26 15 |
| 43 | 23 18 | 13 20 | 02 55 | 13 41 | 26 13 |
| 44 | 23 06 | 12 51 | 02 04 | 13 11 | 26 12 |
| 45 | 22 53 | 12 21 | 01 12 | 12 39 | 26 11 |
| 46 | 22 40 | 11 50 | 00 17 | 12 06 | 26 09 |
| 47 | 22 27 | 11 18 | 29♐21 | 11 30 | 26 08 |
| 48 | 22 13 | 10 45 | 28 22 | 10 52 | 26 06 |
| 49 | 21 59 | 10 11 | 27 21 | 10 12 | 26 05 |
| 50 | 21 44 | 09 35 | 26 18 | 09 29 | 26 03 |
| 51 | 21 28 | 08 58 | 25 12 | 08 43 | 26 01 |
| 52 | 21 12 | 08 20 | 24 03 | 07 53 | 25 59 |
| 53 | 20 55 | 07 40 | 22 52 | 07 00 | 25 57 |
| 54 | 20 38 | 06 58 | 21 38 | 06 02 | 25 55 |
| 55 | 20 20 | 06 15 | 20 20 | 04 59 | 25 53 |
| 56 | 20 00 | 05 29 | 18 59 | 03 50 | 25 50 |
| 57 | 19 40 | 04 41 | 17 35 | 02 34 | 25 48 |
| 58 | 19 19 | 03 51 | 16 07 | 01 10 | 25 45 |
| 59 | 18 56 | 02 58 | 14 35 | 29♑36 | 25 42 |
| 60 | 18♏32 | 02♐03 | 12♐59 | 27♑50 | 25♓38 |

# Placidus Table of Houses for Latitudes 0° to 60° North

**13h 52m 0s — 208° 0' 0" — 00 ♏ 06**

| LAT. | 11 | 12 | ASC | 2 | 3 |
|---|---|---|---|---|---|
| 0 | 00♐11 | 28♐10 | 26♑00 | 25♒44 | 27♓49 |
| 5 | 29♏35 | 26 50 | 24 09 | 24 56 | 27 48 |
| 10 | 29 00 | 25 29 | 22 13 | 24 04 | 27 46 |
| 15 | 28 24 | 24 06 | 20 09 | 23 09 | 27 44 |
| 20 | 27 46 | 22 39 | 17 57 | 22 08 | 27 42 |
| 21 | 27 39 | 22 21 | 17 29 | 21 55 | 27 42 |
| 22 | 27 31 | 22 03 | 17 00 | 21 41 | 27 41 |
| 23 | 27 23 | 21 45 | 16 31 | 21 28 | 27 41 |
| 24 | 27 15 | 21 26 | 16 01 | 21 14 | 27 40 |
| 25 | 27 07 | 21 07 | 15 31 | 20 59 | 27 40 |
| 26 | 26 59 | 20 48 | 15 00 | 20 45 | 27 39 |
| 27 | 26 50 | 20 28 | 14 29 | 20 29 | 27 39 |
| 28 | 26 42 | 20 08 | 13 56 | 20 14 | 27 38 |
| 29 | 26 33 | 19 48 | 13 23 | 19 58 | 27 38 |
| 30 | 26 25 | 19 27 | 12 49 | 19 41 | 27 37 |
| 31 | 26 16 | 19 06 | 12 15 | 19 24 | 27 37 |
| 32 | 26 07 | 18 45 | 11 39 | 19 06 | 27 36 |
| 33 | 25 57 | 18 23 | 11 03 | 18 48 | 27 36 |
| 34 | 25 48 | 18 00 | 10 25 | 18 29 | 27 35 |
| 35 | 25 38 | 17 37 | 09 46 | 18 09 | 27 34 |
| 36 | 25 28 | 17 14 | 09 07 | 17 48 | 27 34 |
| 37 | 25 18 | 16 50 | 08 26 | 17 27 | 27 33 |
| 38 | 25 08 | 16 25 | 07 44 | 17 05 | 27 33 |
| 39 | 24 57 | 16 00 | 07 00 | 16 41 | 27 32 |
| 40 | 24 46 | 15 34 | 06 16 | 16 17 | 27 31 |
| 41 | 24 35 | 15 07 | 05 29 | 15 52 | 27 30 |
| 42 | 24 23 | 14 40 | 04 41 | 15 25 | 27 30 |
| 43 | 24 12 | 14 11 | 03 52 | 14 57 | 27 29 |
| 44 | 23 59 | 13 42 | 03 01 | 14 27 | 27 28 |
| 45 | 23 47 | 13 12 | 02 08 | 13 56 | 27 27 |
| 46 | 23 34 | 12 41 | 01 13 | 13 23 | 27 26 |
| 47 | 23 20 | 12 08 | 00 16 | 12 48 | 27 25 |
| 48 | 23 06 | 11 35 | 29♐16 | 12 10 | 27 24 |
| 49 | 22 52 | 11 00 | 28 15 | 11 31 | 27 23 |
| 50 | 22 36 | 10 24 | 27 11 | 10 48 | 27 22 |
| 51 | 22 21 | 09 47 | 26 04 | 10 03 | 27 21 |
| 52 | 22 04 | 09 08 | 24 55 | 09 14 | 27 20 |
| 53 | 21 47 | 08 28 | 23 43 | 08 21 | 27 18 |
| 54 | 21 29 | 07 45 | 22 27 | 07 24 | 27 17 |
| 55 | 21 11 | 07 01 | 21 09 | 06 21 | 27 15 |
| 56 | 20 51 | 06 15 | 19 47 | 05 13 | 27 14 |
| 57 | 20 31 | 05 27 | 18 21 | 03 58 | 27 12 |
| 58 | 20 09 | 04 36 | 16 52 | 02 35 | 27 10 |
| 59 | 19 46 | 03 42 | 15 19 | 01 01 | 27 08 |
| 60 | 19♏22 | 02♐46 | 13♐41 | 29♑16 | 27♓06 |

**13h 56m 0s — 209° 0' 0" — 01 ♏ 08**

| LAT. | 11 | 12 | ASC | 2 | 3 |
|---|---|---|---|---|---|
| 0 | 01♐08 | 29♐05 | 26♑57 | 26♒47 | 28♓55 |
| 5 | 00 33 | 27 45 | 25 07 | 25 59 | 28 54 |
| 10 | 29♏57 | 26 24 | 23 11 | 25 09 | 28 53 |
| 15 | 29 21 | 25 01 | 21 08 | 24 15 | 28 52 |
| 20 | 28 43 | 23 34 | 18 56 | 23 15 | 28 51 |
| 21 | 28 35 | 23 16 | 18 28 | 23 02 | 28 51 |
| 22 | 28 27 | 22 58 | 17 59 | 22 49 | 28 51 |
| 23 | 28 19 | 22 39 | 17 30 | 22 36 | 28 50 |
| 24 | 28 11 | 22 20 | 17 01 | 22 22 | 28 50 |
| 25 | 28 03 | 22 01 | 16 31 | 22 08 | 28 50 |
| 26 | 27 55 | 21 42 | 16 00 | 21 54 | 28 50 |
| 27 | 27 46 | 21 22 | 15 28 | 21 39 | 28 49 |
| 28 | 27 38 | 21 02 | 14 56 | 21 24 | 28 49 |
| 29 | 27 29 | 20 42 | 14 23 | 21 08 | 28 49 |
| 30 | 27 20 | 20 21 | 13 49 | 20 52 | 28 49 |
| 31 | 27 11 | 20 00 | 13 14 | 20 35 | 28 48 |
| 32 | 27 02 | 19 38 | 12 38 | 20 18 | 28 48 |
| 33 | 26 52 | 19 16 | 12 02 | 20 00 | 28 48 |
| 34 | 26 43 | 18 53 | 11 24 | 19 41 | 28 48 |
| 35 | 26 33 | 18 30 | 10 45 | 19 22 | 28 47 |
| 36 | 26 23 | 18 07 | 10 06 | 19 01 | 28 47 |
| 37 | 26 13 | 17 42 | 09 25 | 18 40 | 28 47 |
| 38 | 26 02 | 17 18 | 08 42 | 18 19 | 28 46 |
| 39 | 25 52 | 16 52 | 07 59 | 17 56 | 28 46 |
| 40 | 25 41 | 16 26 | 07 14 | 17 32 | 28 46 |
| 41 | 25 29 | 15 59 | 06 27 | 17 07 | 28 45 |
| 42 | 25 17 | 15 31 | 05 39 | 16 41 | 28 45 |
| 43 | 25 05 | 15 03 | 04 49 | 16 13 | 28 44 |
| 44 | 24 53 | 14 33 | 03 58 | 15 44 | 28 44 |
| 45 | 24 40 | 14 03 | 03 04 | 15 13 | 28 44 |
| 46 | 24 27 | 13 31 | 02 09 | 14 41 | 28 43 |
| 47 | 24 13 | 12 59 | 01 11 | 14 06 | 28 43 |
| 48 | 23 59 | 12 25 | 00 11 | 13 29 | 28 42 |
| 49 | 23 44 | 11 50 | 29♐09 | 12 50 | 28 42 |
| 50 | 23 29 | 11 14 | 28 05 | 12 09 | 28 41 |
| 51 | 23 13 | 10 36 | 26 57 | 11 24 | 28 40 |
| 52 | 22 56 | 09 57 | 25 47 | 10 35 | 28 40 |
| 53 | 22 39 | 09 16 | 24 34 | 09 43 | 28 39 |
| 54 | 22 21 | 08 33 | 23 18 | 08 47 | 28 38 |
| 55 | 22 02 | 07 48 | 21 58 | 07 45 | 28 38 |
| 56 | 21 42 | 07 01 | 20 35 | 06 38 | 28 37 |
| 57 | 21 21 | 06 12 | 19 08 | 05 23 | 28 36 |
| 58 | 20 59 | 05 21 | 17 37 | 04 01 | 28 35 |
| 59 | 20 36 | 04 27 | 16 02 | 02 29 | 28 34 |
| 60 | 20♏11 | 03♐30 | 14♐23 | 00♒44 | 28♓33 |

**14h 0m 0s — 210° 0' 0" — 02 ♏ 11**

| LAT. | 11 | 12 | ASC | 2 | 3 |
|---|---|---|---|---|---|
| 0 | 02♐05 | 00♑00 | 27♑55 | 27♒49 | 00♈00 |
| 5 | 01 30 | 28♐40 | 26 05 | 27 03 | 00 00 |
| 10 | 00 54 | 27 19 | 24 10 | 26 14 | 00 00 |
| 15 | 00 17 | 25 56 | 22 08 | 25 21 | 00 00 |
| 20 | 29♏39 | 24 28 | 19 55 | 24 23 | 00 00 |
| 21 | 29 31 | 24 10 | 19 28 | 24 10 | 00 00 |
| 22 | 29 23 | 23 52 | 18 59 | 23 58 | 00 00 |
| 23 | 29 15 | 23 33 | 18 30 | 23 45 | 00 00 |
| 24 | 29 07 | 23 14 | 18 01 | 23 31 | 00 00 |
| 25 | 28 59 | 22 55 | 17 30 | 23 18 | 00 00 |
| 26 | 28 50 | 22 36 | 17 00 | 23 04 | 00 00 |
| 27 | 28 42 | 22 16 | 16 28 | 22 49 | 00 00 |
| 28 | 28 33 | 21 56 | 15 56 | 22 34 | 00 00 |
| 29 | 28 24 | 21 35 | 15 23 | 22 19 | 00 00 |
| 30 | 28 15 | 21 15 | 14 49 | 22 03 | 00 00 |
| 31 | 28 06 | 20 53 | 14 14 | 21 46 | 00 00 |
| 32 | 27 57 | 20 32 | 13 38 | 21 29 | 00 00 |
| 33 | 27 47 | 20 09 | 13 01 | 21 12 | 00 00 |
| 34 | 27 38 | 19 47 | 12 24 | 20 54 | 00 00 |
| 35 | 27 28 | 19 23 | 11 45 | 20 35 | 00 00 |
| 36 | 27 18 | 19 00 | 11 05 | 20 15 | 00 00 |
| 37 | 27 07 | 18 35 | 10 24 | 19 54 | 00 00 |
| 38 | 26 57 | 18 10 | 09 41 | 19 33 | 00 00 |
| 39 | 26 46 | 17 45 | 08 58 | 19 11 | 00 00 |
| 40 | 26 35 | 17 18 | 08 12 | 18 47 | 00 00 |
| 41 | 26 23 | 16 51 | 07 25 | 18 23 | 00 00 |
| 42 | 26 11 | 16 23 | 06 37 | 17 57 | 00 00 |
| 43 | 25 59 | 15 54 | 05 47 | 17 30 | 00 00 |
| 44 | 25 47 | 15 25 | 04 55 | 17 01 | 00 00 |
| 45 | 25 34 | 14 54 | 04 01 | 16 31 | 00 00 |
| 46 | 25 20 | 14 22 | 03 05 | 15 59 | 00 00 |
| 47 | 25 06 | 13 49 | 02 07 | 15 25 | 00 00 |
| 48 | 24 52 | 13 15 | 01 07 | 14 49 | 00 00 |
| 49 | 24 37 | 12 40 | 00 04 | 14 11 | 00 00 |
| 50 | 24 21 | 12 03 | 28♐59 | 13 30 | 00 00 |
| 51 | 24 05 | 11 25 | 27 51 | 12 46 | 00 00 |
| 52 | 23 48 | 10 45 | 26 40 | 11 58 | 00 00 |
| 53 | 23 31 | 10 04 | 25 26 | 11 07 | 00 00 |
| 54 | 23 12 | 09 20 | 24 08 | 10 11 | 00 00 |
| 55 | 22 53 | 08 35 | 22 48 | 09 10 | 00 00 |
| 56 | 22 33 | 07 48 | 21 23 | 08 04 | 00 00 |
| 57 | 22 12 | 06 58 | 19 55 | 06 50 | 00 00 |
| 58 | 21 49 | 06 06 | 18 23 | 05 29 | 00 00 |
| 59 | 21 26 | 05 11 | 16 47 | 03 57 | 00 00 |
| 60 | 21♏00 | 04♐13 | 15♐06 | 02♒14 | 00♈00 |

**14h 4m 0s — 211° 0' 0" — 03 ♏ 13**

| LAT. | 11 | 12 | ASC | 2 | 3 |
|---|---|---|---|---|---|
| 0 | 03♐03 | 00♑55 | 28♑52 | 28♒52 | 01♈05 |
| 5 | 02 27 | 29♐35 | 27 03 | 28 07 | 01 06 |
| 10 | 01 50 | 28 14 | 25 09 | 27 19 | 01 07 |
| 15 | 01 13 | 26 51 | 23 07 | 26 27 | 01 08 |
| 20 | 00 35 | 25 23 | 20 55 | 25 31 | 01 09 |
| 21 | 00 27 | 25 05 | 20 28 | 25 19 | 01 09 |
| 22 | 00 19 | 24 46 | 19 59 | 25 06 | 01 09 |
| 23 | 00 11 | 24 28 | 19 30 | 24 54 | 01 10 |
| 24 | 00 03 | 24 09 | 19 01 | 24 41 | 01 10 |
| 25 | 29♏54 | 23 50 | 18 31 | 24 27 | 01 10 |
| 26 | 29 46 | 23 30 | 18 00 | 24 14 | 01 10 |
| 27 | 29 37 | 23 10 | 17 28 | 23 59 | 01 11 |
| 28 | 29 29 | 22 50 | 16 56 | 23 45 | 01 11 |
| 29 | 29 20 | 22 29 | 16 23 | 23 30 | 01 11 |
| 30 | 29 11 | 22 08 | 15 49 | 23 14 | 01 11 |
| 31 | 29 01 | 21 47 | 15 14 | 22 58 | 01 12 |
| 32 | 28 52 | 21 25 | 14 38 | 22 42 | 01 12 |
| 33 | 28 42 | 21 03 | 14 02 | 22 24 | 01 12 |
| 34 | 28 33 | 20 40 | 13 24 | 22 07 | 01 12 |
| 35 | 28 23 | 20 17 | 12 45 | 21 48 | 01 13 |
| 36 | 28 12 | 19 53 | 12 05 | 21 29 | 01 13 |
| 37 | 28 02 | 19 28 | 11 23 | 21 09 | 01 13 |
| 38 | 27 51 | 19 03 | 10 41 | 20 48 | 01 14 |
| 39 | 27 40 | 18 37 | 09 57 | 20 26 | 01 14 |
| 40 | 27 29 | 18 11 | 09 11 | 20 03 | 01 14 |
| 41 | 27 17 | 17 43 | 08 24 | 19 39 | 01 15 |
| 42 | 27 05 | 17 15 | 07 36 | 19 14 | 01 15 |
| 43 | 26 53 | 16 46 | 06 45 | 18 47 | 01 16 |
| 44 | 26 40 | 16 16 | 05 53 | 18 19 | 01 16 |
| 45 | 26 27 | 15 45 | 04 59 | 17 50 | 01 16 |
| 46 | 26 13 | 15 13 | 04 02 | 17 18 | 01 17 |
| 47 | 25 59 | 14 40 | 03 04 | 16 45 | 01 17 |
| 48 | 25 45 | 14 06 | 02 03 | 16 10 | 01 18 |
| 49 | 25 30 | 13 30 | 00 59 | 15 32 | 01 18 |
| 50 | 25 14 | 12 53 | 29♐53 | 14 52 | 01 19 |
| 51 | 24 58 | 12 14 | 28 45 | 14 08 | 01 20 |
| 52 | 24 40 | 11 34 | 27 33 | 13 22 | 01 20 |
| 53 | 24 23 | 10 52 | 26 18 | 12 31 | 01 21 |
| 54 | 24 04 | 10 08 | 24 59 | 11 36 | 01 22 |
| 55 | 23 44 | 09 22 | 23 38 | 10 37 | 01 22 |
| 56 | 23 24 | 08 34 | 22 12 | 09 31 | 01 23 |
| 57 | 23 02 | 07 44 | 20 43 | 08 19 | 01 24 |
| 58 | 22 39 | 06 51 | 19 09 | 06 58 | 01 25 |
| 59 | 22 15 | 05 55 | 17 31 | 05 28 | 01 26 |
| 60 | 21♏50 | 04♐56 | 15♐49 | 03♒46 | 01♈27 |

**14h 8m 0s — 212° 0' 0" — 04 ♏ 16**

| LAT. | 11 | 12 | ASC | 2 | 3 |
|---|---|---|---|---|---|
| 0 | 04♐00 | 01♑50 | 29♑49 | 29♒54 | 02♈11 |
| 5 | 03 23 | 00 30 | 28 01 | 29 11 | 02 12 |
| 10 | 02 47 | 29♐09 | 26 08 | 28 24 | 02 14 |
| 15 | 02 10 | 27 45 | 24 07 | 27 34 | 02 16 |
| 20 | 01 31 | 26 18 | 21 56 | 26 39 | 02 18 |
| 21 | 01 23 | 25 59 | 21 28 | 26 27 | 02 18 |
| 22 | 01 15 | 25 41 | 21 00 | 26 15 | 02 19 |
| 23 | 01 07 | 25 22 | 20 31 | 26 03 | 02 19 |
| 24 | 00 58 | 25 03 | 20 01 | 25 50 | 02 20 |
| 25 | 00 50 | 24 44 | 19 31 | 25 37 | 02 20 |
| 26 | 00 41 | 24 24 | 19 00 | 25 24 | 02 21 |
| 27 | 00 33 | 24 04 | 18 29 | 25 10 | 02 21 |
| 28 | 00 24 | 23 44 | 17 57 | 24 56 | 02 22 |
| 29 | 00 15 | 23 23 | 17 23 | 24 41 | 02 22 |
| 30 | 00 06 | 23 02 | 16 50 | 24 26 | 02 23 |
| 31 | 29♏56 | 22 41 | 16 15 | 24 11 | 02 23 |
| 32 | 29 47 | 22 19 | 15 39 | 23 54 | 02 24 |
| 33 | 29 37 | 21 56 | 15 02 | 23 38 | 02 24 |
| 34 | 29 27 | 21 33 | 14 24 | 23 20 | 02 25 |
| 35 | 29 17 | 21 10 | 13 45 | 23 02 | 02 26 |
| 36 | 29 07 | 20 46 | 13 05 | 22 43 | 02 26 |
| 37 | 28 56 | 20 21 | 12 24 | 22 24 | 02 27 |
| 38 | 28 46 | 19 56 | 11 41 | 22 03 | 02 27 |
| 39 | 28 34 | 19 30 | 10 57 | 21 42 | 02 28 |
| 40 | 28 23 | 19 03 | 10 11 | 21 19 | 02 29 |
| 41 | 28 11 | 18 36 | 09 24 | 20 56 | 02 30 |
| 42 | 27 59 | 18 07 | 08 35 | 20 31 | 02 30 |
| 43 | 27 47 | 17 38 | 07 44 | 20 05 | 02 31 |
| 44 | 27 34 | 17 08 | 06 51 | 19 38 | 02 32 |
| 45 | 27 20 | 16 37 | 05 57 | 19 09 | 02 33 |
| 46 | 27 07 | 16 04 | 05 00 | 18 38 | 02 34 |
| 47 | 26 52 | 15 31 | 04 01 | 18 06 | 02 35 |
| 48 | 26 38 | 14 56 | 02 59 | 17 31 | 02 36 |
| 49 | 26 22 | 14 20 | 01 55 | 16 54 | 02 37 |
| 50 | 26 06 | 13 43 | 00 49 | 16 15 | 02 38 |
| 51 | 25 50 | 13 04 | 29♐39 | 15 32 | 02 39 |
| 52 | 25 32 | 12 23 | 28 26 | 14 46 | 02 40 |
| 53 | 25 14 | 11 41 | 27 11 | 13 57 | 02 42 |
| 54 | 24 55 | 10 56 | 25 51 | 13 03 | 02 43 |
| 55 | 24 35 | 10 10 | 24 28 | 12 04 | 02 45 |
| 56 | 24 15 | 09 21 | 23 02 | 11 00 | 02 46 |
| 57 | 23 53 | 08 30 | 21 31 | 09 48 | 02 48 |
| 58 | 23 29 | 07 36 | 19 56 | 08 29 | 02 50 |
| 59 | 23 05 | 06 40 | 18 16 | 07 00 | 02 52 |
| 60 | 22♏39 | 05♐40 | 16♐32 | 05♒19 | 02♈54 |

**14h 12m 0s — 213° 0' 0" — 05 ♏ 18**

| LAT. | 11 | 12 | ASC | 2 | 3 |
|---|---|---|---|---|---|
| 0 | 04♐57 | 02♑45 | 00♒47 | 00♓57 | 03♈16 |
| 5 | 04 20 | 01 25 | 29♑00 | 00 15 | 03 19 |
| 10 | 03 43 | 00 04 | 27 07 | 29♒30 | 03 21 |
| 15 | 03 06 | 28♐40 | 25 07 | 28 41 | 03 24 |
| 20 | 02 27 | 27 12 | 22 56 | 27 48 | 03 27 |
| 21 | 02 19 | 26 54 | 22 28 | 27 36 | 03 28 |
| 22 | 02 10 | 26 36 | 22 00 | 27 25 | 03 28 |
| 23 | 02 02 | 26 17 | 21 31 | 27 13 | 03 29 |
| 24 | 01 54 | 25 58 | 21 02 | 27 00 | 03 30 |
| 25 | 01 45 | 25 38 | 20 32 | 26 48 | 03 30 |
| 26 | 01 37 | 25 19 | 20 01 | 26 35 | 03 31 |
| 27 | 01 28 | 24 59 | 19 30 | 26 21 | 03 32 |
| 28 | 01 19 | 24 38 | 18 58 | 26 07 | 03 32 |
| 29 | 01 10 | 24 18 | 18 24 | 25 53 | 03 33 |
| 30 | 01 01 | 23 56 | 17 51 | 25 38 | 03 34 |
| 31 | 00 51 | 23 35 | 17 16 | 25 23 | 03 35 |
| 32 | 00 42 | 23 13 | 16 40 | 25 07 | 03 36 |
| 33 | 00 32 | 22 50 | 16 03 | 24 51 | 03 36 |
| 34 | 00 22 | 22 27 | 15 25 | 24 34 | 03 37 |
| 35 | 00 12 | 22 03 | 14 46 | 24 17 | 03 38 |
| 36 | 00 01 | 21 39 | 14 06 | 23 58 | 03 39 |
| 37 | 29♏51 | 21 14 | 13 24 | 23 39 | 03 40 |
| 38 | 29 40 | 20 49 | 12 41 | 23 19 | 03 41 |
| 39 | 29 29 | 20 23 | 11 57 | 22 58 | 03 42 |
| 40 | 29 17 | 19 56 | 11 11 | 22 36 | 03 43 |
| 41 | 29 05 | 19 28 | 10 24 | 22 14 | 03 44 |
| 42 | 28 53 | 18 59 | 09 34 | 21 49 | 03 45 |
| 43 | 28 40 | 18 30 | 08 43 | 21 24 | 03 47 |
| 44 | 28 27 | 18 00 | 07 50 | 20 57 | 03 48 |
| 45 | 28 14 | 17 28 | 06 55 | 20 29 | 03 49 |
| 46 | 28 00 | 16 56 | 05 58 | 19 59 | 03 51 |
| 47 | 27 45 | 16 22 | 04 58 | 19 27 | 03 52 |
| 48 | 27 30 | 15 47 | 03 56 | 18 54 | 03 54 |
| 49 | 27 15 | 15 10 | 02 52 | 18 17 | 03 55 |
| 50 | 26 59 | 14 33 | 01 44 | 17 39 | 03 57 |
| 51 | 26 42 | 13 53 | 00 34 | 16 57 | 03 59 |
| 52 | 26 24 | 13 12 | 29♐21 | 16 12 | 04 01 |
| 53 | 26 06 | 12 29 | 28 04 | 15 23 | 04 03 |
| 54 | 25 47 | 11 44 | 26 44 | 14 31 | 04 05 |
| 55 | 25 27 | 10 57 | 25 20 | 13 33 | 04 07 |
| 56 | 25 05 | 10 08 | 23 52 | 12 30 | 04 10 |
| 57 | 24 43 | 09 16 | 22 20 | 11 19 | 04 12 |
| 58 | 24 19 | 08 22 | 20 43 | 10 01 | 04 15 |
| 59 | 23 55 | 07 24 | 19 02 | 08 34 | 04 18 |
| 60 | 23♏28 | 06♐24 | 17♐16 | 06♒55 | 04♈22 |

**14h 16m 0s — 214° 0' 0" — 06 ♏ 19**

| LAT. | 11 | 12 | ASC | 2 | 3 |
|---|---|---|---|---|---|
| 0 | 05♐54 | 03♑40 | 01♒45 | 02♓00 | 04♈22 |
| 5 | 05 17 | 02 20 | 29♑59 | 01 19 | 04 25 |
| 10 | 04 40 | 00 59 | 28 07 | 00 36 | 04 28 |
| 15 | 04 02 | 29♐35 | 26 07 | 29♒49 | 04 32 |
| 20 | 03 22 | 28 07 | 23 57 | 28 57 | 04 36 |
| 21 | 03 14 | 27 49 | 23 29 | 28 46 | 04 37 |
| 22 | 03 06 | 27 30 | 23 01 | 28 34 | 04 38 |
| 23 | 02 58 | 27 11 | 22 33 | 28 23 | 04 39 |
| 24 | 02 49 | 26 52 | 22 03 | 28 11 | 04 39 |
| 25 | 02 41 | 26 33 | 21 33 | 27 58 | 04 40 |
| 26 | 02 32 | 26 13 | 21 03 | 27 46 | 04 41 |
| 27 | 02 23 | 25 53 | 20 31 | 27 33 | 04 42 |
| 28 | 02 14 | 25 33 | 19 59 | 27 19 | 04 43 |
| 29 | 02 05 | 25 12 | 19 26 | 27 05 | 04 44 |
| 30 | 01 56 | 24 51 | 18 52 | 26 51 | 04 45 |
| 31 | 01 46 | 24 29 | 18 17 | 26 36 | 04 46 |
| 32 | 01 37 | 24 07 | 17 41 | 26 21 | 04 47 |
| 33 | 01 27 | 23 44 | 17 04 | 26 05 | 04 49 |
| 34 | 01 17 | 23 21 | 16 26 | 25 49 | 04 50 |
| 35 | 01 06 | 22 57 | 15 47 | 25 31 | 04 51 |
| 36 | 00 56 | 22 33 | 15 07 | 25 14 | 04 52 |
| 37 | 00 45 | 22 08 | 14 25 | 24 55 | 04 53 |
| 38 | 00 34 | 21 42 | 13 42 | 24 36 | 04 55 |
| 39 | 00 23 | 21 16 | 12 58 | 24 15 | 04 56 |
| 40 | 00 11 | 20 49 | 12 12 | 23 54 | 04 58 |
| 41 | 29♏59 | 20 21 | 11 24 | 23 32 | 04 59 |
| 42 | 29 47 | 19 52 | 10 34 | 23 08 | 05 01 |
| 43 | 29 34 | 19 22 | 09 43 | 22 44 | 05 02 |
| 44 | 29 21 | 18 52 | 08 50 | 22 17 | 05 04 |
| 45 | 29 07 | 18 20 | 07 54 | 21 50 | 05 06 |
| 46 | 28 53 | 17 47 | 06 57 | 21 21 | 05 07 |
| 47 | 28 38 | 17 13 | 05 57 | 20 50 | 05 09 |
| 48 | 28 23 | 16 38 | 04 54 | 20 17 | 05 11 |
| 49 | 28 07 | 16 01 | 03 49 | 19 41 | 05 14 |
| 50 | 27 51 | 15 23 | 02 41 | 19 03 | 05 16 |
| 51 | 27 34 | 14 43 | 01 30 | 18 23 | 05 18 |
| 52 | 27 16 | 14 01 | 00 16 | 17 39 | 05 21 |
| 53 | 26 58 | 13 18 | 28♐58 | 16 51 | 05 23 |
| 54 | 26 38 | 12 33 | 27 37 | 15 59 | 05 26 |
| 55 | 26 18 | 11 45 | 26 11 | 15 03 | 05 29 |
| 56 | 25 56 | 10 55 | 24 42 | 14 01 | 05 33 |
| 57 | 25 33 | 10 03 | 23 09 | 12 52 | 05 36 |
| 58 | 25 10 | 09 08 | 21 31 | 11 35 | 05 40 |
| 59 | 24 44 | 08 09 | 19 48 | 10 10 | 05 44 |
| 60 | 24♏17 | 07♐08 | 18♐00 | 08♒32 | 05♈49 |

**14h 20m 0s — 215° 0' 0" — 07 ♏ 21**

| LAT. | 11 | 12 | ASC | 2 | 3 |
|---|---|---|---|---|---|
| 0 | 06♐50 | 04♑35 | 02♒43 | 03♓03 | 05♈27 |
| 5 | 06 13 | 03 16 | 00 58 | 02 24 | 05 31 |
| 10 | 05 36 | 01 54 | 29♑06 | 01 42 | 05 35 |
| 15 | 04 58 | 00 30 | 27 07 | 00 56 | 05 40 |
| 20 | 04 18 | 29♐02 | 24 58 | 00 06 | 05 45 |
| 21 | 04 10 | 28 44 | 24 31 | 29♒55 | 05 46 |
| 22 | 04 02 | 28 25 | 24 03 | 29 44 | 05 47 |
| 23 | 03 53 | 28 06 | 23 34 | 29 33 | 05 48 |
| 24 | 03 45 | 27 47 | 23 05 | 29 21 | 05 49 |
| 25 | 03 36 | 27 28 | 22 35 | 29 09 | 05 50 |
| 26 | 03 27 | 27 08 | 22 04 | 28 57 | 05 52 |
| 27 | 03 18 | 26 48 | 21 33 | 28 44 | 05 53 |
| 28 | 03 09 | 26 27 | 21 01 | 28 31 | 05 54 |
| 29 | 03 00 | 26 06 | 20 28 | 28 18 | 05 55 |
| 30 | 02 51 | 25 45 | 19 54 | 28 04 | 05 57 |
| 31 | 02 41 | 25 23 | 19 19 | 27 50 | 05 58 |
| 32 | 02 31 | 25 01 | 18 43 | 27 35 | 05 59 |
| 33 | 02 22 | 24 38 | 18 06 | 27 19 | 06 01 |
| 34 | 02 11 | 24 15 | 17 28 | 27 03 | 06 02 |
| 35 | 02 01 | 23 51 | 16 49 | 26 47 | 06 04 |
| 36 | 01 50 | 23 26 | 16 09 | 26 29 | 06 05 |
| 37 | 01 39 | 23 01 | 15 27 | 26 11 | 06 07 |
| 38 | 01 28 | 22 35 | 14 44 | 25 53 | 06 08 |
| 39 | 01 17 | 22 09 | 13 59 | 25 33 | 06 10 |
| 40 | 01 05 | 21 42 | 13 13 | 25 12 | 06 12 |
| 41 | 00 53 | 21 14 | 12 25 | 24 50 | 06 14 |
| 42 | 00 40 | 20 45 | 11 35 | 24 28 | 06 16 |
| 43 | 00 27 | 20 15 | 10 44 | 24 04 | 06 18 |
| 44 | 00 14 | 19 44 | 09 50 | 23 38 | 06 20 |
| 45 | 00 00 | 19 12 | 08 54 | 23 11 | 06 22 |
| 46 | 29♏46 | 18 39 | 07 56 | 22 43 | 06 24 |
| 47 | 29 31 | 18 04 | 06 56 | 22 13 | 06 27 |
| 48 | 29 16 | 17 29 | 05 53 | 21 40 | 06 29 |
| 49 | 29 00 | 16 52 | 04 47 | 21 06 | 06 32 |
| 50 | 28 43 | 16 13 | 03 38 | 20 29 | 06 35 |
| 51 | 28 26 | 15 33 | 02 26 | 19 49 | 06 38 |
| 52 | 28 08 | 14 51 | 01 11 | 19 06 | 06 41 |
| 53 | 27 49 | 14 07 | 29♐53 | 18 20 | 06 44 |
| 54 | 27 29 | 13 21 | 28 30 | 17 29 | 06 48 |
| 55 | 27 09 | 12 33 | 27 04 | 16 34 | 06 52 |
| 56 | 26 47 | 11 42 | 25 33 | 15 33 | 06 56 |
| 57 | 26 24 | 10 49 | 23 58 | 14 26 | 07 00 |
| 58 | 26 00 | 09 53 | 22 19 | 13 11 | 07 05 |
| 59 | 25 34 | 08 54 | 20 35 | 11 47 | 07 10 |
| 60 | 25♏06 | 07♐52 | 18♐45 | 10♒11 | 07♈16 |

# Placidus Table of Houses for Latitudes 0° to 60° North

| 14h 24m 0s | 08 ♏ 23 | 216° 0' 0" | | | |
|---|---|---|---|---|---|
| 11 | 12 | ASC | 2 | 3 | LAT. |
| 07♐47 | 05♑30 | 03♒41 | 04♓07 | 06♈32 | 0 |
| 07 10 | 04 11 | 01 57 | 03 29 | 06 37 | 5 |
| 06 32 | 02 50 | 00 06 | 02 48 | 06 42 | 10 |
| 05 54 | 01 25 | 28♑08 | 02 04 | 06 48 | 15 |
| 05 14 | 29♐57 | 26 00 | 01 15 | 06 54 | 20 |
| 05 05 | 29 39 | 25 32 | 01 05 | 06 55 | 21 |
| 04 57 | 29 20 | 25 04 | 00 54 | 06 56 | 22 |
| 04 49 | 29 01 | 24 36 | 00 43 | 06 58 | 23 |
| 04 40 | 28 42 | 24 07 | 00 32 | 06 59 | 24 |
| 04 31 | 28 22 | 23 37 | 00 21 | 07 00 | 25 |
| 04 23 | 28 02 | 23 06 | 00 09 | 07 02 | 26 |
| 04 14 | 27 42 | 22 35 | 29♒56 | 07 03 | 27 |
| 04 04 | 27 22 | 22 03 | 29 44 | 07 05 | 28 |
| 03 55 | 27 01 | 21 30 | 29 31 | 07 06 | 29 |
| 03 46 | 26 39 | 20 56 | 29 17 | 07 08 | 30 |
| 03 36 | 26 17 | 20 21 | 29 04 | 07 09 | 31 |
| 03 26 | 25 55 | 19 46 | 28 49 | 07 11 | 32 |
| 03 16 | 25 32 | 19 09 | 28 34 | 07 13 | 33 |
| 03 06 | 25 09 | 18 31 | 28 19 | 07 14 | 34 |
| 02 55 | 24 45 | 17 52 | 28 03 | 07 16 | 35 |
| 02 45 | 24 20 | 17 11 | 27 46 | 07 18 | 36 |
| 02 34 | 23 55 | 16 29 | 27 28 | 07 20 | 37 |
| 02 22 | 23 29 | 15 46 | 27 10 | 07 22 | 38 |
| 02 11 | 23 02 | 15 01 | 26 51 | 07 24 | 39 |
| 01 59 | 22 35 | 14 15 | 26 31 | 07 26 | 40 |
| 01 47 | 22 07 | 13 27 | 26 10 | 07 28 | 41 |
| 01 34 | 21 37 | 12 37 | 25 48 | 07 31 | 42 |
| 01 21 | 21 07 | 11 45 | 25 24 | 07 33 | 43 |
| 01 07 | 20 36 | 10 51 | 25 00 | 07 35 | 44 |
| 00 53 | 20 04 | 09 55 | 24 33 | 07 38 | 45 |
| 00 39 | 19 31 | 08 56 | 24 06 | 07 41 | 46 |
| 00 24 | 18 56 | 07 55 | 23 36 | 07 44 | 47 |
| 00 09 | 18 20 | 06 52 | 23 05 | 07 47 | 48 |
| 29♏52 | 17 43 | 05 45 | 22 32 | 07 50 | 49 |
| 29 36 | 17 04 | 04 36 | 21 56 | 07 53 | 50 |
| 29 18 | 16 23 | 03 23 | 21 17 | 07 57 | 51 |
| 29 00 | 15 41 | 02 07 | 20 35 | 08 01 | 52 |
| 28 41 | 14 56 | 00 48 | 19 50 | 08 05 | 53 |
| 28 21 | 14 10 | 29♐24 | 19 01 | 08 09 | 54 |
| 28 00 | 13 21 | 27 57 | 18 07 | 08 14 | 55 |
| 27 38 | 12 30 | 26 25 | 17 07 | 08 19 | 56 |
| 27 14 | 11 36 | 24 49 | 16 01 | 08 24 | 57 |
| 26 50 | 10 39 | 23 08 | 14 48 | 08 30 | 58 |
| 26 23 | 09 40 | 21 22 | 13 26 | 08 36 | 59 |
| 25♏56 | 08♐36 | 19♐30 | 11♒52 | 08♈43 | 60 |

| 14h 28m 0s | 09 ♏ 24 | 217° 0' 0" | | | |
|---|---|---|---|---|---|
| 11 | 12 | ASC | 2 | 3 | LAT. |
| 08♐43 | 06♑26 | 04♒39 | 05♓10 | 07♈37 | 0 |
| 08 06 | 05 06 | 02 56 | 04 33 | 07 43 | 5 |
| 07 28 | 03 45 | 01 07 | 03 54 | 07 49 | 10 |
| 06 49 | 02 21 | 29♑09 | 03 12 | 07 56 | 15 |
| 06 09 | 00 52 | 27 01 | 02 25 | 08 03 | 20 |
| 06 01 | 00 34 | 26 34 | 02 15 | 08 04 | 21 |
| 05 52 | 00 15 | 26 06 | 02 05 | 08 06 | 22 |
| 05 44 | 29♐56 | 25 38 | 01 54 | 08 07 | 23 |
| 05 35 | 29 37 | 25 09 | 01 43 | 08 09 | 24 |
| 05 27 | 29 17 | 24 39 | 01 32 | 08 10 | 25 |
| 05 18 | 28 57 | 24 09 | 01 21 | 08 12 | 26 |
| 05 09 | 28 37 | 23 38 | 01 09 | 08 14 | 27 |
| 04 59 | 28 16 | 23 06 | 00 57 | 08 15 | 28 |
| 04 50 | 27 55 | 22 33 | 00 44 | 08 17 | 29 |
| 04 40 | 27 34 | 21 59 | 00 31 | 08 19 | 30 |
| 04 31 | 27 12 | 21 24 | 00 18 | 08 21 | 31 |
| 04 21 | 26 49 | 20 48 | 00 04 | 08 23 | 32 |
| 04 11 | 26 26 | 20 12 | 29♒49 | 08 25 | 33 |
| 04 00 | 26 03 | 19 34 | 29 34 | 08 27 | 34 |
| 03 50 | 25 39 | 18 54 | 29 19 | 08 29 | 35 |
| 03 39 | 25 14 | 18 14 | 29 03 | 08 31 | 36 |
| 03 28 | 24 49 | 17 32 | 28 46 | 08 33 | 37 |
| 03 16 | 24 23 | 16 49 | 28 28 | 08 35 | 38 |
| 03 05 | 23 56 | 16 04 | 28 09 | 08 38 | 39 |
| 02 53 | 23 28 | 15 17 | 27 50 | 08 40 | 40 |
| 02 40 | 23 00 | 14 29 | 27 30 | 08 43 | 41 |
| 02 27 | 22 30 | 13 39 | 27 08 | 08 45 | 42 |
| 02 14 | 22 00 | 12 47 | 26 45 | 08 48 | 43 |
| 02 01 | 21 29 | 11 52 | 26 22 | 08 51 | 44 |
| 01 47 | 20 56 | 10 56 | 25 56 | 08 54 | 45 |
| 01 32 | 20 23 | 09 57 | 25 29 | 08 57 | 46 |
| 01 17 | 19 48 | 08 56 | 25 01 | 09 01 | 47 |
| 01 01 | 19 11 | 07 52 | 24 31 | 09 04 | 48 |
| 00 45 | 18 34 | 06 45 | 23 58 | 09 08 | 49 |
| 00 28 | 17 54 | 05 34 | 23 23 | 09 12 | 50 |
| 00 10 | 17 13 | 04 21 | 22 45 | 09 16 | 51 |
| 29♏52 | 16 31 | 03 04 | 22 05 | 09 21 | 52 |
| 29 32 | 15 46 | 01 44 | 21 21 | 09 25 | 53 |
| 29 12 | 14 59 | 00 19 | 20 33 | 09 30 | 54 |
| 28 51 | 14 10 | 28♐51 | 19 40 | 09 36 | 55 |
| 28 28 | 13 18 | 27 18 | 18 42 | 09 41 | 56 |
| 28 05 | 12 23 | 25 40 | 17 38 | 09 48 | 57 |
| 27 40 | 11 26 | 23 57 | 16 27 | 09 54 | 58 |
| 27 13 | 10 25 | 22 09 | 15 06 | 10 01 | 59 |
| 26♏45 | 09♐21 | 20♐16 | 13♒35 | 10♈09 | 60 |

| 14h 32m 0s | 10 ♏ 25 | 218° 0' 0" | | | |
|---|---|---|---|---|---|
| 11 | 12 | ASC | 2 | 3 | LAT. |
| 09♐40 | 07♑21 | 05♒38 | 06♓14 | 08♈43 | 0 |
| 09 02 | 06 01 | 03 56 | 05 39 | 08 49 | 5 |
| 08 24 | 04 40 | 02 07 | 05 01 | 08 56 | 10 |
| 07 45 | 03 16 | 00 11 | 04 20 | 09 03 | 15 |
| 07 05 | 01 47 | 28♑03 | 03 35 | 09 11 | 20 |
| 06 56 | 01 29 | 27 36 | 03 25 | 09 13 | 21 |
| 06 48 | 01 10 | 27 09 | 03 15 | 09 15 | 22 |
| 06 39 | 00 51 | 26 41 | 03 05 | 09 17 | 23 |
| 06 30 | 00 32 | 26 12 | 02 55 | 09 18 | 24 |
| 06 22 | 00 12 | 25 42 | 02 44 | 09 20 | 25 |
| 06 13 | 29♐52 | 25 12 | 02 33 | 09 22 | 26 |
| 06 04 | 29 32 | 24 41 | 02 22 | 09 24 | 27 |
| 05 54 | 29 11 | 24 09 | 02 10 | 09 26 | 28 |
| 05 45 | 28 50 | 23 36 | 01 58 | 09 28 | 29 |
| 05 35 | 28 28 | 23 02 | 01 45 | 09 30 | 30 |
| 05 25 | 28 06 | 22 28 | 01 32 | 09 32 | 31 |
| 05 15 | 27 44 | 21 52 | 01 19 | 09 34 | 32 |
| 05 05 | 27 21 | 21 15 | 01 05 | 09 36 | 33 |
| 04 55 | 26 57 | 20 37 | 00 50 | 09 39 | 34 |
| 04 44 | 26 33 | 19 58 | 00 35 | 09 41 | 35 |
| 04 33 | 26 08 | 19 17 | 00 20 | 09 43 | 36 |
| 04 22 | 25 43 | 18 35 | 00 03 | 09 46 | 37 |
| 04 10 | 25 16 | 17 52 | 29♒46 | 09 49 | 38 |
| 03 59 | 24 50 | 17 07 | 29 28 | 09 51 | 39 |
| 03 46 | 24 22 | 16 20 | 29 10 | 09 54 | 40 |
| 03 34 | 23 53 | 15 32 | 28 50 | 09 57 | 41 |
| 03 21 | 23 24 | 14 41 | 28 29 | 10 00 | 42 |
| 03 08 | 22 53 | 13 49 | 28 07 | 10 03 | 43 |
| 02 54 | 22 21 | 12 55 | 27 44 | 10 07 | 44 |
| 02 40 | 21 49 | 11 58 | 27 20 | 10 10 | 45 |
| 02 25 | 21 15 | 10 58 | 26 54 | 10 14 | 46 |
| 02 10 | 20 40 | 09 57 | 26 26 | 10 18 | 47 |
| 01 54 | 20 03 | 08 52 | 25 57 | 10 22 | 48 |
| 01 37 | 19 25 | 07 44 | 25 25 | 10 26 | 49 |
| 01 20 | 18 45 | 06 34 | 24 51 | 10 31 | 50 |
| 01 02 | 18 04 | 05 20 | 24 15 | 10 35 | 51 |
| 00 44 | 17 21 | 04 02 | 23 35 | 10 40 | 52 |
| 00 24 | 16 35 | 02 41 | 22 53 | 10 46 | 53 |
| 00 03 | 15 48 | 01 15 | 22 06 | 10 51 | 54 |
| 29♏42 | 14 58 | 29♐45 | 21 15 | 10 58 | 55 |
| 29 19 | 14 06 | 28 11 | 20 19 | 11 04 | 56 |
| 28 55 | 13 10 | 26 31 | 19 17 | 11 11 | 57 |
| 28 30 | 12 12 | 24 47 | 18 07 | 11 19 | 58 |
| 28 03 | 11 11 | 22 57 | 16 49 | 11 27 | 59 |
| 27♏34 | 10♐05 | 21♐02 | 15♒20 | 11♈36 | 60 |

| 14h 36m 0s | 11 ♏ 26 | 219° 0' 0" | | | |
|---|---|---|---|---|---|
| 11 | 12 | ASC | 2 | 3 | LAT. |
| 10♐36 | 08♑16 | 06♒37 | 07♓18 | 09♈48 | 0 |
| 09 58 | 06 57 | 04 55 | 06 44 | 09 55 | 5 |
| 09 20 | 05 36 | 03 08 | 06 08 | 10 03 | 10 |
| 08 41 | 04 11 | 01 12 | 05 28 | 10 11 | 15 |
| 08 00 | 02 43 | 29♑06 | 04 45 | 10 20 | 20 |
| 07 52 | 02 24 | 28 39 | 04 36 | 10 22 | 21 |
| 07 43 | 02 05 | 28 12 | 04 26 | 10 24 | 22 |
| 07 34 | 01 46 | 27 44 | 04 17 | 10 26 | 23 |
| 07 26 | 01 27 | 27 15 | 04 07 | 10 28 | 24 |
| 07 17 | 01 07 | 26 45 | 03 56 | 10 30 | 25 |
| 07 08 | 00 47 | 26 15 | 03 46 | 10 32 | 26 |
| 06 58 | 00 27 | 25 44 | 03 35 | 10 34 | 27 |
| 06 49 | 00 06 | 25 12 | 03 23 | 10 36 | 28 |
| 06 40 | 29♐45 | 24 40 | 03 12 | 10 38 | 29 |
| 06 30 | 29 23 | 24 06 | 03 00 | 10 41 | 30 |
| 06 20 | 29 01 | 23 31 | 02 47 | 10 43 | 31 |
| 06 10 | 28 39 | 22 56 | 02 34 | 10 46 | 32 |
| 06 00 | 28 15 | 22 19 | 02 21 | 10 48 | 33 |
| 05 49 | 27 52 | 21 41 | 02 07 | 10 51 | 34 |
| 05 38 | 27 27 | 21 02 | 01 52 | 10 53 | 35 |
| 05 27 | 27 02 | 20 21 | 01 37 | 10 56 | 36 |
| 05 16 | 26 37 | 19 39 | 01 22 | 10 59 | 37 |
| 05 04 | 26 11 | 18 56 | 01 05 | 11 02 | 38 |
| 04 53 | 25 43 | 18 11 | 00 48 | 11 05 | 39 |
| 04 40 | 25 15 | 17 24 | 00 30 | 11 08 | 40 |
| 04 28 | 24 47 | 16 35 | 00 11 | 11 11 | 41 |
| 04 15 | 24 17 | 15 45 | 29♒51 | 11 15 | 42 |
| 04 01 | 23 46 | 14 52 | 29 30 | 11 18 | 43 |
| 03 47 | 23 14 | 13 57 | 29 07 | 11 22 | 44 |
| 03 33 | 22 42 | 13 00 | 28 44 | 11 26 | 45 |
| 03 18 | 22 07 | 12 01 | 28 19 | 11 30 | 46 |
| 03 03 | 21 32 | 10 58 | 27 52 | 11 35 | 47 |
| 02 47 | 20 55 | 09 53 | 27 24 | 11 39 | 48 |
| 02 30 | 20 17 | 08 45 | 26 53 | 11 44 | 49 |
| 02 13 | 19 37 | 07 34 | 26 20 | 11 49 | 50 |
| 01 54 | 18 55 | 06 19 | 25 45 | 11 54 | 51 |
| 01 35 | 18 11 | 05 00 | 25 07 | 12 00 | 52 |
| 01 16 | 17 25 | 03 38 | 24 26 | 12 06 | 53 |
| 00 55 | 16 37 | 02 11 | 23 41 | 12 12 | 54 |
| 00 33 | 15 47 | 00 40 | 22 51 | 12 19 | 55 |
| 00 10 | 14 54 | 29♐05 | 21 57 | 12 27 | 56 |
| 29♏45 | 13 58 | 27 24 | 20 56 | 12 34 | 57 |
| 29 20 | 12 59 | 25 38 | 19 49 | 12 43 | 58 |
| 28 52 | 11 56 | 23 46 | 18 33 | 12 52 | 59 |
| 28♏23 | 10♐50 | 21♐49 | 17♒07 | 13♈02 | 60 |

| 14h 40m 0s | 12 ♏ 27 | 220° 0' 0" | | | |
|---|---|---|---|---|---|
| 11 | 12 | ASC | 2 | 3 | LAT. |
| 11♐32 | 09♑11 | 07♒35 | 08♓22 | 10♈53 | 0 |
| 10 54 | 07 52 | 05 55 | 07 49 | 11 01 | 5 |
| 10 16 | 06 31 | 04 09 | 07 15 | 11 10 | 10 |
| 09 36 | 05 07 | 02 14 | 06 37 | 11 19 | 15 |
| 08 55 | 03 38 | 00 09 | 05 56 | 11 29 | 20 |
| 08 47 | 03 20 | 29♑42 | 05 47 | 11 31 | 21 |
| 08 38 | 03 01 | 29 15 | 05 38 | 11 33 | 22 |
| 08 29 | 02 42 | 28 47 | 05 28 | 11 35 | 23 |
| 08 21 | 02 22 | 28 18 | 05 19 | 11 37 | 24 |
| 08 12 | 02 03 | 27 49 | 05 09 | 11 39 | 25 |
| 08 03 | 01 43 | 27 19 | 04 59 | 11 42 | 26 |
| 07 53 | 01 22 | 26 48 | 04 48 | 11 44 | 27 |
| 07 44 | 01 01 | 26 16 | 04 37 | 11 47 | 28 |
| 07 34 | 00 40 | 25 44 | 04 26 | 11 49 | 29 |
| 07 25 | 00 18 | 25 10 | 04 15 | 11 52 | 30 |
| 07 15 | 29♐56 | 24 36 | 04 03 | 11 54 | 31 |
| 07 05 | 29 33 | 24 00 | 03 50 | 11 57 | 32 |
| 06 54 | 29 10 | 23 23 | 03 37 | 12 00 | 33 |
| 06 44 | 28 46 | 22 45 | 03 24 | 12 03 | 34 |
| 06 33 | 28 22 | 22 06 | 03 10 | 12 05 | 35 |
| 06 22 | 27 57 | 21 26 | 02 55 | 12 09 | 36 |
| 06 10 | 27 31 | 20 44 | 02 40 | 12 12 | 37 |
| 05 58 | 27 05 | 20 00 | 02 24 | 12 15 | 38 |
| 05 46 | 26 38 | 19 15 | 02 08 | 12 18 | 39 |
| 05 34 | 26 09 | 18 28 | 01 51 | 12 22 | 40 |
| 05 21 | 25 40 | 17 39 | 01 32 | 12 26 | 41 |
| 05 08 | 25 11 | 16 49 | 01 13 | 12 29 | 42 |
| 04 55 | 24 40 | 15 56 | 00 53 | 12 33 | 43 |
| 04 41 | 24 08 | 15 01 | 00 31 | 12 37 | 44 |
| 04 26 | 23 34 | 14 04 | 00 09 | 12 42 | 45 |
| 04 11 | 23 00 | 13 04 | 29♒44 | 12 46 | 46 |
| 03 55 | 22 24 | 12 01 | 29 19 | 12 51 | 47 |
| 03 39 | 21 47 | 10 55 | 28 51 | 12 56 | 48 |
| 03 22 | 21 08 | 09 47 | 28 22 | 13 01 | 49 |
| 03 05 | 20 28 | 08 35 | 27 50 | 13 07 | 50 |
| 02 47 | 19 46 | 07 19 | 27 16 | 13 13 | 51 |
| 02 27 | 19 02 | 06 00 | 26 40 | 13 19 | 52 |
| 02 07 | 18 16 | 04 36 | 26 00 | 13 26 | 53 |
| 01 46 | 17 27 | 03 09 | 25 16 | 13 33 | 54 |
| 01 24 | 16 36 | 01 36 | 24 28 | 13 41 | 55 |
| 01 01 | 15 42 | 29♐59 | 23 36 | 13 49 | 56 |
| 00 36 | 14 46 | 28 17 | 22 37 | 13 58 | 57 |
| 00 10 | 13 46 | 26 29 | 21 32 | 14 07 | 58 |
| 29♏42 | 12 42 | 24 36 | 20 19 | 14 17 | 59 |
| 29♏12 | 11♐35 | 22♐36 | 18♒55 | 14♈28 | 60 |

| 14h 44m 0s | 13 ♏ 27 | 221° 0' 0" | | | |
|---|---|---|---|---|---|
| 11 | 12 | ASC | 2 | 3 | LAT. |
| 12♐28 | 10♑07 | 08♒34 | 09♓26 | 11♈58 | 0 |
| 11 50 | 08 48 | 06 55 | 08 55 | 12 07 | 5 |
| 11 11 | 07 27 | 05 10 | 08 22 | 12 16 | 10 |
| 10 32 | 06 02 | 03 17 | 07 46 | 12 26 | 15 |
| 09 50 | 04 34 | 01 12 | 07 06 | 12 37 | 20 |
| 09 42 | 04 15 | 00 46 | 06 58 | 12 39 | 21 |
| 09 33 | 03 56 | 00 18 | 06 49 | 12 42 | 22 |
| 09 25 | 03 37 | 29♑51 | 06 40 | 12 44 | 23 |
| 09 16 | 03 18 | 29 22 | 06 31 | 12 47 | 24 |
| 09 07 | 02 58 | 28 53 | 06 21 | 12 49 | 25 |
| 08 57 | 02 38 | 28 23 | 06 12 | 12 52 | 26 |
| 08 48 | 02 17 | 27 52 | 06 02 | 12 54 | 27 |
| 08 39 | 01 57 | 27 21 | 05 51 | 12 57 | 28 |
| 08 29 | 01 35 | 26 48 | 05 41 | 12 59 | 29 |
| 08 19 | 01 14 | 26 15 | 05 30 | 13 02 | 30 |
| 08 09 | 00 51 | 25 41 | 05 18 | 13 05 | 31 |
| 07 59 | 00 29 | 25 05 | 05 06 | 13 08 | 32 |
| 07 49 | 00 05 | 24 28 | 04 54 | 13 11 | 33 |
| 07 38 | 29♐41 | 23 50 | 04 41 | 13 14 | 34 |
| 07 27 | 29 17 | 23 11 | 04 28 | 13 18 | 35 |
| 07 16 | 28 52 | 22 31 | 04 14 | 13 21 | 36 |
| 07 04 | 28 26 | 21 49 | 03 59 | 13 24 | 37 |
| 06 52 | 27 59 | 21 05 | 03 44 | 13 28 | 38 |
| 06 40 | 27 32 | 20 20 | 03 28 | 13 32 | 39 |
| 06 28 | 27 04 | 19 33 | 03 12 | 13 36 | 40 |
| 06 15 | 26 35 | 18 44 | 02 54 | 13 40 | 41 |
| 06 02 | 26 04 | 17 53 | 02 36 | 13 44 | 42 |
| 05 48 | 25 33 | 17 01 | 02 16 | 13 48 | 43 |
| 05 34 | 25 01 | 16 05 | 01 56 | 13 53 | 44 |
| 05 19 | 24 28 | 15 08 | 01 34 | 13 57 | 45 |
| 05 04 | 23 53 | 14 07 | 01 11 | 14 02 | 46 |
| 04 48 | 23 17 | 13 04 | 00 46 | 14 08 | 47 |
| 04 32 | 22 40 | 11 58 | 00 20 | 14 13 | 48 |
| 04 15 | 22 01 | 10 49 | 29♒52 | 14 19 | 49 |
| 03 57 | 21 20 | 09 36 | 29 21 | 14 25 | 50 |
| 03 39 | 20 37 | 08 20 | 28 49 | 14 32 | 51 |
| 03 19 | 19 53 | 07 00 | 28 13 | 14 38 | 52 |
| 02 59 | 19 06 | 05 35 | 27 35 | 14 46 | 53 |
| 02 37 | 18 17 | 04 07 | 26 53 | 14 54 | 54 |
| 02 15 | 17 25 | 02 33 | 26 07 | 15 02 | 55 |
| 01 51 | 16 31 | 00 55 | 25 16 | 15 11 | 56 |
| 01 26 | 15 34 | 29♐11 | 24 20 | 15 20 | 57 |
| 01 00 | 14 33 | 27 21 | 23 17 | 15 31 | 58 |
| 00 31 | 13 29 | 25 26 | 22 06 | 15 42 | 59 |
| 00♐01 | 12♐20 | 23♐24 | 20♒45 | 15♈54 | 60 |

| 14h 48m 0s | 14 ♏ 28 | 222° 0' 0" | | | |
|---|---|---|---|---|---|
| 11 | 12 | ASC | 2 | 3 | LAT. |
| 13♐24 | 11♑02 | 09♒34 | 10♓30 | 13♈03 | 0 |
| 12 46 | 09 43 | 07 56 | 10 00 | 13 13 | 5 |
| 12 07 | 08 22 | 06 11 | 09 29 | 13 23 | 10 |
| 11 27 | 06 58 | 04 19 | 08 55 | 13 34 | 15 |
| 10 46 | 05 29 | 02 16 | 08 17 | 13 46 | 20 |
| 10 37 | 05 11 | 01 49 | 08 09 | 13 48 | 21 |
| 10 28 | 04 52 | 01 22 | 08 01 | 13 51 | 22 |
| 10 20 | 04 33 | 00 55 | 07 52 | 13 53 | 23 |
| 10 11 | 04 13 | 00 27 | 07 43 | 13 56 | 24 |
| 10 02 | 03 54 | 29♑58 | 07 34 | 13 58 | 25 |
| 09 52 | 03 34 | 29 28 | 07 25 | 14 01 | 26 |
| 09 43 | 03 13 | 28 57 | 07 16 | 14 04 | 27 |
| 09 33 | 02 52 | 28 26 | 07 06 | 14 07 | 28 |
| 09 24 | 02 31 | 27 53 | 06 56 | 14 10 | 29 |
| 09 14 | 02 09 | 27 20 | 06 45 | 14 13 | 30 |
| 09 04 | 01 47 | 26 46 | 06 34 | 14 16 | 31 |
| 08 53 | 01 24 | 26 10 | 06 23 | 14 19 | 32 |
| 08 43 | 01 00 | 25 34 | 06 11 | 14 23 | 33 |
| 08 32 | 00 36 | 24 56 | 05 59 | 14 26 | 34 |
| 08 21 | 00 12 | 24 17 | 05 46 | 14 29 | 35 |
| 08 10 | 29♐47 | 23 37 | 05 33 | 14 33 | 36 |
| 07 58 | 29 21 | 22 55 | 05 19 | 14 37 | 37 |
| 07 46 | 28 54 | 22 11 | 05 04 | 14 41 | 38 |
| 07 34 | 28 26 | 21 26 | 04 49 | 14 45 | 39 |
| 07 22 | 27 58 | 20 39 | 04 33 | 14 49 | 40 |
| 07 09 | 27 29 | 19 50 | 04 17 | 14 53 | 41 |
| 06 55 | 26 58 | 18 59 | 03 59 | 14 58 | 42 |
| 06 41 | 26 27 | 18 06 | 03 40 | 15 03 | 43 |
| 06 27 | 25 55 | 17 10 | 03 21 | 15 08 | 44 |
| 06 12 | 25 21 | 16 12 | 03 00 | 15 13 | 45 |
| 05 57 | 24 46 | 15 12 | 02 38 | 15 18 | 46 |
| 05 41 | 24 10 | 14 08 | 02 14 | 15 24 | 47 |
| 05 25 | 23 32 | 13 02 | 01 49 | 15 30 | 48 |
| 05 07 | 22 53 | 11 52 | 01 22 | 15 36 | 49 |
| 04 49 | 22 12 | 10 39 | 00 53 | 15 43 | 50 |
| 04 31 | 21 29 | 09 22 | 00 22 | 15 50 | 51 |
| 04 11 | 20 44 | 08 01 | 29♒48 | 15 57 | 52 |
| 03 50 | 19 57 | 06 36 | 29 11 | 16 05 | 53 |
| 03 29 | 19 07 | 05 06 | 28 31 | 16 14 | 54 |
| 03 06 | 18 15 | 03 31 | 27 46 | 16 23 | 55 |
| 02 42 | 17 20 | 01 51 | 26 58 | 16 33 | 56 |
| 02 17 | 16 22 | 00 06 | 26 04 | 16 43 | 57 |
| 01 50 | 15 20 | 28♐14 | 25 03 | 16 54 | 58 |
| 01 21 | 14 15 | 26 17 | 23 55 | 17 07 | 59 |
| 00♐50 | 13♐06 | 24♐13 | 22♒37 | 17♈20 | 60 |

| 14h 52m 0s | 15 ♏ 28 | 223° 0' 0" | | | |
|---|---|---|---|---|---|
| 11 | 12 | ASC | 2 | 3 | LAT. |
| 14♐20 | 11♑58 | 10♒33 | 11♓34 | 14♈07 | 0 |
| 13 41 | 10 39 | 08 56 | 11 06 | 14 18 | 5 |
| 13 02 | 09 18 | 07 13 | 10 36 | 14 29 | 10 |
| 12 22 | 07 54 | 05 22 | 10 04 | 14 41 | 15 |
| 11 41 | 06 25 | 03 20 | 09 28 | 14 54 | 20 |
| 11 32 | 06 07 | 02 53 | 09 21 | 14 56 | 21 |
| 11 23 | 05 48 | 02 27 | 09 13 | 14 59 | 22 |
| 11 14 | 05 29 | 01 59 | 09 05 | 15 02 | 23 |
| 11 05 | 05 09 | 01 31 | 08 56 | 15 05 | 24 |
| 10 56 | 04 49 | 01 02 | 08 48 | 15 08 | 25 |
| 10 47 | 04 29 | 00 33 | 08 39 | 15 11 | 26 |
| 10 38 | 04 09 | 00 03 | 08 30 | 15 14 | 27 |
| 10 28 | 03 48 | 29♑31 | 08 20 | 15 17 | 28 |
| 10 18 | 03 26 | 28 59 | 08 11 | 15 20 | 29 |
| 10 08 | 03 04 | 28 26 | 08 01 | 15 23 | 30 |
| 09 58 | 02 42 | 27 52 | 07 50 | 15 27 | 31 |
| 09 48 | 02 19 | 27 16 | 07 40 | 15 30 | 32 |
| 09 37 | 01 56 | 26 40 | 07 28 | 15 34 | 33 |
| 09 26 | 01 32 | 26 02 | 07 17 | 15 37 | 34 |
| 09 15 | 01 07 | 25 23 | 07 05 | 15 41 | 35 |
| 09 04 | 00 42 | 24 43 | 06 52 | 15 45 | 36 |
| 08 52 | 00 16 | 24 01 | 06 39 | 15 49 | 37 |
| 08 40 | 29♐49 | 23 17 | 06 25 | 15 53 | 38 |
| 08 28 | 29 21 | 22 32 | 06 11 | 15 58 | 39 |
| 08 15 | 28 53 | 21 45 | 05 56 | 16 02 | 40 |
| 08 02 | 28 23 | 20 56 | 05 40 | 16 07 | 41 |
| 07 49 | 27 53 | 20 05 | 05 23 | 16 12 | 42 |
| 07 35 | 27 21 | 19 12 | 05 05 | 16 17 | 43 |
| 07 20 | 26 49 | 18 16 | 04 46 | 16 22 | 44 |
| 07 05 | 26 15 | 17 18 | 04 26 | 16 28 | 45 |
| 06 50 | 25 40 | 16 17 | 04 05 | 16 34 | 46 |
| 06 34 | 25 03 | 15 13 | 03 43 | 16 40 | 47 |
| 06 17 | 24 25 | 14 06 | 03 19 | 16 46 | 48 |
| 06 00 | 23 46 | 12 56 | 02 53 | 16 53 | 49 |
| 05 42 | 23 04 | 11 42 | 02 25 | 17 00 | 50 |
| 05 23 | 22 21 | 10 25 | 01 55 | 17 08 | 51 |
| 05 03 | 21 35 | 09 03 | 01 23 | 17 16 | 52 |
| 04 42 | 20 48 | 07 36 | 00 48 | 17 25 | 53 |
| 04 20 | 19 58 | 06 06 | 00 09 | 17 34 | 54 |
| 03 57 | 19 05 | 04 30 | 29♒27 | 17 44 | 55 |
| 03 33 | 18 09 | 02 48 | 28 40 | 17 54 | 56 |
| 03 07 | 17 11 | 01 01 | 27 49 | 18 06 | 57 |
| 02 40 | 16 08 | 29♐08 | 26 51 | 18 18 | 58 |
| 02 11 | 15 02 | 27 09 | 25 45 | 18 31 | 59 |
| 01♐39 | 13♐52 | 25♐02 | 24♒31 | 18♈45 | 60 |

# Placidus Table of Houses for Latitudes 0° to 60° North

**14h 56m 0s — 224° 0' 0" — 16 ♏ 28**

| LAT. | 11 | 12 | ASC | 2 | 3 |
|---|---|---|---|---|---|
| 0 | 15♐16 | 12♑53 | 11♒32 | 12♓39 | 15♈12 |
| 5 | 14 37 | 11 35 | 09 57 | 12 12 | 15 24 |
| 10 | 13 58 | 10 14 | 08 15 | 11 44 | 15 36 |
| 15 | 13 18 | 08 50 | 06 25 | 11 13 | 15 48 |
| 20 | 12 36 | 07 21 | 04 24 | 10 40 | 16 02 |
| 21 | 12 27 | 07 03 | 03 58 | 10 32 | 16 05 |
| 22 | 12 18 | 06 44 | 03 31 | 10 25 | 16 08 |
| 23 | 12 09 | 06 25 | 03 04 | 10 17 | 16 11 |
| 24 | 12 00 | 06 05 | 02 36 | 10 09 | 16 14 |
| 25 | 11 51 | 05 45 | 02 08 | 10 01 | 16 17 |
| 26 | 11 42 | 05 25 | 01 38 | 09 53 | 16 20 |
| 27 | 11 32 | 05 05 | 01 08 | 09 44 | 16 23 |
| 28 | 11 23 | 04 44 | 00 37 | 09 35 | 16 27 |
| 29 | 11 13 | 04 22 | 00 05 | 09 26 | 16 30 |
| 30 | 11 03 | 04 00 | 29♑32 | 09 17 | 16 34 |
| 31 | 10 53 | 03 38 | 28 58 | 09 07 | 16 37 |
| 32 | 10 42 | 03 15 | 28 23 | 08 57 | 16 41 |
| 33 | 10 32 | 02 51 | 27 47 | 08 46 | 16 45 |
| 34 | 10 21 | 02 27 | 27 09 | 08 35 | 16 49 |
| 35 | 10 09 | 02 02 | 26 30 | 08 24 | 16 53 |
| 36 | 09 58 | 01 37 | 25 50 | 08 12 | 16 57 |
| 37 | 09 46 | 01 11 | 25 08 | 07 59 | 17 01 |
| 38 | 09 34 | 00 44 | 24 25 | 07 46 | 17 06 |
| 39 | 09 22 | 00 16 | 23 39 | 07 32 | 17 11 |
| 40 | 09 09 | 29♐48 | 22 52 | 07 18 | 17 15 |
| 41 | 08 56 | 29 18 | 22 03 | 07 03 | 17 21 |
| 42 | 08 42 | 28 47 | 21 12 | 06 47 | 17 26 |
| 43 | 08 28 | 28 16 | 20 19 | 06 30 | 17 31 |
| 44 | 08 14 | 27 43 | 19 23 | 06 12 | 17 37 |
| 45 | 07 59 | 27 09 | 18 25 | 05 54 | 17 43 |
| 46 | 07 43 | 26 34 | 17 23 | 05 33 | 17 49 |
| 47 | 07 27 | 25 57 | 16 19 | 05 12 | 17 56 |
| 48 | 07 10 | 25 18 | 15 12 | 04 49 | 18 03 |
| 49 | 06 52 | 24 38 | 14 01 | 04 25 | 18 10 |
| 50 | 06 34 | 23 57 | 12 47 | 03 58 | 18 18 |
| 51 | 06 15 | 23 13 | 11 28 | 03 30 | 18 26 |
| 52 | 05 55 | 22 27 | 10 06 | 02 59 | 18 35 |
| 53 | 05 34 | 21 39 | 08 38 | 02 26 | 18 44 |
| 54 | 05 12 | 20 48 | 07 06 | 01 49 | 18 54 |
| 55 | 04 48 | 19 55 | 05 29 | 01 09 | 19 04 |
| 56 | 04 24 | 18 59 | 03 46 | 00 24 | 19 16 |
| 57 | 03 58 | 17 59 | 01 58 | 29♒35 | 19 28 |
| 58 | 03 30 | 16 56 | 00 03 | 28 40 | 19 41 |
| 59 | 03 00 | 15 49 | 28♐01 | 27 37 | 19 55 |
| 60 | 02♐29 | 14♐38 | 25♐53 | 26♒26 | 20♈10 |

**15h 0m 0s — 225° 0' 0" — 17 ♏ 28**

| LAT. | 11 | 12 | ASC | 2 | 3 |
|---|---|---|---|---|---|
| 0 | 16♐11 | 13♑49 | 12♒32 | 13♓43 | 16♈17 |
| 5 | 15 33 | 12 30 | 10 58 | 13 18 | 16 29 |
| 10 | 14 53 | 11 10 | 09 17 | 12 52 | 16 42 |
| 15 | 14 13 | 09 46 | 07 29 | 12 23 | 16 55 |
| 20 | 13 31 | 08 17 | 05 28 | 11 51 | 17 10 |
| 21 | 13 22 | 07 59 | 05 03 | 11 44 | 17 13 |
| 22 | 13 13 | 07 40 | 04 37 | 11 37 | 17 16 |
| 23 | 13 04 | 07 21 | 04 10 | 11 30 | 17 19 |
| 24 | 12 55 | 07 01 | 03 42 | 11 23 | 17 23 |
| 25 | 12 46 | 06 41 | 03 14 | 11 15 | 17 26 |
| 26 | 12 37 | 06 21 | 02 44 | 11 07 | 17 29 |
| 27 | 12 27 | 06 01 | 02 14 | 10 59 | 17 33 |
| 28 | 12 17 | 05 40 | 01 44 | 10 51 | 17 36 |
| 29 | 12 07 | 05 18 | 01 12 | 10 42 | 17 40 |
| 30 | 11 57 | 04 56 | 00 39 | 10 33 | 17 44 |
| 31 | 11 47 | 04 34 | 00 05 | 10 24 | 17 48 |
| 32 | 11 37 | 04 11 | 29♑30 | 10 14 | 17 52 |
| 33 | 11 26 | 03 47 | 28 54 | 10 04 | 17 56 |
| 34 | 11 15 | 03 23 | 28 17 | 09 54 | 18 00 |
| 35 | 11 04 | 02 58 | 27 38 | 09 43 | 18 04 |
| 36 | 10 52 | 02 33 | 26 58 | 09 32 | 18 09 |
| 37 | 10 40 | 02 06 | 26 16 | 09 20 | 18 13 |
| 38 | 10 28 | 01 39 | 25 32 | 09 08 | 18 18 |
| 39 | 10 16 | 01 11 | 24 47 | 08 55 | 18 23 |
| 40 | 10 03 | 00 43 | 24 00 | 08 41 | 18 28 |
| 41 | 09 49 | 00 13 | 23 11 | 08 27 | 18 34 |
| 42 | 09 36 | 29♐42 | 22 20 | 08 12 | 18 39 |
| 43 | 09 22 | 29 10 | 21 26 | 07 56 | 18 45 |
| 44 | 09 07 | 28 37 | 20 31 | 07 39 | 18 51 |
| 45 | 08 52 | 28 03 | 19 32 | 07 21 | 18 58 |
| 46 | 08 36 | 27 28 | 18 30 | 07 02 | 19 05 |
| 47 | 08 20 | 26 51 | 17 26 | 06 42 | 19 12 |
| 48 | 08 03 | 26 12 | 16 18 | 06 20 | 19 19 |
| 49 | 07 45 | 25 32 | 15 07 | 05 57 | 19 27 |
| 50 | 07 26 | 24 50 | 13 52 | 05 32 | 19 35 |
| 51 | 07 07 | 24 06 | 12 33 | 05 05 | 19 44 |
| 52 | 06 47 | 23 19 | 11 09 | 04 36 | 19 53 |
| 53 | 06 25 | 22 31 | 09 41 | 04 04 | 20 03 |
| 54 | 06 03 | 21 40 | 08 08 | 03 30 | 20 13 |
| 55 | 05 39 | 20 46 | 06 30 | 02 51 | 20 25 |
| 56 | 05 15 | 19 49 | 04 45 | 02 09 | 20 37 |
| 57 | 04 48 | 18 49 | 02 55 | 01 22 | 20 50 |
| 58 | 04 20 | 17 45 | 00 58 | 00 30 | 21 03 |
| 59 | 03 50 | 16 37 | 28♐55 | 29♒31 | 21 19 |
| 60 | 03♐18 | 15♐24 | 26♐44 | 28♒24 | 21♈35 |

**15h 4m 0s — 226° 0' 0" — 18 ♏ 28**

| LAT. | 11 | 12 | ASC | 2 | 3 |
|---|---|---|---|---|---|
| 0 | 17♐07 | 14♑44 | 13♒32 | 14♓48 | 17♈21 |
| 5 | 16 28 | 13 26 | 11 59 | 14 25 | 17 34 |
| 10 | 15 49 | 12 06 | 10 20 | 14 00 | 17 48 |
| 15 | 15 08 | 10 42 | 08 32 | 13 33 | 18 02 |
| 20 | 14 26 | 09 13 | 06 34 | 13 03 | 18 18 |
| 21 | 14 17 | 08 55 | 06 08 | 12 56 | 18 21 |
| 22 | 14 08 | 08 36 | 05 42 | 12 50 | 18 24 |
| 23 | 13 59 | 08 17 | 05 15 | 12 43 | 18 28 |
| 24 | 13 50 | 07 57 | 04 48 | 12 36 | 18 31 |
| 25 | 13 41 | 07 38 | 04 20 | 12 29 | 18 35 |
| 26 | 13 31 | 07 17 | 03 51 | 12 22 | 18 38 |
| 27 | 13 22 | 06 57 | 03 21 | 12 14 | 18 42 |
| 28 | 13 12 | 06 36 | 02 50 | 12 06 | 18 46 |
| 29 | 13 02 | 06 14 | 02 19 | 11 58 | 18 50 |
| 30 | 12 52 | 05 52 | 01 46 | 11 50 | 18 54 |
| 31 | 12 41 | 05 30 | 01 13 | 11 41 | 18 58 |
| 32 | 12 31 | 05 07 | 00 38 | 11 32 | 19 02 |
| 33 | 12 20 | 04 43 | 00 02 | 11 22 | 19 06 |
| 34 | 12 09 | 04 19 | 29♑25 | 11 13 | 19 11 |
| 35 | 11 58 | 03 54 | 28 46 | 11 03 | 19 16 |
| 36 | 11 46 | 03 28 | 28 06 | 10 52 | 19 20 |
| 37 | 11 34 | 03 02 | 27 24 | 10 41 | 19 25 |
| 38 | 11 22 | 02 35 | 26 41 | 10 29 | 19 30 |
| 39 | 11 09 | 02 07 | 25 56 | 10 17 | 19 36 |
| 40 | 10 56 | 01 38 | 25 09 | 10 04 | 19 41 |
| 41 | 10 43 | 01 08 | 24 20 | 09 51 | 19 47 |
| 42 | 10 29 | 00 37 | 23 29 | 09 37 | 19 53 |
| 43 | 10 15 | 00 05 | 22 35 | 09 22 | 19 59 |
| 44 | 10 00 | 29♐32 | 21 39 | 09 06 | 20 06 |
| 45 | 09 45 | 28 58 | 20 40 | 08 49 | 20 12 |
| 46 | 09 29 | 28 22 | 19 39 | 08 31 | 20 20 |
| 47 | 09 12 | 27 45 | 18 34 | 08 12 | 20 27 |
| 48 | 08 55 | 27 06 | 17 26 | 07 52 | 20 35 |
| 49 | 08 37 | 26 25 | 16 14 | 07 30 | 20 43 |
| 50 | 08 19 | 25 43 | 14 58 | 07 07 | 20 52 |
| 51 | 07 59 | 24 58 | 13 39 | 06 41 | 21 01 |
| 52 | 07 39 | 24 12 | 12 14 | 06 14 | 21 11 |
| 53 | 07 17 | 23 23 | 10 45 | 05 44 | 21 21 |
| 54 | 06 55 | 22 31 | 09 11 | 05 11 | 21 33 |
| 55 | 06 31 | 21 37 | 07 31 | 04 35 | 21 44 |
| 56 | 06 06 | 20 39 | 05 46 | 03 55 | 21 57 |
| 57 | 05 39 | 19 38 | 03 54 | 03 11 | 22 11 |
| 58 | 05 10 | 18 33 | 01 55 | 02 22 | 22 26 |
| 59 | 04 40 | 17 24 | 29♐49 | 01 26 | 22 42 |
| 60 | 04♐07 | 16♐11 | 27♐36 | 00♓22 | 23♈00 |

**15h 8m 0s — 227° 0' 0" — 19 ♏ 27**

| LAT. | 11 | 12 | ASC | 2 | 3 |
|---|---|---|---|---|---|
| 0 | 18♐02 | 15♑40 | 14♒32 | 15♓53 | 18♈26 |
| 5 | 17 23 | 14 22 | 13 01 | 15 31 | 18 40 |
| 10 | 16 44 | 13 02 | 11 23 | 15 08 | 18 54 |
| 15 | 16 03 | 11 39 | 09 36 | 14 43 | 19 09 |
| 20 | 15 21 | 10 10 | 07 39 | 14 15 | 19 26 |
| 21 | 15 12 | 09 51 | 07 14 | 14 09 | 19 29 |
| 22 | 15 03 | 09 33 | 06 48 | 14 03 | 19 32 |
| 23 | 14 54 | 09 13 | 06 22 | 13 56 | 19 36 |
| 24 | 14 45 | 08 54 | 05 54 | 13 50 | 19 40 |
| 25 | 14 35 | 08 34 | 05 27 | 13 43 | 19 43 |
| 26 | 14 26 | 08 14 | 04 58 | 13 36 | 19 47 |
| 27 | 14 16 | 07 53 | 04 28 | 13 29 | 19 51 |
| 28 | 14 06 | 07 32 | 03 58 | 13 22 | 19 55 |
| 29 | 13 56 | 07 11 | 03 27 | 13 14 | 19 59 |
| 30 | 13 46 | 06 49 | 02 54 | 13 06 | 20 04 |
| 31 | 13 36 | 06 26 | 02 21 | 12 58 | 20 08 |
| 32 | 13 25 | 06 03 | 01 46 | 12 50 | 20 12 |
| 33 | 13 14 | 05 39 | 01 10 | 12 41 | 20 17 |
| 34 | 13 03 | 05 15 | 00 33 | 12 32 | 20 22 |
| 35 | 12 52 | 04 50 | 29♑55 | 12 23 | 20 27 |
| 36 | 12 40 | 04 24 | 29 15 | 12 13 | 20 32 |
| 37 | 12 28 | 03 58 | 28 33 | 12 02 | 20 37 |
| 38 | 12 16 | 03 31 | 27 50 | 11 51 | 20 42 |
| 39 | 12 03 | 03 03 | 27 05 | 11 40 | 20 48 |
| 40 | 11 50 | 02 34 | 26 18 | 11 28 | 20 54 |
| 41 | 11 37 | 02 04 | 25 29 | 11 16 | 21 00 |
| 42 | 11 23 | 01 33 | 24 38 | 11 02 | 21 06 |
| 43 | 11 08 | 01 01 | 23 44 | 10 48 | 21 13 |
| 44 | 10 53 | 00 27 | 22 48 | 10 34 | 21 20 |
| 45 | 10 38 | 29♐53 | 21 49 | 10 18 | 21 27 |
| 46 | 10 22 | 29 17 | 20 47 | 10 01 | 21 34 |
| 47 | 10 05 | 28 39 | 19 42 | 09 43 | 21 42 |
| 48 | 09 48 | 28 00 | 18 34 | 09 24 | 21 51 |
| 49 | 09 30 | 27 19 | 17 22 | 09 04 | 21 59 |
| 50 | 09 11 | 26 36 | 16 06 | 08 42 | 22 09 |
| 51 | 08 51 | 25 52 | 14 45 | 08 18 | 22 18 |
| 52 | 08 31 | 25 04 | 13 20 | 07 52 | 22 29 |
| 53 | 08 09 | 24 15 | 11 50 | 07 24 | 22 40 |
| 54 | 07 46 | 23 23 | 10 15 | 06 54 | 22 52 |
| 55 | 07 22 | 22 28 | 08 34 | 06 20 | 23 04 |
| 56 | 06 56 | 21 30 | 06 47 | 05 43 | 23 18 |
| 57 | 06 29 | 20 28 | 04 53 | 05 01 | 23 32 |
| 58 | 06 00 | 19 22 | 02 52 | 04 15 | 23 48 |
| 59 | 05 30 | 18 12 | 00 44 | 03 22 | 24 05 |
| 60 | 04♐57 | 16♐58 | 28♐28 | 02♓22 | 24♈24 |

**15h 12m 0s — 228° 0' 0" — 20 ♏ 26**

| LAT. | 11 | 12 | ASC | 2 | 3 |
|---|---|---|---|---|---|
| 0 | 18♐58 | 16♑36 | 15♒32 | 16♓57 | 19♈30 |
| 5 | 18 19 | 15 18 | 14 02 | 16 37 | 19 45 |
| 10 | 17 39 | 13 59 | 12 26 | 16 16 | 20 00 |
| 15 | 16 58 | 12 35 | 10 41 | 15 53 | 20 16 |
| 20 | 16 16 | 11 07 | 08 45 | 15 27 | 20 33 |
| 21 | 16 07 | 10 48 | 08 20 | 15 21 | 20 37 |
| 22 | 15 58 | 10 29 | 07 54 | 15 16 | 20 40 |
| 23 | 15 49 | 10 10 | 07 28 | 15 10 | 20 44 |
| 24 | 15 39 | 09 51 | 07 01 | 15 04 | 20 48 |
| 25 | 15 30 | 09 31 | 06 34 | 14 57 | 20 52 |
| 26 | 15 21 | 09 10 | 06 05 | 14 51 | 20 56 |
| 27 | 15 11 | 08 50 | 05 36 | 14 45 | 21 00 |
| 28 | 15 01 | 08 29 | 05 06 | 14 38 | 21 04 |
| 29 | 14 51 | 08 07 | 04 35 | 14 31 | 21 09 |
| 30 | 14 41 | 07 45 | 04 03 | 14 23 | 21 13 |
| 31 | 14 30 | 07 23 | 03 29 | 14 16 | 21 18 |
| 32 | 14 20 | 06 59 | 02 55 | 14 08 | 21 22 |
| 33 | 14 09 | 06 36 | 02 19 | 14 00 | 21 27 |
| 34 | 13 57 | 06 11 | 01 43 | 13 52 | 21 32 |
| 35 | 13 46 | 05 46 | 01 04 | 13 43 | 21 37 |
| 36 | 13 34 | 05 21 | 00 25 | 13 34 | 21 43 |
| 37 | 13 22 | 04 54 | 29♑43 | 13 24 | 21 48 |
| 38 | 13 10 | 04 27 | 29 00 | 13 14 | 21 54 |
| 39 | 12 57 | 03 59 | 28 15 | 13 03 | 22 00 |
| 40 | 12 44 | 03 30 | 27 28 | 12 52 | 22 06 |
| 41 | 12 30 | 02 59 | 26 39 | 12 41 | 22 12 |
| 42 | 12 16 | 02 28 | 25 48 | 12 28 | 22 19 |
| 43 | 12 02 | 01 56 | 24 55 | 12 15 | 22 26 |
| 44 | 11 47 | 01 23 | 23 58 | 12 02 | 22 33 |
| 45 | 11 31 | 00 48 | 22 59 | 11 47 | 22 41 |
| 46 | 11 15 | 00 12 | 21 57 | 11 31 | 22 49 |
| 47 | 10 58 | 29♐34 | 20 52 | 11 15 | 22 57 |
| 48 | 10 41 | 28 54 | 19 43 | 10 57 | 23 06 |
| 49 | 10 23 | 28 13 | 18 31 | 10 38 | 23 15 |
| 50 | 10 04 | 27 30 | 17 14 | 10 18 | 23 25 |
| 51 | 09 44 | 26 45 | 15 53 | 09 56 | 23 35 |
| 52 | 09 23 | 25 58 | 14 27 | 09 32 | 23 46 |
| 53 | 09 01 | 25 08 | 12 57 | 09 05 | 23 58 |
| 54 | 08 38 | 24 15 | 11 20 | 08 37 | 24 10 |
| 55 | 08 13 | 23 19 | 09 38 | 08 05 | 24 23 |
| 56 | 07 47 | 22 21 | 07 49 | 07 31 | 24 38 |
| 57 | 07 20 | 21 18 | 05 54 | 06 52 | 24 53 |
| 58 | 06 51 | 20 12 | 03 51 | 06 09 | 25 10 |
| 59 | 06 19 | 19 01 | 01 41 | 05 20 | 25 28 |
| 60 | 05♐46 | 17♐45 | 29♐22 | 04♓24 | 25♈47 |

**15h 16m 0s — 229° 0' 0" — 21 ♏ 26**

| LAT. | 11 | 12 | ASC | 2 | 3 |
|---|---|---|---|---|---|
| 0 | 19♐53 | 17♑32 | 16♒33 | 18♓02 | 20♈34 |
| 5 | 19 14 | 16 15 | 15 04 | 17 44 | 20 50 |
| 10 | 18 34 | 14 55 | 13 29 | 17 24 | 21 06 |
| 15 | 17 53 | 13 32 | 11 46 | 17 03 | 21 22 |
| 20 | 17 10 | 12 03 | 09 51 | 16 39 | 21 40 |
| 21 | 17 02 | 11 45 | 09 26 | 16 34 | 21 44 |
| 22 | 16 53 | 11 26 | 09 01 | 16 29 | 21 48 |
| 23 | 16 43 | 11 07 | 08 35 | 16 23 | 21 52 |
| 24 | 16 34 | 10 47 | 08 09 | 16 18 | 21 56 |
| 25 | 16 25 | 10 28 | 07 41 | 16 12 | 22 00 |
| 26 | 16 15 | 10 07 | 07 13 | 16 06 | 22 05 |
| 27 | 16 05 | 09 47 | 06 44 | 16 00 | 22 09 |
| 28 | 15 56 | 09 26 | 06 14 | 15 54 | 22 13 |
| 29 | 15 45 | 09 04 | 05 43 | 15 47 | 22 18 |
| 30 | 15 35 | 08 42 | 05 12 | 15 41 | 22 23 |
| 31 | 15 25 | 08 19 | 04 39 | 15 34 | 22 27 |
| 32 | 15 14 | 07 56 | 04 05 | 15 27 | 22 32 |
| 33 | 15 03 | 07 32 | 03 29 | 15 19 | 22 37 |
| 34 | 14 52 | 07 08 | 02 53 | 15 11 | 22 43 |
| 35 | 14 40 | 06 43 | 02 14 | 15 03 | 22 48 |
| 36 | 14 28 | 06 17 | 01 35 | 14 55 | 22 54 |
| 37 | 14 16 | 05 51 | 00 54 | 14 46 | 22 59 |
| 38 | 14 04 | 05 23 | 00 11 | 14 37 | 23 05 |
| 39 | 13 51 | 04 55 | 29♑26 | 14 27 | 23 12 |
| 40 | 13 38 | 04 26 | 28 39 | 14 17 | 23 18 |
| 41 | 13 24 | 03 56 | 27 51 | 14 06 | 23 25 |
| 42 | 13 10 | 03 24 | 26 59 | 13 55 | 23 32 |
| 43 | 12 55 | 02 52 | 26 06 | 13 43 | 23 39 |
| 44 | 12 40 | 02 18 | 25 10 | 13 30 | 23 47 |
| 45 | 12 24 | 01 43 | 24 11 | 13 17 | 23 55 |
| 46 | 12 08 | 01 07 | 23 08 | 13 02 | 24 03 |
| 47 | 11 51 | 00 29 | 22 03 | 12 47 | 24 12 |
| 48 | 11 34 | 29♐49 | 20 54 | 12 31 | 24 21 |
| 49 | 11 15 | 29 08 | 19 41 | 12 13 | 24 31 |
| 50 | 10 56 | 28 24 | 18 24 | 11 54 | 24 41 |
| 51 | 10 36 | 27 39 | 17 02 | 11 34 | 24 52 |
| 52 | 10 15 | 26 51 | 15 36 | 11 11 | 25 03 |
| 53 | 09 53 | 26 01 | 14 04 | 10 47 | 25 15 |
| 54 | 09 29 | 25 08 | 12 27 | 10 21 | 25 29 |
| 55 | 09 05 | 24 11 | 10 43 | 09 52 | 25 42 |
| 56 | 08 38 | 23 12 | 08 53 | 09 20 | 25 57 |
| 57 | 08 11 | 22 09 | 06 56 | 08 44 | 26 14 |
| 58 | 07 41 | 21 01 | 04 51 | 08 04 | 26 31 |
| 59 | 07 09 | 19 50 | 02 38 | 07 18 | 26 50 |
| 60 | 06♐35 | 18♐33 | 00♑17 | 06♓27 | 27♈11 |

**15h 20m 0s — 230° 0' 0" — 22 ♏ 25**

| LAT. | 11 | 12 | ASC | 2 | 3 |
|---|---|---|---|---|---|
| 0 | 20♐49 | 18♑28 | 17♒33 | 19♓07 | 21♈38 |
| 5 | 20 09 | 17 11 | 16 06 | 18 50 | 21 54 |
| 10 | 19 29 | 15 52 | 14 33 | 18 33 | 22 11 |
| 15 | 18 48 | 14 29 | 12 51 | 18 13 | 22 29 |
| 20 | 18 05 | 13 00 | 10 58 | 17 51 | 22 48 |
| 21 | 17 56 | 12 42 | 10 33 | 17 47 | 22 52 |
| 22 | 17 47 | 12 23 | 10 08 | 17 42 | 22 56 |
| 23 | 17 38 | 12 04 | 09 43 | 17 37 | 23 00 |
| 24 | 17 29 | 11 44 | 09 17 | 17 32 | 23 04 |
| 25 | 17 19 | 11 25 | 08 49 | 17 27 | 23 09 |
| 26 | 17 10 | 11 04 | 08 22 | 17 21 | 23 13 |
| 27 | 17 00 | 10 44 | 07 53 | 17 16 | 23 18 |
| 28 | 16 50 | 10 23 | 07 23 | 17 10 | 23 22 |
| 29 | 16 40 | 10 01 | 06 53 | 17 04 | 23 27 |
| 30 | 16 30 | 09 39 | 06 21 | 16 58 | 23 32 |
| 31 | 16 19 | 09 16 | 05 48 | 16 52 | 23 37 |
| 32 | 16 08 | 08 53 | 05 15 | 16 45 | 23 42 |
| 33 | 15 57 | 08 29 | 04 40 | 16 38 | 23 47 |
| 34 | 15 46 | 08 05 | 04 03 | 16 31 | 23 53 |
| 35 | 15 34 | 07 40 | 03 25 | 16 24 | 23 59 |
| 36 | 15 22 | 07 14 | 02 46 | 16 16 | 24 04 |
| 37 | 15 10 | 06 47 | 02 05 | 16 08 | 24 10 |
| 38 | 14 58 | 06 20 | 01 22 | 16 00 | 24 17 |
| 39 | 14 45 | 05 52 | 00 38 | 15 51 | 24 23 |
| 40 | 14 31 | 05 22 | 29♑51 | 15 41 | 24 30 |
| 41 | 14 18 | 04 52 | 29 03 | 15 32 | 24 37 |
| 42 | 14 03 | 04 21 | 28 12 | 15 21 | 24 44 |
| 43 | 13 49 | 03 48 | 27 18 | 15 10 | 24 52 |
| 44 | 13 33 | 03 14 | 26 22 | 14 59 | 25 00 |
| 45 | 13 18 | 02 39 | 25 23 | 14 46 | 25 08 |
| 46 | 13 01 | 02 02 | 24 20 | 14 33 | 25 17 |
| 47 | 12 44 | 01 24 | 23 15 | 14 19 | 25 26 |
| 48 | 12 27 | 00 44 | 22 06 | 14 04 | 25 36 |
| 49 | 12 08 | 00 03 | 20 52 | 13 48 | 25 46 |
| 50 | 11 49 | 29♐19 | 19 35 | 13 31 | 25 57 |
| 51 | 11 28 | 28 33 | 18 13 | 13 12 | 26 08 |
| 52 | 11 07 | 27 45 | 16 45 | 12 52 | 26 20 |
| 53 | 10 45 | 26 54 | 15 13 | 12 30 | 26 33 |
| 54 | 10 21 | 26 00 | 13 34 | 12 06 | 26 47 |
| 55 | 09 56 | 25 04 | 11 49 | 11 39 | 27 01 |
| 56 | 09 30 | 24 04 | 09 58 | 11 10 | 27 17 |
| 57 | 09 01 | 23 00 | 07 59 | 10 37 | 27 34 |
| 58 | 08 31 | 21 51 | 05 52 | 10 00 | 27 52 |
| 59 | 07 59 | 20 39 | 03 37 | 09 18 | 28 12 |
| 60 | 07♐25 | 19♐21 | 01♑13 | 08♓31 | 28♈34 |

**15h 24m 0s — 231° 0' 0" — 23 ♏ 23**

| LAT. | 11 | 12 | ASC | 2 | 3 |
|---|---|---|---|---|---|
| 0 | 21♐44 | 19♑24 | 18♒34 | 20♓12 | 22♈42 |
| 5 | 21 04 | 18 07 | 17 08 | 19 57 | 22 59 |
| 10 | 20 24 | 16 48 | 15 36 | 19 41 | 23 17 |
| 15 | 19 43 | 15 26 | 13 56 | 19 23 | 23 35 |
| 20 | 19 00 | 13 57 | 12 05 | 19 04 | 23 55 |
| 21 | 18 51 | 13 39 | 11 41 | 19 00 | 23 59 |
| 22 | 18 42 | 13 20 | 11 16 | 18 55 | 24 03 |
| 23 | 18 33 | 13 01 | 10 51 | 18 51 | 24 08 |
| 24 | 18 24 | 12 42 | 10 25 | 18 46 | 24 12 |
| 25 | 18 14 | 12 22 | 09 58 | 18 42 | 24 17 |
| 26 | 18 04 | 12 02 | 09 30 | 18 37 | 24 21 |
| 27 | 17 55 | 11 41 | 09 02 | 18 32 | 24 26 |
| 28 | 17 45 | 11 20 | 08 33 | 18 27 | 24 31 |
| 29 | 17 34 | 10 58 | 08 03 | 18 21 | 24 36 |
| 30 | 17 24 | 10 36 | 07 31 | 18 16 | 24 41 |
| 31 | 17 13 | 10 14 | 06 59 | 18 10 | 24 46 |
| 32 | 17 03 | 09 50 | 06 25 | 18 04 | 24 52 |
| 33 | 16 51 | 09 27 | 05 51 | 17 58 | 24 57 |
| 34 | 16 40 | 09 02 | 05 14 | 17 52 | 25 03 |
| 35 | 16 28 | 08 37 | 04 37 | 17 45 | 25 09 |
| 36 | 16 16 | 08 11 | 03 58 | 17 38 | 25 15 |
| 37 | 16 04 | 07 44 | 03 17 | 17 31 | 25 21 |
| 38 | 15 51 | 07 17 | 02 35 | 17 23 | 25 28 |
| 39 | 15 38 | 06 48 | 01 50 | 17 15 | 25 35 |
| 40 | 15 25 | 06 19 | 01 04 | 17 06 | 25 42 |
| 41 | 15 11 | 05 49 | 00 15 | 16 58 | 25 49 |
| 42 | 14 57 | 05 17 | 29♑25 | 16 48 | 25 57 |
| 43 | 14 42 | 04 44 | 28 31 | 16 38 | 26 05 |
| 44 | 14 27 | 04 11 | 27 35 | 16 28 | 26 13 |
| 45 | 14 11 | 03 35 | 26 36 | 16 17 | 26 22 |
| 46 | 13 54 | 02 58 | 25 34 | 16 05 | 26 31 |
| 47 | 13 37 | 02 20 | 24 28 | 15 52 | 26 40 |
| 48 | 13 19 | 01 40 | 23 18 | 15 39 | 26 50 |
| 49 | 13 01 | 00 58 | 22 05 | 15 24 | 27 01 |
| 50 | 12 41 | 00 14 | 20 47 | 15 08 | 27 12 |
| 51 | 12 21 | 29♐28 | 19 24 | 14 51 | 27 24 |
| 52 | 11 59 | 28 39 | 17 56 | 14 33 | 27 36 |
| 53 | 11 37 | 27 48 | 16 23 | 14 13 | 27 50 |
| 54 | 11 13 | 26 54 | 14 43 | 13 51 | 28 04 |
| 55 | 10 48 | 25 56 | 12 57 | 13 27 | 28 19 |
| 56 | 10 21 | 24 56 | 11 04 | 13 00 | 28 36 |
| 57 | 09 52 | 23 51 | 09 03 | 12 30 | 28 54 |
| 58 | 09 22 | 22 42 | 06 54 | 11 57 | 29 13 |
| 59 | 08 49 | 21 28 | 04 37 | 11 19 | 29 33 |
| 60 | 08♐14 | 20♐09 | 02♑10 | 10♓36 | 29♈56 |

# Placidus Table of Houses for Latitudes 0° to 60° North

15h 28m 0s — 232° 0' 0" — 24 ♏ 22

| LAT. | 11 | 12 | ASC | 2 | 3 |
|---|---|---|---|---|---|
| 0 | 22♐39 | 20♑20 | 19♒35 | 21♓17 | 23♈46 |
| 5 | 22 00 | 19 04 | 18 11 | 21 04 | 24 04 |
| 10 | 21 20 | 17 45 | 16 41 | 20 50 | 24 22 |
| 15 | 20 38 | 16 23 | 15 02 | 20 34 | 24 41 |
| 20 | 19 55 | 14 55 | 13 12 | 20 16 | 25 02 |
| 21 | 19 46 | 14 36 | 12 48 | 20 13 | 25 06 |
| 22 | 19 37 | 14 18 | 12 24 | 20 09 | 25 10 |
| 23 | 19 28 | 13 59 | 11 59 | 20 05 | 25 15 |
| 24 | 19 18 | 13 39 | 11 33 | 20 01 | 25 20 |
| 25 | 19 09 | 13 19 | 11 07 | 19 57 | 25 24 |
| 26 | 18 59 | 12 59 | 10 40 | 19 52 | 25 29 |
| 27 | 18 49 | 12 38 | 10 12 | 19 48 | 25 34 |
| 28 | 18 39 | 12 17 | 09 43 | 19 43 | 25 39 |
| 29 | 18 29 | 11 56 | 09 13 | 19 39 | 25 44 |
| 30 | 18 18 | 11 34 | 08 42 | 19 34 | 25 50 |
| 31 | 18 08 | 11 11 | 08 10 | 19 29 | 25 55 |
| 32 | 17 57 | 10 48 | 07 37 | 19 23 | 26 01 |
| 33 | 17 46 | 10 24 | 07 02 | 19 18 | 26 07 |
| 34 | 17 34 | 09 59 | 06 26 | 19 12 | 26 13 |
| 35 | 17 23 | 09 34 | 05 49 | 19 06 | 26 19 |
| 36 | 17 11 | 09 08 | 05 10 | 19 00 | 26 25 |
| 37 | 16 58 | 08 42 | 04 30 | 18 53 | 26 32 |
| 38 | 16 45 | 08 14 | 03 48 | 18 46 | 26 39 |
| 39 | 16 32 | 07 46 | 03 04 | 18 39 | 26 46 |
| 40 | 16 19 | 07 16 | 02 18 | 18 32 | 26 53 |
| 41 | 16 05 | 06 46 | 01 29 | 18 24 | 27 01 |
| 42 | 15 51 | 06 14 | 00 38 | 18 15 | 27 09 |
| 43 | 15 36 | 05 41 | 29♑45 | 18 07 | 27 17 |
| 44 | 15 20 | 05 07 | 28 49 | 17 57 | 27 25 |
| 45 | 15 04 | 04 32 | 27 50 | 17 47 | 27 35 |
| 46 | 14 48 | 03 55 | 26 48 | 17 37 | 27 44 |
| 47 | 14 30 | 03 16 | 25 42 | 17 25 | 27 54 |
| 48 | 14 12 | 02 36 | 24 32 | 17 13 | 28 04 |
| 49 | 13 54 | 01 54 | 23 18 | 17 00 | 28 15 |
| 50 | 13 34 | 01 09 | 22 00 | 16 46 | 28 27 |
| 51 | 13 13 | 00 23 | 20 37 | 16 31 | 28 39 |
| 52 | 12 52 | 29♐34 | 19 08 | 16 15 | 28 53 |
| 53 | 12 29 | 28 42 | 17 34 | 15 57 | 29 07 |
| 54 | 12 05 | 27 47 | 15 54 | 15 37 | 29 21 |
| 55 | 11 39 | 26 50 | 14 06 | 15 16 | 29 37 |
| 56 | 11 12 | 25 48 | 12 12 | 14 52 | 29 54 |
| 57 | 10 43 | 24 43 | 10 09 | 14 25 | 00♉13 |
| 58 | 10 13 | 23 33 | 07 58 | 13 55 | 00 33 |
| 59 | 09 40 | 22 18 | 05 38 | 13 21 | 00 54 |
| 60 | 09♐04 | 20♐58 | 03♑09 | 12♓43 | 01♉18 |

15h 32m 0s — 233° 0' 0" — 25 ♏ 21

| LAT. | 11 | 12 | ASC | 2 | 3 |
|---|---|---|---|---|---|
| 0 | 23♐34 | 21♑17 | 20♒36 | 22♓23 | 24♈50 |
| 5 | 22 55 | 20 01 | 19 14 | 22 11 | 25 08 |
| 10 | 22 15 | 18 42 | 17 45 | 21 58 | 25 27 |
| 15 | 21 33 | 17 20 | 16 08 | 21 44 | 25 47 |
| 20 | 20 50 | 15 52 | 14 20 | 21 29 | 26 08 |
| 21 | 20 41 | 15 34 | 13 56 | 21 26 | 26 13 |
| 22 | 20 32 | 15 15 | 13 33 | 21 22 | 26 17 |
| 23 | 20 22 | 14 56 | 13 08 | 21 19 | 26 22 |
| 24 | 20 13 | 14 37 | 12 43 | 21 15 | 26 27 |
| 25 | 20 03 | 14 17 | 12 17 | 21 12 | 26 32 |
| 26 | 19 54 | 13 57 | 11 50 | 21 08 | 26 37 |
| 27 | 19 44 | 13 36 | 11 22 | 21 04 | 26 42 |
| 28 | 19 34 | 13 15 | 10 53 | 21 00 | 26 47 |
| 29 | 19 23 | 12 53 | 10 24 | 20 56 | 26 53 |
| 30 | 19 13 | 12 31 | 09 53 | 20 52 | 26 58 |
| 31 | 19 02 | 12 09 | 09 22 | 20 47 | 27 04 |
| 32 | 18 51 | 11 46 | 08 49 | 20 42 | 27 10 |
| 33 | 18 40 | 11 22 | 08 15 | 20 38 | 27 16 |
| 34 | 18 28 | 10 57 | 07 39 | 20 33 | 27 22 |
| 35 | 18 17 | 10 32 | 07 02 | 20 27 | 27 28 |
| 36 | 18 05 | 10 06 | 06 24 | 20 22 | 27 35 |
| 37 | 17 52 | 09 39 | 05 44 | 20 16 | 27 42 |
| 38 | 17 39 | 09 12 | 05 02 | 20 10 | 27 49 |
| 39 | 17 26 | 08 43 | 04 18 | 20 04 | 27 56 |
| 40 | 17 13 | 08 14 | 03 32 | 19 57 | 28 04 |
| 41 | 16 59 | 07 43 | 02 44 | 19 50 | 28 12 |
| 42 | 16 44 | 07 11 | 01 53 | 19 43 | 28 20 |
| 43 | 16 29 | 06 38 | 01 00 | 19 35 | 28 29 |
| 44 | 16 14 | 06 04 | 00 04 | 19 27 | 28 38 |
| 45 | 15 58 | 05 29 | 29♑05 | 19 18 | 28 47 |
| 46 | 15 41 | 04 51 | 28 03 | 19 09 | 28 57 |
| 47 | 15 24 | 04 13 | 26 57 | 18 59 | 29 07 |
| 48 | 15 05 | 03 32 | 25 47 | 18 48 | 29 18 |
| 49 | 14 46 | 02 50 | 24 33 | 18 37 | 29 30 |
| 50 | 14 27 | 02 05 | 23 15 | 18 25 | 29 42 |
| 51 | 14 06 | 01 18 | 21 51 | 18 11 | 29 55 |
| 52 | 13 44 | 00 29 | 20 22 | 17 57 | 00♉08 |
| 53 | 13 21 | 29♐37 | 18 47 | 17 41 | 00 23 |
| 54 | 12 57 | 28 42 | 17 06 | 17 24 | 00 38 |
| 55 | 12 31 | 27 43 | 15 17 | 17 05 | 00 55 |
| 56 | 12 03 | 26 41 | 13 21 | 16 44 | 01 13 |
| 57 | 11 34 | 25 35 | 11 17 | 16 20 | 01 32 |
| 58 | 11 03 | 24 24 | 09 04 | 15 54 | 01 53 |
| 59 | 10 30 | 23 09 | 06 41 | 15 24 | 02 15 |
| 60 | 09♐54 | 21♐47 | 04♑08 | 14♓50 | 02♉40 |

15h 36m 0s — 234° 0' 0" — 26 ♏ 19

| LAT. | 11 | 12 | ASC | 2 | 3 |
|---|---|---|---|---|---|
| 0 | 24♐30 | 22♑13 | 21♒37 | 23♓28 | 25♈53 |
| 5 | 23 50 | 20 58 | 20 17 | 23 18 | 26 12 |
| 10 | 23 10 | 19 40 | 18 50 | 23 07 | 26 32 |
| 15 | 22 28 | 18 18 | 17 14 | 22 55 | 26 53 |
| 20 | 21 45 | 16 50 | 15 28 | 22 42 | 27 15 |
| 21 | 21 35 | 16 32 | 15 05 | 22 39 | 27 20 |
| 22 | 21 26 | 16 13 | 14 41 | 22 36 | 27 24 |
| 23 | 21 17 | 15 54 | 14 17 | 22 33 | 27 29 |
| 24 | 21 08 | 15 35 | 13 52 | 22 30 | 27 34 |
| 25 | 20 58 | 15 15 | 13 27 | 22 27 | 27 39 |
| 26 | 20 48 | 14 55 | 13 00 | 22 24 | 27 44 |
| 27 | 20 38 | 14 34 | 12 33 | 22 20 | 27 50 |
| 28 | 20 28 | 14 13 | 12 05 | 22 17 | 27 55 |
| 29 | 20 18 | 13 51 | 11 35 | 22 13 | 28 01 |
| 30 | 20 07 | 13 29 | 11 05 | 22 10 | 28 07 |
| 31 | 19 57 | 13 07 | 10 34 | 22 06 | 28 13 |
| 32 | 19 46 | 12 44 | 10 01 | 22 02 | 28 19 |
| 33 | 19 34 | 12 20 | 09 28 | 21 58 | 28 25 |
| 34 | 19 23 | 11 55 | 08 52 | 21 53 | 28 31 |
| 35 | 19 11 | 11 30 | 08 16 | 21 49 | 28 38 |
| 36 | 18 59 | 11 04 | 07 38 | 21 44 | 28 45 |
| 37 | 18 46 | 10 37 | 06 58 | 21 39 | 28 52 |
| 38 | 18 33 | 10 09 | 06 16 | 21 34 | 28 59 |
| 39 | 18 20 | 09 41 | 05 33 | 21 29 | 29 07 |
| 40 | 18 07 | 09 11 | 04 47 | 21 23 | 29 15 |
| 41 | 17 53 | 08 41 | 04 00 | 21 17 | 29 23 |
| 42 | 17 38 | 08 09 | 03 09 | 21 11 | 29 32 |
| 43 | 17 23 | 07 36 | 02 16 | 21 04 | 29 41 |
| 44 | 17 07 | 07 02 | 01 21 | 20 57 | 29 50 |
| 45 | 16 51 | 06 26 | 00 22 | 20 49 | 00♉00 |
| 46 | 16 34 | 05 48 | 29♑20 | 20 41 | 00 10 |
| 47 | 16 17 | 05 10 | 28 14 | 20 33 | 00 21 |
| 48 | 15 58 | 04 29 | 27 04 | 20 24 | 00 32 |
| 49 | 15 39 | 03 46 | 25 50 | 20 14 | 00 44 |
| 50 | 15 19 | 03 01 | 24 31 | 20 03 | 00 56 |
| 51 | 14 58 | 02 14 | 23 07 | 19 52 | 01 10 |
| 52 | 14 36 | 01 24 | 21 37 | 19 39 | 01 24 |
| 53 | 14 13 | 00 32 | 20 01 | 19 26 | 01 39 |
| 54 | 13 49 | 29♐36 | 18 19 | 19 11 | 01 55 |
| 55 | 13 23 | 28 37 | 16 29 | 18 54 | 02 12 |
| 56 | 12 55 | 27 35 | 14 32 | 18 36 | 02 30 |
| 57 | 12 25 | 26 28 | 12 26 | 18 16 | 02 50 |
| 58 | 11 54 | 25 16 | 10 10 | 17 53 | 03 12 |
| 59 | 11 20 | 24 00 | 07 45 | 17 28 | 03 35 |
| 60 | 10♐44 | 22♐37 | 05♑10 | 16♓59 | 04♉01 |

15h 40m 0s — 235° 0' 0" — 27 ♏ 17

| LAT. | 11 | 12 | ASC | 2 | 3 |
|---|---|---|---|---|---|
| 0 | 25♐25 | 23♑10 | 22♒39 | 24♓33 | 26♈57 |
| 5 | 24 45 | 21 55 | 21 20 | 24 25 | 27 16 |
| 10 | 24 05 | 20 37 | 19 55 | 24 16 | 27 37 |
| 15 | 23 23 | 19 15 | 18 21 | 24 06 | 27 58 |
| 20 | 22 39 | 17 48 | 16 36 | 23 55 | 28 21 |
| 21 | 22 30 | 17 30 | 16 14 | 23 52 | 28 26 |
| 22 | 22 21 | 17 11 | 15 51 | 23 50 | 28 31 |
| 23 | 22 12 | 16 52 | 15 27 | 23 48 | 28 36 |
| 24 | 22 02 | 16 33 | 15 02 | 23 45 | 28 41 |
| 25 | 21 53 | 16 13 | 14 37 | 23 42 | 28 46 |
| 26 | 21 43 | 15 53 | 14 11 | 23 40 | 28 52 |
| 27 | 21 33 | 15 32 | 13 44 | 23 37 | 28 57 |
| 28 | 21 23 | 15 11 | 13 16 | 23 34 | 29 03 |
| 29 | 21 12 | 14 50 | 12 47 | 23 31 | 29 09 |
| 30 | 21 02 | 14 28 | 12 18 | 23 28 | 29 15 |
| 31 | 20 51 | 14 05 | 11 47 | 23 25 | 29 21 |
| 32 | 20 40 | 13 42 | 11 15 | 23 21 | 29 27 |
| 33 | 20 29 | 13 18 | 10 41 | 23 18 | 29 34 |
| 34 | 20 17 | 12 53 | 10 07 | 23 14 | 29 40 |
| 35 | 20 05 | 12 28 | 09 30 | 23 10 | 29 47 |
| 36 | 19 53 | 12 02 | 08 53 | 23 07 | 29 54 |
| 37 | 19 40 | 11 35 | 08 13 | 23 02 | 00♉02 |
| 38 | 19 28 | 11 08 | 07 32 | 22 58 | 00 09 |
| 39 | 19 14 | 10 39 | 06 49 | 22 54 | 00 17 |
| 40 | 19 01 | 10 09 | 06 04 | 22 49 | 00 25 |
| 41 | 18 46 | 09 39 | 05 16 | 22 44 | 00 34 |
| 42 | 18 32 | 09 07 | 04 26 | 22 39 | 00 43 |
| 43 | 18 17 | 08 34 | 03 34 | 22 33 | 00 52 |
| 44 | 18 01 | 07 59 | 02 38 | 22 27 | 01 02 |
| 45 | 17 45 | 07 23 | 01 39 | 22 21 | 01 12 |
| 46 | 17 28 | 06 46 | 00 37 | 22 14 | 01 22 |
| 47 | 17 10 | 06 07 | 29♑32 | 22 07 | 01 33 |
| 48 | 16 52 | 05 26 | 28 22 | 21 59 | 01 45 |
| 49 | 16 32 | 04 43 | 27 07 | 21 51 | 01 57 |
| 50 | 16 12 | 03 58 | 25 48 | 21 42 | 02 10 |
| 51 | 15 51 | 03 10 | 24 24 | 21 33 | 02 24 |
| 52 | 15 29 | 02 20 | 22 54 | 21 22 | 02 39 |
| 53 | 15 05 | 01 27 | 21 17 | 21 11 | 02 54 |
| 54 | 14 41 | 00 31 | 19 34 | 20 58 | 03 11 |
| 55 | 14 14 | 29♐32 | 17 43 | 20 45 | 03 29 |
| 56 | 13 46 | 28 28 | 15 44 | 20 29 | 03 48 |
| 57 | 13 17 | 27 21 | 13 36 | 20 13 | 04 08 |
| 58 | 12 45 | 26 09 | 11 19 | 19 54 | 04 31 |
| 59 | 12 11 | 24 51 | 08 51 | 19 32 | 04 55 |
| 60 | 11♐34 | 23♐27 | 06♑12 | 19♓08 | 05♉22 |

15h 44m 0s — 236° 0' 0" — 28 ♏ 15

| LAT. | 11 | 12 | ASC | 2 | 3 |
|---|---|---|---|---|---|
| 0 | 26♐20 | 24♑06 | 23♒41 | 25♓38 | 28♈00 |
| 5 | 25 40 | 22 52 | 22 23 | 25 32 | 28 20 |
| 10 | 25 00 | 21 34 | 21 00 | 25 24 | 28 41 |
| 15 | 24 18 | 20 13 | 19 28 | 25 17 | 29 03 |
| 20 | 23 34 | 18 46 | 17 45 | 25 08 | 29 27 |
| 21 | 23 25 | 18 28 | 17 23 | 25 06 | 29 32 |
| 22 | 23 16 | 18 09 | 17 00 | 25 04 | 29 37 |
| 23 | 23 06 | 17 50 | 16 37 | 25 02 | 29 43 |
| 24 | 22 57 | 17 31 | 16 13 | 25 00 | 29 48 |
| 25 | 22 47 | 17 11 | 15 48 | 24 58 | 29 53 |
| 26 | 22 38 | 16 51 | 15 22 | 24 56 | 29 59 |
| 27 | 22 28 | 16 31 | 14 56 | 24 53 | 00♉05 |
| 28 | 22 17 | 16 10 | 14 28 | 24 51 | 00 11 |
| 29 | 22 07 | 15 48 | 14 00 | 24 49 | 00 17 |
| 30 | 21 56 | 15 26 | 13 31 | 24 46 | 00 23 |
| 31 | 21 45 | 15 04 | 13 00 | 24 44 | 00 29 |
| 32 | 21 34 | 14 40 | 12 29 | 24 41 | 00 35 |
| 33 | 21 23 | 14 17 | 11 56 | 24 38 | 00 42 |
| 34 | 21 11 | 13 52 | 11 21 | 24 35 | 00 49 |
| 35 | 21 00 | 13 27 | 10 46 | 24 32 | 00 56 |
| 36 | 20 47 | 13 01 | 10 08 | 24 29 | 01 03 |
| 37 | 20 35 | 12 34 | 09 29 | 24 26 | 01 11 |
| 38 | 20 22 | 12 06 | 08 48 | 24 22 | 01 19 |
| 39 | 20 08 | 11 38 | 08 06 | 24 19 | 01 27 |
| 40 | 19 55 | 11 08 | 07 21 | 24 15 | 01 36 |
| 41 | 19 40 | 10 37 | 06 34 | 24 11 | 01 44 |
| 42 | 19 26 | 10 05 | 05 44 | 24 07 | 01 54 |
| 43 | 19 10 | 09 32 | 04 52 | 24 02 | 02 03 |
| 44 | 18 55 | 08 57 | 03 57 | 23 57 | 02 13 |
| 45 | 18 38 | 08 21 | 02 58 | 23 52 | 02 23 |
| 46 | 18 21 | 07 44 | 01 56 | 23 47 | 02 34 |
| 47 | 18 03 | 07 04 | 00 51 | 23 41 | 02 46 |
| 48 | 17 45 | 06 23 | 29♑41 | 23 35 | 02 58 |
| 49 | 17 25 | 05 40 | 28 26 | 23 29 | 03 11 |
| 50 | 17 05 | 04 55 | 27 07 | 23 21 | 03 24 |
| 51 | 16 44 | 04 07 | 25 43 | 23 14 | 03 38 |
| 52 | 16 21 | 03 17 | 24 12 | 23 05 | 03 53 |
| 53 | 15 58 | 02 23 | 22 35 | 22 56 | 04 09 |
| 54 | 15 33 | 01 27 | 20 51 | 22 46 | 04 27 |
| 55 | 15 06 | 00 27 | 18 59 | 22 35 | 04 45 |
| 56 | 14 38 | 29♐23 | 16 59 | 22 23 | 05 05 |
| 57 | 14 08 | 28 15 | 14 49 | 22 09 | 05 26 |
| 58 | 13 36 | 27 02 | 12 29 | 21 54 | 05 49 |
| 59 | 13 01 | 25 43 | 09 59 | 21 37 | 06 14 |
| 60 | 12♐24 | 24♐18 | 07♑17 | 21♓17 | 06♉42 |

15h 48m 0s — 237° 0' 0" — 29 ♏ 13

| LAT. | 11 | 12 | ASC | 2 | 3 |
|---|---|---|---|---|---|
| 0 | 27♐15 | 25♑03 | 24♒42 | 26♓44 | 29♈03 |
| 5 | 26 35 | 23 49 | 23 27 | 26 39 | 29 24 |
| 10 | 25 55 | 22 32 | 22 05 | 26 33 | 29 45 |
| 15 | 25 13 | 21 11 | 20 35 | 26 27 | 00♉08 |
| 20 | 24 29 | 19 45 | 18 55 | 26 21 | 00 33 |
| 21 | 24 20 | 19 26 | 18 33 | 26 19 | 00 38 |
| 22 | 24 11 | 19 08 | 18 11 | 26 18 | 00 44 |
| 23 | 24 01 | 18 49 | 17 48 | 26 16 | 00 49 |
| 24 | 23 52 | 18 30 | 17 24 | 26 15 | 00 54 |
| 25 | 23 42 | 18 10 | 17 00 | 26 13 | 01 00 |
| 26 | 23 32 | 17 50 | 16 34 | 26 12 | 01 06 |
| 27 | 23 22 | 17 30 | 16 08 | 26 10 | 01 12 |
| 28 | 23 12 | 17 09 | 15 41 | 26 08 | 01 18 |
| 29 | 23 02 | 16 47 | 15 13 | 26 06 | 01 24 |
| 30 | 22 51 | 16 25 | 14 44 | 26 05 | 01 30 |
| 31 | 22 40 | 16 02 | 14 14 | 26 03 | 01 37 |
| 32 | 22 29 | 15 39 | 13 43 | 26 01 | 01 44 |
| 33 | 22 17 | 15 15 | 13 11 | 25 59 | 01 50 |
| 34 | 22 06 | 14 51 | 12 37 | 25 56 | 01 58 |
| 35 | 21 54 | 14 26 | 12 02 | 25 54 | 02 05 |
| 36 | 21 42 | 14 00 | 11 25 | 25 52 | 02 12 |
| 37 | 21 29 | 13 33 | 10 46 | 25 49 | 02 20 |
| 38 | 21 16 | 13 05 | 10 06 | 25 47 | 02 28 |
| 39 | 21 02 | 12 36 | 09 23 | 25 44 | 02 37 |
| 40 | 20 49 | 12 07 | 08 39 | 25 41 | 02 45 |
| 41 | 20 34 | 11 36 | 07 52 | 25 38 | 02 55 |
| 42 | 20 20 | 11 04 | 07 03 | 25 35 | 03 04 |
| 43 | 20 04 | 10 31 | 06 11 | 25 32 | 03 14 |
| 44 | 19 48 | 09 56 | 05 16 | 25 28 | 03 24 |
| 45 | 19 32 | 09 20 | 04 18 | 25 24 | 03 35 |
| 46 | 19 15 | 08 42 | 03 16 | 25 20 | 03 46 |
| 47 | 18 57 | 08 03 | 02 11 | 25 16 | 03 58 |
| 48 | 18 38 | 07 21 | 01 01 | 25 11 | 04 10 |
| 49 | 18 19 | 06 38 | 29♑47 | 25 06 | 04 24 |
| 50 | 17 58 | 05 52 | 28 28 | 25 01 | 04 37 |
| 51 | 17 37 | 05 04 | 27 03 | 24 55 | 04 52 |
| 52 | 17 14 | 04 14 | 25 32 | 24 49 | 05 08 |
| 53 | 16 50 | 03 20 | 23 54 | 24 42 | 05 24 |
| 54 | 16 25 | 02 23 | 22 09 | 24 34 | 05 42 |
| 55 | 15 58 | 01 22 | 20 16 | 24 26 | 06 01 |
| 56 | 15 30 | 00 18 | 18 15 | 24 17 | 06 21 |
| 57 | 15 00 | 29♐09 | 16 03 | 24 07 | 06 43 |
| 58 | 14 27 | 27 55 | 13 41 | 23 55 | 07 07 |
| 59 | 13 52 | 26 35 | 11 08 | 23 42 | 07 33 |
| 60 | 13♐14 | 25♐09 | 08♑23 | 23♓28 | 08♉01 |

15h 52m 0s — 238° 0' 0" — 00 ♐ 11

| LAT. | 11 | 12 | ASC | 2 | 3 |
|---|---|---|---|---|---|
| 0 | 28♐10 | 26♑00 | 25♒44 | 27♓49 | 00♉06 |
| 5 | 27 30 | 24 46 | 24 31 | 27 46 | 00 27 |
| 10 | 26 50 | 23 30 | 23 11 | 27 42 | 00 50 |
| 15 | 26 08 | 22 09 | 21 43 | 27 38 | 01 13 |
| 20 | 25 24 | 20 43 | 20 04 | 27 34 | 01 39 |
| 21 | 25 15 | 20 25 | 19 43 | 27 33 | 01 44 |
| 22 | 25 05 | 20 07 | 19 21 | 27 32 | 01 50 |
| 23 | 24 56 | 19 48 | 18 59 | 27 31 | 01 55 |
| 24 | 24 46 | 19 29 | 18 35 | 27 30 | 02 01 |
| 25 | 24 37 | 19 09 | 18 11 | 27 29 | 02 07 |
| 26 | 24 27 | 18 49 | 17 47 | 27 28 | 02 13 |
| 27 | 24 17 | 18 29 | 17 21 | 27 27 | 02 19 |
| 28 | 24 07 | 18 08 | 16 55 | 27 25 | 02 25 |
| 29 | 23 56 | 17 46 | 16 27 | 27 24 | 02 31 |
| 30 | 23 45 | 17 24 | 15 59 | 27 23 | 02 38 |
| 31 | 23 35 | 17 02 | 15 29 | 27 22 | 02 44 |
| 32 | 23 23 | 16 38 | 14 58 | 27 20 | 02 51 |
| 33 | 23 12 | 16 15 | 14 26 | 27 19 | 02 58 |
| 34 | 23 00 | 15 50 | 13 53 | 27 18 | 03 06 |
| 35 | 22 48 | 15 25 | 13 18 | 27 16 | 03 13 |
| 36 | 22 36 | 14 59 | 12 42 | 27 14 | 03 21 |
| 37 | 22 23 | 14 32 | 12 04 | 27 13 | 03 29 |
| 38 | 22 10 | 14 04 | 11 24 | 27 11 | 03 37 |
| 39 | 21 57 | 13 36 | 10 42 | 27 09 | 03 46 |
| 40 | 21 43 | 13 06 | 09 58 | 27 07 | 03 55 |
| 41 | 21 28 | 12 35 | 09 12 | 27 05 | 04 04 |
| 42 | 21 14 | 12 03 | 08 23 | 27 03 | 04 14 |
| 43 | 20 58 | 11 30 | 07 32 | 27 01 | 04 24 |
| 44 | 20 42 | 10 55 | 06 37 | 26 59 | 04 35 |
| 45 | 20 26 | 10 19 | 05 39 | 26 56 | 04 46 |
| 46 | 20 08 | 09 41 | 04 38 | 26 53 | 04 58 |
| 47 | 19 50 | 09 01 | 03 33 | 26 50 | 05 10 |
| 48 | 19 32 | 08 20 | 02 23 | 26 47 | 05 23 |
| 49 | 19 12 | 07 36 | 01 09 | 26 44 | 05 36 |
| 50 | 18 51 | 06 50 | 29♑50 | 26 41 | 05 50 |
| 51 | 18 30 | 06 02 | 28 25 | 26 37 | 06 05 |
| 52 | 18 07 | 05 11 | 26 54 | 26 32 | 06 21 |
| 53 | 17 43 | 04 17 | 25 16 | 26 28 | 06 39 |
| 54 | 17 18 | 03 20 | 23 30 | 26 23 | 06 57 |
| 55 | 16 51 | 02 18 | 21 36 | 26 17 | 07 16 |
| 56 | 16 22 | 01 13 | 19 33 | 26 11 | 07 37 |
| 57 | 15 51 | 00 04 | 17 20 | 26 04 | 08 00 |
| 58 | 15 18 | 28♐49 | 14 56 | 25 57 | 08 25 |
| 59 | 14 43 | 27 28 | 12 20 | 25 48 | 08 51 |
| 60 | 14♐04 | 26♐01 | 09♑31 | 25♓38 | 09♉21 |

15h 56m 0s — 239° 0' 0" — 01 ♐ 08

| LAT. | 11 | 12 | ASC | 2 | 3 |
|---|---|---|---|---|---|
| 0 | 29♐05 | 26♑57 | 26♒47 | 28♓55 | 01♉08 |
| 5 | 28 25 | 25 44 | 25 35 | 28 53 | 01 31 |
| 10 | 27 45 | 24 28 | 24 17 | 28 51 | 01 54 |
| 15 | 27 03 | 23 08 | 22 51 | 28 49 | 02 18 |
| 20 | 26 19 | 21 42 | 21 15 | 28 47 | 02 44 |
| 21 | 26 10 | 21 24 | 20 54 | 28 46 | 02 50 |
| 22 | 26 00 | 21 06 | 20 32 | 28 46 | 02 55 |
| 23 | 25 51 | 20 47 | 20 10 | 28 45 | 03 01 |
| 24 | 25 41 | 20 28 | 19 47 | 28 45 | 03 07 |
| 25 | 25 32 | 20 08 | 19 24 | 28 44 | 03 13 |
| 26 | 25 22 | 19 48 | 19 00 | 28 44 | 03 19 |
| 27 | 25 12 | 19 28 | 18 34 | 28 43 | 03 25 |
| 28 | 25 01 | 19 07 | 18 08 | 28 43 | 03 32 |
| 29 | 24 51 | 18 46 | 17 41 | 28 42 | 03 38 |
| 30 | 24 40 | 18 24 | 17 14 | 28 41 | 03 45 |
| 31 | 24 29 | 18 01 | 16 44 | 28 41 | 03 52 |
| 32 | 24 18 | 17 38 | 16 14 | 28 40 | 03 59 |
| 33 | 24 07 | 17 14 | 15 43 | 28 39 | 04 06 |
| 34 | 23 55 | 16 50 | 15 10 | 28 39 | 04 14 |
| 35 | 23 43 | 16 25 | 14 36 | 28 38 | 04 21 |
| 36 | 23 30 | 15 59 | 14 00 | 28 37 | 04 29 |
| 37 | 23 18 | 15 32 | 13 22 | 28 36 | 04 38 |
| 38 | 23 04 | 15 04 | 12 43 | 28 36 | 04 46 |
| 39 | 22 51 | 14 35 | 12 02 | 28 35 | 04 55 |
| 40 | 22 37 | 14 05 | 11 18 | 28 34 | 05 04 |
| 41 | 22 23 | 13 34 | 10 32 | 28 33 | 05 14 |
| 42 | 22 08 | 13 02 | 09 44 | 28 32 | 05 24 |
| 43 | 21 52 | 12 29 | 08 53 | 28 30 | 05 34 |
| 44 | 21 36 | 11 54 | 07 59 | 28 29 | 05 45 |
| 45 | 21 19 | 11 18 | 07 02 | 28 28 | 05 57 |
| 46 | 21 02 | 10 40 | 06 01 | 28 27 | 06 09 |
| 47 | 20 44 | 10 00 | 04 56 | 28 26 | 06 21 |
| 48 | 20 25 | 09 19 | 03 47 | 28 24 | 06 34 |
| 49 | 20 05 | 08 35 | 02 33 | 28 22 | 06 48 |
| 50 | 19 45 | 07 49 | 01 13 | 28 21 | 07 03 |
| 51 | 19 23 | 07 00 | 29♑48 | 28 18 | 07 18 |
| 52 | 19 00 | 06 09 | 28 17 | 28 16 | 07 35 |
| 53 | 18 36 | 05 14 | 26 39 | 28 14 | 07 52 |
| 54 | 18 10 | 04 17 | 24 52 | 28 11 | 08 11 |
| 55 | 17 43 | 03 15 | 22 57 | 28 09 | 08 31 |
| 56 | 17 14 | 02 09 | 20 53 | 28 06 | 08 53 |
| 57 | 16 43 | 00 59 | 18 38 | 28 02 | 09 16 |
| 58 | 16 10 | 29♐43 | 16 12 | 27 58 | 09 42 |
| 59 | 15 34 | 28 22 | 13 34 | 27 54 | 10 09 |
| 60 | 14♐55 | 26♐54 | 10♑42 | 27♓49 | 10♉39 |

# Placidus Table of Houses for Latitudes 0° to 60° North

**16h 0m 0s — 240° 0' 0" — 02 ♐ 05**

| LAT. | 11 | 12 | ASC | 2 | 3 |
|---|---|---|---|---|---|
| 0 | 00♑00 | 27♑55 | 27♒49 | 00♈00 | 02♉11 |
| 5 | 29♐20 | 26 42 | 26 39 | 00 00 | 02 34 |
| 10 | 28 40 | 25 26 | 25 23 | 00 00 | 02 58 |
| 15 | 27 58 | 24 07 | 23 59 | 00 00 | 03 23 |
| 20 | 27 14 | 22 41 | 22 25 | 00 00 | 03 49 |
| 21 | 27 04 | 22 23 | 22 05 | 00 00 | 03 55 |
| 22 | 26 55 | 22 05 | 21 44 | 00 00 | 04 01 |
| 23 | 26 46 | 21 46 | 21 22 | 00 00 | 04 07 |
| 24 | 26 36 | 21 27 | 21 00 | 00 00 | 04 13 |
| 25 | 26 26 | 21 08 | 20 37 | 00 00 | 04 19 |
| 26 | 26 16 | 20 48 | 20 13 | 00 00 | 04 25 |
| 27 | 26 06 | 20 27 | 19 48 | 00 00 | 04 32 |
| 28 | 25 56 | 20 07 | 19 23 | 00 00 | 04 38 |
| 29 | 25 46 | 19 45 | 18 56 | 00 00 | 04 45 |
| 30 | 25 35 | 19 23 | 18 29 | 00 00 | 04 52 |
| 31 | 25 24 | 19 01 | 18 00 | 00 00 | 04 59 |
| 32 | 25 13 | 18 38 | 17 31 | 00 00 | 05 06 |
| 33 | 25 01 | 18 14 | 17 00 | 00 00 | 05 14 |
| 34 | 24 49 | 17 50 | 16 28 | 00 00 | 05 21 |
| 35 | 24 37 | 17 24 | 15 54 | 00 00 | 05 29 |
| 36 | 24 25 | 16 58 | 15 19 | 00 00 | 05 38 |
| 37 | 24 12 | 16 32 | 14 42 | 00 00 | 05 46 |
| 38 | 23 59 | 16 04 | 14 03 | 00 00 | 05 55 |
| 39 | 23 45 | 15 35 | 13 22 | 00 00 | 06 04 |
| 40 | 23 31 | 15 05 | 12 39 | 00 00 | 06 13 |
| 41 | 23 17 | 14 34 | 11 54 | 00 00 | 06 23 |
| 42 | 23 02 | 14 02 | 11 06 | 00 00 | 06 34 |
| 43 | 22 46 | 13 29 | 10 16 | 00 00 | 06 44 |
| 44 | 22 30 | 12 54 | 09 22 | 00 00 | 06 55 |
| 45 | 22 13 | 12 18 | 08 25 | 00 00 | 07 07 |
| 46 | 21 56 | 11 40 | 07 25 | 00 00 | 07 19 |
| 47 | 21 38 | 11 00 | 06 21 | 00 00 | 07 32 |
| 48 | 21 19 | 10 18 | 05 12 | 00 00 | 07 46 |
| 49 | 20 59 | 09 34 | 03 58 | 00 00 | 08 00 |
| 50 | 20 38 | 08 48 | 02 39 | 00 00 | 08 15 |
| 51 | 20 16 | 07 59 | 01 14 | 00 00 | 08 31 |
| 52 | 19 53 | 07 07 | 29♑42 | 00 00 | 08 48 |
| 53 | 19 29 | 06 13 | 28 04 | 00 00 | 09 06 |
| 54 | 19 03 | 05 14 | 26 17 | 00 00 | 09 25 |
| 55 | 18 35 | 04 12 | 24 21 | 00 00 | 09 46 |
| 56 | 18 06 | 03 06 | 22 16 | 00 00 | 10 08 |
| 57 | 17 35 | 01 55 | 19 59 | 00 00 | 10 32 |
| 58 | 17 01 | 00 39 | 17 31 | 00 00 | 10 58 |
| 59 | 16 25 | 29♐16 | 14 49 | 00 00 | 11 26 |
| 60 | 15♐46 | 27♐47 | 11♑54 | 00♈00 | 11♉58 |

**16h 4m 0s — 241° 0' 0" — 03 ♐ 03**

| LAT. | 11 | 12 | ASC | 2 | 3 |
|---|---|---|---|---|---|
| 0 | 00♑55 | 28♑52 | 28♒52 | 01♈05 | 03♉13 |
| 5 | 00 15 | 27 40 | 27 43 | 01 07 | 03 37 |
| 10 | 29♐35 | 26 25 | 26 30 | 01 09 | 04 01 |
| 15 | 28 53 | 25 05 | 25 08 | 01 11 | 04 27 |
| 20 | 28 08 | 23 40 | 23 36 | 01 13 | 04 54 |
| 21 | 27 59 | 23 22 | 23 16 | 01 14 | 05 00 |
| 22 | 27 50 | 23 04 | 22 56 | 01 14 | 05 06 |
| 23 | 27 41 | 22 46 | 22 34 | 01 15 | 05 12 |
| 24 | 27 31 | 22 27 | 22 13 | 01 15 | 05 18 |
| 25 | 27 21 | 22 07 | 21 50 | 01 16 | 05 25 |
| 26 | 27 11 | 21 47 | 21 27 | 01 16 | 05 31 |
| 27 | 27 01 | 21 27 | 21 03 | 01 17 | 05 38 |
| 28 | 26 51 | 21 06 | 20 38 | 01 17 | 05 44 |
| 29 | 26 40 | 20 45 | 20 12 | 01 18 | 05 51 |
| 30 | 26 30 | 20 23 | 19 45 | 01 19 | 05 58 |
| 31 | 26 19 | 20 01 | 19 17 | 01 19 | 06 06 |
| 32 | 26 07 | 19 38 | 18 48 | 01 20 | 06 13 |
| 33 | 25 56 | 19 14 | 18 18 | 01 21 | 06 21 |
| 34 | 25 44 | 18 50 | 17 46 | 01 21 | 06 29 |
| 35 | 25 32 | 18 25 | 17 13 | 01 22 | 06 37 |
| 36 | 25 19 | 17 59 | 16 38 | 01 23 | 06 45 |
| 37 | 25 06 | 17 32 | 16 02 | 01 24 | 06 54 |
| 38 | 24 53 | 17 04 | 15 24 | 01 24 | 07 03 |
| 39 | 24 40 | 16 35 | 14 44 | 01 25 | 07 12 |
| 40 | 24 26 | 16 06 | 14 01 | 01 26 | 07 22 |
| 41 | 24 11 | 15 35 | 13 17 | 01 27 | 07 32 |
| 42 | 23 56 | 15 03 | 12 30 | 01 28 | 07 43 |
| 43 | 23 40 | 14 29 | 11 40 | 01 30 | 07 54 |
| 44 | 23 24 | 13 54 | 10 47 | 01 31 | 08 05 |
| 45 | 23 07 | 13 18 | 09 51 | 01 32 | 08 17 |
| 46 | 22 50 | 12 40 | 08 51 | 01 33 | 08 30 |
| 47 | 22 32 | 12 00 | 07 47 | 01 35 | 08 43 |
| 48 | 22 12 | 11 18 | 06 38 | 01 36 | 08 57 |
| 49 | 21 52 | 10 34 | 05 25 | 01 38 | 09 11 |
| 50 | 21 32 | 09 47 | 04 06 | 01 40 | 09 27 |
| 51 | 21 09 | 08 58 | 02 41 | 01 42 | 09 43 |
| 52 | 20 46 | 08 06 | 01 10 | 01 44 | 10 01 |
| 53 | 20 22 | 07 11 | 29♑31 | 01 46 | 10 19 |
| 54 | 19 56 | 06 13 | 27 43 | 01 49 | 10 39 |
| 55 | 19 28 | 05 10 | 25 47 | 01 51 | 11 00 |
| 56 | 18 58 | 04 03 | 23 40 | 01 54 | 11 23 |
| 57 | 18 27 | 02 52 | 21 22 | 01 58 | 11 47 |
| 58 | 17 53 | 01 34 | 18 52 | 02 02 | 12 14 |
| 59 | 17 16 | 00 11 | 16 08 | 02 06 | 12 43 |
| 60 | 16♐37 | 28♐40 | 13♑09 | 02♈11 | 13♉15 |

**16h 8m 0s — 242° 0' 0" — 04 ♐ 00**

| LAT. | 11 | 12 | ASC | 2 | 3 |
|---|---|---|---|---|---|
| 0 | 01♑50 | 29♑49 | 29♒54 | 02♈11 | 04♉16 |
| 5 | 01 10 | 28 38 | 28 48 | 02 14 | 04 40 |
| 10 | 00 30 | 27 23 | 27 36 | 02 18 | 05 05 |
| 15 | 29♐48 | 26 05 | 26 17 | 02 22 | 05 31 |
| 20 | 29 03 | 24 40 | 24 47 | 02 26 | 05 59 |
| 21 | 28 54 | 24 22 | 24 28 | 02 27 | 06 05 |
| 22 | 28 45 | 24 04 | 24 08 | 02 28 | 06 11 |
| 23 | 28 36 | 23 45 | 23 47 | 02 29 | 06 17 |
| 24 | 28 26 | 23 27 | 23 26 | 02 30 | 06 24 |
| 25 | 28 16 | 23 07 | 23 04 | 02 31 | 06 30 |
| 26 | 28 06 | 22 48 | 22 41 | 02 32 | 06 37 |
| 27 | 27 56 | 22 27 | 22 18 | 02 33 | 06 43 |
| 28 | 27 46 | 22 07 | 21 53 | 02 35 | 06 50 |
| 29 | 27 35 | 21 45 | 21 28 | 02 36 | 06 57 |
| 30 | 27 24 | 21 24 | 21 02 | 02 37 | 07 05 |
| 31 | 27 13 | 21 01 | 20 34 | 02 38 | 07 12 |
| 32 | 27 02 | 20 38 | 20 06 | 02 40 | 07 20 |
| 33 | 26 50 | 20 15 | 19 36 | 02 41 | 07 28 |
| 34 | 26 39 | 19 50 | 19 05 | 02 42 | 07 36 |
| 35 | 26 26 | 19 25 | 18 33 | 02 44 | 07 44 |
| 36 | 26 14 | 18 59 | 17 59 | 02 46 | 07 53 |
| 37 | 26 01 | 18 33 | 17 23 | 02 47 | 08 02 |
| 38 | 25 48 | 18 05 | 16 45 | 02 49 | 08 11 |
| 39 | 25 34 | 17 36 | 16 06 | 02 51 | 08 21 |
| 40 | 25 20 | 17 06 | 15 24 | 02 53 | 08 31 |
| 41 | 25 05 | 16 35 | 14 41 | 02 55 | 08 41 |
| 42 | 24 50 | 16 03 | 13 54 | 02 57 | 08 52 |
| 43 | 24 35 | 15 30 | 13 05 | 02 59 | 09 03 |
| 44 | 24 18 | 14 55 | 12 13 | 03 01 | 09 15 |
| 45 | 24 02 | 14 18 | 11 17 | 03 04 | 09 27 |
| 46 | 23 44 | 13 40 | 10 18 | 03 07 | 09 40 |
| 47 | 23 26 | 13 00 | 09 14 | 03 10 | 09 53 |
| 48 | 23 06 | 12 18 | 08 06 | 03 13 | 10 07 |
| 49 | 22 46 | 11 34 | 06 53 | 03 16 | 10 22 |
| 50 | 22 25 | 10 47 | 05 35 | 03 19 | 10 38 |
| 51 | 22 03 | 09 58 | 04 10 | 03 23 | 10 55 |
| 52 | 21 40 | 09 06 | 02 39 | 03 28 | 11 13 |
| 53 | 21 15 | 08 10 | 01 00 | 03 32 | 11 32 |
| 54 | 20 49 | 07 12 | 29♑12 | 03 37 | 11 52 |
| 55 | 20 21 | 06 09 | 27 15 | 03 43 | 12 14 |
| 56 | 19 51 | 05 01 | 25 07 | 03 49 | 12 37 |
| 57 | 19 19 | 03 49 | 22 48 | 03 56 | 13 02 |
| 58 | 18 45 | 02 31 | 20 16 | 04 03 | 13 30 |
| 59 | 18 08 | 01 06 | 17 29 | 04 12 | 13 59 |
| 60 | 17♐28 | 29♐35 | 14♑26 | 04♈22 | 14♉32 |

**16h 12m 0s — 243° 0' 0" — 04 ♐ 57**

| LAT. | 11 | 12 | ASC | 2 | 3 |
|---|---|---|---|---|---|
| 0 | 02♑45 | 00♒47 | 00♓57 | 03♈16 | 05♉18 |
| 5 | 02 05 | 29♑36 | 29♒53 | 03 21 | 05 42 |
| 10 | 01 25 | 28 22 | 28 43 | 03 27 | 06 08 |
| 15 | 00 43 | 27 04 | 27 26 | 03 33 | 06 35 |
| 20 | 29♐58 | 25 40 | 25 59 | 03 39 | 07 04 |
| 21 | 29 49 | 25 22 | 25 40 | 03 41 | 07 10 |
| 22 | 29 40 | 25 04 | 25 21 | 03 42 | 07 16 |
| 23 | 29 31 | 24 46 | 25 00 | 03 44 | 07 22 |
| 24 | 29 21 | 24 27 | 24 40 | 03 45 | 07 29 |
| 25 | 29 11 | 24 08 | 24 18 | 03 47 | 07 35 |
| 26 | 29 01 | 23 48 | 23 56 | 03 48 | 07 42 |
| 27 | 28 51 | 23 28 | 23 33 | 03 50 | 07 49 |
| 28 | 28 41 | 23 07 | 23 09 | 03 52 | 07 56 |
| 29 | 28 30 | 22 46 | 22 45 | 03 54 | 08 03 |
| 30 | 28 19 | 22 24 | 22 19 | 03 55 | 08 11 |
| 31 | 28 08 | 22 02 | 21 52 | 03 57 | 08 18 |
| 32 | 27 57 | 21 39 | 21 24 | 03 59 | 08 26 |
| 33 | 27 45 | 21 16 | 20 55 | 04 01 | 08 34 |
| 34 | 27 33 | 20 51 | 20 25 | 04 04 | 08 43 |
| 35 | 27 21 | 20 26 | 19 53 | 04 06 | 08 51 |
| 36 | 27 09 | 20 00 | 19 20 | 04 08 | 09 00 |
| 37 | 26 56 | 19 34 | 18 45 | 04 11 | 09 09 |
| 38 | 26 42 | 19 06 | 18 08 | 04 13 | 09 19 |
| 39 | 26 29 | 18 37 | 17 29 | 04 16 | 09 28 |
| 40 | 26 15 | 18 08 | 16 48 | 04 19 | 09 39 |
| 41 | 26 00 | 17 37 | 16 05 | 04 22 | 09 49 |
| 42 | 25 45 | 17 05 | 15 20 | 04 25 | 10 00 |
| 43 | 25 29 | 16 31 | 14 31 | 04 28 | 10 12 |
| 44 | 25 13 | 15 56 | 13 40 | 04 32 | 10 24 |
| 45 | 24 56 | 15 19 | 12 45 | 04 36 | 10 36 |
| 46 | 24 38 | 14 41 | 11 46 | 04 40 | 10 49 |
| 47 | 24 20 | 14 01 | 10 43 | 04 44 | 11 03 |
| 48 | 24 00 | 13 19 | 09 36 | 04 49 | 11 18 |
| 49 | 23 40 | 12 35 | 08 24 | 04 54 | 11 33 |
| 50 | 23 19 | 11 48 | 07 06 | 04 59 | 11 49 |
| 51 | 22 57 | 10 58 | 05 41 | 05 05 | 12 06 |
| 52 | 22 33 | 10 06 | 04 10 | 05 11 | 12 25 |
| 53 | 22 08 | 09 10 | 02 31 | 05 18 | 12 44 |
| 54 | 21 42 | 08 11 | 00 43 | 05 26 | 13 05 |
| 55 | 21 14 | 07 08 | 28♑46 | 05 34 | 13 27 |
| 56 | 20 44 | 06 00 | 26 37 | 05 43 | 13 51 |
| 57 | 20 11 | 04 47 | 24 17 | 05 53 | 14 16 |
| 58 | 19 37 | 03 28 | 21 42 | 06 05 | 14 45 |
| 59 | 18 59 | 02 03 | 18 53 | 06 18 | 15 15 |
| 60 | 18♐19 | 00♑30 | 15♑47 | 06♈32 | 15♉49 |

**16h 16m 0s — 244° 0' 0" — 05 ♐ 54**

| LAT. | 11 | 12 | ASC | 2 | 3 |
|---|---|---|---|---|---|
| 0 | 03♑40 | 01♒45 | 02♓00 | 04♈22 | 06♉19 |
| 5 | 03 00 | 00 35 | 00 58 | 04 28 | 06 45 |
| 10 | 02 20 | 29♑21 | 29♒50 | 04 36 | 07 11 |
| 15 | 01 38 | 28 03 | 28 36 | 04 43 | 07 39 |
| 20 | 00 54 | 26 40 | 27 11 | 04 52 | 08 08 |
| 21 | 00 44 | 26 22 | 26 53 | 04 54 | 08 14 |
| 22 | 00 35 | 26 04 | 26 34 | 04 56 | 08 21 |
| 23 | 00 26 | 25 46 | 26 14 | 04 58 | 08 27 |
| 24 | 00 16 | 25 27 | 25 54 | 05 00 | 08 34 |
| 25 | 00 06 | 25 08 | 25 33 | 05 02 | 08 40 |
| 26 | 29♐56 | 24 49 | 25 11 | 05 04 | 08 47 |
| 27 | 29 46 | 24 28 | 24 49 | 05 07 | 08 54 |
| 28 | 29 36 | 24 08 | 24 26 | 05 09 | 09 02 |
| 29 | 29 25 | 23 47 | 24 02 | 05 11 | 09 09 |
| 30 | 29 14 | 23 25 | 23 37 | 05 14 | 09 17 |
| 31 | 29 03 | 23 03 | 23 11 | 05 16 | 09 24 |
| 32 | 28 52 | 22 40 | 22 43 | 05 19 | 09 32 |
| 33 | 28 40 | 22 17 | 22 15 | 05 22 | 09 41 |
| 34 | 28 28 | 21 53 | 21 45 | 05 25 | 09 49 |
| 35 | 28 16 | 21 28 | 21 14 | 05 28 | 09 58 |
| 36 | 28 03 | 21 02 | 20 42 | 05 31 | 10 07 |
| 37 | 27 50 | 20 35 | 20 08 | 05 34 | 10 16 |
| 38 | 27 37 | 20 08 | 19 32 | 05 38 | 10 26 |
| 39 | 27 23 | 19 39 | 18 54 | 05 41 | 10 36 |
| 40 | 27 09 | 19 09 | 18 14 | 05 45 | 10 46 |
| 41 | 26 55 | 18 38 | 17 31 | 05 49 | 10 57 |
| 42 | 26 39 | 18 06 | 16 46 | 05 53 | 11 08 |
| 43 | 26 24 | 17 33 | 15 59 | 05 58 | 11 20 |
| 44 | 26 07 | 16 58 | 15 08 | 06 03 | 11 32 |
| 45 | 25 50 | 16 21 | 14 14 | 06 08 | 11 45 |
| 46 | 25 32 | 15 43 | 13 16 | 06 13 | 11 59 |
| 47 | 25 14 | 15 03 | 12 14 | 06 19 | 12 13 |
| 48 | 24 54 | 14 20 | 11 07 | 06 25 | 12 28 |
| 49 | 24 34 | 13 36 | 09 56 | 06 31 | 12 43 |
| 50 | 24 13 | 12 49 | 08 38 | 06 39 | 13 00 |
| 51 | 23 50 | 11 59 | 07 14 | 06 46 | 13 17 |
| 52 | 23 27 | 11 07 | 05 44 | 06 55 | 13 36 |
| 53 | 23 02 | 10 11 | 04 05 | 07 04 | 13 56 |
| 54 | 22 35 | 09 11 | 02 17 | 07 14 | 14 17 |
| 55 | 22 07 | 08 07 | 00 19 | 07 25 | 14 39 |
| 56 | 21 36 | 06 59 | 28♑10 | 07 37 | 15 04 |
| 57 | 21 04 | 05 45 | 25 48 | 07 51 | 15 30 |
| 58 | 20 29 | 04 26 | 23 12 | 08 06 | 15 59 |
| 59 | 19 51 | 03 00 | 20 20 | 08 23 | 16 30 |
| 60 | 19♐10 | 01♑26 | 17♑10 | 08♈43 | 17♉05 |

**16h 20m 0s — 245° 0' 0" — 06 ♐ 50**

| LAT. | 11 | 12 | ASC | 2 | 3 |
|---|---|---|---|---|---|
| 0 | 04♑35 | 02♒43 | 03♓03 | 05♈27 | 07♉21 |
| 5 | 03 56 | 01 33 | 02 03 | 05 35 | 07 47 |
| 10 | 03 15 | 00 20 | 00 58 | 05 44 | 08 14 |
| 15 | 02 33 | 29♑03 | 29♒45 | 05 54 | 08 42 |
| 20 | 01 49 | 27 40 | 28 23 | 06 05 | 09 12 |
| 21 | 01 39 | 27 23 | 28 06 | 06 08 | 09 19 |
| 22 | 01 30 | 27 05 | 27 47 | 06 10 | 09 25 |
| 23 | 01 21 | 26 47 | 27 28 | 06 12 | 09 32 |
| 24 | 01 11 | 26 28 | 27 09 | 06 15 | 09 38 |
| 25 | 01 01 | 26 09 | 26 48 | 06 18 | 09 45 |
| 26 | 00 51 | 25 49 | 26 27 | 06 20 | 09 52 |
| 27 | 00 41 | 25 30 | 26 06 | 06 23 | 10 00 |
| 28 | 00 31 | 25 09 | 25 43 | 06 26 | 10 07 |
| 29 | 00 20 | 24 48 | 25 20 | 06 29 | 10 14 |
| 30 | 00 09 | 24 27 | 24 55 | 06 32 | 10 22 |
| 31 | 29♐58 | 24 05 | 24 30 | 06 35 | 10 30 |
| 32 | 29 47 | 23 42 | 24 03 | 06 39 | 10 38 |
| 33 | 29 35 | 23 18 | 23 36 | 06 42 | 10 47 |
| 34 | 29 23 | 22 54 | 23 07 | 06 46 | 10 55 |
| 35 | 29 11 | 22 29 | 22 36 | 06 50 | 11 04 |
| 36 | 28 58 | 22 04 | 22 05 | 06 53 | 11 14 |
| 37 | 28 45 | 21 37 | 21 31 | 06 58 | 11 23 |
| 38 | 28 32 | 21 09 | 20 56 | 07 02 | 11 33 |
| 39 | 28 18 | 20 41 | 20 19 | 07 06 | 11 43 |
| 40 | 28 04 | 20 11 | 19 40 | 07 11 | 11 54 |
| 41 | 27 49 | 19 40 | 18 58 | 07 16 | 12 05 |
| 42 | 27 34 | 19 08 | 18 14 | 07 21 | 12 16 |
| 43 | 27 18 | 18 35 | 17 27 | 07 27 | 12 28 |
| 44 | 27 02 | 18 00 | 16 37 | 07 33 | 12 41 |
| 45 | 26 45 | 17 23 | 15 44 | 07 39 | 12 54 |
| 46 | 26 27 | 16 45 | 14 47 | 07 46 | 13 08 |
| 47 | 26 08 | 16 05 | 13 46 | 07 53 | 13 22 |
| 48 | 25 49 | 15 22 | 12 40 | 08 01 | 13 37 |
| 49 | 25 28 | 14 38 | 11 29 | 08 09 | 13 53 |
| 50 | 25 07 | 13 51 | 10 13 | 08 18 | 14 10 |
| 51 | 24 44 | 13 01 | 08 50 | 08 27 | 14 28 |
| 52 | 24 20 | 12 08 | 07 19 | 08 38 | 14 47 |
| 53 | 23 55 | 11 12 | 05 41 | 08 49 | 15 07 |
| 54 | 23 28 | 10 12 | 03 53 | 09 02 | 15 29 |
| 55 | 23 00 | 09 08 | 01 55 | 09 15 | 15 52 |
| 56 | 22 29 | 07 59 | 29♑45 | 09 31 | 16 17 |
| 57 | 21 57 | 06 45 | 27 22 | 09 47 | 16 44 |
| 58 | 21 22 | 05 25 | 24 44 | 10 06 | 17 13 |
| 59 | 20 43 | 03 57 | 21 50 | 10 28 | 17 45 |
| 60 | 20♐02 | 02♑22 | 18♑37 | 10♈52 | 18♉20 |

**16h 24m 0s — 246° 0' 0" — 07 ♐ 47**

| LAT. | 11 | 12 | ASC | 2 | 3 |
|---|---|---|---|---|---|
| 0 | 05♑30 | 03♒41 | 04♓07 | 06♈32 | 08♉23 |
| 5 | 04 51 | 02 32 | 03 09 | 06 42 | 08 49 |
| 10 | 04 10 | 01 20 | 02 06 | 06 53 | 09 16 |
| 15 | 03 28 | 00 03 | 00 55 | 07 05 | 09 45 |
| 20 | 02 44 | 28♑41 | 29♒36 | 07 18 | 10 16 |
| 21 | 02 35 | 28 23 | 29 19 | 07 21 | 10 23 |
| 22 | 02 25 | 28 06 | 29 01 | 07 24 | 10 29 |
| 23 | 02 16 | 27 47 | 28 43 | 07 27 | 10 36 |
| 24 | 02 06 | 27 29 | 28 24 | 07 30 | 10 43 |
| 25 | 01 56 | 27 10 | 28 04 | 07 33 | 10 50 |
| 26 | 01 46 | 26 51 | 27 44 | 07 36 | 10 57 |
| 27 | 01 36 | 26 31 | 27 23 | 07 40 | 11 04 |
| 28 | 01 26 | 26 11 | 27 01 | 07 43 | 11 12 |
| 29 | 01 15 | 25 50 | 26 38 | 07 47 | 11 20 |
| 30 | 01 04 | 25 28 | 26 14 | 07 50 | 11 27 |
| 31 | 00 53 | 25 06 | 25 49 | 07 54 | 11 36 |
| 32 | 00 42 | 24 44 | 25 24 | 07 58 | 11 44 |
| 33 | 00 30 | 24 20 | 24 57 | 08 02 | 11 52 |
| 34 | 00 18 | 23 56 | 24 29 | 08 07 | 12 01 |
| 35 | 00 06 | 23 31 | 23 59 | 08 11 | 12 10 |
| 36 | 29♐53 | 23 06 | 23 28 | 08 16 | 12 20 |
| 37 | 29 40 | 22 39 | 22 56 | 08 21 | 12 30 |
| 38 | 29 27 | 22 12 | 22 21 | 08 26 | 12 40 |
| 39 | 29 13 | 21 43 | 21 45 | 08 31 | 12 50 |
| 40 | 28 59 | 21 14 | 21 07 | 08 37 | 13 01 |
| 41 | 28 44 | 20 43 | 20 26 | 08 43 | 13 12 |
| 42 | 28 29 | 20 11 | 19 43 | 08 49 | 13 24 |
| 43 | 28 13 | 19 37 | 18 57 | 08 56 | 13 36 |
| 44 | 27 56 | 19 02 | 18 08 | 09 03 | 13 49 |
| 45 | 27 39 | 18 26 | 17 16 | 09 11 | 14 02 |
| 46 | 27 21 | 17 47 | 16 20 | 09 19 | 14 16 |
| 47 | 27 03 | 17 07 | 15 20 | 09 27 | 14 31 |
| 48 | 26 43 | 16 25 | 14 15 | 09 36 | 14 46 |
| 49 | 26 23 | 15 40 | 13 05 | 09 46 | 15 02 |
| 50 | 26 01 | 14 53 | 11 49 | 09 57 | 15 20 |
| 51 | 25 38 | 14 03 | 10 27 | 10 08 | 15 38 |
| 52 | 25 14 | 13 10 | 08 57 | 10 21 | 15 57 |
| 53 | 24 49 | 12 14 | 07 19 | 10 34 | 16 18 |
| 54 | 24 22 | 11 13 | 05 32 | 10 49 | 16 40 |
| 55 | 23 53 | 10 09 | 03 34 | 11 06 | 17 03 |
| 56 | 23 23 | 09 00 | 01 24 | 11 24 | 17 29 |
| 57 | 22 50 | 07 45 | 29♑00 | 11 44 | 17 56 |
| 58 | 22 14 | 06 24 | 26 20 | 12 07 | 18 26 |
| 59 | 21 36 | 04 56 | 23 23 | 12 32 | 18 59 |
| 60 | 20♐54 | 03♑20 | 20♑07 | 13♈01 | 19♉35 |

**16h 28m 0s — 247° 0' 0" — 08 ♐ 43**

| LAT. | 11 | 12 | ASC | 2 | 3 |
|---|---|---|---|---|---|
| 0 | 06♑26 | 04♒39 | 05♓10 | 07♈37 | 09♉24 |
| 5 | 05 46 | 03 31 | 04 14 | 07 49 | 09 51 |
| 10 | 05 05 | 02 19 | 03 13 | 08 02 | 10 19 |
| 15 | 04 23 | 01 04 | 02 06 | 08 16 | 10 48 |
| 20 | 03 39 | 29♑42 | 00 49 | 08 31 | 11 20 |
| 21 | 03 30 | 29 24 | 00 32 | 08 34 | 11 26 |
| 22 | 03 21 | 29 07 | 00 15 | 08 38 | 11 33 |
| 23 | 03 11 | 28 49 | 29♒57 | 08 41 | 11 40 |
| 24 | 03 01 | 28 30 | 29 39 | 08 45 | 11 47 |
| 25 | 02 52 | 28 12 | 29 20 | 08 48 | 11 54 |
| 26 | 02 42 | 27 52 | 29 00 | 08 52 | 12 01 |
| 27 | 02 31 | 27 33 | 28 40 | 08 56 | 12 09 |
| 28 | 02 21 | 27 12 | 28 19 | 09 00 | 12 17 |
| 29 | 02 10 | 26 52 | 27 57 | 09 04 | 12 24 |
| 30 | 01 59 | 26 30 | 27 34 | 09 08 | 12 32 |
| 31 | 01 48 | 26 08 | 27 10 | 09 13 | 12 41 |
| 32 | 01 37 | 25 46 | 26 45 | 09 18 | 12 49 |
| 33 | 01 25 | 25 23 | 26 19 | 09 22 | 12 58 |
| 34 | 01 13 | 24 59 | 25 51 | 09 27 | 13 07 |
| 35 | 01 01 | 24 34 | 25 23 | 09 33 | 13 16 |
| 36 | 00 48 | 24 08 | 24 52 | 09 38 | 13 26 |
| 37 | 00 35 | 23 42 | 24 21 | 09 44 | 13 36 |
| 38 | 00 22 | 23 15 | 23 47 | 09 50 | 13 46 |
| 39 | 00 08 | 22 46 | 23 12 | 09 56 | 13 57 |
| 40 | 29♐54 | 22 17 | 22 35 | 10 03 | 14 08 |
| 41 | 29 39 | 21 46 | 21 55 | 10 10 | 14 19 |
| 42 | 29 24 | 21 14 | 21 13 | 10 17 | 14 31 |
| 43 | 29 08 | 20 40 | 20 28 | 10 25 | 14 44 |
| 44 | 28 51 | 20 06 | 19 40 | 10 33 | 14 56 |
| 45 | 28 34 | 19 29 | 18 49 | 10 42 | 15 10 |
| 46 | 28 16 | 18 51 | 17 54 | 10 51 | 15 24 |
| 47 | 27 57 | 18 10 | 16 55 | 11 01 | 15 39 |
| 48 | 27 38 | 17 28 | 15 51 | 11 12 | 15 55 |
| 49 | 27 17 | 16 43 | 14 43 | 11 23 | 16 12 |
| 50 | 26 55 | 15 56 | 13 28 | 11 35 | 16 29 |
| 51 | 26 33 | 15 06 | 12 07 | 11 49 | 16 48 |
| 52 | 26 08 | 14 13 | 10 38 | 12 03 | 17 07 |
| 53 | 25 43 | 13 16 | 09 00 | 12 19 | 17 28 |
| 54 | 25 16 | 12 16 | 07 14 | 12 36 | 17 51 |
| 55 | 24 47 | 11 11 | 05 16 | 12 55 | 18 15 |
| 56 | 24 16 | 10 01 | 03 05 | 13 16 | 18 41 |
| 57 | 23 43 | 08 46 | 00 41 | 13 40 | 19 09 |
| 58 | 23 07 | 07 24 | 28♑00 | 14 06 | 19 39 |
| 59 | 22 28 | 05 55 | 25 01 | 14 36 | 20 13 |
| 60 | 21♐46 | 04♑18 | 21♑41 | 15♈10 | 20♉50 |

# Placidus Table of Houses for Latitudes 0° to 60° North

**16h 32m 0s — 248° 0' 0" — 09 ♐ 40**

| LAT. | 11 | 12 | ASC | 2 | 3 |
|---|---|---|---|---|---|
| 0 | 07♑21 | 05♒38 | 06♓14 | 08♈43 | 10♉25 |
| 5 | 06 41 | 04 30 | 05 20 | 08 56 | 10 53 |
| 10 | 06 01 | 03 19 | 04 22 | 09 10 | 11 21 |
| 15 | 05 19 | 02 04 | 03 17 | 09 26 | 11 51 |
| 20 | 04 34 | 00 43 | 02 03 | 09 44 | 12 23 |
| 21 | 04 25 | 00 26 | 01 46 | 09 47 | 12 30 |
| 22 | 04 16 | 00 08 | 01 30 | 09 51 | 12 37 |
| 23 | 04 06 | 29♑50 | 01 13 | 09 55 | 12 44 |
| 24 | 03 57 | 29 32 | 00 55 | 09 59 | 12 51 |
| 25 | 03 47 | 29 13 | 00 37 | 10 03 | 12 58 |
| 26 | 03 37 | 28 54 | 00 18 | 10 08 | 13 06 |
| 27 | 03 27 | 28 35 | 29♒58 | 10 12 | 13 13 |
| 28 | 03 16 | 28 15 | 29 37 | 10 17 | 13 21 |
| 29 | 03 06 | 27 54 | 29 16 | 10 21 | 13 29 |
| 30 | 02 55 | 27 33 | 28 54 | 10 26 | 13 37 |
| 31 | 02 44 | 27 11 | 28 31 | 10 31 | 13 46 |
| 32 | 02 32 | 26 48 | 28 06 | 10 37 | 13 54 |
| 33 | 02 21 | 26 25 | 27 41 | 10 42 | 14 03 |
| 34 | 02 09 | 26 02 | 27 15 | 10 48 | 14 12 |
| 35 | 01 56 | 25 37 | 26 47 | 10 54 | 14 22 |
| 36 | 01 44 | 25 11 | 26 18 | 11 00 | 14 32 |
| 37 | 01 31 | 24 45 | 25 47 | 11 07 | 14 42 |
| 38 | 01 17 | 24 18 | 25 14 | 11 14 | 14 52 |
| 39 | 01 03 | 23 49 | 24 40 | 11 21 | 15 03 |
| 40 | 00 49 | 23 20 | 24 04 | 11 28 | 15 14 |
| 41 | 00 34 | 22 49 | 23 25 | 11 36 | 15 26 |
| 42 | 00 19 | 22 17 | 22 44 | 11 45 | 15 38 |
| 43 | 00 03 | 21 44 | 22 00 | 11 53 | 15 51 |
| 44 | 29♐46 | 21 09 | 21 14 | 12 03 | 16 04 |
| 45 | 29 29 | 20 33 | 20 24 | 12 13 | 16 18 |
| 46 | 29 11 | 19 54 | 19 30 | 12 23 | 16 32 |
| 47 | 28 52 | 19 14 | 18 32 | 12 35 | 16 47 |
| 48 | 28 32 | 18 32 | 17 30 | 12 47 | 17 03 |
| 49 | 28 12 | 17 47 | 16 22 | 13 00 | 17 20 |
| 50 | 27 50 | 17 00 | 15 08 | 13 14 | 17 38 |
| 51 | 27 27 | 16 09 | 13 48 | 13 29 | 17 57 |
| 52 | 27 03 | 15 16 | 12 21 | 13 45 | 18 17 |
| 53 | 26 37 | 14 19 | 10 44 | 14 03 | 18 38 |
| 54 | 26 10 | 13 19 | 08 58 | 14 23 | 19 01 |
| 55 | 25 41 | 12 13 | 07 01 | 14 44 | 19 26 |
| 56 | 25 10 | 11 03 | 04 50 | 15 08 | 19 52 |
| 57 | 24 36 | 09 48 | 02 25 | 15 35 | 20 21 |
| 58 | 24 00 | 08 25 | 29♑44 | 16 05 | 20 52 |
| 59 | 23 21 | 06 56 | 26 42 | 16 39 | 21 26 |
| 60 | 22♐38 | 05♑17 | 23♑19 | 17♈17 | 22♉03 |

**16h 36m 0s — 249° 0' 0" — 10 ♐ 36**

| LAT. | 11 | 12 | ASC | 2 | 3 |
|---|---|---|---|---|---|
| 0 | 08♑16 | 06♒37 | 07♓18 | 09♈48 | 11♉26 |
| 5 | 07 36 | 05 29 | 06 26 | 10 03 | 11 54 |
| 10 | 06 56 | 04 19 | 05 30 | 10 19 | 12 23 |
| 15 | 06 14 | 03 05 | 04 27 | 10 37 | 12 54 |
| 20 | 05 30 | 01 44 | 03 16 | 10 56 | 13 26 |
| 21 | 05 21 | 01 27 | 03 01 | 11 00 | 13 33 |
| 22 | 05 11 | 01 10 | 02 45 | 11 05 | 13 40 |
| 23 | 05 02 | 00 52 | 02 28 | 11 09 | 13 47 |
| 24 | 04 52 | 00 34 | 02 11 | 11 14 | 13 54 |
| 25 | 04 42 | 00 15 | 01 54 | 11 18 | 14 02 |
| 26 | 04 32 | 29♑56 | 01 35 | 11 23 | 14 09 |
| 27 | 04 22 | 29 37 | 01 16 | 11 28 | 14 17 |
| 28 | 04 12 | 29 17 | 00 56 | 11 33 | 14 25 |
| 29 | 04 01 | 28 56 | 00 36 | 11 39 | 14 33 |
| 30 | 03 50 | 28 35 | 00 14 | 11 44 | 14 42 |
| 31 | 03 39 | 28 14 | 29♒52 | 11 50 | 14 50 |
| 32 | 03 28 | 27 51 | 29 29 | 11 56 | 14 59 |
| 33 | 03 16 | 27 28 | 29 04 | 12 02 | 15 08 |
| 34 | 03 04 | 27 05 | 28 39 | 12 08 | 15 17 |
| 35 | 02 52 | 26 40 | 28 12 | 12 15 | 15 27 |
| 36 | 02 39 | 26 15 | 27 43 | 12 22 | 15 37 |
| 37 | 02 26 | 25 49 | 27 14 | 12 29 | 15 47 |
| 38 | 02 12 | 25 21 | 26 42 | 12 37 | 15 58 |
| 39 | 01 58 | 24 53 | 26 09 | 12 45 | 16 09 |
| 40 | 01 44 | 24 24 | 25 34 | 12 54 | 16 20 |
| 41 | 01 29 | 23 53 | 24 56 | 13 02 | 16 32 |
| 42 | 01 14 | 23 21 | 24 16 | 13 12 | 16 44 |
| 43 | 00 58 | 22 48 | 23 34 | 13 22 | 16 57 |
| 44 | 00 41 | 22 13 | 22 48 | 13 32 | 17 11 |
| 45 | 00 24 | 21 37 | 22 00 | 13 43 | 17 25 |
| 46 | 00 06 | 20 59 | 21 07 | 13 55 | 17 39 |
| 47 | 29♐47 | 20 18 | 20 11 | 14 08 | 17 55 |
| 48 | 29 27 | 19 36 | 19 10 | 14 21 | 18 11 |
| 49 | 29 06 | 18 51 | 18 03 | 14 36 | 18 28 |
| 50 | 28 45 | 18 04 | 16 51 | 14 52 | 18 46 |
| 51 | 28 22 | 17 14 | 15 32 | 15 09 | 19 06 |
| 52 | 27 57 | 16 20 | 14 06 | 15 27 | 19 26 |
| 53 | 27 32 | 15 23 | 12 31 | 15 47 | 19 48 |
| 54 | 27 04 | 14 22 | 10 45 | 16 09 | 20 11 |
| 55 | 26 35 | 13 17 | 08 49 | 16 33 | 20 36 |
| 56 | 26 04 | 12 06 | 06 39 | 17 00 | 21 03 |
| 57 | 25 30 | 10 50 | 04 14 | 17 30 | 21 32 |
| 58 | 24 54 | 09 27 | 01 31 | 18 03 | 22 04 |
| 59 | 24 14 | 07 57 | 28♑28 | 18 41 | 22 38 |
| 60 | 23♐31 | 06♑17 | 25♑02 | 19♈24 | 23♉17 |

**16h 40m 0s — 250° 0' 0" — 11 ♐ 32**

| LAT. | 11 | 12 | ASC | 2 | 3 |
|---|---|---|---|---|---|
| 0 | 09♑11 | 07♒35 | 08♓22 | 10♈53 | 12♉27 |
| 5 | 08 32 | 06 29 | 07 32 | 11 10 | 12 55 |
| 10 | 07 51 | 05 20 | 06 39 | 11 27 | 13 25 |
| 15 | 07 10 | 04 06 | 05 39 | 11 47 | 13 56 |
| 20 | 06 25 | 02 46 | 04 30 | 12 09 | 14 29 |
| 21 | 06 16 | 02 29 | 04 16 | 12 13 | 14 36 |
| 22 | 06 07 | 02 12 | 04 00 | 12 18 | 14 43 |
| 23 | 05 57 | 01 54 | 03 44 | 12 23 | 14 50 |
| 24 | 05 48 | 01 36 | 03 28 | 12 28 | 14 58 |
| 25 | 05 38 | 01 18 | 03 11 | 12 33 | 15 05 |
| 26 | 05 28 | 00 59 | 02 53 | 12 39 | 15 13 |
| 27 | 05 18 | 00 40 | 02 35 | 12 44 | 15 21 |
| 28 | 05 07 | 00 20 | 02 16 | 12 50 | 15 29 |
| 29 | 04 57 | 29♑59 | 01 56 | 12 56 | 15 37 |
| 30 | 04 46 | 29 39 | 01 36 | 13 02 | 15 46 |
| 31 | 04 34 | 29 17 | 01 14 | 13 08 | 15 55 |
| 32 | 04 23 | 28 55 | 00 52 | 13 15 | 16 03 |
| 33 | 04 11 | 28 32 | 00 28 | 13 22 | 16 13 |
| 34 | 03 59 | 28 08 | 00 03 | 13 29 | 16 22 |
| 35 | 03 47 | 27 44 | 29♒37 | 13 36 | 16 32 |
| 36 | 03 34 | 27 19 | 29 10 | 13 44 | 16 42 |
| 37 | 03 21 | 26 53 | 28 41 | 13 52 | 16 52 |
| 38 | 03 08 | 26 26 | 28 11 | 14 00 | 17 03 |
| 39 | 02 54 | 25 57 | 27 39 | 14 09 | 17 14 |
| 40 | 02 39 | 25 28 | 27 05 | 14 19 | 17 26 |
| 41 | 02 25 | 24 58 | 26 28 | 14 28 | 17 38 |
| 42 | 02 09 | 24 26 | 25 50 | 14 39 | 17 51 |
| 43 | 01 53 | 23 53 | 25 09 | 14 50 | 18 04 |
| 44 | 01 36 | 23 18 | 24 25 | 15 01 | 18 17 |
| 45 | 01 19 | 22 42 | 23 37 | 15 14 | 18 32 |
| 46 | 01 01 | 22 03 | 22 46 | 15 27 | 18 47 |
| 47 | 00 42 | 21 23 | 21 51 | 15 41 | 19 02 |
| 48 | 00 22 | 20 41 | 20 51 | 15 56 | 19 19 |
| 49 | 00 01 | 19 56 | 19 47 | 16 12 | 19 36 |
| 50 | 29♐39 | 19 09 | 18 36 | 16 29 | 19 55 |
| 51 | 29 16 | 18 19 | 17 19 | 16 48 | 20 14 |
| 52 | 28 52 | 17 25 | 15 54 | 17 08 | 20 35 |
| 53 | 28 26 | 16 28 | 14 20 | 17 30 | 20 57 |
| 54 | 27 59 | 15 27 | 12 36 | 17 54 | 21 20 |
| 55 | 27 29 | 14 21 | 10 40 | 18 21 | 21 46 |
| 56 | 26 58 | 13 10 | 08 31 | 18 50 | 22 13 |
| 57 | 26 24 | 11 53 | 06 06 | 19 23 | 22 43 |
| 58 | 25 47 | 10 30 | 03 23 | 20 00 | 23 15 |
| 59 | 25 07 | 08 59 | 00 18 | 20 42 | 23 50 |
| 60 | 24♐24 | 07♑18 | 26♑50 | 21♈29 | 24♉29 |

**16h 44m 0s — 251° 0' 0" — 12 ♐ 28**

| LAT. | 11 | 12 | ASC | 2 | 3 |
|---|---|---|---|---|---|
| 0 | 10♑07 | 08♒34 | 09♓26 | 11♈58 | 13♉27 |
| 5 | 09 27 | 07 29 | 08 39 | 12 16 | 13 56 |
| 10 | 08 47 | 06 20 | 07 47 | 12 36 | 14 26 |
| 15 | 08 05 | 05 07 | 06 50 | 12 57 | 14 58 |
| 20 | 07 21 | 03 48 | 05 45 | 13 21 | 15 32 |
| 21 | 07 12 | 03 31 | 05 31 | 13 26 | 15 39 |
| 22 | 07 02 | 03 14 | 05 16 | 13 31 | 15 46 |
| 23 | 06 53 | 02 57 | 05 01 | 13 37 | 15 53 |
| 24 | 06 43 | 02 39 | 04 45 | 13 42 | 16 01 |
| 25 | 06 33 | 02 21 | 04 29 | 13 48 | 16 09 |
| 26 | 06 23 | 02 02 | 04 12 | 13 54 | 16 16 |
| 27 | 06 13 | 01 43 | 03 54 | 14 00 | 16 24 |
| 28 | 06 03 | 01 23 | 03 36 | 14 06 | 16 33 |
| 29 | 05 52 | 01 03 | 03 17 | 14 13 | 16 41 |
| 30 | 05 41 | 00 42 | 02 57 | 14 19 | 16 50 |
| 31 | 05 30 | 00 21 | 02 37 | 14 26 | 16 59 |
| 32 | 05 19 | 29♑59 | 02 15 | 14 33 | 17 08 |
| 33 | 05 07 | 29 36 | 01 52 | 14 41 | 17 17 |
| 34 | 04 55 | 29 12 | 01 29 | 14 49 | 17 27 |
| 35 | 04 43 | 28 48 | 01 04 | 14 57 | 17 37 |
| 36 | 04 30 | 28 23 | 00 37 | 15 05 | 17 47 |
| 37 | 04 17 | 27 57 | 00 10 | 15 14 | 17 57 |
| 38 | 04 03 | 27 30 | 29♒41 | 15 23 | 18 08 |
| 39 | 03 49 | 27 02 | 29 10 | 15 33 | 18 20 |
| 40 | 03 35 | 26 33 | 28 37 | 15 43 | 18 31 |
| 41 | 03 20 | 26 03 | 28 02 | 15 54 | 18 44 |
| 42 | 03 05 | 25 31 | 27 24 | 16 05 | 18 56 |
| 43 | 02 48 | 24 58 | 26 45 | 16 17 | 19 10 |
| 44 | 02 32 | 24 23 | 26 02 | 16 30 | 19 24 |
| 45 | 02 14 | 23 47 | 25 16 | 16 43 | 19 38 |
| 46 | 01 56 | 23 09 | 24 26 | 16 58 | 19 53 |
| 47 | 01 37 | 22 29 | 23 33 | 17 13 | 20 09 |
| 48 | 01 17 | 21 46 | 22 35 | 17 29 | 20 26 |
| 49 | 00 56 | 21 02 | 21 32 | 17 47 | 20 44 |
| 50 | 00 35 | 20 14 | 20 23 | 18 06 | 21 02 |
| 51 | 00 11 | 19 24 | 19 07 | 18 26 | 21 22 |
| 52 | 29♐47 | 18 31 | 17 44 | 18 49 | 21 43 |
| 53 | 29 21 | 17 33 | 16 12 | 19 13 | 22 05 |
| 54 | 28 53 | 16 32 | 14 29 | 19 39 | 22 29 |
| 55 | 28 24 | 15 26 | 12 35 | 20 08 | 22 55 |
| 56 | 27 52 | 14 15 | 10 27 | 20 40 | 23 23 |
| 57 | 27 18 | 12 58 | 08 03 | 21 16 | 23 53 |
| 58 | 26 41 | 11 34 | 05 19 | 21 56 | 24 26 |
| 59 | 26 01 | 10 02 | 02 14 | 22 42 | 25 02 |
| 60 | 25♐17 | 08♑20 | 28♑42 | 23♈33 | 25♉41 |

**16h 48m 0s — 252° 0' 0" — 13 ♐ 24**

| LAT. | 11 | 12 | ASC | 2 | 3 |
|---|---|---|---|---|---|
| 0 | 11♑02 | 09♒34 | 10♓30 | 13♈03 | 14♉28 |
| 5 | 10 23 | 08 29 | 09 45 | 13 23 | 14 57 |
| 10 | 09 42 | 07 21 | 08 56 | 13 44 | 15 28 |
| 15 | 09 01 | 06 09 | 08 02 | 14 07 | 16 00 |
| 20 | 08 17 | 04 50 | 07 00 | 14 33 | 16 34 |
| 21 | 08 07 | 04 34 | 06 46 | 14 39 | 16 41 |
| 22 | 07 58 | 04 17 | 06 32 | 14 44 | 16 49 |
| 23 | 07 49 | 03 59 | 06 17 | 14 50 | 16 56 |
| 24 | 07 39 | 03 42 | 06 02 | 14 56 | 17 04 |
| 25 | 07 29 | 03 24 | 05 47 | 15 03 | 17 12 |
| 26 | 07 19 | 03 05 | 05 31 | 15 09 | 17 20 |
| 27 | 07 09 | 02 46 | 05 14 | 15 15 | 17 28 |
| 28 | 06 58 | 02 26 | 04 57 | 15 22 | 17 36 |
| 29 | 06 48 | 02 06 | 04 38 | 15 29 | 17 45 |
| 30 | 06 37 | 01 46 | 04 20 | 15 37 | 17 53 |
| 31 | 06 26 | 01 25 | 04 00 | 15 44 | 18 02 |
| 32 | 06 14 | 01 03 | 03 39 | 15 52 | 18 12 |
| 33 | 06 03 | 00 40 | 03 17 | 16 00 | 18 21 |
| 34 | 05 51 | 00 17 | 02 55 | 16 08 | 18 31 |
| 35 | 05 38 | 29♑53 | 02 31 | 16 17 | 18 41 |
| 36 | 05 26 | 29 28 | 02 06 | 16 26 | 18 51 |
| 37 | 05 12 | 29 02 | 01 39 | 16 36 | 19 02 |
| 38 | 04 59 | 28 35 | 01 11 | 16 46 | 19 13 |
| 39 | 04 45 | 28 07 | 00 41 | 16 57 | 19 25 |
| 40 | 04 31 | 27 38 | 00 10 | 17 08 | 19 37 |
| 41 | 04 16 | 27 08 | 29♒36 | 17 19 | 19 49 |
| 42 | 04 00 | 26 37 | 29 00 | 17 32 | 20 02 |
| 43 | 03 44 | 26 04 | 28 22 | 17 45 | 20 15 |
| 44 | 03 27 | 25 29 | 27 40 | 17 58 | 20 29 |
| 45 | 03 10 | 24 53 | 26 56 | 18 13 | 20 44 |
| 46 | 02 52 | 24 15 | 26 08 | 18 29 | 20 59 |
| 47 | 02 33 | 23 35 | 25 16 | 18 45 | 21 16 |
| 48 | 02 13 | 22 53 | 24 20 | 19 03 | 21 33 |
| 49 | 01 52 | 22 08 | 23 19 | 19 22 | 21 51 |
| 50 | 01 30 | 21 21 | 22 12 | 19 42 | 22 10 |
| 51 | 01 07 | 20 30 | 20 58 | 20 04 | 22 30 |
| 52 | 00 42 | 19 37 | 19 37 | 20 28 | 22 51 |
| 53 | 00 16 | 18 39 | 18 07 | 20 55 | 23 14 |
| 54 | 29♐48 | 17 38 | 16 26 | 21 23 | 23 38 |
| 55 | 29 18 | 16 32 | 14 34 | 21 55 | 24 04 |
| 56 | 28 47 | 15 21 | 12 27 | 22 29 | 24 32 |
| 57 | 28 12 | 14 03 | 10 04 | 23 08 | 25 03 |
| 58 | 27 35 | 12 39 | 07 21 | 23 51 | 25 36 |
| 59 | 26 55 | 11 06 | 04 15 | 24 40 | 26 12 |
| 60 | 26♐10 | 09♑24 | 00♒41 | 25♈36 | 26♉53 |

**16h 52m 0s — 253° 0' 0" — 14 ♐ 20**

| LAT. | 11 | 12 | ASC | 2 | 3 |
|---|---|---|---|---|---|
| 0 | 11♑58 | 10♒33 | 11♓34 | 14♈07 | 15♉28 |
| 5 | 11 18 | 09 29 | 10 52 | 14 29 | 15 58 |
| 10 | 10 38 | 08 22 | 10 05 | 14 52 | 16 29 |
| 15 | 09 56 | 07 10 | 09 14 | 15 17 | 17 02 |
| 20 | 09 12 | 05 53 | 08 15 | 15 45 | 17 36 |
| 21 | 09 03 | 05 36 | 08 02 | 15 51 | 17 44 |
| 22 | 08 54 | 05 20 | 07 48 | 15 57 | 17 51 |
| 23 | 08 44 | 05 02 | 07 34 | 16 04 | 17 59 |
| 24 | 08 35 | 04 45 | 07 20 | 16 10 | 18 06 |
| 25 | 08 25 | 04 27 | 07 05 | 16 17 | 18 14 |
| 26 | 08 15 | 04 09 | 06 50 | 16 24 | 18 22 |
| 27 | 08 05 | 03 50 | 06 34 | 16 31 | 18 30 |
| 28 | 07 54 | 03 30 | 06 18 | 16 38 | 18 39 |
| 29 | 07 44 | 03 10 | 06 00 | 16 46 | 18 48 |
| 30 | 07 33 | 02 50 | 05 42 | 16 54 | 18 57 |
| 31 | 07 22 | 02 29 | 05 23 | 17 02 | 19 06 |
| 32 | 07 10 | 02 07 | 05 04 | 17 10 | 19 15 |
| 33 | 06 59 | 01 45 | 04 43 | 17 19 | 19 25 |
| 34 | 06 47 | 01 22 | 04 21 | 17 28 | 19 35 |
| 35 | 06 34 | 00 58 | 03 58 | 17 37 | 19 45 |
| 36 | 06 21 | 00 33 | 03 34 | 17 47 | 19 55 |
| 37 | 06 08 | 00 07 | 03 09 | 17 58 | 20 06 |
| 38 | 05 55 | 29♑41 | 02 42 | 18 09 | 20 18 |
| 39 | 05 41 | 29 13 | 02 14 | 18 20 | 20 29 |
| 40 | 05 26 | 28 44 | 01 43 | 18 32 | 20 41 |
| 41 | 05 11 | 28 14 | 01 11 | 18 44 | 20 54 |
| 42 | 04 56 | 27 43 | 00 37 | 18 58 | 21 07 |
| 43 | 04 40 | 27 10 | 00 00 | 19 12 | 21 21 |
| 44 | 04 23 | 26 36 | 29♒20 | 19 26 | 21 35 |
| 45 | 04 06 | 26 00 | 28 38 | 19 42 | 21 50 |
| 46 | 03 47 | 25 22 | 27 52 | 19 59 | 22 05 |
| 47 | 03 28 | 24 42 | 27 02 | 20 17 | 22 22 |
| 48 | 03 08 | 24 00 | 26 07 | 20 36 | 22 39 |
| 49 | 02 47 | 23 15 | 25 08 | 20 56 | 22 57 |
| 50 | 02 25 | 22 28 | 24 03 | 21 18 | 23 16 |
| 51 | 02 02 | 21 37 | 22 52 | 21 42 | 23 37 |
| 52 | 01 37 | 20 44 | 21 32 | 22 08 | 23 58 |
| 53 | 01 11 | 19 46 | 20 04 | 22 36 | 24 21 |
| 54 | 00 43 | 18 45 | 18 26 | 23 06 | 24 46 |
| 55 | 00 13 | 17 39 | 16 36 | 23 40 | 25 13 |
| 56 | 29♐41 | 16 27 | 14 31 | 24 17 | 25 41 |
| 57 | 29 07 | 15 09 | 12 09 | 24 59 | 26 12 |
| 58 | 28 30 | 13 44 | 09 27 | 25 45 | 26 46 |
| 59 | 27 49 | 12 11 | 06 21 | 26 38 | 27 23 |
| 60 | 27♐04 | 10♑28 | 02♒46 | 27♈38 | 28♉04 |

**16h 56m 0s — 254° 0' 0" — 15 ♐ 16**

| LAT. | 11 | 12 | ASC | 2 | 3 |
|---|---|---|---|---|---|
| 0 | 12♑53 | 11♒32 | 12♓39 | 15♈12 | 16♉28 |
| 5 | 12 14 | 10 29 | 11 59 | 15 35 | 16 59 |
| 10 | 11 34 | 09 23 | 11 15 | 16 00 | 17 30 |
| 15 | 10 52 | 08 12 | 10 26 | 16 27 | 18 03 |
| 20 | 10 08 | 06 56 | 09 30 | 16 57 | 18 38 |
| 21 | 09 59 | 06 39 | 09 18 | 17 04 | 18 46 |
| 22 | 09 50 | 06 23 | 09 05 | 17 10 | 18 53 |
| 23 | 09 40 | 06 06 | 08 52 | 17 17 | 19 01 |
| 24 | 09 31 | 05 48 | 08 38 | 17 24 | 19 09 |
| 25 | 09 21 | 05 31 | 08 24 | 17 31 | 19 17 |
| 26 | 09 11 | 05 12 | 08 10 | 17 38 | 19 25 |
| 27 | 09 01 | 04 54 | 07 55 | 17 46 | 19 33 |
| 28 | 08 50 | 04 35 | 07 39 | 17 54 | 19 42 |
| 29 | 08 40 | 04 15 | 07 22 | 18 02 | 19 51 |
| 30 | 08 29 | 03 55 | 07 05 | 18 10 | 20 00 |
| 31 | 08 18 | 03 34 | 06 47 | 18 19 | 20 09 |
| 32 | 08 06 | 03 12 | 06 29 | 18 28 | 20 18 |
| 33 | 07 55 | 02 50 | 06 09 | 18 38 | 20 28 |
| 34 | 07 43 | 02 27 | 05 48 | 18 47 | 20 38 |
| 35 | 07 30 | 02 03 | 05 27 | 18 57 | 20 49 |
| 36 | 07 17 | 01 39 | 05 04 | 19 08 | 20 59 |
| 37 | 07 04 | 01 13 | 04 40 | 19 19 | 21 10 |
| 38 | 06 51 | 00 47 | 04 14 | 19 31 | 21 22 |
| 39 | 06 37 | 00 19 | 03 47 | 19 43 | 21 34 |
| 40 | 06 22 | 29♑51 | 03 18 | 19 56 | 21 46 |
| 41 | 06 07 | 29 21 | 02 47 | 20 09 | 21 59 |
| 42 | 05 52 | 28 49 | 02 14 | 20 23 | 22 12 |
| 43 | 05 36 | 28 17 | 01 39 | 20 38 | 22 26 |
| 44 | 05 19 | 27 43 | 01 01 | 20 54 | 22 40 |
| 45 | 05 02 | 27 07 | 00 20 | 21 11 | 22 55 |
| 46 | 04 43 | 26 29 | 29♒36 | 21 29 | 23 11 |
| 47 | 04 24 | 25 49 | 28 48 | 21 48 | 23 28 |
| 48 | 04 04 | 25 07 | 27 56 | 22 08 | 23 45 |
| 49 | 03 43 | 24 23 | 26 59 | 22 30 | 24 03 |
| 50 | 03 21 | 23 35 | 25 56 | 22 53 | 24 23 |
| 51 | 02 58 | 22 45 | 24 47 | 23 19 | 24 43 |
| 52 | 02 33 | 21 52 | 23 31 | 23 46 | 25 05 |
| 53 | 02 07 | 20 54 | 22 05 | 24 16 | 25 29 |
| 54 | 01 39 | 19 53 | 20 29 | 24 49 | 25 54 |
| 55 | 01 09 | 18 46 | 18 42 | 25 25 | 26 20 |
| 56 | 00 37 | 17 35 | 16 39 | 26 05 | 26 49 |
| 57 | 00 02 | 16 16 | 14 19 | 26 49 | 27 21 |
| 58 | 29♐24 | 14 51 | 11 39 | 27 38 | 27 55 |
| 59 | 28 43 | 13 17 | 08 34 | 28 34 | 28 32 |
| 60 | 27♐58 | 11♑33 | 04♒58 | 29♈38 | 29♉14 |

**17h 0m 0s — 255° 0' 0" — 16 ♐ 11**

| LAT. | 11 | 12 | ASC | 2 | 3 |
|---|---|---|---|---|---|
| 0 | 13♑49 | 12♒32 | 13♓43 | 16♈17 | 17♉28 |
| 5 | 13 10 | 11 30 | 13 05 | 16 42 | 17 59 |
| 10 | 12 30 | 10 24 | 12 24 | 17 08 | 18 31 |
| 15 | 11 48 | 09 15 | 11 38 | 17 37 | 19 04 |
| 20 | 11 04 | 07 59 | 10 45 | 18 09 | 19 40 |
| 21 | 10 55 | 07 43 | 10 34 | 18 16 | 19 48 |
| 22 | 10 46 | 07 26 | 10 22 | 18 23 | 19 55 |
| 23 | 10 36 | 07 10 | 10 10 | 18 30 | 20 03 |
| 24 | 10 27 | 06 52 | 09 57 | 18 37 | 20 11 |
| 25 | 10 17 | 06 35 | 09 44 | 18 45 | 20 19 |
| 26 | 10 07 | 06 17 | 09 30 | 18 53 | 20 27 |
| 27 | 09 57 | 05 58 | 09 16 | 19 01 | 20 36 |
| 28 | 09 46 | 05 39 | 09 01 | 19 09 | 20 45 |
| 29 | 09 36 | 05 20 | 08 45 | 19 18 | 20 53 |
| 30 | 09 25 | 05 00 | 08 29 | 19 27 | 21 03 |
| 31 | 09 14 | 04 39 | 08 12 | 19 36 | 21 12 |
| 32 | 09 02 | 04 18 | 07 54 | 19 46 | 21 21 |
| 33 | 08 51 | 03 56 | 07 36 | 19 56 | 21 31 |
| 34 | 08 39 | 03 33 | 07 16 | 20 06 | 21 42 |
| 35 | 08 26 | 03 09 | 06 56 | 20 17 | 21 52 |
| 36 | 08 14 | 02 45 | 06 34 | 20 28 | 22 03 |
| 37 | 08 00 | 02 20 | 06 11 | 20 40 | 22 14 |
| 38 | 07 47 | 01 53 | 05 47 | 20 52 | 22 26 |
| 39 | 07 33 | 01 26 | 05 21 | 21 05 | 22 38 |
| 40 | 07 19 | 00 57 | 04 54 | 21 19 | 22 50 |
| 41 | 07 04 | 00 28 | 04 24 | 21 33 | 23 03 |
| 42 | 06 48 | 29♑57 | 03 53 | 21 48 | 23 16 |
| 43 | 06 32 | 29 24 | 03 19 | 22 04 | 23 30 |
| 44 | 06 15 | 28 50 | 02 43 | 22 21 | 23 45 |
| 45 | 05 58 | 28 14 | 02 04 | 22 39 | 24 00 |
| 46 | 05 39 | 27 37 | 01 22 | 22 58 | 24 16 |
| 47 | 05 20 | 26 57 | 00 37 | 23 18 | 24 33 |
| 48 | 05 00 | 26 15 | 29♒47 | 23 40 | 24 51 |
| 49 | 04 39 | 25 31 | 28 52 | 24 03 | 25 09 |
| 50 | 04 17 | 24 44 | 27 52 | 24 28 | 25 29 |
| 51 | 03 53 | 23 54 | 26 45 | 24 55 | 25 50 |
| 52 | 03 29 | 23 00 | 25 31 | 25 24 | 26 12 |
| 53 | 03 02 | 22 03 | 24 09 | 25 56 | 26 36 |
| 54 | 02 34 | 21 01 | 22 36 | 26 30 | 27 01 |
| 55 | 02 04 | 19 55 | 20 51 | 27 09 | 27 28 |
| 56 | 01 32 | 18 43 | 18 52 | 27 51 | 27 57 |
| 57 | 00 57 | 17 25 | 16 35 | 28 38 | 28 29 |
| 58 | 00 19 | 15 59 | 13 57 | 29 30 | 29 04 |
| 59 | 29♐38 | 14 25 | 10 52 | 00♉29 | 29 42 |
| 60 | 28♐53 | 12♑40 | 07♒17 | 01♉36 | 00♊24 |

# Placidus Table of Houses for Latitudes 0° to 60° North

**17h 4m 0s — 256° 0' 0" — 17 ♐ 07**

| LAT. | 11 | 12 | ASC | 2 | 3 |
|---|---|---|---|---|---|
| 0 | 14♑44 | 13♒32 | 14♓48 | 17♈21 | 18♉28 |
| 5 | 14 05 | 12 31 | 14 12 | 17 48 | 18 59 |
| 10 | 13 26 | 11 26 | 13 34 | 18 16 | 19 31 |
| 15 | 12 44 | 10 17 | 12 51 | 18 47 | 20 05 |
| 20 | 12 00 | 09 02 | 12 01 | 19 20 | 20 42 |
| 21 | 11 51 | 08 46 | 11 50 | 19 28 | 20 49 |
| 22 | 11 42 | 08 30 | 11 39 | 19 35 | 20 57 |
| 23 | 11 33 | 08 14 | 11 28 | 19 43 | 21 05 |
| 24 | 11 23 | 07 57 | 11 16 | 19 51 | 21 13 |
| 25 | 11 13 | 07 39 | 11 03 | 19 59 | 21 21 |
| 26 | 11 03 | 07 21 | 10 50 | 20 07 | 21 29 |
| 27 | 10 53 | 07 03 | 10 37 | 20 16 | 21 38 |
| 28 | 10 43 | 06 44 | 10 23 | 20 25 | 21 47 |
| 29 | 10 32 | 06 25 | 10 08 | 20 34 | 21 56 |
| 30 | 10 21 | 06 05 | 09 53 | 20 43 | 22 05 |
| 31 | 10 10 | 05 45 | 09 37 | 20 53 | 22 15 |
| 32 | 09 59 | 05 23 | 09 20 | 21 03 | 22 24 |
| 33 | 09 47 | 05 02 | 09 03 | 21 14 | 22 34 |
| 34 | 09 35 | 04 39 | 08 44 | 21 25 | 22 45 |
| 35 | 09 23 | 04 16 | 08 25 | 21 36 | 22 55 |
| 36 | 09 10 | 03 51 | 08 05 | 21 48 | 23 06 |
| 37 | 08 57 | 03 26 | 07 43 | 22 01 | 23 17 |
| 38 | 08 43 | 03 00 | 07 20 | 22 14 | 23 29 |
| 39 | 08 29 | 02 33 | 06 56 | 22 28 | 23 41 |
| 40 | 08 15 | 02 05 | 06 30 | 22 42 | 23 54 |
| 41 | 08 00 | 01 35 | 06 02 | 22 57 | 24 07 |
| 42 | 07 44 | 01 05 | 05 33 | 23 13 | 24 20 |
| 43 | 07 28 | 00 32 | 05 01 | 23 30 | 24 35 |
| 44 | 07 11 | 29♑58 | 04 27 | 23 48 | 24 49 |
| 45 | 06 54 | 29 23 | 03 50 | 24 06 | 25 05 |
| 46 | 06 36 | 28 45 | 03 10 | 24 27 | 25 21 |
| 47 | 06 16 | 28 06 | 02 26 | 24 48 | 25 38 |
| 48 | 05 56 | 27 24 | 01 39 | 25 11 | 25 56 |
| 49 | 05 35 | 26 40 | 00 47 | 25 35 | 26 15 |
| 50 | 05 13 | 25 53 | 29♒49 | 26 02 | 26 35 |
| 51 | 04 50 | 25 03 | 28 46 | 26 30 | 26 56 |
| 52 | 04 25 | 24 10 | 27 35 | 27 01 | 27 18 |
| 53 | 03 58 | 23 13 | 26 16 | 27 34 | 27 42 |
| 54 | 03 30 | 22 11 | 24 46 | 28 11 | 28 07 |
| 55 | 03 00 | 21 05 | 23 05 | 28 51 | 28 35 |
| 56 | 02 28 | 19 52 | 21 09 | 29 36 | 29 05 |
| 57 | 01 53 | 18 34 | 18 55 | 00♉25 | 29 37 |
| 58 | 01 15 | 17 08 | 16 20 | 01 20 | 00♊12 |
| 59 | 00 33 | 15 33 | 13 18 | 02 23 | 00 50 |
| 60 | 29♐47 | 13♑48 | 09♒44 | 03♉34 | 01♊33 |

**17h 8m 0s — 257° 0' 0" — 18 ♐ 02**

| LAT. | 11 | 12 | ASC | 2 | 3 |
|---|---|---|---|---|---|
| 0 | 15♑40 | 14♒32 | 15♓53 | 18♈26 | 19♉27 |
| 5 | 15 01 | 13 32 | 15 20 | 18 54 | 19 59 |
| 10 | 14 22 | 12 28 | 14 44 | 19 24 | 20 32 |
| 15 | 13 40 | 11 20 | 14 03 | 19 56 | 21 06 |
| 20 | 12 57 | 10 06 | 13 17 | 20 32 | 21 43 |
| 21 | 12 48 | 09 50 | 13 07 | 20 39 | 21 50 |
| 22 | 12 38 | 09 34 | 12 57 | 20 47 | 21 58 |
| 23 | 12 29 | 09 18 | 12 46 | 20 55 | 22 06 |
| 24 | 12 19 | 09 01 | 12 35 | 21 04 | 22 14 |
| 25 | 12 09 | 08 44 | 12 23 | 21 12 | 22 23 |
| 26 | 12 00 | 08 26 | 12 11 | 21 21 | 22 31 |
| 27 | 11 49 | 08 08 | 11 58 | 21 30 | 22 40 |
| 28 | 11 39 | 07 50 | 11 45 | 21 40 | 22 49 |
| 29 | 11 28 | 07 30 | 11 32 | 21 49 | 22 58 |
| 30 | 11 18 | 07 11 | 11 17 | 21 59 | 23 07 |
| 31 | 11 06 | 06 51 | 11 03 | 22 10 | 23 17 |
| 32 | 10 55 | 06 30 | 10 47 | 22 20 | 23 27 |
| 33 | 10 43 | 06 08 | 10 31 | 22 32 | 23 37 |
| 34 | 10 31 | 05 46 | 10 13 | 22 43 | 23 47 |
| 35 | 10 19 | 05 22 | 09 55 | 22 55 | 23 58 |
| 36 | 10 06 | 04 59 | 09 36 | 23 08 | 24 09 |
| 37 | 09 53 | 04 34 | 09 16 | 23 21 | 24 20 |
| 38 | 09 40 | 04 08 | 08 54 | 23 35 | 24 32 |
| 39 | 09 26 | 03 41 | 08 31 | 23 49 | 24 45 |
| 40 | 09 11 | 03 13 | 08 07 | 24 04 | 24 57 |
| 41 | 08 56 | 02 44 | 07 41 | 24 20 | 25 10 |
| 42 | 08 41 | 02 13 | 07 13 | 24 37 | 25 24 |
| 43 | 08 25 | 01 41 | 06 43 | 24 55 | 25 38 |
| 44 | 08 08 | 01 07 | 06 11 | 25 14 | 25 53 |
| 45 | 07 50 | 00 32 | 05 36 | 25 34 | 26 09 |
| 46 | 07 32 | 29♑55 | 04 59 | 25 55 | 26 25 |
| 47 | 07 13 | 29 15 | 04 18 | 26 17 | 26 43 |
| 48 | 06 53 | 28 34 | 03 33 | 26 41 | 27 01 |
| 49 | 06 32 | 27 50 | 02 43 | 27 07 | 27 20 |
| 50 | 06 09 | 27 03 | 01 49 | 27 35 | 27 40 |
| 51 | 05 46 | 26 13 | 00 48 | 28 05 | 28 01 |
| 52 | 05 21 | 25 20 | 29♒41 | 28 37 | 28 24 |
| 53 | 04 54 | 24 23 | 28 25 | 29 12 | 28 48 |
| 54 | 04 26 | 23 21 | 27 00 | 29 51 | 29 14 |
| 55 | 03 56 | 22 15 | 25 22 | 00♉33 | 29 42 |
| 56 | 03 23 | 21 03 | 23 30 | 01 20 | 00♊11 |
| 57 | 02 48 | 19 44 | 21 21 | 02 11 | 00 44 |
| 58 | 02 10 | 18 18 | 18 49 | 03 09 | 01 19 |
| 59 | 01 28 | 16 43 | 15 51 | 04 15 | 01 58 |
| 60 | 00♑42 | 14♑57 | 12♒19 | 05♉29 | 02♊42 |

**17h 12m 0s — 258° 0' 0" — 18 ♐ 58**

| LAT. | 11 | 12 | ASC | 2 | 3 |
|---|---|---|---|---|---|
| 0 | 16♑36 | 15♒32 | 16♓57 | 19♈30 | 20♉26 |
| 5 | 15 57 | 14 33 | 16 27 | 20 00 | 20 59 |
| 10 | 15 18 | 13 30 | 15 54 | 20 31 | 21 32 |
| 15 | 14 37 | 12 23 | 15 16 | 21 05 | 22 07 |
| 20 | 13 53 | 11 10 | 14 33 | 21 43 | 22 44 |
| 21 | 13 44 | 10 55 | 14 24 | 21 51 | 22 52 |
| 22 | 13 35 | 10 39 | 14 14 | 21 59 | 23 00 |
| 23 | 13 25 | 10 23 | 14 04 | 22 08 | 23 08 |
| 24 | 13 16 | 10 06 | 13 54 | 22 17 | 23 16 |
| 25 | 13 06 | 09 49 | 13 43 | 22 26 | 23 24 |
| 26 | 12 56 | 09 32 | 13 32 | 22 35 | 23 33 |
| 27 | 12 46 | 09 14 | 13 20 | 22 44 | 23 42 |
| 28 | 12 36 | 08 55 | 13 08 | 22 54 | 23 51 |
| 29 | 12 25 | 08 36 | 12 55 | 23 04 | 24 00 |
| 30 | 12 14 | 08 17 | 12 42 | 23 15 | 24 09 |
| 31 | 12 03 | 07 57 | 12 28 | 23 26 | 24 19 |
| 32 | 11 52 | 07 36 | 12 14 | 23 37 | 24 29 |
| 33 | 11 40 | 07 15 | 11 59 | 23 49 | 24 39 |
| 34 | 11 28 | 06 53 | 11 43 | 24 01 | 24 50 |
| 35 | 11 16 | 06 30 | 11 26 | 24 14 | 25 00 |
| 36 | 11 03 | 06 06 | 11 08 | 24 27 | 25 12 |
| 37 | 10 50 | 05 41 | 10 49 | 24 41 | 25 23 |
| 38 | 10 36 | 05 16 | 10 29 | 24 56 | 25 35 |
| 39 | 10 22 | 04 49 | 10 08 | 25 11 | 25 48 |
| 40 | 10 08 | 04 21 | 09 45 | 25 27 | 26 00 |
| 41 | 09 53 | 03 52 | 09 21 | 25 43 | 26 14 |
| 42 | 09 38 | 03 22 | 08 55 | 26 01 | 26 28 |
| 43 | 09 21 | 02 50 | 08 27 | 26 20 | 26 42 |
| 44 | 09 05 | 02 17 | 07 57 | 26 39 | 26 57 |
| 45 | 08 47 | 01 42 | 07 24 | 27 00 | 27 13 |
| 46 | 08 29 | 01 05 | 06 49 | 27 22 | 27 29 |
| 47 | 08 10 | 00 26 | 06 10 | 27 46 | 27 47 |
| 48 | 07 49 | 29♑44 | 05 28 | 28 11 | 28 05 |
| 49 | 07 28 | 29 01 | 04 42 | 28 38 | 28 24 |
| 50 | 07 06 | 28 14 | 03 50 | 29 07 | 28 45 |
| 51 | 06 42 | 27 24 | 02 53 | 29 38 | 29 06 |
| 52 | 06 17 | 26 31 | 01 49 | 00♉12 | 29 29 |
| 53 | 05 51 | 25 34 | 00 38 | 00 49 | 29 53 |
| 54 | 05 23 | 24 33 | 29♒16 | 01 29 | 00♊20 |
| 55 | 04 52 | 23 27 | 27 43 | 02 14 | 00 48 |
| 56 | 04 20 | 22 14 | 25 56 | 03 02 | 01 18 |
| 57 | 03 44 | 20 56 | 23 52 | 03 56 | 01 51 |
| 58 | 03 06 | 19 29 | 21 25 | 04 57 | 02 27 |
| 59 | 02 24 | 17 54 | 18 31 | 06 05 | 03 06 |
| 60 | 01♑38 | 16♑08 | 15♒03 | 07♉23 | 03♊50 |

**17h 16m 0s — 259° 0' 0" — 19 ♐ 53**

| LAT. | 11 | 12 | ASC | 2 | 3 |
|---|---|---|---|---|---|
| 0 | 17♑32 | 16♒33 | 18♓02 | 20♈34 | 21♉26 |
| 5 | 16 53 | 15 34 | 17 34 | 21 05 | 21 58 |
| 10 | 16 14 | 14 32 | 17 04 | 21 38 | 22 32 |
| 15 | 15 33 | 13 26 | 16 29 | 22 14 | 23 07 |
| 20 | 14 49 | 12 14 | 15 50 | 22 54 | 23 45 |
| 21 | 14 40 | 11 59 | 15 41 | 23 02 | 23 52 |
| 22 | 14 31 | 11 44 | 15 32 | 23 11 | 24 01 |
| 23 | 14 22 | 11 28 | 15 23 | 23 20 | 24 09 |
| 24 | 14 12 | 11 11 | 15 13 | 23 29 | 24 17 |
| 25 | 14 03 | 10 54 | 15 04 | 23 39 | 24 26 |
| 26 | 13 53 | 10 37 | 14 53 | 23 48 | 24 34 |
| 27 | 13 43 | 10 20 | 14 42 | 23 58 | 24 43 |
| 28 | 13 32 | 10 01 | 14 31 | 24 09 | 24 52 |
| 29 | 13 22 | 09 43 | 14 20 | 24 19 | 25 01 |
| 30 | 13 11 | 09 24 | 14 07 | 24 30 | 25 11 |
| 31 | 13 00 | 09 04 | 13 55 | 24 42 | 25 21 |
| 32 | 12 48 | 08 43 | 13 41 | 24 54 | 25 31 |
| 33 | 12 37 | 08 22 | 13 27 | 25 06 | 25 41 |
| 34 | 12 25 | 08 00 | 13 12 | 25 19 | 25 52 |
| 35 | 12 12 | 07 38 | 12 57 | 25 32 | 26 03 |
| 36 | 12 00 | 07 14 | 12 40 | 25 46 | 26 14 |
| 37 | 11 47 | 06 50 | 12 22 | 26 01 | 26 26 |
| 38 | 11 33 | 06 24 | 12 04 | 26 16 | 26 38 |
| 39 | 11 19 | 05 58 | 11 45 | 26 32 | 26 50 |
| 40 | 11 05 | 05 30 | 11 24 | 26 48 | 27 03 |
| 41 | 10 50 | 05 02 | 11 01 | 27 06 | 27 17 |
| 42 | 10 34 | 04 31 | 10 37 | 27 24 | 27 31 |
| 43 | 10 18 | 04 00 | 10 11 | 27 44 | 27 45 |
| 44 | 10 01 | 03 27 | 09 43 | 28 04 | 28 01 |
| 45 | 09 44 | 02 52 | 09 13 | 28 26 | 28 17 |
| 46 | 09 26 | 02 15 | 08 40 | 28 49 | 28 33 |
| 47 | 09 06 | 01 37 | 08 04 | 29 14 | 28 51 |
| 48 | 08 46 | 00 55 | 07 25 | 29 40 | 29 09 |
| 49 | 08 25 | 00 12 | 06 41 | 00♉08 | 29 29 |
| 50 | 08 03 | 29♑26 | 05 54 | 00 39 | 29 49 |
| 51 | 07 39 | 28 36 | 05 00 | 01 11 | 00♊11 |
| 52 | 07 14 | 27 43 | 04 00 | 01 47 | 00 34 |
| 53 | 06 48 | 26 47 | 02 53 | 02 25 | 00 59 |
| 54 | 06 19 | 25 45 | 01 36 | 03 07 | 01 25 |
| 55 | 05 49 | 24 39 | 00 08 | 03 53 | 01 53 |
| 56 | 05 16 | 23 27 | 28♒27 | 04 44 | 02 24 |
| 57 | 04 41 | 22 08 | 26 28 | 05 40 | 02 57 |
| 58 | 04 02 | 20 42 | 24 08 | 06 43 | 03 33 |
| 59 | 03 20 | 19 06 | 21 20 | 07 54 | 04 13 |
| 60 | 02♑34 | 17♑20 | 17♒56 | 09♉15 | 04♊57 |

**17h 20m 0s — 260° 0' 0" — 20 ♐ 49**

| LAT. | 11 | 12 | ASC | 2 | 3 |
|---|---|---|---|---|---|
| 0 | 18♑28 | 17♒33 | 19♓07 | 21♈38 | 22♉25 |
| 5 | 17 50 | 16 36 | 18 42 | 22 11 | 22 58 |
| 10 | 17 10 | 15 35 | 18 14 | 22 45 | 23 32 |
| 15 | 16 29 | 14 30 | 17 42 | 23 23 | 24 07 |
| 20 | 15 46 | 13 19 | 17 06 | 24 04 | 24 45 |
| 21 | 15 37 | 13 04 | 16 59 | 24 13 | 24 53 |
| 22 | 15 28 | 12 49 | 16 50 | 24 22 | 25 01 |
| 23 | 15 19 | 12 33 | 16 42 | 24 32 | 25 10 |
| 24 | 15 09 | 12 17 | 16 33 | 24 41 | 25 18 |
| 25 | 14 59 | 12 00 | 16 24 | 24 51 | 25 27 |
| 26 | 14 49 | 11 43 | 16 15 | 25 01 | 25 35 |
| 27 | 14 39 | 11 26 | 16 05 | 25 12 | 25 44 |
| 28 | 14 29 | 11 08 | 15 55 | 25 23 | 25 53 |
| 29 | 14 18 | 10 50 | 15 44 | 25 34 | 26 03 |
| 30 | 14 08 | 10 31 | 15 33 | 25 45 | 26 12 |
| 31 | 13 57 | 10 11 | 15 21 | 25 57 | 26 22 |
| 32 | 13 45 | 09 51 | 15 09 | 26 10 | 26 32 |
| 33 | 13 34 | 09 30 | 14 56 | 26 23 | 26 43 |
| 34 | 13 22 | 09 08 | 14 43 | 26 36 | 26 54 |
| 35 | 13 09 | 08 46 | 14 28 | 26 50 | 27 05 |
| 36 | 12 57 | 08 23 | 14 13 | 27 05 | 27 16 |
| 37 | 12 44 | 07 58 | 13 57 | 27 20 | 27 28 |
| 38 | 12 30 | 07 33 | 13 40 | 27 36 | 27 40 |
| 39 | 12 16 | 07 07 | 13 22 | 27 52 | 27 53 |
| 40 | 12 02 | 06 40 | 13 03 | 28 09 | 28 06 |
| 41 | 11 47 | 06 11 | 12 42 | 28 28 | 28 19 |
| 42 | 11 32 | 05 42 | 12 20 | 28 47 | 28 34 |
| 43 | 11 15 | 05 10 | 11 56 | 29 07 | 28 48 |
| 44 | 10 59 | 04 38 | 11 31 | 29 29 | 29 04 |
| 45 | 10 41 | 04 03 | 11 03 | 29 51 | 29 20 |
| 46 | 10 23 | 03 27 | 10 32 | 00♉16 | 29 37 |
| 47 | 10 04 | 02 48 | 09 59 | 00 41 | 29 54 |
| 48 | 09 43 | 02 07 | 09 23 | 01 09 | 00♊13 |
| 49 | 09 22 | 01 24 | 08 43 | 01 38 | 00 32 |
| 50 | 09 00 | 00 38 | 07 59 | 02 10 | 00 53 |
| 51 | 08 36 | 29♑49 | 07 09 | 02 44 | 01 15 |
| 52 | 08 11 | 28 56 | 06 14 | 03 20 | 01 38 |
| 53 | 07 45 | 28 00 | 05 11 | 04 00 | 02 03 |
| 54 | 07 16 | 26 59 | 03 59 | 04 44 | 02 30 |
| 55 | 06 46 | 25 53 | 02 37 | 05 32 | 02 58 |
| 56 | 06 13 | 24 41 | 01 02 | 06 24 | 03 29 |
| 57 | 05 38 | 23 22 | 29♒09 | 07 23 | 04 03 |
| 58 | 04 59 | 21 56 | 26 56 | 08 28 | 04 39 |
| 59 | 04 17 | 20 20 | 24 16 | 09 41 | 05 19 |
| 60 | 03♑30 | 18♑33 | 20♒59 | 11♉05 | 06♊04 |

**17h 24m 0s — 261° 0' 0" — 21 ♐ 44**

| LAT. | 11 | 12 | ASC | 2 | 3 |
|---|---|---|---|---|---|
| 0 | 19♑24 | 18♒34 | 20♓12 | 22♈42 | 23♉23 |
| 5 | 18 46 | 17 37 | 19 49 | 23 16 | 23 57 |
| 10 | 18 07 | 16 38 | 19 24 | 23 52 | 24 31 |
| 15 | 17 26 | 15 34 | 18 56 | 24 32 | 25 07 |
| 20 | 16 43 | 14 24 | 18 23 | 25 15 | 25 46 |
| 21 | 16 34 | 14 09 | 18 16 | 25 24 | 25 54 |
| 22 | 16 25 | 13 54 | 18 09 | 25 34 | 26 02 |
| 23 | 16 15 | 13 39 | 18 01 | 25 43 | 26 10 |
| 24 | 16 06 | 13 23 | 17 53 | 25 53 | 26 19 |
| 25 | 15 56 | 13 06 | 17 45 | 26 04 | 26 27 |
| 26 | 15 46 | 12 50 | 17 37 | 26 14 | 26 36 |
| 27 | 15 36 | 12 33 | 17 28 | 26 25 | 26 45 |
| 28 | 15 26 | 12 15 | 17 18 | 26 37 | 26 54 |
| 29 | 15 16 | 11 57 | 17 09 | 26 48 | 27 04 |
| 30 | 15 05 | 11 38 | 16 59 | 27 00 | 27 14 |
| 31 | 14 54 | 11 19 | 16 48 | 27 13 | 27 24 |
| 32 | 14 42 | 10 59 | 16 37 | 27 26 | 27 34 |
| 33 | 14 31 | 10 38 | 16 25 | 27 39 | 27 44 |
| 34 | 14 19 | 10 17 | 16 13 | 27 53 | 27 55 |
| 35 | 14 07 | 09 55 | 16 00 | 28 08 | 28 06 |
| 36 | 13 54 | 09 32 | 15 46 | 28 23 | 28 18 |
| 37 | 13 41 | 09 08 | 15 32 | 28 38 | 28 30 |
| 38 | 13 28 | 08 43 | 15 17 | 28 55 | 28 42 |
| 39 | 13 14 | 08 17 | 15 00 | 29 12 | 28 55 |
| 40 | 12 59 | 07 50 | 14 43 | 29 30 | 29 08 |
| 41 | 12 44 | 07 22 | 14 24 | 29 49 | 29 22 |
| 42 | 12 29 | 06 52 | 14 04 | 00♉09 | 29 36 |
| 43 | 12 13 | 06 21 | 13 42 | 00 30 | 29 51 |
| 44 | 11 56 | 05 49 | 13 19 | 00 53 | 00♊06 |
| 45 | 11 38 | 05 15 | 12 54 | 01 16 | 00 23 |
| 46 | 11 20 | 04 39 | 12 26 | 01 41 | 00 40 |
| 47 | 11 01 | 04 00 | 11 56 | 02 08 | 00 57 |
| 48 | 10 41 | 03 20 | 11 23 | 02 36 | 01 16 |
| 49 | 10 20 | 02 37 | 10 46 | 03 07 | 01 36 |
| 50 | 09 57 | 01 51 | 10 06 | 03 40 | 01 57 |
| 51 | 09 34 | 01 02 | 09 20 | 04 15 | 02 19 |
| 52 | 09 09 | 00 10 | 08 29 | 04 53 | 02 42 |
| 53 | 08 42 | 29♑14 | 07 32 | 05 34 | 03 07 |
| 54 | 08 14 | 28 13 | 06 26 | 06 19 | 03 34 |
| 55 | 07 43 | 27 07 | 05 09 | 07 09 | 04 03 |
| 56 | 07 10 | 25 56 | 03 41 | 08 03 | 04 34 |
| 57 | 06 35 | 24 37 | 01 56 | 09 04 | 05 08 |
| 58 | 05 56 | 23 11 | 29♒51 | 10 11 | 05 45 |
| 59 | 05 14 | 21 35 | 27 20 | 11 27 | 06 25 |
| 60 | 04♑27 | 19♑48 | 24♒13 | 12♉53 | 07♊10 |

**17h 28m 0s — 262° 0' 0" — 22 ♐ 39**

| LAT. | 11 | 12 | ASC | 2 | 3 |
|---|---|---|---|---|---|
| 0 | 20♑20 | 19♒35 | 21♓17 | 23♈46 | 24♉22 |
| 5 | 19 42 | 18 39 | 20 57 | 24 21 | 24 56 |
| 10 | 19 03 | 17 41 | 20 34 | 24 59 | 25 30 |
| 15 | 18 23 | 16 38 | 20 09 | 25 40 | 26 07 |
| 20 | 17 40 | 15 29 | 19 40 | 26 25 | 26 46 |
| 21 | 17 31 | 15 15 | 19 34 | 26 35 | 26 54 |
| 22 | 17 22 | 15 00 | 19 27 | 26 45 | 27 02 |
| 23 | 17 12 | 14 45 | 19 21 | 26 55 | 27 10 |
| 24 | 17 03 | 14 29 | 19 14 | 27 05 | 27 19 |
| 25 | 16 53 | 14 13 | 19 06 | 27 16 | 27 28 |
| 26 | 16 43 | 13 56 | 18 59 | 27 27 | 27 37 |
| 27 | 16 33 | 13 40 | 18 51 | 27 38 | 27 46 |
| 28 | 16 23 | 13 22 | 18 42 | 27 50 | 27 55 |
| 29 | 16 13 | 13 04 | 18 34 | 28 02 | 28 05 |
| 30 | 16 02 | 12 46 | 18 25 | 28 15 | 28 15 |
| 31 | 15 51 | 12 27 | 18 15 | 28 28 | 28 25 |
| 32 | 15 40 | 12 07 | 18 05 | 28 41 | 28 35 |
| 33 | 15 28 | 11 47 | 17 55 | 28 55 | 28 46 |
| 34 | 15 16 | 11 26 | 17 44 | 29 10 | 28 57 |
| 35 | 15 04 | 11 04 | 17 32 | 29 25 | 29 08 |
| 36 | 14 51 | 10 41 | 17 20 | 29 40 | 29 19 |
| 37 | 14 38 | 10 18 | 17 07 | 29 57 | 29 31 |
| 38 | 14 25 | 09 53 | 16 53 | 00♉14 | 29 44 |
| 39 | 14 11 | 09 27 | 16 39 | 00 32 | 29 57 |
| 40 | 13 57 | 09 01 | 16 23 | 00 50 | 00♊10 |
| 41 | 13 42 | 08 33 | 16 06 | 01 10 | 00 24 |
| 42 | 13 26 | 08 04 | 15 48 | 01 31 | 00 38 |
| 43 | 13 10 | 07 33 | 15 29 | 01 53 | 00 53 |
| 44 | 12 54 | 07 01 | 15 08 | 02 16 | 01 09 |
| 45 | 12 36 | 06 27 | 14 45 | 02 40 | 01 25 |
| 46 | 12 18 | 05 51 | 14 20 | 03 06 | 01 42 |
| 47 | 11 59 | 05 13 | 13 53 | 03 34 | 02 00 |
| 48 | 11 38 | 04 33 | 13 24 | 04 03 | 02 19 |
| 49 | 11 17 | 03 51 | 12 51 | 04 35 | 02 39 |
| 50 | 10 55 | 03 05 | 12 14 | 05 09 | 03 00 |
| 51 | 10 31 | 02 17 | 11 33 | 05 45 | 03 22 |
| 52 | 10 06 | 01 25 | 10 47 | 06 25 | 03 46 |
| 53 | 09 40 | 00 29 | 09 55 | 07 07 | 04 11 |
| 54 | 09 11 | 29♑29 | 08 55 | 07 54 | 04 38 |
| 55 | 08 41 | 28 23 | 07 45 | 08 45 | 05 07 |
| 56 | 08 08 | 27 12 | 06 24 | 09 41 | 05 39 |
| 57 | 07 32 | 25 53 | 04 48 | 10 43 | 06 13 |
| 58 | 06 54 | 24 27 | 02 53 | 11 53 | 06 50 |
| 59 | 06 11 | 22 51 | 00 32 | 13 11 | 07 31 |
| 60 | 05♑24 | 21♑04 | 27♒36 | 14♉40 | 08♊16 |

**17h 32m 0s — 263° 0' 0" — 23 ♐ 34**

| LAT. | 11 | 12 | ASC | 2 | 3 |
|---|---|---|---|---|---|
| 0 | 21♑17 | 20♒36 | 22♓23 | 24♈50 | 25♉21 |
| 5 | 20 39 | 19 42 | 22 05 | 25 27 | 25 55 |
| 10 | 20 00 | 18 44 | 21 45 | 26 06 | 26 30 |
| 15 | 19 20 | 17 43 | 21 23 | 26 48 | 27 06 |
| 20 | 18 37 | 16 35 | 20 57 | 27 35 | 27 46 |
| 21 | 18 28 | 16 21 | 20 52 | 27 45 | 27 54 |
| 22 | 18 19 | 16 06 | 20 46 | 27 55 | 28 02 |
| 23 | 18 10 | 15 51 | 20 40 | 28 06 | 28 11 |
| 24 | 18 00 | 15 36 | 20 34 | 28 17 | 28 19 |
| 25 | 17 51 | 15 20 | 20 28 | 28 28 | 28 28 |
| 26 | 17 41 | 15 04 | 20 21 | 28 39 | 28 37 |
| 27 | 17 31 | 14 47 | 20 14 | 28 51 | 28 46 |
| 28 | 17 21 | 14 30 | 20 07 | 29 03 | 28 56 |
| 29 | 17 10 | 14 12 | 19 59 | 29 16 | 29 05 |
| 30 | 16 59 | 13 54 | 19 51 | 29 29 | 29 15 |
| 31 | 16 48 | 13 35 | 19 43 | 29 42 | 29 25 |
| 32 | 16 37 | 13 16 | 19 34 | 29 56 | 29 36 |
| 33 | 16 26 | 12 56 | 19 25 | 00♉11 | 29 47 |
| 34 | 16 14 | 12 35 | 19 15 | 00 26 | 29 58 |
| 35 | 16 02 | 12 13 | 19 05 | 00 41 | 00♊09 |
| 36 | 15 49 | 11 51 | 18 54 | 00 57 | 00 21 |
| 37 | 15 36 | 11 27 | 18 43 | 01 14 | 00 33 |
| 38 | 15 23 | 11 04 | 18 31 | 01 32 | 00 45 |
| 39 | 15 09 | 10 38 | 18 18 | 01 51 | 00 58 |
| 40 | 14 54 | 10 12 | 18 04 | 02 10 | 01 12 |
| 41 | 14 40 | 09 45 | 17 49 | 02 30 | 01 26 |
| 42 | 14 24 | 09 16 | 17 33 | 02 52 | 01 40 |
| 43 | 14 08 | 08 45 | 17 16 | 03 15 | 01 55 |
| 44 | 13 51 | 08 14 | 16 58 | 03 38 | 02 11 |
| 45 | 13 34 | 07 40 | 16 38 | 04 04 | 02 27 |
| 46 | 13 16 | 07 05 | 16 16 | 04 31 | 02 45 |
| 47 | 12 56 | 06 27 | 15 52 | 04 59 | 03 03 |
| 48 | 12 36 | 05 48 | 15 26 | 05 29 | 03 22 |
| 49 | 12 15 | 05 05 | 14 56 | 06 02 | 03 42 |
| 50 | 11 53 | 04 20 | 14 24 | 06 37 | 04 03 |
| 51 | 11 29 | 03 32 | 13 48 | 07 15 | 04 25 |
| 52 | 11 04 | 02 41 | 13 07 | 07 55 | 04 49 |
| 53 | 10 38 | 01 45 | 12 20 | 08 39 | 05 15 |
| 54 | 10 09 | 00 45 | 11 26 | 09 27 | 05 42 |
| 55 | 09 39 | 29♑40 | 10 24 | 10 20 | 06 11 |
| 56 | 09 06 | 28 29 | 09 12 | 11 18 | 06 43 |
| 57 | 08 30 | 27 11 | 07 45 | 12 22 | 07 17 |
| 58 | 07 51 | 25 45 | 06 01 | 13 33 | 07 54 |
| 59 | 07 09 | 24 09 | 03 52 | 14 52 | 08 36 |
| 60 | 06♑22 | 22♑22 | 01♓10 | 16♉25 | 09♊21 |

# Placidus Table of Houses for Latitudes 0° to 60° North

**17h 36m 0s — 264° 0' 0" — 24 ♐ 30**

| LAT. | 11 | 12 | ASC | 2 | 3 |
|---|---|---|---|---|---|
| 0 | 22♑13 | 21♒37 | 23♓28 | 25♈53 | 26♉19 |
| 5 | 21 36 | 20 44 | 23 12 | 26 31 | 26 53 |
| 10 | 20 57 | 19 48 | 22 56 | 27 12 | 27 29 |
| 15 | 20 17 | 18 47 | 22 37 | 27 56 | 28 06 |
| 20 | 19 34 | 17 41 | 22 15 | 28 45 | 28 45 |
| 21 | 19 25 | 17 27 | 22 10 | 28 55 | 28 53 |
| 22 | 19 16 | 17 12 | 22 05 | 29 06 | 29 02 |
| 23 | 19 07 | 16 58 | 22 00 | 29 17 | 29 10 |
| 24 | 18 57 | 16 43 | 21 55 | 29 28 | 29 19 |
| 25 | 18 48 | 16 27 | 21 49 | 29 39 | 29 28 |
| 26 | 18 38 | 16 11 | 21 43 | 29 51 | 29 37 |
| 27 | 18 28 | 15 55 | 21 37 | 00♉04 | 29 47 |
| 28 | 18 18 | 15 38 | 21 31 | 00 16 | 29 56 |
| 29 | 18 08 | 15 20 | 21 25 | 00 29 | 00♊06 |
| 30 | 17 57 | 15 03 | 21 18 | 00 43 | 00 16 |
| 31 | 17 46 | 14 44 | 21 11 | 00 56 | 00 26 |
| 32 | 17 35 | 14 25 | 21 03 | 01 11 | 00 36 |
| 33 | 17 23 | 14 05 | 20 55 | 01 26 | 00 47 |
| 34 | 17 11 | 13 45 | 20 47 | 01 41 | 00 58 |
| 35 | 16 59 | 13 24 | 20 38 | 01 57 | 01 10 |
| 36 | 16 47 | 13 02 | 20 29 | 02 14 | 01 22 |
| 37 | 16 34 | 12 39 | 20 19 | 02 32 | 01 34 |
| 38 | 16 20 | 12 15 | 20 09 | 02 50 | 01 46 |
| 39 | 16 07 | 11 50 | 19 57 | 03 09 | 01 59 |
| 40 | 15 52 | 11 24 | 19 46 | 03 29 | 02 13 |
| 41 | 15 38 | 10 57 | 19 33 | 03 50 | 02 27 |
| 42 | 15 22 | 10 28 | 19 19 | 04 12 | 02 42 |
| 43 | 15 06 | 09 58 | 19 04 | 04 36 | 02 57 |
| 44 | 14 49 | 09 27 | 18 48 | 05 00 | 03 13 |
| 45 | 14 32 | 08 54 | 18 31 | 05 27 | 03 29 |
| 46 | 14 14 | 08 19 | 18 12 | 05 54 | 03 47 |
| 47 | 13 55 | 07 42 | 17 51 | 06 24 | 04 05 |
| 48 | 13 35 | 07 03 | 17 28 | 06 55 | 04 24 |
| 49 | 13 13 | 06 21 | 17 03 | 07 28 | 04 44 |
| 50 | 12 51 | 05 36 | 16 35 | 08 04 | 05 05 |
| 51 | 12 28 | 04 49 | 16 04 | 08 43 | 05 28 |
| 52 | 12 03 | 03 57 | 15 28 | 09 25 | 05 52 |
| 53 | 11 36 | 03 02 | 14 47 | 10 10 | 06 18 |
| 54 | 11 07 | 02 03 | 14 01 | 10 59 | 06 45 |
| 55 | 10 37 | 00 58 | 13 06 | 11 53 | 07 15 |
| 56 | 10 04 | 29♑47 | 12 03 | 12 53 | 07 46 |
| 57 | 09 28 | 28 30 | 10 46 | 13 59 | 08 21 |
| 58 | 08 50 | 27 04 | 09 14 | 15 12 | 08 58 |
| 59 | 08 07 | 25 29 | 07 20 | 16 34 | 09 40 |
| 60 | 07♑20 | 23♑41 | 04♓55 | 18♉08 | 10♊26 |

**17h 40m 0s — 265° 0' 0" — 25 ♐ 25**

| LAT. | 11 | 12 | ASC | 2 | 3 |
|---|---|---|---|---|---|
| 0 | 23♑10 | 22♒39 | 24♓33 | 26♈57 | 27♉17 |
| 5 | 22 32 | 21 47 | 24 20 | 27 36 | 27 52 |
| 10 | 21 54 | 20 52 | 24 06 | 28 18 | 28 27 |
| 15 | 21 14 | 19 52 | 23 50 | 29 04 | 29 05 |
| 20 | 20 31 | 18 47 | 23 32 | 29 54 | 29 45 |
| 21 | 20 23 | 18 33 | 23 28 | 00♉05 | 29 53 |
| 22 | 20 14 | 18 19 | 23 24 | 00 16 | 00♊02 |
| 23 | 20 04 | 18 05 | 23 20 | 00 27 | 00 10 |
| 24 | 19 55 | 17 50 | 23 15 | 00 39 | 00 19 |
| 25 | 19 46 | 17 35 | 23 11 | 00 51 | 00 28 |
| 26 | 19 36 | 17 19 | 23 06 | 01 03 | 00 37 |
| 27 | 19 26 | 17 03 | 23 01 | 01 16 | 00 46 |
| 28 | 19 16 | 16 46 | 22 56 | 01 29 | 00 56 |
| 29 | 19 05 | 16 29 | 22 50 | 01 42 | 01 06 |
| 30 | 18 55 | 16 12 | 22 44 | 01 56 | 01 16 |
| 31 | 18 44 | 15 53 | 22 38 | 02 10 | 01 26 |
| 32 | 18 33 | 15 35 | 22 32 | 02 25 | 01 37 |
| 33 | 18 21 | 15 15 | 22 26 | 02 41 | 01 48 |
| 34 | 18 09 | 14 55 | 22 19 | 02 57 | 01 59 |
| 35 | 17 57 | 14 34 | 22 11 | 03 13 | 02 10 |
| 36 | 17 45 | 14 13 | 22 04 | 03 31 | 02 22 |
| 37 | 17 32 | 13 50 | 21 55 | 03 49 | 02 35 |
| 38 | 17 19 | 13 26 | 21 47 | 04 07 | 02 47 |
| 39 | 17 05 | 13 02 | 21 37 | 04 27 | 03 00 |
| 40 | 16 51 | 12 36 | 21 27 | 04 48 | 03 14 |
| 41 | 16 36 | 12 10 | 21 17 | 05 10 | 03 28 |
| 42 | 16 20 | 11 41 | 21 05 | 05 32 | 03 43 |
| 43 | 16 04 | 11 12 | 20 53 | 05 56 | 03 58 |
| 44 | 15 48 | 10 41 | 20 39 | 06 22 | 04 14 |
| 45 | 15 30 | 10 08 | 20 25 | 06 49 | 04 31 |
| 46 | 15 12 | 09 34 | 20 09 | 07 17 | 04 48 |
| 47 | 14 53 | 08 57 | 19 52 | 07 47 | 05 07 |
| 48 | 14 33 | 08 18 | 19 32 | 08 20 | 05 26 |
| 49 | 14 12 | 07 37 | 19 11 | 08 54 | 05 46 |
| 50 | 13 50 | 06 53 | 18 47 | 09 31 | 06 08 |
| 51 | 13 26 | 06 06 | 18 21 | 10 11 | 06 30 |
| 52 | 13 01 | 05 15 | 17 51 | 10 54 | 06 55 |
| 53 | 12 34 | 04 20 | 17 16 | 11 40 | 07 20 |
| 54 | 12 06 | 03 21 | 16 37 | 12 31 | 07 48 |
| 55 | 11 36 | 02 17 | 15 51 | 13 26 | 08 17 |
| 56 | 11 03 | 01 07 | 14 57 | 14 27 | 08 49 |
| 57 | 10 27 | 29♑50 | 13 52 | 15 34 | 09 24 |
| 58 | 09 48 | 28 24 | 12 33 | 16 49 | 10 02 |
| 59 | 09 05 | 26 49 | 10 54 | 18 13 | 10 44 |
| 60 | 08♑18 | 25♑03 | 08♓48 | 19♉49 | 11♊30 |

**17h 44m 0s — 266° 0' 0" — 26 ♐ 20**

| LAT. | 11 | 12 | ASC | 2 | 3 |
|---|---|---|---|---|---|
| 0 | 24♑06 | 23♒41 | 25♓38 | 28♈00 | 28♉15 |
| 5 | 23 29 | 22 50 | 25 28 | 28 41 | 28 50 |
| 10 | 22 51 | 21 56 | 25 17 | 29 24 | 29 26 |
| 15 | 22 11 | 20 57 | 25 04 | 00♉11 | 00♊04 |
| 20 | 21 29 | 19 54 | 24 50 | 01 03 | 00 44 |
| 21 | 21 20 | 19 40 | 24 46 | 01 14 | 00 52 |
| 22 | 21 11 | 19 26 | 24 43 | 01 26 | 01 01 |
| 23 | 21 02 | 19 12 | 24 40 | 01 37 | 01 10 |
| 24 | 20 53 | 18 57 | 24 36 | 01 49 | 01 18 |
| 25 | 20 43 | 18 43 | 24 32 | 02 02 | 01 28 |
| 26 | 20 34 | 18 27 | 24 28 | 02 14 | 01 37 |
| 27 | 20 24 | 18 11 | 24 24 | 02 27 | 01 46 |
| 28 | 20 14 | 17 55 | 24 20 | 02 41 | 01 56 |
| 29 | 20 03 | 17 38 | 24 16 | 02 55 | 02 06 |
| 30 | 19 53 | 17 21 | 24 11 | 03 09 | 02 16 |
| 31 | 19 42 | 17 03 | 24 07 | 03 24 | 02 26 |
| 32 | 19 31 | 16 45 | 24 02 | 03 39 | 02 37 |
| 33 | 19 19 | 16 26 | 23 56 | 03 55 | 02 48 |
| 34 | 19 08 | 16 06 | 23 51 | 04 11 | 02 59 |
| 35 | 18 55 | 15 45 | 23 45 | 04 29 | 03 11 |
| 36 | 18 43 | 15 24 | 23 39 | 04 46 | 03 23 |
| 37 | 18 30 | 15 02 | 23 32 | 05 05 | 03 35 |
| 38 | 18 17 | 14 39 | 23 25 | 05 24 | 03 48 |
| 39 | 18 03 | 14 15 | 23 17 | 05 45 | 04 01 |
| 40 | 17 49 | 13 49 | 23 09 | 06 06 | 04 15 |
| 41 | 17 34 | 13 23 | 23 01 | 06 28 | 04 29 |
| 42 | 17 19 | 12 55 | 22 52 | 06 52 | 04 44 |
| 43 | 17 03 | 12 26 | 22 42 | 07 16 | 04 59 |
| 44 | 16 46 | 11 56 | 22 31 | 07 43 | 05 15 |
| 45 | 16 29 | 11 23 | 22 19 | 08 10 | 05 32 |
| 46 | 16 11 | 10 49 | 22 06 | 08 39 | 05 50 |
| 47 | 15 52 | 10 13 | 21 52 | 09 10 | 06 08 |
| 48 | 15 32 | 09 35 | 21 37 | 09 43 | 06 27 |
| 49 | 15 11 | 08 54 | 21 20 | 10 19 | 06 48 |
| 50 | 14 48 | 08 10 | 21 01 | 10 57 | 07 09 |
| 51 | 14 25 | 07 24 | 20 39 | 11 37 | 07 32 |
| 52 | 14 00 | 06 34 | 20 15 | 12 21 | 07 57 |
| 53 | 13 33 | 05 40 | 19 47 | 13 09 | 08 23 |
| 54 | 13 05 | 04 41 | 19 15 | 14 01 | 08 50 |
| 55 | 12 35 | 03 37 | 18 38 | 14 57 | 09 20 |
| 56 | 12 02 | 02 28 | 17 54 | 15 59 | 09 52 |
| 57 | 11 26 | 01 11 | 17 01 | 17 08 | 10 27 |
| 58 | 10 47 | 29♑46 | 15 56 | 18 25 | 11 05 |
| 59 | 10 04 | 28 12 | 14 35 | 19 50 | 11 47 |
| 60 | 09♑17 | 26♑25 | 12♓51 | 21♉28 | 12♊33 |

**17h 48m 0s — 267° 0' 0" — 27 ♐ 15**

| LAT. | 11 | 12 | ASC | 2 | 3 |
|---|---|---|---|---|---|
| 0 | 25♑03 | 24♒42 | 26♓44 | 29♈03 | 29♉13 |
| 5 | 24 26 | 23 53 | 26 36 | 29 45 | 29 48 |
| 10 | 23 48 | 23 00 | 26 28 | 00♉30 | 00♊24 |
| 15 | 23 09 | 22 03 | 26 18 | 01 19 | 01 03 |
| 20 | 22 27 | 21 01 | 26 07 | 02 12 | 01 43 |
| 21 | 22 18 | 20 47 | 26 05 | 02 24 | 01 51 |
| 22 | 22 09 | 20 34 | 26 02 | 02 35 | 02 00 |
| 23 | 22 00 | 20 20 | 26 00 | 02 47 | 02 09 |
| 24 | 21 51 | 20 05 | 25 57 | 03 00 | 02 18 |
| 25 | 21 41 | 19 51 | 25 54 | 03 12 | 02 27 |
| 26 | 21 32 | 19 36 | 25 51 | 03 25 | 02 36 |
| 27 | 21 22 | 19 20 | 25 48 | 03 39 | 02 46 |
| 28 | 21 12 | 19 04 | 25 45 | 03 53 | 02 55 |
| 29 | 21 01 | 18 48 | 25 42 | 04 07 | 03 05 |
| 30 | 20 51 | 18 31 | 25 38 | 04 22 | 03 16 |
| 31 | 20 40 | 18 13 | 25 35 | 04 37 | 03 26 |
| 32 | 20 29 | 17 55 | 25 31 | 04 53 | 03 37 |
| 33 | 20 18 | 17 37 | 25 27 | 05 09 | 03 48 |
| 34 | 20 06 | 17 17 | 25 23 | 05 26 | 03 59 |
| 35 | 19 54 | 16 57 | 25 18 | 05 43 | 04 11 |
| 36 | 19 41 | 16 36 | 25 14 | 06 02 | 04 23 |
| 37 | 19 29 | 16 14 | 25 09 | 06 21 | 04 35 |
| 38 | 19 15 | 15 51 | 25 04 | 06 41 | 04 48 |
| 39 | 19 02 | 15 28 | 24 58 | 07 02 | 05 01 |
| 40 | 18 48 | 15 03 | 24 52 | 07 24 | 05 15 |
| 41 | 18 33 | 14 37 | 24 45 | 07 46 | 05 30 |
| 42 | 18 18 | 14 10 | 24 38 | 08 11 | 05 44 |
| 43 | 18 02 | 13 41 | 24 31 | 08 36 | 06 00 |
| 44 | 17 45 | 13 11 | 24 23 | 09 03 | 06 16 |
| 45 | 17 28 | 12 39 | 24 14 | 09 31 | 06 33 |
| 46 | 17 10 | 12 06 | 24 04 | 10 01 | 06 51 |
| 47 | 16 51 | 11 30 | 23 54 | 10 33 | 07 09 |
| 48 | 16 31 | 10 52 | 23 42 | 11 06 | 07 29 |
| 49 | 16 10 | 10 12 | 23 29 | 11 43 | 07 49 |
| 50 | 15 48 | 09 29 | 23 15 | 12 21 | 08 11 |
| 51 | 15 24 | 08 43 | 22 59 | 13 03 | 08 34 |
| 52 | 14 59 | 07 53 | 22 40 | 13 48 | 08 58 |
| 53 | 14 33 | 07 00 | 22 19 | 14 37 | 09 24 |
| 54 | 14 04 | 06 02 | 21 55 | 15 29 | 09 52 |
| 55 | 13 34 | 04 59 | 21 27 | 16 27 | 10 22 |
| 56 | 13 01 | 03 50 | 20 53 | 17 30 | 10 54 |
| 57 | 12 25 | 02 34 | 20 13 | 18 41 | 11 29 |
| 58 | 11 47 | 01 10 | 19 24 | 19 59 | 12 08 |
| 59 | 11 04 | 29♑36 | 18 21 | 21 26 | 12 50 |
| 60 | 10♑16 | 27♑50 | 17♓01 | 23♉05 | 13♊37 |

**17h 52m 0s — 268° 0' 0" — 28 ♐ 10**

| LAT. | 11 | 12 | ASC | 2 | 3 |
|---|---|---|---|---|---|
| 0 | 26♑00 | 25♒44 | 27♓49 | 00♉06 | 00♊11 |
| 5 | 25 24 | 24 56 | 27 44 | 00 49 | 00 46 |
| 10 | 24 46 | 24 04 | 27 38 | 01 36 | 01 23 |
| 15 | 24 06 | 23 09 | 27 32 | 02 26 | 02 01 |
| 20 | 23 25 | 22 08 | 27 25 | 03 21 | 02 42 |
| 21 | 23 16 | 21 55 | 27 23 | 03 33 | 02 50 |
| 22 | 23 07 | 21 41 | 27 21 | 03 45 | 02 59 |
| 23 | 22 58 | 21 28 | 27 20 | 03 57 | 03 08 |
| 24 | 22 49 | 21 14 | 27 18 | 04 10 | 03 17 |
| 25 | 22 39 | 20 59 | 27 16 | 04 23 | 03 26 |
| 26 | 22 30 | 20 45 | 27 14 | 04 36 | 03 35 |
| 27 | 22 20 | 20 29 | 27 12 | 04 50 | 03 45 |
| 28 | 22 10 | 20 14 | 27 10 | 05 04 | 03 55 |
| 29 | 22 00 | 19 58 | 27 08 | 05 19 | 04 05 |
| 30 | 21 49 | 19 41 | 27 06 | 05 34 | 04 15 |
| 31 | 21 39 | 19 24 | 27 03 | 05 49 | 04 26 |
| 32 | 21 27 | 19 06 | 27 01 | 06 06 | 04 36 |
| 33 | 21 16 | 18 48 | 26 58 | 06 22 | 04 47 |
| 34 | 21 04 | 18 29 | 26 55 | 06 40 | 04 59 |
| 35 | 20 52 | 18 09 | 26 52 | 06 58 | 05 11 |
| 36 | 20 40 | 17 48 | 26 49 | 07 17 | 05 23 |
| 37 | 20 27 | 17 27 | 26 46 | 07 36 | 05 35 |
| 38 | 20 14 | 17 05 | 26 42 | 07 57 | 05 48 |
| 39 | 20 01 | 16 41 | 26 38 | 08 18 | 06 02 |
| 40 | 19 46 | 16 17 | 26 34 | 08 41 | 06 15 |
| 41 | 19 32 | 15 52 | 26 30 | 09 04 | 06 30 |
| 42 | 19 17 | 15 25 | 26 26 | 09 29 | 06 45 |
| 43 | 19 01 | 14 57 | 26 21 | 09 55 | 07 00 |
| 44 | 18 44 | 14 27 | 26 15 | 10 22 | 07 17 |
| 45 | 18 27 | 13 56 | 26 09 | 10 51 | 07 34 |
| 46 | 18 09 | 13 23 | 26 03 | 11 22 | 07 51 |
| 47 | 17 50 | 12 48 | 25 56 | 11 54 | 08 10 |
| 48 | 17 30 | 12 10 | 25 48 | 12 29 | 08 30 |
| 49 | 17 09 | 11 31 | 25 39 | 13 06 | 08 50 |
| 50 | 16 47 | 10 48 | 25 30 | 13 45 | 09 12 |
| 51 | 16 24 | 10 03 | 25 19 | 14 28 | 09 35 |
| 52 | 15 59 | 09 14 | 25 06 | 15 14 | 10 00 |
| 53 | 15 32 | 08 21 | 24 52 | 16 03 | 10 26 |
| 54 | 15 04 | 07 24 | 24 36 | 16 57 | 10 54 |
| 55 | 14 34 | 06 21 | 24 17 | 17 56 | 11 24 |
| 56 | 14 01 | 05 13 | 23 54 | 19 00 | 11 56 |
| 57 | 13 25 | 03 58 | 23 27 | 20 12 | 12 31 |
| 58 | 12 46 | 02 35 | 22 54 | 21 31 | 13 10 |
| 59 | 12 04 | 01 01 | 22 12 | 23 00 | 13 52 |
| 60 | 11♑16 | 29♑16 | 21♓17 | 24♉41 | 14♊39 |

**17h 56m 0s — 269° 0' 0" — 29 ♐ 05**

| LAT. | 11 | 12 | ASC | 2 | 3 |
|---|---|---|---|---|---|
| 0 | 26♑57 | 26♒47 | 28♓55 | 01♉08 | 01♊08 |
| 5 | 26 21 | 25 59 | 28 52 | 01 53 | 01 44 |
| 10 | 25 43 | 25 09 | 28 49 | 02 41 | 02 21 |
| 15 | 25 04 | 24 15 | 28 46 | 03 33 | 02 59 |
| 20 | 24 23 | 23 15 | 28 42 | 04 29 | 03 41 |
| 21 | 24 14 | 23 02 | 28 42 | 04 41 | 03 49 |
| 22 | 24 05 | 22 49 | 28 41 | 04 54 | 03 58 |
| 23 | 23 56 | 22 36 | 28 40 | 05 06 | 04 07 |
| 24 | 23 47 | 22 22 | 28 39 | 05 19 | 04 16 |
| 25 | 23 38 | 22 08 | 28 38 | 05 33 | 04 25 |
| 26 | 23 28 | 21 54 | 28 37 | 05 46 | 04 34 |
| 27 | 23 18 | 21 39 | 28 36 | 06 01 | 04 44 |
| 28 | 23 08 | 21 24 | 28 35 | 06 15 | 04 54 |
| 29 | 22 58 | 21 08 | 28 34 | 06 30 | 05 04 |
| 30 | 22 48 | 20 52 | 28 33 | 06 46 | 05 14 |
| 31 | 22 37 | 20 35 | 28 32 | 07 02 | 05 25 |
| 32 | 22 26 | 20 18 | 28 30 | 07 18 | 05 36 |
| 33 | 22 15 | 20 00 | 28 29 | 07 36 | 05 47 |
| 34 | 22 03 | 19 41 | 28 28 | 07 53 | 05 58 |
| 35 | 21 51 | 19 22 | 28 26 | 08 12 | 06 10 |
| 36 | 21 39 | 19 01 | 28 25 | 08 31 | 06 22 |
| 37 | 21 26 | 18 40 | 28 23 | 08 51 | 06 35 |
| 38 | 21 13 | 18 19 | 28 21 | 09 12 | 06 48 |
| 39 | 21 00 | 17 56 | 28 19 | 09 34 | 07 01 |
| 40 | 20 46 | 17 32 | 28 17 | 09 57 | 07 15 |
| 41 | 20 31 | 17 07 | 28 15 | 10 21 | 07 30 |
| 42 | 20 16 | 16 41 | 28 13 | 10 46 | 07 45 |
| 43 | 20 00 | 16 13 | 28 10 | 11 13 | 08 01 |
| 44 | 19 44 | 15 44 | 28 07 | 11 41 | 08 17 |
| 45 | 19 26 | 15 13 | 28 05 | 12 10 | 08 34 |
| 46 | 19 08 | 14 41 | 28 01 | 12 42 | 08 52 |
| 47 | 18 49 | 14 06 | 27 58 | 13 15 | 09 10 |
| 48 | 18 30 | 13 29 | 27 54 | 13 50 | 09 30 |
| 49 | 18 09 | 12 50 | 27 50 | 14 28 | 09 51 |
| 50 | 17 47 | 12 09 | 27 45 | 15 08 | 10 13 |
| 51 | 17 23 | 11 24 | 27 39 | 15 52 | 10 36 |
| 52 | 16 59 | 10 35 | 27 33 | 16 38 | 11 01 |
| 53 | 16 32 | 09 43 | 27 26 | 17 29 | 11 27 |
| 54 | 16 04 | 08 47 | 27 18 | 18 24 | 11 55 |
| 55 | 15 34 | 07 45 | 27 08 | 19 23 | 12 25 |
| 56 | 15 01 | 06 38 | 26 57 | 20 29 | 12 58 |
| 57 | 14 25 | 05 23 | 26 43 | 21 41 | 13 33 |
| 58 | 13 47 | 04 01 | 26 26 | 23 02 | 14 11 |
| 59 | 13 04 | 02 29 | 26 05 | 24 32 | 14 54 |
| 60 | 12♑17 | 00♒44 | 25♓38 | 26♉14 | 15♊41 |

**18h 0m 0s — 270° 0' 0" — 00 ♑ 00**

| LAT. | 11 | 12 | ASC | 2 | 3 |
|---|---|---|---|---|---|
| 0 | 27♑55 | 27♒49 | 00♈00 | 02♉11 | 02♊05 |
| 5 | 27 18 | 27 03 | 00 00 | 02 57 | 02 42 |
| 10 | 26 41 | 26 14 | 00 00 | 03 46 | 03 19 |
| 15 | 26 02 | 25 21 | 00 00 | 04 39 | 03 58 |
| 20 | 25 21 | 24 23 | 00 00 | 05 37 | 04 39 |
| 21 | 25 12 | 24 10 | 00 00 | 05 50 | 04 48 |
| 22 | 25 04 | 23 58 | 00 00 | 06 02 | 04 56 |
| 23 | 24 55 | 23 45 | 00 00 | 06 15 | 05 05 |
| 24 | 24 46 | 23 31 | 00 00 | 06 29 | 05 14 |
| 25 | 24 36 | 23 18 | 00 00 | 06 42 | 05 24 |
| 26 | 24 27 | 23 04 | 00 00 | 06 56 | 05 33 |
| 27 | 24 17 | 22 49 | 00 00 | 07 11 | 05 43 |
| 28 | 24 07 | 22 34 | 00 00 | 07 26 | 05 53 |
| 29 | 23 57 | 22 19 | 00 00 | 07 41 | 06 03 |
| 30 | 23 47 | 22 03 | 00 00 | 07 57 | 06 13 |
| 31 | 23 36 | 21 46 | 00 00 | 08 14 | 06 24 |
| 32 | 23 25 | 21 29 | 00 00 | 08 31 | 06 35 |
| 33 | 23 14 | 21 12 | 00 00 | 08 48 | 06 46 |
| 34 | 23 02 | 20 54 | 00 00 | 09 06 | 06 58 |
| 35 | 22 50 | 20 35 | 00 00 | 09 25 | 07 10 |
| 36 | 22 38 | 20 15 | 00 00 | 09 45 | 07 22 |
| 37 | 22 26 | 19 54 | 00 00 | 10 06 | 07 34 |
| 38 | 22 12 | 19 33 | 00 00 | 10 27 | 07 48 |
| 39 | 21 59 | 19 11 | 00 00 | 10 49 | 08 01 |
| 40 | 21 45 | 18 47 | 00 00 | 11 13 | 08 15 |
| 41 | 21 30 | 18 23 | 00 00 | 11 37 | 08 30 |
| 42 | 21 15 | 17 57 | 00 00 | 12 03 | 08 45 |
| 43 | 21 00 | 17 30 | 00 00 | 12 30 | 09 00 |
| 44 | 20 43 | 17 01 | 00 00 | 12 59 | 09 17 |
| 45 | 20 26 | 16 31 | 00 00 | 13 29 | 09 34 |
| 46 | 20 08 | 15 59 | 00 00 | 14 01 | 09 52 |
| 47 | 19 49 | 15 25 | 00 00 | 14 35 | 10 11 |
| 48 | 19 30 | 14 49 | 00 00 | 15 11 | 10 30 |
| 49 | 19 09 | 14 11 | 00 00 | 15 49 | 10 51 |
| 50 | 18 47 | 13 30 | 00 00 | 16 30 | 11 13 |
| 51 | 18 24 | 12 46 | 00 00 | 17 14 | 11 36 |
| 52 | 17 59 | 11 58 | 00 00 | 18 02 | 12 01 |
| 53 | 17 33 | 11 07 | 00 00 | 18 53 | 12 27 |
| 54 | 17 04 | 10 11 | 00 00 | 19 49 | 12 56 |
| 55 | 16 34 | 09 10 | 00 00 | 20 50 | 13 26 |
| 56 | 16 01 | 08 04 | 00 00 | 21 56 | 13 59 |
| 57 | 15 26 | 06 50 | 00 00 | 23 10 | 14 34 |
| 58 | 14 47 | 05 29 | 00 00 | 24 31 | 15 13 |
| 59 | 14 05 | 03 57 | 00 00 | 25 59 | 15 55 |
| 60 | 13♑18 | 02♒14 | 00♈00 | 27♉46 | 16♊42 |

**18h 4m 0s — 271° 0' 0" — 00 ♑ 55**

| LAT. | 11 | 12 | ASC | 2 | 3 |
|---|---|---|---|---|---|
| 0 | 28♑52 | 28♒52 | 01♈05 | 03♉13 | 03♊03 |
| 5 | 28 16 | 28 07 | 01 08 | 04 01 | 03 39 |
| 10 | 27 39 | 27 19 | 01 11 | 04 51 | 04 17 |
| 15 | 27 01 | 26 27 | 01 14 | 05 45 | 04 56 |
| 20 | 26 19 | 25 31 | 01 18 | 06 45 | 05 37 |
| 21 | 26 11 | 25 19 | 01 18 | 06 58 | 05 46 |
| 22 | 26 02 | 25 06 | 01 19 | 07 11 | 05 55 |
| 23 | 25 53 | 24 54 | 01 20 | 07 24 | 06 04 |
| 24 | 25 44 | 24 41 | 01 21 | 07 38 | 06 13 |
| 25 | 25 35 | 24 27 | 01 22 | 07 52 | 06 22 |
| 26 | 25 26 | 24 14 | 01 23 | 08 06 | 06 32 |
| 27 | 25 16 | 23 59 | 01 24 | 08 21 | 06 42 |
| 28 | 25 06 | 23 45 | 01 25 | 08 36 | 06 52 |
| 29 | 24 56 | 23 30 | 01 26 | 08 52 | 07 02 |
| 30 | 24 46 | 23 14 | 01 27 | 09 08 | 07 12 |
| 31 | 24 35 | 22 58 | 01 28 | 09 25 | 07 23 |
| 32 | 24 24 | 22 41 | 01 30 | 09 42 | 07 34 |
| 33 | 24 13 | 22 24 | 01 31 | 10 00 | 07 45 |
| 34 | 24 02 | 22 07 | 01 32 | 10 19 | 07 57 |
| 35 | 23 50 | 21 48 | 01 34 | 10 38 | 08 09 |
| 36 | 23 38 | 21 29 | 01 35 | 10 59 | 08 21 |
| 37 | 23 25 | 21 09 | 01 37 | 11 20 | 08 34 |
| 38 | 23 12 | 20 48 | 01 39 | 11 41 | 08 47 |
| 39 | 22 59 | 20 26 | 01 41 | 12 04 | 09 00 |
| 40 | 22 45 | 20 03 | 01 43 | 12 28 | 09 14 |
| 41 | 22 30 | 19 39 | 01 45 | 12 53 | 09 29 |
| 42 | 22 15 | 19 14 | 01 47 | 13 19 | 09 44 |
| 43 | 21 59 | 18 47 | 01 50 | 13 47 | 10 00 |
| 44 | 21 43 | 18 19 | 01 53 | 14 16 | 10 16 |
| 45 | 21 26 | 17 50 | 01 55 | 14 47 | 10 34 |
| 46 | 21 08 | 17 18 | 01 59 | 15 19 | 10 52 |
| 47 | 20 50 | 16 45 | 02 02 | 15 54 | 11 11 |
| 48 | 20 30 | 16 10 | 02 06 | 16 31 | 11 30 |
| 49 | 20 09 | 15 32 | 02 10 | 17 10 | 11 51 |
| 50 | 19 47 | 14 52 | 02 15 | 17 51 | 12 13 |
| 51 | 19 24 | 14 08 | 02 21 | 18 36 | 12 37 |
| 52 | 18 59 | 13 22 | 02 27 | 19 25 | 13 01 |
| 53 | 18 33 | 12 31 | 02 34 | 20 17 | 13 28 |
| 54 | 18 05 | 11 36 | 02 42 | 21 13 | 13 56 |
| 55 | 17 35 | 10 37 | 02 52 | 22 15 | 14 26 |
| 56 | 17 02 | 09 31 | 03 03 | 23 22 | 14 59 |
| 57 | 16 27 | 08 19 | 03 17 | 24 37 | 15 35 |
| 58 | 15 49 | 06 58 | 03 34 | 25 59 | 16 13 |
| 59 | 15 06 | 05 28 | 03 55 | 27 31 | 16 56 |
| 60 | 14♑19 | 03♒46 | 04♈22 | 29♉16 | 17♊43 |

# Placidus Table of Houses for Latitudes 0° to 60° North

**18h 8m 0s — 272° 0' 0" — 01 ♑ 50**

| LAT. | 11 | 12 | ASC | 2 | 3 |
|---|---|---|---|---|---|
| 0 | 29♑49 | 29♒54 | 02♈11 | 04♉16 | 04♊00 |
| 5 | 29 14 | 29 11 | 02 16 | 05 04 | 04 36 |
| 10 | 28 37 | 28 24 | 02 22 | 05 56 | 05 14 |
| 15 | 27 59 | 27 34 | 02 28 | 06 51 | 05 54 |
| 20 | 27 18 | 26 39 | 02 35 | 07 52 | 06 35 |
| 21 | 27 10 | 26 27 | 02 37 | 08 05 | 06 44 |
| 22 | 27 01 | 26 15 | 02 39 | 08 19 | 06 53 |
| 23 | 26 52 | 26 03 | 02 40 | 08 32 | 07 02 |
| 24 | 26 43 | 25 50 | 02 42 | 08 46 | 07 11 |
| 25 | 26 34 | 25 37 | 02 44 | 09 01 | 07 21 |
| 26 | 26 25 | 25 24 | 02 46 | 09 15 | 07 30 |
| 27 | 26 15 | 25 10 | 02 48 | 09 31 | 07 40 |
| 28 | 26 05 | 24 56 | 02 50 | 09 46 | 07 50 |
| 29 | 25 55 | 24 41 | 02 52 | 10 02 | 08 00 |
| 30 | 25 45 | 24 26 | 02 54 | 10 19 | 08 11 |
| 31 | 25 34 | 24 11 | 02 57 | 10 36 | 08 21 |
| 32 | 25 24 | 23 54 | 02 59 | 10 54 | 08 33 |
| 33 | 25 13 | 23 38 | 03 02 | 11 12 | 08 44 |
| 34 | 25 01 | 23 20 | 03 05 | 11 31 | 08 56 |
| 35 | 24 49 | 23 02 | 03 08 | 11 51 | 09 08 |
| 36 | 24 37 | 22 43 | 03 11 | 12 12 | 09 20 |
| 37 | 24 25 | 22 24 | 03 14 | 12 33 | 09 33 |
| 38 | 24 12 | 22 03 | 03 18 | 12 55 | 09 46 |
| 39 | 23 58 | 21 42 | 03 22 | 13 19 | 09 59 |
| 40 | 23 45 | 21 19 | 03 26 | 13 43 | 10 14 |
| 41 | 23 30 | 20 56 | 03 30 | 14 08 | 10 28 |
| 42 | 23 15 | 20 31 | 03 34 | 14 35 | 10 43 |
| 43 | 23 00 | 20 05 | 03 39 | 15 03 | 10 59 |
| 44 | 22 43 | 19 38 | 03 45 | 15 33 | 11 16 |
| 45 | 22 26 | 19 09 | 03 51 | 16 04 | 11 33 |
| 46 | 22 09 | 18 38 | 03 57 | 16 37 | 11 51 |
| 47 | 21 50 | 18 06 | 04 04 | 17 12 | 12 10 |
| 48 | 21 30 | 17 31 | 04 12 | 17 50 | 12 30 |
| 49 | 21 10 | 16 54 | 04 21 | 18 29 | 12 51 |
| 50 | 20 48 | 16 15 | 04 30 | 19 12 | 13 13 |
| 51 | 20 25 | 15 32 | 04 41 | 19 57 | 13 36 |
| 52 | 20 00 | 14 46 | 04 54 | 20 46 | 14 01 |
| 53 | 19 34 | 13 57 | 05 08 | 21 39 | 14 28 |
| 54 | 19 06 | 13 03 | 05 24 | 22 36 | 14 56 |
| 55 | 18 36 | 12 04 | 05 43 | 23 39 | 15 26 |
| 56 | 18 04 | 11 00 | 06 06 | 24 47 | 15 59 |
| 57 | 17 29 | 09 48 | 06 33 | 26 02 | 16 35 |
| 58 | 16 50 | 08 29 | 07 06 | 27 25 | 17 14 |
| 59 | 16 08 | 07 00 | 07 48 | 28 59 | 17 56 |
| 60 | 15♑21 | 05♒19 | 08♈43 | 00♊44 | 18♊44 |

**18h 12m 0s — 273° 0' 0" — 02 ♑ 45**

| LAT. | 11 | 12 | ASC | 2 | 3 |
|---|---|---|---|---|---|
| 0 | 00♒47 | 00♓57 | 03♈16 | 05♉18 | 04♊57 |
| 5 | 00 12 | 00 15 | 03 24 | 06 07 | 05 34 |
| 10 | 29♑36 | 29♒30 | 03 32 | 07 00 | 06 12 |
| 15 | 28 57 | 28 41 | 03 42 | 07 57 | 06 51 |
| 20 | 28 17 | 27 48 | 03 53 | 08 59 | 07 33 |
| 21 | 28 09 | 27 36 | 03 55 | 09 13 | 07 42 |
| 22 | 28 00 | 27 25 | 03 58 | 09 26 | 07 51 |
| 23 | 27 51 | 27 13 | 04 00 | 09 40 | 08 00 |
| 24 | 27 42 | 27 00 | 04 03 | 09 55 | 08 09 |
| 25 | 27 33 | 26 48 | 04 06 | 10 09 | 08 19 |
| 26 | 27 24 | 26 35 | 04 09 | 10 24 | 08 28 |
| 27 | 27 14 | 26 21 | 04 12 | 10 40 | 08 38 |
| 28 | 27 05 | 26 07 | 04 15 | 10 56 | 08 48 |
| 29 | 26 55 | 25 53 | 04 18 | 11 12 | 08 59 |
| 30 | 26 44 | 25 38 | 04 22 | 11 29 | 09 09 |
| 31 | 26 34 | 25 23 | 04 25 | 11 47 | 09 20 |
| 32 | 26 23 | 25 07 | 04 29 | 12 05 | 09 31 |
| 33 | 26 12 | 24 51 | 04 33 | 12 23 | 09 42 |
| 34 | 26 01 | 24 34 | 04 37 | 12 43 | 09 54 |
| 35 | 25 49 | 24 17 | 04 42 | 13 03 | 10 06 |
| 36 | 25 37 | 23 58 | 04 46 | 13 24 | 10 19 |
| 37 | 25 25 | 23 39 | 04 51 | 13 46 | 10 31 |
| 38 | 25 12 | 23 19 | 04 56 | 14 09 | 10 45 |
| 39 | 24 59 | 22 58 | 05 02 | 14 32 | 10 58 |
| 40 | 24 45 | 22 36 | 05 08 | 14 57 | 11 12 |
| 41 | 24 30 | 22 14 | 05 15 | 15 23 | 11 27 |
| 42 | 24 16 | 21 49 | 05 22 | 15 50 | 11 42 |
| 43 | 24 00 | 21 24 | 05 29 | 16 19 | 11 58 |
| 44 | 23 44 | 20 57 | 05 37 | 16 49 | 12 15 |
| 45 | 23 27 | 20 29 | 05 46 | 17 21 | 12 32 |
| 46 | 23 09 | 19 59 | 05 56 | 17 54 | 12 50 |
| 47 | 22 51 | 19 27 | 06 06 | 18 30 | 13 09 |
| 48 | 22 31 | 18 54 | 06 18 | 19 08 | 13 29 |
| 49 | 22 11 | 18 17 | 06 31 | 19 48 | 13 50 |
| 50 | 21 49 | 17 39 | 06 45 | 20 31 | 14 12 |
| 51 | 21 26 | 16 57 | 07 01 | 21 17 | 14 36 |
| 52 | 21 02 | 16 12 | 07 20 | 22 07 | 15 01 |
| 53 | 20 36 | 15 23 | 07 41 | 23 00 | 15 27 |
| 54 | 20 08 | 14 31 | 08 05 | 23 58 | 15 56 |
| 55 | 19 38 | 13 33 | 08 33 | 25 01 | 16 26 |
| 56 | 19 06 | 12 30 | 09 07 | 26 10 | 16 59 |
| 57 | 18 31 | 11 19 | 09 47 | 27 26 | 17 35 |
| 58 | 17 52 | 10 01 | 10 36 | 28 50 | 18 13 |
| 59 | 17 10 | 08 34 | 11 39 | 00♊24 | 18 56 |
| 60 | 16♑23 | 06♒55 | 12♈59 | 02♊10 | 19♊44 |

**18h 16m 0s — 274° 0' 0" — 03 ♑ 40**

| LAT. | 11 | 12 | ASC | 2 | 3 |
|---|---|---|---|---|---|
| 0 | 01♒45 | 02♓00 | 04♈22 | 06♉19 | 05♊54 |
| 5 | 01 10 | 01 19 | 04 32 | 07 10 | 06 31 |
| 10 | 00 34 | 00 36 | 04 43 | 08 04 | 07 09 |
| 15 | 29♑56 | 29♒49 | 04 56 | 09 03 | 07 49 |
| 20 | 29 16 | 28 57 | 05 10 | 10 06 | 08 31 |
| 21 | 29 08 | 28 46 | 05 14 | 10 20 | 08 40 |
| 22 | 28 59 | 28 34 | 05 17 | 10 34 | 08 49 |
| 23 | 28 50 | 28 23 | 05 20 | 10 48 | 08 58 |
| 24 | 28 42 | 28 11 | 05 24 | 11 03 | 09 07 |
| 25 | 28 32 | 27 58 | 05 28 | 11 17 | 09 17 |
| 26 | 28 23 | 27 46 | 05 32 | 11 33 | 09 26 |
| 27 | 28 14 | 27 33 | 05 36 | 11 49 | 09 36 |
| 28 | 28 04 | 27 19 | 05 40 | 12 05 | 09 46 |
| 29 | 27 54 | 27 05 | 05 44 | 12 22 | 09 57 |
| 30 | 27 44 | 26 51 | 05 49 | 12 39 | 10 07 |
| 31 | 27 34 | 26 36 | 05 53 | 12 57 | 10 18 |
| 32 | 27 23 | 26 21 | 05 58 | 13 15 | 10 29 |
| 33 | 27 12 | 26 05 | 06 04 | 13 34 | 10 41 |
| 34 | 27 01 | 25 49 | 06 09 | 13 54 | 10 52 |
| 35 | 26 49 | 25 31 | 06 15 | 14 15 | 11 05 |
| 36 | 26 37 | 25 14 | 06 21 | 14 36 | 11 17 |
| 37 | 26 25 | 24 55 | 06 28 | 14 58 | 11 30 |
| 38 | 26 12 | 24 36 | 06 35 | 15 21 | 11 43 |
| 39 | 25 59 | 24 15 | 06 43 | 15 45 | 11 57 |
| 40 | 25 45 | 23 54 | 06 51 | 16 11 | 12 11 |
| 41 | 25 31 | 23 32 | 06 59 | 16 37 | 12 26 |
| 42 | 25 16 | 23 08 | 07 08 | 17 05 | 12 41 |
| 43 | 25 01 | 22 44 | 07 18 | 17 34 | 12 57 |
| 44 | 24 45 | 22 17 | 07 29 | 18 04 | 13 14 |
| 45 | 24 28 | 21 50 | 07 41 | 18 37 | 13 31 |
| 46 | 24 10 | 21 21 | 07 54 | 19 11 | 13 49 |
| 47 | 23 52 | 20 50 | 08 08 | 19 47 | 14 08 |
| 48 | 23 33 | 20 17 | 08 23 | 20 25 | 14 28 |
| 49 | 23 12 | 19 41 | 08 40 | 21 06 | 14 49 |
| 50 | 22 51 | 19 03 | 08 59 | 21 50 | 15 12 |
| 51 | 22 28 | 18 23 | 09 21 | 22 36 | 15 35 |
| 52 | 22 03 | 17 39 | 09 45 | 23 26 | 16 00 |
| 53 | 21 37 | 16 51 | 10 13 | 24 20 | 16 27 |
| 54 | 21 10 | 15 59 | 10 45 | 25 19 | 16 55 |
| 55 | 20 40 | 15 03 | 11 22 | 26 23 | 17 25 |
| 56 | 20 08 | 14 01 | 12 06 | 27 32 | 17 58 |
| 57 | 19 33 | 12 52 | 12 59 | 28 49 | 18 34 |
| 58 | 18 55 | 11 35 | 14 04 | 00♊14 | 19 13 |
| 59 | 18 13 | 10 10 | 15 25 | 01 48 | 19 56 |
| 60 | 17♑27 | 08♒32 | 17♈09 | 03♊35 | 20♊43 |

**18h 20m 0s — 275° 0' 0" — 04 ♑ 35**

| LAT. | 11 | 12 | ASC | 2 | 3 |
|---|---|---|---|---|---|
| 0 | 02♒43 | 03♓03 | 05♈27 | 07♉21 | 06♊50 |
| 5 | 02 08 | 02 24 | 05 40 | 08 13 | 07 28 |
| 10 | 01 33 | 01 42 | 05 54 | 09 08 | 08 06 |
| 15 | 00 55 | 00 56 | 06 10 | 10 08 | 08 46 |
| 20 | 00 15 | 00 06 | 06 28 | 11 13 | 09 29 |
| 21 | 00 07 | 29♒55 | 06 32 | 11 27 | 09 37 |
| 22 | 29♑58 | 29 44 | 06 36 | 11 41 | 09 46 |
| 23 | 29 50 | 29 33 | 06 40 | 11 55 | 09 56 |
| 24 | 29 41 | 29 21 | 06 45 | 12 10 | 10 05 |
| 25 | 29 32 | 29 09 | 06 49 | 12 25 | 10 14 |
| 26 | 29 23 | 28 57 | 06 54 | 12 41 | 10 24 |
| 27 | 29 14 | 28 44 | 06 59 | 12 57 | 10 34 |
| 28 | 29 04 | 28 31 | 07 04 | 13 14 | 10 44 |
| 29 | 28 54 | 28 18 | 07 10 | 13 31 | 10 55 |
| 30 | 28 44 | 28 04 | 07 16 | 13 48 | 11 05 |
| 31 | 28 34 | 27 50 | 07 22 | 14 07 | 11 16 |
| 32 | 28 23 | 27 35 | 07 28 | 14 25 | 11 27 |
| 33 | 28 12 | 27 19 | 07 34 | 14 45 | 11 39 |
| 34 | 28 01 | 27 03 | 07 41 | 15 05 | 11 51 |
| 35 | 27 50 | 26 47 | 07 49 | 15 26 | 12 03 |
| 36 | 27 38 | 26 29 | 07 56 | 15 47 | 12 15 |
| 37 | 27 25 | 26 11 | 08 05 | 16 10 | 12 28 |
| 38 | 27 13 | 25 53 | 08 13 | 16 34 | 12 41 |
| 39 | 27 00 | 25 33 | 08 23 | 16 58 | 12 55 |
| 40 | 26 46 | 25 12 | 08 33 | 17 24 | 13 09 |
| 41 | 26 32 | 24 50 | 08 43 | 17 50 | 13 24 |
| 42 | 26 17 | 24 28 | 08 55 | 18 19 | 13 40 |
| 43 | 26 02 | 24 04 | 09 07 | 18 48 | 13 56 |
| 44 | 25 46 | 23 38 | 09 21 | 19 19 | 14 12 |
| 45 | 25 29 | 23 11 | 09 35 | 19 52 | 14 30 |
| 46 | 25 12 | 22 43 | 09 51 | 20 26 | 14 48 |
| 47 | 24 53 | 22 13 | 10 08 | 21 03 | 15 07 |
| 48 | 24 34 | 21 40 | 10 28 | 21 42 | 15 27 |
| 49 | 24 14 | 21 06 | 10 49 | 22 23 | 15 48 |
| 50 | 23 52 | 20 29 | 11 13 | 23 07 | 16 10 |
| 51 | 23 30 | 19 49 | 11 39 | 23 54 | 16 34 |
| 52 | 23 05 | 19 06 | 12 09 | 24 45 | 16 59 |
| 53 | 22 40 | 18 20 | 12 44 | 25 40 | 17 26 |
| 54 | 22 12 | 17 29 | 13 23 | 26 39 | 17 54 |
| 55 | 21 43 | 16 34 | 14 09 | 27 43 | 18 24 |
| 56 | 21 11 | 15 33 | 15 03 | 28 53 | 18 57 |
| 57 | 20 36 | 14 26 | 16 08 | 00♊10 | 19 33 |
| 58 | 19 58 | 13 11 | 17 27 | 01 36 | 20 12 |
| 59 | 19 16 | 11 47 | 19 06 | 03 11 | 20 55 |
| 60 | 18♑30 | 10♒11 | 21♈12 | 04♊57 | 21♊42 |

**18h 24m 0s — 276° 0' 0" — 05 ♑ 30**

| LAT. | 11 | 12 | ASC | 2 | 3 |
|---|---|---|---|---|---|
| 0 | 03♒41 | 04♓07 | 06♈32 | 08♉23 | 07♊47 |
| 5 | 03 07 | 03 29 | 06 48 | 09 16 | 08 24 |
| 10 | 02 31 | 02 48 | 07 04 | 10 12 | 09 03 |
| 15 | 01 54 | 02 04 | 07 23 | 11 13 | 09 43 |
| 20 | 01 15 | 01 15 | 07 45 | 12 19 | 10 26 |
| 21 | 01 07 | 01 05 | 07 50 | 12 33 | 10 35 |
| 22 | 00 58 | 00 54 | 07 55 | 12 48 | 10 44 |
| 23 | 00 50 | 00 43 | 08 00 | 13 02 | 10 53 |
| 24 | 00 41 | 00 32 | 08 05 | 13 17 | 11 03 |
| 25 | 00 32 | 00 21 | 08 11 | 13 33 | 11 12 |
| 26 | 00 23 | 00 09 | 08 17 | 13 49 | 11 22 |
| 27 | 00 13 | 29♒56 | 08 23 | 14 05 | 11 32 |
| 28 | 00 04 | 29 44 | 08 29 | 14 22 | 11 42 |
| 29 | 29♑54 | 29 31 | 08 35 | 14 40 | 11 52 |
| 30 | 29 44 | 29 17 | 08 42 | 14 57 | 12 03 |
| 31 | 29 34 | 29 04 | 08 49 | 15 16 | 12 14 |
| 32 | 29 24 | 28 49 | 08 57 | 15 35 | 12 25 |
| 33 | 29 13 | 28 34 | 09 05 | 15 55 | 12 37 |
| 34 | 29 02 | 28 19 | 09 13 | 16 15 | 12 49 |
| 35 | 28 50 | 28 03 | 09 22 | 16 36 | 13 01 |
| 36 | 28 38 | 27 46 | 09 31 | 16 58 | 13 13 |
| 37 | 28 26 | 27 28 | 09 41 | 17 21 | 13 26 |
| 38 | 28 14 | 27 10 | 09 51 | 17 45 | 13 40 |
| 39 | 28 01 | 26 51 | 10 03 | 18 10 | 13 53 |
| 40 | 27 47 | 26 31 | 10 14 | 18 36 | 14 08 |
| 41 | 27 33 | 26 10 | 10 27 | 19 03 | 14 22 |
| 42 | 27 18 | 25 48 | 10 41 | 19 32 | 14 38 |
| 43 | 27 03 | 25 24 | 10 56 | 20 02 | 14 54 |
| 44 | 26 47 | 25 00 | 11 12 | 20 33 | 15 11 |
| 45 | 26 31 | 24 33 | 11 29 | 21 06 | 15 28 |
| 46 | 26 13 | 24 06 | 11 48 | 21 41 | 15 46 |
| 47 | 25 55 | 23 36 | 12 09 | 22 18 | 16 05 |
| 48 | 25 36 | 23 05 | 12 32 | 22 57 | 16 25 |
| 49 | 25 16 | 22 32 | 12 57 | 23 39 | 16 47 |
| 50 | 24 55 | 21 56 | 13 25 | 24 24 | 17 09 |
| 51 | 24 32 | 21 17 | 13 56 | 25 11 | 17 32 |
| 52 | 24 08 | 20 35 | 14 32 | 26 03 | 17 57 |
| 53 | 23 42 | 19 50 | 15 13 | 26 58 | 18 24 |
| 54 | 23 15 | 19 01 | 15 59 | 27 57 | 18 53 |
| 55 | 22 45 | 18 07 | 16 54 | 29 02 | 19 23 |
| 56 | 22 14 | 17 07 | 17 57 | 00♊13 | 19 56 |
| 57 | 21 39 | 16 01 | 19 14 | 01 30 | 20 32 |
| 58 | 21 02 | 14 48 | 20 46 | 02 56 | 21 10 |
| 59 | 20 20 | 13 26 | 22 40 | 04 31 | 21 53 |
| 60 | 19♑34 | 11♒52 | 25♈05 | 06♊19 | 22♊40 |

**18h 28m 0s — 277° 0' 0" — 06 ♑ 26**

| LAT. | 11 | 12 | ASC | 2 | 3 |
|---|---|---|---|---|---|
| 0 | 04♒39 | 05♓10 | 07♈37 | 09♉24 | 08♊43 |
| 5 | 04 05 | 04 33 | 07 55 | 10 18 | 09 21 |
| 10 | 03 30 | 03 54 | 08 15 | 11 16 | 10 00 |
| 15 | 02 54 | 03 12 | 08 37 | 12 17 | 10 40 |
| 20 | 02 14 | 02 25 | 09 03 | 13 25 | 11 23 |
| 21 | 02 06 | 02 15 | 09 08 | 13 39 | 11 32 |
| 22 | 01 58 | 02 05 | 09 14 | 13 54 | 11 41 |
| 23 | 01 49 | 01 54 | 09 20 | 14 09 | 11 50 |
| 24 | 01 41 | 01 43 | 09 26 | 14 24 | 12 00 |
| 25 | 01 32 | 01 32 | 09 32 | 14 40 | 12 09 |
| 26 | 01 23 | 01 21 | 09 39 | 14 56 | 12 19 |
| 27 | 01 14 | 01 09 | 09 46 | 15 13 | 12 29 |
| 28 | 01 04 | 00 57 | 09 53 | 15 30 | 12 39 |
| 29 | 00 55 | 00 44 | 10 01 | 15 48 | 12 50 |
| 30 | 00 45 | 00 31 | 10 09 | 16 06 | 13 01 |
| 31 | 00 35 | 00 18 | 10 17 | 16 25 | 13 12 |
| 32 | 00 24 | 00 04 | 10 26 | 16 44 | 13 23 |
| 33 | 00 13 | 29♒49 | 10 35 | 17 04 | 13 34 |
| 34 | 00 02 | 29 34 | 10 45 | 17 25 | 13 46 |
| 35 | 29♑51 | 29 19 | 10 55 | 17 47 | 13 58 |
| 36 | 29 39 | 29 03 | 11 06 | 18 09 | 14 11 |
| 37 | 29 27 | 28 46 | 11 17 | 18 32 | 14 24 |
| 38 | 29 15 | 28 28 | 11 29 | 18 56 | 14 37 |
| 39 | 29 02 | 28 09 | 11 42 | 19 22 | 14 51 |
| 40 | 28 48 | 27 50 | 11 56 | 19 48 | 15 06 |
| 41 | 28 34 | 27 30 | 12 11 | 20 15 | 15 20 |
| 42 | 28 20 | 27 08 | 12 27 | 20 44 | 15 36 |
| 43 | 28 05 | 26 45 | 12 44 | 21 15 | 15 52 |
| 44 | 27 49 | 26 22 | 13 02 | 21 46 | 16 09 |
| 45 | 27 33 | 25 56 | 13 22 | 22 20 | 16 26 |
| 46 | 27 15 | 25 29 | 13 44 | 22 55 | 16 44 |
| 47 | 26 57 | 25 01 | 14 08 | 23 33 | 17 04 |
| 48 | 26 38 | 24 31 | 14 34 | 24 12 | 17 24 |
| 49 | 26 18 | 23 58 | 15 04 | 24 55 | 17 45 |
| 50 | 25 57 | 23 23 | 15 36 | 25 40 | 18 07 |
| 51 | 25 35 | 22 45 | 16 12 | 26 28 | 18 31 |
| 52 | 25 11 | 22 05 | 16 53 | 27 19 | 18 56 |
| 53 | 24 45 | 21 21 | 17 40 | 28 15 | 19 22 |
| 54 | 24 18 | 20 33 | 18 34 | 29 15 | 19 51 |
| 55 | 23 49 | 19 40 | 19 36 | 00♊20 | 20 21 |
| 56 | 23 17 | 18 42 | 20 48 | 01 31 | 20 54 |
| 57 | 22 43 | 17 38 | 22 15 | 02 49 | 21 30 |
| 58 | 22 06 | 16 27 | 23 59 | 04 15 | 22 09 |
| 59 | 21 24 | 15 06 | 26 08 | 05 51 | 22 51 |
| 60 | 20♑39 | 13♒35 | 28♈50 | 07♊38 | 23♊38 |

**18h 32m 0s — 278° 0' 0" — 07 ♑ 21**

| LAT. | 11 | 12 | ASC | 2 | 3 |
|---|---|---|---|---|---|
| 0 | 05♒38 | 06♓14 | 08♈43 | 10♉25 | 09♊40 |
| 5 | 05 04 | 05 39 | 09 03 | 11 21 | 10 18 |
| 10 | 04 30 | 05 01 | 09 26 | 12 19 | 10 57 |
| 15 | 03 53 | 04 20 | 09 51 | 13 22 | 11 37 |
| 20 | 03 14 | 03 35 | 10 20 | 14 31 | 12 20 |
| 21 | 03 06 | 03 25 | 10 26 | 14 45 | 12 29 |
| 22 | 02 58 | 03 15 | 10 33 | 15 00 | 12 38 |
| 23 | 02 50 | 03 05 | 10 39 | 15 15 | 12 48 |
| 24 | 02 41 | 02 55 | 10 46 | 15 31 | 12 57 |
| 25 | 02 32 | 02 44 | 10 54 | 15 47 | 13 07 |
| 26 | 02 23 | 02 33 | 11 01 | 16 04 | 13 17 |
| 27 | 02 14 | 02 22 | 11 09 | 16 20 | 13 27 |
| 28 | 02 05 | 02 10 | 11 18 | 16 38 | 13 37 |
| 29 | 01 55 | 01 58 | 11 26 | 16 56 | 13 47 |
| 30 | 01 45 | 01 45 | 11 35 | 17 14 | 13 58 |
| 31 | 01 35 | 01 32 | 11 45 | 17 33 | 14 09 |
| 32 | 01 25 | 01 19 | 11 55 | 17 53 | 14 20 |
| 33 | 01 14 | 01 05 | 12 05 | 18 13 | 14 32 |
| 34 | 01 03 | 00 50 | 12 16 | 18 34 | 14 44 |
| 35 | 00 52 | 00 35 | 12 28 | 18 56 | 14 56 |
| 36 | 00 41 | 00 20 | 12 40 | 19 19 | 15 09 |
| 37 | 00 29 | 00 03 | 12 53 | 19 42 | 15 22 |
| 38 | 00 16 | 29♒46 | 13 07 | 20 07 | 15 35 |
| 39 | 00 03 | 29 28 | 13 21 | 20 33 | 15 49 |
| 40 | 29♑50 | 29 10 | 13 37 | 20 59 | 16 03 |
| 41 | 29 36 | 28 50 | 13 54 | 21 27 | 16 18 |
| 42 | 29 22 | 28 29 | 14 12 | 21 56 | 16 34 |
| 43 | 29 07 | 28 07 | 14 31 | 22 27 | 16 50 |
| 44 | 28 51 | 27 44 | 14 52 | 22 59 | 17 06 |
| 45 | 28 35 | 27 20 | 15 15 | 23 33 | 17 24 |
| 46 | 28 18 | 26 54 | 15 40 | 24 09 | 17 42 |
| 47 | 28 00 | 26 26 | 16 07 | 24 47 | 18 01 |
| 48 | 27 41 | 25 57 | 16 36 | 25 27 | 18 22 |
| 49 | 27 21 | 25 25 | 17 09 | 26 09 | 18 43 |
| 50 | 27 00 | 24 51 | 17 46 | 26 55 | 19 05 |
| 51 | 26 38 | 24 15 | 18 27 | 27 43 | 19 29 |
| 52 | 26 14 | 23 35 | 19 13 | 28 35 | 19 54 |
| 53 | 25 49 | 22 53 | 20 05 | 29 31 | 20 20 |
| 54 | 25 22 | 22 06 | 21 05 | 00♊31 | 20 49 |
| 55 | 24 53 | 21 15 | 22 15 | 01 37 | 21 19 |
| 56 | 24 21 | 20 19 | 23 36 | 02 48 | 21 52 |
| 57 | 23 47 | 19 17 | 25 12 | 04 07 | 22 28 |
| 58 | 23 10 | 18 07 | 27 07 | 05 33 | 23 06 |
| 59 | 22 29 | 16 49 | 29 28 | 07 09 | 23 49 |
| 60 | 21♑44 | 15♒20 | 02♉24 | 08♊56 | 24♊36 |

**18h 36m 0s — 279° 0' 0" — 08 ♑ 16**

| LAT. | 11 | 12 | ASC | 2 | 3 |
|---|---|---|---|---|---|
| 0 | 06♒37 | 07♓18 | 09♈48 | 11♉26 | 10♊36 |
| 5 | 06 03 | 06 44 | 10 11 | 12 23 | 11 14 |
| 10 | 05 29 | 06 08 | 10 36 | 13 22 | 11 53 |
| 15 | 04 53 | 05 28 | 11 04 | 14 26 | 12 34 |
| 20 | 04 14 | 04 45 | 11 37 | 15 36 | 13 17 |
| 21 | 04 06 | 04 36 | 11 44 | 15 51 | 13 26 |
| 22 | 03 58 | 04 26 | 11 51 | 16 06 | 13 35 |
| 23 | 03 50 | 04 17 | 11 59 | 16 21 | 13 45 |
| 24 | 03 41 | 04 07 | 12 07 | 16 37 | 13 54 |
| 25 | 03 33 | 03 56 | 12 15 | 16 54 | 14 04 |
| 26 | 03 24 | 03 46 | 12 23 | 17 10 | 14 14 |
| 27 | 03 15 | 03 35 | 12 32 | 17 27 | 14 24 |
| 28 | 03 06 | 03 23 | 12 42 | 17 45 | 14 34 |
| 29 | 02 56 | 03 12 | 12 51 | 18 03 | 14 44 |
| 30 | 02 46 | 03 00 | 13 01 | 18 22 | 14 55 |
| 31 | 02 36 | 02 47 | 13 12 | 18 41 | 15 06 |
| 32 | 02 26 | 02 34 | 13 23 | 19 01 | 15 18 |
| 33 | 02 16 | 02 21 | 13 35 | 19 22 | 15 29 |
| 34 | 02 05 | 02 07 | 13 47 | 19 43 | 15 41 |
| 35 | 01 54 | 01 52 | 14 00 | 20 05 | 15 53 |
| 36 | 01 42 | 01 37 | 14 14 | 20 28 | 16 06 |
| 37 | 01 30 | 01 22 | 14 28 | 20 52 | 16 19 |
| 38 | 01 18 | 01 05 | 14 43 | 21 17 | 16 32 |
| 39 | 01 05 | 00 48 | 15 00 | 21 43 | 16 46 |
| 40 | 00 52 | 00 30 | 15 17 | 22 10 | 17 01 |
| 41 | 00 38 | 00 11 | 15 36 | 22 38 | 17 16 |
| 42 | 00 24 | 29♒51 | 15 56 | 23 08 | 17 31 |
| 43 | 00 09 | 29 30 | 16 18 | 23 39 | 17 47 |
| 44 | 29♑54 | 29 07 | 16 41 | 24 11 | 18 04 |
| 45 | 29 37 | 28 44 | 17 06 | 24 45 | 18 22 |
| 46 | 29 20 | 28 19 | 17 34 | 25 21 | 18 40 |
| 47 | 29 03 | 27 52 | 18 04 | 26 00 | 18 59 |
| 48 | 28 44 | 27 24 | 18 37 | 26 40 | 19 19 |
| 49 | 28 24 | 26 53 | 19 14 | 27 23 | 19 40 |
| 50 | 28 03 | 26 20 | 19 54 | 28 09 | 20 03 |
| 51 | 27 41 | 25 45 | 20 40 | 28 58 | 20 26 |
| 52 | 27 18 | 25 07 | 21 31 | 29 50 | 20 51 |
| 53 | 26 53 | 24 26 | 22 28 | 00♊46 | 21 18 |
| 54 | 26 26 | 23 41 | 23 34 | 01 47 | 21 46 |
| 55 | 25 57 | 22 51 | 24 51 | 02 53 | 22 17 |
| 56 | 25 26 | 21 57 | 26 19 | 04 04 | 22 50 |
| 57 | 24 52 | 20 56 | 28 04 | 05 23 | 23 25 |
| 58 | 24 15 | 19 49 | 00♉09 | 06 49 | 24 04 |
| 59 | 23 35 | 18 33 | 02 40 | 08 25 | 24 46 |
| 60 | 22♑50 | 17♒07 | 05♉47 | 10♊12 | 25♊33 |

# Placidus Table of Houses for Latitudes 0° to 60° North

**18h 40m 0s — 280° 0' 0" — 09 ♑ 11**

| LAT. | 11 | 12 | ASC | 2 | 3 |
|---|---|---|---|---|---|
| 0 | 07♒35 | 08♓22 | 10♈53 | 12♉27 | 11♊32 |
| 5 | 07 02 | 07 49 | 11 18 | 13 24 | 12 10 |
| 10 | 06 28 | 07 15 | 11 46 | 14 25 | 12 50 |
| 15 | 05 53 | 06 37 | 12 18 | 15 30 | 13 31 |
| 20 | 05 15 | 05 56 | 12 54 | 16 41 | 14 14 |
| 21 | 05 07 | 05 47 | 13 01 | 16 56 | 14 23 |
| 22 | 04 59 | 05 38 | 13 10 | 17 11 | 14 32 |
| 23 | 04 50 | 05 28 | 13 18 | 17 27 | 14 41 |
| 24 | 04 42 | 05 19 | 13 27 | 17 43 | 14 51 |
| 25 | 04 33 | 05 09 | 13 36 | 18 00 | 15 01 |
| 26 | 04 25 | 04 59 | 13 45 | 18 17 | 15 11 |
| 27 | 04 16 | 04 48 | 13 55 | 18 34 | 15 21 |
| 28 | 04 07 | 04 37 | 14 05 | 18 52 | 15 31 |
| 29 | 03 57 | 04 26 | 14 16 | 19 10 | 15 42 |
| 30 | 03 48 | 04 15 | 14 27 | 19 29 | 15 52 |
| 31 | 03 38 | 04 03 | 14 39 | 19 49 | 16 03 |
| 32 | 03 28 | 03 50 | 14 51 | 20 09 | 16 15 |
| 33 | 03 17 | 03 37 | 15 04 | 20 30 | 16 26 |
| 34 | 03 06 | 03 24 | 15 17 | 20 52 | 16 38 |
| 35 | 02 55 | 03 10 | 15 32 | 21 14 | 16 51 |
| 36 | 02 44 | 02 55 | 15 47 | 21 37 | 17 03 |
| 37 | 02 32 | 02 40 | 16 03 | 22 02 | 17 16 |
| 38 | 02 20 | 02 24 | 16 20 | 22 27 | 17 30 |
| 39 | 02 07 | 02 08 | 16 38 | 22 53 | 17 44 |
| 40 | 01 54 | 01 51 | 16 57 | 23 20 | 17 58 |
| 41 | 01 41 | 01 32 | 17 18 | 23 49 | 18 13 |
| 42 | 01 26 | 01 13 | 17 40 | 24 18 | 18 28 |
| 43 | 01 12 | 00 53 | 18 04 | 24 50 | 18 45 |
| 44 | 00 56 | 00 31 | 18 29 | 25 22 | 19 01 |
| 45 | 00 40 | 00 09 | 18 57 | 25 57 | 19 19 |
| 46 | 00 23 | 29♒44 | 19 28 | 26 33 | 19 37 |
| 47 | 00 06 | 29 19 | 20 01 | 27 12 | 19 56 |
| 48 | 29♑47 | 28 51 | 20 37 | 27 53 | 20 17 |
| 49 | 29 28 | 28 22 | 21 17 | 28 36 | 20 38 |
| 50 | 29 07 | 27 50 | 22 01 | 29 22 | 21 00 |
| 51 | 28 45 | 27 16 | 22 51 | 00♊11 | 21 24 |
| 52 | 28 22 | 26 40 | 23 46 | 01 04 | 21 49 |
| 53 | 27 57 | 26 00 | 24 49 | 02 00 | 22 15 |
| 54 | 27 30 | 25 16 | 26 01 | 03 01 | 22 44 |
| 55 | 27 02 | 24 28 | 27 23 | 04 07 | 23 14 |
| 56 | 26 31 | 23 36 | 28 58 | 05 19 | 23 47 |
| 57 | 25 57 | 22 37 | 00♉51 | 06 38 | 24 22 |
| 58 | 25 21 | 21 32 | 03 04 | 08 04 | 25 01 |
| 59 | 24 41 | 20 19 | 05 44 | 09 40 | 25 43 |
| 60 | 23♑56 | 18♒55 | 09♉01 | 11♊27 | 26♊30 |

**18h 44m 0s — 281° 0' 0" — 10 ♑ 07**

| LAT. | 11 | 12 | ASC | 2 | 3 |
|---|---|---|---|---|---|
| 0 | 08♒34 | 09♓26 | 11♈58 | 13♉27 | 12♊28 |
| 5 | 08 02 | 08 55 | 12 26 | 14 26 | 13 07 |
| 10 | 07 28 | 08 22 | 12 56 | 15 28 | 13 46 |
| 15 | 06 53 | 07 46 | 13 31 | 16 34 | 14 27 |
| 20 | 06 15 | 07 06 | 14 10 | 17 46 | 15 11 |
| 21 | 06 08 | 06 58 | 14 19 | 18 01 | 15 20 |
| 22 | 05 59 | 06 49 | 14 28 | 18 16 | 15 29 |
| 23 | 05 51 | 06 40 | 14 37 | 18 32 | 15 38 |
| 24 | 05 43 | 06 31 | 14 47 | 18 49 | 15 48 |
| 25 | 05 34 | 06 21 | 14 56 | 19 06 | 15 57 |
| 26 | 05 26 | 06 12 | 15 07 | 19 23 | 16 07 |
| 27 | 05 17 | 06 02 | 15 18 | 19 40 | 16 17 |
| 28 | 05 08 | 05 51 | 15 29 | 19 59 | 16 28 |
| 29 | 04 59 | 05 41 | 15 40 | 20 17 | 16 38 |
| 30 | 04 49 | 05 30 | 15 53 | 20 36 | 16 49 |
| 31 | 04 39 | 05 18 | 16 05 | 20 56 | 17 00 |
| 32 | 04 29 | 05 06 | 16 19 | 21 17 | 17 12 |
| 33 | 04 19 | 04 54 | 16 33 | 21 38 | 17 23 |
| 34 | 04 08 | 04 41 | 16 48 | 22 00 | 17 35 |
| 35 | 03 57 | 04 28 | 17 03 | 22 22 | 17 48 |
| 36 | 03 46 | 04 14 | 17 20 | 22 46 | 18 00 |
| 37 | 03 34 | 03 59 | 17 37 | 23 10 | 18 13 |
| 38 | 03 22 | 03 44 | 17 56 | 23 36 | 18 27 |
| 39 | 03 10 | 03 28 | 18 15 | 24 02 | 18 41 |
| 40 | 02 57 | 03 12 | 18 36 | 24 30 | 18 55 |
| 41 | 02 43 | 02 54 | 18 59 | 24 58 | 19 10 |
| 42 | 02 29 | 02 36 | 19 23 | 25 29 | 19 26 |
| 43 | 02 15 | 02 16 | 19 49 | 26 00 | 19 42 |
| 44 | 01 59 | 01 56 | 20 17 | 26 33 | 19 59 |
| 45 | 01 43 | 01 34 | 20 47 | 27 08 | 20 16 |
| 46 | 01 27 | 01 11 | 21 20 | 27 45 | 20 34 |
| 47 | 01 09 | 00 46 | 21 56 | 28 23 | 20 54 |
| 48 | 00 51 | 00 20 | 22 35 | 29 05 | 21 14 |
| 49 | 00 31 | 29♒52 | 23 19 | 29 48 | 21 35 |
| 50 | 00 11 | 29 21 | 24 06 | 00♊34 | 21 57 |
| 51 | 29♑49 | 28 49 | 25 00 | 01 24 | 22 21 |
| 52 | 29 26 | 28 13 | 26 00 | 02 17 | 22 46 |
| 53 | 29 01 | 27 35 | 27 07 | 03 13 | 23 12 |
| 54 | 28 35 | 26 53 | 28 24 | 04 15 | 23 41 |
| 55 | 28 07 | 26 07 | 29 52 | 05 21 | 24 11 |
| 56 | 27 36 | 25 16 | 01♉33 | 06 33 | 24 44 |
| 57 | 27 03 | 24 20 | 03 32 | 07 52 | 25 19 |
| 58 | 26 27 | 23 17 | 05 52 | 09 18 | 25 58 |
| 59 | 25 47 | 22 06 | 08 40 | 10 54 | 26 40 |
| 60 | 25♑03 | 20♒45 | 12♉04 | 12♊40 | 27♊26 |

**18h 48m 0s — 282° 0' 0" — 11 ♑ 02**

| LAT. | 11 | 12 | ASC | 2 | 3 |
|---|---|---|---|---|---|
| 0 | 09♒34 | 10♓30 | 13♈03 | 14♉28 | 13♊24 |
| 5 | 09 01 | 10 00 | 13 33 | 15 27 | 14 03 |
| 10 | 08 28 | 09 29 | 14 06 | 16 30 | 14 42 |
| 15 | 07 53 | 08 55 | 14 44 | 17 37 | 15 23 |
| 20 | 07 16 | 08 17 | 15 27 | 18 50 | 16 07 |
| 21 | 07 08 | 08 09 | 15 36 | 19 05 | 16 16 |
| 22 | 07 00 | 08 01 | 15 46 | 19 21 | 16 25 |
| 23 | 06 52 | 07 52 | 15 56 | 19 37 | 16 35 |
| 24 | 06 44 | 07 43 | 16 06 | 19 54 | 16 44 |
| 25 | 06 36 | 07 34 | 16 17 | 20 11 | 16 54 |
| 26 | 06 27 | 07 25 | 16 28 | 20 28 | 17 04 |
| 27 | 06 18 | 07 16 | 16 40 | 20 46 | 17 14 |
| 28 | 06 09 | 07 06 | 16 52 | 21 05 | 17 24 |
| 29 | 06 00 | 06 56 | 17 05 | 21 24 | 17 35 |
| 30 | 05 51 | 06 45 | 17 18 | 21 43 | 17 46 |
| 31 | 05 41 | 06 34 | 17 32 | 22 03 | 17 57 |
| 32 | 05 31 | 06 23 | 17 46 | 22 24 | 18 08 |
| 33 | 05 21 | 06 11 | 18 01 | 22 45 | 18 20 |
| 34 | 05 10 | 05 59 | 18 17 | 23 07 | 18 32 |
| 35 | 05 00 | 05 46 | 18 34 | 23 30 | 18 44 |
| 36 | 04 48 | 05 33 | 18 52 | 23 54 | 18 57 |
| 37 | 04 37 | 05 19 | 19 11 | 24 19 | 19 10 |
| 38 | 04 25 | 05 04 | 19 31 | 24 44 | 19 24 |
| 39 | 04 12 | 04 49 | 19 52 | 25 11 | 19 38 |
| 40 | 04 00 | 04 33 | 20 15 | 25 39 | 19 52 |
| 41 | 03 46 | 04 17 | 20 39 | 26 08 | 20 07 |
| 42 | 03 32 | 03 59 | 21 05 | 26 38 | 20 22 |
| 43 | 03 18 | 03 40 | 21 33 | 27 10 | 20 39 |
| 44 | 03 03 | 03 21 | 22 03 | 27 43 | 20 55 |
| 45 | 02 47 | 03 00 | 22 36 | 28 18 | 21 13 |
| 46 | 02 31 | 02 38 | 23 11 | 28 55 | 21 31 |
| 47 | 02 13 | 02 14 | 23 50 | 29 34 | 21 50 |
| 48 | 01 55 | 01 49 | 24 32 | 00♊16 | 22 11 |
| 49 | 01 36 | 01 22 | 25 18 | 00 59 | 22 32 |
| 50 | 01 15 | 00 53 | 26 10 | 01 46 | 22 54 |
| 51 | 00 54 | 00 22 | 27 07 | 02 36 | 23 18 |
| 52 | 00 31 | 29♒48 | 28 11 | 03 29 | 23 43 |
| 53 | 00 07 | 29 11 | 29 22 | 04 26 | 24 09 |
| 54 | 29♑40 | 28 31 | 00♉44 | 05 27 | 24 37 |
| 55 | 29 12 | 27 46 | 02 17 | 06 33 | 25 08 |
| 56 | 28 42 | 26 58 | 04 04 | 07 46 | 25 40 |
| 57 | 28 09 | 26 04 | 06 08 | 09 04 | 26 16 |
| 58 | 27 33 | 25 03 | 08 35 | 10 31 | 26 54 |
| 59 | 26 54 | 23 55 | 11 29 | 12 06 | 27 36 |
| 60 | 26♑10 | 22♒37 | 14♉57 | 13♊52 | 28♊22 |

**18h 52m 0s — 283° 0' 0" — 11 ♑ 58**

| LAT. | 11 | 12 | ASC | 2 | 3 |
|---|---|---|---|---|---|
| 0 | 10♒33 | 11♓34 | 14♈07 | 15♉28 | 14♊20 |
| 5 | 10 01 | 11 06 | 14 40 | 16 28 | 14 59 |
| 10 | 09 28 | 10 36 | 15 16 | 17 32 | 15 38 |
| 15 | 08 54 | 10 04 | 15 57 | 18 40 | 16 20 |
| 20 | 08 17 | 09 28 | 16 43 | 19 54 | 17 03 |
| 21 | 08 10 | 09 21 | 16 53 | 20 10 | 17 12 |
| 22 | 08 02 | 09 13 | 17 03 | 20 26 | 17 22 |
| 23 | 07 54 | 09 05 | 17 14 | 20 42 | 17 31 |
| 24 | 07 46 | 08 56 | 17 25 | 20 59 | 17 41 |
| 25 | 07 37 | 08 48 | 17 37 | 21 16 | 17 51 |
| 26 | 07 29 | 08 39 | 17 49 | 21 34 | 18 00 |
| 27 | 07 20 | 08 30 | 18 02 | 21 52 | 18 11 |
| 28 | 07 11 | 08 20 | 18 15 | 22 10 | 18 21 |
| 29 | 07 02 | 08 11 | 18 28 | 22 30 | 18 32 |
| 30 | 06 53 | 08 01 | 18 43 | 22 49 | 18 42 |
| 31 | 06 43 | 07 50 | 18 57 | 23 09 | 18 54 |
| 32 | 06 33 | 07 40 | 19 13 | 23 30 | 19 05 |
| 33 | 06 23 | 07 28 | 19 29 | 23 52 | 19 17 |
| 34 | 06 13 | 07 17 | 19 47 | 24 14 | 19 29 |
| 35 | 06 02 | 07 05 | 20 05 | 24 38 | 19 41 |
| 36 | 05 51 | 06 52 | 20 24 | 25 01 | 19 54 |
| 37 | 05 40 | 06 39 | 20 44 | 25 26 | 20 07 |
| 38 | 05 28 | 06 25 | 21 06 | 25 52 | 20 20 |
| 39 | 05 15 | 06 11 | 21 29 | 26 19 | 20 34 |
| 40 | 05 03 | 05 56 | 21 53 | 26 47 | 20 49 |
| 41 | 04 50 | 05 40 | 22 19 | 27 16 | 21 04 |
| 42 | 04 36 | 05 23 | 22 47 | 27 47 | 21 19 |
| 43 | 04 22 | 05 05 | 23 17 | 28 19 | 21 35 |
| 44 | 04 07 | 04 46 | 23 49 | 28 53 | 21 52 |
| 45 | 03 51 | 04 26 | 24 24 | 29 28 | 22 10 |
| 46 | 03 35 | 04 05 | 25 01 | 00♊05 | 22 28 |
| 47 | 03 17 | 03 43 | 25 42 | 00 45 | 22 47 |
| 48 | 02 59 | 03 19 | 26 27 | 01 26 | 23 07 |
| 49 | 02 40 | 02 53 | 27 17 | 02 10 | 23 28 |
| 50 | 02 20 | 02 25 | 28 11 | 02 57 | 23 51 |
| 51 | 01 59 | 01 55 | 29 12 | 03 47 | 24 14 |
| 52 | 01 36 | 01 23 | 00♉19 | 04 40 | 24 39 |
| 53 | 01 12 | 00 48 | 01 35 | 05 37 | 25 06 |
| 54 | 00 46 | 00 09 | 03 00 | 06 39 | 25 34 |
| 55 | 00 18 | 29♒27 | 04 38 | 07 45 | 26 04 |
| 56 | 29♑49 | 28 40 | 06 30 | 08 57 | 26 37 |
| 57 | 29 16 | 27 49 | 08 39 | 10 16 | 27 12 |
| 58 | 28 41 | 26 51 | 11 11 | 11 42 | 27 50 |
| 59 | 28 02 | 25 45 | 14 09 | 13 17 | 28 32 |
| 60 | 27♑18 | 24♒31 | 17♉41 | 15♊03 | 29♊18 |

**18h 56m 0s — 284° 0' 0" — 12 ♑ 53**

| LAT. | 11 | 12 | ASC | 2 | 3 |
|---|---|---|---|---|---|
| 0 | 11♒32 | 12♓39 | 15♈12 | 16♉28 | 15♊16 |
| 5 | 11 01 | 12 12 | 15 48 | 17 29 | 15 55 |
| 10 | 10 29 | 11 44 | 16 26 | 18 34 | 16 34 |
| 15 | 09 55 | 11 13 | 17 09 | 19 43 | 17 16 |
| 20 | 09 18 | 10 40 | 17 59 | 20 58 | 18 00 |
| 21 | 09 11 | 10 32 | 18 10 | 21 14 | 18 09 |
| 22 | 09 03 | 10 25 | 18 21 | 21 30 | 18 18 |
| 23 | 08 55 | 10 17 | 18 32 | 21 46 | 18 27 |
| 24 | 08 47 | 10 09 | 18 44 | 22 03 | 18 37 |
| 25 | 08 39 | 10 01 | 18 57 | 22 21 | 18 47 |
| 26 | 08 31 | 09 53 | 19 10 | 22 39 | 18 57 |
| 27 | 08 22 | 09 44 | 19 23 | 22 57 | 19 07 |
| 28 | 08 13 | 09 35 | 19 37 | 23 16 | 19 17 |
| 29 | 08 04 | 09 26 | 19 52 | 23 35 | 19 28 |
| 30 | 07 55 | 09 17 | 20 07 | 23 55 | 19 39 |
| 31 | 07 45 | 09 07 | 20 23 | 24 15 | 19 50 |
| 32 | 07 36 | 08 57 | 20 40 | 24 37 | 20 01 |
| 33 | 07 26 | 08 46 | 20 57 | 24 58 | 20 13 |
| 34 | 07 15 | 08 35 | 21 16 | 25 21 | 20 25 |
| 35 | 07 05 | 08 24 | 21 35 | 25 44 | 20 37 |
| 36 | 06 54 | 08 12 | 21 55 | 26 09 | 20 50 |
| 37 | 06 43 | 07 59 | 22 17 | 26 34 | 21 03 |
| 38 | 06 31 | 07 46 | 22 40 | 27 00 | 21 17 |
| 39 | 06 19 | 07 32 | 23 04 | 27 27 | 21 31 |
| 40 | 06 06 | 07 18 | 23 30 | 27 55 | 21 45 |
| 41 | 05 53 | 07 03 | 23 58 | 28 25 | 22 00 |
| 42 | 05 40 | 06 47 | 24 27 | 28 55 | 22 16 |
| 43 | 05 25 | 06 30 | 24 59 | 29 28 | 22 32 |
| 44 | 05 11 | 06 12 | 25 33 | 00♊02 | 22 49 |
| 45 | 04 55 | 05 54 | 26 10 | 00 37 | 23 06 |
| 46 | 04 39 | 05 33 | 26 50 | 01 15 | 23 24 |
| 47 | 04 22 | 05 12 | 27 34 | 01 54 | 23 44 |
| 48 | 04 04 | 04 49 | 28 21 | 02 36 | 24 04 |
| 49 | 03 45 | 04 25 | 29 13 | 03 20 | 24 25 |
| 50 | 03 25 | 03 58 | 00♉11 | 04 07 | 24 47 |
| 51 | 03 04 | 03 30 | 01 14 | 04 57 | 25 10 |
| 52 | 02 42 | 02 59 | 02 25 | 05 50 | 25 35 |
| 53 | 02 18 | 02 26 | 03 44 | 06 47 | 26 02 |
| 54 | 01 53 | 01 49 | 05 14 | 07 49 | 26 30 |
| 55 | 01 25 | 01 09 | 06 55 | 08 55 | 27 00 |
| 56 | 00 55 | 00 24 | 08 51 | 10 08 | 27 32 |
| 57 | 00 23 | 29♒35 | 11 05 | 11 26 | 28 07 |
| 58 | 29♑48 | 28 40 | 13 40 | 12 52 | 28 45 |
| 59 | 29 10 | 27 37 | 16 42 | 14 27 | 29 27 |
| 60 | 28♑27 | 26♒26 | 20♉16 | 16♊12 | 00♋13 |

**19h 0m 0s — 285° 0' 0" — 13 ♑ 49**

| LAT. | 11 | 12 | ASC | 2 | 3 |
|---|---|---|---|---|---|
| 0 | 12♒32 | 13♓43 | 16♈17 | 17♉28 | 16♊11 |
| 5 | 12 01 | 13 18 | 16 55 | 18 30 | 16 50 |
| 10 | 11 29 | 12 52 | 17 36 | 19 36 | 17 30 |
| 15 | 10 56 | 12 23 | 18 22 | 20 45 | 18 12 |
| 20 | 10 20 | 11 51 | 19 15 | 22 01 | 18 56 |
| 21 | 10 12 | 11 44 | 19 26 | 22 17 | 19 05 |
| 22 | 10 05 | 11 37 | 19 38 | 22 34 | 19 14 |
| 23 | 09 57 | 11 30 | 19 50 | 22 50 | 19 24 |
| 24 | 09 49 | 11 23 | 20 03 | 23 08 | 19 33 |
| 25 | 09 41 | 11 15 | 20 16 | 23 25 | 19 43 |
| 26 | 09 33 | 11 07 | 20 30 | 23 43 | 19 53 |
| 27 | 09 24 | 10 59 | 20 44 | 24 02 | 20 03 |
| 28 | 09 15 | 10 51 | 20 59 | 24 21 | 20 14 |
| 29 | 09 07 | 10 42 | 21 15 | 24 40 | 20 24 |
| 30 | 08 57 | 10 33 | 21 31 | 25 00 | 20 35 |
| 31 | 08 48 | 10 24 | 21 48 | 25 21 | 20 46 |
| 32 | 08 39 | 10 14 | 22 06 | 25 42 | 20 58 |
| 33 | 08 29 | 10 04 | 22 24 | 26 04 | 21 09 |
| 34 | 08 18 | 09 54 | 22 44 | 26 27 | 21 21 |
| 35 | 08 08 | 09 43 | 23 04 | 26 51 | 21 34 |
| 36 | 07 57 | 09 32 | 23 26 | 27 15 | 21 46 |
| 37 | 07 46 | 09 20 | 23 49 | 27 40 | 22 00 |
| 38 | 07 34 | 09 08 | 24 13 | 28 07 | 22 13 |
| 39 | 07 22 | 08 55 | 24 39 | 28 34 | 22 27 |
| 40 | 07 10 | 08 41 | 25 06 | 29 03 | 22 41 |
| 41 | 06 57 | 08 27 | 25 36 | 29 32 | 22 56 |
| 42 | 06 44 | 08 12 | 26 07 | 00♊03 | 23 12 |
| 43 | 06 30 | 07 56 | 26 41 | 00 36 | 23 28 |
| 44 | 06 15 | 07 39 | 27 17 | 01 10 | 23 45 |
| 45 | 06 00 | 07 21 | 27 56 | 01 46 | 24 02 |
| 46 | 05 44 | 07 02 | 28 38 | 02 23 | 24 21 |
| 47 | 05 27 | 06 42 | 29 23 | 03 03 | 24 40 |
| 48 | 05 09 | 06 20 | 00♉13 | 03 45 | 25 00 |
| 49 | 04 51 | 05 57 | 01 08 | 04 29 | 25 21 |
| 50 | 04 31 | 05 32 | 02 08 | 05 16 | 25 43 |
| 51 | 04 10 | 05 05 | 03 15 | 06 06 | 26 07 |
| 52 | 03 48 | 04 36 | 04 29 | 07 00 | 26 31 |
| 53 | 03 24 | 04 04 | 05 51 | 07 57 | 26 58 |
| 54 | 02 59 | 03 30 | 07 24 | 08 59 | 27 26 |
| 55 | 02 32 | 02 51 | 09 09 | 10 05 | 27 56 |
| 56 | 02 03 | 02 09 | 11 08 | 11 17 | 28 28 |
| 57 | 01 31 | 01 22 | 13 25 | 12 35 | 29 03 |
| 58 | 00 56 | 00 30 | 16 03 | 14 01 | 29 41 |
| 59 | 00 18 | 29♒31 | 19 08 | 15 35 | 00♋22 |
| 60 | 29♑36 | 28♒24 | 22♉43 | 17♊20 | 01♋07 |

**19h 4m 0s — 286° 0' 0" — 14 ♑ 44**

| LAT. | 11 | 12 | ASC | 2 | 3 |
|---|---|---|---|---|---|
| 0 | 13♒32 | 14♓48 | 17♈21 | 18♉28 | 17♊07 |
| 5 | 13 01 | 14 25 | 18 01 | 19 31 | 17 46 |
| 10 | 12 30 | 14 00 | 18 45 | 20 37 | 18 26 |
| 15 | 11 57 | 13 33 | 19 34 | 21 48 | 19 08 |
| 20 | 11 22 | 13 03 | 20 30 | 23 04 | 19 52 |
| 21 | 11 14 | 12 56 | 20 42 | 23 21 | 20 01 |
| 22 | 11 07 | 12 50 | 20 55 | 23 37 | 20 10 |
| 23 | 10 59 | 12 43 | 21 08 | 23 54 | 20 20 |
| 24 | 10 51 | 12 36 | 21 22 | 24 12 | 20 29 |
| 25 | 10 43 | 12 29 | 21 36 | 24 29 | 20 39 |
| 26 | 10 35 | 12 22 | 21 50 | 24 48 | 20 49 |
| 27 | 10 27 | 12 14 | 22 05 | 25 06 | 20 59 |
| 28 | 10 18 | 12 06 | 22 21 | 25 25 | 21 10 |
| 29 | 10 09 | 11 58 | 22 38 | 25 45 | 21 20 |
| 30 | 10 00 | 11 50 | 22 55 | 26 05 | 21 31 |
| 31 | 09 51 | 11 41 | 23 13 | 26 26 | 21 42 |
| 32 | 09 42 | 11 32 | 23 31 | 26 48 | 21 54 |
| 33 | 09 32 | 11 22 | 23 51 | 27 10 | 22 05 |
| 34 | 09 22 | 11 13 | 24 12 | 27 33 | 22 17 |
| 35 | 09 11 | 11 03 | 24 33 | 27 57 | 22 30 |
| 36 | 09 01 | 10 52 | 24 56 | 28 21 | 22 43 |
| 37 | 08 50 | 10 41 | 25 20 | 28 47 | 22 56 |
| 38 | 08 38 | 10 29 | 25 46 | 29 13 | 23 09 |
| 39 | 08 26 | 10 17 | 26 13 | 29 41 | 23 23 |
| 40 | 08 14 | 10 04 | 26 42 | 00♊09 | 23 38 |
| 41 | 08 01 | 09 51 | 27 13 | 00 39 | 23 53 |
| 42 | 07 48 | 09 37 | 27 46 | 01 11 | 24 08 |
| 43 | 07 34 | 09 22 | 28 21 | 01 43 | 24 24 |
| 44 | 07 20 | 09 06 | 28 59 | 02 17 | 24 41 |
| 45 | 07 05 | 08 49 | 29 40 | 02 53 | 24 58 |
| 46 | 06 49 | 08 31 | 00♉24 | 03 31 | 25 17 |
| 47 | 06 32 | 08 12 | 01 12 | 04 11 | 25 36 |
| 48 | 06 15 | 07 52 | 02 04 | 04 53 | 25 56 |
| 49 | 05 57 | 07 30 | 03 01 | 05 37 | 26 17 |
| 50 | 05 37 | 07 07 | 04 04 | 06 25 | 26 39 |
| 51 | 05 17 | 06 41 | 05 13 | 07 15 | 27 02 |
| 52 | 04 55 | 06 14 | 06 29 | 08 08 | 27 27 |
| 53 | 04 31 | 05 44 | 07 55 | 09 06 | 27 53 |
| 54 | 04 06 | 05 11 | 09 31 | 10 07 | 28 21 |
| 55 | 03 40 | 04 35 | 11 18 | 11 14 | 28 51 |
| 56 | 03 11 | 03 55 | 13 21 | 12 25 | 29 23 |
| 57 | 02 39 | 03 11 | 15 41 | 13 44 | 29 58 |
| 58 | 02 05 | 02 22 | 18 21 | 15 09 | 00♋36 |
| 59 | 01 28 | 01 26 | 21 26 | 16 43 | 01 17 |
| 60 | 00♒46 | 00♓22 | 25♉02 | 18♊27 | 02♋02 |

**19h 8m 0s — 287° 0' 0" — 15 ♑ 40**

| LAT. | 11 | 12 | ASC | 2 | 3 |
|---|---|---|---|---|---|
| 0 | 14♒32 | 15♓53 | 18♈26 | 19♉27 | 18♊02 |
| 5 | 14 02 | 15 31 | 19 08 | 20 31 | 18 42 |
| 10 | 13 31 | 15 08 | 19 55 | 21 38 | 19 22 |
| 15 | 12 58 | 14 43 | 20 46 | 22 50 | 20 04 |
| 20 | 12 24 | 14 15 | 21 45 | 24 07 | 20 48 |
| 21 | 12 16 | 14 09 | 21 58 | 24 24 | 20 57 |
| 22 | 12 09 | 14 03 | 22 12 | 24 40 | 21 06 |
| 23 | 12 01 | 13 56 | 22 26 | 24 58 | 21 16 |
| 24 | 11 54 | 13 50 | 22 40 | 25 15 | 21 25 |
| 25 | 11 46 | 13 43 | 22 55 | 25 33 | 21 35 |
| 26 | 11 38 | 13 36 | 23 10 | 25 51 | 21 45 |
| 27 | 11 29 | 13 29 | 23 26 | 26 10 | 21 55 |
| 28 | 11 21 | 13 22 | 23 42 | 26 30 | 22 06 |
| 29 | 11 12 | 13 14 | 24 00 | 26 50 | 22 16 |
| 30 | 11 03 | 13 06 | 24 18 | 27 10 | 22 27 |
| 31 | 10 54 | 12 58 | 24 37 | 27 31 | 22 38 |
| 32 | 10 45 | 12 50 | 24 56 | 27 53 | 22 50 |
| 33 | 10 35 | 12 41 | 25 17 | 28 15 | 23 01 |
| 34 | 10 25 | 12 32 | 25 39 | 28 38 | 23 13 |
| 35 | 10 15 | 12 23 | 26 02 | 29 02 | 23 26 |
| 36 | 10 05 | 12 13 | 26 26 | 29 27 | 23 39 |
| 37 | 09 54 | 12 02 | 26 51 | 29 53 | 23 52 |
| 38 | 09 42 | 11 51 | 27 18 | 00♊19 | 24 05 |
| 39 | 09 31 | 11 40 | 27 46 | 00 47 | 24 19 |
| 40 | 09 19 | 11 28 | 28 17 | 01 16 | 24 34 |
| 41 | 09 06 | 11 16 | 28 49 | 01 46 | 24 49 |
| 42 | 08 53 | 11 02 | 29 23 | 02 17 | 25 04 |
| 43 | 08 39 | 10 48 | 00♉00 | 02 50 | 25 20 |
| 44 | 08 25 | 10 34 | 00 40 | 03 24 | 25 37 |
| 45 | 08 10 | 10 18 | 01 22 | 04 00 | 25 54 |
| 46 | 07 55 | 10 01 | 02 08 | 04 38 | 26 13 |
| 47 | 07 38 | 09 43 | 02 58 | 05 18 | 26 32 |
| 48 | 07 21 | 09 24 | 03 53 | 06 00 | 26 52 |
| 49 | 07 03 | 09 04 | 04 52 | 06 45 | 27 13 |
| 50 | 06 44 | 08 42 | 05 57 | 07 32 | 27 35 |
| 51 | 06 23 | 08 18 | 07 08 | 08 23 | 27 58 |
| 52 | 06 02 | 07 52 | 08 28 | 09 16 | 28 23 |
| 53 | 05 39 | 07 24 | 09 56 | 10 14 | 28 49 |
| 54 | 05 14 | 06 54 | 11 34 | 11 15 | 29 17 |
| 55 | 04 47 | 06 20 | 13 24 | 12 21 | 29 47 |
| 56 | 04 19 | 05 43 | 15 29 | 13 33 | 00♋19 |
| 57 | 03 48 | 05 01 | 17 51 | 14 51 | 00 53 |
| 58 | 03 14 | 04 15 | 20 33 | 16 16 | 01 30 |
| 59 | 02 37 | 03 22 | 23 39 | 17 49 | 02 11 |
| 60 | 01♒56 | 02♓22 | 27♉14 | 19♊32 | 02♋56 |

# Placidus Table of Houses for Latitudes 0° to 60° North

**19h 12m 0s — 288° 0' 0" — 16 ♑ 36**

| LAT. | 11 | 12 | ASC | 2 | 3 |
|---|---|---|---|---|---|
| 0 | 15♒32 | 16♓57 | 19♈30 | 20♉26 | 18♊58 |
| 5 | 15 03 | 16 37 | 20 15 | 21 31 | 19 37 |
| 10 | 14 32 | 16 16 | 21 04 | 22 39 | 20 18 |
| 15 | 14 00 | 15 53 | 21 58 | 23 51 | 20 59 |
| 20 | 13 26 | 15 27 | 23 00 | 25 10 | 21 43 |
| 21 | 13 19 | 15 21 | 23 14 | 25 26 | 21 53 |
| 22 | 13 11 | 15 16 | 23 28 | 25 43 | 22 02 |
| 23 | 13 04 | 15 10 | 23 43 | 26 01 | 22 11 |
| 24 | 12 56 | 15 04 | 23 58 | 26 18 | 22 21 |
| 25 | 12 48 | 14 57 | 24 13 | 26 36 | 22 31 |
| 26 | 12 40 | 14 51 | 24 29 | 26 55 | 22 41 |
| 27 | 12 32 | 14 45 | 24 46 | 27 14 | 22 51 |
| 28 | 12 24 | 14 38 | 25 03 | 27 34 | 23 02 |
| 29 | 12 15 | 14 31 | 25 22 | 27 54 | 23 12 |
| 30 | 12 07 | 14 23 | 25 40 | 28 14 | 23 23 |
| 31 | 11 58 | 14 16 | 26 00 | 28 35 | 23 34 |
| 32 | 11 48 | 14 08 | 26 21 | 28 57 | 23 46 |
| 33 | 11 39 | 14 00 | 26 43 | 29 20 | 23 57 |
| 34 | 11 29 | 13 52 | 27 05 | 29 43 | 24 09 |
| 35 | 11 19 | 13 43 | 27 29 | 00♊07 | 24 22 |
| 36 | 11 09 | 13 34 | 27 54 | 00 32 | 24 34 |
| 37 | 10 58 | 13 24 | 28 21 | 00 58 | 24 48 |
| 38 | 10 47 | 13 14 | 28 49 | 01 25 | 25 01 |
| 39 | 10 35 | 13 03 | 29 19 | 01 53 | 25 15 |
| 40 | 10 23 | 12 52 | 29 50 | 02 22 | 25 29 |
| 41 | 10 11 | 12 41 | 00♉24 | 02 52 | 25 44 |
| 42 | 09 58 | 12 28 | 01 00 | 03 23 | 26 00 |
| 43 | 09 45 | 12 15 | 01 38 | 03 56 | 26 16 |
| 44 | 09 31 | 12 02 | 02 20 | 04 31 | 26 33 |
| 45 | 09 16 | 11 47 | 03 04 | 05 07 | 26 50 |
| 46 | 09 01 | 11 31 | 03 52 | 05 45 | 27 08 |
| 47 | 08 44 | 11 15 | 04 44 | 06 25 | 27 27 |
| 48 | 08 27 | 10 57 | 05 40 | 07 07 | 27 47 |
| 49 | 08 09 | 10 38 | 06 41 | 07 52 | 28 08 |
| 50 | 07 50 | 10 18 | 07 48 | 08 39 | 28 30 |
| 51 | 07 30 | 09 56 | 09 02 | 09 30 | 28 53 |
| 52 | 07 09 | 09 32 | 10 23 | 10 23 | 29 18 |
| 53 | 06 46 | 09 05 | 11 53 | 11 21 | 29 44 |
| 54 | 06 22 | 08 37 | 13 34 | 12 22 | 00♋12 |
| 55 | 05 56 | 08 05 | 15 26 | 13 28 | 00 42 |
| 56 | 05 28 | 07 31 | 17 33 | 14 39 | 01 13 |
| 57 | 04 57 | 06 52 | 19 56 | 15 57 | 01 48 |
| 58 | 04 24 | 06 09 | 22 39 | 17 21 | 02 25 |
| 59 | 03 48 | 05 20 | 25 45 | 18 54 | 03 05 |
| 60 | 03♒07 | 04♓24 | 29♉19 | 20♊36 | 03♋50 |

**19h 16m 0s — 289° 0' 0" — 17 ♑ 32**

| LAT. | 11 | 12 | ASC | 2 | 3 |
|---|---|---|---|---|---|
| 0 | 16♒33 | 18♓02 | 20♈34 | 21♉26 | 19♊53 |
| 5 | 16 04 | 17 44 | 21 21 | 22 31 | 20 33 |
| 10 | 15 34 | 17 24 | 22 13 | 23 40 | 21 13 |
| 15 | 15 02 | 17 03 | 23 10 | 24 53 | 21 55 |
| 20 | 14 28 | 16 39 | 24 15 | 26 12 | 22 39 |
| 21 | 14 21 | 16 34 | 24 29 | 26 29 | 22 48 |
| 22 | 14 14 | 16 29 | 24 44 | 26 46 | 22 58 |
| 23 | 14 07 | 16 23 | 24 59 | 27 03 | 23 07 |
| 24 | 13 59 | 16 18 | 25 15 | 27 21 | 23 17 |
| 25 | 13 51 | 16 12 | 25 31 | 27 39 | 23 27 |
| 26 | 13 44 | 16 06 | 25 48 | 27 58 | 23 37 |
| 27 | 13 36 | 16 00 | 26 06 | 28 17 | 23 47 |
| 28 | 13 27 | 15 54 | 26 24 | 28 37 | 23 57 |
| 29 | 13 19 | 15 47 | 26 43 | 28 57 | 24 08 |
| 30 | 13 10 | 15 41 | 27 03 | 29 18 | 24 19 |
| 31 | 13 01 | 15 34 | 27 23 | 29 39 | 24 30 |
| 32 | 12 52 | 15 27 | 27 45 | 00♊01 | 24 41 |
| 33 | 12 43 | 15 19 | 28 08 | 00 24 | 24 53 |
| 34 | 12 33 | 15 11 | 28 31 | 00 48 | 25 05 |
| 35 | 12 23 | 15 03 | 28 56 | 01 12 | 25 17 |
| 36 | 12 13 | 14 55 | 29 23 | 01 37 | 25 30 |
| 37 | 12 03 | 14 46 | 29 50 | 02 03 | 25 43 |
| 38 | 11 52 | 14 37 | 00♉19 | 02 30 | 25 57 |
| 39 | 11 40 | 14 27 | 00 50 | 02 58 | 26 11 |
| 40 | 11 29 | 14 17 | 01 23 | 03 27 | 26 25 |
| 41 | 11 16 | 14 06 | 01 58 | 03 57 | 26 40 |
| 42 | 11 04 | 13 55 | 02 36 | 04 29 | 26 55 |
| 43 | 10 50 | 13 43 | 03 15 | 05 02 | 27 12 |
| 44 | 10 36 | 13 30 | 03 58 | 05 37 | 27 28 |
| 45 | 10 22 | 13 17 | 04 44 | 06 13 | 27 46 |
| 46 | 10 07 | 13 02 | 05 34 | 06 51 | 28 04 |
| 47 | 09 51 | 12 47 | 06 27 | 07 31 | 28 23 |
| 48 | 09 34 | 12 31 | 07 25 | 08 14 | 28 43 |
| 49 | 09 16 | 12 13 | 08 28 | 08 58 | 29 04 |
| 50 | 08 58 | 11 54 | 09 37 | 09 46 | 29 25 |
| 51 | 08 38 | 11 34 | 10 53 | 10 36 | 29 49 |
| 52 | 08 17 | 11 11 | 12 16 | 11 29 | 00♋13 |
| 53 | 07 55 | 10 47 | 13 48 | 12 27 | 00 39 |
| 54 | 07 31 | 10 21 | 15 31 | 13 28 | 01 07 |
| 55 | 07 05 | 09 52 | 17 25 | 14 34 | 01 36 |
| 56 | 06 37 | 09 20 | 19 33 | 15 45 | 02 08 |
| 57 | 06 07 | 08 44 | 21 57 | 17 02 | 02 42 |
| 58 | 05 34 | 08 04 | 24 41 | 18 26 | 03 19 |
| 59 | 04 58 | 07 18 | 27 46 | 19 58 | 03 59 |
| 60 | 04♒19 | 06♓27 | 01♊18 | 21♊40 | 04♋43 |

**19h 20m 0s — 290° 0' 0" — 18 ♑ 28**

| LAT. | 11 | 12 | ASC | 2 | 3 |
|---|---|---|---|---|---|
| 0 | 17♒33 | 19♓07 | 21♈38 | 22♉25 | 20♊49 |
| 5 | 17 05 | 18 50 | 22 28 | 23 31 | 21 28 |
| 10 | 16 35 | 18 33 | 23 21 | 24 40 | 22 09 |
| 15 | 16 04 | 18 13 | 24 21 | 25 54 | 22 50 |
| 20 | 15 31 | 17 51 | 25 30 | 27 14 | 23 35 |
| 21 | 15 24 | 17 47 | 25 44 | 27 31 | 23 44 |
| 22 | 15 17 | 17 42 | 26 00 | 27 48 | 23 53 |
| 23 | 15 10 | 17 37 | 26 16 | 28 06 | 24 03 |
| 24 | 15 02 | 17 32 | 26 32 | 28 24 | 24 12 |
| 25 | 14 55 | 17 27 | 26 49 | 28 42 | 24 22 |
| 26 | 14 47 | 17 21 | 27 07 | 29 01 | 24 32 |
| 27 | 14 39 | 17 16 | 27 25 | 29 20 | 24 42 |
| 28 | 14 31 | 17 10 | 27 44 | 29 40 | 24 53 |
| 29 | 14 23 | 17 04 | 28 04 | 00♊01 | 25 03 |
| 30 | 14 14 | 16 58 | 28 24 | 00 21 | 25 14 |
| 31 | 14 05 | 16 52 | 28 46 | 00 43 | 25 26 |
| 32 | 13 57 | 16 45 | 29 08 | 01 05 | 25 37 |
| 33 | 13 47 | 16 38 | 29 32 | 01 28 | 25 49 |
| 34 | 13 38 | 16 31 | 29 57 | 01 52 | 26 01 |
| 35 | 13 28 | 16 24 | 00♉23 | 02 16 | 26 13 |
| 36 | 13 18 | 16 16 | 00 50 | 02 41 | 26 26 |
| 37 | 13 08 | 16 08 | 01 19 | 03 07 | 26 39 |
| 38 | 12 57 | 16 00 | 01 49 | 03 34 | 26 52 |
| 39 | 12 46 | 15 51 | 02 21 | 04 03 | 27 06 |
| 40 | 12 34 | 15 41 | 02 55 | 04 32 | 27 21 |
| 41 | 12 22 | 15 32 | 03 32 | 05 02 | 27 35 |
| 42 | 12 09 | 15 21 | 04 10 | 05 34 | 27 51 |
| 43 | 11 56 | 15 10 | 04 51 | 06 07 | 28 07 |
| 44 | 11 43 | 14 59 | 05 35 | 06 42 | 28 24 |
| 45 | 11 28 | 14 46 | 06 23 | 07 18 | 28 41 |
| 46 | 11 13 | 14 33 | 07 14 | 07 57 | 28 59 |
| 47 | 10 58 | 14 19 | 08 09 | 08 37 | 29 18 |
| 48 | 10 41 | 14 04 | 09 09 | 09 19 | 29 38 |
| 49 | 10 24 | 13 48 | 10 13 | 10 04 | 29 59 |
| 50 | 10 05 | 13 31 | 11 24 | 10 51 | 00♋21 |
| 51 | 09 46 | 13 12 | 12 41 | 11 41 | 00 44 |
| 52 | 09 25 | 12 52 | 14 06 | 12 35 | 01 08 |
| 53 | 09 03 | 12 30 | 15 40 | 13 32 | 01 34 |
| 54 | 08 40 | 12 06 | 17 24 | 14 33 | 02 01 |
| 55 | 08 14 | 11 39 | 19 20 | 15 39 | 02 31 |
| 56 | 07 47 | 11 10 | 21 29 | 16 50 | 03 02 |
| 57 | 07 17 | 10 37 | 23 54 | 18 07 | 03 36 |
| 58 | 06 45 | 10 00 | 26 37 | 19 30 | 04 13 |
| 59 | 06 10 | 09 18 | 29 42 | 21 01 | 04 53 |
| 60 | 05♒31 | 08♓31 | 03♊10 | 22♊42 | 05♋36 |

**19h 24m 0s — 291° 0' 0" — 19 ♑ 24**

| LAT. | 11 | 12 | ASC | 2 | 3 |
|---|---|---|---|---|---|
| 0 | 18♒34 | 20♓12 | 22♈42 | 23♉23 | 21♊44 |
| 5 | 18 06 | 19 57 | 23 34 | 24 31 | 22 24 |
| 10 | 17 37 | 19 41 | 24 30 | 25 41 | 23 04 |
| 15 | 17 06 | 19 23 | 25 33 | 26 55 | 23 46 |
| 20 | 16 34 | 19 04 | 26 44 | 28 16 | 24 30 |
| 21 | 16 27 | 19 00 | 26 59 | 28 33 | 24 39 |
| 22 | 16 20 | 18 55 | 27 15 | 28 50 | 24 49 |
| 23 | 16 13 | 18 51 | 27 32 | 29 08 | 24 58 |
| 24 | 16 06 | 18 46 | 27 49 | 29 26 | 25 08 |
| 25 | 15 58 | 18 42 | 28 06 | 29 45 | 25 18 |
| 26 | 15 51 | 18 37 | 28 25 | 00♊04 | 25 28 |
| 27 | 15 43 | 18 32 | 28 44 | 00 23 | 25 38 |
| 28 | 15 35 | 18 27 | 29 04 | 00 43 | 25 48 |
| 29 | 15 27 | 18 21 | 29 24 | 01 04 | 25 59 |
| 30 | 15 18 | 18 16 | 29 46 | 01 25 | 26 10 |
| 31 | 15 10 | 18 10 | 00♉08 | 01 46 | 26 21 |
| 32 | 15 01 | 18 04 | 00 31 | 02 09 | 26 32 |
| 33 | 14 52 | 17 58 | 00 56 | 02 32 | 26 44 |
| 34 | 14 43 | 17 52 | 01 21 | 02 55 | 26 56 |
| 35 | 14 33 | 17 45 | 01 48 | 03 20 | 27 08 |
| 36 | 14 23 | 17 38 | 02 17 | 03 45 | 27 21 |
| 37 | 14 13 | 17 31 | 02 46 | 04 11 | 27 34 |
| 38 | 14 02 | 17 23 | 03 18 | 04 39 | 27 48 |
| 39 | 13 51 | 17 15 | 03 51 | 05 07 | 28 02 |
| 40 | 13 40 | 17 06 | 04 26 | 05 36 | 28 16 |
| 41 | 13 28 | 16 58 | 05 04 | 06 07 | 28 31 |
| 42 | 13 16 | 16 48 | 05 44 | 06 39 | 28 46 |
| 43 | 13 03 | 16 38 | 06 26 | 07 12 | 29 02 |
| 44 | 12 49 | 16 28 | 07 12 | 07 47 | 29 19 |
| 45 | 12 35 | 16 17 | 08 00 | 08 23 | 29 36 |
| 46 | 12 21 | 16 05 | 08 53 | 09 01 | 29 54 |
| 47 | 12 05 | 15 52 | 09 49 | 09 42 | 00♋13 |
| 48 | 11 49 | 15 39 | 10 50 | 10 24 | 00 33 |
| 49 | 11 32 | 15 24 | 11 57 | 11 09 | 00 54 |
| 50 | 11 14 | 15 08 | 13 09 | 11 56 | 01 15 |
| 51 | 10 54 | 14 51 | 14 28 | 12 46 | 01 38 |
| 52 | 10 34 | 14 33 | 15 54 | 13 40 | 02 03 |
| 53 | 10 12 | 14 13 | 17 29 | 14 37 | 02 28 |
| 54 | 09 49 | 13 51 | 19 15 | 15 38 | 02 56 |
| 55 | 09 24 | 13 27 | 21 11 | 16 43 | 03 25 |
| 56 | 08 57 | 13 00 | 23 21 | 17 54 | 03 56 |
| 57 | 08 28 | 12 30 | 25 46 | 19 10 | 04 30 |
| 58 | 07 56 | 11 57 | 28 29 | 20 33 | 05 06 |
| 59 | 07 22 | 11 19 | 01♊32 | 22 03 | 05 46 |
| 60 | 06♒43 | 10♓36 | 04♊58 | 23♊43 | 06♋29 |

**19h 28m 0s — 292° 0' 0" — 20 ♑ 20**

| LAT. | 11 | 12 | ASC | 2 | 3 |
|---|---|---|---|---|---|
| 0 | 19♒35 | 21♓17 | 23♈46 | 24♉22 | 22♊39 |
| 5 | 19 07 | 21 04 | 24 40 | 25 30 | 23 19 |
| 10 | 18 39 | 20 50 | 25 38 | 26 41 | 23 59 |
| 15 | 18 09 | 20 34 | 26 43 | 27 56 | 24 41 |
| 20 | 17 37 | 20 16 | 27 57 | 29 17 | 25 26 |
| 21 | 17 30 | 20 13 | 28 14 | 29 34 | 25 35 |
| 22 | 17 23 | 20 09 | 28 30 | 29 52 | 25 44 |
| 23 | 17 16 | 20 05 | 28 47 | 00♊10 | 25 54 |
| 24 | 17 09 | 20 01 | 29 05 | 00 28 | 26 03 |
| 25 | 17 02 | 19 57 | 29 23 | 00 47 | 26 13 |
| 26 | 16 54 | 19 52 | 29 42 | 01 06 | 26 23 |
| 27 | 16 47 | 19 48 | 00♉02 | 01 25 | 26 33 |
| 28 | 16 39 | 19 43 | 00 23 | 01 45 | 26 44 |
| 29 | 16 31 | 19 39 | 00 44 | 02 06 | 26 54 |
| 30 | 16 23 | 19 34 | 01 06 | 02 27 | 27 05 |
| 31 | 16 14 | 19 29 | 01 29 | 02 49 | 27 16 |
| 32 | 16 06 | 19 23 | 01 54 | 03 12 | 27 28 |
| 33 | 15 57 | 19 18 | 02 19 | 03 35 | 27 39 |
| 34 | 15 48 | 19 12 | 02 45 | 03 58 | 27 51 |
| 35 | 15 38 | 19 06 | 03 13 | 04 23 | 28 04 |
| 36 | 15 28 | 19 00 | 03 42 | 04 49 | 28 16 |
| 37 | 15 18 | 18 53 | 04 13 | 05 15 | 28 29 |
| 38 | 15 08 | 18 46 | 04 46 | 05 42 | 28 43 |
| 39 | 14 57 | 18 39 | 05 20 | 06 11 | 28 57 |
| 40 | 14 46 | 18 32 | 05 56 | 06 40 | 29 11 |
| 41 | 14 34 | 18 24 | 06 35 | 07 11 | 29 26 |
| 42 | 14 22 | 18 15 | 07 16 | 07 43 | 29 41 |
| 43 | 14 09 | 18 07 | 08 00 | 08 16 | 29 57 |
| 44 | 13 56 | 17 57 | 08 46 | 08 51 | 00♋14 |
| 45 | 13 42 | 17 47 | 09 36 | 09 27 | 00 31 |
| 46 | 13 28 | 17 37 | 10 30 | 10 06 | 00 49 |
| 47 | 13 13 | 17 25 | 11 28 | 10 46 | 01 08 |
| 48 | 12 57 | 17 13 | 12 30 | 11 28 | 01 28 |
| 49 | 12 40 | 17 00 | 13 38 | 12 13 | 01 48 |
| 50 | 12 22 | 16 46 | 14 52 | 13 00 | 02 10 |
| 51 | 12 03 | 16 31 | 16 12 | 13 51 | 02 33 |
| 52 | 11 43 | 16 15 | 17 39 | 14 44 | 02 57 |
| 53 | 11 22 | 15 57 | 19 16 | 15 41 | 03 23 |
| 54 | 10 59 | 15 37 | 21 02 | 16 41 | 03 50 |
| 55 | 10 34 | 15 16 | 22 59 | 17 47 | 04 19 |
| 56 | 10 08 | 14 52 | 25 10 | 18 57 | 04 50 |
| 57 | 09 39 | 14 25 | 27 35 | 20 12 | 05 24 |
| 58 | 09 08 | 13 55 | 00♊16 | 21 35 | 06 00 |
| 59 | 08 34 | 13 21 | 03 18 | 23 04 | 06 39 |
| 60 | 07♒57 | 12♓43 | 06♊41 | 24♊43 | 07♋22 |

**19h 32m 0s — 293° 0' 0" — 21 ♑ 17**

| LAT. | 11 | 12 | ASC | 2 | 3 |
|---|---|---|---|---|---|
| 0 | 20♒36 | 22♓23 | 24♈50 | 25♉21 | 23♊34 |
| 5 | 20 09 | 22 11 | 25 46 | 26 29 | 24 14 |
| 10 | 19 41 | 21 58 | 26 47 | 27 41 | 24 55 |
| 15 | 19 12 | 21 44 | 27 54 | 28 56 | 25 37 |
| 20 | 18 40 | 21 29 | 29 11 | 00♊18 | 26 21 |
| 21 | 18 34 | 21 26 | 29 28 | 00 36 | 26 30 |
| 22 | 18 27 | 21 22 | 29 45 | 00 53 | 26 39 |
| 23 | 18 20 | 21 19 | 00♉03 | 01 11 | 26 49 |
| 24 | 18 13 | 21 15 | 00 21 | 01 30 | 26 59 |
| 25 | 18 06 | 21 12 | 00 40 | 01 48 | 27 08 |
| 26 | 17 59 | 21 08 | 01 00 | 02 08 | 27 18 |
| 27 | 17 51 | 21 04 | 01 20 | 02 27 | 27 29 |
| 28 | 17 43 | 21 00 | 01 41 | 02 48 | 27 39 |
| 29 | 17 36 | 20 56 | 02 03 | 03 08 | 27 50 |
| 30 | 17 28 | 20 52 | 02 26 | 03 30 | 28 01 |
| 31 | 17 19 | 20 47 | 02 50 | 03 52 | 28 12 |
| 32 | 17 11 | 20 42 | 03 15 | 04 14 | 28 23 |
| 33 | 17 02 | 20 38 | 03 41 | 04 37 | 28 35 |
| 34 | 16 53 | 20 33 | 04 09 | 05 01 | 28 47 |
| 35 | 16 44 | 20 27 | 04 37 | 05 26 | 28 59 |
| 36 | 16 34 | 20 22 | 05 08 | 05 52 | 29 12 |
| 37 | 16 24 | 20 16 | 05 39 | 06 18 | 29 25 |
| 38 | 16 14 | 20 10 | 06 13 | 06 45 | 29 38 |
| 39 | 16 03 | 20 04 | 06 48 | 07 14 | 29 52 |
| 40 | 15 52 | 19 57 | 07 25 | 07 43 | 00♋06 |
| 41 | 15 41 | 19 50 | 08 05 | 08 14 | 00 21 |
| 42 | 15 29 | 19 43 | 08 47 | 08 46 | 00 36 |
| 43 | 15 16 | 19 35 | 09 32 | 09 20 | 00 52 |
| 44 | 15 04 | 19 27 | 10 20 | 09 54 | 01 09 |
| 45 | 14 50 | 19 18 | 11 11 | 10 31 | 01 26 |
| 46 | 14 36 | 19 09 | 12 06 | 11 09 | 01 44 |
| 47 | 14 21 | 18 59 | 13 05 | 11 50 | 02 03 |
| 48 | 14 05 | 18 48 | 14 09 | 12 32 | 02 22 |
| 49 | 13 48 | 18 37 | 15 17 | 13 17 | 02 43 |
| 50 | 13 31 | 18 25 | 16 32 | 14 04 | 03 05 |
| 51 | 13 12 | 18 11 | 17 53 | 14 54 | 03 27 |
| 52 | 12 53 | 17 57 | 19 22 | 15 47 | 03 52 |
| 53 | 12 32 | 17 41 | 21 00 | 16 44 | 04 17 |
| 54 | 12 09 | 17 24 | 22 46 | 17 44 | 04 44 |
| 55 | 11 45 | 17 05 | 24 44 | 18 49 | 05 13 |
| 56 | 11 19 | 16 44 | 26 55 | 19 59 | 05 44 |
| 57 | 10 51 | 16 20 | 29 19 | 21 14 | 06 17 |
| 58 | 10 21 | 15 54 | 02♊00 | 22 36 | 06 53 |
| 59 | 09 47 | 15 24 | 04 59 | 24 05 | 07 32 |
| 60 | 09♒10 | 14♓50 | 08♊19 | 25♊42 | 08♋14 |

**19h 36m 0s — 294° 0' 0" — 22 ♑ 13**

| LAT. | 11 | 12 | ASC | 2 | 3 |
|---|---|---|---|---|---|
| 0 | 21♒37 | 23♓28 | 25♈53 | 26♉19 | 24♊30 |
| 5 | 21 11 | 23 18 | 26 51 | 27 28 | 25 09 |
| 10 | 20 44 | 23 07 | 27 54 | 28 40 | 25 50 |
| 15 | 20 15 | 22 55 | 29 05 | 29 57 | 26 32 |
| 20 | 19 44 | 22 42 | 00♉24 | 01♊19 | 27 16 |
| 21 | 19 37 | 22 39 | 00 41 | 01 37 | 27 25 |
| 22 | 19 31 | 22 36 | 00 59 | 01 54 | 27 35 |
| 23 | 19 24 | 22 33 | 01 17 | 02 13 | 27 44 |
| 24 | 19 17 | 22 30 | 01 36 | 02 31 | 27 54 |
| 25 | 19 10 | 22 27 | 01 56 | 02 50 | 28 04 |
| 26 | 19 03 | 22 24 | 02 16 | 03 09 | 28 14 |
| 27 | 18 56 | 22 20 | 02 37 | 03 29 | 28 24 |
| 28 | 18 48 | 22 17 | 02 59 | 03 49 | 28 34 |
| 29 | 18 40 | 22 13 | 03 22 | 04 10 | 28 45 |
| 30 | 18 33 | 22 10 | 03 46 | 04 32 | 28 56 |
| 31 | 18 24 | 22 06 | 04 11 | 04 54 | 29 07 |
| 32 | 18 16 | 22 02 | 04 36 | 05 16 | 29 18 |
| 33 | 18 08 | 21 58 | 05 03 | 05 40 | 29 30 |
| 34 | 17 59 | 21 53 | 05 31 | 06 04 | 29 42 |
| 35 | 17 50 | 21 49 | 06 01 | 06 29 | 29 54 |
| 36 | 17 40 | 21 44 | 06 32 | 06 54 | 00♋07 |
| 37 | 17 30 | 21 39 | 07 04 | 07 21 | 00 20 |
| 38 | 17 20 | 21 34 | 07 39 | 07 48 | 00 33 |
| 39 | 17 10 | 21 29 | 08 15 | 08 17 | 00 47 |
| 40 | 16 59 | 21 23 | 08 53 | 08 46 | 01 01 |
| 41 | 16 48 | 21 17 | 09 34 | 09 17 | 01 16 |
| 42 | 16 36 | 21 11 | 10 17 | 09 49 | 01 31 |
| 43 | 16 24 | 21 04 | 11 03 | 10 23 | 01 47 |
| 44 | 16 11 | 20 57 | 11 52 | 10 58 | 02 04 |
| 45 | 15 58 | 20 49 | 12 44 | 11 34 | 02 21 |
| 46 | 15 44 | 20 41 | 13 40 | 12 13 | 02 39 |
| 47 | 15 29 | 20 33 | 14 40 | 12 53 | 02 57 |
| 48 | 15 14 | 20 24 | 15 45 | 13 35 | 03 17 |
| 49 | 14 58 | 20 14 | 16 55 | 14 20 | 03 37 |
| 50 | 14 40 | 20 03 | 18 11 | 15 07 | 03 59 |
| 51 | 14 22 | 19 52 | 19 33 | 15 57 | 04 22 |
| 52 | 14 03 | 19 39 | 21 03 | 16 50 | 04 46 |
| 53 | 13 42 | 19 26 | 22 41 | 17 46 | 05 11 |
| 54 | 13 20 | 19 11 | 24 28 | 18 47 | 05 38 |
| 55 | 12 57 | 18 54 | 26 26 | 19 51 | 06 07 |
| 56 | 12 31 | 18 36 | 28 36 | 21 00 | 06 37 |
| 57 | 12 04 | 18 16 | 01♊00 | 22 15 | 07 10 |
| 58 | 11 34 | 17 53 | 03 40 | 23 36 | 07 46 |
| 59 | 11 01 | 17 28 | 06 37 | 25 04 | 08 24 |
| 60 | 10♒25 | 16♓59 | 09♊53 | 26♊40 | 09♋06 |

**19h 40m 0s — 295° 0' 0" — 23 ♑ 10**

| LAT. | 11 | 12 | ASC | 2 | 3 |
|---|---|---|---|---|---|
| 0 | 22♒39 | 24♓33 | 26♈57 | 27♉17 | 25♊25 |
| 5 | 22 13 | 24 25 | 27 57 | 28 27 | 26 04 |
| 10 | 21 46 | 24 16 | 29 02 | 29 40 | 26 45 |
| 15 | 21 18 | 24 06 | 00♉15 | 00♊57 | 27 27 |
| 20 | 20 48 | 23 55 | 01 37 | 02 20 | 28 11 |
| 21 | 20 41 | 23 52 | 01 54 | 02 37 | 28 21 |
| 22 | 20 35 | 23 50 | 02 13 | 02 55 | 28 30 |
| 23 | 20 28 | 23 48 | 02 32 | 03 13 | 28 39 |
| 24 | 20 22 | 23 45 | 02 51 | 03 32 | 28 49 |
| 25 | 20 15 | 23 42 | 03 12 | 03 51 | 28 59 |
| 26 | 20 08 | 23 40 | 03 33 | 04 11 | 29 09 |
| 27 | 20 00 | 23 37 | 03 54 | 04 30 | 29 19 |
| 28 | 19 53 | 23 34 | 04 17 | 04 51 | 29 29 |
| 29 | 19 46 | 23 31 | 04 40 | 05 12 | 29 40 |
| 30 | 19 38 | 23 28 | 05 05 | 05 33 | 29 51 |
| 31 | 19 30 | 23 25 | 05 30 | 05 55 | 00♋02 |
| 32 | 19 22 | 23 21 | 05 57 | 06 18 | 00 13 |
| 33 | 19 13 | 23 18 | 06 24 | 06 42 | 00 25 |
| 34 | 19 05 | 23 14 | 06 53 | 07 06 | 00 37 |
| 35 | 18 56 | 23 10 | 07 24 | 07 31 | 00 49 |
| 36 | 18 46 | 23 07 | 07 55 | 07 56 | 01 02 |
| 37 | 18 37 | 23 02 | 08 29 | 08 23 | 01 15 |
| 38 | 18 27 | 22 58 | 09 04 | 08 51 | 01 28 |
| 39 | 18 17 | 22 54 | 09 41 | 09 19 | 01 42 |
| 40 | 18 06 | 22 49 | 10 20 | 09 49 | 01 56 |
| 41 | 17 55 | 22 44 | 11 02 | 10 20 | 02 11 |
| 42 | 17 44 | 22 39 | 11 46 | 10 52 | 02 26 |
| 43 | 17 32 | 22 33 | 12 33 | 11 25 | 02 42 |
| 44 | 17 19 | 22 27 | 13 23 | 12 00 | 02 58 |
| 45 | 17 06 | 22 21 | 14 16 | 12 37 | 03 15 |
| 46 | 16 52 | 22 14 | 15 13 | 13 15 | 03 33 |
| 47 | 16 38 | 22 07 | 16 14 | 13 55 | 03 52 |
| 48 | 16 23 | 21 59 | 17 20 | 14 38 | 04 11 |
| 49 | 16 07 | 21 51 | 18 31 | 15 22 | 04 32 |
| 50 | 15 50 | 21 42 | 19 47 | 16 09 | 04 53 |
| 51 | 15 32 | 21 33 | 21 10 | 16 59 | 05 16 |
| 52 | 15 13 | 21 22 | 22 41 | 17 52 | 05 40 |
| 53 | 14 53 | 21 11 | 24 19 | 18 48 | 06 05 |
| 54 | 14 31 | 20 58 | 26 07 | 19 48 | 06 32 |
| 55 | 14 08 | 20 45 | 28 05 | 20 52 | 07 00 |
| 56 | 13 43 | 20 29 | 00♊15 | 22 01 | 07 31 |
| 57 | 13 16 | 20 13 | 02 38 | 23 15 | 08 03 |
| 58 | 12 47 | 19 54 | 05 16 | 24 35 | 08 38 |
| 59 | 12 15 | 19 32 | 08 10 | 26 03 | 09 17 |
| 60 | 11♒40 | 19♓08 | 11♊23 | 27♊38 | 09♋58 |

# Placidus Table of Houses for Latitudes 0° to 60° North

19h 44m 0s — 296° 0' 0" — 24 ♑ 06

| LAT. | 11 | 12 | ASC | 2 | 3 |
|---|---|---|---|---|---|
| 0 | 23♒41 | 25♓38 | 28♈00 | 28♉15 | 26♊20 |
| 5 | 23 15 | 25 32 | 29 02 | 29 25 | 27 00 |
| 10 | 22 49 | 25 24 | 00♉10 | 00♊39 | 27 40 |
| 15 | 22 21 | 25 17 | 01 24 | 01 57 | 28 22 |
| 20 | 21 52 | 25 08 | 02 49 | 03 20 | 29 06 |
| 21 | 21 46 | 25 06 | 03 07 | 03 38 | 29 16 |
| 22 | 21 39 | 25 04 | 03 26 | 03 56 | 29 25 |
| 23 | 21 33 | 25 02 | 03 46 | 04 14 | 29 34 |
| 24 | 21 26 | 25 00 | 04 06 | 04 33 | 29 44 |
| 25 | 21 20 | 24 58 | 04 27 | 04 52 | 29 54 |
| 26 | 21 13 | 24 56 | 04 49 | 05 11 | 00♋04 |
| 27 | 21 06 | 24 53 | 05 11 | 05 32 | 00 14 |
| 28 | 20 58 | 24 51 | 05 34 | 05 52 | 00 24 |
| 29 | 20 51 | 24 49 | 05 58 | 06 13 | 00 35 |
| 30 | 20 43 | 24 46 | 06 23 | 06 35 | 00 46 |
| 31 | 20 36 | 24 44 | 06 49 | 06 57 | 00 57 |
| 32 | 20 28 | 24 41 | 07 17 | 07 20 | 01 08 |
| 33 | 20 19 | 24 38 | 07 45 | 07 43 | 01 20 |
| 34 | 20 11 | 24 35 | 08 15 | 08 07 | 01 32 |
| 35 | 20 02 | 24 32 | 08 46 | 08 32 | 01 44 |
| 36 | 19 53 | 24 29 | 09 18 | 08 58 | 01 57 |
| 37 | 19 44 | 24 26 | 09 52 | 09 25 | 02 10 |
| 38 | 19 34 | 24 22 | 10 28 | 09 52 | 02 23 |
| 39 | 19 24 | 24 19 | 11 06 | 10 21 | 02 37 |
| 40 | 19 14 | 24 15 | 11 46 | 10 51 | 02 51 |
| 41 | 19 03 | 24 11 | 12 29 | 11 22 | 03 05 |
| 42 | 18 52 | 24 07 | 13 14 | 11 54 | 03 21 |
| 43 | 18 40 | 24 02 | 14 01 | 12 27 | 03 36 |
| 44 | 18 28 | 23 57 | 14 52 | 13 02 | 03 53 |
| 45 | 18 15 | 23 52 | 15 46 | 13 39 | 04 10 |
| 46 | 18 01 | 23 47 | 16 44 | 14 17 | 04 28 |
| 47 | 17 47 | 23 41 | 17 46 | 14 57 | 04 46 |
| 48 | 17 32 | 23 35 | 18 53 | 15 40 | 05 06 |
| 49 | 17 17 | 23 29 | 20 04 | 16 24 | 05 26 |
| 50 | 17 00 | 23 21 | 21 22 | 17 11 | 05 47 |
| 51 | 16 43 | 23 14 | 22 46 | 18 01 | 06 10 |
| 52 | 16 24 | 23 05 | 24 16 | 18 53 | 06 33 |
| 53 | 16 04 | 22 56 | 25 55 | 19 49 | 06 58 |
| 54 | 15 43 | 22 46 | 27 43 | 20 49 | 07 25 |
| 55 | 15 21 | 22 35 | 29 41 | 21 53 | 07 53 |
| 56 | 14 56 | 22 23 | 01♊50 | 23 01 | 08 24 |
| 57 | 14 30 | 22 09 | 04 12 | 24 15 | 08 56 |
| 58 | 14 01 | 21 54 | 06 48 | 25 34 | 09 31 |
| 59 | 13 30 | 21 37 | 09 40 | 27 00 | 10 09 |
| 60 | 12♒55 | 21♓17 | 12♊50 | 28♊34 | 10♋50 |

19h 48m 0s — 297° 0' 0" — 25 ♑ 03

| LAT. | 11 | 12 | ASC | 2 | 3 |
|---|---|---|---|---|---|
| 0 | 24♒42 | 26♓44 | 29♈03 | 29♉13 | 27♊15 |
| 5 | 24 18 | 26 39 | 00♉07 | 00♊24 | 27 55 |
| 10 | 23 52 | 26 33 | 01 17 | 01 38 | 28 35 |
| 15 | 23 25 | 26 27 | 02 34 | 02 56 | 29 17 |
| 20 | 22 56 | 26 21 | 04 01 | 04 20 | 00♋02 |
| 21 | 22 50 | 26 19 | 04 20 | 04 38 | 00 11 |
| 22 | 22 44 | 26 18 | 04 39 | 04 56 | 00 20 |
| 23 | 22 38 | 26 16 | 05 00 | 05 14 | 00 29 |
| 24 | 22 31 | 26 15 | 05 20 | 05 33 | 00 39 |
| 25 | 22 25 | 26 13 | 05 42 | 05 52 | 00 49 |
| 26 | 22 18 | 26 12 | 06 04 | 06 12 | 00 59 |
| 27 | 22 11 | 26 10 | 06 27 | 06 32 | 01 09 |
| 28 | 22 04 | 26 08 | 06 51 | 06 53 | 01 19 |
| 29 | 21 57 | 26 06 | 07 15 | 07 14 | 01 30 |
| 30 | 21 49 | 26 05 | 07 41 | 07 36 | 01 41 |
| 31 | 21 42 | 26 03 | 08 08 | 07 58 | 01 52 |
| 32 | 21 34 | 26 01 | 08 36 | 08 21 | 02 03 |
| 33 | 21 26 | 25 59 | 09 05 | 08 44 | 02 15 |
| 34 | 21 17 | 25 56 | 09 35 | 09 09 | 02 27 |
| 35 | 21 09 | 25 54 | 10 07 | 09 34 | 02 39 |
| 36 | 21 00 | 25 52 | 10 40 | 10 00 | 02 51 |
| 37 | 20 51 | 25 49 | 11 15 | 10 26 | 03 04 |
| 38 | 20 41 | 25 47 | 11 52 | 10 54 | 03 18 |
| 39 | 20 32 | 25 44 | 12 31 | 11 23 | 03 31 |
| 40 | 20 21 | 25 41 | 13 12 | 11 52 | 03 45 |
| 41 | 20 11 | 25 38 | 13 55 | 12 23 | 04 00 |
| 42 | 20 00 | 25 35 | 14 40 | 12 55 | 04 15 |
| 43 | 19 48 | 25 32 | 15 29 | 13 29 | 04 31 |
| 44 | 19 36 | 25 28 | 16 20 | 14 04 | 04 47 |
| 45 | 19 24 | 25 24 | 17 15 | 14 41 | 05 04 |
| 46 | 19 11 | 25 20 | 18 14 | 15 19 | 05 22 |
| 47 | 18 57 | 25 16 | 19 17 | 15 59 | 05 40 |
| 48 | 18 42 | 25 11 | 20 24 | 16 41 | 06 00 |
| 49 | 18 27 | 25 06 | 21 36 | 17 25 | 06 20 |
| 50 | 18 11 | 25 01 | 22 54 | 18 12 | 06 41 |
| 51 | 17 54 | 24 55 | 24 19 | 19 02 | 07 03 |
| 52 | 17 35 | 24 49 | 25 50 | 19 54 | 07 27 |
| 53 | 17 16 | 24 42 | 27 29 | 20 50 | 07 52 |
| 54 | 16 55 | 24 34 | 29 17 | 21 49 | 08 18 |
| 55 | 16 33 | 24 26 | 01♊14 | 22 52 | 08 46 |
| 56 | 16 09 | 24 17 | 03 23 | 24 00 | 09 16 |
| 57 | 15 44 | 24 07 | 05 43 | 25 13 | 09 49 |
| 58 | 15 15 | 23 55 | 08 18 | 26 32 | 10 23 |
| 59 | 14 45 | 23 42 | 11 07 | 27 57 | 11 01 |
| 60 | 14♒11 | 23♓28 | 14♊13 | 29♊30 | 11♋41 |

19h 52m 0s — 298° 0' 0" — 26 ♑ 00

| LAT. | 11 | 12 | ASC | 2 | 3 |
|---|---|---|---|---|---|
| 0 | 25♒44 | 27♓49 | 00♉06 | 00♊11 | 28♊10 |
| 5 | 25 20 | 27 46 | 01 12 | 01 22 | 28 50 |
| 10 | 24 55 | 27 42 | 02 24 | 02 37 | 29 30 |
| 15 | 24 29 | 27 38 | 03 43 | 03 55 | 00♋12 |
| 20 | 24 01 | 27 34 | 05 13 | 05 20 | 00 57 |
| 21 | 23 55 | 27 33 | 05 32 | 05 38 | 01 06 |
| 22 | 23 49 | 27 32 | 05 52 | 05 56 | 01 15 |
| 23 | 23 43 | 27 31 | 06 13 | 06 15 | 01 24 |
| 24 | 23 36 | 27 30 | 06 34 | 06 33 | 01 34 |
| 25 | 23 30 | 27 29 | 06 56 | 06 53 | 01 44 |
| 26 | 23 23 | 27 28 | 07 19 | 07 12 | 01 54 |
| 27 | 23 17 | 27 27 | 07 42 | 07 33 | 02 04 |
| 28 | 23 10 | 27 25 | 08 07 | 07 53 | 02 14 |
| 29 | 23 03 | 27 24 | 08 32 | 08 15 | 02 25 |
| 30 | 22 55 | 27 23 | 08 58 | 08 36 | 02 36 |
| 31 | 22 48 | 27 22 | 09 26 | 08 59 | 02 47 |
| 32 | 22 40 | 27 20 | 09 54 | 09 22 | 02 58 |
| 33 | 22 32 | 27 19 | 10 24 | 09 45 | 03 10 |
| 34 | 22 24 | 27 18 | 10 55 | 10 10 | 03 21 |
| 35 | 22 16 | 27 16 | 11 27 | 10 35 | 03 34 |
| 36 | 22 07 | 27 14 | 12 01 | 11 01 | 03 46 |
| 37 | 21 58 | 27 13 | 12 37 | 11 27 | 03 59 |
| 38 | 21 49 | 27 11 | 13 15 | 11 55 | 04 12 |
| 39 | 21 39 | 27 09 | 13 54 | 12 24 | 04 26 |
| 40 | 21 29 | 27 07 | 14 36 | 12 54 | 04 40 |
| 41 | 21 19 | 27 05 | 15 19 | 13 25 | 04 55 |
| 42 | 21 08 | 27 03 | 16 06 | 13 57 | 05 10 |
| 43 | 20 57 | 27 01 | 16 55 | 14 30 | 05 25 |
| 44 | 20 45 | 26 59 | 17 47 | 15 05 | 05 42 |
| 45 | 20 33 | 26 56 | 18 43 | 15 42 | 05 58 |
| 46 | 20 20 | 26 53 | 19 42 | 16 20 | 06 16 |
| 47 | 20 07 | 26 50 | 20 46 | 17 00 | 06 34 |
| 48 | 19 53 | 26 47 | 21 54 | 17 42 | 06 54 |
| 49 | 19 38 | 26 44 | 23 07 | 18 26 | 07 14 |
| 50 | 19 22 | 26 41 | 24 25 | 19 13 | 07 35 |
| 51 | 19 05 | 26 37 | 25 50 | 20 02 | 07 57 |
| 52 | 18 47 | 26 32 | 27 21 | 20 54 | 08 20 |
| 53 | 18 28 | 26 28 | 29 00 | 21 50 | 08 45 |
| 54 | 18 08 | 26 23 | 00♊48 | 22 48 | 09 11 |
| 55 | 17 46 | 26 17 | 02 45 | 23 51 | 09 39 |
| 56 | 17 23 | 26 11 | 04 53 | 24 59 | 10 09 |
| 57 | 16 58 | 26 04 | 07 12 | 26 11 | 10 41 |
| 58 | 16 30 | 25 57 | 09 44 | 27 29 | 11 15 |
| 59 | 16 01 | 25 48 | 12 31 | 28 54 | 11 52 |
| 60 | 15♒28 | 25♓38 | 15♊34 | 00♋25 | 12♋32 |

19h 56m 0s — 299° 0' 0" — 26 ♑ 57

| LAT. | 11 | 12 | ASC | 2 | 3 |
|---|---|---|---|---|---|
| 0 | 26♒47 | 28♓55 | 01♉08 | 01♊08 | 29♊05 |
| 5 | 26 23 | 28 53 | 02 17 | 02 20 | 29 45 |
| 10 | 25 59 | 28 51 | 03 30 | 03 35 | 00♋25 |
| 15 | 25 33 | 28 49 | 04 52 | 04 55 | 01 07 |
| 20 | 25 06 | 28 47 | 06 24 | 06 20 | 01 52 |
| 21 | 25 00 | 28 46 | 06 44 | 06 38 | 02 01 |
| 22 | 24 54 | 28 46 | 07 04 | 06 56 | 02 10 |
| 23 | 24 48 | 28 45 | 07 26 | 07 14 | 02 19 |
| 24 | 24 42 | 28 45 | 07 47 | 07 33 | 02 29 |
| 25 | 24 35 | 28 44 | 08 10 | 07 53 | 02 39 |
| 26 | 24 29 | 28 44 | 08 33 | 08 13 | 02 49 |
| 27 | 24 22 | 28 43 | 08 57 | 08 33 | 02 59 |
| 28 | 24 16 | 28 43 | 09 22 | 08 54 | 03 09 |
| 29 | 24 09 | 28 42 | 09 48 | 09 15 | 03 20 |
| 30 | 24 02 | 28 41 | 10 15 | 09 37 | 03 30 |
| 31 | 23 54 | 28 41 | 10 43 | 09 59 | 03 41 |
| 32 | 23 47 | 28 40 | 11 12 | 10 22 | 03 53 |
| 33 | 23 39 | 28 39 | 11 42 | 10 46 | 04 04 |
| 34 | 23 31 | 28 39 | 12 14 | 11 10 | 04 16 |
| 35 | 23 23 | 28 38 | 12 47 | 11 35 | 04 28 |
| 36 | 23 15 | 28 37 | 13 22 | 12 01 | 04 41 |
| 37 | 23 06 | 28 36 | 13 58 | 12 28 | 04 54 |
| 38 | 22 57 | 28 36 | 14 36 | 12 56 | 05 07 |
| 39 | 22 48 | 28 35 | 15 16 | 13 25 | 05 20 |
| 40 | 22 38 | 28 34 | 15 59 | 13 54 | 05 34 |
| 41 | 22 28 | 28 33 | 16 43 | 14 25 | 05 49 |
| 42 | 22 17 | 28 32 | 17 30 | 14 57 | 06 04 |
| 43 | 22 06 | 28 30 | 18 20 | 15 31 | 06 20 |
| 44 | 21 55 | 28 29 | 19 13 | 16 06 | 06 36 |
| 45 | 21 43 | 28 28 | 20 09 | 16 42 | 06 53 |
| 46 | 21 30 | 28 27 | 21 09 | 17 20 | 07 10 |
| 47 | 21 17 | 28 25 | 22 13 | 18 00 | 07 28 |
| 48 | 21 03 | 28 24 | 23 22 | 18 42 | 07 48 |
| 49 | 20 49 | 28 22 | 24 35 | 19 26 | 08 08 |
| 50 | 20 33 | 28 20 | 25 54 | 20 13 | 08 28 |
| 51 | 20 17 | 28 18 | 27 19 | 21 02 | 08 51 |
| 52 | 19 59 | 28 16 | 28 50 | 21 54 | 09 14 |
| 53 | 19 41 | 28 14 | 00♊29 | 22 49 | 09 38 |
| 54 | 19 21 | 28 11 | 02 17 | 23 47 | 10 04 |
| 55 | 19 00 | 28 09 | 04 13 | 24 50 | 10 32 |
| 56 | 18 37 | 28 06 | 06 20 | 25 57 | 11 02 |
| 57 | 18 13 | 28 02 | 08 38 | 27 08 | 11 33 |
| 58 | 17 46 | 27 58 | 11 08 | 28 26 | 12 07 |
| 59 | 17 17 | 27 54 | 13 52 | 29 49 | 12 44 |
| 60 | 16♒45 | 27♓49 | 16♊51 | 01♋20 | 13♋23 |

20h 0m 0s — 300° 0' 0" — 27 ♑ 55

| LAT. | 11 | 12 | ASC | 2 | 3 |
|---|---|---|---|---|---|
| 0 | 27♒49 | 00♈00 | 02♉11 | 02♊05 | 00♋00 |
| 5 | 27 26 | 00 00 | 03 21 | 03 18 | 00 40 |
| 10 | 27 02 | 00 00 | 04 37 | 04 34 | 01 20 |
| 15 | 26 37 | 00 00 | 06 01 | 05 53 | 02 02 |
| 20 | 26 11 | 00 00 | 07 35 | 07 19 | 02 46 |
| 21 | 26 05 | 00 00 | 07 55 | 07 37 | 02 56 |
| 22 | 25 59 | 00 00 | 08 16 | 07 55 | 03 05 |
| 23 | 25 53 | 00 00 | 08 38 | 08 14 | 03 14 |
| 24 | 25 47 | 00 00 | 09 00 | 08 33 | 03 24 |
| 25 | 25 41 | 00 00 | 09 23 | 08 52 | 03 34 |
| 26 | 25 35 | 00 00 | 09 47 | 09 12 | 03 44 |
| 27 | 25 28 | 00 00 | 10 12 | 09 33 | 03 54 |
| 28 | 25 22 | 00 00 | 10 37 | 09 53 | 04 04 |
| 29 | 25 15 | 00 00 | 11 04 | 10 15 | 04 14 |
| 30 | 25 08 | 00 00 | 11 31 | 10 37 | 04 25 |
| 31 | 25 01 | 00 00 | 12 00 | 10 59 | 04 36 |
| 32 | 24 54 | 00 00 | 12 29 | 11 22 | 04 47 |
| 33 | 24 46 | 00 00 | 13 00 | 11 46 | 04 59 |
| 34 | 24 39 | 00 00 | 13 32 | 12 10 | 05 11 |
| 35 | 24 31 | 00 00 | 14 06 | 12 36 | 05 23 |
| 36 | 24 22 | 00 00 | 14 41 | 13 02 | 05 35 |
| 37 | 24 14 | 00 00 | 15 18 | 13 28 | 05 48 |
| 38 | 24 05 | 00 00 | 15 57 | 13 56 | 06 01 |
| 39 | 23 56 | 00 00 | 16 38 | 14 25 | 06 15 |
| 40 | 23 47 | 00 00 | 17 21 | 14 55 | 06 29 |
| 41 | 23 37 | 00 00 | 18 06 | 15 26 | 06 43 |
| 42 | 23 26 | 00 00 | 18 54 | 15 58 | 06 58 |
| 43 | 23 16 | 00 00 | 19 44 | 16 31 | 07 14 |
| 44 | 23 05 | 00 00 | 20 38 | 17 06 | 07 30 |
| 45 | 22 53 | 00 00 | 21 35 | 17 42 | 07 47 |
| 46 | 22 41 | 00 00 | 22 35 | 18 20 | 08 04 |
| 47 | 22 28 | 00 00 | 23 39 | 19 00 | 08 22 |
| 48 | 22 14 | 00 00 | 24 48 | 19 42 | 08 41 |
| 49 | 22 00 | 00 00 | 26 02 | 20 26 | 09 01 |
| 50 | 21 45 | 00 00 | 27 21 | 21 12 | 09 22 |
| 51 | 21 29 | 00 00 | 28 46 | 22 01 | 09 44 |
| 52 | 21 12 | 00 00 | 00♊18 | 22 53 | 10 07 |
| 53 | 20 54 | 00 00 | 01 56 | 23 47 | 10 31 |
| 54 | 20 35 | 00 00 | 03 43 | 24 46 | 10 57 |
| 55 | 20 14 | 00 00 | 05 39 | 25 48 | 11 25 |
| 56 | 19 52 | 00 00 | 07 44 | 26 54 | 11 54 |
| 57 | 19 28 | 00 00 | 10 01 | 28 05 | 12 25 |
| 58 | 19 02 | 00 00 | 12 29 | 29 21 | 12 59 |
| 59 | 18 34 | 00 00 | 15 11 | 00♋44 | 13 35 |
| 60 | 18♒02 | 00♈00 | 18♊06 | 02♋13 | 14♋14 |

20h 4m 0s — 301° 0' 0" — 28 ♑ 52

| LAT. | 11 | 12 | ASC | 2 | 3 |
|---|---|---|---|---|---|
| 0 | 28♒52 | 01♈05 | 03♉13 | 03♊03 | 00♋55 |
| 5 | 28 29 | 01 07 | 04 25 | 04 16 | 01 35 |
| 10 | 28 06 | 01 09 | 05 43 | 05 32 | 02 15 |
| 15 | 27 42 | 01 11 | 07 09 | 06 52 | 02 57 |
| 20 | 27 16 | 01 13 | 08 45 | 08 18 | 03 41 |
| 21 | 27 10 | 01 14 | 09 06 | 08 36 | 03 50 |
| 22 | 27 05 | 01 14 | 09 28 | 08 54 | 04 00 |
| 23 | 26 59 | 01 15 | 09 50 | 09 13 | 04 09 |
| 24 | 26 53 | 01 15 | 10 13 | 09 32 | 04 19 |
| 25 | 26 47 | 01 16 | 10 36 | 09 52 | 04 28 |
| 26 | 26 41 | 01 16 | 11 00 | 10 12 | 04 38 |
| 27 | 26 35 | 01 17 | 11 26 | 10 32 | 04 48 |
| 28 | 26 28 | 01 17 | 11 52 | 10 53 | 04 59 |
| 29 | 26 22 | 01 18 | 12 19 | 11 14 | 05 09 |
| 30 | 26 15 | 01 19 | 12 46 | 11 36 | 05 20 |
| 31 | 26 08 | 01 19 | 13 16 | 11 59 | 05 31 |
| 32 | 26 01 | 01 20 | 13 46 | 12 22 | 05 42 |
| 33 | 25 54 | 01 21 | 14 17 | 12 46 | 05 53 |
| 34 | 25 46 | 01 21 | 14 50 | 13 10 | 06 05 |
| 35 | 25 39 | 01 22 | 15 24 | 13 35 | 06 17 |
| 36 | 25 31 | 01 23 | 16 00 | 14 01 | 06 30 |
| 37 | 25 22 | 01 24 | 16 38 | 14 28 | 06 42 |
| 38 | 25 14 | 01 24 | 17 17 | 14 56 | 06 56 |
| 39 | 25 05 | 01 25 | 17 58 | 15 25 | 07 09 |
| 40 | 24 56 | 01 26 | 18 42 | 15 55 | 07 23 |
| 41 | 24 46 | 01 27 | 19 28 | 16 26 | 07 37 |
| 42 | 24 36 | 01 28 | 20 16 | 16 58 | 07 52 |
| 43 | 24 26 | 01 30 | 21 07 | 17 31 | 08 08 |
| 44 | 24 15 | 01 31 | 22 01 | 18 06 | 08 24 |
| 45 | 24 03 | 01 32 | 22 58 | 18 42 | 08 41 |
| 46 | 23 51 | 01 33 | 23 59 | 19 20 | 08 58 |
| 47 | 23 39 | 01 35 | 25 04 | 20 00 | 09 16 |
| 48 | 23 26 | 01 36 | 26 13 | 20 41 | 09 35 |
| 49 | 23 12 | 01 38 | 27 27 | 21 25 | 09 55 |
| 50 | 22 57 | 01 40 | 28 47 | 22 11 | 10 15 |
| 51 | 22 42 | 01 42 | 00♊12 | 23 00 | 10 37 |
| 52 | 22 25 | 01 44 | 01 43 | 23 51 | 11 00 |
| 53 | 22 08 | 01 46 | 03 21 | 24 46 | 11 24 |
| 54 | 21 49 | 01 49 | 05 08 | 25 43 | 11 50 |
| 55 | 21 29 | 01 51 | 07 03 | 26 45 | 12 17 |
| 56 | 21 07 | 01 54 | 09 07 | 27 51 | 12 46 |
| 57 | 20 44 | 01 58 | 11 22 | 29 01 | 13 17 |
| 58 | 20 18 | 02 02 | 13 48 | 00♋17 | 13 50 |
| 59 | 19 51 | 02 06 | 16 26 | 01 38 | 14 26 |
| 60 | 19♒21 | 02♈11 | 19♊18 | 03♋06 | 15♋05 |

20h 8m 0s — 302° 0' 0" — 29 ♑ 49

| LAT. | 11 | 12 | ASC | 2 | 3 |
|---|---|---|---|---|---|
| 0 | 29♒54 | 02♈11 | 04♉16 | 04♊00 | 01♋50 |
| 5 | 29 33 | 02 14 | 05 29 | 05 14 | 02 30 |
| 10 | 29 10 | 02 18 | 06 49 | 06 30 | 03 10 |
| 15 | 28 47 | 02 22 | 08 17 | 07 51 | 03 52 |
| 20 | 28 21 | 02 26 | 09 56 | 09 17 | 04 36 |
| 21 | 28 16 | 02 27 | 10 17 | 09 35 | 04 45 |
| 22 | 28 10 | 02 28 | 10 39 | 09 53 | 04 55 |
| 23 | 28 05 | 02 29 | 11 01 | 10 12 | 05 04 |
| 24 | 27 59 | 02 30 | 11 25 | 10 31 | 05 14 |
| 25 | 27 53 | 02 31 | 11 49 | 10 51 | 05 23 |
| 26 | 27 47 | 02 32 | 12 13 | 11 11 | 05 33 |
| 27 | 27 41 | 02 33 | 12 39 | 11 31 | 05 43 |
| 28 | 27 35 | 02 35 | 13 05 | 11 52 | 05 53 |
| 29 | 27 29 | 02 36 | 13 33 | 12 14 | 06 04 |
| 30 | 27 22 | 02 37 | 14 01 | 12 36 | 06 15 |
| 31 | 27 16 | 02 38 | 14 31 | 12 58 | 06 25 |
| 32 | 27 09 | 02 40 | 15 02 | 13 22 | 06 37 |
| 33 | 27 02 | 02 41 | 15 34 | 13 45 | 06 48 |
| 34 | 26 54 | 02 42 | 16 07 | 14 10 | 07 00 |
| 35 | 26 47 | 02 44 | 16 42 | 14 35 | 07 12 |
| 36 | 26 39 | 02 46 | 17 18 | 15 01 | 07 24 |
| 37 | 26 31 | 02 47 | 17 56 | 15 28 | 07 37 |
| 38 | 26 23 | 02 49 | 18 36 | 15 56 | 07 50 |
| 39 | 26 14 | 02 51 | 19 18 | 16 24 | 08 03 |
| 40 | 26 05 | 02 53 | 20 02 | 16 54 | 08 17 |
| 41 | 25 56 | 02 55 | 20 48 | 17 25 | 08 32 |
| 42 | 25 46 | 02 57 | 21 37 | 17 57 | 08 46 |
| 43 | 25 36 | 02 59 | 22 28 | 18 30 | 09 02 |
| 44 | 25 25 | 03 01 | 23 23 | 19 05 | 09 18 |
| 45 | 25 14 | 03 04 | 24 21 | 19 41 | 09 34 |
| 46 | 25 02 | 03 07 | 25 22 | 20 19 | 09 52 |
| 47 | 24 50 | 03 10 | 26 27 | 20 59 | 10 10 |
| 48 | 24 37 | 03 13 | 27 37 | 21 40 | 10 28 |
| 49 | 24 24 | 03 16 | 28 51 | 22 24 | 10 48 |
| 50 | 24 10 | 03 19 | 00♊10 | 23 10 | 11 09 |
| 51 | 23 55 | 03 23 | 01 35 | 23 58 | 11 30 |
| 52 | 23 39 | 03 28 | 03 06 | 24 49 | 11 53 |
| 53 | 23 21 | 03 32 | 04 44 | 25 43 | 12 17 |
| 54 | 23 03 | 03 37 | 06 30 | 26 40 | 12 42 |
| 55 | 22 44 | 03 43 | 08 24 | 27 42 | 13 09 |
| 56 | 22 23 | 03 49 | 10 27 | 28 47 | 13 38 |
| 57 | 22 00 | 03 56 | 12 40 | 29 56 | 14 09 |
| 58 | 21 35 | 04 03 | 15 04 | 01♋11 | 14 42 |
| 59 | 21 09 | 04 12 | 17 40 | 02 32 | 15 17 |
| 60 | 20♒39 | 04♈22 | 20♊29 | 03♋59 | 15♋56 |

20h 12m 0s — 303° 0' 0" — 00 ♒ 47

| LAT. | 11 | 12 | ASC | 2 | 3 |
|---|---|---|---|---|---|
| 0 | 00♓57 | 03♈16 | 05♉18 | 04♊57 | 02♋45 |
| 5 | 00 36 | 03 21 | 06 33 | 06 11 | 03 25 |
| 10 | 00 15 | 03 27 | 07 55 | 07 28 | 04 05 |
| 15 | 29♒52 | 03 33 | 09 25 | 08 49 | 04 47 |
| 20 | 29 27 | 03 39 | 11 05 | 10 15 | 05 31 |
| 21 | 29 22 | 03 41 | 11 27 | 10 34 | 05 40 |
| 22 | 29 16 | 03 42 | 11 49 | 10 52 | 05 49 |
| 23 | 29 11 | 03 44 | 12 12 | 11 11 | 05 59 |
| 24 | 29 06 | 03 45 | 12 36 | 11 30 | 06 08 |
| 25 | 29 00 | 03 47 | 13 00 | 11 50 | 06 18 |
| 26 | 28 54 | 03 48 | 13 26 | 12 10 | 06 28 |
| 27 | 28 48 | 03 50 | 13 52 | 12 30 | 06 38 |
| 28 | 28 42 | 03 52 | 14 19 | 12 51 | 06 48 |
| 29 | 28 36 | 03 54 | 14 47 | 13 13 | 06 58 |
| 30 | 28 30 | 03 55 | 15 16 | 13 35 | 07 09 |
| 31 | 28 23 | 03 57 | 15 46 | 13 58 | 07 20 |
| 32 | 28 16 | 03 59 | 16 17 | 14 21 | 07 31 |
| 33 | 28 10 | 04 01 | 16 49 | 14 45 | 07 43 |
| 34 | 28 02 | 04 04 | 17 23 | 15 09 | 07 54 |
| 35 | 27 55 | 04 06 | 17 58 | 15 34 | 08 06 |
| 36 | 27 48 | 04 08 | 18 35 | 16 00 | 08 18 |
| 37 | 27 40 | 04 11 | 19 14 | 16 27 | 08 31 |
| 38 | 27 32 | 04 13 | 19 54 | 16 55 | 08 44 |
| 39 | 27 23 | 04 16 | 20 37 | 17 24 | 08 58 |
| 40 | 27 15 | 04 19 | 21 21 | 17 53 | 09 11 |
| 41 | 27 05 | 04 22 | 22 08 | 18 24 | 09 26 |
| 42 | 26 56 | 04 25 | 22 57 | 18 56 | 09 40 |
| 43 | 26 46 | 04 28 | 23 49 | 19 29 | 09 56 |
| 44 | 26 36 | 04 32 | 24 44 | 20 04 | 10 12 |
| 45 | 26 25 | 04 36 | 25 42 | 20 40 | 10 28 |
| 46 | 26 14 | 04 40 | 26 44 | 21 18 | 10 45 |
| 47 | 26 02 | 04 44 | 27 49 | 21 57 | 11 03 |
| 48 | 25 50 | 04 49 | 28 59 | 22 39 | 11 22 |
| 49 | 25 36 | 04 54 | 00♊13 | 23 22 | 11 41 |
| 50 | 25 23 | 04 59 | 01 32 | 24 08 | 12 02 |
| 51 | 25 08 | 05 05 | 02 57 | 24 56 | 12 23 |
| 52 | 24 52 | 05 11 | 04 28 | 25 46 | 12 46 |
| 53 | 24 36 | 05 18 | 06 06 | 26 40 | 13 10 |
| 54 | 24 18 | 05 26 | 07 51 | 27 37 | 13 35 |
| 55 | 23 59 | 05 34 | 09 44 | 28 38 | 14 02 |
| 56 | 23 39 | 05 43 | 11 45 | 29 42 | 14 30 |
| 57 | 23 17 | 05 53 | 13 57 | 00♋51 | 15 00 |
| 58 | 22 53 | 06 05 | 16 19 | 02 05 | 15 33 |
| 59 | 22 27 | 06 18 | 18 52 | 03 25 | 16 08 |
| 60 | 21♒59 | 06♈32 | 21♊37 | 04♋51 | 16♋46 |

# Placidus Table of Houses for Latitudes 0° to 60° North

20h 16m 0s — 304° 0' 0" — 01 ♒ 45

| LAT. | 11 | 12 | ASC | 2 | 3 |
|---|---|---|---|---|---|
| 0 | 02♓00 | 04♈22 | 06♉19 | 05♊54 | 03♋40 |
| 5 | 01 40 | 04 28 | 07 37 | 07 08 | 04 20 |
| 10 | 01 19 | 04 36 | 09 00 | 08 26 | 05 00 |
| 15 | 00 57 | 04 43 | 10 32 | 09 47 | 05 42 |
| 20 | 00 33 | 04 52 | 12 15 | 11 14 | 06 26 |
| 21 | 00 28 | 04 54 | 12 37 | 11 32 | 06 35 |
| 22 | 00 23 | 04 56 | 13 00 | 11 51 | 06 44 |
| 23 | 00 17 | 04 58 | 13 23 | 12 10 | 06 54 |
| 24 | 00 12 | 05 00 | 13 47 | 12 29 | 07 03 |
| 25 | 00 07 | 05 02 | 14 12 | 12 49 | 07 13 |
| 26 | 00 01 | 05 04 | 14 38 | 13 09 | 07 22 |
| 27 | 29♒55 | 05 07 | 15 04 | 13 29 | 07 32 |
| 28 | 29 49 | 05 09 | 15 32 | 13 50 | 07 43 |
| 29 | 29 43 | 05 11 | 16 00 | 14 12 | 07 53 |
| 30 | 29 37 | 05 14 | 16 29 | 14 34 | 08 04 |
| 31 | 29 31 | 05 16 | 17 00 | 14 56 | 08 15 |
| 32 | 29 25 | 05 19 | 17 31 | 15 20 | 08 26 |
| 33 | 29 18 | 05 22 | 18 04 | 15 43 | 08 37 |
| 34 | 29 11 | 05 25 | 18 39 | 16 08 | 08 49 |
| 35 | 29 04 | 05 28 | 19 14 | 16 33 | 09 00 |
| 36 | 28 57 | 05 31 | 19 52 | 16 59 | 09 13 |
| 37 | 28 49 | 05 34 | 20 31 | 17 26 | 09 25 |
| 38 | 28 41 | 05 38 | 21 12 | 17 54 | 09 38 |
| 39 | 28 33 | 05 41 | 21 54 | 18 22 | 09 52 |
| 40 | 28 24 | 05 45 | 22 39 | 18 52 | 10 05 |
| 41 | 28 16 | 05 49 | 23 26 | 19 23 | 10 20 |
| 42 | 28 06 | 05 53 | 24 16 | 19 55 | 10 34 |
| 43 | 27 57 | 05 58 | 25 08 | 20 28 | 10 50 |
| 44 | 27 47 | 06 03 | 26 03 | 21 03 | 11 05 |
| 45 | 27 37 | 06 08 | 27 02 | 21 39 | 11 22 |
| 46 | 27 26 | 06 13 | 28 04 | 22 16 | 11 39 |
| 47 | 27 14 | 06 19 | 29 09 | 22 56 | 11 57 |
| 48 | 27 02 | 06 25 | 00♊19 | 23 37 | 12 15 |
| 49 | 26 49 | 06 31 | 01 34 | 24 20 | 12 35 |
| 50 | 26 36 | 06 39 | 02 53 | 25 05 | 12 55 |
| 51 | 26 22 | 06 46 | 04 17 | 25 53 | 13 16 |
| 52 | 26 07 | 06 55 | 05 48 | 26 43 | 13 39 |
| 53 | 25 51 | 07 04 | 07 25 | 27 37 | 14 02 |
| 54 | 25 33 | 07 14 | 09 09 | 28 33 | 14 27 |
| 55 | 25 15 | 07 25 | 11 01 | 29 33 | 14 54 |
| 56 | 24 55 | 07 37 | 13 01 | 00♋37 | 15 22 |
| 57 | 24 34 | 07 51 | 15 11 | 01 45 | 15 52 |
| 58 | 24 11 | 08 06 | 17 31 | 02 58 | 16 24 |
| 59 | 23 46 | 08 23 | 20 01 | 04 17 | 16 59 |
| 60 | 23♒18 | 08♈43 | 22♊43 | 05♋42 | 17♋36 |

20h 20m 0s — 305° 0' 0" — 02 ♒ 43

| LAT. | 11 | 12 | ASC | 2 | 3 |
|---|---|---|---|---|---|
| 0 | 03♓03 | 05♈27 | 07♉21 | 06♊50 | 04♋35 |
| 5 | 02 44 | 05 35 | 08 40 | 08 05 | 05 15 |
| 10 | 02 23 | 05 44 | 10 05 | 09 23 | 05 55 |
| 15 | 02 02 | 05 54 | 11 39 | 10 45 | 06 37 |
| 20 | 01 39 | 06 05 | 13 24 | 12 12 | 07 21 |
| 21 | 01 34 | 06 08 | 13 46 | 12 30 | 07 30 |
| 22 | 01 29 | 06 10 | 14 09 | 12 49 | 07 39 |
| 23 | 01 24 | 06 12 | 14 33 | 13 08 | 07 48 |
| 24 | 01 19 | 06 15 | 14 58 | 13 27 | 07 58 |
| 25 | 01 14 | 06 18 | 15 23 | 13 47 | 08 07 |
| 26 | 01 08 | 06 20 | 15 49 | 14 07 | 08 17 |
| 27 | 01 03 | 06 23 | 16 16 | 14 28 | 08 27 |
| 28 | 00 57 | 06 26 | 16 44 | 14 49 | 08 37 |
| 29 | 00 51 | 06 29 | 17 13 | 15 10 | 08 48 |
| 30 | 00 45 | 06 32 | 17 42 | 15 32 | 08 58 |
| 31 | 00 39 | 06 35 | 18 13 | 15 55 | 09 09 |
| 32 | 00 33 | 06 39 | 18 45 | 16 18 | 09 20 |
| 33 | 00 26 | 06 42 | 19 19 | 16 42 | 09 31 |
| 34 | 00 20 | 06 46 | 19 53 | 17 07 | 09 43 |
| 35 | 00 13 | 06 50 | 20 30 | 17 32 | 09 55 |
| 36 | 00 06 | 06 53 | 21 07 | 17 58 | 10 07 |
| 37 | 29♒58 | 06 58 | 21 47 | 18 25 | 10 20 |
| 38 | 29 51 | 07 02 | 22 28 | 18 52 | 10 32 |
| 39 | 29 43 | 07 06 | 23 11 | 19 21 | 10 46 |
| 40 | 29 35 | 07 11 | 23 56 | 19 51 | 10 59 |
| 41 | 29 26 | 07 16 | 24 44 | 20 21 | 11 14 |
| 42 | 29 17 | 07 21 | 25 34 | 20 53 | 11 28 |
| 43 | 29 08 | 07 27 | 26 26 | 21 26 | 11 43 |
| 44 | 28 58 | 07 33 | 27 22 | 22 01 | 11 59 |
| 45 | 28 48 | 07 39 | 28 21 | 22 37 | 12 15 |
| 46 | 28 38 | 07 46 | 29 23 | 23 14 | 12 32 |
| 47 | 28 27 | 07 53 | 00♊28 | 23 53 | 12 50 |
| 48 | 28 15 | 08 01 | 01 38 | 24 34 | 13 08 |
| 49 | 28 03 | 08 09 | 02 53 | 25 17 | 13 28 |
| 50 | 27 50 | 08 18 | 04 12 | 26 02 | 13 48 |
| 51 | 27 36 | 08 27 | 05 36 | 26 50 | 14 09 |
| 52 | 27 21 | 08 38 | 07 06 | 27 40 | 14 31 |
| 53 | 27 06 | 08 49 | 08 43 | 28 33 | 14 55 |
| 54 | 26 49 | 09 02 | 10 26 | 29 29 | 15 19 |
| 55 | 26 31 | 09 15 | 12 17 | 00♋28 | 15 46 |
| 56 | 26 12 | 09 31 | 14 16 | 01 32 | 16 14 |
| 57 | 25 52 | 09 47 | 16 24 | 02 39 | 16 43 |
| 58 | 25 29 | 10 06 | 18 41 | 03 51 | 17 15 |
| 59 | 25 05 | 10 28 | 21 09 | 05 09 | 17 49 |
| 60 | 24♒38 | 10♈52 | 23♊48 | 06♋33 | 18♋26 |

20h 24m 0s — 306° 0' 0" — 03 ♒ 41

| LAT. | 11 | 12 | ASC | 2 | 3 |
|---|---|---|---|---|---|
| 0 | 04♓07 | 06♈32 | 08♉23 | 07♊47 | 05♋30 |
| 5 | 03 48 | 06 42 | 09 43 | 09 02 | 06 10 |
| 10 | 03 28 | 06 53 | 11 10 | 10 20 | 06 50 |
| 15 | 03 07 | 07 05 | 12 46 | 11 42 | 07 32 |
| 20 | 02 45 | 07 18 | 14 32 | 13 10 | 08 15 |
| 21 | 02 40 | 07 21 | 14 55 | 13 28 | 08 25 |
| 22 | 02 36 | 07 24 | 15 19 | 13 47 | 08 34 |
| 23 | 02 31 | 07 27 | 15 43 | 14 06 | 08 43 |
| 24 | 02 26 | 07 30 | 16 08 | 14 25 | 08 52 |
| 25 | 02 21 | 07 33 | 16 33 | 14 45 | 09 02 |
| 26 | 02 16 | 07 36 | 17 00 | 15 05 | 09 12 |
| 27 | 02 10 | 07 40 | 17 27 | 15 26 | 09 22 |
| 28 | 02 05 | 07 43 | 17 55 | 15 47 | 09 32 |
| 29 | 01 59 | 07 47 | 18 25 | 16 09 | 09 42 |
| 30 | 01 53 | 07 50 | 18 55 | 16 31 | 09 53 |
| 31 | 01 47 | 07 54 | 19 26 | 16 53 | 10 03 |
| 32 | 01 41 | 07 58 | 19 59 | 17 16 | 10 14 |
| 33 | 01 35 | 08 02 | 20 32 | 17 40 | 10 26 |
| 34 | 01 29 | 08 07 | 21 08 | 18 05 | 10 37 |
| 35 | 01 22 | 08 11 | 21 44 | 18 30 | 10 49 |
| 36 | 01 15 | 08 16 | 22 22 | 18 56 | 11 01 |
| 37 | 01 08 | 08 21 | 23 02 | 19 23 | 11 14 |
| 38 | 01 01 | 08 26 | 23 44 | 19 51 | 11 27 |
| 39 | 00 53 | 08 31 | 24 27 | 20 19 | 11 40 |
| 40 | 00 45 | 08 37 | 25 13 | 20 49 | 11 53 |
| 41 | 00 37 | 08 43 | 26 00 | 21 19 | 12 07 |
| 42 | 00 28 | 08 49 | 26 51 | 21 51 | 12 22 |
| 43 | 00 19 | 08 56 | 27 44 | 22 24 | 12 37 |
| 44 | 00 10 | 09 03 | 28 39 | 22 58 | 12 53 |
| 45 | 00 00 | 09 11 | 29 38 | 23 34 | 13 09 |
| 46 | 29♒50 | 09 19 | 00♊40 | 24 12 | 13 26 |
| 47 | 29 39 | 09 27 | 01 46 | 24 50 | 13 43 |
| 48 | 29 28 | 09 36 | 02 56 | 25 31 | 14 02 |
| 49 | 29 16 | 09 46 | 04 10 | 26 14 | 14 21 |
| 50 | 29 04 | 09 57 | 05 29 | 26 59 | 14 41 |
| 51 | 28 50 | 10 08 | 06 53 | 27 46 | 15 02 |
| 52 | 28 36 | 10 21 | 08 23 | 28 36 | 15 24 |
| 53 | 28 21 | 10 34 | 09 59 | 29 28 | 15 47 |
| 54 | 28 05 | 10 49 | 11 41 | 00♋24 | 16 11 |
| 55 | 27 48 | 11 06 | 13 31 | 01 23 | 16 37 |
| 56 | 27 30 | 11 24 | 15 28 | 02 25 | 17 05 |
| 57 | 27 10 | 11 44 | 17 34 | 03 32 | 17 35 |
| 58 | 26 48 | 12 07 | 19 50 | 04 44 | 18 06 |
| 59 | 26 25 | 12 32 | 22 15 | 06 00 | 18 40 |
| 60 | 25♒59 | 13♈01 | 24♊50 | 07♋23 | 19♋16 |

20h 28m 0s — 307° 0' 0" — 04 ♒ 39

| LAT. | 11 | 12 | ASC | 2 | 3 |
|---|---|---|---|---|---|
| 0 | 05♓10 | 07♈37 | 09♉24 | 08♊43 | 06♋26 |
| 5 | 04 52 | 07 49 | 10 46 | 09 59 | 07 05 |
| 10 | 04 33 | 08 02 | 12 15 | 11 18 | 07 45 |
| 15 | 04 13 | 08 16 | 13 52 | 12 40 | 08 27 |
| 20 | 03 52 | 08 31 | 15 40 | 14 08 | 09 10 |
| 21 | 03 47 | 08 34 | 16 04 | 14 26 | 09 19 |
| 22 | 03 43 | 08 38 | 16 27 | 14 45 | 09 28 |
| 23 | 03 38 | 08 41 | 16 52 | 15 04 | 09 38 |
| 24 | 03 33 | 08 45 | 17 17 | 15 23 | 09 47 |
| 25 | 03 28 | 08 48 | 17 43 | 15 43 | 09 57 |
| 26 | 03 23 | 08 52 | 18 10 | 16 03 | 10 06 |
| 27 | 03 18 | 08 56 | 18 38 | 16 24 | 10 16 |
| 28 | 03 13 | 09 00 | 19 07 | 16 45 | 10 26 |
| 29 | 03 07 | 09 04 | 19 36 | 17 07 | 10 37 |
| 30 | 03 02 | 09 08 | 20 07 | 17 29 | 10 47 |
| 31 | 02 56 | 09 13 | 20 38 | 17 51 | 10 58 |
| 32 | 02 50 | 09 18 | 21 11 | 18 14 | 11 09 |
| 33 | 02 44 | 09 22 | 21 45 | 18 38 | 11 20 |
| 34 | 02 38 | 09 27 | 22 21 | 19 03 | 11 32 |
| 35 | 02 32 | 09 33 | 22 58 | 19 28 | 11 43 |
| 36 | 02 25 | 09 38 | 23 36 | 19 54 | 11 55 |
| 37 | 02 18 | 09 44 | 24 16 | 20 21 | 12 08 |
| 38 | 02 11 | 09 50 | 24 58 | 20 48 | 12 21 |
| 39 | 02 04 | 09 56 | 25 42 | 21 17 | 12 34 |
| 40 | 01 56 | 10 03 | 26 28 | 21 46 | 12 47 |
| 41 | 01 48 | 10 10 | 27 16 | 22 17 | 13 01 |
| 42 | 01 40 | 10 17 | 28 07 | 22 49 | 13 16 |
| 43 | 01 31 | 10 25 | 29 00 | 23 22 | 13 31 |
| 44 | 01 22 | 10 33 | 29 56 | 23 56 | 13 46 |
| 45 | 01 13 | 10 42 | 00♊55 | 24 31 | 14 02 |
| 46 | 01 03 | 10 51 | 01 57 | 25 09 | 14 19 |
| 47 | 00 53 | 11 01 | 03 03 | 25 47 | 14 36 |
| 48 | 00 42 | 11 12 | 04 13 | 26 28 | 14 55 |
| 49 | 00 30 | 11 23 | 05 27 | 27 10 | 15 14 |
| 50 | 00 18 | 11 35 | 06 45 | 27 55 | 15 33 |
| 51 | 00 05 | 11 49 | 08 09 | 28 42 | 15 54 |
| 52 | 29♒52 | 12 03 | 09 38 | 29 31 | 16 16 |
| 53 | 29 37 | 12 19 | 11 13 | 00♋23 | 16 39 |
| 54 | 29 22 | 12 36 | 12 54 | 01 18 | 17 03 |
| 55 | 29 05 | 12 55 | 14 43 | 02 17 | 17 29 |
| 56 | 28 47 | 13 16 | 16 39 | 03 19 | 17 57 |
| 57 | 28 28 | 13 40 | 18 43 | 04 25 | 18 26 |
| 58 | 28 07 | 14 06 | 20 56 | 05 36 | 18 57 |
| 59 | 27 45 | 14 36 | 23 19 | 06 51 | 19 30 |
| 60 | 27♒20 | 15♈10 | 25♊52 | 08♋13 | 20♋06 |

20h 32m 0s — 308° 0' 0" — 05 ♒ 38

| LAT. | 11 | 12 | ASC | 2 | 3 |
|---|---|---|---|---|---|
| 0 | 06♓14 | 08♈43 | 10♉25 | 09♊40 | 07♋21 |
| 5 | 05 56 | 08 56 | 11 49 | 10 56 | 08 00 |
| 10 | 05 38 | 09 10 | 13 19 | 12 15 | 08 40 |
| 15 | 05 19 | 09 26 | 14 58 | 13 37 | 09 22 |
| 20 | 04 58 | 09 44 | 16 48 | 15 05 | 10 05 |
| 21 | 04 54 | 09 47 | 17 12 | 15 24 | 10 14 |
| 22 | 04 50 | 09 51 | 17 36 | 15 42 | 10 23 |
| 23 | 04 45 | 09 55 | 18 01 | 16 01 | 10 32 |
| 24 | 04 40 | 09 59 | 18 27 | 16 21 | 10 42 |
| 25 | 04 36 | 10 03 | 18 53 | 16 41 | 10 51 |
| 26 | 04 31 | 10 08 | 19 20 | 17 01 | 11 01 |
| 27 | 04 26 | 10 12 | 19 48 | 17 22 | 11 11 |
| 28 | 04 21 | 10 17 | 20 17 | 17 43 | 11 21 |
| 29 | 04 16 | 10 21 | 20 47 | 18 04 | 11 31 |
| 30 | 04 10 | 10 26 | 21 18 | 18 26 | 11 42 |
| 31 | 04 05 | 10 31 | 21 50 | 18 49 | 11 52 |
| 32 | 03 59 | 10 37 | 22 23 | 19 12 | 12 03 |
| 33 | 03 53 | 10 42 | 22 58 | 19 36 | 12 14 |
| 34 | 03 47 | 10 48 | 23 34 | 20 01 | 12 26 |
| 35 | 03 41 | 10 54 | 24 11 | 20 26 | 12 37 |
| 36 | 03 35 | 11 00 | 24 50 | 20 52 | 12 49 |
| 37 | 03 28 | 11 07 | 25 30 | 21 18 | 13 02 |
| 38 | 03 21 | 11 14 | 26 12 | 21 46 | 13 15 |
| 39 | 03 14 | 11 21 | 26 56 | 22 14 | 13 28 |
| 40 | 03 07 | 11 28 | 27 42 | 22 44 | 13 41 |
| 41 | 02 59 | 11 36 | 28 31 | 23 14 | 13 55 |
| 42 | 02 51 | 11 45 | 29 22 | 23 46 | 14 09 |
| 43 | 02 43 | 11 53 | 00♊15 | 24 19 | 14 24 |
| 44 | 02 35 | 12 03 | 01 11 | 24 53 | 14 40 |
| 45 | 02 25 | 12 13 | 02 10 | 25 28 | 14 56 |
| 46 | 02 16 | 12 23 | 03 12 | 26 05 | 15 12 |
| 47 | 02 06 | 12 35 | 04 18 | 26 44 | 15 30 |
| 48 | 01 56 | 12 47 | 05 28 | 27 24 | 15 48 |
| 49 | 01 45 | 13 00 | 06 42 | 28 06 | 16 06 |
| 50 | 01 33 | 13 14 | 08 00 | 28 51 | 16 26 |
| 51 | 01 21 | 13 29 | 09 23 | 29 37 | 16 47 |
| 52 | 01 07 | 13 45 | 10 52 | 00♋26 | 17 08 |
| 53 | 00 53 | 14 03 | 12 26 | 01 18 | 17 31 |
| 54 | 00 39 | 14 23 | 14 06 | 02 13 | 17 55 |
| 55 | 00 23 | 14 44 | 15 54 | 03 10 | 18 21 |
| 56 | 00 06 | 15 08 | 17 48 | 04 12 | 18 48 |
| 57 | 29♒47 | 15 35 | 19 51 | 05 17 | 19 17 |
| 58 | 29 27 | 16 05 | 22 02 | 06 27 | 19 47 |
| 59 | 29 06 | 16 39 | 24 22 | 07 42 | 20 20 |
| 60 | 28♒42 | 17♈17 | 26♊51 | 09♋02 | 20♋56 |

20h 36m 0s — 309° 0' 0" — 06 ♒ 37

| LAT. | 11 | 12 | ASC | 2 | 3 |
|---|---|---|---|---|---|
| 0 | 07♓18 | 09♈48 | 11♉26 | 10♊36 | 08♋16 |
| 5 | 07 01 | 10 03 | 12 52 | 11 53 | 08 56 |
| 10 | 06 43 | 10 19 | 14 24 | 13 12 | 09 36 |
| 15 | 06 25 | 10 37 | 16 04 | 14 34 | 10 17 |
| 20 | 06 05 | 10 56 | 17 55 | 16 03 | 11 00 |
| 21 | 06 01 | 11 00 | 18 19 | 16 21 | 11 09 |
| 22 | 05 57 | 11 05 | 18 44 | 16 40 | 11 18 |
| 23 | 05 52 | 11 09 | 19 09 | 16 59 | 11 27 |
| 24 | 05 48 | 11 14 | 19 35 | 17 18 | 11 36 |
| 25 | 05 43 | 11 18 | 20 02 | 17 38 | 11 46 |
| 26 | 05 39 | 11 23 | 20 30 | 17 58 | 11 56 |
| 27 | 05 34 | 11 28 | 20 58 | 18 19 | 12 05 |
| 28 | 05 29 | 11 33 | 21 27 | 18 40 | 12 15 |
| 29 | 05 24 | 11 39 | 21 57 | 19 02 | 12 26 |
| 30 | 05 19 | 11 44 | 22 29 | 19 24 | 12 36 |
| 31 | 05 14 | 11 50 | 23 01 | 19 46 | 12 47 |
| 32 | 05 08 | 11 56 | 23 35 | 20 10 | 12 57 |
| 33 | 05 03 | 12 02 | 24 09 | 20 33 | 13 08 |
| 34 | 04 57 | 12 08 | 24 46 | 20 58 | 13 20 |
| 35 | 04 51 | 12 15 | 25 23 | 21 23 | 13 32 |
| 36 | 04 45 | 12 22 | 26 02 | 21 49 | 13 44 |
| 37 | 04 39 | 12 29 | 26 43 | 22 16 | 13 56 |
| 38 | 04 32 | 12 37 | 27 25 | 22 43 | 14 09 |
| 39 | 04 25 | 12 45 | 28 10 | 23 12 | 14 22 |
| 40 | 04 18 | 12 54 | 28 56 | 23 41 | 14 35 |
| 41 | 04 11 | 13 02 | 29 45 | 24 11 | 14 49 |
| 42 | 04 03 | 13 12 | 00♊35 | 24 43 | 15 03 |
| 43 | 03 55 | 13 22 | 01 29 | 25 16 | 15 18 |
| 44 | 03 47 | 13 32 | 02 25 | 25 49 | 15 33 |
| 45 | 03 38 | 13 43 | 03 24 | 26 25 | 15 49 |
| 46 | 03 29 | 13 55 | 04 26 | 27 02 | 16 06 |
| 47 | 03 20 | 14 08 | 05 32 | 27 40 | 16 23 |
| 48 | 03 10 | 14 21 | 06 42 | 28 20 | 16 41 |
| 49 | 02 59 | 14 36 | 07 55 | 29 02 | 16 59 |
| 50 | 02 48 | 14 52 | 09 13 | 29 46 | 17 19 |
| 51 | 02 36 | 15 09 | 10 36 | 00♋32 | 17 39 |
| 52 | 02 24 | 15 27 | 12 04 | 01 21 | 18 01 |
| 53 | 02 10 | 15 47 | 13 37 | 02 12 | 18 23 |
| 54 | 01 56 | 16 09 | 15 17 | 03 06 | 18 47 |
| 55 | 01 41 | 16 33 | 17 03 | 04 04 | 19 12 |
| 56 | 01 24 | 17 00 | 18 56 | 05 04 | 19 39 |
| 57 | 01 06 | 17 30 | 20 57 | 06 09 | 20 08 |
| 58 | 00 47 | 18 03 | 23 06 | 07 18 | 20 38 |
| 59 | 00 27 | 18 41 | 25 23 | 08 32 | 21 11 |
| 60 | 00♓04 | 19♈24 | 27♊50 | 09♋51 | 21♋46 |

20h 40m 0s — 310° 0' 0" — 07 ♒ 35

| LAT. | 11 | 12 | ASC | 2 | 3 |
|---|---|---|---|---|---|
| 0 | 08♓22 | 10♈53 | 12♉27 | 11♊32 | 09♋11 |
| 5 | 08 06 | 11 10 | 13 54 | 12 49 | 09 51 |
| 10 | 07 49 | 11 27 | 15 27 | 14 08 | 10 31 |
| 15 | 07 31 | 11 47 | 17 09 | 15 31 | 11 12 |
| 20 | 07 12 | 12 09 | 19 02 | 17 00 | 11 55 |
| 21 | 07 08 | 12 13 | 19 27 | 17 18 | 12 04 |
| 22 | 07 04 | 12 18 | 19 52 | 17 37 | 12 13 |
| 23 | 07 00 | 12 23 | 20 17 | 17 56 | 12 22 |
| 24 | 06 56 | 12 28 | 20 43 | 18 16 | 12 31 |
| 25 | 06 51 | 12 33 | 21 11 | 18 35 | 12 41 |
| 26 | 06 47 | 12 39 | 21 38 | 18 56 | 12 50 |
| 27 | 06 42 | 12 44 | 22 07 | 19 16 | 13 00 |
| 28 | 06 38 | 12 50 | 22 37 | 19 37 | 13 10 |
| 29 | 06 33 | 12 56 | 23 07 | 19 59 | 13 20 |
| 30 | 06 28 | 13 02 | 23 39 | 20 21 | 13 30 |
| 31 | 06 23 | 13 08 | 24 12 | 20 44 | 13 41 |
| 32 | 06 18 | 13 15 | 24 45 | 21 07 | 13 52 |
| 33 | 06 13 | 13 22 | 25 20 | 21 31 | 14 03 |
| 34 | 06 07 | 13 29 | 25 57 | 21 55 | 14 14 |
| 35 | 06 01 | 13 36 | 26 35 | 22 20 | 14 26 |
| 36 | 05 56 | 13 44 | 27 14 | 22 46 | 14 38 |
| 37 | 05 50 | 13 52 | 27 55 | 23 13 | 14 50 |
| 38 | 05 43 | 14 00 | 28 38 | 23 40 | 15 02 |
| 39 | 05 37 | 14 09 | 29 22 | 24 08 | 15 15 |
| 40 | 05 30 | 14 19 | 00♊09 | 24 38 | 15 29 |
| 41 | 05 23 | 14 28 | 00 57 | 25 08 | 15 42 |
| 42 | 05 16 | 14 39 | 01 48 | 25 39 | 15 57 |
| 43 | 05 08 | 14 50 | 02 42 | 26 12 | 16 11 |
| 44 | 05 00 | 15 01 | 03 38 | 26 46 | 16 27 |
| 45 | 04 52 | 15 14 | 04 37 | 27 21 | 16 42 |
| 46 | 04 43 | 15 27 | 05 40 | 27 58 | 16 59 |
| 47 | 04 34 | 15 41 | 06 45 | 28 36 | 17 16 |
| 48 | 04 24 | 15 56 | 07 54 | 29 16 | 17 33 |
| 49 | 04 14 | 16 12 | 09 08 | 29 57 | 17 52 |
| 50 | 04 03 | 16 29 | 10 25 | 00♋41 | 18 11 |
| 51 | 03 52 | 16 48 | 11 47 | 01 27 | 18 32 |
| 52 | 03 40 | 17 08 | 13 15 | 02 15 | 18 53 |
| 53 | 03 27 | 17 30 | 14 47 | 03 06 | 19 15 |
| 54 | 03 13 | 17 54 | 16 26 | 04 00 | 19 39 |
| 55 | 02 59 | 18 21 | 18 11 | 04 56 | 20 04 |
| 56 | 02 43 | 18 50 | 20 02 | 05 56 | 20 30 |
| 57 | 02 26 | 19 23 | 22 01 | 07 00 | 20 59 |
| 58 | 02 08 | 20 00 | 24 08 | 08 09 | 21 29 |
| 59 | 01 48 | 20 42 | 26 23 | 09 21 | 22 01 |
| 60 | 01♓26 | 21♈29 | 28♊47 | 10♋39 | 22♋35 |

20h 44m 0s — 311° 0' 0" — 08 ♒ 34

| LAT. | 11 | 12 | ASC | 2 | 3 |
|---|---|---|---|---|---|
| 0 | 09♓26 | 11♈58 | 13♉27 | 12♊28 | 10♋07 |
| 5 | 09 10 | 12 16 | 14 56 | 13 45 | 10 46 |
| 10 | 08 54 | 12 36 | 16 31 | 15 05 | 11 26 |
| 15 | 08 38 | 12 57 | 18 14 | 16 28 | 12 07 |
| 20 | 08 20 | 13 21 | 20 09 | 17 57 | 12 50 |
| 21 | 08 16 | 13 26 | 20 34 | 18 15 | 12 58 |
| 22 | 08 12 | 13 31 | 20 59 | 18 34 | 13 07 |
| 23 | 08 08 | 13 37 | 21 25 | 18 53 | 13 17 |
| 24 | 08 04 | 13 42 | 21 51 | 19 13 | 13 26 |
| 25 | 08 00 | 13 48 | 22 19 | 19 32 | 13 35 |
| 26 | 07 55 | 13 54 | 22 47 | 19 53 | 13 45 |
| 27 | 07 51 | 14 00 | 23 16 | 20 13 | 13 55 |
| 28 | 07 47 | 14 06 | 23 46 | 20 34 | 14 04 |
| 29 | 07 42 | 14 13 | 24 17 | 20 56 | 14 15 |
| 30 | 07 37 | 14 19 | 24 48 | 21 18 | 14 25 |
| 31 | 07 33 | 14 26 | 25 21 | 21 41 | 14 35 |
| 32 | 07 28 | 14 33 | 25 55 | 22 04 | 14 46 |
| 33 | 07 23 | 14 41 | 26 31 | 22 28 | 14 57 |
| 34 | 07 17 | 14 49 | 27 07 | 22 52 | 15 08 |
| 35 | 07 12 | 14 57 | 27 46 | 23 17 | 15 20 |
| 36 | 07 06 | 15 05 | 28 25 | 23 43 | 15 32 |
| 37 | 07 01 | 15 14 | 29 06 | 24 09 | 15 44 |
| 38 | 06 55 | 15 23 | 29 49 | 24 37 | 15 56 |
| 39 | 06 48 | 15 33 | 00♊34 | 25 05 | 16 09 |
| 40 | 06 42 | 15 43 | 01 21 | 25 34 | 16 22 |
| 41 | 06 35 | 15 54 | 02 09 | 26 04 | 16 36 |
| 42 | 06 28 | 16 05 | 03 01 | 26 36 | 16 50 |
| 43 | 06 21 | 16 17 | 03 54 | 27 08 | 17 05 |
| 44 | 06 13 | 16 30 | 04 50 | 27 42 | 17 20 |
| 45 | 06 05 | 16 43 | 05 49 | 28 17 | 17 36 |
| 46 | 05 57 | 16 58 | 06 52 | 28 53 | 17 52 |
| 47 | 05 48 | 17 13 | 07 57 | 29 31 | 18 09 |
| 48 | 05 39 | 17 29 | 09 06 | 00♋11 | 18 26 |
| 49 | 05 29 | 17 47 | 10 19 | 00 52 | 18 45 |
| 50 | 05 19 | 18 06 | 11 36 | 01 36 | 19 04 |
| 51 | 05 08 | 18 26 | 12 58 | 02 21 | 19 24 |
| 52 | 04 57 | 18 49 | 14 24 | 03 09 | 19 45 |
| 53 | 04 45 | 19 13 | 15 56 | 03 59 | 20 07 |
| 54 | 04 31 | 19 39 | 17 33 | 04 52 | 20 31 |
| 55 | 04 18 | 20 08 | 19 17 | 05 49 | 20 55 |
| 56 | 04 03 | 20 40 | 21 07 | 06 48 | 21 22 |
| 57 | 03 46 | 21 16 | 23 04 | 07 51 | 21 49 |
| 58 | 03 29 | 21 56 | 25 09 | 08 59 | 22 19 |
| 59 | 03 10 | 22 42 | 27 22 | 10 10 | 22 51 |
| 60 | 02♓49 | 23♈33 | 29♊43 | 11♋27 | 23♋25 |

# Placidus Table of Houses for Latitudes 0° to 60° North

20h 48m 0s — 312° 0' 0" — 09 ♒ 34

| LAT. | 11 | 12 | ASC | 2 | 3 |
|---|---|---|---|---|---|
| 0 | 10♓30 | 13♈03 | 14♉28 | 13♊24 | 11♋02 |
| 5 | 10 15 | 13 23 | 15 58 | 14 42 | 11 41 |
| 10 | 10 00 | 13 44 | 17 34 | 16 01 | 12 21 |
| 15 | 09 44 | 14 07 | 19 19 | 17 25 | 13 02 |
| 20 | 09 27 | 14 33 | 21 15 | 18 53 | 13 44 |
| 21 | 09 23 | 14 39 | 21 40 | 19 12 | 13 53 |
| 22 | 09 20 | 14 44 | 22 06 | 19 31 | 14 02 |
| 23 | 09 16 | 14 50 | 22 32 | 19 50 | 14 11 |
| 24 | 09 12 | 14 56 | 22 59 | 20 09 | 14 21 |
| 25 | 09 08 | 15 03 | 23 26 | 20 29 | 14 30 |
| 26 | 09 04 | 15 09 | 23 55 | 20 50 | 14 39 |
| 27 | 09 00 | 15 15 | 24 24 | 21 10 | 14 49 |
| 28 | 08 56 | 15 22 | 24 54 | 21 31 | 14 59 |
| 29 | 08 51 | 15 29 | 25 25 | 21 53 | 15 09 |
| 30 | 08 47 | 15 37 | 25 57 | 22 15 | 15 19 |
| 31 | 08 42 | 15 44 | 26 31 | 22 37 | 15 30 |
| 32 | 08 38 | 15 52 | 27 05 | 23 01 | 15 40 |
| 33 | 08 33 | 16 00 | 27 41 | 23 24 | 15 51 |
| 34 | 08 28 | 16 08 | 28 17 | 23 49 | 16 03 |
| 35 | 08 23 | 16 17 | 28 56 | 24 14 | 16 14 |
| 36 | 08 17 | 16 26 | 29 35 | 24 39 | 16 26 |
| 37 | 08 12 | 16 36 | 00♊17 | 25 06 | 16 38 |
| 38 | 08 06 | 16 46 | 01 00 | 25 33 | 16 50 |
| 39 | 08 00 | 16 57 | 01 45 | 26 01 | 17 03 |
| 40 | 07 54 | 17 08 | 02 32 | 26 30 | 17 16 |
| 41 | 07 48 | 17 19 | 03 21 | 27 01 | 17 30 |
| 42 | 07 41 | 17 32 | 04 12 | 27 32 | 17 44 |
| 43 | 07 34 | 17 45 | 05 05 | 28 04 | 17 58 |
| 44 | 07 27 | 17 58 | 06 02 | 28 37 | 18 13 |
| 45 | 07 19 | 18 13 | 07 01 | 29 12 | 18 29 |
| 46 | 07 11 | 18 29 | 08 03 | 29 48 | 18 45 |
| 47 | 07 03 | 18 45 | 09 08 | 00♋26 | 19 02 |
| 48 | 06 54 | 19 03 | 10 17 | 01 06 | 19 19 |
| 49 | 06 45 | 19 22 | 11 29 | 01 47 | 19 37 |
| 50 | 06 35 | 19 42 | 12 46 | 02 30 | 19 56 |
| 51 | 06 25 | 20 04 | 14 07 | 03 15 | 20 16 |
| 52 | 06 14 | 20 28 | 15 33 | 04 02 | 20 37 |
| 53 | 06 02 | 20 55 | 17 03 | 04 52 | 20 59 |
| 54 | 05 50 | 21 23 | 18 40 | 05 45 | 21 22 |
| 55 | 05 37 | 21 55 | 20 22 | 06 41 | 21 47 |
| 56 | 05 22 | 22 29 | 22 11 | 07 39 | 22 13 |
| 57 | 05 07 | 23 08 | 24 06 | 08 42 | 22 40 |
| 58 | 04 50 | 23 51 | 26 09 | 09 48 | 23 09 |
| 59 | 04 32 | 24 40 | 28 19 | 10 59 | 23 41 |
| 60 | 04♓13 | 25♈36 | 00♋38 | 12♋15 | 24♋14 |

20h 52m 0s — 313° 0' 0" — 10 ♒ 33

| LAT. | 11 | 12 | ASC | 2 | 3 |
|---|---|---|---|---|---|
| 0 | 11♓34 | 14♈07 | 15♉28 | 14♊20 | 11♋58 |
| 5 | 11 20 | 14 29 | 16 59 | 15 38 | 12 37 |
| 10 | 11 06 | 14 52 | 18 37 | 16 58 | 13 16 |
| 15 | 10 51 | 15 17 | 20 24 | 18 21 | 13 57 |
| 20 | 10 34 | 15 45 | 22 21 | 19 50 | 14 39 |
| 21 | 10 31 | 15 51 | 22 46 | 20 09 | 14 48 |
| 22 | 10 28 | 15 57 | 23 12 | 20 27 | 14 57 |
| 23 | 10 24 | 16 04 | 23 38 | 20 47 | 15 06 |
| 24 | 10 20 | 16 10 | 24 06 | 21 06 | 15 15 |
| 25 | 10 17 | 16 17 | 24 33 | 21 26 | 15 25 |
| 26 | 10 13 | 16 24 | 25 02 | 21 46 | 15 34 |
| 27 | 10 09 | 16 31 | 25 32 | 22 07 | 15 44 |
| 28 | 10 05 | 16 38 | 26 02 | 22 28 | 15 54 |
| 29 | 10 01 | 16 46 | 26 33 | 22 49 | 16 04 |
| 30 | 09 56 | 16 54 | 27 06 | 23 11 | 16 14 |
| 31 | 09 52 | 17 02 | 27 39 | 23 34 | 16 24 |
| 32 | 09 48 | 17 10 | 28 14 | 23 57 | 16 35 |
| 33 | 09 43 | 17 19 | 28 50 | 24 21 | 16 46 |
| 34 | 09 38 | 17 28 | 29 27 | 24 45 | 16 57 |
| 35 | 09 33 | 17 37 | 00♊05 | 25 10 | 17 08 |
| 36 | 09 28 | 17 47 | 00 45 | 25 36 | 17 20 |
| 37 | 09 23 | 17 58 | 01 27 | 26 02 | 17 32 |
| 38 | 09 18 | 18 09 | 02 10 | 26 29 | 17 44 |
| 39 | 09 12 | 18 20 | 02 55 | 26 57 | 17 57 |
| 40 | 09 06 | 18 32 | 03 42 | 27 26 | 18 10 |
| 41 | 09 00 | 18 44 | 04 31 | 27 56 | 18 23 |
| 42 | 08 54 | 18 58 | 05 22 | 28 27 | 18 37 |
| 43 | 08 47 | 19 12 | 06 16 | 28 59 | 18 52 |
| 44 | 08 40 | 19 26 | 07 12 | 29 33 | 19 07 |
| 45 | 08 33 | 19 42 | 08 11 | 00♋07 | 19 22 |
| 46 | 08 26 | 19 59 | 09 13 | 00 43 | 19 38 |
| 47 | 08 18 | 20 17 | 10 18 | 01 21 | 19 55 |
| 48 | 08 09 | 20 36 | 11 26 | 02 00 | 20 12 |
| 49 | 08 01 | 20 56 | 12 38 | 02 41 | 20 30 |
| 50 | 07 51 | 21 18 | 13 54 | 03 24 | 20 49 |
| 51 | 07 42 | 21 42 | 15 15 | 04 08 | 21 09 |
| 52 | 07 31 | 22 08 | 16 40 | 04 56 | 21 29 |
| 53 | 07 20 | 22 36 | 18 10 | 05 45 | 21 51 |
| 54 | 07 08 | 23 06 | 19 45 | 06 37 | 22 14 |
| 55 | 06 56 | 23 40 | 21 26 | 07 32 | 22 38 |
| 56 | 06 42 | 24 17 | 23 13 | 08 30 | 23 04 |
| 57 | 06 28 | 24 59 | 25 07 | 09 32 | 23 31 |
| 58 | 06 12 | 25 45 | 27 08 | 10 38 | 24 00 |
| 59 | 05 55 | 26 38 | 29 16 | 11 48 | 24 30 |
| 60 | 05♓36 | 27♈38 | 01♋32 | 13♋02 | 25♋03 |

20h 56m 0s — 314° 0' 0" — 11 ♒ 32

| LAT. | 11 | 12 | ASC | 2 | 3 |
|---|---|---|---|---|---|
| 0 | 12♓39 | 15♈12 | 16♉28 | 15♊16 | 12♋53 |
| 5 | 12 26 | 15 35 | 18 01 | 16 34 | 13 32 |
| 10 | 12 12 | 16 00 | 19 40 | 17 54 | 14 11 |
| 15 | 11 58 | 16 27 | 21 28 | 19 18 | 14 52 |
| 20 | 11 42 | 16 57 | 23 26 | 20 47 | 15 34 |
| 21 | 11 39 | 17 04 | 23 52 | 21 05 | 15 43 |
| 22 | 11 36 | 17 10 | 24 18 | 21 24 | 15 52 |
| 23 | 11 32 | 17 17 | 24 45 | 21 43 | 16 01 |
| 24 | 11 29 | 17 24 | 25 12 | 22 03 | 16 10 |
| 25 | 11 25 | 17 31 | 25 40 | 22 22 | 16 19 |
| 26 | 11 22 | 17 38 | 26 09 | 22 43 | 16 29 |
| 27 | 11 18 | 17 46 | 26 39 | 23 03 | 16 38 |
| 28 | 11 14 | 17 54 | 27 10 | 23 24 | 16 48 |
| 29 | 11 10 | 18 02 | 27 41 | 23 46 | 16 58 |
| 30 | 11 06 | 18 10 | 28 14 | 24 08 | 17 08 |
| 31 | 11 02 | 18 19 | 28 47 | 24 30 | 17 19 |
| 32 | 10 58 | 18 28 | 29 22 | 24 53 | 17 29 |
| 33 | 10 54 | 18 38 | 29 58 | 25 17 | 17 40 |
| 34 | 10 49 | 18 47 | 00♊35 | 25 41 | 17 51 |
| 35 | 10 44 | 18 57 | 01 14 | 26 06 | 18 02 |
| 36 | 10 40 | 19 08 | 01 54 | 26 32 | 18 14 |
| 37 | 10 35 | 19 19 | 02 36 | 26 58 | 18 26 |
| 38 | 10 30 | 19 31 | 03 19 | 27 25 | 18 38 |
| 39 | 10 24 | 19 43 | 04 04 | 27 53 | 18 51 |
| 40 | 10 19 | 19 56 | 04 51 | 28 22 | 19 04 |
| 41 | 10 13 | 20 09 | 05 40 | 28 52 | 19 17 |
| 42 | 10 07 | 20 23 | 06 31 | 29 23 | 19 31 |
| 43 | 10 01 | 20 38 | 07 25 | 29 55 | 19 45 |
| 44 | 09 54 | 20 54 | 08 21 | 00♋28 | 20 00 |
| 45 | 09 48 | 21 11 | 09 20 | 01 02 | 20 15 |
| 46 | 09 40 | 21 29 | 10 21 | 01 38 | 20 31 |
| 47 | 09 33 | 21 48 | 11 26 | 02 15 | 20 48 |
| 48 | 09 25 | 22 08 | 12 34 | 02 54 | 21 05 |
| 49 | 09 17 | 22 30 | 13 46 | 03 35 | 21 23 |
| 50 | 09 08 | 22 53 | 15 02 | 04 17 | 21 41 |
| 51 | 08 59 | 23 19 | 16 21 | 05 02 | 22 01 |
| 52 | 08 49 | 23 46 | 17 46 | 05 48 | 22 21 |
| 53 | 08 39 | 24 16 | 19 15 | 06 37 | 22 43 |
| 54 | 08 27 | 24 49 | 20 49 | 07 29 | 23 05 |
| 55 | 08 16 | 25 25 | 22 29 | 08 23 | 23 29 |
| 56 | 08 03 | 26 05 | 24 14 | 09 21 | 23 55 |
| 57 | 07 49 | 26 49 | 26 06 | 10 22 | 24 21 |
| 58 | 07 34 | 27 38 | 28 05 | 11 27 | 24 50 |
| 59 | 07 18 | 28 34 | 00♋11 | 12 36 | 25 20 |
| 60 | 07♓00 | 29♈38 | 02♋24 | 13♋49 | 25♋53 |

21h 0m 0s — 315° 0' 0" — 12 ♒ 32

| LAT. | 11 | 12 | ASC | 2 | 3 |
|---|---|---|---|---|---|
| 0 | 13♓43 | 16♈17 | 17♉28 | 16♊11 | 13♋49 |
| 5 | 13 31 | 16 42 | 19 02 | 17 30 | 14 27 |
| 10 | 13 18 | 17 08 | 20 43 | 18 50 | 15 07 |
| 15 | 13 05 | 17 37 | 22 31 | 20 14 | 15 47 |
| 20 | 12 50 | 18 09 | 24 32 | 21 43 | 16 29 |
| 21 | 12 47 | 18 16 | 24 57 | 22 01 | 16 38 |
| 22 | 12 44 | 18 23 | 25 23 | 22 20 | 16 47 |
| 23 | 12 41 | 18 30 | 25 50 | 22 39 | 16 56 |
| 24 | 12 37 | 18 37 | 26 18 | 22 59 | 17 05 |
| 25 | 12 34 | 18 45 | 26 46 | 23 19 | 17 14 |
| 26 | 12 31 | 18 53 | 27 16 | 23 39 | 17 23 |
| 27 | 12 27 | 19 01 | 27 46 | 23 59 | 17 33 |
| 28 | 12 24 | 19 09 | 28 16 | 24 20 | 17 43 |
| 29 | 12 20 | 19 18 | 28 48 | 24 42 | 17 53 |
| 30 | 12 16 | 19 27 | 29 21 | 25 04 | 18 03 |
| 31 | 12 12 | 19 36 | 29 55 | 25 26 | 18 13 |
| 32 | 12 08 | 19 46 | 00♊30 | 25 49 | 18 23 |
| 33 | 12 04 | 19 56 | 01 06 | 26 13 | 18 34 |
| 34 | 12 00 | 20 06 | 01 43 | 26 37 | 18 45 |
| 35 | 11 56 | 20 17 | 02 22 | 27 02 | 18 56 |
| 36 | 11 51 | 20 28 | 03 02 | 27 27 | 19 08 |
| 37 | 11 47 | 20 40 | 03 44 | 27 54 | 19 20 |
| 38 | 11 42 | 20 52 | 04 28 | 28 21 | 19 32 |
| 39 | 11 37 | 21 05 | 05 13 | 28 49 | 19 44 |
| 40 | 11 32 | 21 19 | 06 00 | 29 17 | 19 57 |
| 41 | 11 26 | 21 33 | 06 49 | 29 47 | 20 11 |
| 42 | 11 21 | 21 48 | 07 40 | 00♋18 | 20 24 |
| 43 | 11 15 | 22 04 | 08 34 | 00 50 | 20 38 |
| 44 | 11 09 | 22 21 | 09 29 | 01 23 | 20 53 |
| 45 | 11 02 | 22 39 | 10 28 | 01 57 | 21 08 |
| 46 | 10 55 | 22 58 | 11 30 | 02 32 | 21 24 |
| 47 | 10 48 | 23 18 | 12 34 | 03 09 | 21 40 |
| 48 | 10 41 | 23 40 | 13 42 | 03 48 | 21 57 |
| 49 | 10 33 | 24 03 | 14 53 | 04 28 | 22 15 |
| 50 | 10 25 | 24 28 | 16 08 | 05 10 | 22 34 |
| 51 | 10 16 | 24 55 | 17 27 | 05 54 | 22 53 |
| 52 | 10 07 | 25 24 | 18 51 | 06 41 | 23 13 |
| 53 | 09 57 | 25 56 | 20 19 | 07 29 | 23 35 |
| 54 | 09 47 | 26 30 | 21 52 | 08 20 | 23 57 |
| 55 | 09 35 | 27 09 | 23 30 | 09 14 | 24 21 |
| 56 | 09 23 | 27 51 | 25 15 | 10 11 | 24 45 |
| 57 | 09 10 | 28 38 | 27 05 | 11 11 | 25 12 |
| 58 | 08 57 | 29 30 | 29 02 | 12 15 | 25 40 |
| 59 | 08 41 | 00♉29 | 01♋05 | 13 23 | 26 10 |
| 60 | 08♓25 | 01♉36 | 03♋16 | 14♋36 | 26♋42 |

21h 4m 0s — 316° 0' 0" — 13 ♒ 32

| LAT. | 11 | 12 | ASC | 2 | 3 |
|---|---|---|---|---|---|
| 0 | 14♓48 | 17♈21 | 18♉28 | 17♊07 | 14♋44 |
| 5 | 14 36 | 17 48 | 20 03 | 18 25 | 15 23 |
| 10 | 14 24 | 18 16 | 21 45 | 19 46 | 16 02 |
| 15 | 14 12 | 18 47 | 23 35 | 21 10 | 16 42 |
| 20 | 13 58 | 19 20 | 25 36 | 22 39 | 17 24 |
| 21 | 13 55 | 19 28 | 26 02 | 22 57 | 17 33 |
| 22 | 13 52 | 19 35 | 26 29 | 23 16 | 17 42 |
| 23 | 13 49 | 19 43 | 26 56 | 23 35 | 17 51 |
| 24 | 13 46 | 19 51 | 27 24 | 23 55 | 18 00 |
| 25 | 13 43 | 19 59 | 27 52 | 24 15 | 18 09 |
| 26 | 13 40 | 20 07 | 28 22 | 24 35 | 18 18 |
| 27 | 13 37 | 20 16 | 28 52 | 24 55 | 18 28 |
| 28 | 13 33 | 20 25 | 29 23 | 25 16 | 18 37 |
| 29 | 13 30 | 20 34 | 29 55 | 25 38 | 18 47 |
| 30 | 13 26 | 20 43 | 00♊28 | 26 00 | 18 57 |
| 31 | 13 23 | 20 53 | 01 02 | 26 22 | 19 07 |
| 32 | 13 19 | 21 03 | 01 37 | 26 45 | 19 18 |
| 33 | 13 15 | 21 14 | 02 13 | 27 09 | 19 28 |
| 34 | 13 11 | 21 25 | 02 51 | 27 33 | 19 39 |
| 35 | 13 07 | 21 36 | 03 30 | 27 58 | 19 51 |
| 36 | 13 03 | 21 48 | 04 10 | 28 23 | 20 02 |
| 37 | 12 59 | 22 01 | 04 52 | 28 49 | 20 14 |
| 38 | 12 54 | 22 14 | 05 35 | 29 16 | 20 26 |
| 39 | 12 49 | 22 28 | 06 21 | 29 44 | 20 38 |
| 40 | 12 45 | 22 42 | 07 08 | 00♋12 | 20 51 |
| 41 | 12 39 | 22 57 | 07 57 | 00 42 | 21 04 |
| 42 | 12 34 | 23 13 | 08 48 | 01 13 | 21 18 |
| 43 | 12 29 | 23 30 | 09 41 | 01 44 | 21 32 |
| 44 | 12 23 | 23 48 | 10 37 | 02 17 | 21 46 |
| 45 | 12 17 | 24 06 | 11 35 | 02 51 | 22 01 |
| 46 | 12 11 | 24 27 | 12 37 | 03 26 | 22 17 |
| 47 | 12 04 | 24 48 | 13 41 | 04 03 | 22 33 |
| 48 | 11 57 | 25 11 | 14 48 | 04 42 | 22 50 |
| 49 | 11 50 | 25 35 | 15 59 | 05 22 | 23 08 |
| 50 | 11 42 | 26 02 | 17 13 | 06 03 | 23 26 |
| 51 | 11 34 | 26 30 | 18 32 | 06 47 | 23 45 |
| 52 | 11 25 | 27 01 | 19 54 | 07 33 | 24 05 |
| 53 | 11 16 | 27 34 | 21 22 | 08 21 | 24 26 |
| 54 | 11 06 | 28 11 | 22 54 | 09 12 | 24 48 |
| 55 | 10 56 | 28 51 | 24 31 | 10 05 | 25 12 |
| 56 | 10 44 | 29 36 | 26 14 | 11 01 | 25 36 |
| 57 | 10 32 | 00♉25 | 28 02 | 12 01 | 26 02 |
| 58 | 10 19 | 01 20 | 29 57 | 13 04 | 26 30 |
| 59 | 10 05 | 02 23 | 01♋59 | 14 11 | 27 00 |
| 60 | 09♓50 | 03♉34 | 04♋07 | 15♋22 | 27♋31 |

21h 8m 0s — 317° 0' 0" — 14 ♒ 32

| LAT. | 11 | 12 | ASC | 2 | 3 |
|---|---|---|---|---|---|
| 0 | 15♓53 | 18♈26 | 19♉27 | 18♊02 | 15♋40 |
| 5 | 15 42 | 18 54 | 21 04 | 19 21 | 16 19 |
| 10 | 15 31 | 19 24 | 22 47 | 20 42 | 16 58 |
| 15 | 15 19 | 19 56 | 24 38 | 22 06 | 17 38 |
| 20 | 15 06 | 20 32 | 26 40 | 23 35 | 18 19 |
| 21 | 15 04 | 20 39 | 27 07 | 23 53 | 18 28 |
| 22 | 15 01 | 20 47 | 27 33 | 24 12 | 18 37 |
| 23 | 14 58 | 20 55 | 28 01 | 24 31 | 18 46 |
| 24 | 14 55 | 21 04 | 28 29 | 24 51 | 18 55 |
| 25 | 14 52 | 21 12 | 28 58 | 25 11 | 19 04 |
| 26 | 14 49 | 21 21 | 29 27 | 25 31 | 19 13 |
| 27 | 14 46 | 21 30 | 29 57 | 25 51 | 19 22 |
| 28 | 14 43 | 21 40 | 00♊29 | 26 12 | 19 32 |
| 29 | 14 40 | 21 49 | 01 01 | 26 34 | 19 42 |
| 30 | 14 37 | 21 59 | 01 34 | 26 56 | 19 52 |
| 31 | 14 33 | 22 10 | 02 08 | 27 18 | 20 02 |
| 32 | 14 30 | 22 20 | 02 44 | 27 41 | 20 12 |
| 33 | 14 26 | 22 32 | 03 20 | 28 04 | 20 23 |
| 34 | 14 23 | 22 43 | 03 58 | 28 28 | 20 34 |
| 35 | 14 19 | 22 55 | 04 37 | 28 53 | 20 45 |
| 36 | 14 15 | 23 08 | 05 17 | 29 18 | 20 56 |
| 37 | 14 11 | 23 21 | 05 59 | 29 44 | 21 08 |
| 38 | 14 07 | 23 35 | 06 43 | 00♋11 | 21 20 |
| 39 | 14 02 | 23 49 | 07 28 | 00 39 | 21 32 |
| 40 | 13 58 | 24 04 | 08 15 | 01 07 | 21 45 |
| 41 | 13 53 | 24 20 | 09 04 | 01 37 | 21 58 |
| 42 | 13 48 | 24 37 | 09 55 | 02 07 | 22 11 |
| 43 | 13 43 | 24 55 | 10 48 | 02 39 | 22 25 |
| 44 | 13 38 | 25 14 | 11 44 | 03 11 | 22 40 |
| 45 | 13 32 | 25 34 | 12 42 | 03 45 | 22 55 |
| 46 | 13 26 | 25 55 | 13 43 | 04 20 | 23 10 |
| 47 | 13 20 | 26 17 | 14 47 | 04 57 | 23 26 |
| 48 | 13 14 | 26 41 | 15 54 | 05 35 | 23 43 |
| 49 | 13 07 | 27 07 | 17 04 | 06 14 | 24 00 |
| 50 | 13 00 | 27 35 | 18 18 | 06 56 | 24 18 |
| 51 | 12 52 | 28 05 | 19 35 | 07 39 | 24 37 |
| 52 | 12 44 | 28 37 | 20 57 | 08 25 | 24 57 |
| 53 | 12 35 | 29 12 | 22 24 | 09 12 | 25 18 |
| 54 | 12 26 | 29 51 | 23 54 | 10 02 | 25 39 |
| 55 | 12 16 | 00♉33 | 25 30 | 10 55 | 26 03 |
| 56 | 12 06 | 01 20 | 27 12 | 11 51 | 26 27 |
| 57 | 11 54 | 02 11 | 28 59 | 12 49 | 26 53 |
| 58 | 11 42 | 03 09 | 00♋52 | 13 52 | 27 20 |
| 59 | 11 29 | 04 15 | 02 51 | 14 58 | 27 49 |
| 60 | 11♓15 | 05♉29 | 04♋58 | 16♋08 | 28♋21 |

21h 12m 0s — 318° 0' 0" — 15 ♒ 32

| LAT. | 11 | 12 | ASC | 2 | 3 |
|---|---|---|---|---|---|
| 0 | 16♓57 | 19♈30 | 20♉26 | 18♊58 | 16♋36 |
| 5 | 16 47 | 20 00 | 22 04 | 20 17 | 17 14 |
| 10 | 16 37 | 20 31 | 23 49 | 21 38 | 17 53 |
| 15 | 16 26 | 21 05 | 25 41 | 23 02 | 18 33 |
| 20 | 16 14 | 21 43 | 27 44 | 24 31 | 19 14 |
| 21 | 16 12 | 21 51 | 28 11 | 24 49 | 19 23 |
| 22 | 16 09 | 21 59 | 28 38 | 25 08 | 19 32 |
| 23 | 16 07 | 22 08 | 29 05 | 25 27 | 19 40 |
| 24 | 16 04 | 22 17 | 29 33 | 25 47 | 19 49 |
| 25 | 16 02 | 22 26 | 00♊02 | 26 06 | 19 58 |
| 26 | 15 59 | 22 35 | 00 32 | 26 26 | 20 08 |
| 27 | 15 56 | 22 44 | 01 03 | 26 47 | 20 17 |
| 28 | 15 53 | 22 54 | 01 34 | 27 08 | 20 27 |
| 29 | 15 50 | 23 04 | 02 07 | 27 29 | 20 36 |
| 30 | 15 47 | 23 15 | 02 40 | 27 51 | 20 46 |
| 31 | 15 44 | 23 26 | 03 14 | 28 13 | 20 56 |
| 32 | 15 41 | 23 37 | 03 50 | 28 36 | 21 07 |
| 33 | 15 37 | 23 49 | 04 26 | 29 00 | 21 17 |
| 34 | 15 34 | 24 01 | 05 04 | 29 24 | 21 28 |
| 35 | 15 31 | 24 14 | 05 43 | 29 48 | 21 39 |
| 36 | 15 27 | 24 27 | 06 24 | 00♋13 | 21 50 |
| 37 | 15 23 | 24 41 | 07 05 | 00 39 | 22 02 |
| 38 | 15 19 | 24 56 | 07 49 | 01 06 | 22 14 |
| 39 | 15 15 | 25 11 | 08 34 | 01 34 | 22 26 |
| 40 | 15 11 | 25 27 | 09 21 | 02 02 | 22 38 |
| 41 | 15 07 | 25 43 | 10 10 | 02 31 | 22 51 |
| 42 | 15 02 | 26 01 | 11 01 | 03 02 | 23 05 |
| 43 | 14 57 | 26 20 | 11 54 | 03 33 | 23 19 |
| 44 | 14 52 | 26 39 | 12 50 | 04 05 | 23 33 |
| 45 | 14 47 | 27 00 | 13 48 | 04 39 | 23 48 |
| 46 | 14 42 | 27 22 | 14 48 | 05 14 | 24 03 |
| 47 | 14 36 | 27 46 | 15 52 | 05 50 | 24 19 |
| 48 | 14 30 | 28 11 | 16 58 | 06 28 | 24 35 |
| 49 | 14 24 | 28 38 | 18 08 | 07 07 | 24 53 |
| 50 | 14 17 | 29 07 | 19 21 | 07 48 | 25 11 |
| 51 | 14 10 | 29 38 | 20 38 | 08 31 | 25 29 |
| 52 | 14 03 | 00♉12 | 21 59 | 09 16 | 25 49 |
| 53 | 13 55 | 00 49 | 23 24 | 10 03 | 26 10 |
| 54 | 13 46 | 01 29 | 24 54 | 10 53 | 26 31 |
| 55 | 13 37 | 02 14 | 26 29 | 11 45 | 26 54 |
| 56 | 13 27 | 03 02 | 28 09 | 12 40 | 27 18 |
| 57 | 13 17 | 03 56 | 29 54 | 13 38 | 27 43 |
| 58 | 13 06 | 04 57 | 01♋46 | 14 40 | 28 10 |
| 59 | 12 53 | 06 05 | 03 43 | 15 45 | 28 39 |
| 60 | 12♓40 | 07♉23 | 05♋47 | 16♋54 | 29♋10 |

21h 16m 0s — 319° 0' 0" — 16 ♒ 33

| LAT. | 11 | 12 | ASC | 2 | 3 |
|---|---|---|---|---|---|
| 0 | 18♓02 | 20♈34 | 21♉26 | 19♊53 | 17♋32 |
| 5 | 17 53 | 21 05 | 23 05 | 21 12 | 18 10 |
| 10 | 17 44 | 21 38 | 24 50 | 22 33 | 18 49 |
| 15 | 17 34 | 22 14 | 26 43 | 23 58 | 19 28 |
| 20 | 17 23 | 22 54 | 28 48 | 25 26 | 20 10 |
| 21 | 17 21 | 23 02 | 29 14 | 25 45 | 20 18 |
| 22 | 17 18 | 23 11 | 29 42 | 26 04 | 20 27 |
| 23 | 17 16 | 23 20 | 00♊09 | 26 23 | 20 35 |
| 24 | 17 13 | 23 29 | 00 38 | 26 42 | 20 44 |
| 25 | 17 11 | 23 39 | 01 07 | 27 02 | 20 53 |
| 26 | 17 08 | 23 48 | 01 37 | 27 22 | 21 03 |
| 27 | 17 06 | 23 58 | 02 08 | 27 43 | 21 12 |
| 28 | 17 03 | 24 09 | 02 39 | 28 03 | 21 21 |
| 29 | 17 01 | 24 19 | 03 12 | 28 25 | 21 31 |
| 30 | 16 58 | 24 30 | 03 45 | 28 46 | 21 41 |
| 31 | 16 55 | 24 42 | 04 19 | 29 09 | 21 51 |
| 32 | 16 52 | 24 54 | 04 55 | 29 31 | 22 01 |
| 33 | 16 49 | 25 06 | 05 32 | 29 55 | 22 11 |
| 34 | 16 46 | 25 19 | 06 10 | 00♋19 | 22 22 |
| 35 | 16 42 | 25 32 | 06 49 | 00 43 | 22 33 |
| 36 | 16 39 | 25 46 | 07 29 | 01 08 | 22 44 |
| 37 | 16 36 | 26 01 | 08 11 | 01 34 | 22 56 |
| 38 | 16 32 | 26 16 | 08 55 | 02 01 | 23 08 |
| 39 | 16 28 | 26 32 | 09 40 | 02 28 | 23 20 |
| 40 | 16 24 | 26 48 | 10 27 | 02 56 | 23 32 |
| 41 | 16 20 | 27 06 | 11 16 | 03 25 | 23 45 |
| 42 | 16 16 | 27 24 | 12 07 | 03 56 | 23 58 |
| 43 | 16 12 | 27 44 | 12 59 | 04 27 | 24 12 |
| 44 | 16 07 | 28 04 | 13 55 | 04 59 | 24 26 |
| 45 | 16 03 | 28 26 | 14 52 | 05 32 | 24 41 |
| 46 | 15 58 | 28 49 | 15 53 | 06 07 | 24 56 |
| 47 | 15 52 | 29 14 | 16 56 | 06 43 | 25 12 |
| 48 | 15 47 | 29 40 | 18 02 | 07 20 | 25 28 |
| 49 | 15 41 | 00♉08 | 19 11 | 07 59 | 25 45 |
| 50 | 15 35 | 00 39 | 20 24 | 08 40 | 26 03 |
| 51 | 15 28 | 01 11 | 21 40 | 09 23 | 26 21 |
| 52 | 15 22 | 01 47 | 23 00 | 10 07 | 26 41 |
| 53 | 15 14 | 02 25 | 24 25 | 10 54 | 27 01 |
| 54 | 15 06 | 03 07 | 25 53 | 11 43 | 27 23 |
| 55 | 14 58 | 03 53 | 27 27 | 12 35 | 27 45 |
| 56 | 14 49 | 04 44 | 29 05 | 13 29 | 28 09 |
| 57 | 14 40 | 05 40 | 00♋49 | 14 26 | 28 34 |
| 58 | 14 29 | 06 43 | 02 39 | 15 27 | 29 00 |
| 59 | 14 18 | 07 54 | 04 34 | 16 31 | 29 29 |
| 60 | 14♓06 | 09♉15 | 06♋36 | 17♋40 | 29♋59 |

# Placidus Table of Houses for Latitudes 0° to 60° North

**21h 20m 0s — 320° 0' 0" — 17♒33**

| LAT. | 11 | 12 | ASC | 2 | 3 |
|---|---|---|---|---|---|
| 0 | 19♓07 | 21♈38 | 22♉25 | 20♊49 | 18♋28 |
| 5 | 18 59 | 22 11 | 24 05 | 22 08 | 19 06 |
| 10 | 18 50 | 22 45 | 25 51 | 23 29 | 19 44 |
| 15 | 18 41 | 23 23 | 27 46 | 24 53 | 20 24 |
| 20 | 18 31 | 24 04 | 29 51 | 26 22 | 21 05 |
| 21 | 18 29 | 24 13 | 00♊18 | 26 40 | 21 13 |
| 22 | 18 27 | 24 22 | 00 45 | 26 59 | 21 22 |
| 23 | 18 25 | 24 32 | 01 13 | 27 18 | 21 31 |
| 24 | 18 23 | 24 41 | 01 42 | 27 38 | 21 39 |
| 25 | 18 21 | 24 51 | 02 11 | 27 57 | 21 48 |
| 26 | 18 18 | 25 01 | 02 41 | 28 17 | 21 57 |
| 27 | 18 16 | 25 12 | 03 12 | 28 38 | 22 07 |
| 28 | 18 13 | 25 23 | 03 44 | 28 59 | 22 16 |
| 29 | 18 11 | 25 34 | 04 16 | 29 20 | 22 26 |
| 30 | 18 08 | 25 45 | 04 50 | 29 42 | 22 35 |
| 31 | 18 06 | 25 57 | 05 24 | 00♋04 | 22 45 |
| 32 | 18 03 | 26 10 | 06 00 | 00 27 | 22 55 |
| 33 | 18 00 | 26 23 | 06 37 | 00 50 | 23 06 |
| 34 | 17 57 | 26 36 | 07 15 | 01 14 | 23 16 |
| 35 | 17 55 | 26 50 | 07 54 | 01 38 | 23 27 |
| 36 | 17 51 | 27 05 | 08 34 | 02 03 | 23 38 |
| 37 | 17 48 | 27 20 | 09 16 | 02 29 | 23 50 |
| 38 | 17 45 | 27 36 | 10 00 | 02 55 | 24 02 |
| 39 | 17 42 | 27 52 | 10 45 | 03 22 | 24 14 |
| 40 | 17 38 | 28 09 | 11 32 | 03 51 | 24 26 |
| 41 | 17 34 | 28 28 | 12 21 | 04 20 | 24 39 |
| 42 | 17 31 | 28 47 | 13 11 | 04 49 | 24 52 |
| 43 | 17 27 | 29 07 | 14 04 | 05 20 | 25 05 |
| 44 | 17 23 | 29 29 | 14 59 | 05 52 | 25 19 |
| 45 | 17 18 | 29 51 | 15 56 | 06 26 | 25 34 |
| 46 | 17 14 | 00♉16 | 16 56 | 07 00 | 25 49 |
| 47 | 17 09 | 00 41 | 17 59 | 07 36 | 26 05 |
| 48 | 17 04 | 01 09 | 19 05 | 08 13 | 26 21 |
| 49 | 16 59 | 01 38 | 20 13 | 08 52 | 26 38 |
| 50 | 16 53 | 02 10 | 21 25 | 09 32 | 26 55 |
| 51 | 16 47 | 02 44 | 22 41 | 10 14 | 27 13 |
| 52 | 16 41 | 03 20 | 24 00 | 10 58 | 27 33 |
| 53 | 16 34 | 04 00 | 25 24 | 11 44 | 27 53 |
| 54 | 16 27 | 04 44 | 26 51 | 12 33 | 28 14 |
| 55 | 16 19 | 05 32 | 28 24 | 13 24 | 28 36 |
| 56 | 16 11 | 06 24 | 00♋01 | 14 18 | 28 59 |
| 57 | 16 02 | 07 23 | 01 43 | 15 14 | 29 24 |
| 58 | 15 53 | 08 28 | 03 31 | 16 14 | 29 50 |
| 59 | 15 43 | 09 41 | 05 24 | 17 18 | 00♌18 |
| 60 | 15♓32 | 11♉05 | 07♋24 | 18♋25 | 00♌48 |

**21h 24m 0s — 321° 0' 0" — 18♒34**

| LAT. | 11 | 12 | ASC | 2 | 3 |
|---|---|---|---|---|---|
| 0 | 20♓12 | 22♈42 | 23♉23 | 21♊44 | 19♋24 |
| 5 | 20 05 | 23 16 | 25 05 | 23 03 | 20 02 |
| 10 | 19 57 | 23 52 | 26 52 | 24 24 | 20 40 |
| 15 | 19 49 | 24 32 | 28 48 | 25 49 | 21 19 |
| 20 | 19 40 | 25 15 | 00♊54 | 27 17 | 22 00 |
| 21 | 19 38 | 25 24 | 01 21 | 27 36 | 22 08 |
| 22 | 19 36 | 25 34 | 01 48 | 27 55 | 22 17 |
| 23 | 19 34 | 25 43 | 02 16 | 28 14 | 22 26 |
| 24 | 19 32 | 25 53 | 02 45 | 28 33 | 22 34 |
| 25 | 19 30 | 26 04 | 03 15 | 28 53 | 22 43 |
| 26 | 19 28 | 26 14 | 03 45 | 29 13 | 22 52 |
| 27 | 19 26 | 26 25 | 04 16 | 29 33 | 23 02 |
| 28 | 19 24 | 26 37 | 04 48 | 29 54 | 23 11 |
| 29 | 19 22 | 26 48 | 05 20 | 00♋15 | 23 20 |
| 30 | 19 19 | 27 00 | 05 54 | 00 37 | 23 30 |
| 31 | 19 17 | 27 13 | 06 29 | 00 59 | 23 40 |
| 32 | 19 14 | 27 26 | 07 04 | 01 21 | 23 50 |
| 33 | 19 12 | 27 39 | 07 41 | 01 45 | 24 00 |
| 34 | 19 09 | 27 53 | 08 19 | 02 08 | 24 11 |
| 35 | 19 07 | 28 08 | 08 58 | 02 33 | 24 22 |
| 36 | 19 04 | 28 23 | 09 39 | 02 58 | 24 33 |
| 37 | 19 01 | 28 38 | 10 21 | 03 23 | 24 44 |
| 38 | 18 58 | 28 55 | 11 04 | 03 49 | 24 56 |
| 39 | 18 55 | 29 12 | 11 49 | 04 17 | 25 07 |
| 40 | 18 52 | 29 30 | 12 36 | 04 45 | 25 20 |
| 41 | 18 49 | 29 49 | 13 25 | 05 13 | 25 32 |
| 42 | 18 45 | 00♉09 | 14 15 | 05 43 | 25 45 |
| 43 | 18 42 | 00 30 | 15 08 | 06 14 | 25 59 |
| 44 | 18 38 | 00 53 | 16 03 | 06 46 | 26 13 |
| 45 | 18 34 | 01 16 | 17 00 | 07 18 | 26 27 |
| 46 | 18 30 | 01 41 | 17 59 | 07 53 | 26 42 |
| 47 | 18 25 | 02 08 | 19 02 | 08 28 | 26 57 |
| 48 | 18 21 | 02 36 | 20 07 | 09 05 | 27 13 |
| 49 | 18 16 | 03 07 | 21 15 | 09 43 | 27 30 |
| 50 | 18 11 | 03 40 | 22 26 | 10 23 | 27 47 |
| 51 | 18 06 | 04 15 | 23 41 | 11 05 | 28 06 |
| 52 | 18 00 | 04 53 | 25 00 | 11 49 | 28 25 |
| 53 | 17 54 | 05 34 | 26 22 | 12 35 | 28 44 |
| 54 | 17 48 | 06 19 | 27 49 | 13 23 | 29 05 |
| 55 | 17 41 | 07 09 | 29 20 | 14 13 | 29 27 |
| 56 | 17 33 | 08 03 | 00♋55 | 15 06 | 29 50 |
| 57 | 17 26 | 09 04 | 02 36 | 16 02 | 00♌15 |
| 58 | 17 17 | 10 11 | 04 22 | 17 01 | 00 40 |
| 59 | 17 08 | 11 27 | 06 14 | 18 04 | 01 08 |
| 60 | 16♓58 | 12♉53 | 08♋11 | 19♋10 | 01♌37 |

**21h 28m 0s — 322° 0' 0" — 19♒35**

| LAT. | 11 | 12 | ASC | 2 | 3 |
|---|---|---|---|---|---|
| 0 | 21♓17 | 23♈46 | 24♉22 | 22♊39 | 20♋20 |
| 5 | 21 11 | 24 21 | 26 04 | 23 59 | 20 58 |
| 10 | 21 04 | 24 59 | 27 53 | 25 20 | 21 36 |
| 15 | 20 57 | 25 40 | 29 49 | 26 44 | 22 15 |
| 20 | 20 49 | 26 25 | 01♊57 | 28 13 | 22 55 |
| 21 | 20 47 | 26 35 | 02 24 | 28 31 | 23 04 |
| 22 | 20 45 | 26 45 | 02 51 | 28 50 | 23 12 |
| 23 | 20 43 | 26 55 | 03 19 | 29 09 | 23 21 |
| 24 | 20 42 | 27 05 | 03 48 | 29 28 | 23 30 |
| 25 | 20 40 | 27 16 | 04 18 | 29 48 | 23 38 |
| 26 | 20 38 | 27 27 | 04 48 | 00♋08 | 23 47 |
| 27 | 20 36 | 27 38 | 05 19 | 00 28 | 23 56 |
| 28 | 20 34 | 27 50 | 05 51 | 00 49 | 24 06 |
| 29 | 20 32 | 28 02 | 06 24 | 01 10 | 24 15 |
| 30 | 20 30 | 28 15 | 06 58 | 01 32 | 24 25 |
| 31 | 20 28 | 28 28 | 07 32 | 01 54 | 24 35 |
| 32 | 20 26 | 28 41 | 08 08 | 02 16 | 24 45 |
| 33 | 20 24 | 28 55 | 08 45 | 02 39 | 24 55 |
| 34 | 20 21 | 29 10 | 09 23 | 03 03 | 25 05 |
| 35 | 20 19 | 29 25 | 10 02 | 03 27 | 25 16 |
| 36 | 20 17 | 29 40 | 10 43 | 03 52 | 25 27 |
| 37 | 20 14 | 29 57 | 11 25 | 04 17 | 25 38 |
| 38 | 20 11 | 00♉14 | 12 08 | 04 44 | 25 50 |
| 39 | 20 09 | 00 32 | 12 53 | 05 10 | 26 01 |
| 40 | 20 06 | 00 50 | 13 40 | 05 38 | 26 14 |
| 41 | 20 03 | 01 10 | 14 28 | 06 07 | 26 26 |
| 42 | 20 00 | 01 31 | 15 19 | 06 36 | 26 39 |
| 43 | 19 57 | 01 53 | 16 11 | 07 07 | 26 52 |
| 44 | 19 53 | 02 16 | 17 05 | 07 39 | 27 06 |
| 45 | 19 50 | 02 40 | 18 02 | 08 11 | 27 20 |
| 46 | 19 46 | 03 06 | 19 02 | 08 45 | 27 35 |
| 47 | 19 42 | 03 34 | 20 03 | 09 20 | 27 50 |
| 48 | 19 38 | 04 03 | 21 08 | 09 57 | 28 06 |
| 49 | 19 34 | 04 35 | 22 16 | 10 35 | 28 23 |
| 50 | 19 29 | 05 09 | 23 26 | 11 15 | 28 40 |
| 51 | 19 25 | 05 45 | 24 40 | 11 56 | 28 58 |
| 52 | 19 20 | 06 25 | 25 58 | 12 39 | 29 16 |
| 53 | 19 14 | 07 07 | 27 19 | 13 25 | 29 36 |
| 54 | 19 09 | 07 54 | 28 45 | 14 12 | 29 57 |
| 55 | 19 02 | 08 45 | 00♋15 | 15 02 | 00♌18 |
| 56 | 18 56 | 09 41 | 01 49 | 15 54 | 00 41 |
| 57 | 18 49 | 10 43 | 03 29 | 16 50 | 01 05 |
| 58 | 18 41 | 11 53 | 05 13 | 17 48 | 01 30 |
| 59 | 18 33 | 13 11 | 07 03 | 18 49 | 01 57 |
| 60 | 18♓24 | 14♉40 | 08♋58 | 19♋55 | 02♌26 |

**21h 32m 0s — 323° 0' 0" — 20♒36**

| LAT. | 11 | 12 | ASC | 2 | 3 |
|---|---|---|---|---|---|
| 0 | 22♓23 | 24♈50 | 25♉21 | 23♊34 | 21♋17 |
| 5 | 22 17 | 25 27 | 27 04 | 24 54 | 21 54 |
| 10 | 22 11 | 26 06 | 28 53 | 26 15 | 22 32 |
| 15 | 22 04 | 26 48 | 00♊51 | 27 39 | 23 11 |
| 20 | 21 57 | 27 35 | 02 59 | 29 08 | 23 51 |
| 21 | 21 56 | 27 45 | 03 26 | 29 26 | 23 59 |
| 22 | 21 54 | 27 55 | 03 54 | 29 45 | 24 08 |
| 23 | 21 53 | 28 06 | 04 22 | 00♋04 | 24 16 |
| 24 | 21 51 | 28 17 | 04 51 | 00 23 | 24 25 |
| 25 | 21 50 | 28 28 | 05 21 | 00 43 | 24 33 |
| 26 | 21 48 | 28 39 | 05 51 | 01 03 | 24 42 |
| 27 | 21 46 | 28 51 | 06 22 | 01 23 | 24 51 |
| 28 | 21 45 | 29 03 | 06 54 | 01 44 | 25 01 |
| 29 | 21 43 | 29 16 | 07 27 | 02 05 | 25 10 |
| 30 | 21 41 | 29 29 | 08 01 | 02 26 | 25 20 |
| 31 | 21 39 | 29 42 | 08 36 | 02 48 | 25 29 |
| 32 | 21 37 | 29 56 | 09 12 | 03 11 | 25 39 |
| 33 | 21 35 | 00♉11 | 09 48 | 03 34 | 25 49 |
| 34 | 21 33 | 00 26 | 10 26 | 03 57 | 26 00 |
| 35 | 21 31 | 00 41 | 11 06 | 04 21 | 26 10 |
| 36 | 21 29 | 00 57 | 11 46 | 04 46 | 26 21 |
| 37 | 21 27 | 01 14 | 12 28 | 05 11 | 26 32 |
| 38 | 21 25 | 01 32 | 13 11 | 05 37 | 26 44 |
| 39 | 21 22 | 01 51 | 13 56 | 06 04 | 26 55 |
| 40 | 21 20 | 02 10 | 14 43 | 06 32 | 27 07 |
| 41 | 21 17 | 02 30 | 15 31 | 07 00 | 27 20 |
| 42 | 21 15 | 02 52 | 16 21 | 07 30 | 27 33 |
| 43 | 21 12 | 03 15 | 17 13 | 08 00 | 27 46 |
| 44 | 21 09 | 03 38 | 18 08 | 08 31 | 27 59 |
| 45 | 21 06 | 04 04 | 19 04 | 09 04 | 28 13 |
| 46 | 21 03 | 04 31 | 20 03 | 09 37 | 28 28 |
| 47 | 20 59 | 04 59 | 21 04 | 10 12 | 28 43 |
| 48 | 20 56 | 05 29 | 22 08 | 10 49 | 28 59 |
| 49 | 20 52 | 06 02 | 23 15 | 11 26 | 29 15 |
| 50 | 20 48 | 06 37 | 24 26 | 12 06 | 29 32 |
| 51 | 20 44 | 07 15 | 25 39 | 12 47 | 29 50 |
| 52 | 20 39 | 07 55 | 26 56 | 13 29 | 00♌08 |
| 53 | 20 35 | 08 39 | 28 16 | 14 14 | 00 28 |
| 54 | 20 30 | 09 27 | 29 41 | 15 01 | 00 48 |
| 55 | 20 24 | 10 20 | 01♋09 | 15 50 | 01 09 |
| 56 | 20 19 | 11 18 | 02 42 | 16 42 | 01 32 |
| 57 | 20 12 | 12 22 | 04 20 | 17 37 | 01 55 |
| 58 | 20 06 | 13 33 | 06 03 | 18 34 | 02 20 |
| 59 | 19 59 | 14 54 | 07 51 | 19 35 | 02 47 |
| 60 | 19♓51 | 16♉25 | 09♋44 | 20♋39 | 03♌15 |

**21h 36m 0s — 324° 0' 0" — 21♒37**

| LAT. | 11 | 12 | ASC | 2 | 3 |
|---|---|---|---|---|---|
| 0 | 23♓28 | 25♈53 | 26♉19 | 24♊30 | 22♋13 |
| 5 | 23 23 | 26 31 | 28 03 | 25 49 | 22 50 |
| 10 | 23 18 | 27 12 | 29 54 | 27 10 | 23 28 |
| 15 | 23 12 | 27 56 | 01♊52 | 28 35 | 24 06 |
| 20 | 23 06 | 28 45 | 04 00 | 00♋03 | 24 46 |
| 21 | 23 05 | 28 55 | 04 28 | 00 21 | 24 55 |
| 22 | 23 04 | 29 06 | 04 56 | 00 40 | 25 03 |
| 23 | 23 02 | 29 17 | 05 24 | 00 59 | 25 11 |
| 24 | 23 01 | 29 28 | 05 53 | 01 18 | 25 20 |
| 25 | 23 00 | 29 39 | 06 23 | 01 38 | 25 29 |
| 26 | 22 58 | 29 51 | 06 54 | 01 58 | 25 37 |
| 27 | 22 57 | 00♉04 | 07 25 | 02 18 | 25 46 |
| 28 | 22 55 | 00 16 | 07 57 | 02 38 | 25 56 |
| 29 | 22 54 | 00 29 | 08 30 | 02 59 | 26 05 |
| 30 | 22 52 | 00 43 | 09 04 | 03 21 | 26 14 |
| 31 | 22 51 | 00 56 | 09 39 | 03 43 | 26 24 |
| 32 | 22 49 | 01 11 | 10 14 | 04 05 | 26 34 |
| 33 | 22 47 | 01 26 | 10 51 | 04 28 | 26 44 |
| 34 | 22 46 | 01 41 | 11 29 | 04 51 | 26 54 |
| 35 | 22 44 | 01 57 | 12 08 | 05 15 | 27 05 |
| 36 | 22 42 | 02 14 | 12 49 | 05 40 | 27 15 |
| 37 | 22 40 | 02 32 | 13 31 | 06 05 | 27 26 |
| 38 | 22 38 | 02 50 | 14 14 | 06 31 | 27 38 |
| 39 | 22 36 | 03 09 | 14 59 | 06 58 | 27 49 |
| 40 | 22 34 | 03 29 | 15 45 | 07 25 | 28 01 |
| 41 | 22 32 | 03 50 | 16 33 | 07 53 | 28 13 |
| 42 | 22 29 | 04 12 | 17 23 | 08 23 | 28 26 |
| 43 | 22 27 | 04 36 | 18 15 | 08 53 | 28 39 |
| 44 | 22 25 | 05 00 | 19 09 | 09 24 | 28 53 |
| 45 | 22 22 | 05 27 | 20 05 | 09 56 | 29 07 |
| 46 | 22 19 | 05 54 | 21 04 | 10 29 | 29 21 |
| 47 | 22 16 | 06 24 | 22 05 | 11 04 | 29 36 |
| 48 | 22 13 | 06 55 | 23 08 | 11 40 | 29 51 |
| 49 | 22 10 | 07 28 | 24 15 | 12 17 | 00♌08 |
| 50 | 22 07 | 08 04 | 25 24 | 12 56 | 00 24 |
| 51 | 22 03 | 08 43 | 26 37 | 13 37 | 00 42 |
| 52 | 21 59 | 09 25 | 27 53 | 14 19 | 01 00 |
| 53 | 21 55 | 10 10 | 29 12 | 15 04 | 01 19 |
| 54 | 21 51 | 10 59 | 00♋36 | 15 50 | 01 39 |
| 55 | 21 46 | 11 53 | 02 03 | 16 39 | 02 00 |
| 56 | 21 41 | 12 53 | 03 35 | 17 30 | 02 22 |
| 57 | 21 36 | 13 59 | 05 11 | 18 24 | 02 46 |
| 58 | 21 30 | 15 12 | 06 52 | 19 21 | 03 10 |
| 59 | 21 24 | 16 34 | 08 38 | 20 20 | 03 37 |
| 60 | 21♓17 | 18♉08 | 10♋30 | 21♋24 | 04♌04 |

**21h 40m 0s — 325° 0' 0" — 22♒39**

| LAT. | 11 | 12 | ASC | 2 | 3 |
|---|---|---|---|---|---|
| 0 | 24♓33 | 26♈57 | 27♉17 | 25♊25 | 23♋10 |
| 5 | 24 29 | 27 36 | 29 02 | 26 44 | 23 47 |
| 10 | 24 25 | 28 18 | 00♊54 | 28 06 | 24 24 |
| 15 | 24 20 | 29 04 | 02 53 | 29 30 | 25 02 |
| 20 | 24 15 | 29 54 | 05 02 | 00♋58 | 25 42 |
| 21 | 24 14 | 00♉05 | 05 29 | 01 16 | 25 50 |
| 22 | 24 13 | 00 16 | 05 57 | 01 35 | 25 58 |
| 23 | 24 12 | 00 27 | 06 26 | 01 54 | 26 07 |
| 24 | 24 11 | 00 39 | 06 55 | 02 13 | 26 15 |
| 25 | 24 10 | 00 51 | 07 25 | 02 32 | 26 24 |
| 26 | 24 08 | 01 03 | 07 56 | 02 52 | 26 33 |
| 27 | 24 07 | 01 16 | 08 27 | 03 12 | 26 42 |
| 28 | 24 06 | 01 29 | 08 59 | 03 33 | 26 51 |
| 29 | 24 05 | 01 42 | 09 32 | 03 54 | 27 00 |
| 30 | 24 03 | 01 56 | 10 06 | 04 15 | 27 09 |
| 31 | 24 02 | 02 10 | 10 41 | 04 37 | 27 19 |
| 32 | 24 01 | 02 25 | 11 17 | 04 59 | 27 29 |
| 33 | 23 59 | 02 41 | 11 54 | 05 22 | 27 38 |
| 34 | 23 58 | 02 57 | 12 32 | 05 45 | 27 49 |
| 35 | 23 56 | 03 13 | 13 11 | 06 09 | 27 59 |
| 36 | 23 55 | 03 31 | 13 51 | 06 34 | 28 10 |
| 37 | 23 53 | 03 49 | 14 33 | 06 59 | 28 21 |
| 38 | 23 52 | 04 07 | 15 16 | 07 25 | 28 32 |
| 39 | 23 50 | 04 27 | 16 01 | 07 51 | 28 43 |
| 40 | 23 48 | 04 48 | 16 47 | 08 18 | 28 55 |
| 41 | 23 46 | 05 10 | 17 35 | 08 46 | 29 07 |
| 42 | 23 44 | 05 32 | 18 25 | 09 15 | 29 20 |
| 43 | 23 42 | 05 56 | 19 16 | 09 45 | 29 33 |
| 44 | 23 40 | 06 22 | 20 10 | 10 16 | 29 46 |
| 45 | 23 38 | 06 49 | 21 06 | 10 48 | 00♌00 |
| 46 | 23 36 | 07 17 | 22 04 | 11 21 | 00 14 |
| 47 | 23 33 | 07 47 | 23 04 | 11 56 | 00 29 |
| 48 | 23 31 | 08 20 | 24 07 | 12 31 | 00 44 |
| 49 | 23 28 | 08 54 | 25 13 | 13 08 | 01 00 |
| 50 | 23 25 | 09 31 | 26 22 | 13 47 | 01 17 |
| 51 | 23 22 | 10 11 | 27 34 | 14 27 | 01 34 |
| 52 | 23 19 | 10 54 | 28 49 | 15 09 | 01 52 |
| 53 | 23 16 | 11 40 | 00♋07 | 15 53 | 02 11 |
| 54 | 23 12 | 12 31 | 01 30 | 16 39 | 02 30 |
| 55 | 23 08 | 13 26 | 02 56 | 17 27 | 02 51 |
| 56 | 23 04 | 14 27 | 04 27 | 18 18 | 03 13 |
| 57 | 23 00 | 15 34 | 06 02 | 19 11 | 03 36 |
| 58 | 22 55 | 16 49 | 07 41 | 20 07 | 04 00 |
| 59 | 22 50 | 18 13 | 09 25 | 21 06 | 04 26 |
| 60 | 22♓44 | 19♉49 | 11♋15 | 22♋08 | 04♌54 |

**21h 44m 0s — 326° 0' 0" — 23♒41**

| LAT. | 11 | 12 | ASC | 2 | 3 |
|---|---|---|---|---|---|
| 0 | 25♓38 | 28♈00 | 28♉15 | 26♊20 | 24♋06 |
| 5 | 25 35 | 28 41 | 00♊01 | 27 40 | 24 43 |
| 10 | 25 32 | 29 24 | 01 53 | 29 01 | 25 20 |
| 15 | 25 28 | 00♉11 | 03 53 | 00♋25 | 25 58 |
| 20 | 25 24 | 01 03 | 06 03 | 01 53 | 26 38 |
| 21 | 25 23 | 01 14 | 06 31 | 02 11 | 26 46 |
| 22 | 25 22 | 01 26 | 06 59 | 02 30 | 26 54 |
| 23 | 25 21 | 01 37 | 07 27 | 02 49 | 27 02 |
| 24 | 25 21 | 01 49 | 07 57 | 03 08 | 27 11 |
| 25 | 25 20 | 02 02 | 08 27 | 03 27 | 27 19 |
| 26 | 25 19 | 02 14 | 08 57 | 03 47 | 27 28 |
| 27 | 25 18 | 02 27 | 09 29 | 04 07 | 27 37 |
| 28 | 25 17 | 02 41 | 10 01 | 04 27 | 27 46 |
| 29 | 25 16 | 02 55 | 10 34 | 04 48 | 27 55 |
| 30 | 25 15 | 03 09 | 11 08 | 05 09 | 28 04 |
| 31 | 25 14 | 03 24 | 11 43 | 05 31 | 28 14 |
| 32 | 25 13 | 03 39 | 12 19 | 05 53 | 28 23 |
| 33 | 25 11 | 03 55 | 12 56 | 06 16 | 28 33 |
| 34 | 25 10 | 04 11 | 13 34 | 06 39 | 28 43 |
| 35 | 25 09 | 04 29 | 14 13 | 07 03 | 28 54 |
| 36 | 25 08 | 04 46 | 14 53 | 07 27 | 29 04 |
| 37 | 25 07 | 05 05 | 15 35 | 07 52 | 29 15 |
| 38 | 25 05 | 05 24 | 16 18 | 08 18 | 29 26 |
| 39 | 25 04 | 05 45 | 17 02 | 08 44 | 29 37 |
| 40 | 25 02 | 06 06 | 17 48 | 09 11 | 29 49 |
| 41 | 25 01 | 06 28 | 18 36 | 09 39 | 00♌01 |
| 42 | 24 59 | 06 52 | 19 26 | 10 08 | 00 13 |
| 43 | 24 58 | 07 16 | 20 17 | 10 38 | 00 26 |
| 44 | 24 56 | 07 43 | 21 10 | 11 08 | 00 39 |
| 45 | 24 54 | 08 10 | 22 06 | 11 40 | 00 53 |
| 46 | 24 53 | 08 39 | 23 03 | 12 13 | 01 07 |
| 47 | 24 51 | 09 10 | 24 03 | 12 47 | 01 22 |
| 48 | 24 49 | 09 43 | 25 06 | 13 22 | 01 37 |
| 49 | 24 46 | 10 19 | 26 11 | 13 59 | 01 53 |
| 50 | 24 44 | 10 57 | 27 19 | 14 37 | 02 09 |
| 51 | 24 42 | 11 37 | 28 30 | 15 17 | 02 26 |
| 52 | 24 39 | 12 21 | 29 44 | 15 59 | 02 44 |
| 53 | 24 37 | 13 09 | 01♋02 | 16 42 | 03 02 |
| 54 | 24 34 | 14 01 | 02 23 | 17 27 | 03 22 |
| 55 | 24 31 | 14 57 | 03 49 | 18 15 | 03 42 |
| 56 | 24 27 | 15 59 | 05 18 | 19 05 | 04 04 |
| 57 | 24 24 | 17 08 | 06 51 | 19 57 | 04 27 |
| 58 | 24 20 | 18 25 | 08 29 | 20 52 | 04 50 |
| 59 | 24 16 | 19 50 | 10 12 | 21 51 | 05 16 |
| 60 | 24♓11 | 21♉28 | 12♋00 | 22♋52 | 05♌43 |

**21h 48m 0s — 327° 0' 0" — 24♒42**

| LAT. | 11 | 12 | ASC | 2 | 3 |
|---|---|---|---|---|---|
| 0 | 26♓44 | 29♈03 | 29♉13 | 27♊15 | 25♋03 |
| 5 | 26 41 | 29 45 | 01♊00 | 28 35 | 25 40 |
| 10 | 26 39 | 00♉30 | 02 53 | 29 56 | 26 17 |
| 15 | 26 36 | 01 19 | 04 53 | 01♋20 | 26 54 |
| 20 | 26 33 | 02 12 | 07 04 | 02 48 | 27 33 |
| 21 | 26 32 | 02 24 | 07 32 | 03 06 | 27 41 |
| 22 | 26 32 | 02 35 | 08 00 | 03 24 | 27 50 |
| 23 | 26 31 | 02 47 | 08 29 | 03 43 | 27 58 |
| 24 | 26 30 | 03 00 | 08 58 | 04 02 | 28 06 |
| 25 | 26 30 | 03 12 | 09 28 | 04 22 | 28 15 |
| 26 | 26 29 | 03 25 | 09 59 | 04 41 | 28 23 |
| 27 | 26 28 | 03 39 | 10 30 | 05 01 | 28 32 |
| 28 | 26 28 | 03 53 | 11 02 | 05 22 | 28 41 |
| 29 | 26 27 | 04 07 | 11 36 | 05 42 | 28 50 |
| 30 | 26 26 | 04 22 | 12 09 | 06 04 | 28 59 |
| 31 | 26 25 | 04 37 | 12 44 | 06 25 | 29 09 |
| 32 | 26 24 | 04 53 | 13 20 | 06 47 | 29 18 |
| 33 | 26 24 | 05 09 | 13 57 | 07 10 | 29 28 |
| 34 | 26 23 | 05 26 | 14 35 | 07 33 | 29 38 |
| 35 | 26 22 | 05 43 | 15 14 | 07 57 | 29 48 |
| 36 | 26 21 | 06 02 | 15 54 | 08 21 | 29 59 |
| 37 | 26 20 | 06 21 | 16 36 | 08 46 | 00♌09 |
| 38 | 26 19 | 06 41 | 17 19 | 09 11 | 00 20 |
| 39 | 26 18 | 07 02 | 18 03 | 09 37 | 00 31 |
| 40 | 26 17 | 07 24 | 18 49 | 10 04 | 00 43 |
| 41 | 26 16 | 07 46 | 19 36 | 10 32 | 00 55 |
| 42 | 26 15 | 08 11 | 20 26 | 11 01 | 01 07 |
| 43 | 26 13 | 08 36 | 21 17 | 11 30 | 01 20 |
| 44 | 26 12 | 09 03 | 22 10 | 12 00 | 01 33 |
| 45 | 26 11 | 09 31 | 23 05 | 12 32 | 01 46 |
| 46 | 26 09 | 10 01 | 24 02 | 13 04 | 02 00 |
| 47 | 26 08 | 10 33 | 25 02 | 13 38 | 02 15 |
| 48 | 26 06 | 11 06 | 26 04 | 14 13 | 02 30 |
| 49 | 26 05 | 11 43 | 27 08 | 14 50 | 02 45 |
| 50 | 26 03 | 12 21 | 28 16 | 15 27 | 03 01 |
| 51 | 26 01 | 13 03 | 29 26 | 16 07 | 03 18 |
| 52 | 25 59 | 13 48 | 00♋39 | 16 48 | 03 36 |
| 53 | 25 57 | 14 37 | 01 56 | 17 31 | 03 54 |
| 54 | 25 55 | 15 29 | 03 16 | 18 16 | 04 13 |
| 55 | 25 53 | 16 27 | 04 40 | 19 03 | 04 33 |
| 56 | 25 50 | 17 30 | 06 08 | 19 52 | 04 55 |
| 57 | 25 48 | 18 41 | 07 40 | 20 44 | 05 17 |
| 58 | 25 45 | 19 59 | 09 17 | 21 38 | 05 41 |
| 59 | 25 42 | 21 26 | 10 58 | 22 36 | 06 05 |
| 60 | 25♓38 | 23♉05 | 12♋44 | 23♋36 | 06♌32 |

# Placidus Table of Houses for Latitudes 0° to 60° North

**21h 52m 0s — 328° 0' 0" — 25 ♒ 44**

| LAT. | 11 | 12 | ASC | 2 | 3 |
|---|---|---|---|---|---|
| 0 | 27♓49 | 00♉06 | 00♊11 | 28♊10 | 26♋00 |
| 5 | 27 48 | 00 49 | 01 59 | 29 30 | 26 37 |
| 10 | 27 46 | 01 36 | 03 52 | 00♋51 | 27 13 |
| 15 | 27 44 | 02 26 | 05 53 | 02 15 | 27 50 |
| 20 | 27 42 | 03 21 | 08 04 | 03 42 | 28 29 |
| 21 | 27 42 | 03 33 | 08 32 | 04 01 | 28 37 |
| 22 | 27 41 | 03 45 | 09 00 | 04 19 | 28 45 |
| 23 | 27 41 | 03 57 | 09 29 | 04 38 | 28 53 |
| 24 | 27 40 | 04 10 | 09 59 | 04 57 | 29 02 |
| 25 | 27 40 | 04 23 | 10 29 | 05 16 | 29 10 |
| 26 | 27 39 | 04 36 | 11 00 | 05 36 | 29 19 |
| 27 | 27 39 | 04 50 | 11 31 | 05 56 | 29 27 |
| 28 | 27 38 | 05 04 | 12 03 | 06 16 | 29 36 |
| 29 | 27 38 | 05 19 | 12 37 | 06 37 | 29 45 |
| 30 | 27 37 | 05 34 | 13 10 | 06 58 | 29 54 |
| 31 | 27 37 | 05 49 | 13 45 | 07 19 | 00♌04 |
| 32 | 27 36 | 06 06 | 14 21 | 07 41 | 00 13 |
| 33 | 27 36 | 06 22 | 14 58 | 08 04 | 00 23 |
| 34 | 27 35 | 06 40 | 15 36 | 08 27 | 00 33 |
| 35 | 27 34 | 06 58 | 16 15 | 08 50 | 00 43 |
| 36 | 27 34 | 07 17 | 16 55 | 09 14 | 00 53 |
| 37 | 27 33 | 07 36 | 17 36 | 09 39 | 01 04 |
| 38 | 27 33 | 07 57 | 18 19 | 10 04 | 01 14 |
| 39 | 27 32 | 08 18 | 19 03 | 10 30 | 01 26 |
| 40 | 27 31 | 08 41 | 19 49 | 10 57 | 01 37 |
| 41 | 27 30 | 09 04 | 20 36 | 11 24 | 01 49 |
| 42 | 27 30 | 09 29 | 21 25 | 11 53 | 02 01 |
| 43 | 27 29 | 09 55 | 22 16 | 12 22 | 02 13 |
| 44 | 27 28 | 10 22 | 23 09 | 12 52 | 02 26 |
| 45 | 27 27 | 10 51 | 24 03 | 13 23 | 02 40 |
| 46 | 27 26 | 11 22 | 25 00 | 13 56 | 02 53 |
| 47 | 27 25 | 11 54 | 25 59 | 14 29 | 03 08 |
| 48 | 27 24 | 12 29 | 27 01 | 15 04 | 03 22 |
| 49 | 27 23 | 13 06 | 28 05 | 15 40 | 03 38 |
| 50 | 27 22 | 13 45 | 29 11 | 16 17 | 03 54 |
| 51 | 27 21 | 14 28 | 00♋21 | 16 56 | 04 10 |
| 52 | 27 20 | 15 14 | 01 34 | 17 37 | 04 28 |
| 53 | 27 18 | 16 03 | 02 49 | 18 19 | 04 46 |
| 54 | 27 17 | 16 57 | 04 09 | 19 04 | 05 05 |
| 55 | 27 15 | 17 56 | 05 32 | 19 50 | 05 25 |
| 56 | 27 14 | 19 00 | 06 58 | 20 39 | 05 45 |
| 57 | 27 12 | 20 12 | 08 29 | 21 30 | 06 07 |
| 58 | 27 10 | 21 31 | 10 04 | 22 24 | 06 31 |
| 59 | 27 08 | 23 00 | 11 44 | 23 20 | 06 55 |
| 60 | 27♓06 | 24♉41 | 13♋28 | 24♋20 | 07♌21 |

**21h 56m 0s — 329° 0' 0" — 26 ♒ 47**

| LAT. | 11 | 12 | ASC | 2 | 3 |
|---|---|---|---|---|---|
| 0 | 28♓55 | 01♉08 | 01♊08 | 29♊05 | 26♋57 |
| 5 | 28 54 | 01 53 | 02 57 | 00♋25 | 27 33 |
| 10 | 28 53 | 02 41 | 04 51 | 01 46 | 28 10 |
| 15 | 28 52 | 03 33 | 06 53 | 03 09 | 28 47 |
| 20 | 28 51 | 04 29 | 09 05 | 04 37 | 29 25 |
| 21 | 28 51 | 04 41 | 09 32 | 04 55 | 29 33 |
| 22 | 28 51 | 04 54 | 10 01 | 05 14 | 29 41 |
| 23 | 28 50 | 05 06 | 10 30 | 05 32 | 29 49 |
| 24 | 28 50 | 05 19 | 10 59 | 05 51 | 29 57 |
| 25 | 28 50 | 05 33 | 11 29 | 06 10 | 00♌06 |
| 26 | 28 50 | 05 46 | 12 00 | 06 30 | 00 14 |
| 27 | 28 49 | 06 01 | 12 32 | 06 50 | 00 23 |
| 28 | 28 49 | 06 15 | 13 04 | 07 10 | 00 31 |
| 29 | 28 49 | 06 30 | 13 37 | 07 31 | 00 40 |
| 30 | 28 49 | 06 46 | 14 11 | 07 52 | 00 49 |
| 31 | 28 48 | 07 02 | 14 46 | 08 13 | 00 59 |
| 32 | 28 48 | 07 18 | 15 22 | 08 35 | 01 08 |
| 33 | 28 48 | 07 36 | 15 58 | 08 57 | 01 18 |
| 34 | 28 48 | 07 53 | 16 36 | 09 20 | 01 27 |
| 35 | 28 47 | 08 12 | 17 15 | 09 43 | 01 37 |
| 36 | 28 47 | 08 31 | 17 55 | 10 07 | 01 48 |
| 37 | 28 47 | 08 51 | 18 37 | 10 32 | 01 58 |
| 38 | 28 46 | 09 12 | 19 19 | 10 57 | 02 09 |
| 39 | 28 46 | 09 34 | 20 03 | 11 23 | 02 20 |
| 40 | 28 46 | 09 57 | 20 49 | 11 49 | 02 31 |
| 41 | 28 45 | 10 21 | 21 36 | 12 17 | 02 43 |
| 42 | 28 45 | 10 46 | 22 24 | 12 45 | 02 55 |
| 43 | 28 44 | 11 13 | 23 15 | 13 14 | 03 07 |
| 44 | 28 44 | 11 41 | 24 07 | 13 44 | 03 20 |
| 45 | 28 44 | 12 10 | 25 01 | 14 15 | 03 33 |
| 46 | 28 43 | 12 42 | 25 58 | 14 47 | 03 47 |
| 47 | 28 43 | 13 15 | 26 56 | 15 20 | 04 01 |
| 48 | 28 42 | 13 50 | 27 57 | 15 54 | 04 15 |
| 49 | 28 42 | 14 28 | 29 01 | 16 30 | 04 30 |
| 50 | 28 41 | 15 08 | 00♋07 | 17 07 | 04 46 |
| 51 | 28 40 | 15 52 | 01 15 | 17 46 | 05 02 |
| 52 | 28 40 | 16 38 | 02 27 | 18 26 | 05 20 |
| 53 | 28 39 | 17 29 | 03 42 | 19 08 | 05 37 |
| 54 | 28 38 | 18 24 | 05 01 | 19 52 | 05 56 |
| 55 | 28 38 | 19 23 | 06 22 | 20 38 | 06 16 |
| 56 | 28 37 | 20 29 | 07 48 | 21 26 | 06 36 |
| 57 | 28 36 | 21 41 | 09 17 | 22 16 | 06 58 |
| 58 | 28 35 | 23 02 | 10 51 | 23 09 | 07 21 |
| 59 | 28 34 | 24 32 | 12 29 | 24 05 | 07 45 |
| 60 | 28♓33 | 26♉14 | 14♋11 | 25♋04 | 08♌10 |

**22h 0m 0s — 330° 0' 0" — 27 ♒ 49**

| LAT. | 11 | 12 | ASC | 2 | 3 |
|---|---|---|---|---|---|
| 0 | 00♈00 | 02♉11 | 02♊05 | 00♋00 | 27♋55 |
| 5 | 00 00 | 02 57 | 03 55 | 01 20 | 28 30 |
| 10 | 00 00 | 03 46 | 05 50 | 02 41 | 29 06 |
| 15 | 00 00 | 04 39 | 07 52 | 04 04 | 29 43 |
| 20 | 00 00 | 05 37 | 10 05 | 05 32 | 00♌21 |
| 21 | 00 00 | 05 50 | 10 32 | 05 50 | 00 29 |
| 22 | 00 00 | 06 02 | 11 01 | 06 08 | 00 37 |
| 23 | 00 00 | 06 15 | 11 30 | 06 27 | 00 45 |
| 24 | 00 00 | 06 29 | 11 59 | 06 46 | 00 53 |
| 25 | 00 00 | 06 42 | 12 30 | 07 05 | 01 01 |
| 26 | 00 00 | 06 56 | 13 00 | 07 24 | 01 10 |
| 27 | 00 00 | 07 11 | 13 32 | 07 44 | 01 18 |
| 28 | 00 00 | 07 26 | 14 04 | 08 04 | 01 27 |
| 29 | 00 00 | 07 41 | 14 37 | 08 25 | 01 36 |
| 30 | 00 00 | 07 57 | 15 11 | 08 45 | 01 45 |
| 31 | 00 00 | 08 14 | 15 46 | 09 07 | 01 54 |
| 32 | 00 00 | 08 31 | 16 22 | 09 28 | 02 03 |
| 33 | 00 00 | 08 48 | 16 59 | 09 51 | 02 13 |
| 34 | 00 00 | 09 06 | 17 36 | 10 13 | 02 22 |
| 35 | 00 00 | 09 25 | 18 15 | 10 37 | 02 32 |
| 36 | 00 00 | 09 45 | 18 55 | 11 00 | 02 42 |
| 37 | 00 00 | 10 06 | 19 36 | 11 25 | 02 53 |
| 38 | 00 00 | 10 27 | 20 19 | 11 50 | 03 03 |
| 39 | 00 00 | 10 49 | 21 02 | 12 15 | 03 14 |
| 40 | 00 00 | 11 13 | 21 48 | 12 42 | 03 25 |
| 41 | 00 00 | 11 37 | 22 35 | 13 09 | 03 37 |
| 42 | 00 00 | 12 03 | 23 23 | 13 37 | 03 49 |
| 43 | 00 00 | 12 30 | 24 13 | 14 06 | 04 01 |
| 44 | 00 00 | 12 59 | 25 05 | 14 35 | 04 13 |
| 45 | 00 00 | 13 29 | 25 59 | 15 06 | 04 26 |
| 46 | 00 00 | 14 01 | 26 55 | 15 38 | 04 40 |
| 47 | 00 00 | 14 35 | 27 53 | 16 11 | 04 54 |
| 48 | 00 00 | 15 11 | 28 53 | 16 45 | 05 08 |
| 49 | 00 00 | 15 49 | 29 56 | 17 20 | 05 23 |
| 50 | 00 00 | 16 30 | 01♋01 | 17 57 | 05 39 |
| 51 | 00 00 | 17 14 | 02 09 | 18 35 | 05 55 |
| 52 | 00 00 | 18 02 | 03 20 | 19 15 | 06 12 |
| 53 | 00 00 | 18 53 | 04 34 | 19 56 | 06 29 |
| 54 | 00 00 | 19 49 | 05 52 | 20 40 | 06 48 |
| 55 | 00 00 | 20 50 | 07 12 | 21 25 | 07 07 |
| 56 | 00 00 | 21 56 | 08 37 | 22 12 | 07 27 |
| 57 | 00 00 | 23 10 | 10 05 | 23 02 | 07 48 |
| 58 | 00 00 | 24 31 | 11 37 | 23 54 | 08 11 |
| 59 | 00 00 | 26 03 | 13 13 | 24 49 | 08 34 |
| 60 | 00♈00 | 27♉46 | 14♋54 | 25♋47 | 09♌00 |

**22h 4m 0s — 331° 0' 0" — 28 ♒ 52**

| LAT. | 11 | 12 | ASC | 2 | 3 |
|---|---|---|---|---|---|
| 0 | 01♈05 | 03♉13 | 03♊03 | 00♋55 | 28♋52 |
| 5 | 01 06 | 04 01 | 04 53 | 02 15 | 29 27 |
| 10 | 01 07 | 04 51 | 06 49 | 03 36 | 00♌03 |
| 15 | 01 08 | 05 45 | 08 52 | 04 59 | 00 39 |
| 20 | 01 09 | 06 45 | 11 04 | 06 26 | 01 17 |
| 21 | 01 09 | 06 58 | 11 32 | 06 44 | 01 25 |
| 22 | 01 09 | 07 11 | 12 01 | 07 02 | 01 33 |
| 23 | 01 10 | 07 24 | 12 30 | 07 21 | 01 41 |
| 24 | 01 10 | 07 38 | 12 59 | 07 40 | 01 49 |
| 25 | 01 10 | 07 52 | 13 29 | 07 59 | 01 57 |
| 26 | 01 10 | 08 06 | 14 00 | 08 18 | 02 05 |
| 27 | 01 11 | 08 21 | 14 32 | 08 38 | 02 14 |
| 28 | 01 11 | 08 36 | 15 04 | 08 58 | 02 22 |
| 29 | 01 11 | 08 52 | 15 37 | 09 18 | 02 31 |
| 30 | 01 11 | 09 08 | 16 11 | 09 39 | 02 40 |
| 31 | 01 12 | 09 25 | 16 46 | 10 00 | 02 49 |
| 32 | 01 12 | 09 42 | 17 22 | 10 22 | 02 58 |
| 33 | 01 12 | 10 00 | 17 58 | 10 44 | 03 08 |
| 34 | 01 12 | 10 19 | 18 36 | 11 07 | 03 17 |
| 35 | 01 13 | 10 38 | 19 15 | 11 30 | 03 27 |
| 36 | 01 13 | 10 59 | 19 54 | 11 53 | 03 37 |
| 37 | 01 13 | 11 20 | 20 35 | 12 18 | 03 47 |
| 38 | 01 14 | 11 41 | 21 18 | 12 42 | 03 58 |
| 39 | 01 14 | 12 04 | 22 01 | 13 08 | 04 08 |
| 40 | 01 14 | 12 28 | 22 46 | 13 34 | 04 19 |
| 41 | 01 15 | 12 53 | 23 33 | 14 01 | 04 31 |
| 42 | 01 15 | 13 19 | 24 21 | 14 29 | 04 43 |
| 43 | 01 16 | 13 47 | 25 11 | 14 57 | 04 55 |
| 44 | 01 16 | 14 16 | 26 02 | 15 27 | 05 07 |
| 45 | 01 16 | 14 47 | 26 56 | 15 57 | 05 20 |
| 46 | 01 17 | 15 19 | 27 51 | 16 29 | 05 33 |
| 47 | 01 17 | 15 54 | 28 49 | 17 01 | 05 47 |
| 48 | 01 18 | 16 31 | 29 49 | 17 35 | 06 01 |
| 49 | 01 18 | 17 10 | 00♋51 | 18 10 | 06 16 |
| 50 | 01 19 | 17 51 | 01 55 | 18 46 | 06 31 |
| 51 | 01 20 | 18 36 | 03 03 | 19 24 | 06 47 |
| 52 | 01 20 | 19 25 | 04 13 | 20 03 | 07 04 |
| 53 | 01 21 | 20 17 | 05 26 | 20 44 | 07 21 |
| 54 | 01 22 | 21 13 | 06 42 | 21 27 | 07 39 |
| 55 | 01 22 | 22 15 | 08 02 | 22 12 | 07 58 |
| 56 | 01 23 | 23 22 | 09 25 | 22 59 | 08 18 |
| 57 | 01 24 | 24 37 | 10 52 | 23 48 | 08 39 |
| 58 | 01 25 | 25 59 | 12 23 | 24 39 | 09 01 |
| 59 | 01 26 | 27 31 | 13 58 | 25 33 | 09 24 |
| 60 | 01♈27 | 29♉16 | 15♋37 | 26♋30 | 09♌49 |

**22h 8m 0s — 332° 0' 0" — 29 ♒ 54**

| LAT. | 11 | 12 | ASC | 2 | 3 |
|---|---|---|---|---|---|
| 0 | 02♈11 | 04♉16 | 04♊00 | 01♋50 | 29♋49 |
| 5 | 02 12 | 05 04 | 05 51 | 03 10 | 00♌25 |
| 10 | 02 14 | 05 56 | 07 47 | 04 31 | 01 00 |
| 15 | 02 16 | 06 51 | 09 51 | 05 54 | 01 36 |
| 20 | 02 18 | 07 52 | 12 03 | 07 21 | 02 14 |
| 21 | 02 18 | 08 05 | 12 31 | 07 39 | 02 21 |
| 22 | 02 19 | 08 19 | 13 00 | 07 57 | 02 29 |
| 23 | 02 19 | 08 32 | 13 29 | 08 15 | 02 37 |
| 24 | 02 20 | 08 46 | 13 59 | 08 34 | 02 45 |
| 25 | 02 20 | 09 01 | 14 29 | 08 53 | 02 53 |
| 26 | 02 21 | 09 15 | 15 00 | 09 12 | 03 01 |
| 27 | 02 21 | 09 31 | 15 31 | 09 32 | 03 10 |
| 28 | 02 22 | 09 46 | 16 04 | 09 52 | 03 18 |
| 29 | 02 22 | 10 02 | 16 37 | 10 12 | 03 27 |
| 30 | 02 23 | 10 19 | 17 11 | 10 33 | 03 35 |
| 31 | 02 23 | 10 36 | 17 45 | 10 54 | 03 44 |
| 32 | 02 24 | 10 54 | 18 21 | 11 15 | 03 53 |
| 33 | 02 24 | 11 12 | 18 57 | 11 37 | 04 03 |
| 34 | 02 25 | 11 31 | 19 35 | 12 00 | 04 12 |
| 35 | 02 26 | 11 51 | 20 14 | 12 23 | 04 22 |
| 36 | 02 26 | 12 12 | 20 53 | 12 46 | 04 32 |
| 37 | 02 27 | 12 33 | 21 34 | 13 10 | 04 42 |
| 38 | 02 27 | 12 55 | 22 16 | 13 35 | 04 52 |
| 39 | 02 28 | 13 19 | 23 00 | 14 00 | 05 03 |
| 40 | 02 29 | 13 43 | 23 44 | 14 26 | 05 14 |
| 41 | 02 30 | 14 08 | 24 31 | 14 53 | 05 25 |
| 42 | 02 30 | 14 35 | 25 19 | 15 20 | 05 37 |
| 43 | 02 31 | 15 03 | 26 08 | 15 49 | 05 48 |
| 44 | 02 32 | 15 33 | 26 59 | 16 18 | 06 01 |
| 45 | 02 33 | 16 04 | 27 52 | 16 48 | 06 13 |
| 46 | 02 34 | 16 37 | 28 47 | 17 19 | 06 26 |
| 47 | 02 35 | 17 12 | 29 44 | 17 52 | 06 40 |
| 48 | 02 36 | 17 50 | 00♋44 | 18 25 | 06 54 |
| 49 | 02 37 | 18 29 | 01 45 | 19 00 | 07 08 |
| 50 | 02 38 | 19 12 | 02 49 | 19 36 | 07 24 |
| 51 | 02 39 | 19 57 | 03 56 | 20 13 | 07 39 |
| 52 | 02 40 | 20 46 | 05 05 | 20 52 | 07 56 |
| 53 | 02 42 | 21 39 | 06 17 | 21 32 | 08 13 |
| 54 | 02 43 | 22 36 | 07 33 | 22 15 | 08 31 |
| 55 | 02 45 | 23 39 | 08 51 | 22 59 | 08 49 |
| 56 | 02 46 | 24 47 | 10 13 | 23 45 | 09 09 |
| 57 | 02 48 | 26 02 | 11 39 | 24 33 | 09 29 |
| 58 | 02 50 | 27 25 | 13 08 | 25 24 | 09 51 |
| 59 | 02 52 | 28 59 | 14 41 | 26 18 | 10 14 |
| 60 | 02♈54 | 00♊44 | 16♋19 | 27♋14 | 10♌38 |

**22h 12m 0s — 333° 0' 0" — 00 ♓ 57**

| LAT. | 11 | 12 | ASC | 2 | 3 |
|---|---|---|---|---|---|
| 0 | 03♈16 | 05♉18 | 04♊57 | 02♋45 | 00♌47 |
| 5 | 03 19 | 06 07 | 06 49 | 04 05 | 01 22 |
| 10 | 03 21 | 07 00 | 08 45 | 05 25 | 01 57 |
| 15 | 03 24 | 07 57 | 10 49 | 06 48 | 02 33 |
| 20 | 03 27 | 08 59 | 13 03 | 08 15 | 03 10 |
| 21 | 03 28 | 09 13 | 13 31 | 08 33 | 03 17 |
| 22 | 03 28 | 09 26 | 13 59 | 08 51 | 03 25 |
| 23 | 03 29 | 09 40 | 14 28 | 09 09 | 03 33 |
| 24 | 03 30 | 09 55 | 14 58 | 09 28 | 03 41 |
| 25 | 03 30 | 10 09 | 15 28 | 09 47 | 03 49 |
| 26 | 03 31 | 10 24 | 15 59 | 10 06 | 03 57 |
| 27 | 03 32 | 10 40 | 16 30 | 10 26 | 04 05 |
| 28 | 03 32 | 10 56 | 17 03 | 10 45 | 04 14 |
| 29 | 03 33 | 11 12 | 17 36 | 11 06 | 04 22 |
| 30 | 03 34 | 11 29 | 18 10 | 11 26 | 04 31 |
| 31 | 03 35 | 11 47 | 18 44 | 11 47 | 04 40 |
| 32 | 03 36 | 12 05 | 19 20 | 12 09 | 04 49 |
| 33 | 03 36 | 12 23 | 19 56 | 12 30 | 04 58 |
| 34 | 03 37 | 12 43 | 20 34 | 12 53 | 05 07 |
| 35 | 03 38 | 13 03 | 21 12 | 13 15 | 05 17 |
| 36 | 03 39 | 13 24 | 21 52 | 13 39 | 05 27 |
| 37 | 03 40 | 13 46 | 22 32 | 14 03 | 05 37 |
| 38 | 03 41 | 14 09 | 23 14 | 14 27 | 05 47 |
| 39 | 03 42 | 14 32 | 23 57 | 14 52 | 05 57 |
| 40 | 03 43 | 14 57 | 24 42 | 15 18 | 06 08 |
| 41 | 03 44 | 15 23 | 25 28 | 15 45 | 06 19 |
| 42 | 03 45 | 15 50 | 26 16 | 16 12 | 06 31 |
| 43 | 03 47 | 16 19 | 27 05 | 16 40 | 06 42 |
| 44 | 03 48 | 16 49 | 27 56 | 17 09 | 06 54 |
| 45 | 03 49 | 17 21 | 28 48 | 17 39 | 07 07 |
| 46 | 03 51 | 17 54 | 29 43 | 18 10 | 07 20 |
| 47 | 03 52 | 18 30 | 00♋39 | 18 42 | 07 33 |
| 48 | 03 54 | 19 08 | 01 38 | 19 15 | 07 47 |
| 49 | 03 55 | 19 48 | 02 39 | 19 49 | 08 01 |
| 50 | 03 57 | 20 31 | 03 42 | 20 25 | 08 16 |
| 51 | 03 59 | 21 17 | 04 48 | 21 02 | 08 32 |
| 52 | 04 01 | 22 07 | 05 57 | 21 40 | 08 48 |
| 53 | 04 03 | 23 00 | 07 08 | 22 20 | 09 05 |
| 54 | 04 05 | 23 58 | 08 22 | 23 02 | 09 22 |
| 55 | 04 07 | 25 01 | 09 40 | 23 45 | 09 40 |
| 56 | 04 10 | 26 10 | 11 01 | 24 31 | 10 00 |
| 57 | 04 12 | 27 26 | 12 25 | 25 19 | 10 20 |
| 58 | 04 15 | 28 50 | 13 53 | 26 09 | 10 41 |
| 59 | 04 18 | 00♊24 | 15 25 | 27 02 | 11 04 |
| 60 | 04♈22 | 02♊10 | 17♋01 | 27♋57 | 11♌28 |

**22h 16m 0s — 334° 0' 0" — 02 ♓ 00**

| LAT. | 11 | 12 | ASC | 2 | 3 |
|---|---|---|---|---|---|
| 0 | 04♈22 | 06♉19 | 05♊54 | 03♋40 | 01♌45 |
| 5 | 04 25 | 07 10 | 07 46 | 05 00 | 02 20 |
| 10 | 04 28 | 08 04 | 09 44 | 06 20 | 02 54 |
| 15 | 04 32 | 09 03 | 11 48 | 07 43 | 03 30 |
| 20 | 04 36 | 10 06 | 14 01 | 09 09 | 04 06 |
| 21 | 04 37 | 10 20 | 14 29 | 09 27 | 04 14 |
| 22 | 04 38 | 10 34 | 14 58 | 09 45 | 04 21 |
| 23 | 04 39 | 10 48 | 15 27 | 10 03 | 04 29 |
| 24 | 04 39 | 11 03 | 15 57 | 10 22 | 04 37 |
| 25 | 04 40 | 11 17 | 16 27 | 10 41 | 04 45 |
| 26 | 04 41 | 11 33 | 16 58 | 11 00 | 04 53 |
| 27 | 04 42 | 11 49 | 17 29 | 11 19 | 05 01 |
| 28 | 04 43 | 12 05 | 18 02 | 11 39 | 05 09 |
| 29 | 04 44 | 12 22 | 18 35 | 11 59 | 05 18 |
| 30 | 04 45 | 12 39 | 19 08 | 12 20 | 05 26 |
| 31 | 04 46 | 12 57 | 19 43 | 12 40 | 05 35 |
| 32 | 04 47 | 13 15 | 20 18 | 13 02 | 05 44 |
| 33 | 04 49 | 13 34 | 20 55 | 13 23 | 05 53 |
| 34 | 04 50 | 13 54 | 21 32 | 13 46 | 06 02 |
| 35 | 04 51 | 14 15 | 22 10 | 14 08 | 06 12 |
| 36 | 04 52 | 14 36 | 22 50 | 14 31 | 06 21 |
| 37 | 04 53 | 14 58 | 23 30 | 14 55 | 06 31 |
| 38 | 04 55 | 15 21 | 24 12 | 15 19 | 06 41 |
| 39 | 04 56 | 15 45 | 24 55 | 15 44 | 06 52 |
| 40 | 04 58 | 16 11 | 25 39 | 16 10 | 07 02 |
| 41 | 04 59 | 16 37 | 26 25 | 16 36 | 07 13 |
| 42 | 05 01 | 17 05 | 27 12 | 17 03 | 07 25 |
| 43 | 05 02 | 17 34 | 28 01 | 17 31 | 07 36 |
| 44 | 05 04 | 18 04 | 28 51 | 18 00 | 07 48 |
| 45 | 05 06 | 18 37 | 29 44 | 18 30 | 08 00 |
| 46 | 05 07 | 19 11 | 00♋38 | 19 00 | 08 13 |
| 47 | 05 09 | 19 47 | 01 34 | 19 32 | 08 26 |
| 48 | 05 11 | 20 25 | 02 32 | 20 05 | 08 40 |
| 49 | 05 14 | 21 06 | 03 32 | 20 38 | 08 54 |
| 50 | 05 16 | 21 50 | 04 35 | 21 14 | 09 09 |
| 51 | 05 18 | 22 36 | 05 40 | 21 50 | 09 24 |
| 52 | 05 21 | 23 26 | 06 48 | 22 28 | 09 40 |
| 53 | 05 23 | 24 20 | 07 58 | 23 08 | 09 56 |
| 54 | 05 26 | 25 19 | 09 12 | 23 49 | 10 14 |
| 55 | 05 29 | 26 23 | 10 28 | 24 32 | 10 32 |
| 56 | 05 33 | 27 32 | 11 48 | 25 17 | 10 51 |
| 57 | 05 36 | 28 49 | 13 11 | 26 04 | 11 11 |
| 58 | 05 40 | 00♊14 | 14 38 | 26 54 | 11 32 |
| 59 | 05 44 | 01 48 | 16 08 | 27 45 | 11 54 |
| 60 | 05♈49 | 03♊35 | 17♋42 | 28♋40 | 12♌17 |

**22h 20m 0s — 335° 0' 0" — 03 ♓ 03**

| LAT. | 11 | 12 | ASC | 2 | 3 |
|---|---|---|---|---|---|
| 0 | 05♈27 | 07♉21 | 06♊50 | 04♋35 | 02♌43 |
| 5 | 05 31 | 08 13 | 08 43 | 05 55 | 03 17 |
| 10 | 05 35 | 09 08 | 10 41 | 07 15 | 03 52 |
| 15 | 05 40 | 10 08 | 12 46 | 08 38 | 04 27 |
| 20 | 05 45 | 11 13 | 15 00 | 10 04 | 05 03 |
| 21 | 05 46 | 11 27 | 15 28 | 10 21 | 05 10 |
| 22 | 05 47 | 11 41 | 15 56 | 10 39 | 05 18 |
| 23 | 05 48 | 11 55 | 16 26 | 10 58 | 05 26 |
| 24 | 05 49 | 12 10 | 16 55 | 11 16 | 05 33 |
| 25 | 05 50 | 12 25 | 17 25 | 11 35 | 05 41 |
| 26 | 05 52 | 12 41 | 17 56 | 11 54 | 05 49 |
| 27 | 05 53 | 12 57 | 18 28 | 12 13 | 05 57 |
| 28 | 05 54 | 13 14 | 19 00 | 12 33 | 06 05 |
| 29 | 05 55 | 13 31 | 19 33 | 12 53 | 06 14 |
| 30 | 05 57 | 13 48 | 20 07 | 13 13 | 06 22 |
| 31 | 05 58 | 14 07 | 20 41 | 13 34 | 06 31 |
| 32 | 05 59 | 14 25 | 21 16 | 13 55 | 06 39 |
| 33 | 06 01 | 14 45 | 21 53 | 14 16 | 06 48 |
| 34 | 06 02 | 15 05 | 22 30 | 14 38 | 06 58 |
| 35 | 06 04 | 15 26 | 23 08 | 15 01 | 07 07 |
| 36 | 06 05 | 15 47 | 23 47 | 15 24 | 07 16 |
| 37 | 06 07 | 16 10 | 24 28 | 15 47 | 07 26 |
| 38 | 06 08 | 16 34 | 25 09 | 16 12 | 07 36 |
| 39 | 06 10 | 16 58 | 25 52 | 16 36 | 07 46 |
| 40 | 06 12 | 17 24 | 26 36 | 17 02 | 07 57 |
| 41 | 06 14 | 17 50 | 27 21 | 17 28 | 08 08 |
| 42 | 06 16 | 18 19 | 28 08 | 17 55 | 08 19 |
| 43 | 06 18 | 18 48 | 28 57 | 18 22 | 08 30 |
| 44 | 06 20 | 19 19 | 29 47 | 18 51 | 08 42 |
| 45 | 06 22 | 19 52 | 00♋39 | 19 20 | 08 54 |
| 46 | 06 24 | 20 26 | 01 32 | 19 50 | 09 07 |
| 47 | 06 27 | 21 03 | 02 28 | 20 22 | 09 20 |
| 48 | 06 29 | 21 42 | 03 25 | 20 54 | 09 33 |
| 49 | 06 32 | 22 23 | 04 25 | 21 28 | 09 47 |
| 50 | 06 35 | 23 07 | 05 27 | 22 03 | 10 01 |
| 51 | 06 38 | 23 54 | 06 31 | 22 39 | 10 16 |
| 52 | 06 41 | 24 45 | 07 38 | 23 16 | 10 32 |
| 53 | 06 44 | 25 40 | 08 48 | 23 55 | 10 48 |
| 54 | 06 48 | 26 39 | 10 00 | 24 36 | 11 05 |
| 55 | 06 52 | 27 43 | 11 16 | 25 19 | 11 23 |
| 56 | 06 56 | 28 53 | 12 34 | 26 03 | 11 42 |
| 57 | 07 00 | 00♊10 | 13 56 | 26 49 | 12 01 |
| 58 | 07 05 | 01 36 | 15 22 | 27 38 | 12 22 |
| 59 | 07 10 | 03 11 | 16 51 | 28 29 | 12 44 |
| 60 | 07♈16 | 04♊57 | 18♋24 | 29♋23 | 13♌06 |

# Placidus Table of Houses for Latitudes 0° to 60° North

**22h 24m 0s — 336° 0' 0" — 04 ♓ 07**

| LAT. | 11 | 12 | ASC | 2 | 3 |
|---|---|---|---|---|---|
| 0 | 06♈32 | 08♉23 | 07♊47 | 05♋30 | 03♌41 |
| 5 | 06 37 | 09 16 | 09 41 | 06 50 | 04 15 |
| 10 | 06 42 | 10 12 | 11 39 | 08 10 | 04 49 |
| 15 | 06 48 | 11 13 | 13 44 | 09 32 | 05 24 |
| 20 | 06 54 | 12 19 | 15 58 | 10 58 | 06 00 |
| 21 | 06 55 | 12 33 | 16 26 | 11 15 | 06 07 |
| 22 | 06 56 | 12 48 | 16 55 | 11 33 | 06 14 |
| 23 | 06 58 | 13 02 | 17 24 | 11 52 | 06 22 |
| 24 | 06 59 | 13 17 | 17 53 | 12 10 | 06 30 |
| 25 | 07 00 | 13 33 | 18 24 | 12 29 | 06 37 |
| 26 | 07 02 | 13 49 | 18 54 | 12 47 | 06 45 |
| 27 | 07 03 | 14 05 | 19 26 | 13 07 | 06 53 |
| 28 | 07 05 | 14 22 | 19 58 | 13 26 | 07 01 |
| 29 | 07 06 | 14 40 | 20 31 | 13 46 | 07 10 |
| 30 | 07 08 | 14 57 | 21 05 | 14 06 | 07 18 |
| 31 | 07 09 | 15 16 | 21 39 | 14 27 | 07 26 |
| 32 | 07 11 | 15 35 | 22 14 | 14 48 | 07 35 |
| 33 | 07 13 | 15 55 | 22 50 | 15 09 | 07 44 |
| 34 | 07 14 | 16 15 | 23 27 | 15 31 | 07 53 |
| 35 | 07 16 | 16 36 | 24 05 | 15 53 | 08 02 |
| 36 | 07 18 | 16 58 | 24 44 | 16 16 | 08 12 |
| 37 | 07 20 | 17 21 | 25 25 | 16 40 | 08 21 |
| 38 | 07 22 | 17 45 | 26 06 | 17 04 | 08 31 |
| 39 | 07 24 | 18 10 | 26 48 | 17 28 | 08 41 |
| 40 | 07 26 | 18 36 | 27 32 | 17 53 | 08 51 |
| 41 | 07 28 | 19 03 | 28 17 | 18 19 | 09 02 |
| 42 | 07 31 | 19 32 | 29 04 | 18 46 | 09 13 |
| 43 | 07 33 | 20 02 | 29 52 | 19 13 | 09 24 |
| 44 | 07 35 | 20 33 | 00♋42 | 19 41 | 09 36 |
| 45 | 07 38 | 21 06 | 01 33 | 20 11 | 09 48 |
| 46 | 07 41 | 21 41 | 02 26 | 20 41 | 10 00 |
| 47 | 07 44 | 22 18 | 03 21 | 21 12 | 10 13 |
| 48 | 07 47 | 22 57 | 04 18 | 21 44 | 10 26 |
| 49 | 07 50 | 23 39 | 05 17 | 22 17 | 10 40 |
| 50 | 07 53 | 24 24 | 06 19 | 22 51 | 10 54 |
| 51 | 07 57 | 25 11 | 07 22 | 23 27 | 11 09 |
| 52 | 08 01 | 26 03 | 08 28 | 24 04 | 11 24 |
| 53 | 08 05 | 26 58 | 09 37 | 24 43 | 11 40 |
| 54 | 08 09 | 27 57 | 10 49 | 25 23 | 11 57 |
| 55 | 08 14 | 29 02 | 12 03 | 26 05 | 12 14 |
| 56 | 08 19 | 00♊13 | 13 21 | 26 49 | 12 33 |
| 57 | 08 24 | 01 30 | 14 42 | 27 35 | 12 52 |
| 58 | 08 30 | 02 56 | 16 06 | 28 23 | 13 12 |
| 59 | 08 36 | 04 31 | 17 33 | 29 13 | 13 33 |
| 60 | 08♈43 | 06♊19 | 19♋05 | 00♌06 | 13♌56 |

**22h 28m 0s — 337° 0' 0" — 05 ♓ 10**

| LAT. | 11 | 12 | ASC | 2 | 3 |
|---|---|---|---|---|---|
| 0 | 07♈37 | 09♉24 | 08♊43 | 06♋26 | 04♌39 |
| 5 | 07 43 | 10 18 | 10 38 | 07 45 | 05 13 |
| 10 | 07 49 | 11 16 | 12 37 | 09 05 | 05 47 |
| 15 | 07 56 | 12 17 | 14 42 | 10 27 | 06 21 |
| 20 | 08 03 | 13 25 | 16 56 | 11 52 | 06 56 |
| 21 | 08 04 | 13 39 | 17 24 | 12 10 | 07 04 |
| 22 | 08 06 | 13 54 | 17 53 | 12 27 | 07 11 |
| 23 | 08 07 | 14 09 | 18 22 | 12 45 | 07 19 |
| 24 | 08 09 | 14 24 | 18 51 | 13 04 | 07 26 |
| 25 | 08 10 | 14 40 | 19 22 | 13 22 | 07 34 |
| 26 | 08 12 | 14 56 | 19 52 | 13 41 | 07 41 |
| 27 | 08 14 | 15 13 | 20 24 | 14 00 | 07 49 |
| 28 | 08 15 | 15 30 | 20 56 | 14 20 | 07 57 |
| 29 | 08 17 | 15 48 | 21 29 | 14 39 | 08 05 |
| 30 | 08 19 | 16 06 | 22 02 | 14 59 | 08 14 |
| 31 | 08 21 | 16 25 | 22 37 | 15 20 | 08 22 |
| 32 | 08 23 | 16 44 | 23 12 | 15 41 | 08 31 |
| 33 | 08 25 | 17 04 | 23 48 | 16 02 | 08 39 |
| 34 | 08 27 | 17 25 | 24 25 | 16 24 | 08 48 |
| 35 | 08 29 | 17 47 | 25 02 | 16 46 | 08 57 |
| 36 | 08 31 | 18 09 | 25 41 | 17 09 | 09 07 |
| 37 | 08 33 | 18 32 | 26 21 | 17 32 | 09 16 |
| 38 | 08 35 | 18 56 | 27 02 | 17 56 | 09 26 |
| 39 | 08 38 | 19 22 | 27 45 | 18 20 | 09 36 |
| 40 | 08 40 | 19 48 | 28 28 | 18 45 | 09 46 |
| 41 | 08 43 | 20 15 | 29 13 | 19 11 | 09 57 |
| 42 | 08 45 | 20 44 | 29 59 | 19 37 | 10 07 |
| 43 | 08 48 | 21 15 | 00♋47 | 20 04 | 10 18 |
| 44 | 08 51 | 21 46 | 01 36 | 20 32 | 10 30 |
| 45 | 08 54 | 22 20 | 02 27 | 21 01 | 10 42 |
| 46 | 08 57 | 22 55 | 03 20 | 21 31 | 10 54 |
| 47 | 09 01 | 23 33 | 04 14 | 22 01 | 11 06 |
| 48 | 09 04 | 24 12 | 05 11 | 22 33 | 11 19 |
| 49 | 09 08 | 24 55 | 06 09 | 23 06 | 11 33 |
| 50 | 09 12 | 25 40 | 07 10 | 23 40 | 11 47 |
| 51 | 09 16 | 26 28 | 08 13 | 24 15 | 12 01 |
| 52 | 09 21 | 27 19 | 09 18 | 24 52 | 12 17 |
| 53 | 09 25 | 28 15 | 10 26 | 25 30 | 12 32 |
| 54 | 09 30 | 29 15 | 11 37 | 26 10 | 12 49 |
| 55 | 09 36 | 00♊20 | 12 50 | 26 51 | 13 06 |
| 56 | 09 41 | 01 31 | 14 07 | 27 34 | 13 24 |
| 57 | 09 48 | 02 49 | 15 26 | 28 20 | 13 43 |
| 58 | 09 54 | 04 15 | 16 49 | 29 07 | 14 03 |
| 59 | 10 01 | 05 51 | 18 16 | 29 56 | 14 23 |
| 60 | 10♈09 | 07♊38 | 19♋46 | 00♌49 | 14♌45 |

**22h 32m 0s — 338° 0' 0" — 06 ♓ 14**

| LAT. | 11 | 12 | ASC | 2 | 3 |
|---|---|---|---|---|---|
| 0 | 08♈43 | 10♉25 | 09♊40 | 07♋21 | 05♌38 |
| 5 | 08 49 | 11 21 | 11 35 | 08 40 | 06 11 |
| 10 | 08 56 | 12 19 | 13 34 | 10 00 | 06 44 |
| 15 | 09 03 | 13 22 | 15 39 | 11 21 | 07 18 |
| 20 | 09 11 | 14 31 | 17 54 | 12 46 | 07 53 |
| 21 | 09 13 | 14 45 | 18 22 | 13 04 | 08 01 |
| 22 | 09 15 | 15 00 | 18 50 | 13 21 | 08 08 |
| 23 | 09 17 | 15 15 | 19 19 | 13 39 | 08 15 |
| 24 | 09 18 | 15 31 | 19 49 | 13 58 | 08 23 |
| 25 | 09 20 | 15 47 | 20 19 | 14 16 | 08 30 |
| 26 | 09 22 | 16 04 | 20 50 | 14 35 | 08 38 |
| 27 | 09 24 | 16 20 | 21 21 | 14 54 | 08 46 |
| 28 | 09 26 | 16 38 | 21 53 | 15 13 | 08 54 |
| 29 | 09 28 | 16 56 | 22 26 | 15 33 | 09 02 |
| 30 | 09 30 | 17 14 | 23 00 | 15 53 | 09 10 |
| 31 | 09 32 | 17 33 | 23 34 | 16 13 | 09 18 |
| 32 | 09 34 | 17 53 | 24 09 | 16 34 | 09 26 |
| 33 | 09 36 | 18 13 | 24 45 | 16 55 | 09 35 |
| 34 | 09 39 | 18 34 | 25 21 | 17 16 | 09 44 |
| 35 | 09 41 | 18 56 | 25 59 | 17 38 | 09 53 |
| 36 | 09 43 | 19 19 | 26 38 | 18 01 | 10 02 |
| 37 | 09 46 | 19 42 | 27 18 | 18 24 | 10 11 |
| 38 | 09 49 | 20 07 | 27 58 | 18 47 | 10 21 |
| 39 | 09 51 | 20 33 | 28 40 | 19 12 | 10 31 |
| 40 | 09 54 | 20 59 | 29 24 | 19 36 | 10 41 |
| 41 | 09 57 | 21 27 | 00♋08 | 20 02 | 10 51 |
| 42 | 10 00 | 21 56 | 00 54 | 20 28 | 11 02 |
| 43 | 10 03 | 22 27 | 01 41 | 20 55 | 11 13 |
| 44 | 10 07 | 22 59 | 02 30 | 21 23 | 11 24 |
| 45 | 10 10 | 23 33 | 03 21 | 21 51 | 11 36 |
| 46 | 10 14 | 24 09 | 04 13 | 22 20 | 11 48 |
| 47 | 10 18 | 24 47 | 05 07 | 22 51 | 12 00 |
| 48 | 10 22 | 25 27 | 06 03 | 23 22 | 12 13 |
| 49 | 10 26 | 26 09 | 07 01 | 23 55 | 12 26 |
| 50 | 10 31 | 26 55 | 08 01 | 24 28 | 12 40 |
| 51 | 10 35 | 27 43 | 09 03 | 25 03 | 12 54 |
| 52 | 10 40 | 28 35 | 10 08 | 25 40 | 13 09 |
| 53 | 10 46 | 29 31 | 11 15 | 26 17 | 13 24 |
| 54 | 10 51 | 00♊31 | 12 24 | 26 56 | 13 41 |
| 55 | 10 58 | 01 37 | 13 37 | 27 37 | 13 57 |
| 56 | 11 04 | 02 48 | 14 52 | 28 20 | 14 15 |
| 57 | 11 11 | 04 07 | 16 11 | 29 05 | 14 34 |
| 58 | 11 19 | 05 33 | 17 32 | 29 51 | 14 53 |
| 59 | 11 27 | 07 09 | 18 58 | 00♌40 | 15 13 |
| 60 | 11♈36 | 08♊56 | 20♋26 | 01♌31 | 15♌35 |

**22h 36m 0s — 339° 0' 0" — 07 ♓ 18**

| LAT. | 11 | 12 | ASC | 2 | 3 |
|---|---|---|---|---|---|
| 0 | 09♈48 | 11♉26 | 10♊36 | 08♋16 | 06♌37 |
| 5 | 09 55 | 12 23 | 12 31 | 09 35 | 07 09 |
| 10 | 10 03 | 13 22 | 14 31 | 10 54 | 07 42 |
| 15 | 10 11 | 14 26 | 16 37 | 12 16 | 08 16 |
| 20 | 10 20 | 15 36 | 18 51 | 13 40 | 08 50 |
| 21 | 10 22 | 15 51 | 19 19 | 13 58 | 08 58 |
| 22 | 10 24 | 16 06 | 19 48 | 14 15 | 09 05 |
| 23 | 10 26 | 16 21 | 20 17 | 14 33 | 09 12 |
| 24 | 10 28 | 16 37 | 20 46 | 14 51 | 09 19 |
| 25 | 10 30 | 16 54 | 21 17 | 15 10 | 09 27 |
| 26 | 10 32 | 17 10 | 21 47 | 15 28 | 09 34 |
| 27 | 10 34 | 17 27 | 22 19 | 15 47 | 09 42 |
| 28 | 10 36 | 17 45 | 22 51 | 16 06 | 09 50 |
| 29 | 10 38 | 18 03 | 23 23 | 16 26 | 09 58 |
| 30 | 10 41 | 18 22 | 23 57 | 16 46 | 10 06 |
| 31 | 10 43 | 18 41 | 24 31 | 17 06 | 10 14 |
| 32 | 10 46 | 19 01 | 25 06 | 17 26 | 10 22 |
| 33 | 10 48 | 19 22 | 25 41 | 17 47 | 10 31 |
| 34 | 10 51 | 19 43 | 26 18 | 18 09 | 10 39 |
| 35 | 10 53 | 20 05 | 26 55 | 18 31 | 10 48 |
| 36 | 10 56 | 20 28 | 27 34 | 18 53 | 10 57 |
| 37 | 10 59 | 20 52 | 28 13 | 19 16 | 11 07 |
| 38 | 11 02 | 21 17 | 28 54 | 19 39 | 11 16 |
| 39 | 11 05 | 21 43 | 29 36 | 20 03 | 11 26 |
| 40 | 11 08 | 22 10 | 00♋19 | 20 28 | 11 36 |
| 41 | 11 11 | 22 38 | 01 03 | 20 53 | 11 46 |
| 42 | 11 15 | 23 08 | 01 48 | 21 19 | 11 56 |
| 43 | 11 18 | 23 39 | 02 35 | 21 46 | 12 07 |
| 44 | 11 22 | 24 11 | 03 24 | 22 13 | 12 18 |
| 45 | 11 26 | 24 45 | 04 14 | 22 41 | 12 30 |
| 46 | 11 30 | 25 21 | 05 06 | 23 10 | 12 41 |
| 47 | 11 35 | 26 00 | 05 59 | 23 40 | 12 53 |
| 48 | 11 39 | 26 40 | 06 54 | 24 11 | 13 06 |
| 49 | 11 44 | 27 23 | 07 52 | 24 44 | 13 19 |
| 50 | 11 49 | 28 09 | 08 51 | 25 17 | 13 33 |
| 51 | 11 54 | 28 58 | 09 53 | 25 51 | 13 47 |
| 52 | 12 00 | 29 50 | 10 57 | 26 27 | 14 01 |
| 53 | 12 06 | 00♊46 | 12 03 | 27 04 | 14 17 |
| 54 | 12 12 | 01 47 | 13 12 | 27 43 | 14 32 |
| 55 | 12 19 | 02 53 | 14 23 | 28 23 | 14 49 |
| 56 | 12 27 | 04 04 | 15 38 | 29 05 | 15 06 |
| 57 | 12 34 | 05 23 | 16 55 | 29 49 | 15 24 |
| 58 | 12 43 | 06 49 | 18 15 | 00♌35 | 15 44 |
| 59 | 12 52 | 08 25 | 19 39 | 01 23 | 16 04 |
| 60 | 13♈02 | 10♊12 | 21♋06 | 02♌14 | 16♌25 |

**22h 40m 0s — 340° 0' 0" — 08 ♓ 22**

| LAT. | 11 | 12 | ASC | 2 | 3 |
|---|---|---|---|---|---|
| 0 | 10♈53 | 12♉27 | 11♊32 | 09♋11 | 07♌35 |
| 5 | 11 01 | 13 24 | 13 28 | 10 30 | 08 08 |
| 10 | 11 10 | 14 25 | 15 28 | 11 49 | 08 40 |
| 15 | 11 19 | 15 30 | 17 34 | 13 10 | 09 13 |
| 20 | 11 29 | 16 41 | 19 48 | 14 34 | 09 48 |
| 21 | 11 31 | 16 56 | 20 16 | 14 52 | 09 55 |
| 22 | 11 33 | 17 11 | 20 45 | 15 09 | 10 02 |
| 23 | 11 35 | 17 27 | 21 14 | 15 27 | 10 09 |
| 24 | 11 37 | 17 43 | 21 44 | 15 45 | 10 16 |
| 25 | 11 39 | 18 00 | 22 14 | 16 03 | 10 24 |
| 26 | 11 42 | 18 17 | 22 44 | 16 22 | 10 31 |
| 27 | 11 44 | 18 34 | 23 16 | 16 41 | 10 39 |
| 28 | 11 47 | 18 52 | 23 47 | 17 00 | 10 46 |
| 29 | 11 49 | 19 10 | 24 20 | 17 19 | 10 54 |
| 30 | 11 52 | 19 29 | 24 53 | 17 39 | 11 02 |
| 31 | 11 54 | 19 49 | 25 27 | 17 59 | 11 10 |
| 32 | 11 57 | 20 09 | 26 02 | 18 19 | 11 18 |
| 33 | 12 00 | 20 30 | 26 38 | 18 40 | 11 27 |
| 34 | 12 03 | 20 52 | 27 14 | 19 01 | 11 35 |
| 35 | 12 05 | 21 14 | 27 51 | 19 23 | 11 44 |
| 36 | 12 09 | 21 37 | 28 30 | 19 45 | 11 53 |
| 37 | 12 12 | 22 02 | 29 09 | 20 08 | 12 02 |
| 38 | 12 15 | 22 27 | 29 49 | 20 31 | 12 11 |
| 39 | 12 18 | 22 53 | 00♋31 | 20 55 | 12 21 |
| 40 | 12 22 | 23 20 | 01 13 | 21 19 | 12 30 |
| 41 | 12 26 | 23 49 | 01 57 | 21 44 | 12 40 |
| 42 | 12 29 | 24 18 | 02 43 | 22 10 | 12 51 |
| 43 | 12 33 | 24 50 | 03 29 | 22 36 | 13 01 |
| 44 | 12 37 | 25 22 | 04 17 | 23 03 | 13 12 |
| 45 | 12 42 | 25 57 | 05 07 | 23 31 | 13 24 |
| 46 | 12 46 | 26 33 | 05 58 | 24 00 | 13 35 |
| 47 | 12 51 | 27 12 | 06 51 | 24 30 | 13 47 |
| 48 | 12 56 | 27 53 | 07 46 | 25 00 | 13 59 |
| 49 | 13 01 | 28 36 | 08 42 | 25 32 | 14 12 |
| 50 | 13 07 | 29 22 | 09 41 | 26 05 | 14 26 |
| 51 | 13 13 | 00♊11 | 10 42 | 26 39 | 14 39 |
| 52 | 13 19 | 01 04 | 11 45 | 27 15 | 14 54 |
| 53 | 13 26 | 02 00 | 12 51 | 27 51 | 15 09 |
| 54 | 13 33 | 03 01 | 13 58 | 28 29 | 15 24 |
| 55 | 13 41 | 04 07 | 15 09 | 29 09 | 15 41 |
| 56 | 13 49 | 05 19 | 16 22 | 29 51 | 15 58 |
| 57 | 13 58 | 06 38 | 17 39 | 00♌34 | 16 15 |
| 58 | 14 07 | 08 04 | 18 58 | 01 19 | 16 34 |
| 59 | 14 17 | 09 40 | 20 21 | 02 07 | 16 54 |
| 60 | 14♈28 | 11♊27 | 21♋46 | 02♌56 | 17♌14 |

**22h 44m 0s — 341° 0' 0" — 09 ♓ 26**

| LAT. | 11 | 12 | ASC | 2 | 3 |
|---|---|---|---|---|---|
| 0 | 11♈58 | 13♉27 | 12♊28 | 10♋07 | 08♌34 |
| 5 | 12 07 | 14 26 | 14 24 | 11 25 | 09 06 |
| 10 | 12 16 | 15 28 | 16 25 | 12 44 | 09 39 |
| 15 | 12 26 | 16 34 | 18 31 | 14 05 | 10 11 |
| 20 | 12 37 | 17 46 | 20 45 | 15 29 | 10 45 |
| 21 | 12 39 | 18 01 | 21 13 | 15 46 | 10 52 |
| 22 | 12 42 | 18 16 | 21 42 | 16 03 | 10 59 |
| 23 | 12 44 | 18 32 | 22 11 | 16 21 | 11 06 |
| 24 | 12 47 | 18 49 | 22 41 | 16 39 | 11 13 |
| 25 | 12 49 | 19 06 | 23 11 | 16 57 | 11 20 |
| 26 | 12 52 | 19 23 | 23 41 | 17 15 | 11 28 |
| 27 | 12 54 | 19 40 | 24 12 | 17 34 | 11 35 |
| 28 | 12 57 | 19 59 | 24 44 | 17 53 | 11 43 |
| 29 | 12 59 | 20 17 | 25 17 | 18 12 | 11 50 |
| 30 | 13 02 | 20 36 | 25 50 | 18 32 | 11 58 |
| 31 | 13 05 | 20 56 | 26 24 | 18 52 | 12 06 |
| 32 | 13 08 | 21 17 | 26 58 | 19 12 | 12 14 |
| 33 | 13 11 | 21 38 | 27 34 | 19 33 | 12 22 |
| 34 | 13 14 | 22 00 | 28 10 | 19 54 | 12 31 |
| 35 | 13 18 | 22 22 | 28 47 | 20 15 | 12 39 |
| 36 | 13 21 | 22 46 | 29 25 | 20 37 | 12 48 |
| 37 | 13 24 | 23 10 | 00♋04 | 21 00 | 12 57 |
| 38 | 13 28 | 23 36 | 00 44 | 21 23 | 13 06 |
| 39 | 13 32 | 24 02 | 01 25 | 21 46 | 13 16 |
| 40 | 13 36 | 24 30 | 02 08 | 22 10 | 13 25 |
| 41 | 13 40 | 24 58 | 02 51 | 22 35 | 13 35 |
| 42 | 13 44 | 25 29 | 03 36 | 23 00 | 13 45 |
| 43 | 13 48 | 26 00 | 04 23 | 23 27 | 13 56 |
| 44 | 13 53 | 26 33 | 05 10 | 23 53 | 14 07 |
| 45 | 13 57 | 27 08 | 05 59 | 24 21 | 14 18 |
| 46 | 14 02 | 27 45 | 06 50 | 24 50 | 14 29 |
| 47 | 14 08 | 28 23 | 07 43 | 25 19 | 14 41 |
| 48 | 14 13 | 29 05 | 08 37 | 25 49 | 14 53 |
| 49 | 14 19 | 29 48 | 09 33 | 26 21 | 15 06 |
| 50 | 14 25 | 00♊34 | 10 31 | 26 53 | 15 19 |
| 51 | 14 32 | 01 24 | 11 31 | 27 27 | 15 32 |
| 52 | 14 38 | 02 17 | 12 33 | 28 02 | 15 46 |
| 53 | 14 46 | 03 13 | 13 38 | 28 38 | 16 01 |
| 54 | 14 54 | 04 15 | 14 45 | 29 16 | 16 16 |
| 55 | 15 02 | 05 21 | 15 55 | 29 55 | 16 32 |
| 56 | 15 11 | 06 33 | 17 07 | 00♌36 | 16 49 |
| 57 | 15 20 | 07 52 | 18 22 | 01 19 | 17 06 |
| 58 | 15 31 | 09 18 | 19 40 | 02 03 | 17 25 |
| 59 | 15 42 | 10 54 | 21 02 | 02 50 | 17 44 |
| 60 | 15♈54 | 12♊40 | 22♋26 | 03♌39 | 18♌04 |

**22h 48m 0s — 342° 0' 0" — 10 ♓ 30**

| LAT. | 11 | 12 | ASC | 2 | 3 |
|---|---|---|---|---|---|
| 0 | 13♈03 | 14♉28 | 13♊24 | 11♋02 | 09♌34 |
| 5 | 13 13 | 15 27 | 15 21 | 12 20 | 10 05 |
| 10 | 13 23 | 16 30 | 17 21 | 13 39 | 10 37 |
| 15 | 13 34 | 17 37 | 19 28 | 14 59 | 11 09 |
| 20 | 13 46 | 18 50 | 21 42 | 16 23 | 11 42 |
| 21 | 13 48 | 19 05 | 22 10 | 16 40 | 11 49 |
| 22 | 13 51 | 19 21 | 22 39 | 16 57 | 11 56 |
| 23 | 13 53 | 19 37 | 23 08 | 17 15 | 12 03 |
| 24 | 13 56 | 19 54 | 23 37 | 17 33 | 12 10 |
| 25 | 13 58 | 20 11 | 24 07 | 17 51 | 12 17 |
| 26 | 14 01 | 20 28 | 24 38 | 18 09 | 12 25 |
| 27 | 14 04 | 20 46 | 25 09 | 18 27 | 12 32 |
| 28 | 14 07 | 21 05 | 25 40 | 18 46 | 12 39 |
| 29 | 14 10 | 21 24 | 26 13 | 19 05 | 12 47 |
| 30 | 14 13 | 21 43 | 26 46 | 19 25 | 12 55 |
| 31 | 14 16 | 22 03 | 27 20 | 19 44 | 13 02 |
| 32 | 14 19 | 22 24 | 27 54 | 20 05 | 13 10 |
| 33 | 14 23 | 22 45 | 28 29 | 20 25 | 13 19 |
| 34 | 14 26 | 23 07 | 29 05 | 20 46 | 13 27 |
| 35 | 14 29 | 23 30 | 29 42 | 21 07 | 13 35 |
| 36 | 14 33 | 23 54 | 00♋20 | 21 29 | 13 44 |
| 37 | 14 37 | 24 19 | 00 59 | 21 51 | 13 53 |
| 38 | 14 41 | 24 44 | 01 39 | 22 14 | 14 02 |
| 39 | 14 45 | 25 11 | 02 20 | 22 38 | 14 11 |
| 40 | 14 49 | 25 39 | 03 02 | 23 01 | 14 20 |
| 41 | 14 53 | 26 08 | 03 45 | 23 26 | 14 30 |
| 42 | 14 58 | 26 38 | 04 30 | 23 51 | 14 40 |
| 43 | 15 03 | 27 10 | 05 15 | 24 17 | 14 50 |
| 44 | 15 08 | 27 43 | 06 03 | 24 44 | 15 01 |
| 45 | 15 13 | 28 18 | 06 51 | 25 11 | 15 12 |
| 46 | 15 18 | 28 55 | 07 42 | 25 39 | 15 23 |
| 47 | 15 24 | 29 34 | 08 34 | 26 08 | 15 35 |
| 48 | 15 30 | 00♊16 | 09 27 | 26 38 | 15 47 |
| 49 | 15 36 | 00 59 | 10 23 | 27 09 | 15 59 |
| 50 | 15 43 | 01 46 | 11 20 | 27 41 | 16 12 |
| 51 | 15 50 | 02 36 | 12 20 | 28 15 | 16 25 |
| 52 | 15 57 | 03 29 | 13 21 | 28 49 | 16 39 |
| 53 | 16 05 | 04 26 | 14 25 | 29 25 | 16 53 |
| 54 | 16 14 | 05 27 | 15 31 | 00♌02 | 17 08 |
| 55 | 16 23 | 06 33 | 16 40 | 00 41 | 17 24 |
| 56 | 16 33 | 07 46 | 17 51 | 01 21 | 17 40 |
| 57 | 16 43 | 09 04 | 19 06 | 02 03 | 17 57 |
| 58 | 16 54 | 10 31 | 20 23 | 02 47 | 18 15 |
| 59 | 17 07 | 12 06 | 21 43 | 03 33 | 18 34 |
| 60 | 17♈20 | 13♊52 | 23♋06 | 04♌21 | 18♌54 |

**22h 52m 0s — 343° 0' 0" — 11 ♓ 34**

| LAT. | 11 | 12 | ASC | 2 | 3 |
|---|---|---|---|---|---|
| 0 | 14♈07 | 15♉28 | 14♊20 | 11♋58 | 10♌33 |
| 5 | 14 18 | 16 28 | 16 17 | 13 16 | 11 04 |
| 10 | 14 29 | 17 32 | 18 18 | 14 34 | 11 35 |
| 15 | 14 41 | 18 40 | 20 24 | 15 54 | 12 07 |
| 20 | 14 54 | 19 54 | 22 39 | 17 17 | 12 40 |
| 21 | 14 56 | 20 10 | 23 07 | 17 34 | 12 47 |
| 22 | 14 59 | 20 26 | 23 35 | 17 51 | 12 53 |
| 23 | 15 02 | 20 42 | 24 04 | 18 09 | 13 00 |
| 24 | 15 05 | 20 59 | 24 34 | 18 26 | 13 07 |
| 25 | 15 08 | 21 16 | 25 03 | 18 44 | 13 14 |
| 26 | 15 11 | 21 34 | 25 34 | 19 02 | 13 21 |
| 27 | 15 14 | 21 52 | 26 05 | 19 21 | 13 29 |
| 28 | 15 17 | 22 10 | 26 36 | 19 39 | 13 36 |
| 29 | 15 20 | 22 30 | 27 09 | 19 58 | 13 44 |
| 30 | 15 23 | 22 49 | 27 42 | 20 18 | 13 51 |
| 31 | 15 27 | 23 09 | 28 15 | 20 37 | 13 59 |
| 32 | 15 30 | 23 30 | 28 50 | 20 57 | 14 07 |
| 33 | 15 34 | 23 52 | 29 25 | 21 18 | 14 15 |
| 34 | 15 37 | 24 14 | 00♋01 | 21 38 | 14 23 |
| 35 | 15 41 | 24 38 | 00 37 | 21 59 | 14 31 |
| 36 | 15 45 | 25 01 | 01 15 | 22 21 | 14 40 |
| 37 | 15 49 | 25 26 | 01 54 | 22 43 | 14 48 |
| 38 | 15 53 | 25 52 | 02 33 | 23 06 | 14 57 |
| 39 | 15 58 | 26 19 | 03 14 | 23 29 | 15 06 |
| 40 | 16 02 | 26 47 | 03 56 | 23 53 | 15 16 |
| 41 | 16 07 | 27 16 | 04 38 | 24 17 | 15 25 |
| 42 | 16 12 | 27 47 | 05 23 | 24 42 | 15 35 |
| 43 | 16 17 | 28 19 | 06 08 | 25 07 | 15 45 |
| 44 | 16 22 | 28 53 | 06 55 | 25 34 | 15 55 |
| 45 | 16 28 | 29 28 | 07 43 | 26 01 | 16 06 |
| 46 | 16 34 | 00♊05 | 08 33 | 26 29 | 16 17 |
| 47 | 16 40 | 00 45 | 09 24 | 26 57 | 16 28 |
| 48 | 16 46 | 01 26 | 10 18 | 27 27 | 16 40 |
| 49 | 16 53 | 02 10 | 11 12 | 27 58 | 16 52 |
| 50 | 17 00 | 02 57 | 12 09 | 28 29 | 17 05 |
| 51 | 17 08 | 03 47 | 13 08 | 29 02 | 17 18 |
| 52 | 17 16 | 04 40 | 14 09 | 29 36 | 17 32 |
| 53 | 17 25 | 05 37 | 15 12 | 00♌12 | 17 46 |
| 54 | 17 34 | 06 39 | 16 17 | 00 48 | 18 00 |
| 55 | 17 44 | 07 45 | 17 25 | 01 27 | 18 16 |
| 56 | 17 54 | 08 57 | 18 35 | 02 06 | 18 32 |
| 57 | 18 06 | 10 16 | 19 49 | 02 48 | 18 49 |
| 58 | 18 18 | 11 42 | 21 04 | 03 31 | 19 06 |
| 59 | 18 31 | 13 17 | 22 23 | 04 16 | 19 25 |
| 60 | 18♈45 | 15♊03 | 23♋45 | 05♌04 | 19♌44 |

# Placidus Table of Houses for Latitudes 0° to 60° North

22h 56m 0s — 344° 0' 0" — 12 ♓ 39

| LAT. | 11 | 12 | ASC | 2 | 3 |
|---|---|---|---|---|---|
| 0 | 15♈12 | 16♉28 | 15♊16 | 12♋53 | 11♌32 |
| 5 | 15 24 | 17 29 | 17 13 | 14 11 | 12 03 |
| 10 | 15 36 | 18 34 | 19 14 | 15 29 | 12 34 |
| 15 | 15 48 | 19 43 | 21 21 | 16 48 | 13 05 |
| 20 | 16 02 | 20 58 | 23 35 | 18 11 | 13 38 |
| 21 | 16 05 | 21 14 | 24 03 | 18 28 | 13 44 |
| 22 | 16 08 | 21 30 | 24 32 | 18 45 | 13 51 |
| 23 | 16 11 | 21 46 | 25 00 | 19 02 | 13 58 |
| 24 | 16 14 | 22 03 | 25 30 | 19 20 | 14 05 |
| 25 | 16 17 | 22 21 | 26 00 | 19 38 | 14 12 |
| 26 | 16 20 | 22 39 | 26 30 | 19 56 | 14 19 |
| 27 | 16 23 | 22 57 | 27 01 | 20 14 | 14 26 |
| 28 | 16 27 | 23 16 | 27 32 | 20 33 | 14 33 |
| 29 | 16 30 | 23 35 | 28 04 | 20 51 | 14 40 |
| 30 | 16 34 | 23 55 | 28 37 | 21 10 | 14 48 |
| 31 | 16 37 | 24 15 | 29 11 | 21 30 | 14 55 |
| 32 | 16 41 | 24 37 | 29 45 | 21 50 | 15 03 |
| 33 | 16 45 | 24 58 | 00♋20 | 22 10 | 15 11 |
| 34 | 16 49 | 25 21 | 00 55 | 22 31 | 15 19 |
| 35 | 16 53 | 25 44 | 01 32 | 22 51 | 15 27 |
| 36 | 16 57 | 26 09 | 02 09 | 23 13 | 15 35 |
| 37 | 17 01 | 26 34 | 02 48 | 23 35 | 15 44 |
| 38 | 17 06 | 27 00 | 03 27 | 23 57 | 15 53 |
| 39 | 17 11 | 27 27 | 04 07 | 24 20 | 16 02 |
| 40 | 17 15 | 27 55 | 04 49 | 24 44 | 16 11 |
| 41 | 17 21 | 28 25 | 05 32 | 25 08 | 16 20 |
| 42 | 17 26 | 28 55 | 06 15 | 25 32 | 16 30 |
| 43 | 17 31 | 29 28 | 07 00 | 25 58 | 16 40 |
| 44 | 17 37 | 00♊02 | 07 47 | 26 24 | 16 50 |
| 45 | 17 43 | 00 37 | 08 35 | 26 50 | 17 00 |
| 46 | 17 49 | 01 15 | 09 24 | 27 18 | 17 11 |
| 47 | 17 56 | 01 54 | 10 15 | 27 46 | 17 22 |
| 48 | 18 03 | 02 36 | 11 07 | 28 16 | 17 34 |
| 49 | 18 10 | 03 20 | 12 02 | 28 46 | 17 46 |
| 50 | 18 18 | 04 07 | 12 58 | 29 17 | 17 58 |
| 51 | 18 26 | 04 57 | 13 56 | 29 50 | 18 11 |
| 52 | 18 35 | 05 50 | 14 56 | 00♌23 | 18 24 |
| 53 | 18 44 | 06 47 | 15 58 | 00 58 | 18 38 |
| 54 | 18 54 | 07 49 | 17 01 | 01 35 | 18 53 |
| 55 | 19 04 | 08 55 | 18 10 | 02 12 | 19 08 |
| 56 | 19 16 | 10 08 | 19 19 | 02 51 | 19 23 |
| 57 | 19 28 | 11 26 | 20 31 | 03 32 | 19 40 |
| 58 | 19 41 | 12 52 | 21 46 | 04 15 | 19 57 |
| 59 | 19 55 | 14 27 | 23 04 | 05 00 | 20 15 |
| 60 | 20♈10 | 16♊12 | 24♋25 | 05♌46 | 20♌34 |

23h 0m 0s — 345° 0' 0" — 13 ♓ 43

| LAT. | 11 | 12 | ASC | 2 | 3 |
|---|---|---|---|---|---|
| 0 | 16♈17 | 17♉28 | 16♊11 | 13♋49 | 12♌32 |
| 5 | 16 29 | 18 30 | 18 09 | 15 06 | 13 02 |
| 10 | 16 42 | 19 36 | 20 10 | 16 24 | 13 33 |
| 15 | 16 55 | 20 45 | 22 17 | 17 43 | 14 04 |
| 20 | 17 10 | 22 01 | 24 31 | 19 05 | 14 35 |
| 21 | 17 13 | 22 17 | 24 59 | 19 22 | 14 42 |
| 22 | 17 16 | 22 34 | 25 28 | 19 39 | 14 49 |
| 23 | 17 19 | 22 50 | 25 56 | 19 56 | 14 55 |
| 24 | 17 23 | 23 08 | 26 26 | 20 14 | 15 02 |
| 25 | 17 26 | 23 25 | 26 55 | 20 31 | 15 09 |
| 26 | 17 29 | 23 43 | 27 26 | 20 49 | 15 16 |
| 27 | 17 33 | 24 02 | 27 56 | 21 07 | 15 23 |
| 28 | 17 36 | 24 21 | 28 28 | 21 26 | 15 30 |
| 29 | 17 40 | 24 40 | 29 00 | 21 44 | 15 37 |
| 30 | 17 44 | 25 00 | 29 32 | 22 03 | 15 44 |
| 31 | 17 48 | 25 21 | 00♋06 | 22 23 | 15 52 |
| 32 | 17 52 | 25 42 | 00 40 | 22 42 | 15 59 |
| 33 | 17 56 | 26 04 | 01 15 | 23 02 | 16 07 |
| 34 | 18 00 | 26 27 | 01 50 | 23 23 | 16 15 |
| 35 | 18 04 | 26 51 | 02 26 | 23 44 | 16 23 |
| 36 | 18 09 | 27 15 | 03 04 | 24 05 | 16 31 |
| 37 | 18 13 | 27 40 | 03 42 | 24 26 | 16 40 |
| 38 | 18 18 | 28 07 | 04 21 | 24 49 | 16 48 |
| 39 | 18 23 | 28 34 | 05 01 | 25 11 | 16 57 |
| 40 | 18 28 | 29 03 | 05 42 | 25 34 | 17 06 |
| 41 | 18 34 | 29 32 | 06 24 | 25 58 | 17 15 |
| 42 | 18 39 | 00♊03 | 07 08 | 26 23 | 17 25 |
| 43 | 18 45 | 00 36 | 07 52 | 26 48 | 17 34 |
| 44 | 18 51 | 01 10 | 08 38 | 27 14 | 17 44 |
| 45 | 18 58 | 01 46 | 09 26 | 27 40 | 17 55 |
| 46 | 19 05 | 02 23 | 10 15 | 28 07 | 18 05 |
| 47 | 19 12 | 03 03 | 11 05 | 28 35 | 18 16 |
| 48 | 19 19 | 03 45 | 11 57 | 29 04 | 18 28 |
| 49 | 19 27 | 04 29 | 12 51 | 29 34 | 18 39 |
| 50 | 19 35 | 05 16 | 13 46 | 00♌05 | 18 51 |
| 51 | 19 44 | 06 06 | 14 44 | 00 37 | 19 04 |
| 52 | 19 53 | 07 00 | 15 43 | 01 11 | 19 17 |
| 53 | 20 03 | 07 57 | 16 44 | 01 45 | 19 31 |
| 54 | 20 13 | 08 59 | 17 48 | 02 21 | 19 45 |
| 55 | 20 25 | 10 05 | 18 54 | 02 58 | 19 59 |
| 56 | 20 37 | 11 17 | 20 03 | 03 36 | 20 15 |
| 57 | 20 50 | 12 35 | 21 14 | 04 17 | 20 31 |
| 58 | 21 03 | 14 01 | 22 28 | 04 59 | 20 48 |
| 59 | 21 19 | 15 35 | 23 44 | 05 43 | 21 05 |
| 60 | 21♈35 | 17♊20 | 25♋04 | 06♌29 | 21♌24 |

23h 4m 0s — 346° 0' 0" — 14 ♓ 48

| LAT. | 11 | 12 | ASC | 2 | 3 |
|---|---|---|---|---|---|
| 0 | 17♈21 | 18♉28 | 17♊07 | 14♋44 | 13♌32 |
| 5 | 17 34 | 19 31 | 19 05 | 16 01 | 14 02 |
| 10 | 17 48 | 20 37 | 21 07 | 17 19 | 14 32 |
| 15 | 18 02 | 21 48 | 23 13 | 18 38 | 15 02 |
| 20 | 18 18 | 23 04 | 25 27 | 19 59 | 15 33 |
| 21 | 18 21 | 23 21 | 25 55 | 20 16 | 15 40 |
| 22 | 18 24 | 23 37 | 26 23 | 20 33 | 15 46 |
| 23 | 18 28 | 23 54 | 26 52 | 20 50 | 15 53 |
| 24 | 18 31 | 24 12 | 27 21 | 21 07 | 16 00 |
| 25 | 18 35 | 24 29 | 27 51 | 21 25 | 16 06 |
| 26 | 18 38 | 24 48 | 28 21 | 21 43 | 16 13 |
| 27 | 18 42 | 25 06 | 28 52 | 22 01 | 16 20 |
| 28 | 18 46 | 25 25 | 29 23 | 22 19 | 16 27 |
| 29 | 18 50 | 25 45 | 29 55 | 22 37 | 16 34 |
| 30 | 18 54 | 26 05 | 00♋28 | 22 56 | 16 41 |
| 31 | 18 58 | 26 26 | 01 01 | 23 15 | 16 49 |
| 32 | 19 02 | 26 48 | 01 34 | 23 35 | 16 56 |
| 33 | 19 06 | 27 10 | 02 09 | 23 55 | 17 04 |
| 34 | 19 11 | 27 33 | 02 44 | 24 15 | 17 11 |
| 35 | 19 16 | 27 57 | 03 20 | 24 35 | 17 19 |
| 36 | 19 20 | 28 21 | 03 57 | 24 57 | 17 27 |
| 37 | 19 25 | 28 47 | 04 35 | 25 18 | 17 36 |
| 38 | 19 30 | 29 13 | 05 14 | 25 40 | 17 44 |
| 39 | 19 36 | 29 41 | 05 54 | 26 02 | 17 53 |
| 40 | 19 41 | 00♊09 | 06 35 | 26 25 | 18 01 |
| 41 | 19 47 | 00 39 | 07 17 | 26 49 | 18 10 |
| 42 | 19 53 | 01 11 | 08 00 | 27 13 | 18 20 |
| 43 | 19 59 | 01 43 | 08 44 | 27 38 | 18 29 |
| 44 | 20 06 | 02 17 | 09 30 | 28 03 | 18 39 |
| 45 | 20 12 | 02 53 | 10 17 | 28 30 | 18 49 |
| 46 | 20 20 | 03 31 | 11 05 | 28 57 | 19 00 |
| 47 | 20 27 | 04 11 | 11 55 | 29 24 | 19 10 |
| 48 | 20 35 | 04 53 | 12 46 | 29 53 | 19 21 |
| 49 | 20 43 | 05 37 | 13 39 | 00♌23 | 19 33 |
| 50 | 20 52 | 06 25 | 14 34 | 00 53 | 19 45 |
| 51 | 21 01 | 07 15 | 15 31 | 01 25 | 19 57 |
| 52 | 21 11 | 08 08 | 16 30 | 01 58 | 20 10 |
| 53 | 21 21 | 09 06 | 17 30 | 02 31 | 20 23 |
| 54 | 21 33 | 10 07 | 18 33 | 03 07 | 20 37 |
| 55 | 21 44 | 11 14 | 19 38 | 03 43 | 20 51 |
| 56 | 21 57 | 12 25 | 20 46 | 04 21 | 21 06 |
| 57 | 22 11 | 13 44 | 21 56 | 05 01 | 21 22 |
| 58 | 22 26 | 15 09 | 23 09 | 05 42 | 21 39 |
| 59 | 22 42 | 16 43 | 24 24 | 06 26 | 21 56 |
| 60 | 23♈00 | 18♊27 | 25♋43 | 07♌11 | 22♌14 |

23h 8m 0s — 347° 0' 0" — 15 ♓ 53

| LAT. | 11 | 12 | ASC | 2 | 3 |
|---|---|---|---|---|---|
| 0 | 18♈26 | 19♉27 | 18♊02 | 15♋40 | 14♌32 |
| 5 | 18 40 | 20 31 | 20 01 | 16 57 | 15 01 |
| 10 | 18 54 | 21 38 | 22 02 | 18 14 | 15 31 |
| 15 | 19 09 | 22 50 | 24 09 | 19 32 | 16 01 |
| 20 | 19 26 | 24 07 | 26 23 | 20 53 | 16 32 |
| 21 | 19 29 | 24 24 | 26 51 | 21 10 | 16 38 |
| 22 | 19 32 | 24 40 | 27 19 | 21 27 | 16 44 |
| 23 | 19 36 | 24 58 | 27 48 | 21 44 | 16 51 |
| 24 | 19 40 | 25 15 | 28 17 | 22 01 | 16 57 |
| 25 | 19 43 | 25 33 | 28 46 | 22 18 | 17 04 |
| 26 | 19 47 | 25 51 | 29 17 | 22 36 | 17 10 |
| 27 | 19 51 | 26 10 | 29 47 | 22 54 | 17 17 |
| 28 | 19 55 | 26 30 | 00♋18 | 23 12 | 17 24 |
| 29 | 19 59 | 26 50 | 00 50 | 23 30 | 17 31 |
| 30 | 20 04 | 27 10 | 01 22 | 23 49 | 17 38 |
| 31 | 20 08 | 27 31 | 01 55 | 24 08 | 17 45 |
| 32 | 20 12 | 27 53 | 02 29 | 24 27 | 17 53 |
| 33 | 20 17 | 28 15 | 03 03 | 24 47 | 18 00 |
| 34 | 20 22 | 28 38 | 03 38 | 25 07 | 18 08 |
| 35 | 20 27 | 29 02 | 04 14 | 25 27 | 18 16 |
| 36 | 20 32 | 29 27 | 04 51 | 25 48 | 18 23 |
| 37 | 20 37 | 29 53 | 05 29 | 26 10 | 18 32 |
| 38 | 20 42 | 00♊19 | 06 07 | 26 31 | 18 40 |
| 39 | 20 48 | 00 47 | 06 47 | 26 54 | 18 48 |
| 40 | 20 54 | 01 16 | 07 27 | 27 16 | 18 57 |
| 41 | 21 00 | 01 46 | 08 09 | 27 40 | 19 06 |
| 42 | 21 06 | 02 17 | 08 52 | 28 03 | 19 15 |
| 43 | 21 13 | 02 50 | 09 35 | 28 28 | 19 24 |
| 44 | 21 20 | 03 24 | 10 21 | 28 53 | 19 34 |
| 45 | 21 27 | 04 00 | 11 07 | 29 19 | 19 44 |
| 46 | 21 34 | 04 38 | 11 55 | 29 46 | 19 54 |
| 47 | 21 42 | 05 18 | 12 44 | 00♌13 | 20 05 |
| 48 | 21 51 | 06 00 | 13 35 | 00 42 | 20 15 |
| 49 | 21 59 | 06 45 | 14 28 | 01 11 | 20 27 |
| 50 | 22 09 | 07 32 | 15 22 | 01 41 | 20 38 |
| 51 | 22 18 | 08 23 | 16 18 | 02 12 | 20 50 |
| 52 | 22 29 | 09 16 | 17 16 | 02 44 | 21 03 |
| 53 | 22 40 | 10 14 | 18 16 | 03 18 | 21 16 |
| 54 | 22 52 | 11 15 | 19 18 | 03 53 | 21 29 |
| 55 | 23 04 | 12 21 | 20 22 | 04 29 | 21 43 |
| 56 | 23 18 | 13 33 | 21 29 | 05 06 | 21 58 |
| 57 | 23 32 | 14 51 | 22 38 | 05 45 | 22 14 |
| 58 | 23 48 | 16 16 | 23 50 | 06 26 | 22 30 |
| 59 | 24 05 | 17 49 | 25 04 | 07 09 | 22 47 |
| 60 | 24♈24 | 19♊32 | 26♋21 | 07♌53 | 23♌04 |

23h 12m 0s — 348° 0' 0" — 16 ♓ 57

| LAT. | 11 | 12 | ASC | 2 | 3 |
|---|---|---|---|---|---|
| 0 | 19♈30 | 20♉26 | 18♊58 | 16♋36 | 15♌32 |
| 5 | 19 45 | 21 31 | 20 57 | 17 52 | 16 01 |
| 10 | 20 00 | 22 39 | 22 58 | 19 09 | 16 30 |
| 15 | 20 16 | 23 51 | 25 05 | 20 27 | 17 00 |
| 20 | 20 33 | 25 10 | 27 19 | 21 48 | 17 30 |
| 21 | 20 37 | 25 26 | 27 46 | 22 04 | 17 36 |
| 22 | 20 40 | 25 43 | 28 15 | 22 21 | 17 42 |
| 23 | 20 44 | 26 01 | 28 43 | 22 38 | 17 49 |
| 24 | 20 48 | 26 18 | 29 12 | 22 55 | 17 55 |
| 25 | 20 52 | 26 36 | 29 42 | 23 12 | 18 01 |
| 26 | 20 56 | 26 55 | 00♋12 | 23 29 | 18 08 |
| 27 | 21 00 | 27 14 | 00 42 | 23 47 | 18 15 |
| 28 | 21 04 | 27 34 | 01 13 | 24 05 | 18 21 |
| 29 | 21 09 | 27 54 | 01 45 | 24 23 | 18 28 |
| 30 | 21 13 | 28 14 | 02 17 | 24 42 | 18 35 |
| 31 | 21 18 | 28 35 | 02 50 | 25 01 | 18 42 |
| 32 | 21 22 | 28 57 | 03 23 | 25 20 | 18 50 |
| 33 | 21 27 | 29 20 | 03 57 | 25 39 | 18 57 |
| 34 | 21 32 | 29 43 | 04 32 | 25 59 | 19 04 |
| 35 | 21 37 | 00♊07 | 05 08 | 26 19 | 19 12 |
| 36 | 21 43 | 00 32 | 05 44 | 26 40 | 19 20 |
| 37 | 21 48 | 00 58 | 06 22 | 27 01 | 19 28 |
| 38 | 21 54 | 01 25 | 07 00 | 27 23 | 19 36 |
| 39 | 22 00 | 01 53 | 07 39 | 27 45 | 19 44 |
| 40 | 22 06 | 02 22 | 08 19 | 28 07 | 19 52 |
| 41 | 22 12 | 02 52 | 09 01 | 28 30 | 20 01 |
| 42 | 22 19 | 03 23 | 09 43 | 28 54 | 20 10 |
| 43 | 22 26 | 03 56 | 10 27 | 29 18 | 20 19 |
| 44 | 22 33 | 04 31 | 11 11 | 29 43 | 20 29 |
| 45 | 22 41 | 05 07 | 11 57 | 00♌09 | 20 38 |
| 46 | 22 49 | 05 45 | 12 45 | 00 35 | 20 48 |
| 47 | 22 57 | 06 25 | 13 34 | 01 02 | 20 59 |
| 48 | 23 06 | 07 07 | 14 24 | 01 30 | 21 09 |
| 49 | 23 15 | 07 52 | 15 16 | 01 59 | 21 20 |
| 50 | 23 25 | 08 39 | 16 10 | 02 29 | 21 32 |
| 51 | 23 35 | 09 30 | 17 05 | 02 59 | 21 44 |
| 52 | 23 46 | 10 23 | 18 02 | 03 31 | 21 56 |
| 53 | 23 58 | 11 21 | 19 01 | 04 04 | 22 09 |
| 54 | 24 10 | 12 22 | 20 03 | 04 39 | 22 22 |
| 55 | 24 23 | 13 28 | 21 06 | 05 14 | 22 36 |
| 56 | 24 38 | 14 39 | 22 12 | 05 51 | 22 50 |
| 57 | 24 53 | 15 57 | 23 20 | 06 30 | 23 05 |
| 58 | 25 10 | 17 21 | 24 31 | 07 10 | 23 21 |
| 59 | 25 28 | 18 54 | 25 44 | 07 52 | 23 37 |
| 60 | 25♈47 | 20♊36 | 27♋00 | 08♌35 | 23♌55 |

23h 16m 0s — 349° 0' 0" — 18 ♓ 02

| LAT. | 11 | 12 | ASC | 2 | 3 |
|---|---|---|---|---|---|
| 0 | 20♈34 | 21♉26 | 19♊53 | 17♋32 | 16♌33 |
| 5 | 20 50 | 22 31 | 21 52 | 18 48 | 17 01 |
| 10 | 21 06 | 23 40 | 23 54 | 20 04 | 17 30 |
| 15 | 21 22 | 24 53 | 26 01 | 21 22 | 17 58 |
| 20 | 21 40 | 26 12 | 28 14 | 22 42 | 18 28 |
| 21 | 21 44 | 26 29 | 28 42 | 22 58 | 18 34 |
| 22 | 21 48 | 26 46 | 29 10 | 23 15 | 18 40 |
| 23 | 21 52 | 27 03 | 29 38 | 23 31 | 18 47 |
| 24 | 21 56 | 27 21 | 00♋07 | 23 48 | 18 53 |
| 25 | 22 00 | 27 39 | 00 37 | 24 05 | 18 59 |
| 26 | 22 05 | 27 58 | 01 07 | 24 23 | 19 06 |
| 27 | 22 09 | 28 17 | 01 37 | 24 40 | 19 12 |
| 28 | 22 13 | 28 37 | 02 08 | 24 58 | 19 19 |
| 29 | 22 18 | 28 57 | 02 39 | 25 16 | 19 26 |
| 30 | 22 23 | 29 18 | 03 11 | 25 35 | 19 32 |
| 31 | 22 27 | 29 39 | 03 44 | 25 53 | 19 39 |
| 32 | 22 32 | 00♊01 | 04 17 | 26 12 | 19 46 |
| 33 | 22 37 | 00 24 | 04 51 | 26 32 | 19 54 |
| 34 | 22 43 | 00 48 | 05 26 | 26 51 | 20 01 |
| 35 | 22 48 | 01 12 | 06 01 | 27 11 | 20 08 |
| 36 | 22 54 | 01 37 | 06 38 | 27 32 | 20 16 |
| 37 | 22 59 | 02 03 | 07 15 | 27 53 | 20 24 |
| 38 | 23 05 | 02 30 | 07 53 | 28 14 | 20 32 |
| 39 | 23 12 | 02 58 | 08 31 | 28 36 | 20 40 |
| 40 | 23 18 | 03 27 | 09 11 | 28 58 | 20 48 |
| 41 | 23 25 | 03 57 | 09 52 | 29 21 | 20 57 |
| 42 | 23 32 | 04 29 | 10 34 | 29 44 | 21 05 |
| 43 | 23 39 | 05 02 | 11 17 | 00♌08 | 21 14 |
| 44 | 23 47 | 05 37 | 12 02 | 00 33 | 21 24 |
| 45 | 23 55 | 06 13 | 12 47 | 00 58 | 21 33 |
| 46 | 24 03 | 06 51 | 13 34 | 01 24 | 21 43 |
| 47 | 24 12 | 07 31 | 14 23 | 01 51 | 21 53 |
| 48 | 24 21 | 08 14 | 15 12 | 02 18 | 22 03 |
| 49 | 24 31 | 08 58 | 16 04 | 02 47 | 22 14 |
| 50 | 24 41 | 09 46 | 16 57 | 03 16 | 22 25 |
| 51 | 24 52 | 10 36 | 17 52 | 03 47 | 22 37 |
| 52 | 25 03 | 11 29 | 18 48 | 04 18 | 22 49 |
| 53 | 25 15 | 12 27 | 19 47 | 04 51 | 23 01 |
| 54 | 25 29 | 13 28 | 20 47 | 05 24 | 23 14 |
| 55 | 25 42 | 14 34 | 21 50 | 06 00 | 23 28 |
| 56 | 25 57 | 15 45 | 22 55 | 06 36 | 23 42 |
| 57 | 26 14 | 17 02 | 24 02 | 07 14 | 23 57 |
| 58 | 26 31 | 18 26 | 25 11 | 07 53 | 24 12 |
| 59 | 26 50 | 19 58 | 26 24 | 08 35 | 24 28 |
| 60 | 27♈11 | 21♊40 | 27♋39 | 09♌18 | 24♌45 |

23h 20m 0s — 350° 0' 0" — 19 ♓ 07

| LAT. | 11 | 12 | ASC | 2 | 3 |
|---|---|---|---|---|---|
| 0 | 21♈38 | 22♉25 | 20♊49 | 18♋28 | 17♌33 |
| 5 | 21 54 | 23 31 | 22 48 | 19 44 | 18 01 |
| 10 | 22 11 | 24 40 | 24 50 | 21 00 | 18 29 |
| 15 | 22 29 | 25 54 | 26 56 | 22 17 | 18 58 |
| 20 | 22 48 | 27 14 | 29 09 | 23 36 | 19 27 |
| 21 | 22 52 | 27 31 | 29 37 | 23 52 | 19 33 |
| 22 | 22 56 | 27 48 | 00♋05 | 24 09 | 19 39 |
| 23 | 23 00 | 28 06 | 00 33 | 24 25 | 19 45 |
| 24 | 23 04 | 28 24 | 01 02 | 24 42 | 19 51 |
| 25 | 23 09 | 28 42 | 01 32 | 24 59 | 19 57 |
| 26 | 23 13 | 29 01 | 02 01 | 25 16 | 20 04 |
| 27 | 23 18 | 29 20 | 02 31 | 25 34 | 20 10 |
| 28 | 23 22 | 29 40 | 03 02 | 25 51 | 20 16 |
| 29 | 23 27 | 00♊01 | 03 33 | 26 09 | 20 23 |
| 30 | 23 32 | 00 21 | 04 05 | 26 27 | 20 30 |
| 31 | 23 37 | 00 43 | 04 38 | 26 46 | 20 37 |
| 32 | 23 42 | 01 05 | 05 11 | 27 05 | 20 43 |
| 33 | 23 47 | 01 28 | 05 45 | 27 24 | 20 50 |
| 34 | 23 53 | 01 52 | 06 19 | 27 43 | 20 58 |
| 35 | 23 59 | 02 16 | 06 54 | 28 03 | 21 05 |
| 36 | 24 04 | 02 41 | 07 30 | 28 23 | 21 12 |
| 37 | 24 10 | 03 07 | 08 07 | 28 44 | 21 20 |
| 38 | 24 17 | 03 34 | 08 45 | 29 05 | 21 28 |
| 39 | 24 23 | 04 03 | 09 23 | 29 27 | 21 36 |
| 40 | 24 30 | 04 32 | 10 03 | 29 49 | 21 44 |
| 41 | 24 37 | 05 02 | 10 44 | 00♌11 | 21 52 |
| 42 | 24 44 | 05 34 | 11 25 | 00 34 | 22 01 |
| 43 | 24 52 | 06 07 | 12 08 | 00 58 | 22 10 |
| 44 | 25 00 | 06 42 | 12 52 | 01 22 | 22 19 |
| 45 | 25 08 | 07 18 | 13 37 | 01 47 | 22 28 |
| 46 | 25 17 | 07 57 | 14 24 | 02 13 | 22 38 |
| 47 | 25 26 | 08 37 | 15 11 | 02 40 | 22 47 |
| 48 | 25 36 | 09 19 | 16 01 | 03 07 | 22 58 |
| 49 | 25 46 | 10 04 | 16 51 | 03 35 | 23 08 |
| 50 | 25 57 | 10 51 | 17 44 | 04 04 | 23 19 |
| 51 | 26 08 | 11 41 | 18 38 | 04 34 | 23 30 |
| 52 | 26 20 | 12 35 | 19 34 | 05 05 | 23 42 |
| 53 | 26 33 | 13 32 | 20 32 | 05 37 | 23 54 |
| 54 | 26 47 | 14 33 | 21 31 | 06 10 | 24 07 |
| 55 | 27 01 | 15 39 | 22 33 | 06 45 | 24 20 |
| 56 | 27 17 | 16 50 | 23 37 | 07 21 | 24 34 |
| 57 | 27 34 | 18 07 | 24 43 | 07 58 | 24 48 |
| 58 | 27 52 | 19 30 | 25 52 | 08 37 | 25 03 |
| 59 | 28 12 | 21 01 | 27 03 | 09 17 | 25 19 |
| 60 | 28♈34 | 22♊42 | 28♋17 | 10♌00 | 25♌35 |

23h 24m 0s — 351° 0' 0" — 20 ♓ 12

| LAT. | 11 | 12 | ASC | 2 | 3 |
|---|---|---|---|---|---|
| 0 | 22♈42 | 23♉23 | 21♊44 | 19♋24 | 18♌34 |
| 5 | 22 59 | 24 31 | 23 43 | 20 39 | 19 01 |
| 10 | 23 17 | 25 41 | 25 45 | 21 55 | 19 29 |
| 15 | 23 35 | 26 55 | 27 52 | 23 11 | 19 57 |
| 20 | 23 55 | 28 16 | 00♋05 | 24 30 | 20 25 |
| 21 | 23 59 | 28 33 | 00 32 | 24 46 | 20 31 |
| 22 | 24 03 | 28 50 | 01 00 | 25 03 | 20 37 |
| 23 | 24 08 | 29 08 | 01 28 | 25 19 | 20 43 |
| 24 | 24 12 | 29 26 | 01 57 | 25 36 | 20 49 |
| 25 | 24 17 | 29 45 | 02 26 | 25 53 | 20 55 |
| 26 | 24 21 | 00♊04 | 02 56 | 26 10 | 21 01 |
| 27 | 24 26 | 00 23 | 03 26 | 26 27 | 21 08 |
| 28 | 24 31 | 00 43 | 03 56 | 26 44 | 21 14 |
| 29 | 24 36 | 01 04 | 04 28 | 27 02 | 21 21 |
| 30 | 24 41 | 01 25 | 04 59 | 27 20 | 21 27 |
| 31 | 24 46 | 01 46 | 05 32 | 27 39 | 21 34 |
| 32 | 24 52 | 02 09 | 06 04 | 27 57 | 21 41 |
| 33 | 24 57 | 02 32 | 06 38 | 28 16 | 21 47 |
| 34 | 25 03 | 02 55 | 07 12 | 28 35 | 21 54 |
| 35 | 25 09 | 03 20 | 07 47 | 28 55 | 22 02 |
| 36 | 25 15 | 03 45 | 08 23 | 29 15 | 22 09 |
| 37 | 25 21 | 04 11 | 09 00 | 29 35 | 22 16 |
| 38 | 25 28 | 04 39 | 09 37 | 29 56 | 22 24 |
| 39 | 25 35 | 05 07 | 10 15 | 00♌18 | 22 32 |
| 40 | 25 42 | 05 36 | 10 54 | 00 39 | 22 40 |
| 41 | 25 49 | 06 07 | 11 35 | 01 02 | 22 48 |
| 42 | 25 57 | 06 39 | 12 16 | 01 25 | 22 56 |
| 43 | 26 05 | 07 12 | 12 58 | 01 48 | 23 05 |
| 44 | 26 13 | 07 47 | 13 42 | 02 12 | 23 14 |
| 45 | 26 22 | 08 23 | 14 27 | 02 37 | 23 23 |
| 46 | 26 31 | 09 01 | 15 12 | 03 02 | 23 32 |
| 47 | 26 40 | 09 42 | 16 00 | 03 28 | 23 42 |
| 48 | 26 50 | 10 24 | 16 49 | 03 55 | 23 52 |
| 49 | 27 01 | 11 09 | 17 39 | 04 23 | 24 02 |
| 50 | 27 12 | 11 56 | 18 31 | 04 51 | 24 13 |
| 51 | 27 24 | 12 46 | 19 24 | 05 21 | 24 24 |
| 52 | 27 36 | 13 40 | 20 19 | 05 52 | 24 35 |
| 53 | 27 50 | 14 37 | 21 16 | 06 23 | 24 47 |
| 54 | 28 04 | 15 38 | 22 15 | 06 56 | 24 59 |
| 55 | 28 19 | 16 43 | 23 16 | 07 30 | 25 12 |
| 56 | 28 36 | 17 54 | 24 19 | 08 05 | 25 26 |
| 57 | 28 54 | 19 10 | 25 24 | 08 42 | 25 40 |
| 58 | 29 13 | 20 33 | 26 32 | 09 20 | 25 54 |
| 59 | 29 33 | 22 03 | 27 42 | 10 00 | 26 10 |
| 60 | 29♈56 | 23♊43 | 28♋55 | 10♌42 | 26♌26 |

# Placidus Table of Houses for Latitudes 0° to 60° North

23h 28m 0s — 352° 0' 0" — 21 ♓ 17

| LAT. | 11 | 12 | ASC | 2 | 3 |
|---|---|---|---|---|---|
| 0 | 23♈46 | 24♉22 | 22♊39 | 20♋20 | 19♌35 |
| 5 | 24 04 | 25 30 | 24 39 | 21 35 | 20 02 |
| 10 | 24 22 | 26 41 | 26 41 | 22 50 | 20 29 |
| 15 | 24 41 | 27 56 | 28 47 | 24 06 | 20 56 |
| 20 | 25 02 | 29 17 | 00♋59 | 25 24 | 21 24 |
| 21 | 25 06 | 29 34 | 01 27 | 25 40 | 21 30 |
| 22 | 25 10 | 29 52 | 01 55 | 25 57 | 21 36 |
| 23 | 25 15 | 00♊10 | 02 23 | 26 13 | 21 42 |
| 24 | 25 20 | 00 28 | 02 52 | 26 29 | 21 47 |
| 25 | 25 24 | 00 47 | 03 21 | 26 46 | 21 53 |
| 26 | 25 29 | 01 06 | 03 50 | 27 03 | 22 00 |
| 27 | 25 34 | 01 25 | 04 20 | 27 20 | 22 06 |
| 28 | 25 39 | 01 45 | 04 50 | 27 38 | 22 12 |
| 29 | 25 44 | 02 06 | 05 21 | 27 55 | 22 18 |
| 30 | 25 50 | 02 27 | 05 53 | 28 13 | 22 25 |
| 31 | 25 55 | 02 49 | 06 25 | 28 31 | 22 31 |
| 32 | 26 01 | 03 12 | 06 58 | 28 50 | 22 38 |
| 33 | 26 07 | 03 35 | 07 31 | 29 08 | 22 45 |
| 34 | 26 13 | 03 58 | 08 05 | 29 27 | 22 51 |
| 35 | 26 19 | 04 23 | 08 40 | 29 47 | 22 58 |
| 36 | 26 25 | 04 49 | 09 15 | 00♌07 | 23 06 |
| 37 | 26 32 | 05 15 | 09 52 | 00 27 | 23 13 |
| 38 | 26 39 | 05 42 | 10 29 | 00 47 | 23 20 |
| 39 | 26 46 | 06 11 | 11 07 | 01 09 | 23 28 |
| 40 | 26 53 | 06 40 | 11 46 | 01 30 | 23 36 |
| 41 | 27 01 | 07 11 | 12 26 | 01 52 | 23 44 |
| 42 | 27 09 | 07 43 | 13 06 | 02 15 | 23 52 |
| 43 | 27 17 | 08 16 | 13 48 | 02 38 | 24 00 |
| 44 | 27 25 | 08 51 | 14 31 | 03 02 | 24 09 |
| 45 | 27 35 | 09 27 | 15 16 | 03 26 | 24 18 |
| 46 | 27 44 | 10 06 | 16 01 | 03 51 | 24 27 |
| 47 | 27 54 | 10 46 | 16 48 | 04 17 | 24 36 |
| 48 | 28 04 | 11 28 | 17 36 | 04 43 | 24 46 |
| 49 | 28 15 | 12 13 | 18 26 | 05 11 | 24 56 |
| 50 | 28 27 | 13 00 | 19 17 | 05 39 | 25 07 |
| 51 | 28 39 | 13 51 | 20 10 | 06 08 | 25 17 |
| 52 | 28 53 | 14 44 | 21 04 | 06 38 | 25 29 |
| 53 | 29 07 | 15 41 | 22 01 | 07 10 | 25 40 |
| 54 | 29 21 | 16 41 | 22 59 | 07 42 | 25 52 |
| 55 | 29 37 | 17 47 | 23 59 | 08 15 | 26 05 |
| 56 | 29 54 | 18 57 | 25 01 | 08 50 | 26 18 |
| 57 | 00♉13 | 20 12 | 26 06 | 09 26 | 26 31 |
| 58 | 00 33 | 21 35 | 27 12 | 10 04 | 26 46 |
| 59 | 00 54 | 23 04 | 28 21 | 10 43 | 27 01 |
| 60 | 01♉18 | 24♊43 | 29♋33 | 11♌24 | 27♌16 |

23h 32m 0s — 353° 0' 0" — 22 ♓ 23

| LAT. | 11 | 12 | ASC | 2 | 3 |
|---|---|---|---|---|---|
| 0 | 24♈50 | 25♉21 | 23♊34 | 21♋17 | 20♌36 |
| 5 | 25 08 | 26 29 | 25 34 | 22 31 | 21 03 |
| 10 | 25 27 | 27 41 | 27 36 | 23 46 | 21 29 |
| 15 | 25 47 | 28 56 | 29 42 | 25 01 | 21 56 |
| 20 | 26 08 | 00♊18 | 01♋54 | 26 19 | 22 23 |
| 21 | 26 13 | 00 36 | 02 22 | 26 35 | 22 29 |
| 22 | 26 17 | 00 53 | 02 49 | 26 51 | 22 34 |
| 23 | 26 22 | 01 11 | 03 17 | 27 07 | 22 40 |
| 24 | 26 27 | 01 30 | 03 46 | 27 23 | 22 46 |
| 25 | 26 32 | 01 48 | 04 15 | 27 40 | 22 52 |
| 26 | 26 37 | 02 08 | 04 44 | 27 57 | 22 58 |
| 27 | 26 42 | 02 27 | 05 14 | 28 13 | 23 04 |
| 28 | 26 47 | 02 48 | 05 44 | 28 31 | 23 10 |
| 29 | 26 53 | 03 08 | 06 15 | 28 48 | 23 16 |
| 30 | 26 58 | 03 30 | 06 46 | 29 06 | 23 22 |
| 31 | 27 04 | 03 52 | 07 18 | 29 24 | 23 29 |
| 32 | 27 10 | 04 14 | 07 51 | 29 42 | 23 35 |
| 33 | 27 16 | 04 37 | 08 24 | 00♌01 | 23 42 |
| 34 | 27 22 | 05 01 | 08 58 | 00 19 | 23 48 |
| 35 | 27 28 | 05 26 | 09 32 | 00 39 | 23 55 |
| 36 | 27 35 | 05 52 | 10 08 | 00 58 | 24 02 |
| 37 | 27 42 | 06 18 | 10 44 | 01 18 | 24 09 |
| 38 | 27 49 | 06 45 | 11 20 | 01 39 | 24 17 |
| 39 | 27 56 | 07 14 | 11 58 | 02 00 | 24 24 |
| 40 | 28 04 | 07 43 | 12 37 | 02 21 | 24 32 |
| 41 | 28 12 | 08 14 | 13 16 | 02 43 | 24 40 |
| 42 | 28 20 | 08 46 | 13 57 | 03 05 | 24 48 |
| 43 | 28 29 | 09 20 | 14 38 | 03 28 | 24 56 |
| 44 | 28 38 | 09 54 | 15 21 | 03 51 | 25 04 |
| 45 | 28 47 | 10 31 | 16 05 | 04 15 | 25 13 |
| 46 | 28 57 | 11 09 | 16 50 | 04 40 | 25 22 |
| 47 | 29 07 | 11 50 | 17 36 | 05 05 | 25 31 |
| 48 | 29 18 | 12 32 | 18 24 | 05 32 | 25 41 |
| 49 | 29 30 | 13 17 | 19 13 | 05 59 | 25 50 |
| 50 | 29 42 | 14 04 | 20 03 | 06 27 | 26 01 |
| 51 | 29 55 | 14 54 | 20 56 | 06 55 | 26 11 |
| 52 | 00♉08 | 15 47 | 21 49 | 07 25 | 26 22 |
| 53 | 00 23 | 16 44 | 22 45 | 07 56 | 26 33 |
| 54 | 00 38 | 17 44 | 23 42 | 08 28 | 26 45 |
| 55 | 00 55 | 18 49 | 24 42 | 09 01 | 26 57 |
| 56 | 01 13 | 19 59 | 25 43 | 09 35 | 27 10 |
| 57 | 01 32 | 21 14 | 26 47 | 10 10 | 27 23 |
| 58 | 01 53 | 22 36 | 27 52 | 10 47 | 27 37 |
| 59 | 02 15 | 24 05 | 29 01 | 11 26 | 27 52 |
| 60 | 02♉40 | 25♊42 | 00♌11 | 12♌06 | 28♌07 |

23h 36m 0s — 354° 0' 0" — 23 ♓ 28

| LAT. | 11 | 12 | ASC | 2 | 3 |
|---|---|---|---|---|---|
| 0 | 25♈53 | 26♉19 | 24♊30 | 22♋13 | 21♌37 |
| 5 | 26 12 | 27 28 | 26 29 | 23 27 | 22 03 |
| 10 | 26 32 | 28 40 | 28 31 | 24 41 | 22 29 |
| 15 | 26 53 | 29 57 | 00♋37 | 25 56 | 22 55 |
| 20 | 27 15 | 01♊19 | 02 49 | 27 13 | 23 22 |
| 21 | 27 20 | 01 37 | 03 16 | 27 29 | 23 28 |
| 22 | 27 24 | 01 54 | 03 44 | 27 45 | 23 33 |
| 23 | 27 29 | 02 13 | 04 12 | 28 01 | 23 39 |
| 24 | 27 34 | 02 31 | 04 40 | 28 17 | 23 44 |
| 25 | 27 39 | 02 50 | 05 09 | 28 33 | 23 50 |
| 26 | 27 44 | 03 09 | 05 38 | 28 50 | 23 56 |
| 27 | 27 50 | 03 29 | 06 08 | 29 07 | 24 02 |
| 28 | 27 55 | 03 49 | 06 38 | 29 24 | 24 08 |
| 29 | 28 01 | 04 10 | 07 09 | 29 41 | 24 14 |
| 30 | 28 07 | 04 32 | 07 40 | 29 59 | 24 20 |
| 31 | 28 13 | 04 54 | 08 12 | 00♌16 | 24 26 |
| 32 | 28 19 | 05 16 | 08 44 | 00 34 | 24 33 |
| 33 | 28 25 | 05 40 | 09 17 | 00 53 | 24 39 |
| 34 | 28 31 | 06 04 | 09 50 | 01 12 | 24 46 |
| 35 | 28 38 | 06 29 | 10 25 | 01 31 | 24 52 |
| 36 | 28 45 | 06 54 | 11 00 | 01 50 | 24 59 |
| 37 | 28 52 | 07 21 | 11 35 | 02 10 | 25 06 |
| 38 | 28 59 | 07 48 | 12 12 | 02 30 | 25 13 |
| 39 | 29 07 | 08 17 | 12 49 | 02 50 | 25 21 |
| 40 | 29 15 | 08 46 | 13 27 | 03 11 | 25 28 |
| 41 | 29 23 | 09 17 | 14 07 | 03 33 | 25 36 |
| 42 | 29 32 | 09 49 | 14 47 | 03 55 | 25 43 |
| 43 | 29 41 | 10 23 | 15 28 | 04 18 | 25 51 |
| 44 | 29 50 | 10 58 | 16 10 | 04 41 | 26 00 |
| 45 | 00♉00 | 11 34 | 16 53 | 05 05 | 26 08 |
| 46 | 00 10 | 12 13 | 17 38 | 05 29 | 26 17 |
| 47 | 00 21 | 12 53 | 18 24 | 05 54 | 26 26 |
| 48 | 00 32 | 13 35 | 19 11 | 06 20 | 26 35 |
| 49 | 00 44 | 14 20 | 19 59 | 06 47 | 26 45 |
| 50 | 00 56 | 15 07 | 20 49 | 07 14 | 26 55 |
| 51 | 01 10 | 15 57 | 21 41 | 07 42 | 27 05 |
| 52 | 01 24 | 16 50 | 22 34 | 08 12 | 27 15 |
| 53 | 01 39 | 17 46 | 23 29 | 08 42 | 27 26 |
| 54 | 01 55 | 18 47 | 24 26 | 09 13 | 27 38 |
| 55 | 02 12 | 19 51 | 25 24 | 09 46 | 27 50 |
| 56 | 02 30 | 21 00 | 26 25 | 10 19 | 28 02 |
| 57 | 02 50 | 22 15 | 27 27 | 10 55 | 28 15 |
| 58 | 03 12 | 23 36 | 28 32 | 11 31 | 28 29 |
| 59 | 03 35 | 25 04 | 29 39 | 12 09 | 28 43 |
| 60 | 04♉01 | 26♊40 | 00♌49 | 12♌48 | 28♌58 |

23h 40m 0s — 355° 0' 0" — 24 ♓ 33

| LAT. | 11 | 12 | ASC | 2 | 3 |
|---|---|---|---|---|---|
| 0 | 26♈57 | 27♉17 | 25♊25 | 23♋10 | 22♌39 |
| 5 | 27 16 | 28 27 | 27 24 | 24 23 | 23 04 |
| 10 | 27 37 | 29 40 | 29 26 | 25 37 | 23 30 |
| 15 | 27 58 | 00♊57 | 01♋32 | 26 51 | 23 55 |
| 20 | 28 21 | 02 20 | 03 43 | 28 08 | 24 21 |
| 21 | 28 26 | 02 37 | 04 11 | 28 23 | 24 27 |
| 22 | 28 31 | 02 55 | 04 38 | 28 39 | 24 32 |
| 23 | 28 36 | 03 13 | 05 06 | 28 55 | 24 38 |
| 24 | 28 41 | 03 32 | 05 34 | 29 11 | 24 43 |
| 25 | 28 46 | 03 51 | 06 03 | 29 27 | 24 49 |
| 26 | 28 52 | 04 11 | 06 32 | 29 44 | 24 54 |
| 27 | 28 57 | 04 30 | 07 02 | 00♌00 | 25 00 |
| 28 | 29 03 | 04 51 | 07 32 | 00 17 | 25 06 |
| 29 | 29 09 | 05 12 | 08 02 | 00 34 | 25 12 |
| 30 | 29 15 | 05 33 | 08 33 | 00 51 | 25 18 |
| 31 | 29 21 | 05 55 | 09 04 | 01 09 | 25 24 |
| 32 | 29 27 | 06 18 | 09 37 | 01 27 | 25 30 |
| 33 | 29 34 | 06 42 | 10 09 | 01 45 | 25 36 |
| 34 | 29 40 | 07 06 | 10 43 | 02 04 | 25 43 |
| 35 | 29 47 | 07 31 | 11 17 | 02 22 | 25 49 |
| 36 | 29 54 | 07 56 | 11 51 | 02 42 | 25 56 |
| 37 | 00♉02 | 08 23 | 12 27 | 03 01 | 26 03 |
| 38 | 00 09 | 08 51 | 13 03 | 03 21 | 26 10 |
| 39 | 00 17 | 09 19 | 13 40 | 03 41 | 26 17 |
| 40 | 00 25 | 09 49 | 14 18 | 04 02 | 26 24 |
| 41 | 00 34 | 10 20 | 14 57 | 04 23 | 26 32 |
| 42 | 00 43 | 10 52 | 15 36 | 04 45 | 26 39 |
| 43 | 00 52 | 11 25 | 16 17 | 05 07 | 26 47 |
| 44 | 01 02 | 12 00 | 16 59 | 05 30 | 26 55 |
| 45 | 01 12 | 12 37 | 17 42 | 05 54 | 27 03 |
| 46 | 01 22 | 13 15 | 18 26 | 06 18 | 27 12 |
| 47 | 01 33 | 13 55 | 19 11 | 06 43 | 27 21 |
| 48 | 01 45 | 14 38 | 19 58 | 07 08 | 27 30 |
| 49 | 01 57 | 15 22 | 20 46 | 07 34 | 27 39 |
| 50 | 02 10 | 16 09 | 21 35 | 08 01 | 27 49 |
| 51 | 02 24 | 16 59 | 22 26 | 08 29 | 27 59 |
| 52 | 02 39 | 17 52 | 23 19 | 08 58 | 28 09 |
| 53 | 02 54 | 18 48 | 24 13 | 09 28 | 28 20 |
| 54 | 03 11 | 19 48 | 25 09 | 09 59 | 28 31 |
| 55 | 03 29 | 20 52 | 26 07 | 10 31 | 28 42 |
| 56 | 03 48 | 22 01 | 27 06 | 11 04 | 28 54 |
| 57 | 04 08 | 23 15 | 28 08 | 11 39 | 29 07 |
| 58 | 04 31 | 24 35 | 29 12 | 12 14 | 29 20 |
| 59 | 04 55 | 26 03 | 00♌18 | 12 52 | 29 34 |
| 60 | 05♉22 | 27♊38 | 01♌27 | 13♌31 | 29♌48 |

23h 44m 0s — 356° 0' 0" — 25 ♓ 38

| LAT. | 11 | 12 | ASC | 2 | 3 |
|---|---|---|---|---|---|
| 0 | 28♈00 | 28♉15 | 26♊20 | 24♋06 | 23♌41 |
| 5 | 28 20 | 29 25 | 28 19 | 25 20 | 24 05 |
| 10 | 28 41 | 00♊39 | 00♋21 | 26 33 | 24 30 |
| 15 | 29 03 | 01 57 | 02 27 | 27 46 | 24 55 |
| 20 | 29 27 | 03 20 | 04 38 | 29 02 | 25 21 |
| 21 | 29 32 | 03 38 | 05 05 | 29 17 | 25 26 |
| 22 | 29 37 | 03 56 | 05 32 | 29 33 | 25 31 |
| 23 | 29 43 | 04 14 | 06 00 | 29 49 | 25 37 |
| 24 | 29 48 | 04 33 | 06 28 | 00♌05 | 25 42 |
| 25 | 29 53 | 04 52 | 06 57 | 00 21 | 25 47 |
| 26 | 29 59 | 05 11 | 07 26 | 00 37 | 25 53 |
| 27 | 00♉05 | 05 32 | 07 55 | 00 54 | 25 59 |
| 28 | 00 11 | 05 52 | 08 25 | 01 10 | 26 04 |
| 29 | 00 17 | 06 13 | 08 55 | 01 27 | 26 10 |
| 30 | 00 23 | 06 35 | 09 26 | 01 44 | 26 16 |
| 31 | 00 29 | 06 57 | 09 57 | 02 02 | 26 22 |
| 32 | 00 35 | 07 20 | 10 29 | 02 19 | 26 28 |
| 33 | 00 42 | 07 43 | 11 02 | 02 37 | 26 34 |
| 34 | 00 49 | 08 07 | 11 35 | 02 56 | 26 40 |
| 35 | 00 56 | 08 32 | 12 08 | 03 14 | 26 47 |
| 36 | 01 03 | 08 58 | 12 43 | 03 33 | 26 53 |
| 37 | 01 11 | 09 25 | 13 18 | 03 52 | 27 00 |
| 38 | 01 19 | 09 52 | 13 54 | 04 12 | 27 07 |
| 39 | 01 27 | 10 21 | 14 31 | 04 32 | 27 13 |
| 40 | 01 36 | 10 51 | 15 08 | 04 53 | 27 21 |
| 41 | 01 44 | 11 22 | 15 47 | 05 14 | 27 28 |
| 42 | 01 54 | 11 54 | 16 26 | 05 35 | 27 35 |
| 43 | 02 03 | 12 27 | 17 06 | 05 57 | 27 43 |
| 44 | 02 13 | 13 02 | 17 48 | 06 20 | 27 51 |
| 45 | 02 23 | 13 39 | 18 30 | 06 43 | 27 59 |
| 46 | 02 34 | 14 17 | 19 14 | 07 07 | 28 07 |
| 47 | 02 46 | 14 57 | 19 59 | 07 31 | 28 16 |
| 48 | 02 58 | 15 40 | 20 45 | 07 56 | 28 24 |
| 49 | 03 11 | 16 24 | 21 32 | 08 22 | 28 33 |
| 50 | 03 24 | 17 11 | 22 21 | 08 49 | 28 43 |
| 51 | 03 38 | 18 01 | 23 11 | 09 16 | 28 52 |
| 52 | 03 53 | 18 53 | 24 03 | 09 45 | 29 03 |
| 53 | 04 09 | 19 49 | 24 57 | 10 14 | 29 13 |
| 54 | 04 27 | 20 49 | 25 52 | 10 45 | 29 24 |
| 55 | 04 45 | 21 53 | 26 49 | 11 16 | 29 35 |
| 56 | 05 05 | 23 01 | 27 48 | 11 49 | 29 47 |
| 57 | 05 26 | 24 15 | 28 49 | 12 23 | 29 59 |
| 58 | 05 49 | 25 34 | 29 52 | 12 58 | 00♍12 |
| 59 | 06 14 | 27 00 | 00♌57 | 13 35 | 00 25 |
| 60 | 06♉42 | 28♊34 | 02♌04 | 14♌13 | 00♍39 |

23h 48m 0s — 357° 0' 0" — 26 ♓ 44

| LAT. | 11 | 12 | ASC | 2 | 3 |
|---|---|---|---|---|---|
| 0 | 29♈03 | 29♉13 | 27♊15 | 25♋03 | 24♌42 |
| 5 | 29 24 | 00♊24 | 29 15 | 26 16 | 25 07 |
| 10 | 29 45 | 01 38 | 01♋16 | 27 28 | 25 31 |
| 15 | 00♉08 | 02 56 | 03 21 | 28 42 | 25 55 |
| 20 | 00 33 | 04 20 | 05 32 | 29 56 | 26 20 |
| 21 | 00 38 | 04 38 | 05 59 | 00♌12 | 26 25 |
| 22 | 00 44 | 04 56 | 06 26 | 00 27 | 26 30 |
| 23 | 00 49 | 05 14 | 06 54 | 00 43 | 26 36 |
| 24 | 00 54 | 05 33 | 07 22 | 00 59 | 26 41 |
| 25 | 01 00 | 05 52 | 07 50 | 01 15 | 26 46 |
| 26 | 01 06 | 06 12 | 08 19 | 01 31 | 26 52 |
| 27 | 01 12 | 06 32 | 08 48 | 01 47 | 26 57 |
| 28 | 01 18 | 06 53 | 09 18 | 02 04 | 27 03 |
| 29 | 01 24 | 07 14 | 09 48 | 02 20 | 27 08 |
| 30 | 01 30 | 07 36 | 10 19 | 02 37 | 27 14 |
| 31 | 01 37 | 07 58 | 10 50 | 02 54 | 27 20 |
| 32 | 01 44 | 08 21 | 11 22 | 03 12 | 27 26 |
| 33 | 01 50 | 08 44 | 11 54 | 03 30 | 27 32 |
| 34 | 01 58 | 09 09 | 12 27 | 03 48 | 27 38 |
| 35 | 02 05 | 09 34 | 13 00 | 04 06 | 27 44 |
| 36 | 02 12 | 10 00 | 13 34 | 04 25 | 27 50 |
| 37 | 02 20 | 10 26 | 14 09 | 04 44 | 27 57 |
| 38 | 02 28 | 10 54 | 14 45 | 05 03 | 28 03 |
| 39 | 02 37 | 11 23 | 15 21 | 05 23 | 28 10 |
| 40 | 02 45 | 11 52 | 15 58 | 05 43 | 28 17 |
| 41 | 02 55 | 12 23 | 16 36 | 06 04 | 28 24 |
| 42 | 03 04 | 12 55 | 17 15 | 06 25 | 28 31 |
| 43 | 03 14 | 13 29 | 17 55 | 06 47 | 28 39 |
| 44 | 03 24 | 14 04 | 18 36 | 07 09 | 28 46 |
| 45 | 03 35 | 14 41 | 19 18 | 07 32 | 28 54 |
| 46 | 03 46 | 15 19 | 20 02 | 07 56 | 29 02 |
| 47 | 03 58 | 15 59 | 20 46 | 08 20 | 29 10 |
| 48 | 04 10 | 16 41 | 21 32 | 08 45 | 29 19 |
| 49 | 04 24 | 17 25 | 22 18 | 09 10 | 29 28 |
| 50 | 04 37 | 18 12 | 23 07 | 09 36 | 29 37 |
| 51 | 04 52 | 19 02 | 23 56 | 10 03 | 29 46 |
| 52 | 05 08 | 19 54 | 24 47 | 10 31 | 29 56 |
| 53 | 05 24 | 20 50 | 25 40 | 11 00 | 00♍06 |
| 54 | 05 42 | 21 49 | 26 35 | 11 30 | 00 17 |
| 55 | 06 01 | 22 52 | 27 31 | 12 01 | 00 28 |
| 56 | 06 21 | 24 00 | 28 29 | 12 33 | 00 39 |
| 57 | 06 43 | 25 13 | 29 29 | 13 07 | 00 51 |
| 58 | 07 07 | 26 32 | 00♌31 | 13 41 | 01 04 |
| 59 | 07 33 | 27 57 | 01 36 | 14 17 | 01 16 |
| 60 | 08♉01 | 29♊30 | 02♌42 | 14♌55 | 01♍30 |

23h 52m 0s — 358° 0' 0" — 27 ♓ 49

| LAT. | 11 | 12 | ASC | 2 | 3 |
|---|---|---|---|---|---|
| 0 | 00♉06 | 00♊11 | 28♊10 | 26♋00 | 25♌44 |
| 5 | 00 27 | 01 22 | 00♋10 | 27 12 | 26 08 |
| 10 | 00 50 | 02 37 | 02 11 | 28 24 | 26 32 |
| 15 | 01 13 | 03 55 | 04 16 | 29 37 | 26 55 |
| 20 | 01 39 | 05 20 | 06 26 | 00♌51 | 27 20 |
| 21 | 01 44 | 05 38 | 06 53 | 01 06 | 27 25 |
| 22 | 01 50 | 05 56 | 07 20 | 01 22 | 27 30 |
| 23 | 01 55 | 06 15 | 07 48 | 01 37 | 27 35 |
| 24 | 02 01 | 06 33 | 08 16 | 01 53 | 27 40 |
| 25 | 02 07 | 06 53 | 08 44 | 02 08 | 27 45 |
| 26 | 02 13 | 07 12 | 09 13 | 02 24 | 27 50 |
| 27 | 02 19 | 07 33 | 09 42 | 02 40 | 27 56 |
| 28 | 02 25 | 07 53 | 10 11 | 02 57 | 28 01 |
| 29 | 02 31 | 08 15 | 10 41 | 03 13 | 28 07 |
| 30 | 02 38 | 08 36 | 11 11 | 03 30 | 28 12 |
| 31 | 02 44 | 08 59 | 11 42 | 03 47 | 28 18 |
| 32 | 02 51 | 09 22 | 12 14 | 04 04 | 28 24 |
| 33 | 02 58 | 09 45 | 12 46 | 04 22 | 28 29 |
| 34 | 03 06 | 10 10 | 13 18 | 04 40 | 28 35 |
| 35 | 03 13 | 10 35 | 13 52 | 04 58 | 28 41 |
| 36 | 03 21 | 11 01 | 14 25 | 05 16 | 28 48 |
| 37 | 03 29 | 11 27 | 15 00 | 05 35 | 28 54 |
| 38 | 03 37 | 11 55 | 15 35 | 05 55 | 29 00 |
| 39 | 03 46 | 12 24 | 16 11 | 06 14 | 29 07 |
| 40 | 03 55 | 12 54 | 16 48 | 06 34 | 29 13 |
| 41 | 04 04 | 13 25 | 17 26 | 06 55 | 29 20 |
| 42 | 04 14 | 13 57 | 18 05 | 07 16 | 29 27 |
| 43 | 04 24 | 14 30 | 18 44 | 07 37 | 29 35 |
| 44 | 04 35 | 15 05 | 19 25 | 07 59 | 29 42 |
| 45 | 04 46 | 15 42 | 20 06 | 08 21 | 29 50 |
| 46 | 04 58 | 16 20 | 20 49 | 08 45 | 29 57 |
| 47 | 05 10 | 17 00 | 21 33 | 09 08 | 00♍06 |
| 48 | 05 23 | 17 42 | 22 18 | 09 33 | 00 14 |
| 49 | 05 36 | 18 26 | 23 04 | 09 58 | 00 22 |
| 50 | 05 50 | 19 13 | 23 52 | 10 24 | 00 31 |
| 51 | 06 05 | 20 02 | 24 41 | 10 50 | 00 40 |
| 52 | 06 21 | 20 54 | 25 32 | 11 18 | 00 50 |
| 53 | 06 39 | 21 50 | 26 24 | 11 46 | 01 00 |
| 54 | 06 57 | 22 48 | 27 17 | 12 16 | 01 10 |
| 55 | 07 16 | 23 51 | 28 13 | 12 46 | 01 21 |
| 56 | 07 37 | 24 59 | 29 10 | 13 18 | 01 32 |
| 57 | 08 00 | 26 11 | 00♌09 | 13 51 | 01 43 |
| 58 | 08 25 | 27 29 | 01 11 | 14 25 | 01 55 |
| 59 | 08 51 | 28 54 | 02 14 | 15 00 | 02 08 |
| 60 | 09♉21 | 00♋25 | 03♌20 | 15♌37 | 02♍21 |

23h 56m 0s — 359° 0' 0" — 28 ♓ 55

| LAT. | 11 | 12 | ASC | 2 | 3 |
|---|---|---|---|---|---|
| 0 | 01♉08 | 01♊08 | 29♊05 | 26♋57 | 26♌47 |
| 5 | 01 31 | 02 20 | 01♋05 | 28 09 | 27 10 |
| 10 | 01 54 | 03 35 | 03 06 | 29 20 | 27 33 |
| 15 | 02 18 | 04 55 | 05 11 | 00♌32 | 27 56 |
| 20 | 02 44 | 06 20 | 07 20 | 01 46 | 28 19 |
| 21 | 02 50 | 06 38 | 07 47 | 02 01 | 28 24 |
| 22 | 02 55 | 06 56 | 08 14 | 02 16 | 28 29 |
| 23 | 03 01 | 07 14 | 08 42 | 02 31 | 28 34 |
| 24 | 03 07 | 07 33 | 09 09 | 02 47 | 28 39 |
| 25 | 03 13 | 07 53 | 09 37 | 03 02 | 28 44 |
| 26 | 03 19 | 08 13 | 10 06 | 03 18 | 28 49 |
| 27 | 03 25 | 08 33 | 10 35 | 03 34 | 28 55 |
| 28 | 03 32 | 08 54 | 11 04 | 03 50 | 29 00 |
| 29 | 03 38 | 09 15 | 11 34 | 04 06 | 29 05 |
| 30 | 03 45 | 09 37 | 12 04 | 04 23 | 29 11 |
| 31 | 03 52 | 09 59 | 12 35 | 04 40 | 29 16 |
| 32 | 03 59 | 10 22 | 13 06 | 04 57 | 29 22 |
| 33 | 04 06 | 10 46 | 13 38 | 05 14 | 29 27 |
| 34 | 04 14 | 11 10 | 14 10 | 05 32 | 29 33 |
| 35 | 04 21 | 11 35 | 14 43 | 05 50 | 29 39 |
| 36 | 04 29 | 12 01 | 15 17 | 06 08 | 29 45 |
| 37 | 04 38 | 12 28 | 15 51 | 06 27 | 29 51 |
| 38 | 04 46 | 12 56 | 16 26 | 06 46 | 29 57 |
| 39 | 04 55 | 13 25 | 17 02 | 07 05 | 00♍04 |
| 40 | 05 04 | 13 54 | 17 38 | 07 25 | 00 10 |
| 41 | 05 14 | 14 25 | 18 15 | 07 45 | 00 17 |
| 42 | 05 24 | 14 57 | 18 54 | 08 06 | 00 24 |
| 43 | 05 34 | 15 31 | 19 33 | 08 27 | 00 31 |
| 44 | 05 45 | 16 06 | 20 13 | 08 48 | 00 38 |
| 45 | 05 57 | 16 42 | 20 54 | 09 11 | 00 45 |
| 46 | 06 09 | 17 20 | 21 36 | 09 33 | 00 53 |
| 47 | 06 21 | 18 00 | 22 20 | 09 57 | 01 01 |
| 48 | 06 34 | 18 42 | 23 04 | 10 21 | 01 09 |
| 49 | 06 48 | 19 26 | 23 50 | 10 46 | 01 17 |
| 50 | 07 03 | 20 13 | 24 37 | 11 11 | 01 26 |
| 51 | 07 18 | 21 02 | 25 26 | 11 37 | 01 35 |
| 52 | 07 35 | 21 54 | 26 16 | 12 04 | 01 44 |
| 53 | 07 52 | 22 49 | 27 07 | 12 32 | 01 53 |
| 54 | 08 11 | 23 47 | 28 00 | 13 01 | 02 03 |
| 55 | 08 31 | 24 50 | 28 55 | 13 31 | 02 14 |
| 56 | 08 53 | 25 57 | 29 51 | 14 03 | 02 24 |
| 57 | 09 16 | 27 08 | 00♌50 | 14 35 | 02 35 |
| 58 | 09 42 | 28 26 | 01 50 | 15 08 | 02 47 |
| 59 | 10 09 | 29 49 | 02 52 | 15 43 | 02 59 |
| 60 | 10♉39 | 01♋20 | 03♌57 | 16♌19 | 03♍12 |

# Table I Time Zones of the World

| STANDARD TIME NAME | MERIDIAN | h m |
|---|---|---|
| GREENWICH UNIVERSAL TIME (UT) | 0°W | 0 |
| WEST AFRICA | 15 | 1 |
| AZORES | 30 | 2 |
| BRAZIL ZONE 2 | 45 | 3 |
| NEWFOUNDLAND | 52°W 30' | 3:30 |
| ATLANTIC | 60 | 4 |
| EASTERN | 75 | 5 |
| CENTRAL | 90 | 6 |
| MOUNTAIN | 105 | 7 |
| PACIFIC | 120 | 8 |
| YUKON | 135 | 9 |
| ALASKA-HAWAII | 150 | 10 |
| HAWAIIAN | 157°W 30' | 10:30 |
| BERING (SAMOA) | 165 | 11 |
| INT'L DATE LINE | 180°W | 12 |

| STANDARD TIME NAME | MERIDIAN | h m |
|---|---|---|
| CENTRAL EUROPEAN | 15°E | 1 |
| MIDDLE EUROPEAN | 15 | 1 |
| EASTERN EUROPEAN | 30 | 2 |
| BAGHDAD | 45 | 3 |
| (NO AGREED NAME) | 60 | 4 |
| (NO AGREED NAME) | 75 | 5 |
| INDIAN | 82°E 30' | 5:30 |
| (NO AGREED NAME) | 90 | 6 |
| NORTH SUMATRA (BURMA) | 97°E 30' | 6:30 |
| SOUTH SUMATRA | 105 | 7 |
| JAVA | 112°E 30' | 7:30 |
| CHINA COAST | 120 | 8 |
| JAPAN | 135 | 9 |
| SOUTH AUSTRALIA | 142°E 30' | 9:30 |
| GUAM | 150 | 10 |
| (NO AGREED NAME) | 165 | 11 |
| NEW ZEALAND | 180°E | 12 |

# Table II Solar-Sidereal Time Correction – Use GMT birth time

| | 0h | 1h | 2h | 3h | 4h | 5h | 6h | 7h | 8h | 9h | 10h | 11h | 12h | 13h | 14h | 15h | 16h | 17h | 18h | 19h | 20h | 21h | 22h | 23h | |
|---|---|---|---|---|---|---|---|---|---|---|---|---|---|---|---|---|---|---|---|---|---|---|---|---|---|
| MIN | m s | m s | m s | m s | m s | m s | m s | m s | m s | m s | m s | m s | m s | m s | m s | m s | m s | m s | m s | m s | m s | m s | m s | m s | MIN |
| 0 | 0 0 | 0 10 | 0 20 | 0 30 | 0 39 | 0 49 | 0 59 | 1 9 | 1 19 | 1 29 | 1 39 | 1 48 | 1 58 | 2 8 | 2 18 | 2 28 | 2 38 | 2 48 | 2 57 | 3 7 | 3 17 | 3 27 | 3 37 | 3 47 | 0 |
| 1 | 0 0 | 0 10 | 0 20 | 0 30 | 0 40 | 0 49 | 0 59 | 1 9 | 1 19 | 1 29 | 1 39 | 1 49 | 1 58 | 2 8 | 2 18 | 2 28 | 2 38 | 2 48 | 2 58 | 3 7 | 3 17 | 3 27 | 3 37 | 3 47 | 1 |
| 2 | 0 0 | 0 10 | 0 20 | 0 30 | 0 40 | 0 50 | 0 59 | 1 9 | 1 19 | 1 29 | 1 39 | 1 49 | 1 59 | 2 8 | 2 18 | 2 28 | 2 38 | 2 48 | 2 58 | 3 8 | 3 17 | 3 27 | 3 37 | 3 47 | 2 |
| 3 | 0 0 | 0 10 | 0 20 | 0 30 | 0 40 | 0 50 | 0 60 | 1 9 | 1 19 | 1 29 | 1 39 | 1 49 | 1 59 | 2 9 | 2 18 | 2 28 | 2 38 | 2 48 | 2 58 | 3 8 | 3 18 | 3 27 | 3 37 | 3 47 | 3 |
| 4 | 0 1 | 0 11 | 0 20 | 0 30 | 0 40 | 0 50 | 0 60 | 1 10 | 1 20 | 1 29 | 1 39 | 1 49 | 1 59 | 2 9 | 2 19 | 2 29 | 2 38 | 2 48 | 2 58 | 3 8 | 3 18 | 3 28 | 3 37 | 3 47 | 4 |
| 5 | 0 1 | 0 11 | 0 21 | 0 30 | 0 40 | 0 50 | 0 60 | 1 10 | 1 20 | 1 30 | 1 39 | 1 49 | 1 59 | 2 9 | 2 19 | 2 29 | 2 39 | 2 48 | 2 58 | 3 8 | 3 18 | 3 28 | 3 38 | 3 48 | 5 |
| 6 | 0 1 | 0 11 | 0 21 | 0 31 | 0 40 | 0 50 | 1 0 | 1 10 | 1 20 | 1 30 | 1 40 | 1 49 | 1 59 | 2 9 | 2 19 | 2 29 | 2 39 | 2 49 | 2 58 | 3 8 | 3 18 | 3 28 | 3 38 | 3 48 | 6 |
| 7 | 0 1 | 0 11 | 0 21 | 0 31 | 0 41 | 0 50 | 1 0 | 1 10 | 1 20 | 1 30 | 1 40 | 1 50 | 1 59 | 2 9 | 2 19 | 2 29 | 2 39 | 2 49 | 2 59 | 3 8 | 3 18 | 3 28 | 3 38 | 3 48 | 7 |
| 8 | 0 1 | 0 11 | 0 21 | 0 31 | 0 41 | 0 51 | 1 0 | 1 10 | 1 20 | 1 30 | 1 40 | 1 50 | 1 60 | 2 9 | 2 19 | 2 29 | 2 39 | 2 49 | 2 59 | 3 9 | 3 18 | 3 28 | 3 38 | 3 48 | 8 |
| 9 | 0 1 | 0 11 | 0 21 | 0 31 | 0 41 | 0 51 | 1 1 | 1 10 | 1 20 | 1 30 | 1 40 | 1 50 | 1 60 | 2 10 | 2 19 | 2 29 | 2 39 | 2 49 | 2 59 | 3 9 | 3 19 | 3 28 | 3 38 | 3 48 | 9 |
| 10 | 0 2 | 0 11 | 0 21 | 0 31 | 0 41 | 0 51 | 1 1 | 1 11 | 1 20 | 1 30 | 1 40 | 1 50 | 1 60 | 2 10 | 2 20 | 2 29 | 2 39 | 2 49 | 2 59 | 3 9 | 3 19 | 3 29 | 3 38 | 3 48 | 10 |
| 11 | 0 2 | 0 12 | 0 22 | 0 31 | 0 41 | 0 51 | 1 1 | 1 11 | 1 21 | 1 31 | 1 40 | 1 50 | 2 0 | 2 10 | 2 20 | 2 30 | 2 40 | 2 49 | 2 59 | 3 9 | 3 19 | 3 29 | 3 39 | 3 49 | 11 |
| 12 | 0 2 | 0 12 | 0 22 | 0 32 | 0 41 | 0 51 | 1 1 | 1 11 | 1 21 | 1 31 | 1 41 | 1 50 | 2 0 | 2 10 | 2 20 | 2 30 | 2 40 | 2 50 | 2 59 | 3 9 | 3 19 | 3 29 | 3 39 | 3 49 | 12 |
| 13 | 0 2 | 0 12 | 0 22 | 0 32 | 0 42 | 0 51 | 1 1 | 1 11 | 1 21 | 1 31 | 1 41 | 1 51 | 2 0 | 2 10 | 2 20 | 2 30 | 2 40 | 2 50 | 2 60 | 3 9 | 3 19 | 3 29 | 3 39 | 3 49 | 13 |
| 14 | 0 2 | 0 12 | 0 22 | 0 32 | 0 42 | 0 52 | 1 1 | 1 11 | 1 21 | 1 31 | 1 41 | 1 51 | 2 1 | 2 10 | 2 20 | 2 30 | 2 40 | 2 50 | 2 60 | 3 0 | 3 19 | 3 29 | 3 39 | 3 49 | 14 |
| 15 | 0 2 | 0 12 | 0 22 | 0 32 | 0 42 | 0 52 | 1 2 | 1 11 | 1 21 | 1 31 | 1 41 | 1 51 | 2 1 | 2 11 | 2 20 | 2 30 | 2 40 | 2 50 | 2 60 | 3 0 | 3 20 | 3 29 | 3 39 | 3 49 | 15 |
| 16 | 0 3 | 0 12 | 0 22 | 0 32 | 0 42 | 0 52 | 1 2 | 1 12 | 1 21 | 1 31 | 1 41 | 1 51 | 2 1 | 2 11 | 2 21 | 2 30 | 2 40 | 2 50 | 3 0 | 3 0 | 3 20 | 3 30 | 3 39 | 3 49 | 16 |
| 17 | 0 3 | 0 13 | 0 23 | 0 32 | 0 42 | 0 52 | 1 2 | 1 12 | 1 22 | 1 32 | 1 41 | 1 51 | 2 1 | 2 11 | 2 21 | 2 31 | 2 40 | 2 50 | 3 0 | 3 0 | 3 20 | 3 30 | 3 40 | 3 49 | 17 |
| 18 | 0 3 | 0 13 | 0 23 | 0 33 | 0 42 | 0 52 | 1 2 | 1 12 | 1 22 | 1 32 | 1 42 | 1 51 | 2 1 | 2 11 | 2 21 | 2 31 | 2 41 | 2 51 | 3 0 | 3 0 | 3 20 | 3 30 | 3 40 | 3 50 | 18 |
| 19 | 0 3 | 0 13 | 0 23 | 0 33 | 0 43 | 0 52 | 1 2 | 1 12 | 1 22 | 1 32 | 1 42 | 1 52 | 2 1 | 2 11 | 2 21 | 2 31 | 2 41 | 2 51 | 3 1 | 3 0 | 3 20 | 3 30 | 3 40 | 3 50 | 19 |
| 20 | 0 3 | 0 13 | 0 23 | 0 33 | 0 43 | 0 53 | 1 2 | 1 12 | 1 22 | 1 32 | 1 42 | 1 52 | 2 2 | 2 11 | 2 21 | 2 31 | 2 41 | 2 51 | 3 1 | 3 11 | 3 20 | 3 30 | 3 40 | 3 50 | 20 |
| 21 | 0 3 | 0 13 | 0 23 | 0 33 | 0 43 | 0 53 | 1 3 | 1 12 | 1 22 | 1 32 | 1 42 | 1 52 | 2 2 | 2 12 | 2 21 | 2 31 | 2 41 | 2 51 | 3 1 | 3 11 | 3 21 | 3 30 | 3 40 | 3 50 | 21 |
| 22 | 0 4 | 0 13 | 0 23 | 0 33 | 0 43 | 0 53 | 1 3 | 1 13 | 1 22 | 1 32 | 1 43 | 1 52 | 2 2 | 2 12 | 2 22 | 2 31 | 2 41 | 2 51 | 3 1 | 3 11 | 3 21 | 3 31 | 3 40 | 3 50 | 22 |
| 23 | 0 4 | 0 14 | 0 24 | 0 33 | 0 43 | 0 53 | 1 3 | 1 13 | 1 23 | 1 32 | 1 42 | 1 52 | 2 2 | 2 12 | 2 22 | 2 32 | 2 41 | 2 51 | 3 1 | 3 11 | 3 21 | 3 31 | 3 41 | 3 50 | 23 |
| 24 | 0 4 | 0 14 | 0 24 | 0 34 | 0 43 | 0 53 | 1 3 | 1 13 | 1 23 | 1 33 | 1 43 | 1 52 | 2 2 | 2 12 | 2 22 | 2 32 | 2 42 | 2 52 | 3 1 | 3 11 | 3 21 | 3 31 | 3 41 | 3 51 | 24 |
| 25 | 0 4 | 0 14 | 0 24 | 0 34 | 0 44 | 0 53 | 1 3 | 1 13 | 1 23 | 1 33 | 1 43 | 1 53 | 2 2 | 2 12 | 2 22 | 2 32 | 2 42 | 2 52 | 3 2 | 3 11 | 3 21 | 3 31 | 3 41 | 3 51 | 25 |
| 26 | 0 4 | 0 14 | 0 24 | 0 34 | 0 44 | 0 54 | 1 3 | 1 13 | 1 23 | 1 33 | 1 43 | 1 53 | 2 3 | 2 12 | 2 22 | 2 32 | 2 42 | 2 52 | 3 2 | 3 12 | 3 21 | 3 31 | 3 41 | 3 51 | 26 |
| 27 | 0 4 | 0 14 | 0 24 | 0 34 | 0 44 | 0 54 | 1 4 | 1 13 | 1 23 | 1 33 | 1 43 | 1 53 | 2 3 | 2 13 | 2 22 | 2 32 | 2 42 | 2 52 | 3 2 | 3 12 | 3 22 | 3 31 | 3 41 | 3 51 | 27 |
| 28 | 0 5 | 0 14 | 0 24 | 0 34 | 0 44 | 0 54 | 1 4 | 1 14 | 1 23 | 1 33 | 1 43 | 1 53 | 2 3 | 2 13 | 2 23 | 2 32 | 2 42 | 2 52 | 3 2 | 3 12 | 3 22 | 3 32 | 3 41 | 3 51 | 28 |
| 29 | 0 5 | 0 15 | 0 25 | 0 34 | 0 44 | 0 54 | 1 4 | 1 14 | 1 24 | 1 33 | 1 43 | 1 53 | 2 3 | 2 13 | 2 23 | 2 33 | 2 42 | 2 52 | 3 2 | 3 12 | 3 22 | 3 32 | 3 42 | 3 51 | 29 |
| 30 | 0 5 | 0 15 | 0 25 | 0 34 | 0 44 | 0 54 | 1 4 | 1 14 | 1 24 | 1 34 | 1 43 | 1 53 | 2 3 | 2 13 | 2 23 | 2 33 | 2 43 | 2 52 | 3 2 | 3 12 | 3 22 | 3 32 | 3 42 | 3 52 | 30 |
| 31 | 0 5 | 0 15 | 0 25 | 0 35 | 0 45 | 0 54 | 1 4 | 1 14 | 1 24 | 1 34 | 1 44 | 1 54 | 2 3 | 2 13 | 2 23 | 2 33 | 2 43 | 2 53 | 3 3 | 3 12 | 3 22 | 3 32 | 3 42 | 3 52 | 31 |
| 32 | 0 5 | 0 15 | 0 25 | 0 35 | 0 45 | 0 55 | 1 4 | 1 14 | 1 24 | 1 34 | 1 44 | 1 54 | 2 4 | 2 13 | 2 23 | 2 33 | 2 43 | 2 53 | 3 3 | 3 13 | 3 22 | 3 32 | 3 42 | 3 52 | 32 |
| 33 | 0 5 | 0 15 | 0 25 | 0 35 | 0 45 | 0 55 | 1 5 | 1 14 | 1 24 | 1 34 | 1 44 | 1 54 | 2 4 | 2 14 | 2 23 | 2 33 | 2 43 | 2 53 | 3 3 | 3 13 | 3 23 | 3 32 | 3 42 | 3 52 | 33 |
| 34 | 0 6 | 0 16 | 0 25 | 0 35 | 0 45 | 0 55 | 1 5 | 1 15 | 1 24 | 1 34 | 1 44 | 1 54 | 2 4 | 2 14 | 2 24 | 2 33 | 2 43 | 2 53 | 3 3 | 3 13 | 3 23 | 3 33 | 3 42 | 3 52 | 34 |
| 35 | 0 6 | 0 16 | 0 26 | 0 35 | 0 45 | 0 55 | 1 5 | 1 15 | 1 25 | 1 34 | 1 44 | 1 54 | 2 4 | 2 14 | 2 24 | 2 34 | 2 43 | 2 53 | 3 3 | 3 13 | 3 23 | 3 33 | 3 43 | 3 52 | 35 |
| 36 | 0 6 | 0 16 | 0 26 | 0 35 | 0 45 | 0 55 | 1 5 | 1 15 | 1 25 | 1 35 | 1 44 | 1 54 | 2 4 | 2 14 | 2 24 | 2 34 | 2 44 | 2 53 | 3 3 | 3 13 | 3 23 | 3 33 | 3 43 | 3 53 | 36 |
| 37 | 0 6 | 0 16 | 0 26 | 0 36 | 0 46 | 0 55 | 1 5 | 1 15 | 1 25 | 1 35 | 1 45 | 1 54 | 2 4 | 2 14 | 2 24 | 2 34 | 2 44 | 2 54 | 3 3 | 3 13 | 3 23 | 3 33 | 3 43 | 3 53 | 37 |
| 38 | 0 6 | 0 16 | 0 26 | 0 36 | 0 46 | 0 56 | 1 5 | 1 15 | 1 25 | 1 35 | 1 45 | 1 55 | 2 5 | 2 14 | 2 24 | 2 34 | 2 44 | 2 54 | 3 4 | 3 14 | 3 23 | 3 33 | 3 43 | 3 53 | 38 |
| 39 | 0 6 | 0 16 | 0 26 | 0 36 | 0 46 | 0 56 | 1 6 | 1 15 | 1 25 | 1 35 | 1 45 | 1 55 | 2 5 | 2 15 | 2 24 | 2 34 | 2 44 | 2 54 | 3 4 | 3 14 | 3 24 | 3 33 | 3 43 | 3 53 | 39 |
| 40 | 0 7 | 0 16 | 0 26 | 0 36 | 0 46 | 0 56 | 1 6 | 1 16 | 1 25 | 1 35 | 1 45 | 1 55 | 2 5 | 2 15 | 2 25 | 2 34 | 2 44 | 2 54 | 3 4 | 3 14 | 3 24 | 3 34 | 3 43 | 3 53 | 40 |
| 41 | 0 7 | 0 17 | 0 27 | 0 36 | 0 46 | 0 56 | 1 6 | 1 16 | 1 26 | 1 35 | 1 45 | 1 55 | 2 5 | 2 15 | 2 25 | 2 35 | 2 44 | 2 54 | 3 4 | 3 14 | 3 24 | 3 34 | 3 44 | 3 53 | 41 |
| 42 | 0 7 | 0 17 | 0 27 | 0 36 | 0 46 | 0 56 | 1 6 | 1 16 | 1 26 | 1 36 | 1 45 | 1 55 | 2 5 | 2 15 | 2 25 | 2 35 | 2 45 | 2 54 | 3 4 | 3 14 | 3 24 | 3 34 | 3 44 | 3 54 | 42 |
| 43 | 0 7 | 0 17 | 0 27 | 0 37 | 0 46 | 0 56 | 1 6 | 1 16 | 1 26 | 1 36 | 1 46 | 1 55 | 2 5 | 2 15 | 2 25 | 2 35 | 2 45 | 2 55 | 3 4 | 3 14 | 3 24 | 3 34 | 3 44 | 3 54 | 43 |
| 44 | 0 7 | 0 17 | 0 27 | 0 37 | 0 47 | 0 57 | 1 6 | 1 16 | 1 26 | 1 36 | 1 46 | 1 56 | 2 6 | 2 15 | 2 25 | 2 35 | 2 45 | 2 55 | 3 5 | 3 15 | 3 24 | 3 34 | 3 44 | 3 54 | 44 |
| 45 | 0 7 | 0 17 | 0 27 | 0 37 | 0 47 | 0 57 | 1 7 | 1 16 | 1 26 | 1 36 | 1 46 | 1 56 | 2 6 | 2 16 | 2 25 | 2 35 | 2 45 | 2 55 | 3 5 | 3 15 | 3 25 | 3 34 | 3 44 | 3 54 | 45 |
| 46 | 0 8 | 0 18 | 0 27 | 0 37 | 0 47 | 0 57 | 1 7 | 1 17 | 1 26 | 1 36 | 1 46 | 1 56 | 2 6 | 2 16 | 2 26 | 2 35 | 2 45 | 2 55 | 3 5 | 3 15 | 3 25 | 3 35 | 3 45 | 3 54 | 46 |
| 47 | 0 8 | 0 18 | 0 28 | 0 37 | 0 47 | 0 57 | 1 7 | 1 17 | 1 27 | 1 36 | 1 46 | 1 56 | 2 6 | 2 16 | 2 26 | 2 36 | 2 45 | 2 55 | 3 5 | 3 15 | 3 25 | 3 35 | 3 45 | 3 54 | 47 |
| 48 | 0 8 | 0 18 | 0 28 | 0 37 | 0 47 | 0 57 | 1 7 | 1 17 | 1 27 | 1 37 | 1 46 | 1 56 | 2 6 | 2 16 | 2 26 | 2 36 | 2 46 | 2 55 | 3 5 | 3 15 | 3 25 | 3 35 | 3 45 | 3 55 | 48 |
| 49 | 0 8 | 0 18 | 0 28 | 0 38 | 0 47 | 0 57 | 1 7 | 1 17 | 1 27 | 1 37 | 1 47 | 1 56 | 2 6 | 2 16 | 2 26 | 2 36 | 2 46 | 2 56 | 3 5 | 3 15 | 3 25 | 3 35 | 3 45 | 3 55 | 49 |
| 50 | 0 8 | 0 18 | 0 28 | 0 38 | 0 48 | 0 57 | 1 7 | 1 17 | 1 27 | 1 37 | 1 47 | 1 57 | 2 6 | 2 16 | 2 26 | 2 36 | 2 46 | 2 56 | 3 6 | 3 15 | 3 25 | 3 35 | 3 45 | 3 55 | 50 |
| 51 | 0 8 | 0 18 | 0 28 | 0 38 | 0 48 | 0 58 | 1 8 | 1 17 | 1 27 | 1 37 | 1 47 | 1 57 | 2 7 | 2 17 | 2 26 | 2 36 | 2 46 | 2 56 | 3 6 | 3 16 | 3 26 | 3 35 | 3 45 | 3 55 | 51 |
| 52 | 0 9 | 0 18 | 0 28 | 0 38 | 0 48 | 0 58 | 1 8 | 1 18 | 1 27 | 1 37 | 1 47 | 1 57 | 2 7 | 2 17 | 2 27 | 2 36 | 2 46 | 2 56 | 3 6 | 3 16 | 3 26 | 3 36 | 3 45 | 3 55 | 52 |
| 53 | 0 9 | 0 19 | 0 29 | 0 38 | 0 48 | 0 58 | 1 8 | 1 18 | 1 28 | 1 37 | 1 47 | 1 57 | 2 7 | 2 17 | 2 27 | 2 37 | 2 46 | 2 56 | 3 6 | 3 16 | 3 26 | 3 36 | 3 46 | 3 55 | 53 |
| 54 | 0 9 | 0 19 | 0 29 | 0 38 | 0 48 | 0 58 | 1 8 | 1 18 | 1 28 | 1 38 | 1 47 | 1 57 | 2 7 | 2 17 | 2 27 | 2 37 | 2 47 | 2 56 | 3 6 | 3 16 | 3 26 | 3 36 | 3 46 | 3 56 | 54 |
| 55 | 0 9 | 0 19 | 0 29 | 0 39 | 0 48 | 0 58 | 1 8 | 1 18 | 1 28 | 1 38 | 1 48 | 1 57 | 2 7 | 2 17 | 2 27 | 2 37 | 2 47 | 2 57 | 3 6 | 3 16 | 3 26 | 3 36 | 3 46 | 3 56 | 55 |
| 56 | 0 9 | 0 19 | 0 29 | 0 39 | 0 49 | 0 58 | 1 8 | 1 18 | 1 28 | 1 38 | 1 48 | 1 58 | 2 7 | 2 17 | 2 27 | 2 37 | 2 47 | 2 57 | 3 7 | 3 16 | 3 26 | 3 36 | 3 46 | 3 56 | 56 |
| 57 | 0 9 | 0 19 | 0 29 | 0 39 | 0 49 | 0 59 | 1 9 | 1 18 | 1 28 | 1 38 | 1 48 | 1 58 | 2 8 | 2 17 | 2 27 | 2 37 | 2 47 | 2 57 | 3 7 | 3 17 | 3 26 | 3 36 | 3 46 | 3 56 | 57 |
| 58 | 0 10 | 0 19 | 0 29 | 0 39 | 0 49 | 0 59 | 1 9 | 1 19 | 1 28 | 1 38 | 1 48 | 1 58 | 2 8 | 2 18 | 2 28 | 2 37 | 2 47 | 2 57 | 3 7 | 3 17 | 3 27 | 3 37 | 3 46 | 3 56 | 58 |
| 59 | 0 10 | 0 20 | 0 29 | 0 39 | 0 49 | 0 59 | 1 9 | 1 19 | 1 29 | 1 38 | 1 48 | 1 58 | 2 8 | 2 18 | 2 28 | 2 38 | 2 47 | 2 57 | 3 7 | 3 17 | 3 27 | 3 37 | 3 47 | 3 56 | 59 |
| 60 | 0 10 | 0 20 | 0 30 | 0 39 | 0 49 | 0 59 | 1 9 | 1 19 | 1 29 | 1 39 | 1 48 | 1 58 | 2 8 | 2 18 | 2 28 | 2 38 | 2 48 | 2 57 | 3 7 | 3 17 | 3 27 | 3 37 | 3 47 | 3 57 | 60 |

## Table III
## Time Correction for Longitude

| ° | h m | ° | h m | ° | h m | ' | m s |
|---|-----|---|-----|---|-----|---|-----|
| 1 | 0 4 | 61 | 4 4 | 121 | 8 4 | 1 | 0 4 |
| 2 | 0 8 | 62 | 4 8 | 122 | 8 8 | 2 | 0 8 |
| 3 | 0 12 | 63 | 4 12 | 123 | 8 12 | 3 | 0 12 |
| 4 | 0 16 | 64 | 4 16 | 124 | 8 16 | 4 | 0 16 |
| 5 | 0 20 | 65 | 4 20 | 125 | 8 20 | 5 | 0 20 |
| 6 | 0 24 | 66 | 4 24 | 126 | 8 24 | 6 | 0 24 |
| 7 | 0 28 | 67 | 4 28 | 127 | 8 28 | 7 | 0 28 |
| 8 | 0 32 | 68 | 4 32 | 128 | 8 32 | 8 | 0 32 |
| 9 | 0 36 | 69 | 4 36 | 129 | 8 36 | 9 | 0 36 |
| 10 | 0 40 | 70 | 4 40 | 130 | 8 40 | 10 | 0 40 |
| 11 | 0 44 | 71 | 4 44 | 131 | 8 44 | 11 | 0 44 |
| 12 | 0 48 | 72 | 4 48 | 132 | 8 48 | 12 | 0 48 |
| 13 | 0 52 | 73 | 4 52 | 133 | 8 52 | 13 | 0 52 |
| 14 | 0 56 | 74 | 4 56 | 134 | 8 56 | 14 | 0 56 |
| 15 | 1 0 | 75 | 5 0 | 135 | 9 0 | 15 | 1 0 |
| 16 | 1 4 | 76 | 5 4 | 136 | 9 4 | 16 | 1 4 |
| 17 | 1 8 | 77 | 5 8 | 137 | 9 8 | 17 | 1 8 |
| 18 | 1 12 | 78 | 5 12 | 138 | 9 12 | 18 | 1 12 |
| 19 | 1 16 | 79 | 5 16 | 139 | 9 16 | 19 | 1 16 |
| 20 | 1 20 | 80 | 5 20 | 140 | 9 20 | 20 | 1 20 |
| 21 | 1 24 | 81 | 24 | 141 | 9 24 | 21 | 1 24 |
| 22 | 1 28 | 82 | 5 28 | 142 | 9 28 | 22 | 1 28 |
| 23 | 1 32 | 83 | 5 32 | 143 | 9 32 | 23 | 1 32 |
| 24 | 1 36 | 84 | 5 36 | 144 | 9 36 | 24 | 1 36 |
| 25 | 1 40 | 85 | 5 40 | 145 | 9 40 | 25 | 1 40 |
| 26 | 1 44 | 86 | 5 44 | 146 | 9 44 | 26 | 1 44 |
| 27 | 1 48 | 87 | 5 48 | 147 | 9 48 | 27 | 1 48 |
| 28 | 1 52 | 88 | 5 52 | 148 | 9 52 | 28 | 1 52 |
| 29 | 1 56 | 89 | 5 56 | 149 | 9 56 | 29 | 1 56 |
| 30 | 2 0 | 90 | 6 0 | 150 | 10 0 | 30 | 2 0 |
| 31 | 2 4 | 91 | 6 4 | 151 | 10 4 | 31 | 2 4 |
| 32 | 2 8 | 92 | 6 8 | 152 | 10 8 | 32 | 2 8 |
| 33 | 2 12 | 93 | 6 12 | 153 | 10 12 | 33 | 2 12 |
| 34 | 2 16 | 94 | 6 16 | 154 | 10 16 | 34 | 2 16 |
| 35 | 2 20 | 95 | 6 20 | 155 | 10 20 | 35 | 2 20 |
| 36 | 2 24 | 96 | 6 24 | 156 | 10 24 | 36 | 2 24 |
| 37 | 2 28 | 97 | 6 28 | 157 | 10 28 | 37 | 2 28 |
| 38 | 2 32 | 98 | 6 32 | 158 | 10 32 | 38 | 2 32 |
| 39 | 2 36 | 99 | 6 36 | 159 | 10 36 | 39 | 2 36 |
| 40 | 2 40 | 100 | 6 40 | 160 | 10 40 | 40 | 2 40 |
| 41 | 2 44 | 101 | 6 44 | 161 | 10 44 | 41 | 2 44 |
| 42 | 2 48 | 102 | 6 48 | 162 | 10 48 | 42 | 2 48 |
| 43 | 2 52 | 103 | 6 52 | 163 | 10 52 | 43 | 2 52 |
| 44 | 2 56 | 104 | 6 56 | 164 | 10 56 | 44 | 2 56 |
| 45 | 3 0 | 105 | 7 0 | 165 | 11 0 | 45 | 3 0 |
| 46 | 3 4 | 106 | 7 4 | 166 | 11 4 | 46 | 3 4 |
| 47 | 3 8 | 107 | 7 8 | 167 | 11 8 | 47 | 3 8 |
| 48 | 3 12 | 108 | 7 12 | 168 | 11 12 | 48 | 3 12 |
| 49 | 3 16 | 109 | 7 16 | 169 | 11 16 | 49 | 3 16 |
| 50 | 3 20 | 110 | 7 20 | 170 | 11 20 | 50 | 3 20 |
| 51 | 3 24 | 111 | 7 24 | 171 | 11 24 | 51 | 3 24 |
| 52 | 3 28 | 112 | 7 28 | 172 | 11 28 | 52 | 3 28 |
| 53 | 3 32 | 113 | 7 32 | 173 | 11 32 | 53 | 3 32 |
| 54 | 3 36 | 114 | 7 36 | 174 | 11 36 | 54 | 3 36 |
| 55 | 3 40 | 115 | 7 40 | 175 | 11 40 | 55 | 3 40 |
| 56 | 3 44 | 116 | 7 44 | 176 | 11 44 | 56 | 3 44 |
| 57 | 3 48 | 117 | 7 48 | 177 | 11 48 | 57 | 3 48 |
| 58 | 3 52 | 118 | 7 52 | 178 | 11 52 | 58 | 3 52 |
| 59 | 3 56 | 119 | 7 56 | 179 | 11 56 | 59 | 3 56 |
| 60 | 4 0 | 120 | 8 0 | 180 | 12 0 | 60 | 4 0 |

## Table IV
## Universal to Ephemeris
## Time Correction (ΔT)

ADD TO UNIVERSAL TIME ENTRIES FOR JANUARY 1st

| YEAR | SECONDS | YEAR | SECONDS | YEAR | SECONDS |
|------|---------|------|---------|------|---------|
| 1860 | 8 | 1910 | 10 | 1955 | 31 |
| 1861 | 8 | 1911 | 12 | 1956 | 31 |
| 1862 | 8 | 1912 | 13 | 1957 | 32 |
| 1863 | 7 | 1913 | 15 | 1958 | 32 |
| 1864 | 6 | 1914 | 16 | 1959 | 33 |
| 1865 | 6 | 1915 | 17 | 1960 | 33 |
| 1866 | 5 | 1916 | 18 | 1961 | 34 |
| 1867 | 4 | 1917 | 19 | 1962 | 34 |
| 1868 | 3 | 1918 | 20 | 1963 | 34 |
| 1869 | 2 | 1919 | 21 | 1964 | 35 |
| 1870 | 2 | 1920 | 21 | 1965 | 36 |
| 1871 | 0 | 1921 | 22 | 1966 | 37 |
| 1872 | -1 | 1922 | 22 | 1967 | 37 |
| 1873 | -1 | 1923 | 23 | 1968 | 38 |
| 1874 | -3 | 1924 | 23 | 1969 | 39 |
| 1875 | -3 | 1925 | 24 | 1970 | 40 |
| 1876 | -4 | 1926 | 24 | 1971 | 41 |
| 1877 | -5 | 1927 | 24 | 1972 | 42 |
| 1878 | -5 | 1928 | 24 | 1973 | 43 |
| 1879 | -5 | 1929 | 24 | 1974 | 44 |
| 1880 | -5 | 1930 | 24 | 1975 | 45 |
| 1881 | -5 | 1931 | 24 | 1976 | 46 |
| 1882 | -5 | 1932 | 24 | 1977 | 48 |
| 1883 | -5 | 1933 | 24 | 1978 | 49 |
| 1884 | -5 | 1934 | 24 | 1979 | 50 |
| 1885 | -6 | 1935 | 24 | 1980 | 51 |
| 1886 | -6 | 1936 | 24 | 1981 | 51 |
| 1887 | -6 | 1937 | 24 | 1982 | 52 |
| 1888 | -6 | 1938 | 24 | 1983 | 53 |
| 1889 | -6 | 1939 | 24 | 1984 | 54 |
| 1890 | -6 | 1940 | 24 | 1985 | 55 |
| 1891 | -6 | 1941 | 25 | 1986 | 55 |
| 1892 | -6 | 1942 | 25 | 1987 | 55 |
| 1893 | -7 | 1943 | 26 | 1988 | 56 |
| 1894 | -6 | 1944 | 26 | 1989 | 56 |
| 1895 | -6 | 1945 | 27 | 1990 | 57 |
| 1896 | -6 | 1946 | 27 | 1991 | 58 |
| 1897 | -6 | 1947 | 28 | 1992 | 58 |
| 1898 | -5 | 1948 | 28 | 1993 | 59 |
| 1899 | -4 | 1949 | 29 | 1994 | 60 |
| 1900 | -3 | 1950 | 29 | 1995 | 61 |
| 1901 | -2 | 1951 | 30 | 1996 | 62 |
| 1902 | 0 | 1952 | 30 | 1997 | 63 |
| 1903 | 1 | 1953 | 30 | | |
| 1904 | 3 | 1954 | 31 | | |
| 1905 | 4 | | | | |
| 1906 | 5 | | | | |
| 1907 | 6 | | | | |
| 1908 | 8 | | | | |
| 1909 | 9 | | | | |

Pre-1995 figures are based on astronomical measurements. Due to revisions in 1987, what appears above may differ slightly from figures in earlier editions.

# Table V Diurnal Motion of the Sun

24 HOUR TRAVEL

| TIME | 57 12 | 57 14 | 57 16 | 57 18 | 57 20 | 57 22 | 57 24 | 57 26 | 57 28 | 57 30 | 57 32 | 57 34 | 57 36 | 57 38 | 57 40 | 57 42 | 57 44 | 57 46 | 57 48 | 57 50 | TIME |
|---|---|---|---|---|---|---|---|---|---|---|---|---|---|---|---|---|---|---|---|---|---|
| M 1 | 2 | 2 | 2 | 2 | 2 | 2 | 2 | 2 | 2 | 2 | 2 | 2 | 2 | 2 | 2 | 2 | 2 | 2 | 2 | 2 | 1 M |
| I 2 | 5 | 5 | 5 | 5 | 5 | 5 | 5 | 5 | 5 | 5 | 5 | 5 | 5 | 5 | 5 | 5 | 5 | 5 | 5 | 5 | 2 I |
| N 3 | 7 | 7 | 7 | 7 | 7 | 7 | 7 | 7 | 7 | 7 | 7 | 7 | 7 | 7 | 7 | 7 | 7 | 7 | 7 | 7 | 3 N |
| U 4 | 10 | 10 | 10 | 10 | 10 | 10 | 10 | 10 | 10 | 10 | 10 | 10 | 10 | 10 | 10 | 10 | 10 | 10 | 10 | 10 | 4 U |
| T 5 | 12 | 12 | 12 | 12 | 12 | 12 | 12 | 12 | 12 | 12 | 12 | 12 | 12 | 12 | 12 | 12 | 12 | 12 | 12 | 12 | 5 T |
| E S 6 | 14 | 14 | 14 | 14 | 14 | 14 | 14 | 14 | 14 | 14 | 14 | 14 | 14 | 14 | 14 | 14 | 14 | 14 | 14 | 14 | E 6 S |
| 7 | 17 | 17 | 17 | 17 | 17 | 17 | 17 | 17 | 17 | 17 | 17 | 17 | 17 | 17 | 17 | 17 | 17 | 17 | 17 | 17 | 7 |
| 8 | 19 | 19 | 19 | 19 | 19 | 19 | 19 | 19 | 19 | 19 | 19 | 19 | 19 | 19 | 19 | 19 | 19 | 19 | 19 | 19 | 8 |
| 9 | 21 | 21 | 21 | 21 | 22 | 22 | 22 | 22 | 22 | 22 | 22 | 22 | 22 | 22 | 22 | 22 | 22 | 22 | 22 | 22 | 9 |
| 10 | 24 | 24 | 24 | 24 | 24 | 24 | 24 | 24 | 24 | 24 | 24 | 24 | 24 | 24 | 24 | 24 | 24 | 24 | 24 | 24 | 10 |
| 11 | 26 | 26 | 26 | 26 | 26 | 26 | 26 | 26 | 26 | 26 | 26 | 26 | 26 | 26 | 26 | 26 | 26 | 26 | 26 | 27 | 11 |
| 12 | 29 | 29 | 29 | 29 | 29 | 29 | 29 | 29 | 29 | 29 | 29 | 29 | 29 | 29 | 29 | 29 | 29 | 29 | 29 | 29 | 12 |
| 13 | 31 | 31 | 31 | 31 | 31 | 31 | 31 | 31 | 31 | 31 | 31 | 31 | 31 | 31 | 31 | 31 | 31 | 31 | 31 | 31 | 13 |
| 14 | 33 | 33 | 33 | 33 | 33 | 33 | 33 | 34 | 34 | 34 | 34 | 34 | 34 | 34 | 34 | 34 | 34 | 34 | 34 | 34 | 14 |
| 15 | 36 | 36 | 36 | 36 | 36 | 36 | 36 | 36 | 36 | 36 | 36 | 36 | 36 | 36 | 36 | 36 | 36 | 36 | 36 | 36 | 15 |
| 16 | 38 | 38 | 38 | 38 | 38 | 38 | 38 | 38 | 38 | 38 | 38 | 38 | 38 | 38 | 38 | 38 | 38 | 39 | 39 | 39 | 16 |
| 17 | 41 | 41 | 41 | 41 | 41 | 41 | 41 | 41 | 41 | 41 | 41 | 41 | 41 | 41 | 41 | 41 | 41 | 41 | 41 | 41 | 17 |
| 18 | 43 | 43 | 43 | 43 | 43 | 43 | 43 | 43 | 43 | 43 | 43 | 43 | 43 | 43 | 43 | 43 | 43 | 43 | 43 | 43 | 18 |
| 19 | 45 | 45 | 45 | 45 | 45 | 45 | 45 | 45 | 45 | 46 | 46 | 46 | 46 | 46 | 46 | 46 | 46 | 46 | 46 | 46 | 19 |
| 20 | 48 | 48 | 48 | 48 | 48 | 48 | 48 | 48 | 48 | 48 | 48 | 48 | 48 | 48 | 48 | 48 | 48 | 48 | 48 | 48 | 20 |
| 21 | 50 | 50 | 50 | 50 | 50 | 50 | 50 | 50 | 50 | 50 | 50 | 50 | 50 | 50 | 50 | 50 | 51 | 51 | 51 | 51 | 21 |
| 22 | 52 | 52 | 52 | 53 | 53 | 53 | 53 | 53 | 53 | 53 | 53 | 53 | 53 | 53 | 53 | 53 | 53 | 53 | 53 | 53 | 22 |
| 23 | 55 | 55 | 55 | 55 | 55 | 55 | 55 | 55 | 55 | 55 | 55 | 55 | 55 | 55 | 55 | 55 | 55 | 55 | 55 | 55 | 23 |
| 24 | 57 | 57 | 57 | 57 | 57 | 57 | 57 | 57 | 57 | 58 | 58 | 58 | 58 | 58 | 58 | 58 | 58 | 58 | 58 | 58 | 24 |
| 25 | 1 0 | 1 0 | 1 0 | 1 0 | 1 0 | 1 0 | 1 0 | 1 0 | 1 0 | 1 0 | 1 0 | 1 0 | 1 0 | 1 0 | 1 0 | 1 0 | 1 0 | 1 0 | 1 0 | 1 0 | 25 |
| 26 | 1 2 | 1 2 | 1 2 | 1 2 | 1 2 | 1 2 | 1 2 | 1 2 | 1 2 | 1 2 | 1 2 | 1 2 | 1 2 | 1 2 | 1 2 | 1 3 | 1 3 | 1 3 | 1 3 | 1 3 | 26 |
| 27 | 1 4 | 1 4 | 1 4 | 1 4 | 1 5 | 1 5 | 1 5 | 1 5 | 1 5 | 1 5 | 1 5 | 1 5 | 1 5 | 1 5 | 1 5 | 1 5 | 1 5 | 1 5 | 1 5 | 1 5 | 27 |
| 28 | 1 7 | 1 7 | 1 7 | 1 7 | 1 7 | 1 7 | 1 7 | 1 7 | 1 7 | 1 7 | 1 7 | 1 7 | 1 7 | 1 7 | 1 7 | 1 7 | 1 7 | 1 7 | 1 7 | 1 7 | 28 |
| 29 | 1 9 | 1 9 | 1 9 | 1 9 | 1 9 | 1 9 | 1 9 | 1 9 | 1 9 | 1 9 | 1 10 | 1 10 | 1 10 | 1 10 | 1 10 | 1 10 | 1 10 | 1 10 | 1 10 | 1 10 | 29 |
| 30 | 1 12 | 1 12 | 1 12 | 1 12 | 1 12 | 1 12 | 1 12 | 1 12 | 1 12 | 1 12 | 1 12 | 1 12 | 1 12 | 1 12 | 1 12 | 1 12 | 1 12 | 1 12 | 1 12 | 1 12 | 30 |
| 31 | 1 14 | 1 14 | 1 14 | 1 14 | 1 14 | 1 14 | 1 14 | 1 14 | 1 14 | 1 14 | 1 14 | 1 14 | 1 14 | 1 14 | 1 14 | 1 15 | 1 15 | 1 15 | 1 15 | 1 15 | 31 |
| 32 | 1 16 | 1 16 | 1 16 | 1 16 | 1 16 | 1 16 | 1 17 | 1 17 | 1 17 | 1 17 | 1 17 | 1 17 | 1 17 | 1 17 | 1 17 | 1 17 | 1 17 | 1 17 | 1 17 | 1 17 | 32 |
| 33 | 1 19 | 1 19 | 1 19 | 1 19 | 1 19 | 1 19 | 1 19 | 1 19 | 1 19 | 1 19 | 1 19 | 1 19 | 1 19 | 1 19 | 1 19 | 1 19 | 1 19 | 1 19 | 1 19 | 1 20 | 33 |
| 34 | 1 21 | 1 21 | 1 21 | 1 21 | 1 21 | 1 21 | 1 21 | 1 21 | 1 21 | 1 21 | 1 22 | 1 22 | 1 22 | 1 22 | 1 22 | 1 22 | 1 22 | 1 22 | 1 22 | 1 22 | 34 |
| 35 | 1 23 | 1 23 | 1 24 | 1 24 | 1 24 | 1 24 | 1 24 | 1 24 | 1 24 | 1 24 | 1 24 | 1 24 | 1 24 | 1 24 | 1 24 | 1 24 | 1 24 | 1 24 | 1 24 | 1 24 | 35 |
| 36 | 1 26 | 1 26 | 1 26 | 1 26 | 1 26 | 1 26 | 1 26 | 1 26 | 1 26 | 1 26 | 1 26 | 1 26 | 1 26 | 1 26 | 1 27 | 1 27 | 1 27 | 1 27 | 1 27 | 1 27 | 36 |
| 37 | 1 28 | 1 28 | 1 28 | 1 28 | 1 28 | 1 28 | 1 28 | 1 29 | 1 29 | 1 29 | 1 29 | 1 29 | 1 29 | 1 29 | 1 29 | 1 29 | 1 29 | 1 29 | 1 29 | 1 29 | 37 |
| 38 | 1 31 | 1 31 | 1 31 | 1 31 | 1 31 | 1 31 | 1 31 | 1 31 | 1 31 | 1 31 | 1 31 | 1 31 | 1 31 | 1 31 | 1 31 | 1 31 | 1 31 | 1 31 | 1 32 | 1 32 | 38 |
| 39 | 1 33 | 1 33 | 1 33 | 1 33 | 1 33 | 1 33 | 1 33 | 1 33 | 1 33 | 1 33 | 1 33 | 1 34 | 1 34 | 1 34 | 1 34 | 1 34 | 1 34 | 1 34 | 1 34 | 1 34 | 39 |
| 40 | 1 35 | 1 35 | 1 35 | 1 36 | 1 36 | 1 36 | 1 36 | 1 36 | 1 36 | 1 36 | 1 36 | 1 36 | 1 36 | 1 36 | 1 36 | 1 36 | 1 36 | 1 36 | 1 36 | 1 36 | 40 |
| 41 | 1 38 | 1 38 | 1 38 | 1 38 | 1 38 | 1 38 | 1 38 | 1 38 | 1 38 | 1 38 | 1 38 | 1 38 | 1 38 | 1 38 | 1 39 | 1 39 | 1 39 | 1 39 | 1 39 | 1 39 | 41 |
| 42 | 1 40 | 1 40 | 1 40 | 1 40 | 1 40 | 1 40 | 1 40 | 1 41 | 1 41 | 1 41 | 1 41 | 1 41 | 1 41 | 1 41 | 1 41 | 1 41 | 1 41 | 1 41 | 1 41 | 1 41 | 42 |
| 43 | 1 42 | 1 43 | 1 43 | 1 43 | 1 43 | 1 43 | 1 43 | 1 43 | 1 43 | 1 43 | 1 43 | 1 43 | 1 43 | 1 43 | 1 43 | 1 43 | 1 43 | 1 43 | 1 44 | 1 44 | 43 |
| 44 | 1 45 | 1 45 | 1 45 | 1 45 | 1 45 | 1 45 | 1 45 | 1 45 | 1 45 | 1 45 | 1 45 | 1 46 | 1 46 | 1 46 | 1 46 | 1 46 | 1 46 | 1 46 | 1 46 | 1 46 | 44 |
| 45 | 1 47 | 1 47 | 1 47 | 1 47 | 1 48 | 1 48 | 1 48 | 1 48 | 1 48 | 1 48 | 1 48 | 1 48 | 1 48 | 1 48 | 1 48 | 1 48 | 1 48 | 1 48 | 1 48 | 1 48 | 45 |
| 46 | 1 50 | 1 50 | 1 50 | 1 50 | 1 50 | 1 50 | 1 50 | 1 50 | 1 50 | 1 50 | 1 50 | 1 50 | 1 50 | 1 50 | 1 51 | 1 51 | 1 51 | 1 51 | 1 51 | 1 51 | 46 |
| 47 | 1 52 | 1 52 | 1 52 | 1 52 | 1 52 | 1 52 | 1 52 | 1 52 | 1 53 | 1 53 | 1 53 | 1 53 | 1 53 | 1 53 | 1 53 | 1 53 | 1 53 | 1 53 | 1 53 | 1 53 | 47 |
| 48 | 1 54 | 1 54 | 1 55 | 1 55 | 1 55 | 1 55 | 1 55 | 1 55 | 1 55 | 1 55 | 1 55 | 1 55 | 1 55 | 1 55 | 1 55 | 1 55 | 1 55 | 1 56 | 1 56 | 1 56 | 48 |
| 49 | 1 57 | 1 57 | 1 57 | 1 57 | 1 57 | 1 57 | 1 57 | 1 57 | 1 57 | 1 57 | 1 57 | 1 58 | 1 58 | 1 58 | 1 58 | 1 58 | 1 58 | 1 58 | 1 58 | 1 58 | 49 |
| 50 | 1 59 | 1 59 | 1 59 | 1 59 | 1 59 | 2 0 | 2 0 | 2 0 | 2 0 | 2 0 | 2 0 | 2 0 | 2 0 | 2 0 | 2 0 | 2 0 | 2 0 | 2 0 | 2 0 | 2 0 | 50 |
| 51 | 2 2 | 2 2 | 2 2 | 2 2 | 2 2 | 2 2 | 2 2 | 2 2 | 2 2 | 2 2 | 2 2 | 2 2 | 2 2 | 2 2 | 2 3 | 2 3 | 2 3 | 2 3 | 2 3 | 2 3 | 51 |
| 52 | 2 4 | 2 4 | 2 4 | 2 4 | 2 4 | 2 4 | 2 4 | 2 4 | 2 5 | 2 5 | 2 5 | 2 5 | 2 5 | 2 5 | 2 5 | 2 5 | 2 5 | 2 5 | 2 5 | 2 5 | 52 |
| 53 | 2 6 | 2 6 | 2 6 | 2 7 | 2 7 | 2 7 | 2 7 | 2 7 | 2 7 | 2 7 | 2 7 | 2 7 | 2 7 | 2 7 | 2 7 | 2 7 | 2 7 | 2 8 | 2 8 | 2 8 | 53 |
| 54 | 2 9 | 2 9 | 2 9 | 2 9 | 2 9 | 2 9 | 2 9 | 2 9 | 2 9 | 2 9 | 2 9 | 2 10 | 2 10 | 2 10 | 2 10 | 2 10 | 2 10 | 2 10 | 2 10 | 2 10 | 54 |
| 55 | 2 11 | 2 11 | 2 11 | 2 11 | 2 11 | 2 11 | 2 12 | 2 12 | 2 12 | 2 12 | 2 12 | 2 12 | 2 12 | 2 12 | 2 12 | 2 12 | 2 12 | 2 12 | 2 12 | 2 13 | 55 |
| 56 | 2 13 | 2 14 | 2 14 | 2 14 | 2 14 | 2 14 | 2 14 | 2 14 | 2 14 | 2 14 | 2 14 | 2 14 | 2 14 | 2 14 | 2 15 | 2 15 | 2 15 | 2 15 | 2 15 | 2 15 | 56 |
| 57 | 2 16 | 2 16 | 2 16 | 2 16 | 2 16 | 2 16 | 2 16 | 2 16 | 2 16 | 2 17 | 2 17 | 2 17 | 2 17 | 2 17 | 2 17 | 2 17 | 2 17 | 2 17 | 2 17 | 2 17 | 57 |
| 58 | 2 18 | 2 18 | 2 18 | 2 18 | 2 19 | 2 19 | 2 19 | 2 19 | 2 19 | 2 19 | 2 19 | 2 19 | 2 19 | 2 19 | 2 19 | 2 19 | 2 20 | 2 20 | 2 20 | 2 20 | 58 |
| 59 | 2 21 | 2 21 | 2 21 | 2 21 | 2 21 | 2 21 | 2 21 | 2 21 | 2 21 | 2 21 | 2 21 | 2 22 | 2 22 | 2 22 | 2 22 | 2 22 | 2 22 | 2 22 | 2 22 | 2 22 | 59 |
| 60 | 2 23 | 2 23 | 2 23 | 2 23 | 2 23 | 2 23 | 2 24 | 2 24 | 2 24 | 2 24 | 2 24 | 2 24 | 2 24 | 2 24 | 2 24 | 2 24 | 2 24 | 2 24 | 2 25 | 2 25 | 60 |
| H 1 | 2 23 | 2 23 | 2 23 | 2 23 | 2 23 | 2 23 | 2 24 | 2 24 | 2 24 | 2 24 | 2 24 | 2 24 | 2 24 | 2 24 | 2 24 | 2 24 | 2 24 | 2 24 | 2 25 | 2 25 | 1 H |
| O 2 | 4 46 | 4 46 | 4 46 | 4 47 | 4 47 | 4 47 | 4 47 | 4 47 | 4 47 | 4 48 | 4 48 | 4 48 | 4 48 | 4 48 | 4 48 | 4 49 | 4 49 | 4 49 | 4 49 | 4 49 | 2 O |
| U 3 | 7 9 | 7 9 | 7 10 | 7 10 | 7 10 | 7 10 | 7 11 | 7 11 | 7 11 | 7 11 | 7 12 | 7 12 | 7 12 | 7 12 | 7 13 | 7 13 | 7 13 | 7 13 | 7 14 | 7 14 | 3 U |
| R 4 | 9 32 | 9 32 | 9 33 | 9 33 | 9 33 | 9 34 | 9 34 | 9 34 | 9 35 | 9 35 | 9 35 | 9 36 | 9 36 | 9 36 | 9 37 | 9 37 | 9 37 | 9 38 | 9 38 | 9 38 | 4 R |
| S 5 | 11 55 | 11 55 | 11 56 | 11 56 | 11 57 | 11 57 | 11 58 | 11 58 | 11 58 | 11 59 | 11 59 | 12 0 | 12 0 | 12 0 | 12 1 | 12 1 | 12 2 | 12 2 | 12 3 | 12 3 | 5 S |
| 6 | 14 18 | 14 19 | 14 19 | 14 20 | 14 20 | 14 21 | 14 21 | 14 22 | 14 22 | 14 23 | 14 23 | 14 24 | 14 24 | 14 25 | 14 25 | 14 26 | 14 26 | 14 27 | 14 27 | 14 28 | 6 |
| 7 | 16 41 | 16 42 | 16 42 | 16 43 | 16 43 | 16 44 | 16 45 | 16 45 | 16 46 | 16 46 | 16 47 | 16 47 | 16 48 | 16 49 | 16 49 | 16 50 | 16 50 | 16 51 | 16 52 | 16 52 | 7 |
| 8 | 19 4 | 19 5 | 19 5 | 19 6 | 19 7 | 19 7 | 19 8 | 19 9 | 19 9 | 19 10 | 19 11 | 19 11 | 19 12 | 19 13 | 19 13 | 19 14 | 19 15 | 19 15 | 19 16 | 19 17 | 8 |
| 9 | 21 27 | 21 28 | 21 29 | 21 29 | 21 30 | 21 31 | 21 32 | 21 32 | 21 33 | 21 34 | 21 35 | 21 35 | 21 36 | 21 37 | 21 38 | 21 38 | 21 39 | 21 40 | 21 41 | 21 41 | 9 |
| 10 | 23 50 | 23 51 | 23 52 | 23 53 | 23 53 | 23 54 | 23 55 | 23 56 | 23 57 | 23 58 | 23 58 | 23 59 | 24 0 | 24 1 | 24 2 | 24 3 | 24 3 | 24 4 | 24 5 | 24 6 | 10 |
| 11 | 26 13 | 26 14 | 26 15 | 26 16 | 26 17 | 26 18 | 26 19 | 26 19 | 26 20 | 26 21 | 26 22 | 26 23 | 26 24 | 26 25 | 26 26 | 26 27 | 26 28 | 26 29 | 26 30 | 26 30 | 11 |
| 12 | 28 36 | 28 37 | 28 38 | 28 39 | 28 40 | 28 41 | 28 42 | 28 43 | 28 44 | 28 45 | 28 46 | 28 47 | 28 48 | 28 49 | 28 50 | 28 51 | 28 52 | 28 53 | 28 54 | 28 55 | 12 |
| 13 | 30 59 | 31 0 | 31 1 | 31 2 | 31 3 | 31 4 | 31 6 | 31 7 | 31 8 | 31 9 | 31 10 | 31 11 | 31 12 | 31 13 | 31 14 | 31 15 | 31 16 | 31 17 | 31 19 | 31 20 | 13 |
| 14 | 33 22 | 33 23 | 33 24 | 33 26 | 33 27 | 33 28 | 33 29 | 33 30 | 33 31 | 33 33 | 33 34 | 33 35 | 33 36 | 33 37 | 33 38 | 33 40 | 33 41 | 33 42 | 33 43 | 33 44 | 14 |
| 15 | 35 45 | 35 46 | 35 48 | 35 49 | 35 50 | 35 51 | 35 53 | 35 54 | 35 55 | 35 56 | 35 58 | 35 59 | 36 0 | 36 1 | 36 3 | 36 4 | 36 5 | 36 6 | 36 8 | 36 9 | 15 |
| 16 | 38 8 | 38 9 | 38 11 | 38 12 | 38 13 | 38 15 | 38 16 | 38 17 | 38 19 | 38 20 | 38 21 | 38 23 | 38 24 | 38 25 | 38 27 | 38 28 | 38 29 | 38 31 | 38 32 | 38 33 | 16 |
| 17 | 40 31 | 40 32 | 40 34 | 40 35 | 40 37 | 40 38 | 40 40 | 40 41 | 40 42 | 40 44 | 40 45 | 40 47 | 40 48 | 40 49 | 40 51 | 40 52 | 40 54 | 40 55 | 40 57 | 40 58 | 17 |
| 18 | 42 54 | 42 56 | 42 57 | 42 59 | 43 0 | 43 2 | 43 3 | 43 5 | 43 6 | 43 8 | 43 9 | 43 11 | 43 12 | 43 14 | 43 15 | 43 17 | 43 18 | 43 20 | 43 21 | 43 23 | 18 |
| 19 | 45 17 | 45 19 | 45 20 | 45 22 | 45 23 | 45 25 | 45 27 | 45 28 | 45 30 | 45 31 | 45 33 | 45 34 | 45 36 | 45 38 | 45 39 | 45 41 | 45 42 | 45 44 | 45 46 | 45 47 | 19 |
| 20 | 47 40 | 47 42 | 47 43 | 47 45 | 47 47 | 47 48 | 47 50 | 47 52 | 47 53 | 47 55 | 47 57 | 47 58 | 48 0 | 48 2 | 48 3 | 48 5 | 48 7 | 48 8 | 48 10 | 48 12 | 20 |
| 21 | 50 3 | 50 5 | 50 7 | 50 8 | 50 10 | 50 12 | 50 14 | 50 15 | 50 17 | 50 19 | 50 21 | 50 22 | 50 24 | 50 26 | 50 28 | 50 29 | 50 31 | 50 33 | 50 35 | 50 36 | 21 |
| 22 | 52 26 | 52 28 | 52 30 | 52 32 | 52 33 | 52 35 | 52 37 | 52 39 | 52 41 | 52 43 | 52 44 | 52 46 | 52 48 | 52 50 | 52 52 | 52 54 | 52 55 | 52 57 | 52 59 | 53 1 | 22 |
| 23 | 54 49 | 54 51 | 54 53 | 54 55 | 54 57 | 54 59 | 55 1 | 55 2 | 55 4 | 55 6 | 55 8 | 55 10 | 55 12 | 55 14 | 55 16 | 55 18 | 55 20 | 55 22 | 55 24 | 55 25 | 23 |
| 24 | 57 12 | 57 14 | 57 16 | 57 18 | 57 20 | 57 22 | 57 24 | 57 26 | 57 28 | 57 30 | 57 32 | 57 34 | 57 36 | 57 38 | 57 40 | 57 42 | 57 44 | 57 46 | 57 48 | 57 50 | 24 |

# Table V Diurnal Motion of the Sun

| TIME | 24 HOUR TRAVEL | | | | | | | | | | | | | | | | | | | | TIME |
|---|---|---|---|---|---|---|---|---|---|---|---|---|---|---|---|---|---|---|---|---|---|
| | 57 52 | 57 54 | 57 56 | 57 58 | 58 0 | 58 2 | 58 4 | 58 6 | 58 8 | 58 10 | 58 12 | 58 14 | 58 16 | 58 18 | 58 20 | 58 22 | 58 24 | 58 26 | 58 28 | 58 30 | |
| MINUTES | | | | | | | | | | | | | | | | | | | | | MINUTES |
| 1 | 2 | 2 | 2 | 2 | 2 | 2 | 2 | 2 | 2 | 2 | 2 | 2 | 2 | 2 | 2 | 2 | 2 | 2 | 2 | 2 | 1 |
| 2 | 5 | 5 | 5 | 5 | 5 | 5 | 5 | 5 | 5 | 5 | 5 | 5 | 5 | 5 | 5 | 5 | 5 | 5 | 5 | 5 | 2 |
| 3 | 7 | 7 | 7 | 7 | 7 | 7 | 7 | 7 | 7 | 7 | 7 | 7 | 7 | 7 | 7 | 7 | 7 | 7 | 7 | 7 | 3 |
| 4 | 10 | 10 | 10 | 10 | 10 | 10 | 10 | 10 | 10 | 10 | 10 | 10 | 10 | 10 | 10 | 10 | 10 | 10 | 10 | 10 | 4 |
| 5 | 12 | 12 | 12 | 12 | 12 | 12 | 12 | 12 | 12 | 12 | 12 | 12 | 12 | 12 | 12 | 12 | 12 | 12 | 12 | 12 | 5 |
| 6 | 14 | 14 | 14 | 14 | 15 | 15 | 15 | 15 | 15 | 15 | 15 | 15 | 15 | 15 | 15 | 15 | 15 | 15 | 15 | 15 | 6 |
| 7 | 17 | 17 | 17 | 17 | 17 | 17 | 17 | 17 | 17 | 17 | 17 | 17 | 17 | 17 | 17 | 17 | 17 | 17 | 17 | 17 | 7 |
| 8 | 19 | 19 | 19 | 19 | 19 | 19 | 19 | 19 | 19 | 19 | 19 | 19 | 19 | 19 | 19 | 19 | 19 | 19 | 19 | 20 | 8 |
| 9 | 22 | 22 | 22 | 22 | 22 | 22 | 22 | 22 | 22 | 22 | 22 | 22 | 22 | 22 | 22 | 22 | 22 | 22 | 22 | 22 | 9 |
| 10 | 24 | 24 | 24 | 24 | 24 | 24 | 24 | 24 | 24 | 24 | 24 | 24 | 24 | 24 | 24 | 24 | 24 | 24 | 24 | 24 | 10 |
| 11 | 27 | 27 | 27 | 27 | 27 | 27 | 27 | 27 | 27 | 27 | 27 | 27 | 27 | 27 | 27 | 27 | 27 | 27 | 27 | 27 | 11 |
| 12 | 29 | 29 | 29 | 29 | 29 | 29 | 29 | 29 | 29 | 29 | 29 | 29 | 29 | 29 | 29 | 29 | 29 | 29 | 29 | 29 | 12 |
| 13 | 31 | 31 | 31 | 31 | 31 | 31 | 31 | 31 | 31 | 32 | 32 | 32 | 32 | 32 | 32 | 32 | 32 | 32 | 32 | 32 | 13 |
| 14 | 34 | 34 | 34 | 34 | 34 | 34 | 34 | 34 | 34 | 34 | 34 | 34 | 34 | 34 | 34 | 34 | 34 | 34 | 34 | 34 | 14 |
| 15 | 36 | 36 | 36 | 36 | 36 | 36 | 36 | 36 | 36 | 36 | 36 | 36 | 36 | 36 | 36 | 36 | 37 | 37 | 37 | 37 | 15 |
| 16 | 39 | 39 | 39 | 39 | 39 | 39 | 39 | 39 | 39 | 39 | 39 | 39 | 39 | 39 | 39 | 39 | 39 | 39 | 39 | 39 | 16 |
| 17 | 41 | 41 | 41 | 41 | 41 | 41 | 41 | 41 | 41 | 41 | 41 | 41 | 41 | 41 | 41 | 41 | 41 | 41 | 41 | 41 | 17 |
| 18 | 43 | 43 | 43 | 43 | 44 | 44 | 44 | 44 | 44 | 44 | 44 | 44 | 44 | 44 | 44 | 44 | 44 | 44 | 44 | 44 | 18 |
| 19 | 46 | 46 | 46 | 46 | 46 | 46 | 46 | 46 | 46 | 46 | 46 | 46 | 46 | 46 | 46 | 46 | 46 | 46 | 46 | 46 | 19 |
| 20 | 48 | 48 | 48 | 48 | 48 | 48 | 48 | 48 | 48 | 48 | 49 | 49 | 49 | 49 | 49 | 49 | 49 | 49 | 49 | 49 | 20 |
| 21 | 51 | 51 | 51 | 51 | 51 | 51 | 51 | 51 | 51 | 51 | 51 | 51 | 51 | 51 | 51 | 51 | 51 | 51 | 51 | 51 | 21 |
| 22 | 53 | 53 | 53 | 53 | 53 | 53 | 53 | 53 | 53 | 53 | 53 | 53 | 53 | 53 | 53 | 54 | 54 | 54 | 54 | 54 | 22 |
| 23 | 55 | 55 | 56 | 56 | 56 | 56 | 56 | 56 | 56 | 56 | 56 | 56 | 56 | 56 | 56 | 56 | 56 | 56 | 56 | 56 | 23 |
| 24 | 58 | 58 | 58 | 58 | 58 | 58 | 58 | 58 | 58 | 58 | 58 | 58 | 58 | 58 | 58 | 58 | 58 | 58 | 58 | 59 | 24 |
| 25 | 1 0 | 1 0 | 1 0 | 1 0 | 1 0 | 1 0 | 1 0 | 1 1 | 1 1 | 1 1 | 1 1 | 1 1 | 1 1 | 1 1 | 1 1 | 1 1 | 1 1 | 1 1 | 1 1 | 1 1 | 25 |
| 26 | 1 3 | 1 3 | 1 3 | 1 3 | 1 3 | 1 3 | 1 3 | 1 3 | 1 3 | 1 3 | 1 3 | 1 3 | 1 3 | 1 3 | 1 3 | 1 3 | 1 3 | 1 3 | 1 3 | 1 3 | 26 |
| 27 | 1 5 | 1 5 | 1 5 | 1 5 | 1 5 | 1 5 | 1 5 | 1 5 | 1 5 | 1 5 | 1 5 | 1 6 | 1 6 | 1 6 | 1 6 | 1 6 | 1 6 | 1 6 | 1 6 | 1 6 | 27 |
| 28 | 1 8 | 1 8 | 1 8 | 1 8 | 1 8 | 1 8 | 1 8 | 1 8 | 1 8 | 1 8 | 1 8 | 1 8 | 1 8 | 1 8 | 1 8 | 1 8 | 1 8 | 1 8 | 1 8 | 1 8 | 28 |
| 29 | 1 10 | 1 10 | 1 10 | 1 10 | 1 10 | 1 10 | 1 10 | 1 10 | 1 10 | 1 10 | 1 10 | 1 10 | 1 10 | 1 10 | 1 10 | 1 11 | 1 11 | 1 11 | 1 11 | 1 11 | 29 |
| 30 | 1 12 | 1 12 | 1 12 | 1 12 | 1 13 | 1 13 | 1 13 | 1 13 | 1 13 | 1 13 | 1 13 | 1 13 | 1 13 | 1 13 | 1 13 | 1 13 | 1 13 | 1 13 | 1 13 | 1 13 | 30 |
| 31 | 1 15 | 1 15 | 1 15 | 1 15 | 1 15 | 1 15 | 1 15 | 1 15 | 1 15 | 1 15 | 1 15 | 1 15 | 1 15 | 1 15 | 1 15 | 1 15 | 1 15 | 1 15 | 1 16 | 1 16 | 31 |
| 32 | 1 17 | 1 17 | 1 17 | 1 17 | 1 17 | 1 17 | 1 17 | 1 17 | 1 18 | 1 18 | 1 18 | 1 18 | 1 18 | 1 18 | 1 18 | 1 18 | 1 18 | 1 18 | 1 18 | 1 18 | 32 |
| 33 | 1 20 | 1 20 | 1 20 | 1 20 | 1 20 | 1 20 | 1 20 | 1 20 | 1 20 | 1 20 | 1 20 | 1 20 | 1 20 | 1 20 | 1 20 | 1 20 | 1 20 | 1 20 | 1 20 | 1 20 | 33 |
| 34 | 1 22 | 1 22 | 1 22 | 1 22 | 1 22 | 1 22 | 1 22 | 1 22 | 1 22 | 1 22 | 1 22 | 1 22 | 1 23 | 1 23 | 1 23 | 1 23 | 1 23 | 1 23 | 1 23 | 1 23 | 34 |
| 35 | 1 24 | 1 24 | 1 24 | 1 25 | 1 25 | 1 25 | 1 25 | 1 25 | 1 25 | 1 25 | 1 25 | 1 25 | 1 25 | 1 25 | 1 25 | 1 25 | 1 25 | 1 25 | 1 25 | 1 25 | 35 |
| 36 | 1 27 | 1 27 | 1 27 | 1 27 | 1 27 | 1 27 | 1 27 | 1 27 | 1 27 | 1 27 | 1 27 | 1 27 | 1 27 | 1 27 | 1 28 | 1 28 | 1 28 | 1 28 | 1 28 | 1 28 | 36 |
| 37 | 1 29 | 1 29 | 1 29 | 1 29 | 1 29 | 1 29 | 1 30 | 1 30 | 1 30 | 1 30 | 1 30 | 1 30 | 1 30 | 1 30 | 1 30 | 1 30 | 1 30 | 1 30 | 1 30 | 1 30 | 37 |
| 38 | 1 32 | 1 32 | 1 32 | 1 32 | 1 32 | 1 32 | 1 32 | 1 32 | 1 32 | 1 32 | 1 32 | 1 32 | 1 32 | 1 32 | 1 32 | 1 32 | 1 32 | 1 33 | 1 33 | 1 33 | 38 |
| 39 | 1 34 | 1 34 | 1 34 | 1 34 | 1 34 | 1 34 | 1 34 | 1 34 | 1 34 | 1 35 | 1 35 | 1 35 | 1 35 | 1 35 | 1 35 | 1 35 | 1 35 | 1 35 | 1 35 | 1 35 | 39 |
| 40 | 1 36 | 1 37 | 1 37 | 1 37 | 1 37 | 1 37 | 1 37 | 1 37 | 1 37 | 1 37 | 1 37 | 1 37 | 1 37 | 1 37 | 1 37 | 1 37 | 1 37 | 1 37 | 1 37 | 1 38 | 40 |
| 41 | 1 39 | 1 39 | 1 39 | 1 39 | 1 39 | 1 39 | 1 39 | 1 39 | 1 39 | 1 39 | 1 39 | 1 39 | 1 40 | 1 40 | 1 40 | 1 40 | 1 40 | 1 40 | 1 40 | 1 40 | 41 |
| 42 | 1 41 | 1 41 | 1 41 | 1 41 | 1 42 | 1 42 | 1 42 | 1 42 | 1 42 | 1 42 | 1 42 | 1 42 | 1 42 | 1 42 | 1 42 | 1 42 | 1 42 | 1 42 | 1 42 | 1 42 | 42 |
| 43 | 1 44 | 1 44 | 1 44 | 1 44 | 1 44 | 1 44 | 1 44 | 1 44 | 1 44 | 1 44 | 1 44 | 1 44 | 1 44 | 1 44 | 1 45 | 1 45 | 1 45 | 1 45 | 1 45 | 1 45 | 43 |
| 44 | 1 46 | 1 46 | 1 46 | 1 46 | 1 46 | 1 46 | 1 46 | 1 47 | 1 47 | 1 47 | 1 47 | 1 47 | 1 47 | 1 47 | 1 47 | 1 47 | 1 47 | 1 47 | 1 47 | 1 47 | 44 |
| 45 | 1 49 | 1 49 | 1 49 | 1 49 | 1 49 | 1 49 | 1 49 | 1 49 | 1 49 | 1 49 | 1 49 | 1 49 | 1 49 | 1 49 | 1 49 | 1 49 | 1 50 | 1 50 | 1 50 | 1 50 | 45 |
| 46 | 1 51 | 1 51 | 1 51 | 1 51 | 1 51 | 1 51 | 1 51 | 1 51 | 1 51 | 1 51 | 1 52 | 1 52 | 1 52 | 1 52 | 1 52 | 1 52 | 1 52 | 1 52 | 1 52 | 1 52 | 46 |
| 47 | 1 53 | 1 53 | 1 53 | 1 54 | 1 54 | 1 54 | 1 54 | 1 54 | 1 54 | 1 54 | 1 54 | 1 54 | 1 54 | 1 54 | 1 54 | 1 54 | 1 54 | 1 54 | 1 54 | 1 55 | 47 |
| 48 | 1 56 | 1 56 | 1 56 | 1 56 | 1 56 | 1 56 | 1 56 | 1 56 | 1 56 | 1 56 | 1 56 | 1 56 | 1 57 | 1 57 | 1 57 | 1 57 | 1 57 | 1 57 | 1 57 | 1 57 | 48 |
| 49 | 1 58 | 1 58 | 1 58 | 1 58 | 1 58 | 1 58 | 1 59 | 1 59 | 1 59 | 1 59 | 1 59 | 1 59 | 1 59 | 1 59 | 1 59 | 1 59 | 1 59 | 1 59 | 1 59 | 1 59 | 49 |
| 50 | 2 1 | 2 1 | 2 1 | 2 1 | 2 1 | 2 1 | 2 1 | 2 1 | 2 1 | 2 1 | 2 1 | 2 1 | 2 1 | 2 1 | 2 2 | 2 2 | 2 2 | 2 2 | 2 2 | 2 2 | 50 |
| 51 | 2 3 | 2 3 | 2 3 | 2 3 | 2 3 | 2 3 | 2 3 | 2 3 | 2 4 | 2 4 | 2 4 | 2 4 | 2 4 | 2 4 | 2 4 | 2 4 | 2 4 | 2 4 | 2 4 | 2 4 | 51 |
| 52 | 2 5 | 2 5 | 2 6 | 2 6 | 2 6 | 2 6 | 2 6 | 2 6 | 2 6 | 2 6 | 2 6 | 2 6 | 2 6 | 2 6 | 2 6 | 2 6 | 2 7 | 2 7 | 2 7 | 2 7 | 52 |
| 53 | 2 8 | 2 8 | 2 8 | 2 8 | 2 8 | 2 8 | 2 8 | 2 8 | 2 8 | 2 8 | 2 9 | 2 9 | 2 9 | 2 9 | 2 9 | 2 9 | 2 9 | 2 9 | 2 9 | 2 9 | 53 |
| 54 | 2 10 | 2 10 | 2 10 | 2 10 | 2 11 | 2 11 | 2 11 | 2 11 | 2 11 | 2 11 | 2 11 | 2 11 | 2 11 | 2 11 | 2 11 | 2 11 | 2 11 | 2 11 | 2 12 | 2 12 | 54 |
| 55 | 2 13 | 2 13 | 2 13 | 2 13 | 2 13 | 2 13 | 2 13 | 2 13 | 2 13 | 2 13 | 2 13 | 2 13 | 2 14 | 2 14 | 2 14 | 2 14 | 2 14 | 2 14 | 2 14 | 2 14 | 55 |
| 56 | 2 15 | 2 15 | 2 15 | 2 15 | 2 15 | 2 15 | 2 15 | 2 16 | 2 16 | 2 16 | 2 16 | 2 16 | 2 16 | 2 16 | 2 16 | 2 16 | 2 16 | 2 16 | 2 16 | 2 17 | 56 |
| 57 | 2 17 | 2 18 | 2 18 | 2 18 | 2 18 | 2 18 | 2 18 | 2 18 | 2 18 | 2 18 | 2 18 | 2 18 | 2 18 | 2 18 | 2 19 | 2 19 | 2 19 | 2 19 | 2 19 | 2 19 | 57 |
| 58 | 2 20 | 2 20 | 2 20 | 2 20 | 2 20 | 2 20 | 2 20 | 2 20 | 2 20 | 2 21 | 2 21 | 2 21 | 2 21 | 2 21 | 2 21 | 2 21 | 2 21 | 2 21 | 2 21 | 2 21 | 58 |
| 59 | 2 22 | 2 22 | 2 22 | 2 23 | 2 23 | 2 23 | 2 23 | 2 23 | 2 23 | 2 23 | 2 23 | 2 23 | 2 23 | 2 23 | 2 23 | 2 23 | 2 24 | 2 24 | 2 24 | 2 24 | 59 |
| 60 | 2 25 | 2 25 | 2 25 | 2 25 | 2 25 | 2 25 | 2 25 | 2 25 | 2 25 | 2 25 | 2 26 | 2 26 | 2 26 | 2 26 | 2 26 | 2 26 | 2 26 | 2 26 | 2 26 | 2 26 | 60 |
| HOURS | | | | | | | | | | | | | | | | | | | | | HOURS |
| 1 | 2 25 | 2 25 | 2 25 | 2 25 | 2 25 | 2 25 | 2 25 | 2 25 | 2 25 | 2 25 | 2 26 | 2 26 | 2 26 | 2 26 | 2 26 | 2 26 | 2 26 | 2 26 | 2 26 | 2 26 | 1 |
| 2 | 4 49 | 4 50 | 4 50 | 4 50 | 4 50 | 4 50 | 4 50 | 4 51 | 4 51 | 4 51 | 4 51 | 4 51 | 4 51 | 4 52 | 4 52 | 4 52 | 4 52 | 4 52 | 4 52 | 4 53 | 2 |
| 3 | 7 14 | 7 14 | 7 15 | 7 15 | 7 15 | 7 15 | 7 16 | 7 16 | 7 16 | 7 16 | 7 17 | 7 17 | 7 17 | 7 17 | 7 18 | 7 18 | 7 18 | 7 18 | 7 19 | 7 19 | 3 |
| 4 | 9 39 | 9 39 | 9 39 | 9 40 | 9 40 | 9 40 | 9 41 | 9 41 | 9 41 | 9 42 | 9 42 | 9 42 | 9 43 | 9 43 | 9 43 | 9 44 | 9 44 | 9 44 | 9 45 | 9 45 | 4 |
| 5 | 12 3 | 12 4 | 12 4 | 12 5 | 12 5 | 12 5 | 12 6 | 12 6 | 12 7 | 12 7 | 12 8 | 12 8 | 12 8 | 12 9 | 12 9 | 12 10 | 12 10 | 12 10 | 12 11 | 12 11 | 5 |
| 6 | 14 28 | 14 29 | 14 29 | 14 30 | 14 30 | 14 31 | 14 31 | 14 32 | 14 32 | 14 33 | 14 33 | 14 34 | 14 34 | 14 35 | 14 35 | 14 36 | 14 36 | 14 37 | 14 37 | 14 38 | 6 |
| 7 | 16 53 | 16 53 | 16 54 | 16 54 | 16 55 | 16 56 | 16 56 | 16 57 | 16 57 | 16 58 | 16 59 | 16 59 | 17 0 | 17 0 | 17 1 | 17 1 | 17 2 | 17 3 | 17 3 | 17 4 | 7 |
| 8 | 19 17 | 19 18 | 19 19 | 19 19 | 19 20 | 19 21 | 19 21 | 19 22 | 19 23 | 19 23 | 19 24 | 19 25 | 19 25 | 19 26 | 19 27 | 19 27 | 19 28 | 19 29 | 19 29 | 19 30 | 8 |
| 9 | 21 42 | 21 43 | 21 44 | 21 44 | 21 45 | 21 46 | 21 47 | 21 47 | 21 48 | 21 49 | 21 50 | 21 50 | 21 51 | 21 52 | 21 53 | 21 53 | 21 54 | 21 55 | 21 56 | 21 56 | 9 |
| 10 | 24 7 | 24 8 | 24 8 | 24 9 | 24 10 | 24 11 | 24 12 | 24 13 | 24 13 | 24 14 | 24 15 | 24 16 | 24 17 | 24 18 | 24 18 | 24 19 | 24 20 | 24 21 | 24 22 | 24 23 | 10 |
| 11 | 26 31 | 26 32 | 26 33 | 26 34 | 26 35 | 26 36 | 26 37 | 26 38 | 26 39 | 26 40 | 26 41 | 26 41 | 26 42 | 26 43 | 26 44 | 26 45 | 26 46 | 26 47 | 26 48 | 26 49 | 11 |
| 12 | 28 56 | 28 57 | 28 58 | 28 59 | 29 0 | 29 1 | 29 2 | 29 3 | 29 4 | 29 5 | 29 6 | 29 7 | 29 8 | 29 9 | 29 10 | 29 11 | 29 12 | 29 13 | 29 14 | 29 15 | 12 |
| 13 | 31 21 | 31 22 | 31 23 | 31 24 | 31 25 | 31 26 | 31 27 | 31 28 | 31 29 | 31 30 | 31 32 | 31 33 | 31 34 | 31 35 | 31 36 | 31 37 | 31 38 | 31 39 | 31 40 | 31 41 | 13 |
| 14 | 33 45 | 33 47 | 33 48 | 33 49 | 33 50 | 33 51 | 33 52 | 33 54 | 33 55 | 33 56 | 33 57 | 33 58 | 33 59 | 34 1 | 34 2 | 34 3 | 34 4 | 34 5 | 34 6 | 34 8 | 14 |
| 15 | 36 10 | 36 11 | 36 13 | 36 14 | 36 15 | 36 16 | 36 18 | 36 19 | 36 20 | 36 21 | 36 23 | 36 24 | 36 25 | 36 26 | 36 28 | 36 29 | 36 30 | 36 31 | 36 33 | 36 34 | 15 |
| 16 | 38 35 | 38 36 | 38 37 | 38 39 | 38 40 | 38 41 | 38 43 | 38 44 | 38 45 | 38 47 | 38 48 | 38 49 | 38 51 | 38 52 | 38 53 | 38 55 | 38 56 | 38 57 | 38 59 | 39 0 | 16 |
| 17 | 40 59 | 41 1 | 41 2 | 41 4 | 41 5 | 41 6 | 41 8 | 41 9 | 41 11 | 41 12 | 41 14 | 41 15 | 41 16 | 41 18 | 41 19 | 41 21 | 41 22 | 41 23 | 41 25 | 41 26 | 17 |
| 18 | 43 24 | 43 26 | 43 27 | 43 29 | 43 30 | 43 32 | 43 33 | 43 35 | 43 36 | 43 38 | 43 39 | 43 41 | 43 42 | 43 44 | 43 45 | 43 47 | 43 48 | 43 50 | 43 51 | 43 53 | 18 |
| 19 | 45 49 | 45 50 | 45 52 | 45 53 | 45 55 | 45 57 | 45 58 | 46 0 | 46 1 | 46 3 | 46 5 | 46 6 | 46 8 | 46 9 | 46 11 | 46 12 | 46 14 | 46 16 | 46 17 | 46 19 | 19 |
| 20 | 48 13 | 48 15 | 48 17 | 48 18 | 48 20 | 48 22 | 48 23 | 48 25 | 48 27 | 48 28 | 48 30 | 48 32 | 48 33 | 48 35 | 48 37 | 48 38 | 48 40 | 48 42 | 48 43 | 48 45 | 20 |
| 21 | 50 38 | 50 40 | 50 42 | 50 43 | 50 45 | 50 47 | 50 49 | 50 50 | 50 52 | 50 54 | 50 56 | 50 57 | 50 59 | 51 1 | 51 3 | 51 4 | 51 6 | 51 8 | 51 10 | 51 11 | 21 |
| 22 | 53 3 | 53 5 | 53 6 | 53 8 | 53 10 | 53 12 | 53 14 | 53 16 | 53 17 | 53 19 | 53 21 | 53 23 | 53 25 | 53 27 | 53 28 | 53 30 | 53 32 | 53 34 | 53 36 | 53 38 | 22 |
| 23 | 55 27 | 55 29 | 55 31 | 55 33 | 55 35 | 55 37 | 55 39 | 55 41 | 55 43 | 55 45 | 55 47 | 55 48 | 55 50 | 55 52 | 55 54 | 55 56 | 55 58 | 56 0 | 56 2 | 56 4 | 23 |
| 24 | 57 52 | 57 54 | 57 56 | 57 58 | 58 0 | 58 2 | 58 4 | 58 6 | 58 8 | 58 10 | 58 12 | 58 14 | 58 16 | 58 18 | 58 20 | 58 22 | 58 24 | 58 26 | 58 28 | 58 30 | 24 |

# Table V Diurnal Motion of the Sun

| TIME | 24 HOUR TRAVEL | | | | | | | | | | | | | | | | | | | | TIME |
|---|---|---|---|---|---|---|---|---|---|---|---|---|---|---|---|---|---|---|---|---|---|
| | 58 32 | 58 34 | 58 36 | 58 38 | 58 40 | 58 42 | 58 44 | 58 46 | 58 48 | 58 50 | 58 52 | 58 54 | 58 56 | 58 58 | 59 0 | 59 2 | 59 4 | 59 6 | 59 8 | 59 10 | |
| MINUTES | | | | | | | | | | | | | | | | | | | | | MINUTES |
| 1 | 2 | 2 | 2 | 2 | 2 | 2 | 2 | 2 | 2 | 2 | 2 | 2 | 2 | 2 | 2 | 2 | 2 | 2 | 2 | 2 | 1 |
| 2 | 5 | 5 | 5 | 5 | 5 | 5 | 5 | 5 | 5 | 5 | 5 | 5 | 5 | 5 | 5 | 5 | 5 | 5 | 5 | 5 | 2 |
| 3 | 7 | 7 | 7 | 7 | 7 | 7 | 7 | 7 | 7 | 7 | 7 | 7 | 7 | 7 | 7 | 7 | 7 | 7 | 7 | 7 | 3 |
| 4 | 10 | 10 | 10 | 10 | 10 | 10 | 10 | 10 | 10 | 10 | 10 | 10 | 10 | 10 | 10 | 10 | 10 | 10 | 10 | 10 | 4 |
| 5 | 12 | 12 | 12 | 12 | 12 | 12 | 12 | 12 | 12 | 12 | 12 | 12 | 12 | 12 | 12 | 12 | 12 | 12 | 12 | 12 | 5 |
| 6 | 15 | 15 | 15 | 15 | 15 | 15 | 15 | 15 | 15 | 15 | 15 | 15 | 15 | 15 | 15 | 15 | 15 | 15 | 15 | 15 | 6 |
| 7 | 17 | 17 | 17 | 17 | 17 | 17 | 17 | 17 | 17 | 17 | 17 | 17 | 17 | 17 | 17 | 17 | 17 | 17 | 17 | 17 | 7 |
| 8 | 20 | 20 | 20 | 20 | 20 | 20 | 20 | 20 | 20 | 20 | 20 | 20 | 20 | 20 | 20 | 20 | 20 | 20 | 20 | 20 | 8 |
| 9 | 22 | 22 | 22 | 22 | 22 | 22 | 22 | 22 | 22 | 22 | 22 | 22 | 22 | 22 | 22 | 22 | 22 | 22 | 22 | 22 | 9 |
| 10 | 24 | 24 | 24 | 24 | 24 | 24 | 24 | 24 | 25 | 25 | 25 | 25 | 25 | 25 | 25 | 25 | 25 | 25 | 25 | 25 | 10 |
| 11 | 27 | 27 | 27 | 27 | 27 | 27 | 27 | 27 | 27 | 27 | 27 | 27 | 27 | 27 | 27 | 27 | 27 | 27 | 27 | 27 | 11 |
| 12 | 29 | 29 | 29 | 29 | 29 | 29 | 29 | 29 | 29 | 29 | 29 | 29 | 29 | 29 | 30 | 30 | 30 | 30 | 30 | 30 | 12 |
| 13 | 32 | 32 | 32 | 32 | 32 | 32 | 32 | 32 | 32 | 32 | 32 | 32 | 32 | 32 | 32 | 32 | 32 | 32 | 32 | 32 | 13 |
| 14 | 34 | 34 | 34 | 34 | 34 | 34 | 34 | 34 | 34 | 34 | 34 | 34 | 34 | 34 | 34 | 34 | 34 | 34 | 34 | 35 | 14 |
| 15 | 37 | 37 | 37 | 37 | 37 | 37 | 37 | 37 | 37 | 37 | 37 | 37 | 37 | 37 | 37 | 37 | 37 | 37 | 37 | 37 | 15 |
| 16 | 39 | 39 | 39 | 39 | 39 | 39 | 39 | 39 | 39 | 39 | 39 | 39 | 39 | 39 | 39 | 39 | 39 | 39 | 39 | 39 | 16 |
| 17 | 41 | 41 | 42 | 42 | 42 | 42 | 42 | 42 | 42 | 42 | 42 | 42 | 42 | 42 | 42 | 42 | 42 | 42 | 42 | 42 | 17 |
| 18 | 44 | 44 | 44 | 44 | 44 | 44 | 44 | 44 | 44 | 44 | 44 | 44 | 44 | 44 | 44 | 44 | 44 | 44 | 44 | 44 | 18 |
| 19 | 46 | 46 | 46 | 46 | 46 | 46 | 46 | 47 | 47 | 47 | 47 | 47 | 47 | 47 | 47 | 47 | 47 | 47 | 47 | 47 | 19 |
| 20 | 49 | 49 | 49 | 49 | 49 | 49 | 49 | 49 | 49 | 49 | 49 | 49 | 49 | 49 | 49 | 49 | 49 | 49 | 49 | 49 | 20 |
| 21 | 51 | 51 | 51 | 51 | 51 | 51 | 51 | 51 | 51 | 51 | 52 | 52 | 52 | 52 | 52 | 52 | 52 | 52 | 52 | 52 | 21 |
| 22 | 54 | 54 | 54 | 54 | 54 | 54 | 54 | 54 | 54 | 54 | 54 | 54 | 54 | 54 | 54 | 54 | 54 | 54 | 54 | 54 | 22 |
| 23 | 56 | 56 | 56 | 56 | 56 | 56 | 56 | 56 | 56 | 56 | 56 | 56 | 56 | 57 | 57 | 57 | 57 | 57 | 57 | 57 | 23 |
| 24 | 59 | 59 | 59 | 59 | 59 | 59 | 59 | 59 | 59 | 59 | 59 | 59 | 59 | 59 | 59 | 59 | 59 | 59 | 59 | 59 | 24 |
| 25 | 1 1 | 1 1 | 1 1 | 1 1 | 1 1 | 1 1 | 1 1 | 1 1 | 1 1 | 1 1 | 1 1 | 1 1 | 1 1 | 1 1 | 1 1 | 1 1 | 1 2 | 1 2 | 1 2 | 1 2 | 25 |
| 26 | 1 3 | 1 3 | 1 3 | 1 4 | 1 4 | 1 4 | 1 4 | 1 4 | 1 4 | 1 4 | 1 4 | 1 4 | 1 4 | 1 4 | 1 4 | 1 4 | 1 4 | 1 4 | 1 4 | 1 4 | 26 |
| 27 | 1 6 | 1 6 | 1 6 | 1 6 | 1 6 | 1 6 | 1 6 | 1 6 | 1 6 | 1 6 | 1 6 | 1 6 | 1 6 | 1 6 | 1 6 | 1 6 | 1 6 | 1 6 | 1 7 | 1 7 | 27 |
| 28 | 1 8 | 1 8 | 1 8 | 1 8 | 1 8 | 1 8 | 1 9 | 1 9 | 1 9 | 1 9 | 1 9 | 1 9 | 1 9 | 1 9 | 1 9 | 1 9 | 1 9 | 1 9 | 1 9 | 1 9 | 28 |
| 29 | 1 11 | 1 11 | 1 11 | 1 11 | 1 11 | 1 11 | 1 11 | 1 11 | 1 11 | 1 11 | 1 11 | 1 11 | 1 11 | 1 11 | 1 11 | 1 11 | 1 11 | 1 11 | 1 11 | 1 11 | 29 |
| 30 | 1 13 | 1 13 | 1 13 | 1 13 | 1 13 | 1 13 | 1 13 | 1 13 | 1 14 | 1 14 | 1 14 | 1 14 | 1 14 | 1 14 | 1 14 | 1 14 | 1 14 | 1 14 | 1 14 | 1 14 | 30 |
| 31 | 1 16 | 1 16 | 1 16 | 1 16 | 1 16 | 1 16 | 1 16 | 1 16 | 1 16 | 1 16 | 1 16 | 1 16 | 1 16 | 1 16 | 1 16 | 1 16 | 1 16 | 1 16 | 1 16 | 1 16 | 31 |
| 32 | 1 18 | 1 18 | 1 18 | 1 18 | 1 18 | 1 18 | 1 18 | 1 18 | 1 18 | 1 18 | 1 18 | 1 19 | 1 19 | 1 19 | 1 19 | 1 19 | 1 19 | 1 19 | 1 19 | 1 19 | 32 |
| 33 | 1 20 | 1 21 | 1 21 | 1 21 | 1 21 | 1 21 | 1 21 | 1 21 | 1 21 | 1 21 | 1 21 | 1 21 | 1 21 | 1 21 | 1 21 | 1 21 | 1 21 | 1 21 | 1 21 | 1 21 | 33 |
| 34 | 1 23 | 1 23 | 1 23 | 1 23 | 1 23 | 1 23 | 1 23 | 1 23 | 1 23 | 1 23 | 1 23 | 1 23 | 1 23 | 1 24 | 1 24 | 1 24 | 1 24 | 1 24 | 1 24 | 1 24 | 34 |
| 35 | 1 25 | 1 25 | 1 25 | 1 26 | 1 26 | 1 26 | 1 26 | 1 26 | 1 26 | 1 26 | 1 26 | 1 26 | 1 26 | 1 26 | 1 26 | 1 26 | 1 26 | 1 26 | 1 26 | 1 26 | 35 |
| 36 | 1 28 | 1 28 | 1 28 | 1 28 | 1 28 | 1 28 | 1 28 | 1 28 | 1 28 | 1 28 | 1 28 | 1 28 | 1 28 | 1 28 | 1 29 | 1 29 | 1 29 | 1 29 | 1 29 | 1 29 | 36 |
| 37 | 1 30 | 1 30 | 1 30 | 1 30 | 1 30 | 1 30 | 1 31 | 1 31 | 1 31 | 1 31 | 1 31 | 1 31 | 1 31 | 1 31 | 1 31 | 1 31 | 1 31 | 1 31 | 1 31 | 1 31 | 37 |
| 38 | 1 33 | 1 33 | 1 33 | 1 33 | 1 33 | 1 33 | 1 33 | 1 33 | 1 33 | 1 33 | 1 33 | 1 33 | 1 33 | 1 33 | 1 33 | 1 33 | 1 34 | 1 34 | 1 34 | 1 34 | 38 |
| 39 | 1 35 | 1 35 | 1 35 | 1 35 | 1 35 | 1 35 | 1 35 | 1 35 | 1 36 | 1 36 | 1 36 | 1 36 | 1 36 | 1 36 | 1 36 | 1 36 | 1 36 | 1 36 | 1 36 | 1 36 | 39 |
| 40 | 1 38 | 1 38 | 1 38 | 1 38 | 1 38 | 1 38 | 1 38 | 1 38 | 1 38 | 1 38 | 1 38 | 1 38 | 1 38 | 1 38 | 1 38 | 1 38 | 1 38 | 1 39 | 1 39 | 1 39 | 40 |
| 41 | 1 40 | 1 40 | 1 40 | 1 40 | 1 40 | 1 40 | 1 40 | 1 40 | 1 40 | 1 41 | 1 41 | 1 41 | 1 41 | 1 41 | 1 41 | 1 41 | 1 41 | 1 41 | 1 41 | 1 41 | 41 |
| 42 | 1 42 | 1 42 | 1 43 | 1 43 | 1 43 | 1 43 | 1 43 | 1 43 | 1 43 | 1 43 | 1 43 | 1 43 | 1 43 | 1 43 | 1 43 | 1 43 | 1 43 | 1 43 | 1 43 | 1 44 | 42 |
| 43 | 1 45 | 1 45 | 1 45 | 1 45 | 1 45 | 1 45 | 1 45 | 1 45 | 1 45 | 1 45 | 1 45 | 1 46 | 1 46 | 1 46 | 1 46 | 1 46 | 1 46 | 1 46 | 1 46 | 1 46 | 43 |
| 44 | 1 47 | 1 47 | 1 47 | 1 47 | 1 48 | 1 48 | 1 48 | 1 48 | 1 48 | 1 48 | 1 48 | 1 48 | 1 48 | 1 48 | 1 48 | 1 48 | 1 48 | 1 48 | 1 48 | 1 48 | 44 |
| 45 | 1 50 | 1 50 | 1 50 | 1 50 | 1 50 | 1 50 | 1 50 | 1 50 | 1 50 | 1 50 | 1 50 | 1 50 | 1 51 | 1 51 | 1 51 | 1 51 | 1 51 | 1 51 | 1 51 | 1 51 | 45 |
| 46 | 1 52 | 1 52 | 1 52 | 1 52 | 1 52 | 1 53 | 1 53 | 1 53 | 1 53 | 1 53 | 1 53 | 1 53 | 1 53 | 1 53 | 1 53 | 1 53 | 1 53 | 1 53 | 1 53 | 1 53 | 46 |
| 47 | 1 55 | 1 55 | 1 55 | 1 55 | 1 55 | 1 55 | 1 55 | 1 55 | 1 55 | 1 55 | 1 55 | 1 55 | 1 55 | 1 55 | 1 56 | 1 56 | 1 56 | 1 56 | 1 56 | 1 56 | 47 |
| 48 | 1 57 | 1 57 | 1 57 | 1 57 | 1 57 | 1 57 | 1 57 | 1 58 | 1 58 | 1 58 | 1 58 | 1 58 | 1 58 | 1 58 | 1 58 | 1 58 | 1 58 | 1 58 | 1 58 | 1 58 | 48 |
| 49 | 2 0 | 2 0 | 2 0 | 2 0 | 2 0 | 2 0 | 2 0 | 2 0 | 2 0 | 2 0 | 2 0 | 2 0 | 2 0 | 2 0 | 2 0 | 2 1 | 2 1 | 2 1 | 2 1 | 2 1 | 49 |
| 50 | 2 2 | 2 2 | 2 2 | 2 2 | 2 2 | 2 2 | 2 2 | 2 2 | 2 3 | 2 3 | 2 3 | 2 3 | 2 3 | 2 3 | 2 3 | 2 3 | 2 3 | 2 3 | 2 3 | 2 3 | 50 |
| 51 | 2 4 | 2 4 | 2 5 | 2 5 | 2 5 | 2 5 | 2 5 | 2 5 | 2 5 | 2 5 | 2 5 | 2 5 | 2 5 | 2 5 | 2 5 | 2 5 | 2 6 | 2 6 | 2 6 | 2 6 | 51 |
| 52 | 2 7 | 2 7 | 2 7 | 2 7 | 2 7 | 2 7 | 2 7 | 2 7 | 2 7 | 2 7 | 2 8 | 2 8 | 2 8 | 2 8 | 2 8 | 2 8 | 2 8 | 2 8 | 2 8 | 2 8 | 52 |
| 53 | 2 9 | 2 9 | 2 9 | 2 9 | 2 10 | 2 10 | 2 10 | 2 10 | 2 10 | 2 10 | 2 10 | 2 10 | 2 10 | 2 10 | 2 10 | 2 10 | 2 10 | 2 11 | 2 11 | 2 11 | 53 |
| 54 | 2 12 | 2 12 | 2 12 | 2 12 | 2 12 | 2 12 | 2 12 | 2 12 | 2 12 | 2 12 | 2 12 | 2 13 | 2 13 | 2 13 | 2 13 | 2 13 | 2 13 | 2 13 | 2 13 | 2 13 | 54 |
| 55 | 2 14 | 2 14 | 2 14 | 2 14 | 2 14 | 2 15 | 2 15 | 2 15 | 2 15 | 2 15 | 2 15 | 2 15 | 2 15 | 2 15 | 2 15 | 2 15 | 2 15 | 2 15 | 2 16 | 2 16 | 55 |
| 56 | 2 17 | 2 17 | 2 17 | 2 17 | 2 17 | 2 17 | 2 17 | 2 17 | 2 17 | 2 17 | 2 17 | 2 17 | 2 18 | 2 18 | 2 18 | 2 18 | 2 18 | 2 18 | 2 18 | 2 18 | 56 |
| 57 | 2 19 | 2 19 | 2 19 | 2 19 | 2 19 | 2 19 | 2 19 | 2 20 | 2 20 | 2 20 | 2 20 | 2 20 | 2 20 | 2 20 | 2 20 | 2 20 | 2 20 | 2 20 | 2 20 | 2 21 | 57 |
| 58 | 2 21 | 2 22 | 2 22 | 2 22 | 2 22 | 2 22 | 2 22 | 2 22 | 2 22 | 2 22 | 2 22 | 2 22 | 2 22 | 2 23 | 2 23 | 2 23 | 2 23 | 2 23 | 2 23 | 2 23 | 58 |
| 59 | 2 24 | 2 24 | 2 24 | 2 24 | 2 24 | 2 24 | 2 24 | 2 24 | 2 25 | 2 25 | 2 25 | 2 25 | 2 25 | 2 25 | 2 25 | 2 25 | 2 25 | 2 25 | 2 25 | 2 25 | 59 |
| 60 | 2 26 | 2 26 | 2 27 | 2 27 | 2 27 | 2 27 | 2 27 | 2 27 | 2 27 | 2 27 | 2 27 | 2 27 | 2 27 | 2 27 | 2 28 | 2 28 | 2 28 | 2 28 | 2 28 | 2 28 | 60 |
| HOURS | | | | | | | | | | | | | | | | | | | | | HOURS |
| 1 | 2 26 | 2 26 | 2 27 | 2 27 | 2 27 | 2 27 | 2 27 | 2 27 | 2 27 | 2 27 | 2 27 | 2 27 | 2 27 | 2 27 | 2 28 | 2 28 | 2 28 | 2 28 | 2 28 | 2 28 | 1 |
| 2 | 4 53 | 4 53 | 4 53 | 4 53 | 4 53 | 4 54 | 4 54 | 4 54 | 4 54 | 4 54 | 4 54 | 4 55 | 4 55 | 4 55 | 4 55 | 4 55 | 4 55 | 4 56 | 4 56 | 4 56 | 2 |
| 3 | 7 19 | 7 19 | 7 20 | 7 20 | 7 20 | 7 20 | 7 21 | 7 21 | 7 21 | 7 21 | 7 22 | 7 22 | 7 22 | 7 22 | 7 23 | 7 23 | 7 23 | 7 23 | 7 24 | 7 24 | 3 |
| 4 | 9 45 | 9 46 | 9 46 | 9 46 | 9 47 | 9 47 | 9 47 | 9 48 | 9 48 | 9 48 | 9 49 | 9 49 | 9 49 | 9 50 | 9 50 | 9 50 | 9 51 | 9 51 | 9 51 | 9 52 | 4 |
| 5 | 12 12 | 12 12 | 12 13 | 12 13 | 12 13 | 12 14 | 12 14 | 12 15 | 12 15 | 12 15 | 12 16 | 12 16 | 12 17 | 12 17 | 12 18 | 12 18 | 12 18 | 12 19 | 12 19 | 12 20 | 5 |
| 6 | 14 38 | 14 39 | 14 39 | 14 40 | 14 40 | 14 41 | 14 41 | 14 42 | 14 42 | 14 43 | 14 43 | 14 44 | 14 44 | 14 45 | 14 45 | 14 46 | 14 46 | 14 47 | 14 47 | 14 48 | 6 |
| 7 | 17 4 | 17 5 | 17 6 | 17 6 | 17 7 | 17 7 | 17 8 | 17 8 | 17 9 | 17 10 | 17 10 | 17 11 | 17 11 | 17 12 | 17 13 | 17 13 | 17 14 | 17 14 | 17 15 | 17 15 | 7 |
| 8 | 19 31 | 19 31 | 19 32 | 19 33 | 19 33 | 19 34 | 19 35 | 19 35 | 19 36 | 19 37 | 19 37 | 19 38 | 19 39 | 19 39 | 19 40 | 19 41 | 19 41 | 19 42 | 19 43 | 19 43 | 8 |
| 9 | 21 57 | 21 58 | 21 59 | 21 59 | 22 0 | 22 1 | 22 2 | 22 2 | 22 3 | 22 4 | 22 5 | 22 5 | 22 6 | 22 7 | 22 8 | 22 8 | 22 9 | 22 10 | 22 11 | 22 11 | 9 |
| 10 | 24 23 | 24 24 | 24 25 | 24 26 | 24 27 | 24 28 | 24 28 | 24 29 | 24 30 | 24 31 | 24 32 | 24 33 | 24 33 | 24 34 | 24 35 | 24 36 | 24 37 | 24 38 | 24 38 | 24 39 | 10 |
| 11 | 26 50 | 26 51 | 26 52 | 26 52 | 26 53 | 26 54 | 26 55 | 26 56 | 26 57 | 26 58 | 26 59 | 27 0 | 27 1 | 27 2 | 27 3 | 27 3 | 27 4 | 27 5 | 27 6 | 27 7 | 11 |
| 12 | 29 16 | 29 17 | 29 18 | 29 19 | 29 20 | 29 21 | 29 22 | 29 23 | 29 24 | 29 25 | 29 26 | 29 27 | 29 28 | 29 29 | 29 30 | 29 31 | 29 32 | 29 33 | 29 34 | 29 35 | 12 |
| 13 | 31 42 | 31 43 | 31 45 | 31 46 | 31 47 | 31 48 | 31 49 | 31 50 | 31 51 | 31 52 | 31 53 | 31 54 | 31 55 | 31 56 | 31 58 | 31 59 | 32 0 | 32 1 | 32 2 | 32 3 | 13 |
| 14 | 34 9 | 34 10 | 34 11 | 34 12 | 34 13 | 34 15 | 34 16 | 34 17 | 34 18 | 34 19 | 34 20 | 34 22 | 34 23 | 34 24 | 34 25 | 34 26 | 34 27 | 34 29 | 34 30 | 34 31 | 14 |
| 15 | 36 35 | 36 36 | 36 38 | 36 39 | 36 40 | 36 41 | 36 43 | 36 44 | 36 45 | 36 46 | 36 48 | 36 49 | 36 50 | 36 51 | 36 53 | 36 54 | 36 55 | 36 56 | 36 58 | 36 59 | 15 |
| 16 | 39 1 | 39 3 | 39 4 | 39 5 | 39 7 | 39 8 | 39 9 | 39 11 | 39 12 | 39 13 | 39 15 | 39 16 | 39 17 | 39 19 | 39 20 | 39 21 | 39 23 | 39 24 | 39 25 | 39 27 | 16 |
| 17 | 41 28 | 41 29 | 41 31 | 41 32 | 41 33 | 41 35 | 41 36 | 41 38 | 41 39 | 41 40 | 41 42 | 41 43 | 41 45 | 41 46 | 41 48 | 41 49 | 41 50 | 41 52 | 41 53 | 41 55 | 17 |
| 18 | 43 54 | 43 56 | 43 57 | 43 59 | 44 0 | 44 2 | 44 3 | 44 5 | 44 6 | 44 8 | 44 9 | 44 11 | 44 12 | 44 14 | 44 15 | 44 17 | 44 18 | 44 20 | 44 21 | 44 23 | 18 |
| 19 | 46 20 | 46 22 | 46 24 | 46 25 | 46 27 | 46 28 | 46 30 | 46 31 | 46 33 | 46 35 | 46 36 | 46 38 | 46 39 | 46 41 | 46 43 | 46 44 | 46 46 | 46 47 | 46 49 | 46 50 | 19 |
| 20 | 48 47 | 48 48 | 48 50 | 48 52 | 48 53 | 48 55 | 48 57 | 48 58 | 49 0 | 49 2 | 49 3 | 49 5 | 49 7 | 49 8 | 49 10 | 49 12 | 49 13 | 49 15 | 49 17 | 49 18 | 20 |
| 21 | 51 13 | 51 15 | 51 17 | 51 18 | 51 20 | 51 22 | 51 24 | 51 25 | 51 27 | 51 29 | 51 31 | 51 32 | 51 34 | 51 36 | 51 38 | 51 39 | 51 41 | 51 43 | 51 45 | 51 46 | 21 |
| 22 | 53 39 | 53 41 | 53 43 | 53 45 | 53 47 | 53 49 | 53 50 | 53 52 | 53 54 | 53 56 | 53 58 | 54 0 | 54 1 | 54 3 | 54 5 | 54 7 | 54 9 | 54 11 | 54 12 | 54 14 | 22 |
| 23 | 56 6 | 56 8 | 56 10 | 56 11 | 56 13 | 56 15 | 56 17 | 56 19 | 56 21 | 56 23 | 56 25 | 56 27 | 56 29 | 56 31 | 56 33 | 56 34 | 56 36 | 56 38 | 56 40 | 56 42 | 23 |
| 24 | 58 32 | 58 34 | 58 36 | 58 38 | 58 40 | 58 42 | 58 44 | 58 46 | 58 48 | 58 50 | 58 52 | 58 54 | 58 56 | 58 58 | 59 0 | 59 2 | 59 4 | 59 6 | 59 8 | 59 10 | 24 |

# Table V Diurnal Motion of the Sun

| TIME | 24 HOUR TRAVEL | | | | | | | | | | | | | | | | | | | | TIME |
|---|---|---|---|---|---|---|---|---|---|---|---|---|---|---|---|---|---|---|---|---|---|
| | 59 12 | 59 14 | 59 16 | 59 18 | 59 20 | 59 22 | 59 24 | 59 26 | 59 28 | 59 30 | 59 32 | 59 34 | 59 36 | 59 38 | 59 40 | 59 42 | 59 44 | 59 46 | 59 48 | 59 50 | |
| MINUTES | | | | | | | | | | | | | | | | | | | | | MINUTES |
| 1 | 2 | 2 | 2 | 2 | 2 | 2 | 2 | 2 | 2 | 2 | 2 | 2 | 2 | 2 | 2 | 2 | 2 | 2 | 2 | 2 | 1 |
| 2 | 5 | 5 | 5 | 5 | 5 | 5 | 5 | 5 | 5 | 5 | 5 | 5 | 5 | 5 | 5 | 5 | 5 | 5 | 5 | 5 | 2 |
| 3 | 7 | 7 | 7 | 7 | 7 | 7 | 7 | 7 | 7 | 7 | 7 | 7 | 7 | 7 | 7 | 7 | 7 | 7 | 7 | 7 | 3 |
| 4 | 10 | 10 | 10 | 10 | 10 | 10 | 10 | 10 | 10 | 10 | 10 | 10 | 10 | 10 | 10 | 10 | 10 | 10 | 10 | 10 | 4 |
| 5 | 12 | 12 | 12 | 12 | 12 | 12 | 12 | 12 | 12 | 12 | 12 | 12 | 12 | 12 | 12 | 12 | 12 | 12 | 12 | 12 | 5 |
| 6 | 15 | 15 | 15 | 15 | 15 | 15 | 15 | 15 | 15 | 15 | 15 | 15 | 15 | 15 | 15 | 15 | 15 | 15 | 15 | 15 | 6 |
| 7 | 17 | 17 | 17 | 17 | 17 | 17 | 17 | 17 | 17 | 17 | 17 | 17 | 17 | 17 | 17 | 17 | 17 | 17 | 17 | 17 | 7 |
| 8 | 20 | 20 | 20 | 20 | 20 | 20 | 20 | 20 | 20 | 20 | 20 | 20 | 20 | 20 | 20 | 20 | 20 | 20 | 20 | 20 | 8 |
| 9 | 22 | 22 | 22 | 22 | 22 | 22 | 22 | 22 | 22 | 22 | 22 | 22 | 22 | 22 | 22 | 22 | 22 | 22 | 22 | 22 | 9 |
| 10 | 25 | 25 | 25 | 25 | 25 | 25 | 25 | 25 | 25 | 25 | 25 | 25 | 25 | 25 | 25 | 25 | 25 | 25 | 25 | 25 | 10 |
| 11 | 27 | 27 | 27 | 27 | 27 | 27 | 27 | 27 | 27 | 27 | 27 | 27 | 27 | 27 | 27 | 27 | 27 | 27 | 27 | 27 | 11 |
| 12 | 30 | 30 | 30 | 30 | 30 | 30 | 30 | 30 | 30 | 30 | 30 | 30 | 30 | 30 | 30 | 30 | 30 | 30 | 30 | 30 | 12 |
| 13 | 32 | 32 | 32 | 32 | 32 | 32 | 32 | 32 | 32 | 32 | 32 | 32 | 32 | 32 | 32 | 32 | 32 | 32 | 32 | 32 | 13 |
| 14 | 35 | 35 | 35 | 35 | 35 | 35 | 35 | 35 | 35 | 35 | 35 | 35 | 35 | 35 | 35 | 35 | 35 | 35 | 35 | 35 | 14 |
| 15 | 37 | 37 | 37 | 37 | 37 | 37 | 37 | 37 | 37 | 37 | 37 | 37 | 37 | 37 | 37 | 37 | 37 | 37 | 37 | 37 | 15 |
| 16 | 39 | 39 | 40 | 40 | 40 | 40 | 40 | 40 | 40 | 40 | 40 | 40 | 40 | 40 | 40 | 40 | 40 | 40 | 40 | 40 | 16 |
| 17 | 42 | 42 | 42 | 42 | 42 | 42 | 42 | 42 | 42 | 42 | 42 | 42 | 42 | 42 | 42 | 42 | 42 | 42 | 42 | 42 | 17 |
| 18 | 44 | 44 | 44 | 44 | 45 | 45 | 45 | 45 | 45 | 45 | 45 | 45 | 45 | 45 | 45 | 45 | 45 | 45 | 45 | 45 | 18 |
| 19 | 47 | 47 | 47 | 47 | 47 | 47 | 47 | 47 | 47 | 47 | 47 | 47 | 47 | 47 | 47 | 47 | 47 | 47 | 47 | 47 | 19 |
| 20 | 49 | 49 | 49 | 49 | 49 | 49 | 50 | 50 | 50 | 50 | 50 | 50 | 50 | 50 | 50 | 50 | 50 | 50 | 50 | 50 | 20 |
| 21 | 52 | 52 | 52 | 52 | 52 | 52 | 52 | 52 | 52 | 52 | 52 | 52 | 52 | 52 | 52 | 52 | 52 | 52 | 52 | 52 | 21 |
| 22 | 54 | 54 | 54 | 54 | 54 | 54 | 54 | 54 | 55 | 55 | 55 | 55 | 55 | 55 | 55 | 55 | 55 | 55 | 55 | 55 | 22 |
| 23 | 57 | 57 | 57 | 57 | 57 | 57 | 57 | 57 | 57 | 57 | 57 | 57 | 57 | 57 | 57 | 57 | 57 | 57 | 57 | 57 | 23 |
| 24 | 59 | 59 | 59 | 59 | 59 | 59 | 59 | 59 | 59 | 1 0 | 1 0 | 1 0 | 1 0 | 1 0 | 1 0 | 1 0 | 1 0 | 1 0 | 1 0 | 1 0 | 24 |
| 25 | 1 2 | 1 2 | 1 2 | 1 2 | 1 2 | 1 2 | 1 2 | 1 2 | 1 2 | 1 2 | 1 2 | 1 2 | 1 2 | 1 2 | 1 2 | 1 2 | 1 2 | 1 2 | 1 2 | 1 2 | 25 |
| 26 | 1 4 | 1 4 | 1 4 | 1 4 | 1 4 | 1 4 | 1 4 | 1 4 | 1 4 | 1 4 | 1 4 | 1 5 | 1 5 | 1 5 | 1 5 | 1 5 | 1 5 | 1 5 | 1 5 | 1 5 | 26 |
| 27 | 1 7 | 1 7 | 1 7 | 1 7 | 1 7 | 1 7 | 1 7 | 1 7 | 1 7 | 1 7 | 1 7 | 1 7 | 1 7 | 1 7 | 1 7 | 1 7 | 1 7 | 1 7 | 1 7 | 1 7 | 27 |
| 28 | 1 9 | 1 9 | 1 9 | 1 9 | 1 9 | 1 9 | 1 9 | 1 9 | 1 9 | 1 9 | 1 9 | 1 9 | 1 10 | 1 10 | 1 10 | 1 10 | 1 10 | 1 10 | 1 10 | 1 10 | 28 |
| 29 | 1 12 | 1 12 | 1 12 | 1 12 | 1 12 | 1 12 | 1 12 | 1 12 | 1 12 | 1 12 | 1 12 | 1 12 | 1 12 | 1 12 | 1 12 | 1 12 | 1 12 | 1 12 | 1 12 | 1 12 | 29 |
| 30 | 1 14 | 1 14 | 1 14 | 1 14 | 1 14 | 1 14 | 1 14 | 1 14 | 1 14 | 1 14 | 1 14 | 1 14 | 1 15 | 1 15 | 1 15 | 1 15 | 1 15 | 1 15 | 1 15 | 1 15 | 30 |
| 31 | 1 16 | 1 17 | 1 17 | 1 17 | 1 17 | 1 17 | 1 17 | 1 17 | 1 17 | 1 17 | 1 17 | 1 17 | 1 17 | 1 17 | 1 17 | 1 17 | 1 17 | 1 17 | 1 17 | 1 17 | 31 |
| 32 | 1 19 | 1 19 | 1 19 | 1 19 | 1 19 | 1 19 | 1 19 | 1 19 | 1 19 | 1 19 | 1 19 | 1 19 | 1 19 | 1 20 | 1 20 | 1 20 | 1 20 | 1 20 | 1 20 | 1 20 | 32 |
| 33 | 1 21 | 1 21 | 1 21 | 1 22 | 1 22 | 1 22 | 1 22 | 1 22 | 1 22 | 1 22 | 1 22 | 1 22 | 1 22 | 1 22 | 1 22 | 1 22 | 1 22 | 1 22 | 1 22 | 1 22 | 33 |
| 34 | 1 24 | 1 24 | 1 24 | 1 24 | 1 24 | 1 24 | 1 24 | 1 24 | 1 24 | 1 24 | 1 24 | 1 24 | 1 24 | 1 24 | 1 25 | 1 25 | 1 25 | 1 25 | 1 25 | 1 25 | 34 |
| 35 | 1 26 | 1 26 | 1 26 | 1 26 | 1 27 | 1 27 | 1 27 | 1 27 | 1 27 | 1 27 | 1 27 | 1 27 | 1 27 | 1 27 | 1 27 | 1 27 | 1 27 | 1 27 | 1 27 | 1 27 | 35 |
| 36 | 1 29 | 1 29 | 1 29 | 1 29 | 1 29 | 1 29 | 1 29 | 1 29 | 1 29 | 1 29 | 1 29 | 1 29 | 1 29 | 1 29 | 1 30 | 1 30 | 1 30 | 1 30 | 1 30 | 1 30 | 36 |
| 37 | 1 31 | 1 31 | 1 31 | 1 31 | 1 31 | 1 32 | 1 32 | 1 32 | 1 32 | 1 32 | 1 32 | 1 32 | 1 32 | 1 32 | 1 32 | 1 32 | 1 32 | 1 32 | 1 32 | 1 32 | 37 |
| 38 | 1 34 | 1 34 | 1 34 | 1 34 | 1 34 | 1 34 | 1 34 | 1 34 | 1 34 | 1 34 | 1 34 | 1 34 | 1 34 | 1 34 | 1 34 | 1 35 | 1 35 | 1 35 | 1 35 | 1 35 | 38 |
| 39 | 1 36 | 1 36 | 1 36 | 1 36 | 1 36 | 1 36 | 1 37 | 1 37 | 1 37 | 1 37 | 1 37 | 1 37 | 1 37 | 1 37 | 1 37 | 1 37 | 1 37 | 1 37 | 1 37 | 1 37 | 39 |
| 40 | 1 39 | 1 39 | 1 39 | 1 39 | 1 39 | 1 39 | 1 39 | 1 39 | 1 39 | 1 39 | 1 39 | 1 39 | 1 39 | 1 39 | 1 39 | 1 40 | 1 40 | 1 40 | 1 40 | 1 40 | 40 |
| 41 | 1 41 | 1 41 | 1 41 | 1 41 | 1 41 | 1 41 | 1 41 | 1 42 | 1 42 | 1 42 | 1 42 | 1 42 | 1 42 | 1 42 | 1 42 | 1 42 | 1 42 | 1 42 | 1 42 | 1 42 | 41 |
| 42 | 1 44 | 1 44 | 1 44 | 1 44 | 1 44 | 1 44 | 1 44 | 1 44 | 1 44 | 1 44 | 1 44 | 1 44 | 1 44 | 1 44 | 1 44 | 1 44 | 1 45 | 1 45 | 1 45 | 1 45 | 42 |
| 43 | 1 46 | 1 46 | 1 46 | 1 46 | 1 46 | 1 46 | 1 46 | 1 46 | 1 47 | 1 47 | 1 47 | 1 47 | 1 47 | 1 47 | 1 47 | 1 47 | 1 47 | 1 47 | 1 47 | 1 47 | 43 |
| 44 | 1 49 | 1 49 | 1 49 | 1 49 | 1 49 | 1 49 | 1 49 | 1 49 | 1 49 | 1 49 | 1 49 | 1 49 | 1 49 | 1 49 | 1 49 | 1 49 | 1 50 | 1 50 | 1 50 | 1 50 | 44 |
| 45 | 1 51 | 1 51 | 1 51 | 1 51 | 1 51 | 1 51 | 1 51 | 1 51 | 1 52 | 1 52 | 1 52 | 1 52 | 1 52 | 1 52 | 1 52 | 1 52 | 1 52 | 1 52 | 1 52 | 1 52 | 45 |
| 46 | 1 53 | 1 54 | 1 54 | 1 54 | 1 54 | 1 54 | 1 54 | 1 54 | 1 54 | 1 54 | 1 54 | 1 54 | 1 54 | 1 54 | 1 54 | 1 54 | 1 54 | 1 55 | 1 55 | 1 55 | 46 |
| 47 | 1 56 | 1 56 | 1 56 | 1 56 | 1 56 | 1 56 | 1 56 | 1 56 | 1 56 | 1 57 | 1 57 | 1 57 | 1 57 | 1 57 | 1 57 | 1 57 | 1 57 | 1 57 | 1 57 | 1 57 | 47 |
| 48 | 1 58 | 1 58 | 1 59 | 1 59 | 1 59 | 1 59 | 1 59 | 1 59 | 1 59 | 1 59 | 1 59 | 1 59 | 1 59 | 1 59 | 1 59 | 1 59 | 1 59 | 2 0 | 2 0 | 2 0 | 48 |
| 49 | 2 1 | 2 1 | 2 1 | 2 1 | 2 1 | 2 1 | 2 1 | 2 1 | 2 1 | 2 1 | 2 2 | 2 2 | 2 2 | 2 2 | 2 2 | 2 2 | 2 2 | 2 2 | 2 2 | 2 2 | 49 |
| 50 | 2 3 | 2 3 | 2 3 | 2 4 | 2 4 | 2 4 | 2 4 | 2 4 | 2 4 | 2 4 | 2 4 | 2 4 | 2 4 | 2 4 | 2 4 | 2 4 | 2 4 | 2 5 | 2 5 | 2 5 | 50 |
| 51 | 2 6 | 2 6 | 2 6 | 2 6 | 2 6 | 2 6 | 2 6 | 2 6 | 2 6 | 2 6 | 2 7 | 2 7 | 2 7 | 2 7 | 2 7 | 2 7 | 2 7 | 2 7 | 2 7 | 2 7 | 51 |
| 52 | 2 8 | 2 8 | 2 8 | 2 8 | 2 9 | 2 9 | 2 9 | 2 9 | 2 9 | 2 9 | 2 9 | 2 9 | 2 9 | 2 9 | 2 9 | 2 9 | 2 9 | 2 9 | 2 10 | 2 10 | 52 |
| 53 | 2 11 | 2 11 | 2 11 | 2 11 | 2 11 | 2 11 | 2 11 | 2 11 | 2 11 | 2 11 | 2 11 | 2 12 | 2 12 | 2 12 | 2 12 | 2 12 | 2 12 | 2 12 | 2 12 | 2 12 | 53 |
| 54 | 2 13 | 2 13 | 2 13 | 2 13 | 2 14 | 2 14 | 2 14 | 2 14 | 2 14 | 2 14 | 2 14 | 2 14 | 2 14 | 2 14 | 2 14 | 2 14 | 2 14 | 2 14 | 2 15 | 2 15 | 54 |
| 55 | 2 16 | 2 16 | 2 16 | 2 16 | 2 16 | 2 16 | 2 16 | 2 16 | 2 16 | 2 16 | 2 16 | 2 17 | 2 17 | 2 17 | 2 17 | 2 17 | 2 17 | 2 17 | 2 17 | 2 17 | 55 |
| 56 | 2 18 | 2 18 | 2 18 | 2 18 | 2 18 | 2 19 | 2 19 | 2 19 | 2 19 | 2 19 | 2 19 | 2 19 | 2 19 | 2 19 | 2 19 | 2 19 | 2 19 | 2 19 | 2 20 | 2 20 | 56 |
| 57 | 2 21 | 2 21 | 2 21 | 2 21 | 2 21 | 2 21 | 2 21 | 2 21 | 2 21 | 2 21 | 2 21 | 2 21 | 2 22 | 2 22 | 2 22 | 2 22 | 2 22 | 2 22 | 2 22 | 2 22 | 57 |
| 58 | 2 23 | 2 23 | 2 23 | 2 23 | 2 23 | 2 23 | 2 24 | 2 24 | 2 24 | 2 24 | 2 24 | 2 24 | 2 24 | 2 24 | 2 24 | 2 24 | 2 24 | 2 24 | 2 25 | 2 25 | 58 |
| 59 | 2 26 | 2 26 | 2 26 | 2 26 | 2 26 | 2 26 | 2 26 | 2 26 | 2 26 | 2 26 | 2 26 | 2 26 | 2 27 | 2 27 | 2 27 | 2 27 | 2 27 | 2 27 | 2 27 | 2 27 | 59 |
| 60 | 2 28 | 2 28 | 2 28 | 2 28 | 2 28 | 2 28 | 2 29 | 2 29 | 2 29 | 2 29 | 2 29 | 2 29 | 2 29 | 2 29 | 2 29 | 2 29 | 2 29 | 2 29 | 2 30 | 2 30 | 60 |
| HOURS | | | | | | | | | | | | | | | | | | | | | HOURS |
| 1 | 2 28 | 2 28 | 2 28 | 2 28 | 2 28 | 2 28 | 2 29 | 2 29 | 2 29 | 2 29 | 2 29 | 2 29 | 2 29 | 2 29 | 2 29 | 2 29 | 2 29 | 2 29 | 2 30 | 2 30 | 1 |
| 2 | 4 56 | 4 56 | 4 56 | 4 57 | 4 57 | 4 57 | 4 57 | 4 57 | 4 57 | 4 58 | 4 58 | 4 58 | 4 58 | 4 58 | 4 58 | 4 59 | 4 59 | 4 59 | 4 59 | 4 59 | 2 |
| 3 | 7 24 | 7 24 | 7 25 | 7 25 | 7 25 | 7 25 | 7 26 | 7 26 | 7 26 | 7 26 | 7 27 | 7 27 | 7 27 | 7 27 | 7 28 | 7 28 | 7 28 | 7 28 | 7 29 | 7 29 | 3 |
| 4 | 9 52 | 9 52 | 9 53 | 9 53 | 9 53 | 9 54 | 9 54 | 9 54 | 9 55 | 9 55 | 9 55 | 9 56 | 9 56 | 9 56 | 9 57 | 9 57 | 9 57 | 9 58 | 9 58 | 9 58 | 4 |
| 5 | 12 20 | 12 20 | 12 21 | 12 21 | 12 22 | 12 22 | 12 23 | 12 23 | 12 23 | 12 24 | 12 24 | 12 25 | 12 25 | 12 25 | 12 26 | 12 26 | 12 27 | 12 27 | 12 28 | 12 28 | 5 |
| 6 | 14 48 | 14 49 | 14 49 | 14 50 | 14 50 | 14 51 | 14 51 | 14 52 | 14 52 | 14 53 | 14 53 | 14 54 | 14 54 | 14 55 | 14 55 | 14 56 | 14 56 | 14 57 | 14 57 | 14 58 | 6 |
| 7 | 17 16 | 17 17 | 17 17 | 17 18 | 17 18 | 17 19 | 17 20 | 17 20 | 17 21 | 17 21 | 17 22 | 17 22 | 17 23 | 17 24 | 17 24 | 17 25 | 17 25 | 17 26 | 17 27 | 17 27 | 7 |
| 8 | 19 44 | 19 45 | 19 45 | 19 46 | 19 47 | 19 47 | 19 48 | 19 49 | 19 49 | 19 50 | 19 51 | 19 51 | 19 52 | 19 53 | 19 53 | 19 54 | 19 55 | 19 55 | 19 56 | 19 57 | 8 |
| 9 | 22 12 | 22 13 | 22 14 | 22 14 | 22 15 | 22 16 | 22 17 | 22 17 | 22 18 | 22 19 | 22 20 | 22 20 | 22 21 | 22 22 | 22 23 | 22 23 | 22 24 | 22 25 | 22 26 | 22 26 | 9 |
| 10 | 24 40 | 24 41 | 24 42 | 24 43 | 24 43 | 24 44 | 24 45 | 24 46 | 24 47 | 24 48 | 24 48 | 24 49 | 24 50 | 24 51 | 24 52 | 24 53 | 24 53 | 24 54 | 24 55 | 24 56 | 10 |
| 11 | 27 8 | 27 9 | 27 10 | 27 11 | 27 12 | 27 13 | 27 14 | 27 14 | 27 15 | 27 16 | 27 17 | 27 18 | 27 19 | 27 20 | 27 21 | 27 22 | 27 23 | 27 24 | 27 25 | 27 25 | 11 |
| 12 | 29 36 | 29 37 | 29 38 | 29 39 | 29 40 | 29 41 | 29 42 | 29 43 | 29 44 | 29 45 | 29 46 | 29 47 | 29 48 | 29 49 | 29 50 | 29 51 | 29 52 | 29 53 | 29 54 | 29 55 | 12 |
| 13 | 32 4 | 32 5 | 32 6 | 32 7 | 32 8 | 32 9 | 32 11 | 32 12 | 32 13 | 32 14 | 32 15 | 32 16 | 32 17 | 32 18 | 32 19 | 32 20 | 32 21 | 32 22 | 32 24 | 32 25 | 13 |
| 14 | 34 32 | 34 33 | 34 34 | 34 36 | 34 37 | 34 38 | 34 39 | 34 40 | 34 41 | 34 43 | 34 44 | 34 45 | 34 46 | 34 47 | 34 48 | 34 50 | 34 51 | 34 52 | 34 53 | 34 54 | 14 |
| 15 | 37 0 | 37 1 | 37 3 | 37 4 | 37 5 | 37 6 | 37 8 | 37 9 | 37 10 | 37 11 | 37 13 | 37 14 | 37 15 | 37 16 | 37 18 | 37 19 | 37 20 | 37 21 | 37 23 | 37 24 | 15 |
| 16 | 39 28 | 39 29 | 39 31 | 39 32 | 39 33 | 39 35 | 39 36 | 39 37 | 39 39 | 39 40 | 39 41 | 39 43 | 39 44 | 39 45 | 39 47 | 39 48 | 39 49 | 39 51 | 39 52 | 39 53 | 16 |
| 17 | 41 56 | 41 57 | 41 59 | 42 0 | 42 2 | 42 3 | 42 5 | 42 6 | 42 7 | 42 9 | 42 10 | 42 12 | 42 13 | 42 14 | 42 16 | 42 17 | 42 19 | 42 20 | 42 22 | 42 23 | 17 |
| 18 | 44 24 | 44 26 | 44 27 | 44 29 | 44 30 | 44 32 | 44 33 | 44 35 | 44 36 | 44 38 | 44 39 | 44 41 | 44 42 | 44 44 | 44 45 | 44 47 | 44 48 | 44 50 | 44 51 | 44 53 | 18 |
| 19 | 46 52 | 46 54 | 46 55 | 46 57 | 46 58 | 47 0 | 47 2 | 47 3 | 47 5 | 47 6 | 47 8 | 47 9 | 47 11 | 47 13 | 47 14 | 47 16 | 47 17 | 47 19 | 47 21 | 47 22 | 19 |
| 20 | 49 20 | 49 22 | 49 23 | 49 25 | 49 27 | 49 28 | 49 30 | 49 32 | 49 33 | 49 35 | 49 37 | 49 38 | 49 40 | 49 42 | 49 43 | 49 45 | 49 47 | 49 48 | 49 50 | 49 52 | 20 |
| 21 | 51 48 | 51 50 | 51 52 | 51 53 | 51 55 | 51 57 | 51 59 | 52 0 | 52 2 | 52 4 | 52 6 | 52 7 | 52 9 | 52 11 | 52 13 | 52 14 | 52 16 | 52 18 | 52 20 | 52 21 | 21 |
| 22 | 54 16 | 54 18 | 54 20 | 54 22 | 54 23 | 54 25 | 54 27 | 54 29 | 54 31 | 54 33 | 54 34 | 54 36 | 54 38 | 54 40 | 54 42 | 54 44 | 54 45 | 54 47 | 54 49 | 54 51 | 22 |
| 23 | 56 44 | 56 46 | 56 48 | 56 50 | 56 52 | 56 54 | 56 56 | 56 57 | 56 59 | 57 1 | 57 3 | 57 5 | 57 7 | 57 9 | 57 11 | 57 13 | 57 15 | 57 17 | 57 19 | 57 20 | 23 |
| 24 | 59 12 | 59 14 | 59 16 | 59 18 | 59 20 | 59 22 | 59 24 | 59 26 | 59 28 | 59 30 | 59 32 | 59 34 | 59 36 | 59 38 | 59 40 | 59 42 | 59 44 | 59 46 | 59 48 | 59 50 | 24 |

# Table V Diurnal Motion of the Sun

| TIME | 24 HOUR TRAVEL | | | | | | | | | | | | | | | | | | | | TIME |
|---|---|---|---|---|---|---|---|---|---|---|---|---|---|---|---|---|---|---|---|---|---|
| | 59' 52'' | 59' 54'' | 59' 56'' | 59' 58'' | 60' 0'' | 60' 2'' | 60' 4'' | 60' 6'' | 60' 8'' | 60' 10'' | 60' 12'' | 60' 14'' | 60' 16'' | 60' 18'' | 60' 20'' | 60' 22'' | 60' 24'' | 60' 26'' | 60' 28'' | 60' 30'' | |
| MINUTES | ' '' | ' '' | ' '' | ' '' | ' '' | ' '' | ' '' | ' '' | ' '' | ' '' | ' '' | ' '' | ' '' | ' '' | ' '' | ' '' | ' '' | ' '' | ' '' | ' '' | MINUTES |
| 1 | 2 | 2 | 2 | 2 | 3 | 3 | 3 | 3 | 3 | 3 | 3 | 3 | 3 | 3 | 3 | 3 | 3 | 3 | 3 | 3 | 1 |
| 2 | 5 | 5 | 5 | 5 | 5 | 5 | 5 | 5 | 5 | 5 | 5 | 5 | 5 | 5 | 5 | 5 | 5 | 5 | 5 | 5 | 2 |
| 3 | 7 | 7 | 7 | 7 | 8 | 8 | 8 | 8 | 8 | 8 | 8 | 8 | 8 | 8 | 8 | 8 | 8 | 8 | 8 | 8 | 3 |
| 4 | 10 | 10 | 10 | 10 | 10 | 10 | 10 | 10 | 10 | 10 | 10 | 10 | 10 | 10 | 10 | 10 | 10 | 10 | 10 | 10 | 4 |
| 5 | 12 | 12 | 12 | 12 | 13 | 13 | 13 | 13 | 13 | 13 | 13 | 13 | 13 | 13 | 13 | 13 | 13 | 13 | 13 | 13 | 5 |
| 6 | 15 | 15 | 15 | 15 | 15 | 15 | 15 | 15 | 15 | 15 | 15 | 15 | 15 | 15 | 15 | 15 | 15 | 15 | 15 | 15 | 6 |
| 7 | 17 | 17 | 17 | 17 | 18 | 18 | 18 | 18 | 18 | 18 | 18 | 18 | 18 | 18 | 18 | 18 | 18 | 18 | 18 | 18 | 7 |
| 8 | 20 | 20 | 20 | 20 | 20 | 20 | 20 | 20 | 20 | 20 | 20 | 20 | 20 | 20 | 20 | 20 | 20 | 20 | 20 | 20 | 8 |
| 9 | 22 | 22 | 22 | 22 | 23 | 23 | 23 | 23 | 23 | 23 | 23 | 23 | 23 | 23 | 23 | 23 | 23 | 23 | 23 | 23 | 9 |
| 10 | 25 | 25 | 25 | 25 | 25 | 25 | 25 | 25 | 25 | 25 | 25 | 25 | 25 | 25 | 25 | 25 | 25 | 25 | 25 | 25 | 10 |
| 11 | 27 | 27 | 27 | 27 | 28 | 28 | 28 | 28 | 28 | 28 | 28 | 28 | 28 | 28 | 28 | 28 | 28 | 28 | 28 | 28 | 11 |
| 12 | 30 | 30 | 30 | 30 | 30 | 30 | 30 | 30 | 30 | 30 | 30 | 30 | 30 | 30 | 30 | 30 | 30 | 30 | 30 | 30 | 12 |
| 13 | 32 | 32 | 32 | 32 | 33 | 33 | 33 | 33 | 33 | 33 | 33 | 33 | 33 | 33 | 33 | 33 | 33 | 33 | 33 | 33 | 13 |
| 14 | 35 | 35 | 35 | 35 | 35 | 35 | 35 | 35 | 35 | 35 | 35 | 35 | 35 | 35 | 35 | 35 | 35 | 35 | 35 | 35 | 14 |
| 15 | 37 | 37 | 37 | 37 | 38 | 38 | 38 | 38 | 38 | 38 | 38 | 38 | 38 | 38 | 38 | 38 | 38 | 38 | 38 | 38 | 15 |
| 16 | 40 | 40 | 40 | 40 | 40 | 40 | 40 | 40 | 40 | 40 | 40 | 40 | 40 | 40 | 40 | 40 | 40 | 40 | 40 | 40 | 16 |
| 17 | 42 | 42 | 42 | 42 | 43 | 43 | 43 | 43 | 43 | 43 | 43 | 43 | 43 | 43 | 43 | 43 | 43 | 43 | 43 | 43 | 17 |
| 18 | 45 | 45 | 45 | 45 | 45 | 45 | 45 | 45 | 45 | 45 | 45 | 45 | 45 | 45 | 45 | 45 | 45 | 45 | 45 | 45 | 18 |
| 19 | 47 | 47 | 47 | 47 | 48 | 48 | 48 | 48 | 48 | 48 | 48 | 48 | 48 | 48 | 48 | 48 | 48 | 48 | 48 | 48 | 19 |
| 20 | 50 | 50 | 50 | 50 | 50 | 50 | 50 | 50 | 50 | 50 | 50 | 50 | 50 | 50 | 50 | 50 | 50 | 50 | 50 | 50 | 20 |
| 21 | 52 | 52 | 52 | 52 | 53 | 53 | 53 | 53 | 53 | 53 | 53 | 53 | 53 | 53 | 53 | 53 | 53 | 53 | 53 | 53 | 21 |
| 22 | 55 | 55 | 55 | 55 | 55 | 55 | 55 | 55 | 55 | 55 | 55 | 55 | 55 | 55 | 55 | 55 | 55 | 55 | 55 | 55 | 22 |
| 23 | 57 | 57 | 57 | 57 | 58 | 58 | 58 | 58 | 58 | 58 | 58 | 58 | 58 | 58 | 58 | 58 | 58 | 58 | 58 | 58 | 23 |
| 24 | 1 0 | 1 0 | 1 0 | 1 0 | 1 0 | 1 0 | 1 0 | 1 0 | 1 0 | 1 0 | 1 0 | 1 0 | 1 0 | 1 0 | 1 0 | 1 0 | 1 0 | 1 0 | 1 0 | 1 1 | 24 |
| 25 | 1 2 | 1 2 | 1 2 | 1 2 | 1 3 | 1 3 | 1 3 | 1 3 | 1 3 | 1 3 | 1 3 | 1 3 | 1 3 | 1 3 | 1 3 | 1 3 | 1 3 | 1 3 | 1 3 | 1 3 | 25 |
| 26 | 1 5 | 1 5 | 1 5 | 1 5 | 1 5 | 1 5 | 1 5 | 1 5 | 1 5 | 1 5 | 1 5 | 1 5 | 1 5 | 1 5 | 1 5 | 1 5 | 1 5 | 1 5 | 1 6 | 1 6 | 26 |
| 27 | 1 7 | 1 7 | 1 7 | 1 7 | 1 8 | 1 8 | 1 8 | 1 8 | 1 8 | 1 8 | 1 8 | 1 8 | 1 8 | 1 8 | 1 8 | 1 8 | 1 8 | 1 8 | 1 8 | 1 8 | 27 |
| 28 | 1 10 | 1 10 | 1 10 | 1 10 | 1 10 | 1 10 | 1 10 | 1 10 | 1 10 | 1 10 | 1 10 | 1 10 | 1 10 | 1 10 | 1 10 | 1 10 | 1 10 | 1 11 | 1 11 | 1 11 | 28 |
| 29 | 1 12 | 1 12 | 1 12 | 1 12 | 1 13 | 1 13 | 1 13 | 1 13 | 1 13 | 1 13 | 1 13 | 1 13 | 1 13 | 1 13 | 1 13 | 1 13 | 1 13 | 1 13 | 1 13 | 1 13 | 29 |
| 30 | 1 15 | 1 15 | 1 15 | 1 15 | 1 15 | 1 15 | 1 15 | 1 15 | 1 15 | 1 15 | 1 15 | 1 15 | 1 15 | 1 15 | 1 15 | 1 15 | 1 16 | 1 16 | 1 16 | 1 16 | 30 |
| 31 | 1 17 | 1 17 | 1 17 | 1 17 | 1 18 | 1 18 | 1 18 | 1 18 | 1 18 | 1 18 | 1 18 | 1 18 | 1 18 | 1 18 | 1 18 | 1 18 | 1 18 | 1 18 | 1 18 | 1 18 | 31 |
| 32 | 1 20 | 1 20 | 1 20 | 1 20 | 1 20 | 1 20 | 1 20 | 1 20 | 1 20 | 1 20 | 1 20 | 1 20 | 1 20 | 1 20 | 1 20 | 1 20 | 1 21 | 1 21 | 1 21 | 1 21 | 32 |
| 33 | 1 22 | 1 22 | 1 22 | 1 22 | 1 23 | 1 23 | 1 23 | 1 23 | 1 23 | 1 23 | 1 23 | 1 23 | 1 23 | 1 23 | 1 23 | 1 23 | 1 23 | 1 23 | 1 23 | 1 23 | 33 |
| 34 | 1 25 | 1 25 | 1 25 | 1 25 | 1 25 | 1 25 | 1 25 | 1 25 | 1 25 | 1 25 | 1 25 | 1 25 | 1 25 | 1 25 | 1 25 | 1 26 | 1 26 | 1 26 | 1 26 | 1 26 | 34 |
| 35 | 1 27 | 1 27 | 1 27 | 1 27 | 1 28 | 1 28 | 1 28 | 1 28 | 1 28 | 1 28 | 1 28 | 1 28 | 1 28 | 1 28 | 1 28 | 1 28 | 1 28 | 1 28 | 1 28 | 1 28 | 35 |
| 36 | 1 30 | 1 30 | 1 30 | 1 30 | 1 30 | 1 30 | 1 30 | 1 30 | 1 30 | 1 30 | 1 30 | 1 30 | 1 30 | 1 30 | 1 31 | 1 31 | 1 31 | 1 31 | 1 31 | 1 31 | 36 |
| 37 | 1 32 | 1 32 | 1 32 | 1 32 | 1 33 | 1 33 | 1 33 | 1 33 | 1 33 | 1 33 | 1 33 | 1 33 | 1 33 | 1 33 | 1 33 | 1 33 | 1 33 | 1 33 | 1 33 | 1 33 | 37 |
| 38 | 1 35 | 1 35 | 1 35 | 1 35 | 1 35 | 1 35 | 1 35 | 1 35 | 1 35 | 1 35 | 1 35 | 1 35 | 1 35 | 1 35 | 1 36 | 1 36 | 1 36 | 1 36 | 1 36 | 1 36 | 38 |
| 39 | 1 37 | 1 37 | 1 37 | 1 37 | 1 38 | 1 38 | 1 38 | 1 38 | 1 38 | 1 38 | 1 38 | 1 38 | 1 38 | 1 38 | 1 38 | 1 38 | 1 38 | 1 38 | 1 38 | 1 38 | 39 |
| 40 | 1 40 | 1 40 | 1 40 | 1 40 | 1 40 | 1 40 | 1 40 | 1 40 | 1 40 | 1 40 | 1 40 | 1 40 | 1 40 | 1 41 | 1 41 | 1 41 | 1 41 | 1 41 | 1 41 | 1 41 | 40 |
| 41 | 1 42 | 1 42 | 1 42 | 1 42 | 1 43 | 1 43 | 1 43 | 1 43 | 1 43 | 1 43 | 1 43 | 1 43 | 1 43 | 1 43 | 1 43 | 1 43 | 1 43 | 1 43 | 1 43 | 1 43 | 41 |
| 42 | 1 45 | 1 45 | 1 45 | 1 45 | 1 45 | 1 45 | 1 45 | 1 45 | 1 45 | 1 45 | 1 45 | 1 45 | 1 45 | 1 46 | 1 46 | 1 46 | 1 46 | 1 46 | 1 46 | 1 46 | 42 |
| 43 | 1 47 | 1 47 | 1 47 | 1 47 | 1 48 | 1 48 | 1 48 | 1 48 | 1 48 | 1 48 | 1 48 | 1 48 | 1 48 | 1 48 | 1 48 | 1 48 | 1 48 | 1 48 | 1 48 | 1 48 | 43 |
| 44 | 1 50 | 1 50 | 1 50 | 1 50 | 1 50 | 1 50 | 1 50 | 1 50 | 1 50 | 1 50 | 1 50 | 1 50 | 1 50 | 1 51 | 1 51 | 1 51 | 1 51 | 1 51 | 1 51 | 1 51 | 44 |
| 45 | 1 52 | 1 52 | 1 52 | 1 52 | 1 53 | 1 53 | 1 53 | 1 53 | 1 53 | 1 53 | 1 53 | 1 53 | 1 53 | 1 53 | 1 53 | 1 53 | 1 53 | 1 53 | 1 53 | 1 53 | 45 |
| 46 | 1 55 | 1 55 | 1 55 | 1 55 | 1 55 | 1 55 | 1 55 | 1 55 | 1 55 | 1 55 | 1 55 | 1 55 | 1 56 | 1 56 | 1 56 | 1 56 | 1 56 | 1 56 | 1 56 | 1 56 | 46 |
| 47 | 1 57 | 1 57 | 1 57 | 1 57 | 1 58 | 1 58 | 1 58 | 1 58 | 1 58 | 1 58 | 1 58 | 1 58 | 1 58 | 1 58 | 1 58 | 1 58 | 1 58 | 1 58 | 1 58 | 1 58 | 47 |
| 48 | 2 0 | 2 0 | 2 0 | 2 0 | 2 0 | 2 0 | 2 0 | 2 0 | 2 0 | 2 0 | 2 0 | 2 0 | 2 1 | 2 1 | 2 1 | 2 1 | 2 1 | 2 1 | 2 1 | 2 1 | 48 |
| 49 | 2 2 | 2 2 | 2 2 | 2 2 | 2 3 | 2 3 | 2 3 | 2 3 | 2 3 | 2 3 | 2 3 | 2 3 | 2 3 | 2 3 | 2 3 | 2 3 | 2 3 | 2 3 | 2 3 | 2 4 | 49 |
| 50 | 2 5 | 2 5 | 2 5 | 2 5 | 2 5 | 2 5 | 2 5 | 2 5 | 2 5 | 2 5 | 2 5 | 2 5 | 2 6 | 2 6 | 2 6 | 2 6 | 2 6 | 2 6 | 2 6 | 2 6 | 50 |
| 51 | 2 7 | 2 7 | 2 7 | 2 7 | 2 8 | 2 8 | 2 8 | 2 8 | 2 8 | 2 8 | 2 8 | 2 8 | 2 8 | 2 8 | 2 8 | 2 8 | 2 8 | 2 8 | 2 8 | 2 9 | 51 |
| 52 | 2 10 | 2 10 | 2 10 | 2 10 | 2 10 | 2 10 | 2 10 | 2 10 | 2 10 | 2 10 | 2 10 | 2 11 | 2 11 | 2 11 | 2 11 | 2 11 | 2 11 | 2 11 | 2 11 | 2 11 | 52 |
| 53 | 2 12 | 2 12 | 2 12 | 2 12 | 2 13 | 2 13 | 2 13 | 2 13 | 2 13 | 2 13 | 2 13 | 2 13 | 2 13 | 2 13 | 2 13 | 2 13 | 2 13 | 2 13 | 2 14 | 2 14 | 53 |
| 54 | 2 15 | 2 15 | 2 15 | 2 15 | 2 15 | 2 15 | 2 15 | 2 15 | 2 15 | 2 15 | 2 15 | 2 16 | 2 16 | 2 16 | 2 16 | 2 16 | 2 16 | 2 16 | 2 16 | 2 16 | 54 |
| 55 | 2 17 | 2 17 | 2 17 | 2 17 | 2 18 | 2 18 | 2 18 | 2 18 | 2 18 | 2 18 | 2 18 | 2 18 | 2 18 | 2 18 | 2 18 | 2 18 | 2 18 | 2 18 | 2 19 | 2 19 | 55 |
| 56 | 2 20 | 2 20 | 2 20 | 2 20 | 2 20 | 2 20 | 2 20 | 2 20 | 2 20 | 2 20 | 2 20 | 2 21 | 2 21 | 2 21 | 2 21 | 2 21 | 2 21 | 2 21 | 2 21 | 2 21 | 56 |
| 57 | 2 22 | 2 22 | 2 22 | 2 22 | 2 23 | 2 23 | 2 23 | 2 23 | 2 23 | 2 23 | 2 23 | 2 23 | 2 23 | 2 23 | 2 23 | 2 23 | 2 23 | 2 24 | 2 24 | 2 24 | 57 |
| 58 | 2 25 | 2 25 | 2 25 | 2 25 | 2 25 | 2 25 | 2 25 | 2 25 | 2 25 | 2 25 | 2 25 | 2 26 | 2 26 | 2 26 | 2 26 | 2 26 | 2 26 | 2 26 | 2 26 | 2 26 | 58 |
| 59 | 2 27 | 2 27 | 2 27 | 2 27 | 2 28 | 2 28 | 2 28 | 2 28 | 2 28 | 2 28 | 2 28 | 2 28 | 2 28 | 2 28 | 2 28 | 2 28 | 2 28 | 2 29 | 2 29 | 2 29 | 59 |
| 60 | 2 30 | 2 30 | 2 30 | 2 30 | 2 30 | 2 30 | 2 30 | 2 30 | 2 30 | 2 30 | 2 31 | 2 31 | 2 31 | 2 31 | 2 31 | 2 31 | 2 31 | 2 31 | 2 31 | 2 31 | 60 |
| HOURS | | | | | | | | | | | | | | | | | | | | | HOURS |
| 1 | 2 30 | 2 30 | 2 30 | 2 30 | 2 30 | 2 30 | 2 30 | 2 30 | 2 30 | 2 30 | 2 31 | 2 31 | 2 31 | 2 31 | 2 31 | 2 31 | 2 31 | 2 31 | 2 31 | 2 31 | 1 |
| 2 | 4 59 | 5 0 | 5 0 | 5 0 | 5 0 | 5 0 | 5 0 | 5 1 | 5 1 | 5 1 | 5 1 | 5 1 | 5 1 | 5 2 | 5 2 | 5 2 | 5 2 | 5 2 | 5 2 | 5 3 | 2 |
| 3 | 7 29 | 7 29 | 7 30 | 7 30 | 7 30 | 7 30 | 7 31 | 7 31 | 7 31 | 7 31 | 7 32 | 7 32 | 7 32 | 7 32 | 7 33 | 7 33 | 7 33 | 7 33 | 7 34 | 7 34 | 3 |
| 4 | 9 59 | 9 59 | 9 59 | 10 0 | 10 0 | 10 0 | 10 1 | 10 1 | 10 1 | 10 2 | 10 2 | 10 2 | 10 3 | 10 3 | 10 3 | 10 4 | 10 4 | 10 4 | 10 5 | 10 5 | 4 |
| 5 | 12 28 | 12 29 | 12 29 | 12 30 | 12 30 | 12 30 | 12 31 | 12 31 | 12 32 | 12 32 | 12 33 | 12 33 | 12 33 | 12 34 | 12 34 | 12 35 | 12 35 | 12 35 | 12 36 | 12 36 | 5 |
| 6 | 14 58 | 14 59 | 14 59 | 15 0 | 15 0 | 15 1 | 15 1 | 15 2 | 15 2 | 15 3 | 15 3 | 15 4 | 15 4 | 15 5 | 15 5 | 15 6 | 15 6 | 15 7 | 15 7 | 15 8 | 6 |
| 7 | 17 28 | 17 28 | 17 29 | 17 29 | 17 30 | 17 31 | 17 31 | 17 32 | 17 32 | 17 33 | 17 34 | 17 34 | 17 35 | 17 35 | 17 36 | 17 36 | 17 37 | 17 38 | 17 38 | 17 39 | 7 |
| 8 | 19 57 | 19 58 | 19 59 | 19 59 | 20 0 | 20 1 | 20 1 | 20 2 | 20 3 | 20 3 | 20 4 | 20 5 | 20 5 | 20 6 | 20 7 | 20 7 | 20 8 | 20 9 | 20 9 | 20 10 | 8 |
| 9 | 22 27 | 22 28 | 22 29 | 22 29 | 22 30 | 22 31 | 22 32 | 22 32 | 22 33 | 22 34 | 22 35 | 22 35 | 22 36 | 22 37 | 22 38 | 22 38 | 22 39 | 22 40 | 22 41 | 22 41 | 9 |
| 10 | 24 57 | 24 58 | 24 58 | 24 59 | 25 0 | 25 1 | 25 2 | 25 3 | 25 3 | 25 4 | 25 5 | 25 6 | 25 7 | 25 8 | 25 8 | 25 9 | 25 10 | 25 11 | 25 12 | 25 13 | 10 |
| 11 | 27 26 | 27 27 | 27 28 | 27 29 | 27 30 | 27 31 | 27 32 | 27 33 | 27 34 | 27 35 | 27 36 | 27 36 | 27 37 | 27 38 | 27 39 | 27 40 | 27 41 | 27 42 | 27 43 | 27 44 | 11 |
| 12 | 29 56 | 29 57 | 29 58 | 29 59 | 30 0 | 30 1 | 30 2 | 30 3 | 30 4 | 30 5 | 30 6 | 30 7 | 30 8 | 30 9 | 30 10 | 30 11 | 30 12 | 30 13 | 30 14 | 30 15 | 12 |
| 13 | 32 26 | 32 27 | 32 28 | 32 29 | 32 30 | 32 31 | 32 32 | 32 33 | 32 34 | 32 35 | 32 37 | 32 38 | 32 39 | 32 40 | 32 41 | 32 42 | 32 43 | 32 44 | 32 45 | 32 46 | 13 |
| 14 | 34 55 | 34 57 | 34 58 | 34 59 | 35 0 | 35 1 | 35 2 | 35 4 | 35 5 | 35 6 | 35 7 | 35 8 | 35 9 | 35 11 | 35 12 | 35 13 | 35 14 | 35 15 | 35 16 | 35 18 | 14 |
| 15 | 37 25 | 37 26 | 37 28 | 37 29 | 37 30 | 37 31 | 37 33 | 37 34 | 37 35 | 37 36 | 37 38 | 37 39 | 37 40 | 37 41 | 37 43 | 37 44 | 37 45 | 37 46 | 37 48 | 37 49 | 15 |
| 16 | 39 55 | 39 56 | 39 57 | 39 59 | 40 0 | 40 1 | 40 3 | 40 4 | 40 5 | 40 7 | 40 8 | 40 9 | 40 11 | 40 12 | 40 13 | 40 15 | 40 16 | 40 17 | 40 19 | 40 20 | 16 |
| 17 | 42 24 | 42 26 | 42 27 | 42 29 | 42 30 | 42 31 | 42 33 | 42 34 | 42 36 | 42 37 | 42 39 | 42 40 | 42 41 | 42 43 | 42 44 | 42 46 | 42 47 | 42 48 | 42 50 | 42 51 | 17 |
| 18 | 44 54 | 44 56 | 44 57 | 44 59 | 45 0 | 45 2 | 45 3 | 45 5 | 45 6 | 45 8 | 45 9 | 45 11 | 45 12 | 45 14 | 45 15 | 45 17 | 45 18 | 45 20 | 45 21 | 45 23 | 18 |
| 19 | 47 24 | 47 25 | 47 27 | 47 28 | 47 30 | 47 32 | 47 33 | 47 35 | 47 36 | 47 38 | 47 40 | 47 41 | 47 43 | 47 44 | 47 46 | 47 47 | 47 49 | 47 51 | 47 52 | 47 54 | 19 |
| 20 | 49 53 | 49 55 | 49 57 | 49 58 | 50 0 | 50 2 | 50 3 | 50 5 | 50 7 | 50 8 | 50 10 | 50 12 | 50 13 | 50 15 | 50 17 | 50 18 | 50 20 | 50 22 | 50 23 | 50 25 | 20 |
| 21 | 52 23 | 52 25 | 52 27 | 52 28 | 52 30 | 52 32 | 52 34 | 52 35 | 52 37 | 52 39 | 52 41 | 52 42 | 52 44 | 52 46 | 52 48 | 52 49 | 52 51 | 52 53 | 52 55 | 52 56 | 21 |
| 22 | 54 53 | 54 55 | 54 56 | 54 58 | 55 0 | 55 2 | 55 4 | 55 6 | 55 7 | 55 9 | 55 11 | 55 13 | 55 15 | 55 17 | 55 18 | 55 20 | 55 22 | 55 24 | 55 26 | 55 28 | 22 |
| 23 | 57 22 | 57 24 | 57 26 | 57 28 | 57 30 | 57 32 | 57 34 | 57 36 | 57 38 | 57 40 | 57 42 | 57 43 | 57 45 | 57 47 | 57 49 | 57 51 | 57 53 | 57 55 | 57 57 | 57 59 | 23 |
| 24 | 59 52 | 59 54 | 59 56 | 59 58 | 60 0 | 60 2 | 60 4 | 60 6 | 60 8 | 60 10 | 60 12 | 60 14 | 60 16 | 60 18 | 60 20 | 60 22 | 60 24 | 60 26 | 60 28 | 60 30 | 24 |

# Table V Diurnal Motion of the Sun

| TIME | 24 HOUR TRAVEL | | | | | | | | | | | | | | | | | | | | TIME |
|---|---|---|---|---|---|---|---|---|---|---|---|---|---|---|---|---|---|---|---|---|---|
| | ° ' | ° ' | ° ' | ° ' | ° ' | ° ' | ° ' | ° ' | ° ' | ° ' | ° ' | ° ' | ° ' | ° ' | ° ' | ° ' | ° ' | ° ' | ° ' | ° ' | |
| TIME | 60 32 | 60 34 | 60 36 | 60 38 | 60 40 | 60 42 | 60 44 | 60 46 | 60 48 | 60 50 | 60 52 | 60 54 | 60 56 | 60 58 | 61 0 | 61 2 | 61 4 | 61 6 | 61 8 | 61 10 | TIME |
| MINUTES | ° ' | ° ' | ° ' | ° ' | ° ' | ° ' | ° ' | ° ' | ° ' | ° ' | ° ' | ° ' | ° ' | ° ' | ° ' | ° ' | ° ' | ° ' | ° ' | ° ' | MINUTES |
| 1 | 3 | 3 | 3 | 3 | 3 | 3 | 3 | 3 | 3 | 3 | 3 | 3 | 3 | 3 | 3 | 3 | 3 | 3 | 3 | 3 | 1 |
| 2 | 5 | 5 | 5 | 5 | 5 | 5 | 5 | 5 | 5 | 5 | 5 | 5 | 5 | 5 | 5 | 5 | 5 | 5 | 5 | 5 | 2 |
| 3 | 8 | 8 | 8 | 8 | 8 | 8 | 8 | 8 | 8 | 8 | 8 | 8 | 8 | 8 | 8 | 8 | 8 | 8 | 8 | 8 | 3 |
| 4 | 10 | 10 | 10 | 10 | 10 | 10 | 10 | 10 | 10 | 10 | 10 | 10 | 10 | 10 | 10 | 10 | 10 | 10 | 10 | 10 | 4 |
| 5 | 13 | 13 | 13 | 13 | 13 | 13 | 13 | 13 | 13 | 13 | 13 | 13 | 13 | 13 | 13 | 13 | 13 | 13 | 13 | 13 | 5 |
| 6 | 15 | 15 | 15 | 15 | 15 | 15 | 15 | 15 | 15 | 15 | 15 | 15 | 15 | 15 | 15 | 15 | 15 | 15 | 15 | 15 | 6 |
| 7 | 18 | 18 | 18 | 18 | 18 | 18 | 18 | 18 | 18 | 18 | 18 | 18 | 18 | 18 | 18 | 18 | 18 | 18 | 18 | 18 | 7 |
| 8 | 20 | 20 | 20 | 20 | 20 | 20 | 20 | 20 | 20 | 20 | 20 | 20 | 20 | 20 | 20 | 20 | 20 | 20 | 20 | 20 | 8 |
| 9 | 23 | 23 | 23 | 23 | 23 | 23 | 23 | 23 | 23 | 23 | 23 | 23 | 23 | 23 | 23 | 23 | 23 | 23 | 23 | 23 | 9 |
| 10 | 25 | 25 | 25 | 25 | 25 | 25 | 25 | 25 | 25 | 25 | 25 | 25 | 25 | 25 | 25 | 25 | 25 | 25 | 25 | 25 | 10 |
| 11 | 28 | 28 | 28 | 28 | 28 | 28 | 28 | 28 | 28 | 28 | 28 | 28 | 28 | 28 | 28 | 28 | 28 | 28 | 28 | 28 | 11 |
| 12 | 30 | 30 | 30 | 30 | 30 | 30 | 30 | 30 | 30 | 30 | 30 | 30 | 30 | 30 | 31 | 31 | 31 | 31 | 31 | 31 | 12 |
| 13 | 33 | 33 | 33 | 33 | 33 | 33 | 33 | 33 | 33 | 33 | 33 | 33 | 33 | 33 | 33 | 33 | 33 | 33 | 33 | 33 | 13 |
| 14 | 35 | 35 | 35 | 35 | 35 | 35 | 35 | 35 | 35 | 35 | 36 | 36 | 36 | 36 | 36 | 36 | 36 | 36 | 36 | 36 | 14 |
| 15 | 38 | 38 | 38 | 38 | 38 | 38 | 38 | 38 | 38 | 38 | 38 | 38 | 38 | 38 | 38 | 38 | 38 | 38 | 38 | 38 | 15 |
| 16 | 40 | 40 | 40 | 40 | 40 | 40 | 40 | 41 | 41 | 41 | 41 | 41 | 41 | 41 | 41 | 41 | 41 | 41 | 41 | 41 | 16 |
| 17 | 43 | 43 | 43 | 43 | 43 | 43 | 43 | 43 | 43 | 43 | 43 | 43 | 43 | 43 | 43 | 43 | 43 | 43 | 43 | 43 | 17 |
| 18 | 45 | 45 | 45 | 45 | 46 | 46 | 46 | 46 | 46 | 46 | 46 | 46 | 46 | 46 | 46 | 46 | 46 | 46 | 46 | 46 | 18 |
| 19 | 48 | 48 | 48 | 48 | 48 | 48 | 48 | 48 | 48 | 48 | 48 | 48 | 48 | 48 | 48 | 48 | 48 | 48 | 48 | 48 | 19 |
| 20 | 50 | 50 | 51 | 51 | 51 | 51 | 51 | 51 | 51 | 51 | 51 | 51 | 51 | 51 | 51 | 51 | 51 | 51 | 51 | 51 | 20 |
| 21 | 53 | 53 | 53 | 53 | 53 | 53 | 53 | 53 | 53 | 53 | 53 | 53 | 53 | 53 | 53 | 53 | 53 | 53 | 53 | 54 | 21 |
| 22 | 55 | 56 | 56 | 56 | 56 | 56 | 56 | 56 | 56 | 56 | 56 | 56 | 56 | 56 | 56 | 56 | 56 | 56 | 56 | 56 | 22 |
| 23 | 58 | 58 | 58 | 58 | 58 | 58 | 58 | 58 | 58 | 58 | 58 | 58 | 58 | 58 | 58 | 58 | 59 | 59 | 59 | 59 | 23 |
| 24 | 1 1 | 1 1 | 1 1 | 1 1 | 1 1 | 1 1 | 1 1 | 1 1 | 1 1 | 1 1 | 1 1 | 1 1 | 1 1 | 1 1 | 1 1 | 1 1 | 1 1 | 1 1 | 1 1 | 1 1 | 24 |
| 25 | 1 3 | 1 3 | 1 3 | 1 3 | 1 3 | 1 3 | 1 3 | 1 3 | 1 3 | 1 3 | 1 3 | 1 3 | 1 3 | 1 4 | 1 4 | 1 4 | 1 4 | 1 4 | 1 4 | 1 4 | 25 |
| 26 | 1 6 | 1 6 | 1 6 | 1 6 | 1 6 | 1 6 | 1 6 | 1 6 | 1 6 | 1 6 | 1 6 | 1 6 | 1 6 | 1 6 | 1 6 | 1 6 | 1 6 | 1 6 | 1 6 | 1 6 | 26 |
| 27 | 1 8 | 1 8 | 1 8 | 1 8 | 1 8 | 1 8 | 1 8 | 1 8 | 1 8 | 1 8 | 1 8 | 1 9 | 1 9 | 1 9 | 1 9 | 1 9 | 1 9 | 1 9 | 1 9 | 1 9 | 27 |
| 28 | 1 11 | 1 11 | 1 11 | 1 11 | 1 11 | 1 11 | 1 11 | 1 11 | 1 11 | 1 11 | 1 11 | 1 11 | 1 11 | 1 11 | 1 11 | 1 11 | 1 11 | 1 11 | 1 11 | 1 11 | 28 |
| 29 | 1 13 | 1 13 | 1 13 | 1 13 | 1 13 | 1 13 | 1 13 | 1 13 | 1 13 | 1 14 | 1 14 | 1 14 | 1 14 | 1 14 | 1 14 | 1 14 | 1 14 | 1 14 | 1 14 | 1 14 | 29 |
| 30 | 1 16 | 1 16 | 1 16 | 1 16 | 1 16 | 1 16 | 1 16 | 1 16 | 1 16 | 1 16 | 1 16 | 1 16 | 1 16 | 1 16 | 1 16 | 1 16 | 1 16 | 1 16 | 1 16 | 1 16 | 30 |
| 31 | 1 18 | 1 18 | 1 18 | 1 18 | 1 18 | 1 18 | 1 18 | 1 18 | 1 19 | 1 19 | 1 19 | 1 19 | 1 19 | 1 19 | 1 19 | 1 19 | 1 19 | 1 19 | 1 19 | 1 19 | 31 |
| 32 | 1 21 | 1 21 | 1 21 | 1 21 | 1 21 | 1 21 | 1 21 | 1 21 | 1 21 | 1 21 | 1 21 | 1 21 | 1 21 | 1 21 | 1 21 | 1 21 | 1 21 | 1 21 | 1 22 | 1 22 | 32 |
| 33 | 1 23 | 1 23 | 1 23 | 1 23 | 1 23 | 1 23 | 1 24 | 1 24 | 1 24 | 1 24 | 1 24 | 1 24 | 1 24 | 1 24 | 1 24 | 1 24 | 1 24 | 1 24 | 1 24 | 1 24 | 33 |
| 34 | 1 26 | 1 26 | 1 26 | 1 26 | 1 26 | 1 26 | 1 26 | 1 26 | 1 26 | 1 26 | 1 26 | 1 26 | 1 26 | 1 26 | 1 26 | 1 26 | 1 27 | 1 27 | 1 27 | 1 27 | 34 |
| 35 | 1 28 | 1 28 | 1 28 | 1 28 | 1 28 | 1 29 | 1 29 | 1 29 | 1 29 | 1 29 | 1 29 | 1 29 | 1 29 | 1 29 | 1 29 | 1 29 | 1 29 | 1 29 | 1 29 | 1 29 | 35 |
| 36 | 1 31 | 1 31 | 1 31 | 1 31 | 1 31 | 1 31 | 1 31 | 1 31 | 1 31 | 1 31 | 1 31 | 1 31 | 1 31 | 1 31 | 1 32 | 1 32 | 1 32 | 1 32 | 1 32 | 1 32 | 36 |
| 37 | 1 33 | 1 33 | 1 33 | 1 33 | 1 34 | 1 34 | 1 34 | 1 34 | 1 34 | 1 34 | 1 34 | 1 34 | 1 34 | 1 34 | 1 34 | 1 34 | 1 34 | 1 34 | 1 34 | 1 34 | 37 |
| 38 | 1 36 | 1 36 | 1 36 | 1 36 | 1 36 | 1 36 | 1 36 | 1 36 | 1 36 | 1 36 | 1 36 | 1 36 | 1 36 | 1 37 | 1 37 | 1 37 | 1 37 | 1 37 | 1 37 | 1 37 | 38 |
| 39 | 1 38 | 1 38 | 1 38 | 1 39 | 1 39 | 1 39 | 1 39 | 1 39 | 1 39 | 1 39 | 1 39 | 1 39 | 1 39 | 1 39 | 1 39 | 1 39 | 1 39 | 1 39 | 1 39 | 1 39 | 39 |
| 40 | 1 41 | 1 41 | 1 41 | 1 41 | 1 41 | 1 41 | 1 41 | 1 41 | 1 41 | 1 41 | 1 41 | 1 42 | 1 42 | 1 42 | 1 42 | 1 42 | 1 42 | 1 42 | 1 42 | 1 42 | 40 |
| 41 | 1 43 | 1 43 | 1 44 | 1 44 | 1 44 | 1 44 | 1 44 | 1 44 | 1 44 | 1 44 | 1 44 | 1 44 | 1 44 | 1 44 | 1 44 | 1 44 | 1 44 | 1 44 | 1 44 | 1 44 | 41 |
| 42 | 1 46 | 1 46 | 1 46 | 1 46 | 1 46 | 1 46 | 1 46 | 1 46 | 1 46 | 1 46 | 1 47 | 1 47 | 1 47 | 1 47 | 1 47 | 1 47 | 1 47 | 1 47 | 1 47 | 1 47 | 42 |
| 43 | 1 48 | 1 49 | 1 49 | 1 49 | 1 49 | 1 49 | 1 49 | 1 49 | 1 49 | 1 49 | 1 49 | 1 49 | 1 49 | 1 49 | 1 49 | 1 49 | 1 49 | 1 49 | 1 50 | 1 50 | 43 |
| 44 | 1 51 | 1 51 | 1 51 | 1 51 | 1 51 | 1 51 | 1 51 | 1 51 | 1 51 | 1 52 | 1 52 | 1 52 | 1 52 | 1 52 | 1 52 | 1 52 | 1 52 | 1 52 | 1 52 | 1 52 | 44 |
| 45 | 1 54 | 1 54 | 1 54 | 1 54 | 1 54 | 1 54 | 1 54 | 1 54 | 1 54 | 1 54 | 1 54 | 1 54 | 1 54 | 1 54 | 1 54 | 1 54 | 1 55 | 1 55 | 1 55 | 1 55 | 45 |
| 46 | 1 56 | 1 56 | 1 56 | 1 56 | 1 56 | 1 56 | 1 56 | 1 56 | 1 57 | 1 57 | 1 57 | 1 57 | 1 57 | 1 57 | 1 57 | 1 57 | 1 57 | 1 57 | 1 57 | 1 57 | 46 |
| 47 | 1 59 | 1 59 | 1 59 | 1 59 | 1 59 | 1 59 | 1 59 | 1 59 | 1 59 | 1 59 | 1 59 | 1 59 | 1 59 | 1 59 | 1 59 | 2 0 | 2 0 | 2 0 | 2 0 | 2 0 | 47 |
| 48 | 2 1 | 2 1 | 2 1 | 2 1 | 2 1 | 2 1 | 2 1 | 2 2 | 2 2 | 2 2 | 2 2 | 2 2 | 2 2 | 2 2 | 2 2 | 2 2 | 2 2 | 2 2 | 2 2 | 2 2 | 48 |
| 49 | 2 4 | 2 4 | 2 4 | 2 4 | 2 4 | 2 4 | 2 4 | 2 4 | 2 4 | 2 4 | 2 4 | 2 4 | 2 4 | 2 4 | 2 5 | 2 5 | 2 5 | 2 5 | 2 5 | 2 5 | 49 |
| 50 | 2 6 | 2 6 | 2 6 | 2 6 | 2 6 | 2 6 | 2 7 | 2 7 | 2 7 | 2 7 | 2 7 | 2 7 | 2 7 | 2 7 | 2 7 | 2 7 | 2 7 | 2 7 | 2 7 | 2 7 | 50 |
| 51 | 2 9 | 2 9 | 2 9 | 2 9 | 2 9 | 2 9 | 2 9 | 2 9 | 2 9 | 2 9 | 2 9 | 2 9 | 2 9 | 2 10 | 2 10 | 2 10 | 2 10 | 2 10 | 2 10 | 2 10 | 51 |
| 52 | 2 11 | 2 11 | 2 11 | 2 11 | 2 11 | 2 12 | 2 12 | 2 12 | 2 12 | 2 12 | 2 12 | 2 12 | 2 12 | 2 12 | 2 12 | 2 12 | 2 12 | 2 12 | 2 12 | 2 13 | 52 |
| 53 | 2 14 | 2 14 | 2 14 | 2 14 | 2 14 | 2 14 | 2 14 | 2 14 | 2 14 | 2 14 | 2 14 | 2 14 | 2 15 | 2 15 | 2 15 | 2 15 | 2 15 | 2 15 | 2 15 | 2 15 | 53 |
| 54 | 2 16 | 2 16 | 2 16 | 2 16 | 2 17 | 2 17 | 2 17 | 2 17 | 2 17 | 2 17 | 2 17 | 2 17 | 2 17 | 2 17 | 2 17 | 2 17 | 2 17 | 2 17 | 2 18 | 2 18 | 54 |
| 55 | 2 19 | 2 19 | 2 19 | 2 19 | 2 19 | 2 19 | 2 19 | 2 19 | 2 19 | 2 19 | 2 19 | 2 20 | 2 20 | 2 20 | 2 20 | 2 20 | 2 20 | 2 20 | 2 20 | 2 20 | 55 |
| 56 | 2 21 | 2 21 | 2 21 | 2 21 | 2 22 | 2 22 | 2 22 | 2 22 | 2 22 | 2 22 | 2 22 | 2 22 | 2 22 | 2 22 | 2 22 | 2 22 | 2 22 | 2 23 | 2 23 | 2 23 | 56 |
| 57 | 2 24 | 2 24 | 2 24 | 2 24 | 2 24 | 2 24 | 2 24 | 2 24 | 2 24 | 2 24 | 2 25 | 2 25 | 2 25 | 2 25 | 2 25 | 2 25 | 2 25 | 2 25 | 2 25 | 2 25 | 57 |
| 58 | 2 26 | 2 26 | 2 26 | 2 27 | 2 27 | 2 27 | 2 27 | 2 27 | 2 27 | 2 27 | 2 27 | 2 27 | 2 27 | 2 27 | 2 27 | 2 27 | 2 28 | 2 28 | 2 28 | 2 28 | 58 |
| 59 | 2 29 | 2 29 | 2 29 | 2 29 | 2 29 | 2 29 | 2 29 | 2 29 | 2 29 | 2 30 | 2 30 | 2 30 | 2 30 | 2 30 | 2 30 | 2 30 | 2 30 | 2 30 | 2 30 | 2 30 | 59 |
| 60 | 2 31 | 2 31 | 2 32 | 2 32 | 2 32 | 2 32 | 2 32 | 2 32 | 2 32 | 2 32 | 2 32 | 2 32 | 2 32 | 2 32 | 2 33 | 2 33 | 2 33 | 2 33 | 2 33 | 2 33 | 60 |
| HOURS | | | | | | | | | | | | | | | | | | | | | HOURS |
| 1 | 2 31 | 2 31 | 2 32 | 2 32 | 2 32 | 2 32 | 2 32 | 2 32 | 2 32 | 2 32 | 2 32 | 2 32 | 2 32 | 2 32 | 2 33 | 2 33 | 2 33 | 2 33 | 2 33 | 2 33 | 1 |
| 2 | 5 3 | 5 3 | 5 3 | 5 3 | 5 3 | 5 4 | 5 4 | 5 4 | 5 4 | 5 4 | 5 4 | 5 5 | 5 5 | 5 5 | 5 5 | 5 5 | 5 5 | 5 6 | 5 6 | 5 6 | 2 |
| 3 | 7 34 | 7 34 | 7 35 | 7 35 | 7 35 | 7 35 | 7 36 | 7 36 | 7 36 | 7 36 | 7 37 | 7 37 | 7 37 | 7 37 | 7 38 | 7 38 | 7 38 | 7 38 | 7 39 | 7 39 | 3 |
| 4 | 10 5 | 10 6 | 10 6 | 10 6 | 10 7 | 10 7 | 10 7 | 10 8 | 10 8 | 10 8 | 10 9 | 10 9 | 10 9 | 10 10 | 10 10 | 10 10 | 10 11 | 10 11 | 10 11 | 10 12 | 4 |
| 5 | 12 37 | 12 37 | 12 38 | 12 38 | 12 38 | 12 39 | 12 39 | 12 40 | 12 40 | 12 40 | 12 41 | 12 41 | 12 42 | 12 42 | 12 43 | 12 43 | 12 43 | 12 44 | 12 44 | 12 45 | 5 |
| 6 | 15 8 | 15 9 | 15 9 | 15 10 | 15 10 | 15 11 | 15 11 | 15 12 | 15 12 | 15 13 | 15 13 | 15 14 | 15 14 | 15 15 | 15 15 | 15 16 | 15 16 | 15 17 | 15 17 | 15 18 | 6 |
| 7 | 17 39 | 17 40 | 17 41 | 17 41 | 17 42 | 17 42 | 17 43 | 17 43 | 17 44 | 17 45 | 17 45 | 17 46 | 17 46 | 17 47 | 17 48 | 17 48 | 17 49 | 17 49 | 17 50 | 17 50 | 7 |
| 8 | 20 11 | 20 11 | 20 12 | 20 13 | 20 13 | 20 14 | 20 15 | 20 15 | 20 16 | 20 17 | 20 17 | 20 18 | 20 19 | 20 19 | 20 20 | 20 21 | 20 21 | 20 22 | 20 23 | 20 23 | 8 |
| 9 | 22 42 | 22 43 | 22 44 | 22 44 | 22 45 | 22 46 | 22 47 | 22 47 | 22 48 | 22 49 | 22 50 | 22 50 | 22 51 | 22 52 | 22 53 | 22 53 | 22 54 | 22 55 | 22 56 | 22 56 | 9 |
| 10 | 25 13 | 25 14 | 25 15 | 25 16 | 25 17 | 25 18 | 25 18 | 25 19 | 25 20 | 25 21 | 25 22 | 25 23 | 25 23 | 25 24 | 25 25 | 25 26 | 25 27 | 25 28 | 25 28 | 25 29 | 10 |
| 11 | 27 45 | 27 46 | 27 47 | 27 47 | 27 48 | 27 49 | 27 50 | 27 51 | 27 52 | 27 53 | 27 54 | 27 55 | 27 56 | 27 57 | 27 58 | 27 58 | 27 59 | 28 0 | 28 1 | 28 2 | 11 |
| 12 | 30 16 | 30 17 | 30 18 | 30 19 | 30 20 | 30 21 | 30 22 | 30 23 | 30 24 | 30 25 | 30 26 | 30 27 | 30 28 | 30 29 | 30 30 | 30 31 | 30 32 | 30 33 | 30 34 | 30 35 | 12 |
| 13 | 32 47 | 32 48 | 32 50 | 32 51 | 32 52 | 32 53 | 32 54 | 32 55 | 32 56 | 32 57 | 32 58 | 32 59 | 33 0 | 33 1 | 33 3 | 33 4 | 33 5 | 33 6 | 33 7 | 33 8 | 13 |
| 14 | 35 19 | 35 20 | 35 21 | 35 22 | 35 23 | 35 25 | 35 26 | 35 27 | 35 28 | 35 29 | 35 30 | 35 32 | 35 33 | 35 34 | 35 35 | 35 36 | 35 37 | 35 39 | 35 40 | 35 41 | 14 |
| 15 | 37 50 | 37 51 | 37 53 | 37 54 | 37 55 | 37 56 | 37 58 | 37 59 | 38 0 | 38 1 | 38 3 | 38 4 | 38 5 | 38 6 | 38 8 | 38 9 | 38 10 | 38 11 | 38 13 | 38 14 | 15 |
| 16 | 40 21 | 40 23 | 40 24 | 40 25 | 40 27 | 40 28 | 40 29 | 40 31 | 40 32 | 40 33 | 40 35 | 40 36 | 40 37 | 40 39 | 40 40 | 40 41 | 40 43 | 40 44 | 40 45 | 40 47 | 16 |
| 17 | 42 53 | 42 54 | 42 56 | 42 57 | 42 58 | 43 0 | 43 1 | 43 3 | 43 4 | 43 5 | 43 7 | 43 8 | 43 10 | 43 11 | 43 13 | 43 14 | 43 15 | 43 17 | 43 18 | 43 20 | 17 |
| 18 | 45 24 | 45 26 | 45 27 | 45 29 | 45 30 | 45 32 | 45 33 | 45 35 | 45 36 | 45 38 | 45 39 | 45 41 | 45 42 | 45 44 | 45 45 | 45 47 | 45 48 | 45 50 | 45 51 | 45 53 | 18 |
| 19 | 47 55 | 47 57 | 47 59 | 48 0 | 48 2 | 48 3 | 48 5 | 48 6 | 48 8 | 48 10 | 48 11 | 48 13 | 48 14 | 48 16 | 48 18 | 48 19 | 48 21 | 48 22 | 48 24 | 48 25 | 19 |
| 20 | 50 27 | 50 28 | 50 30 | 50 32 | 50 33 | 50 35 | 50 37 | 50 38 | 50 40 | 50 42 | 50 43 | 50 45 | 50 47 | 50 48 | 50 50 | 50 52 | 50 53 | 50 55 | 50 57 | 50 58 | 20 |
| 21 | 52 58 | 53 0 | 53 2 | 53 3 | 53 5 | 53 7 | 53 9 | 53 10 | 53 12 | 53 14 | 53 16 | 53 17 | 53 19 | 53 21 | 53 23 | 53 24 | 53 26 | 53 28 | 53 30 | 53 31 | 21 |
| 22 | 55 29 | 55 31 | 55 33 | 55 35 | 55 37 | 55 39 | 55 40 | 55 42 | 55 44 | 55 46 | 55 48 | 55 50 | 55 51 | 55 53 | 55 55 | 55 57 | 55 59 | 56 1 | 56 2 | 56 4 | 22 |
| 23 | 58 1 | 58 3 | 58 5 | 58 6 | 58 8 | 58 10 | 58 12 | 58 14 | 58 16 | 58 18 | 58 20 | 58 22 | 58 24 | 58 26 | 58 28 | 58 29 | 58 31 | 58 33 | 58 35 | 58 37 | 23 |
| 24 | 60 32 | 60 34 | 60 36 | 60 38 | 60 40 | 60 42 | 60 44 | 60 46 | 60 48 | 60 50 | 60 52 | 60 54 | 60 56 | 60 58 | 61 0 | 61 2 | 61 4 | 61 6 | 61 8 | 61 10 | 24 |

# Table VI Semidiurnal Motion of the Moon

Values are given as minutes and seconds (and degrees, minutes, seconds for the Hours section).

| TIME | 5°55' | 5°56' | 5°57' | 5°58' | 5°59' | 6°0' | 6°1' | 6°2' | 6°3' | 6°4' | 6°5' | 6°6' | 6°7' | 6°8' | 6°9' | TIME |
|---|---|---|---|---|---|---|---|---|---|---|---|---|---|---|---|---|
| **MINUTES** | | | | | | 12 HOUR TRAVEL | | | | | | | | | | **MINUTES** |
| 1 | 0 30 | 0 30 | 0 30 | 0 30 | 0 30 | 0 30 | 0 30 | 0 30 | 0 30 | 0 30 | 0 30 | 0 31 | 0 31 | 0 31 | 0 31 | 1 |
| 2 | 0 59 | 0 59 | 1 0 | 1 0 | 1 0 | 1 0 | 1 0 | 1 0 | 1 0 | 1 1 | 1 1 | 1 1 | 1 1 | 1 1 | 1 2 | 2 |
| 3 | 1 29 | 1 29 | 1 29 | 1 30 | 1 30 | 1 30 | 1 30 | 1 31 | 1 31 | 1 31 | 1 31 | 1 32 | 1 32 | 1 32 | 1 32 | 3 |
| 4 | 1 58 | 1 58 | 1 59 | 1 59 | 1 59 | 2 0 | 2 0 | 2 0 | 2 1 | 2 1 | 2 1 | 2 2 | 2 2 | 2 2 | 2 3 | 4 |
| 5 | 2 28 | 2 28 | 2 29 | 2 29 | 2 30 | 2 30 | 2 30 | 2 31 | 2 31 | 2 32 | 2 32 | 2 33 | 2 33 | 2 33 | 2 34 | 5 |
| 6 | 2 58 | 2 58 | 2 59 | 2 59 | 3 0 | 3 0 | 3 1 | 3 1 | 3 2 | 3 2 | 3 3 | 3 3 | 3 4 | 3 4 | 3 5 | 6 |
| 7 | 3 27 | 3 28 | 3 28 | 3 29 | 3 29 | 3 30 | 3 31 | 3 31 | 3 32 | 3 32 | 3 33 | 3 34 | 3 34 | 3 35 | 3 35 | 7 |
| 8 | 3 57 | 3 57 | 3 58 | 3 58 | 3 59 | 4 0 | 4 1 | 4 1 | 4 2 | 4 3 | 4 3 | 4 4 | 4 5 | 4 5 | 4 6 | 8 |
| 9 | 4 26 | 4 27 | 4 28 | 4 29 | 4 29 | 4 30 | 4 31 | 4 32 | 4 32 | 4 33 | 4 34 | 4 35 | 4 35 | 4 36 | 4 37 | 9 |
| 10 | 4 56 | 4 57 | 4 58 | 4 58 | 4 59 | 5 0 | 5 1 | 5 2 | 5 3 | 5 3 | 5 4 | 5 5 | 5 6 | 5 7 | 5 8 | 10 |
| 11 | 5 25 | 5 26 | 5 27 | 5 28 | 5 29 | 5 30 | 5 31 | 5 32 | 5 33 | 5 34 | 5 35 | 5 36 | 5 36 | 5 37 | 5 38 | 11 |
| 12 | 5 55 | 5 56 | 5 57 | 5 58 | 5 59 | 6 0 | 6 1 | 6 2 | 6 3 | 6 4 | 6 5 | 6 6 | 6 7 | 6 8 | 6 9 | 12 |
| 13 | 6 25 | 6 26 | 6 27 | 6 28 | 6 29 | 6 30 | 6 31 | 6 32 | 6 33 | 6 34 | 6 35 | 6 37 | 6 38 | 6 39 | 6 40 | 13 |
| 14 | 6 54 | 6 55 | 6 57 | 6 58 | 6 59 | 7 0 | 7 1 | 7 2 | 7 4 | 7 5 | 7 6 | 7 7 | 7 8 | 7 9 | 7 11 | 14 |
| 15 | 7 24 | 7 25 | 7 26 | 7 28 | 7 29 | 7 30 | 7 31 | 7 33 | 7 34 | 7 35 | 7 36 | 7 38 | 7 39 | 7 40 | 7 41 | 15 |
| 16 | 7 53 | 7 55 | 7 56 | 7 57 | 7 59 | 8 0 | 8 1 | 8 3 | 8 4 | 8 5 | 8 7 | 8 8 | 8 9 | 8 11 | 8 12 | 16 |
| 17 | 8 23 | 8 24 | 8 26 | 8 27 | 8 29 | 8 30 | 8 31 | 8 33 | 8 34 | 8 36 | 8 37 | 8 39 | 8 40 | 8 41 | 8 43 | 17 |
| 18 | 8 53 | 8 54 | 8 56 | 8 57 | 8 59 | 9 0 | 9 2 | 9 3 | 9 5 | 9 6 | 9 8 | 9 9 | 9 11 | 9 12 | 9 14 | 18 |
| 19 | 9 22 | 9 24 | 9 25 | 9 27 | 9 28 | 9 30 | 9 32 | 9 33 | 9 35 | 9 36 | 9 38 | 9 40 | 9 41 | 9 43 | 9 44 | 19 |
| 20 | 9 52 | 9 53 | 9 55 | 9 57 | 9 58 | 10 0 | 10 2 | 10 3 | 10 5 | 10 7 | 10 8 | 10 10 | 10 12 | 10 13 | 10 15 | 20 |
| 21 | 10 21 | 10 23 | 10 25 | 10 27 | 10 28 | 10 30 | 10 32 | 10 34 | 10 35 | 10 37 | 10 39 | 10 41 | 10 42 | 10 44 | 10 46 | 21 |
| 22 | 10 51 | 10 53 | 10 55 | 10 56 | 10 58 | 11 0 | 11 2 | 11 4 | 11 6 | 11 7 | 11 9 | 11 11 | 11 13 | 11 15 | 11 17 | 22 |
| 23 | 11 20 | 11 22 | 11 24 | 11 26 | 11 28 | 11 30 | 11 32 | 11 34 | 11 36 | 11 38 | 11 40 | 11 42 | 11 43 | 11 45 | 11 47 | 23 |
| 24 | 11 50 | 11 52 | 11 54 | 11 56 | 11 58 | 12 0 | 12 2 | 12 4 | 12 6 | 12 8 | 12 10 | 12 12 | 12 14 | 12 16 | 12 18 | 24 |
| 25 | 12 20 | 12 22 | 12 24 | 12 26 | 12 28 | 12 30 | 12 32 | 12 34 | 12 36 | 12 38 | 12 40 | 12 43 | 12 45 | 12 47 | 12 49 | 25 |
| 26 | 12 49 | 12 51 | 12 54 | 12 56 | 12 58 | 13 0 | 13 2 | 13 4 | 13 7 | 13 9 | 13 11 | 13 13 | 13 15 | 13 17 | 13 20 | 26 |
| 27 | 13 19 | 13 21 | 13 23 | 13 26 | 13 28 | 13 30 | 13 32 | 13 35 | 13 37 | 13 39 | 13 41 | 13 44 | 13 46 | 13 48 | 13 50 | 27 |
| 28 | 13 48 | 13 51 | 13 53 | 13 55 | 13 58 | 14 0 | 14 2 | 14 5 | 14 7 | 14 9 | 14 12 | 14 14 | 14 16 | 14 19 | 14 21 | 28 |
| 29 | 14 18 | 14 20 | 14 23 | 14 25 | 14 28 | 14 30 | 14 32 | 14 35 | 14 37 | 14 40 | 14 42 | 14 45 | 14 47 | 14 49 | 14 52 | 29 |
| 30 | 14 48 | 14 50 | 14 53 | 14 55 | 14 58 | 15 0 | 15 3 | 15 5 | 15 8 | 15 10 | 15 13 | 15 15 | 15 18 | 15 20 | 15 23 | 30 |
| 31 | 15 17 | 15 20 | 15 22 | 15 25 | 15 27 | 15 30 | 15 33 | 15 35 | 15 38 | 15 40 | 15 43 | 15 46 | 15 48 | 15 51 | 15 53 | 31 |
| 32 | 15 47 | 15 49 | 15 52 | 15 55 | 15 57 | 16 0 | 16 3 | 16 5 | 16 8 | 16 11 | 16 13 | 16 16 | 16 19 | 16 21 | 16 24 | 32 |
| 33 | 16 16 | 16 19 | 16 22 | 16 25 | 16 27 | 16 30 | 16 33 | 16 36 | 16 38 | 16 41 | 16 44 | 16 47 | 16 49 | 16 52 | 16 55 | 33 |
| 34 | 16 46 | 16 49 | 16 52 | 16 54 | 16 57 | 17 0 | 17 3 | 17 6 | 17 9 | 17 11 | 17 14 | 17 17 | 17 20 | 17 23 | 17 26 | 34 |
| 35 | 17 15 | 17 18 | 17 21 | 17 24 | 17 27 | 17 30 | 17 33 | 17 36 | 17 39 | 17 42 | 17 45 | 17 48 | 17 50 | 17 53 | 17 56 | 35 |
| 36 | 17 45 | 17 48 | 17 51 | 17 54 | 17 57 | 18 0 | 18 3 | 18 6 | 18 9 | 18 12 | 18 15 | 18 18 | 18 21 | 18 24 | 18 27 | 36 |
| 37 | 18 15 | 18 18 | 18 21 | 18 24 | 18 27 | 18 30 | 18 33 | 18 36 | 18 39 | 18 42 | 18 45 | 18 49 | 18 52 | 18 55 | 18 58 | 37 |
| 38 | 18 44 | 18 47 | 18 51 | 18 54 | 18 57 | 19 0 | 19 3 | 19 6 | 19 10 | 19 13 | 19 16 | 19 19 | 19 22 | 19 25 | 19 29 | 38 |
| 39 | 19 14 | 19 17 | 19 20 | 19 24 | 19 27 | 19 30 | 19 33 | 19 37 | 19 40 | 19 43 | 19 46 | 19 50 | 19 53 | 19 56 | 19 59 | 39 |
| 40 | 19 43 | 19 47 | 19 50 | 19 53 | 19 57 | 20 0 | 20 3 | 20 7 | 20 10 | 20 13 | 20 17 | 20 20 | 20 23 | 20 27 | 20 30 | 40 |
| 41 | 20 13 | 20 16 | 20 20 | 20 23 | 20 27 | 20 30 | 20 33 | 20 37 | 20 40 | 20 44 | 20 47 | 20 51 | 20 54 | 20 57 | 21 1 | 41 |
| 42 | 20 43 | 20 46 | 20 50 | 20 53 | 20 57 | 21 0 | 21 4 | 21 7 | 21 11 | 21 14 | 21 18 | 21 21 | 21 25 | 21 28 | 21 32 | 42 |
| 43 | 21 12 | 21 16 | 21 19 | 21 23 | 21 26 | 21 30 | 21 34 | 21 37 | 21 41 | 21 44 | 21 48 | 21 52 | 21 55 | 21 59 | 22 2 | 43 |
| 44 | 21 42 | 21 45 | 21 49 | 21 53 | 21 56 | 22 0 | 22 4 | 22 7 | 22 11 | 22 15 | 22 18 | 22 22 | 22 26 | 22 29 | 22 33 | 44 |
| 45 | 22 11 | 22 15 | 22 19 | 22 23 | 22 26 | 22 30 | 22 34 | 22 38 | 22 41 | 22 45 | 22 49 | 22 53 | 22 56 | 23 0 | 23 4 | 45 |
| 46 | 22 41 | 22 45 | 22 49 | 22 52 | 22 56 | 23 0 | 23 4 | 23 8 | 23 12 | 23 15 | 23 19 | 23 23 | 23 27 | 23 31 | 23 35 | 46 |
| 47 | 23 10 | 23 14 | 23 18 | 23 22 | 23 26 | 23 30 | 23 34 | 23 38 | 23 42 | 23 46 | 23 50 | 23 54 | 23 57 | 24 1 | 24 5 | 47 |
| 48 | 23 40 | 23 44 | 23 48 | 23 52 | 23 56 | 24 0 | 24 4 | 24 8 | 24 12 | 24 16 | 24 20 | 24 24 | 24 28 | 24 32 | 24 36 | 48 |
| 49 | 24 10 | 24 14 | 24 18 | 24 22 | 24 26 | 24 30 | 24 34 | 24 38 | 24 42 | 24 46 | 24 50 | 24 55 | 24 59 | 25 3 | 25 7 | 49 |
| 50 | 24 39 | 24 43 | 24 48 | 24 52 | 24 56 | 25 0 | 25 4 | 25 8 | 25 13 | 25 17 | 25 21 | 25 25 | 25 29 | 25 33 | 25 38 | 50 |
| 51 | 25 9 | 25 13 | 25 17 | 25 22 | 25 26 | 25 30 | 25 34 | 25 39 | 25 43 | 25 47 | 25 51 | 25 56 | 26 0 | 26 4 | 26 8 | 51 |
| 52 | 25 38 | 25 43 | 25 47 | 25 51 | 25 56 | 26 0 | 26 4 | 26 9 | 26 13 | 26 17 | 26 22 | 26 26 | 26 30 | 26 35 | 26 39 | 52 |
| 53 | 26 8 | 26 12 | 26 17 | 26 21 | 26 26 | 26 30 | 26 34 | 26 39 | 26 43 | 26 48 | 26 52 | 26 57 | 27 1 | 27 5 | 27 10 | 53 |
| 54 | 26 38 | 26 42 | 26 47 | 26 51 | 26 56 | 27 0 | 27 5 | 27 9 | 27 14 | 27 18 | 27 23 | 27 27 | 27 32 | 27 36 | 27 41 | 54 |
| 55 | 27 7 | 27 12 | 27 16 | 27 21 | 27 25 | 27 30 | 27 35 | 27 39 | 27 44 | 27 48 | 27 53 | 27 58 | 28 2 | 28 7 | 28 11 | 55 |
| 56 | 27 37 | 27 41 | 27 46 | 27 51 | 27 55 | 28 0 | 28 5 | 28 9 | 28 14 | 28 19 | 28 23 | 28 28 | 28 33 | 28 37 | 28 42 | 56 |
| 57 | 28 6 | 28 11 | 28 16 | 28 21 | 28 25 | 28 30 | 28 35 | 28 40 | 28 44 | 28 49 | 28 54 | 28 59 | 29 3 | 29 8 | 29 13 | 57 |
| 58 | 28 36 | 28 41 | 28 46 | 28 50 | 28 55 | 29 0 | 29 5 | 29 10 | 29 15 | 29 19 | 29 24 | 29 29 | 29 34 | 29 39 | 29 44 | 58 |
| 59 | 29 5 | 29 10 | 29 15 | 29 20 | 29 25 | 29 30 | 29 35 | 29 40 | 29 45 | 29 50 | 29 55 | 30 0 | 30 4 | 30 9 | 30 14 | 59 |
| 60 | 29 35 | 29 40 | 29 45 | 29 50 | 29 55 | 30 0 | 30 5 | 30 10 | 30 15 | 30 20 | 30 25 | 30 30 | 30 35 | 30 40 | 30 45 | 60 |
| **HOURS 1** | 29 35 | 29 40 | 29 45 | 29 50 | 29 55 | 30 0 | 30 5 | 30 10 | 30 15 | 30 20 | 30 25 | 30 30 | 30 35 | 30 40 | 30 45 | 1 **HOURS** |
| 2 | 59 10 | 59 20 | 59 30 | 59 40 | 59 50 | 1 0 0 | 1 0 10 | 1 0 20 | 1 0 30 | 1 0 40 | 1 0 50 | 1 1 0 | 1 1 10 | 1 1 20 | 1 1 30 | 2 |
| 3 | 1 28 45 | 1 29 0 | 1 29 15 | 1 29 30 | 1 29 45 | 1 30 0 | 1 30 15 | 1 30 30 | 1 30 45 | 1 31 0 | 1 31 15 | 1 31 30 | 1 31 45 | 1 32 0 | 1 32 15 | 3 |
| 4 | 1 58 20 | 1 58 40 | 1 59 0 | 1 59 20 | 1 59 40 | 2 0 0 | 2 0 20 | 2 0 40 | 2 1 0 | 2 1 20 | 2 1 40 | 2 2 0 | 2 2 20 | 2 2 40 | 2 3 0 | 4 |
| 5 | 2 27 55 | 2 28 20 | 2 28 45 | 2 29 10 | 2 29 35 | 2 30 0 | 2 30 25 | 2 30 50 | 2 31 15 | 2 31 40 | 2 32 5 | 2 32 30 | 2 32 55 | 2 33 20 | 2 33 45 | 5 |
| 6 | 2 57 30 | 2 58 0 | 2 58 30 | 2 59 0 | 2 59 30 | 3 0 0 | 3 0 30 | 3 1 0 | 3 1 30 | 3 2 0 | 3 2 30 | 3 3 0 | 3 3 30 | 3 4 0 | 3 4 30 | 6 |
| 7 | 3 27 5 | 3 27 40 | 3 28 15 | 3 28 50 | 3 29 25 | 3 30 0 | 3 30 35 | 3 31 10 | 3 31 45 | 3 32 20 | 3 32 55 | 3 33 30 | 3 34 5 | 3 34 40 | 3 35 15 | 7 |
| 8 | 3 56 40 | 3 57 20 | 3 58 0 | 3 58 40 | 3 59 20 | 4 0 0 | 4 0 40 | 4 1 20 | 4 2 0 | 4 2 40 | 4 3 20 | 4 4 0 | 4 4 40 | 4 5 20 | 4 6 0 | 8 |
| 9 | 4 26 15 | 4 27 0 | 4 27 45 | 4 28 30 | 4 29 15 | 4 30 0 | 4 30 45 | 4 31 30 | 4 32 15 | 4 33 0 | 4 33 45 | 4 34 30 | 4 35 15 | 4 36 0 | 4 36 45 | 9 |
| 10 | 4 55 50 | 4 56 40 | 4 57 30 | 4 58 20 | 4 59 10 | 5 0 0 | 5 0 50 | 5 1 40 | 5 2 30 | 5 3 20 | 5 4 10 | 5 5 0 | 5 5 50 | 5 6 40 | 5 7 30 | 10 |
| 11 | 5 25 25 | 5 26 20 | 5 27 15 | 5 28 10 | 5 29 5 | 5 30 0 | 5 30 55 | 5 31 50 | 5 32 45 | 5 33 40 | 5 34 35 | 5 35 30 | 5 36 25 | 5 37 20 | 5 38 15 | 11 |
| 12 | 5 55 0 | 5 56 0 | 5 57 0 | 5 58 0 | 5 59 0 | 6 0 0 | 6 1 0 | 6 2 0 | 6 3 0 | 6 4 0 | 6 5 0 | 6 6 0 | 6 7 0 | 6 8 0 | 6 9 0 | 12 |

# Table VI Semidiurnal Motion of the Moon

| 12 HOUR TRAVEL |||||||||||||||||

| TIME | 6° 10' | 6° 11' | 6° 12' | 6° 13' | 6° 14' | 6° 15' | 6° 16' | 6° 17' | 6° 18' | 6° 19' | 6° 20' | 6° 21' | 6° 22' | 6° 23' | 6° 24' | TIME |
|---|---|---|---|---|---|---|---|---|---|---|---|---|---|---|---|---|
| **MINUTES** | ° ' | ° ' | ° ' | ° ' | ° ' | ° ' | ° ' | ° ' | ° ' | ° ' | ° ' | ° ' | ° ' | ° ' | ° ' | **MINUTES** |
| 1 | 0 31 | 0 31 | 0 31 | 0 31 | 0 31 | 0 31 | 0 31 | 0 31 | 0 32 | 0 32 | 0 32 | 0 32 | 0 32 | 0 32 | 0 32 | 1 |
| 2 | 1 2 | 1 2 | 1 2 | 1 2 | 1 2 | 1 3 | 1 3 | 1 3 | 1 3 | 1 3 | 1 3 | 1 4 | 1 4 | 1 4 | 1 4 | 2 |
| 3 | 1 33 | 1 33 | 1 33 | 1 33 | 1 34 | 1 34 | 1 34 | 1 34 | 1 35 | 1 35 | 1 35 | 1 35 | 1 36 | 1 36 | 1 36 | 3 |
| 4 | 2 3 | 2 4 | 2 4 | 2 4 | 2 5 | 2 5 | 2 5 | 2 6 | 2 6 | 2 6 | 2 7 | 2 7 | 2 7 | 2 8 | 2 8 | 4 |
| 5 | 2 34 | 2 35 | 2 35 | 2 35 | 2 36 | 2 36 | 2 37 | 2 37 | 2 38 | 2 38 | 2 38 | 2 39 | 2 39 | 2 40 | 2 40 | 5 |
| 6 | 3 5 | 3 6 | 3 6 | 3 7 | 3 7 | 3 8 | 3 8 | 3 9 | 3 9 | 3 10 | 3 10 | 3 11 | 3 11 | 3 12 | 3 12 | 6 |
| 7 | 3 36 | 3 36 | 3 37 | 3 38 | 3 38 | 3 39 | 3 39 | 3 40 | 3 41 | 3 41 | 3 42 | 3 42 | 3 43 | 3 43 | 3 44 | 7 |
| 8 | 4 7 | 4 7 | 4 8 | 4 9 | 4 9 | 4 10 | 4 11 | 4 11 | 4 12 | 4 13 | 4 13 | 4 14 | 4 15 | 4 15 | 4 16 | 8 |
| 9 | 4 38 | 4 38 | 4 39 | 4 40 | 4 41 | 4 41 | 4 42 | 4 43 | 4 44 | 4 44 | 4 45 | 4 46 | 4 47 | 4 47 | 4 48 | 9 |
| 10 | 5 8 | 5 9 | 5 10 | 5 11 | 5 12 | 5 13 | 5 13 | 5 14 | 5 15 | 5 16 | 5 17 | 5 18 | 5 18 | 5 19 | 5 20 | 10 |
| 11 | 5 39 | 5 40 | 5 41 | 5 42 | 5 43 | 5 44 | 5 45 | 5 46 | 5 47 | 5 47 | 5 48 | 5 49 | 5 50 | 5 51 | 5 52 | 11 |
| 12 | 6 10 | 6 11 | 6 12 | 6 13 | 6 14 | 6 15 | 6 16 | 6 17 | 6 18 | 6 19 | 6 20 | 6 21 | 6 22 | 6 23 | 6 24 | 12 |
| 13 | 6 41 | 6 42 | 6 43 | 6 44 | 6 45 | 6 46 | 6 47 | 6 48 | 6 50 | 6 51 | 6 52 | 6 53 | 6 54 | 6 55 | 6 56 | 13 |
| 14 | 7 12 | 7 13 | 7 14 | 7 15 | 7 16 | 7 18 | 7 19 | 7 20 | 7 21 | 7 22 | 7 23 | 7 25 | 7 26 | 7 27 | 7 28 | 14 |
| 15 | 7 43 | 7 44 | 7 45 | 7 46 | 7 48 | 7 49 | 7 50 | 7 51 | 7 53 | 7 54 | 7 55 | 7 56 | 7 58 | 7 59 | 8 0 | 15 |
| 16 | 8 13 | 8 15 | 8 16 | 8 17 | 8 19 | 8 20 | 8 21 | 8 23 | 8 24 | 8 25 | 8 27 | 8 28 | 8 29 | 8 31 | 8 32 | 16 |
| 17 | 8 44 | 8 46 | 8 47 | 8 48 | 8 50 | 8 51 | 8 53 | 8 54 | 8 56 | 8 57 | 8 58 | 9 0 | 9 1 | 9 3 | 9 4 | 17 |
| 18 | 9 15 | 9 17 | 9 18 | 9 20 | 9 21 | 9 23 | 9 24 | 9 26 | 9 27 | 9 29 | 9 30 | 9 32 | 9 33 | 9 35 | 9 36 | 18 |
| 19 | 9 46 | 9 47 | 9 49 | 9 51 | 9 52 | 9 54 | 9 55 | 9 57 | 9 59 | 10 0 | 10 2 | 10 3 | 10 5 | 10 6 | 10 8 | 19 |
| 20 | 10 17 | 10 18 | 10 20 | 10 22 | 10 23 | 10 25 | 10 27 | 10 28 | 10 30 | 10 32 | 10 33 | 10 35 | 10 37 | 10 38 | 10 40 | 20 |
| 21 | 10 48 | 10 49 | 10 51 | 10 53 | 10 55 | 10 56 | 10 58 | 11 0 | 11 2 | 11 3 | 11 5 | 11 7 | 11 9 | 11 10 | 11 12 | 21 |
| 22 | 11 18 | 11 20 | 11 22 | 11 24 | 11 26 | 11 28 | 11 29 | 11 31 | 11 33 | 11 35 | 11 37 | 11 39 | 11 40 | 11 42 | 11 44 | 22 |
| 23 | 11 49 | 11 51 | 11 53 | 11 55 | 11 57 | 11 59 | 12 1 | 12 3 | 12 5 | 12 6 | 12 8 | 12 10 | 12 12 | 12 14 | 12 16 | 23 |
| 24 | 12 20 | 12 22 | 12 24 | 12 26 | 12 28 | 12 30 | 12 32 | 12 34 | 12 36 | 12 38 | 12 40 | 12 42 | 12 44 | 12 46 | 12 48 | 24 |
| 25 | 12 51 | 12 53 | 12 55 | 12 57 | 12 59 | 13 1 | 13 3 | 13 5 | 13 8 | 13 10 | 13 12 | 13 14 | 13 16 | 13 18 | 13 20 | 25 |
| 26 | 13 22 | 13 24 | 13 26 | 13 28 | 13 30 | 13 33 | 13 35 | 13 37 | 13 39 | 13 41 | 13 43 | 13 46 | 13 48 | 13 50 | 13 52 | 26 |
| 27 | 13 53 | 13 55 | 13 57 | 13 59 | 14 2 | 14 4 | 14 6 | 14 8 | 14 11 | 14 13 | 14 15 | 14 17 | 14 20 | 14 22 | 14 24 | 27 |
| 28 | 14 23 | 14 26 | 14 28 | 14 30 | 14 33 | 14 35 | 14 37 | 14 40 | 14 42 | 14 44 | 14 47 | 14 49 | 14 51 | 14 54 | 14 56 | 28 |
| 29 | 14 54 | 14 57 | 14 59 | 15 1 | 15 4 | 15 6 | 15 9 | 15 11 | 15 14 | 15 16 | 15 18 | 15 21 | 15 23 | 15 26 | 15 28 | 29 |
| 30 | 15 25 | 15 28 | 15 30 | 15 33 | 15 35 | 15 38 | 15 40 | 15 43 | 15 45 | 15 48 | 15 50 | 15 53 | 15 55 | 15 58 | 16 0 | 30 |
| 31 | 15 56 | 15 58 | 16 1 | 16 4 | 16 6 | 16 9 | 16 11 | 16 14 | 16 17 | 16 19 | 16 22 | 16 24 | 16 27 | 16 29 | 16 32 | 31 |
| 32 | 16 27 | 16 29 | 16 32 | 16 35 | 16 37 | 16 40 | 16 43 | 16 45 | 16 48 | 16 51 | 16 53 | 16 56 | 16 59 | 17 1 | 17 4 | 32 |
| 33 | 16 58 | 17 0 | 17 3 | 17 6 | 17 9 | 17 11 | 17 14 | 17 17 | 17 20 | 17 22 | 17 25 | 17 28 | 17 31 | 17 33 | 17 36 | 33 |
| 34 | 17 28 | 17 31 | 17 34 | 17 37 | 17 40 | 17 43 | 17 45 | 17 48 | 17 51 | 17 54 | 17 57 | 18 0 | 18 2 | 18 5 | 18 8 | 34 |
| 35 | 17 59 | 18 2 | 18 5 | 18 8 | 18 11 | 18 14 | 18 17 | 18 20 | 18 23 | 18 25 | 18 28 | 18 31 | 18 34 | 18 37 | 18 40 | 35 |
| 36 | 18 30 | 18 33 | 18 36 | 18 39 | 18 42 | 18 45 | 18 48 | 18 51 | 18 54 | 18 57 | 19 0 | 19 3 | 19 6 | 19 9 | 19 12 | 36 |
| 37 | 19 1 | 19 4 | 19 7 | 19 10 | 19 13 | 19 16 | 19 19 | 19 22 | 19 26 | 19 29 | 19 32 | 19 35 | 19 38 | 19 41 | 19 44 | 37 |
| 38 | 19 32 | 19 35 | 19 38 | 19 41 | 19 44 | 19 48 | 19 51 | 19 54 | 19 57 | 20 0 | 20 3 | 20 7 | 20 10 | 20 13 | 20 16 | 38 |
| 39 | 20 3 | 20 6 | 20 9 | 20 12 | 20 16 | 20 19 | 20 22 | 20 25 | 20 29 | 20 32 | 20 35 | 20 38 | 20 42 | 20 45 | 20 48 | 39 |
| 40 | 20 33 | 20 37 | 20 40 | 20 43 | 20 47 | 20 50 | 20 53 | 20 57 | 21 0 | 21 3 | 21 7 | 21 10 | 21 13 | 21 17 | 21 20 | 40 |
| 41 | 21 4 | 21 8 | 21 11 | 21 14 | 21 18 | 21 21 | 21 25 | 21 28 | 21 32 | 21 35 | 21 38 | 21 42 | 21 45 | 21 49 | 21 52 | 41 |
| 42 | 21 35 | 21 39 | 21 42 | 21 46 | 21 49 | 21 53 | 21 56 | 22 0 | 22 3 | 22 7 | 22 10 | 22 14 | 22 17 | 22 21 | 22 24 | 42 |
| 43 | 22 6 | 22 9 | 22 13 | 22 17 | 22 20 | 22 24 | 22 27 | 22 31 | 22 35 | 22 38 | 22 42 | 22 45 | 22 49 | 22 52 | 22 56 | 43 |
| 44 | 22 37 | 22 40 | 22 44 | 22 48 | 22 51 | 22 55 | 22 59 | 23 2 | 23 6 | 23 10 | 23 13 | 23 17 | 23 21 | 23 24 | 23 28 | 44 |
| 45 | 23 8 | 23 11 | 23 15 | 23 19 | 23 23 | 23 26 | 23 30 | 23 34 | 23 38 | 23 41 | 23 45 | 23 49 | 23 53 | 23 56 | 24 0 | 45 |
| 46 | 23 38 | 23 42 | 23 46 | 23 50 | 23 54 | 23 58 | 24 1 | 24 5 | 24 9 | 24 13 | 24 17 | 24 21 | 24 24 | 24 28 | 24 32 | 46 |
| 47 | 24 9 | 24 13 | 24 17 | 24 21 | 24 25 | 24 29 | 24 33 | 24 37 | 24 41 | 24 44 | 24 48 | 24 52 | 24 56 | 25 0 | 25 4 | 47 |
| 48 | 24 40 | 24 44 | 24 48 | 24 52 | 24 56 | 25 0 | 25 4 | 25 8 | 25 12 | 25 16 | 25 20 | 25 24 | 25 28 | 25 32 | 25 36 | 48 |
| 49 | 25 11 | 25 15 | 25 19 | 25 23 | 25 27 | 25 31 | 25 35 | 25 39 | 25 44 | 25 48 | 25 52 | 25 56 | 26 0 | 26 4 | 26 8 | 49 |
| 50 | 25 42 | 25 46 | 25 50 | 25 54 | 25 58 | 26 3 | 26 7 | 26 11 | 26 15 | 26 19 | 26 23 | 26 28 | 26 32 | 26 36 | 26 40 | 50 |
| 51 | 26 13 | 26 17 | 26 21 | 26 25 | 26 30 | 26 34 | 26 38 | 26 42 | 26 47 | 26 51 | 26 55 | 26 59 | 27 4 | 27 8 | 27 12 | 51 |
| 52 | 26 43 | 26 48 | 26 52 | 26 56 | 27 1 | 27 5 | 27 9 | 27 14 | 27 18 | 27 22 | 27 27 | 27 31 | 27 35 | 27 40 | 27 44 | 52 |
| 53 | 27 14 | 27 19 | 27 23 | 27 27 | 27 32 | 27 36 | 27 41 | 27 45 | 27 50 | 27 54 | 27 58 | 28 3 | 28 7 | 28 12 | 28 16 | 53 |
| 54 | 27 45 | 27 50 | 27 54 | 27 59 | 28 3 | 28 8 | 28 12 | 28 17 | 28 21 | 28 26 | 28 30 | 28 35 | 28 39 | 28 44 | 28 48 | 54 |
| 55 | 28 16 | 28 20 | 28 25 | 28 30 | 28 34 | 28 39 | 28 43 | 28 48 | 28 53 | 28 57 | 29 2 | 29 6 | 29 11 | 29 15 | 29 20 | 55 |
| 56 | 28 47 | 28 51 | 28 56 | 29 1 | 29 5 | 29 10 | 29 15 | 29 19 | 29 24 | 29 29 | 29 33 | 29 38 | 29 43 | 29 47 | 29 52 | 56 |
| 57 | 29 18 | 29 22 | 29 27 | 29 32 | 29 37 | 29 41 | 29 46 | 29 51 | 29 56 | 30 0 | 30 5 | 30 10 | 30 15 | 30 19 | 30 24 | 57 |
| 58 | 29 48 | 29 53 | 29 58 | 30 3 | 30 8 | 30 13 | 30 17 | 30 22 | 30 27 | 30 32 | 30 37 | 30 42 | 30 46 | 30 51 | 30 56 | 58 |
| 59 | 30 19 | 30 24 | 30 29 | 30 34 | 30 39 | 30 44 | 30 49 | 30 54 | 30 59 | 31 3 | 31 8 | 31 13 | 31 18 | 31 23 | 31 28 | 59 |
| 60 | 30 50 | 30 55 | 31 0 | 31 5 | 31 10 | 31 15 | 31 20 | 31 25 | 31 30 | 31 35 | 31 40 | 31 45 | 31 50 | 31 55 | 32 0 | 60 |
| **HOURS** 1 | 30 50 | 30 55 | 31 0 | 31 5 | 31 10 | 31 15 | 31 20 | 31 25 | 31 30 | 31 35 | 31 40 | 31 45 | 31 50 | 31 55 | 32 0 | 1 **HOURS** |
| 2 | 1 1 40 | 1 1 50 | 1 2 0 | 1 2 10 | 1 2 20 | 1 2 30 | 1 2 40 | 1 2 50 | 1 3 0 | 1 3 10 | 1 3 20 | 1 3 30 | 1 3 40 | 1 3 50 | 1 4 0 | 2 |
| 3 | 1 32 30 | 1 32 45 | 1 33 0 | 1 33 15 | 1 33 30 | 1 33 45 | 1 34 0 | 1 34 15 | 1 34 30 | 1 34 45 | 1 35 0 | 1 35 15 | 1 35 30 | 1 35 45 | 1 36 0 | 3 |
| 4 | 2 3 20 | 2 3 40 | 2 4 0 | 2 4 20 | 2 4 40 | 2 5 0 | 2 5 20 | 2 5 40 | 2 6 0 | 2 6 20 | 2 6 40 | 2 7 0 | 2 7 20 | 2 7 40 | 2 8 0 | 4 |
| 5 | 2 34 10 | 2 34 35 | 2 35 0 | 2 35 25 | 2 35 50 | 2 36 15 | 2 36 40 | 2 37 5 | 2 37 30 | 2 37 55 | 2 38 20 | 2 38 45 | 2 39 10 | 2 39 35 | 2 40 0 | 5 |
| 6 | 3 5 0 | 3 5 30 | 3 6 0 | 3 6 30 | 3 7 0 | 3 7 30 | 3 8 0 | 3 8 30 | 3 9 0 | 3 9 30 | 3 10 0 | 3 10 30 | 3 11 0 | 3 11 30 | 3 12 0 | 6 |
| 7 | 3 35 50 | 3 36 25 | 3 37 0 | 3 37 35 | 3 38 10 | 3 38 45 | 3 39 20 | 3 39 55 | 3 40 30 | 3 41 5 | 3 41 40 | 3 42 15 | 3 42 50 | 3 43 25 | 3 44 0 | 7 |
| 8 | 4 6 40 | 4 7 20 | 4 8 0 | 4 8 40 | 4 9 20 | 4 10 0 | 4 10 40 | 4 11 20 | 4 12 0 | 4 12 40 | 4 13 20 | 4 14 0 | 4 14 40 | 4 15 20 | 4 16 0 | 8 |
| 9 | 4 37 30 | 4 38 15 | 4 39 0 | 4 39 45 | 4 40 30 | 4 41 15 | 4 42 0 | 4 42 45 | 4 43 30 | 4 44 15 | 4 45 0 | 4 45 45 | 4 46 30 | 4 47 15 | 4 48 0 | 9 |
| 10 | 5 8 20 | 5 9 10 | 5 10 0 | 5 10 50 | 5 11 40 | 5 12 30 | 5 13 20 | 5 14 10 | 5 15 0 | 5 15 50 | 5 16 40 | 5 17 30 | 5 18 20 | 5 19 10 | 5 20 0 | 10 |
| 11 | 5 39 10 | 5 40 5 | 5 41 0 | 5 41 55 | 5 42 50 | 5 43 45 | 5 44 40 | 5 45 35 | 5 46 30 | 5 47 25 | 5 48 20 | 5 49 15 | 5 50 10 | 5 51 5 | 5 52 0 | 11 |
| 12 | 6 10 0 | 6 11 0 | 6 12 0 | 6 13 0 | 6 14 0 | 6 15 0 | 6 16 0 | 6 17 0 | 6 18 0 | 6 19 0 | 6 20 0 | 6 21 0 | 6 22 0 | 6 23 0 | 6 24 0 | 12 |

# Table VI Semidiurnal Motion of the Moon

**12 HOUR TRAVEL**

### MINUTES

| TIME | 6°25' | 6°26' | 6°27' | 6°28' | 6°29' | 6°30' | 6°31' | 6°32' | 6°33' | 6°34' | 6°35' | 6°36' | 6°37' | 6°38' | 6°39' | TIME |
|---|---|---|---|---|---|---|---|---|---|---|---|---|---|---|---|---|
| 1 | 0 32 | 0 32 | 0 32 | 0 32 | 0 32 | 0 33 | 0 33 | 0 33 | 0 33 | 0 33 | 0 33 | 0 33 | 0 33 | 0 33 | 0 33 | 1 |
| 2 | 1 4 | 1 4 | 1 5 | 1 5 | 1 5 | 1 5 | 1 5 | 1 5 | 1 6 | 1 6 | 1 6 | 1 6 | 1 6 | 1 6 | 1 7 | 2 |
| 3 | 1 36 | 1 37 | 1 37 | 1 37 | 1 37 | 1 38 | 1 38 | 1 38 | 1 38 | 1 39 | 1 39 | 1 39 | 1 39 | 1 40 | 1 40 | 3 |
| 4 | 2 8 | 2 9 | 2 9 | 2 9 | 2 10 | 2 10 | 2 10 | 2 11 | 2 11 | 2 11 | 2 12 | 2 12 | 2 12 | 2 13 | 2 13 | 4 |
| 5 | 2 40 | 2 41 | 2 41 | 2 42 | 2 42 | 2 43 | 2 43 | 2 43 | 2 44 | 2 44 | 2 45 | 2 45 | 2 45 | 2 46 | 2 46 | 5 |
| 6 | 3 13 | 3 13 | 3 14 | 3 14 | 3 15 | 3 15 | 3 16 | 3 16 | 3 17 | 3 17 | 3 18 | 3 18 | 3 19 | 3 19 | 3 20 | 6 |
| 7 | 3 45 | 3 45 | 3 46 | 3 46 | 3 47 | 3 48 | 3 48 | 3 49 | 3 49 | 3 50 | 3 50 | 3 51 | 3 52 | 3 52 | 3 53 | 7 |
| 8 | 4 17 | 4 17 | 4 18 | 4 19 | 4 19 | 4 20 | 4 21 | 4 21 | 4 22 | 4 23 | 4 23 | 4 24 | 4 25 | 4 25 | 4 26 | 8 |
| 9 | 4 49 | 4 50 | 4 50 | 4 51 | 4 52 | 4 53 | 4 53 | 4 54 | 4 55 | 4 56 | 4 56 | 4 57 | 4 58 | 4 59 | 4 59 | 9 |
| 10 | 5 21 | 5 22 | 5 23 | 5 23 | 5 24 | 5 25 | 5 26 | 5 27 | 5 28 | 5 28 | 5 29 | 5 30 | 5 31 | 5 32 | 5 33 | 10 |
| 11 | 5 53 | 5 54 | 5 55 | 5 56 | 5 57 | 5 58 | 5 58 | 5 59 | 6 0 | 6 1 | 6 2 | 6 3 | 6 4 | 6 5 | 6 6 | 11 |
| 12 | 6 25 | 6 26 | 6 27 | 6 28 | 6 29 | 6 30 | 6 31 | 6 32 | 6 33 | 6 34 | 6 35 | 6 36 | 6 37 | 6 38 | 6 39 | 12 |
| 13 | 6 57 | 6 58 | 6 59 | 7 0 | 7 1 | 7 3 | 7 4 | 7 5 | 7 6 | 7 7 | 7 8 | 7 9 | 7 10 | 7 11 | 7 12 | 13 |
| 14 | 7 29 | 7 30 | 7 32 | 7 33 | 7 34 | 7 35 | 7 36 | 7 37 | 7 39 | 7 40 | 7 41 | 7 42 | 7 43 | 7 44 | 7 46 | 14 |
| 15 | 8 1 | 8 3 | 8 4 | 8 5 | 8 6 | 8 8 | 8 9 | 8 10 | 8 11 | 8 13 | 8 14 | 8 15 | 8 16 | 8 18 | 8 19 | 15 |
| 16 | 8 33 | 8 35 | 8 36 | 8 37 | 8 39 | 8 40 | 8 41 | 8 43 | 8 44 | 8 45 | 8 47 | 8 48 | 8 49 | 8 51 | 8 52 | 16 |
| 17 | 9 5 | 9 7 | 9 8 | 9 10 | 9 11 | 9 13 | 9 14 | 9 15 | 9 17 | 9 18 | 9 20 | 9 21 | 9 22 | 9 24 | 9 25 | 17 |
| 18 | 9 38 | 9 39 | 9 41 | 9 42 | 9 44 | 9 45 | 9 47 | 9 48 | 9 50 | 9 51 | 9 53 | 9 54 | 9 56 | 9 57 | 9 59 | 18 |
| 19 | 10 10 | 10 11 | 10 13 | 10 14 | 10 16 | 10 18 | 10 19 | 10 21 | 10 22 | 10 24 | 10 25 | 10 27 | 10 29 | 10 30 | 10 32 | 19 |
| 20 | 10 42 | 10 43 | 10 45 | 10 47 | 10 48 | 10 50 | 10 52 | 10 53 | 10 55 | 10 57 | 10 58 | 11 0 | 11 2 | 11 3 | 11 5 | 20 |
| 21 | 11 14 | 11 16 | 11 17 | 11 19 | 11 21 | 11 23 | 11 24 | 11 26 | 11 28 | 11 30 | 11 31 | 11 33 | 11 35 | 11 37 | 11 38 | 21 |
| 22 | 11 46 | 11 48 | 11 50 | 11 51 | 11 53 | 11 55 | 11 57 | 11 59 | 12 1 | 12 2 | 12 4 | 12 6 | 12 8 | 12 10 | 12 12 | 22 |
| 23 | 12 18 | 12 20 | 12 22 | 12 24 | 12 26 | 12 28 | 12 29 | 12 31 | 12 33 | 12 35 | 12 37 | 12 39 | 12 41 | 12 43 | 12 45 | 23 |
| 24 | 12 50 | 12 52 | 12 54 | 12 56 | 12 58 | 13 0 | 13 2 | 13 4 | 13 6 | 13 8 | 13 10 | 13 12 | 13 14 | 13 16 | 13 18 | 24 |
| 25 | 13 22 | 13 24 | 13 26 | 13 28 | 13 30 | 13 33 | 13 35 | 13 37 | 13 39 | 13 41 | 13 43 | 13 45 | 13 47 | 13 49 | 13 51 | 25 |
| 26 | 13 54 | 13 56 | 13 59 | 14 1 | 14 3 | 14 5 | 14 7 | 14 9 | 14 12 | 14 14 | 14 16 | 14 18 | 14 20 | 14 22 | 14 25 | 26 |
| 27 | 14 26 | 14 29 | 14 31 | 14 33 | 14 35 | 14 38 | 14 40 | 14 42 | 14 44 | 14 47 | 14 49 | 14 51 | 14 53 | 14 56 | 14 58 | 27 |
| 28 | 14 58 | 15 1 | 15 3 | 15 5 | 15 8 | 15 10 | 15 12 | 15 15 | 15 17 | 15 19 | 15 22 | 15 24 | 15 26 | 15 29 | 15 31 | 28 |
| 29 | 15 30 | 15 33 | 15 35 | 15 38 | 15 40 | 15 43 | 15 45 | 15 47 | 15 50 | 15 52 | 15 55 | 15 57 | 15 59 | 16 2 | 16 4 | 29 |
| 30 | 16 3 | 16 5 | 16 8 | 16 10 | 16 13 | 16 15 | 16 18 | 16 20 | 16 23 | 16 25 | 16 28 | 16 30 | 16 33 | 16 35 | 16 38 | 30 |
| 31 | 16 35 | 16 37 | 16 40 | 16 42 | 16 45 | 16 48 | 16 50 | 16 53 | 16 55 | 16 58 | 17 0 | 17 3 | 17 6 | 17 8 | 17 11 | 31 |
| 32 | 17 7 | 17 9 | 17 12 | 17 15 | 17 17 | 17 20 | 17 23 | 17 25 | 17 28 | 17 31 | 17 33 | 17 36 | 17 39 | 17 41 | 17 44 | 32 |
| 33 | 17 39 | 17 42 | 17 44 | 17 47 | 17 50 | 17 53 | 17 55 | 17 58 | 18 1 | 18 4 | 18 6 | 18 9 | 18 12 | 18 15 | 18 17 | 33 |
| 34 | 18 11 | 18 14 | 18 17 | 18 19 | 18 22 | 18 25 | 18 28 | 18 31 | 18 34 | 18 36 | 18 39 | 18 42 | 18 45 | 18 48 | 18 51 | 34 |
| 35 | 18 43 | 18 46 | 18 49 | 18 52 | 18 55 | 18 58 | 19 0 | 19 3 | 19 6 | 19 9 | 19 12 | 19 15 | 19 18 | 19 21 | 19 24 | 35 |
| 36 | 19 15 | 19 18 | 19 21 | 19 24 | 19 27 | 19 30 | 19 33 | 19 36 | 19 39 | 19 42 | 19 45 | 19 48 | 19 51 | 19 54 | 19 57 | 36 |
| 37 | 19 47 | 19 50 | 19 53 | 19 56 | 19 59 | 20 3 | 20 6 | 20 9 | 20 12 | 20 15 | 20 18 | 20 21 | 20 24 | 20 27 | 20 30 | 37 |
| 38 | 20 19 | 20 22 | 20 26 | 20 29 | 20 32 | 20 35 | 20 38 | 20 41 | 20 45 | 20 48 | 20 51 | 20 54 | 20 57 | 21 0 | 21 4 | 38 |
| 39 | 20 51 | 20 55 | 20 58 | 21 1 | 21 4 | 21 8 | 21 11 | 21 14 | 21 17 | 21 21 | 21 24 | 21 27 | 21 30 | 21 34 | 21 37 | 39 |
| 40 | 21 23 | 21 27 | 21 30 | 21 33 | 21 37 | 21 40 | 21 43 | 21 47 | 21 50 | 21 53 | 21 57 | 22 0 | 22 3 | 22 7 | 22 10 | 40 |
| 41 | 21 55 | 21 59 | 22 2 | 22 6 | 22 9 | 22 13 | 22 16 | 22 19 | 22 23 | 22 26 | 22 30 | 22 33 | 22 36 | 22 40 | 22 43 | 41 |
| 42 | 22 28 | 22 31 | 22 35 | 22 38 | 22 42 | 22 45 | 22 49 | 22 52 | 22 56 | 22 59 | 23 3 | 23 6 | 23 10 | 23 13 | 23 17 | 42 |
| 43 | 23 0 | 23 3 | 23 7 | 23 10 | 23 14 | 23 18 | 23 21 | 23 25 | 23 28 | 23 32 | 23 35 | 23 39 | 23 43 | 23 46 | 23 50 | 43 |
| 44 | 23 32 | 23 35 | 23 39 | 23 43 | 23 46 | 23 50 | 23 54 | 23 57 | 24 1 | 24 5 | 24 8 | 24 12 | 24 16 | 24 19 | 24 23 | 44 |
| 45 | 24 4 | 24 8 | 24 11 | 24 15 | 24 19 | 24 23 | 24 26 | 24 30 | 24 34 | 24 38 | 24 41 | 24 45 | 24 49 | 24 53 | 24 56 | 45 |
| 46 | 24 36 | 24 40 | 24 44 | 24 47 | 24 51 | 24 55 | 24 59 | 25 3 | 25 7 | 25 10 | 25 14 | 25 18 | 25 22 | 25 26 | 25 30 | 46 |
| 47 | 25 8 | 25 12 | 25 16 | 25 20 | 25 24 | 25 28 | 25 31 | 25 35 | 25 39 | 25 43 | 25 47 | 25 51 | 25 55 | 25 59 | 26 3 | 47 |
| 48 | 25 40 | 25 44 | 25 48 | 25 52 | 25 56 | 26 0 | 26 4 | 26 8 | 26 12 | 26 16 | 26 20 | 26 24 | 26 28 | 26 32 | 26 36 | 48 |
| 49 | 26 12 | 26 16 | 26 20 | 26 24 | 26 28 | 26 33 | 26 37 | 26 41 | 26 45 | 26 49 | 26 53 | 26 57 | 27 1 | 27 5 | 27 9 | 49 |
| 50 | 26 44 | 26 48 | 26 53 | 26 57 | 27 1 | 27 5 | 27 9 | 27 13 | 27 18 | 27 22 | 27 26 | 27 30 | 27 34 | 27 38 | 27 43 | 50 |
| 51 | 27 16 | 27 21 | 27 25 | 27 29 | 27 33 | 27 38 | 27 42 | 27 46 | 27 50 | 27 55 | 27 59 | 28 3 | 28 7 | 28 12 | 28 16 | 51 |
| 52 | 27 48 | 27 53 | 27 57 | 28 1 | 28 6 | 28 10 | 28 14 | 28 19 | 28 23 | 28 27 | 28 32 | 28 36 | 28 40 | 28 45 | 28 49 | 52 |
| 53 | 28 20 | 28 25 | 28 29 | 28 34 | 28 38 | 28 43 | 28 47 | 28 51 | 28 56 | 29 0 | 29 5 | 29 9 | 29 13 | 29 18 | 29 22 | 53 |
| 54 | 28 53 | 28 57 | 29 2 | 29 6 | 29 11 | 29 15 | 29 20 | 29 24 | 29 29 | 29 33 | 29 38 | 29 42 | 29 47 | 29 51 | 29 56 | 54 |
| 55 | 29 25 | 29 29 | 29 34 | 29 38 | 29 43 | 29 48 | 29 52 | 29 57 | 30 1 | 30 6 | 30 10 | 30 15 | 30 20 | 30 24 | 30 29 | 55 |
| 56 | 29 57 | 30 1 | 30 6 | 30 11 | 30 15 | 30 20 | 30 25 | 30 29 | 30 34 | 30 39 | 30 43 | 30 48 | 30 53 | 30 57 | 31 2 | 56 |
| 57 | 30 29 | 30 34 | 30 38 | 30 43 | 30 48 | 30 53 | 30 57 | 31 2 | 31 7 | 31 12 | 31 16 | 31 21 | 31 26 | 31 31 | 31 35 | 57 |
| 58 | 31 1 | 31 6 | 31 11 | 31 15 | 31 20 | 31 25 | 31 30 | 31 35 | 31 40 | 31 44 | 31 49 | 31 54 | 31 59 | 32 4 | 32 9 | 58 |
| 59 | 31 33 | 31 38 | 31 43 | 31 48 | 31 53 | 31 58 | 32 2 | 32 7 | 32 12 | 32 17 | 32 22 | 32 27 | 32 32 | 32 37 | 32 42 | 59 |
| 60 | 32 5 | 32 10 | 32 15 | 32 20 | 32 25 | 32 30 | 32 35 | 32 40 | 32 45 | 32 50 | 32 55 | 33 0 | 33 5 | 33 10 | 33 15 | 60 |

### HOURS

| TIME | 6°25' | 6°26' | 6°27' | 6°28' | 6°29' | 6°30' | 6°31' | 6°32' | 6°33' | 6°34' | 6°35' | 6°36' | 6°37' | 6°38' | 6°39' | TIME |
|---|---|---|---|---|---|---|---|---|---|---|---|---|---|---|---|---|
| 1 | 32 5 | 32 10 | 32 15 | 32 20 | 32 25 | 32 30 | 32 35 | 32 40 | 32 45 | 32 50 | 32 55 | 33 0 | 33 5 | 33 10 | 33 15 | 1 |
| 2 | 1 4 10 | 1 4 20 | 1 4 30 | 1 4 40 | 1 4 50 | 1 5 0 | 1 5 10 | 1 5 20 | 1 5 30 | 1 5 40 | 1 5 50 | 1 6 0 | 1 6 10 | 1 6 20 | 1 6 30 | 2 |
| 3 | 1 36 15 | 1 36 30 | 1 36 45 | 1 37 0 | 1 37 15 | 1 37 30 | 1 37 45 | 1 38 0 | 1 38 15 | 1 38 30 | 1 38 45 | 1 39 0 | 1 39 15 | 1 39 30 | 1 39 45 | 3 |
| 4 | 2 8 20 | 2 8 40 | 2 9 0 | 2 9 20 | 2 9 40 | 2 10 0 | 2 10 20 | 2 10 40 | 2 11 0 | 2 11 20 | 2 11 40 | 2 12 0 | 2 12 20 | 2 12 40 | 2 13 0 | 4 |
| 5 | 2 40 25 | 2 40 50 | 2 41 15 | 2 41 40 | 2 42 5 | 2 42 30 | 2 42 55 | 2 43 20 | 2 43 45 | 2 44 10 | 2 44 35 | 2 45 0 | 2 45 25 | 2 45 50 | 2 46 15 | 5 |
| 6 | 3 12 30 | 3 13 0 | 3 13 30 | 3 14 0 | 3 14 30 | 3 15 0 | 3 15 30 | 3 16 0 | 3 16 30 | 3 17 0 | 3 17 30 | 3 18 0 | 3 18 30 | 3 19 0 | 3 19 30 | 6 |
| 7 | 3 44 35 | 3 45 10 | 3 45 45 | 3 46 20 | 3 46 55 | 3 47 30 | 3 48 5 | 3 48 40 | 3 49 15 | 3 49 50 | 3 50 25 | 3 51 0 | 3 51 35 | 3 52 10 | 3 52 45 | 7 |
| 8 | 4 16 40 | 4 17 20 | 4 18 0 | 4 18 40 | 4 19 20 | 4 20 0 | 4 20 40 | 4 21 20 | 4 22 0 | 4 22 40 | 4 23 20 | 4 24 0 | 4 24 40 | 4 25 20 | 4 26 0 | 8 |
| 9 | 4 48 45 | 4 49 30 | 4 50 15 | 4 51 0 | 4 51 45 | 4 52 30 | 4 53 15 | 4 54 0 | 4 54 45 | 4 55 30 | 4 56 15 | 4 57 0 | 4 57 45 | 4 58 30 | 4 59 15 | 9 |
| 10 | 5 20 50 | 5 21 40 | 5 22 30 | 5 23 20 | 5 24 10 | 5 25 0 | 5 25 50 | 5 26 40 | 5 27 30 | 5 28 20 | 5 29 10 | 5 30 0 | 5 30 50 | 5 31 40 | 5 32 30 | 10 |
| 11 | 5 52 55 | 5 53 50 | 5 54 45 | 5 55 40 | 5 56 35 | 5 57 30 | 5 58 25 | 5 59 20 | 6 0 15 | 6 1 10 | 6 2 5 | 6 3 0 | 6 3 55 | 6 4 50 | 6 5 45 | 11 |
| 12 | 6 25 0 | 6 26 0 | 6 27 0 | 6 28 0 | 6 29 0 | 6 30 0 | 6 31 0 | 6 32 0 | 6 33 0 | 6 34 0 | 6 35 0 | 6 36 0 | 6 37 0 | 6 38 0 | 6 39 0 | 12 |

# Table VI Semidiurnal Motion of the Moon

| TIME (MINUTES) | 6° 40' | 6° 41' | 6° 42' | 6° 43' | 6° 44' | 6° 45' | 6° 46' | 6° 47' | 6° 48' | 6° 49' | 6° 50' | 6° 51' | 6° 52' | 6° 53' | 6° 54' | TIME (MINUTES) |
|---|---|---|---|---|---|---|---|---|---|---|---|---|---|---|---|---|
| 1 | 0 33 | 0 33 | 0 34 | 0 34 | 0 34 | 0 34 | 0 34 | 0 34 | 0 34 | 0 34 | 0 34 | 0 34 | 0 34 | 0 34 | 0 35 | 1 |
| 2 | 1 7 | 1 7 | 1 7 | 1 7 | 1 7 | 1 7 | 1 8 | 1 8 | 1 8 | 1 8 | 1 8 | 1 9 | 1 9 | 1 9 | 1 9 | 2 |
| 3 | 1 40 | 1 40 | 1 41 | 1 41 | 1 41 | 1 41 | 1 42 | 1 42 | 1 42 | 1 42 | 1 43 | 1 43 | 1 43 | 1 43 | 1 44 | 3 |
| 4 | 2 13 | 2 14 | 2 14 | 2 14 | 2 15 | 2 15 | 2 15 | 2 16 | 2 16 | 2 16 | 2 17 | 2 17 | 2 17 | 2 18 | 2 18 | 4 |
| 5 | 2 47 | 2 47 | 2 48 | 2 48 | 2 48 | 2 49 | 2 49 | 2 50 | 2 50 | 2 50 | 2 51 | 2 51 | 2 52 | 2 52 | 2 53 | 5 |
| 6 | 3 20 | 3 21 | 3 21 | 3 22 | 3 22 | 3 23 | 3 23 | 3 24 | 3 24 | 3 25 | 3 25 | 3 26 | 3 26 | 3 27 | 3 27 | 6 |
| 7 | 3 53 | 3 54 | 3 55 | 3 55 | 3 56 | 3 56 | 3 57 | 3 57 | 3 58 | 3 59 | 3 59 | 4 0 | 4 0 | 4 1 | 4 2 | 7 |
| 8 | 4 27 | 4 27 | 4 28 | 4 29 | 4 29 | 4 30 | 4 31 | 4 31 | 4 32 | 4 33 | 4 33 | 4 34 | 4 35 | 4 35 | 4 36 | 8 |
| 9 | 5 0 | 5 1 | 5 2 | 5 2 | 5 3 | 5 4 | 5 5 | 5 5 | 5 6 | 5 7 | 5 8 | 5 8 | 5 9 | 5 10 | 5 11 | 9 |
| 10 | 5 33 | 5 34 | 5 35 | 5 36 | 5 37 | 5 38 | 5 38 | 5 39 | 5 40 | 5 41 | 5 42 | 5 43 | 5 43 | 5 44 | 5 45 | 10 |
| 11 | 6 7 | 6 8 | 6 9 | 6 9 | 6 10 | 6 11 | 6 12 | 6 13 | 6 14 | 6 15 | 6 16 | 6 17 | 6 18 | 6 19 | 6 20 | 11 |
| 12 | 6 40 | 6 41 | 6 42 | 6 43 | 6 44 | 6 45 | 6 46 | 6 47 | 6 48 | 6 49 | 6 50 | 6 51 | 6 52 | 6 53 | 6 54 | 12 |
| 13 | 7 13 | 7 14 | 7 16 | 7 17 | 7 18 | 7 19 | 7 20 | 7 21 | 7 22 | 7 23 | 7 24 | 7 25 | 7 26 | 7 27 | 7 29 | 13 |
| 14 | 7 47 | 7 48 | 7 49 | 7 50 | 7 51 | 7 53 | 7 54 | 7 55 | 7 56 | 7 57 | 7 58 | 8 0 | 8 1 | 8 2 | 8 3 | 14 |
| 15 | 8 20 | 8 21 | 8 23 | 8 24 | 8 25 | 8 26 | 8 28 | 8 29 | 8 30 | 8 31 | 8 33 | 8 34 | 8 35 | 8 36 | 8 38 | 15 |
| 16 | 8 53 | 8 55 | 8 56 | 8 57 | 8 59 | 9 0 | 9 1 | 9 3 | 9 4 | 9 5 | 9 7 | 9 8 | 9 9 | 9 11 | 9 12 | 16 |
| 17 | 9 27 | 9 28 | 9 30 | 9 31 | 9 32 | 9 34 | 9 35 | 9 37 | 9 38 | 9 39 | 9 41 | 9 42 | 9 44 | 9 45 | 9 47 | 17 |
| 18 | 10 0 | 10 2 | 10 3 | 10 5 | 10 6 | 10 8 | 10 9 | 10 11 | 10 12 | 10 14 | 10 15 | 10 17 | 10 18 | 10 20 | 10 21 | 18 |
| 19 | 10 33 | 10 35 | 10 37 | 10 38 | 10 40 | 10 41 | 10 43 | 10 44 | 10 46 | 10 48 | 10 49 | 10 51 | 10 52 | 10 54 | 10 56 | 19 |
| 20 | 11 7 | 11 8 | 11 10 | 11 12 | 11 13 | 11 15 | 11 17 | 11 18 | 11 20 | 11 22 | 11 23 | 11 25 | 11 27 | 11 28 | 11 30 | 20 |
| 21 | 11 40 | 11 42 | 11 44 | 11 45 | 11 47 | 11 49 | 11 51 | 11 52 | 11 54 | 11 56 | 11 58 | 11 59 | 12 1 | 12 3 | 12 5 | 21 |
| 22 | 12 13 | 12 15 | 12 17 | 12 19 | 12 21 | 12 23 | 12 24 | 12 26 | 12 28 | 12 30 | 12 32 | 12 34 | 12 35 | 12 37 | 12 39 | 22 |
| 23 | 12 47 | 12 49 | 12 51 | 12 52 | 12 54 | 12 56 | 12 58 | 13 0 | 13 2 | 13 4 | 13 6 | 13 8 | 13 10 | 13 12 | 13 14 | 23 |
| 24 | 13 20 | 13 22 | 13 24 | 13 26 | 13 28 | 13 30 | 13 32 | 13 34 | 13 36 | 13 38 | 13 40 | 13 42 | 13 44 | 13 46 | 13 48 | 24 |
| 25 | 13 53 | 13 55 | 13 58 | 14 0 | 14 2 | 14 4 | 14 6 | 14 8 | 14 10 | 14 12 | 14 14 | 14 16 | 14 18 | 14 20 | 14 23 | 25 |
| 26 | 14 27 | 14 29 | 14 31 | 14 33 | 14 35 | 14 38 | 14 40 | 14 42 | 14 44 | 14 46 | 14 48 | 14 51 | 14 53 | 14 55 | 14 57 | 26 |
| 27 | 15 0 | 15 2 | 15 5 | 15 7 | 15 9 | 15 11 | 15 14 | 15 16 | 15 18 | 15 20 | 15 23 | 15 25 | 15 27 | 15 29 | 15 32 | 27 |
| 28 | 15 33 | 15 36 | 15 38 | 15 40 | 15 43 | 15 45 | 15 47 | 15 50 | 15 52 | 15 54 | 15 57 | 15 59 | 16 1 | 16 4 | 16 6 | 28 |
| 29 | 16 7 | 16 9 | 16 12 | 16 14 | 16 16 | 16 19 | 16 21 | 16 24 | 16 26 | 16 28 | 16 31 | 16 33 | 16 36 | 16 38 | 16 41 | 29 |
| 30 | 16 40 | 16 43 | 16 45 | 16 48 | 16 50 | 16 53 | 16 55 | 16 58 | 17 0 | 17 3 | 17 5 | 17 8 | 17 10 | 17 13 | 17 15 | 30 |
| 31 | 17 13 | 17 16 | 17 19 | 17 21 | 17 24 | 17 26 | 17 29 | 17 31 | 17 34 | 17 37 | 17 39 | 17 42 | 17 44 | 17 47 | 17 50 | 31 |
| 32 | 17 47 | 17 49 | 17 52 | 17 55 | 17 57 | 18 0 | 18 3 | 18 5 | 18 8 | 18 11 | 18 13 | 18 16 | 18 19 | 18 21 | 18 24 | 32 |
| 33 | 18 20 | 18 23 | 18 26 | 18 28 | 18 31 | 18 34 | 18 37 | 18 39 | 18 42 | 18 45 | 18 48 | 18 50 | 18 53 | 18 56 | 18 59 | 33 |
| 34 | 18 53 | 18 56 | 18 59 | 19 2 | 19 5 | 19 8 | 19 10 | 19 13 | 19 16 | 19 19 | 19 22 | 19 25 | 19 27 | 19 30 | 19 33 | 34 |
| 35 | 19 27 | 19 30 | 19 33 | 19 35 | 19 38 | 19 41 | 19 44 | 19 47 | 19 50 | 19 53 | 19 56 | 19 59 | 20 2 | 20 5 | 20 8 | 35 |
| 36 | 20 0 | 20 3 | 20 6 | 20 9 | 20 12 | 20 15 | 20 18 | 20 21 | 20 24 | 20 27 | 20 30 | 20 33 | 20 36 | 20 39 | 20 42 | 36 |
| 37 | 20 33 | 20 36 | 20 40 | 20 43 | 20 46 | 20 49 | 20 52 | 20 55 | 20 58 | 21 1 | 21 4 | 21 7 | 21 10 | 21 13 | 21 17 | 37 |
| 38 | 21 7 | 21 10 | 21 13 | 21 16 | 21 19 | 21 23 | 21 26 | 21 29 | 21 32 | 21 35 | 21 38 | 21 42 | 21 45 | 21 48 | 21 51 | 38 |
| 39 | 21 40 | 21 43 | 21 47 | 21 50 | 21 53 | 21 56 | 22 0 | 22 3 | 22 6 | 22 9 | 22 13 | 22 16 | 22 19 | 22 22 | 22 26 | 39 |
| 40 | 22 13 | 22 17 | 22 20 | 22 23 | 22 27 | 22 30 | 22 33 | 22 37 | 22 40 | 22 43 | 22 47 | 22 50 | 22 53 | 22 57 | 23 0 | 40 |
| 41 | 22 47 | 22 50 | 22 54 | 22 57 | 23 0 | 23 4 | 23 7 | 23 11 | 23 14 | 23 17 | 23 21 | 23 24 | 23 28 | 23 31 | 23 35 | 41 |
| 42 | 23 20 | 23 24 | 23 27 | 23 31 | 23 34 | 23 38 | 23 41 | 23 45 | 23 48 | 23 52 | 23 55 | 23 59 | 24 2 | 24 6 | 24 9 | 42 |
| 43 | 23 53 | 23 57 | 24 1 | 24 4 | 24 8 | 24 11 | 24 15 | 24 18 | 24 22 | 24 26 | 24 29 | 24 33 | 24 36 | 24 40 | 24 44 | 43 |
| 44 | 24 27 | 24 30 | 24 34 | 24 38 | 24 41 | 24 45 | 24 49 | 24 52 | 24 56 | 25 0 | 25 3 | 25 7 | 25 11 | 25 14 | 25 18 | 44 |
| 45 | 25 0 | 25 4 | 25 8 | 25 11 | 25 15 | 25 19 | 25 23 | 25 26 | 25 30 | 25 34 | 25 38 | 25 41 | 25 45 | 25 49 | 25 53 | 45 |
| 46 | 25 33 | 25 37 | 25 41 | 25 45 | 25 49 | 25 53 | 25 56 | 26 0 | 26 4 | 26 8 | 26 12 | 26 16 | 26 19 | 26 23 | 26 27 | 46 |
| 47 | 26 7 | 26 11 | 26 15 | 26 18 | 26 22 | 26 26 | 26 30 | 26 34 | 26 38 | 26 42 | 26 46 | 26 50 | 26 54 | 26 58 | 27 2 | 47 |
| 48 | 26 40 | 26 44 | 26 48 | 26 52 | 26 56 | 27 0 | 27 4 | 27 8 | 27 12 | 27 16 | 27 20 | 27 24 | 27 28 | 27 32 | 27 36 | 48 |
| 49 | 27 13 | 27 17 | 27 22 | 27 26 | 27 30 | 27 34 | 27 38 | 27 42 | 27 46 | 27 50 | 27 54 | 27 58 | 28 2 | 28 6 | 28 11 | 49 |
| 50 | 27 47 | 27 51 | 27 55 | 27 59 | 28 3 | 28 8 | 28 12 | 28 16 | 28 20 | 28 24 | 28 28 | 28 33 | 28 37 | 28 41 | 28 45 | 50 |
| 51 | 28 20 | 28 24 | 28 29 | 28 33 | 28 37 | 28 41 | 28 46 | 28 50 | 28 54 | 28 58 | 29 3 | 29 7 | 29 11 | 29 15 | 29 20 | 51 |
| 52 | 28 53 | 28 58 | 29 2 | 29 6 | 29 11 | 29 15 | 29 19 | 29 24 | 29 28 | 29 32 | 29 37 | 29 41 | 29 45 | 29 50 | 29 54 | 52 |
| 53 | 29 27 | 29 31 | 29 36 | 29 40 | 29 44 | 29 49 | 29 53 | 29 58 | 30 2 | 30 6 | 30 11 | 30 15 | 30 20 | 30 24 | 30 29 | 53 |
| 54 | 30 0 | 30 5 | 30 9 | 30 14 | 30 18 | 30 23 | 30 27 | 30 32 | 30 36 | 30 41 | 30 45 | 30 50 | 30 54 | 30 59 | 31 3 | 54 |
| 55 | 30 33 | 30 38 | 30 43 | 30 47 | 30 52 | 30 56 | 31 1 | 31 5 | 31 10 | 31 15 | 31 19 | 31 24 | 31 28 | 31 33 | 31 38 | 55 |
| 56 | 31 7 | 31 11 | 31 16 | 31 21 | 31 25 | 31 30 | 31 35 | 31 39 | 31 44 | 31 49 | 31 53 | 31 58 | 32 3 | 32 7 | 32 12 | 56 |
| 57 | 31 40 | 31 45 | 31 50 | 31 54 | 31 59 | 32 4 | 32 9 | 32 13 | 32 18 | 32 23 | 32 28 | 32 32 | 32 37 | 32 42 | 32 47 | 57 |
| 58 | 32 13 | 32 18 | 32 23 | 32 28 | 32 33 | 32 38 | 32 42 | 32 47 | 32 52 | 32 57 | 33 2 | 33 7 | 33 11 | 33 16 | 33 21 | 58 |
| 59 | 32 47 | 32 52 | 32 57 | 33 1 | 33 6 | 33 11 | 33 16 | 33 21 | 33 26 | 33 31 | 33 36 | 33 41 | 33 46 | 33 51 | 33 56 | 59 |
| 60 | 33 20 | 33 25 | 33 30 | 33 35 | 33 40 | 33 45 | 33 50 | 33 55 | 34 0 | 34 5 | 34 10 | 34 15 | 34 20 | 34 25 | 34 30 | 60 |

| TIME (HOURS) | 6° 40' | 6° 41' | 6° 42' | 6° 43' | 6° 44' | 6° 45' | 6° 46' | 6° 47' | 6° 48' | 6° 49' | 6° 50' | 6° 51' | 6° 52' | 6° 53' | 6° 54' | TIME (HOURS) |
|---|---|---|---|---|---|---|---|---|---|---|---|---|---|---|---|---|
| 1 | 33 20 | 33 25 | 33 30 | 33 35 | 33 40 | 33 45 | 33 50 | 33 55 | 34 0 | 34 5 | 34 10 | 34 15 | 34 20 | 34 25 | 34 30 | 1 |
| 2 | 1 6 40 | 1 6 50 | 1 7 0 | 1 7 10 | 1 7 20 | 1 7 30 | 1 7 40 | 1 7 50 | 1 8 0 | 1 8 10 | 1 8 20 | 1 8 30 | 1 8 40 | 1 8 50 | 1 9 0 | 2 |
| 3 | 1 40 0 | 1 40 15 | 1 40 30 | 1 40 45 | 1 41 0 | 1 41 15 | 1 41 30 | 1 41 45 | 1 42 0 | 1 42 15 | 1 42 30 | 1 42 45 | 1 43 0 | 1 43 15 | 1 43 30 | 3 |
| 4 | 2 13 20 | 2 13 40 | 2 14 0 | 2 14 20 | 2 14 40 | 2 15 0 | 2 15 20 | 2 15 40 | 2 16 0 | 2 16 20 | 2 16 40 | 2 17 0 | 2 17 20 | 2 17 40 | 2 18 0 | 4 |
| 5 | 2 46 40 | 2 47 5 | 2 47 30 | 2 47 55 | 2 48 20 | 2 48 45 | 2 49 10 | 2 49 35 | 2 50 0 | 2 50 25 | 2 50 50 | 2 51 15 | 2 51 40 | 2 52 5 | 2 52 30 | 5 |
| 6 | 3 20 0 | 3 20 30 | 3 21 0 | 3 21 30 | 3 22 0 | 3 22 30 | 3 23 0 | 3 23 30 | 3 24 0 | 3 24 30 | 3 25 0 | 3 25 30 | 3 26 0 | 3 26 30 | 3 27 0 | 6 |
| 7 | 3 53 20 | 3 53 55 | 3 54 30 | 3 55 5 | 3 55 40 | 3 56 15 | 3 56 50 | 3 57 25 | 3 58 0 | 3 58 35 | 3 59 10 | 3 59 45 | 4 0 20 | 4 0 55 | 4 1 30 | 7 |
| 8 | 4 26 40 | 4 27 20 | 4 28 0 | 4 28 40 | 4 29 20 | 4 30 0 | 4 30 40 | 4 31 20 | 4 32 0 | 4 32 40 | 4 33 20 | 4 34 0 | 4 34 40 | 4 35 20 | 4 36 0 | 8 |
| 9 | 5 0 0 | 5 0 45 | 5 1 30 | 5 2 15 | 5 3 0 | 5 3 45 | 5 4 30 | 5 5 15 | 5 6 0 | 5 6 45 | 5 7 30 | 5 8 15 | 5 9 0 | 5 9 45 | 5 10 30 | 9 |
| 10 | 5 33 20 | 5 34 10 | 5 35 0 | 5 35 50 | 5 36 40 | 5 37 30 | 5 38 20 | 5 39 10 | 5 40 0 | 5 40 50 | 5 41 40 | 5 42 30 | 5 43 20 | 5 44 10 | 5 45 0 | 10 |
| 11 | 6 6 40 | 6 7 35 | 6 8 30 | 6 9 25 | 6 10 20 | 6 11 15 | 6 12 10 | 6 13 5 | 6 14 0 | 6 14 55 | 6 15 50 | 6 16 45 | 6 17 40 | 6 18 35 | 6 19 30 | 11 |
| 12 | 6 40 0 | 6 41 0 | 6 42 0 | 6 43 0 | 6 44 0 | 6 45 0 | 6 46 0 | 6 47 0 | 6 48 0 | 6 49 0 | 6 50 0 | 6 51 0 | 6 52 0 | 6 53 0 | 6 54 0 | 12 |

# Table VI Semidiurnal Motion of the Moon

| TIME | 6° 55' | 6° 56' | 6° 57' | 6° 58' | 6° 59' | 7° 0' | 7° 1' | 7° 2' | 7° 3' | 7° 4' | 7° 5' | 7° 6' | 7° 7' | 7° 8' | 7° 9' | TIME |
|---|---|---|---|---|---|---|---|---|---|---|---|---|---|---|---|---|
| **12 HOUR TRAVEL** | | | | | | | | | | | | | | | | |
| **MINUTES 1** | 0 35 | 0 35 | 0 35 | 0 35 | 0 35 | 0 35 | 0 35 | 0 35 | 0 35 | 0 35 | 0 35 | 0 36 | 0 36 | 0 36 | 0 36 | **1 MINUTES** |
| 2 | 1 9 | 1 9 | 1 10 | 1 10 | 1 10 | 1 10 | 1 10 | 1 10 | 1 11 | 1 11 | 1 11 | 1 11 | 1 11 | 1 11 | 1 12 | 2 |
| 3 | 1 44 | 1 44 | 1 44 | 1 45 | 1 45 | 1 45 | 1 45 | 1 46 | 1 46 | 1 46 | 1 46 | 1 47 | 1 47 | 1 47 | 1 47 | 3 |
| 4 | 2 18 | 2 19 | 2 19 | 2 19 | 2 20 | 2 20 | 2 20 | 2 21 | 2 21 | 2 21 | 2 21 | 2 22 | 2 22 | 2 23 | 2 23 | 4 |
| 5 | 2 53 | 2 53 | 2 54 | 2 54 | 2 55 | 2 55 | 2 55 | 2 56 | 2 56 | 2 57 | 2 57 | 2 58 | 2 58 | 2 58 | 2 59 | 5 |
| 6 | 3 28 | 3 28 | 3 29 | 3 29 | 3 30 | 3 30 | 3 31 | 3 31 | 3 32 | 3 32 | 3 33 | 3 33 | 3 34 | 3 34 | 3 35 | 6 |
| 7 | 4 2 | 4 3 | 4 3 | 4 4 | 4 4 | 4 5 | 4 6 | 4 6 | 4 7 | 4 7 | 4 8 | 4 9 | 4 9 | 4 10 | 4 10 | 7 |
| 8 | 4 37 | 4 37 | 4 38 | 4 39 | 4 39 | 4 40 | 4 41 | 4 41 | 4 42 | 4 43 | 4 43 | 4 44 | 4 45 | 4 45 | 4 46 | 8 |
| 9 | 5 11 | 5 12 | 5 13 | 5 14 | 5 14 | 5 15 | 5 16 | 5 17 | 5 17 | 5 18 | 5 19 | 5 20 | 5 20 | 5 21 | 5 22 | 9 |
| 10 | 5 46 | 5 47 | 5 48 | 5 48 | 5 49 | 5 50 | 5 51 | 5 52 | 5 53 | 5 53 | 5 54 | 5 55 | 5 56 | 5 57 | 5 58 | 10 |
| 11 | 6 20 | 6 21 | 6 22 | 6 23 | 6 24 | 6 25 | 6 26 | 6 27 | 6 28 | 6 29 | 6 30 | 6 31 | 6 31 | 6 32 | 6 33 | 11 |
| 12 | 6 55 | 6 56 | 6 57 | 6 58 | 6 59 | 7 0 | 7 1 | 7 2 | 7 3 | 7 4 | 7 5 | 7 6 | 7 7 | 7 8 | 7 9 | 12 |
| 13 | 7 30 | 7 31 | 7 32 | 7 33 | 7 34 | 7 35 | 7 36 | 7 37 | 7 38 | 7 39 | 7 40 | 7 42 | 7 43 | 7 44 | 7 45 | 13 |
| 14 | 8 4 | 8 5 | 8 7 | 8 8 | 8 9 | 8 10 | 8 11 | 8 12 | 8 14 | 8 15 | 8 16 | 8 17 | 8 18 | 8 19 | 8 21 | 14 |
| 15 | 8 39 | 8 40 | 8 41 | 8 43 | 8 44 | 8 45 | 8 46 | 8 48 | 8 49 | 8 50 | 8 51 | 8 53 | 8 54 | 8 55 | 8 56 | 15 |
| 16 | 9 13 | 9 15 | 9 16 | 9 17 | 9 19 | 9 20 | 9 21 | 9 23 | 9 24 | 9 25 | 9 27 | 9 28 | 9 29 | 9 31 | 9 32 | 16 |
| 17 | 9 48 | 9 49 | 9 51 | 9 52 | 9 54 | 9 55 | 9 56 | 9 58 | 9 59 | 10 1 | 10 2 | 10 4 | 10 5 | 10 6 | 10 8 | 17 |
| 18 | 10 23 | 10 24 | 10 26 | 10 27 | 10 29 | 10 30 | 10 32 | 10 33 | 10 35 | 10 36 | 10 38 | 10 39 | 10 41 | 10 42 | 10 44 | 18 |
| 19 | 10 57 | 10 59 | 11 0 | 11 2 | 11 3 | 11 5 | 11 7 | 11 8 | 11 10 | 11 11 | 11 13 | 11 15 | 11 16 | 11 18 | 11 19 | 19 |
| 20 | 11 32 | 11 33 | 11 35 | 11 37 | 11 38 | 11 40 | 11 42 | 11 43 | 11 45 | 11 47 | 11 48 | 11 50 | 11 52 | 11 53 | 11 55 | 20 |
| 21 | 12 6 | 12 8 | 12 10 | 12 12 | 12 13 | 12 15 | 12 17 | 12 19 | 12 20 | 12 22 | 12 24 | 12 26 | 12 27 | 12 29 | 12 31 | 21 |
| 22 | 12 41 | 12 43 | 12 45 | 12 46 | 12 48 | 12 50 | 12 52 | 12 54 | 12 56 | 12 57 | 12 59 | 13 1 | 13 3 | 13 5 | 13 7 | 22 |
| 23 | 13 15 | 13 17 | 13 19 | 13 21 | 13 23 | 13 25 | 13 27 | 13 29 | 13 31 | 13 33 | 13 35 | 13 37 | 13 38 | 13 40 | 13 42 | 23 |
| 24 | 13 50 | 13 52 | 13 54 | 13 56 | 13 58 | 14 0 | 14 2 | 14 4 | 14 6 | 14 8 | 14 10 | 14 12 | 14 14 | 14 16 | 14 18 | 24 |
| 25 | 14 25 | 14 27 | 14 29 | 14 31 | 14 33 | 14 35 | 14 37 | 14 39 | 14 41 | 14 43 | 14 45 | 14 48 | 14 50 | 14 52 | 14 54 | 25 |
| 26 | 14 59 | 15 1 | 15 4 | 15 6 | 15 8 | 15 10 | 15 12 | 15 14 | 15 17 | 15 19 | 15 21 | 15 23 | 15 25 | 15 27 | 15 30 | 26 |
| 27 | 15 34 | 15 36 | 15 38 | 15 41 | 15 43 | 15 45 | 15 47 | 15 50 | 15 52 | 15 54 | 15 56 | 15 59 | 16 1 | 16 3 | 16 5 | 27 |
| 28 | 16 8 | 16 11 | 16 13 | 16 15 | 16 18 | 16 20 | 16 22 | 16 25 | 16 27 | 16 29 | 16 32 | 16 34 | 16 36 | 16 39 | 16 41 | 28 |
| 29 | 16 43 | 16 45 | 16 48 | 16 50 | 16 53 | 16 55 | 16 57 | 17 0 | 17 2 | 17 5 | 17 7 | 17 10 | 17 12 | 17 14 | 17 17 | 29 |
| 30 | 17 18 | 17 20 | 17 23 | 17 25 | 17 28 | 17 30 | 17 33 | 17 35 | 17 38 | 17 40 | 17 43 | 17 45 | 17 48 | 17 50 | 17 53 | 30 |
| 31 | 17 52 | 17 55 | 17 57 | 18 0 | 18 2 | 18 5 | 18 8 | 18 10 | 18 13 | 18 15 | 18 18 | 18 21 | 18 23 | 18 26 | 18 28 | 31 |
| 32 | 18 27 | 18 29 | 18 32 | 18 35 | 18 37 | 18 40 | 18 43 | 18 45 | 18 48 | 18 51 | 18 53 | 18 56 | 18 59 | 19 1 | 19 4 | 32 |
| 33 | 19 1 | 19 4 | 19 7 | 19 10 | 19 12 | 19 15 | 19 18 | 19 21 | 19 23 | 19 26 | 19 29 | 19 32 | 19 34 | 19 37 | 19 40 | 33 |
| 34 | 19 36 | 19 39 | 19 42 | 19 44 | 19 47 | 19 50 | 19 53 | 19 56 | 19 59 | 20 1 | 20 4 | 20 7 | 20 10 | 20 13 | 20 16 | 34 |
| 35 | 20 10 | 20 13 | 20 16 | 20 19 | 20 22 | 20 25 | 20 28 | 20 31 | 20 34 | 20 37 | 20 40 | 20 43 | 20 45 | 20 48 | 20 51 | 35 |
| 36 | 20 45 | 20 48 | 20 51 | 20 54 | 20 57 | 21 0 | 21 3 | 21 6 | 21 9 | 21 12 | 21 15 | 21 18 | 21 21 | 21 24 | 21 27 | 36 |
| 37 | 21 20 | 21 23 | 21 26 | 21 29 | 21 32 | 21 35 | 21 38 | 21 41 | 21 44 | 21 47 | 21 50 | 21 54 | 21 57 | 22 0 | 22 3 | 37 |
| 38 | 21 54 | 21 57 | 22 1 | 22 4 | 22 7 | 22 10 | 22 13 | 22 16 | 22 20 | 22 23 | 22 26 | 22 29 | 22 32 | 22 35 | 22 39 | 38 |
| 39 | 22 29 | 22 32 | 22 35 | 22 39 | 22 42 | 22 45 | 22 48 | 22 52 | 22 55 | 22 58 | 23 1 | 23 5 | 23 8 | 23 11 | 23 14 | 39 |
| 40 | 23 3 | 23 7 | 23 10 | 23 13 | 23 17 | 23 20 | 23 23 | 23 27 | 23 30 | 23 33 | 23 37 | 23 40 | 23 43 | 23 47 | 23 50 | 40 |
| 41 | 23 38 | 23 41 | 23 45 | 23 48 | 23 52 | 23 55 | 23 58 | 24 2 | 24 5 | 24 9 | 24 12 | 24 16 | 24 19 | 24 22 | 24 26 | 41 |
| 42 | 24 13 | 24 16 | 24 20 | 24 23 | 24 27 | 24 30 | 24 34 | 24 37 | 24 41 | 24 44 | 24 48 | 24 51 | 24 55 | 24 58 | 25 2 | 42 |
| 43 | 24 47 | 24 51 | 24 54 | 24 58 | 25 1 | 25 5 | 25 9 | 25 12 | 25 16 | 25 19 | 25 23 | 25 27 | 25 30 | 25 34 | 25 37 | 43 |
| 44 | 25 22 | 25 25 | 25 29 | 25 33 | 25 36 | 25 40 | 25 44 | 25 47 | 25 51 | 25 55 | 25 58 | 26 2 | 26 6 | 26 9 | 26 13 | 44 |
| 45 | 25 56 | 26 0 | 26 4 | 26 8 | 26 11 | 26 15 | 26 19 | 26 23 | 26 26 | 26 30 | 26 34 | 26 38 | 26 41 | 26 45 | 26 49 | 45 |
| 46 | 26 31 | 26 35 | 26 39 | 26 42 | 26 46 | 26 50 | 26 54 | 26 58 | 27 2 | 27 5 | 27 9 | 27 13 | 27 17 | 27 21 | 27 25 | 46 |
| 47 | 27 5 | 27 9 | 27 13 | 27 17 | 27 21 | 27 25 | 27 29 | 27 33 | 27 37 | 27 41 | 27 45 | 27 49 | 27 52 | 27 56 | 28 0 | 47 |
| 48 | 27 40 | 27 44 | 27 48 | 27 52 | 27 56 | 28 0 | 28 4 | 28 8 | 28 12 | 28 16 | 28 20 | 28 24 | 28 28 | 28 32 | 28 36 | 48 |
| 49 | 28 15 | 28 19 | 28 23 | 28 27 | 28 31 | 28 35 | 28 39 | 28 43 | 28 47 | 28 51 | 28 55 | 29 0 | 29 4 | 29 8 | 29 12 | 49 |
| 50 | 28 49 | 28 53 | 28 58 | 29 2 | 29 6 | 29 10 | 29 14 | 29 18 | 29 23 | 29 27 | 29 31 | 29 35 | 29 39 | 29 43 | 29 48 | 50 |
| 51 | 29 24 | 29 28 | 29 32 | 29 37 | 29 41 | 29 45 | 29 49 | 29 54 | 29 58 | 30 2 | 30 6 | 30 11 | 30 15 | 30 19 | 30 23 | 51 |
| 52 | 29 58 | 30 3 | 30 7 | 30 11 | 30 16 | 30 20 | 30 24 | 30 29 | 30 33 | 30 37 | 30 42 | 30 46 | 30 50 | 30 55 | 30 59 | 52 |
| 53 | 30 33 | 30 37 | 30 42 | 30 46 | 30 51 | 30 55 | 30 59 | 31 4 | 31 8 | 31 13 | 31 17 | 31 22 | 31 26 | 31 30 | 31 35 | 53 |
| 54 | 31 8 | 31 12 | 31 17 | 31 21 | 31 26 | 31 30 | 31 35 | 31 39 | 31 44 | 31 48 | 31 53 | 31 57 | 32 2 | 32 6 | 32 11 | 54 |
| 55 | 31 42 | 31 47 | 31 51 | 31 56 | 32 0 | 32 5 | 32 10 | 32 14 | 32 19 | 32 23 | 32 28 | 32 33 | 32 37 | 32 42 | 32 46 | 55 |
| 56 | 32 17 | 32 21 | 32 26 | 32 31 | 32 35 | 32 40 | 32 45 | 32 49 | 32 54 | 32 59 | 33 3 | 33 8 | 33 13 | 33 17 | 33 22 | 56 |
| 57 | 32 51 | 32 56 | 33 1 | 33 6 | 33 10 | 33 15 | 33 20 | 33 25 | 33 29 | 33 34 | 33 39 | 33 44 | 33 48 | 33 53 | 33 58 | 57 |
| 58 | 33 26 | 33 31 | 33 36 | 33 40 | 33 45 | 33 50 | 33 55 | 34 0 | 34 5 | 34 9 | 34 14 | 34 19 | 34 24 | 34 29 | 34 33 | 58 |
| 59 | 34 0 | 34 5 | 34 10 | 34 15 | 34 20 | 34 25 | 34 30 | 34 35 | 34 40 | 34 45 | 34 50 | 34 55 | 34 59 | 35 4 | 35 9 | 59 |
| 60 | 34 35 | 34 40 | 34 45 | 34 50 | 34 55 | 35 0 | 35 5 | 35 10 | 35 15 | 35 20 | 35 25 | 35 30 | 35 35 | 35 40 | 35 45 | 60 |
| **HOURS 1** | 34 35 | 34 40 | 34 45 | 34 50 | 34 55 | 35 0 | 35 5 | 35 10 | 35 15 | 35 20 | 35 25 | 35 30 | 35 35 | 35 40 | 35 45 | **1 HOURS** |
| 2 | 1 9 10 | 1 9 20 | 1 9 30 | 1 9 40 | 1 9 50 | 1 10 0 | 1 10 10 | 1 10 20 | 1 10 30 | 1 10 40 | 1 10 50 | 1 11 0 | 1 11 10 | 1 11 20 | 1 11 30 | 2 |
| 3 | 1 43 45 | 1 44 0 | 1 44 15 | 1 44 30 | 1 44 45 | 1 45 0 | 1 45 15 | 1 45 30 | 1 45 45 | 1 46 0 | 1 46 15 | 1 46 30 | 1 46 45 | 1 47 0 | 1 47 15 | 3 |
| 4 | 2 18 20 | 2 18 40 | 2 19 0 | 2 19 20 | 2 19 40 | 2 20 0 | 2 20 20 | 2 20 40 | 2 21 0 | 2 21 20 | 2 21 40 | 2 22 0 | 2 22 20 | 2 22 40 | 2 23 0 | 4 |
| 5 | 2 52 55 | 2 53 20 | 2 53 45 | 2 54 10 | 2 54 35 | 2 55 0 | 2 55 25 | 2 55 50 | 2 56 15 | 2 56 40 | 2 57 5 | 2 57 30 | 2 57 55 | 2 58 20 | 2 58 45 | 5 |
| 6 | 3 27 30 | 3 28 0 | 3 28 30 | 3 29 0 | 3 29 30 | 3 30 0 | 3 30 30 | 3 31 0 | 3 31 30 | 3 32 0 | 3 32 30 | 3 33 0 | 3 33 30 | 3 34 0 | 3 34 30 | 6 |
| 7 | 4 2 5 | 4 2 40 | 4 3 15 | 4 3 50 | 4 4 25 | 4 5 0 | 4 5 35 | 4 6 10 | 4 6 45 | 4 7 20 | 4 7 55 | 4 8 30 | 4 9 5 | 4 9 40 | 4 10 15 | 7 |
| 8 | 4 36 40 | 4 37 20 | 4 38 0 | 4 38 40 | 4 39 20 | 4 40 0 | 4 40 40 | 4 41 20 | 4 42 0 | 4 42 40 | 4 43 20 | 4 44 0 | 4 44 40 | 4 45 20 | 4 46 0 | 8 |
| 9 | 5 11 15 | 5 12 0 | 5 12 45 | 5 13 30 | 5 14 15 | 5 15 0 | 5 15 45 | 5 16 30 | 5 17 15 | 5 18 0 | 5 18 45 | 5 19 30 | 5 20 15 | 5 21 0 | 5 21 45 | 9 |
| 10 | 5 45 50 | 5 46 40 | 5 47 30 | 5 48 20 | 5 49 10 | 5 50 0 | 5 50 50 | 5 51 40 | 5 52 30 | 5 53 20 | 5 54 10 | 5 55 0 | 5 55 50 | 5 56 40 | 5 57 30 | 10 |
| 11 | 6 20 25 | 6 21 20 | 6 22 15 | 6 23 10 | 6 24 5 | 6 25 0 | 6 25 55 | 6 26 50 | 6 27 45 | 6 28 40 | 6 29 35 | 6 30 30 | 6 31 25 | 6 32 20 | 6 33 15 | 11 |
| 12 | 6 55 0 | 6 56 0 | 6 57 0 | 6 58 0 | 6 59 0 | 7 0 0 | 7 1 0 | 7 2 0 | 7 3 0 | 7 4 0 | 7 5 0 | 7 6 0 | 7 7 0 | 7 8 0 | 7 9 0 | 12 |

# Table VI Semidiurnal Motion of the Moon

**12 HOUR TRAVEL**

| TIME | 7° 10' | 7° 11' | 7° 12' | 7° 13' | 7° 14' | 7° 15' | 7° 16' | 7° 17' | 7° 18' | 7° 19' | 7° 20' | 7° 21' | 7° 22' | 7° 23' | 7° 24' | TIME |
|---|---|---|---|---|---|---|---|---|---|---|---|---|---|---|---|---|
| **MINUTES 1** | 0 36 | 0 36 | 0 36 | 0 36 | 0 36 | 0 36 | 0 36 | 0 36 | 0 37 | 0 37 | 0 37 | 0 37 | 0 37 | 0 37 | 0 37 | 1 |
| 2 | 1 12 | 1 12 | 1 12 | 1 12 | 1 12 | 1 13 | 1 13 | 1 13 | 1 13 | 1 13 | 1 13 | 1 14 | 1 14 | 1 14 | 1 14 | 2 |
| 3 | 1 48 | 1 48 | 1 48 | 1 48 | 1 49 | 1 49 | 1 49 | 1 49 | 1 50 | 1 50 | 1 50 | 1 50 | 1 51 | 1 51 | 1 51 | 3 |
| 4 | 2 23 | 2 24 | 2 24 | 2 24 | 2 25 | 2 25 | 2 25 | 2 26 | 2 26 | 2 26 | 2 27 | 2 27 | 2 27 | 2 28 | 2 28 | 4 |
| 5 | 2 59 | 3 0 | 3 0 | 3 0 | 3 1 | 3 1 | 3 2 | 3 2 | 3 3 | 3 3 | 3 3 | 3 4 | 3 4 | 3 5 | 3 5 | 5 |
| 6 | 3 35 | 3 36 | 3 36 | 3 37 | 3 37 | 3 38 | 3 38 | 3 39 | 3 39 | 3 40 | 3 40 | 3 41 | 3 41 | 3 42 | 3 42 | 6 |
| 7 | 4 11 | 4 11 | 4 12 | 4 13 | 4 13 | 4 14 | 4 14 | 4 15 | 4 16 | 4 16 | 4 17 | 4 17 | 4 18 | 4 18 | 4 19 | 7 |
| 8 | 4 47 | 4 47 | 4 48 | 4 49 | 4 49 | 4 50 | 4 51 | 4 51 | 4 52 | 4 53 | 4 53 | 4 54 | 4 55 | 4 55 | 4 56 | 8 |
| 9 | 5 23 | 5 23 | 5 24 | 5 25 | 5 26 | 5 26 | 5 27 | 5 28 | 5 29 | 5 29 | 5 30 | 5 31 | 5 32 | 5 32 | 5 33 | 9 |
| 10 | 5 58 | 5 59 | 6 0 | 6 1 | 6 2 | 6 3 | 6 3 | 6 4 | 6 5 | 6 6 | 6 7 | 6 8 | 6 8 | 6 9 | 6 10 | 10 |
| 11 | 6 34 | 6 35 | 6 36 | 6 37 | 6 38 | 6 39 | 6 40 | 6 41 | 6 42 | 6 42 | 6 43 | 6 44 | 6 45 | 6 46 | 6 47 | 11 |
| 12 | 7 10 | 7 11 | 7 12 | 7 13 | 7 14 | 7 15 | 7 16 | 7 17 | 7 18 | 7 19 | 7 20 | 7 21 | 7 22 | 7 23 | 7 24 | 12 |
| 13 | 7 46 | 7 47 | 7 48 | 7 49 | 7 50 | 7 51 | 7 52 | 7 53 | 7 55 | 7 55 | 7 56 | 7 57 | 7 58 | 7 59 | 8 0 | 13 |
| 14 | 8 22 | 8 23 | 8 24 | 8 25 | 8 26 | 8 28 | 8 29 | 8 30 | 8 31 | 8 32 | 8 33 | 8 35 | 8 36 | 8 37 | 8 38 | 14 |
| 15 | 8 58 | 8 59 | 9 0 | 9 1 | 9 3 | 9 4 | 9 5 | 9 6 | 9 8 | 9 9 | 9 10 | 9 11 | 9 13 | 9 14 | 9 15 | 15 |
| 16 | 9 33 | 9 35 | 9 36 | 9 37 | 9 39 | 9 40 | 9 41 | 9 43 | 9 44 | 9 45 | 9 47 | 9 48 | 9 49 | 9 51 | 9 52 | 16 |
| 17 | 10 9 | 10 11 | 10 12 | 10 13 | 10 15 | 10 16 | 10 18 | 10 19 | 10 21 | 10 22 | 10 23 | 10 25 | 10 26 | 10 28 | 10 29 | 17 |
| 18 | 10 45 | 10 47 | 10 48 | 10 50 | 10 51 | 10 53 | 10 54 | 10 56 | 10 57 | 10 59 | 11 0 | 11 2 | 11 3 | 11 5 | 11 6 | 18 |
| 19 | 11 21 | 11 22 | 11 24 | 11 26 | 11 27 | 11 29 | 11 30 | 11 32 | 11 34 | 11 35 | 11 37 | 11 38 | 11 40 | 11 41 | 11 43 | 19 |
| 20 | 11 57 | 11 58 | 12 0 | 12 2 | 12 3 | 12 5 | 12 7 | 12 8 | 12 10 | 12 12 | 12 13 | 12 15 | 12 17 | 12 18 | 12 20 | 20 |
| 21 | 12 33 | 12 34 | 12 36 | 12 38 | 12 40 | 12 41 | 12 43 | 12 45 | 12 47 | 12 48 | 12 50 | 12 52 | 12 54 | 12 55 | 12 57 | 21 |
| 22 | 13 8 | 13 10 | 13 12 | 13 14 | 13 16 | 13 18 | 13 19 | 13 21 | 13 23 | 13 25 | 13 27 | 13 29 | 13 30 | 13 32 | 13 34 | 22 |
| 23 | 13 44 | 13 46 | 13 48 | 13 50 | 13 52 | 13 54 | 13 56 | 13 58 | 14 0 | 14 1 | 14 3 | 14 5 | 14 7 | 14 9 | 14 11 | 23 |
| 24 | 14 20 | 14 22 | 14 24 | 14 26 | 14 28 | 14 30 | 14 32 | 14 34 | 14 36 | 14 38 | 14 40 | 14 42 | 14 44 | 14 46 | 14 48 | 24 |
| 25 | 14 56 | 14 58 | 15 0 | 15 2 | 15 4 | 15 6 | 15 8 | 15 10 | 15 13 | 15 15 | 15 17 | 15 19 | 15 21 | 15 23 | 15 25 | 25 |
| 26 | 15 32 | 15 34 | 15 36 | 15 38 | 15 40 | 15 43 | 15 45 | 15 47 | 15 49 | 15 51 | 15 53 | 15 56 | 15 58 | 16 0 | 16 2 | 26 |
| 27 | 16 8 | 16 10 | 16 12 | 16 14 | 16 17 | 16 19 | 16 21 | 16 23 | 16 26 | 16 28 | 16 30 | 16 32 | 16 35 | 16 37 | 16 39 | 27 |
| 28 | 16 43 | 16 46 | 16 48 | 16 50 | 16 53 | 16 55 | 16 57 | 17 0 | 17 2 | 17 4 | 17 7 | 17 9 | 17 11 | 17 14 | 17 16 | 28 |
| 29 | 17 19 | 17 22 | 17 24 | 17 26 | 17 29 | 17 31 | 17 34 | 17 36 | 17 39 | 17 41 | 17 43 | 17 46 | 17 48 | 17 51 | 17 53 | 29 |
| 30 | 17 55 | 17 58 | 18 0 | 18 3 | 18 5 | 18 8 | 18 10 | 18 13 | 18 15 | 18 18 | 18 20 | 18 23 | 18 25 | 18 28 | 18 30 | 30 |
| 31 | 18 31 | 18 33 | 18 36 | 18 39 | 18 41 | 18 44 | 18 46 | 18 49 | 18 52 | 18 54 | 18 57 | 18 59 | 19 2 | 19 4 | 19 7 | 31 |
| 32 | 19 7 | 19 9 | 19 12 | 19 15 | 19 17 | 19 20 | 19 23 | 19 25 | 19 28 | 19 31 | 19 33 | 19 36 | 19 39 | 19 41 | 19 44 | 32 |
| 33 | 19 43 | 19 45 | 19 48 | 19 51 | 19 54 | 19 56 | 19 59 | 20 2 | 20 5 | 20 7 | 20 10 | 20 13 | 20 16 | 20 18 | 20 21 | 33 |
| 34 | 20 18 | 20 21 | 20 24 | 20 27 | 20 30 | 20 33 | 20 35 | 20 38 | 20 41 | 20 44 | 20 47 | 20 50 | 20 52 | 20 55 | 20 58 | 34 |
| 35 | 20 54 | 20 57 | 21 0 | 21 3 | 21 6 | 21 9 | 21 12 | 21 15 | 21 18 | 21 20 | 21 23 | 21 26 | 21 29 | 21 32 | 21 35 | 35 |
| 36 | 21 30 | 21 33 | 21 36 | 21 39 | 21 42 | 21 45 | 21 48 | 21 51 | 21 54 | 21 57 | 22 0 | 22 3 | 22 6 | 22 9 | 22 12 | 36 |
| 37 | 22 6 | 22 9 | 22 12 | 22 15 | 22 18 | 22 21 | 22 24 | 22 27 | 22 31 | 22 34 | 22 37 | 22 40 | 22 43 | 22 46 | 22 49 | 37 |
| 38 | 22 42 | 22 45 | 22 48 | 22 51 | 22 54 | 22 58 | 23 1 | 23 4 | 23 7 | 23 10 | 23 13 | 23 17 | 23 20 | 23 23 | 23 26 | 38 |
| 39 | 23 18 | 23 21 | 23 24 | 23 27 | 23 31 | 23 34 | 23 37 | 23 40 | 23 44 | 23 47 | 23 50 | 23 53 | 23 57 | 24 0 | 24 3 | 39 |
| 40 | 23 53 | 23 57 | 24 0 | 24 3 | 24 7 | 24 10 | 24 13 | 24 17 | 24 20 | 24 23 | 24 27 | 24 30 | 24 33 | 24 37 | 24 40 | 40 |
| 41 | 24 29 | 24 33 | 24 36 | 24 39 | 24 43 | 24 46 | 24 50 | 24 53 | 24 57 | 25 0 | 25 3 | 25 7 | 25 10 | 25 14 | 25 17 | 41 |
| 42 | 25 5 | 25 9 | 25 12 | 25 16 | 25 19 | 25 23 | 25 26 | 25 30 | 25 33 | 25 37 | 25 40 | 25 44 | 25 47 | 25 51 | 25 54 | 42 |
| 43 | 25 41 | 25 44 | 25 48 | 25 52 | 25 55 | 25 59 | 26 2 | 26 6 | 26 10 | 26 13 | 26 17 | 26 20 | 26 24 | 26 27 | 26 31 | 43 |
| 44 | 26 17 | 26 20 | 26 24 | 26 28 | 26 31 | 26 35 | 26 39 | 26 42 | 26 46 | 26 50 | 26 53 | 26 57 | 27 1 | 27 4 | 27 8 | 44 |
| 45 | 26 53 | 26 56 | 27 0 | 27 4 | 27 8 | 27 11 | 27 15 | 27 19 | 27 23 | 27 26 | 27 30 | 27 34 | 27 38 | 27 41 | 27 45 | 45 |
| 46 | 27 28 | 27 32 | 27 36 | 27 40 | 27 44 | 27 48 | 27 51 | 27 55 | 27 59 | 28 3 | 28 7 | 28 11 | 28 14 | 28 18 | 28 22 | 46 |
| 47 | 28 4 | 28 8 | 28 12 | 28 16 | 28 20 | 28 24 | 28 28 | 28 32 | 28 36 | 28 39 | 28 43 | 28 47 | 28 51 | 28 55 | 28 59 | 47 |
| 48 | 28 40 | 28 44 | 28 48 | 28 52 | 28 56 | 29 0 | 29 4 | 29 8 | 29 12 | 29 16 | 29 20 | 29 24 | 29 28 | 29 32 | 29 36 | 48 |
| 49 | 29 16 | 29 20 | 29 24 | 29 28 | 29 32 | 29 36 | 29 40 | 29 44 | 29 49 | 29 53 | 29 57 | 30 1 | 30 5 | 30 9 | 30 13 | 49 |
| 50 | 29 52 | 29 56 | 30 0 | 30 4 | 30 8 | 30 13 | 30 17 | 30 21 | 30 25 | 30 29 | 30 33 | 30 38 | 30 42 | 30 46 | 30 50 | 50 |
| 51 | 30 28 | 30 32 | 30 36 | 30 40 | 30 45 | 30 49 | 30 53 | 30 57 | 31 2 | 31 6 | 31 10 | 31 14 | 31 19 | 31 23 | 31 27 | 51 |
| 52 | 31 3 | 31 8 | 31 12 | 31 16 | 31 21 | 31 25 | 31 29 | 31 34 | 31 38 | 31 42 | 31 47 | 31 51 | 31 55 | 32 0 | 32 4 | 52 |
| 53 | 31 39 | 31 44 | 31 48 | 31 52 | 31 57 | 32 1 | 32 6 | 32 10 | 32 15 | 32 19 | 32 23 | 32 28 | 32 32 | 32 37 | 32 41 | 53 |
| 54 | 32 15 | 32 20 | 32 24 | 32 29 | 32 33 | 32 38 | 32 42 | 32 47 | 32 51 | 32 56 | 33 0 | 33 5 | 33 9 | 33 14 | 33 18 | 54 |
| 55 | 32 51 | 32 55 | 33 0 | 33 5 | 33 9 | 33 14 | 33 18 | 33 23 | 33 28 | 33 32 | 33 37 | 33 41 | 33 46 | 33 50 | 33 55 | 55 |
| 56 | 33 27 | 33 31 | 33 36 | 33 41 | 33 45 | 33 50 | 33 55 | 33 59 | 34 4 | 34 9 | 34 13 | 34 18 | 34 23 | 34 27 | 34 32 | 56 |
| 57 | 34 3 | 34 7 | 34 12 | 34 17 | 34 22 | 34 26 | 34 31 | 34 36 | 34 41 | 34 45 | 34 50 | 34 55 | 35 0 | 35 4 | 35 9 | 57 |
| 58 | 34 38 | 34 43 | 34 48 | 34 53 | 34 58 | 35 3 | 35 7 | 35 12 | 35 17 | 35 22 | 35 27 | 35 32 | 35 36 | 35 41 | 35 46 | 58 |
| 59 | 35 14 | 35 19 | 35 24 | 35 29 | 35 34 | 35 39 | 35 44 | 35 49 | 35 54 | 35 58 | 36 3 | 36 8 | 36 13 | 36 18 | 36 23 | 59 |
| 60 | 35 50 | 35 55 | 36 0 | 36 5 | 36 10 | 36 15 | 36 20 | 36 25 | 36 30 | 36 35 | 36 40 | 36 45 | 36 50 | 36 55 | 37 0 | 60 |
| **HOURS 1** | 35 50 | 35 55 | 36 0 | 36 5 | 36 10 | 36 15 | 36 20 | 36 25 | 36 30 | 36 35 | 36 40 | 36 45 | 36 50 | 36 55 | 37 0 | 1 |
| 2 | 1 11 40 | 1 11 50 | 1 12 0 | 1 12 10 | 1 12 20 | 1 12 30 | 1 12 40 | 1 12 50 | 1 13 0 | 1 13 10 | 1 13 20 | 1 13 30 | 1 13 40 | 1 13 50 | 1 14 0 | 2 |
| 3 | 1 47 30 | 1 47 45 | 1 48 0 | 1 48 15 | 1 48 30 | 1 48 45 | 1 49 0 | 1 49 15 | 1 49 30 | 1 49 45 | 1 50 0 | 1 50 15 | 1 50 30 | 1 50 45 | 1 51 0 | 3 |
| 4 | 2 23 20 | 2 23 40 | 2 24 0 | 2 24 20 | 2 24 40 | 2 25 0 | 2 25 20 | 2 25 40 | 2 26 0 | 2 26 20 | 2 26 40 | 2 27 0 | 2 27 20 | 2 27 40 | 2 28 0 | 4 |
| 5 | 2 59 10 | 2 59 35 | 3 0 0 | 3 0 25 | 3 0 50 | 3 1 15 | 3 1 40 | 3 2 5 | 3 2 30 | 3 2 55 | 3 3 20 | 3 3 45 | 3 4 10 | 3 4 35 | 3 5 0 | 5 |
| 6 | 3 35 0 | 3 35 30 | 3 36 0 | 3 36 30 | 3 37 0 | 3 37 30 | 3 38 0 | 3 38 30 | 3 39 0 | 3 39 30 | 3 40 0 | 3 40 30 | 3 41 0 | 3 41 30 | 3 42 0 | 6 |
| 7 | 4 10 50 | 4 11 25 | 4 12 0 | 4 12 35 | 4 13 10 | 4 13 45 | 4 14 20 | 4 14 55 | 4 15 30 | 4 16 5 | 4 16 40 | 4 17 15 | 4 17 50 | 4 18 25 | 4 19 0 | 7 |
| 8 | 4 46 40 | 4 47 20 | 4 48 0 | 4 48 40 | 4 49 20 | 4 50 0 | 4 50 40 | 4 51 20 | 4 52 0 | 4 52 40 | 4 53 20 | 4 54 0 | 4 54 40 | 4 55 20 | 4 56 0 | 8 |
| 9 | 5 22 30 | 5 23 15 | 5 24 0 | 5 24 45 | 5 25 30 | 5 26 15 | 5 27 0 | 5 27 45 | 5 28 30 | 5 29 15 | 5 30 0 | 5 30 45 | 5 31 30 | 5 32 15 | 5 33 0 | 9 |
| 10 | 5 58 20 | 5 59 10 | 6 0 0 | 6 0 50 | 6 1 40 | 6 2 30 | 6 3 20 | 6 4 10 | 6 5 0 | 6 5 50 | 6 6 40 | 6 7 30 | 6 8 20 | 6 9 10 | 6 10 0 | 10 |
| 11 | 6 34 10 | 6 35 5 | 6 36 0 | 6 36 55 | 6 37 50 | 6 38 45 | 6 39 40 | 6 40 35 | 6 41 30 | 6 42 25 | 6 43 20 | 6 44 15 | 6 45 10 | 6 46 5 | 6 47 0 | 11 |
| 12 | 7 10 0 | 7 11 0 | 7 12 0 | 7 13 0 | 7 14 0 | 7 15 0 | 7 16 0 | 7 17 0 | 7 18 0 | 7 19 0 | 7 20 0 | 7 21 0 | 7 22 0 | 7 23 0 | 7 24 0 | 12 |

# Table VI Semidiurnal Motion of the Moon

**12 HOUR TRAVEL**

## MINUTES

| TIME | 7° 25' | 7° 26' | 7° 27' | 7° 28' | 7° 29' | 7° 30' | 7° 31' | 7° 32' | 7° 33' | 7° 34' | 7° 35' | 7° 36' | 7° 37' | 7° 38' | 7° 39' | TIME |
|---|---|---|---|---|---|---|---|---|---|---|---|---|---|---|---|---|
| 1 | 0 37 | 0 37 | 0 37 | 0 37 | 0 37 | 0 38 | 0 38 | 0 38 | 0 38 | 0 38 | 0 38 | 0 38 | 0 38 | 0 38 | 0 38 | 1 |
| 2 | 1 14 | 1 14 | 1 15 | 1 15 | 1 15 | 1 15 | 1 15 | 1 15 | 1 16 | 1 16 | 1 16 | 1 16 | 1 16 | 1 16 | 1 17 | 2 |
| 3 | 1 51 | 1 52 | 1 52 | 1 52 | 1 52 | 1 53 | 1 53 | 1 53 | 1 53 | 1 53 | 1 54 | 1 54 | 1 54 | 1 55 | 1 55 | 3 |
| 4 | 2 28 | 2 29 | 2 29 | 2 29 | 2 30 | 2 30 | 2 30 | 2 31 | 2 31 | 2 31 | 2 32 | 2 32 | 2 32 | 2 33 | 2 33 | 4 |
| 5 | 3 5 | 3 6 | 3 6 | 3 7 | 3 7 | 3 8 | 3 8 | 3 8 | 3 9 | 3 9 | 3 10 | 3 10 | 3 10 | 3 11 | 3 11 | 5 |
| 6 | 3 43 | 3 43 | 3 44 | 3 44 | 3 45 | 3 45 | 3 46 | 3 46 | 3 47 | 3 47 | 3 48 | 3 48 | 3 49 | 3 49 | 3 50 | 6 |
| 7 | 4 20 | 4 20 | 4 21 | 4 21 | 4 22 | 4 23 | 4 23 | 4 24 | 4 24 | 4 25 | 4 25 | 4 26 | 4 27 | 4 27 | 4 28 | 7 |
| 8 | 4 57 | 4 57 | 4 58 | 4 59 | 4 59 | 5 0 | 5 1 | 5 1 | 5 2 | 5 3 | 5 3 | 5 4 | 5 5 | 5 5 | 5 6 | 8 |
| 9 | 5 34 | 5 35 | 5 35 | 5 36 | 5 37 | 5 38 | 5 38 | 5 39 | 5 40 | 5 41 | 5 41 | 5 42 | 5 43 | 5 44 | 5 44 | 9 |
| 10 | 6 11 | 6 12 | 6 13 | 6 13 | 6 14 | 6 15 | 6 16 | 6 17 | 6 18 | 6 18 | 6 19 | 6 20 | 6 21 | 6 22 | 6 23 | 10 |
| 11 | 6 48 | 6 49 | 6 50 | 6 51 | 6 52 | 6 53 | 6 53 | 6 54 | 6 55 | 6 56 | 6 57 | 6 58 | 6 59 | 7 0 | 7 1 | 11 |
| 12 | 7 25 | 7 26 | 7 27 | 7 28 | 7 29 | 7 30 | 7 31 | 7 32 | 7 33 | 7 34 | 7 35 | 7 36 | 7 37 | 7 38 | 7 39 | 12 |
| 13 | 8 2 | 8 3 | 8 4 | 8 5 | 8 6 | 8 8 | 8 9 | 8 10 | 8 11 | 8 12 | 8 13 | 8 14 | 8 15 | 8 16 | 8 17 | 13 |
| 14 | 8 39 | 8 40 | 8 42 | 8 43 | 8 44 | 8 45 | 8 46 | 8 47 | 8 49 | 8 50 | 8 51 | 8 52 | 8 53 | 8 54 | 8 56 | 14 |
| 15 | 9 16 | 9 18 | 9 19 | 9 20 | 9 21 | 9 23 | 9 24 | 9 25 | 9 26 | 9 28 | 9 29 | 9 30 | 9 31 | 9 33 | 9 34 | 15 |
| 16 | 9 53 | 9 55 | 9 56 | 9 57 | 9 59 | 10 0 | 10 1 | 10 3 | 10 4 | 10 5 | 10 7 | 10 8 | 10 9 | 10 11 | 10 12 | 16 |
| 17 | 10 30 | 10 32 | 10 33 | 10 35 | 10 36 | 10 38 | 10 39 | 10 40 | 10 42 | 10 43 | 10 45 | 10 46 | 10 47 | 10 49 | 10 50 | 17 |
| 18 | 11 8 | 11 9 | 11 11 | 11 12 | 11 14 | 11 15 | 11 17 | 11 18 | 11 20 | 11 21 | 11 23 | 11 24 | 11 26 | 11 27 | 11 29 | 18 |
| 19 | 11 45 | 11 46 | 11 48 | 11 49 | 11 51 | 11 53 | 11 54 | 11 56 | 11 57 | 11 59 | 12 0 | 12 2 | 12 4 | 12 5 | 12 7 | 19 |
| 20 | 12 22 | 12 23 | 12 25 | 12 27 | 12 28 | 12 30 | 12 32 | 12 33 | 12 35 | 12 37 | 12 38 | 12 40 | 12 42 | 12 43 | 12 45 | 20 |
| 21 | 12 59 | 13 1 | 13 2 | 13 4 | 13 6 | 13 8 | 13 9 | 13 11 | 13 13 | 13 15 | 13 16 | 13 18 | 13 20 | 13 22 | 13 23 | 21 |
| 22 | 13 36 | 13 38 | 13 40 | 13 41 | 13 43 | 13 45 | 13 47 | 13 49 | 13 51 | 13 52 | 13 54 | 13 56 | 13 58 | 14 0 | 14 2 | 22 |
| 23 | 14 13 | 14 15 | 14 17 | 14 19 | 14 21 | 14 23 | 14 24 | 14 26 | 14 28 | 14 30 | 14 32 | 14 34 | 14 36 | 14 38 | 14 40 | 23 |
| 24 | 14 50 | 14 52 | 14 54 | 14 56 | 14 58 | 15 0 | 15 2 | 15 4 | 15 5 | 15 8 | 15 10 | 15 12 | 15 14 | 15 16 | 15 18 | 24 |
| 25 | 15 27 | 15 29 | 15 31 | 15 33 | 15 35 | 15 38 | 15 40 | 15 42 | 15 44 | 15 46 | 15 48 | 15 50 | 15 52 | 15 54 | 15 56 | 25 |
| 26 | 16 4 | 16 6 | 16 9 | 16 11 | 16 13 | 16 15 | 16 17 | 16 19 | 16 22 | 16 24 | 16 26 | 16 28 | 16 30 | 16 32 | 16 35 | 26 |
| 27 | 16 41 | 16 44 | 16 46 | 16 48 | 16 50 | 16 53 | 16 55 | 16 57 | 16 59 | 17 2 | 17 4 | 17 6 | 17 8 | 17 11 | 17 13 | 27 |
| 28 | 17 18 | 17 21 | 17 23 | 17 25 | 17 28 | 17 30 | 17 32 | 17 35 | 17 37 | 17 39 | 17 42 | 17 44 | 17 46 | 17 49 | 17 51 | 28 |
| 29 | 17 55 | 17 58 | 18 0 | 18 3 | 18 5 | 18 8 | 18 10 | 18 12 | 18 15 | 18 17 | 18 20 | 18 22 | 18 24 | 18 27 | 18 29 | 29 |
| 30 | 18 33 | 18 35 | 18 38 | 18 40 | 18 43 | 18 45 | 18 48 | 18 50 | 18 53 | 18 55 | 18 58 | 19 0 | 19 3 | 19 5 | 19 8 | 30 |
| 31 | 19 10 | 19 12 | 19 15 | 19 17 | 19 20 | 19 23 | 19 25 | 19 28 | 19 30 | 19 33 | 19 35 | 19 38 | 19 41 | 19 43 | 19 46 | 31 |
| 32 | 19 47 | 19 49 | 19 52 | 19 55 | 19 57 | 20 0 | 20 3 | 20 5 | 20 8 | 20 11 | 20 13 | 20 16 | 20 19 | 20 21 | 20 24 | 32 |
| 33 | 20 24 | 20 27 | 20 29 | 20 32 | 20 35 | 20 38 | 20 40 | 20 43 | 20 46 | 20 49 | 20 51 | 20 54 | 20 57 | 21 0 | 21 2 | 33 |
| 34 | 21 1 | 21 4 | 21 7 | 21 9 | 21 12 | 21 15 | 21 18 | 21 21 | 21 24 | 21 26 | 21 29 | 21 32 | 21 35 | 21 38 | 21 41 | 34 |
| 35 | 21 38 | 21 41 | 21 44 | 21 47 | 21 50 | 21 53 | 21 55 | 21 58 | 22 1 | 22 4 | 22 7 | 22 10 | 22 13 | 22 16 | 22 19 | 35 |
| 36 | 22 15 | 22 18 | 22 21 | 22 24 | 22 27 | 22 30 | 22 33 | 22 36 | 22 39 | 22 42 | 22 45 | 22 48 | 22 51 | 22 54 | 22 57 | 36 |
| 37 | 22 52 | 22 55 | 22 58 | 23 1 | 23 4 | 23 8 | 23 11 | 23 14 | 23 17 | 23 20 | 23 23 | 23 26 | 23 29 | 23 32 | 23 35 | 37 |
| 38 | 23 29 | 23 32 | 23 36 | 23 39 | 23 42 | 23 45 | 23 48 | 23 51 | 23 55 | 23 58 | 24 1 | 24 4 | 24 7 | 24 10 | 24 14 | 38 |
| 39 | 24 6 | 24 10 | 24 13 | 24 16 | 24 19 | 24 23 | 24 26 | 24 29 | 24 32 | 24 36 | 24 39 | 24 42 | 24 45 | 24 49 | 24 52 | 39 |
| 40 | 24 43 | 24 47 | 24 50 | 24 53 | 24 57 | 25 0 | 25 3 | 25 7 | 25 10 | 25 13 | 25 17 | 25 20 | 25 23 | 25 27 | 25 30 | 40 |
| 41 | 25 20 | 25 24 | 25 27 | 25 31 | 25 34 | 25 38 | 25 41 | 25 44 | 25 48 | 25 51 | 25 55 | 25 58 | 26 1 | 26 5 | 26 8 | 41 |
| 42 | 25 58 | 26 1 | 26 5 | 26 8 | 26 12 | 26 15 | 26 19 | 26 22 | 26 26 | 26 29 | 26 33 | 26 36 | 26 40 | 26 43 | 26 47 | 42 |
| 43 | 26 35 | 26 38 | 26 42 | 26 45 | 26 49 | 26 53 | 26 56 | 27 0 | 27 3 | 27 7 | 27 10 | 27 14 | 27 18 | 27 21 | 27 25 | 43 |
| 44 | 27 12 | 27 15 | 27 19 | 27 23 | 27 26 | 27 30 | 27 34 | 27 37 | 27 41 | 27 45 | 27 48 | 27 52 | 27 56 | 28 3 | 28 4 | 44 |
| 45 | 27 49 | 27 53 | 27 56 | 28 0 | 28 4 | 28 8 | 28 11 | 28 15 | 28 19 | 28 23 | 28 26 | 28 30 | 28 34 | 28 38 | 28 41 | 45 |
| 46 | 28 26 | 28 30 | 28 34 | 28 37 | 28 41 | 28 45 | 28 49 | 28 53 | 28 57 | 29 0 | 29 4 | 29 8 | 29 12 | 29 16 | 29 20 | 46 |
| 47 | 29 3 | 29 7 | 29 11 | 29 15 | 29 19 | 29 23 | 29 26 | 29 30 | 29 34 | 29 38 | 29 42 | 29 46 | 29 50 | 29 54 | 29 58 | 47 |
| 48 | 29 40 | 29 44 | 29 48 | 29 52 | 29 56 | 30 0 | 30 4 | 30 8 | 30 12 | 30 16 | 30 20 | 30 24 | 30 28 | 30 32 | 30 36 | 48 |
| 49 | 30 17 | 30 21 | 30 25 | 30 29 | 30 33 | 30 38 | 30 42 | 30 46 | 30 50 | 30 54 | 30 58 | 31 2 | 31 6 | 31 10 | 31 14 | 49 |
| 50 | 30 54 | 30 58 | 31 3 | 31 7 | 31 11 | 31 15 | 31 19 | 31 23 | 31 28 | 31 32 | 31 36 | 31 40 | 31 44 | 31 48 | 31 53 | 50 |
| 51 | 31 31 | 31 36 | 31 40 | 31 44 | 31 48 | 31 53 | 31 57 | 32 1 | 32 5 | 32 10 | 32 14 | 32 18 | 32 22 | 32 27 | 32 31 | 51 |
| 52 | 32 8 | 32 13 | 32 17 | 32 21 | 32 26 | 32 30 | 32 34 | 32 39 | 32 43 | 32 47 | 32 52 | 32 56 | 33 0 | 33 5 | 33 9 | 52 |
| 53 | 32 45 | 32 50 | 32 54 | 32 59 | 33 3 | 33 8 | 33 12 | 33 16 | 33 21 | 33 25 | 33 30 | 33 34 | 33 38 | 33 43 | 33 47 | 53 |
| 54 | 33 23 | 33 27 | 33 32 | 33 36 | 33 41 | 33 45 | 33 50 | 33 54 | 33 59 | 34 3 | 34 8 | 34 12 | 34 17 | 34 21 | 34 26 | 54 |
| 55 | 34 0 | 34 4 | 34 9 | 34 13 | 34 18 | 34 23 | 34 27 | 34 32 | 34 36 | 34 41 | 34 45 | 34 50 | 34 55 | 34 59 | 35 4 | 55 |
| 56 | 34 37 | 34 41 | 34 46 | 34 51 | 34 55 | 35 0 | 35 5 | 35 9 | 35 14 | 35 19 | 35 23 | 35 28 | 35 33 | 35 37 | 35 42 | 56 |
| 57 | 35 14 | 35 19 | 35 23 | 35 28 | 35 33 | 35 38 | 35 42 | 35 47 | 35 52 | 35 57 | 36 1 | 36 6 | 36 11 | 36 16 | 36 20 | 57 |
| 58 | 35 51 | 35 56 | 36 1 | 36 5 | 36 10 | 36 15 | 36 20 | 36 25 | 36 30 | 36 34 | 36 39 | 36 44 | 36 49 | 36 54 | 36 59 | 58 |
| 59 | 36 28 | 36 33 | 36 38 | 36 43 | 36 48 | 36 53 | 36 57 | 37 2 | 37 7 | 37 12 | 37 17 | 37 22 | 37 27 | 37 32 | 37 37 | 59 |
| 60 | 37 5 | 37 10 | 37 15 | 37 20 | 37 25 | 37 30 | 37 35 | 37 40 | 37 45 | 37 50 | 37 55 | 38 0 | 38 5 | 38 10 | 38 15 | 60 |

## HOURS

| TIME | 7° 25' | 7° 26' | 7° 27' | 7° 28' | 7° 29' | 7° 30' | 7° 31' | 7° 32' | 7° 33' | 7° 34' | 7° 35' | 7° 36' | 7° 37' | 7° 38' | 7° 39' | TIME |
|---|---|---|---|---|---|---|---|---|---|---|---|---|---|---|---|---|
| 1 | 37 5 | 37 10 | 37 15 | 37 20 | 37 25 | 37 30 | 37 35 | 37 40 | 37 45 | 37 50 | 37 55 | 38 0 | 38 5 | 38 10 | 38 15 | 1 |
| 2 | 1 14 10 | 1 14 20 | 1 14 30 | 1 14 40 | 1 14 50 | 1 15 0 | 1 15 10 | 1 15 20 | 1 15 30 | 1 15 40 | 1 15 50 | 1 16 0 | 1 16 10 | 1 16 20 | 1 16 30 | 2 |
| 3 | 1 51 15 | 1 51 30 | 1 51 45 | 1 52 0 | 1 52 15 | 1 52 30 | 1 52 45 | 1 53 0 | 1 53 15 | 1 53 30 | 1 53 45 | 1 54 0 | 1 54 15 | 1 54 30 | 1 54 45 | 3 |
| 4 | 2 28 20 | 2 28 40 | 2 29 0 | 2 29 20 | 2 29 40 | 2 30 0 | 2 30 20 | 2 30 40 | 2 31 0 | 2 31 20 | 2 31 40 | 2 32 0 | 2 32 20 | 2 32 40 | 2 33 0 | 4 |
| 5 | 3 5 25 | 3 5 50 | 3 6 15 | 3 6 40 | 3 7 5 | 3 7 30 | 3 7 55 | 3 8 20 | 3 8 45 | 3 9 10 | 3 9 35 | 3 10 0 | 3 10 25 | 3 10 50 | 3 11 15 | 5 |
| 6 | 3 42 30 | 3 43 0 | 3 43 30 | 3 44 0 | 3 44 30 | 3 45 0 | 3 45 30 | 3 46 0 | 3 46 30 | 3 47 0 | 3 47 30 | 3 48 0 | 3 48 30 | 3 49 0 | 3 49 30 | 6 |
| 7 | 4 19 35 | 4 20 10 | 4 20 45 | 4 21 20 | 4 21 55 | 4 22 30 | 4 23 5 | 4 23 40 | 4 24 15 | 4 24 50 | 4 25 25 | 4 26 0 | 4 26 35 | 4 27 10 | 4 27 45 | 7 |
| 8 | 4 56 40 | 4 57 20 | 4 58 0 | 4 58 40 | 4 59 20 | 5 0 0 | 5 0 40 | 5 1 20 | 5 2 0 | 5 2 40 | 5 3 20 | 5 4 0 | 5 4 40 | 5 5 20 | 5 6 0 | 8 |
| 9 | 5 33 45 | 5 34 30 | 5 35 15 | 5 36 0 | 5 36 45 | 5 37 30 | 5 38 15 | 5 39 0 | 5 39 45 | 5 40 30 | 5 41 15 | 5 42 0 | 5 42 45 | 5 43 30 | 5 44 15 | 9 |
| 10 | 6 10 50 | 6 11 40 | 6 12 30 | 6 13 20 | 6 14 10 | 6 15 0 | 6 15 50 | 6 16 40 | 6 17 30 | 6 18 20 | 6 19 10 | 6 20 0 | 6 20 50 | 6 21 40 | 6 22 30 | 10 |
| 11 | 6 47 55 | 6 48 50 | 6 49 45 | 6 50 40 | 6 51 35 | 6 52 30 | 6 53 25 | 6 54 20 | 6 55 15 | 6 56 10 | 6 57 5 | 6 58 0 | 6 58 55 | 6 59 50 | 7 0 45 | 11 |
| 12 | 7 25 0 | 7 26 0 | 7 27 0 | 7 28 0 | 7 29 0 | 7 30 0 | 7 31 0 | 7 32 0 | 7 33 0 | 7 34 0 | 7 35 0 | 7 36 0 | 7 37 0 | 7 38 0 | 7 39 0 | 12 |

# Table VII Diurnal Motion of the Planets

**24 HOUR TRAVEL**

Each cell shows degrees/minutes value pair (arcminutes and arcseconds). Left column = TIME (MINUTES 1–60, then HOURS 1–24).

| TIME | 0° 1' | 0° 2' | 0° 3' | 0° 4' | 0° 5' | 0° 6' | 0° 7' | 0° 8' | 0° 9' | 0° 10' | 0° 11' | 0° 12' | 0° 13' | 0° 14' | 0° 15' | TIME |
|---|---|---|---|---|---|---|---|---|---|---|---|---|---|---|---|---|
| **MINUTES** | | | | | | | | | | | | | | | | |
| 1 | 0 0 | 0 0 | 0 0 | 0 0 | 0 0 | 0 0 | 0 0 | 0 0 | 0 0 | 0 0 | 0 0 | 0 1 | 0 1 | 0 1 | 0 1 | 1 |
| 2 | 0 0 | 0 0 | 0 0 | 0 0 | 0 0 | 0 1 | 0 1 | 0 1 | 0 1 | 0 1 | 0 1 | 0 1 | 0 1 | 0 1 | 0 1 | 2 |
| 3 | 0 0 | 0 0 | 0 0 | 0 1 | 0 1 | 0 1 | 0 1 | 0 1 | 0 1 | 0 1 | 0 1 | 0 2 | 0 2 | 0 2 | 0 2 | 3 |
| 4 | 0 0 | 0 0 | 0 1 | 0 1 | 0 1 | 0 1 | 0 1 | 0 1 | 0 2 | 0 2 | 0 2 | 0 2 | 0 2 | 0 2 | 0 3 | 4 |
| 5 | 0 0 | 0 0 | 0 1 | 0 1 | 0 1 | 0 1 | 0 1 | 0 2 | 0 2 | 0 2 | 0 2 | 0 3 | 0 3 | 0 3 | 0 3 | 5 |
| 6 | 0 0 | 0 1 | 0 1 | 0 1 | 0 1 | 0 2 | 0 2 | 0 2 | 0 2 | 0 3 | 0 3 | 0 3 | 0 3 | 0 4 | 0 4 | 6 |
| 7 | 0 0 | 0 1 | 0 1 | 0 1 | 0 1 | 0 2 | 0 2 | 0 2 | 0 3 | 0 3 | 0 3 | 0 4 | 0 4 | 0 4 | 0 4 | 7 |
| 8 | 0 0 | 0 1 | 0 1 | 0 1 | 0 2 | 0 2 | 0 2 | 0 3 | 0 3 | 0 3 | 0 4 | 0 4 | 0 4 | 0 5 | 0 5 | 8 |
| 9 | 0 0 | 0 1 | 0 1 | 0 2 | 0 2 | 0 2 | 0 3 | 0 3 | 0 3 | 0 4 | 0 4 | 0 5 | 0 5 | 0 5 | 0 6 | 9 |
| 10 | 0 0 | 0 1 | 0 1 | 0 2 | 0 2 | 0 3 | 0 3 | 0 3 | 0 4 | 0 4 | 0 5 | 0 5 | 0 5 | 0 6 | 0 6 | 10 |
| 11 | 0 0 | 0 1 | 0 1 | 0 2 | 0 2 | 0 3 | 0 3 | 0 4 | 0 4 | 0 5 | 0 5 | 0 6 | 0 6 | 0 6 | 0 7 | 11 |
| 12 | 0 1 | 0 1 | 0 2 | 0 2 | 0 3 | 0 3 | 0 4 | 0 4 | 0 5 | 0 5 | 0 6 | 0 6 | 0 7 | 0 7 | 0 8 | 12 |
| 13 | 0 1 | 0 1 | 0 2 | 0 2 | 0 3 | 0 3 | 0 4 | 0 4 | 0 5 | 0 5 | 0 6 | 0 7 | 0 7 | 0 8 | 0 8 | 13 |
| 14 | 0 1 | 0 1 | 0 2 | 0 2 | 0 3 | 0 4 | 0 4 | 0 5 | 0 5 | 0 6 | 0 6 | 0 7 | 0 8 | 0 8 | 0 9 | 14 |
| 15 | 0 1 | 0 1 | 0 2 | 0 3 | 0 3 | 0 4 | 0 4 | 0 5 | 0 6 | 0 6 | 0 7 | 0 8 | 0 8 | 0 9 | 0 9 | 15 |
| 16 | 0 1 | 0 1 | 0 2 | 0 3 | 0 3 | 0 4 | 0 5 | 0 5 | 0 6 | 0 7 | 0 7 | 0 8 | 0 9 | 0 9 | 0 10 | 16 |
| 17 | 0 1 | 0 1 | 0 2 | 0 3 | 0 4 | 0 4 | 0 5 | 0 6 | 0 6 | 0 7 | 0 8 | 0 9 | 0 9 | 0 10 | 0 11 | 17 |
| 18 | 0 1 | 0 2 | 0 2 | 0 3 | 0 4 | 0 5 | 0 5 | 0 6 | 0 7 | 0 8 | 0 8 | 0 9 | 0 10 | 0 11 | 0 11 | 18 |
| 19 | 0 1 | 0 2 | 0 2 | 0 3 | 0 4 | 0 5 | 0 6 | 0 6 | 0 7 | 0 8 | 0 9 | 0 10 | 0 10 | 0 11 | 0 12 | 19 |
| 20 | 0 1 | 0 2 | 0 3 | 0 3 | 0 4 | 0 5 | 0 6 | 0 7 | 0 8 | 0 8 | 0 9 | 0 10 | 0 11 | 0 12 | 0 13 | 20 |
| 21 | 0 1 | 0 2 | 0 3 | 0 4 | 0 4 | 0 5 | 0 6 | 0 7 | 0 8 | 0 9 | 0 10 | 0 11 | 0 11 | 0 12 | 0 13 | 21 |
| 22 | 0 1 | 0 2 | 0 3 | 0 4 | 0 5 | 0 6 | 0 6 | 0 7 | 0 8 | 0 9 | 0 10 | 0 11 | 0 12 | 0 13 | 0 14 | 22 |
| 23 | 0 1 | 0 2 | 0 3 | 0 4 | 0 5 | 0 6 | 0 7 | 0 8 | 0 9 | 0 10 | 0 11 | 0 12 | 0 12 | 0 13 | 0 14 | 23 |
| 24 | 0 1 | 0 2 | 0 3 | 0 4 | 0 5 | 0 6 | 0 7 | 0 8 | 0 9 | 0 10 | 0 11 | 0 12 | 0 13 | 0 14 | 0 15 | 24 |
| 25 | 0 1 | 0 2 | 0 3 | 0 4 | 0 5 | 0 6 | 0 7 | 0 8 | 0 9 | 0 10 | 0 11 | 0 13 | 0 14 | 0 15 | 0 16 | 25 |
| 26 | 0 1 | 0 2 | 0 3 | 0 4 | 0 5 | 0 7 | 0 8 | 0 9 | 0 10 | 0 11 | 0 12 | 0 13 | 0 14 | 0 15 | 0 16 | 26 |
| 27 | 0 1 | 0 2 | 0 3 | 0 5 | 0 6 | 0 7 | 0 8 | 0 9 | 0 10 | 0 11 | 0 12 | 0 14 | 0 15 | 0 16 | 0 17 | 27 |
| 28 | 0 1 | 0 2 | 0 4 | 0 5 | 0 6 | 0 7 | 0 8 | 0 9 | 0 11 | 0 12 | 0 13 | 0 14 | 0 15 | 0 16 | 0 18 | 28 |
| 29 | 0 1 | 0 2 | 0 4 | 0 5 | 0 6 | 0 7 | 0 8 | 0 10 | 0 11 | 0 12 | 0 13 | 0 15 | 0 16 | 0 17 | 0 18 | 29 |
| 30 | 0 1 | 0 3 | 0 4 | 0 5 | 0 6 | 0 8 | 0 9 | 0 10 | 0 11 | 0 13 | 0 14 | 0 15 | 0 16 | 0 18 | 0 19 | 30 |
| 31 | 0 1 | 0 3 | 0 4 | 0 5 | 0 6 | 0 8 | 0 9 | 0 10 | 0 12 | 0 13 | 0 14 | 0 16 | 0 17 | 0 18 | 0 19 | 31 |
| 32 | 0 1 | 0 3 | 0 4 | 0 5 | 0 7 | 0 8 | 0 9 | 0 11 | 0 12 | 0 13 | 0 15 | 0 16 | 0 17 | 0 19 | 0 20 | 32 |
| 33 | 0 1 | 0 3 | 0 4 | 0 6 | 0 7 | 0 8 | 0 10 | 0 11 | 0 12 | 0 14 | 0 15 | 0 17 | 0 18 | 0 19 | 0 21 | 33 |
| 34 | 0 1 | 0 3 | 0 4 | 0 6 | 0 7 | 0 9 | 0 10 | 0 11 | 0 13 | 0 14 | 0 16 | 0 17 | 0 18 | 0 20 | 0 21 | 34 |
| 35 | 0 1 | 0 3 | 0 4 | 0 6 | 0 7 | 0 9 | 0 10 | 0 12 | 0 13 | 0 15 | 0 16 | 0 18 | 0 19 | 0 20 | 0 22 | 35 |
| 36 | 0 2 | 0 3 | 0 5 | 0 6 | 0 8 | 0 9 | 0 11 | 0 12 | 0 14 | 0 15 | 0 17 | 0 18 | 0 20 | 0 21 | 0 23 | 36 |
| 37 | 0 2 | 0 3 | 0 5 | 0 6 | 0 8 | 0 9 | 0 11 | 0 12 | 0 14 | 0 15 | 0 17 | 0 19 | 0 20 | 0 22 | 0 23 | 37 |
| 38 | 0 2 | 0 3 | 0 5 | 0 6 | 0 8 | 0 10 | 0 11 | 0 13 | 0 14 | 0 16 | 0 17 | 0 19 | 0 21 | 0 22 | 0 24 | 38 |
| 39 | 0 2 | 0 3 | 0 5 | 0 7 | 0 8 | 0 10 | 0 11 | 0 13 | 0 15 | 0 16 | 0 18 | 0 20 | 0 21 | 0 23 | 0 24 | 39 |
| 40 | 0 2 | 0 3 | 0 5 | 0 7 | 0 8 | 0 10 | 0 12 | 0 13 | 0 15 | 0 17 | 0 18 | 0 20 | 0 22 | 0 23 | 0 25 | 40 |
| 41 | 0 2 | 0 3 | 0 5 | 0 7 | 0 9 | 0 10 | 0 12 | 0 14 | 0 15 | 0 17 | 0 19 | 0 21 | 0 22 | 0 24 | 0 26 | 41 |
| 42 | 0 2 | 0 4 | 0 5 | 0 7 | 0 9 | 0 11 | 0 12 | 0 14 | 0 16 | 0 18 | 0 19 | 0 21 | 0 23 | 0 25 | 0 26 | 42 |
| 43 | 0 2 | 0 4 | 0 5 | 0 7 | 0 9 | 0 11 | 0 13 | 0 14 | 0 16 | 0 18 | 0 20 | 0 22 | 0 23 | 0 25 | 0 27 | 43 |
| 44 | 0 2 | 0 4 | 0 6 | 0 7 | 0 9 | 0 11 | 0 13 | 0 15 | 0 17 | 0 18 | 0 20 | 0 22 | 0 24 | 0 26 | 0 28 | 44 |
| 45 | 0 2 | 0 4 | 0 6 | 0 8 | 0 9 | 0 11 | 0 13 | 0 15 | 0 17 | 0 19 | 0 21 | 0 23 | 0 24 | 0 26 | 0 28 | 45 |
| 46 | 0 2 | 0 4 | 0 6 | 0 8 | 0 10 | 0 12 | 0 13 | 0 15 | 0 17 | 0 19 | 0 21 | 0 23 | 0 25 | 0 27 | 0 29 | 46 |
| 47 | 0 2 | 0 4 | 0 6 | 0 8 | 0 10 | 0 12 | 0 14 | 0 16 | 0 18 | 0 20 | 0 22 | 0 24 | 0 25 | 0 27 | 0 29 | 47 |
| 48 | 0 2 | 0 4 | 0 6 | 0 8 | 0 10 | 0 12 | 0 14 | 0 16 | 0 18 | 0 20 | 0 22 | 0 24 | 0 26 | 0 28 | 0 30 | 48 |
| 49 | 0 2 | 0 4 | 0 6 | 0 8 | 0 10 | 0 12 | 0 14 | 0 16 | 0 18 | 0 20 | 0 22 | 0 25 | 0 27 | 0 29 | 0 31 | 49 |
| 50 | 0 2 | 0 4 | 0 6 | 0 8 | 0 10 | 0 13 | 0 15 | 0 17 | 0 19 | 0 21 | 0 23 | 0 25 | 0 27 | 0 29 | 0 31 | 50 |
| 51 | 0 2 | 0 4 | 0 6 | 0 9 | 0 11 | 0 13 | 0 15 | 0 17 | 0 19 | 0 21 | 0 23 | 0 26 | 0 28 | 0 30 | 0 32 | 51 |
| 52 | 0 2 | 0 4 | 0 7 | 0 9 | 0 11 | 0 13 | 0 15 | 0 17 | 0 20 | 0 22 | 0 24 | 0 26 | 0 28 | 0 30 | 0 33 | 52 |
| 53 | 0 2 | 0 4 | 0 7 | 0 9 | 0 11 | 0 13 | 0 15 | 0 18 | 0 20 | 0 22 | 0 24 | 0 27 | 0 29 | 0 31 | 0 33 | 53 |
| 54 | 0 2 | 0 5 | 0 7 | 0 9 | 0 11 | 0 14 | 0 16 | 0 18 | 0 20 | 0 23 | 0 25 | 0 27 | 0 29 | 0 32 | 0 34 | 54 |
| 55 | 0 2 | 0 5 | 0 7 | 0 9 | 0 11 | 0 14 | 0 16 | 0 18 | 0 21 | 0 23 | 0 25 | 0 28 | 0 30 | 0 32 | 0 34 | 55 |
| 56 | 0 2 | 0 5 | 0 7 | 0 9 | 0 12 | 0 14 | 0 16 | 0 19 | 0 21 | 0 23 | 0 26 | 0 28 | 0 30 | 0 33 | 0 35 | 56 |
| 57 | 0 2 | 0 5 | 0 7 | 0 10 | 0 12 | 0 14 | 0 17 | 0 19 | 0 21 | 0 24 | 0 26 | 0 29 | 0 31 | 0 33 | 0 36 | 57 |
| 58 | 0 2 | 0 5 | 0 7 | 0 10 | 0 12 | 0 15 | 0 17 | 0 19 | 0 22 | 0 24 | 0 27 | 0 29 | 0 31 | 0 34 | 0 36 | 58 |
| 59 | 0 2 | 0 5 | 0 7 | 0 10 | 0 12 | 0 15 | 0 17 | 0 20 | 0 22 | 0 25 | 0 27 | 0 30 | 0 32 | 0 34 | 0 37 | 59 |
| 60 | 0 3 | 0 5 | 0 8 | 0 10 | 0 13 | 0 15 | 0 18 | 0 20 | 0 23 | 0 25 | 0 28 | 0 30 | 0 33 | 0 35 | 0 38 | 60 |
| **HOURS** | | | | | | | | | | | | | | | | |
| 1 | 0 3 | 0 5 | 0 8 | 0 10 | 0 13 | 0 15 | 0 18 | 0 20 | 0 23 | 0 25 | 0 28 | 0 30 | 0 33 | 0 35 | 0 38 | 1 |
| 2 | 0 5 | 0 10 | 0 15 | 0 20 | 0 25 | 0 30 | 0 35 | 0 40 | 0 45 | 0 50 | 0 55 | 1 0 | 1 5 | 1 10 | 1 15 | 2 |
| 3 | 0 8 | 0 15 | 0 23 | 0 30 | 0 38 | 0 45 | 0 53 | 1 0 | 1 8 | 1 15 | 1 23 | 1 30 | 1 38 | 1 45 | 1 53 | 3 |
| 4 | 0 10 | 0 20 | 0 30 | 0 40 | 0 50 | 1 0 | 1 10 | 1 20 | 1 30 | 1 40 | 1 50 | 2 0 | 2 10 | 2 20 | 2 30 | 4 |
| 5 | 0 13 | 0 25 | 0 38 | 0 50 | 1 3 | 1 15 | 1 28 | 1 40 | 1 53 | 2 5 | 2 18 | 2 30 | 2 43 | 2 55 | 3 8 | 5 |
| 6 | 0 15 | 0 30 | 0 45 | 1 0 | 1 15 | 1 30 | 1 45 | 2 0 | 2 15 | 2 30 | 2 45 | 3 0 | 3 15 | 3 30 | 3 45 | 6 |
| 7 | 0 18 | 0 35 | 0 53 | 1 10 | 1 28 | 1 45 | 2 3 | 2 20 | 2 38 | 2 55 | 3 13 | 3 30 | 3 48 | 4 5 | 4 23 | 7 |
| 8 | 0 20 | 0 40 | 1 0 | 1 20 | 1 40 | 2 0 | 2 20 | 2 40 | 3 0 | 3 20 | 3 40 | 4 0 | 4 20 | 4 40 | 5 0 | 8 |
| 9 | 0 23 | 0 45 | 1 8 | 1 30 | 1 53 | 2 15 | 2 38 | 3 0 | 3 23 | 3 45 | 4 8 | 4 30 | 4 53 | 5 15 | 5 38 | 9 |
| 10 | 0 25 | 0 50 | 1 15 | 1 40 | 2 5 | 2 30 | 2 55 | 3 20 | 3 45 | 4 10 | 4 35 | 5 0 | 5 25 | 5 50 | 6 15 | 10 |
| 11 | 0 28 | 0 55 | 1 23 | 1 50 | 2 18 | 2 45 | 3 13 | 3 40 | 4 8 | 4 35 | 5 3 | 5 30 | 5 58 | 6 25 | 6 53 | 11 |
| 12 | 0 30 | 1 0 | 1 30 | 2 0 | 2 30 | 3 0 | 3 30 | 4 0 | 4 30 | 5 0 | 5 30 | 6 0 | 6 30 | 7 0 | 7 30 | 12 |
| 13 | 0 33 | 1 5 | 1 38 | 2 10 | 2 43 | 3 15 | 3 48 | 4 20 | 4 53 | 5 25 | 5 58 | 6 30 | 7 3 | 7 35 | 8 8 | 13 |
| 14 | 0 35 | 1 10 | 1 45 | 2 20 | 2 55 | 3 30 | 4 5 | 4 40 | 5 15 | 5 50 | 6 25 | 7 0 | 7 35 | 8 10 | 8 45 | 14 |
| 15 | 0 38 | 1 15 | 1 53 | 2 30 | 3 8 | 3 45 | 4 23 | 5 0 | 5 38 | 6 15 | 6 53 | 7 30 | 8 8 | 8 45 | 9 23 | 15 |
| 16 | 0 40 | 1 20 | 2 0 | 2 40 | 3 20 | 4 0 | 4 40 | 5 20 | 6 0 | 6 40 | 7 20 | 8 0 | 8 40 | 9 20 | 10 0 | 16 |
| 17 | 0 43 | 1 25 | 2 8 | 2 50 | 3 33 | 4 15 | 4 58 | 5 40 | 6 23 | 7 5 | 7 48 | 8 30 | 9 13 | 9 55 | 10 38 | 17 |
| 18 | 0 45 | 1 30 | 2 15 | 3 0 | 3 45 | 4 30 | 5 15 | 6 0 | 6 45 | 7 30 | 8 15 | 9 0 | 9 45 | 10 30 | 11 15 | 18 |
| 19 | 0 48 | 1 35 | 2 23 | 3 10 | 3 58 | 4 45 | 5 33 | 6 20 | 7 8 | 7 55 | 8 43 | 9 30 | 10 18 | 11 5 | 11 53 | 19 |
| 20 | 0 50 | 1 40 | 2 30 | 3 20 | 4 10 | 5 0 | 5 50 | 6 40 | 7 30 | 8 20 | 9 10 | 10 0 | 10 50 | 11 40 | 12 30 | 20 |
| 21 | 0 53 | 1 45 | 2 38 | 3 30 | 4 23 | 5 15 | 6 8 | 7 0 | 7 53 | 8 45 | 9 38 | 10 30 | 11 23 | 12 15 | 13 8 | 21 |
| 22 | 0 55 | 1 50 | 2 45 | 3 40 | 4 35 | 5 30 | 6 25 | 7 20 | 8 15 | 9 10 | 10 5 | 11 0 | 11 55 | 12 50 | 13 45 | 22 |
| 23 | 0 58 | 1 55 | 2 53 | 3 50 | 4 48 | 5 45 | 6 43 | 7 40 | 8 38 | 9 35 | 10 33 | 11 30 | 12 28 | 13 25 | 14 23 | 23 |
| 24 | 1 0 | 2 0 | 3 0 | 4 0 | 5 0 | 6 0 | 7 0 | 8 0 | 9 0 | 10 0 | 11 0 | 12 0 | 13 0 | 14 0 | 15 0 | 24 |

# Table VII Diurnal Motion of the Planets

**24 HOUR TRAVEL**

*(Each cell below gives degrees and minutes, e.g. "0 1" = 0° 1'.)*

| TIME | 0°16' | 0°17' | 0°18' | 0°19' | 0°20' | 0°21' | 0°22' | 0°23' | 0°24' | 0°25' | 0°26' | 0°27' | 0°28' | 0°29' | 0°30' | TIME |
|---|---|---|---|---|---|---|---|---|---|---|---|---|---|---|---|---|
| **MINUTES 1** | 0 1 | 0 1 | 0 1 | 0 1 | 0 1 | 0 1 | 0 1 | 0 1 | 0 1 | 0 1 | 0 1 | 0 1 | 0 1 | 0 1 | 0 1 | 1 **MINUTES** |
| 2 | 0 1 | 0 1 | 0 2 | 0 2 | 0 2 | 0 2 | 0 2 | 0 2 | 0 2 | 0 2 | 0 2 | 0 2 | 0 2 | 0 2 | 0 3 | 2 |
| 3 | 0 2 | 0 2 | 0 2 | 0 2 | 0 3 | 0 3 | 0 3 | 0 3 | 0 3 | 0 3 | 0 3 | 0 3 | 0 4 | 0 4 | 0 4 | 3 |
| 4 | 0 3 | 0 3 | 0 3 | 0 3 | 0 3 | 0 4 | 0 4 | 0 4 | 0 4 | 0 4 | 0 4 | 0 5 | 0 5 | 0 5 | 0 5 | 4 |
| 5 | 0 3 | 0 4 | 0 4 | 0 4 | 0 4 | 0 4 | 0 5 | 0 5 | 0 5 | 0 5 | 0 5 | 0 6 | 0 6 | 0 6 | 0 6 | 5 |
| 6 | 0 4 | 0 4 | 0 5 | 0 5 | 0 5 | 0 5 | 0 6 | 0 6 | 0 6 | 0 6 | 0 7 | 0 7 | 0 7 | 0 7 | 0 8 | 6 |
| 7 | 0 5 | 0 5 | 0 5 | 0 6 | 0 6 | 0 6 | 0 6 | 0 7 | 0 7 | 0 7 | 0 8 | 0 8 | 0 8 | 0 9 | 0 9 | 7 |
| 8 | 0 5 | 0 6 | 0 6 | 0 6 | 0 7 | 0 7 | 0 7 | 0 8 | 0 8 | 0 8 | 0 9 | 0 9 | 0 9 | 0 10 | 0 10 | 8 |
| 9 | 0 6 | 0 6 | 0 7 | 0 7 | 0 8 | 0 8 | 0 8 | 0 9 | 0 9 | 0 9 | 0 10 | 0 10 | 0 11 | 0 11 | 0 11 | 9 |
| 10 | 0 7 | 0 7 | 0 8 | 0 8 | 0 8 | 0 9 | 0 9 | 0 10 | 0 10 | 0 11 | 0 11 | 0 11 | 0 12 | 0 12 | 0 13 | 10 |
| 11 | 0 7 | 0 8 | 0 8 | 0 9 | 0 9 | 0 10 | 0 10 | 0 11 | 0 11 | 0 12 | 0 12 | 0 12 | 0 13 | 0 13 | 0 14 | 11 |
| 12 | 0 8 | 0 9 | 0 9 | 0 10 | 0 10 | 0 11 | 0 11 | 0 12 | 0 12 | 0 13 | 0 13 | 0 14 | 0 14 | 0 15 | 0 15 | 12 |
| 13 | 0 9 | 0 9 | 0 10 | 0 10 | 0 11 | 0 11 | 0 12 | 0 13 | 0 13 | 0 14 | 0 14 | 0 15 | 0 15 | 0 16 | 0 16 | 13 |
| 14 | 0 9 | 0 10 | 0 11 | 0 11 | 0 12 | 0 12 | 0 13 | 0 14 | 0 14 | 0 15 | 0 15 | 0 16 | 0 16 | 0 17 | 0 18 | 14 |
| 15 | 0 10 | 0 11 | 0 11 | 0 12 | 0 13 | 0 13 | 0 14 | 0 15 | 0 15 | 0 16 | 0 16 | 0 17 | 0 18 | 0 18 | 0 19 | 15 |
| 16 | 0 11 | 0 11 | 0 12 | 0 13 | 0 13 | 0 14 | 0 15 | 0 15 | 0 16 | 0 17 | 0 17 | 0 18 | 0 19 | 0 19 | 0 20 | 16 |
| 17 | 0 11 | 0 12 | 0 13 | 0 14 | 0 14 | 0 15 | 0 16 | 0 16 | 0 17 | 0 18 | 0 18 | 0 19 | 0 20 | 0 21 | 0 21 | 17 |
| 18 | 0 12 | 0 13 | 0 14 | 0 14 | 0 15 | 0 16 | 0 17 | 0 17 | 0 18 | 0 19 | 0 20 | 0 20 | 0 21 | 0 22 | 0 23 | 18 |
| 19 | 0 13 | 0 13 | 0 14 | 0 15 | 0 16 | 0 17 | 0 17 | 0 18 | 0 19 | 0 20 | 0 21 | 0 22 | 0 22 | 0 23 | 0 24 | 19 |
| 20 | 0 13 | 0 14 | 0 15 | 0 16 | 0 17 | 0 18 | 0 18 | 0 19 | 0 20 | 0 21 | 0 22 | 0 23 | 0 23 | 0 24 | 0 25 | 20 |
| 21 | 0 14 | 0 15 | 0 16 | 0 17 | 0 18 | 0 19 | 0 19 | 0 20 | 0 21 | 0 22 | 0 23 | 0 24 | 0 25 | 0 26 | 0 26 | 21 |
| 22 | 0 15 | 0 16 | 0 17 | 0 18 | 0 18 | 0 19 | 0 20 | 0 21 | 0 22 | 0 23 | 0 24 | 0 25 | 0 26 | 0 27 | 0 28 | 22 |
| 23 | 0 15 | 0 16 | 0 17 | 0 18 | 0 19 | 0 20 | 0 21 | 0 22 | 0 23 | 0 24 | 0 25 | 0 26 | 0 27 | 0 28 | 0 29 | 23 |
| 24 | 0 16 | 0 17 | 0 18 | 0 19 | 0 20 | 0 21 | 0 22 | 0 23 | 0 24 | 0 25 | 0 26 | 0 27 | 0 28 | 0 29 | 0 30 | 24 |
| 25 | 0 17 | 0 18 | 0 19 | 0 20 | 0 21 | 0 22 | 0 23 | 0 24 | 0 25 | 0 26 | 0 27 | 0 28 | 0 29 | 0 30 | 0 31 | 25 |
| 26 | 0 17 | 0 18 | 0 20 | 0 21 | 0 22 | 0 23 | 0 24 | 0 25 | 0 26 | 0 27 | 0 28 | 0 29 | 0 30 | 0 32 | 0 33 | 26 |
| 27 | 0 18 | 0 19 | 0 20 | 0 22 | 0 23 | 0 24 | 0 25 | 0 26 | 0 27 | 0 28 | 0 29 | 0 31 | 0 32 | 0 33 | 0 34 | 27 |
| 28 | 0 19 | 0 20 | 0 21 | 0 22 | 0 23 | 0 25 | 0 26 | 0 27 | 0 28 | 0 29 | 0 30 | 0 32 | 0 33 | 0 34 | 0 35 | 28 |
| 29 | 0 19 | 0 21 | 0 22 | 0 23 | 0 24 | 0 26 | 0 27 | 0 28 | 0 29 | 0 30 | 0 31 | 0 33 | 0 34 | 0 35 | 0 36 | 29 |
| 30 | 0 20 | 0 21 | 0 23 | 0 24 | 0 25 | 0 26 | 0 28 | 0 29 | 0 30 | 0 31 | 0 33 | 0 34 | 0 35 | 0 36 | 0 38 | 30 |
| 31 | 0 21 | 0 22 | 0 23 | 0 25 | 0 26 | 0 27 | 0 28 | 0 30 | 0 31 | 0 33 | 0 34 | 0 35 | 0 36 | 0 38 | 0 39 | 31 |
| 32 | 0 21 | 0 23 | 0 24 | 0 26 | 0 27 | 0 28 | 0 29 | 0 31 | 0 32 | 0 34 | 0 35 | 0 36 | 0 37 | 0 39 | 0 40 | 32 |
| 33 | 0 22 | 0 23 | 0 25 | 0 26 | 0 28 | 0 29 | 0 30 | 0 32 | 0 33 | 0 35 | 0 36 | 0 37 | 0 39 | 0 40 | 0 41 | 33 |
| 34 | 0 23 | 0 24 | 0 26 | 0 27 | 0 28 | 0 30 | 0 31 | 0 33 | 0 34 | 0 36 | 0 37 | 0 39 | 0 40 | 0 41 | 0 43 | 34 |
| 35 | 0 23 | 0 25 | 0 26 | 0 28 | 0 29 | 0 31 | 0 32 | 0 34 | 0 35 | 0 37 | 0 38 | 0 40 | 0 41 | 0 43 | 0 44 | 35 |
| 36 | 0 24 | 0 26 | 0 27 | 0 29 | 0 30 | 0 32 | 0 33 | 0 35 | 0 36 | 0 38 | 0 39 | 0 41 | 0 42 | 0 44 | 0 45 | 36 |
| 37 | 0 25 | 0 26 | 0 28 | 0 30 | 0 31 | 0 33 | 0 34 | 0 36 | 0 37 | 0 39 | 0 40 | 0 42 | 0 43 | 0 45 | 0 46 | 37 |
| 38 | 0 25 | 0 27 | 0 29 | 0 30 | 0 32 | 0 34 | 0 35 | 0 37 | 0 38 | 0 40 | 0 41 | 0 43 | 0 44 | 0 46 | 0 48 | 38 |
| 39 | 0 26 | 0 28 | 0 29 | 0 31 | 0 33 | 0 34 | 0 36 | 0 38 | 0 39 | 0 41 | 0 42 | 0 44 | 0 46 | 0 47 | 0 49 | 39 |
| 40 | 0 27 | 0 28 | 0 30 | 0 32 | 0 33 | 0 35 | 0 37 | 0 39 | 0 40 | 0 42 | 0 43 | 0 45 | 0 47 | 0 48 | 0 50 | 40 |
| 41 | 0 27 | 0 29 | 0 31 | 0 33 | 0 34 | 0 36 | 0 38 | 0 40 | 0 41 | 0 43 | 0 44 | 0 46 | 0 48 | 0 50 | 0 51 | 41 |
| 42 | 0 28 | 0 30 | 0 32 | 0 34 | 0 35 | 0 37 | 0 39 | 0 41 | 0 42 | 0 44 | 0 46 | 0 48 | 0 49 | 0 51 | 0 53 | 42 |
| 43 | 0 29 | 0 30 | 0 32 | 0 34 | 0 36 | 0 38 | 0 39 | 0 42 | 0 43 | 0 45 | 0 47 | 0 49 | 0 50 | 0 52 | 0 54 | 43 |
| 44 | 0 29 | 0 31 | 0 33 | 0 35 | 0 37 | 0 39 | 0 40 | 0 43 | 0 44 | 0 46 | 0 48 | 0 50 | 0 51 | 0 54 | 0 55 | 44 |
| 45 | 0 30 | 0 32 | 0 34 | 0 36 | 0 38 | 0 40 | 0 41 | 0 44 | 0 45 | 0 47 | 0 49 | 0 51 | 0 53 | 0 55 | 0 56 | 45 |
| 46 | 0 31 | 0 33 | 0 35 | 0 37 | 0 38 | 0 41 | 0 42 | 0 44 | 0 46 | 0 48 | 0 50 | 0 52 | 0 54 | 0 56 | 0 58 | 46 |
| 47 | 0 31 | 0 33 | 0 35 | 0 38 | 0 39 | 0 42 | 0 43 | 0 45 | 0 47 | 0 49 | 0 51 | 0 53 | 0 55 | 0 57 | 0 59 | 47 |
| 48 | 0 32 | 0 34 | 0 36 | 0 38 | 0 40 | 0 42 | 0 44 | 0 46 | 0 48 | 0 50 | 0 52 | 0 54 | 0 56 | 0 58 | 1 0 | 48 |
| 49 | 0 33 | 0 35 | 0 37 | 0 39 | 0 41 | 0 43 | 0 45 | 0 47 | 0 49 | 0 51 | 0 53 | 0 56 | 0 57 | 1 0 | 1 1 | 49 |
| 50 | 0 33 | 0 35 | 0 38 | 0 40 | 0 42 | 0 44 | 0 46 | 0 48 | 0 50 | 0 52 | 0 54 | 0 56 | 0 58 | 1 0 | 1 3 | 50 |
| 51 | 0 34 | 0 36 | 0 38 | 0 41 | 0 43 | 0 45 | 0 47 | 0 49 | 0 51 | 0 53 | 0 55 | 0 58 | 1 0 | 1 2 | 1 4 | 51 |
| 52 | 0 35 | 0 37 | 0 39 | 0 42 | 0 43 | 0 46 | 0 48 | 0 50 | 0 52 | 0 54 | 0 56 | 0 59 | 1 1 | 1 3 | 1 5 | 52 |
| 53 | 0 35 | 0 38 | 0 40 | 0 42 | 0 44 | 0 47 | 0 49 | 0 51 | 0 53 | 0 55 | 0 57 | 1 0 | 1 2 | 1 4 | 1 6 | 53 |
| 54 | 0 36 | 0 38 | 0 41 | 0 43 | 0 45 | 0 48 | 0 50 | 0 52 | 0 54 | 0 56 | 0 59 | 1 1 | 1 3 | 1 5 | 1 8 | 54 |
| 55 | 0 37 | 0 39 | 0 41 | 0 44 | 0 46 | 0 48 | 0 50 | 0 53 | 0 55 | 0 57 | 1 0 | 1 2 | 1 4 | 1 6 | 1 9 | 55 |
| 56 | 0 37 | 0 40 | 0 42 | 0 45 | 0 47 | 0 49 | 0 51 | 0 54 | 0 56 | 0 58 | 1 1 | 1 3 | 1 5 | 1 8 | 1 10 | 56 |
| 57 | 0 38 | 0 40 | 0 43 | 0 45 | 0 48 | 0 50 | 0 52 | 0 55 | 0 57 | 0 59 | 1 2 | 1 4 | 1 7 | 1 9 | 1 11 | 57 |
| 58 | 0 39 | 0 41 | 0 44 | 0 46 | 0 48 | 0 51 | 0 53 | 0 56 | 0 58 | 1 0 | 1 3 | 1 5 | 1 8 | 1 10 | 1 13 | 58 |
| 59 | 0 39 | 0 42 | 0 44 | 0 47 | 0 49 | 0 52 | 0 54 | 0 57 | 0 59 | 1 1 | 1 4 | 1 6 | 1 9 | 1 11 | 1 14 | 59 |
| 60 | 0 40 | 0 43 | 0 45 | 0 48 | 0 50 | 0 53 | 0 55 | 0 58 | 1 0 | 1 3 | 1 5 | 1 8 | 1 10 | 1 13 | 1 15 | 60 |
| **HOURS 1** | 0 40 | 0 43 | 0 45 | 0 48 | 0 50 | 0 53 | 0 55 | 0 58 | 1 0 | 1 3 | 1 5 | 1 8 | 1 10 | 1 13 | 1 15 | 1 **HOURS** |
| 2 | 1 20 | 1 25 | 1 30 | 1 35 | 1 40 | 1 45 | 1 50 | 1 55 | 2 0 | 2 5 | 2 10 | 2 15 | 2 20 | 2 25 | 2 30 | 2 |
| 3 | 2 0 | 2 8 | 2 15 | 2 23 | 2 30 | 2 38 | 2 45 | 2 53 | 3 0 | 3 8 | 3 15 | 3 23 | 3 30 | 3 38 | 3 45 | 3 |
| 4 | 2 40 | 2 50 | 3 0 | 3 10 | 3 20 | 3 30 | 3 40 | 3 50 | 4 0 | 4 10 | 4 20 | 4 30 | 4 40 | 4 50 | 5 0 | 4 |
| 5 | 3 20 | 3 33 | 3 45 | 3 58 | 4 10 | 4 23 | 4 35 | 4 48 | 5 0 | 5 13 | 5 25 | 5 38 | 5 50 | 6 3 | 6 15 | 5 |
| 6 | 4 0 | 4 15 | 4 30 | 4 45 | 5 0 | 5 15 | 5 30 | 5 45 | 6 0 | 6 15 | 6 30 | 6 45 | 7 0 | 7 15 | 7 30 | 6 |
| 7 | 4 40 | 4 58 | 5 15 | 5 33 | 5 50 | 6 8 | 6 25 | 6 43 | 7 0 | 7 18 | 7 35 | 7 53 | 8 10 | 8 28 | 8 45 | 7 |
| 8 | 5 20 | 5 40 | 6 0 | 6 20 | 6 40 | 7 0 | 7 20 | 7 40 | 8 0 | 8 20 | 8 40 | 9 0 | 9 20 | 9 40 | 10 0 | 8 |
| 9 | 6 0 | 6 23 | 6 45 | 7 8 | 7 30 | 7 53 | 8 15 | 8 38 | 9 0 | 9 23 | 9 45 | 10 8 | 10 30 | 10 53 | 11 15 | 9 |
| 10 | 6 40 | 7 5 | 7 30 | 7 55 | 8 20 | 8 45 | 9 10 | 9 35 | 10 0 | 10 25 | 10 50 | 11 15 | 11 40 | 12 5 | 12 30 | 10 |
| 11 | 7 20 | 7 48 | 8 15 | 8 43 | 9 10 | 9 38 | 10 5 | 10 33 | 11 0 | 11 28 | 11 55 | 12 23 | 12 50 | 13 18 | 13 45 | 11 |
| 12 | 8 0 | 8 30 | 9 0 | 9 30 | 10 0 | 10 30 | 11 0 | 11 30 | 12 0 | 12 30 | 13 0 | 13 30 | 14 0 | 14 30 | 15 0 | 12 |
| 13 | 8 40 | 9 13 | 9 45 | 10 18 | 10 50 | 11 23 | 11 55 | 12 28 | 13 0 | 13 33 | 14 5 | 14 38 | 15 10 | 15 43 | 16 15 | 13 |
| 14 | 9 20 | 9 55 | 10 30 | 11 5 | 11 40 | 12 15 | 12 50 | 13 25 | 14 0 | 14 35 | 15 10 | 15 45 | 16 20 | 16 55 | 17 30 | 14 |
| 15 | 10 0 | 10 38 | 11 15 | 11 53 | 12 30 | 13 8 | 13 45 | 14 23 | 15 0 | 15 38 | 16 15 | 16 53 | 17 30 | 18 8 | 18 45 | 15 |
| 16 | 10 40 | 11 20 | 12 0 | 12 40 | 13 20 | 14 0 | 14 40 | 15 20 | 16 0 | 16 40 | 17 20 | 18 0 | 18 40 | 19 20 | 20 0 | 16 |
| 17 | 11 20 | 12 3 | 12 45 | 13 28 | 14 10 | 14 53 | 15 35 | 16 18 | 17 0 | 17 43 | 18 25 | 19 8 | 19 50 | 20 33 | 21 15 | 17 |
| 18 | 12 0 | 12 45 | 13 30 | 14 15 | 15 0 | 15 45 | 16 30 | 17 15 | 18 0 | 18 45 | 19 30 | 20 15 | 21 0 | 21 45 | 22 30 | 18 |
| 19 | 12 40 | 13 28 | 14 15 | 15 3 | 15 50 | 16 38 | 17 25 | 18 13 | 19 0 | 19 48 | 20 35 | 21 23 | 22 10 | 22 58 | 23 45 | 19 |
| 20 | 13 20 | 14 10 | 15 0 | 15 50 | 16 40 | 17 30 | 18 20 | 19 10 | 20 0 | 20 50 | 21 40 | 22 30 | 23 20 | 24 10 | 25 0 | 20 |
| 21 | 14 0 | 14 53 | 15 45 | 16 38 | 17 30 | 18 23 | 19 15 | 20 8 | 21 0 | 21 53 | 22 45 | 23 38 | 24 30 | 25 23 | 26 15 | 21 |
| 22 | 14 40 | 15 35 | 16 30 | 17 25 | 18 20 | 19 15 | 20 10 | 21 5 | 22 0 | 22 55 | 23 50 | 24 45 | 25 40 | 26 35 | 27 30 | 22 |
| 23 | 15 20 | 16 18 | 17 15 | 18 13 | 19 10 | 20 8 | 21 5 | 22 3 | 23 0 | 23 58 | 24 55 | 25 53 | 26 50 | 27 48 | 28 45 | 23 |
| 24 | 16 0 | 17 0 | 18 0 | 19 0 | 20 0 | 21 0 | 22 0 | 23 0 | 24 0 | 25 0 | 26 0 | 27 0 | 28 0 | 29 0 | 30 0 | 24 |

# Table VII Diurnal Motion of the Planets

| TIME | 0°31' | 0°32' | 0°33' | 0°34' | 0°35' | 0°36' | 0°37' | 0°38' | 0°39' | 0°40' | 0°41' | 0°42' | 0°43' | 0°44' | 0°45' | TIME |
|---|---|---|---|---|---|---|---|---|---|---|---|---|---|---|---|---|
| **MINUTES 1** | 0 1 | 0 1 | 0 1 | 0 1 | 0 1 | 0 2 | 0 2 | 0 2 | 0 2 | 0 2 | 0 2 | 0 2 | 0 2 | 0 2 | 0 2 | 1 |
| 2 | 0 3 | 0 3 | 0 3 | 0 3 | 0 3 | 0 3 | 0 3 | 0 3 | 0 3 | 0 3 | 0 3 | 0 4 | 0 4 | 0 4 | 0 4 | 2 |
| 3 | 0 4 | 0 4 | 0 4 | 0 4 | 0 4 | 0 5 | 0 5 | 0 5 | 0 5 | 0 5 | 0 5 | 0 5 | 0 5 | 0 6 | 0 6 | 3 |
| 4 | 0 5 | 0 5 | 0 6 | 0 6 | 0 6 | 0 6 | 0 6 | 0 6 | 0 6 | 0 7 | 0 7 | 0 7 | 0 7 | 0 7 | 0 8 | 4 |
| 5 | 0 6 | 0 7 | 0 7 | 0 7 | 0 7 | 0 8 | 0 8 | 0 8 | 0 8 | 0 8 | 0 8 | 0 9 | 0 9 | 0 9 | 0 9 | 5 |
| 6 | 0 8 | 0 8 | 0 8 | 0 9 | 0 9 | 0 9 | 0 9 | 0 10 | 0 10 | 0 10 | 0 10 | 0 10 | 0 11 | 0 11 | 0 11 | 6 |
| 7 | 0 9 | 0 9 | 0 10 | 0 10 | 0 10 | 0 11 | 0 11 | 0 11 | 0 11 | 0 12 | 0 12 | 0 12 | 0 13 | 0 13 | 0 13 | 7 |
| 8 | 0 10 | 0 11 | 0 11 | 0 11 | 0 12 | 0 12 | 0 12 | 0 13 | 0 13 | 0 13 | 0 14 | 0 14 | 0 14 | 0 15 | 0 15 | 8 |
| 9 | 0 12 | 0 12 | 0 12 | 0 13 | 0 13 | 0 14 | 0 14 | 0 14 | 0 15 | 0 15 | 0 15 | 0 16 | 0 16 | 0 17 | 0 17 | 9 |
| 10 | 0 13 | 0 13 | 0 14 | 0 14 | 0 15 | 0 15 | 0 15 | 0 16 | 0 16 | 0 17 | 0 17 | 0 18 | 0 18 | 0 18 | 0 19 | 10 |
| 11 | 0 14 | 0 15 | 0 15 | 0 16 | 0 16 | 0 17 | 0 17 | 0 17 | 0 18 | 0 18 | 0 19 | 0 19 | 0 20 | 0 20 | 0 21 | 11 |
| 12 | 0 16 | 0 16 | 0 17 | 0 17 | 0 18 | 0 18 | 0 19 | 0 19 | 0 20 | 0 20 | 0 21 | 0 21 | 0 22 | 0 22 | 0 23 | 12 |
| 13 | 0 17 | 0 17 | 0 18 | 0 18 | 0 19 | 0 20 | 0 20 | 0 21 | 0 21 | 0 22 | 0 22 | 0 23 | 0 23 | 0 24 | 0 24 | 13 |
| 14 | 0 18 | 0 19 | 0 19 | 0 20 | 0 20 | 0 21 | 0 22 | 0 22 | 0 23 | 0 23 | 0 24 | 0 25 | 0 25 | 0 26 | 0 26 | 14 |
| 15 | 0 19 | 0 20 | 0 21 | 0 21 | 0 22 | 0 23 | 0 23 | 0 24 | 0 24 | 0 25 | 0 26 | 0 26 | 0 27 | 0 28 | 0 28 | 15 |
| 16 | 0 21 | 0 21 | 0 22 | 0 23 | 0 23 | 0 24 | 0 25 | 0 25 | 0 26 | 0 27 | 0 27 | 0 28 | 0 29 | 0 29 | 0 30 | 16 |
| 17 | 0 22 | 0 23 | 0 23 | 0 24 | 0 25 | 0 26 | 0 26 | 0 27 | 0 28 | 0 28 | 0 29 | 0 30 | 0 30 | 0 31 | 0 32 | 17 |
| 18 | 0 23 | 0 24 | 0 25 | 0 26 | 0 26 | 0 27 | 0 28 | 0 29 | 0 29 | 0 30 | 0 31 | 0 32 | 0 32 | 0 33 | 0 34 | 18 |
| 19 | 0 25 | 0 25 | 0 26 | 0 27 | 0 28 | 0 29 | 0 29 | 0 30 | 0 31 | 0 32 | 0 32 | 0 33 | 0 34 | 0 35 | 0 36 | 19 |
| 20 | 0 26 | 0 27 | 0 28 | 0 28 | 0 29 | 0 30 | 0 31 | 0 32 | 0 33 | 0 33 | 0 34 | 0 35 | 0 36 | 0 37 | 0 38 | 20 |
| 21 | 0 27 | 0 28 | 0 29 | 0 30 | 0 31 | 0 32 | 0 32 | 0 33 | 0 34 | 0 35 | 0 36 | 0 37 | 0 38 | 0 39 | 0 39 | 21 |
| 22 | 0 28 | 0 29 | 0 30 | 0 31 | 0 32 | 0 33 | 0 34 | 0 35 | 0 36 | 0 37 | 0 38 | 0 39 | 0 39 | 0 40 | 0 41 | 22 |
| 23 | 0 30 | 0 31 | 0 32 | 0 33 | 0 34 | 0 35 | 0 35 | 0 36 | 0 37 | 0 38 | 0 39 | 0 40 | 0 41 | 0 42 | 0 43 | 23 |
| 24 | 0 31 | 0 32 | 0 33 | 0 34 | 0 35 | 0 36 | 0 37 | 0 38 | 0 39 | 0 40 | 0 41 | 0 42 | 0 43 | 0 44 | 0 45 | 24 |
| 25 | 0 32 | 0 33 | 0 34 | 0 35 | 0 36 | 0 38 | 0 39 | 0 40 | 0 41 | 0 42 | 0 43 | 0 44 | 0 45 | 0 46 | 0 47 | 25 |
| 26 | 0 34 | 0 35 | 0 36 | 0 37 | 0 38 | 0 39 | 0 40 | 0 41 | 0 42 | 0 43 | 0 44 | 0 46 | 0 47 | 0 48 | 0 49 | 26 |
| 27 | 0 35 | 0 36 | 0 37 | 0 38 | 0 39 | 0 41 | 0 42 | 0 43 | 0 44 | 0 45 | 0 46 | 0 47 | 0 48 | 0 50 | 0 51 | 27 |
| 28 | 0 36 | 0 37 | 0 39 | 0 40 | 0 41 | 0 42 | 0 43 | 0 44 | 0 46 | 0 47 | 0 48 | 0 49 | 0 50 | 0 51 | 0 53 | 28 |
| 29 | 0 37 | 0 39 | 0 40 | 0 41 | 0 42 | 0 44 | 0 45 | 0 46 | 0 47 | 0 48 | 0 50 | 0 51 | 0 52 | 0 53 | 0 54 | 29 |
| 30 | 0 39 | 0 40 | 0 41 | 0 43 | 0 44 | 0 45 | 0 46 | 0 48 | 0 49 | 0 50 | 0 51 | 0 53 | 0 54 | 0 55 | 0 56 | 30 |
| 31 | 0 40 | 0 41 | 0 43 | 0 44 | 0 45 | 0 47 | 0 48 | 0 49 | 0 50 | 0 52 | 0 53 | 0 54 | 0 56 | 0 57 | 0 58 | 31 |
| 32 | 0 41 | 0 43 | 0 44 | 0 45 | 0 47 | 0 48 | 0 49 | 0 51 | 0 52 | 0 52 | 0 55 | 0 56 | 0 57 | 0 59 | 1 0 | 32 |
| 33 | 0 43 | 0 44 | 0 45 | 0 47 | 0 48 | 0 50 | 0 51 | 0 52 | 0 54 | 0 54 | 0 55 | 0 56 | 0 58 | 1 1 | 1 2 | 33 |
| 34 | 0 44 | 0 45 | 0 47 | 0 48 | 0 50 | 0 51 | 0 52 | 0 54 | 0 55 | 0 57 | 0 58 | 1 0 | 1 1 | 1 2 | 1 4 | 34 |
| 35 | 0 45 | 0 47 | 0 48 | 0 50 | 0 51 | 0 53 | 0 54 | 0 55 | 0 57 | 0 58 | 1 0 | 1 1 | 1 3 | 1 4 | 1 6 | 35 |
| 36 | 0 47 | 0 48 | 0 50 | 0 51 | 0 53 | 0 54 | 0 56 | 0 57 | 0 59 | 1 0 | 1 2 | 1 3 | 1 5 | 1 6 | 1 8 | 36 |
| 37 | 0 48 | 0 49 | 0 51 | 0 52 | 0 54 | 0 56 | 0 57 | 0 59 | 1 0 | 1 2 | 1 3 | 1 5 | 1 6 | 1 8 | 1 9 | 37 |
| 38 | 0 49 | 0 51 | 0 52 | 0 54 | 0 55 | 0 57 | 0 59 | 1 0 | 1 2 | 1 3 | 1 5 | 1 7 | 1 8 | 1 10 | 1 11 | 38 |
| 39 | 0 50 | 0 52 | 0 54 | 0 55 | 0 57 | 0 59 | 1 0 | 1 2 | 1 3 | 1 5 | 1 7 | 1 8 | 1 10 | 1 12 | 1 13 | 39 |
| 40 | 0 52 | 0 53 | 0 55 | 0 57 | 0 58 | 1 0 | 1 2 | 1 3 | 1 5 | 1 7 | 1 8 | 1 10 | 1 12 | 1 13 | 1 15 | 40 |
| 41 | 0 53 | 0 55 | 0 56 | 0 58 | 1 0 | 1 2 | 1 3 | 1 5 | 1 7 | 1 8 | 1 10 | 1 12 | 1 13 | 1 15 | 1 17 | 41 |
| 42 | 0 54 | 0 56 | 0 58 | 1 0 | 1 1 | 1 3 | 1 5 | 1 7 | 1 8 | 1 10 | 1 12 | 1 14 | 1 15 | 1 17 | 1 19 | 42 |
| 43 | 0 56 | 0 57 | 0 59 | 1 1 | 1 3 | 1 5 | 1 6 | 1 8 | 1 10 | 1 12 | 1 13 | 1 15 | 1 17 | 1 19 | 1 21 | 43 |
| 44 | 0 57 | 0 59 | 1 1 | 1 2 | 1 4 | 1 6 | 1 8 | 1 10 | 1 12 | 1 13 | 1 15 | 1 17 | 1 19 | 1 21 | 1 23 | 44 |
| 45 | 0 58 | 1 0 | 1 2 | 1 4 | 1 6 | 1 8 | 1 9 | 1 11 | 1 13 | 1 15 | 1 17 | 1 19 | 1 21 | 1 23 | 1 24 | 45 |
| 46 | 0 59 | 1 1 | 1 3 | 1 5 | 1 7 | 1 9 | 1 11 | 1 13 | 1 15 | 1 17 | 1 19 | 1 21 | 1 22 | 1 24 | 1 26 | 46 |
| 47 | 1 1 | 1 3 | 1 5 | 1 7 | 1 9 | 1 11 | 1 12 | 1 14 | 1 16 | 1 18 | 1 20 | 1 22 | 1 24 | 1 26 | 1 28 | 47 |
| 48 | 1 2 | 1 4 | 1 6 | 1 8 | 1 10 | 1 12 | 1 14 | 1 16 | 1 18 | 1 20 | 1 22 | 1 24 | 1 26 | 1 28 | 1 30 | 48 |
| 49 | 1 3 | 1 5 | 1 7 | 1 9 | 1 11 | 1 14 | 1 16 | 1 18 | 1 20 | 1 22 | 1 24 | 1 26 | 1 28 | 1 30 | 1 32 | 49 |
| 50 | 1 5 | 1 7 | 1 9 | 1 11 | 1 13 | 1 15 | 1 17 | 1 19 | 1 21 | 1 23 | 1 25 | 1 28 | 1 30 | 1 32 | 1 34 | 50 |
| 51 | 1 6 | 1 8 | 1 10 | 1 12 | 1 14 | 1 17 | 1 19 | 1 21 | 1 23 | 1 25 | 1 27 | 1 29 | 1 31 | 1 34 | 1 36 | 51 |
| 52 | 1 7 | 1 9 | 1 12 | 1 14 | 1 16 | 1 18 | 1 20 | 1 22 | 1 25 | 1 27 | 1 29 | 1 31 | 1 33 | 1 35 | 1 38 | 52 |
| 53 | 1 8 | 1 11 | 1 13 | 1 15 | 1 17 | 1 20 | 1 22 | 1 24 | 1 26 | 1 28 | 1 31 | 1 33 | 1 35 | 1 37 | 1 39 | 53 |
| 54 | 1 10 | 1 12 | 1 14 | 1 17 | 1 19 | 1 21 | 1 23 | 1 26 | 1 28 | 1 30 | 1 32 | 1 35 | 1 37 | 1 39 | 1 41 | 54 |
| 55 | 1 11 | 1 13 | 1 16 | 1 18 | 1 20 | 1 23 | 1 25 | 1 27 | 1 29 | 1 32 | 1 34 | 1 36 | 1 39 | 1 41 | 1 43 | 55 |
| 56 | 1 12 | 1 15 | 1 17 | 1 19 | 1 22 | 1 24 | 1 26 | 1 29 | 1 31 | 1 33 | 1 36 | 1 38 | 1 40 | 1 43 | 1 45 | 56 |
| 57 | 1 14 | 1 16 | 1 18 | 1 21 | 1 23 | 1 26 | 1 28 | 1 30 | 1 33 | 1 35 | 1 37 | 1 40 | 1 42 | 1 45 | 1 47 | 57 |
| 58 | 1 15 | 1 17 | 1 20 | 1 22 | 1 25 | 1 27 | 1 29 | 1 32 | 1 34 | 1 37 | 1 39 | 1 42 | 1 44 | 1 46 | 1 49 | 58 |
| 59 | 1 16 | 1 19 | 1 21 | 1 24 | 1 26 | 1 29 | 1 31 | 1 33 | 1 36 | 1 38 | 1 41 | 1 43 | 1 46 | 1 48 | 1 51 | 59 |
| 60 | 1 18 | 1 20 | 1 23 | 1 25 | 1 28 | 1 30 | 1 33 | 1 35 | 1 38 | 1 40 | 1 43 | 1 45 | 1 48 | 1 50 | 1 53 | 60 |
| **HOURS 1** | 1 18 | 1 20 | 1 23 | 1 25 | 1 28 | 1 30 | 1 33 | 1 35 | 1 38 | 1 40 | 1 43 | 1 45 | 1 48 | 1 50 | 1 53 | 1 |
| 2 | 2 35 | 2 40 | 2 45 | 2 50 | 2 55 | 3 0 | 3 5 | 3 10 | 3 15 | 3 20 | 3 25 | 3 30 | 3 35 | 3 40 | 3 45 | 2 |
| 3 | 3 53 | 4 0 | 4 8 | 4 15 | 4 23 | 4 30 | 4 38 | 4 45 | 4 53 | 5 0 | 5 8 | 5 15 | 5 23 | 5 30 | 5 38 | 3 |
| 4 | 5 10 | 5 20 | 5 30 | 5 40 | 5 50 | 6 0 | 6 10 | 6 20 | 6 30 | 6 40 | 6 50 | 7 0 | 7 10 | 7 20 | 7 30 | 4 |
| 5 | 6 28 | 6 40 | 6 53 | 7 5 | 7 18 | 7 30 | 7 43 | 7 55 | 8 8 | 8 20 | 8 33 | 8 45 | 8 58 | 9 10 | 9 23 | 5 |
| 6 | 7 45 | 8 0 | 8 15 | 8 30 | 8 45 | 9 0 | 9 15 | 9 30 | 9 45 | 10 0 | 10 15 | 10 30 | 10 45 | 11 0 | 11 15 | 6 |
| 7 | 9 3 | 9 20 | 9 38 | 9 55 | 10 13 | 10 30 | 10 48 | 11 5 | 11 23 | 11 40 | 11 58 | 12 15 | 12 33 | 12 50 | 13 8 | 7 |
| 8 | 10 20 | 10 40 | 11 0 | 11 20 | 11 40 | 12 0 | 12 20 | 12 40 | 13 0 | 13 20 | 13 40 | 14 0 | 14 20 | 14 40 | 15 0 | 8 |
| 9 | 11 38 | 12 0 | 12 23 | 12 45 | 13 8 | 13 30 | 13 53 | 14 15 | 14 38 | 15 0 | 15 23 | 15 45 | 16 8 | 16 30 | 16 53 | 9 |
| 10 | 12 55 | 13 20 | 13 45 | 14 10 | 14 35 | 15 0 | 15 25 | 15 50 | 16 15 | 16 40 | 17 5 | 17 30 | 17 55 | 18 20 | 18 45 | 10 |
| 11 | 14 13 | 14 40 | 15 8 | 15 35 | 16 3 | 16 30 | 16 58 | 17 25 | 17 53 | 18 20 | 18 48 | 19 15 | 19 43 | 20 10 | 20 38 | 11 |
| 12 | 15 30 | 16 0 | 16 30 | 17 0 | 17 30 | 18 0 | 18 30 | 19 0 | 19 30 | 20 0 | 20 30 | 21 0 | 21 30 | 22 0 | 22 30 | 12 |
| 13 | 16 48 | 17 20 | 17 53 | 18 25 | 18 58 | 19 30 | 20 3 | 20 35 | 21 8 | 21 40 | 22 13 | 22 45 | 23 18 | 23 50 | 24 23 | 13 |
| 14 | 18 5 | 18 40 | 19 15 | 19 50 | 20 25 | 21 0 | 21 35 | 22 10 | 22 45 | 23 20 | 23 55 | 24 30 | 25 5 | 25 40 | 26 15 | 14 |
| 15 | 19 23 | 20 0 | 20 38 | 21 15 | 21 53 | 22 30 | 23 8 | 23 45 | 24 23 | 25 0 | 25 38 | 26 15 | 26 53 | 27 30 | 28 8 | 15 |
| 16 | 20 40 | 21 20 | 22 0 | 22 40 | 23 20 | 24 0 | 24 40 | 25 20 | 26 0 | 26 40 | 27 20 | 28 0 | 28 40 | 29 20 | 30 0 | 16 |
| 17 | 21 58 | 22 40 | 23 23 | 24 5 | 24 48 | 25 30 | 26 13 | 26 55 | 27 38 | 28 20 | 29 3 | 29 45 | 30 28 | 31 10 | 31 53 | 17 |
| 18 | 23 15 | 24 0 | 24 45 | 25 30 | 26 15 | 27 0 | 27 45 | 28 30 | 29 15 | 30 0 | 30 45 | 31 30 | 32 15 | 33 0 | 33 45 | 18 |
| 19 | 24 33 | 25 20 | 26 8 | 26 55 | 27 43 | 28 30 | 29 18 | 30 5 | 30 53 | 31 40 | 32 28 | 33 15 | 34 3 | 34 50 | 35 38 | 19 |
| 20 | 25 50 | 26 40 | 27 30 | 28 20 | 29 10 | 30 0 | 30 50 | 31 40 | 32 30 | 33 20 | 34 10 | 35 0 | 35 50 | 36 40 | 37 30 | 20 |
| 21 | 27 8 | 28 0 | 28 53 | 29 45 | 30 38 | 31 30 | 32 23 | 33 15 | 34 8 | 35 0 | 35 53 | 36 45 | 37 38 | 38 30 | 39 23 | 21 |
| 22 | 28 25 | 29 20 | 30 15 | 31 10 | 32 5 | 33 0 | 33 55 | 34 50 | 35 45 | 36 40 | 37 35 | 38 30 | 39 25 | 40 20 | 41 15 | 22 |
| 23 | 29 43 | 30 40 | 31 38 | 32 35 | 33 33 | 34 30 | 35 28 | 36 25 | 37 23 | 38 20 | 39 18 | 40 15 | 41 13 | 42 10 | 43 8 | 23 |
| 24 | 31 0 | 32 0 | 33 0 | 34 0 | 35 0 | 36 0 | 37 0 | 38 0 | 39 0 | 40 0 | 41 0 | 42 0 | 43 0 | 44 0 | 45 0 | 24 |

# Table VII Diurnal Motion of the Planets

| TIME | 0° 46' | 0° 47' | 0° 48' | 0° 49' | 0° 50' | 0° 51' | 0° 52' | 0° 53' | 0° 54' | 0° 55' | 0° 56' | 0° 57' | 0° 58' | 0° 59' | 1° 0' | TIME |
|---|---|---|---|---|---|---|---|---|---|---|---|---|---|---|---|---|
| | | | | | | | 24 HOUR TRAVEL | | | | | | | | | |
| MINUTES 1 | 0 2 | 0 2 | 0 2 | 0 2 | 0 2 | 0 2 | 0 2 | 0 2 | 0 2 | 0 2 | 0 2 | 0 2 | 0 2 | 0 2 | 0 3 | 1 MINUTES |
| 2 | 0 4 | 0 4 | 0 4 | 0 4 | 0 4 | 0 4 | 0 4 | 0 4 | 0 5 | 0 5 | 0 5 | 0 5 | 0 5 | 0 5 | 0 5 | 2 |
| 3 | 0 6 | 0 6 | 0 6 | 0 6 | 0 6 | 0 6 | 0 7 | 0 7 | 0 7 | 0 7 | 0 7 | 0 7 | 0 7 | 0 7 | 0 8 | 3 |
| 4 | 0 8 | 0 8 | 0 8 | 0 8 | 0 8 | 0 9 | 0 9 | 0 9 | 0 9 | 0 9 | 0 9 | 0 10 | 0 10 | 0 10 | 0 10 | 4 |
| 5 | 0 10 | 0 10 | 0 10 | 0 10 | 0 10 | 0 11 | 0 11 | 0 11 | 0 11 | 0 11 | 0 12 | 0 12 | 0 12 | 0 12 | 0 13 | 5 |
| 6 | 0 12 | 0 12 | 0 12 | 0 12 | 0 13 | 0 13 | 0 13 | 0 13 | 0 14 | 0 14 | 0 14 | 0 14 | 0 15 | 0 15 | 0 15 | 6 |
| 7 | 0 13 | 0 14 | 0 14 | 0 14 | 0 15 | 0 15 | 0 15 | 0 15 | 0 16 | 0 16 | 0 16 | 0 17 | 0 17 | 0 17 | 0 18 | 7 |
| 8 | 0 15 | 0 16 | 0 16 | 0 16 | 0 17 | 0 17 | 0 17 | 0 18 | 0 18 | 0 18 | 0 19 | 0 19 | 0 19 | 0 20 | 0 20 | 8 |
| 9 | 0 17 | 0 18 | 0 18 | 0 18 | 0 19 | 0 19 | 0 20 | 0 20 | 0 20 | 0 21 | 0 21 | 0 21 | 0 22 | 0 22 | 0 23 | 9 |
| 10 | 0 19 | 0 20 | 0 20 | 0 20 | 0 21 | 0 21 | 0 22 | 0 22 | 0 23 | 0 23 | 0 23 | 0 24 | 0 24 | 0 25 | 0 25 | 10 |
| 11 | 0 21 | 0 22 | 0 22 | 0 22 | 0 23 | 0 23 | 0 24 | 0 24 | 0 25 | 0 25 | 0 26 | 0 26 | 0 27 | 0 27 | 0 28 | 11 |
| 12 | 0 23 | 0 24 | 0 24 | 0 25 | 0 25 | 0 26 | 0 26 | 0 27 | 0 27 | 0 28 | 0 28 | 0 29 | 0 29 | 0 30 | 0 30 | 12 |
| 13 | 0 25 | 0 25 | 0 26 | 0 27 | 0 27 | 0 28 | 0 28 | 0 29 | 0 29 | 0 30 | 0 30 | 0 31 | 0 31 | 0 32 | 0 33 | 13 |
| 14 | 0 27 | 0 27 | 0 28 | 0 29 | 0 29 | 0 30 | 0 30 | 0 31 | 0 32 | 0 32 | 0 33 | 0 33 | 0 34 | 0 34 | 0 35 | 14 |
| 15 | 0 29 | 0 29 | 0 30 | 0 31 | 0 31 | 0 32 | 0 33 | 0 33 | 0 34 | 0 34 | 0 35 | 0 36 | 0 36 | 0 37 | 0 38 | 15 |
| 16 | 0 31 | 0 31 | 0 32 | 0 33 | 0 33 | 0 34 | 0 35 | 0 35 | 0 36 | 0 37 | 0 37 | 0 38 | 0 39 | 0 39 | 0 40 | 16 |
| 17 | 0 33 | 0 33 | 0 34 | 0 35 | 0 35 | 0 36 | 0 37 | 0 38 | 0 38 | 0 39 | 0 40 | 0 40 | 0 41 | 0 42 | 0 43 | 17 |
| 18 | 0 35 | 0 35 | 0 36 | 0 37 | 0 38 | 0 38 | 0 39 | 0 40 | 0 41 | 0 41 | 0 42 | 0 43 | 0 44 | 0 44 | 0 45 | 18 |
| 19 | 0 36 | 0 37 | 0 38 | 0 39 | 0 40 | 0 40 | 0 41 | 0 42 | 0 43 | 0 44 | 0 44 | 0 45 | 0 46 | 0 47 | 0 48 | 19 |
| 20 | 0 38 | 0 39 | 0 40 | 0 41 | 0 42 | 0 43 | 0 43 | 0 44 | 0 45 | 0 46 | 0 47 | 0 48 | 0 48 | 0 49 | 0 50 | 20 |
| 21 | 0 40 | 0 41 | 0 42 | 0 43 | 0 44 | 0 45 | 0 46 | 0 46 | 0 47 | 0 48 | 0 49 | 0 50 | 0 51 | 0 52 | 0 53 | 21 |
| 22 | 0 42 | 0 43 | 0 44 | 0 45 | 0 46 | 0 47 | 0 48 | 0 49 | 0 50 | 0 50 | 0 51 | 0 52 | 0 53 | 0 54 | 0 55 | 22 |
| 23 | 0 44 | 0 45 | 0 46 | 0 47 | 0 48 | 0 49 | 0 50 | 0 51 | 0 52 | 0 53 | 0 54 | 0 55 | 0 56 | 0 57 | 0 58 | 23 |
| 24 | 0 46 | 0 47 | 0 48 | 0 49 | 0 50 | 0 51 | 0 52 | 0 53 | 0 54 | 0 55 | 0 56 | 0 57 | 0 58 | 0 59 | 1 0 | 24 |
| 25 | 0 48 | 0 49 | 0 50 | 0 51 | 0 52 | 0 53 | 0 54 | 0 55 | 0 56 | 0 57 | 0 58 | 0 59 | 1 0 | 1 1 | 1 3 | 25 |
| 26 | 0 50 | 0 51 | 0 52 | 0 53 | 0 54 | 0 55 | 0 56 | 0 57 | 0 59 | 1 0 | 1 1 | 1 2 | 1 3 | 1 4 | 1 5 | 26 |
| 27 | 0 52 | 0 53 | 0 54 | 0 55 | 0 56 | 0 57 | 0 59 | 1 0 | 1 1 | 1 2 | 1 3 | 1 4 | 1 5 | 1 6 | 1 8 | 27 |
| 28 | 0 54 | 0 55 | 0 56 | 0 57 | 0 58 | 1 0 | 1 1 | 1 2 | 1 3 | 1 4 | 1 5 | 1 7 | 1 8 | 1 9 | 1 10 | 28 |
| 29 | 0 56 | 0 57 | 0 58 | 0 59 | 1 0 | 1 2 | 1 3 | 1 4 | 1 5 | 1 6 | 1 8 | 1 9 | 1 10 | 1 11 | 1 13 | 29 |
| 30 | 0 58 | 0 59 | 1 0 | 1 1 | 1 3 | 1 4 | 1 5 | 1 6 | 1 8 | 1 9 | 1 10 | 1 11 | 1 13 | 1 14 | 1 15 | 30 |
| 31 | 0 59 | 1 1 | 1 2 | 1 3 | 1 5 | 1 6 | 1 7 | 1 8 | 1 10 | 1 11 | 1 12 | 1 14 | 1 15 | 1 16 | 1 18 | 31 |
| 32 | 1 1 | 1 3 | 1 4 | 1 5 | 1 7 | 1 8 | 1 9 | 1 11 | 1 12 | 1 13 | 1 15 | 1 16 | 1 17 | 1 19 | 1 20 | 32 |
| 33 | 1 3 | 1 5 | 1 6 | 1 7 | 1 9 | 1 10 | 1 12 | 1 13 | 1 14 | 1 16 | 1 17 | 1 18 | 1 20 | 1 21 | 1 23 | 33 |
| 34 | 1 5 | 1 7 | 1 8 | 1 9 | 1 11 | 1 12 | 1 14 | 1 15 | 1 17 | 1 18 | 1 19 | 1 21 | 1 22 | 1 24 | 1 25 | 34 |
| 35 | 1 7 | 1 9 | 1 10 | 1 11 | 1 13 | 1 14 | 1 16 | 1 17 | 1 19 | 1 20 | 1 22 | 1 23 | 1 25 | 1 26 | 1 28 | 35 |
| 36 | 1 9 | 1 11 | 1 12 | 1 14 | 1 15 | 1 17 | 1 18 | 1 20 | 1 21 | 1 23 | 1 24 | 1 26 | 1 27 | 1 29 | 1 30 | 36 |
| 37 | 1 11 | 1 12 | 1 14 | 1 16 | 1 17 | 1 19 | 1 20 | 1 22 | 1 23 | 1 25 | 1 26 | 1 28 | 1 29 | 1 31 | 1 33 | 37 |
| 38 | 1 13 | 1 14 | 1 16 | 1 18 | 1 19 | 1 21 | 1 22 | 1 24 | 1 26 | 1 27 | 1 29 | 1 30 | 1 32 | 1 33 | 1 35 | 38 |
| 39 | 1 15 | 1 16 | 1 18 | 1 20 | 1 21 | 1 23 | 1 25 | 1 26 | 1 28 | 1 29 | 1 31 | 1 33 | 1 34 | 1 36 | 1 38 | 39 |
| 40 | 1 17 | 1 18 | 1 20 | 1 22 | 1 23 | 1 25 | 1 27 | 1 28 | 1 30 | 1 32 | 1 33 | 1 35 | 1 37 | 1 38 | 1 40 | 40 |
| 41 | 1 19 | 1 20 | 1 22 | 1 24 | 1 25 | 1 27 | 1 29 | 1 31 | 1 32 | 1 34 | 1 36 | 1 37 | 1 39 | 1 41 | 1 43 | 41 |
| 42 | 1 21 | 1 22 | 1 24 | 1 26 | 1 28 | 1 29 | 1 31 | 1 33 | 1 35 | 1 36 | 1 38 | 1 40 | 1 42 | 1 43 | 1 45 | 42 |
| 43 | 1 22 | 1 24 | 1 26 | 1 28 | 1 30 | 1 31 | 1 33 | 1 35 | 1 37 | 1 39 | 1̇ 40 | 1 42 | 1 44 | 1 46 | 1 48 | 43 |
| 44 | 1 24 | 1 26 | 1 28 | 1 30 | 1 32 | 1 34 | 1 35 | 1 37 | 1 39 | 1 41 | 1 43 | 1 45 | 1 46 | 1 48 | 1 50 | 44 |
| 45 | 1 26 | 1 28 | 1 30 | 1 32 | 1 34 | 1 36 | 1 38 | 1 39 | 1 41 | 1 43 | 1 45 | 1 47 | 1 49 | 1 51 | 1 53 | 45 |
| 46 | 1 28 | 1 30 | 1 32 | 1 34 | 1 36 | 1 38 | 1 40 | 1 42 | 1 44 | 1 45 | 1 47 | 1 49 | 1 51 | 1 53 | 1 55 | 46 |
| 47 | 1 30 | 1 32 | 1 34 | 1 36 | 1 38 | 1 40 | 1 42 | 1 44 | 1 46 | 1 48 | 1 50 | 1 52 | 1 54 | 1 56 | 1 58 | 47 |
| 48 | 1 32 | 1 34 | 1 36 | 1 38 | 1 40 | 1 42 | 1 44 | 1 46 | 1 48 | 1 50 | 1 52 | 1 54 | 1 56 | 1 58 | 2 0 | 48 |
| 49 | 1 34 | 1 36 | 1 38 | 1 40 | 1 42 | 1 44 | 1 46 | 1 48 | 1 50 | 1 52 | 1 54 | 1 56 | 1 58 | 2 0 | 2 3 | 49 |
| 50 | 1 36 | 1 38 | 1 40 | 1 42 | 1 44 | 1 46 | 1 48 | 1 50 | 1 53 | 1 55 | 1 57 | 1 59 | 2 1 | 2 3 | 2 5 | 50 |
| 51 | 1 38 | 1 40 | 1 42 | 1 44 | 1 46 | 1 48 | 1 51 | 1 53 | 1 55 | 1 57 | 1 59 | 2 1 | 2 3 | 2 5 | 2 8 | 51 |
| 52 | 1 40 | 1 42 | 1 44 | 1 46 | 1 48 | 1 51 | 1 53 | 1 55 | 1 57 | 1 59 | 2 1 | 2 4 | 2 6 | 2 8 | 2 10 | 52 |
| 53 | 1 42 | 1 44 | 1 46 | 1 48 | 1 50 | 1 53 | 1 55 | 1 57 | 1 59 | 2 1 | 2 4 | 2 6 | 2 8 | 2 10 | 2 13 | 53 |
| 54 | 1 44 | 1 46 | 1 48 | 1 50 | 1 53 | 1 55 | 1 57 | 1 59 | 2 2 | 2 4 | 2 6 | 2 8 | 2 11 | 2 13 | 2 15 | 54 |
| 55 | 1 45 | 1 48 | 1 50 | 1 52 | 1 55 | 1 57 | 1 59 | 2 1 | 2 4 | 2 6 | 2 8 | 2 11 | 2 13 | 2 15 | 2 18 | 55 |
| 56 | 1 47 | 1 50 | 1 52 | 1 54 | 1 57 | 1 59 | 2 1 | 2 4 | 2 6 | 2 8 | 2 11 | 2 13 | 2 15 | 2 18 | 2 20 | 56 |
| 57 | 1 49 | 1 52 | 1 54 | 1 56 | 1 59 | 2 1 | 2 4 | 2 6 | 2 8 | 2 11 | 2 13 | 2 15 | 2 18 | 2 20 | 2 23 | 57 |
| 58 | 1 51 | 1 54 | 1 56 | 1 58 | 2 1 | 2 3 | 2 6 | 2 8 | 2 10 | 2 13 | 2 15 | 2 18 | 2 20 | 2 23 | 2 25 | 58 |
| 59 | 1 53 | 1 56 | 1 58 | 2 0 | 2 3 | 2 5 | 2 8 | 2 10 | 2 13 | 2 15 | 2 18 | 2 20 | 2 23 | 2 25 | 2 28 | 59 |
| 60 | 1 55 | 1 58 | 2 0 | 2 3 | 2 5 | 2 8 | 2 10 | 2 13 | 2 15 | 2 18 | 2 20 | 2 23 | 2 25 | 2 28 | 2 30 | 60 |
| HOURS 1 | 1 55 | 1 58 | 2 0 | 2 3 | 2 5 | 2 8 | 2 10 | 2 13 | 2 15 | 2 18 | 2 20 | 2 23 | 2 25 | 2 28 | 2 30 | 1 HOURS |
| 2 | 3 50 | 3 55 | 4 0 | 4 5 | 4 10 | 4 15 | 4 20 | 4 25 | 4 30 | 4 35 | 4 40 | 4 45 | 4 50 | 4 55 | 5 0 | 2 |
| 3 | 5 45 | 5 53 | 6 0 | 6 8 | 6 15 | 6 23 | 6 30 | 6 38 | 6 45 | 6 53 | 7 0 | 7 8 | 7 15 | 7 23 | 7 30 | 3 |
| 4 | 7 40 | 7 50 | 8 0 | 8 10 | 8 20 | 8 30 | 8 40 | 8 50 | 9 0 | 9 10 | 9 20 | 9 30 | 9 40 | 9 50 | 10 0 | 4 |
| 5 | 9 35 | 9 48 | 10 0 | 10 13 | 10 25 | 10 38 | 10 50 | 11 3 | 11 15 | 11 28 | 11 40 | 11 53 | 12 5 | 12 18 | 12 30 | 5 |
| 6 | 11 30 | 11 45 | 12 0 | 12 15 | 12 30 | 12 45 | 13 0 | 13 15 | 13 30 | 13 45 | 14 0 | 14 15 | 14 30 | 14 45 | 15 0 | 6 |
| 7 | 13 25 | 13 43 | 14 0 | 14 18 | 14 35 | 14 53 | 15 10 | 15 28 | 15 45 | 16 3 | 16 20 | 16 38 | 16 55 | 17 13 | 17 30 | 7 |
| 8 | 15 20 | 15 40 | 16 0 | 16 20 | 16 40 | 17 0 | 17 20 | 17 40 | 18 0 | 18 20 | 18 40 | 19 0 | 19 20 | 19 40 | 20 0 | 8 |
| 9 | 17 15 | 17 38 | 18 0 | 18 23 | 18 45 | 19 8 | 19 30 | 19 53 | 20 15 | 20 38 | 21 0 | 21 23 | 21 45 | 22 8 | 22 30 | 9 |
| 10 | 19 10 | 19 35 | 20 0 | 20 25 | 20 50 | 21 15 | 21 40 | 22 5 | 22 30 | 22 55 | 23 20 | 23 45 | 24 10 | 24 35 | 25 0 | 10 |
| 11 | 21 5 | 21 33 | 22 0 | 22 28 | 22 55 | 23 23 | 23 50 | 24 18 | 24 45 | 25 13 | 25 40 | 26 8 | 26 35 | 27 3 | 27 30 | 11 |
| 12 | 23 0 | 23 30 | 24 0 | 24 30 | 25 0 | 25 30 | 26 0 | 26 30 | 27 0 | 27 30 | 28 0 | 28 30 | 29 0 | 29 30 | 30 0 | 12 |
| 13 | 24 55 | 25 28 | 26 0 | 26 33 | 27 5 | 27 38 | 28 10 | 28 43 | 29 15 | 29 48 | 30 20 | 30 53 | 31 25 | 31 58 | 32 30 | 13 |
| 14 | 26 50 | 27 25 | 28 0 | 28 35 | 29 10 | 29 45 | 30 20 | 30 55 | 31 30 | 32 5 | 32 40 | 33 15 | 33 50 | 34 25 | 35 0 | 14 |
| 15 | 28 45 | 29 23 | 30 0 | 30 38 | 31 15 | 31 53 | 32 30 | 33 8 | 33 45 | 34 23 | 35 0 | 35 38 | 36 15 | 36 53 | 37 30 | 15 |
| 16 | 30 40 | 31 20 | 32 0 | 32 40 | 33 20 | 34 0 | 34 40 | 35 20 | 36 0 | 36 40 | 37 20 | 38 0 | 38 40 | 39 20 | 40 0 | 16 |
| 17 | 32 35 | 33 18 | 34 0 | 34 43 | 35 25 | 36 8 | 36 50 | 37 33 | 38 15 | 38 58 | 39 40 | 40 23 | 41 5 | 41 48 | 42 30 | 17 |
| 18 | 34 30 | 35 15 | 36 0 | 36 45 | 37 30 | 38 15 | 39 0 | 39 45 | 40 30 | 41 15 | 42 0 | 42 45 | 43 30 | 44 15 | 45 0 | 18 |
| 19 | 36 25 | 37 13 | 38 0 | 38 48 | 39 35 | 40 23 | 41 10 | 41 58 | 42 45 | 43 33 | 44 20 | 45 8 | 45 55 | 46 43 | 47 30 | 19 |
| 20 | 38 20 | 39 10 | 40 0 | 40 50 | 41 40 | 42 30 | 43 20 | 44 10 | 45 0 | 45 50 | 46 40 | 47 30 | 48 20 | 49 10 | 50 0 | 20 |
| 21 | 40 15 | 41 8 | 42 0 | 42 53 | 43 45 | 44 38 | 45 30 | 46 23 | 47 15 | 48 8 | 49 0 | 49 53 | 50 45 | 51 38 | 52 30 | 21 |
| 22 | 42 10 | 43 5 | 44 0 | 44 55 | 45 50 | 46 45 | 47 40 | 48 35 | 49 30 | 50 25 | 51 20 | 52 15 | 53 10 | 54 5 | 55 0 | 22 |
| 23 | 44 5 | 45 3 | 46 0 | 46 58 | 47 55 | 48 53 | 49 50 | 50 48 | 51 45 | 52 43 | 53 40 | 54 38 | 55 35 | 56 33 | 57 30 | 23 |
| 24 | 46 0 | 47 0 | 48 0 | 49 0 | 50 0 | 51 0 | 52 0 | 53 0 | 54 0 | 55 0 | 56 0 | 57 0 | 58 0 | 59 0 | 1 0 0 | 24 |

# Table VII Diurnal Motion of the Planets

**24 HOUR TRAVEL**

Each cell gives the interpolated motion. In the MINUTES section values are arcminutes and arcseconds ('  "); in the HOURS section values are arcminutes/arcseconds or degrees/minutes/seconds (°  '  ") once the value exceeds 60'.

## MINUTES

| TIME | 1° 1' | 1° 2' | 1° 3' | 1° 4' | 1° 5' | 1° 6' | 1° 7' | 1° 8' | 1° 9' | 1° 10' | 1° 11' | 1° 12' | 1° 13' | 1° 14' | 1° 15' |
|---|---|---|---|---|---|---|---|---|---|---|---|---|---|---|---|
| 1 | 0 3 | 0 3 | 0 3 | 0 3 | 0 3 | 0 3 | 0 3 | 0 3 | 0 3 | 0 3 | 0 3 | 0 3 | 0 3 | 0 3 | 0 3 |
| 2 | 0 5 | 0 5 | 0 5 | 0 5 | 0 5 | 0 6 | 0 6 | 0 6 | 0 6 | 0 6 | 0 6 | 0 6 | 0 6 | 0 6 | 0 6 |
| 3 | 0 8 | 0 8 | 0 8 | 0 8 | 0 8 | 0 8 | 0 8 | 0 9 | 0 9 | 0 9 | 0 9 | 0 9 | 0 9 | 0 9 | 0 9 |
| 4 | 0 10 | 0 10 | 0 11 | 0 11 | 0 11 | 0 11 | 0 11 | 0 11 | 0 12 | 0 12 | 0 12 | 0 12 | 0 12 | 0 12 | 0 13 |
| 5 | 0 13 | 0 13 | 0 13 | 0 13 | 0 14 | 0 14 | 0 14 | 0 14 | 0 14 | 0 15 | 0 15 | 0 15 | 0 15 | 0 15 | 0 16 |
| 6 | 0 15 | 0 16 | 0 16 | 0 16 | 0 16 | 0 17 | 0 17 | 0 17 | 0 17 | 0 18 | 0 18 | 0 18 | 0 18 | 0 19 | 0 19 |
| 7 | 0 18 | 0 18 | 0 18 | 0 19 | 0 19 | 0 19 | 0 20 | 0 20 | 0 20 | 0 20 | 0 21 | 0 21 | 0 21 | 0 22 | 0 22 |
| 8 | 0 20 | 0 21 | 0 21 | 0 21 | 0 22 | 0 22 | 0 22 | 0 23 | 0 23 | 0 23 | 0 24 | 0 24 | 0 24 | 0 25 | 0 25 |
| 9 | 0 23 | 0 23 | 0 24 | 0 24 | 0 24 | 0 25 | 0 25 | 0 26 | 0 26 | 0 26 | 0 27 | 0 27 | 0 27 | 0 28 | 0 28 |
| 10 | 0 25 | 0 26 | 0 26 | 0 27 | 0 27 | 0 28 | 0 28 | 0 28 | 0 29 | 0 29 | 0 30 | 0 30 | 0 30 | 0 31 | 0 31 |
| 11 | 0 28 | 0 28 | 0 29 | 0 29 | 0 30 | 0 30 | 0 31 | 0 31 | 0 32 | 0 32 | 0 33 | 0 33 | 0 33 | 0 34 | 0 34 |
| 12 | 0 31 | 0 31 | 0 32 | 0 32 | 0 33 | 0 33 | 0 34 | 0 34 | 0 35 | 0 35 | 0 36 | 0 36 | 0 37 | 0 37 | 0 38 |
| 13 | 0 33 | 0 34 | 0 34 | 0 35 | 0 35 | 0 36 | 0 36 | 0 37 | 0 37 | 0 38 | 0 38 | 0 39 | 0 40 | 0 40 | 0 41 |
| 14 | 0 36 | 0 36 | 0 37 | 0 37 | 0 38 | 0 39 | 0 39 | 0 40 | 0 40 | 0 41 | 0 41 | 0 42 | 0 43 | 0 43 | 0 44 |
| 15 | 0 38 | 0 39 | 0 39 | 0 40 | 0 41 | 0 41 | 0 42 | 0 43 | 0 43 | 0 44 | 0 44 | 0 45 | 0 46 | 0 46 | 0 47 |
| 16 | 0 41 | 0 41 | 0 42 | 0 43 | 0 43 | 0 44 | 0 45 | 0 45 | 0 46 | 0 47 | 0 47 | 0 48 | 0 49 | 0 49 | 0 50 |
| 17 | 0 43 | 0 44 | 0 45 | 0 45 | 0 46 | 0 47 | 0 47 | 0 48 | 0 49 | 0 50 | 0 50 | 0 51 | 0 52 | 0 52 | 0 53 |
| 18 | 0 46 | 0 47 | 0 47 | 0 48 | 0 49 | 0 50 | 0 50 | 0 51 | 0 52 | 0 52 | 0 53 | 0 54 | 0 55 | 0 56 | 0 56 |
| 19 | 0 48 | 0 49 | 0 50 | 0 51 | 0 51 | 0 52 | 0 53 | 0 54 | 0 55 | 0 55 | 0 56 | 0 57 | 0 58 | 0 59 | 0 59 |
| 20 | 0 51 | 0 52 | 0 53 | 0 53 | 0 54 | 0 55 | 0 56 | 0 57 | 0 58 | 0 58 | 0 59 | 1 0 | 1 1 | 1 2 | 1 3 |
| 21 | 0 53 | 0 54 | 0 55 | 0 56 | 0 57 | 0 58 | 0 59 | 1 0 | 1 0 | 1 1 | 1 2 | 1 3 | 1 4 | 1 5 | 1 6 |
| 22 | 0 56 | 0 57 | 0 58 | 0 59 | 1 0 | 1 1 | 1 1 | 1 2 | 1 3 | 1 4 | 1 5 | 1 6 | 1 7 | 1 8 | 1 9 |
| 23 | 0 58 | 0 59 | 1 0 | 1 1 | 1 2 | 1 3 | 1 4 | 1 5 | 1 6 | 1 7 | 1 8 | 1 9 | 1 10 | 1 11 | 1 12 |
| 24 | 1 1 | 1 2 | 1 3 | 1 4 | 1 5 | 1 6 | 1 7 | 1 8 | 1 9 | 1 10 | 1 11 | 1 12 | 1 13 | 1 14 | 1 15 |
| 25 | 1 4 | 1 5 | 1 6 | 1 7 | 1 8 | 1 9 | 1 10 | 1 11 | 1 12 | 1 13 | 1 14 | 1 15 | 1 16 | 1 17 | 1 18 |
| 26 | 1 6 | 1 7 | 1 8 | 1 9 | 1 10 | 1 12 | 1 13 | 1 14 | 1 15 | 1 16 | 1 17 | 1 18 | 1 19 | 1 20 | 1 21 |
| 27 | 1 9 | 1 10 | 1 11 | 1 12 | 1 13 | 1 14 | 1 15 | 1 17 | 1 18 | 1 19 | 1 20 | 1 21 | 1 22 | 1 23 | 1 24 |
| 28 | 1 11 | 1 12 | 1 14 | 1 15 | 1 16 | 1 17 | 1 18 | 1 19 | 1 21 | 1 22 | 1 23 | 1 24 | 1 25 | 1 26 | 1 28 |
| 29 | 1 14 | 1 15 | 1 16 | 1 17 | 1 19 | 1 20 | 1 21 | 1 22 | 1 23 | 1 25 | 1 26 | 1 27 | 1 28 | 1 29 | 1 31 |
| 30 | 1 16 | 1 18 | 1 19 | 1 20 | 1 21 | 1 23 | 1 24 | 1 25 | 1 26 | 1 28 | 1 29 | 1 30 | 1 31 | 1 33 | 1 34 |
| 31 | 1 19 | 1 20 | 1 21 | 1 23 | 1 24 | 1 25 | 1 27 | 1 28 | 1 29 | 1 30 | 1 32 | 1 33 | 1 34 | 1 36 | 1 37 |
| 32 | 1 21 | 1 23 | 1 24 | 1 25 | 1 27 | 1 28 | 1 29 | 1 31 | 1 32 | 1 33 | 1 35 | 1 36 | 1 37 | 1 39 | 1 40 |
| 33 | 1 24 | 1 25 | 1 27 | 1 28 | 1 29 | 1 31 | 1 32 | 1 34 | 1 35 | 1 36 | 1 38 | 1 39 | 1 40 | 1 42 | 1 43 |
| 34 | 1 26 | 1 28 | 1 29 | 1 31 | 1 32 | 1 34 | 1 35 | 1 36 | 1 38 | 1 39 | 1 41 | 1 42 | 1 43 | 1 45 | 1 46 |
| 35 | 1 29 | 1 30 | 1 32 | 1 33 | 1 35 | 1 36 | 1 38 | 1 39 | 1 41 | 1 42 | 1 44 | 1 45 | 1 46 | 1 48 | 1 49 |
| 36 | 1 32 | 1 33 | 1 35 | 1 36 | 1 38 | 1 39 | 1 41 | 1 42 | 1 44 | 1 45 | 1 47 | 1 48 | 1 50 | 1 51 | 1 53 |
| 37 | 1 34 | 1 36 | 1 37 | 1 39 | 1 40 | 1 42 | 1 43 | 1 45 | 1 46 | 1 48 | 1 49 | 1 51 | 1 53 | 1 54 | 1 56 |
| 38 | 1 37 | 1 38 | 1 40 | 1 41 | 1 43 | 1 45 | 1 46 | 1 48 | 1 49 | 1 51 | 1 52 | 1 54 | 1 56 | 1 57 | 1 59 |
| 39 | 1 39 | 1 41 | 1 42 | 1 44 | 1 46 | 1 47 | 1 49 | 1 51 | 1 52 | 1 54 | 1 55 | 1 57 | 1 59 | 2 0 | 2 2 |
| 40 | 1 42 | 1 43 | 1 45 | 1 47 | 1 48 | 1 50 | 1 52 | 1 53 | 1 55 | 1 57 | 1 58 | 2 0 | 2 2 | 2 3 | 2 5 |
| 41 | 1 44 | 1 46 | 1 48 | 1 49 | 1 51 | 1 53 | 1 54 | 1 56 | 1 58 | 2 0 | 2 1 | 2 3 | 2 5 | 2 6 | 2 8 |
| 42 | 1 47 | 1 49 | 1 50 | 1 52 | 1 54 | 1 56 | 1 57 | 1 59 | 2 1 | 2 3 | 2 4 | 2 6 | 2 8 | 2 10 | 2 11 |
| 43 | 1 49 | 1 51 | 1 53 | 1 55 | 1 56 | 1 58 | 2 0 | 2 2 | 2 4 | 2 5 | 2 7 | 2 9 | 2 11 | 2 13 | 2 14 |
| 44 | 1 52 | 1 54 | 1 56 | 1 57 | 1 59 | 2 1 | 2 3 | 2 5 | 2 7 | 2 8 | 2 10 | 2 12 | 2 14 | 2 16 | 2 18 |
| 45 | 1 54 | 1 56 | 1 58 | 2 0 | 2 2 | 2 4 | 2 6 | 2 8 | 2 9 | 2 11 | 2 13 | 2 15 | 2 17 | 2 19 | 2 21 |
| 46 | 1 57 | 1 59 | 2 1 | 2 3 | 2 5 | 2 7 | 2 8 | 2 10 | 2 12 | 2 14 | 2 16 | 2 18 | 2 20 | 2 22 | 2 24 |
| 47 | 1 59 | 2 1 | 2 3 | 2 5 | 2 7 | 2 9 | 2 11 | 2 13 | 2 15 | 2 17 | 2 19 | 2 21 | 2 23 | 2 25 | 2 27 |
| 48 | 2 2 | 2 4 | 2 6 | 2 8 | 2 10 | 2 12 | 2 14 | 2 16 | 2 18 | 2 20 | 2 22 | 2 24 | 2 26 | 2 28 | 2 30 |
| 49 | 2 5 | 2 7 | 2 9 | 2 11 | 2 13 | 2 15 | 2 17 | 2 19 | 2 21 | 2 23 | 2 25 | 2 27 | 2 29 | 2 31 | 2 33 |
| 50 | 2 7 | 2 9 | 2 11 | 2 13 | 2 15 | 2 18 | 2 20 | 2 22 | 2 24 | 2 26 | 2 28 | 2 30 | 2 32 | 2 34 | 2 36 |
| 51 | 2 10 | 2 12 | 2 14 | 2 16 | 2 18 | 2 20 | 2 22 | 2 25 | 2 27 | 2 29 | 2 31 | 2 33 | 2 35 | 2 37 | 2 39 |
| 52 | 2 12 | 2 14 | 2 17 | 2 19 | 2 21 | 2 23 | 2 25 | 2 27 | 2 30 | 2 32 | 2 34 | 2 36 | 2 38 | 2 40 | 2 43 |
| 53 | 2 15 | 2 17 | 2 19 | 2 21 | 2 24 | 2 26 | 2 28 | 2 30 | 2 32 | 2 35 | 2 37 | 2 39 | 2 41 | 2 43 | 2 46 |
| 54 | 2 17 | 2 20 | 2 22 | 2 24 | 2 26 | 2 29 | 2 31 | 2 33 | 2 35 | 2 38 | 2 40 | 2 42 | 2 44 | 2 47 | 2 49 |
| 55 | 2 20 | 2 22 | 2 24 | 2 27 | 2 29 | 2 31 | 2 34 | 2 36 | 2 38 | 2 40 | 2 43 | 2 45 | 2 47 | 2 50 | 2 52 |
| 56 | 2 22 | 2 25 | 2 27 | 2 29 | 2 32 | 2 34 | 2 36 | 2 39 | 2 41 | 2 43 | 2 46 | 2 48 | 2 50 | 2 53 | 2 55 |
| 57 | 2 25 | 2 27 | 2 30 | 2 32 | 2 34 | 2 37 | 2 39 | 2 42 | 2 44 | 2 46 | 2 49 | 2 51 | 2 53 | 2 56 | 2 58 |
| 58 | 2 27 | 2 30 | 2 32 | 2 35 | 2 37 | 2 40 | 2 42 | 2 44 | 2 47 | 2 49 | 2 52 | 2 54 | 2 56 | 2 59 | 3 1 |
| 59 | 2 30 | 2 32 | 2 35 | 2 37 | 2 40 | 2 42 | 2 45 | 2 47 | 2 50 | 2 52 | 2 55 | 2 57 | 2 59 | 3 2 | 3 4 |
| 60 | 2 33 | 2 35 | 2 38 | 2 40 | 2 43 | 2 45 | 2 48 | 2 50 | 2 53 | 2 55 | 2 58 | 3 0 | 3 3 | 3 5 | 3 8 |

## HOURS

| TIME | 1° 1' | 1° 2' | 1° 3' | 1° 4' | 1° 5' | 1° 6' | 1° 7' | 1° 8' | 1° 9' | 1° 10' | 1° 11' | 1° 12' | 1° 13' | 1° 14' | 1° 15' |
|---|---|---|---|---|---|---|---|---|---|---|---|---|---|---|---|
| 1 | 2 33 | 2 35 | 2 38 | 2 40 | 2 43 | 2 45 | 2 48 | 2 50 | 2 53 | 2 55 | 2 58 | 3 0 | 3 3 | 3 5 | 3 8 |
| 2 | 5 5 | 5 10 | 5 15 | 5 20 | 5 25 | 5 30 | 5 35 | 5 40 | 5 45 | 5 50 | 5 55 | 6 0 | 6 5 | 6 10 | 6 15 |
| 3 | 7 38 | 7 45 | 7 53 | 8 0 | 8 8 | 8 15 | 8 23 | 8 30 | 8 38 | 8 45 | 8 53 | 9 0 | 9 8 | 9 15 | 9 23 |
| 4 | 10 10 | 10 20 | 10 30 | 10 40 | 10 50 | 11 0 | 11 10 | 11 20 | 11 30 | 11 40 | 11 50 | 12 0 | 12 10 | 12 20 | 12 30 |
| 5 | 12 43 | 12 55 | 13 8 | 13 20 | 13 33 | 13 45 | 13 58 | 14 10 | 14 23 | 14 35 | 14 48 | 15 0 | 15 13 | 15 25 | 15 38 |
| 6 | 15 15 | 15 30 | 15 45 | 16 0 | 16 15 | 16 30 | 16 45 | 17 0 | 17 15 | 17 30 | 17 45 | 18 0 | 18 15 | 18 30 | 18 45 |
| 7 | 17 48 | 18 5 | 18 23 | 18 40 | 18 58 | 19 15 | 19 33 | 19 50 | 20 8 | 20 25 | 20 43 | 21 0 | 21 18 | 21 35 | 21 53 |
| 8 | 20 20 | 20 40 | 21 0 | 21 20 | 21 40 | 22 0 | 22 20 | 22 40 | 23 0 | 23 20 | 23 40 | 24 0 | 24 20 | 24 40 | 25 0 |
| 9 | 22 53 | 23 15 | 23 38 | 24 0 | 24 23 | 24 45 | 25 8 | 25 30 | 25 53 | 26 15 | 26 38 | 27 0 | 27 23 | 27 45 | 28 8 |
| 10 | 25 25 | 25 50 | 26 15 | 26 40 | 27 5 | 27 30 | 27 55 | 28 20 | 28 45 | 29 10 | 29 35 | 30 0 | 30 25 | 30 50 | 31 15 |
| 11 | 27 58 | 28 25 | 28 53 | 29 20 | 29 48 | 30 15 | 30 43 | 31 10 | 31 38 | 32 5 | 32 33 | 33 0 | 33 28 | 33 55 | 34 23 |
| 12 | 30 30 | 31 0 | 31 30 | 32 0 | 32 30 | 33 0 | 33 30 | 34 0 | 34 30 | 35 0 | 35 30 | 36 0 | 36 30 | 37 0 | 37 30 |
| 13 | 33 3 | 33 35 | 34 8 | 34 40 | 35 13 | 35 45 | 36 18 | 36 50 | 37 23 | 37 55 | 38 28 | 39 0 | 39 33 | 40 5 | 40 38 |
| 14 | 35 35 | 36 10 | 36 45 | 37 20 | 37 55 | 38 30 | 39 5 | 39 40 | 40 15 | 40 50 | 41 25 | 42 0 | 42 35 | 43 10 | 43 45 |
| 15 | 38 8 | 38 45 | 39 23 | 40 0 | 40 38 | 41 15 | 41 53 | 42 30 | 43 8 | 43 45 | 44 23 | 45 0 | 45 38 | 46 15 | 46 53 |
| 16 | 40 40 | 41 20 | 42 0 | 42 40 | 43 20 | 44 0 | 44 40 | 45 20 | 46 0 | 46 40 | 47 20 | 48 0 | 48 40 | 49 20 | 50 0 |
| 17 | 43 13 | 43 55 | 44 38 | 45 20 | 46 3 | 46 45 | 47 28 | 48 10 | 48 53 | 49 35 | 50 18 | 51 0 | 51 43 | 52 25 | 53 8 |
| 18 | 45 45 | 46 30 | 47 15 | 48 0 | 48 45 | 49 30 | 50 15 | 51 0 | 51 45 | 52 30 | 53 15 | 54 0 | 54 45 | 55 30 | 56 15 |
| 19 | 48 18 | 49 5 | 49 53 | 50 40 | 51 28 | 52 15 | 53 3 | 53 50 | 54 38 | 55 25 | 56 13 | 57 0 | 57 48 | 58 35 | 59 23 |
| 20 | 50 50 | 51 40 | 52 30 | 53 20 | 54 10 | 55 0 | 55 50 | 56 40 | 57 30 | 58 20 | 59 10 | 1 0 0 | 1 0 50 | 1 1 40 | 1 2 30 |
| 21 | 53 23 | 54 15 | 55 8 | 56 0 | 56 53 | 57 45 | 58 38 | 59 30 | 1 0 23 | 1 1 15 | 1 2 8 | 1 3 0 | 1 3 53 | 1 4 45 | 1 5 38 |
| 22 | 55 55 | 56 50 | 57 45 | 58 40 | 59 35 | 1 0 30 | 1 1 25 | 1 2 20 | 1 3 15 | 1 4 10 | 1 5 5 | 1 6 0 | 1 6 55 | 1 7 50 | 1 8 45 |
| 23 | 58 28 | 59 25 | 1 0 23 | 1 1 20 | 1 2 18 | 1 3 15 | 1 4 13 | 1 5 10 | 1 6 8 | 1 7 5 | 1 8 3 | 1 9 0 | 1 9 58 | 1 10 55 | 1 11 53 |
| 24 | 1 1 0 | 1 2 0 | 1 3 0 | 1 4 0 | 1 5 0 | 1 6 0 | 1 7 0 | 1 8 0 | 1 9 0 | 1 10 0 | 1 11 0 | 1 12 0 | 1 13 0 | 1 14 0 | 1 15 0 |

# Table VII Diurnal Motion of the Planets

**24 HOUR TRAVEL**

### Minutes

| TIME (min) | 1° 16' | 1° 17' | 1° 18' | 1° 19' | 1° 20' | 1° 21' | 1° 22' | 1° 23' | 1° 24' | 1° 25' | 1° 26' | 1° 27' | 1° 28' | 1° 29' | 1° 30' |
|---|---|---|---|---|---|---|---|---|---|---|---|---|---|---|---|
| 1 | 0 3 | 0 3 | 0 3 | 0 3 | 0 3 | 0 3 | 0 3 | 0 3 | 0 4 | 0 4 | 0 4 | 0 4 | 0 4 | 0 4 | 0 4 |
| 2 | 0 6 | 0 6 | 0 7 | 0 7 | 0 7 | 0 7 | 0 7 | 0 7 | 0 7 | 0 7 | 0 7 | 0 7 | 0 7 | 0 7 | 0 8 |
| 3 | 0 10 | 0 10 | 0 10 | 0 10 | 0 10 | 0 10 | 0 10 | 0 10 | 0 11 | 0 11 | 0 11 | 0 11 | 0 11 | 0 11 | 0 11 |
| 4 | 0 13 | 0 13 | 0 13 | 0 13 | 0 13 | 0 14 | 0 14 | 0 14 | 0 14 | 0 14 | 0 14 | 0 15 | 0 15 | 0 15 | 0 15 |
| 5 | 0 16 | 0 16 | 0 16 | 0 16 | 0 17 | 0 17 | 0 17 | 0 17 | 0 18 | 0 18 | 0 18 | 0 18 | 0 18 | 0 19 | 0 19 |
| 6 | 0 19 | 0 19 | 0 20 | 0 20 | 0 20 | 0 20 | 0 21 | 0 21 | 0 21 | 0 21 | 0 22 | 0 22 | 0 22 | 0 22 | 0 23 |
| 7 | 0 22 | 0 22 | 0 23 | 0 23 | 0 23 | 0 24 | 0 24 | 0 24 | 0 25 | 0 25 | 0 25 | 0 25 | 0 26 | 0 26 | 0 26 |
| 8 | 0 25 | 0 26 | 0 26 | 0 26 | 0 27 | 0 27 | 0 27 | 0 28 | 0 28 | 0 28 | 0 29 | 0 29 | 0 29 | 0 30 | 0 30 |
| 9 | 0 29 | 0 29 | 0 29 | 0 30 | 0 30 | 0 30 | 0 31 | 0 31 | 0 32 | 0 32 | 0 32 | 0 33 | 0 33 | 0 33 | 0 34 |
| 10 | 0 32 | 0 32 | 0 33 | 0 33 | 0 33 | 0 34 | 0 34 | 0 35 | 0 35 | 0 35 | 0 36 | 0 36 | 0 37 | 0 37 | 0 38 |
| 11 | 0 35 | 0 35 | 0 36 | 0 36 | 0 37 | 0 37 | 0 38 | 0 38 | 0 39 | 0 39 | 0 39 | 0 40 | 0 40 | 0 41 | 0 41 |
| 12 | 0 38 | 0 39 | 0 39 | 0 40 | 0 40 | 0 41 | 0 41 | 0 42 | 0 42 | 0 43 | 0 43 | 0 44 | 0 44 | 0 45 | 0 45 |
| 13 | 0 41 | 0 42 | 0 42 | 0 43 | 0 43 | 0 44 | 0 44 | 0 45 | 0 46 | 0 46 | 0 47 | 0 47 | 0 48 | 0 48 | 0 49 |
| 14 | 0 44 | 0 45 | 0 46 | 0 46 | 0 47 | 0 47 | 0 48 | 0 48 | 0 49 | 0 50 | 0 50 | 0 51 | 0 51 | 0 52 | 0 53 |
| 15 | 0 48 | 0 48 | 0 49 | 0 49 | 0 50 | 0 51 | 0 51 | 0 52 | 0 53 | 0 53 | 0 54 | 0 54 | 0 55 | 0 56 | 0 56 |
| 16 | 0 51 | 0 51 | 0 52 | 0 53 | 0 53 | 0 54 | 0 55 | 0 55 | 0 56 | 0 57 | 0 57 | 0 58 | 0 59 | 0 59 | 1 0 |
| 17 | 0 54 | 0 55 | 0 55 | 0 56 | 0 57 | 0 57 | 0 58 | 0 59 | 1 0 | 1 0 | 1 1 | 1 2 | 1 2 | 1 3 | 1 4 |
| 18 | 0 57 | 0 58 | 0 59 | 0 59 | 1 0 | 1 1 | 1 2 | 1 2 | 1 3 | 1 4 | 1 5 | 1 5 | 1 6 | 1 7 | 1 8 |
| 19 | 1 0 | 1 1 | 1 2 | 1 3 | 1 3 | 1 4 | 1 5 | 1 6 | 1 7 | 1 7 | 1 8 | 1 9 | 1 10 | 1 10 | 1 11 |
| 20 | 1 3 | 1 4 | 1 5 | 1 6 | 1 7 | 1 8 | 1 8 | 1 9 | 1 10 | 1 11 | 1 12 | 1 13 | 1 13 | 1 14 | 1 15 |
| 21 | 1 7 | 1 7 | 1 8 | 1 9 | 1 10 | 1 11 | 1 12 | 1 13 | 1 14 | 1 14 | 1 15 | 1 16 | 1 17 | 1 18 | 1 19 |
| 22 | 1 10 | 1 11 | 1 12 | 1 12 | 1 13 | 1 14 | 1 15 | 1 16 | 1 17 | 1 18 | 1 19 | 1 20 | 1 21 | 1 22 | 1 23 |
| 23 | 1 13 | 1 14 | 1 15 | 1 16 | 1 17 | 1 18 | 1 19 | 1 20 | 1 21 | 1 21 | 1 22 | 1 23 | 1 24 | 1 25 | 1 26 |
| 24 | 1 16 | 1 17 | 1 18 | 1 19 | 1 20 | 1 21 | 1 22 | 1 23 | 1 24 | 1 25 | 1 26 | 1 27 | 1 28 | 1 29 | 1 30 |
| 25 | 1 19 | 1 20 | 1 21 | 1 22 | 1 23 | 1 24 | 1 25 | 1 26 | 1 28 | 1 29 | 1 30 | 1 31 | 1 32 | 1 33 | 1 34 |
| 26 | 1 22 | 1 23 | 1 25 | 1 26 | 1 27 | 1 28 | 1 29 | 1 30 | 1 31 | 1 32 | 1 33 | 1 34 | 1 35 | 1 36 | 1 38 |
| 27 | 1 26 | 1 27 | 1 28 | 1 29 | 1 30 | 1 31 | 1 32 | 1 33 | 1 35 | 1 36 | 1 37 | 1 38 | 1 39 | 1 40 | 1 41 |
| 28 | 1 29 | 1 30 | 1 31 | 1 32 | 1 33 | 1 35 | 1 36 | 1 37 | 1 38 | 1 39 | 1 40 | 1 42 | 1 43 | 1 44 | 1 45 |
| 29 | 1 32 | 1 33 | 1 34 | 1 35 | 1 37 | 1 38 | 1 39 | 1 40 | 1 42 | 1 43 | 1 44 | 1 45 | 1 46 | 1 48 | 1 49 |
| 30 | 1 35 | 1 36 | 1 38 | 1 39 | 1 40 | 1 41 | 1 43 | 1 44 | 1 45 | 1 46 | 1 48 | 1 49 | 1 50 | 1 51 | 1 53 |
| 31 | 1 38 | 1 39 | 1 41 | 1 42 | 1 43 | 1 45 | 1 46 | 1 47 | 1 49 | 1 50 | 1 51 | 1 52 | 1 54 | 1 55 | 1 56 |
| 32 | 1 41 | 1 43 | 1 44 | 1 45 | 1 47 | 1 48 | 1 49 | 1 51 | 1 52 | 1 53 | 1 55 | 1 56 | 1 57 | 1 59 | 2 0 |
| 33 | 1 45 | 1 46 | 1 47 | 1 49 | 1 50 | 1 51 | 1 53 | 1 54 | 1 56 | 1 57 | 1 58 | 2 0 | 2 1 | 2 2 | 2 4 |
| 34 | 1 48 | 1 49 | 1 51 | 1 52 | 1 53 | 1 55 | 1 56 | 1 58 | 1 59 | 2 0 | 2 2 | 2 3 | 2 5 | 2 6 | 2 8 |
| 35 | 1 51 | 1 52 | 1 54 | 1 55 | 1 57 | 1 58 | 2 0 | 2 1 | 2 3 | 2 4 | 2 5 | 2 7 | 2 8 | 2 10 | 2 11 |
| 36 | 1 54 | 1 56 | 1 57 | 1 59 | 2 0 | 2 2 | 2 3 | 2 5 | 2 6 | 2 8 | 2 9 | 2 11 | 2 12 | 2 14 | 2 15 |
| 37 | 1 57 | 1 59 | 2 0 | 2 2 | 2 3 | 2 5 | 2 6 | 2 8 | 2 10 | 2 11 | 2 13 | 2 14 | 2 16 | 2 17 | 2 19 |
| 38 | 2 0 | 2 2 | 2 4 | 2 5 | 2 7 | 2 8 | 2 10 | 2 11 | 2 13 | 2 15 | 2 16 | 2 18 | 2 19 | 2 21 | 2 23 |
| 39 | 2 4 | 2 5 | 2 7 | 2 8 | 2 10 | 2 12 | 2 13 | 2 15 | 2 17 | 2 18 | 2 20 | 2 21 | 2 23 | 2 25 | 2 26 |
| 40 | 2 7 | 2 8 | 2 10 | 2 12 | 2 13 | 2 15 | 2 17 | 2 18 | 2 20 | 2 22 | 2 23 | 2 25 | 2 27 | 2 28 | 2 30 |
| 41 | 2 10 | 2 12 | 2 13 | 2 15 | 2 17 | 2 18 | 2 20 | 2 22 | 2 24 | 2 25 | 2 27 | 2 29 | 2 30 | 2 32 | 2 34 |
| 42 | 2 13 | 2 15 | 2 17 | 2 18 | 2 20 | 2 22 | 2 24 | 2 25 | 2 27 | 2 29 | 2 31 | 2 32 | 2 34 | 2 36 | 2 38 |
| 43 | 2 16 | 2 18 | 2 20 | 2 22 | 2 23 | 2 25 | 2 27 | 2 29 | 2 31 | 2 32 | 2 34 | 2 36 | 2 38 | 2 39 | 2 41 |
| 44 | 2 19 | 2 21 | 2 23 | 2 25 | 2 27 | 2 29 | 2 30 | 2 32 | 2 34 | 2 36 | 2 38 | 2 40 | 2 41 | 2 43 | 2 45 |
| 45 | 2 23 | 2 24 | 2 26 | 2 28 | 2 30 | 2 32 | 2 34 | 2 36 | 2 38 | 2 39 | 2 41 | 2 43 | 2 45 | 2 47 | 2 49 |
| 46 | 2 26 | 2 28 | 2 30 | 2 31 | 2 33 | 2 35 | 2 37 | 2 39 | 2 41 | 2 43 | 2 45 | 2 47 | 2 49 | 2 51 | 2 53 |
| 47 | 2 29 | 2 31 | 2 33 | 2 35 | 2 37 | 2 39 | 2 41 | 2 43 | 2 45 | 2 46 | 2 48 | 2 50 | 2 52 | 2 54 | 2 56 |
| 48 | 2 32 | 2 34 | 2 36 | 2 38 | 2 40 | 2 42 | 2 44 | 2 46 | 2 48 | 2 50 | 2 52 | 2 54 | 2 56 | 2 58 | 3 0 |
| 49 | 2 35 | 2 37 | 2 39 | 2 41 | 2 43 | 2 45 | 2 47 | 2 49 | 2 52 | 2 54 | 2 56 | 2 58 | 3 0 | 3 2 | 3 4 |
| 50 | 2 38 | 2 40 | 2 43 | 2 45 | 2 47 | 2 49 | 2 51 | 2 53 | 2 55 | 2 57 | 2 59 | 3 1 | 3 3 | 3 5 | 3 8 |
| 51 | 2 42 | 2 44 | 2 46 | 2 48 | 2 50 | 2 52 | 2 54 | 2 56 | 2 59 | 3 1 | 3 3 | 3 5 | 3 7 | 3 9 | 3 11 |
| 52 | 2 45 | 2 47 | 2 49 | 2 51 | 2 53 | 2 56 | 2 58 | 3 0 | 3 2 | 3 4 | 3 6 | 3 8 | 3 10 | 3 12 | 3 15 |
| 53 | 2 48 | 2 50 | 2 52 | 2 54 | 2 57 | 2 59 | 3 1 | 3 3 | 3 6 | 3 8 | 3 10 | 3 12 | 3 14 | 3 17 | 3 19 |
| 54 | 2 51 | 2 53 | 2 56 | 2 58 | 3 0 | 3 2 | 3 5 | 3 7 | 3 9 | 3 11 | 3 14 | 3 16 | 3 18 | 3 20 | 3 23 |
| 55 | 2 54 | 2 56 | 2 59 | 3 1 | 3 3 | 3 6 | 3 8 | 3 10 | 3 13 | 3 15 | 3 17 | 3 19 | 3 22 | 3 24 | 3 26 |
| 56 | 2 57 | 3 0 | 3 2 | 3 4 | 3 7 | 3 9 | 3 11 | 3 14 | 3 16 | 3 18 | 3 21 | 3 23 | 3 25 | 3 28 | 3 30 |
| 57 | 3 1 | 3 3 | 3 5 | 3 8 | 3 10 | 3 12 | 3 15 | 3 17 | 3 20 | 3 22 | 3 24 | 3 27 | 3 29 | 3 31 | 3 34 |
| 58 | 3 4 | 3 6 | 3 9 | 3 11 | 3 13 | 3 16 | 3 18 | 3 21 | 3 23 | 3 25 | 3 28 | 3 30 | 3 33 | 3 35 | 3 38 |
| 59 | 3 7 | 3 9 | 3 12 | 3 14 | 3 17 | 3 19 | 3 22 | 3 24 | 3 27 | 3 29 | 3 31 | 3 34 | 3 36 | 3 39 | 3 41 |
| 60 | 3 10 | 3 13 | 3 15 | 3 18 | 3 20 | 3 23 | 3 25 | 3 28 | 3 30 | 3 33 | 3 35 | 3 38 | 3 40 | 3 43 | 3 45 |

### Hours

| TIME (hr) | 1° 16' | 1° 17' | 1° 18' | 1° 19' | 1° 20' | 1° 21' | 1° 22' | 1° 23' | 1° 24' | 1° 25' | 1° 26' | 1° 27' | 1° 28' | 1° 29' | 1° 30' |
|---|---|---|---|---|---|---|---|---|---|---|---|---|---|---|---|
| 1 | 3 10 | 3 13 | 3 15 | 3 18 | 3 20 | 3 23 | 3 25 | 3 28 | 3 30 | 3 33 | 3 35 | 3 38 | 3 40 | 3 43 | 3 45 |
| 2 | 6 20 | 6 25 | 6 30 | 6 35 | 6 40 | 6 45 | 6 50 | 6 55 | 7 0 | 7 5 | 7 10 | 7 15 | 7 20 | 7 25 | 7 30 |
| 3 | 9 30 | 9 38 | 9 45 | 9 53 | 10 0 | 10 8 | 10 15 | 10 23 | 10 30 | 10 38 | 10 45 | 10 53 | 11 0 | 11 8 | 11 15 |
| 4 | 12 40 | 12 50 | 13 0 | 13 10 | 13 20 | 13 30 | 13 40 | 13 50 | 14 0 | 14 10 | 14 20 | 14 30 | 14 40 | 14 50 | 15 0 |
| 5 | 15 50 | 16 3 | 16 15 | 16 28 | 16 40 | 16 53 | 17 5 | 17 18 | 17 30 | 17 43 | 17 55 | 18 8 | 18 20 | 18 33 | 18 45 |
| 6 | 19 0 | 19 15 | 19 30 | 19 45 | 20 0 | 20 15 | 20 30 | 20 45 | 21 0 | 21 15 | 21 30 | 21 45 | 22 0 | 22 15 | 22 30 |
| 7 | 22 10 | 22 28 | 22 45 | 23 3 | 23 20 | 23 38 | 23 55 | 24 13 | 24 30 | 24 48 | 25 5 | 25 23 | 25 40 | 25 58 | 26 15 |
| 8 | 25 20 | 25 40 | 26 0 | 26 20 | 26 40 | 27 0 | 27 20 | 27 40 | 28 0 | 28 20 | 28 40 | 29 0 | 29 20 | 29 40 | 30 0 |
| 9 | 28 30 | 28 53 | 29 15 | 29 38 | 30 0 | 30 23 | 30 45 | 31 8 | 31 30 | 31 53 | 32 15 | 32 38 | 33 0 | 33 23 | 33 45 |
| 10 | 31 40 | 32 5 | 32 30 | 32 55 | 33 20 | 33 45 | 34 10 | 34 35 | 35 0 | 35 25 | 35 50 | 36 15 | 36 40 | 37 5 | 37 30 |
| 11 | 34 50 | 35 18 | 35 45 | 36 13 | 36 40 | 37 8 | 37 35 | 38 3 | 38 30 | 38 58 | 39 25 | 39 53 | 40 20 | 40 48 | 41 15 |
| 12 | 38 0 | 38 30 | 39 0 | 39 30 | 40 0 | 40 30 | 41 0 | 41 30 | 42 0 | 42 30 | 43 0 | 43 30 | 44 0 | 44 30 | 45 0 |
| 13 | 41 10 | 41 43 | 42 15 | 42 48 | 43 20 | 43 53 | 44 25 | 44 58 | 45 30 | 46 3 | 46 35 | 47 8 | 47 40 | 48 13 | 48 45 |
| 14 | 44 20 | 44 55 | 45 30 | 46 5 | 46 40 | 47 15 | 47 50 | 48 25 | 49 0 | 49 35 | 50 10 | 50 45 | 51 20 | 51 55 | 52 30 |
| 15 | 47 30 | 48 8 | 48 45 | 49 23 | 50 0 | 50 38 | 51 15 | 51 53 | 52 30 | 53 8 | 53 45 | 54 23 | 55 0 | 55 38 | 56 15 |
| 16 | 50 40 | 51 20 | 52 0 | 52 40 | 53 20 | 54 0 | 54 40 | 55 20 | 56 0 | 56 40 | 57 20 | 58 0 | 58 40 | 59 20 | 1 0 0 |
| 17 | 53 50 | 54 33 | 55 15 | 55 58 | 56 40 | 57 23 | 58 5 | 58 48 | 59 30 | 1 0 13 | 1 0 55 | 1 1 38 | 1 2 20 | 1 3 3 | 1 3 45 |
| 18 | 57 0 | 57 45 | 58 30 | 59 15 | 1 0 0 | 1 0 45 | 1 1 30 | 1 2 15 | 1 3 0 | 1 3 45 | 1 4 30 | 1 5 15 | 1 6 0 | 1 6 45 | 1 7 30 |
| 19 | 1 0 10 | 1 0 58 | 1 1 45 | 1 2 33 | 1 3 20 | 1 4 8 | 1 4 55 | 1 5 43 | 1 6 30 | 1 7 18 | 1 8 5 | 1 8 53 | 1 9 40 | 1 10 28 | 1 11 15 |
| 20 | 1 3 20 | 1 4 10 | 1 5 0 | 1 5 50 | 1 6 40 | 1 7 30 | 1 8 20 | 1 9 10 | 1 10 0 | 1 10 50 | 1 11 40 | 1 12 30 | 1 13 20 | 1 14 10 | 1 15 0 |
| 21 | 1 6 30 | 1 7 23 | 1 8 15 | 1 9 8 | 1 10 0 | 1 10 53 | 1 11 45 | 1 12 38 | 1 13 30 | 1 14 23 | 1 15 15 | 1 16 8 | 1 17 0 | 1 17 53 | 1 18 45 |
| 22 | 1 9 40 | 1 10 35 | 1 11 30 | 1 12 25 | 1 13 20 | 1 14 15 | 1 15 10 | 1 16 5 | 1 17 0 | 1 17 55 | 1 18 50 | 1 19 45 | 1 20 40 | 1 21 35 | 1 22 30 |
| 23 | 1 12 50 | 1 13 48 | 1 14 45 | 1 15 43 | 1 16 40 | 1 17 38 | 1 18 35 | 1 19 33 | 1 20 30 | 1 21 28 | 1 22 25 | 1 23 23 | 1 24 20 | 1 25 18 | 1 26 15 |
| 24 | 1 16 0 | 1 17 0 | 1 18 0 | 1 19 0 | 1 20 0 | 1 21 0 | 1 22 0 | 1 23 0 | 1 24 0 | 1 25 0 | 1 26 0 | 1 27 0 | 1 28 0 | 1 29 0 | 1 30 0 |

# Table VII Diurnal Motion of the Planets

| 24 HOUR TRAVEL | | | | | | | | | | | | | | | |
|---|---|---|---|---|---|---|---|---|---|---|---|---|---|---|---|
| TIME | 1°31' | 1°32' | 1°33' | 1°34' | 1°35' | 1°36' | 1°37' | 1°38' | 1°39' | 1°40' | 1°41' | 1°42' | 1°43' | 1°44' | 1°45' |
| **MINUTES 1** | 0 4 | 0 4 | 0 4 | 0 4 | 0 4 | 0 4 | 0 4 | 0 4 | 0 4 | 0 4 | 0 4 | 0 4 | 0 4 | 0 4 | 0 4 |
| 2 | 0 8 | 0 8 | 0 8 | 0 8 | 0 8 | 0 8 | 0 8 | 0 8 | 0 8 | 0 8 | 0 8 | 0 9 | 0 9 | 0 9 | 0 9 |
| 3 | 0 11 | 0 12 | 0 12 | 0 12 | 0 12 | 0 12 | 0 12 | 0 12 | 0 12 | 0 12 | 0 13 | 0 13 | 0 13 | 0 13 | 0 13 |
| 4 | 0 15 | 0 15 | 0 16 | 0 16 | 0 16 | 0 16 | 0 16 | 0 16 | 0 16 | 0 17 | 0 17 | 0 17 | 0 17 | 0 17 | 0 18 |
| 5 | 0 19 | 0 19 | 0 19 | 0 20 | 0 20 | 0 20 | 0 20 | 0 20 | 0 20 | 0 21 | 0 21 | 0 21 | 0 21 | 0 22 | 0 22 |
| 6 | 0 23 | 0 23 | 0 23 | 0 24 | 0 24 | 0 24 | 0 24 | 0 25 | 0 25 | 0 25 | 0 25 | 0 26 | 0 26 | 0 26 | 0 26 |
| 7 | 0 27 | 0 27 | 0 27 | 0 27 | 0 28 | 0 28 | 0 28 | 0 29 | 0 29 | 0 29 | 0 29 | 0 30 | 0 30 | 0 30 | 0 31 |
| 8 | 0 30 | 0 31 | 0 31 | 0 31 | 0 32 | 0 32 | 0 32 | 0 33 | 0 33 | 0 33 | 0 34 | 0 34 | 0 34 | 0 35 | 0 35 |
| 9 | 0 34 | 0 35 | 0 35 | 0 35 | 0 36 | 0 36 | 0 36 | 0 37 | 0 37 | 0 38 | 0 38 | 0 38 | 0 39 | 0 39 | 0 39 |
| 10 | 0 38 | 0 38 | 0 39 | 0 39 | 0 40 | 0 40 | 0 40 | 0 41 | 0 41 | 0 42 | 0 42 | 0 43 | 0 43 | 0 43 | 0 44 |
| 11 | 0 42 | 0 42 | 0 43 | 0 43 | 0 44 | 0 44 | 0 44 | 0 45 | 0 45 | 0 46 | 0 46 | 0 47 | 0 47 | 0 48 | 0 48 |
| 12 | 0 46 | 0 46 | 0 47 | 0 47 | 0 48 | 0 48 | 0 49 | 0 49 | 0 49 | 0 50 | 0 50 | 0 51 | 0 51 | 0 52 | 0 52 |
| 13 | 0 49 | 0 50 | 0 50 | 0 51 | 0 51 | 0 52 | 0 53 | 0 53 | 0 54 | 0 54 | 0 55 | 0 55 | 0 56 | 0 56 | 0 57 |
| 14 | 0 53 | 0 54 | 0 54 | 0 55 | 0 55 | 0 56 | 0 57 | 0 57 | 0 58 | 0 58 | 0 59 | 0 59 | 1 0 | 1 1 | 1 1 |
| 15 | 0 57 | 0 58 | 0 58 | 0 59 | 0 59 | 1 0 | 1 1 | 1 1 | 1 2 | 1 3 | 1 3 | 1 4 | 1 4 | 1 5 | 1 6 |
| 16 | 1 1 | 1 1 | 1 2 | 1 3 | 1 3 | 1 4 | 1 5 | 1 5 | 1 6 | 1 7 | 1 7 | 1 8 | 1 9 | 1 9 | 1 10 |
| 17 | 1 4 | 1 5 | 1 6 | 1 7 | 1 7 | 1 8 | 1 9 | 1 9 | 1 10 | 1 11 | 1 12 | 1 12 | 1 13 | 1 14 | 1 14 |
| 18 | 1 8 | 1 9 | 1 10 | 1 11 | 1 11 | 1 12 | 1 13 | 1 14 | 1 14 | 1 15 | 1 16 | 1 17 | 1 17 | 1 18 | 1 19 |
| 19 | 1 12 | 1 13 | 1 14 | 1 14 | 1 15 | 1 16 | 1 17 | 1 18 | 1 18 | 1 19 | 1 20 | 1 21 | 1 22 | 1 22 | 1 23 |
| 20 | 1 16 | 1 17 | 1 18 | 1 18 | 1 19 | 1 20 | 1 21 | 1 22 | 1 23 | 1 23 | 1 24 | 1 25 | 1 26 | 1 27 | 1 28 |
| 21 | 1 20 | 1 21 | 1 21 | 1 22 | 1 23 | 1 24 | 1 25 | 1 26 | 1 27 | 1 28 | 1 28 | 1 29 | 1 30 | 1 31 | 1 32 |
| 22 | 1 23 | 1 24 | 1 25 | 1 26 | 1 27 | 1 28 | 1 29 | 1 30 | 1 31 | 1 32 | 1 33 | 1 34 | 1 34 | 1 35 | 1 36 |
| 23 | 1 27 | 1 28 | 1 29 | 1 30 | 1 31 | 1 32 | 1 33 | 1 34 | 1 35 | 1 36 | 1 37 | 1 38 | 1 39 | 1 40 | 1 41 |
| 24 | 1 31 | 1 32 | 1 33 | 1 34 | 1 35 | 1 36 | 1 37 | 1 38 | 1 39 | 1 40 | 1 41 | 1 42 | 1 43 | 1 44 | 1 45 |
| 25 | 1 35 | 1 36 | 1 37 | 1 38 | 1 39 | 1 40 | 1 41 | 1 42 | 1 43 | 1 44 | 1 45 | 1 46 | 1 47 | 1 48 | 1 49 |
| 26 | 1 39 | 1 40 | 1 41 | 1 42 | 1 43 | 1 44 | 1 45 | 1 46 | 1 47 | 1 48 | 1 49 | 1 51 | 1 52 | 1 53 | 1 54 |
| 27 | 1 42 | 1 44 | 1 45 | 1 46 | 1 47 | 1 48 | 1 49 | 1 50 | 1 51 | 1 53 | 1 54 | 1 55 | 1 56 | 1 57 | 1 58 |
| 28 | 1 46 | 1 47 | 1 49 | 1 50 | 1 51 | 1 52 | 1 53 | 1 54 | 1 56 | 1 57 | 1 58 | 1 59 | 2 0 | 2 1 | 2 3 |
| 29 | 1 50 | 1 51 | 1 52 | 1 54 | 1 55 | 1 56 | 1 57 | 1 58 | 2 0 | 2 1 | 2 2 | 2 3 | 2 4 | 2 6 | 2 7 |
| 30 | 1 54 | 1 55 | 1 56 | 1 58 | 1 59 | 2 0 | 2 1 | 2 3 | 2 4 | 2 5 | 2 6 | 2 8 | 2 9 | 2 10 | 2 11 |
| 31 | 1 58 | 1 59 | 2 0 | 2 1 | 2 3 | 2 4 | 2 5 | 2 7 | 2 8 | 2 9 | 2 10 | 2 12 | 2 13 | 2 14 | 2 16 |
| 32 | 2 1 | 2 3 | 2 4 | 2 5 | 2 7 | 2 8 | 2 9 | 2 11 | 2 12 | 2 13 | 2 15 | 2 16 | 2 17 | 2 19 | 2 20 |
| 33 | 2 5 | 2 7 | 2 8 | 2 9 | 2 11 | 2 12 | 2 13 | 2 15 | 2 16 | 2 18 | 2 19 | 2 20 | 2 22 | 2 23 | 2 24 |
| 34 | 2 9 | 2 10 | 2 12 | 2 13 | 2 15 | 2 16 | 2 17 | 2 19 | 2 20 | 2 22 | 2 23 | 2 25 | 2 26 | 2 27 | 2 29 |
| 35 | 2 13 | 2 14 | 2 16 | 2 17 | 2 19 | 2 20 | 2 21 | 2 23 | 2 24 | 2 26 | 2 27 | 2 29 | 2 30 | 2 32 | 2 33 |
| 36 | 2 17 | 2 18 | 2 20 | 2 21 | 2 23 | 2 24 | 2 26 | 2 27 | 2 29 | 2 30 | 2 32 | 2 33 | 2 35 | 2 36 | 2 38 |
| 37 | 2 20 | 2 22 | 2 23 | 2 25 | 2 26 | 2 28 | 2 30 | 2 31 | 2 33 | 2 34 | 2 36 | 2 37 | 2 39 | 2 40 | 2 42 |
| 38 | 2 24 | 2 26 | 2 27 | 2 29 | 2 30 | 2 32 | 2 34 | 2 35 | 2 37 | 2 38 | 2 40 | 2 42 | 2 43 | 2 45 | 2 46 |
| 39 | 2 28 | 2 30 | 2 31 | 2 33 | 2 34 | 2 36 | 2 38 | 2 39 | 2 41 | 2 43 | 2 44 | 2 46 | 2 47 | 2 49 | 2 51 |
| 40 | 2 32 | 2 33 | 2 35 | 2 37 | 2 38 | 2 40 | 2 42 | 2 43 | 2 45 | 2 47 | 2 48 | 2 50 | 2 52 | 2 53 | 2 55 |
| 41 | 2 35 | 2 37 | 2 39 | 2 41 | 2 42 | 2 44 | 2 46 | 2 47 | 2 49 | 2 51 | 2 53 | 2 54 | 2 56 | 2 58 | 2 59 |
| 42 | 2 39 | 2 41 | 2 43 | 2 45 | 2 46 | 2 48 | 2 50 | 2 52 | 2 53 | 2 55 | 2 57 | 2 59 | 3 0 | 3 2 | 3 4 |
| 43 | 2 43 | 2 45 | 2 47 | 2 48 | 2 50 | 2 52 | 2 54 | 2 56 | 2 57 | 2 59 | 3 1 | 3 3 | 3 5 | 3 6 | 3 8 |
| 44 | 2 47 | 2 49 | 2 51 | 2 52 | 2 54 | 2 56 | 2 58 | 3 0 | 3 2 | 3 3 | 3 5 | 3 7 | 3 9 | 3 11 | 3 13 |
| 45 | 2 51 | 2 53 | 2 54 | 2 56 | 2 58 | 3 0 | 3 2 | 3 4 | 3 6 | 3 8 | 3 9 | 3 11 | 3 13 | 3 15 | 3 17 |
| 46 | 2 54 | 2 56 | 2 58 | 3 0 | 3 2 | 3 4 | 3 6 | 3 8 | 3 10 | 3 12 | 3 14 | 3 16 | 3 17 | 3 19 | 3 21 |
| 47 | 2 58 | 3 0 | 3 2 | 3 4 | 3 6 | 3 8 | 3 10 | 3 12 | 3 14 | 3 16 | 3 18 | 3 20 | 3 22 | 3 24 | 3 26 |
| 48 | 3 2 | 3 4 | 3 6 | 3 8 | 3 10 | 3 12 | 3 14 | 3 16 | 3 18 | 3 20 | 3 22 | 3 24 | 3 26 | 3 28 | 3 30 |
| 49 | 3 6 | 3 8 | 3 10 | 3 12 | 3 14 | 3 16 | 3 18 | 3 20 | 3 22 | 3 24 | 3 26 | 3 28 | 3 30 | 3 32 | 3 34 |
| 50 | 3 10 | 3 12 | 3 14 | 3 16 | 3 18 | 3 20 | 3 22 | 3 24 | 3 26 | 3 28 | 3 30 | 3 33 | 3 35 | 3 37 | 3 39 |
| 51 | 3 13 | 3 16 | 3 18 | 3 20 | 3 22 | 3 24 | 3 26 | 3 28 | 3 30 | 3 33 | 3 35 | 3 37 | 3 39 | 3 41 | 3 43 |
| 52 | 3 17 | 3 19 | 3 22 | 3 24 | 3 26 | 3 28 | 3 30 | 3 32 | 3 35 | 3 37 | 3 39 | 3 41 | 3 43 | 3 45 | 3 48 |
| 53 | 3 21 | 3 23 | 3 25 | 3 28 | 3 30 | 3 32 | 3 34 | 3 36 | 3 39 | 3 41 | 3 43 | 3 45 | 3 47 | 3 50 | 3 52 |
| 54 | 3 25 | 3 27 | 3 29 | 3 32 | 3 34 | 3 36 | 3 38 | 3 41 | 3 43 | 3 45 | 3 47 | 3 50 | 3 52 | 3 54 | 3 56 |
| 55 | 3 29 | 3 31 | 3 33 | 3 35 | 3 38 | 3 40 | 3 42 | 3 45 | 3 47 | 3 49 | 3 51 | 3 54 | 3 56 | 3 58 | 4 1 |
| 56 | 3 32 | 3 35 | 3 37 | 3 39 | 3 42 | 3 44 | 3 46 | 3 49 | 3 51 | 3 53 | 3 56 | 3 58 | 4 0 | 4 3 | 4 5 |
| 57 | 3 36 | 3 39 | 3 41 | 3 43 | 3 46 | 3 48 | 3 50 | 3 53 | 3 55 | 3 58 | 4 0 | 4 2 | 4 5 | 4 7 | 4 9 |
| 58 | 3 40 | 3 42 | 3 45 | 3 47 | 3 50 | 3 52 | 3 54 | 3 57 | 3 59 | 4 2 | 4 4 | 4 7 | 4 9 | 4 11 | 4 14 |
| 59 | 3 44 | 3 46 | 3 49 | 3 51 | 3 54 | 3 56 | 3 58 | 4 1 | 4 3 | 4 6 | 4 8 | 4 11 | 4 13 | 4 16 | 4 18 |
| 60 | 3 48 | 3 50 | 3 53 | 3 55 | 3 58 | 4 0 | 4 3 | 4 5 | 4 8 | 4 10 | 4 13 | 4 15 | 4 18 | 4 20 | 4 23 |
| **HOURS 1** | 3 48 | 3 50 | 3 53 | 3 55 | 3 58 | 4 0 | 4 3 | 4 5 | 4 8 | 4 10 | 4 13 | 4 15 | 4 18 | 4 20 | 4 23 |
| 2 | 7 35 | 7 40 | 7 45 | 7 50 | 7 55 | 8 0 | 8 5 | 8 10 | 8 15 | 8 20 | 8 25 | 8 30 | 8 35 | 8 40 | 8 45 |
| 3 | 11 23 | 11 30 | 11 38 | 11 45 | 11 53 | 12 0 | 12 8 | 12 15 | 12 23 | 12 30 | 12 38 | 12 45 | 12 53 | 13 0 | 13 8 |
| 4 | 15 10 | 15 20 | 15 30 | 15 40 | 15 50 | 16 0 | 16 10 | 16 20 | 16 30 | 16 40 | 16 50 | 17 0 | 17 10 | 17 20 | 17 30 |
| 5 | 18 58 | 19 10 | 19 23 | 19 35 | 19 48 | 20 0 | 20 13 | 20 25 | 20 38 | 20 50 | 21 3 | 21 15 | 21 28 | 21 40 | 21 53 |
| 6 | 22 45 | 23 0 | 23 15 | 23 30 | 23 45 | 24 0 | 24 15 | 24 30 | 24 45 | 25 0 | 25 15 | 25 30 | 25 45 | 26 0 | 26 15 |
| 7 | 26 33 | 26 50 | 27 8 | 27 25 | 27 43 | 28 0 | 28 18 | 28 35 | 28 53 | 29 10 | 29 28 | 29 45 | 30 3 | 30 20 | 30 38 |
| 8 | 30 20 | 30 40 | 31 0 | 31 20 | 31 40 | 32 0 | 32 20 | 32 40 | 33 0 | 33 20 | 33 40 | 34 0 | 34 20 | 34 40 | 35 0 |
| 9 | 34 8 | 34 30 | 34 53 | 35 15 | 35 38 | 36 0 | 36 23 | 36 45 | 37 8 | 37 30 | 37 53 | 38 15 | 38 38 | 39 0 | 39 23 |
| 10 | 37 55 | 38 20 | 38 45 | 39 10 | 39 35 | 40 0 | 40 25 | 40 50 | 41 15 | 41 40 | 42 5 | 42 30 | 42 55 | 43 20 | 43 45 |
| 11 | 41 43 | 42 10 | 42 38 | 43 5 | 43 33 | 44 0 | 44 28 | 44 55 | 45 23 | 45 50 | 46 18 | 46 45 | 47 13 | 47 40 | 48 8 |
| 12 | 45 30 | 46 0 | 46 30 | 47 0 | 47 30 | 48 0 | 48 30 | 49 0 | 49 30 | 50 0 | 50 30 | 51 0 | 51 30 | 52 0 | 52 30 |
| 13 | 49 18 | 49 50 | 50 23 | 50 55 | 51 28 | 52 0 | 52 33 | 53 5 | 53 38 | 54 10 | 54 43 | 55 15 | 55 48 | 56 20 | 56 53 |
| 14 | 53 5 | 53 40 | 54 15 | 54 50 | 55 25 | 56 0 | 56 35 | 57 10 | 57 45 | 58 20 | 58 55 | 59 30 | 1 0 5 | 1 0 40 | 1 1 15 |
| 15 | 56 53 | 57 30 | 58 8 | 58 45 | 59 23 | 1 0 0 | 1 0 38 | 1 1 15 | 1 1 53 | 1 2 30 | 1 3 8 | 1 3 45 | 1 4 23 | 1 5 0 | 1 5 38 |
| 16 | 1 0 40 | 1 1 20 | 1 2 0 | 1 2 40 | 1 3 20 | 1 4 0 | 1 4 40 | 1 5 20 | 1 6 0 | 1 6 40 | 1 7 20 | 1 8 0 | 1 8 40 | 1 9 20 | 1 10 0 |
| 17 | 1 4 28 | 1 5 10 | 1 5 53 | 1 6 35 | 1 7 18 | 1 8 0 | 1 8 43 | 1 9 25 | 1 10 8 | 1 10 50 | 1 11 33 | 1 12 15 | 1 12 58 | 1 13 40 | 1 14 23 |
| 18 | 1 8 15 | 1 9 0 | 1 9 45 | 1 10 30 | 1 11 15 | 1 12 0 | 1 12 45 | 1 13 30 | 1 14 15 | 1 15 0 | 1 15 45 | 1 16 30 | 1 17 15 | 1 18 0 | 1 18 45 |
| 19 | 1 12 3 | 1 12 50 | 1 13 38 | 1 14 25 | 1 15 13 | 1 16 0 | 1 16 48 | 1 17 35 | 1 18 23 | 1 19 10 | 1 19 58 | 1 20 45 | 1 21 33 | 1 22 20 | 1 23 8 |
| 20 | 1 15 50 | 1 16 40 | 1 17 30 | 1 18 20 | 1 19 10 | 1 20 0 | 1 20 50 | 1 21 40 | 1 22 30 | 1 23 20 | 1 24 10 | 1 25 0 | 1 25 50 | 1 26 40 | 1 27 30 |
| 21 | 1 19 38 | 1 20 30 | 1 21 23 | 1 22 15 | 1 23 8 | 1 24 0 | 1 24 53 | 1 25 45 | 1 26 38 | 1 27 30 | 1 28 23 | 1 29 15 | 1 30 8 | 1 31 0 | 1 31 53 |
| 22 | 1 23 25 | 1 24 20 | 1 25 15 | 1 26 10 | 1 27 5 | 1 28 0 | 1 28 55 | 1 29 50 | 1 30 45 | 1 31 40 | 1 32 35 | 1 33 30 | 1 34 25 | 1 35 20 | 1 36 15 |
| 23 | 1 27 13 | 1 28 10 | 1 29 8 | 1 30 5 | 1 31 3 | 1 32 0 | 1 32 58 | 1 33 55 | 1 34 53 | 1 35 50 | 1 36 48 | 1 37 45 | 1 38 43 | 1 39 40 | 1 40 38 |
| 24 | 1 31 0 | 1 32 0 | 1 33 0 | 1 34 0 | 1 35 0 | 1 36 0 | 1 37 0 | 1 38 0 | 1 39 0 | 1 40 0 | 1 41 0 | 1 42 0 | 1 43 0 | 1 44 0 | 1 45 0 |

# Table VII Diurnal Motion of the Planets

**24 HOUR TRAVEL**

| TIME | 1° 46' | 1° 47' | 1° 48' | 1° 49' | 1° 50' | 1° 51' | 1° 52' | 1° 53' | 1° 54' | 1° 55' | 1° 56' | 1° 57' | 1° 58' | 1° 59' | 2° 0' | TIME |
|---|---|---|---|---|---|---|---|---|---|---|---|---|---|---|---|---|
| **MINUTES** | | | | | | | | | | | | | | | | |
| 1 | 0 4 | 0 4 | 0 5 | 0 5 | 0 5 | 0 5 | 0 5 | 0 5 | 0 5 | 0 5 | 0 5 | 0 5 | 0 5 | 0 5 | 0 5 | 1 |
| 2 | 0 9 | 0 9 | 0 9 | 0 9 | 0 9 | 0 9 | 0 9 | 0 9 | 0 10 | 0 10 | 0 10 | 0 10 | 0 10 | 0 10 | 0 10 | 2 |
| 3 | 0 13 | 0 13 | 0 14 | 0 14 | 0 14 | 0 14 | 0 14 | 0 14 | 0 14 | 0 14 | 0 15 | 0 15 | 0 15 | 0 15 | 0 15 | 3 |
| 4 | 0 18 | 0 18 | 0 18 | 0 18 | 0 18 | 0 19 | 0 19 | 0 19 | 0 19 | 0 19 | 0 19 | 0 20 | 0 20 | 0 20 | 0 20 | 4 |
| 5 | 0 22 | 0 22 | 0 23 | 0 23 | 0 23 | 0 23 | 0 23 | 0 23 | 0 24 | 0 24 | 0 24 | 0 24 | 0 24 | 0 25 | 0 25 | 5 |
| 6 | 0 27 | 0 27 | 0 27 | 0 27 | 0 28 | 0 28 | 0 28 | 0 28 | 0 29 | 0 29 | 0 29 | 0 29 | 0 30 | 0 30 | 0 30 | 6 |
| 7 | 0 31 | 0 31 | 0 32 | 0 32 | 0 32 | 0 32 | 0 33 | 0 33 | 0 33 | 0 34 | 0 34 | 0 34 | 0 34 | 0 35 | 0 35 | 7 |
| 8 | 0 35 | 0 36 | 0 36 | 0 36 | 0 37 | 0 37 | 0 37 | 0 38 | 0 38 | 0 38 | 0 39 | 0 39 | 0 39 | 0 40 | 0 40 | 8 |
| 9 | 0 40 | 0 40 | 0 41 | 0 41 | 0 41 | 0 42 | 0 42 | 0 42 | 0 43 | 0 43 | 0 44 | 0 44 | 0 44 | 0 45 | 0 45 | 9 |
| 10 | 0 44 | 0 45 | 0 45 | 0 45 | 0 46 | 0 46 | 0 47 | 0 47 | 0 48 | 0 48 | 0 48 | 0 49 | 0 49 | 0 50 | 0 50 | 10 |
| 11 | 0 49 | 0 49 | 0 50 | 0 50 | 0 50 | 0 51 | 0 51 | 0 52 | 0 52 | 0 53 | 0 53 | 0 54 | 0 54 | 0 55 | 0 55 | 11 |
| 12 | 0 53 | 0 54 | 0 54 | 0 55 | 0 55 | 0 56 | 0 56 | 0 57 | 0 57 | 0 58 | 0 58 | 0 59 | 0 59 | 1 0 | 1 0 | 12 |
| 13 | 0 57 | 0 58 | 0 59 | 0 59 | 1 0 | 1 0 | 1 1 | 1 1 | 1 2 | 1 2 | 1 3 | 1 3 | 1 4 | 1 4 | 1 5 | 13 |
| 14 | 1 2 | 1 2 | 1 3 | 1 4 | 1 4 | 1 5 | 1 5 | 1 6 | 1 7 | 1 7 | 1 8 | 1 8 | 1 9 | 1 9 | 1 10 | 14 |
| 15 | 1 6 | 1 7 | 1 8 | 1 8 | 1 9 | 1 9 | 1 10 | 1 11 | 1 11 | 1 12 | 1 13 | 1 13 | 1 14 | 1 14 | 1 15 | 15 |
| 16 | 1 11 | 1 11 | 1 12 | 1 13 | 1 13 | 1 14 | 1 15 | 1 15 | 1 16 | 1 17 | 1 17 | 1 18 | 1 19 | 1 19 | 1 20 | 16 |
| 17 | 1 15 | 1 16 | 1 17 | 1 17 | 1 18 | 1 19 | 1 19 | 1 20 | 1 21 | 1 21 | 1 22 | 1 23 | 1 24 | 1 24 | 1 25 | 17 |
| 18 | 1 20 | 1 20 | 1 21 | 1 22 | 1 23 | 1 23 | 1 24 | 1 25 | 1 26 | 1 26 | 1 27 | 1 28 | 1 29 | 1 29 | 1 30 | 18 |
| 19 | 1 24 | 1 25 | 1 26 | 1 26 | 1 27 | 1 28 | 1 29 | 1 29 | 1 30 | 1 31 | 1 32 | 1 33 | 1 33 | 1 34 | 1 35 | 19 |
| 20 | 1 28 | 1 29 | 1 30 | 1 31 | 1 32 | 1 33 | 1 33 | 1 34 | 1 35 | 1 36 | 1 37 | 1 38 | 1 38 | 1 39 | 1 40 | 20 |
| 21 | 1 33 | 1 34 | 1 35 | 1 35 | 1 36 | 1 37 | 1 38 | 1 39 | 1 40 | 1 41 | 1 42 | 1 42 | 1 43 | 1 44 | 1 45 | 21 |
| 22 | 1 37 | 1 38 | 1 39 | 1 40 | 1 41 | 1 42 | 1 43 | 1 44 | 1 45 | 1 45 | 1 46 | 1 47 | 1 48 | 1 49 | 1 50 | 22 |
| 23 | 1 42 | 1 43 | 1 44 | 1 44 | 1 45 | 1 46 | 1 47 | 1 48 | 1 49 | 1 50 | 1 51 | 1 52 | 1 53 | 1 54 | 1 55 | 23 |
| 24 | 1 46 | 1 47 | 1 48 | 1 49 | 1 50 | 1 51 | 1 52 | 1 53 | 1 54 | 1 55 | 1 56 | 1 57 | 1 58 | 1 59 | 2 0 | 24 |
| 25 | 1 50 | 1 51 | 1 53 | 1 54 | 1 55 | 1 56 | 1 57 | 1 58 | 1 59 | 2 0 | 2 1 | 2 2 | 2 3 | 2 4 | 2 5 | 25 |
| 26 | 1 55 | 1 56 | 1 57 | 1 58 | 1 59 | 2 0 | 2 1 | 2 2 | 2 4 | 2 5 | 2 6 | 2 7 | 2 8 | 2 9 | 2 10 | 26 |
| 27 | 1 59 | 2 0 | 2 2 | 2 3 | 2 4 | 2 5 | 2 6 | 2 7 | 2 8 | 2 9 | 2 11 | 2 12 | 2 13 | 2 14 | 2 15 | 27 |
| 28 | 2 4 | 2 5 | 2 6 | 2 7 | 2 8 | 2 10 | 2 11 | 2 12 | 2 13 | 2 14 | 2 15 | 2 17 | 2 18 | 2 19 | 2 20 | 28 |
| 29 | 2 8 | 2 9 | 2 11 | 2 12 | 2 13 | 2 14 | 2 15 | 2 17 | 2 18 | 2 19 | 2 20 | 2 21 | 2 23 | 2 24 | 2 25 | 29 |
| 30 | 2 13 | 2 14 | 2 15 | 2 16 | 2 18 | 2 19 | 2 20 | 2 21 | 2 23 | 2 24 | 2 25 | 2 26 | 2 28 | 2 29 | 2 30 | 30 |
| 31 | 2 17 | 2 18 | 2 20 | 2 21 | 2 22 | 2 23 | 2 25 | 2 26 | 2 27 | 2 29 | 2 30 | 2 31 | 2 32 | 2 34 | 2 35 | 31 |
| 32 | 2 21 | 2 23 | 2 24 | 2 25 | 2 27 | 2 28 | 2 29 | 2 31 | 2 32 | 2 33 | 2 35 | 2 36 | 2 37 | 2 39 | 2 40 | 32 |
| 33 | 2 26 | 2 27 | 2 29 | 2 30 | 2 31 | 2 33 | 2 34 | 2 35 | 2 37 | 2 38 | 2 40 | 2 41 | 2 42 | 2 44 | 2 45 | 33 |
| 34 | 2 30 | 2 32 | 2 33 | 2 34 | 2 36 | 2 37 | 2 39 | 2 40 | 2 42 | 2 43 | 2 44 | 2 46 | 2 47 | 2 49 | 2 50 | 34 |
| 35 | 2 35 | 2 36 | 2 38 | 2 39 | 2 40 | 2 42 | 2 43 | 2 45 | 2 46 | 2 48 | 2 49 | 2 51 | 2 52 | 2 54 | 2 55 | 35 |
| 36 | 2 39 | 2 41 | 2 42 | 2 44 | 2 45 | 2 47 | 2 48 | 2 50 | 2 51 | 2 53 | 2 54 | 2 56 | 2 57 | 2 59 | 3 0 | 36 |
| 37 | 2 43 | 2 45 | 2 47 | 2 48 | 2 50 | 2 51 | 2 53 | 2 54 | 2 56 | 2 57 | 2 59 | 3 0 | 3 2 | 3 3 | 3 5 | 37 |
| 38 | 2 48 | 2 49 | 2 51 | 2 53 | 2 54 | 2 56 | 2 57 | 2 59 | 3 1 | 3 2 | 3 4 | 3 5 | 3 7 | 3 8 | 3 10 | 38 |
| 39 | 2 52 | 2 54 | 2 56 | 2 57 | 2 59 | 3 0 | 3 2 | 3 4 | 3 5 | 3 7 | 3 9 | 3 10 | 3 12 | 3 13 | 3 15 | 39 |
| 40 | 2 57 | 2 58 | 3 0 | 3 2 | 3 3 | 3 5 | 3 7 | 3 8 | 3 10 | 3 12 | 3 13 | 3 15 | 3 17 | 3 18 | 3 20 | 40 |
| 41 | 3 1 | 3 3 | 3 5 | 3 6 | 3 8 | 3 10 | 3 11 | 3 13 | 3 15 | 3 16 | 3 18 | 3 20 | 3 22 | 3 23 | 3 25 | 41 |
| 42 | 3 6 | 3 7 | 3 9 | 3 11 | 3 13 | 3 14 | 3 16 | 3 18 | 3 20 | 3 21 | 3 23 | 3 25 | 3 27 | 3 28 | 3 30 | 42 |
| 43 | 3 10 | 3 12 | 3 14 | 3 15 | 3 17 | 3 19 | 3 21 | 3 22 | 3 24 | 3 26 | 3 28 | 3 30 | 3 31 | 3 33 | 3 35 | 43 |
| 44 | 3 14 | 3 16 | 3 18 | 3 20 | 3 22 | 3 24 | 3 25 | 3 27 | 3 29 | 3 31 | 3 33 | 3 35 | 3 36 | 3 38 | 3 40 | 44 |
| 45 | 3 19 | 3 21 | 3 23 | 3 24 | 3 26 | 3 28 | 3 30 | 3 32 | 3 34 | 3 36 | 3 38 | 3 39 | 3 41 | 3 43 | 3 45 | 45 |
| 46 | 3 23 | 3 25 | 3 27 | 3 29 | 3 31 | 3 33 | 3 35 | 3 37 | 3 39 | 3 40 | 3 42 | 3 44 | 3 46 | 3 48 | 3 50 | 46 |
| 47 | 3 28 | 3 30 | 3 32 | 3 33 | 3 35 | 3 37 | 3 39 | 3 41 | 3 43 | 3 45 | 3 47 | 3 49 | 3 51 | 3 53 | 3 55 | 47 |
| 48 | 3 32 | 3 34 | 3 36 | 3 38 | 3 40 | 3 42 | 3 44 | 3 46 | 3 48 | 3 50 | 3 52 | 3 54 | 3 56 | 3 58 | 4 0 | 48 |
| 49 | 3 36 | 3 38 | 3 41 | 3 43 | 3 45 | 3 47 | 3 49 | 3 51 | 3 53 | 3 55 | 3 57 | 3 59 | 4 1 | 4 3 | 4 5 | 49 |
| 50 | 3 41 | 3 43 | 3 45 | 3 47 | 3 49 | 3 51 | 3 53 | 3 55 | 3 58 | 4 0 | 4 2 | 4 4 | 4 6 | 4 8 | 4 10 | 50 |
| 51 | 3 45 | 3 47 | 3 50 | 3 52 | 3 54 | 3 56 | 3 58 | 4 0 | 4 2 | 4 4 | 4 7 | 4 9 | 4 11 | 4 13 | 4 15 | 51 |
| 52 | 3 50 | 3 52 | 3 54 | 3 56 | 3 58 | 4 1 | 4 3 | 4 5 | 4 7 | 4 9 | 4 11 | 4 14 | 4 16 | 4 18 | 4 20 | 52 |
| 53 | 3 54 | 3 56 | 3 59 | 4 1 | 4 3 | 4 5 | 4 7 | 4 10 | 4 12 | 4 14 | 4 16 | 4 18 | 4 21 | 4 23 | 4 25 | 53 |
| 54 | 3 59 | 4 1 | 4 3 | 4 5 | 4 8 | 4 10 | 4 12 | 4 14 | 4 17 | 4 19 | 4 21 | 4 24 | 4 26 | 4 28 | 4 30 | 54 |
| 55 | 4 3 | 4 5 | 4 8 | 4 10 | 4 12 | 4 14 | 4 17 | 4 19 | 4 21 | 4 24 | 4 26 | 4 28 | 4 30 | 4 33 | 4 35 | 55 |
| 56 | 4 7 | 4 10 | 4 12 | 4 14 | 4 17 | 4 19 | 4 21 | 4 24 | 4 26 | 4 28 | 4 31 | 4 33 | 4 35 | 4 38 | 4 40 | 56 |
| 57 | 4 12 | 4 14 | 4 17 | 4 19 | 4 21 | 4 24 | 4 26 | 4 28 | 4 31 | 4 33 | 4 36 | 4 38 | 4 40 | 4 43 | 4 45 | 57 |
| 58 | 4 16 | 4 19 | 4 21 | 4 23 | 4 26 | 4 28 | 4 31 | 4 33 | 4 36 | 4 38 | 4 40 | 4 43 | 4 45 | 4 48 | 4 50 | 58 |
| 59 | 4 21 | 4 23 | 4 26 | 4 28 | 4 30 | 4 33 | 4 35 | 4 38 | 4 40 | 4 43 | 4 45 | 4 48 | 4 50 | 4 53 | 4 55 | 59 |
| 60 | 4 25 | 4 28 | 4 30 | 4 33 | 4 35 | 4 38 | 4 40 | 4 43 | 4 45 | 4 48 | 4 50 | 4 53 | 4 55 | 4 58 | 5 0 | 60 |
| **HOURS** | | | | | | | | | | | | | | | | |
| 1 | 4 25 | 4 28 | 4 30 | 4 33 | 4 35 | 4 38 | 4 40 | 4 43 | 4 45 | 4 48 | 4 50 | 4 53 | 4 55 | 4 58 | 5 0 | 1 |
| 2 | 8 50 | 8 55 | 9 0 | 9 5 | 9 10 | 9 15 | 9 20 | 9 25 | 9 30 | 9 35 | 9 40 | 9 45 | 9 50 | 9 55 | 10 0 | 2 |
| 3 | 13 15 | 13 23 | 13 30 | 13 38 | 13 45 | 13 53 | 14 0 | 14 8 | 14 15 | 14 23 | 14 30 | 14 38 | 14 45 | 14 53 | 15 0 | 3 |
| 4 | 17 40 | 17 50 | 18 0 | 18 10 | 18 20 | 18 30 | 18 40 | 18 50 | 19 0 | 19 10 | 19 20 | 19 30 | 19 40 | 19 50 | 20 0 | 4 |
| 5 | 22 5 | 22 18 | 22 30 | 22 43 | 22 55 | 23 8 | 23 20 | 23 33 | 23 45 | 23 58 | 24 10 | 24 23 | 24 35 | 24 48 | 25 0 | 5 |
| 6 | 26 30 | 26 45 | 27 0 | 27 15 | 27 30 | 27 45 | 28 0 | 28 15 | 28 30 | 28 45 | 29 0 | 29 15 | 29 30 | 29 45 | 30 0 | 6 |
| 7 | 30 55 | 31 13 | 31 30 | 31 48 | 32 5 | 32 23 | 32 40 | 32 58 | 33 15 | 33 33 | 33 50 | 34 8 | 34 25 | 34 43 | 35 0 | 7 |
| 8 | 35 20 | 35 40 | 36 0 | 36 20 | 36 40 | 37 0 | 37 20 | 37 40 | 38 0 | 38 20 | 38 40 | 39 0 | 39 20 | 39 40 | 40 0 | 8 |
| 9 | 39 45 | 40 8 | 40 30 | 40 53 | 41 15 | 41 38 | 42 0 | 42 23 | 42 45 | 43 8 | 43 30 | 43 53 | 44 15 | 44 38 | 45 0 | 9 |
| 10 | 44 10 | 44 35 | 45 0 | 45 25 | 45 50 | 46 15 | 46 40 | 47 5 | 47 30 | 47 55 | 48 20 | 48 45 | 49 10 | 49 35 | 50 0 | 10 |
| 11 | 48 35 | 49 3 | 49 30 | 49 58 | 50 25 | 50 53 | 51 20 | 51 48 | 52 15 | 52 43 | 53 10 | 53 38 | 54 5 | 54 33 | 55 0 | 11 |
| 12 | 53 0 | 53 30 | 54 0 | 54 30 | 55 0 | 55 30 | 56 0 | 56 30 | 57 0 | 57 30 | 58 0 | 58 30 | 59 0 | 59 30 | 1 0 0 | 12 |
| 13 | 57 25 | 57 58 | 58 30 | 59 3 | 59 35 | 1 0 8 | 1 0 40 | 1 1 13 | 1 1 45 | 1 2 18 | 1 2 50 | 1 3 23 | 1 3 55 | 1 4 28 | 1 5 0 | 13 |
| 14 | 1 1 50 | 1 2 25 | 1 3 0 | 1 3 35 | 1 4 10 | 1 4 45 | 1 5 20 | 1 5 55 | 1 6 30 | 1 7 5 | 1 7 40 | 1 8 15 | 1 8 50 | 1 9 25 | 1 10 0 | 14 |
| 15 | 1 6 15 | 1 6 53 | 1 7 30 | 1 8 8 | 1 8 45 | 1 9 23 | 1 10 0 | 1 10 38 | 1 11 15 | 1 11 53 | 1 12 30 | 1 13 8 | 1 13 45 | 1 14 23 | 1 15 0 | 15 |
| 16 | 1 10 40 | 1 11 20 | 1 12 0 | 1 12 40 | 1 13 20 | 1 14 0 | 1 14 40 | 1 15 20 | 1 16 0 | 1 16 40 | 1 17 20 | 1 18 0 | 1 18 40 | 1 19 20 | 1 20 0 | 16 |
| 17 | 1 15 5 | 1 15 48 | 1 16 30 | 1 17 13 | 1 17 55 | 1 18 38 | 1 19 20 | 1 20 3 | 1 20 45 | 1 21 28 | 1 22 10 | 1 22 53 | 1 23 35 | 1 24 15 | 1 25 0 | 17 |
| 18 | 1 19 30 | 1 20 15 | 1 21 0 | 1 21 45 | 1 22 30 | 1 23 15 | 1 24 0 | 1 24 45 | 1 25 30 | 1 26 15 | 1 27 0 | 1 27 45 | 1 28 30 | 1 29 15 | 1 30 0 | 18 |
| 19 | 1 23 55 | 1 24 43 | 1 25 30 | 1 26 18 | 1 27 5 | 1 27 53 | 1 28 40 | 1 29 28 | 1 30 15 | 1 31 3 | 1 31 50 | 1 32 38 | 1 33 25 | 1 34 13 | 1 35 0 | 19 |
| 20 | 1 28 20 | 1 29 10 | 1 30 0 | 1 30 50 | 1 31 40 | 1 32 30 | 1 33 20 | 1 34 10 | 1 35 0 | 1 35 50 | 1 36 40 | 1 37 30 | 1 38 20 | 1 39 10 | 1 40 0 | 20 |
| 21 | 1 32 45 | 1 33 38 | 1 34 30 | 1 35 23 | 1 36 15 | 1 37 8 | 1 38 0 | 1 38 53 | 1 39 45 | 1 40 38 | 1 41 30 | 1 42 23 | 1 43 15 | 1 44 8 | 1 45 0 | 21 |
| 22 | 1 37 10 | 1 38 5 | 1 39 0 | 1 39 55 | 1 40 50 | 1 41 45 | 1 42 40 | 1 43 35 | 1 44 30 | 1 45 25 | 1 46 20 | 1 47 15 | 1 48 10 | 1 49 5 | 1 50 0 | 22 |
| 23 | 1 41 35 | 1 42 33 | 1 43 30 | 1 44 28 | 1 45 25 | 1 46 23 | 1 47 20 | 1 48 18 | 1 49 15 | 1 50 13 | 1 51 10 | 1 52 8 | 1 53 5 | 1 54 3 | 1 55 0 | 23 |
| 24 | 1 46 0 | 1 47 0 | 1 48 0 | 1 49 0 | 1 50 0 | 1 51 0 | 1 52 0 | 1 53 0 | 1 54 0 | 1 55 0 | 1 56 0 | 1 57 0 | 1 58 0 | 1 59 0 | 2 0 0 | 24 |

# Table VII Diurnal Motion of the Planets

**24 HOUR TRAVEL**

| TIME | 2° 1' | 2° 2' | 2° 3' | 2° 4' | 2° 5' | 2° 6' | 2° 7' | 2° 8' | 2° 9' | 2° 10' | 2° 11' | 2° 12' | 2° 13' | 2° 14' | 2° 15' | TIME |
|---|---|---|---|---|---|---|---|---|---|---|---|---|---|---|---|---|
| **MINUTES 1** | 0 5 | 0 5 | 0 5 | 0 5 | 0 5 | 0 5 | 0 5 | 0 5 | 0 5 | 0 5 | 0 5 | 0 6 | 0 6 | 0 6 | 0 6 | 1 |
| 2 | 0 10 | 0 10 | 0 10 | 0 10 | 0 10 | 0 11 | 0 11 | 0 11 | 0 11 | 0 11 | 0 11 | 0 11 | 0 11 | 0 11 | 0 11 | 2 |
| 3 | 0 15 | 0 15 | 0 15 | 0 16 | 0 16 | 0 16 | 0 16 | 0 16 | 0 16 | 0 16 | 0 16 | 0 17 | 0 17 | 0 17 | 0 17 | 3 |
| 4 | 0 20 | 0 20 | 0 21 | 0 21 | 0 21 | 0 21 | 0 21 | 0 21 | 0 22 | 0 22 | 0 22 | 0 22 | 0 22 | 0 22 | 0 23 | 4 |
| 5 | 0 25 | 0 25 | 0 26 | 0 26 | 0 26 | 0 26 | 0 26 | 0 27 | 0 27 | 0 27 | 0 27 | 0 28 | 0 28 | 0 28 | 0 28 | 5 |
| 6 | 0 30 | 0 31 | 0 31 | 0 31 | 0 31 | 0 32 | 0 32 | 0 32 | 0 32 | 0 33 | 0 33 | 0 33 | 0 33 | 0 34 | 0 34 | 6 |
| 7 | 0 35 | 0 36 | 0 36 | 0 36 | 0 36 | 0 37 | 0 37 | 0 37 | 0 38 | 0 38 | 0 38 | 0 39 | 0 39 | 0 39 | 0 39 | 7 |
| 8 | 0 40 | 0 41 | 0 41 | 0 41 | 0 42 | 0 42 | 0 42 | 0 43 | 0 43 | 0 43 | 0 44 | 0 44 | 0 44 | 0 45 | 0 45 | 8 |
| 9 | 0 45 | 0 46 | 0 46 | 0 47 | 0 47 | 0 47 | 0 48 | 0 48 | 0 48 | 0 49 | 0 49 | 0 50 | 0 50 | 0 50 | 0 51 | 9 |
| 10 | 0 50 | 0 51 | 0 51 | 0 52 | 0 52 | 0 53 | 0 53 | 0 53 | 0 54 | 0 54 | 0 55 | 0 55 | 0 55 | 0 56 | 0 56 | 10 |
| 11 | 0 55 | 0 56 | 0 56 | 0 57 | 0 57 | 0 58 | 0 58 | 0 58 | 0 59 | 0 59 | 1 0 | 1 0 | 1 1 | 1 1 | 1 2 | 11 |
| 12 | 1 1 | 1 1 | 1 2 | 1 2 | 1 3 | 1 3 | 1 4 | 1 4 | 1 5 | 1 5 | 1 6 | 1 6 | 1 7 | 1 7 | 1 8 | 12 |
| 13 | 1 6 | 1 6 | 1 7 | 1 7 | 1 8 | 1 8 | 1 9 | 1 9 | 1 10 | 1 10 | 1 11 | 1 12 | 1 12 | 1 13 | 1 13 | 13 |
| 14 | 1 11 | 1 11 | 1 12 | 1 12 | 1 13 | 1 14 | 1 14 | 1 15 | 1 15 | 1 16 | 1 16 | 1 17 | 1 18 | 1 18 | 1 19 | 14 |
| 15 | 1 16 | 1 16 | 1 17 | 1 18 | 1 18 | 1 19 | 1 19 | 1 20 | 1 21 | 1 21 | 1 22 | 1 23 | 1 23 | 1 24 | 1 24 | 15 |
| 16 | 1 21 | 1 21 | 1 22 | 1 23 | 1 23 | 1 24 | 1 25 | 1 25 | 1 26 | 1 27 | 1 27 | 1 28 | 1 29 | 1 29 | 1 30 | 16 |
| 17 | 1 26 | 1 26 | 1 27 | 1 28 | 1 29 | 1 29 | 1 30 | 1 31 | 1 31 | 1 32 | 1 33 | 1 34 | 1 34 | 1 35 | 1 36 | 17 |
| 18 | 1 31 | 1 32 | 1 32 | 1 33 | 1 34 | 1 35 | 1 35 | 1 36 | 1 37 | 1 38 | 1 38 | 1 39 | 1 40 | 1 41 | 1 41 | 18 |
| 19 | 1 36 | 1 37 | 1 37 | 1 38 | 1 39 | 1 40 | 1 41 | 1 41 | 1 42 | 1 43 | 1 44 | 1 45 | 1 45 | 1 46 | 1 47 | 19 |
| 20 | 1 41 | 1 42 | 1 43 | 1 43 | 1 44 | 1 45 | 1 46 | 1 47 | 1 48 | 1 48 | 1 49 | 1 50 | 1 51 | 1 52 | 1 53 | 20 |
| 21 | 1 46 | 1 47 | 1 48 | 1 49 | 1 49 | 1 50 | 1 51 | 1 52 | 1 53 | 1 54 | 1 55 | 1 56 | 1 56 | 1 57 | 1 58 | 21 |
| 22 | 1 51 | 1 52 | 1 53 | 1 54 | 1 55 | 1 56 | 1 56 | 1 57 | 1 58 | 1 59 | 2 0 | 2 1 | 2 2 | 2 3 | 2 4 | 22 |
| 23 | 1 56 | 1 57 | 1 58 | 1 59 | 2 0 | 2 1 | 2 2 | 2 3 | 2 4 | 2 5 | 2 6 | 2 7 | 2 7 | 2 8 | 2 9 | 23 |
| 24 | 2 1 | 2 2 | 2 3 | 2 4 | 2 5 | 2 6 | 2 7 | 2 8 | 2 9 | 2 10 | 2 11 | 2 12 | 2 13 | 2 14 | 2 15 | 24 |
| 25 | 2 6 | 2 7 | 2 8 | 2 9 | 2 10 | 2 11 | 2 12 | 2 13 | 2 14 | 2 15 | 2 16 | 2 18 | 2 19 | 2 20 | 2 21 | 25 |
| 26 | 2 11 | 2 12 | 2 13 | 2 14 | 2 15 | 2 17 | 2 18 | 2 19 | 2 20 | 2 21 | 2 22 | 2 23 | 2 24 | 2 25 | 2 26 | 26 |
| 27 | 2 16 | 2 17 | 2 18 | 2 20 | 2 21 | 2 22 | 2 23 | 2 24 | 2 25 | 2 26 | 2 27 | 2 29 | 2 30 | 2 31 | 2 32 | 27 |
| 28 | 2 21 | 2 22 | 2 24 | 2 25 | 2 26 | 2 27 | 2 28 | 2 29 | 2 31 | 2 32 | 2 33 | 2 34 | 2 35 | 2 36 | 2 38 | 28 |
| 29 | 2 26 | 2 27 | 2 29 | 2 30 | 2 31 | 2 32 | 2 33 | 2 35 | 2 36 | 2 37 | 2 38 | 2 40 | 2 41 | 2 42 | 2 43 | 29 |
| 30 | 2 31 | 2 33 | 2 34 | 2 35 | 2 36 | 2 38 | 2 39 | 2 40 | 2 41 | 2 43 | 2 44 | 2 45 | 2 46 | 2 48 | 2 49 | 30 |
| 31 | 2 36 | 2 38 | 2 39 | 2 40 | 2 41 | 2 43 | 2 44 | 2 45 | 2 47 | 2 48 | 2 49 | 2 51 | 2 52 | 2 53 | 2 54 | 31 |
| 32 | 2 41 | 2 43 | 2 44 | 2 45 | 2 47 | 2 48 | 2 49 | 2 51 | 2 52 | 2 53 | 2 55 | 2 56 | 2 57 | 2 59 | 3 0 | 32 |
| 33 | 2 46 | 2 48 | 2 49 | 2 51 | 2 52 | 2 53 | 2 55 | 2 56 | 2 57 | 2 59 | 3 0 | 3 2 | 3 3 | 3 4 | 3 6 | 33 |
| 34 | 2 51 | 2 53 | 2 54 | 2 56 | 2 57 | 2 59 | 3 0 | 3 1 | 3 3 | 3 4 | 3 6 | 3 7 | 3 8 | 3 10 | 3 11 | 34 |
| 35 | 2 56 | 2 58 | 2 59 | 3 1 | 3 2 | 3 4 | 3 5 | 3 7 | 3 8 | 3 10 | 3 11 | 3 13 | 3 14 | 3 15 | 3 17 | 35 |
| 36 | 3 2 | 3 3 | 3 5 | 3 6 | 3 8 | 3 9 | 3 11 | 3 12 | 3 14 | 3 15 | 3 17 | 3 18 | 3 20 | 3 21 | 3 23 | 36 |
| 37 | 3 7 | 3 8 | 3 10 | 3 11 | 3 13 | 3 14 | 3 16 | 3 17 | 3 19 | 3 20 | 3 22 | 3 24 | 3 25 | 3 27 | 3 28 | 37 |
| 38 | 3 12 | 3 13 | 3 15 | 3 16 | 3 18 | 3 20 | 3 21 | 3 23 | 3 24 | 3 26 | 3 27 | 3 29 | 3 31 | 3 32 | 3 34 | 38 |
| 39 | 3 17 | 3 18 | 3 20 | 3 22 | 3 23 | 3 25 | 3 26 | 3 28 | 3 30 | 3 31 | 3 33 | 3 35 | 3 36 | 3 38 | 3 39 | 39 |
| 40 | 3 22 | 3 23 | 3 25 | 3 27 | 3 28 | 3 30 | 3 32 | 3 33 | 3 35 | 3 37 | 3 38 | 3 40 | 3 42 | 3 43 | 3 45 | 40 |
| 41 | 3 27 | 3 28 | 3 30 | 3 32 | 3 34 | 3 35 | 3 37 | 3 39 | 3 40 | 3 42 | 3 44 | 3 46 | 3 47 | 3 49 | 3 51 | 41 |
| 42 | 3 32 | 3 34 | 3 35 | 3 37 | 3 39 | 3 41 | 3 42 | 3 44 | 3 46 | 3 48 | 3 49 | 3 51 | 3 53 | 3 55 | 3 56 | 42 |
| 43 | 3 37 | 3 39 | 3 40 | 3 42 | 3 44 | 3 46 | 3 48 | 3 49 | 3 51 | 3 53 | 3 55 | 3 57 | 3 58 | 4 0 | 4 2 | 43 |
| 44 | 3 42 | 3 44 | 3 46 | 3 47 | 3 49 | 3 51 | 3 53 | 3 55 | 3 57 | 3 58 | 4 0 | 4 2 | 4 4 | 4 6 | 4 8 | 44 |
| 45 | 3 47 | 3 49 | 3 51 | 3 53 | 3 54 | 3 56 | 3 58 | 4 0 | 4 2 | 4 4 | 4 6 | 4 8 | 4 9 | 4 11 | 4 13 | 45 |
| 46 | 3 52 | 3 54 | 3 56 | 3 58 | 4 0 | 4 2 | 4 3 | 4 5 | 4 7 | 4 9 | 4 11 | 4 13 | 4 15 | 4 17 | 4 19 | 46 |
| 47 | 3 57 | 3 59 | 4 1 | 4 3 | 4 5 | 4 7 | 4 9 | 4 11 | 4 13 | 4 15 | 4 17 | 4 19 | 4 20 | 4 22 | 4 24 | 47 |
| 48 | 4 2 | 4 4 | 4 6 | 4 8 | 4 10 | 4 12 | 4 14 | 4 16 | 4 18 | 4 20 | 4 22 | 4 24 | 4 26 | 4 28 | 4 30 | 48 |
| 49 | 4 7 | 4 9 | 4 11 | 4 13 | 4 15 | 4 17 | 4 19 | 4 21 | 4 23 | 4 25 | 4 27 | 4 30 | 4 32 | 4 34 | 4 36 | 49 |
| 50 | 4 12 | 4 14 | 4 16 | 4 18 | 4 20 | 4 23 | 4 25 | 4 27 | 4 29 | 4 31 | 4 33 | 4 35 | 4 37 | 4 39 | 4 41 | 50 |
| 51 | 4 17 | 4 19 | 4 21 | 4 24 | 4 26 | 4 28 | 4 30 | 4 32 | 4 34 | 4 36 | 4 38 | 4 41 | 4 43 | 4 45 | 4 47 | 51 |
| 52 | 4 22 | 4 24 | 4 27 | 4 29 | 4 31 | 4 33 | 4 35 | 4 37 | 4 40 | 4 42 | 4 44 | 4 46 | 4 48 | 4 50 | 4 53 | 52 |
| 53 | 4 27 | 4 29 | 4 32 | 4 34 | 4 36 | 4 38 | 4 40 | 4 43 | 4 45 | 4 47 | 4 49 | 4 52 | 4 54 | 4 56 | 4 58 | 53 |
| 54 | 4 32 | 4 35 | 4 37 | 4 39 | 4 41 | 4 44 | 4 46 | 4 48 | 4 50 | 4 53 | 4 55 | 4 57 | 4 59 | 5 2 | 5 4 | 54 |
| 55 | 4 37 | 4 40 | 4 42 | 4 44 | 4 46 | 4 49 | 4 51 | 4 53 | 4 56 | 4 58 | 5 0 | 5 3 | 5 5 | 5 7 | 5 9 | 55 |
| 56 | 4 42 | 4 45 | 4 47 | 4 49 | 4 52 | 4 54 | 4 56 | 4 59 | 5 1 | 5 3 | 5 6 | 5 8 | 5 10 | 5 13 | 5 15 | 56 |
| 57 | 4 47 | 4 50 | 4 52 | 4 55 | 4 57 | 4 59 | 5 2 | 5 4 | 5 6 | 5 9 | 5 11 | 5 14 | 5 16 | 5 18 | 5 21 | 57 |
| 58 | 4 52 | 4 55 | 4 57 | 5 0 | 5 2 | 5 5 | 5 7 | 5 9 | 5 12 | 5 14 | 5 17 | 5 19 | 5 21 | 5 24 | 5 26 | 58 |
| 59 | 4 57 | 5 0 | 5 2 | 5 5 | 5 7 | 5 10 | 5 12 | 5 15 | 5 17 | 5 20 | 5 22 | 5 25 | 5 27 | 5 29 | 5 32 | 59 |
| 60 | 5 3 | 5 5 | 5 8 | 5 10 | 5 13 | 5 15 | 5 18 | 5 20 | 5 23 | 5 25 | 5 28 | 5 30 | 5 33 | 5 35 | 5 38 | 60 |
| **HOURS 1** | 5 3 | 5 5 | 5 8 | 5 10 | 5 13 | 5 15 | 5 18 | 5 20 | 5 23 | 5 25 | 5 28 | 5 30 | 5 33 | 5 35 | 5 38 | 1 |
| 2 | 10 5 | 10 10 | 10 15 | 10 20 | 10 25 | 10 30 | 10 35 | 10 40 | 10 45 | 10 50 | 10 55 | 11 0 | 11 5 | 11 10 | 11 15 | 2 |
| 3 | 15 8 | 15 15 | 15 23 | 15 30 | 15 38 | 15 45 | 15 53 | 16 0 | 16 8 | 16 15 | 16 23 | 16 30 | 16 38 | 16 45 | 16 53 | 3 |
| 4 | 20 10 | 20 20 | 20 30 | 20 40 | 20 50 | 21 0 | 21 10 | 21 20 | 21 30 | 21 40 | 21 50 | 22 0 | 22 10 | 22 20 | 22 30 | 4 |
| 5 | 25 13 | 25 25 | 25 38 | 25 50 | 26 3 | 26 15 | 26 28 | 26 40 | 26 53 | 27 5 | 27 18 | 27 30 | 27 43 | 27 55 | 28 8 | 5 |
| 6 | 30 15 | 30 30 | 30 45 | 31 0 | 31 15 | 31 30 | 31 45 | 32 0 | 32 15 | 32 30 | 32 45 | 33 0 | 33 15 | 33 30 | 33 45 | 6 |
| 7 | 35 18 | 35 35 | 35 53 | 36 10 | 36 28 | 36 45 | 37 3 | 37 20 | 37 38 | 37 55 | 38 13 | 38 30 | 38 48 | 39 5 | 39 23 | 7 |
| 8 | 40 20 | 40 40 | 41 0 | 41 20 | 41 40 | 42 0 | 42 20 | 42 40 | 43 0 | 43 20 | 43 40 | 44 0 | 44 20 | 44 40 | 45 0 | 8 |
| 9 | 45 23 | 45 45 | 46 8 | 46 30 | 46 53 | 47 15 | 47 38 | 48 0 | 48 23 | 48 45 | 49 8 | 49 30 | 49 53 | 50 15 | 50 38 | 9 |
| 10 | 50 25 | 50 50 | 51 15 | 51 40 | 52 5 | 52 30 | 52 55 | 53 20 | 53 45 | 54 10 | 54 35 | 55 0 | 55 25 | 55 50 | 56 15 | 10 |
| 11 | 55 28 | 55 55 | 56 23 | 56 50 | 57 18 | 57 45 | 58 13 | 58 40 | 59 8 | 59 35 | 1 0 3 | 1 0 30 | 1 0 58 | 1 1 25 | 1 1 53 | 11 |
| 12 | 1 0 30 | 1 1 0 | 1 1 30 | 1 2 0 | 1 2 30 | 1 3 0 | 1 3 30 | 1 4 0 | 1 4 30 | 1 5 0 | 1 5 30 | 1 6 0 | 1 6 30 | 1 7 0 | 1 7 30 | 12 |
| 13 | 1 5 33 | 1 6 5 | 1 6 38 | 1 7 10 | 1 7 43 | 1 8 15 | 1 8 48 | 1 9 20 | 1 9 53 | 1 10 25 | 1 10 58 | 1 11 30 | 1 12 3 | 1 12 35 | 1 13 8 | 13 |
| 14 | 1 10 35 | 1 11 10 | 1 11 45 | 1 12 20 | 1 12 55 | 1 13 30 | 1 14 5 | 1 14 40 | 1 15 15 | 1 15 50 | 1 16 25 | 1 17 0 | 1 17 35 | 1 18 10 | 1 18 45 | 14 |
| 15 | 1 15 38 | 1 16 15 | 1 16 53 | 1 17 30 | 1 18 8 | 1 18 45 | 1 19 23 | 1 20 0 | 1 20 38 | 1 21 15 | 1 21 53 | 1 22 30 | 1 23 8 | 1 23 45 | 1 24 23 | 15 |
| 16 | 1 20 40 | 1 21 20 | 1 22 0 | 1 22 40 | 1 23 20 | 1 24 0 | 1 24 40 | 1 25 20 | 1 26 0 | 1 26 40 | 1 27 20 | 1 28 0 | 1 28 40 | 1 29 20 | 1 30 0 | 16 |
| 17 | 1 25 43 | 1 26 25 | 1 27 8 | 1 27 50 | 1 28 33 | 1 29 15 | 1 29 58 | 1 30 40 | 1 31 23 | 1 32 5 | 1 32 48 | 1 33 30 | 1 34 13 | 1 34 55 | 1 35 38 | 17 |
| 18 | 1 30 45 | 1 31 30 | 1 32 15 | 1 33 0 | 1 33 45 | 1 34 30 | 1 35 15 | 1 36 0 | 1 36 45 | 1 37 30 | 1 38 15 | 1 39 0 | 1 39 45 | 1 40 30 | 1 41 15 | 18 |
| 19 | 1 35 48 | 1 36 35 | 1 37 23 | 1 38 10 | 1 38 58 | 1 39 45 | 1 40 33 | 1 41 20 | 1 42 8 | 1 42 55 | 1 43 43 | 1 44 30 | 1 45 18 | 1 46 5 | 1 46 53 | 19 |
| 20 | 1 40 50 | 1 41 40 | 1 42 30 | 1 43 20 | 1 44 10 | 1 45 0 | 1 45 50 | 1 46 40 | 1 47 30 | 1 48 20 | 1 49 10 | 1 50 0 | 1 50 50 | 1 51 40 | 1 52 30 | 20 |
| 21 | 1 45 53 | 1 46 45 | 1 47 38 | 1 48 30 | 1 49 23 | 1 50 15 | 1 51 8 | 1 52 0 | 1 52 53 | 1 53 45 | 1 54 38 | 1 55 30 | 1 56 23 | 1 57 15 | 1 58 8 | 21 |
| 22 | 1 50 55 | 1 51 50 | 1 52 45 | 1 53 40 | 1 54 35 | 1 55 30 | 1 56 25 | 1 57 20 | 1 58 15 | 1 59 10 | 2 0 5 | 2 1 0 | 2 1 55 | 2 2 50 | 2 3 45 | 22 |
| 23 | 1 55 58 | 1 56 55 | 1 57 53 | 1 58 50 | 1 59 48 | 2 0 45 | 2 1 43 | 2 2 40 | 2 3 38 | 2 4 35 | 2 5 33 | 2 6 30 | 2 7 28 | 2 8 25 | 2 9 23 | 23 |
| 24 | 2 1 0 | 2 2 0 | 2 3 0 | 2 4 0 | 2 5 0 | 2 6 0 | 2 7 0 | 2 8 0 | 2 9 0 | 2 10 0 | 2 11 0 | 2 12 0 | 2 13 0 | 2 14 0 | 2 15 0 | 24 |

# Table VIII Second Difference Interpolation for the Moon

## 12 HOUR INTERVAL

| TIME INTVL | 1' ' " | 2' ' " | 3' ' " | 4' ' " | 5' ' " | 6' ' " | 7' ' " | 8' ' " | 9' ' " | 10' ' " | TIME INTVL |
|---|---|---|---|---|---|---|---|---|---|---|---|
| | MEAN SECOND DIFFERENCE | | | | | | | | | | |
| 0-1 | 0 1 | 0 2 | 0 4 | 0 5 | 0 6 | 0 7 | 0 8 | 0 10 | 0 11 | 0 12 | 11-12 |
| 1-2 | 0 3 | 0 7 | 0 10 | 0 13 | 0 16 | 0 20 | 0 23 | 0 26 | 0 30 | 0 33 | 10-11 |
| 2-3 | 0 5 | 0 10 | 0 15 | 0 20 | 0 25 | 0 30 | 0 35 | 0 40 | 0 45 | 0 49 | 9-10 |
| 3-4 | 0 6 | 0 12 | 0 19 | 0 25 | 0 31 | 0 37 | 0 43 | 0 50 | 0 56 | 1 2 | 8-9 |
| 4-5 | 0 7 | 0 14 | 0 21 | 0 28 | 0 35 | 0 42 | 0 49 | 0 56 | 1 3 | 1 10 | 7-8 |
| 5-6 | 0 7 | 0 15 | 0 22 | 0 30 | 0 37 | 0 45 | 0 52 | 0 60 | 1 7 | 1 14 | 6-7 |

| TIME INTVL | 11' ' " | 12' ' " | 13' ' " | 14' ' " | 15' ' " | 16' ' " | 17' ' " | 18' ' " | 19' ' " | 20' ' " | TIME INTVL |
|---|---|---|---|---|---|---|---|---|---|---|---|
| | MEAN SECOND DIFFERENCE | | | | | | | | | | |
| 0-1 | 0 13 | 0 14 | 0 16 | 0 17 | 0 18 | 0 19 | 0 20 | 0 22 | 0 23 | 0 24 | 11-12 |
| 1-2 | 0 36 | 0 39 | 0 43 | 0 46 | 0 49 | 0 52 | 0 56 | 0 59 | 1 2 | 1 6 | 10-11 |
| 2-3 | 0 54 | 0 59 | 1 4 | 1 9 | 1 14 | 1 19 | 1 24 | 1 29 | 1 34 | 1 39 | 9-10 |
| 3-4 | 1 8 | 1 14 | 1 21 | 1 27 | 1 33 | 1 39 | 1 45 | 1 52 | 1 58 | 2 4 | 8-9 |
| 4-5 | 1 17 | 1 24 | 1 31 | 1 38 | 1 45 | 1 52 | 1 60 | 2 7 | 2 14 | 2 21 | 7-8 |
| 5-6 | 1 22 | 1 29 | 1 37 | 1 44 | 1 52 | 1 59 | 2 7 | 2 14 | 2 22 | 2 29 | 6-7 |

## 24 HOUR INTERVAL

| TIME INTVL | 1' ' " | 2' ' " | 3' ' " | 4' ' " | 5' ' " | 6' ' " | 7' ' " | 8' ' " | 9' ' " | 10' ' " | 11' ' " | 12' ' " | 13' ' " | 14' ' " | 15' ' " | TIME INTVL |
|---|---|---|---|---|---|---|---|---|---|---|---|---|---|---|---|---|
| | MEAN SECOND DIFFERENCE | | | | | | | | | | | | | | | |
| 0-1 | 0 1 | 0 1 | 0 2 | 0 2 | 0 3 | 0 4 | 0 4 | 0 5 | 0 6 | 0 6 | 0 7 | 0 7 | 0 8 | 0 9 | 0 9 | 23-24 |
| 1-2 | 0 2 | 0 4 | 0 5 | 0 7 | 0 9 | 0 11 | 0 12 | 0 14 | 0 16 | 0 18 | 0 19 | 0 21 | 0 23 | 0 25 | 0 26 | 22-23 |
| 2-3 | 0 3 | 0 6 | 0 8 | 0 11 | 0 14 | 0 17 | 0 20 | 0 22 | 0 25 | 0 28 | 0 31 | 0 34 | 0 36 | 0 39 | 0 42 | 21-22 |
| 3-4 | 0 4 | 0 7 | 0 11 | 0 15 | 0 19 | 0 22 | 0 26 | 0 30 | 0 34 | 0 37 | 0 41 | 0 45 | 0 49 | 0 52 | 0 56 | 20-21 |
| 4-5 | 0 5 | 0 9 | 0 14 | 0 18 | 0 23 | 0 27 | 0 32 | 0 37 | 0 41 | 0 46 | 0 50 | 0 55 | 0 59 | 1 4 | 1 9 | 19-20 |
| 5-6 | 0 5 | 0 11 | 0 16 | 0 21 | 0 26 | 0 32 | 0 37 | 0 42 | 0 48 | 0 53 | 0 58 | 1 4 | 1 9 | 1 14 | 1 19 | 18-19 |
| 6-7 | 0 6 | 0 12 | 0 18 | 0 24 | 0 30 | 0 36 | 0 41 | 0 47 | 0 53 | 0 59 | 1 5 | 1 11 | 1 17 | 1 23 | 1 29 | 17-18 |
| 7-8 | 0 6 | 0 13 | 0 19 | 0 26 | 0 32 | 0 39 | 0 45 | 0 52 | 0 58 | 1 4 | 1 11 | 1 17 | 1 24 | 1 30 | 1 37 | 16-17 |
| 8-9 | 0 7 | 0 14 | 0 21 | 0 27 | 0 34 | 0 41 | 0 48 | 0 55 | 1 2 | 1 9 | 1 15 | 1 22 | 1 29 | 1 36 | 1 43 | 15-16 |
| 9-10 | 0 7 | 0 14 | 0 22 | 0 29 | 0 36 | 0 43 | 0 50 | 0 57 | 1 5 | 1 12 | 1 19 | 1 26 | 1 33 | 1 40 | 1 48 | 14-15 |
| 10-11 | 0 7 | 0 15 | 0 22 | 0 30 | 0 37 | 0 4 | 0 52 | 0 59 | 1 6 | 1 14 | 1 21 | 1 29 | 1 36 | 1 43 | 1 51 | 13-14 |
| 11-12 | 0 7 | 0 15 | 0 22 | 0 30 | 0 37 | 0 45 | 0 52 | 0 60 | 1 7 | 1 15 | 1 22 | 1 30 | 1 37 | 1 45 | 1 52 | 12-13 |

| TIME INTVL | 16' ' " | 17' ' " | 18' ' " | 19' ' " | 20' ' " | 21' ' " | 22' ' " | 23' ' " | 24' ' " | 25' ' " | 26' ' " | 27' ' " | 28' ' " | 29' ' " | 30' ' " | TIME INTVL |
|---|---|---|---|---|---|---|---|---|---|---|---|---|---|---|---|---|
| | MEAN SECOND DIFFERENCE | | | | | | | | | | | | | | | |
| 0-1 | 0 10 | 0 10 | 0 11 | 0 12 | 0 12 | 0 13 | 0 13 | 0 14 | 0 15 | 0 15 | 0 16 | 0 17 | 0 17 | 0 18 | 0 18 | 23-24 |
| 1-2 | 0 28 | 0 30 | 0 32 | 0 33 | 0 35 | 0 37 | 0 39 | 0 40 | 0 42 | 0 44 | 0 46 | 0 47 | 0 49 | 0 51 | 0 53 | 22-23 |
| 2-3 | 0 45 | 0 48 | 0 50 | 0 53 | 0 56 | 0 59 | 1 2 | 1 4 | 1 7 | 1 10 | 0 13 | 1 18 | 1 18 | 1 21 | 1 24 | 21-22 |
| 3-4 | 0 60 | 1 4 | 1 7 | 1 11 | 1 15 | 1 18 | 1 22 | 1 26 | 1 30 | 1 33 | 1 37 | 1 45 | 1 45 | 1 48 | 1 52 | 20-21 |
| 4-5 | 1 13 | 1 18 | 1 22 | 1 27 | 1 31 | 1 36 | 1 41 | 1 45 | 1 50 | 1 54 | 1 59 | 2 8 | 2 8 | 2 13 | 2 17 | 19-20 |
| 5-6 | 1 25 | 1 30 | 1 35 | 1 41 | 1 46 | 1 51 | 1 57 | 2 2 | 2 7 | 2 12 | 2 18 | 2 23 | 2 28 | 2 34 | 2 39 | 18-19 |
| 6-7 | 1 35 | 1 41 | 1 47 | 1 53 | 0 58 | 2 4 | 2 10 | 2 16 | 2 22 | 2 28 | 2 34 | 2 40 | 2 46 | 2 52 | 2 58 | 17-18 |
| 7-8 | 1 43 | 1 50 | 1 56 | 2 2 | 2 9 | 2 15 | 2 22 | 2 28 | 2 35 | 2 41 | 2 48 | 2 54 | 3 0 | 3 7 | 3 13 | 16-17 |
| 8-9 | 1 50 | 1 57 | 2 4 | 2 10 | 2 17 | 2 24 | 2 31 | 2 38 | 2 45 | 2 52 | 2 58 | 3 5 | 3 12 | 3 19 | 3 26 | 15-16 |
| 9-10 | 1 55 | 2 2 | 2 9 | 2 16 | 2 23 | 2 31 | 2 38 | 2 45 | 2 52 | 2 59 | 3 7 | 3 14 | 3 21 | 3 28 | 3 35 | 14-15 |
| 10-11 | 1 58 | 2 6 | 2 13 | 2 20 | 2 28 | 2 35 | 2 42 | 2 50 | 2 57 | 3 5 | 3 12 | 3 19 | 3 27 | 3 34 | 3 41 | 13-14 |
| 11-12 | 1 60 | 2 7 | 2 15 | 2 22 | 2 30 | 2 37 | 2 45 | 2 52 | 2 60 | 3 7 | 3 15 | 3 22 | 3 30 | 3 37 | 3 45 | 12-13 |

# Table IX Diurnal Motion Logarithms, 0 to 24 Hours/Degrees

HOURS or DEGREES

| MINUTES OF TIME OR ARC | 0 | 1 | 2 | 3 | 4 | 5 | 6 | 7 | 8 | 9 | 10 | 11 | 12 | 13 | 14 | 15 | 16 | 17 | 18 | 19 | 20 | 21 | 22 | 23 | MINUTES OF TIME OR ARC |
|---|---|---|---|---|---|---|---|---|---|---|---|---|---|---|---|---|---|---|---|---|---|---|---|---|---|
| 0 | INFINITE | 1.38021 | 1.07918 | .90309 | .77815 | .68124 | .60206 | .53511 | .47712 | .42597 | .38021 | .33882 | .30103 | .26627 | .23408 | .20412 | .17609 | .14976 | .12494 | .10146 | .07918 | .05799 | .03779 | .01848 | 0 |
| 1 | 3.15836 | 1.37303 | 1.07558 | .90068 | .77635 | .67980 | .60086 | .53408 | .47622 | .42517 | .37949 | .33816 | .30043 | .26571 | .23357 | .20364 | .17564 | .14934 | .12454 | .10108 | .07882 | .05765 | .03746 | .01817 | 1 |
| 2 | 2.85733 | 1.36597 | 1.07200 | .89829 | .77455 | .67836 | .59965 | .53305 | .47532 | .42436 | .37877 | .33750 | .29983 | .26516 | .23305 | .20316 | .17519 | .14891 | .12414 | .10070 | .07846 | .05730 | .03713 | .01785 | 2 |
| 3 | 2.68124 | 1.35902 | 1.06846 | .89591 | .77276 | .67692 | .59846 | .53202 | .47442 | .42356 | .37805 | .33685 | .29922 | .26460 | .23253 | .20267 | .17474 | .14849 | .12373 | .10032 | .07810 | .05696 | .03680 | .01754 | 3 |
| 4 | 2.55630 | 1.35218 | 1.06494 | .89354 | .77097 | .67549 | .59726 | .53100 | .47352 | .42276 | .37733 | .33619 | .29862 | .26405 | .23202 | .20219 | .17429 | .14806 | .12333 | .09994 | .07774 | .05662 | .03647 | .01723 | 4 |
| 5 | 2.45939 | 1.34545 | 1.06145 | .89119 | .76920 | .67406 | .59607 | .52997 | .47262 | .42197 | .37661 | .33554 | .29802 | .26349 | .23151 | .20171 | .17384 | .14764 | .12293 | .09956 | .07738 | .05627 | .03615 | .01691 | 5 |
| 6 | 2.38021 | 1.33882 | 1.05799 | .88885 | .76743 | .67264 | .59488 | .52895 | .47173 | .42117 | .37589 | .33489 | .29743 | .26294 | .23099 | .20123 | .17339 | .14722 | .12253 | .09918 | .07702 | .05593 | .03582 | .01660 | 6 |
| 7 | 2.31326 | 1.33229 | 1.05456 | .88652 | .76567 | .67122 | .59370 | .52793 | .47083 | .42038 | .37517 | .33424 | .29683 | .26239 | .23048 | .20076 | .17294 | .14679 | .12213 | .09880 | .07666 | .05559 | .03549 | .01629 | 7 |
| 8 | 2.25527 | 1.32585 | 1.05115 | .88420 | .76391 | .66981 | .59251 | .52692 | .46994 | .41958 | .37446 | .33359 | .29623 | .26184 | .22997 | .20028 | .17249 | .14637 | .12173 | .09842 | .07630 | .05524 | .03516 | .01597 | 8 |
| 9 | 2.20412 | 1.31951 | 1.04777 | .88190 | .76216 | .66840 | .59134 | .52591 | .46905 | .41879 | .37375 | .33294 | .29563 | .26129 | .22945 | .19980 | .17204 | .14595 | .12133 | .09804 | .07594 | .05490 | .03484 | .01566 | 9 |
| 10 | 2.15836 | 1.31326 | 1.04442 | .87961 | .76042 | .66700 | .59016 | .52489 | .46817 | .41800 | .37303 | .33229 | .29504 | .26074 | .22894 | .19932 | .17159 | .14553 | .12094 | .09766 | .07558 | .05456 | .03451 | .01535 | 10 |
| 11 | 2.11697 | 1.30710 | 1.04109 | .87733 | .75869 | .66560 | .58899 | .52389 | .46728 | .41721 | .37232 | .33164 | .29445 | .26019 | .22843 | .19884 | .17114 | .14510 | .12054 | .09729 | .07522 | .05422 | .03418 | .01504 | 11 |
| 12 | 2.07918 | 1.30103 | 1.03779 | .87506 | .75696 | .66421 | .58782 | .52288 | .46640 | .41642 | .37161 | .33099 | .29385 | .25964 | .22792 | .19837 | .17070 | .14468 | .12014 | .09691 | .07486 | .05388 | .03386 | .01472 | 12 |
| 13 | 2.04442 | 1.29504 | 1.03451 | .87281 | .75524 | .66282 | .58665 | .52187 | .46552 | .41564 | .37090 | .33035 | .29326 | .25909 | .22741 | .19789 | .17025 | .14426 | .11974 | .09653 | .07450 | .05353 | .03353 | .01441 | 13 |
| 14 | 2.01223 | 1.28913 | 1.03126 | .87056 | .75353 | .66143 | .58549 | .52087 | .46464 | .41485 | .37019 | .32970 | .29267 | .25854 | .22690 | .19742 | .16980 | .14384 | .11935 | .09616 | .07414 | .05319 | .03321 | .01410 | 14 |
| 15 | 1.98227 | 1.28330 | 1.02803 | .86833 | .75182 | .66005 | .58433 | .51987 | .46376 | .41407 | .36949 | .32906 | .29208 | .25800 | .22640 | .19694 | .16936 | .14342 | .11895 | .09578 | .07379 | .05285 | .03288 | .01379 | 15 |
| 16 | 1.95424 | 1.27755 | 1.02482 | .86611 | .75012 | .65868 | .58317 | .51888 | .46288 | .41329 | .36878 | .32842 | .29148 | .25745 | .22589 | .19647 | .16891 | .14300 | .11855 | .09540 | .07343 | .05251 | .03256 | .01348 | 16 |
| 17 | 1.92791 | 1.27187 | 1.02164 | .86390 | .74843 | .65730 | .58202 | .51788 | .46201 | .41251 | .36808 | .32777 | .29090 | .25690 | .22538 | .19599 | .16847 | .14258 | .11816 | .09503 | .07307 | .05217 | .03223 | .01317 | 17 |
| 18 | 1.90309 | 1.26627 | 1.01848 | .86170 | .74674 | .65594 | .58087 | .51689 | .46113 | .41173 | .36737 | .32713 | .29031 | .25636 | .22488 | .19552 | .16802 | .14217 | .11776 | .09465 | .07272 | .05183 | .03191 | .01286 | 18 |
| 19 | 1.87961 | 1.26074 | 1.01535 | .85951 | .74506 | .65457 | .57972 | .51590 | .46026 | .41095 | .36667 | .32649 | .28972 | .25582 | .22437 | .19505 | .16758 | .14175 | .11736 | .09428 | .07236 | .05149 | .03158 | .01254 | 19 |
| 20 | 1.85733 | 1.25527 | 1.01223 | .85733 | .74339 | .65321 | .57858 | .51491 | .45939 | .41017 | .36597 | .32585 | .28913 | .25527 | .22386 | .19457 | .16714 | .14133 | .11697 | .09390 | .07200 | .05115 | .03126 | .01223 | 20 |
| 21 | 1.83614 | 1.24988 | 1.00914 | .85517 | .74172 | .65186 | .57744 | .51392 | .45852 | .40940 | .36527 | .32522 | .28854 | .25473 | .22336 | .19410 | .16669 | .14091 | .11658 | .09353 | .07165 | .05081 | .03093 | .01192 | 21 |
| 22 | 1.81594 | 1.24455 | 1.00607 | .85301 | .74006 | .65051 | .57630 | .51294 | .45766 | .40863 | .36457 | .32458 | .28796 | .25419 | .22286 | .19363 | .16625 | .14049 | .11618 | .09316 | .07129 | .05047 | .03061 | .01161 | 22 |
| 23 | 1.79663 | 1.23928 | 1.00303 | .85087 | .73841 | .64916 | .57516 | .51196 | .45679 | .40785 | .36387 | .32394 | .28737 | .25365 | .22235 | .19316 | .16581 | .14008 | .11579 | .09278 | .07094 | .05014 | .03029 | .01130 | 23 |
| 24 | 1.77815 | 1.23408 | 1.00000 | .84873 | .73676 | .64782 | .57403 | .51098 | .45593 | .40708 | .36318 | .32331 | .28679 | .25311 | .22185 | .19269 | .16537 | .13966 | .11539 | .09241 | .07058 | .04980 | .02996 | .01100 | 24 |
| 25 | 1.76042 | 1.22894 | .99699 | .84661 | .73512 | .64648 | .57290 | .51000 | .45507 | .40631 | .36248 | .32267 | .28621 | .25257 | .22135 | .19222 | .16493 | .13925 | .11500 | .09204 | .07023 | .04946 | .02964 | .01069 | 25 |
| 26 | 1.74339 | 1.22386 | .99401 | .84450 | .73348 | .64514 | .57178 | .50903 | .45421 | .40555 | .36179 | .32204 | .28562 | .25203 | .22084 | .19175 | .16449 | .13883 | .11461 | .09166 | .06987 | .04912 | .02932 | .01038 | 26 |
| 27 | 1.72700 | 1.21884 | .99105 | .84239 | .73185 | .64381 | .57065 | .50805 | .45335 | .40478 | .36109 | .32141 | .28504 | .25149 | .22034 | .19128 | .16405 | .13842 | .11421 | .09129 | .06952 | .04878 | .02899 | .01007 | 27 |
| 28 | 1.71120 | 1.21388 | .98810 | .84030 | .73023 | .64249 | .56953 | .50708 | .45250 | .40401 | .36040 | .32077 | .28446 | .25095 | .21984 | .19081 | .16361 | .13800 | .11382 | .09092 | .06916 | .04845 | .02867 | .00976 | 28 |
| 29 | 1.69596 | 1.20897 | .98518 | .83822 | .72861 | .64117 | .56841 | .50612 | .45164 | .40325 | .35971 | .32014 | .28388 | .25041 | .21934 | .19035 | .16317 | .13759 | .11343 | .09055 | .06881 | .04811 | .02835 | .00945 | 29 |
| 30 | 1.68124 | 1.20412 | .98227 | .83614 | .72700 | .63985 | .56730 | .50515 | .45079 | .40249 | .35902 | .31951 | .28330 | .24988 | .21884 | .18988 | .16273 | .13717 | .11304 | .09018 | .06846 | .04777 | .02803 | .00914 | 30 |
| 31 | 1.66700 | 1.19932 | .97939 | .83408 | .72539 | .63853 | .56619 | .50419 | .44994 | .40173 | .35833 | .31888 | .28272 | .24934 | .21834 | .18941 | .16229 | .13676 | .11265 | .08981 | .06810 | .04744 | .02771 | .00884 | 31 |
| 32 | 1.65321 | 1.19457 | .97652 | .83203 | .72379 | .63722 | .56508 | .50322 | .44909 | .40097 | .35765 | .31826 | .28214 | .24881 | .21785 | .18895 | .16185 | .13635 | .11226 | .08943 | .06775 | .04710 | .02739 | .00853 | 32 |
| 33 | 1.63985 | 1.18988 | .97367 | .82998 | .72220 | .63592 | .56397 | .50226 | .44825 | .40021 | .35696 | .31763 | .28157 | .24827 | .21735 | .18848 | .16141 | .13593 | .11187 | .08906 | .06740 | .04676 | .02706 | .00822 | 33 |
| 34 | 1.62688 | 1.18523 | .97084 | .82795 | .72061 | .63462 | .56287 | .50131 | .44740 | .39945 | .35627 | .31700 | .28099 | .24774 | .21685 | .18802 | .16098 | .13552 | .11148 | .08869 | .06705 | .04643 | .02674 | .00791 | 34 |
| 35 | 1.61429 | 1.18064 | .96803 | .82592 | .71903 | .63332 | .56177 | .50035 | .44656 | .39869 | .35559 | .31638 | .28042 | .24720 | .21635 | .18755 | .16054 | .13511 | .11109 | .08832 | .06670 | .04609 | .02642 | .00761 | 35 |
| 36 | 1.60206 | 1.17609 | .96524 | .82391 | .71745 | .63202 | .56067 | .49940 | .44571 | .39794 | .35491 | .31575 | .27984 | .24667 | .21586 | .18709 | .16010 | .13470 | .11070 | .08796 | .06634 | .04576 | .02610 | .00730 | 36 |
| 37 | 1.59016 | 1.17159 | .96246 | .82190 | .71588 | .63073 | .55957 | .49845 | .44487 | .39719 | .35422 | .31513 | .27927 | .24614 | .21536 | .18662 | .15967 | .13429 | .11031 | .08759 | .06599 | .04542 | .02578 | .00699 | 37 |
| 38 | 1.57858 | 1.16714 | .95971 | .81991 | .71432 | .62945 | .55848 | .49750 | .44403 | .39643 | .35354 | .31451 | .27869 | .24561 | .21487 | .18616 | .15923 | .13388 | .10992 | .08722 | .06564 | .04509 | .02546 | .00669 | 38 |
| 39 | 1.56730 | 1.16273 | .95697 | .81792 | .71276 | .62816 | .55739 | .49655 | .44320 | .39568 | .35286 | .31389 | .27812 | .24508 | .21437 | .18570 | .15880 | .13347 | .10953 | .08685 | .06529 | .04475 | .02514 | .00638 | 39 |
| 40 | 1.55630 | 1.15836 | .95424 | .81594 | .71120 | .62688 | .55630 | .49560 | .44236 | .39493 | .35218 | .31326 | .27755 | .24455 | .21388 | .18523 | .15836 | .13306 | .10914 | .08648 | .06494 | .04442 | .02482 | .00607 | 40 |
| 41 | 1.54558 | 1.15404 | .95154 | .81397 | .70966 | .62561 | .55522 | .49466 | .44152 | .39419 | .35150 | .31264 | .27698 | .24402 | .21339 | .18477 | .15793 | .13265 | .10876 | .08611 | .06459 | .04409 | .02450 | .00577 | 41 |
| 42 | 1.53511 | 1.14976 | .94885 | .81201 | .70811 | .62434 | .55414 | .49372 | .44069 | .39344 | .35083 | .31203 | .27641 | .24349 | .21289 | .18431 | .15749 | .13224 | .10837 | .08575 | .06424 | .04375 | .02419 | .00546 | 42 |
| 43 | 1.52489 | 1.14553 | .94617 | .81006 | .70658 | .62307 | .55306 | .49278 | .43986 | .39269 | .35015 | .31141 | .27584 | .24296 | .21240 | .18385 | .15706 | .13183 | .10798 | .08538 | .06389 | .04342 | .02387 | .00516 | 43 |
| 44 | 1.51491 | 1.14133 | .94352 | .80811 | .70504 | .62180 | .55198 | .49184 | .43903 | .39195 | .34948 | .31079 | .27527 | .24244 | .21191 | .18339 | .15663 | .13142 | .10760 | .08501 | .06354 | .04308 | .02355 | .00485 | 44 |
| 45 | 1.50515 | 1.13717 | .94088 | .80618 | .70352 | .62054 | .55091 | .49091 | .43820 | .39121 | .34880 | .31017 | .27470 | .24191 | .21142 | .18293 | .15620 | .13101 | .10721 | .08464 | .06319 | .04275 | .02323 | .00455 | 45 |
| 46 | 1.49560 | 1.13306 | .93825 | .80425 | .70200 | .61929 | .54984 | .48998 | .43738 | .39046 | .34813 | .30956 | .27413 | .24138 | .21093 | .18247 | .15576 | .13061 | .10682 | .08428 | .06284 | .04242 | .02291 | .00424 | 46 |
| 47 | 1.48626 | 1.12898 | .93565 | .80234 | .70048 | .61803 | .54877 | .48905 | .43655 | .38972 | .34746 | .30894 | .27357 | .24086 | .21044 | .18201 | .15533 | .13020 | .10644 | .08391 | .06250 | .04209 | .02259 | .00394 | 47 |
| 48 | 1.47712 | 1.12494 | .93305 | .80043 | .69897 | .61678 | .54770 | .48812 | .43573 | .38899 | .34679 | .30833 | .27300 | .24033 | .20995 | .18155 | .15490 | .12979 | .10605 | .08355 | .06215 | .04175 | .02228 | .00363 | 48 |
| 49 | 1.46817 | 1.12094 | .93048 | .79853 | .69746 | .61554 | .54664 | .48719 | .43491 | .38825 | .34612 | .30772 | .27244 | .23981 | .20946 | .18110 | .15447 | .12938 | .10567 | .08318 | .06180 | .04142 | .02196 | .00333 | 49 |
| 50 | 1.45939 | 1.11697 | .92791 | .79663 | .69596 | .61429 | .54558 | .48626 | .43409 | .38751 | .34545 | .30710 | .27187 | .23928 | .20897 | .18064 | .15404 | .12898 | .10528 | .08282 | .06145 | .04109 | .02164 | .00303 | 50 |
| 51 | 1.45079 | 1.11304 | .92537 | .79475 | .69447 | .61306 | .54452 | .48534 | .43327 | .38678 | .34478 | .30649 | .27131 | .23876 | .20848 | .18018 | .15361 | .12857 | .10490 | .08245 | .06111 | .04076 | .02133 | .00272 | 51 |
| 52 | 1.44236 | 1.10914 | .92283 | .79287 | .69298 | .61182 | .54347 | .48442 | .43245 | .38604 | .34411 | .30588 | .27075 | .23824 | .20800 | .17973 | .15318 | .12817 | .10452 | .08209 | .06076 | .04043 | .02101 | .00242 | 52 |
| 53 | 1.43409 | 1.10528 | .92032 | .79101 | .69149 | .61059 | .54241 | .48350 | .43164 | .38531 | .34345 | .30527 | .27018 | .23772 | .20751 | .17927 | .15275 | .12776 | .10413 | .08172 | .06041 | .04010 | .02069 | .00212 | 53 |
| 54 | 1.42597 | 1.10146 | .91781 | .78915 | .69002 | .60936 | .54136 | .48258 | .43082 | .38458 | .34278 | .30466 | .26962 | .23720 | .20702 | .17881 | .15232 | .12736 | .10375 | .08136 | .06006 | .03977 | .02038 | .00181 | 54 |
| 55 | 1.41800 | 1.09766 | .91532 | .78729 | .68854 | .60813 | .54031 | .48167 | .43001 | .38385 | .34212 | .30406 | .26906 | .23668 | .20654 | .17836 | .15190 | .12695 | .10337 | .08099 | .05972 | .03944 | .02006 | .00151 | 55 |
| 56 | 1.41017 | 1.09390 | .91285 | .78545 | .68707 | .60691 | .53927 | .48076 | .42920 | .38312 | .34146 | .30345 | .26850 | .23616 | .20605 | .17790 | .15147 | .12655 | .10298 | .08063 | .05937 | .03911 | .01974 | .00121 | 56 |
| 57 | 1.40249 | 1.09018 | .91039 | .78361 | .68561 | .60569 | .53823 | .47984 | .42839 | .38239 | .34080 | .30284 | .26794 | .23564 | .20557 | .17745 | .15104 | .12615 | .10260 | .08027 | .05903 | .03878 | .01943 | .00091 | 57 |
| 58 | 1.39493 | 1.08648 | .90794 | .78179 | .68415 | .60448 | .53719 | .47893 | .42758 | .38166 | .34014 | .30224 | .26738 | .23512 | .20509 | .17700 | .15061 | .12574 | .10222 | .07991 | .05868 | .03845 | .01911 | .00060 | 58 |
| 59 | 1.38751 | 1.08282 | .90551 | .77996 | .68269 | .60327 | .53615 | .47803 | .42677 | .38094 | .33948 | .30163 | .26683 | .23460 | .20460 | .17654 | .15019 | .12534 | .10184 | .07954 | .05834 | .03812 | .01880 | .00030 | 59 |
| 60 | 1.38021 | 1.07918 | .90309 | .77815 | .68124 | .60206 | .53511 | .47712 | .42597 | .38021 | .33882 | .30103 | .26627 | .23408 | .20412 | .17609 | .14976 | .12494 | .10146 | .07918 | .05799 | .03779 | .01848 | .00000 | 60 |

# Table X Diurnal Motion Logarithms, 0 to 2 Hours/Degrees

SECONDS OF TIME OR ARC (rows) — DEGREES or HOURS and MINUTES (columns)

| Sec | 0°19' | 0°18' | 0°17' | 0°16' | 0°15' | 0°14' | 0°13' | 0°12' | 0°11' | 0°10' | 0°9' | 0°8' | 0°7' | 0°6' | 0°5' | 0°4' | 0°3' | 0°2' | 0°1' | 0°0' |
|---|---|---|---|---|---|---|---|---|---|---|---|---|---|---|---|---|---|---|---|---|
| 0 | 1.87961 | 1.90309 | 1.92791 | 1.95424 | 1.98227 | 2.01223 | 2.04442 | 2.07918 | 2.11697 | 2.15836 | 2.20412 | 2.25527 | 2.31326 | 2.38021 | 2.45939 | 2.55630 | 2.68124 | 2.85733 | 3.15836 | INFINITE |
| 1 | 1.87923 | 1.90269 | 1.92749 | 1.95379 | 1.98179 | 2.01172 | 2.04386 | 2.07858 | 2.11631 | 2.15764 | 2.20332 | 2.25437 | 2.31223 | 2.37901 | 2.45795 | 2.55450 | 2.67884 | 2.85373 | 3.15118 | 4.93651 |
| 2 | 1.87885 | 1.90229 | 1.92706 | 1.95334 | 1.98131 | 2.01120 | 2.04331 | 2.07798 | 2.11566 | 2.15692 | 2.20251 | 2.25347 | 2.31120 | 2.37781 | 2.45651 | 2.55270 | 2.67644 | 2.85015 | 3.14412 | 4.63548 |
| 3 | 1.87847 | 1.90189 | 1.92664 | 1.95289 | 1.98083 | 2.01069 | 2.04275 | 2.07738 | 2.11500 | 2.15620 | 2.20171 | 2.25257 | 2.31017 | 2.37661 | 2.45507 | 2.55091 | 2.67406 | 2.84661 | 3.13717 | 4.45939 |
| 4 | 1.87809 | 1.90148 | 1.92621 | 1.95244 | 1.98035 | 2.01017 | 2.04220 | 2.07678 | 2.11435 | 2.15548 | 2.20091 | 2.25167 | 2.30915 | 2.37541 | 2.45364 | 2.54912 | 2.67170 | 2.84309 | 3.13033 | 4.33445 |
| 5 | 1.87771 | 1.90108 | 1.92579 | 1.95199 | 1.97987 | 2.00966 | 2.04164 | 2.07618 | 2.11369 | 2.15476 | 2.20012 | 2.25077 | 2.30812 | 2.37422 | 2.45221 | 2.54735 | 2.66934 | 2.83960 | 3.12360 | 4.23754 |
| 6 | 1.87733 | 1.90068 | 1.92537 | 1.95154 | 1.97939 | 2.00914 | 2.04109 | 2.07558 | 2.11304 | 2.15404 | 2.19932 | 2.24988 | 2.30710 | 2.37303 | 2.45079 | 2.54558 | 2.66700 | 2.83614 | 3.11697 | 4.15836 |
| 7 | 1.87695 | 1.90028 | 1.92494 | 1.95109 | 1.97891 | 2.00863 | 2.04054 | 2.07498 | 2.11239 | 2.15333 | 2.19853 | 2.24898 | 2.30609 | 2.37185 | 2.44938 | 2.54382 | 2.66467 | 2.83271 | 3.11044 | 4.09142 |
| 8 | 1.87657 | 1.89988 | 1.92452 | 1.95064 | 1.97843 | 2.00812 | 2.03999 | 2.07438 | 2.11174 | 2.15261 | 2.19773 | 2.24809 | 2.30507 | 2.37067 | 2.44796 | 2.54206 | 2.66236 | 2.82930 | 3.10400 | 4.03342 |
| 9 | 1.87619 | 1.89949 | 1.92410 | 1.95019 | 1.97795 | 2.00761 | 2.03944 | 2.07379 | 2.11109 | 2.15190 | 2.19694 | 2.24720 | 2.30406 | 2.36949 | 2.44656 | 2.54031 | 2.66005 | 2.82592 | 3.09766 | 3.98227 |
| 10 | 1.87582 | 1.89909 | 1.92368 | 1.94974 | 1.97747 | 2.00709 | 2.03889 | 2.07319 | 2.11044 | 2.15118 | 2.19615 | 2.24632 | 2.30305 | 2.36831 | 2.44515 | 2.53857 | 2.65776 | 2.82257 | 3.09142 | 3.93651 |
| 11 | 1.87544 | 1.89869 | 1.92326 | 1.94929 | 1.97700 | 2.00658 | 2.03834 | 2.07260 | 2.10979 | 2.15047 | 2.19536 | 2.24543 | 2.30204 | 2.36714 | 2.44375 | 2.53684 | 2.65548 | 2.81924 | 3.08526 | 3.89512 |
| 12 | 1.87506 | 1.89829 | 1.92283 | 1.94885 | 1.97652 | 2.00607 | 2.03779 | 2.07200 | 2.10914 | 2.14976 | 2.19457 | 2.24455 | 2.30103 | 2.36597 | 2.44236 | 2.53511 | 2.65321 | 2.81594 | 3.07919 | 3.85733 |
| 13 | 1.87468 | 1.89789 | 1.92241 | 1.94840 | 1.97604 | 2.00556 | 2.03724 | 2.07141 | 2.10850 | 2.14905 | 2.19378 | 2.24367 | 2.30003 | 2.36480 | 2.44097 | 2.53339 | 2.65096 | 2.81266 | 3.07319 | 3.82257 |
| 14 | 1.87431 | 1.89750 | 1.92199 | 1.94795 | 1.97557 | 2.00506 | 2.03669 | 2.07082 | 2.10785 | 2.14835 | 2.19300 | 2.24279 | 2.29902 | 2.36364 | 2.43958 | 2.53168 | 2.64871 | 2.80941 | 3.06728 | 3.79039 |
| 15 | 1.87393 | 1.89710 | 1.92157 | 1.94751 | 1.97509 | 2.00455 | 2.03615 | 2.07023 | 2.10721 | 2.14764 | 2.19222 | 2.24191 | 2.29802 | 2.36248 | 2.43820 | 2.52997 | 2.64648 | 2.80618 | 3.06145 | 3.76042 |
| 16 | 1.87356 | 1.89670 | 1.92115 | 1.94706 | 1.97462 | 2.00404 | 2.03560 | 2.06964 | 2.10657 | 2.14693 | 2.19144 | 2.24103 | 2.29703 | 2.36133 | 2.43683 | 2.52827 | 2.64426 | 2.80297 | 3.05570 | 3.73239 |
| 17 | 1.87318 | 1.89631 | 1.92073 | 1.94662 | 1.97414 | 2.00353 | 2.03506 | 2.06905 | 2.10593 | 2.14623 | 2.19066 | 2.24016 | 2.29603 | 2.36017 | 2.43545 | 2.52658 | 2.64205 | 2.79979 | 3.05002 | 3.70606 |
| 18 | 1.87281 | 1.89591 | 1.92032 | 1.94617 | 1.97367 | 2.00303 | 2.03451 | 2.06846 | 2.10528 | 2.14553 | 2.18988 | 2.23928 | 2.29504 | 2.35902 | 2.43409 | 2.52489 | 2.63985 | 2.79663 | 3.04442 | 3.68124 |
| 19 | 1.87243 | 1.89552 | 1.91990 | 1.94573 | 1.97320 | 2.00252 | 2.03397 | 2.06787 | 2.10464 | 2.14482 | 2.18910 | 2.23841 | 2.29405 | 2.35787 | 2.43272 | 2.52321 | 2.63766 | 2.79350 | 3.03889 | 3.65776 |
| 20 | 1.87206 | 1.89512 | 1.91948 | 1.94529 | 1.97273 | 2.00202 | 2.03342 | 2.06728 | 2.10400 | 2.14412 | 2.18833 | 2.23754 | 2.29306 | 2.35673 | 2.43136 | 2.52154 | 2.63548 | 2.79039 | 3.03342 | 3.63548 |
| 21 | 1.87168 | 1.89473 | 1.91906 | 1.94484 | 1.97225 | 2.00151 | 2.03288 | 2.06670 | 2.10337 | 2.14342 | 2.18755 | 2.23668 | 2.29208 | 2.35559 | 2.43001 | 2.51987 | 2.63332 | 2.78729 | 3.02803 | 3.61429 |
| 22 | 1.87131 | 1.89433 | 1.91865 | 1.94440 | 1.97178 | 2.00101 | 2.03234 | 2.06611 | 2.10273 | 2.14272 | 2.18678 | 2.23581 | 2.29109 | 2.35445 | 2.42866 | 2.51821 | 2.63116 | 2.78423 | 3.02270 | 3.59409 |
| 23 | 1.87093 | 1.89394 | 1.91823 | 1.94396 | 1.97131 | 2.00050 | 2.03180 | 2.06552 | 2.10209 | 2.14203 | 2.18601 | 2.23495 | 2.29011 | 2.35331 | 2.42731 | 2.51656 | 2.62902 | 2.78118 | 3.01744 | 3.57479 |
| 24 | 1.87056 | 1.89354 | 1.91781 | 1.94352 | 1.97084 | 2.00000 | 2.03126 | 2.06494 | 2.10146 | 2.14133 | 2.18523 | 2.23408 | 2.28913 | 2.35218 | 2.42597 | 2.51491 | 2.62688 | 2.77815 | 3.01223 | 3.55630 |
| 25 | 1.87019 | 1.89315 | 1.91740 | 1.94308 | 1.97037 | 1.99950 | 2.03072 | 2.06436 | 2.10082 | 2.14063 | 2.18447 | 2.23322 | 2.28815 | 2.35105 | 2.42463 | 2.51327 | 2.62476 | 2.77515 | 3.00709 | 3.53857 |
| 26 | 1.86982 | 1.89276 | 1.91698 | 1.94264 | 1.96990 | 1.99899 | 2.03018 | 2.06377 | 2.10019 | 2.13994 | 2.18370 | 2.23236 | 2.28718 | 2.34993 | 2.42330 | 2.51163 | 2.62265 | 2.77216 | 3.00202 | 3.52154 |
| 27 | 1.86944 | 1.89237 | 1.91657 | 1.94220 | 1.96943 | 1.99849 | 2.02964 | 2.06319 | 2.09956 | 2.13925 | 2.18293 | 2.23151 | 2.28621 | 2.34880 | 2.42197 | 2.51000 | 2.62054 | 2.76920 | 2.99699 | 3.50515 |
| 28 | 1.86907 | 1.89197 | 1.91615 | 1.94176 | 1.96897 | 1.99799 | 2.02910 | 2.06261 | 2.09893 | 2.13855 | 2.18217 | 2.23065 | 2.28524 | 2.34768 | 2.42064 | 2.50838 | 2.61845 | 2.76625 | 2.99203 | 3.48936 |
| 29 | 1.86870 | 1.89158 | 1.91574 | 1.94132 | 1.96850 | 1.99749 | 2.02857 | 2.06203 | 2.09829 | 2.13786 | 2.18140 | 2.22980 | 2.28427 | 2.34656 | 2.41932 | 2.50676 | 2.61637 | 2.76333 | 2.98712 | 3.47412 |
| 30 | 1.86833 | 1.89119 | 1.91532 | 1.94088 | 1.96803 | 1.99699 | 2.02803 | 2.06145 | 2.09766 | 2.13717 | 2.18064 | 2.22894 | 2.28330 | 2.34545 | 2.41800 | 2.50515 | 2.61429 | 2.76042 | 2.98227 | 3.45939 |
| 31 | 1.86796 | 1.89080 | 1.91491 | 1.94044 | 1.96756 | 1.99650 | 2.02749 | 2.06087 | 2.09704 | 2.13648 | 2.17988 | 2.22809 | 2.28234 | 2.34434 | 2.41669 | 2.50354 | 2.61223 | 2.75754 | 2.97747 | 3.44515 |
| 32 | 1.86759 | 1.89041 | 1.91450 | 1.94000 | 1.96710 | 1.99600 | 2.02696 | 2.06030 | 2.09641 | 2.13580 | 2.17912 | 2.22724 | 2.28138 | 2.34323 | 2.41538 | 2.50194 | 2.61018 | 2.75467 | 2.97273 | 3.43136 |
| 33 | 1.86722 | 1.89002 | 1.91409 | 1.93956 | 1.96663 | 1.99550 | 2.02642 | 2.05972 | 2.09578 | 2.13511 | 2.17836 | 2.22640 | 2.28042 | 2.34212 | 2.41407 | 2.50035 | 2.60813 | 2.75182 | 2.96803 | 3.41800 |
| 34 | 1.86685 | 1.88963 | 1.91367 | 1.93913 | 1.96617 | 1.99500 | 2.02589 | 2.05914 | 2.09515 | 2.13442 | 2.17760 | 2.22555 | 2.27946 | 2.34102 | 2.41277 | 2.49876 | 2.60610 | 2.74899 | 2.96339 | 3.40503 |
| 35 | 1.86648 | 1.88924 | 1.91326 | 1.93869 | 1.96570 | 1.99451 | 2.02535 | 2.05857 | 2.09453 | 2.13374 | 2.17685 | 2.22471 | 2.27850 | 2.33992 | 2.41147 | 2.49718 | 2.60408 | 2.74618 | 2.95879 | 3.39245 |
| 36 | 1.86611 | 1.88885 | 1.91285 | 1.93825 | 1.96524 | 1.99401 | 2.02482 | 2.05799 | 2.09390 | 2.13306 | 2.17609 | 2.22386 | 2.27755 | 2.33882 | 2.41017 | 2.49560 | 2.60206 | 2.74339 | 2.95424 | 3.38021 |
| 37 | 1.86574 | 1.88846 | 1.91244 | 1.93782 | 1.96477 | 1.99351 | 2.02429 | 2.05742 | 2.09328 | 2.13237 | 2.17534 | 2.22302 | 2.27660 | 2.33772 | 2.40888 | 2.49403 | 2.60005 | 2.74061 | 2.94974 | 3.36831 |
| 38 | 1.86537 | 1.88807 | 1.91203 | 1.93738 | 1.96431 | 1.99302 | 2.02376 | 2.05684 | 2.09266 | 2.13169 | 2.17459 | 2.22218 | 2.27565 | 2.33663 | 2.40760 | 2.49247 | 2.59806 | 2.73786 | 2.94529 | 3.35673 |
| 39 | 1.86500 | 1.88768 | 1.91162 | 1.93695 | 1.96385 | 1.99252 | 2.02323 | 2.05627 | 2.09204 | 2.13101 | 2.17384 | 2.22135 | 2.27470 | 2.33554 | 2.40631 | 2.49091 | 2.59607 | 2.73512 | 2.94088 | 3.34545 |
| 40 | 1.86463 | 1.88730 | 1.91121 | 1.93651 | 1.96339 | 1.99203 | 2.02270 | 2.05570 | 2.09142 | 2.13033 | 2.17309 | 2.22051 | 2.27376 | 2.33445 | 2.40503 | 2.48936 | 2.59409 | 2.73239 | 2.93651 | 3.33445 |
| 41 | 1.86426 | 1.88691 | 1.91080 | 1.93608 | 1.96292 | 1.99154 | 2.02217 | 2.05513 | 2.09080 | 2.12966 | 2.17234 | 2.21968 | 2.27281 | 2.33337 | 2.40376 | 2.48781 | 2.59212 | 2.72969 | 2.93219 | 3.32373 |
| 42 | 1.86390 | 1.88652 | 1.91039 | 1.93565 | 1.96246 | 1.99105 | 2.02164 | 2.05456 | 2.09018 | 2.12898 | 2.17159 | 2.21884 | 2.27187 | 2.33229 | 2.40249 | 2.48626 | 2.59016 | 2.72700 | 2.92791 | 3.31326 |
| 43 | 1.86353 | 1.88613 | 1.90998 | 1.93521 | 1.96200 | 1.99055 | 2.02111 | 2.05399 | 2.08956 | 2.12830 | 2.17085 | 2.21801 | 2.27093 | 2.33121 | 2.40122 | 2.48473 | 2.58821 | 2.72433 | 2.92368 | 3.30305 |
| 44 | 1.86316 | 1.88575 | 1.90957 | 1.93478 | 1.96154 | 1.99006 | 2.02059 | 2.05342 | 2.08894 | 2.12763 | 2.17010 | 2.21718 | 2.27000 | 2.33013 | 2.39996 | 2.48320 | 2.58627 | 2.72167 | 2.91948 | 3.29306 |
| 45 | 1.86280 | 1.88536 | 1.90916 | 1.93435 | 1.96108 | 1.98957 | 2.02006 | 2.05285 | 2.08832 | 2.12695 | 2.16936 | 2.21635 | 2.26906 | 2.32906 | 2.39869 | 2.48167 | 2.58433 | 2.71903 | 2.91532 | 3.28330 |
| 46 | 1.86243 | 1.88498 | 1.90876 | 1.93392 | 1.96062 | 1.98908 | 2.01953 | 2.05228 | 2.08771 | 2.12628 | 2.16862 | 2.21553 | 2.26813 | 2.32799 | 2.39744 | 2.48015 | 2.58241 | 2.71641 | 2.91121 | 3.27376 |
| 47 | 1.86206 | 1.88459 | 1.90835 | 1.93348 | 1.96016 | 1.98859 | 2.01901 | 2.05172 | 2.08709 | 2.12561 | 2.16788 | 2.21470 | 2.26720 | 2.32692 | 2.39618 | 2.47863 | 2.58049 | 2.71380 | 2.90713 | 3.26442 |
| 48 | 1.86170 | 1.88420 | 1.90794 | 1.93305 | 1.95971 | 1.98810 | 2.01848 | 2.05115 | 2.08648 | 2.12494 | 2.16714 | 2.21388 | 2.26627 | 2.32585 | 2.39493 | 2.47712 | 2.57858 | 2.71120 | 2.90309 | 3.25527 |
| 49 | 1.86133 | 1.88382 | 1.90754 | 1.93262 | 1.95925 | 1.98761 | 2.01796 | 2.05059 | 2.08587 | 2.12427 | 2.16640 | 2.21306 | 2.26534 | 2.32479 | 2.39369 | 2.47562 | 2.57668 | 2.70863 | 2.89909 | 3.24632 |
| 50 | 1.86097 | 1.88344 | 1.90713 | 1.93219 | 1.95879 | 1.98712 | 2.01744 | 2.05002 | 2.08526 | 2.12360 | 2.16566 | 2.21224 | 2.26442 | 2.32373 | 2.39245 | 2.47412 | 2.57479 | 2.70606 | 2.89512 | 3.23754 |
| 51 | 1.86060 | 1.88305 | 1.90672 | 1.93176 | 1.95833 | 1.98664 | 2.01691 | 2.04946 | 2.08464 | 2.12293 | 2.16493 | 2.21142 | 2.26349 | 2.32267 | 2.39121 | 2.47262 | 2.57290 | 2.70352 | 2.89119 | 3.22894 |
| 52 | 1.86024 | 1.88267 | 1.90632 | 1.93133 | 1.95788 | 1.98615 | 2.01639 | 2.04889 | 2.08403 | 2.12227 | 2.16419 | 2.21060 | 2.26257 | 2.32162 | 2.38997 | 2.47113 | 2.57103 | 2.70099 | 2.88730 | 3.22051 |
| 53 | 1.85987 | 1.88228 | 1.90591 | 1.93090 | 1.95742 | 1.98566 | 2.01587 | 2.04833 | 2.08342 | 2.12160 | 2.16346 | 2.20979 | 2.26165 | 2.32056 | 2.38874 | 2.46965 | 2.56916 | 2.69847 | 2.88344 | 3.21224 |
| 54 | 1.85951 | 1.88190 | 1.90551 | 1.93048 | 1.95697 | 1.98518 | 2.01535 | 2.04777 | 2.08282 | 2.12094 | 2.16273 | 2.20897 | 2.26074 | 2.31951 | 2.38751 | 2.46817 | 2.56730 | 2.69596 | 2.87961 | 3.20412 |
| 55 | 1.85915 | 1.88152 | 1.90511 | 1.93005 | 1.95651 | 1.98469 | 2.01483 | 2.04721 | 2.08221 | 2.12027 | 2.16200 | 2.20816 | 2.25982 | 2.31847 | 2.38629 | 2.46669 | 2.56545 | 2.69348 | 2.87582 | 3.19615 |
| 56 | 1.85878 | 1.88114 | 1.90470 | 1.92962 | 1.95606 | 1.98421 | 2.01431 | 2.04665 | 2.08160 | 2.11961 | 2.16127 | 2.20735 | 2.25891 | 2.31742 | 2.38506 | 2.46522 | 2.56360 | 2.69100 | 2.87206 | 3.18833 |
| 57 | 1.85842 | 1.88075 | 1.90430 | 1.92919 | 1.95560 | 1.98372 | 2.01379 | 2.04609 | 2.08099 | 2.11895 | 2.16054 | 2.20654 | 2.25800 | 2.31638 | 2.38385 | 2.46376 | 2.56177 | 2.68854 | 2.86833 | 3.18064 |
| 58 | 1.85806 | 1.88037 | 1.90389 | 1.92877 | 1.95515 | 1.98324 | 2.01327 | 2.04553 | 2.08039 | 2.11829 | 2.15981 | 2.20573 | 2.25709 | 2.31534 | 2.38263 | 2.46230 | 2.55994 | 2.68609 | 2.86463 | 3.17309 |
| 59 | 1.85769 | 1.87999 | 1.90349 | 1.92834 | 1.95470 | 1.98275 | 2.01275 | 2.04498 | 2.07978 | 2.11763 | 2.15909 | 2.20492 | 2.25618 | 2.31430 | 2.38142 | 2.46084 | 2.55812 | 2.68366 | 2.86097 | 3.16566 |
| 60 | 1.85733 | 1.87961 | 1.90309 | 1.92791 | 1.95424 | 1.98227 | 2.01223 | 2.04442 | 2.07918 | 2.11697 | 2.15836 | 2.20412 | 2.25527 | 2.31326 | 2.38021 | 2.45939 | 2.55630 | 2.68124 | 2.85733 | 3.15836 |

# Table X Diurnal Motion Logarithms, 0 to 2 Hours/Degrees

DEGREES or HOURS and MINUTES

SECONDS OF TIME OR ARC

| S | 0°39' | 0°38' | 0°37' | 0°36' | 0°35' | 0°34' | 0°33' | 0°32' | 0°31' | 0°30' | 0°29' | 0°28' | 0°27' | 0°26' | 0°25' | 0°24' | 0°23' | 0°22' | 0°21' | 0°20' |
|---|---|---|---|---|---|---|---|---|---|---|---|---|---|---|---|---|---|---|---|---|
| 0 | 1.56730 | 1.57858 | 1.59016 | 1.60206 | 1.61429 | 1.62688 | 1.63985 | 1.65321 | 1.66700 | 1.68124 | 1.69596 | 1.71120 | 1.72700 | 1.74339 | 1.76042 | 1.77815 | 1.79663 | 1.81594 | 1.83614 | 1.85733 |
| 1 | 1.56711 | 1.57839 | 1.58997 | 1.60186 | 1.61409 | 1.62667 | 1.63963 | 1.65299 | 1.66677 | 1.68100 | 1.69571 | 1.71095 | 1.72673 | 1.74311 | 1.76013 | 1.77785 | 1.79632 | 1.81561 | 1.83580 | 1.85697 |
| 2 | 1.56693 | 1.57820 | 1.58977 | 1.60166 | 1.61388 | 1.62646 | 1.63941 | 1.65276 | 1.66653 | 1.68076 | 1.69547 | 1.71069 | 1.72646 | 1.74283 | 1.75984 | 1.77755 | 1.79601 | 1.81528 | 1.83545 | 1.85661 |
| 3 | 1.56674 | 1.57801 | 1.58957 | 1.60146 | 1.61367 | 1.62625 | 1.63919 | 1.65253 | 1.66630 | 1.68052 | 1.69522 | 1.71043 | 1.72620 | 1.74255 | 1.75955 | 1.77725 | 1.79569 | 1.81495 | 1.83511 | 1.85625 |
| 4 | 1.56656 | 1.57782 | 1.58938 | 1.60126 | 1.61347 | 1.62603 | 1.63897 | 1.65231 | 1.66607 | 1.68028 | 1.69497 | 1.71017 | 1.72593 | 1.74228 | 1.75927 | 1.77695 | 1.79538 | 1.81463 | 1.83477 | 1.85589 |
| 5 | 1.56637 | 1.57763 | 1.58918 | 1.60106 | 1.61326 | 1.62582 | 1.63875 | 1.65208 | 1.66583 | 1.68004 | 1.69472 | 1.70991 | 1.72566 | 1.74200 | 1.75898 | 1.77665 | 1.79506 | 1.81430 | 1.83442 | 1.85553 |
| 6 | 1.56619 | 1.57744 | 1.58899 | 1.60086 | 1.61306 | 1.62561 | 1.63853 | 1.65186 | 1.66560 | 1.67980 | 1.69447 | 1.70966 | 1.72539 | 1.74172 | 1.75869 | 1.77635 | 1.79475 | 1.81397 | 1.83408 | 1.85517 |
| 7 | 1.56600 | 1.57725 | 1.58879 | 1.60065 | 1.61285 | 1.62540 | 1.63832 | 1.65163 | 1.66537 | 1.67956 | 1.69422 | 1.70940 | 1.72513 | 1.74144 | 1.75840 | 1.77605 | 1.79444 | 1.81364 | 1.83374 | 1.85481 |
| 8 | 1.56582 | 1.57706 | 1.58860 | 1.60045 | 1.61264 | 1.62518 | 1.63810 | 1.65141 | 1.66514 | 1.67932 | 1.69397 | 1.70914 | 1.72486 | 1.74117 | 1.75811 | 1.77575 | 1.79412 | 1.81332 | 1.83339 | 1.85445 |
| 9 | 1.56563 | 1.57687 | 1.58840 | 1.60025 | 1.61244 | 1.62497 | 1.63788 | 1.65118 | 1.66490 | 1.67908 | 1.69372 | 1.70888 | 1.72459 | 1.74089 | 1.75782 | 1.77545 | 1.79381 | 1.81299 | 1.83305 | 1.85409 |
| 10 | 1.56545 | 1.57668 | 1.58821 | 1.60005 | 1.61223 | 1.62476 | 1.63766 | 1.65096 | 1.66467 | 1.67884 | 1.69348 | 1.70863 | 1.72433 | 1.74061 | 1.75754 | 1.77515 | 1.79350 | 1.81266 | 1.83271 | 1.85373 |
| 11 | 1.56526 | 1.57649 | 1.58801 | 1.59985 | 1.61203 | 1.62455 | 1.63744 | 1.65073 | 1.66444 | 1.67860 | 1.69323 | 1.70837 | 1.72406 | 1.74034 | 1.75725 | 1.77485 | 1.79319 | 1.81234 | 1.83237 | 1.85337 |
| 12 | 1.56508 | 1.57630 | 1.58782 | 1.59965 | 1.61182 | 1.62434 | 1.63722 | 1.65051 | 1.66421 | 1.67836 | 1.69298 | 1.70811 | 1.72379 | 1.74006 | 1.75696 | 1.77455 | 1.79287 | 1.81201 | 1.83203 | 1.85301 |
| 13 | 1.56489 | 1.57611 | 1.58763 | 1.59945 | 1.61161 | 1.62412 | 1.63701 | 1.65028 | 1.66398 | 1.67812 | 1.69273 | 1.70786 | 1.72353 | 1.73978 | 1.75667 | 1.77425 | 1.79256 | 1.81168 | 1.83169 | 1.85265 |
| 14 | 1.56471 | 1.57592 | 1.58743 | 1.59925 | 1.61141 | 1.62391 | 1.63679 | 1.65006 | 1.66374 | 1.67788 | 1.69248 | 1.70760 | 1.72326 | 1.73951 | 1.75639 | 1.77395 | 1.79225 | 1.81136 | 1.83134 | 1.85230 |
| 15 | 1.56452 | 1.57573 | 1.58724 | 1.59905 | 1.61120 | 1.62370 | 1.63657 | 1.64983 | 1.66351 | 1.67764 | 1.69224 | 1.70734 | 1.72300 | 1.73923 | 1.75610 | 1.77365 | 1.79194 | 1.81103 | 1.83100 | 1.85194 |
| 16 | 1.56434 | 1.57554 | 1.58704 | 1.59885 | 1.61100 | 1.62349 | 1.63635 | 1.64961 | 1.66328 | 1.67740 | 1.69199 | 1.70709 | 1.72273 | 1.73896 | 1.75581 | 1.77335 | 1.79163 | 1.81071 | 1.83066 | 1.85158 |
| 17 | 1.56415 | 1.57535 | 1.58685 | 1.59866 | 1.61079 | 1.62328 | 1.63613 | 1.64938 | 1.66305 | 1.67716 | 1.69174 | 1.70683 | 1.72247 | 1.73868 | 1.75553 | 1.77305 | 1.79132 | 1.81038 | 1.83032 | 1.85122 |
| 18 | 1.56397 | 1.57516 | 1.58665 | 1.59846 | 1.61059 | 1.62307 | 1.63592 | 1.64916 | 1.66282 | 1.67692 | 1.69149 | 1.70658 | 1.72220 | 1.73841 | 1.75524 | 1.77276 | 1.79101 | 1.81006 | 1.82998 | 1.85087 |
| 19 | 1.56379 | 1.57497 | 1.58646 | 1.59826 | 1.61038 | 1.62286 | 1.63570 | 1.64894 | 1.66259 | 1.67668 | 1.69125 | 1.70632 | 1.72193 | 1.73813 | 1.75496 | 1.77246 | 1.79070 | 1.80973 | 1.82964 | 1.85051 |
| 20 | 1.56360 | 1.57479 | 1.58627 | 1.59806 | 1.61018 | 1.62265 | 1.63548 | 1.64871 | 1.66236 | 1.67644 | 1.69100 | 1.70606 | 1.72167 | 1.73786 | 1.75467 | 1.77216 | 1.79039 | 1.80941 | 1.82930 | 1.85015 |
| 21 | 1.56342 | 1.57460 | 1.58607 | 1.59786 | 1.60997 | 1.62244 | 1.63527 | 1.64849 | 1.66212 | 1.67620 | 1.69075 | 1.70581 | 1.72141 | 1.73758 | 1.75438 | 1.77186 | 1.79008 | 1.80908 | 1.82896 | 1.84980 |
| 22 | 1.56323 | 1.57441 | 1.58588 | 1.59766 | 1.60977 | 1.62223 | 1.63505 | 1.64826 | 1.66189 | 1.67597 | 1.69051 | 1.70555 | 1.72114 | 1.73731 | 1.75410 | 1.77157 | 1.78977 | 1.80876 | 1.82863 | 1.84944 |
| 23 | 1.56305 | 1.57422 | 1.58568 | 1.59746 | 1.60956 | 1.62201 | 1.63483 | 1.64804 | 1.66166 | 1.67573 | 1.69026 | 1.70530 | 1.72088 | 1.73703 | 1.75381 | 1.77127 | 1.78946 | 1.80844 | 1.82829 | 1.84909 |
| 24 | 1.56287 | 1.57403 | 1.58549 | 1.59726 | 1.60936 | 1.62180 | 1.63462 | 1.64782 | 1.66143 | 1.67549 | 1.69002 | 1.70504 | 1.72061 | 1.73676 | 1.75353 | 1.77097 | 1.78915 | 1.80811 | 1.82795 | 1.84873 |
| 25 | 1.56268 | 1.57384 | 1.58530 | 1.59706 | 1.60915 | 1.62159 | 1.63440 | 1.64759 | 1.66120 | 1.67525 | 1.68977 | 1.70479 | 1.72035 | 1.73648 | 1.75324 | 1.77068 | 1.78884 | 1.80779 | 1.82761 | 1.84838 |
| 26 | 1.56250 | 1.57365 | 1.58510 | 1.59686 | 1.60895 | 1.62138 | 1.63418 | 1.64737 | 1.66097 | 1.67501 | 1.68952 | 1.70453 | 1.72008 | 1.73621 | 1.75296 | 1.77038 | 1.78853 | 1.80747 | 1.82727 | 1.84802 |
| 27 | 1.56232 | 1.57347 | 1.58491 | 1.59666 | 1.60875 | 1.62117 | 1.63397 | 1.64715 | 1.66074 | 1.67478 | 1.68928 | 1.70428 | 1.71982 | 1.73594 | 1.75267 | 1.77008 | 1.78822 | 1.80715 | 1.82694 | 1.84767 |
| 28 | 1.56213 | 1.57328 | 1.58472 | 1.59647 | 1.60854 | 1.62096 | 1.63375 | 1.64692 | 1.66051 | 1.67454 | 1.68903 | 1.70403 | 1.71956 | 1.73566 | 1.75239 | 1.76979 | 1.78791 | 1.80682 | 1.82660 | 1.84732 |
| 29 | 1.56195 | 1.57309 | 1.58452 | 1.59627 | 1.60834 | 1.62075 | 1.63353 | 1.64670 | 1.66028 | 1.67430 | 1.68879 | 1.70377 | 1.71929 | 1.73539 | 1.75211 | 1.76949 | 1.78760 | 1.80650 | 1.82626 | 1.84696 |
| 30 | 1.56177 | 1.57290 | 1.58433 | 1.59607 | 1.60813 | 1.62054 | 1.63332 | 1.64648 | 1.66005 | 1.67406 | 1.68854 | 1.70352 | 1.71903 | 1.73512 | 1.75182 | 1.76920 | 1.78729 | 1.80618 | 1.82592 | 1.84661 |
| 31 | 1.56158 | 1.57271 | 1.58414 | 1.59587 | 1.60793 | 1.62033 | 1.63310 | 1.64626 | 1.65982 | 1.67383 | 1.68830 | 1.70326 | 1.71877 | 1.73484 | 1.75154 | 1.76890 | 1.78699 | 1.80586 | 1.82559 | 1.84626 |
| 32 | 1.56140 | 1.57253 | 1.58395 | 1.59567 | 1.60773 | 1.62012 | 1.63289 | 1.64603 | 1.65959 | 1.67359 | 1.68805 | 1.70301 | 1.71850 | 1.73457 | 1.75125 | 1.76861 | 1.78668 | 1.80554 | 1.82525 | 1.84590 |
| 33 | 1.56122 | 1.57234 | 1.58375 | 1.59548 | 1.60752 | 1.61991 | 1.63267 | 1.64581 | 1.65936 | 1.67335 | 1.68781 | 1.70276 | 1.71824 | 1.73430 | 1.75097 | 1.76831 | 1.78637 | 1.80522 | 1.82492 | 1.84555 |
| 34 | 1.56103 | 1.57215 | 1.58356 | 1.59528 | 1.60732 | 1.61970 | 1.63245 | 1.64559 | 1.65913 | 1.67311 | 1.68756 | 1.70250 | 1.71798 | 1.73403 | 1.75069 | 1.76802 | 1.78606 | 1.80490 | 1.82458 | 1.84520 |
| 35 | 1.56085 | 1.57196 | 1.58337 | 1.59508 | 1.60712 | 1.61950 | 1.63224 | 1.64537 | 1.65890 | 1.67288 | 1.68732 | 1.70225 | 1.71772 | 1.73375 | 1.75041 | 1.76772 | 1.78576 | 1.80457 | 1.82424 | 1.84485 |
| 36 | 1.56067 | 1.57178 | 1.58317 | 1.59488 | 1.60691 | 1.61929 | 1.63202 | 1.64514 | 1.65868 | 1.67264 | 1.68707 | 1.70200 | 1.71745 | 1.73348 | 1.75012 | 1.76743 | 1.78545 | 1.80425 | 1.82391 | 1.84450 |
| 37 | 1.56048 | 1.57159 | 1.58298 | 1.59468 | 1.60671 | 1.61908 | 1.63181 | 1.64492 | 1.65845 | 1.67240 | 1.68683 | 1.70174 | 1.71719 | 1.73321 | 1.74984 | 1.76713 | 1.78514 | 1.80393 | 1.82357 | 1.84414 |
| 38 | 1.56030 | 1.57140 | 1.58279 | 1.59449 | 1.60651 | 1.61887 | 1.63159 | 1.64470 | 1.65822 | 1.67217 | 1.68658 | 1.70149 | 1.71693 | 1.73294 | 1.74956 | 1.76684 | 1.78484 | 1.80361 | 1.82324 | 1.84379 |
| 39 | 1.56012 | 1.57121 | 1.58260 | 1.59429 | 1.60630 | 1.61866 | 1.63138 | 1.64448 | 1.65799 | 1.67193 | 1.68634 | 1.70124 | 1.71667 | 1.73267 | 1.74928 | 1.76655 | 1.78453 | 1.80329 | 1.82290 | 1.84344 |
| 40 | 1.55994 | 1.57103 | 1.58241 | 1.59409 | 1.60610 | 1.61845 | 1.63116 | 1.64426 | 1.65776 | 1.67170 | 1.68609 | 1.70099 | 1.71641 | 1.73239 | 1.74899 | 1.76625 | 1.78423 | 1.80297 | 1.82257 | 1.84309 |
| 41 | 1.55975 | 1.57084 | 1.58221 | 1.59389 | 1.60590 | 1.61824 | 1.63095 | 1.64404 | 1.65753 | 1.67146 | 1.68585 | 1.70073 | 1.71614 | 1.73212 | 1.74871 | 1.76596 | 1.78392 | 1.80266 | 1.82224 | 1.84274 |
| 42 | 1.55957 | 1.57065 | 1.58202 | 1.59370 | 1.60569 | 1.61803 | 1.63073 | 1.64381 | 1.65730 | 1.67122 | 1.68561 | 1.70048 | 1.71588 | 1.73185 | 1.74843 | 1.76567 | 1.78361 | 1.80234 | 1.82190 | 1.84239 |
| 43 | 1.55939 | 1.57046 | 1.58183 | 1.59350 | 1.60549 | 1.61782 | 1.63052 | 1.64359 | 1.65707 | 1.67099 | 1.68536 | 1.70023 | 1.71562 | 1.73158 | 1.74815 | 1.76537 | 1.78331 | 1.80202 | 1.82157 | 1.84204 |
| 44 | 1.55921 | 1.57028 | 1.58164 | 1.59330 | 1.60529 | 1.61762 | 1.63030 | 1.64337 | 1.65685 | 1.67075 | 1.68512 | 1.69998 | 1.71536 | 1.73131 | 1.74787 | 1.76508 | 1.78300 | 1.80170 | 1.82124 | 1.84169 |
| 45 | 1.55903 | 1.57009 | 1.58145 | 1.59311 | 1.60509 | 1.61741 | 1.63009 | 1.64315 | 1.65662 | 1.67052 | 1.68488 | 1.69972 | 1.71510 | 1.73104 | 1.74759 | 1.76479 | 1.78270 | 1.80138 | 1.82090 | 1.84134 |
| 46 | 1.55884 | 1.56990 | 1.58125 | 1.59291 | 1.60488 | 1.61720 | 1.62987 | 1.64293 | 1.65639 | 1.67028 | 1.68463 | 1.69947 | 1.71484 | 1.73077 | 1.74730 | 1.76449 | 1.78239 | 1.80106 | 1.82057 | 1.84100 |
| 47 | 1.55866 | 1.56972 | 1.58106 | 1.59271 | 1.60468 | 1.61699 | 1.62966 | 1.64271 | 1.65616 | 1.67005 | 1.68439 | 1.69922 | 1.71458 | 1.73050 | 1.74702 | 1.76420 | 1.78209 | 1.80075 | 1.82024 | 1.84065 |
| 48 | 1.55848 | 1.56953 | 1.58087 | 1.59251 | 1.60448 | 1.61678 | 1.62945 | 1.64249 | 1.65594 | 1.66981 | 1.68415 | 1.69897 | 1.71432 | 1.73023 | 1.74674 | 1.76391 | 1.78178 | 1.80043 | 1.81991 | 1.84030 |
| 49 | 1.55830 | 1.56934 | 1.58068 | 1.59232 | 1.60428 | 1.61658 | 1.62923 | 1.64227 | 1.65571 | 1.66958 | 1.68390 | 1.69872 | 1.71406 | 1.72996 | 1.74646 | 1.76362 | 1.78148 | 1.80011 | 1.81957 | 1.83995 |
| 50 | 1.55812 | 1.56916 | 1.58049 | 1.59212 | 1.60408 | 1.61637 | 1.62902 | 1.64205 | 1.65548 | 1.66934 | 1.68366 | 1.69847 | 1.71380 | 1.72969 | 1.74618 | 1.76333 | 1.78118 | 1.79979 | 1.81924 | 1.83960 |
| 51 | 1.55793 | 1.56897 | 1.58030 | 1.59192 | 1.60387 | 1.61616 | 1.62880 | 1.64183 | 1.65525 | 1.66911 | 1.68342 | 1.69822 | 1.71354 | 1.72942 | 1.74590 | 1.76304 | 1.78087 | 1.79948 | 1.81891 | 1.83926 |
| 52 | 1.55775 | 1.56879 | 1.58011 | 1.59173 | 1.60367 | 1.61595 | 1.62859 | 1.64161 | 1.65503 | 1.66887 | 1.68318 | 1.69797 | 1.71328 | 1.72915 | 1.74562 | 1.76274 | 1.78057 | 1.79916 | 1.81858 | 1.83891 |
| 53 | 1.55757 | 1.56860 | 1.57991 | 1.59153 | 1.60347 | 1.61574 | 1.62838 | 1.64139 | 1.65480 | 1.66864 | 1.68293 | 1.69772 | 1.71302 | 1.72888 | 1.74534 | 1.76245 | 1.78027 | 1.79884 | 1.81825 | 1.83856 |
| 54 | 1.55739 | 1.56841 | 1.57972 | 1.59134 | 1.60327 | 1.61554 | 1.62816 | 1.64117 | 1.65457 | 1.66840 | 1.68269 | 1.69746 | 1.71276 | 1.72861 | 1.74506 | 1.76216 | 1.77996 | 1.79852 | 1.81792 | 1.83822 |
| 55 | 1.55721 | 1.56823 | 1.57953 | 1.59114 | 1.60307 | 1.61533 | 1.62795 | 1.64095 | 1.65434 | 1.66817 | 1.68245 | 1.69721 | 1.71250 | 1.72834 | 1.74478 | 1.76187 | 1.77966 | 1.79821 | 1.81759 | 1.83787 |
| 56 | 1.55703 | 1.56804 | 1.57934 | 1.59094 | 1.60286 | 1.61512 | 1.62774 | 1.64073 | 1.65412 | 1.66794 | 1.68221 | 1.69696 | 1.71224 | 1.72807 | 1.74450 | 1.76158 | 1.77936 | 1.79790 | 1.81726 | 1.83752 |
| 57 | 1.55685 | 1.56786 | 1.57915 | 1.59075 | 1.60266 | 1.61492 | 1.62752 | 1.64051 | 1.65389 | 1.66770 | 1.68197 | 1.69671 | 1.71198 | 1.72780 | 1.74423 | 1.76129 | 1.77906 | 1.79758 | 1.81693 | 1.83718 |
| 58 | 1.55666 | 1.56767 | 1.57896 | 1.59055 | 1.60246 | 1.61471 | 1.62731 | 1.64029 | 1.65366 | 1.66747 | 1.68172 | 1.69646 | 1.71172 | 1.72754 | 1.74395 | 1.76100 | 1.77875 | 1.79727 | 1.81660 | 1.83683 |
| 59 | 1.55648 | 1.56748 | 1.57877 | 1.59036 | 1.60226 | 1.61450 | 1.62709 | 1.64007 | 1.65344 | 1.66723 | 1.68148 | 1.69621 | 1.71146 | 1.72727 | 1.74367 | 1.76071 | 1.77845 | 1.79695 | 1.81627 | 1.83649 |
| 60 | 1.55630 | 1.56730 | 1.57858 | 1.59016 | 1.60206 | 1.61429 | 1.62688 | 1.63985 | 1.65321 | 1.66700 | 1.68124 | 1.69596 | 1.71120 | 1.72700 | 1.74339 | 1.76042 | 1.77815 | 1.79663 | 1.81594 | 1.83614 |

SECONDS OF TIME OR ARC

# Table X Diurnal Motion Logarithms, 0 to 2 Hours/Degrees

SECONDS OF TIME OR ARC / DEGREES or HOURS and MINUTES

| Sec | 0° 59' | 0° 58' | 0° 57' | 0° 56' | 0° 55' | 0° 54' | 0° 53' | 0° 52' | 0° 51' | 0° 50' | 0° 49' | 0° 48' | 0° 47' | 0° 46' | 0° 45' | 0° 44' | 0° 43' | 0° 42' | 0° 41' | 0° 40' |
|---|---|---|---|---|---|---|---|---|---|---|---|---|---|---|---|---|---|---|---|---|
| 0 | 1.38751 | 1.39493 | 1.40249 | 1.41017 | 1.41800 | 1.42597 | 1.43409 | 1.44236 | 1.45079 | 1.45939 | 1.46817 | 1.47712 | 1.48626 | 1.49560 | 1.50515 | 1.51491 | 1.52489 | 1.53511 | 1.54558 | 1.55630 |
| 1 | 1.38739 | 1.39481 | 1.40236 | 1.41005 | 1.41787 | 1.42583 | 1.43395 | 1.44222 | 1.45065 | 1.45925 | 1.46802 | 1.47697 | 1.48611 | 1.49545 | 1.50499 | 1.51475 | 1.52473 | 1.53494 | 1.54540 | 1.55612 |
| 2 | 1.38727 | 1.39468 | 1.40223 | 1.40992 | 1.41774 | 1.42570 | 1.43381 | 1.44208 | 1.45051 | 1.45910 | 1.46787 | 1.47682 | 1.48596 | 1.49529 | 1.50483 | 1.51458 | 1.52456 | 1.53477 | 1.54523 | 1.55594 |
| 3 | 1.38714 | 1.39456 | 1.40211 | 1.40979 | 1.41761 | 1.42557 | 1.43368 | 1.44194 | 1.45037 | 1.45896 | 1.46772 | 1.47667 | 1.48580 | 1.49513 | 1.50467 | 1.51442 | 1.52439 | 1.53460 | 1.54505 | 1.55576 |
| 4 | 1.38702 | 1.39444 | 1.40198 | 1.40966 | 1.41747 | 1.42543 | 1.43354 | 1.44180 | 1.45022 | 1.45881 | 1.46758 | 1.47652 | 1.48565 | 1.49498 | 1.50451 | 1.51425 | 1.52422 | 1.53442 | 1.54487 | 1.55558 |
| 5 | 1.38690 | 1.39431 | 1.40185 | 1.40953 | 1.41734 | 1.42530 | 1.43340 | 1.44166 | 1.45008 | 1.45867 | 1.46743 | 1.47637 | 1.48550 | 1.49482 | 1.50435 | 1.51409 | 1.52405 | 1.53425 | 1.54470 | 1.55540 |
| 6 | 1.38678 | 1.39419 | 1.40173 | 1.40940 | 1.41721 | 1.42517 | 1.43327 | 1.44152 | 1.44994 | 1.45852 | 1.46728 | 1.47622 | 1.48534 | 1.49466 | 1.50419 | 1.51392 | 1.52389 | 1.53408 | 1.54452 | 1.55522 |
| 7 | 1.38665 | 1.39406 | 1.40160 | 1.40927 | 1.41708 | 1.42503 | 1.43313 | 1.44139 | 1.44980 | 1.45838 | 1.46713 | 1.47607 | 1.48519 | 1.49450 | 1.50403 | 1.51376 | 1.52372 | 1.53391 | 1.54434 | 1.55504 |
| 8 | 1.38653 | 1.39394 | 1.40147 | 1.40914 | 1.41695 | 1.42490 | 1.43300 | 1.44125 | 1.44966 | 1.45824 | 1.46699 | 1.47592 | 1.48503 | 1.49435 | 1.50387 | 1.51360 | 1.52355 | 1.53374 | 1.54417 | 1.55486 |
| 9 | 1.38641 | 1.39381 | 1.40135 | 1.40901 | 1.41682 | 1.42476 | 1.43286 | 1.44111 | 1.44952 | 1.45809 | 1.46684 | 1.47577 | 1.48488 | 1.49419 | 1.50370 | 1.51343 | 1.52338 | 1.53356 | 1.54399 | 1.55468 |
| 10 | 1.38629 | 1.39369 | 1.40122 | 1.40888 | 1.41669 | 1.42463 | 1.43272 | 1.44097 | 1.44938 | 1.45795 | 1.46669 | 1.47562 | 1.48473 | 1.49403 | 1.50354 | 1.51327 | 1.52321 | 1.53339 | 1.54382 | 1.55450 |
| 11 | 1.38616 | 1.39356 | 1.40109 | 1.40875 | 1.41655 | 1.42450 | 1.43259 | 1.44083 | 1.44923 | 1.45780 | 1.46654 | 1.47547 | 1.48457 | 1.49388 | 1.50338 | 1.51310 | 1.52305 | 1.53322 | 1.54364 | 1.55432 |
| 12 | 1.38604 | 1.39344 | 1.40097 | 1.40863 | 1.41642 | 1.42436 | 1.43245 | 1.44069 | 1.44909 | 1.45766 | 1.46640 | 1.47532 | 1.48442 | 1.49372 | 1.50322 | 1.51294 | 1.52288 | 1.53305 | 1.54347 | 1.55414 |
| 13 | 1.38592 | 1.39332 | 1.40084 | 1.40850 | 1.41629 | 1.42423 | 1.43231 | 1.44055 | 1.44895 | 1.45751 | 1.46625 | 1.47517 | 1.48427 | 1.49356 | 1.50306 | 1.51278 | 1.52271 | 1.53288 | 1.54329 | 1.55396 |
| 14 | 1.38580 | 1.39319 | 1.40071 | 1.40837 | 1.41616 | 1.42410 | 1.43218 | 1.44041 | 1.44881 | 1.45737 | 1.46610 | 1.47502 | 1.48411 | 1.49341 | 1.50290 | 1.51261 | 1.52254 | 1.53271 | 1.54311 | 1.55378 |
| 15 | 1.38567 | 1.39307 | 1.40059 | 1.40824 | 1.41603 | 1.42396 | 1.43204 | 1.44028 | 1.44867 | 1.45723 | 1.46596 | 1.47487 | 1.48396 | 1.49325 | 1.50274 | 1.51245 | 1.52238 | 1.53254 | 1.54294 | 1.55360 |
| 16 | 1.38555 | 1.39294 | 1.40046 | 1.40811 | 1.41590 | 1.42383 | 1.43191 | 1.44014 | 1.44853 | 1.45708 | 1.46581 | 1.47472 | 1.48381 | 1.49309 | 1.50258 | 1.51229 | 1.52221 | 1.53236 | 1.54276 | 1.55342 |
| 17 | 1.38543 | 1.39282 | 1.40033 | 1.40798 | 1.41577 | 1.42370 | 1.43177 | 1.44000 | 1.44839 | 1.45694 | 1.46566 | 1.47457 | 1.48365 | 1.49294 | 1.50242 | 1.51212 | 1.52204 | 1.53219 | 1.54259 | 1.55324 |
| 18 | 1.38531 | 1.39269 | 1.40021 | 1.40785 | 1.41564 | 1.42356 | 1.43164 | 1.43986 | 1.44825 | 1.45679 | 1.46552 | 1.47442 | 1.48350 | 1.49278 | 1.50226 | 1.51196 | 1.52187 | 1.53202 | 1.54241 | 1.55306 |
| 19 | 1.38519 | 1.39257 | 1.40008 | 1.40773 | 1.41551 | 1.42343 | 1.43150 | 1.43972 | 1.44811 | 1.45665 | 1.46537 | 1.47427 | 1.48335 | 1.49263 | 1.50210 | 1.51180 | 1.52171 | 1.53185 | 1.54224 | 1.55288 |
| 20 | 1.38506 | 1.39245 | 1.39996 | 1.40760 | 1.41538 | 1.42330 | 1.43136 | 1.43958 | 1.44796 | 1.45651 | 1.46522 | 1.47412 | 1.48320 | 1.49247 | 1.50194 | 1.51163 | 1.52154 | 1.53168 | 1.54206 | 1.55270 |
| 21 | 1.38494 | 1.39232 | 1.39983 | 1.40747 | 1.41524 | 1.42316 | 1.43123 | 1.43945 | 1.44782 | 1.45636 | 1.46508 | 1.47397 | 1.48304 | 1.49231 | 1.50179 | 1.51147 | 1.52137 | 1.53151 | 1.54189 | 1.55252 |
| 22 | 1.38482 | 1.39220 | 1.39970 | 1.40734 | 1.41511 | 1.42303 | 1.43109 | 1.43931 | 1.44768 | 1.45622 | 1.46493 | 1.47382 | 1.48289 | 1.49216 | 1.50163 | 1.51131 | 1.52121 | 1.53134 | 1.54171 | 1.55234 |
| 23 | 1.38470 | 1.39207 | 1.39958 | 1.40721 | 1.41498 | 1.42290 | 1.43096 | 1.43917 | 1.44754 | 1.45608 | 1.46478 | 1.47367 | 1.48274 | 1.49200 | 1.50147 | 1.51114 | 1.52104 | 1.53117 | 1.54154 | 1.55216 |
| 24 | 1.38458 | 1.39195 | 1.39945 | 1.40708 | 1.41485 | 1.42276 | 1.43082 | 1.43903 | 1.44740 | 1.45593 | 1.46464 | 1.47352 | 1.48258 | 1.49184 | 1.50131 | 1.51098 | 1.52087 | 1.53100 | 1.54136 | 1.55198 |
| 25 | 1.38445 | 1.39183 | 1.39932 | 1.40696 | 1.41472 | 1.42263 | 1.43069 | 1.43889 | 1.44726 | 1.45579 | 1.46449 | 1.47337 | 1.48243 | 1.49169 | 1.50115 | 1.51082 | 1.52071 | 1.53083 | 1.54119 | 1.55180 |
| 26 | 1.38433 | 1.39170 | 1.39920 | 1.40683 | 1.41459 | 1.42250 | 1.43055 | 1.43876 | 1.44712 | 1.45564 | 1.46434 | 1.47322 | 1.48228 | 1.49153 | 1.50099 | 1.51065 | 1.52054 | 1.53066 | 1.54101 | 1.55162 |
| 27 | 1.38421 | 1.39158 | 1.39907 | 1.40670 | 1.41446 | 1.42236 | 1.43041 | 1.43862 | 1.44698 | 1.45550 | 1.46420 | 1.47307 | 1.48213 | 1.49138 | 1.50083 | 1.51049 | 1.52037 | 1.53048 | 1.54084 | 1.55144 |
| 28 | 1.38409 | 1.39145 | 1.39895 | 1.40657 | 1.41433 | 1.42223 | 1.43028 | 1.43848 | 1.44684 | 1.45536 | 1.46405 | 1.47292 | 1.48197 | 1.49122 | 1.50067 | 1.51033 | 1.52021 | 1.53031 | 1.54066 | 1.55127 |
| 29 | 1.38397 | 1.39133 | 1.39882 | 1.40644 | 1.41420 | 1.42210 | 1.43014 | 1.43834 | 1.44670 | 1.45521 | 1.46390 | 1.47277 | 1.48182 | 1.49107 | 1.50051 | 1.51017 | 1.52004 | 1.53014 | 1.54049 | 1.55109 |
| 30 | 1.38385 | 1.39121 | 1.39869 | 1.40631 | 1.41407 | 1.42197 | 1.43001 | 1.43820 | 1.44656 | 1.45507 | 1.46376 | 1.47262 | 1.48167 | 1.49091 | 1.50035 | 1.51000 | 1.51987 | 1.52997 | 1.54031 | 1.55091 |
| 31 | 1.38372 | 1.39108 | 1.39857 | 1.40619 | 1.41394 | 1.42183 | 1.42987 | 1.43807 | 1.44641 | 1.45493 | 1.46361 | 1.47247 | 1.48152 | 1.49075 | 1.50019 | 1.50984 | 1.51971 | 1.52980 | 1.54014 | 1.55073 |
| 32 | 1.38360 | 1.39096 | 1.39844 | 1.40606 | 1.41381 | 1.42170 | 1.42974 | 1.43793 | 1.44627 | 1.45478 | 1.46346 | 1.47232 | 1.48136 | 1.49060 | 1.50003 | 1.50968 | 1.51954 | 1.52963 | 1.53997 | 1.55055 |
| 33 | 1.38348 | 1.39084 | 1.39832 | 1.40593 | 1.41368 | 1.42157 | 1.42960 | 1.43779 | 1.44613 | 1.45464 | 1.46332 | 1.47217 | 1.48121 | 1.49044 | 1.49987 | 1.50951 | 1.51937 | 1.52946 | 1.53979 | 1.55037 |
| 34 | 1.38336 | 1.39071 | 1.39819 | 1.40580 | 1.41355 | 1.42144 | 1.42947 | 1.43765 | 1.44599 | 1.45450 | 1.46317 | 1.47202 | 1.48106 | 1.49029 | 1.49972 | 1.50935 | 1.51921 | 1.52929 | 1.53962 | 1.55019 |
| 35 | 1.38324 | 1.39059 | 1.39807 | 1.40567 | 1.41342 | 1.42130 | 1.42933 | 1.43751 | 1.44585 | 1.45436 | 1.46303 | 1.47188 | 1.48091 | 1.49013 | 1.49956 | 1.50919 | 1.51904 | 1.52912 | 1.53944 | 1.55001 |
| 36 | 1.38312 | 1.39046 | 1.39794 | 1.40555 | 1.41329 | 1.42117 | 1.42920 | 1.43738 | 1.44571 | 1.45421 | 1.46288 | 1.47173 | 1.48076 | 1.48998 | 1.49940 | 1.50903 | 1.51888 | 1.52895 | 1.53927 | 1.54984 |
| 37 | 1.38299 | 1.39034 | 1.39781 | 1.40542 | 1.41316 | 1.42104 | 1.42906 | 1.43724 | 1.44557 | 1.45407 | 1.46273 | 1.47158 | 1.48060 | 1.48982 | 1.49924 | 1.50887 | 1.51871 | 1.52878 | 1.53910 | 1.54966 |
| 38 | 1.38287 | 1.39022 | 1.39769 | 1.40529 | 1.41303 | 1.42090 | 1.42893 | 1.43710 | 1.44543 | 1.45393 | 1.46259 | 1.47143 | 1.48045 | 1.48967 | 1.49908 | 1.50870 | 1.51854 | 1.52861 | 1.53892 | 1.54948 |
| 39 | 1.38275 | 1.39009 | 1.39756 | 1.40516 | 1.41290 | 1.42077 | 1.42879 | 1.43696 | 1.44529 | 1.45378 | 1.46244 | 1.47128 | 1.48030 | 1.48951 | 1.49892 | 1.50854 | 1.51838 | 1.52844 | 1.53875 | 1.54930 |
| 40 | 1.38263 | 1.38997 | 1.39744 | 1.40503 | 1.41277 | 1.42064 | 1.42866 | 1.43683 | 1.44515 | 1.45364 | 1.46230 | 1.47113 | 1.48015 | 1.48936 | 1.49876 | 1.50838 | 1.51821 | 1.52827 | 1.53857 | 1.54912 |
| 41 | 1.38251 | 1.38985 | 1.39731 | 1.40491 | 1.41264 | 1.42051 | 1.42852 | 1.43669 | 1.44501 | 1.45350 | 1.46215 | 1.47098 | 1.48000 | 1.48920 | 1.49860 | 1.50822 | 1.51805 | 1.52810 | 1.53840 | 1.54895 |
| 42 | 1.38239 | 1.38972 | 1.39719 | 1.40478 | 1.41251 | 1.42038 | 1.42839 | 1.43655 | 1.44487 | 1.45335 | 1.46201 | 1.47083 | 1.47984 | 1.48905 | 1.49845 | 1.50805 | 1.51788 | 1.52793 | 1.53823 | 1.54877 |
| 43 | 1.38227 | 1.38960 | 1.39706 | 1.40465 | 1.41238 | 1.42024 | 1.42825 | 1.43641 | 1.44473 | 1.45321 | 1.46186 | 1.47068 | 1.47969 | 1.48889 | 1.49829 | 1.50789 | 1.51772 | 1.52777 | 1.53805 | 1.54859 |
| 44 | 1.38215 | 1.38948 | 1.39694 | 1.40452 | 1.41225 | 1.42011 | 1.42812 | 1.43628 | 1.44459 | 1.45307 | 1.46171 | 1.47053 | 1.47954 | 1.48874 | 1.49813 | 1.50773 | 1.51755 | 1.52760 | 1.53788 | 1.54841 |
| 45 | 1.38202 | 1.38935 | 1.39681 | 1.40440 | 1.41212 | 1.41998 | 1.42798 | 1.43614 | 1.44445 | 1.45293 | 1.46157 | 1.47039 | 1.47939 | 1.48858 | 1.49797 | 1.50757 | 1.51738 | 1.52743 | 1.53771 | 1.54823 |
| 46 | 1.38190 | 1.38923 | 1.39669 | 1.40427 | 1.41199 | 1.41985 | 1.42785 | 1.43600 | 1.44431 | 1.45278 | 1.46142 | 1.47024 | 1.47924 | 1.48843 | 1.49781 | 1.50741 | 1.51722 | 1.52726 | 1.53753 | 1.54806 |
| 47 | 1.38178 | 1.38911 | 1.39656 | 1.40414 | 1.41186 | 1.41971 | 1.42771 | 1.43587 | 1.44417 | 1.45264 | 1.46128 | 1.47009 | 1.47909 | 1.48827 | 1.49766 | 1.50725 | 1.51705 | 1.52709 | 1.53736 | 1.54788 |
| 48 | 1.38166 | 1.38899 | 1.39643 | 1.40401 | 1.41173 | 1.41958 | 1.42758 | 1.43573 | 1.44403 | 1.45250 | 1.46113 | 1.46994 | 1.47893 | 1.48812 | 1.49750 | 1.50708 | 1.51689 | 1.52692 | 1.53719 | 1.54770 |
| 49 | 1.38154 | 1.38886 | 1.39631 | 1.40389 | 1.41160 | 1.41945 | 1.42745 | 1.43559 | 1.44389 | 1.45236 | 1.46099 | 1.46979 | 1.47878 | 1.48796 | 1.49734 | 1.50692 | 1.51672 | 1.52675 | 1.53701 | 1.54752 |
| 50 | 1.38142 | 1.38874 | 1.39618 | 1.40376 | 1.41147 | 1.41932 | 1.42731 | 1.43545 | 1.44375 | 1.45221 | 1.46084 | 1.46965 | 1.47863 | 1.48781 | 1.49718 | 1.50676 | 1.51656 | 1.52658 | 1.53684 | 1.54735 |
| 51 | 1.38130 | 1.38862 | 1.39606 | 1.40363 | 1.41134 | 1.41919 | 1.42718 | 1.43532 | 1.44361 | 1.45207 | 1.46070 | 1.46950 | 1.47848 | 1.48765 | 1.49702 | 1.50660 | 1.51639 | 1.52641 | 1.53667 | 1.54717 |
| 52 | 1.38118 | 1.38849 | 1.39593 | 1.40350 | 1.41121 | 1.41905 | 1.42704 | 1.43518 | 1.44347 | 1.45193 | 1.46055 | 1.46935 | 1.47833 | 1.48750 | 1.49687 | 1.50644 | 1.51623 | 1.52624 | 1.53649 | 1.54699 |
| 53 | 1.38106 | 1.38837 | 1.39581 | 1.40338 | 1.41108 | 1.41892 | 1.42691 | 1.43504 | 1.44333 | 1.45179 | 1.46041 | 1.46920 | 1.47818 | 1.48734 | 1.49671 | 1.50628 | 1.51606 | 1.52607 | 1.53632 | 1.54682 |
| 54 | 1.38094 | 1.38825 | 1.39568 | 1.40325 | 1.41095 | 1.41879 | 1.42677 | 1.43491 | 1.44320 | 1.45164 | 1.46026 | 1.46905 | 1.47803 | 1.48719 | 1.49655 | 1.50612 | 1.51590 | 1.52591 | 1.53615 | 1.54664 |
| 55 | 1.38081 | 1.38812 | 1.39556 | 1.40312 | 1.41082 | 1.41866 | 1.42664 | 1.43477 | 1.44306 | 1.45150 | 1.46012 | 1.46891 | 1.47788 | 1.48704 | 1.49639 | 1.50595 | 1.51573 | 1.52574 | 1.53598 | 1.54646 |
| 56 | 1.38069 | 1.38800 | 1.39543 | 1.40300 | 1.41069 | 1.41853 | 1.42651 | 1.43463 | 1.44292 | 1.45136 | 1.45997 | 1.46876 | 1.47772 | 1.48688 | 1.49623 | 1.50579 | 1.51557 | 1.52557 | 1.53580 | 1.54629 |
| 57 | 1.38057 | 1.38788 | 1.39531 | 1.40287 | 1.41056 | 1.41839 | 1.42637 | 1.43450 | 1.44278 | 1.45122 | 1.45983 | 1.46861 | 1.47757 | 1.48673 | 1.49608 | 1.50563 | 1.51540 | 1.52540 | 1.53563 | 1.54611 |
| 58 | 1.38045 | 1.38776 | 1.39518 | 1.40274 | 1.41043 | 1.41826 | 1.42624 | 1.43436 | 1.44264 | 1.45108 | 1.45968 | 1.46846 | 1.47742 | 1.48657 | 1.49592 | 1.50547 | 1.51524 | 1.52523 | 1.53546 | 1.54593 |
| 59 | 1.38033 | 1.38763 | 1.39506 | 1.40261 | 1.41030 | 1.41813 | 1.42610 | 1.43422 | 1.44250 | 1.45093 | 1.45954 | 1.46831 | 1.47727 | 1.48642 | 1.49576 | 1.50531 | 1.51507 | 1.52506 | 1.53529 | 1.54576 |
| 60 | 1.38021 | 1.38751 | 1.39493 | 1.40249 | 1.41017 | 1.41800 | 1.42597 | 1.43409 | 1.44236 | 1.45079 | 1.45939 | 1.46817 | 1.47712 | 1.48626 | 1.49560 | 1.50515 | 1.51491 | 1.52489 | 1.53511 | 1.54558 |

SECONDS OF TIME OR ARC

# Table X Diurnal Motion Logarithms, 0 to 2 Hours/Degrees

DEGREES or HOURS and MINUTES — SECONDS OF TIME OR ARC

| Sec | 1°19' | 1°18' | 1°17' | 1°16' | 1°15' | 1°14' | 1°13' | 1°12' | 1°11' | 1°10' | 1°9' | 1°8' | 1°7' | 1°6' | 1°5' | 1°4' | 1°3' | 1°2' | 1°1' | 1°0' |
|---|---|---|---|---|---|---|---|---|---|---|---|---|---|---|---|---|---|---|---|---|
| 0 | 1.26074 | 1.26627 | 1.27187 | 1.27755 | 1.28330 | 1.28913 | 1.29504 | 1.30103 | 1.30710 | 1.31326 | 1.31951 | 1.32585 | 1.33229 | 1.33882 | 1.34545 | 1.35218 | 1.35902 | 1.36597 | 1.37303 | 1.38021 |
| 1 | 1.26064 | 1.26618 | 1.27178 | 1.27745 | 1.28320 | 1.28903 | 1.29494 | 1.30093 | 1.30700 | 1.31316 | 1.31941 | 1.32575 | 1.33218 | 1.33871 | 1.34534 | 1.35207 | 1.35891 | 1.36585 | 1.37291 | 1.38009 |
| 2 | 1.26055 | 1.26608 | 1.27168 | 1.27736 | 1.28311 | 1.28894 | 1.29484 | 1.30083 | 1.30690 | 1.31306 | 1.31930 | 1.32564 | 1.33207 | 1.33860 | 1.34523 | 1.35196 | 1.35879 | 1.36574 | 1.37280 | 1.37997 |
| 3 | 1.26046 | 1.26599 | 1.27159 | 1.27726 | 1.28301 | 1.28884 | 1.29474 | 1.30073 | 1.30680 | 1.31295 | 1.31920 | 1.32553 | 1.33196 | 1.33849 | 1.34512 | 1.35184 | 1.35868 | 1.36562 | 1.37268 | 1.37985 |
| 4 | 1.26037 | 1.26590 | 1.27150 | 1.27717 | 1.28292 | 1.28874 | 1.29464 | 1.30063 | 1.30670 | 1.31285 | 1.31909 | 1.32543 | 1.33186 | 1.33838 | 1.34500 | 1.35173 | 1.35856 | 1.36550 | 1.37256 | 1.37973 |
| 5 | 1.26028 | 1.26580 | 1.27140 | 1.27707 | 1.28282 | 1.28864 | 1.29454 | 1.30053 | 1.30659 | 1.31275 | 1.31899 | 1.32532 | 1.33175 | 1.33827 | 1.34489 | 1.35162 | 1.35845 | 1.36539 | 1.37244 | 1.37961 |
| 6 | 1.26019 | 1.26571 | 1.27131 | 1.27698 | 1.28272 | 1.28854 | 1.29445 | 1.30043 | 1.30649 | 1.31264 | 1.31888 | 1.32522 | 1.33164 | 1.33816 | 1.34478 | 1.35150 | 1.35833 | 1.36527 | 1.37232 | 1.37949 |
| 7 | 1.26009 | 1.26562 | 1.27121 | 1.27688 | 1.28263 | 1.28845 | 1.29435 | 1.30033 | 1.30639 | 1.31254 | 1.31878 | 1.32511 | 1.33153 | 1.33805 | 1.34467 | 1.35139 | 1.35822 | 1.36515 | 1.37220 | 1.37937 |
| 8 | 1.26000 | 1.26553 | 1.27112 | 1.27679 | 1.28253 | 1.28835 | 1.29425 | 1.30023 | 1.30629 | 1.31244 | 1.31867 | 1.32500 | 1.33142 | 1.33794 | 1.34456 | 1.35128 | 1.35810 | 1.36504 | 1.37208 | 1.37925 |
| 9 | 1.25991 | 1.26543 | 1.27103 | 1.27669 | 1.28243 | 1.28825 | 1.29415 | 1.30013 | 1.30619 | 1.31233 | 1.31857 | 1.32490 | 1.33132 | 1.33783 | 1.34445 | 1.35117 | 1.35799 | 1.36492 | 1.37197 | 1.37913 |
| 10 | 1.25982 | 1.26534 | 1.27093 | 1.27660 | 1.28234 | 1.28815 | 1.29405 | 1.30003 | 1.30609 | 1.31223 | 1.31847 | 1.32479 | 1.33121 | 1.33772 | 1.34434 | 1.35105 | 1.35787 | 1.36480 | 1.37185 | 1.37901 |
| 11 | 1.25973 | 1.26525 | 1.27084 | 1.27650 | 1.28224 | 1.28806 | 1.29395 | 1.29993 | 1.30598 | 1.31213 | 1.31836 | 1.32468 | 1.33110 | 1.33761 | 1.34423 | 1.35094 | 1.35776 | 1.36469 | 1.37173 | 1.37889 |
| 12 | 1.25964 | 1.26516 | 1.27075 | 1.27641 | 1.28214 | 1.28796 | 1.29385 | 1.29983 | 1.30588 | 1.31203 | 1.31826 | 1.32458 | 1.33099 | 1.33750 | 1.34411 | 1.35083 | 1.35765 | 1.36457 | 1.37161 | 1.37877 |
| 13 | 1.25955 | 1.26506 | 1.27065 | 1.27631 | 1.28205 | 1.28786 | 1.29375 | 1.29973 | 1.30578 | 1.31192 | 1.31815 | 1.32447 | 1.33089 | 1.33740 | 1.34400 | 1.35071 | 1.35753 | 1.36446 | 1.37149 | 1.37865 |
| 14 | 1.25945 | 1.26497 | 1.27056 | 1.27622 | 1.28195 | 1.28776 | 1.29365 | 1.29962 | 1.30568 | 1.31182 | 1.31805 | 1.32437 | 1.33078 | 1.33729 | 1.34389 | 1.35060 | 1.35742 | 1.36434 | 1.37137 | 1.37853 |
| 15 | 1.25936 | 1.26488 | 1.27046 | 1.27612 | 1.28186 | 1.28767 | 1.29355 | 1.29952 | 1.30558 | 1.31172 | 1.31794 | 1.32426 | 1.33067 | 1.33718 | 1.34378 | 1.35049 | 1.35730 | 1.36422 | 1.37126 | 1.37841 |
| 16 | 1.25927 | 1.26479 | 1.27037 | 1.27603 | 1.28176 | 1.28757 | 1.29346 | 1.29942 | 1.30548 | 1.31161 | 1.31784 | 1.32415 | 1.33056 | 1.33707 | 1.34367 | 1.35038 | 1.35719 | 1.36411 | 1.37114 | 1.37829 |
| 17 | 1.25918 | 1.26469 | 1.27028 | 1.27593 | 1.28166 | 1.28747 | 1.29336 | 1.29932 | 1.30537 | 1.31151 | 1.31773 | 1.32405 | 1.33045 | 1.33696 | 1.34356 | 1.35026 | 1.35707 | 1.36399 | 1.37102 | 1.37817 |
| 18 | 1.25909 | 1.26460 | 1.27018 | 1.27584 | 1.28157 | 1.28737 | 1.29326 | 1.29922 | 1.30527 | 1.31141 | 1.31763 | 1.32394 | 1.33035 | 1.33685 | 1.34345 | 1.35015 | 1.35696 | 1.36387 | 1.37090 | 1.37805 |
| 19 | 1.25900 | 1.26451 | 1.27009 | 1.27574 | 1.28147 | 1.28728 | 1.29316 | 1.29912 | 1.30517 | 1.31130 | 1.31752 | 1.32384 | 1.33024 | 1.33674 | 1.34334 | 1.35004 | 1.35684 | 1.36376 | 1.37078 | 1.37793 |
| 20 | 1.25891 | 1.26442 | 1.27000 | 1.27565 | 1.28138 | 1.28718 | 1.29306 | 1.29902 | 1.30507 | 1.31120 | 1.31742 | 1.32373 | 1.33013 | 1.33663 | 1.34323 | 1.34993 | 1.35673 | 1.36364 | 1.37067 | 1.37781 |
| 21 | 1.25882 | 1.26432 | 1.26990 | 1.27555 | 1.28128 | 1.28708 | 1.29296 | 1.29892 | 1.30497 | 1.31110 | 1.31732 | 1.32362 | 1.33002 | 1.33652 | 1.34312 | 1.34981 | 1.35662 | 1.36353 | 1.37055 | 1.37769 |
| 22 | 1.25872 | 1.26423 | 1.26981 | 1.27546 | 1.28118 | 1.28698 | 1.29286 | 1.29882 | 1.30487 | 1.31100 | 1.31721 | 1.32352 | 1.32992 | 1.33641 | 1.34301 | 1.34970 | 1.35650 | 1.36341 | 1.37043 | 1.37757 |
| 23 | 1.25863 | 1.26414 | 1.26972 | 1.27536 | 1.28109 | 1.28689 | 1.29277 | 1.29872 | 1.30477 | 1.31089 | 1.31711 | 1.32341 | 1.32981 | 1.33630 | 1.34290 | 1.34959 | 1.35639 | 1.36329 | 1.37031 | 1.37745 |
| 24 | 1.25854 | 1.26405 | 1.26962 | 1.27527 | 1.28099 | 1.28679 | 1.29267 | 1.29862 | 1.30466 | 1.31079 | 1.31700 | 1.32331 | 1.32970 | 1.33619 | 1.34278 | 1.34948 | 1.35627 | 1.36318 | 1.37019 | 1.37733 |
| 25 | 1.25845 | 1.26395 | 1.26953 | 1.27517 | 1.28090 | 1.28669 | 1.29257 | 1.29852 | 1.30456 | 1.31069 | 1.31690 | 1.32320 | 1.32960 | 1.33609 | 1.34267 | 1.34936 | 1.35616 | 1.36306 | 1.37008 | 1.37721 |
| 26 | 1.25836 | 1.26386 | 1.26943 | 1.27508 | 1.28080 | 1.28660 | 1.29247 | 1.29842 | 1.30446 | 1.31058 | 1.31679 | 1.32309 | 1.32949 | 1.33598 | 1.34256 | 1.34925 | 1.35604 | 1.36295 | 1.36996 | 1.37709 |
| 27 | 1.25827 | 1.26377 | 1.26934 | 1.27499 | 1.28070 | 1.28650 | 1.29237 | 1.29832 | 1.30436 | 1.31048 | 1.31669 | 1.32298 | 1.32938 | 1.33587 | 1.34245 | 1.34914 | 1.35593 | 1.36283 | 1.36984 | 1.37697 |
| 28 | 1.25818 | 1.26368 | 1.26925 | 1.27489 | 1.28061 | 1.28640 | 1.29227 | 1.29822 | 1.30426 | 1.31038 | 1.31659 | 1.32288 | 1.32927 | 1.33576 | 1.34234 | 1.34903 | 1.35582 | 1.36271 | 1.36972 | 1.37685 |
| 29 | 1.25809 | 1.26359 | 1.26915 | 1.27480 | 1.28051 | 1.28630 | 1.29217 | 1.29812 | 1.30416 | 1.31028 | 1.31648 | 1.32277 | 1.32917 | 1.33565 | 1.34223 | 1.34892 | 1.35570 | 1.36260 | 1.36961 | 1.37673 |
| 30 | 1.25800 | 1.26349 | 1.26906 | 1.27470 | 1.28042 | 1.28621 | 1.29208 | 1.29802 | 1.30406 | 1.31017 | 1.31638 | 1.32267 | 1.32906 | 1.33554 | 1.34212 | 1.34880 | 1.35559 | 1.36248 | 1.36949 | 1.37661 |
| 31 | 1.25790 | 1.26340 | 1.26897 | 1.27461 | 1.28032 | 1.28611 | 1.29198 | 1.29792 | 1.30396 | 1.31007 | 1.31627 | 1.32257 | 1.32895 | 1.33543 | 1.34201 | 1.34869 | 1.35547 | 1.36237 | 1.36937 | 1.37649 |
| 32 | 1.25781 | 1.26331 | 1.26887 | 1.27451 | 1.28022 | 1.28601 | 1.29188 | 1.29782 | 1.30385 | 1.30997 | 1.31617 | 1.32246 | 1.32884 | 1.33532 | 1.34190 | 1.34858 | 1.35536 | 1.36225 | 1.36925 | 1.37637 |
| 33 | 1.25772 | 1.26322 | 1.26878 | 1.27442 | 1.28013 | 1.28591 | 1.29178 | 1.29773 | 1.30375 | 1.30987 | 1.31606 | 1.32236 | 1.32874 | 1.33521 | 1.34179 | 1.34847 | 1.35525 | 1.36214 | 1.36913 | 1.37625 |
| 34 | 1.25763 | 1.26312 | 1.26869 | 1.27432 | 1.28003 | 1.28582 | 1.29168 | 1.29763 | 1.30365 | 1.30976 | 1.31596 | 1.32225 | 1.32863 | 1.33511 | 1.34168 | 1.34835 | 1.35513 | 1.36202 | 1.36902 | 1.37613 |
| 35 | 1.25754 | 1.26303 | 1.26859 | 1.27423 | 1.27994 | 1.28572 | 1.29158 | 1.29753 | 1.30355 | 1.30966 | 1.31586 | 1.32214 | 1.32852 | 1.33500 | 1.34157 | 1.34824 | 1.35502 | 1.36190 | 1.36890 | 1.37601 |
| 36 | 1.25745 | 1.26294 | 1.26850 | 1.27413 | 1.27984 | 1.28562 | 1.29148 | 1.29743 | 1.30345 | 1.30956 | 1.31575 | 1.32204 | 1.32842 | 1.33489 | 1.34146 | 1.34813 | 1.35491 | 1.36179 | 1.36878 | 1.37589 |
| 37 | 1.25736 | 1.26285 | 1.26841 | 1.27404 | 1.27974 | 1.28553 | 1.29139 | 1.29733 | 1.30335 | 1.30946 | 1.31565 | 1.32193 | 1.32831 | 1.33478 | 1.34135 | 1.34802 | 1.35479 | 1.36167 | 1.36866 | 1.37577 |
| 38 | 1.25727 | 1.26276 | 1.26831 | 1.27394 | 1.27965 | 1.28543 | 1.29129 | 1.29723 | 1.30325 | 1.30935 | 1.31555 | 1.32183 | 1.32820 | 1.33467 | 1.34124 | 1.34791 | 1.35468 | 1.36156 | 1.36855 | 1.37565 |
| 39 | 1.25718 | 1.26266 | 1.26822 | 1.27385 | 1.27955 | 1.28533 | 1.29119 | 1.29713 | 1.30315 | 1.30925 | 1.31544 | 1.32172 | 1.32809 | 1.33456 | 1.34113 | 1.34779 | 1.35456 | 1.36144 | 1.36843 | 1.37553 |
| 40 | 1.25709 | 1.26257 | 1.26813 | 1.27376 | 1.27946 | 1.28524 | 1.29109 | 1.29703 | 1.30305 | 1.30915 | 1.31534 | 1.32162 | 1.32799 | 1.33445 | 1.34102 | 1.34768 | 1.35445 | 1.36133 | 1.36831 | 1.37541 |
| 41 | 1.25699 | 1.26248 | 1.26803 | 1.27366 | 1.27936 | 1.28514 | 1.29099 | 1.29693 | 1.30294 | 1.30905 | 1.31523 | 1.32151 | 1.32788 | 1.33435 | 1.34091 | 1.34757 | 1.35434 | 1.36121 | 1.36819 | 1.37529 |
| 42 | 1.25690 | 1.26239 | 1.26794 | 1.27357 | 1.27927 | 1.28504 | 1.29090 | 1.29683 | 1.30284 | 1.30894 | 1.31513 | 1.32141 | 1.32777 | 1.33424 | 1.34080 | 1.34746 | 1.35422 | 1.36109 | 1.36808 | 1.37517 |
| 43 | 1.25681 | 1.26230 | 1.26785 | 1.27347 | 1.27917 | 1.28495 | 1.29080 | 1.29673 | 1.30274 | 1.30884 | 1.31503 | 1.32130 | 1.32767 | 1.33413 | 1.34069 | 1.34735 | 1.35411 | 1.36098 | 1.36796 | 1.37505 |
| 44 | 1.25672 | 1.26220 | 1.26776 | 1.27338 | 1.27908 | 1.28485 | 1.29070 | 1.29663 | 1.30264 | 1.30874 | 1.31492 | 1.32120 | 1.32756 | 1.33402 | 1.34058 | 1.34723 | 1.35400 | 1.36086 | 1.36784 | 1.37494 |
| 45 | 1.25663 | 1.26211 | 1.26766 | 1.27328 | 1.27898 | 1.28475 | 1.29060 | 1.29653 | 1.30254 | 1.30864 | 1.31482 | 1.32109 | 1.32745 | 1.33391 | 1.34047 | 1.34712 | 1.35388 | 1.36075 | 1.36773 | 1.37482 |
| 46 | 1.25654 | 1.26202 | 1.26757 | 1.27319 | 1.27888 | 1.28465 | 1.29050 | 1.29643 | 1.30244 | 1.30853 | 1.31471 | 1.32098 | 1.32735 | 1.33380 | 1.34036 | 1.34701 | 1.35377 | 1.36063 | 1.36761 | 1.37470 |
| 47 | 1.25645 | 1.26193 | 1.26748 | 1.27310 | 1.27879 | 1.28456 | 1.29040 | 1.29633 | 1.30234 | 1.30843 | 1.31461 | 1.32088 | 1.32724 | 1.33369 | 1.34025 | 1.34690 | 1.35366 | 1.36052 | 1.36749 | 1.37458 |
| 48 | 1.25636 | 1.26184 | 1.26738 | 1.27300 | 1.27869 | 1.28446 | 1.29031 | 1.29623 | 1.30224 | 1.30833 | 1.31451 | 1.32077 | 1.32713 | 1.33359 | 1.34014 | 1.34679 | 1.35354 | 1.36040 | 1.36737 | 1.37446 |
| 49 | 1.25627 | 1.26174 | 1.26729 | 1.27291 | 1.27860 | 1.28436 | 1.29021 | 1.29613 | 1.30214 | 1.30823 | 1.31440 | 1.32067 | 1.32703 | 1.33348 | 1.34003 | 1.34668 | 1.35343 | 1.36029 | 1.36726 | 1.37434 |
| 50 | 1.25618 | 1.26165 | 1.26720 | 1.27281 | 1.27850 | 1.28427 | 1.29011 | 1.29603 | 1.30204 | 1.30812 | 1.31430 | 1.32056 | 1.32692 | 1.33337 | 1.33992 | 1.34656 | 1.35331 | 1.36017 | 1.36714 | 1.37422 |
| 51 | 1.25609 | 1.26156 | 1.26710 | 1.27272 | 1.27841 | 1.28417 | 1.29001 | 1.29593 | 1.30194 | 1.30802 | 1.31420 | 1.32046 | 1.32681 | 1.33326 | 1.33981 | 1.34645 | 1.35320 | 1.36006 | 1.36702 | 1.37410 |
| 52 | 1.25600 | 1.26147 | 1.26701 | 1.27262 | 1.27831 | 1.28407 | 1.28991 | 1.29583 | 1.30183 | 1.30792 | 1.31409 | 1.32035 | 1.32671 | 1.33315 | 1.33970 | 1.34634 | 1.35309 | 1.35994 | 1.36691 | 1.37398 |
| 53 | 1.25591 | 1.26138 | 1.26692 | 1.27253 | 1.27822 | 1.28398 | 1.28982 | 1.29573 | 1.30173 | 1.30782 | 1.31399 | 1.32025 | 1.32660 | 1.33304 | 1.33959 | 1.34623 | 1.35297 | 1.35983 | 1.36679 | 1.37386 |
| 54 | 1.25582 | 1.26129 | 1.26683 | 1.27244 | 1.27812 | 1.28388 | 1.28972 | 1.29563 | 1.30163 | 1.30772 | 1.31389 | 1.32014 | 1.32649 | 1.33294 | 1.33948 | 1.34612 | 1.35286 | 1.35971 | 1.36667 | 1.37375 |
| 55 | 1.25573 | 1.26119 | 1.26673 | 1.27234 | 1.27803 | 1.28378 | 1.28962 | 1.29554 | 1.30153 | 1.30761 | 1.31378 | 1.32004 | 1.32639 | 1.33283 | 1.33937 | 1.34601 | 1.35275 | 1.35960 | 1.36655 | 1.37363 |
| 56 | 1.25563 | 1.26110 | 1.26664 | 1.27225 | 1.27793 | 1.28369 | 1.28952 | 1.29544 | 1.30143 | 1.30751 | 1.31368 | 1.31993 | 1.32628 | 1.33272 | 1.33926 | 1.34589 | 1.35264 | 1.35948 | 1.36644 | 1.37351 |
| 57 | 1.25554 | 1.26101 | 1.26655 | 1.27215 | 1.27783 | 1.28359 | 1.28942 | 1.29534 | 1.30133 | 1.30741 | 1.31357 | 1.31983 | 1.32617 | 1.33261 | 1.33915 | 1.34578 | 1.35252 | 1.35937 | 1.36632 | 1.37339 |
| 58 | 1.25545 | 1.26092 | 1.26645 | 1.27206 | 1.27774 | 1.28349 | 1.28933 | 1.29524 | 1.30123 | 1.30731 | 1.31347 | 1.31972 | 1.32607 | 1.33250 | 1.33904 | 1.34567 | 1.35241 | 1.35925 | 1.36620 | 1.37327 |
| 59 | 1.25536 | 1.26083 | 1.26636 | 1.27197 | 1.27764 | 1.28340 | 1.28923 | 1.29514 | 1.30113 | 1.30721 | 1.31337 | 1.31962 | 1.32596 | 1.33240 | 1.33893 | 1.34556 | 1.35230 | 1.35914 | 1.36609 | 1.37315 |
| 60 | 1.25527 | 1.26074 | 1.26627 | 1.27187 | 1.27755 | 1.28330 | 1.28913 | 1.29504 | 1.30103 | 1.30710 | 1.31326 | 1.31951 | 1.32585 | 1.33229 | 1.33882 | 1.34545 | 1.35218 | 1.35902 | 1.36597 | 1.37303 |

# Table X Diurnal Motion Logarithms, 0 to 2 Hours/Degrees

| SECONDS OF TIME OR ARC | DEGREES or HOURS and MINUTES | | | | | | | | | | | | | | | | | | | |
|---|---|---|---|---|---|---|---|---|---|---|---|---|---|---|---|---|---|---|---|---|
| | 1° 20' | 1° 21' | 1° 22' | 1° 23' | 1° 24' | 1° 25' | 1° 26' | 1° 27' | 1° 28' | 1° 29' | 1° 30' | 1° 31' | 1° 32' | 1° 33' | 1° 34' | 1° 35' | 1° 36' | 1° 37' | 1° 38' | 1° 39' |
| 0 | 1.25527 | 1.24988 | 1.24455 | 1.23928 | 1.23408 | 1.22894 | 1.22386 | 1.21884 | 1.21388 | 1.20897 | 1.20412 | 1.19932 | 1.19457 | 1.18988 | 1.18523 | 1.18064 | 1.17609 | 1.17159 | 1.16714 | 1.16273 |
| 1 | 1.25518 | 1.24979 | 1.24446 | 1.23920 | 1.23400 | 1.22886 | 1.22378 | 1.21876 | 1.21380 | 1.20889 | 1.20404 | 1.19924 | 1.19450 | 1.18980 | 1.18516 | 1.18056 | 1.17602 | 1.17152 | 1.16706 | 1.16265 |
| 2 | 1.25509 | 1.24970 | 1.24437 | 1.23911 | 1.23391 | 1.22877 | 1.22370 | 1.21868 | 1.21372 | 1.20881 | 1.20396 | 1.19916 | 1.19442 | 1.18972 | 1.18508 | 1.18049 | 1.17594 | 1.17144 | 1.16699 | 1.16258 |
| 3 | 1.25500 | 1.24961 | 1.24428 | 1.23902 | 1.23382 | 1.22869 | 1.22361 | 1.21859 | 1.21363 | 1.20873 | 1.20388 | 1.19908 | 1.19434 | 1.18965 | 1.18500 | 1.18041 | 1.17587 | 1.17137 | 1.16691 | 1.16251 |
| 4 | 1.25491 | 1.24952 | 1.24420 | 1.23894 | 1.23374 | 1.22860 | 1.22353 | 1.21851 | 1.21355 | 1.20865 | 1.20380 | 1.19900 | 1.19426 | 1.18957 | 1.18493 | 1.18033 | 1.17579 | 1.17129 | 1.16684 | 1.16243 |
| 5 | 1.25482 | 1.24943 | 1.24411 | 1.23885 | 1.23365 | 1.22852 | 1.22344 | 1.21843 | 1.21347 | 1.20857 | 1.20372 | 1.19892 | 1.19418 | 1.18949 | 1.18485 | 1.18026 | 1.17571 | 1.17122 | 1.16677 | 1.16236 |
| 6 | 1.25473 | 1.24934 | 1.24402 | 1.23876 | 1.23357 | 1.22843 | 1.22336 | 1.21834 | 1.21339 | 1.20848 | 1.20364 | 1.19884 | 1.19410 | 1.18941 | 1.18477 | 1.18018 | 1.17564 | 1.17114 | 1.16669 | 1.16229 |
| 7 | 1.25464 | 1.24925 | 1.24393 | 1.23867 | 1.23348 | 1.22835 | 1.22328 | 1.21826 | 1.21330 | 1.20840 | 1.20356 | 1.19876 | 1.19402 | 1.18934 | 1.18470 | 1.18011 | 1.17556 | 1.17107 | 1.16662 | 1.16222 |
| 8 | 1.25455 | 1.24916 | 1.24384 | 1.23859 | 1.23339 | 1.22826 | 1.22319 | 1.21818 | 1.21322 | 1.20832 | 1.20348 | 1.19869 | 1.19395 | 1.18926 | 1.18462 | 1.18003 | 1.17549 | 1.17099 | 1.16655 | 1.16214 |
| 9 | 1.25446 | 1.24907 | 1.24375 | 1.23850 | 1.23331 | 1.22818 | 1.22311 | 1.21810 | 1.21314 | 1.20824 | 1.20340 | 1.19861 | 1.19387 | 1.18918 | 1.18454 | 1.17995 | 1.17541 | 1.17092 | 1.16647 | 1.16207 |
| 10 | 1.25437 | 1.24898 | 1.24367 | 1.23841 | 1.23322 | 1.22809 | 1.22302 | 1.21801 | 1.21306 | 1.20816 | 1.20332 | 1.19853 | 1.19379 | 1.18910 | 1.18447 | 1.17988 | 1.17534 | 1.17085 | 1.16640 | 1.16200 |
| 11 | 1.25428 | 1.24890 | 1.24358 | 1.23833 | 1.23314 | 1.22801 | 1.22294 | 1.21793 | 1.21298 | 1.20808 | 1.20324 | 1.19845 | 1.19371 | 1.18902 | 1.18439 | 1.17980 | 1.17526 | 1.17077 | 1.16632 | 1.16192 |
| 12 | 1.25419 | 1.24881 | 1.24349 | 1.23824 | 1.23305 | 1.22792 | 1.22286 | 1.21785 | 1.21289 | 1.20800 | 1.20316 | 1.19837 | 1.19363 | 1.18895 | 1.18431 | 1.17973 | 1.17519 | 1.17070 | 1.16625 | 1.16185 |
| 13 | 1.25410 | 1.24872 | 1.24340 | 1.23815 | 1.23296 | 1.22784 | 1.22277 | 1.21776 | 1.21281 | 1.20792 | 1.20308 | 1.19829 | 1.19355 | 1.18887 | 1.18423 | 1.17965 | 1.17511 | 1.17062 | 1.16618 | 1.16178 |
| 14 | 1.25401 | 1.24863 | 1.24331 | 1.23807 | 1.23288 | 1.22775 | 1.22269 | 1.21768 | 1.21273 | 1.20784 | 1.20300 | 1.19821 | 1.19347 | 1.18879 | 1.18416 | 1.17957 | 1.17504 | 1.17055 | 1.16610 | 1.16170 |
| 15 | 1.25392 | 1.24854 | 1.24323 | 1.23798 | 1.23279 | 1.22767 | 1.22260 | 1.21760 | 1.21265 | 1.20775 | 1.20292 | 1.19813 | 1.19340 | 1.18871 | 1.18408 | 1.17950 | 1.17496 | 1.17047 | 1.16603 | 1.16163 |
| 16 | 1.25383 | 1.24845 | 1.24314 | 1.23789 | 1.23271 | 1.22758 | 1.22252 | 1.21751 | 1.21257 | 1.20767 | 1.20284 | 1.19805 | 1.19332 | 1.18864 | 1.18400 | 1.17942 | 1.17489 | 1.17040 | 1.16596 | 1.16156 |
| 17 | 1.25374 | 1.24836 | 1.24305 | 1.23780 | 1.23262 | 1.22750 | 1.22244 | 1.21743 | 1.21248 | 1.20759 | 1.20275 | 1.19797 | 1.19324 | 1.18856 | 1.18393 | 1.17935 | 1.17481 | 1.17032 | 1.16588 | 1.16149 |
| 18 | 1.25365 | 1.24827 | 1.24296 | 1.23772 | 1.23253 | 1.22741 | 1.22235 | 1.21735 | 1.21240 | 1.20751 | 1.20267 | 1.19789 | 1.19316 | 1.18848 | 1.18385 | 1.17927 | 1.17474 | 1.17025 | 1.16581 | 1.16141 |
| 19 | 1.25356 | 1.24818 | 1.24287 | 1.23763 | 1.23245 | 1.22733 | 1.22227 | 1.21727 | 1.21232 | 1.20743 | 1.20259 | 1.19781 | 1.19308 | 1.18840 | 1.18377 | 1.17919 | 1.17466 | 1.17018 | 1.16574 | 1.16134 |
| 20 | 1.25347 | 1.24809 | 1.24279 | 1.23754 | 1.23236 | 1.22724 | 1.22218 | 1.21718 | 1.21224 | 1.20735 | 1.20251 | 1.19773 | 1.19300 | 1.18833 | 1.18370 | 1.17912 | 1.17459 | 1.17010 | 1.16566 | 1.16127 |
| 21 | 1.25338 | 1.24800 | 1.24270 | 1.23746 | 1.23228 | 1.22716 | 1.22210 | 1.21710 | 1.21216 | 1.20727 | 1.20243 | 1.19765 | 1.19293 | 1.18825 | 1.18362 | 1.17904 | 1.17451 | 1.17003 | 1.16559 | 1.16119 |
| 22 | 1.25329 | 1.24792 | 1.24261 | 1.23737 | 1.23219 | 1.22707 | 1.22202 | 1.21702 | 1.21207 | 1.20719 | 1.20235 | 1.19757 | 1.19285 | 1.18817 | 1.18354 | 1.17897 | 1.17444 | 1.16995 | 1.16551 | 1.16112 |
| 23 | 1.25320 | 1.24783 | 1.24252 | 1.23728 | 1.23211 | 1.22699 | 1.22193 | 1.21693 | 1.21199 | 1.20711 | 1.20227 | 1.19750 | 1.19277 | 1.18809 | 1.18347 | 1.17889 | 1.17436 | 1.16988 | 1.16544 | 1.16105 |
| 24 | 1.25311 | 1.24774 | 1.24244 | 1.23720 | 1.23202 | 1.22690 | 1.22185 | 1.21685 | 1.21191 | 1.20702 | 1.20219 | 1.19742 | 1.19269 | 1.18802 | 1.18339 | 1.17881 | 1.17429 | 1.16980 | 1.16537 | 1.16098 |
| 25 | 1.25302 | 1.24765 | 1.24235 | 1.23711 | 1.23193 | 1.22682 | 1.22176 | 1.21677 | 1.21183 | 1.20694 | 1.20211 | 1.19734 | 1.19261 | 1.18794 | 1.18331 | 1.17874 | 1.17421 | 1.16973 | 1.16529 | 1.16090 |
| 26 | 1.25293 | 1.24756 | 1.24226 | 1.23702 | 1.23185 | 1.22674 | 1.22168 | 1.21669 | 1.21175 | 1.20686 | 1.20203 | 1.19726 | 1.19253 | 1.18786 | 1.18324 | 1.17866 | 1.17414 | 1.16965 | 1.16522 | 1.16083 |
| 27 | 1.25284 | 1.24747 | 1.24217 | 1.23694 | 1.23176 | 1.22665 | 1.22160 | 1.21660 | 1.21166 | 1.20678 | 1.20195 | 1.19718 | 1.19246 | 1.18778 | 1.18316 | 1.17859 | 1.17406 | 1.16958 | 1.16515 | 1.16076 |
| 28 | 1.25275 | 1.24738 | 1.24208 | 1.23685 | 1.23168 | 1.22657 | 1.22151 | 1.21652 | 1.21158 | 1.20670 | 1.20187 | 1.19710 | 1.19238 | 1.18771 | 1.18308 | 1.17851 | 1.17399 | 1.16951 | 1.16507 | 1.16068 |
| 29 | 1.25266 | 1.24729 | 1.24200 | 1.23676 | 1.23159 | 1.22648 | 1.22143 | 1.21644 | 1.21150 | 1.20662 | 1.20179 | 1.19702 | 1.19230 | 1.18763 | 1.18301 | 1.17843 | 1.17391 | 1.16943 | 1.16500 | 1.16061 |
| 30 | 1.25257 | 1.24720 | 1.24191 | 1.23668 | 1.23151 | 1.22640 | 1.22135 | 1.21635 | 1.21142 | 1.20654 | 1.20171 | 1.19694 | 1.19222 | 1.18755 | 1.18293 | 1.17836 | 1.17384 | 1.16936 | 1.16493 | 1.16054 |
| 31 | 1.25248 | 1.24712 | 1.24182 | 1.23659 | 1.23142 | 1.22631 | 1.22126 | 1.21627 | 1.21134 | 1.20646 | 1.20163 | 1.19686 | 1.19214 | 1.18747 | 1.18285 | 1.17828 | 1.17376 | 1.16928 | 1.16485 | 1.16047 |
| 32 | 1.25239 | 1.24703 | 1.24173 | 1.23650 | 1.23133 | 1.22623 | 1.22118 | 1.21619 | 1.21126 | 1.20638 | 1.20155 | 1.19678 | 1.19206 | 1.18740 | 1.18278 | 1.17821 | 1.17369 | 1.16921 | 1.16478 | 1.16039 |
| 33 | 1.25230 | 1.24694 | 1.24165 | 1.23642 | 1.23125 | 1.22614 | 1.22110 | 1.21611 | 1.21117 | 1.20630 | 1.20147 | 1.19670 | 1.19199 | 1.18732 | 1.18270 | 1.17813 | 1.17361 | 1.16914 | 1.16471 | 1.16032 |
| 34 | 1.25221 | 1.24685 | 1.24156 | 1.23633 | 1.23116 | 1.22606 | 1.22101 | 1.21602 | 1.21109 | 1.20622 | 1.20139 | 1.19663 | 1.19191 | 1.18724 | 1.18262 | 1.17806 | 1.17354 | 1.16906 | 1.16463 | 1.16025 |
| 35 | 1.25212 | 1.24676 | 1.24147 | 1.23624 | 1.23108 | 1.22597 | 1.22093 | 1.21594 | 1.21101 | 1.20614 | 1.20131 | 1.19655 | 1.19183 | 1.18716 | 1.18255 | 1.17798 | 1.17346 | 1.16899 | 1.16456 | 1.16018 |
| 36 | 1.25203 | 1.24667 | 1.24138 | 1.23616 | 1.23099 | 1.22589 | 1.22084 | 1.21586 | 1.21093 | 1.20605 | 1.20123 | 1.19647 | 1.19175 | 1.18709 | 1.18247 | 1.17790 | 1.17339 | 1.16891 | 1.16449 | 1.16010 |
| 37 | 1.25194 | 1.24658 | 1.24129 | 1.23607 | 1.23091 | 1.22580 | 1.22076 | 1.21578 | 1.21085 | 1.20597 | 1.20115 | 1.19639 | 1.19167 | 1.18701 | 1.18239 | 1.17783 | 1.17331 | 1.16884 | 1.16441 | 1.16003 |
| 38 | 1.25185 | 1.24649 | 1.24121 | 1.23598 | 1.23082 | 1.22572 | 1.22068 | 1.21569 | 1.21077 | 1.20589 | 1.20107 | 1.19631 | 1.19160 | 1.18693 | 1.18232 | 1.17775 | 1.17324 | 1.16876 | 1.16434 | 1.15996 |
| 39 | 1.25176 | 1.24641 | 1.24112 | 1.23590 | 1.23074 | 1.22564 | 1.22059 | 1.21561 | 1.21068 | 1.20581 | 1.20099 | 1.19623 | 1.19152 | 1.18685 | 1.18224 | 1.17768 | 1.17316 | 1.16869 | 1.16427 | 1.15989 |
| 40 | 1.25167 | 1.24632 | 1.24103 | 1.23581 | 1.23065 | 1.22555 | 1.22051 | 1.21553 | 1.21060 | 1.20573 | 1.20091 | 1.19615 | 1.19144 | 1.18678 | 1.18217 | 1.17760 | 1.17309 | 1.16862 | 1.16419 | 1.15981 |
| 41 | 1.25158 | 1.24623 | 1.24094 | 1.23572 | 1.23056 | 1.22547 | 1.22043 | 1.21545 | 1.21052 | 1.20565 | 1.20084 | 1.19607 | 1.19136 | 1.18670 | 1.18209 | 1.17753 | 1.17301 | 1.16854 | 1.16412 | 1.15974 |
| 42 | 1.25149 | 1.24614 | 1.24086 | 1.23564 | 1.23048 | 1.22538 | 1.22034 | 1.21536 | 1.21044 | 1.20557 | 1.20076 | 1.19599 | 1.19128 | 1.18662 | 1.18201 | 1.17745 | 1.17294 | 1.16847 | 1.16405 | 1.15967 |
| 43 | 1.25140 | 1.24605 | 1.24077 | 1.23555 | 1.23039 | 1.22530 | 1.22026 | 1.21528 | 1.21036 | 1.20549 | 1.20068 | 1.19591 | 1.19120 | 1.18655 | 1.18194 | 1.17737 | 1.17286 | 1.16839 | 1.16397 | 1.15959 |
| 44 | 1.25131 | 1.24596 | 1.24068 | 1.23546 | 1.23031 | 1.22521 | 1.22018 | 1.21520 | 1.21028 | 1.20541 | 1.20060 | 1.19584 | 1.19113 | 1.18647 | 1.18186 | 1.17730 | 1.17279 | 1.16832 | 1.16390 | 1.15952 |
| 45 | 1.25122 | 1.24587 | 1.24059 | 1.23538 | 1.23022 | 1.22513 | 1.22009 | 1.21512 | 1.21019 | 1.20533 | 1.20052 | 1.19576 | 1.19105 | 1.18639 | 1.18178 | 1.17722 | 1.17271 | 1.16825 | 1.16383 | 1.15945 |
| 46 | 1.25113 | 1.24579 | 1.24051 | 1.23529 | 1.23014 | 1.22504 | 1.22001 | 1.21503 | 1.21011 | 1.20525 | 1.20044 | 1.19568 | 1.19097 | 1.18631 | 1.18171 | 1.17715 | 1.17264 | 1.16817 | 1.16375 | 1.15938 |
| 47 | 1.25104 | 1.24570 | 1.24042 | 1.23520 | 1.23005 | 1.22496 | 1.21993 | 1.21495 | 1.21003 | 1.20517 | 1.20036 | 1.19560 | 1.19089 | 1.18624 | 1.18163 | 1.17707 | 1.17256 | 1.16810 | 1.16368 | 1.15930 |
| 48 | 1.25095 | 1.24561 | 1.24033 | 1.23512 | 1.22997 | 1.22488 | 1.21984 | 1.21487 | 1.20995 | 1.20509 | 1.20028 | 1.19552 | 1.19081 | 1.18616 | 1.18155 | 1.17700 | 1.17249 | 1.16802 | 1.16361 | 1.15923 |
| 49 | 1.25086 | 1.24552 | 1.24024 | 1.23503 | 1.22988 | 1.22479 | 1.21976 | 1.21479 | 1.20987 | 1.20501 | 1.20020 | 1.19544 | 1.19074 | 1.18608 | 1.18148 | 1.17692 | 1.17241 | 1.16795 | 1.16353 | 1.15916 |
| 50 | 1.25077 | 1.24543 | 1.24016 | 1.23495 | 1.22980 | 1.22471 | 1.21968 | 1.21470 | 1.20979 | 1.20492 | 1.20012 | 1.19536 | 1.19066 | 1.18601 | 1.18140 | 1.17685 | 1.17234 | 1.16788 | 1.16346 | 1.15909 |
| 51 | 1.25068 | 1.24534 | 1.24007 | 1.23486 | 1.22971 | 1.22462 | 1.21959 | 1.21462 | 1.20971 | 1.20484 | 1.20004 | 1.19528 | 1.19058 | 1.18593 | 1.18133 | 1.17677 | 1.17226 | 1.16780 | 1.16339 | 1.15901 |
| 52 | 1.25059 | 1.24526 | 1.23998 | 1.23477 | 1.22963 | 1.22454 | 1.21951 | 1.21454 | 1.20962 | 1.20476 | 1.19996 | 1.19520 | 1.19050 | 1.18585 | 1.18125 | 1.17669 | 1.17219 | 1.16773 | 1.16331 | 1.15894 |
| 53 | 1.25050 | 1.24517 | 1.23990 | 1.23469 | 1.22954 | 1.22445 | 1.21943 | 1.21446 | 1.20954 | 1.20468 | 1.19988 | 1.19513 | 1.19042 | 1.18577 | 1.18117 | 1.17662 | 1.17211 | 1.16765 | 1.16324 | 1.15887 |
| 54 | 1.25041 | 1.24508 | 1.23981 | 1.23460 | 1.22945 | 1.22437 | 1.21934 | 1.21437 | 1.20946 | 1.20460 | 1.19980 | 1.19505 | 1.19035 | 1.18570 | 1.18110 | 1.17654 | 1.17204 | 1.16758 | 1.16317 | 1.15880 |
| 55 | 1.25032 | 1.24499 | 1.23972 | 1.23451 | 1.22937 | 1.22429 | 1.21926 | 1.21429 | 1.20938 | 1.20452 | 1.19972 | 1.19497 | 1.19027 | 1.18562 | 1.18102 | 1.17647 | 1.17196 | 1.16751 | 1.16309 | 1.15872 |
| 56 | 1.25024 | 1.24490 | 1.23963 | 1.23443 | 1.22928 | 1.22420 | 1.21918 | 1.21421 | 1.20930 | 1.20444 | 1.19964 | 1.19489 | 1.19019 | 1.18554 | 1.18094 | 1.17639 | 1.17189 | 1.16743 | 1.16302 | 1.15865 |
| 57 | 1.25015 | 1.24481 | 1.23955 | 1.23434 | 1.22920 | 1.22412 | 1.21909 | 1.21413 | 1.20922 | 1.20436 | 1.19956 | 1.19481 | 1.19011 | 1.18547 | 1.18087 | 1.17632 | 1.17181 | 1.16736 | 1.16295 | 1.15858 |
| 58 | 1.25006 | 1.24473 | 1.23946 | 1.23426 | 1.22911 | 1.22403 | 1.21901 | 1.21404 | 1.20914 | 1.20428 | 1.19948 | 1.19473 | 1.19004 | 1.18539 | 1.18079 | 1.17624 | 1.17174 | 1.16728 | 1.16287 | 1.15851 |
| 59 | 1.24997 | 1.24464 | 1.23937 | 1.23417 | 1.22903 | 1.22395 | 1.21893 | 1.21396 | 1.20905 | 1.20420 | 1.19940 | 1.19465 | 1.18996 | 1.18531 | 1.18072 | 1.17617 | 1.17167 | 1.16721 | 1.16280 | 1.15843 |
| 60 | 1.24988 | 1.24455 | 1.23928 | 1.23408 | 1.22894 | 1.22386 | 1.21884 | 1.21388 | 1.20897 | 1.20412 | 1.19932 | 1.19457 | 1.18988 | 1.18523 | 1.18064 | 1.17609 | 1.17159 | 1.16714 | 1.16273 | 1.15836 |

# Table X Diurnal Motion Logarithms, 0 to 2 Hours/Degrees

DEGREES or HOURS and MINUTES

| Seconds of Time or Arc | 1° 40' | 1° 41' | 1° 42' | 1° 43' | 1° 44' | 1° 45' | 1° 46' | 1° 47' | 1° 48' | 1° 49' |
|---|---|---|---|---|---|---|---|---|---|---|
| 0 | 1.15836 | 1.15404 | 1.14976 | 1.14553 | 1.14133 | 1.13717 | 1.13306 | 1.12898 | 1.12494 | 1.12094 |
| 1 | 1.15829 | 1.15397 | 1.14969 | 1.14545 | 1.14126 | 1.13710 | 1.13299 | 1.12891 | 1.12487 | 1.12087 |
| 2 | 1.15822 | 1.15390 | 1.14962 | 1.14538 | 1.14119 | 1.13704 | 1.13292 | 1.12884 | 1.12480 | 1.12080 |
| 3 | 1.15815 | 1.15383 | 1.14955 | 1.14531 | 1.14112 | 1.13697 | 1.13285 | 1.12878 | 1.12474 | 1.12074 |
| 4 | 1.15807 | 1.15375 | 1.14948 | 1.14524 | 1.14105 | 1.13690 | 1.13278 | 1.12871 | 1.12467 | 1.12067 |
| 5 | 1.15800 | 1.15368 | 1.14941 | 1.14517 | 1.14098 | 1.13683 | 1.13272 | 1.12864 | 1.12460 | 1.12060 |
| 6 | 1.15793 | 1.15361 | 1.14934 | 1.14510 | 1.14091 | 1.13676 | 1.13265 | 1.12857 | 1.12454 | 1.12054 |
| 7 | 1.15786 | 1.15354 | 1.14927 | 1.14503 | 1.14084 | 1.13669 | 1.13258 | 1.12851 | 1.12447 | 1.12047 |
| 8 | 1.15778 | 1.15347 | 1.14919 | 1.14496 | 1.14077 | 1.13662 | 1.13251 | 1.12844 | 1.12440 | 1.12041 |
| 9 | 1.15771 | 1.15340 | 1.14912 | 1.14489 | 1.14070 | 1.13655 | 1.13244 | 1.12837 | 1.12434 | 1.12034 |
| 10 | 1.15764 | 1.15333 | 1.14905 | 1.14482 | 1.14063 | 1.13648 | 1.13237 | 1.12830 | 1.12427 | 1.12027 |
| 11 | 1.15757 | 1.15325 | 1.14898 | 1.14475 | 1.14056 | 1.13642 | 1.13231 | 1.12824 | 1.12420 | 1.12021 |
| 12 | 1.15749 | 1.15318 | 1.14891 | 1.14468 | 1.14049 | 1.13635 | 1.13224 | 1.12817 | 1.12414 | 1.12014 |
| 13 | 1.15742 | 1.15311 | 1.14884 | 1.14461 | 1.14043 | 1.13628 | 1.13217 | 1.12810 | 1.12407 | 1.12007 |
| 14 | 1.15735 | 1.15304 | 1.14877 | 1.14454 | 1.14036 | 1.13621 | 1.13210 | 1.12803 | 1.12400 | 1.12001 |
| 15 | 1.15728 | 1.15297 | 1.14870 | 1.14447 | 1.14029 | 1.13614 | 1.13203 | 1.12797 | 1.12393 | 1.11994 |
| 16 | 1.15721 | 1.15290 | 1.14863 | 1.14440 | 1.14022 | 1.13607 | 1.13197 | 1.12790 | 1.12387 | 1.11987 |
| 17 | 1.15713 | 1.15282 | 1.14856 | 1.14433 | 1.14015 | 1.13600 | 1.13190 | 1.12783 | 1.12380 | 1.11981 |
| 18 | 1.15706 | 1.15275 | 1.14849 | 1.14426 | 1.14008 | 1.13593 | 1.13183 | 1.12776 | 1.12373 | 1.11974 |
| 19 | 1.15699 | 1.15268 | 1.14842 | 1.14419 | 1.14001 | 1.13587 | 1.13176 | 1.12770 | 1.12367 | 1.11968 |
| 20 | 1.15692 | 1.15261 | 1.14835 | 1.14412 | 1.13994 | 1.13580 | 1.13169 | 1.12763 | 1.12360 | 1.11961 |
| 21 | 1.15685 | 1.15254 | 1.14827 | 1.14405 | 1.13987 | 1.13573 | 1.13162 | 1.12756 | 1.12353 | 1.11954 |
| 22 | 1.15677 | 1.15247 | 1.14820 | 1.14398 | 1.13980 | 1.13566 | 1.13156 | 1.12749 | 1.12347 | 1.11948 |
| 23 | 1.15670 | 1.15240 | 1.14813 | 1.14391 | 1.13973 | 1.13559 | 1.13149 | 1.12743 | 1.12340 | 1.11941 |
| 24 | 1.15663 | 1.15232 | 1.14806 | 1.14384 | 1.13966 | 1.13552 | 1.13142 | 1.12736 | 1.12333 | 1.11935 |
| 25 | 1.15656 | 1.15225 | 1.14799 | 1.14377 | 1.13959 | 1.13545 | 1.13135 | 1.12729 | 1.12327 | 1.11928 |
| 26 | 1.15648 | 1.15218 | 1.14792 | 1.14370 | 1.13952 | 1.13538 | 1.13128 | 1.12722 | 1.12320 | 1.11921 |
| 27 | 1.15641 | 1.15211 | 1.14785 | 1.14363 | 1.13945 | 1.13532 | 1.13122 | 1.12716 | 1.12313 | 1.11915 |
| 28 | 1.15634 | 1.15204 | 1.14778 | 1.14356 | 1.13938 | 1.13525 | 1.13115 | 1.12709 | 1.12307 | 1.11908 |
| 29 | 1.15627 | 1.15197 | 1.14771 | 1.14349 | 1.13932 | 1.13518 | 1.13108 | 1.12702 | 1.12300 | 1.11901 |
| 30 | 1.15620 | 1.15190 | 1.14764 | 1.14342 | 1.13925 | 1.13511 | 1.13101 | 1.12695 | 1.12293 | 1.11895 |
| 31 | 1.15612 | 1.15183 | 1.14757 | 1.14335 | 1.13918 | 1.13504 | 1.13094 | 1.12689 | 1.12287 | 1.11888 |
| 32 | 1.15605 | 1.15175 | 1.14750 | 1.14328 | 1.13911 | 1.13497 | 1.13088 | 1.12682 | 1.12280 | 1.11882 |
| 33 | 1.15598 | 1.15168 | 1.14743 | 1.14321 | 1.13904 | 1.13490 | 1.13081 | 1.12675 | 1.12273 | 1.11875 |
| 34 | 1.15591 | 1.15161 | 1.14736 | 1.14314 | 1.13897 | 1.13484 | 1.13074 | 1.12668 | 1.12267 | 1.11868 |
| 35 | 1.15584 | 1.15154 | 1.14729 | 1.14307 | 1.13890 | 1.13477 | 1.13067 | 1.12662 | 1.12260 | 1.11862 |
| 36 | 1.15576 | 1.15147 | 1.14722 | 1.14300 | 1.13883 | 1.13470 | 1.13061 | 1.12655 | 1.12253 | 1.11855 |
| 37 | 1.15569 | 1.15140 | 1.14714 | 1.14293 | 1.13876 | 1.13463 | 1.13054 | 1.12648 | 1.12247 | 1.11849 |
| 38 | 1.15562 | 1.15133 | 1.14707 | 1.14286 | 1.13869 | 1.13456 | 1.13047 | 1.12642 | 1.12240 | 1.11842 |
| 39 | 1.15555 | 1.15126 | 1.14700 | 1.14279 | 1.13862 | 1.13449 | 1.13040 | 1.12635 | 1.12233 | 1.11835 |
| 40 | 1.15548 | 1.15118 | 1.14693 | 1.14272 | 1.13855 | 1.13442 | 1.13033 | 1.12628 | 1.12227 | 1.11829 |
| 41 | 1.15540 | 1.15111 | 1.14686 | 1.14265 | 1.13848 | 1.13436 | 1.13027 | 1.12621 | 1.12220 | 1.11822 |
| 42 | 1.15533 | 1.15104 | 1.14679 | 1.14258 | 1.13842 | 1.13429 | 1.13020 | 1.12615 | 1.12213 | 1.11816 |
| 43 | 1.15526 | 1.15097 | 1.14672 | 1.14251 | 1.13835 | 1.13422 | 1.13013 | 1.12608 | 1.12207 | 1.11809 |
| 44 | 1.15519 | 1.15090 | 1.14665 | 1.14244 | 1.13828 | 1.13415 | 1.13006 | 1.12601 | 1.12200 | 1.11802 |
| 45 | 1.15512 | 1.15083 | 1.14658 | 1.14237 | 1.13821 | 1.13408 | 1.12999 | 1.12595 | 1.12193 | 1.11796 |
| 46 | 1.15505 | 1.15076 | 1.14651 | 1.14230 | 1.13814 | 1.13401 | 1.12993 | 1.12588 | 1.12187 | 1.11789 |
| 47 | 1.15497 | 1.15069 | 1.14644 | 1.14223 | 1.13807 | 1.13395 | 1.12986 | 1.12581 | 1.12180 | 1.11783 |
| 48 | 1.15490 | 1.15061 | 1.14637 | 1.14217 | 1.13800 | 1.13388 | 1.12979 | 1.12574 | 1.12173 | 1.11776 |
| 49 | 1.15483 | 1.15054 | 1.14630 | 1.14210 | 1.13793 | 1.13381 | 1.12972 | 1.12568 | 1.12167 | 1.11769 |
| 50 | 1.15476 | 1.15047 | 1.14623 | 1.14203 | 1.13786 | 1.13374 | 1.12966 | 1.12561 | 1.12160 | 1.11763 |
| 51 | 1.15469 | 1.15040 | 1.14616 | 1.14196 | 1.13779 | 1.13367 | 1.12959 | 1.12554 | 1.12153 | 1.11756 |
| 52 | 1.15461 | 1.15033 | 1.14609 | 1.14189 | 1.13773 | 1.13360 | 1.12952 | 1.12548 | 1.12147 | 1.11750 |
| 53 | 1.15454 | 1.15026 | 1.14602 | 1.14182 | 1.13766 | 1.13353 | 1.12945 | 1.12541 | 1.12140 | 1.11743 |
| 54 | 1.15447 | 1.15019 | 1.14595 | 1.14175 | 1.13759 | 1.13347 | 1.12938 | 1.12534 | 1.12133 | 1.11736 |
| 55 | 1.15440 | 1.15012 | 1.14588 | 1.14168 | 1.13752 | 1.13340 | 1.12932 | 1.12527 | 1.12127 | 1.11730 |
| 56 | 1.15433 | 1.15005 | 1.14581 | 1.14161 | 1.13745 | 1.13333 | 1.12925 | 1.12521 | 1.12120 | 1.11723 |
| 57 | 1.15426 | 1.14998 | 1.14574 | 1.14154 | 1.13738 | 1.13326 | 1.12918 | 1.12514 | 1.12114 | 1.11717 |
| 58 | 1.15418 | 1.14990 | 1.14567 | 1.14147 | 1.13731 | 1.13319 | 1.12911 | 1.12507 | 1.12107 | 1.11710 |
| 59 | 1.15411 | 1.14983 | 1.14560 | 1.14140 | 1.13724 | 1.13312 | 1.12905 | 1.12501 | 1.12100 | 1.11704 |
| 60 | 1.15404 | 1.14976 | 1.14553 | 1.14133 | 1.13717 | 1.13306 | 1.12898 | 1.12494 | 1.12094 | 1.11697 |

| Seconds of Time or Arc | 1° 50' | 1° 51' | 1° 52' | 1° 53' | 1° 54' | 1° 55' | 1° 56' | 1° 57' | 1° 58' | 1° 59' |
|---|---|---|---|---|---|---|---|---|---|---|
| 0 | 1.11697 | 1.11304 | 1.10914 | 1.10528 | 1.10146 | 1.09766 | 1.09390 | 1.09018 | 1.08648 | 1.08282 |
| 1 | 1.11690 | 1.11297 | 1.10908 | 1.10522 | 1.10139 | 1.09760 | 1.09384 | 1.09011 | 1.08642 | 1.08275 |
| 2 | 1.11684 | 1.11291 | 1.10902 | 1.10516 | 1.10133 | 1.09754 | 1.09378 | 1.09005 | 1.08636 | 1.08269 |
| 3 | 1.11677 | 1.11284 | 1.10895 | 1.10509 | 1.10127 | 1.09748 | 1.09372 | 1.08999 | 1.08630 | 1.08263 |
| 4 | 1.11671 | 1.11278 | 1.10889 | 1.10503 | 1.10120 | 1.09741 | 1.09365 | 1.08993 | 1.08624 | 1.08257 |
| 5 | 1.11664 | 1.11271 | 1.10882 | 1.10496 | 1.10114 | 1.09735 | 1.09359 | 1.08987 | 1.08617 | 1.08251 |
| 6 | 1.11658 | 1.11265 | 1.10876 | 1.10490 | 1.10108 | 1.09729 | 1.09353 | 1.08981 | 1.08611 | 1.08245 |
| 7 | 1.11651 | 1.11258 | 1.10869 | 1.10484 | 1.10101 | 1.09722 | 1.09347 | 1.08974 | 1.08605 | 1.08239 |
| 8 | 1.11644 | 1.11252 | 1.10863 | 1.10477 | 1.10095 | 1.09716 | 1.09341 | 1.08968 | 1.08599 | 1.08233 |
| 9 | 1.11638 | 1.11245 | 1.10856 | 1.10471 | 1.10089 | 1.09710 | 1.09334 | 1.08962 | 1.08593 | 1.08227 |
| 10 | 1.11631 | 1.11239 | 1.10850 | 1.10464 | 1.10082 | 1.09704 | 1.09328 | 1.08956 | 1.08587 | 1.08221 |
| 11 | 1.11625 | 1.11232 | 1.10843 | 1.10458 | 1.10076 | 1.09697 | 1.09322 | 1.08950 | 1.08581 | 1.08215 |
| 12 | 1.11618 | 1.11226 | 1.10837 | 1.10452 | 1.10070 | 1.09691 | 1.09316 | 1.08943 | 1.08575 | 1.08209 |
| 13 | 1.11612 | 1.11219 | 1.10831 | 1.10445 | 1.10063 | 1.09685 | 1.09309 | 1.08937 | 1.08568 | 1.08203 |
| 14 | 1.11605 | 1.11213 | 1.10824 | 1.10439 | 1.10057 | 1.09678 | 1.09303 | 1.08931 | 1.08562 | 1.08196 |
| 15 | 1.11598 | 1.11206 | 1.10818 | 1.10432 | 1.10051 | 1.09672 | 1.09297 | 1.08925 | 1.08556 | 1.08190 |
| 16 | 1.11592 | 1.11200 | 1.10811 | 1.10426 | 1.10044 | 1.09666 | 1.09291 | 1.08919 | 1.08550 | 1.08184 |
| 17 | 1.11585 | 1.11193 | 1.10805 | 1.10420 | 1.10038 | 1.09660 | 1.09285 | 1.08913 | 1.08544 | 1.08178 |
| 18 | 1.11579 | 1.11187 | 1.10798 | 1.10413 | 1.10032 | 1.09653 | 1.09278 | 1.08906 | 1.08538 | 1.08172 |
| 19 | 1.11572 | 1.11180 | 1.10792 | 1.10407 | 1.10025 | 1.09647 | 1.09272 | 1.08900 | 1.08532 | 1.08166 |
| 20 | 1.11566 | 1.11174 | 1.10785 | 1.10400 | 1.10019 | 1.09641 | 1.09266 | 1.08894 | 1.08526 | 1.08160 |
| 21 | 1.11559 | 1.11167 | 1.10779 | 1.10394 | 1.10013 | 1.09634 | 1.09260 | 1.08888 | 1.08519 | 1.08154 |
| 22 | 1.11552 | 1.11161 | 1.10772 | 1.10388 | 1.10006 | 1.09628 | 1.09253 | 1.08882 | 1.08513 | 1.08148 |
| 23 | 1.11546 | 1.11154 | 1.10766 | 1.10381 | 1.10000 | 1.09622 | 1.09247 | 1.08876 | 1.08507 | 1.08142 |
| 24 | 1.11539 | 1.11148 | 1.10760 | 1.10375 | 1.09994 | 1.09616 | 1.09241 | 1.08869 | 1.08501 | 1.08136 |
| 25 | 1.11533 | 1.11141 | 1.10753 | 1.10369 | 1.09987 | 1.09609 | 1.09235 | 1.08863 | 1.08495 | 1.08130 |
| 26 | 1.11526 | 1.11135 | 1.10747 | 1.10362 | 1.09981 | 1.09603 | 1.09229 | 1.08857 | 1.08489 | 1.08124 |
| 27 | 1.11520 | 1.11128 | 1.10740 | 1.10356 | 1.09975 | 1.09597 | 1.09222 | 1.08851 | 1.08483 | 1.08118 |
| 28 | 1.11513 | 1.11122 | 1.10734 | 1.10349 | 1.09968 | 1.09591 | 1.09216 | 1.08845 | 1.08477 | 1.08112 |
| 29 | 1.11507 | 1.11115 | 1.10727 | 1.10343 | 1.09962 | 1.09584 | 1.09210 | 1.08839 | 1.08471 | 1.08106 |
| 30 | 1.11500 | 1.11109 | 1.10721 | 1.10337 | 1.09956 | 1.09578 | 1.09204 | 1.08832 | 1.08464 | 1.08099 |
| 31 | 1.11493 | 1.11102 | 1.10715 | 1.10330 | 1.09949 | 1.09572 | 1.09197 | 1.08826 | 1.08458 | 1.08093 |
| 32 | 1.11487 | 1.11096 | 1.10708 | 1.10324 | 1.09943 | 1.09566 | 1.09191 | 1.08820 | 1.08452 | 1.08087 |
| 33 | 1.11480 | 1.11089 | 1.10702 | 1.10318 | 1.09937 | 1.09559 | 1.09185 | 1.08814 | 1.08446 | 1.08081 |
| 34 | 1.11474 | 1.11083 | 1.10695 | 1.10311 | 1.09930 | 1.09553 | 1.09179 | 1.08808 | 1.08440 | 1.08075 |
| 35 | 1.11467 | 1.11076 | 1.10689 | 1.10305 | 1.09924 | 1.09547 | 1.09173 | 1.08802 | 1.08434 | 1.08069 |
| 36 | 1.11461 | 1.11070 | 1.10682 | 1.10298 | 1.09918 | 1.09540 | 1.09166 | 1.08796 | 1.08428 | 1.08063 |
| 37 | 1.11454 | 1.11063 | 1.10676 | 1.10292 | 1.09911 | 1.09534 | 1.09160 | 1.08789 | 1.08422 | 1.08057 |
| 38 | 1.11448 | 1.11057 | 1.10670 | 1.10286 | 1.09905 | 1.09528 | 1.09154 | 1.08783 | 1.08416 | 1.08051 |
| 39 | 1.11441 | 1.11050 | 1.10663 | 1.10279 | 1.09899 | 1.09522 | 1.09148 | 1.08777 | 1.08409 | 1.08045 |
| 40 | 1.11435 | 1.11044 | 1.10657 | 1.10273 | 1.09893 | 1.09515 | 1.09142 | 1.08771 | 1.08403 | 1.08039 |
| 41 | 1.11428 | 1.11037 | 1.10650 | 1.10267 | 1.09886 | 1.09509 | 1.09135 | 1.08765 | 1.08397 | 1.08033 |
| 42 | 1.11421 | 1.11031 | 1.10644 | 1.10260 | 1.09880 | 1.09503 | 1.09129 | 1.08759 | 1.08391 | 1.08027 |
| 43 | 1.11415 | 1.11024 | 1.10637 | 1.10254 | 1.09874 | 1.09497 | 1.09123 | 1.08752 | 1.08385 | 1.08021 |
| 44 | 1.11408 | 1.11018 | 1.10631 | 1.10247 | 1.09867 | 1.09490 | 1.09117 | 1.08746 | 1.08379 | 1.08015 |
| 45 | 1.11402 | 1.11011 | 1.10625 | 1.10241 | 1.09861 | 1.09484 | 1.09111 | 1.08740 | 1.08373 | 1.08009 |
| 46 | 1.11395 | 1.11005 | 1.10618 | 1.10235 | 1.09855 | 1.09478 | 1.09104 | 1.08734 | 1.08367 | 1.08003 |
| 47 | 1.11389 | 1.10999 | 1.10612 | 1.10228 | 1.09848 | 1.09472 | 1.09098 | 1.08728 | 1.08361 | 1.07997 |
| 48 | 1.11382 | 1.10992 | 1.10605 | 1.10222 | 1.09842 | 1.09465 | 1.09092 | 1.08722 | 1.08355 | 1.07991 |
| 49 | 1.11376 | 1.10986 | 1.10599 | 1.10216 | 1.09836 | 1.09459 | 1.09086 | 1.08716 | 1.08349 | 1.07985 |
| 50 | 1.11369 | 1.10979 | 1.10593 | 1.10209 | 1.09829 | 1.09453 | 1.09080 | 1.08709 | 1.08342 | 1.07978 |
| 51 | 1.11363 | 1.10973 | 1.10586 | 1.10203 | 1.09823 | 1.09447 | 1.09073 | 1.08703 | 1.08336 | 1.07972 |
| 52 | 1.11356 | 1.10966 | 1.10580 | 1.10197 | 1.09817 | 1.09440 | 1.09067 | 1.08697 | 1.08330 | 1.07966 |
| 53 | 1.11350 | 1.10960 | 1.10573 | 1.10190 | 1.09811 | 1.09434 | 1.09061 | 1.08691 | 1.08324 | 1.07960 |
| 54 | 1.11343 | 1.10953 | 1.10567 | 1.10184 | 1.09804 | 1.09428 | 1.09055 | 1.08685 | 1.08318 | 1.07954 |
| 55 | 1.11337 | 1.10947 | 1.10560 | 1.10178 | 1.09798 | 1.09422 | 1.09049 | 1.08679 | 1.08312 | 1.07948 |
| 56 | 1.11330 | 1.10940 | 1.10554 | 1.10171 | 1.09792 | 1.09415 | 1.09042 | 1.08673 | 1.08306 | 1.07942 |
| 57 | 1.11324 | 1.10934 | 1.10548 | 1.10165 | 1.09785 | 1.09409 | 1.09036 | 1.08666 | 1.08300 | 1.07936 |
| 58 | 1.11317 | 1.10927 | 1.10541 | 1.10158 | 1.09779 | 1.09403 | 1.09030 | 1.08660 | 1.08294 | 1.07930 |
| 59 | 1.11310 | 1.10921 | 1.10535 | 1.10152 | 1.09773 | 1.09397 | 1.09024 | 1.08654 | 1.08288 | 1.07924 |
| 60 | 1.11304 | 1.10914 | 1.10528 | 1.10146 | 1.09766 | 1.09390 | 1.09018 | 1.08648 | 1.08282 | 1.07918 |

# Table XI House Cusp Interpolation Between Sidereal Times

| CUSP INTVL | LOCAL SIDEREAL TIME INCREMENT<br>m 0 s 4 | m 0 s 8 | m 0 s 12 | m 0 s 16 | m 0 s 20 | m 0 s 24 | m 0 s 28 | m 0 s 32 | m 0 s 36 | m 0 s 40 | m 0 s 44 | m 0 s 48 | m 0 s 52 | m 0 s 56 | m 1 s 0 | m 1 s 4 | m 1 s 8 | m 1 s 12 | m 1 s 16 | m 1 s 20 | CUSP INTVL |
|---|---|---|---|---|---|---|---|---|---|---|---|---|---|---|---|---|---|---|---|---|---|
| ° ' | ° ' | ° ' | ° ' | ° ' | ° ' | ° ' | ° ' | ° ' | ° ' | ° ' | ° ' | ° ' | ° ' | ° ' | ° ' | ° ' | ° ' | ° ' | ° ' | ° ' | ° ' |
| 0 31 | 0 1 | 0 1 | 0 2 | 0 2 | 0 3 | 0 3 | 0 4 | 0 4 | 0 5 | 0 5 | 0 6 | 0 6 | 0 7 | 0 7 | 0 8 | 0 8 | 0 9 | 0 9 | 0 10 | 0 10 | 0 31 |
| 0 32 | 0 1 | 0 1 | 0 2 | 0 2 | 0 3 | 0 3 | 0 4 | 0 4 | 0 5 | 0 5 | 0 6 | 0 6 | 0 7 | 0 7 | 0 8 | 0 8 | 0 9 | 0 10 | 0 10 | 0 11 | 0 32 |
| 0 33 | 0 1 | 0 1 | 0 2 | 0 2 | 0 3 | 0 3 | 0 4 | 0 4 | 0 5 | 0 6 | 0 6 | 0 7 | 0 7 | 0 8 | 0 8 | 0 9 | 0 9 | 0 10 | 0 10 | 0 11 | 0 33 |
| 0 34 | 0 1 | 0 1 | 0 2 | 0 2 | 0 3 | 0 3 | 0 4 | 0 5 | 0 5 | 0 6 | 0 6 | 0 7 | 0 7 | 0 8 | 0 9 | 0 9 | 0 10 | 0 10 | 0 11 | 0 11 | 0 34 |
| 0 35 | 0 1 | 0 1 | 0 2 | 0 2 | 0 3 | 0 4 | 0 4 | 0 5 | 0 5 | 0 6 | 0 6 | 0 7 | 0 8 | 0 8 | 0 9 | 0 9 | 0 10 | 0 11 | 0 11 | 0 12 | 0 35 |
| 0 36 | 0 1 | 0 1 | 0 2 | 0 2 | 0 3 | 0 4 | 0 4 | 0 5 | 0 5 | 0 6 | 0 7 | 0 7 | 0 8 | 0 8 | 0 9 | 0 10 | 0 10 | 0 11 | 0 11 | 0 12 | 0 36 |
| 0 37 | 0 1 | 0 1 | 0 2 | 0 2 | 0 3 | 0 4 | 0 4 | 0 5 | 0 6 | 0 6 | 0 7 | 0 7 | 0 8 | 0 9 | 0 9 | 0 10 | 0 10 | 0 11 | 0 12 | 0 12 | 0 37 |
| 0 38 | 0 1 | 0 1 | 0 2 | 0 3 | 0 3 | 0 4 | 0 4 | 0 5 | 0 6 | 0 6 | 0 7 | 0 8 | 0 8 | 0 9 | 0 10 | 0 10 | 0 11 | 0 11 | 0 12 | 0 13 | 0 38 |
| 0 39 | 0 1 | 0 1 | 0 2 | 0 3 | 0 3 | 0 4 | 0 5 | 0 5 | 0 6 | 0 7 | 0 7 | 0 8 | 0 8 | 0 9 | 0 10 | 0 10 | 0 11 | 0 12 | 0 12 | 0 13 | 0 39 |
| 0 40 | 0 1 | 0 1 | 0 2 | 0 3 | 0 3 | 0 4 | 0 5 | 0 5 | 0 6 | 0 7 | 0 7 | 0 8 | 0 9 | 0 9 | 0 10 | 0 11 | 0 11 | 0 12 | 0 13 | 0 13 | 0 40 |
| 0 41 | 0 1 | 0 1 | 0 2 | 0 3 | 0 3 | 0 4 | 0 5 | 0 5 | 0 6 | 0 7 | 0 8 | 0 8 | 0 9 | 0 10 | 0 10 | 0 11 | 0 12 | 0 12 | 0 13 | 0 14 | 0 41 |
| 0 42 | 0 1 | 0 1 | 0 2 | 0 3 | 0 4 | 0 4 | 0 5 | 0 6 | 0 6 | 0 7 | 0 8 | 0 8 | 0 9 | 0 10 | 0 11 | 0 11 | 0 12 | 0 13 | 0 13 | 0 14 | 0 42 |
| 0 43 | 0 1 | 0 1 | 0 2 | 0 3 | 0 4 | 0 4 | 0 5 | 0 6 | 0 6 | 0 7 | 0 8 | 0 9 | 0 9 | 0 10 | 0 11 | 0 11 | 0 12 | 0 13 | 0 14 | 0 14 | 0 43 |
| 0 44 | 0 1 | 0 1 | 0 2 | 0 3 | 0 4 | 0 4 | 0 5 | 0 6 | 0 7 | 0 7 | 0 8 | 0 9 | 0 10 | 0 10 | 0 11 | 0 12 | 0 12 | 0 13 | 0 14 | 0 15 | 0 44 |
| 0 45 | 0 1 | 0 2 | 0 2 | 0 3 | 0 4 | 0 5 | 0 5 | 0 6 | 0 7 | 0 8 | 0 8 | 0 9 | 0 10 | 0 11 | 0 11 | 0 12 | 0 13 | 0 14 | 0 14 | 0 15 | 0 45 |
| 0 46 | 0 1 | 0 2 | 0 2 | 0 3 | 0 4 | 0 5 | 0 5 | 0 6 | 0 7 | 0 8 | 0 8 | 0 9 | 0 10 | 0 11 | 0 12 | 0 12 | 0 13 | 0 14 | 0 15 | 0 15 | 0 46 |
| 0 47 | 0 1 | 0 2 | 0 2 | 0 3 | 0 4 | 0 5 | 0 5 | 0 6 | 0 7 | 0 8 | 0 9 | 0 9 | 0 10 | 0 11 | 0 12 | 0 13 | 0 13 | 0 14 | 0 15 | 0 16 | 0 47 |
| 0 48 | 0 1 | 0 2 | 0 2 | 0 3 | 0 4 | 0 5 | 0 6 | 0 6 | 0 7 | 0 8 | 0 9 | 0 10 | 0 10 | 0 11 | 0 12 | 0 13 | 0 14 | 0 14 | 0 15 | 0 16 | 0 48 |
| 0 49 | 0 1 | 0 2 | 0 2 | 0 3 | 0 4 | 0 5 | 0 6 | 0 7 | 0 7 | 0 8 | 0 9 | 0 10 | 0 11 | 0 11 | 0 12 | 0 13 | 0 14 | 0 15 | 0 16 | 0 16 | 0 49 |
| 0 50 | 0 1 | 0 2 | 0 3 | 0 3 | 0 4 | 0 5 | 0 6 | 0 7 | 0 8 | 0 8 | 0 9 | 0 10 | 0 11 | 0 12 | 0 13 | 0 13 | 0 14 | 0 15 | 0 16 | 0 17 | 0 50 |
| 0 51 | 0 1 | 0 2 | 0 3 | 0 3 | 0 4 | 0 5 | 0 6 | 0 7 | 0 8 | 0 9 | 0 9 | 0 10 | 0 11 | 0 12 | 0 13 | 0 14 | 0 14 | 0 15 | 0 16 | 0 17 | 0 51 |
| 0 52 | 0 1 | 0 2 | 0 3 | 0 3 | 0 4 | 0 5 | 0 6 | 0 7 | 0 8 | 0 9 | 0 10 | 0 10 | 0 11 | 0 12 | 0 13 | 0 14 | 0 15 | 0 16 | 0 16 | 0 17 | 0 52 |
| 0 53 | 0 1 | 0 2 | 0 3 | 0 4 | 0 4 | 0 5 | 0 6 | 0 7 | 0 8 | 0 9 | 0 10 | 0 11 | 0 11 | 0 12 | 0 13 | 0 14 | 0 15 | 0 16 | 0 17 | 0 18 | 0 53 |
| 0 54 | 0 1 | 0 2 | 0 3 | 0 4 | 0 5 | 0 5 | 0 6 | 0 7 | 0 8 | 0 9 | 0 10 | 0 11 | 0 12 | 0 13 | 0 14 | 0 14 | 0 15 | 0 16 | 0 17 | 0 18 | 0 54 |
| 0 55 | 0 1 | 0 2 | 0 3 | 0 4 | 0 5 | 0 6 | 0 6 | 0 7 | 0 8 | 0 9 | 0 10 | 0 11 | 0 12 | 0 13 | 0 14 | 0 15 | 0 16 | 0 17 | 0 17 | 0 18 | 0 55 |
| 0 56 | 0 1 | 0 2 | 0 3 | 0 4 | 0 5 | 0 6 | 0 7 | 0 7 | 0 8 | 0 9 | 0 10 | 0 11 | 0 12 | 0 13 | 0 14 | 0 15 | 0 16 | 0 17 | 0 18 | 0 19 | 0 56 |
| 0 57 | 0 1 | 0 2 | 0 3 | 0 4 | 0 5 | 0 6 | 0 7 | 0 8 | 0 9 | 0 10 | 0 10 | 0 11 | 0 12 | 0 13 | 0 14 | 0 15 | 0 16 | 0 17 | 0 18 | 0 19 | 0 57 |
| 0 58 | 0 1 | 0 2 | 0 3 | 0 4 | 0 5 | 0 6 | 0 7 | 0 8 | 0 9 | 0 10 | 0 11 | 0 12 | 0 13 | 0 14 | 0 15 | 0 15 | 0 16 | 0 17 | 0 18 | 0 19 | 0 58 |
| 0 59 | 0 1 | 0 2 | 0 3 | 0 4 | 0 5 | 0 6 | 0 7 | 0 8 | 0 9 | 0 10 | 0 11 | 0 12 | 0 13 | 0 14 | 0 15 | 0 16 | 0 17 | 0 18 | 0 19 | 0 20 | 0 59 |
| 1 0 | 0 1 | 0 2 | 0 3 | 0 4 | 0 5 | 0 6 | 0 7 | 0 8 | 0 9 | 0 10 | 0 11 | 0 12 | 0 13 | 0 14 | 0 15 | 0 16 | 0 17 | 0 18 | 0 19 | 0 20 | 1 0 |
| 1 1 | 0 1 | 0 2 | 0 3 | 0 4 | 0 5 | 0 6 | 0 7 | 0 8 | 0 9 | 0 10 | 0 11 | 0 12 | 0 13 | 0 14 | 0 15 | 0 16 | 0 17 | 0 18 | 0 19 | 0 20 | 1 1 |
| 1 2 | 0 1 | 0 2 | 0 3 | 0 4 | 0 5 | 0 6 | 0 7 | 0 8 | 0 9 | 0 10 | 0 11 | 0 12 | 0 13 | 0 14 | 0 16 | 0 17 | 0 18 | 0 19 | 0 20 | 0 21 | 1 2 |
| 1 3 | 0 1 | 0 2 | 0 3 | 0 4 | 0 5 | 0 6 | 0 7 | 0 8 | 0 9 | 0 11 | 0 12 | 0 13 | 0 14 | 0 15 | 0 16 | 0 17 | 0 18 | 0 19 | 0 20 | 0 21 | 1 3 |
| 1 4 | 0 1 | 0 2 | 0 3 | 0 4 | 0 5 | 0 6 | 0 7 | 0 9 | 0 10 | 0 11 | 0 12 | 0 13 | 0 14 | 0 15 | 0 16 | 0 17 | 0 18 | 0 19 | 0 20 | 0 21 | 1 4 |
| 1 5 | 0 1 | 0 2 | 0 3 | 0 4 | 0 5 | 0 7 | 0 8 | 0 9 | 0 10 | 0 11 | 0 12 | 0 13 | 0 14 | 0 15 | 0 16 | 0 17 | 0 18 | 0 20 | 0 21 | 0 22 | 1 5 |
| 1 6 | 0 1 | 0 2 | 0 3 | 0 4 | 0 6 | 0 7 | 0 8 | 0 9 | 0 10 | 0 11 | 0 12 | 0 13 | 0 14 | 0 15 | 0 17 | 0 18 | 0 19 | 0 20 | 0 21 | 0 22 | 1 6 |
| 1 7 | 0 1 | 0 2 | 0 3 | 0 4 | 0 6 | 0 7 | 0 8 | 0 9 | 0 10 | 0 11 | 0 12 | 0 13 | 0 15 | 0 16 | 0 17 | 0 18 | 0 19 | 0 20 | 0 21 | 0 22 | 1 7 |
| 1 8 | 0 1 | 0 2 | 0 3 | 0 5 | 0 6 | 0 7 | 0 8 | 0 9 | 0 10 | 0 11 | 0 12 | 0 14 | 0 15 | 0 16 | 0 17 | 0 18 | 0 19 | 0 20 | 0 22 | 0 23 | 1 8 |
| 1 9 | 0 1 | 0 2 | 0 3 | 0 5 | 0 6 | 0 7 | 0 8 | 0 9 | 0 10 | 0 12 | 0 13 | 0 14 | 0 15 | 0 16 | 0 17 | 0 18 | 0 20 | 0 21 | 0 22 | 0 23 | 1 9 |
| 1 10 | 0 1 | 0 2 | 0 4 | 0 5 | 0 6 | 0 7 | 0 8 | 0 9 | 0 11 | 0 12 | 0 13 | 0 14 | 0 15 | 0 16 | 0 18 | 0 19 | 0 20 | 0 21 | 0 22 | 0 23 | 1 10 |
| 1 11 | 0 1 | 0 2 | 0 4 | 0 5 | 0 6 | 0 7 | 0 8 | 0 9 | 0 11 | 0 12 | 0 13 | 0 14 | 0 15 | 0 17 | 0 18 | 0 19 | 0 20 | 0 21 | 0 22 | 0 24 | 1 11 |
| 1 12 | 0 1 | 0 2 | 0 4 | 0 5 | 0 6 | 0 7 | 0 8 | 0 10 | 0 11 | 0 12 | 0 13 | 0 14 | 0 16 | 0 17 | 0 18 | 0 19 | 0 20 | 0 22 | 0 23 | 0 24 | 1 12 |
| 1 13 | 0 1 | 0 2 | 0 4 | 0 5 | 0 6 | 0 7 | 0 9 | 0 10 | 0 11 | 0 12 | 0 13 | 0 15 | 0 16 | 0 17 | 0 18 | 0 19 | 0 21 | 0 22 | 0 23 | 0 24 | 1 13 |
| 1 14 | 0 1 | 0 2 | 0 4 | 0 5 | 0 6 | 0 7 | 0 9 | 0 10 | 0 11 | 0 12 | 0 14 | 0 15 | 0 16 | 0 17 | 0 19 | 0 20 | 0 21 | 0 22 | 0 23 | 0 25 | 1 14 |
| 1 15 | 0 1 | 0 3 | 0 4 | 0 5 | 0 6 | 0 8 | 0 9 | 0 10 | 0 11 | 0 13 | 0 14 | 0 15 | 0 16 | 0 18 | 0 19 | 0 20 | 0 21 | 0 23 | 0 24 | 0 25 | 1 15 |
| 1 16 | 0 1 | 0 3 | 0 4 | 0 5 | 0 6 | 0 8 | 0 9 | 0 10 | 0 11 | 0 13 | 0 14 | 0 15 | 0 16 | 0 18 | 0 19 | 0 20 | 0 22 | 0 23 | 0 24 | 0 25 | 1 16 |
| 1 17 | 0 1 | 0 3 | 0 4 | 0 5 | 0 6 | 0 8 | 0 9 | 0 10 | 0 12 | 0 13 | 0 14 | 0 15 | 0 17 | 0 18 | 0 19 | 0 21 | 0 22 | 0 23 | 0 24 | 0 26 | 1 17 |
| 1 18 | 0 1 | 0 3 | 0 4 | 0 5 | 0 7 | 0 8 | 0 9 | 0 10 | 0 12 | 0 13 | 0 14 | 0 16 | 0 17 | 0 18 | 0 20 | 0 21 | 0 22 | 0 23 | 0 25 | 0 26 | 1 18 |
| 1 19 | 0 1 | 0 3 | 0 4 | 0 5 | 0 7 | 0 8 | 0 9 | 0 11 | 0 12 | 0 13 | 0 14 | 0 16 | 0 17 | 0 18 | 0 20 | 0 21 | 0 22 | 0 24 | 0 25 | 0 26 | 1 19 |
| 1 20 | 0 1 | 0 3 | 0 4 | 0 5 | 0 7 | 0 8 | 0 9 | 0 11 | 0 12 | 0 13 | 0 15 | 0 16 | 0 17 | 0 19 | 0 20 | 0 21 | 0 23 | 0 24 | 0 25 | 0 27 | 1 20 |
| 1 21 | 0 1 | 0 3 | 0 4 | 0 5 | 0 7 | 0 8 | 0 9 | 0 11 | 0 12 | 0 14 | 0 15 | 0 16 | 0 18 | 0 19 | 0 20 | 0 22 | 0 23 | 0 24 | 0 26 | 0 27 | 1 21 |
| 1 22 | 0 1 | 0 3 | 0 4 | 0 5 | 0 7 | 0 8 | 0 10 | 0 11 | 0 12 | 0 14 | 0 15 | 0 16 | 0 18 | 0 19 | 0 21 | 0 22 | 0 23 | 0 25 | 0 26 | 0 27 | 1 22 |
| 1 23 | 0 1 | 0 3 | 0 4 | 0 6 | 0 7 | 0 8 | 0 10 | 0 11 | 0 12 | 0 14 | 0 15 | 0 17 | 0 18 | 0 19 | 0 21 | 0 22 | 0 24 | 0 25 | 0 26 | 0 28 | 1 23 |
| 1 24 | 0 1 | 0 3 | 0 4 | 0 6 | 0 7 | 0 8 | 0 10 | 0 11 | 0 13 | 0 14 | 0 15 | 0 17 | 0 18 | 0 20 | 0 21 | 0 22 | 0 24 | 0 25 | 0 27 | 0 28 | 1 24 |
| 1 25 | 0 1 | 0 3 | 0 4 | 0 6 | 0 7 | 0 9 | 0 10 | 0 11 | 0 13 | 0 14 | 0 16 | 0 17 | 0 18 | 0 20 | 0 21 | 0 23 | 0 24 | 0 26 | 0 27 | 0 28 | 1 25 |
| 1 26 | 0 1 | 0 3 | 0 4 | 0 6 | 0 7 | 0 9 | 0 10 | 0 11 | 0 13 | 0 14 | 0 16 | 0 17 | 0 19 | 0 20 | 0 22 | 0 23 | 0 24 | 0 26 | 0 27 | 0 29 | 1 26 |
| 1 27 | 0 1 | 0 3 | 0 4 | 0 6 | 0 7 | 0 9 | 0 10 | 0 12 | 0 13 | 0 15 | 0 16 | 0 17 | 0 19 | 0 20 | 0 22 | 0 23 | 0 25 | 0 26 | 0 28 | 0 29 | 1 27 |
| 1 28 | 0 1 | 0 3 | 0 4 | 0 6 | 0 7 | 0 9 | 0 10 | 0 12 | 0 13 | 0 15 | 0 16 | 0 18 | 0 19 | 0 21 | 0 22 | 0 23 | 0 25 | 0 26 | 0 28 | 0 29 | 1 28 |
| 1 29 | 0 1 | 0 3 | 0 4 | 0 6 | 0 7 | 0 9 | 0 10 | 0 12 | 0 13 | 0 15 | 0 16 | 0 18 | 0 19 | 0 21 | 0 22 | 0 24 | 0 25 | 0 27 | 0 28 | 0 30 | 1 29 |
| 1 30 | 0 2 | 0 3 | 0 5 | 0 6 | 0 8 | 0 9 | 0 11 | 0 12 | 0 14 | 0 15 | 0 17 | 0 18 | 0 20 | 0 21 | 0 23 | 0 24 | 0 26 | 0 27 | 0 29 | 0 30 | 1 30 |
| 1 31 | 0 2 | 0 3 | 0 5 | 0 6 | 0 8 | 0 9 | 0 11 | 0 12 | 0 14 | 0 15 | 0 17 | 0 18 | 0 20 | 0 21 | 0 23 | 0 24 | 0 26 | 0 27 | 0 29 | 0 30 | 1 31 |
| 1 32 | 0 2 | 0 3 | 0 5 | 0 6 | 0 8 | 0 9 | 0 11 | 0 12 | 0 14 | 0 15 | 0 17 | 0 18 | 0 20 | 0 21 | 0 23 | 0 25 | 0 26 | 0 28 | 0 29 | 0 31 | 1 32 |
| 1 33 | 0 2 | 0 3 | 0 5 | 0 6 | 0 8 | 0 9 | 0 11 | 0 12 | 0 14 | 0 16 | 0 17 | 0 19 | 0 20 | 0 22 | 0 23 | 0 25 | 0 26 | 0 28 | 0 29 | 0 31 | 1 33 |
| 1 34 | 0 2 | 0 3 | 0 5 | 0 6 | 0 8 | 0 9 | 0 11 | 0 13 | 0 14 | 0 16 | 0 17 | 0 19 | 0 20 | 0 22 | 0 24 | 0 25 | 0 27 | 0 28 | 0 30 | 0 31 | 1 34 |
| 1 35 | 0 2 | 0 3 | 0 5 | 0 6 | 0 8 | 0 10 | 0 11 | 0 13 | 0 14 | 0 16 | 0 17 | 0 19 | 0 21 | 0 22 | 0 24 | 0 25 | 0 27 | 0 29 | 0 30 | 0 32 | 1 35 |
| 1 36 | 0 2 | 0 3 | 0 5 | 0 6 | 0 8 | 0 10 | 0 11 | 0 13 | 0 14 | 0 16 | 0 18 | 0 19 | 0 21 | 0 22 | 0 24 | 0 26 | 0 27 | 0 29 | 0 30 | 0 32 | 1 36 |
| 1 37 | 0 2 | 0 3 | 0 5 | 0 6 | 0 8 | 0 10 | 0 11 | 0 13 | 0 15 | 0 16 | 0 18 | 0 19 | 0 21 | 0 23 | 0 24 | 0 26 | 0 27 | 0 29 | 0 31 | 0 32 | 1 37 |
| 1 38 | 0 2 | 0 3 | 0 5 | 0 7 | 0 8 | 0 10 | 0 11 | 0 13 | 0 15 | 0 16 | 0 18 | 0 20 | 0 21 | 0 23 | 0 25 | 0 26 | 0 28 | 0 29 | 0 31 | 0 33 | 1 38 |
| 1 39 | 0 2 | 0 3 | 0 5 | 0 7 | 0 8 | 0 10 | 0 12 | 0 13 | 0 15 | 0 17 | 0 18 | 0 20 | 0 21 | 0 23 | 0 25 | 0 26 | 0 28 | 0 30 | 0 31 | 0 33 | 1 39 |
| 1 40 | 0 2 | 0 3 | 0 5 | 0 7 | 0 8 | 0 10 | 0 12 | 0 13 | 0 15 | 0 17 | 0 18 | 0 20 | 0 22 | 0 23 | 0 25 | 0 27 | 0 28 | 0 30 | 0 32 | 0 33 | 1 40 |
| 1 41 | 0 2 | 0 3 | 0 5 | 0 7 | 0 8 | 0 10 | 0 12 | 0 13 | 0 15 | 0 17 | 0 19 | 0 20 | 0 22 | 0 24 | 0 25 | 0 27 | 0 29 | 0 30 | 0 32 | 0 34 | 1 41 |
| 1 42 | 0 2 | 0 3 | 0 5 | 0 7 | 0 9 | 0 10 | 0 12 | 0 14 | 0 15 | 0 17 | 0 19 | 0 20 | 0 22 | 0 24 | 0 26 | 0 27 | 0 29 | 0 31 | 0 32 | 0 34 | 1 42 |
| 1 43 | 0 2 | 0 3 | 0 5 | 0 7 | 0 9 | 0 10 | 0 12 | 0 14 | 0 15 | 0 17 | 0 19 | 0 21 | 0 22 | 0 24 | 0 26 | 0 27 | 0 29 | 0 31 | 0 33 | 0 34 | 1 43 |
| 1 44 | 0 2 | 0 3 | 0 5 | 0 7 | 0 9 | 0 10 | 0 12 | 0 14 | 0 16 | 0 17 | 0 19 | 0 21 | 0 23 | 0 24 | 0 26 | 0 28 | 0 29 | 0 31 | 0 33 | 0 35 | 1 44 |
| 1 45 | 0 2 | 0 4 | 0 5 | 0 7 | 0 9 | 0 11 | 0 12 | 0 14 | 0 16 | 0 18 | 0 19 | 0 21 | 0 23 | 0 25 | 0 26 | 0 28 | 0 30 | 0 32 | 0 33 | 0 35 | 1 45 |
| 1 46 | 0 2 | 0 4 | 0 5 | 0 7 | 0 9 | 0 11 | 0 12 | 0 14 | 0 16 | 0 18 | 0 19 | 0 21 | 0 23 | 0 25 | 0 27 | 0 28 | 0 30 | 0 32 | 0 34 | 0 35 | 1 46 |
| 1 47 | 0 2 | 0 4 | 0 5 | 0 7 | 0 9 | 0 11 | 0 12 | 0 14 | 0 16 | 0 18 | 0 20 | 0 21 | 0 23 | 0 25 | 0 27 | 0 29 | 0 30 | 0 32 | 0 34 | 0 36 | 1 47 |
| 1 48 | 0 2 | 0 4 | 0 5 | 0 7 | 0 9 | 0 11 | 0 13 | 0 14 | 0 16 | 0 18 | 0 20 | 0 22 | 0 23 | 0 25 | 0 27 | 0 29 | 0 31 | 0 32 | 0 34 | 0 36 | 1 48 |
| 1 49 | 0 2 | 0 4 | 0 5 | 0 7 | 0 9 | 0 11 | 0 13 | 0 15 | 0 16 | 0 18 | 0 20 | 0 22 | 0 24 | 0 25 | 0 27 | 0 29 | 0 31 | 0 33 | 0 35 | 0 36 | 1 49 |
| 1 50 | 0 2 | 0 4 | 0 6 | 0 7 | 0 9 | 0 11 | 0 13 | 0 15 | 0 17 | 0 18 | 0 20 | 0 22 | 0 24 | 0 26 | 0 28 | 0 29 | 0 31 | 0 33 | 0 35 | 0 37 | 1 50 |
| 1 51 | 0 2 | 0 4 | 0 6 | 0 7 | 0 9 | 0 11 | 0 13 | 0 15 | 0 17 | 0 19 | 0 20 | 0 22 | 0 24 | 0 26 | 0 28 | 0 30 | 0 31 | 0 33 | 0 35 | 0 37 | 1 51 |
| 1 52 | 0 2 | 0 4 | 0 6 | 0 7 | 0 9 | 0 11 | 0 13 | 0 15 | 0 17 | 0 19 | 0 21 | 0 22 | 0 24 | 0 26 | 0 28 | 0 30 | 0 32 | 0 34 | 0 35 | 0 37 | 1 52 |
| 1 53 | 0 2 | 0 4 | 0 6 | 0 8 | 0 9 | 0 11 | 0 13 | 0 15 | 0 17 | 0 19 | 0 21 | 0 23 | 0 24 | 0 26 | 0 28 | 0 30 | 0 32 | 0 34 | 0 36 | 0 38 | 1 53 |
| 1 54 | 0 2 | 0 4 | 0 6 | 0 8 | 0 10 | 0 11 | 0 13 | 0 15 | 0 17 | 0 19 | 0 21 | 0 23 | 0 25 | 0 27 | 0 29 | 0 30 | 0 32 | 0 34 | 0 36 | 0 38 | 1 54 |
| 1 55 | 0 2 | 0 4 | 0 6 | 0 8 | 0 10 | 0 12 | 0 13 | 0 15 | 0 17 | 0 19 | 0 21 | 0 23 | 0 25 | 0 27 | 0 29 | 0 31 | 0 33 | 0 35 | 0 36 | 0 38 | 1 55 |
| 1 56 | 0 2 | 0 4 | 0 6 | 0 8 | 0 10 | 0 12 | 0 14 | 0 15 | 0 17 | 0 19 | 0 21 | 0 23 | 0 25 | 0 27 | 0 29 | 0 31 | 0 33 | 0 35 | 0 37 | 0 39 | 1 56 |
| 1 57 | 0 2 | 0 4 | 0 6 | 0 8 | 0 10 | 0 12 | 0 14 | 0 16 | 0 18 | 0 20 | 0 21 | 0 23 | 0 25 | 0 27 | 0 29 | 0 31 | 0 33 | 0 35 | 0 37 | 0 39 | 1 57 |
| 1 58 | 0 2 | 0 4 | 0 6 | 0 8 | 0 10 | 0 12 | 0 14 | 0 16 | 0 18 | 0 20 | 0 22 | 0 24 | 0 26 | 0 28 | 0 30 | 0 31 | 0 33 | 0 35 | 0 37 | 0 39 | 1 58 |
| 1 59 | 0 2 | 0 4 | 0 6 | 0 8 | 0 10 | 0 12 | 0 14 | 0 16 | 0 18 | 0 20 | 0 22 | 0 24 | 0 26 | 0 28 | 0 30 | 0 32 | 0 34 | 0 36 | 0 38 | 0 40 | 1 59 |
| 2 0 | 0 2 | 0 4 | 0 6 | 0 8 | 0 10 | 0 12 | 0 14 | 0 16 | 0 18 | 0 20 | 0 22 | 0 24 | 0 26 | 0 28 | 0 30 | 0 32 | 0 34 | 0 36 | 0 38 | 0 40 | 2 0 |

# Table XI House Cusp Interpolation Between Sidereal Times

LOCAL SIDEREAL TIME INCREMENT

| CUSP INTVL | m s<br>1 24 | m s<br>1 28 | m s<br>1 32 | m s<br>1 36 | m s<br>1 40 | m s<br>1 44 | m s<br>1 48 | m s<br>1 52 | m s<br>1 56 | m s<br>2 0 | m s<br>2 4 | m s<br>2 8 | m s<br>2 12 | m s<br>2 16 | m s<br>2 20 | m s<br>2 24 | m s<br>2 28 | m s<br>2 32 | m s<br>2 36 | m s<br>2 40 | CUSP INTVL |
|---|---|---|---|---|---|---|---|---|---|---|---|---|---|---|---|---|---|---|---|---|---|
| ° ' | ° ' | ° ' | ° ' | ° ' | ° ' | ° ' | ° ' | ° ' | ° ' | ° ' | ° ' | ° ' | ° ' | ° ' | ° ' | ° ' | ° ' | ° ' | ° ' | ° ' | ° ' |
| 0 31 | 0 11 | 0 11 | 0 12 | 0 12 | 0 13 | 0 13 | 0 14 | 0 14 | 0 15 | 0 16 | 0 16 | 0 17 | 0 17 | 0 18 | 0 18 | 0 19 | 0 19 | 0 20 | 0 20 | 0 21 | 0 31 |
| 0 32 | 0 11 | 0 12 | 0 12 | 0 13 | 0 13 | 0 14 | 0 14 | 0 15 | 0 15 | 0 16 | 0 17 | 0 17 | 0 18 | 0 18 | 0 19 | 0 19 | 0 20 | 0 20 | 0 21 | 0 21 | 0 32 |
| 0 33 | 0 12 | 0 12 | 0 13 | 0 13 | 0 14 | 0 14 | 0 15 | 0 15 | 0 16 | 0 17 | 0 17 | 0 18 | 0 18 | 0 19 | 0 19 | 0 20 | 0 20 | 0 21 | 0 21 | 0 22 | 0 33 |
| 0 34 | 0 12 | 0 12 | 0 13 | 0 13 | 0 14 | 0 15 | 0 15 | 0 16 | 0 16 | 0 17 | 0 18 | 0 18 | 0 19 | 0 19 | 0 20 | 0 20 | 0 21 | 0 22 | 0 22 | 0 23 | 0 34 |
| 0 35 | 0 12 | 0 13 | 0 13 | 0 14 | 0 15 | 0 15 | 0 16 | 0 16 | 0 17 | 0 18 | 0 18 | 0 19 | 0 19 | 0 20 | 0 20 | 0 21 | 0 22 | 0 22 | 0 23 | 0 23 | 0 35 |
| 0 36 | 0 13 | 0 13 | 0 14 | 0 14 | 0 15 | 0 16 | 0 16 | 0 17 | 0 17 | 0 18 | 0 19 | 0 19 | 0 20 | 0 20 | 0 21 | 0 22 | 0 22 | 0 23 | 0 23 | 0 24 | 0 36 |
| 0 37 | 0 13 | 0 14 | 0 14 | 0 15 | 0 15 | 0 16 | 0 17 | 0 17 | 0 18 | 0 19 | 0 19 | 0 20 | 0 20 | 0 21 | 0 22 | 0 22 | 0 23 | 0 23 | 0 24 | 0 25 | 0 37 |
| 0 38 | 0 13 | 0 14 | 0 15 | 0 15 | 0 16 | 0 16 | 0 17 | 0 18 | 0 18 | 0 19 | 0 20 | 0 20 | 0 21 | 0 22 | 0 22 | 0 23 | 0 23 | 0 24 | 0 25 | 0 25 | 0 38 |
| 0 39 | 0 14 | 0 14 | 0 15 | 0 16 | 0 16 | 0 17 | 0 18 | 0 18 | 0 19 | 0 20 | 0 20 | 0 21 | 0 21 | 0 22 | 0 23 | 0 23 | 0 24 | 0 25 | 0 25 | 0 26 | 0 39 |
| 0 40 | 0 14 | 0 15 | 0 15 | 0 16 | 0 17 | 0 17 | 0 18 | 0 19 | 0 19 | 0 20 | 0 21 | 0 21 | 0 22 | 0 23 | 0 23 | 0 24 | 0 25 | 0 25 | 0 26 | 0 27 | 0 40 |
| 0 41 | 0 14 | 0 15 | 0 16 | 0 16 | 0 17 | 0 18 | 0 18 | 0 19 | 0 20 | 0 21 | 0 21 | 0 22 | 0 23 | 0 23 | 0 24 | 0 25 | 0 25 | 0 26 | 0 27 | 0 27 | 0 41 |
| 0 42 | 0 15 | 0 15 | 0 16 | 0 17 | 0 18 | 0 18 | 0 19 | 0 20 | 0 20 | 0 21 | 0 22 | 0 22 | 0 23 | 0 24 | 0 25 | 0 25 | 0 26 | 0 27 | 0 27 | 0 28 | 0 42 |
| 0 43 | 0 15 | 0 16 | 0 16 | 0 17 | 0 18 | 0 19 | 0 19 | 0 20 | 0 21 | 0 22 | 0 22 | 0 23 | 0 24 | 0 24 | 0 25 | 0 26 | 0 27 | 0 27 | 0 28 | 0 29 | 0 43 |
| 0 44 | 0 15 | 0 16 | 0 17 | 0 18 | 0 18 | 0 19 | 0 20 | 0 21 | 0 21 | 0 22 | 0 23 | 0 23 | 0 24 | 0 25 | 0 26 | 0 26 | 0 27 | 0 28 | 0 29 | 0 29 | 0 44 |
| 0 45 | 0 16 | 0 17 | 0 17 | 0 18 | 0 19 | 0 20 | 0 20 | 0 21 | 0 22 | 0 23 | 0 23 | 0 24 | 0 25 | 0 26 | 0 26 | 0 27 | 0 28 | 0 29 | 0 29 | 0 30 | 0 45 |
| 0 46 | 0 16 | 0 17 | 0 18 | 0 18 | 0 19 | 0 20 | 0 21 | 0 21 | 0 22 | 0 23 | 0 24 | 0 25 | 0 25 | 0 26 | 0 27 | 0 28 | 0 28 | 0 29 | 0 30 | 0 31 | 0 46 |
| 0 47 | 0 16 | 0 17 | 0 18 | 0 19 | 0 20 | 0 20 | 0 21 | 0 22 | 0 23 | 0 24 | 0 24 | 0 25 | 0 26 | 0 27 | 0 27 | 0 28 | 0 29 | 0 30 | 0 31 | 0 31 | 0 47 |
| 0 48 | 0 17 | 0 18 | 0 18 | 0 19 | 0 20 | 0 21 | 0 22 | 0 22 | 0 23 | 0 24 | 0 25 | 0 26 | 0 26 | 0 27 | 0 28 | 0 29 | 0 30 | 0 30 | 0 31 | 0 32 | 0 48 |
| 0 49 | 0 17 | 0 18 | 0 19 | 0 20 | 0 20 | 0 21 | 0 22 | 0 23 | 0 24 | 0 25 | 0 25 | 0 26 | 0 27 | 0 28 | 0 29 | 0 29 | 0 30 | 0 31 | 0 32 | 0 33 | 0 49 |
| 0 50 | 0 18 | 0 18 | 0 19 | 0 20 | 0 21 | 0 22 | 0 23 | 0 23 | 0 24 | 0 25 | 0 26 | 0 27 | 0 28 | 0 28 | 0 29 | 0 30 | 0 31 | 0 32 | 0 33 | 0 33 | 0 50 |
| 0 51 | 0 18 | 0 19 | 0 20 | 0 20 | 0 21 | 0 22 | 0 23 | 0 24 | 0 25 | 0 26 | 0 26 | 0 27 | 0 28 | 0 29 | 0 30 | 0 31 | 0 31 | 0 32 | 0 33 | 0 34 | 0 51 |
| 0 52 | 0 18 | 0 19 | 0 20 | 0 21 | 0 22 | 0 23 | 0 23 | 0 24 | 0 25 | 0 26 | 0 27 | 0 28 | 0 29 | 0 29 | 0 30 | 0 31 | 0 32 | 0 33 | 0 34 | 0 35 | 0 52 |
| 0 53 | 0 19 | 0 19 | 0 20 | 0 21 | 0 22 | 0 23 | 0 24 | 0 25 | 0 26 | 0 27 | 0 27 | 0 28 | 0 29 | 0 30 | 0 31 | 0 32 | 0 33 | 0 34 | 0 34 | 0 35 | 0 53 |
| 0 54 | 0 19 | 0 20 | 0 21 | 0 22 | 0 23 | 0 23 | 0 24 | 0 25 | 0 26 | 0 27 | 0 28 | 0 29 | 0 30 | 0 31 | 0 32 | 0 32 | 0 33 | 0 34 | 0 35 | 0 36 | 0 54 |
| 0 55 | 0 19 | 0 20 | 0 21 | 0 22 | 0 23 | 0 24 | 0 25 | 0 26 | 0 27 | 0 28 | 0 28 | 0 29 | 0 30 | 0 31 | 0 32 | 0 33 | 0 34 | 0 35 | 0 36 | 0 37 | 0 55 |
| 0 56 | 0 20 | 0 21 | 0 21 | 0 22 | 0 23 | 0 24 | 0 25 | 0 26 | 0 27 | 0 28 | 0 29 | 0 30 | 0 31 | 0 32 | 0 33 | 0 34 | 0 35 | 0 35 | 0 36 | 0 37 | 0 56 |
| 0 57 | 0 20 | 0 21 | 0 22 | 0 23 | 0 24 | 0 25 | 0 26 | 0 27 | 0 28 | 0 29 | 0 29 | 0 30 | 0 31 | 0 32 | 0 33 | 0 34 | 0 35 | 0 36 | 0 37 | 0 38 | 0 57 |
| 0 58 | 0 20 | 0 21 | 0 22 | 0 23 | 0 24 | 0 25 | 0 26 | 0 27 | 0 28 | 0 29 | 0 30 | 0 31 | 0 32 | 0 33 | 0 34 | 0 35 | 0 36 | 0 37 | 0 38 | 0 39 | 0 58 |
| 0 59 | 0 21 | 0 22 | 0 23 | 0 24 | 0 25 | 0 26 | 0 27 | 0 28 | 0 29 | 0 30 | 0 30 | 0 31 | 0 32 | 0 33 | 0 34 | 0 35 | 0 36 | 0 37 | 0 38 | 0 39 | 0 59 |
| 1 0 | 0 21 | 0 22 | 0 23 | 0 24 | 0 25 | 0 26 | 0 27 | 0 28 | 0 29 | 0 30 | 0 31 | 0 32 | 0 33 | 0 34 | 0 35 | 0 36 | 0 37 | 0 38 | 0 39 | 0 40 | 1 0 |
| 1 1 | 0 21 | 0 22 | 0 23 | 0 24 | 0 25 | 0 26 | 0 27 | 0 28 | 0 29 | 0 31 | 0 32 | 0 33 | 0 34 | 0 35 | 0 36 | 0 37 | 0 38 | 0 39 | 0 40 | 0 41 | 1 1 |
| 1 2 | 0 22 | 0 23 | 0 24 | 0 25 | 0 26 | 0 27 | 0 28 | 0 29 | 0 30 | 0 31 | 0 32 | 0 33 | 0 34 | 0 35 | 0 36 | 0 37 | 0 38 | 0 39 | 0 40 | 0 41 | 1 2 |
| 1 3 | 0 22 | 0 23 | 0 24 | 0 25 | 0 26 | 0 27 | 0 28 | 0 29 | 0 30 | 0 32 | 0 33 | 0 34 | 0 35 | 0 36 | 0 37 | 0 38 | 0 39 | 0 40 | 0 41 | 0 42 | 1 3 |
| 1 4 | 0 22 | 0 23 | 0 25 | 0 26 | 0 27 | 0 28 | 0 29 | 0 30 | 0 31 | 0 32 | 0 33 | 0 34 | 0 35 | 0 36 | 0 37 | 0 38 | 0 39 | 0 41 | 0 42 | 0 43 | 1 4 |
| 1 5 | 0 23 | 0 24 | 0 25 | 0 26 | 0 27 | 0 28 | 0 29 | 0 30 | 0 31 | 0 33 | 0 34 | 0 35 | 0 36 | 0 37 | 0 38 | 0 39 | 0 40 | 0 41 | 0 42 | 0 43 | 1 5 |
| 1 6 | 0 23 | 0 24 | 0 25 | 0 26 | 0 28 | 0 29 | 0 30 | 0 31 | 0 32 | 0 33 | 0 34 | 0 35 | 0 36 | 0 37 | 0 39 | 0 40 | 0 41 | 0 42 | 0 43 | 0 44 | 1 6 |
| 1 7 | 0 23 | 0 25 | 0 26 | 0 27 | 0 28 | 0 29 | 0 30 | 0 31 | 0 32 | 0 34 | 0 35 | 0 36 | 0 37 | 0 38 | 0 39 | 0 40 | 0 41 | 0 42 | 0 44 | 0 45 | 1 7 |
| 1 8 | 0 24 | 0 25 | 0 26 | 0 27 | 0 28 | 0 29 | 0 31 | 0 32 | 0 33 | 0 34 | 0 35 | 0 36 | 0 37 | 0 39 | 0 40 | 0 41 | 0 42 | 0 43 | 0 44 | 0 45 | 1 8 |
| 1 9 | 0 24 | 0 25 | 0 26 | 0 28 | 0 29 | 0 30 | 0 31 | 0 32 | 0 33 | 0 35 | 0 36 | 0 37 | 0 38 | 0 39 | 0 40 | 0 41 | 0 43 | 0 44 | 0 45 | 0 46 | 1 9 |
| 1 10 | 0 25 | 0 26 | 0 27 | 0 28 | 0 29 | 0 30 | 0 32 | 0 33 | 0 34 | 0 35 | 0 36 | 0 37 | 0 39 | 0 40 | 0 41 | 0 42 | 0 43 | 0 44 | 0 46 | 0 47 | 1 10 |
| 1 11 | 0 25 | 0 26 | 0 27 | 0 28 | 0 30 | 0 31 | 0 32 | 0 33 | 0 34 | 0 36 | 0 37 | 0 38 | 0 39 | 0 40 | 0 41 | 0 43 | 0 44 | 0 45 | 0 46 | 0 47 | 1 11 |
| 1 12 | 0 25 | 0 26 | 0 28 | 0 29 | 0 30 | 0 31 | 0 32 | 0 34 | 0 35 | 0 36 | 0 37 | 0 38 | 0 40 | 0 41 | 0 42 | 0 43 | 0 44 | 0 46 | 0 47 | 0 48 | 1 12 |
| 1 13 | 0 26 | 0 27 | 0 28 | 0 29 | 0 30 | 0 32 | 0 33 | 0 34 | 0 35 | 0 37 | 0 38 | 0 39 | 0 40 | 0 41 | 0 43 | 0 44 | 0 45 | 0 46 | 0 47 | 0 49 | 1 13 |
| 1 14 | 0 26 | 0 27 | 0 28 | 0 30 | 0 31 | 0 32 | 0 33 | 0 35 | 0 36 | 0 37 | 0 38 | 0 39 | 0 41 | 0 42 | 0 43 | 0 44 | 0 46 | 0 47 | 0 48 | 0 49 | 1 14 |
| 1 15 | 0 26 | 0 28 | 0 29 | 0 30 | 0 31 | 0 33 | 0 34 | 0 35 | 0 36 | 0 38 | 0 39 | 0 40 | 0 41 | 0 43 | 0 44 | 0 45 | 0 46 | 0 48 | 0 49 | 0 50 | 1 15 |
| 1 16 | 0 27 | 0 28 | 0 29 | 0 30 | 0 32 | 0 33 | 0 34 | 0 35 | 0 37 | 0 38 | 0 39 | 0 41 | 0 42 | 0 43 | 0 44 | 0 46 | 0 47 | 0 48 | 0 49 | 0 51 | 1 16 |
| 1 17 | 0 27 | 0 28 | 0 30 | 0 31 | 0 32 | 0 33 | 0 35 | 0 36 | 0 37 | 0 39 | 0 40 | 0 41 | 0 42 | 0 44 | 0 45 | 0 46 | 0 47 | 0 49 | 0 50 | 0 51 | 1 17 |
| 1 18 | 0 27 | 0 29 | 0 30 | 0 31 | 0 33 | 0 34 | 0 35 | 0 36 | 0 38 | 0 39 | 0 40 | 0 42 | 0 43 | 0 44 | 0 46 | 0 47 | 0 48 | 0 49 | 0 51 | 0 52 | 1 18 |
| 1 19 | 0 28 | 0 29 | 0 30 | 0 32 | 0 33 | 0 34 | 0 36 | 0 37 | 0 38 | 0 40 | 0 41 | 0 42 | 0 43 | 0 45 | 0 46 | 0 47 | 0 49 | 0 50 | 0 51 | 0 53 | 1 19 |
| 1 20 | 0 28 | 0 29 | 0 31 | 0 32 | 0 33 | 0 35 | 0 36 | 0 37 | 0 39 | 0 40 | 0 41 | 0 43 | 0 44 | 0 45 | 0 47 | 0 48 | 0 49 | 0 51 | 0 52 | 0 53 | 1 20 |
| 1 21 | 0 28 | 0 30 | 0 31 | 0 32 | 0 34 | 0 35 | 0 36 | 0 38 | 0 39 | 0 41 | 0 42 | 0 43 | 0 45 | 0 46 | 0 47 | 0 49 | 0 50 | 0 51 | 0 53 | 0 54 | 1 21 |
| 1 22 | 0 29 | 0 30 | 0 31 | 0 33 | 0 34 | 0 36 | 0 37 | 0 38 | 0 40 | 0 41 | 0 42 | 0 44 | 0 45 | 0 46 | 0 48 | 0 49 | 0 51 | 0 52 | 0 53 | 0 55 | 1 22 |
| 1 23 | 0 29 | 0 30 | 0 32 | 0 33 | 0 35 | 0 36 | 0 37 | 0 39 | 0 40 | 0 42 | 0 43 | 0 44 | 0 46 | 0 47 | 0 48 | 0 50 | 0 51 | 0 53 | 0 54 | 0 55 | 1 23 |
| 1 24 | 0 29 | 0 31 | 0 32 | 0 34 | 0 35 | 0 36 | 0 38 | 0 39 | 0 41 | 0 42 | 0 43 | 0 45 | 0 46 | 0 48 | 0 49 | 0 50 | 0 52 | 0 53 | 0 55 | 0 56 | 1 24 |
| 1 25 | 0 30 | 0 31 | 0 33 | 0 34 | 0 35 | 0 37 | 0 38 | 0 40 | 0 41 | 0 43 | 0 44 | 0 45 | 0 47 | 0 48 | 0 50 | 0 51 | 0 52 | 0 54 | 0 55 | 0 57 | 1 25 |
| 1 26 | 0 30 | 0 32 | 0 33 | 0 34 | 0 36 | 0 37 | 0 39 | 0 40 | 0 42 | 0 43 | 0 44 | 0 46 | 0 47 | 0 49 | 0 50 | 0 52 | 0 53 | 0 54 | 0 56 | 0 57 | 1 26 |
| 1 27 | 0 30 | 0 32 | 0 33 | 0 35 | 0 36 | 0 38 | 0 39 | 0 41 | 0 42 | 0 44 | 0 45 | 0 46 | 0 48 | 0 49 | 0 51 | 0 52 | 0 54 | 0 55 | 0 57 | 0 58 | 1 27 |
| 1 28 | 0 31 | 0 32 | 0 34 | 0 35 | 0 37 | 0 38 | 0 40 | 0 41 | 0 43 | 0 44 | 0 45 | 0 47 | 0 48 | 0 50 | 0 51 | 0 53 | 0 54 | 0 56 | 0 57 | 0 59 | 1 28 |
| 1 29 | 0 31 | 0 33 | 0 34 | 0 36 | 0 37 | 0 39 | 0 40 | 0 42 | 0 43 | 0 45 | 0 46 | 0 47 | 0 49 | 0 50 | 0 52 | 0 53 | 0 55 | 0 56 | 0 58 | 0 59 | 1 29 |
| 1 30 | 0 32 | 0 33 | 0 35 | 0 36 | 0 38 | 0 39 | 0 41 | 0 42 | 0 44 | 0 45 | 0 47 | 0 48 | 0 50 | 0 51 | 0 53 | 0 54 | 0 56 | 0 57 | 0 59 | 1 0 | 1 30 |
| 1 31 | 0 32 | 0 33 | 0 35 | 0 36 | 0 38 | 0 39 | 0 41 | 0 42 | 0 44 | 0 46 | 0 47 | 0 49 | 0 50 | 0 52 | 0 53 | 0 55 | 0 56 | 0 58 | 0 59 | 1 1 | 1 31 |
| 1 32 | 0 32 | 0 34 | 0 35 | 0 37 | 0 38 | 0 40 | 0 41 | 0 43 | 0 44 | 0 46 | 0 48 | 0 49 | 0 51 | 0 52 | 0 54 | 0 55 | 0 57 | 0 58 | 1 0 | 1 1 | 1 32 |
| 1 33 | 0 33 | 0 34 | 0 36 | 0 37 | 0 39 | 0 40 | 0 42 | 0 43 | 0 45 | 0 47 | 0 48 | 0 50 | 0 51 | 0 53 | 0 54 | 0 56 | 0 57 | 0 59 | 1 0 | 1 2 | 1 33 |
| 1 34 | 0 33 | 0 34 | 0 36 | 0 38 | 0 39 | 0 41 | 0 42 | 0 44 | 0 45 | 0 47 | 0 49 | 0 50 | 0 52 | 0 53 | 0 55 | 0 56 | 0 58 | 1 0 | 1 1 | 1 3 | 1 34 |
| 1 35 | 0 33 | 0 35 | 0 36 | 0 38 | 0 40 | 0 41 | 0 43 | 0 44 | 0 46 | 0 48 | 0 49 | 0 51 | 0 52 | 0 54 | 0 55 | 0 57 | 0 59 | 1 0 | 1 2 | 1 3 | 1 35 |
| 1 36 | 0 34 | 0 35 | 0 37 | 0 38 | 0 40 | 0 42 | 0 43 | 0 45 | 0 46 | 0 48 | 0 50 | 0 51 | 0 53 | 0 54 | 0 56 | 0 58 | 0 59 | 1 1 | 1 2 | 1 4 | 1 36 |
| 1 37 | 0 34 | 0 36 | 0 37 | 0 39 | 0 40 | 0 42 | 0 44 | 0 45 | 0 47 | 0 49 | 0 50 | 0 52 | 0 53 | 0 55 | 0 57 | 0 58 | 1 0 | 1 1 | 1 3 | 1 5 | 1 37 |
| 1 38 | 0 34 | 0 36 | 0 38 | 0 39 | 0 41 | 0 42 | 0 44 | 0 46 | 0 47 | 0 49 | 0 51 | 0 52 | 0 54 | 0 56 | 0 57 | 0 59 | 1 0 | 1 2 | 1 4 | 1 5 | 1 38 |
| 1 39 | 0 35 | 0 36 | 0 38 | 0 40 | 0 41 | 0 43 | 0 45 | 0 46 | 0 48 | 0 50 | 0 51 | 0 53 | 0 54 | 0 56 | 0 58 | 0 59 | 1 1 | 1 3 | 1 4 | 1 6 | 1 39 |
| 1 40 | 0 35 | 0 37 | 0 38 | 0 40 | 0 42 | 0 43 | 0 45 | 0 47 | 0 48 | 0 50 | 0 52 | 0 53 | 0 55 | 0 57 | 0 58 | 1 0 | 1 2 | 1 3 | 1 5 | 1 7 | 1 40 |
| 1 41 | 0 35 | 0 37 | 0 39 | 0 40 | 0 42 | 0 44 | 0 45 | 0 47 | 0 49 | 0 51 | 0 52 | 0 54 | 0 56 | 0 57 | 0 59 | 1 1 | 1 2 | 1 4 | 1 6 | 1 7 | 1 41 |
| 1 42 | 0 36 | 0 37 | 0 39 | 0 41 | 0 43 | 0 44 | 0 46 | 0 48 | 0 49 | 0 51 | 0 53 | 0 54 | 0 56 | 0 58 | 1 0 | 1 1 | 1 3 | 1 5 | 1 6 | 1 8 | 1 42 |
| 1 43 | 0 36 | 0 38 | 0 39 | 0 41 | 0 43 | 0 45 | 0 46 | 0 48 | 0 50 | 0 52 | 0 53 | 0 55 | 0 57 | 0 58 | 1 0 | 1 2 | 1 4 | 1 5 | 1 7 | 1 9 | 1 43 |
| 1 44 | 0 36 | 0 38 | 0 40 | 0 42 | 0 43 | 0 45 | 0 47 | 0 49 | 0 50 | 0 52 | 0 54 | 0 55 | 0 57 | 0 59 | 1 1 | 1 2 | 1 4 | 1 6 | 1 8 | 1 9 | 1 44 |
| 1 45 | 0 37 | 0 39 | 0 40 | 0 42 | 0 44 | 0 46 | 0 47 | 0 49 | 0 51 | 0 53 | 0 54 | 0 56 | 0 58 | 1 0 | 1 1 | 1 3 | 1 5 | 1 7 | 1 8 | 1 10 | 1 45 |
| 1 46 | 0 37 | 0 39 | 0 41 | 0 42 | 0 44 | 0 46 | 0 48 | 0 49 | 0 51 | 0 53 | 0 55 | 0 57 | 0 58 | 1 0 | 1 2 | 1 4 | 1 5 | 1 7 | 1 9 | 1 11 | 1 46 |
| 1 47 | 0 37 | 0 39 | 0 41 | 0 43 | 0 45 | 0 46 | 0 48 | 0 50 | 0 52 | 0 54 | 0 55 | 0 57 | 0 59 | 1 1 | 1 2 | 1 4 | 1 6 | 1 8 | 1 10 | 1 11 | 1 47 |
| 1 48 | 0 38 | 0 40 | 0 41 | 0 43 | 0 45 | 0 47 | 0 49 | 0 50 | 0 52 | 0 54 | 0 56 | 0 58 | 0 59 | 1 1 | 1 3 | 1 5 | 1 7 | 1 8 | 1 10 | 1 12 | 1 48 |
| 1 49 | 0 38 | 0 40 | 0 42 | 0 44 | 0 45 | 0 47 | 0 49 | 0 51 | 0 53 | 0 55 | 0 56 | 0 58 | 1 0 | 1 2 | 1 4 | 1 5 | 1 7 | 1 9 | 1 11 | 1 13 | 1 49 |
| 1 50 | 0 39 | 0 40 | 0 42 | 0 44 | 0 46 | 0 48 | 0 50 | 0 51 | 0 53 | 0 55 | 0 57 | 0 59 | 1 1 | 1 2 | 1 4 | 1 6 | 1 8 | 1 10 | 1 12 | 1 13 | 1 50 |
| 1 51 | 0 39 | 0 41 | 0 43 | 0 44 | 0 46 | 0 48 | 0 50 | 0 52 | 0 54 | 0 56 | 0 57 | 0 59 | 1 1 | 1 3 | 1 5 | 1 7 | 1 8 | 1 10 | 1 12 | 1 14 | 1 51 |
| 1 52 | 0 39 | 0 41 | 0 43 | 0 45 | 0 47 | 0 49 | 0 50 | 0 52 | 0 54 | 0 56 | 0 58 | 1 0 | 1 2 | 1 3 | 1 5 | 1 7 | 1 9 | 1 11 | 1 13 | 1 15 | 1 52 |
| 1 53 | 0 40 | 0 41 | 0 43 | 0 45 | 0 47 | 0 49 | 0 51 | 0 53 | 0 55 | 0 57 | 0 58 | 1 0 | 1 2 | 1 4 | 1 6 | 1 8 | 1 10 | 1 12 | 1 13 | 1 15 | 1 53 |
| 1 54 | 0 40 | 0 42 | 0 44 | 0 46 | 0 48 | 0 49 | 0 51 | 0 53 | 0 55 | 0 57 | 0 59 | 1 1 | 1 3 | 1 5 | 1 7 | 1 8 | 1 10 | 1 12 | 1 14 | 1 16 | 1 54 |
| 1 55 | 0 40 | 0 42 | 0 44 | 0 46 | 0 48 | 0 50 | 0 52 | 0 54 | 0 56 | 0 58 | 0 59 | 1 1 | 1 3 | 1 5 | 1 7 | 1 9 | 1 11 | 1 13 | 1 15 | 1 17 | 1 55 |
| 1 56 | 0 41 | 0 43 | 0 44 | 0 46 | 0 48 | 0 50 | 0 52 | 0 54 | 0 56 | 0 58 | 1 0 | 1 2 | 1 4 | 1 6 | 1 8 | 1 10 | 1 12 | 1 13 | 1 15 | 1 17 | 1 56 |
| 1 57 | 0 41 | 0 43 | 0 45 | 0 47 | 0 49 | 0 51 | 0 53 | 0 55 | 0 57 | 0 59 | 1 0 | 1 2 | 1 4 | 1 6 | 1 8 | 1 10 | 1 12 | 1 14 | 1 16 | 1 18 | 1 57 |
| 1 58 | 0 41 | 0 43 | 0 45 | 0 47 | 0 49 | 0 51 | 0 53 | 0 55 | 0 57 | 0 59 | 1 1 | 1 3 | 1 5 | 1 7 | 1 9 | 1 11 | 1 13 | 1 15 | 1 17 | 1 19 | 1 58 |
| 1 59 | 0 42 | 0 44 | 0 46 | 0 48 | 0 50 | 0 52 | 0 54 | 0 56 | 0 58 | 1 0 | 1 1 | 1 3 | 1 5 | 1 7 | 1 9 | 1 11 | 1 13 | 1 15 | 1 17 | 1 19 | 1 59 |
| 2 0 | 0 42 | 0 44 | 0 46 | 0 48 | 0 50 | 0 52 | 0 54 | 0 56 | 0 58 | 1 0 | 1 2 | 1 4 | 1 6 | 1 8 | 1 10 | 1 12 | 1 14 | 1 16 | 1 18 | 1 20 | 2 0 |

# Table XI House Cusp Interpolation Between Sidereal Times

| | LOCAL SIDEREAL TIME INCREMENT | | | | | | | | | | | | | | | | | | | | |
|---|---|---|---|---|---|---|---|---|---|---|---|---|---|---|---|---|---|---|---|---|---|
| CUSP INTVL | m s 2 44 | m s 2 48 | m s 2 52 | m s 2 56 | m s 3 0 | m s 3 4 | m s 3 8 | m s 3 12 | m s 3 16 | m s 3 20 | m s 3 24 | m s 3 28 | m s 3 32 | m s 3 36 | m s 3 40 | m s 3 44 | m s 3 48 | m s 3 52 | m s 3 56 | m s 4 0 | CUSP INTVL |
| ° ' | ° ' | ° ' | ° ' | ° ' | ° ' | ° ' | ° ' | ° ' | ° ' | ° ' | ° ' | ° ' | ° ' | ° ' | ° ' | ° ' | ° ' | ° ' | ° ' | ° ' | ° ' |
| 0 31 | 0 21 | 0 22 | 0 22 | 0 23 | 0 23 | 0 24 | 0 24 | 0 25 | 0 25 | 0 26 | 0 26 | 0 27 | 0 27 | 0 28 | 0 28 | 0 29 | 0 29 | 0 30 | 0 30 | 0 31 | 0 31 |
| 0 32 | 0 22 | 0 22 | 0 23 | 0 23 | 0 24 | 0 25 | 0 25 | 0 26 | 0 26 | 0 27 | 0 27 | 0 28 | 0 28 | 0 29 | 0 29 | 0 30 | 0 30 | 0 31 | 0 31 | 0 32 | 0 32 |
| 0 33 | 0 23 | 0 23 | 0 24 | 0 24 | 0 25 | 0 25 | 0 26 | 0 26 | 0 27 | 0 28 | 0 28 | 0 29 | 0 29 | 0 30 | 0 30 | 0 31 | 0 31 | 0 32 | 0 32 | 0 33 | 0 33 |
| 0 34 | 0 23 | 0 24 | 0 24 | 0 25 | 0 26 | 0 26 | 0 27 | 0 27 | 0 28 | 0 28 | 0 29 | 0 29 | 0 30 | 0 31 | 0 31 | 0 32 | 0 32 | 0 33 | 0 33 | 0 34 | 0 34 |
| 0 35 | 0 24 | 0 25 | 0 25 | 0 26 | 0 26 | 0 27 | 0 27 | 0 28 | 0 29 | 0 29 | 0 30 | 0 30 | 0 31 | 0 32 | 0 32 | 0 33 | 0 33 | 0 34 | 0 34 | 0 35 | 0 35 |
| 0 36 | 0 25 | 0 25 | 0 26 | 0 26 | 0 27 | 0 28 | 0 28 | 0 29 | 0 29 | 0 30 | 0 31 | 0 31 | 0 32 | 0 32 | 0 33 | 0 34 | 0 34 | 0 35 | 0 35 | 0 36 | 0 36 |
| 0 37 | 0 25 | 0 26 | 0 27 | 0 27 | 0 28 | 0 28 | 0 29 | 0 30 | 0 30 | 0 31 | 0 31 | 0 32 | 0 33 | 0 33 | 0 34 | 0 35 | 0 35 | 0 36 | 0 36 | 0 37 | 0 37 |
| 0 38 | 0 26 | 0 27 | 0 27 | 0 28 | 0 29 | 0 29 | 0 30 | 0 30 | 0 31 | 0 32 | 0 32 | 0 33 | 0 34 | 0 34 | 0 35 | 0 35 | 0 36 | 0 37 | 0 37 | 0 38 | 0 38 |
| 0 39 | 0 27 | 0 27 | 0 28 | 0 29 | 0 29 | 0 30 | 0 31 | 0 31 | 0 32 | 0 33 | 0 33 | 0 34 | 0 34 | 0 35 | 0 36 | 0 36 | 0 37 | 0 38 | 0 38 | 0 39 | 0 39 |
| 0 40 | 0 27 | 0 28 | 0 29 | 0 29 | 0 30 | 0 31 | 0 31 | 0 32 | 0 33 | 0 33 | 0 34 | 0 35 | 0 35 | 0 36 | 0 37 | 0 37 | 0 38 | 0 39 | 0 39 | 0 40 | 0 40 |
| 0 41 | 0 28 | 0 29 | 0 29 | 0 30 | 0 31 | 0 31 | 0 32 | 0 33 | 0 33 | 0 34 | 0 35 | 0 36 | 0 36 | 0 37 | 0 38 | 0 38 | 0 39 | 0 40 | 0 40 | 0 41 | 0 41 |
| 0 42 | 0 29 | 0 29 | 0 30 | 0 31 | 0 32 | 0 32 | 0 33 | 0 34 | 0 34 | 0 35 | 0 36 | 0 36 | 0 37 | 0 38 | 0 39 | 0 39 | 0 40 | 0 41 | 0 41 | 0 42 | 0 42 |
| 0 43 | 0 29 | 0 30 | 0 31 | 0 32 | 0 32 | 0 33 | 0 34 | 0 34 | 0 35 | 0 36 | 0 37 | 0 37 | 0 38 | 0 39 | 0 39 | 0 40 | 0 41 | 0 42 | 0 42 | 0 43 | 0 43 |
| 0 44 | 0 30 | 0 31 | 0 32 | 0 32 | 0 33 | 0 34 | 0 34 | 0 35 | 0 36 | 0 37 | 0 37 | 0 38 | 0 39 | 0 40 | 0 40 | 0 41 | 0 42 | 0 43 | 0 43 | 0 44 | 0 44 |
| 0 45 | 0 31 | 0 32 | 0 32 | 0 33 | 0 34 | 0 35 | 0 35 | 0 36 | 0 37 | 0 38 | 0 38 | 0 39 | 0 40 | 0 41 | 0 41 | 0 42 | 0 43 | 0 44 | 0 44 | 0 45 | 0 45 |
| 0 46 | 0 31 | 0 32 | 0 33 | 0 34 | 0 35 | 0 35 | 0 36 | 0 37 | 0 38 | 0 38 | 0 39 | 0 40 | 0 41 | 0 41 | 0 42 | 0 43 | 0 44 | 0 44 | 0 45 | 0 46 | 0 46 |
| 0 47 | 0 32 | 0 33 | 0 34 | 0 34 | 0 35 | 0 36 | 0 37 | 0 38 | 0 38 | 0 39 | 0 40 | 0 41 | 0 42 | 0 42 | 0 43 | 0 44 | 0 45 | 0 45 | 0 46 | 0 47 | 0 47 |
| 0 48 | 0 33 | 0 34 | 0 34 | 0 35 | 0 36 | 0 37 | 0 38 | 0 38 | 0 39 | 0 40 | 0 41 | 0 42 | 0 42 | 0 43 | 0 44 | 0 45 | 0 46 | 0 46 | 0 47 | 0 48 | 0 48 |
| 0 49 | 0 33 | 0 34 | 0 35 | 0 36 | 0 37 | 0 38 | 0 38 | 0 39 | 0 40 | 0 41 | 0 42 | 0 42 | 0 43 | 0 44 | 0 45 | 0 46 | 0 47 | 0 47 | 0 48 | 0 49 | 0 49 |
| 0 50 | 0 34 | 0 35 | 0 36 | 0 37 | 0 38 | 0 38 | 0 39 | 0 40 | 0 41 | 0 42 | 0 43 | 0 43 | 0 44 | 0 45 | 0 46 | 0 47 | 0 48 | 0 48 | 0 49 | 0 50 | 0 50 |
| 0 51 | 0 35 | 0 36 | 0 37 | 0 37 | 0 38 | 0 39 | 0 40 | 0 41 | 0 42 | 0 43 | 0 43 | 0 44 | 0 45 | 0 46 | 0 47 | 0 48 | 0 48 | 0 49 | 0 50 | 0 51 | 0 51 |
| 0 52 | 0 36 | 0 36 | 0 37 | 0 38 | 0 39 | 0 40 | 0 41 | 0 42 | 0 42 | 0 43 | 0 44 | 0 45 | 0 46 | 0 47 | 0 48 | 0 49 | 0 49 | 0 50 | 0 51 | 0 52 | 0 52 |
| 0 53 | 0 36 | 0 37 | 0 38 | 0 39 | 0 40 | 0 41 | 0 42 | 0 42 | 0 43 | 0 44 | 0 45 | 0 46 | 0 47 | 0 48 | 0 49 | 0 49 | 0 50 | 0 51 | 0 52 | 0 53 | 0 53 |
| 0 54 | 0 37 | 0 38 | 0 39 | 0 40 | 0 41 | 0 41 | 0 42 | 0 43 | 0 44 | 0 45 | 0 46 | 0 47 | 0 48 | 0 49 | 0 50 | 0 50 | 0 51 | 0 52 | 0 53 | 0 54 | 0 54 |
| 0 55 | 0 38 | 0 39 | 0 39 | 0 40 | 0 41 | 0 42 | 0 43 | 0 44 | 0 45 | 0 46 | 0 47 | 0 48 | 0 49 | 0 50 | 0 50 | 0 51 | 0 52 | 0 53 | 0 54 | 0 55 | 0 55 |
| 0 56 | 0 38 | 0 39 | 0 40 | 0 41 | 0 42 | 0 43 | 0 44 | 0 45 | 0 46 | 0 47 | 0 48 | 0 49 | 0 49 | 0 50 | 0 51 | 0 52 | 0 53 | 0 54 | 0 55 | 0 56 | 0 56 |
| 0 57 | 0 39 | 0 40 | 0 41 | 0 42 | 0 43 | 0 44 | 0 45 | 0 46 | 0 47 | 0 48 | 0 48 | 0 49 | 0 50 | 0 51 | 0 52 | 0 53 | 0 54 | 0 55 | 0 56 | 0 57 | 0 57 |
| 0 58 | 0 40 | 0 41 | 0 42 | 0 43 | 0 44 | 0 44 | 0 45 | 0 46 | 0 47 | 0 48 | 0 49 | 0 50 | 0 51 | 0 52 | 0 53 | 0 54 | 0 55 | 0 56 | 0 57 | 0 58 | 0 58 |
| 0 59 | 0 40 | 0 41 | 0 42 | 0 43 | 0 44 | 0 45 | 0 46 | 0 47 | 0 48 | 0 49 | 0 50 | 0 51 | 0 52 | 0 53 | 0 54 | 0 55 | 0 56 | 0 57 | 0 58 | 0 59 | 0 59 |
| 1 0 | 0 41 | 0 42 | 0 43 | 0 44 | 0 45 | 0 46 | 0 47 | 0 48 | 0 49 | 0 50 | 0 51 | 0 52 | 0 53 | 0 54 | 0 55 | 0 56 | 0 57 | 0 58 | 0 59 | 1 0 | 1 0 |
| 1 1 | 0 42 | 0 43 | 0 44 | 0 45 | 0 46 | 0 47 | 0 48 | 0 49 | 0 50 | 0 51 | 0 52 | 0 53 | 0 54 | 0 55 | 0 56 | 0 57 | 0 58 | 0 59 | 1 0 | 1 1 | 1 1 |
| 1 2 | 0 42 | 0 43 | 0 44 | 0 45 | 0 47 | 0 48 | 0 49 | 0 50 | 0 51 | 0 52 | 0 53 | 0 54 | 0 55 | 0 56 | 0 57 | 0 58 | 0 59 | 1 0 | 1 1 | 1 2 | 1 2 |
| 1 3 | 0 43 | 0 44 | 0 45 | 0 46 | 0 47 | 0 48 | 0 49 | 0 50 | 0 51 | 0 53 | 0 54 | 0 55 | 0 56 | 0 57 | 0 58 | 0 59 | 1 0 | 1 1 | 1 2 | 1 3 | 1 3 |
| 1 4 | 0 44 | 0 45 | 0 46 | 0 47 | 0 48 | 0 49 | 0 50 | 0 51 | 0 52 | 0 53 | 0 54 | 0 55 | 0 57 | 0 58 | 0 59 | 1 0 | 1 1 | 1 2 | 1 3 | 1 4 | 1 4 |
| 1 5 | 0 44 | 0 46 | 0 47 | 0 48 | 0 49 | 0 50 | 0 51 | 0 52 | 0 53 | 0 54 | 0 55 | 0 56 | 0 57 | 0 59 | 1 0 | 1 1 | 1 2 | 1 3 | 1 4 | 1 5 | 1 5 |
| 1 6 | 0 45 | 0 46 | 0 47 | 0 48 | 0 50 | 0 51 | 0 52 | 0 53 | 0 54 | 0 55 | 0 56 | 0 57 | 0 58 | 0 59 | 1 1 | 1 2 | 1 3 | 1 4 | 1 5 | 1 6 | 1 6 |
| 1 7 | 0 46 | 0 47 | 0 48 | 0 49 | 0 50 | 0 51 | 0 52 | 0 54 | 0 55 | 0 56 | 0 57 | 0 58 | 0 59 | 1 0 | 1 1 | 1 3 | 1 4 | 1 5 | 1 6 | 1 7 | 1 7 |
| 1 8 | 0 46 | 0 48 | 0 49 | 0 50 | 0 51 | 0 52 | 0 53 | 0 54 | 0 56 | 0 57 | 0 58 | 0 59 | 1 0 | 1 1 | 1 2 | 1 3 | 1 5 | 1 6 | 1 7 | 1 8 | 1 8 |
| 1 9 | 0 47 | 0 48 | 0 49 | 0 51 | 0 52 | 0 53 | 0 54 | 0 55 | 0 56 | 0 58 | 0 59 | 1 0 | 1 1 | 1 2 | 1 3 | 1 4 | 1 6 | 1 7 | 1 8 | 1 9 | 1 9 |
| 1 10 | 0 48 | 0 49 | 0 50 | 0 51 | 0 53 | 0 54 | 0 55 | 0 56 | 0 57 | 0 58 | 1 0 | 1 1 | 1 2 | 1 3 | 1 4 | 1 5 | 1 7 | 1 8 | 1 9 | 1 10 | 1 10 |
| 1 11 | 0 49 | 0 50 | 0 51 | 0 52 | 0 53 | 0 54 | 0 56 | 0 57 | 0 58 | 0 59 | 1 0 | 1 2 | 1 3 | 1 4 | 1 5 | 1 6 | 1 7 | 1 9 | 1 10 | 1 11 | 1 11 |
| 1 12 | 0 49 | 0 50 | 0 52 | 0 53 | 0 54 | 0 55 | 0 56 | 0 58 | 0 59 | 1 0 | 1 1 | 1 2 | 1 4 | 1 5 | 1 6 | 1 7 | 1 8 | 1 10 | 1 11 | 1 12 | 1 12 |
| 1 13 | 0 50 | 0 51 | 0 52 | 0 54 | 0 55 | 0 56 | 0 57 | 0 58 | 1 0 | 1 1 | 1 2 | 1 3 | 1 4 | 1 6 | 1 7 | 1 8 | 1 9 | 1 11 | 1 12 | 1 13 | 1 13 |
| 1 14 | 0 51 | 0 52 | 0 53 | 0 54 | 0 56 | 0 57 | 0 58 | 0 59 | 1 0 | 1 2 | 1 3 | 1 4 | 1 5 | 1 7 | 1 8 | 1 9 | 1 10 | 1 12 | 1 13 | 1 14 | 1 14 |
| 1 15 | 0 51 | 0 53 | 0 54 | 0 55 | 0 56 | 0 58 | 0 59 | 1 0 | 1 1 | 1 3 | 1 4 | 1 5 | 1 6 | 1 8 | 1 9 | 1 10 | 1 11 | 1 13 | 1 14 | 1 15 | 1 15 |
| 1 16 | 0 52 | 0 53 | 0 54 | 0 56 | 0 57 | 0 58 | 1 0 | 1 1 | 1 2 | 1 3 | 1 5 | 1 6 | 1 7 | 1 8 | 1 10 | 1 11 | 1 12 | 1 13 | 1 15 | 1 16 | 1 16 |
| 1 17 | 0 53 | 0 54 | 0 55 | 0 56 | 0 58 | 0 59 | 1 0 | 1 2 | 1 3 | 1 4 | 1 5 | 1 7 | 1 8 | 1 9 | 1 11 | 1 12 | 1 13 | 1 14 | 1 16 | 1 17 | 1 17 |
| 1 18 | 0 53 | 0 55 | 0 56 | 0 57 | 0 59 | 1 0 | 1 1 | 1 2 | 1 4 | 1 5 | 1 6 | 1 8 | 1 9 | 1 10 | 1 12 | 1 13 | 1 14 | 1 15 | 1 17 | 1 18 | 1 18 |
| 1 19 | 0 54 | 0 55 | 0 57 | 0 58 | 0 59 | 1 1 | 1 2 | 1 3 | 1 5 | 1 6 | 1 7 | 1 8 | 1 10 | 1 11 | 1 12 | 1 14 | 1 15 | 1 16 | 1 18 | 1 19 | 1 19 |
| 1 20 | 0 55 | 0 56 | 0 57 | 0 59 | 1 0 | 1 1 | 1 3 | 1 4 | 1 5 | 1 7 | 1 8 | 1 9 | 1 11 | 1 12 | 1 13 | 1 15 | 1 16 | 1 17 | 1 19 | 1 20 | 1 20 |
| 1 21 | 0 55 | 0 57 | 0 58 | 0 59 | 1 1 | 1 2 | 1 3 | 1 5 | 1 6 | 1 8 | 1 9 | 1 10 | 1 12 | 1 13 | 1 14 | 1 16 | 1 17 | 1 18 | 1 20 | 1 21 | 1 21 |
| 1 22 | 0 56 | 0 57 | 0 59 | 1 0 | 1 2 | 1 3 | 1 4 | 1 6 | 1 7 | 1 8 | 1 10 | 1 11 | 1 12 | 1 14 | 1 15 | 1 17 | 1 18 | 1 19 | 1 21 | 1 22 | 1 22 |
| 1 23 | 0 57 | 0 58 | 0 59 | 1 1 | 1 2 | 1 4 | 1 5 | 1 6 | 1 8 | 1 9 | 1 11 | 1 12 | 1 13 | 1 15 | 1 16 | 1 17 | 1 19 | 1 20 | 1 22 | 1 23 | 1 23 |
| 1 24 | 0 57 | 0 59 | 1 0 | 1 2 | 1 3 | 1 4 | 1 6 | 1 7 | 1 9 | 1 10 | 1 11 | 1 13 | 1 14 | 1 16 | 1 17 | 1 18 | 1 20 | 1 21 | 1 23 | 1 24 | 1 24 |
| 1 25 | 0 58 | 1 0 | 1 1 | 1 2 | 1 4 | 1 5 | 1 7 | 1 8 | 1 9 | 1 11 | 1 12 | 1 14 | 1 15 | 1 17 | 1 18 | 1 19 | 1 21 | 1 22 | 1 24 | 1 25 | 1 25 |
| 1 26 | 0 59 | 1 0 | 1 2 | 1 3 | 1 5 | 1 6 | 1 7 | 1 9 | 1 10 | 1 12 | 1 13 | 1 15 | 1 16 | 1 17 | 1 19 | 1 20 | 1 22 | 1 23 | 1 25 | 1 26 | 1 26 |
| 1 27 | 0 59 | 1 1 | 1 2 | 1 4 | 1 5 | 1 7 | 1 8 | 1 10 | 1 11 | 1 13 | 1 14 | 1 15 | 1 17 | 1 18 | 1 20 | 1 21 | 1 23 | 1 24 | 1 26 | 1 27 | 1 27 |
| 1 28 | 1 0 | 1 2 | 1 3 | 1 5 | 1 6 | 1 7 | 1 9 | 1 10 | 1 12 | 1 13 | 1 15 | 1 16 | 1 18 | 1 19 | 1 21 | 1 22 | 1 24 | 1 25 | 1 27 | 1 28 | 1 28 |
| 1 29 | 1 1 | 1 2 | 1 4 | 1 5 | 1 7 | 1 8 | 1 10 | 1 11 | 1 13 | 1 14 | 1 16 | 1 17 | 1 19 | 1 20 | 1 22 | 1 23 | 1 25 | 1 26 | 1 28 | 1 29 | 1 29 |
| 1 30 | 1 2 | 1 3 | 1 5 | 1 6 | 1 8 | 1 9 | 1 11 | 1 12 | 1 14 | 1 15 | 1 17 | 1 18 | 1 20 | 1 21 | 1 23 | 1 24 | 1 26 | 1 27 | 1 29 | 1 30 | 1 30 |
| 1 31 | 1 2 | 1 4 | 1 5 | 1 7 | 1 8 | 1 10 | 1 11 | 1 13 | 1 14 | 1 16 | 1 17 | 1 19 | 1 20 | 1 22 | 1 23 | 1 25 | 1 26 | 1 28 | 1 29 | 1 31 | 1 31 |
| 1 32 | 1 3 | 1 4 | 1 6 | 1 7 | 1 9 | 1 11 | 1 12 | 1 14 | 1 15 | 1 17 | 1 18 | 1 20 | 1 21 | 1 23 | 1 24 | 1 26 | 1 27 | 1 29 | 1 30 | 1 32 | 1 32 |
| 1 33 | 1 4 | 1 5 | 1 7 | 1 8 | 1 10 | 1 11 | 1 13 | 1 14 | 1 16 | 1 18 | 1 19 | 1 21 | 1 22 | 1 24 | 1 25 | 1 27 | 1 28 | 1 30 | 1 31 | 1 33 | 1 33 |
| 1 34 | 1 4 | 1 6 | 1 7 | 1 9 | 1 11 | 1 12 | 1 14 | 1 15 | 1 17 | 1 18 | 1 20 | 1 21 | 1 23 | 1 25 | 1 26 | 1 28 | 1 29 | 1 31 | 1 32 | 1 34 | 1 34 |
| 1 35 | 1 5 | 1 7 | 1 8 | 1 10 | 1 11 | 1 13 | 1 14 | 1 16 | 1 18 | 1 19 | 1 21 | 1 22 | 1 24 | 1 26 | 1 27 | 1 29 | 1 30 | 1 32 | 1 33 | 1 35 | 1 35 |
| 1 36 | 1 6 | 1 7 | 1 9 | 1 10 | 1 12 | 1 14 | 1 15 | 1 17 | 1 18 | 1 20 | 1 22 | 1 23 | 1 25 | 1 26 | 1 28 | 1 30 | 1 31 | 1 33 | 1 34 | 1 36 | 1 36 |
| 1 37 | 1 6 | 1 8 | 1 10 | 1 11 | 1 13 | 1 14 | 1 16 | 1 18 | 1 19 | 1 21 | 1 22 | 1 24 | 1 26 | 1 27 | 1 29 | 1 31 | 1 32 | 1 34 | 1 35 | 1 37 | 1 37 |
| 1 38 | 1 7 | 1 9 | 1 10 | 1 12 | 1 14 | 1 15 | 1 17 | 1 18 | 1 20 | 1 22 | 1 23 | 1 25 | 1 27 | 1 28 | 1 30 | 1 31 | 1 33 | 1 35 | 1 36 | 1 38 | 1 38 |
| 1 39 | 1 8 | 1 9 | 1 11 | 1 13 | 1 14 | 1 16 | 1 18 | 1 19 | 1 21 | 1 23 | 1 24 | 1 26 | 1 27 | 1 29 | 1 31 | 1 32 | 1 34 | 1 36 | 1 37 | 1 39 | 1 39 |
| 1 40 | 1 8 | 1 10 | 1 12 | 1 13 | 1 15 | 1 17 | 1 18 | 1 20 | 1 22 | 1 23 | 1 25 | 1 27 | 1 28 | 1 30 | 1 32 | 1 33 | 1 35 | 1 37 | 1 38 | 1 40 | 1 40 |
| 1 41 | 1 9 | 1 11 | 1 12 | 1 14 | 1 16 | 1 17 | 1 19 | 1 21 | 1 22 | 1 24 | 1 26 | 1 28 | 1 29 | 1 31 | 1 33 | 1 34 | 1 36 | 1 38 | 1 39 | 1 41 | 1 41 |
| 1 42 | 1 10 | 1 11 | 1 13 | 1 15 | 1 17 | 1 18 | 1 20 | 1 22 | 1 23 | 1 25 | 1 27 | 1 28 | 1 30 | 1 32 | 1 34 | 1 35 | 1 37 | 1 39 | 1 40 | 1 42 | 1 42 |
| 1 43 | 1 10 | 1 12 | 1 14 | 1 16 | 1 17 | 1 19 | 1 21 | 1 22 | 1 24 | 1 26 | 1 28 | 1 29 | 1 31 | 1 33 | 1 34 | 1 36 | 1 38 | 1 40 | 1 41 | 1 43 | 1 43 |
| 1 44 | 1 11 | 1 13 | 1 15 | 1 16 | 1 18 | 1 20 | 1 21 | 1 23 | 1 25 | 1 27 | 1 28 | 1 30 | 1 32 | 1 34 | 1 35 | 1 37 | 1 39 | 1 41 | 1 42 | 1 44 | 1 44 |
| 1 45 | 1 12 | 1 14 | 1 15 | 1 17 | 1 19 | 1 21 | 1 22 | 1 24 | 1 26 | 1 28 | 1 29 | 1 31 | 1 33 | 1 35 | 1 36 | 1 38 | 1 40 | 1 42 | 1 43 | 1 45 | 1 45 |
| 1 46 | 1 12 | 1 14 | 1 16 | 1 18 | 1 20 | 1 21 | 1 23 | 1 25 | 1 27 | 1 28 | 1 30 | 1 32 | 1 34 | 1 35 | 1 37 | 1 39 | 1 41 | 1 42 | 1 44 | 1 46 | 1 46 |
| 1 47 | 1 13 | 1 15 | 1 17 | 1 18 | 1 20 | 1 22 | 1 24 | 1 26 | 1 27 | 1 29 | 1 31 | 1 33 | 1 35 | 1 36 | 1 38 | 1 40 | 1 42 | 1 43 | 1 45 | 1 47 | 1 47 |
| 1 48 | 1 14 | 1 16 | 1 17 | 1 19 | 1 21 | 1 23 | 1 25 | 1 26 | 1 28 | 1 30 | 1 32 | 1 34 | 1 35 | 1 37 | 1 39 | 1 41 | 1 43 | 1 44 | 1 46 | 1 48 | 1 48 |
| 1 49 | 1 14 | 1 16 | 1 18 | 1 20 | 1 22 | 1 24 | 1 25 | 1 27 | 1 29 | 1 31 | 1 33 | 1 34 | 1 36 | 1 38 | 1 40 | 1 42 | 1 44 | 1 45 | 1 47 | 1 49 | 1 49 |
| 1 50 | 1 15 | 1 17 | 1 19 | 1 21 | 1 23 | 1 24 | 1 26 | 1 28 | 1 30 | 1 32 | 1 34 | 1 35 | 1 37 | 1 39 | 1 41 | 1 43 | 1 45 | 1 46 | 1 48 | 1 50 | 1 50 |
| 1 51 | 1 16 | 1 18 | 1 20 | 1 21 | 1 23 | 1 25 | 1 27 | 1 29 | 1 31 | 1 33 | 1 34 | 1 36 | 1 38 | 1 40 | 1 42 | 1 44 | 1 45 | 1 47 | 1 49 | 1 51 | 1 51 |
| 1 52 | 1 17 | 1 18 | 1 20 | 1 22 | 1 24 | 1 26 | 1 28 | 1 30 | 1 31 | 1 33 | 1 35 | 1 37 | 1 39 | 1 41 | 1 43 | 1 45 | 1 46 | 1 48 | 1 50 | 1 52 | 1 52 |
| 1 53 | 1 17 | 1 19 | 1 21 | 1 23 | 1 25 | 1 27 | 1 29 | 1 30 | 1 32 | 1 34 | 1 36 | 1 38 | 1 40 | 1 42 | 1 44 | 1 45 | 1 47 | 1 49 | 1 51 | 1 53 | 1 53 |
| 1 54 | 1 18 | 1 20 | 1 22 | 1 24 | 1 26 | 1 27 | 1 29 | 1 31 | 1 33 | 1 35 | 1 37 | 1 39 | 1 41 | 1 43 | 1 45 | 1 46 | 1 48 | 1 50 | 1 52 | 1 54 | 1 54 |
| 1 55 | 1 19 | 1 21 | 1 22 | 1 24 | 1 26 | 1 28 | 1 30 | 1 32 | 1 34 | 1 36 | 1 38 | 1 40 | 1 42 | 1 44 | 1 45 | 1 47 | 1 49 | 1 51 | 1 53 | 1 55 | 1 55 |
| 1 56 | 1 19 | 1 21 | 1 23 | 1 25 | 1 27 | 1 29 | 1 31 | 1 33 | 1 35 | 1 37 | 1 39 | 1 41 | 1 42 | 1 44 | 1 46 | 1 48 | 1 50 | 1 52 | 1 54 | 1 56 | 1 56 |
| 1 57 | 1 20 | 1 22 | 1 24 | 1 26 | 1 28 | 1 30 | 1 32 | 1 34 | 1 36 | 1 38 | 1 39 | 1 41 | 1 43 | 1 45 | 1 47 | 1 49 | 1 51 | 1 53 | 1 55 | 1 57 | 1 57 |
| 1 58 | 1 21 | 1 23 | 1 25 | 1 27 | 1 29 | 1 30 | 1 32 | 1 34 | 1 36 | 1 38 | 1 40 | 1 42 | 1 44 | 1 46 | 1 48 | 1 50 | 1 52 | 1 54 | 1 56 | 1 58 | 1 58 |
| 1 59 | 1 21 | 1 23 | 1 25 | 1 27 | 1 29 | 1 31 | 1 33 | 1 35 | 1 37 | 1 39 | 1 41 | 1 43 | 1 45 | 1 47 | 1 49 | 1 51 | 1 53 | 1 55 | 1 57 | 1 59 | 1 59 |
| 2 0 | 1 22 | 1 24 | 1 26 | 1 28 | 1 30 | 1 32 | 1 34 | 1 36 | 1 38 | 1 40 | 1 42 | 1 44 | 1 46 | 1 48 | 1 50 | 1 52 | 1 54 | 1 56 | 1 58 | 2 0 | 2 0 |

# Table XII House Cusp Interpolation Between Latitudes

| LAT INC | HOUSE CUSP INTERVAL | | | | | | | | | | | | | | | | | | | | | | | | | | | | | | LAT INC |
|---|---|---|---|---|---|---|---|---|---|---|---|---|---|---|---|---|---|---|---|---|---|---|---|---|---|---|---|---|---|---|---|
| | 1 | 2 | 3 | 4 | 5 | 6 | 7 | 8 | 9 | 10 | 11 | 12 | 13 | 14 | 15 | 16 | 17 | 18 | 19 | 20 | 21 | 22 | 23 | 24 | 25 | 26 | 27 | 28 | 29 | 30 | |
| 1 | 0 | 0 | 0 | 0 | 0 | 0 | 0 | 0 | 0 | 0 | 0 | 0 | 0 | 0 | 0 | 0 | 0 | 0 | 0 | 0 | 0 | 0 | 0 | 0 | 0 | 0 | 0 | 0 | 0 | 1 | 1 |
| 2 | 0 | 0 | 0 | 0 | 0 | 0 | 0 | 0 | 0 | 0 | 0 | 0 | 0 | 0 | 1 | 1 | 1 | 1 | 1 | 1 | 1 | 1 | 1 | 1 | 1 | 1 | 1 | 1 | 1 | 1 | 2 |
| 3 | 0 | 0 | 0 | 0 | 0 | 0 | 0 | 0 | 0 | 1 | 1 | 1 | 1 | 1 | 1 | 1 | 1 | 1 | 1 | 1 | 1 | 1 | 1 | 1 | 1 | 1 | 1 | 1 | 1 | 2 | 3 |
| 4 | 0 | 0 | 0 | 0 | 0 | 0 | 0 | 1 | 1 | 1 | 1 | 1 | 1 | 1 | 1 | 1 | 1 | 1 | 1 | 1 | 1 | 1 | 2 | 2 | 2 | 2 | 2 | 2 | 2 | 2 | 4 |
| 5 | 0 | 0 | 0 | 0 | 0 | 1 | 1 | 1 | 1 | 1 | 1 | 1 | 1 | 1 | 1 | 1 | 1 | 2 | 2 | 2 | 2 | 2 | 2 | 2 | 2 | 2 | 2 | 2 | 2 | 3 | 5 |
| 6 | 0 | 0 | 0 | 0 | 1 | 1 | 1 | 1 | 1 | 1 | 1 | 1 | 1 | 1 | 2 | 2 | 2 | 2 | 2 | 2 | 2 | 2 | 2 | 2 | 3 | 3 | 3 | 3 | 3 | 3 | 6 |
| 7 | 0 | 0 | 0 | 0 | 1 | 1 | 1 | 1 | 1 | 1 | 1 | 1 | 2 | 2 | 2 | 2 | 2 | 2 | 2 | 2 | 2 | 3 | 3 | 3 | 3 | 3 | 3 | 3 | 3 | 4 | 7 |
| 8 | 0 | 0 | 0 | 1 | 1 | 1 | 1 | 1 | 1 | 1 | 1 | 2 | 2 | 2 | 2 | 2 | 2 | 2 | 3 | 3 | 3 | 3 | 3 | 3 | 3 | 3 | 4 | 4 | 4 | 4 | 8 |
| 9 | 0 | 0 | 0 | 1 | 1 | 1 | 1 | 1 | 1 | 2 | 2 | 2 | 2 | 2 | 2 | 2 | 3 | 3 | 3 | 3 | 3 | 3 | 3 | 4 | 4 | 4 | 4 | 4 | 4 | 5 | 9 |
| 10 | 0 | 0 | 1 | 1 | 1 | 1 | 1 | 1 | 2 | 2 | 2 | 2 | 2 | 2 | 3 | 3 | 3 | 3 | 3 | 3 | 4 | 4 | 4 | 4 | 4 | 4 | 5 | 5 | 5 | 5 | 10 |
| 11 | 0 | 0 | 1 | 1 | 1 | 1 | 1 | 1 | 2 | 2 | 2 | 2 | 2 | 3 | 3 | 3 | 3 | 3 | 3 | 4 | 4 | 4 | 4 | 4 | 5 | 5 | 5 | 5 | 5 | 6 | 11 |
| 12 | 0 | 0 | 1 | 1 | 1 | 1 | 1 | 2 | 2 | 2 | 2 | 2 | 3 | 3 | 3 | 3 | 3 | 4 | 4 | 4 | 4 | 4 | 5 | 5 | 5 | 5 | 5 | 6 | 6 | 6 | 12 |
| 13 | 0 | 0 | 1 | 1 | 1 | 1 | 2 | 2 | 2 | 2 | 2 | 3 | 3 | 3 | 3 | 3 | 4 | 4 | 4 | 4 | 5 | 5 | 5 | 5 | 5 | 6 | 6 | 6 | 6 | 7 | 13 |
| 14 | 0 | 0 | 1 | 1 | 1 | 1 | 2 | 2 | 2 | 2 | 3 | 3 | 3 | 3 | 4 | 4 | 4 | 4 | 4 | 5 | 5 | 5 | 5 | 6 | 6 | 6 | 6 | 7 | 7 | 7 | 14 |
| 15 | 0 | 1 | 1 | 1 | 1 | 2 | 2 | 2 | 2 | 3 | 3 | 3 | 3 | 4 | 4 | 4 | 4 | 5 | 5 | 5 | 5 | 6 | 6 | 6 | 6 | 7 | 7 | 7 | 7 | 8 | 15 |
| 16 | 0 | 1 | 1 | 1 | 1 | 2 | 2 | 2 | 2 | 3 | 3 | 3 | 3 | 4 | 4 | 4 | 5 | 5 | 5 | 5 | 6 | 6 | 6 | 6 | 7 | 7 | 7 | 7 | 8 | 8 | 16 |
| 17 | 0 | 1 | 1 | 1 | 1 | 2 | 2 | 2 | 3 | 3 | 3 | 3 | 4 | 4 | 4 | 5 | 5 | 5 | 5 | 6 | 6 | 6 | 7 | 7 | 7 | 7 | 8 | 8 | 8 | 9 | 17 |
| 18 | 0 | 1 | 1 | 1 | 2 | 2 | 2 | 2 | 3 | 3 | 3 | 4 | 4 | 4 | 5 | 5 | 5 | 5 | 6 | 6 | 6 | 7 | 7 | 7 | 8 | 8 | 8 | 8 | 9 | 9 | 18 |
| 19 | 0 | 1 | 1 | 1 | 2 | 2 | 2 | 3 | 3 | 3 | 3 | 4 | 4 | 4 | 5 | 5 | 5 | 6 | 6 | 6 | 7 | 7 | 7 | 8 | 8 | 8 | 9 | 9 | 9 | 10 | 19 |
| 20 | 0 | 1 | 1 | 1 | 2 | 2 | 2 | 3 | 3 | 3 | 4 | 4 | 4 | 5 | 5 | 5 | 6 | 6 | 6 | 7 | 7 | 7 | 8 | 8 | 8 | 9 | 9 | 9 | 10 | 10 | 20 |
| 21 | 0 | 1 | 1 | 1 | 2 | 2 | 2 | 3 | 3 | 4 | 4 | 4 | 5 | 5 | 5 | 6 | 6 | 6 | 7 | 7 | 7 | 8 | 8 | 8 | 9 | 9 | 9 | 10 | 10 | 11 | 21 |
| 22 | 0 | 1 | 1 | 1 | 2 | 2 | 3 | 3 | 3 | 4 | 4 | 4 | 5 | 5 | 6 | 6 | 6 | 7 | 7 | 7 | 8 | 8 | 8 | 9 | 9 | 10 | 10 | 10 | 11 | 11 | 22 |
| 23 | 0 | 1 | 1 | 2 | 2 | 2 | 3 | 3 | 3 | 4 | 4 | 5 | 5 | 5 | 6 | 6 | 7 | 7 | 7 | 8 | 8 | 8 | 9 | 9 | 10 | 10 | 10 | 11 | 11 | 12 | 23 |
| 24 | 0 | 1 | 1 | 2 | 2 | 2 | 3 | 3 | 4 | 4 | 4 | 5 | 5 | 6 | 6 | 6 | 7 | 7 | 8 | 8 | 8 | 9 | 9 | 10 | 10 | 10 | 11 | 11 | 12 | 12 | 24 |
| 25 | 0 | 1 | 1 | 2 | 2 | 3 | 3 | 3 | 4 | 4 | 5 | 5 | 5 | 6 | 6 | 7 | 7 | 8 | 8 | 8 | 9 | 9 | 10 | 10 | 10 | 11 | 11 | 12 | 12 | 13 | 25 |
| 26 | 0 | 1 | 1 | 2 | 2 | 3 | 3 | 3 | 4 | 4 | 5 | 5 | 6 | 6 | 7 | 7 | 7 | 8 | 8 | 9 | 9 | 10 | 10 | 10 | 11 | 11 | 12 | 12 | 13 | 13 | 26 |
| 27 | 0 | 1 | 1 | 2 | 2 | 3 | 3 | 4 | 4 | 5 | 5 | 5 | 6 | 6 | 7 | 7 | 8 | 8 | 9 | 9 | 9 | 10 | 10 | 11 | 11 | 12 | 12 | 13 | 13 | 14 | 27 |
| 28 | 0 | 1 | 1 | 2 | 2 | 3 | 3 | 4 | 4 | 5 | 5 | 6 | 6 | 7 | 7 | 7 | 8 | 8 | 9 | 9 | 10 | 10 | 11 | 11 | 12 | 12 | 13 | 13 | 14 | 14 | 28 |
| 29 | 0 | 1 | 1 | 2 | 2 | 3 | 3 | 4 | 4 | 5 | 5 | 6 | 6 | 7 | 7 | 8 | 8 | 9 | 9 | 10 | 10 | 11 | 11 | 12 | 12 | 13 | 13 | 14 | 14 | 15 | 29 |
| 30 | 1 | 1 | 2 | 2 | 3 | 3 | 4 | 4 | 5 | 5 | 6 | 6 | 7 | 7 | 8 | 8 | 9 | 9 | 10 | 10 | 11 | 11 | 12 | 12 | 13 | 13 | 14 | 14 | 15 | 15 | 30 |
| 31 | 1 | 1 | 2 | 2 | 3 | 3 | 4 | 4 | 5 | 5 | 6 | 6 | 7 | 7 | 8 | 8 | 9 | 9 | 10 | 10 | 11 | 11 | 12 | 12 | 13 | 13 | 14 | 14 | 15 | 16 | 31 |
| 32 | 1 | 1 | 2 | 2 | 3 | 3 | 4 | 4 | 5 | 5 | 6 | 6 | 7 | 7 | 8 | 9 | 9 | 10 | 10 | 11 | 11 | 12 | 12 | 13 | 13 | 14 | 14 | 15 | 15 | 16 | 32 |
| 33 | 1 | 1 | 2 | 2 | 3 | 3 | 4 | 4 | 5 | 6 | 6 | 7 | 7 | 8 | 8 | 9 | 9 | 10 | 10 | 11 | 12 | 12 | 13 | 13 | 14 | 14 | 15 | 15 | 16 | 17 | 33 |
| 34 | 1 | 1 | 2 | 2 | 3 | 3 | 4 | 5 | 5 | 6 | 6 | 7 | 7 | 8 | 9 | 9 | 10 | 10 | 11 | 11 | 12 | 12 | 13 | 14 | 14 | 15 | 15 | 16 | 16 | 17 | 34 |
| 35 | 1 | 1 | 2 | 2 | 3 | 4 | 4 | 5 | 5 | 6 | 6 | 7 | 8 | 8 | 9 | 9 | 10 | 11 | 11 | 12 | 12 | 13 | 13 | 14 | 15 | 15 | 16 | 16 | 17 | 18 | 35 |
| 36 | 1 | 1 | 2 | 2 | 3 | 4 | 4 | 5 | 5 | 6 | 7 | 7 | 8 | 8 | 9 | 10 | 10 | 11 | 11 | 12 | 13 | 13 | 14 | 14 | 15 | 16 | 16 | 17 | 17 | 18 | 36 |
| 37 | 1 | 1 | 2 | 2 | 3 | 4 | 4 | 5 | 6 | 6 | 7 | 7 | 8 | 9 | 9 | 10 | 10 | 11 | 12 | 12 | 13 | 14 | 14 | 15 | 15 | 16 | 17 | 17 | 18 | 19 | 37 |
| 38 | 1 | 1 | 2 | 3 | 3 | 4 | 4 | 5 | 6 | 6 | 7 | 8 | 8 | 9 | 10 | 10 | 11 | 11 | 12 | 13 | 13 | 14 | 15 | 15 | 16 | 16 | 17 | 18 | 18 | 19 | 38 |
| 39 | 1 | 1 | 2 | 3 | 3 | 4 | 5 | 5 | 6 | 7 | 7 | 8 | 8 | 9 | 10 | 10 | 11 | 12 | 12 | 13 | 14 | 14 | 15 | 16 | 16 | 17 | 18 | 18 | 19 | 20 | 39 |
| 40 | 1 | 1 | 2 | 3 | 3 | 4 | 5 | 5 | 6 | 7 | 7 | 8 | 9 | 9 | 10 | 11 | 11 | 12 | 13 | 13 | 14 | 15 | 15 | 16 | 17 | 17 | 18 | 19 | 19 | 20 | 40 |
| 41 | 1 | 1 | 2 | 3 | 3 | 4 | 5 | 5 | 6 | 7 | 8 | 8 | 9 | 10 | 10 | 11 | 12 | 12 | 13 | 14 | 14 | 15 | 16 | 16 | 17 | 18 | 18 | 19 | 20 | 21 | 41 |
| 42 | 1 | 1 | 2 | 3 | 4 | 4 | 5 | 6 | 6 | 7 | 8 | 8 | 9 | 10 | 11 | 11 | 12 | 13 | 13 | 14 | 15 | 15 | 16 | 17 | 18 | 18 | 19 | 20 | 20 | 21 | 42 |
| 43 | 1 | 1 | 2 | 3 | 4 | 4 | 5 | 6 | 6 | 7 | 8 | 9 | 9 | 10 | 11 | 11 | 12 | 13 | 14 | 14 | 15 | 16 | 16 | 17 | 18 | 19 | 19 | 20 | 21 | 22 | 43 |
| 44 | 1 | 1 | 2 | 3 | 4 | 4 | 5 | 6 | 7 | 7 | 8 | 9 | 10 | 10 | 11 | 12 | 12 | 13 | 14 | 15 | 15 | 16 | 17 | 18 | 18 | 19 | 20 | 21 | 21 | 22 | 44 |
| 45 | 1 | 2 | 2 | 3 | 4 | 5 | 5 | 6 | 7 | 8 | 8 | 9 | 10 | 11 | 11 | 12 | 13 | 14 | 14 | 15 | 16 | 17 | 17 | 18 | 19 | 20 | 20 | 21 | 22 | 23 | 45 |
| 46 | 1 | 2 | 2 | 3 | 4 | 5 | 5 | 6 | 7 | 8 | 8 | 9 | 10 | 11 | 12 | 12 | 13 | 14 | 15 | 15 | 16 | 17 | 18 | 18 | 19 | 20 | 21 | 21 | 22 | 23 | 46 |
| 47 | 1 | 2 | 2 | 3 | 4 | 5 | 5 | 6 | 7 | 8 | 9 | 9 | 10 | 11 | 12 | 13 | 13 | 14 | 15 | 16 | 16 | 17 | 18 | 19 | 20 | 20 | 21 | 22 | 23 | 24 | 47 |
| 48 | 1 | 2 | 2 | 3 | 4 | 5 | 6 | 6 | 7 | 8 | 9 | 10 | 10 | 11 | 12 | 13 | 14 | 14 | 15 | 16 | 17 | 18 | 18 | 19 | 20 | 21 | 22 | 22 | 23 | 24 | 48 |
| 49 | 1 | 2 | 2 | 3 | 4 | 5 | 6 | 7 | 7 | 8 | 9 | 10 | 11 | 11 | 12 | 13 | 14 | 15 | 16 | 16 | 17 | 18 | 19 | 20 | 20 | 21 | 22 | 23 | 24 | 25 | 49 |
| 50 | 1 | 2 | 3 | 3 | 4 | 5 | 6 | 7 | 8 | 8 | 9 | 10 | 11 | 12 | 13 | 13 | 14 | 15 | 16 | 17 | 18 | 18 | 19 | 20 | 21 | 22 | 23 | 23 | 24 | 25 | 50 |
| 51 | 1 | 2 | 3 | 3 | 4 | 5 | 6 | 7 | 8 | 9 | 9 | 10 | 11 | 12 | 13 | 14 | 14 | 15 | 16 | 17 | 18 | 19 | 20 | 20 | 21 | 22 | 23 | 24 | 25 | 26 | 51 |
| 52 | 1 | 2 | 3 | 3 | 4 | 5 | 6 | 7 | 8 | 9 | 10 | 10 | 11 | 12 | 13 | 14 | 15 | 16 | 16 | 17 | 18 | 19 | 20 | 21 | 22 | 23 | 23 | 24 | 25 | 26 | 52 |
| 53 | 1 | 2 | 3 | 4 | 4 | 5 | 6 | 7 | 8 | 9 | 10 | 11 | 11 | 12 | 13 | 14 | 15 | 16 | 17 | 18 | 19 | 19 | 20 | 21 | 22 | 23 | 24 | 25 | 26 | 27 | 53 |
| 54 | 1 | 2 | 3 | 4 | 5 | 5 | 6 | 7 | 8 | 9 | 10 | 11 | 12 | 13 | 14 | 14 | 15 | 16 | 17 | 18 | 19 | 20 | 21 | 22 | 23 | 23 | 24 | 25 | 26 | 27 | 54 |
| 55 | 1 | 2 | 3 | 4 | 5 | 6 | 6 | 7 | 8 | 9 | 10 | 11 | 12 | 13 | 14 | 15 | 16 | 17 | 17 | 18 | 19 | 20 | 21 | 22 | 23 | 24 | 25 | 26 | 27 | 28 | 55 |
| 56 | 1 | 2 | 3 | 4 | 5 | 6 | 7 | 7 | 8 | 9 | 10 | 11 | 12 | 13 | 14 | 15 | 16 | 17 | 18 | 19 | 20 | 21 | 21 | 22 | 23 | 24 | 25 | 26 | 27 | 28 | 56 |
| 57 | 1 | 2 | 3 | 4 | 5 | 6 | 7 | 8 | 9 | 10 | 10 | 11 | 12 | 13 | 14 | 15 | 16 | 17 | 18 | 19 | 20 | 21 | 22 | 23 | 24 | 25 | 26 | 27 | 28 | 29 | 57 |
| 58 | 1 | 2 | 3 | 4 | 5 | 6 | 7 | 8 | 9 | 10 | 11 | 12 | 13 | 14 | 15 | 15 | 16 | 17 | 18 | 19 | 20 | 21 | 22 | 23 | 24 | 25 | 26 | 27 | 28 | 29 | 58 |
| 59 | 1 | 2 | 3 | 4 | 5 | 6 | 7 | 8 | 9 | 10 | 11 | 12 | 13 | 14 | 15 | 16 | 17 | 18 | 19 | 20 | 21 | 22 | 23 | 24 | 25 | 26 | 27 | 28 | 29 | 30 | 59 |

# Table XII House Cusp Interpolation Between Latitudes

HOUSE CUSP INTERVAL

| LAT INC | 31 | 32 | 33 | 34 | 35 | 36 | 37 | 38 | 39 | 40 | 41 | 42 | 43 | 44 | 45 | 46 | 47 | 48 | 49 | 50 | 51 | 52 | 53 | 54 | 55 | 56 | 57 | 58 | 59 | 60 | LAT INC |
|---|---|---|---|---|---|---|---|---|---|---|---|---|---|---|---|---|---|---|---|---|---|---|---|---|---|---|---|---|---|---|---|
| 1 | 1 | 1 | 1 | 1 | 1 | 1 | 1 | 1 | 1 | 1 | 1 | 1 | 1 | 1 | 1 | 1 | 1 | 1 | 1 | 1 | 1 | 1 | 1 | 1 | 1 | 1 | 1 | 1 | 1 | 1 | 1 |
| 2 | 1 | 1 | 1 | 1 | 1 | 1 | 1 | 1 | 1 | 1 | 1 | 1 | 1 | 1 | 2 | 2 | 2 | 2 | 2 | 2 | 2 | 2 | 2 | 2 | 2 | 2 | 2 | 2 | 2 | 2 | 2 |
| 3 | 2 | 2 | 2 | 2 | 2 | 2 | 2 | 2 | 2 | 2 | 2 | 2 | 2 | 2 | 2 | 2 | 2 | 2 | 2 | 3 | 3 | 3 | 3 | 3 | 3 | 3 | 3 | 3 | 3 | 3 | 3 |
| 4 | 2 | 2 | 2 | 2 | 2 | 2 | 2 | 3 | 3 | 3 | 3 | 3 | 3 | 3 | 3 | 3 | 3 | 3 | 3 | 3 | 3 | 3 | 4 | 4 | 4 | 4 | 4 | 4 | 4 | 4 | 4 |
| 5 | 3 | 3 | 3 | 3 | 3 | 3 | 3 | 3 | 3 | 3 | 3 | 4 | 4 | 4 | 4 | 4 | 4 | 4 | 4 | 4 | 4 | 4 | 4 | 5 | 5 | 5 | 5 | 5 | 5 | 5 | 5 |
| 6 | 3 | 3 | 3 | 3 | 4 | 4 | 4 | 4 | 4 | 4 | 4 | 4 | 4 | 4 | 5 | 5 | 5 | 5 | 5 | 5 | 5 | 5 | 5 | 5 | 6 | 6 | 6 | 6 | 6 | 6 | 6 |
| 7 | 4 | 4 | 4 | 4 | 4 | 4 | 4 | 4 | 5 | 5 | 5 | 5 | 5 | 5 | 5 | 5 | 5 | 6 | 6 | 6 | 6 | 6 | 6 | 6 | 6 | 7 | 7 | 7 | 7 | 7 | 7 |
| 8 | 4 | 4 | 4 | 5 | 5 | 5 | 5 | 5 | 5 | 5 | 5 | 6 | 6 | 6 | 6 | 6 | 6 | 6 | 7 | 7 | 7 | 7 | 7 | 7 | 7 | 7 | 8 | 8 | 8 | 8 | 8 |
| 9 | 5 | 5 | 5 | 5 | 5 | 5 | 6 | 6 | 6 | 6 | 6 | 6 | 6 | 7 | 7 | 7 | 7 | 7 | 7 | 8 | 8 | 8 | 8 | 8 | 8 | 8 | 9 | 9 | 9 | 9 | 9 |
| 10 | 5 | 5 | 6 | 6 | 6 | 6 | 6 | 6 | 7 | 7 | 7 | 7 | 7 | 7 | 8 | 8 | 8 | 8 | 8 | 8 | 9 | 9 | 9 | 9 | 9 | 9 | 10 | 10 | 10 | 10 | 10 |
| 11 | 6 | 6 | 6 | 6 | 6 | 7 | 7 | 7 | 7 | 7 | 8 | 8 | 8 | 8 | 8 | 8 | 9 | 9 | 9 | 9 | 9 | 10 | 10 | 10 | 10 | 10 | 10 | 11 | 11 | 11 | 11 |
| 12 | 6 | 6 | 7 | 7 | 7 | 7 | 7 | 8 | 8 | 8 | 8 | 8 | 9 | 9 | 9 | 9 | 9 | 10 | 10 | 10 | 10 | 10 | 11 | 11 | 11 | 11 | 11 | 12 | 12 | 12 | 12 |
| 13 | 7 | 7 | 7 | 7 | 8 | 8 | 8 | 8 | 8 | 9 | 9 | 9 | 9 | 10 | 10 | 10 | 10 | 10 | 11 | 11 | 11 | 11 | 11 | 12 | 12 | 12 | 12 | 13 | 13 | 13 | 13 |
| 14 | 7 | 7 | 8 | 8 | 8 | 8 | 9 | 9 | 9 | 9 | 10 | 10 | 10 | 10 | 11 | 11 | 11 | 11 | 11 | 12 | 12 | 12 | 12 | 13 | 13 | 13 | 13 | 14 | 14 | 14 | 14 |
| 15 | 8 | 8 | 8 | 9 | 9 | 9 | 9 | 10 | 10 | 10 | 10 | 11 | 11 | 11 | 11 | 12 | 12 | 12 | 12 | 13 | 13 | 13 | 13 | 14 | 14 | 14 | 14 | 15 | 15 | 15 | 15 |
| 16 | 8 | 9 | 9 | 9 | 9 | 10 | 10 | 10 | 10 | 11 | 11 | 11 | 11 | 12 | 12 | 12 | 13 | 13 | 13 | 13 | 14 | 14 | 14 | 14 | 15 | 15 | 15 | 15 | 16 | 16 | 16 |
| 17 | 9 | 9 | 9 | 10 | 10 | 10 | 10 | 11 | 11 | 11 | 12 | 12 | 12 | 12 | 13 | 13 | 13 | 14 | 14 | 14 | 14 | 15 | 15 | 15 | 16 | 16 | 16 | 16 | 17 | 17 | 17 |
| 18 | 9 | 10 | 10 | 10 | 11 | 11 | 11 | 11 | 12 | 12 | 12 | 13 | 13 | 13 | 14 | 14 | 14 | 14 | 15 | 15 | 15 | 16 | 16 | 16 | 17 | 17 | 17 | 17 | 18 | 18 | 18 |
| 19 | 10 | 10 | 10 | 11 | 11 | 11 | 12 | 12 | 12 | 13 | 13 | 13 | 14 | 14 | 14 | 15 | 15 | 15 | 16 | 16 | 16 | 16 | 17 | 17 | 17 | 18 | 18 | 18 | 19 | 19 | 19 |
| 20 | 10 | 11 | 11 | 11 | 12 | 12 | 12 | 13 | 13 | 13 | 14 | 14 | 14 | 15 | 15 | 15 | 16 | 16 | 16 | 17 | 17 | 17 | 18 | 18 | 18 | 19 | 19 | 19 | 20 | 20 | 20 |
| 21 | 11 | 11 | 12 | 12 | 12 | 13 | 13 | 13 | 14 | 14 | 14 | 15 | 15 | 15 | 16 | 16 | 16 | 17 | 17 | 18 | 18 | 18 | 19 | 19 | 19 | 20 | 20 | 20 | 21 | 21 | 21 |
| 22 | 11 | 12 | 12 | 12 | 13 | 13 | 14 | 14 | 14 | 15 | 15 | 15 | 16 | 16 | 17 | 17 | 17 | 18 | 18 | 18 | 19 | 19 | 19 | 20 | 20 | 21 | 21 | 21 | 22 | 22 | 22 |
| 23 | 12 | 12 | 13 | 13 | 13 | 14 | 14 | 15 | 15 | 15 | 16 | 16 | 16 | 17 | 17 | 18 | 18 | 18 | 19 | 19 | 20 | 20 | 20 | 21 | 21 | 21 | 22 | 22 | 23 | 23 | 23 |
| 24 | 12 | 13 | 13 | 14 | 14 | 14 | 15 | 15 | 16 | 16 | 16 | 17 | 17 | 18 | 18 | 18 | 19 | 19 | 20 | 20 | 20 | 21 | 21 | 22 | 22 | 22 | 23 | 23 | 24 | 24 | 24 |
| 25 | 13 | 13 | 14 | 14 | 15 | 15 | 15 | 16 | 16 | 17 | 17 | 18 | 18 | 18 | 19 | 19 | 20 | 20 | 20 | 21 | 21 | 22 | 22 | 23 | 23 | 23 | 24 | 24 | 25 | 25 | 25 |
| 26 | 13 | 14 | 14 | 15 | 15 | 16 | 16 | 16 | 17 | 17 | 18 | 18 | 19 | 19 | 20 | 20 | 20 | 21 | 21 | 22 | 22 | 23 | 23 | 23 | 24 | 24 | 25 | 25 | 26 | 26 | 26 |
| 27 | 14 | 14 | 15 | 15 | 16 | 16 | 17 | 17 | 18 | 18 | 18 | 19 | 19 | 20 | 20 | 21 | 21 | 22 | 22 | 23 | 23 | 23 | 24 | 24 | 25 | 25 | 26 | 26 | 27 | 27 | 27 |
| 28 | 14 | 15 | 15 | 16 | 16 | 17 | 17 | 18 | 18 | 19 | 19 | 20 | 20 | 21 | 21 | 21 | 22 | 22 | 23 | 23 | 24 | 24 | 25 | 25 | 26 | 26 | 27 | 27 | 28 | 28 | 28 |
| 29 | 15 | 15 | 16 | 16 | 17 | 17 | 18 | 18 | 19 | 19 | 20 | 20 | 21 | 21 | 22 | 22 | 23 | 23 | 24 | 24 | 25 | 25 | 26 | 26 | 27 | 27 | 28 | 28 | 29 | 29 | 29 |
| 30 | 16 | 16 | 17 | 17 | 18 | 18 | 19 | 19 | 20 | 20 | 21 | 21 | 22 | 22 | 23 | 23 | 24 | 24 | 25 | 25 | 26 | 26 | 27 | 27 | 28 | 28 | 29 | 29 | 30 | 30 | 30 |
| 31 | 16 | 17 | 17 | 18 | 18 | 19 | 19 | 20 | 20 | 21 | 21 | 22 | 22 | 23 | 23 | 24 | 24 | 25 | 25 | 26 | 26 | 27 | 27 | 28 | 28 | 29 | 29 | 30 | 30 | 31 | 31 |
| 32 | 17 | 17 | 18 | 18 | 19 | 19 | 20 | 20 | 21 | 21 | 22 | 22 | 23 | 23 | 24 | 25 | 25 | 26 | 26 | 27 | 27 | 28 | 28 | 29 | 29 | 30 | 30 | 31 | 31 | 32 | 32 |
| 33 | 17 | 18 | 18 | 19 | 19 | 20 | 20 | 21 | 21 | 22 | 23 | 23 | 24 | 24 | 25 | 25 | 26 | 26 | 27 | 28 | 28 | 29 | 29 | 30 | 30 | 31 | 31 | 32 | 32 | 33 | 33 |
| 34 | 18 | 18 | 19 | 19 | 20 | 20 | 21 | 22 | 22 | 23 | 23 | 24 | 24 | 25 | 26 | 26 | 27 | 27 | 28 | 28 | 29 | 29 | 30 | 31 | 31 | 32 | 32 | 33 | 33 | 34 | 34 |
| 35 | 18 | 19 | 19 | 20 | 20 | 21 | 22 | 22 | 23 | 23 | 24 | 25 | 25 | 26 | 26 | 27 | 27 | 28 | 29 | 29 | 30 | 30 | 31 | 32 | 32 | 33 | 33 | 34 | 34 | 35 | 35 |
| 36 | 19 | 19 | 20 | 20 | 21 | 22 | 22 | 23 | 23 | 24 | 25 | 25 | 26 | 26 | 27 | 28 | 28 | 29 | 29 | 30 | 31 | 31 | 32 | 32 | 33 | 34 | 34 | 35 | 35 | 36 | 36 |
| 37 | 19 | 20 | 20 | 21 | 22 | 22 | 23 | 23 | 24 | 25 | 25 | 26 | 27 | 27 | 28 | 28 | 29 | 30 | 30 | 31 | 31 | 32 | 33 | 33 | 34 | 35 | 35 | 36 | 36 | 37 | 37 |
| 38 | 20 | 20 | 21 | 22 | 22 | 23 | 23 | 24 | 25 | 25 | 26 | 27 | 27 | 28 | 29 | 29 | 30 | 30 | 31 | 32 | 32 | 33 | 34 | 34 | 35 | 35 | 36 | 37 | 37 | 38 | 38 |
| 39 | 20 | 21 | 21 | 22 | 23 | 23 | 24 | 25 | 25 | 26 | 27 | 27 | 28 | 29 | 29 | 30 | 31 | 31 | 32 | 33 | 33 | 34 | 34 | 35 | 36 | 36 | 37 | 38 | 38 | 39 | 39 |
| 40 | 21 | 21 | 22 | 23 | 23 | 24 | 25 | 25 | 26 | 27 | 27 | 28 | 29 | 29 | 30 | 31 | 31 | 32 | 33 | 33 | 34 | 35 | 35 | 36 | 37 | 37 | 38 | 39 | 39 | 40 | 40 |
| 41 | 21 | 22 | 23 | 23 | 24 | 25 | 25 | 26 | 27 | 27 | 28 | 29 | 29 | 30 | 31 | 31 | 32 | 33 | 33 | 34 | 35 | 36 | 36 | 37 | 38 | 38 | 39 | 40 | 40 | 41 | 41 |
| 42 | 22 | 22 | 23 | 24 | 25 | 25 | 26 | 27 | 27 | 28 | 29 | 29 | 30 | 31 | 32 | 32 | 33 | 34 | 34 | 35 | 36 | 36 | 37 | 38 | 39 | 39 | 40 | 41 | 41 | 42 | 42 |
| 43 | 22 | 23 | 24 | 24 | 25 | 26 | 27 | 27 | 28 | 29 | 29 | 30 | 31 | 32 | 32 | 33 | 34 | 34 | 35 | 36 | 37 | 37 | 38 | 39 | 39 | 40 | 41 | 42 | 42 | 43 | 43 |
| 44 | 23 | 23 | 24 | 25 | 26 | 26 | 27 | 28 | 29 | 29 | 30 | 31 | 32 | 32 | 33 | 34 | 34 | 35 | 36 | 37 | 37 | 38 | 39 | 40 | 40 | 41 | 42 | 43 | 43 | 44 | 44 |
| 45 | 23 | 24 | 25 | 26 | 26 | 27 | 28 | 29 | 29 | 30 | 31 | 32 | 32 | 33 | 34 | 35 | 35 | 36 | 37 | 38 | 38 | 39 | 40 | 41 | 41 | 42 | 43 | 44 | 44 | 45 | 45 |
| 46 | 24 | 25 | 25 | 26 | 27 | 28 | 28 | 29 | 30 | 31 | 31 | 32 | 33 | 34 | 35 | 35 | 36 | 37 | 38 | 38 | 39 | 40 | 41 | 41 | 42 | 43 | 44 | 44 | 45 | 46 | 46 |
| 47 | 24 | 25 | 26 | 27 | 27 | 28 | 29 | 30 | 31 | 31 | 32 | 33 | 34 | 34 | 35 | 36 | 37 | 38 | 38 | 39 | 40 | 41 | 42 | 42 | 43 | 44 | 45 | 45 | 46 | 47 | 47 |
| 48 | 25 | 26 | 26 | 27 | 28 | 29 | 30 | 30 | 31 | 32 | 33 | 34 | 34 | 35 | 36 | 37 | 38 | 38 | 39 | 40 | 41 | 42 | 42 | 43 | 44 | 45 | 46 | 46 | 47 | 48 | 48 |
| 49 | 25 | 26 | 27 | 28 | 29 | 29 | 30 | 31 | 32 | 33 | 33 | 34 | 35 | 36 | 37 | 38 | 38 | 39 | 40 | 41 | 42 | 42 | 43 | 44 | 45 | 46 | 47 | 47 | 48 | 49 | 49 |
| 50 | 26 | 27 | 28 | 28 | 29 | 30 | 31 | 32 | 33 | 33 | 34 | 35 | 36 | 37 | 38 | 38 | 39 | 40 | 41 | 42 | 43 | 43 | 44 | 45 | 46 | 47 | 48 | 48 | 49 | 50 | 50 |
| 51 | 26 | 27 | 28 | 29 | 30 | 31 | 31 | 32 | 33 | 34 | 35 | 36 | 37 | 37 | 38 | 39 | 40 | 41 | 42 | 43 | 43 | 44 | 45 | 46 | 47 | 48 | 48 | 49 | 50 | 51 | 51 |
| 52 | 27 | 28 | 29 | 29 | 30 | 31 | 32 | 33 | 34 | 35 | 36 | 36 | 37 | 38 | 39 | 40 | 41 | 42 | 42 | 43 | 44 | 45 | 46 | 47 | 48 | 49 | 49 | 50 | 51 | 52 | 52 |
| 53 | 27 | 28 | 29 | 30 | 31 | 32 | 33 | 34 | 34 | 35 | 36 | 37 | 38 | 39 | 40 | 41 | 42 | 42 | 43 | 44 | 45 | 46 | 47 | 48 | 49 | 49 | 50 | 51 | 52 | 53 | 53 |
| 54 | 28 | 29 | 30 | 31 | 32 | 32 | 33 | 34 | 35 | 36 | 37 | 38 | 39 | 40 | 41 | 41 | 42 | 43 | 44 | 45 | 46 | 47 | 48 | 49 | 50 | 50 | 51 | 52 | 53 | 54 | 54 |
| 55 | 28 | 29 | 30 | 31 | 32 | 33 | 34 | 35 | 36 | 37 | 38 | 39 | 39 | 40 | 41 | 42 | 43 | 44 | 45 | 46 | 47 | 48 | 49 | 50 | 50 | 51 | 52 | 53 | 54 | 55 | 55 |
| 56 | 29 | 30 | 31 | 32 | 33 | 34 | 35 | 35 | 36 | 37 | 38 | 39 | 40 | 41 | 42 | 43 | 44 | 45 | 46 | 47 | 48 | 49 | 49 | 50 | 51 | 52 | 53 | 54 | 55 | 56 | 56 |
| 57 | 29 | 30 | 31 | 32 | 33 | 34 | 35 | 36 | 37 | 38 | 39 | 40 | 41 | 42 | 43 | 44 | 45 | 46 | 47 | 48 | 48 | 49 | 50 | 51 | 52 | 53 | 54 | 55 | 56 | 57 | 57 |
| 58 | 30 | 31 | 32 | 33 | 34 | 35 | 36 | 37 | 38 | 39 | 40 | 41 | 42 | 43 | 44 | 44 | 45 | 46 | 47 | 48 | 49 | 50 | 51 | 52 | 53 | 54 | 55 | 56 | 57 | 58 | 58 |
| 59 | 30 | 31 | 32 | 33 | 34 | 35 | 36 | 37 | 38 | 39 | 40 | 41 | 42 | 43 | 44 | 45 | 46 | 47 | 48 | 49 | 50 | 51 | 52 | 53 | 54 | 55 | 56 | 57 | 58 | 59 | 59 |

# Table XII House Cusp Interpolation Between Latitudes

HOUSE CUSP INTERVAL

Values are given in degrees and minutes (e.g. "0 5" = 0°5'). Column headings are house cusp intervals of 1° plus the indicated minutes.

| LAT INC | 1°1' | 1°2' | 1°3' | 1°4' | 1°5' | 1°6' | 1°7' | 1°8' | 1°9' | 1°10' | 1°11' | 1°12' | 1°13' | 1°14' | 1°15' | 1°16' | 1°17' | 1°18' | 1°19' | 1°20' | 1°21' | 1°22' | 1°23' | 1°24' | LAT INC |
|---|---|---|---|---|---|---|---|---|---|---|---|---|---|---|---|---|---|---|---|---|---|---|---|---|---|
| 1 | 0 1 | 0 1 | 0 1 | 0 1 | 0 1 | 0 1 | 0 1 | 0 1 | 0 1 | 0 1 | 0 1 | 0 1 | 0 1 | 0 1 | 0 1 | 0 1 | 0 1 | 0 1 | 0 1 | 0 1 | 0 1 | 0 1 | 0 1 | 0 1 | 1 |
| 2 | 0 2 | 0 2 | 0 2 | 0 2 | 0 2 | 0 2 | 0 2 | 0 2 | 0 2 | 0 2 | 0 2 | 0 2 | 0 2 | 0 2 | 0 3 | 0 3 | 0 3 | 0 3 | 0 3 | 0 3 | 0 3 | 0 3 | 0 3 | 0 3 | 2 |
| 3 | 0 3 | 0 3 | 0 3 | 0 3 | 0 3 | 0 3 | 0 3 | 0 3 | 0 3 | 0 4 | 0 4 | 0 4 | 0 4 | 0 4 | 0 4 | 0 4 | 0 4 | 0 4 | 0 4 | 0 4 | 0 4 | 0 4 | 0 4 | 0 4 | 3 |
| 4 | 0 4 | 0 4 | 0 4 | 0 4 | 0 4 | 0 4 | 0 4 | 0 5 | 0 5 | 0 5 | 0 5 | 0 5 | 0 5 | 0 5 | 0 5 | 0 5 | 0 5 | 0 5 | 0 5 | 0 5 | 0 5 | 0 5 | 0 6 | 0 6 | 4 |
| 5 | 0 5 | 0 5 | 0 5 | 0 5 | 0 5 | 0 6 | 0 6 | 0 6 | 0 6 | 0 6 | 0 6 | 0 6 | 0 6 | 0 6 | 0 6 | 0 6 | 0 6 | 0 7 | 0 7 | 0 7 | 0 7 | 0 7 | 0 7 | 0 7 | 5 |
| 6 | 0 6 | 0 6 | 0 6 | 0 6 | 0 7 | 0 7 | 0 7 | 0 7 | 0 7 | 0 7 | 0 7 | 0 7 | 0 7 | 0 7 | 0 8 | 0 8 | 0 8 | 0 8 | 0 8 | 0 8 | 0 8 | 0 8 | 0 8 | 0 8 | 6 |
| 7 | 0 7 | 0 7 | 0 7 | 0 7 | 0 8 | 0 8 | 0 8 | 0 8 | 0 8 | 0 8 | 0 8 | 0 8 | 0 9 | 0 9 | 0 9 | 0 9 | 0 9 | 0 9 | 0 9 | 0 9 | 0 9 | 0 10 | 0 10 | 0 10 | 7 |
| 8 | 0 8 | 0 8 | 0 8 | 0 9 | 0 9 | 0 9 | 0 9 | 0 9 | 0 9 | 0 9 | 0 9 | 0 10 | 0 10 | 0 10 | 0 10 | 0 10 | 0 10 | 0 10 | 0 11 | 0 11 | 0 11 | 0 11 | 0 11 | 0 11 | 8 |
| 9 | 0 9 | 0 9 | 0 9 | 0 10 | 0 10 | 0 10 | 0 10 | 0 10 | 0 10 | 0 11 | 0 11 | 0 11 | 0 11 | 0 11 | 0 11 | 0 11 | 0 12 | 0 12 | 0 12 | 0 12 | 0 12 | 0 12 | 0 12 | 0 13 | 9 |
| 10 | 0 10 | 0 10 | 0 11 | 0 11 | 0 11 | 0 11 | 0 11 | 0 11 | 0 12 | 0 12 | 0 12 | 0 12 | 0 12 | 0 12 | 0 13 | 0 13 | 0 13 | 0 13 | 0 13 | 0 13 | 0 14 | 0 14 | 0 14 | 0 14 | 10 |
| 11 | 0 11 | 0 11 | 0 12 | 0 12 | 0 12 | 0 12 | 0 12 | 0 12 | 0 13 | 0 13 | 0 13 | 0 13 | 0 13 | 0 14 | 0 14 | 0 14 | 0 14 | 0 14 | 0 14 | 0 15 | 0 15 | 0 15 | 0 15 | 0 15 | 11 |
| 12 | 0 12 | 0 12 | 0 13 | 0 13 | 0 13 | 0 13 | 0 13 | 0 14 | 0 14 | 0 14 | 0 14 | 0 14 | 0 15 | 0 15 | 0 15 | 0 15 | 0 15 | 0 16 | 0 16 | 0 16 | 0 16 | 0 16 | 0 17 | 0 17 | 12 |
| 13 | 0 13 | 0 13 | 0 14 | 0 14 | 0 14 | 0 14 | 0 15 | 0 15 | 0 15 | 0 15 | 0 15 | 0 16 | 0 16 | 0 16 | 0 16 | 0 16 | 0 17 | 0 17 | 0 17 | 0 17 | 0 18 | 0 18 | 0 18 | 0 18 | 13 |
| 14 | 0 14 | 0 14 | 0 15 | 0 15 | 0 15 | 0 15 | 0 16 | 0 16 | 0 16 | 0 16 | 0 17 | 0 17 | 0 17 | 0 17 | 0 18 | 0 18 | 0 18 | 0 18 | 0 18 | 0 19 | 0 19 | 0 19 | 0 19 | 0 20 | 14 |
| 15 | 0 15 | 0 16 | 0 16 | 0 16 | 0 16 | 0 17 | 0 17 | 0 17 | 0 17 | 0 18 | 0 18 | 0 18 | 0 18 | 0 19 | 0 19 | 0 19 | 0 19 | 0 20 | 0 20 | 0 20 | 0 20 | 0 21 | 0 21 | 0 21 | 15 |
| 16 | 0 16 | 0 17 | 0 17 | 0 17 | 0 17 | 0 18 | 0 18 | 0 18 | 0 19 | 0 19 | 0 19 | 0 19 | 0 20 | 0 20 | 0 20 | 0 21 | 0 21 | 0 21 | 0 21 | 0 22 | 0 22 | 0 22 | 0 22 | 0 22 | 16 |
| 17 | 0 17 | 0 18 | 0 18 | 0 18 | 0 18 | 0 19 | 0 19 | 0 19 | 0 20 | 0 20 | 0 20 | 0 20 | 0 21 | 0 21 | 0 21 | 0 22 | 0 22 | 0 22 | 0 22 | 0 23 | 0 23 | 0 23 | 0 24 | 0 24 | 17 |
| 18 | 0 18 | 0 19 | 0 19 | 0 19 | 0 20 | 0 20 | 0 20 | 0 20 | 0 21 | 0 21 | 0 21 | 0 22 | 0 22 | 0 22 | 0 23 | 0 23 | 0 23 | 0 23 | 0 24 | 0 24 | 0 24 | 0 25 | 0 25 | 0 25 | 18 |
| 19 | 0 19 | 0 20 | 0 20 | 0 20 | 0 21 | 0 21 | 0 21 | 0 22 | 0 22 | 0 22 | 0 22 | 0 23 | 0 23 | 0 23 | 0 24 | 0 24 | 0 24 | 0 25 | 0 25 | 0 25 | 0 26 | 0 26 | 0 26 | 0 27 | 19 |
| 20 | 0 20 | 0 21 | 0 21 | 0 21 | 0 22 | 0 22 | 0 22 | 0 23 | 0 23 | 0 23 | 0 24 | 0 24 | 0 24 | 0 25 | 0 25 | 0 25 | 0 26 | 0 26 | 0 26 | 0 27 | 0 27 | 0 27 | 0 28 | 0 28 | 20 |
| 21 | 0 21 | 0 22 | 0 22 | 0 22 | 0 23 | 0 23 | 0 23 | 0 24 | 0 24 | 0 25 | 0 25 | 0 25 | 0 26 | 0 26 | 0 26 | 0 27 | 0 27 | 0 27 | 0 28 | 0 28 | 0 28 | 0 29 | 0 29 | 0 29 | 21 |
| 22 | 0 22 | 0 23 | 0 23 | 0 23 | 0 24 | 0 24 | 0 25 | 0 25 | 0 25 | 0 26 | 0 26 | 0 26 | 0 27 | 0 27 | 0 28 | 0 28 | 0 28 | 0 29 | 0 29 | 0 29 | 0 30 | 0 30 | 0 30 | 0 31 | 22 |
| 23 | 0 23 | 0 24 | 0 24 | 0 25 | 0 25 | 0 25 | 0 26 | 0 26 | 0 26 | 0 27 | 0 27 | 0 28 | 0 28 | 0 28 | 0 29 | 0 29 | 0 30 | 0 30 | 0 30 | 0 31 | 0 31 | 0 31 | 0 32 | 0 32 | 23 |
| 24 | 0 24 | 0 25 | 0 25 | 0 26 | 0 26 | 0 26 | 0 27 | 0 27 | 0 28 | 0 28 | 0 28 | 0 29 | 0 29 | 0 30 | 0 30 | 0 30 | 0 31 | 0 31 | 0 32 | 0 32 | 0 32 | 0 33 | 0 33 | 0 34 | 24 |
| 25 | 0 25 | 0 26 | 0 26 | 0 27 | 0 27 | 0 28 | 0 28 | 0 28 | 0 29 | 0 29 | 0 30 | 0 30 | 0 30 | 0 31 | 0 31 | 0 32 | 0 32 | 0 33 | 0 33 | 0 33 | 0 34 | 0 34 | 0 35 | 0 35 | 25 |
| 26 | 0 26 | 0 27 | 0 27 | 0 28 | 0 28 | 0 29 | 0 29 | 0 29 | 0 30 | 0 30 | 0 31 | 0 31 | 0 32 | 0 32 | 0 33 | 0 33 | 0 33 | 0 34 | 0 34 | 0 35 | 0 35 | 0 36 | 0 36 | 0 36 | 26 |
| 27 | 0 27 | 0 28 | 0 28 | 0 29 | 0 29 | 0 30 | 0 30 | 0 31 | 0 31 | 0 32 | 0 32 | 0 32 | 0 33 | 0 33 | 0 34 | 0 34 | 0 35 | 0 35 | 0 36 | 0 36 | 0 36 | 0 37 | 0 37 | 0 38 | 27 |
| 28 | 0 28 | 0 29 | 0 29 | 0 30 | 0 30 | 0 31 | 0 31 | 0 32 | 0 32 | 0 33 | 0 33 | 0 34 | 0 34 | 0 35 | 0 35 | 0 35 | 0 36 | 0 36 | 0 37 | 0 37 | 0 38 | 0 38 | 0 39 | 0 39 | 28 |
| 29 | 0 29 | 0 30 | 0 30 | 0 31 | 0 31 | 0 32 | 0 32 | 0 33 | 0 33 | 0 34 | 0 34 | 0 35 | 0 35 | 0 36 | 0 36 | 0 37 | 0 37 | 0 38 | 0 38 | 0 39 | 0 39 | 0 40 | 0 40 | 0 41 | 29 |
| 30 | 0 31 | 0 31 | 0 32 | 0 32 | 0 33 | 0 33 | 0 34 | 0 34 | 0 35 | 0 35 | 0 36 | 0 36 | 0 37 | 0 37 | 0 38 | 0 38 | 0 39 | 0 39 | 0 40 | 0 40 | 0 41 | 0 41 | 0 42 | 0 42 | 30 |
| 31 | 0 32 | 0 32 | 0 33 | 0 33 | 0 34 | 0 34 | 0 35 | 0 35 | 0 36 | 0 36 | 0 37 | 0 37 | 0 38 | 0 38 | 0 39 | 0 39 | 0 40 | 0 40 | 0 41 | 0 41 | 0 42 | 0 42 | 0 43 | 0 43 | 31 |
| 32 | 0 33 | 0 33 | 0 34 | 0 34 | 0 35 | 0 35 | 0 36 | 0 36 | 0 37 | 0 37 | 0 38 | 0 38 | 0 39 | 0 39 | 0 40 | 0 41 | 0 41 | 0 42 | 0 42 | 0 43 | 0 43 | 0 44 | 0 44 | 0 45 | 32 |
| 33 | 0 34 | 0 34 | 0 35 | 0 35 | 0 36 | 0 36 | 0 37 | 0 37 | 0 38 | 0 39 | 0 39 | 0 40 | 0 40 | 0 41 | 0 41 | 0 42 | 0 42 | 0 43 | 0 43 | 0 44 | 0 45 | 0 45 | 0 46 | 0 46 | 33 |
| 34 | 0 35 | 0 35 | 0 36 | 0 36 | 0 37 | 0 37 | 0 38 | 0 39 | 0 39 | 0 40 | 0 40 | 0 41 | 0 41 | 0 42 | 0 43 | 0 43 | 0 44 | 0 44 | 0 45 | 0 45 | 0 46 | 0 46 | 0 47 | 0 48 | 34 |
| 35 | 0 36 | 0 36 | 0 37 | 0 37 | 0 38 | 0 39 | 0 39 | 0 40 | 0 40 | 0 41 | 0 41 | 0 42 | 0 43 | 0 43 | 0 44 | 0 44 | 0 45 | 0 46 | 0 46 | 0 47 | 0 47 | 0 48 | 0 48 | 0 49 | 35 |
| 36 | 0 37 | 0 37 | 0 38 | 0 38 | 0 39 | 0 40 | 0 40 | 0 41 | 0 41 | 0 42 | 0 43 | 0 43 | 0 44 | 0 44 | 0 45 | 0 46 | 0 46 | 0 47 | 0 47 | 0 48 | 0 49 | 0 49 | 0 50 | 0 50 | 36 |
| 37 | 0 38 | 0 38 | 0 39 | 0 39 | 0 40 | 0 41 | 0 41 | 0 42 | 0 43 | 0 43 | 0 44 | 0 44 | 0 45 | 0 46 | 0 46 | 0 47 | 0 47 | 0 48 | 0 49 | 0 49 | 0 50 | 0 51 | 0 51 | 0 52 | 37 |
| 38 | 0 39 | 0 39 | 0 40 | 0 41 | 0 41 | 0 42 | 0 42 | 0 43 | 0 44 | 0 44 | 0 45 | 0 46 | 0 46 | 0 47 | 0 48 | 0 48 | 0 49 | 0 49 | 0 50 | 0 51 | 0 51 | 0 52 | 0 53 | 0 53 | 38 |
| 39 | 0 40 | 0 40 | 0 41 | 0 42 | 0 42 | 0 43 | 0 44 | 0 44 | 0 45 | 0 46 | 0 46 | 0 47 | 0 47 | 0 48 | 0 49 | 0 49 | 0 50 | 0 51 | 0 51 | 0 52 | 0 53 | 0 53 | 0 54 | 0 55 | 39 |
| 40 | 0 41 | 0 41 | 0 42 | 0 43 | 0 43 | 0 44 | 0 45 | 0 45 | 0 46 | 0 47 | 0 47 | 0 48 | 0 49 | 0 49 | 0 50 | 0 51 | 0 51 | 0 52 | 0 53 | 0 53 | 0 54 | 0 55 | 0 55 | 0 56 | 40 |
| 41 | 0 42 | 0 42 | 0 43 | 0 44 | 0 44 | 0 45 | 0 46 | 0 46 | 0 47 | 0 48 | 0 49 | 0 49 | 0 50 | 0 51 | 0 51 | 0 52 | 0 53 | 0 53 | 0 54 | 0 55 | 0 55 | 0 56 | 0 57 | 0 57 | 41 |
| 42 | 0 43 | 0 43 | 0 44 | 0 45 | 0 46 | 0 46 | 0 47 | 0 48 | 0 48 | 0 49 | 0 50 | 0 50 | 0 51 | 0 52 | 0 53 | 0 53 | 0 54 | 0 55 | 0 55 | 0 56 | 0 57 | 0 57 | 0 58 | 0 59 | 42 |
| 43 | 0 44 | 0 44 | 0 45 | 0 46 | 0 47 | 0 47 | 0 48 | 0 49 | 0 49 | 0 50 | 0 51 | 0 52 | 0 52 | 0 53 | 0 54 | 0 54 | 0 55 | 0 56 | 0 57 | 0 57 | 0 58 | 0 59 | 0 59 | 1 0 | 43 |
| 44 | 0 45 | 0 45 | 0 46 | 0 47 | 0 48 | 0 48 | 0 49 | 0 50 | 0 51 | 0 51 | 0 52 | 0 53 | 0 54 | 0 54 | 0 55 | 0 56 | 0 56 | 0 57 | 0 58 | 0 59 | 0 59 | 1 0 | 1 1 | 1 2 | 44 |
| 45 | 0 46 | 0 47 | 0 47 | 0 48 | 0 49 | 0 50 | 0 50 | 0 51 | 0 52 | 0 53 | 0 53 | 0 54 | 0 55 | 0 56 | 0 56 | 0 57 | 0 58 | 0 59 | 0 59 | 1 0 | 1 1 | 1 2 | 1 2 | 1 3 | 45 |
| 46 | 0 47 | 0 48 | 0 48 | 0 49 | 0 50 | 0 51 | 0 51 | 0 52 | 0 53 | 0 54 | 0 54 | 0 55 | 0 56 | 0 57 | 0 58 | 0 58 | 0 59 | 1 0 | 1 1 | 1 1 | 1 2 | 1 3 | 1 4 | 1 4 | 46 |
| 47 | 0 48 | 0 49 | 0 49 | 0 50 | 0 51 | 0 52 | 0 52 | 0 53 | 0 54 | 0 55 | 0 56 | 0 56 | 0 57 | 0 58 | 0 59 | 1 0 | 1 0 | 1 1 | 1 2 | 1 3 | 1 3 | 1 4 | 1 5 | 1 6 | 47 |
| 48 | 0 49 | 0 50 | 0 50 | 0 51 | 0 52 | 0 53 | 0 54 | 0 54 | 0 55 | 0 56 | 0 57 | 0 58 | 0 58 | 0 59 | 1 0 | 1 1 | 1 2 | 1 2 | 1 3 | 1 4 | 1 5 | 1 6 | 1 6 | 1 7 | 48 |
| 49 | 0 50 | 0 51 | 0 51 | 0 52 | 0 53 | 0 54 | 0 55 | 0 56 | 0 56 | 0 57 | 0 58 | 0 59 | 1 0 | 1 0 | 1 1 | 1 2 | 1 3 | 1 4 | 1 5 | 1 5 | 1 6 | 1 7 | 1 8 | 1 9 | 49 |
| 50 | 0 51 | 0 52 | 0 53 | 0 53 | 0 54 | 0 55 | 0 56 | 0 57 | 0 58 | 0 58 | 0 59 | 1 0 | 1 1 | 1 2 | 1 3 | 1 3 | 1 4 | 1 5 | 1 6 | 1 7 | 1 8 | 1 8 | 1 9 | 1 10 | 50 |
| 51 | 0 52 | 0 53 | 0 54 | 0 54 | 0 55 | 0 56 | 0 57 | 0 58 | 0 59 | 1 0 | 1 0 | 1 1 | 1 2 | 1 3 | 1 4 | 1 5 | 1 5 | 1 6 | 1 7 | 1 8 | 1 9 | 1 10 | 1 11 | 1 11 | 51 |
| 52 | 0 53 | 0 54 | 0 55 | 0 55 | 0 56 | 0 57 | 0 58 | 0 59 | 1 0 | 1 1 | 1 2 | 1 2 | 1 3 | 1 4 | 1 5 | 1 6 | 1 7 | 1 8 | 1 8 | 1 9 | 1 10 | 1 11 | 1 12 | 1 13 | 52 |
| 53 | 0 54 | 0 55 | 0 56 | 0 57 | 0 57 | 0 58 | 0 59 | 1 0 | 1 1 | 1 2 | 1 3 | 1 4 | 1 4 | 1 5 | 1 6 | 1 7 | 1 8 | 1 9 | 1 10 | 1 11 | 1 12 | 1 12 | 1 13 | 1 14 | 53 |
| 54 | 0 55 | 0 56 | 0 57 | 0 58 | 0 59 | 0 59 | 1 0 | 1 1 | 1 2 | 1 3 | 1 4 | 1 5 | 1 6 | 1 7 | 1 8 | 1 8 | 1 9 | 1 10 | 1 11 | 1 12 | 1 13 | 1 14 | 1 15 | 1 16 | 54 |
| 55 | 0 56 | 0 57 | 0 58 | 0 59 | 1 0 | 1 1 | 1 1 | 1 2 | 1 3 | 1 4 | 1 5 | 1 6 | 1 7 | 1 8 | 1 9 | 1 10 | 1 11 | 1 12 | 1 12 | 1 13 | 1 14 | 1 15 | 1 16 | 1 17 | 55 |
| 56 | 0 57 | 0 58 | 0 59 | 1 0 | 1 1 | 1 2 | 1 3 | 1 3 | 1 4 | 1 5 | 1 6 | 1 7 | 1 8 | 1 9 | 1 10 | 1 11 | 1 12 | 1 13 | 1 14 | 1 15 | 1 16 | 1 17 | 1 17 | 1 18 | 56 |
| 57 | 0 58 | 0 59 | 1 0 | 1 1 | 1 2 | 1 3 | 1 4 | 1 5 | 1 6 | 1 7 | 1 7 | 1 8 | 1 9 | 1 10 | 1 11 | 1 12 | 1 13 | 1 14 | 1 15 | 1 16 | 1 17 | 1 18 | 1 19 | 1 20 | 57 |
| 58 | 0 59 | 1 0 | 1 1 | 1 2 | 1 3 | 1 4 | 1 5 | 1 6 | 1 7 | 1 8 | 1 9 | 1 10 | 1 11 | 1 12 | 1 13 | 1 13 | 1 14 | 1 15 | 1 16 | 1 17 | 1 18 | 1 19 | 1 20 | 1 21 | 58 |
| 59 | 1 0 | 1 1 | 1 2 | 1 3 | 1 4 | 1 5 | 1 6 | 1 7 | 1 8 | 1 9 | 1 10 | 1 11 | 1 12 | 1 13 | 1 14 | 1 15 | 1 16 | 1 17 | 1 18 | 1 19 | 1 20 | 1 21 | 1 22 | 1 23 | 59 |

# Table XII House Cusp Interpolation Between Latitudes

HOUSE CUSP INTERVAL

Values are given in degrees and minutes (e.g. "0 1" = 0°1'). The LAT INC column is the latitude increment.

| LAT INC | 1°25' | 1°26' | 1°27' | 1°28' | 1°29' | 1°30' | 1°31' | 1°32' | 1°33' | 1°34' | 1°35' | 1°36' | 1°37' | 1°38' | 1°39' | 1°40' | 1°41' | 1°42' | 1°43' | 1°44' | 1°45' | 1°46' | 1°47' | 1°48' | LAT INC |
|---|---|---|---|---|---|---|---|---|---|---|---|---|---|---|---|---|---|---|---|---|---|---|---|---|---|
| 1 | 0 1 | 0 1 | 0 1 | 0 1 | 0 1 | 0 2 | 0 2 | 0 2 | 0 2 | 0 2 | 0 2 | 0 2 | 0 2 | 0 2 | 0 2 | 0 2 | 0 2 | 0 2 | 0 2 | 0 2 | 0 2 | 0 2 | 0 2 | 0 2 | 1 |
| 2 | 0 3 | 0 3 | 0 3 | 0 3 | 0 3 | 0 3 | 0 3 | 0 3 | 0 3 | 0 3 | 0 3 | 0 3 | 0 3 | 0 3 | 0 3 | 0 3 | 0 3 | 0 3 | 0 3 | 0 3 | 0 4 | 0 4 | 0 4 | 0 4 | 2 |
| 3 | 0 4 | 0 4 | 0 4 | 0 4 | 0 4 | 0 5 | 0 5 | 0 5 | 0 5 | 0 5 | 0 5 | 0 5 | 0 5 | 0 5 | 0 5 | 0 5 | 0 5 | 0 5 | 0 5 | 0 5 | 0 5 | 0 5 | 0 5 | 0 5 | 3 |
| 4 | 0 6 | 0 6 | 0 6 | 0 6 | 0 6 | 0 6 | 0 6 | 0 6 | 0 6 | 0 6 | 0 6 | 0 6 | 0 6 | 0 7 | 0 7 | 0 7 | 0 7 | 0 7 | 0 7 | 0 7 | 0 7 | 0 7 | 0 7 | 0 7 | 4 |
| 5 | 0 7 | 0 7 | 0 7 | 0 7 | 0 7 | 0 8 | 0 8 | 0 8 | 0 8 | 0 8 | 0 8 | 0 8 | 0 8 | 0 8 | 0 8 | 0 8 | 0 8 | 0 9 | 0 9 | 0 9 | 0 9 | 0 9 | 0 9 | 0 9 | 5 |
| 6 | 0 9 | 0 9 | 0 9 | 0 9 | 0 9 | 0 9 | 0 9 | 0 9 | 0 9 | 0 9 | 0 10 | 0 10 | 0 10 | 0 10 | 0 10 | 0 10 | 0 10 | 0 10 | 0 10 | 0 10 | 0 11 | 0 11 | 0 11 | 0 11 | 6 |
| 7 | 0 10 | 0 10 | 0 10 | 0 10 | 0 10 | 0 11 | 0 11 | 0 11 | 0 11 | 0 11 | 0 11 | 0 11 | 0 11 | 0 11 | 0 12 | 0 12 | 0 12 | 0 12 | 0 12 | 0 12 | 0 12 | 0 12 | 0 12 | 0 13 | 7 |
| 8 | 0 11 | 0 11 | 0 12 | 0 12 | 0 12 | 0 12 | 0 12 | 0 12 | 0 12 | 0 13 | 0 13 | 0 13 | 0 13 | 0 13 | 0 13 | 0 13 | 0 13 | 0 14 | 0 14 | 0 14 | 0 14 | 0 14 | 0 14 | 0 14 | 8 |
| 9 | 0 13 | 0 13 | 0 13 | 0 13 | 0 13 | 0 14 | 0 14 | 0 14 | 0 14 | 0 14 | 0 14 | 0 14 | 0 15 | 0 15 | 0 15 | 0 15 | 0 15 | 0 15 | 0 15 | 0 16 | 0 16 | 0 16 | 0 16 | 0 16 | 9 |
| 10 | 0 14 | 0 14 | 0 15 | 0 15 | 0 15 | 0 15 | 0 15 | 0 15 | 0 16 | 0 16 | 0 16 | 0 16 | 0 16 | 0 16 | 0 17 | 0 17 | 0 17 | 0 17 | 0 17 | 0 17 | 0 18 | 0 18 | 0 18 | 0 18 | 10 |
| 11 | 0 16 | 0 16 | 0 16 | 0 16 | 0 16 | 0 17 | 0 17 | 0 17 | 0 17 | 0 17 | 0 17 | 0 18 | 0 18 | 0 18 | 0 18 | 0 18 | 0 19 | 0 19 | 0 19 | 0 19 | 0 19 | 0 19 | 0 20 | 0 20 | 11 |
| 12 | 0 17 | 0 17 | 0 17 | 0 18 | 0 18 | 0 18 | 0 18 | 0 18 | 0 19 | 0 19 | 0 19 | 0 19 | 0 19 | 0 20 | 0 20 | 0 20 | 0 20 | 0 20 | 0 21 | 0 21 | 0 21 | 0 21 | 0 21 | 0 22 | 12 |
| 13 | 0 18 | 0 19 | 0 19 | 0 19 | 0 19 | 0 20 | 0 20 | 0 20 | 0 20 | 0 20 | 0 21 | 0 21 | 0 21 | 0 21 | 0 21 | 0 22 | 0 22 | 0 22 | 0 22 | 0 23 | 0 23 | 0 23 | 0 23 | 0 23 | 13 |
| 14 | 0 20 | 0 20 | 0 20 | 0 21 | 0 21 | 0 21 | 0 21 | 0 21 | 0 22 | 0 22 | 0 22 | 0 22 | 0 23 | 0 23 | 0 23 | 0 23 | 0 24 | 0 24 | 0 24 | 0 24 | 0 25 | 0 25 | 0 25 | 0 25 | 14 |
| 15 | 0 21 | 0 22 | 0 22 | 0 22 | 0 22 | 0 23 | 0 23 | 0 23 | 0 23 | 0 24 | 0 24 | 0 24 | 0 24 | 0 25 | 0 25 | 0 25 | 0 25 | 0 26 | 0 26 | 0 26 | 0 26 | 0 27 | 0 27 | 0 27 | 15 |
| 16 | 0 23 | 0 23 | 0 23 | 0 23 | 0 24 | 0 24 | 0 24 | 0 25 | 0 25 | 0 25 | 0 25 | 0 26 | 0 26 | 0 26 | 0 26 | 0 27 | 0 27 | 0 27 | 0 27 | 0 28 | 0 28 | 0 28 | 0 29 | 0 29 | 16 |
| 17 | 0 24 | 0 24 | 0 25 | 0 25 | 0 25 | 0 26 | 0 26 | 0 26 | 0 26 | 0 27 | 0 27 | 0 27 | 0 27 | 0 28 | 0 28 | 0 28 | 0 29 | 0 29 | 0 29 | 0 29 | 0 30 | 0 30 | 0 30 | 0 31 | 17 |
| 18 | 0 26 | 0 26 | 0 26 | 0 26 | 0 27 | 0 27 | 0 27 | 0 28 | 0 28 | 0 28 | 0 29 | 0 29 | 0 29 | 0 29 | 0 30 | 0 30 | 0 30 | 0 31 | 0 31 | 0 31 | 0 32 | 0 32 | 0 32 | 0 32 | 18 |
| 19 | 0 27 | 0 27 | 0 28 | 0 28 | 0 28 | 0 29 | 0 29 | 0 29 | 0 29 | 0 30 | 0 30 | 0 30 | 0 31 | 0 31 | 0 31 | 0 32 | 0 32 | 0 32 | 0 33 | 0 33 | 0 33 | 0 34 | 0 34 | 0 34 | 19 |
| 20 | 0 28 | 0 29 | 0 29 | 0 29 | 0 30 | 0 30 | 0 30 | 0 31 | 0 31 | 0 31 | 0 32 | 0 32 | 0 32 | 0 33 | 0 33 | 0 33 | 0 34 | 0 34 | 0 34 | 0 35 | 0 35 | 0 35 | 0 36 | 0 36 | 20 |
| 21 | 0 30 | 0 30 | 0 30 | 0 31 | 0 31 | 0 32 | 0 32 | 0 32 | 0 33 | 0 33 | 0 33 | 0 34 | 0 34 | 0 34 | 0 35 | 0 35 | 0 35 | 0 36 | 0 36 | 0 36 | 0 37 | 0 37 | 0 37 | 0 38 | 21 |
| 22 | 0 31 | 0 32 | 0 32 | 0 32 | 0 33 | 0 33 | 0 33 | 0 34 | 0 34 | 0 34 | 0 35 | 0 35 | 0 36 | 0 36 | 0 36 | 0 37 | 0 37 | 0 37 | 0 38 | 0 38 | 0 39 | 0 39 | 0 39 | 0 40 | 22 |
| 23 | 0 33 | 0 33 | 0 33 | 0 34 | 0 34 | 0 35 | 0 35 | 0 35 | 0 36 | 0 36 | 0 36 | 0 37 | 0 37 | 0 38 | 0 38 | 0 38 | 0 39 | 0 39 | 0 39 | 0 40 | 0 40 | 0 41 | 0 41 | 0 41 | 23 |
| 24 | 0 34 | 0 34 | 0 35 | 0 35 | 0 36 | 0 36 | 0 36 | 0 37 | 0 37 | 0 38 | 0 38 | 0 38 | 0 39 | 0 39 | 0 40 | 0 40 | 0 40 | 0 41 | 0 41 | 0 42 | 0 42 | 0 42 | 0 43 | 0 43 | 24 |
| 25 | 0 35 | 0 36 | 0 36 | 0 37 | 0 37 | 0 38 | 0 38 | 0 38 | 0 39 | 0 39 | 0 40 | 0 40 | 0 40 | 0 41 | 0 41 | 0 42 | 0 42 | 0 43 | 0 43 | 0 43 | 0 44 | 0 44 | 0 45 | 0 45 | 25 |
| 26 | 0 37 | 0 37 | 0 38 | 0 38 | 0 39 | 0 39 | 0 39 | 0 40 | 0 40 | 0 41 | 0 41 | 0 42 | 0 42 | 0 42 | 0 43 | 0 43 | 0 44 | 0 44 | 0 45 | 0 45 | 0 46 | 0 46 | 0 46 | 0 47 | 26 |
| 27 | 0 38 | 0 39 | 0 39 | 0 40 | 0 40 | 0 41 | 0 41 | 0 41 | 0 42 | 0 42 | 0 43 | 0 43 | 0 44 | 0 44 | 0 45 | 0 45 | 0 45 | 0 46 | 0 46 | 0 47 | 0 47 | 0 48 | 0 48 | 0 49 | 27 |
| 28 | 0 40 | 0 40 | 0 41 | 0 41 | 0 42 | 0 42 | 0 42 | 0 43 | 0 43 | 0 44 | 0 44 | 0 45 | 0 45 | 0 46 | 0 46 | 0 47 | 0 47 | 0 48 | 0 48 | 0 49 | 0 49 | 0 49 | 0 50 | 0 50 | 28 |
| 29 | 0 41 | 0 42 | 0 42 | 0 43 | 0 43 | 0 44 | 0 44 | 0 44 | 0 45 | 0 45 | 0 46 | 0 46 | 0 47 | 0 47 | 0 48 | 0 48 | 0 49 | 0 49 | 0 50 | 0 50 | 0 51 | 0 51 | 0 52 | 0 52 | 29 |
| 30 | 0 43 | 0 43 | 0 44 | 0 44 | 0 45 | 0 45 | 0 46 | 0 46 | 0 47 | 0 47 | 0 48 | 0 48 | 0 49 | 0 49 | 0 50 | 0 50 | 0 51 | 0 51 | 0 52 | 0 52 | 0 53 | 0 53 | 0 54 | 0 54 | 30 |
| 31 | 0 44 | 0 44 | 0 45 | 0 45 | 0 46 | 0 47 | 0 47 | 0 48 | 0 48 | 0 49 | 0 49 | 0 50 | 0 50 | 0 51 | 0 51 | 0 52 | 0 52 | 0 53 | 0 53 | 0 54 | 0 54 | 0 55 | 0 55 | 0 56 | 31 |
| 32 | 0 45 | 0 46 | 0 46 | 0 47 | 0 47 | 0 48 | 0 49 | 0 49 | 0 50 | 0 50 | 0 51 | 0 51 | 0 52 | 0 52 | 0 53 | 0 53 | 0 54 | 0 54 | 0 55 | 0 55 | 0 56 | 0 57 | 0 57 | 0 58 | 32 |
| 33 | 0 47 | 0 47 | 0 48 | 0 48 | 0 49 | 0 50 | 0 50 | 0 51 | 0 51 | 0 52 | 0 52 | 0 53 | 0 53 | 0 54 | 0 54 | 0 55 | 0 56 | 0 56 | 0 57 | 0 57 | 0 58 | 0 58 | 0 59 | 0 59 | 33 |
| 34 | 0 48 | 0 49 | 0 49 | 0 50 | 0 50 | 0 51 | 0 52 | 0 52 | 0 53 | 0 53 | 0 54 | 0 54 | 0 55 | 0 56 | 0 56 | 0 57 | 0 57 | 0 58 | 0 58 | 0 59 | 1 0 | 1 0 | 1 1 | 1 1 | 34 |
| 35 | 0 50 | 0 50 | 0 51 | 0 51 | 0 52 | 0 53 | 0 53 | 0 54 | 0 54 | 0 55 | 0 55 | 0 56 | 0 57 | 0 57 | 0 58 | 0 58 | 0 59 | 1 0 | 1 0 | 1 1 | 1 1 | 1 2 | 1 2 | 1 3 | 35 |
| 36 | 0 51 | 0 52 | 0 52 | 0 53 | 0 53 | 0 54 | 0 55 | 0 55 | 0 56 | 0 56 | 0 57 | 0 58 | 0 58 | 0 58 | 0 59 | 1 0 | 1 1 | 1 1 | 1 2 | 1 2 | 1 3 | 1 4 | 1 4 | 1 5 | 36 |
| 37 | 0 52 | 0 53 | 0 54 | 0 54 | 0 55 | 0 56 | 0 56 | 0 57 | 0 57 | 0 58 | 0 59 | 0 59 | 1 0 | 1 0 | 1 1 | 1 2 | 1 2 | 1 3 | 1 4 | 1 4 | 1 5 | 1 5 | 1 6 | 1 7 | 37 |
| 38 | 0 54 | 0 54 | 0 55 | 0 56 | 0 56 | 0 57 | 0 58 | 0 58 | 0 59 | 1 0 | 1 0 | 1 1 | 1 1 | 1 2 | 1 3 | 1 3 | 1 4 | 1 5 | 1 5 | 1 6 | 1 7 | 1 7 | 1 8 | 1 8 | 38 |
| 39 | 0 55 | 0 56 | 0 57 | 0 57 | 0 58 | 0 59 | 0 59 | 1 0 | 1 0 | 1 1 | 1 2 | 1 2 | 1 3 | 1 4 | 1 4 | 1 5 | 1 6 | 1 6 | 1 7 | 1 8 | 1 8 | 1 9 | 1 10 | 1 10 | 39 |
| 40 | 0 57 | 0 57 | 0 58 | 0 59 | 0 59 | 1 0 | 1 1 | 1 1 | 1 2 | 1 3 | 1 3 | 1 4 | 1 5 | 1 5 | 1 6 | 1 7 | 1 7 | 1 8 | 1 9 | 1 9 | 1 10 | 1 11 | 1 11 | 1 12 | 40 |
| 41 | 0 58 | 0 59 | 0 59 | 1 0 | 1 1 | 1 2 | 1 2 | 1 3 | 1 4 | 1 4 | 1 5 | 1 6 | 1 6 | 1 7 | 1 8 | 1 8 | 1 9 | 1 10 | 1 10 | 1 11 | 1 12 | 1 12 | 1 13 | 1 14 | 41 |
| 42 | 1 0 | 1 0 | 1 1 | 1 2 | 1 2 | 1 3 | 1 4 | 1 4 | 1 5 | 1 6 | 1 7 | 1 7 | 1 8 | 1 9 | 1 9 | 1 10 | 1 11 | 1 11 | 1 12 | 1 13 | 1 14 | 1 14 | 1 15 | 1 16 | 42 |
| 43 | 1 1 | 1 2 | 1 2 | 1 3 | 1 4 | 1 5 | 1 5 | 1 6 | 1 7 | 1 7 | 1 8 | 1 9 | 1 10 | 1 10 | 1 11 | 1 12 | 1 12 | 1 13 | 1 14 | 1 15 | 1 15 | 1 16 | 1 17 | 1 17 | 43 |
| 44 | 1 2 | 1 3 | 1 4 | 1 5 | 1 5 | 1 6 | 1 7 | 1 7 | 1 8 | 1 9 | 1 10 | 1 10 | 1 11 | 1 12 | 1 13 | 1 13 | 1 14 | 1 15 | 1 16 | 1 16 | 1 17 | 1 18 | 1 18 | 1 19 | 44 |
| 45 | 1 4 | 1 5 | 1 5 | 1 6 | 1 7 | 1 8 | 1 8 | 1 9 | 1 10 | 1 11 | 1 11 | 1 12 | 1 13 | 1 14 | 1 14 | 1 15 | 1 16 | 1 17 | 1 17 | 1 18 | 1 19 | 1 20 | 1 20 | 1 21 | 45 |
| 46 | 1 5 | 1 6 | 1 7 | 1 7 | 1 8 | 1 9 | 1 10 | 1 11 | 1 11 | 1 12 | 1 13 | 1 14 | 1 14 | 1 15 | 1 16 | 1 17 | 1 17 | 1 18 | 1 19 | 1 20 | 1 21 | 1 21 | 1 22 | 1 23 | 46 |
| 47 | 1 7 | 1 7 | 1 8 | 1 9 | 1 10 | 1 11 | 1 11 | 1 12 | 1 13 | 1 14 | 1 14 | 1 15 | 1 16 | 1 17 | 1 18 | 1 18 | 1 19 | 1 20 | 1 21 | 1 21 | 1 22 | 1 23 | 1 24 | 1 25 | 47 |
| 48 | 1 8 | 1 9 | 1 10 | 1 10 | 1 11 | 1 12 | 1 13 | 1 14 | 1 14 | 1 15 | 1 16 | 1 17 | 1 18 | 1 18 | 1 19 | 1 20 | 1 21 | 1 22 | 1 22 | 1 23 | 1 24 | 1 25 | 1 26 | 1 26 | 48 |
| 49 | 1 9 | 1 10 | 1 11 | 1 12 | 1 13 | 1 14 | 1 14 | 1 15 | 1 16 | 1 17 | 1 18 | 1 18 | 1 19 | 1 20 | 1 21 | 1 22 | 1 22 | 1 23 | 1 24 | 1 25 | 1 26 | 1 27 | 1 27 | 1 28 | 49 |
| 50 | 1 11 | 1 12 | 1 13 | 1 13 | 1 14 | 1 15 | 1 16 | 1 17 | 1 18 | 1 18 | 1 19 | 1 20 | 1 21 | 1 22 | 1 23 | 1 23 | 1 24 | 1 25 | 1 26 | 1 27 | 1 28 | 1 28 | 1 29 | 1 30 | 50 |
| 51 | 1 12 | 1 13 | 1 14 | 1 15 | 1 16 | 1 17 | 1 17 | 1 18 | 1 19 | 1 20 | 1 21 | 1 22 | 1 22 | 1 23 | 1 24 | 1 25 | 1 26 | 1 27 | 1 28 | 1 28 | 1 29 | 1 30 | 1 31 | 1 32 | 51 |
| 52 | 1 14 | 1 15 | 1 15 | 1 16 | 1 17 | 1 18 | 1 19 | 1 20 | 1 21 | 1 21 | 1 22 | 1 23 | 1 24 | 1 25 | 1 26 | 1 27 | 1 28 | 1 28 | 1 29 | 1 30 | 1 31 | 1 32 | 1 33 | 1 34 | 52 |
| 53 | 1 15 | 1 16 | 1 17 | 1 18 | 1 19 | 1 20 | 1 20 | 1 21 | 1 22 | 1 23 | 1 24 | 1 25 | 1 26 | 1 27 | 1 27 | 1 28 | 1 29 | 1 30 | 1 31 | 1 32 | 1 33 | 1 34 | 1 35 | 1 35 | 53 |
| 54 | 1 17 | 1 17 | 1 18 | 1 19 | 1 20 | 1 21 | 1 22 | 1 23 | 1 24 | 1 25 | 1 26 | 1 26 | 1 27 | 1 28 | 1 29 | 1 30 | 1 31 | 1 32 | 1 33 | 1 34 | 1 35 | 1 35 | 1 36 | 1 37 | 54 |
| 55 | 1 18 | 1 19 | 1 20 | 1 21 | 1 22 | 1 23 | 1 23 | 1 24 | 1 25 | 1 26 | 1 27 | 1 28 | 1 29 | 1 30 | 1 31 | 1 32 | 1 33 | 1 34 | 1 34 | 1 35 | 1 36 | 1 37 | 1 38 | 1 39 | 55 |
| 56 | 1 19 | 1 20 | 1 21 | 1 22 | 1 23 | 1 24 | 1 25 | 1 26 | 1 27 | 1 28 | 1 29 | 1 30 | 1 31 | 1 31 | 1 32 | 1 33 | 1 34 | 1 35 | 1 36 | 1 37 | 1 38 | 1 39 | 1 40 | 1 41 | 56 |
| 57 | 1 21 | 1 22 | 1 23 | 1 24 | 1 25 | 1 26 | 1 26 | 1 27 | 1 28 | 1 29 | 1 30 | 1 31 | 1 32 | 1 33 | 1 34 | 1 35 | 1 36 | 1 37 | 1 38 | 1 39 | 1 40 | 1 41 | 1 42 | 1 43 | 57 |
| 58 | 1 22 | 1 23 | 1 24 | 1 25 | 1 26 | 1 27 | 1 28 | 1 29 | 1 30 | 1 31 | 1 32 | 1 33 | 1 34 | 1 35 | 1 36 | 1 37 | 1 38 | 1 39 | 1 40 | 1 41 | 1 42 | 1 42 | 1 43 | 1 44 | 58 |
| 59 | 1 24 | 1 25 | 1 26 | 1 27 | 1 28 | 1 29 | 1 29 | 1 30 | 1 31 | 1 32 | 1 33 | 1 34 | 1 35 | 1 36 | 1 37 | 1 38 | 1 39 | 1 40 | 1 41 | 1 42 | 1 43 | 1 44 | 1 45 | 1 46 | 59 |

# Table XII House Cusp Interpolation Between Latitudes

HOUSE CUSP INTERVAL

Column headers are given in degrees (°) and minutes ('). Each cell value is degrees and minutes.

| LAT INC | 1 49 | 1 50 | 1 51 | 1 52 | 1 53 | 1 54 | 1 55 | 1 56 | 1 57 | 1 58 | 1 59 | 2 0 | 2 1 | 2 2 | 2 3 | 2 4 | 2 5 | 2 6 | 2 7 | 2 8 | 2 9 | 2 10 | 2 11 | 2 12 | LAT INC |
|---|---|---|---|---|---|---|---|---|---|---|---|---|---|---|---|---|---|---|---|---|---|---|---|---|---|
| 1 | 0 2 | 0 2 | 0 2 | 0 2 | 0 2 | 0 2 | 0 2 | 0 2 | 0 2 | 0 2 | 0 2 | 0 2 | 0 2 | 0 2 | 0 2 | 0 2 | 0 2 | 0 2 | 0 2 | 0 2 | 0 2 | 0 2 | 0 2 | 0 2 | 1 |
| 2 | 0 4 | 0 4 | 0 4 | 0 4 | 0 4 | 0 4 | 0 4 | 0 4 | 0 4 | 0 4 | 0 4 | 0 4 | 0 4 | 0 4 | 0 4 | 0 4 | 0 4 | 0 4 | 0 4 | 0 4 | 0 4 | 0 4 | 0 4 | 0 4 | 2 |
| 3 | 0 5 | 0 6 | 0 6 | 0 6 | 0 6 | 0 6 | 0 6 | 0 6 | 0 6 | 0 6 | 0 6 | 0 6 | 0 6 | 0 6 | 0 6 | 0 6 | 0 6 | 0 6 | 0 6 | 0 6 | 0 6 | 0 7 | 0 7 | 0 7 | 3 |
| 4 | 0 7 | 0 7 | 0 7 | 0 7 | 0 8 | 0 8 | 0 8 | 0 8 | 0 8 | 0 8 | 0 8 | 0 8 | 0 8 | 0 8 | 0 8 | 0 8 | 0 8 | 0 8 | 0 8 | 0 9 | 0 9 | 0 9 | 0 9 | 0 9 | 4 |
| 5 | 0 9 | 0 9 | 0 9 | 0 9 | 0 9 | 0 10 | 0 10 | 0 10 | 0 10 | 0 10 | 0 10 | 0 10 | 0 10 | 0 10 | 0 10 | 0 10 | 0 10 | 0 10 | 0 10 | 0 11 | 0 11 | 0 11 | 0 11 | 0 11 | 5 |
| 6 | 0 11 | 0 11 | 0 11 | 0 11 | 0 11 | 0 11 | 0 12 | 0 12 | 0 12 | 0 12 | 0 12 | 0 12 | 0 12 | 0 12 | 0 12 | 0 12 | 0 12 | 0 13 | 0 13 | 0 13 | 0 13 | 0 13 | 0 13 | 0 13 | 6 |
| 7 | 0 13 | 0 13 | 0 13 | 0 13 | 0 13 | 0 13 | 0 14 | 0 14 | 0 14 | 0 14 | 0 14 | 0 14 | 0 14 | 0 14 | 0 15 | 0 15 | 0 15 | 0 15 | 0 15 | 0 15 | 0 15 | 0 15 | 0 15 | 0 15 | 7 |
| 8 | 0 15 | 0 15 | 0 15 | 0 15 | 0 15 | 0 15 | 0 16 | 0 16 | 0 16 | 0 16 | 0 16 | 0 16 | 0 16 | 0 16 | 0 17 | 0 17 | 0 17 | 0 17 | 0 17 | 0 17 | 0 17 | 0 17 | 0 17 | 0 18 | 8 |
| 9 | 0 16 | 0 17 | 0 17 | 0 17 | 0 17 | 0 17 | 0 17 | 0 18 | 0 18 | 0 18 | 0 18 | 0 18 | 0 18 | 0 18 | 0 19 | 0 19 | 0 19 | 0 19 | 0 19 | 0 19 | 0 20 | 0 20 | 0 20 | 0 20 | 9 |
| 10 | 0 18 | 0 18 | 0 19 | 0 19 | 0 19 | 0 19 | 0 19 | 0 20 | 0 20 | 0 20 | 0 20 | 0 20 | 0 20 | 0 20 | 0 21 | 0 21 | 0 21 | 0 21 | 0 21 | 0 21 | 0 22 | 0 22 | 0 22 | 0 22 | 10 |
| 11 | 0 20 | 0 20 | 0 20 | 0 21 | 0 21 | 0 21 | 0 21 | 0 21 | 0 21 | 0 22 | 0 22 | 0 22 | 0 22 | 0 22 | 0 23 | 0 23 | 0 23 | 0 23 | 0 23 | 0 23 | 0 24 | 0 24 | 0 24 | 0 24 | 11 |
| 12 | 0 22 | 0 22 | 0 22 | 0 22 | 0 23 | 0 23 | 0 23 | 0 23 | 0 24 | 0 24 | 0 24 | 0 24 | 0 24 | 0 25 | 0 25 | 0 25 | 0 25 | 0 25 | 0 26 | 0 26 | 0 26 | 0 26 | 0 26 | 0 26 | 12 |
| 13 | 0 24 | 0 24 | 0 24 | 0 24 | 0 24 | 0 25 | 0 25 | 0 25 | 0 25 | 0 26 | 0 26 | 0 26 | 0 26 | 0 26 | 0 27 | 0 27 | 0 27 | 0 27 | 0 28 | 0 28 | 0 28 | 0 28 | 0 28 | 0 29 | 13 |
| 14 | 0 25 | 0 26 | 0 26 | 0 26 | 0 26 | 0 27 | 0 27 | 0 27 | 0 27 | 0 28 | 0 28 | 0 28 | 0 28 | 0 29 | 0 29 | 0 29 | 0 29 | 0 30 | 0 30 | 0 30 | 0 30 | 0 31 | 0 31 | 0 31 | 14 |
| 15 | 0 27 | 0 28 | 0 28 | 0 28 | 0 28 | 0 29 | 0 29 | 0 29 | 0 29 | 0 30 | 0 30 | 0 30 | 0 30 | 0 31 | 0 31 | 0 31 | 0 31 | 0 32 | 0 32 | 0 32 | 0 32 | 0 33 | 0 33 | 0 33 | 15 |
| 16 | 0 29 | 0 29 | 0 30 | 0 30 | 0 30 | 0 30 | 0 31 | 0 31 | 0 31 | 0 31 | 0 32 | 0 32 | 0 32 | 0 33 | 0 33 | 0 33 | 0 33 | 0 34 | 0 34 | 0 34 | 0 34 | 0 35 | 0 35 | 0 35 | 16 |
| 17 | 0 31 | 0 31 | 0 31 | 0 32 | 0 32 | 0 32 | 0 33 | 0 33 | 0 33 | 0 33 | 0 34 | 0 34 | 0 34 | 0 35 | 0 35 | 0 35 | 0 35 | 0 36 | 0 36 | 0 36 | 0 37 | 0 37 | 0 37 | 0 37 | 17 |
| 18 | 0 33 | 0 33 | 0 33 | 0 34 | 0 34 | 0 35 | 0 35 | 0 35 | 0 35 | 0 36 | 0 36 | 0 36 | 0 37 | 0 37 | 0 37 | 0 37 | 0 38 | 0 38 | 0 38 | 0 39 | 0 39 | 0 39 | 0 40 | 0 40 | 18 |
| 19 | 0 35 | 0 35 | 0 35 | 0 35 | 0 36 | 0 36 | 0 36 | 0 37 | 0 37 | 0 37 | 0 38 | 0 38 | 0 38 | 0 39 | 0 39 | 0 39 | 0 40 | 0 40 | 0 40 | 0 41 | 0 41 | 0 41 | 0 41 | 0 42 | 19 |
| 20 | 0 36 | 0 37 | 0 37 | 0 37 | 0 38 | 0 38 | 0 38 | 0 39 | 0 39 | 0 39 | 0 40 | 0 40 | 0 40 | 0 41 | 0 41 | 0 41 | 0 42 | 0 42 | 0 42 | 0 43 | 0 43 | 0 43 | 0 44 | 0 44 | 20 |
| 21 | 0 38 | 0 39 | 0 39 | 0 39 | 0 40 | 0 40 | 0 41 | 0 41 | 0 41 | 0 42 | 0 42 | 0 42 | 0 43 | 0 43 | 0 43 | 0 44 | 0 44 | 0 44 | 0 45 | 0 45 | 0 46 | 0 46 | 0 46 | 0 46 | 21 |
| 22 | 0 40 | 0 40 | 0 41 | 0 41 | 0 42 | 0 42 | 0 43 | 0 43 | 0 43 | 0 44 | 0 44 | 0 44 | 0 45 | 0 45 | 0 45 | 0 46 | 0 46 | 0 47 | 0 47 | 0 47 | 0 48 | 0 48 | 0 48 | 0 48 | 22 |
| 23 | 0 42 | 0 42 | 0 43 | 0 43 | 0 43 | 0 44 | 0 44 | 0 44 | 0 45 | 0 45 | 0 46 | 0 46 | 0 46 | 0 47 | 0 47 | 0 48 | 0 48 | 0 48 | 0 49 | 0 49 | 0 49 | 0 50 | 0 50 | 0 51 | 23 |
| 24 | 0 44 | 0 44 | 0 44 | 0 45 | 0 45 | 0 46 | 0 46 | 0 46 | 0 47 | 0 47 | 0 48 | 0 48 | 0 48 | 0 49 | 0 49 | 0 50 | 0 50 | 0 51 | 0 51 | 0 51 | 0 52 | 0 52 | 0 52 | 0 53 | 24 |
| 25 | 0 45 | 0 46 | 0 46 | 0 47 | 0 47 | 0 48 | 0 48 | 0 48 | 0 49 | 0 49 | 0 50 | 0 50 | 0 50 | 0 51 | 0 51 | 0 52 | 0 52 | 0 53 | 0 53 | 0 53 | 0 54 | 0 54 | 0 55 | 0 55 | 25 |
| 26 | 0 47 | 0 48 | 0 48 | 0 49 | 0 49 | 0 49 | 0 50 | 0 50 | 0 51 | 0 51 | 0 52 | 0 52 | 0 52 | 0 53 | 0 53 | 0 54 | 0 54 | 0 55 | 0 55 | 0 55 | 0 56 | 0 56 | 0 57 | 0 57 | 26 |
| 27 | 0 49 | 0 50 | 0 50 | 0 50 | 0 51 | 0 52 | 0 52 | 0 53 | 0 53 | 0 54 | 0 54 | 0 54 | 0 55 | 0 55 | 0 56 | 0 56 | 0 57 | 0 57 | 0 58 | 0 58 | 0 59 | 0 59 | 0 59 | 1 0 | 27 |
| 28 | 0 51 | 0 51 | 0 52 | 0 52 | 0 53 | 0 53 | 0 54 | 0 54 | 0 55 | 0 55 | 0 56 | 0 56 | 0 56 | 0 57 | 0 57 | 0 58 | 0 58 | 0 59 | 0 59 | 1 0 | 1 0 | 1 1 | 1 1 | 1 2 | 28 |
| 29 | 0 53 | 0 53 | 0 54 | 0 54 | 0 55 | 0 55 | 0 56 | 0 56 | 0 57 | 0 57 | 0 58 | 0 58 | 0 59 | 0 59 | 1 0 | 1 0 | 1 1 | 1 1 | 1 2 | 1 2 | 1 3 | 1 3 | 1 4 | 1 4 | 29 |
| 30 | 0 55 | 0 55 | 0 56 | 0 56 | 0 57 | 0 57 | 0 58 | 0 58 | 0 59 | 0 59 | 1 0 | 1 0 | 1 1 | 1 1 | 1 2 | 1 2 | 1 3 | 1 3 | 1 4 | 1 4 | 1 5 | 1 5 | 1 6 | 1 6 | 30 |
| 31 | 0 56 | 0 57 | 0 57 | 0 58 | 0 58 | 0 59 | 0 59 | 1 0 | 1 0 | 1 1 | 1 1 | 1 2 | 1 3 | 1 3 | 1 4 | 1 4 | 1 5 | 1 5 | 1 6 | 1 6 | 1 7 | 1 7 | 1 8 | 1 8 | 31 |
| 32 | 0 58 | 0 59 | 0 59 | 1 0 | 1 0 | 1 1 | 1 1 | 1 2 | 1 2 | 1 3 | 1 3 | 1 4 | 1 5 | 1 5 | 1 6 | 1 6 | 1 7 | 1 7 | 1 8 | 1 8 | 1 9 | 1 9 | 1 10 | 1 10 | 32 |
| 33 | 1 0 | 1 1 | 1 1 | 1 2 | 1 2 | 1 3 | 1 4 | 1 4 | 1 5 | 1 5 | 1 6 | 1 7 | 1 7 | 1 8 | 1 8 | 1 9 | 1 10 | 1 10 | 1 11 | 1 11 | 1 12 | 1 12 | 1 13 | 1 13 | 33 |
| 34 | 1 2 | 1 2 | 1 3 | 1 3 | 1 4 | 1 5 | 1 5 | 1 6 | 1 6 | 1 7 | 1 7 | 1 8 | 1 9 | 1 9 | 1 10 | 1 10 | 1 11 | 1 11 | 1 12 | 1 13 | 1 13 | 1 14 | 1 14 | 1 15 | 34 |
| 35 | 1 4 | 1 4 | 1 5 | 1 5 | 1 6 | 1 7 | 1 7 | 1 8 | 1 8 | 1 9 | 1 9 | 1 10 | 1 11 | 1 11 | 1 12 | 1 12 | 1 13 | 1 14 | 1 14 | 1 15 | 1 15 | 1 16 | 1 16 | 1 17 | 35 |
| 36 | 1 5 | 1 6 | 1 7 | 1 7 | 1 8 | 1 8 | 1 9 | 1 10 | 1 10 | 1 11 | 1 11 | 1 12 | 1 13 | 1 13 | 1 14 | 1 14 | 1 15 | 1 16 | 1 16 | 1 17 | 1 17 | 1 18 | 1 19 | 1 19 | 36 |
| 37 | 1 7 | 1 8 | 1 8 | 1 9 | 1 10 | 1 10 | 1 11 | 1 12 | 1 12 | 1 13 | 1 13 | 1 14 | 1 15 | 1 15 | 1 16 | 1 16 | 1 17 | 1 18 | 1 18 | 1 19 | 1 20 | 1 20 | 1 21 | 1 21 | 37 |
| 38 | 1 9 | 1 10 | 1 10 | 1 11 | 1 12 | 1 12 | 1 13 | 1 13 | 1 14 | 1 15 | 1 15 | 1 16 | 1 17 | 1 17 | 1 18 | 1 19 | 1 19 | 1 20 | 1 20 | 1 21 | 1 22 | 1 22 | 1 23 | 1 24 | 38 |
| 39 | 1 11 | 1 12 | 1 12 | 1 13 | 1 13 | 1 14 | 1 15 | 1 15 | 1 16 | 1 17 | 1 17 | 1 18 | 1 19 | 1 19 | 1 20 | 1 21 | 1 21 | 1 22 | 1 23 | 1 23 | 1 24 | 1 25 | 1 25 | 1 26 | 39 |
| 40 | 1 13 | 1 13 | 1 14 | 1 15 | 1 15 | 1 16 | 1 17 | 1 17 | 1 18 | 1 19 | 1 19 | 1 20 | 1 21 | 1 21 | 1 22 | 1 23 | 1 23 | 1 24 | 1 25 | 1 25 | 1 26 | 1 27 | 1 27 | 1 28 | 40 |
| 41 | 1 14 | 1 15 | 1 16 | 1 17 | 1 17 | 1 18 | 1 19 | 1 19 | 1 20 | 1 21 | 1 21 | 1 22 | 1 23 | 1 23 | 1 24 | 1 25 | 1 25 | 1 26 | 1 27 | 1 27 | 1 28 | 1 29 | 1 30 | 1 30 | 41 |
| 42 | 1 16 | 1 17 | 1 18 | 1 18 | 1 19 | 1 20 | 1 21 | 1 21 | 1 22 | 1 23 | 1 23 | 1 24 | 1 25 | 1 25 | 1 26 | 1 27 | 1 28 | 1 28 | 1 29 | 1 30 | 1 30 | 1 31 | 1 32 | 1 32 | 42 |
| 43 | 1 18 | 1 19 | 1 20 | 1 20 | 1 21 | 1 22 | 1 22 | 1 23 | 1 24 | 1 25 | 1 25 | 1 26 | 1 27 | 1 27 | 1 28 | 1 29 | 1 30 | 1 30 | 1 31 | 1 32 | 1 32 | 1 33 | 1 34 | 1 35 | 43 |
| 44 | 1 20 | 1 21 | 1 21 | 1 22 | 1 23 | 1 24 | 1 24 | 1 25 | 1 26 | 1 27 | 1 27 | 1 28 | 1 29 | 1 29 | 1 30 | 1 31 | 1 32 | 1 32 | 1 33 | 1 34 | 1 35 | 1 35 | 1 36 | 1 37 | 44 |
| 45 | 1 22 | 1 23 | 1 23 | 1 24 | 1 25 | 1 26 | 1 26 | 1 27 | 1 28 | 1 29 | 1 29 | 1 30 | 1 31 | 1 32 | 1 32 | 1 33 | 1 34 | 1 35 | 1 35 | 1 36 | 1 37 | 1 38 | 1 38 | 1 39 | 45 |
| 46 | 1 24 | 1 24 | 1 25 | 1 26 | 1 27 | 1 27 | 1 28 | 1 29 | 1 30 | 1 30 | 1 31 | 1 32 | 1 33 | 1 34 | 1 34 | 1 35 | 1 36 | 1 37 | 1 37 | 1 38 | 1 39 | 1 40 | 1 40 | 1 41 | 46 |
| 47 | 1 25 | 1 26 | 1 27 | 1 28 | 1 29 | 1 29 | 1 30 | 1 31 | 1 32 | 1 32 | 1 33 | 1 34 | 1 35 | 1 36 | 1 36 | 1 37 | 1 38 | 1 39 | 1 39 | 1 40 | 1 41 | 1 42 | 1 43 | 1 43 | 47 |
| 48 | 1 27 | 1 28 | 1 29 | 1 30 | 1 30 | 1 31 | 1 32 | 1 33 | 1 34 | 1 34 | 1 35 | 1 36 | 1 37 | 1 38 | 1 38 | 1 39 | 1 40 | 1 41 | 1 42 | 1 42 | 1 43 | 1 44 | 1 45 | 1 46 | 48 |
| 49 | 1 29 | 1 30 | 1 31 | 1 31 | 1 32 | 1 33 | 1 34 | 1 35 | 1 36 | 1 36 | 1 37 | 1 38 | 1 39 | 1 40 | 1 40 | 1 41 | 1 42 | 1 43 | 1 44 | 1 45 | 1 45 | 1 46 | 1 47 | 1 48 | 49 |
| 50 | 1 31 | 1 32 | 1 33 | 1 33 | 1 34 | 1 35 | 1 36 | 1 37 | 1 38 | 1 38 | 1 39 | 1 40 | 1 41 | 1 42 | 1 43 | 1 43 | 1 44 | 1 45 | 1 46 | 1 47 | 1 48 | 1 48 | 1 49 | 1 50 | 50 |
| 51 | 1 33 | 1 34 | 1 34 | 1 35 | 1 36 | 1 37 | 1 38 | 1 39 | 1 39 | 1 40 | 1 41 | 1 42 | 1 43 | 1 44 | 1 45 | 1 45 | 1 46 | 1 47 | 1 48 | 1 49 | 1 50 | 1 51 | 1 51 | 1 52 | 51 |
| 52 | 1 34 | 1 35 | 1 36 | 1 37 | 1 38 | 1 39 | 1 40 | 1 41 | 1 41 | 1 42 | 1 43 | 1 44 | 1 45 | 1 46 | 1 47 | 1 47 | 1 48 | 1 49 | 1 50 | 1 51 | 1 52 | 1 53 | 1 54 | 1 54 | 52 |
| 53 | 1 36 | 1 37 | 1 38 | 1 39 | 1 40 | 1 41 | 1 42 | 1 42 | 1 43 | 1 44 | 1 45 | 1 46 | 1 47 | 1 48 | 1 49 | 1 50 | 1 50 | 1 51 | 1 52 | 1 53 | 1 54 | 1 55 | 1 56 | 1 57 | 53 |
| 54 | 1 38 | 1 39 | 1 40 | 1 41 | 1 42 | 1 43 | 1 44 | 1 44 | 1 45 | 1 46 | 1 47 | 1 48 | 1 49 | 1 50 | 1 51 | 1 52 | 1 53 | 1 53 | 1 54 | 1 55 | 1 56 | 1 57 | 1 58 | 1 59 | 54 |
| 55 | 1 40 | 1 41 | 1 42 | 1 43 | 1 44 | 1 45 | 1 45 | 1 46 | 1 47 | 1 48 | 1 49 | 1 50 | 1 51 | 1 52 | 1 53 | 1 54 | 1 55 | 1 56 | 1 56 | 1 57 | 1 58 | 1 59 | 2 0 | 2 1 | 55 |
| 56 | 1 42 | 1 43 | 1 44 | 1 45 | 1 45 | 1 46 | 1 47 | 1 48 | 1 49 | 1 50 | 1 51 | 1 52 | 1 53 | 1 54 | 1 55 | 1 56 | 1 57 | 1 58 | 1 59 | 1 59 | 2 0 | 2 1 | 2 2 | 2 3 | 56 |
| 57 | 1 44 | 1 45 | 1 45 | 1 46 | 1 47 | 1 48 | 1 49 | 1 50 | 1 51 | 1 52 | 1 53 | 1 53 | 1 54 | 1 55 | 1 56 | 1 57 | 1 58 | 1 59 | 2 0 | 2 1 | 2 2 | 2 3 | 2 4 | 2 5 | 57 |
| 58 | 1 45 | 1 46 | 1 47 | 1 48 | 1 49 | 1 50 | 1 51 | 1 52 | 1 53 | 1 54 | 1 55 | 1 56 | 1 57 | 1 58 | 1 59 | 2 0 | 2 1 | 2 2 | 2 3 | 2 4 | 2 5 | 2 6 | 2 7 | 2 8 | 58 |
| 59 | 1 47 | 1 48 | 1 49 | 1 50 | 1 51 | 1 52 | 1 53 | 1 54 | 1 55 | 1 56 | 1 57 | 1 58 | 1 59 | 2 0 | 2 1 | 2 2 | 2 3 | 2 4 | 2 5 | 2 6 | 2 7 | 2 8 | 2 9 | 2 10 | 59 |

Longitude Correction in time – (Subtract if West / Add if East)

# Longitudes and Latitudes of Major U.S. Cities

| City | Long | Lat | Time | City | Long | Lat | Time | City | Long | Lat | Time |
|---|---|---|---|---|---|---|---|---|---|---|---|
| Abbeville, LA | 92W08 | 29N58 | 06:08:32 | Barrow, AK | 156W47 | 71N17 | 10:27:09 | Broken Arrow, OK | 95W47 | 36N03 | 06:23:10 |
| Aberdeen, MD | 76W10 | 39N31 | 05:04:39 | Barstow, CA | 117W01 | 34N54 | 07:48:05 | Broken Bow, NE | 99W38 | 41N24 | 06:38:33 |
| Aberdeen, SD | 98W29 | 45N28 | 06:33:57 | Bartlesville, OK | 95W59 | 36N45 | 06:23:55 | Brookfield, IL | 87W51 | 41N49 | 05:51:24 |
| Aberdeen, WA | 123W49 | 46N59 | 08:15:15 | Bartlett, NE | 98W33 | 41N53 | 06:34:12 | Brookfield, WI | 88W06 | 43N04 | 05:52:26 |
| Abilene, TX | 99W44 | 32N27 | 06:38:56 | Bartlett, TN | 89W52 | 35N12 | 05:59:30 | Brookline, MA | 71W07 | 42N20 | 04:44:29 |
| Ada, OK | 96W41 | 34N46 | 06:26:43 | Batavia, NY | 78W11 | 42N60 | 05:12:45 | Brooklyn Park, MN | 93W21 | 45N06 | 06:13:25 |
| Agoura Hills, CA | 118W44 | 34N09 | 07:54:57 | Baton Rouge, LA | 91W09 | 30N27 | 06:04:37 | Brookside, DE | 75W44 | 39N40 | 05:02:55 |
| Akron, OH | 81W31 | 41N05 | 05:26:05 | Battle Creek, MI | 85W11 | 42N19 | 05:40:43 | Brownsville, TX | 97W30 | 25N54 | 06:29:59 |
| Alameda, CA | 122W14 | 37N46 | 08:08:58 | Bay City, MI | 83W53 | 43N36 | 05:35:33 | Brunswick, ME | 69W58 | 43N55 | 04:39:52 |
| Alamogordo, NM | 105W58 | 32N54 | 07:03:50 | Bay City, TX | 95W58 | 28N59 | 06:23:53 | Brunswick, OH | 81W51 | 41N14 | 05:27:22 |
| Albany, CA | 122W18 | 37N53 | 08:09:11 | Bay Shore, NY | 73W15 | 40N44 | 04:52:59 | Bryn Mawr, WA | 122W14 | 47N30 | 08:08:56 |
| Albany, GA | 84W09 | 31N35 | 05:36:37 | Bayonne, NJ | 74W07 | 40N40 | 04:56:28 | Buena Park, CA | 117W60 | 33N52 | 07:51:59 |
| Albany, NY | 73W45 | 42N39 | 04:55:02 | Baytown, TX | 94W59 | 29N44 | 06:19:55 | Buffalo Grove, IL | 87W58 | 42N09 | 05:51:50 |
| Albion, MI | 84W45 | 42N15 | 05:39:01 | Beacon, NY | 73W58 | 41N30 | 04:55:53 | Buffalo, NY | 78W53 | 42N53 | 05:15:31 |
| Albuquerque, NM | 106W39 | 35N05 | 07:06:36 | Beaumont, TX | 94W06 | 30N05 | 06:16:24 | Bullhead City, AZ | 114W34 | 35N09 | 07:38:16 |
| Alexandria, LA | 92W27 | 31N19 | 06:09:47 | Beaver Dam, WI | 88W50 | 43N27 | 05:55:21 | Bunker Hill, CT | 73W04 | 41N34 | 04:52:15 |
| Alexandria, VA | 77W03 | 38N48 | 05:08:11 | Beaverton, OR | 122W48 | 45N29 | 08:11:13 | Burbank, CA | 118W18 | 34N11 | 07:53:14 |
| Algonquin, IL | 88W18 | 42N10 | 05:53:11 | Beckley, WV | 81W11 | 37N47 | 05:24:45 | Burlingame, CA | 122W22 | 37N35 | 08:09:28 |
| Allentown, PA | 75W29 | 40N37 | 05:01:56 | Bedford, OH | 81W32 | 41N24 | 05:26:09 | Burlington, CO | 102W16 | 39N18 | 06:49:05 |
| Allouez, WI | 88W01 | 44N29 | 05:52:04 | Beech Grove, IN | 86W05 | 39N43 | 05:44:22 | Burlington, MA | 71W12 | 42N30 | 04:44:47 |
| Alpharetta, GA | 84W18 | 34N05 | 05:37:11 | Belle Fourche, SD | 103W51 | 44N40 | 06:55:24 | Burlington, NC | 79W26 | 36N06 | 05:17:45 |
| Altamonte Springs, FL | 81W22 | 28N40 | 05:25:28 | Bellefontaine, OH | 83W46 | 40N22 | 05:35:02 | Burlington, VT | 73W13 | 44N29 | 04:52:51 |
| Altoona, PA | 78W24 | 40N31 | 05:13:35 | Belleville, NJ | 74W09 | 40N48 | 04:56:36 | Burnsville, MN | 93W17 | 44N46 | 06:13:07 |
| Amarillo, TX | 101W50 | 35N13 | 06:47:19 | Bellevue, WA | 122W12 | 47N37 | 08:08:48 | Butler, MO | 94W20 | 38N16 | 06:17:19 |
| American Fork, UT | 111W48 | 40N23 | 07:27:11 | Bellingham, WA | 122W29 | 48N46 | 08:09:57 | Butte, MT | 112W32 | 46N00 | 07:30:08 |
| Americus, GA | 84W14 | 32N04 | 05:36:56 | Bellmawr, NJ | 75W06 | 39N52 | 05:00:23 | Cadillac, MI | 85W24 | 44N15 | 05:41:36 |
| Ames, IA | 93W37 | 42N02 | 06:14:29 | Bellview, FL | 87W19 | 30N28 | 05:49:16 | Calexico, CA | 115W30 | 32N41 | 07:41:60 |
| Amherst, MA | 72W31 | 42N22 | 04:50:05 | Bellwood, IL | 87W53 | 41N53 | 05:51:32 | Calumet City, IL | 87W32 | 41N37 | 05:50:07 |
| Amherst, OH | 82W13 | 41N24 | 05:28:53 | Belmont, CA | 122W16 | 37N31 | 08:09:06 | Calverton, MD | 76W56 | 39N03 | 05:07:45 |
| Anaheim, CA | 117W55 | 33N50 | 07:51:39 | Belmont, MA | 71W11 | 42N24 | 04:44:43 | Camarillo, CA | 119W02 | 34N13 | 07:56:09 |
| Anchorage, AK | 149W54 | 61N13 | 09:59:36 | Belmont, NY | 78W02 | 42N13 | 05:12:08 | Cambridge, MA | 71W06 | 42N22 | 04:44:24 |
| Anderson, SC | 82W39 | 34N30 | 05:30:36 | Beloit, WI | 89W02 | 42N31 | 05:56:08 | Camden, NJ | 75W07 | 39N56 | 05:00:29 |
| Andover, MN | 93W17 | 45N14 | 06:13:10 | Belton, MO | 94W32 | 38N49 | 06:18:08 | Camp Pendleton, CA | 117W18 | 33N19 | 07:49:12 |
| Ann Arbor, MI | 83W45 | 42N17 | 05:34:59 | Belvidere, IL | 88W51 | 42N16 | 05:55:23 | Camp Springs, MD | 76W54 | 38N48 | 05:07:38 |
| Annandale, VA | 77W12 | 38N50 | 05:08:47 | Bend, OR | 121W19 | 44N04 | 08:05:15 | Campbell, CA | 121W57 | 37N17 | 08:07:48 |
| Annapolis, MD | 76W30 | 38N59 | 05:05:58 | Bennington, VT | 73W12 | 42N53 | 04:52:47 | Canton, IL | 90W02 | 40N33 | 06:00:08 |
| Anoka, MN | 93W23 | 45N12 | 06:13:33 | Benton Harbor, MI | 86W27 | 42N07 | 05:45:49 | Canton, MI | 83W28 | 42N19 | 05:33:52 |
| Ansonia, CT | 73W05 | 41N21 | 04:52:19 | Benton, AR | 92W35 | 34N34 | 06:10:21 | Canton, OH | 81W23 | 40N48 | 05:25:31 |
| Antioch, CA | 121W48 | 38N00 | 08:07:13 | Bentonville, AR | 94W13 | 36N22 | 06:16:50 | Cape Coral, FL | 81W57 | 26N34 | 05:27:48 |
| Apache Junction, AZ | 111W33 | 33N25 | 07:26:12 | Berkeley, CA | 122W16 | 37N52 | 08:09:05 | Cape Girardeau, MO | 89W31 | 37N18 | 05:58:04 |
| Apple Valley, CA | 117W11 | 34N30 | 07:48:44 | Berwick, PA | 76W14 | 41N03 | 05:04:56 | Cape May, NJ | 74W54 | 38N56 | 04:59:38 |
| Appleton, WI | 88W25 | 44N16 | 05:53:40 | Berwyn, IL | 87W48 | 41N51 | 05:51:10 | Capitola, CA | 121W57 | 36N59 | 08:07:49 |
| Arcadia, CA | 118W02 | 34N08 | 07:52:08 | Bethel Park, PA | 80W01 | 40N20 | 05:20:04 | Carbondale, IL | 89W13 | 37N44 | 05:56:52 |
| Arcata, CA | 124W05 | 40N52 | 08:16:20 | Bethesda, MD | 77W06 | 38N59 | 05:08:24 | Carbondale, PA | 75W30 | 41N34 | 05:02:01 |
| Ardmore, OK | 97W09 | 34N10 | 06:28:34 | Bethlehem, PA | 75W22 | 40N38 | 05:01:29 | Caribou, ME | 68W01 | 46N52 | 04:32:03 |
| Arlington, MA | 71W09 | 42N25 | 04:44:38 | Bethpage, NY | 73W29 | 40N45 | 04:53:56 | Carlisle, PA | 77W11 | 40N12 | 05:08:45 |
| Arlington, VA | 77W07 | 38N53 | 05:08:28 | Beverly Hills, CA | 118W24 | 34N04 | 07:53:36 | Carlsbad, CA | 117W21 | 33N09 | 07:49:24 |
| Arroyo Grande, CA | 120W35 | 35N07 | 08:02:22 | Big Rapids, MI | 85W29 | 43N42 | 05:41:56 | Carlsbad, NM | 104W14 | 32N25 | 06:56:55 |
| Arvada, CO | 105W05 | 39N48 | 07:00:21 | Billings, MT | 108W30 | 45N47 | 07:14:00 | Carrollton, GA | 85W05 | 33N35 | 05:40:20 |
| Asbury Park, NJ | 74W01 | 40N13 | 04:56:03 | Biloxi, MS | 88W53 | 30N24 | 05:55:32 | Carson City, NV | 119W46 | 39N10 | 07:59:04 |
| Asheboro, NC | 79W49 | 35N42 | 05:19:15 | Binghamton, NY | 75W55 | 42N06 | 05:03:40 | Carteret, NJ | 74W14 | 40N35 | 04:56:55 |
| Asheville, NC | 82W33 | 35N36 | 05:30:13 | Birmingham, AL | 86W48 | 33N31 | 05:47:13 | Carthage, MO | 94W19 | 37N11 | 06:17:14 |
| Ashland, KY | 82W38 | 38N29 | 05:30:33 | Birmingham, MI | 83W13 | 42N33 | 05:32:51 | Casa Grande, AZ | 111W45 | 32N53 | 07:27:02 |
| Ashland, OH | 82W19 | 40N52 | 05:29:16 | Bisbee, AZ | 109W56 | 31N27 | 07:19:43 | Casper, WY | 106W19 | 42N52 | 07:05:15 |
| Ashland, OR | 122W43 | 42N12 | 08:10:50 | Bismarck, ND | 100W47 | 46N49 | 06:43:08 | Castro Valley, CA | 122W05 | 37N42 | 08:08:20 |
| Ashland, WI | 90W53 | 46N36 | 06:03:32 | Bison, SD | 102W28 | 45N31 | 06:49:51 | Cayce, SC | 81W04 | 33N58 | 05:24:18 |
| Ashtabula, OH | 80W47 | 41N52 | 05:23:10 | Bloomfield, MI | 83W14 | 42N32 | 05:32:56 | Cedar City, UT | 113W04 | 37N41 | 07:32:15 |
| Aspen, CO | 106W49 | 39N11 | 07:07:16 | Bloomfield, NJ | 74W11 | 40N48 | 04:56:45 | Cedar Falls, IA | 92W27 | 42N32 | 06:09:47 |
| Astoria, OR | 123W50 | 46N11 | 08:15:19 | Bloomington, IL | 88W60 | 40N29 | 05:55:58 | Cedar Rapids, IA | 91W39 | 42N01 | 06:06:35 |
| Atascadero, CA | 120W40 | 35N29 | 08:02:41 | Bloomington, IN | 86W32 | 39N10 | 05:46:06 | Centerville, UT | 111W52 | 40N55 | 07:27:29 |
| Atchison, KS | 95W07 | 39N34 | 06:20:29 | Blue Ash, OH | 84W23 | 39N14 | 05:37:31 | Cerritos, CA | 118W05 | 33N52 | 07:52:20 |
| Athens, GA | 83W23 | 33N58 | 05:33:31 | Bluefield, WV | 81W13 | 37N16 | 05:24:53 | Chalmette, LA | 89W57 | 29N57 | 05:59:51 |
| Athens, OH | 82W06 | 39N20 | 05:28:24 | Boca Raton, FL | 80W05 | 26N22 | 05:20:20 | Champaign, IL | 88W15 | 40N07 | 05:52:58 |
| Athens, TN | 84W36 | 35N27 | 05:38:22 | Boise, ID | 116W12 | 43N37 | 07:44:49 | Chandler, AZ | 111W50 | 33N18 | 07:27:22 |
| Athens, TX | 95W51 | 32N12 | 06:23:25 | Boone, NC | 81W40 | 36N13 | 05:26:42 | Chantilly, VA | 77W26 | 38N54 | 05:09:44 |
| Atlanta, GA | 84W23 | 33N45 | 05:37:33 | Boston, MA | 71W04 | 42N22 | 04:44:14 | Chapel Hill, NC | 79W03 | 35N55 | 05:16:13 |
| Atlantic Beach, FL | 81W24 | 30N20 | 05:25:36 | Bottineau, ND | 100W27 | 48N50 | 06:41:47 | Charleston, SC | 79W56 | 32N47 | 05:19:43 |
| Atlantic City, NJ | 74W25 | 39N22 | 04:57:42 | Boulder City, NV | 114W50 | 35N59 | 07:39:20 | Charleston, WV | 81W38 | 38N21 | 05:26:32 |
| Attleboro, MA | 71W17 | 41N57 | 04:45:09 | Boulder, CO | 105W16 | 40N01 | 07:01:05 | Charlotte, NC | 80W51 | 35N14 | 05:23:22 |
| Auburn, AL | 85W29 | 32N37 | 05:41:55 | Bountiful, UT | 111W53 | 40N53 | 07:27:31 | Charlottesville, VA | 78W29 | 38N02 | 05:13:54 |
| Auburn, CA | 121W05 | 38N54 | 08:04:18 | Bowbells, ND | 102W15 | 48N48 | 06:48:59 | Chattanooga, TN | 85W19 | 35N03 | 05:41:14 |
| Auburn, ME | 70W14 | 44N06 | 04:40:56 | Bowie, MD | 76W47 | 39N00 | 05:07:07 | Cheboygan, MI | 84W28 | 45N39 | 05:37:54 |
| Auburn, NY | 76W34 | 42N56 | 05:06:16 | Bowling Green, KY | 86W27 | 36N59 | 05:45:46 | Chelsea, MA | 71W02 | 42N24 | 04:44:07 |
| Auburn, WA | 122W14 | 47N18 | 08:08:55 | Bowling Green, OH | 83W39 | 41N22 | 05:34:36 | Cherry Hill, NJ | 75W02 | 39N56 | 05:00:07 |
| Augusta, GA | 82W01 | 33N28 | 05:28:04 | Bowman, ND | 103W24 | 46N11 | 06:53:35 | Chesapeake, VA | 76W17 | 36N49 | 05:05:06 |
| Augusta, ME | 69W47 | 44N19 | 04:39:07 | Bozeman, MT | 111W02 | 45N41 | 07:24:09 | Chester, PA | 75W21 | 39N51 | 05:01:25 |
| Aurora, CO | 104W50 | 39N44 | 06:59:20 | Brainerd, MN | 94W12 | 46N21 | 06:16:48 | Chester, VA | 77W27 | 37N21 | 05:09:46 |
| Aurora, IL | 88W19 | 41N46 | 05:53:17 | Braintree, MA | 71W00 | 42N13 | 04:44:00 | Cheyenne, WY | 104W49 | 41N08 | 06:59:16 |
| Austin, TX | 97W41 | 30N16 | 06:30:58 | Brandon, FL | 82W17 | 27N56 | 05:29:09 | Chicago, IL | 87W39 | 41N51 | 05:50:36 |
| Avenel, NJ | 74W17 | 40N35 | 04:57:09 | Brawley, CA | 115W32 | 32N59 | 07:42:07 | Chickasha, OK | 97W56 | 35N03 | 06:31:45 |
| Babylon, NY | 73W20 | 40N42 | 04:53:18 | Brea, CA | 117W54 | 33N55 | 07:51:36 | Chico, CA | 121W50 | 39N44 | 08:07:21 |
| Bainbridge, GA | 84W35 | 30N54 | 05:38:18 | Bremerton, WA | 122W38 | 47N34 | 08:10:32 | Chillicothe, MO | 93W33 | 39N48 | 06:14:13 |
| Baker, OR | 117W50 | 44N47 | 07:51:19 | Brentwood, TN | 86W47 | 36N02 | 05:47:08 | Chillicothe, OH | 82W59 | 39N20 | 05:31:56 |
| Bakersfield, CA | 119W01 | 35N22 | 07:56:04 | Bridgeport, CT | 73W12 | 41N10 | 04:52:49 | Chippewa Falls, WI | 91W24 | 44N56 | 06:05:34 |
| Baldwin, NY | 73W37 | 40N39 | 04:54:26 | Brigham City, UT | 112W01 | 41N31 | 07:28:04 | Cicero, IL | 87W45 | 41N51 | 05:51:01 |
| Baltimore, MD | 76W37 | 39N17 | 05:06:27 | Bristol, CT | 72W57 | 41N40 | 04:51:48 | Cincinnati, OH | 84W30 | 39N10 | 05:37:50 |
| Bangor, ME | 68W47 | 44N48 | 04:35:07 | Bristol, RI | 71W16 | 41N41 | 04:45:05 | Claremont, CA | 117W43 | 34N06 | 07:50:53 |
| Banning, CA | 116W53 | 33N56 | 07:47:30 | Bristol, TN | 82W11 | 36N36 | 05:28:45 | Claremont, NH | 72W21 | 43N23 | 04:49:23 |

# Longitudes and Latitudes of Major U.S. Cities

| City | Long. | Lat. | Time | City | Long. | Lat. | Time | City | Long. | Lat. | Time |
|---|---|---|---|---|---|---|---|---|---|---|---|
| Clarksburg, WV | 80W21 | 39N17 | 05:21:23 | Dodge City, KS | 100W01 | 37N45 | 06:40:04 | Florence, KY | 84W38 | 38N60 | 05:38:30 |
| Clarksville, TN | 87W22 | 36N32 | 05:49:26 | Dover, DE | 75W31 | 39N09 | 05:02:06 | Florence, SC | 79W46 | 34N12 | 05:19:03 |
| Clearfield, UT | 112W02 | 41N07 | 07:28:06 | Dover, NH | 70W52 | 43N12 | 04:43:30 | Folsom, CA | 121W11 | 38N41 | 08:04:42 |
| Clearwater, FL | 82W48 | 27N58 | 05:31:12 | Dover, NJ | 74W34 | 40N53 | 04:58:15 | Fond du Lac, WI | 88W27 | 43N46 | 05:53:47 |
| Clemson, SC | 82W50 | 34N41 | 05:31:21 | Dover, OH | 81W28 | 40N31 | 05:25:54 | Fontana, CA | 117W26 | 34N06 | 07:49:44 |
| Cleveland, OH | 81W42 | 41N30 | 05:26:47 | Downers Grove, IL | 88W01 | 41N49 | 05:52:03 | Forest Hill, TX | 97W16 | 32N40 | 06:29:05 |
| Clifton, CO | 108W27 | 39N06 | 07:13:48 | Drexel Hill, PA | 75W18 | 39N57 | 05:01:10 | Forest Hills, MI | 85W35 | 42N56 | 05:42:20 |
| Clifton, NJ | 74W10 | 40N52 | 04:56:39 | Dublin, CA | 121W56 | 37N42 | 08:07:44 | Forest Park, IL | 87W49 | 41N53 | 05:51:15 |
| Clinton, IA | 90W11 | 41N51 | 06:00:45 | Dublin, GA | 82W54 | 32N32 | 05:31:37 | Fort Atkinson, WI | 88W50 | 42N56 | 05:55:21 |
| Clovis, NM | 103W12 | 34N24 | 06:52:49 | Dublin, OH | 83W07 | 40N06 | 05:32:27 | Fort Benning, GA | 84W58 | 32N21 | 05:39:53 |
| Coachella, CA | 116W10 | 33N41 | 07:44:42 | Dubois, IN | 86W48 | 38N27 | 05:47:13 | Fort Bliss, TX | 106W25 | 31N48 | 07:05:40 |
| Cocoa Beach, FL | 80W36 | 28N19 | 05:22:26 | Dubuque, IA | 90W40 | 42N30 | 06:02:39 | Fort Bragg, NC | 79W00 | 35N09 | 05:16:00 |
| Cocoa, FL | 80W45 | 28N23 | 05:22:58 | Duluth, MN | 92W06 | 46N47 | 06:08:26 | Fort Carson, CO | 104W47 | 38N45 | 06:59:08 |
| Cody, WY | 109W03 | 44N32 | 07:16:13 | Duncan, OK | 97W57 | 34N30 | 06:31:50 | Fort Collins, CO | 105W05 | 40N35 | 07:00:20 |
| Coeur d'Alene, ID | 116W47 | 47N41 | 07:47:07 | Durango, CO | 107W53 | 37N17 | 07:11:31 | Fort Dix, NJ | 74W37 | 40N02 | 04:58:29 |
| College Park, GA | 84W27 | 33N39 | 05:37:48 | Durant, OK | 96W22 | 33N59 | 06:25:30 | Fort Dodge, IA | 94W10 | 42N30 | 06:16:40 |
| College Park, MD | 76W56 | 38N59 | 05:07:45 | Durham, NC | 78W54 | 35N60 | 05:15:36 | Fort Hood, TX | 97W45 | 31N08 | 06:31:00 |
| Collingswood, NJ | 75W04 | 39N55 | 05:00:17 | Dyer, IN | 87W31 | 41N30 | 05:50:05 | Fort Hunt, VA | 77W04 | 38N43 | 05:08:16 |
| Colorado Springs, CO | 104W49 | 38N50 | 06:59:17 | Dyersburg, TN | 89W23 | 36N02 | 05:57:33 | Fort Knox, KY | 85W57 | 37N54 | 05:43:48 |
| Colton, CA | 117W19 | 34N04 | 07:49:15 | East Brunswick, NJ | 74W25 | 40N26 | 04:57:40 | Fort Lauderdale, FL | 80W09 | 26N07 | 05:20:34 |
| Columbia, MD | 76W50 | 39N14 | 05:07:22 | East Haven, CT | 72W52 | 41N17 | 04:51:29 | Fort Lee, NJ | 73W58 | 40N51 | 04:55:53 |
| Columbia, MO | 92W20 | 38N57 | 06:09:20 | Eau Claire, WI | 91W30 | 44N49 | 06:05:60 | Fort Leonard Wood, MO | 92W12 | 37N50 | 06:08:48 |
| Columbia, PA | 76W30 | 40N02 | 05:06:01 | Eden, NC | 79W46 | 36N29 | 05:19:04 | Fort Lewis, WA | 122W35 | 47N06 | 08:10:20 |
| Columbia, SC | 81W02 | 34N00 | 05:24:08 | Edina, MN | 93W21 | 44N53 | 06:13:24 | Fort Madison, IA | 91W19 | 40N38 | 06:05:16 |
| Columbus, GA | 84W59 | 32N28 | 05:39:57 | Edison, NJ | 74W25 | 39N31 | 04:57:39 | Fort Meade, MD | 76W44 | 39N07 | 05:06:55 |
| Columbus, NE | 97W22 | 41N26 | 06:29:28 | Edmond, OK | 97W29 | 35N39 | 06:29:55 | Fort Myers, FL | 81W52 | 26N38 | 05:27:29 |
| Columbus, OH | 82W60 | 39N58 | 05:31:60 | Edmonds, WA | 122W23 | 47N49 | 08:09:30 | Fort Pierce, FL | 80W20 | 27N27 | 05:21:18 |
| Concord, CA | 122W02 | 37N59 | 08:08:07 | El Centro, CA | 115W34 | 32N48 | 07:42:15 | Fort Polk, LA | 93W11 | 31N04 | 06:12:44 |
| Concord, NC | 80W35 | 35N25 | 05:22:19 | El Cerrito, CA | 122W19 | 37N55 | 08:09:15 | Fort Riley, KS | 96W47 | 39N04 | 06:27:08 |
| Concord, NH | 71W32 | 43N12 | 04:46:09 | El Dorado, KS | 96W52 | 37N49 | 06:27:27 | Fort Sill, OK | 98W26 | 34N41 | 06:33:44 |
| Conway, NH | 71W07 | 43N59 | 04:44:29 | El Paso, TX | 106W29 | 31N46 | 07:05:57 | Fort Smith, AR | 94W24 | 35N23 | 06:17:36 |
| Coos Bay, OR | 124W13 | 43N22 | 08:16:52 | El Segundo, CA | 118W25 | 33N55 | 07:53:40 | Fort Thomas, KY | 84W27 | 39N05 | 05:37:47 |
| Coral Gables, FL | 80W16 | 25N43 | 05:21:04 | El Toro, CA | 117W42 | 33N38 | 07:50:46 | Fort Wayne, IN | 85W08 | 41N08 | 05:40:31 |
| Coral Springs, FL | 80W15 | 26N16 | 05:21:00 | Elgin, IL | 88W17 | 42N02 | 05:53:07 | Fort Worth, TX | 97W19 | 32N44 | 06:29:17 |
| Corinth, MS | 88W31 | 34N56 | 05:54:05 | Elizabeth, NJ | 74W13 | 40N40 | 04:56:51 | Fountain Hills, AZ | 111W43 | 33N37 | 07:26:52 |
| Corning, NY | 77W03 | 42N09 | 05:08:13 | Elk City, OK | 99W24 | 35N25 | 06:37:37 | Fountain Valley, CA | 117W57 | 33N43 | 07:51:49 |
| Corona, CA | 117W34 | 33N53 | 07:50:16 | Elk River, MN | 93W34 | 45N18 | 06:14:16 | Four Corners, OR | 122W59 | 44N56 | 08:11:56 |
| Corpus Christi, TX | 97W24 | 27N48 | 06:29:35 | Elkhart, IN | 85W59 | 41N41 | 05:43:54 | Framingham, MA | 71W25 | 42N17 | 04:45:40 |
| Corsicana, TX | 96W28 | 32N06 | 06:25:52 | Elkins, WV | 79W51 | 38N56 | 05:19:23 | Franklin Park, IL | 87W52 | 41N56 | 05:51:28 |
| Corvallis, OR | 123W16 | 44N34 | 08:13:03 | Ellicott City, MD | 76W48 | 39N16 | 05:07:12 | Franklin, OH | 84W18 | 39N34 | 05:37:13 |
| Costa Mesa, CA | 117W55 | 33N38 | 07:51:40 | Elmhurst, IL | 87W56 | 41N54 | 05:51:46 | Franklin, WI | 88W02 | 42N53 | 05:52:09 |
| Cottonwood, UT | 109W11 | 39N04 | 07:16:43 | Elmira, NY | 76W48 | 42N05 | 05:07:14 | Frederick, MD | 77W25 | 39N25 | 05:09:39 |
| Council Bluffs, IA | 95W52 | 41N16 | 06:23:27 | Elmont, NY | 73W43 | 40N42 | 04:54:51 | Fredericksburg, VA | 77W28 | 38N18 | 05:09:51 |
| Covina, CA | 117W53 | 34N05 | 07:51:33 | Elmwood Park, IL | 87W49 | 41N55 | 05:51:14 | Fredonia, NY | 79W20 | 42N26 | 05:17:20 |
| Covington, KY | 84W31 | 39N05 | 05:38:02 | Elmwood Park, NJ | 74W07 | 40N54 | 04:56:29 | Freeport, NY | 73W35 | 40N39 | 04:54:20 |
| Cudahy, WI | 87W52 | 42N58 | 05:51:27 | Ely, NV | 114W53 | 39N15 | 07:39:33 | Freeport, TX | 95W22 | 28N57 | 06:21:26 |
| Cupertino, CA | 122W02 | 37N19 | 08:08:07 | Elyria, OH | 82W06 | 41N22 | 05:28:26 | Fremont, CA | 121W59 | 37N33 | 08:07:57 |
| Cuyahoga Falls, OH | 81W29 | 41N08 | 05:25:56 | Emporia, KS | 96W11 | 38N24 | 06:24:44 | Fremont, NE | 96W30 | 41N26 | 06:25:59 |
| Cypress, CA | 118W02 | 33N49 | 07:52:09 | Encinitas, CA | 117W17 | 33N02 | 07:49:10 | Fremont, OH | 83W07 | 41N21 | 05:32:29 |
| Dakota City, NE | 96W25 | 42N25 | 06:25:40 | Englewood, CO | 104W59 | 39N39 | 06:59:57 | French Lick, IN | 86W37 | 38N33 | 05:46:29 |
| Dallas, TX | 96W48 | 32N47 | 06:27:12 | Englewood, NJ | 73W58 | 40N54 | 04:55:54 | Frenchville, ME | 68W20 | 46N41 | 04:33:20 |
| Daly City, CA | 122W32 | 37N43 | 08:10:06 | Enid, OK | 97W53 | 36N24 | 06:31:31 | Fresno, CA | 119W46 | 36N45 | 07:59:05 |
| Danbury, CT | 73W27 | 41N24 | 04:53:49 | Ennis, TX | 96W38 | 32N20 | 06:26:30 | Front Royal, VA | 78W12 | 38N55 | 05:12:47 |
| Danvers, MA | 70W56 | 42N35 | 04:43:43 | Erie, PA | 80W05 | 42N08 | 05:20:20 | Fullerton, CA | 117W55 | 33N52 | 07:51:42 |
| Danville, CA | 121W60 | 37N49 | 08:07:60 | Escondido, CA | 117W05 | 33N07 | 07:48:21 | Fulton, MO | 91W57 | 38N51 | 06:07:47 |
| Danville, IL | 87W38 | 40N07 | 05:50:31 | Essex, MD | 76W29 | 39N19 | 05:05:54 | Gadsden, AL | 86W00 | 34N01 | 05:44:02 |
| Danville, VA | 79W24 | 36N35 | 05:17:35 | Euclid, OH | 81W32 | 41N36 | 05:26:06 | Gaffney, SC | 81W39 | 35N04 | 05:26:36 |
| Darby, PA | 75W16 | 39N55 | 05:01:02 | Eugene, OR | 123W05 | 44N03 | 08:12:21 | Gainesville, FL | 82W20 | 29N39 | 05:29:18 |
| Darien, CT | 73W28 | 41N05 | 04:53:53 | Eureka, CA | 124W10 | 40N48 | 08:16:39 | Gaithersburg, MD | 77W12 | 39N09 | 05:08:48 |
| Darien, IL | 87W58 | 41N45 | 05:51:52 | Evanston, IL | 87W41 | 42N02 | 05:50:46 | Gallatin, TN | 86W27 | 36N23 | 05:45:47 |
| Davenport, IA | 90W35 | 41N31 | 06:02:19 | Evanston, WY | 110W58 | 41N16 | 07:23:51 | Gallup, NM | 108W45 | 35N32 | 07:14:58 |
| Davie, FL | 80W14 | 26N04 | 05:20:56 | Everett, MA | 71W03 | 42N25 | 04:44:13 | Galveston, TX | 94W48 | 29N18 | 06:19:12 |
| Davis, CA | 121W44 | 38N33 | 08:06:57 | Everett, WA | 122W12 | 47N59 | 08:08:48 | Garden City, KS | 100W52 | 37N58 | 06:43:29 |
| Dayton, OH | 84W12 | 39N46 | 05:36:46 | Evergreen, WA | 122W35 | 45N39 | 08:10:20 | Garden City, NY | 73W38 | 40N44 | 04:54:32 |
| Daytona Beach, FL | 81W01 | 29N13 | 05:24:06 | Exeter, NH | 70W57 | 42N59 | 04:43:48 | Garden Grove, CA | 117W56 | 33N46 | 07:51:46 |
| De Kalb, IL | 88W45 | 41N56 | 05:55:00 | Fair Lawn, NJ | 74W08 | 40N56 | 04:56:32 | Garland, TX | 96W38 | 32N55 | 06:26:33 |
| De Soto, TX | 96W51 | 32N35 | 06:27:26 | Fair Oaks, CA | 121W16 | 38N39 | 08:05:05 | Gary, IN | 87W21 | 41N36 | 05:49:23 |
| De Witt, AR | 91W20 | 34N18 | 06:05:21 | Fairbanks, AK | 147W43 | 64N50 | 09:50:52 | Gastonia, NC | 81W11 | 35N16 | 05:24:45 |
| Dearborn, MI | 83W11 | 42N19 | 05:32:42 | Fairbury, NE | 97W11 | 40N08 | 06:28:43 | Gautier, MS | 88W37 | 30N23 | 05:54:27 |
| Decatur, AL | 86W59 | 34N36 | 05:47:56 | Fairfax, VA | 77W18 | 38N51 | 05:09:14 | Geneva, NY | 76W59 | 42N52 | 05:07:55 |
| Decatur, GA | 84W18 | 33N46 | 05:37:11 | Fairmont, WV | 80W09 | 39N29 | 05:20:34 | Georgetown, KY | 84W34 | 38N13 | 05:38:14 |
| Decatur, IL | 88W57 | 39N50 | 05:55:49 | Fairmount, NY | 76W14 | 43N03 | 05:04:57 | Germantown, MD | 77W16 | 39N10 | 05:09:05 |
| Deerfield Beach, FL | 80W06 | 26N19 | 05:20:24 | Fairview Heights, IL | 90W00 | 38N36 | 06:00:00 | Germantown, TN | 89W49 | 35N05 | 05:59:14 |
| Deerfield, IL | 87W51 | 42N10 | 05:51:23 | Fairview, NJ | 73W60 | 40N49 | 04:55:60 | Germantown, WI | 88W07 | 43N14 | 05:52:26 |
| Defiance, OH | 84W21 | 41N17 | 05:37:25 | Fall River, MA | 71W09 | 41N42 | 04:44:36 | Gillette, WY | 105W30 | 44N17 | 07:02:00 |
| Del Rio, TX | 100W54 | 29N22 | 06:43:35 | Fallbrook, CA | 117W15 | 33N23 | 07:49:00 | Gilroy, CA | 121W34 | 37N00 | 08:06:16 |
| Delray Beach, FL | 80W04 | 26N28 | 05:20:18 | Falls City, NE | 95W36 | 40N04 | 06:22:24 | Girard, OH | 80W42 | 41N09 | 05:22:48 |
| Deltona, FL | 81W16 | 28N54 | 05:25:03 | Fargo, ND | 96W47 | 46N53 | 06:27:09 | Glen Burnie, MD | 76W38 | 39N10 | 05:06:30 |
| Deming, NM | 107W45 | 32N16 | 07:11:02 | Farmington, MI | 83W23 | 42N28 | 05:33:30 | Glen Cove, NY | 73W38 | 40N52 | 04:54:32 |
| Denton, TX | 97W08 | 33N13 | 06:28:32 | Farmingville, NY | 73W02 | 40N50 | 04:52:07 | Glen Ellyn, IL | 88W04 | 41N53 | 05:52:16 |
| Denver, CO | 104W59 | 39N44 | 06:59:56 | Farragut, TN | 84W09 | 35N53 | 05:36:37 | Glendale, AZ | 112W11 | 33N32 | 07:28:44 |
| Depew, NY | 78W42 | 42N54 | 05:14:46 | Fayetteville, AR | 94W09 | 36N04 | 06:16:38 | Glenmont, MD | 77W03 | 39N03 | 05:08:12 |
| Derby, CT | 73W05 | 41N19 | 04:52:21 | Fayetteville, NC | 78W53 | 35N03 | 05:15:31 | Glenview, IL | 87W47 | 42N04 | 05:51:09 |
| Des Moines, IA | 93W37 | 41N36 | 06:14:26 | Ferndale, MD | 76W38 | 39N11 | 05:06:34 | Gloucester, MA | 70W40 | 42N37 | 04:42:34 |
| Des Plaines, IL | 87W53 | 42N02 | 05:51:32 | Ferndale, MI | 83W08 | 42N28 | 05:32:32 | Golden Valley, MN | 93W21 | 45N01 | 06:13:24 |
| Desert Hot Springs, CA | 116W30 | 33N58 | 07:46:00 | Fitchburg, WI | 89W28 | 42N58 | 05:57:53 | Golden, CO | 105W13 | 39N45 | 07:00:53 |
| Detroit, MI | 83W03 | 42N20 | 05:32:11 | Flagstaff, AZ | 111W39 | 35N12 | 07:26:36 | Goldsboro, NC | 77W60 | 35N23 | 05:11:58 |
| Dickinson, ND | 102W47 | 46N53 | 06:51:09 | Flint, MI | 83W41 | 43N01 | 05:34:45 | Grafton, ND | 97W25 | 48N25 | 06:29:38 |

# Longitudes and Latitudes of Major U.S. Cities

| | | | |
|---|---|---|---|
| Graham, NC | 79W24 | 36N04 | 05:17:36 |
| Grand Forks, ND | 97W02 | 47N56 | 06:28:08 |
| Grand Island, NE | 98W21 | 40N56 | 06:33:22 |
| Grand Junction, CO | 108W33 | 39N04 | 07:14:12 |
| Grand Prairie, TX | 96W60 | 32N45 | 06:27:59 |
| Grand Rapids, MI | 85W40 | 42N58 | 05:42:40 |
| Grand Rapids, MN | 93W32 | 47N14 | 06:14:07 |
| Grangeville, ID | 116W07 | 45N56 | 07:44:29 |
| Grants Pass, OR | 123W20 | 42N26 | 08:13:19 |
| Grapevine, TX | 97W05 | 32N56 | 06:28:19 |
| Great Falls, MT | 111W18 | 47N30 | 07:25:12 |
| Greeley, CO | 104W43 | 40N25 | 06:58:50 |
| Green Bay, WI | 88W01 | 44N31 | 05:52:05 |
| Green River, WY | 109W28 | 41N32 | 07:17:52 |
| Green Valley, AZ | 110W60 | 31N52 | 07:23:58 |
| Greenacres City, FL | 80W08 | 26N37 | 05:20:30 |
| Greenbelt, MD | 76W53 | 39N00 | 05:07:30 |
| Greensboro, AL | 87W36 | 32N42 | 05:50:23 |
| Greensboro, NC | 79W48 | 36N04 | 05:19:10 |
| Greenville, MS | 91W04 | 33N25 | 06:04:15 |
| Greenville, SC | 82W24 | 34N51 | 05:29:35 |
| Greenwood, MS | 90W11 | 33N31 | 06:00:43 |
| Greenwood, SC | 82W10 | 34N12 | 05:28:39 |
| Gretna, LA | 90W03 | 29N55 | 06:00:13 |
| Griffin, GA | 84W16 | 33N15 | 05:37:03 |
| Grosse Pointe Farms, MI | 82W54 | 42N25 | 05:31:34 |
| Groves, TX | 93W55 | 29N57 | 06:15:40 |
| Gulf Gate Estates, FL | 82W31 | 27N16 | 05:30:04 |
| Gulfport, FL | 82W42 | 27N45 | 05:30:49 |
| Gulfport, MS | 89W06 | 30N22 | 05:56:22 |
| Guthrie, OK | 97W26 | 35N53 | 06:29:42 |
| Hacienda Heights, CA | 117W58 | 34N00 | 07:51:51 |
| Hackensack, NJ | 74W03 | 40N53 | 04:56:11 |
| Hagerstown, MD | 77W43 | 39N39 | 05:10:53 |
| Halawa, HI | 157W56 | 21N23 | 10:31:44 |
| Hamilton, MT | 114W10 | 46N15 | 07:36:38 |
| Hamilton, OH | 84W34 | 39N24 | 05:38:15 |
| Hammond, IN | 87W30 | 41N35 | 05:50:00 |
| Hammond, LA | 90W28 | 30N30 | 06:01:51 |
| Hampton, VA | 76W21 | 37N02 | 05:05:23 |
| Hana, HI | 155W59 | 20N45 | 10:23:58 |
| Hanalei, HI | 159W30 | 22N12 | 10:38:01 |
| Hannibal, MO | 91W22 | 39N43 | 06:05:26 |
| Hanover, PA | 76W59 | 39N48 | 05:07:56 |
| Harrisburg, PA | 76W53 | 40N16 | 05:07:32 |
| Hartford, CT | 72W41 | 41N46 | 04:50:45 |
| Haslett, MI | 84W24 | 42N45 | 05:37:36 |
| Hastings, MN | 92W51 | 44N45 | 06:11:25 |
| Hastings, NE | 98W23 | 40N35 | 06:33:33 |
| Hattiesburg, MS | 89W17 | 31N20 | 05:57:10 |
| Hauppauge, NY | 73W12 | 40N50 | 04:52:49 |
| Havelock, NC | 76W54 | 34N53 | 05:07:36 |
| Haverhill, MA | 71W05 | 42N47 | 04:44:19 |
| Havre, MT | 109W41 | 48N33 | 07:18:44 |
| Hawthorne, CA | 118W21 | 33N55 | 07:53:24 |
| Hayward, CA | 122W05 | 37N40 | 08:08:19 |
| Hazel Park, MI | 83W06 | 42N28 | 05:32:25 |
| Helena, MT | 112W02 | 46N36 | 07:28:08 |
| Hemet, CA | 116W58 | 33N45 | 07:47:53 |
| Hempstead, NY | 73W37 | 40N42 | 04:54:29 |
| Henderson, KY | 87W35 | 37N50 | 05:50:22 |
| Henderson, NV | 114W59 | 36N02 | 07:39:55 |
| Henderson, TN | 88W38 | 35N26 | 05:54:34 |
| Hendersonville, TN | 86W37 | 36N18 | 05:46:29 |
| Hermosa Beach, CA | 118W24 | 33N52 | 07:53:36 |
| Hershey, PA | 76W39 | 40N17 | 05:06:36 |
| Hesperia, CA | 117W18 | 34N26 | 07:49:12 |
| Hialeah, FL | 80W17 | 25N51 | 05:21:07 |
| Hickory, NC | 81W20 | 35N44 | 05:25:22 |
| High Point, FL | 82W42 | 27N55 | 05:30:49 |
| High Point, NC | 80W00 | 35N57 | 05:20:01 |
| Hillsboro, OR | 122W59 | 45N31 | 08:11:57 |
| Hillsborough, CA | 122W23 | 37N34 | 08:09:31 |
| Hilo, HI | 155W05 | 19N44 | 10:20:22 |
| Hilton Head Island, SC | 80W45 | 32N13 | 05:23:01 |
| Hinsdale, IL | 87W56 | 41N48 | 05:51:45 |
| Hoboken, NJ | 74W02 | 40N45 | 04:56:08 |
| Hoffman Estates, IL | 88W05 | 42N03 | 05:52:19 |
| Holbrook, MA | 71W01 | 42N09 | 04:44:02 |
| Holiday, FL | 82W44 | 28N11 | 05:30:58 |
| Holland, MI | 86W07 | 42N47 | 05:44:26 |
| Holly Hill, FL | 81W02 | 29N15 | 05:24:09 |
| Hollywood, FL | 80W09 | 26N01 | 05:20:36 |
| Holyoke, MA | 72W37 | 42N12 | 04:50:28 |
| Homestead, FL | 80W29 | 25N28 | 05:21:55 |
| Homewood, AL | 86W48 | 33N28 | 05:47:12 |
| Homewood, IL | 87W40 | 41N33 | 05:50:40 |
| Honolulu, HI | 157W52 | 21N18 | 10:31:26 |
| Hope, AR | 93W35 | 33N40 | 06:14:22 |
| Hopewell, VA | 77W17 | 37N18 | 05:09:09 |
| Hot Springs, AR | 93W03 | 34N30 | 06:12:13 |
| Hot Springs, SD | 103W28 | 43N26 | 06:53:54 |
| Houghton, MI | 88W34 | 47N07 | 05:54:17 |
| Houston, TX | 95W22 | 29N46 | 06:21:27 |
| Hudson, MA | 71W34 | 42N24 | 04:46:16 |
| Hull, MA | 70W55 | 42N18 | 04:43:38 |
| Huntington Beach, CA | 117W60 | 33N40 | 07:51:60 |
| Huntington, NY | 73W26 | 40N52 | 04:53:42 |
| Huntington, WV | 82W27 | 38N25 | 05:29:47 |
| Huntsville, AL | 86W35 | 34N44 | 05:46:21 |
| Huntsville, TX | 95W33 | 30N43 | 06:22:12 |
| Huron, SD | 98W13 | 44N22 | 06:32:51 |
| Hutchinson, KS | 97W56 | 38N04 | 06:31:43 |
| Hyannis, MA | 70W17 | 41N39 | 04:41:08 |
| Hyattsville, MD | 76W57 | 38N57 | 05:07:47 |
| Idaho Falls, ID | 112W02 | 43N28 | 07:28:08 |
| Idylwood, VA | 77W13 | 38N54 | 05:08:51 |
| Independence, KS | 95W42 | 37N13 | 06:22:50 |
| Independence, KY | 84W33 | 38N57 | 05:38:11 |
| Independence, MO | 94W25 | 39N05 | 06:17:40 |
| Indianapolis, IN | 86W09 | 39N46 | 05:44:38 |
| Indio, CA | 116W13 | 33N43 | 07:44:52 |
| Inglewood, CA | 118W21 | 33N58 | 07:53:25 |
| Iowa City, IA | 91W32 | 41N40 | 06:06:07 |
| Irvine, CA | 117W49 | 33N40 | 07:51:17 |
| Irving, TX | 96W57 | 32N49 | 06:27:48 |
| Isla Vista, CA | 119W51 | 34N25 | 07:59:24 |
| Islip, NY | 73W13 | 40N44 | 04:52:51 |
| Ithaca, NY | 76W30 | 42N26 | 05:05:59 |
| Jackson, MI | 84W24 | 42N15 | 05:37:36 |
| Jackson, MS | 90W11 | 32N18 | 06:00:44 |
| Jackson, TN | 88W49 | 35N37 | 05:55:15 |
| Jackson, WY | 110W46 | 43N29 | 07:23:03 |
| Jacksonville, AL | 85W46 | 33N49 | 05:43:03 |
| Jacksonville, FL | 81W39 | 30N20 | 05:26:37 |
| Jacksonville, NC | 77W26 | 34N45 | 05:09:43 |
| Jamestown, NY | 79W14 | 42N06 | 05:16:57 |
| Jamestown, VA | 76W46 | 37N12 | 05:07:06 |
| Janesville, WI | 89W01 | 42N41 | 05:56:04 |
| Jasper, FL | 82W57 | 30N31 | 05:31:48 |
| Jasper, IN | 86W56 | 38N23 | 05:47:43 |
| Jefferson City, MO | 92W10 | 38N35 | 06:08:42 |
| Jefferson Valley, NY | 73W47 | 41N20 | 04:55:10 |
| Jefferson, LA | 90W10 | 29N58 | 06:00:40 |
| Jefferson, VA | 77W54 | 37N37 | 05:11:37 |
| Jeffersontown, KY | 85W34 | 38N12 | 05:42:15 |
| Jeffersonville, IN | 85W45 | 38N17 | 05:43:00 |
| Jericho, NY | 73W32 | 40N48 | 04:54:10 |
| Jersey City, NJ | 74W05 | 40N44 | 04:56:19 |
| Johnson City, TN | 82W21 | 36N19 | 05:29:25 |
| Joliet, IL | 88W05 | 41N32 | 05:52:20 |
| Jonesboro, AR | 90W42 | 35N51 | 06:02:49 |
| Jonesboro, LA | 92W43 | 32N14 | 06:10:52 |
| Joplin, MO | 94W31 | 37N05 | 06:18:03 |
| Junction City, KS | 96W50 | 39N02 | 06:27:19 |
| Junction, UT | 112W13 | 38N14 | 07:28:53 |
| Juneau, AK | 134W25 | 58N18 | 08:57:41 |
| Jupiter, FL | 80W06 | 26N56 | 05:20:23 |
| Kahului, HI | 156W28 | 20N54 | 10:25:53 |
| Kailua, HI | 157W44 | 21N24 | 10:30:57 |
| Kalamazoo, MI | 85W35 | 42N18 | 05:42:21 |
| Kalaupapa, HI | 156W59 | 21N12 | 10:27:57 |
| Kalispell, MT | 114W19 | 48N12 | 07:37:15 |
| Kaneohe, HI | 157W48 | 21N25 | 10:31:13 |
| Kankakee, IL | 87W52 | 41N07 | 05:51:27 |
| Kansas City, KS | 94W38 | 39N07 | 06:18:31 |
| Kansas City, MO | 94W35 | 39N06 | 06:18:19 |
| Kawaihae, HI | 155W50 | 20N02 | 10:23:19 |
| Kaysville, UT | 111W56 | 41N02 | 07:27:45 |
| Kearney, NE | 99W05 | 40N42 | 06:36:19 |
| Keene, NH | 72W17 | 42N56 | 04:49:07 |
| Kelso, WA | 122W54 | 46N09 | 08:11:38 |
| Kennewick, WA | 119W08 | 46N13 | 07:56:33 |
| Kenosha, WI | 87W49 | 42N35 | 05:51:17 |
| Kent, OH | 81W21 | 41N09 | 05:25:26 |
| Kent, WA | 122W14 | 47N23 | 08:08:56 |
| Key Largo, FL | 80W25 | 25N08 | 05:21:40 |
| Key West, FL | 81W47 | 24N33 | 05:27:08 |
| Keyser, WV | 78W58 | 39N26 | 05:15:54 |
| Kihei, HI | 156W28 | 20N47 | 10:25:52 |
| King Cove, AK | 162W19 | 55N03 | 10:49:16 |
| King of Prussia, PA | 75W24 | 40N05 | 05:01:35 |
| Kingman, AZ | 114W03 | 35N11 | 07:36:13 |
| Kings Park, NY | 73W15 | 40N53 | 04:53:02 |
| Kingsgate, WA | 122W12 | 47N41 | 08:08:48 |
| Kingsport, TN | 82W34 | 36N33 | 05:30:15 |
| Kingston, NY | 73W60 | 41N56 | 04:55:59 |
| Kingston, PA | 75W54 | 41N16 | 05:03:35 |
| Kirkland, WA | 122W12 | 47N41 | 08:08:50 |
| Kissimmee, FL | 81W24 | 28N18 | 05:25:38 |
| Klamath Falls, OR | 121W47 | 42N14 | 08:07:07 |
| Knox, IN | 86W38 | 41N18 | 05:46:30 |
| Knoxville, TN | 83W55 | 35N58 | 05:35:41 |
| Kodiak, AK | 152W24 | 57N47 | 10:09:38 |
| La Canada, CA | 118W12 | 34N12 | 07:52:48 |
| La Crescenta, CA | 118W14 | 34N13 | 07:52:57 |
| La Crosse, WI | 91W14 | 43N48 | 06:04:57 |
| La Grande, OR | 118W05 | 45N19 | 07:52:21 |
| La Grange, GA | 85W02 | 33N02 | 05:40:08 |
| La Grange, IL | 87W52 | 41N48 | 05:51:29 |
| La Junta, CO | 103W33 | 37N59 | 06:54:10 |
| La Porte, IN | 86W43 | 41N37 | 05:46:53 |
| La Verne, CA | 117W46 | 34N06 | 07:51:04 |
| Lacey, WA | 122W49 | 47N02 | 08:11:17 |
| Laconia, NH | 71W28 | 43N32 | 04:45:53 |
| Lafayette, CA | 122W07 | 37N53 | 08:08:28 |
| Lafayette, CO | 105W05 | 39N60 | 07:00:21 |
| Lafayette, IN | 86W53 | 40N25 | 05:47:30 |
| Lafayette, LA | 92W01 | 30N13 | 06:08:05 |
| Laguna Beach, CA | 117W47 | 33N33 | 07:51:08 |
| Lake Charles, LA | 93W13 | 30N14 | 06:12:52 |
| Lake Elsinore, CA | 117W44 | 33N55 | 07:50:56 |
| Lake Forest, IL | 87W53 | 42N13 | 05:51:33 |
| Lake Havasu City, AZ | 114W19 | 34N29 | 07:37:17 |
| Lake Oswego, OR | 122W40 | 45N25 | 08:10:41 |
| Lake Placid, NY | 73W59 | 44N17 | 04:55:55 |
| Lake Tahoe, NV | 119W57 | 39N01 | 07:59:48 |
| Lakeland, FL | 81W57 | 28N03 | 05:27:48 |
| Lakeside, FL | 84W18 | 30N23 | 05:37:12 |
| Lakewood, CO | 105W05 | 39N42 | 07:00:19 |
| Lakewood, NJ | 74W13 | 40N06 | 04:56:52 |
| Lakewood, WA | 122W12 | 48N09 | 08:08:49 |
| Lanai City, HI | 156W55 | 20N50 | 10:27:41 |
| Lancaster, CA | 118W08 | 34N42 | 07:52:33 |
| Lancaster, NH | 71W34 | 44N29 | 04:46:17 |
| Lancaster, OH | 82W36 | 39N43 | 05:30:24 |
| Lancaster, PA | 76W18 | 40N02 | 05:05:13 |
| Lancaster, SC | 80W46 | 34N43 | 05:23:05 |
| Lancaster, WI | 90W43 | 42N51 | 06:02:51 |
| Langdon, ND | 98W22 | 48N46 | 06:33:28 |
| Langley Park, MD | 76W59 | 38N59 | 05:07:56 |
| Lansdowne, MD | 76W40 | 39N15 | 05:06:39 |
| Lansdowne, PA | 75W16 | 39N56 | 05:01:05 |
| Lansing, MI | 84W33 | 42N44 | 05:38:13 |
| Laplace, LA | 90W29 | 30N04 | 06:01:55 |
| LaQuinta, CA | 116W19 | 33N40 | 07:45:14 |
| Laramie, WY | 105W35 | 41N19 | 07:02:22 |
| Laredo, TX | 99W30 | 27N30 | 06:38:02 |
| Largo, FL | 82W47 | 27N55 | 05:31:09 |
| Larkspur, CA | 122W32 | 37N56 | 08:10:08 |
| Las Cruces, NM | 106W47 | 32N19 | 07:07:07 |
| Las Vegas, NV | 115W08 | 36N11 | 07:40:33 |
| Latham, NY | 73W46 | 42N45 | 04:55:02 |
| Laurel, MD | 76W51 | 39N06 | 05:07:24 |
| Laurel, MS | 89W08 | 31N42 | 05:56:31 |
| Lawrence, KS | 95W14 | 38N58 | 06:20:56 |
| Lawrence, MA | 71W10 | 42N42 | 04:44:39 |
| Lawrenceburg, TN | 87W20 | 35N15 | 05:49:20 |
| Lawrenceville, GA | 83W59 | 33N57 | 05:35:57 |
| Lawton, OK | 98W23 | 34N37 | 06:33:34 |
| Leavenworth, KS | 94W55 | 39N19 | 06:19:41 |
| Lebanon, IN | 86W28 | 40N03 | 05:45:53 |
| Lebanon, NH | 72W15 | 43N39 | 04:49:01 |
| Lebanon, OH | 84W12 | 39N26 | 05:36:49 |
| Lebanon, OR | 122W54 | 44N32 | 08:11:37 |
| Lebanon, PA | 76W25 | 40N20 | 05:05:39 |
| Lee's Summit, MO | 94W23 | 38N55 | 06:17:32 |
| Leesburg, FL | 81W53 | 28N49 | 05:27:31 |
| Leesburg, VA | 77W34 | 39N07 | 05:10:15 |
| Leisure City, FL | 80W26 | 25N30 | 05:21:43 |
| Levittown, NY | 73W31 | 40N44 | 04:54:04 |
| Levittown, PA | 74W50 | 40N09 | 04:59:19 |
| Lewes, DE | 75W08 | 38N46 | 05:00:34 |
| Lewiston, ID | 117W01 | 46N25 | 07:48:04 |
| Lewiston, ME | 70W13 | 44N06 | 04:40:52 |
| Lewistown, MT | 109W26 | 47N04 | 07:17:43 |
| Lewisville, TX | 96W60 | 33N03 | 06:27:59 |
| Lexington, KY | 84W30 | 38N03 | 05:38:00 |
| Lexington, MA | 71W14 | 42N27 | 04:44:54 |
| Liberal, KS | 100W55 | 37N03 | 06:43:41 |
| Liberty, MO | 94W25 | 39N15 | 06:17:41 |
| Lihue, HI | 159W22 | 21N59 | 10:37:29 |
| Lima, OH | 84W06 | 40N45 | 05:36:25 |
| Lincoln, IL | 89W22 | 40N09 | 05:57:28 |

# Longitudes and Latitudes of Major U.S. Cities

| City | Longitude | Latitude | Time |
|---|---|---|---|
| Lincoln, NE | 96W40 | 40N48 | 06:26:40 |
| Lincolnia, VA | 77W09 | 38N49 | 05:08:34 |
| Lisle, IL | 88W04 | 41N48 | 05:52:18 |
| Little Rock, AR | 92W17 | 34N45 | 06:09:09 |
| Littleton, CO | 105W01 | 39N37 | 07:00:04 |
| Live Oak, CA | 121W40 | 39N17 | 08:06:38 |
| Livermore, CA | 121W46 | 37N41 | 08:07:04 |
| Livingston, NJ | 74W19 | 40N48 | 04:57:16 |
| Livonia, MI | 83W21 | 42N22 | 05:33:25 |
| Lockhart, FL | 81W27 | 28N37 | 05:25:46 |
| Lodi, CA | 121W16 | 38N08 | 08:05:05 |
| Logan, UT | 111W50 | 41N44 | 07:27:20 |
| Loma Linda, CA | 117W16 | 34N03 | 07:49:02 |
| Lombard, IL | 88W00 | 41N53 | 05:52:02 |
| Lompoc, CA | 120W27 | 34N38 | 08:01:50 |
| Londonderry, NH | 71W22 | 42N52 | 04:45:30 |
| Long Beach, CA | 118W11 | 33N46 | 07:52:45 |
| Long Branch, NJ | 73W60 | 40N18 | 04:55:58 |
| Longmont, CO | 105W06 | 40N10 | 07:00:24 |
| Longview, TX | 94W44 | 32N30 | 06:18:58 |
| Longwood, FL | 81W20 | 28N42 | 05:25:21 |
| Lorton, VA | 77W14 | 38N42 | 05:08:55 |
| Los Alamitos, CA | 118W04 | 33N48 | 07:52:17 |
| Los Alamos, NM | 106W19 | 35N53 | 07:05:16 |
| Los Altos, CA | 122W07 | 37N23 | 08:08:27 |
| Los Angeles, CA | 118W15 | 34N03 | 07:52:58 |
| Los Gatos, CA | 121W58 | 37N14 | 08:07:54 |
| Los Osos, CA | 120W50 | 35N19 | 08:03:20 |
| Louisville, KY | 85W46 | 38N15 | 05:43:02 |
| Loveland, CO | 105W04 | 40N24 | 07:00:18 |
| Lowell, MA | 71W19 | 42N38 | 04:45:16 |
| Lubbock, TX | 101W51 | 33N35 | 06:47:25 |
| Lutz, FL | 82W28 | 28N09 | 05:29:51 |
| Lynchburg, VA | 79W09 | 37N25 | 05:16:34 |
| Lynn, MA | 70W57 | 42N28 | 04:43:48 |
| Lynnfield, MA | 71W03 | 42N32 | 04:44:12 |
| Macon, GA | 83W38 | 32N50 | 05:34:32 |
| Madera, CA | 120W04 | 36N58 | 08:00:14 |
| Madison, WI | 89W24 | 43N04 | 05:57:36 |
| Madisonville, KY | 87W30 | 37N20 | 05:49:60 |
| Magnolia, AR | 93W14 | 33N16 | 06:12:57 |
| Malden, MA | 71W04 | 42N26 | 04:44:16 |
| Manassas, VA | 77W29 | 38N45 | 05:09:54 |
| Manchester, CT | 72W31 | 41N47 | 04:50:05 |
| Manchester, NH | 71W27 | 42N60 | 04:45:49 |
| Mandan, ND | 100W53 | 46N50 | 06:43:33 |
| Manhattan Beach, CA | 118W25 | 33N53 | 07:53:38 |
| Manhattan, KS | 96W34 | 39N11 | 06:26:17 |
| Manitowoc, WI | 87W39 | 44N05 | 05:50:38 |
| Mankato, MN | 93W60 | 44N10 | 06:15:60 |
| Maple Grove, MN | 93W27 | 45N04 | 06:13:49 |
| Maplewood, NJ | 74W16 | 40N46 | 04:57:06 |
| Marblehead, MA | 70W52 | 42N30 | 04:43:26 |
| Margate, FL | 80W12 | 26N15 | 05:20:50 |
| Marietta, GA | 84W33 | 33N57 | 05:38:12 |
| Marion, IA | 91W36 | 42N02 | 06:06:23 |
| Marion, OH | 83W08 | 40N35 | 05:32:31 |
| Marion, VA | 81W31 | 36N50 | 05:26:04 |
| Marlborough, MA | 71W33 | 42N21 | 04:46:13 |
| Marquette, MI | 87W24 | 46N33 | 05:49:35 |
| Marshall, MO | 93W12 | 39N07 | 06:12:47 |
| Martinez, CA | 122W08 | 38N01 | 08:08:32 |
| Martinez, GA | 82W05 | 33N31 | 05:28:18 |
| Martinsburg, WV | 77W58 | 39N27 | 05:11:51 |
| Martinsville, VA | 79W52 | 36N41 | 05:19:29 |
| Marysville, CA | 121W35 | 39N09 | 08:06:22 |
| Marysville, WA | 122W11 | 48N03 | 08:08:42 |
| Maryville, MO | 94W52 | 40N21 | 06:19:29 |
| Maryville, TN | 83W58 | 35N45 | 05:35:53 |
| Mauldin, SC | 82W19 | 34N47 | 05:29:14 |
| Maynard, MA | 71W27 | 42N26 | 04:45:48 |
| Maywood, IL | 87W51 | 41N53 | 05:51:22 |
| McComb, MS | 90W27 | 31N15 | 06:01:49 |
| McKeesport, PA | 79W52 | 40N21 | 05:19:27 |
| McKinleyville, CA | 124W06 | 40N57 | 08:16:24 |
| McLean, VA | 77W11 | 38N56 | 05:08:43 |
| Mechanicsville, VA | 77W22 | 37N37 | 05:09:30 |
| Medford, MA | 71W06 | 42N25 | 04:44:26 |
| Medford, OR | 122W52 | 42N20 | 08:11:30 |
| Medicine Bow, WY | 106W12 | 41N54 | 07:04:49 |
| Melbourne, FL | 80W36 | 28N05 | 05:22:25 |
| Melrose Park, IL | 87W51 | 41N54 | 05:51:26 |
| Melville, NY | 73W25 | 40N48 | 04:53:40 |
| Memphis, TN | 90W03 | 35N09 | 06:00:12 |
| Menlo Park, CA | 122W11 | 37N27 | 08:08:43 |
| Menomonee Falls, WI | 88W07 | 43N11 | 05:52:28 |
| Menomonie, WI | 91W55 | 44N53 | 06:07:41 |
| Mentor, OH | 81W20 | 41N40 | 05:25:22 |
| Merced, CA | 120W29 | 37N18 | 08:01:56 |
| Mercedes, TX | 97W55 | 26N09 | 06:31:39 |
| Mercer Island, WA | 122W13 | 47N34 | 08:08:53 |
| Meriden, CT | 72W48 | 41N32 | 04:51:14 |
| Meridian, MS | 88W42 | 32N22 | 05:54:49 |
| Meridian, WA | 122W20 | 47N40 | 08:09:19 |
| Merrick, NY | 73W33 | 40N40 | 04:54:12 |
| Mesa, AZ | 111W49 | 33N25 | 07:27:17 |
| Mesquite, TX | 96W36 | 32N46 | 06:26:24 |
| Metairie, LA | 90W09 | 29N59 | 06:00:37 |
| Metuchen, NJ | 74W22 | 40N33 | 04:57:27 |
| Miami, FL | 80W12 | 25N46 | 05:20:47 |
| Middlesex, NJ | 74W30 | 40N34 | 04:57:58 |
| Middleton, WI | 89W30 | 43N06 | 05:58:01 |
| Middletown, CT | 72W39 | 41N34 | 04:50:36 |
| Middletown, NY | 74W25 | 41N27 | 04:57:42 |
| Middletown, OH | 84W24 | 39N31 | 05:37:36 |
| Midland, TX | 102W05 | 31N60 | 06:48:19 |
| Milford, CT | 73W03 | 41N13 | 04:52:14 |
| Milford, MA | 71W31 | 42N08 | 04:46:04 |
| Mill Valley, CA | 122W33 | 37N54 | 08:10:11 |
| Millbrae, CA | 122W23 | 37N36 | 08:09:33 |
| Milpitas, CA | 121W54 | 37N26 | 08:07:37 |
| Milton, MA | 71W04 | 42N15 | 04:44:16 |
| Milwaukee, WI | 87W54 | 43N02 | 05:51:38 |
| Mineola, NY | 73W38 | 40N45 | 04:54:34 |
| Minneapolis, MN | 93W16 | 44N59 | 06:13:03 |
| Minnetonka, MN | 93W30 | 44N55 | 06:14:01 |
| Minot, ND | 101W18 | 48N14 | 06:45:11 |
| Miramar, FL | 80W14 | 25N59 | 05:20:56 |
| Mission Viejo, CA | 117W40 | 33N36 | 07:50:41 |
| Missoula, MT | 113W60 | 46N52 | 07:35:58 |
| Missouri City, TX | 95W32 | 29N37 | 06:22:09 |
| Moab, UT | 109W33 | 38N34 | 07:18:12 |
| Mobile, AL | 88W03 | 30N42 | 05:52:10 |
| Modesto, CA | 120W60 | 37N38 | 08:03:59 |
| Moline, IL | 90W31 | 41N30 | 06:02:04 |
| Monroe, LA | 92W07 | 32N31 | 06:08:29 |
| Monroe, NC | 80W33 | 34N59 | 05:22:12 |
| Monroe, WI | 89W38 | 42N36 | 05:58:33 |
| Monroeville, AL | 87W19 | 31N32 | 05:49:18 |
| Monroeville, PA | 79W45 | 40N26 | 05:19:00 |
| Monrovia, CA | 117W60 | 34N09 | 07:51:60 |
| Montclair, NJ | 74W13 | 40N50 | 04:56:50 |
| Monterey, CA | 121W54 | 36N36 | 08:07:34 |
| Montgomery, AL | 86W18 | 32N22 | 05:45:12 |
| Montpelier, VT | 72W35 | 44N16 | 04:50:18 |
| Moraga, CA | 122W08 | 37N50 | 08:08:31 |
| Morgantown, WV | 79W57 | 39N38 | 05:19:49 |
| Morristown, NJ | 74W29 | 40N48 | 04:57:56 |
| Morristown, TN | 83W18 | 36N13 | 05:33:11 |
| Morton Grove, IL | 87W47 | 42N02 | 05:51:08 |
| Moscow, ID | 116W60 | 46N44 | 07:47:60 |
| Moundsville, WV | 80W45 | 39N55 | 05:22:58 |
| Mount Clemens, MI | 82W53 | 42N36 | 05:31:31 |
| Mount Holly, NJ | 74W47 | 39N60 | 04:59:09 |
| Mount Pleasant, MI | 84W46 | 43N36 | 05:39:04 |
| Mount Pleasant, SC | 79W52 | 32N48 | 05:19:27 |
| Mount Prospect, IL | 87W56 | 42N04 | 05:51:45 |
| Mount Vernon, IL | 88W54 | 38N19 | 05:55:37 |
| Mount Vernon, NY | 73W50 | 40N55 | 04:55:21 |
| Mount Vernon, VA | 77W05 | 38N42 | 05:08:21 |
| Mountain View, CA | 122W05 | 37N23 | 08:08:20 |
| Muncie, IN | 85W23 | 40N12 | 05:41:33 |
| Muskegon, MI | 86W15 | 43N14 | 05:44:60 |
| Muskogee, OK | 95W22 | 35N45 | 06:21:29 |
| Mustang, OK | 97W43 | 35N23 | 06:30:54 |
| Myrtle Beach, SC | 78W53 | 33N41 | 05:15:33 |
| Myrtle Grove, FL | 87W18 | 30N25 | 05:49:14 |
| Nacogdoches, TX | 94W39 | 31N36 | 06:18:37 |
| Napa, CA | 122W17 | 38N18 | 08:09:08 |
| Naples, FL | 81W48 | 26N09 | 05:27:11 |
| Nashua, NH | 71W28 | 42N46 | 04:45:52 |
| Nashville, TN | 86W47 | 36N10 | 05:47:08 |
| Natchez, LA | 93W03 | 31N41 | 06:12:11 |
| Needham, MA | 71W14 | 42N17 | 04:44:56 |
| Nevada City, CA | 121W01 | 39N16 | 08:04:04 |
| New Bedford, MA | 70W56 | 41N38 | 04:43:44 |
| New Bern, NC | 77W03 | 35N07 | 05:08:11 |
| New Brunswick, NJ | 74W27 | 40N29 | 04:57:49 |
| New Carrollton, MD | 76W53 | 38N58 | 05:07:31 |
| New Castle, PA | 80W21 | 41N00 | 05:21:23 |
| New Haven, CT | 72W56 | 41N18 | 04:51:43 |
| New Hope, MN | 93W23 | 45N02 | 06:13:33 |
| New Iberia, LA | 91W49 | 30N00 | 06:07:16 |
| New Kensington, PA | 79W46 | 40N34 | 05:19:04 |
| New London, CT | 72W06 | 41N21 | 04:48:24 |
| New Milford, NJ | 74W01 | 40N56 | 04:56:05 |
| New Orleans, LA | 90W05 | 29N57 | 06:00:18 |
| New Port Richey, FL | 82W43 | 28N15 | 05:30:53 |
| New Providence, NJ | 74W24 | 40N42 | 04:57:36 |
| New Rochelle, NY | 73W47 | 40N55 | 04:55:08 |
| New Smyrna Beach, FL | 80W56 | 29N02 | 05:23:43 |
| New York, NY | 74W00 | 40N43 | 04:56:02 |
| Newark, CA | 122W02 | 37N32 | 08:08:09 |
| Newark, DE | 75W45 | 39N41 | 05:03:00 |
| Newark, NJ | 74W10 | 40N44 | 04:56:41 |
| Newberry, SC | 81W37 | 34N16 | 05:26:29 |
| Newburg, KY | 85W40 | 38N10 | 05:42:38 |
| Newington, VA | 77W11 | 38N44 | 05:08:44 |
| Newport Beach, CA | 117W56 | 33N37 | 07:51:43 |
| Newport News, VA | 76W26 | 36N59 | 05:05:43 |
| Newport, RI | 71W19 | 41N29 | 04:45:15 |
| Newport, VT | 72W12 | 44N56 | 04:48:49 |
| Newton, IA | 93W03 | 41N42 | 06:12:11 |
| Newton, KS | 97W21 | 38N03 | 06:29:23 |
| Newton, MA | 71W13 | 42N20 | 04:44:50 |
| Newton, NJ | 74W45 | 41N03 | 04:59:01 |
| Niagara Falls, NY | 79W03 | 43N06 | 05:16:14 |
| Niles, MI | 86W15 | 41N50 | 05:45:01 |
| Niles, OH | 80W46 | 41N11 | 05:23:04 |
| Nogales, AZ | 110W56 | 31N20 | 07:23:44 |
| Nome, AK | 165W24 | 64N30 | 11:01:38 |
| Norfolk, VA | 76W17 | 36N51 | 05:05:09 |
| Normal, IL | 88W59 | 40N31 | 05:55:58 |
| Norman, OK | 97W26 | 35N13 | 06:29:45 |
| Norristown, PA | 75W20 | 40N07 | 05:01:22 |
| North Haven, CT | 72W52 | 41N23 | 04:51:26 |
| North Little Rock, AR | 92W16 | 34N46 | 06:09:04 |
| North Platte, NE | 100W46 | 41N07 | 06:43:04 |
| Northbrook, IL | 87W50 | 42N08 | 05:51:19 |
| Norton, OH | 83W04 | 40N26 | 05:32:18 |
| Norwalk, CA | 118W05 | 33N54 | 07:52:19 |
| Norwalk, CT | 73W25 | 41N07 | 04:53:38 |
| Norwalk, OH | 82W37 | 41N15 | 05:30:28 |
| Norwich, CT | 72W05 | 41N31 | 04:48:18 |
| Norwood, OH | 84W28 | 39N09 | 05:37:50 |
| Novato, CA | 122W34 | 38N06 | 08:10:16 |
| Nutley, NJ | 74W10 | 40N49 | 04:56:38 |
| Oak Forest, IL | 87W45 | 41N36 | 05:50:59 |
| Oak Grove, OR | 122W38 | 45N25 | 08:10:33 |
| Oak Harbor, WA | 122W39 | 48N18 | 08:10:34 |
| Oak Lawn, IL | 87W45 | 41N43 | 05:51:01 |
| Oak Park, IL | 87W47 | 41N53 | 05:51:08 |
| Oak Park, MI | 83W11 | 42N28 | 05:32:44 |
| Oak Ridge, TN | 84W16 | 36N01 | 05:37:05 |
| Oakdale, MN | 92W58 | 44N59 | 06:11:52 |
| Oakland, CA | 122W16 | 37N48 | 08:09:05 |
| Oakland, NJ | 79W24 | 39N24 | 05:17:38 |
| Ocala, FL | 82W08 | 29N11 | 05:28:34 |
| Ocean City, MD | 75W05 | 38N20 | 05:00:20 |
| Ocean City, NJ | 74W35 | 39N17 | 04:58:18 |
| Oceanside, CA | 117W23 | 33N12 | 07:49:31 |
| Odessa, TX | 102W22 | 31N51 | 06:49:28 |
| Ogallala, NE | 101W43 | 41N08 | 06:46:53 |
| Ogden, UT | 111W58 | 41N13 | 07:27:54 |
| Oil City, PA | 79W42 | 41N26 | 05:18:50 |
| Oklahoma City, OK | 97W31 | 35N28 | 06:30:04 |
| Olney, MD | 77W04 | 39N09 | 05:08:16 |
| Olympia, WA | 122W54 | 47N02 | 08:11:36 |
| Omaha, NE | 95W56 | 41N16 | 06:23:45 |
| Oneida, NY | 75W39 | 43N06 | 05:02:36 |
| Oneonta, NY | 75W04 | 42N27 | 05:00:15 |
| Ontario, CA | 117W39 | 34N04 | 07:50:36 |
| Opportunity, WA | 117W14 | 47N39 | 07:48:57 |
| Orange, CA | 117W51 | 33N47 | 07:51:25 |
| Orange, CT | 73W02 | 41N17 | 04:52:06 |
| Orange, NJ | 74W14 | 40N46 | 04:56:56 |
| Orangeburg, SC | 80W51 | 33N30 | 05:23:25 |
| Oregon City, OR | 122W36 | 45N21 | 08:10:25 |
| Oregon, OH | 83W29 | 41N39 | 05:33:57 |
| Orem, UT | 111W42 | 40N18 | 07:26:47 |
| Orinda, CA | 122W11 | 37N53 | 08:08:43 |
| Orlando, FL | 81W23 | 28N32 | 05:25:31 |
| Ormond Beach, FL | 81W03 | 29N17 | 05:24:13 |
| Oshkosh, WI | 88W33 | 44N01 | 05:54:10 |
| Oswego, NY | 76W31 | 43N27 | 05:06:03 |
| Ottawa, KS | 95W16 | 38N37 | 06:21:04 |
| Overlook, OH | 84W06 | 39N46 | 05:36:24 |
| Oxford, OH | 84W45 | 39N30 | 05:38:59 |
| Oxnard, CA | 119W11 | 34N12 | 07:56:42 |
| Ozark, AL | 85W38 | 31N28 | 05:42:34 |
| Pacific Grove, CA | 121W55 | 36N37 | 08:07:40 |
| Pacifica, CA | 122W29 | 37N37 | 08:09:57 |
| Palestine, TX | 95W38 | 31N46 | 06:22:31 |
| Palisades Park, NJ | 73W60 | 40N51 | 04:55:60 |

# Longitudes and Latitudes of Major U.S. Cities

| | | | |
|---|---|---|---|
| Palm Beach Gardens, FL | 80W06 | 26N50 | 05:20:24 |
| Palm Desert, CA | 116W23 | 33N43 | 07:45:33 |
| Palm Harbor, FL | 82W46 | 28N05 | 05:31:03 |
| Palm Springs, CA | 116W33 | 33N50 | 07:46:11 |
| Palmdale, CA | 118W07 | 34N35 | 07:52:28 |
| Palmetto Estates, FL | 80W22 | 25N36 | 05:21:28 |
| Palo Alto, CA | 122W09 | 37N27 | 08:08:34 |
| Palos Verdes Estates, CA | 118W23 | 33N48 | 07:53:33 |
| Panama City, FL | 85W40 | 30N10 | 05:42:38 |
| Paradise Valley, AZ | 111W57 | 33N32 | 07:27:46 |
| Paradise, CA | 121W38 | 39N45 | 08:06:33 |
| Paramus, NJ | 74W05 | 40N57 | 04:56:18 |
| Paris, TN | 88W20 | 36N18 | 05:53:18 |
| Paris, TX | 95W33 | 33N40 | 06:22:13 |
| Park Forest, IL | 87W40 | 41N29 | 05:50:42 |
| Park Ridge, IL | 87W50 | 42N01 | 05:51:22 |
| Parkersburg, WV | 81W34 | 39N16 | 05:26:15 |
| Parkville, MD | 76W32 | 39N23 | 05:06:10 |
| Parma, OH | 81W43 | 41N24 | 05:26:54 |
| Pasadena, CA | 118W09 | 34N09 | 07:52:34 |
| Pascagoula, MS | 88W33 | 30N22 | 05:54:13 |
| Passaic, NJ | 74W08 | 40N51 | 04:56:31 |
| Pawtucket, RI | 71W23 | 41N53 | 04:45:32 |
| Peabody, MA | 70W56 | 42N32 | 04:43:43 |
| Pecos, TX | 103W30 | 31N25 | 06:53:58 |
| Peekskill, NY | 73W55 | 41N17 | 04:55:41 |
| Pekin, IL | 89W38 | 40N34 | 05:58:34 |
| Pensacola, FL | 87W13 | 30N25 | 05:48:52 |
| Peoria, IL | 89W35 | 40N42 | 05:58:21 |
| Perth Amboy, NJ | 74W16 | 40N30 | 04:57:04 |
| Petaluma, CA | 122W38 | 38N14 | 08:10:33 |
| Philadelphia, PA | 75W10 | 39N57 | 05:00:39 |
| Phoenix, AZ | 112W04 | 33N27 | 07:28:18 |
| Picayune, MS | 89W41 | 30N32 | 05:58:43 |
| Pico Rivera, CA | 118W06 | 33N59 | 07:52:23 |
| Piedmont, CA | 122W14 | 37N49 | 08:08:55 |
| Pierre, SD | 100W21 | 44N22 | 06:41:24 |
| Pine Bluff, AR | 92W00 | 34N14 | 06:08:01 |
| Pine City, MN | 92W58 | 45N50 | 06:11:52 |
| Pineville, KY | 83W42 | 36N46 | 05:34:47 |
| Pineville, LA | 92W26 | 31N19 | 06:09:44 |
| Pinewood, FL | 80W13 | 25N54 | 05:20:52 |
| Pinole, CA | 122W18 | 38N00 | 08:09:11 |
| Pioche, NV | 114W27 | 37N56 | 07:37:48 |
| Pittsburgh, PA | 79W60 | 40N26 | 05:19:59 |
| Pittsfield, MA | 73W15 | 42N27 | 04:52:59 |
| Placentia, CA | 117W52 | 33N52 | 07:51:29 |
| Plainfield, NJ | 74W24 | 40N38 | 04:57:38 |
| Plainview, NY | 73W28 | 40N47 | 04:53:52 |
| Plano, TX | 96W42 | 33N01 | 06:26:48 |
| Plantation, FL | 80W14 | 26N08 | 05:20:56 |
| Plattsburgh, NY | 73W27 | 44N42 | 04:53:49 |
| Pleasant Grove, UT | 111W44 | 40N22 | 07:26:57 |
| Pleasant Hill, CA | 122W04 | 37N57 | 08:08:14 |
| Pleasanton, CA | 121W52 | 37N40 | 08:07:30 |
| Pleasure Ridge Park, KY | 85W49 | 38N09 | 05:43:16 |
| Plum, PA | 79W47 | 40N29 | 05:19:08 |
| Plymouth, MA | 70W40 | 41N58 | 04:42:40 |
| Plymouth, MI | 83W28 | 42N22 | 05:33:53 |
| Pocatello, ID | 112W27 | 42N52 | 07:29:47 |
| Pomona, CA | 117W45 | 34N03 | 07:51:00 |
| Pompano Beach, FL | 80W08 | 26N14 | 05:20:30 |
| Pontiac, MI | 83W17 | 42N38 | 05:33:10 |
| Poplar Bluff, MO | 90W24 | 36N45 | 06:01:34 |
| Port Angeles, WA | 123W26 | 48N07 | 08:13:43 |
| Port Arthur, TX | 93W56 | 29N54 | 06:15:43 |
| Port Chester, NY | 73W40 | 41N00 | 04:54:40 |
| Port Hueneme, CA | 119W12 | 34N09 | 07:56:47 |
| Port Huron, MI | 82W26 | 42N58 | 05:29:42 |
| Port Royal, SC | 80W42 | 32N23 | 05:22:46 |
| Port Washington, NY | 73W42 | 40N50 | 04:54:48 |
| Portage Lakes, OH | 81W32 | 41N00 | 05:26:08 |
| Portales, NM | 103W20 | 34N11 | 06:53:20 |
| Porterville, CA | 119W01 | 36N04 | 07:56:04 |
| Portland, ME | 70W15 | 43N40 | 04:41:01 |
| Portland, OR | 122W41 | 45N31 | 08:10:42 |
| Portsmouth, NH | 70W46 | 43N04 | 04:43:03 |
| Portsmouth, OH | 82W60 | 38N44 | 05:31:59 |
| Portsmouth, VA | 76W18 | 36N50 | 05:05:12 |
| Potomac, MD | 77W13 | 39N01 | 05:08:50 |
| Potsdam, NY | 74W59 | 44N40 | 04:59:56 |
| Pottstown, PA | 75W39 | 40N15 | 05:02:36 |
| Pottsville, PA | 76W12 | 40N41 | 05:04:47 |
| Poughkeepsie, NY | 73W55 | 41N42 | 04:55:41 |
| Poway, CA | 117W02 | 32N58 | 07:48:08 |
| Prescott, AZ | 112W28 | 34N32 | 07:29:52 |
| Presque Isle, ME | 68W01 | 46N41 | 04:32:04 |
| Princess Anne, MD | 75W42 | 38N12 | 05:02:46 |

| | | | |
|---|---|---|---|
| Princeton, NJ | 74W40 | 40N21 | 04:58:38 |
| Providence, RI | 71W25 | 41N49 | 04:45:39 |
| Provo, UT | 111W39 | 40N14 | 07:26:38 |
| Pueblo, CO | 104W37 | 38N15 | 06:58:26 |
| Pullman, WA | 117W11 | 46N44 | 07:48:43 |
| Punta Gorda, FL | 82W03 | 26N56 | 05:28:11 |
| Quincy, IL | 91W25 | 39N56 | 06:05:38 |
| Quincy, MA | 71W00 | 42N15 | 04:44:01 |
| Racine, WI | 87W47 | 42N44 | 05:51:08 |
| Radcliff, KY | 85W57 | 37N50 | 05:43:48 |
| Radford, VA | 80W35 | 37N08 | 05:22:18 |
| Rahway, NJ | 74W17 | 40N36 | 04:57:07 |
| Raleigh, NC | 78W38 | 35N46 | 05:14:33 |
| Ramona, CA | 116W52 | 33N03 | 07:47:28 |
| Ramsey, MN | 92W58 | 43N43 | 06:11:53 |
| Rancho Cucamonga, CA | 117W36 | 34N06 | 07:50:22 |
| Randallstown, MD | 76W48 | 39N22 | 05:07:11 |
| Randolph, MA | 71W03 | 42N10 | 04:44:10 |
| Rapid City, SD | 103W14 | 44N05 | 06:52:55 |
| Ravenna, OH | 81W15 | 41N09 | 05:24:58 |
| Rawlins, WY | 107W14 | 41N47 | 07:08:57 |
| Reading, MA | 71W06 | 42N32 | 04:44:23 |
| Reading, OH | 84W27 | 39N13 | 05:37:46 |
| Reading, PA | 75W56 | 40N20 | 05:03:43 |
| Red Bank, TN | 85W18 | 35N07 | 05:41:11 |
| Red Bluff, CA | 122W14 | 40N11 | 08:08:56 |
| Red Wing, MN | 92W32 | 44N34 | 06:10:08 |
| Redding, CA | 122W23 | 40N35 | 08:09:34 |
| Redland, MD | 77W09 | 39N09 | 05:08:35 |
| Redlands, CA | 117W11 | 34N04 | 07:48:44 |
| Redmond, WA | 122W07 | 47N40 | 08:08:29 |
| Redondo Beach, CA | 118W23 | 33N51 | 07:53:33 |
| Redwood City, CA | 122W14 | 37N29 | 08:08:56 |
| Reidsville, NC | 79W40 | 36N21 | 05:18:40 |
| Reno, NV | 119W49 | 39N32 | 07:59:15 |
| Renton, WA | 122W13 | 47N29 | 08:08:52 |
| Revere, MA | 71W01 | 42N25 | 04:44:03 |
| Richfield, MN | 93W17 | 44N53 | 06:13:08 |
| Richland, WA | 119W17 | 46N17 | 07:57:08 |
| Richmond, CA | 122W21 | 37N56 | 08:09:23 |
| Richmond, KY | 84W18 | 37N45 | 05:37:11 |
| Richmond, VA | 77W28 | 37N33 | 05:09:51 |
| Ridgewood, NJ | 74W07 | 40N59 | 04:56:28 |
| River Forest, IL | 87W49 | 41N54 | 05:51:15 |
| Riverside, CA | 117W24 | 33N57 | 07:49:35 |
| Riverview, MI | 83W11 | 42N10 | 05:32:43 |
| Riviera Beach, FL | 80W04 | 26N47 | 05:20:14 |
| Roanoke Rapids, NC | 77W39 | 36N28 | 05:10:37 |
| Roanoke, VA | 79W57 | 37N16 | 05:19:46 |
| Rochester, MI | 83W08 | 42N41 | 05:32:32 |
| Rochester, MN | 92W28 | 44N01 | 06:09:53 |
| Rochester, NY | 77W37 | 43N09 | 05:10:28 |
| Rock Hill, SC | 81W02 | 34N55 | 05:24:06 |
| Rockford, IL | 89W06 | 42N16 | 05:56:23 |
| Rockville, MD | 77W09 | 39N05 | 05:08:37 |
| Rocky Mount, NC | 77W47 | 35N56 | 05:11:10 |
| Rohnert Park, CA | 122W42 | 38N20 | 08:10:48 |
| Rome, GA | 85W10 | 34N15 | 05:40:40 |
| Romulus, MI | 83W24 | 42N13 | 05:33:35 |
| Roosevelt, NY | 73W35 | 40N41 | 04:54:21 |
| Rose Hill, VA | 77W07 | 38N47 | 05:08:28 |
| Roseburg, OR | 123W20 | 43N13 | 08:13:22 |
| Rosedale, MD | 76W31 | 39N19 | 05:06:04 |
| Roselle, IL | 88W05 | 41N59 | 05:52:19 |
| Roselle, NJ | 74W16 | 40N40 | 04:57:03 |
| Rosemont, CA | 121W22 | 38N33 | 08:05:27 |
| Roseville, CA | 121W17 | 38N45 | 08:05:09 |
| Roseville, MN | 93W09 | 45N00 | 06:12:38 |
| Roswell, GA | 84W22 | 34N01 | 05:37:27 |
| Roswell, NM | 104W31 | 33N24 | 06:58:05 |
| Rotterdam, NY | 74W01 | 42N49 | 04:56:04 |
| Rowland Heights, CA | 117W54 | 33N59 | 07:51:37 |
| Royal Oak, MI | 83W09 | 42N29 | 05:32:35 |
| Royal Palm Beach, FL | 80W15 | 26N41 | 05:21:00 |
| Rugby, ND | 99W60 | 48N22 | 06:39:59 |
| Rutherford, NJ | 74W06 | 40N50 | 04:56:26 |
| Rutland, VT | 72W58 | 43N37 | 04:51:54 |
| Rye, NY | 73W41 | 40N59 | 04:54:44 |
| Sacramento, CA | 121W30 | 38N35 | 08:05:58 |
| Saginaw, MI | 83W57 | 43N25 | 05:35:48 |
| Saint Albans, VT | 73W05 | 44N49 | 04:52:20 |
| Saint Albans, WV | 81W50 | 38N23 | 05:27:21 |
| Saint Andrews, SC | 80W56 | 33N51 | 05:23:44 |
| Saint Augustine, FL | 81W19 | 29N54 | 05:25:16 |
| Saint Charles, MO | 90W29 | 38N47 | 06:01:55 |
| Saint Clair Shores, MI | 82W53 | 42N30 | 05:31:33 |
| Saint Cloud, MN | 94W10 | 45N34 | 06:16:39 |
| Saint George, UT | 113W35 | 37N06 | 07:34:20 |

| | | | |
|---|---|---|---|
| Saint Joseph, MO | 94W51 | 39N46 | 06:19:23 |
| Saint Louis, MO | 90W12 | 38N38 | 06:00:47 |
| Saint Matthews, KY | 85W39 | 38N15 | 05:42:37 |
| Saint Paul, MN | 93W06 | 44N57 | 06:12:22 |
| Saint Peters, MO | 90W38 | 38N48 | 06:02:30 |
| Saint Petersburg, FL | 82W41 | 27N46 | 05:30:43 |
| Saint Simons, GA | 81W23 | 31N08 | 05:25:34 |
| Salem, MA | 70W54 | 42N31 | 04:43:35 |
| Salem, OR | 123W02 | 44N57 | 08:12:08 |
| Salem, VA | 80W03 | 37N18 | 05:20:13 |
| Salina, KS | 97W37 | 38N50 | 06:30:27 |
| Salinas, CA | 121W39 | 36N41 | 08:06:37 |
| Salisbury, MD | 75W36 | 38N22 | 05:02:24 |
| Salisbury, NC | 80W28 | 35N40 | 05:21:54 |
| Salisbury, NY | 74W49 | 43N08 | 04:59:18 |
| Salmon, ID | 113W54 | 45N11 | 07:35:35 |
| Salt Lake City, UT | 111W53 | 40N46 | 07:27:34 |
| San Angelo, TX | 100W26 | 31N28 | 06:41:45 |
| San Anselmo, CA | 122W34 | 37N58 | 08:10:15 |
| San Antonio, TX | 98W30 | 29N25 | 06:33:58 |
| San Benito, TX | 97W38 | 26N08 | 06:30:31 |
| San Bernardino, CA | 117W18 | 34N07 | 07:49:13 |
| San Bruno, CA | 122W25 | 37N38 | 08:09:38 |
| San Carlos, CA | 122W16 | 37N30 | 08:09:02 |
| San Clemente, CA | 117W37 | 33N26 | 07:50:27 |
| San Diego, CA | 117W09 | 32N43 | 07:48:38 |
| San Fernando, CA | 118W26 | 34N17 | 07:53:45 |
| San Francisco, CA | 122W25 | 37N47 | 08:09:40 |
| San Jacinto, CA | 116W57 | 33N47 | 07:47:50 |
| San Jose, CA | 121W54 | 37N20 | 08:07:35 |
| San Juan Capistrano, CA | 117W40 | 33N30 | 07:50:39 |
| San Juan, PR | 66W06 | 18N28 | 04:24:25 |
| San Juan, TX | 98W09 | 26N11 | 06:32:37 |
| San Luis Obispo, CA | 120W40 | 35N17 | 08:02:38 |
| San Marcos, CA | 117W10 | 33N09 | 07:48:40 |
| San Marcos, TX | 97W56 | 29N53 | 06:31:46 |
| San Mateo, CA | 122W19 | 37N34 | 08:09:18 |
| San Pablo, CA | 122W21 | 37N58 | 08:09:23 |
| San Rafael, CA | 122W32 | 37N58 | 08:10:07 |
| San Ramon, CA | 121W59 | 37N47 | 08:07:54 |
| Sand Springs, OK | 96W07 | 36N08 | 06:24:26 |
| Sandusky, OH | 82W42 | 41N27 | 05:30:50 |
| Sandy Springs, GA | 84W23 | 33N55 | 05:37:31 |
| Sandy, UT | 111W53 | 40N36 | 07:27:32 |
| Sanford, NC | 79W11 | 35N29 | 05:16:43 |
| Santa Ana, CA | 117W52 | 33N45 | 07:51:28 |
| Santa Barbara, CA | 119W42 | 34N25 | 07:58:49 |
| Santa Clara, CA | 121W16 | 37N21 | 08:05:04 |
| Santa Cruz, CA | 122W02 | 36N58 | 08:08:07 |
| Santa Fe Springs, CA | 118W05 | 33N57 | 07:52:20 |
| Santa Fe, NM | 105W56 | 35N41 | 07:03:45 |
| Santa Maria, CA | 120W26 | 34N57 | 08:01:44 |
| Santa Monica, CA | 118W29 | 34N01 | 07:53:58 |
| Santa Paula, CA | 119W04 | 34N21 | 07:56:14 |
| Santa Rosa, CA | 122W43 | 38N26 | 08:10:51 |
| Santee, CA | 116W58 | 32N50 | 07:47:54 |
| Sarasota, FL | 82W32 | 27N20 | 05:30:07 |
| Saratoga Springs, NY | 73W47 | 43N05 | 04:55:08 |
| Saratoga, CA | 122W01 | 37N16 | 08:08:05 |
| Sault Sainte Marie, MI | 84W21 | 46N30 | 05:37:23 |
| Savannah, GA | 81W06 | 32N05 | 05:24:24 |
| Scarsdale, NY | 73W47 | 41N00 | 04:55:08 |
| Schaumburg, IL | 88W05 | 42N02 | 05:52:20 |
| Schenectady, NY | 73W56 | 42N49 | 04:55:46 |
| Scottsbluff, NE | 103W40 | 41N52 | 06:54:40 |
| Scottsboro, AL | 86W02 | 34N40 | 05:44:08 |
| Scottsdale, AZ | 111W54 | 33N31 | 07:27:36 |
| Scranton, PA | 75W40 | 41N25 | 05:02:39 |
| Seabrook, MD | 76W51 | 38N58 | 05:07:23 |
| Seaford, NY | 73W29 | 40N40 | 04:53:57 |
| Seal Beach, CA | 118W06 | 33N44 | 07:52:25 |
| Seaside, CA | 121W51 | 36N37 | 08:07:24 |
| Seattle, WA | 122W20 | 47N36 | 08:09:19 |
| Secaucus, NJ | 74W03 | 40N47 | 04:56:14 |
| Selma, AL | 87W01 | 32N24 | 05:48:05 |
| Seven Hills, OH | 81W41 | 41N24 | 05:26:42 |
| Severn, MD | 76W42 | 39N08 | 05:06:48 |
| Severna Park, MD | 76W33 | 39N04 | 05:06:11 |
| Shaker Heights, OH | 81W32 | 41N28 | 05:26:09 |
| Sharonville, OH | 84W25 | 39N16 | 05:37:39 |
| Shawnee, KS | 94W43 | 39N03 | 06:18:53 |
| Shawnee, OK | 96W56 | 35N20 | 06:27:42 |
| Sheboygan, WI | 87W43 | 43N45 | 05:50:51 |
| Sheffield, AL | 87W42 | 34N46 | 05:50:48 |
| Shelby, MT | 111W51 | 48N30 | 07:27:25 |
| Shelby, NC | 81W32 | 35N18 | 05:26:09 |
| Shelbyville, IN | 85W47 | 39N31 | 05:43:06 |
| Shelbyville, TN | 86W28 | 35N29 | 05:45:50 |

# Longitudes and Latitudes of Major U.S. Cities

| | | | |
|---|---|---|---|
| Sheridan, WY | 106W57 | 44N48 | 07:07:49 |
| Sherwood, AR | 92W13 | 34N49 | 06:08:54 |
| Shiloh, OH | 84W14 | 39N49 | 05:36:55 |
| Shoreview, MN | 93W09 | 45N05 | 06:12:35 |
| Shreveport, LA | 93W45 | 32N32 | 06:15:00 |
| Sierra Madre, CA | 118W03 | 34N10 | 07:52:12 |
| Silver Spring, MD | 77W02 | 38N59 | 05:08:06 |
| Simi Valley, CA | 118W45 | 34N16 | 07:55:00 |
| Sioux City, IA | 96W24 | 42N30 | 06:25:36 |
| Sioux Falls, SD | 96W42 | 43N33 | 06:26:48 |
| Skokie, IL | 87W44 | 42N02 | 05:50:56 |
| Slidell, LA | 89W47 | 30N17 | 05:59:07 |
| Smyrna, GA | 84W31 | 33N53 | 05:38:03 |
| Smyrna, TN | 86W31 | 35N59 | 05:46:04 |
| Socorro, NM | 106W53 | 34N04 | 07:07:34 |
| Solana Beach, CA | 117W16 | 32N59 | 07:49:05 |
| Somerset, KY | 84W36 | 37N06 | 05:38:25 |
| Somerville, MA | 71W06 | 42N23 | 04:44:24 |
| Sonora, TX | 100W39 | 30N34 | 06:42:34 |
| South Bend, IN | 86W15 | 41N41 | 05:45:00 |
| South Charleston, WV | 81W42 | 38N22 | 05:26:48 |
| South Lake Tahoe, CA | 119W58 | 38N57 | 07:59:53 |
| Spanish Fork, UT | 111W39 | 40N07 | 07:26:37 |
| Spanish Lake, MO | 90W13 | 38N47 | 06:00:52 |
| Sparks, NV | 119W45 | 39N32 | 07:59:00 |
| Sparta, NC | 81W07 | 36N30 | 05:24:29 |
| Spartanburg, SC | 81W56 | 34N57 | 05:27:44 |
| Spencer, IA | 95W09 | 43N08 | 06:20:35 |
| Spokane, WA | 117W26 | 47N40 | 07:49:42 |
| Spring Hill, FL | 82W27 | 28N33 | 05:29:48 |
| Spring Valley, CA | 116W60 | 32N45 | 07:47:60 |
| Springdale, OH | 84W29 | 39N17 | 05:37:56 |
| Springfield, IL | 89W39 | 39N48 | 05:58:34 |
| Springfield, MA | 72W35 | 42N06 | 04:50:22 |
| Springfield, MO | 93W18 | 37N13 | 06:13:12 |
| Springfield, NJ | 74W19 | 40N43 | 04:57:15 |
| Springfield, OH | 83W49 | 39N55 | 05:35:14 |
| Springfield, OR | 123W01 | 44N03 | 08:12:05 |
| Springfield, PA | 75W19 | 39N56 | 05:01:17 |
| Springfield, VA | 77W11 | 38N47 | 05:08:45 |
| Springfield, VT | 72W29 | 43N18 | 04:49:56 |
| Stamford, CT | 73W32 | 41N03 | 04:54:09 |
| Stanford, CA | 122W10 | 37N25 | 08:08:40 |
| State College, PA | 77W52 | 40N48 | 05:11:26 |
| Staunton, VA | 79W04 | 38N09 | 05:16:17 |
| Steamboat Springs, CO | 106W50 | 40N29 | 07:07:19 |
| Sterling Heights, MI | 83W02 | 42N35 | 05:32:07 |
| Sterling, VA | 77W26 | 39N00 | 05:09:43 |
| Steubenville, OH | 80W38 | 40N22 | 05:22:32 |
| Stillwater, MN | 92W48 | 45N03 | 06:11:13 |
| Stillwater, OK | 97W03 | 36N07 | 06:28:14 |
| Stockton, CA | 121W17 | 37N57 | 08:05:10 |
| Stoneham, MA | 71W06 | 42N29 | 04:44:24 |
| Stony Brook, NY | 73W08 | 40N56 | 04:52:34 |
| Stow, OH | 81W26 | 41N10 | 05:25:46 |
| Stratford, CT | 73W08 | 41N11 | 04:52:32 |
| Stratton, ME | 70W26 | 45N08 | 04:41:46 |
| Stuttgart, AR | 91W33 | 34N30 | 06:06:13 |
| Suffolk, VA | 76W35 | 36N44 | 05:06:20 |
| Sugar Land, TX | 95W38 | 29N37 | 06:22:32 |
| Sulphur Springs, TX | 95W36 | 33N08 | 06:22:24 |
| Sulphur, LA | 93W23 | 30N14 | 06:13:31 |
| Summit, NJ | 74W22 | 40N44 | 04:57:26 |
| Sumter, SC | 80W21 | 33N55 | 05:21:22 |
| Sun City, AZ | 112W16 | 33N36 | 07:29:05 |
| Sun City, CA | 117W12 | 33N43 | 07:48:47 |
| Sun Prairie, WI | 89W13 | 43N11 | 05:56:51 |
| Sunnyvale, CA | 122W02 | 37N22 | 08:08:08 |
| Sunrise, FL | 80W07 | 26N08 | 05:20:27 |
| Superior, WI | 92W06 | 46N43 | 06:08:25 |
| Susanville, CA | 120W39 | 40N25 | 08:02:36 |
| Sweetwater, FL | 80W22 | 25N46 | 05:21:30 |
| Sweetwater, TX | 100W24 | 32N28 | 06:41:37 |
| Sylvania, OH | 83W43 | 41N43 | 05:34:51 |
| Syracuse, NY | 76W09 | 43N03 | 05:04:35 |
| Tacoma, WA | 122W27 | 47N15 | 08:09:46 |
| Takoma Park, MD | 77W00 | 38N59 | 05:08:02 |
| Tallahassee, FL | 84W17 | 30N26 | 05:37:07 |
| Tallmadge, OH | 81W27 | 41N06 | 05:25:46 |
| Tampa, FL | 82W28 | 27N57 | 05:29:50 |
| Tarpon Springs, FL | 82W45 | 28N09 | 05:31:02 |
| Tarrytown, NY | 73W52 | 41N05 | 04:55:26 |
| Taunton, MA | 71W05 | 41N54 | 04:44:22 |
| Taylor, TX | 97W25 | 30N34 | 06:29:38 |
| Teaneck, NJ | 74W01 | 40N54 | 04:56:04 |
| Temecula, CA | 117W09 | 33N30 | 07:48:35 |
| Tempe, AZ | 111W55 | 33N25 | 07:27:38 |
| Terre Haute, IN | 87W25 | 39N28 | 05:49:39 |
| Tewksbury, MA | 71W14 | 42N37 | 04:44:56 |
| Texarkana, AR | 94W02 | 33N27 | 06:16:09 |
| Texarkana, TX | 94W03 | 33N26 | 06:16:11 |
| Texas City, TX | 94W54 | 29N23 | 06:19:37 |
| The Colony, TX | 96W52 | 33N05 | 06:27:28 |
| Thibodaux, LA | 90W49 | 29N48 | 06:03:17 |
| Thomasville, GA | 83W59 | 30N50 | 05:35:55 |
| Thomasville, NC | 80W05 | 35N53 | 05:20:20 |
| Thousand Oaks, CA | 118W50 | 34N10 | 07:55:21 |
| Timberlake, VA | 79W15 | 37N19 | 05:17:02 |
| Timonium, MD | 76W37 | 39N26 | 05:06:29 |
| Toledo, OH | 83W33 | 41N40 | 05:34:13 |
| Tonawanda, NY | 78W53 | 43N01 | 05:15:31 |
| Topeka, KS | 95W41 | 39N03 | 06:22:43 |
| Torrington, CT | 73W07 | 41N48 | 04:52:29 |
| Torrington, WY | 104W11 | 42N04 | 06:56:43 |
| Towson, MD | 76W36 | 39N24 | 05:06:25 |
| Tracy, CA | 121W25 | 37N44 | 08:05:42 |
| Trenton, NJ | 74W45 | 40N13 | 04:58:58 |
| Tribune, KS | 101W45 | 38N28 | 06:47:01 |
| Trinidad, CO | 104W30 | 37N10 | 06:58:00 |
| Troy, AL | 85W58 | 31N49 | 05:43:53 |
| Troy, MI | 83W09 | 42N36 | 05:32:36 |
| Troy, NY | 73W42 | 42N44 | 04:54:46 |
| Troy, OH | 84W12 | 40N02 | 05:36:49 |
| Tucson, AZ | 110W56 | 32N13 | 07:23:42 |
| Tucumcari, NM | 103W43 | 35N10 | 06:54:54 |
| Tulare, CA | 119W21 | 36N12 | 07:57:23 |
| Tulsa, OK | 95W60 | 36N09 | 06:23:58 |
| Tupelo, MS | 88W42 | 34N15 | 05:54:49 |
| Turlock, CA | 120W51 | 37N30 | 08:03:23 |
| Tuscaloosa, AL | 87W34 | 33N13 | 05:50:17 |
| Tuskegee, AL | 85W42 | 32N25 | 05:42:46 |
| Tustin, CA | 117W50 | 33N45 | 07:51:18 |
| Twentynine Palms, CA | 116W03 | 34N08 | 07:44:13 |
| Twin Falls, ID | 114W28 | 42N34 | 07:37:50 |
| Two Rivers, WI | 87W34 | 44N09 | 05:50:17 |
| Tyler, TX | 95W18 | 32N21 | 06:21:12 |
| Tysons Corner, VA | 77W14 | 38N55 | 05:08:56 |
| Ukiah, CA | 123W12 | 39N09 | 08:12:50 |
| Union City (Alvarado), CA | 122W05 | 37N36 | 08:08:19 |
| Union City, TN | 89W03 | 36N25 | 05:56:14 |
| Union, MO | 91W00 | 38N27 | 06:04:01 |
| Union, NJ | 74W16 | 40N42 | 04:57:03 |
| Uniontown, PA | 79W44 | 39N54 | 05:18:56 |
| University Heights, OH | 81W32 | 41N30 | 05:26:09 |
| Upland, CA | 117W39 | 34N06 | 07:50:35 |
| Upper Arlington, OH | 84W23 | 39N31 | 05:37:30 |
| Upper Marlboro, MD | 76W45 | 38N49 | 05:07:00 |
| Urbana, IL | 88W12 | 40N07 | 05:52:50 |
| Urbana, OH | 83W45 | 40N07 | 05:35:01 |
| Urbandale, IA | 93W43 | 41N38 | 06:14:51 |
| Utica, NY | 75W14 | 43N06 | 05:00:56 |
| Vacaville, CA | 121W59 | 38N21 | 08:07:57 |
| Vadnais Heights, MN | 93W04 | 45N03 | 06:12:18 |
| Valdosta, GA | 83W17 | 30N50 | 05:33:07 |
| Valentine, NE | 100W33 | 42N52 | 06:42:12 |
| Vallejo, CA | 122W15 | 38N06 | 08:09:01 |
| Valley Falls, RI | 71W23 | 41N54 | 04:45:34 |
| Valley Station, KY | 85W52 | 38N07 | 05:43:29 |
| Valparaiso, IN | 87W04 | 41N28 | 05:48:15 |
| Van Buren, AR | 94W21 | 35N26 | 06:17:24 |
| Vancouver, WA | 122W40 | 45N38 | 08:10:38 |
| Vandalia, OH | 84W12 | 39N53 | 05:36:48 |
| Venice, FL | 82W27 | 27N06 | 05:29:49 |
| Ventura, CA | 119W18 | 34N17 | 07:57:10 |
| Vermillion, SD | 96W56 | 42N47 | 06:27:43 |
| Vernal, UT | 109W32 | 40N27 | 07:18:07 |
| Vero Beach, FL | 80W24 | 27N38 | 05:21:35 |
| Versailles, IN | 85W15 | 39N04 | 05:41:00 |
| Vicksburg, MS | 90W53 | 32N21 | 06:03:31 |
| Victorville, CA | 117W17 | 34N32 | 07:49:10 |
| Vidalia, GA | 82W25 | 32N13 | 05:29:39 |
| Vienna, WV | 81W33 | 39N20 | 05:26:12 |
| Vincennes, IN | 87W32 | 38N41 | 05:50:07 |
| Virginia Beach, VA | 75W59 | 36N51 | 05:03:55 |
| Visalia, CA | 119W17 | 36N20 | 07:57:10 |
| Vista, CA | 117W15 | 33N12 | 07:48:58 |
| Wabash, IN | 85W49 | 40N48 | 05:43:17 |
| Waco, TX | 97W09 | 31N33 | 06:28:35 |
| Wadsworth, OH | 81W44 | 41N02 | 05:26:55 |
| Wahiawa, HI | 158W01 | 21N30 | 10:32:06 |
| Wailuku, HI | 156W30 | 20N53 | 10:26:01 |
| Waimalu, HI | 157W57 | 21N24 | 10:31:48 |
| Waipahu, HI | 158W01 | 21N23 | 10:32:02 |
| Waipio, HI | 155W36 | 20N07 | 10:22:24 |
| Wakefield, MA | 71W04 | 42N30 | 04:44:18 |
| Waldorf, MD | 76W56 | 38N37 | 05:07:45 |
| Walla Walla, WA | 118W21 | 46N04 | 07:53:22 |
| Walnut Creek, CA | 122W04 | 37N54 | 08:08:15 |
| Walnut, CA | 117W52 | 34N01 | 07:51:27 |
| Waltham, MA | 71W14 | 42N23 | 04:44:57 |
| Warren, AR | 92W04 | 33N37 | 06:08:15 |
| Warren, OH | 80W49 | 41N14 | 05:23:16 |
| Warren, PA | 79W09 | 41N51 | 05:16:35 |
| Warrensburg, MO | 93W44 | 38N46 | 06:14:57 |
| Warsaw, IN | 85W51 | 41N14 | 05:43:25 |
| Washington, DC | 77W02 | 38N54 | 05:08:09 |
| Watauga, TX | 97W15 | 32N51 | 06:29:01 |
| Waterbury, CT | 73W03 | 41N33 | 04:52:12 |
| Waterloo, IA | 92W21 | 42N30 | 06:09:22 |
| Watertown, MA | 71W11 | 42N22 | 04:44:44 |
| Watertown, NY | 75W55 | 43N58 | 05:03:39 |
| Watertown, SD | 97W07 | 44N54 | 06:28:28 |
| Watertown, WI | 88W44 | 43N12 | 05:54:55 |
| Waterville, ME | 69W38 | 44N33 | 04:38:32 |
| Waterville, WA | 120W04 | 47N39 | 08:00:17 |
| Watsonville, CA | 121W45 | 36N55 | 08:07:01 |
| Waukegan, IL | 87W51 | 42N22 | 05:51:23 |
| Waukesha, WI | 88W14 | 43N01 | 05:52:56 |
| Waycross, GA | 82W21 | 31N13 | 05:29:25 |
| Wayne, MI | 83W23 | 42N17 | 05:33:33 |
| Webster Springs, WV | 80W25 | 38N29 | 05:21:39 |
| Webster, MA | 71W53 | 42N03 | 04:47:31 |
| Welby, CO | 104W58 | 39N50 | 06:59:50 |
| Wellesley, MA | 71W18 | 42N18 | 04:45:10 |
| Wenatchee, WA | 120W19 | 47N25 | 08:01:14 |
| Wendover, UT | 114W02 | 40N44 | 07:36:09 |
| West Haven, CT | 72W57 | 41N16 | 04:51:47 |
| West Memphis, AR | 90W11 | 35N09 | 06:00:44 |
| West Monroe, LA | 92W09 | 32N31 | 06:08:35 |
| West Palm Beach, FL | 80W03 | 26N43 | 05:20:13 |
| Westbrook, ME | 70W22 | 43N41 | 04:41:29 |
| Westerly, RI | 71W50 | 41N23 | 04:47:19 |
| Westminster, CA | 118W00 | 33N46 | 07:52:01 |
| Westport, CT | 73W22 | 41N08 | 04:53:26 |
| Wethersfield, CT | 72W39 | 41N43 | 04:50:37 |
| Weymouth, MA | 70W56 | 42N13 | 04:43:46 |
| Wheaton, IL | 88W06 | 41N52 | 05:52:26 |
| Wheaton, MD | 77W03 | 39N02 | 05:08:13 |
| Wheeling, IL | 87W56 | 42N08 | 05:51:43 |
| Wheeling, WV | 80W43 | 40N04 | 05:22:53 |
| White Bear Lake, MN | 93W01 | 45N05 | 06:12:02 |
| White Oak, MD | 76W60 | 39N02 | 05:07:58 |
| White Oak, OH | 84W36 | 39N13 | 05:38:24 |
| White Plains, NY | 73W46 | 41N02 | 04:55:03 |
| White River, SD | 100W45 | 43N34 | 06:42:59 |
| Whitefish Bay, WI | 87W54 | 43N07 | 05:51:36 |
| Whitehall, OH | 82W53 | 39N58 | 05:31:33 |
| Whitehall, PA | 75W30 | 40N39 | 05:02:00 |
| Whitewater, WI | 88W44 | 42N50 | 05:54:56 |
| Whittier, CA | 118W02 | 33N59 | 07:52:08 |
| Wichita Falls, TX | 98W30 | 33N55 | 06:33:58 |
| Wichita, KS | 97W20 | 37N42 | 06:29:21 |
| Wilkes-Barre, PA | 75W53 | 41N15 | 05:03:32 |
| Williamsburg, VA | 76W42 | 37N16 | 05:06:50 |
| Williston, ND | 103W38 | 48N08 | 06:54:32 |
| Willoughby, OH | 81W24 | 41N38 | 05:25:38 |
| Wilmette, IL | 87W43 | 42N04 | 05:50:53 |
| Wilmington, DE | 75W33 | 39N45 | 05:02:11 |
| Winchester, KY | 84W11 | 37N59 | 05:36:43 |
| Winchester, MA | 71W08 | 42N27 | 04:44:33 |
| Windsor, CA | 122W49 | 38N33 | 08:11:16 |
| Winnetka, IL | 87W44 | 42N06 | 05:50:57 |
| Winona, MN | 91W38 | 44N03 | 06:06:33 |
| Winston-Salem, NC | 80W15 | 36N06 | 05:20:59 |
| Winter Haven, FL | 81W44 | 28N01 | 05:26:56 |
| Winter Park, FL | 81W20 | 28N36 | 05:25:21 |
| Winter Springs, FL | 81W19 | 28N42 | 05:25:14 |
| Winthrop, MA | 70W59 | 42N23 | 04:43:56 |
| Woburn, MA | 71W09 | 42N29 | 04:44:37 |
| Woodland, CA | 121W46 | 38N41 | 08:07:05 |
| Woodlawn, MD | 76W44 | 39N19 | 05:06:55 |
| Woonsocket, RI | 71W31 | 42N00 | 04:46:04 |
| Wooster, OH | 81W56 | 40N48 | 05:27:44 |
| Worcester, MA | 71W48 | 42N16 | 04:47:13 |
| Worthington, OH | 83W01 | 40N06 | 05:32:04 |
| Wray, CO | 102W13 | 40N05 | 06:48:53 |
| Wyandotte, MI | 83W09 | 42N13 | 05:32:36 |
| Wyckoff, NJ | 74W10 | 41N01 | 04:56:42 |
| Xenia, OH | 83W56 | 39N41 | 05:35:43 |
| Yakima, WA | 120W30 | 46N36 | 08:02:01 |
| Yankton, SD | 97W24 | 42N52 | 06:29:35 |
| Yazoo City, MS | 90W24 | 32N51 | 06:01:37 |
| Yeadon, PA | 75W15 | 39N56 | 05:01:01 |

# Longitudes and Latitudes of Major Cities

| City | Longitude | Latitude | Offset |
|---|---|---|---|
| Yonkers, NY | 73W54 | 40N56 | 04:55:36 |
| Yorba Linda, CA | 117W49 | 33N53 | 07:51:15 |
| York, PA | 76W44 | 39N58 | 05:06:55 |
| Yorktown, NY | 73W49 | 41N18 | 04:55:14 |
| Youngstown, OH | 80W39 | 41N06 | 05:22:36 |
| Ypsilanti, MI | 83W37 | 42N14 | 05:34:27 |
| Yreka, CA | 122W38 | 41N44 | 08:10:32 |
| Yuba City, CA | 121W37 | 39N08 | 08:06:28 |
| Yucaipa, CA | 117W03 | 34N02 | 07:48:10 |
| Yucca Valley, CA | 116W27 | 34N07 | 07:45:47 |
| Yukon, OK | 97W46 | 35N30 | 06:31:03 |
| Yuma, AZ | 114W37 | 32N44 | 07:38:30 |
| Zanesville, OH | 82W01 | 39N56 | 05:28:03 |
| Zion, IL | 87W50 | 42N27 | 05:51:20 |

## ——— International Cities ———

| City | Longitude | Latitude | Offset |
|---|---|---|---|
| Aberdeen, SCOT | 2W04 | 57N10 | 00:08:16 |
| Abidjan, IVC | 4W02 | 5N19 | 00:16:08 |
| Abu Dhabi, UAE | 54E22 | 24N28 | -03:37:28 |
| Acapulco (de Juárez), MEX | 99W55 | 16N51 | 06:39:40 |
| Accra, GHANA | 0W13 | 5N33 | 00:00:52 |
| Adamstown, PIT | 130W05 | 25S04 | 08:40:20 |
| Addis Ababa > Adis Abeba, ETH | 38E42 | 9N02 | -02:34:48 |
| Adelaide, AUSTL | 138E35 | 34S55 | -09:14:20 |
| Aden, YEMEN | 45E12 | 12N45 | -03:00:48 |
| Agana, GUAM | 144E45 | 13N28 | -09:39:00 |
| Akita, JAPAN | 140E07 | 39N43 | -09:20:28 |
| Al-Kuwayt, KUW | 47E59 | 29N20 | -03:11:56 |
| Al-Manamah, BAHR | 50E35 | 26N13 | -03:22:20 |
| Alexandria > Al-Iskandar, EGYPT | 29E54 | 31N12 | -01:59:36 |
| Algiers > Alger, ALG | 3E03 | 36N47 | -00:12:12 |
| Alofi, NIUE | 169W55 | 19S01 | 11:19:40 |
| Amiens, FR | 2E18 | 49N54 | -00:09:12 |
| 'Amman, JOR | 35E56 | 31N57 | -02:23:44 |
| Amsterdam, NETH | 4E54 | 52N22 | -00:19:36 |
| Andorra, AND | 1E31 | 42N30 | -00:06:04 |
| Ankara, TUR | 32E52 | 39N56 | -02:11:28 |
| Antananarivo, MADA | 47E31 | 18S55 | -03:10:04 |
| Antwerp > Antwerpen, BEL | 4E25 | 51N13 | -00:17:40 |
| Apia, WSAM | 171W44 | 13S50 | 11:26:56 |
| Århus, DEN | 10E13 | 56N09 | -00:40:52 |
| Asmera, ETH | 38E53 | 15N20 | -02:35:32 |
| Asunción, PAR | 57W40 | 25S16 | 03:50:40 |
| Athens > Athínai, GRC | 23E43 | 37N58 | -01:34:52 |
| Auckland, NZ | 174E46 | 36S52 | -11:39:04 |
| Avarua, CKIS | 159W46 | 21S12 | 10:39:04 |
| Baghdad, IRAQ | 44E25 | 33N21 | -02:57:40 |
| Bahía Blanca, ARG | 62W17 | 38S43 | 04:09:08 |
| Bairiki, KIRI | 173E01 | 1N20 | -11:32:04 |
| Bamako, MALI | 8W00 | 12N39 | 00:32:00 |
| Bandar Seri Begawan, BRU | 114E55 | 4N56 | -07:39:40 |
| Bangalore, INDIA | 77E35 | 12N59 | -05:10:20 |
| Banghazi, LIBYA | 20E04 | 32N07 | -01:20:16 |
| Bangkok > Krung Thep, THAI | 100E31 | 13N45 | -06:42:04 |
| Bangui, CAR | 18E35 | 4N22 | -01:14:20 |
| Banjul, GAM | 16W39 | 13N28 | 01:06:36 |
| Barcelona, SPAIN | 2E11 | 41N23 | -00:08:44 |
| Basel (Bêle), SWTZ | 7E35 | 47N33 | -00:30:20 |
| Basse-Terre, GUAD | 61W44 | 16N00 | 04:06:56 |
| Basseterre, STKN | 62W43 | 17N18 | 04:10:52 |
| Beijing (Peking), CHINA | 116E25 | 39N55 | -07:45:40 |
| Beirut > Bayrut, LEB | 35E30 | 33N53 | -02:22:00 |
| Belém, BRZ | 48W29 | 1S27 | 03:13:56 |
| Belfast, NIRE | 5W55 | 54N35 | 00:23:40 |
| Belgrade > Beograd, YUG | 20E30 | 44N50 | -01:22:00 |
| Belize City, BLZ | 88W12 | 17N30 | 05:52:48 |
| Belo Horizonte, BRZ | 43W56 | 19S55 | 02:55:44 |
| Berlin, GER | 13E22 | 52N30 | -00:53:28 |
| Bern (Berne), SWTZ | 7E26 | 46N57 | -00:29:44 |
| Birmingham, ENG | 1W50 | 52N30 | 00:07:20 |
| Bissau, GUBI | 15W35 | 11N51 | 01:02:20 |
| Bitburg, GER | 6E31 | 49N58 | -00:26:04 |
| Blantyre, MALW | 35E00 | 15S47 | -02:20:00 |
| Bobo Dioulasso, BKF | 4W18 | 11N12 | 00:17:12 |
| Bogotá, COL | 74W05 | 4N36 | 04:56:20 |
| Bologna, ITALY | 11E20 | 44N29 | -00:45:20 |
| Bombay, INDIA | 72E50 | 18N58 | -04:51:20 |
| Bonn, GER | 7E05 | 50N44 | -00:28:20 |
| Bordeaux, FR | 0W34 | 44N50 | 00:02:16 |
| Brandon, CAN | 99W57 | 49N50 | 06:39:48 |
| Brasília, BRZ | 47W55 | 15S47 | 03:11:40 |
| Bratislava, CZEC | 17E07 | 48N09 | -01:08:28 |
| Brazzaville, CONGO | 15E17 | 4S16 | -01:01:08 |
| Bremen, GER | 8E49 | 53N04 | -00:35:16 |
| Bridgetown, BARB | 59W37 | 13N06 | 03:58:28 |
| Brighton, ENG | 0W08 | 50N50 | 00:00:32 |
| Brisbane, AUSTL | 153E02 | 27S28 | -10:12:08 |
| Bristol, ENG | 2W35 | 51N27 | 00:10:20 |
| Brno, CZEC | 16E37 | 49N12 | -01:06:28 |
| Brugge (Bruges), BEL | 3E14 | 51N13 | -00:12:56 |
| Brussels > Bruxelles, BEL | 4E20 | 50N50 | -00:17:20 |
| Bucharest > Bucuresti, ROM | 26E06 | 44N26 | -01:44:24 |
| Budapest, HUN | 19E05 | 47N30 | -01:16:20 |
| Buenos Aires, ARG | 58W27 | 34S36 | 03:53:48 |
| Builth Wells, WALES | 3W24 | 52N09 | 00:13:36 |
| Bujumbura, BDI | 29E22 | 3S23 | -01:57:28 |
| Burgas, BULG | 27E28 | 42N30 | -01:49:52 |
| Cádiz, SPAIN | 6W18 | 36N32 | 00:25:12 |
| Cairns, AUSTL | 145E46 | 16S55 | -09:43:04 |
| Cairo > Al-Qahirah, EGYPT | 31E15 | 30N03 | -02:05:00 |
| Calais, FR | 1E50 | 50N57 | -00:07:20 |
| Calcutta, INDIA | 88E22 | 22N32 | -05:53:28 |
| Calgary, CAN | 114W05 | 51N03 | 07:36:20 |
| Cali, COL | 76W31 | 3N27 | 05:06:04 |
| Cambridge (Galt), CAN | 80W19 | 43N22 | 05:21:16 |
| Canberra, AUSTL | 149E08 | 35S17 | -09:56:32 |
| Canton > Guangzhou, CHINA | 113E16 | 23N06 | -07:33:04 |
| Cape Town (Kaapstad), SAFR | 18E22 | 33S55 | -01:13:28 |
| Caracas, VEN | 66W56 | 10N30 | 04:27:44 |
| Cardigan, WALES | 4W40 | 52N06 | 00:18:40 |
| Carlisle, ENG | 2W55 | 54N54 | 00:11:40 |
| Casablanca (Dar-El-Beida, MOR | 7W35 | 33N39 | 00:30:20 |
| Castries, STLU | 61W00 | 14N01 | 04:04:00 |
| Cayenne, FRGU | 52W20 | 4N56 | 03:29:20 |
| Changchun, CHINA | 125E19 | 43N53 | -08:21:16 |
| Charlotte Amalie, VI | 64W56 | 18N21 | 04:19:44 |
| Chengdu (Chengtu), CHINA | 104E04 | 30N39 | -06:56:16 |
| Cherbourg, FR | 1W39 | 49N39 | 00:06:36 |
| Chicoutimi, CAN | 71W04 | 48N26 | 04:44:16 |
| Chifeng (Ulanhad), CHINA | 119E00 | 42N18 | -07:56:00 |
| Chittagong, BANG | 91E50 | 22N20 | -06:07:20 |
| Christchurch, NZ | 172E38 | 43S32 | -11:30:32 |
| Chungking > Chongqing, CHINA | 106E35 | 29N34 | -07:06:20 |
| Ciudad Juárez, MEX | 106W29 | 31N44 | 07:05:56 |
| Cologne > Köln, GER | 6E59 | 50N56 | -00:27:56 |
| Colombo, SLAN | 79E51 | 6N56 | -05:19:24 |
| Conakry, GUIN | 13W43 | 9N31 | 00:54:52 |
| Concepción, CHILE | 73W03 | 36S50 | 04:52:12 |
| Copenhagen > København, DEN | 12E35 | 55N40 | -00:50:20 |
| Coral Harbour, CAN | 83W10 | 64N08 | 05:32:40 |
| Córdoba, ARG | 64W11 | 31S24 | 04:16:44 |
| Córdoba, SPAIN | 4W46 | 37N53 | 00:19:04 |
| Cork, IRE | 8W28 | 51N54 | 00:33:52 |
| Corner Brook, CAN | 57W57 | 48N57 | 03:51:48 |
| Cremona, ITALY | 10E02 | 45N07 | -00:40:08 |
| Curitiba, BRZ | 49W15 | 25S25 | 03:17:00 |
| Dacca, BANG | 90E25 | 23N43 | -06:01:40 |
| Dakar, SEN | 17W26 | 14N40 | 01:09:44 |
| Damascus > Dimashq, SYRIA | 36E18 | 33N30 | -02:25:12 |
| Dar es Salaam, TANZ | 39E17 | 6S48 | -02:37:08 |
| Darwin, AUSTL | 130E50 | 12S28 | -08:43:20 |
| Dawson, CAN | 139W25 | 64N04 | 09:17:40 |
| Delhi, INDIA | 77E13 | 28N40 | -05:08:52 |
| Djibouti, DJB | 43E09 | 11N36 | -02:52:36 |
| Doha > Ad-Dawhah, QATAR | 51E32 | 25N17 | -03:26:08 |
| Douglas, IMAN | 4W28 | 54N09 | 00:17:52 |
| Dover, ENG | 1E19 | 51N08 | -00:05:16 |
| Dresden, GER | 13E44 | 51N03 | -00:54:56 |
| Dublin (Baile Átha Cliath), IRE | 6W15 | 53N20 | 00:25:00 |
| Dulan (Chahanwusu), CHINA | 98E28 | 36N16 | -06:33:52 |
| Dumfries, SCOT | 3W37 | 55N04 | 00:14:28 |
| Durango, MEX | 104W40 | 24N02 | 06:58:40 |
| Durban, SAFR | 30E56 | 29S55 | -02:03:44 |
| Dzaoudzi, MAYT | 45E17 | 12S47 | -03:01:08 |
| Edinburgh, SCOT | 3W13 | 55N57 | 00:12:52 |
| Edmonton, CAN | 113W28 | 53N33 | 07:33:52 |
| Ensenada, MEX | 116W37 | 31N52 | 07:46:28 |
| Essen, GER | 7E01 | 51N28 | -00:28:04 |
| Faisalabad (Lyallpur), PAK | 73E05 | 31N25 | -04:52:20 |
| Fakaofo Island, TOK | 171W14 | 9S22 | 11:24:56 |
| Florence > Firenze, ITALY | 11E15 | 43N46 | -00:45:00 |
| Fort-de-France, MART | 61W05 | 14N36 | 04:04:20 |
| Fortaleza, BRZ | 38W30 | 3S43 | 02:34:00 |
| Frankfurt am Main, GER | 8E40 | 50N07 | -00:34:40 |
| Freetown, SL | 13W15 | 8N30 | 00:53:00 |
| Fukuoka, JAPAN | 130E24 | 33N35 | -08:41:36 |
| Funafuti Island, TUV | 179E13 | 8S31 | -11:56:52 |
| Fuzhou, CHINA | 116E20 | 28N01 | -07:45:20 |
| Gaborone, BOTS | 25E55 | 24S45 | -01:43:40 |
| Ganzhou > Zhangye, CHINA | 100E27 | 38N56 | -06:41:48 |
| Gdansk (Danzig), POL | 18E40 | 54N23 | -01:14:40 |
| Geneva > Genäve, SWTZ | 6E09 | 46N12 | -00:24:36 |
| Genoa > Genova, ITALY | 8E57 | 44N25 | -00:35:48 |
| George Town (Pinang), MLYS | 100E20 | 5N25 | -06:41:20 |
| Georgetown, CAYI | 81W23 | 19N18 | 05:25:32 |
| Georgetown, GUY | 58W10 | 6N48 | 03:52:40 |
| Gibraltar, GIB | 5W21 | 36N08 | 00:21:24 |
| Glasgow, SCOT | 4W15 | 55N53 | 00:17:00 |
| Goose Bay, CAN | 60W25 | 53N20 | 04:01:40 |
| Gorky > Gor'kij, USSR | 44E00 | 56N20 | -02:56:00 |
| Göteborg (Gothenburg), SWED | 11E58 | 57N43 | -00:47:52 |
| Grand Turk, TCI | 71W08 | 21N28 | 04:44:32 |
| Graz, AUS | 15E27 | 47N05 | -01:01:48 |
| Grytviken, SGEO | 36W32 | 54S16 | 02:26:08 |
| Guadalajara, MEX | 103W20 | 20N40 | 06:53:20 |
| Guatemala, GUAT | 90W31 | 14N38 | 06:02:04 |
| Ha-Noi, VIET | 105E51 | 21N02 | -07:03:24 |
| Halifax, CAN | 63W36 | 44N39 | 04:14:24 |
| Hamburg, GER | 9E59 | 53N33 | -00:39:56 |
| Hamilton, BER | 64W46 | 32N17 | 04:19:04 |
| Hamilton, CAN | 79W51 | 43N15 | 05:19:24 |
| Hannover, GER | 9E44 | 52N24 | -00:38:56 |
| Harrogate, ENG | 1W33 | 54N00 | 00:06:12 |
| Havana > La Habana, CUBA | 82W22 | 23N08 | 05:29:28 |
| Helsinki (Helsingfors), FIN | 24E58 | 60N10 | -01:39:52 |
| Herat, AFG | 62E12 | 34N20 | -04:08:48 |
| Hermosillo, MEX | 110W58 | 29N04 | 07:23:52 |
| Hiroshima, JAPAN | 132E27 | 34N24 | -08:49:48 |
| Hobart, AUSTL | 147E19 | 42S53 | -09:49:16 |
| Honiara, SOLIS | 159E57 | 9S26 | -10:39:48 |
| Hyderabad, INDIA | 78E29 | 17N23 | -05:13:56 |
| Hyderabad, PAK | 68E22 | 25N22 | -04:33:28 |
| Ibadan, NIG | 3E30 | 7N17 | -00:14:00 |
| Innsbruck, AUS | 11E24 | 47N16 | -00:45:36 |
| Inverness, SCOT | 4W15 | 57N27 | 00:17:00 |
| Ipswich, ENG | 1E10 | 52N04 | -00:04:40 |
| Istanbul, TUR | 28E58 | 41N01 | -01:55:52 |
| Jaipur, INDIA | 75E49 | 26N55 | -05:03:16 |
| Jakarta, INDSA | 106E48 | 6S10 | -07:07:12 |
| Jamestown, STHEL | 5W42 | 15S55 | 00:22:48 |
| Jerusalem > Yerushalayim, ISRL | 35E14 | 31N46 | -02:20:56 |
| Johannesburg, SAFR | 28E00 | 26S15 | -01:52:00 |
| Kabul, AFG | 69E12 | 34N31 | -04:36:48 |
| Kaliningrad (Königsberg), USSR | 20E30 | 54N43 | -01:22:00 |
| Kampala, UG | 32E25 | 0N19 | -02:09:40 |
| Karachi, PAK | 67E03 | 24N52 | -04:28:12 |
| Karamay > Kelamayi, CHINA | 84E55 | 45N30 | -05:39:40 |
| Kashi (Shufu) (Kashgar), CHINA | 75E59 | 39N29 | -05:03:56 |
| Kathmandu, NEPAL | 85E19 | 27N43 | -05:41:16 |
| Kawasaki, JAPAN | 139E43 | 35N32 | -09:18:52 |
| Khartoum > Al-Khartum, SUDAN | 32E32 | 15N36 | -02:10:08 |
| Kiev > Kijev, UKR | 30E31 | 50N26 | -02:02:04 |
| Kigali, RW | 30E04 | 1S57 | -02:00:16 |
| Kingston, JAM | 76W48 | 18N00 | 05:07:12 |
| Kingston, NORF | 167E58 | 29S03 | -11:11:52 |
| Kingston, STVI | 61W14 | 13N09 | 04:04:56 |
| Kinshasa (Léopoldville), ZAIRE | 15E18 | 4S18 | -01:01:12 |
| Klerksdorp, SAFR | 26E39 | 26S58 | -01:46:36 |
| Kraków, POL | 19E58 | 50N03 | -01:19:52 |
| Kuala Lumpur, MLYS | 101E42 | 3N10 | -06:46:48 |
| Kyoto, JAPAN | 135E45 | 35N00 | -09:03:00 |
| La Paz, BOL | 68W09 | 16S30 | 04:32:36 |
| La Paz, MEX | 110W18 | 24N10 | 07:21:12 |
| Lagos, NIG | 3E24 | 6N27 | -00:13:36 |
| Le Mans, FR | 0E12 | 48N00 | -00:00:48 |

# Longitudes and Latitudes of Major Cities

| City | Longitude | Latitude | Offset |
|---|---|---|---|
| Leipzig, GER | 12E20 | 51N19 | -00:49:20 |
| Leningrad, USSR | 30E15 | 59N55 | -02:01:00 |
| Levkosía (Nicosia), CYP | 33E22 | 35N10 | -02:13:28 |
| Libreville, GABON | 9E27 | 0N23 | -00:37:48 |
| Lima, PERU | 77W03 | 12S03 | 05:08:12 |
| Limoges, FR | 1E16 | 45N50 | -00:05:04 |
| Linz, AUS | 14E18 | 48N18 | -00:57:12 |
| Lisbon > Lisboa, PORT | 9W08 | 38N43 | 00:36:32 |
| Liverpool, ENG | 2W55 | 53N25 | 00:11:40 |
| Lobito, ANG | 13E34 | 12S20 | -00:54:16 |
| Lomé, TOGO | 1E13 | 6N08 | -00:04:52 |
| London, ENG | 0W10 | 51N30 | 00:00:40 |
| Londonderry, NIRE | 7W19 | 55N00 | 00:29:16 |
| Lourdes, FR | 0W03 | 43N06 | 00:00:12 |
| Luanda, ANG | 13E14 | 8S48 | -00:52:56 |
| Lusaka, ZAM | 28E17 | 15S25 | -01:53:08 |
| Luxembourg, LUX | 6E09 | 49N36 | -00:24:36 |
| Lyon, FR | 4E51 | 45N45 | -00:19:24 |
| Macau, MACAU | 113E35 | 22N14 | -07:34:20 |
| Madras, INDIA | 80E17 | 13N05 | -05:21:08 |
| Madrid, SPAIN | 3W41 | 40N24 | 00:14:44 |
| Malabo, EQGU | 8E47 | 3N45 | -00:35:08 |
| Málaga, SPAIN | 4W25 | 36N43 | 00:17:40 |
| Malang, INDSA | 112E37 | 7S59 | -07:30:28 |
| Male, MALD | 73E30 | 4N10 | -04:54:00 |
| Managua, NIC | 86W17 | 12N09 | 05:45:08 |
| Manaus, BRZ | 60W01 | 3S08 | 04:00:04 |
| Manchester, ENG | 2W15 | 53N30 | 00:09:00 |
| Mandalay, BURMA | 96E05 | 22N00 | -06:24:20 |
| Manila, PHIL | 121E00 | 14N35 | -08:04:00 |
| Manzanillo, MEX | 104W20 | 19N03 | 06:57:20 |
| Mar del Plata, ARG | 57W33 | 38S00 | 03:50:12 |
| Marrakech, MOR | 8W00 | 31N38 | 00:32:00 |
| Marseille, FR | 5E24 | 43N18 | -00:21:36 |
| Maseru, LESO | 27E30 | 29S28 | -01:50:00 |
| Masqat (Muscat), OMAN | 58E25 | 23N37 | -03:54:20 |
| Mbabane, SWAZ | 31E06 | 26S18 | -02:04:24 |
| Mecca > Makkah, SAUDI | 39E49 | 21N27 | -02:39:16 |
| Medellín, COL | 75W35 | 6N15 | 05:02:20 |
| Medicine Hat, CAN | 110W40 | 50N03 | 07:22:40 |
| Medina > Al-Madinah, SAUDI | 39E36 | 24N28 | -02:38:24 |
| Melbourne, AUSTL | 144E58 | 37S49 | -09:39:52 |
| Mendoza, ARG | 68W49 | 32S53 | 04:35:16 |
| Mérida, MEX | 89W37 | 20N58 | 05:58:28 |
| Metz, FR | 6E10 | 49N08 | -00:24:40 |
| Mexicali, MEX | 115W29 | 32N40 | 07:41:56 |
| Mexico City > Ciudad de, MEX | 99W09 | 19N24 | 06:36:36 |
| Midway Naval Station, MIDW | 177W26 | 28N13 | 11:49:44 |
| Milan > Milano, ITALY | 9E12 | 45N28 | -00:36:48 |
| Minsk, USSR | 27E34 | 53N54 | -01:50:16 |
| Mogadishu > Muqdisho, SOM | 45E22 | 2N04 | -03:01:28 |
| Mombasa, KENYA | 39E40 | 4S03 | -02:38:40 |
| Monaco, MONACO | 7E23 | 43N42 | -00:29:32 |
| Moncton, CAN | 64W47 | 46N06 | 04:19:08 |
| Monrovia, LIBR | 10W47 | 6N18 | 00:43:08 |
| Monterrey, MEX | 93W23 | 16N05 | 06:13:32 |
| Montevideo, UR | 56W11 | 34S53 | 03:44:44 |
| Montréal, CAN | 73W34 | 45N31 | 04:54:16 |
| Moose Jaw, CAN | 105W32 | 50N23 | 07:02:08 |
| Moroni, COMI | 43E16 | 11S41 | -02:53:04 |
| Moscow > Moskva, USSR | 37E35 | 55N45 | -02:30:20 |
| Munich > München, GER | 11E34 | 48N08 | -00:46:16 |
| Nairobi, KENYA | 36E49 | 1S17 | -02:27:16 |
| Nantes, FR | 1W33 | 47N13 | 00:06:12 |
| Naples > Napoli, ITALY | 14E17 | 40N51 | -00:57:08 |
| Nassau, BA | 77W21 | 25N05 | 05:09:24 |
| Natal, BRZ | 35W13 | 5S47 | 02:20:52 |
| Ndjamena, CHAD | 15E03 | 12N07 | -01:00:12 |
| Nelson, NZ | 173E17 | 41S17 | -11:33:08 |
| Newcastle, ENG | 3W06 | 52N26 | 00:12:24 |
| Niamey, NIGER | 2E07 | 13N31 | -00:08:28 |
| Nice, FR | 7E15 | 43N42 | -00:29:00 |
| Nogales, MEX | 110W56 | 31N20 | 07:23:44 |
| Nouakchott, MAUR | 15W57 | 18N06 | 01:03:48 |
| Nouméa, NCAL | 166E27 | 22S16 | -11:05:48 |
| Nukualofa, TONGA | 175W12 | 21S08 | 11:40:48 |
| Nürnberg, GER | 11E04 | 49N27 | -00:44:16 |
| Oaxaca (de Juárez), MEX | 96W43 | 17N03 | 06:26:52 |
| Ocampo, MEX | 108W23 | 28N11 | 07:13:32 |
| Odense, DEN | 10E23 | 55N24 | -00:41:32 |
| Odessa, USSR | 30E44 | 46N28 | -02:02:56 |
| Omsk, USSR | 73E24 | 55N00 | -04:53:36 |
| Oran (Ouahran), ALG | 0W43 | 35N43 | 00:02:52 |
| Osaka, JAPAN | 135E30 | 34N40 | -09:02:00 |
| Oslo, NOR | 10E45 | 59N55 | -00:43:00 |
| Ostrava, CZEC | 18E17 | 49N50 | -01:13:08 |
| Ottawa, CAN | 75W42 | 45N25 | 05:02:48 |
| Ouagadougou, BKF | 1W31 | 12N22 | 00:06:04 |
| P'yongyang, NKOR | 125E45 | 39N01 | -08:23:00 |
| Pago Pago, ASAM | 170W42 | 14S16 | 11:22:48 |
| Palembang, INDSA | 104E45 | 2S55 | -06:59:00 |
| Palermo, ITALY | 13E22 | 38N07 | -00:53:28 |
| Pamplona, SPAIN | 1W38 | 42N49 | 00:06:32 |
| Panamá, PAN | 79W32 | 8N58 | 05:18:08 |
| Papeete, FRPO | 149W34 | 17S32 | 09:58:16 |
| Paramaribo, SUR | 55W10 | 5N50 | 03:40:40 |
| Paris, FR | 2E20 | 48N52 | -00:09:20 |
| Penzance, ENG | 5W33 | 50N07 | 00:22:12 |
| Perth, AUSTL | 115E51 | 31S57 | -07:43:24 |
| Perugia, ITALY | 12E22 | 43N08 | -00:49:28 |
| Phnom Penh > Phnum Pénh, CAMB | 104E55 | 11N33 | -06:59:40 |
| Plovdiv, BULG | 24E45 | 42N09 | -01:39:00 |
| Plymouth, ENG | 4W10 | 50N23 | 00:16:40 |
| Plymouth, MONTS | 62W13 | 16N42 | 04:08:52 |
| Port Louis, MAUS | 57E30 | 20S10 | -03:50:00 |
| Port Moresby, PAPUA | 147E10 | 9S30 | -09:48:40 |
| Port of Spain, TRIN | 61W31 | 10N39 | 04:06:04 |
| Port Said > Bur Sa'Id, EGYPT | 32E18 | 31N16 | -02:09:12 |
| Port Vila, VANU | 168E19 | 17S44 | -11:13:16 |
| Port-au-Prince, HAITI | 72W20 | 18N32 | 04:49:20 |
| Portmadoc, WALES | 4W08 | 52N55 | 00:16:32 |
| Porto Alegre, BRZ | 51W11 | 30S04 | 03:24:44 |
| Porto-Novo, BENIN | 2E37 | 6N29 | -00:10:28 |
| Prague > Praha, CZEC | 14E26 | 50N05 | -00:57:44 |
| Praia, CV | 23W31 | 14N55 | 01:34:04 |
| Pretoria, SAFR | 28E10 | 25S45 | -01:52:40 |
| Prince George, CAN | 122W45 | 53N55 | 08:11:00 |
| Prince Rupert, CAN | 130W19 | 54N19 | 08:41:16 |
| Puerto Vallarta, MEX | 105W15 | 20N37 | 07:01:00 |
| Qingyang, CHINA | 107E47 | 36N06 | -07:11:08 |
| Québec, CAN | 71W14 | 46N49 | 04:44:56 |
| Queenstown, AUSTL | 145E33 | 42S05 | -09:42:12 |
| Quito, EC | 78W30 | 0S13 | 05:14:00 |
| Rabat, MOR | 6W51 | 34N02 | 00:27:24 |
| Rangoon, BURMA | 96E10 | 16N47 | -06:24:40 |
| Recife, BRZ | 34W54 | 8S03 | 02:19:36 |
| Regina, CAN | 104W39 | 50N25 | 06:58:36 |
| Reykjavík, ICE | 21W51 | 64N09 | 01:27:24 |
| Riga, LATV | 24E06 | 56N57 | -01:36:24 |
| Rio de Janeiro, BRZ | 43W14 | 22S54 | 02:52:56 |
| Riyadh > Ar-Riyad, SAUDI | 46E43 | 24N38 | -03:06:52 |
| Rockhampton, AUSTL | 150E31 | 23S23 | -10:02:04 |
| Rome > Roma, ITALY | 12E29 | 41N54 | -00:49:56 |
| Rosario, ARG | 60W40 | 32S57 | 04:02:40 |
| Rotterdam, NETH | 4E28 | 51N55 | -00:17:52 |
| Rouen, FR | 1E05 | 49N26 | -00:04:20 |
| Saint George's, GREN | 61W45 | 12N03 | 04:07:00 |
| Saint Helier, FR | 2W37 | 49N12 | 00:10:28 |
| Saint John's, CAN | 52W43 | 47N34 | 03:30:52 |
| Saint Johns, ATG | 61W51 | 17N06 | 04:07:24 |
| Saint Peter Port, GUER | 2W32 | 49N27 | 00:10:08 |
| Saint-Denis, REU | 55E28 | 20S52 | -03:41:52 |
| Saint-Pierre, STPM | 56W10 | 46N40 | 03:44:40 |
| Saipan, PITT | 134E08 | 6N54 | -08:56:32 |
| Salvador, BRZ | 38W31 | 12S59 | 02:34:04 |
| Salzburg, AUS | 13E02 | 47N48 | -00:52:08 |
| San Cristóbal, ARG | 61W14 | 30S19 | 04:04:56 |
| San José, CR | 84W05 | 9N56 | 05:36:20 |
| San Juan, PR | 66W06 | 18N28 | 04:24:24 |
| San Marino, SMAR | 12E28 | 43N55 | -00:49:52 |
| San Miguel de Tucuman, ARG | 65W13 | 26S49 | 04:20:52 |
| San Salvador, ELS | 89W12 | 13N42 | 05:56:48 |
| Santa Cruz, BOL | 63W10 | 17S48 | 04:12:40 |
| Santa Fe, ARG | 60W42 | 31S38 | 04:02:48 |
| Santiago, CHILE | 70W40 | 33S27 | 04:42:40 |
| Santo Domingo, DR | 69W54 | 18N28 | 04:39:36 |
| Santos, BRZ | 46W20 | 23S57 | 03:05:20 |
| Sao Paulo, BRZ | 46W37 | 23S32 | 03:06:28 |
| Sao Tomé, SAOT | 6E44 | 0N20 | -00:26:56 |
| Saskatoon, CAN | 106W38 | 52N07 | 07:06:32 |
| Semarang, INDSA | 110E25 | 6S58 | -07:21:40 |
| Seoul > Soul, SKOR | 126E58 | 37N33 | -08:27:52 |
| Settlement, WAKE | 166E37 | 19N18 | -11:06:28 |
| Seville > Sevilla, SPAIN | 5W59 | 37N23 | 00:23:56 |
| Singapore, SING | 103E51 | 1N17 | -06:55:24 |
| Sofia > Sofija, BULG | 23E19 | 42N41 | -01:33:16 |
| Stanley, FLI | 57W51 | 51S42 | 03:51:24 |
| Stockholm, SWED | 18E03 | 59N20 | -01:12:12 |
| Strasbourg, FR | 7E45 | 48N35 | -00:31:00 |
| Stuttgart, GER | 9E11 | 48N46 | -00:36:44 |
| Sucre, BOL | 65W17 | 19S02 | 04:21:08 |
| Sudbury, CAN | 81W00 | 46N30 | 05:24:00 |
| Suez > As-Suways, EGYPT | 32E33 | 29N58 | -02:10:12 |
| Surabaya, INDSA | 112E45 | 7S15 | -07:31:00 |
| Suva, FIJI | 178E25 | 18S08 | -11:53:40 |
| Sydney, AUSTL | 151E13 | 33S52 | -10:04:52 |
| T'aipei, TAIW | 121E30 | 25N03 | -08:06:00 |
| Tallinn, ESTON | 24E45 | 59N25 | -01:39:00 |
| Tampere, FIN | 23E45 | 61N30 | -01:35:00 |
| Tampico, MEX | 97W51 | 22N13 | 06:31:24 |
| Tegucigalpa, HON | 87W13 | 14N06 | 05:48:52 |
| Tehran, IRAN | 51E26 | 35N40 | -03:25:44 |
| Tel Aviv, ISRL | 34E46 | 32N04 | -02:19:04 |
| The Valley, ANGU | 63W04 | 18N13 | 04:12:16 |
| Thimbu, BHU | 89E39 | 27N28 | -05:58:36 |
| Thohoyandou, VENDA | 30E29 | 23S00 | -02:01:56 |
| Thunder Bay, CAN | 89W15 | 48N23 | 05:57:00 |
| Tientsin > Tianjin, CHINA | 117E12 | 39N08 | -07:48:48 |
| Tijuana, MEX | 117W01 | 32N32 | 07:48:04 |
| Tiranâ, ALB | 19E50 | 41N20 | -01:19:20 |
| Tokyo, JAPAN | 139E46 | 35N42 | -09:19:04 |
| Torino (Turin), ITALY | 7E40 | 45N03 | -00:30:40 |
| Toronto, CAN | 79W23 | 43N39 | 05:17:32 |
| Torreón, MEX | 103W26 | 25N33 | 06:53:44 |
| Tórshavn, FRI | 6W46 | 62N01 | 00:27:04 |
| Toulouse, FR | 1E26 | 43N36 | -00:05:44 |
| Trieste (Triest), ITALY | 13E46 | 45N40 | -00:55:04 |
| Tripoli > Tarabulus, LIBYA | 13E11 | 32N54 | -00:52:44 |
| Tshidilamolomo, BOPH | 24E41 | 25S50 | -01:38:44 |
| Tunis, TUN | 10E11 | 36N48 | -00:40:44 |
| Turku (èbo), FIN | 22E17 | 60N27 | -01:29:08 |
| Uaboe, NAURU | 166E55 | 0S31 | -11:07:40 |
| Ulan Bator > Ulaan Baata, MONG | 106E53 | 47N55 | -07:07:32 |
| Umtata, TRNSK | 28E47 | 31S35 | -01:55:08 |
| Vaduz, LICT | 9E31 | 47N09 | -00:38:04 |
| Valencia, SPAIN | 0W22 | 39N28 | 00:01:28 |
| Valletta, MALTA | 14E31 | 35N54 | -00:58:04 |
| Valparaíso, CHILE | 71W38 | 33S02 | 04:46:32 |
| Vancouver, CAN | 123W07 | 49N16 | 08:12:28 |
| Varna, BULG | 27E55 | 43N13 | -01:51:40 |
| Venice > Venezia, ITALY | 12E21 | 45N27 | -00:49:24 |
| Victoria (Xianggang), HK | 114E09 | 22N17 | -07:36:36 |
| Victoria, CAN | 123W22 | 48N25 | 08:13:28 |
| Victoria, SEY | 55E27 | 4S38 | -03:41:48 |
| Vienna > Wien, AUS | 16E20 | 48N13 | -01:05:20 |
| Vientiane > Viangchan, LAOS | 102E36 | 17N58 | -06:50:24 |
| Vila > Vilnius, LITH | 25E19 | 54N41 | -01:41:16 |
| Vladivostok, USSR | 131E56 | 43N10 | -08:47:44 |
| Volgograd (Stalingrad), USSR | 44E25 | 48N44 | -02:57:40 |
| Vordingborg, DEN | 11E55 | 55N01 | -00:47:40 |
| Wallis, Üles, WALF | 176W10 | 13S18 | 11:44:40 |
| Warsaw > Warszawa, POL | 21E00 | 52N15 | -01:24:00 |
| Wellington, NZ | 174E47 | 41S18 | -11:39:08 |
| Wenzhou, CHINA | 120E39 | 28N01 | -08:02:36 |
| Whitehorse, CAN | 135W03 | 60N43 | 09:00:12 |
| Willemstad, NANT | 68W56 | 12N06 | 04:35:44 |
| Windhoek, NAM | 17E06 | 22S34 | -01:08:24 |
| Winnipeg, CAN | 97W09 | 49N53 | 06:28:36 |
| Wuhan, CHINA | 114E17 | 30N36 | -07:37:08 |
| Yichun, CHINA | 114E23 | 27N50 | -07:37:32 |
| Zürich, SWTZ | 8E32 | 47N23 | -00:34:08 |

## Also by ACS Publications

# Best-Selling Reference Books

## The American Ephemeris for the 21st Century, Expanded 2nd Ed.

**Compiled and Programmed by Neil F. Michelsen**
**Revisions by Rique Pottenger**

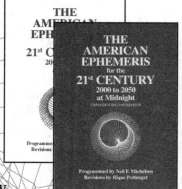

The millennium is here, and it's time to look ahead! This book contains the years 2000 through 2050 with the same accuracy of data and format as The American Ephemeris for the 20th Century.

An absolute **MUST** for every astrologer's library!

**Now including the year 2,000!**

B106X-BMBT Midnight ................. **$18.95**
BAE21N-BMBT Noon ................. **$18.95**

## The American Ephemeris for the 20th Century

**Compiled and Programmed by Neil F. Michelsen**
**Revisions by Rique Pottenger**

No astrologer's library can be complete without the ephemeris with the latest data from NASA's Jet Propulsion Laboratory. *The American Ephemeris* is the most accurate ephemeris in the world today. In addition to planetary positions for every day in the entire 20th century, it includes a wealth of data, such as solar and lunar eclipses, aspectarian of Jupiter through Pluto, Chiron, Synetic Vernal Point, Moon phases and more.

ACS's ephemeris is used by computer programmers and ephemeris makers to measure the accuracy of their work. It is available in two versions, Noon or Midnight.

B104X-BMBT Midnight ................. **$21.95**
B105X-BMBT Noon ......................... **$26.95**

## The Asteroid Ephemeris 1900 to 2050

*Including Chiron and the Black Moon Lilith*

**By Neil F. Michelsen**
**Revised by Rique Pottenger**
**Introduction by Zipporah Dobyns**

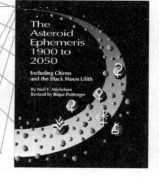

This unique ephemeris provides daily longitudes, weekly declinations and stations for the asteroids Ceres, Pallas, Juno and Vesta. Longitudes for Chiron and the Black Moon Lilith (True and Mean) make this the only source for these astrological factors. All calculations are, of course, at ACS's high standards for accuracy and precision.

Use this reference to add specificity and detail to your astrological work. Gain insight into issues of mother love, work, wisdom, marriage, and the use and abuse of power. See the important connections between parents and children. Explore the significance of Chiron — teacher, healer, idealist — in your horoscope. Investigate the Black Moon Lilith — widely used in Europe, now available in an American Ephemeris.

- 150 years of positions (1900-2050)
- Longitudes and declinations
- Station times and mean positions
- Retrogrades clearly marked

BASTE-BMBT ............................... **$26.95**

**Astro Communications Services, Inc.**
**5521 Ruffin Road • San Diego, CA 92123-1314**
**Orders: (800)888-9983 • Fax: (858)492-9917**
**E-mail: sales@astrocom.com**
**For a complete list of astrological products & services,**
**visit Astro's web site at www.astrocom.com.**

**ASTRO**
When it comes to Astrology,
we wrote the book.